PETERSON'S®
GRADUATE PROGRAMS
IN ENGINEERING
& APPLIED SCIENCES

2021

About Peterson's®

Peterson's® has been your trusted educational publisher for over 50 years. It's a milestone we're quite proud of, as we continue to offer the most accurate, dependable, high-quality educational content in the field, providing you with everything you need to succeed. No matter where you are on your academic or professional path, you can rely on Peterson's for its books, online information, expert test-prep tools, the most up-to-date education exploration data, and the highest quality career success resources—everything you need to achieve your education goals. For our complete line of products, visit **www.petersons.com**.

For more information about Peterson's range of educational products, contact Peterson's, 4380 S. Syracuse Street, Suite 200, Denver CO 80237, or find us online at **www.petersons.com**.

ISSN 1093-8443
ISBN: 978-0-7689-4556-0

Printed in the United States of America

10 9 8 7 6 5 4 3 2 1   22 21 20

Fifty-fifth Edition

CONTENTS

CONTENTS

A Note from the Peterson's Editors

The six volumes of Peterson's *Graduate and Professional Programs*, the only annually updated reference work of its kind, provide wide-ranging information on the graduate and professional programs offered by accredited colleges and universities in the United States, U.S. territories, and Canada and by those institutions outside the United States that are accredited by U.S. accrediting bodies. More than 44,000 individual academic and professional programs at nearly 2,300 institutions are listed. Peterson's *Graduate and Professional Programs* have been used for more than fifty years by prospective graduate and professional students, placement counselors, faculty advisers, and all others interested in postbaccalaureate education.

Graduate & Professional Programs: An Overview contains information on institutions as a whole, while the other books in the series are devoted to specific academic and professional fields:

- *Graduate Programs in the Biological/Biomedical Sciences & Health-Related Medical Professions*

- *Graduate Programs in Business, Education, Information Studies, Law & Social Work*

- *Graduate Programs in Engineering & Applied Sciences*

- *Graduate Programs in the Humanities, Arts & Social Sciences*

- *Graduate Programs in the Physical Sciences, Mathematics, Agricultural Sciences, the Environment & Natural Resources*

The books may be used individually or as a set. For example, if you have chosen a field of study but do not know what institution you want to attend or if you have a college or university in mind but have not chosen an academic field of study, it is best to begin with the Overview guide.

Graduate & Professional Programs: An Overview presents several directories to help you identify programs of study that might interest you; you can then research those programs further in the other books in the series by using the Directory of Graduate and Professional Programs by Field, which lists 500 fields and gives the names of those institutions that offer graduate degree programs in each.

For geographical or financial reasons, you may be interested in attending a particular institution and will want to know what it has to offer. You should turn to the Directory of Institutions and Their Offerings, which lists the degree programs available at each institution. As in the Directory of Graduate and Professional Programs by Field, the level of degrees offered is also indicated.

All books in the series include advice on graduate education, including topics such as admissions tests, financial aid, and accreditation. **The Graduate Adviser** includes two essays and information about accreditation. The first essay, "The Admissions Process," discusses general admission requirements, admission tests, factors to consider when selecting a graduate school or program, when and how to apply, and how admission decisions are made. Special information for international students and tips for minority students are also included. The second essay, "Financial Support," is an overview of the broad range of support available at the graduate level. Fellowships, scholarships, and grants; assistantships and internships; federal and private loan programs, as well as Federal Work-Study; and the GI bill are detailed. This essay concludes with advice on applying for need-based financial aid. "Accreditation and Accrediting Agencies" gives information on accreditation and its purpose and lists institutional accrediting agencies first and then specialized accrediting agencies relevant to each volume's specific fields of study.

With information on more than 40,000 graduate programs in more than 500 disciplines, Peterson's *Graduate and Professional Programs* give you all the information you need about the programs that are of interest to you in three formats: **Profiles** (capsule summaries of basic information), **Displays** (information that an institution or program wants to emphasize), and **Close-Ups** (written by administrators, with more expansive information than the **Profiles**, emphasizing different aspects of the programs). By using these various formats of program information, coupled with **Appendixes** and **Indexes** covering directories and subject areas for all six books, you will find that these guides provide the most comprehensive, accurate, and up-to-date graduate study information available.

Peterson's publishes a full line of resources with information you need to guide you through the graduate admissions process. Peterson's publications can be found at college libraries and career centers and your local bookstore or library—or visit us on the Web at www.petersons.com.

Colleges and universities will be pleased to know that Peterson's helped you in your selection. Admissions staff members are more than happy to answer questions, address specific problems, and help in any way they can. The editors at Peterson's wish you great success in your graduate program search!

THE GRADUATE ADVISER

The Admissions Process

Generalizations about graduate admissions practices are not always helpful because each institution has its own set of guidelines and procedures. Nevertheless, some broad statements can be made about the admissions process that may help you plan your strategy.

Factors Involved in Selecting a Graduate School or Program

Selecting a graduate school and a specific program of study is a complex matter. Quality of the faculty; program and course offerings; the nature, size, and location of the institution; admission requirements; cost; and the availability of financial assistance are among the many factors that affect one's choice of institution. Other considerations are job placement and achievements of the program's graduates and the institution's resources, such as libraries, laboratories, and computer facilities. If you are to make the best possible choice, you need to learn as much as you can about the schools and programs you are considering before you apply.

The following steps may help you narrow your choices.

- Talk to alumni of the programs or institutions you are considering to get their impressions of how well they were prepared for work in their fields of study.
- Remember that graduate school requirements change, so be sure to get the most up-to-date information possible.
- Talk to department faculty members and the graduate adviser at your undergraduate institution. They often have information about programs of study at other institutions.
- Visit the websites of the graduate schools in which you are interested to request a graduate catalog. Contact the department chair in your chosen field of study for additional information about the department and the field.
- Visit as many campuses as possible. Call ahead for an appointment with the graduate adviser in your field of interest and be sure to check out the facilities and talk to students.

General Requirements

Graduate schools and departments have requirements that applicants for admission must meet. Typically, these requirements include undergraduate transcripts (which provide information about undergraduate grade point average and course work applied toward a major), admission test scores, and letters of recommendation. Most graduate programs also ask for an essay or personal statement that describes your personal reasons for seeking graduate study. In some fields, such as art and music, portfolios or auditions may be required in addition to other evidence of talent. Some institutions require that the applicant have an undergraduate degree in the same subject as the intended graduate major.

Most institutions evaluate each applicant on the basis of the applicant's total record, and the weight accorded any given factor varies widely from institution to institution and from program to program.

The Application Process

You should begin the application process at least one year before you expect to begin your graduate study. Find out the application deadline for each institution (many are provided in the **Profile** section of this guide). Go to the institution's website and find out if you can apply online. If not, request a paper application form. Fill out this form thoroughly and neatly. Assume that the school needs all the information it is requesting and that the admissions officer will be sensitive to the neatness and overall quality of what you submit. Do not supply more information than the school requires.

The institution may ask at least one question that will require a three- or four-paragraph answer. Compose your response on the assumption that the admissions officer is interested in both what you think and how you express yourself. Keep your statement brief and to the point, but, at the same time, include all pertinent information about your past experiences and your educational goals. Individual statements vary greatly in style and content, which helps admissions officers differentiate among applicants. Many graduate departments give considerable weight to the statement in making their admissions decisions, so be sure to take the time to prepare a thoughtful and concise statement.

If recommendations are a part of the admissions requirements, carefully choose the individuals you ask to write them. It is generally best to ask current or former professors to write the recommendations, provided they are able to attest to your intellectual ability and motivation for doing the work required of a graduate student. It is advisable to provide stamped, preaddressed envelopes to people being asked to submit recommendations on your behalf.

Completed applications, including references, transcripts, and admission test scores, should be received at the institution by the specified date.

Be advised that institutions do not usually make admissions decisions until all materials have been received. Enclose a self-addressed postcard with your application, requesting confirmation of receipt. Allow at least ten days for the return of the postcard before making further inquiries.

If you plan to apply for financial support, it is imperative that you file your application early.

ADMISSION TESTS

The major testing program used in graduate admissions is the Graduate Record Examinations (GRE®) testing program, sponsored by the GRE Board and administered by Educational Testing Service, Princeton, New Jersey.

The Graduate Record Examinations testing program consists of a General Test and six Subject Tests. The General Test measures critical thinking, verbal reasoning, quantitative reasoning, and analytical writing skills. It is offered as an Internet-based test (iBT) in the United States, Canada, and many other countries.

The GRE® revised General Test's questions were designed to reflect the kind of thinking that students need to do in graduate or business school and demonstrate that students are indeed ready for graduate-level work.

- **Verbal Reasoning**—Measures ability to analyze and evaluate written material and synthesize information obtained from it, analyze relationships among component parts of sentences, and recognize relationships among words and concepts.
- **Quantitative Reasoning**—Measures problem-solving ability, focusing on basic concepts of arithmetic, algebra, geometry, and data analysis.
- **Analytical Writing**—Measures critical thinking and analytical writing skills, specifically the ability to articulate and support complex ideas clearly and effectively.

The computer-delivered GRE® revised General Test is offered year-round at Prometric™ test centers and on specific dates at testing locations outside of the Prometric test center network. Appointments are scheduled on a first-come, first-served basis. The GRE® revised General Test is also offered as a paper-based test three times a year in areas where computer-based testing is not available.

You can take the computer-delivered GRE® revised General Test once every twenty-one days, up to five times within any continuous rolling twelve-month period (365 days)—even if you canceled your scores on a previously taken test. You may take the paper-based GRE® revised General Test as often as it is offered.

Three scores are reported on the revised General Test:

1. A **Verbal Reasoning score** is reported on a 130–170 score scale, in 1-point increments.

2. A **Quantitative Reasoning score** is reported on a 130–170 score scale, in 1-point increments.

3. An **Analytical Writing score** is reported on a 0–6 score level, in half-point increments.

The GRE® Subject Tests measure achievement and assume undergraduate majors or extensive background in the following six disciplines:

- Biology
- Chemistry
- Literature in English
- Mathematics
- Physics
- Psychology

The Subject Tests are available three times per year as paper-based administrations around the world. Testing time is approximately 2 hours and 50 minutes. You can obtain more information about the GRE® by visiting the ETS website at **www.ets.org** or consulting the *GRE® Information Bulletin*. The *Bulletin* can be obtained at many undergraduate colleges. You can also download it from the ETS website or obtain it by contacting Graduate Record Examinations, Educational Testing Service, P.O. Box 6000, Princeton, NJ 08541-6000; phone: 609-771-7670 or 866-473-4373.

If you expect to apply for admission to a program that requires any of the GRE® tests, you should select a test date well in advance of the application deadline. Scores on the computer-based General Test are reported within ten to fifteen days; scores on the paper-based Subject Tests are reported within six weeks.

Another testing program, the Miller Analogies Test® (MAT®), is administered at more than 500 Controlled Testing Centers in the United States, Canada, and other countries. The MAT® computer-based test is now available. Testing time is 60 minutes. The test consists of 120 partial analogies. You can obtain the *Candidate Information Booklet,* which contains a list of test centers and instructions for taking the test, from **www.milleranalogies.com** or by calling 800-328-5999 (toll-free).

Check the specific requirements of the programs to which you are applying.

How Admission Decisions Are Made

The program you apply to is directly involved in the admissions process. Although the final decision is usually made by the graduate dean (or an associate) or the faculty admissions committee, recommendations from faculty members in your intended field are important. At some institutions, an interview is incorporated into the decision process.

A Special Note for International Students

In addition to the steps already described, there are some special considerations for international students who intend to apply for graduate study in the United States. All graduate schools require an indication of competence in English. The purpose of the Test of English as a Foreign Language (TOEFL®) is to evaluate the English proficiency of people who are nonnative speakers of English and want to study at colleges and universities where English is the language of instruction. The TOEFL® is administered by Educational Testing Service (ETS) under the general direction of a policy board established by the College Board and the Graduate Record Examinations Board.

The TOEFL iBT® assesses four basic language skills: listening, reading, writing, and speaking. The Internet-based test is administered at secure, official test centers. The testing time is approximately 4 hours.

The TOEFL® is also offered in a paper-based format in areas of the world where internet-based testing is not available. In 2017, ETS launched a revised TOEFL® paper-based Test, that more closely aligned to the TOEFL iBT® test. This revised paper-based test consists of three sections—listening, reading, and writing. The testing time is approximately 3 hours.

You can obtain more information for both versions of the TOEFL® by visiting the ETS website at **www.ets.org/toefl**. Information can also be obtained by contacting TOEFL® Services, Educational Testing Service, P.O. Box 6151, Princeton, NJ 08541-6151. Phone: 609-771-7100 or 877-863-3546 (toll free).

International students should apply especially early because of the number of steps required to complete the admissions process. Furthermore, many United States graduate schools have a limited number of spaces for international students, and many more students apply than the schools can accommodate.

International students may find financial assistance from institutions very limited. The U.S. government requires international applicants to submit a certification of support, which is a statement attesting to the applicant's financial resources. In addition, international students *must* have health insurance coverage.

Tips for Minority Students

Indicators of a university's values in terms of diversity are found both in its recruitment programs and its resources directed to student success. Important questions: Does the institution vigorously recruit minorities for its graduate programs? Is there funding available to help with the costs associated with visiting the school? Are minorities represented in the institution's brochures or website or on their faculty rolls? What campus-based resources or services (including assistance in locating housing or career counseling and placement) are available? Is funding available to members of underrepresented groups?

At the program level, it is particularly important for minority students to investigate the "climate" of a program under consideration. How many minority students are enrolled and how many have graduated? What opportunities are there to work with diverse faculty and mentors whose research interests match yours? How are conflicts resolved or concerns addressed? How interested are faculty in building strong and supportive relations with students? "Climate" concerns should be addressed by posing questions to various individuals, including faculty members, current students, and alumni.

Information is also available through various organizations, such as the Hispanic Association of Colleges & Universities (HACU), and publications such as *Diverse Issues in Higher Education* and *Hispanic Outlook* magazine. There are also books devoted to this topic, such as *The Multicultural Student's Guide to Colleges* by Robert Mitchell.

Financial Support

The range of financial support at the graduate level is very broad. The following descriptions will give you a general idea of what you might expect and what will be expected of you as a financial support recipient.

Fellowships, Scholarships, and Grants

These are usually outright awards of a few hundred to many thousands of dollars with no service to the institution required in return. Fellowships and scholarships are usually awarded on the basis of merit and are highly competitive. Grants are made on the basis of financial need or special talent in a field of study. Many fellowships, scholarships, and grants not only cover tuition, fees, and supplies but also include stipends for living expenses with allowances for dependents. However, the terms of each should be examined because some do not permit recipients to supplement their income with outside work. Fellowships, scholarships, and grants may vary in the number of years for which they are awarded.

In addition to the availability of these funds at the university or program level, many excellent fellowship programs are available at the national level and may be applied for before and during enrollment in a graduate program. A listing of many of these programs can be found at the Council of Graduate Schools' website, **https://cgsnet.org/**. There is a wealth of information in the "Programs" and "Awards" sections.

Assistantships and Internships

Many graduate students receive financial support through assistantships, particularly involving teaching or research duties. It is important to recognize that such appointments should not be viewed simply as employment relationships but rather should constitute an integral and important part of a student's graduate education. As such, the appointments should be accompanied by strong faculty mentoring and increasingly responsible apprenticeship experiences. The specific nature of these appointments in a given program should be considered in selecting that graduate program.

TEACHING ASSISTANTSHIPS

These usually provide a salary and full or partial tuition remission and may also provide health benefits. Unlike fellowships, scholarships, and grants, which require no service to the institution, teaching assistantships require recipients to provide the institution with a specific amount of undergraduate teaching, ideally related to the student's field of study. Some teaching assistants are limited to grading papers, compiling bibliographies, taking notes, or monitoring laboratories. At some graduate schools, teaching assistants must carry lighter course loads than regular full-time students.

RESEARCH ASSISTANTSHIPS

These are very similar to teaching assistantships in the manner in which financial assistance is provided. The difference is that recipients are given basic research assignments in their disciplines rather than teaching responsibilities. The work required is normally related to the student's field of study; in most instances, the assistantship supports the student's thesis or dissertation research.

ADMINISTRATIVE INTERNSHIPS

These are similar to assistantships in application of financial assistance funds, but the student is given an assignment on a part-time basis, usually as a special assistant with one of the university's administrative offices. The assignment may not necessarily be directly related to the recipient's discipline.

RESIDENCE HALL AND COUNSELING ASSISTANTSHIPS

These assistantships are frequently assigned to graduate students in psychology, counseling, and social work, but they may be offered to students in other disciplines, especially if the student has worked in this capacity during his or her undergraduate years. Duties can vary from being available in a dean's office for a specific number of hours for consultation with undergraduates to living in campus residences and being responsible for both counseling and administrative tasks or advising student activity groups. Residence hall assistantships often include a room and board allowance and, in some cases, tuition assistance and stipends. Contact the Housing and Student Life Office for more information.

Health Insurance

The availability and affordability of health insurance is an important issue and one that should be considered in an applicant's choice of institution and program. While often included with assistantships and fellowships, this is not always the case and, even if provided, the benefits may be limited. It is important to note that the U.S. government requires international students to have health insurance.

The GI Bill

This provides financial assistance for students who are veterans of the United States armed forces. If you are a veteran, contact your local Veterans Administration office to determine your eligibility and to get full details about benefits. There are a number of programs that offer educational benefits to current military enlistees. Some states have tuition assistance programs for members of the National Guard. Contact the VA office at the college for more information.

Federal Work-Study Program (FWS)

Employment is another way some students finance their graduate studies. The federally funded Federal Work-Study Program provides eligible students with employment opportunities, usually in public and private nonprofit organizations. Federal funds pay up to 75 percent of the wages, with the remainder paid by the employing agency. FWS is available to graduate students who demonstrate financial need. Not all schools have these funds, and some only award them to undergraduates. Each school sets its application deadline and workstudy earnings limits. Wages vary and are related to the type of work done. You must file the Free Application for Federal Student Aid (FAFSA) to be eligible for this program.

Loans

Many graduate students borrow to finance their graduate programs when other sources of assistance (which do not have to be repaid) prove insufficient. You should always read and understand the terms of any loan program before submitting your application.

FEDERAL DIRECT LOANS

Federal Direct Loans. The Federal Direct Loan Program offers a variable-fixed interest rate loan to graduate students with the Department of Education acting as the lender. Students receive a new rate with each new loan, but that rate is fixed for the life of the loan. Beginning with loans made on or after July 1, 2013, the interest rate for loans made each July 1st to June 30th period are determined based on the last 10-year Treasury note auction prior to June 1st of that year, plus an added percentage. The interest rate can be no higher than 9.5%.

Beginning July 1, 2012, the Federal Direct Loan for graduate students is an unsubsidized loan. Under the *unsubsidized* program, the grad borrower pays the interest on the loan from the day proceeds are issued and is responsible for paying interest during all periods. If the borrower chooses not to pay the interest while in school, or during the grace periods, deferment, or forbearance, the interest accrues and will be capitalized.

Graduate students may borrow up to $20,500 per year through the Direct Loan Program, up to a cumulative maximum of $138,500, including undergraduate borrowing. No more than $65,500 of the $138,500 can be from subsidized loans, including loans the grad borrower may have received for periods of enrollment that began before July 1, 2012, or for prior undergraduate borrowing. You may borrow up to the cost of attendance at the school in which you are enrolled or will attend, minus estimated financial assistance from other federal, state, and private sources, up to a maximum of $20,500. Grad borrowers who reach the aggregate loan limit over the course of their education cannot receive additional loans; however, if they repay some of their loans to bring the outstanding balance below the aggregate limit, they could be eligible to borrow again, up to that limit.

Under the *subsidized* Federal Direct Loan Program, repayment begins six months after your last date of enrollment on at least a half-time basis. Under the *unsubsidized* program, repayment of interest begins within thirty days from disbursement of the loan proceeds, and repayment of the principal begins six months after your last enrollment on at least a half-time basis. Some borrowers may choose to defer interest payments while they are in school. The accrued interest is added to the loan balance when the borrower begins repayment. There are several repayment options.

Federal Perkins Loans. The Federal Perkins Loan is available to students demonstrating financial need and is administered directly by the school. Not all schools have these funds, and some may award them to undergraduates only. Eligibility is determined from the information you provide on the FAFSA. The school will notify you of your eligibility.

Eligible graduate students may borrow up to $8,000 per year, up to a maximum of $60,000, including undergraduate borrowing (even if your previous Perkins Loans have been repaid). The interest rate for Federal Perkins Loans is 5 percent, and no interest accrues while you remain in school at least half-time. Students who are attending less than half-time need to check with their school to determine the length of their grace period. There are no guarantee, loan, or disbursement fees. Repayment begins nine months after your last date of enrollment on at least a half-time basis and may extend over a maximum of ten years with no prepayment penalty.

Federal Direct Graduate PLUS Loans. Effective July 1, 2006, graduate and professional students are eligible for Graduate PLUS loans. This program allows students to borrow up to the cost of attendance, less any other aid received. These loans have a fixed interest rate (7.08% for loans first disbursed on or after July 1, 2019, and before July 1, 2020) and interest begins to accrue at the time of disbursement. Beginning with loans made on or after July 1, 2013, the interest rate for loans made each July 1st to June 30th period are determined based on the last 10-year Treasury note auction prior to June 1st of that year. The interest rate can be no higher than 10.5%. The PLUS loans do involve a credit check; a PLUS borrower may obtain a loan with a cosigner if his or her credit is not good enough. Grad PLUS loans may be deferred while a student is in school and for the six months following a drop below half-time enrollment. For more information, you should contact a representative in your college's financial aid office.

Deferring Your Federal Loan Repayments. If you borrowed under the Federal Direct Loan Program, Federal Direct PLUS Loan Program, or the Federal Perkins Loan Program for previous undergraduate or graduate study, your payments may be deferred when you return to graduate school, depending on when you borrowed and under which program.

There are other deferment options available if you are temporarily unable to repay your loan. Information about these deferments is provided at your entrance and exit interviews. If you believe you are eligible for a deferment of your loan payments, you must contact your lender or loan servicer to request a deferment. The deferment must be filed prior to the time your payment is due, and it must be re-filed when it expires if you remain eligible for deferment at that time.

SUPPLEMENTAL (PRIVATE) LOANS

Many lending institutions offer supplemental loan programs and other financing plans, such as the ones described here, to students seeking additional assistance in meeting their education expenses. Some loan programs target all types of graduate students; others are designed specifically for business, law, or medical students. In addition, you can use private loans not specifically designed for education to help finance your graduate degree.

If you are considering borrowing through a supplemental or private loan program, you should carefully consider the terms and be sure to read the fine print. Check with the program sponsor for the most current terms that will be applicable to the amounts you intend to borrow for graduate study. Most supplemental loan programs for graduate study offer unsubsidized, credit-based loans. In general, a credit-ready borrower is one who has a satisfactory credit history or no credit history at all. A creditworthy borrower generally must pass a credit test to be eligible to borrow or act as a cosigner for the loan funds.

Many supplemental loan programs have minimum and maximum annual loan limits. Some offer amounts equal to the cost of attendance minus any other aid you will receive for graduate study. If you are planning to borrow for several years of graduate study, consider whether there is a cumulative or aggregate limit on the amount you may borrow. Often this cumulative or aggregate limit will include any amounts you borrowed and have not repaid for undergraduate or previous graduate study.

The combination of the annual interest rate, loan fees, and the repayment terms you choose will determine how much you will repay over time. Compare these features in combination before you decide which loan program to use. Some loans offer interest rates that are adjusted monthly, quarterly, or annually. Some offer interest rates that are lower during the in-school, grace, and deferment periods and then increase when you begin repayment. Some programs include a loan origination fee, which is usually deducted from the principal amount you receive when the loan is disbursed and must be repaid along with the interest and other principal when you graduate, withdraw from school, or drop below half-time study. Sometimes the loan fees are reduced if you borrow with a qualified cosigner. Some programs allow you to defer interest and/or principal payments while you are enrolled in graduate school. Many programs allow you to capitalize your interest payments; the interest due on your loan is added to the outstanding balance of your loan, so you don't have to repay immediately, but this increases the amount you owe. Other programs allow you to pay the interest as you go, which reduces the amount you later have to repay. The private loan market is very competitive, and your financial aid office can help you evaluate these programs.

Applying for Need-Based Financial Aid

Schools that award federal and institutional financial assistance based on need will require you to complete the FAFSA and, in some cases, an institutional financial aid application.

If you are applying for federal student assistance, you **must** complete the FAFSA. A service of the U.S. Department of Education, the FAFSA is free to all applicants. Most applicants apply online at **www.fafsa.ed.gov**. Paper applications are available at the financial aid office of your local college.

After your FAFSA information has been processed, you will receive a Student Aid Report (SAR). If you provided an e-mail address on the FAFSA, this will be sent to you electronically; otherwise, it will be mailed to your home address.

Follow the instructions on the SAR if you need to correct information reported on your original application. If your situation changes after you file your FAFSA, contact your financial aid officer to discuss amending your information. You can also appeal your financial aid award if you have extenuating circumstances.

If you would like more information on federal student financial aid, visit the FAFSA website or download the most recent version of *Do You Need Money for College* at www.studentaid.ed.gov/sites/default/files/2019-20-do-you-need-money.pdf. This guide is also available in Spanish.

The U.S. Department of Education also has a toll-free number for questions concerning federal student aid programs. The number is 1-800-4-FED AID (1-800-433-3243). If you are hearing impaired, call toll-free, 1-800-730-8913.

Summary

Remember that these are generalized statements about financial assistance at the graduate level. Because each institution allots its aid differently, you should communicate directly with the school and the specific department of interest to you. It is not unusual, for example, to find that an endowment vested within a specific department supports one or more fellowships. You may fit its requirements and specifications precisely.

Accreditation and Accrediting Agencies

Colleges and universities in the United States, and their individual academic and professional programs, are accredited by nongovernmental agencies concerned with monitoring the quality of education in this country. Agencies with both regional and national jurisdictions grant accreditation to institutions as a whole, while specialized bodies acting on a nationwide basis—often national professional associations—grant accreditation to departments and programs in specific fields.

Institutional and specialized accrediting agencies share the same basic concerns: the purpose an academic unit—whether university or program—has set for itself and how well it fulfills that purpose, the adequacy of its financial and other resources, the quality of its academic offerings, and the level of services it provides. Agencies that grant institutional accreditation take a broader view, of course, and examine university-wide or college-wide services with which a specialized agency may not concern itself.

Both types of agencies follow the same general procedures when considering an application for accreditation. The academic unit prepares a self-evaluation, focusing on the concerns mentioned above and usually including an assessment of both its strengths and weaknesses; a team of representatives of the accrediting body reviews this evaluation, visits the campus, and makes its own report; and finally, the accrediting body makes a decision on the application. Often, even when accreditation is granted, the agency makes a recommendation regarding how the institution or program can improve. All institutions and programs are also reviewed every few years to determine whether they continue to meet established standards; if they do not, they may lose their accreditation.

Accrediting agencies themselves are reviewed and evaluated periodically by the U.S. Department of Education and the Council for Higher Education Accreditation (CHEA). Recognized agencies adhere to certain standards and practices, and their authority in matters of accreditation is widely accepted in the educational community.

This does not mean, however, that accreditation is a simple matter, either for schools wishing to become accredited or for students deciding where to apply. Indeed, in certain fields the very meaning and methods of accreditation are the subject of a good deal of debate. For their part, those applying to graduate school should be aware of the safeguards provided by regional accreditation, especially in terms of degree acceptance and institutional longevity. Beyond this, applicants should understand the role that specialized accreditation plays in their field, as this varies considerably from one discipline to another. In certain professional fields, it is necessary to have graduated from a program that is accredited in order to be eligible for a license to practice, and in some fields the federal government also makes this a hiring requirement. In other disciplines, however, accreditation is not as essential, and there can be excellent programs that are not accredited. In fact, some programs choose not to seek accreditation, although most do.

Institutions and programs that present themselves for accreditation are sometimes granted the status of candidate for accreditation, or what is known as "preaccreditation." This may happen, for example, when an academic unit is too new to have met all the requirements for accreditation. Such status signifies initial recognition and indicates that the school or program in question is working to fulfill all requirements; it does not, however, guarantee that accreditation will be granted.

Institutional Accrediting Agencies—Regional

MIDDLE STATES COMMISSION ON HIGHER EDUCATION

Accredits institutions in Delaware, District of Columbia, Maryland, New Jersey, New York, Pennsylvania, Puerto Rico, and the Virgin Islands.

Dr. Elizabeth Sibolski, President
Middle States Commission on Higher Education
3624 Market Street, Second Floor West
Philadelphia, Pennsylvania 19104
Phone: 267-284-5000
Fax: 215-662-5501
E-mail: info@msche.org
Website: www.msche.org

NEW ENGLAND ASSOCIATION OF SCHOOLS AND COLLEGES

Accredits institutions in Connecticut, Maine, Massachusetts, New Hampshire, Rhode Island, and Vermont.

Dr. Barbara E. Brittingham, President/Director
Commission on Institutions of Higher Education
3 Burlington Woods Drive, Suite 100
Burlington, Massachusetts 01803-4531
Phone: 855-886-3272 or 781-425-7714
Fax: 781-425-1001
E-mail: cihe@neasc.org
Website: https://cihe.neasc.org

THE HIGHER LEARNING COMMISSION

Accredits institutions in Arizona, Arkansas, Colorado, Illinois, Indiana, Iowa, Kansas, Michigan, Minnesota, Missouri, Nebraska, New Mexico, North Dakota, Ohio, Oklahoma, South Dakota, West Virginia, Wisconsin, and Wyoming.

Dr. Barbara Gellman-Danley, President
The Higher Learning Commission
230 South LaSalle Street, Suite 7-500
Chicago, Illinois 60604-1413
Phone: 800-621-7440 or 312-263-0456
Fax: 312-263-7462
E-mail: info@hlcommission.org
Website: www.hlcommission.org

NORTHWEST COMMISSION ON COLLEGES AND UNIVERSITIES

Accredits institutions in Alaska, Idaho, Montana, Nevada, Oregon, Utah, and Washington.

Dr. Sandra E. Elman, President
8060 165th Avenue, NE, Suite 100
Redmond, Washington 98052
Phone: 425-558-4224
Fax: 425-376-0596
E-mail: selman@nwccu.org
Website: www.nwccu.org

SOUTHERN ASSOCIATION OF COLLEGES AND SCHOOLS

Accredits institutions in Alabama, Florida, Georgia, Kentucky, Louisiana, Mississippi, North Carolina, South Carolina, Tennessee, Texas, and Virginia.

Dr. Belle S. Wheelan, President
Commission on Colleges
1866 Southern Lane
Decatur, Georgia 30033-4097
Phone: 404-679-4500 Ext. 4504
Fax: 404-679-4558
E-mail: questions@sacscoc.org
Website: www.sacscoc.org

WESTERN ASSOCIATION OF SCHOOLS AND COLLEGES

Accredits institutions in California, Guam, and Hawaii.

Jamienne S. Studley, President
WASC Senior College and University Commission
985 Atlantic Avenue, Suite 100
Alameda, California 94501
Phone: 510-748-9001
Fax: 510-748-9797
E-mail: wasc@wscuc.org
Website: https://www.wscuc.org/

Institutional Accrediting Agencies—Other

ACCREDITING COUNCIL FOR INDEPENDENT COLLEGES AND SCHOOLS
Michelle Edwards, President
750 First Street NE, Suite 980
Washington, DC 20002-4223
Phone: 202-336-6780
Fax: 202-842-2593
E-mail: info@acics.org
Website: www.acics.org

DISTANCE EDUCATION ACCREDITING COMMISSION (DEAC)
Leah Matthews, Executive Director
1101 17th Street NW, Suite 808
Washington, DC 20036-4704
Phone: 202-234-5100
Fax: 202-332-1386
E-mail: info@deac.org
Website: www.deac.org

Specialized Accrediting Agencies

ACUPUNCTURE AND ORIENTAL MEDICINE
Mark S. McKenzie, LAc MsOM DiplOM, Executive Director
Accreditation Commission for Acupuncture and Oriental Medicine
8941 Aztec Drive, Suite 2
Eden Prairie, Minnesota 55347
Phone: 952-212-2434
Fax: 301-313-0912
E-mail: info@acaom.org
Website: www.acaom.org

ALLIED HEALTH
Kathleen Megivern, Executive Director
Commission on Accreditation of Allied Health Education Programs (CAAHEP)
25400 US Hwy 19 North, Suite 158
Clearwater, Florida 33763
Phone: 727-210-2350
Fax: 727-210-2354
E-mail: mail@caahep.org
Website: www.caahep.org

ART AND DESIGN
Karen P. Moynahan, Executive Director
National Association of Schools of Art and Design (NASAD)
Commission on Accreditation
11250 Roger Bacon Drive, Suite 21
Reston, Virginia 20190-5248
Phone: 703-437-0700
Fax: 703-437-6312
E-mail: info@arts-accredit.org
Website: http://nasad.arts-accredit.org

ATHLETIC TRAINING EDUCATION
Pamela Hansen, CAATE Director of Accreditation
Commission on Accreditation of Athletic Training Education (CAATE)
6850 Austin Center Blvd., Suite 100
Austin, Texas 78731-3184
Phone: 512-733-9700
E-mail: pamela@caate.net
Website: www.caate.net

AUDIOLOGY EDUCATION
Meggan Olek, Director
Accreditation Commission for Audiology Education (ACAE)
11480 Commerce Park Drive, Suite 220
Reston, Virginia 20191
Phone: 202-986-9500
Fax: 202-986-9550
E-mail: info@acaeaccred.org
Website: https://acaeaccred.org/

AVIATION
Dr. Gary J. Northam, President
Aviation Accreditation Board International (AABI)
3410 Skyway Drive
Auburn, Alabama 36830
Phone: 334-844-2431
Fax: 334-844-2432
E-mail: gary.northam@auburn.edu
Website: www.aabi.aero

BUSINESS
Stephanie Bryant, Executive Vice President and Chief Accreditation Officer
AACSB International—The Association to Advance Collegiate Schools of Business
777 South Harbour Island Boulevard, Suite 750
Tampa, Florida 33602
Phone: 813-769-6500
Fax: 813-769-6559
E-mail: stephanie.bryant@aacsb.edu
Website: www.aacsb.edu

BUSINESS EDUCATION
Dr. Phyllis Okrepkie, President
International Assembly for Collegiate Business Education (IACBE)
11374 Strang Line Road
Lenexa, Kansas 66215
Phone: 913-631-3009
Fax: 913-631-9154
E-mail: iacbe@iacbe.org
Website: www.iacbe.org

CHIROPRACTIC
Dr. Craig S. Little, President
Council on Chiropractic Education (CCE)
Commission on Accreditation
8049 North 85th Way
Scottsdale, Arizona 85258-4321
Phone: 480-443-8877 or 888-443-3506
Fax: 480-483-7333
E-mail: cce@cce-usa.org
Website: www.cce-usa.org

CLINICAL LABORATORY SCIENCES
Dianne M. Cearlock, Ph.D., Chief Executive Officer
National Accrediting Agency for Clinical Laboratory Sciences
5600 North River Road, Suite 720
Rosemont, Illinois 60018-5119
Phone: 773-714-8880 or 847-939-3597
Fax: 773-714-8886
E-mail: info@naacls.org
Website: www.naacls.org

CLINICAL PASTORAL EDUCATION
Trace Haythorn, Ph.D., Executive Director/CEO
Association for Clinical Pastoral Education, Inc.
One West Court Square, Suite 325
Decatur, Georgia 30030-2576
Phone: 678-363-6226
Fax: 404-320-0849
E-mail: acpe@acpe.edu
Website: www.acpe.edu

DANCE
Karen P. Moynahan, Executive Director
National Association of Schools of Dance (NASD)
Commission on Accreditation
11250 Roger Bacon Drive, Suite 21
Reston, Virginia 20190-5248
Phone: 703-437-0700
Fax: 703-437-6312
E-mail: info@arts-accredit.org
Website: http://nasd.arts-accredit.org

DENTISTRY
Dr. Kathleen T. O'Loughlin, Executive Director
Commission on Dental Accreditation
American Dental Association
211 East Chicago Avenue
Chicago, Illinois 60611
Phone: 312-440-2500
E-mail: accreditation@ada.org
Website: www.ada.org

DIETETICS AND NUTRITION
Mary B. Gregoire, Ph.D., Executive Director; RD, FADA, FAND
Academy of Nutrition and Dietetics
Accreditation Council for Education in Nutrition and Dietetics (ACEND)
120 South Riverside Plaza
Chicago, Illinois 60606-6995
Phone: 800-877-1600 or 312-899-0040
E-mail: acend@eatright.org
Website: www.eatright.org/cade

EDUCATION PREPARATION
Christopher Koch, President
Council for the Accreditation of Educator Preparation (CAEP)
1140 19th Street NW, Suite 400
Washington, DC 20036
Phone: 202-223-0077
Fax: 202-296-6620
E-mail: caep@caepnet.org
Website: www.caepnet.org

ENGINEERING
Michael Milligan, Ph.D., PE, Executive Director
Accreditation Board for Engineering and Technology, Inc. (ABET)
415 North Charles Street
Baltimore, Maryland 21201
Phone: 410-347-7700
E-mail: accreditation@abet.org
Website: www.abet.org

FORENSIC SCIENCES
Nancy J. Jackson, Director of Development and Accreditation
American Academy of Forensic Sciences (AAFS)
Forensic Science Education Program Accreditation Commission (FEPAC)
410 North 21st Street
Colorado Springs, Colorado 80904
Phone: 719-636-1100
Fax: 719-636-1993
E-mail: njackson@aafs.org
Website: www.fepac-edu.org

FORESTRY
Carol L. Redelsheimer
Director of Science and Education
Society of American Foresters
10100 Laureate Way
Bethesda, Maryland 20814-2198
Phone: 301-897-8720 or 866-897-8720
Fax: 301-897-3690
E-mail: membership@safnet.org
Website: www.eforester.com

HEALTHCARE MANAGEMENT
Commission on Accreditation of Healthcare Management Education (CAHME)
Anthony Stanowski, President and CEO
6110 Executive Boulevard, Suite 614
Rockville, Maryland 20852
Phone: 301-298-1820
E-mail: info@cahme.org
Website: www.cahme.org

HEALTH INFORMATICS AND HEALTH MANAGEMENT
Angela Kennedy, EdD, MBA, RHIA, Chief Executive Officer
Commission on Accreditation for Health Informatics and Information Management Education (CAHIIM)
233 North Michigan Avenue, 21st Floor
Chicago, Illinois 60601-5800
Phone: 312-233-1134
Fax: 312-233-1948
E-mail: info@cahiim.org
Website: www.cahiim.org

HUMAN SERVICE EDUCATION
Dr. Elaine Green, President
Council for Standards in Human Service Education (CSHSE)
3337 Duke Street
Alexandria, Virginia 22314
Phone: 571-257-3959
E-mail: info@cshse.org
Website: www.cshse.org

INTERIOR DESIGN
Holly Mattson, Executive Director
Council for Interior Design Accreditation
206 Grandview Avenue, Suite 350
Grand Rapids, Michigan 49503-4014
Phone: 616-458-0400
Fax: 616-458-0460
E-mail: info@accredit-id.org
Website: www.accredit-id.org

JOURNALISM AND MASS COMMUNICATIONS
Patricia Thompson, Executive Director
Accrediting Council on Education in Journalism and Mass Communications (ACEJMC)
201 Bishop Hall
P.O. Box 1848
University, MS 38677-1848
Phone: 662-915-5504
E-mail: pthomps1@olemiss.edu
Website: www.acejmc.org

LANDSCAPE ARCHITECTURE
Nancy Somerville, Executive Vice President, CEO
American Society of Landscape Architects (ASLA)
636 Eye Street, NW
Washington, DC 20001-3736
Phone: 202-898-2444
Fax: 202-898-1185
E-mail: info@asla.org
Website: www.asla.org

LAW
Barry Currier, Managing Director of Accreditation & Legal Education
American Bar Association
321 North Clark Street, 21st Floor
Chicago, Illinois 60654
Phone: 312-988-6738
Fax: 312-988-5681
E-mail: legaled@americanbar.org
Website: https://www.americanbar.org/groups/legal_education/accreditation.html

LIBRARY
Karen O'Brien, Director
Office for Accreditation
American Library Association
50 East Huron Street
Chicago, Illinois 60611-2795
Phone: 800-545-2433, ext. 2432 or 312-280-2432
Fax: 312-280-2433
E-mail: accred@ala.org
Website: http://www.ala.org/aboutala/offices/accreditation/

MARRIAGE AND FAMILY THERAPY
Tanya A. Tamarkin, Director of Educational Affairs
Commission on Accreditation for Marriage and Family Therapy
    Education (COAMFTE)
American Association for Marriage and Family Therapy
112 South Alfred Street
Alexandria, Virginia 22314-3061
Phone: 703-838-9808
Fax: 703-838-9805
E-mail: coa@aamft.org
Website: www.aamft.org

MEDICAL ILLUSTRATION
Kathleen Megivern, Executive Director
Commission on Accreditation of Allied Health Education Programs
    (CAAHEP)
25400 US Highway 19 North, Suite 158
Clearwater, Florida 33756
Phone: 727-210-2350
Fax: 727-210-2354
E-mail: mail@caahep.org
Website: www.caahep.org

MEDICINE
Liaison Committee on Medical Education (LCME)
Robert B. Hash, M.D., LCME Secretary
American Medical Association
Council on Medical Education
330 North Wabash Avenue, Suite 39300
Chicago, Illinois 60611-5885
Phone: 312-464-4933
E-mail: lcme@aamc.org
Website: www.ama-assn.org

Liaison Committee on Medical Education (LCME)
Heather Lent, M.A., Director
Accreditation Services
Association of American Medical Colleges
655 K Street, NW
Washington, DC 20001-2399
Phone: 202-828-0596
E-mail: lcme@aamc.org
Website: www.lcme.org

MUSIC
Karen P. Moynahan, Executive Director
National Association of Schools of Music (NASM)
Commission on Accreditation
11250 Roger Bacon Drive, Suite 21
Reston, Virginia 20190-5248
Phone: 703-437-0700
Fax: 703-437-6312
E-mail: info@arts-accredit.org
Website: http://nasm.arts-accredit.org/

NATUROPATHIC MEDICINE
Daniel Seitz, J.D., Ed.D., Executive Director
Council on Naturopathic Medical Education
P.O. Box 178
Great Barrington, Massachusetts 01230
Phone: 413-528-8877
E-mail: https://cnme.org/contact-us/
Website: www.cnme.org

NURSE ANESTHESIA
Francis R.Gerbasi, Ph.D., CRNA, COA Executive Director
Council on Accreditation of Nurse Anesthesia Educational Programs
    (CoA-NAEP)
American Association of Nurse Anesthetists
222 South Prospect Avenue
Park Ridge, Illinois 60068-4001
Phone: 847-655-1160
Fax: 847-692-7137
E-mail: accreditation@coa.us.com
Website: http://www.coacrna.org

NURSE EDUCATION
Jennifer L. Butlin, Executive Director
Commission on Collegiate Nursing Education (CCNE)
One Dupont Circle, NW, Suite 530
Washington, DC 20036-1120
Phone: 202-887-6791
Fax: 202-887-8476
E-mail: jbutlin@aacn.nche.edu
Website: www.aacn.nche.edu/accreditation

Marsal P. Stoll, Chief Executive Officer
Accreditation Commission for Education in Nursing (ACEN)
3343 Peachtree Road, NE, Suite 850
Atlanta, Georgia 30326
Phone: 404-975-5000
Fax: 404-975-5020
E-mail: mstoll@acenursing.org
Website: www.acenursing.org

NURSE MIDWIFERY
Heather L. Maurer, M.A., Executive Director
Accreditation Commission for Midwifery Education (ACME)
American College of Nurse-Midwives
8403 Colesville Road, Suite 1550
Silver Spring, Maryland 20910
Phone: 240-485-1800
Fax: 240-485-1818
E-mail: info@acnm.org
Website: www.midwife.org/Program-Accreditation

NURSE PRACTITIONER
Gay Johnson, CEO
National Association of Nurse Practitioners in Women's Health
Council on Accreditation
505 C Street, NE
Washington, DC 20002
Phone: 202-543-9693 Ext. 1
Fax: 202-543-9858
E-mail: info@npwh.org
Website: www.npwh.org

NURSING
Marsal P. Stoll, Chief Executive Director
Accreditation Commission for Education in Nursing (ACEN)
3343 Peachtree Road, NE, Suite 850
Atlanta, Georgia 30326
Phone: 404-975-5000
Fax: 404-975-5020
E-mail: info@acenursing.org
Website: www.acenursing.org

OCCUPATIONAL THERAPY
Heather Stagliano, DHSc, OTR/L, Executive Director
The American Occupational Therapy Association, Inc.
4720 Montgomery Lane, Suite 200
Bethesda, Maryland 20814-3449
Phone: 301-652-6611 Ext. 2682
TDD: 800-377-8555
Fax: 240-762-5150
E-mail: accred@aota.org
Website: www.aoteonline.org

OPTOMETRY
Joyce L. Urbeck, Administrative Director
Accreditation Council on Optometric Education (ACOE)
American Optometric Association
243 North Lindbergh Boulevard
St. Louis, Missouri 63141-7881
Phone: 314-991-4100, Ext. 4246
Fax: 314-991-4101
E-mail: accredit@aoa.org
Website: www.theacoe.org

OSTEOPATHIC MEDICINE
Director, Department of Accreditation
Commission on Osteopathic College Accreditation (COCA)
American Osteopathic Association
142 East Ontario Street
Chicago, Illinois 60611
Phone: 312-202-8048
Fax: 312-202-8202
E-mail: predoc@osteopathic.org
Website: www.aoacoca.org

PHARMACY
Peter H. Vlasses, PharmD, Executive Director
Accreditation Council for Pharmacy Education
135 South LaSalle Street, Suite 4100
Chicago, Illinois 60603-4810
Phone: 312-664-3575
Fax: 312-664-4652
E-mail: csinfo@acpe-accredit.org
Website: www.acpe-accredit.org

PHYSICAL THERAPY
Sandra Wise, Senior Director
Commission on Accreditation in Physical Therapy Education (CAPTE)
American Physical Therapy Association (APTA)
1111 North Fairfax Street
Alexandria, Virginia 22314-1488
Phone: 703-706-3245
Fax: 703-706-3387
E-mail: accreditation@apta.org
Website: www.capteonline.org

PHYSICIAN ASSISTANT STUDIES
Sharon L. Luke, Executive Director
Accredittion Review Commission on Education for the Physician
    Assistant, Inc. (ARC-PA)
12000 Findley Road, Suite 275
Johns Creek, Georgia 30097
Phone: 770-476-1224
Fax: 770-476-1738
E-mail: arc-pa@arc-pa.org
Website: www.arc-pa.org

PLANNING
Jesmarie Soto Johnson, Executive Director
American Institute of Certified Planners/Association of Collegiate
    Schools of Planning/American Planning Association
Planning Accreditation Board (PAB)
2334 West Lawrence Avenue, Suite 209
Chicago, Illinois 60625
Phone: 773-334-7200
E-mail: smerits@planningaccreditationboard.org
Website: www.planningaccreditationboard.org

PODIATRIC MEDICINE
Heather Stagliano, OTR/L, DHSc, Executive Director
Council on Podiatric Medical Education (CPME)
American Podiatric Medical Association (APMA)
9312 Old Georgetown Road
Bethesda, Maryland 20814-1621
Phone: 301-581-9200
Fax: 301-571-4903
Website: www.cpme.org

PSYCHOLOGY AND COUNSELING
Jacqueline Remondet, Associate Executive Director, CEO of the
Accrediting Unit,
Office of Program Consultation and Accreditation
American Psychological Association
750 First Street, NE
Washington, DC 20002-4202
Phone: 202-336-5979 or 800-374-2721
TDD/TTY: 202-336-6123
Fax: 202-336-5978
E-mail: apaaccred@apa.org
Website: www.apa.org/ed/accreditation

Kelly Coker, Executive Director
Council for Accreditation of Counseling and Related Educational
    Programs (CACREP)
1001 North Fairfax Street, Suite 510
Alexandria, Virginia 22314
Phone: 703-535-5990
Fax: 703-739-6209
E-mail: cacrep@cacrep.org
Website: www.cacrep.org

Richard M. McFall, Executive Director
Psychological Clinical Science Accreditation System (PCSAS)
1101 East Tenth Street
IU Psychology Building
Bloomington, Indiana 47405-7007
Phone: 812-856-2570
Fax: 812-322-5545
E-mail: rmmcfall@pcsas.org
Website: www.pcsas.org

PUBLIC HEALTH
Laura Rasar King, M.P.H., MCHES, Executive Director
Council on Education for Public Health
1010 Wayne Avenue, Suite 220
Silver Spring, Maryland 20910
Phone: 202-789-1050
Fax: 202-789-1895
E-mail: Lking@ceph.org
Website: www.ceph.org

PUBLIC POLICY, AFFAIRS AND ADMINISTRATION
Crystal Calarusse, Chief Accreditation Officer
Commission on Peer Review and Accreditation
Network of Schools of Public Policy, Affairs, and Administration
(NASPAA-COPRA)
1029 Vermont Avenue, NW, Suite 1100
Washington, DC 20005
Phone: 202-628-8965
Fax: 202-626-4978
E-mail: copra@naspaa.org
Website: accreditation.naspaa.org

RADIOLOGIC TECHNOLOGY
Leslie Winter, Chief Executive Officer Joint Review Committee on
Education in Radiologic Technology (JRCERT)
20 North Wacker Drive, Suite 2850
Chicago, Illinois 60606-3182
Phone: 312-704-5300
Fax: 312-704-5304
E-mail: mail@jrcert.org
Website: www.jrcert.org

REHABILITATION EDUCATION
Frank Lane, Ph.D., Executive Director
Council for Accreditation of Counseling and Related Educational
    Programs (CACREP)
1001 North Fairfax Street, Suite 510
Alexandria, Virginia 22314
Phone: 703-535-5990
Fax: 703-739-6209
E-mail: cacrep@cacrep.org
Website: www.cacrep.org

RESPIRATORY CARE
Thomas Smalling, Executive Director
Commission on Accreditation for Respiratory Care (CoARC)
1248 Harwood Road
Bedford, Texas 76021-4244
Phone: 817-283-2835
Fax: 817-354-8519
E-mail: tom@coarc.com
Website: www.coarc.com

SOCIAL WORK
Dr. Stacey Borasky, Director of Accreditation
Office of Social Work Accreditation
Council on Social Work Education
1701 Duke Street, Suite 200
Alexandria, Virginia 22314
Phone: 703-683-8080
Fax: 703-519-2078
E-mail: info@cswe.org
Website: www.cswe.org

SPEECH-LANGUAGE PATHOLOGY AND AUDIOLOGY
Kimberlee Moore, Accreditation Executive Director
American Speech-Language-Hearing Association
Council on Academic Accreditation in Audiology and Speech-Language
    Pathology
2200 Research Boulevard #310
Rockville, Maryland 20850-3289
Phone: 301-296-5700
Fax: 301-296-8750
E-mail: accreditation@asha.org
Website: http://caa.asha.org

TEACHER EDUCATION
Christopher A. Koch, President
National Council for Accreditation of Teacher Education (NCATE)
Teacher Education Accreditation Council (TEAC)
1140 19th Street, Suite 400
Washington, DC 20036
Phone: 202-223-0077
Fax: 202-296-6620
E-mail: caep@caepnet.org
Website: www.ncate.org

TECHNOLOGY
Michale S. McComis, Ed.D., Executive Director
Accrediting Commission of Career Schools and Colleges
2101 Wilson Boulevard, Suite 302
Arlington, Virginia 22201
Phone: 703-247-4212
Fax: 703-247-4533
E-mail: mccomis@accsc.org
Website: www.accsc.org

TECHNOLOGY, MANAGEMENT, AND APPLIED ENGINEERING
Kelly Schild, Director of Accreditation
The Association of Technology, Management, and Applied Engineering
(ATMAE)
275 N. York Street, Suite 401
Elmhurst, Illinois 60126
Phone: 630-433-4514
Fax: 630-563-9181
E-mail: Kelly@atmae.org
Website: www.atmae.org

THEATER
Karen P. Moynahan, Executive Director
National Association of Schools of Theatre Commission on
    Accreditation
11250 Roger Bacon Drive, Suite 21
Reston, Virginia 20190
Phone: 703-437-0700
Fax: 703-437-6312
E-mail: info@arts-accredit.org
Website: http://nast.arts-accredit.org/

THEOLOGY
Dr. Bernard Fryshman, Executive VP
Emeritus and Interim Executive Director
Association of Advanced Rabbinical and Talmudic Schools (AARTS)
Accreditation Commission
11 Broadway, Suite 405
New York, New York 10004
Phone: 212-363-1991
Fax: 212-533-5335
E-mail: k.sharfman.aarts@gmail.com

Frank Yamada, Executive Director
Association of Theological Schools in the United States and Canada
    (ATS)
Commission on Accrediting
10 Summit Park Drive
Pittsburgh, Pennsylvania 15275
Phone: 412-788-6505
Fax: 412-788-6510
E-mail: ats@ats.edu
Website: www.ats.edu

Dr. Timothy Eaton, President
Transnational Association of Christian Colleges and Schools (TRACS)
Accreditation Commission
15935 Forest Road
Forest, Virginia 24551
Phone: 434-525-9539
Fax: 434-525-9538
E-mail: info@tracs.org
Website: www.tracs.org

VETERINARY MEDICINE
Dr. Karen Brandt, Director of Education and Research
American Veterinary Medical Association (AVMA)
Council on Education
1931 North Meacham Road, Suite 100
Schaumburg, Illinois 60173-4360
Phone: 847-925-8070 Ext. 6674
Fax: 847-285-5732
E-mail: info@avma.org
Website: www.avma.org

How to Use These Guides

As you identify the particular programs and institutions that interest you, you can use both the *Graduate & Professional Programs: An Overview* volume and the specialized volumes in the series to obtain detailed information.

- *Graduate Programs in the Biological/Biomedical Sciences & Health-Related Professions*
- *Graduate Programs in Business, Education, Information Studies, Law & Social Work*
- *Graduate Programs in Engineering & Applied Sciences*
- *Graduate Programs the Humanities, Arts & Social Sciences*
- *Graduate Programs in the Physical Sciences, Mathematics, Agricultural Sciences, the Environment & Natural Resources*

Each of the specialized volumes in the series is divided into sections that contain one or more directories devoted to programs in a particular field. If you do not find a directory devoted to your field of interest in a specific volume, consult "Directories and Subject Areas" (located at the end of each volume). After you have identified the correct volume, consult the "Directories and Subject Areas in This Book" index, which shows (as does the more general directory) what directories cover subjects not specifically named in a directory or section title.

Each of the specialized volumes in the series has a number of general directories. These directories have entries for the largest unit at an institution granting graduate degrees in that field. For example, the general Engineering and Applied Sciences directory in the *Graduate Programs in Engineering & Applied Sciences* volume consists of **Profiles** for colleges, schools, and departments of engineering and applied sciences.

General directories are followed by other directories, or sections, that give more detailed information about programs in particular areas of the general field that has been covered. The general Engineering and Applied Sciences directory, in the previous example, is followed by nineteen sections with directories in specific areas of engineering, such as Chemical Engineering, Industrial/Management Engineering, and Mechanical Engineering.

Because of the broad nature of many fields, any system of organization is bound to involve a certain amount of overlap. Environmental studies, for example, is a field whose various aspects are studied in several types of departments and schools. Readers interested in such studies will find information on relevant programs in the *Graduate Programs in the Biological/Biomedical Sciences & Health-Related Professions* volume under Ecology and Environmental Biology and Environmental and Occupational Health; in the *Graduate Programs in the Physical Sciences, Mathematics, Agricultural Sciences, the Environment & Natural Resources* volume under Environmental Management and Policy and Natural Resources; and in the *Graduate Programs in Engineering & Applied Sciences* volume under Energy Management and Policy and Environmental Engineering. To help you find all of the programs of interest to you, the introduction to each section within the specialized volumes includes, if applicable, a paragraph suggesting other sections and directories with information on related areas of study.

Directory of Institutions with Programs in Engineering and Applied Sciences

This directory lists institutions in alphabetical order and includes beneath each name the academic fields in which each institution offers graduate programs. The degree level in each field is also indicated, provided that the institution has supplied that information in response to Peterson's Annual Survey of Graduate and Professional Institutions.

An M indicates that a master's degree program is offered; a D indicates that a doctoral degree program is offered; an O signifies that other advanced degrees (e.g., certificates or specialist degrees) are offered; and an * (asterisk) indicates that a **Close-Up** and/or **Display** is located in this volume. See the index, "Close-Ups and Displays," for the specific page number.

Profiles of Academic and Professional Programs in the Specialized Volumes

Each section of **Profiles** has a table of contents that lists the Program Directories, **Displays**, and **Close-Ups**. Program Directories consist of the **Profiles** of programs in the relevant fields, with **Displays** following if programs have chosen to include them. **Close-Ups,** which are more individualized statements, are also listed for those graduate schools or programs that have chosen to submit them.

The **Profiles** found in the 500 directories in the specialized volumes provide basic data about the graduate units in capsule form for quick reference. To make these directories as useful as possible, **Profiles** are generally listed for an institution's smallest academic unit within a subject area. In other words, if an institution has a College of Liberal Arts that administers many related programs, the **Profile** for the individual program (e.g., Program in History), not the entire College, appears in the directory.

Some institutions maintain a "Premium Profile" at Peterson's where prospective students can find more in-depth school programs descriptions and information. You can learn more about those schools by visiting **www.petersons.com.**

There are some programs that do not fit into any current directory and are not given individual **Profiles**. The directory structure is reviewed annually in order to keep this number to a minimum and to accommodate major trends in graduate education.

The following outline describes the **Profile** information found in the guides and explains how best to use that information. Any item that does not apply to or was not provided by a graduate unit is omitted from its listing. The format of the **Profiles** is constant, making it easy to compare one institution with another and one program with another.

Identifying Information. The institution's name, in boldface type, is followed by a complete listing of the administrative structure for that field of study. (For example, University of Akron, Buchtel College of Arts and Sciences, Department of Theoretical and Applied Mathematics, Program in Mathematics.) The last unit listed is the one to which all information in the **Profile** pertains. The institution's city, state, and ZIP code follow.

Offerings. Each field of study offered by the unit is listed with all postbaccalaureate degrees awarded. Degrees that are not preceded by a specific concentration are awarded in the general field listed in the unit name. Frequently, fields of study are broken down into subspecializations, and those appear following the degrees awarded; for example, "Offerings in secondary education (M.Ed.), including English education, mathematics education, science education." Students enrolled in the M.Ed. program would be able to specialize in any of the three fields mentioned.

Professional Accreditation. Some **Profiles** indicate whether a program is professionally accredited. Because it is possible for a program to receive or lose professional accreditation at any time, students entering fields in which accreditation is important to a career should verify the status of programs by contacting either the chairperson or the appropriate accrediting association.

Jointly Offered Degrees. Explanatory statements concerning programs that are offered in cooperation with other institutions are included in the list of degrees offered. This occurs most commonly on a regional basis (for example, two state universities offering a cooperative Ph.D. in special education) or where the specialized nature of the institutions encourages joint efforts (a J.D./M.B.A. offered by a law school at an institution with no formal business programs and an institution with a business school but lacking a law school). Only programs that are truly cooperative are listed; those involving only limited course work at another institution are not. Interested students should contact the heads of such units for further information.

Program Availability. This may include the following: part-time, evening/weekend, online only, blended/hybrid learning, and/or minimal on-campus study. When information regarding the availability of part-time or evening/weekend study appears in the **Profile**, it means that students are able to earn a degree exclusively through such study. Blended/hybrid learning describes those courses in which some traditional in-class time has been replaced by online learning activities. Hybrid courses take advantage of the best features of both face-to-face and online learning.

Faculty. Figures on the number of faculty members actively involved with graduate students through teaching or research are separated into full- and part-time as well as men and women whenever the information has been supplied.

Students. Figures for the number of students enrolled in graduate and professional programs pertain to the semester of highest enrollment from the 2019-20 academic year. These figures are broken down into full- and part-time and men and women whenever the data have been supplied. Information on the number of matriculated students enrolled in the unit who are members of a minority group or are international students appears here. The average age of the matriculated students is followed by the number of applicants, the percentage accepted, and the number enrolled for fall 2019.

Degrees Awarded. The number of degrees awarded in the calendar year is listed. Many doctoral programs offer a terminal master's degree if students leave the program after completing only part of the requirements for a doctoral degree; that is indicated here. All degrees are classified into one of four types: master's, doctoral, first professional, and other advanced degrees. A unit may award one or several degrees at a given level; however, the data are only collected by type and may therefore represent several different degree programs.

Degree Requirements. The information in this section is also broken down by type of degree, and all information for a degree level pertains to all degrees of that type unless otherwise specified. Degree requirements are collected in a simplified form to provide some very basic information on the nature of the program and on foreign language, thesis or dissertation, comprehensive exam, and registration requirements. Many units also provide a short list of additional requirements, such as fieldwork or an internship. For complete information on graduation requirements, contact the graduate school or program directly.

Entrance Requirements. Entrance requirements are broken down into the four degree levels of master's, doctoral, first professional, and other advanced degrees. Within each level, information may be provided in two basic categories: entrance exams and other requirements. The entrance exams are identified by the standard acronyms used by the testing agencies, unless they are not well known. Other entrance requirements are quite varied, but they often contain an undergraduate or graduate grade point average (GPA). Unless otherwise stated, the GPA is calculated on a 4.0 scale and is listed as a minimum required for admission. Additional exam requirements/recommendations for international students may be listed here. Application deadlines for domestic and international students, the application fee, and whether electronic applications are accepted may be listed here. Note that the deadline should be used for reference only; these dates are subject to change, and students interested in applying should always contact the graduate unit directly about application procedures and deadlines.

Expenses. The typical cost of study for the 2019-20 academic year (2018-19 if 2019-20 figures were not available) is given in two basic categories: tuition and fees. Cost of study may be quite complex at a graduate institution. There are often sliding scales for part-time study, a different cost for first-year students, and other variables that make it impossible to completely cover the cost of study for each graduate program. To provide the most usable information, figures are given for full-time study for a full year where available and for part-time study in terms of a per-unit rate (per credit, per semester hour, etc.). Occasionally, variances may be noted in tuition and fees for reasons such as the type of program, whether courses are taken during the day or evening, whether courses are at the master's or doctoral level, or other institution-specific reasons. Respondents were also given the opportunity to provide more specific and detailed tuition and fees information at the unit level. When provided, this information will appear in

place of any typical costs entered elsewhere on the university-level survey. Expenses are usually subject to change; for exact costs at any given time, contact your chosen schools and programs directly. Keep in mind that the tuition of Canadian institutions is usually given in Canadian dollars.

Financial Support. This section contains data on the number of awards administered by the institution and given to graduate students during the 2019-20 academic year. The first figure given represents the total number of students receiving financial support enrolled in that unit. If the unit has provided information on graduate appointments, these are broken down into three major categories: fellowships give money to graduate students to cover the cost of study and living expenses and are not based on a work obligation or research commitment, research assistantships provide stipends to graduate students for assistance in a formal research project with a faculty member, and teaching assistantships provide stipends to graduate students for teaching or for assisting faculty members in teaching undergraduate classes. Within each category, figures are given for the total number of awards, the average yearly amount per award, and whether full or partial tuition reimbursements are awarded. In addition to graduate appointments, the availability of several other financial aid sources is covered in this section. Tuition waivers are routinely part of a graduate appointment, but units sometimes waive part or all of a student's tuition even if a graduate appointment is not available. Federal Work Study is made available to students who demonstrate need and meet the federal guidelines; this form of aid normally includes 10 or more hours of work per week in an office of the institution. Institutionally sponsored loans are low-interest loans available to graduate students to cover both educational and living expenses. Career-related internships or fieldwork offer money to students who are participating in a formal off-campus research project or practicum. Grants, scholarships, traineeships, unspecified assistantships, and other awards may also be noted. The availability of financial support to part-time students is also indicated here.

Some programs list the financial aid application deadline and the forms that need to be completed for students to be eligible for financial awards. There are two forms: FAFSA, the Free Application for Federal Student Aid, which is required for federal aid, and the CSS PROFILE®.

Faculty Research. Each unit has the opportunity to list several keyword phrases describing the current research involving faculty members and graduate students. Space limitations prevent the unit from listing complete information on all research programs. The total expenditure for funded research from the previous academic year may also be included.

Unit Head and Application Contact. The head of the graduate program for each unit may be listed with academic title, phone and fax numbers, and e-mail address. In addition to the unit head's contact information, many graduate programs also list a separate contact for application and admission information, followed by the graduate school, program, or department's website. If no unit head or application contact is given, you should contact the overall institution for information on graduate admissions.

Displays and Close-Ups

Any **Displays** and **Close-Ups** are supplementary insertions submitted by deans, chairs, and other administrators who wish to offer an additional, more individualized statement to readers. A number of graduate school and program administrators have attached a **Display** ad near the **Profile** listing. Here you will find information that an institution or program wants to emphasize. The **Close-Ups** are by their very nature more expansive and flexible than the **Profiles**, and the administrators who have written them may emphasize different aspects of their programs. All of the **Close-Ups** are organized in the same way (with the exception of a few that describe research and training opportunities instead of degree programs), and in each one you will find information on the same basic topics, such as programs of study, research facilities, tuition and fees, financial aid, and application procedures. If an institution or program has submitted a **Close-Up**, a boldface cross-reference appears below its **Profile**. As with the **Displays**, all of the **Close-Ups** in the guides have been submitted by choice; the absence of a **Display** or **Close-Up** does not reflect any type of editorial judgment on the part of Peterson's, and their presence in the guides should not be taken as an indication of status, quality, or approval. Statements regarding a university's objectives and accomplishments are a reflection of its own beliefs and are not the opinions of the Peterson's editors.

Appendixes

This section contains two appendixes. The first, "Institutional Changes Since the 2020 Edition," lists institutions that have closed, merged, or changed their name or status since the last edition of the guides. The second, "Abbreviations Used in the Guides," gives abbreviations of degree names, along with what those abbreviations stand for. These appendixes are identical in all six volumes of **Peterson's Graduate and Professional Programs**.

Indexes

There are three indexes presented here typically. When present, the first index, "Close-Ups and Displays," gives page references for all programs that have chosen to place **Close-Ups** and **Displays** in this volume. It is arranged alphabetically by institution; within institutions, the arrangement is alphabetical by subject area. It is not an index to all programs in the book's directories of **Profiles**; readers must refer to the directories themselves for **Profile** information on programs that have not submitted the additional, more individualized statements. The next index, "Directories and Subject Areas in Other Books in This Series", gives book references for the directories in the specialized volumes and also includes cross-references for subject area names not used in the directory structure, for example, "Computing Technology (see Computer Science)." The last index, "Directories and Subject Areas in This Book," gives page references for the directories in this volume and cross-references for subject area names not used in this volume's directory structure.

Data Collection Procedures

The information published in the directories and Profiles of all the books is collected through Peterson's Annual Survey of Graduate and Professional Institutions. The survey is sent each spring to nearly 2,300 institutions offering postbaccalaureate degree programs, including accredited institutions in the United States, U.S. territories, and Canada and those institutions outside the United States that are accredited by U.S. accrediting bodies. Deans and other administrators complete these surveys, providing information on programs in the 500 academic and professional fields covered in the guides as well as overall institutional information. While every effort has been made to ensure the accuracy and completeness of the data, information is sometimes unavailable or changes occur after publication deadlines. All usable information received in time for publication has been included. The omission of any particular item from a directory or Profile signifies either that the item is not applicable to the institution or program or that information was not available. Profiles of programs scheduled to begin during the 2019-20 academic year cannot, obviously, include statistics on enrollment or, in many cases, the number of faculty members. If no usable data were submitted by an institution, its name, address, and program name appear in order to indicate the availability of graduate work.

Criteria for Inclusion in This Guide

To be included in this guide, an institution must have full accreditation or be a candidate for accreditation (preaccreditation) status by an institutional or specialized accrediting body recognized by the U.S. Department of Education or the Council for Higher Education Accreditation (CHEA). Institutional accrediting bodies, which review each institution as a whole, include the six regional associations of schools and colleges (Middle States, New England, North Central, Northwest, Southern, and Western), each of which is responsible for a specified portion of the United States and its territories. Other institutional accrediting bodies are national in scope and accredit specific kinds of institutions (e.g., Bible colleges, independent colleges, and rabbinical and Talmudic schools). Program registration by the New York State Board of Regents is considered to be the equivalent of institutional accreditation, since the board requires that all programs offered by an institution meet its standards before recognition is granted. A Canadian institution must be chartered and authorized to grant degrees by the provincial government, affiliated with a chartered institution, or accredited by a recognized U.S. accrediting body. This guide also includes institutions outside the United States that are accredited by these U.S. accrediting bodies. There are recognized specialized or professional accrediting bodies in more than fifty different fields, each of which is authorized to accredit institutions or specific programs in its particular field. For specialized institutions that offer programs in one field only, we designate this to be the equivalent of institutional accreditation. A full explanation of the accrediting process and complete information on recognized institutional (regional and national) and specialized accrediting bodies can be found online at **www.chea.org** or at **www.ed.gov/admins/finaid/accred/index.html.**

DIRECTORY OF INSTITUTIONS WITH PROGRAMS IN ENGINEERING & APPLIED SCIENCES

ACADEMY OF ART UNIVERSITY
Game Design and
   Development — M

ACADIA UNIVERSITY
Computer Science — M

ADELPHI UNIVERSITY
Biotechnology — M
Health Informatics — M,O

AIR FORCE INSTITUTE OF TECHNOLOGY
Aerospace/Aeronautical
   Engineering — M,D
Computer Engineering — M,D
Computer Science — M,D
Electrical Engineering — M,D
Engineering and Applied
   Sciences—General — M,D
Engineering Management — M
Engineering Physics — M,D
Environmental Engineering — M
Management of Technology — M,D
Materials Sciences — M,D
Nuclear Engineering — M,D
Operations Research — M,D
Systems Engineering — M,D

ALABAMA AGRICULTURAL AND MECHANICAL UNIVERSITY
Computer Science — M
Engineering and Applied
   Sciences—General — M,D
Materials Engineering — M
Materials Sciences — M,D

ALASKA PACIFIC UNIVERSITY
Telecommunications
   Management — M

ALCORN STATE UNIVERSITY
Computer Science — M
Information Science — M

ALFRED UNIVERSITY
Bioengineering — M,D
Ceramic Sciences and
   Engineering — M,D
Electrical Engineering — M,D
Engineering and Applied
   Sciences—General — M,D
Materials Sciences — M,D
Mechanical Engineering — M,D

AMERICAN COLLEGE DUBLIN
Energy Management and
   Policy — M

AMERICAN INTERCONTINENTAL UNIVERSITY ATLANTA
Information Science — M

AMERICAN INTERCONTINENTAL UNIVERSITY ONLINE
Computer and Information
   Systems Security — M
Information Science — M

AMERICAN PUBLIC UNIVERSITY SYSTEM
Computer and Information
   Systems Security — M
Health Informatics — M,D

AMERICAN SENTINEL UNIVERSITY
Computer Science — M
Health Informatics — M

AMERICAN UNIVERSITY
Biotechnology — M
Data Science/Data Analytics — M,O

THE AMERICAN UNIVERSITY IN CAIRO
Artificial Intelligence/Robotics — M,D,O
Biotechnology — M,D,O
Computer Science — M,D,O
Construction Engineering — M,D,O
Electrical Engineering — M,D,O
Engineering and Applied
   Sciences—General — M,D,O
Environmental Engineering — M,D,O
Mechanical Engineering — M,D,O
Nanotechnology — M,D,O

THE AMERICAN UNIVERSITY IN DUBAI
Construction Management — M

AMERICAN UNIVERSITY OF ARMENIA
Computer Science — M
Energy Management and
   Policy — M
Industrial/Management
   Engineering — M
Information Science — M
Manufacturing Engineering — M

AMERICAN UNIVERSITY OF SHARJAH
Biomedical Engineering — M,D
Chemical Engineering — M,D
Civil Engineering — M,D
Computer Engineering — M,D
Electrical Engineering — M,D
Engineering Management — M,D
Mechanical Engineering — M,D

APPALACHIAN STATE UNIVERSITY
Computer Science — M
Energy and Power
   Engineering — M

ARIZONA STATE UNIVERSITY AT TEMPE
Aerospace/Aeronautical
   Engineering — M,D
Bioinformatics — M,D
Biomedical Engineering — M,D
Biotechnology — M,D
Chemical Engineering — M,D
Civil Engineering — M,D
Computer Engineering — M,D
Computer Science — M,D
Construction Engineering — M,D
Construction Management — M,D
Electrical Engineering — M,D,O
Energy and Power
   Engineering — M,D
Engineering and Applied
   Sciences—General — M,D,O
Environmental Engineering — M,D
Ergonomics and Human
   Factors — M
Geological Engineering — M,D
Industrial/Management
   Engineering — M,D
Information Science — M
Management of Technology — M
Manufacturing Engineering — M
Materials Engineering — M,D
Materials Sciences — M,D
Mechanical Engineering — M,D
Medical Informatics — M,D
Modeling and Simulation — M,D
Nanotechnology — M,D
Nuclear Engineering — M,D,O
Reliability Engineering — M

Software Engineering — M,D
Systems Engineering — M
Systems Science — M,D
Technology and Public Policy — M
Transportation and Highway
   Engineering — M,D,O

ARKANSAS STATE UNIVERSITY
Biotechnology — M,O
Computer Science — M
Engineering and Applied
   Sciences—General — M
Engineering Management — M

ARKANSAS TECH UNIVERSITY
Electrical Engineering — M
Engineering and Applied
   Sciences—General — M
Health Informatics — M
Information Science — M
Mechanical Engineering — M

ARTCENTER COLLEGE OF DESIGN
Transportation and Highway
   Engineering — M

ASPEN UNIVERSITY
Information Science — M,O

ATHABASCA UNIVERSITY
Management of Technology — M,D,O

ATLANTIS UNIVERSITY
Computer Engineering — M
Engineering and Applied
   Sciences—General — M
Management of Technology — M

AUBURN UNIVERSITY
Aerospace/Aeronautical
   Engineering — M,D
Biosystems Engineering — M,D
Chemical Engineering — M,D
Civil Engineering — M,D
Computer Engineering — M,D
Computer Science — M,D
Construction Engineering — M
Electrical Engineering — M,D
Engineering and Applied
   Sciences—General — M,D,O
Industrial/Management
   Engineering — M,D,O
Materials Engineering — M,D
Mechanical Engineering — M,D
Software Engineering — M,D
Systems Engineering — M,D,O

AUGUSTA UNIVERSITY
Computer and Information
   Systems Security — M
Health Informatics — M

AUSTIN PEAY STATE UNIVERSITY
Computer and Information
   Systems Security — M
Data Science/Data Analytics — M

AZUSA PACIFIC UNIVERSITY
Biotechnology — M
Data Science/Data Analytics — M

BALL STATE UNIVERSITY
Computer Science — M
Information Science — M,O
Telecommunications — M

BARRY UNIVERSITY
Health Informatics — O

Information Science — M

BARUCH COLLEGE OF THE CITY UNIVERSITY OF NEW YORK
Financial Engineering — M

BAYLOR COLLEGE OF MEDICINE
Bioengineering — D
Biomedical Engineering — D

BAYLOR UNIVERSITY
Biomedical Engineering — M,D
Computer Engineering — M,D
Computer Science — M,D
Electrical Engineering — M,D
Engineering and Applied
   Sciences—General — M,D
Mechanical Engineering — M,D

BAY PATH UNIVERSITY
Computer and Information
   Systems Security — M
Health Informatics — M

BELLEVUE UNIVERSITY
Information Science — M

BELMONT UNIVERSITY
Health Informatics — D

BENEDICTINE UNIVERSITY
Computer and Information
   Systems Security — M
Health Informatics — M

BENTLEY UNIVERSITY
Ergonomics and Human
   Factors — M
Information Science — M

BINGHAMTON UNIVERSITY, STATE UNIVERSITY OF NEW YORK
Biomedical Engineering — M,D
Computer Science — M,D
Electrical Engineering — M,D
Engineering and Applied
   Sciences—General — M,D
Industrial/Management
   Engineering — M,D
Materials Engineering — M,D
Materials Sciences — M,D
Mechanical Engineering — M,D
Systems Science — M,D

BOISE STATE UNIVERSITY
Civil Engineering — M
Computer Engineering — M,D
Computer Science — M,O
Electrical Engineering — M,D
Engineering and Applied
   Sciences—General — M,D,O
Materials Engineering — M,D
Mechanical Engineering — M

BOSTON UNIVERSITY
Bioinformatics — M,D
Biomedical Engineering — M,D
Computer and Information
   Systems Security — M,D,O
Computer Engineering — M,D,O
Computer Science — M,D,O
Data Science/Data Analytics — M,O
Electrical Engineering — M,D
Energy Management and
   Policy — M,D
Engineering and Applied
   Sciences—General — M,D
Health Informatics — M,O
Management of Technology — M

Manufacturing Engineering	M,D
Materials Engineering	M,D
Materials Sciences	M,D
Mechanical Engineering	M,D
Software Engineering	M,O
Systems Engineering	M,D
Telecommunications Management	M,O
Telecommunications	M,O

BOWIE STATE UNIVERSITY

| Computer Science | M,D |

BOWLING GREEN STATE UNIVERSITY

Computer Science	M
Operations Research	M
Software Engineering	M

BRADLEY UNIVERSITY

Civil Engineering	M
Computer Science	M
Construction Engineering	M
Electrical Engineering	M
Engineering and Applied Sciences—General	M
Industrial/Management Engineering	M
Information Science	M
Manufacturing Engineering	M
Mechanical Engineering	M

BRANDEIS UNIVERSITY

Artificial Intelligence/Robotics	M
Bioinformatics	M
Biotechnology	M
Computer and Information Systems Security	M
Computer Science	M,D
Health Informatics	M
Human-Computer Interaction	M
Medical Informatics	M
Software Engineering	M

BRANDMAN UNIVERSITY

| Data Science/Data Analytics | M |

BRIDGEWATER STATE UNIVERSITY

| Computer Science | M |

BRIGHAM YOUNG UNIVERSITY

Biotechnology	M,D
Chemical Engineering	M,D
Civil Engineering	M,D
Computer Engineering	M,D
Computer Science	M,D
Construction Management	M
Electrical Engineering	M,D
Engineering and Applied Sciences—General	M,D
Information Science	M
Manufacturing Engineering	M
Mechanical Engineering	M,D

BROCK UNIVERSITY

| Biotechnology | M,D |
| Computer Science | M |

BROOKLYN COLLEGE OF THE CITY UNIVERSITY OF NEW YORK

Computer Science	M,O
Health Informatics	M,O
Information Science	M,O

BROWN UNIVERSITY

| Biochemical Engineering | M,D |
| Biomedical Engineering | M,D |

Biotechnology	M,D
Chemical Engineering	M,D
Computer Engineering	M,D
Computer Science	M,D
Electrical Engineering	M,D
Engineering and Applied Sciences—General	M,D
Materials Sciences	M,D
Mechanical Engineering	M,D
Mechanics	M,D

BUCKNELL UNIVERSITY

Chemical Engineering	M
Civil Engineering	M
Computer Engineering	M
Electrical Engineering	M
Engineering and Applied Sciences—General	M
Mechanical Engineering	M

BUFFALO STATE COLLEGE, STATE UNIVERSITY OF NEW YORK

Data Science/Data Analytics	M
Industrial/Management Engineering	M
Manufacturing Engineering	M
Mechanical Engineering	M

CALIFORNIA BAPTIST UNIVERSITY

| Construction Management | M |

CALIFORNIA INSTITUTE OF TECHNOLOGY

Aerospace/Aeronautical Engineering	M,D,O
Bioengineering	M,D
Chemical Engineering	M,D
Civil Engineering	M,D,O
Computer Science	M,D
Electrical Engineering	M,D,O
Engineering and Applied Sciences—General	M,D,O
Environmental Engineering	M,D
Materials Sciences	M,D
Mechanical Engineering	M,D,O
Mechanics	M,D
Systems Engineering	M,D

CALIFORNIA LUTHERAN UNIVERSITY

| Management of Technology | M,O |

CALIFORNIA MIRAMAR UNIVERSITY

| Telecommunications Management | M |
| Telecommunications | M |

CALIFORNIA POLYTECHNIC STATE UNIVERSITY, SAN LUIS OBISPO

Aerospace/Aeronautical Engineering	M
Architectural Engineering	M
Biomedical Engineering	M
Civil Engineering	M
Computer Science	M
Electrical Engineering	M
Engineering and Applied Sciences—General	M
Environmental Engineering	M
Industrial/Management Engineering	M
Mechanical Engineering	M
Polymer Science and Engineering	M

CALIFORNIA STATE POLYTECHNIC UNIVERSITY, POMONA

Aerospace/Aeronautical Engineering	M
Civil Engineering	M
Computer Science	M
Electrical Engineering	M
Engineering Management	M
Mechanical Engineering	M
Systems Engineering	M

CALIFORNIA STATE UNIVERSITY CHANNEL ISLANDS

| Computer Science | M |

CALIFORNIA STATE UNIVERSITY, CHICO

Computer Engineering	M
Computer Science	M
Construction Management	M
Electrical Engineering	M
Engineering and Applied Sciences—General	M

CALIFORNIA STATE UNIVERSITY, DOMINGUEZ HILLS

| Bioinformatics | M |
| Computer Science | M |

CALIFORNIA STATE UNIVERSITY, EAST BAY

Computer Science	M
Construction Management	M
Engineering and Applied Sciences—General	M
Engineering Management	M

CALIFORNIA STATE UNIVERSITY, FRESNO

Civil Engineering	M
Computer Engineering	M
Computer Science	M
Electrical Engineering	M
Engineering and Applied Sciences—General	M
Industrial/Management Engineering	M
Mechanical Engineering	M

CALIFORNIA STATE UNIVERSITY, FULLERTON

Architectural Engineering	M
Biotechnology	M
Civil Engineering	M
Computer Engineering	M
Computer Science	M
Electrical Engineering	M
Engineering and Applied Sciences—General	M
Environmental Engineering	M
Information Science	M
Mechanical Engineering	M
Software Engineering	M
Systems Engineering	M

CALIFORNIA STATE UNIVERSITY, LONG BEACH

Civil Engineering	M
Computer Engineering	M
Computer Science	M
Electrical Engineering	M
Engineering Management	M,D
Ergonomics and Human Factors	M
Mechanical Engineering	M,D

CALIFORNIA STATE UNIVERSITY, LOS ANGELES

Civil Engineering	M
Computer Science	M
Electrical Engineering	M
Engineering and Applied Sciences—General	M
Management of Technology	M
Mechanical Engineering	M

CALIFORNIA STATE UNIVERSITY MARITIME ACADEMY

| Engineering Management | M |

CALIFORNIA STATE UNIVERSITY, NORTHRIDGE

Artificial Intelligence/Robotics	M
Civil Engineering	M
Computer Science	M
Construction Management	M
Electrical Engineering	M
Engineering and Applied Sciences—General	M
Engineering Management	M
Industrial/Management Engineering	M
Manufacturing Engineering	M
Materials Engineering	M
Mechanical Engineering	M
Software Engineering	M
Structural Engineering	M
Systems Engineering	M

CALIFORNIA STATE UNIVERSITY, SACRAMENTO

Civil Engineering	M
Computer Science	M
Electrical Engineering	M
Engineering and Applied Sciences—General	M
Mechanical Engineering	M
Software Engineering	M

CALIFORNIA STATE UNIVERSITY, SAN BERNARDINO

| Computer and Information Systems Security | M |
| Computer Science | M |

CALIFORNIA STATE UNIVERSITY, SAN MARCOS

Biotechnology	M
Computer and Information Systems Security	M
Computer Science	M

CALIFORNIA UNIVERSITY OF PENNSYLVANIA

| Computer and Information Systems Security | M |

CAMBRIDGE COLLEGE

| Management of Technology | M |

CAMPBELLSVILLE UNIVERSITY

| Management of Technology | M,D |

CANISIUS COLLEGE

| Health Informatics | M,O |

CAPELLA UNIVERSITY

Computer and Information Systems Security	M,D
Health Informatics	M
Management of Technology	M,D
Operations Research	M

M—masters degree; D—doctorate; O—other advanced degree; *—Close-Up and/or Display

CAPITOL TECHNOLOGY UNIVERSITY

Computer and Information Systems Security	M
Computer Science	M
Electrical Engineering	M
Information Science	M
Telecommunications Management	M

CARDINAL STRITCH UNIVERSITY

Computer and Information Systems Security	M

CARLETON UNIVERSITY

Aerospace/Aeronautical Engineering	M,D
Biomedical Engineering	M
Civil Engineering	M,D
Computer Science	M,D
Electrical Engineering	M,D
Engineering and Applied Sciences—General	M,D
Environmental Engineering	M,D
Information Science	M,D
Management of Technology	M
Materials Engineering	M,D
Mechanical Engineering	M,D
Systems Engineering	M,D
Systems Science	M,D

CARNEGIE MELLON UNIVERSITY

Architectural Engineering	M,D
Artificial Intelligence/Robotics	M,D
Bioengineering	M,D
Biomedical Engineering	M,D
Biotechnology	M
Chemical Engineering	M,D
Civil Engineering	M,D
Computer and Information Systems Security	M
Computer Engineering	M,D
Computer Science	M,D
Construction Management	M,D
Electrical Engineering	M,D
Energy and Power Engineering	M,D
Environmental Engineering	M,D
Human-Computer Interaction	M,D
Information Science	M,D
Materials Engineering	M,D
Materials Sciences	M,D
Mechanical Engineering	M,D
Mechanics	M,D
Modeling and Simulation	M,D
Nanotechnology	D
Operations Research	D
Polymer Science and Engineering	M
Software Engineering	M,D
Systems Engineering	M,D
Technology and Public Policy	M,D
Telecommunications Management	M
Water Resources Engineering	M,D

CARROLL UNIVERSITY

Software Engineering	M

CASE WESTERN RESERVE UNIVERSITY

Aerospace/Aeronautical Engineering	M,D
Biomedical Engineering	M,D
Chemical Engineering	M,D
Civil Engineering	M,D
Computer Engineering	M,D
Computer Science	M,D
Electrical Engineering	M,D
Engineering and Applied Sciences—General	M,D
Engineering Management	M
Information Science	M,D

Materials Engineering	M,D
Materials Sciences	M,D
Mechanical Engineering	M,D
Operations Research	M,D
Polymer Science and Engineering	M,D
Systems Engineering	M,D

THE CATHOLIC UNIVERSITY OF AMERICA

Biomedical Engineering	M,D
Biotechnology	M,D
Civil Engineering	M,D,O
Computer Science	M,D
Electrical Engineering	M,D
Energy and Power Engineering	M,D
Engineering and Applied Sciences—General	M,D,O
Engineering Management	M,O
Environmental Engineering	M,D
Ergonomics and Human Factors	M,D
Management of Technology	M,O
Materials Engineering	M
Materials Sciences	M
Mechanical Engineering	M,D
Systems Engineering	M,O
Transportation and Highway Engineering	M,D,O

CENTRAL CONNECTICUT STATE UNIVERSITY

Computer Science	M,O
Construction Management	M,O
Engineering and Applied Sciences—General	M
Management of Technology	M,O

CENTRAL EUROPEAN UNIVERSITY

Data Science/Data Analytics	D
Management of Technology	M,D

CENTRAL MICHIGAN UNIVERSITY

Computer and Information Systems Security	O
Computer Science	M
Engineering and Applied Sciences—General	M
Engineering Management	M,O
Materials Sciences	D

CHAMPLAIN COLLEGE

Computer and Information Systems Security	M
Management of Technology	M

CHATHAM UNIVERSITY

Health Informatics	M

CHICAGO STATE UNIVERSITY

Computer Science	M

CHRISTIAN BROTHERS UNIVERSITY

Engineering and Applied Sciences—General	M

CHRISTOPHER NEWPORT UNIVERSITY

Computer Science	M

THE CITADEL, THE MILITARY COLLEGE OF SOUTH CAROLINA

Aerospace/Aeronautical Engineering	M,O
Civil Engineering	M,O
Computer Engineering	M,O
Electrical Engineering	M,O

Engineering and Applied Sciences—General	M,O
Engineering Management	M,O
Geotechnical Engineering	M,O
Information Science	M
Manufacturing Engineering	M,O
Mechanical Engineering	M,O
Structural Engineering	M,O
Systems Engineering	M,O
Transportation and Highway Engineering	M,O

CITY COLLEGE OF THE CITY UNIVERSITY OF NEW YORK

Biomedical Engineering	M,D
Chemical Engineering	M,D
Civil Engineering	M,D
Computer Science	M,D
Electrical Engineering	M,D
Engineering and Applied Sciences—General	M,D
Mechanical Engineering	M,D

CITY UNIVERSITY OF SEATTLE

Computer and Information Systems Security	M,O
Computer Science	M,O
Management of Technology	M,O

CLAFLIN UNIVERSITY

Biotechnology	M

CLAREMONT GRADUATE UNIVERSITY

Computer and Information Systems Security	M,D,O
Data Science/Data Analytics	M,D,O
Financial Engineering	M
Health Informatics	M,D,O
Information Science	M,D,O
Operations Research	M,D
Systems Science	M,D,O
Telecommunications	M,D,O

CLARK ATLANTA UNIVERSITY

Computer Science	M
Information Science	M

CLARKSON UNIVERSITY

Biotechnology	M,D
Civil Engineering	M,D
Computer Science	M,D
Electrical Engineering	M
Energy and Power Engineering	M
Energy Management and Policy	M,O
Engineering and Applied Sciences—General	M,D,O
Engineering Management	M
Environmental Engineering	M,D
Health Informatics	M
Materials Engineering	D
Materials Sciences	D

CLARK UNIVERSITY

Information Science	M

CLEMSON UNIVERSITY

Automotive Engineering	M,D,O
Bioengineering	M,D,O
Bioinformatics	M,D,O
Biomedical Engineering	M,D,O
Biosystems Engineering	M,D
Chemical Engineering	M,D
Civil Engineering	M,D
Computer Engineering	M,D
Computer Science	M,D
Construction Engineering	M,D
Construction Management	M,D
Electrical Engineering	M,D

Engineering and Applied Sciences—General	M,D,O
Environmental Engineering	M,D
Ergonomics and Human Factors	M,D
Geotechnical Engineering	M,D
Industrial/Management Engineering	M,D
Materials Engineering	M,D
Materials Sciences	M,D
Mechanical Engineering	M,D
Structural Engineering	M,D
Transportation and Highway Engineering	M,D
Water Resources Engineering	M,D

CLEVELAND STATE UNIVERSITY

Biomedical Engineering	D
Chemical Engineering	M,D
Civil Engineering	M,D
Electrical Engineering	M,D
Engineering and Applied Sciences—General	M,D
Environmental Engineering	M,D
Mechanical Engineering	M,D
Software Engineering	M,D

COASTAL CAROLINA UNIVERSITY

Computer Science	M,D,O

COLLEGE FOR CREATIVE STUDIES

Automotive Engineering	M
Transportation and Highway Engineering	M

COLLEGE OF CHARLESTON

Computer Science	M

COLLEGE OF SAINT ELIZABETH

Computer and Information Systems Security	M,O
Data Science/Data Analytics	M

THE COLLEGE OF SAINT ROSE

Computer Science	M,O
Information Science	M,O

THE COLLEGE OF ST. SCHOLASTICA

Health Informatics	M,O

COLLEGE OF STATEN ISLAND OF THE CITY UNIVERSITY OF NEW YORK

Artificial Intelligence/Robotics	M
Biotechnology	M
Computer and Information Systems Security	M
Computer Science	M
Data Science/Data Analytics	M,O
Electrical Engineering	M
Software Engineering	M

COLORADO CHRISTIAN UNIVERSITY

Computer and Information Systems Security	M

COLORADO MESA UNIVERSITY

Health Informatics	M,D,O

COLORADO SCHOOL OF MINES

Bioengineering	M,D
Chemical Engineering	M,D
Civil Engineering	M,D
Computer Science	M,D
Construction Engineering	M,D
Electrical Engineering	M,D
Electronic Materials	M,D

Energy Management and
   Policy — M,D
Engineering and Applied
   Sciences—General — M,D,O
Engineering Management — M,D
Environmental Engineering — M,D
Geological Engineering — M,D
Management of Technology — M,D
Materials Engineering — M,D
Materials Sciences — M,D
Mechanical Engineering — M,D
Metallurgical Engineering and
   Metallurgy — M,D
Mineral/Mining Engineering — M,D
Nuclear Engineering — M,D
Operations Research — M,D
Petroleum Engineering — M,D

COLORADO STATE UNIVERSITY
Bioengineering — M,D
Biomedical Engineering — M,D
Chemical Engineering — M,D
Civil Engineering — M,D
Computer Science — M,D
Construction Management — M
Electrical Engineering — M,D
Energy Management and
   Policy — M
Engineering and Applied
   Sciences—General — M,D
Materials Sciences — M,D
Mechanical Engineering — M,D
Systems Engineering — M,D

COLORADO STATE UNIVERSITY-PUEBLO
Applied Science and
   Technology — M
Engineering and Applied
   Sciences—General — M
Industrial/Management
   Engineering — M
Systems Engineering — M

**COLORADO TECHNICAL
UNIVERSITY AURORA**
Computer and Information
   Systems Security — M
Computer Engineering — M
Computer Science — M
Data Science/Data Analytics — M
Electrical Engineering — M
Management of Technology — M
Software Engineering — M
Systems Engineering — M

**COLORADO TECHNICAL
UNIVERSITY COLORADO
SPRINGS**
Computer and Information
   Systems Security — M,D
Computer Engineering — M
Computer Science — M,D
Data Science/Data Analytics — M,D
Electrical Engineering — M
Management of Technology — M,D
Software Engineering — M,D
Systems Engineering — M

COLUMBIA UNIVERSITY
Biomedical Engineering — M,D
Biotechnology — M,D
Chemical Engineering — M,D
Civil Engineering — M,D
Computer Engineering — M,D
Computer Science — M,D
Construction Engineering — M,D
Construction Management — M,D
Data Science/Data Analytics — M

Electrical Engineering — M,D
Engineering and Applied
   Sciences—General — M,D
Environmental Engineering — M,D
Financial Engineering — M,D
Industrial/Management
   Engineering — M,D
Management of Technology — M
Materials Engineering — M,D
Materials Sciences — M,D
Mechanical Engineering — M,D
Mechanics — M,D
Medical Informatics — M,D,O
Operations Research — M,D

COLUMBUS STATE UNIVERSITY
Computer and Information
   Systems Security — M,O
Computer Science — M,O
Modeling and Simulation — M,O

**CONCORDIA UNIVERSITY
(CANADA)**
Aerospace/Aeronautical
   Engineering — M
Biotechnology — M,D,O
Civil Engineering — M,D,O
Computer and Information
   Systems Security — M,D,O
Computer Engineering — M,D
Computer Science — M,D,O
Construction Engineering — M,D,O
Electrical Engineering — M,D
Engineering and Applied
   Sciences—General — M,D,O
Environmental Engineering — M,D,O
Game Design and
   Development — M,D,O
Industrial/Management
   Engineering — M,D,O
Mechanical Engineering — M,D,O
Software Engineering — M,D,O
Systems Engineering — M,D,O
Telecommunications
   Management — M,D,O

**CONCORDIA UNIVERSITY,
NEBRASKA**
Computer and Information
   Systems Security — M
Computer Science — M

**CONCORDIA UNIVERSITY OF
EDMONTON**
Computer and Information
   Systems Security — M

**CONCORDIA UNIVERSITY, ST.
PAUL**
Computer and Information
   Systems Security — M

**COOPER UNION FOR THE
ADVANCEMENT OF SCIENCE AND
ART**
Chemical Engineering — M
Civil Engineering — M
Electrical Engineering — M
Engineering and Applied
   Sciences—General — M
Mechanical Engineering — M

CORNELL UNIVERSITY
Aerospace/Aeronautical
   Engineering — M,D
Agricultural Engineering — M,D
Artificial Intelligence/Robotics — M,D
Biochemical Engineering — M,D

Bioengineering — M,D
Biomedical Engineering — M,D
Biotechnology — M,D
Chemical Engineering — M,D
Civil Engineering — M,D
Computer Engineering — M,D
Computer Science — M,D
Electrical Engineering — M,D
Energy and Power
   Engineering — M,D
Engineering and Applied
   Sciences—General — M,D
Engineering Management — M,D
Engineering Physics — M,D
Environmental Engineering — M,D
Ergonomics and Human
   Factors — M
Geotechnical Engineering — M,D
Human-Computer Interaction — M,D
Industrial/Management
   Engineering — M,D
Information Science — D
Manufacturing Engineering — M,D
Materials Engineering — M,D
Materials Sciences — M,D
Mechanical Engineering — M,D
Mechanics — M,D
Nanotechnology — M,D
Operations Research — M,D
Polymer Science and
   Engineering — M,D
Structural Engineering — M,D
Systems Engineering — M,D
Textile Sciences and
   Engineering — M,D
Transportation and Highway
   Engineering — M,D
Water Resources Engineering — M,D

DAKOTA STATE UNIVERSITY
Computer Science — M,D,O
Health Informatics — M,D,O
Information Science — M,D,O

DALHOUSIE UNIVERSITY
Bioengineering — M,D
Bioinformatics — M,D
Biomedical Engineering — M,D
Chemical Engineering — M,D
Civil Engineering — M,D
Computer Engineering — M,D
Computer Science — M,D
Electrical Engineering — M,D
Engineering and Applied
   Sciences—General — M,D
Environmental Engineering — M,D
Human-Computer Interaction — M,D
Industrial/Management
   Engineering — M,D
Internet Engineering — M,D
Mechanical Engineering — M,D
Medical Informatics — M,D
Mineral/Mining Engineering — M,D

DARTMOUTH COLLEGE
Biomedical Engineering — M,D
Chemical Engineering — M,D
Computer Engineering — M,D
Computer Science — M,D
Electrical Engineering — M,D
Energy and Power
   Engineering — M,D
Engineering and Applied
   Sciences—General — M,D
Engineering Management — M
Health Informatics — M,D
Materials Engineering — M,D
Materials Sciences — M,D
Mechanical Engineering — M,D
Systems Engineering — M,D

DAVENPORT UNIVERSITY
Computer and Information
   Systems Security — M

DEPAUL UNIVERSITY
Computer and Information
   Systems Security — M,D
Computer Science — M,D
Data Science/Data Analytics — M,D
Game Design and
   Development — M,D
Health Informatics — M,D
Human-Computer Interaction — M,D
Information Science — M,D
Polymer Science and
   Engineering — M,D
Software Engineering — M,D

DESALES UNIVERSITY
Computer and Information
   Systems Security — M,O
Data Science/Data Analytics — M,O
Health Informatics — M,O

**DIGIPEN INSTITUTE OF
TECHNOLOGY**
Computer Science — M

DREXEL UNIVERSITY
Architectural Engineering — M,D
Biochemical Engineering — M
Biomedical Engineering — M,D
Chemical Engineering — M,D
Civil Engineering — M,D
Computer Engineering — M
Computer Science — M,D,O
Construction Management — M
Electrical Engineering — M
Engineering and Applied
   Sciences—General — M,D,O
Engineering Management — M,O
Environmental Engineering — M,D
Geotechnical Engineering — M,D
Hydraulics — M,D
Information Science — M,D,O
Materials Engineering — M,D
Mechanical Engineering — M,D
Mechanics — M,D
Software Engineering — M,D,O
Structural Engineering — M,D
Telecommunications — M

DRURY UNIVERSITY
Computer and Information
   Systems Security — O

DUKE UNIVERSITY
Bioinformatics — D,O
Biomedical Engineering — M,D
Civil Engineering — M,D
Computer Engineering — M,D
Computer Science — M,D
Electrical Engineering — M,D
Engineering and Applied
   Sciences—General — M
Engineering Management — M
Environmental Engineering — M,D
Health Informatics — M
Materials Engineering — M
Materials Sciences — M,D
Mechanical Engineering — M,D

DUQUESNE UNIVERSITY
Biotechnology — M

EAST CAROLINA UNIVERSITY
Biomedical Engineering — M
Biotechnology — M

M—masters degree; D—doctorate; O—other advanced degree; *—Close-Up and/or Display

Computer and Information Systems Security	M,D,O
Computer Engineering	M,D,O
Computer Science	M,D,O
Construction Management	M,O
Health Informatics	M,O
Management of Technology	M,D,O
Software Engineering	M
Telecommunications Management	M,D,O

EASTERN ILLINOIS UNIVERSITY

Computer and Information Systems Security	M
Computer Science	M
Energy Management and Policy	M
Engineering and Applied Sciences—General	M,O
Systems Science	M,O

EASTERN KENTUCKY UNIVERSITY

Industrial/Management Engineering	M
Manufacturing Engineering	M

EASTERN MICHIGAN UNIVERSITY

Computer and Information Systems Security	O
Computer Science	M,O
Construction Management	M,O
Engineering and Applied Sciences—General	M
Engineering Management	M
Management of Technology	D
Polymer Science and Engineering	M,O
Technology and Public Policy	M

EASTERN VIRGINIA MEDICAL SCHOOL

Biotechnology	M

EASTERN WASHINGTON UNIVERSITY

Computer Science	M

EAST STROUDSBURG UNIVERSITY OF PENNSYLVANIA

Computer Science	M

EAST TENNESSEE STATE UNIVERSITY

Computer Science	M,O
Information Science	M,O
Manufacturing Engineering	M

EC-COUNCIL UNIVERSITY

Computer and Information Systems Security	M

ECPI UNIVERSITY

Computer and Information Systems Security	M

ELIZABETH CITY STATE UNIVERSITY

Computer Science	M

ELMHURST UNIVERSITY

Data Science/Data Analytics	M

EMBRY-RIDDLE AERONAUTICAL UNIVERSITY–DAYTONA

Aerospace/Aeronautical Engineering	M,D
Aviation	M
Civil Engineering	M

Computer and Information Systems Security	M
Electrical Engineering	M
Engineering Physics	M,D
Ergonomics and Human Factors	M,D
Mechanical Engineering	M,D
Software Engineering	M
Systems Engineering	M

EMBRY-RIDDLE AERONAUTICAL UNIVERSITY–PRESCOTT

Aviation	M
Safety Engineering	M

EMBRY-RIDDLE AERONAUTICAL UNIVERSITY–WORLDWIDE

Aerospace/Aeronautical Engineering	M
Computer and Information Systems Security	M
Engineering Management	M
Management of Technology	M
Systems Engineering	M

EMORY UNIVERSITY

Bioinformatics	M,D
Computer Science	M,D
Health Informatics	M,D

ENDICOTT COLLEGE

Computer and Information Systems Security	M,O

EVERGLADES UNIVERSITY

Aviation	M

FAIRFIELD UNIVERSITY

Computer and Information Systems Security	M,O
Computer Engineering	M,O
Data Science/Data Analytics	M,O
Electrical Engineering	M,O
Engineering and Applied Sciences—General	M,O
Management of Technology	M,O
Mechanical Engineering	M,O
Software Engineering	M,O
Telecommunications	M,O

FAIRLEIGH DICKINSON UNIVERSITY, FLORHAM CAMPUS

Chemical Engineering	M,O
Computer Science	M
Management of Technology	M,O

FAIRLEIGH DICKINSON UNIVERSITY, METROPOLITAN CAMPUS

Computer Engineering	M
Computer Science	M
Electrical Engineering	M
Engineering and Applied Sciences—General	M
Systems Science	M

FARMINGDALE STATE COLLEGE

Construction Management	M
Electrical Engineering	M
Management of Technology	M
Mechanical Engineering	M

FITCHBURG STATE UNIVERSITY

Computer Science	M
Data Science/Data Analytics	M

FLORIDA AGRICULTURAL AND MECHANICAL UNIVERSITY

Biomedical Engineering	M,D
Chemical Engineering	M,D

Civil Engineering	M,D
Electrical Engineering	M,D
Engineering and Applied Sciences—General	M,D
Industrial/Management Engineering	M,D
Mechanical Engineering	M,D
Software Engineering	M

FLORIDA ATLANTIC UNIVERSITY

Bioengineering	M,D
Civil Engineering	M
Computer Engineering	M,D
Computer Science	M,D
Electrical Engineering	M,D
Engineering and Applied Sciences—General	M,D
Environmental Engineering	M
Mechanical Engineering	M,D
Ocean Engineering	M,D

FLORIDA INSTITUTE OF TECHNOLOGY

Aerospace/Aeronautical Engineering	M,D
Aviation	M,D
Biomedical Engineering	M,D
Biotechnology	M,D
Chemical Engineering	M,D
Civil Engineering	M,D
Computer and Information Systems Security	M
Computer Engineering	M,D
Computer Science	M,D
Electrical Engineering	M,D
Engineering and Applied Sciences—General	M,D
Engineering Management	M
Ergonomics and Human Factors	M
Human-Computer Interaction	M
Information Science	M
Mechanical Engineering	M,D
Ocean Engineering	M,D
Operations Research	M,D
Safety Engineering	M
Software Engineering	M
Systems Engineering	M,D

FLORIDA INTERNATIONAL UNIVERSITY

Biomedical Engineering	M,D
Civil Engineering	M,D
Computer and Information Systems Security	M,D
Computer Engineering	M,D
Computer Science	M,D
Construction Management	M
Data Science/Data Analytics	M,D
Electrical Engineering	M,D
Engineering and Applied Sciences—General	M,D
Engineering Management	M
Environmental Engineering	M,D
Information Science	M,D
Materials Engineering	M,D
Materials Sciences	M,D
Mechanical Engineering	M,D
Telecommunications	M,D

FLORIDA POLYTECHNIC UNIVERSITY

Computer Science	M
Engineering and Applied Sciences—General	M

FLORIDA STATE UNIVERSITY

Biomedical Engineering	M,D
Chemical Engineering	M,D
Civil Engineering	M,D
Computer and Information Systems Security	M,D
Electrical Engineering	M,D

Energy and Power Engineering	M,D
Engineering and Applied Sciences—General	M,D
Environmental Engineering	M,D
Industrial/Management Engineering	M,D
Manufacturing Engineering	M,D
Materials Engineering	M,D
Materials Sciences	M,D
Mechanical Engineering	M,D

FONTBONNE UNIVERSITY

Computer Science	M

FORDHAM UNIVERSITY

Computer Science	M
Data Science/Data Analytics	M

FRANKLIN PIERCE UNIVERSITY

Energy Management and Policy	M,D,O
Telecommunications	M,D,O

FRANKLIN UNIVERSITY

Computer Science	M

FROSTBURG STATE UNIVERSITY

Computer Science	M

FULL SAIL UNIVERSITY

Game Design and Development	M

GANNON UNIVERSITY

Computer Science	M
Electrical Engineering	M
Engineering Management	M
Environmental Engineering	M
Information Science	M
Mechanical Engineering	M
Software Engineering	M

GEORGE MASON UNIVERSITY

Bioengineering	D
Bioinformatics	M,D,O
Civil Engineering	M,D
Computer and Information Systems Security	M
Computer Engineering	M,D,O
Computer Science	M,D,O
Construction Engineering	M,D
Data Science/Data Analytics	M,D,O
Electrical Engineering	M,D,O
Engineering and Applied Sciences—General	M,D,O
Health Informatics	M,D,O
Information Science	M,D,O
Management of Technology	M
Operations Research	M,D,O
Systems Engineering	M,D,O
Transportation and Highway Engineering	M,D

GEORGETOWN UNIVERSITY

Bioinformatics	M,O
Computer Science	M,D
Management of Technology	M,D
Materials Sciences	D
Systems Engineering	M,D

THE GEORGE WASHINGTON UNIVERSITY

Aerospace/Aeronautical Engineering	M,D,O
Biomedical Engineering	M,D
Biotechnology	M,D,O
Civil Engineering	M,D,O
Computer and Information Systems Security	M,D,O

Computer Engineering	M,D,O
Computer Science	M,D,O
Electrical Engineering	M,D,O
Engineering and Applied Sciences—General	M,D,O
Engineering Management	M,D,O
Environmental Engineering	M,D,O
Management of Technology	M,D
Materials Sciences	M,D
Mechanical Engineering	M,D,O
Systems Engineering	M,D,O
Technology and Public Policy	M,O
Telecommunications	M,D,O

GEORGIA INSTITUTE OF TECHNOLOGY

Aerospace/Aeronautical Engineering	M,D
Biomedical Engineering	D
Chemical Engineering	M,D
Civil Engineering	M,D
Computer Engineering	M,D
Electrical Engineering	M,D
Engineering and Applied Sciences—General	M,D
Environmental Engineering	M,D
Industrial/Management Engineering	M,D
Materials Engineering	M,D
Mechanical Engineering	M,D
Mechanics	M,D
Nuclear Engineering	M,D
Operations Research	M,D

GEORGIA SOUTHERN UNIVERSITY

Civil Engineering	M
Computer and Information Systems Security	M,O
Construction Management	M
Electrical Engineering	M
Energy and Power Engineering	M
Engineering and Applied Sciences—General	M,O
Engineering Management	M,O
Manufacturing Engineering	M,O
Mechanical Engineering	M
Systems Engineering	M

GEORGIA SOUTHWESTERN STATE UNIVERSITY

Computer Science	M,O
Health Informatics	M,O

GEORGIA STATE UNIVERSITY

Bioinformatics	M,D
Computer Science	M,D
Health Informatics	M,D,O
Information Science	M,D,O
Operations Research	M,D

GOLDEN GATE UNIVERSITY

Management of Technology	M,D,O

GONZAGA UNIVERSITY

Engineering and Applied Sciences—General	M,O

GOVERNORS STATE UNIVERSITY

Computer Science	M

THE GRADUATE CENTER, CITY UNIVERSITY OF NEW YORK

Computer Science	D
Data Science/Data Analytics	M

GRAND CANYON UNIVERSITY

Data Science/Data Analytics	D
Health Informatics	M,D,O
Management of Technology	M

GRAND VALLEY STATE UNIVERSITY

Bioinformatics	M
Computer Engineering	M
Computer Science	M
Electrical Engineering	M
Engineering and Applied Sciences—General	M
Information Science	M
Manufacturing Engineering	M
Mechanical Engineering	M
Medical Informatics	M

GRANTHAM UNIVERSITY

Engineering and Applied Sciences—General	M

HAMPTON UNIVERSITY

Computer and Information Systems Security	M
Computer Science	M

HARDIN-SIMMONS UNIVERSITY

Information Science	M

HARRISBURG UNIVERSITY OF SCIENCE AND TECHNOLOGY

Computer and Information Systems Security	M
Human-Computer Interaction	M
Management of Technology	M
Software Engineering	M
Systems Engineering	M
Systems Science	M

HARVARD UNIVERSITY

Applied Science and Technology	M,O
Bioengineering	M,D
Biomedical Engineering	D
Biotechnology	M,O
Computer Science	M,D
Electrical Engineering	M,D
Engineering and Applied Sciences—General	M,D
Engineering Design	M,D
Environmental Engineering	M,D
Ergonomics and Human Factors	M,D
Information Science	M,D,O
Management of Technology	D
Materials Sciences	M,D
Mechanical Engineering	M,D

HEC MONTREAL

Data Science/Data Analytics	D
Financial Engineering	M,D
Operations Research	O

HERZING UNIVERSITY ONLINE

Management of Technology	M

HOFSTRA UNIVERSITY

Computer and Information Systems Security	M
Engineering and Applied Sciences—General	M
Health Informatics	M,O

HOOD COLLEGE

Bioinformatics	M,O
Computer and Information Systems Security	M,O

Computer Science	M,O
Information Science	M,O
Systems Science	M

HOWARD UNIVERSITY

Biotechnology	M,D
Chemical Engineering	M
Civil Engineering	M
Computer Science	M
Electrical Engineering	M,D
Engineering and Applied Sciences—General	M,D
Mechanical Engineering	M,D

HUMBOLDT STATE UNIVERSITY

Hazardous Materials Management	M

HUNTER COLLEGE OF THE CITY UNIVERSITY OF NEW YORK

Bioinformatics	M

HUSSON UNIVERSITY

Biotechnology	M

IDAHO STATE UNIVERSITY

Civil Engineering	M
Engineering and Applied Sciences—General	M,D,O
Environmental Engineering	M
Mechanical Engineering	M
Nuclear Engineering	M,D
Operations Research	M

IGLOBAL UNIVERSITY

Data Science/Data Analytics	M

ILLINOIS INSTITUTE OF TECHNOLOGY

Aerospace/Aeronautical Engineering	M,D
Agricultural Engineering	M
Architectural Engineering	M,D
Artificial Intelligence/Robotics	M,D
Bioengineering	M,D
Biomedical Engineering	M,D
Chemical Engineering	M,D
Civil Engineering	M,D
Computer and Information Systems Security	M,D
Computer Engineering	M,D
Computer Science	M,D
Construction Engineering	M,D
Construction Management	M,D
Data Science/Data Analytics	M,D
Electrical Engineering	M,D
Engineering and Applied Sciences—General	M,D
Environmental Engineering	M,D
Geotechnical Engineering	M,D
Manufacturing Engineering	M,D
Materials Engineering	M,D
Materials Sciences	M,D
Mechanical Engineering	M,D
Software Engineering	M,D
Structural Engineering	M,D
Telecommunications	M,D
Transportation and Highway Engineering	M,D

ILLINOIS STATE UNIVERSITY

Biotechnology	M
Industrial/Management Engineering	M
Management of Technology	M

INDIANA STATE UNIVERSITY

Computer Engineering	M

Computer Science	M
Engineering and Applied Sciences—General	M
Management of Technology	M,D

INDIANA TECH

Engineering Management	M

INDIANA UNIVERSITY BLOOMINGTON

Artificial Intelligence/Robotics	D
Bioinformatics	M,D,O
Biotechnology	M,D
Computer and Information Systems Security	M,D
Computer Science	M,D,O
Data Science/Data Analytics	M,O
Energy Management and Policy	M,D,O
Ergonomics and Human Factors	M,D
Hazardous Materials Management	M,D,O
Health Informatics	M,D
Human-Computer Interaction	M,D
Information Science	M,D,O
Materials Sciences	M,D
Safety Engineering	M,D
Systems Engineering	D
Water Resources Engineering	M,D,O

INDIANA UNIVERSITY OF PENNSYLVANIA

Nanotechnology	M

INDIANA UNIVERSITY-PURDUE UNIVERSITY INDIANAPOLIS

Bioinformatics	M,D
Biomedical Engineering	M,D
Computer and Information Systems Security	M,D,O
Computer Engineering	M,D
Computer Science	M,D,O
Data Science/Data Analytics	M,D,O
Electrical Engineering	M,D
Health Informatics	M,D
Human-Computer Interaction	M,D
Information Science	M
Management of Technology	M
Mechanical Engineering	M,D
Software Engineering	M,D,O

INDIANA UNIVERSITY SOUTH BEND

Computer Science	M,O

THE INSTITUTE OF WORLD POLITICS

Computer and Information Systems Security	M,D,O

INSTITUTO CENTROAMERICANO DE ADMINISTRACION DE EMPRESAS

Management of Technology	M

INSTITUTO TECNOLOGICO DE SANTO DOMINGO

Construction Management	M,O
Energy and Power Engineering	M,D,O
Energy Management and Policy	M,D,O
Engineering and Applied Sciences—General	M,O
Environmental Engineering	M,O
Industrial/Management Engineering	M,O
Information Science	M,O

*M—masters degree; D—doctorate; O—other advanced degree; *—Close-Up and/or Display*

Software Engineering	M,O
Structural Engineering	M,O
Telecommunications	M,O

INSTITUTO TECNOLÓGICO Y DE ESTUDIOS SUPERIORES DE MONTERREY, CAMPUS CENTRAL DE VERACRUZ

Computer Science	M

INSTITUTO TECNOLÓGICO Y DE ESTUDIOS SUPERIORES DE MONTERREY, CAMPUS CHIHUAHUA

Computer Engineering	M,O
Electrical Engineering	M,O
Engineering Management	M,O
Industrial/Management Engineering	M,O
Mechanical Engineering	M,O
Systems Engineering	M,O

INSTITUTO TECNOLÓGICO Y DE ESTUDIOS SUPERIORES DE MONTERREY, CAMPUS CIUDAD DE MÉXICO

Computer Science	M,D
Environmental Engineering	M,D
Industrial/Management Engineering	M,D
Telecommunications Management	M

INSTITUTO TECNOLÓGICO Y DE ESTUDIOS SUPERIORES DE MONTERREY, CAMPUS CIUDAD OBREGÓN

Engineering and Applied Sciences—General	M
Telecommunications Management	M

INSTITUTO TECNOLÓGICO Y DE ESTUDIOS SUPERIORES DE MONTERREY, CAMPUS CUERNAVACA

Computer Science	M,D
Information Science	M,D
Management of Technology	M,D

INSTITUTO TECNOLÓGICO Y DE ESTUDIOS SUPERIORES DE MONTERREY, CAMPUS ESTADO DE MÉXICO

Computer Science	M,D
Information Science	M,D
Materials Engineering	M,D
Materials Sciences	M,D
Telecommunications Management	M,D

INSTITUTO TECNOLÓGICO Y DE ESTUDIOS SUPERIORES DE MONTERREY, CAMPUS IRAPUATO

Computer Science	M,D
Information Science	M,D
Management of Technology	M,D
Telecommunications Management	M,D

INSTITUTO TECNOLÓGICO Y DE ESTUDIOS SUPERIORES DE MONTERREY, CAMPUS LAGUNA

Industrial/Management Engineering	M

INSTITUTO TECNOLÓGICO Y DE ESTUDIOS SUPERIORES DE MONTERREY, CAMPUS MONTERREY

Agricultural Engineering	M,D
Artificial Intelligence/Robotics	M,D
Biotechnology	M,D
Chemical Engineering	M,D
Civil Engineering	M,D
Computer Science	M,D
Electrical Engineering	M,D
Engineering and Applied Sciences—General	M,D
Environmental Engineering	M,D
Industrial/Management Engineering	M,D
Information Science	M,D
Manufacturing Engineering	M,D
Mechanical Engineering	M,D
Systems Engineering	M,D

INSTITUTO TECNOLÓGICO Y DE ESTUDIOS SUPERIORES DE MONTERREY, CAMPUS SONORA NORTE

Information Science	M

INTER AMERICAN UNIVERSITY OF PUERTO RICO, BARRANQUITAS CAMPUS

Biotechnology	M

INTER AMERICAN UNIVERSITY OF PUERTO RICO, BAYAMÓN CAMPUS

Aerospace/Aeronautical Engineering	M
Biotechnology	M
Electrical Engineering	M
Energy and Power Engineering	M
Mechanical Engineering	M

INTER AMERICAN UNIVERSITY OF PUERTO RICO, FAJARDO CAMPUS

Computer Science	M

INTER AMERICAN UNIVERSITY OF PUERTO RICO, GUAYAMA CAMPUS

Computer and Information Systems Security	M
Computer Science	M

INTER AMERICAN UNIVERSITY OF PUERTO RICO, METROPOLITAN CAMPUS

Computer Science	M

INTERNATIONAL TECHNOLOGICAL UNIVERSITY

Computer Engineering	M
Electrical Engineering	M,D
Engineering Management	M
Software Engineering	M

THE INTERNATIONAL UNIVERSITY OF MONACO

Financial Engineering	M

IONA COLLEGE

Computer and Information Systems Security	M,O
Computer Science	M
Game Design and Development	M
Management of Technology	M,O

IOWA STATE UNIVERSITY OF SCIENCE AND TECHNOLOGY

Aerospace/Aeronautical Engineering	M,D
Agricultural Engineering	M,D
Bioinformatics	M,D

Chemical Engineering	M,D
Civil Engineering	M,D
Computer Engineering	M,D
Computer Science	M,D
Construction Engineering	M,D
Electrical Engineering	M,D
Environmental Engineering	M,D
Geotechnical Engineering	M,D
Human-Computer Interaction	M,D
Industrial/Management Engineering	M,D
Information Science	M
Materials Engineering	M,D
Materials Sciences	M,D
Mechanical Engineering	M,D
Mechanics	M,D
Operations Research	M,D
Structural Engineering	M,D
Systems Engineering	M
Transportation and Highway Engineering	M,D

JACKSON STATE UNIVERSITY

Civil Engineering	M,D
Computer Science	M
Environmental Engineering	M,D
Hazardous Materials Management	M,D
Materials Sciences	M,D

JACKSONVILLE STATE UNIVERSITY

Computer Science	M
Software Engineering	M

JACKSONVILLE UNIVERSITY

Health Informatics	M

JAMES MADISON UNIVERSITY

Computer and Information Systems Security	M
Computer Science	M
Engineering and Applied Sciences—General	M

JOHN F. KENNEDY UNIVERSITY

Management of Technology	M

JOHNS HOPKINS UNIVERSITY

Aerospace/Aeronautical Engineering	M
Artificial Intelligence/Robotics	M
Bioengineering	M,D
Bioinformatics	M
Biomedical Engineering	M,D,O
Biotechnology	M
Chemical Engineering	M,D
Civil Engineering	M,D,O
Computer and Information Systems Security	M,O
Computer Engineering	M,D,O
Computer Science	M,D,O
Electrical Engineering	M,D,O
Energy Management and Policy	M,O
Engineering and Applied Sciences—General	M,D,O
Engineering Management	M
Environmental Engineering	M,D,O
Health Informatics	M,D,O
Management of Technology	M,O
Materials Engineering	M,D
Materials Sciences	M,D
Mechanical Engineering	M,D,O
Mechanics	M
Medical Informatics	M,D,O
Nanotechnology	M
Operations Research	M,D
Systems Engineering	M,O

JOHNSON & WALES UNIVERSITY

Computer and Information Systems Security	M
Data Science/Data Analytics	M

KANSAS STATE UNIVERSITY

Agricultural Engineering	M,D
Applied Science and Technology	M,O
Architectural Engineering	M
Bioengineering	M,D
Chemical Engineering	M,D,O
Civil Engineering	M,D
Computer Engineering	M,D
Computer Science	M,D
Data Science/Data Analytics	M,O
Electrical Engineering	M,D
Energy and Power Engineering	M,D
Energy Management and Policy	M,D
Engineering and Applied Sciences—General	M,D,O
Engineering Management	M,D
Environmental Engineering	M,D
Geotechnical Engineering	M,D
Industrial/Management Engineering	M,D
Management of Technology	M
Manufacturing Engineering	M,D
Mechanical Engineering	M,D
Nuclear Engineering	M,D
Operations Research	M,D
Structural Engineering	M,D
Transportation and Highway Engineering	M,D
Water Resources Engineering	M,D

KEAN UNIVERSITY

Biotechnology	M

KECK GRADUATE INSTITUTE

Data Science/Data Analytics	M

KEISER UNIVERSITY

Computer and Information Systems Security	M
Management of Technology	M

KENNESAW STATE UNIVERSITY

Civil Engineering	M
Computer and Information Systems Security	M,O
Computer Science	M
Construction Management	M
Data Science/Data Analytics	M,D,O
Electrical Engineering	M
Engineering and Applied Sciences—General	M
Engineering Management	M
Environmental Engineering	M
Geotechnical Engineering	M
Health Informatics	M,O
Information Science	M,O
Management of Technology	M
Mechanical Engineering	M
Software Engineering	M,O
Structural Engineering	M
Systems Engineering	M
Transportation and Highway Engineering	M
Water Resources Engineering	M

KENT STATE UNIVERSITY

Aerospace/Aeronautical Engineering	M
Computer and Information Systems Security	M
Computer Science	M,D
Health Informatics	M
Information Science	M

KETTERING UNIVERSITY
Electrical Engineering — M
Engineering Management — M
Manufacturing Engineering — M
Mechanical Engineering — M

KUTZTOWN UNIVERSITY OF PENNSYLVANIA
Computer Science — M

LAKEHEAD UNIVERSITY
Computer Engineering — M
Computer Science — M
Electrical Engineering — M
Engineering and Applied
   Sciences—General — M
Environmental Engineering — M

LAMAR UNIVERSITY
Chemical Engineering — M,D
Computer Science — M
Electrical Engineering — M,D
Engineering and Applied
   Sciences—General — M,D
Mechanical Engineering — M,D

LA SALLE UNIVERSITY
Computer Science — M,O
Management of Technology — M,O

LAURENTIAN UNIVERSITY
Engineering and Applied
   Sciences—General — M,D
Mineral/Mining Engineering — M,D

LAWRENCE TECHNOLOGICAL UNIVERSITY
Architectural Engineering — M,D
Artificial Intelligence/Robotics — M,O
Automotive Engineering — M,D
Bioinformatics — M,O
Biomedical Engineering — M,D
Civil Engineering — M,D
Computer and Information
   Systems Security — M,D,O
Computer Engineering — M,D
Computer Science — M,O
Construction Engineering — M,D
Data Science/Data Analytics — M,O
Electrical Engineering — M,D
Energy and Power
   Engineering — M,D
Engineering and Applied
   Sciences—General — M,D
Engineering Management — M,D
Industrial/Management
   Engineering — M,D
Information Science — M,D,O
Manufacturing Engineering — M,D
Mechanical Engineering — M,D
Water Resources Engineering — M,D

LEBANESE AMERICAN UNIVERSITY
Computer Science — M

LEHIGH UNIVERSITY
Biochemical Engineering — M,D
Bioengineering — M,D
Chemical Engineering — M,D
Civil Engineering — M,D
Computer Engineering — M,D
Computer Science — M,D
Electrical Engineering — M,D
Energy and Power
   Engineering — M
Engineering and Applied
   Sciences—General — M,D,O
Engineering Management — M,D,O

Environmental Engineering — M,D
Industrial/Management
   Engineering — M,D,O
Information Science — M
Materials Engineering — M,D
Materials Sciences — M,D
Mechanical Engineering — M,D
Mechanics — M,D
Polymer Science and
   Engineering — M,D
Systems Engineering — M,D,O

LEHMAN COLLEGE OF THE CITY UNIVERSITY OF NEW YORK
Computer Science — M

LETOURNEAU UNIVERSITY
Engineering and Applied
   Sciences—General — M
Engineering Management — M

LEWIS UNIVERSITY
Bioinformatics — M
Computer and Information
   Systems Security — M
Computer Science — M
Management of Technology — M
Software Engineering — M

LIBERTY UNIVERSITY
Computer and Information
   Systems Security — M,D
Health Informatics — M,D

LINDENWOOD UNIVERSITY
Computer and Information
   Systems Security — M,O

LIPSCOMB UNIVERSITY
Computer and Information
   Systems Security — M,O
Data Science/Data Analytics — M,O
Health Informatics — M,D
Management of Technology — M,O
Software Engineering — M,O

LOGAN UNIVERSITY
Health Informatics — M,D

LONDON METROPOLITAN UNIVERSITY
Computer and Information
   Systems Security — M,D
Data Science/Data Analytics — M,D
Management of Technology — M,D

LONG ISLAND UNIVERSITY - BROOKLYN
Computer Science — M,O

LONG ISLAND UNIVERSITY - POST
Engineering Management — M
Game Design and
   Development — M

LONG ISLAND UNIVERSITY - RIVERHEAD
Computer and Information
   Systems Security — M,O

LOUISIANA STATE UNIVERSITY AND AGRICULTURAL & MECHANICAL COLLEGE
Agricultural Engineering — M,D
Applied Science and
   Technology — M

Bioengineering — M,D
Chemical Engineering — M,D
Civil Engineering — M,D
Computer Engineering — M,D
Computer Science — M,D
Construction Management — M,D
Electrical Engineering — M,D
Engineering and Applied
   Sciences—General — M,D
Environmental Engineering — M,D
Geotechnical Engineering — M,D
Mechanical Engineering — M,D
Mechanics — M,D
Petroleum Engineering — M,D
Structural Engineering — M,D
Systems Science — M,D
Transportation and Highway
   Engineering — M,D
Water Resources Engineering — M,D

LOUISIANA STATE UNIVERSITY IN SHREVEPORT
Computer Science — M
Systems Science — M

LOUISIANA TECH UNIVERSITY
Biomedical Engineering — M,D,O
Computer and Information
   Systems Security — M,D
Computer Science — M,D,O
Engineering and Applied
   Sciences—General — M,D,O
Engineering Management — M,D,O
Engineering Physics — M,D,O
Health Informatics — M,D,O
Management of Technology — M,D,O
Materials Sciences — M,D,O
Nanotechnology — M,D,O

LOYOLA MARYMOUNT UNIVERSITY
Civil Engineering — M
Electrical Engineering — M
Engineering Management
Mechanical Engineering — M
Systems Engineering — M

LOYOLA UNIVERSITY CHICAGO
Bioinformatics — M
Computer Science — M
Information Science — M
Software Engineering — M

MAHARISHI INTERNATIONAL UNIVERSITY
Computer Science — M

MANHATTAN COLLEGE
Chemical Engineering — M
Civil Engineering — M
Computer Engineering — M
Construction Management — M
Data Science/Data Analytics — M
Electrical Engineering — M
Engineering and Applied
   Sciences—General — M
Environmental Engineering — M
Mechanical Engineering — M

MARIST COLLEGE
Computer Science — M,O
Software Engineering — M,O

MARQUETTE UNIVERSITY
Bioinformatics — M,D
Biomedical Engineering — M,D
Civil Engineering — M,D,O
Computer Engineering — M,D,O
Computer Science — M,D

Construction Engineering — M,D,O
Construction Management — M,D,O
Electrical Engineering — M,D,O
Engineering and Applied
   Sciences—General — M,D,O
Engineering Management — M,D,O
Environmental Engineering — M,D,O
Hazardous Materials
   Management — M,D,O
Management of Technology — M,D
Mechanical Engineering — M,D,O
Structural Engineering — M,D,O
Transportation and Highway
   Engineering — M,D,O
Water Resources Engineering — M,D,O

MARSHALL UNIVERSITY
Computer Engineering — M
Computer Science — M
Electrical Engineering — M
Engineering and Applied
   Sciences—General — M,O
Engineering Management — M
Environmental Engineering — M
Health Informatics — M
Information Science — M
Management of Technology — M,O
Mechanical Engineering — M
Transportation and Highway
   Engineering — M

MARYMOUNT UNIVERSITY
Computer and Information
   Systems Security — M,D,O
Health Informatics — M,O
Software Engineering — M,O

MARYVILLE UNIVERSITY OF SAINT LOUIS
Computer and Information
   Systems Security — M,O
Data Science/Data Analytics — M
Information Science — M,O

MARYWOOD UNIVERSITY
Biotechnology — M
Computer and Information
   Systems Security — M

MASSACHUSETTS INSTITUTE OF TECHNOLOGY
Aerospace/Aeronautical
   Engineering — M,D,O
Bioengineering — M,D
Bioinformatics — M,D
Biomedical Engineering — M,D
Chemical Engineering — M,D
Civil Engineering — M,D,O
Computer Engineering — M,D,O
Computer Science — M,D,O
Construction Engineering — M,D,O
Electrical Engineering — M,D,O
Engineering and Applied
   Sciences—General — M,D,O
Engineering Management — M
Environmental Engineering — M,D,O
Geotechnical Engineering — M,D,O
Information Science — M,D,O
Manufacturing Engineering — M,D,O
Materials Engineering — M,D,O
Materials Sciences — M,D,O
Mechanical Engineering — M,D,O
Nuclear Engineering — M,D,O
Ocean Engineering — M,D,O
Operations Research — M,D
Structural Engineering — M,D,O
Systems Engineering — M,D
Technology and Public Policy — M,D
Transportation and Highway
   Engineering — M,D,O

---

*M—masters degree; D—doctorate; O—other advanced degree; *—Close-Up and/or Display*

MAYO CLINIC GRADUATE SCHOOL OF BIOMEDICAL SCIENCES
Biomedical Engineering — M,D

MCGILL UNIVERSITY
Aerospace/Aeronautical Engineering — M,D
Agricultural Engineering — M,D
Bioengineering — M,D
Bioinformatics — M,D
Biomedical Engineering — M,D
Biotechnology — M,D,O
Chemical Engineering — M,D
Civil Engineering — M,D
Computer Engineering — M,D
Computer Science — M,D
Electrical Engineering — M,D
Engineering and Applied Sciences—General — M,D,O
Environmental Engineering — M,D
Geotechnical Engineering — M,D
Hydraulics — M,D
Materials Engineering — M,D,O
Mechanical Engineering — M,D
Mechanics — M,D
Mineral/Mining Engineering — M,D,O
Structural Engineering — M,D
Water Resources Engineering — M,D

MCMASTER UNIVERSITY
Chemical Engineering — M,D
Civil Engineering — M,D
Computer Science — M,D
Electrical Engineering — M,D
Engineering and Applied Sciences—General — M,D
Engineering Physics — M,D
Materials Engineering — M,D
Materials Sciences — M,D
Mechanical Engineering — M,D
Nuclear Engineering — M,D
Software Engineering — M,D

MCNEESE STATE UNIVERSITY
Chemical Engineering — M
Civil Engineering — M
Computer Science — M
Electrical Engineering — M
Engineering and Applied Sciences—General — M
Engineering Management — M
Mechanical Engineering — M

MEMORIAL UNIVERSITY OF NEWFOUNDLAND
Civil Engineering — M,D
Computer Engineering — M,D
Computer Science — M,D
Electrical Engineering — M,D
Engineering and Applied Sciences—General — M,D
Environmental Engineering — M
Mechanical Engineering — M,D
Ocean Engineering — M,D

MERCER UNIVERSITY
Biomedical Engineering — M
Computer Engineering — M
Electrical Engineering — M
Engineering and Applied Sciences—General — M
Engineering Management — M
Environmental Engineering — M
Health Informatics — M,D
Management of Technology — M
Mechanical Engineering — M
Software Engineering — M

MERCY COLLEGE
Computer and Information Systems Security — M

MERCYHURST UNIVERSITY
Computer and Information Systems Security — M

MERRIMACK COLLEGE
Civil Engineering — M
Computer Science — M
Data Science/Data Analytics — M
Engineering and Applied Sciences—General — M
Engineering Management — M
Mechanical Engineering — M

METROPOLITAN STATE UNIVERSITY
Computer and Information Systems Security — M,D,O
Computer Science — M
Data Science/Data Analytics — M,D,O

MIAMI UNIVERSITY
Chemical Engineering — M
Computer Engineering — M
Electrical Engineering — M
Engineering and Applied Sciences—General — M
Mechanical Engineering — M
Systems Science — M

MICHIGAN STATE UNIVERSITY
Biosystems Engineering — M,D
Chemical Engineering — M,D
Civil Engineering — M,D
Computer Science — M,D
Construction Management — M,D
Electrical Engineering — M,D
Engineering and Applied Sciences—General — M,D
Environmental Engineering — M,D
Game Design and Development — M
Manufacturing Engineering — M,D
Materials Engineering — M,D
Materials Sciences — M,D
Mechanical Engineering — M,D
Mechanics — M,D

MICHIGAN TECHNOLOGICAL UNIVERSITY
Biomedical Engineering — M,D
Chemical Engineering — M,D
Civil Engineering — M,D
Computer Engineering — M,D,O
Data Science/Data Analytics — M,D,O
Electrical Engineering — M,D,O
Engineering and Applied Sciences—General — M,D,O
Environmental Engineering — M,D
Ergonomics and Human Factors — M,D,O
Materials Engineering — M,D
Mechanical Engineering — M,D,O
Mechanics — M,D,O
Metallurgical Engineering and Metallurgy — M,D

MIDDLE GEORGIA STATE UNIVERSITY
Computer and Information Systems Security — M
Health Informatics — M

MIDDLE TENNESSEE STATE UNIVERSITY
Aerospace/Aeronautical Engineering — M
Biotechnology — M
Computer Science — M
Engineering Management — M
Medical Informatics — M

MIDWESTERN STATE UNIVERSITY
Computer Science — M
Health Informatics — M,O

MILLENNIA ATLANTIC UNIVERSITY
Health Informatics — M

MILLS COLLEGE
Computer Science — M,O

MILWAUKEE SCHOOL OF ENGINEERING
Architectural Engineering — M
Civil Engineering — M
Engineering and Applied Sciences—General — M
Engineering Management — M

MINNESOTA STATE UNIVERSITY MANKATO
Automotive Engineering — M
Computer Science — M,O
Information Science — M,O
Manufacturing Engineering — M

MISSISSIPPI COLLEGE
Computer and Information Systems Security — M
Computer Science — M

MISSISSIPPI STATE UNIVERSITY
Aerospace/Aeronautical Engineering — M,D
Bioengineering — M,D
Biomedical Engineering — M,D
Chemical Engineering — M,D
Civil Engineering — M,D
Computer Engineering — M,D
Computer Science — M,D
Electrical Engineering — M,D
Engineering and Applied Sciences—General — M,D
Ergonomics and Human Factors — M,D
Industrial/Management Engineering — M,D
Mechanical Engineering — M,D
Operations Research — M,D
Systems Engineering — M,D

MISSOURI STATE UNIVERSITY
Applied Science and Technology — M,O
Computer Science — M
Construction Management — M
Materials Sciences — M

MISSOURI UNIVERSITY OF SCIENCE AND TECHNOLOGY
Aerospace/Aeronautical Engineering — M,D
Ceramic Sciences and Engineering — M,D
Chemical Engineering — M,D
Civil Engineering — M,D
Computer Engineering — M,D
Computer Science — M,D
Electrical Engineering — M,D
Engineering Management — M,D
Environmental Engineering — M,D
Geological Engineering — M,D
Geotechnical Engineering — M
Information Science — M
Manufacturing Engineering — M,D
Materials Engineering — M,D
Materials Sciences — M,D
Mechanical Engineering — M,D
Metallurgical Engineering and Metallurgy — M,D
Mineral/Mining Engineering — M,D

Nuclear Engineering — M,D
Petroleum Engineering — M,D
Systems Engineering — M,D

MISSOURI WESTERN STATE UNIVERSITY
Computer and Information Systems Security — M
Engineering and Applied Sciences—General — M

MONMOUTH UNIVERSITY
Computer Science — M
Software Engineering — M,O

MONROE COLLEGE
Computer Science — M
Information Science — M

MONTANA STATE UNIVERSITY
Chemical Engineering — M,D
Civil Engineering — M,D
Computer Engineering — M,D
Computer Science — M,D
Construction Engineering — M,D
Electrical Engineering — M,D
Engineering and Applied Sciences—General — M,D
Environmental Engineering — M,D
Industrial/Management Engineering — M,D
Mechanical Engineering — M,D
Mechanics — M,D

MONTANA TECHNOLOGICAL UNIVERSITY
Electrical Engineering — M
Engineering and Applied Sciences—General — M
Environmental Engineering — M
Geological Engineering — M
Health Informatics — O
Industrial/Management Engineering — M
Materials Sciences — D
Metallurgical Engineering and Metallurgy — M
Mineral/Mining Engineering — M
Petroleum Engineering — M

MONTCLAIR STATE UNIVERSITY
Computer Science — M,O
Data Science/Data Analytics — O
Management of Technology — M

MORGAN STATE UNIVERSITY
Bioinformatics — M
Civil Engineering — M,D,O
Computer Science — M
Electrical Engineering — M,D,O
Engineering and Applied Sciences—General — M,D,O
Industrial/Management Engineering — M,D,O
Transportation and Highway Engineering — M,D,O

MOUNT ST. MARY'S UNIVERSITY (MD)
Biotechnology — M

MURRAY STATE UNIVERSITY
Computer Science — M
Safety Engineering — M
Telecommunications Management — M

NATIONAL TEST PILOT SCHOOL
Aviation — M

NATIONAL UNIVERSITY

Computer and Information Systems Security	M
Computer Science	M
Data Science/Data Analytics	M
Electrical Engineering	M
Engineering and Applied Sciences—General	M
Engineering Management	M
Health Informatics	M,O
Management of Technology	M

NAVAL POSTGRADUATE SCHOOL

Aerospace/Aeronautical Engineering	M,D,O
Applied Science and Technology	M,D
Computer and Information Systems Security	M,D
Computer Engineering	M,D,O
Computer Science	M,D,O
Electrical Engineering	M,D
Engineering Management	M,D,O
Information Science	M,D,O
Mechanical Engineering	M,D,O
Modeling and Simulation	M,D
Operations Research	M,D
Software Engineering	M,D
Systems Engineering	M,D,O

NEW COLLEGE OF FLORIDA

Data Science/Data Analytics	M

NEW ENGLAND INSTITUTE OF TECHNOLOGY

Construction Management	M
Engineering Management	M

NEW JERSEY CITY UNIVERSITY

Computer and Information Systems Security	M,D,O

NEW JERSEY INSTITUTE OF TECHNOLOGY

Biomedical Engineering	M,D
Chemical Engineering	M,D
Computer and Information Systems Security	M,D,O
Computer Engineering	M,D
Computer Science	M,D,O
Data Science/Data Analytics	M,D,O
Electrical Engineering	M,D
Energy and Power Engineering	M,D
Engineering and Applied Sciences—General	M,D
Engineering Management	M,D
Environmental Engineering	M,D
Industrial/Management Engineering	M,D
Information Science	M,D,O
Internet Engineering	M,D
Management of Technology	M,D,O
Manufacturing Engineering	M,D
Materials Engineering	M,D,O
Materials Sciences	M,D,O
Mechanical Engineering	M,D
Pharmaceutical Engineering	M,D
Safety Engineering	M,D
Software Engineering	M,D,O
Telecommunications	M,D
Transportation and Highway Engineering	M,D

NEW MEXICO HIGHLANDS UNIVERSITY

Computer Science	M

NEW MEXICO INSTITUTE OF MINING AND TECHNOLOGY

Computer Science	M,D
Electrical Engineering	M
Engineering Management	M
Environmental Engineering	M
Geological Engineering	M
Hazardous Materials Management	M
Materials Engineering	M,D
Mechanical Engineering	M
Mechanics	M
Mineral/Mining Engineering	M
Operations Research	M,D
Petroleum Engineering	M,D
Systems Engineering	M
Water Resources Engineering	M

NEW MEXICO STATE UNIVERSITY

Bioinformatics	M,D
Biotechnology	M,D
Engineering and Applied Sciences—General	M,D,O
Environmental Engineering	M,D
Systems Engineering	M,D,O

THE NEW SCHOOL

Data Science/Data Analytics	M

NEWSCHOOL OF ARCHITECTURE AND DESIGN

Construction Management	M

NEW YORK INSTITUTE OF TECHNOLOGY

Computer and Information Systems Security	M
Computer Engineering	M
Computer Science	M
Electrical Engineering	M
Energy and Power Engineering	O
Energy Management and Policy	O
Engineering and Applied Sciences—General	M,O
Environmental Engineering	M
Mechanical Engineering	M

NEW YORK UNIVERSITY

Artificial Intelligence/Robotics	M
Bioinformatics	M
Biomedical Engineering	M,D
Biotechnology	M
Chemical Engineering	M,D
Civil Engineering	M,D
Computer and Information Systems Security	M
Computer Engineering	M
Computer Science	M,D
Construction Management	M
Data Science/Data Analytics	M
Electrical Engineering	M,D
Engineering and Applied Sciences—General	M,D,O
Environmental Engineering	M
Financial Engineering	M
Game Design and Development	M
Industrial/Management Engineering	M
Management of Technology	M,D
Manufacturing Engineering	M
Mechanical Engineering	M,D
Software Engineering	O
Transportation and Highway Engineering	M,D

NIAGARA UNIVERSITY

Computer and Information Systems Security	M

NORFOLK STATE UNIVERSITY

Computer Engineering	M
Computer Science	M
Electrical Engineering	M
Materials Sciences	M

NORTH CAROLINA AGRICULTURAL AND TECHNICAL STATE UNIVERSITY

Bioengineering	M
Chemical Engineering	M
Civil Engineering	M
Computer Engineering	M,D
Computer Science	M,D
Electrical Engineering	M,D
Energy and Power Engineering	M,D
Engineering and Applied Sciences—General	M,D
Industrial/Management Engineering	M,D
Mechanical Engineering	M,D
Systems Engineering	M,D

NORTH CAROLINA STATE UNIVERSITY

Aerospace/Aeronautical Engineering	M,D
Agricultural Engineering	M,D,O
Bioengineering	M,D,O
Chemical Engineering	M,D
Civil Engineering	M,D
Computer Engineering	M,D
Computer Science	M,D
Electrical Engineering	M,D
Engineering and Applied Sciences—General	M,D
Ergonomics and Human Factors	D
Financial Engineering	M
Industrial/Management Engineering	M,D
Management of Technology	M,D
Manufacturing Engineering	M
Materials Engineering	M,D
Materials Sciences	M,D
Mechanical Engineering	M,D
Nuclear Engineering	M,D
Operations Research	M,D
Polymer Science and Engineering	M,D
Textile Sciences and Engineering	M,D

NORTH CENTRAL COLLEGE

Computer Science	M

NORTHCENTRAL UNIVERSITY

Computer and Information Systems Security	M,D,O
Computer Science	M,D,O
Data Science/Data Analytics	M,D,O

NORTH DAKOTA STATE UNIVERSITY

Agricultural Engineering	M,D
Bioinformatics	M,D
Biosystems Engineering	M,D
Civil Engineering	M,D
Computer Engineering	M,D
Computer Science	M,D,O
Construction Management	M,O
Electrical Engineering	M,D
Engineering and Applied Sciences—General	M,D,O
Environmental Engineering	M,D
Industrial/Management Engineering	M,D
Manufacturing Engineering	M,D
Materials Sciences	M,D
Mechanical Engineering	M,D
Nanotechnology	M,D
Polymer Science and Engineering	M,D
Software Engineering	M,D,O
Transportation and Highway Engineering	D

NORTHEASTERN ILLINOIS UNIVERSITY

Computer Science	M

NORTHEASTERN UNIVERSITY

Bioengineering	M,D
Bioinformatics	M,D
Biotechnology	M,D
Chemical Engineering	M,D,O
Civil Engineering	M,D,O
Computer and Information Systems Security	M,D,O
Computer Engineering	M,D,O
Computer Science	M,D
Data Science/Data Analytics	M,D
Electrical Engineering	M,D,O
Energy and Power Engineering	M,D,O
Engineering and Applied Sciences—General	M,D,O
Engineering Management	M,D,O
Environmental Engineering	M,D,O
Health Informatics	M,D
Industrial/Management Engineering	M,D,O
Mechanical Engineering	M,D,O
Operations Research	M,D,O
Systems Engineering	M,D,O
Telecommunications	M,D,O

NORTHERN ARIZONA UNIVERSITY

Bioengineering	M,D
Civil Engineering	M
Computer Engineering	M,D
Computer Science	M,D
Electrical Engineering	M,D
Engineering and Applied Sciences—General	M,D,O
Mechanical Engineering	M,D

NORTHERN ILLINOIS UNIVERSITY

Computer Science	M
Electrical Engineering	M
Engineering and Applied Sciences—General	M
Industrial/Management Engineering	M
Mechanical Engineering	M

NORTHERN KENTUCKY UNIVERSITY

Computer and Information Systems Security	M,O
Computer Science	M,O
Health Informatics	M,O
Information Science	M,O
Management of Technology	M
Software Engineering	M,O

NORTHWESTERN POLYTECHNIC UNIVERSITY

Computer Engineering	M,D
Computer Science	M,D
Electrical Engineering	M,D
Engineering and Applied Sciences—General	M,D

*M—masters degree; D—doctorate; O—other advanced degree; *—Close-Up and/or Display*

NORTHWESTERN UNIVERSITY

Artificial Intelligence/Robotics	M
Bioengineering	D
Biomedical Engineering	M,D
Biotechnology	M,D
Chemical Engineering	M,D
Civil Engineering	M,D
Computer and Information Systems Security	M
Computer Engineering	M,D
Computer Science	M,D
Data Science/Data Analytics	M
Electrical Engineering	M,D
Engineering and Applied Sciences—General	M,D,O
Engineering Design	M
Engineering Management	M
Environmental Engineering	M,D
Geotechnical Engineering	M,D
Health Informatics	M,D
Industrial/Management Engineering	M,D
Information Science	M
Materials Engineering	M,D,O
Materials Sciences	M,D,O
Mechanical Engineering	M,D
Mechanics	M,D
Medical Informatics	M,D
Software Engineering	M
Structural Engineering	M,D
Transportation and Highway Engineering	M,D

NORTHWEST MISSOURI STATE UNIVERSITY

Computer Science	M

NORWICH UNIVERSITY

Civil Engineering	M
Computer and Information Systems Security	M
Construction Management	M
Energy Management and Policy	M
Environmental Engineering	M
Geotechnical Engineering	M
Structural Engineering	M

NOTRE DAME COLLEGE (OH)

Computer Science	M,O

NOVA SOUTHEASTERN UNIVERSITY

Bioinformatics	M,D,O
Computer and Information Systems Security	M,D
Computer Science	M,D
Health Informatics	M,D,O
Information Science	M,D
Medical Informatics	M,D,O

OAKLAND UNIVERSITY

Computer Engineering	M,D
Computer Science	M,D
Electrical Engineering	M,D
Engineering and Applied Sciences—General	M,D,O
Engineering Management	M
Mechanical Engineering	M,D
Software Engineering	M,D
Systems Engineering	M,D
Systems Science	M,D

OHIO DOMINICAN UNIVERSITY

Data Science/Data Analytics	M
Engineering Design	M

THE OHIO STATE UNIVERSITY

Aerospace/Aeronautical Engineering	M,D
Agricultural Engineering	M,D
Bioengineering	M,D
Biomedical Engineering	M,D
Chemical Engineering	M,D
Civil Engineering	M,D
Computer Engineering	M,D
Computer Science	M,D
Electrical Engineering	M,D
Engineering and Applied Sciences—General	M,D
Industrial/Management Engineering	M,D
Materials Engineering	M,D
Materials Sciences	M,D
Mechanical Engineering	M,D
Metallurgical Engineering and Metallurgy	M,D
Nuclear Engineering	M,D
Operations Research	M
Systems Engineering	M,D

OHIO UNIVERSITY

Biomedical Engineering	M
Chemical Engineering	M,D
Civil Engineering	M,D
Computer Science	M,D
Construction Engineering	M,D
Electrical Engineering	M,D
Engineering and Applied Sciences—General	M,D
Environmental Engineering	M,D
Geotechnical Engineering	M,D
Industrial/Management Engineering	M,D
Mechanical Engineering	M
Mechanics	M,D
Structural Engineering	M,D
Systems Engineering	M
Telecommunications	M
Transportation and Highway Engineering	M,D
Water Resources Engineering	M,D

OKLAHOMA BAPTIST UNIVERSITY

Energy Management and Policy	M

OKLAHOMA CHRISTIAN UNIVERSITY

Computer Engineering	M
Computer Science	M
Electrical Engineering	M
Engineering and Applied Sciences—General	M
Engineering Management	M
Mechanical Engineering	M
Software Engineering	M

OKLAHOMA CITY UNIVERSITY

Computer Science	M
Energy Management and Policy	M

OKLAHOMA STATE UNIVERSITY

Agricultural Engineering	M,D
Aviation	M,D,O
Bioengineering	M,D
Chemical Engineering	M,D
Civil Engineering	M,D
Computer Engineering	M,D
Computer Science	M,D
Electrical Engineering	M,D
Engineering and Applied Sciences—General	M,D
Environmental Engineering	M,D
Fire Protection Engineering	M,D
Industrial/Management Engineering	M,D
Information Science	M,D
Materials Engineering	M,D
Materials Sciences	M,D
Mechanical Engineering	M,D
Telecommunications Management	M,D,O

OLD DOMINION UNIVERSITY

Aerospace/Aeronautical Engineering	M,D
Biomedical Engineering	M,D
Civil Engineering	M,D
Computer Engineering	M,D
Computer Science	M,D
Electrical Engineering	M,D
Engineering and Applied Sciences—General	M,D
Engineering Management	M,D
Environmental Engineering	M,D
Ergonomics and Human Factors	D
Geotechnical Engineering	M
Hydraulics	M
Information Science	D
Mechanical Engineering	M,D
Modeling and Simulation	M,D
Structural Engineering	M
Systems Engineering	M,D
Transportation and Highway Engineering	M

OPEN UNIVERSITY

Engineering and Applied Sciences—General	M

OREGON HEALTH & SCIENCE UNIVERSITY

Bioinformatics	M,D,O
Biomedical Engineering	M,D
Computer Engineering	M,D
Computer Science	M,D
Electrical Engineering	M,D
Environmental Engineering	M,D
Health Informatics	M,D,O
Medical Informatics	M,D,O

OREGON INSTITUTE OF TECHNOLOGY

Manufacturing Engineering	M

OREGON STATE UNIVERSITY

Agricultural Engineering	M,D
Artificial Intelligence/Robotics	M,D
Bioengineering	M,D
Bioinformatics	D
Biotechnology	M,D
Chemical Engineering	M,D
Civil Engineering	M,D
Computer Engineering	M,D
Computer Science	M,D
Construction Engineering	M,D
Data Science/Data Analytics	M
Electrical Engineering	M,D
Engineering and Applied Sciences—General	M,D
Engineering Management	M,D
Environmental Engineering	M,D
Geotechnical Engineering	M,D
Industrial/Management Engineering	M,D
Manufacturing Engineering	M,D
Materials Sciences	M,D
Mechanical Engineering	M,D
Nuclear Engineering	M,D
Ocean Engineering	M,D
Structural Engineering	M,D
Systems Engineering	M,D
Transportation and Highway Engineering	M,D
Water Resources Engineering	M,D

OUR LADY OF THE LAKE UNIVERSITY

Computer and Information Systems Security	M

PACE UNIVERSITY

Computer and Information Systems Security	M,D,O
Computer Science	M,D,O
Information Science	M,D,O
Software Engineering	M,D,O
Telecommunications	M,D,O

PACIFIC STATES UNIVERSITY

Computer Science	M
Management of Technology	M,O

PENN STATE GREAT VALLEY

Computer and Information Systems Security	M,O
Data Science/Data Analytics	M,O
Engineering and Applied Sciences—General	M,O
Engineering Management	M,O
Information Science	M,O
Software Engineering	M,O
Systems Engineering	M,O

PENN STATE HARRISBURG

Civil Engineering	M,O
Computer Science	M,O
Electrical Engineering	M,O
Engineering and Applied Sciences—General	M,O
Engineering Management	M,O
Environmental Engineering	M,O
Mechanical Engineering	M,O
Structural Engineering	M,O

PENN STATE HERSHEY MEDICAL CENTER

Bioinformatics	M,D

PENN STATE UNIVERSITY PARK

Aerospace/Aeronautical Engineering	M,D
Agricultural Engineering	M,D
Architectural Engineering	M,D
Bioengineering	M,D
Biotechnology	M,D
Chemical Engineering	M,D
Civil Engineering	M,D
Computer Engineering	M,D
Computer Science	M,D*
Electrical Engineering	M,D
Engineering and Applied Sciences—General	M,D
Engineering Design	M
Environmental Engineering	M,D
Geotechnical Engineering	M,D
Industrial/Management Engineering	M,D
Information Science	M,D
Materials Engineering	M,D
Materials Sciences	M,D
Mechanical Engineering	M,D
Mechanics	M,D
Mineral/Mining Engineering	M,D
Nuclear Engineering	M,D

PITTSBURG STATE UNIVERSITY

Construction Engineering	M
Construction Management	M,O
Electrical Engineering	M
Management of Technology	M,O
Manufacturing Engineering	M
Mechanical Engineering	M
Polymer Science and Engineering	M

POINT PARK UNIVERSITY

Engineering Management	M

POLYTECHNIC UNIVERSITY OF PUERTO RICO

Civil Engineering	M
Computer Engineering	M
Computer Science	M
Electrical Engineering	M

Engineering Management M
Management of Technology M
Manufacturing Engineering M
Mechanical Engineering M

POLYTECHNIC UNIVERSITY OF PUERTO RICO, MIAMI CAMPUS
Construction Management M
Environmental Engineering M

POLYTECHNIC UNIVERSITY OF PUERTO RICO, ORLANDO CAMPUS
Construction Management M
Engineering Management M
Environmental Engineering M
Management of Technology M

POLYTECHNIQUE MONTRÉAL
Aerospace/Aeronautical
  Engineering M,D,O
Biomedical Engineering M,D,O
Chemical Engineering M,D,O
Civil Engineering M,D,O
Computer Engineering M,D,O
Computer Science M,D,O
Electrical Engineering M,D,O
Engineering and Applied
  Sciences—General M,D,O
Engineering Physics M,D,O
Environmental Engineering M,D,O
Geotechnical Engineering M,D,O
Hydraulics M,D,O
Industrial/Management
  Engineering M,D,O
Management of Technology M,D,O
Mechanical Engineering M,D,O
Mechanics M,D,O
Nuclear Engineering M,D,O
Operations Research M,D,O
Structural Engineering M,D,O
Transportation and Highway
  Engineering M,D,O

PONTIFICAL JOHN PAUL II INSTITUTE FOR STUDIES ON MARRIAGE AND FAMILY
Biotechnology M,D,O

PONTIFICIA UNIVERSIDAD CATOLICA MADRE Y MAESTRA
Engineering and Applied
  Sciences—General M
Structural Engineering M

PORTLAND STATE UNIVERSITY
Artificial Intelligence/Robotics M,D,O
Civil Engineering M,D,O
Computer and Information
  Systems Security M,D,O
Computer Engineering M,D
Computer Science M,D,O
Electrical Engineering M,D
Energy Management and
  Policy M,D,O
Engineering and Applied
  Sciences—General M,D,O
Engineering Management M,D,O
Environmental Engineering M,D
Management of Technology M,D
Materials Engineering M,D
Mechanical Engineering M,D,O
Modeling and Simulation M,D,O
Systems Science M,D,O

PRAIRIE VIEW A&M UNIVERSITY
Computer Science M,D
Electrical Engineering M,D

Engineering and Applied
  Sciences—General M,D

PRINCETON UNIVERSITY
Aerospace/Aeronautical
  Engineering M,D
Bioengineering M,D
Chemical Engineering M,D
Civil Engineering M,D
Computer Science M,D
Electrical Engineering M,D
Electronic Materials D
Engineering and Applied
  Sciences—General M,D
Environmental Engineering M,D
Financial Engineering M,D
Materials Sciences D
Mechanical Engineering M,D
Ocean Engineering D
Operations Research M,D

PURDUE UNIVERSITY
Aerospace/Aeronautical
  Engineering M,D
Agricultural Engineering M,D
Biomedical Engineering M,D
Biotechnology D
Chemical Engineering M,D
Civil Engineering M,D
Computer and Information
  Systems Security M
Computer Engineering M,D
Computer Science M,D
Construction Management M
Electrical Engineering M,D
Engineering and Applied
  Sciences—General M,D,O
Environmental Engineering M,D
Ergonomics and Human
  Factors M,D
Industrial/Management
  Engineering M,D
Management of Technology M,D
Materials Engineering M,D
Mechanical Engineering M,D,O
Nuclear Engineering M,D

PURDUE UNIVERSITY FORT WAYNE
Civil Engineering M
Computer Engineering M
Computer Science M
Construction Management M
Electrical Engineering M
Engineering and Applied
  Sciences—General M,O
Industrial/Management
  Engineering M
Information Science M
Mechanical Engineering M
Operations Research M,O
Systems Engineering M

PURDUE UNIVERSITY GLOBAL
Computer and Information
  Systems Security M

PURDUE UNIVERSITY NORTHWEST
Biotechnology M
Computer Engineering M
Computer Science M
Electrical Engineering M
Engineering and Applied
  Sciences—General M
Mechanical Engineering M

QUEENS COLLEGE OF THE CITY UNIVERSITY OF NEW YORK
Computer Science M
Data Science/Data Analytics M

QUEEN'S UNIVERSITY AT KINGSTON
Artificial Intelligence/Robotics M
Chemical Engineering M,D
Civil Engineering M,D
Computer Engineering M,D
Computer Science M,D
Electrical Engineering M,D
Engineering and Applied
  Sciences—General M,D
Engineering Physics M,D
Ergonomics and Human
  Factors M,D
Materials Engineering M,D
Mechanical Engineering M,D
Mineral/Mining Engineering M,D

QUINNIPIAC UNIVERSITY
Computer and Information
  Systems Security M

RADFORD UNIVERSITY
Data Science/Data Analytics M

REGENT UNIVERSITY
Computer and Information
  Systems Security M

REGIS UNIVERSITY
Computer and Information
  Systems Security M,O
Computer Science M,O
Data Science/Data Analytics M,O
Health Informatics M,O
Information Science M,O
Medical Informatics M,O
Software Engineering M,O
Systems Engineering M,O

RENSSELAER AT HARTFORD
Computer Engineering M
Computer Science M
Electrical Engineering M
Engineering and Applied
  Sciences—General M
Information Science M
Mechanical Engineering M
Systems Science M

RENSSELAER POLYTECHNIC INSTITUTE
Aerospace/Aeronautical
  Engineering M,D
Biomedical Engineering M,D
Chemical Engineering M,D
Civil Engineering M,D
Computer Engineering M,D
Computer Science M,D
Electrical Engineering M,D
Engineering and Applied
  Sciences—General M,D
Engineering Physics M,D
Environmental Engineering M,D
Financial Engineering M
Industrial/Management
  Engineering M,D
Information Science M
Materials Engineering M,D
Mechanical Engineering M,D
Nuclear Engineering M,D
Systems Engineering M,D
Technology and Public Policy M,D
Transportation and Highway
  Engineering M,D

RICE UNIVERSITY
Bioengineering M,D
Bioinformatics M,D
Biomedical Engineering M,D
Chemical Engineering M,D
Civil Engineering M,D
Computer Engineering M,D
Computer Science M,D
Electrical Engineering M,D
Energy Management and
  Policy M,D
Engineering and Applied
  Sciences—General M,D
Environmental Engineering M,D
Materials Sciences M,D
Mechanical Engineering M,D

RIVIER UNIVERSITY
Computer Science M

ROBERT MORRIS UNIVERSITY
Computer and Information
  Systems Security M,D
Data Science/Data Analytics M,D
Engineering and Applied
  Sciences—General M
Engineering Management M
Information Science M

ROBERT MORRIS UNIVERSITY ILLINOIS
Computer and Information
  Systems Security M

ROBERTS WESLEYAN COLLEGE
Health Informatics M

ROCHESTER INSTITUTE OF TECHNOLOGY
Bioinformatics M
Computer and Information
  Systems Security M,O
Computer Engineering M
Computer Science M,D
Data Science/Data Analytics O
Electrical Engineering M
Engineering and Applied
  Sciences—General M,D,O
Engineering Design M
Engineering Management M
Game Design and
  Development M
Health Informatics M
Human-Computer Interaction M
Industrial/Management
  Engineering M
Information Science M,D
Manufacturing Engineering M
Materials Engineering M
Materials Sciences M
Mechanical Engineering M
Modeling and Simulation D
Safety Engineering M
Software Engineering M
Systems Engineering M,D
Technology and Public Policy M
Telecommunications M

ROCKHURST UNIVERSITY
Data Science/Data Analytics M,O

ROGER WILLIAMS UNIVERSITY
Computer and Information
  Systems Security M

ROOSEVELT UNIVERSITY
Biotechnology M
Computer Science M

---

*M—masters degree; D—doctorate; O—other advanced degree; *—Close-Up and/or Display*

ROSE-HULMAN INSTITUTE OF TECHNOLOGY

Biomedical Engineering	M
Chemical Engineering	M
Civil Engineering	M
Computer Engineering	M
Electrical Engineering	M
Engineering and Applied Sciences—General	M
Engineering Management	M
Environmental Engineering	M
Mechanical Engineering	M
Systems Engineering	M

ROWAN UNIVERSITY

Bioinformatics	M
Chemical Engineering	M
Civil Engineering	M
Computer and Information Systems Security	O
Computer Science	M
Electrical Engineering	M
Engineering and Applied Sciences—General	M
Mechanical Engineering	M

ROYAL MILITARY COLLEGE OF CANADA

Chemical Engineering	M,D
Civil Engineering	M,D
Computer Engineering	M,D
Computer Science	M
Electrical Engineering	M,D
Engineering and Applied Sciences—General	M,D
Mechanical Engineering	M,D
Software Engineering	M,D

RUTGERS UNIVERSITY - CAMDEN

Computer Science	M

RUTGERS UNIVERSITY - NEWARK

Bioinformatics	M,D
Biomedical Engineering	O
Management of Technology	D
Medical Informatics	M,D,O

RUTGERS UNIVERSITY - NEW BRUNSWICK

Aerospace/Aeronautical Engineering	M,D
Biochemical Engineering	M,D
Biomedical Engineering	M,D
Chemical Engineering	M,D
Civil Engineering	M,D
Computer Engineering	M,D
Computer Science	M,D
Electrical Engineering	M,D
Environmental Engineering	M,D
Hazardous Materials Management	M,D
Health Informatics	M
Industrial/Management Engineering	M,D
Information Science	M
Materials Engineering	M,D
Materials Sciences	M,D
Mechanical Engineering	M,D
Mechanics	M,D
Operations Research	D
Reliability Engineering	M,D
Systems Engineering	M,D

RYERSON UNIVERSITY

Management of Technology	M

SACRED HEART UNIVERSITY

Computer and Information Systems Security	M
Computer Science	M
Game Design and Development	M

Health Informatics	M
Information Science	M

SAGINAW VALLEY STATE UNIVERSITY

Computer and Information Systems Security	M
Computer Science	M
Energy and Power Engineering	M
Engineering and Applied Sciences—General	M

ST. AMBROSE UNIVERSITY

Management of Technology	M

ST. CATHERINE UNIVERSITY

Health Informatics	M

ST. CLOUD STATE UNIVERSITY

Biomedical Engineering	M,O
Computer and Information Systems Security	M
Computer Science	M,O
Electrical Engineering	M
Engineering and Applied Sciences—General	M,O

ST. FRANCIS XAVIER UNIVERSITY

Computer Science	M

ST. JOHN'S UNIVERSITY (NY)

Biotechnology	M
Data Science/Data Analytics	M
Information Science	

ST. JOSEPH'S COLLEGE, LONG ISLAND CAMPUS

Health Informatics	M

ST. JOSEPH'S COLLEGE, NEW YORK

Health Informatics	M

SAINT JOSEPH'S UNIVERSITY

Computer Science	M,O
Health Informatics	M

SAINT LEO UNIVERSITY

Computer and Information Systems Security	M,D

SAINT LOUIS UNIVERSITY

Bioinformatics	M
Biomedical Engineering	M,D
Computer Science	M
Software Engineering	M

SAINT MARTIN'S UNIVERSITY

Civil Engineering	M
Engineering Management	M
Mechanical Engineering	M

SAINT MARY'S UNIVERSITY (CANADA)

Applied Science and Technology	M

ST. MARY'S UNIVERSITY (UNITED STATES)

Computer and Information Systems Security	M,O
Computer Engineering	M
Computer Science	M
Electrical Engineering	M
Engineering Management	M
Industrial/Management Engineering	M

Information Science	M
Software Engineering	M,O

SAINT MARY'S UNIVERSITY OF MINNESOTA

Computer and Information Systems Security	M
Data Science/Data Analytics	M

SAINT PETER'S UNIVERSITY

Data Science/Data Analytics	M

SAINT XAVIER UNIVERSITY

Computer Science	M

SALEM INTERNATIONAL UNIVERSITY

Computer and Information Systems Security	M

SALVE REGINA UNIVERSITY

Computer and Information Systems Security	M,O

SAMFORD UNIVERSITY

Energy Management and Policy	M
Health Informatics	M

SAM HOUSTON STATE UNIVERSITY

Computer and Information Systems Security	M,D
Computer Science	M,D
Information Science	M,D

SAN DIEGO STATE UNIVERSITY

Aerospace/Aeronautical Engineering	M,D
Civil Engineering	M
Computer Science	M
Electrical Engineering	M
Engineering and Applied Sciences—General	M,D
Engineering Design	M,D
Mechanical Engineering	M,D
Mechanics	M,D
Telecommunications Management	M

SAN FRANCISCO STATE UNIVERSITY

Biotechnology	M
Computer Science	M
Electrical Engineering	M
Energy and Power Engineering	M
Engineering and Applied Sciences—General	M

SAN JOSE STATE UNIVERSITY

Aerospace/Aeronautical Engineering	M
Chemical Engineering	M
Civil Engineering	M
Computer Engineering	M
Electrical Engineering	M
Industrial/Management Engineering	M
Materials Engineering	M
Mechanical Engineering	M
Software Engineering	M
Systems Engineering	M

THE SANS TECHNOLOGY INSTITUTE

Computer and Information Systems Security	M

SANTA CLARA UNIVERSITY

Bioengineering	M,D,O
Civil Engineering	M,D,O
Computer Engineering	M,D,O
Computer Science	M,D,O
Electrical Engineering	M,D,O
Energy and Power Engineering	M,D,O
Engineering and Applied Sciences—General	M,D,O
Engineering Management	M,D,O
Mechanical Engineering	M,D,O
Software Engineering	M,D,O

SAVANNAH COLLEGE OF ART AND DESIGN

Game Design and Development	M

SEATTLE PACIFIC UNIVERSITY

Computer and Information Systems Security	M
Data Science/Data Analytics	M

SEATTLE UNIVERSITY

Computer Science	M
Engineering and Applied Sciences—General	M

SETON HALL UNIVERSITY

Management of Technology	M,O

SHIPPENSBURG UNIVERSITY OF PENNSYLVANIA

Computer Science	M,O
Information Science	M,O
Software Engineering	M,O

SIMON FRASER UNIVERSITY

Bioinformatics	M,D,O
Biotechnology	M,D,O
Computer Science	M,D
Engineering and Applied Sciences—General	M,D
Management of Technology	M,D,O
Mechanical Engineering	M,D
Operations Research	M,D
Systems Engineering	M,D

SIT GRADUATE INSTITUTE

Energy Management and Policy	M

SLIPPERY ROCK UNIVERSITY OF PENNSYLVANIA

Data Science/Data Analytics	M
Health Informatics	M

SOFIA UNIVERSITY

Computer Science	M,D

SOUTH CAROLINA STATE UNIVERSITY

Civil Engineering	M
Mechanical Engineering	M
Transportation and Highway Engineering	M

SOUTH DAKOTA SCHOOL OF MINES AND TECHNOLOGY

Artificial Intelligence/Robotics	M
Bioengineering	D
Biomedical Engineering	M,D
Chemical Engineering	M,D
Civil Engineering	M,D
Construction Management	M
Electrical Engineering	M
Engineering and Applied Sciences—General	M,D
Engineering Management	M

Geological Engineering	M,D
Management of Technology	M
Materials Engineering	M,D
Materials Sciences	M,D
Mechanical Engineering	M,D
Mineral/Mining Engineering	M
Nanotechnology	D

SOUTH DAKOTA STATE UNIVERSITY

Agricultural Engineering	M,D
Biosystems Engineering	M,D
Civil Engineering	M
Electrical Engineering	M,D
Engineering and Applied Sciences—General	M,D
Mechanical Engineering	M,D
Operations Research	M

SOUTHEASTERN LOUISIANA UNIVERSITY

Applied Science and Technology	M

SOUTHEASTERN OKLAHOMA STATE UNIVERSITY

Aviation	M
Biotechnology	M

SOUTHEAST MISSOURI STATE UNIVERSITY

Management of Technology	M

SOUTHERN ADVENTIST UNIVERSITY

Computer Science	M

SOUTHERN ARKANSAS UNIVERSITY–MAGNOLIA

Computer and Information Systems Security	M
Computer Science	M
Data Science/Data Analytics	M

SOUTHERN CONNECTICUT STATE UNIVERSITY

Computer Science	M

SOUTHERN ILLINOIS UNIVERSITY CARBONDALE

Biomedical Engineering	M
Civil Engineering	M,D
Computer Engineering	M,D
Computer Science	M,D
Electrical Engineering	M,D
Energy and Power Engineering	D
Engineering and Applied Sciences—General	M,D
Engineering Management	M
Environmental Engineering	D
Mechanical Engineering	M,D
Mechanics	M
Mineral/Mining Engineering	M,D

SOUTHERN ILLINOIS UNIVERSITY EDWARDSVILLE

Civil Engineering	M
Computer Science	M
Electrical Engineering	M
Engineering and Applied Sciences—General	M
Environmental Engineering	M
Geotechnical Engineering	M
Health Informatics	M
Industrial/Management Engineering	M
Mechanical Engineering	M

Operations Research	M
Structural Engineering	M
Transportation and Highway Engineering	M

SOUTHERN METHODIST UNIVERSITY

Civil Engineering	M,D
Computer Engineering	M,D
Computer Science	M,D
Data Science/Data Analytics	M,D
Electrical Engineering	M,D
Engineering and Applied Sciences—General	M,D
Engineering Management	M,D
Environmental Engineering	M,D
Geotechnical Engineering	M,D
Information Science	M,D
Manufacturing Engineering	M,D
Mechanical Engineering	M,D
Operations Research	M,D
Software Engineering	M,D
Structural Engineering	M,D
Systems Engineering	M,D
Telecommunications	M,D
Transportation and Highway Engineering	M,D

SOUTHERN NEW HAMPSHIRE UNIVERSITY

Computer and Information Systems Security	M
Data Science/Data Analytics	M,D,O
Engineering Management	M,D,O
Health Informatics	M,D,O

SOUTHERN OREGON UNIVERSITY

Computer Science	M

SOUTHERN STATES UNIVERSITY

Information Science	M

SOUTHERN UNIVERSITY AND AGRICULTURAL AND MECHANICAL COLLEGE

Computer Science	M
Engineering and Applied Sciences—General	M

SOUTHERN UTAH UNIVERSITY

Computer and Information Systems Security	M

STANFORD UNIVERSITY

Bioengineering	M,D
Chemical Engineering	M,D
Computer Science	M,D
Construction Engineering	M,D,O
Electrical Engineering	M,D
Energy and Power Engineering	M,D,O
Engineering and Applied Sciences—General	M,D,O
Engineering Management	M,D
Engineering Physics	M,D
Industrial/Management Engineering	M,D
Materials Engineering	M,D,O
Materials Sciences	M,D,O
Mechanical Engineering	M,D,O
Mechanics	M,D,O
Medical Informatics	M,D
Structural Engineering	M,D,O

STATE UNIVERSITY OF NEW YORK AT OSWEGO

Bioinformatics	M
Health Informatics	M

Human-Computer Interaction	M

STATE UNIVERSITY OF NEW YORK COLLEGE OF ENVIRONMENTAL SCIENCE AND FORESTRY

Environmental Engineering	M,D
Materials Sciences	M,D,O
Paper and Pulp Engineering	M,D,O
Water Resources Engineering	M,D

STATE UNIVERSITY OF NEW YORK DOWNSTATE MEDICAL CENTER

Biomedical Engineering	M,D

STATE UNIVERSITY OF NEW YORK POLYTECHNIC INSTITUTE

Computer and Information Systems Security	M
Computer Science	M
Information Science	M
Management of Technology	M
Nanotechnology	M,D

STEPHEN F. AUSTIN STATE UNIVERSITY

Biotechnology	M
Computer and Information Systems Security	M

STEPHENS COLLEGE

Health Informatics	M,O

STEVENS INSTITUTE OF TECHNOLOGY

Aerospace/Aeronautical Engineering	M,O
Artificial Intelligence/Robotics	M,D,O
Biomedical Engineering	M,D,O
Chemical Engineering	M,D,O
Civil Engineering	M,D,O
Computer and Information Systems Security	M,O
Computer Engineering	M,D,O
Computer Science	M,D,O
Construction Engineering	M,O
Construction Management	M,O
Electrical Engineering	M,D,O
Engineering and Applied Sciences—General	M,D,O
Engineering Design	M
Engineering Management	M,D,O
Environmental Engineering	M,D,O
Financial Engineering	M,D,O
Hydraulics	M,D,O
Information Science	M,O
Management of Technology	M,D,O
Manufacturing Engineering	M
Materials Engineering	M,D
Materials Sciences	M,D
Mechanical Engineering	M,D,O
Modeling and Simulation	M,D,O
Ocean Engineering	M,D
Software Engineering	M,O
Structural Engineering	M,D,O
Systems Engineering	M,D,O
Systems Science	M,D
Telecommunications Management	M,D,O
Telecommunications	M,D,O
Transportation and Highway Engineering	M,D,O
Water Resources Engineering	M,D,O

STEVENSON UNIVERSITY

Computer and Information Systems Security	M
Management of Technology	M

STOCKTON UNIVERSITY

Data Science/Data Analytics	M

STONY BROOK UNIVERSITY, STATE UNIVERSITY OF NEW YORK

Bioinformatics	M,D,O
Biomedical Engineering	M,D,O
Civil Engineering	M,D,O
Computer Engineering	M,D
Computer Science	M,D,O
Electrical Engineering	M,D
Energy Management and Policy	M
Engineering and Applied Sciences—General	M,D,O
Health Informatics	M,D,O
Management of Technology	M
Materials Engineering	M,D
Materials Sciences	M,D
Mechanical Engineering	M,D
Systems Engineering	M
Telecommunications	M,D,O

STRATFORD UNIVERSITY (VA)

Computer and Information Systems Security	M,D
Computer Science	M,D
Management of Technology	M,D
Software Engineering	M,D
Telecommunications	M,D

STRAYER UNIVERSITY

Computer and Information Systems Security	M
Information Science	M
Software Engineering	M
Systems Science	M
Telecommunications Management	M

SUFFOLK UNIVERSITY

Data Science/Data Analytics	M

SYRACUSE UNIVERSITY

Aerospace/Aeronautical Engineering	M,D
Bioengineering	M,D
Chemical Engineering	M,D
Civil Engineering	M,D
Computer and Information Systems Security	M,O
Computer Engineering	M,D
Computer Science	M
Data Science/Data Analytics	M,O
Electrical Engineering	M,D
Engineering and Applied Sciences—General	M,D,O
Engineering Management	M
Environmental Engineering	M
Information Science	M,D
Mechanical Engineering	M,D

TARLETON STATE UNIVERSITY

Engineering Management	M

TEMPLE UNIVERSITY

Artificial Intelligence/Robotics	M,D
Bioengineering	M,D
Biotechnology	M,D
Civil Engineering	M,O
Computer and Information Systems Security	M,D
Computer Science	M,D
Electrical Engineering	M,D
Environmental Engineering	M,O
Financial Engineering	M
Health Informatics	M,D
Information Science	M,D

M—masters degree; D—doctorate; O—other advanced degree; *—Close-Up and/or Display

Mechanical Engineering M

TENNESSEE STATE UNIVERSITY
Biomedical Engineering M,D
Biotechnology M,D
Civil Engineering M,D
Computer Engineering M,D
Electrical Engineering M,D
Engineering and Applied
   Sciences—General M,D
Environmental Engineering M,D
Manufacturing Engineering M,D
Mechanical Engineering M,D
Systems Engineering M,D

TENNESSEE TECHNOLOGICAL UNIVERSITY
Chemical Engineering M
Civil Engineering M
Computer Science M,D
Electrical Engineering M
Engineering and Applied
   Sciences—General M,D
Mechanical Engineering M

TEXAS A&M UNIVERSITY
Aerospace/Aeronautical
   Engineering M,D
Agricultural Engineering M,D
Bioengineering M,D
Biomedical Engineering M,D
Chemical Engineering M,D
Civil Engineering M,D
Computer Engineering M,D
Computer Science M,D
Construction Management M
Electrical Engineering M,D
Engineering Management M,D
Industrial/Management
   Engineering M,D
Manufacturing Engineering M
Materials Engineering M,D
Materials Sciences M,D
Mechanical Engineering M,D
Nuclear Engineering M,D
Petroleum Engineering M,D

TEXAS A&M UNIVERSITY–COMMERCE
Management of Technology M,O

TEXAS A&M UNIVERSITY–CORPUS CHRISTI
Computer Science M

TEXAS A&M UNIVERSITY–KINGSVILLE
Chemical Engineering M
Civil Engineering M
Computer Science M
Electrical Engineering M
Energy and Power
   Engineering D
Engineering and Applied
   Sciences—General M,D
Environmental Engineering M,D
Industrial/Management
   Engineering M
Mechanical Engineering M
Petroleum Engineering M
Systems Engineering D

TEXAS SOUTHERN UNIVERSITY
Computer Science M
Industrial/Management
   Engineering M
Transportation and Highway
   Engineering M

TEXAS STATE UNIVERSITY
Civil Engineering M

Computer Science M,D
Electrical Engineering M
Engineering and Applied
   Sciences—General M
Health Informatics M
Industrial/Management
   Engineering M
Management of Technology M
Manufacturing Engineering M
Materials Engineering D
Materials Sciences D
Mechanical Engineering M
Software Engineering M

TEXAS TECH UNIVERSITY
Biotechnology M,D
Data Science/Data Analytics M,D
Energy and Power
   Engineering M,D
Engineering and Applied
   Sciences—General M,D
Engineering Management M,D
Software Engineering M,D

TEXAS TECH UNIVERSITY HEALTH SCIENCES CENTER
Biotechnology M

TEXAS WOMAN'S UNIVERSITY
Information Science M

THOMAS EDISON STATE UNIVERSITY
Applied Science and
   Technology M,O
Computer and Information
   Systems Security M,O
Information Science M,O

THOMAS JEFFERSON UNIVERSITY
Biotechnology M
Construction Management M
Textile Sciences and
   Engineering M,D

TOWSON UNIVERSITY
Computer Science M
Information Science M,D,O
Management of Technology M,O

TOYOTA TECHNOLOGICAL INSTITUTE AT CHICAGO
Computer Science D

TRENT UNIVERSITY
Computer Science M
Materials Sciences M
Modeling and Simulation M,D

TREVECCA NAZARENE UNIVERSITY
Information Science M,O

TRIDENT UNIVERSITY INTERNATIONAL
Computer and Information
   Systems Security M,D
Health Informatics M,D,O

TRINE UNIVERSITY
Engineering Management M

TROY UNIVERSITY
Computer Science M

TUFTS UNIVERSITY
Artificial Intelligence/Robotics M,D
Bioengineering M,D,O

Bioinformatics M,D
Biomedical Engineering M,D
Biotechnology M,D,O
Chemical Engineering M,D
Civil Engineering M,D
Computer Science M,D,O
Data Science/Data Analytics M,D
Electrical Engineering M,D,O
Engineering and Applied
   Sciences—General M,D
Engineering Management M
Environmental Engineering M,D
Ergonomics and Human
   Factors M,D
Geotechnical Engineering M,D
Human-Computer Interaction O
Manufacturing Engineering O
Mechanical Engineering M,D
Structural Engineering M,D
Water Resources Engineering M,D

TULANE UNIVERSITY
Biomedical Engineering M,D
Chemical Engineering M,D
Energy Management and
   Policy M,D

TUSKEGEE UNIVERSITY
Computer and Information
   Systems Security M
Electrical Engineering M
Engineering and Applied
   Sciences—General M,D
Materials Engineering D
Mechanical Engineering M

UNITED STATES MERCHANT MARINE ACADEMY
Civil Engineering M

UNIVERSIDAD AUTONOMA DE GUADALAJARA
Computer Science M,D
Energy and Power
   Engineering M,D
Manufacturing Engineering M,D
Systems Science M,D

UNIVERSIDAD CENTRAL DEL ESTE
Environmental Engineering M

UNIVERSIDAD DE LAS AMÉRICAS PUEBLA
Biotechnology M
Chemical Engineering M
Computer Science M,D
Construction Management M
Electrical Engineering M
Engineering and Applied
   Sciences—General M,D
Industrial/Management
   Engineering M
Manufacturing Engineering M

UNIVERSIDAD DEL ESTE
Computer and Information
   Systems Security M

UNIVERSIDAD DEL TURABO
Computer Engineering M
Electrical Engineering M
Engineering and Applied
   Sciences—General M
Mechanical Engineering M
Telecommunications M

UNIVERSIDAD NACIONAL PEDRO HENRIQUEZ URENA
Environmental Engineering M

UNIVERSITÉ DE MONCTON
Civil Engineering M
Computer Science M,O
Electrical Engineering M
Engineering and Applied
   Sciences—General M
Industrial/Management
   Engineering M
Mechanical Engineering M

UNIVERSITÉ DE MONTRÉAL
Bioinformatics M,D
Biomedical Engineering M,D,O
Computer Science M,D
Ergonomics and Human
   Factors O

UNIVERSITÉ DE SHERBROOKE
Chemical Engineering M,D
Civil Engineering M,D
Computer and Information
   Systems Security M
Electrical Engineering M,D
Engineering and Applied
   Sciences—General M,D,O
Engineering Management M,O
Environmental Engineering M
Information Science M,D
Mechanical Engineering M,D

UNIVERSITÉ DU QUÉBEC À CHICOUTIMI
Engineering and Applied
   Sciences—General M,D

UNIVERSITÉ DU QUÉBEC À MONTRÉAL
Ergonomics and Human
   Factors O

UNIVERSITÉ DU QUÉBEC À RIMOUSKI
Engineering and Applied
   Sciences—General M

UNIVERSITÉ DU QUÉBEC À TROIS-RIVIÈRES
Computer Science M
Electrical Engineering M,D
Industrial/Management
   Engineering M,O

UNIVERSITÉ DU QUÉBEC, ÉCOLE DE TECHNOLOGIE SUPÉRIEURE
Engineering and Applied
   Sciences—General M,D,O

UNIVERSITÉ DU QUÉBEC EN ABITIBI-TÉMISCAMINGUE
Engineering and Applied
   Sciences—General M,O
Mineral/Mining Engineering M,O

UNIVERSITÉ DU QUÉBEC EN OUTAOUAIS
Computer Science M,D,O

UNIVERSITÉ DU QUÉBEC, INSTITUT NATIONAL DE LA RECHERCHE SCIENTIFIQUE
Energy Management and
   Policy M,D
Materials Sciences M,D
Telecommunications M,D

UNIVERSITY AT ALBANY, STATE UNIVERSITY OF NEW YORK
Computer and Information
   Systems Security M,D,O
Computer Science M,D

Engineering and Applied
    Sciences—General   M,D,O
Information Science   M,D

UNIVERSITY AT BUFFALO, THE STATE UNIVERSITY OF NEW YORK

Aerospace/Aeronautical Engineering	M,D
Bioengineering	M,D,O
Bioinformatics	M,D
Biomedical Engineering	M,D
Biotechnology	M
Chemical Engineering	M,D,O
Civil Engineering	M,D
Computer Science	M,D
Data Science/Data Analytics	M,D
Electrical Engineering	M,D
Energy and Power Engineering	M,D
Engineering and Applied Sciences—General	M,D,O
Engineering Management	M,D,O
Environmental Engineering	M,D
Industrial/Management Engineering	M,D,O
Manufacturing Engineering	M,D,O
Materials Sciences	M,D
Mechanical Engineering	M,D
Medical Informatics	M,D
Modeling and Simulation	M,D
Nanotechnology	M,D,O
Structural Engineering	M,D
Water Resources Engineering	M,D

UNIVERSITY OF ADVANCING TECHNOLOGY

Computer and Information Systems Security	M
Computer Science	M
Game Design and Development	M
Management of Technology	M

THE UNIVERSITY OF AKRON

Biomedical Engineering	M,D
Chemical Engineering	M,D
Civil Engineering	M,D
Computer Engineering	M,D
Computer Science	M
Electrical Engineering	M,D
Engineering and Applied Sciences—General	M,D
Geological Engineering	M
Mechanical Engineering	M,D
Polymer Science and Engineering	M,D

THE UNIVERSITY OF ALABAMA

Aerospace/Aeronautical Engineering	M,D
Chemical Engineering	M,D
Civil Engineering	M,D
Computer Engineering	M,D
Computer Science	M,D
Construction Engineering	M,D
Electrical Engineering	M,D
Engineering and Applied Sciences—General	M,D
Environmental Engineering	M,D
Ergonomics and Human Factors	M
Materials Engineering	M,D
Mechanical Engineering	M,D
Mechanics	M,D
Metallurgical Engineering and Metallurgy	M,D

THE UNIVERSITY OF ALABAMA AT BIRMINGHAM

Bioinformatics	D
Biomedical Engineering	M,D
Biotechnology	M
Civil Engineering	M,D
Computer and Information Systems Security	M
Computer Engineering	M,D
Computer Science	M,D
Construction Engineering	M
Construction Management	M
Electrical Engineering	M,D
Engineering and Applied Sciences—General	D
Engineering Design	M
Engineering Management	M
Health Informatics	M
Information Science	M,D
Materials Engineering	M,D
Mechanical Engineering	M
Safety Engineering	M
Structural Engineering	M

THE UNIVERSITY OF ALABAMA IN HUNTSVILLE

Aerospace/Aeronautical Engineering	M,D
Biotechnology	M,D
Chemical Engineering	M,D
Civil Engineering	M,D
Computer and Information Systems Security	M,D,O
Computer Engineering	M,D
Computer Science	M,D,O
Electrical Engineering	M,D
Engineering and Applied Sciences—General	M,D
Environmental Engineering	M,D
Industrial/Management Engineering	M,D
Management of Technology	M,O
Materials Sciences	M,D
Mechanical Engineering	M,D
Modeling and Simulation	M,D,O
Operations Research	M,D
Software Engineering	M,D,O
Systems Engineering	M,D

UNIVERSITY OF ALASKA FAIRBANKS

Civil Engineering	M,D,O
Computer Science	M
Construction Management	M,D,O
Electrical Engineering	M
Engineering and Applied Sciences—General	D
Environmental Engineering	M,D,O
Geological Engineering	M
Mechanical Engineering	M
Mineral/Mining Engineering	M
Petroleum Engineering	M

UNIVERSITY OF ALBERTA

Biomedical Engineering	M,D
Biotechnology	M,D
Chemical Engineering	M,D
Civil Engineering	M,D
Computer Engineering	M,D
Computer Science	M,D
Construction Engineering	M,D
Electrical Engineering	M,D
Energy and Power Engineering	M,D
Engineering Management	M,D
Environmental Engineering	M,D
Geotechnical Engineering	M,D
Materials Engineering	M,D
Mechanical Engineering	M,D
Mineral/Mining Engineering	M,D
Nanotechnology	M,D

Petroleum Engineering	M,D
Structural Engineering	M,D
Systems Engineering	M,D
Telecommunications	M,D
Water Resources Engineering	M,D

THE UNIVERSITY OF ARIZONA

Aerospace/Aeronautical Engineering	M,D
Agricultural Engineering	M,D
Biomedical Engineering	M,D
Biosystems Engineering	M,D
Chemical Engineering	M,D
Computer Engineering	M,D
Computer Science	M,D
Data Science/Data Analytics	M
Electrical Engineering	M,D
Engineering and Applied Sciences—General	M,D,O
Engineering Management	M,D,O
Environmental Engineering	M,D
Geological Engineering	M,D,O
Industrial/Management Engineering	M,D,O
Materials Engineering	M,D
Materials Sciences	M,D
Mechanical Engineering	M,D
Medical Informatics	M,D,O
Mineral/Mining Engineering	M,D,O
Systems Engineering	M,D,O

UNIVERSITY OF ARKANSAS

Agricultural Engineering	M,D
Bioengineering	M
Biomedical Engineering	M
Chemical Engineering	M,D
Civil Engineering	M,D
Computer Engineering	M,D
Computer Science	M,D
Electrical Engineering	M,D
Electronic Materials	M,D
Engineering and Applied Sciences—General	M,D
Environmental Engineering	M,D
Industrial/Management Engineering	M,D
Mechanical Engineering	M,D
Telecommunications	M,D
Transportation and Highway Engineering	M,D

UNIVERSITY OF ARKANSAS AT LITTLE ROCK

Applied Science and Technology	M,D
Bioinformatics	M,D
Computer Science	M,D
Construction Management	M
Information Science	M,D,O
Systems Engineering	M,D,O

UNIVERSITY OF ARKANSAS FOR MEDICAL SCIENCES

Bioinformatics	M,D,O

UNIVERSITY OF BALTIMORE

Human-Computer Interaction	M

UNIVERSITY OF BRIDGEPORT

Biomedical Engineering	M
Computer Engineering	M,D
Computer Science	M,D
Electrical Engineering	M
Engineering and Applied Sciences—General	M,D
Management of Technology	M,D
Mechanical Engineering	M

THE UNIVERSITY OF BRITISH COLUMBIA

Bioengineering	M,D
Bioinformatics	M,D
Biomedical Engineering	M,D
Chemical Engineering	M,D
Civil Engineering	M,D
Computer Engineering	M,D
Computer Science	M,D
Electrical Engineering	M,D
Energy and Power Engineering	M
Engineering and Applied Sciences—General	M,D
Geological Engineering	M,D
Materials Engineering	M,D
Mechanical Engineering	M,D
Mineral/Mining Engineering	M,D

UNIVERSITY OF CALGARY

Biomedical Engineering	M,D
Biotechnology	M
Chemical Engineering	M,D
Civil Engineering	M,D
Computer Engineering	M,D
Computer Science	M,D
Electrical Engineering	M,D
Energy and Power Engineering	M,D
Energy Management and Policy	M,D
Engineering and Applied Sciences—General	M,D
Environmental Engineering	M,D
Geotechnical Engineering	M,D
Manufacturing Engineering	M,D
Materials Sciences	M,D
Mechanical Engineering	M,D
Mechanics	M,D
Petroleum Engineering	M,D
Software Engineering	M,D
Structural Engineering	M,D
Transportation and Highway Engineering	M,D

UNIVERSITY OF CALIFORNIA, BERKELEY

Applied Science and Technology	D
Bioengineering	M,D
Chemical Engineering	M,D
Civil Engineering	M,D
Computer Science	M,D
Construction Management	O
Data Science/Data Analytics	M
Electrical Engineering	M,D
Energy Management and Policy	M,D
Engineering and Applied Sciences—General	M,D,O
Engineering Management	M,D
Environmental Engineering	M,D
Financial Engineering	M
Geotechnical Engineering	M,D
Industrial/Management Engineering	M,D
Materials Engineering	M,D
Materials Sciences	M,D
Mechanical Engineering	M,D
Mechanics	M,D
Nuclear Engineering	M,D
Operations Research	M,D
Structural Engineering	M,D
Transportation and Highway Engineering	M,D
Water Resources Engineering	M,D

UNIVERSITY OF CALIFORNIA, DAVIS

Aerospace/Aeronautical Engineering	M,D,O

---

*M—masters degree; D—doctorate; O—other advanced degree; *—Close-Up and/or Display*

Applied Science and Technology	M,D
Bioengineering	M,D
Biomedical Engineering	M,D
Chemical Engineering	M,D
Civil Engineering	M,D,O
Computer Engineering	M,D
Computer Science	M,D
Electrical Engineering	M,D
Engineering and Applied Sciences—General	M,D,O
Environmental Engineering	M,D,O
Materials Engineering	M,D
Materials Sciences	M,D
Mechanical Engineering	M,D,O
Medical Informatics	M
Transportation and Highway Engineering	M,D

UNIVERSITY OF CALIFORNIA, IRVINE

Aerospace/Aeronautical Engineering	M,D
Biochemical Engineering	M,D
Biomedical Engineering	M,D
Biotechnology	M
Chemical Engineering	M,D
Civil Engineering	M,D
Computer Science	M,D
Electrical Engineering	M,D
Engineering and Applied Sciences—General	M,D
Engineering Management	M
Environmental Engineering	M,D
Information Science	M,D
Manufacturing Engineering	M,D
Materials Engineering	M,D
Materials Sciences	M,D
Mechanical Engineering	M,D
Transportation and Highway Engineering	M,D

UNIVERSITY OF CALIFORNIA, LOS ANGELES

Aerospace/Aeronautical Engineering	M,D
Bioengineering	M,D
Bioinformatics	M,D
Biomedical Engineering	M,D
Chemical Engineering	M,D
Civil Engineering	M,D
Computer Engineering	M,D
Computer Science	M,D
Electrical Engineering	M,D
Engineering and Applied Sciences—General	M,D
Environmental Engineering	M,D
Financial Engineering	M,D
Management of Technology	M,D
Manufacturing Engineering	M
Materials Engineering	M,D
Materials Sciences	M,D
Mechanical Engineering	M,D

UNIVERSITY OF CALIFORNIA, MERCED

Bioengineering	M,D
Computer Science	M,D
Electrical Engineering	M,D
Engineering and Applied Sciences—General	M,D
Environmental Engineering	M,D
Information Science	M,D
Mechanical Engineering	M,D
Mechanics	M,D
Systems Engineering	M,D

UNIVERSITY OF CALIFORNIA, RIVERSIDE

Artificial Intelligence/Robotics	M,D
Bioengineering	M,D
Bioinformatics	D
Chemical Engineering	M,D

Computer Engineering	M
Computer Science	M,D
Electrical Engineering	M,D
Environmental Engineering	M,D
Materials Engineering	M
Materials Sciences	M
Mechanical Engineering	M,D
Nanotechnology	M

UNIVERSITY OF CALIFORNIA, SAN DIEGO

Aerospace/Aeronautical Engineering	M,D
Architectural Engineering	M
Artificial Intelligence/Robotics	M,D
Bioengineering	M,D
Bioinformatics	D
Chemical Engineering	M,D
Computer Engineering	M,D
Computer Science	M,D
Data Science/Data Analytics	M
Electrical Engineering	M,D
Energy Management and Policy	M
Engineering Physics	M,D
Materials Sciences	M,D
Mechanical Engineering	M,D
Mechanics	M,D
Modeling and Simulation	M,D
Nanotechnology	M,D
Ocean Engineering	M,D
Structural Engineering	M,D
Telecommunications	M,D

UNIVERSITY OF CALIFORNIA, SAN FRANCISCO

Bioengineering	D
Bioinformatics	D

UNIVERSITY OF CALIFORNIA, SANTA BARBARA

Bioengineering	M,D
Chemical Engineering	M,D
Computer Engineering	M,D
Computer Science	M,D
Electrical Engineering	M,D
Engineering and Applied Sciences—General	M,D
Management of Technology	M
Materials Engineering	M,D
Materials Sciences	M,D
Mechanical Engineering	M,D

UNIVERSITY OF CALIFORNIA, SANTA CRUZ

Bioinformatics	M,D
Computer Science	M,D
Electrical Engineering	M,D
Engineering and Applied Sciences—General	M,D
Game Design and Development	M,D

UNIVERSITY OF CENTRAL ARKANSAS

Computer Science	M

UNIVERSITY OF CENTRAL FLORIDA

Aerospace/Aeronautical Engineering	M
Civil Engineering	M,D,O
Computer Engineering	M,D
Computer Science	M,D
Electrical Engineering	M,D
Engineering and Applied Sciences—General	M,D,O
Environmental Engineering	M,D
Health Informatics	M,O
Industrial/Management Engineering	M,D,O
Materials Engineering	M,D

Materials Sciences	M,D
Mechanical Engineering	M,D
Modeling and Simulation	M,D,O
Structural Engineering	M,D,O
Transportation and Highway Engineering	M,D,O

UNIVERSITY OF CENTRAL MISSOURI

Aerospace/Aeronautical Engineering	M,D,O
Computer Science	M,D,O
Information Science	M,D,O
Management of Technology	M,D,O

UNIVERSITY OF CENTRAL OKLAHOMA

Biomedical Engineering	M
Computer Science	M
Electrical Engineering	M
Engineering and Applied Sciences—General	M
Engineering Physics	M
Mechanical Engineering	M

UNIVERSITY OF CHICAGO

Bioengineering	D
Bioinformatics	M
Computer Science	M,D

UNIVERSITY OF CINCINNATI

Aerospace/Aeronautical Engineering	M,D
Bioinformatics	D,O
Biomedical Engineering	M,D
Chemical Engineering	M,D
Civil Engineering	M,D
Computer Engineering	M,D
Computer Science	M,D
Electrical Engineering	M,D
Engineering and Applied Sciences—General	M,D
Environmental Engineering	M,D
Ergonomics and Human Factors	M,D
Health Informatics	M
Industrial/Management Engineering	M,D
Information Science	M,O
Materials Engineering	M,D
Materials Sciences	M,D
Mechanical Engineering	M,D
Mechanics	M,D
Nuclear Engineering	M,D

UNIVERSITY OF COLORADO BOULDER

Aerospace/Aeronautical Engineering	M,D
Architectural Engineering	M,D
Chemical Engineering	M,D
Civil Engineering	M,D
Computer Engineering	M,D
Computer Science	M,D
Electrical Engineering	M,D
Engineering and Applied Sciences—General	M,D
Engineering Management	M
Environmental Engineering	M,D
Information Science	D
Materials Engineering	M,D
Materials Sciences	M,D
Mechanical Engineering	M,D
Telecommunications Management	M
Telecommunications	M

UNIVERSITY OF COLORADO COLORADO SPRINGS

Aerospace/Aeronautical Engineering	M,D

Computer and Information Systems Security	M,D
Energy and Power Engineering	M,D
Engineering and Applied Sciences—General	M,D
Software Engineering	M,D
Systems Engineering	M,D

UNIVERSITY OF COLORADO DENVER

Applied Science and Technology	M
Bioengineering	M,D
Bioinformatics	D
Civil Engineering	M,D
Computer Science	M,D
Data Science/Data Analytics	M
Electrical Engineering	M,D
Energy Management and Policy	M
Engineering and Applied Sciences—General	M,D
Environmental Engineering	M,D
Geotechnical Engineering	M,D
Hazardous Materials Management	M
Health Informatics	M
Hydraulics	M,D
Information Science	M
Management of Technology	M
Mechanical Engineering	M
Mechanics	M
Medical Informatics	M,D
Operations Research	M,D
Structural Engineering	M,D
Transportation and Highway Engineering	M,D

UNIVERSITY OF CONNECTICUT

Biochemical Engineering	M,D
Biomedical Engineering	M,D
Chemical Engineering	M,D
Civil Engineering	M,D
Computer Engineering	M,D
Computer Science	M,D
Electrical Engineering	M,D
Engineering and Applied Sciences—General	M,D
Environmental Engineering	M,D
Materials Engineering	M
Materials Sciences	M,D
Mechanical Engineering	M,D
Polymer Science and Engineering	M,D
Software Engineering	M,D

UNIVERSITY OF DALLAS

Computer and Information Systems Security	M,D
Management of Technology	M,D

UNIVERSITY OF DAYTON

Aerospace/Aeronautical Engineering	M,D
Bioengineering	M
Chemical Engineering	M
Civil Engineering	M
Computer and Information Systems Security	M
Computer Engineering	M,D
Computer Science	M
Electrical Engineering	M,D
Engineering Management	M
Environmental Engineering	M
Geotechnical Engineering	M
Materials Engineering	M,D
Mechanical Engineering	M,D
Mechanics	M
Structural Engineering	M
Transportation and Highway Engineering	M
Water Resources Engineering	M

UNIVERSITY OF DELAWARE

Biotechnology	M,D
Chemical Engineering	M,D
Civil Engineering	M,D
Computer Engineering	M,D
Computer Science	M,D
Electrical Engineering	M,D
Energy Management and Policy	M,D
Engineering and Applied Sciences—General	M,D
Environmental Engineering	M,D
Geotechnical Engineering	M,D
Information Science	M,D
Management of Technology	M
Materials Engineering	M,D
Materials Sciences	M,D
Mechanical Engineering	M,D
Ocean Engineering	M,D
Operations Research	M
Structural Engineering	M,D
Transportation and Highway Engineering	M,D
Water Resources Engineering	M,D

UNIVERSITY OF DENVER

Bioengineering	M,D
Computer and Information Systems Security	M,D
Computer Engineering	M,D
Computer Science	M,D
Construction Management	M
Data Science/Data Analytics	M,D
Electrical Engineering	M,D
Engineering and Applied Sciences—General	M,D
Engineering Management	M,D
Information Science	M,O
Materials Engineering	M,D
Materials Sciences	M,D
Mechanical Engineering	M,D

UNIVERSITY OF DETROIT MERCY

Architectural Engineering	M
Civil Engineering	M,D
Computer and Information Systems Security	M,D,O
Computer Engineering	M,D
Computer Science	M,D,O
Electrical Engineering	M,D
Engineering and Applied Sciences—General	M,D
Engineering Management	M,D
Environmental Engineering	M,D
Mechanical Engineering	M,D
Software Engineering	M,D

UNIVERSITY OF FAIRFAX

Computer and Information Systems Security	M,D
Computer Science	M,D
Information Science	M,D

THE UNIVERSITY OF FINDLAY

Health Informatics	M,D

UNIVERSITY OF FLORIDA

Aerospace/Aeronautical Engineering	M,D
Agricultural Engineering	M,D,O
Bioengineering	M,D,O
Biomedical Engineering	M,D,O
Chemical Engineering	M,D,O
Civil Engineering	M,D
Computer Engineering	M,D
Computer Science	M,D
Construction Management	M,D
Electrical Engineering	M,D
Engineering and Applied Sciences—General	M,D,O

Environmental Engineering	M,D,O
Industrial/Management Engineering	M,D,O
Information Science	M,D
Materials Engineering	M,D
Materials Sciences	M,D
Mechanical Engineering	M,D
Nuclear Engineering	M,D
Ocean Engineering	M,D
Systems Engineering	M,D,O
Telecommunications	M,D

UNIVERSITY OF GEORGIA

Artificial Intelligence/Robotics	M
Biochemical Engineering	M
Bioinformatics	M
Computer Science	M,D
Environmental Engineering	M

UNIVERSITY OF GUELPH

Bioengineering	M,D
Biotechnology	M,D
Computer Science	M,D
Engineering and Applied Sciences—General	M,D
Environmental Engineering	M,D
Water Resources Engineering	M,D

UNIVERSITY OF HARTFORD

Engineering and Applied Sciences—General	M

UNIVERSITY OF HAWAII AT MANOA

Bioengineering	M
Civil Engineering	M,D
Computer Science	M,D,O
Electrical Engineering	M,D
Engineering and Applied Sciences—General	M,D
Environmental Engineering	M,D
Geological Engineering	M,D
Information Science	M,D
Mechanical Engineering	M,D
Ocean Engineering	M,D
Telecommunications	O

UNIVERSITY OF HOUSTON

Biomedical Engineering	D
Chemical Engineering	M,D
Civil Engineering	M,D
Computer and Information Systems Security	M
Computer Science	M,D
Construction Management	M
Electrical Engineering	M,D
Engineering and Applied Sciences—General	M,D
Industrial/Management Engineering	M,D
Information Science	M,D
Mechanical Engineering	M,D
Petroleum Engineering	M,D
Telecommunications	M

UNIVERSITY OF HOUSTON–CLEAR LAKE

Biotechnology	M
Computer Engineering	M
Computer Science	M
Information Science	M
Software Engineering	M
Systems Engineering	M

UNIVERSITY OF HOUSTON - DOWNTOWN

Data Science/Data Analytics	M

UNIVERSITY OF HOUSTON–VICTORIA

Computer Science	M

UNIVERSITY OF IDAHO

Bioengineering	M,D
Bioinformatics	M,D
Chemical Engineering	M,D
Civil Engineering	M,D
Computer Science	M,D
Electrical Engineering	M,D
Engineering and Applied Sciences—General	M,D
Geological Engineering	M,D
Materials Sciences	M,D
Mechanical Engineering	M,D
Nuclear Engineering	M,D
Water Resources Engineering	M,D

UNIVERSITY OF ILLINOIS AT CHICAGO

Bioengineering	M,D
Bioinformatics	M,D
Chemical Engineering	M,D
Civil Engineering	M,D
Computer Engineering	M,D
Computer Science	M,D
Electrical Engineering	M,D
Engineering and Applied Sciences—General	M,D
Health Informatics	M,O
Industrial/Management Engineering	M,D
Materials Engineering	M,D
Mechanical Engineering	M,D
Operations Research	M,D

UNIVERSITY OF ILLINOIS AT SPRINGFIELD

Computer Science	M
Data Science/Data Analytics	M

UNIVERSITY OF ILLINOIS AT URBANA-CHAMPAIGN

Aerospace/Aeronautical Engineering	M,D
Agricultural Engineering	M,D
Bioengineering	M,D
Bioinformatics	M,D,O
Chemical Engineering	M,D
Civil Engineering	M,D
Computer Engineering	M,D
Computer Science	M,D
Electrical Engineering	M,D
Energy and Power Engineering	M,D
Energy Management and Policy	M
Engineering and Applied Sciences—General	M,D
Environmental Engineering	M,D
Financial Engineering	M
Health Informatics	M,D,O
Human-Computer Interaction	M,D,O
Industrial/Management Engineering	M,D
Information Science	M,D,O
Management of Technology	M,D
Materials Engineering	M,D
Materials Sciences	M,D
Mechanical Engineering	M,D
Mechanics	M,D
Medical Informatics	M,D,O
Nuclear Engineering	M,D
Systems Engineering	M,D

THE UNIVERSITY OF IOWA

Biochemical Engineering	M,D
Bioinformatics	M,D,O
Biomedical Engineering	M,D

Chemical Engineering	M,D
Civil Engineering	M,D
Computer Engineering	M,D
Computer Science	M,D
Electrical Engineering	M,D
Energy and Power Engineering	M,D
Engineering and Applied Sciences—General	M,D
Environmental Engineering	M,D
Ergonomics and Human Factors	M,D,O
Health Informatics	M,D,O
Hydraulics	M,D
Industrial/Management Engineering	M,D
Information Science	M,D,O
Manufacturing Engineering	M,D
Materials Engineering	M,D
Mechanical Engineering	M,D
Operations Research	M,D
Transportation and Highway Engineering	M,D
Water Resources Engineering	M,D

THE UNIVERSITY OF KANSAS

Aerospace/Aeronautical Engineering	M,D
Architectural Engineering	M
Bioengineering	M,D
Biotechnology	M
Chemical Engineering	M,D,O
Civil Engineering	M,D
Computer Engineering	M
Computer Science	M
Construction Management	M
Electrical Engineering	M,D
Engineering and Applied Sciences—General	M,D,O
Engineering Management	M,O
Environmental Engineering	M,D
Health Informatics	M,O
Mechanical Engineering	M,D
Medical Informatics	M,D,O
Petroleum Engineering	M,D,O

UNIVERSITY OF KENTUCKY

Agricultural Engineering	M,D
Biomedical Engineering	M,D
Chemical Engineering	M,D
Civil Engineering	M,D
Computer Science	M,D
Electrical Engineering	M,D
Engineering and Applied Sciences—General	M,D
Information Science	M,D
Manufacturing Engineering	M
Materials Engineering	M,D
Materials Sciences	M,D
Mechanical Engineering	M,D
Mineral/Mining Engineering	M,D

UNIVERSITY OF LETHBRIDGE

Computer Science	M,D

UNIVERSITY OF LOUISIANA AT LAFAYETTE

Architectural Engineering	M
Chemical Engineering	M
Civil Engineering	M
Electrical Engineering	M,D
Mechanical Engineering	M
Petroleum Engineering	M
Systems Engineering	M,D

UNIVERSITY OF LOUISVILLE

Bioengineering	M,D
Bioinformatics	M,D
Chemical Engineering	M,D
Civil Engineering	M,D

*M—masters degree; D—doctorate; O—other advanced degree; *—Close-Up and/or Display*

Computer and Information Systems Security	M,D,O
Computer Engineering	M,D,O
Computer Science	M,D,O
Data Science/Data Analytics	M,D,O
Electrical Engineering	M,D
Engineering and Applied Sciences—General	M,D,O
Engineering Management	M,D,O
Industrial/Management Engineering	M,D,O
Mechanical Engineering	M,D

UNIVERSITY OF LYNCHBURG

Health Informatics	O

UNIVERSITY OF MAINE

Bioinformatics	M,D
Biomedical Engineering	M,D
Chemical Engineering	M,D
Civil Engineering	M,D
Computer Engineering	M,D
Computer Science	M,D,O
Electrical Engineering	M,D
Engineering and Applied Sciences—General	M,D
Information Science	M,D,O
Mechanical Engineering	M,D

UNIVERSITY OF MANAGEMENT AND TECHNOLOGY

Computer Science	M,O
Engineering Management	M
Software Engineering	M,O

THE UNIVERSITY OF MANCHESTER

Aerospace/Aeronautical Engineering	M,D
Biochemical Engineering	M,D
Bioinformatics	M,D
Biotechnology	M,D
Chemical Engineering	M,D
Civil Engineering	M,D
Computer Science	M,D
Electrical Engineering	M,D
Engineering Management	M,D
Environmental Engineering	M,D
Hazardous Materials Management	M,D
Materials Sciences	M,D
Mechanical Engineering	M,D
Metallurgical Engineering and Metallurgy	M,D
Modeling and Simulation	M,D
Nuclear Engineering	M,D
Paper and Pulp Engineering	M,D
Polymer Science and Engineering	M,D
Structural Engineering	M,D

UNIVERSITY OF MANITOBA

Biosystems Engineering	M,D
Civil Engineering	M,D
Computer Engineering	M,D
Computer Science	M,D
Electrical Engineering	M,D
Engineering and Applied Sciences—General	M,D
Industrial/Management Engineering	M,D
Manufacturing Engineering	M,D
Mechanical Engineering	M,D

UNIVERSITY OF MARY

Energy Management and Policy	M

UNIVERSITY OF MARYLAND, BALTIMORE COUNTY

Biochemical Engineering	M,D,O

Biotechnology	M,O
Chemical Engineering	M,D
Computer and Information Systems Security	M,O
Computer Engineering	M,D
Computer Science	M,D
Data Science/Data Analytics	M
Electrical Engineering	M,D
Engineering and Applied Sciences—General	M,D,O
Engineering Management	M,O
Environmental Engineering	M,D
Health Informatics	M
Information Science	M,D
Management of Technology	M
Mechanical Engineering	M,D
Mechanics	O
Systems Engineering	M,O

UNIVERSITY OF MARYLAND, COLLEGE PARK

Aerospace/Aeronautical Engineering	M,D
Bioengineering	M,D
Bioinformatics	D
Chemical Engineering	M,D
Civil Engineering	M,D
Computer Engineering	M,D
Computer Science	M,D
Electrical Engineering	M,D
Engineering and Applied Sciences—General	M
Environmental Engineering	M,D
Fire Protection Engineering	M
Manufacturing Engineering	M,D
Materials Engineering	M,D
Materials Sciences	M,D
Mechanical Engineering	M,D
Mechanics	M,D
Nuclear Engineering	M,D
Reliability Engineering	M,D
Systems Engineering	M
Telecommunications	M

UNIVERSITY OF MARYLAND EASTERN SHORE

Computer Science	M

UNIVERSITY OF MARYLAND GLOBAL CAMPUS

Biotechnology	M,O
Computer and Information Systems Security	M,O
Data Science/Data Analytics	M,O
Health Informatics	M
Information Science	M

UNIVERSITY OF MASSACHUSETTS AMHERST

Architectural Engineering	M,D
Biotechnology	M,D
Chemical Engineering	M,D
Civil Engineering	M,D
Computer Engineering	M,D
Computer Science	M,D
Electrical Engineering	M,D
Engineering and Applied Sciences—General	M,D
Environmental Engineering	M,D
Geotechnical Engineering	M,D
Industrial/Management Engineering	M,D
Mechanical Engineering	M,D
Mechanics	M,D
Operations Research	M,D
Polymer Science and Engineering	M,D
Structural Engineering	M,D
Transportation and Highway Engineering	M,D
Water Resources Engineering	M,D

UNIVERSITY OF MASSACHUSETTS BOSTON

Biomedical Engineering	D
Biotechnology	M,D
Computer Science	M,D

UNIVERSITY OF MASSACHUSETTS DARTMOUTH

Biomedical Engineering	D
Biotechnology	D
Civil Engineering	M
Computer Engineering	M,D,O
Computer Science	M,O
Data Science/Data Analytics	M
Electrical Engineering	M,D,O
Engineering and Applied Sciences—General	D
Industrial/Management Engineering	M,O
Management of Technology	M
Mechanical Engineering	M,O
Software Engineering	M,O
Systems Engineering	M,O
Telecommunications	M,D,O

UNIVERSITY OF MASSACHUSETTS LOWELL

Chemical Engineering	M,D
Civil Engineering	M,D
Computer Engineering	M,D
Computer Science	M,D
Electrical Engineering	M,D
Energy and Power Engineering	M,D
Engineering and Applied Sciences—General	M,D
Environmental Engineering	M,D
Industrial/Management Engineering	D
Mechanical Engineering	M,D
Nuclear Engineering	M,D
Polymer Science and Engineering	M,D

UNIVERSITY OF MASSACHUSETTS MEDICAL SCHOOL

Bioinformatics	M,D

UNIVERSITY OF MEMPHIS

Bioinformatics	M,D
Biomedical Engineering	M,D
Civil Engineering	M,D,O
Computer Engineering	M,D,O
Computer Science	M,D
Electrical Engineering	M,D,O
Electronic Materials	M,O
Energy and Power Engineering	M,D,O
Engineering and Applied Sciences—General	M,D,O
Environmental Engineering	M,D,O
Geotechnical Engineering	M,D,O
Mechanical Engineering	M,D,O
Structural Engineering	M,D,O
Transportation and Highway Engineering	M,D,O
Water Resources Engineering	M,D,O

UNIVERSITY OF MIAMI

Aerospace/Aeronautical Engineering	M,D
Architectural Engineering	M,D
Biomedical Engineering	M,D
Civil Engineering	M,D
Computer Engineering	M,D
Computer Science	M,D
Electrical Engineering	M,D
Engineering and Applied Sciences—General	M,D
Ergonomics and Human Factors	M

Industrial/Management Engineering	M,D
Management of Technology	M,D
Mechanical Engineering	M,D

UNIVERSITY OF MICHIGAN

Aerospace/Aeronautical Engineering	M,D
Artificial Intelligence/Robotics	M,D
Automotive Engineering	M,D
Bioinformatics	M,D
Biomedical Engineering	M,D
Chemical Engineering	M,D,O
Civil Engineering	M,D,O
Computer Engineering	M,D
Computer Science	M,D
Construction Engineering	M,D,O
Data Science/Data Analytics	M,D,O
Electrical Engineering	M,D
Energy and Power Engineering	M,D
Engineering and Applied Sciences—General	M,D,O
Engineering Design	M,D
Environmental Engineering	M,D,O
Health Informatics	M,D
Industrial/Management Engineering	M,D
Information Science	M,D
Manufacturing Engineering	M,D
Materials Engineering	M,D
Materials Sciences	M,D
Mechanical Engineering	M,D
Nuclear Engineering	M,D,O
Ocean Engineering	M,D,O
Operations Research	M,D
Pharmaceutical Engineering	M,D
Structural Engineering	M,D,O
Systems Engineering	M,D
Systems Science	M,D

UNIVERSITY OF MICHIGAN–DEARBORN

Automotive Engineering	M
Bioengineering	M
Computer and Information Systems Security	D
Computer Engineering	M,D
Computer Science	D
Data Science/Data Analytics	M,D
Electrical Engineering	M,D
Energy and Power Engineering	M
Engineering and Applied Sciences—General	M,D
Engineering Management	M
Health Informatics	M
Industrial/Management Engineering	M,D
Information Science	M,D
Manufacturing Engineering	M
Mechanical Engineering	M,D
Software Engineering	M,D
Systems Engineering	M,D

UNIVERSITY OF MICHIGAN–FLINT

Computer Science	M
Health Informatics	M
Information Science	M
Mechanical Engineering	M

UNIVERSITY OF MINNESOTA, DULUTH

Computer Engineering	M
Computer Science	M
Electrical Engineering	M
Engineering Management	M
Safety Engineering	M

UNIVERSITY OF MINNESOTA ROCHESTER

Bioinformatics	M,D

UNIVERSITY OF MINNESOTA, TWIN CITIES CAMPUS

Aerospace/Aeronautical Engineering	M,D
Biomedical Engineering	M,D
Biosystems Engineering	M,D
Biotechnology	M
Chemical Engineering	M,D
Civil Engineering	M,D,O
Computer and Information Systems Security	M
Computer Engineering	M,D
Computer Science	M,D
Data Science/Data Analytics	M
Electrical Engineering	M,D
Engineering and Applied Sciences—General	M,D,O
Geological Engineering	M,D
Health Informatics	M,D
Industrial/Management Engineering	M,D
Management of Technology	M
Materials Engineering	M,D
Materials Sciences	M,D
Mechanical Engineering	M,D
Mechanics	M,D
Paper and Pulp Engineering	M,D
Software Engineering	M
Technology and Public Policy	M

UNIVERSITY OF MISSISSIPPI

Applied Science and Technology	M,D
Chemical Engineering	M,D
Civil Engineering	M,D
Computer Science	M,D
Data Science/Data Analytics	M,D
Electrical Engineering	M,D
Engineering and Applied Sciences—General	M,D
Environmental Engineering	M,D
Geological Engineering	M,D
Mechanical Engineering	M,D
Telecommunications	M,D

UNIVERSITY OF MISSISSIPPI MEDICAL CENTER

Materials Sciences	M,D

UNIVERSITY OF MISSOURI

Aerospace/Aeronautical Engineering	M,D
Bioengineering	M,D
Bioinformatics	M
Chemical Engineering	M,D
Civil Engineering	M,D
Computer Engineering	M,D
Computer Science	M,D
Electrical Engineering	M,D
Engineering and Applied Sciences—General	M,D,O
Environmental Engineering	M,D
Health Informatics	M,O
Industrial/Management Engineering	M,D
Manufacturing Engineering	M,D
Mechanical Engineering	M,D

UNIVERSITY OF MISSOURI–KANSAS CITY

Bioinformatics	M,D,O
Civil Engineering	M,D,O
Computer Engineering	M,D,O
Computer Science	M,D,O
Construction Engineering	M,D,O
Electrical Engineering	M,D,O
Engineering and Applied Sciences—General	M,D,O
Engineering Management	M,D,O
Mechanical Engineering	M,D,O

Polymer Science and Engineering	M,D
Software Engineering	M,D,O
Telecommunications	M,D,O

UNIVERSITY OF MISSOURI–ST. LOUIS

Biotechnology	M,D
Computer and Information Systems Security	M,D,O
Computer Science	M,D

UNIVERSITY OF MONTANA

Computer Science	M

UNIVERSITY OF NEBRASKA AT OMAHA

Artificial Intelligence/Robotics	M,O
Bioinformatics	M,D
Computer and Information Systems Security	M,D,O
Computer Science	M,D
Data Science/Data Analytics	M,D,O
Information Science	M,D,O
Software Engineering	M,O
Systems Engineering	M,O

UNIVERSITY OF NEBRASKA–LINCOLN

Agricultural Engineering	M,D
Architectural Engineering	M,D
Bioengineering	M,D
Bioinformatics	M,D
Biomedical Engineering	M,D
Chemical Engineering	M,D
Civil Engineering	M,D
Computer Engineering	M,D
Computer Science	M,D
Electrical Engineering	M,D
Engineering and Applied Sciences—General	M,D
Engineering Management	M,D
Environmental Engineering	M,D
Industrial/Management Engineering	M,D
Information Science	M,D
Manufacturing Engineering	M,D
Materials Engineering	M,D
Materials Sciences	M,D
Mechanical Engineering	M,D
Mechanics	M,D
Metallurgical Engineering and Metallurgy	M,D

UNIVERSITY OF NEBRASKA MEDICAL CENTER

Bioinformatics	M,D

UNIVERSITY OF NEVADA, LAS VEGAS

Aerospace/Aeronautical Engineering	M,D,O
Biomedical Engineering	M,D,O
Computer and Information Systems Security	M,D,O
Data Science/Data Analytics	M,O
Engineering and Applied Sciences—General	M,D,O
Materials Engineering	M,D,O
Nuclear Engineering	M,D,O
Transportation and Highway Engineering	M,D

UNIVERSITY OF NEVADA, RENO

Biomedical Engineering	M,D
Biotechnology	M
Chemical Engineering	M,D
Civil Engineering	M,D
Computer Engineering	M,D

Computer Science	M,D
Electrical Engineering	M,D
Engineering and Applied Sciences—General	M,D
Geological Engineering	M,D
Materials Engineering	M,D
Mechanical Engineering	M,D
Metallurgical Engineering and Metallurgy	M,D
Mineral/Mining Engineering	M,D

UNIVERSITY OF NEW BRUNSWICK FREDERICTON

Chemical Engineering	M,D
Civil Engineering	M,D
Computer Engineering	M,D
Construction Engineering	M,D
Electrical Engineering	M,D
Engineering and Applied Sciences—General	M,D,O
Engineering Management	M
Environmental Engineering	M,D
Geotechnical Engineering	M,D
Materials Sciences	M,D
Mechanical Engineering	M,D
Mechanics	M,D
Structural Engineering	M,D
Surveying Science and Engineering	M,D
Transportation and Highway Engineering	M,D

UNIVERSITY OF NEW ENGLAND

Health Informatics	M,D,O

UNIVERSITY OF NEW HAMPSHIRE

Chemical Engineering	M,D
Civil Engineering	M,D
Computer and Information Systems Security	M,O
Computer Science	M,D
Electrical Engineering	M,D,O
Environmental Engineering	M,D
Materials Engineering	M,D
Materials Sciences	M,D
Mechanical Engineering	M,D
Ocean Engineering	M,D,O

UNIVERSITY OF NEW HAVEN

Biomedical Engineering	M
Civil Engineering	M
Computer and Information Systems Security	M
Computer Engineering	M
Computer Science	M,O
Electrical Engineering	M
Engineering and Applied Sciences—General	M,O
Engineering Management	M,O
Environmental Engineering	M
Fire Protection Engineering	M,O
Hazardous Materials Management	M
Industrial/Management Engineering	M,O
Mechanical Engineering	M
Software Engineering	M,O
Water Resources Engineering	M

UNIVERSITY OF NEW MEXICO

Biomedical Engineering	M,D
Chemical Engineering	M,D
Civil Engineering	M,D
Computer and Information Systems Security	M
Computer Engineering	M,D
Computer Science	M,D
Construction Management	M,D
Electrical Engineering	M,D

Engineering and Applied Sciences—General	M,D
Management of Technology	M
Manufacturing Engineering	M
Mechanical Engineering	M,D
Nanotechnology	M,D
Nuclear Engineering	M,D
Systems Engineering	M,D

UNIVERSITY OF NEW ORLEANS

Civil Engineering	M
Computer Science	M,D
Electrical Engineering	M
Engineering and Applied Sciences—General	M,D
Engineering Management	M
Mechanical Engineering	M

UNIVERSITY OF NORTH ALABAMA

Information Science	M

THE UNIVERSITY OF NORTH CAROLINA AT CHAPEL HILL

Bioinformatics	D
Computer Science	M,D
Environmental Engineering	M,D
Operations Research	M,D
Telecommunications	M,D,O

THE UNIVERSITY OF NORTH CAROLINA AT CHARLOTTE

Bioinformatics	D
Computer and Information Systems Security	M,O
Computer Science	D
Energy and Power Engineering	M,O
Engineering and Applied Sciences—General	M,D,O
Environmental Engineering	M,D
Fire Protection Engineering	M,O
Game Design and Development	M,O
Information Science	M,O
Systems Engineering	M,D

THE UNIVERSITY OF NORTH CAROLINA AT GREENSBORO

Computer Science	M

THE UNIVERSITY OF NORTH CAROLINA WILMINGTON

Computer Science	M
Data Science/Data Analytics	M

UNIVERSITY OF NORTH DAKOTA

Aviation	M
Chemical Engineering	M,D
Civil Engineering	M,D
Computer Science	M
Electrical Engineering	M,D
Engineering and Applied Sciences—General	D
Environmental Engineering	M,D
Geological Engineering	M,D
Mechanical Engineering	M,D

UNIVERSITY OF NORTHERN BRITISH COLUMBIA

Computer Science	M,D,O

UNIVERSITY OF NORTH FLORIDA

Civil Engineering	M
Computer Science	M
Construction Management	M
Electrical Engineering	M
Mechanical Engineering	M

---

*M—masters degree; D—doctorate; O—other advanced degree; *—Close-Up and/or Display*

Software Engineering — M

UNIVERSITY OF NORTH TEXAS
Biomedical Engineering	M,D,O
Computer Engineering	M,D,O
Computer Science	M,D,O
Electrical Engineering	M,D,O
Energy and Power Engineering	M,D,O
Engineering and Applied Sciences—General	M,D,O
Information Science	M,D,O
Mechanical Engineering	M,D,O

UNIVERSITY OF NORTH TEXAS HEALTH SCIENCE CENTER AT FORT WORTH
Biotechnology	M,D

UNIVERSITY OF NOTRE DAME
Aerospace/Aeronautical Engineering	M,D
Bioengineering	M,D
Chemical Engineering	M,D
Civil Engineering	M,D
Computer Engineering	M,D
Computer Science	M,D
Electrical Engineering	M,D
Engineering and Applied Sciences—General	M,D
Environmental Engineering	M,D
Mechanical Engineering	M,D

UNIVERSITY OF OKLAHOMA
Aerospace/Aeronautical Engineering	M,D
Biomedical Engineering	M,D
Chemical Engineering	M,D
Civil Engineering	M,D
Computer Engineering	M,D
Computer Science	M,D
Construction Management	M,D
Electrical Engineering	M,D
Engineering Physics	M,D
Environmental Engineering	M,D
Geological Engineering	M,D,O
Industrial/Management Engineering	M,D
Mechanical Engineering	M,D
Petroleum Engineering	M,D,O
Telecommunications	M,D

UNIVERSITY OF OREGON
Computer Science	M,D
Information Science	M,D

UNIVERSITY OF OTTAWA
Aerospace/Aeronautical Engineering	M,D
Bioengineering	M,D
Biomedical Engineering	M
Chemical Engineering	M,D
Civil Engineering	M,D
Computer Engineering	M,D
Computer Science	M,D
Electrical Engineering	M,D
Engineering and Applied Sciences—General	M,D,O
Engineering Management	M,O
Information Science	M,O
Mechanical Engineering	M,D
Systems Science	M,D,O

UNIVERSITY OF PENNSYLVANIA
Artificial Intelligence/Robotics	M
Bioengineering	M,D
Biotechnology	M
Chemical Engineering	M,D
Computer Science	M,D
Data Science/Data Analytics	M
Electrical Engineering	M,D

Engineering and Applied Sciences—General	M,D
Game Design and Development	M,D
Information Science	M,D
Materials Engineering	M,D
Materials Sciences	M,D
Mechanical Engineering	M,D
Mechanics	M,D
Nanotechnology	M
Systems Engineering	M,D

UNIVERSITY OF PHOENIX - BAY AREA CAMPUS
Energy Management and Policy	M,D
Management of Technology	M,D

UNIVERSITY OF PHOENIX - CENTRAL VALLEY CAMPUS
Management of Technology	M

UNIVERSITY OF PHOENIX - DALLAS CAMPUS
Management of Technology	M

UNIVERSITY OF PHOENIX - HAWAII CAMPUS
Management of Technology	M

UNIVERSITY OF PHOENIX - HOUSTON CAMPUS
Management of Technology	M

UNIVERSITY OF PHOENIX - LAS VEGAS CAMPUS
Management of Technology	M

UNIVERSITY OF PHOENIX–ONLINE CAMPUS
Energy Management and Policy	M,O
Health Informatics	M,O
Management of Technology	M,O

UNIVERSITY OF PHOENIX - PHOENIX CAMPUS
Energy Management and Policy	M,O
Management of Technology	M,O
Medical Informatics	M,O

UNIVERSITY OF PHOENIX - SACRAMENTO VALLEY CAMPUS
Management of Technology	M

UNIVERSITY OF PHOENIX - SAN ANTONIO CAMPUS
Management of Technology	M

UNIVERSITY OF PHOENIX - SAN DIEGO CAMPUS
Management of Technology	M

UNIVERSITY OF PITTSBURGH
Artificial Intelligence/Robotics	M,D
Bioengineering	M,D
Bioinformatics	M,D,O
Chemical Engineering	M,D
Civil Engineering	M,D
Computer Engineering	M,D
Computer Science	M,D
Data Science/Data Analytics	M,D,O
Electrical Engineering	M,D
Energy Management and Policy	M
Engineering and Applied Sciences—General	M,D
Environmental Engineering	M,D

Health Informatics	M
Industrial/Management Engineering	M,D
Information Science	M,D,O
Materials Sciences	M,D
Mechanical Engineering	M,D
Petroleum Engineering	M,D

UNIVERSITY OF PORTLAND
Biomedical Engineering	M
Civil Engineering	M
Computer Science	M
Electrical Engineering	M
Engineering and Applied Sciences—General	M
Management of Technology	M
Mechanical Engineering	M

UNIVERSITY OF PUERTO RICO AT MAYAGÜEZ
Aerospace/Aeronautical Engineering	M,D
Bioengineering	M,D
Chemical Engineering	M,D
Civil Engineering	M,D
Computer Engineering	M,D
Computer Science	M,D
Construction Engineering	M,D
Electrical Engineering	M,D
Energy and Power Engineering	M,D
Engineering and Applied Sciences—General	M,D
Engineering Management	M,D
Environmental Engineering	M,D
Geotechnical Engineering	M,D
Industrial/Management Engineering	M
Information Science	M,D
Manufacturing Engineering	M,D
Materials Engineering	M,D
Materials Sciences	M,D
Mechanical Engineering	M,D
Structural Engineering	M,D
Transportation and Highway Engineering	M,D

UNIVERSITY OF PUERTO RICO AT RIO PIEDRAS
Information Science	M,O

UNIVERSITY OF PUERTO RICO - MEDICAL SCIENCES CAMPUS
Health Informatics	M

UNIVERSITY OF REGINA
Computer Engineering	M,D
Computer Science	M,D
Engineering and Applied Sciences—General	M,D
Engineering Management	M,O
Environmental Engineering	M,D
Industrial/Management Engineering	M,D
Petroleum Engineering	M,D
Software Engineering	M,D
Systems Engineering	M,D

UNIVERSITY OF RHODE ISLAND
Biomedical Engineering	M,D
Biotechnology	M,D
Chemical Engineering	M,D,O
Civil Engineering	M,D
Computer and Information Systems Security	M,D,O
Computer Engineering	M,D
Computer Science	M,D,O
Electrical Engineering	M,D
Engineering and Applied Sciences—General	M,D,O
Environmental Engineering	M,D
Geotechnical Engineering	M,D

Industrial/Management Engineering	M,D
Ocean Engineering	M,D
Systems Engineering	M,D

UNIVERSITY OF ROCHESTER
Artificial Intelligence/Robotics	M,D
Bioinformatics	M,D
Biomedical Engineering	M,D
Chemical Engineering	M,D
Computer Engineering	M,D
Computer Science	M,D
Data Science/Data Analytics	M
Electrical Engineering	M,D
Engineering and Applied Sciences—General	M,D
Human-Computer Interaction	M,D
Materials Sciences	M,D
Mechanical Engineering	M,D

UNIVERSITY OF ST. AUGUSTINE FOR HEALTH SCIENCES
Health Informatics	M

UNIVERSITY OF ST. THOMAS (MN)
Data Science/Data Analytics	M,D
Electrical Engineering	M,O
Engineering and Applied Sciences—General	M,O
Engineering Management	M,O
Information Science	M,O
Management of Technology	M,O
Manufacturing Engineering	M,O
Mechanical Engineering	M,O
Software Engineering	M,O
Systems Engineering	M,O

UNIVERSITY OF SAN DIEGO
Computer and Information Systems Security	M
Computer Engineering	M
Health Informatics	M,D

UNIVERSITY OF SAN FRANCISCO
Biotechnology	M
Computer Science	M
Data Science/Data Analytics	M
Energy Management and Policy	M
Health Informatics	M

UNIVERSITY OF SASKATCHEWAN
Bioengineering	M,D
Biomedical Engineering	M,D,O
Chemical Engineering	M,D
Civil Engineering	M,D
Computer Science	M,D
Electrical Engineering	M,D,O
Engineering and Applied Sciences—General	M,D,O
Engineering Physics	M,D
Geological Engineering	M,D
Mechanical Engineering	M,D

THE UNIVERSITY OF SCRANTON
Software Engineering	M

UNIVERSITY OF SOUTH AFRICA
Chemical Engineering	M
Engineering and Applied Sciences—General	M
Information Science	M,D
Technology and Public Policy	M,D
Telecommunications Management	M,D

UNIVERSITY OF SOUTH ALABAMA
Chemical Engineering	M
Civil Engineering	M
Computer Engineering	M
Computer Science	M,D

Electrical Engineering	M
Engineering and Applied Sciences—General	M,D
Environmental Engineering	M
Mechanical Engineering	M
Systems Engineering	D

UNIVERSITY OF SOUTH CAROLINA

Chemical Engineering	M,D
Civil Engineering	M,D
Computer Engineering	M,D
Computer Science	M,D
Electrical Engineering	M,D
Engineering and Applied Sciences—General	M,D
Hazardous Materials Management	M,D
Mechanical Engineering	M,D
Nuclear Engineering	M,D
Software Engineering	M,D

UNIVERSITY OF SOUTH CAROLINA UPSTATE

Health Informatics	M
Information Science	M

UNIVERSITY OF SOUTH DAKOTA

Computer Science	M

UNIVERSITY OF SOUTHERN CALIFORNIA

Aerospace/Aeronautical Engineering	M,D,O
Artificial Intelligence/Robotics	M,D
Bioinformatics	D
Biomedical Engineering	M,D
Biotechnology	M
Chemical Engineering	M,D,O
Civil Engineering	M,D,O
Computer and Information Systems Security	M,D
Computer Engineering	M,D,O
Computer Science	M,D
Construction Management	M,D,O
Electrical Engineering	M,D,O
Engineering and Applied Sciences—General	M,D,O
Engineering Management	M,D,O
Environmental Engineering	M,D,O
Game Design and Development	M,D
Geotechnical Engineering	M,D,O
Hazardous Materials Management	M,D,O
Industrial/Management Engineering	M,D,O
Manufacturing Engineering	M,D,O
Materials Engineering	M,D,O
Materials Sciences	M,D,O
Mechanical Engineering	M,D,O
Mechanics	M,D,O
Modeling and Simulation	M,D
Operations Research	M,D,O
Petroleum Engineering	M,D,O
Safety Engineering	M,D,O
Software Engineering	M,D
Systems Engineering	M,D,O
Telecommunications	M,D,O
Transportation and Highway Engineering	M,D,O

UNIVERSITY OF SOUTHERN INDIANA

Data Science/Data Analytics	M
Engineering and Applied Sciences—General	M,D
Engineering Management	M

UNIVERSITY OF SOUTHERN MAINE

Computer Science	M,O
Software Engineering	M,O

UNIVERSITY OF SOUTHERN MISSISSIPPI

Computer Science	M,D
Information Science	M,O
Polymer Science and Engineering	M,D

UNIVERSITY OF SOUTH FLORIDA

Bioinformatics	M,D,O
Biomedical Engineering	M,D,O
Biotechnology	O
Chemical Engineering	M,D,O
Civil Engineering	M,D,O
Computer and Information Systems Security	M
Computer Engineering	M,D
Computer Science	M,D
Data Science/Data Analytics	O
Electrical Engineering	M,D
Engineering and Applied Sciences—General	M,D,O
Engineering Management	M,D
Environmental Engineering	M,D
Geotechnical Engineering	M,D
Health Informatics	O
Industrial/Management Engineering	M,D,O
Information Science	M
Management of Technology	O
Materials Engineering	M,D,O
Materials Sciences	O
Mechanical Engineering	M,D
Nanotechnology	M,D
Structural Engineering	M,D
Systems Engineering	O
Transportation and Highway Engineering	M,D,O
Water Resources Engineering	M,D,O

THE UNIVERSITY OF TAMPA

Computer and Information Systems Security	M,O

THE UNIVERSITY OF TENNESSEE

Aerospace/Aeronautical Engineering	M,D
Agricultural Engineering	M
Aviation	M
Biomedical Engineering	M,D
Biosystems Engineering	M,D
Chemical Engineering	M,D
Civil Engineering	M,D
Computer Engineering	M,D
Computer Science	M,D
Data Science/Data Analytics	D
Electrical Engineering	M,D
Energy and Power Engineering	D
Engineering and Applied Sciences—General	M,D
Engineering Management	M,D
Environmental Engineering	M
Industrial/Management Engineering	M,D
Information Science	M,D
Materials Engineering	M,D
Materials Sciences	M,D
Mechanical Engineering	M,D
Nuclear Engineering	M,D
Reliability Engineering	M,D

THE UNIVERSITY OF TENNESSEE AT CHATTANOOGA

Automotive Engineering	M
Bioinformatics	M,O

Chemical Engineering	M
Civil Engineering	M
Computer Science	M,O
Construction Management	M,O
Electrical Engineering	M
Energy and Power Engineering	M,O
Engineering Management	M,O
Mechanical Engineering	.

THE UNIVERSITY OF TENNESSEE HEALTH SCIENCE CENTER

Biomedical Engineering	M,D
Health Informatics	M,D

THE UNIVERSITY OF TEXAS AT ARLINGTON

Aerospace/Aeronautical Engineering	M,D
Bioengineering	M,D
Civil Engineering	M,D
Computer Engineering	M,D
Computer Science	M,D
Construction Management	M,D
Electrical Engineering	M,D
Engineering and Applied Sciences—General	M,D
Engineering Management	M
Industrial/Management Engineering	M,D
Materials Engineering	M,D
Materials Sciences	M,D
Mechanical Engineering	M,D
Software Engineering	M,D
Systems Engineering	M

THE UNIVERSITY OF TEXAS AT AUSTIN

Aerospace/Aeronautical Engineering	M,D
Architectural Engineering	M
Biomedical Engineering	M,D
Chemical Engineering	M,D
Civil Engineering	M,D
Computer and Information Systems Security	M,D
Computer Engineering	M,D
Computer Science	M,D
Electrical Engineering	M,D
Engineering and Applied Sciences—General	M,D
Environmental Engineering	M,D
Geotechnical Engineering	M,D
Industrial/Management Engineering	M,D
Materials Engineering	M,D
Materials Sciences	M,D
Mechanical Engineering	M,D
Mechanics	M,D
Mineral/Mining Engineering	M
Operations Research	M,D
Petroleum Engineering	M,D
Technology and Public Policy	M
Textile Sciences and Engineering	M
Water Resources Engineering	M,D

THE UNIVERSITY OF TEXAS AT DALLAS

Biomedical Engineering	M,D
Biotechnology	M,D
Computer Engineering	M,D
Computer Science	M,D
Data Science/Data Analytics	M,D
Electrical Engineering	M,D
Engineering and Applied Sciences—General	M,D
Management of Technology	M
Materials Engineering	M,D
Materials Sciences	M,D
Mechanical Engineering	M,D

Software Engineering	M,D
Systems Engineering	M,D
Telecommunications	M,D

THE UNIVERSITY OF TEXAS AT EL PASO

Bioinformatics	M,D
Civil Engineering	M,D,O
Computer and Information Systems Security	M,D,O
Computer Engineering	M,D,O
Computer Science	M,D,O
Construction Management	M,D,O
Electrical Engineering	M,D,O
Energy and Power Engineering	M,D,O
Engineering and Applied Sciences—General	M,D,O
Environmental Engineering	M,D,O
Industrial/Management Engineering	M
Information Science	M,D,O
Manufacturing Engineering	M
Materials Engineering	M,D
Materials Sciences	M,D
Mechanical Engineering	M,D
Metallurgical Engineering and Metallurgy	M,D
Software Engineering	M,D,O
Systems Engineering	M

THE UNIVERSITY OF TEXAS AT SAN ANTONIO

Biomedical Engineering	M,D
Biotechnology	M,D
Civil Engineering	M,D
Computer and Information Systems Security	M,D,O
Computer Engineering	M,D
Computer Science	M,D
Electrical Engineering	M,D
Engineering and Applied Sciences—General	M,D
Environmental Engineering	M,D
Information Science	M,D,O
Management of Technology	M,D,O
Manufacturing Engineering	M,D
Materials Engineering	M,D
Mechanical Engineering	M,D

THE UNIVERSITY OF TEXAS AT TYLER

Civil Engineering	M
Computer and Information Systems Security	M
Computer Science	M
Electrical Engineering	M
Energy Management and Policy	M
Engineering Management	M
Environmental Engineering	M
Mechanical Engineering	M
Structural Engineering	M
Transportation and Highway Engineering	M
Water Resources Engineering	M

THE UNIVERSITY OF TEXAS HEALTH SCIENCE CENTER AT HOUSTON

Bioinformatics	M,D,O
Data Science/Data Analytics	M,D,O
Health Informatics	M,D,O

THE UNIVERSITY OF TEXAS HEALTH SCIENCE CENTER AT SAN ANTONIO

Biomedical Engineering	M,D

---

*M—masters degree; D—doctorate; O—other advanced degree; *—Close-Up and/or Display*

THE UNIVERSITY OF TEXAS HEALTH SCIENCE CENTER AT TYLER

Biotechnology	M

THE UNIVERSITY OF TEXAS MEDICAL BRANCH

Bioinformatics	D

THE UNIVERSITY OF TEXAS OF THE PERMIAN BASIN

Computer Science	M

THE UNIVERSITY OF TEXAS RIO GRANDE VALLEY

Computer Science	M
Electrical Engineering	M
Engineering Management	M
Manufacturing Engineering	M
Mechanical Engineering	M
Systems Engineering	M

THE UNIVERSITY OF TEXAS SOUTHWESTERN MEDICAL CENTER

Biomedical Engineering	M,D

UNIVERSITY OF THE DISTRICT OF COLUMBIA

Computer Science	M
Electrical Engineering	M
Engineering and Applied Sciences—General	M

UNIVERSITY OF THE PACIFIC

Engineering and Applied Sciences—General	M

UNIVERSITY OF THE SACRED HEART

Information Science	O

UNIVERSITY OF THE SCIENCES

Bioinformatics	M
Biotechnology	M

THE UNIVERSITY OF TOLEDO

Bioengineering	M,D
Bioinformatics	M,O
Biomedical Engineering	D
Chemical Engineering	M,D
Civil Engineering	M,D
Computer Science	M,D
Electrical Engineering	M,D
Engineering and Applied Sciences—General	M
Industrial/Management Engineering	M,D
Materials Sciences	M,D
Mechanical Engineering	M,D

UNIVERSITY OF TORONTO

Aerospace/Aeronautical Engineering	M,D
Biomedical Engineering	M,D
Biotechnology	M
Chemical Engineering	M,D
Civil Engineering	M,D
Computer Engineering	M,D
Computer Science	M,D
Electrical Engineering	M,D
Engineering and Applied Sciences—General	M
Health Informatics	M
Industrial/Management Engineering	M,D
Management of Technology	M
Manufacturing Engineering	M
Materials Engineering	M,D
Materials Sciences	M,D

Mechanical Engineering	M,D

THE UNIVERSITY OF TULSA

Chemical Engineering	M,D
Computer and Information Systems Security	M,D
Computer Science	M,D
Electrical Engineering	M,D
Energy Management and Policy	M
Engineering and Applied Sciences—General	M,D
Mechanical Engineering	M,D
Petroleum Engineering	M,D

UNIVERSITY OF UTAH

Bioengineering	M,D
Bioinformatics	M,D,O
Biotechnology	M
Chemical Engineering	M,D
Civil Engineering	M,D
Computer and Information Systems Security	M,O
Computer Engineering	M,D
Computer Science	M,D
Electrical Engineering	M,D
Engineering and Applied Sciences—General	M,D
Environmental Engineering	M,D
Game Design and Development	M
Geological Engineering	M,D
Materials Engineering	M,D
Materials Sciences	M,D
Mechanical Engineering	M,D
Mineral/Mining Engineering	M,D
Nuclear Engineering	M,D
Petroleum Engineering	M,D
Software Engineering	M,D,O
Systems Engineering	M,O

UNIVERSITY OF VERMONT

Bioengineering	D
Biomedical Engineering	M
Civil Engineering	M,D
Computer Science	M,D
Data Science/Data Analytics	M,D
Electrical Engineering	M,D
Engineering and Applied Sciences—General	M,D
Engineering Management	M
Environmental Engineering	M,D
Materials Sciences	M,D
Mechanical Engineering	M,D

UNIVERSITY OF VICTORIA

Computer Engineering	M,D
Computer Science	M,D
Electrical Engineering	M,D
Engineering and Applied Sciences—General	M,D
Health Informatics	M
Mechanical Engineering	M,D

UNIVERSITY OF VIRGINIA

Aerospace/Aeronautical Engineering	M,D
Biomedical Engineering	M,D
Chemical Engineering	M,D
Civil Engineering	M,D
Computer Engineering	M,D
Computer Science	M,D
Construction Engineering	D
Data Science/Data Analytics	M
Electrical Engineering	M,D
Engineering and Applied Sciences—General	M,D
Engineering Physics	M,D
Health Informatics	M
Management of Technology	M
Materials Sciences	M,D
Mechanical Engineering	M,D
Systems Engineering	M,D

UNIVERSITY OF WASHINGTON

Aerospace/Aeronautical Engineering	M,D
Bioengineering	M,D
Bioinformatics	M,D
Biotechnology	D
Chemical Engineering	M,D
Civil Engineering	M,D
Computer and Information Systems Security	M,D
Computer Engineering	M,D
Computer Science	M,D
Construction Engineering	M,D
Construction Management	M
Data Science/Data Analytics	M,D
Electrical Engineering	M,D
Engineering and Applied Sciences—General	M,D,O
Environmental Engineering	M,D
Geotechnical Engineering	M,D
Health Informatics	M,D
Human-Computer Interaction	M,D,O
Industrial/Management Engineering	M,D
Information Science	M,D
Management of Technology	M,D
Materials Engineering	M,D
Materials Sciences	M,D
Mechanical Engineering	M,D
Mechanics	M,D
Medical Informatics	M,D
Nanotechnology	M,D
Structural Engineering	M,D
Systems Engineering	M,D
Transportation and Highway Engineering	M,D

UNIVERSITY OF WASHINGTON, BOTHELL

Computer Engineering	M
Software Engineering	M

UNIVERSITY OF WASHINGTON, TACOMA

Computer Engineering	M
Software Engineering	M

UNIVERSITY OF WATERLOO

Chemical Engineering	M,D
Civil Engineering	M,D
Computer Engineering	M,D
Computer Science	M,D
Electrical Engineering	M,D
Engineering and Applied Sciences—General	M,D
Engineering Management	M,D
Environmental Engineering	M,D
Health Informatics	M,D
Information Science	M,D
Management of Technology	M,D
Mechanical Engineering	M,D
Operations Research	M,D
Software Engineering	M,D
Systems Engineering	M,D

THE UNIVERSITY OF WESTERN ONTARIO

Biochemical Engineering	M,D
Chemical Engineering	M,D
Civil Engineering	M,D
Computer Engineering	M,D
Computer Science	M,D
Electrical Engineering	M,D
Engineering and Applied Sciences—General	M,D
Environmental Engineering	M,D
Materials Engineering	M,D
Mechanical Engineering	M,D

UNIVERSITY OF WEST FLORIDA

Computer and Information Systems Security	M
Computer Science	M

Data Science/Data Analytics	M
Software Engineering	M

UNIVERSITY OF WINDSOR

Civil Engineering	M,D
Computer Science	M,D
Electrical Engineering	M,D
Engineering and Applied Sciences—General	M,D
Environmental Engineering	M,D
Industrial/Management Engineering	M,D
Manufacturing Engineering	M,D
Materials Engineering	M,D
Mechanical Engineering	M,D

UNIVERSITY OF WISCONSIN–LA CROSSE

Data Science/Data Analytics	M
Software Engineering	M

UNIVERSITY OF WISCONSIN–MADISON

Agricultural Engineering	M,D
Automotive Engineering	M,D
Bioinformatics	M,D
Biomedical Engineering	M,D
Chemical Engineering	D
Civil Engineering	M
Computer and Information Systems Security	M
Computer Science	M,D
Construction Engineering	M
Electrical Engineering	M,D
Engineering and Applied Sciences—General	M,D
Engineering Physics	M,D
Environmental Engineering	M
Ergonomics and Human Factors	M,D
Geological Engineering	M,D
Geotechnical Engineering	M
Industrial/Management Engineering	M,D
Management of Technology	M
Manufacturing Engineering	M
Materials Engineering	M,D
Mechanical Engineering	M,D
Mechanics	M,D
Nuclear Engineering	M,D
Structural Engineering	M,D
Systems Engineering	M,D
Transportation and Highway Engineering	M
Water Resources Engineering	M

UNIVERSITY OF WISCONSIN–MILWAUKEE

Biomedical Engineering	M,D
Civil Engineering	M,D
Computer Engineering	M,D
Computer Science	M,D
Electrical Engineering	M,D
Engineering and Applied Sciences—General	M,D
Ergonomics and Human Factors	M
Health Informatics	M,D
Industrial/Management Engineering	M,D
Management of Technology	M,O
Manufacturing Engineering	M,D
Materials Engineering	M,D
Mechanical Engineering	M,D
Mechanics	M,D
Medical Informatics	M

UNIVERSITY OF WISCONSIN–PARKSIDE

Computer Science	M
Information Science	M

UNIVERSITY OF WISCONSIN–PLATTEVILLE

Computer Science	M
Engineering and Applied Sciences—General	M

UNIVERSITY OF WISCONSIN–STEVENS POINT

Data Science/Data Analytics	M

UNIVERSITY OF WISCONSIN–STOUT

Construction Management	M
Industrial/Management Engineering	M
Information Science	M
Manufacturing Engineering	M
Telecommunications Management	M

UNIVERSITY OF WYOMING

Architectural Engineering	M,D
Biotechnology	D
Chemical Engineering	M,D
Civil Engineering	M,D
Computer Science	M,D
Electrical Engineering	M,D
Engineering and Applied Sciences—General	M,D
Environmental Engineering	M
Mechanical Engineering	M,D
Petroleum Engineering	M,D

UNIVERSITÉ LAVAL

Aerospace/Aeronautical Engineering	M
Agricultural Engineering	M
Chemical Engineering	M,D
Civil Engineering	M,D,O
Computer Science	M,D
Electrical Engineering	M,D
Engineering and Applied Sciences—General	M,D,O
Environmental Engineering	M,D
Industrial/Management Engineering	O
Mechanical Engineering	M,D
Metallurgical Engineering and Metallurgy	M,D
Mineral/Mining Engineering	M,D
Modeling and Simulation	M,O
Software Engineering	O

UNIVERSITÉ TÉLUQ

Computer Science	M,D

UTAH STATE UNIVERSITY

Aerospace/Aeronautical Engineering	M,D
Bioengineering	M,D
Civil Engineering	M,D,O
Computer Science	M,D
Electrical Engineering	M,D
Engineering and Applied Sciences—General	M,D,O
Environmental Engineering	M,D,O
Mechanical Engineering	M,D

UTAH VALLEY UNIVERSITY

Computer and Information Systems Security	O

UTICA COLLEGE

Computer and Information Systems Security	M

VALPARAISO UNIVERSITY

Computer and Information Systems Security	M
Engineering Management	M,O

VANDERBILT UNIVERSITY

Bioinformatics	M,D
Biomedical Engineering	M,D
Chemical Engineering	M,D
Civil Engineering	M,D
Computer and Information Systems Security	M
Computer Science	M,D
Electrical Engineering	M,D
Engineering and Applied Sciences—General	M,D
Environmental Engineering	M,D
Materials Sciences	M,D
Mechanical Engineering	M,D

VERMONT LAW SCHOOL

Energy Management and Policy	M

VERMONT TECHNICAL COLLEGE

Software Engineering	M

VILLANOVA UNIVERSITY

Artificial Intelligence/Robotics	M,O
Biochemical Engineering	M,O
Chemical Engineering	M,O
Civil Engineering	M
Computer Engineering	M,O
Computer Science	M,O
Electrical Engineering	M,O
Engineering and Applied Sciences—General	M,D,O
Environmental Engineering	M,O
Manufacturing Engineering	M,O
Mechanical Engineering	M,O
Water Resources Engineering	M,O

VIRGINIA COMMONWEALTH UNIVERSITY

Biomedical Engineering	M,D
Computer Science	M,D
Engineering and Applied Sciences—General	M,D
Mechanical Engineering	M,D
Nanotechnology	M,D
Nuclear Engineering	M,D

VIRGINIA INTERNATIONAL UNIVERSITY

Computer and Information Systems Security	M,O
Computer Science	M,O
Data Science/Data Analytics	M,O
Game Design and Development	M,O
Health Informatics	M,O
Software Engineering	M,O

VIRGINIA POLYTECHNIC INSTITUTE AND STATE UNIVERSITY

Aerospace/Aeronautical Engineering	M,D,O
Agricultural Engineering	M,D
Bioengineering	M,D
Bioinformatics	M,D
Biomedical Engineering	M,D
Biotechnology	M,D
Chemical Engineering	M,D
Civil Engineering	M,D,O
Computer and Information Systems Security	M,O
Computer Engineering	M,D,O
Computer Science	M,D,O

Electrical Engineering	M,D,O
Engineering and Applied Sciences—General	M,D
Engineering Management	M,O
Environmental Engineering	M,O
Industrial/Management Engineering	M,O
Ocean Engineering	M,O
Software Engineering	M,O
Systems Engineering	M,O
Transportation and Highway Engineering	M,O

WAKE FOREST UNIVERSITY

Biomedical Engineering	M,D
Computer Science	M

WALDEN UNIVERSITY

Computer and Information Systems Security	M,D,O
Health Informatics	M,D,O

WALSH COLLEGE OF ACCOUNTANCY AND BUSINESS ADMINISTRATION

Computer and Information Systems Security	M
Data Science/Data Analytics	M
Management of Technology	M

WASHINGTON STATE UNIVERSITY

Agricultural Engineering	M,D
Bioengineering	M,D
Chemical Engineering	M,D
Civil Engineering	M,D
Computer Engineering	M,D
Computer Science	M,D
Electrical Engineering	M,D
Energy and Power Engineering	M,D
Engineering and Applied Sciences—General	M,D,O
Engineering Management	M,O
Environmental Engineering	M,D
Management of Technology	M,O
Materials Engineering	M,D
Materials Sciences	M,D
Mechanical Engineering	M,D

WASHINGTON UNIVERSITY IN ST. LOUIS

Aerospace/Aeronautical Engineering	M,D
Biomedical Engineering	M,D
Chemical Engineering	M,D
Computer Engineering	M,D
Computer Science	M,D
Data Science/Data Analytics	M
Engineering and Applied Sciences—General	M,D
Environmental Engineering	M,D
Materials Sciences	M,D
Mechanical Engineering	M,D

WAYNESBURG UNIVERSITY

Energy Management and Policy	M,D

WAYNE STATE UNIVERSITY

Automotive Engineering	M,O
Bioinformatics	M,D
Biomedical Engineering	M,D,O
Chemical Engineering	M,D,O
Civil Engineering	M,D
Computer Engineering	M,D
Computer Science	M,D
Data Science/Data Analytics	M,D,O
Electrical Engineering	M,D
Electronic Materials	M

WEBER STATE UNIVERSITY

Energy and Power Engineering	M,O
Engineering and Applied Sciences—General	M,D,O
Engineering Management	M,D,O
Industrial/Management Engineering	M,D,O
Manufacturing Engineering	M,D,O
Materials Sciences	M,D,O
Mechanical Engineering	M,D
Polymer Science and Engineering	M,D,O
Systems Engineering	M,D,O

WEBER STATE UNIVERSITY

Computer Engineering	M

WEBSTER UNIVERSITY

Aerospace/Aeronautical Engineering	M,D,O
Computer and Information Systems Security	M
Computer Science	M
Management of Technology	M,D,O

WEILL CORNELL MEDICINE

Data Science/Data Analytics	M
Health Informatics	M

WENTWORTH INSTITUTE OF TECHNOLOGY

Civil Engineering	M
Computer Science	M
Construction Engineering	M
Construction Management	M
Management of Technology	M
Transportation and Highway Engineering	M

WESLEYAN UNIVERSITY

Bioinformatics	D
Computer Science	M,D

WESTERN CAROLINA UNIVERSITY

Construction Management	M
Industrial/Management Engineering	M

WESTERN GOVERNORS UNIVERSITY

Computer and Information Systems Security	M
Data Science/Data Analytics	M
Information Science	M

WESTERN ILLINOIS UNIVERSITY

Computer Science	M
Manufacturing Engineering	M

WESTERN KENTUCKY UNIVERSITY

Computer Science	M
Management of Technology	M

WESTERN MICHIGAN UNIVERSITY

Aerospace/Aeronautical Engineering	M,D
Chemical Engineering	M,D
Civil Engineering	M
Computer Engineering	M,D
Computer Science	M,D
Electrical Engineering	M,D
Engineering and Applied Sciences—General	M,D
Engineering Management	M,D
Industrial/Management Engineering	M,D

*M—masters degree; D—doctorate; O—other advanced degree; *—Close-Up and/or Display*

Manufacturing Engineering	M
Mechanical Engineering	M,D
Paper and Pulp Engineering	M,D

WESTERN NEW ENGLAND UNIVERSITY

Civil Engineering	M
Electrical Engineering	M
Engineering and Applied Sciences—General	M,D
Engineering Management	M,D
Industrial/Management Engineering	M
Manufacturing Engineering	M
Mechanical Engineering	M

WESTERN WASHINGTON UNIVERSITY

Computer Science	M

WEST TEXAS A&M UNIVERSITY

Engineering and Applied Sciences—General	M

WEST VIRGINIA STATE UNIVERSITY

Biotechnology	M

WEST VIRGINIA UNIVERSITY

Aerospace/Aeronautical Engineering	M,D
Chemical Engineering	M,D
Civil Engineering	M,D
Computer and Information Systems Security	M,D,O
Computer Engineering	M,D
Computer Science	M,D
Electrical Engineering	M,D
Energy and Power Engineering	M,D
Engineering and Applied Sciences—General	M,D
Industrial/Management Engineering	M,D

Materials Engineering	M,D
Materials Sciences	M,D
Mechanical Engineering	M,D
Mineral/Mining Engineering	M,D
Petroleum Engineering	M,D
Safety Engineering	M,D
Software Engineering	M,D

WICHITA STATE UNIVERSITY

Aerospace/Aeronautical Engineering	M,D
Biomedical Engineering	M
Computer Engineering	M,D
Computer Science	M,D
Electrical Engineering	M,D
Engineering and Applied Sciences—General	M,D
Engineering Management	M,D
Industrial/Management Engineering	M,D
Manufacturing Engineering	M,D
Mechanical Engineering	M,D

WIDENER UNIVERSITY

Biomedical Engineering	M
Chemical Engineering	M
Civil Engineering	M
Electrical Engineering	M
Engineering and Applied Sciences—General	M
Engineering Management	M
Mechanical Engineering	M

WILFRID LAURIER UNIVERSITY

Management of Technology	M,D

WILMINGTON UNIVERSITY

Computer and Information Systems Security	M
Internet Engineering	M

WINSTON-SALEM STATE UNIVERSITY

Computer Science	M

WOODS HOLE OCEANOGRAPHIC INSTITUTION

Ocean Engineering	D

WORCESTER POLYTECHNIC INSTITUTE

Aerospace/Aeronautical Engineering	M,D
Artificial Intelligence/Robotics	M,D
Bioinformatics	M,D
Biomedical Engineering	M,D,O
Biotechnology	M,D
Chemical Engineering	M,D
Civil Engineering	M,D,O
Computer Engineering	M,D,O
Computer Science	M,D,O
Data Science/Data Analytics	M,D,O
Electrical Engineering	M,D,O
Energy and Power Engineering	M,D,O
Engineering and Applied Sciences—General	M,D,O
Engineering Design	M,D,O
Environmental Engineering	M,D,O
Fire Protection Engineering	M,D,O
Game Design and Development	M
Manufacturing Engineering	M,D
Materials Engineering	M,D
Materials Sciences	M,D
Mechanical Engineering	M,D,O
Modeling and Simulation	M,D,O
Nuclear Engineering	M,D,O
Systems Engineering	M,D,O
Systems Science	M,D,O

WORCESTER STATE UNIVERSITY

Biotechnology	M

WRIGHT STATE UNIVERSITY

Aerospace/Aeronautical Engineering	M
Biomedical Engineering	M
Computer Engineering	M,D
Computer Science	M,D

Electrical Engineering	M
Engineering and Applied Sciences—General	M,D
Ergonomics and Human Factors	M,D
Industrial/Management Engineering	M
Materials Engineering	M
Materials Sciences	M
Mechanical Engineering	M

YALE UNIVERSITY

Bioinformatics	D
Biomedical Engineering	M,D
Chemical Engineering	M,D
Computer Science	M,D
Electrical Engineering	M,D
Engineering and Applied Sciences—General	M,D
Engineering Physics	M,D
Environmental Engineering	M,D
Mechanical Engineering	M,D

YESHIVA UNIVERSITY

Biotechnology	M
Data Science/Data Analytics	M

YORK UNIVERSITY

Computer Science	M,D

YOUNGSTOWN STATE UNIVERSITY

Civil Engineering	M
Computer Engineering	M
Computer Science	M
Electrical Engineering	M
Engineering and Applied Sciences—General	M,O
Environmental Engineering	M
Industrial/Management Engineering	M
Information Science	M
Mechanical Engineering	M
Systems Engineering	M

ACADEMIC AND PROFESSIONAL PROGRAMS IN PROGRAMS IN ENGINEERING & APPLIED SCIENCES

Section 1
Engineering and Applied Sciences

This section contains a directory of institutions offering graduate work in engineering and applied sciences, followed by in-depth entries submitted by institutions that chose to prepare detailed program descriptions. Additional information about programs listed in the directory but not augmented by an in-depth entry may be obtained by writing directly to the dean of a graduate school or chair of a department at the address given in the directory.

For programs in specific areas of engineering, see all other sections in this book. In the other guides in this series:

Graduate Programs in the Humanities, Arts & Social Sciences
See *Applied Arts and Design (Industrial Design)* and *Architecture (Environmental Design)*

Graduate Programs in the Biological/Biomedical Sciences & Health-Related Medical Professions
See *Ecology, Environmental Biology,* and *Evolutionary Biology*

Graduate Programs in the Physical Sciences, Mathematics, Agricultural Sciences, the Environment & Natural Resources
See *Agricultural and Food Sciences* and *Natural Resources*

CONTENTS

Program Directories

Featured School: Display and Close-Up

Engineering and Applied Sciences—General

Air Force Institute of Technology, Graduate School of Engineering and Management, Dayton, OH 45433-7765. Offers MS, PhD. *Accreditation:* ABET (one or more programs are accredited). *Program availability:* Part-time. *Degree requirements:* For master's, thesis; for doctorate, thesis/dissertation. *Entrance requirements:* For master's, GRE General Test, minimum GPA of 3.0; for doctorate, GRE General Test.

Alabama Agricultural and Mechanical University, School of Graduate Studies, College of Engineering, Technology, and Physical Sciences, Huntsville, AL 35811. Offers M Eng, MS, PhD. *Program availability:* Part-time, evening/weekend. *Degree requirements:* For master's, comprehensive exam, thesis optional. *Entrance requirements:* For master's, GRE General Test. Additional exam requirements/recommendations for international students: required—TOEFL (minimum score 500 paper-based; 61 iBT). Electronic applications accepted.

Alfred University, Graduate School, College of Ceramics, Inamori School of Engineering, Alfred, NY 14802-1205. Offers biomaterials engineering (MS); ceramic engineering (MS, PhD); electrical engineering (MS); glass science (MS, PhD); materials science and engineering (MS, PhD); mechanical engineering (MS). *Program availability:* Part-time. *Faculty:* 27 full-time (4 women), 2 part-time/adjunct (both women). *Students:* 30 full-time (11 women), 15 part-time (5 women); includes 2 minority (both Asian, non-Hispanic/Latino), 12 international. Average age 28. 24 applicants, 83% accepted, 18 enrolled. In 2019, 8 master's, 5 doctorates awarded. *Degree requirements:* For master's, comprehensive exam, thesis; for doctorate, comprehensive exam, thesis/dissertation. *Entrance requirements:* Additional exam requirements/recommendations for international students: required—TOEFL (minimum score 590 paper-based; 90 iBT), IELTS (minimum score 6.5). *Application deadline:* For fall admission, 3/1 priority date for domestic students, 3/15 for international students; for spring admission, 10/1 priority date for domestic students, 10/1 for international students. Applications are processed on a rolling basis. Application fee: $60. Electronic applications accepted. Application fee is waived when completed online. *Expenses:* $23,530 per year. *Financial support:* In 2019–20, 31 students received support. Fellowships with full tuition reimbursements available, research assistantships with full tuition reimbursements available, teaching assistantships with full tuition reimbursements available, tuition waivers (full and partial), and unspecified assistantships available. Financial award application deadline: 3/15; financial award applicants required to submit FAFSA. *Unit head:* Dr. Gabrielle Gaustad, Dean, 607-871-2953, E-mail: gaustad@alfred.edu. *Application contact:* Lindsey Gertin, Assistant Director of Graduate Admissions, 607-871-2017, Fax: 607-871-2198, E-mail: gradinquiry@alfred.edu.
Website: http://engineering.alfred.edu/grad/

The American University in Cairo, School of Sciences and Engineering, Cairo, Egypt. Offers biotechnology (MS); chemistry (MS); computer science (MS); computing (M Comp); construction engineering (M Eng, MS); electronics and communications engineering (M Eng); environmental engineering (MS); environmental system design (M Eng); mechanical engineering (M Eng, MS); nanotechnology (MS); physics (MS); robotics, control and smart systems (MS); sciences and engineering (PhD); sustainable development (MS, Graduate Diploma). *Program availability:* Part-time, evening/weekend. *Degree requirements:* For master's, comprehensive exam (for some programs), thesis (for some programs); for doctorate, comprehensive exam (for some programs), thesis/dissertation. *Entrance requirements:* Additional exam requirements/recommendations for international students: required—TOEFL (minimum score 450 paper-based; 45 iBT), IELTS (minimum score 5). Electronic applications accepted.

Arizona State University at Tempe, Ira A. Fulton Schools of Engineering, Tempe, AZ 85287-9309. Offers M Eng, MA, MCS, MS, MSE, PSM, PhD, Graduate Certificate. *Program availability:* Part-time, evening/weekend, online learning. Terminal master's awarded for partial completion of doctoral program. *Degree requirements:* For master's, comprehensive exam (for some programs), thesis (for some programs), interactive Program of Study (iPOS) submitted before completing 50 percent of required credit hours; for doctorate, comprehensive exam, thesis/dissertation, interactive Program of Study (iPOS) submitted before completing 50 percent of required credit hours. *Entrance requirements:* For master's and doctorate, GRE, minimum GPA of 3.0 or equivalent in last 2 years of work leading to bachelor's degree. Additional exam requirements/recommendations for international students: required—TOEFL, IELTS, or PTE. Electronic applications accepted. *Expenses:* Contact institution.

Arkansas State University, Graduate School, College of Engineering, State University, AR 72467. Offers engineering (MS Eng); engineering management (MEM). *Program availability:* Part-time. *Degree requirements:* For master's, comprehensive exam. *Entrance requirements:* For master's, GRE, appropriate bachelor's degree, official transcript, letters of recommendation, resume, immunization records. Additional exam requirements/recommendations for international students: required—TOEFL (minimum score 550 paper-based; 79 iBT), IELTS (minimum score 6), PTE (minimum score 56). Electronic applications accepted. *Expenses:* Contact institution.

Arkansas Tech University, College of Engineering and Applied Sciences, Russellville, AR 72801. Offers electrical engineering (M Engr); emergency management (MS); information technology (MS); mechanical engineering (M Engr). *Program availability:* Part-time, evening/weekend, 100% online, blended/hybrid learning. *Students:* 38 full-time (11 women), 45 part-time (22 women); includes 13 minority (10 Black or African American, non-Hispanic/Latino; 1 Asian, non-Hispanic/Latino; 1 Hispanic/Latino; 1 Two or more races, non-Hispanic/Latino), 24 international. Average age 32. In 2019, 26 master's awarded. *Degree requirements:* For master's, comprehensive exam (for some programs), thesis (for some programs). *Entrance requirements:* Additional exam requirements/recommendations for international students: required—TOEFL (minimum score 550 paper-based; 79 iBT), IELTS (minimum score 6.5), PTE (minimum score 58). *Application deadline:* For fall admission, 3/1 priority date for domestic students, 5/1 priority date for international students; for spring admission, 10/1 priority date for domestic and international students. Applications are processed on a rolling basis. Application fee: $40 ($90 for international students). Electronic applications accepted. *Expenses: Tuition, area resident:* Full-time $7008; part-time $292 per credit hour. Tuition, state resident: full-time $7008; part-time $292 per credit hour. Tuition, nonresident: full-time $14,016; part-time $584 per credit hour. *International tuition:* $14,016 full-time. *Required fees:* $343 per term. *Financial support:* In 2019–20, research assistantships with full and partial tuition reimbursements (averaging $4,800 per year), teaching assistantships with full and partial tuition reimbursements (averaging $4,800 per year) were awarded; career-related internships or fieldwork, Federal Work-Study, scholarships/grants, health care benefits, and unspecified assistantships also available. Support available to part-time students. Financial award application deadline: 4/15; financial award applicants required to submit FAFSA. *Unit head:* Dr. Judy Cezeaux, Dean, 479-968-0353, E-mail: jcezeaux@atu.edu. *Application contact:* Dr. Richard Schoephoerster, Dean of Graduate College and Research, 479-968-0398, Fax: 479-964-0542, E-mail: gradcollege@atu.edu.
Website: http://www.atu.edu/appliedsci/

Atlantis University, School of Engineering, Miami, FL 33132. Offers computer engineering (MS).

Auburn University, Graduate School, Samuel Ginn College of Engineering, Auburn, AL 36849. Offers M Ch E, M Mtl E, MAE, MCE, MEE, MISE, MME, MS, MSWE, PhD, Graduate Certificate. *Program availability:* Part-time. *Faculty:* 185 full-time (18 women), 16 part-time/adjunct (2 women). *Students:* 585 full-time (155 women), 418 part-time (97 women); includes 92 minority (33 Black or African American, non-Hispanic/Latino; 1 American Indian or Alaska Native, non-Hispanic/Latino; 23 Asian, non-Hispanic/Latino; 28 Hispanic/Latino; 7 Two or more races, non-Hispanic/Latino), 537 international. Average age 29. 1,028 applicants, 53% accepted, 215 enrolled. In 2019, 229 master's, 70 doctorates, 20 other advanced degrees awarded. *Degree requirements:* For master's, thesis (for some programs); for doctorate, thesis/dissertation. *Entrance requirements:* For master's and doctorate, GRE General Test. Additional exam requirements/recommendations for international students: required—TOEFL (minimum score 550 paper-based; 79 iBT); recommended—IELTS (minimum score 6.5). *Application deadline:* For fall admission, 3/31 priority date for domestic and international students; for spring admission, 9/30 priority date for domestic and international students. Applications are processed on a rolling basis. Application fee: $60 ($70 for international students). Electronic applications accepted. *Expenses: Tuition, area resident:* Full-time $9828; part-time $546 per credit hour. Tuition, state resident: full-time $9828; part-time $546 per credit hour. Tuition, nonresident: full-time $29,484; part-time $1638 per credit hour. *International tuition:* $29,744 full-time. Tuition and fees vary according to course load, program and reciprocity agreements. *Financial support:* In 2019–20, 68 research assistantships (averaging $15,750 per year), 18 teaching assistantships (averaging $10,182 per year) were awarded; fellowships and Federal Work-Study also available. Support available to part-time students. Financial award application deadline: 3/15; financial award applicants required to submit FAFSA. *Unit head:* Dr. Christopher Roberts, Dean, 334-844-2308, E-mail: robercr@auburn.edu. *Application contact:* Dr. George Flowers, Dean of the Graduate School, 334-844-2125.
Website: http://www.eng.auburn.edu/

Baylor University, Graduate School, School of Engineering and Computer Science, Department of Engineering, Waco, TX 76798. Offers biomedical engineering (MSBME); electrical and computer engineering (MSECE, PhD); engineering (ME); mechanical engineering (MSME).

Binghamton University, State University of New York, Graduate School, Thomas J. Watson School of Engineering and Applied Science, Binghamton, NY 13902-6000. Offers M Eng, MS, PhD. *Program availability:* Part-time, evening/weekend, online learning. *Degree requirements:* For master's, comprehensive exam (for some programs), thesis (for some programs); for doctorate, comprehensive exam (for some programs), thesis/dissertation. *Entrance requirements:* For master's and doctorate, GRE General Test. Additional exam requirements/recommendations for international students: required—TOEFL (minimum score 550 paper-based; 80 iBT). Electronic applications accepted. *Expenses:* Contact institution.

Boise State University, College of Engineering, Boise, ID 83725-0399. Offers M Engr, MS, PhD, Graduate Certificate. *Program availability:* Part-time, online learning. *Students:* 173 full-time (53 women), 234 part-time (117 women); includes 48 minority (10 Black or African American, non-Hispanic/Latino; 2 American Indian or Alaska Native, non-Hispanic/Latino; 15 Asian, non-Hispanic/Latino; 13 Hispanic/Latino; 1 Native Hawaiian or other Pacific Islander, non-Hispanic/Latino; 7 Two or more races, non-Hispanic/Latino), 100 international. *Degree requirements:* For master's, comprehensive exam (for some programs), thesis (for some programs); for doctorate, comprehensive exam, thesis/dissertation. *Entrance requirements:* For master's, GRE General Test, minimum GPA of 3.0. Additional exam requirements/recommendations for international students: required—TOEFL, IELTS. Electronic applications accepted. *Expenses: Tuition, area resident:* Full-time $7110; part-time $470 per credit hour. Tuition, state resident: full-time $7110; part-time $470 per credit hour. Tuition, nonresident: full-time $24,030; part-time $827 per credit hour. *International tuition:* $827 full-time. *Required fees:* $2536. Tuition and fees vary according to course load and program. *Financial support:* Research assistantships, teaching assistantships with partial tuition reimbursements, scholarships/grants, and unspecified assistantships available. Financial award applicants required to submit FAFSA. *Unit head:* Dr. JoAnn Lighty, Dean, 208-426-4844, E-mail: joannlighty@boisestate.edu. *Application contact:* Hao Chen, Program Coordinator, 208-426-1020, E-mail: haochen@boisestate.edu.
Website: https://www.boisestate.edu/coen/academics/graduate-students/

Boston University, College of Engineering, Boston, MA 02215. Offers M Eng, MS, PhD, MD/PhD, MS/MBA. *Program availability:* Part-time, blended/hybrid learning. *Faculty:* 112 full-time (12 women), 9 part-time/adjunct (1 woman). *Students:* 849 full-time (282 women), 177 part-time (44 women); includes 151 minority (12 Black or African American, non-Hispanic/Latino; 83 Asian, non-Hispanic/Latino; 33 Hispanic/Latino; 23 Two or more races, non-Hispanic/Latino), 536 international. Average age 25. 4,014 applicants, 39% accepted, 348 enrolled. In 2019, 327 master's, 59 doctorates awarded. Terminal master's awarded for partial completion of doctoral program. *Degree requirements:* For master's, thesis (for some programs); for doctorate, comprehensive exam, thesis/dissertation. *Entrance requirements:* For master's and doctorate, GRE General Test. Additional exam requirements/recommendations for international students: required—TOEFL (minimum score 90 iBT), IELTS (minimum score 7). *Application deadline:* For fall admission, 12/15 for domestic and international students; for spring admission, 10/1 for domestic and international students. Application fee: $95. Electronic applications accepted. *Expenses:* $27,360 tuition, $172 student services fee, $25 community service/program fee, $219 health and wellness fee. *Financial support:* In 2019–20, 458 students received support, including 115 fellowships with full tuition reimbursements available (averaging $33,000 per year), 246 research assistantships with full tuition reimbursements available (averaging $33,000 per year), 7 teaching assistantships with full tuition reimbursements available (averaging $22,000 per year); scholarships/grants and unspecified assistantships also available. Support available to part-time students. Financial award application deadline: 1/15; financial award applicants required to submit FAFSA. *Unit head:* Dr. Kenneth R. Lutchen, Dean, 617-353-2800, Fax: 617-358-3468, E-mail: klutch@bu.edu. *Application contact:* Andrew Butler, Assistant Director, Enrollment Operations, 617-353-9760, E-mail: enggrad@bu.edu.
Website: http://www.bu.edu/eng/

Bradley University, The Graduate School, Caterpillar College of Engineering and Technology, Peoria, IL 61625-0002. Offers MS, MSCE, MSEE, MSME. *Program availability:* Part-time, evening/weekend. *Faculty:* 45 full-time (6 women), 1 part-time/adjunct (0 women). *Students:* 30 full-time (7 women), 22 part-time (3 women); includes 2 minority (both Black or African American, non-Hispanic/Latino), 46 international. Average age 27. 128 applicants, 58% accepted, 14 enrolled. In 2019, 34 master's awarded. *Degree requirements:* For master's, comprehensive exam, thesis optional.

Entrance requirements: Additional exam requirements/recommendations for international students: required—TOEFL (minimum score 550 paper-based; 79 iBT), IELTS (minimum score 6.5), PTE (minimum score 58). *Application deadline:* For fall admission, 5/15 priority date for domestic and international students; for spring admission, 10/15 priority date for domestic and international students. Applications are processed on a rolling basis. Application fee: $40 ($50 for international students). Electronic applications accepted. *Expenses:* Contact institution. *Financial support:* In 2019–20, 23 students received support, including 8 teaching assistantships with full and partial tuition reimbursements available (averaging $4,847 per year); research assistantships, institutionally sponsored loans, scholarships/grants, tuition waivers (full and partial), and unspecified assistantships also available. Support available to part-time students. Financial award application deadline: 4/1. *Unit head:* Lex Akers, Dean, 309-677-2721, E-mail: lakers@bradley.edu. *Application contact:* Rachel Webb, Director of On-Campus Graduate Admissions and International Student and Scholar Services, 309-677-2375, E-mail: rkwebb@bradley.edu.
Website: http://www.bradley.edu/academic/colleges/egt/

Brigham Young University, Graduate Studies, Ira A. Fulton College of Engineering, Provo, UT 84602. Offers MS, PhD. *Faculty:* 104 full-time (4 women), 2 part-time/adjunct (1 woman). *Students:* 330 full-time (37 women); includes 20 minority (5 Asian, non-Hispanic/Latino; 2 Hispanic/Latino; 13 Two or more races, non-Hispanic/Latino), 59 international. Average age 28. 191 applicants, 45% accepted, 86 enrolled. In 2019, 102 master's, 24 doctorates awarded. *Degree requirements:* For master's, comprehensive exam (for some programs), thesis (for some programs); for doctorate, comprehensive exam (for some programs), thesis/dissertation (for some programs). *Entrance requirements:* For master's and doctorate, GRE, At least 3 letters of recommendation, transcripts from each institution attended, ecclesiastical endorsement, minimum cumulative GPA of 3.0 in last 60 hours of coursework. Additional exam requirements/recommendations for international students: required—TOEFL (minimum score 580 paper-based; 85 iBT), IELTS (minimum score 7). *Application deadline:* For fall admission, 1/15 for domestic and international students; for winter admission, 6/15 for domestic and international students; for spring admission, 2/5 for domestic and international students; for summer admission, 2/5 for domestic and international students. Application fee: $50. Electronic applications accepted. *Financial support:* In 2019–20, 486 students received support, including 16 fellowships with full and partial tuition reimbursements available (averaging $23,224 per year), 360 research assistantships with full and partial tuition reimbursements available (averaging $18,726 per year), 136 teaching assistantships with full and partial tuition reimbursements available (averaging $13,740 per year); scholarships/grants and health care benefits also available. Financial award application deadline: 1/1; financial award applicants required to submit FAFSA. *Unit head:* Dr. Michael A. Jensen, Dean, 801-422-5736, Fax: 801-422-0218, E-mail: college@et.byu.edu. *Application contact:* Claire A. DeWitt, Adviser, 801-422-4541, Fax: 801-422-0270, E-mail: gradstudies@byu.edu.
Website: http://www.et.byu.edu/

Brown University, Graduate School, School of Engineering, Providence, RI 02912. Offers biomedical engineering (Sc M, PhD); chemical and biochemical engineering (Sc M, PhD); electrical sciences and computer engineering (Sc M, PhD); fluid and thermal sciences (Sc M, PhD); materials science and engineering (Sc M, PhD); mechanics of solids and structures (Sc M, PhD). *Degree requirements:* For doctorate, thesis/dissertation, preliminary exam.

Bucknell University, Graduate Studies, College of Engineering, Lewisburg, PA 17837. Offers MS Ch E, MSCE, MSEE, MSEV, MSME. *Program availability:* Part-time. *Degree requirements:* For master's, thesis. *Entrance requirements:* For master's, GRE General Test, minimum GPA of 3.0. Additional exam requirements/recommendations for international students: required—TOEFL (minimum score 600 paper-based).

California Institute of Technology, Division of Engineering and Applied Science, Pasadena, CA 91125. Offers aeronautics (MS, PhD, Engr); applied and computational mathematics (MS, PhD); applied mechanics (MS, PhD); applied physics (MS, PhD); bioengineering (MS, PhD); civil engineering (MS, PhD, Engr); computation and neural systems (MS, PhD); computer science (MS, PhD); control and dynamical systems (MS, PhD); electrical engineering (MS, PhD, Engr); environmental science and engineering (MS, PhD); materials science (MS, PhD); mechanical engineering (MS, PhD, Engr). Terminal master's awarded for partial completion of doctoral program. *Degree requirements:* For doctorate, thesis/dissertation. *Entrance requirements:* For master's and doctorate, GRE (strongly recommended), minimum GPA of 3.5. Additional exam requirements/recommendations for international students: required—TOEFL; recommended—TWE (minimum score 5). Electronic applications accepted.

California Polytechnic State University, San Luis Obispo, College of Engineering, Department of General Engineering, San Luis Obispo, CA 93407. Offers MS. Electronic applications accepted. Application fee is waived when completed online. *Expenses:* Tuition, state resident: full-time $7176; part-time $4164 per year. Tuition, nonresident: full-time $18,690; part-time $8916 per year. *Required fees:* $4206; $3185 per unit. $1061 per term.

California State University, Chico, Office of Graduate Studies, College of Engineering, Computer Science, and Construction Management, Chico, CA 95929-0722. Offers MS. *Program availability:* Part-time, online learning. *Degree requirements:* For master's, thesis or project or comprehensive exam. *Entrance requirements:* For master's, GRE, fall admissions only; 2 letters of recommendation, statement of purpose, departmental letter of recommendation access waiver form. Additional exam requirements/recommendations for international students: required—TOEFL (minimum score 550 paper-based; 80 iBT), IELTS (minimum score 6.5), PTE (minimum score 59). Electronic applications accepted.

California State University, East Bay, Office of Graduate Studies, College of Science, School of Engineering, Hayward, CA 94542-3000. Offers construction management (MS); engineering management (MS). *Degree requirements:* For master's, comprehensive exam (for some programs), research project or exam. *Entrance requirements:* For master's, GRE or GMAT, minimum GPA of 2.5; personal statement; 2 letters of recommendation; resume; college algebra/trigonometry or equivalent. Additional exam requirements/recommendations for international students: required—TOEFL (minimum score 550 paper-based). Electronic applications accepted.

California State University, Fresno, Division of Research and Graduate Studies, Lyles College of Engineering, Fresno, CA 93740-8027. Offers MS, MSE. *Program availability:* Part-time, evening/weekend. *Degree requirements:* For master's, thesis or alternative. *Entrance requirements:* For master's, GRE General Test, minimum GPA of 2.7. Additional exam requirements/recommendations for international students: required—TOEFL. Electronic applications accepted. *Expenses:* Tuition, state resident: full-time $4012; part-time $2506 per semester.

California State University, Fullerton, Graduate Studies, College of Engineering and Computer Science, Fullerton, CA 92831-3599. Offers MS. *Program availability:* Part-time. *Degree requirements:* For master's, comprehensive exam, project or thesis. *Entrance requirements:* For master's, minimum undergraduate GPA of 2.5.

California State University, Los Angeles, Graduate Studies, College of Engineering, Computer Science, and Technology, Los Angeles, CA 90032-8530. Offers MA, MS.

Program availability: Part-time, evening/weekend. *Entrance requirements:* Additional exam requirements/recommendations for international students: required—TOEFL (minimum score 550 paper-based). Electronic applications accepted. *Expenses: Tuition, area resident:* Full-time $7176; part-time $4164 per year. Tuition, state resident: full-time $7176; part-time $4164 per year. Tuition, nonresident: full-time $14,304; part-time $8916 per year. *International tuition:* $14,304 full-time. *Required fees:* $1037.76; $1037.76 per unit. Tuition and fees vary according to degree level and program.

California State University, Northridge, Graduate Studies, College of Engineering and Computer Science, Northridge, CA 91330. Offers MS. *Program availability:* Part-time, evening/weekend. *Entrance requirements:* For master's, GRE General Test, minimum GPA of 2.5. Additional exam requirements/recommendations for international students: required—TOEFL.

California State University, Sacramento, College of Engineering and Computer Science, Sacramento, CA 95819. Offers MS. *Program availability:* Part-time, evening/weekend. *Students:* 228 full-time (85 women), 175 part-time (55 women); includes 92 minority (14 Black or African American, non-Hispanic/Latino; 1 American Indian or Alaska Native, non-Hispanic/Latino; 49 Asian, non-Hispanic/Latino; 24 Hispanic/Latino; 4 Native Hawaiian or other Pacific Islander, non-Hispanic/Latino), 211 international. Average age 28. 641 applicants, 44% accepted, 92 enrolled. In 2019, 106 master's awarded. *Degree requirements:* For master's, comprehensive exam (for some programs), thesis (for some programs), thesis/project; writing proficiency exam. *Entrance requirements:* Additional exam requirements/recommendations for international students: required—TOEFL (minimum score 550 paper-based; 80 iBT); recommended—IELTS (minimum score 7). *Application deadline:* For fall admission, 3/1 for domestic students, 2/1 for international students. Applications are processed on a rolling basis. Application fee: $70. Electronic applications accepted. *Expenses:* Contact institution. *Financial support:* Teaching assistantships, career-related internships or fieldwork, Federal Work-Study, and scholarships/grants available. Support available to part-time students. Financial award application deadline: 3/1; financial award applicants required to submit FAFSA. *Unit head:* Dr. Lorenzo M. Smith, Dean, 916-278-6127, Fax: 916-278-5949, E-mail: lsmith@csus.edu. *Application contact:* Jose Martinez, Graduate Admissions Supervisor, 916-278-7871, E-mail: martinj@skymail.csus.edu.
Website: http://www.hera.ecs.csus.edu

Carleton University, Faculty of Graduate Studies, Faculty of Engineering and Design, Ottawa, ON K1S 5B6, Canada. Offers M Arch, M Des, M Eng, M Sc, MA Sc, PhD. *Degree requirements:* For doctorate, thesis/dissertation. *Entrance requirements:* For master's, honors degree; for doctorate, MA Sc or M Eng. Additional exam requirements/recommendations for international students: required—TOEFL.

Case Western Reserve University, School of Graduate Studies, Case School of Engineering, Cleveland, OH 44106. Offers ME, MEM, MS, PhD, MD/MS, MD/PhD. *Program availability:* Part-time, evening/weekend, 100% online, blended/hybrid learning. Terminal master's awarded for partial completion of doctoral program. *Degree requirements:* For master's, thesis (for some programs); for doctorate, thesis/dissertation, qualifying exam, teaching experience. *Entrance requirements:* For master's and doctorate, GRE General Test. Additional exam requirements/recommendations for international students: required—TOEFL (minimum score 577 paper-based; 90 iBT), IELTS (minimum score 7). Electronic applications accepted.

The Catholic University of America, School of Engineering, Washington, DC 20064. Offers MBE, MCE, MEE, MME, MS, MSCS, MSE, PhD, Certificate. *Program availability:* Part-time. *Faculty:* 33 full-time (2 women), 31 part-time/adjunct (21 women). *Students:* 70 full-time (26 women), 161 part-time (58 women); includes 50 minority (18 Black or African American, non-Hispanic/Latino; 9 Asian, non-Hispanic/Latino; 7 Hispanic/Latino; 16 Two or more races, non-Hispanic/Latino), 114 international. Average age 31. 224 applicants, 77% accepted, 74 enrolled. In 2019, 73 master's, 13 doctorates awarded. *Degree requirements:* For master's, thesis optional; for doctorate, comprehensive exam, thesis/dissertation. *Entrance requirements:* For master's and doctorate, statement of purpose, official copies of academic transcripts, three letters of recommendation. Additional exam requirements/recommendations for international students: required—TOEFL (minimum score 550 paper-based; 80 iBT). *Application deadline:* For fall admission, 7/15 priority date for domestic students, 7/1 for international students; for spring admission, 11/15 priority date for domestic students, 11/1 for international students. Applications are processed on a rolling basis. Application fee: $55. Electronic applications accepted. *Expenses:* Contact institution. *Financial support:* Fellowships, research assistantships, teaching assistantships, Federal Work-Study, scholarships/grants, tuition waivers (full and partial), and unspecified assistantships available. Financial award application deadline: 2/1; financial award applicants required to submit FAFSA. *Unit head:* Dr. John Judge, Dean, 202-319-5127, Fax: 202-319-4499, E-mail: judge@cua.edu. *Application contact:* Dr. Steven Brown, Director of Graduate Admissions, 202-319-5057, Fax: 202-319-6533, E-mail: cua-admissions@cua.edu.
Website: https://engineering.catholic.edu/

Central Connecticut State University, School of Graduate Studies, School of Engineering, Science and Technology, Department of Engineering, New Britain, CT 06050-4010. Offers MS. *Program availability:* Part-time, evening/weekend. *Degree requirements:* For master's, thesis or alternative, special project. *Entrance requirements:* For master's, minimum undergraduate GPA of 2.7; four-year BS program in engineering technology, engineering or other programs with specific courses. Additional exam requirements/recommendations for international students: required—TOEFL (minimum score 550 paper-based; 79 iBT); recommended—IELTS (minimum score 6.5). Electronic applications accepted.

Central Connecticut State University, School of Graduate Studies, School of Engineering, Science and Technology, Department of Technology and Engineering Education, New Britain, CT 06050-4010. Offers MS. *Program availability:* Part-time, evening/weekend. *Degree requirements:* For master's, thesis or alternative, special project. *Entrance requirements:* For master's, minimum undergraduate GPA of 2.7. Additional exam requirements/recommendations for international students: required—TOEFL (minimum score 550 paper-based; 79 iBT); recommended—IELTS (minimum score 6.5). Electronic applications accepted.

Central Michigan University, College of Graduate Studies, College of Science and Engineering, School of Engineering and Technology, Mount Pleasant, MI 48859. Offers industrial management and technology (MA). *Program availability:* Part-time. *Degree requirements:* For master's, thesis or alternative. Electronic applications accepted. *Expenses: Tuition, area resident:* Full-time $12,267; part-time $8178 per year. Tuition, state resident: full-time $12,267; part-time $8178 per year. Tuition, nonresident: full-time $12,267; part-time $8178 per year. *International tuition:* $16,110 full-time. *Required fees:* $225 per semester. Tuition and fees vary according to degree level and program.

Christian Brothers University, School of Engineering, Memphis, TN 38104-5581. Offers MEM, MSEM. *Program availability:* Part-time, evening/weekend, online learning. *Degree requirements:* For master's, engineering management project. *Entrance requirements:* For master's, GRE. Additional exam requirements/recommendations for international students: required—TOEFL.

The Citadel, The Military College of South Carolina, Citadel Graduate College, School of Engineering, Charleston, SC 29409. Offers MS, Graduate Certificate.

Engineering and Applied Sciences—General

Program availability: Part-time, evening/weekend. *Entrance requirements:* Additional exam requirements/recommendations for international students: required—TOEFL (minimum score 550 paper-based; 79 iBT). Electronic applications accepted.

City College of the City University of New York, Graduate School, Grove School of Engineering, New York, NY 10031-9198. Offers ME, MIS, MS, PhD. *Program availability:* Part-time. Terminal master's awarded for partial completion of doctoral program. *Degree requirements:* For master's, thesis optional; for doctorate, one foreign language, comprehensive exam, thesis/dissertation. *Entrance requirements:* For master's, GRE General Test, minimum B average in undergraduate coursework; for doctorate, GRE General Test, minimum GPA of 3.5. Additional exam requirements/recommendations for international students: required—TOEFL (minimum score 500 paper-based; 61 iBT).

Clarkson University, Wallace H. Coulter School of Engineering, Potsdam, NY 13699. Offers ME, MS, PhD, Advanced Certificate. *Faculty:* 70 full-time (12 women), 21 part-time/adjunct (5 women). *Students:* 132 full-time (29 women), 117 part-time (22 women); includes 27 minority (2 Black or African American, non-Hispanic/Latino; 1 American Indian or Alaska Native, non-Hispanic/Latino; 12 Asian, non-Hispanic/Latino; 6 Hispanic/Latino; 6 Two or more races, non-Hispanic/Latino), 83 international. In 2019, 63 master's, 19 doctorates, 45 other advanced degrees awarded. *Expenses: Tuition:* Full-time $24,984; part-time $1388. *Required fees:* $225. Tuition and fees vary according to campus/location and program. *Unit head:* Dr. William Jemison, Dean of Engineering, 315-268-6446, E-mail: wjemison@clarkson.edu. *Application contact:* Daniel Capogna, Director of Graduate Admissions & Recruitment, 518-631-9910, E-mail: graduate@clarkson.edu.
Website: https://www.clarkson.edu/academics/graduate

Clemson University, Graduate School, College of Engineering, Computing and Applied Sciences, Clemson, SC 29634. Offers M Engr, MFA, MS, PhD, Certificate. *Faculty:* 292 full-time (61 women), 13 part-time/adjunct (5 women). *Students:* 1,364 full-time (335 women), 282 part-time (67 women); includes 124 minority (38 Black or African American, non-Hispanic/Latino; 1 American Indian or Alaska Native, non-Hispanic/Latino; 36 Asian, non-Hispanic/Latino; 30 Hispanic/Latino; 1 Native Hawaiian or other Pacific Islander, non-Hispanic/Latino; 18 Two or more races, non-Hispanic/Latino), 969 international. Average age 26. 2,751 applicants, 60% accepted, 679 enrolled. In 2019, 392 master's, 87 doctorates, 59 other advanced degrees awarded. Terminal master's awarded for partial completion of doctoral program. *Expenses:* Full-Time Student per Semester: Tuition: $5300 (in-state), $11025 (out-of-state), Fees: $598; Graduate Assistant Per Semester: $1144; Part-Time Student Per Credit Hour: $724 (in-state), $1451 (out-of-state), Fees: $617; other fees apply depending on program, credit hours, campus & residency. Doctoral Base Fee per Semester: $4938 (in-state), $10405 (out-of-state). *Financial support:* In 2019–20, 982 students received support, including 116 fellowships with full and partial tuition reimbursements available (averaging $9,990 per year), 402 research assistantships with full and partial tuition reimbursements available (averaging $21,740 per year), 225 teaching assistantships with full and partial tuition reimbursements available (averaging $20,686 per year); career-related internships or fieldwork and unspecified assistantships also available. *Unit head:* Dr. Anand Gramopadhye, Dean, 864-656-3200, E-mail: agrampo@clemson.edu. *Application contact:* Dr. Douglas Hirt, Associate Dean for Research and Graduate Studies, 864-656-3201, E-mail: hirtd@clemson.edu.
Website: http://www.clemson.edu/cecas/

Cleveland State University, College of Graduate Studies, Fenn College of Engineering, Cleveland, OH 44115. Offers MS, D Eng. *Program availability:* Part-time, evening/weekend. *Faculty:* 54 full-time (5 women), 12 part-time/adjunct (0 women). *Students:* 202 full-time (60 women), 153 part-time (41 women); includes 34 minority (7 Black or African American, non-Hispanic/Latino; 17 Asian, non-Hispanic/Latino; 6 Hispanic/Latino; 4 Two or more races, non-Hispanic/Latino), 169 international. Average age 26. 1,037 applicants, 48% accepted, 143 enrolled. In 2019, 157 master's, 8 doctorates awarded. *Entrance requirements:* For master's, GRE General Test, BS in engineering, minimum GPA of 3.0 (2.75 for students from ABET-/EAC-accredited programs from the U.S. and Canada); for doctorate, GRE General Test, MS in engineering, minimum GPA of 3.25. Additional exam requirements/recommendations for international students: required—TOEFL (minimum score 550 paper-based; 78 iBT). *Application deadline:* Applications are processed on a rolling basis. Application fee: $30. Electronic applications accepted. *Expenses:* Tuition, state resident: full-time $10,215; part-time $6810 per credit hour. Tuition, nonresident: full-time $17,496; part-time $11,664 per credit hour. *International tuition:* $19,316 full-time. Tuition and fees vary according to degree level and program. *Financial support:* Fellowships, research assistantships, teaching assistantships, career-related internships or fieldwork, institutionally sponsored loans, scholarships/grants, tuition waivers (full and partial), and unspecified assistantships available. Support available to part-time students. Financial award application deadline: 3/30; financial award applicants required to submit FAFSA. *Unit head:* Dr. Paul P. Lin, Associate Dean, 216-687-2556, Fax: 216-687-9280, E-mail: p.lin@csuohio.edu. *Application contact:* Deborah L. Brown, Interim Assistant Director, Graduate Admissions, 216-523-7572, Fax: 216-687-9214, E-mail: d.l.brown@csuohio.edu.
Website: http://www.csuohio.edu/engineering/

Colorado School of Mines, Office of Graduate Studies, Golden, CO 80401. Offers ME, MIPER, MP, MS, PMS, PhD, Graduate Certificate. *Program availability:* Part-time. *Degree requirements:* For master's, thesis (for some programs); for doctorate, comprehensive exam, thesis/dissertation. *Entrance requirements:* For master's, doctorate, and Graduate Certificate, GRE General Test. Additional exam requirements/recommendations for international students: required—TOEFL (minimum score 550 paper-based; 79 iBT). Electronic applications accepted. *Expenses:* Tuition, state resident: full-time $16,650; part-time $925 per credit hour. Tuition, nonresident: full-time $37,350; part-time $2075 per credit hour. *International tuition:* $37,350 full-time. *Required fees:* $2412.

Colorado State University, Walter Scott, Jr. College of Engineering, Fort Collins, CO 80523-1301. Offers ME, MS, PhD. *Program availability:* Part-time, evening/weekend, 100% online, blended/hybrid learning. *Faculty:* 188 full-time (49 women), 40 part-time/adjunct (9 women). *Students:* 317 full-time (85 women), 669 part-time (149 women); includes 133 minority (32 Black or African American, non-Hispanic/Latino; 1 American Indian or Alaska Native, non-Hispanic/Latino; 33 Asian, non-Hispanic/Latino; 54 Hispanic/Latino; 13 Two or more races, non-Hispanic/Latino), 311 international. Average age 30. 1,206 applicants, 38% accepted, 234 enrolled. In 2019, 206 master's, 60 doctorates awarded. Terminal master's awarded for partial completion of doctoral program. *Degree requirements:* For master's, comprehensive exam (for some programs), thesis (for some programs); for doctorate, comprehensive exam (for some programs), thesis/dissertation. Application fee: $60 ($70 for international students). Electronic applications accepted. *Expenses:* Contact institution. *Financial support:* In 2019–20, 294 research assistantships (averaging $24,920 per year), 69 teaching assistantships (averaging $17,643 per year) were awarded; scholarships/grants, traineeships, health care benefits, and unspecified assistantships also available. *Unit head:* Dr. David McLean, Dean, 970-491-3366, E-mail: david.mclean@colostate.edu. *Application contact:* Dr. Anthony Marchese, Associate Dean of Academic and Student Affairs, 970-491-6220, Fax: 970-491-3429, E-mail: anthony.marchese@colostate.edu.
Website: https://www.engr.colostate.edu/

Colorado State University-Pueblo, College of Education, Engineering and Professional Studies, Pueblo, CO 81001-4901. Offers M Ed, MS. *Program availability:* Part-time, evening/weekend. *Degree requirements:* For master's, thesis optional. *Entrance requirements:* For master's, GRE General Test. Additional exam requirements/recommendations for international students: required—TOEFL (minimum score 500 paper-based). Electronic applications accepted. *Expenses:* Contact institution.

Columbia University, Fu Foundation School of Engineering and Applied Science, New York, NY 10027. Offers MS, Eng Sc D, PhD, MS/MBA, MS/PhD. *Program availability:* Part-time, 100% online. Terminal master's awarded for partial completion of doctoral program. *Degree requirements:* For master's, comprehensive exam (for some programs), thesis (for some programs); for doctorate, comprehensive exam (for some programs), thesis/dissertation, qualifying exam. *Entrance requirements:* For master's, GRE General Test; for doctorate, GRE General Test, GRE Subject Test (applied physics program only). Additional exam requirements/recommendations for international students: required—TOEFL (minimum score 590 paper-based; 96 iBT), IELTS (minimum score 6.5), PTE. Electronic applications accepted. *Expenses: Tuition:* Full-time $47,600; part-time $1880 per credit. One-time fee: $105.

Concordia University, School of Graduate Studies, Faculty of Engineering and Computer Science, Montréal, QC H3G 1M8, Canada. Offers M App Comp Sc, M Comp Sc, M Eng, MA Sc, PhD, Certificate, Diploma. *Degree requirements:* For doctorate, comprehensive exam, thesis/dissertation. *Expenses:* Contact institution.

Cooper Union for the Advancement of Science and Art, Albert Nerken School of Engineering, New York, NY 10003. Offers chemical engineering (ME); civil engineering (ME); electrical engineering (ME); mechanical engineering (ME). *Program availability:* Part-time. *Degree requirements:* For master's, thesis (for some programs), thesis or special project. *Entrance requirements:* For master's, BE or BS in an engineering discipline; official copies of school transcripts including secondary (high school), college and university work; two letters of recommendation; resume. Additional exam requirements/recommendations for international students: required—TOEFL (minimum score 600 paper-based; 100 iBT). Electronic applications accepted.

Cornell University, Graduate School, Graduate Fields of Engineering, Ithaca, NY 14853. Offers M Eng, MPS, MS, PhD, M Eng/MBA. *Degree requirements:* For doctorate, comprehensive exam, thesis/dissertation. *Entrance requirements:* Additional exam requirements/recommendations for international students: required—TOEFL. Electronic applications accepted.

Dalhousie University, Faculty of Engineering, Halifax, NS B3H 4R2, Canada. Offers M Eng, M Sc, MA Sc, PhD, M Eng/M Plan, MA Sc/M Plan, MBA/M Eng. *Entrance requirements:* Additional exam requirements/recommendations for international students: required—1 of 5 approved tests: TOEFL, IELTS, CANTEST, CAEL, Michigan English Language Assessment Battery.

Dartmouth College, Dartmouth Engineering - Thayer School of Engineering, Hanover, NH 03755. Offers M Eng, MEM, MS, PhD, MD/MS, MD/PhD. *Faculty:* 54 full-time (10 women), 17 part-time/adjunct (2 women). *Students:* 219 full-time (75 women); includes 25 minority (2 Black or African American, non-Hispanic/Latino; 14 Asian, non-Hispanic/Latino; 4 Hispanic/Latino; 5 Two or more races, non-Hispanic/Latino), 124 international. Average age 26. 698 applicants, 22% accepted, 86 enrolled. In 2019, 65 master's, 22 doctorates awarded. Terminal master's awarded for partial completion of doctoral program. *Degree requirements:* For master's, thesis (for some programs); for doctorate, thesis/dissertation, six terms in residence. *Entrance requirements:* For master's and doctorate, GRE General Test. Additional exam requirements/recommendations for international students: required—TOEFL, IELTS. *Application deadline:* For fall admission, 1/1 priority date for domestic and international students. Applications are processed on a rolling basis. Application fee: $45. Electronic applications accepted. *Financial support:* In 2019–20, 27 fellowships with full tuition reimbursements (averaging $28,320 per year), 81 research assistantships with full tuition reimbursements (averaging $28,320 per year), 13 teaching assistantships with partial tuition reimbursements (averaging $8,640 per year) were awarded; career-related internships or fieldwork, institutionally sponsored loans, scholarships/grants, and tuition waivers (full and partial) also available. Financial award application deadline: 2/15; financial award applicants required to submit CSS PROFILE. *Unit head:* Dr. Alexis R. Abramson, Dean, 603-646-2238, Fax: 603-646-2580, E-mail: Alexis.R.Abramson@Dartmouth.edu. *Application contact:* Candace S. Potter, Graduate Admissions & Financial Aid Administrator, 603-646-3844, Fax: 603-646-1620, E-mail: candace.s.potter@dartmouth.edu.
Website: http://engineering.dartmouth.edu/

Drexel University, College of Engineering, Philadelphia, PA 19104-2875. Offers MS, MSEE, MSSE, PhD, Certificate. *Program availability:* Part-time, evening/weekend. *Degree requirements:* For doctorate, thesis/dissertation. *Entrance requirements:* Additional exam requirements/recommendations for international students: required—TOEFL. Electronic applications accepted.

Drexel University, Goodwin College of Professional Studies, School of Technology and Professional Studies, Philadelphia, PA 19104-2875. Offers construction management (MS); creativity and innovation (MS); engineering technology (MS); food science (MS); hospitality management (MS); professional studies: creativity studies (MS); professional studies: e-learning leadership (MS); professional studies: homeland security management (MS); project management (MS); property management (MS); sport management (MS). *Program availability:* Part-time, evening/weekend. *Entrance requirements:* Additional exam requirements/recommendations for international students: required—TOEFL, IELTS. Electronic applications accepted. Application fee is waived when completed online.

Duke University, Graduate School, Pratt School of Engineering, Master of Engineering Program, Durham, NC 27708-0271. Offers biomedical engineering (M Eng); civil engineering (M Eng); computational mechanics and scientific computing (M Eng); electrical and computer engineering (M Eng); environmental engineering (M Eng); materials science and engineering (M Eng); mechanical engineering (M Eng); photonics and optical sciences (M Eng); risk engineering (M Eng). *Program availability:* Part-time. *Entrance requirements:* For master's, GRE General Test, resume, 3 letters of recommendation, statement of purpose, transcripts. Additional exam requirements/recommendations for international students: required—TOEFL. Electronic applications accepted.

Eastern Illinois University, Graduate School, Lumpkin College of Business and Technology, School of Technology, Charleston, IL 61920. Offers computer technology (Certificate); cybersecurity (MS); quality systems (Certificate); sustainable energy (MS); technology (MS); technology security (Certificate); work performance improvement (Certificate); MS/MBA; MS/MS. *Program availability:* Part-time, evening/weekend.

Eastern Michigan University, Graduate School, College of Engineering and Technology, School of Engineering, Programs in Computer Aided Engineering, Ypsilanti, MI 48197. Offers CAD/CAM (MS); computer-aided technology (MS). *Program availability:* Part-time, evening/weekend, online learning. *Students:* 10 full-time (2 women), 5 part-time (0 women); includes 3 minority (all Asian, non-Hispanic/Latino), 7 international. Average age 29. 30 applicants, 50% accepted, 5 enrolled. In 2019, 10 master's awarded. *Entrance requirements:* Additional exam requirements/recommendations for international students: required—TOEFL. *Application deadline:* Applications are processed on a rolling basis. Application fee: $45. *Financial support:* Fellowships, research assistantships with full tuition reimbursements, teaching assistantships with full tuition reimbursements, and tuition waivers (partial) available. Financial award applicants required to submit FAFSA. *Application contact:* Dr. Tony Shay, Program Coordinator, 734-487-2040, Fax: 734-487-8755, E-mail: tshay@emich.edu.

Fairfield University, School of Engineering, Fairfield, CT 06824. Offers database management (CAS); electrical and computer engineering (MS); information security (CAS); management of technology (MS); mechanical engineering (MS); network technology (CAS); software engineering (MS); Web application development (CAS). *Program availability:* Part-time, evening/weekend. *Faculty:* 10 full-time (2 women), 15 part-time/adjunct (1 woman). *Students:* 46 full-time (24 women), 57 part-time (10 women); includes 23 minority (5 Black or African American, non-Hispanic/Latino; 9 Asian, non-Hispanic/Latino; 9 Hispanic/Latino), 33 international. Average age 29. 68 applicants, 62% accepted, 30 enrolled. In 2019, 100 master's awarded. *Degree requirements:* For master's, capstone course. *Entrance requirements:* For master's, resume, 2 recommendations. Additional exam requirements/recommendations for international students: required—TOEFL (minimum score 550 paper-based; 80 iBT), IELTS (minimum score 6.5), TOEFL (minimum score 550 paper-based; 80 iBT) or IELTS (minimum score 6.5). *Application deadline:* For fall admission, 5/15 for international students; for spring admission, 10/15 for international students. Applications are processed on a rolling basis. Application fee: $60. Electronic applications accepted. *Expenses:* Tuition $900/credit hour; Registration Fee $50/semester; Graduate Student Activity Fee (Fall and Spring) $65/semester. *Financial support:* In 2019–20, 20 students received support. Scholarships/grants and unspecified assistantships available. Financial award applicants required to submit FAFSA. *Unit head:* Richard Heist, Dean, 203-254-4147, Fax: 203-254-4013, E-mail: rheist@fairfield.edu. *Application contact:* Melanie Rogers, Director of Graduate Admission, 203-254-4184, Fax: 203-254-4073, E-mail: gradadmis@fairfield.edu. Website: http://www.fairfield.edu/soe

Fairleigh Dickinson University, Metropolitan Campus, University College: Arts, Sciences, and Professional Studies, School of Computer Sciences and Engineering, Teaneck, NJ 07666-1914. Offers computer engineering (MS); computer science (MS); e-commerce (MS); electrical engineering (MSEE); management information systems (MS); mathematical foundation (MS).

Florida Agricultural and Mechanical University, Division of Graduate Studies, Research, and Continuing Education, FAMU-FSU College of Engineering, Tallahassee, FL 32307-3200. Offers M Eng, MS, PhD. *Entrance requirements:* For master's, GRE General Test, minimum GPA of 3.0. Additional exam requirements/recommendations for international students: required—TOEFL (minimum score 550 paper-based).

Florida Atlantic University, College of Engineering and Computer Science, Boca Raton, FL 33431-0991. Offers MS, PhD. *Program availability:* Part-time, evening/weekend, online learning. *Faculty:* 75 full-time (9 women), 1 part-time/adjunct (0 women). *Students:* 172 full-time (43 women), 209 part-time (48 women); includes 127 minority (26 Black or African American, non-Hispanic/Latino; 27 Asian, non-Hispanic/Latino; 65 Hispanic/Latino; 9 Two or more races, non-Hispanic/Latino), 115 international. Average age 31. 357 applicants, 53% accepted, 134 enrolled. In 2019, 120 master's, 24 doctorates awarded. Terminal master's awarded for partial completion of doctoral program. *Degree requirements:* For master's, thesis optional; for doctorate, thesis/dissertation, qualifying exam. *Entrance requirements:* For master's, GRE General Test, minimum GPA of 3.0; for doctorate, GRE General Test. Additional exam requirements/recommendations for international students: required—TOEFL (minimum score 500 paper-based; 61 iBT), IELTS (minimum score 6). *Application deadline:* For fall admission, 7/1 for domestic students, 2/15 for international students; for spring admission, 11/1 for domestic students, 7/15 for international students. Applications are processed on a rolling basis. Application fee: $30. *Expenses:* Tuition: Full-time $20,536; part-time $371.82 per credit hour. Tuition and fees vary according to program. *Financial support:* Fellowships, research assistantships with partial tuition reimbursements, teaching assistantships with partial tuition reimbursements, career-related internships or fieldwork, Federal Work-Study, and unspecified assistantships available. Support available to part-time students. Financial award applicants required to submit FAFSA. *Unit head:* Dr. Stella Batalama, Dean, 561-297-3426, E-mail: sbatalama@fau.edu. *Application contact:* Dr. Stella Batalama, Dean, 561-297-3426, E-mail: sbatalama@fau.edu. Website: http://www.eng.fau.edu/

Florida Institute of Technology, College of Engineering and Science, Melbourne, FL 32901-6975. Offers MS, PhD. *Program availability:* Part-time. Terminal master's awarded for partial completion of doctoral program. *Degree requirements:* For master's, comprehensive exam (for some programs), thesis (for some programs), thesis or final exam; for doctorate, thesis/dissertation. *Entrance requirements:* For master's, GRE, minimum GPA of 3.0, 3 letters of recommendation, resume, statement of objectives; for doctorate, GRE, minimum GPA of 3.2, 3 letters of recommendation, resume, statement of objectives. Additional exam requirements/recommendations for international students: required—TOEFL (minimum score 550 paper-based; 79 iBT). Electronic applications accepted.

Florida International University, College of Engineering and Computing, Miami, FL 33175. Offers MS, PMS, PhD. *Program availability:* Part-time, evening/weekend, online learning. *Faculty:* 152 full-time (30 women), 90 part-time/adjunct (14 women). *Students:* 690 full-time (190 women), 378 part-time (103 women); includes 471 minority (67 Black or African American, non-Hispanic/Latino; 1 American Indian or Alaska Native, non-Hispanic/Latino; 35 Asian, non-Hispanic/Latino; 347 Hispanic/Latino; 1 Native Hawaiian or other Pacific Islander, non-Hispanic/Latino; 20 Two or more races, non-Hispanic/Latino), 515 international. Average age 29. 1,218 applicants, 52% accepted, 310 enrolled. In 2019, 274 master's, 46 doctorates awarded. Terminal master's awarded for partial completion of doctoral program. *Degree requirements:* For master's, thesis (for some programs); for doctorate, comprehensive exam, thesis/dissertation. *Entrance requirements:* For master's, GRE (depending on program), minimum GPA of 3.0; for doctorate, GRE General Test, minimum GPA of 3.0. Additional exam requirements/recommendations for international students: required—TOEFL (minimum score 550 paper-based; 80 iBT). *Application deadline:* For fall admission, 6/1 for domestic students, 4/1 for international students; for spring admission, 10/1 for domestic students, 9/1 for international students. Applications are processed on a rolling basis. Application fee: $30. Electronic applications accepted. *Expenses: Tuition, area resident:* Full-time $8912; part-time $446 per credit hour. Tuition, state resident: full-time $8912; part-time $446 per credit hour. Tuition, nonresident: full-time $21,393; part-time $992 per credit hour. *Required fees:* $2194. *Financial support:* Career-related internships or fieldwork, Federal Work-Study, institutionally sponsored loans, scholarships/grants, and unspecified assistantships available. Financial award application deadline: 3/1; financial award applicants required to submit FAFSA. *Unit head:* Dr. John Volakis, Dean, 305-

348-0273, Fax: 305-348-0127, E-mail: grad_eng@fiu.edu. *Application contact:* Nanett Rojas, Manager, Admissions Operations, 305-348-7464, Fax: 305-348-7441, E-mail: gradadm@fiu.edu.

Florida Polytechnic University, Graduate Programs, Lakeland, FL 33805. Offers computer science (MS); engineering (MS).

Florida State University, The Graduate School, FAMU-FSU College of Engineering, Tallahassee, FL 32310-6046. Offers M Eng, MS, PhD. *Program availability:* Part-time, 100% online. *Faculty:* 92 full-time (16 women). *Students:* 258 full-time (62 women), 68 part-time (17 women); includes 57 minority (33 Black or African American, non-Hispanic/Latino; 2 Asian, non-Hispanic/Latino; 13 Hispanic/Latino; 9 Two or more races, non-Hispanic/Latino), 176 international. Average age 29. 692 applicants, 44% accepted, 101 enrolled. In 2019, 78 master's, 31 doctorates awarded. Terminal master's awarded for partial completion of doctoral program. *Degree requirements:* For master's, comprehensive exam (for some programs), thesis (for some programs); for doctorate, thesis/dissertation, preliminary exam, qualifying exam. *Entrance requirements:* For master's and doctorate, GRE General Test. Additional exam requirements/recommendations for international students: required—TOEFL (minimum score 550 paper-based; 80 iBT). *Application deadline:* For fall admission, 7/1 for domestic and international students; for spring admission, 11/1 for domestic and international students; for summer admission, 3/1 for domestic and international students. Applications are processed on a rolling basis. Application fee: $30. Electronic applications accepted. *Financial support:* In 2019–20, 261 students received support, including 22 fellowships with full tuition reimbursements available, 135 research assistantships with full tuition reimbursements available, 104 teaching assistantships with full tuition reimbursements available; career-related internships or fieldwork, scholarships/grants, tuition waivers (full), and unspecified assistantships also available. Financial award application deadline: 1/15; financial award applicants required to submit FAFSA. *Unit head:* Dr. John Murray Gibson, Dean/Professor, 850-410-6161, Fax: 850-410-6546, E-mail: dean@eng.famu.fsu.edu. *Application contact:* Deborah Gautier, Director, Graduate Studies, 850-410-6613, E-mail: gradstudies@eng.famu.fsu.edu. Website: https://www.eng.famu.fsu.edu/

George Mason University, Volgenau School of Engineering, Fairfax, VA 22030. Offers MS, PhD, Certificate. *Program availability:* Part-time, evening/weekend, 100% online. *Degree requirements:* For master's, thesis optional; for doctorate, thesis/dissertation, comprehensive oral and written exams. *Entrance requirements:* For master's, minimum GPA of 3.0 in last 60 hours of course work; for doctorate, GRE General Test, minimum graduate GPA of 3.5. Additional exam requirements/recommendations for international students: required—TOEFL (minimum score 575 paper-based; 88 iBT), IELTS (minimum score 6.5), PTE (minimum score 59). Electronic applications accepted. *Expenses:* Contact institution.

The George Washington University, School of Engineering and Applied Science, Washington, DC 20052. Offers MS, D Sc, PhD, App Sc, Engr, Graduate Certificate. *Program availability:* Part-time, evening/weekend. *Degree requirements:* For master's, thesis optional; for doctorate, thesis/dissertation, qualifying exam. *Entrance requirements:* For master's, appropriate bachelor's degree; for doctorate, GRE (if highest earned degree is BS), appropriate bachelor's or master's degree; for other advanced degree, appropriate master's degree. Additional exam requirements/recommendations for international students: required—TOEFL or The George Washington University English as a Foreign Language Test.

Georgia Institute of Technology, Graduate Studies, College of Engineering, Atlanta, GA 30332-0360. Offers MS, MSMP, MSNE, PhD, MD/PhD. *Program availability:* Part-time, 100% online. *Faculty:* 3 full-time (1 woman). *Students:* 93 part-time (24 women); includes 26 minority (5 Black or African American, non-Hispanic/Latino; 3 Asian, non-Hispanic/Latino; 15 Hispanic/Latino; 3 Two or more races, non-Hispanic/Latino), 6 international. Average age 35. 74 applicants, 82% accepted, 49 enrolled. In 2019, 37 master's awarded. Terminal master's awarded for partial completion of doctoral program. *Degree requirements:* For doctorate, thesis/dissertation. *Entrance requirements:* For master's and doctorate, GRE. Additional exam requirements/recommendations for international students: required—TOEFL (minimum score 577 paper-based; 90 iBT), IELTS (minimum score 7), TOEFL is the preferred method with the requirements shown on the programs. *Application deadline:* Applications are processed on a rolling basis. Application fee: $75 ($85 for international students). Electronic applications accepted. *Expenses: Tuition, area resident:* Full-time $14,064; part-time $586 per credit hour. Tuition, state resident: full-time $14,064; part-time $586 per credit hour. Tuition, nonresident: full-time $29,140; part-time $1215 per credit hour. *International tuition:* $29,140 full-time. *Required fees:* $2024; $840 per semester. $2096. Tuition and fees vary according to course load. *Financial support:* Fellowships, research assistantships, teaching assistantships, career-related internships or fieldwork, Federal Work-Study, institutionally sponsored loans, tuition waivers (full and partial), and unspecified assistantships available. Support available to part-time students. Financial award application deadline: 7/1; financial award applicants required to submit FAFSA. *Unit head:* Steven McLaughlin, Dean, 404-894-3350, Fax: 404-894-0168, E-mail: steve.mclaughlin@coe.gatech.edu. *Application contact:* Marla Bruner, Director of Graduate Studies, 404-894-1610, Fax: 404-894-1609, E-mail: gradinfo@mail.gatech.edu. Website: http://www.coe.gatech.edu

Georgia Southern University, Jack N. Averitt College of Graduate Studies, Allen E. Paulson College of Engineering and Computing, Statesboro, GA 30458. Offers MS, MSAE, Graduate Certificate. *Program availability:* Part-time, blended/hybrid learning. *Faculty:* 92 full-time (9 women), 1 part-time/adjunct (0 women). *Students:* 77 full-time (11 women), 49 part-time (11 women); includes 32 minority (16 Black or African American, non-Hispanic/Latino; 5 Asian, non-Hispanic/Latino; 9 Hispanic/Latino; 2 Two or more races, non-Hispanic/Latino), 50 international. Average age 28. 156 applicants, 75% accepted, 40 enrolled. In 2019, 53 master's, 1 other advanced degree awarded. *Degree requirements:* For master's, comprehensive exam, thesis optional. *Entrance requirements:* For master's, GRE, undergraduate major or equivalent in proposed study area. Additional exam requirements/recommendations for international students: required—TOEFL (minimum score 550 paper-based; 80 iBT), IELTS (minimum score 6). *Application deadline:* For fall admission, 3/1 priority date for domestic students, 6/1 for international students; for spring admission, 10/1 priority date for domestic students, 10/1 for international students. Applications are processed on a rolling basis. Application fee: $50. Electronic applications accepted. *Expenses: Tuition, area resident:* Full-time $4986; part-time $277 per credit hour. Tuition, nonresident: full-time $19,890; part-time $1105 per credit hour. *International tuition:* $19,890 full-time. *Required fees:* $2114; $1057 per semester. $1057 per semester. Tuition and fees vary according to course load, campus/location and program. *Financial support:* In 2019–20, 84 students received support, including 3 research assistantships with full tuition reimbursements available (averaging $7,750 per year), 4 teaching assistantships with full tuition reimbursements available (averaging $7,750 per year); Federal Work-Study, scholarships/grants, tuition waivers (full), and unspecified assistantships also available. Financial award applicants required to submit FAFSA. *Unit head:* Dr. Mohammad S. Davoud, Dean, 912-478-8046, E-mail: mdavoud@georgiasouthern.edu. *Application contact:* Dr. Mohammad S. Davoud, Dean, 912-478-8046, E-mail: mdavoud@

georgiasouthern.edu.
Website: https://cec.georgiasouthern.edu/

Gonzaga University, School of Engineering and Applied Science, Spokane, WA 99258. Offers transmission and distribution engineering (M Eng, Certificate). *Program availability:* Part-time-only, evening/weekend, online only, 100% online. *Degree requirements:* For master's, portfolio, capstone course. *Entrance requirements:* For master's, GRE, letter of intent, two letters of recommendation, transcripts, resume/curriculum vitae. Electronic applications accepted. *Expenses:* Contact institution.

Grand Valley State University, Padnos College of Engineering and Computing, School of Engineering, Allendale, MI 49401-9403. Offers electrical and computer engineering (MSE); mechanical engineering (MSE); product design and manufacturing engineering (MSE). *Program availability:* Part-time, evening/weekend. *Faculty:* 22 full-time (6 women), 1 part-time/adjunct (0 women). *Students:* 23 full-time (2 women), 35 part-time (5 women); includes 4 minority (2 Asian, non-Hispanic/Latino; 1 Hispanic/Latino; 1 Two or more races, non-Hispanic/Latino), 25 international. Average age 27. 46 applicants, 78% accepted, 10 enrolled. In 2019, 32 master's awarded. *Degree requirements:* For master's, capstone experience. *Entrance requirements:* For master's, engineering degree, minimum GPA of 3.0, resume, 3 confidential letters of recommendation, 1-2 page essay, base of underlying relevant knowledge/evidence from academic records or relevant wok experience. Additional exam requirements/recommendations for international students: required—Michigan English Language Assessment Battery (minimum score 77), TOEFL (minimum iBT score of 80), or IELTS (6.5); GRE. *Application deadline:* Applications are processed on a rolling basis. Application fee: $30. Electronic applications accepted. *Expenses:* $733 per credit hour, 33 credit hours. *Financial support:* In 2019–20, 40 students received support, including 8 fellowships, 34 research assistantships with full and partial tuition reimbursements available (averaging $4,000 per year); career-related internships or fieldwork, Federal Work-Study, institutionally sponsored loans, scholarships/grants, and unspecified assistantships also available. *Unit head:* Dr. Wael Mokhtar, Director, 616-331-6015, Fax: 616-331-7215, E-mail: mokhtarw@gvsu.edu. *Application contact:* Dr. Shabbir Choudhuri, Graduate Program Director, 616-331-6845, Fax: 616-331-7215, E-mail: choudhus@gvsu.edu.
Website: http://www.engineer.gvsu.edu/

Grantham University, College of Engineering and Computer Science, Lenexa, KS 66219. Offers information management (MS), including project management; information management technology (MS); information technology (MS). *Program availability:* Part-time, evening/weekend, online only, 100% online. *Students:* 118 full-time (28 women), 45 part-time (11 women); includes 94 minority (55 Black or African American, non-Hispanic/Latino; 8 Asian, non-Hispanic/Latino; 19 Hispanic/Latino; 1 Native Hawaiian or other Pacific Islander, non-Hispanic/Latino; 11 Two or more races, non-Hispanic/Latino). Average age 40. 20 applicants, 95% accepted, 17 enrolled. In 2019, 96 master's awarded. *Degree requirements:* For master's, comprehensive exam (for some programs), Project Management: PMP Prep Exam (for information management). *Entrance requirements:* For master's, Graduate: A minimum score of 530 on the paper-based TOEFL, or 71 on the internet-based TOEFL, 6.5 on the IELTS, or 50 on the PTE Academic Score Report, baccalaureate or master's degree with minimum cumulative GPA of 2.5 from institution accredited by agency recognized by U.S. ED or foreign equivalent; official transcripts showing proof of degree. Additional exam requirements/recommendations for international students: required—TOEFL (minimum score 530 paper-based; 71 iBT), IELTS (minimum score 6.5), PTE (minimum score 50). *Application deadline:* Applications are processed on a rolling basis. Application fee: $0. Electronic applications accepted. *Expenses:* Contact institution. *Financial support:* Scholarships/grants available. Financial award applicants required to submit FAFSA. *Unit head:* Dr. Nancy Miller, Dean of the College of Engineering and Computer Science, 913-309-4738, Fax: 855-681-5201, E-mail: nmiller@grantham.edu. *Application contact:* Lauren Cook, Director of Admissions, 800-955-2527 Ext. 803, Fax: 877-304-4467, E-mail: admissions@grantham.edu.
Website: http://www.grantham.edu/engineering-and-computer-science/

Harvard University, Graduate School of Arts and Sciences, Harvard John A. Paulson School of Engineering and Applied Sciences, Cambridge, MA 02138. Offers applied mathematics (PhD); applied physics (PhD); computational science and engineering (ME, SM); computer science (PhD); data science (SM); design engineering (MDE); engineering science (ME), including electrical engineering (ME, SM, PhD); engineering sciences (SM, PhD), including bioengineering (PhD), electrical engineering (ME, SM, PhD), environmental science and engineering (PhD), materials science and mechanical engineering (PhD). *Program availability:* Part-time. Terminal master's awarded for partial completion of doctoral program. *Degree requirements:* For master's, thesis (for ME); for doctorate, comprehensive exam, thesis/dissertation. *Entrance requirements:* For master's and doctorate, GRE General Test, GRE Subject Test (recommended), 3 letters of recommendation. Additional exam requirements/recommendations for international students: required—TOEFL (minimum score 80 iBT). Electronic applications accepted. *Expenses:* Contact institution.

Hofstra University, Fred DeMatteis School of Engineering and Applied Sciences, Hempstead, NY 11549. Offers computer science (MS). *Program availability:* Part-time, evening/weekend, blended/hybrid learning. *Faculty:* 8 full-time (2 women), 6 part-time/adjunct (0 women). *Students:* 26 full-time (7 women), 34 part-time (7 women); includes 19 minority (3 Black or African American, non-Hispanic/Latino; 1 American Indian or Alaska Native, non-Hispanic/Latino; 6 Asian, non-Hispanic/Latino; 8 Hispanic/Latino; 1 Native Hawaiian or other Pacific Islander, non-Hispanic/Latino), 19 international. Average age 28. 107 applicants, 63% accepted, 26 enrolled. In 2019, 17 master's awarded. *Degree requirements:* For master's, thesis optional, 30 credits, minimum GPA of 3.0. *Entrance requirements:* For master's, GRE, minimum GPA of 3.0. Additional exam requirements/recommendations for international students: required—TOEFL (minimum score 550 paper-based; 80 iBT); recommended—IELTS (minimum score 6.5). *Application deadline:* Applications are processed on a rolling basis. Application fee: $75. Electronic applications accepted. *Expenses: Tuition:* Full-time $25,164; part-time $1398 per credit. *Required fees:* $580; $165 per semester. Tuition and fees vary according to course load, degree level and program. *Financial support:* In 2019–20, 29 students received support, including 22 fellowships with full and partial tuition reimbursements available (averaging $3,686 per year), 2 research assistantships with full and partial tuition reimbursements available (averaging $6,675 per year); career-related internships or fieldwork, Federal Work-Study, institutionally sponsored loans, scholarships/grants, tuition waivers (full and partial), unspecified assistantships, and scholarships and endowed scholarships also available. Support available to part-time students. Financial award applicants required to submit FAFSA. *Unit head:* Dr. Sina Rabbany, Dean, 516-463-6672, E-mail: sina.y.rabbany@hofstra.edu. *Application contact:* Sunil Samuel, Assistant Vice President of Admissions, 516-463-4723, Fax: 516-463-4664, E-mail: graduateadmission@hofstra.edu.
Website: http://www.hofstra.edu/academics/colleges/seas/

Howard University, College of Engineering, Architecture, and Computer Sciences, School of Engineering and Computer Science, Washington, DC 20059-0002. Offers M Eng, MCS, MS, PhD. *Program availability:* Part-time. Terminal master's awarded for partial completion of doctoral program. *Degree requirements:* For doctorate, one foreign language, thesis/dissertation, preliminary exam. *Entrance requirements:* For master's and doctorate, GRE General Test, minimum GPA of 3.0. Additional exam requirements/recommendations for international students: required—TOEFL. Electronic applications accepted.

Idaho State University, Graduate School, College of Science and Engineering, Pocatello, ID 83209-8060. Offers MA, MNS, MS, DA, PhD, Postbaccalaureate Certificate. *Program availability:* Part-time. *Degree requirements:* For master's, comprehensive exam (for some programs), thesis, thesis project, 2 semesters of seminar; for doctorate, comprehensive exam, thesis/dissertation, oral presentation and defense of research, oral examination; for Postbaccalaureate Certificate, comprehensive exam (for some programs), thesis optional, oral exam or thesis defense. *Entrance requirements:* For master's, GRE General Test, minimum GPA of 3.0 in upper-division undergraduate classes; for doctorate, GRE General Test, master's degree in engineering or physics, 1-page statement of research interests, resume, 3 letters of reference, 1-page statement of career interests; for Postbaccalaureate Certificate, GRE (if GPA between 2.0 and 3.0), bachelor's degree, minimum GPA of 3.0 in upper-division courses. Additional exam requirements/recommendations for international students: required—TOEFL (minimum score 550 paper-based; 80 iBT). Electronic applications accepted.

Illinois Institute of Technology, Graduate College, Armour College of Engineering, Chicago, IL 60616. Offers M Arch E, M Env E, M Geoenv E, M Trans E, MAS, MCEM, MGE, MPW, MS, MSE, PhD, MS/MAS, MS/MS. *Program availability:* Part-time, evening/weekend, online learning. Terminal master's awarded for partial completion of doctoral program. *Degree requirements:* For master's, comprehensive exam (for some programs), thesis (for some programs); for doctorate, comprehensive exam, thesis/dissertation. *Entrance requirements:* For master's and doctorate, GRE General Test, minimum undergraduate GPA of 3.0. Additional exam requirements/recommendations for international students: required—TOEFL (minimum score 550 paper-based; 80 iBT); recommended—IELTS (minimum score 5.5). Electronic applications accepted.

Indiana State University, College of Graduate and Professional Studies, College of Technology, Terre Haute, IN 47809. Offers MS, MA/MS. *Entrance requirements:* For master's, bachelor's degree in industrial technology or related field. Additional exam requirements/recommendations for international students: required—TOEFL. Electronic applications accepted.

Instituto Tecnologico de Santo Domingo, Graduate School, Area of Engineering, Santo Domingo, Dominican Republic. Offers construction administration (MS, Certificate); data telecommunications (M Eng, MS, Certificate); industrial engineering (M Eng, Certificate); industrial management (M Mgmt); information technology (Certificate); maintenance engineering (M Eng); occupational hazard prevention (M Mgmt); production management (Certificate); quantitative methods (Certificate); sanitary and environmental engineering (M Eng); structural engineering (M Eng); systems engineering and electronic data processing (Certificate); transportation (Certificate).

Instituto Tecnológico y de Estudios Superiores de Monterrey, Campus Ciudad Obregón, Program in Engineering, Ciudad Obregón, Mexico. Offers ME.

Instituto Tecnológico y de Estudios Superiores de Monterrey, Campus Monterrey, Graduate and Research Division, Programs in Engineering, Monterrey, Mexico. Offers applied statistics (M Eng); artificial intelligence (PhD); automation engineering (M Eng); chemical engineering (M Eng); civil engineering (M Eng); electrical engineering (M Eng); electronic engineering (M Eng); environmental engineering (M Eng); industrial engineering (M Eng, PhD); manufacturing engineering (M Eng); mechanical engineering (M Eng); systems and quality engineering (M Eng). *Program availability:* Part-time, evening/weekend. Terminal master's awarded for partial completion of doctoral program. *Degree requirements:* For master's, one foreign language, thesis; for doctorate, one foreign language, thesis/dissertation. *Entrance requirements:* For master's, EXADEP; for doctorate, GRE, master's degree in related field. Additional exam requirements/recommendations for international students: required—TOEFL.

James Madison University, The Graduate School, College of Integrated Science and Engineering, Harrisonburg, VA 22807. Offers MS. *Accreditation:* AOTA. *Program availability:* Part-time, evening/weekend, 100% online, blended/hybrid learning, study abroad. *Faculty:* 76. *Students:* 3 full-time (1 woman), 55 part-time (11 women); includes 14 minority (8 Black or African American, non-Hispanic/Latino; 3 Asian, non-Hispanic/Latino; 3 Hispanic/Latino), 3 international. Average age 30. In 2019, 19 master's awarded. Application fee: $60. Electronic applications accepted. *Financial support:* In 2019–20, 2 students received support. Career-related internships or fieldwork, Federal Work-Study, and assistantships (averaging $7911) available. Financial award application deadline: 3/1; financial award applicants required to submit FAFSA. *Unit head:* Dr. Robert A. Kolvoord, Dean, 540-568-2752, E-mail: kolvoora@jmu.edu. *Application contact:* Lynette D. Michael, Director of Graduate Admissions, 540-568-6395, Fax: 540-568-7860, E-mail: michaeld@jmu.edu.
Website: http://www.jmu.edu/cise/

Johns Hopkins University, Engineering Program for Professionals, Baltimore, MD 21218. Offers M Ch E, M Mat SE, MCE, MEE, MEM, MME, MS, MSE, D Eng, Graduate Certificate, Post Master's Certificate, Post-Master's Certificate. *Program availability:* Part-time, evening/weekend, 100% online, blended/hybrid learning. *Degree requirements:* For master's, thesis optional, 10 courses. *Entrance requirements:* For master's, Applicants typically have earned a grade point average of at least 3.0 on a 4.0 scale (B or above) in the latter half of their undergraduate studies. Significant relevant work experience or a graduate degree in a relevant technical discipline may be considered in lieu of meeting the GPA guideline. Additional exam requirements/recommendations for international students: required—TOEFL (minimum score 600 paper-based; 100 iBT). Electronic applications accepted. *Expenses:* Contact institution.

Johns Hopkins University, G. W. C. Whiting School of Engineering, Baltimore, MD 21218. Offers M Ch E, M Mat SE, MA, MEE, MME, MS, MSE, MSEM, MSSI, PhD, Certificate, Post-Master's Certificate. Terminal master's awarded for partial completion of doctoral program. *Degree requirements:* For master's, comprehensive exam (for some programs), thesis (for some programs); for doctorate, comprehensive exam, thesis/dissertation, oral exam. *Entrance requirements:* For master's, GRE General Test, letters of recommendation, transcripts; for doctorate, GRE General Test, letters of recommendation. Additional exam requirements/recommendations for international students: required—TOEFL (minimum score 600 paper-based; 100 iBT) or IELTS (minimum score 7). Electronic applications accepted. *Expenses:* Contact institution.

Kansas State University, Graduate School, College of Engineering, Manhattan, KS 66506. Offers MEM, MS, MSE, PhD, Graduate Certificate. *Program availability:* Part-time, online learning. *Degree requirements:* For doctorate, thesis/dissertation. *Entrance requirements:* For master's and doctorate, GRE. Additional exam requirements/recommendations for international students: required—TOEFL. Electronic applications accepted.

Kennesaw State University, Southern Polytechnic College of Engineering and Engineering Technology, Kennesaw, GA 30144. Offers MS. *Program availability:* Part-time, evening/weekend, online learning. *Students:* 30 full-time (9 women), 192 part-time (50 women); includes 90 minority (42 Black or African American, non-Hispanic/Latino;

20 Asian, non-Hispanic/Latino; 24 Hispanic/Latino; 4 Two or more races, non-Hispanic/Latino), 10 international. Average age 35. 88 applicants, 95% accepted, 58 enrolled. In 2019, 52 master's awarded. *Degree requirements:* For master's, thesis optional. *Entrance requirements:* Additional exam requirements/recommendations for international students: required—TOEFL (minimum score 80 iBT), IELTS (minimum score 6.5). *Application deadline:* For fall admission, 7/1 priority date for domestic and international students; for spring admission, 11/1 priority date for domestic and international students. Applications are processed on a rolling basis. Application fee: $60. Electronic applications accepted. *Expenses: Tuition, area resident:* Full-time $7104; part-time $296 per credit hour. Tuition, state resident: full-time $7104; part-time $296 per credit hour. Tuition, nonresident: full-time $25,584; part-time $1066 per credit hour. *International tuition:* $25,584 full-time. *Required fees:* $2006; $1706 per unit. $853 per semester. *Financial support:* Applicants required to submit FAFSA. *Application contact:* Admissions Counselor, 470-578-4377, E-mail: ksugrad@kennesaw.edu.
Website: http://engineering.kennesaw.edu/

Lakehead University, Graduate Studies, Faculty of Engineering, Thunder Bay, ON P7B 5E1, Canada. Offers control engineering (M Sc Engr); electrical/computer engineering (M Sc Engr); environmental engineering (M Sc Engr). *Program availability:* Part-time. *Degree requirements:* For master's, thesis. *Entrance requirements:* For master's, bachelor's degree in chemical, electrical or mechanical engineering, minimum B average. Additional exam requirements/recommendations for international students: required—TOEFL.

Lamar University, College of Graduate Studies, College of Engineering, Beaumont, TX 77710. Offers ME, MEM, MES, MS, DE, PhD. *Program availability:* Part-time, evening/weekend. *Faculty:* 50 full-time (7 women), 4 part-time/adjunct (1 woman). *Students:* 108 full-time (14 women), 91 part-time (21 women); includes 32 minority (3 Black or African American, non-Hispanic/Latino; 1 American Indian or Alaska Native, non-Hispanic/Latino; 13 Asian, non-Hispanic/Latino; 13 Hispanic/Latino; 2 Two or more races, non-Hispanic/Latino), 144 international. Average age 29. 288 applicants, 82% accepted, 47 enrolled. In 2019, 107 master's, 15 doctorates awarded. Terminal master's awarded for partial completion of doctoral program. *Degree requirements:* For doctorate, thesis/dissertation. *Entrance requirements:* For master's and doctorate, GRE General Test. Additional exam requirements/recommendations for international students: required—TOEFL (minimum score 550 paper-based; 79 iBT), IELTS (minimum score 6.5). *Application deadline:* Applications are processed on a rolling basis. Application fee: $25 ($50 for international students). Electronic applications accepted. *Expenses: Tuition, area resident:* Full-time $6324; part-time $351 per credit. Tuition, state resident: full-time $6324; part-time $351 per credit. Tuition, nonresident: full-time $13,920; part-time $773 per credit. *International tuition:* $13,920 full-time. *Required fees:* $2462; $327 per credit. Tuition and fees vary according to course load, campus/location and reciprocity agreements. *Financial support:* In 2019–20, 14 students received support. Fellowships with partial tuition reimbursements available, research assistantships with partial tuition reimbursements available, teaching assistantships with partial tuition reimbursements available, career-related internships or fieldwork, Federal Work-Study, institutionally sponsored loans, scholarships/grants, tuition waivers (full and partial), and laboratory assistantships available. Support available to part-time students. Financial award applicants required to submit FAFSA. *Unit head:* Dr. Brian Craig, Dean, 409-880-8784, Fax: 409-880-2197. *Application contact:* Celeste Contreas, Director, Admissions and Academic Services, 409-880-8888, Fax: 409-880-7419, E-mail: gradmissions@lamar.edu.
Website: http://engineering.lamar.edu

Laurentian University, School of Graduate Studies and Research, School of Engineering, Sudbury, ON P3E 2C6, Canada. Offers mineral resources engineering (M Eng, MA Sc); natural resources engineering (PhD). *Program availability:* Part-time.

Lawrence Technological University, College of Engineering, Southfield, MI 48075-1058. Offers architectural engineering (MS); automotive engineering (MS); biomedical engineering (MS); civil engineering (MA, MS, PhD), including environmental engineering (MS), geotechnical engineering (MS), structural engineering (MS), transportation engineering (MS), water resource engineering (MS); construction engineering management (MA); electrical and computer engineering (MS); engineering management (MEM); engineering technology (MS); fire engineering (MS); industrial engineering (MS), including healthcare systems; manufacturing systems (ME); mechanical engineering (MS, DE, PhD), including automotive engineering (MS), energy engineering (MS), manufacturing (DE), solid mechanics (MS), thermal/fluid systems (MS); mechatronic systems engineering (MS). *Program availability:* Part-time, evening/weekend. *Faculty:* 23 full-time (2 women), 20 part-time/adjunct (1 woman). *Students:* 14 full-time (5 women), 286 part-time (54 women); includes 26 minority (13 Black or African American, non-Hispanic/Latino; 8 Asian, non-Hispanic/Latino; 3 Hispanic/Latino; 2 Two or more races, non-Hispanic/Latino), 150 international. Average age 29. 384 applicants, 58% accepted, 74 enrolled. In 2019, 223 master's, 7 doctorates awarded. Terminal master's awarded for partial completion of doctoral program. *Degree requirements:* For master's, thesis optional; for doctorate, comprehensive exam, thesis/dissertation optional. *Entrance requirements:* Additional exam requirements/recommendations for international students: required—TOEFL (minimum score 550 paper-based; 79 iBT), IELTS (minimum score 6.5). *Application deadline:* For fall admission, 5/24 for international students; for spring admission, 10/13 for international students; for summer admission, 2/18 for international students. Applications are processed on a rolling basis. Application fee: $50. Electronic applications accepted. *Expenses: Tuition:* Full-time $16,618; part-time $8309 per year. *Required fees:* $600; $600. *Financial support:* In 2019–20, 21 students received support. Unspecified assistantships available. Financial award application deadline: 4/1; financial award applicants required to submit FAFSA. *Unit head:* Dr. Nabil Grace, Dean, 248-204-2500, Fax: 248-204-2509, E-mail: engrdean@ltu.edu. *Application contact:* Jane Rohrback, Director of Admissions, 248-204-3160, Fax: 248-204-2228, E-mail: admissions@ltu.edu.
Website: http://www.ltu.edu/engineering/index.asp

Lehigh University, P.C. Rossin College of Engineering and Applied Science, Bethlehem, PA 18015. Offers M Eng, MS, PhD, Certificate, MBA/E. *Program availability:* Part-time, 100% online, blended/hybrid learning. *Faculty:* 134 full-time (24 women), 9 part-time/adjunct (1 woman). *Students:* 654 full-time (174 women), 124 part-time (50 women); includes 58 minority (10 Black or African American, non-Hispanic/Latino; 24 Asian, non-Hispanic/Latino; 20 Hispanic/Latino; 1 Native Hawaiian or other Pacific Islander, non-Hispanic/Latino; 3 Two or more races, non-Hispanic/Latino), 387 international. Average age 27. 1,501 applicants, 40% accepted, 184 enrolled. In 2019, 205 master's, 55 doctorates, 5 other advanced degrees awarded. Terminal master's awarded for partial completion of doctoral program. *Degree requirements:* For master's, comprehensive exam (for some programs), thesis (for some programs); for doctorate, comprehensive exam (for some programs), thesis/dissertation. *Entrance requirements:* For master's and doctorate, GRE General Test, BS. Additional exam requirements/recommendations for international students: required—TOEFL (minimum score 79 iBT), IELTS (minimum score 6.5). *Application deadline:* For fall admission, 7/15 for domestic students; for spring admission, 12/1 for domestic students. Application fee: $75. Electronic applications accepted. *Financial support:* In 2019–20, 48 fellowships with tuition reimbursements (averaging $22,050 per year), 129 research assistantships with tuition reimbursements (averaging $29,400 per year), 50 teaching assistantships with tuition reimbursements (averaging $22,050 per year) were awarded; tuition waivers (full and partial) and unspecified assistantships also available. Financial award application deadline: 1/15. *Unit head:* Dr. Stephen P. DeWeerth, Dean, 610-758-5308, Fax: 610-758-5623, E-mail: steve.deweerth@lehigh.edu. *Application contact:* Brianne Lisk, Manager of Graduate Programs, 610-758-6310, Fax: 610-758-5623, E-mail: brie.lisk@lehigh.edu.
Website: https://engineering.lehigh.edu

LeTourneau University, Graduate Programs, Longview, TX 75607-7001. Offers business administration (MBA); counseling (MA); curriculum and instruction (M Ed); educational administration (M Ed); engineering (ME, MS); engineering management (MEM); health care administration (MS); marriage and family therapy (MA); psychology (MA); strategic leadership (MSL); teacher leadership (M Ed); teaching and learning (M Ed). *Program availability:* Part-time, 100% online, blended/hybrid learning. *Students:* 45 full-time (34 women), 243 part-time (186 women); includes 142 minority (89 Black or African American, non-Hispanic/Latino; 1 Asian, non-Hispanic/Latino; 26 Hispanic/Latino; 26 Two or more races, non-Hispanic/Latino), 2 international. Average age 37. In 2019, 143 master's awarded. *Entrance requirements:* Additional exam requirements/recommendations for international students: required—TOEFL (minimum score 525 paper-based; 80 iBT), IELTS (minimum score 6), Either a TOEFL or IELTS is required for graduate students. One or the other. *Application deadline:* Applications are processed on a rolling basis. Application fee: $0. Electronic applications accepted. *Financial support:* Unspecified assistantships and employee tuition waivers and institutionally sponsored loans available. Financial award applicants required to submit FAFSA.
Website: http://www.letu.edu

Louisiana State University and Agricultural & Mechanical College, Graduate School, College of Engineering, Department of Biological and Agricultural Engineering, Baton Rouge, LA 70803. Offers biological and agricultural engineering (MSBAE); engineering science (MS, PhD).

Louisiana State University and Agricultural & Mechanical College, Graduate School, College of Engineering, Interdepartmental Program in Engineering Science, Baton Rouge, LA 70803. Offers MSES, PhD.

Louisiana Tech University, Graduate School, College of Engineering and Science, Ruston, LA 71272. Offers applied physics (MS); biomedical engineering (PhD); computer science (MS); engineering (MS, PhD), including cyberspace engineering (PhD), engineering education (PhD), engineering physics (PhD), materials and infrastructure systems (PhD), micro/nanoscale systems (PhD); engineering and technology management (MS); mathematics (MS); molecular science and nanotechnology (MS, PhD). *Program availability:* Part-time-only. Terminal master's awarded for partial completion of doctoral program. *Degree requirements:* For master's, thesis (for some programs); for doctorate, thesis/dissertation. *Entrance requirements:* For master's and Graduate Certificate, GRE General Test, minimum GPA of 3.0 in last 60 hours. Additional exam requirements/recommendations for international students: required—TOEFL (minimum score 550 paper-based; 80 iBT), IELTS (minimum score 6.5). Electronic applications accepted. *Expenses: Tuition, area resident:* Full-time $6592; part-time $400 per credit. Tuition, state resident: full-time $6592; part-time $400 per credit. Tuition, nonresident: full-time $13,333; part-time $681 per credit. *International tuition:* $13,333 full-time. *Required fees:* $3011; $3011 per unit.

Manhattan College, Graduate Programs, School of Engineering, Riverdale, NY 10471. Offers chemical engineering (MS), including chemical engineering, cosmetic engineering; civil engineering (MS); computer engineering (MS); construction management (MS); electrical engineering (MS); environmental engineering (ME, MS); mechanical engineering (MS). *Program availability:* Part-time, evening/weekend. *Degree requirements:* For master's, thesis or alternative. *Entrance requirements:* For master's, GRE (recommended), minimum GPA of 3.0. Additional exam requirements/recommendations for international students: required—TOEFL (minimum score 550 paper-based; 80 iBT), IELTS (minimum score 6). *Expenses:* Contact institution.

Marquette University, Graduate School, College of Engineering, Milwaukee, WI 53201-1881. Offers ME, MS, MSEM, PhD, Certificate. *Program availability:* Part-time, evening/weekend. *Degree requirements:* For doctorate, thesis/dissertation. *Entrance requirements:* For master's, minimum GPA of 3.0; for doctorate, GRE General Test, minimum GPA of 3.0. Additional exam requirements/recommendations for international students: required—TOEFL (minimum score 530 paper-based). Electronic applications accepted.

Marshall University, Academic Affairs Division, College of Information Technology and Engineering, Huntington, WV 25755. Offers MS, MSE, MSEE, MSME, Certificate. *Program availability:* Part-time, evening/weekend. *Expenses:* Contact institution.

Massachusetts Institute of Technology, School of Engineering, Cambridge, MA 02139. Offers M Eng, SM, PhD, Sc D, CE, EAA, ECS, EE, Mat E, Mech E, NE, Naval E, SM/MBA. *Degree requirements:* For master's, thesis (for some programs); for doctorate, comprehensive exam, thesis/dissertation; for other advanced degree, thesis. Electronic applications accepted.

McGill University, Faculty of Graduate and Postdoctoral Studies, Faculty of Engineering, Montréal, QC H3A 2T5, Canada. Offers M Arch I, M Arch II, M Eng, M Sc, MMM, MUP, PhD, Diploma.

McGill University, Faculty of Graduate and Postdoctoral Studies, Faculty of Science, Department of Mathematics and Statistics, Montréal, QC H3A 2T5, Canada. Offers computational science and engineering (M Sc); mathematics and statistics (M Sc, MA, PhD), including applied mathematics (M Sc, MA), pure mathematics (M Sc, MA), statistics (M Sc, MA).

McMaster University, School of Graduate Studies, Faculty of Engineering, Hamilton, ON L8S 4M2, Canada. Offers M Eng, M Sc, MA Sc, PhD. *Program availability:* Part-time. *Degree requirements:* For doctorate, comprehensive exam, thesis/dissertation. *Entrance requirements:* Additional exam requirements/recommendations for international students: required—TOEFL (minimum score 550 paper-based).

McNeese State University, Doré School of Graduate Studies, College of Engineering and Computer Science, Lake Charles, LA 70609. Offers chemical engineering (M Eng). *Program availability:* Part-time, evening/weekend. *Entrance requirements:* For master's, GRE, minimum undergraduate GPA of 3.0. Additional exam requirements/recommendations for international students: required—TOEFL (minimum score 560 paper-based; 83 iBT).

Memorial University of Newfoundland, School of Graduate Studies, Faculty of Engineering and Applied Science, St. John's, NL A1C 5S7, Canada. Offers civil engineering (M Eng, PhD); electrical and computer engineering (M Eng, PhD); mechanical engineering (M Eng, PhD); ocean and naval architecture engineering (M Eng, PhD). *Program availability:* Part-time. *Degree requirements:* For master's, thesis; for doctorate, comprehensive exam, thesis/dissertation, oral thesis defense. *Entrance requirements:* For master's, 2nd class degree; for doctorate, master's degree in engineering. Electronic applications accepted.

Engineering and Applied Sciences—General

Mercer University, Graduate Studies, Macon Campus, School of Engineering, Macon, GA 31207. Offers biomedical engineering (MSE); computer engineering (MSE); electrical engineering (MSE); engineering management (MSE); environmental engineering (MSE); environmental systems (MS); mechanical engineering (MSE); software engineering (MSE); software systems (MS); technical communications management (MS); technical management (MS). *Program availability:* Part-time-only, evening/weekend, online learning. *Faculty:* 27 full-time (9 women), 2 part-time/adjunct (0 women). *Students:* 38 full-time (10 women), 51 part-time (20 women); includes 22 minority (5 Black or African American, non-Hispanic/Latino; 11 Asian, non-Hispanic/Latino; 4 Hispanic/Latino; 2 Two or more races, non-Hispanic/Latino), 2 international. Average age 26. In 2019, 70 master's awarded. *Degree requirements:* For master's, thesis or alternative. *Entrance requirements:* For master's, GRE (minimum score 300), minimum undergraduate GPA of 3.0. Additional exam requirements/recommendations for international students: required—TOEFL (minimum score 550 paper-based; 80 iBT). *Application deadline:* For fall admission, 4/1 priority date for domestic and international students; for spring admission, 11/1 priority date for domestic and international students. Applications are processed on a rolling basis. Application fee: $75. *Expenses:* Tuition: $938.00 ($700.00 for Technical Communication Management program) per credit hour; Facility and Technology Fee: $17.00 per credit hour. *Financial support:* Federal Work-Study available. Financial award applicants required to submit FAFSA. *Unit head:* Dr. Laura W. Lackey, Dean, 478-301-4106, Fax: 478-301-5593, E-mail: lackey_l@mercer.edu. *Application contact:* Dr. Sinjae Hyun, Program Director, 478-301-2214, Fax: 478-301-5593, E-mail: hyun_s@mercer.edu.
Website: http://engineering.mercer.edu/

Merrimack College, School of Science and Engineering, North Andover, MA 01845-5800. Offers civil engineering (MS); computer science (MS); data science (MS); engineering management (MS); mechanical engineering (MS), including engineering management. *Program availability:* Part-time, evening/weekend, 100% online. *Degree requirements:* For master's, comprehensive exam, thesis optional, internship or capstone (for some programs). *Entrance requirements:* For master's, official college transcripts, resume, personal statement, 2 recommendations. Additional exam requirements/recommendations for international students: required—TOEFL (minimum score 84 iBT), IELTS (minimum score 6.5), PTE (minimum score 56). Electronic applications accepted. Application fee is waived when completed online. *Expenses:* Contact institution.

Miami University, College of Engineering and Computing, Oxford, OH 45056. Offers MCS, MS.

Michigan State University, The Graduate School, College of Engineering, East Lansing, MI 48824. Offers MS, PhD. *Program availability:* Part-time. Electronic applications accepted.

Michigan Technological University, Graduate School, College of Engineering, Houghton, MI 49931. Offers MS, PhD, Graduate Certificate. *Program availability:* Part-time, 100% online, blended/hybrid learning. *Faculty:* 247 full-time (42 women), 93 part-time/adjunct (19 women). *Students:* 549 full-time (116 women), 163 part-time (35 women); includes 24 minority (7 Black or African American, non-Hispanic/Latino; 7 Asian, non-Hispanic/Latino; 5 Hispanic/Latino; 5 Two or more races, non-Hispanic/Latino), 473 international. Average age 27. 2,262 applicants, 40% accepted, 230 enrolled. In 2019, 269 master's, 46 doctorates, 20 other advanced degrees awarded. Terminal master's awarded for partial completion of doctoral program. *Degree requirements:* For master's, thesis (for some programs), 30 credits; for doctorate, comprehensive exam, thesis/dissertation, 30 credits beyond master's degree. *Entrance requirements:* For master's and doctorate, GRE, statement of purpose, personal statement, official transcripts, 2-3 letters of recommendation; for Graduate Certificate, statement of purpose, personal statement, official transcripts. Additional exam requirements/recommendations for international students: required—TOEFL/IELTS. *Application deadline:* Applications are processed on a rolling basis. Application fee: $0. Electronic applications accepted. *Expenses:* $1,212 per credit. *Financial support:* In 2019–20, 497 students received support, including 58 fellowships with tuition reimbursements available (averaging $16,590 per year), 119 research assistantships with tuition reimbursements available (averaging $16,590 per year), 76 teaching assistantships with tuition reimbursements available (averaging $16,590 per year); career-related internships or fieldwork, Federal Work-Study, scholarships/grants, health care benefits, unspecified assistantships, and cooperative program also available. Financial award applicants required to submit FAFSA. *Unit head:* Dr. Janet Callahan, Dean, 906-487-2005, E-mail: callahan@mtu.edu. *Application contact:* Ashli Wells, Assistant Director of Graduate Enrollment Services, 906-487-3513, Fax: 906-487-2284, E-mail: gradadms@mtu.edu.
Website: http://www.mtu.edu/engineering/

Milwaukee School of Engineering, MS Program in Engineering, Milwaukee, WI 53202-3109. Offers MS. *Program availability:* Part-time, evening/weekend. *Degree requirements:* For master's, thesis or alternative, design project or capstone. *Entrance requirements:* For master's, GRE General Test if undergraduate GPA is less than 2.8, BS in engineering, engineering technology, or closely-related area; 2 letters of recommendation. Additional exam requirements/recommendations for international students: required—TOEFL (minimum score 90 iBT), IELTS (minimum score 7). Electronic applications accepted.

Mississippi State University, Bagley College of Engineering, Mississippi State, MS 39762. Offers M Eng, MS, PhD. *Program availability:* Part-time, 100% online. *Faculty:* 100 full-time (15 women), 7 part-time/adjunct (2 women). *Students:* 329 full-time (109 women), 352 part-time (75 women); includes 108 minority (37 Black or African American, non-Hispanic/Latino; 35 Asian, non-Hispanic/Latino; 30 Hispanic/Latino; 6 Two or more races, non-Hispanic/Latino), 218 international. Average age 31. 509 applicants, 57% accepted, 122 enrolled. In 2019, 117 master's, 47 doctorates awarded. *Degree requirements:* For master's, comprehensive exam (for some programs), thesis; for doctorate, comprehensive exam (for some programs), thesis/dissertation. *Entrance requirements:* For master's, GRE, minimum GPA of 2.75; for doctorate, GRE. Additional exam requirements/recommendations for international students: required—TOEFL (minimum score 477 paper-based; 53 iBT); recommended—IELTS (minimum score 4.5). *Application deadline:* For fall admission, 7/1 for domestic students, 5/1 for international students; for spring admission, 11/1 for domestic students, 9/1 for international students. Applications are processed on a rolling basis. Application fee: $60 ($80 for international students). Electronic applications accepted. *Expenses: Tuition, area resident:* Full-time $8880; part-time $456 per credit hour. Tuition, state resident: full-time $8880. Tuition, nonresident: full-time $23,840; part-time $1236 per credit hour. *Required fees:* $110; $11.12 per credit hour. Tuition and fees vary according to course load. *Financial support:* In 2019–20, 179 research assistantships with full tuition reimbursements (averaging $17,054 per year), 60 teaching assistantships with full tuition reimbursements (averaging $15,495 per year) were awarded; Federal Work-Study, institutionally sponsored loans, scholarships/grants, and unspecified assistantships also available. Financial award application deadline: 4/1; financial award applicants required to submit FAFSA. *Unit head:* Dr. Jason Keith, Dean, 662-325-7183, Fax: 662-325-8573, E-mail: keith@bagley.msstate.edu. *Application contact:* Angie Campbell, Admissions and Enrollment Assistant, 662-325-9514, E-mail: acampbell@grad.msstate.edu.
Website: https://www.bagley.msstate.edu/

Missouri Western State University, Program in Applied Science, St. Joseph, MO 64507-2294. Offers chemistry (MAS); engineering technology management (MAS); industrial life science (MAS); sport and fitness management (MAS). *Accreditation:* AACSB. *Program availability:* Part-time. *Students:* 24 full-time (10 women), 21 part-time (5 women); includes 11 minority (3 Black or African American, non-Hispanic/Latino; 1 American Indian or Alaska Native, non-Hispanic/Latino; 1 Hispanic/Latino; 6 Two or more races, non-Hispanic/Latino), 8 international. Average age 26. 19 applicants, 89% accepted, 15 enrolled. In 2019, 18 master's awarded. *Entrance requirements:* Additional exam requirements/recommendations for international students: recommended—TOEFL (minimum score 79 iBT), IELTS (minimum score 6). *Application deadline:* For fall admission, 7/15 for domestic and international students; for spring admission, 11/1 for domestic and international students; for summer admission, 4/29 for domestic and international students. Applications are processed on a rolling basis. Application fee: $45 ($50 for international students). Electronic applications accepted. *Expenses:* Tuition, state resident: full-time $6469.02; part-time $359.39 per credit hour. Tuition, nonresident: full-time $11,581; part-time $643.39 per credit hour. *Required fees:* $345.20; $99.10 per credit hour. Tuition and fees vary according to course load, campus/location and program. *Financial support:* Scholarships/grants and unspecified assistantships available. Support available to part-time students. *Unit head:* Dr. Susan Bashinski, Dean of the Graduate School, 816-271-4394, Fax: 816-271-4525, E-mail: graduate@missouriwestern.edu. *Application contact:* Dr. Susan Bashinski, Dean of the Graduate School, 816-271-4394, Fax: 816-271-4525, E-mail: graduate@missouriwestern.edu.

Montana State University, The Graduate School, College of Engineering, Department of Chemical and Biological Engineering, Bozeman, MT 59717. Offers chemical engineering (MS); engineering (PhD), including chemical engineering option, environmental engineering option; environmental engineering (MS). *Program availability:* Part-time. *Degree requirements:* For master's, comprehensive exam, thesis (for some programs); for doctorate, comprehensive exam, thesis/dissertation. *Entrance requirements:* For master's and doctorate, GRE General Test. Additional exam requirements/recommendations for international students: required—TOEFL (minimum score 550 paper-based). Electronic applications accepted.

Montana State University, The Graduate School, College of Engineering, Department of Civil Engineering, Bozeman, MT 59717. Offers civil engineering (MS); construction engineering management (MCEM); engineering (PhD), including applied mechanics option, civil engineering option. *Program availability:* Part-time. *Degree requirements:* For master's, comprehensive exam, thesis (for some programs); for doctorate, comprehensive exam, thesis/dissertation. *Entrance requirements:* For master's and doctorate, GRE General Test. Additional exam requirements/recommendations for international students: required—TOEFL (minimum score 550 paper-based). Electronic applications accepted.

Montana State University, The Graduate School, College of Engineering, Department of Mechanical and Industrial Engineering, Bozeman, MT 59717. Offers engineering (PhD), including industrial engineering, mechanical engineering; industrial and management engineering (MS); mechanical engineering (MS). *Program availability:* Part-time. *Degree requirements:* For master's, comprehensive exam, thesis, oral exams; for doctorate, comprehensive exam, thesis/dissertation, qualifying exam. *Entrance requirements:* For master's, GRE, official transcript, minimum GPA of 3.0, demonstrated potential for success, statement of goals, three letters of recommendation, proof of funds affidavit; for doctorate, minimum undergraduate GPA of 3.0, 3.2 graduate; three letters of recommendation; statement of objectives. Additional exam requirements/recommendations for international students: required—TOEFL or IELTS. Electronic applications accepted.

Montana Technological University, Department of General Engineering, Butte, MT 59701-8997. Offers MS. *Program availability:* Part-time. *Faculty:* 9 full-time (1 woman), 4 part-time/adjunct (0 women). *Students:* 9 full-time (0 women), 1 part-time (0 women), 1 international. Average age 25. 6 applicants, 67% accepted, 3 enrolled. In 2019, 8 master's awarded. *Degree requirements:* For master's, comprehensive exam (for some programs), thesis optional. *Entrance requirements:* For master's, minimum GPA of 3.0. Additional exam requirements/recommendations for international students: required—TOEFL (minimum score 545 paper-based; 78 iBT), IELTS (minimum score 6.5). *Application deadline:* For fall admission, 4/1 priority date for domestic students, 3/1 priority date for international students; for spring admission, 10/1 priority date for domestic students, 6/1 priority date for international students. Applications are processed on a rolling basis. Application fee: $50. Electronic applications accepted. *Financial support:* In 2019–20, 9 students received support, including 11 teaching assistantships with partial tuition reimbursements available (averaging $3,500 per year); research assistantships with partial tuition reimbursements available, career-related internships or fieldwork, tuition waivers (full and partial), and unspecified assistantships also available. Financial award application deadline: 4/1; financial award applicants required to submit FAFSA. *Unit head:* Dr. Jack Skinner, Department Head, 406-496-4460, Fax: 406-496-4650, E-mail: JSkinner@mtech.edu. *Application contact:* Daniel Stirling, Administrator, Graduate School, 406-496-4304, Fax: 406-496-4710, E-mail: gradschool@mtech.edu.
Website: http://www.mtech.edu/academics/gradschool/degreeprograms/degrees-general-engineering.htm

Morgan State University, School of Graduate Studies, Clarence M. Mitchell, Jr. School of Engineering, Baltimore, MD 21251. Offers civil engineering (M Eng, D Eng); electrical and computer engineering (M Eng, MS, D Eng); industrial and systems engineering (M Eng, D Eng); transportation and urban infrastructure studies (MS, PhD, Postbaccalaureate Certificate), including transportation. *Program availability:* Part-time, evening/weekend. *Faculty:* 35 full-time (8 women), 19 part-time/adjunct (4 women). *Students:* 113 full-time (34 women), 24 part-time (4 women); includes 88 minority (75 Black or African American, non-Hispanic/Latino; 8 Asian, non-Hispanic/Latino; 2 Hispanic/Latino; 3 Two or more races, non-Hispanic/Latino), 36 international. Average age 35. 78 applicants, 83% accepted, 26 enrolled. In 2019, 23 master's, 11 doctorates awarded. *Degree requirements:* For master's, thesis optional, comprehensive exam or equivalent; for doctorate, thesis/dissertation, comprehensive exam or equivalent. *Entrance requirements:* For master's, GRE, minimum undergraduate GPA of 2.5; for doctorate, GRE, minimum GPA of 3.0. Additional exam requirements/recommendations for international students: required—TOEFL (minimum score 550 paper-based). *Application deadline:* For fall admission, 2/1 priority date for domestic students; for spring admission, 10/1 priority date for domestic students. Applications are processed on a rolling basis. Application fee: $50 ($70 for international students). Electronic applications accepted. *Expenses:* Tuition, state resident: full-time $455; part-time $455 per credit hour. Tuition, nonresident: full-time $894; part-time $894 per credit hour. *Required fees:* $82; $82 per credit hour. *Financial support:* In 2019–20, 35 students received support. Fellowships with full and partial tuition reimbursements available, research assistantships with full and partial tuition reimbursements available, teaching assistantships with full and partial tuition reimbursements available, career-related internships or fieldwork, scholarships/grants, and unspecified assistantships available.

Financial award application deadline: 2/1. *Unit head:* Dr. Craig Scott, Interim Dean, 443-885-3231, E-mail: craig.scott@morgan.edu. *Application contact:* Dr. Jahmaine Smith, Director of Admissions, 443-885-3185, Fax: 443-885-8226, E-mail: gradapply@morgan.edu.
Website: https://morgan.edu/soe

National University, School of Engineering and Computing, La Jolla, CA 92037-1011. Offers computer science (MS), including advanced computing; cyber security and information assurance (MS); data analytics (MS); electrical engineering (MS); engineering management (MS); information technology management (MS); management information systems (MS); sustainability management (MS). *Program availability:* Part-time, evening/weekend, 100% online, blended/hybrid learning. *Degree requirements:* For master's, thesis (for some programs). *Entrance requirements:* For master's, interview, minimum GPA of 2.5. Additional exam requirements/recommendations for international students: required—TOEFL (minimum score 550 paper-based; 79 iBT), IELTS (minimum score 6). Electronic applications accepted. *Expenses: Tuition:* Full-time $442; part-time $442 per unit.

New Jersey Institute of Technology, Newark College of Engineering, Newark, NJ 07102. Offers biomedical engineering (MS, PhD); biopharmaceutical engineering (MS); chemical engineering (MS, PhD); civil engineering (MS, PhD); computer engineering (MS); critical infrastructure systems (MS); electrical engineering (MS, PhD); engineering management (MS); engineering science (MS); environmental engineering (MS, PhD); healthcare systems management (MS); industrial engineering (MS, PhD); internet engineering (MS); manufacturing systems engineering (MS); materials science & engineering (PhD); materials science and engineering (MS); mechanical engineering (MS, PhD); occupational safety and health engineering (MS). *Program availability:* Part-time, evening/weekend. *Faculty:* 151 full-time (29 women), 135 part-time/adjunct (15 women). *Students:* 576 full-time (161 women), 528 part-time (111 women); includes 366 minority (61 Black or African American, non-Hispanic/Latino; 1 American Indian or Alaska Native, non-Hispanic/Latino; 166 Asian, non-Hispanic/Latino; 115 Hispanic/Latino; 23 Two or more races, non-Hispanic/Latino), 450 international. Average age 28. 2,053 applicants, 67% accepted, 338 enrolled. In 2019, 474 master's, 30 doctorates awarded. Terminal master's awarded for partial completion of doctoral program. *Degree requirements:* For master's, thesis (for some programs); for doctorate, thesis/dissertation. *Entrance requirements:* For master's, GRE General Test, minimum GPA 2.8, personal statement, 1 letter of recommendation, transcripts; for doctorate, GRE General Test, minimum GPA of 3.5, personal statement, 3 letters of recommendation, transcripts. Additional exam requirements/recommendations for international students: required—TOEFL (minimum score 550 paper-based; 79 iBT), IELTS (minimum score 6.5). *Application deadline:* For fall admission, 6/1 priority date for domestic students, 5/1 priority date for international students; for spring admission, 11/15 priority date for domestic and international students. Applications are processed on a rolling basis. Application fee: $75. Electronic applications accepted. *Expenses:* $23,828 per year (in-state), $33,744 per year (out-of-state). *Financial support:* In 2019–20, 352 students received support, including 33 fellowships with full tuition reimbursements available (averaging $24,000 per year), 89 research assistantships with full tuition reimbursements available (averaging $24,000 per year), 112 teaching assistantships with full tuition reimbursements available (averaging $24,000 per year); career-related internships or fieldwork, Federal Work-Study, scholarships/grants, and unspecified assistantships also available. Financial award application deadline: 1/15. *Unit head:* Dr. Moshe Kam, Dean, 973-596-5534, Fax: 973-596-2316, E-mail: moshe.kam@njit.edu. *Application contact:* Stephen Eck, Executive Director of University Admissions, 973-596-3300, Fax: 973-596-3461, E-mail: admissions@njit.edu.
Website: http://engineering.njit.edu/

New Mexico State University, College of Engineering, Las Cruces, NM 88003-8001. Offers aerospace engineering (MSAE); chemical engineering (MS Ch E); civil engineering (MSCE); electrical & computer engineering (MSEE); environmental engineering (MS Env E); industrial engineering (MSIE); mechanical engineering (MSME). *Program availability:* Part-time, online learning. *Faculty:* 63 full-time (11 women), 4 part-time/adjunct (0 women). *Students:* 212 full-time (51 women), 82 part-time (21 women); includes 98 minority (5 Black or African American, non-Hispanic/Latino; 1 American Indian or Alaska Native, non-Hispanic/Latino; 13 Asian, non-Hispanic/Latino; 70 Hispanic/Latino; 9 Two or more races, non-Hispanic/Latino), 117 international. Average age 30. 220 applicants, 63% accepted, 57 enrolled. In 2019, 112 master's, 21 doctorates, 6 other advanced degrees awarded. *Degree requirements:* For master's, comprehensive exam; for doctorate, comprehensive exam, thesis/dissertation. *Entrance requirements:* For master's and doctorate, GRE (for some engineering programs). Additional exam requirements/recommendations for international students: required—TOEFL (minimum score 550 paper-based; 79 iBT), IELTS (minimum score 6.5). *Application deadline:* For fall admission, 7/1 priority date for domestic students; for spring admission, 11/1 for domestic students. Applications are processed on a rolling basis. Application fee: $40 ($50 for international students). Electronic applications accepted. *Financial support:* In 2019–20, 228 students received support, including 13 fellowships (averaging $3,752 per year), 94 research assistantships (averaging $15,692 per year), 59 teaching assistantships (averaging $13,560 per year); career-related internships or fieldwork, Federal Work-Study, scholarships/grants, traineeships, health care benefits, and unspecified assistantships also available. Support available to part-time students. Financial award application deadline: 3/1. *Unit head:* Dr. Lakshmi Reddi, Dean, 575-646-7234, Fax: 575-646-3549, E-mail: engrdean@nmsu.edu. *Application contact:* Graduate Admissions, 575-646-3121, E-mail: admissions@nmsu.edu.
Website: http://engr.nmsu.edu/

New York Institute of Technology, College of Engineering and Computing Sciences, Old Westbury, NY 11568-8000. Offers MS, Advanced Certificate. *Program availability:* Part-time, evening/weekend, 100% online, blended/hybrid learning. *Degree requirements:* For master's, thesis (for some programs). *Entrance requirements:* Additional exam requirements/recommendations for international students: required—TOEFL (minimum score 79 iBT), IELTS (minimum score 6), PTE (minimum score 53). Electronic applications accepted. *Expenses: Tuition:* Full-time $23,760; part-time $1320 per credit. *Required fees:* $260; $220 per unit. Full-time tuition and fees vary according to degree level and program. Part-time tuition and fees vary according to course load and program.

New York University, Tandon School of Engineering, Brooklyn, NY 11201. Offers applied physics (Advanced Certificate); biomedical engineering (MS); biotechnology (PhD). *Program availability:* Part-time, 100% online, blended/hybrid learning. *Entrance requirements:* Additional exam requirements/recommendations for international students: required—TOEFL (minimum score 550 paper-based; 90 iBT); recommended—IELTS (minimum score 7). Electronic applications accepted. *Expenses:* Contact institution.

North Carolina Agricultural and Technical State University, The Graduate College, College of Engineering, Greensboro, NC 27411. Offers MS, MSCE, MSCS, MSE, MSEE, MSIE, MSME, PhD. *Program availability:* Part-time.

North Carolina State University, Graduate School, College of Engineering, Raleigh, NC 27695. Offers M Ch E, M Eng, MC Sc, MCE, MIE, MIMS, MMSE, MNAE, MNE, MOR, MS, PhD. *Program availability:* Part-time. Terminal master's awarded for partial completion of doctoral program. *Degree requirements:* For doctorate, thesis/dissertation. Electronic applications accepted.

North Dakota State University, College of Graduate and Interdisciplinary Studies, College of Engineering, Fargo, ND 58102. Offers M Eng, MCM, MS, PhD, Graduate Certificate. *Program availability:* Part-time. Terminal master's awarded for partial completion of doctoral program. *Degree requirements:* For master's, thesis; for doctorate, comprehensive exam, thesis/dissertation. *Entrance requirements:* For master's and doctorate, minimum GPA of 3.0. Additional exam requirements/recommendations for international students: required—TOEFL. Electronic applications accepted. *Expenses:* Contact institution.

Northeastern University, College of Engineering, Boston, MA 02115-5096. Offers bioengineering (MS, PhD); chemical engineering (MS, PhD); civil engineering (MS, PhD); computer engineering (PhD); computer systems engineering (MS); electrical and computer engineering (MS); electrical and computer engineering leadership (MS); electrical engineering (PhD); energy systems (MS); engineering and public policy (MS); engineering management (MS, Certificate); environmental engineering (MS); industrial engineering (MS, PhD); information assurance (PhD); information systems (MS); interdisciplinary engineering (PhD); mechanical engineering (PhD); operations research (MS); telecommunication systems management (MS). *Program availability:* Part-time, online learning. Electronic applications accepted. *Expenses:* Contact institution.

Northern Arizona University, College of Environment, Forestry, and Natural Sciences, Flagstaff, AZ 86011. Offers M Eng, MA, MAT, MF, MS, MSF, PhD, Graduate Certificate. *Program availability:* Part-time, 100% online, blended/hybrid learning. *Degree requirements:* For master's, variable foreign language requirement, comprehensive exam (for some programs), thesis (for some programs); for doctorate, variable foreign language requirement, comprehensive exam (for some programs), thesis/dissertation (for some programs); for Graduate Certificate, comprehensive exam (for some programs). *Entrance requirements:* Additional exam requirements/recommendations for international students: required—TOEFL (minimum score 80 iBT), IELTS (minimum score 6.5). Electronic applications accepted.

Northern Illinois University, Graduate School, College of Engineering and Engineering Technology, De Kalb, IL 60115-2854. Offers MS. *Program availability:* Part-time, evening/weekend. *Faculty:* 36 full-time (2 women), 2 part-time/adjunct (0 women). *Students:* 125 full-time (32 women), 138 part-time (23 women); includes 36 minority (4 Black or African American, non-Hispanic/Latino; 14 Asian, non-Hispanic/Latino; 12 Hispanic/Latino; 6 Two or more races, non-Hispanic/Latino), 140 international. Average age 28. 274 applicants, 66% accepted, 55 enrolled. In 2019, 128 master's awarded. *Degree requirements:* For master's, comprehensive exam, thesis optional. *Entrance requirements:* For master's, GRE General Test, minimum GPA of 2.75. Additional exam requirements/recommendations for international students: required—TOEFL (minimum score 550 paper-based). *Application deadline:* For fall admission, 6/1 for domestic students, 5/1 for international students; for spring admission, 11/1 for domestic students, 10/1 for international students. Applications are processed on a rolling basis. Application fee: $40. Electronic applications accepted. *Financial support:* In 2019–20, 48 research assistantships with full tuition reimbursements, 90 teaching assistantships with full tuition reimbursements were awarded; fellowships with full tuition reimbursements, career-related internships or fieldwork, Federal Work-Study, scholarships/grants, tuition waivers (full), and unspecified assistantships also available. Support available to part-time students. Financial award applicants required to submit FAFSA. *Unit head:* Dr. Donald R Peterson, Dean, 815-753-1281, Fax: 815-753-1310, E-mail: drpeterson@niu.edu. *Application contact:* Graduate School Office, 815-753-0395, E-mail: gradsch@niu.edu.
Website: http://www.niu.edu/CEET/

Northwestern Polytechnic University, School of Engineering, Fremont, CA 94539-7482. Offers computer engineering (DCE); computer science (MS); computer systems engineering (MS); electrical engineering (MS). *Program availability:* Part-time, evening/weekend. *Degree requirements:* For master's, thesis optional; for doctorate, thesis/dissertation. *Entrance requirements:* For master's, minimum GPA of 3.0. Additional exam requirements/recommendations for international students: required—TOEFL (minimum score 550 paper-based; 79 iBT).

Northwestern University, McCormick School of Engineering and Applied Science, Evanston, IL 60208. Offers MBA, MEM, MIT, MME, MMM, MPD, MS, PhD, Certificate, MBA/MEM. *Program availability:* Part-time, evening/weekend. Terminal master's awarded for partial completion of doctoral program. *Degree requirements:* For master's, comprehensive exam (for some programs), thesis (for some programs); for doctorate, comprehensive exam, thesis/dissertation. *Entrance requirements:* For master's and doctorate, GRE General Test. Additional exam requirements/recommendations for international students: required—TOEFL (minimum score 577 paper-based; 90 iBT) or IELTS (minimum score 7). Electronic applications accepted.

Oakland University, Graduate Study and Lifelong Learning, School of Engineering and Computer Science, Rochester, MI 48309-4401. Offers MS, PhD, Graduate Certificate. *Program availability:* Part-time, evening/weekend. *Degree requirements:* For doctorate, thesis/dissertation. *Entrance requirements:* For master's and doctorate, minimum GPA of 3.0. Additional exam requirements/recommendations for international students: required—TOEFL (minimum score 550 paper-based). Electronic applications accepted. *Expenses:* Contact institution.

The Ohio State University, Graduate School, College of Engineering, Columbus, OH 43210. Offers M Arch, M Land Arch, MCRP, MS, PhD. *Program availability:* Part-time, evening/weekend. *Entrance requirements:* For master's and doctorate, GRE. Additional exam requirements/recommendations for international students: required—TOEFL (minimum score 600 paper-based; 100 iBT), Michigan English Language Assessment Battery (minimum score 86); recommended—IELTS (minimum score 8). Electronic applications accepted.

Ohio University, Graduate College, Russ College of Engineering and Technology, Athens, OH 45701-2979. Offers M Eng Mgt, MS, PhD. *Program availability:* Part-time. *Degree requirements:* For master's, comprehensive exam (for some programs), thesis (for some programs); for doctorate, comprehensive exam, thesis/dissertation. *Entrance requirements:* For master's, GRE General Test, BS in engineering or related field; for doctorate, GRE General Test, MS in engineering or related field. Additional exam requirements/recommendations for international students: required—TOEFL or IELTS. Electronic applications accepted. *Expenses:* Contact institution.

Oklahoma Christian University, Graduate School of Engineering and Computer Science, Oklahoma City, OK 73136-1100. Offers electrical and computer engineering (MSE); engineering management (MSE); mechanical engineering (MSE); software engineering (MSCS, MSE). *Program availability:* Part-time. *Entrance requirements:* Additional exam requirements/recommendations for international students: required—TOEFL (minimum score 550 paper-based). Electronic applications accepted. *Expenses:* Contact institution.

Oklahoma State University, College of Engineering, Architecture and Technology, Stillwater, OK 74078. Offers MS, PhD. *Program availability:* Online learning. *Faculty:* 127 full-time (16 women), 3 part-time/adjunct (1 woman). *Students:* 135 full-time (23

women), 377 part-time (58 women); includes 62 minority (7 Black or African American, non-Hispanic/Latino; 9 American Indian or Alaska Native, non-Hispanic/Latino; 13 Asian, non-Hispanic/Latino; 14 Hispanic/Latino; 19 Two or more races, non-Hispanic/Latino), 222 international. Average age 30. 511 applicants, 41% accepted, 149 enrolled. In 2019, 122 master's, 35 doctorates awarded. *Degree requirements:* For master's, thesis (for some programs); for doctorate, comprehensive exam, thesis/dissertation. *Entrance requirements:* For master's and doctorate, GRE or GMAT. Additional exam requirements/recommendations for international students: required—TOEFL (minimum score 550 paper-based; 79 iBT). *Application deadline:* For fall admission, 3/1 priority date for domestic and international students; for spring admission, 8/1 priority date for domestic and international students. Applications are processed on a rolling basis. Application fee: $50 ($75 for international students). Electronic applications accepted. *Expenses: Tuition, area resident:* Full-time $4148.10; part-time $2765.40. Tuition, state resident: full-time $4148.10; part-time $2765.40. Tuition, nonresident: full-time $15,775; part-time $10,516.80. *International tuition:* $15,775.20 full-time. *Required fees:* $2196.90; $122.05 per credit hour. Tuition and fees vary according to course load, campus/location and program. *Financial support:* In 2019–20, 169 research assistantships (averaging $1,928 per year), 132 teaching assistantships (averaging $1,636 per year) were awarded; career-related internships or fieldwork, Federal Work-Study, scholarships/grants, health care benefits, tuition waivers (partial), and unspecified assistantships also available. Support available to part-time students. Financial award application deadline: 3/1; financial award applicants required to submit FAFSA. *Unit head:* Dr. Paul Tikalsky, Dean, 405-744-5140, E-mail: paul.tikalsky@okstate.edu. *Application contact:* Dr. Sheryl Tucker, Dean, 405-744-6368, Fax: 405-744-0355, E-mail: gradi@okstate.edu.
Website: http://ceat.okstate.edu

Old Dominion University, Frank Batten College of Engineering and Technology, Norfolk, VA 23529. Offers ME, MS, D Eng, PhD. *Program availability:* Part-time, evening/weekend, 100% online, blended/hybrid learning. *Degree requirements:* For master's, comprehensive exam, thesis (for some programs); for doctorate, comprehensive exam, thesis/dissertation, candidacy exam. *Entrance requirements:* For master's, GRE, minimum GPA of 3.0; for doctorate, GRE, minimum GPA of 3.5. Additional exam requirements/recommendations for international students: required—TOEFL (minimum score 550 paper-based). Electronic applications accepted. *Expenses:* Contact institution.

Open University, Graduate Programs, Milton Keynes, United Kingdom. Offers business (MBA); education (M Ed); engineering (M Eng); history (MA); music (MA); philosophy (MA).

Oregon State University, College of Engineering, Corvallis, OR 97331. Offers M Eng, MHP, MMP, MS, PhD. *Program availability:* Part-time, 100% online. Terminal master's awarded for partial completion of doctoral program. *Expenses:* Contact institution.

Penn State Great Valley, Graduate Studies, Engineering Division, Malvern, PA 19355-1488. Offers engineering management (MEM); software engineering (MSE); systems engineering (M Eng, Certificate).

Penn State Harrisburg, Graduate School, School of Science, Engineering and Technology, Middletown, PA 17057. Offers civil engineering (MS); computer science (MS); electrical engineering (M Eng, MS); engineering management (MPS); engineering science (M Eng); environmental engineering (M Eng); environmental pollution control (MEPC, MS); mechanical engineering (MS); structural engineering (Certificate). *Program availability:* Part-time, evening/weekend.

Penn State University Park, Graduate School, College of Engineering, University Park, PA 16802. Offers M Eng, MAE, MFR, MS, PhD. *Program availability:* Part-time, evening/weekend. *Entrance requirements:* Additional exam requirements/recommendations for international students: required—TOEFL (minimum score 550 paper-based; 80 iBT), IELTS. Electronic applications accepted. *Expenses:* Contact institution.

Polytechnique Montréal, Graduate Programs, Montréal, QC H3C 3A7, Canada. Offers M Eng, M Sc A, PhD, DESS. *Program availability:* Part-time, evening/weekend. Terminal master's awarded for partial completion of doctoral program. *Degree requirements:* For master's, one foreign language, thesis; for doctorate, one foreign language, thesis/dissertation. *Entrance requirements:* For master's, minimum GPA of 2.75; for doctorate, minimum GPA of 3.0. Electronic applications accepted.

Pontificia Universidad Catolica Madre y Maestra, Graduate School, Faculty of Engineering Sciences, Santiago, Dominican Republic. Offers earthquake engineering (ME); logistics management (ME).

Portland State University, Graduate Studies, Maseeh College of Engineering and Computer Science, Portland, OR 97207-0751. Offers M Eng, MS, MSME, MSMSE, PhD, Certificate, MS/MBA, MS/MS. *Program availability:* Part-time, evening/weekend. *Faculty:* 96 full-time (18 women), 39 part-time/adjunct (3 women). *Students:* 388 full-time (120 women), 372 part-time (111 women); includes 135 minority (14 Black or African American, non-Hispanic/Latino; 67 Asian, non-Hispanic/Latino; 31 Hispanic/Latino; 1 Native Hawaiian or other Pacific Islander, non-Hispanic/Latino; 22 Two or more races, non-Hispanic/Latino), 325 international. Average age 31. 585 applicants, 70% accepted, 189 enrolled. In 2019, 308 master's, 25 doctorates awarded. *Degree requirements:* For doctorate, one foreign language, thesis/dissertation. *Entrance requirements:* Additional exam requirements/recommendations for international students: required—TOEFL (minimum score 550 paper-based; 80 iBT). *Application deadline:* For fall admission, 4/1 for domestic students, 3/1 for international students; for winter admission, 9/1 for domestic and international students; for spring admission, 2/1 for domestic and international students. Application fee: $65. *Expenses:* Contact institution. *Financial support:* In 2019–20, 181 students received support, including 40 research assistantships (averaging $17,176 per year), 71 teaching assistantships (averaging $11,956 per year); career-related internships or fieldwork, Federal Work-Study, scholarships/grants, and unspecified assistantships also available. Support available to part-time students. Financial award application deadline: 3/1; financial award applicants required to submit FAFSA. *Unit head:* Dr. Richard Corsi, Dean, 503-725-2816, Fax: 503-725-2825, E-mail: engdean@pdx.edu. *Application contact:* Dr. Richard Corsi, Dean, 503-725-2816, Fax: 503-725-2825, E-mail: engdean@pdx.edu.
Website: http://www.pdx.edu/cecs/

Prairie View A&M University, College of Engineering, Prairie View, TX 77446. Offers computer information systems (MSCIS); computer science (MSCS); electrical engineering (MSEE, PhDEE); general engineering (MS Engr). *Program availability:* Part-time, evening/weekend. *Faculty:* 30 full-time (8 women), 1 part-time/adjunct (0 women). *Students:* 121 full-time (38 women), 55 part-time (14 women); includes 82 minority (61 Black or African American, non-Hispanic/Latino; 14 Asian, non-Hispanic/Latino; 7 Hispanic/Latino), 77 international. Average age 32. 139 applicants, 84% accepted, 40 enrolled. In 2019, 78 master's, 2 doctorates awarded. *Degree requirements:* For master's, thesis optional; for doctorate, comprehensive exam, thesis/dissertation. *Entrance requirements:* For master's, GRE General Test (minimum score of 900), bachelor's degree in engineering from ABET-accredited institution; for doctorate, minimum GPA of 3.0. Additional exam requirements/recommendations for international students: required—TOEFL (minimum score 550 paper-based; 79 iBT). *Application deadline:* For fall admission, 5/1 priority date for domestic and international students; for spring admission, 10/1 priority date for domestic students, 9/1 priority date for international students; for summer admission, 3/1 priority date for domestic students, 2/1 priority date for international students. Applications are processed on a rolling basis. Application fee: $50. Electronic applications accepted. *Expenses: Tuition, area resident:* Full-time $5479.68. Tuition, state resident: full-time $5479.68. Tuition, nonresident: full-time $15,439. *International tuition:* $15,438.74 full-time. *Required fees:* $2149.32. *Financial support:* In 2019–20, 64 students received support, including 64 research assistantships (averaging $14,400 per year), 8 teaching assistantships (averaging $14,400 per year); career-related internships or fieldwork, institutionally sponsored loans, scholarships/grants, health care benefits, tuition waivers (full), and unspecified assistantships also available. Financial award application deadline: 4/1; financial award applicants required to submit FAFSA. *Unit head:* Dr. Pamela H Obiomon, Dean, 936-261-9890, Fax: 936-261-9868, E-mail: phobiomon@pvamu.edu. *Application contact:* Pauline Walker, Administrative Assistant II, Research and Graduate Studies, 936-261-3521, Fax: 936-261-3529, E-mail: gradadmissions@pvamu.edu.

Princeton University, Graduate School, School of Engineering and Applied Science, Princeton, NJ 08544-1019. Offers M Eng, MSE, PhD. Terminal master's awarded for partial completion of doctoral program. *Degree requirements:* For master's, thesis (for some programs); for doctorate, thesis/dissertation, research requirement, teaching requirement, general exam. *Entrance requirements:* For master's and doctorate, GRE General Test, official transcript(s), 3 letters of recommendation, personal statement. Additional exam requirements/recommendations for international students: required—TOEFL. Electronic applications accepted.

Purdue University, College of Engineering, West Lafayette, IN 47906-3105. Offers MS, MSABE, MSBME, MSCE, MSChE, MSE, MSECE, MSIE, MSME, MSMSE, MSNE, PhD, Certificate, MD/PhD. *Program availability:* Part-time, 100% online, blended/hybrid learning. *Faculty:* 513. *Students:* 3,628. Terminal master's awarded for partial completion of doctoral program. *Degree requirements:* For doctorate, thesis/dissertation. *Application deadline:* Applications are processed on a rolling basis. Application fee: $60 ($75 for international students). Electronic applications accepted. *Expenses:* Contact institution. *Financial support:* Fellowships with full and partial tuition reimbursements, research assistantships with full and partial tuition reimbursements, teaching assistantships with full and partial tuition reimbursements, career-related internships or fieldwork, scholarships/grants, health care benefits, and unspecified assistantships available. *Unit head:* Dr. Dana Weinstein, Associate Dean for Graduate Education, E-mail: engrgrad@purdue.edu. *Application contact:* Dr. Jacqueline McDermott, Asst Director of Graduate Recruitment and Retention, E-mail: engrgrad@purdue.edu.
Website: https://engineering.purdue.edu/Engr

Purdue University Fort Wayne, College of Engineering, Technology, and Computer Science, Fort Wayne, IN 46805-1499. Offers MS, MSE, Certificate. *Program availability:* Part-time. *Entrance requirements:* For master's, GRE General Test, minimum GPA of 3.0. Additional exam requirements/recommendations for international students: required—TOEFL (minimum score 550 paper-based; 79 iBT); recommended—TWE. Electronic applications accepted.

Purdue University Northwest, Graduate Studies Office, School of Engineering, Mathematics, and Science, Department of Engineering, Hammond, IN 46323-2094. Offers computer engineering (MSE); electrical engineering (MSE); engineering (MS); mechanical engineering (MSE). *Program availability:* Evening/weekend. *Entrance requirements:* Additional exam requirements/recommendations for international students: required—TOEFL.

Purdue University Northwest, Graduate Studies Office, School of Technology, Hammond, IN 46323-2094. Offers MS.

Queen's University at Kingston, School of Graduate Studies, Faculty of Engineering and Applied Science, Kingston, ON K7L 3N6, Canada. Offers M Eng, M Sc, M Sc Eng, PhD. *Program availability:* Part-time. *Degree requirements:* For doctorate, comprehensive exam, thesis/dissertation. *Entrance requirements:* Additional exam requirements/recommendations for international students: required—TOEFL. Electronic applications accepted.

Rensselaer at Hartford, Department of Engineering, Hartford, CT 06120-2991. Offers ME, MS. *Program availability:* Part-time, evening/weekend. *Entrance requirements:* For master's, GRE. Additional exam requirements/recommendations for international students: required—TOEFL (minimum score 600 paper-based; 100 iBT). Electronic applications accepted.

Rensselaer Polytechnic Institute, Graduate School, School of Engineering, Troy, NY 12180-3590. Offers M Eng, MS, D Eng, PhD. *Program availability:* Part-time. *Faculty:* 179 full-time (28 women), 8 part-time/adjunct (0 women). *Students:* 582 full-time (162 women), 95 part-time (16 women); includes 99 minority (12 Black or African American, non-Hispanic/Latino; 1 American Indian or Alaska Native, non-Hispanic/Latino; 40 Asian, non-Hispanic/Latino; 20 Hispanic/Latino; 26 Two or more races, non-Hispanic/Latino), 319 international. Average age 26. 1,367 applicants, 46% accepted, 214 enrolled. In 2019, 128 master's, 89 doctorates awarded. Terminal master's awarded for partial completion of doctoral program. *Degree requirements:* For master's, comprehensive exam (for some programs), thesis (for some programs); for doctorate, comprehensive exam (for some programs), thesis/dissertation. *Entrance requirements:* For master's and doctorate, GRE. Additional exam requirements/recommendations for international students: required—TOEFL (minimum score 570 paper-based; 88 iBT), IELTS (minimum score 6.5), PTE (minimum score 60). *Application deadline:* For fall admission, 1/1 priority date for domestic and international students; for spring admission, 8/15 priority date for domestic and international students; for summer admission, 1/1 priority date for domestic and international students. Applications are processed on a rolling basis. Application fee: $75. Electronic applications accepted. *Financial support:* In 2019–20, 462 students received support, including research assistantships (averaging $23,000 per year), teaching assistantships (averaging $23,000 per year); fellowships also available. Financial award application deadline: 1/1. *Unit head:* Shekhar Garde, Dean, 518-276-6298, E-mail: gardes@rpi.edu. *Application contact:* Jarron Decker, Director of Graduate Admissions, 518-276-6216, Fax: 518-276-4072, E-mail: gradadmissions@rpi.edu.
Website: http://www.eng.rpi.edu/

Rice University, Graduate Programs, George R. Brown School of Engineering, Houston, TX 77251-1892. Offers M Ch E, M Stat, MA, MBE, MCAM, MCE, MCS, MEE, MEE, MES, MME, MMS, MS, PhD, MBA/M Stat, MBA/ME, MBA/MEE, MD/PhD. *Program availability:* Part-time. Terminal master's awarded for partial completion of doctoral program. *Degree requirements:* For master's, comprehensive exam (for some programs), thesis (for some programs); for doctorate, comprehensive exam (for some programs), thesis/dissertation. *Entrance requirements:* For master's and doctorate, GRE General Test. Additional exam requirements/recommendations for international students: required—TOEFL (minimum score 600 paper-based). Electronic applications accepted.

Robert Morris University, School of Engineering, Mathematics and Science, Moon Township, PA 15108. Offers engineering management (MS). *Program availability:* Part-time-only, evening/weekend, 100% online. *Faculty:* 6 full-time (1 woman), 1 part-time/

adjunct (0 women). *Students:* 20 part-time (8 women); includes 4 minority (1 Black or African American, non-Hispanic/Latino; 2 Asian, non-Hispanic/Latino; 1 Two or more races, non-Hispanic/Latino), 6 international. Average age 28. In 2019, 20 master's awarded. *Degree requirements:* For master's, Completion of 30 credits. *Entrance requirements:* For master's, letters of recommendation. Additional exam requirements/recommendations for international students: required—TOEFL (minimum score 550 paper-based; 79 iBT). *Application deadline:* For fall admission, 7/1 priority date for domestic and international students; for spring admission, 11/1 priority date for domestic and international students. Applications are processed on a rolling basis. Application fee: $35. Electronic applications accepted. *Expenses:* $1,020 per credit tuition plus $85 per credit fees. *Financial support:* Federal Work-Study, institutionally sponsored loans, and unspecified assistantships available. Financial award application deadline: 5/1; financial award applicants required to submit FAFSA. *Unit head:* Dr. Maria V. Kalevitch, Dean, 412-397-4020, E-mail: kalevitch@rmu.edu. *Application contact:* Kellie Laurenzi, Associate Vice President, Enrollment Management, 412-397-5200, E-mail: graduateadmissions@rmu.edu.
Website: https://www.rmu.edu/academics/schools/sems

Rochester Institute of Technology, Graduate Enrollment Services, Kate Gleason College of Engineering, Rochester, NY 14623-5603. Offers ME, MS, PhD, Advanced Certificate. *Program availability:* Part-time, evening/weekend, 100% online. Terminal master's awarded for partial completion of doctoral program. *Entrance requirements:* For master's and doctorate, GRE, minimum GPA of 3.0 (recommended); for Advanced Certificate, minimum GPA of 3.0 (recommended). Electronic applications accepted. *Expenses:* Contact institution.

Rose-Hulman Institute of Technology, Graduate Studies, Terre Haute, IN 47803-3999. Offers M Eng, MS, MD/MS. *Program availability:* Part-time. *Students:* Average age 25. 57 applicants, 60% accepted, 21 enrolled. In 2019, 33 master's awarded. *Entrance requirements:* For master's, GRE, minimum GPA of 3.0. Additional exam requirements/recommendations for international students: required—TOEFL (minimum score 580 paper-based; 94 iBT), IELTS (minimum score 7). *Application deadline:* For fall admission, 2/1 priority date for domestic and international students; for winter admission, 10/1 for domestic students, 8/1 for international students; for spring admission, 1/15 for domestic students, 11/1 for international students. Applications are processed on a rolling basis. Application fee: $0. Electronic applications accepted. *Financial support:* In 2019–20, 49 students received support. Fellowships, research assistantships, institutionally sponsored loans, scholarships/grants, and tuition waivers (full and partial) available. Financial award application deadline: 2/1; financial award applicants required to submit FAFSA. *Unit head:* Dr. Craig Downing, Associate Dean of Lifelong Learning, 812-877-8822, E-mail: downing@rose-hulman.edu. *Application contact:* Dr. Craig Downing, Associate Dean of Lifelong Learning, 812-877-8822, E-mail: downing@rose-hulman.edu.
Website: https://www.rose-hulman.edu/academics/degrees-and-programs/graduate-studies/index.html

Rowan University, Graduate School, College of Engineering, Program in Engineering, Glassboro, NJ 08028-1701. Offers MSE. *Program availability:* Part-time, evening/weekend. *Degree requirements:* For master's, thesis (for some programs). *Entrance requirements:* For master's, GRE General Test. Additional exam requirements/recommendations for international students: required—TOEFL. Electronic applications accepted. *Expenses: Tuition, area resident:* Part-time $715.50 per semester hour. Tuition, state resident: part-time $715.50 per semester hour. Tuition, nonresident: part-time $715.50 per semester hour. *Required fees:* $161.55 per semester hour.

Royal Military College of Canada, Division of Graduate Studies, Faculty of Engineering, Kingston, ON K7K 7B4, Canada. Offers M Eng, M Sc, MA Sc, PhD. *Degree requirements:* For master's, thesis; for doctorate, comprehensive exam, thesis/dissertation. *Entrance requirements:* For master's, honours degree with second-class standing; for doctorate, master's degree. Electronic applications accepted.

Saginaw Valley State University, College of Science, Engineering, and Technology, University Center, MI 48710. Offers computer science and information systems (MS); energy and materials (MS). *Program availability:* Part-time, evening/weekend. *Faculty:* 6 full-time (1 woman), 1 part-time/adjunct (0 women). *Students:* 7 full-time (2 women), 11 part-time (1 woman); includes 2 minority (both Asian, non-Hispanic/Latino), 4 international. Average age 32. 29 applicants, 62% accepted, 4 enrolled. In 2019, 4 master's awarded. *Degree requirements:* For master's, field project or thesis work. *Entrance requirements:* For master's, minimum GPA of 3.0. Additional exam requirements/recommendations for international students: required—TOEFL (minimum score 550 paper-based; 79 iBT). *Application deadline:* For fall admission, 7/15 for international students; for winter admission, 11/15 for international students; for spring admission, 4/15 for international students. Applications are processed on a rolling basis. Application fee: $30 ($90 for international students). Electronic applications accepted. *Expenses: Tuition, area resident:* Full-time $11,212; part-time $622.90 per credit hour. Tuition, state resident: full-time $11,212; part-time $622.90 per credit hour. Tuition, nonresident: full-time $11,212; part-time $1253 per credit hour. *Required fees:* $263; $14.60 per credit hour. Tuition and fees vary according to course load, degree level and program. *Financial support:* Federal Work-Study and scholarships/grants available. Support available to part-time students. Financial award application deadline: 4/1; financial award applicants required to submit FAFSA. *Unit head:* Dr. Robert Tuttle, Program Coordinator, 989-964-4144, Fax: 989-964-2717. *Application contact:* Jenna Briggs, Director, Graduate and International Admissions, 989-964-6096, Fax: 989-964-2788, E-mail: gradadm@svsu.edu.
Website: http://www.svsu.edu/collegeofscienceengineeringtechnology/

St. Cloud State University, School of Graduate Studies, College of Science and Engineering, St. Cloud, MN 56301-4498. Offers MA, MS, Graduate Certificate. *Degree requirements:* For master's, thesis or alternative. *Entrance requirements:* For master's, GRE General Test, minimum GPA of 2.75. Additional exam requirements/recommendations for international students: required—TOEFL (minimum score 550 paper-based). Electronic applications accepted.

San Diego State University, Graduate and Research Affairs, College of Engineering, San Diego, CA 92182. Offers MS, PhD. *Program availability:* Part-time, evening/weekend. Terminal master's awarded for partial completion of doctoral program. *Degree requirements:* For master's, thesis optional; for doctorate, thesis/dissertation. *Entrance requirements:* For master's, GRE General Test; for doctorate, GRE, 3 letters of recommendation. Additional exam requirements/recommendations for international students: required—TOEFL. Electronic applications accepted.

San Francisco State University, Division of Graduate Studies, College of Science and Engineering, School of Engineering, San Francisco, CA 94132-1722. Offers embedded electrical and computer systems (MS); energy systems (MS); structural/earthquake engineering (MS). *Program availability:* Part-time. *Application deadline:* Applications are processed on a rolling basis. Electronic applications accepted. *Expenses: Tuition, area resident:* Full-time $7176; part-time $4164 per year. Tuition, state resident: full-time $7176; part-time $4164 per year. Tuition, nonresident: full-time $16,680; part-time $396 per unit. *International tuition:* $16,680 full-time. *Required fees:* $1524; $1524 per unit. $762 per semester. Tuition and fees vary according to degree level and program. *Unit head:* Dr. Kwok-Siong Teh, Director, 415-338-1228, Fax: 415-338-0525, E-mail: ksteh@sfsu.edu. *Application contact:* Dr. Hamid Shahnasser, Graduate Coordinator, 415-338-2124, Fax: 415-338-0525, E-mail: hamid@sfsu.edu.
Website: http://engineering.sfsu.edu/

Santa Clara University, School of Engineering, Santa Clara, CA 95053. Offers applied mathematics (MS); bioengineering (MS); civil, environmental, and sustainable engineering (MS); computer science and engineering (MS, PhD, Engineer); electrical engineering (MS, PhD, Engineer); engineering management and leadership (MS); mechanical engineering (MS, PhD, Engineer); power systems and sustainable energy (MS); software engineering (MS). *Program availability:* Part-time. *Entrance requirements:* For master's, GRE, official transcript; for doctorate, GRE, Official transcript, 500 word statement of purpose, three letters of recommendation. Additional exam requirements/recommendations for international students: required—TOEFL (minimum score 79 iBT), IELTS (minimum score 6.5). Electronic applications accepted.

Seattle University, College of Science and Engineering, Seattle, WA 98122-1090. Offers MSCS. *Program availability:* Part-time, evening/weekend. *Faculty:* 104 full-time (42 women), 15 part-time/adjunct (7 women). *Students:* 81 full-time (35 women), 75 part-time (22 women); includes 31 minority (16 Asian, non-Hispanic/Latino; 10 Hispanic/Latino; 5 Two or more races, non-Hispanic/Latino), 67 international. Average age 28. 136 applicants, 57% accepted, 56 enrolled. In 2019, 32 master's awarded. *Entrance requirements:* For master's, GRE General Test, 2 years of related work experience. *Application deadline:* For fall admission, 7/1 for domestic students. Application fee: $55. *Expenses:* Contact institution. *Financial support:* In 2019–20, 14 students received support. Career-related internships or fieldwork and Federal Work-Study available. Support available to part-time students. Financial award applicants required to submit FAFSA. *Unit head:* Dr. Michael Quinn, Dean, 206-296-5500, Fax: 206-296-2071. *Application contact:* Janet Shandley, Director of Graduate Admissions, 206-296-5900, Fax: 206-298-5656, E-mail: grad_admissions@seattleu.edu.
Website: https://www.seattleu.edu/scieng/

Simon Fraser University, Office of Graduate Studies and Postdoctoral Fellows, Faculty of Applied Sciences, School of Engineering Science, Burnaby, BC V5A 1S6, Canada. Offers M Eng, MA Sc, PhD. *Program availability:* Part-time. *Degree requirements:* For master's, thesis (for some programs); for doctorate, thesis/dissertation, qualifying exam, seminar presentations. *Entrance requirements:* For master's, minimum GPA of 3.0 (on scale of 4.33) or 3.33 based on last 60 credits of undergraduate courses; for doctorate, minimum GPA of 3.5 (on scale of 4.33). Additional exam requirements/recommendations for international students: recommended—TOEFL (minimum score 580 paper-based; 93 iBT), IELTS (minimum score 7), TWE (minimum score 5). Electronic applications accepted.

South Dakota School of Mines and Technology, Graduate Division, College of Engineering, Rapid City, SD 57701-3995. Offers MS, PhD. *Program availability:* Part-time, online learning. *Degree requirements:* For doctorate, thesis/dissertation. *Entrance requirements:* For doctorate, minimum graduate GPA of 3.0. Additional exam requirements/recommendations for international students: required—TOEFL (minimum score 520 paper-based; 68 iBT), TWE. Electronic applications accepted.

South Dakota State University, Graduate School, Jerome J. Lohr College of Engineering, Brookings, SD 57007. Offers MS, PhD. *Program availability:* Part-time. *Degree requirements:* For master's, thesis, oral exam; for doctorate, thesis/dissertation, preliminary oral and written exams. *Entrance requirements:* Additional exam requirements/recommendations for international students: required—TOEFL.

Southern Illinois University Carbondale, Graduate School, College of Engineering, Carbondale, IL 62901-4701. Offers ME, MS, PhD, JD/MS. *Degree requirements:* For master's, comprehensive exam; for doctorate, thesis/dissertation. *Entrance requirements:* For master's, GRE, minimum GPA of 2.7; for doctorate, GRE General Test, minimum GPA of 3.5. Additional exam requirements/recommendations for international students: required—TOEFL.

Southern Illinois University Edwardsville, Graduate School, School of Engineering, Edwardsville, IL 62026. Offers MS. *Program availability:* Part-time, evening/weekend. *Degree requirements:* For master's, thesis (for some programs), research paper, final exam. *Entrance requirements:* Additional exam requirements/recommendations for international students: required—TOEFL (minimum score 550 paper-based; 79 iBT), IELTS (minimum score 6.5). Electronic applications accepted.

Southern Methodist University, Lyle School of Engineering, Dallas, TX 75275. Offers MA, MS, MSIEM, DE, PhD. *Program availability:* Part-time, evening/weekend, online learning. Terminal master's awarded for partial completion of doctoral program. *Degree requirements:* For master's, thesis optional; for doctorate, thesis/dissertation, oral and written qualifying exams. *Entrance requirements:* For master's, GRE General Test, minimum GPA of 3.0 in last 2 years; bachelor's degree in engineering, mathematics, or sciences; for doctorate, bachelor's degree in related field. Additional exam requirements/recommendations for international students: required—TOEFL (minimum score 550 paper-based). *Expenses:* Contact institution.

Southern University and Agricultural and Mechanical College, Graduate School, College of Sciences and Engineering, Baton Rouge, LA 70813. Offers MA, ME, MS. *Program availability:* Part-time. *Entrance requirements:* For master's, GRE General Test. Additional exam requirements/recommendations for international students: required—TOEFL (minimum score 525 paper-based).

Stanford University, School of Engineering, Stanford, CA 94305-2004. Offers MS, MSE, PhD, Engr. *Expenses: Tuition:* Full-time $52,479; part-time $34,110 per unit. *Required fees:* $672; $224 per quarter. Tuition and fees vary according to program and student level.
Website: http://soe.stanford.edu/

Stevens Institute of Technology, Graduate School, Charles V. Schaefer Jr. School of Engineering and Science, Hoboken, NJ 07030. Offers M Eng, MS, PhD, Certificate, Engr. *Program availability:* Part-time, evening/weekend, 100% online, blended/hybrid learning. *Faculty:* 159 full-time (36 women), 92 part-time/adjunct (10 women). *Students:* 1,352 full-time (319 women), 269 part-time (71 women); includes 141 minority (25 Black or African American, non-Hispanic/Latino; 4 American Indian or Alaska Native, non-Hispanic/Latino; 103 Asian, non-Hispanic/Latino; 9 Hispanic/Latino), 1,148 international. Average age 26. In 2019, 718 master's, 39 doctorates, 112 other advanced degrees awarded. Terminal master's awarded for partial completion of doctoral program. *Entrance requirements:* For master's, International applicants must submit TOEFL/IELTS scores and fulfill the English Language Proficiency Requirement. Applicants to full-time programs who do not qualify for a score waiver are required to submit GRE/GMAT scores. Additional exam requirements/recommendations for international students: required—TOEFL (minimum score 74 iBT), IELTS (minimum score 6). *Application deadline:* For fall admission, 4/15 for domestic and international students; for spring admission, 11/1 for domestic and international students; for summer admission, 5/1 for domestic students. Applications are processed on a rolling basis. Application fee: $60. Electronic applications accepted. *Expenses: Tuition:* Full-time $52,134. *Required fees:* $1880. Tuition and fees vary according to course load. *Financial support:* Fellowships, research assistantships, teaching assistantships, career-related

Engineering and Applied Sciences—General

internships or fieldwork, Federal Work-Study, scholarships/grants, and unspecified assistantships available. Financial award application deadline: 2/15; financial award applicants required to submit FAFSA. *Unit head:* Dr. Jean Zu, Dean, 201-216-2833, E-mail: jean.zu@stevens.edu. *Application contact:* Graduate Admissions, 888-783-8367, Fax: 888-555-1306, E-mail: graduate@stevens.edu.
Website: http://www.stevens.edu/ses/

Stony Brook University, State University of New York, Graduate School, College of Engineering and Applied Sciences, Stony Brook, NY 11794. Offers MS, PhD, AGC, Advanced Certificate, Certificate, Graduate Certificate. *Program availability:* Part-time, evening/weekend. *Faculty:* 169 full-time (27 women), 38 part-time/adjunct (8 women). *Students:* 1,276 full-time (309 women), 295 part-time (74 women); includes 186 minority (21 Black or African American, non-Hispanic/Latino; 120 Asian, non-Hispanic/Latino; 34 Hispanic/Latino; 11 Two or more races, non-Hispanic/Latino), 1,179 international. Average age 26. 3,500 applicants, 47% accepted, 594 enrolled. In 2019, 743 master's, 109 doctorates, 21 other advanced degrees awarded. *Degree requirements:* For doctorate, comprehensive exam, thesis/dissertation. *Entrance requirements:* For doctorate, GRE General Test. Additional exam requirements/recommendations for international students: required—TOEFL (minimum score 90 iBT). *Application deadline:* For fall admission, 1/15 for domestic students; for spring admission, 10/1 for domestic students. Application fee: $100. *Expenses:* Contact institution. *Financial support:* In 2019–20, 24 fellowships, 248 research assistantships, 248 teaching assistantships were awarded; career-related internships or fieldwork also available. *Unit head:* Dr. Fotis Sotiropoulos, Dean, 631-632-8380, Fax: 631-632-8205, E-mail: fotis.sotiropoulos@stonybrook.edu. *Application contact:* Melissa Jordan, Assistant Dean for Records and Admission, 631-632-9712, Fax: 631-632-7243, E-mail: gradadmissions@stonybrook.edu.
Website: http://www.ceas.sunysb.edu/

Syracuse University, College of Engineering and Computer Science, Syracuse, NY 13244. Offers MS, PhD, CAS. *Program availability:* Part-time, evening/weekend. *Degree requirements:* For master's, comprehensive exam (for some programs), thesis (for some programs); for doctorate, comprehensive exam, thesis/dissertation. *Entrance requirements:* For master's, doctorate, and CAS, GRE General Test, resume, official transcripts, personal statement, three letters of recommendation. Additional exam requirements/recommendations for international students: required—TOEFL, IELTS. Electronic applications accepted.

Temple University, College of Engineering.

See Display below and Close-Up on page 69.

Tennessee State University, The School of Graduate Studies and Research, College of Engineering, Nashville, TN 37209-1561. Offers biomedical engineering (ME); civil engineering (ME); computer and information systems engineering (MS, PhD); electrical engineering (ME); environmental engineering (ME); manufacturing engineering (ME); mathematical sciences (MS); mechanical engineering (ME). *Program availability:* Part-time, evening/weekend. *Degree requirements:* For master's, project; for doctorate, comprehensive exam, thesis/dissertation. *Entrance requirements:* For doctorate, minimum GPA of 3.3.

Tennessee Technological University, College of Graduate Studies, College of Engineering, Cookeville, TN 38505. Offers MS, PhD. *Program availability:* Part-time. *Faculty:* 76 full-time (2 women). *Students:* 58 full-time (10 women), 153 part-time (30 women); includes 8 minority (3 Black or African American, non-Hispanic/Latino; 4 Asian, non-Hispanic/Latino; 1 Hispanic/Latino), 100 international. 205 applicants, 62% accepted, 44 enrolled. In 2019, 32 master's, 15 doctorates awarded. *Degree requirements:* For master's, comprehensive exam, thesis; for doctorate, comprehensive exam, thesis/dissertation. *Entrance requirements:* For master's, GRE General Test; for doctorate, GRE, minimum GPA of 3.5. Additional exam requirements/recommendations for international students: required—TOEFL (minimum score 550 paper-based; 79 iBT), IELTS (minimum score 5.5), PTE (minimum score 53), or TOEIC (Test of English as an International Communication). *Application deadline:* For fall admission, 8/1 for domestic students, 5/1 for international students; for spring admission, 12/1 for domestic students, 10/1 for international students. Applications are processed on a rolling basis. Application fee: $35 ($40 for international students). Electronic applications accepted. *Expenses: Tuition, area resident:* Part-time $597 per credit hour. Tuition, state resident: part-time $597 per credit hour. Tuition, nonresident: part-time $1323 per credit hour. *Financial support:* Fellowships, research assistantships, teaching assistantships, and career-related internships or fieldwork available. Support available to part-time students. Financial award application deadline: 4/1. *Unit head:* Dr. Joseph Slater, Dean, 931-372-3172, Fax: 931-372-6172, E-mail: jslater@tntech.edu. *Application contact:* Shelia K. Kendrick, Coordinator of Graduate Studies, 931-372-3808, Fax: 931-372-3497, E-mail: skendrick@tntech.edu.

Texas A&M University–Kingsville, College of Graduate Studies, Frank H. Dotterweich College of Engineering, Kingsville, TX 78363. Offers ME, MS, PhD. *Degree requirements:* For master's, variable foreign language requirement, comprehensive exam, thesis (for some programs); for doctorate, variable foreign language requirement, comprehensive exam, thesis/dissertation (for some programs). *Entrance requirements:* For master's and doctorate, GRE, MAT, GMAT. Additional exam requirements/recommendations for international students: required—TOEFL (minimum score 550 paper-based; 79 iBT). Electronic applications accepted.

Texas State University, The Graduate College, College of Science and Engineering, Program in Engineering, San Marcos, TX 78666. Offers civil engineering (MS); electrical engineering (MS); industrial engineering (MS); mechanical and manufacturing engineering (MS). *Program availability:* Part-time. *Degree requirements:* For master's, comprehensive exam, thesis (for some programs), thesis or research project. *Entrance requirements:* For master's, official GRE (general test only) required with competitive scores in the verbal reasoning and quantitative reasoning sections, baccalaureate degree from regionally-accredited university in engineering, computer science, physics, technology, or closely-related field with minimum GPA of 3.0 on last 60 undergraduate semester hours; resume or curriculum vitae; 2 letters of recommendation; statement of purpose conveying research interest and professional aspirations. Additional exam requirements/recommendations for international students: required—TOEFL (minimum score 550 paper-based; 78 iBT), IELTS (minimum score 6.5). Electronic applications accepted.

Texas Tech University, Graduate School, Edward E. Whitacre Jr. College of Engineering, Lubbock, TX 79409-3103. Offers engineering (M Engr); JD/M Engr. *Program availability:* Part-time, evening/weekend, 100% online, blended/hybrid learning. *Faculty:* 182 full-time (33 women), 20 part-time/adjunct (5 women). *Students:* 640 full-time (175 women), 205 part-time (35 women); includes 117 minority (24 Black or African American, non-Hispanic/Latino; 27 Asian, non-Hispanic/Latino; 51 Hispanic/Latino; 15 Two or more races, non-Hispanic/Latino), 514 international. Average age 29. 1,036 applicants, 58% accepted, 241 enrolled. In 2019, 155 master's, 72 doctorates awarded. *Degree requirements:* For master's, comprehensive exam, thesis (for some programs); for doctorate, comprehensive exam, thesis/dissertation. *Entrance requirements:* For master's, GRE (Verbal and Quantitative), minimum GPA of 3.0. Additional exam requirements/recommendations for international students: required—TOEFL (minimum

score 550 paper-based; 79 iBT), IELTS (minimum score 6.5). *Application deadline:* For fall admission, 6/1 priority date for domestic students, 1/15 priority date for international students; for spring admission, 9/1 priority date for domestic students, 6/15 priority date for international students. Applications are processed on a rolling basis. Application fee: $65. Electronic applications accepted. *Expenses:* Contact institution. *Financial support:* In 2019–20, 683 students received support, including 614 fellowships (averaging $3,437 per year), 268 research assistantships (averaging $23,055 per year), 129 teaching assistantships (averaging $22,516 per year); scholarships/grants, health care benefits, and unspecified assistantships also available. Financial award application deadline: 4/15; financial award applicants required to submit FAFSA. *Unit head:* Dr. Albert Sacco, Jr., Dean, Edward E. Whitacre Jr. College of Engineering, 806-742-3451, Fax: 806-742-3493, E-mail: al.sacco-jr@ttu.edu. *Application contact:* Dr. Brandon Weeks, Associate Dean of Research and Graduate Programs, Edward E. Whitacre Jr. College of Engineering, 806-834-7450, Fax: 806-742-3493, E-mail: brandon.weeks@ttu.edu.
Website: www.coe.ttu.edu

Tufts University, School of Engineering, Medford, MA 02155. Offers MS, MSEM, PhD, PhD/PhD. *Program availability:* Part-time. Terminal master's awarded for partial completion of doctoral program. *Degree requirements:* For master's, thesis (for some programs); for doctorate, thesis/dissertation. *Entrance requirements:* For master's and doctorate, GRE General Test. Additional exam requirements/recommendations for international students: required—TOEFL (minimum score 550 paper-based; 90 iBT), IELTS (minimum score 6.5). Electronic applications accepted. Full-time tuition and fees vary according to degree level, program and student level. Part-time tuition and fees vary according to course load.

Tuskegee University, Graduate Programs, College of Engineering, Tuskegee, AL 36088. Offers MSEE, MSME, PhD. *Degree requirements:* For master's, thesis or alternative. *Entrance requirements:* For master's, GRE General Test, GRE Subject Test. Additional exam requirements/recommendations for international students: required—TOEFL (minimum score 500 paper-based).

Universidad de las Américas Puebla, Division of Graduate Studies, School of Engineering, Puebla, Mexico. Offers M Adm, MS, PhD. *Program availability:* Part-time, evening/weekend. *Degree requirements:* For master's, one foreign language, thesis.

Universidad del Turabo, Graduate Programs, School of Engineering, Gurabo, PR 00778-3030. Offers computer engineering (M Eng); electrical engineering (M Eng); mechanical engineering (M Eng); telecommunications and network systems administration (M Eng). *Entrance requirements:* For master's, GRE, EXADEP or GMAT, interview, essay, official transcript, recommendation letters. Electronic applications accepted.

Université de Moncton, Faculty of Engineering, Moncton, NB E1A 3E9, Canada. Offers civil engineering (M Sc A); electrical engineering (M Sc A); industrial engineering (M Sc A); mechanical engineering (M Sc A). *Degree requirements:* For master's, thesis, proficiency in French.

Université de Sherbrooke, Faculty of Engineering, Sherbrooke, QC J1K 2R1, Canada. Offers M Eng, M Env, M Sc A, PhD, Diploma. *Program availability:* Part-time. *Degree requirements:* For master's, one foreign language, thesis; for doctorate, comprehensive exam, thesis/dissertation. *Entrance requirements:* For master's, bachelor's degree in engineering or equivalent. Electronic applications accepted.

Université du Québec à Chicoutimi, Graduate Programs, Program in Engineering, Chicoutimi, QC G7H 2B1, Canada. Offers M Sc A, PhD. *Program availability:* Part-time. *Degree requirements:* For master's, thesis; for doctorate, thesis/dissertation. *Entrance requirements:* For master's, appropriate bachelor's degree, proficiency in French.

Université du Québec à Rimouski, Graduate Programs, Program in Engineering, Rimouski, QC G5L 3A1, Canada. Offers M Sc A.

Université du Québec, École de technologie supérieure, Graduate Programs, Montréal, QC H3C 1K3, Canada. Offers M Eng, PhD, Diploma. *Program availability:* Online learning. *Entrance requirements:* For master's and Diploma, appropriate bachelor's degree, proficiency in French; for doctorate, appropriate master's degree, proficiency in French.

Université du Québec en Abitibi-Témiscamingue, Graduate Programs, Program in Engineering, Rouyn-Noranda, QC J9X 5E4, Canada. Offers engineering (ME); mineral engineering (ME); mining engineering (DESS).

University at Albany, State University of New York, College of Engineering and Applied Sciences, Albany, NY 12222. Offers MS, PhD, CAS. *Accreditation:* ALA (one or more programs are accredited). *Program availability:* Part-time, blended/hybrid learning. *Faculty:* 37 full-time (8 women), 7 part-time/adjunct (0 women). *Students:* 188 full-time (48 women), 69 part-time (22 women); includes 15 minority (2 Black or African American, non-Hispanic/Latino; 11 Asian, non-Hispanic/Latino; 1 Hispanic/Latino; 1 Two or more races, non-Hispanic/Latino), 120 international. Average age 27. 381 applicants, 51% accepted, 59 enrolled. In 2019, 147 master's, 3 doctorates awarded. *Degree requirements:* For doctorate, thesis/dissertation. *Entrance requirements:* For master's, GRE, transcripts from all schools attended, 3 letters of recommendation, resume, personal statement; for doctorate, GRE General Test, transcripts from all schools attended, 3 letters of recommendation, resume, personal statement. Additional exam requirements/recommendations for international students: required—TOEFL (minimum score 550 paper-based). *Application deadline:* For fall admission, 1/15 for domestic students; for spring admission, 11/15 for domestic students. Application fee: $75. Electronic applications accepted. *Expenses: Tuition, area resident:* Full-time $11,530; part-time $480 per credit hour. Tuition, nonresident: full-time $23,530; part-time $980 per credit hour. *International tuition:* $23,530 full-time. *Required fees:* $2185; $96 per credit hour. Part-time tuition and fees vary according to course load and program. *Financial support:* Fellowships, research assistantships, teaching assistantships, and Federal Work-Study available. Financial award application deadline: 4/1. *Unit head:* Kim L. Boyer, Dean, 518-956-8240, Fax: 518-442-5367, E-mail: ceasinfo@albany.edu. *Application contact:* Kim L. Boyer, Dean, 518-956-8240, Fax: 518-442-5367, E-mail: ceasinfo@albany.edu.
Website: http://www.albany.edu/ceas/

University at Buffalo, the State University of New York, Graduate School, School of Engineering and Applied Sciences, Buffalo, NY 14260. Offers ME, MS, PhD, Certificate. *Program availability:* Part-time, evening/weekend, 100% online, blended/hybrid learning. Terminal master's awarded for partial completion of doctoral program. *Degree requirements:* For master's, minimum of 30 credits; for doctorate, minimum of 72 credits; for Certificate, minimum of 12 credits. *Entrance requirements:* For master's and doctorate, GRE General Test, transcripts, curriculum vitae/resume, statement of purpose, letters of recommendation. Additional exam requirements/recommendations for international students: required—TOEFL (minimum score 79 iBT), IELTS. Electronic applications accepted. *Expenses: Tuition, area resident:* Full-time $11,310; part-time $471 per credit hour. Tuition, state resident: full-time $11,310; part-time $471 per credit hour. Tuition, nonresident: full-time $23,100; part-time $963 per credit hour. *International tuition:* $23,100 full-time. *Required fees:* $2820.

The University of Akron, Graduate School, College of Engineering, Akron, OH 44325. Offers MS, PhD. *Program availability:* Part-time, evening/weekend. Terminal master's awarded for partial completion of doctoral program. *Degree requirements:* For master's, thesis optional; for doctorate, one foreign language, thesis/dissertation, candidacy exam, qualifying exam. *Entrance requirements:* For master's, GRE, minimum GPA of 2.75, letters of recommendation, statement of purpose, resume; for doctorate, GRE, minimum GPA of 3.0 with bachelor's degree, 3.5 with master's degree; letters of recommendation; personal statement; resume. Additional exam requirements/recommendations for international students: required—TOEFL (minimum score 550 paper-based; 79 iBT), IELTS (minimum score 6.5). Electronic applications accepted.

The University of Alabama, Graduate School, College of Engineering, Tuscaloosa, AL 35487. Offers MS, MS Ch E, MS Met E, MSAEM, MSCE, PhD. *Program availability:* Part-time, online learning. *Faculty:* 123 full-time (15 women). *Students:* 254 full-time (46 women), 50 part-time (5 women); includes 21 minority (11 Black or African American, non-Hispanic/Latino; 3 Asian, non-Hispanic/Latino; 4 Hispanic/Latino; 3 Two or more races, non-Hispanic/Latino), 152 international. Average age 27. 327 applicants, 39% accepted, 65 enrolled. In 2019, 57 master's, 36 doctorates awarded. Terminal master's awarded for partial completion of doctoral program. *Degree requirements:* For master's, comprehensive exam; for doctorate, thesis/dissertation. *Entrance requirements:* For master's and doctorate, minimum GPA of 3.0. Additional exam requirements/recommendations for international students: required—TOEFL (minimum score 550 paper-based). *Application deadline:* For fall admission, 7/1 for domestic students, 4/15 for international students; for spring admission, 11/15 for domestic students, 9/1 for international students. Applications are processed on a rolling basis. Application fee: $50 ($60 for international students). Electronic applications accepted. *Expenses: Tuition, area resident:* Full-time $10,780; part-time $440 per credit hour. Tuition, nonresident: full-time $30,250; part-time $1550 per credit hour. *Financial support:* In 2019–20, 229 students received support, including fellowships with full tuition reimbursements available (averaging $16,022 per year), research assistantships with full tuition reimbursements available (averaging $16,022 per year), teaching assistantships with full tuition reimbursements available (averaging $16,022 per year); career-related internships or fieldwork, Federal Work-Study, and institutionally sponsored loans also available. Financial award application deadline: 2/15. *Unit head:* Dr. Charles Karr, Dean, 205-348-6405, Fax: 205-348-8573. *Application contact:* Dr. Susan Carvalho, Dean, 205-348-8280, Fax: 205-348-0400, E-mail: secarvalho@ua.edu.
Website: http://coeweb.eng.ua.edu/

The University of Alabama at Birmingham, School of Engineering, Program in Interdisciplinary Engineering, Birmingham, AL 35294. Offers computational engineering (PhD). *Program availability:* Part-time. *Faculty:* 2 full-time (0 women), 1 (woman) part-time/adjunct. *Students:* 6 full-time (1 woman), 17 part-time (4 women); includes 6 minority (4 Black or African American, non-Hispanic/Latino; 1 Asian, non-Hispanic/Latino; 1 Two or more races, non-Hispanic/Latino), 7 international. 8 applicants, 75% accepted, 1 enrolled. In 2019, 2 doctorates awarded. *Degree requirements:* For doctorate, comprehensive exam, thesis/dissertation, publication of three first-author original research articles in peer-reviewed journal. *Entrance requirements:* For doctorate, GRE general test (minimum score of 156 or higher on the quantitative section of the GRE to be considered for admission), undergraduate or graduate degree in engineering, minimum 3.0 on a 4.0 scale on most recent degree, personal statement identifying research interest, CV/résumé, 3 recommendations from academic or professional contact. Additional exam requirements/recommendations for international students: required—TOEFL (minimum score 80 iBT); recommended—IELTS (minimum score 6.5). *Application deadline:* For fall admission, 8/1 for domestic and international students; for spring admission, 12/1 for domestic and international students; for summer admission, 5/1 for domestic and international students. Applications are processed on a rolling basis. Application fee: $50 ($60 for international students). Electronic applications accepted. *Unit head:* Dr. Gregg Janowski, Program Director, 205-934-8524, E-mail: janowski@uab.edu. *Application contact:* Jesse Keppley, Director of Student and Academic Services, 205-996-5696, E-mail: gradschool@uab.edu.
Website: http://www.uab.edu/engineering/home/

The University of Alabama in Huntsville, School of Graduate Studies, College of Engineering, Huntsville, AL 35899. Offers MS, MSE, MSOR, MSSE, PhD. *Program availability:* Part-time. *Degree requirements:* For master's, comprehensive exam, thesis or alternative, oral and written exams; for doctorate, comprehensive exam, thesis/dissertation, oral and written exams. *Entrance requirements:* For master's and doctorate, GRE General Test, minimum GPA of 3.0. Additional exam requirements/recommendations for international students: required—TOEFL (minimum score 500 paper-based; 80 iBT), IELTS (minimum score 6.5). Electronic applications accepted.

University of Alaska Fairbanks, College of Engineering and Mines, PhD Programs in Engineering, Fairbanks, AK 99775-7520. Offers PhD. *Program availability:* Part-time. *Degree requirements:* For doctorate, comprehensive exam, thesis/dissertation, oral defense of dissertation. *Entrance requirements:* For doctorate, GRE General Test, minimum cumulative GPA of 3.0. Additional exam requirements/recommendations for international students: required—TOEFL (minimum score 550 paper-based; 79 iBT), IELTS (minimum score 6.5). Electronic applications accepted. *Expenses:* Contact institution.

The University of Arizona, College of Engineering, Tucson, AZ 85721. Offers ME, MS, PhD, Certificate. *Program availability:* Part-time, online learning. *Degree requirements:* For doctorate, thesis/dissertation. *Entrance requirements:* Additional exam requirements/recommendations for international students: required—TOEFL (minimum score 550 paper-based; 79 iBT). Electronic applications accepted.

University of Arkansas, Graduate School, College of Engineering, Fayetteville, AR 72701. Offers MS, MS Cmp E, MS Ch E, MS En E, MS Tc E, MSBE, MSBME, MSCE, MSE, MSEE, MSIE, MSME, MSTE, PhD. *Students:* 390 full-time (121 women), 472 part-time (116 women); includes 137 minority (42 Black or African American, non-Hispanic/Latino; 8 American Indian or Alaska Native, non-Hispanic/Latino; 26 Asian, non-Hispanic/Latino; 43 Hispanic/Latino; 2 Native Hawaiian or other Pacific Islander, non-Hispanic/Latino; 16 Two or more races, non-Hispanic/Latino), 276 international. 401 applicants, 82% accepted. In 2019, 235 master's, 33 doctorates awarded. *Degree requirements:* For doctorate, one foreign language, thesis/dissertation. *Application deadline:* For fall admission, 8/1 for domestic students, 4/1 for international students; for spring admission, 12/1 for domestic students, 10/1 for international students; for summer admission, 4/15 for domestic students, 3/1 for international students. Applications are processed on a rolling basis. Application fee: $60. Electronic applications accepted. *Financial support:* In 2019–20, 198 research assistantships, 21 teaching assistantships were awarded; fellowships with tuition reimbursements, career-related internships or fieldwork, and Federal Work-Study also available. Support available to part-time students. Financial award application deadline: 4/1; financial award applicants required to submit FAFSA. *Unit head:* Dr. John R. English, Dean, 479-575-7455, E-mail: jre@uark.edu. *Application contact:* Dr. Norman Dennis, Senior Associate Dean and University Professor, 479-575-6011, E-mail: ndennis@uark.edu.
Website: https://engineering.uark.edu

University of Bridgeport, School of Engineering, Bridgeport, CT 06604. Offers MS, PhD. *Program availability:* Part-time, evening/weekend, online learning. *Degree requirements:* For master's, thesis optional; for doctorate, thesis/dissertation. *Entrance requirements:* Additional exam requirements/recommendations for international students: recommended—TOEFL (minimum score 550 paper-based; 80 iBT), IELTS (minimum score 6.5). Electronic applications accepted. *Expenses:* Contact institution.

The University of British Columbia, Faculty of Applied Science, Vancouver, BC V6T 1Z4, Canada. Offers M Arch, M Eng, M Sc, M Sc P, MA Sc, MAP, MASA, MASLA, MCRP, MEL, MLA, MN, MSN, MUD, PhD, M Arch/MLA. *Program availability:* Part-time. *Degree requirements:* For master's, comprehensive exam (for some programs), thesis (for some programs); for doctorate, comprehensive exam, thesis/dissertation. *Entrance requirements:* Additional exam requirements/recommendations for international students: required—TOEFL (minimum score 550 paper-based; 90 iBT), IELTS. Electronic applications accepted. *Expenses:* Contact institution.

University of Calgary, Faculty of Graduate Studies, Schulich School of Engineering, Calgary, AB T2N 1N4, Canada. Offers M Eng, M Sc, MPM, PhD. *Program availability:* Part-time, evening/weekend. *Degree requirements:* For doctorate, comprehensive exam, thesis/dissertation. *Entrance requirements:* Additional exam requirements/recommendations for international students: required—TOEFL, IELTS. Electronic applications accepted.

University of California, Berkeley, Graduate Division, College of Engineering, Berkeley, CA 94720. Offers M Eng, MS, MTM, PhD, M Arch/MS, MCP/MS, MPP/MS. *Program availability:* Part-time, 100% online, blended/hybrid learning. Terminal master's awarded for partial completion of doctoral program. *Degree requirements:* For master's, comprehensive exam (for some programs), thesis (for some programs); for doctorate, thesis/dissertation, qualifying exam. *Entrance requirements:* For master's and doctorate, GRE General Test, minimum GPA of 3.0, 3 letters of recommendation. Additional exam requirements/recommendations for international students: required—TOEFL (minimum score 570 paper-based; 90 iBT). Electronic applications accepted.

University of California, Berkeley, UC Berkeley Extension, Certificate Programs in Engineering, Construction and Facilities Management, Berkeley, CA 94720. Offers construction management (Certificate); HVAC (Certificate); integrated circuit design and techniques (online) (Certificate). *Program availability:* Online learning.

University of California, Davis, College of Engineering, Davis, CA 95616. Offers M Engr, MS, D Engr, PhD, Certificate, M Engr/MBA. *Program availability:* Part-time. Terminal master's awarded for partial completion of doctoral program. *Degree requirements:* For master's, comprehensive exam (for some programs), thesis (for some programs); for doctorate, comprehensive exam, thesis/dissertation. *Entrance requirements:* For doctorate, GRE. Additional exam requirements/recommendations for international students: required—TOEFL (minimum score 550 paper-based). Electronic applications accepted.

University of California, Irvine, Samueli School of Engineering, Irvine, CA 92697. Offers MS, PhD. *Program availability:* Part-time. *Students:* 877 full-time (283 women), 37 part-time (13 women); includes 178 minority (16 Black or African American, non-Hispanic/Latino; 119 Asian, non-Hispanic/Latino; 33 Hispanic/Latino; 1 Native Hawaiian or other Pacific Islander, non-Hispanic/Latino; 9 Two or more races, non-Hispanic/Latino), 526 international. Average age 26. 3,710 applicants, 33% accepted, 281 enrolled. In 2019, 282 master's, 97 doctorates awarded. Terminal master's awarded for partial completion of doctoral program. *Entrance requirements:* For master's and doctorate, GRE General Test, minimum GPA of 3.0, 3 letters of recommendation. Additional exam requirements/recommendations for international students: required—TOEFL (minimum score 550 paper-based). *Application deadline:* For fall admission, 1/15 priority date for domestic students, 1/15 for international students. Applications are processed on a rolling basis. Application fee: $120 ($140 for international students). Electronic applications accepted. *Financial support:* Fellowships with tuition reimbursements, research assistantships with full tuition reimbursements, teaching assistantships with tuition reimbursements, institutionally sponsored loans, traineeships, health care benefits, and unspecified assistantships available. Financial award application deadline: 3/1; financial award applicants required to submit FAFSA. *Unit head:* Gregory N. Washington, Dean, 949-824-4333, Fax: 949-824-8200, E-mail: engineering@uci.edu. *Application contact:* Jean Bennett, Director of Graduate Student Affairs, 949-824-6475, Fax: 949-824-8200, E-mail: jean.bennett@uci.edu.
Website: http://www.eng.uci.edu/

University of California, Los Angeles, Graduate Division, Henry Samueli School of Engineering and Applied Science, Los Angeles, CA 90095-1601. Offers MS, PhD, MBA/MS. *Program availability:* Evening/weekend, blended/hybrid learning. *Degree requirements:* For master's, comprehensive exam or thesis; for doctorate, thesis/dissertation, qualifying exams. *Entrance requirements:* For master's, GRE General Test, minimum GPA of 3.0 depending on department/major; for doctorate, GRE General Test, minimum GPA of 3.25 (depending on department/major). Additional exam requirements/recommendations for international students: required—TOEFL (minimum score 560 paper-based; 87 iBT), IELTS (minimum score 7). Electronic applications accepted.

University of California, Merced, Graduate Division, School of Engineering, Merced, CA 95343. Offers biological engineering and small scale technologies (MS, PhD); electrical engineering and computer science (MS, PhD); environmental systems (MS, PhD); management of innovation, sustainability, and technology (MM); mechanical engineering (MS, PhD). *Faculty:* 60 full-time (16 women). *Students:* 244 full-time (83 women), 1 (woman) part-time; includes 56 minority (2 Black or African American, non-Hispanic/Latino; 20 Asian, non-Hispanic/Latino; 30 Hispanic/Latino; 1 Native Hawaiian or other Pacific Islander, non-Hispanic/Latino; 3 Two or more races, non-Hispanic/Latino), 153 international. Average age 28. 330 applicants, 32% accepted, 67 enrolled. In 2019, 30 master's, 17 doctorates awarded. Terminal master's awarded for partial completion of doctoral program. *Degree requirements:* For master's, variable foreign language requirement, comprehensive exam, thesis or alternative, oral defense; for doctorate, variable foreign language requirement, comprehensive exam, thesis/dissertation, oral defense. *Entrance requirements:* For master's and doctorate, GRE. Additional exam requirements/recommendations for international students: required—TOEFL (minimum score 550 paper-based; 80 iBT); recommended—IELTS (minimum score 6.5). *Application deadline:* For fall admission, 1/15 for domestic and international students. Application fee: $105 ($125 for international students). Electronic applications accepted. *Expenses: Tuition, area resident:* Full-time $11,442; part-time $5721. Tuition, state resident: full-time $11,442; part-time $5721. Tuition, nonresident: full-time $26,544; part-time $13,272. *International tuition:* $26,544 full-time. *Required fees:* $564 per semester. *Financial support:* In 2019–20, 205 students received support, including 6 fellowships with full tuition reimbursements available (averaging $22,005 per year), 76 research assistantships with full tuition reimbursements available (averaging $21,420 per year), 123 teaching assistantships with full tuition reimbursements available (averaging $21,911 per year); scholarships/grants, traineeships, and health care benefits also available. *Unit head:* Dr. Mark Matsumoto, Dean, 209-228-4047, Fax: 209-228-4047, E-mail: mmatsumoto@ucmerced.edu. *Application contact:* Tsu Ya, Director of Admissions and Academic Services, 209-228-4521, Fax: 209-228-6906, E-mail: tya@ucmerced.edu.

University of California, Santa Barbara, Graduate Division, College of Engineering, Santa Barbara, CA 93106-5130. Offers MS, MTM, PhD, MS/PhD. Terminal master's awarded for partial completion of doctoral program. *Degree requirements:* For doctorate, thesis/dissertation. *Entrance requirements:* For master's, GRE, 3 letters of recommendation, resume/curriculum vitae; for doctorate, GRE, 3 letters of recommendation, statement of purpose, personal achievements/contributions statement, resume/curriculum vitae, transcripts for post-secondary institutions attended. Additional exam requirements/recommendations for international students: required—TOEFL, IELTS. Electronic applications accepted.

University of California, Santa Cruz, Jack Baskin School of Engineering, Santa Cruz, CA 95064. Offers MS, PhD. *Program availability:* Part-time. *Faculty:* 107 full-time (22 women), 13 part-time/adjunct (1 woman). *Students:* 626 full-time (201 women), 38 part-time (8 women); includes 122 minority (9 Black or African American, non-Hispanic/Latino; 4 American Indian or Alaska Native, non-Hispanic/Latino; 65 Asian, non-Hispanic/Latino; 34 Hispanic/Latino; 10 Native Hawaiian or other Pacific Islander, non-Hispanic/Latino), 366 international. 2,083 applicants, 32% accepted, 223 enrolled. In 2019, 181 master's, 46 doctorates awarded. *Entrance requirements:* Additional exam requirements/recommendations for international students: required—TOEFL (minimum score 570 paper-based; 89 iBT); recommended—IELTS (minimum score 8). Application fee: $105 ($125 for international students). Electronic applications accepted. *Financial support:* Fellowships, research assistantships, teaching assistantships, institutionally sponsored loans, scholarships/grants, traineeships, health care benefits, and tuition waivers (full and partial) available. Financial award applicants required to submit FAFSA. *Unit head:* Dr. Alexander Wolf, Dean, E-mail: alw@ucsc.edu. *Application contact:* BSOE Graduate Student Affairs Office, 831-459-3531, E-mail: bsoe-ga@rt.ucsc.edu.
Website: https://www.soe.ucsc.edu/

University of Central Florida, College of Engineering and Computer Science, Orlando, FL 32816. Offers MS, MS Cp E, MS Env E, MSAE, MSCE, MSEE, MSEM, MSIE, MSME, MSMSE, PhD, Certificate. *Program availability:* Part-time, evening/weekend. *Faculty:* 208 full-time (29 women), 50 part-time/adjunct (3 women). *Students:* 999 full-time (232 women), 770 part-time (193 women); includes 455 minority (82 Black or African American, non-Hispanic/Latino; 2 American Indian or Alaska Native, non-Hispanic/Latino; 106 Asian, non-Hispanic/Latino; 240 Hispanic/Latino; 25 Two or more races, non-Hispanic/Latino), 682 international. Average age 30. 1,826 applicants, 67% accepted, 555 enrolled. In 2019, 390 master's, 108 doctorates, 28 other advanced degrees awarded. *Degree requirements:* For master's, thesis or alternative; for doctorate, thesis/dissertation, candidacy exam, departmental qualifying exam. *Entrance requirements:* For master's, resume, letters of recommendation; for doctorate, GRE, resume, letters of recommendation. Additional exam requirements/recommendations for international students: required—TOEFL. *Application deadline:* For fall admission, 7/15 for domestic students; for spring admission, 12/1 for domestic students. Application fee: $30. Electronic applications accepted. *Financial support:* In 2019–20, 602 students received support, including 170 fellowships with partial tuition reimbursements available (averaging $11,677 per year), 436 research assistantships with partial tuition reimbursements available (averaging $8,253 per year), 176 teaching assistantships with partial tuition reimbursements available (averaging $8,249 per year); career-related internships or fieldwork, Federal Work-Study, tuition waivers (partial), and unspecified assistantships also available. Financial award application deadline: 3/1; financial award applicants required to submit FAFSA. *Unit head:* Dr. Michael Georgiopoulos, Dean, 407-823-2156, E-mail: michaelg@ucf.edu. *Application contact:* Associate Director, Graduate Admissions, 407-823-2766, Fax: 407-823-6442, E-mail: gradadmissions@ucf.edu.
Website: http://www.cecs.ucf.edu/

University of Central Oklahoma, The Jackson College of Graduate Studies, College of Mathematics and Science, Department of Engineering and Physics, Edmond, OK 73034-5209. Offers engineering physics (MS), including biomedical engineering, electrical engineering, mechanical systems, physics. *Program availability:* Part-time. *Degree requirements:* For master's, thesis optional. *Entrance requirements:* For master's, GRE, 24 hours of course work in physics or equivalent, mathematics through differential equations, minimum GPA of 2.75 overall and 3.0 in last 60 hours attempted, two letters of recommendation. Additional exam requirements/recommendations for international students: required—TOEFL (minimum score 550 paper-based; 79 iBT), IELTS (minimum score 6.5). Electronic applications accepted.

University of Cincinnati, Graduate School, College of Engineering and Applied Science, Cincinnati, OH 45221. Offers M Eng, MS, PhD. *Program availability:* Part-time, 100% online. Terminal master's awarded for partial completion of doctoral program. *Degree requirements:* For master's, thesis or alternative, Thesis for MS students; capstone for MEng students; for doctorate, comprehensive exam, thesis/dissertation. *Entrance requirements:* For master's and doctorate, GRE General Test-some students may be exempt. Additional exam requirements/recommendations for international students: required—Required to take one exam to demonstrate proficiency: TOEFL (minimum score 92 iBT), IELTS (6.5), or PTE (47). Electronic applications accepted. *Expenses:* Contact institution.

University of Colorado Boulder, Graduate School, College of Engineering and Applied Science, Boulder, CO 80309. Offers ME, MS, PhD, JD/MS, MBA/MS. *Degree requirements:* For doctorate, thesis/dissertation. *Entrance requirements:* For master's, minimum undergraduate GPA of 2.75. Electronic applications accepted. Application fee is waived when completed online. *Expenses:* Contact institution.

University of Colorado Colorado Springs, College of Engineering and Applied Science, Colorado Springs, CO 80918. Offers computer science (MS, PhD); engineering (ME). *Program availability:* Part-time, evening/weekend. *Faculty:* 50 full-time (11 women), 34 part-time/adjunct (6 women). *Students:* 23 full-time (4 women), 256 part-time (52 women); includes 55 minority (9 Black or African American, non-Hispanic/Latino; 18 Asian, non-Hispanic/Latino; 17 Hispanic/Latino; 11 Two or more races, non-Hispanic/Latino), 75 international. Average age 33. 169 applicants, 67% accepted, 64 enrolled. In 2019, 61 master's, 13 doctorates awarded. *Degree requirements:* For master's, comprehensive exam (for some programs), thesis or alternative; for doctorate, comprehensive exam, thesis/dissertation. *Entrance requirements:* For master's, GRE General Test, minimum GPA of 3.0; for doctorate, GRE General Test, minimum GPA of 3.3. Additional exam requirements/recommendations for international students: required—TOEFL (minimum score 80 iBT), IELTS (minimum score 6.5). *Application deadline:* For fall admission, 6/1 for domestic students, 4/1 for international students; for spring admission, 11/1 for domestic students, 10/1 for international students. Applications are processed on a rolling basis. Application fee: $60 ($100 for international students). *Expenses:* Contact institution. *Financial support:* In 2019–20, 44 students received support, including 43 research assistantships (averaging $20,000 per year), 50 teaching assistantships (averaging $4,970 per year); career-related internships or fieldwork, Federal Work-Study, institutionally sponsored loans, scholarships/grants, traineeships, and unspecified assistantships also available. Support available to part-time students. Financial award application deadline: 3/1; financial award applicants required to submit FAFSA. *Unit head:* Dr. Donald Rabern, Dean, 719-255-3543, E-mail: drabern@uccs.edu. *Application contact:* Ali Langfels, Office of Student Support, 719-255-3544, E-mail: alangfel@uccs.edu.
Website: https://www.uccs.edu/eas/

University of Colorado Denver, College of Engineering, Design and Computing, Denver, CO 80217. Offers comp sci and info systems, bioengineering, civil engineering (PhD); electrical, mechanical, civil engineering (M Eng); electrical, mechanical, civil, computer science, bioengineering (MS). *Program availability:* Part-time, evening/weekend. Electronic applications accepted. *Expenses:* Contact institution.

University of Connecticut, Graduate School, School of Engineering, Storrs, CT 06269. Offers M Eng, MS, PhD. Terminal master's awarded for partial completion of doctoral program. *Degree requirements:* For master's, comprehensive exam; for doctorate, thesis/dissertation. *Entrance requirements:* For master's and doctorate, GRE General Test. Additional exam requirements/recommendations for international students: required—TOEFL (minimum score 550 paper-based). Electronic applications accepted.

University of Delaware, College of Engineering, Newark, DE 19716. Offers M Ch E, MAS, MCE, MEM, MMSE, MS, MSECE, MSME, PhD. *Program availability:* Part-time, evening/weekend, online learning. Terminal master's awarded for partial completion of doctoral program. *Degree requirements:* For master's, thesis (for some programs); for doctorate, thesis/dissertation. *Entrance requirements:* For master's and doctorate, GRE General Test. Additional exam requirements/recommendations for international students: required—TOEFL (minimum score 550 paper-based). Electronic applications accepted.

University of Denver, Daniel Felix Ritchie School of Engineering and Computer Science, Denver, CO 80208. Offers MS, PhD. *Faculty:* 42 full-time (7 women), 8 part-time/adjunct (3 women). *Students:* 30 full-time (11 women), 249 part-time (63 women); includes 60 minority (8 Black or African American, non-Hispanic/Latino; 16 Asian, non-Hispanic/Latino; 26 Hispanic/Latino; 10 Two or more races, non-Hispanic/Latino), 78 international. Average age 29. 462 applicants, 71% accepted, 149 enrolled. In 2019, 86 master's, 14 doctorates awarded. *Degree requirements:* For master's, thesis (for some programs); for doctorate, variable foreign language requirement, comprehensive exam, thesis/dissertation. *Entrance requirements:* For master's, GRE General Test, bachelor's degree, transcripts, three letters of recommendation, personal statement, resume; for doctorate, GRE General Test, master's degree, transcripts, three letters of recommendation, personal statement, resume. Additional exam requirements/recommendations for international students: required—TOEFL (minimum score 550 paper-based; 80 iBT). *Application deadline:* Applications are processed on a rolling basis. Application fee: $65. Electronic applications accepted. *Expenses:* Contact institution. *Financial support:* In 2019–20, 139 students received support, including 20 research assistantships with tuition reimbursements available (averaging $14,559 per year), 33 teaching assistantships with tuition reimbursements available (averaging $15,152 per year); Federal Work-Study, institutionally sponsored loans, scholarships/grants, health care benefits, and unspecified assistantships also available. Financial award application deadline: 2/15; financial award applicants required to submit FAFSA. *Unit head:* JB Holston, Dean, 303-871-3787, E-mail: jb.holston@du.edu. *Application contact:* Information Contact, 303-871-3787, E-mail: ritchieschool@du.edu. Website: http://ritchieschool.du.edu/

University of Detroit Mercy, College of Engineering and Science, Detroit, MI 48221. Offers chemistry (MS); civil and environmental engineering (DE); electrical and computer engineering (ME); electrical engineering (DE); engineering management (M Eng Mgt); environmental engineering (MEE); mechanical engineering (MME, DE); product development (MS); software engineering (MSSE); teaching of mathematics (MATM). *Program availability:* Part-time, evening/weekend. *Degree requirements:* For doctorate, thesis/dissertation. Electronic applications accepted. Application fee is waived when completed online. *Expenses:* Contact institution.

University of Florida, Graduate School, Herbert Wertheim College of Engineering, Gainesville, FL 32611. Offers ME, MS, PhD, Certificate, Engr, JD/MS, MD/PhD, MSM/MS. *Program availability:* Part-time, online learning. *Degree requirements:* For doctorate, thesis/dissertation. *Entrance requirements:* For master's and doctorate, minimum GPA of 3.0; for other advanced degree, GRE General Test. Additional exam requirements/recommendations for international students: required—TOEFL (minimum score 550 paper-based; 80 iBT), IELTS (minimum score 6). Electronic applications accepted.

University of Guelph, Office of Graduate and Postdoctoral Studies, College of Physical and Engineering Science, School of Engineering, Guelph, ON N1G 2W1, Canada. Offers biological engineering (M Eng, M Sc, MA Sc, PhD); engineering systems and computing (M Eng, M Sc, MA Sc, PhD); environmental engineering (M Eng, M Sc, MA Sc, PhD); water resources engineering (M Eng, M Sc, MA Sc, PhD). *Program availability:* Part-time. *Degree requirements:* For master's, thesis (for some programs); for doctorate, comprehensive exam, thesis/dissertation. *Entrance requirements:* For master's, minimum B- average during previous 2 years of course work; for doctorate, minimum B average. Additional exam requirements/recommendations for international students: required—TOEFL (minimum score 550 paper-based; 89 iBT), IELTS (minimum score 6.5). Electronic applications accepted.

University of Hartford, College of Engineering, Technology and Architecture, Program in Engineering, West Hartford, CT 06117-1599. Offers M Eng. *Faculty:* 11 full-time (0 women), 10 part-time/adjunct (1 woman). *Students:* 27 full-time (7 women), 72 part-time (9 women); includes 22 minority (7 Black or African American, non-Hispanic/Latino; 1 American Indian or Alaska Native, non-Hispanic/Latino; 2 Asian, non-Hispanic/Latino; 11 Hispanic/Latino; 1 Two or more races, non-Hispanic/Latino), 18 international. Average age 29. 72 applicants, 67% accepted, 25 enrolled. In 2019, 37 master's awarded. *Entrance requirements:* Additional exam requirements/recommendations for international students: required—TOEFL. *Application deadline:* Applications are processed on a rolling basis. Application fee: $45. *Expenses:* Tuition: Full-time $23,700; part-time $645 per credit. *Required fees:* $510; $510 per unit. Tuition and fees vary according to course load, degree level and program. *Financial support:* In 2019–20, 24 fellowships (averaging $2,500 per year) were awarded; unspecified assistantships also available. *Unit head:* Laurie Granstrand, Manager of Student Services, 860-768-4858, E-mail: granstran@hartford.edu. *Application contact:* Laurie Granstrand, Manager of Student Services, 860-768-4858, E-mail: granstran@hartford.edu.

University of Hawaii at Manoa, Office of Graduate Education, College of Engineering, Honolulu, HI 96822. Offers MS, PhD. *Accreditation:* ABET (one or more programs are accredited). *Program availability:* Part-time. *Entrance requirements:* Additional exam requirements/recommendations for international students: required—TOEFL or IELTS.

University of Houston, Cullen College of Engineering, Houston, TX 77204. Offers M Pet E, MCE, MCHE, MEE, MIE, MME, MSEE, MSME, PhD. *Program availability:* Part-time. Terminal master's awarded for partial completion of doctoral program. *Degree requirements:* For master's, thesis (for some programs); for doctorate, thesis/dissertation, departmental qualifying exam. *Entrance requirements:* For master's and doctorate, GRE General Test.

University of Idaho, College of Graduate Studies, College of Engineering, Moscow, ID 83844-2282. Offers M Engr, MS, PhD. *Faculty:* 83. *Students:* 230 full-time (35 women), 210 part-time (30 women). Average age 33. 397 applicants, 55% accepted, 93 enrolled. In 2019, 81 master's, 11 doctorates awarded. *Degree requirements:* For doctorate, thesis/dissertation. *Entrance requirements:* For master's, minimum GPA of 3.0. Additional exam requirements/recommendations for international students: required—TOEFL. *Application deadline:* For fall admission, 7/30 for domestic students; for spring admission, 12/1 for domestic students. Applications are processed on a rolling basis. Application fee: $60. Electronic applications accepted. *Expenses:* Tuition, state

resident: full-time $7753.80; part-time $502 per credit hour. Tuition, nonresident: full-time $26,990; part-time $1571 per credit hour. *Required fees:* $2122.20; $47 per credit hour. *Financial support:* Fellowships, research assistantships, teaching assistantships, career-related internships or fieldwork, and Federal Work-Study available. Support available to part-time students. Financial award applicants required to submit FAFSA. *Unit head:* Dr. Larry Stauffer, Dean, 208-885-6470, E-mail: deanengr@uidaho.edu. *Application contact:* Dr. Larry Stauffer, Dean, 208-885-6470, E-mail: deanengr@uidaho.edu. Website: https://www.uidaho.edu/engr

University of Illinois at Chicago, College of Engineering, Chicago, IL 60607-7128. Offers M Eng, MEE, MS, PhD. *Program availability:* Part-time, evening/weekend. Terminal master's awarded for partial completion of doctoral program. *Degree requirements:* For doctorate, thesis/dissertation. *Entrance requirements:* For doctorate, GRE. Additional exam requirements/recommendations for international students: required—TOEFL. Electronic applications accepted. *Expenses:* Contact institution.

University of Illinois at Urbana-Champaign, Graduate College, College of Engineering, Champaign, IL 61820. Offers M Eng, MCS, MS, PhD, M Arch/MS, MBA/MS, MCS/JD, MCS/M Arch, MCS/MBA, MS/MBA, PhD/MBA. *Program availability:* Part-time, evening/weekend, online learning. *Expenses:* Contact institution.

The University of Iowa, Graduate College, College of Engineering, Iowa City, IA 52242-1527. Offers MS, PhD. *Degree requirements:* For master's, comprehensive exam (for some programs), oral exam and/or thesis; for doctorate, comprehensive exam, thesis/dissertation. *Entrance requirements:* For master's and doctorate, GRE, official academic records/transcripts, 3 letters of recommendation, resume, statement of purpose. Additional exam requirements/recommendations for international students: required—TOEFL (minimum score 550 paper-based; 81 iBT), IELTS (minimum score 7). Electronic applications accepted. *Expenses:* Contact institution.

The University of Kansas, Graduate Studies, School of Engineering, Lawrence, KS 66045. Offers MCE, MCM, ME, MS, DE, PhD, Certificate. *Program availability:* Part-time, evening/weekend, online learning. *Students:* 376 full-time (99 women), 211 part-time (69 women); includes 84 minority (16 Black or African American, non-Hispanic/Latino; 3 American Indian or Alaska Native, non-Hispanic/Latino; 25 Asian, non-Hispanic/Latino; 25 Hispanic/Latino; 15 Two or more races, non-Hispanic/Latino), 214 international. Average age 29. 525 applicants, 61% accepted, 143 enrolled. In 2019, 160 master's, 45 doctorates, 12 other advanced degrees awarded. Terminal master's awarded for partial completion of doctoral program. *Entrance requirements:* For master's and doctorate, GRE, minimum GPA of 3.0, 3 letters of recommendation, official transcripts, statement of purpose. Additional exam requirements/recommendations for international students: required—TOEFL, IELTS. Application fee: $65 ($85 for international students). Electronic applications accepted. *Expenses:* Tuition, state resident: full-time $9989. Tuition, nonresident: full-time $23,950. *International tuition:* $23,950 full-time. *Required fees:* $984; $81.99 per credit hour. Tuition and fees vary according to course load, campus/location and program. *Financial support:* Fellowships, research assistantships, teaching assistantships, career-related internships or fieldwork, Federal Work-Study, scholarships/grants, and unspecified assistantships available. *Unit head:* Dr. Arvin Agah, Dean, 785-864-2930, E-mail: agah@ku.edu. *Application contact:* Amy Wierman, Assistant to the Dean, 785-864-2930, E-mail: awierman@ku.edu. Website: http://www.engr.ku.edu/

University of Kentucky, Graduate School, College of Engineering, Lexington, KY 40506-0032. Offers M Eng, MCE, MME, MS, MS Ch E, MS Min, MSCE, MSEE, MSEM, MSMAE, MSME, MSMSE, PhD. *Program availability:* Part-time. *Degree requirements:* For master's, comprehensive exam; for doctorate, comprehensive exam, thesis/dissertation. *Entrance requirements:* For master's, GRE General Test, minimum undergraduate GPA of 2.75; for doctorate, GRE General Test, minimum undergraduate GPA of 3.0. Additional exam requirements/recommendations for international students: required—TOEFL (minimum score 550 paper-based). Electronic applications accepted.

University of Louisville, J. B. Speed School of Engineering, Louisville, KY 40292-0001. Offers M Eng, MS, PhD, Certificate. *Accreditation:* ABET (one or more programs are accredited). *Program availability:* 100% online, blended/hybrid learning. *Faculty:* 110 full-time (19 women), 29 part-time/adjunct (6 women). *Students:* 313 full-time (70 women), 352 part-time (98 women); includes 117 minority (33 Black or African American, non-Hispanic/Latino; 1 American Indian or Alaska Native, non-Hispanic/Latino; 35 Asian, non-Hispanic/Latino; 23 Hispanic/Latino; 25 Two or more races, non-Hispanic/Latino), 173 international. Average age 29. 301 applicants, 53% accepted, 123 enrolled. In 2019, 259 master's, 25 doctorates, 26 other advanced degrees awarded. Terminal master's awarded for partial completion of doctoral program. *Degree requirements:* For master's, thesis optional; for doctorate, comprehensive exam, thesis/dissertation. *Entrance requirements:* For master's, letters of recommendation, official transcripts, personal statement; for doctorate, GRE, letters of recommendation, official transcripts, personal statement. Additional exam requirements/recommendations for international students: required—TOEFL (minimum score 550 paper-based; 80 iBT), IELTS (minimum score 6.5). *Application deadline:* For fall admission, 5/1 priority date for domestic and international students; for spring admission, 11/1 priority date for domestic and international students; for summer admission, 3/1 priority date for domestic and international students. Applications are processed on a rolling basis. Application fee: $65. Electronic applications accepted. *Expenses: Tuition, area resident:* Full-time $13,000; part-time $723 per credit hour. Tuition, state resident: full-time $13,000; part-time $723 per credit hour. Tuition, nonresident: full-time $27,114; part-time $1507 per credit hour. *International tuition:* $27,114 full-time. *Required fees:* $196. Tuition and fees vary according to program and reciprocity agreements. *Financial support:* In 2019–20, 251 students received support. Fellowships, research assistantships, teaching assistantships, scholarships/grants, health care benefits, and unspecified assistantships available. Financial award application deadline: 1/1. *Unit head:* Dr. Kevin Walsh, Associate Dean for Research and Graduate Studies, 502-852-0826, E-mail: kevin.walsh@louisville.edu. *Application contact:* Dr. Katherine Markuson, Director of Graduate Affairs, 502-852-6278, E-mail: katherine.markuson@louisville.edu. Website: http://louisville.edu/speed/

University of Maine, Graduate School, College of Engineering, Orono, ME 04469. Offers ME, MS, PSM, PhD. *Program availability:* Part-time. *Faculty:* 52 full-time (8 women), 5 part-time/adjunct (0 women). *Students:* 108 full-time (29 women), 30 part-time (5 women); includes 11 minority (2 Black or African American, non-Hispanic/Latino; 1 American Indian or Alaska Native, non-Hispanic/Latino; 3 Asian, non-Hispanic/Latino; 4 Hispanic/Latino; 1 Two or more races, non-Hispanic/Latino), 54 international. Average age 29. 116 applicants, 76% accepted, 41 enrolled. In 2019, 25 master's, 3 doctorates awarded. Terminal master's awarded for partial completion of doctoral program. *Degree requirements:* For master's, thesis (for some programs); for doctorate, comprehensive exam, thesis/dissertation. *Entrance requirements:* For master's and doctorate, GRE General Test. Additional exam requirements/recommendations for international students: required—TOEFL. *Application deadline:* For fall admission, 2/1 priority date for domestic students. Applications are processed on a rolling basis. Application fee: $65. Electronic applications accepted. *Expenses: Tuition, area resident:* Full-time $8100; part-time $450 per credit hour. Tuition, state resident: full-time $8100; part-time $450

per credit hour. Tuition, nonresident: full-time $26,388; part-time $1466 per credit hour. *International tuition:* $26,388 full-time. *Required fees:* $1257; $278 per semester. Tuition and fees vary according to course load. *Financial support:* In 2019–20, 120 students received support, including 4 fellowships (averaging $22,650 per year), 48 research assistantships (averaging $20,700 per year), 22 teaching assistantships (averaging $16,300 per year); Federal Work-Study, institutionally sponsored loans, scholarships/grants, tuition waivers (full and partial), and unspecified assistantships also available. Financial award application deadline: 3/1. *Unit head:* Dr. Dana Humphrey, Dean, 207-581-2217, Fax: 207-581-2220, E-mail: dana.humphrey@umit.maine.edu. *Application contact:* Scott G. Delcourt, Assistant Vice President for Graduate Studies and Senior Associate Dean, 207-581-3291, Fax: 207-581-3232, E-mail: graduate@maine.edu.
Website: http://engineering.umaine.edu

University of Manitoba, Faculty of Graduate Studies, Faculty of Engineering, Winnipeg, MB R3T 2N2, Canada. Offers M Eng, M Sc, PhD.

University of Maryland, Baltimore County, The Graduate School, College of Engineering and Information Technology, Baltimore, MD 21250. Offers MPS, MS, PhD, Postbaccalaureate Certificate. *Program availability:* Part-time. *Faculty:* 125 full-time (39 women), 110 part-time/adjunct (21 women). *Students:* 712 full-time (265 women), 625 part-time (223 women); includes 367 minority (144 Black or African American, non-Hispanic/Latino; 2 American Indian or Alaska Native, non-Hispanic/Latino; 157 Asian, non-Hispanic/Latino; 44 Hispanic/Latino; 1 Native Hawaiian or other Pacific Islander, non-Hispanic/Latino; 19 Two or more races, non-Hispanic/Latino), 585 international. Average age 30. 1,739 applicants, 63% accepted, 438 enrolled. In 2019, 347 master's, 36 doctorates, 66 other advanced degrees awarded. Terminal master's awarded for partial completion of doctoral program. *Degree requirements:* For master's, comprehensive exam (for some programs), thesis (for some programs); for doctorate, comprehensive exam, thesis/dissertation. *Entrance requirements:* Additional exam requirements/recommendations for international students: required—TOEFL (minimum score 550 paper-based; 80 iBT). *Application deadline:* For fall admission, 6/1 for domestic students, 1/1 for international students; for spring admission, 11/1 for domestic students, 6/1 for international students. Applications are processed on a rolling basis. Application fee: $70. Electronic applications accepted. *Expenses:* Contact institution. *Financial support:* In 2019–20, 296 students received support, including 11 fellowships with full tuition reimbursements available (averaging $21,750 per year), 155 research assistantships with full tuition reimbursements available (averaging $19,250 per year), 130 teaching assistantships with full tuition reimbursements available (averaging $16,750 per year); career-related internships or fieldwork, Federal Work-Study, scholarships/grants, health care benefits, tuition waivers (partial), and unspecified assistantships also available. Support available to part-time students. Financial award application deadline: 6/30; financial award applicants required to submit FAFSA. *Unit head:* Dr. Keith J. Bowman, Dean and Professor, 410-455-3270, Fax: 410-455-3559, E-mail: kjb@umbc.edu. *Application contact:* Kathryn Nee, Coordinator of Domestic Admissions, 410-455-2944, E-mail: nee@umbc.edu.
Website: https://coeit.umbc.edu/

University of Maryland, College Park, Academic Affairs, A. James Clark School of Engineering and School of Public Policy, Program in Engineering and Public Policy, College Park, MD 20742. Offers MS.

University of Massachusetts Amherst, Graduate School, College of Engineering, Amherst, MA 01003. Offers MS, MS Env E, MSCE, MSChE, MSECE, MSEM, MSIE, MSME, PhD. *Program availability:* Part-time. Terminal master's awarded for partial completion of doctoral program. *Degree requirements:* For master's, thesis (for some programs); for doctorate, comprehensive exam, thesis/dissertation. *Entrance requirements:* For master's and doctorate, GRE General Test. Additional exam requirements/recommendations for international students: required—TOEFL (minimum score 550 paper-based; 80 iBT), IELTS (minimum score 6.5). Electronic applications accepted.

University of Massachusetts Dartmouth, Graduate School, College of Engineering, Program in Engineering and Applied Science, North Dartmouth, MA 02747-2300. Offers engineering and applied science (PhD). *Program availability:* Part-time. *Degree requirements:* For doctorate, comprehensive exam, thesis/dissertation. *Entrance requirements:* For doctorate, GRE, statement of purpose (minimum of 300 words), resume, 3 letters of recommendation, official transcripts. Additional exam requirements/recommendations for international students: required—TOEFL (minimum score 550 paper-based; 79 iBT). Electronic applications accepted.

University of Massachusetts Lowell, Francis College of Engineering, Lowell, MA 01854. Offers MS, MS Eng, PhD. *Program availability:* Part-time, evening/weekend. Terminal master's awarded for partial completion of doctoral program. *Degree requirements:* For doctorate, thesis/dissertation. *Entrance requirements:* For master's and doctorate, GRE General Test.

University of Memphis, Graduate School, Herff College of Engineering, Memphis, TN 38152. Offers MS, PhD, Graduate Certificate. *Program availability:* Part-time. *Faculty:* 39 full-time (6 women), 5 part-time/adjunct (1 woman). *Students:* 99 full-time (26 women), 90 part-time (22 women); includes 31 minority (7 Black or African American, non-Hispanic/Latino; 1 American Indian or Alaska Native, non-Hispanic/Latino; 17 Asian, non-Hispanic/Latino; 5 Hispanic/Latino; 1 Two or more races, non-Hispanic/Latino), 98 international. Average age 30. 104 applicants, 75% accepted, 43 enrolled. In 2019, 27 master's, 7 doctorates, 3 other advanced degrees awarded. *Degree requirements:* For master's, comprehensive exam, thesis optional, 30-36 hours of course work, completion of course work within 6 years, continuous enrollment; for doctorate, comprehensive exam, thesis/dissertation, completion of degree within 12 years, residency, continuous enrollment. *Entrance requirements:* For master's and doctorate, GRE, MAT, GMAT, three letters of recommendation. Additional exam requirements/recommendations for international students: required—TOEFL (minimum score 550 paper-based; 79 iBT). *Application deadline:* For fall admission, 8/1 for domestic students, 5/1 for international students; for spring admission, 12/1 for domestic students, 9/15 for international students; for summer admission, 5/1 for domestic students. Application fee: $35 ($60 for international students). Electronic applications accepted. *Expenses: Tuition, area resident:* Full-time $9216; part-time $512 per credit hour. Tuition, state resident: full-time $9216; part-time $512 per credit hour. Tuition, nonresident: full-time $12,672; part-time $704 per credit hour. *International tuition:* $16,128 full-time. *Required fees:* $1530; $85 per credit hour. Tuition and fees vary according to program. *Financial support:* Fellowships with full tuition reimbursements, research assistantships with full tuition reimbursements, teaching assistantships with full tuition reimbursements, career-related internships or fieldwork, Federal Work-Study, scholarships/grants, tuition waivers (full and partial), and unspecified assistantships available. Financial award application deadline: 2/1; financial award applicants required to submit FAFSA. *Unit head:* Dr. Richard Joseph Sweigard, Dean, 901-678-4306, Fax: 901-678-4180, E-mail: rjswgard@memphis.edu. *Application contact:* Dr. Russell Deaton, Associate Dean of Academic Affairs and Administration, 901-678-2175, Fax: 901-678-5030, E-mail: rjdeaton@memphis.edu.
Website: https://www.memphis.edu/herff/

University of Miami, Graduate School, College of Engineering, Coral Gables, FL 33124. Offers MS, MSAE, MSBE, MSCE, MSECE, MSIE, MSME, MSOES, PhD, MBA/MSIE. *Program availability:* Part-time, evening/weekend. *Degree requirements:* For master's, thesis (for some programs); for doctorate, comprehensive exam, thesis/dissertation. *Entrance requirements:* For master's and doctorate, GRE General Test, minimum GPA of 3.0. Additional exam requirements/recommendations for international students: required—TOEFL (minimum score 550 paper-based; 59 iBT). Electronic applications accepted.

University of Michigan, College of Engineering, Ann Arbor, MI 48109. Offers M Eng, MS, MSE, D Eng, PhD, CE, Certificate, Ch E, Mar Eng, Nav Arch, Nuc E, M Arch/M Eng, M Arch/MSE, MBA/M Eng, MBA/MS, MBA/MSE, MSE/MS. *Program availability:* Part-time, 100% online, blended/hybrid learning. Electronic applications accepted. *Expenses:* Contact institution.

University of Michigan–Dearborn, College of Engineering and Computer Science, Dearborn, MI 48128. Offers MS, MSE, PhD, MBA/MSE. *Program availability:* Part-time, evening/weekend, 100% online. *Faculty:* 80 full-time (11 women), 42 part-time/adjunct (4 women). *Students:* 333 full-time (104 women), 1,007 part-time (229 women); includes 192 minority (46 Black or African American, non-Hispanic/Latino; 2 American Indian or Alaska Native, non-Hispanic/Latino; 90 Asian, non-Hispanic/Latino; 41 Hispanic/Latino; 13 Two or more races, non-Hispanic/Latino), 511 international. Average age 28. 1,700 applicants, 48% accepted, 328 enrolled. In 2019, 455 master's, 4 doctorates awarded. *Degree requirements:* For master's, thesis optional; for doctorate, comprehensive exam, thesis/dissertation. *Entrance requirements:* For doctorate, GRE. Additional exam requirements/recommendations for international students: required—TOEFL (minimum score 560 paper-based; 84 iBT), IELTS (minimum score 6.5). *Application deadline:* For fall admission, 8/1 priority date for domestic students, 5/1 priority date for international students; for winter admission, 12/1 priority date for domestic students, 9/1 priority date for international students; for spring admission, 4/1 priority date for domestic students, 1/1 priority date for international students. Applications are processed on a rolling basis. Application fee: $60. Electronic applications accepted. *Financial support:* In 2019–20, 327 students received support. Research assistantships with full tuition reimbursements available, teaching assistantships with full tuition reimbursements available, career-related internships or fieldwork, scholarships/grants, health care benefits, and non-residential student scholarships available. Support available to part-time students. Financial award application deadline: 3/1; financial award applicants required to submit FAFSA. *Unit head:* Dr. Anthony England, Dean, 313-593-5290, E-mail: cecsdeansoffice@umich.edu. *Application contact:* Office of Graduate Studies Staff, 313-583-6321, E-mail: umd-graduatestudies@umich.edu.
Website: http://umdearborn.edu/cecs/

University of Minnesota, Twin Cities Campus, College of Science and Engineering, Minneapolis, MN 55455. Offers M Ch E, M Geo E, M Mat SE, MA, MCE, MCS, MFM, MS, MS Ch E, MS Mat SE, MSEE, MSME, MSMOT, MSSE, MSST, PhD, Certificate, MD/PhD. *Program availability:* Part-time, evening/weekend, 100% online, blended/hybrid learning. Terminal master's awarded for partial completion of doctoral program. *Degree requirements:* For master's, thesis (for some programs); for doctorate, thesis/dissertation. *Entrance requirements:* Additional exam requirements/recommendations for international students: required—TOEFL (minimum score 550 paper-based; 79 iBT). Electronic applications accepted.

University of Mississippi, Graduate School, School of Engineering, University, MS 38677. Offers aeroacoustics (MS, PhD); chemical engineering (MS, PhD); civil engineering (MS, PhD); computational hydroscience (MS, PhD); computer science (MS, PhD); electrical engineering (MS, PhD); electromagnetics (MS, PhD); environmental engineering (MS, PhD); geology and geological engineering (MS, PhD); hydrology (MS); material science (MS); mechanical engineering (MS, PhD); telecommunications (MS). *Students:* 104 full-time (23 women), 19 part-time (5 women); includes 10 minority (3 Black or African American, non-Hispanic/Latino; 6 Asian, non-Hispanic/Latino; 1 Hispanic/Latino), 72 international. Average age 30. In 2019, 36 master's, 17 doctorates awarded. *Expenses:* Tuition, state resident: full-time $8718; part-time $484.25 per credit hour. Tuition, nonresident: full-time $24,990; part-time $1388.25 per credit hour. *Required fees:* $100; $4.16 per credit hour. *Unit head:* Dr. David Puleo, Dean, 662-915-5780, Fax: 662-915-5387, E-mail: engineer@olemiss.edu. *Application contact:* Temeka Smith, Graduate Activities Specialist for Admissions, 662-915-7474, Fax: 662-915-7577, E-mail: gschool@olemiss.edu.

University of Missouri, Office of Research and Graduate Studies, College of Engineering, Columbia, MO 65211. Offers ME, MS, MSCE, MSEE, PhD, Certificate, MS/MHA. *Program availability:* Part-time. *Entrance requirements:* For master's and doctorate, GRE General Test. Additional exam requirements/recommendations for international students: required—TOEFL, IELTS.

University of Missouri–Kansas City, School of Computing and Engineering, Kansas City, MO 64110-2499. Offers civil engineering (MS); computer and electrical engineering (PhD); computer science (MS), including bioinformatics, software engineering, telecommunications networking; computer science and informatics (PhD); computing (PhD); electrical engineering (MS); engineering (PhD); engineering and construction management (Graduate Certificate); mechanical engineering (MS); telecommunications and computer networking (PhD). *Program availability:* Part-time. *Degree requirements:* For doctorate, thesis/dissertation. *Entrance requirements:* For master's, GRE General Test, minimum GPA of 3.0, 3 letters of recommendation from professors; for doctorate, GRE General Test, minimum GPA of 3.5. Additional exam requirements/recommendations for international students: required—TOEFL (minimum score 550 paper-based; 80 iBT).

University of Nebraska–Lincoln, Graduate College, College of Engineering, Lincoln, NE 68588. Offers M Eng, MAE, MEE, MS, PhD. *Degree requirements:* For doctorate, comprehensive exam, thesis/dissertation. *Entrance requirements:* For master's and doctorate, GRE General Test. Additional exam requirements/recommendations for international students: required—TOEFL. Electronic applications accepted.

University of Nevada, Las Vegas, Graduate College, Howard R. Hughes College of Engineering, Las Vegas, NV 89154-4005. Offers civil & environmental engineering and construction, computer science, electrical and computer engineering, mechanical engineering (PhD); MS/MS; MS/PhD. *Program availability:* Part-time. *Faculty:* 66 full-time (10 women), 4 part-time/adjunct (1 woman). *Students:* 166 full-time (48 women), 91 part-time (21 women); includes 72 minority (9 Black or African American, non-Hispanic/Latino; 1 American Indian or Alaska Native, non-Hispanic/Latino; 21 Asian, non-Hispanic/Latino; 30 Hispanic/Latino; 11 Two or more races, non-Hispanic/Latino), 111 international. Average age 30. 182 applicants, 75% accepted, 64 enrolled. In 2019, 65 master's, 12 doctorates, 1 other advanced degree awarded. *Degree requirements:* For master's, comprehensive exam (for some programs), thesis (for some programs); for doctorate, comprehensive exam, thesis/dissertation. *Entrance requirements:* For master's, GRE General Test; for doctorate, GRE General Test, 3 letters of recommendation; statement of purpose. Additional exam requirements/recommendations for international students: required—TOEFL (minimum score 550 paper-based; 80 iBT), IELTS (minimum score 7). Application fee: $60 ($95 for international students). Electronic applications accepted. *Expenses:* Contact institution.

Financial support: In 2019–20, 153 students received support, including 3 fellowships with full tuition reimbursements available (averaging $21,667 per year), 52 research assistantships with full tuition reimbursements available (averaging $16,202 per year), 98 teaching assistantships with full tuition reimbursements available (averaging $16,903 per year); institutionally sponsored loans, scholarships/grants, health care benefits, and unspecified assistantships also available. Financial award application deadline: 3/15; financial award applicants required to submit FAFSA. *Unit head:* Dr. Rama Venkat, Dean, 702-895-3699, Fax: 702-895-4059, E-mail: engineering.dean@unlv.edu. *Application contact:* Dr. Rama Venkat, Dean, 702-895-3699, Fax: 702-895-4059, E-mail: engineering.dean@unlv.edu.
Website: http://engineering.unlv.edu/

University of Nevada, Reno, Graduate School, College of Engineering, Reno, NV 89557. Offers MS, PhD. Terminal master's awarded for partial completion of doctoral program. *Degree requirements:* For master's, thesis optional; for doctorate, thesis/dissertation. *Entrance requirements:* For master's, GRE General Test, minimum GPA of 2.75; for doctorate, GRE General Test, minimum GPA of 3.0. Additional exam requirements/recommendations for international students: required—TOEFL (minimum score 500 paper-based; 61 iBT), IELTS (minimum score 6). Electronic applications accepted.

University of New Brunswick Fredericton, School of Graduate Studies, Faculty of Engineering, Fredericton, NB E3B 5A3, Canada. Offers M Eng, M Sc E, PhD, Certificate. *Program availability:* Part-time. *Faculty:* 76 full-time (10 women). *Students:* 222 full-time (50 women), 36 part-time (6 women), 136 international. Average age 29. In 2019, 54 master's, 9 doctorates awarded. *Degree requirements:* For master's, thesis; for doctorate, comprehensive exam, thesis/dissertation, qualifying exam. *Entrance requirements:* For master's, minimum GPA of 3.0. Additional exam requirements/recommendations for international students: required—TOEFL, TWE. *Application deadline:* For fall admission, 3/1 priority date for domestic students. Applications are processed on a rolling basis. Application fee: $50 Canadian dollars. Electronic applications accepted. *Expenses: Tuition, area resident:* Full-time $6975 Canadian dollars; part-time $3423 Canadian dollars per year. Tuition, state resident: full-time $6975 Canadian dollars; part-time $3423 Canadian dollars per year. Tuition, Canadian resident: full-time $6975 Canadian dollars; part-time $3423 Canadian dollars per year. *International tuition:* $12,435 Canadian dollars full-time. *Required fees:* $92.25 Canadian dollars per term. Full-time tuition and fees vary according to degree level, campus/location, program, reciprocity agreements and student level. *Financial support:* Fellowships, research assistantships, teaching assistantships, and career-related internships or fieldwork available. Financial award application deadline: 1/15. *Unit head:* Dr. Chris Diduch, Dean, 506-453-4570, Fax: 506-453-5003, E-mail: diduch@unb.ca. *Application contact:* Dr. Chris Diduch, Dean, 506-453-4570, Fax: 506-453-5003, E-mail: diduch@unb.ca.
Website: http://www.unbf.ca/eng/

University of New Haven, Graduate School, Tagliatela College of Engineering, West Haven, CT 06516. Offers MS, MSIE, Graduate Certificate, MBA/MSIE. *Program availability:* Part-time, evening/weekend. *Students:* 463 full-time (129 women), 143 part-time (41 women); includes 50 minority (16 Black or African American, non-Hispanic/Latino; 1 American Indian or Alaska Native, non-Hispanic/Latino; 22 Asian, non-Hispanic/Latino; 10 Hispanic/Latino; 1 Two or more races, non-Hispanic/Latino), 445 international. Average age 26. 1,825 applicants, 72% accepted, 188 enrolled. In 2019, 213 master's, 1 other advanced degree awarded. *Entrance requirements:* Additional exam requirements/recommendations for international students: required—TOEFL (minimum score 75 iBT), IELTS, PTE (minimum score 50). *Application deadline:* Applications are processed on a rolling basis. Application fee: $50. Electronic applications accepted. Application fee is waived when completed online. *Financial support:* Research assistantships with partial tuition reimbursements, teaching assistantships with partial tuition reimbursements, Federal Work-Study, scholarships/grants, and unspecified assistantships available. Support available to part-time students. Financial award applicants required to submit FAFSA. *Unit head:* Dr. Ronald Harichandran, Dean and Vice Provost for Research, 203-932-7167, E-mail: rharichandran@newhaven.edu. *Application contact:* Selina O'Toole, Senior Associate Director of Graduate Admissions, 203-932-7337, E-mail: SOToole@newhaven.edu.
Website: http://www.newhaven.edu/engineering/

University of New Mexico, Graduate Studies, School of Engineering, Albuquerque, NM 87131. Offers M Eng, MCM, MEME, MS, MSCE, PhD, MBA/MEME. *Program availability:* Part-time, 100% online, blended/hybrid learning. *Faculty:* 94 full-time (18 women), 42 part-time/adjunct (7 women). *Students:* 746 full-time (170 women); includes 211 minority (16 Black or African American, non-Hispanic/Latino; 8 American Indian or Alaska Native, non-Hispanic/Latino; 31 Asian, non-Hispanic/Latino; 142 Hispanic/Latino; 1 Native Hawaiian or other Pacific Islander, non-Hispanic/Latino; 13 Two or more races, non-Hispanic/Latino), 241 international. Average age 32. 559 applicants, 60% accepted, 178 enrolled. In 2019, 211 master's, 56 doctorates awarded. Terminal master's awarded for partial completion of doctoral program. *Degree requirements:* For master's, comprehensive exam (for some programs), thesis or alternative; for doctorate, comprehensive exam, thesis/dissertation. *Entrance requirements:* For master's, GRE, GMAT, letters of recommendation; letter of intent; for doctorate, GRE, letters of recommendation; letter of intent. Additional exam requirements/recommendations for international students: required—TOEFL (minimum score 550 paper-based; 79 iBT), IELTS, PTE, Official English language proficiency results from either the TOEFL, IELTS, PTE-Academic, or Cambridge CPE or CAE. *Application deadline:* For fall admission, 1/15 priority date for domestic and international students; for spring admission, 7/14 priority date for domestic and international students. Applications are processed on a rolling basis. Application fee: $50 ($70 for international students). Electronic applications accepted. *Expenses:* $421/cr resident; $1102/cr non-resident; $72/cr mandatory fees; $100/cr differential tuition. *Financial support:* In 2019–20, 7 fellowships with full and partial tuition reimbursements (averaging $25,715 per year), 280 research assistantships with full and partial tuition reimbursements (averaging $27,408 per year), 62 teaching assistantships with full and partial tuition reimbursements (averaging $24,945 per year) were awarded; career-related internships or fieldwork, Federal Work-Study, scholarships/grants, health care benefits, tuition waivers (full and partial), and unspecified assistantships also available. Financial award application deadline: 3/1; financial award applicants required to submit FAFSA. *Unit head:* Christos Christodoulou, Dean, 505-277-5522, Fax: 505-277-1422, E-mail: christos@unm.edu. *Application contact:* Prof. Charles Fleddermann, Associate Dean for Academic Affairs and Community Engagement, 505-277-5522, Fax: 505-277-1422, E-mail: cbf@unm.edu.
Website: http://engineering.unm.edu/

University of New Orleans, Graduate School, College of Engineering, New Orleans, LA 70148. Offers MS, PhD. *Program availability:* Part-time. Terminal master's awarded for partial completion of doctoral program. *Degree requirements:* For master's, comprehensive exam, thesis optional; for doctorate, comprehensive exam, thesis/dissertation. *Entrance requirements:* For master's, GRE General Test, minimum GPA of 3.0; for doctorate, GRE General Test. Additional exam requirements/recommendations for international students: required—TOEFL (minimum score 550 paper-based; 79 iBT). Electronic applications accepted.

The University of North Carolina at Charlotte, William States Lee College of Engineering, Charlotte, NC 28223-0001. Offers applied energy and electromechanical systems engineering (Graduate Certificate); civil engineering (MSCE), including environmental and water resources, geo-environmental, geo-technical, structural, and transportation; construction and facilities management (MS); electrical engineering (MSEE); engineering (MSE); engineering management (MSEM), including energy analytics, lean logistics/supply chains, systems analytics; mechanical engineering (MSME), including metrology & manufacturing, thermal science & fluid mechanics, solid mechanics & materials science, motorsports engineering, dynamics &. *Program availability:* Part-time, evening/weekend, blended/hybrid learning. *Faculty:* 122 full-time (22 women), 8 part-time/adjunct (2 women). *Students:* 335 full-time (83 women), 181 part-time (31 women); includes 56 minority (16 Black or African American, non-Hispanic/Latino; 3 American Indian or Alaska Native, non-Hispanic/Latino; 16 Asian, non-Hispanic/Latino; 16 Hispanic/Latino; 5 Two or more races, non-Hispanic/Latino), 308 international. Average age 28. 619 applicants, 69% accepted, 126 enrolled. In 2019, 209 master's, 39 doctorates, 5 other advanced degrees awarded. Terminal master's awarded for partial completion of doctoral program. *Degree requirements:* For master's, thesis (for some programs); for doctorate, comprehensive exam, thesis/dissertation. *Entrance requirements:* For master's, GRE, bachelor's degree, or its U.S. equivalent, from regionally-accredited college or university; minimum overall GPA of 3.0 on all previous work beyond high school; statement of purpose (essay); at least three recommendation forms; for doctorate, GRE, bachelor's degree (or its U.S. equivalent) from regionally-accredited college or university; minimum overall GPA of 3.5 in master's degree program; letters of recommendation; statement of purpose; for Graduate Certificate, bachelor's degree from regionally-accredited university; minimum GPA of 2.75 on all post-secondary work attempted; transcripts; personal statement outlining why the applicant seeks admission to the program. Additional exam requirements/recommendations for international students: required—TOEFL (minimum score 557 paper-based; 83 iBT), IELTS (minimum score 6.5), TOEFL (minimum score 557 paper-based, 83 iBT) or IELTS (6.5). *Application deadline:* Applications are processed on a rolling basis. Application fee: $75. Electronic applications accepted. *Expenses:* Contact institution. *Financial support:* In 2019–20, 251 students received support, including 7 fellowships (averaging $46,500 per year), 136 research assistantships (averaging $9,241 per year), 106 teaching assistantships (averaging $9,072 per year); career-related internships or fieldwork, institutionally sponsored loans, scholarships/grants, and unspecified assistantships also available. Support available to part-time students. Financial award application deadline: 3/1; financial award applicants required to submit FAFSA. *Unit head:* Dr. Ronald E. Smelser, Interim Dean, 704-687-8244, E-mail: rsmelser@uncc.edu. *Application contact:* Kathy B. Giddings, Director of Graduate Admissions, 704-687-5503, Fax: 704-687-1668, E-mail: gradadm@uncc.edu.
Website: http://engr.uncc.edu/

University of North Dakota, Graduate School, School of Engineering and Mines, Program in Engineering, Grand Forks, ND 58202. Offers PhD. *Degree requirements:* For doctorate, comprehensive exam, thesis/dissertation, final exam. *Entrance requirements:* For doctorate, minimum GPA of 3.0. Additional exam requirements/recommendations for international students: required—TOEFL (minimum score 550 paper-based; 79 iBT), IELTS (minimum score 6.5). Electronic applications accepted.

University of North Texas, Toulouse Graduate School, Denton, TX 76203-5459. Offers accounting (MS); applied anthropology (MA, MS); applied behavior analysis (Certificate); applied geography (MA); applied technology and performance improvement (M Ed, MS); art education (MA); art history (MA); arts leadership (Certificate); audiology (Au D); behavior analysis (MS); behavioral science (PhD); biochemistry and molecular biology (MS); biology (MA, MS); biomedical engineering (MS); business analysis (MS); chemistry (MS); clinical health psychology (PhD); communication studies (MA, MS); computer engineering (MS); computer science (MS); counseling (M Ed, MS), including clinical mental health counseling (MS), college and university counseling, elementary school counseling, secondary school counseling; creative writing (MA); criminal justice (MS); curriculum and instruction (M Ed); decision sciences (MBA); design (MA, MFA), including fashion design (MFA), innovation studies, interior design (MFA); early childhood studies (MS); economics (MS); educational leadership (M Ed, Ed D); educational psychology (MS, PhD), including family studies (MS), gifted and talented (MS), human development (MS), learning and cognition (MS), research, measurement and evaluation (MS); electrical engineering (MS); emergency management (MPA); engineering technology (MS); English (MA); English as a second language (MA); environmental science (MS); finance (MBA, MS); financial management (MPA); French (MA); health services management (MBA); higher education (M Ed, Ed D); history (MA, MS); hospitality management (MS); human resources management (MPA); information science (MS); information systems (PhD); information technologies (MBA); interdisciplinary studies (MA, MS); international studies (MA); international sustainable tourism (MS); jazz studies (MM); journalism (MA, MJ, Graduate Certificate), including interactive and virtual digital communication (Graduate Certificate), narrative journalism (Graduate Certificate), public relations (Graduate Certificate); kinesiology (MS); linguistics (MA); local government management (MPA); logistics (PhD); logistics and supply chain management (MBA); long-term care, senior housing, and aging services (MA); management (PhD); marketing (MBA); mathematics (MA, MS); mechanical and energy engineering (MS, PhD); music (MA), including ethnomusicology, music theory, musicology, performance; music composition (PhD); music education (MM Ed, PhD); nonprofit management (MPA); operations and supply chain management (MBA); performance (MM, DMA); philosophy (MA); political science (MA); professional and technical communication (MA); radio, television and film (MA, MFA); rehabilitation counseling (Certificate); sociology (MA); Spanish (MA); special education (M Ed); speech-language pathology (MA); strategic management (MBA); studio art (MFA); teaching (M Ed); MBA/MS. *Program availability:* Part-time, evening/weekend, online learning. Terminal master's awarded for partial completion of doctoral program. *Degree requirements:* For master's, variable foreign language requirement, comprehensive exam (for some programs), thesis (for some programs); for doctorate, variable foreign language requirement, comprehensive exam (for some programs), thesis/dissertation; for other advanced degree, variable foreign language requirement, comprehensive exam (for some programs). *Entrance requirements:* For master's and doctorate, GRE, GMAT. Additional exam requirements/recommendations for international students: required—TOEFL (minimum score 550 paper-based; 79 iBT). Electronic applications accepted.

University of Notre Dame, The Graduate School, College of Engineering, Notre Dame, IN 46556. Offers M Eng, MEME, MS, MS Aero E, MS Bio E, MS Ch E, MS Env E, MSCE, MSCSE, MSEE, MSME, PhD. Terminal master's awarded for partial completion of doctoral program. *Degree requirements:* For master's, comprehensive exam; for doctorate, thesis/dissertation. *Entrance requirements:* For master's and doctorate, GRE General Test. Additional exam requirements/recommendations for international students: required—TOEFL. Electronic applications accepted.

University of Ottawa, Faculty of Graduate and Postdoctoral Studies, Faculty of Engineering, Ottawa, ON K1N 6N5, Canada. Offers M Eng, MA Sc, MCS, PhD, Certificate. *Degree requirements:* For master's, thesis or alternative; for doctorate, thesis/dissertation. *Entrance requirements:* For master's, honors degree or equivalent, minimum B average. Electronic applications accepted.

Engineering and Applied Sciences—General

University of Pennsylvania, School of Engineering and Applied Science, Philadelphia, PA 19104. Offers MBT, MCIT, MIPD, MSE, PhD, MSE/MBA, PhD/MD, VMD/PhD. *Program availability:* Part-time. *Faculty:* 124 full-time (22 women), 27 part-time/adjunct (4 women). *Students:* 1,630 full-time (556 women), 593 part-time (229 women); includes 456 minority (40 Black or African American, non-Hispanic/Latino; 1 American Indian or Alaska Native, non-Hispanic/Latino; 298 Asian, non-Hispanic/Latino; 77 Hispanic/Latino; 40 Two or more races, non-Hispanic/Latino), 1,216 international. Average age 25. 10,541 applicants, 23% accepted, 1,062 enrolled. In 2019, 661 master's, 65 doctorates awarded. Terminal master's awarded for partial completion of doctoral program. *Degree requirements:* For master's, comprehensive exam, thesis optional; for doctorate, comprehensive exam, thesis/dissertation. *Entrance requirements:* For master's and doctorate, GRE, bachelor's degree, letters of recommendation, resume, personal statement. Additional exam requirements/recommendations for international students: required—TOEFL (minimum score 100 iBT), IELTS (minimum score 7). *Application deadline:* For fall admission, 12/15 for domestic and international students. Application fee: $80. Electronic applications accepted. *Expenses:* Contact institution. *Unit head:* Vijay Kumar, Dean, E-mail: seasdean@seas.upenn.edu. *Application contact:* Associate director of Graduate Admissions, 215- 898-4542, Fax: 215- 573-5577, E-mail: admissions1@seas.upenn.edu.
Website: http://www.seas.upenn.edu

University of Pittsburgh, Katz Graduate School of Business, MBA/Master of Science in Engineering Joint Degree Program, Pittsburgh, PA 15260. Offers MBA/MSE. *Accreditation:* AACSB. *Program availability:* Part-time, evening/weekend. *Faculty:* 95 full-time (30 women), 30 part-time/adjunct (10 women). *Students:* 8 full-time (2 women), 6 part-time (1 woman); includes 4 minority (1 Asian, non-Hispanic/Latino; 3 Hispanic/Latino), 1 international. Average age 28. 18 applicants, 61% accepted, 5 enrolled. *Entrance requirements:* Additional exam requirements/recommendations for international students: required—TOEFL (minimum score 100 iBT). *Application deadline:* For fall admission, 4/1 priority date for domestic students, 2/1 priority date for international students. Application fee: $50. Electronic applications accepted. *Financial support:* Research assistantships, teaching assistantships, Federal Work-Study, scholarships/grants, health care benefits, and unspecified assistantships available. Financial award application deadline: 6/1; financial award applicants required to submit FAFSA. *Unit head:* Dr. Arjang A. Assad, Dean, 412-648-1552, Fax: 412-648-1552, E-mail: aassad@katz.pitt.edu. *Application contact:* Thomas Keller, Director of Admissions, 412-648-1700, Fax: 412-648-1659, E-mail: admissions@katz.pitt.edu.
Website: https://www.katz.business.pitt.edu/mba/joint-and-dual/engineering#section-1

University of Pittsburgh, Swanson School of Engineering, Pittsburgh, PA 15260. Offers MS, MS Ch E, MSBENG, MSCEE, MSIE, MSME, MSNE, MSPE, PhD, MD/PhD, MS Ch E/MSPE. *Program availability:* Part-time. Terminal master's awarded for partial completion of doctoral program. *Degree requirements:* For doctorate, comprehensive exam, thesis/dissertation, final oral exams. *Entrance requirements:* For master's and doctorate, minimum GPA of 3.0. Additional exam requirements/recommendations for international students: required—TOEFL (minimum score 550 paper-based; 80 iBT). Electronic applications accepted. *Expenses:* Contact institution.

University of Portland, Shiley School of Engineering, Portland, OR 97203-5798. Offers biomedical engineering (MBME); civil engineering (ME); computer science (ME); electrical engineering (ME); mechanical engineering (ME). *Program availability:* Part-time, evening/weekend. *Degree requirements:* For master's, thesis optional. *Entrance requirements:* For master's, GRE General Test, minimum GPA of 3.0, 2 letters of recommendation, resume, statement of goals, official transcripts. Additional exam requirements/recommendations for international students: required—TOEFL (minimum score 80 iBT), IELTS (minimum score 7). Electronic applications accepted. *Expenses:* Contact institution.

University of Puerto Rico at Mayagüez, Graduate Studies, College of Engineering, Mayagüez, PR 00681-9000. Offers ME, MS, PhD. *Program availability:* Part-time. *Degree requirements:* For master's, one foreign language, comprehensive exam, thesis. Electronic applications accepted.

University of Regina, Faculty of Graduate Studies and Research, Faculty of Engineering and Applied Science, Regina, SK S4S 0A2, Canada. Offers electronic systems engineering (M Eng, MA Sc, PhD), including electronic systems; environmental systems engineering (M Eng, MA Sc, PhD), including environmental systems; industrial systems engineering (M Eng, MA Sc, PhD), including industrial systems; petroleum systems engineering (M Eng, MA Sc, PhD), including petroleum systems; process systems engineering (M Eng, MA Sc, PhD), including process systems; software systems engineering (M Eng, MA Sc, PhD), including software systems. *Program availability:* Part-time. *Faculty:* 47 full-time (6 women), 21 part-time/adjunct (2 women). *Students:* 262 full-time (70 women), 42 part-time (13 women). Average age 30. 689 applicants, 14% accepted. In 2019, 80 master's, 12 doctorates awarded. *Degree requirements:* For master's, thesis, project report, course work, co-op workplacement; for doctorate, comprehensive exam, thesis/dissertation. *Entrance requirements:* For master's, 4 years bachelor degree, at least 70 percent from a four-year baccalaureate degree (or equivalent). Additional exam requirements/recommendations for international students: required—TOEFL (minimum score 550 paper-based; 80 iBT), IELTS (minimum score 6.5), PTE (minimum score 59), Other options are MELAB, CANTEST, CAEL and Uof R ESL. *Application deadline:* For fall admission, 1/31 for domestic and international students; for winter admission, 7/31 for domestic and international students. Applications are processed on a rolling basis. Application fee: $100. Electronic applications accepted. *Expenses:* 11,036.50 -This amount is based on three semesters tuition, registered in 6 credit hours per semester. Plus one year student fees and books. There is additional 438.75 if student is in Co-op route. *Financial support:* In 2019–20, 318 students received support, including 180 fellowships with tuition reimbursements available, 70 teaching assistantships (averaging $2,552 per year); research assistantships, career-related internships or fieldwork, Federal Work-Study, scholarships/grants, traineeships, unspecified assistantships, and Graduate scholarship base funds, SIES and other donor funded schols also available. Support available to part-time students. Financial award application deadline: 9/30. *Unit head:* Dr. Amr Henni, Acting Dean, 306-585-4960, Fax: 306-585-4556, E-mail: Amr.Henni@uregina.ca. *Application contact:* Colleen Walsh, Graduate and Co-operative Education Coordinator, 306-585-5416, Fax: 306-585-4556, E-mail: engg@uregina.ca.
Website: http://www.uregina.ca/engineering/

University of Rhode Island, Graduate School, College of Engineering, Kingston, RI 02881. Offers MS, PhD, Graduate Certificate, Postbaccalaureate Certificate. *Program availability:* Part-time. *Faculty:* 67 full-time (14 women), 1 part-time/adjunct (0 women). *Students:* 127 full-time (32 women), 81 part-time (16 women); includes 21 minority (6 Black or African American, non-Hispanic/Latino; 1 American Indian or Alaska Native, non-Hispanic/Latino; 6 Asian, non-Hispanic/Latino; 5 Hispanic/Latino; 3 Two or more races, non-Hispanic/Latino), 76 international. 144 applicants, 71% accepted, 62 enrolled. In 2019, 79 master's, 16 doctorates, 2 other advanced degrees awarded. *Entrance requirements:* Additional exam requirements/recommendations for international students: required—TOEFL. Application fee: $65. Electronic applications accepted. *Expenses: Tuition, area resident:* Full-time $13,734; part-time $763 per credit. Tuition, state resident: full-time $13,734; part-time $763 per credit. Tuition, nonresident: full-time $26,512; part-time $1473 per credit. *International tuition:* $26,512 full-time. *Required fees:* $1780; $52 per credit. $35 per term. One-time fee: $165. *Financial support:* In 2019–20, 50 research assistantships with full tuition reimbursements (averaging $9,726 per year), 31 teaching assistantships with full tuition reimbursements (averaging $10,292 per year) were awarded. Financial award applicants required to submit FAFSA. *Unit head:* Dr. Raymond Wright, Dean, 401-874-2186, Fax: 401-782-1066, E-mail: dean@egr.uri.edu. *Application contact:* Dr. Raymond Wright, Dean, 401-874-2186, Fax: 401-782-1066, E-mail: dean@egr.uri.edu.
Website: http://www.egr.uri.edu/

University of Rochester, Hajim School of Engineering and Applied Sciences, Rochester, NY 14627. Offers MS, PhD. *Faculty:* 98 full-time (16 women). *Students:* 624 full-time (158 women), 14 part-time (4 women); includes 66 minority (14 Black or African American, non-Hispanic/Latino; 1 American Indian or Alaska Native, non-Hispanic/Latino; 26 Asian, non-Hispanic/Latino; 16 Hispanic/Latino; 9 Two or more races, non-Hispanic/Latino), 396 international. Average age 26. 2,368 applicants, 37% accepted, 216 enrolled. In 2019, 202 master's, 36 doctorates awarded. Terminal master's awarded for partial completion of doctoral program. *Degree requirements:* For master's, comprehensive exam (for some programs), thesis (for some programs); for doctorate, comprehensive exam (for some programs), thesis/dissertation. *Entrance requirements:* For master's, personal statement, three letters of recommendation, transcripts; for doctorate, GRE, personal statement, three letters of recommendation, transcripts. Additional exam requirements/recommendations for international students: required—TOEFL. Application fee: $60. Electronic applications accepted. *Financial support:* Fellowships, research assistantships, teaching assistantships, career-related internships or fieldwork, scholarships/grants, traineeships, health care benefits, tuition waivers, and unspecified assistantships available. Support available to part-time students. *Unit head:* Dr. Wendi Heinzelman, Dean, Hajim School of Engineering and Applied Sciences/Professor of Electrical and Computer Engineering, 585-273-3958, E-mail: wendi.heinzelman@rochester.edu. *Application contact:* Gretchen Briscoe, Assistant Dean of Graduate Education and Postdoctoral Affairs, AS&E, 585-275-2059, E-mail: gretchen.briscoe@rochester.edu.
Website: https://www.hajim.rochester.edu/

University of St. Thomas, School of Engineering, St. Paul, MN 55105. Offers data science (MS); electrical engineering (MS); information technology (MS); manufacturing engineering (MS); manufacturing systems (Certificate); mechanical engineering (MS); medical device development (Certificate); regulatory science (MS); software engineering (MS); software management (MS); systems engineering (MS); technology leadership (Certificate); technology management (MS). *Program availability:* Part-time, evening/weekend. *Entrance requirements:* For master's, resume, official transcripts. Additional exam requirements/recommendations for international students: required—TOEFL (minimum score 80 iBT), IELTS (minimum score 6.5). Electronic applications accepted. *Expenses:* Contact institution.

University of Saskatchewan, College of Graduate and Postdoctoral Studies, College of Engineering, Saskatoon, SK S7N 5E5, Canada. Offers M Eng, M Sc, PhD, PGD. *Program availability:* Part-time. *Degree requirements:* For master's, 30 credits (for M Eng); thesis and 12 credits (for MS); for doctorate, comprehensive exam, thesis/dissertation, qualifying exam, 18 credits. *Entrance requirements:* For master's and doctorate, GRE. Additional exam requirements/recommendations for international students: required—TOEFL (minimum iBT score of 80), IELTS (6.5), CanTEST (4.5), or PTE (59). Electronic applications accepted.

University of South Africa, College of Science, Engineering and Technology, Pretoria, South Africa. Offers chemical engineering (M Tech); information technology (M Tech).

University of South Alabama, College of Engineering, Mobile, AL 36688-0002. Offers MS Ch E, MSCE, MSEE, MSME, D Sc. *Program availability:* Part-time. *Faculty:* 20 full-time (2 women), 1 part-time/adjunct (0 women). *Students:* 48 full-time (14 women), 29 part-time (6 women); includes 11 minority (4 Black or African American, non-Hispanic/Latino; 3 Asian, non-Hispanic/Latino; 3 Hispanic/Latino; 1 Two or more races, non-Hispanic/Latino), 18 international. Average age 30. 62 applicants, 79% accepted, 27 enrolled. In 2019, 24 master's, 4 doctorates awarded. *Degree requirements:* For master's, comprehensive exam, thesis optional; for doctorate, comprehensive exam, thesis/dissertation. *Entrance requirements:* For master's and doctorate, GRE. Additional exam requirements/recommendations for international students: required—TOEFL (minimum score 550 paper-based; 79 iBT), IELTS (minimum score 6.5). *Application deadline:* For fall admission, 7/1 priority date for domestic students, 6/15 priority date for international students; for spring admission, 12/1 priority date for domestic students, 11/1 priority date for international students; for summer admission, 5/1 priority date for domestic students, 4/1 priority date for international students. Applications are processed on a rolling basis. Application fee: $35. Electronic applications accepted. *Expenses:* Contact institution. *Financial support:* Fellowships, research assistantships, teaching assistantships, career-related internships or fieldwork, Federal Work-Study, institutionally sponsored loans, scholarships/grants, and unspecified assistantships available. Support available to part-time students. Financial award application deadline: 3/31; financial award applicants required to submit FAFSA. *Unit head:* Dr. John Usher, Dean, College of Engineering, 251-460-6140, Fax: 251-460-6343, E-mail: engineering@southalabama.edu. *Application contact:* Brenda Poole, Academic Records Specialist, 251-460-6140, Fax: 251-460-6343, E-mail: engineering@southalabama.edu.
Website: https://www.southalabama.edu/colleges/engineering/

University of South Carolina, The Graduate School, College of Engineering and Computing, Columbia, SC 29208. Offers ME, MS, PhD. *Program availability:* Part-time, evening/weekend, online learning. *Degree requirements:* For master's, thesis (for some programs); for doctorate, thesis/dissertation. *Entrance requirements:* For master's and doctorate, GRE General Test. Additional exam requirements/recommendations for international students: required—TOEFL. Electronic applications accepted.

University of Southern California, Graduate School, Viterbi School of Engineering, Los Angeles, CA 90089. Offers MCM, ME, MS, PhD, Engr, Graduate Certificate, MS/MBA. *Program availability:* Part-time, online learning. Terminal master's awarded for partial completion of doctoral program. *Degree requirements:* For doctorate, comprehensive exam, thesis/dissertation. *Entrance requirements:* For master's and doctorate, GRE. Additional exam requirements/recommendations for international students: recommended—TOEFL. Electronic applications accepted. *Expenses:* Contact institution.

University of Southern Indiana, Graduate Studies, Pott College of Science, Engineering, and Education, Evansville, IN 47712-3590. Offers MSE, MSIM, MSSM, Ed D. *Program availability:* Part-time, evening/weekend. *Degree requirements:* For master's, project. *Entrance requirements:* For master's, GRE General Test, NTE, PRAXIS I, minimum GPA of 2.5 and BS in engineering or engineering technology (MSIM); minimum GPA of 3.0 and teaching license (MSE). Additional exam requirements/recommendations for international students: required—TOEFL (minimum score 550 paper-based; 79 iBT), IELTS (minimum score 6). Electronic applications accepted.

University of South Florida, College of Engineering, Tampa, FL 33620-9951. Offers MCE, MEVE, MSBE, MSCE, MSCH, MSCP, MSCS, MSEE, MSEM, MSEV, MSIE,

MSIT, MSME, MSMSE, PhD, Graduate Certificate, MSBE/MS. *Program availability:* Part-time, evening/weekend. *Faculty:* 136 full-time (22 women), 1 part-time/adjunct (0 women). *Students:* 842 full-time (237 women), 256 part-time (55 women); includes 156 minority (37 Black or African American, non-Hispanic/Latino; 36 Asian, non-Hispanic/Latino; 72 Hispanic/Latino; 11 Two or more races, non-Hispanic/Latino), 759 international. Average age 27. 1,915 applicants, 44% accepted, 277 enrolled. In 2019, 454 master's, 62 doctorates awarded. Terminal master's awarded for partial completion of doctoral program. *Degree requirements:* For master's, comprehensive exam, thesis (for some programs); for doctorate, comprehensive exam, thesis/dissertation. *Entrance requirements:* For master's, GRE General Test, minimum GPA of 3.0 in last 60 hours of coursework; for doctorate, GRE General Test, minimum GPA of 3.3 in last 60 hours of coursework. Additional exam requirements/recommendations for international students: required—TOEFL (minimum score 550 paper-based; 79 iBT), IELTS (minimum score 6.5). *Application deadline:* For fall admission, 2/15 for domestic students, 1/2 priority date for international students; for spring admission, 10/15 for domestic students, 6/1 priority date for international students. Applications are processed on a rolling basis. Application fee: $30. Electronic applications accepted. *Financial support:* In 2019–20, 169 students received support. Career-related internships or fieldwork, Federal Work-Study, scholarships/grants, health care benefits, and unspecified assistantships available. Financial award application deadline: 3/1. *Unit head:* Dr. Robert Bishop, Dean, 813-974-3864, Fax: 813-974-5094, E-mail: robertbishop@usf.edu. *Application contact:* Dr. Sanjukta Bhanja, Associate Dean for Academic Affairs, 813-974-4755, Fax: 813-974-5094, E-mail: bhanja@usf.edu.
Website: http://www2.eng.usf.edu/

The University of Tennessee, Graduate School, Tickle College of Engineering, Knoxville, TN 37996. Offers MS, PhD, MS/MBA, MS/PhD. *Program availability:* Part-time, online learning. *Faculty:* 209 full-time (29 women), 13 part-time/adjunct (1 woman). *Students:* 893 full-time (197 women), 217 part-time (44 women); includes 128 minority (30 Black or African American, non-Hispanic/Latino; 2 American Indian or Alaska Native, non-Hispanic/Latino; 43 Asian, non-Hispanic/Latino; 33 Hispanic/Latino; 1 Native Hawaiian or other Pacific Islander, non-Hispanic/Latino; 19 Two or more races, non-Hispanic/Latino), 365 international. Average age 29. 990 applicants, 39% accepted, 226 enrolled. In 2019, 215 master's, 108 doctorates awarded. *Degree requirements:* For master's, thesis or alternative; for doctorate, comprehensive exam, thesis/dissertation. *Entrance requirements:* For master's, GRE General Test (for MS students pursuing research thesis), minimum GPA of 2.7 (for U.S. degree holders), 3.0 (for international degree holders); 3 references; statement of purpose; for doctorate, GRE General Test, minimum GPA of 3.0 on previous graduate course work; 3 references; statement of purpose. Additional exam requirements/recommendations for international students: required—TOEFL (minimum score 550 paper-based; 80 iBT), IELTS (minimum score 6.5). *Application deadline:* For fall admission, 2/1 priority date for domestic and international students; for spring admission, 6/15 for domestic and international students; for summer admission, 10/15 for domestic and international students. Applications are processed on a rolling basis. Application fee: $60. Electronic applications accepted. *Expenses:* Contact institution. *Financial support:* In 2019–20, 949 students received support, including 176 fellowships with full tuition reimbursements available (averaging $18,134 per year), 561 research assistantships with full tuition reimbursements available (averaging $23,396 per year), 212 teaching assistantships with full tuition reimbursements available (averaging $19,998 per year); career-related internships or fieldwork, Federal Work-Study, institutionally sponsored loans, health care benefits, and unspecified assistantships also available. Financial award application deadline: 2/1; financial award applicants required to submit FAFSA. *Unit head:* Dr. Janis P. Terpenny, Dean, 865-974-5321, Fax: 865-974-8890, E-mail: terpenny@utk.edu. *Application contact:* Dr. Ozlem Kilic, Associate Dean of Student Affairs, 865-974-2454, Fax: 865-974-9871, E-mail: okilic@utk.edu.

The University of Texas at Arlington, Graduate School, College of Engineering, Arlington, TX 76019. Offers M Engr, MCM, MS, PhD. *Program availability:* Part-time, evening/weekend, online learning. Terminal master's awarded for partial completion of doctoral program. *Degree requirements:* For master's, thesis optional; for doctorate, thesis/dissertation. *Entrance requirements:* For master's, GRE General Test, minimum GPA of 3.0 in last 60 hours of coursework; for doctorate, GRE General Test. Additional exam requirements/recommendations for international students: required—TOEFL (minimum score 550 paper-based).

The University of Texas at Austin, Graduate School, Cockrell School of Engineering, Austin, TX 78712-1111. Offers MA, MS, MSE, PhD, MBA/MSE, MD/PhD, MP Aff/MSE. *Program availability:* Part-time, evening/weekend. *Entrance requirements:* For master's and doctorate, GRE General Test. Additional exam requirements/recommendations for international students: required—TOEFL (minimum score 550 paper-based). Electronic applications accepted.

The University of Texas at Dallas, Erik Jonsson School of Engineering and Computer Science, Richardson, TX 75080. Offers MS, MSCS, MSEE, MSTE, PhD. *Program availability:* Part-time, evening/weekend. *Faculty:* 152 full-time (17 women), 41 part-time/adjunct (8 women). *Students:* 1,711 full-time (492 women), 538 part-time (140 women); includes 249 minority (32 Black or African American, non-Hispanic/Latino; 139 Asian, non-Hispanic/Latino; 64 Hispanic/Latino; 14 Two or more races, non-Hispanic/Latino), 1,706 international. Average age 27. 6,263 applicants, 23% accepted, 635 enrolled. In 2019, 774 master's, 89 doctorates awarded. *Degree requirements:* For master's, thesis optional; for doctorate, thesis/dissertation. *Entrance requirements:* For master's, GRE General Test, minimum GPA of 3.0 in related bachelor's course work; for doctorate, GRE General Test, minimum GPA of 3.5. Additional exam requirements/recommendations for international students: required—TOEFL (minimum score 550 paper-based). *Application deadline:* For fall admission, 7/15 for domestic students, 5/1 priority date for international students; for spring admission, 11/15 for domestic students, 9/1 priority date for international students. Applications are processed on a rolling basis. Application fee: $50 ($100 for international students). Electronic applications accepted. *Expenses: Tuition, area resident:* Full-time $16,504. Tuition, state resident: full-time $16,504. Tuition, nonresident: full-time $34,266. Tuition and fees vary according to course load. *Financial support:* In 2019–20, 608 students received support, including 43 fellowships (averaging $4,082 per year), 373 research assistantships with partial tuition reimbursements available (averaging $24,016 per year), 217 teaching assistantships with partial tuition reimbursements available (averaging $17,130 per year); career-related internships or fieldwork, Federal Work-Study, institutionally sponsored loans, scholarships/grants, and unspecified assistantships also available. Support available to part-time students. Financial award application deadline: 4/30; financial award applicants required to submit FAFSA. *Unit head:* Dr. Stephanie G Adams, Dean, 972-883-2974, Fax: 972-883-2813, E-mail: sgadams@utdallas.edu. *Application contact:* Dr. Stephanie G Adams, Dean, 972-883-2974, Fax: 972-883-2813, E-mail: sgadams@utdallas.edu.
Website: http://engineering.utdallas.edu/

The University of Texas at El Paso, Graduate School, College of Engineering, El Paso, TX 79968-0001. Offers M Eng, MEENE, MS, MSENE, MSIT, PhD, Certificate, Graduate Certificate. *Program availability:* Part-time, evening/weekend. *Degree requirements:* For master's, thesis optional; for doctorate, thesis/dissertation. *Entrance requirements:* For master's, GRE, minimum GPA of 3.0, letters of reference; for doctorate, GRE, statement of purpose, letters of reference. Additional exam requirements/recommendations for international students: required—TOEFL; recommended—IELTS. Electronic applications accepted. *Expenses:* Contact institution.

The University of Texas at San Antonio, College of Engineering, San Antonio, TX 78249-0617. Offers MCE, MS, MSCE, MSEE, PhD. *Program availability:* Part-time, evening/weekend. Terminal master's awarded for partial completion of doctoral program. *Degree requirements:* For master's, variable foreign language requirement, comprehensive exam, thesis optional, completion of all course work requirements within six-year time limit; no courses with grade of less than C; minimum GPA of 3.0; for doctorate, variable foreign language requirement, comprehensive exam, thesis/dissertation, continuous enrollment until time of graduation; all completed coursework included in the final program of study must have been taken within the preceding eight years to include successful completion and defense of the dissertation. *Entrance requirements:* For master's, GRE, baccalaureate degree in related field from regionally-accredited college or university in the U.S. or proof of equivalent training at foreign institution; minimum GPA of 3.0 in last 60 semester credit hours or foreign institution equivalent of coursework taken; for doctorate, GRE, baccalaureate degree or MS in related field from regionally-accredited college or university in the U.S. or proof of equivalent training at foreign institution; minimum GPA of 3.0, 3.3 in upper-division/graduate courses. Additional exam requirements/recommendations for international students: required—TOEFL (minimum score 550 paper-based; 79 iBT), IELTS (minimum score 6.5). Electronic applications accepted. *Expenses:* Contact institution.

University of the District of Columbia, School of Engineering and Applied Sciences, Washington, DC 20008-1175. Offers MSCS, MSEE.

University of the Pacific, School of Engineering and Computer Science, Stockton, CA 95211-0197. Offers engineering science (MS). *Entrance requirements:* For master's, GRE, three references; official transcripts; personal statement; bachelor's degree in engineering, computer science, or a closely related discipline. Additional exam requirements/recommendations for international students: required—TOEFL. Electronic applications accepted.

The University of Toledo, College of Graduate Studies, College of Engineering, Program in Engineering, Toledo, OH 43606-3390. Offers general engineering (MS). *Entrance requirements:* For master's, GRE General Test, minimum GPA of 2.7, industrial experience.

University of Toronto, School of Graduate Studies, Faculty of Applied Science and Engineering, Toronto, ON M5S 1A1, Canada. Offers M Eng, MA Sc, MH Sc, PhD. *Program availability:* Part-time. *Degree requirements:* For doctorate, thesis/dissertation. *Expenses:* Contact institution.

The University of Tulsa, Graduate School, College of Engineering and Natural Sciences, Tulsa, OK 74104-3189. Offers ME, MS, MSE, MTA, PhD, JD/MS, MBA/MS, MSF/MSAM. *Program availability:* Part-time. Terminal master's awarded for partial completion of doctoral program. *Degree requirements:* For master's, thesis (for some programs); for doctorate, comprehensive exam, thesis/dissertation. *Entrance requirements:* For master's and doctorate, GRE General Test. Additional exam requirements/recommendations for international students: required—TOEFL (minimum score 550 paper-based), IELTS (minimum score 6). Electronic applications accepted. *Expenses: Tuition:* Full-time $22,896; part-time $1272 per credit hour. *Required fees:* $6 per credit hour. Tuition and fees vary according to course load and program.

University of Utah, Graduate School, College of Engineering, Salt Lake City, UT 84112. Offers ME, MEAE, MS, PhD, MS/MBA. *Program availability:* Part-time. *Faculty:* 202 full-time (29 women), 15 part-time/adjunct (1 woman). *Students:* 960 full-time (212 women), 330 part-time (49 women); includes 134 minority (6 Black or African American, non-Hispanic/Latino; 1 American Indian or Alaska Native, non-Hispanic/Latino; 60 Asian, non-Hispanic/Latino; 41 Hispanic/Latino; 2 Native Hawaiian or other Pacific Islander, non-Hispanic/Latino; 24 Two or more races, non-Hispanic/Latino), 541 international. Average age 28. 1,779 applicants, 37% accepted, 360 enrolled. In 2019, 370 master's, 111 doctorates awarded. Terminal master's awarded for partial completion of doctoral program. *Degree requirements:* For master's, comprehensive exam (for some programs), thesis (for some programs); for doctorate, comprehensive exam (for some programs), thesis/dissertation (for some programs). *Entrance requirements:* For master's and doctorate, minimum GPA of 3.0. Additional exam requirements/recommendations for international students: required—TOEFL (minimum score 550 paper-based; 80 iBT), IELTS (minimum score 6.5). *Application deadline:* For fall admission, 12/15 priority date for domestic and international students. Applications are processed on a rolling basis. Application fee: $30 ($45 for international students). Electronic applications accepted. *Expenses:* Contact institution. *Financial support:* In 2019–20, 228 students received support, including 49 fellowships (averaging $11,184 per year), 547 research assistantships (averaging $13,718 per year), 195 teaching assistantships (averaging $11,949 per year); tuition waivers and unspecified assistantships also available. Financial award application deadline: 12/15. *Unit head:* Dr. Richard B. Brown, Dean, 801-581-6912, Fax: 801-581-6912, E-mail: brown@utah.edu. *Application contact:* Amy Arkwright, Academic Program Coordinator, 801-585-0370, Fax: 801-581-8692, E-mail: amy.arkwright@utah.edu.
Website: http://www.coe.utah.edu/

University of Vermont, Graduate College, College of Engineering and Mathematical Sciences, Burlington, VT 05405-0156. Offers MS, MST, PhD. *Program availability:* Part-time. *Degree requirements:* For master's, thesis (for some programs); for doctorate, thesis/dissertation. *Entrance requirements:* Additional exam requirements/recommendations for international students: required—TOEFL (minimum score 550 paper-based; 90 iBT), IELTS (minimum score 6.5). Electronic applications accepted.

University of Victoria, Faculty of Graduate Studies, Faculty of Engineering, Victoria, BC V8W 2Y2, Canada. Offers M Eng, M Sc, MA Sc, PhD.

University of Virginia, School of Engineering and Applied Science, Charlottesville, VA 22903. Offers MCS, ME, MEP, MMSE, MS, PhD, ME/MBA. *Program availability:* Part-time, online learning. Terminal master's awarded for partial completion of doctoral program. *Degree requirements:* For doctorate, comprehensive exam, thesis/dissertation. *Entrance requirements:* For master's, GRE General Test, 3 letters of recommendation; for doctorate, GRE General Test, 3 letters of recommendation, essay. Additional exam requirements/recommendations for international students: required—TOEFL (minimum score 600 paper-based; 90 iBT), IELTS (minimum score 7). Electronic applications accepted. *Expenses:* Contact institution.

University of Washington, Graduate School, College of Engineering, Seattle, WA 98195-2180. Offers MAB, MAE, MISE, MS, MSAA, MSCE, MSE, MSME, PhD, Certificate. *Program availability:* Part-time, online learning. *Students:* 1,787 full-time (591 women), 1,026 part-time (326 women); includes 610 minority (44 Black or African American, non-Hispanic/Latino; 3 American Indian or Alaska Native, non-Hispanic/Latino; 343 Asian, non-Hispanic/Latino; 119 Hispanic/Latino; 3 Native Hawaiian or other Pacific Islander, non-Hispanic/Latino; 98 Two or more races, non-Hispanic/Latino), 1,091 international. Average age 27. 8,636 applicants, 30% accepted, 968 enrolled. In 2019, 724 master's, 184 doctorates awarded. Terminal master's awarded for partial

completion of doctoral program. *Degree requirements:* For master's, comprehensive exam (for some programs), thesis (for some programs); for doctorate, comprehensive exam, thesis/dissertation. *Entrance requirements:* Additional exam requirements/ recommendations for international students: required—TOEFL. Application fee: $85. Electronic applications accepted. *Expenses:* Contact institution. *Financial support:* In 2019–20, 115 fellowships with full tuition reimbursements (averaging $33,540 per year), 761 research assistantships with full tuition reimbursements (averaging $34,990 per year), 297 teaching assistantships with full tuition reimbursements (averaging $33,460 per year) were awarded; Federal Work-Study, institutionally sponsored loans, scholarships/grants, health care benefits, tuition waivers (full), unspecified assistantships, and stipend supplements also available. Support available to part-time students. *Unit head:* Dr. Nancy Allbritton, Frank & Julie Jungers Dean of Engineering, 206-543-1829, Fax: 206-685-0666, E-mail: nlallbr@uw.edu. *Application contact:* Mike Engh, Assistant Director, Academic Affairs, 206-685-3714, Fax: 206-685-0666, E-mail: enghmw@uw.edu.
Website: http://www.engr.washington.edu/

University of Waterloo, Graduate Studies and Postdoctoral Affairs, Faculty of Engineering, Waterloo, ON N2L 3G1, Canada. Offers M Arch, M Eng, MA Sc, MBET, MMS, PhD. *Program availability:* Part-time, evening/weekend, online learning. *Degree requirements:* For master's, research paper or thesis; for doctorate, comprehensive exam, thesis/dissertation. *Entrance requirements:* For master's, honors degree; for doctorate, master's degree, minimum A- average. Additional exam requirements/ recommendations for international students: required—TOEFL, IELTS, PTE. Electronic applications accepted.

The University of Western Ontario, School of Graduate and Postdoctoral Studies, Physical Sciences Division, Faculty of Engineering, London, ON N6A 3K7, Canada. Offers chemical and biochemical engineering (ME Sc, PhD); civil and environmental engineering (M Eng, ME Sc, PhD); electrical and computer engineering (M Eng, ME Sc, PhD); mechanical and materials engineering (M Eng, ME Sc, PhD). *Program availability:* Part-time. Terminal master's awarded for partial completion of doctoral program. *Degree requirements:* For master's, thesis; for doctorate, thesis/dissertation. *Entrance requirements:* For master's, minimum B average; for doctorate, minimum B+ average.

University of Windsor, Faculty of Graduate Studies, Faculty of Engineering, Windsor, ON N9B 3P4, Canada. Offers M Eng, MA Sc, PhD. *Program availability:* Part-time. *Degree requirements:* For doctorate, comprehensive exam, thesis/dissertation. *Entrance requirements:* For master's, minimum B average; for doctorate, master's degree. Additional exam requirements/recommendations for international students: required—TOEFL. Electronic applications accepted.

University of Wisconsin–Madison, Graduate School, College of Engineering, Madison, WI 53706-1380. Offers MS, PhD. *Program availability:* Part-time, 100% online, blended/hybrid learning. *Faculty:* 204 full-time (40 women). *Students:* 1,373 full-time (349 women), 485 part-time (101 women); includes 226 minority (30 Black or African American, non-Hispanic/Latino; 1 American Indian or Alaska Native, non-Hispanic/ Latino; 87 Asian, non-Hispanic/Latino; 79 Hispanic/Latino; 1 Native Hawaiian or other Pacific Islander, non-Hispanic/Latino; 28 Two or more races, non-Hispanic/Latino), 897 international. Average age 27. 5,754 applicants, 30% accepted, 510 enrolled. In 2019, 497 master's, 166 doctorates awarded. Terminal master's awarded for partial completion of doctoral program. *Degree requirements:* For master's, thesis (for some programs); for doctorate, thesis/dissertation. *Entrance requirements:* For master's and doctorate, GRE. Additional exam requirements/recommendations for international students: required—TOEFL (minimum score 580 paper-based; 92 iBT), IELTS (minimum score 7). *Application deadline:* Applications are processed on a rolling basis. Application fee: $75 ($81 for international students). Electronic applications accepted. *Financial support:* In 2019–20, 1,197 students received support, including 75 fellowships with full tuition reimbursements available, 725 research assistantships with full tuition reimbursements available, 351 teaching assistantships with full tuition reimbursements available; career-related internships or fieldwork, Federal Work-Study, institutionally sponsored loans, scholarships/grants, health care benefits, and unspecified assistantships also available. Support available to part-time students. Financial award application deadline: 12/1; financial award applicants required to submit FAFSA. *Unit head:* Dr. Ian M. Robertson, Dean, 608-262-3482, Fax: 608-262-6400, E-mail: engr-dean_engr@wisc.edu. *Application contact:* Information Contact, 608-262-2433, Fax: 608-265-9505, E-mail: admissions@grad.wisc.edu.
Website: http://www.engr.wisc.edu/

University of Wisconsin–Milwaukee, Graduate School, College of Engineering and Applied Science, Milwaukee, WI 53201. Offers MS, PhD. *Program availability:* Part-time. *Degree requirements:* For master's, comprehensive exam (for some programs), thesis or alternative; for doctorate, thesis/dissertation, internship. *Entrance requirements:* For master's, GRE, minimum GPA of 2.75; for doctorate, GRE, minimum GPA of 3.5. Additional exam requirements/recommendations for international students: required—TOEFL (minimum score 550 paper-based; 79 iBT), IELTS (minimum score 6.5). Electronic applications accepted.

University of Wisconsin–Platteville, School of Graduate Studies, Distance Learning Center, Online Master of Science in Engineering Program, Platteville, WI 53818-3099. Offers MS. *Program availability:* Part-time. *Degree requirements:* For master's, thesis or alternative. *Entrance requirements:* Additional exam requirements/recommendations for international students: required—TOEFL (minimum score 550 paper-based; 79 iBT), IELTS (minimum score 6.5). Electronic applications accepted. *Expenses:* Contact institution.

University of Wyoming, College of Engineering and Applied Science, Laramie, WY 82071. Offers MS, PhD. *Program availability:* Part-time. *Entrance requirements:* For master's and doctorate, GRE General Test, minimum GPA of 3.0. Additional exam requirements/recommendations for international students: required—TOEFL. Electronic applications accepted.

Université Laval, Faculty of Sciences and Engineering, Québec, QC G1K 7P4, Canada. Offers M Sc, PhD, Diploma. *Program availability:* Part-time. *Degree requirements:* For doctorate, thesis/dissertation. Electronic applications accepted.

Utah State University, School of Graduate Studies, College of Engineering, Logan, UT 84322. Offers MCS, ME, MS, PhD, CE. *Program availability:* Part-time, evening/ weekend. Terminal master's awarded for partial completion of doctoral program. *Degree requirements:* For master's, thesis (for some programs); for doctorate, thesis/ dissertation. *Entrance requirements:* For master's and doctorate, GRE General Test, minimum GPA of 3.0. Additional exam requirements/recommendations for international students: required—TOEFL. Electronic applications accepted.

Vanderbilt University, School of Engineering, Nashville, TN 37235. Offers M Eng, MS, PhD, MD/PhD. *Program availability:* Part-time. Terminal master's awarded for partial completion of doctoral program. *Degree requirements:* For master's, comprehensive exam (for some programs), thesis (for some programs); for doctorate, comprehensive exam (for some programs), thesis/dissertation. *Entrance requirements:* For master's and doctorate, GRE General Test. Additional exam requirements/recommendations for international students: required—TOEFL. Electronic applications accepted. Application fee is waived when completed online. *Expenses: Tuition:* Full-time $51,018; part-time $2087 per hour. *Required fees:* $542. Tuition and fees vary according to program.

Villanova University, College of Engineering, Villanova, PA 19085-1699. Offers MSCPE, MSChE, MSEE, MSME, MSWREE, PhD, Certificate. *Program availability:* Part-time, evening/weekend, online learning. Terminal master's awarded for partial completion of doctoral program. *Degree requirements:* For master's, thesis optional; for doctorate, thesis/dissertation. *Entrance requirements:* For master's, GRE General Test (for applicants with degrees from foreign universities), minimum GPA of 3.0; for doctorate, GRE General Test. Additional exam requirements/recommendations for international students: required—TOEFL (minimum score 600 paper-based; 100 iBT). Electronic applications accepted. *Expenses:* Contact institution.

Virginia Commonwealth University, Graduate School, School of Engineering, Richmond, VA 23284-9005. Offers MS, PhD. *Degree requirements:* For doctorate, thesis/dissertation, comprehensive oral and written exams. *Entrance requirements:* For master's and doctorate, GRE General Test. Additional exam requirements/ recommendations for international students: required—TOEFL (minimum score 600 paper-based; 100 iBT). Electronic applications accepted.

Virginia Polytechnic Institute and State University, Graduate School, College of Engineering, Blacksburg, VA 24061. Offers aerospace engineering (PhD, M Eng/MS); biological systems engineering (PhD); biomedical engineering (MS, PhD); chemical engineering (PhD); civil engineering (PhD); computer engineering (PhD); computer science and applications (MS); electrical engineering (PhD); engineering education (PhD); M Eng/MS. *Faculty:* 447 full-time (90 women), 6 part-time/adjunct (2 women). *Students:* 1,881 full-time (495 women), 326 part-time (70 women); includes 264 minority (51 Black or African American, non-Hispanic/Latino; 2 American Indian or Alaska Native, non-Hispanic/Latino; 96 Asian, non-Hispanic/Latino; 69 Hispanic/Latino; 46 Two or more races, non-Hispanic/Latino), 1,247 international. Average age 27. 4,014 applicants, 44% accepted, 658 enrolled. In 2019, 489 master's, 200 doctorates awarded. *Degree requirements:* For master's, comprehensive exam (for some programs), thesis (for some programs); for doctorate, comprehensive exam (for some programs), thesis/dissertation (for some programs). *Entrance requirements:* For master's and doctorate, GRE/GMAT. Additional exam requirements/recommendations for international students: required—TOEFL (minimum score 90 iBT). *Application deadline:* For fall admission, 8/1 for domestic students, 4/1 for international students; for spring admission, 1/1 for domestic students, 9/1 for international students. Applications are processed on a rolling basis. Application fee: $75. Electronic applications accepted. *Expenses:* Tuition, state resident: full-time $13,700; part-time $761.25 per credit hour. Tuition, nonresident: full-time $27,614; part-time $1534 per credit hour. *Required fees:* $886.50 per term. Tuition and fees vary according to campus/location and program. *Financial support:* In 2019–20, 47 fellowships with full tuition reimbursements (averaging $19,703 per year), 1,163 research assistantships with full tuition reimbursements (averaging $20,602 per year), 554 teaching assistantships with full tuition reimbursements (averaging $16,333 per year) were awarded; scholarships/grants and unspecified assistantships also available. Financial award application deadline: 3/1; financial award applicants required to submit FAFSA. *Unit head:* Dr. Julia Ross, Dean, 540-231-9752, Fax: 540-231-3031, E-mail: rjulie@vt.edu. *Application contact:* Linda Perkins, Executive Assistant, 540-231-9752, Fax: 540-231-3031, E-mail: lperkins@vt.edu.
Website: http://www.eng.vt.edu/

Washington State University, Voiland College of Engineering and Architecture, Pullman, WA 99164-2714. Offers M Arch, METM, MS, PhD, Certificate. Terminal master's awarded for partial completion of doctoral program. *Degree requirements:* For master's, comprehensive exam (for some programs), thesis (for some programs), oral exam; for doctorate, comprehensive exam, thesis/dissertation, oral exam. *Entrance requirements:* For master's, GRE, minimum GPA of 3.0, 3 letters of recommendation; for doctorate, GRE, minimum GPA of 3.4, 3 letters of recommendation. Additional exam requirements/recommendations for international students: required—TOEFL (minimum score 520 paper-based).

Washington University in St. Louis, School of Engineering and Applied Science, Saint Louis, MO 63130-4899. Offers M Eng, MCE, MCM, MEM, MIM, MPM, MS, MSEE, MSEE, MSI, D Sc, PhD. *Program availability:* Part-time, evening/weekend. Terminal master's awarded for partial completion of doctoral program. *Degree requirements:* For master's, comprehensive exam (for some programs), thesis (for some programs); for doctorate, comprehensive exam, thesis/dissertation. *Entrance requirements:* For master's and doctorate, GRE. Additional exam requirements/recommendations for international students: required—TOEFL (minimum score 550 paper-based; 90 iBT), IELTS (minimum score 6.5) or TWE. Electronic applications accepted.

Wayne State University, College of Engineering, Detroit, MI 48202. Offers MS, MSET, PhD, Certificate, Graduate Certificate, Postbaccalaureate Certificate. *Program availability:* Part-time, evening/weekend. *Faculty:* 118. *Students:* 601 full-time (178 women), 388 part-time (107 women); includes 137 minority (50 Black or African American, non-Hispanic/Latino; 57 Asian, non-Hispanic/Latino; 19 Hispanic/Latino; 11 Two or more races, non-Hispanic/Latino), 536 international. Average age 29. 1,774 applicants, 34% accepted, 203 enrolled. In 2019, 423 master's, 43 doctorates, 5 other advanced degrees awarded. Terminal master's awarded for partial completion of doctoral program. *Degree requirements:* For master's, thesis (for some programs), project (engineering management and engineering technology); for doctorate, thesis/ dissertation. *Entrance requirements:* For master's, minimum GPA of 2.8 from ABET-accredited institution and in all upper-division courses; for doctorate, minimum overall GPA of 3.2, 3.5 in last two years as undergraduate student if being admitted directly from a bachelor's program, or master's degree with minimum GPA of 3.5 (preferred); for other advanced degree, minimum GPA of 3.0 from ABET-accredited institution and in all upper-division courses. Additional exam requirements/recommendations for international students: required—TOEFL (minimum score 550 paper-based; 79 iBT), TWE (minimum score 5.5); recommended—IELTS (minimum score 6.5). *Application deadline:* For fall admission, 7/15 priority date for domestic students, 5/15 priority date for international students; for winter admission, 11/1 priority date for domestic students, 10/1 priority date for international students; for spring admission, 2/1 priority date for domestic students, 1/1 priority date for international students. Applications are processed on a rolling basis. Application fee: $50. Electronic applications accepted. *Expenses:* $790 per credit hour in-state tuition, $1579 per credit hour out-of-state tuition. *Financial support:* In 2019–20, 484 students received support, including 22 fellowships with tuition reimbursements available (averaging $20,144 per year), 72 research assistantships with tuition reimbursements available (averaging $21,706 per year), 86 teaching assistantships with tuition reimbursements available (averaging $20,780 per year); Federal Work-Study, scholarships/grants, health care benefits, tuition waivers (full and partial), and unspecified assistantships also available. Support available to part-time students. Financial award applicants required to submit FAFSA. *Unit head:* Dr. Farshad Fotouhi, Dean, 313-577-3776, E-mail: fotouhi@wayne.edu. *Application contact:* Graduate Program Coordinator, E-mail: engineeringgradadmissions@eng.wayne.edu.
Website: http://engineering.wayne.edu/

Western Michigan University, Graduate College, College of Engineering and Applied Sciences, Kalamazoo, MI 49008. Offers MS, MSE, PhD. *Program availability:* Part-time. *Degree requirements:* For doctorate, thesis/dissertation.

Western New England University, College of Engineering, Springfield, MA 01119. Offers MS, MSEE, MSEM, MSME, PhD, MSEM/MBA. *Program availability:* Part-time, evening/weekend, online learning. *Degree requirements:* For master's, comprehensive exam (for some programs), thesis optional; for doctorate, comprehensive exam, thesis/dissertation. *Entrance requirements:* For master's, bachelor's degree in engineering or related field, official transcript, two letters of recommendation, resume; for doctorate, GRE, official transcript, master's or bachelor's degree in engineering or closely-related discipline, two letters of recommendation. Additional exam requirements/recommendations for international students: required—TOEFL (minimum score 79 iBT). Electronic applications accepted. *Expenses:* Contact institution.

West Texas A&M University, School of Engineering, Computer Science and Mathematics, Program in Engineering Technology, Canyon, TX 79015. Offers MS. *Program availability:* Part-time, evening/weekend. *Degree requirements:* For master's, comprehensive exam, thesis optional. *Entrance requirements:* For master's, GRE General Test. Additional exam requirements/recommendations for international students: required—TOEFL (minimum score 550 paper-based). Electronic applications accepted.

West Virginia University, Statler College of Engineering and Mineral Resources, Morgantown, WV 26506. Offers aerospace engineering (MSAE, PhD); chemical engineering (MS Ch E, PhD); civil engineering (MSCE, PhD); computer engineering (PhD); computer science (MSCS, PhD); electrical engineering (MSEE, PhD); energy systems engineering (MSESE); engineering (MSE); industrial engineering (MSIE, PhD); industrial hygiene (MS); material science and engineering (MSMSE, PhD); mechanical engineering (MSME, PhD); mining engineering (MS Min E, PhD); petroleum and natural gas engineering (MSPNGE, PhD); safety management (MS); software engineering (MSSE). *Program availability:* Part-time. Terminal master's awarded for partial completion of doctoral program. *Degree requirements:* For master's, thesis optional; for doctorate, comprehensive exam, thesis/dissertation. *Entrance requirements:* Additional exam requirements/recommendations for international students: required—TOEFL (minimum score 550 paper-based). Electronic applications accepted. *Expenses:* Contact institution.

Wichita State University, Graduate School, College of Engineering, Wichita, KS 67260. Offers MEM, MS, PhD. *Program availability:* Part-time, evening/weekend.

Widener University, Graduate Programs in Engineering, Chester, PA 19013. Offers M Eng, ME/MBA. *Program availability:* Part-time, evening/weekend. *Degree requirements:* For master's, thesis optional. *Entrance requirements:* Additional exam requirements/recommendations for international students: required—TOEFL (minimum score 550 paper-based). Electronic applications accepted. *Expenses:* Contact institution.

Worcester Polytechnic Institute, Graduate Admissions, Worcester, MA 01609-2280. Offers M Eng, MBA, ME, MME, MS, PhD, Advanced Certificate, Graduate Certificate. *Program availability:* Part-time, evening/weekend, 100% online, blended/hybrid learning. Terminal master's awarded for partial completion of doctoral program. *Degree requirements:* For master's, thesis (for some programs); for doctorate, comprehensive exam, thesis/dissertation. *Entrance requirements:* For master's and doctorate, 3 letters of recommendation. Additional exam requirements/recommendations for international students: required—TOEFL (minimum score 563 paper-based; 84 iBT), IELTS (minimum score 7). Electronic applications accepted.

Wright State University, Graduate School, College of Engineering and Computer Science, Dayton, OH 45435. Offers MS, PhD. *Program availability:* Part-time, evening/weekend. *Degree requirements:* For master's, thesis optional; for doctorate, thesis/dissertation, candidacy and general exams. *Entrance requirements:* For doctorate, GRE General Test, minimum GPA of 3.3. Additional exam requirements/recommendations for international students: required—TOEFL.

Yale University, Graduate School of Arts and Sciences, School of Engineering and Applied Science, New Haven, CT 06520. Offers MS, PhD. *Program availability:* Part-time. Terminal master's awarded for partial completion of doctoral program. *Degree requirements:* For doctorate, thesis/dissertation, exam. *Entrance requirements:* For master's and doctorate, GRE General Test. Additional exam requirements/recommendations for international students: required—TOEFL.

Youngstown State University, College of Graduate Studies, College of Science, Technology, Engineering and Mathematics, Youngstown, OH 44555-0001. Offers MCIS, MS, MSE, Certificate. *Program availability:* Part-time, evening/weekend. *Degree requirements:* For master's, thesis optional. *Entrance requirements:* For master's, minimum GPA of 2.75 in field. Additional exam requirements/recommendations for international students: required—TOEFL.

Applied Science and Technology

Colorado State University-Pueblo, College of Science and Mathematics, Pueblo, CO 81001-4901. Offers applied natural science (MS), including biochemistry, biology, chemistry. *Program availability:* Part-time, evening/weekend. *Degree requirements:* For master's, comprehensive exam (for some programs), thesis (for some programs), internship report (if non-thesis). *Entrance requirements:* For master's, GRE General Test (minimum score 1000), 2 letters of reference, minimum GPA of 3.0. Additional exam requirements/recommendations for international students: required—TOEFL (minimum score 500 paper-based), IELTS (minimum score 5).

Harvard University, Extension School, Cambridge, MA 02138-3722. Offers applied sciences (CAS); biotechnology (ALM); educational technologies (ALM); educational technology (CET); English for graduate and professional studies (DGP); environmental management (ALM, CEM); information technology (ALM); journalism (ALM); liberal arts (ALM); management (ALM, CM); mathematics for teaching (ALM); museum studies (ALM); premedical studies (Diploma); publication and communication (CPC). *Program availability:* Part-time, evening/weekend. *Degree requirements:* For master's, thesis. *Entrance requirements:* For master's, 3 completed graduate courses with grade of B or higher. Additional exam requirements/recommendations for international students: required—TOEFL (minimum score 600 paper-based), TWE (minimum score 5). *Expenses:* Contact institution.

Kansas State University, Graduate School, School of Applied and Interdisciplinary Studies, Olathe, KS 66061. Offers applied science and technology (PSM); professional interdisciplinary sciences (Graduate Certificate); professional skills for STEM practitioners (Graduate Certificate). *Program availability:* Part-time, 100% online, blended/hybrid learning. *Degree requirements:* For master's, capstone experience and/or internship. *Entrance requirements:* Additional exam requirements/recommendations for international students: required—TOEFL (minimum score 550 paper-based; 79 iBT), IELTS (minimum score 6.5), PTE (minimum score 58). Electronic applications accepted.

Louisiana State University and Agricultural & Mechanical College, Graduate School, College of Science, Master of Natural Sciences Program, Baton Rouge, LA 70803. Offers MNS.

Missouri State University, Graduate College, College of Natural and Applied Sciences, Department of Biology, Springfield, MO 65897. Offers biology (MS); natural and applied science (MNAS), including biology (MNAS, MS Ed); secondary education (MS Ed), including biology (MNAS, MS Ed). *Degree requirements:* For master's, comprehensive exam, thesis or alternative. *Entrance requirements:* For master's, GRE (MS, MNAS), 24 hours of course work in biology (MS); minimum GPA of 3.0 (MS, MNAS); 9-12 teacher certification (MS Ed). Additional exam requirements/recommendations for international students: required—TOEFL (minimum score 550 paper-based; 79 iBT), IELTS (minimum score 6). Electronic applications accepted. *Expenses: Tuition, area resident:* Full-time $2600; part-time $1735 per credit hour. Tuition, nonresident: full-time $5240; part-time $3495 per credit hour. *International tuition:* $5240 full-time. *Required fees:* $530; $438 per credit hour. Tuition and fees vary according to class time, course level, course load, degree level, campus/location and program.

Missouri State University, Graduate College, College of Natural and Applied Sciences, Department of Chemistry, Springfield, MO 65897. Offers chemistry (MS); natural and applied science (MNAS), including chemistry (MNAS, MS Ed); secondary education (MS Ed), including chemistry (MNAS, MS Ed). *Program availability:* Part-time. *Degree requirements:* For master's, comprehensive exam, thesis. *Entrance requirements:* For master's, GRE General Test (MS, MNAS), minimum undergraduate GPA of 3.0 (MS and MNAS), 9-12 teacher certification (MS Ed). Additional exam requirements/recommendations for international students: required—TOEFL (minimum score 550 paper-based; 79 iBT), IELTS (minimum score 6). Electronic applications accepted. *Expenses: Tuition, area resident:* Full-time $2600; part-time $1735 per credit hour. Tuition, nonresident: full-time $5240; part-time $3495 per credit hour. *International tuition:* $5240 full-time. *Required fees:* $530; $438 per credit hour. Tuition and fees vary according to class time, course level, course load, degree level, campus/location and program.

Missouri State University, Graduate College, College of Natural and Applied Sciences, Department of Computer Science, Springfield, MO 65897. Offers natural and applied science (MNAS), including computer science. *Program availability:* Part-time. *Degree requirements:* For master's, comprehensive exam, thesis or alternative. *Entrance requirements:* For master's, GRE, minimum GPA of 3.0. Additional exam requirements/recommendations for international students: required—TOEFL (minimum score 550 paper-based; 79 iBT), IELTS (minimum score 6). Electronic applications accepted. *Expenses: Tuition, area resident:* Full-time $2600; part-time $1735 per credit hour. Tuition, nonresident: full-time $5240; part-time $3495 per credit hour. *International tuition:* $5240 full-time. *Required fees:* $530; $438 per credit hour. Tuition and fees vary according to class time, course level, course load, degree level, campus/location and program.

Missouri State University, Graduate College, College of Natural and Applied Sciences, Department of Geography, Geology, and Planning, Springfield, MO 65897. Offers geography, geology, and planning (Certificate); natural and applied science (MNAS), including geography, geology and planning; secondary education (MS Ed), including earth science, physical geography. *Program availability:* Part-time, evening/weekend. *Degree requirements:* For master's, comprehensive exam, thesis (for some programs). *Entrance requirements:* For master's, GRE General Test (MS, MNAS), minimum undergraduate GPA of 3.0 (MS, MNAS), 9-12 teacher certification (MS Ed). Additional exam requirements/recommendations for international students: required—TOEFL (minimum score 550 paper-based; 79 iBT), IELTS (minimum score 6). Electronic applications accepted. *Expenses: Tuition, area resident:* Full-time $2600; part-time $1735 per credit hour. Tuition, nonresident: full-time $5240; part-time $3495 per credit hour. *International tuition:* $5240 full-time. *Required fees:* $530; $438 per credit hour. Tuition and fees vary according to class time, course level, course load, degree level, campus/location and program.

Missouri State University, Graduate College, College of Natural and Applied Sciences, Department of Mathematics, Springfield, MO 65897. Offers mathematics (MS); natural and applied science (MNAS), including mathematics (MNAS, MS Ed); secondary education (MS Ed), including mathematics (MNAS, MS Ed). *Program availability:* Part-time. *Degree requirements:* For master's, comprehensive exam, thesis or alternative. *Entrance requirements:* For master's, GRE (MS, MNAS), minimum undergraduate GPA of 3.0 (MS, MNAS), 9-12 teacher certification (MS Ed). Additional exam requirements/recommendations for international students: required—TOEFL (minimum score 550 paper-based; 79 iBT), IELTS (minimum score 6). Electronic applications accepted. *Expenses: Tuition, area resident:* Full-time $2600; part-time $1735 per credit hour. Tuition, nonresident: full-time $5240; part-time $3495 per credit hour. *International tuition:* $5240 full-time. *Required fees:* $530; $438 per credit hour. Tuition and fees vary according to class time, course level, course load, degree level, campus/location and program.

Missouri State University, Graduate College, College of Natural and Applied Sciences, Department of Physics, Astronomy, and Materials Science, Springfield, MO 65897. Offers materials science (MS); natural and applied science (MNAS), including physics (MNAS, MS Ed); secondary education (MS Ed), including physics (MNAS, MS Ed). *Program availability:* Part-time. *Degree requirements:* For master's, comprehensive exam, thesis. *Entrance requirements:* For master's, GRE (MS, MNAS), minimum undergraduate GPA of 3.0 (MS and MNAS), 9-12 teaching certification (MS Ed). Additional exam requirements/recommendations for international students: required—TOEFL (minimum score 550 paper-based; 79 iBT), IELTS (minimum score 6). Electronic applications accepted. *Expenses: Tuition, area resident:* Full-time $2600; part-time $1735 per credit hour. Tuition, nonresident: full-time $5240; part-time $3495 per credit hour. *International tuition:* $5240 full-time. *Required fees:* $530; $438 per credit hour. Tuition and fees vary according to class time, course level, course load, degree level, campus/location and program.

Naval Postgraduate School, Departments and Academic Groups, Department of Operations Research, Monterey, CA 93943. Offers applied science (MS), including operations research; cost estimating analysis (MS); human systems integration (MS); operations research (MS, PhD); systems analysis (MS). *Program availability:* Part-time. *Degree requirements:* For master's, thesis (for some programs); for doctorate, thesis/dissertation.

Naval Postgraduate School, Departments and Academic Groups, Undersea Warfare Academic Group, Monterey, CA 93943. Offers applied mathematics (MS); applied physics (MS); applied science (MS), including acoustics, operations research, physical oceanography, signal processing; electrical engineering (MS); engineering acoustics (MS, PhD); engineering science (MS), including electrical engineering, mechanical engineering; mechanical engineer (ME); mechanical engineering (MS, MSME); meteorology (MS); operations research (MS); physical oceanography (MS). *Program availability:* Part-time. *Degree requirements:* For master's, thesis.

Saint Mary's University, Faculty of Science, Interdisciplinary Program in Applied Science, Halifax, NS B3H 3C3, Canada. Offers M Sc.

Southeastern Louisiana University, College of Science and Technology, Program in Integrated Science and Technology, Hammond, LA 70402. Offers integrated science and technology (MS). *Program availability:* Part-time. *Faculty:* 9 full-time (2 women). *Students:* 9 full-time (4 women), 5 part-time (1 woman); includes 3 minority (1 Black or African American, non-Hispanic/Latino; 2 Hispanic/Latino), 3 international. Average age 28. 7 applicants, 100% accepted, 3 enrolled. In 2019, 3 master's awarded. *Degree requirements:* For master's, thesis optional, 33 hours of classes for generalist option, 36 hours of classes for specialist option. *Entrance requirements:* For master's, GRE (minimum combined Verbal and Quantitative score of 290), undergraduate degree; at least 30 semester hours in any combination of chemistry, computer science, industrial technology, mathematics, or physics; letter of application; 2 letters of recommendation; cumulative undergraduate GPA of 2.75. Additional exam requirements/recommendations for international students: required—TOEFL (minimum score 500 paper-based; 61 iBT). *Application deadline:* For fall admission, 7/15 priority date for domestic students, 6/1 priority date for international students; for spring admission, 12/1 priority date for domestic students, 10/1 priority date for international students. Applications are processed on a rolling basis. Application fee: $20 ($30 for international students). Electronic applications accepted. *Expenses: Tuition, area resident:* Full-time $6684; part-time $489 per credit hour. Tuition, state resident: full-time $6684; part-time $489 per credit hour. Tuition, nonresident: full-time $19,162; part-time $1183 per credit hour. *International tuition:* $19,162 full-time. *Required fees:* $2124. *Financial support:* In 2019–20, 11 students received support, including 4 research assistantships with tuition reimbursements available (averaging $10,100 per year); career-related internships or fieldwork, institutionally sponsored loans, and unspecified assistantships also available. Financial award application deadline: 5/1; financial award applicants required to submit FAFSA. *Unit head:* Dr. David Gurney, Program Co-Coordinator, 985-549-5903, E-mail: dgurney@southeastern.edu. *Application contact:* Dr. David Gurney, Program Co-Coordinator, 985-549-5903, E-mail: dgurney@southeastern.edu.
Website: http://www.southeastern.edu/acad_research/programs/isat/index.html

Thomas Edison State University, School of Applied Science and Technology, Trenton, NJ 08608. Offers clinical trials management (MS); cybersecurity (Graduate Certificate); information technology (MS); nuclear energy technology management (MS); technical studies (MS). *Program availability:* Part-time, online learning. *Degree requirements:* For master's, project. *Entrance requirements:* Additional exam requirements/recommendations for international students: required—TOEFL (minimum score 550 paper-based; 79 iBT). Electronic applications accepted.

University of Arkansas at Little Rock, Graduate School, George W. Donaghey College of Engineering and Information Technology, Department of Applied Science, Little Rock, AR 72204-1099. Offers MS, PhD. *Program availability:* Part-time. *Degree*

requirements: For master's, comprehensive exam, thesis optional, oral exams; for doctorate, thesis/dissertation, 2 semesters of residency, candidacy exams. *Entrance requirements:* For master's, GRE General Test, interview, minimum GPA of 3.0; for doctorate, GRE General Test, interview, minimum graduate GPA of 3.5. Additional exam requirements/recommendations for international students: required—TOEFL.

University of California, Berkeley, Graduate Division, College of Engineering, Group in Applied Science and Technology, Berkeley, CA 94720. Offers PhD. Terminal master's awarded for partial completion of doctoral program. *Degree requirements:* For doctorate, thesis/dissertation, preliminary exam, qualifying exam. *Entrance requirements:* For doctorate, GRE General Test, BA or BS in engineering, physics, mathematics, chemistry, or related field; minimum GPA of 3.0, 3 letters of recommendation. Additional exam requirements/recommendations for international students: required—TOEFL (minimum score 570 paper-based; 90 iBT). Electronic applications accepted. Application fee is waived when completed online.

University of California, Davis, College of Engineering, Program in Applied Science, Davis, CA 95616. Offers MS, PhD. Terminal master's awarded for partial completion of doctoral program. *Degree requirements:* For master's, comprehensive exam (for some programs), thesis (for some programs); for doctorate, thesis/dissertation. *Entrance requirements:* For master's and doctorate, GRE General Test, minimum GPA of 3.3. Additional exam requirements/recommendations for international students: required—TOEFL (minimum score 550 paper-based). Electronic applications accepted.

University of Colorado Denver, College of Liberal Arts and Sciences, Program in Integrated Sciences, Denver, CO 80217. Offers applied science (MIS); computer science (MIS); mathematics (MIS). *Program availability:* Part-time, evening/weekend. *Entrance requirements:* For master's, GRE if undergraduate GPA is 3.0 or less, minimum of 40 semester hours in mathematics, computer science, physics, biology, chemistry and/or geology; essay; three letters of recommendation. Tuition and fees vary according to course load, program and reciprocity agreements.

University of Mississippi, Graduate School, School of Applied Sciences, University, MS 38677. Offers communicative disorders (MS); criminal justice (MCJ); exercise science (MS); food and nutrition services (MS); health and kinesiology (PhD); health promotion (MS); nutrition and hospitality management (PhD); park and recreation management (MA); social welfare (PhD); social work (MSW). *Students:* 188 full-time (149 women), 37 part-time (18 women); includes 47 minority (35 Black or African American, non-Hispanic/Latino; 2 American Indian or Alaska Native, non-Hispanic/Latino; 1 Asian, non-Hispanic/Latino; 5 Hispanic/Latino; 1 Native Hawaiian or other Pacific Islander, non-Hispanic/Latino; 3 Two or more races, non-Hispanic/Latino), 23 international. Average age 26. *Expenses:* Tuition, state resident: full-time $8718; part-time $484.25 per credit hour. Tuition, nonresident: full-time $24,990; part-time $1388.25 per credit hour. *Required fees:* $100; $4.16 per credit hour. *Unit head:* Dr. Peter Grandjean, Dean of Applied Sciences, 662-915-7900, Fax: 662-915-7901, E-mail: applsci@olemiss.edu. *Application contact:* Temeka Smith, Graduate Activities Specialist for Admissions, 662-915-7474, Fax: 662-915-7577, E-mail: gschool@olemiss.edu.
Website: applsci@olemiss.edu

TEMPLE UNIVERSITY
College of Engineering

College of Engineering

Programs of Study

Established in 1969, the College of Engineering at Temple University is a rising institution with an intimate and diverse community. You will have access to faculty performing top-tier research, both within the College and collaboratively with Temple's dental, medical and other professional schools. Temple Engineers show their work, demonstrating their skills and reaching their goals in engineering and in their careers.

- Bioengineering, MS and PhD
- Civil Engineering, MS and PhD
- Computer & Systems Security, Graduate Certificate
- Electrical Engineering, MS and PhD
- Engineering Management, MS and Graduate Certificate
- Environmental Engineering, MS and PhD
- Mechanical Engineering, MS and PhD
- Stormwater Management, Graduate Certificate

The MS programs require 30 semester hours that can be completed on a part-time or full-time basis. Each program has core coursework with the remainder completed with elective course work, allowing for customization for your interests. Students enrolled in the program can choose to complete coursework only, project, or thesis study tracks.

The PhD degree requires 30 semester hours beyond the master's degree -- 15 semester hours are associated with didactic coursework and the remaining 15 semester hours are associated with PhD examinations and dissertation research. Students entering with a bachelor's degree complete 60 credits to earn the PhD. The programs are highly individualized; students work closely with their adviser on creating a plan of study through to the conclusion of their dissertation proposal, dissertation writing, and then defense of the dissertation.

Research Facilities

Faculty members engage in cutting-edge research funded by grants through such organizations as the National Institutes of Health, the American Heart Association, the National Science Foundation, and PennDOT. The College's faculty work in the 15+ advanced laboratories and centers supported by a thriving graduate student population and team of post-doctoral fellows and research scientists.

Research is critical in graduate-level education. It is through research activities that graduate students can apply what they have learned in their undergraduate- and graduate-level coursework to solve real-world problems. Graduate students have opportunities to participate at the College in addition to interdisciplinary research being conducted with other colleges and schools at Temple University, such as the College of Science and Technology, School of Podiatry, College of Public Health, and the Lewis Katz School of Medicine.

Financial Aid

The College of Engineering makes every effort to provide graduate students with the resources necessary for an affordable education. Eligible PhD students are awarded teaching and research assistantships and are automatically reviewed at the time of application. Students awarded an assistantship receive a stipend, tuition remission, and health insurance in exchange for conducting research or assisting faculty in the classroom. Preference is given to those applicants who already have MS degrees. In addition, PhD students are eligible for University-wide fellowships, which typically provide a stipend, tuition remission, and health insurance coverage.

In the master's programs there are a limited amount of merit-based scholarships available for competitive applicants. Students are automatically considered and will be notified at time of admission if they have received such an award.

All U.S. citizens and permanent residents are eligible to apply for need-based aid by completing the Free Application for Federal Student Aid (FAFSA) at www.fafsa.ed.gov.

Cost of Study

Tuition for the 2020-2021 academic year is $1,135 per semester credit for Pennsylvania residents and $1,490 per semester credit for out-of-state residents.

Location

The College of Engineering is located at Temple University's main campus, in the thriving city of Philadelphia—a city at the forefront of science and technology. Graduate students can take advantage of a vibrant arts and culture scene, restaurants, sports and recreation activities in a city easily navigated by walking, biking, or through an array of public transportation options.

Philadelphia is a multicultural city, providing numerous opportunities for students to immerse themselves in the city's diverse neighborhoods and traditions. With a thriving student culture, the Greater Philadelphia region is home to over 25 colleges and universities and boasts an affordable cost of living.

The University

Temple University is many things to many people. A place to pursue life's passions. A nurturing learning environment. A hotbed of research. An engine of employment. A melting pot of ideas and innovation. An incubator for tomorrow's leaders. The University is a R1 rated Carnegie classification for research activity.

Temple's 17 schools and colleges, eight campuses, hundreds of degree programs, and nearly 40,000 students combine to create one of the nation's most comprehensive and diverse learning environments. In neighborhoods, across disciplines, and on a global stage, members of the Temple community are making things happen.

The Faculty

Graduate-level instruction and research are guided by a talented faculty. College of Engineering graduate faculty members explore new and innovative research, publish in peer-reviewed journals, participate in top conference proceedings, and receive grants from prestigious funding sources such as the U.S. Army, the National Science Foundation, the National Institutes of Health, and many others. Faculty members are engaged in areas of research including, but not limited to water resources engineering, sustainability, network securities, artificial intelligence, rehabilitation engineering, tissue engineering, targeted drug delivery, biomaterials, and materials science engineering.

A complete list of faculty members and their areas of research can be found at https://engineering.temple.edu.

Temple University

Applying

The College of Engineering at Temple University welcomes applications to its doctoral, master's, and certificate programs. The College of Engineering admits for both the fall and spring semesters with the following recommended deadlines:

PhD PROGRAMS

Fall Entry
- December 15—Fellowship Consideration Deadline
- January 15—Priority Deadline for Departmental Funding Consideration*
- March 1—Regular Decision Deadline

Spring Entry
- August 1

MASTER'S PROGRAMS

Fall Entry
- June 1—Domestic Students
- March 1—International Students

Spring Entry
- November 1—Domestic Students
- August 1—International Students

Upon receiving all of the required credentials, the application will be reviewed individually by the appropriate department. Please note that the Certificate in Computer and Systems Security admits for Fall only.

To apply for a PhD or MS degree program, students must have:
- An undergraduate degree in engineering from an ABET-accredited or equivalent institution.
- For applicants to the doctoral program, a master's degree is preferred, though not required.
- Competitive applicants will have an undergraduate GPA of at least 3.0 and GREs of at least the 50th percentile in each section.
- For applicants whose native language is not English, the TOEFL or IELTS exam is required with the following minimum scores: 79 on the internet based TOEFL or 6.5 on the academic version of the IELTS.

The following credentials must be submitted for doctoral or master's degree programs:
- Completed graduate application and submission of the application fee.
- Official transcripts from all post-secondary institutions attended;
- Three letters of reference from academic or professional sources
- Statement of Goals
- Resume/CV
- Official GRE score report sent directly from the Educational Testing Agency (ETS). Temple University's institutional code is 2906.
- For applicants whose native language is not English, the TOEFL or the academic version of the IELTS exam is required. TOEFL scores must be submitted directly from the testing agency.

Correspondence and Information

Office of Admissions and Graduate Student Services
College of Engineering
Temple University
1947 N. 12th Street
Philadelphia, Pennsylvania 19122
Phone: 215-204-7800
E-mail: gradengr@temple.edu
Website: engineering.temple.edu

Section 2
Aerospace/Aeronautical Engineering

This section contains a directory of institutions offering graduate work in aerospace/aeronautical engineering. Additional information about programs listed in the directory may be obtained by writing directly to the dean of a graduate school or chair of a department at the address given in the directory.

For programs offering related work, see also in this book *Engineering and Applied Sciences* and *Mechanical Engineering and Mechanics.* In another guide in this series:

Graduate Programs in the Physical Sciences, Mathematics, Agricultural Sciences, the Environment & Natural Resources
See *Geosciences* and *Physics*

CONTENTS

Program Directories

Aerospace/Aeronautical Engineering

Air Force Institute of Technology, Graduate School of Engineering and Management, Department of Aeronautics and Astronautics, Dayton, OH 45433-7765. Offers aeronautical engineering (MS, PhD); astronautical engineering (MS, PhD); materials science (MS, PhD); space operations (MS); systems engineering (MS, PhD). *Accreditation:* ABET (one or more programs are accredited). *Program availability:* Part-time. *Degree requirements:* For master's, thesis; for doctorate, thesis/dissertation. *Entrance requirements:* For master's and doctorate, GRE General Test, minimum GPA of 3.0, U.S. citizenship.

Arizona State University at Tempe, Ira A. Fulton Schools of Engineering, School for Engineering of Matter, Transport and Energy, Tempe, AZ 85281. Offers aerospace engineering (MS, PhD); chemical engineering (MS, PhD); materials science and engineering (MS, PhD); mechanical engineering (MS, PhD); solar energy engineering and commercialization (PSM). *Program availability:* Part-time, evening/weekend, online learning. Terminal master's awarded for partial completion of doctoral program. *Degree requirements:* For master's, thesis and oral defense (MS); applied project or comprehensive exam (MSE); interactive Program of Study (iPOS) submitted before completing 50 percent of required credit hours; for doctorate, comprehensive exam, thesis/dissertation, interactive Program of Study (iPOS) submitted before completing 50 percent of required credit hours. *Entrance requirements:* For master's, GRE, minimum GPA of 3.0 or equivalent in last 2 years of work leading to bachelor's degree; for doctorate, GRE, minimum GPA of 3.0 in last 2 years of work leading to bachelor's degree. Additional exam requirements/recommendations for international students: required—TOEFL, IELTS, or PTE. Electronic applications accepted. *Expenses:* Contact institution.

Auburn University, Graduate School, Samuel Ginn College of Engineering, Department of Aerospace Engineering, Auburn University, AL 36849. Offers MAE, MS, PhD. *Program availability:* Part-time. *Faculty:* 16 full-time (1 woman), 2 part-time/adjunct (0 women). *Students:* 35 full-time (8 women), 35 part-time (10 women); includes 8 minority (1 Black or African American, non-Hispanic/Latino; 3 Asian, non-Hispanic/Latino; 3 Hispanic/Latino; 1 Two or more races, non-Hispanic/Latino), 24 international. Average age 28. 86 applicants, 51% accepted, 23 enrolled. In 2019, 8 master's, 1 doctorate awarded. *Degree requirements:* For master's, thesis, thesis (MS), exam; for doctorate, thesis/dissertation, exams. *Entrance requirements:* For master's and doctorate, GRE General Test. Additional exam requirements/recommendations for international students: required—TOEFL (minimum score 550 paper-based; 79 iBT). *Application deadline:* Applications are processed on a rolling basis. Application fee: $60 ($70 for international students). Electronic applications accepted. *Expenses: Tuition, area resident:* Full-time $9828; part-time $546 per credit hour. Tuition, state resident: full-time $9828; part-time $546 per credit hour. Tuition, nonresident: full-time $29,484; part-time $1638 per credit hour. *International tuition:* $29,744 full-time. Tuition and fees vary according to course load, program and reciprocity agreements. *Financial support:* In 2019–20, 48 fellowships (averaging $33,600 per year), 26 research assistantships (averaging $16,700 per year), 14 teaching assistantships (averaging $13,029 per year) were awarded; Federal Work-Study also available. Support available to part-time students. Financial award application deadline: 3/15; financial award applicants required to submit FAFSA. *Unit head:* Dr. Brian Thurow, Chair, 334-844-6827, E-mail: thurobs@auburn.edu. *Application contact:* Dr. George Flowers, Dean of the Graduate School, 334-844-2125.
Website: http://www.eng.auburn.edu/department/ae/

California Institute of Technology, Division of Engineering and Applied Science, Option in Aeronautics, Pasadena, CA 91125-0001. Offers MS, PhD, Engr. Terminal master's awarded for partial completion of doctoral program. *Degree requirements:* For doctorate, thesis/dissertation.

California Polytechnic State University, San Luis Obispo, College of Engineering, Department of Aerospace Engineering, San Luis Obispo, CA 93407. Offers MS. *Program availability:* Part-time. *Faculty:* 7 full-time (3 women). *Students:* 27 full-time (2 women), 12 part-time (2 women); includes 6 minority (2 Asian, non-Hispanic/Latino; 2 Hispanic/Latino; 2 Two or more races, non-Hispanic/Latino), 5 international. Average age 24. 61 applicants, 61% accepted, 28 enrolled. In 2019, 14 master's awarded. *Entrance requirements:* For master's, GRE. Additional exam requirements/recommendations for international students: required—TOEFL (minimum score 80 iBT). *Application deadline:* For fall admission, 1/4 for domestic and international students. Applications are processed on a rolling basis. Application fee: $55. Electronic applications accepted. *Expenses:* Tuition, state resident: full-time $7176; part-time $4164 per year. Tuition, nonresident: full-time $18,690; part-time $8916 per year. *Required fees:* $4206; $3185 per unit. $1061 per term. *Financial support:* Fellowships, research assistantships, teaching assistantships, career-related internships or fieldwork, scholarships/grants, and unspecified assistantships available. Financial award application deadline: 3/2; financial award applicants required to submit FAFSA. *Unit head:* Dr. Aaron Drake, Graduate Coordinator, 805-756-2577, E-mail: agdrake@calpoly.edu. *Application contact:* Dr. Aaron Drake, Graduate Coordinator, 805-756-2577, E-mail: agdrake@calpoly.edu.
Website: http://aero.calpoly.edu

California State Polytechnic University, Pomona, Program in Engineering, Pomona, CA 91768-2557. Offers engineering (MSE). *Program availability:* Part-time, evening/weekend. *Entrance requirements:* Additional exam requirements/recommendations for international students: required—TOEFL (minimum score 550 paper-based). Electronic applications accepted. *Expenses:* Contact institution.

Carleton University, Faculty of Graduate Studies, Faculty of Engineering and Design, Department of Mechanical and Aerospace Engineering, Ottawa, ON K1S 5B6, Canada. Offers aerospace engineering (M Eng, MA Sc, PhD); materials engineering (M Eng, MA Sc); mechanical engineering (M Eng, MA Sc, PhD). *Degree requirements:* For master's, thesis optional; for doctorate, thesis/dissertation. *Entrance requirements:* For master's, honors degree; for doctorate, MA Sc or M Eng. Additional exam requirements/recommendations for international students: required—TOEFL.

Case Western Reserve University, School of Graduate Studies, Case School of Engineering, Department of Mechanical and Aerospace Engineering, Cleveland, OH 44106. Offers MS, PhD. *Program availability:* Part-time, 100% online. *Degree requirements:* For master's, thesis (for some programs); for doctorate, thesis/dissertation, qualifying exam, teaching experience. *Entrance requirements:* For master's and doctorate, GRE General Test. Additional exam requirements/recommendations for international students: required—TOEFL.

The Citadel, The Military College of South Carolina, Citadel Graduate College, School of Engineering, Department of Mechanical Engineering, Charleston, SC 29409. Offers aeronautical engineering (Graduate Certificate); composites engineering (Graduate Certificate); manufacturing engineering (Graduate Certificate); mechanical engineering (MS); mechatronics engineering (Graduate Certificate); power and energy (Graduate Certificate). *Program availability:* Part-time, evening/weekend. *Degree requirements:* For master's, 30 hours of coursework with minimum GPA of 3.0 on hours earned at The Citadel. *Entrance requirements:* For master's, GRE, 2 letters of recommendation; official transcript of baccalaureate degree from an ABET accredited engineering program or approved alternative. Additional exam requirements/recommendations for international students: required—TOEFL (minimum score 550 paper-based; 79 iBT). Electronic applications accepted.

Concordia University, School of Graduate Studies, Faculty of Engineering and Computer Science, Program in Aerospace Engineering, Montréal, QC H3G 1M8, Canada. Offers M Eng. *Degree requirements:* For master's, thesis or alternative.

Cornell University, Graduate School, Graduate Fields of Engineering, Field of Aerospace Engineering, Ithaca, NY 14853. Offers M Eng, MS, PhD. Terminal master's awarded for partial completion of doctoral program. *Degree requirements:* For master's, thesis (MS); for doctorate, one foreign language, comprehensive exam, thesis/dissertation. *Entrance requirements:* For master's and doctorate, GRE General Test, 3 letters of recommendation. Additional exam requirements/recommendations for international students: required—TOEFL (minimum score 550 paper-based; 77 iBT). Electronic applications accepted.

Embry-Riddle Aeronautical University–Daytona, Department of Aerospace Engineering, Daytona Beach, FL 32114-3900. Offers aerodynamics and propulsion (MS, PhD); dynamics and control (MS, PhD); structures and materials (MS, PhD). *Degree requirements:* For master's, thesis optional; for doctorate, thesis/dissertation. *Entrance requirements:* For doctorate, GRE, minimum master's cumulative GPA of 3.5. Additional exam requirements/recommendations for international students: required—TOEFL (minimum score 550 paper-based, 79 iBT) or IELTS (6). Electronic applications accepted.

Embry-Riddle Aeronautical University–Daytona, School of Graduate Studies, Daytona Beach, FL 32114-3900. Offers aeronautics (MSA), including air traffic management, aviation safety systems, aviation/aerospace education technology, aviation/aerospace management, aviation/aerospace operations, small unmanned aircraft systems operation; aviation (PhD), including human factors in aviation systems. *Degree requirements:* For master's, thesis or capstone project; for doctorate, comprehensive exam, thesis/dissertation. *Entrance requirements:* Additional exam requirements/recommendations for international students: required—TOEFL (minimum score 550 paper-based, 79 iBT) or IELTS (6). Electronic applications accepted.

Embry-Riddle Aeronautical University–Worldwide, Department of Aeronautics, Graduate Studies, Daytona Beach, FL 32114-3900. Offers aeronautics (MSA); aeronautics and design (MS); aviation & aerospace sustainability (MS); aviation maintenance (MAM); aviation/aerospace research (MS); education (MS); human factors (MSHFS); occupational safety management (MS); operations (MS); safety/emergency response (MS); space systems (MS); unmanned systems (MS). *Program availability:* Part-time, evening/weekend, 100% online. *Degree requirements:* For master's, comprehensive exam, thesis (for some programs), capstone or thesis dependent on degree program. *Entrance requirements:* For master's, GRE required for MSHF. Additional exam requirements/recommendations for international students: required—TOEFL (minimum score 550 paper-based; 79 iBT), IELTS (minimum score 6), TOEFL or IELTS required for Applicants for whom English is not the primary language. Electronic applications accepted.

Embry-Riddle Aeronautical University–Worldwide, Department of Engineering and Technology, Daytona Beach, FL 32114-3900. Offers aerospace engineering (MS); entrepreneurship in technology (MS); systems engineering (M Sys E), including engineering management, technical. *Program availability:* Part-time, evening/weekend, 100% online, blended/hybrid learning. *Entrance requirements:* For master's, GRE (for MS in aerospace engineering). Additional exam requirements/recommendations for international students: required—TOEFL (minimum score 550 paper-based; 79 iBT), IELTS (minimum score 6). Electronic applications accepted. *Expenses:* Contact institution.

Florida Institute of Technology, College of Aeronautics, Melbourne, FL 32901-6975. Offers aviation human factors (MS); aviation safety, applied (MSA); aviation sciences (PhD). *Program availability:* Part-time, evening/weekend, 100% online. *Degree requirements:* For master's, thesis (for some programs), thesis or capstone project; for doctorate, thesis/dissertation (for some programs). *Entrance requirements:* For master's, GRE, minimum GPA of 3.0, 3 letters of recommendation, resume, statement of objectives; for doctorate, GRE, minimum GPA of 3.2; master's degree in an aviation field (for international applicants). Additional exam requirements/recommendations for international students: required—TOEFL (minimum score 550 paper-based; 79 iBT). Electronic applications accepted.

Florida Institute of Technology, College of Engineering and Science, Program in Aerospace Engineering, Melbourne, FL 32901-6975. Offers MS, PhD. *Program availability:* Part-time. Terminal master's awarded for partial completion of doctoral program. *Degree requirements:* For master's, comprehensive exam, 30 credit hours; thesis or additional courses plus final exam; for doctorate, comprehensive exam, thesis/dissertation, 42 credit hours. *Entrance requirements:* For master's, GRE General Test, minimum GPA of 3.0; for doctorate, GRE General Test, minimum GPA of 3.2, 3 letters of recommendation. Additional exam requirements/recommendations for international students: required—TOEFL (minimum score 550 paper-based; 79 iBT). Electronic applications accepted.

Florida Institute of Technology, Eglin Education Center (Florida), Program in Flight Test Engineering, Melbourne, FL 32901-6975. Offers MS. *Program availability:* Part-time. *Degree requirements:* For master's, comprehensive exam (for some programs), thesis optional, 30 credit hours. *Entrance requirements:* For master's, GRE General Test, undergraduate degree in related discipline and coursework in mechanical engineering. Additional exam requirements/recommendations for international students: required—TOEFL (minimum score 550 paper-based; 79 iBT). Electronic applications accepted.

The George Washington University, School of Engineering and Applied Science, Department of Mechanical and Aerospace Engineering, Washington, DC 20052. Offers MS, PhD, App Sc, Engr, Graduate Certificate. *Program availability:* Part-time, evening/weekend. *Degree requirements:* For master's, thesis optional; for doctorate, thesis/dissertation, final and qualifying exams. *Entrance requirements:* For master's, appropriate bachelor's degree, minimum GPA of 3.0; for doctorate, GRE (if highest earned degree is BS), appropriate bachelor's or master's degree, minimum GPA of 3.4; for other advanced degree, appropriate master's degree, minimum GPA of 3.0. Additional exam requirements/recommendations for international students: required—TOEFL or The George Washington University English as a Foreign Language Test.

Georgia Institute of Technology, Graduate Studies, College of Engineering, School of Aerospace Engineering, Atlanta, GA 30332. Offers MS, PhD. *Program availability:* Part-time, 100% online. *Faculty:* 38 full-time (2 women), 2 part-time/adjunct. *Students:* 385 full-time (60 women), 100 part-time (14 women); includes 96 minority (12 Black or African American, non-Hispanic/Latino; 1 American Indian or Alaska Native, non-Hispanic/Latino; 48 Asian, non-Hispanic/Latino; 21 Hispanic/Latino; 14 Two or more races, non-Hispanic/Latino), 176 international. Average age 26. 658 applicants, 31% accepted, 112 enrolled. In 2019, 105 master's, 47 doctorates awarded. Terminal master's awarded for partial completion of doctoral program. *Degree requirements:* For master's, thesis optional; for doctorate, thesis/dissertation, complete 42 credit-hours of coursework beyond the bachelor's degree and must have a minimum GPA of 3.25, develop and execute a unique research program to produce a doctoral dissertation. *Entrance requirements:* For master's and doctorate, GRE. Additional exam requirements/recommendations for international students: required—TOEFL (minimum score 577 paper-based; 90 iBT), IELTS (minimum score 7), TOEFL is the preferred method with the requirements shown on the programs. *Application deadline:* For fall admission, 12/1 for domestic students, 6/1 for international students; for spring admission, 10/1 for domestic and international students; for summer admission, 12/1 for domestic students, 3/1 for international students. Applications are processed on a rolling basis. Application fee: $75 ($85 for international students). Electronic applications accepted. *Expenses: Tuition, area resident:* Full-time $14,064; part-time $586 per credit hour. Tuition, state resident: full-time $14,064; part-time $586 per credit hour. Tuition, nonresident: full-time $29,140; part-time $1215 per credit hour. *International tuition:* $29,140 full-time. *Required fees:* $2024; $840 per semester. $2096. Tuition and fees vary according to course load. *Financial support:* In 2019–20, 14 fellowships, 275 research assistantships, 52 teaching assistantships were awarded; career-related internships or fieldwork, Federal Work-Study, institutionally sponsored loans, tuition waivers (full and partial), and unspecified assistantships also available. Support available to part-time students. Financial award application deadline: 7/1; financial award applicants required to submit FAFSA. *Unit head:* Mark Costello, School Chair, 404-894-3000, Fax: 404-894-2760, E-mail: mark.costello@ae.gatech.edu. *Application contact:* Marla Bruner, Director of Graduate Studies, 404-894-1610, Fax: 404-894-1609, E-mail: gradinfo@mail.gatech.edu.
Website: http://www.ae.gatech.edu

Illinois Institute of Technology, Graduate College, Armour College of Engineering, Department of Mechanical, Materials and Aerospace Engineering, Chicago, IL 60616. Offers manufacturing engineering (MAS, MS); materials science and engineering (MAS, MS, PhD); mechanical and aerospace engineering (MAS, MS, PhD), including economics (MS), energy (MS), environment (MS). *Program availability:* Part-time, evening/weekend, online learning. Terminal master's awarded for partial completion of doctoral program. *Degree requirements:* For master's, comprehensive exam (for some programs), thesis (for some programs); for doctorate, comprehensive exam, thesis/dissertation. *Entrance requirements:* For master's and doctorate, GRE General Test (minimum score 1000 Quantitative and Verbal, 3.0 Analytical Writing), minimum undergraduate GPA of 3.0. Additional exam requirements/recommendations for international students: required—TOEFL (minimum score 550 paper-based; 80 iBT). Electronic applications accepted.

Inter American University of Puerto Rico, Bayamón Campus, Graduate School, Bayamón, PR 00957. Offers biology (MS), including environmental sciences and ecology, molecular biotechnology; electrical engineering (ME), including control system, potence system; human resources (MBA); mechanical engineering (ME, MS), including aerospace, energy. *Program availability:* Part-time, evening/weekend. *Degree requirements:* For master's, comprehensive exam, research project. *Entrance requirements:* For master's, EXADEP, GRE General Test, letters of recommendation. *Expenses: Tuition:* Full-time $3870; part-time $1935 per year. *Required fees:* $735; $642 per unit.

Iowa State University of Science and Technology, Department of Aerospace Engineering and Engineering Mechanics, Ames, IA 50011. Offers aerospace engineering (M Eng, MS, PhD); engineering mechanics (M Eng, MS, PhD). *Degree requirements:* For master's, thesis (for some programs); for doctorate, thesis/dissertation. *Entrance requirements:* For master's and doctorate, GRE General Test, resume. Additional exam requirements/recommendations for international students: required—TOEFL (minimum score 550 paper-based; 80 iBT), IELTS (minimum score 6.5). Electronic applications accepted.

Johns Hopkins University, Engineering Program for Professionals, Part-time Program in Space Systems Engineering, Baltimore, MD 21218. Offers MS. *Program availability:* 100% online, blended/hybrid learning. *Entrance requirements:* For master's, undergraduate degree in a technical discipline; at least two years of experience in the space technology or space science field; minimum of two years of relevant work experience; resume; official transcripts from all college studies. Additional exam requirements/recommendations for international students: required—TOEFL (minimum score 600 paper-based; 100 iBT). Electronic applications accepted.

Kent State University, College of Aeronautics and Engineering, Kent, OH 44242-0001. Offers technology (MTC). *Program availability:* Part-time, 100% online. *Faculty:* 11 full-time (2 women), 3 part-time/adjunct (2 women). *Students:* 15 full-time (5 women), 21 part-time (3 women); includes 4 minority (3 Black or African American, non-Hispanic/Latino; 1 Hispanic/Latino), 12 international. Average age 31. 65 applicants, 54% accepted, 15 enrolled. In 2019, 31 master's awarded. *Degree requirements:* For master's, thesis optional. *Entrance requirements:* For master's, 4-year undergraduate (bachelor's) degree in science or related field from accredited college, university, or institute. Additional exam requirements/recommendations for international students: required—TOEFL (minimum score 71 iBT), IELTS (minimum score 6), PTE (minimum score 50), Michigan English Language Assessment Battery (minimum score 71). *Application deadline:* For fall admission, 7/23 for domestic and international students; for spring admission, 12/14 for domestic and international students; for summer admission, 4/30 for domestic and international students. Applications are processed on a rolling basis. Application fee: $45 ($70 for international students). Electronic applications accepted. *Financial support:* Research assistantships, teaching assistantships, career-related internships or fieldwork, Federal Work-Study, scholarships/grants, and unspecified assistantships available. Financial award application deadline: 2/1; financial award applicants required to submit FAFSA. *Unit head:* Christina Bloebaum, Ph.D., Dean and Professor, 330-672-2892, E-mail: cbloebau@kent.edu. *Application contact:* Richard Mangrum, Ed.D., Coordinator, Graduate Program, 330-672-1933, E-mail: rmangrum@kent.edu.
Website: https://www.kent.edu/cae

Massachusetts Institute of Technology, School of Engineering, Department of Aeronautics and Astronautics, Cambridge, MA 02139. Offers aeronautics and astronautics (SM, PhD, Sc D, EAA); aerospace computational engineering (PhD, Sc D); air transportation systems (PhD, Sc D); air-breathing propulsion (PhD, Sc D); aircraft systems engineering (PhD, Sc D); autonomous systems (PhD, Sc D); communications and networks (PhD, Sc D); controls (PhD, Sc D); humans in aerospace (PhD, Sc D); materials and structures (PhD, Sc D); space propulsion (PhD, Sc D); space systems (PhD, Sc D); SM/MBA. *Degree requirements:* For master's, thesis; for doctorate, comprehensive exam, thesis/dissertation, minimum cumulative GPA of 4.4 on 5.0 scale; for EAA, comprehensive exam, thesis. *Entrance requirements:* For master's and doctorate, GRE General Test. Additional exam requirements/recommendations for international students: required—TOEFL, IELTS. Electronic applications accepted.

McGill University, Faculty of Graduate and Postdoctoral Studies, Faculty of Engineering, Department of Mechanical Engineering, Montréal, QC H3A 2T5, Canada. Offers aerospace (M Eng); manufacturing management (MMM); mechanical engineering (M Eng, M Sc, PhD).

Middle Tennessee State University, College of Graduate Studies, College of Basic and Applied Sciences, Department of Aerospace, Murfreesboro, TN 37132. Offers aerospace education (M Ed); aviation administration (MS). *Program availability:* Part-time, evening/weekend, online learning. *Degree requirements:* For master's, comprehensive exam, thesis optional. *Entrance requirements:* For master's, GRE General Test or MAT. Additional exam requirements/recommendations for international students: required—TOEFL (minimum score 525 paper-based; 71 iBT) or IELTS (minimum score 6). Electronic applications accepted.

Mississippi State University, Bagley College of Engineering, Department of Aerospace Engineering, Mississippi State, MS 39762. Offers aerospace engineering (MS); engineering (PhD), including aerospace engineering. *Program availability:* Part-time. *Faculty:* 9 full-time (1 woman), 3 part-time/adjunct (2 women). *Students:* 36 full-time (13 women), 17 part-time (3 women); includes 4 minority (2 Black or African American, non-Hispanic/Latino; 1 Asian, non-Hispanic/Latino; 1 Hispanic/Latino), 26 international. Average age 27. 27 applicants, 70% accepted, 9 enrolled. In 2019, 15 master's, 5 doctorates awarded. *Degree requirements:* For master's, comprehensive exam, thesis optional, oral exam; for doctorate, comprehensive exam, thesis/dissertation. *Entrance requirements:* For master's, GRE (for graduates from program not accredited by EAC/ABET), bachelor's degree in engineering with minimum GPA of 3.0 from junior and senior years; for doctorate, GRE, bachelor's or master's degree in aerospace engineering or closely-related field. Additional exam requirements/recommendations for international students: required—TOEFL (minimum score 550 paper-based; 79 iBT); recommended—IELTS (minimum score 6.5). *Application deadline:* For fall admission, 7/1 for domestic students, 5/1 for international students; for spring admission, 11/1 for domestic students, 9/1 for international students. Applications are processed on a rolling basis. Application fee: $60 ($80 for international students). Electronic applications accepted. *Expenses: Tuition, area resident:* Full-time $8880; part-time $456 per credit hour. Tuition, state resident: full-time $8880. Tuition, nonresident: full-time $23,840; part-time $1236 per credit hour. *Required fees:* $110; $11.12 per credit hour. Tuition and fees vary according to course load. *Financial support:* In 2019–20, 10 research assistantships with partial tuition reimbursements (averaging $16,508 per year), 6 teaching assistantships with partial tuition reimbursements (averaging $14,400 per year) were awarded; Federal Work-Study, institutionally sponsored loans, and unspecified assistantships also available. Financial award application deadline: 4/1; financial award applicants required to submit FAFSA. *Unit head:* Dr. Davy Belk, Department Head and Professor, 662-325-3623, Fax: 662-325-7730, E-mail: davy.belk@ae.msstate.edu. *Application contact:* Ryan King, Admissions and Enrollment Assistant, 662-325-8951, E-mail: rjk101@grad.msstate.edu.
Website: http://www.ae.msstate.edu/

Missouri University of Science and Technology, Department of Mechanical and Aerospace Engineering, Rolla, MO 65401. Offers aerospace engineering (MS, PhD); manufacturing engineering (M Eng, MS); mechanical engineering (MS, PhD). *Program availability:* Part-time, evening/weekend. Terminal master's awarded for partial completion of doctoral program. *Degree requirements:* For master's, thesis optional; for doctorate, comprehensive exam, thesis/dissertation. *Entrance requirements:* For master's, GRE General Test (minimum score 1100 verbal and quantitative, writing 3.5), minimum GPA of 3.0; for doctorate, GRE General Test (minimum score: verbal and quantitative 1100, writing 3.5), minimum GPA of 3.5. Additional exam requirements/recommendations for international students: required—TOEFL (minimum score 550 paper-based). Electronic applications accepted. *Expenses:* Tuition, state resident: full-time $7839; part-time $435.50 per credit hour. Tuition, nonresident: full-time $22,169; part-time $1231.60 per credit hour. *International tuition:* $18,156.60 full-time. *Required fees:* $649.76. One-time fee: $119. Tuition and fees vary according to course load and program.

Naval Postgraduate School, Departments and Academic Groups, Department of Defense Analysis, Monterey, CA 93943. Offers command and control (MS); communications (MS); defense analysis (MS), including astronautics; financial management (MS); information operations (MS); irregular warfare (MS); national security affairs (MS); operations analysis (MS); special operations (MA, MS), including command and control (MS), communications (MS), financial management (MS), information operations (MS), irregular warfare (MS), national security affairs, operations analysis (MS), tactile missiles (MS), terrorist operations and financing (MS); tactile missiles (MS); terrorist operations and financing (MS). *Program availability:* Part-time. *Degree requirements:* For master's, thesis.

Naval Postgraduate School, Departments and Academic Groups, Department of Mechanical and Aerospace Engineering, Monterey, CA 93943. Offers astronautical engineer (AstE); astronautical engineering (MS); engineering science (MS), including astronautical engineering, mechanical engineering; mechanical and aerospace engineering (PhD); mechanical engineering (MS). *Program availability:* Part-time, online learning. *Degree requirements:* For master's, thesis (for some programs), capstone or research/dissertation paper (for some programs); for doctorate, thesis/dissertation; for AstE, thesis.

Naval Postgraduate School, Departments and Academic Groups, Space Systems Academic Group, Monterey, CA 93943. Offers applied physics (MS); astronautical engineering (MS); computer science (MS); electrical engineering (MS); mechanical engineering (MS); space systems (Engr); space systems operations (MS). *Program availability:* Part-time. *Degree requirements:* For master's and Engr, thesis; for doctorate, thesis/dissertation.

North Carolina State University, Graduate School, College of Engineering, Department of Mechanical and Aerospace Engineering, Program in Aerospace Engineering, Raleigh, NC 27695. Offers MS, PhD. *Program availability:* Online learning. *Degree requirements:* For master's, thesis (for some programs), oral exam; for doctorate, thesis/dissertation, oral and preliminary exams. *Entrance requirements:* For master's and doctorate, GRE General Test. Additional exam requirements/recommendations for international students: required—TOEFL (minimum score 550 paper-based). Electronic applications accepted.

The Ohio State University, Graduate School, College of Engineering, Department of Mechanical and Aerospace Engineering, Columbus, OH 43210. Offers aerospace engineering (MS, PhD); mechanical engineering (MS, PhD); nuclear engineering (MS, PhD). *Entrance requirements:* For master's and doctorate, GRE. Additional exam requirements/recommendations for international students: required—TOEFL (minimum score 550 paper-based; 79 iBT), Michigan English Language Assessment Battery (minimum score 82); recommended—IELTS (minimum score 7). Electronic applications accepted.

Aerospace/Aeronautical Engineering

Old Dominion University, Frank Batten College of Engineering and Technology, Programs in Aerospace Engineering, Norfolk, VA 23529. Offers ME, MS, D Eng, PhD. *Program availability:* Part-time, 100% online, blended/hybrid learning. *Degree requirements:* For master's, comprehensive exam (for some programs), thesis (MS), exam/project (ME); for doctorate, comprehensive exam, thesis/dissertation, candidacy exam, proposal, exam. *Entrance requirements:* For master's, GRE, minimum GPA of 3.0; for doctorate, GRE, minimum GPA of 3.5. Additional exam requirements/recommendations for international students: required—TOEFL (minimum score 550 paper-based; 79 iBT), IELTS (minimum score 6.5). Electronic applications accepted. *Expenses:* Contact institution.

Penn State University Park, Graduate School, College of Engineering, Department of Aerospace Engineering, University Park, PA 16802. Offers M Eng, MS, PhD.

Polytechnique Montréal, Graduate Programs, Department of Mechanical Engineering, Montréal, QC H3C 3A7, Canada. Offers aerothermics (M Eng, M Sc A, PhD); applied mechanics (M Eng, M Sc A, PhD); tool design (M Eng, M Sc A, PhD). *Program availability:* Part-time, evening/weekend. *Degree requirements:* For master's, one foreign language, thesis; for doctorate, one foreign language, thesis/dissertation. *Entrance requirements:* For master's, minimum GPA of 2.75; for doctorate, minimum GPA of 3.0.

Princeton University, Graduate School, School of Engineering and Applied Science, Department of Mechanical and Aerospace Engineering, Princeton, NJ 08544. Offers M Eng, MSE, PhD. Terminal master's awarded for partial completion of doctoral program. *Degree requirements:* For master's, thesis (MSE); for doctorate, thesis/dissertation, general exam. *Entrance requirements:* For master's, GRE General Test, 3 letters of recommendation; for doctorate, GRE General Test, official transcript(s), 3 letters of recommendation, personal statement. Additional exam requirements/recommendations for international students: required—TOEFL. Electronic applications accepted.

Purdue University, College of Engineering, School of Aeronautics and Astronautics, West Lafayette, IN 47907. Offers MS, PhD. *Program availability:* Part-time, 100% online. *Faculty:* 46. *Students:* 550. Terminal master's awarded for partial completion of doctoral program. *Degree requirements:* For master's, thesis optional; for doctorate, thesis/dissertation. *Application deadline:* For fall admission, 12/15 priority date for domestic and international students; for spring admission, 9/15 priority date for domestic and international students. Applications are processed on a rolling basis. Application fee: $60 ($75 for international students). Electronic applications accepted. *Financial support:* Fellowships with full and partial tuition reimbursements, research assistantships with full and partial tuition reimbursements, teaching assistantships with full and partial tuition reimbursements, career-related internships or fieldwork, scholarships/grants, health care benefits, and unspecified assistantships available. *Unit head:* Dr. William Crossley, Department Head, E-mail: crossley@purdue.edu. *Application contact:* Jon Mrozinski, Graduate Administrator, E-mail: jwmrozin@purdue.edu.
Website: https://engineering.purdue.edu/AAE

Rensselaer Polytechnic Institute, Graduate School, School of Engineering, Program in Aeronautical Engineering, Troy, NY 12180-3590. Offers M Eng, MS, PhD. *Faculty:* 55 full-time (6 women), 1 part-time/adjunct (0 women). *Students:* 58 full-time (11 women), 1 part-time; includes 7 minority (3 Asian, non-Hispanic/Latino; 1 Hispanic/Latino; 3 Two or more races, non-Hispanic/Latino), 19 international. Average age 25. 87 applicants, 64% accepted, 23 enrolled. In 2019, 11 master's, 10 doctorates awarded. *Degree requirements:* For master's, thesis (for some programs); for doctorate, thesis/dissertation. *Entrance requirements:* For master's and doctorate, GRE. Additional exam requirements/recommendations for international students: required—TOEFL (minimum score 600 paper-based; 100 iBT), IELTS (minimum score 7), PTE (minimum score 68). *Application deadline:* For fall admission, 1/1 priority date for domestic and international students; for spring admission, 8/15 priority date for domestic and international students; for summer admission, 1/1 priority date for domestic and international students. Applications are processed on a rolling basis. Application fee: $75. Electronic applications accepted. *Financial support:* In 2019–20, research assistantships with full tuition reimbursements (averaging $23,000 per year), teaching assistantships with full tuition reimbursements (averaging $23,000 per year) were awarded; fellowships also available. Financial award application deadline: 1/1. *Unit head:* Dr. Theo Borca-Tasciuc, Graduate Program Director, 518-276-2627, E-mail: borcat@rpi.edu. *Application contact:* Jarron Decker, Director of Graduate Admissions, 518-276-6216, Fax: 518-276-4072, E-mail: gradadmissions@rpi.edu.
Website: http://mane.rpi.edu/graduate/aeronautical-engineering

Rutgers University - New Brunswick, Graduate School-New Brunswick, Program in Mechanical and Aerospace Engineering, Piscataway, NJ 08854-8097. Offers design and control (MS, PhD); fluid mechanics (MS, PhD); solid mechanics (MS, PhD); thermal sciences (MS, PhD). *Program availability:* Part-time, evening/weekend. *Degree requirements:* For master's, thesis (for some programs); for doctorate, thesis/dissertation. *Entrance requirements:* For master's, GRE General Test, BS in mechanical/aerospace engineering or related field; for doctorate, GRE General Test, MS in mechanical/aerospace engineering or related field. Additional exam requirements/recommendations for international students: required—TOEFL. Electronic applications accepted.

San Diego State University, Graduate and Research Affairs, College of Engineering, Department of Aerospace Engineering and Engineering Mechanics, San Diego, CA 92182. Offers aerospace engineering (MS); engineering mechanics (MS); engineering sciences and applied mechanics (PhD); flight dynamics (MS); fluid dynamics (MS). Terminal master's awarded for partial completion of doctoral program. *Degree requirements:* For master's, comprehensive exam (for some programs), thesis (for some programs); for doctorate, thesis/dissertation. *Entrance requirements:* For master's, GRE General Test; for doctorate, GRE, 3 letters of recommendation. Additional exam requirements/recommendations for international students: required—TOEFL. Electronic applications accepted.

San Jose State University, Program in Mechanical and Aerospace Engineering, San Jose, CA 95192-0087. Offers aerospace engineering (MS); mechanical engineering (MS). *Program availability:* Part-time, evening/weekend. *Faculty:* 15 full-time (4 women), 13 part-time/adjunct (0 women). *Students:* Average age 27. 113 applicants, 69% accepted, 51 enrolled. In 2019, 56 master's awarded. *Degree requirements:* For master's, thesis. *Entrance requirements:* For master's, GRE required only if undergraduate degree is not from an accredited U.S./Canadian university. Combined score in Verbal and Quantitative must be equal or greater than 310, and Analytical Writing Score must be 3.0 or above., BS in Mechanical Engineering or closely related STEM field. A 2.5 institutional GPA (from the 0.0-4.0 U.S. grading scale) in the last degree completed, or a 2.5 GPA in the last two years of full time study. Additional exam requirements/recommendations for international students: required—TOEFL (minimum score 550 paper-based; 80 iBT), IELTS (minimum score 6.5), PTE (minimum score 53), International students must only take one required test. *Application deadline:* For fall admission, 6/1 for domestic students, 5/1 for international students; for spring admission, 12/1 for domestic students, 11/1 for international students. Applications are processed on a rolling basis. Application fee: $150. Electronic applications accepted. *Expenses: Tuition, area resident:* Full-time $7176; part-time $4164. Tuition, state resident: full-time $7176; part-time $4164. Tuition, nonresident: full-time $7176; part-time $4165 per credit hour. *International tuition:* $7176 full-time. *Required fees:* $2110; $2110. *Financial support:* In 2019–20, 14 teaching assistantships with full and partial tuition reimbursements (averaging $6,400 per year) were awarded; scholarships/grants also available. *Unit head:* Dr. Nicole Okamoto, Department Chair, 408-924-4054, E-mail: nicole.okamoto@sjsu.edu. *Application contact:* Dr. Nicole Okamoto, Department Chair, 408-924-4054, E-mail: nicole.okamoto@sjsu.edu.
Website: http://www.sjsu.edu/me/

Stevens Institute of Technology, Graduate School, School of Systems and Enterprises, Program in Space Systems Engineering, Hoboken, NJ 07030. Offers M Eng, Certificate. *Program availability:* Part-time, evening/weekend. *Faculty:* 22 full-time (8 women), 15 part-time/adjunct (3 women). *Students:* 6 full-time (1 woman), 21 part-time (6 women); includes 4 minority (3 Black or African American, non-Hispanic/Latino; 1 Asian, non-Hispanic/Latino), 2 international. Average age 30. In 2019, 25 master's, 15 Certificates awarded. *Degree requirements:* For master's, thesis optional, minimum B average in major field and overall; for Certificate, minimum B average. *Entrance requirements:* For master's, International applicants must submit TOEFL/IELTS scores and fulfill the English Language Proficiency Requirement. Applicants to full-time programs who do not qualify for a score waiver are required to submit GRE/GMAT scores. Additional exam requirements/recommendations for international students: required—TOEFL (minimum score 74 iBT), IELTS (minimum score 6). *Application deadline:* For fall admission, 4/15 for domestic and international students; for spring admission, 11/1 for domestic and international students; for summer admission, 5/1 for domestic students. Applications are processed on a rolling basis. Application fee: $60. Electronic applications accepted. *Expenses: Tuition:* Full-time $52,134. *Required fees:* $1880. Tuition and fees vary according to course load. *Financial support:* Fellowships, research assistantships, teaching assistantships, career-related internships or fieldwork, Federal Work-Study, scholarships/grants, and unspecified assistantships available. Financial award application deadline: 2/15; financial award applicants required to submit FAFSA. *Unit head:* Dr. Yehia Massoud, Dean of SSE, 201-216.8025, E-mail: yehia.massoud@stevens.edu. *Application contact:* Graduate Admissions, 888-783-8367, Fax: 888-511-1306, E-mail: graduate@stevens.edu.
Website: https://www.stevens.edu/school-systems-enterprises/masters-degree-programs/space-systems-engineering

Syracuse University, College of Engineering and Computer Science, Programs in Mechanical and Aerospace Engineering, Syracuse, NY 13244. Offers MS, PhD. *Program availability:* Part-time. *Degree requirements:* For master's, project or thesis; for doctorate, comprehensive exam, thesis/dissertation. *Entrance requirements:* For master's and doctorate, GRE General Test, official transcripts, personal statement, three letters of recommendation, resume. Additional exam requirements/recommendations for international students: required—TOEFL (minimum score 100 iBT). Electronic applications accepted.

Texas A&M University, College of Engineering, Department of Aerospace Engineering, College Station, TX 77843. Offers aerospace engineering (M Eng). *Faculty:* 43. *Students:* 167 full-time (18 women), 22 part-time (1 woman); includes 26 minority (1 Black or African American, non-Hispanic/Latino; 7 Asian, non-Hispanic/Latino; 14 Hispanic/Latino; 4 Two or more races, non-Hispanic/Latino), 68 international. Average age 26. 182 applicants, 40% accepted, 42 enrolled. In 2019, 32 master's, 14 doctorates awarded. *Degree requirements:* For master's, thesis optional; for doctorate, comprehensive exam, thesis/dissertation. *Entrance requirements:* For master's and doctorate, GRE General Test. Additional exam requirements/recommendations for international students: required—TOEFL (minimum score 550 paper-based; 80 iBT), IELTS (minimum score 6), PTE (minimum score 53). *Application deadline:* For fall admission, 1/1 priority date for domestic students; for spring admission, 7/1 priority date for domestic students; for summer admission, 12/1 priority date for domestic students. Applications are processed on a rolling basis. Application fee: $65 ($90 for international students). Electronic applications accepted. *Expenses:* Contact institution. *Financial support:* In 2019–20, 166 students received support, including 47 fellowships with tuition reimbursements available (averaging $7,200 per year), 139 research assistantships with tuition reimbursements available (averaging $15,907 per year), 28 teaching assistantships with tuition reimbursements available (averaging $10,154 per year); career-related internships or fieldwork, institutionally sponsored loans, scholarships/grants, traineeships, health care benefits, tuition waivers (full and partial), and unspecified assistantships also available. Support available to part-time students. Financial award application deadline: 3/15; financial award applicants required to submit FAFSA. *Unit head:* Dr. Srinivas Rao Vadali, Interim Department Head, 979-845-3918, E-mail: svadali@tamu.edu. *Application contact:* Gail Rowe, Academic Advisor IV, Graduate Programs, 979-845-5520, Fax: 979-845-6051, E-mail: gradadvising@aero.tamu.edu.
Website: https://engineering.tamu.edu/aerospace/

University at Buffalo, the State University of New York, Graduate School, School of Engineering and Applied Sciences, Department of Mechanical and Aerospace Engineering, Buffalo, NY 14260. Offers aerospace engineering (MS, PhD); mechanical engineering (MS, PhD). *Program availability:* Part-time. Terminal master's awarded for partial completion of doctoral program. *Degree requirements:* For master's, comprehensive exam, project or thesis; for doctorate, thesis/dissertation. *Entrance requirements:* For master's and doctorate, GRE General Test, GRE Subject Test. Additional exam requirements/recommendations for international students: required—TOEFL (minimum score 79 iBT). Electronic applications accepted. *Expenses: Tuition, area resident:* Full-time $11,310; part-time $471 per credit hour. Tuition, state resident: full-time $11,310; part-time $471 per credit hour. Tuition, nonresident: full-time $23,100; part-time $963 per credit hour. *International tuition:* $23,100 full-time. *Required fees:* $2820.

The University of Alabama, Graduate School, College of Engineering, Department of Aerospace Engineering and Mechanics, Tuscaloosa, AL 35487. Offers aerospace engineering (MSAEM); engineering science and mechanics (PhD). *Program availability:* Part-time, online learning. *Faculty:* 23 full-time (4 women). *Students:* 46 full-time (6 women), 63 part-time (8 women); includes 16 minority (1 Black or African American, non-Hispanic/Latino; 2 Asian, non-Hispanic/Latino; 9 Hispanic/Latino; 4 Two or more races, non-Hispanic/Latino), 21 international. Average age 29. 105 applicants, 51% accepted, 25 enrolled. In 2019, 15 master's, 2 doctorates awarded. Terminal master's awarded for partial completion of doctoral program. *Degree requirements:* For master's, comprehensive exam (for some programs), thesis (for some programs), culminating expierence; for doctorate, comprehensive exam, thesis/dissertation, 1-year residency. *Entrance requirements:* For master's and doctorate, GRE (minimum score of 300), Minimum undergraduate GPA of 3.0. Additional exam requirements/recommendations for international students: required—TOEFL (minimum score 550 paper-based; 79 iBT); recommended—IELTS (minimum score 6.5). *Application deadline:* For fall admission, 7/15 priority date for domestic students, 4/30 priority date for international students; for spring admission, 12/1 priority date for domestic students, 9/30 priority date for international students. Applications are processed on a rolling basis. Application fee: $50 ($60 for international students). Electronic applications accepted. *Expenses:*

Tuition, area resident: Full-time $10,780; part-time $440 per credit hour. Tuition, nonresident: full-time $30,250; part-time $1550 per credit hour. *Financial support:* In 2019–20, 33 students received support. Fellowships with full tuition reimbursements available, research assistantships with full tuition reimbursements available, teaching assistantships with full tuition reimbursements available, Federal Work-Study, institutionally sponsored loans, scholarships/grants, health care benefits, and unspecified assistantships available. Financial award application deadline: 1/31; financial award applicants required to submit FAFSA. *Unit head:* Dr. Mark Barkey, Professor/Department Head, 205-348-1621, Fax: 205-348-6959, E-mail: mbarkey@eng.ua.edu. *Application contact:* Dr. James Paul Hubner, Associate Professor, 205-348-1617, Fax: 208-348-7240, E-mail: phubner@eng.ua.edu.
Website: http://aem.eng.ua.edu/

The University of Alabama in Huntsville, School of Graduate Studies, College of Engineering, Department of Mechanical and Aerospace Engineering, Huntsville, AL 35899. Offers aerospace systems engineering (MS, PhD). *Program availability:* Part-time. *Degree requirements:* For master's, comprehensive exam, thesis or alternative, oral and written exams; for doctorate, comprehensive exam, thesis/dissertation, oral and written exams. *Entrance requirements:* For master's, GRE General Test, BSE, minimum GPA of 3.0; for doctorate, GRE General Test, minimum GPA of 3.0. Additional exam requirements/recommendations for international students: required—TOEFL (minimum score 500 paper-based; 80 iBT), IELTS (minimum score 6.5). Electronic applications accepted.

The University of Arizona, College of Engineering, Department of Aerospace and Mechanical Engineering, Tucson, AZ 85721. Offers aerospace engineering (MS, PhD); mechanical engineering (MS, PhD). *Program availability:* Part-time. *Degree requirements:* For master's, thesis or alternative; for doctorate, thesis/dissertation. *Entrance requirements:* For master's, GRE General Test, 3 letters of recommendation; for doctorate, GRE General Test, 3 letters of recommendation, statement of purpose. Additional exam requirements/recommendations for international students: required—TOEFL (minimum score 550 paper-based; 79 iBT). Electronic applications accepted.

University of California, Davis, College of Engineering, Program in Mechanical and Aeronautical Engineering, Davis, CA 95616. Offers aeronautical engineering (M Engr, MS, D Engr, PhD, Certificate); mechanical engineering (M Engr, MS, D Engr, PhD, Certificate); M Engr/MBA. *Degree requirements:* For master's, comprehensive exam (for some programs), thesis (for some programs); for doctorate, thesis/dissertation. *Entrance requirements:* For master's and doctorate, GRE General Test, minimum GPA of 3.0. Additional exam requirements/recommendations for international students: required—TOEFL (minimum score 550 paper-based). Electronic applications accepted.

University of California, Irvine, Samueli School of Engineering, Department of Mechanical and Aerospace Engineering, Irvine, CA 92697. Offers MS, PhD. *Program availability:* Part-time. *Students:* 158 full-time (40 women), 9 part-time (3 women); includes 37 minority (4 Black or African American, non-Hispanic/Latino; 20 Asian, non-Hispanic/Latino; 10 Hispanic/Latino; 3 Two or more races, non-Hispanic/Latino), 88 international. Average age 27. 531 applicants, 29% accepted, 46 enrolled. In 2019, 29 master's, 5 doctorates awarded. Terminal master's awarded for partial completion of doctoral program. *Entrance requirements:* For master's and doctorate, GRE General Test, minimum GPA of 3.0, 3 letters of recommendation. Additional exam requirements/recommendations for international students: required—TOEFL (minimum score 550 paper-based). *Application deadline:* For fall admission, 1/15 priority date for domestic students, 1/15 for international students. Applications are processed on a rolling basis. Application fee: $120 ($140 for international students). Electronic applications accepted. *Financial support:* Fellowships, research assistantships with full tuition reimbursements, teaching assistantships, institutionally sponsored loans, traineeships, health care benefits, and unspecified assistantships available. Financial award application deadline: 3/1; financial award applicants required to submit FAFSA. *Unit head:* Prof. Kenneth Mease, Chair, 949-824-5855, Fax: 949-824-8585, E-mail: kmease@uci.edu. *Application contact:* Prof. Roger Rangel, Graduate Admissions Advisor, 949-824-4033, Fax: 949-824-8585, E-mail: rhrangel@uci.edu.
Website: http://mae.eng.uci.edu/

University of California, Los Angeles, Graduate Division, Henry Samueli School of Engineering and Applied Science, Department of Mechanical and Aerospace Engineering, Program in Aerospace Engineering, Los Angeles, CA 90095-1597. Offers MS, PhD. *Degree requirements:* For master's, comprehensive exam or thesis; for doctorate, thesis/dissertation, qualifying exams. *Entrance requirements:* For master's, GRE General Test, minimum GPA of 3.0; for doctorate, GRE General Test, minimum GPA of 3.25. Additional exam requirements/recommendations for international students: required—TOEFL (minimum score 560 paper-based; 87 iBT), IELTS (minimum score 7). Electronic applications accepted.

University of California, San Diego, Graduate Division, Department of Mechanical and Aerospace Engineering, Program in Aerospace Engineering, La Jolla, CA 92093. Offers MS, PhD. *Students:* 28 full-time (1 woman), 4 part-time (0 women). 112 applicants, 38% accepted, 14 enrolled. In 2019, 6 master's, 1 doctorate awarded. *Degree requirements:* For master's, comprehensive exam (for some programs), thesis (for some programs), comprehensive exam or thesis; for doctorate, comprehensive exam, thesis/dissertation. *Entrance requirements:* For master's and doctorate, GRE General Test, minimum GPA of 3.0. Additional exam requirements/recommendations for international students: required—TOEFL (minimum score 550 paper-based; 80 iBT), IELTS (minimum score 7). *Application deadline:* For fall admission, 12/18 for domestic students. Application fee: $105 ($125 for international students). Electronic applications accepted. *Financial support:* Fellowships, research assistantships, teaching assistantships, scholarships/grants, and unspecified assistantships available. Financial award applicants required to submit FAFSA. *Unit head:* Carlos Coimbra, Chair, 858-534-4285, E-mail: mae-chair-l@ucsd.edu. *Application contact:* Jackie Tam, Graduate Coordinator, 858-534-4387, E-mail: mae-gradadm-l@ucsd.edu.
Website: http://maeweb.ucsd.edu/

University of Central Florida, College of Engineering and Computer Science, Department of Mechanical and Aerospace Engineering, Program in Aerospace Engineering, Orlando, FL 32816. Offers MSAE. *Students:* 51 full-time (4 women), 47 part-time (5 women); includes 40 minority (2 Black or African American, non-Hispanic/Latino; 9 Asian, non-Hispanic/Latino; 25 Hispanic/Latino; 4 Two or more races, non-Hispanic/Latino), 6 international. Average age 26. 105 applicants, 77% accepted, 61 enrolled. In 2019, 23 master's awarded. *Entrance requirements:* For master's, resume, goal statement. Additional exam requirements/recommendations for international students: required—TOEFL. *Application deadline:* For fall admission, 7/15 for domestic students; for spring admission, 12/1 for domestic students. Application fee: $30. Electronic applications accepted. *Financial support:* In 2019–20, 26 students received support, including 12 fellowships with partial tuition reimbursements available (averaging $22,750 per year), 12 research assistantships with partial tuition reimbursements available (averaging $8,036 per year), 6 teaching assistantships with partial tuition reimbursements available (averaging $7,043 per year); career-related internships or fieldwork, institutionally sponsored loans, scholarships/grants, tuition waivers (partial), and unspecified assistantships also available. Financial award application deadline: 3/1; financial award applicants required to submit FAFSA. *Unit head:* Dr. Jihua Gou, Program Coordinator, 407-823-2155, E-mail: jihua.gou@ucf.edu. *Application contact:* Associate Director, Graduate Admissions, 407-823-2766, Fax: 407-823-6442, E-mail: gradadmissions@ucf.edu.
Website: http://mae.ucf.edu/academics/graduate/

University of Central Missouri, The Graduate School, Warrensburg, MO 64093. Offers accountancy (MA); accounting (MBA); applied mathematics (MS); aviation safety (MA); biology (MS); business administration (MBA); career and technology education (MS); college student personnel administration (MS); communication (MA); computer information systems and information technology (MS); computer science (MS); counseling (MS); criminal justice and criminology (MS); educational leadership (Ed S); educational leadership and policy analysis (Ed D); educational technology (MS, Ed S); elementary and early childhood education (MSE); English (MA); english language learners - teaching english as a second language (MA); environmental studies (MA); finance (MBA); history (MA); industrial hygiene (MS); industrial management (MS); information systems (MBA); kinesiology (MS); library science and information services (MS); literacy education (MSE); marketing (MBA); mathematics (MS); music (MA); occupational safety management (MS); professional leadership - adult, career, and technical education (Ed S); professional leadership - counseling (Ed S); psychology (MS); rural family nursing (MS); school administration (MSE); social gerontology (MS); sociology (MA); special education (MSE); speech language pathology (MS); teaching (MAT); technology (MS); technology management (PhD); theatre (MA). *Accreditation:* ASHA. *Program availability:* Part-time, 100% online, blended/hybrid learning. *Faculty:* 236 full-time (113 women), 97 part-time/adjunct (61 women). *Students:* 787 full-time (448 women), 1,459 part-time (997 women); includes 213 minority (72 Black or African American, non-Hispanic/Latino; 5 American Indian or Alaska Native, non-Hispanic/Latino; 27 Asian, non-Hispanic/Latino; 59 Hispanic/Latino; 50 Two or more races, non-Hispanic/Latino), 574 international. Average age 30. 1,477 applicants, 68% accepted, 664 enrolled. In 2019, 831 master's, 93 other advanced degrees awarded. *Degree requirements:* For master's and Ed S, comprehensive exam (for some programs), thesis (for some programs). *Entrance requirements:* For master's, A GRE or GMAT test score may be required by some of the programs, A minimum GPA, letters of recommendation, a statement of purpose may be required by some of the programs; for Ed S, A master's degree is required for the application of an Education Specialist's degree program. Additional exam requirements/recommendations for international students: required—TOEFL (minimum score 550 paper-based; 79 iBT). *Application deadline:* For fall admission, 6/1 priority date for domestic and international students; for spring admission, 10/15 priority date for domestic and international students; for summer admission, 4/1 priority date for domestic and international students. Applications are processed on a rolling basis. Application fee: $30 ($75 for international students). Electronic applications accepted. *Expenses: Tuition, area resident:* Full-time $7524; part-time $313.50 per credit hour. Tuition, state resident: full-time $7524; part-time $313.50 per credit hour. Tuition, nonresident: full-time $15,048; part-time $627 per credit hour. *International tuition:* $15,048 full-time. *Required fees:* $915; $30.50 per credit hour. *Financial support:* In 2019–20, 89 students received support. Research assistantships, teaching assistantships, career-related internships or fieldwork, Federal Work-Study, scholarships/grants, unspecified assistantships, and administrative and laboratory assistantships available. Support available to part-time students. Financial award application deadline: 4/1; financial award applicants required to submit FAFSA. *Unit head:* Shellie Hewitt, Director of Graduate and International Student Services, 660-543-4621, Fax: 660-543-4778, E-mail: hewitt@ucmo.edu. *Application contact:* Shellie Hewitt, Director of Graduate and International Student Services, 660-543-4621, Fax: 660-543-4778, E-mail: hewitt@ucmo.edu.
Website: http://www.ucmo.edu/graduate/

University of Cincinnati, Graduate School, College of Engineering and Applied Science, Department of Aerospace Engineering and Engineering Mechanics, Cincinnati, OH 45221-0070. Offers M Eng, MS, PhD. *Program availability:* Part-time. Terminal master's awarded for partial completion of doctoral program. *Degree requirements:* For master's, thesis; for doctorate, thesis/dissertation. *Entrance requirements:* For master's and doctorate, GRE General Test. Additional exam requirements/recommendations for international students: required—TOEFL (minimum iBT score 90), IELTS (6.5), or PTE (47). Electronic applications accepted.

University of Colorado Boulder, Graduate School, College of Engineering and Applied Science, Department of Aerospace Engineering Sciences, Boulder, CO 80309. Offers MS, PhD. Terminal master's awarded for partial completion of doctoral program. *Degree requirements:* For master's, comprehensive exam, thesis or alternative; for doctorate, comprehensive exam, thesis/dissertation. *Entrance requirements:* For master's, GRE General Test, minimum undergraduate GPA of 3.0; for doctorate, minimum undergraduate GPA of 3.25. Electronic applications accepted. Application fee is waived when completed online.

University of Colorado Colorado Springs, College of Engineering and Applied Science, Program in General Engineering, Colorado Springs, CO 80918. Offers computer science (PhD); cybersecurity (ME); energy engineering (ME); engineering management (ME); engineering systems (ME); software engineering (ME); space operations (ME). *Program availability:* Part-time, evening/weekend, blended/hybrid learning. *Faculty:* 1 full-time (0 women), 12 part-time/adjunct (3 women). *Students:* 2 full-time (1 woman), 88 part-time (22 women); includes 23 minority (3 Black or African American, non-Hispanic/Latino; 6 Asian, non-Hispanic/Latino; 9 Hispanic/Latino; 5 Two or more races, non-Hispanic/Latino), 7 international. Average age 32. 36 applicants, 53% accepted, 15 enrolled. In 2019, 28 master's awarded. *Degree requirements:* For master's, thesis, portfolio, or project. *Entrance requirements:* For master's, GRE may be required based on past academic performance., Professional recommendation letters are required for all applicants.; for doctorate, GRE (minimum score of 148 new grading scale on the quantitative portion if the applicant has not graduated from a program of recognized standing), minimum GPA of 3.3 in the bachelor's or master's degree program attempted. Additional exam requirements/recommendations for international students: required—TOEFL (minimum score 80 iBT), IELTS (minimum score 6). *Application deadline:* For fall admission, 7/1 for domestic and international students; for spring admission, 11/1 for domestic and international students. Applications are processed on a rolling basis. Application fee: $60 ($100 for international students). Electronic applications accepted. *Expenses:* Contact institution. *Financial support:* In 2019–20, 5 students received support. Career-related internships or fieldwork, Federal Work-Study, scholarships/grants, traineeships, health care benefits, and unspecified assistantships available. Support available to part-time students. Financial award application deadline: 3/1; financial award applicants required to submit FAFSA. *Unit head:* Dr. Donald Rabern, Dean of Engineering and Applied Science, 719-255-3543, E-mail: drabern@uccs.edu. *Application contact:* Dawn House, Extended Studies Coordinator, 719-255-3246, E-mail: dhouse@uccs.edu.
Website: https://www.uccs.edu/easonline/degree-programs/engineering-management-degree

University of Dayton, Department of Mechanical and Aerospace Engineering, Dayton, OH 45469. Offers aerospace engineering (MSAE, PhD); mechanical engineering (MSME, PhD); renewable and clean energy (MS). *Program availability:* Part-time, 100% online, blended/hybrid learning. *Degree requirements:* For master's, variable foreign language requirement, comprehensive exam (for some programs), thesis; for doctorate, variable foreign language requirement, comprehensive exam, thesis/dissertation, departmental qualifying exam. *Entrance requirements:* For master's, BS in engineering, math, or physics; minimum GPA of 3.0; for doctorate, GRE. Additional exam requirements/recommendations for international students: required—TOEFL (minimum score 550 paper-based; 80 iBT), IELTS (minimum score 6.5). Electronic applications accepted.

University of Florida, Graduate School, Herbert Wertheim College of Engineering, Department of Mechanical and Aerospace Engineering, Gainesville, FL 32611. Offers aerospace engineering (ME, MS, PhD); mechanical engineering (ME, MS, PhD). *Program availability:* Part-time, online learning. *Degree requirements:* For master's, thesis (for some programs); for doctorate, comprehensive exam, thesis/dissertation. *Entrance requirements:* For master's and doctorate, minimum GPA of 3.0. Additional exam requirements/recommendations for international students: required—TOEFL (minimum score 550 paper-based; 80 iBT), IELTS (minimum score 6). Electronic applications accepted.

University of Illinois at Urbana-Champaign, Graduate College, College of Engineering, Department of Aerospace Engineering, Champaign, IL 61820. Offers MS, PhD. *Program availability:* Part-time, online learning.

The University of Kansas, Graduate Studies, School of Engineering, Program in Aerospace Engineering, Lawrence, KS 66045. Offers ME, MS, DE, PhD. *Program availability:* Part-time. *Students:* 39 full-time (6 women), 1 part-time (0 women); includes 3 minority (1 Asian, non-Hispanic/Latino; 2 Hispanic/Latino), 17 international. Average age 27. 19 applicants, 74% accepted, 8 enrolled. In 2019, 8 master's, 4 doctorates awarded. *Entrance requirements:* For master's, GRE, minimum GPA of 3.0, official transcripts, statement of objectives, three letters of recommendation; Statement of Financial Resources (for international students only); for doctorate, GRE, minimum GPA of 3.5, official transcripts, statement of objectives, three letters of recommendation; Statement of Financial Resources (for international students only). Additional exam requirements/recommendations for international students: required—TOEFL, IELTS. *Application deadline:* For fall admission, 12/1 priority date for domestic and international students; for spring admission, 9/15 priority date for domestic and international students; for summer admission, 9/15 priority date for domestic and international students. Application fee: $65 ($85 for international students). Electronic applications accepted. *Expenses:* Tuition, state resident: full-time $9989. Tuition, nonresident: full-time $23,950. *International tuition:* $23,950 full-time. *Required fees:* $984; $81.99 per credit hour. Tuition and fees vary according to course load, campus/location and program. *Financial support:* Fellowships, research assistantships, teaching assistantships, career-related internships or fieldwork, scholarships/grants, tuition waivers (full and partial), and unspecified assistantships available. Financial award application deadline: 12/1. *Unit head:* Richard Hale, Chair, 785-864-2949, E-mail: rhale@ku.edu. *Application contact:* Amy Borton, Administrative Assistant, 785-864-2963, E-mail: aborton@ku.edu. Website: http://www.ae.engr.ku.edu/

The University of Manchester, School of Materials, Manchester, United Kingdom. Offers advanced aerospace materials engineering (M Sc); advanced metallic systems (PhD); biomedical materials (M Phil, M Sc, PhD); ceramics and glass (M Phil, M Sc, PhD); composite materials (M Sc, PhD); corrosion and protection (M Phil, M Sc, PhD); materials (M Phil, PhD); metallic materials (M Phil, M Sc, PhD); nanostructural materials (M Phil, M Sc, PhD); paper science (M Phil, M Sc, PhD); polymer science and engineering (M Phil, M Sc, PhD); technical textiles (M Sc); textile design, fashion and management (M Phil, M Sc, PhD); textile science and technology (M Phil, M Sc, PhD); textiles (M Phil, PhD); textiles and fashion (M Ent).

The University of Manchester, School of Mechanical, Aerospace and Civil Engineering, Manchester, United Kingdom. Offers advanced manufacturing technology (M Ent); aerospace engineering (M Phil, M Sc, PhD); civil engineering (M Phil, M Sc, PhD); environmental engineering (M Phil, PhD); management of projects (M Phil, M Sc, PhD); mechanical engineering (M Phil, M Sc, PhD); mechanical engineering design (M Ent); nuclear engineering (M Phil, D Eng, PhD).

University of Maryland, College Park, Academic Affairs, A. James Clark School of Engineering, Department of Aerospace Engineering, College Park, MD 20742. Offers M Eng, MS, PhD. *Program availability:* Part-time, evening/weekend, online learning. *Degree requirements:* For master's, thesis optional; for doctorate, thesis/dissertation. *Entrance requirements:* For master's and doctorate, GRE General Test (recommended), 3 letters of recommendation. Electronic applications accepted.

University of Miami, Graduate School, College of Engineering, Department of Mechanical and Aerospace Engineering, Coral Gables, FL 33124. Offers MSME, PhD. *Program availability:* Part-time. *Degree requirements:* For master's, thesis (for some programs); for doctorate, comprehensive exam, thesis/dissertation. *Entrance requirements:* For master's and doctorate, GRE General Test, minimum GPA of 3.0. Additional exam requirements/recommendations for international students: required—TOEFL (minimum score 550 paper-based). Electronic applications accepted.

University of Michigan, College of Engineering, Department of Aerospace Engineering, Ann Arbor, MI 48109. Offers M Eng, MS, MSE, PhD. *Program availability:* Part-time. *Degree requirements:* For doctorate, thesis/dissertation, oral defense of dissertation, preliminary exams. *Entrance requirements:* For master's, GRE General Test; for doctorate, GRE General Test, master's degree. Electronic applications accepted.

University of Michigan, College of Engineering, Department of Climate and Space Sciences and Engineering, Ann Arbor, MI 48109. Offers applied climate (M Eng); atmospheric, oceanic and space sciences (MS, PhD); geoscience and remote sensing (PhD); space and planetary sciences (PhD); space engineering (M Eng). *Program availability:* Part-time. Terminal master's awarded for partial completion of doctoral program. *Degree requirements:* For master's, thesis (for some programs); for doctorate, thesis/dissertation, oral defense of dissertation, preliminary exams. *Entrance requirements:* For master's and doctorate, GRE General Test. Additional exam requirements/recommendations for international students: required—TOEFL. Electronic applications accepted.

University of Minnesota, Twin Cities Campus, College of Science and Engineering, Department of Aerospace Engineering and Mechanics, Minneapolis, MN 55455-0213. Offers MS, PhD. *Program availability:* Part-time. *Degree requirements:* For doctorate, thesis/dissertation. *Entrance requirements:* Additional exam requirements/recommendations for international students: required—TOEFL (minimum score 550 paper-based). Electronic applications accepted.

University of Missouri, Office of Research and Graduate Studies, College of Engineering, Department of Mechanical and Aerospace Engineering, Columbia, MO 65211. Offers ME, MS, PhD. *Entrance requirements:* For master's and doctorate, GRE General Test, minimum GPA of 3.0.

University of Nevada, Las Vegas, Graduate College, Howard R. Hughes College of Engineering, Department of Mechanical Engineering, Las Vegas, NV 89154-4027. Offers aerospace engineering (MS); biomedical engineering (MS); materials and nuclear engineering (MS); mechanical engineering (MS, PhD); nuclear criticality safety engineering (Certificate); nuclear safeguards and security (Certificate). *Program availability:* Part-time. *Faculty:* 18 full-time (2 women), 1 (woman) part-time/adjunct. *Students:* 52 full-time (16 women), 26 part-time (7 women); includes 26 minority (5 Black or African American, non-Hispanic/Latino; 1 American Indian or Alaska Native, non-Hispanic/Latino; 7 Asian, non-Hispanic/Latino; 10 Hispanic/Latino; 3 Two or more races, non-Hispanic/Latino), 22 international. Average age 29. 45 applicants, 76% accepted, 14 enrolled. In 2019, 9 master's, 4 doctorates, 1 other advanced degree awarded. *Degree requirements:* For master's, thesis optional, design project; for doctorate, comprehensive exam, thesis/dissertation. *Entrance requirements:* For master's, GRE General Test, statement of purpose; 2 letters of recommendation; for doctorate, GRE General Test, 3 letters of recommendation; statement of purpose; bachelor's degree with minimum GPA of 3.5/master's degree with minimum GPA of 3.3. Additional exam requirements/recommendations for international students: required—TOEFL (minimum score 550 paper-based; 80 iBT), IELTS (minimum score 7). *Application deadline:* For fall admission, 8/1 for domestic students, 5/1 for international students; for spring admission, 12/1 for domestic students, 10/1 for international students. Application fee: $60 ($95 for international students). Electronic applications accepted. *Expenses:* Contact institution. *Financial support:* In 2019–20, 40 students received support, including 2 fellowships with full tuition reimbursements available (averaging $20,000 per year), 16 research assistantships with full tuition reimbursements available (averaging $16,738 per year), 26 teaching assistantships with full tuition reimbursements available (averaging $18,115 per year); institutionally sponsored loans, scholarships/grants, health care benefits, and unspecified assistantships also available. Financial award application deadline: 3/15; financial award applicants required to submit FAFSA. *Unit head:* Dr. Brendan O'Toole, Chair/Professor, 702-895-3885, Fax: 702-895-3936, E-mail: mechanical.chair@unlv.edu. *Application contact:* Dr. Hui Zhao, Graduate Coordinator, 702-895-1463, Fax: 702-895-3936, E-mail: mechanical.gradcoord@unlv.edu. Website: http://me.unlv.edu/

University of Notre Dame, The Graduate School, College of Engineering, Department of Aerospace and Mechanical Engineering, Notre Dame, IN 46556. Offers aerospace and mechanical engineering (M Eng, PhD); aerospace engineering (MS Aero E); mechanical engineering (MEME, MSME). Terminal master's awarded for partial completion of doctoral program. *Degree requirements:* For master's, comprehensive exam, thesis or alternative; for doctorate, thesis/dissertation, candidacy exam. *Entrance requirements:* For master's and doctorate, GRE General Test. Additional exam requirements/recommendations for international students: required—TOEFL (minimum score 600 paper-based; 80 iBT). Electronic applications accepted.

University of Oklahoma, Gallogly College of Engineering, School of Aerospace and Mechanical Engineering, Norman, OK 73019. Offers aerospace engineering (MS, PhD), including aerospace engineering-general; mechanical engineering (MS, PhD), including mechanical engineering-general. *Program availability:* Part-time. *Degree requirements:* For master's, comprehensive exam (for some programs), thesis (for some programs); for doctorate, comprehensive exam, thesis/dissertation, general exam. *Entrance requirements:* For master's and doctorate, GRE, letters of reference, resume, statement of purpose. Additional exam requirements/recommendations for international students: required—TOEFL (minimum score 79 iBT) or IELTS (minimum score 6.5). Electronic applications accepted. *Expenses:* Tuition, state resident: full-time $6583.20; part-time $274.30 per credit hour. Tuition, nonresident: full-time $21,242; part-time $885.10 per credit hour. *International tuition:* $21,242.40 full-time. *Required fees:* $1994.20; $72.55 per credit hour. $126.50 per semester. Tuition and fees vary according to course load and degree level.

University of Ottawa, Faculty of Graduate and Postdoctoral Studies, Faculty of Engineering, Ottawa-Carleton Institute for Mechanical and Aerospace Engineering, Ottawa, ON K1N 6N5, Canada. Offers M Eng, MA Sc, PhD. *Degree requirements:* For master's, thesis or alternative; for doctorate, thesis/dissertation, seminar series, qualifying exam. *Entrance requirements:* For master's, honors degree or equivalent, minimum B average; for doctorate, master's degree, minimum B+ average. Electronic applications accepted.

University of Puerto Rico at Mayagüez, Graduate Studies, College of Engineering, Department of Mechanical Engineering, Mayagüez, PR 00681-9000. Offers mechanical engineering (ME, MS, PhD), including aerospace and unmanned vehicles (ME), automation/mechatronics, bioengineering, fluid mechanics, heat transfer/energy systems, manufacturing, mechanics of materials, micro and nano engineering. *Program availability:* Part-time. Terminal master's awarded for partial completion of doctoral program. *Degree requirements:* For master's, one foreign language, comprehensive exam, thesis; for doctorate, one foreign language, comprehensive exam, thesis/dissertation. *Entrance requirements:* For master's, BS in mechanical engineering or its equivalent; for doctorate, GRE, BS or MS in mechanical engineering or its equivalent; minimum GPA of 3.0. Additional exam requirements/recommendations for international students: required—TOEFL (minimum score 80 iBT). Electronic applications accepted.

University of Southern California, Graduate School, Viterbi School of Engineering, Department of Aerospace and Mechanical Engineering, Los Angeles, CA 90089. Offers aerospace and mechanical engineering: computational fluid and solid mechanics (MS); aerospace and mechanical engineering: dynamics and control (MS); aerospace engineering (MS, PhD, Engr), including aerospace engineering (PhD, Engr); green technologies (MS); mechanical engineering (MS, PhD, Engr), including energy conversion (MS), mechanical engineering (PhD, Engr), nuclear power (MS); product development engineering (MS). *Program availability:* Part-time, evening/weekend, online learning. Terminal master's awarded for partial completion of doctoral program. *Degree requirements:* For master's, thesis optional; for doctorate, thesis/dissertation. *Entrance requirements:* For master's, doctorate, and Engr, GRE General Test. Additional exam requirements/recommendations for international students: recommended—TOEFL. Electronic applications accepted.

University of Southern California, Graduate School, Viterbi School of Engineering, Department of Astronautical Engineering, Los Angeles, CA 90089. Offers MS, PhD, Engr, Graduate Certificate. *Program availability:* Part-time, evening/weekend, online learning. Terminal master's awarded for partial completion of doctoral program. *Degree requirements:* For master's, thesis optional; for doctorate, thesis/dissertation; for other advanced degree, comprehensive exam (for some programs). *Entrance requirements:* For master's, doctorate, and other advanced degree, GRE General Test. Additional exam requirements/recommendations for international students: recommended—TOEFL. Electronic applications accepted.

The University of Tennessee, Graduate School, Tickle College of Engineering, Department of Mechanical, Aerospace and Biomedical Engineering, Program in Aerospace Engineering, Knoxville, TN 37996-2210. Offers MS, PhD, MS/MBA. *Program availability:* Part-time, online learning. *Faculty:* 10 full-time (2 women), 2 part-time/adjunct (0 women). *Students:* 36 full-time (7 women), 11 part-time (1 woman); includes 5 minority (2 Hispanic/Latino; 3 Two or more races, non-Hispanic/Latino), 5 international. Average age 27. 35 applicants, 54% accepted, 11 enrolled. In 2019, 6 master's, 1 doctorate awarded. *Degree requirements:* For master's, thesis or alternative; for doctorate, comprehensive exam, thesis/dissertation. *Entrance requirements:* For master's, GRE General Test (for MS students pursuing research thesis), minimum GPA of 2.7 (for U.S. degree holders), 3.0 (for international degree holders); 3 references;

statement of purpose; for doctorate, GRE General Test, minimum GPA of 3.0 on previous graduate course work; 3 references; statement of purpose. Additional exam requirements/recommendations for international students: required—TOEFL (minimum score 550 paper-based; 80 iBT), IELTS (minimum score 6.5). *Application deadline:* For fall admission, 2/1 priority date for domestic and international students; for spring admission, 6/15 for domestic and international students; for summer admission, 10/15 for domestic and international students. Applications are processed on a rolling basis. Application fee: $60. Electronic applications accepted. *Financial support:* In 2019–20, 26 students received support, including 5 fellowships with full tuition reimbursements available (averaging $28,704 per year), 14 research assistantships with full tuition reimbursements available (averaging $22,219 per year), 7 teaching assistantships with full tuition reimbursements available (averaging $22,683 per year); career-related internships or fieldwork, Federal Work-Study, institutionally sponsored loans, health care benefits, and unspecified assistantships also available. Financial award application deadline: 2/1; financial award applicants required to submit FAFSA. *Unit head:* Dr. Matthew Mench, Head, 865-974-5115, Fax: 865-974-5274, E-mail: mmench@utk.edu. *Application contact:* Dr. Kivanc Ekici, Professor/Graduate Program Director, 865-974-6016, Fax: 865-974-5274, E-mail: ekici@utk.edu.
Website: http://www.engr.utk.edu/mabe/

The University of Texas at Arlington, Graduate School, College of Engineering, Department of Mechanical and Aerospace Engineering, Program in Aerospace Engineering, Arlington, TX 76019. Offers M Engr, MS, PhD. *Program availability:* Part-time, evening/weekend, online learning. Terminal master's awarded for partial completion of doctoral program. *Degree requirements:* For master's, thesis optional; for doctorate, comprehensive exam, thesis/dissertation. *Entrance requirements:* For master's and doctorate, GRE General Test, minimum GPA of 3.0. Additional exam requirements/recommendations for international students: required—TOEFL (minimum score 550 paper-based).

The University of Texas at Austin, Graduate School, Cockrell School of Engineering, Department of Aerospace Engineering and Engineering Mechanics, Program in Aerospace Engineering, Austin, TX 78712-1111. Offers MSE, PhD. *Entrance requirements:* For master's and doctorate, GRE General Test. Electronic applications accepted.

University of Toronto, School of Graduate Studies, Faculty of Applied Science and Engineering, Institute for Aerospace Studies, Toronto, ON M5S 1A1, Canada. Offers M Eng, MA Sc, PhD. *Program availability:* Part-time. *Degree requirements:* For master's, thesis (for some programs); for doctorate, thesis/dissertation, formal manuscript for publication. *Entrance requirements:* For master's, BA Sc or equivalent in engineering (M Eng); bachelor's degree in physics, mathematics, engineering or chemistry (MA Sc); 2 letters of reference; for doctorate, master's degree in applied science, engineering, mathematics, physics, or chemistry; demonstrated ability to perform advanced research, 2 letters of reference. Additional exam requirements/recommendations for international students: required—TOEFL (minimum score 580 paper-based), TWE (minimum score 5). Electronic applications accepted.

University of Virginia, School of Engineering and Applied Science, Department of Mechanical and Aerospace Engineering, Charlottesville, VA 22903. Offers ME, MS, PhD. *Program availability:* Online learning. *Degree requirements:* For master's, thesis (MS); for doctorate, comprehensive exam, thesis/dissertation. *Entrance requirements:* For master's and doctorate, GRE General Test, 3 letters of recommendation. Additional exam requirements/recommendations for international students: required—TOEFL (minimum score 650 paper-based; 90 iBT), IELTS (minimum score 7). Electronic applications accepted.

University of Washington, Graduate School, College of Engineering, William E. Boeing Department of Aeronautics and Astronautics, Seattle, WA 98195-2400. Offers MAE, MSAA, PhD. *Program availability:* Part-time, online learning. *Students:* 98 full-time (14 women), 122 part-time (22 women); includes 60 minority (3 Black or African American, non-Hispanic/Latino; 32 Asian, non-Hispanic/Latino; 14 Hispanic/Latino; 11 Two or more races, non-Hispanic/Latino), 43 international. Average age 27. 341 applicants, 42% accepted, 69 enrolled. In 2019, 48 master's, 9 doctorates awarded. Terminal master's awarded for partial completion of doctoral program. *Degree requirements:* For master's, thesis optional, completion of all work within 6 years; for doctorate, comprehensive exam, thesis/dissertation, qualifying, general and final exams; completion of all work within 10 years. *Entrance requirements:* For master's and doctorate, GRE General Test, minimum GPA of 3.0, letters of recommendation, statement of objectives, undergraduate degree in aerospace or mechanical engineering. Additional exam requirements/recommendations for international students: required—TOEFL (minimum score 580 paper-based; 92 iBT). *Application deadline:* For fall admission, 12/15 for domestic and international students. Application fee: $85. Electronic applications accepted. *Expenses:* Contact institution. *Financial support:* In 2019–20, 5 fellowships with full tuition reimbursements (averaging $34,800 per year), 44 research assistantships with full tuition reimbursements (averaging $34,800 per year), 21 teaching assistantships with full tuition reimbursements (averaging $34,200 per year) were awarded; Federal Work-Study, institutionally sponsored loans, scholarships/grants, health care benefits, tuition waivers (full), and unspecified assistantships also available. Support available to part-time students. Financial award application deadline: 12/15. *Unit head:* Dr. Kristi Morgansen, Professor and Chair, 206-543-5950, Fax: 206-543-0217, E-mail: morgansen@aa.washington.edu. *Application contact:* Ed Connery, Director of Academic Services, 206-543-6725, Fax: 206-543-0217, E-mail: econnery@uw.edu.
Website: http://www.aa.washington.edu/

Université Laval, Faculty of Sciences and Engineering, Department of Mechanical Engineering, Program in Aerospace Engineering, Québec, QC G1K 7P4, Canada. Offers M Sc. *Program availability:* Part-time. *Entrance requirements:* For master's, knowledge of French and English. Electronic applications accepted.

Utah State University, School of Graduate Studies, College of Engineering, Department of Mechanical and Aerospace Engineering, Logan, UT 84322. Offers aerospace engineering (MS, PhD); mechanical engineering (ME, MS, PhD). Terminal master's awarded for partial completion of doctoral program. *Degree requirements:* For master's, thesis (for some programs); for doctorate, thesis/dissertation. *Entrance requirements:* For master's, GRE General Test, minimum GPA of 3.0; for doctorate, GRE General Test, minimum GPA of 3.3. Additional exam requirements/recommendations for international students: required—TOEFL.

Virginia Polytechnic Institute and State University, Graduate School, College of Engineering, Blacksburg, VA 24061. Offers aerospace engineering (PhD, M Eng/MS); biological systems engineering (PhD); biomedical engineering (MS, PhD); chemical engineering (PhD); civil engineering (PhD); computer engineering (PhD); computer science and applications (MS); electrical engineering (PhD); engineering education (PhD); M Eng/MS. *Faculty:* 447 full-time (90 women), 6 part-time/adjunct (2 women). *Students:* 1,881 full-time (495 women), 326 part-time (70 women); includes 264 minority (51 Black or African American, non-Hispanic/Latino; 2 American Indian or Alaska Native, non-Hispanic/Latino; 96 Asian, non-Hispanic/Latino; 69 Hispanic/Latino; 46 Two or more races, non-Hispanic/Latino), 1,247 international. Average age 27. 4,014 applicants, 44% accepted, 658 enrolled. In 2019, 489 master's, 200 doctorates awarded. *Degree requirements:* For master's, comprehensive exam (for some programs), thesis (for some programs); for doctorate, comprehensive exam (for some programs), thesis/dissertation (for some programs). *Entrance requirements:* For master's and doctorate, GRE/GMAT. Additional exam requirements/recommendations for international students: required—TOEFL (minimum score 90 iBT). *Application deadline:* For fall admission, 8/1 for domestic students, 4/1 for international students; for spring admission, 1/1 for domestic students, 9/1 for international students. Applications are processed on a rolling basis. Application fee: $75. Electronic applications accepted. *Expenses:* Tuition, state resident: full-time $13,700; part-time $761.25 per credit hour. Tuition, nonresident: full-time $27,614; part-time $1534 per credit hour. *Required fees:* $886.50 per term. Tuition and fees vary according to campus/location and program. *Financial support:* In 2019–20, 47 fellowships with full tuition reimbursements (averaging $19,703 per year), 1,163 research assistantships with full tuition reimbursements (averaging $20,602 per year), 554 teaching assistantships with full tuition reimbursements (averaging $16,333 per year) were awarded; scholarships/grants and unspecified assistantships also available. Financial award application deadline: 3/1; financial award applicants required to submit FAFSA. *Unit head:* Dr. Julia Ross, Dean, 540-231-9752, Fax: 540-231-3031, E-mail: rjulie@vt.edu. *Application contact:* Linda Perkins, Executive Assistant, 540-231-9752, Fax: 540-231-3031, E-mail: lperkins@vt.edu.
Website: http://www.eng.vt.edu/

Virginia Polytechnic Institute and State University, VT Online, Blacksburg, VA 24061. Offers advanced transportation systems (Certificate); aerospace engineering (MS); agricultural and life sciences (MSLFS); business information systems (Graduate Certificate); career and technical education (MS); civil engineering (MS); computer engineering (M Eng, MS); decision support systems (Graduate Certificate); eLearning leadership (MA); electrical engineering (M Eng, MS); engineering administration (MEA); environmental engineering (Certificate); environmental politics and policy (Graduate Certificate); environmental sciences and engineering (MS); foundations of political analysis (Graduate Certificate); health product risk management (Graduate Certificate); industrial and systems engineering (MS); information policy and society (Graduate Certificate); information security (Graduate Certificate); information technology (MIT); instructional technology (MA); integrative STEM education (MA Ed); liberal arts (Graduate Certificate); life sciences: health product risk management (MS); natural resources (MNR, Graduate Certificate); networking (Graduate Certificate); nonprofit and nongovernmental organization management (Graduate Certificate); ocean engineering (MS); political science (MA); security studies (Graduate Certificate); software development (Graduate Certificate). *Expenses:* Tuition, state resident: full-time $13,700; part-time $761.25 per credit hour. Tuition, nonresident: full-time $27,614; part-time $1534 per credit hour. *Required fees:* $886.50 per term. Tuition and fees vary according to campus/location and program.

Washington University in St. Louis, School of Engineering and Applied Science, Department of Mechanical Engineering and Materials Science, St. Louis, MO 63130-4899. Offers aerospace engineering (MS, PhD); materials science (MS); mechanical engineering (M Eng, MS, PhD). *Program availability:* Part-time. Terminal master's awarded for partial completion of doctoral program. *Degree requirements:* For master's, thesis optional; for doctorate, thesis/dissertation optional. *Entrance requirements:* For master's, GRE; for doctorate, GRE General Test, departmental qualifying exam.

Webster University, George Herbert Walker School of Business and Technology, Department of Management, St. Louis, MO 63119-3194. Offers business and organizational security management (MA); digital marketing management (Graduate Certificate); government contracting (Graduate Certificate); health administration (MHA); health care management (MA); health services management (MA); human resources development (MA); human resources management (MA); information technology management (MA, MS); management (D Mgt); management and leadership (MA); marketing (MA); nonprofit leadership (MA); nonprofit revenue development (Graduate Certificate); organizational development (Graduate Certificate); procurement and acquisitions management (MA); public administration (MPA); space systems operations management (MS). *Program availability:* Part-time, evening/weekend, online learning. *Degree requirements:* For master's, thesis (for some programs); for doctorate, thesis/dissertation, written exam. *Entrance requirements:* For doctorate, GMAT, 3 years of work experience, MBA. Additional exam requirements/recommendations for international students: required—TOEFL.

Western Michigan University, Graduate College, College of Engineering and Applied Sciences, Department of Mechanical and Aerospace Engineering, Kalamazoo, MI 49008. Offers mechanical engineering (MSE, PhD). *Program availability:* Part-time. *Degree requirements:* For master's, thesis optional; for doctorate, thesis/dissertation.

West Virginia University, Statler College of Engineering and Mineral Resources, Morgantown, WV 26506. Offers aerospace engineering (MSAE, PhD); chemical engineering (MS Ch E, PhD); civil engineering (MSCE, PhD); computer engineering (PhD); computer science (MSCS, PhD); electrical engineering (MSEE, PhD); energy systems engineering (MSESE); engineering (MSE); industrial engineering (MSIE, PhD); industrial hygiene (MS); material science and engineering (MSMSE, PhD); mechanical engineering (MSME, PhD); mining engineering (MS Min E, PhD); petroleum and natural gas engineering (MSPNGE, PhD); safety management (MS); software engineering (MSSE). *Program availability:* Part-time. Terminal master's awarded for partial completion of doctoral program. *Degree requirements:* For master's, thesis optional; for doctorate, comprehensive exam, thesis/dissertation. *Entrance requirements:* Additional exam requirements/recommendations for international students: required—TOEFL (minimum score 550 paper-based). Electronic applications accepted. *Expenses:* Contact institution.

Wichita State University, Graduate School, College of Engineering, Department of Aerospace Engineering, Wichita, KS 67260. Offers MS, PhD. *Program availability:* Part-time.

Worcester Polytechnic Institute, Graduate Admissions, Program in Aerospace Engineering, Worcester, MA 01609-2280. Offers aerospace engineering (MS). *Program availability:* Part-time, evening/weekend. *Entrance requirements:* For master's and doctorate, 3 letters of recommendation. Additional exam requirements/recommendations for international students: required—TOEFL (minimum score 563 paper-based; 84 iBT), IELTS (minimum score 7). Electronic applications accepted.

Wright State University, Graduate School, College of Engineering and Computer Science, Department of Mechanical and Materials Engineering, Dayton, OH 45435. Offers aerospace systems engineering (MS); materials science and engineering (MS); mechanical engineering (MS); renewable and clean energy (MS). *Degree requirements:* For master's, thesis or course option alternative. *Entrance requirements:* Additional exam requirements/recommendations for international students: required—TOEFL.

Aviation

Embry-Riddle Aeronautical University–Daytona, College of Business, Daytona Beach, FL 32114-3900. Offers airline management (MBA); airport management (MBA); aviation finance (MSAF); aviation human resources (MBA); aviation management (MBA-AM); aviation system management (MBA); finance (MBA). *Accreditation:* ACBSP. *Degree requirements:* For master's, thesis (for some programs). *Entrance requirements:* For master's, GRE (for some programs). Additional exam requirements/recommendations for international students: required—TOEFL (minimum score 550 paper-based, 79 iBT) or IELTS (6). Electronic applications accepted.

Embry-Riddle Aeronautical University–Prescott, Behavioral and Safety Sciences Department, Prescott, AZ 86301-3720. Offers aviation safety (MSSS). *Degree requirements:* For master's, research project, capstone, or thesis. *Entrance requirements:* For master's, transcripts, statement of goals, letters of recommendation, resume. Additional exam requirements/recommendations for international students: required—TOEFL (minimum score 550 paper-based; 79 iBT), IELTS (minimum score 6). Electronic applications accepted.

Everglades University, Graduate Programs, Program in Aviation Science, Boca Raton, FL 33431. Offers aviation operations management (MSA); aviation security (MSA); business administration (MSA). *Program availability:* Part-time, evening/weekend, 100% online. *Entrance requirements:* For master's, GMAT (minimum score of 400) or GRE (minimum score of 290), bachelor's or graduate degree from college accredited by an agency recognized by the U.S. Department of Education; minimum cumulative GPA of 2.0 at the baccalaureate level, 3.0 at the master's level. Additional exam requirements/recommendations for international students: recommended—TOEFL (minimum score 500 paper-based). Electronic applications accepted. *Expenses:* Contact institution.

Florida Institute of Technology, College of Aeronautics, Program in Applied Aviation Safety, Melbourne, FL 32901-6975. Offers applied aviation safety (MSA). *Program availability:* Part-time. *Degree requirements:* For master's, comprehensive exam (for some programs), thesis optional, 36 credit hours. *Entrance requirements:* For master's, GRE, 3 letters of recommendation, resume, statement of objectives. Additional exam requirements/recommendations for international students: required—TOEFL (minimum score 550 paper-based; 79 iBT). Electronic applications accepted.

Florida Institute of Technology, College of Aeronautics, Program in Aviation Sciences, Melbourne, FL 32901-6975. Offers aviation science (PhD). *Program availability:* Part-time. *Degree requirements:* For doctorate, thesis/dissertation, 51 semester hours. *Entrance requirements:* Additional exam requirements/recommendations for international students: required—TOEFL (minimum score 550 paper-based; 79 iBT). Electronic applications accepted.

National Test Pilot School, National Flight Institute, Mojave, CA 93502-0658. Offers flight test and evaluation (MS); flight test engineering (MS). *Accreditation:* ABET. *Degree requirements:* For master's, final project. *Entrance requirements:* For master's, undergraduate degree in engineering, physical or computer science, mathematics or technical management.

Oklahoma State University, College of Education, Health and Aviation, Stillwater, OK 74078. Offers MS, Ed D, PhD, Ed S. *Accreditation:* NCATE. *Program availability:* Part-time, online learning. *Faculty:* 91 full-time (63 women), 25 part-time/adjunct (14 women). *Students:* 268 full-time (180 women), 518 part-time (358 women); includes 220 minority (66 Black or African American, non-Hispanic/Latino; 35 American Indian or Alaska Native, non-Hispanic/Latino; 15 Asian, non-Hispanic/Latino; 46 Hispanic/Latino; 58 Two or more races, non-Hispanic/Latino), 45 international. Average age 35. 370 applicants, 70% accepted, 219 enrolled. In 2019, 148 master's, 60 doctorates awarded. *Degree requirements:* For master's, thesis or alternative; for doctorate, comprehensive exam, thesis/dissertation. *Entrance requirements:* For master's and doctorate, GRE or GMAT. Additional exam requirements/recommendations for international students: required—TOEFL (minimum score 550 paper-based; 79 iBT). *Application deadline:* For fall admission, 3/1 priority date for domestic and international students; for spring admission, 8/1 priority date for domestic and international students. Applications are processed on a rolling basis. Application fee: $50 ($75 for international students). Electronic applications accepted. *Expenses: Tuition, area resident:* Full-time $4148.10; part-time $2765.40. Tuition, state resident: full-time $4148.10; part-time $2765.40. Tuition, nonresident: full-time $15,775; part-time $10,516.80. *International tuition:* $15,775.20 full-time. *Required fees:* $2196.90; $122.05 per credit hour. Tuition and fees vary according to course load, campus/location and program. *Financial support:* In 2019–20, 62 research assistantships (averaging $1,223 per year), 78 teaching assistantships (averaging $1,236 per year) were awarded; career-related internships or fieldwork, Federal Work-Study, scholarships/grants, health care benefits, tuition waivers (partial), and unspecified assistantships also available. Support available to part-time students. Financial award application deadline: 3/1; financial award applicants required to submit FAFSA. *Unit head:* Dr. Stephan M Wilson, Interim Dean, 405-744.9805, E-mail: contact.ehs@okstate.edu. *Application contact:* Dr. Sheryl Tucker, Dean, 405-744-6368, Fax: 405-744-0355, E-mail: gradi@okstate.edu. Website: http://education.okstate.edu/

Southeastern Oklahoma State University, Department of Aviation Science, Durant, OK 74701-0609. Offers aerospace administration and logistics (MS). *Program availability:* Part-time, evening/weekend. *Entrance requirements:* For master's, minimum GPA of 3.0 in last 60 hours or 2.75 overall. Additional exam requirements/recommendations for international students: required—TOEFL (minimum score 550 paper-based; 79 iBT). Electronic applications accepted.

University of North Dakota, Graduate School, John D. Odegard School of Aerospace Sciences, Department of Aviation, Grand Forks, ND 58202. Offers MS. *Program availability:* Part-time, online learning. *Degree requirements:* For master's, comprehensive exam. *Entrance requirements:* For master's, GRE General Test, FAA private pilot certificate or foreign equivalent. Additional exam requirements/recommendations for international students: required—TOEFL (minimum score 550 paper-based; 79 iBT), IELTS (minimum score 6.5). Electronic applications accepted.

The University of Tennessee, Graduate School, Intercollegiate Programs, Program in Aviation Systems, Knoxville, TN 37996. Offers MS. *Program availability:* Part-time, online learning. *Degree requirements:* For master's, thesis optional. *Entrance requirements:* For master's, minimum GPA of 2.7. Additional exam requirements/recommendations for international students: required—TOEFL. Electronic applications accepted.

Section 3
Agricultural Engineering and Bioengineering

This section contains a directory of institutions offering graduate work in agricultural engineering and bioengineering, followed by an in-depth entry submitted by an institution that chose to prepare a detailed program description. Additional information about programs listed in the directory but not augmented by an in-depth entry may be obtained by writing directly to the dean of a graduate school or chair of a department at the address given in the directory.

For programs offering related work, see also in this book *Biomedical Engineering and Biotechnology; Civil and Environmental Engineering; Engineering and Applied Sciences;* and *Management of Engineering and Technology.* In the other guides in this series:
Graduate Programs in the Biological/Biomedical Sciences & Health-Related Medical Professions

See *Biological and Biomedical Sciences; Ecology, Environmental Biology, and Evolutionary Biology; Marine Biology; Nutrition;* and *Zoology*
Graduate Programs in the Physical Sciences, Mathematics, Agricultural Sciences, the Environment & Natural Resources
See *Agricultural and Food Sciences* and *Natural Resources*

CONTENTS

Program Directories

Agricultural Engineering

Cornell University, Graduate School, Graduate Fields of Agriculture and Life Sciences and Graduate Fields of Engineering, Field of Biological and Environmental Engineering, Ithaca, NY 14853. Offers bioenergy and integrated energy systems (M Eng, MPS, MS, PhD); biological engineering (M Eng, MPS, MS, PhD); bioprocess engineering (M Eng, MPS, MS, PhD); ecohydrology (M Eng, MPS, MS, PhD); environmental engineering (M Eng, MPS, MS, PhD); environmental management (MPS); food engineering (M Eng, MPS, MS, PhD); industrial biotechnology (M Eng, MPS, MS, PhD); nanobiotechnology (M Eng, MPS, MS, PhD); sustainable systems (M Eng, MPS, MS, PhD); synthetic biology (MS); syntheticbiology (M Eng, MPS, PhD). Terminal master's awarded for partial completion of doctoral program. *Degree requirements:* For master's, thesis (MS); for doctorate, comprehensive exam, thesis/dissertation. *Entrance requirements:* For master's, letters of recommendation (3 for MS, 2 for M Eng and MPS); for doctorate, GRE General Test, 3 letters of recommendation. Additional exam requirements/recommendations for international students: required—TOEFL (minimum score 550 paper-based; 77 iBT). Electronic applications accepted.

Illinois Institute of Technology, Graduate College, School of Applied Technology, Institute for Food Safety and Health, Bedford Park, IL 60501-1957. Offers food process engineering (MFPE, MS); food safety and technology (MFST, MS). *Program availability:* Part-time. *Degree requirements:* For master's, comprehensive exam (for some programs), thesis (for some programs). *Entrance requirements:* For master's, GRE (minimum score 304), minimum undergraduate GPA of 3.0. Additional exam requirements/recommendations for international students: required—TOEFL (minimum score 550 paper-based; 80 iBT). Electronic applications accepted.

Instituto Tecnológico y de Estudios Superiores de Monterrey, Campus Monterrey, Graduate and Research Division, Program in Agriculture, Monterrey, Mexico. Offers agricultural parasitology (PhD); agricultural sciences (MS); farming productivity (MS); food processing engineering (MS); phytopathology (MS). *Program availability:* Part-time. *Degree requirements:* For master's, one foreign language, thesis; for doctorate, one foreign language, thesis/dissertation. *Entrance requirements:* For master's, EXADEP; for doctorate, GMAT or GRE, master's degree in related field. Additional exam requirements/recommendations for international students: required—TOEFL.

Iowa State University of Science and Technology, Program in Agricultural and Biosystems Engineering, Ames, IA 50011. Offers M En, MS, PhD. *Degree requirements:* For master's, thesis (for some programs); for doctorate, thesis/dissertation. *Entrance requirements:* For master's and doctorate, GRE. Additional exam requirements/recommendations for international students: required—TOEFL (minimum score 550 paper-based; 79 iBT), IELTS (minimum score 6.5). Electronic applications accepted.

Kansas State University, Graduate School, College of Agriculture, Department of Grain Science and Industry, Manhattan, KS 66506. Offers MS, PhD. *Program availability:* Part-time. Terminal master's awarded for partial completion of doctoral program. *Degree requirements:* For master's, thesis, oral exam; for doctorate, thesis/dissertation, preliminary exam. *Entrance requirements:* For master's and doctorate, GRE General Test, minimum undergraduate GPA of 3.0. Additional exam requirements/recommendations for international students: required—TOEFL (minimum score 550 paper-based; 79 iBT), IELTS (minimum score 7). Electronic applications accepted.

Kansas State University, Graduate School, College of Engineering, Department of Biological and Agricultural Engineering, Manhattan, KS 66506. Offers MS, PhD. Terminal master's awarded for partial completion of doctoral program. *Degree requirements:* For master's, thesis; for doctorate, thesis/dissertation, preliminary exam. *Entrance requirements:* For master's, GRE, bachelor's degree in biological and agricultural engineering; for doctorate, GRE. Additional exam requirements/recommendations for international students: required—TOEFL (minimum score 550 paper-based; 79 iBT). Electronic applications accepted.

Louisiana State University and Agricultural & Mechanical College, Graduate School, College of Engineering, Department of Biological and Agricultural Engineering, Baton Rouge, LA 70803. Offers biological and agricultural engineering (MSBAE); engineering science (MS, PhD).

McGill University, Faculty of Graduate and Postdoctoral Studies, Faculty of Agricultural and Environmental Sciences, Department of Bioresource Engineering, Montréal, QC H3A 2T5, Canada. Offers computer applications (M Sc, M Sc A, PhD); food engineering (M Sc, M Sc A, PhD); grain drying (M Sc, M Sc A, PhD); irrigation and drainage (M Sc, M Sc A, PhD); machinery (M Sc, M Sc A, PhD); pollution control (M Sc, M Sc A, PhD); post-harvest technology (M Sc, M Sc A, PhD); soil dynamics (M Sc, M Sc A, PhD); structure and environment (M Sc, M Sc A, PhD); vegetable and fruit storage (M Sc, M Sc A, PhD).

North Carolina State University, Graduate School, College of Agriculture and Life Sciences, Department of Biological and Agricultural Engineering, Raleigh, NC 27695. Offers MBAE, MS, PhD, Certificate. *Program availability:* Part-time, online learning. *Degree requirements:* For master's, thesis (for some programs); for doctorate, thesis/dissertation. *Entrance requirements:* For master's and doctorate, GRE. Additional exam requirements/recommendations for international students: required—TOEFL. Electronic applications accepted.

North Dakota State University, College of Graduate and Interdisciplinary Studies, College of Engineering, Department of Agricultural and Biosystems Engineering, Fargo, ND 58102. Offers MS, PhD. *Program availability:* Part-time. *Degree requirements:* For master's, thesis; for doctorate, thesis/dissertation. *Entrance requirements:* For master's and doctorate, BS in engineering or the equivalent, minimum undergraduate GPA of 3.0. Additional exam requirements/recommendations for international students: required—TOEFL (minimum score 550 paper-based; 79 iBT). Electronic applications accepted. Tuition and fees vary according to program and reciprocity agreements.

The Ohio State University, Graduate School, College of Food, Agricultural, and Environmental Sciences, Department of Food, Agricultural, and Biological Engineering, Columbus, OH 43210. Offers MS, PhD. *Entrance requirements:* For master's and doctorate, GRE General Test, GRE Subject Test in engineering (recommended). Additional exam requirements/recommendations for international students: required—TOEFL (minimum score 550 paper-based; 79 iBT), Michigan English Language Assessment Battery (minimum score 82); recommended—IELTS (minimum score 7). Electronic applications accepted.

Oklahoma State University, College of Agricultural Science and Natural Resources, Department of Biosystems and Agricultural Engineering, Stillwater, OK 74078. Offers biosystems engineering (MS, PhD); environmental and natural resources (MS, PhD). *Faculty:* 17 full-time (6 women). *Students:* 8 full-time (3 women), 12 part-time (4 women); includes 1 minority (Black or African American, non-Hispanic/Latino), 13 international. Average age 32. 12 applicants, 25% accepted, 2 enrolled. In 2019, 6 master's, 8 doctorates awarded. *Entrance requirements:* For master's and doctorate, GRE or GMAT. Additional exam requirements/recommendations for international students: required—TOEFL (minimum score 550 paper-based; 79 iBT). *Application deadline:* For fall admission, 3/1 priority date for international students; for spring admission, 8/1 priority date for international students. Applications are processed on a rolling basis. Application fee: $50 ($75 for international students). Electronic applications accepted. *Expenses: Tuition, area resident:* Full-time $4148.10; part-time $2765.40. Tuition, state resident: full-time $4148.10; part-time $2765.40. Tuition, nonresident: full-time $15,775; part-time $10,516.80. *International tuition:* $15,775.20 full-time. *Required fees:* $2196.90; $122.05 per credit hour. Tuition and fees vary according to course load, campus/location and program. *Financial support:* In 2019–20, 19 research assistantships (averaging $1,661 per year), 1 teaching assistantship (averaging $1,000 per year) were awarded; career-related internships or fieldwork, Federal Work-Study, scholarships/grants, health care benefits, tuition waivers (partial), and unspecified assistantships also available. Support available to part-time students. Financial award application deadline: 3/1; financial award applicants required to submit FAFSA. *Unit head:* Dr. John Veenstra, Department Head, 405-744-5431, Fax: 405-744-6059, E-mail: jveenst@okstate.edu. *Application contact:* Dr. Ning Wang, Professor/Graduate Coordinator, 405-744-2877, E-mail: ning.wang@okstate.edu.
Website: http://bae.okstate.edu/

Oregon State University, College of Agricultural Sciences, Program in Food Science and Technology, Corvallis, OR 97331. Offers brewing (MS, PhD); enology (MS, PhD); flavor chemistry (MS, PhD); food and seafood processing (MS, PhD); food chemistry/biochemistry (MS, PhD); food engineering (MS, PhD); food microbiology/biotechnology (MS, PhD); sensory evaluation (MS, PhD). *Entrance requirements:* For master's and doctorate, GRE (minimum Verbal and Quantitative scores of 300), minimum GPA of 3.0 in last 90 hours. Additional exam requirements/recommendations for international students: required—TOEFL (minimum score 80 iBT), IELTS (minimum score 6.5).

Penn State University Park, Graduate School, College of Agricultural Sciences, Department of Agricultural and Biological Engineering, University Park, PA 16802. Offers agricultural and biological engineering (MS, PhD); biorenewable systems (MS, PhD).

Purdue University, College of Engineering, School of Agricultural and Biological Engineering, West Lafayette, IN 47907-2093. Offers MS, MSABE, MSE, PhD. *Program availability:* Part-time. *Faculty:* 39. *Students:* 191. Terminal master's awarded for partial completion of doctoral program. *Degree requirements:* For master's, thesis (for some programs); for doctorate, thesis/dissertation. *Application deadline:* For fall admission, 12/1 for domestic and international students; for spring admission, 9/1 for domestic and international students. Applications are processed on a rolling basis. Application fee: $60 ($75 for international students). Electronic applications accepted. *Financial support:* Fellowships with full and partial tuition reimbursements, research assistantships with full and partial tuition reimbursements, teaching assistantships with full and partial tuition reimbursements, career-related internships or fieldwork, scholarships/grants, health care benefits, unspecified assistantships, and instructorships available. *Unit head:* Nathan Mosier, Interim Head, 765-496-2044, E-mail: mosiern@purdue.edu. *Application contact:* Becky Peer, Assistant to Department Head, 765-494-1181, E-mail: peerb@purdue.edu.
Website: https://engineering.purdue.edu/ABE

South Dakota State University, Graduate School, Jerome J. Lohr College of Engineering, Department of Agricultural and Biosystems Engineering, Brookings, SD 57007. Offers biological sciences (MS, PhD); engineering (MS). *Program availability:* Part-time. *Degree requirements:* For master's, thesis (for some programs), oral exam; for doctorate, thesis/dissertation, preliminary oral and written exams. *Entrance requirements:* For master's and doctorate, engineering degree. Additional exam requirements/recommendations for international students: required—TOEFL (minimum score 550 paper-based; 79 iBT).

Texas A&M University, College of Agriculture and Life Sciences, Department of Biological and Agricultural Engineering, College Station, TX 77843. Offers agricultural systems management (M Agr, MS); biological and agricultural engineering (MS, PhD). *Program availability:* Part-time. *Faculty:* 18. *Students:* 64 full-time (17 women), 8 part-time (4 women); includes 12 minority (4 Black or African American, non-Hispanic/Latino; 2 Asian, non-Hispanic/Latino; 5 Hispanic/Latino; 1 Two or more races, non-Hispanic/Latino), 49 international. Average age 31. 20 applicants, 100% accepted, 11 enrolled. In 2019, 10 master's, 11 doctorates awarded. *Degree requirements:* For master's, thesis (MS), preliminary and final exams; for doctorate, thesis/dissertation, preliminary and final exams. *Entrance requirements:* For master's and doctorate, GRE General Test, statement of purpose, resume, letters of recommendation. Additional exam requirements/recommendations for international students: required—TOEFL (minimum score 550 paper-based; 80 iBT), IELTS (minimum score 6), PTE (minimum score 53). *Application deadline:* For fall admission, 8/15 for domestic students, 7/1 for international students; for spring admission, 12/1 for domestic students, 11/1 for international students; for summer admission, 5/1 for domestic students, 4/1 for international students. Application fee: $65 ($90 for international students). Electronic applications accepted. *Expenses:* Contact institution. *Financial support:* In 2019–20, 70 students received support, including 11 fellowships with tuition reimbursements available (averaging $10,171 per year), 41 research assistantships with tuition reimbursements available (averaging $12,179 per year), 20 teaching assistantships with tuition reimbursements available (averaging $13,004 per year); career-related internships or fieldwork, institutionally sponsored loans, scholarships/grants, traineeships, health care benefits, tuition waivers (full and partial), and unspecified assistantships also available. Support available to part-time students. Financial award application deadline: 3/15; financial award applicants required to submit FAFSA. *Unit head:* Dr. Steve Searcy, Senior Professor and Head, 979-845-3940, Fax: 979-862-3442, E-mail: s-searcy@tamu.edu. *Application contact:* Dr. Sandun Fernando, Director of Graduate Programs, 979-845-9793, E-mail: sfernando@tamu.edu.
Website: http://baen.tamu.edu

The University of Arizona, College of Agriculture and Life Sciences, Department of Agricultural and Biosystems Engineering, Tucson, AZ 85721. Offers MS, PhD. Terminal master's awarded for partial completion of doctoral program. *Degree requirements:* For master's, thesis; for doctorate, thesis/dissertation. *Entrance requirements:* For master's, minimum GPA of 3.0 in last 2 years of undergraduate study, 3 letters of recommendation; for doctorate, minimum GPA of 3.0 in last 2 years of undergraduate study, 3 letters of recommendation, statement of purpose. Additional exam requirements/recommendations for international students: required—TOEFL (minimum score 550 paper-based; 79 iBT). Electronic applications accepted.

University of Arkansas, Graduate School, College of Engineering, Department of Biological and Agricultural Engineering, Fayetteville, AR 72701. Offers biological and agricultural engineering (MSE, PhD); biological engineering (MSBE); biomedical engineering (MSBME). *Students:* 29 full-time (17 women), 17 part-time (6 women);

includes 7 minority (1 Black or African American, non-Hispanic/Latino; 1 American Indian or Alaska Native, non-Hispanic/Latino; 2 Asian, non-Hispanic/Latino; 3 Hispanic/Latino), 13 international. 24 applicants, 63% accepted. In 2019, 6 master's, 4 doctorates awarded. *Degree requirements:* For master's, thesis; for doctorate, one foreign language, thesis/dissertation. *Application deadline:* For fall admission, 8/1 for domestic students, 4/1 for international students; for spring admission, 12/1 for domestic students, 10/1 for international students; for summer admission, 4/15 for domestic students, 3/1 for international students. Applications are processed on a rolling basis. Application fee: $60. Electronic applications accepted. *Financial support:* In 2019–20, 21 research assistantships, 3 teaching assistantships were awarded; fellowships with tuition reimbursements, career-related internships or fieldwork, and Federal Work-Study also available. Support available to part-time students. Financial award application deadline: 4/1; financial award applicants required to submit FAFSA. *Unit head:* Dr. Raj Rao, Department Head, 479-575-6011, E-mail: rajrao@uark.edu. *Application contact:* Dr. kartik Balachandran, Program Coordinator, 479-575-3376, E-mail: kbalacha@uark.edu. Website: https://bio-ag-engineering.uark.edu

University of Florida, Graduate School, Herbert Wertheim College of Engineering and College of Agricultural and Life Sciences, Department of Agricultural and Biological Engineering, Gainesville, FL 32611. Offers agricultural and biological engineering (ME, MS, PhD), including geographic information systems, hydrologic sciences, wetland sciences; biological systems modeling (Certificate). *Program availability:* Part-time. Terminal master's awarded for partial completion of doctoral program. *Degree requirements:* For master's, comprehensive exam, thesis (for some programs); for doctorate, comprehensive exam, thesis/dissertation. *Entrance requirements:* For master's and doctorate, minimum GPA of 3.0, 3 letters of recommendation, statement of purpose. Additional exam requirements/recommendations for international students: required—TOEFL (minimum score 550 paper-based; 80 iBT), IELTS (minimum score 6). Electronic applications accepted.

University of Illinois at Urbana-Champaign, Graduate College, College of Agricultural, Consumer and Environmental Sciences, Department of Agricultural and Biological Engineering, Champaign, IL 61820. Offers agricultural and biological engineering (MS, PhD); technical systems management (MS, PSM).

University of Kentucky, Graduate School, College of Agriculture, Food and Environment, Program in Biosystems and Agricultural Engineering, Lexington, KY 40506-0032. Offers MS, PhD. *Program availability:* Part-time. *Degree requirements:* For master's, comprehensive exam, thesis optional; for doctorate, comprehensive exam, thesis/dissertation. *Entrance requirements:* For master's, GRE General Test, minimum undergraduate GPA of 2.75; for doctorate, GRE General Test, minimum graduate GPA of 3.0. Additional exam requirements/recommendations for international students: required—TOEFL (minimum score 550 paper-based). Electronic applications accepted.

University of Nebraska–Lincoln, Graduate College, College of Engineering, Department of Biological Systems Engineering, Interdepartmental Area of Agricultural and Biological Systems Engineering, Lincoln, NE 68588. Offers MS, PhD. *Degree requirements:* For master's, thesis optional. *Entrance requirements:* Additional exam requirements/recommendations for international students: required—TOEFL (minimum score 550 paper-based). Electronic applications accepted.

The University of Tennessee, Graduate School, College of Agricultural Sciences and Natural Resources, Department of Biosystems Engineering and Environmental Science, Program in Biosystems Engineering Technology, Knoxville, TN 37996. Offers MS. *Degree requirements:* For master's, thesis or alternative. *Entrance requirements:* For master's, GRE General Test, minimum GPA of 2.7. Additional exam requirements/

recommendations for international students: required—TOEFL. Electronic applications accepted.

University of Wisconsin–Madison, Graduate School, College of Agricultural and Life Sciences, Department of Biological Systems Engineering, Madison, WI 53706. Offers MS, PhD. *Program availability:* Part-time. Terminal master's awarded for partial completion of doctoral program. *Degree requirements:* For master's, thesis; for doctorate, thesis/dissertation. *Entrance requirements:* Additional exam requirements/recommendations for international students: required—TOEFL. Electronic applications accepted.

Université Laval, Faculty of Agricultural and Food Sciences, Department of Soils and Agricultural Engineering, Programs in Agri-Food Engineering, Québec, QC G1K 7P4, Canada. Offers agri-food engineering (M Sc); environmental technology (M Sc). *Degree requirements:* For master's, thesis (for some programs). *Entrance requirements:* For master's, knowledge of French. Electronic applications accepted.

Virginia Polytechnic Institute and State University, Graduate School, College of Engineering, Blacksburg, VA 24061. Offers aerospace engineering (PhD, M Eng/MS); biological systems engineering (PhD); biomedical engineering (MS, PhD); chemical engineering (PhD); civil engineering (PhD); computer engineering (PhD); computer science and applications (MS); electrical engineering (PhD); engineering education (PhD); M Eng/MS. *Faculty:* 447 full-time (90 women), 6 part-time/adjunct (2 women). *Students:* 1,881 full-time (495 women), 326 part-time (70 women); includes 264 minority (51 Black or African American, non-Hispanic/Latino; 2 American Indian or Alaska Native, non-Hispanic/Latino; 96 Asian, non-Hispanic/Latino; 69 Hispanic/Latino; 46 Two or more races, non-Hispanic/Latino), 1,247 international. Average age 27. 4,014 applicants, 44% accepted, 658 enrolled. In 2019, 489 master's, 200 doctorates awarded. *Degree requirements:* For master's, comprehensive exam (for some programs), thesis (for some programs); for doctorate, comprehensive exam (for some programs), thesis/dissertation (for some programs). *Entrance requirements:* For master's and doctorate, GRE/GMAT. Additional exam requirements/recommendations for international students: required—TOEFL (minimum score 90 iBT). *Application deadline:* For fall admission, 8/1 for domestic students, 4/1 for international students; for spring admission, 1/1 for domestic students, 9/1 for international students. Applications are processed on a rolling basis. Application fee: $75. Electronic applications accepted. *Expenses:* Tuition, state resident: full-time $13,700; part-time $761.25 per credit hour. Tuition, nonresident: full-time $27,614; part-time $1534 per credit hour. *Required fees:* $886.50 per term. Tuition and fees vary according to campus/location and program. *Financial support:* In 2019–20, 47 fellowships with full tuition reimbursements (averaging $19,703 per year), 1,163 research assistantships with full tuition reimbursements (averaging $20,602 per year), 554 teaching assistantships with full tuition reimbursements (averaging $16,333 per year) were awarded; scholarships/grants and unspecified assistantships also available. Financial award application deadline: 3/1; financial award applicants required to submit FAFSA. *Unit head:* Dr. Julia Ross, Dean, 540-231-9752, Fax: 540-231-3031, E-mail: rjulie@vt.edu. *Application contact:* Linda Perkins, Executive Assistant, 540-231-9752, Fax: 540-231-3031, E-mail: lperkins@vt.edu. Website: http://www.eng.vt.edu/

Washington State University, College of Agricultural, Human, and Natural Resource Sciences, Department of Biological Systems Engineering, Pullman, WA 99164-6120. Offers biological and agricultural engineering (MS, PhD). *Degree requirements:* For master's, comprehensive exam, thesis (for some programs), written and oral exam; for doctorate, comprehensive exam, thesis/dissertation, written and oral exam. *Entrance requirements:* For master's and doctorate, minimum GPA of 3.0, bachelor's degree in engineering or closely-related subject. Additional exam requirements/recommendations for international students: required—TOEFL. Electronic applications accepted.

Bioengineering

Alfred University, Graduate School, College of Ceramics, Inamori School of Engineering, Alfred, NY 14802-1205. Offers biomaterials engineering (MS); ceramic engineering (MS, PhD); electrical engineering (MS); glass science (MS, PhD); materials science and engineering (MS, PhD); mechanical engineering (MS). *Program availability:* Part-time. *Faculty:* 27 full-time (4 women), 2 part-time/adjunct (both women). *Students:* 30 full-time (11 women), 15 part-time (5 women); includes 2 minority (both Asian, non-Hispanic/Latino), 12 international. Average age 28. 24 applicants, 83% accepted, 18 enrolled. In 2019, 8 master's, 5 doctorates awarded. *Degree requirements:* For master's, comprehensive exam, thesis; for doctorate, comprehensive exam, thesis/dissertation. *Entrance requirements:* Additional exam requirements/recommendations for international students: required—TOEFL (minimum score 590 paper-based; 90 iBT), IELTS (minimum score 6.5). *Application deadline:* For fall admission, 3/1 priority date for domestic students, 3/15 for international students; for spring admission, 10/1 priority date for domestic students, 10/1 for international students. Applications are processed on a rolling basis. Application fee: $60. Electronic applications accepted. Application fee is waived when completed online. *Expenses:* $23,530 per year. *Financial support:* In 2019–20, 31 students received support. Fellowships with full tuition reimbursements available, research assistantships with full tuition reimbursements available, teaching assistantships with full tuition reimbursements available, tuition waivers (full and partial), and unspecified assistantships available. Financial award application deadline: 3/15; financial award applicants required to submit FAFSA. *Unit head:* Dr. Gabrielle Gaustad, Dean, 607-871-2953, E-mail: gaustad@alfred.edu. *Application contact:* Lindsey Gertin, Assistant Director of Graduate Admissions, 607-871-2017, Fax: 607-871-2198, E-mail: gradinquiry@alfred.edu.
Website: http://engineering.alfred.edu/grad/

Baylor College of Medicine, Graduate School of Biomedical Sciences, Program in Translational Biology and Molecular Medicine, Houston, TX 77030-3498. Offers PhD. *Degree requirements:* For doctorate, thesis/dissertation, public defense. *Entrance requirements:* For doctorate, GRE, minimum GPA of 3.0. Additional exam requirements/recommendations for international students: required—TOEFL. Electronic applications accepted.

California Institute of Technology, Division of Engineering and Applied Science, Option in Bioengineering, Pasadena, CA 91125-0001. Offers MS, PhD. *Degree requirements:* For master's, thesis; for doctorate, thesis/dissertation.

Carnegie Mellon University, Carnegie Institute of Technology, Biomedical and Health Engineering Program, Pittsburgh, PA 15213-3891. Offers bioengineering (MS, PhD); MD/PhD. *Degree requirements:* For master's, thesis; for doctorate, thesis/dissertation, qualifying exam. *Entrance requirements:* For master's and doctorate, GRE General Test. Additional exam requirements/recommendations for international students: required—TOEFL. Electronic applications accepted.

Clemson University, Graduate School, College of Engineering, Computing and Applied Sciences, Department of Bioengineering, Clemson, SC 29634. Offers bioengineering (MS, PhD); biomedical engineering (M Engr); medical device recycling and reprocessing (Certificate). *Program availability:* Part-time. *Faculty:* 32 full-time (10 women). *Students:* 128 full-time (52 women), 12 part-time (4 women); includes 23 minority (5 Black or African American, non-Hispanic/Latino; 8 Asian, non-Hispanic/Latino; 8 Hispanic/Latino; 2 Two or more races, non-Hispanic/Latino), 28 international. Average age 25. 117 applicants, 71% accepted, 38 enrolled. In 2019, 46 master's, 16 doctorates, 1 other advanced degree awarded. *Degree requirements:* For master's, thesis optional; for doctorate, comprehensive exam, thesis/dissertation. *Entrance requirements:* For master's, doctorate, and Certificate, GRE General Test, unofficial transcripts, letters of recommendation. Additional exam requirements/recommendations for international students: required—TOEFL (minimum score 100 paper-based; 100 iBT); recommended—IELTS (minimum score 7), TSE (minimum score 54). *Application deadline:* For fall admission, 2/15 priority date for domestic students, 1/15 priority date for international students. Applications are processed on a rolling basis. Application fee: $80 ($90 for international students). Electronic applications accepted. *Expenses:* Tuition, area resident: Full-time $10,600; part-time $8688 per semester. Tuition, state resident: full-time $10,600; part-time $8688 per semester. Tuition, nonresident: full-time $22,050; part-time $17,412 per semester. International tuition: $22,050 full-time. *Required fees:* $1196; $617 per semester. $617 per semester. Tuition and fees vary according to course load, degree level, campus/location and program. *Financial support:* In 2019–20, 102 students received support, including 1 fellowship with full and partial tuition reimbursement available (averaging $24,816 per year), 50 research assistantships with full and partial tuition reimbursements available (averaging $23,069 per year), 44 teaching assistantships with full and partial tuition reimbursements available (averaging $22,950 per year); career-related internships or fieldwork and unspecified assistantships also available. Financial award application deadline: 2/15; financial award applicants required to submit FAFSA. *Unit head:* Dr. Martine LaBerge, Department Chair, 864-656-5557, E-mail: laberge@clemson.edu. *Application contact:* Dr. Agneta Simionescu, Graduate Coordinator, 864-650-2575, E-mail: agneta@clemson.edu.
Website: https://www.clemson.edu/cecas/departments/bioe/

Colorado School of Mines, Office of Graduate Studies, Department of Chemical and Biological Engineering, Golden, CO 80401. Offers chemical engineering (MS, PhD). *Program availability:* Part-time. Terminal master's awarded for partial completion of doctoral program. *Degree requirements:* For master's, thesis (for some programs); for doctorate, comprehensive exam, thesis/dissertation. *Entrance requirements:* For master's and doctorate, GRE General Test. Additional exam requirements/recommendations for international students: required—TOEFL (minimum score 550 paper-based; 79 iBT). Electronic applications accepted. *Expenses:* Tuition, state resident: full-time $16,650; part-time $925 per credit hour. Tuition, nonresident: full-time

$37,350; part-time $2075 per credit hour. *International tuition:* $37,350 full-time. *Required fees:* $2412.

Colorado State University, Walter Scott, Jr. College of Engineering, School of Biomedical Engineering, Fort Collins, CO 80523-1376. Offers bioengineering (MS, PhD). *Program availability:* Part-time, online learning. Terminal master's awarded for partial completion of doctoral program. *Degree requirements:* For master's, thesis, minimum of two presentations in seminar series; for doctorate, thesis/dissertation, minimum of two presentations in seminar series. *Entrance requirements:* For master's and doctorate, GRE General Test, minimum GPA of 3.0, resume, statement of purpose, official transcripts, three letters of recommendation. Additional exam requirements/recommendations for international students: required—TOEFL (minimum score 550 paper-based; 80 iBT), IELTS (minimum score 6). Electronic applications accepted. *Expenses:* Contact institution.

Cornell University, Graduate School, Graduate Fields of Agriculture and Life Sciences and Graduate Fields of Engineering, Field of Biological and Environmental Engineering, Ithaca, NY 14853. Offers bioenergy and integrated energy systems (M Eng, MPS, MS, PhD); biological engineering (M Eng, MPS, MS, PhD); bioprocess engineering (M Eng, MPS, MS, PhD); ecohydrology (M Eng, MPS, MS, PhD); environmental engineering (M Eng, MPS, MS, PhD); environmental management (MPS); food engineering (M Eng, MPS, MS, PhD); industrial biotechnology (M Eng, MPS, MS, PhD); nanobiotechnology (M Eng, MPS, MS, PhD); sustainable systems (M Eng, MPS, MS, PhD); synthetic biology (MS); syntheticbiology (M Eng, MPS, PhD). Terminal master's awarded for partial completion of doctoral program. *Degree requirements:* For master's, thesis (MS); for doctorate, comprehensive exam, thesis/dissertation. *Entrance requirements:* For master's, letters of recommendation (3 for MS, 2 for M Eng and MPS); for doctorate, GRE General Test, 3 letters of recommendation. Additional exam requirements/recommendations for international students: required—TOEFL (minimum score 550 paper-based; 77 iBT). Electronic applications accepted.

Dalhousie University, Faculty of Engineering, Department of Process Engineering and Applied Science, Halifax, NS B3J 1Z1, Canada. Offers biological engineering (M Eng, MA Sc, PhD); chemical engineering (M Eng, MA Sc, PhD); food science (M Sc, PhD). *Degree requirements:* For master's, thesis; for doctorate, thesis/dissertation. *Entrance requirements:* Additional exam requirements/recommendations for international students: required—TOEFL, IELTS, CANTEST, CAEL, or Michigan English Language Assessment Battery. Electronic applications accepted.

Florida Atlantic University, College of Engineering and Computer Science, Department of Computer and Electrical Engineering and Computer Science, Boca Raton, FL 33431-0991. Offers bioengineering (MS); computer engineering (MS, PhD); computer science (MS, PhD); electrical engineering (MS, PhD). *Program availability:* Part-time, evening/weekend. *Faculty:* 39 full-time (8 women). *Students:* 112 full-time (26 women), 139 part-time (27 women); includes 104 minority (22 Black or African American, non-Hispanic/Latino; 22 Asian, non-Hispanic/Latino; 52 Hispanic/Latino; 8 Two or more races, non-Hispanic/Latino), 63 international. Average age 32. 231 applicants, 54% accepted, 91 enrolled. In 2019, 67 master's, 14 doctorates awarded. Terminal master's awarded for partial completion of doctoral program. *Degree requirements:* For master's, thesis optional; for doctorate, thesis/dissertation, qualifying exam. *Entrance requirements:* For master's, GRE General Test, minimum GPA of 3.0; for doctorate, GRE General Test, master's degree, minimum GPA of 3.5. Additional exam requirements/recommendations for international students: required—TOEFL (minimum score 500 paper-based; 61 iBT), IELTS (minimum score 6). *Application deadline:* For fall admission, 7/1 priority date for domestic students, 2/15 for international students; for spring admission, 11/1 for domestic students, 7/15 for international students. Applications are processed on a rolling basis. Application fee: $30. *Expenses: Tuition:* Full-time $20,536; part-time $371.82 per credit hour. Tuition and fees vary according to program. *Financial support:* Fellowships, research assistantships with partial tuition reimbursements, teaching assistantships with full tuition reimbursements, career-related internships or fieldwork, and Federal Work-Study available. Support available to part-time students. Financial award application deadline: 4/1; financial award applicants required to submit FAFSA. *Unit head:* Jean Mangiaracina, Graduate Program Administrator, 561-297-6482, E-mail: jmangiar@fau.edu. *Application contact:* Jean Mangiaracina, Graduate Program Administrator, 561-297-6482, E-mail: jmangiar@fau.edu.
Website: http://www.ceecs.fau.edu/

George Mason University, Volgenau School of Engineering, Department of Bioengineering, Fairfax, VA 22030. Offers PhD. *Degree requirements:* For doctorate, comprehensive exam, thesis/dissertation, proposal. *Entrance requirements:* For doctorate, GRE General Test, two copies of official transcripts; goals statement (1000 words maximum); three letters of recommendation; resume. Additional exam requirements/recommendations for international students: required—TOEFL (minimum score 575 paper-based; 88 iBT), IELTS (minimum score 6.5), PTE (minimum score 59). Electronic applications accepted. *Expenses:* Contact institution.

Harvard University, Graduate School of Arts and Sciences, Harvard John A. Paulson School of Engineering and Applied Sciences, Cambridge, MA 02138. Offers applied mathematics (PhD); applied physics (PhD); computational science and engineering (ME, SM); computer science (PhD); data science (SM); design engineering (MDE); engineering science (ME), including electrical engineering (ME, SM, PhD); engineering sciences (SM, PhD), including bioengineering (PhD), electrical engineering (ME, SM, PhD), environmental science and engineering (PhD), materials science and mechanical engineering (PhD). *Program availability:* Part-time. Terminal master's awarded for partial completion of doctoral program. *Degree requirements:* For master's, thesis (for ME); for doctorate, comprehensive exam, thesis/dissertation. *Entrance requirements:* For master's and doctorate, GRE General Test, GRE Subject Test (recommended), 3 letters of recommendation. Additional exam requirements/recommendations for international students: required—TOEFL (minimum score 80 iBT). Electronic applications accepted. *Expenses:* Contact institution.

Illinois Institute of Technology, Graduate College, Armour College of Engineering, Department of Chemical and Biological Engineering, Chicago, IL 60616. Offers biological engineering (MAS); chemical engineering (MAS, MS, PhD); MS/MAS. *Program availability:* Part-time, evening/weekend, online learning. Terminal master's awarded for partial completion of doctoral program. *Degree requirements:* For master's, comprehensive exam (for some programs), thesis (for some programs); for doctorate, comprehensive exam, thesis/dissertation. *Entrance requirements:* For master's, GRE General Test with minimum score of 950 Quantitative and Verbal, 2.5 Analytical Writing (for MAS); GRE General Test with minimum score of 1100 Quantitative and Verbal, 3.0 Analytical Writing (for MS), minimum undergraduate GPA of 3.0; for doctorate, GRE General Test (minimum score 1100 Quantitative and Verbal, 3.0 Analytical Writing), minimum undergraduate GPA of 3.0. Additional exam requirements/recommendations for international students: required—TOEFL (minimum score 550 paper-based; 80 iBT). Electronic applications accepted.

Johns Hopkins University, G. W. C. Whiting School of Engineering and School of Medicine, Department of Biomedical Engineering, Baltimore, MD 21205. Offers bioengineering innovation and design (MSE); biomedical engineering (MSE, PhD). Terminal master's awarded for partial completion of doctoral program. *Degree requirements:* For master's, thesis; for doctorate, comprehensive exam, thesis/dissertation. *Entrance requirements:* For master's and doctorate, GRE General Test, 3 letters of recommendation, statement of purpose, transcripts. Additional exam requirements/recommendations for international students: required—TOEFL (minimum score 600 paper-based, 100 iBT) or IELTS (7). Electronic applications accepted.

Johns Hopkins University, G. W. C. Whiting School of Engineering, Department of Chemical and Biomolecular Engineering, Baltimore, MD 21218. Offers MSE, PhD. Terminal master's awarded for partial completion of doctoral program. *Degree requirements:* For master's, essay presentation; for doctorate, thesis/dissertation, oral exam; thesis presentation. *Entrance requirements:* For master's and doctorate, GRE General Test, 3 letters of recommendation, statement of purpose, transcripts. Additional exam requirements/recommendations for international students: required—TOEFL (minimum score 600 paper-based, 100 iBT) or IELTS (7). Electronic applications accepted.

Kansas State University, Graduate School, College of Engineering, Department of Biological and Agricultural Engineering, Manhattan, KS 66506. Offers MS, PhD. Terminal master's awarded for partial completion of doctoral program. *Degree requirements:* For master's, thesis; for doctorate, thesis/dissertation, preliminary exam. *Entrance requirements:* For master's, GRE, bachelor's degree in biological and agricultural engineering; for doctorate, GRE. Additional exam requirements/recommendations for international students: required—TOEFL (minimum score 550 paper-based; 79 iBT). Electronic applications accepted.

Kansas State University, Graduate School, College of Engineering, Department of Electrical and Computer Engineering, Manhattan, KS 66506. Offers electrical engineering (MS), including bioengineering, communication systems, design of computer systems, electrical engineering, energy and power systems, integrated circuits and devices, real time embedded systems, renewable energy, signal processing. *Program availability:* Part-time, evening/weekend, online learning. *Degree requirements:* For master's, thesis or alternative, final exam; for doctorate, thesis/dissertation, final exam, preliminary exams. *Entrance requirements:* For master's, GRE General Test, bachelor's degree in electrical engineering or computer science, minimum GPA of 3.0; for doctorate, GRE General Test. Additional exam requirements/recommendations for international students: required—TOEFL (minimum score 600 paper-based; 85 iBT). Electronic applications accepted.

Lehigh University, P.C. Rossin College of Engineering and Applied Science, Department of Bioengineering, Bethlehem, PA 18015. Offers MS, PhD. *Faculty:* 13 full-time (7 women). *Students:* 21 full-time (13 women), 2 part-time (1 woman); includes 3 minority (all Asian, non-Hispanic/Latino), 15 international. Average age 26. 53 applicants, 55% accepted, 7 enrolled. In 2019, 3 master's, 1 doctorate awarded. Terminal master's awarded for partial completion of doctoral program. *Degree requirements:* For master's, thesis (for some programs), must attend seminars; for doctorate, comprehensive exam, thesis/dissertation, must attend seminars. *Entrance requirements:* For master's and doctorate, GRE. Additional exam requirements/recommendations for international students: required—TOEFL (minimum score 79 iBT), IELTS (minimum score 6.5), Either TOEFL or IELTS required. *Application deadline:* For fall admission, 7/15 for domestic and international students. Application fee: $75. *Expenses:* 27000. *Financial support:* In 2019–20, 2 fellowships with full tuition reimbursements (averaging $22,050 per year), 12 research assistantships with partial tuition reimbursements (averaging $22,050 per year), 6 teaching assistantships with full tuition reimbursements (averaging $22,050 per year) were awarded; health care benefits and unspecified assistantships also available. Financial award application deadline: 1/15. *Unit head:* Dr. Susan Perry, Faculty Graduate Coordinator in Bioengineering, 610-758-4330, E-mail: sup3@lehigh.edu. *Application contact:* Brianne Lisk, Administrative Coordinator of Graduate Studies and Research, 610-758-6310, Fax: 610-758-5623, E-mail: brc3@lehigh.edu.
Website: http://www.lehigh.edu/~inbioe/graduate/index.html

Louisiana State University and Agricultural & Mechanical College, Graduate School, College of Engineering, Department of Biological and Agricultural Engineering, Baton Rouge, LA 70803. Offers biological and agricultural engineering (MSBAE); engineering science (MS, PhD).

Massachusetts Institute of Technology, School of Engineering, Department of Biological Engineering, Cambridge, MA 02139. Offers applied biosciences (PhD, Sc D); bioengineering (PhD, Sc D); biological engineering (PhD, Sc D); biomedical engineering (M Eng); toxicology (SM); SM/MBA. Terminal master's awarded for partial completion of doctoral program. *Degree requirements:* For master's, thesis; for doctorate, comprehensive exam, thesis/dissertation. *Entrance requirements:* For master's and doctorate, GRE General Test. Additional exam requirements/recommendations for international students: required—IELTS. Electronic applications accepted.

McGill University, Faculty of Graduate and Postdoctoral Studies, Faculty of Agricultural and Environmental Sciences, Department of Bioresource Engineering, Montréal, QC H3A 2T5, Canada. Offers computer applications (M Sc, M Sc A, PhD); food engineering (M Sc, M Sc A, PhD); grain drying (M Sc, M Sc A, PhD); irrigation and drainage (M Sc, M Sc A, PhD); machinery (M Sc, M Sc A, PhD); pollution control (M Sc, M Sc A, PhD); post-harvest technology (M Sc, M Sc A, PhD); soil dynamics (M Sc, M Sc A, PhD); structure and environment (M Sc, M Sc A, PhD); vegetable and fruit storage (M Sc, M Sc A, PhD).

Mississippi State University, College of Agriculture and Life Sciences, Department of Agricultural and Biological Engineering, Mississippi State, MS 39762. Offers biological engineering (MS, PhD); biomedical engineering (MS, PhD). *Faculty:* 15 full-time (4 women). *Students:* 25 full-time (12 women), 12 part-time (3 women); includes 6 minority (3 Black or African American, non-Hispanic/Latino; 2 Asian, non-Hispanic/Latino; 1 Hispanic/Latino), 16 international. Average age 30. 23 applicants, 43% accepted, 6 enrolled. In 2019, 6 master's, 2 doctorates awarded. *Degree requirements:* For master's, thesis (for some programs); for doctorate, thesis/dissertation, preliminary exam. *Entrance requirements:* For master's, GRE General Test, minimum undergraduate GPA of 2.75 (3.0 for biomedical engineering); for doctorate, GRE General Test, minimum GPA of 3.0 (biomedical engineering). Additional exam requirements/recommendations for international students: required—TOEFL (minimum score 550 paper-based; 79 iBT); recommended—IELTS (minimum score 6.5). *Application deadline:* For fall admission, 7/1 for domestic students, 5/1 for international students; for spring admission, 11/1 for domestic students, 9/1 for international students. Applications are processed on a rolling basis. Application fee: $60 ($80 for international students). Electronic applications accepted. *Expenses: Tuition, area resident:* Full-time $8880; part-time $456 per credit hour. Tuition, state resident: full-time $8880. Tuition, nonresident: full-time $23,840; part-time $1236 per credit hour. *Required fees:* $110; $11.12 per credit hour. Tuition and fees vary according to course load. *Financial support:* In 2019–20, 13 research assistantships with partial tuition reimbursements (averaging $17,870 per year), 4 teaching assistantships (averaging $18,160 per year) were awarded; Federal Work-Study, institutionally sponsored loans, and unspecified assistantships also available. Financial award application deadline: 4/1; financial award applicants required to submit FAFSA. *Unit head:* Dr. Wes Burger, Interim Department Head, 662-325-7552, Fax: 662-

325-3853, E-mail: w.burger@msstate.edu. *Application contact:* Ryan King, Admissions and Enrollment Assistant, 662-325-8951, E-mail: rjk101@grad.msstate.edu.
Website: http://www.abe.msstate.edu/

North Carolina Agricultural and Technical State University, The Graduate College, College of Engineering, Department of Chemical, Biological and Bio Engineering, Greensboro, NC 27411. Offers bioengineering (MS); biological engineering (MS); chemical engineering (MS).

North Carolina State University, Graduate School, College of Agriculture and Life Sciences, Department of Biological and Agricultural Engineering, Raleigh, NC 27695. Offers MBAE, MS, PhD, Certificate. *Program availability:* Part-time, online learning. *Degree requirements:* For master's, thesis (for some programs); for doctorate, thesis/dissertation. *Entrance requirements:* For master's and doctorate, GRE. Additional exam requirements/recommendations for international students: required—TOEFL. Electronic applications accepted.

Northeastern University, College of Engineering, Boston, MA 02115-5096. Offers bioengineering (MS, PhD); chemical engineering (MS, PhD); civil engineering (MS, PhD); computer engineering (PhD); computer systems engineering (MS); electrical and computer engineering (MS); electrical and computer engineering leadership (MS); electrical engineering (PhD); energy systems (MS); engineering and public policy (MS); engineering management (MS, Certificate); environmental engineering (MS); industrial engineering (MS, PhD); information assurance (PhD); information systems (MS); interdisciplinary engineering (PhD); mechanical engineering (PhD); operations research (MS); telecommunication systems management (MS). *Program availability:* Part-time, online learning. Electronic applications accepted. *Expenses:* Contact institution.

Northern Arizona University, College of Engineering, Informatics, and Applied Sciences, Department of Mechanical Engineering, Flagstaff, AZ 86011. Offers bioengineering (PhD); engineering (M Eng), including mechanical engineering. *Program availability:* Part-time. *Degree requirements:* For master's, variable foreign language requirement, comprehensive exam (for some programs), thesis (for some programs); for doctorate, variable foreign language requirement, comprehensive exam (for some programs), thesis/dissertation (for some programs). *Entrance requirements:* For master's and doctorate, GRE General Test. Additional exam requirements/recommendations for international students: required—TOEFL (minimum score 80 iBT), IELTS (minimum score 6.5). Electronic applications accepted.

Northwestern University, The Graduate School, Interdisciplinary Biological Sciences Program (IBiS), Evanston, IL 60208. Offers biochemistry (PhD); bioengineering and biotechnology (PhD); biotechnology (PhD); cell and molecular biology (PhD); developmental and systems biology (PhD); nanotechnology (PhD); neurobiology (PhD); structural biology and biophysics (PhD). *Degree requirements:* For doctorate, thesis/dissertation, qualifying exam. *Entrance requirements:* For doctorate, GRE General Test. Additional exam requirements/recommendations for international students: required—TOEFL (minimum score 600 paper-based). Electronic applications accepted.

The Ohio State University, Graduate School, College of Food, Agricultural, and Environmental Sciences, Department of Food, Agricultural, and Biological Engineering, Columbus, OH 43210. Offers MS, PhD. *Entrance requirements:* For master's and doctorate, GRE General Test, GRE Subject Test in engineering (recommended). Additional exam requirements/recommendations for international students: required—TOEFL (minimum score 550 paper-based; 79 iBT), Michigan English Language Assessment Battery (minimum score 82); recommended—IELTS (minimum score 7). Electronic applications accepted.

Oklahoma State University, College of Agricultural Science and Natural Resources, Department of Biosystems and Agricultural Engineering, Stillwater, OK 74078. Offers biosystems engineering (MS, PhD); environmental and natural resources (MS, PhD). *Faculty:* 17 full-time (6 women). *Students:* 8 full-time (3 women), 12 part-time (4 women); includes 1 minority (Black or African American, non-Hispanic/Latino), 13 international. Average age 32. 12 applicants, 25% accepted, 2 enrolled. In 2019, 6 master's, 8 doctorates awarded. *Entrance requirements:* For master's and doctorate, GRE or GMAT. Additional exam requirements/recommendations for international students: required—TOEFL (minimum score 550 paper-based; 79 iBT). *Application deadline:* For fall admission, 3/1 priority date for international students; for spring admission, 8/1 priority date for international students. Applications are processed on a rolling basis. Application fee: $50 ($75 for international students). Electronic applications accepted. *Expenses: Tuition, area resident:* Full-time $4148.10; part-time $2765.40. Tuition, state resident: full-time $4148.10; part-time $2765.40. Tuition, nonresident: full-time $15,775; part-time $10,516.80. *International tuition:* $15,775.20 full-time. *Required fees:* $2196.90; $122.05 per credit hour. Tuition and fees vary according to course load, campus/location and program. *Financial support:* In 2019–20, 19 research assistantships (averaging $1,661 per year), 1 teaching assistantship (averaging $1,000 per year) were awarded; career-related internships or fieldwork, Federal Work-Study, scholarships/grants, health care benefits, tuition waivers (partial), and unspecified assistantships also available. Support available to part-time students. Financial award application deadline: 3/1; financial award applicants required to submit FAFSA. *Unit head:* Dr. John Veenstra, Department Head, 405-744-5431, Fax: 405-744-6059, E-mail: jveenst@okstate.edu. *Application contact:* Dr. Ning Wang, Professor/Graduate Coordinator, 405-744-2877, E-mail: ning.wang@okstate.edu.
Website: http://bae.okstate.edu/

Oregon State University, College of Engineering, Program in Bioengineering, Corvallis, OR 97331. Offers biomaterials (M Eng, MS, PhD); biomedical devices and instrumentation (M Eng, MS, PhD); human performance engineering (M Eng, MS, PhD); medical imaging (M Eng, MS, PhD); systems and computational biology (M Eng, MS, PhD). Electronic applications accepted. *Expenses:* Contact institution.

Oregon State University, College of Engineering, Program in Biological and Ecological Engineering, Corvallis, OR 97331. Offers bio-based products and fuels (M Eng, MS, PhD); biological systems analysis (M Eng, MS, PhD); bioprocessing (M Eng, MS, PhD); ecosystems analysis and modeling (M Eng, MS, PhD); water quality (M Eng, MS, PhD); water resources (M Eng, MS, PhD). Terminal master's awarded for partial completion of doctoral program. *Entrance requirements:* For master's and doctorate, GRE, minimum GPA of 3.0 in last 90 hours. Additional exam requirements/recommendations for international students: required—TOEFL (minimum score 80 iBT), IELTS (minimum score 6.5). *Expenses:* Contact institution.

Penn State University Park, Graduate School, College of Agricultural Sciences, Department of Agricultural and Biological Engineering, University Park, PA 16802. Offers agricultural and biological engineering (MS, PhD); biorenewable systems (MS, PhD).

Penn State University Park, Graduate School, Intercollege Graduate Programs, Intercollege Graduate Program in Bioengineering, University Park, PA 16802. Offers MS, PhD.

Princeton University, Graduate School, School of Engineering and Applied Science, Department of Chemical and Biological Engineering, Princeton, NJ 08544-1019. Offers M Eng, MSE, PhD. Terminal master's awarded for partial completion of doctoral program. *Degree requirements:* For master's, thesis (MSE); for doctorate, thesis/dissertation, general exam. *Entrance requirements:* For master's, GRE General Test, 3 letters of recommendation; for doctorate, GRE General Test, official transcript(s), 3 letters of recommendation, personal statement. Additional exam requirements/recommendations for international students: required—TOEFL. Electronic applications accepted.

Rice University, Graduate Programs, George R. Brown School of Engineering, Department of Bioengineering, Houston, TX 77251-1892. Offers MBE, MS, PhD, MD/PhD. Terminal master's awarded for partial completion of doctoral program. *Degree requirements:* For master's, thesis; for doctorate, thesis/dissertation, qualifying exam, internship. *Entrance requirements:* For master's and doctorate, GRE General Test. Additional exam requirements/recommendations for international students: required—TOEFL (minimum score 600 paper-based; 90 iBT). Electronic applications accepted.

Rice University, Graduate Programs, George R. Brown School of Engineering, Department of Electrical and Computer Engineering, Houston, TX 77251-1892. Offers bioengineering (MS, PhD); circuits, controls, and communication systems (MS, PhD); computer science and engineering (MS, PhD); electrical engineering (MEE); lasers, microwaves, and solid-state electronics (MS, PhD); MBA/MEE. *Program availability:* Part-time. *Degree requirements:* For master's, thesis (for some programs); for doctorate, thesis/dissertation. *Entrance requirements:* For master's and doctorate, GRE General Test, GRE Subject Test, minimum GPA of 3.0. Additional exam requirements/recommendations for international students: required—TOEFL (minimum score 600 paper-based; 90 iBT). Electronic applications accepted.

Santa Clara University, School of Engineering, Santa Clara, CA 95053. Offers applied mathematics (MS); bioengineering (MS); civil, environmental, and sustainable engineering (MS); computer science and engineering (MS, PhD, Engineer); electrical engineering (MS, PhD, Engineer); engineering management and leadership (MS); mechanical engineering (MS, PhD, Engineer); power systems and sustainable energy (MS); software engineering (MS). *Program availability:* Part-time. *Entrance requirements:* For master's, GRE, official transcript; for doctorate, GRE, Official transcript, 500 word statement of purpose, three letters of recommendation. Additional exam requirements/recommendations for international students: required—TOEFL (minimum score 79 iBT), IELTS (minimum score 6.5). Electronic applications accepted.

South Dakota School of Mines and Technology, Graduate Division, Program in Chemical and Biological Engineering, Rapid City, SD 57701-3995. Offers PhD. *Program availability:* Part-time. *Degree requirements:* For doctorate, thesis/dissertation. *Entrance requirements:* Additional exam requirements/recommendations for international students: required—TOEFL (minimum score 520 paper-based; 68 iBT). Electronic applications accepted.

Stanford University, School of Medicine, Department of Bioengineering, Stanford, CA 94305-2004. Offers MS, PhD. *Expenses: Tuition:* Full-time $52,479; part-time $34,110 per unit. *Required fees:* $672; $224 per quarter. Tuition and fees vary according to program and student level.
Website: http://bioengineering.stanford.edu/

Syracuse University, College of Engineering and Computer Science, Programs in Bioengineering, Syracuse, NY 13244. Offers MS, PhD. *Program availability:* Part-time. *Degree requirements:* For master's, thesis (for some programs); for doctorate, comprehensive exam, thesis/dissertation. *Entrance requirements:* For master's and doctorate, GRE General Test, three letters of recommendation, resume, personal statement, official transcripts. Additional exam requirements/recommendations for international students: required—TOEFL (minimum score 100 iBT). Electronic applications accepted.

Temple University, College of Engineering, Department of Bioengineering, Philadelphia, PA 19122. Offers MS, PhD. *Program availability:* Part-time, evening/weekend. *Faculty:* 13 full-time (6 women), 6 part-time/adjunct (2 women). *Students:* 30 full-time (13 women), 2 part-time (0 women); includes 7 minority (4 Black or African American, non-Hispanic/Latino; 1 Asian, non-Hispanic/Latino; 1 Hispanic/Latino; 1 Two or more races, non-Hispanic/Latino), 11 international. 49 applicants, 61% accepted, 10 enrolled. In 2019, 7 master's, 4 doctorates awarded. Terminal master's awarded for partial completion of doctoral program. *Degree requirements:* For master's, thesis optional; for doctorate, comprehensive exam, thesis/dissertation, preliminary exam, dissertation proposal and defense. *Entrance requirements:* For master's, GRE General Test. Waivers are considered on a case by case basis for master's applicants. Competitive applicants to the master's programs should have an undergraduate GPA of at least 3.0 and GREs of at least the 50th percentile in each section. Applicants should also possess an undergraduate degree in engineering from an ABET accredited or equivalent institution. Also required: letters of rec, resume, personal statement; for doctorate, GRE General Test, Competitive applicants to the PhD programs should have an undergraduate GPA of at least 3.0 and GREs of at least the 50th percentile in each section. A master's degree in engineering is preferred, but not required. Also required: letters of rec, resume, personal statement. Additional exam requirements/recommendations for international students: required—TOEFL (minimum score 79 iBT), IELTS (minimum score 6.5). *Application deadline:* For fall admission, 6/1 priority date for domestic students, 3/1 priority date for international students; for spring admission, 11/1 priority date for domestic students, 8/1 priority date for international students. Applications are processed on a rolling basis. Application fee: $60. Electronic applications accepted. *Expenses:* 1,135 per credit hour in-state resident; 1,490 per credit hour out-of-state resident. *Financial support:* In 2019–20, 1 fellowship with full tuition reimbursement (averaging $30,000 per year), 26 research assistantships with full tuition reimbursements (averaging $19,739 per year), 17 teaching assistantships with full tuition reimbursements (averaging $19,739 per year) were awarded. Financial award applicants required to submit FAFSA. *Unit head:* Dr. Peter Lelkes, Chair, Department of Bioengineering, 215-204-3307, Fax: 215-204-6936, E-mail: pilelkes@temple.edu. *Application contact:* Colleen Baillie, Director, Enrollment, 215-204-7800, Fax: 215-204-6936, E-mail: gradengr@temple.edu.
Website: http://engineering.temple.edu/bioengineering

Texas A&M University, College of Agriculture and Life Sciences, Department of Biological and Agricultural Engineering, College Station, TX 77843. Offers agricultural systems management (M Agr, MS); biological and agricultural engineering (MS, PhD). *Program availability:* Part-time. *Faculty:* 18. *Students:* 64 full-time (17 women), 8 part-time (4 women); includes 12 minority (4 Black or African American, non-Hispanic/Latino; 2 Asian, non-Hispanic/Latino; 5 Hispanic/Latino; 1 Two or more races, non-Hispanic/Latino), 49 international. Average age 31. 20 applicants, 100% accepted, 11 enrolled. In 2019, 10 master's, 11 doctorates awarded. *Degree requirements:* For master's, thesis (MS), preliminary and final exams; for doctorate, thesis/dissertation, preliminary and final exams. *Entrance requirements:* For master's and doctorate, GRE General Test, statement of purpose, resume, letters of recommendation. Additional exam requirements/recommendations for international students: required—TOEFL (minimum score 550 paper-based; 80 iBT), IELTS (minimum score 6), PTE (minimum score 53). *Application deadline:* For fall admission, 8/15 for domestic students, 7/1 for international students; for spring admission, 12/1 for domestic students, 11/1 for international students; for summer admission, 5/1 for domestic students, 4/1 for international students. Application fee: $65 ($90 for international students). Electronic applications

accepted. *Expenses:* Contact institution. *Financial support:* In 2019–20, 70 students received support, including 11 fellowships with tuition reimbursements available (averaging $10,171 per year), 41 research assistantships with tuition reimbursements available (averaging $12,179 per year), 20 teaching assistantships with tuition reimbursements available (averaging $13,004 per year); career-related internships or fieldwork, institutionally sponsored loans, scholarships/grants, traineeships, health care benefits, tuition waivers (full and partial), and unspecified assistantships also available. Support available to part-time students. Financial award application deadline: 3/15; financial award applicants required to submit FAFSA. *Unit head:* Dr. Steve Searcy, Senior Professor and Head, 979-845-3940, Fax: 979-862-3442, E-mail: s-searcy@ tamu.edu. *Application contact:* Dr. Sandun Fernando, Director of Graduate Programs, 979-845-9793, E-mail: sfernando@tamu.edu.
Website: http://baen.tamu.edu

Tufts University, Graduate School of Arts and Sciences, Graduate Certificate Programs, Program in Bioengineering, Medford, MA 02155. Offers Certificate. *Program availability:* Part-time, evening/weekend. Electronic applications accepted. Full-time tuition and fees vary according to degree level, program and student level. Part-time tuition and fees vary according to course load.

Tufts University, School of Engineering, Department of Biomedical Engineering, Medford, MA 02155. Offers bioengineering (MS), including biomaterials; biomedical engineering (MS, PhD); PhD/PhD. *Program availability:* Part-time. Terminal master's awarded for partial completion of doctoral program. *Degree requirements:* For master's, thesis (for some programs); for doctorate, thesis/dissertation. *Entrance requirements:* For master's and doctorate, GRE General Test. Additional exam requirements/recommendations for international students: required—TOEFL (minimum score 550 paper-based; 80 iBT), IELTS (minimum score 6.5). Electronic applications accepted. Full-time tuition and fees vary according to degree level, program and student level. Part-time tuition and fees vary according to course load.

Tufts University, School of Engineering, Department of Chemical and Biological Engineering, Medford, MA 02155. Offers bioengineering (MS), including cell and bioprocess engineering; biotechnology (PhD); chemical engineering (MS, PhD); PhD/PhD. *Program availability:* Part-time. Terminal master's awarded for partial completion of doctoral program. *Degree requirements:* For master's, thesis (for some programs); for doctorate, thesis/dissertation. *Entrance requirements:* For master's and doctorate, GRE General Test. Additional exam requirements/recommendations for international students: required—TOEFL (minimum score 550 paper-based; 80 iBT), IELTS (minimum score 6.5). Electronic applications accepted. Full-time tuition and fees vary according to degree level, program and student level. Part-time tuition and fees vary according to course load.

Tufts University, School of Engineering, Department of Civil and Environmental Engineering, Medford, MA 02155. Offers bioengineering (MS), including environmental biotechnology; civil and environmental engineering (MS, PhD), including applied data science, environmental and water resources engineering, environmental health, geosystems engineering, structural engineering and mechanics; PhD/PhD. *Program availability:* Part-time. Terminal master's awarded for partial completion of doctoral program. *Degree requirements:* For master's, thesis (for some programs); for doctorate, thesis/dissertation. *Entrance requirements:* For master's and doctorate, GRE General Test. Additional exam requirements/recommendations for international students: required—TOEFL (minimum score 550 paper-based; 80 iBT), IELTS (minimum score 6.5). Electronic applications accepted. Full-time tuition and fees vary according to degree level, program and student level. Part-time tuition and fees vary according to course load.

Tufts University, School of Engineering, Department of Computer Science, Medford, MA 02155. Offers bioengineering (MS), including bioinformatics; cognitive science/computer science (PhD); computer science (MS, PhD); soft material robotics (PhD). *Program availability:* Part-time. Terminal master's awarded for partial completion of doctoral program. *Entrance requirements:* For master's and doctorate, GRE General Test. Additional exam requirements/recommendations for international students: required—TOEFL (minimum score 550 paper-based; 80 iBT), IELTS (minimum score 6.5). Electronic applications accepted. Full-time tuition and fees vary according to degree level, program and student level. Part-time tuition and fees vary according to course load.

Tufts University, School of Engineering, Department of Electrical and Computer Engineering, Medford, MA 02155. Offers bioengineering (MS), including signals and systems; electrical engineering (MS, PhD); PhD/PhD. *Program availability:* Part-time. Terminal master's awarded for partial completion of doctoral program. *Degree requirements:* For master's, thesis or alternative; for doctorate, thesis/dissertation. *Entrance requirements:* For master's and doctorate, GRE General Test. Additional exam requirements/recommendations for international students: required—TOEFL (minimum score 550 paper-based; 80 iBT), IELTS (minimum score 6.5). Electronic applications accepted. Full-time tuition and fees vary according to degree level, program and student level. Part-time tuition and fees vary according to course load.

University at Buffalo, the State University of New York, Graduate School, School of Engineering and Applied Sciences, Department of Chemical and Biological Engineering, Buffalo, NY 14260. Offers bioengineering nanotechnology (Certificate); chemical and biological engineering (ME, MS, PhD); nanomaterials and materials informatics (Certificate). *Program availability:* Part-time. *Degree requirements:* For master's, thesis (for some programs); for doctorate, comprehensive exam, thesis/dissertation. *Entrance requirements:* For master's and doctorate, GRE General Test. Additional exam requirements/recommendations for international students: required—TOEFL (minimum score 550 paper-based; 79 iBT). Electronic applications accepted. *Expenses: Tuition, area resident:* Full-time $11,310; part-time $471 per credit hour. *Tuition, state resident:* full-time $11,310; part-time $471 per credit hour. *Tuition, nonresident:* full-time $23,100; part-time $963 per credit hour. *International tuition:* $23,100 full-time. *Required fees:* $2820.

University of Arkansas, Graduate School, College of Engineering, Department of Biological and Agricultural Engineering, Program in Biological Engineering, Fayetteville, AR 72701. Offers MSBE. *Students:* 7 full-time (6 women), 12 part-time (5 women); includes 2 minority (1 Black or African American, non-Hispanic/Latino; 1 American Indian or Alaska Native, non-Hispanic/Latino), 6 international. 11 applicants, 36% accepted. In 2019, 1 master's awarded. *Application deadline:* For fall admission, 8/1 for domestic students, 4/1 for international students; for spring admission, 12/1 for domestic students, 10/1 for international students; for summer admission, 4/15 for domestic students, 3/1 for international students. Applications are processed on a rolling basis. Application fee: $60. Electronic applications accepted. *Financial support:* In 2019–20, 17 research assistantships, 1 teaching assistantship were awarded; fellowships also available. *Unit head:* Dr. Raj Rao, Department Head, 479-575-6810, E-mail: rajrao@ uark.edu. *Application contact:* Dr. Jin-Woo Kim, Program Coordinator, 479-575-3402, E-mail: jwkim@uark.edu.
Website: https://bio-ag-engineering.uark.edu

The University of British Columbia, Faculty of Applied Science, Department of Chemical and Biological Engineering, Vancouver, BC V6T 1Z3, Canada. Offers M Eng,

M Sc, MA Sc, PhD. *Program availability:* Part-time, evening/weekend. *Degree requirements:* For master's, thesis (for some programs); for doctorate, thesis/dissertation. *Entrance requirements:* Additional exam requirements/recommendations for international students: required—TOEFL, IELTS. Electronic applications accepted. *Expenses:* Contact institution.

University of California, Berkeley, Graduate Division, Bioengineering Graduate Program Berkeley/UCSF, Berkeley, CA 94720-1762. Offers PhD. *Degree requirements:* For doctorate, comprehensive exam, thesis/dissertation. *Entrance requirements:* For doctorate, GRE General Test, minimum GPA of 3.0. Additional exam requirements/recommendations for international students: required—TOEFL (minimum score 570 paper-based; 68 iBT). Electronic applications accepted.

University of California, Berkeley, Graduate Division, College of Engineering, Department of Bioengineering, Berkeley, CA 94720. Offers M Eng, MTM. *Degree requirements:* For master's, comprehensive exam. *Entrance requirements:* Additional exam requirements/recommendations for international students: required—TOEFL (minimum score 570 paper-based; 90 iBT). Electronic applications accepted.

University of California, Davis, College of Engineering, Program in Biological Systems Engineering, Davis, CA 95616. Offers M Engr, MS, D Engr, PhD, M Engr/MBA. Terminal master's awarded for partial completion of doctoral program. *Degree requirements:* For master's, thesis; for doctorate, thesis/dissertation. *Entrance requirements:* For master's, minimum GPA of 3.0; for doctorate, GRE, minimum graduate GPA of 3.25. Additional exam requirements/recommendations for international students: required—TOEFL (minimum score 550 paper-based). Electronic applications accepted.

University of California, Los Angeles, Graduate Division, Henry Samueli School of Engineering and Applied Science, Department of Bioengineering, Los Angeles, CA 90095-1600. Offers MS, PhD. *Degree requirements:* For master's, comprehensive exam or thesis; for doctorate, thesis/dissertation, qualifying exams. *Entrance requirements:* For master's, GRE General Test, minimum GPA of 3.0; for doctorate, GRE General Test, minimum GPA of 3.25. Additional exam requirements/recommendations for international students: required—TOEFL (minimum score 560 paper-based; 87 iBT), IELTS (minimum score 7). Electronic applications accepted.

University of California, Merced, Graduate Division, School of Engineering, Merced, CA 95343. Offers biological engineering and small scale technologies (MS, PhD); electrical engineering and computer science (MS, PhD); environmental systems (MS, PhD); management of innovation, sustainability, and technology (MM); mechanical engineering (MS, PhD). *Faculty:* 60 full-time (16 women). *Students:* 244 full-time (83 women), 1 (woman) part-time; includes 56 minority (2 Black or African American, non-Hispanic/Latino; 20 Asian, non-Hispanic/Latino; 30 Hispanic/Latino; 1 Native Hawaiian or other Pacific Islander, non-Hispanic/Latino; 3 Two or more races, non-Hispanic/Latino), 153 international. Average age 28. 330 applicants, 32% accepted, 67 enrolled. In 2019, 30 master's, 17 doctorates awarded. Terminal master's awarded for partial completion of doctoral program. *Degree requirements:* For master's, variable foreign language requirement, comprehensive exam, thesis or alternative, oral defense; for doctorate, variable foreign language requirement, comprehensive exam, thesis/dissertation, oral defense. *Entrance requirements:* For master's and doctorate, GRE. Additional exam requirements/recommendations for international students: required—TOEFL (minimum score 550 paper-based; 80 iBT); recommended—IELTS (minimum score 6.5). *Application deadline:* For fall admission, 1/15 for domestic and international students. Application fee: $105 ($125 for international students). Electronic applications accepted. *Expenses: Tuition, area resident:* Full-time $11,442; part-time $5721. *Tuition, state resident:* full-time $11,442; part-time $5721. *Tuition, nonresident:* full-time $26,544; part-time $13,272. *International tuition:* $26,544 full-time. *Required fees:* $564 per semester. *Financial support:* In 2019–20, 205 students received support, including 6 fellowships with full tuition reimbursements available (averaging $22,005 per year), 76 research assistantships with full tuition reimbursements available (averaging $21,420 per year), 123 teaching assistantships with full tuition reimbursements available (averaging $21,911 per year); scholarships/grants, traineeships, and health care benefits also available. *Unit head:* Dr. Mark Matsumoto, Dean, 209-228-4047, Fax: 209-228-4047, E-mail: mmatsumoto@ucmerced.edu. *Application contact:* Tsu Ya, Director of Admissions and Academic Services, 209-228-4521, Fax: 209-228-6906, E-mail: tya@ ucmerced.edu.

University of California, Riverside, Graduate Division, Department of Bioengineering, Riverside, CA 92521. Offers MS, PhD. *Degree requirements:* For doctorate, thesis/dissertation, qualifying exams. *Entrance requirements:* Additional exam requirements/recommendations for international students: required—TOEFL (minimum score 550 paper-based; 80 iBT).

University of California, San Diego, Graduate Division, Department of Bioengineering, La Jolla, CA 92093. Offers M Eng, MS, PhD. *Students:* 237 full-time (99 women), 15 part-time (4 women). 733 applicants, 30% accepted, 83 enrolled. In 2019, 35 master's, 24 doctorates awarded. *Degree requirements:* For doctorate, comprehensive exam, thesis/dissertation, 2 quarters teaching 20 hours a week or 4 quarters teaching 10 hours a week. *Entrance requirements:* For master's, GRE General Test, minimum GPA of 3.0 (for M Eng), 3.4 (for MS); for doctorate, GRE General Test, minimum GPA of 3.4. Additional exam requirements/recommendations for international students: required—TOEFL (minimum score 550 paper-based; 80 iBT), IELTS (minimum score 7). *Application deadline:* For fall admission, 12/13 for domestic students. Application fee: $105 ($125 for international students). Electronic applications accepted. *Financial support:* Fellowships, research assistantships, teaching assistantships, scholarships/grants, traineeships, and unspecified assistantships available. Financial award applicants required to submit FAFSA. *Unit head:* Kun Zhang, Chair, 858-822-3441, E-mail: chair@bioeng.ucsd.edu. *Application contact:* Elizabeth Soos, Student Affairs Manager, 858-822-1604, E-mail: esoos@ucsd.edu.
Website: http://www.be.ucsd.edu/prospective-graduate-students

University of California, San Francisco, Graduate Division, Program in Bioengineering, Berkeley, CA 94720-1762. Offers PhD. *Degree requirements:* For doctorate, thesis/dissertation, qualifying exam. *Entrance requirements:* For doctorate, GRE General Test, minimum GPA of 3.0. Additional exam requirements/recommendations for international students: required—TOEFL (minimum score 570 paper-based). Electronic applications accepted.

University of California, Santa Barbara, Graduate Division, College of Engineering, Department of Mechanical Engineering, Santa Barbara, CA 93106-5070. Offers bioengineering (PhD); mechanical engineering (MS); MS/PhD. Terminal master's awarded for partial completion of doctoral program. *Degree requirements:* For master's, thesis optional; for doctorate, comprehensive exam, thesis/dissertation. *Entrance requirements:* For master's and doctorate, GRE. Additional exam requirements/recommendations for international students: required—TOEFL (minimum score 550 paper-based; 80 iBT), IELTS (minimum score 7). Electronic applications accepted.

University of California, Santa Barbara, Graduate Division, College of Letters and Sciences, Division of Mathematics, Life, and Physical Sciences, Department of Statistics and Applied Probability, Santa Barbara, CA 93106-3110. Offers bioengineering (PhD); financial mathematics and statistics (PhD); quantitative methods in the social sciences (PhD); statistics (MA), including applied statistics, mathematical statistics; statistics and applied probability (PhD); MA/PhD. Terminal master's awarded for partial completion of doctoral program. *Degree requirements:* For master's, comprehensive exam, thesis optional; for doctorate, comprehensive exam, thesis/dissertation. *Entrance requirements:* For master's and doctorate, GRE General Test. Additional exam requirements/recommendations for international students: required—TOEFL (minimum score 550 paper-based; 80 iBT), IELTS (minimum score 7). Electronic applications accepted.

University of California, Santa Barbara, Graduate Division, College of Letters and Sciences, Division of Mathematics, Life, and Physical Sciences, Interdepartmental Graduate Program in Biomolecular Science and Engineering, Santa Barbara, CA 93106-2014. Offers biochemistry and molecular biology (PhD), including biochemistry and molecular biology, biophysics and bioengineering. Terminal master's awarded for partial completion of doctoral program. *Degree requirements:* For doctorate, thesis/dissertation. *Entrance requirements:* For doctorate, GRE General Test. Additional exam requirements/recommendations for international students: required—TOEFL (minimum score 630 paper-based; 109 iBT), IELTS (minimum score 7). Electronic applications accepted.

University of Chicago, Institute for Molecular Engineering, Chicago, IL 60637. Offers PhD. *Degree requirements:* For doctorate, thesis/dissertation, qualifying research presentation, teaching requirement. *Entrance requirements:* For doctorate, GRE General Test, transcripts, statement of purpose, 3 letters of recommendation. Additional exam requirements/recommendations for international students: required—TOEFL (minimum score 90 iBT), IELTS (minimum score 7). Electronic applications accepted.

University of Colorado Denver, College of Engineering, Design and Computing, Department of Bioengineering, Aurora, CO 80045-2560. Offers basic research (MS, PhD); biomedical device design (MS); entrepreneurship (PhD); entrepreneurship and regulatory affairs (MS); translational bioengineering (PhD). *Program availability:* Part-time. Terminal master's awarded for partial completion of doctoral program. *Degree requirements:* For master's, thesis or alternative, 30 credit hours; for doctorate, comprehensive exam, 36 credit hours of classwork (18 core, 18 elective), additional 30 hours of thesis work, three formal examinations, approval of dissertations. *Entrance requirements:* For master's and doctorate, GRE, transcripts, three letters of recommendation, resume, statement of purpose. Additional exam requirements/recommendations for international students: required—TOEFL (minimum score 550 paper-based; 79 iBT), TOEFL (minimum score 600 paper-based; 100 iBT) for PhD. Electronic applications accepted. Tuition and fees vary according to course load, program and reciprocity agreements.

University of Dayton, Department of Chemical Engineering, Dayton, OH 45469. Offers bioengineering (MS); chemical engineering (MS Ch E). *Program availability:* Part-time, online learning. *Degree requirements:* For master's, thesis for 33 credit hours. *Entrance requirements:* For master's, GRE (preferred), minimum GPA of 3.0 as undergraduate, transcript, 3 letters of recommendation, bachelor's degree in chemical engineering (preferred). Additional exam requirements/recommendations for international students: required—TOEFL (minimum score 550 paper-based; 80 iBT); recommended—IELTS. Electronic applications accepted. *Expenses:* Contact institution.

University of Denver, Daniel Felix Ritchie School of Engineering and Computer Science, Department of Mechanical and Materials Engineering, Denver, CO 80208. Offers bioengineering (MS); engineering (MS, PhD), including management; materials science (MS, PhD); mechanical engineering (MS, PhD). *Program availability:* Part-time. *Faculty:* 12 full-time (2 women), 3 part-time/adjunct (1 woman). *Students:* 3 full-time (1 woman), 35 part-time (9 women); includes 3 minority (1 Black or African American, non-Hispanic/Latino; 1 Asian, non-Hispanic/Latino; 1 Hispanic/Latino), 16 international. Average age 27. 58 applicants, 81% accepted, 18 enrolled. In 2019, 16 master's, 4 doctorates awarded. Terminal master's awarded for partial completion of doctoral program. *Degree requirements:* For master's, thesis optional; for doctorate, comprehensive exam, thesis/dissertation. *Entrance requirements:* For master's, GRE General Test, bachelor's degree in engineering or closely related field, transcripts, personal statement, resume or curriculum vitae, two letters of recommendation; for doctorate, GRE General Test, master's degree in engineering or closely related field, transcripts, personal statement, resume or curriculum vitae, two letters of recommendation, recommended that applicants find a research advisor before submitting the application. Additional exam requirements/recommendations for international students: required—TOEFL (minimum score 550 paper-based; 80 iBT). *Application deadline:* For fall admission, 1/15 priority date for domestic and international students; for winter admission, 10/25 for domestic and international students; for spring admission, 2/7 for domestic and international students; for summer admission, 4/24 for domestic and international students. Applications are processed on a rolling basis. Application fee: $65. Electronic applications accepted. *Unit head:* Dr. Matt Gordon, Professor and Chair, 303-871-3580, E-mail: matthew.gordon@du.edu. *Application contact:* Chrissy Alexander, Assistant to the Chair, 303-871-3041, E-mail: Christine.Alexander@du.edu.
Website: http://ritchieschool.du.edu/departments/mme/

University of Florida, Graduate School, Herbert Wertheim College of Engineering and College of Agricultural and Life Sciences, Department of Agricultural and Biological Engineering, Gainesville, FL 32611. Offers agricultural and biological engineering (ME, MS, PhD), including geographic information systems, hydrologic sciences, wetland sciences; biological systems modeling (Certificate). *Program availability:* Part-time. Terminal master's awarded for partial completion of doctoral program. *Degree requirements:* For master's, comprehensive exam, thesis (for some programs); for doctorate, comprehensive exam, thesis/dissertation. *Entrance requirements:* For master's and doctorate, minimum GPA of 3.0, 3 letters of recommendation, statement of purpose. Additional exam requirements/recommendations for international students: required—TOEFL (minimum score 550 paper-based; 80 iBT), IELTS (minimum score 6). Electronic applications accepted.

University of Guelph, Office of Graduate and Postdoctoral Studies, College of Physical and Engineering Science, School of Engineering, Guelph, ON N1G 2W1, Canada. Offers biological engineering (M Eng, M Sc, MA Sc, PhD); engineering systems and computing (M Eng, M Sc, MA Sc, PhD); environmental engineering (M Eng, M Sc, MA Sc, PhD); water resources engineering (M Eng, M Sc, MA Sc, PhD). *Program availability:* Part-time. *Degree requirements:* For master's, thesis (for some programs); for doctorate, comprehensive exam, thesis/dissertation. *Entrance requirements:* For master's, minimum B- average during previous 2 years of course work; for doctorate, minimum B average. Additional exam requirements/recommendations for international students: required—TOEFL (minimum score 550 paper-based; 89 iBT), IELTS (minimum score 6.5). Electronic applications accepted.

University of Hawaii at Manoa, Office of Graduate Education, College of Tropical Agriculture and Human Resources, Department of Molecular Biosciences and Bioengineering, Program in Bioengineering, Honolulu, HI 96822. Offers MS. *Program availability:* Part-time. *Degree requirements:* For master's, thesis optional. *Entrance requirements:* For master's, GRE General Test. Additional exam requirements/recommendations for international students: required—TOEFL (minimum score 500 paper-based; 61 iBT), IELTS (minimum score 5).

University of Idaho, College of Graduate Studies, College of Engineering, Department of Biological Engineering, Moscow, ID 83844-2282. Offers M Engr, MS, PhD. *Faculty:* 9. *Students:* 17. Average age 31. In 2019, 1 master's, 2 doctorates awarded. *Entrance requirements:* For master's, minimum GPA of 3.0. Additional exam requirements/recommendations for international students: required—TOEFL (minimum score 79 iBT), IELTS (minimum score 6.5), Michigan English Language Assessment Battery (minimum score of 77). *Application deadline:* For fall admission, 7/30 for domestic students; for spring admission, 12/1 for domestic students. Applications are processed on a rolling basis. Application fee: $60. Electronic applications accepted. *Expenses:* Tuition, state resident: full-time $7753.80; part-time $502 per credit hour. Tuition, nonresident: full-time $26,990; part-time $1571 per credit hour. *Required fees:* $2122.20; $47 per credit hour. *Financial support:* Research assistantships, teaching assistantships, and career-related internships or fieldwork available. Financial award applicants required to submit FAFSA. *Unit head:* Dr. Ching-An Peng, Chair, 208-885-6182, E-mail: chembioeng@uidaho.edu. *Application contact:* Dr. Ching-An Peng, Chair, 208-885-6182, E-mail: chembioeng@uidaho.edu.
Website: http://www.uidaho.edu/engr/departments/be

University of Illinois at Chicago, College of Engineering, Department of Bioengineering, Chicago, IL 60607-7128. Offers MS, PhD. Terminal master's awarded for partial completion of doctoral program. *Degree requirements:* For master's, thesis; for doctorate, thesis/dissertation. *Entrance requirements:* For master's and doctorate, GRE Subject Test, minimum GPA of 3.0. Additional exam requirements/recommendations for international students: required—TOEFL. Electronic applications accepted. *Expenses:* Contact institution.

University of Illinois at Urbana-Champaign, Graduate College, College of Agricultural, Consumer and Environmental Sciences, Department of Agricultural and Biological Engineering, Champaign, IL 61820. Offers agricultural and biological engineering (MS, PhD); technical systems management (MS, PSM).

University of Illinois at Urbana-Champaign, Graduate College, College of Engineering, Department of Bioengineering, Champaign, IL 61820. Offers MS, PhD.

University of Illinois at Urbana-Champaign, Graduate College, College of Liberal Arts and Sciences, School of Chemical Sciences, Department of Chemical and Biomolecular Engineering, Champaign, IL 61820. Offers bioinformatics: chemical and biomolecular engineering (MS); chemical engineering (MS, PhD). *Entrance requirements:* For master's, minimum GPA of 3.0.

The University of Kansas, Graduate Studies, School of Engineering, Program in Bioengineering, Lawrence, KS 66045. Offers MS, PhD. *Program availability:* Part-time. *Students:* 45 full-time (21 women), 3 part-time (1 woman); includes 6 minority (1 Black or African American, non-Hispanic/Latino; 1 American Indian or Alaska Native, non-Hispanic/Latino; 2 Hispanic/Latino; 2 Two or more races, non-Hispanic/Latino), 11 international. Average age 25. 49 applicants, 63% accepted, 7 enrolled. In 2019, 8 master's, 6 doctorates awarded. Terminal master's awarded for partial completion of doctoral program. *Entrance requirements:* For master's and doctorate, GRE, statement of academic objectives, curriculum vitae or resume, official transcripts, 3 letters of recommendation. Additional exam requirements/recommendations for international students: required—TOEFL, IELTS. *Application deadline:* For fall admission, 12/15 for domestic and international students; for spring admission, 9/30 for domestic and international students; for summer admission, 3/15 for domestic and international students. Application fee: $65 ($85 for international students). Electronic applications accepted. *Expenses:* Tuition, state resident: full-time $9989. Tuition, nonresident: full-time $23,950. International tuition: $23,950 full-time. *Required fees:* $984; $81.99 per credit hour. Tuition and fees vary according to course load, campus/location and program. *Financial support:* Fellowships, research assistantships, teaching assistantships, and scholarships/grants available. Financial award application deadline: 12/12. *Unit head:* Dr. Ken Fischer, Director, 785-864-2994, E-mail: fischer@ku.edu. *Application contact:* Denise Birdwell, Program Assistant, 785-864-5258, E-mail: dbridwell@ku.edu.
Website: http://bio.engr.ku.edu/

University of Louisville, J. B. Speed School of Engineering, Department of Bioengineering, Louisville, KY 40292-0001. Offers advancing bioengineering technologies through entrepreneurship (PhD); bioengineering (M Eng, PhD). *Accreditation:* ABET. *Faculty:* 10 full-time (3 women), 2 part-time/adjunct (1 woman). *Students:* 17 full-time (9 women), 14 part-time (7 women); includes 7 minority (1 Black or African American, non-Hispanic/Latino; 2 Asian, non-Hispanic/Latino; 1 Hispanic/Latino; 3 Two or more races, non-Hispanic/Latino). Average age 24. 1 applicant, 1 enrolled. In 2019, 30 master's awarded. *Degree requirements:* For master's, thesis; for doctorate, comprehensive exam, thesis/dissertation. *Entrance requirements:* For master's, 2 letters of recommendation; for doctorate, GRE, Three letters of recommendation, written statement describing previous experience related to bioengineering, a written statement as to how the PhD in Bioengineering will allow the applicant to fulfill their career goals. Additional exam requirements/recommendations for international students: required—TOEFL (minimum score 550 paper-based; 80 iBT), IELTS (minimum score 6.5). *Application deadline:* For fall admission, 5/1 priority date for domestic and international students; for spring admission, 11/1 priority date for domestic and international students; for summer admission, 3/1 priority date for domestic and international students. Applications are processed on a rolling basis. Application fee: $65. Electronic applications accepted. *Expenses: Tuition, area resident:* Full-time $13,000; part-time $723 per credit hour. Tuition, state resident: full-time $13,000; part-time $723 per credit hour. Tuition, nonresident: full-time $27,114; part-time $1507 per credit hour. International tuition: $27,114 full-time. *Required fees:* $196. Tuition and fees vary according to program and reciprocity agreements. *Financial support:* In 2019–20, 16 students received support. Fellowships, research assistantships, teaching assistantships, scholarships/grants, and health care benefits available. *Unit head:* Dr. Ayman El-Baz, Chair, Bioengineering Department, 502-852-5092, E-mail: aymen.elbaz@louisville.edu. *Application contact:* Gina Bertocci, Director of Graduate Studies, 502-852-0296, E-mail: gina.bertocci@louisville.edu.
Website: https://louisville.edu/speed/bioengineering/

University of Maryland, College Park, Academic Affairs, A. James Clark School of Engineering, Department of Chemical and Biomolecular Engineering, College Park, MD 20742. Offers bioengineering (MS, PhD); chemical engineering (M Eng, MS, PhD). *Program availability:* Part-time, evening/weekend. *Degree requirements:* For master's, thesis optional; for doctorate, variable foreign language requirement, thesis/dissertation, exam, oral presentation. *Entrance requirements:* For master's and doctorate, GRE General Test, 3 letters of recommendation. Additional exam requirements/recommendations for international students: required—TOEFL. Electronic applications accepted.

University of Maryland, College Park, Academic Affairs, A. James Clark School of Engineering, Fischell Department of Bioengineering, College Park, MD 20742. Offers MS, PhD. *Degree requirements:* For master's, thesis optional; for doctorate, thesis/dissertation. *Entrance requirements:* For master's, GRE General Test, minimum GPA of 3.0, 3 letters of recommendation. Electronic applications accepted.

Bioengineering

University of Michigan–Dearborn, College of Engineering and Computer Science, MSE Program in Bioengineering, Dearborn, MI 48128. Offers MSE. *Program availability:* Part-time, evening/weekend. *Faculty:* 24 full-time (4 women), 12 part-time/adjunct (2 women). *Students:* 2 full-time (1 woman), 4 part-time (1 woman). Average age 27. 15 applicants, 60% accepted, 2 enrolled. In 2019, 2 master's awarded. *Entrance requirements:* Additional exam requirements/recommendations for international students: required—TOEFL (minimum score 560 paper-based; 84 iBT), IELTS (minimum score 6.5). *Application deadline:* For fall admission, 8/1 for domestic students, 5/1 for international students; for winter admission, 12/1 for domestic students, 9/1 for international students; for spring admission, 4/1 for domestic students, 1/1 for international students. Applications are processed on a rolling basis. Application fee: $60. Electronic applications accepted. *Financial support:* Research assistantships with full tuition reimbursements, scholarships/grants, and non-resident tuition scholarships available. Financial award application deadline: 3/1; financial award applicants required to submit FAFSA. *Unit head:* Dr. Alan Argento, Program Director, 313-593-5241, E-mail: aargento@umich.edu. *Application contact:* Office of Graduate Studies Staff, 313-583-6321, E-mail: umd-graduatestudies@umich.edu.
Website: https://umdearborn.edu/cecs/departments/mechanical-engineering/graduate-programs/mse-bioengineering

University of Missouri, Office of Research and Graduate Studies, College of Engineering, Department of Biomedical, Biological and Chemical Engineering, Columbia, MO 65211. Offers biological engineering (MS, PhD); chemical engineering (MS, PhD). *Entrance requirements:* For master's and doctorate, GRE General Test, minimum GPA of 3.0. Additional exam requirements/recommendations for international students: required—TOEFL.

University of Nebraska–Lincoln, Graduate College, College of Engineering, Department of Biological Systems Engineering, Interdepartmental Area of Agricultural and Biological Systems Engineering, Lincoln, NE 68588. Offers MS, PhD. *Degree requirements:* For master's, thesis optional. *Entrance requirements:* Additional exam requirements/recommendations for international students: required—TOEFL (minimum score 550 paper-based). Electronic applications accepted.

University of Nebraska–Lincoln, Graduate College, College of Engineering, Department of Chemical and Biomolecular Engineering, Lincoln, NE 68588. Offers MS, PhD. *Degree requirements:* For master's, thesis; for doctorate, comprehensive exam, thesis/dissertation. *Entrance requirements:* For master's and doctorate, GRE. Additional exam requirements/recommendations for international students: required—TOEFL (minimum score 550 paper-based). Electronic applications accepted.

University of Notre Dame, The Graduate School, College of Engineering, Department of Civil and Environmental Engineering and Earth Sciences, Notre Dame, IN 46556. Offers bioengineering (MS Bio E); civil engineering (MSCE); civil engineering and geological sciences (PhD); earth sciences (MS); environmental engineering (MS Env E). Terminal master's awarded for partial completion of doctoral program. *Degree requirements:* For master's, comprehensive exam; for doctorate, thesis/dissertation, candidacy exam. *Entrance requirements:* For master's and doctorate, GRE General Test. Additional exam requirements/recommendations for international students: required—TOEFL (minimum score 600 paper-based; 80 iBT). Electronic applications accepted.

University of Ottawa, Faculty of Graduate and Postdoctoral Studies, Faculty of Engineering, Department of Chemical and Biological Engineering, Ottawa, ON K1N 6N5, Canada. Offers M Eng, MA Sc, PhD. *Degree requirements:* For master's, thesis or alternative; for doctorate, comprehensive exam, thesis/dissertation. *Entrance requirements:* For master's, honors degree or equivalent, minimum B average; for doctorate, master's degree, minimum B+ average. Electronic applications accepted.

University of Pennsylvania, School of Engineering and Applied Science, Department of Bioengineering, Philadelphia, PA 19104. Offers MSE, PhD, PhD/MD, VMD/PhD. *Program availability:* Part-time. *Faculty:* 128 full-time (24 women), 28 part-time/adjunct (2 women). *Students:* 193 full-time (94 women), 32 part-time (17 women); includes 77 minority (8 Black or African American, non-Hispanic/Latino; 39 Asian, non-Hispanic/Latino; 19 Hispanic/Latino; 11 Two or more races, non-Hispanic/Latino), 59 international. Average age 26. 665 applicants, 23% accepted, 66 enrolled. In 2019, 50 master's, 10 doctorates awarded. Terminal master's awarded for partial completion of doctoral program. *Degree requirements:* For master's, comprehensive exam, thesis optional; for doctorate, comprehensive exam, thesis/dissertation. *Entrance requirements:* For master's and doctorate, GRE, bachelor's degree, letters of recommendation, resume, personal statement. Additional exam requirements/recommendations for international students: required—TOEFL (minimum score 100 iBT), IELTS (minimum score 7). *Application deadline:* For fall admission, 12/15 priority date for domestic and international students. Application fee: $80. Electronic applications accepted. *Expenses:* Contact institution. *Application contact:* Christina Burton, Assistant Director of Graduate Admissions, 215-898-4542, Fax: 215-573-5577, E-mail: gradstudies@seas.upenn.edu.
Website: http://www.be.seas.upenn.edu/prospective-students/masters/index.php

University of Pennsylvania, School of Engineering and Applied Science, Department of Chemical and Biomolecular Engineering, Philadelphia, PA 19104. Offers MSE, PhD. *Program availability:* Part-time. *Faculty:* 18 full-time (4 women), 7 part-time/adjunct (2 women). *Students:* 115 full-time (32 women), 7 part-time (1 woman); includes 16 minority (2 Black or African American, non-Hispanic/Latino; 1 American Indian or Alaska Native, non-Hispanic/Latino; 7 Asian, non-Hispanic/Latino; 6 Hispanic/Latino), 77 international. Average age 25. 433 applicants, 30% accepted, 34 enrolled. In 2019, 25 master's, 8 doctorates awarded. Terminal master's awarded for partial completion of doctoral program. *Degree requirements:* For master's, comprehensive exam, thesis optional; for doctorate, comprehensive exam, thesis/dissertation. *Entrance requirements:* For master's and doctorate, GRE, bachelor's degree, letters of recommendation, resume, personal statement. Additional exam requirements/recommendations for international students: required—TOEFL (minimum score 100 iBT), IELTS (minimum score 7). *Application deadline:* For fall admission, 12/15 priority date for domestic and international students. Application fee: $80. Electronic applications accepted. *Expenses:* Contact institution. *Application contact:* Associate Director of Graduate Admissions, 215-898-4542, Fax: 215-573-5577, E-mail: admissions2@seas.upenn.edu.
Website: http://www.cbe.seas.upenn.edu/prospective-students/masters/index.php

University of Pittsburgh, Swanson School of Engineering, Department of Bioengineering, Pittsburgh, PA 15260. Offers MSBENG, PhD, MD/PhD. *Program availability:* Part-time, 100% online. Terminal master's awarded for partial completion of doctoral program. *Degree requirements:* For doctorate, comprehensive exam, thesis/dissertation, final oral exams. *Entrance requirements:* For master's and doctorate, GRE General Test, minimum GPA of 3.0. Additional exam requirements/recommendations for international students: required—TOEFL (minimum score 550 paper-based; 80 iBT). Electronic applications accepted. *Expenses:* Contact institution.

University of Puerto Rico at Mayagüez, Graduate Studies, College of Engineering, Department of Mechanical Engineering, Mayagüez, PR 00681-9000. Offers mechanical engineering (ME, MS, PhD), including aerospace and unmanned vehicles (ME), automation/mechatronics, bioengineering, fluid mechanics, heat transfer/energy systems, manufacturing, mechanics of materials, micro and nano engineering. *Program availability:* Part-time. Terminal master's awarded for partial completion of doctoral program. *Degree requirements:* For master's, one foreign language, comprehensive exam, thesis; for doctorate, one foreign language, comprehensive exam, thesis/dissertation. *Entrance requirements:* For master's, BS in mechanical engineering or its equivalent; for doctorate, GRE, BS or MS in mechanical engineering or its equivalent; minimum GPA of 3.0. Additional exam requirements/recommendations for international students: required—TOEFL (minimum score 80 iBT). Electronic applications accepted.

University of Saskatchewan, College of Graduate and Postdoctoral Studies, College of Engineering, Biological Engineering Program, Saskatoon, SK S7N 5E5, Canada. Offers M Sc, PhD. *Program availability:* Part-time. *Degree requirements:* For master's, 30 credits (for M Eng); thesis and 12 credits (for MS); for doctorate, comprehensive exam, thesis/dissertation, qualifying exam, 18 credits. *Entrance requirements:* For master's and doctorate, GRE. Additional exam requirements/recommendations for international students: required—TOEFL (minimum iBT score of 80), IELTS (6.5), CanTEST (4.5), or PTE (59). Electronic applications accepted.

The University of Texas at Arlington, Graduate School, College of Engineering, Bioengineering Department, Arlington, TX 76019. Offers MS, PhD. *Program availability:* Part-time. Terminal master's awarded for partial completion of doctoral program. *Degree requirements:* For master's, comprehensive exam (for some programs), thesis (for some programs); for doctorate, comprehensive exam, thesis/dissertation, qualifying exam. *Entrance requirements:* For master's, GRE General Test (minimum total of 1100 with minimum verbal score of 400), minimum GPA of 3.0 in last 60 hours of course work, 3 letters of recommendation; for doctorate, GRE General Test (minimum total of 1175 with minimum verbal score of 400), minimum GPA of 3.4 in last 60 hours of course work, 3 letters of recommendation. Additional exam requirements/recommendations for international students: required—TOEFL.

The University of Toledo, College of Graduate Studies, College of Engineering, Department of Bioengineering, Toledo, OH 43606-3390. Offers MS, PhD. Terminal master's awarded for partial completion of doctoral program. *Degree requirements:* For master's, thesis optional; for doctorate, thesis/dissertation, qualifying exam. *Entrance requirements:* For master's, GRE General Test, minimum GPA of 3.0; for doctorate, GRE General Test, minimum GPA of 3.3. Additional exam requirements/recommendations for international students: required—TOEFL (minimum score 550 paper-based; 80 iBT). Electronic applications accepted.

University of Utah, Graduate School, College of Engineering, Department of Bioengineering, Salt Lake City, UT 84112-9202. Offers MS, PhD, MS/MBA. Terminal master's awarded for partial completion of doctoral program. *Degree requirements:* For master's, comprehensive exam (for some programs), thesis (for some programs), project presentation, oral exam; for doctorate, comprehensive exam, thesis/dissertation, seminar presentation, TA mentorship. *Entrance requirements:* For master's and doctorate, GRE General Test or MCAT, bachelor's degree from accredited institution, college, or university; minimum undergraduate GPA of 3.0. Additional exam requirements/recommendations for international students: required—TOEFL (minimum score 575 paper-based; 90 iBT); recommended—IELTS (minimum score 7.5). Electronic applications accepted. *Expenses:* Contact institution.

University of Vermont, Graduate College, Cross-College Interdisciplinary Program, Program in Bioengineering, Burlington, VT 05405. Offers PhD. *Entrance requirements:* For doctorate, GRE General Test. Additional exam requirements/recommendations for international students: required—TOEFL (minimum score 550 paper-based; 90 iBT), IELTS (minimum score 6.5). Electronic applications accepted.

University of Washington, Graduate School, College of Engineering and School of Medicine, Department of Bioengineering, Seattle, WA 98195-5061. Offers applied bioengineering (MAB); bioengineering (MS, PhD); bioengineering and nanotechnology (PhD); pharmaceutical bioengineering (MS). *Program availability:* Part-time. *Students:* 157 full-time (73 women), 36 part-time (19 women); includes 53 minority (4 Black or African American, non-Hispanic/Latino; 1 American Indian or Alaska Native, non-Hispanic/Latino; 28 Asian, non-Hispanic/Latino; 13 Hispanic/Latino; 7 Two or more races, non-Hispanic/Latino), 47 international. Average age 26. 1,437 applicants, 13% accepted, 79 enrolled. In 2019, 37 master's, 31 doctorates awarded. *Degree requirements:* For master's, comprehensive exam, thesis; for doctorate, comprehensive exam, thesis/dissertation, qualifying exam, general exam, thesis defense. *Entrance requirements:* For master's and doctorate, GRE General Test (optional), minimum GPA of 3.0, transcripts, statement of purpose, letters of recommendation, resume/curriculum vitae. Additional exam requirements/recommendations for international students: required—TOEFL (minimum score 500 paper-based; 80 iBT). *Application deadline:* For fall admission, 12/3 for domestic and international students. Application fee: $85. Electronic applications accepted. Application fee is waived when completed online. *Expenses:* Contact institution. *Financial support:* In 2019–20, 1 fellowship with full tuition reimbursement (averaging $40,680 per year), 114 research assistantships with full tuition reimbursements (averaging $40,680 per year), 2 teaching assistantships with full tuition reimbursements (averaging $34,800 per year) were awarded; Federal Work-Study, institutionally sponsored loans, scholarships/grants, health care benefits, tuition waivers (full), and unspecified assistantships also available. Support available to part-time students. Financial award application deadline: 12/1; financial award applicants required to submit FAFSA. *Unit head:* Dr. Michael Regnier, Professor/Interim Chair, 206-685-2000, Fax: 206-685-3300, E-mail: mregnier@uw.edu. *Application contact:* Kalei Combs, Graduate Academic Counselor, 206-221-5448, Fax: 206-685-3300, E-mail: kaleic@uw.edu.
Website: https://bioe.uw.edu/

Utah State University, School of Graduate Studies, College of Engineering, Department of Biological Engineering, Logan, UT 84322. Offers MS, PhD. *Program availability:* Part-time. Terminal master's awarded for partial completion of doctoral program. *Degree requirements:* For master's, thesis (for some programs); for doctorate, thesis/dissertation. *Entrance requirements:* For master's and doctorate, GRE General Test, minimum GPA of 3.0. Additional exam requirements/recommendations for international students: required—TOEFL.

Virginia Polytechnic Institute and State University, Graduate School, College of Engineering, Blacksburg, VA 24061. Offers aerospace engineering (PhD, M Eng/MS); biological systems engineering (PhD); biomedical engineering (MS, PhD); chemical engineering (PhD); civil engineering (PhD); computer engineering (PhD); computer science and applications (MS); electrical engineering (PhD); engineering education (PhD); M Eng/MS. *Faculty:* 447 full-time (90 women), 6 part-time/adjunct (2 women). *Students:* 1,881 full-time (495 women), 326 part-time (70 women); includes 264 minority (51 Black or African American, non-Hispanic/Latino; 2 American Indian or Alaska Native, non-Hispanic/Latino; 96 Asian, non-Hispanic/Latino; 69 Hispanic/Latino; 46 Two or more races, non-Hispanic/Latino), 1,247 international. Average age 27. 4,014 applicants, 44% accepted, 658 enrolled. In 2019, 489 master's, 200 doctorates awarded. *Degree requirements:* For master's, comprehensive exam (for some programs), thesis (for some programs); for doctorate, comprehensive exam (for some programs), thesis/dissertation (for some programs). *Entrance requirements:* For master's and doctorate, GRE/GMAT.

Additional exam requirements/recommendations for international students: required—TOEFL (minimum score 90 iBT). *Application deadline:* For fall admission, 8/1 for domestic students, 4/1 for international students; for spring admission, 1/1 for domestic students, 9/1 for international students. Applications are processed on a rolling basis. Application fee: $75. Electronic applications accepted. *Expenses:* Tuition, state resident: full-time $13,700; part-time $761.25 per credit hour. Tuition, nonresident: full-time $27,614; part-time $1534 per credit hour. *Required fees:* $886.50 per term. Tuition and fees vary according to campus/location and program. *Financial support:* In 2019–20, 47 fellowships with full tuition reimbursements (averaging $19,703 per year), 1,163 research assistantships with full tuition reimbursements (averaging $20,602 per year), 554 teaching assistantships with full tuition reimbursements (averaging $16,333 per year) were awarded; scholarships/grants and unspecified assistantships also available. Financial award application deadline: 3/1; financial award applicants required to submit FAFSA. *Unit head:* Dr. Julia Ross, Dean, 540-231-9752, Fax: 540-231-3031, E-mail: rjulie@vt.edu. *Application contact:* Linda Perkins, Executive Assistant, 540-231-9752, Fax: 540-231-3031, E-mail: lperkins@vt.edu. Website: http://www.eng.vt.edu/

Washington State University, College of Agricultural, Human, and Natural Resource Sciences, Department of Biological Systems Engineering, Pullman, WA 99164-6120. Offers biological and agricultural engineering (MS, PhD). *Degree requirements:* For master's, comprehensive exam, thesis (for some programs), written and oral exam; for doctorate, comprehensive exam, thesis/dissertation, written and oral exam. *Entrance requirements:* For master's and doctorate, minimum GPA of 3.0, bachelor's degree in engineering or closely-related subject. Additional exam requirements/recommendations for international students: required—TOEFL. Electronic applications accepted.

Biosystems Engineering

Auburn University, Graduate School, Samuel Ginn College of Engineering, Department of Biosystems Engineering, Auburn, AL 36849. Offers MS, PhD. *Program availability:* Part-time. *Faculty:* 13 full-time (0 women), 2 part-time/adjunct (0 women). *Students:* 22 full-time (10 women), 8 part-time (1 woman); includes 4 minority (1 Asian, non-Hispanic/Latino; 2 Hispanic/Latino; 1 Two or more races, non-Hispanic/Latino), 21 international. Average age 28. 13 applicants, 62% accepted, 5 enrolled. In 2019, 5 master's, 2 doctorates awarded. *Degree requirements:* For master's, thesis; for doctorate, thesis/dissertation. *Entrance requirements:* For master's and doctorate, GRE. Additional exam requirements/recommendations for international students: required—TOEFL (minimum score 550 paper-based; 79 iBT). *Application deadline:* Applications are processed on a rolling basis. Application fee: $60 ($70 for international students). Electronic applications accepted. *Expenses: Tuition, area resident:* Full-time $9828; part-time $546 per credit hour. Tuition, state resident: full-time $9828; part-time $546 per credit hour. Tuition, nonresident: full-time $29,484; part-time $1638 per credit hour. *International tuition:* $29,744 full-time. Tuition and fees vary according to course load, program and reciprocity agreements. *Financial support:* Fellowships and unspecified assistantships available. Financial award application deadline: 3/15; financial award applicants required to submit FAFSA. *Unit head:* Dr. Oladiran Fasina, Head, 334-844-4180, E-mail: fasinoo@auburn.edu. *Application contact:* Dr. George Flowers, Dean of the Graduate School, 334-844-2125. Website: https://www.eng.auburn.edu/bsen/

Clemson University, Graduate School, College of Engineering, Computing and Applied Sciences, Department of Environmental Engineering and Earth Sciences, Anderson, SC 29625. Offers biosystems engineering (MS, PhD); environmental engineering and science (MS, PhD); environmental health physics (MS); hydrogeology (MS). *Program availability:* Part-time. *Faculty:* 30 full-time (9 women), 2 part-time/adjunct (1 woman). *Students:* 80 full-time (31 women), 12 part-time (4 women); includes 5 minority (1 Black or African American, non-Hispanic/Latino; 1 Hispanic/Latino; 1 Native Hawaiian or other Pacific Islander, non-Hispanic/Latino; 2 Two or more races, non-Hispanic/Latino), 34 international. Average age 25. 108 applicants, 65% accepted, 30 enrolled. In 2019, 21 master's, 5 doctorates awarded. *Degree requirements:* For master's, thesis or alternative; for doctorate, comprehensive exam, thesis/dissertation. *Entrance requirements:* For master's and doctorate, GRE General Test, unofficial transcripts, letters of recommendation. Additional exam requirements/recommendations for international students: required—TOEFL (minimum score 80 paper-based; 80 iBT); recommended—IELTS (minimum score 6.5), TSE (minimum score 54). *Application deadline:* For fall admission, 2/15 for domestic and international students. Applications are processed on a rolling basis. Application fee: $80 ($90 for international students). Electronic applications accepted. *Expenses: Tuition, area resident:* Full-time $10,600; part-time $8688 per semester. Tuition, state resident: full-time $10,600; part-time $8688 per semester. Tuition, nonresident: full-time $22,050; part-time $17,412 per semester. *International tuition:* $22,050 full-time. *Required fees:* $1196; $617 per semester. $617 per semester. Tuition and fees vary according to course load, degree level, campus/location and program. *Financial support:* In 2019–20, 47 students received support, including 3 fellowships with full and partial tuition reimbursements available (averaging $16,000 per year), 15 research assistantships with full and partial tuition reimbursements available (averaging $22,327 per year), 24 teaching assistantships with full and partial tuition reimbursements available (averaging $21,681 per year); career-related internships or fieldwork and unspecified assistantships also available. Financial award application deadline: 2/15. *Unit head:* Dr. David Freedman, Department Chair, 864-656-5566, E-mail: dfreedm@clemson.edu. *Application contact:* Dr. Mark Schlautman, Graduate Program Coordinator, 864-656-4059, E-mail: mschlau@clemson.edu. Website: https://www.clemson.edu/cecas/departments/eees/

Michigan State University, The Graduate School, College of Agriculture and Natural Resources and College of Engineering, Department of Biosystems and Agricultural Engineering, East Lansing, MI 48824. Offers biosystems engineering (MS, PhD). *Entrance requirements:* Additional exam requirements/recommendations for international students: required—TOEFL. Electronic applications accepted.

North Dakota State University, College of Graduate and Interdisciplinary Studies, College of Engineering, Department of Agricultural and Biosystems Engineering, Fargo, ND 58102. Offers MS, PhD. *Program availability:* Part-time. *Degree requirements:* For master's, thesis; for doctorate, thesis/dissertation. *Entrance requirements:* For master's and doctorate, BS in engineering or the equivalent, minimum undergraduate GPA of 3.0. Additional exam requirements/recommendations for international students: required—TOEFL (minimum score 550 paper-based; 79 iBT). Electronic applications accepted. Tuition and fees vary according to program and reciprocity agreements.

South Dakota State University, Graduate School, College of Agriculture, Food and Environmental Sciences, Department of Agricultural and Biosystems Engineering, Brookings, SD 57007. Offers MS, PhD. *Program availability:* Part-time. *Degree requirements:* For master's, thesis; for doctorate, comprehensive exam, thesis/dissertation, preliminary oral and written exams. *Entrance requirements:* Additional exam requirements/recommendations for international students: required—TOEFL (minimum score 525 paper-based; 71 iBT).

South Dakota State University, Graduate School, Jerome J. Lohr College of Engineering, Department of Agricultural and Biosystems Engineering, Brookings, SD 57007. Offers biological sciences (MS, PhD); engineering (MS). *Program availability:* Part-time. *Degree requirements:* For master's, thesis (for some programs), oral exam; for doctorate, thesis/dissertation, preliminary oral and written exams. *Entrance requirements:* For master's and doctorate, engineering degree. Additional exam requirements/recommendations for international students: required—TOEFL (minimum score 550 paper-based; 79 iBT).

The University of Arizona, College of Agriculture and Life Sciences, Department of Agricultural and Biosystems Engineering, Tucson, AZ 85721. Offers MS, PhD. Terminal master's awarded for partial completion of doctoral program. *Degree requirements:* For master's, thesis; for doctorate, thesis/dissertation. *Entrance requirements:* For master's, minimum GPA of 3.0 in last 2 years of undergraduate study, 3 letters of recommendation; for doctorate, minimum GPA of 3.0 in last 2 years of undergraduate study, 3 letters of recommendation, statement of purpose. Additional exam requirements/recommendations for international students: required—TOEFL (minimum score 550 paper-based; 79 iBT). Electronic applications accepted.

University of Manitoba, Faculty of Graduate Studies, Faculty of Engineering, Department of Biosystems Engineering, Winnipeg, MB R3T 2N2, Canada. Offers M Eng, M Sc, PhD.

University of Minnesota, Twin Cities Campus, Graduate School, College of Food, Agricultural and Natural Resource Sciences, Bioproducts and Biosystems Science, Engineering and Management Graduate Program, St. Paul, MN 55108. Offers MS, PhD. *Program availability:* Part-time. *Faculty:* 38 full-time (3 women). *Students:* 41 full-time (19 women); includes 12 minority (10 Asian, non-Hispanic/Latino; 2 Hispanic/Latino). Average age 30. 48 applicants, 19% accepted, 8 enrolled. In 2019, 8 master's, 3 doctorates awarded. Terminal master's awarded for partial completion of doctoral program. *Degree requirements:* For master's, comprehensive exam, thesis, written and oral preliminary exams; for doctorate, comprehensive exam, thesis/dissertation, written and oral preliminary exams. *Entrance requirements:* For master's and doctorate, GRE, BS in engineering, mathematics, physical or biological sciences, or related field. Additional exam requirements/recommendations for international students: required—TOEFL (minimum score 550 paper-based; 79 iBT), IELTS (minimum score 6.5). *Application deadline:* For fall admission, 12/15 for domestic and international students; for spring admission, 8/15 for domestic and international students. Applications are processed on a rolling basis. Application fee: $75 ($95 for international students). Electronic applications accepted. *Financial support:* In 2019–20, 6 fellowships with full and partial tuition reimbursements (averaging $40,000 per year), 28 research assistantships with full and partial tuition reimbursements (averaging $40,000 per year), 2 teaching assistantships with full and partial tuition reimbursements (averaging $40,000 per year) were awarded; scholarships/grants, health care benefits, tuition waivers (full and partial), and unspecified assistantships also available. Support available to part-time students. Financial award application deadline: 12/15. *Unit head:* Dr. Roger Ruan, Director of Graduate Studies, 612-625-1710, Fax: 612-624-3005, E-mail: ruanx001@umn.edu. *Application contact:* Sue Olsen, Graduate Coordinator, 612-625-7733, Fax: 612-624-3005, E-mail: olsen005@umn.edu. Website: http://www.bbe.umn.edu/

The University of Tennessee, Graduate School, College of Agricultural Sciences and Natural Resources, Department of Biosystems Engineering and Environmental Science, Program in Biosystems Engineering, Knoxville, TN 37996. Offers MS, PhD. *Degree requirements:* For master's, thesis; for doctorate, thesis/dissertation. *Entrance requirements:* For master's and doctorate, GRE General Test, minimum GPA of 2.7. Additional exam requirements/recommendations for international students: required—TOEFL. Electronic applications accepted.

The University of Tennessee, Graduate School, College of Agricultural Sciences and Natural Resources, Department of Biosystems Engineering and Environmental Science, Program in Biosystems Engineering Technology, Knoxville, TN 37996. Offers MS. *Degree requirements:* For master's, thesis or alternative. *Entrance requirements:* For master's, GRE General Test, minimum GPA of 2.7. Additional exam requirements/recommendations for international students: required—TOEFL. Electronic applications accepted.

Section 4
Architectural Engineering

This section contains a directory of institutions offering graduate work in architectural engineering. Additional information about programs listed in the directory may be obtained by writing directly to the dean of a graduate school or chair of a department at the address given in the directory.

For programs offering related work, see also in this book *Engineering and Applied Sciences* and *Management of Engineering and Technology.* In the other guides in this series:

Graduate Programs in the Humanities, Arts & Social Sciences

See *Applied Arts and Design (Industrial Design and Interior Design), Architecture (Environmental Design), Political Science and International Affairs,* and *Public, Regional, and Industrial Affairs (Urban and Regional Planning and Urban Studies)*

Graduate Programs in the Physical Sciences, Mathematics, Agricultural Sciences, the Environment & Natural Resources

See *Environmental Sciences and Management*

CONTENTS

Program Directory

Architectural Engineering

California Polytechnic State University, San Luis Obispo, College of Architecture and Environmental Design, Department of Architectural Engineering, San Luis Obispo, CA 93407. Offers MS. *Program availability:* Part-time. *Faculty:* 3 full-time (1 woman). *Students:* 13 full-time (5 women), 2 part-time (1 woman); includes 11 minority (3 Asian, non-Hispanic/Latino; 3 Hispanic/Latino; 5 Two or more races, non-Hispanic/Latino). Average age 23. 22 applicants, 68% accepted, 13 enrolled. In 2019, 10 master's awarded. *Entrance requirements:* For master's, GRE. Additional exam requirements/recommendations for international students: required—TOEFL (minimum score 80 iBT). *Application deadline:* For fall admission, 4/1 for domestic and international students. Applications are processed on a rolling basis. Application fee: $55. Electronic applications accepted. *Expenses:* Tuition, state resident: full-time $7176; part-time $4164 per year. Tuition, nonresident: full-time $18,690; part-time $8916 per year. *Required fees:* $4206; $3185 per unit. $1061 per term. *Financial support:* Fellowships, teaching assistantships, scholarships/grants, tuition waivers, and unspecified assistantships available. Financial award application deadline: 3/2; financial award applicants required to submit FAFSA. *Unit head:* Dr. Allen C. Estes, Head, 805-756-1314, Fax: 805-756-6054, E-mail: acestes@calpoly.edu. *Application contact:* Dr. Allen C. Estes, Head, 805-756-1314, Fax: 805-756-6054, E-mail: acestes@calpoly.edu.
Website: http://www.arce.calpoly.edu

California State University, Fullerton, Graduate Studies, College of Engineering and Computer Science, Department of Civil and Environmental Engineering, Fullerton, CA 92831-3599. Offers civil engineering (MS), including architectural engineering, environmental engineering. *Program availability:* Part-time. *Degree requirements:* For master's, comprehensive exam, project or thesis. *Entrance requirements:* For master's, minimum undergraduate GPA of 2.5.

Carnegie Mellon University, College of Fine Arts, School of Architecture, Pittsburgh, PA 15213-3891. Offers architecture (MSA); architecture, engineering, and construction management (PhD); building performance and diagnostics (MS, PhD); computational design (MS, PhD); engineering construction management (MSA); tangible interaction design (MTID); urban design (MUD). Terminal master's awarded for partial completion of doctoral program. *Degree requirements:* For doctorate, thesis/dissertation. *Entrance requirements:* For master's and doctorate, GRE General Test. Additional exam requirements/recommendations for international students: required—TOEFL.

Drexel University, College of Engineering, Department of Civil, Architectural, and Environmental Engineering, Philadelphia, PA 19104-2875. Offers architectural/building systems engineering (MS, PhD); civil engineering (MS, PhD); environmental engineering (MS, PhD); geotechnical, geoenvironmental and geosynthetics engineering (MS, PhD); hydraulics, hydrology and water resources engineering (MS, PhD); structures (MS). *Program availability:* Part-time, evening/weekend. *Degree requirements:* For master's, thesis optional; for doctorate, thesis/dissertation. *Entrance requirements:* For master's, minimum GPA of 3.0; for doctorate, minimum GPA of 3.5, MS in civil engineering. Additional exam requirements/recommendations for international students: required—TOEFL. Electronic applications accepted.

Illinois Institute of Technology, Graduate College, Armour College of Engineering, Department of Civil, Architectural and Environmental Engineering, Chicago, IL 60616. Offers architectural engineering (M Arch E); civil engineering (MS, PhD), including architectural engineering (MS), construction engineering and management (MS), geoenvironmental engineering (MS), geotechnical engineering (MS), structural engineering (MS), transportation engineering (MS); construction engineering and management (MCEM); environmental engineering (M Env E, MS, PhD); geoenvironmental engineering (M Geoenv E); geotechnical engineering (MGE); infrastructure engineering and management (MPW); structural engineering (MSE); transportation engineering (M Trans E). *Program availability:* Part-time, evening/weekend, online learning. Terminal master's awarded for partial completion of doctoral program. *Degree requirements:* For master's, thesis (for some programs); for doctorate, comprehensive exam, thesis/dissertation. *Entrance requirements:* For master's, GRE General Test (minimum score 900 Quantitative and Verbal, 2.5 Analytical Writing), minimum undergraduate GPA of 3.0; for doctorate, GRE General Test (minimum score 1000 Quantitative and Verbal, 3.0 Analytical Writing), minimum undergraduate GPA of 3.0. Additional exam requirements/recommendations for international students: required—TOEFL (minimum score 550 paper-based; 80 iBT). Electronic applications accepted.

Kansas State University, Graduate School, College of Engineering, Department of Architectural Engineering and Construction Science, Manhattan, KS 66506. Offers MS. *Degree requirements:* For master's, thesis or alternative. *Entrance requirements:* For master's, GRE, minimum GPA of 3.0, undergraduate degree (BS) from ABET-accredited engineering program. Additional exam requirements/recommendations for international students: required—TOEFL. Electronic applications accepted.

Lawrence Technological University, College of Engineering, Southfield, MI 48075-1058. Offers architectural engineering (MS); automotive engineering (MS); biomedical engineering (MS); civil engineering (MA, MS, PhD), including environmental engineering (MS), geotechnical engineering (MS), structural engineering (MS), transportation engineering (MS), water resource engineering (MS); construction engineering management (MA); electrical and computer engineering (MS); engineering management (MEM); engineering technology (MS); fire engineering (MS); industrial engineering (MS), including healthcare systems; manufacturing systems (ME); mechanical engineering (MS, DE, PhD), including automotive engineering (MS), energy engineering (MS), manufacturing (DE), solid mechanics (MS), thermal/fluid systems (MS); mechatronic systems engineering (MS). *Program availability:* Part-time, evening/weekend. *Faculty:* 23 full-time (2 women), 20 part-time/adjunct (1 woman). *Students:* 14 full-time (5 women), 286 part-time (54 women); includes 26 minority (13 Black or African American, non-Hispanic/Latino; 8 Asian, non-Hispanic/Latino; 3 Hispanic/Latino; 2 Two or more races, non-Hispanic/Latino), 150 international. Average age 29. 384 applicants, 58% accepted, 74 enrolled. In 2019, 223 master's, 7 doctorates awarded. Terminal master's awarded for partial completion of doctoral program. *Degree requirements:* For master's, thesis optional; for doctorate, comprehensive exam, thesis/dissertation optional. *Entrance requirements:* Additional exam requirements/recommendations for international students: required—TOEFL (minimum score 550 paper-based; 79 iBT), IELTS (minimum score 6.5). *Application deadline:* For fall admission, 5/24 for international students; for spring admission, 10/13 for international students; for summer admission, 2/18 for international students. Applications are processed on a rolling basis. Application fee: $50. Electronic applications accepted. *Expenses: Tuition:* Full-time $16,618; part-time $8309 per year. *Required fees:* $600; $600. *Financial support:* In 2019–20, 21 students received support. Unspecified assistantships available. Financial award application deadline: 4/1; financial award applicants required to submit FAFSA. *Unit head:* Dr. Nabil Grace, Dean, 248-204-2500, Fax: 248-204-2509, E-mail: engrdean@ltu.edu. *Application contact:* Jane Rohrback, Director of Admissions, 248-204-3160, Fax: 248-204-2228, E-mail: admissions@ltu.edu. Website: http://www.ltu.edu/engineering/index.asp

Milwaukee School of Engineering, MS Program in Architectural Engineering, Milwaukee, WI 53202-3109. Offers MS. *Program availability:* Part-time, evening/weekend. *Degree requirements:* For master's, thesis. *Entrance requirements:* For master's, GRE General Test if undergraduate GPA is less than 3.0, 2 letters of recommendation; BS in architectural engineering or closely-related area from ABET-accredited program. Additional exam requirements/recommendations for international students: required—TOEFL (minimum score 90 iBT), IELTS (minimum score 7). Electronic applications accepted.

Penn State University Park, Graduate School, College of Engineering, Department of Architectural Engineering, University Park, PA 16802. Offers architectural engineering (M Eng, MAE, MS, PhD); facilities engineering and management (M Eng).

University of California, San Diego, Graduate Division, Program in Architecture-based Enterprise Systems Engineering, La Jolla, CA 92093. Offers MAS. *Program availability:* Part-time. *Students:* 35 full-time (5 women). 47 applicants, 94% accepted, 38 enrolled. In 2019, 32 master's awarded. *Degree requirements:* For master's, capstone project. *Entrance requirements:* For master's, 2 letters of recommendation, statement of purpose, resume or curriculum vitae. Additional exam requirements/recommendations for international students: required—TOEFL (minimum score 550 paper-based; 80 iBT), IELTS (minimum score 7). *Application deadline:* For fall admission, 7/1 for domestic students. Application fee: $105 ($125 for international students). Electronic applications accepted. *Expenses:* Contact institution. *Financial support:* Applicants required to submit FAFSA. *Unit head:* Harold Sorenson, Director, 858-534-4406, E-mail: hsorenson@ucsd.edu. *Application contact:* Stacey Williams, Coordinator, 858-534-1069, E-mail: staceyw@eng.ucsd.edu. Website: http://maseng.ucsd.edu/aese/

University of Colorado Boulder, Graduate School, College of Engineering and Applied Science, Department of Civil, Environmental, and Architectural Engineering, Boulder, CO 80309. Offers MS, PhD. Terminal master's awarded for partial completion of doctoral program. *Degree requirements:* For master's, comprehensive exam, thesis or alternative; for doctorate, thesis/dissertation. *Entrance requirements:* For master's, GRE General Test, minimum undergraduate GPA of 3.0. Electronic applications accepted. Application fee is waived when completed online.

University of Detroit Mercy, School of Architecture, Detroit, MI 48221. Offers architecture (M Arch); community development (MA). *Entrance requirements:* For master's, BS in architecture, minimum GPA of 3.0, portfolio.

The University of Kansas, Graduate Studies, School of Engineering, Program in Architectural Engineering, Lawrence, KS 66045. Offers MS. *Program availability:* Part-time. *Students:* Average age 27. 1 applicant. In 2019, 7 master's awarded.

Entrance requirements: For master's, GRE, two letters of recommendation, statement of purpose. Additional exam requirements/recommendations for international students: required—TOEFL, IELTS. *Application deadline:* For fall admission, 8/17 for domestic and international students; for spring admission, 1/14 for domestic and international students; for summer admission, 5/26 for domestic and international students. Application fee: $65 ($85 for international students). Electronic applications accepted. *Expenses:* Tuition, state resident: full-time $9989. Tuition, nonresident: full-time $23,950. *International tuition:* $23,950 full-time. *Required fees:* $984; $81.99 per credit hour. Tuition and fees vary according to course load, campus/location and program. *Financial support:* Fellowships, research assistantships, teaching assistantships, career-related internships or fieldwork, and scholarships/grants available. Financial award application deadline: 12/15. *Unit head:* David Darwin, Chair, 785-864-3827, E-mail: daved@ku.edu. *Application contact:* Susan Scott, Graduate Secretary, 785-864-3826, Fax: 785-864-5631, E-mail: s523s307@ku.edu. Website: http://www.ceae.ku.edu/

University of Louisiana at Lafayette, College of the Arts, School of Architecture and Design, Lafayette, LA 70504. Offers M Arch. *Entrance requirements:* For master's, GRE General Test. Additional exam requirements/recommendations for international students: required—TOEFL (minimum score 550 paper-based). Electronic applications accepted. *Expenses: Tuition, area resident:* Full-time $5511. Tuition, state resident: full-time $5511. Tuition, nonresident: full-time $19,239. *Required fees:* $46,637.

University of Massachusetts Amherst, Graduate School, College of Natural Sciences, Department of Environmental Conservation, Amherst, MA 01003. Offers building systems (MS, PhD); environmental policy and human dimensions (MS, PhD); forest resources (MS, PhD); sustainability science (MS); water, wetlands and watersheds (MS, PhD); wildlife and fisheries conservation (MS, PhD). *Program availability:* Part-time. Terminal master's awarded for partial completion of doctoral program. *Degree requirements:* For master's, thesis or alternative; for doctorate, comprehensive exam, thesis/dissertation. *Entrance requirements:* For master's and doctorate, GRE General Test. Additional exam requirements/recommendations for international students: required—TOEFL (minimum score 550 paper-based; 80 iBT), IELTS (minimum score 6.5). Electronic applications accepted.

University of Miami, Graduate School, College of Engineering, Department of Civil, Architectural, and Environmental Engineering, Coral Gables, FL 33124. Offers architectural engineering (MSAE); civil engineering (MSCE, PhD). *Program availability:* Part-time. Terminal master's awarded for partial completion of doctoral program. *Degree requirements:* For master's, thesis (for some programs); for doctorate, comprehensive exam, thesis/dissertation. *Entrance requirements:* For master's, GRE General Test (minimum score 1000 verbal and quantitative), minimum GPA of 3.0; for doctorate, GRE General Test, minimum GPA of 3.5 in preceding degree. Additional exam requirements/recommendations for international students: required—TOEFL (minimum score 550 paper-based). Electronic applications accepted.

University of Nebraska–Lincoln, Graduate College, College of Engineering, Program in Architectural Engineering, Lincoln, NE 68588. Offers M Eng, MAE, MS, PhD. *Entrance requirements:* Additional exam requirements/recommendations for international students: required—TOEFL (minimum score 550 paper-based).

The University of Texas at Austin, Graduate School, Cockrell School of Engineering, Department of Civil, Architectural and Environmental Engineering, Program in Architectural Engineering, Austin, TX 78712-1111. Offers MSE. *Program availability:* Part-time. *Degree requirements:* For master's, thesis. *Entrance requirements:* For master's, GRE General Test. Additional exam requirements/recommendations for international students: required—TOEFL. Electronic applications accepted.

University of Wyoming, College of Engineering and Applied Science, Department of Civil and Architectural Engineering, Laramie, WY 82071. Offers architectural engineering (MS); civil engineering (MS, PhD). *Program availability:* Part-time. Terminal master's awarded for partial completion of doctoral program. *Degree requirements:* For master's, thesis (for some programs); for doctorate, variable foreign language requirement, comprehensive exam, thesis/dissertation. *Entrance requirements:* For master's, GRE General Test (minimum combined score 900), minimum GPA of 3.0; for doctorate, GRE General Test (minimum combined score: 1000), minimum GPA of 3.0. Additional exam requirements/recommendations for international students: required—TOEFL (minimum score 550 paper-based). Electronic applications accepted.

Section 5
Biomedical Engineering and Biotechnology

This section contains a directory of institutions offering graduate work in biomedical engineering and biotechnology, followed by an in-depth entry submitted by an institution that chose to prepare a detailed program description. Additional information about programs listed in the directory but not augmented by an in-depth entry may be obtained by writing directly to the dean of a graduate school or chair of a department at the address given in the directory.

For programs offering related work, see also in this book *Aerospace/Aeronautical Engineering, Engineering and Applied Sciences, Engineering Design, Engineering Physics, Management of Engineering and Technology,* and *Mechanical Engineering and Mechanics.* In the other guides in this series:

Graduate Programs in the Biological/Biomedical Sciences & Health-Related Medical Professions

See *Allied Health, Biological and Biomedical Sciences,* and *Physiology*

Graduate Programs in the Physical Sciences, Mathematics, Agricultural Sciences, the Environment & Natural Resources
See *Mathematical Sciences (Biometrics and Biostatistics)*

CONTENTS

Program Directories

Biomedical Engineering

American University of Sharjah, Graduate Programs, Sharjah, United Arab Emirates. Offers accounting (MS); biomedical engineering (MSBME); business administration (MBA); chemical engineering (MS Ch E); civil engineering (MSCE); computer engineering (MS); electrical engineering (MSEE); engineering systems management (MS, PhD); mathematics (MS); mechanical engineering (MSME); mechatronics engineering (MS); teaching English to speakers of other languages (MA); translation and interpreting (MA); urban planning (MUP). *Program availability:* Part-time, evening/weekend. *Degree requirements:* For master's, thesis (for some programs). *Entrance requirements:* For master's, GMAT (for MBA). Additional exam requirements/recommendations for international students: required—TOEFL (minimum score 550 paper-based; 80 iBT), TWE (minimum score 5); recommended—IELTS (minimum score 6.5). Electronic applications accepted.

Arizona State University at Tempe, Ira A. Fulton Schools of Engineering, School of Biological and Health Systems Engineering, Tempe, AZ 85287-9709. Offers biological design (PhD); biomedical engineering (MS, PhD). *Program availability:* Part-time, evening/weekend. Terminal master's awarded for partial completion of doctoral program. *Degree requirements:* For master's, thesis and oral defense or applied project; interactive Program of Study (iPOS) submitted before completing 50 percent of required credit hours; for doctorate, comprehensive exam, thesis/dissertation, interactive Program of Study (iPOS) submitted before completing 50 percent of required credit hours. *Entrance requirements:* For master's and doctorate, GRE General Test, minimum GPA of 3.0 or equivalent in last 2 years of work leading to bachelor's degree, 3 letters of recommendation, one-page personal statement. Additional exam requirements/recommendations for international students: required—TOEFL (minimum score 580 paper-based; 92 iBT). Electronic applications accepted. *Expenses:* Contact institution.

Baylor College of Medicine, Graduate School of Biomedical Sciences, Program in Translational Biology and Molecular Medicine, Houston, TX 77030-3498. Offers PhD. *Degree requirements:* For doctorate, thesis/dissertation, public defense. *Entrance requirements:* For doctorate, GRE, minimum GPA of 3.0. Additional exam requirements/recommendations for international students: required—TOEFL. Electronic applications accepted.

Baylor University, Graduate School, School of Engineering and Computer Science, Department of Engineering, Waco, TX 76798. Offers biomedical engineering (MSBME); electrical and computer engineering (MSECE, PhD); engineering (ME); mechanical engineering (MSME).

Baylor University, Graduate School, School of Engineering and Computer Science, Department of Mechanical Engineering, Waco, TX 76798. Offers biomedical engineering (MSBME); engineering (ME); mechanical engineering (MS, PhD). *Program availability:* Part-time. *Degree requirements:* For master's, thesis (for some programs), 30 credits including 24 coursework and 6 research (for MS); 33 coursework credits or 6 project credits and 27 coursework credits (for ME); for doctorate, thesis/dissertation (for some programs), 48 semester hours of approved course work and research hours beyond the master's degree. *Entrance requirements:* For master's, GRE. Additional exam requirements/recommendations for international students: required—TOEFL (minimum score 550 paper-based; 80 iBT), IELTS (minimum score 6.5). Electronic applications accepted. *Expenses:* Contact institution.

Binghamton University, State University of New York, Graduate School, Thomas J. Watson School of Engineering and Applied Science, Department of Biomedical Engineering, Binghamton, NY 13902-6000. Offers MS, PhD. *Program availability:* Part-time, online learning. *Degree requirements:* For master's, thesis; for doctorate, comprehensive exam, thesis/dissertation. *Entrance requirements:* For master's and doctorate, GRE General Test. Additional exam requirements/recommendations for international students: required—TOEFL (minimum score 550 paper-based; 80 iBT). Electronic applications accepted. *Expenses:* Contact institution.

Boston University, College of Engineering, Department of Biomedical Engineering, Boston, MA 02215. Offers biomedical engineering (M Eng, MS, PhD); MD/PhD. *Program availability:* Part-time. *Students:* 211 full-time (89 women), 9 part-time (2 women); includes 58 minority (7 Black or African American, non-Hispanic/Latino; 33 Asian, non-Hispanic/Latino; 10 Hispanic/Latino; 8 Two or more races, non-Hispanic/Latino), 64 international. Average age 24. 903 applicants, 38% accepted, 84 enrolled. In 2019, 69 master's, 27 doctorates awarded. Terminal master's awarded for partial completion of doctoral program. *Degree requirements:* For master's, thesis (for some programs); for doctorate, comprehensive exam, thesis/dissertation. *Entrance requirements:* For master's and doctorate, GRE General Test. Additional exam requirements/recommendations for international students: required—TOEFL (minimum score 90 iBT), IELTS (minimum score 7). *Expenses:* Contact institution. *Financial support:* Fellowships with tuition reimbursements, research assistantships, teaching assistantships, career-related internships or fieldwork, Federal Work-Study, scholarships/grants, traineeships, health care benefits, and unspecified assistantships available. Support available to part-time students. Financial award application deadline: 3/15; financial award applicants required to submit FAFSA. *Unit head:* Dr. John White, Chairman, 617-353-2805, Fax: 617-353-6766. *Application contact:* Dr. John White, Chairman, 617-353-2805, Fax: 617-353-6766.
Website: http://www.bu.edu/bme/

Brown University, Graduate School, Division of Biology and Medicine, Department of Molecular Pharmacology, Physiology and Biotechnology, Providence, RI 02912. Offers biomedical engineering (Sc M, PhD); biotechnology (PhD); molecular pharmacology and physiology (PhD); MD/PhD. *Degree requirements:* For doctorate, thesis/dissertation, preliminary exam. *Entrance requirements:* For master's and doctorate, GRE General Test, GRE Subject Test. Additional exam requirements/recommendations for international students: required—TOEFL. Electronic applications accepted.

Brown University, Graduate School, School of Engineering and Division of Biology and Medicine, Center for Biomedical Engineering, Providence, RI 02912. Offers Sc M, PhD. *Degree requirements:* For master's, thesis.

California Polytechnic State University, San Luis Obispo, College of Engineering, Department of Biomedical Engineering, San Luis Obispo, CA 93407. Offers MS, MBA/MS, MCRP/MS. *Program availability:* Part-time. *Faculty:* 10 full-time (2 women), 1 (woman) part-time/adjunct. *Students:* 34 full-time (20 women), 7 part-time (5 women); includes 9 minority (4 Asian, non-Hispanic/Latino; 5 Hispanic/Latino), 2 international. Average age 23. 52 applicants, 60% accepted, 24 enrolled. In 2019, 41 master's awarded. *Entrance requirements:* For master's, GRE. Additional exam requirements/recommendations for international students: required—TOEFL (minimum score 80 iBT). *Application deadline:* For fall admission, 3/1 for domestic and international students. Applications are processed on a rolling basis. Application fee: $55. Electronic applications accepted. *Expenses:* Tuition, state resident: full-time $7176; part-time $4164 per year. Tuition, nonresident: full-time $18,690; part-time $8916 per year. *Required fees:* $4206; $3185 per unit. $1061 per term. *Financial support:* Fellowships, research assistantships, teaching assistantships, and scholarships/grants available. Financial award application deadline: 3/2; financial award applicants required to submit FAFSA. *Unit head:* Dr. David Clague, Graduate Coordinator, 805-756-5145, E-mail: dclague@calpoly.edu. *Application contact:* Dr. David Clague, Graduate Coordinator, 805-756-5145, E-mail: dclague@calpoly.edu.
Website: http://bmed.calpoly.edu/

Carleton University, Faculty of Graduate Studies, Faculty of Engineering and Design, Ottawa-Carleton Institute for Biomedical Engineering, Ottawa, ON K1S 5B6, Canada. Offers MA Sc. *Degree requirements:* For master's, thesis optional. *Entrance requirements:* For master's, honours degree. Additional exam requirements/recommendations for international students: required—TOEFL.

Carnegie Mellon University, Carnegie Institute of Technology, Biomedical and Health Engineering Program, Pittsburgh, PA 15213-3891. Offers bioengineering (MS, PhD); MD/PhD. *Degree requirements:* For master's, thesis; for doctorate, thesis/dissertation, qualifying exam. *Entrance requirements:* For master's and doctorate, GRE General Test. Additional exam requirements/recommendations for international students: required—TOEFL. Electronic applications accepted.

Case Western Reserve University, School of Graduate Studies, Case School of Engineering, Department of Biomedical Engineering, Cleveland, OH 44106. Offers MS, PhD, MD/MS, MD/PhD. *Program availability:* 100% online. Terminal master's awarded for partial completion of doctoral program. *Degree requirements:* For master's, thesis (for some programs); for doctorate, thesis/dissertation, qualifying exam, teaching experience. *Entrance requirements:* For master's and doctorate, GRE General Test. Additional exam requirements/recommendations for international students: required—TOEFL.

The Catholic University of America, School of Engineering, Department of Biomedical Engineering, Washington, DC 20064. Offers MBE, PhD. *Program availability:* Part-time. *Faculty:* 6 full-time (0 women), 2 part-time/adjunct (both women). *Students:* 16 full-time (12 women), 16 part-time (9 women); includes 7 minority (1 Black or African American, non-Hispanic/Latino; 1 Asian, non-Hispanic/Latino; 4 Hispanic/Latino; 1 Two or more races, non-Hispanic/Latino), 20 international. Average age 28. 31 applicants, 87% accepted, 12 enrolled. In 2019, 9 master's, 1 doctorate awarded. *Degree requirements:* For master's, thesis or alternative; for doctorate, comprehensive exam, thesis/dissertation, oral exams. *Entrance requirements:* For master's, minimum GPA of 3.0, statement of purpose, official copies of academic transcripts, three letters of recommendation; for doctorate, minimum GPA of 3.4, statement of purpose, official copies of academic transcripts, three letters of recommendation. Additional exam requirements/recommendations for international students: required—TOEFL (minimum score 550 paper-based; 80 iBT). *Application deadline:* For fall admission, 7/15 priority date for domestic students, 7/1 for international students; for spring admission, 11/15 priority date for domestic students, 11/1 for international students. Applications are processed on a rolling basis. Application fee: $55. Electronic applications accepted. *Expenses:* Contact institution. *Financial support:* Fellowships, research assistantships, teaching assistantships, Federal Work-Study, scholarships/grants, tuition waivers (full and partial), and unspecified assistantships available. Financial award application deadline: 2/1; financial award applicants required to submit FAFSA. *Unit head:* Dr. Peter S. Lum, Chair, 202-319-5181, Fax: 202-319-4287, E-mail: lum@cua.edu. *Application contact:* Dr. Steven Brown, Director of Graduate Admissions, 202-319-5057, Fax: 202-319-6533, E-mail: cua-admissions@cua.edu.
Website: http://biomedical.cua.edu/

City College of the City University of New York, Graduate School, Grove School of Engineering, Department of Biomedical Engineering, New York, NY 10031-9198. Offers MS, PhD. *Entrance requirements:* For master's, GRE. Additional exam requirements/recommendations for international students: required—TOEFL (minimum score 550 paper-based).

Clemson University, Graduate School, College of Engineering, Computing and Applied Sciences, Department of Bioengineering, Clemson, SC 29634. Offers bioengineering (MS, PhD); biomedical engineering (M Engr); medical device recycling and reprocessing (Certificate). *Program availability:* Part-time. *Faculty:* 32 full-time (10 women). *Students:* 128 full-time (52 women), 12 part-time (4 women); includes 23 minority (5 Black or African American, non-Hispanic/Latino; 8 Asian, non-Hispanic/Latino; 8 Hispanic/Latino; 2 Two or more races, non-Hispanic/Latino), 28 international. Average age 25. 117 applicants, 71% accepted, 38 enrolled. In 2019, 46 master's, 16 doctorates, 1 other advanced degree awarded. *Degree requirements:* For master's, thesis optional; for doctorate, comprehensive exam, thesis/dissertation. *Entrance requirements:* For master's, doctorate, and Certificate, GRE General Test, unofficial transcripts, letters of recommendation. Additional exam requirements/recommendations for international students: required—TOEFL (minimum score 100 paper-based; 100 iBT); recommended—IELTS (minimum score 7), TSE (minimum score 54). *Application deadline:* For fall admission, 2/15 priority date for domestic students, 1/15 priority date for international students. Applications are processed on a rolling basis. Application fee: $80 ($90 for international students). Electronic applications accepted. *Expenses: Tuition, area resident:* Full-time $10,600; part-time $8688 per semester. Tuition, state resident: full-time $10,600; part-time $8688 per semester. Tuition, nonresident: full-time $22,050; part-time $17,412 per semester. *International tuition:* $22,050 full-time. *Required fees:* $1196; $617 per semester. $617 per semester. Tuition and fees vary according to course load, degree level, campus/location and program. *Financial support:* In 2019–20, 102 students received support, including 1 fellowship with full and partial tuition reimbursement available (averaging $24,816 per year), 50 research assistantships with full and partial tuition reimbursements available (averaging $23,069 per year), 44 teaching assistantships with full and partial tuition reimbursements available (averaging $22,950 per year); career-related internships or fieldwork and unspecified assistantships also available. Financial award application deadline: 2/15; financial award applicants required to submit FAFSA. *Unit head:* Dr. Martine LaBerge, Department Chair, 864-656-5557, E-mail: laberge@clemson.edu. *Application contact:* Dr. Agneta Simionescu, Graduate Coordinator, 864-650-2575, E-mail: agneta@clemson.edu.
Website: https://www.clemson.edu/cecas/departments/bioe/

Cleveland State University, College of Graduate Studies, Fenn College of Engineering, Department of Chemical and Biomedical Engineering, Program in Applied Biomedical Engineering, Cleveland, OH 44115. Offers D Eng. *Program availability:* Part-time, evening/weekend. *Entrance requirements:* For doctorate, GRE, minimum undergraduate GPA of 2.75, graduate 3.25; degree in engineering. Additional exam requirements/recommendations for international students: required—TOEFL (minimum score 550 paper-based; 78 iBT). Electronic applications accepted. *Expenses:* Tuition, state resident: full-time $10,215; part-time $6810 per credit hour. Tuition, nonresident:

full-time $17,496; part-time $11,664 per credit hour. *International tuition:* $19,316 full-time. Tuition and fees vary according to degree level and program.

Colorado State University, Walter Scott, Jr. College of Engineering, School of Biomedical Engineering, Fort Collins, CO 80523-1376. Offers bioengineering (MS, PhD). *Program availability:* Part-time, online learning. Terminal master's awarded for partial completion of doctoral program. *Degree requirements:* For master's, thesis, minimum of two presentations in seminar series; for doctorate, thesis/dissertation, minimum of two presentations in seminar series. *Entrance requirements:* For master's and doctorate, GRE General Test, minimum GPA of 3.0, resume, statement of purpose, official transcripts, three letters of recommendation. Additional exam requirements/recommendations for international students: required—TOEFL (minimum score 550 paper-based; 80 iBT), IELTS (minimum score 6). Electronic applications accepted. *Expenses:* Contact institution.

Columbia University, Fu Foundation School of Engineering and Applied Science, Department of Biomedical Engineering, New York, NY 10027. Offers MS, Eng Sc D, PhD. *Program availability:* Part-time, online learning. *Degree requirements:* For doctorate, thesis/dissertation, qualifying exam. *Entrance requirements:* For master's and doctorate, GRE General Test. Additional exam requirements/recommendations for international students: required—TOEFL, IELTS, PTE. Electronic applications accepted. *Expenses: Tuition:* Full-time $47,600; part-time $1880 per credit. One-time fee: $105.

Cornell University, Graduate School, Graduate Fields of Engineering, Field of Biomedical Engineering, Ithaca, NY 14853. Offers M Eng, MS, PhD. *Degree requirements:* For master's, thesis; for doctorate, comprehensive exam, thesis/dissertation. *Entrance requirements:* For master's and doctorate, GRE General Test, GRE Subject Test (engineering), 3 letters of recommendation. Additional exam requirements/recommendations for international students: required—TOEFL (minimum score 77 iBT). Electronic applications accepted.

Dalhousie University, Faculty of Engineering and Faculty of Medicine, School of Biomedical Engineering, Halifax, NS B3H3J5, Canada. Offers MA Sc, PhD. *Entrance requirements:* Additional exam requirements/recommendations for international students: required—TOEFL, IELTS, CANTEST, CAEL, or Michigan English Language Assessment Battery. Electronic applications accepted.

Dartmouth College, Dartmouth Engineering - Thayer School of Engineering, Program in Biomedical Engineering, Hanover, NH 03755. Offers MS, PhD, MD/PhD. *Degree requirements:* For master's, thesis; for doctorate, thesis/dissertation, candidacy oral exam. *Entrance requirements:* For master's and doctorate, GRE General Test.

Drexel University, School of Biomedical Engineering, Science and Health Systems, Program in Biomedical Engineering, Philadelphia, PA 19104-2875. Offers MS, PhD. *Degree requirements:* For master's, thesis (for some programs); for doctorate, thesis/dissertation. Electronic applications accepted.

Duke University, Graduate School, Pratt School of Engineering, Department of Biomedical Engineering, Durham, NC 27708. Offers M Eng, MS, PhD. *Degree requirements:* For doctorate, thesis/dissertation. *Entrance requirements:* For master's and doctorate, GRE General Test. Additional exam requirements/recommendations for international students: required—TOEFL (minimum score 90 iBT), IELTS (minimum score 7). Electronic applications accepted.

Duke University, Graduate School, Pratt School of Engineering, Master of Engineering Program, Durham, NC 27708-0271. Offers biomedical engineering (M Eng); civil engineering (M Eng); computational mechanics and scientific computing (M Eng); electrical and computer engineering (M Eng); environmental engineering (M Eng); materials science and engineering (M Eng); mechanical engineering (M Eng); photonics and optical sciences (M Eng); risk engineering (M Eng). *Program availability:* Part-time. *Entrance requirements:* For master's, GRE General Test, resume, 3 letters of recommendation, statement of purpose, transcripts. Additional exam requirements/recommendations for international students: required—TOEFL. Electronic applications accepted.

East Carolina University, Graduate School, College of Engineering and Technology, Department of Engineering, Greenville, NC 27858-4353. Offers biomedical engineering (MS). *Expenses: Tuition, area resident:* Full-time $4749; part-time $185 per credit hour. Tuition, state resident: full-time $4749; part-time $185 per credit hour. Tuition, nonresident: full-time $17,898; part-time $864 per credit hour. *International tuition:* $17,898 full-time. *Required fees:* $2787. *Unit head:* Dr. Barbara Muller-Borer, Chair, 252-744-2546, E-mail: mullerborerb@ecu.edu. *Application contact:* Graduate School Admissions, 252-328-6012, Fax: 252-328-6071, E-mail: gradschool@ecu.edu. Website: https://cet.ecu.edu/engineering/

Florida Agricultural and Mechanical University, Division of Graduate Studies, Research, and Continuing Education, FAMU-FSU College of Engineering, Department of Chemical and Biomedical Engineering, Tallahassee, FL 32307-3200. Offers biomedical engineering (MS, PhD); chemical engineering (MS, PhD). *Degree requirements:* For master's, thesis optional; for doctorate, thesis/dissertation, paper presentation at professional meeting. *Entrance requirements:* For master's, GRE General Test, minimum GPA of 3.3, letters of recommendation (3); for doctorate, minimum GPA of 3.3. Additional exam requirements/recommendations for international students: required—TOEFL (minimum score 550 paper-based).

Florida Institute of Technology, College of Engineering and Science, Program in Biomedical Engineering, Melbourne, FL 32901-6975. Offers MS, PhD. *Program availability:* Part-time. Terminal master's awarded for partial completion of doctoral program. *Degree requirements:* For master's, thesis optional, thesis or supervised project with 6 credits of elective courses; for doctorate, comprehensive exam, thesis/dissertation, 42 credit hours beyond the master's degree, minimum of GPA of 3.2. *Entrance requirements:* For master's, GRE, 3 letters of recommendation, resume, statement of objectives; for doctorate, GRE, minimum GPA of 3.2, 3 letters of recommendation, resume, statement of objectives. Additional exam requirements/recommendations for international students: required—TOEFL (minimum score 550 paper-based; 79 iBT). Electronic applications accepted.

Florida International University, College of Engineering and Computing, Department of Biomedical Engineering, Miami, FL 33175. Offers MS, PhD. *Program availability:* Part-time, evening/weekend. *Faculty:* 15 full-time (2 women), 2 part-time/adjunct (0 women). *Students:* 64 full-time (24 women), 6 part-time (3 women); includes 34 minority (3 Black or African American, non-Hispanic/Latino; 7 Asian, non-Hispanic/Latino; 20 Hispanic/Latino; 4 Two or more races, non-Hispanic/Latino), 28 international. Average age 28. 106 applicants, 49% accepted, 23 enrolled. In 2019, 10 master's awarded. *Degree requirements:* For master's, thesis; for doctorate, comprehensive exam, thesis/dissertation. *Entrance requirements:* For master's, GRE General Test (minimum combined score 1000, verbal 350, quantitative 650), minimum GPA of 3.0; for doctorate, GRE General Test (minimum combined score 1150, verbal 450, quantitative 700), minimum GPA of 3.0, letter of intent, letters of recommendation. Additional exam requirements/recommendations for international students: required—TOEFL (minimum score 550 paper-based; 80 iBT). *Application deadline:* For fall admission, 6/1 for domestic students, 4/1 for international students; for spring admission, 10/1 for domestic students, 9/1 for international students. Applications are processed on a rolling basis.

Application fee: $30. Electronic applications accepted. *Expenses: Tuition, area resident:* Full-time $8912; part-time $446 per credit hour. Tuition, state resident: full-time $8912; part-time $446 per credit hour. Tuition, nonresident: full-time $21,393; part-time $992 per credit hour. *Required fees:* $2194. *Financial support:* Institutionally sponsored loans, scholarships/grants, and unspecified assistantships available. Financial award application deadline: 3/1; financial award applicants required to submit FAFSA. *Unit head:* Dr. Ranu Jung, Chair, 305-348-3722, E-mail: ranu.jung@fiu.edu. *Application contact:* Nanett Rojas, Manager, Admissions Operations, 305-348-7464, Fax: 305-348-7441, E-mail: gradadm@fiu.edu. Website: http://cec.fiu.edu/

Florida State University, The Graduate School, FAMU-FSU College of Engineering, Department of Chemical and Biomedical Engineering, Tallahassee, FL 32310-6046. Offers biomedical engineering (MS, PhD); chemical engineering (MS, PhD). *Program availability:* Part-time. *Faculty:* 17 full-time (2 women), 2 part-time/adjunct (1 woman). *Students:* 46 full-time (13 women); includes 5 minority (3 Black or African American, non-Hispanic/Latino; 2 Hispanic/Latino), 31 international. Average age 25. 125 applicants, 39% accepted, 19 enrolled. In 2019, 10 master's, 8 doctorates awarded. Terminal master's awarded for partial completion of doctoral program. *Degree requirements:* For master's, thesis (for some programs); for doctorate, comprehensive exam, thesis/dissertation, qualifying exam. *Entrance requirements:* For master's, GRE General Test (recommended minimum scores: verbal 151/8th percentile; quantitative: 158/75th percentile), BS in chemical engineering or other physical science/engineering, minimum GPA of 3.0; for doctorate, GRE General Test (recommended minimum scores: verbal 151/8th percentile; quantitative: 158/75th percentile), BS in chemical engineering or other physical science/engineering, minimum GPA of 3.0, or MS in chemical or biomedical engineering. Additional exam requirements/recommendations for international students: required—TOEFL (minimum score 550 paper-based; 80 iBT); recommended—IELTS (minimum score 6.5). *Application deadline:* For fall admission, 3/1 priority date for domestic students, 3/1 for international students; for spring admission, 10/1 for domestic and international students. Applications are processed on a rolling basis. Application fee: $30. Electronic applications accepted. *Financial support:* In 2019–20, 34 students received support, including fellowships with full tuition reimbursements available (averaging $21,500 per year), 22 research assistantships with full tuition reimbursements available (averaging $21,500 per year), 23 teaching assistantships with full tuition reimbursements available (averaging $21,500 per year); scholarships/grants, tuition waivers, and unspecified assistantships also available. Financial award application deadline: 3/1; financial award applicants required to submit FAFSA. *Unit head:* Dr. Teng Ma, Chair and Professor, 850-410-6149, Fax: 850-410-6150, E-mail: teng@eng.famu.fsu.edu. *Application contact:* Lisa Fowler, Office Administrator, 850-410-6151, Fax: 850-410-6150, E-mail: lfowler@eng.famu.fsu.edu. Website: http://www.eng.famu.fsu.edu/cbe

The George Washington University, School of Engineering and Applied Science, Department of Biomedical Engineering, Washington, DC 20052. Offers biomedical engineering (MS, PhD); regulatory biomedical engineering (MS).

Georgia Institute of Technology, Graduate Studies, College of Engineering, Wallace H. Coulter Department of Biomedical Engineering, Atlanta, GA 30332. Offers PhD, MD/PhD. *Program availability:* Part-time. *Faculty:* 63 full-time (15 women), 5 part-time/adjunct (3 women). *Students:* 242 full-time (111 women), 10 part-time (4 women); includes 103 minority (24 Black or African American, non-Hispanic/Latino; 41 Asian, non-Hispanic/Latino; 31 Hispanic/Latino; 1 Native Hawaiian or other Pacific Islander, non-Hispanic/Latino; 6 Two or more races, non-Hispanic/Latino), 52 international. Average age 26. 678 applicants, 34% accepted, 69 enrolled. In 2019, 34 doctorates awarded. *Degree requirements:* For doctorate, thesis/dissertation. *Entrance requirements:* For doctorate, GRE, B.S. in Engineering or Life Sciences; 1 year of calculus based physics; 1 semester of organic chemistry (2 semesters are recommended). Additional exam requirements/recommendations for international students: required—TOEFL (minimum score 600 paper-based; 100 iBT), IELTS, TOEFL is the preferred method with the requirements shown on the programs. *Application deadline:* For fall admission, 12/1 for domestic and international students. Applications are processed on a rolling basis. Application fee: $75 ($85 for international students). Electronic applications accepted. *Expenses: Tuition, area resident:* Full-time $14,064; part-time $586 per credit hour. Tuition, state resident: full-time $14,064; part-time $586 per credit hour. Tuition, nonresident: full-time $29,140; part-time $1215 per credit hour. *International tuition:* $29,140 full-time. *Required fees:* $2024; $840 per semester. $2096. Tuition and fees vary according to course load. *Financial support:* In 2019–20, 41 fellowships, 94 research assistantships, 1 teaching assistantship were awarded; career-related internships or fieldwork, Federal Work-Study, institutionally sponsored loans, tuition waivers (full and partial), and unspecified assistantships also available. Support available to part-time students. Financial award application deadline: 7/1; financial award applicants required to submit FAFSA. *Unit head:* Susan Margulies, School chair, 404-385-0124, Fax: 404-894-4243, E-mail: susan.margulies@gatech.edu. *Application contact:* Marla Bruner, Director of Graduate Studies, 404-894-1610, Fax: 404-894-1609, E-mail: gradinfo@mail.gatech.edu. Website: http://www.bme.gatech.edu/

Harvard University, Graduate School of Arts and Sciences, Department of Physics, Cambridge, MA 02138. Offers experimental physics (PhD); medical engineering/medical physics (PhD), including applied physics, engineering sciences, physics; theoretical physics (PhD). *Degree requirements:* For doctorate, thesis/dissertation, final exams, laboratory experience. *Entrance requirements:* For doctorate, GRE General Test, GRE Subject Test. Additional exam requirements/recommendations for international students: required—TOEFL.

Illinois Institute of Technology, Graduate College, Armour College of Engineering, Department of Biomedical Engineering, Chicago, IL 60616. Offers MAS, MS, PhD. *Program availability:* Part-time. *Degree requirements:* For doctorate, comprehensive exam, thesis/dissertation. *Entrance requirements:* For master's and doctorate, GRE (minimum 1800 combined; 1200 quantitative and verbal; 3.0 analytical writing), minimum cumulative undergraduate GPA of 3.2. Electronic applications accepted.

Indiana University-Purdue University Indianapolis, School of Engineering and Technology, Department of Biomedical Engineering, Indianapolis, IN 46202. Offers MS, PhD. *Program availability:* Part-time, evening/weekend. *Degree requirements:* For master's, thesis optional. *Entrance requirements:* For master's, GRE, minimum B average; for doctorate, GRE General Test. Additional exam requirements/recommendations for international students: required—TOEFL. *Expenses:* Contact institution.

Johns Hopkins University, Engineering Program for Professionals, Part-time Program in Applied Biomedical Engineering, Baltimore, MD 21218. Offers MS, Post-Master's Certificate. *Program availability:* Part-time, evening/weekend, 100% online, blended/hybrid learning. *Entrance requirements:* Additional exam requirements/recommendations for international students: required—TOEFL (minimum score 600 paper-based; 100 iBT). Electronic applications accepted.

Johns Hopkins University, G. W. C. Whiting School of Engineering and School of Medicine, Department of Biomedical Engineering, Baltimore, MD 21205. Offers bioengineering innovation and design (MSE); biomedical engineering (MSE, PhD). Terminal master's awarded for partial completion of doctoral program. *Degree requirements:* For master's, thesis; for doctorate, comprehensive exam, thesis/dissertation. *Entrance requirements:* For master's and doctorate, GRE General Test, 3 letters of recommendation, statement of purpose, transcripts. Additional exam requirements/recommendations for international students: required—TOEFL (minimum score 600 paper-based, 100 iBT) or IELTS (7). Electronic applications accepted.

Lawrence Technological University, College of Engineering, Southfield, MI 48075-1058. Offers architectural engineering (MS); automotive engineering (MS); biomedical engineering (MS); civil engineering (MA, MS, PhD), including environmental engineering (MS), geotechnical engineering (MS), structural engineering (MS), transportation engineering (MS), water resource engineering (MS); construction engineering management (MA); electrical and computer engineering (MS); engineering management (MEM); engineering technology (MS); fire engineering (MS); industrial engineering (MS), including healthcare systems; manufacturing systems (ME); mechanical engineering (MS, DE, PhD), including automotive engineering (MS), energy engineering (MS), manufacturing (DE), solid mechanics (MS), thermal/fluid systems (MS); mechatronic systems engineering (MS). *Program availability:* Part-time, evening/weekend. *Faculty:* 23 full-time (2 women), 20 part-time/adjunct (1 woman). *Students:* 14 full-time (5 women), 286 part-time (54 women); includes 26 minority (13 Black or African American, non-Hispanic/Latino; 8 Asian, non-Hispanic/Latino; 3 Hispanic/Latino; 2 Two or more races, non-Hispanic/Latino), 150 international. Average age 29. 384 applicants, 58% accepted, 74 enrolled. In 2019, 223 master's, 7 doctorates awarded. Terminal master's awarded for partial completion of doctoral program. *Degree requirements:* For master's, thesis optional; for doctorate, comprehensive exam, thesis/dissertation optional. *Entrance requirements:* Additional exam requirements/recommendations for international students: required—TOEFL (minimum score 550 paper-based; 79 iBT), IELTS (minimum score 6.5). *Application deadline:* For fall admission, 5/24 for international students; for spring admission, 10/13 for international students; for summer admission, 2/18 for international students. Applications are processed on a rolling basis. Application fee: $50. Electronic applications accepted. *Expenses: Tuition:* Full-time $16,618; part-time $8309 per year. *Required fees:* $600; $600. *Financial support:* In 2019–20, 21 students received support. Unspecified assistantships available. Financial award application deadline: 4/1; financial award applicants required to submit FAFSA. *Unit head:* Dr. Nabil Grace, Dean, 248-204-2500, Fax: 248-204-2509, E-mail: engrdean@ltu.edu. *Application contact:* Jane Rohrback, Director of Admissions, 248-204-3160, Fax: 248-204-2228, E-mail: admissions@ltu.edu.
Website: http://www.ltu.edu/engineering/index.asp

Louisiana Tech University, Graduate School, College of Engineering and Science, Ruston, LA 71272. Offers applied physics (MS); biomedical engineering (PhD); computer science (MS); engineering (MS, PhD), including cyberspace engineering (PhD), engineering education (PhD), engineering physics (PhD), materials and infrastructure systems (PhD), micro/nanoscale systems (PhD); engineering and technology management (MS); mathematics (MS); molecular science and nanotechnology (MS, PhD). *Program availability:* Part-time-only. Terminal master's awarded for partial completion of doctoral program. *Degree requirements:* For master's, thesis (for some programs); for doctorate, thesis/dissertation. *Entrance requirements:* For master's and Graduate Certificate, GRE General Test, minimum GPA of 3.0 in last 60 hours. Additional exam requirements/recommendations for international students: required—TOEFL (minimum score 550 paper-based; 80 iBT), IELTS (minimum score 6.5). Electronic applications accepted. *Expenses: Tuition, area resident:* Full-time $6592; part-time $400 per credit. Tuition, state resident: full-time $6592; part-time $400 per credit. Tuition, nonresident: full-time $13,333; part-time $681 per credit. *International tuition:* $13,333 full-time. *Required fees:* $3011; $3011 per unit.

Marquette University, Graduate School, College of Engineering, Department of Biomedical Engineering, Milwaukee, WI 53201-1881. Offers biocomputing (ME); bioimaging (ME); bioinstrumentation (ME); bioinstrumentation/computers (MS, PhD); biomechanics (ME); biomechanics/biomaterials (MS, PhD); biorehabilitation (ME); functional imaging (PhD); healthcare technologies management (MS); rehabilitation bioengineering (PhD); systems physiology (MS, PhD). *Program availability:* Part-time, evening/weekend. Terminal master's awarded for partial completion of doctoral program. *Degree requirements:* For master's, comprehensive exam, thesis; for doctorate, comprehensive exam, thesis/dissertation, dissertation defense, qualifying exam. *Entrance requirements:* For master's, GRE General Test, minimum GPA of 3.0, official transcripts from all current and previous colleges/universities except Marquette, three letters of recommendation, brief statement of purpose that includes proposed area of research specialization, interview with program director (for ME), one year of post-baccalaureate professional work experience; for doctorate, GRE General Test, minimum GPA of 3.0, official transcripts from all current and previous colleges/universities except Marquette, three letters of recommendation, brief statement of purpose that includes proposed area of research specialization. Additional exam requirements/recommendations for international students: required—TOEFL (minimum score 530 paper-based). Electronic applications accepted.

Massachusetts Institute of Technology, School of Engineering, Department of Biological Engineering, Cambridge, MA 02139. Offers applied biosciences (PhD, Sc D); bioengineering (PhD, Sc D); biological engineering (PhD, Sc D); biomedical engineering (M Eng); toxicology (SM); SM/MBA. Terminal master's awarded for partial completion of doctoral program. *Degree requirements:* For master's, thesis; for doctorate, comprehensive exam, thesis/dissertation. *Entrance requirements:* For master's and doctorate, GRE General Test. Additional exam requirements/recommendations for international students: required—IELTS. Electronic applications accepted.

Massachusetts Institute of Technology, School of Engineering, Harvard-MIT Health Sciences and Technology Program, Cambridge, MA 02139. Offers health sciences and technology (SM, PhD, Sc D), including bioastronautics (PhD, Sc D), bioinformatics and integrative genomics (PhD, Sc D), medical engineering and medical physics (PhD, Sc D), speech and hearing bioscience and technology (PhD, Sc D). Terminal master's awarded for partial completion of doctoral program. *Degree requirements:* For doctorate, comprehensive exam, thesis/dissertation. *Entrance requirements:* For doctorate, GRE General Test. Additional exam requirements/recommendations for international students: required—TOEFL, IELTS. Electronic applications accepted.

Mayo Clinic Graduate School of Biomedical Sciences, Program in Biomedical Engineering and Physiology, Rochester, MN 55905. Offers MS, PhD. Terminal master's awarded for partial completion of doctoral program. *Degree requirements:* For master's, thesis; for doctorate, comprehensive exam, thesis/dissertation, oral defense of dissertation, qualifying oral and written exam. *Entrance requirements:* For doctorate, GRE, 1 year of chemistry, biology, calculus, and physics; courses in quantitative science and engineering, e.g., signal processing, computer science, instrumentation (encouraged). Additional exam requirements/recommendations for international students: required—TOEFL. Electronic applications accepted.

McGill University, Faculty of Graduate and Postdoctoral Studies, Faculty of Medicine, Department of Biomedical Engineering, Montréal, QC H3A 2T5, Canada. Offers M Eng, PhD.

Mercer University, Graduate Studies, Macon Campus, School of Engineering, Macon, GA 31207. Offers biomedical engineering (MSE); computer engineering (MSE); electrical engineering (MSE); engineering management (MSE); environmental engineering (MSE); environmental systems (MS); mechanical engineering (MSE); software engineering (MSE); software systems (MS); technical communications management (MS); technical management (MS). *Program availability:* Part-time-only, evening/weekend, online learning. *Faculty:* 27 full-time (9 women), 2 part-time/adjunct (0 women). *Students:* 38 full-time (10 women), 51 part-time (20 women); includes 22 minority (5 Black or African American, non-Hispanic/Latino; 11 Asian, non-Hispanic/Latino; 4 Hispanic/Latino; 2 Two or more races, non-Hispanic/Latino), 2 international. Average age 26. In 2019, 70 master's awarded. *Degree requirements:* For master's, thesis or alternative. *Entrance requirements:* For master's, GRE (minimum score 300), minimum undergraduate GPA of 3.0. Additional exam requirements/recommendations for international students: required—TOEFL (minimum score 550 paper-based; 80 iBT). *Application deadline:* For fall admission, 4/1 priority date for domestic and international students; for spring admission, 11/1 priority date for domestic and international students. Applications are processed on a rolling basis. Application fee: $75. *Expenses:* Tuition: $938.00 ($700.00 for Technical Communication Management program) per credit hour; Facility and Technology Fee: $17.00 per credit hour. *Financial support:* Federal Work-Study available. Financial award applicants required to submit FAFSA. *Unit head:* Dr. Laura W. Lackey, Dean, 478-301-4106, Fax: 478-301-5593, E-mail: lackey_l@mercer.edu. *Application contact:* Dr. Sinjae Hyun, Program Director, 478-301-2214, Fax: 478-301-5593, E-mail: hyun_s@mercer.edu.
Website: http://engineering.mercer.edu/

Michigan Technological University, Graduate School, College of Engineering, Department of Biomedical Engineering, Houghton, MI 49931. Offers MS, PhD. *Program availability:* Part-time. *Faculty:* 18 full-time (8 women), 3 part-time/adjunct. *Students:* 24 full-time (11 women), 1 part-time; includes 2 minority (1 Black or African American, non-Hispanic/Latino; 1 Two or more races, non-Hispanic/Latino), 13 international. Average age 29. 114 applicants, 18% accepted, 5 enrolled. In 2019, 12 master's, 2 doctorates awarded. *Degree requirements:* For master's, comprehensive exam (for some programs), thesis (for some programs); for doctorate, comprehensive exam, thesis/dissertation. *Entrance requirements:* For master's, GRE: Recommended scores of (Michigan Tech students are exempt) 160 Quantitative, 153 Verbal, 3.0 Analytical; TOEFL: Recommended Score of 100 iBT (International Students); IELTS: Recommended Overall Band Score of 7.0 (International Students), statement of purpose, personal statement, official transcripts, 3 letters of recommendation, resume/curriculum vitae; for doctorate, GRE: Recommended scores of 85% (Michigan Tech students are exempt) 165 Quantitative, 153 Verbal, 3.0 Analytical; TOEFL: Recommended Score of 110 iBT (International Students); IELTS: Recommended Overall Band Score of 8.0 (International Students), statement of purpose, personal statement, official transcripts, 3 letters of recommendation, resume/curriculum vitae. Additional exam requirements/recommendations for international students: recommended—TOEFL (minimum score 110 iBT), IELTS (minimum score 8). *Application deadline:* Applications are processed on a rolling basis. Application fee: $0. Electronic applications accepted. *Expenses:* $1,212 per credit. *Financial support:* In 2019–20, 20 students received support, including 6 fellowships with tuition reimbursements available (averaging $16,590 per year), 4 research assistantships with tuition reimbursements available (averaging $16,590 per year), 6 teaching assistantships with tuition reimbursements available (averaging $16,590 per year); career-related internships or fieldwork, Federal Work-Study, scholarships/grants, health care benefits, unspecified assistantships, and cooperative program also available. Financial award applicants required to submit FAFSA. *Unit head:* Dr. Sean J. Kirkpatrick, Chair, 906-487-2167, Fax: 906-487-1717, E-mail: sjkirkpa@mtu.edu. *Application contact:* Coreen Dompier, Department Coordinator, 906-487-2772, Fax: 906-487-1717, E-mail: biomed@mtu.edu.
Website: http://www.mtu.edu/biomedical/

Mississippi State University, College of Agriculture and Life Sciences, Department of Agricultural and Biological Engineering, Mississippi State, MS 39762. Offers biological engineering (MS, PhD); biomedical engineering (MS, PhD). *Faculty:* 15 full-time (4 women). *Students:* 25 full-time (12 women), 12 part-time (3 women); includes 6 minority (3 Black or African American, non-Hispanic/Latino; 2 Asian, non-Hispanic/Latino; 1 Hispanic/Latino), 16 international. Average age 30. 23 applicants, 43% accepted, 6 enrolled. In 2019, 6 master's, 2 doctorates awarded. *Degree requirements:* For master's, thesis (for some programs); for doctorate, thesis/dissertation, preliminary exam. *Entrance requirements:* For master's, GRE General Test, minimum undergraduate GPA of 2.75 (3.0 for biomedical engineering); for doctorate, GRE General Test, minimum GPA of 3.0 (biomedical engineering). Additional exam requirements/recommendations for international students: required—TOEFL (minimum score 550 paper-based; 79 iBT); recommended—IELTS (minimum score 6.5). *Application deadline:* For fall admission, 7/1 for domestic students, 5/1 for international students; for spring admission, 11/1 for domestic students, 9/1 for international students. Applications are processed on a rolling basis. Application fee: $60 ($80 for international students). Electronic applications accepted. *Expenses: Tuition, area resident:* Full-time $8880; part-time $456 per credit hour. Tuition, state resident: full-time $8880. Tuition, nonresident: full-time $23,840; part-time $1236 per credit hour. *Required fees:* $110; $11.12 per credit hour. Tuition and fees vary according to course load. *Financial support:* In 2019–20, 13 research assistantships with partial tuition reimbursements (averaging $17,870 per year), 4 teaching assistantships (averaging $18,160 per year) were awarded; Federal Work-Study, institutionally sponsored loans, and unspecified assistantships also available. Financial award application deadline: 4/1; financial award applicants required to submit FAFSA. *Unit head:* Dr. Wes Burger, Interim Department Head, 662-325-7552, Fax: 662-325-3853, E-mail: w.burger@msstate.edu. *Application contact:* Ryan King, Admissions and Enrollment Assistant, 662-325-8951, E-mail: rjk101@grad.msstate.edu.
Website: http://www.abe.msstate.edu/

New Jersey Institute of Technology, Newark College of Engineering, Newark, NJ 07102. Offers biomedical engineering (MS, PhD); biopharmaceutical engineering (MS); chemical engineering (MS, PhD); civil engineering (MS, PhD); computer engineering (MS); critical infrastructure systems (MS); electrical engineering (MS, PhD); engineering management (MS); engineering science (MS); environmental engineering (MS, PhD); healthcare systems management (MS); industrial engineering (MS, PhD); internet engineering (MS); manufacturing systems engineering (MS); materials science & engineering (PhD); materials science and engineering (MS); mechanical engineering (MS, PhD); occupational safety and health engineering (MS). *Program availability:* Part-time, evening/weekend. *Faculty:* 151 full-time (29 women), 135 part-time/adjunct (15 women). *Students:* 576 full-time (161 women), 528 part-time (111 women); includes 366 minority (61 Black or African American, non-Hispanic/Latino; 1 American Indian or Alaska Native, non-Hispanic/Latino; 166 Asian, non-Hispanic/Latino; 115 Hispanic/Latino; 23 Two or more races, non-Hispanic/Latino), 450 international. Average age 28. 2,053 applicants, 67% accepted, 338 enrolled. In 2019, 474 master's, 30 doctorates awarded. Terminal master's awarded for partial completion of doctoral program. *Degree requirements:* For master's, thesis (for some programs); for doctorate, thesis/dissertation. *Entrance requirements:* For master's, GRE General Test, minimum GPA 2.8, personal statement, 1 letter of recommendation, transcripts; for doctorate, GRE

General Test, minimum GPA of 3.5, personal statement, 3 letters of recommendation, transcripts. Additional exam requirements/recommendations for international students: required—TOEFL (minimum score 550 paper-based; 79 iBT), IELTS (minimum score 6.5). *Application deadline:* For fall admission, 6/1 priority date for domestic students, 5/1 priority date for international students; for spring admission, 11/15 priority date for domestic and international students. Applications are processed on a rolling basis. Application fee: $75. Electronic applications accepted. *Expenses:* $23,828 per year (in-state), $33,744 per year (out-of-state). *Financial support:* In 2019–20, 352 students received support, including 33 fellowships with full tuition reimbursements available (averaging $24,000 per year), 89 research assistantships with full tuition reimbursements available (averaging $24,000 per year), 112 teaching assistantships with full tuition reimbursements available (averaging $24,000 per year); career-related internships or fieldwork, Federal Work-Study, scholarships/grants, and unspecified assistantships also available. Financial award application deadline: 1/15. *Unit head:* Dr. Moshe Kam, Dean, 973-596-5534, Fax: 973-596-2316, E-mail: moshe.kam@njit.edu. *Application contact:* Stephen Eck, Executive Director of University Admissions, 973-596-3300, Fax: 973-596-3461, E-mail: admissions@njit.edu.
Website: http://engineering.njit.edu/

New York University, Department of Biomedical Engineering, Major in Biomedical Engineering, New York, NY 10012-1019. Offers biomedical engineering (MS). *Degree requirements:* For master's, comprehensive exam (for some programs), thesis (for some programs); for doctorate, comprehensive exam, thesis/dissertation. *Entrance requirements:* Additional exam requirements/recommendations for international students: required—TOEFL (minimum score 550 paper-based; 90 iBT); recommended—IELTS (minimum score 7). Electronic applications accepted.

Northwestern University, McCormick School of Engineering and Applied Science, Department of Biomedical Engineering, Evanston, IL 60208. Offers MS, PhD. *Program availability:* Part-time. Terminal master's awarded for partial completion of doctoral program. *Degree requirements:* For master's, comprehensive exam, thesis (for some programs); for doctorate, comprehensive exam, thesis/dissertation. *Entrance requirements:* For master's and doctorate, GRE General Test. Additional exam requirements/recommendations for international students: required—TOEFL (minimum score 577 paper-based; 90 iBT), IELTS (minimum score 7). Electronic applications accepted.

The Ohio State University, Graduate School, College of Engineering, Department of Biomedical Engineering, Columbus, OH 43210. Offers MS, PhD. *Program availability:* Evening/weekend. *Entrance requirements:* For master's and doctorate, GRE General Test. Additional exam requirements/recommendations for international students: required—TOEFL (minimum score 550 paper-based; 79 iBT), Michigan English Language Assessment Battery (minimum score 82); recommended—IELTS (minimum score 7). Electronic applications accepted.

Ohio University, Graduate College, Russ College of Engineering and Technology, Department of Chemical and Biomolecular Engineering, Program in Biomedical Engineering, Athens, OH 45701-2979. Offers MS. *Program availability:* Part-time. *Degree requirements:* For master's, thesis. *Entrance requirements:* For master's, GRE General Test. Additional exam requirements/recommendations for international students: required—TOEFL (minimum score 590 paper-based; 96 iBT), IELTS (minimum score 7). Electronic applications accepted.

Ohio University, Graduate College, Russ College of Engineering and Technology, Department of Mechanical Engineering, Athens, OH 45701-2979. Offers biomedical engineering (MS); mechanical engineering (MS), including CAD/CAM, design, energy, manufacturing, materials, robotics, thermofluids. *Program availability:* Part-time. *Degree requirements:* For master's, comprehensive exam (for some programs), thesis. *Entrance requirements:* For master's, GRE, BS in engineering or science, minimum GPA of 2.8. Additional exam requirements/recommendations for international students: required—TOEFL (minimum score 550 paper-based; 80 iBT) or IELTS (minimum score 6.5). Electronic applications accepted.

Old Dominion University, Frank Batten College of Engineering and Technology, Program in Biomedical Engineering, Norfolk, VA 23529. Offers ME, MS, PhD. *Program availability:* Part-time, evening/weekend. Terminal master's awarded for partial completion of doctoral program. *Degree requirements:* For master's, thesis (for some programs); for doctorate, thesis/dissertation, candidacy exam. *Entrance requirements:* For master's, GRE, master's degree, minimum graduate GPA of 3.0, two letters of recommendation, statement of purpose; for doctorate, GRE, master's degree, minimum graduate GPA of 3.5, three letters of recommendation, statement of purpose. Additional exam requirements/recommendations for international students: required—TOEFL (minimum score 550 paper-based; 79 iBT). Electronic applications accepted.

Oregon Health & Science University, School of Medicine, Graduate Programs in Medicine, Department of Biomedical Engineering, Portland, OR 97239-3098. Offers MBI, MS, PhD. *Program availability:* Part-time. *Degree requirements:* For doctorate, comprehensive exam, thesis/dissertation, qualifying exam. *Entrance requirements:* For doctorate, GRE General Test (minimum scores: 153 Verbal/148 Quantitative/4.5 Analytical). Electronic applications accepted.

Polytechnique Montréal, Graduate Programs, Institute of Biomedical Engineering, Montréal, QC H3C 3A7, Canada. Offers M Sc A, PhD, DESS. *Program availability:* Part-time. *Degree requirements:* For master's, one foreign language, thesis; for doctorate, one foreign language, thesis/dissertation. *Entrance requirements:* For master's, minimum GPA of 2.75; for doctorate, minimum GPA of 3.0.

Purdue University, College of Engineering, Weldon School of Biomedical Engineering, West Lafayette, IN 47907-2032. Offers MSBME, PhD, MD/PhD. *Faculty:* 42. *Students:* 133. *Degree requirements:* For master's, thesis optional; for doctorate, thesis/dissertation. *Application deadline:* For fall admission, 12/15 priority date for domestic and international students; for spring admission, 10/31 priority date for domestic students, 10/1 priority date for international students; for summer admission, 2/15 for domestic and international students. Applications are processed on a rolling basis. Application fee: $60 ($75 for international students). Electronic applications accepted. *Financial support:* Fellowships with full and partial tuition reimbursements, research assistantships with full and partial tuition reimbursements, teaching assistantships with full and partial tuition reimbursements, career-related internships or fieldwork, scholarships/grants, health care benefits, and unspecified assistantships available. *Unit head:* Dr. George R. Wodicka, Head of Biomedical Engineering, 765-494-2998, E-mail: wodicka@purdue.edu. *Application contact:* Sandra M. May, Graduate Program Administrative Assistant, 765-494-7054, E-mail: smmay@purdue.edu.
Website: https://engineering.purdue.edu/BME

Rensselaer Polytechnic Institute, Graduate School, School of Engineering, Program in Biomedical Engineering, Troy, NY 12180-3590. Offers M Eng, MS, D Eng, PhD. *Faculty:* 19 full-time (5 women). *Students:* 60 full-time (28 women), 5 part-time (2 women); includes 15 minority (2 Black or African American, non-Hispanic/Latino; 7 Asian, non-Hispanic/Latino; 6 Hispanic/Latino), 12 international. Average age 24. 165 applicants, 48% accepted, 19 enrolled. In 2019, 19 master's, 10 doctorates awarded. Terminal master's awarded for partial completion of doctoral program. *Degree requirements:* For master's, thesis optional; for doctorate, thesis/dissertation. *Entrance*

requirements: For master's and doctorate, GRE. Additional exam requirements/recommendations for international students: required—TOEFL (minimum score 570 paper-based; 88 iBT), IELTS (minimum score 6.5), PTE (minimum score 60). *Application deadline:* For fall admission, 1/1 priority date for domestic and international students; for spring admission, 8/15 priority date for domestic and international students. Applications are processed on a rolling basis. Application fee: $75. Electronic applications accepted. *Financial support:* In 2019–20, research assistantships with full tuition reimbursements (averaging $23,000 per year), teaching assistantships with full tuition reimbursements (averaging $23,000 per year) were awarded; fellowships also available. Financial award application deadline: 1/1. *Unit head:* Dr. Leo Wan, Graduate Program Director, 518-276-2505, E-mail: wanq@rpi.edu. *Application contact:* Jarron Decker, Director of Graduate Admissions, 518-276-6216, Fax: 518-276-4072, E-mail: gradadmissions@rpi.edu.
Website: http://www.bme.rpi.edu/

Rice University, Graduate Programs, George R. Brown School of Engineering, Department of Chemical and Biomolecular Engineering, Houston, TX 77251-1892. Offers chemical and biomolecular engineering (MS, PhD); chemical engineering (M Ch E). *Program availability:* Part-time. *Degree requirements:* For master's, thesis (for some programs); for doctorate, thesis/dissertation. *Entrance requirements:* For master's and doctorate, GRE General Test, minimum GPA of 3.0. Additional exam requirements/recommendations for international students: required—TOEFL (minimum score 600 paper-based; 90 iBT). Electronic applications accepted.

Rose-Hulman Institute of Technology, Graduate Studies, Department of Biology and Biomedical Engineering, Terre Haute, IN 47803-3999. Offers MS, MD/MS. *Program availability:* Part-time. *Faculty:* 11 full-time (6 women). *Students:* 1 full-time (0 women), 1 (woman) part-time. Average age 23. 1 applicant, 100% accepted, 1 enrolled. In 2019, 1 master's awarded. *Degree requirements:* For master's, thesis. *Entrance requirements:* For master's, GRE, minimum GPA of 3.0. Additional exam requirements/recommendations for international students: required—TOEFL (minimum score 580 paper-based; 94 iBT), IELTS (minimum score 7). *Application deadline:* For fall admission, 2/1 priority date for domestic and international students; for winter admission, 10/1 for domestic students, 8/1 for international students; for spring admission, 1/15 for domestic students, 11/1 for international students. Applications are processed on a rolling basis. Application fee: $75. Electronic applications accepted. *Financial support:* In 2019–20, 2 students received support. Fellowships with tuition reimbursements available, research assistantships with tuition reimbursements available, institutionally sponsored loans, scholarships/grants, tuition waivers (full and partial), and unspecified assistantships available. *Unit head:* Dr. Jameel Ahmed, Department Head, 812-872-6033, Fax: 812-877-8545, E-mail: ahmed@rose-hulman.edu. *Application contact:* Dr. Craig Downing, Associate Dean of Lifelong Learning, 812-877-8822, E-mail: downing@rose-hulman.edu.
Website: https://www.rose-hulman.edu/academics/academic-departments/biology-and-biomedical-engineering/index.html

Rutgers University - Newark, Graduate School of Biomedical Sciences, Department of Biomedical Engineering, Newark, NJ 07107. Offers Certificate. *Entrance requirements:* Additional exam requirements/recommendations for international students: required—TOEFL. Electronic applications accepted.

Rutgers University - New Brunswick, Graduate School of Biomedical Sciences, Program in Biomedical Engineering, Piscataway, NJ 08854-5635. Offers MS, PhD, MD/PhD. *Degree requirements:* For master's, thesis, qualifying exam; for doctorate, thesis/dissertation, qualifying exam. *Entrance requirements:* For master's and doctorate, GRE General Test. Additional exam requirements/recommendations for international students: required—TOEFL. Electronic applications accepted.

St. Cloud State University, School of Graduate Studies, College of Science and Engineering, Program in Regulatory Affairs and Services, St. Cloud, MN 56301-4498. Offers MS, Graduate Certificate. *Program availability:* Part-time. *Degree requirements:* For master's, final paper. *Entrance requirements:* For master's, GRE General Test, minimum GPA of 2.75. Additional exam requirements/recommendations for international students: required—TOEFL (minimum score 550 paper-based; 79 iBT), IELTS (minimum score 6.5). *Expenses:* Contact institution.

Saint Louis University, Graduate Programs, Parks College of Engineering, Aviation, and Technology, Department of Biomedical Engineering, St. Louis, MO 63103. Offers MS, MS-R, PhD. *Degree requirements:* For master's, thesis optional; for doctorate, thesis/dissertation. *Entrance requirements:* For master's, GRE General Test, letters of recommendation, resume, interview; for doctorate, GRE General Test, letters of recommendation, resumé, interview, transcripts, goal statement. Additional exam requirements/recommendations for international students: required—TOEFL (minimum score 525 paper-based).

South Dakota School of Mines and Technology, Graduate Division, Program in Biomedical Engineering, Rapid City, SD 57701-3995. Offers MS, PhD. *Program availability:* Part-time. *Degree requirements:* For master's, thesis (for some programs); for doctorate, thesis/dissertation. *Entrance requirements:* For doctorate, GRE General Test, 3 letters of recommendation, minimum GPA of 3.0. Additional exam requirements/recommendations for international students: required—TOEFL (minimum score 520 paper-based; 68 iBT). Electronic applications accepted.

Southern Illinois University Carbondale, Graduate School, College of Engineering, Program in Biomedical Engineering, Carbondale, IL 62901-4701. Offers ME, MS. *Degree requirements:* For master's, thesis. *Entrance requirements:* For master's, GRE. Additional exam requirements/recommendations for international students: required—TOEFL.

State University of New York Downstate Medical Center, School of Graduate Studies, Program in Biomedical Engineering, Brooklyn, NY 11203-2098. Offers bioimaging and neuroengineering (PhD); biomedical engineering (MS); MD/PhD. *Degree requirements:* For doctorate, comprehensive exam, thesis/dissertation.

Stevens Institute of Technology, Graduate School, Charles V. Schaefer Jr. School of Engineering and Science, Department of Chemistry, Chemical Biology and Biomedical Engineering, Program in Biomedical Engineering, Hoboken, NJ 07030. Offers M Eng, PhD, Certificate. *Program availability:* Part-time, evening/weekend. *Faculty:* 11 full-time (4 women), 4 part-time/adjunct (2 women). *Students:* 47 full-time (25 women), 11 part-time (5 women); includes 7 minority (1 Black or African American, non-Hispanic/Latino; 1 American Indian or Alaska Native, non-Hispanic/Latino; 5 Asian, non-Hispanic/Latino), 20 international. Average age 27. In 2019, 20 master's awarded. Terminal master's awarded for partial completion of doctoral program. *Degree requirements:* For master's, thesis optional, minimum B average in major field and overall; for doctorate, comprehensive exam (for some programs), thesis/dissertation; for Certificate, minimum B average. *Entrance requirements:* For master's, International applicants must submit TOEFL/IELTS scores and fulfill the English Language Proficiency Requirement. Applicants to full-time programs who do not qualify for a score waiver are required to submit GRE/GMAT scores. Additional exam requirements/recommendations for international students: required—TOEFL (minimum score 74 iBT), IELTS (minimum score 6). *Application deadline:* For fall admission, 4/15 for domestic and international students; for spring admission, 11/1 for domestic and international students; for summer admission, 6/1 for domestic students. Applications are processed on a rolling basis. Application fee: $60. Electronic applications accepted. *Expenses: Tuition:* Full-time $52,134. *Required fees:* $1880. Tuition and fees vary according to course load. *Financial support:* Fellowships, research assistantships, teaching assistantships, career-related internships or fieldwork, Federal Work-Study, scholarships/grants, and unspecified assistantships available. Financial award application deadline: 2/15; financial award applicants required to submit FAFSA. *Unit head:* Dr. Jean Zu, Dean of SES, 201-216.8233, Fax: 201-216.8372, E-mail: Jean.Zu@stevens.edu. *Application contact:* Graduate Admissions, 888-783-8367, Fax: 888-511-1306, E-mail: graduate@stevens.edu.

Stony Brook University, State University of New York, Graduate School, College of Engineering and Applied Sciences, Department of Biomedical Engineering, Stony Brook, NY 11794. Offers biomedical engineering (MS, PhD, Certificate); medical physics (MS, PhD). *Faculty:* 11 full-time (2 women), 1 (woman) part-time/adjunct. *Students:* 85 full-time (29 women), 6 part-time (1 woman); includes 25 minority (3 Black or African American, non-Hispanic/Latino; 15 Asian, non-Hispanic/Latino; 5 Hispanic/Latino; 2 Two or more races, non-Hispanic/Latino), 31 international. Average age 27. 94 applicants, 64% accepted, 31 enrolled. In 2019, 26 master's, 10 doctorates awarded. *Degree requirements:* For doctorate, thesis/dissertation, qualifying exams. *Entrance requirements:* For master's and doctorate, GRE General Test. Additional exam requirements/recommendations for international students: required—TOEFL (minimum score 90 iBT). *Application deadline:* For fall admission, 1/15 for domestic students; for spring admission, 10/1 for domestic students. Application fee: $100. *Expenses:* Contact institution. *Financial support:* In 2019–20, 3 fellowships, 29 research assistantships, 18 teaching assistantships were awarded. *Unit head:* Dr. Stefan Judex, Professor and Interim Chair, 631-632-1549, E-mail: stefan.judex@stonybrook.edu. *Application contact:* Erica Valdez, Graduate Program Coordinator, 631-632-8375, Fax: 631-632-8577, E-mail: Erica.Valdez@stonybrook.edu.
Website: https://www.stonybrook.edu/bme/

Tennessee State University, The School of Graduate Studies and Research, College of Engineering, Nashville, TN 37209-1561. Offers biomedical engineering (ME); civil engineering (ME); computer and information systems engineering (MS, PhD); electrical engineering (ME); environmental engineering (ME); manufacturing engineering (ME); mathematical sciences (MS); mechanical engineering (ME). *Program availability:* Part-time, evening/weekend. *Degree requirements:* For master's, project; for doctorate, comprehensive exam, thesis/dissertation. *Entrance requirements:* For doctorate, minimum GPA of 3.3.

Texas A&M University, College of Engineering, Department of Biomedical Engineering, College Station, TX 77843. Offers biomedical engineering (PhD). *Program availability:* Part-time. *Faculty:* 31. *Students:* 136 full-time (54 women), 9 part-time (3 women); includes 35 minority (4 Black or African American, non-Hispanic/Latino; 9 Asian, non-Hispanic/Latino; 18 Hispanic/Latino; 4 Two or more races, non-Hispanic/Latino), 51 international. Average age 26. 210 applicants, 34% accepted, 39 enrolled. In 2019, 27 master's, 9 doctorates awarded. *Degree requirements:* For master's, comprehensive exam (for some programs), thesis (for some programs); for doctorate, comprehensive exam, thesis/dissertation. *Entrance requirements:* For master's and doctorate, GRE General Test, leveling courses if non-engineering undergraduate major. Additional exam requirements/recommendations for international students: required—TOEFL (minimum score 550 paper-based; 80 iBT), TWE, PTE (minimum score 53). *Application deadline:* For fall admission, 5/1 for domestic students, 3/1 for international students; for spring admission, 10/1 for domestic students, 7/1 for international students. Applications are processed on a rolling basis. Application fee: $65 ($90 for international students). Electronic applications accepted. *Expenses:* Contact institution. *Financial support:* In 2019–20, 134 students received support, including 20 fellowships with tuition reimbursements available (averaging $25,013 per year), 91 research assistantships with tuition reimbursements available (averaging $16,076 per year), 20 teaching assistantships with tuition reimbursements available (averaging $12,869 per year); career-related internships or fieldwork, institutionally sponsored loans, scholarships/grants, traineeships, health care benefits, tuition waivers (full and partial), and unspecified assistantships also available. Support available to part-time students. Financial award application deadline: 3/15; financial award applicants required to submit FAFSA. *Unit head:* Dr. Mike McShane, Department Head, 979-458-5652, E-mail: bmen@tamu.edu. *Application contact:* Roland R. Kaunas, Associate Professor and Director of Graduate Programs, 979-845-2412, E-mail: rkaunas@tamu.edu.
Website: http://engineering.tamu.edu/biomedical

Tufts University, School of Engineering, Department of Biomedical Engineering, Medford, MA 02155. Offers bioengineering (MS), including biomaterials; biomedical engineering (MS, PhD); PhD/PhD. *Program availability:* Part-time. Terminal master's awarded for partial completion of doctoral program. *Degree requirements:* For master's, thesis (for some programs); for doctorate, thesis/dissertation. *Entrance requirements:* For master's and doctorate, GRE General Test. Additional exam requirements/recommendations for international students: required—TOEFL (minimum score 550 paper-based; 80 iBT), IELTS (minimum score 6.5). Electronic applications accepted. Full-time tuition and fees vary according to degree level, program and student level. Part-time tuition and fees vary according to course load.

Tulane University, School of Science and Engineering, Department of Biomedical Engineering, New Orleans, LA 70118-5669. Offers MS, PhD. *Program availability:* Part-time. Terminal master's awarded for partial completion of doctoral program. *Degree requirements:* For master's, thesis (for some programs); for doctorate, thesis/dissertation. *Entrance requirements:* For master's and doctorate, GRE General Test, minimum B average in undergraduate course work. Additional exam requirements/recommendations for international students: required—TOEFL. Electronic applications accepted. *Expenses: Tuition:* Full-time $57,004; part-time $3167 per credit hour. *Required fees:* $2086; $44.50 per credit hour. $80 per term. Tuition and fees vary according to course load, degree level and program.

Université de Montréal, Faculty of Medicine, Institute of Biomedical Engineering, Montréal, QC H3C 3J7, Canada. Offers M Sc A, PhD, DESS. *Degree requirements:* For master's, thesis; for doctorate, thesis/dissertation, general exam. *Entrance requirements:* For master's and doctorate, proficiency in French, knowledge of English. Electronic applications accepted.

University at Buffalo, the State University of New York, Graduate School, School of Engineering and Applied Sciences, Department of Biomedical Engineering, Buffalo, NY 14260. Offers MS, PhD. *Program availability:* Part-time. *Degree requirements:* For master's, thesis (for some programs); for doctorate, comprehensive exam, thesis/dissertation. *Entrance requirements:* For master's and doctorate, GRE General Test. Additional exam requirements/recommendations for international students: required—TOEFL (minimum score 550 paper-based; 79 iBT). Electronic applications accepted. *Expenses: Tuition, area resident:* Full-time $11,310; part-time $471 per credit hour. Tuition, state resident: full-time $11,310; part-time $471 per credit hour. Tuition, nonresident: full-time $23,100; part-time $963 per credit hour. *International tuition:* $23,100 full-time. *Required fees:* $2820.

The University of Akron, Graduate School, College of Engineering, Department of Biomedical Engineering, Akron, OH 44325. Offers biomedical engineering (MS); engineering (PhD). *Program availability:* Part-time, evening/weekend. *Degree requirements:* For master's, thesis; for doctorate, one foreign language, thesis/dissertation, candidacy exam, qualifying exam. *Entrance requirements:* For master's, GRE, minimum GPA of 2.75, three letters of recommendation, statement of purpose; for doctorate, GRE, minimum GPA of 3.0 with bachelor's degree, 3.5 with master's degree; three letters of recommendation; statement of purpose; resume. Additional exam requirements/recommendations for international students: required—TOEFL (minimum score 590 paper-based; 96 iBT). Electronic applications accepted.

The University of Alabama at Birmingham, School of Engineering, Program in Biomedical Engineering, Birmingham, AL 35294. Offers MSBME, PhD. *Faculty:* 8 full-time (1 woman), 10 part-time/adjunct (3 women). *Students:* 33 full-time (15 women), 2 part-time (1 woman); includes 3 minority (2 Black or African American, non-Hispanic/Latino; 1 Two or more races, non-Hispanic/Latino), 14 international. 56 applicants, 21% accepted, 4 enrolled. In 2019, 3 master's, 2 doctorates awarded. *Degree requirements:* For master's, thesis or alternative; for doctorate, comprehensive exam, thesis/dissertation. *Entrance requirements:* For master's, GRE General Test for all applicants who did not receive a BS degree from a program accredited by the Engineering Accreditation Committee of ABET http://www.abet.org, or from other programs with reciprocal agreement under the Washington Accord http://www.ieagreements.org/accords/washington/.; for doctorate, GRE General Test. Additional exam requirements/recommendations for international students: required—TOEFL (minimum score 80 iBT); recommended—IELTS (minimum score 6.5). *Application deadline:* For fall admission, 1/15 for domestic students. Application fee: $50 ($60 for international students). Electronic applications accepted. *Financial support:* In 2019–20, 34 students received support, including 19 fellowships with full tuition reimbursements available (averaging $25,956 per year), 14 research assistantships with full tuition reimbursements available (averaging $28,429 per year). *Unit head:* Dr. Jianyi Zhang, Chair, 205-934-8420, E-mail: jayzhang@uab.edu. *Application contact:* Jesse Keppley, Director of Student and Academic Services, 205-996-5696, E-mail: gradschool@uab.edu.
Website: https://www.uab.edu/engineering/home/departments-research/bme

University of Alberta, Faculty of Medicine and Dentistry and Faculty of Graduate Studies and Research, Graduate Programs in Medicine, Department of Biomedical Engineering, Edmonton, AB T6G 2E1, Canada. Offers biomedical engineering (M Sc); medical sciences (PhD). *Degree requirements:* For master's, thesis; for doctorate, thesis/dissertation. Electronic applications accepted.

The University of Arizona, Graduate Interdisciplinary Programs, Graduate Interdisciplinary Program in Biomedical Engineering, Tucson, AZ 85721. Offers MS, PhD. *Entrance requirements:* For master's, GRE, 3 letters of recommendation; for doctorate, GRE, 3 letters of recommendation, statement of purpose. Additional exam requirements/recommendations for international students: required—TOEFL (minimum score 600 paper-based). Electronic applications accepted.

University of Arkansas, Graduate School, College of Engineering, Department of Biological and Agricultural Engineering, Program in Biomedical Engineering, Fayetteville, AR 72701. Offers MSBME. *Students:* 22 full-time (11 women), 5 part-time (1 woman); includes 5 minority (1 American Indian or Alaska Native, non-Hispanic/Latino; 1 Asian, non-Hispanic/Latino; 3 Hispanic/Latino), 7 international. 13 applicants, 85% accepted. In 2019, 5 master's awarded. *Application deadline:* For fall admission, 8/1 for domestic students, 4/1 for international students; for spring admission, 12/1 for domestic students, 10/1 for international students; for summer admission, 4/15 for domestic students, 3/1 for international students. Applications are processed on a rolling basis. Application fee: $60. Electronic applications accepted. *Financial support:* In 2019–20, 4 research assistantships, 2 teaching assistantships were awarded; fellowships also available. *Unit head:* Dr. Raj Raghavendra Rao, Department Head, 479-575-8610, E-mail: rajrao@uark.edu. *Application contact:* Dr. Kartik Balachandran, Program Coordinator, 479-575-3376, E-mail: kbalacha@uark.edu.
Website: https://biomedical-engineering.uark.edu/

University of Bridgeport, School of Engineering, Department of Biomedical Engineering, Bridgeport, CT 06604. Offers MS. *Program availability:* Part-time, evening/weekend. *Degree requirements:* For master's, thesis optional. *Entrance requirements:* Additional exam requirements/recommendations for international students: recommended—TOEFL (minimum score 550 paper-based; 80 iBT), IELTS (minimum score 6.5). *Expenses:* Contact institution.

The University of British Columbia, Faculty of Applied Science, School of Biomedical Engineering, Vancouver, BC V6T 1Z1, Canada. Offers M Eng, MA Sc, PhD. *Degree requirements:* For master's, internship (for M Eng); thesis (for MA Sc); for doctorate, thesis/dissertation.

University of Calgary, Faculty of Graduate Studies, Schulich School of Engineering, Program in Biomedical Engineering, Calgary, AB T2N 1N4, Canada. Offers M Sc, PhD. *Degree requirements:* For master's, comprehensive exam, thesis, defense exam; for doctorate, comprehensive exam, thesis/dissertation, defense exam. *Entrance requirements:* For master's, B Sc, minimum GPA of 3.2, confirmed faculty supervisor; for doctorate, M Sc, minimum GPA of 3.5, confirmed faculty supervisor. Additional exam requirements/recommendations for international students: required—TOEFL, IELTS.

University of California, Davis, College of Engineering, Graduate Group in Biomedical Engineering, Davis, CA 95616. Offers MS, PhD. *Degree requirements:* For master's, thesis; for doctorate, thesis/dissertation. *Entrance requirements:* For master's and doctorate, GRE General Test, minimum GPA of 3.25. Additional exam requirements/recommendations for international students: required—TOEFL (minimum score 550 paper-based), IELTS (minimum score 7). Electronic applications accepted.

University of California, Irvine, Samueli School of Engineering, Department of Biomedical Engineering, Irvine, CA 92697. Offers MS, PhD. *Program availability:* Part-time. *Students:* 128 full-time (44 women), 3 part-time (1 woman); includes 44 minority (2 Black or African American, non-Hispanic/Latino; 36 Asian, non-Hispanic/Latino; 5 Hispanic/Latino; 1 Two or more races, non-Hispanic/Latino), 44 international. Average age 26. 381 applicants, 33% accepted, 36 enrolled. In 2019, 44 master's, 22 doctorates awarded. Terminal master's awarded for partial completion of doctoral program. *Entrance requirements:* For master's and doctorate, GRE General Test, minimum GPA of 3.0, 3 letters of recommendation. Additional exam requirements/recommendations for international students: required—TOEFL (minimum score 550 paper-based). *Application deadline:* For fall admission, 1/15 priority date for domestic students, 1/15 for international students. Applications are processed on a rolling basis. Application fee: $120 ($140 for international students). Electronic applications accepted. *Financial support:* Fellowships, research assistantships with full tuition reimbursements, teaching assistantships, institutionally sponsored loans, traineeships, health care benefits, and unspecified assistantships available. Financial award application deadline: 3/1; financial award applicants required to submit FAFSA. *Unit head:* Prof. Abraham P. Lee, Chair, 949-824-8155, Fax: 949-824-1727, E-mail: aplee@uci.edu. *Application contact:* Connie Cheng, Assistant Director of Graduate Student Affairs, 949-824-3562, Fax: 949-824-9096, E-mail: connie.cheng@uci.edu.
Website: http://www.eng.uci.edu/dept/bme

University of California, Los Angeles, Graduate Division, Henry Samueli School of Engineering and Applied Science, Department of Chemical and Biomolecular Engineering, Los Angeles, CA 90095-1592. Offers MS, PhD. *Degree requirements:* For master's, comprehensive exam (for some programs), thesis (for some programs); for doctorate, thesis/dissertation, qualifying exams. *Entrance requirements:* For master's, GRE General Test, minimum GPA of 3.0; for doctorate, GRE General Test, minimum GPA of 3.25. Additional exam requirements/recommendations for international students: required—TOEFL (minimum score 560 paper-based; 87 iBT), IELTS (minimum score 7). Electronic applications accepted.

University of Central Oklahoma, The Jackson College of Graduate Studies, College of Mathematics and Science, Department of Engineering and Physics, Edmond, OK 73034-5209. Offers engineering physics (MS), including biomedical engineering, electrical engineering, mechanical systems, physics. *Program availability:* Part-time. *Degree requirements:* For master's, thesis optional. *Entrance requirements:* For master's, GRE, 24 hours of course work in physics or equivalent, mathematics through differential equations, minimum GPA of 2.75 overall and 3.0 in last 60 hours attempted, two letters of recommendation. Additional exam requirements/recommendations for international students: required—TOEFL (minimum score 550 paper-based; 79 iBT), IELTS (minimum score 6.5). Electronic applications accepted.

University of Cincinnati, Graduate School, College of Engineering and Applied Science, Department of Biomedical, Chemical and Environmental Engineering, Cincinnati, OH 45221. Offers biomechanics (PhD); chemical engineering (MS, PhD); environmental engineering (MS, PhD); environmental sciences (MS, PhD); medical imaging (PhD); tissue engineering (PhD). *Program availability:* Part-time. *Degree requirements:* For master's, thesis or alternative; for doctorate, one foreign language, thesis/dissertation. *Entrance requirements:* For master's and doctorate, GRE General Test. Additional exam requirements/recommendations for international students: required—TOEFL (minimum score 600 paper-based).

University of Connecticut, Graduate School, School of Engineering, Department of Biomedical Engineering, Storrs, CT 06269. Offers MS, PhD. Terminal master's awarded for partial completion of doctoral program. *Degree requirements:* For master's, comprehensive exam, thesis or alternative; for doctorate, thesis/dissertation. *Entrance requirements:* For master's and doctorate, GRE General Test. Additional exam requirements/recommendations for international students: required—TOEFL (minimum score 550 paper-based). Electronic applications accepted.

University of Florida, Graduate School, Herbert Wertheim College of Engineering, J. Crayton Pruitt Family Department of Biomedical Engineering, Gainesville, FL 32611. Offers biomedical engineering (ME, MS, PhD, Certificate); clinical and translational science (PhD); medical physics (MS, PhD); MD/PhD. Terminal master's awarded for partial completion of doctoral program. *Degree requirements:* For master's, comprehensive exam (for some programs), thesis (for some programs); for doctorate, comprehensive exam (for some programs), thesis/dissertation (for some programs). *Entrance requirements:* Additional exam requirements/recommendations for international students: required—TOEFL (minimum score 550 paper-based; 80 iBT), IELTS (minimum score 6). Electronic applications accepted.

University of Houston, Cullen College of Engineering, Department of Biomedical Engineering, Houston, TX 77204. Offers PhD. *Program availability:* Part-time. *Degree requirements:* For doctorate, seminar. *Entrance requirements:* For doctorate, GRE, BS or MS in biomedical engineering or related field, minimum GPA of 3.3 on last 60 hours. Additional exam requirements/recommendations for international students: required—TOEFL (minimum score 580 paper-based; 92 iBT), IELTS (minimum score 6). Electronic applications accepted.

The University of Iowa, Graduate College, College of Engineering, Department of Biomedical Engineering, Iowa City, IA 52242-1316. Offers MS, PhD. *Program availability:* Part-time. Terminal master's awarded for partial completion of doctoral program. *Degree requirements:* For master's, thesis (for some programs), written and oral exam; for doctorate, comprehensive exam, thesis/dissertation, written and oral exam. *Entrance requirements:* For master's, GRE (minimum combined score of 310 on verbal and quantitative), minimum undergraduate GPA of 3.0; for doctorate, GRE (minimum combined score of 310 on verbal and quantitative), minimum undergraduate GPA of 3.25. Additional exam requirements/recommendations for international students: required—TOEFL (minimum score 553 paper-based; 85 iBT), IELTS (minimum score 7). Electronic applications accepted.

University of Kentucky, Graduate School, College of Engineering, Program in Biomedical Engineering, Lexington, KY 40506-0032. Offers MSBE, PBME, PhD. *Degree requirements:* For master's, comprehensive exam, thesis optional; for doctorate, comprehensive exam, thesis/dissertation. *Entrance requirements:* For master's, GRE General Test, minimum undergraduate GPA of 2.75; for doctorate, GRE General Test, minimum graduate GPA of 3.0. Additional exam requirements/recommendations for international students: required—TOEFL (minimum score 550 paper-based). Electronic applications accepted.

University of Maine, Graduate School, Graduate School of Biomedical Science and Engineering, Orono, ME 04469. Offers bioinformatics (PSM); biomedical engineering (PhD); biomedical science (PhD). *Faculty:* 182 full-time (60 women). *Students:* 47 full-time (26 women), 1 part-time (0 women); includes 2 minority (1 Hispanic/Latino; 1 Two or more races, non-Hispanic/Latino), 9 international. Average age 30. 111 applicants, 17% accepted, 15 enrolled. In 2019, 7 doctorates awarded. *Degree requirements:* For doctorate, comprehensive exam, thesis/dissertation. *Entrance requirements:* For doctorate, GRE General Test, master's degree. Additional exam requirements/recommendations for international students: required—TOEFL (minimum score 80 iBT), IELTS (minimum score 6.5), PTE (minimum score 60). *Application deadline:* For fall admission, 1/1 priority date for domestic and international students. Applications are processed on a rolling basis. Application fee: $65. Electronic applications accepted. *Expenses: Tuition, area resident:* Full-time $8100; part-time $450 per credit hour. Tuition, state resident: full-time $8100; part-time $450 per credit hour. Tuition, nonresident: full-time $26,388; part-time $1466 per credit hour. *International tuition:* $26,388 full-time. *Required fees:* $1257; $278 per semester. Tuition and fees vary according to course load. *Financial support:* In 2019–20, 47 students received support, including 1 fellowship with tuition reimbursement available (averaging $34,000 per year), 41 research assistantships with full tuition reimbursements available (averaging $20,000 per year), 5 teaching assistantships with full tuition reimbursements available (averaging $15,825 per year); career-related internships or fieldwork, scholarships/grants, and unspecified assistantships also available. Financial award application deadline: 3/1; financial award applicants required to submit FAFSA. *Unit head:* Scott G Delcourt, Assistant Vice President for Graduate Studies and Senior Associate Dean, 207-581-3291, Fax: 207-581-3232, E-mail: graduate@maine.edu. *Application contact:* Scott G Delcourt, Assistant Vice President for Graduate Studies and Senior Associate Dean, 207-581-3291, Fax: 207-581-3232, E-mail: graduate@maine.edu.
Website: http://gsbse.umaine.edu/

University of Massachusetts Boston, College of Science and Mathematics, Program in Biomedical Engineering and Biotechnology, Boston, MA 02125-3393. Offers PhD.

University of Massachusetts Dartmouth, Graduate School, College of Engineering, Program in Biomedical Engineering and Biotechnology, North Dartmouth, MA 02747-2300. Offers biomedical engineering/biotechnology (PhD). *Program availability:* Part-time. Terminal master's awarded for partial completion of doctoral program. *Degree requirements:* For doctorate, comprehensive exam, thesis/dissertation. *Entrance requirements:* For doctorate, GRE, statement of purpose (minimum of 300 words), resume, 3 letters of recommendation, official transcripts. Additional exam requirements/recommendations for international students: required—TOEFL (minimum score 550 paper-based; 79 iBT), IELTS (minimum score 6.5). Electronic applications accepted.

University of Memphis, Graduate School, Herff College of Engineering, Program in Biomedical Engineering, Memphis, TN 38152. Offers MS, PhD. *Students:* 19 full-time (7 women), 14 part-time (4 women); includes 7 minority (1 Black or African American, non-Hispanic/Latino; 1 American Indian or Alaska Native, non-Hispanic/Latino; 2 Asian, non-Hispanic/Latino; 2 Hispanic/Latino; 1 Two or more races, non-Hispanic/Latino), 6 international. Average age 30. 14 applicants, 79% accepted, 8 enrolled. In 2019, 2 master's awarded. *Degree requirements:* For master's, thesis or alternative, oral exam; for doctorate, comprehensive exam, thesis/dissertation. *Entrance requirements:* For master's, GRE, minimum undergraduate GPA of 3.0, three letters of recommendation; for doctorate, GRE, minimum undergraduate GPA of 3.25 or master's degree in biomedical engineering, three letters of recommendation. Additional exam requirements/recommendations for international students: required—TOEFL (minimum score 550 paper-based; 79 iBT). *Application deadline:* For fall admission, 8/1 priority date for domestic students; for spring admission, 12/1 for domestic students. Applications are processed on a rolling basis. Application fee: $35 ($60 for international students). Electronic applications accepted. *Expenses: Tuition, area resident:* Full-time $9216; part-time $512 per credit hour. Tuition, state resident: full-time $9216; part-time $512 per credit hour. Tuition, nonresident: full-time $12,672; part-time $704 per credit hour. *International tuition:* $16,128 full-time. *Required fees:* $1530; $85 per credit hour. Tuition and fees vary according to program. *Financial support:* Fellowships with full tuition reimbursements, research assistantships with full tuition reimbursements, career-related internships or fieldwork, Federal Work-Study, scholarships/grants, and unspecified assistantships available. Financial award application deadline: 2/1; financial award applicants required to submit FAFSA. *Unit head:* Dr. Joel Bumgardner, Chair, 901-678-5243, E-mail: jbmgrdnr@memphis.edu. *Application contact:* Dr. John Williams, Graduate Coordinator, 901-678-5485, E-mail: jlwllm17@memphis.edu.
Website: http://www.memphis.edu/bme

University of Miami, Graduate School, College of Engineering, Department of Biomedical Engineering, Coral Gables, FL 33124. Offers MSBE, PhD. *Program availability:* Part-time. *Degree requirements:* For master's, thesis (for some programs); for doctorate, comprehensive exam, thesis/dissertation. *Entrance requirements:* For master's and doctorate, GRE General Test, minimum GPA of 3.0. Additional exam requirements/recommendations for international students: required—TOEFL (minimum score 550 paper-based). Electronic applications accepted.

University of Michigan, College of Engineering, Department of Biomedical Engineering, Ann Arbor, MI 48109. Offers MS, MSE, PhD. *Program availability:* Part-time. *Degree requirements:* For master's, thesis optional; for doctorate, comprehensive exam, oral defense of dissertation. *Entrance requirements:* For master's, GRE General Test; for doctorate, GRE General Test, master's degree. Additional exam requirements/recommendations for international students: required—TOEFL. Electronic applications accepted.

University of Minnesota, Twin Cities Campus, College of Science and Engineering and Medical School, Department of Biomedical Engineering, Minneapolis, MN 55455-0213. Offers MS, PhD, MD/PhD. *Program availability:* Part-time. Terminal master's awarded for partial completion of doctoral program. *Degree requirements:* For master's, thesis optional; for doctorate, thesis/dissertation. *Entrance requirements:* For master's and doctorate, GRE General Test. Additional exam requirements/recommendations for international students: required—TOEFL. Electronic applications accepted.

University of Nebraska–Lincoln, Graduate College, College of Engineering, Department of Mechanical and Materials Engineering, Lincoln, NE 68588-0526. Offers biomedical engineering (PhD); engineering mechanics (MS); materials engineering (PhD); mechanical engineering (MS), including materials science engineering, metallurgical engineering; mechanical engineering and applied mechanics (PhD); MS/MS. *Degree requirements:* For master's, thesis optional; for doctorate, comprehensive exam, thesis/dissertation. *Entrance requirements:* For master's and doctorate, GRE General Test. Additional exam requirements/recommendations for international students: required—TOEFL (minimum score 550 paper-based). Electronic applications accepted.

University of Nevada, Las Vegas, Graduate College, Howard R. Hughes College of Engineering, Department of Mechanical Engineering, Las Vegas, NV 89154-4027. Offers aerospace engineering (MS); biomedical engineering (MS); materials and nuclear engineering (MS); mechanical engineering (MS, PhD); nuclear criticality safety engineering (Certificate); nuclear safeguards and security (Certificate). *Program availability:* Part-time. *Faculty:* 18 full-time (2 women), 1 (woman) part-time/adjunct. *Students:* 52 full-time (16 women), 26 part-time (7 women); includes 26 minority (5 Black or African American, non-Hispanic/Latino; 1 American Indian or Alaska Native, non-Hispanic/Latino; 7 Asian, non-Hispanic/Latino; 10 Hispanic/Latino; 3 Two or more races, non-Hispanic/Latino), 22 international. Average age 29. 45 applicants, 76% accepted, 14 enrolled. In 2019, 9 master's, 4 doctorates, 1 other advanced degree awarded. *Degree requirements:* For master's, thesis optional, design project; for doctorate, comprehensive exam, thesis/dissertation. *Entrance requirements:* For master's, GRE General Test, statement of purpose; 2 letters of recommendation; for doctorate, GRE General Test, 3 letters of recommendation; statement of purpose; bachelor's degree with minimum GPA of 3.5/master's degree with minimum GPA of 3.3. Additional exam requirements/recommendations for international students: required—TOEFL (minimum score 550 paper-based; 80 iBT), IELTS (minimum score 7). *Application deadline:* For fall admission, 8/1 for domestic students, 5/1 for international students; for spring admission, 12/1 for domestic students, 10/1 for international students. Application fee: $60 ($95 for international students). Electronic applications accepted. *Expenses:* Contact institution. *Financial support:* In 2019–20, 40 students received support, including 2 fellowships with full tuition reimbursements available (averaging $20,000 per year), 16 research assistantships with full tuition reimbursements available (averaging $16,738 per year), 26 teaching assistantships with full tuition reimbursements available (averaging $18,115 per year); institutionally sponsored loans, scholarships/grants, health care benefits, and unspecified assistantships also available. Financial award application deadline: 3/15; financial award applicants required to submit FAFSA. *Unit head:* Dr. Brendan O'Toole, Chair/Professor, 702-895-3885, Fax: 702-895-3936, E-mail: mechanical.chair@unlv.edu. *Application contact:* Dr. Hui Zhao, Graduate Coordinator, 702-895-1463, Fax: 702-895-3936, E-mail: mechanical.gradcoord@unlv.edu.
Website: http://me.unlv.edu/

University of Nevada, Reno, Graduate School, College of Engineering, Department of Electrical and Biomedical Engineering, Reno, NV 89557. Offers MS, PhD. Terminal master's awarded for partial completion of doctoral program. *Degree requirements:* For master's, thesis optional; for doctorate, thesis/dissertation. *Entrance requirements:* For master's, GRE General Test, minimum GPA of 2.75; for doctorate, GRE General Test, minimum GPA of 3.0. Additional exam requirements/recommendations for international students: required—TOEFL (minimum score 500 paper-based; 61 iBT), IELTS (minimum score 6). Electronic applications accepted.

University of Nevada, Reno, Graduate School, Interdisciplinary Program in Biomedical Engineering, Reno, NV 89557. Offers MS, PhD. Terminal master's awarded for partial completion of doctoral program. *Degree requirements:* For master's, thesis optional; for doctorate, thesis/dissertation. *Entrance requirements:* For master's, GRE General Test (recommended), minimum GPA of 2.75; for doctorate, GRE General Test (recommended), minimum GPA of 3.0. Additional exam requirements/recommendations for international students: required—TOEFL (minimum score 500 paper-based; 61 iBT), IELTS (minimum score 6). Electronic applications accepted.

University of New Haven, Graduate School, Tagliatela College of Engineering, Program in Biomedical Engineering, West Haven, CT 06516. Offers MS. *Students:* 24 full-time (11 women), 9 part-time (5 women); includes 7 minority (5 Black or African American, non-Hispanic/Latino; 2 Asian, non-Hispanic/Latino), 19 international. Average age 26. 47 applicants, 83% accepted, 13 enrolled. In 2019, 18 master's awarded. *Application deadline:* Applications are processed on a rolling basis. Application fee: $50. Electronic applications accepted. *Financial support:* Applicants required to submit FAFSA. *Unit head:* Dr. Kagya Amoako, Assistant Professor, 203-479-4877, E-mail: kamoako@newhaven.edu. *Application contact:* Selina O'Toole, Senior Associate Director of Graduate Admissions, 203-932-7337, E-mail: sotoole@newhaven.edu.
Website: http://www.newhaven.edu/engineering/graduate-programs/biomedical-engineering/index.php

University of New Mexico, Graduate Studies, School of Engineering, Program in Biomedical Engineering, Albuquerque, NM 87131. Offers MS, PhD. *Program availability:* Part-time. *Faculty:* 7 full-time (3 women). *Students:* 22 full-time (9 women), 19 part-time (10 women); includes 18 minority (1 Black or African American, non-Hispanic/Latino; 3 Asian, non-Hispanic/Latino; 14 Hispanic/Latino), 8 international. 37 applicants, 81% accepted, 17 enrolled. In 2019, 20 master's awarded. Terminal master's awarded for partial completion of doctoral program. *Degree requirements:* For master's, thesis (for some programs); for doctorate, comprehensive exam, thesis/dissertation. *Entrance requirements:* For master's and doctorate, GRE General Test, letters of recommendation, letter of intent. Additional exam requirements/recommendations for international students: required—TOEFL, IELTS, TOEFL or IELTS, not both. *Application deadline:* For fall admission, 1/15 priority date for domestic and international students; for spring admission, 8/1 priority date for domestic and international students. Applications are processed on a rolling basis. Application fee: $50. Electronic applications accepted. *Expenses:* Tuition, state resident: full-time $7633; part-time $972 per year. Tuition, nonresident: full-time $22,586; part-time $3840 per year. *International tuition:* $23,292 full-time. *Required fees:* $8608. Tuition and fees vary according to course level, course load, degree level, program and student level. *Financial support:* Research assistantships, teaching assistantships, and scholarships/grants available. Financial award application deadline: 10/1; financial award applicants required to submit FAFSA. *Unit head:* Dr. Shuang Luan, Program Director, 505-277-6824, Fax: 505-277-1979, E-mail: sluan@cs.unm.edu. *Application contact:* Linda Stewart, Academic Advisor, 505-277-6824, Fax: 505-277-1979, E-mail: lbugge@unm.edu.
Website: https://bme.unm.edu/

University of North Texas, Toulouse Graduate School, Denton, TX 76203-5459. Offers accounting (MS); applied anthropology (MA, MS); applied behavior analysis (Certificate); applied geography (MA); applied technology and performance improvement (M Ed, MS); art education (MA); art history (MA); arts leadership (Certificate); audiology (Au D); behavior analysis (MS); behavioral science (PhD); biochemistry and molecular biology (MS); biology (MA, MS); biomedical engineering (MS); business analysis (MS); chemistry (MS); clinical health psychology (PhD); communication studies (MA, MS); computer engineering (MS); computer science (MS); counseling (M Ed, MS), including clinical mental health counseling (MS), college and university counseling, elementary school counseling, secondary school counseling; creative writing (MA); criminal justice (MS); curriculum and instruction (M Ed); decision sciences (MBA); design (MA, MFA), including fashion design (MFA), innovation studies, interior design (MFA); early childhood studies (MS); economics (MS); educational leadership (M Ed, Ed D); educational psychology (MS, PhD), including family studies (MS), gifted and talented (MS), human development (MS), learning and cognition (MS), research, measurement and evaluation (MS); electrical engineering (MS); emergency management (MPA); engineering technology (MS); English (MA); English as a second language (MA); environmental science (MS); finance (MBA, MS); financial management (MPA); French (MA); health services management (MBA); higher education (M Ed, Ed D); history (MA, MS); hospitality management (MS); human resources management (MPA); information science (MS); information systems (PhD); information technologies (MBA); interdisciplinary studies (MA, MS); international studies (MA); international sustainable tourism (MS); jazz studies (MM); journalism (MA, MJ, Graduate Certificate), including interactive and virtual digital communication (Graduate Certificate), narrative journalism (Graduate Certificate), public relations (Graduate Certificate); kinesiology (MS); linguistics (MA); local government management (MPA); logistics (PhD); logistics and supply chain management (MBA); long-term care, senior housing, and aging services (MA); management (PhD); marketing (MBA); mathematics (MA, MS); mechanical and energy engineering (MS, PhD); music (MA), including ethnomusicology, music theory, musicology, performance; music composition (PhD); music education (MM Ed, PhD); nonprofit management (MPA); operations and supply chain management (MBA); performance (MM, DMA); philosophy (MA); political science (MA); professional and technical communication (MA); radio, television and film (MA, MFA); rehabilitation counseling (Certificate); sociology (MA); Spanish (MA); special education (M Ed); speech-language pathology (MA); strategic management (MBA); studio art (MFA); teaching (M Ed); MBA/MS. *Program availability:* Part-time, evening/weekend, online learning. Terminal master's awarded for partial completion of doctoral program. *Degree requirements:* For master's, variable foreign language requirement, comprehensive exam (for some programs), thesis (for some programs); for doctorate, variable foreign language requirement, comprehensive exam (for some programs), thesis/dissertation; for other advanced degree, variable foreign language requirement, comprehensive exam (for some programs). *Entrance requirements:* For master's and doctorate, GRE, GMAT. Additional exam requirements/recommendations for international students: required—TOEFL (minimum score 550 paper-based; 79 iBT). Electronic applications accepted.

University of Oklahoma, Gallogly College of Engineering, Stephenson School of Biomedical Engineering, Norman, OK 73019. Offers MS, PhD. *Program availability:* Part-time. *Degree requirements:* For master's, thesis; for doctorate, comprehensive exam, thesis/dissertation. *Entrance requirements:* For master's and doctorate, GRE. Additional exam requirements/recommendations for international students: required—TOEFL (minimum score 100 iBT) or IELTS (minimum score 7.0). Electronic applications accepted. *Expenses:* Tuition, state resident: full-time $6583.20; part-time $274.30 per credit hour. Tuition, nonresident: full-time $21,242; part-time $885.10 per credit hour. *International tuition:* $21,242.40 full-time. *Required fees:* $1994.20; $72.55 per credit hour. $126.50 per semester. Tuition and fees vary according to course load and degree level.

University of Ottawa, Faculty of Graduate and Postdoctoral Studies, Ottawa—Carlton Joint Program in Biomedical Engineering, Ottawa, ON K1N 6N5, Canada. Offers MA Sc. *Degree requirements:* For master's, thesis or alternative. *Entrance requirements:* For master's, honors degree or equivalent, minimum B average.

University of Portland, Shiley School of Engineering, Portland, OR 97203-5798. Offers biomedical engineering (MBME); civil engineering (ME); computer science (ME); electrical engineering (ME); mechanical engineering (ME). *Program availability:* Part-time, evening/weekend. *Degree requirements:* For master's, thesis optional. *Entrance requirements:* For master's, GRE General Test, minimum GPA of 3.0, 2 letters of recommendation, resume, statement of goals, official transcripts. Additional exam requirements/recommendations for international students: required—TOEFL (minimum score 80 iBT), IELTS (minimum score 7). Electronic applications accepted. *Expenses:* Contact institution.

University of Rhode Island, Graduate School, College of Engineering, Department of Electrical, Computer and Biomedical Engineering, Kingston, RI 02881. Offers acoustics and underwater acoustics (MS, PhD); biomedical engineering (MS, PhD); circuits and devices (MS); communication theory (MS, PhD); computer architectures and digital systems (MS, PhD); computer networks (MS, PhD); digital signal processing (MS); embedded systems and computer applications (MS, PhD); fault-tolerant computing (MS, PhD); materials and optics (MS, PhD); systems theory (MS, PhD). *Program availability:* Part-time. *Faculty:* 20 full-time (4 women), 1 part-time/adjunct (0 women). *Students:* 39 full-time (7 women), 14 part-time (1 woman); includes 7 minority (3 Black or African American, non-Hispanic/Latino; 1 American Indian or Alaska Native, non-Hispanic/Latino; 2 Asian, non-Hispanic/Latino; 1 Hispanic/Latino), 23 international. 31 applicants, 74% accepted, 13 enrolled. In 2019, 13 master's, 3 doctorates awarded. *Entrance requirements:* Additional exam requirements/recommendations for international students: required—TOEFL. *Application deadline:* For fall admission, 7/15 for domestic students, 2/1 for international students; for spring admission, 11/15 for domestic students, 7/15 for international students; for summer admission, 4/15 for domestic students. Application fee: $65. Electronic applications accepted. *Expenses: Tuition, area resident:* Full-time $13,734; part-time $763 per credit. Tuition, state resident: full-time $13,734; part-time $763 per credit. Tuition, nonresident: full-time $26,512; part-time $1473 per credit. *International tuition:* $26,512 full-time. *Required fees:* $1780; $52 per credit. $35 per term. One-time fee: $165. *Financial support:* In 2019–20, 19 research assistantships with tuition reimbursements (averaging $10,247 per year), 9 teaching assistantships with tuition reimbursements (averaging $9,097 per year) were awarded. Financial award application deadline: 2/1; financial award applicants required to submit FAFSA. *Unit head:* Dr. Haibo He, Chair, 401-874-5844, E-mail: he@ele.uri.edu. *Application contact:* Dr. Frederick J. Vetter, Graduate Director, 401-874-5141, E-mail: vetter@ele.uri.edu.
Website: http://www.ele.uri.edu/

University of Rochester, Hajim School of Engineering and Applied Sciences, Department of Biomedical Engineering, Rochester, NY 14627. Offers MS, PhD. *Faculty:* 14 full-time (7 women). *Students:* 95 full-time (42 women), 1 part-time (0 women); includes 23 minority (4 Black or African American, non-Hispanic/Latino; 11 Asian, non-Hispanic/Latino; 5 Hispanic/Latino; 3 Two or more races, non-Hispanic/Latino), 29 international. Average age 26. 274 applicants, 46% accepted, 34 enrolled. In 2019, 30 master's, 8 doctorates awarded. Terminal master's awarded for partial completion of doctoral program. *Degree requirements:* For master's, comprehensive exam (for some programs), thesis (for some programs), teaching assistantship; for doctorate, thesis/dissertation, 1st-year preliminary exam, qualifying exam, 2 teaching assistantships, 3 lab rotations, 39 required course credits. *Entrance requirements:* For master's and doctorate, GRE General Test, curriculum vitae, three letters of recommendations, official transcripts, personal statement. Additional exam requirements/recommendations for international students: required—TOEFL (minimum score 600 paper-based; 100 iBT), IELTS. *Application deadline:* For fall admission, 4/15 for domestic and international students. Application fee: $60. Electronic applications accepted. *Financial support:* In 2019–20, 64 students received support, including 25 fellowships with full tuition reimbursements available (averaging $29,566 per year), 39 research assistantships with full and partial tuition reimbursements available (averaging $29,568 per year); traineeships, health care benefits, tuition waivers (full and partial), and unspecified assistantships also available. Financial award application deadline: 4/15. *Unit head:* Diane Dalecki, Professor and Chair, 585-275-7378, E-mail: diane.dalecki@rochester.edu. *Application contact:* Ania Dworzanski, Graduate Program Coordinator, 585-275-3891, E-mail: anna.dworzanski@ur.rochester.edu.
Website: http://www.hajim.rochester.edu/bme/graduate/index.html

University of Rochester, Hajim School of Engineering and Applied Sciences, Master of Science in Technical Entrepreneurship and Management Program, Rochester, NY 14627. Offers biomedical engineering (MS). *Program availability:* Part-time. *Students:* 36 full-time (14 women), 3 part-time (1 woman); includes 5 minority (1 Black or African American, non-Hispanic/Latino; 3 Hispanic/Latino; 1 Two or more races, non-Hispanic/Latino), 23 international. Average age 25. 216 applicants, 75% accepted, 26 enrolled. In 2019, 29 master's awarded. *Degree requirements:* For master's, comprehensive exam. *Entrance requirements:* For master's, GRE or GMAT (strongly recommended), 3 letters of recommendation, personal statement, official transcript. Additional exam requirements/recommendations for international students: required—TOEFL (minimum score 90 paper-based), IELTS (minimum score 6.5). *Application deadline:* For fall admission, 2/1 for domestic and international students. Application fee: $60. Electronic applications accepted. *Financial support:* In 2019–20, 1 student received support, including 1 fellowship (averaging $2,664 per year); career-related internships or fieldwork, scholarships/grants, health care benefits, and tuition waivers (partial) also available. Support available to part-time students. Financial award application deadline: 2/1. *Unit head:* Duncan T. Moore, Vice Provost for Entrepreneurship, 585-275-5248, E-mail: duncan.moore@rochester.edu. *Application contact:* Andrea Barrett, Executive Director, 585-276-3407, E-mail: andrea.barrett@rochester.edu.
Website: http://www.rochester.edu/team/

University of Saskatchewan, College of Graduate and Postdoctoral Studies, College of Engineering, Biomedical Engineering Program, Saskatoon, SK S7N 5E5, Canada. Offers M Eng, M Sc, PhD, PGD. *Program availability:* Part-time. *Degree requirements:* For master's, 30 credits (for M Eng); thesis and 12 credits (for MS); for doctorate, comprehensive exam, thesis/dissertation, qualifying exam, 18 credits. *Entrance requirements:* For master's and doctorate, GRE. Additional exam requirements/recommendations for international students: required—TOEFL (minimum iBT score of 80), IELTS (6.5), CanTEST (4.5), or PTE (59). Electronic applications accepted.

University of Southern California, Graduate School, Viterbi School of Engineering, Department of Biomedical Engineering, Los Angeles, CA 90089. Offers biomedical engineering (PhD); medical device and diagnostic engineering (MS); medical imaging and imaging informatics (MS). *Program availability:* Online learning. Terminal master's awarded for partial completion of doctoral program. *Degree requirements:* For master's, thesis optional; for doctorate, thesis/dissertation. *Entrance requirements:* For master's and doctorate, GRE General Test. Additional exam requirements/recommendations for international students: recommended—TOEFL. Electronic applications accepted.

University of South Florida, College of Engineering, Department of Chemical and Biomedical Engineering, Tampa, FL 33620. Offers MSBE, MSCH, PhD. *Program availability:* Part-time. *Faculty:* 18 full-time (2 women). *Students:* 50 full-time (13 women), 10 part-time (3 women); includes 5 minority (1 Black or African American, non-Hispanic/Latino; 2 Asian, non-Hispanic/Latino; 1 Hispanic/Latino; 1 Two or more races, non-Hispanic/Latino), 42 international. Average age 27. 61 applicants, 59% accepted, 20 enrolled. In 2019, 19 master's, 2 doctorates awarded. Terminal master's awarded for partial completion of doctoral program. *Degree requirements:* For master's, comprehensive exam, thesis (for some programs); for doctorate, comprehensive exam, thesis/dissertation. *Entrance requirements:* For master's, GRE (preferred minimum scores of Verbal greater than 50% percentile, Quantitative greater than 75th percentile, Analytical Writing of 3.0 or greater; applicants who have successfully completed the Fundamentals of Engineering (FE) Exam offered by the Society of Professional Engineers will be exempted from the GRE requirement, Bachelors or equivalent in Chemical Engineering; 2 letters of reference; statement of research interests; for doctorate, (preferred scores: Verbal greater than 50% percentile, Quantitative greater than 75% percentile, Analytical Writing greater than 4.0), bachelors or equivalent in Chemical Engineering; 3 letters of reference; statement of research interests. Additional exam requirements/recommendations for international students: required—TOEFL, TOEFL (minimum score 550 paper-based; 79 iBT) or IELTS (minimum score 6.5). *Application deadline:* For fall admission, 2/15 for domestic and international students; for spring admission, 10/15 for domestic students, 9/15 for international students; for summer admission, 2/15 for domestic students, 1/15 for international students. Application fee: $30. Electronic applications accepted. *Financial support:* In 2019–20, 10 students received support, including 29 research assistantships with tuition reimbursements available (averaging $13,171 per year), 12 teaching assistantships with tuition reimbursements available (averaging $14,017 per year); unspecified assistantships also available. Financial award applicants required to submit FAFSA. *Unit head:* Dr. Venkat R. Bhethanabotla, Professor and Department Chair, 813-974-3997, E-mail: bhethana@usf.edu. *Application contact:* Dr. Robert Frisina, Jr., Professor and Graduate Program Director, 813-974-4013, Fax: 813-974-3651, E-mail: rfrisina@usf.edu.
Website: http://che.eng.usf.edu/

University of South Florida, Innovative Education, Tampa, FL 33620-9951. Offers adult, career and higher education (Graduate Certificate), including college teaching, leadership in developing human resources, leadership in higher education; Africana studies (Graduate Certificate), including diasporas and health disparities, genocide and human rights; aging studies (Graduate Certificate), including gerontology; art research (Graduate Certificate), including museum studies; business foundations (Graduate Certificate); chemical and biomedical engineering (Graduate Certificate), including materials science and engineering, water, health and sustainability; child and family studies (Graduate Certificate), including positive behavior support; civil and industrial engineering (Graduate Certificate), including transportation systems analysis; community and family health (Graduate Certificate), including maternal and child health, social marketing and public health, violence and injury: prevention and intervention, women's health; criminology (Graduate Certificate), including criminal justice administration; data science for public administration (Graduate Certificate); digital humanities (Graduate Certificate); educational measurement and research (Graduate Certificate), including evaluation; English (Graduate Certificate), including comparative literary studies, creative writing, professional and technical communication; entrepreneurship (Graduate Certificate); environmental health (Graduate Certificate), including safety management; epidemiology and biostatistics (Graduate Certificate), including applied biostatistics, biostatistics, concepts and tools of epidemiology, epidemiology, epidemiology of infectious diseases; geography, environment and planning (Graduate Certificate), including community development, environmental policy and management, geographical information systems; geology (Graduate Certificate), including hydrogeology; global health (Graduate Certificate), including disaster management, global health and Latin American and Caribbean studies, global health practice, humanitarian assistance, infection control; government and international affairs (Graduate Certificate), including Cuban studies, globalization studies; health policy and management (Graduate Certificate), including health management and leadership, public health policy and programs; hearing specialist: early intervention (Graduate Certificate); industrial and management systems engineering (Graduate Certificate), including systems engineering, technology management; information studies (Graduate Certificate), including school library media specialist; information systems/decision sciences (Graduate Certificate), including analytics and business intelligence; instructional technology (Graduate Certificate), including distance education, Florida digital/virtual educator, instructional design, multimedia design, Web design; internal medicine, bioethics and medical humanities (Graduate Certificate), including biomedical ethics; Latin American and Caribbean studies (Graduate Certificate); leadership for coastal resiliency planning (Graduate Certificate); mass communications (Graduate Certificate), including multimedia journalism; mathematics and statistics (Graduate Certificate), including mathematics; medicine (Graduate Certificate), including aging and neuroscience, bioinformatics, biotechnology, brain fitness and memory management, clinical investigation, hand and upper limb rehabilitation, health informatics, health sciences, integrative weight management, intellectual property, medicine and gender, metabolic and nutritional medicine, metabolic cardiology, pharmacy sciences; national and competitive intelligence (Graduate Certificate); nursing (Graduate Certificate), including simulation based academic fellowship in advanced pain management; psychological and social foundations (Graduate Certificate), including career counseling, college teaching, diversity in education, mental health counseling, school counseling; public affairs (Graduate Certificate), including nonprofit management, public management, research administration; public health (Graduate Certificate), including assessing chemical toxicity and public health risks, health equity, pharmacoepidemiology, public health generalist, toxicology, translational research in adolescent behavioral health; public health practices (Graduate Certificate), including planning for healthy communities; rehabilitation and mental health counseling (Graduate Certificate), including integrative mental health care, marriage and family therapy, rehabilitation technology; secondary education (Graduate Certificate), including ESOL, foreign language education: culture and content, foreign language education: professional; social work (Graduate Certificate), including geriatric social work/clinical gerontology; special education (Graduate Certificate), including autism spectrum disorder, disabilities education: severe/profound; world languages (Graduate Certificate), including teaching English as a second language (TESL) or foreign language. *Unit head:* Dr. Cynthia DeLuca, Associate Vice President and Assistant Vice Provost, 813-974-3077, Fax: 813-974-7061, E-mail: deluca@usf.edu. *Application contact:* Owen Hooper, Director, Summer and Alternative Calendar Programs, 813-974-6917, E-mail: hooper@usf.edu.
Website: http://www.usf.edu/innovative-education/

University of South Florida, USF Health Taneja College of Pharmacy, Tampa, FL 33612. Offers pharmaceutical nanotechnology (MS), including biomedical engineering, drug discovery, delivery, development and manufacturing; pharmacy (Pharm D), including pharmacy and health education. *Accreditation:* ACPE. *Program availability:* Part-time, 100% online, blended/hybrid learning. *Faculty:* 32 full-time (18 women), 1 part-time/adjunct (0 women). *Students:* 398 full-time (234 women), 7 part-time (3 women); includes 180 minority (33 Black or African American, non-Hispanic/Latino; 72 Asian, non-Hispanic/Latino; 59 Hispanic/Latino; 2 Native Hawaiian or other Pacific Islander, non-Hispanic/Latino; 14 Two or more races, non-Hispanic/Latino), 13 international. Average age 25. 465 applicants, 44% accepted, 112 enrolled. In 2019, 11 master's, 91 doctorates awarded. *Degree requirements:* For master's, comprehensive exam, thesis optional, capstone or thesis; for doctorate, internship/field experience. *Entrance requirements:* For master's, GRE, MCAT or DAT, bachelor's preferably in biomedical, biological, chemical sciences or engineering; 2 letters of recommendation; resume; professional statement; interview; for doctorate, PCAT, minimum GPA of 2.75 overall (preferred); completion of 72 prerequisite credit hours; U.S. citizenship or permanent resident; interviews; criminal background check and drug screen. Additional exam requirements/recommendations for international students: required—TOEFL (minimum score 550 paper-based; 79 iBT), IELTS (minimum score 6.5). *Application deadline:* For fall admission, 6/1 for domestic and international students; for spring admission, 10/15 for domestic students, 9/15 for international students; for summer admission, 2/15 for domestic and international students. Applications are processed on a rolling basis. Application fee: $30. Electronic applications accepted. *Financial support:* In 2019–20, 159 students received support. Scholarships/grants available. *Unit head:* James Lambert, 813-974-4562, E-mail: jlambert2@usf.edu. *Application contact:* Dr. Amy Schwartz, Admissions Recruiter, 813-974-4652, E-mail: jlambert2@usf.edu.
Website: https://health.usf.edu/pharmacy

The University of Tennessee, Graduate School, Tickle College of Engineering, Department of Mechanical, Aerospace and Biomedical Engineering, Program in Biomedical Engineering, Knoxville, TN 37996-2210. Offers MS, PhD, MS/PhD. *Program availability:* Part-time, online learning. *Faculty:* 9 full-time (2 women), 1 part-time/adjunct (0 women). *Students:* 24 full-time (6 women), 2 part-time (0 women); includes 3 minority (1 Black or African American, non-Hispanic/Latino; 2 Asian, non-Hispanic/Latino), 3 international. Average age 26. 24 applicants, 38% accepted, 4 enrolled. In 2019, 4 master's, 4 doctorates awarded. *Degree requirements:* For master's, thesis or alternative; for doctorate, comprehensive exam, thesis/dissertation. *Entrance requirements:* For master's, GRE General Test (for MS students pursuing research thesis), minimum GPA of 2.7 (for U.S. degree holders), 3.0 (for international degree holders); 3 references; statement of purpose; for doctorate, GRE General Test, minimum GPA of 3.0 on previous graduate course work; 3 references; statement of purpose. Additional exam requirements/recommendations for international students: required—TOEFL (minimum score 550 paper-based; 80 iBT), IELTS (minimum score 6.5). *Application deadline:* For fall admission, 2/1 priority date for domestic and international students; for spring admission, 6/15 for domestic and international students; for summer admission, 10/15 for domestic and international students. Applications are processed on a rolling basis. Application fee: $60. Electronic applications accepted. *Financial support:* In 2019–20, 20 students received support, including 1 fellowship with full tuition reimbursement available (averaging $28,704 per year), 12 research assistantships with full tuition reimbursements available (averaging $22,500 per year), 7 teaching assistantships with full tuition reimbursements available (averaging $24,500 per year); career-related internships or fieldwork, Federal Work-Study, institutionally sponsored loans, health care benefits, and unspecified assistantships also available. Financial award application deadline: 2/1; financial award applicants required to submit FAFSA. *Unit head:* Dr. Matthew Mench, Head, 865-974-5115, Fax: 865-974-5274, E-mail: mmench@utk.edu. *Application contact:* Dr. Kivanc Ekici, Professor/Graduate Program Director, 865-974-6016, Fax: 865-974-5274, E-mail: ekici@utk.edu.
Website: http://www.engr.utk.edu/mabe

The University of Tennessee Health Science Center, College of Graduate Health Sciences, Memphis, TN 38163. Offers biomedical engineering (MS, PhD); biomedical sciences (PhD); dental sciences (MDS); epidemiology (MS); health outcomes and policy research (PhD); laboratory research and management (MS); nursing science (PhD); pharmaceutical sciences (PhD); pharmacology (MS); speech and hearing science (PhD); DDS/PhD; DNP/PhD; MD/PhD; Pharm D/PhD. Terminal master's awarded for partial completion of doctoral program. *Degree requirements:* For master's, comprehensive exam, thesis; for doctorate, thesis/dissertation, oral and written preliminary and comprehensive exams. *Entrance requirements:* For master's and doctorate, GRE General Test, minimum GPA of 3.0. Additional exam requirements/recommendations for international students: recommended—TOEFL (minimum score 79 iBT), IELTS (minimum score 6.5). Electronic applications accepted. *Expenses:* Contact institution.

The University of Texas at Austin, Graduate School, Cockrell School of Engineering, Department of Biomedical Engineering, Austin, TX 78712-1111. Offers MS, PhD, MD/PhD. *Program availability:* Part-time. *Degree requirements:* For master's, thesis optional; for doctorate, comprehensive exam, thesis/dissertation. *Entrance requirements:* For master's and doctorate, GRE General Test. Additional exam requirements/recommendations for international students: required—TOEFL (minimum score 550 paper-based). Electronic applications accepted.

The University of Texas at Dallas, Erik Jonsson School of Engineering and Computer Science, Department of Bioengineering, Richardson, TX 75080. Offers biomedical engineering (MS, PhD). *Faculty:* 15 full-time (3 women), 6 part-time/adjunct (1 woman). *Students:* 119 full-time (71 women), 17 part-time (7 women); includes 32 minority (2 Black or African American, non-Hispanic/Latino; 13 Asian, non-Hispanic/Latino; 15 Hispanic/Latino; 2 Two or more races, non-Hispanic/Latino), 64 international. Average age 28. 184 applicants, 39% accepted, 45 enrolled. In 2019, 30 master's, 8 doctorates awarded. *Degree requirements:* For master's, thesis (for some programs); for doctorate, comprehensive exam, thesis/dissertation. *Entrance requirements:* For master's, GRE (minimum scores of 500 in verbal, 700 in quantitative and 4 in analytical writing), minimum GPA of 3.0 in upper-division quantitative course work; for doctorate, GRE (minimum scores of 500 in verbal, 700 in quantitative and 4 in analytical writing), minimum GPA of 3.5 in upper-division quantitative course work. Additional exam requirements/recommendations for international students: required—TOEFL (minimum score 550 paper-based). *Application deadline:* For fall admission, 7/15 for domestic students, 5/1 priority date for international students; for spring admission, 11/15 for domestic students, 9/1 priority date for international students. Applications are processed on a rolling basis. Application fee: $50 ($100 for international students). Electronic applications accepted. *Expenses: Tuition, area resident:* Full-time $16,504. Tuition, state resident: full-time $16,504. Tuition, nonresident: full-time $34,266. Tuition and fees vary according to course load. *Financial support:* In 2019–20, 90 students received support, including 12 fellowships (averaging $5,458 per year), 65 research assistantships with partial tuition reimbursements available (averaging $26,009 per year), 23 teaching assistantships with partial tuition reimbursements available (averaging $17,393 per year); career-related internships or fieldwork, Federal Work-Study, institutionally sponsored loans, scholarships/grants, and unspecified assistantships also available. Support available to part-time students. Financial award application deadline: 4/30; financial award applicants required to submit FAFSA. *Unit head:* Dr. Shalini Prasad, Department Head, 972-883-4247, E-mail: shalini.prasad@

utdallas.edu. *Application contact:* Dr. Stuart Cogan, Associate Head for Graduate Studies, 972-883-4639, E-mail: sxc149830@utdallas.edu.
Website: http://be.utdallas.edu/

The University of Texas at San Antonio, College of Engineering, Department of Biomedical Engineering, San Antonio, TX 78249. Offers MS, PhD. *Program availability:* Part-time. Terminal master's awarded for partial completion of doctoral program. *Degree requirements:* For master's, comprehensive exam, thesis; for doctorate, comprehensive exam, thesis/dissertation. *Entrance requirements:* For master's, GRE, three letters of recommendation, statement of purpose, BS in any of the science or engineering disciplines; for doctorate, GRE, resume, three letters of recommendation, statement of purpose, BS in any of the science or engineering disciplines. Additional exam requirements/recommendations for international students: required—TOEFL (minimum score 550 paper-based; 79 iBT), IELTS (minimum score 6.5). Electronic applications accepted. *Expenses:* Contact institution.

The University of Texas Health Science Center at San Antonio, Graduate School of Biomedical Sciences, Biomedical Engineering Program, San Antonio, TX 78229-3900. Offers MS, PhD. *Program availability:* Part-time. Terminal master's awarded for partial completion of doctoral program. *Degree requirements:* For master's, comprehensive exam, thesis; for doctorate, comprehensive exam, thesis/dissertation.

The University of Texas Southwestern Medical Center, Southwestern Graduate School of Biomedical Sciences, Division of Basic Science, Biomedical Engineering Program, Dallas, TX 75390. Offers MS, PhD. *Degree requirements:* For master's, comprehensive exam or thesis; for doctorate, comprehensive exam, thesis/dissertation. *Entrance requirements:* For master's, GRE General Test, minimum GPA of 3.0; for doctorate, GRE General Test, minimum GPA of 3.4. Additional exam requirements/ recommendations for international students: required—TOEFL. Electronic applications accepted.

The University of Toledo, College of Graduate Studies, College of Engineering and College of Medicine and Life Sciences, PhD Program in Biomedical Engineering, Toledo, OH 43606-3390. Offers PhD. *Degree requirements:* For doctorate, thesis/ dissertation, qualifying exam. *Entrance requirements:* For doctorate, GRE General Test, minimum GPA of 3.3. Additional exam requirements/recommendations for international students: required—TOEFL (minimum score 550 paper-based; 80 iBT). Electronic applications accepted.

University of Toronto, School of Graduate Studies, Faculty of Applied Science and Engineering, Institute of Biomaterials and Biomedical Engineering, Toronto, ON M5S 1A1, Canada. Offers biomedical engineering (MA Sc, PhD); clinical engineering (MH Sc, PhD). *Program availability:* Part-time. *Degree requirements:* For master's, thesis (for some programs), research project (MH Sc), oral presentation (MA Sc); for doctorate, thesis/dissertation, qualifying exam. *Entrance requirements:* For master's, minimum A-average; bachelor's degree or equivalent in engineering, physical or biological science (for MA Sc), applied science or engineering (for MH Sc); for doctorate, master's degree in engineering, engineering science, medicine, dentistry, or a physical or biological science. Additional exam requirements/recommendations for international students: required—TOEFL (minimum score 600 paper-based), TWE (minimum score 4), IELTS, Michigan English Language Assessment Battery, or COPE. Electronic applications accepted.

University of Vermont, Graduate College, College of Engineering and Mathematical Sciences, Program in Biomedical Engineering, Burlington, VT 05405. Offers MS. *Entrance requirements:* For master's, GRE. Additional exam requirements/ recommendations for international students: required—TOEFL (minimum iBT score of 90) or IELTS (6.5). Electronic applications accepted.

University of Virginia, School of Engineering and Applied Science, Department of Biomedical Engineering, Charlottesville, VA 22903. Offers ME, MS, PhD. *Degree requirements:* For master's, project or thesis; for doctorate, thesis/dissertation. *Entrance requirements:* For master's, GRE General Test, 3 letters of recommendation; for doctorate, GRE General Test, 3 letters of recommendation, essay. Additional exam requirements/recommendations for international students: required—TOEFL (minimum score 600 paper-based; 90 iBT), IELTS (minimum score 7). Electronic applications accepted.

University of Wisconsin–Madison, Graduate School, College of Engineering, Department of Biomedical Engineering, Madison, WI 53706. Offers MS, PhD. *Program availability:* Part-time. Terminal master's awarded for partial completion of doctoral program. *Degree requirements:* For master's, thesis optional, at least 30 credits of coursework; for doctorate, comprehensive exam, thesis/dissertation, 60 credits total, 30 additional credits of coursework beyond MS. *Entrance requirements:* For master's and doctorate, GRE, bachelor degree in engineering (biomedical, chemical, electrical, industrial, mechanical, etc.) or science (biology, biochemistry, chemistry, genetics, immunology, physics, etc.). Additional exam requirements/recommendations for international students: required—TOEFL (minimum score 625 paper-based; 92 iBT). Electronic applications accepted.

University of Wisconsin–Milwaukee, Graduate School, College of Engineering and Applied Science, Program in Engineering, Milwaukee, WI 53201-0413. Offers biomedical engineering (MS); civil engineering (MS, PhD); computer science (PhD); electrical and computer engineering (MS); electrical engineering (PhD); engineering mechanics (MS); industrial and management engineering (MS); industrial engineering (PhD); manufacturing engineering (MS); materials (PhD); materials engineering (MS); mechanical engineering (MS). *Program availability:* Part-time. *Degree requirements:* For master's, comprehensive exam (for some programs), thesis or alternative; for doctorate, comprehensive exam, thesis/dissertation, internship. *Entrance requirements:* For master's, GRE, minimum GPA of 2.75; for doctorate, GRE, minimum GPA of 3.5. Additional exam requirements/recommendations for international students: required—TOEFL (minimum score 550 paper-based; 79 iBT), IELTS (minimum score 6.5).

Vanderbilt University, School of Engineering, Department of Biomedical Engineering, Nashville, TN 37240-1001. Offers M Eng, MS, PhD, MD/PhD. *Degree requirements:* For master's, thesis (for some programs); for doctorate, thesis/dissertation. *Entrance requirements:* For master's, GRE General Test (for all except M Eng); for doctorate, GRE General Test. Additional exam requirements/recommendations for international students: required—TOEFL. Electronic applications accepted. *Expenses: Tuition:* Full-time $51,018; part-time $2087 per hour. *Required fees:* $542. Tuition and fees vary according to program.

Virginia Commonwealth University, Graduate School, School of Engineering, Department of Biomedical Engineering, Richmond, VA 23284-9005. Offers MS, PhD. *Degree requirements:* For master's, thesis; for doctorate, thesis/dissertation, comprehensive oral and written exams. *Entrance requirements:* For master's and doctorate, GRE General Test. Additional exam requirements/recommendations for international students: required—TOEFL (minimum score 600 paper-based; 100 iBT). Electronic applications accepted.

Virginia Polytechnic Institute and State University, Graduate School, College of Engineering, Blacksburg, VA 24061. Offers aerospace engineering (PhD, M Eng/MS); biological systems engineering (PhD); biomedical engineering (MS, PhD); chemical engineering (PhD); civil engineering (PhD); computer engineering (PhD); computer science and applications (MS); electrical engineering (PhD); engineering education (PhD); M Eng/MS. *Faculty:* 447 full-time (90 women), 6 part-time/adjunct (2 women). *Students:* 1,881 full-time (495 women), 326 part-time (70 women); includes 264 minority (51 Black or African American, non-Hispanic/Latino; 2 American Indian or Alaska Native, non-Hispanic/Latino; 96 Asian, non-Hispanic/Latino; 69 Hispanic/Latino; 46 Two or more races, non-Hispanic/Latino), 1,247 international. Average age 27. 4,014 applicants, 44% accepted, 658 enrolled. In 2019, 489 master's, 200 doctorates awarded. *Degree requirements:* For master's, comprehensive exam (for some programs), thesis (for some programs); for doctorate, comprehensive exam (for some programs), thesis/dissertation (for some programs). *Entrance requirements:* For master's and doctorate, GRE/GMAT. Additional exam requirements/recommendations for international students: required—TOEFL (minimum score 90 iBT). *Application deadline:* For fall admission, 8/1 for domestic students, 4/1 for international students; for spring admission, 1/1 for domestic students, 9/1 for international students. Applications are processed on a rolling basis. Application fee: $75. Electronic applications accepted. *Expenses:* Tuition, state resident: full-time $13,700; part-time $761.25 per credit hour. Tuition, nonresident: full-time $27,614; part-time $1534 per credit hour. *Required fees:* $886.50 per term. Tuition and fees vary according to campus/location and program. *Financial support:* In 2019–20, 47 fellowships with full tuition reimbursements (averaging $19,703 per year), 1,163 research assistantships with full tuition reimbursements (averaging $20,602 per year), 554 teaching assistantships with full tuition reimbursements (averaging $16,333 per year) were awarded; scholarships/grants and unspecified assistantships also available. Financial award application deadline: 3/1; financial award applicants required to submit FAFSA. *Unit head:* Dr. Julia Ross, Dean, 540-231-9752, Fax: 540-231-3031, E-mail: rjulie@vt.edu. *Application contact:* Linda Perkins, Executive Assistant, 540-231-9752, Fax: 540-231-3031, E-mail: lperkins@vt.edu.
Website: http://www.eng.vt.edu/

Wake Forest University, Virginia Tech-Wake Forest University School of Biomedical Engineering and Sciences, Winston-Salem, NC 27109. Offers biomedical engineering (MS, PhD); DVM/PhD; MD/PhD. Terminal master's awarded for partial completion of doctoral program. *Degree requirements:* For master's, comprehensive exam, thesis; for doctorate, comprehensive exam, thesis/dissertation. *Entrance requirements:* For master's and doctorate, GRE, 3 letters of recommendation. Additional exam requirements/recommendations for international students: required—TOEFL (minimum score 603 paper-based). Electronic applications accepted.

Washington University in St. Louis, School of Engineering and Applied Science, Department of Biomedical Engineering, St. Louis, MO 63130-4899. Offers MS, D Sc, PhD. Terminal master's awarded for partial completion of doctoral program. *Degree requirements:* For master's, thesis optional; for doctorate, thesis/dissertation. *Entrance requirements:* For master's, GRE, minimum GPA of 3.0; for doctorate, GRE General Test, minimum GPA of 3.5. Additional exam requirements/recommendations for international students: required—TOEFL. Electronic applications accepted.

Wayne State University, College of Engineering, Department of Biomedical Engineering, Detroit, MI 48202. Offers biomedical engineering (MS, PhD), including biomedical imaging (PhD); injury biomechanics (Graduate Certificate). *Faculty:* 17. *Students:* 58 full-time (32 women), 37 part-time (17 women); includes 17 minority (6 Black or African American, non-Hispanic/Latino; 9 Asian, non-Hispanic/Latino; 2 Hispanic/Latino), 31 international. Average age 28. 88 applicants, 33% accepted, 18 enrolled. In 2019, 38 master's, 3 doctorates awarded. Terminal master's awarded for partial completion of doctoral program. *Degree requirements:* For master's, thesis optional; for doctorate, comprehensive exam, thesis/dissertation. *Entrance requirements:* For master's, GRE (recommended), bachelor's degree, minimum undergraduate GPA of 3.0, one-page statement of purpose, completion of prerequisite coursework in calculus and engineering physics; for doctorate, GRE, bachelor's degree in biomedical engineering with minimum undergraduate GPA of 3.5, or master's degree in biomedical engineering with minimum GPA of 3.3; personal statement; three letters of recommendation; for Graduate Certificate, minimum undergraduate GPA of 3.0, bachelor's degree in engineering or in a mathematics-based science program. Additional exam requirements/recommendations for international students: required—TOEFL (minimum score 550 paper-based; 79 iBT), TWE; recommended—IELTS (minimum score 6.5). *Application deadline:* For fall admission, 6/1 priority date for domestic students, 5/1 priority date for international students; for winter admission, 10/1 priority date for domestic students, 9/1 priority date for international students; for spring admission, 2/1 priority date for domestic students, 1/1 priority date for international students. Applications are processed on a rolling basis. Application fee: $50. Electronic applications accepted. *Expenses:* $790 per credit hour in-state tuition, $1579 per credit hour out-of-state tuition. Courses are 1-4 credits, majority 3 credits. Total 32-34 credits for MS program; 90 credits for PhD program. *Financial support:* In 2019–20, 38 students received support, including 4 fellowships with tuition reimbursements available (averaging $21,875 per year), 2 research assistantships with tuition reimbursements available (averaging $24,950 per year), 8 teaching assistantships with tuition reimbursements available (averaging $20,792 per year); Federal Work-Study, scholarships/grants, health care benefits, and unspecified assistantships also available. Support available to part-time students. Financial award applicants required to submit FAFSA. *Unit head:* Dr. Cynthia Bir, Department Chair, 313-577-7821, E-mail: cbir@wayne.edu. *Application contact:* Rob Carlson, Graduate Program Coordinator, 313-577-0409, Fax: 313-577-9615, E-mail: rcarlson@wayne.edu.
Website: http://engineering.wayne.edu/bme/

Wichita State University, Graduate School, College of Engineering, Department of Biomedical Engineering, Wichita, KS 67260. Offers MS. *Entrance requirements:* For master's, GRE, bachelor's degree, transcript, minimum undergraduate GPA of 3.0, statement of purpose, three letters of recommendation. Additional exam requirements/ recommendations for international students: required—TOEFL.

Widener University, Graduate Programs in Engineering, Program in Biomedical Engineering, Chester, PA 19013. Offers M Eng. *Entrance requirements:* For master's, BS in engineering. Electronic applications accepted. *Expenses: Tuition:* Full-time $48,750; part-time $917 per credit hour. Tuition and fees vary according to class time, degree level, campus/location and program.

Worcester Polytechnic Institute, Graduate Admissions, Department of Biomedical Engineering, Worcester, MA 01609-2280. Offers M Eng, MS, PhD, Graduate Certificate. *Program availability:* Part-time, evening/weekend. Terminal master's awarded for partial completion of doctoral program. *Degree requirements:* For master's, thesis optional; for doctorate, comprehensive exam, thesis/dissertation. *Entrance requirements:* For master's and doctorate, GRE General Test, 3 letters of recommendation, statement of purpose. Additional exam requirements/recommendations for international students: required—TOEFL (minimum score 563 paper-based; 84 iBT), IELTS (minimum score 7). Electronic applications accepted.

Wright State University, Graduate School, College of Engineering and Computer Science, Department of Biomedical, Industrial and Human Factors Engineering, Dayton, OH 45435. Offers biomedical engineering (MS); industrial and human factors engineering (MS). *Program availability:* Part-time. *Degree requirements:* For master's, thesis or course option alternative. *Entrance requirements:* Additional exam requirements/recommendations for international students: required—TOEFL.

Yale University, Graduate School of Arts and Sciences, School of Engineering and Applied Science, Department of Biomedical Engineering, New Haven, CT 06520. Offers MS, PhD.

Biotechnology

Adelphi University, College of Arts and Sciences, Department of Biology, Garden City, NY 11530-0701. Offers biology (MS); biotechnology (MS). *Program availability:* Part-time, evening/weekend. *Degree requirements:* For master's, thesis or alternative. *Entrance requirements:* For master's, bachelor's degree in biology or allied sciences, essay, 3 letters of recommendation, official transcripts. Additional exam requirements/recommendations for international students: required—TOEFL (minimum score 550 paper-based; 80 iBT), IELTS (minimum score 6.5). Electronic applications accepted. *Expenses:* Contact institution.

American University, College of Arts and Sciences, Department of Biology, Washington, DC 20016-8007. Offers biology (MS); biotechnology (MA). *Program availability:* Part-time. *Degree requirements:* For master's, comprehensive exam, thesis (for some programs). *Entrance requirements:* For master's, GRE General Test, GRE Subject Test, statement of purpose, transcripts, 2 letters of recommendation, resume. Additional exam requirements/recommendations for international students: required—TOEFL. Electronic applications accepted. *Expenses:* Contact institution.

The American University in Cairo, School of Sciences and Engineering, Cairo, Egypt. Offers biotechnology (MS); chemistry (MS); computer science (MS); computing (M Comp); construction engineering (M Eng, MS); electronics and communications engineering (M Eng); environmental engineering (MS); environmental system design (M Eng); mechanical engineering (M Eng, MS); nanotechnology (MS); physics (MS); robotics, control and smart systems (MS); sciences and engineering (PhD); sustainable development (MS, Graduate Diploma). *Program availability:* Part-time, evening/weekend. *Degree requirements:* For master's, comprehensive exam (for some programs), thesis (for some programs); for doctorate, comprehensive exam (for some programs), thesis/dissertation. *Entrance requirements:* Additional exam requirements/recommendations for international students: required—TOEFL (minimum score 450 paper-based; 45 iBT), IELTS (minimum score 5). Electronic applications accepted.

Arizona State University at Tempe, Sandra Day O'Connor College of Law, Phoenix, AZ 85287-7906. Offers biotechnology and genomics (LL M); law (JD); legal studies (MLS); patent practice (MLS); sports law and business (MSLB); tribal policy, law and government (LL M); JD/MBA; JD/MD; JD/MSW; JD/PhD. *Accreditation:* ABA. *Faculty:* 67 full-time (27 women), 138 part-time/adjunct (37 women). *Students:* 811 full-time (396 women); includes 197 minority (16 Black or African American, non-Hispanic/Latino; 19 American Indian or Alaska Native, non-Hispanic/Latino; 35 Asian, non-Hispanic/Latino; 87 Hispanic/Latino; 2 Native Hawaiian or other Pacific Islander, non-Hispanic/Latino; 38 Two or more races, non-Hispanic/Latino), 22 international. 3,710 applicants, 29% accepted, 272 enrolled. In 2019, 282 doctorates awarded. *Degree requirements:* For doctorate, See www.law.asu.edu for Juris Doctor degree requirements. *Entrance requirements:* For doctorate, LSAT, bachelor's degree. Additional exam requirements/recommendations for international students: required—TOEFL (minimum score 550 paper-based; 80 iBT). *Application deadline:* For fall admission, 3/1 priority date for domestic and international students. Applications are processed on a rolling basis. Application fee: $0. Electronic applications accepted. *Expenses:* Contact institution. *Financial support:* In 2019–20, 648 students received support. Institutionally sponsored loans and scholarships/grants available. Financial award application deadline: 3/15; financial award applicants required to submit FAFSA. *Unit head:* Douglas Sylvester, Dean/Professor, 480-965-6188, Fax: 480-965-6521, E-mail: douglas.sylvester@asu.edu. *Application contact:* Chitra Damania, Director, 480-965-1474, Fax: 480-727-7930, E-mail: law.admissions@asu.edu.
Website: http://www.law.asu.edu/

Arkansas State University, Graduate School, College of Sciences and Mathematics, Department of Biological Sciences, State University, AR 72467. Offers biological sciences (MA); biology (MS); biology education (MSE, SCCT); biotechnology (PSM). *Program availability:* Part-time. *Degree requirements:* For master's, comprehensive exam, thesis (for some programs); for SCCT, comprehensive exam. *Entrance requirements:* For master's, GRE General Test, appropriate bachelor's degree, letters of reference, interview, official transcripts, immunization records, statement of educational objectives and career goals, teaching certificate (for MSE); for SCCT, GRE General Test or MAT, interview, master's degree, letters of reference, official transcript, personal statement, immunization records. Additional exam requirements/recommendations for international students: required—TOEFL (minimum score 550 paper-based; 79 iBT), IELTS (minimum score 6), PTE (minimum score 56). Electronic applications accepted.

Azusa Pacific University, College of Liberal Arts and Sciences, Program in Biotechnology, Azusa, CA 91702-7000. Offers MS.

Brandeis University, Graduate School of Arts and Sciences, Department of Biotechnology, Waltham, MA 02454-9110. Offers PSM, MS/MBA. *Program availability:* Part-time. *Faculty:* 14 full-time (10 women), 2 part-time/adjunct (0 women). *Students:* 20 full-time (12 women); includes 4 minority (1 Asian, non-Hispanic/Latino; 2 Hispanic/Latino; 1 Two or more races, non-Hispanic/Latino), 13 international. Average age 23. 63 applicants, 83% accepted, 10 enrolled. In 2019, 7 master's awarded. *Degree requirements:* For master's, poster presentation; summer internship. *Entrance requirements:* For master's, General GRE, Transcripts, letters of recommendation, resume, and statement of purpose. Additional exam requirements/recommendations for international students: required—TOEFL, IELTS, PTE. *Application deadline:* For fall admission, 1/15 priority date for domestic and international students. Applications are processed on a rolling basis. Application fee: $75. Electronic applications accepted. *Financial support:* Fellowships, scholarships/grants, health care benefits, and tuition waivers available. *Unit head:* Dr. Neil Simister, Director of Graduate Studies, 781-736-2520, E-mail: simister@brandeis.edu. *Application contact:* Maryanna Aldrich, Administrator, 781-736-2352, E-mail: scigradoffice@brandeis.edu.
Website: http://www.brandeis.edu/gsas/programs/biotech.html

Brigham Young University, Graduate Studies, College of Life Sciences, Department of Plant and Wildlife Sciences, Provo, UT 84602-1001. Offers environmental science (MS); genetics and biotechnology (MS); wildlife and wildlands conservation (MS, PhD). *Faculty:* 23 full-time (1 woman). *Students:* 44 full-time (17 women), 13 part-time (4 women); includes 6 minority (1 American Indian or Alaska Native, non-Hispanic/Latino; 5 Hispanic/Latino). Average age 29. 34 applicants, 74% accepted, 22 enrolled. In 2019, 15 master's, 2 doctorates awarded. *Degree requirements:* For master's, thesis, no C grades or below, 30 hours (24 coursework, 6 thesis); for doctorate, comprehensive exam, thesis/dissertation, no C grades or below, 54 hours (18 dissertation, 36 coursework). *Entrance requirements:* For master's, GRE General Test, minimum GPA of 3.2; for doctorate, GRE, minimum GPA of 3.2. Additional exam requirements/recommendations for international students: required—TOEFL (minimum score 580 paper-based; 85 iBT). *Application deadline:* 2/1 for domestic and international students; for summer admission, 2/1 for domestic and international students. Application fee: $50. Electronic applications accepted. *Financial support:* In 2019–20, 57 students received support, including 83 research assistantships with partial tuition reimbursements available (averaging $17,441 per year), 48 teaching assistantships with partial tuition reimbursements available (averaging $16,253 per year); career-related internships or fieldwork and scholarships/grants also available. Financial award application deadline: 3/1. *Unit head:* Neil Hansen, Chair, 801-422-2491, E-mail: neil_hansen@byu.edu. *Application contact:* Bradley D. Geary, Graduate Coordinator, 801-422-1228, Fax: 801-422-0008, E-mail: bradley_geary@byu.edu.
Website: http://pws.byu.edu

Brock University, Faculty of Graduate Studies, Faculty of Mathematics and Science, Program in Biotechnology, St. Catharines, ON L2S 3A1, Canada. Offers M Sc, PhD. *Program availability:* Part-time. *Degree requirements:* For master's, thesis; for doctorate, thesis/dissertation. *Entrance requirements:* For master's, honors B Sc; for doctorate, M Sc. Additional exam requirements/recommendations for international students: required—TOEFL (minimum score 550 paper-based; 80 iBT), IELTS (minimum score 6.5), TWE (minimum score 4). Electronic applications accepted.

Brown University, Graduate School, Division of Biology and Medicine, Department of Molecular Pharmacology, Physiology and Biotechnology, Providence, RI 02912. Offers biomedical engineering (Sc M, PhD); biotechnology (PhD); molecular pharmacology and physiology (PhD); MD/PhD. *Degree requirements:* For doctorate, thesis/dissertation, preliminary exam. *Entrance requirements:* For master's and doctorate, GRE General Test, GRE Subject Test. Additional exam requirements/recommendations for international students: required—TOEFL. Electronic applications accepted.

California State University, Fullerton, Graduate Studies, College of Natural Science and Mathematics, Department of Biological Science, Fullerton, CA 92831-3599. Offers biology (MS); biotechnology (MBT). *Program availability:* Part-time. *Entrance requirements:* For master's, GRE General and Subject Tests, MCAT, or DAT, minimum GPA of 3.0 in biology.

California State University, San Marcos, Program in Biotechnology, San Marcos, CA 92096-0001. Offers PSM. *Expenses: Tuition, area resident:* Full-time $7176. Tuition, state resident: full-time $7176. Tuition, nonresident: full-time $18,640. *International tuition:* $18,640 full-time. *Required fees:* $1960.

Carnegie Mellon University, Heinz College, School of Public Policy and Management, Master of Science Program in Biotechnology and Management, Pittsburgh, PA 15213-3891. Offers MS. *Accreditation:* AACSB. *Entrance requirements:* For master's, GRE or GMAT, college-level course in advanced algebra/pre-calculus; college-level courses in economics and statistics (recommended). Additional exam requirements/recommendations for international students: required—TOEFL or IELTS.

The Catholic University of America, School of Arts and Sciences, Department of Biology, Washington, DC 20064. Offers biotechnology (MS); cell and microbial biology (MS, PhD), including cell biology; clinical laboratory science (MS, PhD); MSLS/MS. *Program availability:* Part-time. *Faculty:* 10 full-time (4 women), 3 part-time/adjunct (1 woman). *Students:* 16 full-time (13 women), 36 part-time (19 women); includes 11 minority (4 Black or African American, non-Hispanic/Latino; 3 Asian, non-Hispanic/Latino; 4 Two or more races, non-Hispanic/Latino), 33 international. Average age 31. 46 applicants, 65% accepted, 12 enrolled. In 2019, 15 master's, 8 doctorates awarded. Terminal master's awarded for partial completion of doctoral program. *Degree requirements:* For master's and doctorate, comprehensive exam. *Entrance requirements:* For master's and doctorate, GRE General Test, GRE Subject Test, statement of purpose, official copies of academic transcripts, three letters of recommendation. Additional exam requirements/recommendations for international students: required—TOEFL (minimum score 550 paper-based; 80 iBT). *Application deadline:* For fall admission, 7/15 priority date for domestic students, 7/1 for international students; for spring admission, 11/15 priority date for domestic students, 11/1 for international students. Applications are processed on a rolling basis. Application fee: $55. Electronic applications accepted. *Expenses:* Contact institution. *Financial support:* Fellowships, research assistantships, teaching assistantships, Federal Work-Study, scholarships/grants, tuition waivers (full and partial), and unspecified assistantships available. Financial award application deadline: 2/1; financial award applicants required to submit FAFSA. *Unit head:* Dr. Venigalla Rao, Chair, 202-319-5271, Fax: 202-319-5721, E-mail: rao@cua.edu. *Application contact:* Dr. Steven Brown, Director of Graduate Admissions, 202-319-5057, Fax: 202-319-6533, E-mail: cua-admissions@cua.edu.
Website: http://biology.cua.edu/

Claflin University, Graduate Programs, Orangeburg, SC 29115. Offers biotechnology (MS); business administration (MBA). *Program availability:* Part-time. *Degree requirements:* For master's, comprehensive exam, thesis. *Entrance requirements:* For master's, GRE, GMAT, baccalaureate degree, 3 letters of recommendation, resume, statement of purpose. Additional exam requirements/recommendations for international students: recommended—TOEFL (minimum score 550 paper-based).

Clarkson University, School of Arts and Sciences, Program in Interdisciplinary Bioscience and Biotechnology, Potsdam, NY 13699. Offers MS, PhD. *Students:* 14 full-time (10 women), 7 international. 42 applicants, 31% accepted, 6 enrolled. In 2019, 2 master's, 3 doctorates awarded. *Degree requirements:* For doctorate, comprehensive exam, thesis/dissertation. *Entrance requirements:* For doctorate, GRE. Additional exam requirements/recommendations for international students: required—TOEFL (minimum score 550 paper-based, 80 iBT) or IELTS (6.5). *Application deadline:* Applications are processed on a rolling basis. Application fee: $50. Electronic applications accepted. *Expenses: Tuition:* Full-time $24,984; part-time $1388. *Required fees:* $225. Tuition and fees vary according to campus/location and program. *Financial support:* Scholarships/grants and unspecified assistantships available. *Unit head:* Dr. Tom Langen, Interim Dean of Arts & Sciences / Professor of Biology, 315-268-2342, E-mail: tlangen@clarkson.edu. *Application contact:* Daniel Capogna, Director of Graduate Admissions & Recruitment, 518-631-9910, E-mail: graduate@clarkson.edu.
Website: https://www.clarkson.edu/academics/graduate

College of Staten Island of the City University of New York, Graduate Programs, Division of Science and Technology, Program in Biology, Staten Island, NY 10314-6600.

Offers biology (MS), including biotechnology, general biology. *Program availability:* Part-time, evening/weekend. *Faculty:* 10. *Students:* 37. 48 applicants, 46% accepted, 13 enrolled. In 2019, 17 master's awarded. *Degree requirements:* For master's, 30 credits (for general biology and biotechnology tracks). *Entrance requirements:* For master's, GRE (recommended), BS in Biology degree from an accredited college, overall GPA of 2.75 (B-), GPA of 3.0 (B) in undergraduate science and mathematics courses, 2 letters of recommendation. Additional exam requirements/recommendations for international students: required—TOEFL (minimum score 550 paper-based; 79 iBT), IELTS (minimum score 6.5). *Application deadline:* For fall admission, 7/1 for domestic students, 4/25 for international students; for spring admission, 11/25 for domestic and international students. Applications are processed on a rolling basis. Application fee: $75. Electronic applications accepted. *Expenses: Tuition, area resident:* Full-time $11,090; part-time $470 per credit. Tuition, state resident: full-time $11,090; part-time $470 per credit. Tuition, nonresident: full-time $20,520; part-time $855 per credit. *International tuition:* $20,520 full-time. *Required fees:* $559; $181 per semester. Tuition and fees vary according to program. *Unit head:* Dr. Jianying Gu, Biotechnology Coordinator, 718-982-4123, E-mail: jianying.gu@csi.cuny.edu. *Application contact:* Sasha Spence, Associate Director for Graduate Admissions, 718-982-2019, Fax: 718-982-2500, E-mail: sasha.spence@csi.cuny.edu.
Website: http://csicuny.smartcatalogiq.com/en/current/Graduate-Catalog/Graduate-Programs-Disciplines-and-Offerings-in-Selected-Disciplines/Biology-MS

Columbia University, Graduate School of Arts and Sciences, New York, NY 10027. Offers African-American studies (MA); American studies (MA); anthropology (MA, PhD); art history and archaeology (MA, PhD); astronomy (PhD); biological sciences (PhD); biotechnology (MA); chemical physics (PhD); chemistry (PhD); classical studies (MA, PhD); classics (MA, PhD); climate and society (MA); conservation biology (MA); earth and environmental sciences (PhD); East Asia: regional studies (MA); East Asian languages and cultures (MA, PhD); ecology, evolution and environmental biology (MA), including conservation biology; ecology, evolution, and environmental biology (PhD), including ecology and evolutionary biology, evolutionary primatology; economics (MA, PhD); English and comparative literature (MA, PhD); French and Romance philology (MA, PhD); Germanic languages (MA, PhD); global French studies (MA); global thought (MA); Hispanic cultural studies (MA); history (PhD); history and literature (MA); human rights studies (MA); Islamic studies (MA); Italian (MA, PhD); Japanese pedagogy (MA); Jewish studies (MA); Latin America and the Caribbean: regional studies (MA); Latin American and Iberian cultures (PhD); mathematics (MA, PhD), including finance (MA); medieval and Renaissance studies (MA); Middle Eastern, South Asian, and African studies (MA, PhD); modern art: critical and curatorial studies (MA); modern European studies (MA); museum anthropology (MA); music (DMA, PhD); oral history (MA); philosophical foundations of physics (MA); philosophy (MA, PhD); physics (PhD); political science (MA, PhD); psychology (PhD); quantitative methods in the social sciences (MA); religion (MA, PhD); Russia, Eurasia and East Europe: regional studies (MA); Russian translation (MA); Slavic cultures (MA); Slavic languages (MA, PhD); sociology (MA, PhD); South Asian studies (MA); statistics (MA, PhD); theatre (PhD). *Program availability:* Part-time. *Students:* 3,506 full-time (1,844 women), 208 part-time (121 women); includes 864 minority (110 Black or African American, non-Hispanic/Latino; 5 American Indian or Alaska Native, non-Hispanic/Latino; 416 Asian, non-Hispanic/Latino; 147 Hispanic/Latino; 6 Native Hawaiian or other Pacific Islander, non-Hispanic/Latino; 180 Two or more races, non-Hispanic/Latino), 2,065 international. 14,545 applicants, 25% accepted, 1,429 enrolled. In 2019, 1,262 master's, 363 doctorates awarded. Terminal master's awarded for partial completion of doctoral program. *Degree requirements:* For master's, variable foreign language requirement, comprehensive exam (for some programs), thesis (for some programs); for doctorate, variable foreign language requirement, comprehensive exam (for some programs), thesis/dissertation. *Entrance requirements:* For master's and doctorate, GRE General Test, GRE Subject Test (for some programs). Additional exam requirements/recommendations for international students: required—TOEFL (minimum score 600 paper-based; 100 iBT), IELTS (minimum score 7.5). Application fee: $115. Electronic applications accepted. *Expenses: Tuition:* Full-time $47,600; part-time $1880 per credit. One-time fee: $105. *Financial support:* Fellowships, research assistantships, teaching assistantships, career-related internships or fieldwork, Federal Work-Study, institutionally sponsored loans, scholarships/grants, traineeships, health care benefits, tuition waivers, and unspecified assistantships available. Support available to part-time students. Financial award application deadline: 12/15. *Unit head:* Dr. Carlos J. Alonso, Dean of the Graduate School of Arts and Sciences and Vice President for Graduate Education, 212-854-2861, E-mail: gsas-dean@columbia.edu. *Application contact:* GSAS Office of Admissions, 212-854-6729, E-mail: gsas-admissions@columbia.edu.
Website: http://gsas.columbia.edu/

Concordia University, School of Graduate Studies, Faculty of Arts and Science, Department of Biology, Montréal, QC H3G 1M8, Canada. Offers biology (M Sc, PhD); biotechnology and genomics (Diploma). *Degree requirements:* For master's, thesis; for doctorate, thesis/dissertation, pedagogical training. *Entrance requirements:* For master's, honors degree in biology; for doctorate, M Sc in life science.

Cornell University, Graduate School, Graduate Fields of Agriculture and Life Sciences and Graduate Fields of Engineering, Field of Biological and Environmental Engineering, Ithaca, NY 14853. Offers bioenergy and integrated energy systems (M Eng, MPS, MS, PhD); biological engineering (M Eng, MPS, MS, PhD); bioprocess engineering (M Eng, MPS, MS, PhD); ecohydrology (M Eng, MPS, MS, PhD); environmental engineering (M Eng, MPS, MS, PhD); environmental management (MPS); food engineering (M Eng, MPS, MS, PhD); industrial biotechnology (M Eng, MPS, MS, PhD); nanobiotechnology (M Eng, MPS, MS, PhD); sustainable systems (M Eng, MPS, MS, PhD); synthetic biology (MS); syntheticbiology (M Eng, MPS, PhD). Terminal master's awarded for partial completion of doctoral program. *Degree requirements:* For master's, thesis (MS); for doctorate, comprehensive exam, thesis/dissertation. *Entrance requirements:* For master's, letters of recommendation (3 for MS, 2 for M Eng and MPS); for doctorate, GRE General Test, 3 letters of recommendation. Additional exam requirements/recommendations for international students: required—TOEFL (minimum score 550 paper-based; 77 iBT). Electronic applications accepted.

Duquesne University, Bayer School of Natural and Environmental Sciences, Program in Biotechnology, Pittsburgh, PA 15282-0001. Offers MS. *Program availability:* Part-time, evening/weekend. *Entrance requirements:* For master's, GRE General Test, statement of purpose, 2 letters of recommendation, official transcripts. Additional exam requirements/recommendations for international students: required—TOEFL (minimum score 80 iBT), TOEFL (minimum score 80 iBT) or IELTS. Electronic applications accepted. *Expenses:* Contact institution.

East Carolina University, Graduate School, Thomas Harriot College of Arts and Sciences, Department of Biology, Greenville, NC 27858-4353. Offers biology (MS); molecular biology and biotechnology (MS). *Program availability:* Part-time. *Application deadline:* For fall admission, 6/1 priority date for domestic students, 3/1 priority date for international students; for spring admission, 10/15 priority date for domestic students. *Expenses: Tuition, area resident:* Full-time $4749; part-time $185 per credit hour. Tuition, state resident: full-time $4749; part-time $185 per credit hour. Tuition, nonresident: full-time $17,898; part-time $864 per credit hour. *International tuition:* $17,898 full-time. *Required fees:* $2787. *Financial support:* Application deadline: 3/1. *Unit head:* Dr. David Chalcraft, Chair, 252-328-2797, E-mail: chalcraftd@ecu.edu. *Application contact:* graduate School Admissions, 252-328-6012, Fax: 252-328-6071, E-mail: gradschool@ecu.edu.
Website: https://biology.ecu.edu/

Eastern Virginia Medical School, Biotechnology Program, Norfolk, VA 23501-1980. Offers MS. *Entrance requirements:* For master's, GRE. Additional exam requirements/recommendations for international students: required—TOEFL. Electronic applications accepted.

Florida Institute of Technology, College of Engineering and Science, Program in Biological Sciences, Melbourne, FL 32901-6975. Offers biological sciences (PhD); biotechnology (MS); ecology (MS). *Program availability:* Part-time. *Degree requirements:* For doctorate, comprehensive exam, thesis/dissertation, dissertations seminar, publications. *Entrance requirements:* For doctorate, GRE General Test, resume, 3 letters of recommendation, minimum GPA of 3.2, statement of objectives. Additional exam requirements/recommendations for international students: required—TOEFL (minimum score 550 paper-based; 79 iBT). Electronic applications accepted.

Florida Institute of Technology, College of Engineering and Science, Program in Biotechnology, Melbourne, FL 32901-6975. Offers MS. *Program availability:* Part-time. *Degree requirements:* For master's, comprehensive exam, thesis, internship. *Entrance requirements:* For master's, GRE General Test, 3 letters of recommendation, stated objectives. Additional exam requirements/recommendations for international students: required—TOEFL (minimum score 550 paper-based; 79 iBT). Electronic applications accepted.

The George Washington University, School of Medicine and Health Sciences, Health Sciences Programs, Washington, DC 20052. Offers clinical practice management (MSHS); clinical research administration (MSHS); emergency services management (MSHS); end-of-life care (MSHS); immunohematology (MSHS); immunohematology and biotechnology (MSHS); physical therapy (DPT); physician assistant (MSHS). *Program availability:* Online learning. *Entrance requirements:* Additional exam requirements/recommendations for international students: required—TOEFL (minimum score 550 paper-based). *Expenses:* Contact institution.

Harvard University, Extension School, Cambridge, MA 02138-3722. Offers applied sciences (CAS); biotechnology (ALM); educational technologies (ALM); educational technology (CET); English for graduate and professional studies (DGP); environmental management (ALM, CEM); information technology (ALM); journalism (ALM); liberal arts (ALM); management (ALM, CM); mathematics for teaching (ALM); museum studies (ALM); premedical studies (Diploma); publication and communication (CPC). *Program availability:* Part-time, evening/weekend. *Degree requirements:* For master's, thesis. *Entrance requirements:* For master's, 3 completed graduate courses with grade of B or higher. Additional exam requirements/recommendations for international students: required—TOEFL (minimum score 600 paper-based), TWE (minimum score 5). *Expenses:* Contact institution.

Howard University, College of Medicine, Department of Biochemistry and Molecular Biology, Washington, DC 20059-0002. Offers biochemistry and molecular biology (PhD); biotechnology (MS); MD/PhD. *Program availability:* Part-time. *Degree requirements:* For master's, externship; for doctorate, comprehensive exam, thesis/dissertation. *Entrance requirements:* For master's and doctorate, GRE General Test, minimum GPA of 3.0.

Husson University, Master of Business Administration Program, Bangor, ME 04401-2999. Offers athletic administration (MBA); biotechnology and innovation (MBA); general business administration (MBA); healthcare management (MBA); hospitality and tourism management (MBA); organizational management (MBA); risk management (MBA). *Program availability:* Part-time, evening/weekend, 100% online, blended/hybrid learning. *Degree requirements:* For master's, comprehensive exam (for some programs), thesis optional. *Entrance requirements:* For master's, minimum GPA of 3.0, letter of recommendation. Additional exam requirements/recommendations for international students: required—TOEFL (minimum score 550 paper-based; 80 iBT), IELTS (minimum score 6.5). Electronic applications accepted. *Expenses:* Contact institution.

Illinois State University, Graduate School, College of Arts and Sciences, School of Biological Sciences, Program in Biotechnology, Normal, IL 61790. Offers MS. *Faculty:* 26 full-time (6 women), 7 part-time/adjunct (2 women). *Students:* 7 full-time (5 women), 5 part-time (1 woman). Average age 25. 20 applicants, 15% accepted, 1 enrolled. In 2019, 5 master's awarded. *Degree requirements:* For master's, thesis or alternative. *Entrance requirements:* For master's, GRE General Test, minimum GPA of 2.6 in last 60 hours of course work. *Application deadline:* Applications are processed on a rolling basis. Application fee: $50. *Expenses: Tuition, area resident:* Full-time $7956. Tuition, nonresident: full-time $9233. *Required fees:* $1797. *Financial support:* Application deadline: 4/1. *Unit head:* Dr. Craig Gatto, School Director, 309-438-3087, E-mail: cgatto@IllinoisState.edu. *Application contact:* Dr. Ben Sadd, Assistant Chair for Graduate Studies, 309-438-5151, E-mail: bmsadd@IllinoisState.edu.
Website: http://www.bio.ilstu.edu/biotech/

Indiana University Bloomington, University Graduate School, College of Arts and Sciences, Department of Biology, Bloomington, IN 47405. Offers biology teaching (MAT); biotechnology (MA); evolution, ecology, and behavior (MA, PhD); genetics (PhD); microbiology (MA, PhD); molecular, cellular, and developmental biology (PhD); plant sciences (MA, PhD); zoology (MA, PhD). Terminal master's awarded for partial completion of doctoral program. *Degree requirements:* For master's, thesis, oral defense; for doctorate, thesis/dissertation, oral defense. *Entrance requirements:* For master's and doctorate, GRE General Test. Additional exam requirements/recommendations for international students: required—TOEFL (minimum score 100 iBT). Electronic applications accepted.

Instituto Tecnológico y de Estudios Superiores de Monterrey, Campus Monterrey, Graduate and Research Division, Program in Natural and Social Sciences, Monterrey, Mexico. Offers biotechnology (MS); chemistry (MS, PhD); communications (MS); education (MA). *Program availability:* Part-time. *Degree requirements:* For master's, one foreign language, thesis; for doctorate, one foreign language, thesis/dissertation. *Entrance requirements:* For master's, EXADEP; for doctorate, EXADEP, master's degree in related field. Additional exam requirements/recommendations for international students: required—TOEFL.

Inter American University of Puerto Rico, Barranquitas Campus, Program in Biotechnology, Barranquitas, PR 00794. Offers general biotechnology (MSB); plants biotechnology (MSB). *Program availability:* Part-time, evening/weekend. *Degree requirements:* For master's, 2 foreign languages, comprehensive exam (for some programs), project research and thesis or additional 9 credits in biotechnology and comprehensive exam. *Entrance requirements:* For master's, GRE or EXADEP, bachelor's degree in natural science or related area, official academic transcript from institution that conferred bachelor's degree, minimum GPA of 2.5, two recommendations letters, interview (for some programs). Electronic applications accepted. *Expenses:* Contact institution.

Inter American University of Puerto Rico, Bayamón Campus, Graduate School, Bayamón, PR 00957. Offers biology (MS), including environmental sciences and ecology, molecular biotechnology; electrical engineering (ME), including control system, potence system; human resources (MBA); mechanical engineering (ME, MS), including aerospace, energy. *Program availability:* Part-time, evening/weekend. *Degree requirements:* For master's, comprehensive exam, research project. *Entrance requirements:* For master's, EXADEP, GRE General Test, letters of recommendation. *Expenses: Tuition:* Full-time $3870; part-time $1935 per year. *Required fees:* $735; $642 per unit.

Johns Hopkins University, Advanced Academic Programs, Program in Biotechnology, Washington, DC 21218. Offers MS, MS/MBA. *Program availability:* Part-time, evening/weekend, 100% online. *Entrance requirements:* For master's, minimum GPA of 3.0; coursework in biology and chemistry. Additional exam requirements/recommendations for international students: required—TOEFL (minimum score 100 iBT). Electronic applications accepted.

Johns Hopkins University, Advanced Academic Programs, Program in Biotechnology Enterprise and Entrepreneurship, Washington, DC 21218. Offers MBEE. *Program availability:* Part-time, evening/weekend, online learning. *Entrance requirements:* For master's, minimum GPA of 3.0, coursework in biochemistry and cell biology. Additional exam requirements/recommendations for international students: required—TOEFL (minimum score 100 iBT). Electronic applications accepted.

Johns Hopkins University, G. W. C. Whiting School of Engineering, Master of Science in Engineering Management Program, Baltimore, MD 21218. Offers biomaterials (MSEM); civil engineering (MSEM); communications science (MSEM); computer science (MSEM); environmental systems analysis, economics and public policy (MSEM); fluid mechanics (MSEM); materials science and engineering (MSEM); mechanical engineering (MSEM); mechanics and materials (MSEM); nanobiotechnology (MSEM); nanomaterials and nanotechnology (MSEM); operations research (MSEM); probability and statistics (MSEM); smart product and device design (MSEM). *Entrance requirements:* For master's, GRE, 3 letters of recommendation, statement of purpose, transcripts. Additional exam requirements/recommendations for international students: required—TOEFL (minimum score 600 paper-based, 100 iBT) or IELTS (7). Electronic applications accepted.

Kean University, New Jersey Center for Science, Technology and Mathematics, Program in Biotechnology Science, Union, NJ 07083. Offers MS. *Program availability:* Part-time. *Faculty:* 9 full-time (1 woman). *Students:* 11 full-time (9 women), 6 part-time (4 women); includes 9 minority (6 Black or African American, non-Hispanic/Latino; 2 Asian, non-Hispanic/Latino; 1 Hispanic/Latino), 2 international. Average age 27. 10 applicants, 100% accepted, 5 enrolled. In 2019, 10 master's awarded. *Degree requirements:* For master's, written research project paper, presentation of research. *Entrance requirements:* For master's, GRE General Test, minimum GPA of 3.0 cumulative and in all science and math courses; official transcripts from all institutions attended; three letters of recommendation; professional resume/curriculum vitae; personal statement. Additional exam requirements/recommendations for international students: required—TOEFL (minimum score 550 paper-based; 79 iBT), IELTS. *Application deadline:* For fall admission, 6/30 for domestic and international students; for spring admission, 12/1 for domestic and international students. Applications are processed on a rolling basis. Application fee: $75. Electronic applications accepted. *Expenses:* Tuition, state resident: full-time $15,326; part-time $748 per credit. Tuition, nonresident: full-time $20,288; part-time $902 per credit. *Required fees:* $2149.50; $91.25 per credit. Tuition and fees vary according to course level, course load, degree level and program. *Financial support:* Scholarships/grants and unspecified assistantships available. Financial award applicants required to submit FAFSA. *Unit head:* Dr. Salvatore Coniglio, Program Coordinator, 908-737-7216, E-mail: coniglsa@kean.edu. *Application contact:* Pedro Lopes, Graduate Admissions Counselor, 908-737-7100, E-mail: gradadmissions@kean.edu.
Website: http://grad.kean.edu/masters-programs/biotechnology

Marywood University, Academic Affairs, Munley College of Liberal Arts and Sciences, Science Department, Scranton, PA 18509-1598. Offers biotechnology (MS). *Program availability:* Part-time. Electronic applications accepted.

McGill University, Faculty of Graduate and Postdoctoral Studies, Faculty of Agricultural and Environmental Sciences, Institute of Parasitology, Montréal, QC H3A 2T5, Canada. Offers biotechnology (M Sc A, Certificate); parasitology (M Sc, PhD).

Middle Tennessee State University, College of Graduate Studies, College of Basic and Applied Sciences, Program in Professional Science, Murfreesboro, TN 37132. Offers actuarial sciences (MS); biostatistics (MS); biotechnology (MS); engineering management (MS); health care informatics (MS). *Program availability:* Part-time, evening/weekend, online learning. *Degree requirements:* For master's, comprehensive exam. *Entrance requirements:* For master's, GRE. Additional exam requirements/recommendations for international students: required—TOEFL (minimum score 525 paper-based; 71 iBT) or IELTS (minimum score 6).

Mount St. Mary's University, Program in Biotechnology and Management, Emmitsburg, MD 21727-7799. Offers MS. *Program availability:* Part-time-only, evening/weekend. *Students:* 4 full-time (2 women), 13 part-time (8 women); includes 4 minority (1 Black or African American, non-Hispanic/Latino; 2 Hispanic/Latino; 1 Two or more races, non-Hispanic/Latino). In 2019, 5 master's awarded. *Degree requirements:* For master's, capstone experience (written paper and formal oral presentation of the project outcomes). *Entrance requirements:* For master's, bachelor's degree in biology or related field, undergraduate transcripts from accredited four-year institution with minimum GPA of 2.75, two letters of recommendation. Additional exam requirements/recommendations for international students: required—TOEFL (minimum score 550 paper-based; 83 iBT). *Application deadline:* Applications are processed on a rolling basis. Electronic applications accepted. *Expenses:* Contact institution. *Financial support:* Unspecified assistantships available. Financial award applicants required to submit FAFSA.
Website: https://msmary.edu/academics/schools-divisions/school-of-natural-science-and-mathematics/index.html

New Mexico State University, College of Arts and Sciences, Department of Biology, Las Cruces, NM 88003-8001. Offers behavioral, ecological & evolutionary biology (PhD); biology (MS); biotechnology (MS). *Program availability:* Part-time. *Faculty:* 19 full-time (9 women). *Students:* 48 full-time (27 women), 5 part-time (3 women); includes 19 minority (1 American Indian or Alaska Native, non-Hispanic/Latino; 5 Asian, non-Hispanic/Latino; 11 Hispanic/Latino; 2 Two or more races, non-Hispanic/Latino), 15 international. Average age 30. 28 applicants, 50% accepted, 8 enrolled. In 2019, 10 master's, 4 doctorates awarded. *Degree requirements:* For master's, thesis (for some programs), defense or oral exam; for doctorate, comprehensive exam, thesis/dissertation, qualifying exam. *Entrance requirements:* For master's and doctorate, GRE. Additional exam requirements/recommendations for international students: required—TOEFL (minimum score 550 paper-based; 79 iBT), IELTS (minimum score 6.5). *Application deadline:* For fall admission, 1/15 priority date for domestic and international students; for spring admission, 9/30 priority date for domestic and international students. Applications are processed on a rolling basis. Application fee: $40 ($50 for international students). Electronic applications accepted. *Financial support:* In 2019–20, 47 students received support, including 6 fellowships (averaging $4,844 per year), 17 research assistantships (averaging $20,182 per year), 31 teaching assistantships (averaging $18,983 per year); career-related internships or fieldwork, Federal Work-Study, scholarships/grants, traineeships, health care benefits, and unspecified assistantships also available. Support available to part-time students. Financial award application deadline: 3/1. *Unit head:* Dr. Michele K. Nishiguchi, Department Head, 575-646-3611, Fax: 575-646-5665, E-mail: nish@nmsu.edu. *Application contact:* Dr. Jennifer Curtiss, Associate Professor, 575-646-3611, Fax: 575-646-5665, E-mail: curtij01@nmsu.edu.
Website: http://bio.nmsu.edu

New York University, Tandon School of Engineering, Department of Chemical and Biomolecular Engineering, Major in Biotechnology, New York, NY 10012-1019. Offers biotechnology (MS). *Entrance requirements:* Additional exam requirements/recommendations for international students: required—TOEFL (minimum score 550 paper-based; 90 iBT); recommended—IELTS (minimum score 7). Electronic applications accepted.

New York University, Tandon School of Engineering, Department of Chemical and Biomolecular Engineering, Major in Biotechnology and Entrepreneurship, New York, NY 10012-1019. Offers biotechnology and entrepreneurship (MS). *Entrance requirements:* Additional exam requirements/recommendations for international students: required—TOEFL (minimum score 550 paper-based; 90 iBT); recommended—IELTS (minimum score 7). Electronic applications accepted.

Northeastern University, College of Science, Boston, MA 02115-5096. Offers applied mathematics (MS); bioinformatics (MS); biology (PhD); biotechnology (MS); chemistry and chemical biology (MS, PhD); environmental science and policy (MS); marine and environmental sciences (PhD); marine biology (MS); mathematics (MS, PhD); operations research (MSOR); physics (MS, PhD); psychology (PhD). *Program availability:* Part-time. Terminal master's awarded for partial completion of doctoral program. *Degree requirements:* For master's, comprehensive exam (for some programs), thesis; for doctorate, comprehensive exam (for some programs), thesis/dissertation. *Entrance requirements:* For master's, GRE General Test. Electronic applications accepted. *Expenses:* Contact institution.

Northwestern University, The Graduate School, Interdisciplinary Biological Sciences Program (IBiS), Evanston, IL 60208. Offers biochemistry (PhD); bioengineering and biotechnology (PhD); biotechnology (PhD); cell and molecular biology (PhD); developmental and systems biology (PhD); nanotechnology (PhD); neurobiology (PhD); structural biology and biophysics (PhD). *Degree requirements:* For doctorate, thesis/dissertation, qualifying exam. *Entrance requirements:* For doctorate, GRE General Test. Additional exam requirements/recommendations for international students: required—TOEFL (minimum score 600 paper-based). Electronic applications accepted.

Northwestern University, McCormick School of Engineering and Applied Science, Department of Chemical and Biological Engineering, MS in Biotechnology Program, Evanston, IL 60208. Offers MS. *Entrance requirements:* For master's, GRE General Test. Additional exam requirements/recommendations for international students: required—TOEFL, IELTS. Electronic applications accepted.

Oregon State University, College of Agricultural Sciences, Program in Food Science and Technology, Corvallis, OR 97331. Offers brewing (MS, PhD); enology (MS, PhD); flavor chemistry (MS, PhD); food and seafood processing (MS, PhD); food chemistry/biochemistry (MS, PhD); food engineering (MS, PhD); food microbiology/biotechnology (MS, PhD); sensory evaluation (MS, PhD). *Entrance requirements:* For master's and doctorate, GRE (minimum Verbal and Quantitative scores of 300), minimum GPA of 3.0 in last 90 hours. Additional exam requirements/recommendations for international students: required—TOEFL (minimum score 80 iBT), IELTS (minimum score 6.5).

Oregon State University, College of Agricultural Sciences, Program in Horticulture, Corvallis, OR 97331. Offers breeding, genetics, and biotechnology (MS, PhD); community and landscape horticultural systems (MS, PhD); sustainable crop production (MS, PhD). *Degree requirements:* For master's, thesis (for some programs); for doctorate, thesis/dissertation. *Entrance requirements:* For master's and doctorate, GRE General Test, minimum GPA of 3.0 in last 90 hours. Additional exam requirements/recommendations for international students: required—TOEFL (minimum score 80 iBT), IELTS (minimum score 6.5).

Oregon State University, Interdisciplinary/Institutional Programs, Program in Molecular and Cellular Biology, Corvallis, OR 97331. Offers bioinformatics (PhD); biotechnology (PhD); genome biology (PhD); molecular virology (PhD); plant molecular biology (PhD). *Degree requirements:* For doctorate, thesis/dissertation, oral and written qualifying exams. *Entrance requirements:* For doctorate, GRE. Additional exam requirements/recommendations for international students: required—TOEFL (minimum score 80 iBT), IELTS (minimum score 6.5).

Penn State University Park, Graduate School, Eberly College of Science, Department of Biochemistry and Molecular Biology, University Park, PA 16802. Offers biochemistry, microbiology, and molecular biology (MS, PhD); biotechnology (MBIOT).

Pontifical John Paul II Institute for Studies on Marriage and Family, Graduate Programs, Washington, DC 20064. Offers biotechnology and ethics (MTS); marriage and family (MTS, STD, STL); theology (PhD).

Purdue University, Graduate School, PULSe - Purdue University Life Sciences Program, West Lafayette, IN 47907. Offers biomolecular structure and biophysics (PhD); biotechnology (PhD); chemical biology (PhD); chromatin and regulation of gene expression (PhD); integrative neuroscience (PhD); integrative plant sciences (PhD); membrane biology (PhD); microbiology (PhD); molecular evolutionary and cancer biology (PhD); molecular evolutionary genetics (PhD); molecular virology (PhD). *Students:* 37 full-time (23 women); includes 7 minority (1 Black or African American, non-Hispanic/Latino; 2 Asian, non-Hispanic/Latino; 4 Hispanic/Latino), 22 international. Average age 25. 162 applicants, 36% accepted, 19 enrolled. *Entrance requirements:* For doctorate, GRE, minimum undergraduate GPA of 3.0. Additional exam requirements/recommendations for international students: required—TOEFL (minimum score 550 paper-based; 77 iBT). *Application deadline:* For fall admission, 1/15 priority date for domestic and international students. Applications are processed on a rolling basis. Application fee: $60 ($75 for international students). Electronic applications accepted. *Financial support:* In 2019–20, research assistantships with tuition reimbursements (averaging $22,500 per year), teaching assistantships with tuition reimbursements (averaging $22,500 per year) were awarded. *Application contact:* Lindsey Springer, Graduate Contact for Admissions, 765-496-9667, E-mail: lbcampbe@purdue.edu.
Website: http://www.gradschool.purdue.edu/pulse

Purdue University Northwest, Graduate Studies Office, School of Engineering, Mathematics, and Science, Department of Biological Sciences, Program in Biotechnology, Hammond, IN 46323-2094. Offers MS. *Degree requirements:* For master's, thesis (for some programs). *Entrance requirements:* For master's, GRE General Test, 3 letters of recommendation.

Roosevelt University, Graduate Division, College of Arts and Sciences, Department of Biological, Chemical, and Physical Sciences, Chicago, IL 60605. Offers biology (MS); biomedical sciences (MA); biotechnology and chemical science (MS), including biotechnology, biotechnology management, chemical science. *Program availability:*

Part-time, evening/weekend. *Degree requirements:* For master's, thesis optional. Electronic applications accepted. *Expenses:* Contact institution.

St. John's University, Institute for Biotechnology, Queens, NY 11439. Offers biological and pharmaceutical biotechnology (MS). *Entrance requirements:* For master's, GRE General Test, letters of recommendation, transcripts, resume, personal statement. Additional exam requirements/recommendations for international students: required—TOEFL (minimum score 80 iBT), IELTS (minimum score 6.5). Electronic applications accepted. *Expenses:* Contact institution.

San Francisco State University, Division of Graduate Studies, College of Science and Engineering, Department of Biology, Professional Science Master's Program, San Francisco, CA 94132-1722. Offers biotechnology (PSM); stem cell science (PSM). *Expenses: Tuition, area resident:* Full-time $7176; part-time $4164 per year. Tuition, state resident: full-time $7176; part-time $4164 per year. Tuition, nonresident: full-time $16,680; part-time $396 per unit. *International tuition:* $16,680 full-time. *Required fees:* $1524; $1524 per unit. $762 per semester. Tuition and fees vary according to degree level and program. *Unit head:* Dr. Lily Chen, Director, 415-338-6763, Fax: 415-338-2295, E-mail: lilychen@sfsu.edu. *Application contact:* Dr. Linda H. Chen, Associate Director and Program Coordinator, 415-338-1696, Fax: 415-338-2295, E-mail: psm@sfsu.edu.
Website: http://psm.sfsu.edu/

Simon Fraser University, Office of Graduate Studies and Postdoctoral Fellows, Faculty of Business Administration, Vancouver, BC V6B 5K3, Canada. Offers business administration (EMBA, PhD, Graduate Diploma); finance (M Sc); management of technology (MBA); management of technology/biotechnology (MBA). *Program availability:* Online learning. *Degree requirements:* For master's, thesis (for some programs); for doctorate, comprehensive exam, thesis/dissertation. *Entrance requirements:* For master's, GMAT, minimum GPA of 3.0 (on scale of 4.33) or 3.33 based on last 60 credits of undergraduate courses; for doctorate, minimum GPA of 3.5 (on scale of 4.33); for Graduate Diploma, minimum GPA of 2.5 (on scale of 4.33) or 2.67 based on last 60 credits of undergraduate courses. Additional exam requirements/recommendations for international students: recommended—TOEFL (minimum score 580 paper-based; 93 iBT), IELTS (minimum score 7), TWE (minimum score 5). *Expenses:* Contact institution.

Southeastern Oklahoma State University, School of Arts and Sciences, Durant, OK 74701-0609. Offers biology (MT); computer information systems (MT); occupational safety and health (MT). *Program availability:* Part-time, evening/weekend. *Degree requirements:* For master's, thesis optional. *Entrance requirements:* For master's, minimum GPA of 3.0 in last 60 hours or 2.75 overall. Additional exam requirements/recommendations for international students: required—TOEFL (minimum score 550 paper-based; 79 iBT). Electronic applications accepted.

Stephen F. Austin State University, Graduate School, College of Sciences and Mathematics, Division of Biotechnology, Nacogdoches, TX 75962. Offers MS. *Degree requirements:* For master's, comprehensive exam, thesis. *Entrance requirements:* For master's, GRE General Test, minimum GPA of 2.8 in last 60 hours, 2.5 overall. Additional exam requirements/recommendations for international students: required—TOEFL.

Temple University, College of Science and Technology, Department of Biology, Philadelphia, PA 19122-6096. Offers biology (MS, PSM, PhD); biotechnology (MS). *Program availability:* Part-time. *Faculty:* 45 full-time (16 women), 1 part-time/adjunct (0 women). *Students:* 95 full-time (47 women), 13 part-time (4 women); includes 30 minority (3 Black or African American, non-Hispanic/Latino; 17 Asian, non-Hispanic/Latino; 8 Hispanic/Latino; 2 Two or more races, non-Hispanic/Latino), 22 international. 99 applicants, 62% accepted, 34 enrolled. In 2019, 29 master's, 3 doctorates awarded. *Degree requirements:* For master's, thesis (for some programs); for doctorate, thesis/dissertation. *Entrance requirements:* For master's, GRE (optional for P.S.M. in Biotechnology), baccalaureate degree in a related discipline, statement of goals, letters of recommendation; for doctorate, GRE, statement of goals, baccalaureate degree in a related discipline, 3 letters of recommendation. Additional exam requirements/recommendations for international students: required—TOEFL (minimum score 90 iBT), IELTS (minimum score 6.5), PTE (minimum score 61), one of three is required. Application fee: $60. *Expenses:* Contact institution. *Financial support:* Fellowships, research assistantships, teaching assistantships, Federal Work-Study, and health care benefits available. Financial award applicants required to submit FAFSA. *Unit head:* Robert W Sanders, Chairperson/Professor, 215-204-2056, E-mail: robert.sanders@temple.edu. *Application contact:* Richard Waring, Graduate Chair, 215-204-7119, E-mail: richard.waring@temple.edu.
Website: https://bio.cst.temple.edu/

Tennessee State University, The School of Graduate Studies and Research, College of Agriculture, Human and Natural Sciences, Nashville, TN 37209-1561. Offers agricultural sciences (MS), including agribusiness, agricultural and extension education, animal science, plant and soil science; biological sciences (MS, PhD); biotechnology (PhD); chemistry (MS). *Program availability:* Part-time, evening/weekend. *Degree requirements:* For master's, thesis. *Entrance requirements:* For master's, GRE General Test, GRE Subject Test, MAT.

Texas Tech University, Graduate School, Interdisciplinary Programs, Lubbock, TX 79409-1030. Offers arid land studies (MS); biotechnology (MS); heritage and museum sciences (MA); interdisciplinary studies (MA, MS); wind science and engineering (PhD); JD/MS. *Program availability:* Part-time, 100% online, blended/hybrid learning. *Faculty:* 5 full-time (3 women). *Students:* 114 full-time (46 women), 94 part-time (59 women); includes 72 minority (30 Black or African American, non-Hispanic/Latino; 3 Asian, non-Hispanic/Latino; 31 Hispanic/Latino; 8 Two or more races, non-Hispanic/Latino), 34 international. Average age 31. 118 applicants, 85% accepted, 66 enrolled. In 2019, 57 master's, 4 doctorates awarded. Terminal master's awarded for partial completion of doctoral program. *Degree requirements:* For master's, comprehensive exam (for some programs), thesis (for some programs); for doctorate, comprehensive exam, thesis/dissertation (for some programs). *Entrance requirements:* Additional exam requirements/recommendations for international students: required—TOEFL (minimum score 550 paper-based; 79 iBT), IELTS (minimum score 6.5), PTE (minimum score 60), Cambridge Advanced (B), Cambridge Proficiency (C), ELS English for Academic Purposes (Level 112), Duolingo English Test (100). *Application deadline:* For fall admission, 6/1 priority date for domestic students, 1/15 priority date for international students; for spring admission, 9/1 priority date for domestic students, 6/15 priority date for international students. Applications are processed on a rolling basis. Application fee: $65. Electronic applications accepted. *Expenses:* Tuition, state resident: full-time $7944; part-time $331 per credit hour. Tuition, nonresident: full-time $17,904; part-time $746 per credit hour. *Required fees:* $2556; $55.50 per credit hour. $612 per semester. Tuition and fees vary according to program. *Financial support:* In 2019–20, 150 students received support, including 138 fellowships (averaging $5,639 per year), 26 research assistantships (averaging $18,634 per year), 16 teaching assistantships (averaging $13,404 per year); scholarships/grants and unspecified assistantships also available. Financial award application deadline: 4/15; financial award applicants required to submit FAFSA. *Unit head:* Dr. Mark A. Sheridan, Vice Provost for Graduate and Postdoctoral Affairs/Dean of the Graduate School, 806-834-5537, Fax: 806-742-1746, E-mail: mark.sheridan@ttu.edu. *Application contact:* Dr. David Doerfert, Associate Dean, 806-834-4477, Fax: 806-742-4038, E-mail: david.doerfert@ttu.edu.
Website: www.gradschool.ttu.edu

Texas Tech University Health Sciences Center, Graduate School of Biomedical Sciences, Program in Biotechnology, Lubbock, TX 79430. Offers MS. *Entrance requirements:* For master's, GRE General Test, minimum GPA of 3.0. Additional exam requirements/recommendations for international students: required—TOEFL (minimum score 550 paper-based).

Thomas Jefferson University, Jefferson College of Health Professions, Department of Medical Laboratory Sciences and Biotechnology, Philadelphia, PA 19107. Offers biotechnology (MS); cytotechnology (MS); medical laboratory science (MS). *Accreditation:* NAACLS. *Program availability:* Part-time. *Degree requirements:* For master's, comprehensive exam. *Entrance requirements:* Additional exam requirements/recommendations for international students: required—TOEFL (minimum score 87 iBT), IELTS (minimum score 6.5). Electronic applications accepted. *Expenses:* Contact institution.

Tufts University, Graduate School of Arts and Sciences, Department of Chemistry, Medford, MA 02155. Offers chemical physics (PhD); chemistry (MS, PhD); chemistry/biotechnology (PhD). Terminal master's awarded for partial completion of doctoral program. *Degree requirements:* For master's, thesis optional; for doctorate, comprehensive exam, thesis/dissertation. *Entrance requirements:* For master's and doctorate, GRE General Test; GRE Subject Test (recommended). Additional exam requirements/recommendations for international students: required—TOEFL (minimum score 550 paper-based; 80 iBT), IELTS (minimum score 6.5). Electronic applications accepted. *Expenses:* Contact institution.

Tufts University, Graduate School of Arts and Sciences, Graduate Certificate Programs, Biotechnology Engineering Program, Medford, MA 02155. Offers Certificate. *Program availability:* Part-time, evening/weekend. Electronic applications accepted. Full-time tuition and fees vary according to degree level, program and student level. Part-time tuition and fees vary according to course load.

Tufts University, Graduate School of Arts and Sciences, Graduate Certificate Programs, Biotechnology Program, Medford, MA 02155. Offers Certificate. *Program availability:* Part-time, evening/weekend. Electronic applications accepted. Full-time tuition and fees vary according to degree level, program and student level. Part-time tuition and fees vary according to course load.

Tufts University, School of Engineering, Department of Chemical and Biological Engineering, Medford, MA 02155. Offers bioengineering (MS), including cell and bioprocess engineering; biotechnology (PhD); chemical engineering (MS, PhD); PhD/PhD. *Program availability:* Part-time. Terminal master's awarded for partial completion of doctoral program. *Degree requirements:* For master's, thesis (for some programs); for doctorate, thesis/dissertation. *Entrance requirements:* For master's and doctorate, GRE General Test. Additional exam requirements/recommendations for international students: required—TOEFL (minimum score 550 paper-based; 80 iBT), IELTS (minimum score 6.5). Electronic applications accepted. Full-time tuition and fees vary according to degree level, program and student level. Part-time tuition and fees vary according to course load.

Tufts University, School of Engineering, Department of Civil and Environmental Engineering, Medford, MA 02155. Offers bioengineering (MS), including environmental biotechnology; civil and environmental engineering (MS, PhD), including applied data science, environmental and water resources engineering, environmental health, geosystems engineering, structural engineering and mechanics; PhD/PhD. *Program availability:* Part-time. Terminal master's awarded for partial completion of doctoral program. *Degree requirements:* For master's, thesis (for some programs); for doctorate, thesis/dissertation. *Entrance requirements:* For master's and doctorate, GRE General Test. Additional exam requirements/recommendations for international students: required—TOEFL (minimum score 550 paper-based; 80 iBT), IELTS (minimum score 6.5). Electronic applications accepted. Full-time tuition and fees vary according to degree level, program and student level. Part-time tuition and fees vary according to course load.

Universidad de las Américas Puebla, Division of Graduate Studies, School of Sciences, Program in Biotechnology, Puebla, Mexico. Offers MS. *Degree requirements:* For master's, one foreign language, thesis.

University at Buffalo, the State University of New York, Graduate School, Jacobs School of Medicine and Biomedical Sciences, Graduate Programs in Medicine and Biomedical Sciences, Department of Biotechnical and Clinical Laboratory Sciences, Buffalo, NY 14214. Offers biotechnology (MS). *Accreditation:* NAACLS. *Program availability:* Part-time. *Faculty:* 6 full-time (2 women). *Students:* 6 full-time (3 women); includes 3 minority (all Asian, non-Hispanic/Latino), 2 international. Average age 27. 57 applicants, 21% accepted, 6 enrolled. In 2019, 6 master's awarded. *Degree requirements:* For master's, thesis. *Entrance requirements:* For master's, minimum GPA of 3.0 or equivalent. Additional exam requirements/recommendations for international students: required—TOEFL (minimum score 79 iBT), IELTS (minimum score 6.5). *Application deadline:* For fall admission, 3/1 priority date for domestic students, 2/1 priority date for international students. Applications are processed on a rolling basis. Application fee: $85. Electronic applications accepted. *Expenses: Tuition, area resident:* Full-time $11,310; part-time $471 per credit hour. Tuition, state resident: full-time $11,310; part-time $471 per credit hour. Tuition, nonresident: full-time $23,100; part-time $963 per credit hour. *International tuition:* $23,100 full-time. *Required fees:* $2820. *Financial support:* In 2019–20, 6 students received support, including 1 research assistantship with tuition reimbursement available (averaging $15,000 per year), 5 teaching assistantships with full tuition reimbursements available (averaging $10,000 per year). Financial award application deadline: 3/1. *Unit head:* Dr. Paul J. Kostyniak, Chair, 716-829-5188, Fax: 716-829-3601, E-mail: pjkost@buffalo.edu. *Application contact:* Dr. Stephen T. Koury, Director of Graduate Studies, 716-829-5188, Fax: 716-829-3601, E-mail: stvkoury@buffalo.edu.
Website: http://www.smbs.buffalo.edu/cls/biotech-ms.html

The University of Alabama at Birmingham, School of Health Professions, Program in Biotechnology, Birmingham, AL 35294. Offers MS. *Students:* 12 full-time (8 women), 3 part-time (2 women); includes 7 minority (5 Black or African American, non-Hispanic/Latino; 1 Asian, non-Hispanic/Latino; 1 Two or more races, non-Hispanic/Latino), 4 international. Average age 26. 67 applicants, 67% accepted, 24 enrolled. In 2019, 17 master's awarded. *Entrance requirements:* For master's, GRE (minimum score of 500 in each area), minimum GPA of 3.0 overall or on last 60 hours attempted, interview. Additional exam requirements/recommendations for international students: required—TOEFL, TWE. *Application deadline:* For fall admission, 5/31 for domestic students. *Unit head:* Dr. Tino Unlap, Interim Program Director, 205-934-7382, E-mail: unlap@uab.edu. *Application contact:* Susan Noblitt Banks, Director of Graduate School Operations, 205-934-8227, Fax: 205-934-8413, E-mail: gradschool@uab.edu.
Website: http://www.uab.edu/shp/cds/biotechnology-m-s-c-l-s-or-certificate

The University of Alabama in Huntsville, School of Graduate Studies, College of Engineering, Department of Chemical and Materials Engineering, Huntsville, AL 35899. Offers biotechnology science and engineering (PhD); chemical and materials engineering (MSE); materials science (PhD); mechanical engineering (PhD), including chemical engineering. *Program availability:* Part-time. *Degree requirements:* For master's, comprehensive exam, thesis or alternative, oral and written exams; for doctorate, comprehensive exam, thesis/dissertation. *Entrance requirements:* For master's, GRE General Test, appropriate bachelor's degree, minimum GPA of 3.0; for doctorate, GRE General Test, minimum GPA of 3.0. Additional exam requirements/recommendations for international students: required—TOEFL (minimum score 500 paper-based; 80 iBT), IELTS (minimum score 6.5). Electronic applications accepted.

The University of Alabama in Huntsville, School of Graduate Studies, College of Science, Department of Biological Sciences, Huntsville, AL 35899. Offers biology (MS); biotechnology science and engineering (PhD); education (MS). *Program availability:* Part-time. *Degree requirements:* For master's, comprehensive exam, thesis or alternative, oral and written exams. *Entrance requirements:* For master's, GRE General Test, previous course work in biochemistry and organic chemistry, minimum GPA of 3.0. Additional exam requirements/recommendations for international students: required—TOEFL (minimum score 550 paper-based; 80 iBT), IELTS (minimum score 6.5). Electronic applications accepted.

The University of Alabama in Huntsville, School of Graduate Studies, College of Science, Department of Chemistry, Huntsville, AL 35899. Offers biotechnology science and engineering (PhD); chemistry (MS); education (MS); materials science (MS, PhD). *Program availability:* Part-time. *Degree requirements:* For master's, comprehensive exam, thesis or alternative, oral and written exams. *Entrance requirements:* For master's, GRE General Test, minimum GPA of 3.0. Additional exam requirements/recommendations for international students: required—TOEFL (minimum score 550 paper-based; 80 iBT), IELTS (minimum score 6.5). Electronic applications accepted.

University of Alberta, Faculty of Graduate Studies and Research, Department of Biological Sciences, Edmonton, AB T6G 2E1, Canada. Offers environmental biology and ecology (M Sc, PhD); microbiology and biotechnology (M Sc, PhD); molecular biology and genetics (M Sc, PhD); physiology and cell biology (M Sc, PhD); plant biology (M Sc, PhD); systematics and evolution (M Sc, PhD). Terminal master's awarded for partial completion of doctoral program. *Degree requirements:* For master's, thesis; for doctorate, thesis/dissertation. *Entrance requirements:* Additional exam requirements/recommendations for international students: required—TOEFL.

University of Calgary, Cumming School of Medicine and Faculty of Graduate Studies, Masters Program in Biomedical Technology, Calgary, AB T2N 1N4, Canada. Offers MBT. *Program availability:* Part-time. *Degree requirements:* For master's, comprehensive exam, practicum. *Entrance requirements:* For master's, minimum GPA of 3.2 in last 2 years, B Sc in biological science. Additional exam requirements/recommendations for international students: required—TOEFL (minimum score 600 paper-based). Electronic applications accepted. *Expenses:* Contact institution.

University of California, Irvine, School of Biological Sciences, Department of Molecular Biology and Biochemistry, Program in Biotechnology, Irvine, CA 92697. Offers MS. *Students:* 22 full-time (13 women); includes 9 minority (6 Asian, non-Hispanic/Latino; 2 Hispanic/Latino; 1 Two or more races, non-Hispanic/Latino), 7 international. Average age 25. 109 applicants, 40% accepted, 11 enrolled. In 2019, 14 master's awarded. *Entrance requirements:* For master's, GRE General Test, GRE Subject Test, minimum GPA of 3.0. *Application deadline:* For fall admission, 3/1 priority date for domestic and international students. Applications are processed on a rolling basis. Application fee: $120 ($140 for international students). Electronic applications accepted. *Financial support:* Application deadline: 3/1; applicants required to submit FAFSA. *Unit head:* Michael G. Cumsky, Director, 949-824-7766, Fax: 949-824-8551, E-mail: mgcumsky@uci.edu. *Application contact:* Morgan Oldham, Administrative Contact, 949-824-6034, Fax: 949-824-8551, E-mail: morgano@uci.edu.

University of California, Irvine, School of Biological Sciences, Department of Molecular Biology and Biochemistry, Program in Biotechnology Management, Irvine, CA 92697. Offers MS. *Students:* 45 full-time (26 women); includes 8 minority (7 Asian, non-Hispanic/Latino; 1 Hispanic/Latino), 31 international. Average age 25. 65 applicants, 62% accepted, 27 enrolled. In 2019, 17 master's awarded. *Application deadline:* For fall admission, 3/15 for domestic students. Application fee: $120 ($140 for international students). *Unit head:* Michael G. Cumsky, Program Director, 949-824-7766, Fax: 949-824-8551, E-mail: mgcumsky@uci.edu. *Application contact:* Morgan Oldham, Student Affairs Assistant, 949-826-6034, Fax: 949-824-8551, E-mail: morgano@uci.edu. Website: http://mbb.bio.uci.edu/graduates/masters-science-degree-biotechnology-management/

University of Delaware, College of Arts and Sciences, Department of Biological Sciences, Newark, DE 19716. Offers biotechnology (MS); cancer biology (MS, PhD); cell and extracellular matrix biology (MS, PhD); cell and systems physiology (MS, PhD); developmental biology (MS, PhD); ecology and evolution (MS, PhD); microbiology (MS, PhD); molecular biology and genetics (MS, PhD). Terminal master's awarded for partial completion of doctoral program. *Degree requirements:* For master's, thesis, preliminary exam; for doctorate, comprehensive exam, thesis/dissertation, preliminary exam. *Entrance requirements:* For master's and doctorate, GRE General Test. Additional exam requirements/recommendations for international students: required—TOEFL (minimum score 600 paper-based); recommended—TWE. Electronic applications accepted.

University of Guelph, Office of Graduate and Postdoctoral Studies, Ontario Agricultural College, Department of Environmental Biology, Guelph, ON N1G 2W1, Canada. Offers entomology (M Sc, PhD); environmental microbiology and biotechnology (M Sc, PhD); environmental toxicology (M Sc, PhD); plant and forest systems (M Sc, PhD); plant pathology (M Sc, PhD). *Program availability:* Part-time. *Degree requirements:* For master's, thesis; for doctorate, comprehensive exam, thesis/dissertation. *Entrance requirements:* For master's, minimum 75% average during previous 2 years of course work; for doctorate, minimum 75% average. Additional exam requirements/recommendations for international students: required—TOEFL or IELTS. Electronic applications accepted.

University of Houston–Clear Lake, School of Science and Computer Engineering, Program in Biotechnology, Houston, TX 77058-1002. Offers MS.

The University of Kansas, University of Kansas Medical Center, School of Health Professions, Department of Clinical Laboratory Sciences, Kansas City, KS 66045. Offers MS. *Faculty:* 10. *Students:* 3 full-time (1 woman), 2 part-time (both women); includes 2 minority (1 Asian, non-Hispanic/Latino; 1 Hispanic/Latino), 1 international. Average age 31. In 2019, 2 master's awarded. *Degree requirements:* For master's, comprehensive exam. *Entrance requirements:* For master's, GRE General Test. Additional exam requirements/recommendations for international students: required—TOEFL, TOEFL or IELTS. *Application deadline:* For fall admission, 2/1 priority date for domestic and international students. Application fee: $60. Electronic applications accepted. *Expenses:* Tuition, state resident: full-time $9989. Tuition, nonresident: full-time $23,950. *International tuition:* $23,950 full-time. *Required fees:* $984; $81.99 per credit hour. Tuition and fees vary according to course load, campus/location and program. *Financial support:* Career-related internships or fieldwork and scholarships/

grants available. Financial award application deadline: 3/1; financial award applicants required to submit FAFSA. *Unit head:* Dr. Eric Elsinghorst, Department Chair and Graduate Director, 913-588-1089, E-mail: eelsinghorst@kumc.edu. *Application contact:* Dr. Eric Elsinghorst, Department Chair and Graduate Director, 913-588-1089, E-mail: eelsinghorst@kumc.edu. Website: http://www.kumc.edu/school-of-health-professions/clinical-laboratory-sciences.html

The University of Manchester, School of Biological Sciences, Manchester, United Kingdom. Offers adaptive organismal biology (M Phil, PhD); animal biology (M Phil, PhD); biochemistry (M Phil, PhD); bioinformatics (M Phil, PhD); biomolecular sciences (M Phil, PhD); biotechnology (M Phil, PhD); cell biology (M Phil, PhD); cell matrix research (M Phil, PhD); channels and transporters (M Phil, PhD); developmental biology (M Phil, PhD); environmental biology (M Phil, PhD); evolutionary biology (M Phil, PhD); gene expression (M Phil, PhD); genetics (M Phil, PhD); history of science, technology and medicine (M Phil, PhD); immunology (M Phil, PhD); integrative neurobiology and behavior (M Phil, PhD); membrane trafficking (M Phil, PhD); microbiology (M Phil, PhD); molecular and cellular neuroscience (M Phil, PhD); molecular biology (M Phil, PhD); molecular cancer studies (M Phil, PhD); neuroscience (M Phil, PhD); ophthalmology (M Phil, PhD); optometry (M Phil, PhD); organelle function (M Phil, PhD); pharmacology (M Phil, PhD); physiology (M Phil, PhD); plant sciences (M Phil, PhD); stem cell research (M Phil, PhD); structural biology (M Phil, PhD); systems neuroscience (M Phil, PhD); toxicology (M Phil, PhD).

University of Maryland, Baltimore County, The Graduate School, College of Natural and Mathematical Sciences, Department of Biological Sciences, Programs in Biotechnology, Baltimore, MD 21250. Offers biotechnology (MPS); biotechnology management (Graduate Certificate). *Program availability:* Part-time, evening/weekend. *Faculty:* 20 part-time/adjunct (9 women). *Students:* 2 full-time (0 women), 7 part-time (4 women); includes 5 minority (1 Black or African American, non-Hispanic/Latino; 3 Asian, non-Hispanic/Latino; 1 Two or more races, non-Hispanic/Latino). Average age 29. 22 applicants, 73% accepted, 7 enrolled. In 2019, 9 master's, 2 other advanced degrees awarded. *Entrance requirements:* Additional exam requirements/recommendations for international students: required—TOEFL (minimum score 99 iBT). *Application deadline:* For fall admission, 8/1 for domestic students, 1/1 for international students; for spring admission, 12/1 for domestic students. Applications are processed on a rolling basis. Application fee: $50. Electronic applications accepted. *Expenses:* $14,382 per year. *Financial support:* In 2019–20, 1 student received support, including 1 teaching assistantship; unspecified assistantships also available. Financial award applicants required to submit FAFSA. *Unit head:* Annica Wayman, Director, Professional Studies, 410-301-738-6092, E-mail: awayman@umbc.edu. *Application contact:* Karina Jenkins, Program Specialist, E-mail: jenkinsk@umbc.edu. Website: http://www.umbc.edu/biotech/

University of Maryland Global Campus, University of Maryland Global Campus, Biotechnology, Adelphi, MD 20783. Offers MS, Certificate. *Program availability:* Part-time, evening/weekend, online learning. *Students:* 3 full-time (1 woman), 556 part-time (351 women); includes 269 minority (141 Black or African American, non-Hispanic/Latino; 1 American Indian or Alaska Native, non-Hispanic/Latino; 56 Asian, non-Hispanic/Latino; 49 Hispanic/Latino; 2 Native Hawaiian or other Pacific Islander, non-Hispanic/Latino; 20 Two or more races, non-Hispanic/Latino), 21 international. Average age 33. 237 applicants, 100% accepted, 94 enrolled. In 2019, 113 master's, 6 other advanced degrees awarded. *Degree requirements:* For master's, thesis or alternative, capstone course. *Application deadline:* Applications are processed on a rolling basis. Application fee: $50. Electronic applications accepted. *Financial support:* Scholarships/grants available. Support available to part-time students. Financial award application deadline: 6/1; financial award applicants required to submit FAFSA. *Unit head:* Roza Selimyan, Program Director, 240-684-2000, E-mail: Roza.Selimyan@umgc.edu. *Application contact:* Admissions, 800-888-8682, E-mail: studentsfirst@umuc.edu. Website: https://www.umgc.edu/academic-programs/masters-degrees/biotechnology/index.cfm

University of Massachusetts Amherst, Graduate School, College of Natural Sciences, Department of Animal Biotechnology and Biomedical Sciences, Amherst, MA 01003. Offers MS, PhD. *Program availability:* Part-time. Terminal master's awarded for partial completion of doctoral program. *Degree requirements:* For master's, thesis or alternative; for doctorate, comprehensive exam, thesis/dissertation. *Entrance requirements:* For doctorate, GRE General Test. Additional exam requirements/recommendations for international students: required—TOEFL (minimum score 550 paper-based; 80 iBT), IELTS (minimum score 6.5). Electronic applications accepted.

University of Massachusetts Boston, College of Science and Mathematics, Program in Biomedical Engineering and Biotechnology, Boston, MA 02125-3393. Offers PhD.

University of Massachusetts Boston, College of Science and Mathematics, Program in Biotechnology and Biomedical Sciences, Boston, MA 02125-3393. Offers MS. *Program availability:* Part-time, evening/weekend. *Entrance requirements:* For master's, GRE General Test, GRE Subject Test, minimum GPA of 2.75, 3.0 in science and math.

University of Massachusetts Dartmouth, Graduate School, College of Engineering, Program in Biomedical Engineering and Biotechnology, North Dartmouth, MA 02747-2300. Offers biomedical engineering/biotechnology (PhD). *Program availability:* Part-time. Terminal master's awarded for partial completion of doctoral program. *Degree requirements:* For doctorate, comprehensive exam, thesis/dissertation. *Entrance requirements:* For doctorate, GRE, statement of purpose (minimum of 300 words), resume, 3 letters of recommendation, official transcripts. Additional exam requirements/recommendations for international students: required—TOEFL (minimum score 550 paper-based; 79 iBT), IELTS (minimum score 6.5). Electronic applications accepted.

University of Minnesota, Twin Cities Campus, Graduate School, Program in Microbial Engineering, Minneapolis, MN 55455-0213. Offers MS. *Program availability:* Part-time. *Degree requirements:* For master's, thesis. *Entrance requirements:* For master's, GRE General Test. Additional exam requirements/recommendations for international students: required—TOEFL.

University of Missouri–St. Louis, College of Arts and Sciences, Department of Chemistry and Biochemistry, St. Louis, MO 63121. Offers biochemistry and biotechnology (MS); chemistry (MS, PhD). *Program availability:* Part-time, evening/weekend. Terminal master's awarded for partial completion of doctoral program. *Degree requirements:* For master's, thesis optional; for doctorate, thesis/dissertation. *Entrance requirements:* For master's, 2 letters of recommendation; for doctorate, GRE General Test, 3 letters of recommendation. Additional exam requirements/recommendations for international students: required—TOEFL (minimum score 550 paper-based; 79 iBT), IELTS (minimum score 6.5). Electronic applications accepted. *Expenses: Tuition, area resident:* Full-time $9005.40; part-time $6003.60 per credit hour. Tuition, state resident: full-time $9005.40; part-time $6003.60 per credit hour. *Tuition, nonresident:* full-time $22,108; part-time $14,738.40 per credit hour. *International tuition:* $22,107.60 full-time. Tuition and fees vary according to course load.

University of Nevada, Reno, Graduate School, College of Agriculture, Biotechnology and Natural Resources, Program in Biotechnology, Reno, NV 89557. Offers MS. *Degree requirements:* For master's, thesis. *Entrance requirements:* For master's, GRE, minimum GPA of 2.75. Additional exam requirements/recommendations for international students: required—TOEFL (minimum score 500 paper-based; 61 iBT), IELTS (minimum score 6). Electronic applications accepted.

University of North Texas Health Science Center at Fort Worth, Graduate School of Biomedical Sciences, Fort Worth, TX 76107-2699. Offers biochemistry and cancer biology (MS, PhD); biotechnology (MS); cell biology, immunology and microbiology (MS, PhD); clinical research management (MS); forensic genetics (MS); genetics (MS, PhD); integrative physiology (MS, PhD); medical sciences (MS); pharmaceutical sciences and pharmacotherapy (MS, PhD); pharmacology and neuroscience (MS, PhD); structural anatomy and rehabilitation sciences (MS, PhD); DO/MS; DO/PhD. Terminal master's awarded for partial completion of doctoral program. *Degree requirements:* For master's, thesis; for doctorate, thesis/dissertation. *Entrance requirements:* For master's and doctorate, GRE General Test. Additional exam requirements/recommendations for international students: required—TOEFL. *Expenses:* Contact institution.

University of Pennsylvania, School of Engineering and Applied Science, Program in Biotechnology, Philadelphia, PA 19104. Offers MBT. *Program availability:* Part-time. *Students:* 64 full-time (45 women), 24 part-time (12 women); includes 10 minority (7 Asian, non-Hispanic/Latino; 1 Hispanic/Latino; 2 Two or more races, non-Hispanic/Latino), 57 international. Average age 24. 191 applicants, 45% accepted, 37 enrolled. In 2019, 40 master's awarded. *Degree requirements:* For master's, comprehensive exam, thesis optional. *Entrance requirements:* For master's, GRE, bachelor's degree, 3 letters of recommendation, resume, personal statement. Additional exam requirements/recommendations for international students: required—TOEFL (minimum score 100 iBT), IELTS (minimum score 7). *Application deadline:* For fall admission, 3/15 priority date for domestic and international students. Application fee: $80. Electronic applications accepted. *Expenses:* Contact institution. *Application contact:* Associate Director of Graduate Admissions, 215-898-4542, Fax: 215-573-5577, E-mail: admissions1@seas.upenn.edu.
Website: http://www.upenn.edu/biotech/

University of Rhode Island, Graduate School, College of the Environment and Life Sciences, Department of Cell and Molecular Biology, Kingston, RI 02881. Offers biochemistry (MS, PhD); clinical laboratory sciences (MS), including biotechnology, clinical laboratory science, cytopathology; microbiology (MS, PhD); molecular genetics (MS, PhD). *Program availability:* Part-time. *Faculty:* 20 full-time (9 women). *Students:* 1 (woman) part-time. In 2019, 16 master's awarded. *Entrance requirements:* Additional exam requirements/recommendations for international students: required—TOEFL. *Application deadline:* For fall admission, 1/15 for domestic and international students. Application fee: $65. Electronic applications accepted. *Expenses: Tuition, area resident:* Full-time $13,734; part-time $763 per credit. Tuition, state resident: full-time $13,734; part-time $763 per credit. Tuition, nonresident: full-time $26,512; part-time $1473 per credit. *International tuition:* $26,512 full-time. *Required fees:* $1780; $52 per credit. $35 per term. One-time fee: $165. *Financial support:* In 2019–20, 11 teaching assistantships with tuition reimbursements (averaging $10,985 per year) were awarded; traineeships also available. Financial award application deadline: 1/15; financial award applicants required to submit FAFSA. *Unit head:* Dr. Joel Chandlee, Chair, E-mail: joelchandlee@uri.edu. *Application contact:* Dr. Steven Gregory, Graduate Program Director, 401-874-5947, E-mail: stgregory@uri.edu.
Website: https://web.uri.edu/cmb/

University of San Francisco, College of Arts and Sciences, Biotechnology Program, San Francisco, CA 94117. Offers PSM. *Program availability:* Part-time, evening/weekend. *Faculty:* 3 full-time, 2 part-time/adjunct (both women). *Students:* 44 full-time (21 women), 3 part-time (all women); includes 22 minority (2 Black or African American, non-Hispanic/Latino; 12 Asian, non-Hispanic/Latino; 3 Hispanic/Latino; 1 Native Hawaiian or other Pacific Islander, non-Hispanic/Latino; 4 Two or more races, non-Hispanic/Latino), 7 international. Average age 25. 122 applicants, 56% accepted, 27 enrolled. In 2019, 14 master's awarded. *Entrance requirements:* For master's, GRE or MCAT, Upper division biology coursework. Additional exam requirements/recommendations for international students: required—TOEFL (minimum score 90 iBT), IELTS (minimum score 6.5), PTE (minimum score 61). *Application deadline:* For fall admission, 4/15 for domestic and international students. Applications are processed on a rolling basis. Application fee: $55. Electronic applications accepted. Application fee is waived when completed online. *Financial support:* Career-related internships or fieldwork and scholarships/grants available. Financial award applicants required to submit FAFSA. *Unit head:* Dr. Cary Lai, Graduate Director, 415-422-6755, E-mail: cklai2@usfca.edu. *Application contact:* Information Contact, 415-422-5101, Fax: 422-, E-mail: asgraduate@usfca.edu.
Website: https://www.usfca.edu/arts-sciences/graduate-programs/biotechnology

University of Southern California, Keck School of Medicine and Graduate School, Graduate Programs in Medicine, Master of Science Program in Translational Biotechnology, Los Angeles, CA 90089. Offers biotechnology (MS). *Program availability:* Part-time. *Degree requirements:* For master's, experiential projects. *Entrance requirements:* For master's, GRE or MCAT. Additional exam requirements/recommendations for international students: recommended—TOEFL (minimum score 90 iBT), IELTS (minimum score 6.5). Electronic applications accepted.

University of South Florida, Innovative Education, Tampa, FL 33620-9951. Offers adult, career and higher education (Graduate Certificate), including college teaching, leadership in developing human resources, leadership in higher education; Africana studies (Graduate Certificate), including diasporas and health disparities, genocide and human rights; aging studies (Graduate Certificate), including gerontology; art research (Graduate Certificate), including museum studies; business foundations (Graduate Certificate); chemical and biomedical engineering (Graduate Certificate), including materials science and engineering, water, health and sustainability; child and family studies (Graduate Certificate), including positive behavior support; civil and industrial engineering (Graduate Certificate), including transportation systems analysis; community and family health (Graduate Certificate), including maternal and child health, social marketing and public health, violence and injury: prevention and intervention, women's health; criminology (Graduate Certificate), including criminal justice administration; data science for public administration (Graduate Certificate); digital humanities (Graduate Certificate); educational measurement and research (Graduate Certificate), including evaluation; English (Graduate Certificate), including comparative literary studies, creative writing, professional and technical communication; entrepreneurship (Graduate Certificate); environmental health (Graduate Certificate), including safety management; epidemiology and biostatistics (Graduate Certificate), including applied biostatistics, biostatistics, concepts and tools of epidemiology, epidemiology, epidemiology of infectious diseases; geography, environment and planning (Graduate Certificate), including community development, environmental policy and management, geographical information systems; geology (Graduate Certificate), including hydrogeology; global health (Graduate Certificate), including disaster management, global health and Latin American and Caribbean studies, global health practice, humanitarian assistance, infection control; government and international affairs (Graduate Certificate), including Cuban studies, globalization studies; health policy and management (Graduate Certificate), including health management and leadership, public health policy and programs; hearing specialist: early intervention (Graduate

Certificate); industrial and management systems engineering (Graduate Certificate), including systems engineering, technology management; information studies (Graduate Certificate), including school library media specialist; information systems/decision sciences (Graduate Certificate), including analytics and business intelligence; instructional technology (Graduate Certificate), including distance education, Florida digital/virtual educator, instructional design, multimedia design, Web design; internal medicine, bioethics and medical humanities (Graduate Certificate), including biomedical ethics; Latin American and Caribbean studies (Graduate Certificate); leadership for coastal resiliency planning (Graduate Certificate); mass communications (Graduate Certificate), including multimedia journalism; mathematics and statistics (Graduate Certificate), including mathematics; medicine (Graduate Certificate), including aging and neuroscience, bioinformatics, biotechnology, brain fitness and memory management, clinical investigation, hand and upper limb rehabilitation, health informatics, health sciences, integrative weight management, intellectual property, medicine and gender, metabolic and nutritional medicine, metabolic cardiology, pharmacy sciences; national and competitive intelligence (Graduate Certificate); nursing (Graduate Certificate), including simulation based academic fellowship in advanced pain management; psychological and social foundations (Graduate Certificate), including career counseling, college teaching, diversity in education, mental health counseling, school counseling; public affairs (Graduate Certificate), including nonprofit management, public management, research administration; public health (Graduate Certificate), including assessing chemical toxicity and public health risks, health equity, pharmacoepidemiology, public health generalist, toxicology, translational research in adolescent behavioral health; public health practices (Graduate Certificate), including planning for healthy communities; rehabilitation and mental health counseling (Graduate Certificate), including integrative mental health care, marriage and family therapy, rehabilitation technology; secondary education (Graduate Certificate), including ESOL, foreign language education: culture and content, foreign language education: professional; social work (Graduate Certificate), including geriatric social work/clinical gerontology; special education (Graduate Certificate), including autism spectrum disorder, disabilities education: severe/profound; world languages (Graduate Certificate), including teaching English as a second language (TESL) or foreign language. *Unit head:* Dr. Cynthia DeLuca, Associate Vice President and Assistant Vice Provost, 813-974-3077, Fax: 813-974-7061, E-mail: deluca@usf.edu. *Application contact:* Owen Hooper, Director, Summer and Alternative Calendar Programs, 813-974-6917, E-mail: hooper@usf.edu.
Website: http://www.usf.edu/innovative-education/

The University of Texas at Dallas, School of Natural Sciences and Mathematics, Department of Biological Sciences, Richardson, TX 75080. Offers bioinformatics and computational biology (MS); biotechnology (MS); molecular and cell biology (MS, PhD). *Program availability:* Part-time, evening/weekend. *Faculty:* 20 full-time (5 women), 6 part-time/adjunct (4 women). *Students:* 128 full-time (81 women), 12 part-time (7 women); includes 29 minority (1 Black or African American, non-Hispanic/Latino; 19 Asian, non-Hispanic/Latino; 7 Hispanic/Latino; 2 Two or more races, non-Hispanic/Latino), 77 international. Average age 28. 309 applicants, 25% accepted, 38 enrolled. In 2019, 36 master's, 7 doctorates awarded. *Degree requirements:* For master's, thesis optional; for doctorate, thesis/dissertation, publishable paper. *Entrance requirements:* For master's and doctorate, GRE (minimum combined score of 1000 on verbal and quantitative). Additional exam requirements/recommendations for international students: required—TOEFL (minimum score 550 paper-based; 80 iBT). *Application deadline:* For fall admission, 7/15 for domestic students, 5/1 priority date for international students; for spring admission, 11/15 for domestic students, 9/1 priority date for international students. Applications are processed on a rolling basis. Application fee: $50 ($100 for international students). Electronic applications accepted. *Expenses: Tuition, area resident:* Full-time $16,504. Tuition, state resident: full-time $16,504. Tuition, nonresident: full-time $34,266. Tuition and fees vary according to course load. *Financial support:* In 2019–20, 86 students received support, including 1 fellowship with partial tuition reimbursement available (averaging $500 per year), 16 research assistantships with partial tuition reimbursements available (averaging $25,200 per year), 69 teaching assistantships with partial tuition reimbursements available (averaging $18,173 per year); career-related internships or fieldwork, Federal Work-Study, institutionally sponsored loans, scholarships/grants, and unspecified assistantships also available. Support available to part-time students. Financial award application deadline: 4/30; financial award applicants required to submit FAFSA. *Unit head:* Dr. Tae Hoon Kim, Department Head, 972-883-6032, Fax: 972-883-4551, E-mail: biology@utdallas.edu. *Application contact:* Nancy Yu, Graduate Support Assistant, 972-883-4794, Fax: 972-883-4551, E-mail: biology@utdallas.edu.
Website: https://biology.utdallas.edu/

The University of Texas at San Antonio, College of Sciences, Department of Biology, San Antonio, TX 78249-0617. Offers biology (MS); biotechnology (MS); cell and molecular biology (PhD); neurobiology (PhD). Terminal master's awarded for partial completion of doctoral program. *Degree requirements:* For master's, comprehensive exam, thesis or alternative; for doctorate, comprehensive exam, thesis/dissertation. *Entrance requirements:* For master's, GRE General Test, bachelor's degree with 18 credit hours in field of study or in another appropriate field of study; for doctorate, GRE General Test, 3 letters of recommendation, statement of purpose, resume. Additional exam requirements/recommendations for international students: required—TOEFL (minimum score 500 paper-based; 100 iBT), IELTS (minimum score 5). Electronic applications accepted.

The University of Texas Health Science Center at Tyler, School of Medical Biological Sciences, Tyler, TX 75708. Offers biotechnology (MS).

University of the Sciences, Program in Cell Biology and Biotechnology, Philadelphia, PA 19104-4495. Offers MS. *Program availability:* Part-time, evening/weekend. *Degree requirements:* For master's, thesis optional. *Entrance requirements:* For master's, GRE General Test. Additional exam requirements/recommendations for international students: required—TOEFL, TWE. *Expenses:* Contact institution.

University of Toronto, School of Graduate Studies, Program in Biotechnology, Toronto, ON M5S 1A1, Canada. Offers MBiotech. *Entrance requirements:* For master's, minimum B+ average in the last two years of study and/or GRE. Additional exam requirements/recommendations for international students: required—TOEFL (minimum score 580 paper-based; 93 iBT), TWE (minimum score 5). Electronic applications accepted.

University of Utah, Graduate School, Professional Master of Science and Technology Program, Salt Lake City, UT 84112. Offers biotechnology (PSM); computational science (PSM); environmental science (PSM); science instrumentation (PSM). *Program availability:* Part-time. *Faculty:* 1 part-time/adjunct (0 women). *Students:* 15 full-time (7 women), 33 part-time (15 women); includes 10 minority (4 Asian, non-Hispanic/Latino; 1 Hispanic/Latino; 5 Two or more races, non-Hispanic/Latino), 1 international. Average age 31. In 2019, 13 master's awarded. *Degree requirements:* For master's, Professional Experience Project. *Entrance requirements:* For master's, An undergraduate GPA of at least 3.0, based on all undergraduate work. If the undergraduate GPA is below 3.0, a GPA will be calculated on the last 60 semester hours (90 quarter hours) of the undergraduate work for admission consideration; A bachelor's degree from a regionally

accredited college or university. *Application deadline:* For fall admission, 2/1 priority date for domestic students, 2/1 for international students. Application fee: $55 ($65 for international students). *Expenses:* Contact institution. *Financial support:* Unspecified assistantships available. *Unit head:* Ray Hoobler, Director, 801-585-5630, E-mail: ray.hoobler@utah.edu. *Application contact:* Ray Hoobler, Director, 801-585-3650, E-mail: ray.hoobler@utah.edu.
Website: http://pmst.utah.edu/

University of Washington, Graduate School, School of Medicine, Graduate Programs in Medicine, Department of Genome Sciences, Seattle, WA 98195. Offers PhD. *Degree requirements:* For doctorate, thesis/dissertation, general exam. *Entrance requirements:* For doctorate, GRE General Test, minimum GPA of 3.0. Additional exam requirements/recommendations for international students: required—TOEFL. Electronic applications accepted.

University of Wyoming, Graduate Program in Molecular and Cellular Life Sciences, Laramie, WY 82071. Offers PhD. *Degree requirements:* For doctorate, thesis/dissertation, four eight-week laboratory rotations, comprehensive basic practical exam, two-part qualifying exam, seminars, symposium.

Virginia Polytechnic Institute and State University, Graduate School, College of Science, Blacksburg, VA 24061. Offers biological sciences (MS, PhD); biomedical technology development and management (MS); chemistry (MS, PhD); data analysis and applied statistics (MA); economics (PhD); geosciences (MS, PhD); mathematics (MS, PhD); physics (MS, PhD); psychology (MS, PhD); statistics (MS, PhD). *Faculty:* 375 full-time (118 women), 2 part-time/adjunct (1 woman). *Students:* 544 full-time (221 women), 37 part-time (15 women); includes 75 minority (14 Black or African American, non-Hispanic/Latino; 1 American Indian or Alaska Native, non-Hispanic/Latino; 20 Asian, non-Hispanic/Latino; 31 Hispanic/Latino; 9 Two or more races, non-Hispanic/Latino), 216 international. Average age 27. 962 applicants, 33% accepted, 138 enrolled. In 2019, 75 master's, 69 doctorates awarded. *Degree requirements:* For master's, comprehensive exam (for some programs), thesis (for some programs); for doctorate, comprehensive exam (for some programs), thesis/dissertation (for some programs). *Entrance requirements:* For master's and doctorate, GRE/GMAT. Additional exam requirements/recommendations for international students: required—TOEFL (minimum score 90 iBT). *Application deadline:* For fall admission, 8/1 for domestic students, 4/1 for international students; for spring admission, 1/1 for domestic students, 9/1 for international students. Applications are processed on a rolling basis. Application fee: $75. Electronic applications accepted. *Expenses:* Tuition, state resident: full-time $13,700; part-time $761.25 per credit hour. Tuition, nonresident: full-time $27,614; part-time $1534 per credit hour. *Required fees:* $886.50 per term. Tuition and fees vary according to campus/location and program. *Financial support:* In 2019–20, 5 fellowships with full tuition reimbursements (averaging $25,988 per year), 281 research assistantships with full tuition reimbursements (averaging $15,597 per year), 370 teaching assistantships with full tuition reimbursements (averaging $18,225 per year) were awarded; unspecified assistantships also available. Financial award application deadline: 3/1; financial award applicants required to submit FAFSA. *Unit head:* Dr. Sally C. Morton, Dean, 540-231-5422, Fax: 540-231-3380, E-mail: scmorton@vt.edu. *Application contact:* Allison Craft, Executive Assistant, 540-231-6394, Fax: 540-231-3380, E-mail: crafta@vt.edu.
Website: http://www.science.vt.edu/

West Virginia State University, Biotechnology Graduate Program, Institute, WV 25112-1000. Offers MA, MS. *Degree requirements:* For master's, comprehensive exam. *Entrance requirements:* For master's, GRE (Verbal 140, Quantitative 150), International Students: Affidavit of Support, Proof of Immunization, TOEFL (80), evaluation of academic transcripts. Additional exam requirements/recommendations for international students: required—TOEFL. Electronic applications accepted.

Worcester Polytechnic Institute, Graduate Admissions, Department of Biology and Biotechnology, Worcester, MA 01609-2280. Offers MS, PhD. *Program availability:* Part-time, blended/hybrid learning. Terminal master's awarded for partial completion of doctoral program. *Degree requirements:* For master's, thesis (for some programs); for doctorate, comprehensive exam, thesis/dissertation, qualifying exam. *Entrance requirements:* For master's and doctorate, GRE General Test, 3 letters of recommendation, statement of purpose. Additional exam requirements/recommendations for international students: required—TOEFL (minimum score 563 paper-based; 84 iBT), IELTS (minimum score 7). Electronic applications accepted.

Worcester State University, Graduate School, Program in Biotechnology, Worcester, MA 01602-2597. Offers MS. *Program availability:* Part-time, evening/weekend. *Faculty:* 7 full-time (4 women), 2 part-time/adjunct. *Students:* 4 full-time (2 women), 15 part-time (8 women); includes 7 minority (3 Black or African American, non-Hispanic/Latino; 2 Asian, non-Hispanic/Latino; 2 Hispanic/Latino), 1 international. Average age 32. 2 applicants, 100% accepted, 2 enrolled. In 2019, 5 master's awarded. *Degree requirements:* For master's, comprehensive exam, thesis, For a detail list in Degree Completion requirements please see the graduate catalog at catalog.worcester.edu. *Entrance requirements:* For master's, GRE General Test or MAT, For a detail list of entrance requirements please see the graduate catalog at catalog.worcester.edu. Additional exam requirements/recommendations for international students: required—TOEFL (minimum score 550 paper-based; 79 iBT), IELTS (minimum score 6). *Application deadline:* For fall admission, 3/1 for domestic and international students; for spring admission, 11/1 for domestic and international students; for summer admission, 3/1 for domestic and international students. Applications are processed on a rolling basis. Application fee: $50. Electronic applications accepted. *Expenses: Tuition, area resident:* Full-time $3042; part-time $169 per credit hour. Tuition, state resident: full-time $3042; part-time $169 per credit hour. Tuition, nonresident: full-time $3042; part-time $169 per credit hour. *International tuition:* $3042 full-time. *Required fees:* $2754; $153 per credit hour. *Financial support:* Career-related internships or fieldwork, scholarships/grants, and unspecified assistantships available. Financial award application deadline: 3/1; financial award applicants required to submit FAFSA. *Unit head:* Dr. Ellen Fynan, Program Coordinator, 508-929-8596, Fax: 508-929-8148, E-mail: efynan@worcester.edu. *Application contact:* Sara Grady, Associate Dean, Graduate and Professional Development, 508-929-8130, Fax: 508-929-8100, E-mail: sara.grady@worcester.edu.

Yeshiva University, The Katz School, Program in Biotechnology Management and Entrepreneurship, New York, NY 10033-3201. Offers MS. *Program availability:* Part-time.

Nanotechnology

The American University in Cairo, School of Sciences and Engineering, Cairo, Egypt. Offers biotechnology (MS); chemistry (MS); computer science (MS); computing (M Comp); construction engineering (M Eng, MS); electronics and communications engineering (M Eng); environmental engineering (MS); environmental system design (M Eng); mechanical engineering (M Eng, MS); nanotechnology (MS); physics (MS); robotics, control and smart systems (MS); sciences and engineering (PhD); sustainable development (MS, Graduate Diploma). *Program availability:* Part-time, evening/weekend. *Degree requirements:* For master's, comprehensive exam (for some programs), thesis (for some programs); for doctorate, comprehensive exam (for some programs), thesis/dissertation. *Entrance requirements:* Additional exam requirements/recommendations for international students: required—TOEFL (minimum score 450 paper-based; 45 iBT), IELTS (minimum score 5). Electronic applications accepted.

Arizona State University at Tempe, College of Liberal Arts and Sciences, Department of Chemistry and Biochemistry, Tempe, AZ 85287-1604. Offers biochemistry (MS, PhD); chemistry (MS, PhD); nanoscience (PSM). Terminal master's awarded for partial completion of doctoral program. *Degree requirements:* For master's, thesis, interactive Program of Study (iPOS) submitted before completing 50 percent of required credit hours; for doctorate, comprehensive exam, thesis/dissertation, interactive Program of Study (iPOS) submitted before completing 50 percent of required credit hours. *Entrance requirements:* For master's and doctorate, GRE, minimum GPA of 3.0 or equivalent in last 2 years of work leading to bachelor's degree. Additional exam requirements/recommendations for international students: required—TOEFL, IELTS, or PTE. Electronic applications accepted.

Arizona State University at Tempe, College of Liberal Arts and Sciences, Department of Physics, Tempe, AZ 85287-1504. Offers nanoscience (PSM); physics (MNS, PhD). *Program availability:* Part-time. Terminal master's awarded for partial completion of doctoral program. *Degree requirements:* For master's, comprehensive exam, thesis or alternative, interactive Program of Study (iPOS) submitted before completing 50 percent of required credit hours; for doctorate, comprehensive exam, thesis/dissertation, interactive Program of Study (iPOS) submitted before completing 50 percent of required credit hours. *Entrance requirements:* For master's and doctorate, GRE, minimum GPA of 3.0 or equivalent in last 2 years of work leading to bachelor's degree. Additional exam requirements/recommendations for international students: required—TOEFL, IELTS, or PTE. Electronic applications accepted. *Expenses:* Contact institution.

Carnegie Mellon University, Mellon College of Science, Department of Chemistry, Pittsburgh, PA 15213-3891. Offers atmospheric chemistry (PhD); bioinorganic chemistry (PhD); bioorganic chemistry and chemical biology (PhD); biophysical chemistry (PhD); catalysis (PhD); green and environmental chemistry (PhD); materials and nanoscience (PhD); renewable energy (PhD); sensors, probes, and imaging (PhD); spectroscopy and single molecule analysis (PhD); theoretical and computational chemistry (PhD). *Program availability:* Part-time. Terminal master's awarded for partial completion of doctoral program. *Degree requirements:* For doctorate, thesis/dissertation, departmental qualifying and oral exams, teaching experience. *Entrance requirements:* For doctorate, GRE General Test, GRE Subject Test. Additional exam requirements/recommendations for international students: required—TOEFL. Electronic applications accepted.

Cornell University, Graduate School, Graduate Fields of Agriculture and Life Sciences and Graduate Fields of Engineering, Field of Biological and Environmental Engineering, Ithaca, NY 14853. Offers bioenergy and integrated energy systems (M Eng, MPS, MS, PhD); biological engineering (M Eng, MPS, MS, PhD); bioprocess engineering (M Eng, MPS, MS, PhD); ecohydrology (M Eng, MPS, MS, PhD); environmental engineering (M Eng, MPS, MS, PhD); environmental management (MPS); food engineering (M Eng, MPS, MS, PhD); industrial biotechnology (M Eng, MPS, MS, PhD); nanobiotechnology (M Eng, MPS, MS, PhD); sustainable systems (M Eng, MPS, MS, PhD); synthetic biology (MS); syntheticbiology (M Eng, MPS, PhD). Terminal master's awarded for partial completion of doctoral program. *Degree requirements:* For master's, thesis (MS); for doctorate, comprehensive exam, thesis/dissertation. *Entrance requirements:* For master's, letters of recommendation (3 for MS, 2 for M Eng and MPS); for doctorate, GRE General Test, 3 letters of recommendation. Additional exam requirements/recommendations for international students: required—TOEFL (minimum score 550 paper-based; 77 iBT). Electronic applications accepted.

Indiana University of Pennsylvania, School of Graduate Studies and Research, College of Natural Sciences and Mathematics, Department of Physics, Program in Nanoscience/Industrial Materials, Indiana, PA 15705. Offers PSM. *Program availability:* Part-time. *Faculty:* 3 full-time (0 women). *Students:* 2 full-time (0 women), 1 part-time (0 women). Average age 25. 4 applicants, 100% accepted, 2 enrolled. In 2019, 1 master's awarded. *Entrance requirements:* For master's, goal statement, official transcripts, letters of recommendation. Additional exam requirements/recommendations for international students: required—TOEFL (minimum score 540 paper-based; 76 iBT), IELTS (minimum score 6), TOEFL or IELTS. *Application deadline:* Applications are processed on a rolling basis. Application fee: $50. Electronic applications accepted. *Expenses: Tuition, area resident:* Full-time $9288; part-time $516 per credit. Tuition, nonresident: full-time $13,932; part-time $774 per credit. *Required fees:* $4454. One-time fee: $115 full-time. Tuition and fees vary according to course load and program. *Financial support:* In 2019–20, 1 research assistantship (averaging $4,800 per year) was awarded; fellowships, career-related internships or fieldwork, Federal Work-Study, and scholarships/grants also available. Support available to part-time students. Financial award application deadline: 4/15; financial award applicants required to submit FAFSA. *Unit head:* Dr. John Bradshaw, Graduate Coordinator, 724-357-7731, E-mail: bradshaw@iup.edu. *Application contact:* Dr. John Bradshaw, Graduate Coordinator, 724-357-7731, E-mail: bradshaw@iup.edu.

Johns Hopkins University, Engineering Program for Professionals, Part-time Program in Materials Science and Engineering, Baltimore, MD 21218. Offers nanotechnology (M Mat SE). *Program availability:* Part-time, evening/weekend. *Entrance requirements:* Additional exam requirements/recommendations for international students: required—TOEFL (minimum score 600 paper-based; 100 iBT). Electronic applications accepted.

Johns Hopkins University, G. W. C. Whiting School of Engineering, Master of Science in Engineering Management Program, Baltimore, MD 21218. Offers biomaterials (MSEM); civil engineering (MSEM); communications science (MSEM); computer science (MSEM); environmental systems analysis, economics and public policy (MSEM); fluid mechanics (MSEM); materials science and engineering (MSEM); mechanical engineering (MSEM); mechanics and materials (MSEM); nano-biotechnology (MSEM); nanomaterials and nanotechnology (MSEM); operations research (MSEM); probability and statistics (MSEM); smart product and device design (MSEM). *Entrance requirements:* For master's, GRE, 3 letters of recommendation, statement of purpose, transcripts. Additional exam requirements/recommendations for international students: required—TOEFL (minimum score 600 paper-based, 100 iBT) or IELTS (7). Electronic applications accepted.

Louisiana Tech University, Graduate School, College of Applied and Natural Sciences, Ruston, LA 71272. Offers biology (MS); dietetics (Graduate Certificate); health informatics (MHI); molecular science and nanotechnology (MS, PhD). *Program availability:* Part-time. *Degree requirements:* For master's, comprehensive exam (for some programs), thesis (for some programs); for doctorate, comprehensive exam, thesis/dissertation. *Entrance requirements:* For master's and doctorate, GRE General Test, transcript with bachelor's degree awarded; for Graduate Certificate, transcript with bachelor's degree awarded. Additional exam requirements/recommendations for international students: required—TOEFL (minimum score 550 paper-based; 80 iBT), IELTS (minimum score 6.5). Electronic applications accepted. *Expenses: Tuition, area resident:* Full-time $6592; part-time $400 per credit. Tuition, state resident: full-time $6592; part-time $400 per credit. Tuition, nonresident: full-time $13,333; part-time $681 per credit. *International tuition:* $13,333 full-time. *Required fees:* $3011; $3011 per unit.

Louisiana Tech University, Graduate School, College of Engineering and Science, Ruston, LA 71272. Offers applied physics (MS); biomedical engineering (PhD); computer science (MS); engineering (MS, PhD), including cyberspace engineering (PhD), engineering education (PhD), engineering physics (PhD), materials and infrastructure systems (PhD), micro/nanoscale systems (PhD); engineering and technology management (MS); mathematics (MS); molecular science and nanotechnology (MS, PhD). *Program availability:* Part-time-only. Terminal master's awarded for partial completion of doctoral program. *Degree requirements:* For master's, thesis (for some programs); for doctorate, thesis/dissertation. *Entrance requirements:* For master's and Graduate Certificate, GRE General Test, minimum GPA of 3.0 in last 60 hours. Additional exam requirements/recommendations for international students: required—TOEFL (minimum score 550 paper-based; 80 iBT), IELTS (minimum score 6.5). Electronic applications accepted. *Expenses: Tuition, area resident:* Full-time $6592; part-time $400 per credit. Tuition, state resident: full-time $6592; part-time $400 per credit. Tuition, nonresident: full-time $13,333; part-time $681 per credit. *International tuition:* $13,333 full-time. *Required fees:* $3011; $3011 per unit.

North Dakota State University, College of Graduate and Interdisciplinary Studies, College of Engineering, Doctoral Program in Engineering, Fargo, ND 58102. Offers environmental and conservation science (PhD); materials and nanotechnology (PhD); natural resource management (PhD); STEM education (PhD); transportation and logistics (PhD). *Degree requirements:* For doctorate, comprehensive exam, thesis/dissertation. *Entrance requirements:* For doctorate, bachelor's degree in engineering, minimum GPA of 3.0. Additional exam requirements/recommendations for international students: required—TOEFL. Electronic applications accepted. *Expenses:* Contact institution.

North Dakota State University, College of Graduate and Interdisciplinary Studies, Interdisciplinary Program in Materials and Nanotechnology, Fargo, ND 58102. Offers MS, PhD. *Entrance requirements:* For doctorate, GRE General Test. Additional exam requirements/recommendations for international students: required—TOEFL. Tuition and fees vary according to program and reciprocity agreements.

South Dakota School of Mines and Technology, Graduate Division, Program in Nanoscience and Nanoengineering, Rapid City, SD 57701-3995. Offers PhD. *Program availability:* Part-time. *Degree requirements:* For doctorate, thesis/dissertation. *Entrance requirements:* Additional exam requirements/recommendations for international students: required—TOEFL (minimum score 520 paper-based; 68 iBT). Electronic applications accepted.

State University of New York Polytechnic Institute, College of Nanoscale Science and Engineering, Albany, NY 13502. Offers nanoscale engineering (PhD); nanoscale science (MS); MD/PhD. *Degree requirements:* For master's, comprehensive exam, thesis, Research Project; for doctorate, comprehensive exam, thesis/dissertation. *Entrance requirements:* For master's, GRE (preferred, not required), background in sciences. Additional exam requirements/recommendations for international students: required—TOEFL (minimum score 79 paper-based), IELTS (minimum score 6.5), PTE (minimum score 53), TOEFL, IELTS, or PTE; GRE. Electronic applications accepted. *Expenses:* Contact institution.

University at Buffalo, the State University of New York, Graduate School, School of Engineering and Applied Sciences, Department of Chemical and Biological Engineering, Buffalo, NY 14260. Offers bioengineering nanotechnology (Certificate); chemical and biological engineering (ME, MS, PhD); nanomaterials and materials informatics (Certificate). *Program availability:* Part-time. *Degree requirements:* For master's, thesis (for some programs); for doctorate, comprehensive exam, thesis/dissertation. *Entrance requirements:* For master's and doctorate, GRE General Test. Additional exam requirements/recommendations for international students: required—TOEFL (minimum score 550 paper-based; 79 iBT). Electronic applications accepted. *Expenses: Tuition, area resident:* Full-time $11,310; part-time $471 per credit hour. Tuition, state resident: full-time $11,310; part-time $471 per credit hour. Tuition, nonresident: full-time $23,100; part-time $963 per credit hour. *International tuition:* $23,100 full-time. *Required fees:* $2820.

University of Alberta, Faculty of Graduate Studies and Research, Department of Electrical and Computer Engineering, Edmonton, AB T6G 2E1, Canada. Offers communications (M Eng, M Sc, PhD); computer engineering (M Eng, M Sc, PhD); electromagnetics (M Eng, M Sc, PhD); nanotechnology and microdevices (M Eng, M Sc, PhD); power/power electronics (M Eng, M Sc, PhD); systems (M Eng, M Sc, PhD). Terminal master's awarded for partial completion of doctoral program. *Degree requirements:* For master's, thesis; for doctorate, thesis/dissertation. *Entrance requirements:* Additional exam requirements/recommendations for international students: required—TOEFL. Electronic applications accepted.

University of California, Riverside, Graduate Division, Materials Science and Engineering Program, Riverside, CA 92521. Offers MS. *Entrance requirements:* For master's, GRE. Additional exam requirements/recommendations for international students: required—TOEFL (minimum score 550 paper-based; 80 iBT). Electronic applications accepted.

University of California, San Diego, Graduate Division, Department of Electrical and Computer Engineering, La Jolla, CA 92093. Offers applied ocean science (MS, PhD); applied physics (MS, PhD); communication theory and systems (MS, PhD); computer engineering (MS, PhD); electronic circuits and systems (MS, PhD); intelligent systems, robotics and control (MS, PhD); medical devices and systems (MS, PhD); nanoscale devices and systems (MS, PhD); photonics (MS, PhD); signal and image processing (MS, PhD). *Students:* 983 full-time (216 women), 80 part-time (15 women). 3,675 applicants, 33% accepted, 430 enrolled. In 2019, 287 master's, 50 doctorates awarded. Terminal master's awarded for partial completion of doctoral program. *Degree requirements:* For master's, comprehensive exam (for some programs), thesis (for some programs); for doctorate, comprehensive exam, thesis/dissertation. *Entrance requirements:* For master's and doctorate, GRE General Test, minimum GPA of 3.0, resume or curriculum vitae (recommended). Additional exam requirements/recommendations for international students: required—TOEFL (minimum score 550 paper-based; 80 iBT), IELTS (minimum score 7), PTE (minimum score 65). *Application deadline:* For fall admission, 12/18 for domestic students. Application fee: $105 ($125 for international students). Electronic applications accepted. *Financial support:* Fellowships, research assistantships, teaching assistantships, scholarships/grants, traineeships, and unspecified assistantships available. Financial award applicants required to submit FAFSA. *Unit head:* Bill Lin, Chair, 858-822-1383, E-mail: billin@ucsd.edu. *Application contact:* Sean Jones, Graduate Admissions Coordinator, 858-534-3213, E-mail: ecegradapps@ece.ucsd.edu.
Website: http://ece.ucsd.edu/

University of California, San Diego, Graduate Division, Department of Nanoengineering, La Jolla, CA 92093. Offers MS, PhD. *Students:* 121 full-time (35 women), 3 part-time (1 woman). 264 applicants, 32% accepted, 38 enrolled. In 2019, 21 master's, 13 doctorates awarded. *Degree requirements:* For master's, comprehensive exam (for some programs), thesis (for some programs), comprehensive exam or thesis; for doctorate, comprehensive exam, thesis/dissertation, 1-quarter teaching assistantship. *Entrance requirements:* For master's and doctorate, GRE General Test, 3 letters of recommendation, statement of purpose, resume. Additional exam requirements/recommendations for international students: required—TOEFL (minimum score 550 paper-based; 80 iBT), IELTS (minimum score 7). *Application deadline:* For fall admission, 12/20 for domestic students. Application fee: $105 ($125 for international students). Electronic applications accepted. *Financial support:* Fellowships, research assistantships, teaching assistantships, and scholarships/grants available. Financial award applicants required to submit FAFSA. *Unit head:* Jonathan Pokorski, Chair, 858-246-3183, E-mail: jpokorski@ucsd.edu. *Application contact:* Dana Jimenez, Graduate Coordinator, 858-822-7981, E-mail: dljimenez@ucsd.edu.
Website: http://nanoengineering.ucsd.edu

University of New Mexico, Graduate Studies, School of Engineering, Program in Nanoscience and Microsystems Engineering, Albuquerque, NM 87131-2039. Offers MS, PhD. *Program availability:* Part-time. *Students:* 18 full-time (6 women), 24 part-time (2 women); includes 8 minority (3 Black or African American, non-Hispanic/Latino; 3 Asian, non-Hispanic/Latino; 2 Hispanic/Latino), 11 international. 11 applicants, 64% accepted, 4 enrolled. In 2019, 7 master's, 7 doctorates awarded. *Degree requirements:* For master's, comprehensive exam, thesis; for doctorate, comprehensive exam, thesis/dissertation. *Entrance requirements:* For master's and doctorate, GRE. Additional exam requirements/recommendations for international students: required—TOEFL (minimum score 550 paper-based; 80 iBT), IELTS (minimum score 6.5), TOEFL or IELTS, not both. *Application deadline:* For fall admission, 7/30 for domestic students, 2/1 for international students; for spring admission, 11/30 for domestic students, 6/1 for international students. Applications are processed on a rolling basis. Application fee: $50. Electronic applications accepted. *Expenses:* Tuition, state resident: full-time $7633; part-time $972 per year. Tuition, nonresident: full-time $22,586; part-time $3840 per year. *International tuition:* $23,292 full-time. *Required fees:* $8608. Tuition and fees vary according to course level, course load, degree level, program and student level. *Financial support:* Applicants required to submit FAFSA. *Unit head:* Dr. Sang M Han, Professor, 505-277-3118, Fax: 505-277-1979, E-mail: meister@unm.edu. *Application contact:* Linda Stewart, Graduate Programs Coordinator, 505-277-6824, Fax: 505-277-1979, E-mail: lbugge@unm.edu.
Website: http://nsme.unm.edu/

University of Pennsylvania, School of Engineering and Applied Science, Program in Nanotechnology, Philadelphia, PA 19104. Offers MSE. *Program availability:* Part-time. *Students:* 25 full-time (5 women), 2 part-time (0 women); includes 3 minority (2 Asian, non-Hispanic/Latino; 1 Hispanic/Latino), 19 international. Average age 24. 57 applicants, 72% accepted, 17 enrolled. In 2019, 11 master's awarded. *Degree requirements:* For master's, comprehensive exam, thesis optional. *Entrance requirements:* For master's, GRE, bachelor's degree, letters of recommendation, resume, personal statement. Additional exam requirements/recommendations for international students: required—TOEFL (minimum score 100 iBT), IELTS (minimum score 7). *Application deadline:* For fall admission, 3/15 priority date for domestic and international students. Application fee: $80. Electronic applications accepted. *Expenses:* Contact institution. *Application contact:* Associate Director of Graduate Admissions, 215-898-4542, Fax: 215-573-5577, E-mail: admissions1@seas.upenn.edu.
Website: http://www.masters.nano.upenn.edu/

University of South Florida, USF Health Taneja College of Pharmacy, Tampa, FL 33612. Offers pharmaceutical nanotechnology (MS), including biomedical engineering, drug discovery, delivery, development and manufacturing; pharmacy (Pharm D), including pharmacy and health education. *Accreditation:* ACPE. *Program availability:* Part-time, 100% online, blended/hybrid learning. *Faculty:* 32 full-time (18 women), 1 part-time/adjunct (0 women). *Students:* 398 full-time (234 women), 7 part-time (3 women); includes 180 minority (33 Black or African American, non-Hispanic/Latino; 72 Asian, non-Hispanic/Latino; 59 Hispanic/Latino; 2 Native Hawaiian or other Pacific Islander, non-Hispanic/Latino; 14 Two or more races, non-Hispanic/Latino), 13 international. Average age 25. 465 applicants, 44% accepted, 112 enrolled. In 2019, 11 master's, 91 doctorates awarded. *Degree requirements:* For master's, comprehensive exam, thesis optional, capstone or thesis; for doctorate, internship/field experience. *Entrance requirements:* For master's, GRE, MCAT or DAT, bachelor's preferably in biomedical, biological, chemical sciences or engineering; 2 letters of recommendation; resume; professional statement; interview; for doctorate, PCAT, minimum GPA of 2.75 overall (preferred); completion of 72 prerequisite credit hours; U.S. citizenship or permanent resident; interviews; criminal background check and drug screen. Additional exam requirements/recommendations for international students: required—TOEFL (minimum score 550 paper-based; 79 iBT), IELTS (minimum score 6.5). *Application deadline:* For fall admission, 6/1 for domestic and international students; for spring admission, 10/15 for domestic students, 9/15 for international students; for summer admission, 2/15 for domestic and international students. Applications are processed on a rolling basis. Application fee: $30. Electronic applications accepted. *Financial support:* In 2019–20, 159 students received support. Scholarships/grants available. *Unit head:* James Lambert, 813-974-4562, E-mail: jlambert2@usf.edu. *Application contact:* Dr. Amy Schwartz, Admissions Recruiter, 813-974-4652, E-mail: jlambert2@usf.edu.
Website: https://health.usf.edu/pharmacy

University of Washington, Graduate School, College of Engineering and School of Medicine, Department of Bioengineering, Seattle, WA 98195-5061. Offers applied bioengineering (MAB); bioengineering (MS, PhD); bioengineering and nanotechnology (PhD); pharmaceutical bioengineering (MS). *Program availability:* Part-time. *Students:* 157 full-time (73 women), 36 part-time (19 women); includes 53 minority (4 Black or African American, non-Hispanic/Latino; 1 American Indian or Alaska Native, non-Hispanic/Latino; 28 Asian, non-Hispanic/Latino; 13 Hispanic/Latino; 7 Two or more races, non-Hispanic/Latino), 47 international. Average age 26. 1,437 applicants, 13% accepted, 79 enrolled. In 2019, 37 master's, 31 doctorates awarded. *Degree requirements:* For master's, comprehensive exam, thesis; for doctorate, comprehensive exam, thesis/dissertation, qualifying exam, general exam, thesis defense. *Entrance requirements:* For master's and doctorate, GRE General Test (optional), minimum GPA of 3.0, transcripts, statement of purpose, letters of recommendation, resume/curriculum vitae. Additional exam requirements/recommendations for international students: required—TOEFL (minimum score 500 paper-based; 80 iBT). *Application deadline:* For

fall admission, 12/3 for domestic and international students. Application fee: $85. Electronic applications accepted. Application fee is waived when completed online. *Expenses:* Contact institution. *Financial support:* In 2019–20, 1 fellowship with full tuition reimbursement (averaging $40,680 per year), 114 research assistantships with full tuition reimbursements (averaging $40,680 per year), 2 teaching assistantships with full tuition reimbursements (averaging $34,800 per year) were awarded; Federal Work-Study, institutionally sponsored loans, scholarships/grants, health care benefits, tuition waivers (full), and unspecified assistantships also available. Support available to part-time students. Financial award application deadline: 12/1; financial award applicants required to submit FAFSA. *Unit head:* Dr. Michael Regnier, Professor/Interim Chair, 206-685-2000, Fax: 206-685-3300, E-mail: mregnier@uw.edu. *Application contact:* Kalei Combs, Graduate Academic Counselor, 206-221-5448, Fax: 206-685-3300, E-mail: kaleic@uw.edu.
Website: https://bioe.uw.edu/

University of Washington, Graduate School, College of Engineering, Department of Chemical Engineering, Seattle, WA 98195-1750. Offers chemical engineering (MS, PhD); chemical engineering and advanced data science (PhD); chemical engineering and nanotechnology (PhD). *Students:* 79 full-time (32 women), 14 part-time (0 women); includes 13 minority (1 Black or African American, non-Hispanic/Latino; 5 Asian, non-Hispanic/Latino; 5 Hispanic/Latino; 2 Two or more races, non-Hispanic/Latino), 45 international. Average age 25. 371 applicants, 35% accepted, 27 enrolled. In 2019, 29 master's, 16 doctorates awarded. Terminal master's awarded for partial completion of doctoral program. *Degree requirements:* For master's, comprehensive exam, thesis optional, final exam, research project, degree completed in 6 years; for doctorate, comprehensive exam, thesis/dissertation, general and final exams, research project, completion of all work within 10 years. *Entrance requirements:* For master's and doctorate, GRE General Test (optional), minimum GPA of 3.0, transcripts, personal statement, 3 letters of recommendation, writing sample (optional). Additional exam requirements/recommendations for international students: required—TOEFL (minimum score 580 paper-based; 92 iBT). *Application deadline:* For fall admission, 1/1 priority date for domestic students, 12/15 priority date for international students. Applications are processed on a rolling basis. Application fee: $85. Electronic applications accepted. *Expenses:* Contact institution. *Financial support:* In 2019–20, 10 fellowships with full tuition reimbursements (averaging $33,960 per year), 40 research assistantships with full tuition reimbursements (averaging $33,960 per year), 12 teaching assistantships with full tuition reimbursements (averaging $33,960 per year) were awarded; Federal Work-Study, institutionally sponsored loans, scholarships/grants, health care benefits, tuition waivers, and unspecified assistantships also available. Support available to part-time students. Financial award application deadline: 1/1. *Unit head:* Dr. Jim Pfaendtner, Professor/Chair, 206-616-8128, Fax: 206-685-3451, E-mail: jpfaendt@uw.edu. *Application contact:* Allison Sherrill, Graduate Program Advisor, 206-685-9785, E-mail: sherra@uw.edu.
Website: http://www.cheme.washington.edu/

University of Washington, Graduate School, College of Engineering, Department of Electrical and Computer Engineering, Seattle, WA 98195-2500. Offers electrical engineering (MS, PhD); electrical engineering and nanotechnology (PhD). *Program availability:* Part-time, evening/weekend. *Students:* 282 full-time (62 women), 149 part-time (34 women); includes 85 minority (7 Black or African American, non-Hispanic/Latino; 56 Asian, non-Hispanic/Latino; 14 Hispanic/Latino; 8 Two or more races, non-Hispanic/Latino), 220 international. Average age 27. 1,356 applicants, 38% accepted, 164 enrolled. In 2019, 83 master's, 30 doctorates awarded. Terminal master's awarded for partial completion of doctoral program. *Degree requirements:* For master's, thesis optional; for doctorate, thesis/dissertation, qualifying, general, and final exams. *Entrance requirements:* For master's and doctorate, minimum GPA of 3.5 (recommended); resume or curriculum vitae, statement of purpose, 3 letters of recommendation, undergraduate and graduate transcripts. Additional exam requirements/recommendations for international students: required—TOEFL (minimum score 600 paper-based; 92 iBT). *Application deadline:* For fall admission, 12/15 for domestic and

international students. Application fee: $85. Electronic applications accepted. *Expenses:* Contact institution. *Financial support:* In 2019–20, 5 fellowships with full tuition reimbursements (averaging $34,080 per year), 100 research assistantships with full tuition reimbursements (averaging $34,080 per year), 50 teaching assistantships with full tuition reimbursements (averaging $33,240 per year) were awarded; Federal Work-Study, institutionally sponsored loans, scholarships/grants, health care benefits, tuition waivers (full), and unspecified assistantships also available. Support available to part-time students. Financial award application deadline: 12/15. *Unit head:* Dr. Erik Klavins, Professor/Chair, 206-616-1743, Fax: 206-543-3842, E-mail: chair@ece.uw.edu. *Application contact:* Brenda Larson, Lead Academic Counselor, Graduate Programs, 206-616-1351, Fax: 206-543-3842, E-mail: grad@ece.uw.edu.
Website: http://www.ece.uw.edu

University of Washington, Graduate School, College of Engineering, Department of Materials Science and Engineering, Seattle, WA 98195-2120. Offers applied materials science and engineering (MS); materials science and engineering (MS, PhD); materials science and engineering and nanotechnology (PhD); materials science and engineering, nanotechnology, and molecular engineering (PhD). *Program availability:* Part-time. *Students:* 118 full-time (27 women), 26 part-time (8 women); includes 31 minority (1 Black or African American, non-Hispanic/Latino; 16 Asian, non-Hispanic/Latino; 9 Hispanic/Latino; 1 Native Hawaiian or other Pacific Islander, non-Hispanic/Latino; 4 Two or more races, non-Hispanic/Latino), 72 international. Average age 25. 435 applicants, 39% accepted, 57 enrolled. In 2019, 44 master's, 9 doctorates awarded. Terminal master's awarded for partial completion of doctoral program. *Degree requirements:* For master's, comprehensive exam, final paper or thesis and presentation; for doctorate, comprehensive exam, thesis/dissertation, qualifying evaluation, general and final exams. *Entrance requirements:* For master's and doctorate, GRE General Test, minimum GPA of 3.0, resume/curriculum vitae, letters of recommendation, statement of purpose, transcripts. Additional exam requirements/recommendations for international students: required—TOEFL (minimum score 92 iBT). *Application deadline:* For fall admission, 1/6 for domestic and international students. Application fee: $85. Electronic applications accepted. *Expenses:* Contact institution. *Financial support:* In 2019–20, 35 research assistantships with full tuition reimbursements (averaging $30,840 per year), 14 teaching assistantships with full tuition reimbursements (averaging $30,840 per year) were awarded; fellowships with full tuition reimbursements, Federal Work-Study, institutionally sponsored loans, scholarships/grants, health care benefits, tuition waivers, unspecified assistantships, and stipend supplements also available. Support available to part-time students. Financial award application deadline: 1/6. *Unit head:* Dr. Jihui Yang, Professor/Chair, 206-543-7090, Fax: 206-221-4934, E-mail: jihuiy@uw.edu. *Application contact:* Karen Wetterhahn, Academic Counselor, 206-543-2740, Fax: 206-543-3100, E-mail: karenlw@uw.edu.
Website: http://mse.washington.edu

Virginia Commonwealth University, Graduate School, College of Humanities and Sciences, Department of Physics, Richmond, VA 23284-9005. Offers medical physics (MS, PhD); nanoscience and nanotechnology (PhD); physics and applied physics (MS). *Program availability:* Part-time. *Degree requirements:* For master's, comprehensive exam, thesis optional. *Entrance requirements:* For master's, GRE. Additional exam requirements/recommendations for international students: required—TOEFL (minimum score 600 paper-based; 100 iBT); recommended—IELTS (minimum score 6.5). Electronic applications accepted.

Virginia Commonwealth University, Graduate School, College of Humanities and Sciences, Program in Nanosciences, Richmond, VA 23284-9005. Offers PhD. *Entrance requirements:* For doctorate, GRE General Test. Additional exam requirements/recommendations for international students: required—TOEFL (minimum score 600 paper-based; 100 iBT); recommended—IELTS (minimum score 6.5). Electronic applications accepted.

Section 6
Chemical Engineering

This section contains a directory of institutions offering graduate work in chemical engineering, followed by an in-depth entry submitted by an institution that chose to prepare a detailed program description. Additional information about programs listed in the directory but not augmented by an in-depth entry may be obtained by writing directly to the dean of a graduate school or chair of a department at the address given in the directory.

For programs offering related work, see also in this book *Engineering and Applied Sciences; Geological, Mineral/Mining, and Petroleum Engineering; Management of Engineering and Technology;* and *Materials Sciences and Engineering.* In the other guides in this series:

Graduate Programs in the Humanities, Arts & Social Sciences
See *Family and Consumer Sciences (Clothing and Textiles)*

Graduate Programs in the Biological/Biomedical Sciences & Health-Related Medical Professions
See *Biochemistry*

Graduate Programs in the Physical Sciences, Mathematics, Agricultural Sciences, the Environment & Natural Resources
See *Chemistry* and *Geosciences (Geochemistry* and *Geology)*

CONTENTS

Program Directories

Biochemical Engineering

Brown University, Graduate School, School of Engineering, Providence, RI 02912. Offers biomedical engineering (Sc M, PhD); chemical and biochemical engineering (Sc M, PhD); electrical sciences and computer engineering (Sc M, PhD); fluid and thermal sciences (Sc M, PhD); materials science and engineering (Sc M, PhD); mechanics of solids and structures (Sc M, PhD). *Degree requirements:* For doctorate, thesis/dissertation, preliminary exam.

Cornell University, Graduate School, Graduate Fields of Engineering, Field of Chemical Engineering, Ithaca, NY 14853. Offers advanced materials processing (M Eng, MS, PhD); applied mathematics and computational methods (M Eng, MS, PhD); biochemical engineering (M Eng, MS, PhD); chemical reaction engineering (M Eng, MS, PhD); classical and statistical thermodynamics (M Eng, MS, PhD); fluid dynamics, rheology and biorheology (M Eng, MS, PhD); heat and mass transfer (M Eng, MS, PhD); kinetics and catalysis (M Eng, MS, PhD); polymers (M Eng, MS, PhD); surface science (M Eng, MS, PhD). *Degree requirements:* For master's, thesis (MS); for doctorate, comprehensive exam, thesis/dissertation. *Entrance requirements:* For master's and doctorate, GRE General Test, 2 letters of recommendation. Additional exam requirements/recommendations for international students: required—TOEFL (minimum score 600 paper-based; 77 iBT). Electronic applications accepted.

Drexel University, College of Engineering, Department of Chemical and Biological Engineering, Program in Biochemical Engineering, Philadelphia, PA 19104-2875. Offers MS. *Program availability:* Part-time, evening/weekend. *Degree requirements:* For master's, thesis. *Entrance requirements:* For master's, minimum GPA of 3.0 in chemical engineering or biological sciences. Additional exam requirements/recommendations for international students: required—TOEFL. Electronic applications accepted.

Lehigh University, P.C. Rossin College of Engineering and Applied Science, Department of Chemical and Biomolecular Engineering, Bethlehem, PA 18015. Offers biological chemical engineering (M Eng); chemical energy engineering (M Eng); chemical engineering (M Eng, MS, PhD); MBA/E. *Program availability:* Part-time, 100% online. *Faculty:* 13 full-time (2 women), 1 part-time/adjunct (0 women). *Students:* 52 full-time (20 women), 26 part-time (10 women); includes 9 minority (8 Asian, non-Hispanic/Latino; 1 Hispanic/Latino), 36 international. Average age 27. 125 applicants, 61% accepted, 28 enrolled. In 2019, 7 master's, 2 doctorates awarded. Terminal master's awarded for partial completion of doctoral program. *Degree requirements:* For master's, thesis (for some programs); for doctorate, comprehensive exam, thesis/dissertation. *Entrance requirements:* For master's and doctorate, GRE General Test. Additional exam requirements/recommendations for international students: required—TOEFL (minimum score 79 iBT), IELTS (minimum score 6.5). *Application deadline:* For fall admission, 7/15 for domestic students, 7/15 priority date for international students; for spring admission, 12/1 for domestic and international students. Applications are processed on a rolling basis. Application fee: $75. Electronic applications accepted. *Financial support:* In 2019–20, 40 students received support, including 4 fellowships with full tuition reimbursements available (averaging $29,400 per year), 30 research assistantships with full tuition reimbursements available (averaging $29,400 per year), 3 teaching assistantships with full tuition reimbursements available (averaging $29,400 per year). Financial award application deadline: 1/15. *Unit head:* Dr. Mayuresh V. Kothare, Chairman, 610-758-6654, Fax: 610-758-5057, E-mail: mvk2@lehigh.edu. *Application contact:* Janine Jekels, Academic Coordinator, 610-758-4260, Fax: 610-758-5057, E-mail: inchegs@lehigh.edu.
Website: https://www.che.lehigh.edu/

Rutgers University - New Brunswick, Graduate School-New Brunswick, Program in Chemical and Biochemical Engineering, Piscataway, NJ 08854-8097. Offers MS, PhD. *Program availability:* Part-time, evening/weekend. Terminal master's awarded for partial completion of doctoral program. *Degree requirements:* For master's, thesis or alternative; for doctorate, thesis/dissertation. *Entrance requirements:* For master's and doctorate, GRE General Test. Additional exam requirements/recommendations for international students: required—TOEFL.

University of California, Irvine, Samueli School of Engineering, Department of Chemical Engineering and Materials Science, Irvine, CA 92697. Offers chemical and biochemical engineering (MS, PhD); materials science and engineering (MS, PhD). *Program availability:* Part-time. *Students:* 139 full-time (58 women), 3 part-time (2 women); includes 40 minority (5 Black or African American, non-Hispanic/Latino; 28 Asian, non-Hispanic/Latino; 6 Hispanic/Latino; 1 Two or more races, non-Hispanic/Latino), 56 international. Average age 26. 435 applicants, 34% accepted, 48 enrolled. In 2019, 30 master's, 26 doctorates awarded. Terminal master's awarded for partial completion of doctoral program. *Entrance requirements:* For master's and doctorate, GRE General Test, minimum GPA of 3.0, 3 letters of recommendation. Additional exam requirements/recommendations for international students: required—TOEFL (minimum score 550 paper-based). *Application deadline:* For fall admission, 1/15 priority date for domestic students, 1/15 for international students. Applications are processed on a rolling basis. Application fee: $120 ($140 for international students). Electronic applications accepted. *Financial support:* Fellowships, research assistantships with full tuition reimbursements, teaching assistantships, institutionally sponsored loans, traineeships, health care benefits, and unspecified assistantships available. Financial award application deadline: 3/1; financial award applicants required to submit FAFSA. *Unit head:* Prof. Vasan Venugopalan, Chair, 949-824-5802, Fax: 949-824-2541, E-mail: vvenugop@uci.edu. *Application contact:* Grace Chau, Academic Program and Graduate Admission Coordinator, 949-824-3887, Fax: 949-824-2541, E-mail: chaug@uci.edu.
Website: http://www.eng.uci.edu/dept/chems

University of Connecticut, Graduate School, School of Engineering, Department of Chemical and Biomolecular Engineering, Storrs, CT 06269. Offers MS, PhD. Terminal master's awarded for partial completion of doctoral program. *Degree requirements:* For master's, comprehensive exam, thesis or alternative; for doctorate, thesis/dissertation.

Entrance requirements: For master's and doctorate, GRE General Test. Additional exam requirements/recommendations for international students: required—TOEFL (minimum score 550 paper-based). Electronic applications accepted.

University of Georgia, College of Engineering, Athens, GA 30602. Offers MS.

The University of Iowa, Graduate College, College of Engineering, Department of Chemical and Biochemical Engineering, Iowa City, IA 52242-1316. Offers MS, PhD. *Program availability:* Part-time. *Degree requirements:* For master's, comprehensive exam (for some programs), thesis (for some programs); for doctorate, comprehensive exam, thesis/dissertation. *Entrance requirements:* For master's and doctorate, GRE (minimum combined score of 310 on verbal and quantitative), minimum undergraduate GPA of 3.0. Additional exam requirements/recommendations for international students: required—TOEFL (minimum score 600 paper-based; 100 iBT), IELTS (minimum score 7). Electronic applications accepted.

The University of Manchester, School of Chemical Engineering and Analytical Science, Manchester, United Kingdom. Offers biocatalysis (M Phil, PhD); chemical engineering (M Phil, PhD); chemical engineering and analytical science (M Phil, D Eng, PhD); colloids, crystals, interfaces and materials (M Phil, PhD); environment and sustainable technology (M Phil, PhD); instrumentation (M Phil, PhD); multi-scale modeling (M Phil, PhD); process integration (M Phil, PhD); systems biology (M Phil, PhD).

University of Maryland, Baltimore County, The Graduate School, College of Engineering and Information Technology, Department of Chemical, Biochemical, and Environmental Engineering, Post Baccalaureate Certificate Program in Biochemical Regulatory Engineering, Baltimore, MD 21250. Offers Postbaccalaureate Certificate. *Program availability:* Part-time. *Students:* 1 (woman) part-time; minority (Black or African American, non-Hispanic/Latino). Average age 25. 5 applicants, 60% accepted, 1 enrolled. In 2019, 9 Postbaccalaureate Certificates awarded. *Application deadline:* For fall admission, 7/1 for domestic and international students; for spring admission, 2/1 for domestic students, 12/1 for international students. Applications are processed on a rolling basis. Application fee: $70. Electronic applications accepted. *Expenses:* $14,382 per year. *Unit head:* Dr. Antonio Moreira, Vice Provost for Academic Affairs, 410-455-6576, E-mail: moreira@umbc.edu. *Application contact:* Dr. Erin Lavik, Professor/Graduate Program Director, 410-455-3428, Fax: 410-455-1049, E-mail: elavik@umbc.edu.
Website: https://cbee.umbc.edu/academics/graduate-degree-programs/graduate-certificate-in-biochemical-regulatory-engineering/

University of Maryland, Baltimore County, The Graduate School, College of Engineering and Information Technology, Department of Chemical, Biochemical, and Environmental Engineering, Program in Chemical and Biochemical Engineering, Baltimore, MD 21250. Offers MS, PhD. *Program availability:* Part-time. *Faculty:* 16 full-time (6 women), 4 part-time/adjunct (1 woman). *Students:* 32 full-time (14 women), 3 part-time (1 woman); includes 9 minority (6 Black or African American, non-Hispanic/Latino; 1 Asian, non-Hispanic/Latino; 1 Hispanic/Latino; 1 Two or more races, non-Hispanic/Latino), 12 international. Average age 27. 40 applicants, 48% accepted, 14 enrolled. In 2019, 6 master's, 3 doctorates awarded. *Degree requirements:* For master's, comprehensive exam (for some programs), thesis (for some programs); for doctorate, comprehensive exam, thesis/dissertation. *Entrance requirements:* For master's, GRE General Test, minimum GPA of 3.0, strong mathematical background; for doctorate, GRE General Test (taken within last 5 years), minimum GPA of 3.0. Additional exam requirements/recommendations for international students: required—TOEFL (minimum score 550 paper-based; 80 iBT). *Application deadline:* For fall admission, 6/1 for domestic students, 1/1 for international students; for spring admission, 11/1 for domestic students, 6/1 for international students. Applications are processed on a rolling basis. Application fee: $70. Electronic applications accepted. Application fee is waived when completed online. *Expenses:* $14,382 per year. *Financial support:* In 2019–20, 23 students received support, including 2 fellowships with full tuition reimbursements available, 18 research assistantships with full tuition reimbursements available, 3 teaching assistantships; career-related internships or fieldwork, Federal Work-Study, scholarships/grants, health care benefits, tuition waivers (partial), and unspecified assistantships also available. Support available to part-time students. Financial award application deadline: 6/30; financial award applicants required to submit FAFSA. *Unit head:* Dr. Mark Marten, Professor and Interim Chair, 410-455-3400, Fax: 410-455-1049, E-mail: marten@umbc.edu. *Application contact:* Dr. Erin Lavik, Professor/Graduate Program Director, 410-455-3428, Fax: 410-455-1049, E-mail: elavik@umbc.edu.
Website: https://cbee.umbc.edu/

The University of Western Ontario, School of Graduate and Postdoctoral Studies, Physical Sciences Division, Faculty of Engineering, London, ON N6A 3K7, Canada. Offers chemical and biochemical engineering (ME Sc, PhD); civil and environmental engineering (M Eng, ME Sc, PhD); electrical and computer engineering (M Eng, ME Sc, PhD); mechanical and materials engineering (M Eng, ME Sc, PhD). *Program availability:* Part-time. Terminal master's awarded for partial completion of doctoral program. *Degree requirements:* For master's, thesis; for doctorate, thesis/dissertation. *Entrance requirements:* For master's, minimum B average; for doctorate, minimum B+ average.

Villanova University, College of Engineering, Department of Chemical Engineering, Villanova, PA 19085-1699. Offers biochemical engineering (Certificate); chemical engineering (MSChE); environmental protection in the chemical process industries (Certificate). *Program availability:* Part-time, evening/weekend. *Degree requirements:* For master's, comprehensive exam, thesis optional. *Entrance requirements:* For master's, GRE General Test (for applicants with degrees from foreign universities), B Ch E, minimum GPA of 3.0. Additional exam requirements/recommendations for international students: required—TOEFL (minimum score 600 paper-based; 100 iBT).

Chemical Engineering

American University of Sharjah, Graduate Programs, Sharjah, United Arab Emirates. Offers accounting (MS); biomedical engineering (MSBME); business administration (MBA); chemical engineering (MS Ch E); civil engineering (MSCE); computer engineering (MS); electrical engineering (MSEE); engineering systems management (MS, PhD); mathematics (MS); mechanical engineering (MSME); mechatronics engineering (MS); teaching English to speakers of other languages (MA); translation and interpreting (MA); urban planning (MUP). *Program availability:* Part-time, evening/weekend. *Degree requirements:* For master's, thesis (for some programs). *Entrance requirements:* For master's, GMAT (for MBA). Additional exam requirements/recommendations for international students: required—TOEFL (minimum score 550 paper-based; 80 iBT), TWE (minimum score 5); recommended—IELTS (minimum score 6.5). Electronic applications accepted.

Arizona State University at Tempe, Ira A. Fulton Schools of Engineering, School for Engineering of Matter, Transport and Energy, Tempe, AZ 85281. Offers aerospace engineering (MS, PhD); chemical engineering (MS, PhD); materials science and engineering (MS, PhD); mechanical engineering (MS, PhD); solar energy engineering and commercialization (PSM). *Program availability:* Part-time, evening/weekend, online learning. Terminal master's awarded for partial completion of doctoral program. *Degree requirements:* For master's, thesis and oral defense (MS); applied project or comprehensive exam (MSE); interactive Program of Study (iPOS) submitted before completing 50 percent of required credit hours; for doctorate, comprehensive exam, thesis/dissertation, interactive Program of Study (iPOS) submitted before completing 50 percent of required credit hours. *Entrance requirements:* For master's, GRE, minimum GPA of 3.0 or equivalent in last 2 years of work leading to bachelor's degree; for doctorate, GRE, minimum GPA of 3.0 in last 2 years of work leading to bachelor's degree. Additional exam requirements/recommendations for international students: required—TOEFL, IELTS, or PTE. Electronic applications accepted. *Expenses:* Contact institution.

Auburn University, Graduate School, Samuel Ginn College of Engineering, Department of Chemical Engineering, Auburn University, AL 36849. Offers M Ch E, MS, PhD. *Program availability:* Part-time. *Faculty:* 22 full-time (5 women), 2 part-time/adjunct (0 women). *Students:* 58 full-time (21 women), 29 part-time (12 women); includes 3 minority (all Black or African American, non-Hispanic/Latino), 57 international. Average age 29. 99 applicants, 28% accepted, 17 enrolled. In 2019, 9 master's, 11 doctorates awarded. *Degree requirements:* For master's, thesis (for some programs); for doctorate, comprehensive exam, thesis/dissertation. *Entrance requirements:* For master's and doctorate, GRE General Test. Additional exam requirements/recommendations for international students: required—TOEFL (minimum score 550 paper-based; 79 iBT). *Application deadline:* For fall admission, 3/31 priority date for domestic and international students; for spring admission, 9/30 priority date for domestic and international students. Applications are processed on a rolling basis. Application fee: $60 ($70 for international students). Electronic applications accepted. *Expenses: Tuition, area resident:* Full-time $9828; part-time $546 per credit hour. Tuition, state resident: full-time $9828; part-time $546 per credit hour. Tuition, nonresident: full-time $29,484; part-time $1638 per credit hour. *International tuition:* $29,744 full-time. Tuition and fees vary according to course load, program and reciprocity agreements. *Financial support:* In 2019–20, 64 research assistantships (averaging $23,391 per year) were awarded; fellowships, teaching assistantships, and Federal Work-Study also available. Support available to part-time students. Financial award application deadline: 3/15; financial award applicants required to submit FAFSA. *Unit head:* Dr. Mario Richard Eden, Chair, 334-844-2064, E-mail: edenmar@auburn.edu. *Application contact:* Dr. George Flowers, Dean of the Graduate School, 334-844-2125.
Website: http://www.eng.auburn.edu/chen/

Brigham Young University, Graduate Studies, Ira A. Fulton College of Engineering, Department of Chemical Engineering, Provo, UT 84602. Offers chemical engineering (MS). *Faculty:* 17 full-time (1 woman). *Students:* 61 full-time (11 women); includes 12 minority (11 Asian, non-Hispanic/Latino; 1 Hispanic/Latino). Average age 29. 26 applicants, 73% accepted, 8 enrolled. In 2019, 6 master's, 9 doctorates awarded. *Degree requirements:* For master's, comprehensive exam, thesis; for doctorate, comprehensive exam, thesis/dissertation. *Entrance requirements:* For master's and doctorate, GRE, BS in chemical engineering or related engineering field, minimum GPA of 3.3. Additional exam requirements/recommendations for international students: required—TOEFL (minimum score 580 paper-based; 85 iBT), IELTS (minimum score 7). *Application deadline:* For fall admission, 1/31 for domestic and international students; for winter admission, 6/15 for domestic and international students; for spring admission, 10/15 for domestic and international students. Application fee: $50. Electronic applications accepted. *Financial support:* In 2019–20, 17 students received support, including 2 fellowships (averaging $10,000 per year), 6 research assistantships with full and partial tuition reimbursements available (averaging $12,000 per year), 10 teaching assistantships with full and partial tuition reimbursements available (averaging $12,000 per year); scholarships/grants also available. Financial award application deadline: 1/15; financial award applicants required to submit FAFSA. *Unit head:* Dr. Thomas H. Fletcher, Chair, 801-422-6236, Fax: 801-422-0151, E-mail: cheme@byu.edu. *Application contact:* Dr. William G. Pitt, Graduate Coordinator, 801-422-2588, Fax: 801-422-0151, E-mail: pitt@byu.edu.
Website: http://www.chemicalengineering.byu.edu

Brown University, Graduate School, School of Engineering, Providence, RI 02912. Offers biomedical engineering (Sc M, PhD); chemical and biochemical engineering (Sc M, PhD); electrical sciences and computer engineering (Sc M, PhD); fluid and thermal sciences (Sc M, PhD); materials science and engineering (Sc M, PhD); mechanics of solids and structures (Sc M, PhD). *Degree requirements:* For doctorate, thesis/dissertation, preliminary exam.

Bucknell University, Graduate Studies, College of Engineering, Department of Chemical Engineering, Lewisburg, PA 17837. Offers MS Ch E. *Degree requirements:* For master's, thesis. *Entrance requirements:* For master's, GRE General Test, minimum GPA of 3.0. Additional exam requirements/recommendations for international students: required—TOEFL (minimum score 600 paper-based).

California Institute of Technology, Division of Chemistry and Chemical Engineering, Program in Chemical Engineering, Pasadena, CA 91106. Offers MS, PhD. Terminal master's awarded for partial completion of doctoral program. *Degree requirements:* For master's, thesis; for doctorate, thesis/dissertation. *Entrance requirements:* For doctorate, GRE, BS. Additional exam requirements/recommendations for international students: required—TOEFL; recommended—IELTS, TWE. Electronic applications accepted.

Carnegie Mellon University, Carnegie Institute of Technology, Department of Chemical Engineering, Pittsburgh, PA 15213-3891. Offers chemical engineering (M Ch E, MS, PhD); colloids, polymers and surfaces (MS). *Program availability:* Part-time, evening/weekend. Terminal master's awarded for partial completion of doctoral program. *Degree requirements:* For doctorate, thesis/dissertation, qualifying exam. *Entrance requirements:* For master's and doctorate, GRE General Test, GRE Subject Test. Additional exam requirements/recommendations for international students: required—TOEFL.

Case Western Reserve University, School of Graduate Studies, Case School of Engineering, Department of Chemical and Biomolecular Engineering, Cleveland, OH 44106. Offers MS, PhD. *Program availability:* Part-time, evening/weekend, blended/hybrid learning. Terminal master's awarded for partial completion of doctoral program. *Degree requirements:* For master's, thesis (for some programs); for doctorate, thesis/dissertation, qualifying exam, research proposal, teaching experience. *Entrance requirements:* For master's and doctorate, GRE General Test. Additional exam requirements/recommendations for international students: required—TOEFL.

City College of the City University of New York, Graduate School, Grove School of Engineering, Department of Chemical Engineering, New York, NY 10031-9198. Offers ME, PhD. *Program availability:* Part-time. *Degree requirements:* For master's, thesis optional; for doctorate, one foreign language, comprehensive exam, thesis/dissertation. *Entrance requirements:* For master's and doctorate, GRE General Test. Additional exam requirements/recommendations for international students: required—TOEFL (minimum score 500 paper-based; 61 iBT).

Clemson University, Graduate School, College of Engineering, Computing and Applied Sciences, Department of Chemical and Biomolecular Engineering, Clemson, SC 29634. Offers chemical engineering (MS, PhD). *Faculty:* 13 full-time (3 women). *Students:* 56 full-time (15 women), 3 part-time (1 woman); includes 8 minority (3 Black or African American, non-Hispanic/Latino; 5 Asian, non-Hispanic/Latino), 29 international. Average age 26. 103 applicants, 60% accepted, 13 enrolled. In 2019, 2 master's, 8 doctorates awarded. *Degree requirements:* For master's, thesis; for doctorate, comprehensive exam, thesis/dissertation. *Entrance requirements:* For master's and doctorate, GRE General Test, unofficial transcripts, letters of recommendation. Additional exam requirements/recommendations for international students: required—TOEFL (minimum score 80 paper-based; 80 iBT); recommended—IELTS (minimum score 6.5), TSE (minimum score 54). *Application deadline:* For fall admission, 2/1 for domestic and international students. Applications are processed on a rolling basis. Application fee: $80 ($90 for international students). Electronic applications accepted. *Expenses: Tuition, area resident:* Full-time $10,600; part-time $8688 per semester. Tuition, state resident: full-time $10,600; part-time $8688 per semester. Tuition, nonresident: full-time $22,050; part-time $17,412 per semester. *International tuition:* $22,050 full-time. *Required fees:* $1196; $617 per semester. $617 per semester. Tuition and fees vary according to course load, degree level, campus/location and program. *Financial support:* In 2019–20, 57 students received support, including 9 fellowships with full and partial tuition reimbursements available (averaging $21,226 per year), 28 research assistantships with full and partial tuition reimbursements available (averaging $24,839 per year), 20 teaching assistantships with full and partial tuition reimbursements available (averaging $26,100 per year); career-related internships or fieldwork also available. Financial award application deadline: 2/1. *Unit head:* Dr. David Bruce, Department Chair, 864-656-5425, E-mail: dbruce@clemson.edu. *Application contact:* Dr. Mark Roberts, Graduate Coordinator, 864-656-6307, E-mail: mrober9@clemson.edu.
Website: https://www.clemson.edu/cecas/departments/chbe/

Cleveland State University, College of Graduate Studies, Fenn College of Engineering, Department of Chemical and Biomedical Engineering, Cleveland, OH 44115. Offers MS, D Eng. *Program availability:* Part-time, evening/weekend. *Faculty:* 12 full-time (1 woman), 26 part-time/adjunct (3 women). *Students:* 40 full-time (15 women), 20 part-time (8 women); includes 8 minority (3 Black or African American, non-Hispanic/Latino; 3 Asian, non-Hispanic/Latino; 2 Hispanic/Latino), 24 international. Average age 26. 126 applicants, 60% accepted, 22 enrolled. In 2019, 27 master's, 4 doctorates awarded. *Entrance requirements:* For master's, GRE General Test, minimum GPA of 2.75; for doctorate, GRE General Test, minimum GPA of 3.25. Additional exam requirements/recommendations for international students: required—TOEFL (minimum score 550 paper-based; 78 iBT). *Application deadline:* Applications are processed on a rolling basis. Application fee: $40. Electronic applications accepted. *Expenses:* Tuition, state resident: full-time $10,215; part-time $6810 per credit hour. Tuition, nonresident: full-time $17,496; part-time $11,664 per credit hour. *International tuition:* $19,316 full-time. Tuition and fees vary according to degree level and program. *Financial support:* In 2019–20, 34 students received support, including 2 research assistantships with tuition reimbursements available (averaging $6,960 per year), 3 teaching assistantships with tuition reimbursements available (averaging $6,960 per year); fellowships, career-related internships or fieldwork, Federal Work-Study, institutionally sponsored loans, scholarships/grants, tuition waivers (full and partial), and unspecified assistantships also available. Financial award application deadline: 3/30. *Unit head:* Dr. Joanne M. Belovich, Chairperson, 216-687-3502, Fax: 216-687-9220, E-mail: j.belovich@csuohio.edu. *Application contact:* Becky Laird, Administrative Coordinator, 216-687-2571, Fax: 216-687-9220, E-mail: b.laird@csuohio.edu.
Website: http://www.csuohio.edu/engineering/chemical/

Colorado School of Mines, Office of Graduate Studies, Department of Chemical and Biological Engineering, Golden, CO 80401. Offers chemical engineering (MS, PhD). *Program availability:* Part-time. Terminal master's awarded for partial completion of doctoral program. *Degree requirements:* For master's, thesis (for some programs); for doctorate, comprehensive exam, thesis/dissertation. *Entrance requirements:* For master's and doctorate, GRE General Test. Additional exam requirements/recommendations for international students: required—TOEFL (minimum score 550 paper-based; 79 iBT). Electronic applications accepted. *Expenses:* Tuition, state resident: full-time $16,650; part-time $925 per credit hour. Tuition, nonresident: full-time $37,350; part-time $2075 per credit hour. *International tuition:* $37,350 full-time. *Required fees:* $2412.

Colorado State University, Walter Scott, Jr. College of Engineering, Department of Chemical and Biological Engineering, Fort Collins, CO 80523-1370. Offers MS, PhD. *Program availability:* Part-time. Terminal master's awarded for partial completion of doctoral program. *Degree requirements:* For master's, thesis (for some programs); for doctorate, thesis/dissertation, oral and written preliminary exam. *Entrance requirements:* For master's and doctorate, GRE General Test, minimum GPA of 3.0; relevant degree; recommendations; transcripts. Additional exam requirements/recommendations for international students: required—TOEFL (minimum score 550 paper-based; 80 iBT), IELTS (minimum score 6.5), PTE (minimum score 58). Electronic applications accepted. *Expenses:* Contact institution.

Columbia University, Fu Foundation School of Engineering and Applied Science, Department of Chemical Engineering, New York, NY 10027. Offers MS, PhD. *Program availability:* Part-time, online learning. *Degree requirements:* For doctorate, thesis/dissertation, qualifying exam. *Entrance requirements:* For master's and doctorate, GRE General Test. Additional exam requirements/recommendations for international students: required—TOEFL, IELTS, PTE. Electronic applications accepted. *Expenses: Tuition:* Full-time $47,600; part-time $1880 per credit. One-time fee: $105.

Cooper Union for the Advancement of Science and Art, Albert Nerken School of Engineering, New York, NY 10003. Offers chemical engineering (ME); civil engineering (ME); electrical engineering (ME); mechanical engineering (ME). *Program availability:* Part-time. *Degree requirements:* For master's, thesis (for some programs), thesis or special project. *Entrance requirements:* For master's, BE or BS in an engineering discipline; official copies of school transcripts including secondary (high school), college and university work; two letters of recommendation; resume. Additional exam requirements/recommendations for international students: required—TOEFL (minimum score 600 paper-based; 100 iBT). Electronic applications accepted.

Cornell University, Graduate School, Graduate Fields of Engineering, Field of Chemical Engineering, Ithaca, NY 14853. Offers advanced materials processing (M Eng, MS, PhD); applied mathematics and computational methods (M Eng, MS, PhD); biochemical engineering (M Eng, MS, PhD); chemical reaction engineering (M Eng, MS, PhD); classical and statistical thermodynamics (M Eng, MS, PhD); fluid dynamics, rheology and biorheology (M Eng, MS, PhD); heat and mass transfer (M Eng, MS, PhD); kinetics and catalysis (M Eng, MS, PhD); polymers (M Eng, MS, PhD); surface science (M Eng, MS, PhD). *Degree requirements:* For master's, thesis (MS); for doctorate, comprehensive exam, thesis/dissertation. *Entrance requirements:* For master's and doctorate, GRE General Test, 2 letters of recommendation. Additional exam requirements/recommendations for international students: required—TOEFL (minimum score 600 paper-based; 77 iBT). Electronic applications accepted.

Dalhousie University, Faculty of Engineering, Department of Process Engineering and Applied Science, Halifax, NS B3J 1Z1, Canada. Offers biological engineering (M Eng, MA Sc, PhD); chemical engineering (M Eng, MA Sc, PhD); food science (M Sc, PhD). *Degree requirements:* For master's, thesis; for doctorate, thesis/dissertation. *Entrance requirements:* Additional exam requirements/recommendations for international students: required—TOEFL, IELTS, CANTEST, CAEL, or Michigan English Language Assessment Battery. Electronic applications accepted.

Dartmouth College, Dartmouth Engineering - Thayer School of Engineering, Program in Biological Engineering, Hanover, NH 03755. Offers MS, PhD. Terminal master's awarded for partial completion of doctoral program. *Degree requirements:* For master's, thesis (for some programs); for doctorate, thesis/dissertation. *Entrance requirements:* For master's and doctorate, GRE General Test. Additional exam requirements/recommendations for international students: required—TOEFL, IELTS. *Application deadline:* For fall admission, 1/1 priority date for domestic students, 1/1 for international students. Applications are processed on a rolling basis. Application fee: $45. Electronic applications accepted. *Financial support:* Fellowships, research assistantships, teaching assistantships, career-related internships or fieldwork, institutionally sponsored loans, scholarships/grants, and tuition waivers (full and partial) available. Financial award application deadline: 2/15; financial award applicants required to submit CSS PROFILE. *Unit head:* Dr. Lee R. Lynd, Paul E. and Joan H. Queneau Distinguished Professor of Engineering, 603-646-2231, E-mail: lee.r.lynd@dartmouth.edu. *Application contact:* Candace S. Potter, Graduate Admissions & Financial Aid Administrator, 603-646-3844, Fax: 603-646-1620, E-mail: candace.s.potter@dartmouth.edu.
Website: http://engineering.dartmouth.edu/

Drexel University, College of Engineering, Department of Chemical and Biological Engineering, Program in Chemical Engineering, Philadelphia, PA 19104-2875. Offers MS, PhD. *Degree requirements:* For doctorate, thesis/dissertation. *Entrance requirements:* For master's, minimum GPA of 3.0; for doctorate, minimum GPA of 3.5, MS in chemical engineering. Additional exam requirements/recommendations for international students: required—TOEFL. Electronic applications accepted.

Fairleigh Dickinson University, Florham Campus, Silberman College of Business, Program in Pharmaceutical Studies, Madison, NJ 07940-1099. Offers MBA, Certificate.

Florida Agricultural and Mechanical University, Division of Graduate Studies, Research, and Continuing Education, FAMU-FSU College of Engineering, Department of Chemical and Biomedical Engineering, Tallahassee, FL 32307-3200. Offers biomedical engineering (MS, PhD); chemical engineering (MS, PhD). *Degree requirements:* For master's, thesis optional; for doctorate, thesis/dissertation, paper presentation at professional meeting. *Entrance requirements:* For master's, GRE General Test, minimum GPA of 3.3, letters of recommendation (3); for doctorate, minimum GPA of 3.3. Additional exam requirements/recommendations for international students: required—TOEFL (minimum score 550 paper-based).

Florida Institute of Technology, College of Engineering and Science, Program in Chemical Engineering, Melbourne, FL 32901-6975. Offers MS, PhD. *Program availability:* Part-time. Terminal master's awarded for partial completion of doctoral program. *Degree requirements:* For master's, comprehensive exam, thesis, 30 credit hours thesis or capstone project with final exam; for doctorate, comprehensive exam, thesis/dissertation, publication in refereed journals, oral and written exams, research project, minimum of 72 credit hours. *Entrance requirements:* For master's, GRE, resume, 3 letters of recommendation, statement of objectives, undergraduate transcripts; for doctorate, GRE, minimum GPA of 3.5, resume, 3 letters of recommendation, statement of objectives. Additional exam requirements/recommendations for international students: required—TOEFL (minimum score 550 paper-based; 79 iBT). Electronic applications accepted.

Florida State University, The Graduate School, FAMU-FSU College of Engineering, Department of Chemical and Biomedical Engineering, Tallahassee, FL 32310-6046. Offers biomedical engineering (MS, PhD); chemical engineering (MS, PhD). *Program availability:* Part-time. *Faculty:* 17 full-time (2 women), 2 part-time/adjunct (1 woman). *Students:* 46 full-time (13 women); includes 5 minority (3 Black or African American, non-Hispanic/Latino; 2 Hispanic/Latino), 31 international. Average age 25. 125 applicants, 39% accepted, 19 enrolled. In 2019, 10 master's, 8 doctorates awarded. Terminal master's awarded for partial completion of doctoral program. *Degree requirements:* For master's, thesis (for some programs); for doctorate, comprehensive exam, thesis/dissertation, qualifying exam. *Entrance requirements:* For master's, GRE General Test (recommended minimum scores: verbal 151/8th percentile; quantitative: 158/75th percentile), BS in chemical engineering or other physical science/engineering, minimum GPA of 3.0; for doctorate, GRE General Test (recommended minimum scores: verbal 151/8th percentile; quantitative: 158/75th percentile), BS in chemical engineering or other physical science/engineering, minimum GPA of 3.0, or MS in chemical or biomedical engineering. Additional exam requirements/recommendations for international students: required—TOEFL (minimum score 550 paper-based; 80 iBT); recommended—IELTS (minimum score 6.5). *Application deadline:* For fall admission, 3/1 priority date for domestic students, 3/1 for international students; for spring admission, 10/1 for domestic and international students. Applications are processed on a rolling basis. Application fee: $30. Electronic applications accepted. *Financial support:* In 2019–20, 34 students received support, including fellowships with full tuition reimbursements available (averaging $21,500 per year), 22 research assistantships with full tuition reimbursements available (averaging $21,500 per year), 23 teaching assistantships with full tuition reimbursements available (averaging $21,500 per year); scholarships/grants, tuition waivers, and unspecified assistantships also available. Financial award application deadline: 3/1; financial award applicants required to submit FAFSA. *Unit head:* Dr. Teng Ma, Chair and Professor, 850-410-6149, Fax: 850-410-6150, E-mail: teng@eng.famu.fsu.edu. *Application contact:* Lisa Fowler, Office Administrator, 850-410-6151, Fax: 850-410-6150, E-mail: lfowler@eng.famu.fsu.edu.
Website: http://www.eng.famu.fsu.edu/cbe

Georgia Institute of Technology, Graduate Studies, College of Engineering, School of Chemical and Biomolecular Engineering, Atlanta, GA 30332. Offers chemical engineering (MS, PhD). *Faculty:* 39 full-time (11 women). *Students:* 215 full-time (82 women), 3 part-time (all women); includes 47 minority (6 Black or African American, non-Hispanic/Latino; 21 Asian, non-Hispanic/Latino; 11 Hispanic/Latino; 9 Two or more races, non-Hispanic/Latino), 101 international. Average age 25. 660 applicants, 25% accepted, 62 enrolled. In 2019, 19 master's, 24 doctorates awarded. Terminal master's awarded for partial completion of doctoral program. *Degree requirements:* For master's, thesis; for doctorate, comprehensive exam, thesis/dissertation. *Entrance requirements:* For master's and doctorate, GRE, Minimum GPA of 3.3. Additional exam requirements/recommendations for international students: required—TOEFL (minimum score 577 paper-based; 90 iBT), IELTS (minimum score 7), TOEFL is the preferred method with the requirements shown on the programs. *Application deadline:* For fall admission, 1/1 for domestic students. Applications are processed on a rolling basis. Application fee: $75 ($85 for international students). Electronic applications accepted. *Expenses: Tuition, area resident:* Full-time $14,064; part-time $586 per credit hour. Tuition, state resident: full-time $14,064; part-time $586 per credit hour. Tuition, nonresident: full-time $29,140; part-time $1215 per credit hour. *International tuition:* $29,140 full-time. *Required fees:* $2024; $840 per semester. $2096. Tuition and fees vary according to course load. *Financial support:* In 2019–20, 11 fellowships with tuition reimbursements, 187 research assistantships with tuition reimbursements were awarded; teaching assistantships with tuition reimbursements, career-related internships or fieldwork, Federal Work-Study, institutionally sponsored loans, tuition waivers (full and partial), and unspecified assistantships also available. Support available to part-time students. Financial award application deadline: 7/1; financial award applicants required to submit FAFSA. *Unit head:* David Sholl, School Chair, 404-894-4002, Fax: 404-894-7452, E-mail: david.sholl@chbe.gatech.edu. *Application contact:* Marla Bruner, Director of Graduate Studies, 404-894-1610, Fax: 404-894-1609, E-mail: gradinfo@mail.gatech.edu.
Website: http://www.chbe.gatech.edu

Howard University, College of Engineering, Architecture, and Computer Sciences, School of Engineering and Computer Science, Department of Chemical Engineering, Washington, DC 20059-0002. Offers MS. *Program availability:* Part-time. *Degree requirements:* For master's, thesis. *Entrance requirements:* For master's, GRE General Test, minimum GPA of 2.75. Additional exam requirements/recommendations for international students: required—TOEFL.

Illinois Institute of Technology, Graduate College, Armour College of Engineering, Department of Chemical and Biological Engineering, Chicago, IL 60616. Offers biological engineering (MAS); chemical engineering (MAS, MS, PhD); MS/MAS. *Program availability:* Part-time, evening/weekend, online learning. Terminal master's awarded for partial completion of doctoral program. *Degree requirements:* For master's, comprehensive exam (for some programs), thesis (for some programs); for doctorate, comprehensive exam, thesis/dissertation. *Entrance requirements:* For master's, GRE General Test with minimum score of 950 Quantitative and Verbal, 2.5 Analytical Writing (for MAS); GRE General Test with minimum score of 1100 Quantitative and Verbal, 3.0 Analytical Writing (for MS), minimum undergraduate GPA of 3.0; for doctorate, GRE General Test (minimum score 1100 Quantitative and Verbal, 3.0 Analytical Writing), minimum undergraduate GPA of 3.0. Additional exam requirements/recommendations for international students: required—TOEFL (minimum score 550 paper-based; 80 iBT). Electronic applications accepted.

Instituto Tecnológico y de Estudios Superiores de Monterrey, Campus Monterrey, Graduate and Research Division, Programs in Engineering, Monterrey, Mexico. Offers applied statistics (M Eng); artificial intelligence (PhD); automation engineering (M Eng); chemical engineering (M Eng); civil engineering (M Eng); electrical engineering (M Eng); electronic engineering (M Eng); environmental engineering (M Eng); industrial engineering (M Eng, PhD); manufacturing engineering (M Eng); mechanical engineering (M Eng); systems and quality engineering (M Eng). *Program availability:* Part-time, evening/weekend. Terminal master's awarded for partial completion of doctoral program. *Degree requirements:* For master's, one foreign language, thesis; for doctorate, one foreign language, thesis/dissertation. *Entrance requirements:* For master's, EXADEP; for doctorate, GRE, master's degree in related field. Additional exam requirements/recommendations for international students: required—TOEFL.

Iowa State University of Science and Technology, Department of Chemical and Biological Engineering, Ames, IA 50011-2230. Offers M Eng, MS, PhD. *Degree requirements:* For master's, thesis (for some programs); for doctorate, thesis/dissertation. *Entrance requirements:* For master's and doctorate, GRE General Test. Additional exam requirements/recommendations for international students: recommended—TOEFL (minimum score 587 paper-based; 94 iBT), IELTS (minimum score 7). Electronic applications accepted.

Johns Hopkins University, Engineering Program for Professionals, Part-time Program in Chemical and Biomolecular Engineering, Baltimore, MD 21218. Offers M Ch E. *Program availability:* Part-time, evening/weekend. *Entrance requirements:* Additional exam requirements/recommendations for international students: required—TOEFL (minimum score 600 paper-based; 100 iBT). Electronic applications accepted.

Johns Hopkins University, G. W. C. Whiting School of Engineering, Department of Chemical and Biomolecular Engineering, Baltimore, MD 21218. Offers MSE, PhD. Terminal master's awarded for partial completion of doctoral program. *Degree requirements:* For master's, essay presentation; for doctorate, thesis/dissertation, oral exam; thesis presentation. *Entrance requirements:* For master's and doctorate, GRE General Test, 3 letters of recommendation, statement of purpose, transcripts. Additional exam requirements/recommendations for international students: required—TOEFL (minimum score 600 paper-based, 100 iBT) or IELTS (7). Electronic applications accepted.

Kansas State University, Graduate School, College of Engineering, Department of Chemical Engineering, Manhattan, KS 66506. Offers MS, PhD, Graduate Certificate. *Program availability:* Online learning. Terminal master's awarded for partial completion of doctoral program. *Degree requirements:* For master's, thesis, 24 hours of coursework; 6 hours of thesis; for doctorate, thesis/dissertation, 90 hours of credit. *Entrance requirements:* For doctorate, GRE. Additional exam requirements/recommendations for international students: required—TOEFL. Electronic applications accepted.

Lamar University, College of Graduate Studies, College of Engineering, Dan F. Smith Department of Chemical Engineering, Beaumont, TX 77710. Offers ME, PhD. *Faculty:* 12 full-time (1 woman). *Students:* 25 full-time (4 women), 13 part-time (2 women); includes 2 minority (1 Asian, non-Hispanic/Latino; 1 Hispanic/Latino), 33 international. Average age 28. 30 applicants, 63% accepted, 4 enrolled. In 2019, 12 master's, 7 doctorates awarded. *Degree requirements:* For master's, comprehensive exam (for some programs), thesis (for some programs); for doctorate, comprehensive exam, thesis/dissertation. *Entrance requirements:* For master's and doctorate, GRE General Test. Additional exam requirements/recommendations for international students: required—TOEFL (minimum score 550 paper-based; 79 iBT), IELTS (minimum score 6.5). *Application deadline:* Applications are processed on a rolling basis. Application fee: $25 ($50 for international students). Electronic applications accepted. *Expenses: Tuition, area resident:* Full-time $6324; part-time $351 per credit. Tuition, state resident: full-time $6324; part-time $351 per credit. Tuition, nonresident: full-time $13,920; part-time $773 per credit. *International tuition:* $13,920 full-time. *Required fees:* $2462; $327 per credit. Tuition and fees vary according to course load, campus/location and reciprocity agreements. *Financial support:* In 2019–20, 1 student received support. Fellowships with partial tuition reimbursements available, research assistantships with partial tuition reimbursements available, teaching assistantships with partial tuition reimbursements available, and tuition waivers (full and partial) available. Financial award applicants required to submit FAFSA. *Unit head:* Dr. Thomas C. Ho, Chair, 409-880-8784, Fax: 409-880-2197, E-mail: che_dept@lamar.edu. *Application contact:* Celeste Contreas, Director, Admissions and Academic Services, 409-880-8888, Fax: 409-880-7419, E-mail: gradmissions@lamar.edu.
Website: http://engineering.lamar.edu/chemical

Lehigh University, P.C. Rossin College of Engineering and Applied Science, Department of Chemical and Biomolecular Engineering, Bethlehem, PA 18015. Offers biological chemical engineering (M Eng); chemical energy engineering (M Eng);

chemical engineering (M Eng, MS, PhD); MBA/E. *Program availability:* Part-time, 100% online. *Faculty:* 13 full-time (2 women), 1 part-time/adjunct (0 women). *Students:* 52 full-time (20 women), 26 part-time (10 women); includes 9 minority (8 Asian, non-Hispanic/Latino; 1 Hispanic/Latino), 36 international. Average age 27. 125 applicants, 61% accepted, 28 enrolled. In 2019, 7 master's, 2 doctorates awarded. Terminal master's awarded for partial completion of doctoral program. *Degree requirements:* For master's, thesis (for some programs); for doctorate, comprehensive exam, thesis/dissertation. *Entrance requirements:* For master's and doctorate, GRE General Test. Additional exam requirements/recommendations for international students: required—TOEFL (minimum score 79 iBT), IELTS (minimum score 6.5). *Application deadline:* For fall admission, 7/15 for domestic students, 7/15 priority date for international students; for spring admission, 12/1 for domestic and international students. Applications are processed on a rolling basis. Application fee: $75. Electronic applications accepted. *Financial support:* In 2019–20, 40 students received support, including 4 fellowships with full tuition reimbursements available (averaging $29,400 per year), 30 research assistantships with full tuition reimbursements available (averaging $29,400 per year), 3 teaching assistantships with full tuition reimbursements available (averaging $29,400 per year). Financial award application deadline: 1/15. *Unit head:* Dr. Mayuresh V. Kothare, Chairman, 610-758-6654, Fax: 610-758-5057, E-mail: mvk2@lehigh.edu. *Application contact:* Janine Jekels, Academic Coordinator, 610-758-4260, Fax: 610-758-5057, E-mail: inchegs@lehigh.edu.
Website: https://www.che.lehigh.edu/

Louisiana State University and Agricultural & Mechanical College, Graduate School, College of Engineering, Cain Department of Chemical Engineering, Baton Rouge, LA 70803. Offers MS Ch E, PhD.

Manhattan College, Graduate Programs, School of Engineering, Program in Chemical Engineering, Riverdale, NY 10471. Offers chemical engineering (MS). *Program availability:* Part-time, evening/weekend. *Degree requirements:* For master's, 30 credits with minimum GPA of 3.0. *Entrance requirements:* For master's, GRE (recommended), minimum GPA of 3.0. Additional exam requirements/recommendations for international students: required—TOEFL (minimum score 550 paper-based; 80 iBT), IELTS (minimum score 6). Electronic applications accepted. *Expenses:* Contact institution.

Massachusetts Institute of Technology, School of Engineering, Department of Chemical Engineering, Cambridge, MA 02139. Offers chemical engineering (PhD, Sc D); chemical engineering practice (SM, PhD); SM/MBA. *Degree requirements:* For master's, thesis (for some programs), one-semester industrial internship; for doctorate, comprehensive exam, thesis/dissertation. *Entrance requirements:* For master's and doctorate, GRE General Test. Additional exam requirements/recommendations for international students: required—TOEFL, IELTS. Electronic applications accepted.

McGill University, Faculty of Graduate and Postdoctoral Studies, Faculty of Engineering, Department of Chemical Engineering, Montréal, QC H3A 2T5, Canada. Offers chemical engineering (M Eng, PhD); environmental engineering (M Eng).

McMaster University, School of Graduate Studies, Faculty of Engineering, Department of Chemical Engineering, Hamilton, ON L8S 4M2, Canada. Offers M Eng, MA Sc, PhD. *Degree requirements:* For master's, thesis; for doctorate, comprehensive exam, thesis/dissertation. *Entrance requirements:* For master's, minimum B average in the last two years. Additional exam requirements/recommendations for international students: required—TOEFL (minimum score 550 paper-based).

McNeese State University, Doré School of Graduate Studies, College of Engineering and Computer Science, Master of Engineering Program, Lake Charles, LA 70609. Offers chemical engineering (M Eng); civil engineering (M Eng); electrical engineering (M Eng); engineering management (M Eng); mechanical engineering (M Eng). *Program availability:* Part-time, evening/weekend. *Entrance requirements:* For master's, GRE, baccalaureate degree, minimum overall GPA of 3.0. Additional exam requirements/recommendations for international students: required—TOEFL (minimum score 560 paper-based; 83 iBT).

Miami University, College of Engineering and Computing, Department of Chemical, Paper and Biomedical Engineering, Oxford, OH 45056. Offers MS.

Michigan State University, The Graduate School, College of Engineering, Department of Chemical Engineering and Materials Science, East Lansing, MI 48824. Offers chemical engineering (MS, PhD); materials science and engineering (MS, PhD). *Entrance requirements:* Additional exam requirements/recommendations for international students: required—TOEFL. Electronic applications accepted.

Michigan Technological University, Graduate School, College of Engineering, Department of Chemical Engineering, Houghton, MI 49931. Offers MS, PhD. *Program availability:* Part-time. *Faculty:* 19 full-time (5 women), 2 part-time/adjunct. *Students:* 28 full-time (9 women), 2 part-time, 20 international. Average age 27. 133 applicants, 26% accepted, 6 enrolled. In 2019, 9 master's, 6 doctorates awarded. Terminal master's awarded for partial completion of doctoral program. *Degree requirements:* For master's, comprehensive exam (for some programs), thesis (for some programs); for doctorate, comprehensive exam, thesis/dissertation. *Entrance requirements:* For master's and doctorate, GRE is only required for international students, statement of purpose, personal statement, official transcripts, 2 letters of recommendation. Additional exam requirements/recommendations for international students: required—TOEFL (minimum score 550 paper-based; 70 iBT), IELTS (minimum score 6.5). *Application deadline:* For fall admission, 1/15 priority date for domestic and international students. Applications are processed on a rolling basis. Application fee: $0. Electronic applications accepted. *Expenses:* $1,212 per credit. *Financial support:* In 2019–20, 27 students received support, including 1 fellowship with tuition reimbursement available (averaging $16,590 per year), 17 research assistantships with tuition reimbursements available (averaging $16,590 per year), 8 teaching assistantships with tuition reimbursements available (averaging $16,590 per year); career-related internships or fieldwork, Federal Work-Study, scholarships/grants, health care benefits, unspecified assistantships, and cooperative program also available. Financial award applicants required to submit FAFSA. *Unit head:* Dr. Pradeep K. Agrawal, Chair, 906-487-1870, Fax: 906-487-3213, E-mail: pkagrawa@mtu.edu. *Application contact:* Taana Blom, Administrative Aide, 906-487-3211, Fax: 906-487-3213, E-mail: taana@mtu.edu.
Website: http://www.mtu.edu/chemical/

Mississippi State University, Bagley College of Engineering, Dave C. Swalm School of Chemical Engineering, Mississippi State, MS 39762. Offers MS, PhD. *Faculty:* 10 full-time (2 women). *Students:* 21 full-time (8 women), 3 part-time (0 women); includes 2 minority (both Asian, non-Hispanic/Latino), 17 international. Average age 29. 9 applicants, 67% accepted, 2 enrolled. In 2019, 3 doctorates awarded. *Degree requirements:* For master's, comprehensive exam or thesis; for doctorate, comprehensive exam, thesis/dissertation. *Entrance requirements:* For master's, GRE, minimum GPA of 3.0 on last 64 undergraduate hours; for doctorate, GRE, minimum GPA of 3.2 on last 64 undergraduate hours. Additional exam requirements/recommendations for international students: required—TOEFL (minimum score 550 paper-based; 79 iBT); recommended—IELTS (minimum score 6.5). *Application deadline:* For fall admission, 4/1 priority date for domestic students, 5/1 for international students; for spring admission, 8/1 priority date for domestic students, 9/1 for international students. Applications are processed on a rolling basis. Application fee:

$60 ($80 for international students). Electronic applications accepted. *Expenses: Tuition, area resident:* Full-time $8880; part-time $456 per credit hour. *Tuition, state resident:* full-time $8880. *Tuition, nonresident:* full-time $23,840; part-time $1236 per credit hour. *Required fees:* $110; $11.12 per credit hour. Tuition and fees vary according to course load. *Financial support:* In 2019–20, 15 research assistantships with full tuition reimbursements (averaging $17,952 per year), 2 teaching assistantships with full tuition reimbursements (averaging $15,705 per year) were awarded; Federal Work-Study, institutionally sponsored loans, and unspecified assistantships also available. Financial award application deadline: 4/1; financial award applicants required to submit FAFSA. *Unit head:* Dr. Bill Elmore, Director/Earnest W. Deavenport Jr. Chair, 662-325-2480, Fax: 662-325-2482, E-mail: elmore@che.msstate.edu. *Application contact:* Angie Campbell, Admissions and Enrollment Assistant, 662-325-9514, E-mail: acampbell@grad.msstate.edu.
Website: http://www.che.msstate.edu/

Missouri University of Science and Technology, Department of Chemical and Biochemical Engineering, Rolla, MO 65409. Offers chemical engineering (MS, PhD). *Degree requirements:* For master's, thesis optional; for doctorate, comprehensive exam. *Entrance requirements:* For master's, GRE (minimum score 1100 verbal and quantitative, 4 writing); for doctorate, GRE (minimum score: verbal and quantitative 1200, writing 4). Additional exam requirements/recommendations for international students: required—TOEFL (minimum score 550 paper-based). Electronic applications accepted. *Expenses:* Tuition, state resident: full-time $7839; part-time $435.50 per credit hour. Tuition, nonresident: full-time $22,169; part-time $1231.60 per credit hour. *International tuition:* $18,156.60 full-time. *Required fees:* $649.76. One-time fee: $119. Tuition and fees vary according to course load and program.

Montana State University, The Graduate School, College of Engineering, Department of Chemical and Biological Engineering, Bozeman, MT 59717. Offers chemical engineering (MS); engineering (PhD), including chemical engineering option, environmental engineering option; environmental engineering (MS). *Program availability:* Part-time. *Degree requirements:* For master's, comprehensive exam, thesis (for some programs); for doctorate, comprehensive exam, thesis/dissertation. *Entrance requirements:* For master's and doctorate, GRE General Test. Additional exam requirements/recommendations for international students: required—TOEFL (minimum score 550 paper-based). Electronic applications accepted.

New Jersey Institute of Technology, Newark College of Engineering, Newark, NJ 07102. Offers biomedical engineering (MS, PhD); biopharmaceutical engineering (MS); chemical engineering (MS, PhD); civil engineering (MS, PhD); computer engineering (MS); critical infrastructure systems (MS); electrical engineering (MS, PhD); engineering management (MS); engineering science (MS); environmental engineering (MS, PhD); healthcare systems management (MS); industrial engineering (MS, PhD); internet engineering (MS); manufacturing systems engineering (MS); materials science & engineering (PhD); materials science and engineering (MS); mechanical engineering (MS, PhD); occupational safety and health engineering (MS). *Program availability:* Part-time, evening/weekend. *Faculty:* 151 full-time (29 women), 135 part-time/adjunct (15 women). *Students:* 576 full-time (161 women), 528 part-time (111 women); includes 366 minority (61 Black or African American, non-Hispanic/Latino; 1 American Indian or Alaska Native, non-Hispanic/Latino; 166 Asian, non-Hispanic/Latino; 115 Hispanic/Latino; 23 Two or more races, non-Hispanic/Latino), 450 international. Average age 28. 2,053 applicants, 67% accepted, 338 enrolled. In 2019, 474 master's, 30 doctorates awarded. Terminal master's awarded for partial completion of doctoral program. *Degree requirements:* For master's, thesis (for some programs); for doctorate, thesis/dissertation. *Entrance requirements:* For master's, GRE General Test, minimum GPA 2.8, personal statement, 1 letter of recommendation, transcripts; for doctorate, GRE General Test, minimum GPA of 3.5, personal statement, 3 letters of recommendation, transcripts. Additional exam requirements/recommendations for international students: required—TOEFL (minimum score 550 paper-based; 79 iBT), IELTS (minimum score 6.5). *Application deadline:* For fall admission, 6/1 priority date for domestic students, 5/1 priority date for international students; for spring admission, 11/15 priority date for domestic and international students. Applications are processed on a rolling basis. Application fee: $75. Electronic applications accepted. *Expenses:* $23,828 per year (in-state), $33,744 per year (out-of-state). *Financial support:* In 2019–20, 352 students received support, including 33 fellowships with full tuition reimbursements available (averaging $24,000 per year), 89 research assistantships with full tuition reimbursements available (averaging $24,000 per year), 112 teaching assistantships with full tuition reimbursements available (averaging $24,000 per year); career-related internships or fieldwork, Federal Work-Study, scholarships/grants, and unspecified assistantships also available. Financial award application deadline: 1/15. *Unit head:* Dr. Moshe Kam, Dean, 973-596-5534, Fax: 973-596-2316, E-mail: moshe.kam@njit.edu. *Application contact:* Stephen Eck, Executive Director of University Admissions, 973-596-3300, Fax: 973-596-3461, E-mail: admissions@njit.edu.
Website: http://engineering.njit.edu/

New York University, Tandon School of Engineering, Department of Chemical and Biomolecular Engineering, Major in Chemical Engineering, New York, NY 10012-1019. Offers chemical engineering (MS). *Program availability:* Part-time, evening/weekend. *Entrance requirements:* For master's, GRE General Test, BS in chemical engineering; for doctorate, GRE General Test. Additional exam requirements/recommendations for international students: required—TOEFL (minimum score 550 paper-based; 90 iBT); recommended—IELTS (minimum score 7). Electronic applications accepted.

North Carolina Agricultural and Technical State University, The Graduate College, College of Engineering, Department of Chemical, Biological and Bio Engineering, Greensboro, NC 27411. Offers bioengineering (MS); biological engineering (MS); chemical engineering (MS).

North Carolina State University, Graduate School, College of Engineering, Department of Chemical and Biomolecular Engineering, Raleigh, NC 27695. Offers chemical engineering (M Ch E, MS, PhD). *Program availability:* Part-time. Terminal master's awarded for partial completion of doctoral program. *Degree requirements:* For master's, thesis optional; for doctorate, thesis/dissertation. *Entrance requirements:* For master's and doctorate, GRE General Test. Additional exam requirements/recommendations for international students: required—TOEFL. Electronic applications accepted.

Northeastern University, College of Engineering, Boston, MA 02115-5096. Offers bioengineering (MS, PhD); chemical engineering (MS, PhD); civil engineering (MS, PhD); computer engineering (PhD); computer systems engineering (MS); electrical and computer engineering (MS); electrical and computer engineering leadership (MS); electrical engineering (PhD); energy systems (MS); engineering and public policy (MS); engineering management (MS, Certificate); environmental engineering (MS); industrial engineering (MS, PhD); information assurance (PhD); information systems (MS); interdisciplinary engineering (PhD); mechanical engineering (PhD); operations research (MS); telecommunication systems management (MS). *Program availability:* Part-time, online learning. Electronic applications accepted. *Expenses:* Contact institution.

Northwestern University, McCormick School of Engineering and Applied Science, Department of Chemical and Biological Engineering, Evanston, IL 60208. Offers biotechnology (MS); chemical engineering (MS, PhD). *Program availability:* Part-time. Terminal master's awarded for partial completion of doctoral program. *Degree requirements:* For master's, comprehensive exam (for some programs), thesis optional; for doctorate, comprehensive exam, thesis/dissertation. *Entrance requirements:* For master's and doctorate, GRE General Test. Additional exam requirements/recommendations for international students: required—TOEFL (minimum score 577 paper-based; 90 iBT), IELTS (minimum score 7). Electronic applications accepted.

The Ohio State University, Graduate School, College of Engineering, Department of Chemical and Biomolecular Engineering, Columbus, OH 43210. Offers chemical engineering (MS, PhD). *Entrance requirements:* For master's, GRE; for doctorate, GRE (highly recommend minimum score of 75% in Verbal and Quantitative and 4.0 in Analytical Writing). Additional exam requirements/recommendations for international students: required—TOEFL (minimum score 600 paper-based; 100 iBT), Michigan English Language Assessment Battery (minimum score 86); recommended—IELTS (minimum score 8). Electronic applications accepted.

Ohio University, Graduate College, Russ College of Engineering and Technology, Department of Chemical and Biomolecular Engineering, Athens, OH 45701-2979. Offers biomedical engineering (MS); chemical engineering (MS, PhD). *Program availability:* Part-time. *Degree requirements:* For master's, comprehensive exam (for some programs), thesis; for doctorate, comprehensive exam, thesis/dissertation, qualifying exams. *Entrance requirements:* For master's and doctorate, GRE General Test. Additional exam requirements/recommendations for international students: required—TOEFL (minimum score 590 paper-based; 96 iBT) or IELTS (minimum score 7). Electronic applications accepted.

Oklahoma State University, College of Engineering, Architecture and Technology, School of Chemical Engineering, Stillwater, OK 74078. Offers MS, PhD. *Faculty:* 18 full-time (4 women). *Students:* 23 full-time (4 women), 26 part-time (4 women); includes 6 minority (2 American Indian or Alaska Native, non-Hispanic/Latino; 1 Asian, non-Hispanic/Latino; 1 Hispanic/Latino; 2 Two or more races, non-Hispanic/Latino), 30 international. Average age 28. 58 applicants, 29% accepted, 16 enrolled. In 2019, 7 master's, 8 doctorates awarded. *Entrance requirements:* For master's and doctorate, GRE or GMAT. Additional exam requirements/recommendations for international students: required—TOEFL (minimum score 550 paper-based; 79 iBT). *Application deadline:* For fall admission, 3/1 priority date for international students; for spring admission, 8/1 priority date for international students. Applications are processed on a rolling basis. Application fee: $50 ($75 for international students). Electronic applications accepted. *Expenses: Tuition, area resident:* Full-time $4148.10; part-time $2765.40. Tuition, state resident: full-time $4148.10; part-time $2765.40. Tuition, nonresident: full-time $15,775; part-time $10,516.80. *International tuition:* $15,775.20 full-time. *Required fees:* $2196.90; $122.05 per credit hour. Tuition and fees vary according to course load, campus/location and program. *Financial support:* In 2019–20, 36 research assistantships (averaging $2,164 per year), 10 teaching assistantships (averaging $2,170 per year) were awarded; career-related internships or fieldwork, Federal Work-Study, scholarships/grants, health care benefits, tuition waivers (partial), and unspecified assistantships also available. Support available to part-time students. Financial award application deadline: 3/1; financial award applicants required to submit FAFSA. *Unit head:* Dr. Gier Hareland, Continental Resources Chair, Professor and Head, 405-744-5280, Fax: 405-744-6338. *Application contact:* Dr. Sheryl Tucker, Dean, 405-744-6368, Fax: 405-744-0355, E-mail: gradi@okstate.edu.
Website: http://che.okstate.edu/

Oregon State University, College of Engineering, Program in Chemical Engineering, Corvallis, OR 97331. Offers M Eng, MS, PhD. *Entrance requirements:* For master's, GRE. Additional exam requirements/recommendations for international students: required—TOEFL (minimum score 92 iBT). *Expenses:* Contact institution.

Penn State University Park, Graduate School, College of Engineering, Department of Chemical Engineering, University Park, PA 16802. Offers MS, PhD.

Polytechnique Montréal, Graduate Programs, Department of Chemical Engineering, Montréal, QC H3C 3A7, Canada. Offers M Eng, M Sc A, PhD, DESS. *Program availability:* Part-time, evening/weekend. Terminal master's awarded for partial completion of doctoral program. *Degree requirements:* For master's, one foreign language, thesis; for doctorate, one foreign language, thesis/dissertation. *Entrance requirements:* For master's, minimum GPA of 2.75; for doctorate, minimum GPA of 3.0. Electronic applications accepted.

Princeton University, Graduate School, School of Engineering and Applied Science, Department of Chemical and Biological Engineering, Princeton, NJ 08544-1019. Offers M Eng, MSE, PhD. Terminal master's awarded for partial completion of doctoral program. *Degree requirements:* For master's, thesis (MSE); for doctorate, thesis/dissertation, general exam. *Entrance requirements:* For master's, GRE General Test, 3 letters of recommendation; for doctorate, GRE General Test, official transcript(s), 3 letters of recommendation, personal statement. Additional exam requirements/recommendations for international students: required—TOEFL. Electronic applications accepted.

Purdue University, College of Engineering, Davidson School of Chemical Engineering, West Lafayette, IN 47907-2100. Offers MSChE, PhD. *Faculty:* 29. *Students:* 207. Terminal master's awarded for partial completion of doctoral program. *Degree requirements:* For master's, thesis optional; for doctorate, thesis/dissertation. *Application deadline:* For fall admission, 12/15 for domestic and international students. Applications are processed on a rolling basis. Application fee: $60 ($75 for international students). Electronic applications accepted. *Financial support:* Fellowships with full and partial tuition reimbursements, research assistantships with full and partial tuition reimbursements, teaching assistantships with full and partial tuition reimbursements, career-related internships or fieldwork, scholarships/grants, health care benefits, and unspecified assistantships available. *Unit head:* Dr. Kim Sangtae, Head of Chemical Engineering/Professor, 765-494-3492, E-mail: kim55@purdue.edu. *Application contact:* Beverly Johnson, Graduate Program Administrator, 765-494-4057, E-mail: bevjohnson@purdue.edu.
Website: https://engineering.purdue.edu/ChE/

Queen's University at Kingston, School of Graduate Studies, Faculty of Engineering and Applied Science, Department of Chemical Engineering, Kingston, ON K7L 3N6, Canada. Offers M Sc, PhD. *Program availability:* Part-time. *Degree requirements:* For master's, thesis or alternative; for doctorate, comprehensive exam, thesis/dissertation. *Entrance requirements:* Additional exam requirements/recommendations for international students: required—TOEFL (minimum score 580 paper-based). Electronic applications accepted.

Rensselaer Polytechnic Institute, Graduate School, School of Engineering, Program in Chemical Engineering, Troy, NY 12180-3590. Offers M Eng, MS, PhD. *Faculty:* 17 full-time (2 women). *Students:* 84 full-time (32 women), 1 part-time; includes 13 minority (6 Asian, non-Hispanic/Latino; 7 Two or more races, non-Hispanic/Latino), 52 international. Average age 25. 170 applicants, 38% accepted, 26 enrolled. In 2019, 5 master's, 15 doctorates awarded. Terminal master's awarded for partial completion of doctoral program. *Entrance requirements:* For master's and doctorate, GRE. Additional exam requirements/recommendations for international students: required—TOEFL (minimum score 570 paper-based; 88 iBT), IELTS (minimum score 6.5), PTE (minimum score 60). *Application deadline:* For fall admission, 1/1 priority date for domestic and international students; for spring admission, 8/15 priority date for domestic and international students. Applications are processed on a rolling basis. Application fee: $75. Electronic applications accepted. *Financial support:* In 2019–20, research assistantships with full tuition reimbursements (averaging $23,000 per year), teaching assistantships with full tuition reimbursements (averaging $23,000 per year) were awarded; fellowships also available. Financial award application deadline: 1/1. *Unit head:* Dr. Patrick Underhill, Graduate Program Director, 518-276-3032, E-mail: underhill@rpi.edu. *Application contact:* Jarron Decker, Director of Graduate Admissions, 518-276-6216, Fax: 518-276-4072, E-mail: gradadmissions@rpi.edu.
Website: http://cbe.rpi.edu/graduate

Rice University, Graduate Programs, George R. Brown School of Engineering, Department of Chemical and Biomolecular Engineering, Houston, TX 77251-1892. Offers chemical and biomolecular engineering (MS, PhD); chemical engineering (M Ch E). *Program availability:* Part-time. *Degree requirements:* For master's, thesis (for some programs); for doctorate, thesis/dissertation. *Entrance requirements:* For master's and doctorate, GRE General Test, minimum GPA of 3.0. Additional exam requirements/recommendations for international students: required—TOEFL (minimum score 600 paper-based; 90 iBT). Electronic applications accepted.

Rose-Hulman Institute of Technology, Graduate Studies, Department of Chemical Engineering, Terre Haute, IN 47803-3999. Offers M Eng, MS. *Program availability:* Part-time. *Faculty:* 11 full-time (5 women), 1 (woman) part-time/adjunct. *Students:* 3 full-time (2 women), 1 part-time (0 women); includes 1 minority (Asian, non-Hispanic/Latino), 2 international. Average age 23. 5 applicants, 100% accepted, 1 enrolled. In 2019, 8 master's awarded. *Degree requirements:* For master's, thesis (for some programs). *Entrance requirements:* For master's, GRE, minimum GPA of 3.0. Additional exam requirements/recommendations for international students: required—TOEFL (minimum score 580 paper-based; 94 iBT), IELTS (minimum score 7). *Application deadline:* For fall admission, 2/1 priority date for domestic and international students; for winter admission, 10/1 for domestic students, 4/1 for international students; for spring admission, 1/15 for domestic students, 11/1 for international students. Applications are processed on a rolling basis. Application fee: $75. Electronic applications accepted. *Financial support:* In 2019–20, 3 students received support. Fellowships with tuition reimbursements available, research assistantships with tuition reimbursements available, institutionally sponsored loans, scholarships/grants, tuition waivers (full and partial), and unspecified assistantships available. *Unit head:* Dr. Adam Nolte, Department Head, 812-877-8096, Fax: 812-877-8992, E-mail: nolte@rose-hulman.edu. *Application contact:* Dr. Craig Downing, Associate Dean of Lifelong Learning, 812-877-8822, E-mail: downing@rose-hulman.edu.
Website: https://www.rose-hulman.edu/academics/academic-departments/chemical-engineering/index.html

Rowan University, Graduate School, College of Engineering, Department of Chemical Engineering, Glassboro, NJ 08028-1701. Offers MS. Electronic applications accepted. *Expenses: Tuition, area resident:* Part-time $715.50 per semester hour. Tuition, state resident: part-time $715.50 per semester hour. Tuition, nonresident: part-time $715.50 per semester hour. *Required fees:* $161.55 per semester hour.

Royal Military College of Canada, Division of Graduate Studies, Faculty of Science, Department of Chemistry and Chemical Engineering, Kingston, ON K7K 7B4, Canada. Offers chemical engineering (M Eng, MA Sc, PhD); chemistry (M Sc, PhD). *Degree requirements:* For master's, thesis; for doctorate, comprehensive exam, thesis/dissertation. *Entrance requirements:* For master's, honour's degree with second-class standing; for doctorate, master's degree. Electronic applications accepted.

Rutgers University - New Brunswick, Graduate School-New Brunswick, Program in Chemical and Biochemical Engineering, Piscataway, NJ 08854-8097. Offers MS, PhD. *Program availability:* Part-time, evening/weekend. Terminal master's awarded for partial completion of doctoral program. *Degree requirements:* For master's, thesis or alternative; for doctorate, thesis/dissertation. *Entrance requirements:* For master's and doctorate, GRE General Test. Additional exam requirements/recommendations for international students: required—TOEFL.

San Jose State University, Program in Chemical & Materials Engineering, San Jose, CA 95192-0082. Offers chemical engineering (MS); materials engineering (MS). *Program availability:* Part-time. *Faculty:* 2 full-time (both women), 5 part-time/adjunct (0 women). *Students:* 23 full-time (6 women), 68 part-time (16 women); includes 59 minority (32 Asian, non-Hispanic/Latino; 11 Hispanic/Latino; 16 Two or more races, non-Hispanic/Latino), 16 international. Average age 29. 68 applicants, 72% accepted, 27 enrolled. In 2019, 23 master's awarded. *Degree requirements:* For master's, thesis optional, Research Project. *Entrance requirements:* For master's, Students with a US BS degree are admitted to classified standing if they have a GPA in the major of 3.0, or better or they are admitted to conditionally classified standing if they have a GPA in the major between 2.7 and 2.99. Additional exam requirements/recommendations for international students: required—TOEFL (minimum score 575 paper-based; 240 iBT), IELTS (minimum score 7.5). *Application deadline:* For fall admission, 7/1 for domestic students, 5/1 for international students; for spring admission, 12/1 for domestic students, 11/1 for international students. Applications are processed on a rolling basis. Application fee: $70. Electronic applications accepted. *Expenses: Tuition, area resident:* Full-time $7176; part-time $4164. Tuition, state resident: full-time $7176; part-time $4164. Tuition, nonresident: full-time $7176; part-time $4165 per credit hour. *International tuition:* $7176 full-time. *Required fees:* $2110; $2110. *Financial support:* In 2019–20, 16 students received support, including 1 fellowship (averaging $4,500 per year), 10 research assistantships (averaging $8,000 per year), 6 teaching assistantships (averaging $14,000 per year); scholarships/grants and health care benefits also available. Financial award application deadline: 5/1; financial award applicants required to submit FAFSA. *Unit head:* Dr. Richard Chung, Department Chair, 408-924-3927, E-mail: richard.chung@sjsu.edu. *Application contact:* Debi Fennern, Administrative Analyst, 408-924-4056, E-mail: debi.fennern@sjsu.edu.
Website: http://www.sjsu.edu/cme/

South Dakota School of Mines and Technology, Graduate Division, Program in Chemical and Biological Engineering, Rapid City, SD 57701-3995. Offers PhD. *Program availability:* Part-time. *Degree requirements:* For doctorate, thesis/dissertation. *Entrance requirements:* Additional exam requirements/recommendations for international students: required—TOEFL (minimum score 520 paper-based; 68 iBT). Electronic applications accepted.

South Dakota School of Mines and Technology, Graduate Division, Program in Chemical Engineering, Rapid City, SD 57701-3995. Offers MS. *Program availability:* Part-time. *Degree requirements:* For master's, thesis. *Entrance requirements:* For master's, GRE General Test. Additional exam requirements/recommendations for international students: required—TOEFL (minimum score 520 paper-based; 68 iBT), TWE. Electronic applications accepted.

Stanford University, School of Engineering, Department of Chemical Engineering, Stanford, CA 94305-2004. Offers MS, PhD. *Expenses: Tuition:* Full-time $52,479; part-time $34,110 per unit. *Required fees:* $672; $224 per quarter. Tuition and fees vary

according to program and student level.
Website: http://cheme.stanford.edu/

Stevens Institute of Technology, Graduate School, Charles V. Schaefer Jr. School of Engineering and Science, Department of Chemical Engineering and Materials Science, Program in Chemical Engineering, Hoboken, NJ 07030. Offers M Eng, PhD, Engr. *Program availability:* Part-time, evening/weekend, 100% online, blended/hybrid learning. *Faculty:* 13 full-time (3 women), 2 part-time/adjunct (0 women). *Students:* 30 full-time (8 women), 4 part-time (1 woman); includes 2 minority (1 Asian, non-Hispanic/Latino; 1 Hispanic/Latino), 23 international. Average age 26. In 2019, 13 master's awarded. Terminal master's awarded for partial completion of doctoral program. *Entrance requirements:* For master's, International applicants must submit TOEFL/IELTS scores and fulfill the English Language Proficiency Requirement. Applicants to full-time programs who do not qualify for a score waiver are required to submit GRE/GMAT scores. Additional exam requirements/recommendations for international students: required—TOEFL (minimum score 74 iBT), IELTS (minimum score 6). *Application deadline:* For fall admission, 4/15 for domestic and international students; for spring admission, 11/1 for domestic and international students; for summer admission, 5/1 for domestic students. Applications are processed on a rolling basis. Application fee: $60. Electronic applications accepted. *Expenses: Tuition:* Full-time $52,134. *Required fees:* $1880. Tuition and fees vary according to course load. *Financial support:* Fellowships, research assistantships, teaching assistantships, career-related internships or fieldwork, Federal Work-Study, scholarships/grants, and unspecified assistantships available. Financial award application deadline: 2/15; financial award applicants required to submit FAFSA. *Unit head:* Dr. Jean Zu, Dean of SES, 201-216.8233, Fax: 201-216.8372, E-mail: Jean.Zu@stevens.edu. *Application contact:* Graduate Admissions, 888-783-8367, Fax: 888-511-1306, E-mail: graduate@stevens.edu.

Syracuse University, College of Engineering and Computer Science, Programs in Chemical Engineering, Syracuse, NY 13244. Offers MS, PhD. *Program availability:* Part-time. *Degree requirements:* For master's, comprehensive exam (for some programs), thesis (for some programs); for doctorate, comprehensive exam, thesis/dissertation. *Entrance requirements:* For master's, GRE General Test, official transcripts, three letters of recommendation, resume, personal statement; for doctorate, GRE General Test. Additional exam requirements/recommendations for international students: required—TOEFL (minimum score 100 iBT). Electronic applications accepted.

Tennessee Technological University, College of Graduate Studies, College of Engineering, Department of Chemical Engineering, Cookeville, TN 38505. Offers MS. *Program availability:* Part-time. *Faculty:* 8 full-time (0 women). *Students:* 3 full-time (1 woman), 10 part-time (5 women), 6 international. 11 applicants, 64% accepted, 3 enrolled. In 2019, 4 master's awarded. *Degree requirements:* For master's, thesis. *Entrance requirements:* For master's, GRE General Test. Additional exam requirements/recommendations for international students: required—TOEFL (minimum score 550 paper-based; 79 iBT), IELTS (minimum score 5.5), PTE (minimum score 53), or TOEIC (Test of English as an International Communication). *Application deadline:* For fall admission, 8/1 for domestic students, 5/1 for international students; for spring admission, 12/1 for domestic students, 10/1 for international students; for summer admission, 5/1 for domestic students, 2/1 for international students. Applications are processed on a rolling basis. Application fee: $35 ($40 for international students). Electronic applications accepted. *Expenses: Tuition, area resident:* Part-time $597 per credit hour. Tuition, state resident: part-time $597 per credit hour. Tuition, nonresident: part-time $1323 per credit hour. *Financial support:* Fellowships, research assistantships, teaching assistantships, and career-related internships or fieldwork available. Financial award application deadline: 4/1. *Unit head:* Dr. Holly Stretz, Interim Chairperson, 931-372-3297, Fax: 931-372-6372, E-mail: hstretz@tntech.edu. *Application contact:* Shelia K. Kendrick, Coordinator of Graduate Studies, 931-372-3808, Fax: 931-372-3497, E-mail: skendrick@tntech.edu.

Texas A&M University, College of Engineering, Artie McFerrin Department of Chemical Engineering, College Station, TX 77843. Offers chemical engineering (MS). *Faculty:* 37. *Students:* 173 full-time (47 women), 39 part-time (12 women); includes 30 minority (5 Black or African American, non-Hispanic/Latino; 15 Asian, non-Hispanic/Latino; 5 Hispanic/Latino; 5 Two or more races, non-Hispanic/Latino), 152 international. Average age 27. 353 applicants, 35% accepted, 50 enrolled. In 2019, 28 master's, 26 doctorates awarded. Terminal master's awarded for partial completion of doctoral program. *Degree requirements:* For master's, comprehensive exam, thesis (for some programs); for doctorate, comprehensive exam, thesis/dissertation. *Entrance requirements:* For master's and doctorate, GRE General Test, letters of recommendation. Additional exam requirements/recommendations for international students: required—TOEFL (minimum score 550 paper-based; 80 iBT), IELTS (minimum score 6), PTE (minimum score 53). *Application deadline:* For fall admission, 12/15 for domestic students, 12/1 priority date for international students; for spring admission, 10/1 for domestic and international students. Applications are processed on a rolling basis. Application fee: $65 ($90 for international students). Electronic applications accepted. *Expenses:* Contact institution. *Financial support:* In 2019–20, 209 students received support, including 12 fellowships with tuition reimbursements available (averaging $10,914 per year), 140 research assistantships with tuition reimbursements available (averaging $16,927 per year), 38 teaching assistantships with tuition reimbursements available (averaging $15,639 per year); career-related internships or fieldwork, institutionally sponsored loans, scholarships/grants, traineeships, health care benefits, tuition waivers (full and partial), and unspecified assistantships also available. Support available to part-time students. Financial award application deadline: 3/15; financial award applicants required to submit FAFSA. *Unit head:* Dr. Arul Jayaraman, Department Head, 979-845-3306, E-mail: arulj@tamu.edu. *Application contact:* Micah Green, Director of the Graduate Program, 979-862-1588, E-mail: micah.green@tamu.edu.
Website: http://engineering.tamu.edu/chemical

Texas A&M University–Kingsville, College of Graduate Studies, Frank H. Dotterweich College of Engineering, Wayne H. King Department of Chemical and Natural Gas Engineering, Program in Chemical Engineering, Kingsville, TX 78363. Offers ME, MS. *Degree requirements:* For master's, variable foreign language requirement, comprehensive exam, thesis (for some programs). *Entrance requirements:* For master's, GRE (minimum quantitative score of 150, verbal 145), MAT, GMAT, minimum GPA of 2.75. Additional exam requirements/recommendations for international students: required—TOEFL (minimum score 550 paper-based; 79 iBT). Electronic applications accepted.

Tufts University, School of Engineering, Department of Chemical and Biological Engineering, Medford, MA 02155. Offers bioengineering (MS), including cell and bioprocess engineering; biotechnology (PhD); chemical engineering (MS, PhD); PhD/PhD. *Program availability:* Part-time. Terminal master's awarded for partial completion of doctoral program. *Degree requirements:* For master's, thesis (for some programs); for doctorate, thesis/dissertation. *Entrance requirements:* For master's and doctorate, GRE General Test. Additional exam requirements/recommendations for international students: required—TOEFL (minimum score 550 paper-based; 80 iBT), IELTS (minimum score 6.5). Electronic applications accepted. Full-time tuition and fees vary according to degree level, program and student level. Part-time tuition and fees vary according to course load.

Tulane University, School of Science and Engineering, Department of Chemical and Biomolecular Engineering, New Orleans, LA 70118-5669. Offers MS, PhD. *Program availability:* Part-time. Terminal master's awarded for partial completion of doctoral program. *Degree requirements:* For master's, thesis (for some programs); for doctorate, thesis/dissertation. *Entrance requirements:* For master's and doctorate, GRE General Test, minimum B average in undergraduate course work. Additional exam requirements/recommendations for international students: required—TOEFL. Electronic applications accepted. *Expenses: Tuition:* Full-time $57,004; part-time $3167 per credit hour. *Required fees:* $2086; $44.50 per credit hour. $80 per term. Tuition and fees vary according to course load, degree level and program.

Universidad de las Américas Puebla, Division of Graduate Studies, School of Engineering, Program in Chemical Engineering, Puebla, Mexico. Offers chemical engineering (MS); food technology (MS). *Program availability:* Part-time, evening/weekend. *Degree requirements:* For master's, one foreign language, thesis.

Université de Sherbrooke, Faculty of Engineering, Department of Chemical Engineering, Sherbrooke, QC J1K 2R1, Canada. Offers M Sc A, PhD. *Degree requirements:* For master's, one foreign language, thesis; for doctorate, comprehensive exam, thesis/dissertation. *Entrance requirements:* For doctorate, master's degree in engineering or equivalent. Electronic applications accepted.

University at Buffalo, the State University of New York, Graduate School, School of Engineering and Applied Sciences, Department of Chemical and Biological Engineering, Buffalo, NY 14260. Offers bioengineering nanotechnology (Certificate); chemical and biological engineering (ME, MS, PhD); nanomaterials and materials informatics (Certificate). *Program availability:* Part-time. *Degree requirements:* For master's, thesis (for some programs); for doctorate, comprehensive exam, thesis/dissertation. *Entrance requirements:* For master's and doctorate, GRE General Test. Additional exam requirements/recommendations for international students: required—TOEFL (minimum score 550 paper-based; 79 iBT). Electronic applications accepted. *Expenses: Tuition, area resident:* Full-time $11,310; part-time $471 per credit hour. Tuition, state resident: full-time $11,310; part-time $471 per credit hour. Tuition, nonresident: full-time $23,100; part-time $963 per credit hour. *International tuition:* $23,100 full-time. *Required fees:* $2820.

The University of Akron, Graduate School, College of Engineering, Department of Chemical and Biomolecular Engineering, Akron, OH 44325. Offers chemical engineering (MS); engineering (PhD). *Program availability:* Part-time, evening/weekend. *Degree requirements:* For master's, thesis optional; for doctorate, one foreign language, thesis/dissertation, candidacy exam, qualifying exam. *Entrance requirements:* For master's, GRE, minimum GPA of 2.75, letters of recommendation, statement of purpose; for doctorate, GRE, minimum GPA of 3.0 with bachelor's degree, 3.5 with master's degree; letters of recommendation; personal statement; resume. Additional exam requirements/recommendations for international students: required—TOEFL (minimum score 79 iBT), IELTS (minimum score 6.5). Electronic applications accepted.

The University of Alabama, Graduate School, College of Engineering, Department of Chemical and Biological Engineering, Tuscaloosa, AL 35487. Offers MS Ch E, PhD. *Faculty:* 18 full-time (3 women). *Students:* 39 full-time (10 women); includes 3 minority (2 Black or African American, non-Hispanic/Latino; 1 Two or more races, non-Hispanic/Latino), 21 international. Average age 26. 65 applicants, 45% accepted, 11 enrolled. In 2019, 7 master's, 4 doctorates awarded. Terminal master's awarded for partial completion of doctoral program. *Degree requirements:* For master's, comprehensive exam, thesis; for doctorate, comprehensive exam, thesis/dissertation. *Entrance requirements:* For master's, GRE, minimum GPA of 3.0 overall; for doctorate, GRE, minimum GPA of 3.0. Additional exam requirements/recommendations for international students: required—TOEFL (minimum score 550 paper-based); recommended—IELTS (minimum score 6.5). *Application deadline:* For fall admission, 5/1 priority date for domestic and international students; for winter admission, 9/15 priority date for domestic and international students. Applications are processed on a rolling basis. Application fee: $50 ($60 for international students). Electronic applications accepted. *Expenses: Tuition, area resident:* Full-time $10,780; part-time $440 per credit hour. Tuition, nonresident: full-time $30,250; part-time $1550 per credit hour. *Financial support:* In 2019–20, 16 students received support. Fellowships with full tuition reimbursements available, research assistantships with full tuition reimbursements available, teaching assistantships with full tuition reimbursements available, and Federal Work-Study available. Financial award application deadline: 3/15. *Unit head:* Dr. C. Heath Turner, Department Head and Professor, 205-348-1733, Fax: 205-348-6579, E-mail: hturner@eng.ua.edu. *Application contact:* Dr. Yuping Bao, Associate Professor, 205-348-9869, Fax: 205-348-7558, E-mail: ybao@eng.ua.edu.
Website: http://che.eng.ua.edu/

The University of Alabama in Huntsville, School of Graduate Studies, College of Engineering, Department of Chemical and Materials Engineering, Huntsville, AL 35899. Offers biotechnology science and engineering (PhD); chemical and materials engineering (MSE); materials science (PhD); mechanical engineering (PhD), including chemical engineering. *Program availability:* Part-time. *Degree requirements:* For master's, comprehensive exam, thesis or alternative, oral and written exams; for doctorate, comprehensive exam, thesis/dissertation. *Entrance requirements:* For master's, GRE General Test, appropriate bachelor's degree, minimum GPA of 3.0; for doctorate, GRE General Test, minimum GPA of 3.0. Additional exam requirements/recommendations for international students: required—TOEFL (minimum score 500 paper-based; 80 iBT), IELTS (minimum score 6.5). Electronic applications accepted.

University of Alberta, Faculty of Graduate Studies and Research, Department of Chemical and Materials Engineering, Edmonton, AB T6G 2E1, Canada. Offers chemical engineering (M Eng, M Sc, PhD); materials engineering (M Eng, M Sc, PhD); process control (M Eng, M Sc, PhD); welding (M Eng). *Program availability:* Part-time, online learning. Terminal master's awarded for partial completion of doctoral program. *Degree requirements:* For master's, thesis; for doctorate, thesis/dissertation.

The University of Arizona, College of Engineering, Department of Chemical and Environmental Engineering, Tucson, AZ 85721-0011. Offers chemical engineering (MS, PhD); environmental engineering (MS, PhD). *Program availability:* Part-time. *Degree requirements:* For master's, thesis; for doctorate, comprehensive exam, thesis/dissertation, departmental qualifying exams. *Entrance requirements:* For master's and doctorate, GRE General Test, 3 letters of recommendation, resume, statement of purpose. Additional exam requirements/recommendations for international students: required—TOEFL (minimum score 550 paper-based; 79 iBT). Electronic applications accepted.

University of Arkansas, Graduate School, College of Engineering, Department of Chemical Engineering, Fayetteville, AR 72701. Offers MS Ch E, MSE, PhD. *Program availability:* Part-time. *Students:* 31 full-time (12 women), 13 part-time (4 women); includes 5 minority (1 Asian, non-Hispanic/Latino; 2 Hispanic/Latino; 2 Two or more races, non-Hispanic/Latino), 27 international. 29 applicants, 79% accepted. In 2019, 6 doctorates awarded. *Degree requirements:* For master's, thesis optional; for doctorate, one foreign language, thesis/dissertation. *Entrance requirements:* For master's and doctorate, GRE General Test. *Application deadline:* For fall admission, 8/1 for domestic students, 4/1 for international students; for spring admission, 12/1 for domestic students,

10/1 for international students; for summer admission, 4/15 for domestic students, 3/1 for international students. Applications are processed on a rolling basis. Application fee: $60. Electronic applications accepted. *Financial support:* In 2019–20, 18 research assistantships were awarded; fellowships with tuition reimbursements, teaching assistantships, career-related internships or fieldwork, and Federal Work-Study also available. Support available to part-time students. Financial award application deadline: 4/1; financial award applicants required to submit FAFSA. *Unit head:* Dr. David M. Ford, Department Head, 479-575-4951, E-mail: daveford@uark.edu. *Application contact:* Dr. Christa Hestekin, Graduate Coordinator, 479-575-3416, E-mail: chesteki@uark.edu.
Website: https://chemical-engineering.uark.edu/

The University of British Columbia, Faculty of Applied Science, Department of Chemical and Biological Engineering, Vancouver, BC V6T 1Z3, Canada. Offers M Eng, M Sc, MA Sc, PhD. *Program availability:* Part-time, evening/weekend. *Degree requirements:* For master's, thesis (for some programs); for doctorate, thesis/dissertation. *Entrance requirements:* Additional exam requirements/recommendations for international students: required—TOEFL, IELTS. Electronic applications accepted. *Expenses:* Contact institution.

University of Calgary, Faculty of Graduate Studies, Schulich School of Engineering, Program in Chemical and Petroleum Engineering, Calgary, AB T2N 1N4, Canada. Offers chemical engineering (M Eng, M Sc, PhD); energy and environment engineering (M Eng, M Sc, PhD); energy and environmental systems (M Eng, M Sc, PhD); environmental engineering (M Eng, M Sc, PhD); petroleum engineering (M Eng, M Sc, PhD); reservoir characterization (M Eng, M Sc). *Program availability:* Part-time. *Degree requirements:* For master's, thesis (for some programs); for doctorate, comprehensive exam, thesis/dissertation, candidacy exam. *Entrance requirements:* For master's, minimum GPA of 3.0 or equivalent; for doctorate, minimum GPA of 3.5 or equivalent. Additional exam requirements/recommendations for international students: required—TOEFL (minimum score 550 paper-based; 80 iBT), IELTS (minimum score 7). Electronic applications accepted.

University of California, Berkeley, Graduate Division, College of Chemistry, Department of Chemical and Biomolecular Engineering, Berkeley, CA 94720. Offers chemical engineering (PhD); product development (MS). Terminal master's awarded for partial completion of doctoral program. *Degree requirements:* For master's, comprehensive exam (for some programs), thesis (for some programs); for doctorate, thesis/dissertation, qualifying exam. *Entrance requirements:* For master's and doctorate, GRE General Test, minimum GPA of 3.0, 3 letters of recommendation. Additional exam requirements/recommendations for international students: required—TOEFL (minimum score 570 paper-based; 90 iBT). Electronic applications accepted.

University of California, Davis, College of Engineering, Program in Chemical Engineering, Davis, CA 95616. Offers MS, PhD. Terminal master's awarded for partial completion of doctoral program. *Degree requirements:* For master's, comprehensive exam (for some programs), thesis (for some programs); for doctorate, thesis/dissertation. *Entrance requirements:* For master's and doctorate, GRE General Test, minimum GPA of 3.0. Additional exam requirements/recommendations for international students: required—TOEFL (minimum score 550 paper-based). Electronic applications accepted.

University of California, Irvine, Samueli School of Engineering, Department of Chemical Engineering and Materials Science, Irvine, CA 92697. Offers chemical and biochemical engineering (MS, PhD); materials science and engineering (MS, PhD). *Program availability:* Part-time. *Students:* 139 full-time (58 women), 3 part-time (2 women); includes 40 minority (5 Black or African American, non-Hispanic/Latino; 28 Asian, non-Hispanic/Latino; 6 Hispanic/Latino; 1 Two or more races, non-Hispanic/Latino), 56 international. Average age 26. 435 applicants, 34% accepted, 48 enrolled. In 2019, 30 master's, 26 doctorates awarded. Terminal master's awarded for partial completion of doctoral program. *Entrance requirements:* For master's and doctorate, GRE General Test, minimum GPA of 3.0, 3 letters of recommendation. Additional exam requirements/recommendations for international students: required—TOEFL (minimum score 550 paper-based). *Application deadline:* For fall admission, 1/15 priority date for domestic students, 1/15 for international students. Applications are processed on a rolling basis. Application fee: $120 ($140 for international students). Electronic applications accepted. *Financial support:* Fellowships, research assistantships with full tuition reimbursements, teaching assistantships, institutionally sponsored loans, traineeships, health care benefits, and unspecified assistantships available. Financial award application deadline: 3/1; financial award applicants required to submit FAFSA. *Unit head:* Prof. Vasan Venugopalan, Chair, 949-824-5802, Fax: 949-824-2541, E-mail: vvenugop@uci.edu. *Application contact:* Grace Chau, Academic Program and Graduate Admission Coordinator, 949-824-3887, Fax: 949-824-2541, E-mail: chaug@uci.edu.
Website: http://www.eng.uci.edu/dept/chems

University of California, Los Angeles, Graduate Division, Henry Samueli School of Engineering and Applied Science, Department of Chemical and Biomolecular Engineering, Los Angeles, CA 90095-1592. Offers MS, PhD. *Degree requirements:* For master's, comprehensive exam (for some programs), thesis (for some programs); for doctorate, thesis/dissertation, qualifying exams. *Entrance requirements:* For master's, GRE General Test, minimum GPA of 3.0; for doctorate, GRE General Test, minimum GPA of 3.25. Additional exam requirements/recommendations for international students: required—TOEFL (minimum score 560 paper-based; 87 iBT), IELTS (minimum score 7). Electronic applications accepted.

University of California, Riverside, Graduate Division, Department of Chemical and Environmental Engineering, Riverside, CA 92521-0102. Offers MS, PhD. *Program availability:* Part-time. Terminal master's awarded for partial completion of doctoral program. *Degree requirements:* For master's, thesis (for some programs); for doctorate, comprehensive exam, thesis/dissertation. *Entrance requirements:* For master's and doctorate, GRE General Test, minimum GPA of 3.0. Additional exam requirements/recommendations for international students: required—TOEFL (minimum score 550 paper-based; 80 iBT). Electronic applications accepted.

University of California, San Diego, Graduate Division, Program in Chemical Engineering, La Jolla, CA 92093. Offers MS, PhD. *Students:* 65 full-time (18 women), 6 part-time (2 women). 217 applicants, 45% accepted, 30 enrolled. In 2019, 22 master's, 1 doctorate awarded. *Degree requirements:* For master's, comprehensive exam (for some programs), thesis (for some programs); for doctorate, comprehensive exam, thesis/dissertation, 1-quarter teaching assistantship. *Entrance requirements:* For master's, GRE General Test; for doctorate, GRE General Test, statement of purpose. Additional exam requirements/recommendations for international students: required—TOEFL (minimum score 550 paper-based; 80 iBT), IELTS (minimum score 7). *Application deadline:* For fall admission, 12/20 for domestic students. Application fee: $105 ($125 for international students). Electronic applications accepted. *Financial support:* Fellowships, research assistantships, teaching assistantships, scholarships/grants, and readerships available. Financial award applicants required to submit FAFSA. *Unit head:* Joseph Wang, Chair, 858-882-7640, E-mail: josephwang@ucsd.edu. *Application contact:* Dana Jimenez, Graduate Coordinator, 858-822-7981, E-mail: dljimenez@ucsd.edu.
Website: http://nanoengineering.ucsd.edu/graduate-programs/degree/chemical-engineering

University of California, Santa Barbara, Graduate Division, College of Engineering, Department of Chemical Engineering, Santa Barbara, CA 93106. Offers MS, PhD. *Degree requirements:* For master's, thesis or comprehensive exam; for doctorate, thesis/dissertation, research progress reports (prior to candidacy), candidacy exam, thesis defense, seminar. *Entrance requirements:* For doctorate, GRE. Additional exam requirements/recommendations for international students: required—TOEFL (minimum score 560 paper-based; 83 iBT), IELTS (minimum score 7). Electronic applications accepted.

University of Cincinnati, Graduate School, College of Engineering and Applied Science, Department of Biomedical, Chemical and Environmental Engineering, Program in Chemical Engineering, Cincinnati, OH 45221. Offers MS, PhD. *Program availability:* Part-time, evening/weekend. Terminal master's awarded for partial completion of doctoral program. *Degree requirements:* For master's, thesis; for doctorate, thesis/dissertation. *Entrance requirements:* For master's and doctorate, GRE General Test. Additional exam requirements/recommendations for international students: required—TOEFL (minimum score 600 paper-based).

University of Colorado Boulder, Graduate School, College of Engineering and Applied Science, Department of Chemical and Biological Engineering, Boulder, CO 80309. Offers ME, MS, PhD. Terminal master's awarded for partial completion of doctoral program. *Degree requirements:* For master's, comprehensive exam, thesis; for doctorate, thesis/dissertation. *Entrance requirements:* For master's, minimum undergraduate GPA of 3.0. Electronic applications accepted. Application fee is waived when completed online.

University of Connecticut, Graduate School, School of Engineering, Department of Chemical and Biomolecular Engineering, Storrs, CT 06269. Offers MS, PhD. Terminal master's awarded for partial completion of doctoral program. *Degree requirements:* For master's, comprehensive exam, thesis or alternative; for doctorate, thesis/dissertation. *Entrance requirements:* For master's and doctorate, GRE General Test. Additional exam requirements/recommendations for international students: required—TOEFL (minimum score 550 paper-based). Electronic applications accepted.

University of Dayton, Department of Chemical Engineering, Dayton, OH 45469. Offers bioengineering (MS); chemical engineering (MS Ch E). *Program availability:* Part-time, online learning. *Degree requirements:* For master's, thesis for 33 credit hours. *Entrance requirements:* For master's, GRE (preferred), minimum GPA of 3.0 as undergraduate, transcript, 3 letters of recommendation, bachelor's degree in chemical engineering (preferred). Additional exam requirements/recommendations for international students: required—TOEFL (minimum score 550 paper-based; 80 iBT); recommended—IELTS. Electronic applications accepted. *Expenses:* Contact institution.

University of Delaware, College of Engineering, Department of Chemical Engineering, Newark, DE 19716. Offers M Ch E, PhD. *Program availability:* Part-time, evening/weekend, online learning. Terminal master's awarded for partial completion of doctoral program. *Degree requirements:* For master's, thesis (for some programs); for doctorate, thesis/dissertation. *Entrance requirements:* For master's and doctorate, GRE General Test. Additional exam requirements/recommendations for international students: required—TOEFL. Electronic applications accepted.

University of Florida, Graduate School, Herbert Wertheim College of Engineering, Department of Chemical Engineering, Gainesville, FL 32611. Offers ME, MS, PhD, Engr. *Program availability:* Part-time. Terminal master's awarded for partial completion of doctoral program. *Degree requirements:* For master's, thesis optional; for doctorate, comprehensive exam, thesis/dissertation. *Entrance requirements:* For master's and doctorate, minimum GPA of 3.0. Additional exam requirements/recommendations for international students: required—TOEFL (minimum score 550 paper-based; 80 iBT), IELTS (minimum score 6). Electronic applications accepted.

University of Houston, Cullen College of Engineering, Department of Chemical and Biomolecular Engineering, Houston, TX 77204. Offers chemical engineering (MCHE, PhD); petroleum engineering (M Pet E). *Program availability:* Part-time. Terminal master's awarded for partial completion of doctoral program. *Entrance requirements:* For master's and doctorate, GRE General Test. Additional exam requirements/recommendations for international students: required—TOEFL (minimum score 550 paper-based; 79 iBT), IELTS (minimum score 6.5).

University of Idaho, College of Graduate Studies, College of Engineering, Department of Chemical and Materials Engineering, Moscow, ID 83844-2282. Offers chemical engineering (M Engr, MS, PhD); materials science and engineering (PhD). *Faculty:* 14. *Students:* 23 full-time, 10 part-time. Average age 30. In 2019, 7 master's, 1 doctorate awarded. *Entrance requirements:* For master's and doctorate, GRE, minimum GPA of 3.0. Additional exam requirements/recommendations for international students: required—TOEFL (minimum score 79 iBT). *Application deadline:* For fall admission, 7/30 for domestic students; for spring admission, 12/1 for domestic students. Applications are processed on a rolling basis. Application fee: $60. Electronic applications accepted. *Expenses:* Tuition, state resident: full-time $7753.80; part-time $502 per credit hour. Tuition, nonresident: full-time $26,990; part-time $1571 per credit hour. *Required fees:* $2122.20; $47 per credit hour. *Financial support:* Fellowships, research assistantships, and teaching assistantships available. Financial award applicants required to submit FAFSA.
Website: https://www.uidaho.edu/engr/departments/cme

University of Illinois at Chicago, College of Engineering, Department of Chemical Engineering, Chicago, IL 60607-7128. Offers MS, PhD. *Program availability:* Part-time. *Degree requirements:* For master's, thesis or project; for doctorate, thesis/dissertation, departmental qualifying exam. *Entrance requirements:* For master's and doctorate, GRE General Test, minimum GPA of 2.75. Additional exam requirements/recommendations for international students: required—TOEFL. *Expenses:* Contact institution.

University of Illinois at Urbana-Champaign, Graduate College, College of Liberal Arts and Sciences, School of Chemical Sciences, Department of Chemical and Biomolecular Engineering, Champaign, IL 61820. Offers bioinformatics: chemical and biomolecular engineering (MS); chemical engineering (MS, PhD). *Entrance requirements:* For master's, minimum GPA of 3.0.

The University of Iowa, Graduate College, College of Engineering, Department of Chemical and Biochemical Engineering, Iowa City, IA 52242-1316. Offers MS, PhD. *Program availability:* Part-time. *Degree requirements:* For master's, comprehensive exam (for some programs), thesis (for some programs); for doctorate, comprehensive exam, thesis/dissertation. *Entrance requirements:* For master's and doctorate, GRE (minimum combined score of 310 on verbal and quantitative), minimum undergraduate GPA of 3.0. Additional exam requirements/recommendations for international students: required—TOEFL (minimum score 600 paper-based; 100 iBT), IELTS (minimum score 7). Electronic applications accepted.

The University of Kansas, Graduate Studies, School of Engineering, Program in Chemical and Petroleum Engineering, Lawrence, KS 66045. Offers chemical and petroleum engineering (PhD); chemical engineering (MS); petroleum engineering (MS); petroleum management (Certificate). *Program availability:* Part-time. *Students:* 44 full-

time (14 women), 4 part-time (0 women), 26 international. Average age 28. 38 applicants, 61% accepted, 5 enrolled. In 2019, 10 master's awarded. *Entrance requirements:* For master's, GRE General Test, minimum GPA of 3.0, resume, personal statement, transcripts, three letters of recommendation; for doctorate, GRE General Test, minimum GPA of 3.5, resume, personal statement, transcripts, three letters of recommendation. Additional exam requirements/recommendations for international students: required—TOEFL, IELTS. *Application deadline:* For fall admission, 12/15 priority date for domestic and international students; for spring admission, 8/31 priority date for domestic and international students. Application fee: $65 ($85 for international students). Electronic applications accepted. *Expenses:* Tuition, state resident: full-time $9989. Tuition, nonresident: full-time $23,950. *International tuition:* $23,950 full-time. *Required fees:* $984; $81.99 per credit hour. Tuition and fees vary according to course load, campus/location and program. *Financial support:* Fellowships, research assistantships, teaching assistantships, career-related internships or fieldwork, Federal Work-Study, scholarships/grants, traineeships, and unspecified assistantships available. Financial award application deadline: 12/15; financial award applicants required to submit FAFSA. *Unit head:* Laurence R Weatherley, Chair, 785-864-3553, E-mail: lweather@ku.edu. *Application contact:* Martha Kehr, Graduate Admission Contact, 785-864-2900, E-mail: cpegrad@ku.edu.
Website: http://www.cpe.engr.ku.edu

The University of Kansas, Graduate Studies, School of Engineering, Program in Chemical Engineering, Lawrence, KS 66045. Offers MS. *Program availability:* Part-time. *Students:* 9 full-time (4 women), 2 part-time (0 women), 7 international. Average age 26. 16 applicants, 56% accepted, 5 enrolled. In 2019, 4 master's awarded. *Entrance requirements:* For master's, GRE, resume, personal statement, transcripts, three letters of recommendation. Additional exam requirements/recommendations for international students: required—TOEFL, IELTS. *Application deadline:* For fall admission, 12/15 priority date for domestic and international students; for spring admission, 8/31 for domestic and international students. Application fee: $65 ($85 for international students). Electronic applications accepted. *Expenses:* Tuition, state resident: full-time $9989. Tuition, nonresident: full-time $23,950. *International tuition:* $23,950 full-time. *Required fees:* $984; $81.99 per credit hour. Tuition and fees vary according to course load, campus/location and program. *Financial support:* Fellowships, research assistantships, teaching assistantships, Federal Work-Study, and scholarships/grants available. Financial award application deadline: 12/15. *Unit head:* Laurence R Weatherley, Chair, 785-864-3553, E-mail: lweather@ku.edu. *Application contact:* Martha Kehr, Graduate Admissions Contact, 785-864-2900, E-mail: cpegrad@ku.edu.
Website: http://www.cpe.engr.ku.edu/

University of Kentucky, Graduate School, College of Engineering, Program in Chemical Engineering, Lexington, KY 40506-0032. Offers MS, PhD. *Degree requirements:* For master's, comprehensive exam, thesis optional; for doctorate, comprehensive exam, thesis/dissertation. *Entrance requirements:* For master's, GRE General Test, minimum undergraduate GPA of 2.75; for doctorate, GRE General Test, minimum undergraduate GPA of 3.0. Additional exam requirements/recommendations for international students: required—TOEFL (minimum score 550 paper-based). Electronic applications accepted.

University of Louisiana at Lafayette, College of Engineering, Department of Chemical Engineering, Lafayette, LA 70504. Offers MSE. *Program availability:* Evening/weekend. *Degree requirements:* For master's, comprehensive exam, thesis or alternative. *Entrance requirements:* For master's, GRE General Test, BS in chemical engineering, minimum GPA of 2.85. Additional exam requirements/recommendations for international students: required—TOEFL (minimum score 550 paper-based). Electronic applications accepted. *Expenses: Tuition, area resident:* Full-time $5511. Tuition, state resident: full-time $5511. Tuition, nonresident: full-time $19,239. *Required fees:* $46,637.

University of Louisville, J. B. Speed School of Engineering, Department of Chemical Engineering, Louisville, KY 40292-0001. Offers M Eng, MS, PhD. *Accreditation:* ABET (one or more programs are accredited). *Faculty:* 10 full-time (1 woman), 1 part-time/adjunct (0 women). *Students:* 36 full-time (9 women), 3 part-time (1 woman); includes 5 minority (1 Black or African American, non-Hispanic/Latino; 2 Hispanic/Latino; 2 Two or more races, non-Hispanic/Latino), 10 international. Average age 27. 16 applicants, 25% accepted, 3 enrolled. In 2019, 10 master's, 4 doctorates awarded. Terminal master's awarded for partial completion of doctoral program. *Degree requirements:* For master's, thesis optional; for doctorate, comprehensive exam, thesis/dissertation. *Entrance requirements:* For master's, Two letters of recommendation. All final official transcripts.; for doctorate, GRE, Two letters of recommendation. All final official transcripts. Additional exam requirements/recommendations for international students: required—TOEFL (minimum score 550 paper-based; 80 iBT), IELTS (minimum score 6.5). *Application deadline:* For fall admission, 5/1 priority date for domestic and international students; for spring admission, 11/1 priority date for domestic and international students; for summer admission, 3/1 priority date for domestic and international students. Applications are processed on a rolling basis. Application fee: $65. Electronic applications accepted. *Expenses: Tuition, area resident:* Full-time $13,000; part-time $723 per credit hour. Tuition, state resident: full-time $13,000; part-time $723 per credit hour. Tuition, nonresident: full-time $27,114; part-time $1507 per credit hour. *International tuition:* $27,114 full-time. *Required fees:* $196. Tuition and fees vary according to program and reciprocity agreements. *Financial support:* In 2019–20, 27 students received support. Fellowships, research assistantships, teaching assistantships, scholarships/grants, and health care benefits available. Financial award application deadline: 1/1. *Unit head:* Dr. Joel R. Fried, Chair, Chemical Engineering Department, 502-852-6347, Fax: 502-852-6355, E-mail: joel.fried@louisville.edu. *Application contact:* R. Eric Berson, Director of Graduate Studies, 502-852-1567, E-mail: eric.berson@louisville.edu.
Website: http://louisville.edu/speed/chemical/

University of Maine, Graduate School, College of Engineering, Chemical and Biomedical Engineering, Orono, ME 04469. Offers chemical engineering (MS, PhD). *Program availability:* Part-time. *Faculty:* 14 full-time (2 women). *Students:* 18 full-time (8 women), 4 part-time (3 women); includes 1 minority (Asian, non-Hispanic/Latino), 8 international. Average age 29. 31 applicants, 32% accepted, 4 enrolled. In 2019, 6 master's, 2 doctorates awarded. Terminal master's awarded for partial completion of doctoral program. *Degree requirements:* For master's, thesis; for doctorate, comprehensive exam, thesis/dissertation. *Entrance requirements:* For master's and doctorate, GRE General Test. Additional exam requirements/recommendations for international students: required—TOEFL. *Application deadline:* For fall admission, 5/1 priority date for domestic students, 3/1 priority date for international students; for spring admission, 10/1 priority date for domestic students, 9/1 priority date for international students; for summer admission, 3/1 for domestic students, 1/1 for international students. Applications are processed on a rolling basis. Application fee: $65. Electronic applications accepted. *Expenses: Tuition, area resident:* Full-time $8100; part-time $450 per credit hour. Tuition, state resident: full-time $8100; part-time $450 per credit hour. Tuition, nonresident: full-time $26,388; part-time $1466 per credit hour. *International tuition:* $26,388 full-time. *Required fees:* $1257; $278 per semester. Tuition and fees vary according to course load. *Financial support:* In 2019–20, 21 students received support, including 15 research assistantships with full tuition reimbursements available

(averaging $9,550 per year), 6 teaching assistantships with full tuition reimbursements available (averaging $15,825 per year); Federal Work-Study, tuition waivers (full and partial), and unspecified assistantships also available. Financial award application deadline: 3/1; financial award applicants required to submit FAFSA. *Unit head:* Dr. Hemant Pendse, Chair, 207-581-2290, Fax: 207-581-2323, E-mail: pendse@maine.edu. *Application contact:* Scott G. Delcourt, Assistant Vice President for Graduate Studies and Senior Associate Dean, 207-581-3291, Fax: 207-581-3232, E-mail: graduate@maine.edu.
Website: https://umaine.edu/chb/

The University of Manchester, School of Chemical Engineering and Analytical Science, Manchester, United Kingdom. Offers biocatalysis (M Phil, PhD); chemical engineering (M Phil, PhD); chemical engineering and analytical science (M Phil, D Eng, PhD); colloids, crystals, interfaces and materials (M Phil, PhD); environment and sustainable technology (M Phil, PhD); instrumentation (M Phil, PhD); multi-scale modeling (M Phil, PhD); process integration (M Phil, PhD); systems biology (M Phil, PhD).

University of Maryland, Baltimore County, The Graduate School, College of Engineering and Information Technology, Department of Chemical, Biochemical, and Environmental Engineering, Program in Chemical and Biochemical Engineering, Baltimore, MD 21250. Offers MS, PhD. *Program availability:* Part-time. *Faculty:* 16 full-time (6 women), 4 part-time/adjunct (1 woman). *Students:* 32 full-time (14 women), 3 part-time (1 woman); includes 9 minority (6 Black or African American, non-Hispanic/Latino; 1 Asian, non-Hispanic/Latino; 1 Hispanic/Latino; 1 Two or more races, non-Hispanic/Latino), 12 international. Average age 27. 40 applicants, 48% accepted, 14 enrolled. In 2019, 6 master's, 3 doctorates awarded. *Degree requirements:* For master's, comprehensive exam (for some programs), thesis (for some programs); for doctorate, comprehensive exam, thesis/dissertation. *Entrance requirements:* For master's, GRE General Test, minimum GPA of 3.0, strong mathematical background; for doctorate, GRE General Test (taken within last 5 years), minimum GPA of 3.0. Additional exam requirements/recommendations for international students: required—TOEFL (minimum score 550 paper-based; 80 iBT). *Application deadline:* For fall admission, 6/1 for domestic students, 1/1 for international students; for spring admission, 11/1 for domestic students, 6/1 for international students. Applications are processed on a rolling basis. Application fee: $70. Electronic applications accepted. Application fee is waived when completed online. *Expenses:* $14,382 per year. *Financial support:* In 2019–20, 23 students received support, including 2 fellowships with full tuition reimbursements available, 18 research assistantships with full tuition reimbursements available, 3 teaching assistantships; career-related internships or fieldwork, Federal Work-Study, scholarships/grants, health care benefits, tuition waivers (partial), and unspecified assistantships also available. Support available to part-time students. Financial award application deadline: 6/30; financial award applicants required to submit FAFSA. *Unit head:* Dr. Mark Marten, Professor and Interim Chair, 410-455-3400, Fax: 410-455-1049, E-mail: marten@umbc.edu. *Application contact:* Dr. Erin Lavik, Professor/Graduate Program Director, 410-455-3428, Fax: 410-455-1049, E-mail: elavik@umbc.edu.
Website: https://cbee.umbc.edu/

University of Maryland, College Park, Academic Affairs, A. James Clark School of Engineering, Department of Chemical and Biomolecular Engineering, College Park, MD 20742. Offers bioengineering (MS, PhD); chemical engineering (M Eng, MS, PhD). *Program availability:* Part-time, evening/weekend. *Degree requirements:* For master's, thesis optional; for doctorate, variable foreign language requirement, thesis/dissertation, exam, oral presentation. *Entrance requirements:* For master's and doctorate, GRE General Test, 3 letters of recommendation. Additional exam requirements/recommendations for international students: required—TOEFL. Electronic applications accepted.

University of Massachusetts Amherst, Graduate School, College of Engineering, Department of Chemical Engineering, Amherst, MA 01003. Offers MSChE, PhD. *Program availability:* Part-time. Terminal master's awarded for partial completion of doctoral program. *Degree requirements:* For master's, thesis; for doctorate, comprehensive exam, thesis/dissertation. *Entrance requirements:* For master's and doctorate, GRE General Test. Additional exam requirements/recommendations for international students: required—TOEFL (minimum score 550 paper-based; 80 iBT), IELTS (minimum score 6.5). Electronic applications accepted.

University of Massachusetts Lowell, Francis College of Engineering, Department of Chemical Engineering, Lowell, MA 01854. Offers MS Eng, PhD. *Program availability:* Part-time. *Degree requirements:* For master's, thesis; for doctorate, thesis/dissertation, seminar, qualifying examination. *Entrance requirements:* For master's, GRE General Test. Electronic applications accepted.

University of Michigan, College of Engineering, Department of Chemical Engineering, Ann Arbor, MI 48109. Offers MSE, PhD, Ch E. *Program availability:* Part-time. Terminal master's awarded for partial completion of doctoral program. *Degree requirements:* For doctorate, thesis/dissertation, oral defense of dissertation, preliminary exams. *Entrance requirements:* For master's and doctorate, GRE General Test. Additional exam requirements/recommendations for international students: required—TOEFL. Electronic applications accepted.

University of Minnesota, Twin Cities Campus, College of Science and Engineering, Department of Chemical Engineering and Materials Science, Program in Chemical Engineering, Minneapolis, MN 55455-0132. Offers M Ch E, MS Ch E, PhD. *Program availability:* Part-time. Terminal master's awarded for partial completion of doctoral program. *Degree requirements:* For master's, thesis; for doctorate, thesis/dissertation. *Entrance requirements:* For master's and doctorate, GRE General Test. Additional exam requirements/recommendations for international students: required—TOEFL. Electronic applications accepted.

University of Mississippi, Graduate School, School of Engineering, University, MS 38677. Offers aeroacoustics (MS, PhD); chemical engineering (MS, PhD); civil engineering (MS, PhD); computational hydroscience (MS, PhD); computer science (MS, PhD); electrical engineering (MS, PhD); electromagnetics (MS, PhD); environmental engineering (MS, PhD); geology and geological engineering (MS, PhD); hydrology (MS); material science (MS); mechanical engineering (MS, PhD); telecommunications (MS). *Students:* 104 full-time (23 women), 19 part-time (5 women); includes 10 minority (3 Black or African American, non-Hispanic/Latino; 6 Asian, non-Hispanic/Latino; 1 Hispanic/Latino), 72 international. Average age 30. In 2019, 36 master's, 17 doctorates awarded. *Expenses:* Tuition, state resident: full-time $8718; part-time $484.25 per credit hour. Tuition, nonresident: full-time $24,990; part-time $1388.25 per credit hour. *Required fees:* $100; $4.16 per credit hour. *Unit head:* Dr. David Puleo, Dean, 662-915-5780, Fax: 662-915-5387, E-mail: engineer@olemiss.edu. *Application contact:* Temeka Smith, Graduate Activities Specialist for Admissions, 662-915-7474, Fax: 662-915-7577, E-mail: gschool@olemiss.edu.

University of Missouri, Office of Research and Graduate Studies, College of Engineering, Department of Biomedical, Biological and Chemical Engineering, Columbia, MO 65211. Offers biological engineering (MS, PhD); chemical engineering (MS, PhD). *Entrance requirements:* For master's and doctorate, GRE General Test, minimum GPA of 3.0. Additional exam requirements/recommendations for international students: required—TOEFL.

University of Nebraska–Lincoln, Graduate College, College of Engineering, Department of Chemical and Biomolecular Engineering, Lincoln, NE 68588. Offers MS, PhD. *Degree requirements:* For master's, thesis; for doctorate, comprehensive exam, thesis/dissertation. *Entrance requirements:* For master's and doctorate, GRE. Additional exam requirements/recommendations for international students: required—TOEFL (minimum score 550 paper-based). Electronic applications accepted.

University of Nevada, Reno, Graduate School, College of Engineering, Department of Chemical and Materials Engineering, Program in Chemical Engineering, Reno, NV 89557. Offers MS, PhD. Terminal master's awarded for partial completion of doctoral program. *Degree requirements:* For master's, comprehensive exam, thesis optional; for doctorate, thesis/dissertation. *Entrance requirements:* For master's, GRE General Test, minimum GPA of 2.75; for doctorate, GRE General Test, minimum GPA of 3.0. Additional exam requirements/recommendations for international students: required—TOEFL (minimum score 500 paper-based; 61 iBT), IELTS (minimum score 6). Electronic applications accepted.

University of New Brunswick Fredericton, School of Graduate Studies, Faculty of Engineering, Department of Chemical Engineering, Fredericton, NB E3B 5A3, Canada. Offers chemical engineering (M Eng, M Sc E, PhD); environmental studies (M Eng). *Program availability:* Part-time. *Faculty:* 13 full-time (3 women). *Students:* 29 full-time (10 women), 8 part-time (4 women), 22 international. Average age 28. In 2019, 10 master's, 3 doctorates awarded. *Degree requirements:* For master's, thesis; for doctorate, comprehensive exam, thesis/dissertation, qualifying exam. *Entrance requirements:* For master's and doctorate, minimum GPA of 3.0. Additional exam requirements/recommendations for international students: required—TOEFL (minimum score 580 paper-based), TWE (minimum score 5), Michigan English Language Assessment Battery (minimum score 85) or CanTest (minimum score 4.5). *Application deadline:* For fall admission, 3/1 for domestic students. Applications are processed on a rolling basis. Application fee: $50 Canadian dollars. Electronic applications accepted. *Expenses: Tuition, area resident:* Full-time $6975 Canadian dollars; part-time $3423 Canadian dollars per year. Tuition, state resident: full-time $6975 Canadian dollars; part-time $3423 Canadian dollars per year. Tuition, Canadian resident: full-time $6975 Canadian dollars; part-time $3423 Canadian dollars per year. *International tuition:* $12,435 Canadian dollars full-time. *Required fees:* $92.25 Canadian dollars per term. Full-time tuition and fees vary according to degree level, campus/location, program, reciprocity agreements and student level. *Financial support:* Fellowships, research assistantships with tuition reimbursements, and teaching assistantships available. Financial award application deadline: 1/15. *Unit head:* Dr. Yonghao Ni, Director of Graduate Studies, 506-451-6857, Fax: 506-453-3591, E-mail: yonghao@unb.ca. *Application contact:* Sylvia Demerson, Graduate Secretary, 506-453-4520, Fax: 506-453-3591, E-mail: sdemerso@unb.ca.
Website: http://go.unb.ca/gradprograms

University of New Hampshire, Graduate School, College of Engineering and Physical Sciences, Department of Chemical Engineering, Durham, NH 03824. Offers M Engr, MS, PhD. *Students:* 14 full-time (3 women), 4 part-time (2 women); includes 1 minority (Hispanic/Latino), 13 international. Average age 26. 21 applicants, 48% accepted, 3 enrolled. In 2019, 1 master's, 3 doctorates awarded. *Entrance requirements:* For master's and doctorate, GRE. Additional exam requirements/recommendations for international students: required—TOEFL (minimum score 550 paper-based; 80 iBT), IELTS, PTE. *Application deadline:* For fall admission, 4/1 for domestic students; for spring admission, 12/1 for domestic students. Application fee: $65. Electronic applications accepted. *Financial support:* In 2019–20, 18 students received support, including 1 fellowship, 6 research assistantships, 10 teaching assistantships; Federal Work-Study, scholarships/grants, and tuition waivers (full and partial) also available. Support available to part-time students. Financial award application deadline: 2/15. *Unit head:* Xiaowei Teng, Chair, 603-862-4245. *Application contact:* Jennie Allen, Administrative Assistant, 603-862-3654, E-mail: jennie.allen@unh.edu.
Website: http://www.ceps.unh.edu/chemical-engineering

University of New Mexico, Graduate Studies, School of Engineering, Program in Chemical Engineering, Albuquerque, NM 87131. Offers MS, PhD. *Program availability:* Part-time. *Faculty:* 8 full-time (1 woman), 3 part-time/adjunct (1 woman). *Students:* 153 full-time (74 women), 13 part-time (6 women); includes 81 minority (3 Black or African American, non-Hispanic/Latino; 10 American Indian or Alaska Native, non-Hispanic/Latino; 8 Asian, non-Hispanic/Latino; 55 Hispanic/Latino; 5 Two or more races, non-Hispanic/Latino), 28 international. 31 applicants, 52% accepted, 8 enrolled. In 2019, 9 master's, 4 doctorates awarded. Terminal master's awarded for partial completion of doctoral program. *Degree requirements:* For master's, thesis (for some programs); for doctorate, comprehensive exam, thesis/dissertation, qualifying exam. *Entrance requirements:* For master's, GRE General Test, minimum GPA of 3.0, 3 letters of reference, letter of intent; for doctorate, GRE General Test, 3 letters of reference, minimum GPA of 3.0, letter of intent. Additional exam requirements/recommendations for international students: required—TOEFL (minimum score 520 paper-based; 68 iBT), IELTS (minimum score 6), TOEFL or IELTS, not both. *Application deadline:* For fall admission, 1/15 priority date for domestic and international students; for spring admission, 7/15 priority date for domestic and international students. Application fee: $50. Electronic applications accepted. *Expenses:* Tuition, state resident: full-time $7633; part-time $972 per year. Tuition, nonresident: full-time $22,586; part-time $3840 per year. *International tuition:* $23,292 full-time. *Required fees:* $8608. Tuition and fees vary according to course level, course load, degree level, program and student level. *Financial support:* In 2019–20, 4 research assistantships with full tuition reimbursements (averaging $24,434 per year) were awarded; fellowships, scholarships/grants, traineeships, and health care benefits also available. Financial award application deadline: 1/15; financial award applicants required to submit FAFSA. *Unit head:* Dr. Abhaya Datye, Chair, 505-277-5431, Fax: 505-277-5433, E-mail: datye@unm.edu. *Application contact:* Sarah Dominguez, Sr. Academic Advisor, 505-277-5606, Fax: 505-277-5433, E-mail: cbe@unm.edu.
Website: https://cbe.unm.edu/

University of North Dakota, Graduate School, School of Engineering and Mines, Department of Chemical Engineering, Grand Forks, ND 58202. Offers M Engr, MS, PhD. *Program availability:* Part-time. *Degree requirements:* For master's, comprehensive exam, thesis or alternative. *Entrance requirements:* For master's, GRE General Test, minimum GPA of 3.0 (MS), 2.5 (M Engr). Additional exam requirements/recommendations for international students: required—TOEFL (minimum score 550 paper-based; 79 iBT), IELTS (minimum score 6.5). Electronic applications accepted.

University of Notre Dame, The Graduate School, College of Engineering, Department of Chemical and Biomolecular Engineering, Notre Dame, IN 46556. Offers MS Ch E, PhD. *Degree requirements:* For master's, comprehensive exam, thesis; for doctorate, comprehensive exam, thesis/dissertation, candidacy exam. *Entrance requirements:* For master's, GRE General Test; for doctorate, GRE General Test, GRE Subject Test (strongly recommended). Additional exam requirements/recommendations for international students: required—TOEFL (minimum score 600 paper-based; 80 iBT). Electronic applications accepted.

University of Oklahoma, Gallogly College of Engineering, School of Chemical, Biological and Materials Engineering, Norman, OK 73019. Offers chemical engineering (MS, PhD). *Program availability:* Part-time. *Degree requirements:* For master's, thesis, oral defense of thesis; for doctorate, comprehensive exam, thesis/dissertation, oral defense of dissertation. *Entrance requirements:* For master's and doctorate, GRE. Additional exam requirements/recommendations for international students: required—TOEFL (minimum score 79 iBT) or IELTS (minimum score 6.5). Electronic applications accepted. *Expenses:* Tuition, state resident: full-time $6583.20; part-time $274.30 per credit hour. Tuition, nonresident: full-time $21,242; part-time $885.10 per credit hour. *International tuition:* $21,242.40 full-time. *Required fees:* $1994.20; $72.55 per credit hour. $126.50 per semester. Tuition and fees vary according to course load and degree level.

University of Ottawa, Faculty of Graduate and Postdoctoral Studies, Faculty of Engineering, Department of Chemical and Biological Engineering, Ottawa, ON K1N 6N5, Canada. Offers M Eng, MA Sc, PhD. *Degree requirements:* For master's, thesis or alternative; for doctorate, comprehensive exam, thesis/dissertation. *Entrance requirements:* For master's, honors degree or equivalent, minimum B average; for doctorate, master's degree, minimum B+ average. Electronic applications accepted.

University of Pennsylvania, School of Engineering and Applied Science, Department of Chemical and Biomolecular Engineering, Philadelphia, PA 19104. Offers MSE, PhD. *Program availability:* Part-time. *Faculty:* 18 full-time (4 women), 7 part-time/adjunct (2 women). *Students:* 115 full-time (32 women), 7 part-time (1 woman); includes 16 minority (2 Black or African American, non-Hispanic/Latino; 1 American Indian or Alaska Native, non-Hispanic/Latino; 7 Asian, non-Hispanic/Latino; 6 Hispanic/Latino), 77 international. Average age 25. 433 applicants, 30% accepted, 34 enrolled. In 2019, 25 master's, 8 doctorates awarded. Terminal master's awarded for partial completion of doctoral program. *Degree requirements:* For master's, comprehensive exam, thesis optional; for doctorate, comprehensive exam, thesis/dissertation. *Entrance requirements:* For master's and doctorate, GRE, bachelor's degree, letters of recommendation, resume, personal statement. Additional exam requirements/recommendations for international students: required—TOEFL (minimum score 100 iBT), IELTS (minimum score 7). *Application deadline:* For fall admission, 12/15 priority date for domestic and international students. Application fee: $80. Electronic applications accepted. *Expenses:* Contact institution. *Application contact:* Associate Director of Graduate Admissions, 215-898-4542, Fax: 215-573-5577, E-mail: admissions2@seas.upenn.edu.
Website: http://www.cbe.seas.upenn.edu/prospective-students/masters/index.php

University of Pittsburgh, Swanson School of Engineering, Department of Chemical and Petroleum Engineering, Pittsburgh, PA 15260. Offers chemical engineering (MS Ch E, PhD); petroleum engineering (MSPE); MS Ch E/MSPE. *Program availability:* Part-time, 100% online. Terminal master's awarded for partial completion of doctoral program. *Degree requirements:* For doctorate, comprehensive exam, thesis/dissertation, final oral exams. *Entrance requirements:* For master's and doctorate, GRE General Test, minimum GPA of 3.0. Additional exam requirements/recommendations for international students: required—TOEFL (minimum score 550 paper-based; 80 iBT). Electronic applications accepted. *Expenses:* Contact institution.

University of Puerto Rico at Mayagüez, Graduate Studies, College of Engineering, Department of Chemical Engineering, Mayagüez, PR 00681-9000. Offers ME, MS, PhD. *Program availability:* Part-time. Terminal master's awarded for partial completion of doctoral program. *Degree requirements:* For master's, one foreign language, comprehensive exam, thesis; for doctorate, one foreign language, comprehensive exam, thesis/dissertation. *Entrance requirements:* For master's, BS in chemical engineering or its equivalent; minimum GPA of 3.0; for doctorate, MS in chemical engineering or its equivalent; minimum GPA of 3.0. Electronic applications accepted.

University of Rhode Island, Graduate School, College of Engineering, Department of Chemical Engineering, Kingston, RI 02881. Offers chemical engineering (MS, PhD); polymer (Postbaccalaureate Certificate). *Program availability:* Part-time. *Faculty:* 9 full-time (2 women). *Students:* 14 full-time (3 women), 3 part-time (1 woman); includes 2 minority (1 Black or African American, non-Hispanic/Latino; 1 Hispanic/Latino), 8 international. 22 applicants, 23% accepted, 3 enrolled. In 2019, 6 master's, 5 doctorates awarded. *Entrance requirements:* Additional exam requirements/recommendations for international students: required—TOEFL. *Application deadline:* For fall admission, 12/1 for domestic and international students; for spring admission, 7/15 for domestic and international students; for summer admission, 12/1 for domestic students. Application fee: $65. Electronic applications accepted. *Expenses: Tuition, area resident:* Full-time $13,734; part-time $763 per credit. Tuition, state resident: full-time $13,734; part-time $763 per credit. Tuition, nonresident: full-time $26,512; part-time $1473 per credit. *International tuition:* $26,512 full-time. *Required fees:* $1780; $52 per credit. $35 per term. One-time fee: $165. *Financial support:* In 2019–20, 5 research assistantships with tuition reimbursements (averaging $7,969 per year), 4 teaching assistantships with tuition reimbursements (averaging $7,711 per year) were awarded. Financial award application deadline: 12/1; financial award applicants required to submit FAFSA. *Unit head:* Dr. Angelo Lucia, Chair, 401-874-4689, E-mail: alucia@uri.edu. *Application contact:* Dr. Michael Greenfield, Associate Professor/Chair of Polymer Engineering, 401-874-9289, E-mail: greenfield@uri.edu.
Website: http://egr.uri.edu/che/

University of Rochester, Hajim School of Engineering and Applied Sciences, Department of Chemical Engineering, Rochester, NY 14627. Offers MS, PhD. *Faculty:* 11 full-time (1 woman). *Students:* 41 full-time (13 women), 1 part-time (0 women); includes 1 minority (Hispanic/Latino), 26 international. Average age 27. 116 applicants, 34% accepted, 15 enrolled. In 2019, 14 master's, 2 doctorates awarded. Terminal master's awarded for partial completion of doctoral program. *Degree requirements:* For master's, comprehensive exam, thesis or alternative; for doctorate, comprehensive exam, thesis/dissertation, qualifying exam. *Entrance requirements:* For master's and doctorate, GRE, curriculum vitae, personal and research statement, three letters of recommendation, official transcript. Additional exam requirements/recommendations for international students: recommended—TOEFL (minimum score 90 iBT), IELTS (minimum score 7). *Application deadline:* For fall admission, 1/15 for domestic and international students. Application fee: $60. Electronic applications accepted. *Financial support:* In 2019–20, 24 students received support, including 2 fellowships with full tuition reimbursements available (averaging $30,000 per year), 4 research assistantships (averaging $33,000 per year), 18 teaching assistantships with full tuition reimbursements available (averaging $28,000 per year); career-related internships or fieldwork, health care benefits, tuition waivers (full and partial), and unspecified assistantships also available. Financial award application deadline: 4/15. *Unit head:* Mitch Anthamatten, Department Chair, 585-273-5526, E-mail: mitchell.anthamatten@rochester.edu. *Application contact:* Victoria Heberling, Graduate Program Coordinator, 585-275-4913, E-mail: victoria.heberling@rochester.edu.
Website: http://www.hajim.rochester.edu/che/graduate/index.html

University of Saskatchewan, College of Graduate and Postdoctoral Studies, College of Engineering, Chemical Engineering Program, Saskatoon, SK S7N 5E5, Canada. Offers M Eng, M Sc, PhD. *Program availability:* Part-time. *Degree requirements:* For master's, 30 credits (for M Eng); thesis and 12 credits (for MS); for doctorate, comprehensive exam, thesis/dissertation, qualifying exam, 18 credits. *Entrance requirements:* For master's and doctorate, GRE. Additional exam requirements/recommendations for international students: required—TOEFL (minimum iBT score of 80), IELTS (6.5), CanTEST (4.5), or PTE (59). Electronic applications accepted.

University of South Africa, College of Science, Engineering and Technology, Pretoria, South Africa. Offers chemical engineering (M Tech); information technology (M Tech).

University of South Alabama, College of Engineering, Department of Chemical and Biomolecular Engineering, Mobile, AL 36688-0002. Offers MS Ch E. *Faculty:* 4 full-time (1 woman). *Students:* 10 full-time (4 women), 2 part-time (both women); includes 2 minority (1 Black or African American, non-Hispanic/Latino; 1 Hispanic/Latino). Average age 25. 4 applicants, 75% accepted, 2 enrolled. In 2019, 4 master's awarded. *Degree requirements:* For master's, comprehensive exam, thesis optional. *Entrance requirements:* For master's, GRE. Additional exam requirements/recommendations for international students: required—TOEFL (minimum score 550 paper-based; 79 iBT), IELTS (minimum score 6.5). *Application deadline:* For fall admission, 7/1 priority date for domestic students, 6/15 priority date for international students; for spring admission, 12/1 priority date for domestic students, 11/1 priority date for international students; for summer admission, 5/1 priority date for domestic students, 4/1 priority date for international students. Applications are processed on a rolling basis. Application fee: $35. Electronic applications accepted. *Expenses:* Contact institution. *Financial support:* Fellowships, research assistantships, teaching assistantships, career-related internships or fieldwork, Federal Work-Study, institutionally sponsored loans, scholarships/grants, and unspecified assistantships available. Support available to part-time students. Financial award application deadline: 3/31; financial award applicants required to submit FAFSA. *Unit head:* Dr. Carl Knopf, Chair, Professor, Department of ChBE, College of Engineering, 251-460-6160, Fax: 251-461-1485, E-mail: cknopf@southalabama.edu. *Application contact:* Brenda Poole, Academic Records Specialist, 251-460-6140, Fax: 251-460-6343, E-mail: engineering@southalabama.edu.
Website: https://www.southalabama.edu/colleges/engineering/chbe/

University of South Carolina, The Graduate School, College of Engineering and Computing, Department of Chemical Engineering, Columbia, SC 29208. Offers ME, MS, PhD. *Program availability:* Part-time, evening/weekend, online learning. *Degree requirements:* For master's, comprehensive exam, thesis (for some programs); for doctorate, comprehensive exam, thesis/dissertation. *Entrance requirements:* For master's and doctorate, GRE General Test. Additional exam requirements/recommendations for international students: required—TOEFL. Electronic applications accepted.

University of Southern California, Graduate School, Viterbi School of Engineering, Mork Family Department of Chemical Engineering and Materials Science, Los Angeles, CA 90089. Offers chemical engineering (MS, PhD, Engr); geoscience technologies (MS); materials engineering (MS); materials science (MS, PhD, Engr); petroleum engineering (MS, PhD, Engr); smart oilfield technologies (MS, Graduate Certificate). Terminal master's awarded for partial completion of doctoral program. *Degree requirements:* For master's, thesis optional; for doctorate, thesis/dissertation. *Entrance requirements:* For master's and doctorate, GRE General Test. Additional exam requirements/recommendations for international students: , recommended—TOEFL. Electronic applications accepted. *Expenses:* Contact institution.

University of South Florida, College of Engineering, Department of Chemical and Biomedical Engineering, Tampa, FL 33620. Offers MSBE, MSCH, PhD. *Program availability:* Part-time. *Faculty:* 18 full-time (2 women). *Students:* 50 full-time (13 women), 10 part-time (3 women); includes 5 minority (1 Black or African American, non-Hispanic/Latino; 2 Asian, non-Hispanic/Latino; 1 Hispanic/Latino; 1 Two or more races, non-Hispanic/Latino), 42 international. Average age 27. 61 applicants, 59% accepted, 20 enrolled. In 2019, 19 master's, 2 doctorates awarded. Terminal master's awarded for partial completion of doctoral program. *Degree requirements:* For master's, comprehensive exam, thesis (for some programs); for doctorate, comprehensive exam, thesis/dissertation. *Entrance requirements:* For master's, GRE (preferred minimum scores of Verbal greater than 50% percentile, Quantitative greater than 75th percentile, Analytical Writing of 3.0 or greater; applicants who have successfully completed the Fundamentals of Engineering (FE) Exam offered by the Society of Professional Engineers will be exempted from the GRE requirement, Bachelors or equivalent in Chemical Engineering; 2 letters of reference; statement of research interests; for doctorate, (preferred scores: Verbal greater than 50% percentile, Quantitative greater than 75% percentile, Analytical Writing greater than 4.0), bachelors or equivalent in Chemical Engineering; 3 letters of reference; statement of research interests. Additional exam requirements/recommendations for international students: required—TOEFL, TOEFL (minimum score 550 paper-based; 79 iBT) or IELTS (minimum score 6.5). *Application deadline:* For fall admission, 2/15 for domestic and international students; for spring admission, 10/15 for domestic students, 9/15 for international students; for summer admission, 2/15 for domestic students, 1/15 for international students. Application fee: $30. Electronic applications accepted. *Financial support:* In 2019–20, 10 students received support, including 29 research assistantships with tuition reimbursements available (averaging $13,171 per year), 12 teaching assistantships with tuition reimbursements available (averaging $14,017 per year); unspecified assistantships also available. Financial award applicants required to submit FAFSA. *Unit head:* Dr. Venkat R. Bhethanabotla, Professor and Department Chair, 813-974-3997, E-mail: bhethana@usf.edu. *Application contact:* Dr. Robert Frisina, Jr., Professor and Graduate Program Director, 813-974-4013, Fax: 813-974-3651, E-mail: rfrisina@usf.edu.
Website: http://che.eng.usf.edu/

University of South Florida, Innovative Education, Tampa, FL 33620-9951. Offers adult, career and higher education (Graduate Certificate), including college teaching, leadership in developing human resources, leadership in higher education; Africana studies (Graduate Certificate), including diasporas and health disparities, genocide and human rights; aging studies (Graduate Certificate), including gerontology; art research (Graduate Certificate), including museum studies; business foundations (Graduate Certificate); chemical and biomedical engineering (Graduate Certificate), including materials science and engineering, water, health and sustainability; child and family studies (Graduate Certificate), including positive behavior support; civil and industrial engineering (Graduate Certificate), including transportation systems analysis; community and family health (Graduate Certificate), including maternal and child health, social marketing and public health, violence and injury: prevention and intervention, women's health; criminology (Graduate Certificate), including criminal justice administration; data science for public administration (Graduate Certificate); digital humanities (Graduate Certificate); educational measurement and research (Graduate Certificate), including evaluation; English (Graduate Certificate), including comparative literary studies, creative writing, professional and technical communication; entrepreneurship (Graduate Certificate); environmental health (Graduate Certificate), including safety management; epidemiology and biostatistics (Graduate Certificate), including applied biostatistics, biostatistics, concepts and tools of epidemiology, epidemiology, epidemiology of infectious diseases; geography, environment and planning (Graduate Certificate), including community development, environmental policy and management, geographical information systems; geology (Graduate Certificate),

including hydrogeology; global health (Graduate Certificate), including disaster management, global health and Latin American and Caribbean studies, global health practice, humanitarian assistance, infection control; government and international affairs (Graduate Certificate), including Cuban studies, globalization studies; health policy and management (Graduate Certificate), including health management and leadership, public health policy and programs; hearing specialist: early intervention (Graduate Certificate); industrial and management systems engineering (Graduate Certificate), including systems engineering, technology management; information studies (Graduate Certificate), including school library media specialist; information systems/decision sciences (Graduate Certificate), including analytics and business intelligence; instructional technology (Graduate Certificate), including distance education, Florida digital/virtual educator, instructional design, multimedia design, Web design; internal medicine, bioethics and medical humanities (Graduate Certificate), including biomedical ethics; Latin American and Caribbean studies (Graduate Certificate); leadership for coastal resiliency planning (Graduate Certificate); mass communications (Graduate Certificate), including multimedia journalism; mathematics and statistics (Graduate Certificate), including mathematics; medicine (Graduate Certificate), including aging and neuroscience, bioinformatics, biotechnology, brain fitness and memory management, clinical investigation, hand and upper limb rehabilitation, health informatics, health sciences, integrative weight management, intellectual property, medicine and gender, metabolic and nutritional medicine, metabolic cardiology, pharmacy sciences; national and competitive intelligence (Graduate Certificate); nursing (Graduate Certificate), including simulation based academic fellowship in advanced pain management; psychological and social foundations (Graduate Certificate), including career counseling, college teaching, diversity in education, mental health counseling, school counseling; public affairs (Graduate Certificate), including nonprofit management, public management, research administration; public health (Graduate Certificate), including assessing chemical toxicity and public health risks, health equity, pharmacoepidemiology, public health generalist, toxicology, translational research in adolescent behavioral health; public health practices (Graduate Certificate), including planning for healthy communities; rehabilitation and mental health counseling (Graduate Certificate), including integrative mental health care, marriage and family therapy, rehabilitation technology; secondary education (Graduate Certificate), including ESOL, foreign language education: culture and content, foreign language education: professional; social work (Graduate Certificate), including geriatric social work/clinical gerontology; special education (Graduate Certificate), including autism spectrum disorder, disabilities education: severe/profound; world languages (Graduate Certificate), including teaching English as a second language (TESL) or foreign language. *Unit head:* Dr. Cynthia DeLuca, Associate Vice President and Assistant Vice Provost, 813-974-3077, Fax: 813-974-7061, E-mail: deluca@usf.edu. *Application contact:* Owen Hooper, Director, Summer and Alternative Calendar Programs, 813-974-6917, E-mail: hooper@usf.edu.
Website: http://www.usf.edu/innovative-education/

The University of Tennessee, Graduate School, Tickle College of Engineering, Department of Chemical and Biomolecular Engineering, Knoxville, TN 37996-2200. Offers chemical engineering (MS, PhD); reliability and maintainability engineering (MS); MS/MBA. *Program availability:* Part-time. *Faculty:* 18 full-time (1 woman). *Students:* 47 full-time (8 women), 3 part-time (0 women); includes 7 minority (2 Black or African American, non-Hispanic/Latino; 1 Asian, non-Hispanic/Latino; 4 Hispanic/Latino), 22 international. Average age 28. 57 applicants, 54% accepted, 11 enrolled. In 2019, 6 master's, 10 doctorates awarded. *Degree requirements:* For master's, thesis or alternative; for doctorate, comprehensive exam, thesis/dissertation. *Entrance requirements:* For master's, GRE General Test (for MS students pursuing research thesis), minimum GPA of 2.7 (for U.S. degree holders), 3.0 (for international degree holders); for doctorate, GRE General Test, minimum GPA of 3.0 on previous graduate course work. Additional exam requirements/recommendations for international students: required—TOEFL (minimum score 550 paper-based; 80 iBT), IELTS (minimum score 6.5). *Application deadline:* For fall admission, 2/1 priority date for domestic and international students; for spring admission, 6/15 for domestic and international students; for summer admission, 10/15 for domestic and international students. Applications are processed on a rolling basis. Application fee: $60. Electronic applications accepted. *Financial support:* In 2019–20, 69 students received support, including 13 fellowships (averaging $9,696 per year), 34 research assistantships with full tuition reimbursements available (averaging $26,620 per year), 22 teaching assistantships with full tuition reimbursements available (averaging $22,999 per year); career-related internships or fieldwork, Federal Work-Study, institutionally sponsored loans, health care benefits, and unspecified assistantships also available. Financial award application deadline: 2/1; financial award applicants required to submit FAFSA. *Unit head:* Dr. Bamin Khomami, Head, 865-974-2421, Fax: 865-974-7076, E-mail: bkhomami@utk.edu. *Application contact:* Dr. Cong Trinh, Graduate Recruiting Director, 865-974-2421, Fax: 865-974-7076, E-mail: ctrinh@utk.edu.
Website: http://www.engr.utk.edu/cbe/

The University of Tennessee at Chattanooga, Program in Engineering, Chattanooga, TN 37403. Offers automotive (MS Engr); chemical (MS Engr); civil (MS Engr); electrical (MS Engr); mechanical (MS Engr). *Program availability:* Part-time. *Students:* 29 full-time (4 women), 27 part-time (3 women); includes 9 minority (4 Black or African American, non-Hispanic/Latino; 2 Asian, non-Hispanic/Latino; 1 Hispanic/Latino; 1 Native Hawaiian or other Pacific Islander, non-Hispanic/Latino; 1 Two or more races, non-Hispanic/Latino), 19 international. Average age 29. 39 applicants, 74% accepted, 16 enrolled. In 2019, 22 master's awarded. *Degree requirements:* For master's, comprehensive exam, thesis or alternative, engineering project. *Entrance requirements:* For master's, GRE General Test, minimum undergraduate GPA of 2.7 or 3.0 in last two years of undergraduate coursework. Additional exam requirements/recommendations for international students: required—TOEFL (minimum score 550 paper-based; 79 iBT), IELTS (minimum score 6). *Application deadline:* For fall admission, 6/15 priority date for domestic students, 7/1 for international students; for spring admission, 11/1 priority date for domestic students, 11/1 for international students. Applications are processed on a rolling basis. Application fee: $35 ($40 for international students). Electronic applications accepted. *Financial support:* Research assistantships, teaching assistantships, career-related internships or fieldwork, scholarships/grants, health care benefits, and unspecified assistantships available. Support available to part-time students. Financial award application deadline: 7/1; financial award applicants required to submit FAFSA. *Unit head:* Dr. Daniel Pack, Dean, 423-425-2256, Fax: 423-425-5311, E-mail: daniel-pack@utc.edu. *Application contact:* Dr. Joanne Romagni, Dean of the Graduate School, 423-425-4478, Fax: 423-425-5223, E-mail: joanne-romagni@utc.edu.
Website: http://www.utc.edu/college-engineering-computer-science/graduate-programs/msengr.php

The University of Texas at Austin, Graduate School, Cockrell School of Engineering, Department of Chemical Engineering, Austin, TX 78712-1111. Offers MSE, PhD. Terminal master's awarded for partial completion of doctoral program. *Degree requirements:* For master's, thesis (for some programs); for doctorate, comprehensive exam, thesis/dissertation. *Entrance requirements:* For master's and doctorate, GRE General Test. Electronic applications accepted.

Chemical Engineering

The University of Toledo, College of Graduate Studies, College of Engineering, Department of Chemical and Environmental Engineering, Toledo, OH 43606-3390. Offers chemical engineering (MS, PhD). *Program availability:* Part-time, evening/weekend. *Degree requirements:* For master's, thesis optional; for doctorate, thesis/dissertation, qualifying exam. *Entrance requirements:* For master's, GRE General Test, minimum GPA of 3.0; for doctorate, GRE General Test, minimum GPA of 3.3. Additional exam requirements/recommendations for international students: required—TOEFL (minimum score 550 paper-based; 80 iBT). Electronic applications accepted.

University of Toronto, School of Graduate Studies, Faculty of Applied Science and Engineering, Department of Chemical Engineering and Applied Chemistry, Toronto, ON M5S 1A1, Canada. Offers M Eng, MA Sc, PhD. *Program availability:* Part-time. *Degree requirements:* For master's, thesis (for some programs); for doctorate, thesis/dissertation. *Entrance requirements:* For master's, minimum B+ average in final 2 years, four-year degree in engineering (M Eng, MA Sc) or physical sciences (MA Sc), 2 letters of reference; for doctorate, research master's degree, minimum B+ average, 2 letters of reference. Additional exam requirements/recommendations for international students: required—TOEFL (minimum score 580 paper-based; 93 iBT), TWE (minimum score 4). Electronic applications accepted.

The University of Tulsa, Graduate School, College of Engineering and Natural Sciences, Department of Chemical Engineering, Tulsa, OK 74104-3189. Offers ME, MSE, PhD. *Program availability:* Part-time. Terminal master's awarded for partial completion of doctoral program. *Degree requirements:* For master's, thesis (for some programs); for doctorate, comprehensive exam, thesis/dissertation. *Entrance requirements:* For master's and doctorate, GRE General Test. Additional exam requirements/recommendations for international students: required—TOEFL (minimum score 550 paper-based; 80 iBT), IELTS (minimum score 6). Electronic applications accepted. *Expenses: Tuition:* Full-time $22,896; part-time $1272 per credit hour. *Required fees:* $6 per credit hour. Tuition and fees vary according to course load and program.

University of Utah, Graduate School, College of Engineering, Department of Chemical Engineering, Salt Lake City, UT 84112. Offers chemical engineering (MS, PhD); petroleum engineering (MS); MS/MBA. *Program availability:* Part-time, blended/hybrid learning. *Faculty:* 19 full-time (2 women), 1 part-time/adjunct (0 women). *Students:* 58 full-time (12 women), 13 part-time (3 women); includes 5 minority (2 Asian, non-Hispanic/Latino; 2 Hispanic/Latino; 1 Two or more races, non-Hispanic/Latino), 41 international. Average age 28. 69 applicants, 48% accepted, 14 enrolled. In 2019, 25 master's, 11 doctorates awarded. *Degree requirements:* For master's, comprehensive exam (for some programs), thesis optional; for doctorate, comprehensive exam, thesis/dissertation, thesis proposal, thesis defense. *Entrance requirements:* For master's and doctorate, GRE, Toefl/IEITS, 3.0 minimum. Additional exam requirements/recommendations for international students: required—TOEFL (minimum score 80 paper-based), IELTS (minimum score 6.5), GRE. *Application deadline:* For fall admission, 1/1 priority date for domestic students, 12/15 priority date for international students; for spring admission, 10/1 priority date for domestic students. Application fee: $30 ($45 for international students). Electronic applications accepted. *Expenses:* 6,575.00 per semester. *Financial support:* In 2019–20, 3 students received support, including 11 fellowships (averaging $13,090 per year), 44 research assistantships with full tuition reimbursements available (averaging $16,227 per year); unspecified assistantships also available. Financial award application deadline: 1/15; financial award applicants required to submit FAFSA. *Unit head:* Dr. Eric G. Eddings, Chair, 801-581-3931, Fax: 801-585-9291, E-mail: eric.eddings@utah.edu. *Application contact:* Wanda Brown, Graduate Coordinator, 801-585-1181, Fax: 801-585-9291, E-mail: wanda.brown@chemeng.utah.edu.
Website: http://www.che.utah.edu/

University of Virginia, School of Engineering and Applied Science, Department of Chemical Engineering, Charlottesville, VA 22903. Offers ME, MS, PhD. *Program availability:* Online learning. *Degree requirements:* For master's, thesis (for some programs); for doctorate, thesis/dissertation. *Entrance requirements:* For master's, GRE General Test, 3 recommendations; for doctorate, GRE General Test, 3 recommendations, essay. Additional exam requirements/recommendations for international students: required—TOEFL (minimum score 600 paper-based; 90 iBT), IELTS (minimum score 7). Electronic applications accepted.

University of Washington, Graduate School, College of Engineering, Department of Chemical Engineering, Seattle, WA 98195-1750. Offers chemical engineering (MS, PhD); chemical engineering and advanced data science (PhD); chemical engineering and nanotechnology (PhD). *Students:* 79 full-time (32 women), 14 part-time (0 women); includes 13 minority (1 Black or African American, non-Hispanic/Latino; 5 Asian, non-Hispanic/Latino; 5 Hispanic/Latino; 2 Two or more races, non-Hispanic/Latino), 45 international. Average age 25. 371 applicants, 35% accepted, 27 enrolled. In 2019, 29 master's, 16 doctorates awarded. Terminal master's awarded for partial completion of doctoral program. *Degree requirements:* For master's, comprehensive exam, thesis optional, final exam, research project, degree completed in 6 years; for doctorate, comprehensive exam, thesis/dissertation, general and final exams, research project, completion of all work within 10 years. *Entrance requirements:* For master's and doctorate, GRE General Test (optional), minimum GPA of 3.0, transcripts, personal statement, 3 letters of recommendation, writing sample (optional). Additional exam requirements/recommendations for international students: required—TOEFL (minimum score 580 paper-based; 92 iBT). *Application deadline:* For fall admission, 1/1 priority date for domestic students, 12/15 priority date for international students. Applications are processed on a rolling basis. Application fee: $85. Electronic applications accepted. *Expenses:* Contact institution. *Financial support:* In 2019–20, 10 fellowships with full tuition reimbursements (averaging $33,960 per year), 40 research assistantships with full tuition reimbursements (averaging $33,960 per year), 12 teaching assistantships with full tuition reimbursements (averaging $33,960 per year) were awarded; Federal Work-Study, institutionally sponsored loans, scholarships/grants, health care benefits, tuition waivers, and unspecified assistantships also available. Support available to part-time students. Financial award application deadline: 1/1. *Unit head:* Dr. Jim Pfaendtner, Professor/Chair, 206-616-8128, Fax: 206-685-3451, E-mail: jpfaendt@uw.edu. *Application contact:* Allison Sherrill, Graduate Program Advisor, 206-685-9785, E-mail: sherra@uw.edu.
Website: http://www.cheme.washington.edu/

University of Waterloo, Graduate Studies and Postdoctoral Affairs, Faculty of Engineering, Department of Chemical Engineering, Waterloo, ON N2L 3G1, Canada. Offers M Eng, MA Sc, PhD. *Program availability:* Part-time. *Degree requirements:* For master's, research project or thesis, seminar; for doctorate, comprehensive exam, thesis/dissertation. *Entrance requirements:* For master's, honors degree, minimum B average; for doctorate, master's degree, minimum A- average. Additional exam requirements/recommendations for international students: required—TOEFL, IELTS, PTE. Electronic applications accepted.

The University of Western Ontario, School of Graduate and Postdoctoral Studies, Physical Sciences Division, Faculty of Engineering, London, ON N6A 3K7, Canada. Offers chemical and biochemical engineering (ME Sc, PhD); civil and environmental engineering (M Eng, ME Sc, PhD); electrical and computer engineering (M Eng, ME Sc, PhD); mechanical and materials engineering (M Eng, ME Sc, PhD). *Program availability:* Part-time. Terminal master's awarded for partial completion of doctoral program. *Degree requirements:* For master's, thesis; for doctorate, thesis/dissertation. *Entrance requirements:* For master's, minimum B average; for doctorate, minimum B+ average.

University of Wisconsin–Madison, Graduate School, College of Engineering, Department of Chemical and Biological Engineering, Madison, WI 53706-0607. Offers chemical engineering (PhD). *Degree requirements:* For doctorate, comprehensive exam, thesis/dissertation, at least 18 credits of coursework, 2 semesters of teaching assistantship. *Entrance requirements:* For doctorate, GRE General Test, bachelor's degree with strong background in chemical engineering; minimum GPA of 3.0 in last 60 semester hours. Additional exam requirements/recommendations for international students: required—TOEFL (minimum score 580 paper-based; 92 iBT). Electronic applications accepted.

University of Wyoming, College of Engineering and Applied Science, Department of Chemical Engineering, Program in Chemical Engineering, Laramie, WY 82071. Offers MS, PhD. *Program availability:* Part-time. Terminal master's awarded for partial completion of doctoral program. *Degree requirements:* For master's, thesis; for doctorate, thesis/dissertation. *Entrance requirements:* For master's and doctorate, GRE General Test, minimum GPA of 3.0. Additional exam requirements/recommendations for international students: required—TOEFL (minimum score 600 paper-based; 76 iBT). Electronic applications accepted.

Université Laval, Faculty of Sciences and Engineering, Department of Chemical Engineering, Programs in Chemical Engineering, Québec, QC G1K 7P4, Canada. Offers M Sc, PhD. Terminal master's awarded for partial completion of doctoral program. *Degree requirements:* For master's, thesis (for some programs); for doctorate, comprehensive exam, thesis/dissertation. *Entrance requirements:* Additional exam requirements/recommendations for international students: required—TOEFL (minimum score 500 paper-based). Electronic applications accepted.

Vanderbilt University, School of Engineering, Department of Chemical and Biomolecular Engineering, Nashville, TN 37240-1001. Offers M Eng, MS, PhD. *Program availability:* Part-time. *Degree requirements:* For master's, thesis; for doctorate, thesis/dissertation. *Entrance requirements:* For master's and doctorate, GRE General Test. Additional exam requirements/recommendations for international students: required—TOEFL. Electronic applications accepted. *Expenses: Tuition:* Full-time $51,018; part-time $2087 per hour. *Required fees:* $542. Tuition and fees vary according to program.

Villanova University, College of Engineering, Department of Chemical Engineering, Villanova, PA 19085-1699. Offers biochemical engineering (Certificate); chemical engineering (MSChE); environmental protection in the chemical process industries (Certificate). *Program availability:* Part-time, evening/weekend. *Degree requirements:* For master's, comprehensive exam, thesis optional. *Entrance requirements:* For master's, GRE General Test (for applicants with degrees from foreign universities), B Ch E, minimum GPA of 3.0. Additional exam requirements/recommendations for international students: required—TOEFL (minimum score 600 paper-based; 100 iBT).

Virginia Polytechnic Institute and State University, Graduate School, College of Engineering, Blacksburg, VA 24061. Offers aerospace engineering (PhD, M Eng/MS); biological systems engineering (PhD); biomedical engineering (MS, PhD); chemical engineering (PhD); civil engineering (PhD); computer engineering (PhD); computer science and applications (MS); electrical engineering (PhD); engineering education (PhD); M Eng/MS. *Faculty:* 447 full-time (90 women), 6 part-time/adjunct (2 women). *Students:* 1,881 full-time (495 women), 326 part-time (70 women); includes 264 minority (51 Black or African American, non-Hispanic/Latino; 2 American Indian or Alaska Native, non-Hispanic/Latino; 96 Asian, non-Hispanic/Latino; 69 Hispanic/Latino; 46 Two or more races, non-Hispanic/Latino), 1,247 international. Average age 27. 4,014 applicants, 44% accepted, 658 enrolled. In 2019, 489 master's, 200 doctorates awarded. *Degree requirements:* For master's, comprehensive exam (for some programs), thesis (for some programs); for doctorate, comprehensive exam (for some programs), thesis/dissertation (for some programs). *Entrance requirements:* For master's and doctorate, GRE/GMAT. Additional exam requirements/recommendations for international students: required—TOEFL (minimum score 90 iBT). *Application deadline:* For fall admission, 8/1 for domestic students, 4/1 for international students; for spring admission, 1/1 for domestic students, 9/1 for international students. Applications are processed on a rolling basis. Application fee: $75. Electronic applications accepted. *Expenses:* Tuition, state resident: full-time $13,700; part-time $761.25 per credit hour. Tuition, nonresident: full-time $27,614; part-time $1534 per credit hour. *Required fees:* $886.50 per term. Tuition and fees vary according to campus/location and program. *Financial support:* In 2019–20, 47 fellowships with full tuition reimbursements (averaging $19,703 per year), 1,163 research assistantships with full tuition reimbursements (averaging $20,602 per year), 554 teaching assistantships with full tuition reimbursements (averaging $16,333 per year) were awarded; scholarships/grants and unspecified assistantships also available. Financial award application deadline: 3/1; financial award applicants required to submit FAFSA. *Unit head:* Dr. Julia Ross, Dean, 540-231-9752, Fax: 540-231-3031, E-mail: rjulie@vt.edu. *Application contact:* Linda Perkins, Executive Assistant, 540-231-9752, Fax: 540-231-3031, E-mail: lperkins@vt.edu.
Website: http://www.eng.vt.edu/

Washington State University, Voiland College of Engineering and Architecture, The Gene and Linda Voiland School of Chemical Engineering and Bioengineering, Pullman, WA 99164-6515. Offers MS, PhD. Terminal master's awarded for partial completion of doctoral program. *Degree requirements:* For master's, comprehensive exam, thesis (for some programs), oral exam; for doctorate, one foreign language, comprehensive exam, thesis/dissertation, oral exam. *Entrance requirements:* For master's and doctorate, minimum GPA of 3.0, 3 letters of recommendation by faculty. Additional exam requirements/recommendations for international students: required—TOEFL (minimum score 580 paper-based).

Washington University in St. Louis, School of Engineering and Applied Science, Department of Energy, Environmental and Chemical Engineering, St. Louis, MO 63130-4899. Offers chemical engineering (MS, D Sc); environmental engineering (MS, D Sc). *Program availability:* Part-time. Terminal master's awarded for partial completion of doctoral program. *Degree requirements:* For master's, thesis optional; for doctorate, thesis/dissertation, preliminary exam, qualifying exam. *Entrance requirements:* For master's and doctorate, GRE, minimum B average during final 2 years of course work. Additional exam requirements/recommendations for international students: required—TOEFL, TWE. Electronic applications accepted.

Wayne State University, College of Engineering, Department of Chemical Engineering and Materials Science, Detroit, MI 48202. Offers chemical engineering (MS, PhD); materials science and engineering (MS, PhD), including materials science and engineering; polymer engineering (Graduate Certificate), including polymer engineering. *Program availability:* Part-time. *Faculty:* 16. *Students:* 36 full-time (12 women), 20 part-time (5 women); includes 5 minority (1 Asian, non-Hispanic/Latino; 3 Hispanic/Latino; 1 Two or more races, non-Hispanic/Latino), 32 international. Average age 28. 128 applicants, 16% accepted, 9 enrolled. In 2019, 20 master's, 4 doctorates, 1 other advanced degree awarded. *Degree requirements:* For master's, thesis optional; for doctorate, comprehensive exam, thesis/dissertation. *Entrance requirements:* For master's, resume (optional); for doctorate, GRE, three letters of recommendation (at least two from the applicant's academic institution); personal statement; resume; for Graduate Certificate, bachelor's degree in engineering or other mathematics-based sciences in exceptional cases. Additional exam requirements/recommendations for international students: required—TOEFL (minimum score 550 paper-based; 79 iBT), TWE (minimum score 5.5), Michigan English Language Assessment Battery (minimum score 85); recommended—IELTS (minimum score 6.5). *Application deadline:* For fall admission, 3/1 priority date for domestic and international students; for winter admission, 10/1 priority date for domestic students, 9/1 priority date for international students; for spring admission, 2/1 priority date for domestic and international students; for summer admission, 2/1 priority date for domestic and international students. Application fee: $50. Electronic applications accepted. *Expenses:* $790 per credit hour in-state tuition, $1579 per credit hour out-of-state tuition. 32 credits to complete the MS; 90 credits total to complete the PhD. *Financial support:* In 2019–20, 35 students received support, including 4 fellowships with tuition reimbursements available (averaging $20,000 per year), 18 research assistantships with tuition reimbursements available (averaging $21,856 per year), 6 teaching assistantships with tuition reimbursements available (averaging $20,792 per year); scholarships/grants, health care benefits, and unspecified assistantships also available. Support available to part-time students. Financial award applicants required to submit FAFSA. *Unit head:* Dr. Jeffrey Potoff, Professor and Interim Chair, 313-577-9357, E-mail: jpotoff@wayne.edu. *Application contact:* Rob Carlson, Graduate Program Coordinator, 313-577-9615, E-mail: rcarlson@wayne.edu. Website: http://engineering.wayne.edu/che/

Western Michigan University, Graduate College, College of Engineering and Applied Sciences, Department of Chemical and Paper Engineering, Kalamazoo, MI 49008. Offers MS, MSE, PhD. *Degree requirements:* For master's, thesis optional; for doctorate, one foreign language, comprehensive exam, thesis/dissertation.

West Virginia University, Statler College of Engineering and Mineral Resources, Morgantown, WV 26506. Offers aerospace engineering (MSAE, PhD); chemical engineering (MS Ch E, PhD); civil engineering (MSCE, PhD); computer engineering (PhD); computer science (MSCS, PhD); electrical engineering (MSEE, PhD); energy systems engineering (MSESE); engineering (MSE); industrial engineering (MSIE, PhD); industrial hygiene (MS); material science and engineering (MSMSE, PhD); mechanical engineering (MSME, PhD); mining engineering (MS Min E, PhD); petroleum and natural gas engineering (MSPNGE, PhD); safety management (MS); software engineering (MSSE). *Program availability:* Part-time. Terminal master's awarded for partial completion of doctoral program. *Degree requirements:* For master's, thesis optional; for doctorate, comprehensive exam, thesis/dissertation. *Entrance requirements:* Additional exam requirements/recommendations for international students: required—TOEFL (minimum score 550 paper-based). Electronic applications accepted. *Expenses:* Contact institution.

Widener University, Graduate Programs in Engineering, Program in Chemical Engineering, Chester, PA 19013. Offers M Eng. *Program availability:* Part-time, evening/weekend. *Degree requirements:* For master's, thesis optional. Electronic applications accepted. *Expenses: Tuition:* Full-time $48,750; part-time $917 per credit hour. Tuition and fees vary according to class time, degree level, campus/location and program.

Worcester Polytechnic Institute, Graduate Admissions, Department of Chemical Engineering, Worcester, MA 01609-2280. Offers MS, PhD. *Program availability:* Part-time, evening/weekend. Terminal master's awarded for partial completion of doctoral program. *Degree requirements:* For master's, thesis (for some programs); for doctorate, comprehensive exam, thesis/dissertation. *Entrance requirements:* For master's and doctorate, GRE (recommended). GRE is required for International students, 3 letters of recommendation. Additional exam requirements/recommendations for international students: required—TOEFL (minimum score 563 paper-based; 84 iBT), IELTS (minimum score 7). Electronic applications accepted.

Yale University, Graduate School of Arts and Sciences, School of Engineering and Applied Science, Department of Chemical Engineering, New Haven, CT 06520. Offers MS, PhD. Terminal master's awarded for partial completion of doctoral program. *Degree requirements:* For doctorate, thesis/dissertation, exam. *Entrance requirements:* For master's and doctorate, GRE General Test. Additional exam requirements/recommendations for international students: required—TOEFL.

Section 7
Civil and Environmental Engineering

This section contains a directory of institutions offering graduate work in civil and environmental engineering. Additional information about programs listed in the directory may be obtained by writing directly to the dean of a graduate school or chair of a department at the address given in the directory.

For programs offering related work, see also in this book *Agricultural Engineering and Bioengineering, Biomedical Engineering and Biotechnology, Engineering and Applied Sciences, Management of Engineering and Technology,* and *Ocean Engineering.* In the other guides in this series:

Graduate Programs in the Humanities, Arts & Social Sciences

See *Public, Regional, and Industrial Affairs (Urban and Regional Planning and Urban Studies)*

Graduate Programs in the Biological/Biomedical Sciences & Health-Related Medical Professions

See *Ecology, Environmental Biology,* and *Evolutionary Biology*

Graduate Programs in the Physical Sciences, Mathematics, Agricultural Sciences, the Environment & Natural Resources

See *Agricultural and Food Sciences, Environmental Sciences and Management, Geosciences,* and *Marine Sciences and Oceanography*

CONTENTS

Program Directories

Civil Engineering

American University of Sharjah, Graduate Programs, Sharjah, United Arab Emirates. Offers accounting (MS); biomedical engineering (MSBME); business administration (MBA); chemical engineering (MS Ch E); civil engineering (MSCE); computer engineering (MS); electrical engineering (MSEE); engineering systems management (MS, PhD); mathematics (MS); mechanical engineering (MSME); mechatronics engineering (MS); teaching English to speakers of other languages (MA); translation and interpreting (MA); urban planning (MUP). *Program availability:* Part-time, evening/weekend. *Degree requirements:* For master's, thesis (for some programs). *Entrance requirements:* For master's, GMAT (for MBA). Additional exam requirements/recommendations for international students: required—TOEFL (minimum score 550 paper-based; 80 iBT), TWE (minimum score 5); recommended—IELTS (minimum score 6.5). Electronic applications accepted.

Arizona State University at Tempe, Ira A. Fulton Schools of Engineering, School of Sustainable Engineering and the Built Environment, Tempe, AZ 85287-5306. Offers civil, environmental and sustainable engineering (MS, MSE, PhD); construction engineering (MSE); construction management (MS, PhD). *Program availability:* Part-time, evening/weekend, online learning. Terminal master's awarded for partial completion of doctoral program. *Degree requirements:* For master's, thesis optional, comprehensive exams (MSE); interactive Program of Study (iPOS) submitted before completing 50 percent of required credit hours; for doctorate, comprehensive exam, thesis/dissertation, interactive Program of Study (iPOS) submitted before completing 50 percent of required credit hours. *Entrance requirements:* For master's, GRE, minimum GPA of 3.0 or equivalent in last 2 years of work leading to bachelor's degree; for doctorate, GRE, minimum GPA of 3.0 in last 2 years of work leading to bachelor's degree, 3.2 in all graduate-level coursework with master's degree; 3 letters of recommendation; resume/curriculum vitae; letter of intent; thesis (if applicable); statement of research interests. Additional exam requirements/recommendations for international students: required—TOEFL, IELTS, or PTE. Electronic applications accepted. *Expenses:* Contact institution.

Auburn University, Graduate School, Samuel Ginn College of Engineering, Department of Civil Engineering, Auburn University, AL 36849. Offers MCE, MS, PhD. *Program availability:* Part-time. *Faculty:* 25 full-time (4 women), 2 part-time/adjunct (0 women). *Students:* 71 full-time (24 women), 55 part-time (10 women); includes 6 minority (1 Black or African American, non-Hispanic/Latino; 1 American Indian or Alaska Native, non-Hispanic/Latino; 1 Asian, non-Hispanic/Latino; 3 Hispanic/Latino), 65 international. Average age 29. 112 applicants, 63% accepted, 27 enrolled. In 2019, 42 master's, 13 doctorates awarded. *Degree requirements:* For master's, thesis (for some programs), project (MCE), thesis (MS); for doctorate, comprehensive exam, thesis/dissertation. *Entrance requirements:* For master's and doctorate, GRE General Test. Additional exam requirements/recommendations for international students: required—TOEFL (minimum score 550 paper-based; 79 iBT). *Application deadline:* For fall admission, 3/31 priority date for domestic and international students; for spring admission, 9/30 priority date for domestic and international students. Applications are processed on a rolling basis. Application fee: $60 ($70 for international students). Electronic applications accepted. *Expenses: Tuition, area resident:* Full-time $9828; part-time $546 per credit hour. Tuition, state resident: full-time $9828; part-time $546 per credit hour. Tuition, nonresident: full-time $29,484; part-time $1638 per credit hour. *International tuition:* $29,744 full-time. Tuition and fees vary according to course load, program and reciprocity agreements. *Financial support:* In 2019–20, 56 research assistantships (averaging $14,882 per year), 18 teaching assistantships (averaging $10,182 per year) were awarded; fellowships and Federal Work-Study also available. Support available to part-time students. Financial award application deadline: 3/15; financial award applicants required to submit FAFSA. *Unit head:* Dr. Andrzej S. Nowak, Head, 334-844-6216, E-mail: asn0007@auburn.edu. *Application contact:* Dr. George Flowers, Dean of the Graduate School, 334-844-2125. Website: https://www.eng.auburn.edu/civil/

Boise State University, College of Engineering, Department of Civil Engineering, Boise, ID 83725-0399. Offers civil engineering (M Engr, MS). *Program availability:* Part-time. *Students:* 12 full-time (5 women), 6 part-time (0 women), 6 international. *Degree requirements:* For master's, comprehensive exam, thesis (for some programs). *Entrance requirements:* For master's, GRE General Test, minimum GPA of 3.0. Additional exam requirements/recommendations for international students: required—TOEFL, IELTS. Electronic applications accepted. *Expenses: Tuition, area resident:* Full-time $7110; part-time $470 per credit hour. Tuition, state resident: full-time $7110; part-time $470 per credit hour. Tuition, nonresident: full-time $24,030; part-time $827 per credit hour. *International tuition:* $827 full-time. *Required fees:* $2536. Tuition and fees vary according to course load and program. *Financial support:* Research assistantships, teaching assistantships, scholarships/grants, and unspecified assistantships available. Financial award applicants required to submit FAFSA. *Unit head:* Dr. Nick Hudyma, Department Chair, 208-426-3743, E-mail: nickhudyma@boisestate.edu. *Application contact:* Dr. Arvin Farid, Graduate Program Coordinator, 208-426-4827, E-mail: arvinfarid@boisestate.edu. Website: https://www.boisestate.edu/coen-ce/

Bradley University, The Graduate School, Caterpillar College of Engineering and Technology, Department of Civil Engineering and Construction, Peoria, IL 61625-0002. Offers construction management, structural engineering, geo-environmental engineering (MSCE). *Program availability:* Part-time, evening/weekend. *Faculty:* 11 full-time (2 women). *Students:* 14 full-time (2 women), 6 part-time (1 woman); includes 2 minority (both Black or African American, non-Hispanic/Latino), 17 international. Average age 24. 42 applicants, 64% accepted, 5 enrolled. In 2019, 11 master's awarded. *Degree requirements:* For master's, comprehensive exam, thesis or alternative, 30 hours. *Entrance requirements:* For master's, minimum GPA of 2.5, Essays, Recommendation letters, Transcripts. Additional exam requirements/recommendations for international students: required—TOEFL (minimum score 550 paper-based; 79 iBT), IELTS (minimum score 6.5), PTE (minimum score 58). *Application deadline:* For fall admission, 5/15 priority date for domestic and international students; for spring admission, 10/15 priority date for domestic and international students. Applications are processed on a rolling basis. Application fee: $40 ($50 for international students). Electronic applications accepted. *Expenses:* Tuition: Part-time $930 per credit hour. *Financial support:* In 2019–20, 13 students received support, including 3 teaching assistantships with partial tuition reimbursements available (averaging $8,370 per year); research assistantships, scholarships/grants, tuition waivers (partial), and unspecified assistantships also available. Support available to part-time students. Financial award application deadline: 4/1. *Unit head:* Souhail Elhouar, Chairman, 309-677-3830, E-mail: selhouar@bradley.edu. *Application contact:* Rachel Webb, Director of On-Campus Graduate Admissions, 309-677-2375, E-mail: bugrad@bradley.edu. Website: http://www.bradley.edu/academic/departments/cec/

Brigham Young University, Graduate Studies, Ira A. Fulton College of Engineering, Department of Civil and Environmental Engineering, Provo, UT 84602. Offers civil engineering (MS, PhD). *Faculty:* 15 full-time (0 women). *Students:* 28 full-time (8 women), 24 part-time (5 women); includes 6 minority (3 Asian, non-Hispanic/Latino; 2 Hispanic/Latino; 1 Two or more races, non-Hispanic/Latino), 12 international. Average age 26. 36 applicants, 78% accepted, 15 enrolled. In 2019, 24 master's, 3 doctorates awarded. *Degree requirements:* For master's, thesis, Fundamentals of Engineering (FE) Exam; for doctorate, comprehensive exam, thesis/dissertation. *Entrance requirements:* For master's, GRE General Test, minimum cumulative GPA of 3.0 in last 60 hours of upper-division course work; for doctorate, GRE General Test, Minimum cumulative GPA of 3.0 in last 60 hours of upper-division course work. Additional exam requirements/recommendations for international students: required—TOEFL (minimum score 580 paper-based; 85 iBT). *Application deadline:* For fall admission, 2/15 for domestic and international students; for winter admission, 9/5 for domestic and international students; for spring admission, 2/5 for domestic and international students; for summer admission, 2/5 for domestic and international students. Application fee: $50. Electronic applications accepted. *Financial support:* In 2019–20, 43 students received support, including 40 fellowships with full and partial tuition reimbursements available (averaging $4,900 per year), 35 research assistantships with partial tuition reimbursements available (averaging $12,000 per year), 30 teaching assistantships (averaging $6,000 per year); scholarships/grants also available. Financial award application deadline: 5/31; financial award applicants required to submit FAFSA. *Unit head:* Dr. Gustavious Paul Williams, Graduate Committee Chair, 801-422-7810, Fax: 801-422-0159, E-mail: gus.williams@byu.edu. *Application contact:* Kim Glade, Graduate Advisor, 801-422-2814, Fax: 801-422-0159, E-mail: kim_glade@byu.edu. Website: http://ceen.et.byu.edu/

Bucknell University, Graduate Studies, College of Engineering, Department of Civil and Environmental Engineering, Lewisburg, PA 17837. Offers MSCE, MSEV. *Degree requirements:* For master's, thesis. *Entrance requirements:* For master's, GRE General Test, minimum GPA of 3.0. Additional exam requirements/recommendations for international students: required—TOEFL (minimum score 600 paper-based).

California Institute of Technology, Division of Engineering and Applied Science, Option in Civil Engineering, Pasadena, CA 91125-0001. Offers MS, PhD, Engr. *Degree requirements:* For doctorate, thesis/dissertation.

California Polytechnic State University, San Luis Obispo, College of Engineering, Department of Civil and Environmental Engineering, San Luis Obispo, CA 93407. Offers MS. *Program availability:* Part-time. *Faculty:* 11 full-time (1 woman), 1 part-time/adjunct (0 women). *Students:* 45 full-time (21 women), 4 part-time (0 women); includes 21 minority (9 Asian, non-Hispanic/Latino; 6 Hispanic/Latino; 6 Two or more races, non-Hispanic/Latino), 5 international. Average age 23. 79 applicants, 78% accepted, 38 enrolled. In 2019, 34 master's awarded. *Degree requirements:* For master's, comprehensive exam (for some programs), thesis (for some programs). *Entrance requirements:* For master's, GRE. Additional exam requirements/recommendations for international students: required—TOEFL (minimum score 80 iBT). *Application deadline:* For fall admission, 1/1 for domestic students, 3/1 priority date for international students. Applications are processed on a rolling basis. Application fee: $55. Electronic applications accepted. *Expenses:* Tuition, state resident: full-time $7176; part-time $4164 per year. Tuition, nonresident: full-time $18,690; part-time $8916 per year. *Required fees:* $4206; $3185 per unit. $1061 per term. *Financial support:* Fellowships, research assistantships, teaching assistantships, career-related internships or fieldwork, and scholarships/grants available. Financial award application deadline: 3/2; financial award applicants required to submit FAFSA. *Unit head:* Dr. Robb Moss, Graduate Coordinator, 805-756-6427, E-mail: rmoss@calpoly.edu. *Application contact:* Dr. Robb Moss, Graduate Coordinator, 805-756-6427, E-mail: rmoss@calpoly.edu. Website: http://ceenve.calpoly.edu

California State Polytechnic University, Pomona, Program in Civil Engineering, Pomona, CA 91768-2557. Offers civil engineering (MS), including environmental and water resources engineering, geotechnical engineering, structural engineering, transportation engineering. *Program availability:* Part-time, evening/weekend. *Degree requirements:* For master's, project or thesis. *Entrance requirements:* Additional exam requirements/recommendations for international students: required—TOEFL (minimum score 550 paper-based). Electronic applications accepted. *Expenses:* Contact institution.

California State University, Fresno, Division of Research and Graduate Studies, Lyles College of Engineering, Department of Civil and Geomatics Engineering, Fresno, CA 93740-8027. Offers MS. *Program availability:* Part-time, evening/weekend. *Degree requirements:* For master's, thesis or alternative. *Entrance requirements:* For master's, GRE General Test, minimum GPA of 2.75. Additional exam requirements/recommendations for international students: required—TOEFL. Electronic applications accepted. *Expenses:* Tuition, state resident: full-time $4012; part-time $2506 per semester.

California State University, Fullerton, Graduate Studies, College of Engineering and Computer Science, Department of Civil and Environmental Engineering, Fullerton, CA 92831-3599. Offers civil engineering (MS), including architectural engineering, environmental engineering. *Program availability:* Part-time. *Degree requirements:* For master's, comprehensive exam, project or thesis. *Entrance requirements:* For master's, minimum undergraduate GPA of 2.5.

California State University, Long Beach, Graduate Studies, College of Engineering, Department of Civil Engineering and Construction Engineering Management, Long Beach, CA 90840. Offers civil engineering (MSCE). *Program availability:* Part-time. *Degree requirements:* For master's, comprehensive exam or thesis. *Entrance requirements:* Additional exam requirements/recommendations for international students: required—TOEFL. Electronic applications accepted.

California State University, Los Angeles, Graduate Studies, College of Engineering, Computer Science, and Technology, Department of Civil Engineering, Los Angeles, CA 90032-8530. Offers MS. *Program availability:* Part-time, evening/weekend. *Degree requirements:* For master's, comprehensive exam or thesis. *Entrance requirements:* For master's, GRE or minimum GPA of 2.4. Additional exam requirements/recommendations for international students: required—TOEFL (minimum score 550 paper-based). *Expenses: Tuition, area resident:* Full-time $7176; part-time $4164 per year. Tuition, state resident: full-time $7176; part-time $4164 per year. Tuition, nonresident: full-time $14,304; part-time $8916 per year. *International tuition:* $14,304 full-time. *Required fees:* $1037.76; $1037.76 per unit. Tuition and fees vary according to degree level and program.

California State University, Northridge, Graduate Studies, College of Engineering and Computer Science, Department of Civil Engineering and Construction Management, Northridge, CA 91330. Offers engineering (MS), including structural engineering.

Program availability: Part-time, evening/weekend. *Degree requirements:* For master's, thesis. *Entrance requirements:* Additional exam requirements/recommendations for international students: required—TOEFL.

California State University, Sacramento, College of Engineering and Computer Science, Department of Civil Engineering, Sacramento, CA 95819. Offers MS. *Program availability:* Part-time, evening/weekend. *Students:* 12 full-time (4 women), 42 part-time (14 women); includes 19 minority (2 Black or African American, non-Hispanic/Latino; 13 Asian, non-Hispanic/Latino; 3 Hispanic/Latino; 1 Native Hawaiian or other Pacific Islander, non-Hispanic/Latino), 5 international. Average age 30. 57 applicants, 67% accepted, 19 enrolled. In 2019, 22 master's awarded. *Degree requirements:* For master's, thesis, thesis, project, or comprehensive exam; writing proficiency exam. *Entrance requirements:* Additional exam requirements/recommendations for international students: required—TOEFL (minimum score 550 paper-based; 80 iBT); recommended—IELTS (minimum score 7). *Application deadline:* For fall admission, 3/1 for domestic students, 2/1 for international students; for spring admission, 9/15 for domestic students, 8/15 for international students. Applications are processed on a rolling basis. Application fee: $70. Electronic applications accepted. *Expenses:* Contact institution. *Financial support:* Teaching assistantships, career-related internships or fieldwork, Federal Work-Study, and scholarships/grants available. Support available to part-time students. Financial award application deadline: 3/1; financial award applicants required to submit FAFSA. *Unit head:* Dr. Benjamin Fell, Chair, 916-278-8139, Fax: 916-278-7957, E-mail: fellb@csus.edu. *Application contact:* Jose Martinez, Graduate Admissions Supervisor, 916-278-7871, E-mail: martinj@skymail.csus.edu. Website: http://www.ecs.csus.edu/ce

Carleton University, Faculty of Graduate Studies, Faculty of Engineering and Design, Department of Civil and Environmental Engineering, Ottawa, ON K1S 5B6, Canada. Offers M Eng, MA Sc, PhD. *Degree requirements:* For master's, thesis optional; for doctorate, thesis/dissertation. *Entrance requirements:* For master's, honors degree; for doctorate, MA Sc or M Eng. Additional exam requirements/recommendations for international students: required—TOEFL.

Carnegie Mellon University, Carnegie Institute of Technology, Department of Civil and Environmental Engineering, Pittsburgh, PA 15213. Offers advanced infrastructure systems (MS, PhD); advanced infrastructure systems technology development and application (MS); air quality engineering and science (MS); civil and environmental engineering (MS, PhD); civil and environmental engineering/engineering and public policy (PhD); civil engineering (MS, PhD); computational mechanics (MS, PhD); computational modeling and monitoring for resilient structural and material systems (MS); energy infrastructure systems (MS); environmental engineering (MS, PhD); environmental management and science (MS, PhD); IT-based sustainable global infrastructure and construction management (MS); sustainability and green design (MS); water quality engineering and science (MS). *Program availability:* Part-time. *Faculty:* 23 full-time (5 women), 12 part-time/adjunct (3 women). *Students:* 261 full-time (109 women); includes 19 minority (7 Black or African American, non-Hispanic/Latino; 8 Asian, non-Hispanic/Latino; 4 Hispanic/Latino), 214 international. Average age 25. 649 applicants, 57% accepted, 106 enrolled. In 2019, 80 master's, 12 doctorates awarded. Terminal master's awarded for partial completion of doctoral program. *Degree requirements:* For master's, thesis optional; for doctorate, comprehensive exam, thesis/ dissertation, two-part qualifying exam, public defense of dissertation. *Entrance requirements:* For master's, GRE General Test, BS in engineering, science, or mathematics; for doctorate, GRE General Test, BS or MS in engineering, science, or mathematics. Additional exam requirements/recommendations for international students: required—TOEFL (minimum score 84 iBT), TOEFL (minimum score 84 iBT) or IELTS (7.0). *Application deadline:* For fall admission, 1/5 priority date for domestic and international students; for spring admission, 9/15 priority date for domestic and international students. Applications are processed on a rolling basis. Application fee: $75. Electronic applications accepted. *Financial support:* In 2019–20, 113 students received support. Fellowships with tuition reimbursements available, research assistantships with tuition reimbursements available, teaching assistantships, scholarships/grants, health care benefits, tuition waivers (full and partial), and unspecified assistantships available. Financial award application deadline: 1/5. *Unit head:* Dr. David A. Dzombak, Professor and Department Head, 412-268-2941, Fax: 412-268-7813, E-mail: dzombak@cmu.edu. *Application contact:* David A. Vey, Director of Graduate Programs, 412-268-2292, Fax: 412-268-7813, E-mail: dvey@andrew.cmu.edu. Website: http://www.cmu.edu/cee/

Case Western Reserve University, School of Graduate Studies, Case School of Engineering, Department of Civil Engineering, Cleveland, OH 44106. Offers civil engineering (MS, PhD). *Program availability:* Part-time. *Degree requirements:* For master's, thesis (for some programs); for doctorate, thesis/dissertation, qualifying exam, teaching experience. *Entrance requirements:* For master's and doctorate, GRE General Test. Additional exam requirements/recommendations for international students: required—TOEFL.

The Catholic University of America, School of Engineering, Department of Civil Engineering, Washington, DC 20064. Offers civil engineering (MS, PhD); transportation and infrastructure systems (Certificate). *Program availability:* Part-time. *Faculty:* 6 full-time (1 woman), 3 part-time/adjunct (1 woman). *Students:* 13 full-time (4 women), 22 part-time (5 women); includes 12 minority (7 Black or African American, non-Hispanic/Latino; 5 Two or more races, non-Hispanic/Latino), 23 international. Average age 32. 43 applicants, 58% accepted, 10 enrolled. In 2019, 15 master's, 1 doctorate awarded. *Degree requirements:* For master's, thesis optional; for doctorate, comprehensive exam, thesis/dissertation. *Entrance requirements:* For master's and doctorate, GRE General Test, statement of purpose, official copies of academic transcripts, three letters of recommendation. Additional exam requirements/recommendations for international students: required—TOEFL (minimum score 550 paper-based; 80 iBT). *Application deadline:* For fall admission, 7/15 priority date for domestic students, 7/1 for international students; for spring admission, 11/15 priority date for domestic students, 11/1 for international students. Applications are processed on a rolling basis. Application fee: $55. Electronic applications accepted. *Expenses:* Contact institution. *Financial support:* Fellowships, research assistantships, teaching assistantships, Federal Work-Study, scholarships/grants, tuition waivers (full and partial), and unspecified assistantships available. Financial award application deadline: 2/1; financial award applicants required to submit FAFSA. *Unit head:* Dr. Arash Massoudieh, Chair, 202-319-5671, Fax: 202-319-6677, E-mail: massoudieh@cua.edu. *Application contact:* Dr. Steven Brown, Director of Graduate Admissions, 202-319-5057, Fax: 202-319-6533, E-mail: cua-admissions@cua.edu. Website: https://engineering.catholic.edu/civil/index.html

The Citadel, The Military College of South Carolina, Citadel Graduate College, School of Engineering, Department of Civil and Environmental Engineering, Charleston, SC 29409. Offers built environment and public health (Graduate Certificate); civil engineering (MS); geotechnical engineering (Graduate Certificate); structural engineering (Graduate Certificate); transportation engineering (Graduate Certificate). *Program availability:* Part-time, evening/weekend. *Degree requirements:* For master's, plan of study outlining intended areas of interest and top four corresponding courses of

interest. *Entrance requirements:* For master's, official transcript of baccalaureate degree from ABET-accredited engineering program or approved alternative; 2 letters of recommendation; for Graduate Certificate, official transcript of baccalaureate degree directly from an accredited college or university. Additional exam requirements/ recommendations for international students: required—TOEFL (minimum score 550 paper-based; 79 iBT). Electronic applications accepted.

City College of the City University of New York, Graduate School, Grove School of Engineering, Department of Civil Engineering, New York, NY 10031-9198. Offers ME, MS, PhD. *Program availability:* Part-time. *Degree requirements:* For master's, thesis optional; for doctorate, one foreign language, comprehensive exam, thesis/dissertation. *Entrance requirements:* For master's and doctorate, GRE General Test. Additional exam requirements/recommendations for international students: required—TOEFL (minimum score 500 paper-based; 61 iBT).

Clarkson University, Wallace H. Coulter School of Engineering, Department of Civil and Environmental Engineering, Potsdam, NY 13699. Offers ME, MS, PhD. *Faculty:* 19 full-time (2 women), 6 part-time/adjunct (1 woman). *Students:* 17 full-time (8 women), 2 part-time (both women); includes 1 minority (Black or African American, non-Hispanic/ Latino), 13 international. 69 applicants, 61% accepted, 3 enrolled. In 2019, 8 master's, 5 doctorates awarded. *Degree requirements:* For master's, thesis (for MS); project (for ME); for doctorate, comprehensive exam, thesis/dissertation. *Entrance requirements:* For master's and doctorate, GRE. Additional exam requirements/recommendations for international students: required—TOEFL (minimum score 550 paper-based, 80 iBT) or IELTS (6.5). *Application deadline:* Applications are processed on a rolling basis. Application fee: $50. Electronic applications accepted. *Expenses: Tuition:* Full-time $24,984; part-time $1388. *Required fees:* $225. Tuition and fees vary according to campus/location and program. *Financial support:* Scholarships/grants and unspecified assistantships available. *Unit head:* Dr. John Dempsey, Chair of Civil and Environmental Engineering, 315-268-6529, E-mail: jdempsey@clarkson.edu. *Application contact:* Daniel Capogna, Director of Graduate Admissions & Recruitment, 518-631-9910, E-mail: graduate@clarkson.edu. Website: https://www.clarkson.edu/academics/graduate

Clemson University, Graduate School, College of Engineering, Computing and Applied Sciences, Glenn Department of Civil Engineering, Clemson, SC 29634. Offers civil engineering (MS, PhD), including construction engineering and management, construction materials, geotechnical engineering, structural engineering, transportation engineering, water resources engineering. *Program availability:* Part-time, 100% online. *Faculty:* 24 full-time (4 women), 3 part-time/adjunct (2 women). *Students:* 101 full-time (20 women), 44 part-time (9 women); includes 9 minority (3 Black or African American, non-Hispanic/Latino; 1 Asian, non-Hispanic/Latino; 2 Hispanic/Latino; 3 Two or more races, non-Hispanic/Latino), 97 international. Average age 29. 248 applicants, 62% accepted, 61 enrolled. In 2019, 43 master's, 11 doctorates awarded. *Degree requirements:* For master's, thesis or alternative, oral exam, seminar; for doctorate, comprehensive exam, thesis/dissertation, oral exam, seminar. *Entrance requirements:* For master's and doctorate, GRE General Test, unofficial transcripts, letters of recommendation, statement of purpose. Additional exam requirements/ recommendations for international students: required—TOEFL (minimum score 80 paper-based; 80 iBT), PTE (minimum score 54); recommended—IELTS (minimum score 6.5). *Application deadline:* For fall admission, 4/15 for domestic and international students; for spring admission, 9/15 for domestic and international students. Applications are processed on a rolling basis. Application fee: $80 ($90 for international students). Electronic applications accepted. *Expenses: Tuition, area resident:* Full-time $10,600; part-time $8688 per semester. Tuition, state resident: full-time $10,600; part-time $8688 per semester. Tuition, nonresident: full-time $22,050; part-time $17,412 per semester. *International tuition:* $22,050 full-time. *Required fees:* $1196; $617 per semester. $617 per semester. Tuition and fees vary according to course load, degree level, campus/location and program. *Financial support:* In 2019–20, 101 students received support, including 2 fellowships with full and partial tuition reimbursements available (averaging $34,000 per year), 61 research assistantships with full and partial tuition reimbursements available (averaging $18,222 per year), 4 teaching assistantships with full and partial tuition reimbursements available (averaging $20,567 per year); career-related internships or fieldwork and unspecified assistantships also available. Financial award application deadline: 4/15. *Unit head:* Dr. Jesus M de la Garza, Department Chair, 864-656-3001, E-mail: jdelaga@clemson.edu. *Application contact:* Dr. Abdul Khan, Graduate Program Coordinator, 864-656-3327, E-mail: abdkhan@clemson.edu. Website: https://www.clemson.edu/cecas/departments/ce/

Cleveland State University, College of Graduate Studies, Fenn College of Engineering, Department of Civil and Environmental Engineering, Cleveland, OH 44115. Offers MS, D Eng. *Program availability:* Part-time, evening/weekend. *Entrance requirements:* For master's, GRE General Test, GRE Subject Test, minimum GPA of 2.75; for doctorate, GRE General Test, GRE Subject Test, minimum GPA of 3.25. Additional exam requirements/recommendations for international students: required— TOEFL (minimum score 550 paper-based; 78 iBT). Electronic applications accepted. *Expenses:* Tuition, state resident: full-time $10,215; part-time $6810 per credit hour. Tuition, nonresident: full-time $17,496; part-time $11,664 per credit hour. *International tuition:* $19,316 full-time. Tuition and fees vary according to degree level and program.

Colorado School of Mines, Office of Graduate Studies, Department of Civil and Environmental Engineering, Golden, CO 80401. Offers civil and environmental engineering (MS, PhD); environmental engineering science (MS, PhD); hydrologic science and engineering (MS, PhD); underground construction and tunneling (MS, PhD). *Program availability:* Part-time. *Degree requirements:* For master's, thesis (for some programs); for doctorate, comprehensive exam, thesis/dissertation. *Entrance requirements:* For master's and doctorate, GRE General Test. Additional exam requirements/recommendations for international students: required—TOEFL (minimum score 550 paper-based; 79 iBT). Electronic applications accepted. *Expenses:* Tuition, state resident: full-time $16,650; part-time $925 per credit hour. Tuition, nonresident: full-time $37,350; part-time $2075 per credit hour. *International tuition:* $37,350 full-time. *Required fees:* $2412.

Colorado State University, Walter Scott, Jr. College of Engineering, Department of Civil and Environmental Engineering, Fort Collins, CO 80523-1372. Offers MS, PhD. *Program availability:* Part-time, online learning. Terminal master's awarded for partial completion of doctoral program. *Degree requirements:* For master's, thesis, publication (for MS); for doctorate, comprehensive exam, thesis/dissertation, journal paper publication. *Entrance requirements:* For master's, GRE, minimum GPA of 3.0; resume; statement of purpose; three letters of recommendation; transcripts; for doctorate, GRE, master's degree; minimum GPA of 3.0; resume; statement of purpose; three letters of recommendation; transcripts. Additional exam requirements/recommendations for international students: required—TOEFL (minimum score 550 paper-based; 80 iBT), IELTS (minimum score 6.5), PTE (minimum score 58). Electronic applications accepted. *Expenses:* Contact institution.

Columbia University, Fu Foundation School of Engineering and Applied Science, Department of Civil Engineering and Engineering Mechanics, New York, NY 10027. Offers civil engineering (MS, Eng Sc D, PhD); construction engineering and management (MS); engineering mechanics (MS, Eng Sc D, PhD). *Program availability:* Part-time, online learning. Terminal master's awarded for partial completion of doctoral program. *Degree requirements:* For doctorate, thesis/dissertation, qualifying exam. *Entrance requirements:* For master's and doctorate, GRE General Test. Additional exam requirements/recommendations for international students: required—TOEFL, IELTS, PTE. Electronic applications accepted. *Expenses: Tuition:* Full-time $47,600; part-time $1880 per credit. One-time fee: $105.

Concordia University, School of Graduate Studies, Faculty of Engineering and Computer Science, Department of Building, Civil and Environmental Engineering, Montréal, QC H3G 1M8, Canada. Offers building engineering (M Eng, MA Sc, PhD, Certificate); civil engineering (M Eng, MA Sc, PhD); environmental engineering (Certificate). *Degree requirements:* For master's, thesis or alternative; for doctorate, comprehensive exam, thesis/dissertation.

Cooper Union for the Advancement of Science and Art, Albert Nerken School of Engineering, New York, NY 10003. Offers chemical engineering (ME); civil engineering (ME); electrical engineering (ME); mechanical engineering (ME). *Program availability:* Part-time. *Degree requirements:* For master's, thesis (for some programs), thesis or special project. *Entrance requirements:* For master's, BE or BS in an engineering discipline; official copies of school transcripts including secondary (high school), college and university work; two letters of recommendation; resume. Additional exam requirements/recommendations for international students: required—TOEFL (minimum score 600 paper-based; 100 iBT). Electronic applications accepted.

Cornell University, Graduate School, Graduate Fields of Engineering, Field of Civil and Environmental Engineering, Ithaca, NY 14853. Offers engineering management (M Eng, MS, PhD); environmental engineering (M Eng, MS, PhD); environmental fluid mechanics and hydrology (M Eng, MS, PhD); environmental systems engineering (M Eng, MS, PhD); geotechnical engineering (M Eng, MS, PhD); remote sensing (M Eng, MS, PhD); structural engineering (M Eng, MS, PhD); structural mechanics (M Eng, MS); transportation engineering (MS, PhD); transportation systems engineering (M Eng); water resource systems (M Eng, MS, PhD). Terminal master's awarded for partial completion of doctoral program. *Degree requirements:* For master's, thesis (MS); for doctorate, comprehensive exam, thesis/dissertation. *Entrance requirements:* For master's and doctorate, GRE General Test (recommended), 2 letters of recommendation. Additional exam requirements/recommendations for international students: required—TOEFL (minimum score 600 paper-based; 77 iBT). Electronic applications accepted.

Dalhousie University, Faculty of Engineering, Department of Civil and Resource Engineering, Halifax, NS B3J 2X4, Canada. Offers civil engineering (M Eng, MA Sc, PhD); environmental engineering (M Eng, MA Sc); mineral resource engineering (M Eng, MA Sc, PhD). *Degree requirements:* For master's, thesis; for doctorate, thesis/dissertation. *Entrance requirements:* Additional exam requirements/recommendations for international students: required—TOEFL, IELTS, CANTEST, CAEL, or Michigan English Language Assessment Battery. Electronic applications accepted.

Drexel University, College of Engineering, Department of Civil, Architectural, and Environmental Engineering, Program in Civil Engineering, Philadelphia, PA 19104-2875. Offers MS, PhD. *Program availability:* Part-time, evening/weekend. *Degree requirements:* For master's, thesis optional; for doctorate, thesis/dissertation. *Entrance requirements:* For master's, minimum GPA of 3.0; for doctorate, minimum GPA of 3.5, MS in civil engineering. Additional exam requirements/recommendations for international students: required—TOEFL. Electronic applications accepted.

Duke University, Graduate School, Pratt School of Engineering, Department of Civil and Environmental Engineering, Durham, NC 27708. Offers civil and environmental engineering (MS, PhD); civil engineering (M Eng); computational mechanics and scientific computing (M Eng); environmental engineering (M Eng, MS, PhD); risk engineering (M Eng). Terminal master's awarded for partial completion of doctoral program. *Degree requirements:* For doctorate, thesis/dissertation. *Entrance requirements:* For master's and doctorate, GRE General Test. Additional exam requirements/recommendations for international students: required—TOEFL (minimum score 550 paper-based; 90 iBT), IELTS (minimum score 7). Electronic applications accepted.

Duke University, Graduate School, Pratt School of Engineering, Master of Engineering Program, Durham, NC 27708-0271. Offers biomedical engineering (M Eng); civil engineering (M Eng); computational mechanics and scientific computing (M Eng); electrical and computer engineering (M Eng); environmental engineering (M Eng); materials science and engineering (M Eng); mechanical engineering (M Eng); photonics and optical sciences (M Eng); risk engineering (M Eng). *Program availability:* Part-time. *Entrance requirements:* For master's, GRE General Test, resume, 3 letters of recommendation, statement of purpose, transcripts. Additional exam requirements/recommendations for international students: required—TOEFL. Electronic applications accepted.

Embry-Riddle Aeronautical University–Daytona, Department of Civil Engineering, Daytona Beach, FL 32114-3900. Offers MS. *Degree requirements:* For master's, thesis optional. *Entrance requirements:* For master's, GRE, minimum cumulative GPA of 3.0. Additional exam requirements/recommendations for international students: required—TOEFL (minimum score 550 paper-based, 79 iBT) or IELTS (6). Electronic applications accepted.

Florida Agricultural and Mechanical University, Division of Graduate Studies, Research, and Continuing Education, FAMU-FSU College of Engineering, Department of Civil and Environmental Engineering, Tallahassee, FL 32307-3200. Offers civil engineering (M Eng, MS, PhD). *Degree requirements:* For master's, comprehensive exam, thesis optional; for doctorate, comprehensive exam, thesis/dissertation. *Entrance requirements:* For master's, GRE General Test, minimum GPA of 3.0; for doctorate, GRE General Test, minimum GPA of 3.0, letters of recommendation (3). Additional exam requirements/recommendations for international students: required—TOEFL (minimum score 550 paper-based).

Florida Atlantic University, College of Engineering and Computer Science, Department of Civil, Environmental and Geomatics Engineering, Boca Raton, FL 33431-0991. Offers civil engineering (MS); environmental engineering (MS). *Program availability:* Part-time, evening/weekend. *Faculty:* 11 full-time (0 women). *Students:* 22 full-time (9 women), 15 part-time (11 women); includes 10 minority (2 Black or African American, non-Hispanic/Latino; 3 Asian, non-Hispanic/Latino; 4 Hispanic/Latino; 1 Two or more races, non-Hispanic/Latino), 18 international. Average age 28. 43 applicants, 42% accepted, 15 enrolled. In 2019, 26 master's awarded. *Entrance requirements:* For master's, GRE General Test, minimum GPA of 3.0 in last 60 hours of undergraduate course work. Additional exam requirements/recommendations for international students: required—TOEFL (minimum score 550 paper-based; 61 iBT), IELTS (minimum score 6). *Application deadline:* For fall admission, 7/1 priority date for domestic students, 2/15 for international students; for spring admission, 11/1 for domestic students, 7/15 for international students. Applications are processed on a rolling basis. Application fee: $30. *Expenses: Tuition:* Full-time $20,536; part-time $371.82 per credit hour. Tuition and fees vary according to program. *Financial support:* Research assistantships with full tuition reimbursements, teaching assistantships with full tuition reimbursements, career-related internships or fieldwork, Federal Work-Study, scholarships/grants, and unspecified assistantships available. Financial award applicants required to submit FAFSA. *Unit head:* Dr. Yan Yong, Chair, 561-297-3445, Fax: 561-297-0493, E-mail: cege@fau.edu. *Application contact:* Dr. Frederick Bloetscher, Associate Dean and Professor, 561-297-0744, E-mail: fbloetsch@fau.edu.
Website: http://www.cege.fau.edu/

Florida Institute of Technology, College of Engineering and Science, Program in Civil Engineering, Melbourne, FL 32901-6975. Offers MS, PhD. *Program availability:* Part-time. *Degree requirements:* For master's, comprehensive exam (for some programs), thesis optional, 30 credit hours; teaching/internship (for thesis) or final examinations (for non-thesis); for doctorate, comprehensive exam, thesis/dissertation, 42 credit hours of coursework beyond the master's degree. *Entrance requirements:* For master's, GRE, 2 letters of recommendation, statement of objectives; for doctorate, GRE, 3 letters of recommendation, minimum GPA of 3.2, resume, statement of objectives, degree from accredited institution. Additional exam requirements/recommendations for international students: required—TOEFL (minimum score 550 paper-based; 79 iBT). Electronic applications accepted.

Florida International University, College of Engineering and Computing, Department of Civil and Environmental Engineering, Miami, FL 33175. Offers civil engineering (MS, PhD); environmental engineering (MS). *Program availability:* Part-time, evening/weekend, online learning. *Faculty:* 25 full-time (7 women), 15 part-time/adjunct (2 women). *Students:* 87 full-time (27 women), 32 part-time (8 women); includes 31 minority (3 Black or African American, non-Hispanic/Latino; 1 Asian, non-Hispanic/Latino; 26 Hispanic/Latino; 1 Two or more races, non-Hispanic/Latino), 81 international. Average age 30. 132 applicants, 48% accepted, 30 enrolled. In 2019, 20 master's, 8 doctorates awarded. Terminal master's awarded for partial completion of doctoral program. *Degree requirements:* For master's, thesis or alternative; for doctorate, comprehensive exam, thesis/dissertation. *Entrance requirements:* For master's, bachelor's degree in related field, 3 letters of recommendation, minimum GPA of 3.0; for doctorate, GRE General Test, minimum graduate GPA of 3.3, 3 letters of recommendation, master's degree, resume, statement of purpose. Additional exam requirements/recommendations for international students: required—TOEFL (minimum score 550 paper-based; 80 iBT). *Application deadline:* For fall admission, 6/1 for domestic students, 4/1 for international students; for spring admission, 10/1 for domestic students, 9/1 for international students. Applications are processed on a rolling basis. Application fee: $30. Electronic applications accepted. *Expenses: Tuition, area resident:* Full-time $8912; part-time $446 per credit hour. Tuition, state resident: full-time $8912; part-time $446 per credit hour. Tuition, nonresident: full-time $21,393; part-time $992 per credit hour. *Required fees:* $2194. *Financial support:* Federal Work-Study, institutionally sponsored loans, scholarships/grants, health care benefits, and unspecified assistantships available. Financial award application deadline: 3/1; financial award applicants required to submit FAFSA. *Unit head:* Dr. Atorod Azizinamini, Chair, 305-348-2824, Fax: 305-348-2802, E-mail: aazizina@fiu.edu. *Application contact:* Nanett Rojas, Manager, Admissions Operations, 305-348-7464, Fax: 305-348-7441, E-mail: gradadm@fiu.edu.
Website: http://cec.fiu.edu

Florida State University, The Graduate School, FAMU-FSU College of Engineering, Department of Civil and Environmental Engineering, Tallahassee, FL 32306. Offers M Eng, MS, PhD. *Program availability:* Part-time. *Faculty:* 17 full-time (2 women), 3 part-time/adjunct (0 women). *Students:* 63 full-time (20 women); includes 10 minority (6 Black or African American, non-Hispanic/Latino; 2 Asian, non-Hispanic/Latino; 2 Hispanic/Latino), 41 international. Average age 23. 182 applicants, 41% accepted, 20 enrolled. In 2019, 10 master's, 4 doctorates awarded. *Degree requirements:* For master's, comprehensive exam, thesis optional; for doctorate, thesis/dissertation. *Entrance requirements:* For master's, GRE General Test (minimum score 1000 in old version), BS in engineering or related field, minimum GPA of 3.0; for doctorate, GRE General Test, master's degree in engineering or related field, minimum GPA of 3.0. Additional exam requirements/recommendations for international students: required—TOEFL (minimum score 550 paper-based; 80 iBT); recommended—IELTS (minimum score 6.5). *Application deadline:* For fall admission, 7/1 for domestic and international students; for spring admission, 11/1 for domestic and international students; for summer admission, 3/1 for domestic and international students. Applications are processed on a rolling basis. Application fee: $30. Electronic applications accepted. *Financial support:* In 2019–20, 55 students received support, including 24 research assistantships with full tuition reimbursements available, 20 teaching assistantships with full tuition reimbursements available; fellowships with full tuition reimbursements available, Federal Work-Study, scholarships/grants, tuition waivers (full), and unspecified assistantships also available. Financial award application deadline: 3/1; financial award applicants required to submit FAFSA. *Unit head:* Dr. Lisa Spainhour, Chair and Professor, 850-410-6143, Fax: 850-410-6142, E-mail: spainhou@eng.famu.fsu.edu. *Application contact:* Mable Johnson, Office Manager, 850-410-6139, Fax: 850-410-6292, E-mail: mjohnson5@eng.famu.fsu.edu.
Website: http://www.eng.famu.fsu.edu/cee/

George Mason University, Volgenau School of Engineering, Sid and Reva Dewberry Department of Civil, Environmental, and Infrastructure Engineering, Fairfax, VA 22030. Offers construction project management (MS); transportation engineering (PhD). *Degree requirements:* For master's, thesis (for some programs), 30 credits, departmental seminars; for doctorate, thesis/dissertation, qualifying exams. *Entrance requirements:* For master's, GRE, photocopy of passport; 2 official college transcripts; resume; official bank statement; proof of financial support; expanded goals statement; self-evaluation form; BS in engineering or other related science; 3 letters of recommendation; for doctorate, GRE (for those who received degree outside of the U.S.), photocopy of passport; 2 official college transcripts; resume; official bank statement; proof of financial support; expanded goals statement; self-evaluation form; baccalaureate degree in engineering or related science; master's degree (preferred); 3 letters of recommendation. Additional exam requirements/recommendations for international students: required—TOEFL (minimum score 575 paper-based; 88 iBT), IELTS (minimum score 6.5), PTE (minimum score 59). Electronic applications accepted. *Expenses:* Contact institution.

The George Washington University, School of Engineering and Applied Science, Department of Civil and Environmental Engineering, Washington, DC 20052. Offers MS, PhD, App Sc, Engr, Graduate Certificate. *Program availability:* Part-time, evening/weekend. *Degree requirements:* For master's, thesis optional; for doctorate, thesis/dissertation, final and qualifying exams. *Entrance requirements:* For master's, appropriate bachelor's degree, minimum GPA of 3.0; for doctorate, GRE (if highest earned degree is BS), appropriate bachelor's or master's degree, minimum GPA of 3.4; for other advanced degree, appropriate master's degree, minimum GPA of 3.0. Additional exam requirements/recommendations for international students: required—TOEFL or The George Washington University English as a Foreign Language Test.

Georgia Institute of Technology, Graduate Studies, College of Engineering, School of Civil and Environmental Engineering, Atlanta, GA 30332. Offers civil engineering (MS, PhD); engineering science and mechanics (MS, PhD); environmental engineering (MS, PhD). *Program availability:* Part-time. *Faculty:* 50 full-time (13 women), 3 part-time/

adjunct (0 women). *Students:* 350 full-time (117 women), 46 part-time (16 women); includes 48 minority (8 Black or African American, non-Hispanic/Latino; 22 Asian, non-Hispanic/Latino; 16 Hispanic/Latino; 2 Two or more races, non-Hispanic/Latino; 260 international. Average age 26. 758 applicants, 55% accepted, 123 enrolled. In 2019, 150 master's, 32 doctorates awarded. Terminal master's awarded for partial completion of doctoral program. *Degree requirements:* For master's, thesis optional; for doctorate, comprehensive exam, thesis/dissertation. *Entrance requirements:* For master's and doctorate, GRE. Additional exam requirements/recommendations for international students: required—TOEFL (minimum score 577 paper-based; 90 iBT), IELTS (minimum score 7), TOEFL is the preferred method with the requirements shown on the programs. *Application deadline:* For fall admission, 12/15 for domestic and international students; for spring admission, 8/31 for domestic and international students; for summer admission, 12/15 for domestic and international students. Applications are processed on a rolling basis. Application fee: $75 ($85 for international students). Electronic applications accepted. *Expenses: Tuition, area resident:* Full-time $14,064; part-time $586 per credit hour. Tuition, state resident: full-time $14,064; part-time $586 per credit hour. Tuition, nonresident: full-time $29,140; part-time $1215 per credit hour. *International tuition:* $29,140 full-time. *Required fees:* $2024; $840 per semester. $2096. Tuition and fees vary according to course load. *Financial support:* In 2019–20, 16 fellowships, 166 research assistantships, 26 teaching assistantships were awarded; career-related internships or fieldwork, Federal Work-Study, institutionally sponsored loans, tuition waivers (full and partial), and unspecified assistantships also available. Support available to part-time students. Financial award application deadline: 7/1; financial award applicants required to submit FAFSA. *Unit head:* Donald Webster, School Chair, 404-894-2201, Fax: 404-894-2278, E-mail: dwebster@ce.gatech.edu. *Application contact:* Marla Bruner, Director of Graduate Studies, 404-894-1610, Fax: 404-894-1609, E-mail: gradinfo@mail.gatech.edu. Website: https://ce.gatech.edu/

Georgia Southern University, Jack N. Averitt College of Graduate Studies, Allen E. Paulson College of Engineering and Computing, Department of Civil Engineering and Construction, Statesboro, GA 30458. Offers MSAE. *Faculty:* 17 full-time (2 women), 1 part-time/adjunct (0 women). *Students:* 8 full-time (1 woman), 6 part-time (3 women); includes 5 minority (3 Black or African American, non-Hispanic/Latino; 1 Hispanic/Latino; 1 Two or more races, non-Hispanic/Latino), 8 international. Average age 27. 12 applicants, 83% accepted, 6 enrolled. In 2019, 4 master's awarded. *Degree requirements:* For master's, comprehensive exam, thesis (for some programs). *Entrance requirements:* For master's, undergraduate major or equivalent in proposed study area. Additional exam requirements/recommendations for international students: required—TOEFL (minimum score 550 paper-based; 80 iBT), IELTS (minimum score 6). *Application deadline:* For fall admission, 3/1 priority date for domestic and international students; for spring admission, 10/1 priority date for domestic students, 10/1 for international students. Applications are processed on a rolling basis. Application fee: $50. Electronic applications accepted. *Expenses: Tuition, area resident:* Full-time $4986; part-time $277 per credit hour. Tuition, nonresident: full-time $19,890; part-time $1105 per credit hour. *International tuition:* $19,890 full-time. *Required fees:* $2114; $1057 per semester. $1057 per semester. Tuition and fees vary according to course load, campus/location and program. *Financial support:* In 2019–20, 11 students received support. Applicants required to submit FAFSA. *Unit head:* Dr. Francisco Cubas, Program Coordinator, 912-478-1894, E-mail: fcubassuazo@georgiasouthern.edu. *Application contact:* Dr. Francisco Cubas, Program Coordinator, 912-478-1894, E-mail: fcubassuazo@georgiasouthern.edu. Website: http://ceit.georgiasouthern.edu/cecm/

Howard University, College of Engineering, Architecture, and Computer Sciences, School of Engineering and Computer Science, Department of Civil Engineering, Washington, DC 20059-0002. Offers M Eng. *Degree requirements:* For master's, comprehensive exam, thesis. *Entrance requirements:* For master's, GRE General Test, minimum GPA of 3.0, bachelor's degree in engineering or related field. Additional exam requirements/recommendations for international students: required—TOEFL. Electronic applications accepted.

Idaho State University, Graduate School, College of Science and Engineering, Department of Civil and Environmental Engineering, Pocatello, ID 83209-8060. Offers civil engineering (MS); environmental engineering (MS); environmental science and management (MS). *Program availability:* Part-time. *Degree requirements:* For master's, comprehensive exam (for some programs), thesis optional, thesis project, 2 semesters of seminar. *Entrance requirements:* For master's, GRE. Additional exam requirements/recommendations for international students: required—TOEFL (minimum score 550 paper-based; 80 iBT). Electronic applications accepted.

Illinois Institute of Technology, Graduate College, Armour College of Engineering, Department of Civil, Architectural and Environmental Engineering, Chicago, IL 60616. Offers architectural engineering (M Arch E); civil engineering (MS, PhD), including architectural engineering (MS), construction engineering and management (MS), geoenvironmental engineering (MS), geotechnical engineering (MS), structural engineering (MS), transportation engineering (MS); construction engineering and management (MCEM); environmental engineering (M Env E, MS, PhD); geoenvironmental engineering (M Geoenv E); geotechnical engineering (MGE); infrastructure engineering and management (MPW); structural engineering (MSE); transportation engineering (M Trans E). *Program availability:* Part-time, evening/weekend, online learning. Terminal master's awarded for partial completion of doctoral program. *Degree requirements:* For master's, thesis (for some programs); for doctorate, comprehensive exam, thesis/dissertation. *Entrance requirements:* For master's, GRE General Test (minimum score 900 Quantitative and Verbal, 2.5 Analytical Writing), minimum undergraduate GPA of 3.0; for doctorate, GRE General Test (minimum score 1000 Quantitative and Verbal, 3.0 Analytical Writing), minimum undergraduate GPA of 3.0. Additional exam requirements/recommendations for international students: required—TOEFL (minimum score 550 paper-based; 80 iBT). Electronic applications accepted.

Instituto Tecnológico y de Estudios Superiores de Monterrey, Campus Monterrey, Graduate and Research Division, Programs in Engineering, Monterrey, Mexico. Offers applied statistics (M Eng); artificial intelligence (PhD); automation engineering (M Eng); chemical engineering (M Eng); civil engineering (M Eng); electrical engineering (M Eng); electronic engineering (M Eng); environmental engineering (M Eng); industrial engineering (M Eng, PhD); manufacturing engineering (M Eng); mechanical engineering (M Eng); systems and quality engineering (M Eng). *Program availability:* Part-time, evening/weekend. Terminal master's awarded for partial completion of doctoral program. *Degree requirements:* For master's, one foreign language, thesis; for doctorate, one foreign language, thesis/dissertation. *Entrance requirements:* For master's, EXADEP; for doctorate, GRE, master's degree in related field. Additional exam requirements/recommendations for international students: required—TOEFL.

Iowa State University of Science and Technology, Department of Civil and Construction Engineering, Ames, IA 50011. Offers civil engineering (MS, PhD), including civil engineering materials, construction engineering and management, environmental engineering, geotechnical engineering, structural engineering, transportation engineering. *Degree requirements:* For master's, thesis or alternative; for doctorate,

thesis/dissertation. *Entrance requirements:* For master's and doctorate, GRE General Test. Additional exam requirements/recommendations for international students: required—TOEFL (minimum score 550 paper-based; 82 iBT), IELTS (minimum score 6.5). Electronic applications accepted.

Jackson State University, Graduate School, College of Science, Engineering and Technology, Department of Civil and Environmental Engineering and Industrial Systems and Technology, Jackson, MS 39217. Offers civil engineering (MS, PhD); coastal engineering (MS, PhD); environmental engineering (MS, PhD); hazardous materials management (MS); technology education (MS Ed). *Program availability:* Part-time, evening/weekend. *Degree requirements:* For master's, comprehensive exam, thesis or alternative. *Entrance requirements:* For master's, GRE General Test. Additional exam requirements/recommendations for international students: required—TOEFL (minimum score 520 paper-based; 67 iBT).

Johns Hopkins University, Engineering Program for Professionals, Part-time Program in Civil Engineering, Baltimore, MD 21218. Offers MCE, Graduate Certificate. *Program availability:* Part-time, evening/weekend, 100% online, blended/hybrid learning. *Entrance requirements:* Additional exam requirements/recommendations for international students: required—TOEFL (minimum score 600 paper-based; 100 iBT). Electronic applications accepted.

Johns Hopkins University, G. W. C. Whiting School of Engineering, Department of Civil Engineering, Baltimore, MD 21218. Offers MSE, PhD. *Degree requirements:* For master's, thesis (for some programs); for doctorate, comprehensive exam, thesis/dissertation, qualifying and oral exams. *Entrance requirements:* For master's and doctorate, GRE General Test, 3 letters of recommendation, statement of purpose, transcripts. Additional exam requirements/recommendations for international students: required—TOEFL (minimum score 600 paper-based, 100 iBT) or IELTS (7). Electronic applications accepted.

Johns Hopkins University, G. W. C. Whiting School of Engineering, Master of Science in Engineering Management Program, Baltimore, MD 21218. Offers biomaterials (MSEM); civil engineering (MSEM); communications science (MSEM); computer science (MSEM); environmental systems analysis, economics and public policy (MSEM); fluid mechanics (MSEM); materials science and engineering (MSEM); mechanical engineering (MSEM); mechanics and materials (MSEM); nano-biotechnology (MSEM); nanomaterials and nanotechnology (MSEM); operations research (MSEM); probability and statistics (MSEM); smart product and device design (MSEM). *Entrance requirements:* For master's, GRE, 3 letters of recommendation, statement of purpose, transcripts. Additional exam requirements/recommendations for international students: required—TOEFL (minimum score 600 paper-based, 100 iBT) or IELTS (7). Electronic applications accepted.

Kansas State University, Graduate School, College of Engineering, Department of Civil Engineering, Manhattan, KS 66506. Offers civil engineering (MS, PhD); environmental engineering (MS, PhD); geotechnical engineering (MS, PhD); structural engineering (MS, PhD); transportation engineering (MS, PhD); water resources engineering (MS, PhD). *Program availability:* Part-time, evening/weekend, online learning. *Degree requirements:* For master's, thesis or alternative; for doctorate, thesis/dissertation. *Entrance requirements:* For master's, GRE General Test, bachelor's degree or course work in related engineering fields; for doctorate, GRE General Test. Additional exam requirements/recommendations for international students: required—TOEFL (minimum score 550 paper-based; 79 iBT). Electronic applications accepted.

Kennesaw State University, Southern Polytechnic College of Engineering and Engineering Technology, Program in Civil Engineering, Kennesaw, GA 30144. Offers environmental engineering (MS); geotechnical engineering (MS); structural engineering (MS); transportation and pavement engineering (MS); water resources engineering (MS). *Program availability:* Online learning. *Students:* 9 full-time (2 women), 30 part-time (4 women); includes 20 minority (9 Black or African American, non-Hispanic/Latino; 5 Asian, non-Hispanic/Latino; 5 Hispanic/Latino; 1 Two or more races, non-Hispanic/Latino), 3 international. Average age 34. 12 applicants, 92% accepted, 8 enrolled. In 2019, 12 master's awarded. *Degree requirements:* For master's, thesis optional. *Entrance requirements:* Additional exam requirements/recommendations for international students: required—TOEFL (minimum score 80 iBT), IELTS (minimum score 6.5). *Application deadline:* For fall admission, 11/1 for domestic and international students; for spring admission, 4/1 for domestic and international students. Applications are processed on a rolling basis. Application fee: $60. Electronic applications accepted. *Expenses: Tuition, area resident:* Full-time $7104; part-time $296 per credit hour. Tuition, state resident: full-time $7104; part-time $296 per credit hour. Tuition, nonresident: full-time $25,584; part-time $1066 per credit hour. *International tuition:* $25,584 full-time. *Required fees:* $2006; $1706 per unit. $853 per semester. *Unit head:* Metin Oguzmert, Coordinator, 470-578-5083, E-mail: moguzmer@kennesaw.edu. *Application contact:* Admissions Counselor, 470-578-4377, E-mail: ksugrad@kennesaw.edu. Website: http://engineering.kennesaw.edu/civil-construction/degrees/ms-civil-engineering.php

Lawrence Technological University, College of Engineering, Southfield, MI 48075-1058. Offers architectural engineering (MS); automotive engineering (MS); biomedical engineering (MS); civil engineering (MA, MS, PhD), including environmental engineering (MS), geotechnical engineering (MS), structural engineering (MS), transportation engineering (MS), water resource engineering (MS); construction engineering management (MA); electrical and computer engineering (MS); engineering management (MEM); engineering technology (MS); fire engineering (MS); industrial engineering (MS), including healthcare systems; manufacturing systems (ME); mechanical engineering (MS, DE, PhD), including automotive engineering (MS), energy engineering (MS), manufacturing (DE), solid mechanics (MS), thermal/fluid systems (MS); mechatronic systems engineering (MS). *Program availability:* Part-time, evening/weekend. *Faculty:* 23 full-time (2 women), 20 part-time/adjunct (1 woman). *Students:* 14 full-time (5 women), 286 part-time (54 women); includes 26 minority (13 Black or African American, non-Hispanic/Latino; 8 Asian, non-Hispanic/Latino; 3 Hispanic/Latino; 2 Two or more races, non-Hispanic/Latino), 150 international. Average age 29. 384 applicants, 58% accepted, 74 enrolled. In 2019, 223 master's, 7 doctorates awarded. Terminal master's awarded for partial completion of doctoral program. *Degree requirements:* For master's, thesis optional; for doctorate, comprehensive exam, thesis/dissertation optional. *Entrance requirements:* Additional exam requirements/recommendations for international students: required—TOEFL (minimum score 550 paper-based; 79 iBT), IELTS (minimum score 6.5). *Application deadline:* For fall admission, 5/24 for international students; for spring admission, 10/13 for international students; for summer admission, 2/18 for international students. Applications are processed on a rolling basis. Application fee: $50. Electronic applications accepted. *Expenses: Tuition:* Full-time $16,618; part-time $8309 per year. *Required fees:* $600; $600. *Financial support:* In 2019–20, 21 students received support. Unspecified assistantships available. Financial award application deadline: 4/1; financial award applicants required to submit FAFSA. *Unit head:* Dr. Nabil Grace, Dean, 248-204-2500, Fax: 248-204-2509, E-mail: engrdean@ltu.edu. *Application contact:* Jane Rohrback, Director of Admissions, 248-204-3160, Fax: 248-204-2228, E-mail: admissions@ltu.edu. Website: http://www.ltu.edu/engineering/index.asp

Civil Engineering

Lehigh University, P.C. Rossin College of Engineering and Applied Science, Department of Civil and Environmental Engineering, Bethlehem, PA 18015. Offers M Eng, MS, PhD. *Program availability:* Part-time, blended/hybrid learning. *Faculty:* 19 full-time (3 women). *Students:* 60 full-time (15 women), 10 part-time (3 women); includes 5 minority (1 Asian, non-Hispanic/Latino; 4 Hispanic/Latino), 47 international. Average age 28. 141 applicants, 46% accepted, 11 enrolled. In 2019, 28 master's, 8 doctorates awarded. *Degree requirements:* For master's, thesis (for some programs); for doctorate, comprehensive exam, thesis/dissertation. *Entrance requirements:* For master's and doctorate, GRE. Additional exam requirements/recommendations for international students: required—TOEFL (minimum score 550 paper-based; 79 iBT), IELTS (minimum score 6.5). *Application deadline:* For fall admission, 7/15 priority date for domestic and international students; for spring admission, 12/1 priority date for domestic and international students; for summer admission, 5/30 priority date for domestic and international students. Application fee: $75. Electronic applications accepted. Application fee is waived when completed online. *Financial support:* In 2019–20, 30 students received support, including 3 fellowships with full tuition reimbursements available (averaging $22,050 per year), 20 research assistantships with full and partial tuition reimbursements available (averaging $29,400 per year), 7 teaching assistantships with full tuition reimbursements available (averaging $22,050 per year); unspecified assistantships also available. Financial award application deadline: 1/15; financial award applicants required to submit FAFSA. *Unit head:* Shamin Pakzad, Chair, 610-758-3566, E-mail: snp208@lehigh.edu. *Application contact:* Renee Keiderling, Graduate Coordinator, 610-758-3530, E-mail: rmk419@lehigh.edu.
Website: http://www.lehigh.edu/~incee/

Louisiana State University and Agricultural & Mechanical College, Graduate School, College of Engineering, Department of Civil and Environmental Engineering, Baton Rouge, LA 70803. Offers environmental engineering (MSCE, PhD); geotechnical engineering (MSCE, PhD); structural engineering and mechanics (MSCE, PhD); transportation engineering (MSCE, PhD); water resources (MSCE, PhD).

Loyola Marymount University, Frank R. Seaver College of Science and Engineering, Program in Civil Engineering, Los Angeles, CA 90045. Offers MSE. *Program availability:* Part-time, evening/weekend. *Students:* 12 full-time (4 women); includes 6 minority (3 Asian, non-Hispanic/Latino; 2 Hispanic/Latino; 1 Two or more races, non-Hispanic/Latino), 3 international. Average age 33. 20 applicants, 25% accepted, 4 enrolled. In 2019, 8 master's awarded. *Entrance requirements:* For master's, graduate admissions application; undergrad GPA of at least 3.0; 2 letters of recommendation; letter of intent; official transcript; college-level calculus and general chemistry; 4 college-level life and physical science courses. Additional exam requirements/recommendations for international students: required—TOEFL, IELTS. *Application deadline:* Applications are processed on a rolling basis. Application fee: $50. Electronic applications accepted. *Financial support:* Fellowships, research assistantships, teaching assistantships, Federal Work-Study, scholarships/grants, and unspecified assistantships available. Support available to part-time students. Financial award applicants required to submit FAFSA. *Unit head:* Dr. Joseph Reichenberger, Graduate Program Director, Civil Engineering and Environmental Science, 310-338-2830, E-mail: joseph.reichenberger@lmu.edu. *Application contact:* Ammar Dalal, Assistant Vice Provost for Graduate Enrollment, 310-338-2721, Fax: 310-338-6086, E-mail: graduateadmission@lmu.edu.

Manhattan College, Graduate Programs, School of Engineering, Program in Civil Engineering, Riverdale, NY 10471. Offers MS. *Program availability:* Part-time, evening/weekend. *Degree requirements:* For master's, thesis or alternative. *Entrance requirements:* For master's, GRE (recommended), minimum GPA of 3.0. Additional exam requirements/recommendations for international students: required—TOEFL (minimum score 550 paper-based; 80 iBT), IELTS (minimum score 6).

Marquette University, Graduate School, College of Engineering, Department of Civil and Environmental Engineering, Milwaukee, WI 53201-1881. Offers construction engineering and management (MS, PhD, Certificate); environmental engineering (MS, PhD); structural design (Certificate); structural engineering and structural mechanics (MS, PhD); transportation (Certificate); transportation engineering and materials (MS, PhD); waste and wastewater treatment processes (Certificate); water resources engineering (Certificate). *Program availability:* Part-time, evening/weekend. Terminal master's awarded for partial completion of doctoral program. *Degree requirements:* For master's, comprehensive exam (for some programs), thesis or alternative; for doctorate, thesis/dissertation. *Entrance requirements:* For master's, GRE General Test (recommended), minimum GPA of 3.0, official transcripts from all current and previous colleges/universities except Marquette, three letters of recommendation; for doctorate, GRE General Test, minimum GPA of 3.0, official transcripts from all current and previous colleges/universities except Marquette, three letters of recommendation, brief statement of purpose, submission of any English language publications authored by applicant (strongly recommended). Additional exam requirements/recommendations for international students: required—TOEFL (minimum score 530 paper-based). Electronic applications accepted.

Massachusetts Institute of Technology, School of Engineering, Department of Civil and Environmental Engineering, Cambridge, MA 02139. Offers biological oceanography (PhD, Sc D); chemical oceanography (PhD, Sc D); civil and environmental engineering (M Eng, SM, PhD, Sc D); civil and environmental systems (PhD, Sc D); civil engineering (PhD, Sc D, CE); civil engineering and computation (PhD); coastal engineering (PhD, Sc D); construction engineering and management (PhD, Sc D); environmental biology (PhD, Sc D); environmental chemistry (PhD, Sc D); environmental engineering (PhD, Sc D); environmental engineering and computation (PhD); environmental fluid mechanics (PhD, Sc D); geotechnical and geoenvironmental engineering (PhD, Sc D); hydrology (PhD, Sc D); information technology (PhD, Sc D); oceanographic engineering (PhD, Sc D); structures and materials (PhD, Sc D); transportation (PhD, Sc D); SM/MBA. *Degree requirements:* For master's, thesis; for doctorate, comprehensive exam, thesis/dissertation; for CE, comprehensive exam, thesis. *Entrance requirements:* For master's, doctorate, and CE, GRE General Test. Additional exam requirements/recommendations for international students: required—TOEFL, IELTS. Electronic applications accepted.

McGill University, Faculty of Graduate and Postdoctoral Studies, Faculty of Engineering, Department of Civil Engineering and Applied Mechanics, Montréal, QC H3A 2T5, Canada. Offers environmental engineering (M Eng, M Sc, PhD); fluid mechanics (M Sc); fluid mechanics and hydraulic engineering (M Eng, PhD); materials engineering (M Eng, PhD); rehabilitation of urban infrastructure (M Eng, PhD); soil behavior (M Eng, PhD); soil mechanics and foundations (M Eng, PhD); structures and structural mechanics (M Eng, PhD); water resources (M Sc); water resources engineering (M Eng, PhD).

McMaster University, School of Graduate Studies, Faculty of Engineering, Department of Civil Engineering, Hamilton, ON L8S 4M2, Canada. Offers M Eng, MA Sc, PhD. *Degree requirements:* For master's, thesis; for doctorate, comprehensive exam, thesis/dissertation. *Entrance requirements:* Additional exam requirements/recommendations for international students: required—TOEFL (minimum score 550 paper-based).

McNeese State University, Doré School of Graduate Studies, College of Engineering and Computer Science, Master of Engineering Program, Lake Charles, LA 70609. Offers chemical engineering (M Eng); civil engineering (M Eng); electrical engineering (M Eng); engineering management (M Eng); mechanical engineering (M Eng). *Program availability:* Part-time, evening/weekend. *Entrance requirements:* For master's, GRE, baccalaureate degree, minimum overall GPA of 3.0. Additional exam requirements/recommendations for international students: required—TOEFL (minimum score 560 paper-based; 83 iBT).

Memorial University of Newfoundland, School of Graduate Studies, Faculty of Engineering and Applied Science, St. John's, NL A1C 5S7, Canada. Offers civil engineering (M Eng, PhD); electrical and computer engineering (M Eng, PhD); mechanical engineering (M Eng, PhD); ocean and naval architecture engineering (M Eng, PhD). *Program availability:* Part-time. *Degree requirements:* For master's, thesis; for doctorate, comprehensive exam, thesis/dissertation, oral thesis defense. *Entrance requirements:* For master's, 2nd class degree; for doctorate, master's degree in engineering. Electronic applications accepted.

Merrimack College, School of Science and Engineering, North Andover, MA 01845-5800. Offers civil engineering (MS); computer science (MS); data science (MS); engineering management (MS); mechanical engineering (MS), including engineering management. *Program availability:* Part-time, evening/weekend, 100% online. *Degree requirements:* For master's, comprehensive exam, thesis optional, internship or capstone (for some programs). *Entrance requirements:* For master's, official college transcripts, resume, personal statement, 2 recommendations. Additional exam requirements/recommendations for international students: required—TOEFL (minimum score 84 iBT), IELTS (minimum score 6.5), PTE (minimum score 56). Electronic applications accepted. Application fee is waived when completed online. *Expenses:* Contact institution.

Michigan State University, The Graduate School, College of Engineering, Department of Civil and Environmental Engineering, East Lansing, MI 48824. Offers civil engineering (MS, PhD); environmental engineering (MS, PhD); environmental engineering-environmental toxicology (PhD). *Program availability:* Part-time. *Entrance requirements:* Additional exam requirements/recommendations for international students: required—TOEFL. Electronic applications accepted.

Michigan Technological University, Graduate School, College of Engineering, Department of Civil and Environmental Engineering, Houghton, MI 49931. Offers civil engineering (MS, PhD); environmental engineering (MS, PhD); environmental engineering science (MS). *Program availability:* Part-time, 100% online. *Faculty:* 37 full-time, 14 part-time/adjunct (4 women). *Students:* 48 full-time (23 women), 22 part-time (7 women); includes 5 minority (2 Black or African American, non-Hispanic/Latino; 1 Hispanic/Latino; 2 Two or more races, non-Hispanic/Latino), 29 international. Average age 28. 297 applicants, 36% accepted, 23 enrolled. In 2019, 37 master's, 3 doctorates awarded. *Degree requirements:* For master's, comprehensive exam (for some programs), thesis (for some programs); for doctorate, comprehensive exam, thesis/dissertation. *Entrance requirements:* For master's and doctorate, GRE (Michigan Tech students exempt), statement of purpose, personal statement, official transcripts, 2 letters of recommendation. Additional exam requirements/recommendations for international students: required—TOEFL (minimum score 100 iBT), IELTS (minimum score 7), TOEFL (recommended minimum score 100 iBT) or IELTS (recommended minimum score of 7.0). *Application deadline:* For fall admission, 1/15 priority date for domestic and international students; for spring admission, 9/15 priority date for domestic and international students; for summer admission, 2/15 priority date for domestic and international students. Applications are processed on a rolling basis. Application fee: $0. Electronic applications accepted. *Expenses:* $1,212 per credit. *Financial support:* In 2019–20, 47 students received support, including 7 fellowships with tuition reimbursements available (averaging $16,590 per year), 16 research assistantships with tuition reimbursements available (averaging $16,590 per year), 5 teaching assistantships with tuition reimbursements available (averaging $16,590 per year); career-related internships or fieldwork, Federal Work-Study, scholarships/grants, health care benefits, unspecified assistantships, and cooperative program also available. Financial award applicants required to submit FAFSA. *Unit head:* Dr. Audra N. Morse, Chair, 906-487-3240, Fax: 906-487-2943, E-mail: anmorse@mtu.edu. *Application contact:* Angela Keranen, Administrative Aide, 906-487-2474, Fax: 906-487-2943, E-mail: amkerane@mtu.edu.
Website: http://www.mtu.edu/cee/

Milwaukee School of Engineering, MS Program in Civil Engineering, Milwaukee, WI 53202-3109. Offers MS. *Program availability:* Part-time, evening/weekend. *Degree requirements:* For master's, thesis. *Entrance requirements:* For master's, GRE General Test if undergraduate GPA is less than 3.0, 2 letters of recommendation; BS in civil engineering or closely-related area from ABET-accredited program. Additional exam requirements/recommendations for international students: required—TOEFL (minimum score 90 iBT), IELTS (minimum score 7). Electronic applications accepted.

Mississippi State University, Bagley College of Engineering, Department of Civil and Environmental Engineering, Mississippi State, MS 39762. Offers MS, PhD. *Program availability:* Part-time, blended/hybrid learning. *Faculty:* 9 full-time (0 women). *Students:* 15 full-time (6 women), 80 part-time (19 women); includes 20 minority (6 Black or African American, non-Hispanic/Latino; 4 Asian, non-Hispanic/Latino; 10 Hispanic/Latino), 15 international. Average age 34. 74 applicants, 42% accepted, 10 enrolled. In 2019, 22 master's, 5 doctorates awarded. Terminal master's awarded for partial completion of doctoral program. *Degree requirements:* For master's, thesis optional; for doctorate, thesis/dissertation, research on an approved topic, minimum 20 hours of dissertation research. *Entrance requirements:* For master's and doctorate, GRE (for graduates from program not accredited by EAC/ABET), minimum GPA of 3.0. Additional exam requirements/recommendations for international students: required—TOEFL (minimum score 550 paper-based; 79 iBT); recommended—IELTS (minimum score 6.5). *Application deadline:* For fall admission, 7/1 for domestic students, 5/1 for international students; for spring admission, 11/1 for domestic students, 9/1 for international students. Applications are processed on a rolling basis. Application fee: $60 ($80 for international students). Electronic applications accepted. *Expenses: Tuition, area resident:* Full-time $8880; part-time $456 per credit hour. Tuition, state resident: full-time $8880. Tuition, nonresident: full-time $23,840; part-time $1236 per credit hour. *Required fees:* $110; $11.12 per credit hour. Tuition and fees vary according to course load. *Financial support:* In 2019–20, 6 research assistantships with full tuition reimbursements (averaging $16,239 per year), 6 teaching assistantships with full tuition reimbursements (averaging $14,854 per year) were awarded; Federal Work-Study, institutionally sponsored loans, and unspecified assistantships also available. Financial award application deadline: 4/1; financial award applicants required to submit FAFSA. *Unit head:* Dr. Dennis D. Truax, Department Head, 662-325-7187, Fax: 662-325-7189, E-mail: truax@cee.msstate.edu. *Application contact:* Angie Campbell, Admissions and Enrollment Assistant, 662-325-9514, E-mail: acampbell@grad.msstate.edu.
Website: http://www.cee.msstate.edu/

Missouri University of Science and Technology, Department of Civil, Architectural, and Environmental Engineering, Rolla, MO 65401. Offers civil engineering (MS, DE, PhD); environmental engineering (MS). *Program availability:* Part-time, evening/weekend. Terminal master's awarded for partial completion of doctoral program. *Degree requirements:* For master's, thesis optional; for doctorate, comprehensive exam, thesis/

dissertation. *Entrance requirements:* For master's, GRE General Test (minimum combined score 1100), minimum GPA of 3.0; for doctorate, GRE General Test (minimum score: verbal and quantitative 400, writing 3.5), minimum GPA of 3.0. Additional exam requirements/recommendations for international students: required—TOEFL (minimum score 550 paper-based). Electronic applications accepted. *Expenses:* Tuition, state resident: full-time $7839; part-time $435.50 per credit hour. Tuition, nonresident: full-time $22,169; part-time $1231.60 per credit hour. *International tuition:* $18,156.60 full-time. *Required fees:* $649.76. One-time fee: $119. Tuition and fees vary according to course load and program.

Montana State University, The Graduate School, College of Engineering, Department of Civil Engineering, Bozeman, MT 59717. Offers civil engineering (MS); construction engineering management (MCEM); engineering (PhD), including applied mechanics option, civil engineering option. *Program availability:* Part-time. *Degree requirements:* For master's, comprehensive exam, thesis (for some programs); for doctorate, comprehensive exam, thesis/dissertation. *Entrance requirements:* For master's and doctorate, GRE General Test. Additional exam requirements/recommendations for international students: required—TOEFL (minimum score 550 paper-based). Electronic applications accepted.

Morgan State University, School of Graduate Studies, Clarence M. Mitchell, Jr. School of Engineering, Baltimore, MD 21251. Offers civil engineering (M Eng, D Eng); electrical and computer engineering (M Eng, MS, D Eng); industrial and systems engineering (M Eng, D Eng); transportation and urban infrastructure studies (MS, PhD, Postbaccalaureate Certificate), including transportation. *Program availability:* Part-time, evening/weekend. *Faculty:* 35 full-time (8 women), 19 part-time/adjunct (4 women). *Students:* 113 full-time (34 women), 24 part-time (4 women); includes 88 minority (75 Black or African American, non-Hispanic/Latino; 8 Asian, non-Hispanic/Latino; 2 Hispanic/Latino; 3 Two or more races, non-Hispanic/Latino), 36 international. Average age 35. 78 applicants, 83% accepted, 26 enrolled. In 2019, 23 master's, 11 doctorates awarded. *Degree requirements:* For master's, thesis optional, comprehensive exam or equivalent; for doctorate, thesis/dissertation, comprehensive exam or equivalent. *Entrance requirements:* For master's, GRE, minimum undergraduate GPA of 2.5; for doctorate, GRE, minimum GPA of 3.0. Additional exam requirements/recommendations for international students: required—TOEFL (minimum score 550 paper-based). *Application deadline:* For fall admission, 2/1 priority date for domestic students; for spring admission, 10/1 priority date for domestic students. Applications are processed on a rolling basis. Application fee: $50 ($70 for international students). Electronic applications accepted. *Expenses:* Tuition, state resident: full-time $455; part-time $455 per credit hour. Tuition, nonresident: full-time $894; part-time $894 per credit hour. *Required fees:* $82; $82 per credit hour. *Financial support:* In 2019–20, 35 students received support. Fellowships with full and partial tuition reimbursements available, research assistantships with full and partial tuition reimbursements available, teaching assistantships with full and partial tuition reimbursements available, career-related internships or fieldwork, scholarships/grants, and unspecified assistantships available. Financial award application deadline: 2/1. *Unit head:* Dr. Craig Scott, Interim Dean, 443-885-3231, E-mail: craig.scott@morgan.edu. *Application contact:* Dr. Jahmaine Smith, Director of Admissions, 443-885-3185, Fax: 443-885-8226, E-mail: gradapply@morgan.edu.
Website: https://morgan.edu/soe

New York University, Tandon School of Engineering, Department of Civil and Urban Engineering, Major in Civil Engineering, New York, NY 10012-1019. Offers MS, PhD. *Program availability:* Part-time, evening/weekend. *Degree requirements:* For master's, comprehensive exam (for some programs); thesis (for some programs); for doctorate, comprehensive exam, thesis/dissertation, qualifying exam. *Entrance requirements:* For doctorate, MS in civil engineering. Additional exam requirements/recommendations for international students: required—TOEFL (minimum score 550 paper-based; 90 iBT); recommended—IELTS (minimum score 7). Electronic applications accepted.

North Carolina Agricultural and Technical State University, The Graduate College, College of Engineering, Department of Civil, Architectural and Environmental Engineering, Greensboro, NC 27411. Offers civil engineering (MSCE). *Program availability:* Part-time. *Degree requirements:* For master's, thesis optional. *Entrance requirements:* For master's, GRE General Test, GRE Subject Test (recommended). Additional exam requirements/recommendations for international students: required—TOEFL.

North Carolina State University, Graduate School, College of Engineering, Department of Civil, Construction, and Environmental Engineering, Raleigh, NC 27695. Offers civil engineering (MCE, MS, PhD); environmental engineering (MS). *Program availability:* Part-time, online learning. *Degree requirements:* For master's, thesis optional, oral exams; for doctorate, thesis/dissertation, oral exams. *Entrance requirements:* For master's, GRE General Test, minimum B average in major; for doctorate, GRE General Test. Additional exam requirements/recommendations for international students: required—TOEFL. Electronic applications accepted.

North Dakota State University, College of Graduate and Interdisciplinary Studies, College of Engineering, Department of Civil and Environmental Engineering, Fargo, ND 58102. Offers civil engineering (MS, PhD); environmental engineering (MS). *Program availability:* Part-time, online learning. *Degree requirements:* For master's, thesis; for doctorate, comprehensive exam, thesis/dissertation. *Entrance requirements:* Additional exam requirements/recommendations for international students: required—TOEFL (minimum score 525 paper-based; 71 iBT). Electronic applications accepted. Tuition and fees vary according to program and reciprocity agreements.

Northeastern University, College of Engineering, Boston, MA 02115-5096. Offers bioengineering (MS, PhD); chemical engineering (MS, PhD); civil engineering (MS, PhD); computer engineering (PhD); computer systems engineering (MS); electrical and computer engineering (MS); electrical and computer engineering leadership (MS); electrical engineering (PhD); energy systems (MS); engineering and public policy (MS); engineering management (MS, Certificate); environmental engineering (MS); industrial engineering (MS, PhD); information assurance (PhD); information systems (MS); interdisciplinary engineering (PhD); mechanical engineering (PhD); operations research (MS); telecommunication systems management (MS). *Program availability:* Part-time, online learning. Electronic applications accepted. *Expenses:* Contact institution.

Northern Arizona University, College of Engineering, Informatics, and Applied Sciences, Department of Civil Engineering, Construction Management and Environmental Engineering, Flagstaff, AZ 86011. Offers engineering (M Eng), including civil engineering, environmental engineering. *Program availability:* Part-time. *Degree requirements:* For master's, variable foreign language requirement, comprehensive exam (for some programs), thesis, individualized research. *Entrance requirements:* Additional exam requirements/recommendations for international students: required—TOEFL (minimum score 80 iBT), IELTS (minimum score 6.5). Electronic applications accepted.

Northwestern University, McCormick School of Engineering and Applied Science, Department of Civil and Environmental Engineering, Evanston, IL 60208-3109. Offers environmental engineering and science (MS, PhD); geotechnical engineering (MS, PhD); mechanics of materials and solids (MS, PhD); project management (MS);

structural engineering and materials (MS, PhD); transportation systems analysis and planning (MS, PhD). *Program availability:* Part-time. Terminal master's awarded for partial completion of doctoral program. *Degree requirements:* For master's, comprehensive exam (for some programs), thesis (for some programs); for doctorate, comprehensive exam, thesis/dissertation. *Entrance requirements:* For master's and doctorate, GRE General Test, minimum 2 letters of recommendation, transcripts from all academic institutions attended. Additional exam requirements/recommendations for international students: required—TOEFL (minimum score 577 paper-based; 90 iBT), IELTS (minimum score 7). Electronic applications accepted.

Norwich University, College of Graduate and Continuing Studies, Master of Civil Engineering Program, Northfield, VT 05663. Offers construction management (MCE); environmental (MCE); geotechnical (MCE); structural (MCE). *Program availability:* Evening/weekend, online only, mostly all online with a week-long residency requirement. *Degree requirements:* For master's, capstone. *Entrance requirements:* For master's, minimum undergraduate GPA of 2.75. Additional exam requirements/recommendations for international students: required—TOEFL (minimum score 550 paper-based; 80 iBT), IELTS (minimum score 6.5). Electronic applications accepted. *Expenses:* Contact institution.

The Ohio State University, Graduate School, College of Engineering, Department of Civil, Environmental and Geodetic Engineering, Columbus, OH 43210. Offers civil engineering (MS, PhD). *Entrance requirements:* For master's and doctorate, GRE General Test (for all applicants whose undergraduate GPA is below 3.0 or whose undergraduate degree is not from an accredited U.S.-ABET or Canadian-CEAB institution). Additional exam requirements/recommendations for international students: required—TOEFL (minimum score 550 paper-based; 79 iBT), Michigan English Language Assessment Battery (minimum score 82); recommended—IELTS (minimum score 7). Electronic applications accepted.

Ohio University, Graduate College, Russ College of Engineering and Technology, Department of Civil Engineering, Athens, OH 45701-2979. Offers civil engineering (PhD); construction engineering and management (MS); environmental (MS); geoenvironmental (MS); geotechnical (MS); mechanics (MS); structures (MS); transportation (MS); water resources (MS). *Program availability:* Part-time. *Degree requirements:* For master's, comprehensive exam (for some programs), thesis or alternative; for doctorate, comprehensive exam, thesis/dissertation. *Entrance requirements:* For master's, GRE General Test, minimum GPA of 3.0, 3 letters of recommendation; for doctorate, GRE General Test. Additional exam requirements/recommendations for international students: required—TOEFL (minimum score 550 paper-based; 80 iBT) or IELTS (minimum score 6.5). Electronic applications accepted.

Oklahoma State University, College of Engineering, Architecture and Technology, School of Civil and Environmental Engineering, Stillwater, OK 74078. Offers civil engineering (MS, PhD). *Faculty:* 16 full-time (1 woman), 1 (woman) part-time/adjunct. *Students:* 30 full-time (7 women), 40 part-time (10 women); includes 5 minority (3 American Indian or Alaska Native, non-Hispanic/Latino; 2 Two or more races, non-Hispanic/Latino), 40 international. Average age 28. 47 applicants, 49% accepted, 18 enrolled. In 2019, 11 master's, 6 doctorates awarded. *Entrance requirements:* For master's and doctorate, GRE or GMAT. Additional exam requirements/recommendations for international students: required—TOEFL (minimum score 550 paper-based; 79 iBT). *Application deadline:* For fall admission, 3/1 priority date for international students; for spring admission, 8/1 priority date for international students. Applications are processed on a rolling basis. Application fee: $50 ($75 for international students). Electronic applications accepted. *Expenses: Tuition, area resident:* Full-time $4148.10; part-time $2765.40. Tuition, state resident: full-time $4148.10; part-time $2765.40. Tuition, nonresident: full-time $15,775; part-time $10,516.80. *International tuition:* $15,775.20 full-time. *Required fees:* $2196.90; $122.05 per credit hour. Tuition and fees vary according to course load, campus/location and program. *Financial support:* In 2019–20, 51 research assistantships (averaging $1,915 per year), 1 teaching assistantship (averaging $2,000 per year) were awarded; career-related internships or fieldwork, Federal Work-Study, scholarships/grants, health care benefits, tuition waivers (partial), and unspecified assistantships also available. Support available to part-time students. Financial award application deadline: 3/1; financial award applicants required to submit FAFSA. *Unit head:* Dr. Norb Delatte, Department Head, 405-744-5190, Fax: 405-744-7554, E-mail: norb.delatte@okstate.edu. *Application contact:* Dr. Sheryl Tucker, Dean, 405-744-6368, Fax: 405-744-0355, E-mail: gradi@okstate.edu.
Website: http://cive.okstate.edu

Old Dominion University, Frank Batten College of Engineering and Technology, Program in Civil and Environmental Engineering, Norfolk, VA 23529. Offers D Eng, PhD. *Program availability:* Part-time, evening/weekend, blended/hybrid learning. *Degree requirements:* For doctorate, comprehensive exam, thesis/dissertation, candidacy exam. *Entrance requirements:* For doctorate, GRE, minimum GPA of 3.5. Electronic applications accepted. *Expenses:* Contact institution.

Old Dominion University, Frank Batten College of Engineering and Technology, Program in Civil Engineering, Norfolk, VA 23529. Offers civil engineering (ME, MS), including coastal engineering, geotechnical engineering, hydraulics and water resources, structural engineering, transportation engineering. *Program availability:* Part-time, evening/weekend, blended/hybrid learning. *Degree requirements:* For master's, comprehensive exam, thesis optional. *Entrance requirements:* For master's, GRE, minimum GPA of 3.0. Additional exam requirements/recommendations for international students: required—TOEFL (minimum score 550 paper-based, 80 iBT) or IELTS (6.5). Electronic applications accepted. *Expenses:* Contact institution.

Oregon State University, College of Engineering, Program in Civil Engineering, Corvallis, OR 97331. Offers civil engineering (M Eng, MS, PhD); coastal and ocean engineering (M Eng, MS, PhD); construction engineering management (M Eng, MS, PhD); engineering education (M Eng, MS, PhD); geomatics (M Eng, MS, PhD); geotechnical engineering (M Eng, MS, PhD); infrastructure materials (M Eng, MS, PhD); structural engineering (M Eng, MS, PhD); transportation engineering (M Eng). *Entrance requirements:* For master's and doctorate, GRE. Additional exam requirements/recommendations for international students: required—TOEFL (minimum score 80 iBT), IELTS (minimum score 6.5). *Expenses:* Contact institution.

Penn State Harrisburg, Graduate School, School of Science, Engineering and Technology, Middletown, PA 17057. Offers civil engineering (MS); computer science (MS); electrical engineering (M Eng, MS); engineering management (MPS); engineering science (M Eng); environmental engineering (M Eng); environmental pollution control (MEPC, MS); mechanical engineering (MS); structural engineering (Certificate). *Program availability:* Part-time, evening/weekend.

Penn State University Park, Graduate School, College of Engineering, Department of Civil and Environmental Engineering, University Park, PA 16802. Offers civil engineering (M Eng, MS, PhD); environmental engineering (M Eng, MS, PhD).

Polytechnic University of Puerto Rico, Graduate School, Hato Rey, PR 00918. Offers business administration (MBA), including computer information systems, general management, management of information systems, management of international enterprises; civil engineering (ME, MS); computer engineering (ME, MS); computer science (MCS, MS); electrical engineering (ME, MS); engineering management (MEM); environmental management (MEM); landscape architecture (M Land Arch); manufacturing competitiveness (MMC, MS); manufacturing engineering (ME, MS); mechanical engineering (M Mech E). *Accreditation:* ASLA. *Program availability:* Part-time, evening/weekend. *Entrance requirements:* For master's, 3 letters of recommendation.

Polytechnique Montréal, Graduate Programs, Department of Civil, Geological and Mining Engineering, Montréal, QC H3C 3A7, Canada. Offers civil, geological and mining engineering (DESS); environmental engineering (M Eng, M Sc A, PhD); geotechnical engineering (M Eng, M Sc A, PhD); hydraulics engineering (M Eng, M Sc A, PhD); structural engineering (M Eng, M Sc A, PhD); transportation engineering (M Eng, M Sc A, PhD). *Program availability:* Part-time. *Degree requirements:* For master's, one foreign language, thesis; for doctorate, one foreign language, thesis/dissertation. *Entrance requirements:* For master's, minimum GPA of 2.75; for doctorate, minimum GPA of 3.0.

Portland State University, Graduate Studies, College of Liberal Arts and Sciences, Systems Science Program, Portland, OR 97207-0751. Offers computational intelligence (Certificate); computer modeling and simulation (Certificate); systems science (MS); systems science/anthropology (PhD); systems science/business administration (PhD); systems science/civil engineering (PhD); systems science/economics (PhD); systems science/engineering management (PhD); systems science/general (PhD); systems science/mathematical sciences (PhD); systems science/mechanical engineering (PhD); systems science/psychology (PhD); systems science/sociology (PhD). *Program availability:* Part-time. *Faculty:* 2 full-time (0 women), 6 part-time/adjunct (1 woman). *Students:* 6 full-time (3 women), 25 part-time (8 women); includes 7 minority (2 Asian, non-Hispanic/Latino; 4 Hispanic/Latino; 1 Two or more races, non-Hispanic/Latino), 2 international. Average age 39. 25 applicants, 80% accepted, 15 enrolled. In 2019, 7 master's, 2 doctorates awarded. Terminal master's awarded for partial completion of doctoral program. *Degree requirements:* For master's, comprehensive exam (for some programs), thesis optional; for doctorate, variable foreign language requirement, comprehensive exam (for some programs), thesis/dissertation. *Entrance requirements:* For master's, GRE/GMAT (recommended), minimum GPA of 3.0 on undergraduate or graduate work, 2 letters of recommendation, statement of interest; for doctorate, GRE required, minimum GPA of 3.0 undergraduate, 3.25 graduate; 3 letters of recommendation; statement of interest. Additional exam requirements/recommendations for international students: required—TOEFL (minimum score 550 paper-based; 80 iBT). *Application deadline:* For fall admission, 3/15 priority date for domestic and international students. Application fee: $65. Electronic applications accepted. *Expenses: Tuition, area resident:* Full-time $13,020; part-time $6510 per year. Tuition, state resident: full-time $13,020; part-time $6510 per year. Tuition, nonresident: full-time $19,830; part-time $9915 per year. *International tuition:* $19,830 full-time. *Required fees:* $1226. One-time fee: $350. Tuition and fees vary according to course load, program and reciprocity agreements. *Financial support:* Research assistantships, teaching assistantships, career-related internships or fieldwork, Federal Work-Study, scholarships/grants, and unspecified assistantships available. Support available to part-time students. Financial award application deadline: 3/1; financial award applicants required to submit FAFSA. *Unit head:* Dr. Wayne Wakeland, Chair, 503-725-4975, E-mail: wakeland@pdx.edu. *Application contact:* Dr. Wayne Wakeland, Chair, 503-725-4975, E-mail: wakeland@pdx.edu.
Website: http://www.pdx.edu/sysc/

Portland State University, Graduate Studies, Maseeh College of Engineering and Computer Science, Department of Civil and Environmental Engineering, Portland, OR 97207-0751. Offers civil and environmental engineering (M Eng, MS, PhD). *Program availability:* Part-time, evening/weekend. *Faculty:* 21 full-time (5 women), 3 part-time/adjunct (0 women). *Students:* 36 full-time (11 women), 35 part-time (12 women); includes 12 minority (2 Black or African American, non-Hispanic/Latino; 3 Asian, non-Hispanic/Latino; 3 Hispanic/Latino; 4 Two or more races, non-Hispanic/Latino), 22 international. Average age 32. 45 applicants, 47% accepted, 9 enrolled. In 2019, 33 master's, 3 doctorates awarded. *Degree requirements:* For master's, comprehensive exam (for some programs), thesis (for some programs); for doctorate, one foreign language, comprehensive exam, thesis/dissertation, oral and written exams. *Entrance requirements:* For master's, BS in an engineering field, science, or closely-related area with minimum GPA of 3.0; for doctorate, MS in an engineering field, science, or closely-related area. Additional exam requirements/recommendations for international students: required—TOEFL (minimum score 550 paper-based). *Application deadline:* For fall admission, 1/4 priority date for domestic and international students; for winter admission, 9/1 for domestic and international students; for spring admission, 11/1 for domestic and international students. Applications are processed on a rolling basis. Application fee: $65. *Expenses:* Contact institution. *Financial support:* In 2019–20, 41 students received support, including 11 research assistantships with tuition reimbursements available (averaging $15,789 per year), 12 teaching assistantships with tuition reimbursements available (averaging $12,750 per year); career-related internships or fieldwork, Federal Work-Study, scholarships/grants, and unspecified assistantships also available. Support available to part-time students. Financial award application deadline: 3/1; financial award applicants required to submit FAFSA. *Unit head:* Dr. Chris Monsere, Chair, 503-725-9746, Fax: 503-725-4298, E-mail: monserec@cecs.pdx.edu. *Application contact:* Sarah Phillips, Department Manager, 503-725-4244, Fax: 503-725-4298, E-mail: sap23@pdx.edu.
Website: http://www.pdx.edu/cee/

Princeton University, Graduate School, School of Engineering and Applied Science, Department of Civil and Environmental Engineering, Princeton, NJ 08544-1019. Offers M Eng, MSE, PhD. Terminal master's awarded for partial completion of doctoral program. *Degree requirements:* For master's, thesis (MSE); for doctorate, thesis/dissertation, general exam. *Entrance requirements:* For master's, GRE General Test, 3 letters of recommendation; for doctorate, GRE General Test, official transcript(s), 3 letters of recommendation, personal statement. Additional exam requirements/recommendations for international students: required—TOEFL. Electronic applications accepted.

Purdue University, College of Engineering, Lyles School of Civil Engineering, West Lafayette, IN 47907-2051. Offers MS, MSCE, MSE, PhD. *Program availability:* Part-time. *Faculty:* 59. *Students:* 346. Terminal master's awarded for partial completion of doctoral program. *Degree requirements:* For master's, thesis optional; for doctorate, thesis/dissertation. *Application deadline:* For fall admission, 5/15 priority date for domestic students, 4/15 priority date for international students; for spring admission, 9/15 for domestic and international students. Applications are processed on a rolling basis. Application fee: $60 ($75 for international students). Electronic applications accepted. *Financial support:* Fellowships with full and partial tuition reimbursements, research assistantships with full and partial tuition reimbursements, teaching assistantships with full and partial tuition reimbursements, career-related internships or fieldwork, scholarships/grants, health care benefits, and unspecified assistantships available. *Unit head:* Dr. Rao Govindaraju, Head/Professor, 765-494-2256, E-mail: govind@purdue.edu. *Application contact:* Jenny Ricksy, Graduate Administrator, 765-494-2436, E-mail: jricksy@purdue.edu.
Website: https://engineering.purdue.edu/CE

Purdue University Fort Wayne, College of Engineering, Technology, and Computer Science, Department of Civil and Mechanical Engineering, Fort Wayne, IN 46805-1499. Offers civil engineering (MSE); mechanical engineering (MSE). *Program availability:* Part-time. *Entrance requirements:* For master's, minimum GPA of 3.0, bachelor's degree in engineering discipline. Additional exam requirements/recommendations for international students: required—TOEFL (minimum score 550 paper-based; 79 iBT); recommended—TWE. Electronic applications accepted.

Queen's University at Kingston, School of Graduate Studies, Faculty of Engineering and Applied Science, Department of Civil Engineering, Kingston, ON K7L 3N6, Canada. Offers M Eng, M Sc Eng, PhD. *Program availability:* Part-time. *Degree requirements:* For master's, thesis (for some programs); for doctorate, comprehensive exam, thesis/dissertation. *Entrance requirements:* Additional exam requirements/recommendations for international students: required—TOEFL.

Rensselaer Polytechnic Institute, Graduate School, School of Engineering, Program in Civil Engineering, Troy, NY 12180-3590. Offers M Eng, MS, PhD. *Program availability:* Part-time. *Faculty:* 18 full-time (3 women), 4 part-time/adjunct (0 women). *Students:* 26 full-time (11 women), 12 international. Average age 25. 62 applicants, 29% accepted, 10 enrolled. In 2019, 6 master's, 1 doctorate awarded. Terminal master's awarded for partial completion of doctoral program. *Degree requirements:* For master's, thesis (for some programs); for doctorate, thesis/dissertation. *Entrance requirements:* For master's and doctorate, GRE. Additional exam requirements/recommendations for international students: required—TOEFL (minimum score 570 paper-based; 88 iBT), IELTS (minimum score 6.5), PTE (minimum score 60). *Application deadline:* For fall admission, 1/1 priority date for domestic and international students; for spring admission, 8/15 priority date for domestic and international students. Applications are processed on a rolling basis. Application fee: $75. Electronic applications accepted. *Financial support:* In 2019–20, 16 students received support, including research assistantships (averaging $23,000 per year), teaching assistantships (averaging $23,000 per year); fellowships also available. Financial award application deadline: 1/1. *Unit head:* Dr. Michael O'Rourke, Graduate Program Director, 518-276-6933, E-mail: orourm@rpi.edu. *Application contact:* Jarron Decker, Director of Graduate Admissions, 518-276-6216, Fax: 518-276-4072, E-mail: gradadmissions@rpi.edu.
Website: http://cee.rpi.edu/graduate

Rice University, Graduate Programs, George R. Brown School of Engineering, Department of Civil and Environmental Engineering, Houston, TX 77251-1892. Offers civil engineering (MCE, MS, PhD); environmental engineering (MEE, MES, MS, PhD); environmental science (MEE, MES, MS, PhD). *Program availability:* Part-time. *Degree requirements:* For master's, thesis (for some programs); for doctorate, thesis/dissertation. *Entrance requirements:* For master's and doctorate, GRE General Test, GRE Subject Test, minimum GPA of 3.25. Additional exam requirements/recommendations for international students: required—TOEFL (minimum score 600 paper-based; 90 iBT). Electronic applications accepted.

Rose-Hulman Institute of Technology, Graduate Studies, Department of Civil and Environmental Engineering, Terre Haute, IN 47803-3999. Offers civil engineering (MS); environmental engineering (MS). *Program availability:* Part-time. *Faculty:* 8 full-time (2 women). *Students:* 2 full-time (1 woman), 1 part-time (0 women). Average age 25. 3 applicants, 100% accepted, 2 enrolled. In 2019, 2 master's awarded. *Degree requirements:* For master's, thesis (for some programs). *Entrance requirements:* For master's, GRE, minimum GPA of 3.0. Additional exam requirements/recommendations for international students: required—TOEFL (minimum score 580 paper-based; 94 iBT), IELTS (minimum score 7). *Application deadline:* For fall admission, 2/1 priority date for domestic and international students; for winter admission, 10/1 for domestic students, 4/1 for international students; for spring admission, 1/15 for domestic students, 11/1 for international students. Applications are processed on a rolling basis. Application fee: $75. Electronic applications accepted. *Financial support:* In 2019–20, 2 students received support. Fellowships with tuition reimbursements available, research assistantships with tuition reimbursements available, institutionally sponsored loans, scholarships/grants, tuition waivers (full and partial), and unspecified assistantships available. *Unit head:* Dr. Kevin Sutterer, Department Head, 812-877-8959, E-mail: sutterer@rose-hulman.edu. *Application contact:* Dr. Craig Downing, Associate Dean of Lifelong Learning, 812-877-8822, E-mail: downing@rose-hulman.edu.
Website: https://www.rose-hulman.edu/academics/academic-departments/civil-and-environmental-engineering/index.html

Rowan University, Graduate School, College of Engineering, Department of Civil Engineering, Glassboro, NJ 08028-1701. Offers MEM, MS. Electronic applications accepted. *Expenses: Tuition, area resident:* Part-time $715.50 per semester hour. Tuition, state resident: part-time $715.50 per semester hour. Tuition, nonresident: part-time $715.50 per semester hour. *Required fees:* $161.55 per semester hour.

Royal Military College of Canada, Division of Graduate Studies, Faculty of Engineering, Department of Civil Engineering, Kingston, ON K7K 7B4, Canada. Offers M Eng, MA Sc, PhD. *Degree requirements:* For master's, thesis; for doctorate, comprehensive exam, thesis/dissertation. *Entrance requirements:* For master's, honours degree with second-class standing; for doctorate, master's degree. Electronic applications accepted.

Rutgers University - New Brunswick, Graduate School-New Brunswick, Department of Civil and Environmental Engineering, Piscataway, NJ 08854-8097. Offers MS, PhD. *Program availability:* Part-time, evening/weekend. Terminal master's awarded for partial completion of doctoral program. *Degree requirements:* For master's, comprehensive exam, thesis or alternative; for doctorate, comprehensive exam, thesis/dissertation. *Entrance requirements:* For master's and doctorate, GRE General Test. Additional exam requirements/recommendations for international students: required—TOEFL (minimum score 580 paper-based). Electronic applications accepted.

Saint Martin's University, Office of Graduate Studies, Program in Civil Engineering, Lacey, WA 98503. Offers MCE. *Program availability:* Part-time. *Students:* 10 full-time (1 woman), 2 part-time (both women); includes 4 minority (3 Asian, non-Hispanic/Latino; 1 Two or more races, non-Hispanic/Latino), 2 international. Average age 35. In 2019, 6 master's awarded. *Degree requirements:* For master's, thesis optional. *Entrance requirements:* For master's, minimum GPA of 2.8 in undergraduate work; BS in civil engineering or other engineering/science with completion of calculus, differential equations, physics, chemistry, statistics, mechanics of materials and dynamics. Additional exam requirements/recommendations for international students: required—TOEFL (minimum score 550 paper-based; 79 iBT); recommended—IELTS (minimum score 6.5). *Application deadline:* For fall admission, 4/1 priority date for domestic students, 4/1 for international students; for spring admission, 11/1 priority date for domestic students, 11/1 for international students. Applications are processed on a rolling basis. Application fee: $50. Electronic applications accepted. *Expenses: Tuition:* Full-time $22,950; part-time $15,300 per year. Tuition and fees vary according to course level, course load, degree level, campus/location and program. *Financial support:* Scholarships/grants and tuition waivers (partial) available. Support available to part-time students. Financial award application deadline: 3/1; financial award applicants required to submit FAFSA. *Unit head:* Dr. Dintie S. Mahamah, Program Chair, 360-688-2755, Fax: 360-438-4548, E-mail: dmahamah@stmartin.edu. *Application contact:* Timothy Greer, Graduate Admissions Recruiter, 360-412-6128, E-mail: tgreer@stmartin.edu. Website: https://www.stmartin.edu/directory/office-graduate-studies

San Diego State University, Graduate and Research Affairs, College of Engineering, Department of Civil and Environmental Engineering, San Diego, CA 92182. Offers civil engineering (MS). *Program availability:* Part-time, evening/weekend. *Degree requirements:* For master's, thesis optional. *Entrance requirements:* For master's, GRE General Test. Additional exam requirements/recommendations for international students: required—TOEFL. Electronic applications accepted.

San Jose State University, Program in Civil & Environmental Engineering, San Jose, CA 95192-0001. Offers civil engineering (MS). *Degree requirements:* For master's, thesis or alternative. *Entrance requirements:* For master's, minimum GPA of 2.7. Electronic applications accepted. *Expenses: Tuition, area resident:* Full-time $7176; part-time $4164. Tuition, state resident: full-time $7176; part-time $4164. Tuition, nonresident: full-time $7176; part-time $4165 per credit hour. *International tuition:* $7176 full-time. *Required fees:* $2110; $2110.

Santa Clara University, School of Engineering, Santa Clara, CA 95053. Offers applied mathematics (MS); bioengineering (MS); civil, environmental, and sustainable engineering (MS); computer science and engineering (MS, PhD, Engineer); electrical engineering (MS, PhD, Engineer); engineering management and leadership (MS); mechanical engineering (MS, PhD, Engineer); power systems and sustainable energy (MS); software engineering (MS). *Program availability:* Part-time. *Entrance requirements:* For master's, GRE, official transcript; for doctorate, GRE, Official transcript, 500 word statement of purpose, three letters of recommendation. Additional exam requirements/recommendations for international students: required—TOEFL (minimum score 79 iBT), IELTS (minimum score 6.5). Electronic applications accepted.

South Carolina State University, College of Graduate and Professional Studies, Department of Civil and Mechanical Engineering Technology, Orangeburg, SC 29117-0001. Offers transportation (MS). *Program availability:* Part-time, evening/weekend. *Degree requirements:* For master's, comprehensive exam, thesis, departmental qualifying exam. *Entrance requirements:* For master's, GRE. Additional exam requirements/recommendations for international students: recommended—TOEFL. Electronic applications accepted.

South Dakota School of Mines and Technology, Graduate Division, Program in Civil and Environmental Engineering, Rapid City, SD 57701-3995. Offers MS, PhD. *Program availability:* Part-time, online learning. *Degree requirements:* For master's, thesis (for some programs). *Entrance requirements:* Additional exam requirements/recommendations for international students: required—TOEFL (minimum score 520 paper-based; 68 iBT), TWE. Electronic applications accepted.

South Dakota State University, Graduate School, Jerome J. Lohr College of Engineering, Department of Civil and Environmental Engineering, Brookings, SD 57007. Offers engineering (MS). *Program availability:* Part-time, online learning. *Degree requirements:* For master's, thesis (for some programs), oral exam. *Entrance requirements:* Additional exam requirements/recommendations for international students: required—TOEFL (minimum score 525 paper-based).

Southern Illinois University Carbondale, Graduate School, College of Engineering, Department of Civil and Environmental Engineering, Carbondale, IL 62901-4701. Offers civil and environmental engineering (ME); civil engineering (MS). *Degree requirements:* For master's, comprehensive exam, thesis. *Entrance requirements:* For master's, GRE, minimum GPA of 2.7. Additional exam requirements/recommendations for international students: required—TOEFL.

Southern Illinois University Carbondale, Graduate School, College of Engineering, Program in Engineering Science, Carbondale, IL 62901-4701. Offers engineering science (PhD), including civil and environmental engineering, electrical and computer engineering, mechanical engineering and energy processes, mining and mineral resources engineering. *Degree requirements:* For doctorate, thesis/dissertation. *Entrance requirements:* For doctorate, GRE General Test, minimum GPA of 3.5. Additional exam requirements/recommendations for international students: required—TOEFL.

Southern Illinois University Edwardsville, Graduate School, School of Engineering, Department of Civil Engineering, Edwardsville, IL 62026. Offers environmental engineering (MS); geotechnical engineering (MS); structural engineering (MS); transportation engineering (MS). *Program availability:* Part-time, evening/weekend. *Degree requirements:* For master's, thesis (for some programs), research paper. *Entrance requirements:* For master's, minimum undergraduate GPA of 2.75 in science, math, and engineering courses. Additional exam requirements/recommendations for international students: required—TOEFL (minimum score 550 paper-based; 79 iBT), IELTS (minimum score 6.5). Electronic applications accepted.

Southern Methodist University, Lyle School of Engineering, Department of Civil and Environmental Engineering, Dallas, TX 75275-0340. Offers civil and environmental engineering (PhD); civil engineering (MS), including geotechnical engineering, structural engineering, transportation systems; environmental engineering (MS); sustainability and development (MA). *Program availability:* Part-time, evening/weekend, online learning. Terminal master's awarded for partial completion of doctoral program. *Degree requirements:* For master's, thesis optional; for doctorate, thesis/dissertation, oral and written qualifying exams. *Entrance requirements:* For master's, GRE General Test, minimum GPA of 3.0 in last 2 years; bachelor's degree in engineering, mathematics, or sciences; for doctorate, GRE, BS and MS in related field, minimum GPA of 3.3. Additional exam requirements/recommendations for international students: required—TOEFL. Electronic applications accepted.

Stevens Institute of Technology, Graduate School, Charles V. Schaefer Jr. School of Engineering and Science, Department of Civil, Environmental, and Ocean Engineering, Program in Civil Engineering, Hoboken, NJ 07030. Offers civil engineering (PhD, Certificate), including geotechnical engineering (Certificate); geotechnical/geoenvironmental engineering (M Eng, Engr); hydrologic modeling (M Eng); stormwater management (M Eng); structural engineering (M Eng, Engr); transportation engineering (M Eng); water resources engineering (M Eng). *Program availability:* Part-time, evening/weekend. *Faculty:* 23 full-time (8 women), 21 part-time/adjunct (2 women). *Students:* 38 full-time (6 women), 19 part-time (6 women); includes 11 minority (2 Black or African American, non-Hispanic/Latino; 1 American Indian or Alaska Native, non-Hispanic/Latino; 8 Asian, non-Hispanic/Latino), 29 international. Average age 25. In 2019, 38 master's, 2 doctorates awarded. Terminal master's awarded for partial completion of doctoral program. *Degree requirements:* For master's, thesis optional, minimum B average in major field and overall; for doctorate, comprehensive exam (for some programs), thesis/dissertation; for other advanced degree, minimum B average. *Entrance requirements:* For master's, International applicants must submit TOEFL/IELTS scores and fulfill the English Language Proficiency Requirement. Applicants to full-time programs who do not qualify for a score waiver are required to submit GRE/GMAT scores. Additional exam requirements/recommendations for international students: required—TOEFL (minimum score 74 iBT), IELTS (minimum score 6). *Application deadline:* For fall admission, 4/15 for domestic and international students; for spring admission, 11/1 for domestic and international students; for summer admission, 5/1 for domestic students. Applications are processed on a rolling basis. Application fee: $60. Electronic applications accepted. *Expenses: Tuition:* Full-time $52,134. *Required fees:* $1880. Tuition and fees vary according to course load. *Financial support:* Fellowships, research assistantships, teaching assistantships, career-related internships or fieldwork, Federal Work-Study, scholarships/grants, and unspecified assistantships available. Financial award application deadline: 2/15; financial award applicants required to submit FAFSA. *Unit head:* Dr. Jean Zu, Dean of SES, 201-216.8233, Fax: 201-216.8372, E-mail: Jean.Zu@stevens.edu. *Application contact:* Graduate Admission, 888-783-8367, Fax: 888-511-1306, E-mail: graduate@stevens.edu.

Stony Brook University, State University of New York, Graduate School, College of Engineering and Applied Sciences, Department of Civil Engineering, Stony Brook, NY 11794. Offers MS, PhD, Graduate Certificate. *Program availability:* Part-time. *Faculty:* 5 full-time (2 women), 3 part-time/adjunct (0 women). *Students:* 18 full-time (6 women), 2 part-time (0 women); includes 1 minority (Black or African American, non-Hispanic/Latino), 14 international. Average age 25. 40 applicants, 45% accepted, 4 enrolled. In 2019, 2 master's awarded. Terminal master's awarded for partial completion of doctoral program. *Degree requirements:* For doctorate, thesis/dissertation, preliminary examination, qualifying examination, teaching requirement. *Entrance requirements:* For doctorate, GRE General Test. Additional exam requirements/recommendations for international students: required—TOEFL (minimum score 90 iBT). *Application deadline:* For fall admission, 1/15 for domestic students; for spring admission, 10/1 for domestic students. Application fee: $100. *Expenses:* Contact institution. *Financial support:* In 2019–20, 8 research assistantships, 4 teaching assistantships were awarded; fellowships also available. *Unit head:* Dr. Burgueno Rigoberto, Chair, 631-632-8315, Fax: 631-632-8110, E-mail: Rigoberto.Burgueno@stonybrook.edu. *Application contact:* Erin Giuliano, 631-632-8777, E-mail: Erin.Giuliano@stonybrook.edu. Website: http://www.stonybrook.edu/commcms/civileng/

Syracuse University, College of Engineering and Computer Science, Programs in Civil Engineering, Syracuse, NY 13244. Offers MS, PhD. *Program availability:* Part-time. *Degree requirements:* For master's, comprehensive exam (for some programs), thesis (for some programs); for doctorate, comprehensive exam, thesis/dissertation. *Entrance requirements:* For master's and doctorate, GRE General Test, official transcripts, resume, three letters of recommendation, personal statement. Additional exam requirements/recommendations for international students: required—TOEFL (minimum score 100 iBT). Electronic applications accepted.

Temple University, College of Engineering, Department of Civil and Environmental Engineering, Philadelphia, PA 19122-6096. Offers civil engineering (MSCE); environmental engineering (MS Env E); storm water management (Graduate Certificate). *Program availability:* Part-time, evening/weekend. *Faculty:* 16 full-time (2 women), 18 part-time/adjunct (4 women). *Students:* 40 full-time (15 women), 7 part-time (1 woman); includes 6 minority (3 Black or African American, non-Hispanic/Latino; 2 Asian, non-Hispanic/Latino; 1 Two or more races, non-Hispanic/Latino), 30 international. 68 applicants, 56% accepted, 14 enrolled. In 2019, 9 master's awarded. Terminal master's awarded for partial completion of doctoral program. *Degree requirements:* For master's, thesis optional. *Entrance requirements:* For master's, GRE General Test. Waivers are considered on a case by case basis for master's applicants. Additional exam requirements/recommendations for international students: required—TOEFL (minimum score 79 iBT), IELTS (minimum score 6.5). *Application deadline:* For fall admission, 6/1 priority date for domestic students, 3/1 priority date for international students; for spring admission, 11/1 priority date for domestic students, 8/1 priority date for international students. Applications are processed on a rolling basis. Application fee: $60. Electronic applications accepted. *Expenses:* 1,135 per credit hour in-state resident; 1,490 per credit hour out-of state resident. *Financial support:* In 2019–20, 16 research assistantships with full tuition reimbursements (averaging $19,739 per year), 18 teaching assistantships with full tuition reimbursements (averaging $19,739 per year) were awarded. Financial award applicants required to submit FAFSA. *Unit head:* Dr. Rominder Suri, Chair, Department of Civil and Environmental Engineering, 215-204-2378, Fax: 215-204-6936, E-mail: rominder.suri@temple.edu. *Application contact:* Colleen Baillie, Director of Enrollment Management, 215-204-7800, Fax: 215-204-6936, E-mail: gradengr@temple.edu.
Website: http://engineering.temple.edu/department/civil-environmental-engineering

Tennessee State University, The School of Graduate Studies and Research, College of Engineering, Nashville, TN 37209-1561. Offers biomedical engineering (ME); civil engineering (ME); computer and information systems engineering (MS, PhD); electrical engineering (ME); environmental engineering (ME); manufacturing engineering (ME); mathematical sciences (MS); mechanical engineering (ME). *Program availability:* Part-time, evening/weekend. *Degree requirements:* For master's, project; for doctorate, comprehensive exam, thesis/dissertation. *Entrance requirements:* For doctorate, minimum GPA of 3.3.

Tennessee Technological University, College of Graduate Studies, College of Engineering, Department of Civil and Environmental Engineering, Cookeville, TN 38505. Offers MS. *Program availability:* Part-time. *Faculty:* 17 full-time (0 women). *Students:* 10 full-time (2 women), 8 part-time (2 women), 9 international. 31 applicants, 48% accepted, 6 enrolled. In 2019, 10 master's awarded. *Degree requirements:* For master's, thesis. *Entrance requirements:* For master's, GRE. Additional exam requirements/recommendations for international students: required—TOEFL (minimum score 550 paper-based; 79 iBT), IELTS (minimum score 5.5), PTE (minimum score 53), or TOEIC (Test of English as an International Communication). *Application deadline:* For fall admission, 8/1 for domestic students, 5/1 for international students; for spring admission, 12/1 for domestic students, 10/1 for international students; for summer admission, 5/1 for domestic students, 2/1 for international students. Applications are processed on a rolling basis. Application fee: $35 ($40 for international students). Electronic applications accepted. *Expenses: Tuition, area resident:* Part-time $597 per credit hour. Tuition, state resident: part-time $597 per credit hour. Tuition, nonresident: part-time $1323 per credit hour. *Financial support:* Research assistantships, teaching assistantships, and career-related internships or fieldwork available. Financial award application deadline: 4/1. *Unit head:* Dr. Ben Mohr, Chairperson, 931-372-3454, Fax: 931-372-6352, E-mail: bmohr@tntech.edu. *Application contact:* Shelia K. Kendrick, Coordinator of Graduate Studies, 931-372-3808, Fax: 931-372-3497, E-mail: skendrick@tntech.edu.

Texas A&M University, College of Engineering, Zachry Department of Civil & Environmental Engineering, College Station, TX 77843. Offers civil engineering (M Eng, MS, PhD). *Program availability:* Part-time. *Faculty:* 61. *Students:* 335 full-time (68 women), 61 part-time (10 women); includes 41 minority (7 Black or African American, non-Hispanic/Latino; 13 Asian, non-Hispanic/Latino; 20 Hispanic/Latino; 1 Two or more races, non-Hispanic/Latino), 278 international. Average age 28. 514 applicants, 52% accepted, 100 enrolled. In 2019, 140 master's, 25 doctorates awarded. *Degree requirements:* For master's, comprehensive exam (for some programs), thesis (for some programs); for doctorate, comprehensive exam, thesis/dissertation. *Entrance requirements:* For master's and doctorate, GRE General Test, letters of

recommendation. Additional exam requirements/recommendations for international students: required—TOEFL (minimum score 550 paper-based; 80 iBT), IELTS (minimum score 6), PTE (minimum score 53). *Application deadline:* For fall admission, 7/15 for domestic students, 4/15 for international students; for spring admission, 10/15 for domestic students, 9/15 for international students. Applications are processed on a rolling basis. Application fee: $65 ($90 for international students). Electronic applications accepted. *Expenses:* Contact institution. *Financial support:* In 2019–20, 320 students received support, including 88 fellowships with tuition reimbursements available (averaging $5,455 per year), 179 research assistantships with tuition reimbursements available (averaging $14,204 per year), 69 teaching assistantships with tuition reimbursements available (averaging $11,031 per year); career-related internships or fieldwork, institutionally sponsored loans, scholarships/grants, traineeships, health care benefits, tuition waivers (full and partial), and unspecified assistantships also available. Support available to part-time students. Financial award application deadline: 3/15; financial award applicants required to submit FAFSA. *Unit head:* Dr. Robin Autenrieth, Department Head, 979-845-2438, E-mail: rautenrieth@civil.tamu.edu. *Application contact:* Chris Grunkemeyer, Academic Advisor, Graduate Student Services, 979-845-2498, E-mail: cgrunk@civil.tamu.edu.
Website: http://engineering.tamu.edu/civil/

Texas A&M University–Kingsville, College of Graduate Studies, Frank H. Dotterweich College of Engineering, Department of Civil and Architectural Engineering, Kingsville, TX 78363. Offers civil engineering (ME, MS). *Degree requirements:* For master's, variable foreign language requirement, comprehensive exam, thesis (for some programs). *Entrance requirements:* For master's, GRE (minimum Quantitative and Verbal score of 950 on old scale), MAT, GMAT, minimum GPA of 2.6. Additional exam requirements/recommendations for international students: required—TOEFL (minimum score 550 paper-based; 79 iBT). Electronic applications accepted.

Texas State University, The Graduate College, College of Science and Engineering, Program in Engineering, San Marcos, TX 78666. Offers civil engineering (MS); electrical engineering (MS); industrial engineering (MS); mechanical and manufacturing engineering (MS). *Program availability:* Part-time. *Degree requirements:* For master's, comprehensive exam, thesis (for some programs), thesis or research project. *Entrance requirements:* For master's, official GRE (general test only) required with competitive scores in the verbal reasoning and quantitative reasoning sections, baccalaureate degree from regionally-accredited university in engineering, computer science, physics, technology, or closely-related field with minimum GPA of 3.0 on last 60 undergraduate semester hours; resume or curriculum vitae; 2 letters of recommendation; statement of purpose conveying research interest and professional aspirations. Additional exam requirements/recommendations for international students: required—TOEFL (minimum score 550 paper-based; 78 iBT), IELTS (minimum score 6.5). Electronic applications accepted.

Tufts University, School of Engineering, Department of Civil and Environmental Engineering, Medford, MA 02155. Offers bioengineering (MS), including environmental biotechnology; civil and environmental engineering (MS, PhD), including applied data science, environmental and water resources engineering, environmental health, geosystems engineering, structural engineering and mechanics; PhD/PhD. *Program availability:* Part-time. Terminal master's awarded for partial completion of doctoral program. *Degree requirements:* For master's, thesis (for some programs); for doctorate, thesis/dissertation. *Entrance requirements:* For master's and doctorate, GRE General Test. Additional exam requirements/recommendations for international students: required—TOEFL (minimum score 550 paper-based; 80 iBT), IELTS (minimum score 6.5). Electronic applications accepted. Full-time tuition and fees vary according to degree level, program and student level. Part-time tuition and fees vary according to course load.

United States Merchant Marine Academy, Graduate Program, Kings Point, NY 11024-1699. Offers MS.

Université de Moncton, Faculty of Engineering, Program in Civil Engineering, Moncton, NB E1A 3E9, Canada. Offers M Sc A. *Degree requirements:* For master's, thesis, proficiency in French.

Université de Sherbrooke, Faculty of Engineering, Department of Civil Engineering, Sherbrooke, QC J1K 2R1, Canada. Offers M Sc A, PhD. *Degree requirements:* For master's, one foreign language, thesis; for doctorate, comprehensive exam, thesis/dissertation. *Entrance requirements:* For master's, bachelor's degree in engineering or equivalent; for doctorate, master's degree in engineering or equivalent. Electronic applications accepted.

University at Buffalo, the State University of New York, Graduate School, School of Engineering and Applied Sciences, Department of Civil, Structural, and Environmental Engineering, Buffalo, NY 14260. Offers civil engineering (MS, PhD); engineering science (MS), including data sciences, green energy, Internet of Things, nanoelectronics; environmental and water resources engineering (MS). *Program availability:* Part-time, online learning. Terminal master's awarded for partial completion of doctoral program. *Degree requirements:* For master's, project, thesis, or comprehensive exam; for doctorate, thesis/dissertation. *Entrance requirements:* For master's and doctorate, GRE General Test, letters of reference. Additional exam requirements/recommendations for international students: required—TOEFL (minimum score 550 paper-based; 79 iBT). Electronic applications accepted. *Expenses: Tuition, area resident:* Full-time $11,310; part-time $471 per credit hour. Tuition, state resident: full-time $11,310; part-time $471 per credit hour. Tuition, nonresident: full-time $23,100; part-time $963 per credit hour. *International tuition:* $23,100 full-time. *Required fees:* $2820.

The University of Akron, Graduate School, College of Engineering, Department of Civil Engineering, Akron, OH 44325. Offers civil engineering (MS); engineering (PhD). *Program availability:* Evening/weekend. *Degree requirements:* For master's, thesis optional; for doctorate, thesis/dissertation, candidacy exam, qualifying exam. *Entrance requirements:* For master's, GRE, minimum GPA of 2.75, statement of purpose, three letters of recommendation; for doctorate, GRE, minimum GPA of 3.0 with bachelor's degree, 3.5 with master's degree; three letters of recommendation; statement of purpose; resume. Additional exam requirements/recommendations for international students: required—TOEFL (minimum score 79 iBT), IELTS (minimum score 6.5). Electronic applications accepted.

The University of Alabama, Graduate School, College of Engineering, Department of Civil, Construction and Environmental Engineering, Tuscaloosa, AL 35487-0205. Offers civil engineering (MSCE, PhD); environmental engineering (MS). *Program availability:* Part-time. *Faculty:* 18 full-time (1 woman). *Students:* 64 full-time (23 women), 5 part-time (2 women); includes 4 minority (2 Asian, non-Hispanic/Latino; 2 Hispanic/Latino), 41 international. Average age 29. 116 applicants, 63% accepted, 17 enrolled. In 2019, 22 master's, 4 doctorates awarded. Terminal master's awarded for partial completion of doctoral program. *Degree requirements:* For master's, thesis or alternative; for doctorate, comprehensive exam, thesis/dissertation. *Entrance requirements:* For master's and doctorate, GRE General Test (minimum combined score of 300), minimum overall GPA of 3.0 in last hours of course work. Additional exam requirements/recommendations for international students: required—TOEFL (minimum score 550 paper-based; 79 iBT), IELTS (minimum score 6.5), PTE (minimum score 59). *Application deadline:* Applications are processed on a rolling basis. Application fee: $50 ($60 for international students). Electronic applications accepted. *Expenses: Tuition, area resident:* Full-time $10,780; part-time $440 per credit hour. Tuition, nonresident: full-time $30,250; part-time $1550 per credit hour. *Financial support:* In 2019–20, 36 students received support. Fellowships with full tuition reimbursements available, research assistantships with full tuition reimbursements available, teaching assistantships with full tuition reimbursements available, scholarships/grants, tuition waivers (partial), and unspecified assistantships available. Financial award application deadline: 1/5. *Unit head:* Dr. W. Edward Back, Head/Professor, 205-348-6550, Fax: 205-348-0783, E-mail: eback@eng.ua.edu. *Application contact:* Dr. Andrew Graettinger, Professor and Graduate Program Director, 205-348-1707, Fax: 205-348-0783, E-mail: andrewg@eng.ua.edu.
Website: http://cce.eng.ua.edu/

The University of Alabama at Birmingham, School of Engineering, Program in Civil Engineering, Birmingham, AL 35294. Offers MSCE, PhD. *Program availability:* Part-time, evening/weekend, online learning. *Faculty:* 7 full-time (1 woman), 3 part-time/adjunct (0 women). *Students:* 19 full-time (10 women), 13 part-time (4 women); includes 2 minority (1 Black or African American, non-Hispanic/Latino; 1 Two or more races, non-Hispanic/Latino), 23 international. 38 applicants, 55% accepted, 3 enrolled. In 2019, 9 master's, 2 doctorates awarded. *Degree requirements:* For master's, comprehensive exam, thesis optional; for doctorate, comprehensive exam, thesis/dissertation. *Entrance requirements:* For master's, GRE general test is required for all applicants who did not receive a BS degree from a program accredited by the Engineering Accreditation Committee of ABET http://www.abet.org, or from other programs with reciprocal agreement under the Washington Accord http://www.ieagreements.org/accords/washington/., minimum GPA of 3.0 in all undergraduate degree major courses attempted, letters of evaluation; for doctorate, GRE. Additional exam requirements/recommendations for international students: required—TOEFL (minimum score 80 iBT), TWE (minimum score 3.5); recommended—IELTS (minimum score 6.5). *Application deadline:* For fall admission, 8/1 for domestic and international students; for spring admission, 12/1 for domestic and international students; for summer admission, 5/1 for domestic and international students. Applications are processed on a rolling basis. Application fee: $50 ($60 for international students). Electronic applications accepted. *Financial support:* In 2019–20, 20 students received support, including 11 fellowships with full tuition reimbursements available (averaging $23,196 per year), 9 research assistantships with full and partial tuition reimbursements available (averaging $13,276 per year). *Unit head:* Dr. Fouad H. Fouad, Chair, 205-934-8430, Fax: 205-934-9855, E-mail: ffouad@uab.edu. *Application contact:* Jesse Keppley, Director of Student and Academic Services, 205-996-5696, Fax: 205-934-8413, E-mail: gradschool@uab.edu.
Website: https://www.uab.edu/engineering/home/graduate-civil

The University of Alabama in Huntsville, School of Graduate Studies, College of Engineering, Department of Civil and Environmental Engineering, Huntsville, AL 35899. Offers civil and environmental engineering (PhD); civil engineering (MSE), including civil engineering. *Program availability:* Part-time. *Degree requirements:* For master's, comprehensive exam, thesis or alternative, oral and written exams; for doctorate, comprehensive exam, thesis/dissertation, oral and written exams. *Entrance requirements:* For master's, GRE General Test, BSE, minimum GPA of 3.0; for doctorate, GRE General Test, minimum GPA of 3.0. Additional exam requirements/recommendations for international students: required—TOEFL (minimum score 500 paper-based; 80 iBT), IELTS (minimum score 6.5). Electronic applications accepted.

University of Alaska Fairbanks, College of Engineering and Mines, Department of Civil and Environmental Engineering, Fairbanks, AK 99775-5900. Offers civil engineering (MS); design and construction management (Graduate Certificate); environmental engineering (PhD). *Program availability:* Part-time. *Degree requirements:* For master's, comprehensive exam, thesis (for some programs), oral defense of project or thesis; for doctorate, comprehensive exam, thesis/dissertation. *Entrance requirements:* For master's, bachelor's degree from accredited institution with minimum cumulative undergraduate and major GPA of 3.0. Additional exam requirements/recommendations for international students: required—TOEFL (minimum score 550 paper-based; 79 iBT), IELTS (minimum score 6.5). Electronic applications accepted. *Expenses:* Contact institution.

University of Alberta, Faculty of Graduate Studies and Research, Department of Civil and Environmental Engineering, Edmonton, AB T6G 2E1, Canada. Offers construction engineering and management (M Eng, M Sc, PhD); environmental engineering (M Eng, M Sc, PhD); environmental science (M Sc, PhD); geoenvironmental engineering (M Eng, M Sc, PhD); geotechnical engineering (M Eng, M Sc, PhD); mining engineering (M Eng, M Sc, PhD); petroleum engineering (M Eng, M Sc, PhD); structural engineering (M Eng, M Sc, PhD); water resources (M Eng, M Sc, PhD). *Program availability:* Part-time, online learning. *Degree requirements:* For master's, thesis (for some programs); for doctorate, thesis/dissertation. *Entrance requirements:* For master's, minimum GPA of 3.0 in last 2 years of undergraduate studies; for doctorate, minimum GPA of 3.0. Additional exam requirements/recommendations for international students: required—TOEFL (minimum score 550 paper-based). Electronic applications accepted.

University of Arkansas, Graduate School, College of Engineering, Department of Civil Engineering, Program in Civil Engineering, Fayetteville, AR 72701. Offers MSCE, MSE, PhD. *Students:* 40 full-time (15 women), 11 part-time (2 women); includes 5 minority (1 Black or African American, non-Hispanic/Latino; 3 Hispanic/Latino; 1 Two or more races, non-Hispanic/Latino), 29 international. 22 applicants, 73% accepted. In 2019, 15 master's, 3 doctorates awarded. *Degree requirements:* For master's, thesis optional; for doctorate, one foreign language, thesis/dissertation. *Application deadline:* For fall admission, 8/1 for domestic students, 4/1 for international students; for spring admission, 12/1 for domestic students, 10/1 for international students; for summer admission, 4/15 for domestic students, 3/1 for international students. Applications are processed on a rolling basis. Application fee: $60. Electronic applications accepted. *Financial support:* In 2019–20, 33 research assistantships, 1 teaching assistantship were awarded; fellowships, career-related internships or fieldwork, and Federal Work-Study also available. Support available to part-time students. Financial award application deadline: 4/1; financial award applicants required to submit FAFSA. *Unit head:* Dr. Micah Hale, Department Head, 479-575-6348, E-mail: micah@uark.edu. *Application contact:* Dr. Julian Fairey, Graduate Coordinator, 479-575-4023, E-mail: julianf@uark.edu.
Website: https://civil-engineering.uark.edu/

The University of British Columbia, Faculty of Applied Science, Department of Civil Engineering, Vancouver, BC V6T 1Z4, Canada. Offers M Eng, MA Sc, PhD. *Program availability:* Part-time. *Degree requirements:* For master's, thesis; for doctorate, thesis/dissertation. *Entrance requirements:* Additional exam requirements/recommendations for international students: required—TOEFL (minimum score 100 iBT), IELTS. Electronic applications accepted. *Expenses:* Contact institution.

University of Calgary, Faculty of Graduate Studies, Schulich School of Engineering, Program in Civil Engineering, Calgary, AB T2N 1N4, Canada. Offers avalanche mechanics (M Sc, PhD); civil engineering (M Eng, M Sc, PhD); energy and environment engineering (M Eng, M Sc, PhD); environmental engineering (M Eng, M Sc, PhD);

geotechnical engineering (M Eng, M Sc, PhD); materials science (M Eng, M Sc, PhD); project management (M Eng, M Sc, PhD); structures and solid mechanics (M Eng, M Sc, PhD); transportation engineering (M Eng, M Sc, PhD); water resources (M Eng, M Sc, PhD). *Program availability:* Part-time. *Degree requirements:* For master's, thesis; for doctorate, thesis/dissertation, written and oral candidacy exam. *Entrance requirements:* For master's, minimum GPA of 3.0; for doctorate, minimum GPA of 3.5. Additional exam requirements/recommendations for international students: required—TOEFL (minimum score 580 paper-based; 93 iBT), IELTS (minimum score 7). Electronic applications accepted.

University of California, Berkeley, Graduate Division, College of Engineering, Department of Civil and Environmental Engineering, Berkeley, CA 94720. Offers engineering and project management (M Eng, MS, PhD); environmental engineering (M Eng, MS, PhD); geoengineering (M Eng, MS, PhD); structural engineering, mechanics and materials (M Eng, MS, PhD); transportation engineering (M Eng, MS, PhD); M Arch/MS; MCP/MS; MPP/MS. Terminal master's awarded for partial completion of doctoral program. *Degree requirements:* For master's, comprehensive exam (for some programs), thesis (for some programs), comprehensive exam or thesis (MS); for doctorate, thesis/dissertation, qualifying exam. *Entrance requirements:* For master's, GRE General Test, minimum GPA of 3.0, 3 letters of recommendation; for doctorate, GRE General Test, minimum GPA of 3.5, 3 letters of recommendation. Additional exam requirements/recommendations for international students: required—TOEFL (minimum score 570 paper-based; 90 iBT). Electronic applications accepted.

University of California, Davis, College of Engineering, Program in Civil and Environmental Engineering, Davis, CA 95616. Offers M Engr, MS, D Engr, PhD, Certificate, M Engr/MBA. *Degree requirements:* For master's, comprehensive exam (for some programs), thesis (for some programs); for doctorate, thesis/dissertation. *Entrance requirements:* For master's, GRE General Test, minimum GPA of 3.0; for doctorate, GRE, minimum graduate GPA of 3.5. Additional exam requirements/recommendations for international students: required—TOEFL (minimum score 550 paper-based). Electronic applications accepted.

University of California, Irvine, Samueli School of Engineering, Department of Civil and Environmental Engineering, Irvine, CA 92697. Offers MS, PhD. *Program availability:* Part-time. *Students:* 132 full-time (57 women), 7 part-time (2 women); includes 25 minority (2 Black or African American, non-Hispanic/Latino; 16 Asian, non-Hispanic/Latino; 6 Hispanic/Latino; 1 Two or more races, non-Hispanic/Latino), 79 international. Average age 27. 434 applicants, 47% accepted, 37 enrolled. In 2019, 49 master's, 16 doctorates awarded. Terminal master's awarded for partial completion of doctoral program. *Entrance requirements:* For master's and doctorate, GRE General Test, minimum GPA of 3.0, 3 letters of recommendation. Additional exam requirements/recommendations for international students: required—TOEFL (minimum score 550 paper-based). *Application deadline:* For fall admission, 1/15 priority date for domestic students, 1/15 for international students. Applications are processed on a rolling basis. Application fee: $120 ($140 for international students). Electronic applications accepted. *Financial support:* Fellowships, research assistantships with full tuition reimbursements, teaching assistantships, institutionally sponsored loans, traineeships, health care benefits, and unspecified assistantships available. Financial award application deadline: 3/1; financial award applicants required to submit FAFSA. *Unit head:* Prof. Brett F. Sanders, Chair and Professor, 949-824-4327, Fax: 949-824-3672, E-mail: bsanders@uci.edu. *Application contact:* Connie Cheng, Assistant Director, 949-824-3562, Fax: 949-824-8200, E-mail: connie.cheng@uci.edu.
Website: http://www.eng.uci.edu/dept/cee

University of California, Los Angeles, Graduate Division, Henry Samueli School of Engineering and Applied Science, Department of Civil and Environmental Engineering, Los Angeles, CA 90095-1593. Offers MS, PhD. *Degree requirements:* For master's, comprehensive exam or thesis; for doctorate, thesis/dissertation, qualifying exams. *Entrance requirements:* For master's, GRE General Test, minimum GPA of 3.0; for doctorate, GRE General Test, minimum GPA of 3.25. Additional exam requirements/recommendations for international students: required—TOEFL (minimum score 560 paper-based; 87 iBT), IELTS (minimum score 7). Electronic applications accepted.

University of Central Florida, College of Engineering and Computer Science, Department of Civil, Environmental, and Construction Engineering, Program in Civil Engineering, Orlando, FL 32816. Offers MS, MSCE, PhD, Certificate. *Program availability:* Part-time, evening/weekend. *Students:* 84 full-time (24 women), 62 part-time (17 women); includes 26 minority (5 Black or African American, non-Hispanic/Latino; 5 Asian, non-Hispanic/Latino; 15 Hispanic/Latino; 1 Two or more races, non-Hispanic/Latino), 74 international. Average age 31. 118 applicants, 45% accepted, 26 enrolled. In 2019, 22 master's, 14 doctorates, 3 other advanced degrees awarded. *Degree requirements:* For master's, thesis or alternative; for doctorate, thesis/dissertation, departmental qualifying exam, candidacy exam. *Entrance requirements:* For master's, minimum GPA of 3.0 in last 60 hours, letters of recommendation, goal statement, resume; for doctorate, GRE General Test, minimum GPA of 3.5 in last 60 hours, letters of recommendation, goal statement, resume. Additional exam requirements/recommendations for international students: required—TOEFL. *Application deadline:* For fall admission, 7/15 priority date for domestic students; for spring admission, 12/1 priority date for domestic students. Application fee: $30. Electronic applications accepted. *Financial support:* In 2019–20, 59 students received support, including 19 fellowships with partial tuition reimbursements available (averaging $12,463 per year), 41 research assistantships with partial tuition reimbursements available (averaging $8,053 per year), 14 teaching assistantships with partial tuition reimbursements available (averaging $6,801 per year); career-related internships or fieldwork, Federal Work-Study, institutionally sponsored loans, health care benefits, tuition waivers (partial), and unspecified assistantships also available. Financial award application deadline: 3/1; financial award applicants required to submit FAFSA. *Unit head:* Dr. Andrew Randall, Graduate Director, 407-823-2841, E-mail: andrew.randall@ucf.edu. *Application contact:* Associate Director, Graduate Admissions, 407-823-2766, Fax: 407-823-6442, E-mail: gradadmissions@ucf.edu.
Website: http://cece.ucf.edu/

University of Cincinnati, Graduate School, College of Engineering and Applied Science, Department of Civil and Architectural Engineering and Construction Management, Program in Civil Engineering, Cincinnati, OH 452210071. Offers M Eng, MS, PhD. *Program availability:* Part-time. *Faculty:* 14 full-time (3 women). *Students:* 35 full-time (6 women), 20 part-time (3 women); includes 4 minority (2 Black or African American, non-Hispanic/Latino; 2 Asian, non-Hispanic/Latino), 33 international. Average age 28. 110 applicants, 51% accepted, 30 enrolled. In 2019, 16 master's, 2 doctorates awarded. Terminal master's awarded for partial completion of doctoral program. *Degree requirements:* For master's, comprehensive exam, thesis (for some programs); for doctorate, comprehensive exam, thesis/dissertation. *Entrance requirements:* For master's and doctorate, GRE General Test (3.0,155,155), minimum 3.0 GPA. Additional exam requirements/recommendations for international students: required—TOEFL (minimum score 96 iBT), IELTS, TOEFL (minimum iBT score 96), IELTS (7.0). *Application deadline:* For fall admission, 1/31 priority date for domestic and international students. Application fee: $75 ($80 for international students). Electronic applications accepted. *Financial support:* In 2019–20, 2 students received support, including 2 fellowships with full tuition reimbursements available (averaging $23,400 per year), 2 research assistantships with full tuition reimbursements available (averaging $23,400 per year), 9 teaching assistantships with full tuition reimbursements available (averaging $23,400 per year); career-related internships or fieldwork, tuition waivers (full and partial), and unspecified assistantships also available. Financial award application deadline: 1/31. *Unit head:* Dr. Richard A Miller, Department Head, 513-556-3744, Fax: 513-556-2599, E-mail: richard.miller@uc.edu. *Application contact:* Dr. Gian A. Rassati, Graduate Program Director, 513-556-3696, Fax: 513-556-2599, E-mail: gian.rassati@uc.edu.
Website: http://ceas.uc.edu/caecm.html

University of Colorado Boulder, Graduate School, College of Engineering and Applied Science, Department of Civil, Environmental, and Architectural Engineering, Boulder, CO 80309. Offers MS, PhD. Terminal master's awarded for partial completion of doctoral program. *Degree requirements:* For master's, comprehensive exam, thesis or alternative; for doctorate, thesis/dissertation. *Entrance requirements:* For master's, GRE General Test, minimum undergraduate GPA of 3.0. Electronic applications accepted. Application fee is waived when completed online.

University of Colorado Denver, College of Engineering, Design and Computing, Department of Civil Engineering, Denver, CO 80217. Offers civil engineering (EASPh D); civil engineering systems (PhD); environmental and sustainability engineering (MS, PhD); geographic information systems (MS); geotechnical engineering (MS, PhD); hydrology and hydraulics (MS, PhD); structural engineering (MS, PhD); transportation engineering (MS, PhD). *Program availability:* Part-time, evening/weekend. *Degree requirements:* For master's, comprehensive exam, 30 credit hours, project or thesis; for doctorate, comprehensive exam, thesis/dissertation, 60 credit hours (30 of which are dissertation research). *Entrance requirements:* For master's, GRE, statement of purpose, transcripts, three references; for doctorate, GRE, statement of purpose, transcripts, references, letter of support from faculty stating willingness to serve as dissertation advisor and outlining plan for financial support. Additional exam requirements/recommendations for international students: required—TOEFL (minimum score 537 paper-based; 75 iBT); recommended—IELTS (minimum score 6.5). Electronic applications accepted. Tuition and fees vary according to course load, program and reciprocity agreements.

University of Colorado Denver, College of Engineering, Design and Computing, Master of Engineering Program, Denver, CO 80217-3364. Offers civil engineering (M Eng), including civil engineering, geographic information systems, transportation systems; electrical engineering (M Eng); mechanical engineering (M Eng). *Program availability:* Part-time. *Entrance requirements:* For master's, GRE (for those with GPA below 2.75), transcripts, references, statement of purpose. Tuition and fees vary according to course load, program and reciprocity agreements.

University of Connecticut, Graduate School, School of Engineering, Department of Civil and Environmental Engineering, Field of Civil Engineering, Storrs, CT 06269. Offers MS, PhD. Terminal master's awarded for partial completion of doctoral program. *Degree requirements:* For master's, comprehensive exam, thesis or alternative; for doctorate, thesis/dissertation. *Entrance requirements:* Additional exam requirements/recommendations for international students: required—TOEFL (minimum score 550 paper-based). Electronic applications accepted.

University of Dayton, Department of Civil and Environmental Engineering and Engineering Mechanics, Dayton, OH 45469. Offers engineering mechanics (MSEM); environmental engineering (MSCE); geotechnical engineering (MSCE); structural engineering (MSCE); transportation engineering (MSCE); water resources engineering (MSCE). *Program availability:* Part-time, blended/hybrid learning. *Degree requirements:* For master's, thesis or alternative. *Entrance requirements:* For master's, minimum GPA of 3.0 in undergraduate work. Additional exam requirements/recommendations for international students: required—TOEFL (minimum score 550 paper-based; 80 iBT); recommended—IELTS (minimum score 6.5), TSE (minimum score 60). Electronic applications accepted.

University of Delaware, College of Engineering, Department of Civil and Environmental Engineering, Newark, DE 19716. Offers environmental engineering (MAS, MCE, PhD); geotechnical engineering (MAS, MCE, PhD); ocean engineering (MAS, MCE, PhD); structural engineering (MAS, MCE, PhD); transportation engineering (MAS, MCE, PhD); water resource engineering (MAS, MCE, PhD). *Program availability:* Part-time. Terminal master's awarded for partial completion of doctoral program. *Degree requirements:* For master's, thesis; for doctorate, thesis/dissertation. *Entrance requirements:* For master's and doctorate, GRE General Test. Additional exam requirements/recommendations for international students: required—TOEFL. Electronic applications accepted.

University of Detroit Mercy, College of Engineering and Science, Detroit, MI 48221. Offers chemistry (MS); civil and environmental engineering (DE); electrical and computer engineering (ME); electrical engineering (DE); engineering management (M Eng Mgt); environmental engineering (MEE); mechanical engineering (MME, DE); product development (MS); software engineering (MSSE); teaching of mathematics (MATM). *Program availability:* Part-time, evening/weekend. *Degree requirements:* For doctorate, thesis/dissertation. Electronic applications accepted. Application fee is waived when completed online. *Expenses:* Contact institution.

University of Florida, Graduate School, Herbert Wertheim College of Engineering, Department of Civil and Coastal Engineering, Gainesville, FL 32611. Offers civil engineering (ME, MS, PhD); coastal and oceanographic engineering (ME, MS, PhD); geographic information systems (ME, MS, PhD); hydrologic sciences (ME, MS, PhD); structural engineering (ME, MS); wetland sciences (ME, MS, PhD). *Program availability:* Part-time, online learning. Terminal master's awarded for partial completion of doctoral program. *Degree requirements:* For master's, thesis (for some programs); for doctorate, comprehensive exam, thesis/dissertation. *Entrance requirements:* For master's and doctorate, minimum GPA of 3.0. Additional exam requirements/recommendations for international students: required—TOEFL (minimum score 550 paper-based; 80 iBT), IELTS (minimum score 6). Electronic applications accepted.

University of Hawaii at Manoa, Office of Graduate Education, College of Engineering, Department of Civil and Environmental Engineering, Honolulu, HI 96822. Offers MS, PhD. *Program availability:* Part-time. *Degree requirements:* For master's, comprehensive exam, thesis; for doctorate, comprehensive exam, thesis/dissertation. *Entrance requirements:* For master's and doctorate, GRE General Test or EIT Exam. Additional exam requirements/recommendations for international students: required—TOEFL (minimum score 540 paper-based; 76 iBT), IELTS (minimum score 5).

University of Houston, Cullen College of Engineering, Department of Civil and Environmental Engineering, Houston, TX 77204. Offers civil engineering (MCE, PhD). *Program availability:* Part-time. Terminal master's awarded for partial completion of doctoral program. *Entrance requirements:* For master's and doctorate, GRE General Test. Additional exam requirements/recommendations for international students: required—TOEFL (minimum score 550 paper-based; 79 iBT), IELTS (minimum score 6.5). Electronic applications accepted.

University of Idaho, College of Graduate Studies, College of Engineering, Department of Civil and Environmental Engineering, Moscow, ID 83844-2282. Offers civil and

environmental engineering (M Engr, PhD); geological engineering (MS). *Faculty:* 11. *Students:* 23 full-time (5 women), 55 part-time (7 women). Average age 34. In 2019, 21 master's, 1 doctorate awarded. *Entrance requirements:* For master's and doctorate, minimum GPA of 3.0. Additional exam requirements/recommendations for international students: required—TOEFL (minimum score 550 paper-based; 79 iBT). *Application deadline:* For fall admission, 7/30 for domestic students; for spring admission, 12/1 for domestic students. Applications are processed on a rolling basis. Application fee: $60. Electronic applications accepted. *Expenses:* Tuition, state resident: full-time $7753.80; part-time $502 per credit hour. Tuition, nonresident: full-time $26,990; part-time $1571 per credit hour. *Required fees:* $2122.20; $47 per credit hour. *Financial support:* Fellowships, research assistantships, teaching assistantships, and career-related internships or fieldwork available. Financial award applicants required to submit FAFSA. *Unit head:* Patricia Colberg, Department Chair, 208-885-6782, E-mail: cee@uidaho.edu. *Application contact:* Patricia Colberg, Department Chair, 208-885-6782, E-mail: cee@uidaho.edu.
Website: http://www.uidaho.edu/engr/cee

University of Illinois at Chicago, College of Engineering, Department of Civil and Materials Engineering, Chicago, IL 60607-7128. Offers MS, PhD. *Program availability:* Evening/weekend. *Degree requirements:* For master's, thesis (for some programs); for doctorate, thesis/dissertation, preliminary and qualifying exams. *Entrance requirements:* For master's and doctorate, GRE General Test, minimum GPA of 3.0. Additional exam requirements/recommendations for international students: required—TOEFL. Electronic applications accepted. *Expenses:* Contact institution.

University of Illinois at Urbana-Champaign, Graduate College, College of Engineering, Department of Civil and Environmental Engineering, Champaign, IL 61820. Offers civil engineering (MS, PhD); environmental engineering in civil engineering (MS, PhD); M Arch/MS; MBA/MS. *Program availability:* Part-time, evening/weekend, online learning.

The University of Iowa, Graduate College, College of Engineering, Department of Civil and Environmental Engineering, Iowa City, IA 52242-1316. Offers environmental engineering and science (MS, PhD); hydraulics and water resources (MS, PhD); structures, mechanics and materials (MS, PhD); sustainable water development (MS, PhD); transportation engineering (MS, PhD). *Program availability:* Part-time. Terminal master's awarded for partial completion of doctoral program. *Degree requirements:* For master's, thesis optional, exam; for doctorate, comprehensive exam, thesis/dissertation, exam. *Entrance requirements:* For master's, GRE (minimum combined score of 301 on verbal and quantitative), minimum undergraduate GPA of 3.0; for doctorate, GRE (minimum combined score of 301 on verbal and quantitative), minimum graduate GPA of 3.0. Additional exam requirements/recommendations for international students: required—TOEFL (minimum score 550 paper-based; 81 iBT), IELTS (minimum score 7). Electronic applications accepted.

The University of Kansas, Graduate Studies, School of Engineering, Program in Civil Engineering, Lawrence, KS 66045. Offers MCE, MS, PhD. *Program availability:* Part-time, evening/weekend. *Students:* 53 full-time (12 women), 30 part-time (11 women); includes 6 minority (2 Black or African American, non-Hispanic/Latino; 2 Hispanic/Latino; 2 Two or more races, non-Hispanic/Latino), 41 international. Average age 28. 47 applicants, 53% accepted, 15 enrolled. In 2019, 33 master's, 11 doctorates awarded. *Entrance requirements:* For master's and doctorate, GRE, BS in engineering, two letters of recommendation, statement of purpose. Additional exam requirements/recommendations for international students: required—TOEFL, IELTS. *Application deadline:* For fall admission, 8/17 priority date for domestic and international students; for spring admission, 1/14 priority date for domestic and international students; for summer admission, 5/26 for domestic and international students. Application fee: $65 ($85 for international students). Electronic applications accepted. *Expenses:* Tuition, state resident: full-time $9989. Tuition, nonresident: full-time $23,950. *International tuition:* $23,950 full-time. *Required fees:* $984; $81.99 per credit hour. Tuition and fees vary according to course load, campus/location and program. *Financial support:* Fellowships, research assistantships, teaching assistantships, and career-related internships or fieldwork available. Financial award application deadline: 12/15. *Unit head:* David Darwin, Chair, 785-864-3827, E-mail: daved@ku.edu. *Application contact:* Susan Scott, Graduate Secretary, 785-864-3826, E-mail: s523s307@ku.edu.
Website: http://www.ceae.ku.edu/

University of Kentucky, Graduate School, College of Engineering, Program in Civil Engineering, Lexington, KY 40506-0032. Offers MSCE, PhD. *Degree requirements:* For master's, comprehensive exam, thesis optional; for doctorate, comprehensive exam, thesis/dissertation. *Entrance requirements:* For master's, GRE General Test, minimum undergraduate GPA of 2.75; for doctorate, GRE General Test, minimum undergraduate GPA of 3.0. Additional exam requirements/recommendations for international students: required—TOEFL (minimum score 550 paper-based). Electronic applications accepted.

University of Louisiana at Lafayette, College of Engineering, Department of Civil Engineering, Lafayette, LA 70504. Offers MSE. *Program availability:* Evening/weekend. *Degree requirements:* For master's, comprehensive exam, thesis or alternative. *Entrance requirements:* For master's, GRE General Test, BS in civil engineering, minimum GPA of 2.85. *Expenses: Tuition, area resident:* Full-time $5511. Tuition, state resident: full-time $5511. Tuition, nonresident: full-time $19,239. *Required fees:* $46,637.

University of Louisville, J. B. Speed School of Engineering, Department of Civil and Environmental Engineering, Louisville, KY 40292-0001. Offers civil engineering (M Eng, MS, PhD). *Accreditation:* ABET (one or more programs are accredited). *Program availability:* 100% online, blended/hybrid learning. *Faculty:* 11 full-time (1 woman), 7 part-time/adjunct (0 women). *Students:* 27 full-time (4 women), 21 part-time (3 women); includes 10 minority (3 Black or African American, non-Hispanic/Latino; 1 Asian, non-Hispanic/Latino; 2 Hispanic/Latino; 4 Two or more races, non-Hispanic/Latino), 13 international. Average age 29. 26 applicants, 38% accepted, 7 enrolled. In 2019, 24 master's, 1 doctorate awarded. Terminal master's awarded for partial completion of doctoral program. *Degree requirements:* For master's, thesis optional; for doctorate, comprehensive exam, thesis/dissertation. *Entrance requirements:* For master's, Two letters of recommendation, official transcripts; for doctorate, GRE, Two letters of recommendation, official transcripts. Additional exam requirements/recommendations for international students: required—TOEFL (minimum score 550 paper-based; 80 iBT), IELTS (minimum score 6.5). *Application deadline:* For fall admission, 5/1 priority date for domestic and international students; for spring admission, 11/1 priority date for domestic and international students; for summer admission, 3/1 priority date for domestic and international students. Applications are processed on a rolling basis. Application fee: $65. Electronic applications accepted. *Expenses: Tuition, area resident:* Full-time $13,000; part-time $723 per credit hour. Tuition, state resident: full-time $13,000; part-time $723 per credit hour. Tuition, nonresident: full-time $27,114; part-time $1507 per credit hour. *International tuition:* $27,114 full-time. *Required fees:* $196. Tuition and fees vary according to program and reciprocity agreements. *Financial support:* In 2019–20, 21 students received support. Fellowships, research assistantships, teaching assistantships, scholarships/grants, health care benefits, and tuition waivers (full) available. Financial award application deadline: 1/1. *Unit head:* Zhihui Sun, Chair, Civil and Environmental Engineering Department, 502-852-4583, Fax: 502-852-8851, E-mail: z.sun@louisville.edu. *Application contact:* Nageshar R. Bhaskar, Director of Graduate Studies, 502-852-4547, E-mail: nageshar.bhaskar@louisville.edu.
Website: http://louisville.edu/speed/civil/

University of Maine, Graduate School, College of Engineering, Department of Civil and Environmental Engineering, Orono, ME 04469. Offers MS, PSM, PhD. *Faculty:* 14 full-time (5 women), 1 part-time/adjunct (0 women). *Students:* 33 full-time (13 women), 6 part-time (1 woman); includes 4 minority (2 Black or African American, non-Hispanic/Latino; 1 American Indian or Alaska Native, non-Hispanic/Latino; 1 Asian, non-Hispanic/Latino), 20 international. Average age 29. 30 applicants, 87% accepted, 13 enrolled. In 2019, 8 master's, 3 doctorates awarded. Terminal master's awarded for partial completion of doctoral program. *Degree requirements:* For master's, thesis (for some programs); for doctorate, comprehensive exam, thesis/dissertation. *Entrance requirements:* For master's and doctorate, GRE General Test. Additional exam requirements/recommendations for international students: required—TOEFL (minimum score 80 iBT), IELTS (minimum score 6.5). *Application deadline:* For fall admission, 2/1 priority date for domestic and international students. Applications are processed on a rolling basis. Application fee: $65. Electronic applications accepted. *Expenses: Tuition, area resident:* Full-time $8100; part-time $450 per credit hour. Tuition, state resident: full-time $8100; part-time $450 per credit hour. Tuition, nonresident: full-time $26,388; part-time $1466 per credit hour. *International tuition:* $26,388 full-time. *Required fees:* $1257; $278 per semester. Tuition and fees vary according to course load. *Financial support:* In 2019–20, 67 students received support, including 1 fellowship with full tuition reimbursement available (averaging $25,500 per year), 28 research assistantships with full tuition reimbursements available (averaging $16,500 per year), 14 teaching assistantships with full tuition reimbursements available (averaging $13,800 per year); Federal Work-Study, institutionally sponsored loans, scholarships/grants, and tuition waivers (full and partial) also available. Financial award application deadline: 3/1; financial award applicants required to submit FAFSA. *Unit head:* Dr. Bill Davids, Chair, 207-581-2170, E-mail: william.davids@umit.maine.edu. *Application contact:* Scott G. Delcourt, Assistant Vice President for Graduate Studies and Senior Associate Dean, 207-581-3291, Fax: 207-581-3232, E-mail: graduate@maine.edu.
Website: http://www.civil.umaine.edu/

The University of Manchester, School of Mechanical, Aerospace and Civil Engineering, Manchester, United Kingdom. Offers advanced manufacturing technology (M Ent); aerospace engineering (M Phil, M Sc, PhD); civil engineering (M Phil, M Sc, PhD); environmental engineering (M Phil, PhD); management of projects (M Phil, M Sc, PhD); mechanical engineering (M Phil, M Sc, PhD); mechanical engineering design (M Ent); nuclear engineering (M Phil, D Eng, PhD).

University of Manitoba, Faculty of Graduate Studies, Faculty of Engineering, Department of Civil Engineering, Winnipeg, MB R3T 2N2, Canada. Offers M Eng, M Sc, PhD. *Degree requirements:* For master's, thesis.

University of Maryland, College Park, Academic Affairs, A. James Clark School of Engineering, Department of Civil and Environmental Engineering, College Park, MD 20742. Offers M Eng, MS, PhD. *Program availability:* Part-time, evening/weekend, online learning. *Degree requirements:* For master's, thesis optional; for doctorate, thesis/dissertation, qualifying exam. *Entrance requirements:* For master's and doctorate, GRE General Test, 3 letters of recommendation. Electronic applications accepted.

University of Massachusetts Amherst, Graduate School, College of Engineering, Department of Civil and Environmental Engineering, Amherst, MA 01003. Offers civil engineering (MSCE, PhD); environmental and water resources engineering (MSCE); geotechnical engineering (MSCE); structural engineering and mechanics (MSCE); transportation engineering (MSCE). *Program availability:* Part-time. Terminal master's awarded for partial completion of doctoral program. *Degree requirements:* For master's, thesis or alternative; for doctorate, comprehensive exam, thesis/dissertation. *Entrance requirements:* For master's and doctorate, GRE General Test. Additional exam requirements/recommendations for international students: required—TOEFL (minimum score 550 paper-based; 80 iBT), IELTS (minimum score 6.5). Electronic applications accepted.

University of Massachusetts Amherst, Graduate School, Interdisciplinary Programs, Dual Degree Programs in Management and Engineering, Amherst, MA 01003. Offers MBA/MIE, MBA/MSEWRE, MSCE/MBA, MSME/MBA. *Program availability:* Part-time. *Entrance requirements:* Additional exam requirements/recommendations for international students: required—TOEFL (minimum score 600 paper-based; 100 iBT), IELTS (minimum score 7). Electronic applications accepted.

University of Massachusetts Dartmouth, Graduate School, College of Engineering, Department of Civil and Environmental Engineering, North Dartmouth, MA 02747-2300. Offers civil engineering (MS). *Program availability:* Part-time. *Degree requirements:* For master's, thesis, thesis or project. *Entrance requirements:* For master's, GRE unless UMass Dartmouth graduate in civil engineering, statement of purpose (minimum of 300 words), resume, 3 letters of recommendation, official transcripts. Additional exam requirements/recommendations for international students: required—TOEFL (minimum score 550 paper-based; 79 iBT), IELTS (minimum score 6.5). Electronic applications accepted.

University of Massachusetts Lowell, Francis College of Engineering, Department of Civil and Environmental Engineering, Lowell, MA 01854. Offers environmental studies (PhD). *Program availability:* Part-time. *Degree requirements:* For master's, thesis optional. *Entrance requirements:* For master's, GRE General Test.

University of Memphis, Graduate School, Herff College of Engineering, Department of Civil Engineering, Memphis, TN 38152. Offers civil engineering (PhD); engineering seismology (MS); environmental engineering (MS); freight transportation (Graduate Certificate); geotechnical engineering (MS); structural engineering (MS); transportation engineering (MS); water resources engineering (MS). *Students:* 15 full-time (4 women), 8 part-time (1 woman); includes 1 minority (Black or African American, non-Hispanic/Latino), 12 international. Average age 27. 26 applicants, 38% accepted, 5 enrolled. In 2019, 11 master's awarded. Terminal master's awarded for partial completion of doctoral program. *Degree requirements:* For master's, comprehensive exam, thesis optional; for doctorate, comprehensive exam, thesis/dissertation. *Entrance requirements:* For master's, GRE General Test, minimum undergraduate GPA of 2.5; bachelor's degree in engineering or a related science or mathematics program; three letters of reference; for doctorate, GRE General Test, bachelor's degree in engineering or engineering science; three letters of reference; for Graduate Certificate, minimum undergraduate GPA of 2.75; bachelor's degree in engineering or engineering science. Additional exam requirements/recommendations for international students: required—TOEFL (minimum score 550 paper-based; 79 iBT). *Application deadline:* For fall admission, 8/1 for domestic students; for spring admission, 12/1 for domestic students. Application fee: $35 ($60 for international students). Electronic applications accepted. *Expenses: Tuition, area resident:* Full-time $9216; part-time $512 per credit hour. Tuition, state resident: full-time $9216; part-time $512 per credit hour. Tuition, nonresident: full-time $12,672; part-time $704 per credit hour. *International tuition:* $16,128 full-time. *Required fees:* $1530; $85 per credit hour. Tuition and fees vary according to program. *Financial support:* Fellowships with full tuition reimbursements, research assistantships with full tuition reimbursements, career-related internships or

fieldwork, Federal Work-Study, scholarships/grants, and unspecified assistantships available. Financial award application deadline: 2/1; financial award applicants required to submit FAFSA. *Unit head:* Dr. Shahram Pezeshk, Chair, 901-678-2746, Fax: 901-678-3026, E-mail: spezeshk@memphis.edu. *Application contact:* Dr. Roger Meier, Graduate Coordinator, 901-678-3284, E-mail: rwmeier@memphis.edu.
Website: https://www.memphis.edu/ce

University of Miami, Graduate School, College of Engineering, Department of Civil, Architectural, and Environmental Engineering, Coral Gables, FL 33124. Offers architectural engineering (MSAE); civil engineering (MSCE, PhD). *Program availability:* Part-time. Terminal master's awarded for partial completion of doctoral program. *Degree requirements:* For master's, thesis (for some programs); for doctorate, comprehensive exam, thesis/dissertation. *Entrance requirements:* For master's, GRE General Test (minimum score 1000 verbal and quantitative), minimum GPA of 3.0; for doctorate, GRE General Test, minimum GPA of 3.5 in preceding degree. Additional exam requirements/recommendations for international students: required—TOEFL (minimum score 550 paper-based). Electronic applications accepted.

University of Michigan, College of Engineering, Department of Civil and Environmental Engineering, Ann Arbor, MI 48109. Offers civil engineering (MSE, PhD, CE); construction engineering and management (M Eng, MSE); environmental engineering (MSE, PhD); structural engineering (M Eng); MBA/MSE. *Program availability:* Part-time. Terminal master's awarded for partial completion of doctoral program. *Degree requirements:* For master's, thesis optional; for doctorate, comprehensive exam, thesis/dissertation, oral defense of dissertation, preliminary and written exams. *Entrance requirements:* For master's and doctorate, GRE General Test. Additional exam requirements/recommendations for international students: required—TOEFL. Electronic applications accepted.

University of Michigan, College of Engineering, Department of Naval Architecture and Marine Engineering, Ann Arbor, MI 48109. Offers MS, MSE, PhD, Mar Eng, Nav Arch, MBA/MSE. *Program availability:* Part-time. Terminal master's awarded for partial completion of doctoral program. *Degree requirements:* For master's, thesis (for some programs); for doctorate, comprehensive exam, thesis/dissertation, oral defense of dissertation, written and oral preliminary exams; for other advanced degree, comprehensive exam, thesis, oral defense of thesis. *Entrance requirements:* For doctorate, GRE General Test, master's degree; for other advanced degree, GRE General Test. Additional exam requirements/recommendations for international students: required—TOEFL. Electronic applications accepted.

University of Minnesota, Twin Cities Campus, College of Science and Engineering, Department of Civil, Environmental, and Geo-Engineering, Minneapolis, MN 55455-0213. Offers civil engineering (MCE, MS, PhD); geological engineering (M Geo E, MS); stream restoration science and engineering (Certificate). *Program availability:* Part-time. *Degree requirements:* For master's, thesis optional; for doctorate, thesis/dissertation. *Entrance requirements:* For master's and doctorate, GRE General Test. Additional exam requirements/recommendations for international students: required—TOEFL. Electronic applications accepted.

University of Mississippi, Graduate School, School of Engineering, University, MS 38677. Offers aeroacoustics (MS, PhD); chemical engineering (MS, PhD); civil engineering (MS, PhD); computational hydroscience (MS, PhD); computer science (MS, PhD); electrical engineering (MS, PhD); electromagnetics (MS, PhD); environmental engineering (MS, PhD); geology and geological engineering (MS, PhD); hydrology (MS); material science (MS); mechanical engineering (MS, PhD); telecommunications (MS). *Students:* 104 full-time (23 women), 19 part-time (5 women); includes 10 minority (3 Black or African American, non-Hispanic/Latino; 6 Asian, non-Hispanic/Latino; 1 Hispanic/Latino), 72 international. Average age 30. In 2019, 36 master's, 17 doctorates awarded. *Expenses:* Tuition, state resident: full-time $8718; part-time $484.25 per credit hour. Tuition, nonresident: full-time $24,990; part-time $1388.25 per credit hour. *Required fees:* $100; $4.16 per credit hour. *Unit head:* Dr. David Puleo, Dean, 662-915-5780, Fax: 662-915-5387, E-mail: engineer@olemiss.edu. *Application contact:* Temeka Smith, Graduate Activities Specialist for Admissions, 662-915-7474, Fax: 662-915-7577, E-mail: gschool@olemiss.edu.

University of Missouri, Office of Research and Graduate Studies, College of Engineering, Department of Civil and Environmental Engineering, Columbia, MO 65211. Offers civil engineering (MS, PhD). *Degree requirements:* For master's, report or thesis. *Entrance requirements:* For master's and doctorate, GRE General Test. Additional exam requirements/recommendations for international students: required—TOEFL (minimum score 550 paper-based; 80 iBT).

University of Missouri–Kansas City, School of Computing and Engineering, Kansas City, MO 64110-2499. Offers civil engineering (MS); computer and electrical engineering (PhD); computer science (MS), including bioinformatics, software engineering, telecommunications networking; computer science and informatics (PhD); computing (PhD); electrical engineering (MS); engineering (PhD); engineering and construction management (Graduate Certificate); mechanical engineering (MS); telecommunications and computer networking (PhD). *Program availability:* Part-time. *Degree requirements:* For doctorate, thesis/dissertation. *Entrance requirements:* For master's, GRE General Test, minimum GPA of 3.0, 3 letters of recommendation from professors; for doctorate, GRE General Test, minimum GPA of 3.5. Additional exam requirements/recommendations for international students: required—TOEFL (minimum score 550 paper-based; 80 iBT).

University of Nebraska–Lincoln, Graduate College, College of Engineering, Department of Civil Engineering, Lincoln, NE 68588. Offers MS, PhD. *Degree requirements:* For master's, thesis optional; for doctorate, comprehensive exam, thesis/dissertation. *Entrance requirements:* For master's and doctorate, GRE General Test. Additional exam requirements/recommendations for international students: required—TOEFL (minimum score 550 paper-based). Electronic applications accepted.

University of Nevada, Reno, Graduate School, College of Engineering, Department of Civil and Environmental Engineering, Reno, NV 89557. Offers MS, PhD. Terminal master's awarded for partial completion of doctoral program. *Degree requirements:* For master's, thesis optional; for doctorate, thesis/dissertation. *Entrance requirements:* For master's, GRE General Test, minimum GPA of 3.0; for doctorate, GRE General Test, minimum GPA of 3.25. Additional exam requirements/recommendations for international students: required—TOEFL (minimum score 500 paper-based; 61 iBT), IELTS (minimum score 6). Electronic applications accepted.

University of New Brunswick Fredericton, School of Graduate Studies, Faculty of Engineering, Department of Civil Engineering, Fredericton, NB E3B 5A3, Canada. Offers construction engineering and management (M Eng, M Sc E, PhD); environmental engineering (M Eng, M Sc E, PhD); environmental studies (M Eng); geotechnical engineering (M Eng, M Sc E, PhD); groundwater/hydrology (M Eng, M Sc E, PhD); materials (M Eng, M Sc E, PhD); pavements (M Eng, M Sc E, PhD); structures (M Eng, M Sc E, PhD); transportation (M Eng, M Sc E, PhD). *Program availability:* Part-time. *Faculty:* 17 full-time (2 women). *Students:* 31 full-time (6 women), 10 part-time (0 women), 12 international. Average age 27. In 2019, 11 master's awarded. *Degree requirements:* For master's, thesis; for doctorate, comprehensive exam, thesis/dissertation, qualifying exam; 27 credit hours of courses. *Entrance requirements:* For master's, minimum GPA of 3.0; B Sc E in civil engineering or related engineering degree; for doctorate, minimum GPA of 3.0; graduate degree in engineering or applied science. Additional exam requirements/recommendations for international students: required—IELTS (minimum score 7.5), TWE (minimum score 4), Michigan English Language Assessment Battery (minimum score 85) or CanTest (minimum score 4.5); recommended—TOEFL (minimum score 580 paper-based). *Application deadline:* For fall admission, 5/1 for domestic students; for winter admission, 11/1 for domestic students. Applications are processed on a rolling basis. Application fee: $50 Canadian dollars. Electronic applications accepted. *Expenses: Tuition, area resident:* Full-time $6975 Canadian dollars; part-time $3423 Canadian dollars per year. Tuition, state resident: full-time $6975 Canadian dollars; part-time $3423 Canadian dollars per year. Tuition, Canadian resident: full-time $6975 Canadian dollars; part-time $3423 Canadian dollars per year. *International tuition:* $12,435 Canadian dollars full-time. *Required fees:* $92.25 Canadian dollars per term. Full-time tuition and fees vary according to degree level, campus/location, program, reciprocity agreements and student level. *Financial support:* Fellowships, research assistantships, teaching assistantships, career-related internships or fieldwork, and scholarships/grants available. Financial award application deadline: 1/15. *Unit head:* Dr. Jeff Rankin, Chair, 506-453-4618, Fax: 506-453-3568, E-mail: ktm@unb.ca. *Application contact:* MaryBeth Nicholson, Graduate Secretary, 506-452-6127, Fax: 506-453-3568, E-mail: mbnich@unb.ca.
Website: http://go.unb.ca/gradprograms

University of New Hampshire, Graduate School, College of Engineering and Physical Sciences, Department of Civil and Environmental Engineering, Durham, NH 03824. Offers M Engr, MS, PhD. *Program availability:* Part-time. *Students:* 30 full-time (16 women), 16 part-time (6 women); includes 2 minority (both Hispanic/Latino), 14 international. Average age 25. 59 applicants, 69% accepted, 21 enrolled. In 2019, 3 master's, 1 doctorate awarded. *Entrance requirements:* For master's and doctorate, GRE. Additional exam requirements/recommendations for international students: required—TOEFL (minimum score 550 paper-based; 80 iBT), IELTS (minimum score 6.5), PTE. *Application deadline:* For fall admission, 7/1 for domestic students, 4/1 for international students; for spring admission, 12/1 for domestic students. Application fee: $65. Electronic applications accepted. *Financial support:* In 2019–20, 30 students received support, including 2 fellowships, 7 research assistantships, 21 teaching assistantships; Federal Work-Study, scholarships/grants, and tuition waivers (full and partial) also available. Support available to part-time students. Financial award application deadline: 2/15. *Unit head:* Dr. Erin Bell, Chair, 603-862-3850. *Application contact:* Kristen Parenteau, Administrative Assistant, 603-862-1440, E-mail: cee.graduate@unh.edu.
Website: http://www.ceps.unh.edu/cee

University of New Haven, Graduate School, Tagliatela College of Engineering, Program in Civil Engineering, West Haven, CT 06516. Offers MS. *Students:* 42 full-time (6 women), 6 part-time (0 women); includes 3 minority (all Asian, non-Hispanic/Latino), 42 international. Average age 25. 117 applicants, 87% accepted, 16 enrolled. In 2019, 4 master's awarded. *Application deadline:* Applications are processed on a rolling basis. Application fee: $50. Electronic applications accepted. *Financial support:* Applicants required to submit FAFSA. *Unit head:* Dr. Goli Nossoni, Associate Professor, 203-479-4173, E-mail: gnossoni@newhaven.edu. *Application contact:* Selina O'Toole, Senior Associate Director of Graduate Admissions, 203-932-7337, E-mail: sotoole@newhaven.edu.
Website: http://www.newhaven.edu/engineering/graduate-programs/civil-engineering/index.php

University of New Mexico, Graduate Studies, School of Engineering, Program in Civil Engineering, Albuquerque, NM 87131-0001. Offers civil engineering (M Eng, MSCE); construction management (MCM); engineering (PhD). *Program availability:* Part-time. *Faculty:* 13 full-time (2 women), 4 part-time/adjunct (1 woman). *Students:* 12 full-time (5 women), 51 part-time (19 women); includes 11 minority (1 Black or African American, non-Hispanic/Latino; 9 Hispanic/Latino; 1 Two or more races, non-Hispanic/Latino), 26 international. 68 applicants, 53% accepted, 22 enrolled. In 2019, 27 master's, 5 doctorates awarded. Terminal master's awarded for partial completion of doctoral program. *Degree requirements:* For master's, comprehensive exam, thesis (for some programs); for doctorate, comprehensive exam, thesis/dissertation. *Entrance requirements:* For master's, GRE General Test (for MSCE and M Eng); GRE or GMAT (for MCM), minimum GPA of 3.0; for doctorate, GRE General Test, minimum GPA of 3.0. Additional exam requirements/recommendations for international students: required—TOEFL (minimum score 550 paper-based; 68 iBT), IELTS (minimum score 6), TOEFL or IELTS, not both. *Application deadline:* For fall admission, 7/15 for domestic students, 3/1 for international students; for spring admission, 11/10 for domestic students, 8/1 for international students. Applications are processed on a rolling basis. Application fee: $50. Electronic applications accepted. *Expenses:* Tuition, state resident: full-time $7633; part-time $972 per year. Tuition, nonresident: full-time $22,586; part-time $3840 per year. *International tuition:* $23,292 full-time. *Required fees:* $8608. Tuition and fees vary according to course level, course load, degree level, program and student level. *Financial support:* In 2019–20, 4 fellowships with full tuition reimbursements, 23 research assistantships with full tuition reimbursements, 5 teaching assistantships with full tuition reimbursements were awarded; scholarships/grants, health care benefits, and unspecified assistantships also available. Support available to part-time students. Financial award application deadline: 3/1; financial award applicants required to submit FAFSA. *Unit head:* Dr. Mahmoud R. Taha, Chair, 505-277-2722, Fax: 505-277-1988, E-mail: mrtaha@unm.edu. *Application contact:* Nicole Bingham, Sr. Academic Advisor, 505-277-2722, Fax: 505-277-1988, E-mail: civil@unm.edu.
Website: http://civil.unm.edu

University of New Orleans, Graduate School, College of Engineering, Program in Engineering, New Orleans, LA 70148. Offers civil engineering (MS); electrical engineering (MS); mechanical engineering (MS); naval architecture and marine engineering (MS). *Degree requirements:* For master's, thesis optional. *Entrance requirements:* For master's, GRE General Test, minimum GPA of 3.0. Additional exam requirements/recommendations for international students: required—TOEFL (minimum score 550 paper-based; 79 iBT). Electronic applications accepted.

University of North Dakota, Graduate School, School of Engineering and Mines, Department of Civil Engineering, Grand Forks, ND 58202. Offers civil engineering (M Engr). *Program availability:* Part-time. *Degree requirements:* For master's, comprehensive exam, thesis or alternative. *Entrance requirements:* For master's, GRE General Test, minimum GPA of 2.5. Additional exam requirements/recommendations for international students: required—TOEFL (minimum score 550 paper-based; 79 iBT), IELTS (minimum score 6.5). Electronic applications accepted.

University of North Florida, College of Computing, Engineering, and Construction, School of Engineering, Jacksonville, FL 32224. Offers MSCE, MSEE, MSME. *Program availability:* Part-time.

University of Notre Dame, The Graduate School, College of Engineering, Department of Civil and Environmental Engineering and Earth Sciences, Notre Dame, IN 46556. Offers bioengineering (MS Bio E); civil engineering (MSCE); civil engineering and geological sciences (PhD); earth sciences (MS); environmental engineering (MS Env E). Terminal master's awarded for partial completion of doctoral program. *Degree* *requirements:* For master's, comprehensive exam; for doctorate, thesis/dissertation, candidacy exam. *Entrance requirements:* For master's and doctorate, GRE General Test. Additional exam requirements/recommendations for international students: required—TOEFL (minimum score 600 paper-based; 80 iBT). Electronic applications accepted.

University of Oklahoma, Gallogly College of Engineering, School of Civil Engineering and Environmental Science, Norman, OK 73019-0390. Offers civil engineering (MS, PhD), including civil engineering; environmental engineering (MS, PhD); environmental science (M Env Sc, PhD), including environmental science. *Program availability:* Part-time. Terminal master's awarded for partial completion of doctoral program. *Degree requirements:* For master's, thesis; for doctorate, comprehensive exam, thesis/dissertation, general exam. *Entrance requirements:* For master's and doctorate, GRE. Additional exam requirements/recommendations for international students: required—TOEFL (minimum score 79 iBT) or IELTS (minimum score 6.5). Electronic applications accepted. *Expenses:* Tuition, state resident: full-time $6583.20; part-time $274.30 per credit hour. Tuition, nonresident: full-time $21,242; part-time $885.10 per credit hour. *International tuition:* $21,242.40 full-time. *Required fees:* $1994.20; $72.55 per credit hour. $126.50 per semester. Tuition and fees vary according to course load and degree level.

University of Ottawa, Faculty of Graduate and Postdoctoral Studies, Faculty of Engineering, Ottawa-Carleton Institute for Civil Engineering, Ottawa, ON K1N 6N5, Canada. Offers M Eng, MA Sc, PhD. *Degree requirements:* For master's, thesis or alternative; for doctorate, comprehensive exam, thesis/dissertation, seminar series. *Entrance requirements:* For master's, honors degree or equivalent, minimum B average; for doctorate, master's degree, minimum B+ average. Electronic applications accepted.

University of Pittsburgh, Swanson School of Engineering, Department of Civil and Environmental Engineering, Pittsburgh, PA 15260. Offers MSCEE, PhD. *Program availability:* Part-time, 100% online. Terminal master's awarded for partial completion of doctoral program. *Degree requirements:* For doctorate, comprehensive exam, thesis/ dissertation, final oral exams. *Entrance requirements:* For master's and doctorate, minimum GPA of 3.0. Additional exam requirements/recommendations for international students: required—TOEFL (minimum score 550 paper-based; 80 iBT). Electronic applications accepted. *Expenses:* Contact institution.

University of Portland, Shiley School of Engineering, Portland, OR 97203-5798. Offers biomedical engineering (MBME); civil engineering (ME); computer science (ME); electrical engineering (ME); mechanical engineering (ME). *Program availability:* Part-time, evening/weekend. *Degree requirements:* For master's, thesis optional. *Entrance requirements:* For master's, GRE General Test, minimum GPA of 3.0, 2 letters of recommendation, resume, statement of goals, official transcripts. Additional exam requirements/recommendations for international students: required—TOEFL (minimum score 80 iBT), IELTS (minimum score 7). Electronic applications accepted. *Expenses:* Contact institution.

University of Puerto Rico at Mayagüez, Graduate Studies, College of Engineering, Department of Civil Engineering and Surveying, Mayagüez, PR 00681-9000. Offers civil engineering (ME, MS, PhD), including construction engineering and management (ME, MS), environmental engineering, geotechnical engineering (ME, MS), structural engineering, transportation engineering. *Program availability:* Part-time. Terminal master's awarded for partial completion of doctoral program. *Degree requirements:* For master's, one foreign language, thesis; for doctorate, one foreign language, comprehensive exam, thesis/dissertation, qualifying exams. *Entrance requirements:* For master's, proficiency in English and Spanish; BS in civil engineering or its equivalent; for doctorate, proficiency in English and Spanish. Electronic applications accepted.

University of Rhode Island, Graduate School, College of Engineering, Department of Civil and Environmental Engineering, Kingston, RI 02881. Offers civil and environmental engineering (MS, PhD), including environmental engineering, geotechnical engineering, structural engineering, transportation engineering. *Program availability:* Part-time. *Faculty:* 12 full-time (3 women). *Students:* 23 full-time (7 women), 11 part-time (3 women); includes 3 minority (2 Asian, non-Hispanic/Latino; 1 Hispanic/Latino), 16 international. 26 applicants, 65% accepted, 10 enrolled. In 2019, 9 master's, 3 doctorates awarded. *Entrance requirements:* Additional exam requirements/ recommendations for international students: required—TOEFL. *Application deadline:* For fall admission, 7/15 for domestic students, 2/1 for international students; for spring admission, 11/15 for domestic students, 7/15 for international students. Application fee: $65. Electronic applications accepted. *Expenses: Tuition, area resident:* Full-time $13,734; part-time $763 per credit. Tuition, state resident: full-time $13,734; part-time $763 per credit. Tuition, nonresident: full-time $26,512; part-time $1473 per credit. *International tuition:* $26,512 full-time. *Required fees:* $1780; $52 per credit. $35 per term. One-time fee: $165. *Financial support:* In 2019–20, 8 research assistantships with tuition reimbursements (averaging $11,061 per year), 5 teaching assistantships with tuition reimbursements (averaging $14,558 per year) were awarded. Financial award application deadline: 2/1; financial award applicants required to submit FAFSA. *Unit head:* Dr. Leon Thiem, Chair, 401-874-2693, Fax: 401-874-2786, E-mail: leonthiem@uri.edu. *Application contact:* Dr. Ali Akanda, Graduate Program Director, 401-874-7050, E-mail: akanda@uri.edu.
Website: http://www.uri.edu/cve/

University of Saskatchewan, College of Graduate and Postdoctoral Studies, College of Engineering, Civil and Geological Engineering Program, Saskatoon, SK S7N 5E5, Canada. Offers M Eng, M Sc, PhD. *Program availability:* Part-time. *Degree requirements:* For master's, 30 credits (for M Eng); thesis and 12 credits (for MS); for doctorate, comprehensive exam, thesis/dissertation, qualifying exam, 18 credits. *Entrance requirements:* For master's, GRE, minimum GPA of 5.0 on an 8.0 scale; for doctorate, GRE. Additional exam requirements/recommendations for international students: required—TOEFL (minimum iBT score of 80), IELTS (6.5), CanTEST (4.5), or PTE (59). Electronic applications accepted.

University of South Alabama, College of Engineering, Department of Civil, Coastal, and Environmental Engineering, Mobile, AL 36688-0002. Offers MSCE. *Faculty:* 3 full-time (0 women). *Students:* 12 full-time (6 women), 1 part-time (0 women), 5 international. Average age 25. 18 applicants, 72% accepted, 5 enrolled. In 2019, 6 master's awarded. *Degree requirements:* For master's, comprehensive exam, thesis optional. *Entrance requirements:* For master's, GRE. Additional exam requirements/ recommendations for international students: required—TOEFL (minimum score 550 paper-based; 79 iBT), IELTS (minimum score 6.5). *Application deadline:* For fall admission, 7/1 priority date for domestic students, 6/15 priority date for international students; for spring admission, 12/1 priority date for domestic students, 11/1 priority date for international students; for summer admission, 5/1 priority date for domestic students, 4/1 priority date for international students. Applications are processed on a rolling basis. Application fee: $35. Electronic applications accepted. *Expenses:* Contact institution. *Financial support:* Fellowships, research assistantships, teaching assistantships, career-related internships or fieldwork, Federal Work-Study, institutionally sponsored loans, scholarships/grants, and unspecified assistantships available. Support available to part-time students. Financial award application deadline: 3/31; financial award applicants required to submit FAFSA. *Unit head:* Dr. Kevin White, Chair, Professor,

Department of Civil, Coastal, and Environmental Engineering, College of Engineering, 251-460-6174, Fax: 251-461-1400, E-mail: kwhite@southalabama.edu. *Application contact:* Brenda Poole, Academic Records Specialist, 251-460-6140, Fax: 251-460-6343, E-mail: engineering@alabama.edu.
Website: https://www.southalabama.edu/colleges/engineering/ce/

University of South Carolina, The Graduate School, College of Engineering and Computing, Department of Civil and Environmental Engineering, Columbia, SC 29208. Offers civil engineering (ME, MS, PhD). *Program availability:* Part-time, evening/ weekend, online learning. *Degree requirements:* For master's, comprehensive exam, thesis (for some programs); for doctorate, thesis/dissertation. *Entrance requirements:* For master's and doctorate, GRE General Test, 2 letters of recommendation. Additional exam requirements/recommendations for international students: required—TOEFL (minimum score 570 paper-based). Electronic applications accepted.

University of Southern California, Graduate School, Viterbi School of Engineering, Sonny Astani Department of Civil and Environmental Engineering, Los Angeles, CA 90089. Offers applied mechanics (MS); civil engineering (MS, PhD); computer-aided engineering (ME, Graduate Certificate); construction management (MCM); engineering technology commercialization (Graduate Certificate); environmental engineering (MS, PhD); environmental quality management (ME); structural design (ME); sustainable cities (Graduate Certificate); transportation systems (MS, Graduate Certificate); water and waste management (MS). *Program availability:* Part-time, evening/weekend. Terminal master's awarded for partial completion of doctoral program. *Degree requirements:* For master's, thesis optional; for doctorate, thesis/dissertation. *Entrance requirements:* For master's and doctorate, GRE General Test. Additional exam requirements/recommendations for international students: recommended—TOEFL. Electronic applications accepted.

University of South Florida, College of Engineering, Department of Civil and Environmental Engineering, Tampa, FL 33620-9951. Offers civil engineering (MCE, MSCE), including geotechnical engineering, materials science and engineering, structures engineering, transportation engineering, water resources; environmental engineering (MEVE, MSEV, PhD), including engineering for international development (MSEV). *Program availability:* Part-time. *Faculty:* 19 full-time (5 women). *Students:* 144 full-time (46 women), 76 part-time (22 women); includes 35 minority (8 Black or African American, non-Hispanic/Latino; 5 Asian, non-Hispanic/Latino; 18 Hispanic/Latino; 4 Two or more races, non-Hispanic/Latino), 123 international. Average age 28. 220 applicants, 65% accepted, 59 enrolled. In 2019, 82 master's, 15 doctorates awarded. Terminal master's awarded for partial completion of doctoral program. *Degree requirements:* For master's, comprehensive exam, thesis (for some programs); for doctorate, comprehensive exam, thesis/dissertation. *Entrance requirements:* For master's, GRE required, bachelor's degree in appropriate field, minimum GPA of 3.0 in major, letters of reference, statement of purpose, resume, intake form; for doctorate, GRE with V (45th percentile), Q (75th percentile), and AW (55th percentile), letters of recommendation, statement of purpose, resume, intake form. Additional exam requirements/ recommendations for international students: required—TOEFL, TOEFL (minimum score 550 paper-based; 79 iBT) or IELTS (minimum score 6.5). *Application deadline:* For fall admission, 2/15 for domestic students, 2/15 priority date for international students; for spring admission, 10/15 for domestic students, 9/15 priority date for international students. Application fee: $30. Electronic applications accepted. *Financial support:* In 2019–20, 45 students received support, including 44 research assistantships (averaging $14,123 per year), 21 teaching assistantships with tuition reimbursements available (averaging $15,329 per year). *Unit head:* Dr. Manjriker Gunaratne, Professor and Department Chair, 813-974-5818, Fax: 813-974-2957, E-mail: gunaratn@usf.edu. *Application contact:* Dr. Sarina J. Ergas, Professor and Graduate Program Coordinator, 813-974-1119, Fax: 813-974-2957, E-mail: sergas@usf.edu.
Website: http://www.usf.edu/engineering/cee/

University of South Florida, Innovative Education, Tampa, FL 33620-9951. Offers adult, career and higher education (Graduate Certificate), including college teaching, leadership in developing human resources, leadership in higher education; Africana studies (Graduate Certificate), including diasporas and health disparities, genocide and human rights; aging studies (Graduate Certificate), including gerontology; art research (Graduate Certificate), including museum studies; business foundations (Graduate Certificate); chemical and biomedical engineering (Graduate Certificate), including materials science and engineering, water, health and sustainability; child and family studies (Graduate Certificate), including positive behavior support; civil and industrial engineering (Graduate Certificate), including transportation systems analysis; community and family health (Graduate Certificate), including maternal and child health, social marketing and public health, violence and injury: prevention and intervention, women's health; criminology (Graduate Certificate), including criminal justice administration; data science for public administration (Graduate Certificate); digital humanities (Graduate Certificate); educational measurement and research (Graduate Certificate), including evaluation; English (Graduate Certificate), including comparative literary studies, creative writing, professional and technical communication; entrepreneurship (Graduate Certificate); environmental health (Graduate Certificate), including safety management; epidemiology and biostatistics (Graduate Certificate), including applied biostatistics, biostatistics, concepts and tools of epidemiology, epidemiology, epidemiology of infectious diseases; geography, environment and planning (Graduate Certificate), including community development, environmental policy and management, geographical information systems; geology (Graduate Certificate), including hydrogeology; global health (Graduate Certificate), including disaster management, global health and Latin American and Caribbean studies, global health practice, humanitarian assistance, infection control; government and international affairs (Graduate Certificate), including Cuban studies, globalization studies; health policy and management (Graduate Certificate), including health management and leadership, public health policy and programs; hearing specialist: early intervention (Graduate Certificate); industrial and management systems engineering (Graduate Certificate), including systems engineering, technology management; information studies (Graduate Certificate), including school library media specialist; information systems/decision sciences (Graduate Certificate), including analytics and business intelligence; instructional technology (Graduate Certificate), including distance education, Florida digital/virtual educator, instructional design, multimedia design, Web design; internal medicine, bioethics and medical humanities (Graduate Certificate), including biomedical ethics; Latin American and Caribbean studies (Graduate Certificate); leadership for coastal resiliency planning (Graduate Certificate); mass communications (Graduate Certificate), including multimedia journalism; mathematics and statistics (Graduate Certificate), including mathematics; medicine (Graduate Certificate), including aging and neuroscience, bioinformatics, biotechnology, brain fitness and memory management, clinical investigation, hand and upper limb rehabilitation, health informatics, health sciences, integrative weight management, intellectual property, medicine and gender, metabolic and nutritional medicine, metabolic cardiology, pharmacy sciences; national and competitive intelligence (Graduate Certificate); nursing (Graduate Certificate), including simulation based academic fellowship in advanced pain management; psychological and social foundations (Graduate Certificate), including career counseling, college teaching, diversity in education, mental health counseling, school counseling; public affairs (Graduate Certificate), including nonprofit management, public

management, research administration; public health (Graduate Certificate), including assessing chemical toxicity and public health risks, health equity, pharmacoepidemiology, public health generalist, toxicology, translational research in adolescent behavioral health; public health practices (Graduate Certificate), including planning for healthy communities; rehabilitation and mental health counseling (Graduate Certificate), including integrative mental health care, marriage and family therapy, rehabilitation technology; secondary education (Graduate Certificate), including ESOL, foreign language education: culture and content, foreign language education: professional; social work (Graduate Certificate), including geriatric social work/clinical gerontology; special education (Graduate Certificate), including autism spectrum disorder, disabilities education: severe/profound; world languages (Graduate Certificate), including teaching English as a second language (TESL) or foreign language. *Unit head:* Dr. Cynthia DeLuca, Associate Vice President and Assistant Vice Provost, 813-974-3077, Fax: 813-974-7061, E-mail: deluca@usf.edu. *Application contact:* Owen Hooper, Director, Summer and Alternative Calendar Programs, 813-974-6917, E-mail: hooper@usf.edu.
Website: http://www.usf.edu/innovative-education/

The University of Tennessee, Graduate School, Tickle College of Engineering, Department of Civil and Environmental Engineering, Program in Civil Engineering, Knoxville, TN 37996-2010. Offers MS, PhD, MS/MBA. *Program availability:* Part-time, online learning. *Faculty:* 27 full-time (6 women), 3 part-time/adjunct (0 women). *Students:* 81 full-time (22 women), 49 part-time (8 women); includes 15 minority (4 Black or African American, non-Hispanic/Latino; 5 Asian, non-Hispanic/Latino; 5 Hispanic/Latino; 1 Native Hawaiian or other Pacific Islander, non-Hispanic/Latino), 55 international. Average age 30. 87 applicants, 55% accepted, 23 enrolled. In 2019, 26 master's, 13 doctorates awarded. *Degree requirements:* For master's, thesis or alternative; for doctorate, comprehensive exam, thesis/dissertation. *Entrance requirements:* For master's, GRE General Test (for MS students pursuing research thesis), minimum GPA of 2.7 (for U.S. degree holders), 3.0 (for international degree holders); 3 references; statement of purpose; resume; for doctorate, GRE General Test, minimum GPA of 3.0 on previous graduate course work; 3 references; statement of purpose; resume. Additional exam requirements/recommendations for international students: required—TOEFL (minimum score 550 paper-based; 80 iBT), IELTS (minimum score 6.5). *Application deadline:* For fall admission, 2/1 priority date for domestic and international students; for spring admission, 6/15 for domestic and international students; for summer admission, 10/15 for domestic and international students. Applications are processed on a rolling basis. Application fee: $60. Electronic applications accepted. *Financial support:* In 2019–20, 109 students received support, including 16 fellowships (averaging $5,940 per year), 71 research assistantships with full tuition reimbursements available (averaging $21,988 per year), 22 teaching assistantships with full tuition reimbursements available (averaging $20,935 per year); career-related internships or fieldwork, Federal Work-Study, institutionally sponsored loans, health care benefits, and unspecified assistantships also available. Financial award application deadline: 2/1; financial award applicants required to submit FAFSA. *Unit head:* Dr. Chris Cox, Head, 865-974-2503, Fax: 865-974-2669, E-mail: ccox9@utk.edu. *Application contact:* Dr. Khalid Alshibli, Associate Head, 865-974-7728, Fax: 865-974-2669, E-mail: alshibli@utk.edu.
Website: http://www.engr.utk.edu/civil

The University of Tennessee at Chattanooga, Program in Engineering, Chattanooga, TN 37403. Offers automotive (MS Engr); chemical (MS Engr); civil (MS Engr); electrical (MS Engr); mechanical (MS Engr). *Program availability:* Part-time. *Students:* 29 full-time (4 women), 27 part-time (3 women); includes 9 minority (4 Black or African American, non-Hispanic/Latino; 2 Asian, non-Hispanic/Latino; 1 Hispanic/Latino; 1 Native Hawaiian or other Pacific Islander, non-Hispanic/Latino; 1 Two or more races, non-Hispanic/Latino), 19 international. Average age 29. 39 applicants, 74% accepted, 16 enrolled. In 2019, 22 master's awarded. *Degree requirements:* For master's, comprehensive exam, thesis or alternative, engineering project. *Entrance requirements:* For master's, GRE General Test, minimum undergraduate GPA of 2.7 or 3.0 in last two years of undergraduate coursework. Additional exam requirements/recommendations for international students: required—TOEFL (minimum score 550 paper-based; 79 iBT), IELTS (minimum score 6). *Application deadline:* For fall admission, 6/15 priority date for domestic students, 7/1 for international students; for spring admission, 11/1 priority date for domestic students, 11/1 for international students. Applications are processed on a rolling basis. Application fee: $35 ($40 for international students). Electronic applications accepted. *Financial support:* Research assistantships, teaching assistantships, career-related internships or fieldwork, scholarships/grants, health care benefits, and unspecified assistantships available. Support available to part-time students. Financial award application deadline: 7/1; financial award applicants required to submit FAFSA. *Unit head:* Dr. Daniel Pack, Dean, 423-425-2256, Fax: 423-425-5311, E-mail: daniel-pack@utc.edu. *Application contact:* Dr. Joanne Romagni, Dean of the Graduate School, 423-425-4478, Fax: 423-425-5223, E-mail: joanne-romagni@utc.edu.
Website: http://www.utc.edu/college-engineering-computer-science/graduate-programs/msengr.php

The University of Texas at Arlington, Graduate School, College of Engineering, Department of Civil Engineering, Arlington, TX 76019. Offers civil engineering (M Engr, MS, PhD); construction management (MCM). *Program availability:* Part-time, evening/weekend, online learning. Terminal master's awarded for partial completion of doctoral program. *Degree requirements:* For master's, comprehensive exam, thesis (for some programs), oral and written exams; for doctorate, comprehensive exam, thesis/dissertation, oral and written defense of dissertation. *Entrance requirements:* For master's, GRE General Test, minimum GPA of 3.0 in last 60 hours of undergraduate course work; for doctorate, GRE General Test, minimum GPA of 3.5. Additional exam requirements/recommendations for international students: required—TOEFL. Electronic applications accepted.

The University of Texas at Austin, Graduate School, Cockrell School of Engineering, Department of Civil, Architectural and Environmental Engineering, Austin, TX 78712-1111. Offers architectural engineering (MSE); civil engineering (MS, PhD); environmental and water resources engineering (MS, PhD). *Program availability:* Part-time. *Degree requirements:* For master's, thesis or alternative; for doctorate, comprehensive exam, thesis/dissertation. *Entrance requirements:* For master's and doctorate, GRE General Test. Additional exam requirements/recommendations for international students: required—TOEFL. Electronic applications accepted.

The University of Texas at El Paso, Graduate School, College of Engineering, Department of Civil Engineering, El Paso, TX 79968-0001. Offers civil engineering (MS, PhD); construction management (MS, Certificate); environmental engineering (MEENE, MSENE). *Program availability:* Part-time, evening/weekend. *Degree requirements:* For master's, comprehensive exam, thesis optional; for doctorate, comprehensive exam, thesis/dissertation. *Entrance requirements:* For master's, GRE, minimum GPA of 3.0; for doctorate, GRE. Additional exam requirements/recommendations for international students: required—TOEFL. Electronic applications accepted.

The University of Texas at San Antonio, College of Engineering, Department of Civil and Environmental Engineering, San Antonio, TX 78249-0617. Offers civil engineering (MCE, MSCE); environmental science and engineering (PhD). *Program availability:*

Part-time. *Degree requirements:* For master's, comprehensive exam, thesis (for some programs); for doctorate, comprehensive exam, thesis/dissertation, written qualifying exam, dissertation proposal. *Entrance requirements:* For master's, GRE General Test, BS in civil engineering or related field from accredited institution, statement of research/specialization interest, recommendation by the Civil Engineering Master's Program Admissions Committee; for doctorate, GRE, BS and MS from accredited institution, minimum GPA of 3.0 in upper-division and graduate courses, three letters of recommendation, letter of research interest, resume/curriculum vitae. Additional exam requirements/recommendations for international students: required—TOEFL (minimum score 550 paper-based; 79 iBT), IELTS (minimum score 6.5). Electronic applications accepted. *Expenses:* Contact institution.

The University of Texas at Tyler, College of Engineering, Department of Civil Engineering, Tyler, TX 75799-0001. Offers environmental engineering (MS); industrial safety (MS); structural engineering (MS); transportation engineering (MS); water resources engineering (MS). *Program availability:* Part-time, evening/weekend. *Faculty:* 5 full-time. *Students:* 7 full-time (0 women), 8 part-time (6 women); includes 4 minority (1 Asian, non-Hispanic/Latino; 3 Hispanic/Latino), 4 international. Average age 28. 14 applicants, 79% accepted, 4 enrolled. In 2019, 6 master's awarded. *Entrance requirements:* For master's, GRE General Test, bachelor's degree in engineering, associated science degree. Additional exam requirements/recommendations for international students: required—TOEFL. *Application deadline:* For fall admission, 8/17 priority date for domestic students, 7/1 priority date for international students; for spring admission, 12/21 priority date for domestic students, 11/1 priority date for international students. Application fee: $25 ($50 for international students). *Financial support:* Application deadline: 7/1. *Unit head:* Dr. Torey Nalbone, Chair, 903-565-5520, E-mail: tnalbone@uttyler.edu. *Application contact:* Dr. Torey Nalbone, Chair, 903-565-5520, E-mail: tnalbone@uttyler.edu.
Website: https://www.uttyler.edu/ce/

The University of Toledo, College of Graduate Studies, College of Engineering, Department of Civil Engineering, Toledo, OH 43606-3390. Offers MS, PhD. *Program availability:* Part-time. Terminal master's awarded for partial completion of doctoral program. *Degree requirements:* For master's, thesis or alternative; for doctorate, thesis/dissertation, qualifying exam. *Entrance requirements:* For master's, GRE General Test, minimum GPA of 3.0; for doctorate, GRE General Test, minimum GPA of 3.3. Additional exam requirements/recommendations for international students: required—TOEFL (minimum score 550 paper-based; 80 iBT). Electronic applications accepted.

University of Toronto, School of Graduate Studies, Faculty of Applied Science and Engineering, Department of Civil Engineering, Toronto, ON M5S 1A1, Canada. Offers M Eng, MA Sc, PhD. *Program availability:* Part-time. *Degree requirements:* For master's, thesis and oral presentation (MA Sc); for doctorate, thesis/dissertation, oral presentation. *Entrance requirements:* For master's, bachelor's degree in civil engineering, proficiency in computer usage, minimum B average in final 2 years, 3 letters of reference; for doctorate, proficiency in computer usage, minimum B average in final 2 years, 3 letters of reference. Additional exam requirements/recommendations for international students: required—TOEFL (minimum score 580 paper-based; 93 iBT). Electronic applications accepted.

University of Utah, Graduate School, College of Engineering, Department of Civil and Environmental Engineering, Salt Lake City, UT 84112. Offers civil and environmental engineering (MS, PhD); nuclear engineering (MS, PhD). *Faculty:* 22 full-time (5 women), 2 part-time/adjunct (1 woman). *Students:* 75 full-time (18 women), 38 part-time (3 women); includes 18 minority (1 Black or African American, non-Hispanic/Latino; 8 Asian, non-Hispanic/Latino; 6 Hispanic/Latino; 3 Two or more races, non-Hispanic/Latino), 44 international. Average age 29. 104 applicants, 36% accepted, 21 enrolled. In 2019, 26 master's, 12 doctorates awarded. Terminal master's awarded for partial completion of doctoral program. *Degree requirements:* For master's, comprehensive exam (for some programs), thesis (for some programs); for doctorate, comprehensive exam, thesis/dissertation. *Entrance requirements:* For master's and doctorate, GRE, Online application completed through ApplyYourself portal, GPA of 3.0+ on 4.0 scale, CV, personal statement, unofficial transcripts, three letters of reference, proof of English proficiency. Additional exam requirements/recommendations for international students: required—TOEFL (minimum score 80 iBT), IELTS (minimum score 6.5), Either IELTS or TOEFL required, not both. *Application deadline:* For fall admission, 1/1 priority date for domestic and international students; for spring admission, 10/1 for domestic and international students. Applications are processed on a rolling basis. Application fee: $0 ($30 for international students). Electronic applications accepted. *Expenses:* $58.29 per credit hour. *Financial support:* In 2019–20, 1 student received support, including 8 fellowships with full tuition reimbursements available (averaging $28,375 per year), 48 research assistantships with full tuition reimbursements available (averaging $24,000 per year), 15 teaching assistantships with full tuition reimbursements available (averaging $24,000 per year); health care benefits and unspecified assistantships also available. Financial award application deadline: 1/1. *Unit head:* Dr. Michael E. Barber, Chair, 801-581-6931, Fax: 801-585-5477, E-mail: barber@civil.utah.edu. *Application contact:* Courtney Phillips, Academic Advisor, 801-581-6678, Fax: 801-585-5477, E-mail: cveen-graduate@utah.edu.
Website: http://www.civil.utah.edu

University of Vermont, Graduate College, College of Engineering and Mathematical Sciences, Department of Civil and Environmental Engineering, Burlington, VT 05405. Offers MS, PhD. *Degree requirements:* For master's, thesis or alternative; for doctorate, thesis/dissertation. *Entrance requirements:* For master's and doctorate, GRE General Test. Additional exam requirements/recommendations for international students: required—TOEFL (minimum score 550 paper-based, 90 iBT) or IELTS (6.5). Electronic applications accepted.

University of Virginia, School of Engineering and Applied Science, Department of Civil and Environmental Engineering, Charlottesville, VA 22903. Offers ME, MS, PhD. *Program availability:* Part-time, online learning. Terminal master's awarded for partial completion of doctoral program. *Degree requirements:* For master's, thesis (for some programs); for doctorate, comprehensive exam, thesis/dissertation. *Entrance requirements:* For master's and doctorate, GRE General Test, 3 letters of recommendation. Additional exam requirements/recommendations for international students: required—TOEFL (minimum score 600 paper-based; 90 iBT), IELTS (minimum score 7). Electronic applications accepted.

University of Washington, Graduate School, College of Engineering, Department of Civil and Environmental Engineering, Seattle, WA 98195-2700. Offers construction engineering (MSCE, PhD); environmental engineering (MSCE, PhD); geotechnical engineering (MSCE, PhD); hydrology and hydrodynamics (MSCE, PhD); structural engineering and mechanics (MSCE, PhD); transportation engineering (MSCE, PhD). *Program availability:* Part-time, 100% online. *Students:* 248 full-time (97 women), 174 part-time (63 women); includes 90 minority (8 Black or African American, non-Hispanic/Latino; 2 American Indian or Alaska Native, non-Hispanic/Latino; 46 Asian, non-Hispanic/Latino; 18 Hispanic/Latino; 16 Two or more races, non-Hispanic/Latino), 118 international. Average age 28. 756 applicants, 59% accepted, 164 enrolled. In 2019, 133 master's, 21 doctorates awarded. Terminal master's awarded for partial completion of doctoral program. *Degree requirements:* For master's, thesis optional; for doctorate,

comprehensive exam, thesis/dissertation, qualifying, general and final exams; completion of degree within 10 years. *Entrance requirements:* For master's, GRE General Test, minimum GPA of 3.0, statement of purpose, letters of recommendation, transcripts; for doctorate, GRE General Test, minimum GPA of 3.5, statement of purpose, letters of recommendation, transcripts, resume. Additional exam requirements/recommendations for international students: required—TOEFL (minimum score 580 paper-based; 92 iBT). *Application deadline:* For fall admission, 12/15 for domestic and international students. Applications are processed on a rolling basis. Application fee: $85. Electronic applications accepted. *Expenses:* Contact institution. *Financial support:* In 2019–20, 21 fellowships with full tuition reimbursements (averaging $30,600 per year), 76 research assistantships with full tuition reimbursements (averaging $30,600 per year), 27 teaching assistantships with full tuition reimbursements (averaging $30,120 per year) were awarded; Federal Work-Study, institutionally sponsored loans, scholarships/grants, health care benefits, tuition waivers, and unspecified assistantships also available. Support available to part-time students. Financial award application deadline: 12/15. *Unit head:* Dr. Laura Lowes, Professor/Chair, 206-685-2563, Fax: 206-543-1543, E-mail: lowes@uw.edu. *Application contact:* Bryan Crockett, Director of Academic Services, 206-616-1891, Fax: 206-543-1543, E-mail: ceginfo@u.washington.edu.
Website: http://www.ce.washington.edu/

University of Waterloo, Graduate Studies and Postdoctoral Affairs, Faculty of Engineering, Department of Civil and Environmental Engineering, Waterloo, ON N2L 3G1, Canada. Offers M Eng, MA Sc, PhD. *Program availability:* Part-time. *Degree requirements:* For master's, research paper or thesis; for doctorate, comprehensive exam, thesis/dissertation. *Entrance requirements:* For master's, honors degree, minimum B average; for doctorate, master's degree, minimum A- average. Additional exam requirements/recommendations for international students: required—TOEFL, IELTS, PTE. Electronic applications accepted.

The University of Western Ontario, School of Graduate and Postdoctoral Studies, Physical Sciences Division, Faculty of Engineering, London, ON N6A 3K7, Canada. Offers chemical and biochemical engineering (ME Sc, PhD); civil and environmental engineering (M Eng, ME Sc, PhD); electrical and computer engineering (M Eng, ME Sc, PhD); mechanical and materials engineering (M Eng, ME Sc, PhD). *Program availability:* Part-time. Terminal master's awarded for partial completion of doctoral program. *Degree requirements:* For master's, thesis; for doctorate, thesis/dissertation. *Entrance requirements:* For master's, minimum B average; for doctorate, minimum B+ average.

University of Windsor, Faculty of Graduate Studies, Faculty of Engineering, Department of Civil and Environmental Engineering, Windsor, ON N9B 3P4, Canada. Offers civil engineering (M Eng, MA Sc, PhD); environmental engineering (M Eng, MA Sc, PhD). *Program availability:* Part-time. *Degree requirements:* For master's, thesis; for doctorate, comprehensive exam, thesis/dissertation. *Entrance requirements:* For master's, minimum B average; for doctorate, master's degree, minimum A average. Additional exam requirements/recommendations for international students: required—TOEFL (minimum score 580 paper-based). Electronic applications accepted.

University of Wisconsin–Madison, Graduate School, College of Engineering, Department of Civil and Environmental Engineering, Madison, WI 53706-1380. Offers construction engineering and management (MS); environmental science and engineering (MS); geological/geotechnical engineering (MS); structural engineering (MS); transportation engineering (MS); water resources engineering (MS). *Program availability:* Part-time. Terminal master's awarded for partial completion of doctoral program. *Degree requirements:* For master's, thesis (for some programs), minimum of 30 credits; minimum overall GPA of 3.0. *Entrance requirements:* For master's, GRE General Test, bachelor's degree; minimum GPA of 3.0 for last 60 credits of course work. Additional exam requirements/recommendations for international students: required—TOEFL (minimum score 580 paper-based; 92 iBT). Electronic applications accepted. *Expenses:* Contact institution.

University of Wisconsin–Milwaukee, Graduate School, College of Engineering and Applied Science, Program in Engineering, Milwaukee, WI 53201-0413. Offers biomedical engineering (MS); civil engineering (MS, PhD); computer science (PhD); electrical and computer engineering (MS); electrical engineering (PhD); engineering mechanics (MS); industrial and management engineering (MS); industrial engineering (PhD); manufacturing engineering (MS); materials (PhD); materials engineering (MS); mechanical engineering (MS). *Program availability:* Part-time. *Degree requirements:* For master's, comprehensive exam (for some programs), thesis or alternative; for doctorate, comprehensive exam, thesis/dissertation, internship. *Entrance requirements:* For master's, GRE, minimum GPA of 2.75; for doctorate, GRE, minimum GPA of 3.5. Additional exam requirements/recommendations for international students: required—TOEFL (minimum score 550 paper-based; 79 iBT), IELTS (minimum score 6.5).

University of Wyoming, College of Engineering and Applied Science, Department of Civil and Architectural Engineering, Laramie, WY 82071. Offers architectural engineering (MS); civil engineering (MS, PhD). *Program availability:* Part-time. Terminal master's awarded for partial completion of doctoral program. *Degree requirements:* For master's, thesis (for some programs); for doctorate, variable foreign language requirement, comprehensive exam, thesis/dissertation. *Entrance requirements:* For master's, GRE General Test (minimum combined score 900), minimum GPA of 3.0; for doctorate, GRE General Test (minimum combined score: 1000), minimum GPA of 3.0. Additional exam requirements/recommendations for international students: required—TOEFL (minimum score 550 paper-based). Electronic applications accepted.

Université Laval, Faculty of Sciences and Engineering, Department of Civil Engineering, Program in Urban Infrastructure Engineering, Québec, QC G1K 7P4, Canada. Offers Diploma. *Program availability:* Part-time, evening/weekend. *Entrance requirements:* For degree, knowledge of French. Electronic applications accepted.

Université Laval, Faculty of Sciences and Engineering, Department of Civil Engineering, Programs in Civil Engineering, Québec, QC G1K 7P4, Canada. Offers civil engineering (M Sc, PhD); environmental technology (M Sc). Terminal master's awarded for partial completion of doctoral program. *Degree requirements:* For master's, thesis (for some programs); for doctorate, comprehensive exam, thesis/dissertation. *Entrance requirements:* For master's and doctorate, knowledge of French and English. Electronic applications accepted.

Utah State University, School of Graduate Studies, College of Engineering, Department of Civil and Environmental Engineering, Logan, UT 84322. Offers ME, MS, PhD, CE. *Degree requirements:* For master's, thesis (for some programs); for doctorate, thesis/dissertation. *Entrance requirements:* For master's and doctorate, GRE General Test, minimum GPA of 3.0. Additional exam requirements/recommendations for international students: required—TOEFL. Electronic applications accepted.

Vanderbilt University, School of Engineering, Department of Civil and Environmental Engineering, Program in Civil Engineering, Nashville, TN 37240-1001. Offers M Eng, MS, PhD. *Program availability:* Part-time. Terminal master's awarded for partial completion of doctoral program. *Degree requirements:* For master's, thesis; for doctorate, thesis/dissertation. *Entrance requirements:* For master's and doctorate, GRE General Test. Additional exam requirements/recommendations for international students: required—TOEFL. Electronic applications accepted. *Expenses: Tuition:* Full-time $51,018; part-time $2087 per hour. *Required fees:* $542. Tuition and fees vary according to program.

Villanova University, College of Engineering, Department of Civil and Environmental Engineering, Program in Civil Engineering, Villanova, PA 19085-1699. Offers MSCE. *Program availability:* Part-time, evening/weekend. *Degree requirements:* For master's, thesis optional. *Entrance requirements:* For master's, GRE General Test (for applicants with degrees from foreign universities), minimum GPA of 3.0. Additional exam requirements/recommendations for international students: required—TOEFL (minimum score 600 paper-based; 100 iBT). Electronic applications accepted.

Virginia Polytechnic Institute and State University, Graduate School, College of Engineering, Blacksburg, VA 24061. Offers aerospace engineering (PhD, M Eng/MS); biological systems engineering (PhD); biomedical engineering (MS, PhD); chemical engineering (PhD); civil engineering (PhD); computer engineering (PhD); computer science and applications (MS); electrical engineering (PhD); engineering education (PhD); M Eng/MS. *Faculty:* 447 full-time (90 women), 6 part-time/adjunct (2 women). *Students:* 1,881 full-time (495 women), 326 part-time (70 women); includes 264 minority (51 Black or African American, non-Hispanic/Latino; 2 American Indian or Alaska Native, non-Hispanic/Latino; 96 Asian, non-Hispanic/Latino; 69 Hispanic/Latino; 46 Two or more races, non-Hispanic/Latino), 1,247 international. Average age 27. 4,014 applicants, 44% accepted, 658 enrolled. In 2019, 489 master's, 200 doctorates awarded. *Degree requirements:* For master's, comprehensive exam (for some programs), thesis (for some programs); for doctorate, comprehensive exam (for some programs), thesis/dissertation (for some programs). *Entrance requirements:* For master's and doctorate, GRE/GMAT. Additional exam requirements/recommendations for international students: required—TOEFL (minimum score 90 iBT). *Application deadline:* For fall admission, 8/1 for domestic students, 4/1 for international students; for spring admission, 1/1 for domestic students, 9/1 for international students. Applications are processed on a rolling basis. Application fee: $75. Electronic applications accepted. *Expenses:* Tuition, state resident: full-time $13,700; part-time $761.25 per credit hour. Tuition, nonresident: full-time $27,614; part-time $1534 per credit hour. *Required fees:* $886.50 per term. Tuition and fees vary according to campus/location and program. *Financial support:* In 2019–20, 47 fellowships with full tuition reimbursements (averaging $19,703 per year), 1,163 research assistantships with full tuition reimbursements (averaging $20,602 per year), 554 teaching assistantships with full tuition reimbursements (averaging $16,333 per year) were awarded; scholarships/grants and unspecified assistantships also available. Financial award application deadline: 3/1; financial award applicants required to submit FAFSA. *Unit head:* Dr. Julia Ross, Dean, 540-231-9752, Fax: 540-231-3031, E-mail: rjulie@vt.edu. *Application contact:* Linda Perkins, Executive Assistant, 540-231-9752, Fax: 540-231-3031, E-mail: lperkins@vt.edu.
Website: http://www.eng.vt.edu/

Virginia Polytechnic Institute and State University, VT Online, Blacksburg, VA 24061. Offers advanced transportation systems (Certificate); aerospace engineering (MS); agricultural and life sciences (MSLFS); business information systems (Graduate Certificate); career and technical education (MS); civil engineering (MS); computer engineering (M Eng, MS); decision support systems (Graduate Certificate); eLearning leadership (MA); electrical engineering (M Eng, MS); engineering administration (MEA); environmental engineering (Certificate); environmental politics and policy (Graduate Certificate); environmental sciences and engineering (MS); foundations of political analysis (Graduate Certificate); health product risk management (Graduate Certificate); industrial and systems engineering (MS); information policy and society (Graduate Certificate); information security (Graduate Certificate); information technology (MIT); instructional technology (MA); integrative STEM education (MA Ed); liberal arts (Graduate Certificate); life sciences: health product risk management (MS); natural resources (MNR, Graduate Certificate); networking (Graduate Certificate); nonprofit and nongovernmental organization management (Graduate Certificate); ocean engineering (MS); political science (MA); security studies (Graduate Certificate); software development (Graduate Certificate). *Expenses:* Tuition, state resident: full-time $13,700; part-time $761.25 per credit hour. Tuition, nonresident: full-time $27,614; part-time $1534 per credit hour. *Required fees:* $886.50 per term. Tuition and fees vary according to campus/location and program.

Washington State University, Voiland College of Engineering and Architecture, Department of Civil and Environmental Engineering, Pullman, WA 99164-2910. Offers civil engineering (MS, PhD); environmental engineering (MS). *Program availability:* Part-time. Terminal master's awarded for partial completion of doctoral program. *Degree requirements:* For master's, comprehensive exam (for some programs), thesis (for some programs), oral exam; for doctorate, comprehensive exam, thesis/dissertation, oral exam, written exam. *Entrance requirements:* For master's, minimum GPA of 3.0, 3 letters of recommendation, statement of purpose; for doctorate, minimum GPA of 3.4, 3 letters of recommendation, statement of purpose. Additional exam requirements/recommendations for international students: required—TOEFL (minimum score 550 paper-based), IELTS. Electronic applications accepted.

Wayne State University, College of Engineering, Department of Civil and Environmental Engineering, Detroit, MI 48202. Offers civil engineering (MS). *Faculty:* 12. *Students:* 38 full-time (9 women), 31 part-time (12 women); includes 6 minority (all Black or African American, non-Hispanic/Latino), 25 international. Average age 30. 128 applicants, 29% accepted, 17 enrolled. In 2019, 24 master's, 6 doctorates awarded. *Degree requirements:* For master's, thesis optional; for doctorate, comprehensive exam, thesis/dissertation. *Entrance requirements:* For master's, BS in civil engineering from ABET-accredited institution with minimum GPA of 3.0, statement of purpose; for doctorate, BS in civil engineering from ABET-accredited institution (or comparable foreign institution) with minimum GPA of 3.3, 3.4 in last two years, or MS in civil engineering with minimum GPA of 3.5 from ABET-accredited institution (or comparable foreign institution). Additional exam requirements/recommendations for international students: required—TOEFL (minimum score 550 paper-based; 79 iBT), TWE (minimum score 5.5), Michigan English Language Assessment Battery (minimum score 85); recommended—IELTS (minimum score 6.5). *Application deadline:* For fall admission, 3/1 priority date for domestic and international students; for winter admission, 10/1 priority date for domestic students, 9/1 priority date for international students; for spring admission, 2/1 priority date for domestic students, 1/1 priority date for international students. Applications are processed on a rolling basis. Application fee: $50. Electronic applications accepted. *Expenses:* $790 per credit hour in-state tuition, $1579 per credit hour out-of-state tuition. MS degree 30 credits; PhD 90 credits. *Financial support:* In 2019–20, 31 students received support, including 2 fellowships with tuition reimbursements available (averaging $17,830 per year), 13 research assistantships with tuition reimbursements available (averaging $21,873 per year), 5 teaching assistantships with tuition reimbursements available (averaging $20,792 per year); scholarships/grants, health care benefits, and unspecified assistantships also available. Support available to part-time students. Financial award applicants required to submit FAFSA. *Unit head:* Dr. William Shuster, Professor and Chair, 313-577-0228, E-mail: wshuster@wayne.edu. *Application contact:* Rob Carlson, Graduate Program Coordinator, 313-577-9615, E-mail: rcarlson@wayne.edu.
Website: http://engineering.wayne.edu/cee/

Wentworth Institute of Technology, Master of Engineering in Civil Engineering Program, Boston, MA 02115-5998. Offers construction engineering (M Eng); infrastructure engineering (M Eng). *Program availability:* Part-time-only, evening/weekend. *Degree requirements:* For master's, thesis optional, capstone course. *Entrance requirements:* For master's, resume, statement of purpose, official transcripts, two professional recommendations, bachelor's degree, minimum GPA of 3.0, one year of professional experience in a technical role and/or technical organization. Additional exam requirements/recommendations for international students: recommended—TOEFL (minimum score 550 paper-based). Electronic applications accepted. *Expenses:* Contact institution.

Western Michigan University, Graduate College, College of Engineering and Applied Sciences, Department of Civil and Construction Engineering, Kalamazoo, MI 49008. Offers MSE.

Western New England University, College of Engineering, Department of Civil and Environmental Engineering, Springfield, MA 01119. Offers civil engineering (MS). *Program availability:* Part-time, evening/weekend. *Degree requirements:* For master's, thesis optional. *Entrance requirements:* For master's, transcript, two letters of recommendations, resume, bachelor's degree in engineering or related field. Additional exam requirements/recommendations for international students: required—TOEFL (minimum score 79 iBT). Electronic applications accepted. *Expenses:* Contact institution.

West Virginia University, Statler College of Engineering and Mineral Resources, Morgantown, WV 26506. Offers aerospace engineering (MSAE, PhD); chemical engineering (MS Ch E, PhD); civil engineering (MSCE, PhD); computer engineering (PhD); computer science (MSCS, PhD); electrical engineering (MSEE, PhD); energy systems engineering (MSESE); engineering (MSE); industrial engineering (MSIE, PhD); industrial hygiene (MS); material science and engineering (MSMSE, PhD); mechanical engineering (MSME, PhD); mining engineering (MS Min E, PhD); petroleum and natural gas engineering (MSPNGE, PhD); safety management (MS); software engineering (MSSE). *Program availability:* Part-time. Terminal master's awarded for partial completion of doctoral program. *Degree requirements:* For master's, thesis optional; for doctorate, comprehensive exam, thesis/dissertation. *Entrance requirements:* Additional exam requirements/recommendations for international students: required—TOEFL (minimum score 550 paper-based). Electronic applications accepted. *Expenses:* Contact institution.

Widener University, Graduate Programs in Engineering, Program in Civil Engineering, Chester, PA 19013. Offers M Eng. *Program availability:* Part-time, evening/weekend. *Degree requirements:* For master's, thesis optional. Electronic applications accepted. *Expenses: Tuition:* Full-time $48,750; part-time $917 per credit hour. Tuition and fees vary according to class time, degree level, campus/location and program.

Worcester Polytechnic Institute, Graduate Admissions, Department of Civil and Environmental Engineering, Worcester, MA 01609-2280. Offers civil engineering (MS); construction project management (Graduate Certificate). *Program availability:* Part-time, evening/weekend, 100% online, blended/hybrid learning. *Degree requirements:* For master's, thesis optional; for doctorate, comprehensive exam, thesis/dissertation. *Entrance requirements:* For master's, required for all international applicants; recommended for all others, 3 letters of recommendation; for doctorate, required for all international applicants; recommended for all others, 3 letters of recommendation, statement of purpose. Additional exam requirements/recommendations for international students: required—TOEFL (minimum score 563 paper-based; 84 iBT), IELTS (minimum score 7). Electronic applications accepted.

Youngstown State University, College of Graduate Studies, College of Science, Technology, Engineering and Mathematics, Department of Civil/Environmental and Chemical Engineering, Youngstown, OH 44555-0001. Offers civil and environmental engineering (MSE). *Program availability:* Part-time, evening/weekend. *Degree requirements:* For master's, thesis optional. *Entrance requirements:* For master's, minimum GPA of 2.75 in field. Additional exam requirements/recommendations for international students: required—TOEFL.

Construction Engineering

The American University in Cairo, School of Sciences and Engineering, Cairo, Egypt. Offers biotechnology (MS); chemistry (MS); computer science (MS); computing (M Comp); construction engineering (M Eng, MS); electronics and communications engineering (M Eng); environmental engineering (MS); environmental system design (M Eng); mechanical engineering (M Eng, MS); nanotechnology (MS); physics (MS); robotics, control and smart systems (MS); sciences and engineering (PhD); sustainable development (MS, Graduate Diploma). *Program availability:* Part-time, evening/weekend. *Degree requirements:* For master's, comprehensive exam (for some programs), thesis (for some programs); for doctorate, comprehensive exam (for some programs), thesis/dissertation. *Entrance requirements:* Additional exam requirements/recommendations for international students: required—TOEFL (minimum score 450 paper-based; 45 iBT), IELTS (minimum score 5). Electronic applications accepted.

Arizona State University at Tempe, Ira A. Fulton Schools of Engineering, School of Sustainable Engineering and the Built Environment, Tempe, AZ 85287-5306. Offers civil, environmental and sustainable engineering (MS, MSE, PhD); construction engineering (MSE); construction management (MS, PhD). *Program availability:* Part-time, evening/weekend, online learning. Terminal master's awarded for partial completion of doctoral program. *Degree requirements:* For master's, thesis optional, comprehensive exams (MSE); interactive Program of Study (iPOS) submitted before completing 50 percent of required credit hours; for doctorate, comprehensive exam, thesis/dissertation, interactive Program of Study (iPOS) submitted before completing 50 percent of required credit hours. *Entrance requirements:* For master's, GRE, minimum GPA of 3.0 or equivalent in last 2 years of work leading to bachelor's degree; for doctorate, GRE, minimum GPA of 3.0 in last 2 years of work leading to bachelor's degree, 3.2 in all graduate-level coursework with master's degree; 3 letters of recommendation; resume/curriculum vitae; letter of intent; thesis (if applicable); statement of research interests. Additional exam requirements/recommendations for international students: required—TOEFL, IELTS, or PTE. Electronic applications accepted. *Expenses:* Contact institution.

Auburn University, Graduate School, College of Architecture, Design, and Construction, McWhorter School of Building Science, Auburn, AL 36849. Offers MBC. *Faculty:* 20 full-time (3 women), 3 part-time/adjunct (2 women). *Students:* 14 full-time (4 women), 71 part-time (15 women); includes 19 minority (7 Black or African American, non-Hispanic/Latino; 1 American Indian or Alaska Native, non-Hispanic/Latino; 4 Asian, non-Hispanic/Latino; 6 Hispanic/Latino; 1 Native Hawaiian or other Pacific Islander, non-Hispanic/Latino), 6 international. Average age 38. 69 applicants, 96% accepted, 38 enrolled. In 2019, 28 master's awarded. *Degree requirements:* For master's, thesis (for some programs). *Entrance requirements:* For master's, GRE General Test. Additional exam requirements/recommendations for international students: required—TOEFL (minimum score 550 paper-based; 79 iBT), iTEP; recommended—IELTS (minimum score 6.5). *Application deadline:* Applications are processed on a rolling basis. Application fee: $60 ($70 for international students). Electronic applications accepted. *Expenses:* $546 per credit hour state resident tuition, $1638 per credit hour nonresident tuition, $680 student services fee for GRA/GTA, $2160 per semester. *Financial support:* In 2019–20, 2 research assistantships (averaging $9,696 per year), 13 teaching assistantships (averaging $7,706 per year) were awarded; fellowships also available. Financial award application deadline: 3/15; financial award applicants required to submit FAFSA. *Unit head:* Dr. Richard Burt, Head, 334-844-5260, E-mail: rab0011@auburn.edu. *Application contact:* Dr. George Flowers, Dean of the Graduate School, 334-844-2125.
Website: http://cadc.auburn.edu/construction

Bradley University, The Graduate School, Caterpillar College of Engineering and Technology, Department of Civil Engineering and Construction, Peoria, IL 61625-0002. Offers construction management, structural engineering, geo-environmental engineering (MSCE). *Program availability:* Part-time, evening/weekend. *Faculty:* 11 full-time (2 women). *Students:* 14 full-time (2 women), 6 part-time (1 woman); includes 2 minority (both Black or African American, non-Hispanic/Latino), 17 international. Average age 24. 42 applicants, 64% accepted, 5 enrolled. In 2019, 11 master's awarded. *Degree requirements:* For master's, comprehensive exam, thesis or alternative, 30 hours. *Entrance requirements:* For master's, minimum GPA of 2.5, Essays, Recommendation letters, Transcripts. Additional exam requirements/recommendations for international students: required—TOEFL (minimum score 550 paper-based; 79 iBT), IELTS (minimum score 6.5), PTE (minimum score 58). *Application deadline:* For fall admission, 5/15 priority date for domestic and international students; for spring admission, 10/15 priority date for domestic and international students. Applications are processed on a rolling basis. Application fee: $40 ($50 for international students). Electronic applications accepted. *Expenses: Tuition:* Part-time $930 per credit hour. *Financial support:* In 2019–20, 13 students received support, including 3 teaching assistantships with partial tuition reimbursements available (averaging $8,370 per year); research assistantships, scholarships/grants, tuition waivers (partial), and unspecified assistantships also available. Support available to part-time students. Financial award application deadline: 4/1. *Unit head:* Souhail Elhouar, Chairman, 309-677-3830, E-mail: selhouar@bradley.edu. *Application contact:* Rachel Webb, Director of On-Campus Graduate Admissions, 309-677-2375, E-mail: bugrad@bradley.edu.
Website: http://www.bradley.edu/academic/departments/cec/

Clemson University, Graduate School, College of Engineering, Computing and Applied Sciences, Glenn Department of Civil Engineering, Clemson, SC 29634. Offers civil engineering (MS, PhD), including construction engineering and management, construction materials, geotechnical engineering, structural engineering, transportation engineering, water resources engineering. *Program availability:* Part-time, 100% online. *Faculty:* 24 full-time (4 women), 3 part-time/adjunct (2 women). *Students:* 101 full-time (20 women), 44 part-time (9 women); includes 9 minority (3 Black or African American, non-Hispanic/Latino; 1 Asian, non-Hispanic/Latino; 2 Hispanic/Latino; 3 Two or more races, non-Hispanic/Latino), 97 international. Average age 29. 248 applicants, 62% accepted, 61 enrolled. In 2019, 43 master's, 11 doctorates awarded. *Degree requirements:* For master's, thesis or alternative, oral exam, seminar; for doctorate, comprehensive exam, thesis/dissertation, oral exam, seminar. *Entrance requirements:* For master's and doctorate, GRE General Test, unofficial transcripts, letters of recommendation, statement of purpose. Additional exam requirements/recommendations for international students: required—TOEFL (minimum score 80 paper-based; 80 iBT), PTE (minimum score 54); recommended—IELTS (minimum score 6.5). *Application deadline:* For fall admission, 4/15 for domestic and international students; for spring admission, 9/15 for domestic and international students. Applications are processed on a rolling basis. Application fee: $80 ($90 for international students). Electronic applications accepted. *Expenses: Tuition, area resident:* Full-time $10,600; part-time $8688 per semester. Tuition, state resident: full-time $10,600; part-time $8688 per semester. Tuition, nonresident: full-time $22,050; part-time $17,412 per semester. *International tuition:* $22,050 full-time. *Required fees:* $1196; $617 per semester. $617 per semester. Tuition and fees vary according to course load, degree level, campus/location and program. *Financial support:* In 2019–20, 101 students received support, including 2 fellowships with full and partial tuition reimbursements available (averaging $34,000 per year), 61 research assistantships with full and partial tuition reimbursements available (averaging $18,222 per year), 4 teaching assistantships with full and partial tuition reimbursements available (averaging $20,567 per year); career-related internships or fieldwork and unspecified assistantships also available. Financial award application deadline: 4/15. *Unit head:* Dr. Jesus M de la Garza, Department Chair, 864-656-3001, E-mail: jdelaga@clemson.edu. *Application contact:* Dr. Abdul Khan, Graduate Program Coordinator, 864-656-3327, E-mail: abdkhan@clemson.edu.
Website: https://www.clemson.edu/cecas/departments/ce/

Colorado School of Mines, Office of Graduate Studies, Department of Civil and Environmental Engineering, Golden, CO 80401. Offers civil and environmental engineering (MS, PhD); environmental engineering science (MS, PhD); hydrologic science and engineering (MS, PhD); underground construction and tunneling (MS, PhD). *Program availability:* Part-time. *Degree requirements:* For master's, thesis (for some programs); for doctorate, comprehensive exam, thesis/dissertation. *Entrance requirements:* For master's and doctorate, GRE General Test. Additional exam requirements/recommendations for international students: required—TOEFL (minimum score 550 paper-based; 79 iBT). Electronic applications accepted. *Expenses:* Tuition, state resident: full-time $16,650; part-time $925 per credit hour. Tuition, nonresident: full-time $37,350; part-time $2075 per credit hour. *International tuition:* $37,350 full-time. *Required fees:* $2412.

Colorado School of Mines, Office of Graduate Studies, Department of Geology and Geological Engineering, Golden, CO 80401. Offers environmental geochemistry (PMS); geochemistry (MS, PhD); geological engineering (ME, MS, PhD); geology (MS, PhD); hydrology (MS, PhD); mineral exploration (PMS); petroleum reservoir systems (PMS); underground construction and tunneling (MS). *Program availability:* Part-time. *Degree requirements:* For master's, thesis (for some programs); for doctorate, comprehensive exam, thesis/dissertation. *Entrance requirements:* For master's and doctorate, GRE General Test. Additional exam requirements/recommendations for international students: required—TOEFL (minimum score 550 paper-based; 79 iBT). Electronic applications accepted. *Expenses:* Tuition, state resident: full-time $16,650; part-time $925 per credit hour. Tuition, nonresident: full-time $37,350; part-time $2075 per credit hour. *International tuition:* $37,350 full-time. *Required fees:* $2412.

Colorado School of Mines, Office of Graduate Studies, Department of Mining Engineering, Golden, CO 80401. Offers mining and earth systems engineering (MS); mining engineering (PhD); underground construction and tunneling (MS, PhD). *Program availability:* Part-time. *Degree requirements:* For master's, thesis (for some programs); for doctorate, comprehensive exam, thesis/dissertation. *Entrance requirements:* For master's and doctorate, GRE General Test. Additional exam requirements/recommendations for international students: required—TOEFL (minimum score 550 paper-based; 79 iBT). Electronic applications accepted. *Expenses:* Tuition, state resident: full-time $16,650; part-time $925 per credit hour. Tuition, nonresident: full-time $37,350; part-time $2075 per credit hour. *International tuition:* $37,350 full-time. *Required fees:* $2412.

Columbia University, Fu Foundation School of Engineering and Applied Science, Department of Civil Engineering and Engineering Mechanics, New York, NY 10027. Offers civil engineering (MS, Eng Sc D, PhD); construction engineering and management (MS); engineering mechanics (MS, Eng Sc D, PhD). *Program availability:* Part-time, online learning. Terminal master's awarded for partial completion of doctoral program. *Degree requirements:* For doctorate, thesis/dissertation, qualifying exam. *Entrance requirements:* For master's and doctorate, GRE General Test. Additional exam requirements/recommendations for international students: required—TOEFL, IELTS, PTE. Electronic applications accepted. *Expenses: Tuition:* Full-time $47,600; part-time $1880 per credit. One-time fee: $105.

Concordia University, School of Graduate Studies, Faculty of Engineering and Computer Science, Department of Building, Civil and Environmental Engineering, Montréal, QC H3G 1M8, Canada. Offers building engineering (M Eng, MA Sc, PhD, Certificate); civil engineering (M Eng, MA Sc, PhD); environmental engineering (Certificate). *Degree requirements:* For master's, thesis or alternative; for doctorate, comprehensive exam, thesis/dissertation.

George Mason University, Volgenau School of Engineering, Sid and Reva Dewberry Department of Civil, Environmental, and Infrastructure Engineering, Fairfax, VA 22030. Offers construction project management (MS); transportation engineering (PhD). *Degree requirements:* For master's, thesis (for some programs), 30 credits, departmental seminars; for doctorate, thesis/dissertation, qualifying exams. *Entrance requirements:* For master's, GRE, photocopy of passport; 2 official college transcripts; resume; official bank statement; proof of financial support; expanded goals statement; self-evaluation form; BS in engineering or other related science; 3 letters of recommendation; for doctorate, GRE (for those who received degree outside of the U.S.), photocopy of passport; 2 official college transcripts; resume; official bank statement; proof of financial support; expanded goals statement; self-evaluation form; baccalaureate degree in engineering or related science; master's degree (preferred); 3 letters of recommendation. Additional exam requirements/recommendations for international students: required—TOEFL (minimum score 575 paper-based; 88 iBT), IELTS (minimum score 6.5), PTE (minimum score 59). Electronic applications accepted. *Expenses:* Contact institution.

Illinois Institute of Technology, Graduate College, Armour College of Engineering, Department of Civil, Architectural and Environmental Engineering, Chicago, IL 60616. Offers architectural engineering (M Arch E); civil engineering (MS, PhD), including architectural engineering (MS), construction engineering and management (MS), geoenvironmental engineering (MS), geotechnical engineering (MS), structural engineering (MS), transportation engineering (MS); construction engineering and management (MCEM); environmental engineering (M Env E, MS, PhD); geoenvironmental engineering (M Geoenv E); geotechnical engineering (MGE); infrastructure engineering and management (MPW); structural engineering (MSE); transportation engineering (M Trans E). *Program availability:* Part-time, evening/weekend, online learning. Terminal master's awarded for partial completion of doctoral program. *Degree requirements:* For master's, thesis (for some programs); for doctorate, comprehensive exam, thesis/dissertation. *Entrance requirements:* For master's, GRE General Test (minimum score 900 Quantitative and Verbal, 2.5 Analytical Writing), minimum undergraduate GPA of 3.0; for doctorate, GRE General Test (minimum score 1000 Quantitative and Verbal, 3.0 Analytical Writing), minimum undergraduate GPA of 3.0. Additional exam requirements/recommendations for international students: required—TOEFL (minimum score 550 paper-based; 80 iBT). Electronic applications accepted.

Iowa State University of Science and Technology, Department of Civil and Construction Engineering, Ames, IA 50011. Offers civil engineering (MS, PhD), including civil engineering materials, construction engineering and management, environmental engineering, geotechnical engineering, structural engineering, transportation engineering. *Degree requirements:* For master's, thesis or alternative; for doctorate, thesis/dissertation. *Entrance requirements:* For master's and doctorate, GRE General Test. Additional exam requirements/recommendations for international students: required—TOEFL (minimum score 550 paper-based; 82 iBT), IELTS (minimum score 6.5). Electronic applications accepted.

Lawrence Technological University, College of Engineering, Southfield, MI 48075-1058. Offers architectural engineering (MS); automotive engineering (MS); biomedical engineering (MS); civil engineering (MA, MS, PhD), including environmental engineering (MS), geotechnical engineering (MS), structural engineering (MS), transportation engineering (MS), water resource engineering (MS); construction engineering management (MA); electrical and computer engineering (MS); engineering management (MEM); engineering technology (MS); fire engineering (MS); industrial engineering (MS), including healthcare systems; manufacturing systems (ME); mechanical engineering (MS, DE, PhD), including automotive engineering (MS), energy engineering (MS), manufacturing (DE), solid mechanics (MS), thermal/fluid systems (MS); mechatronic systems engineering (MS). *Program availability:* Part-time, evening/weekend. *Faculty:* 23 full-time (2 women), 20 part-time/adjunct (1 woman). *Students:* 14 full-time (5 women), 286 part-time (54 women); includes 26 minority (13 Black or African American, non-Hispanic/Latino; 8 Asian, non-Hispanic/Latino; 3 Hispanic/Latino; 2 Two or more races, non-Hispanic/Latino), 150 international. Average age 29. 384 applicants, 58% accepted, 74 enrolled. In 2019, 223 master's, 7 doctorates awarded. Terminal master's awarded for partial completion of doctoral program. *Degree requirements:* For master's, thesis optional; for doctorate, comprehensive exam, thesis/dissertation optional. *Entrance requirements:* Additional exam requirements/recommendations for international students: required—TOEFL (minimum score 550 paper-based; 79 iBT), IELTS (minimum score 6.5). *Application deadline:* For fall admission, 5/24 for international students; for spring admission, 10/13 for international students; for summer admission, 2/18 for international students. Applications are processed on a rolling basis. Application fee: $50. Electronic applications accepted. *Expenses: Tuition:* Full-time $16,618; part-time $8309 per year. *Required fees:* $600; $600. *Financial support:* In 2019–20, 21 students received support. Unspecified assistantships available. Financial award application deadline: 4/1; financial award applicants required to submit FAFSA. *Unit head:* Dr. Nabil Grace, Dean, 248-204-2500, Fax: 248-204-2509, E-mail: engrdean@ltu.edu. *Application contact:* Jane Rohrback, Director of Admissions, 248-204-3160, Fax: 248-204-2228, E-mail: admissions@ltu.edu.
Website: http://www.ltu.edu/engineering/index.asp

Marquette University, Graduate School, College of Engineering, Department of Civil and Environmental Engineering, Milwaukee, WI 53201-1881. Offers construction engineering and management (MS, PhD, Certificate); environmental engineering (MS, PhD); structural design (Certificate); structural engineering and structural mechanics (MS, PhD); transportation (Certificate); transportation engineering and materials (MS, PhD); waste and wastewater treatment processes (Certificate); water resources engineering (Certificate). *Program availability:* Part-time, evening/weekend. Terminal master's awarded for partial completion of doctoral program. *Degree requirements:* For master's, comprehensive exam (for some programs), thesis or alternative; for doctorate, thesis/dissertation. *Entrance requirements:* For master's, GRE General Test (recommended), minimum GPA of 3.0, official transcripts from all current and previous colleges/universities except Marquette, three letters of recommendation; for doctorate, GRE General Test, minimum GPA of 3.0, official transcripts from all current and previous colleges/universities except Marquette, three letters of recommendation, brief statement of purpose, submission of any English language publications authored by applicant (strongly recommended). Additional exam requirements/recommendations for international students: required—TOEFL (minimum score 530 paper-based). Electronic applications accepted.

Massachusetts Institute of Technology, School of Engineering, Department of Civil and Environmental Engineering, Cambridge, MA 02139. Offers biological oceanography (PhD, Sc D); chemical oceanography (PhD, Sc D); civil and environmental engineering (M Eng, SM, PhD, Sc D); civil and environmental systems (PhD, Sc D); civil engineering (PhD, Sc D, CE); civil engineering and computation (PhD); coastal engineering (PhD, Sc D); construction engineering and management (PhD, Sc D); environmental biology (PhD, Sc D); environmental chemistry (PhD, Sc D); environmental engineering (PhD, Sc D); environmental engineering and computation (PhD); environmental fluid mechanics (PhD, Sc D); geotechnical and geoenvironmental engineering (PhD, Sc D); hydrology (PhD, Sc D); information technology (PhD, Sc D); oceanographic engineering (PhD, Sc D); structures and materials (PhD, Sc D); transportation (PhD, Sc D); SM/MBA. *Degree requirements:* For master's, thesis; for doctorate, comprehensive exam, thesis/dissertation; for CE, comprehensive exam, thesis. *Entrance requirements:* For master's, doctorate, and CE, GRE General Test. Additional exam requirements/recommendations for international students: required—TOEFL, IELTS. Electronic applications accepted.

Montana State University, The Graduate School, College of Engineering, Department of Civil Engineering, Bozeman, MT 59717. Offers civil engineering (MS); construction engineering management (MCEM); engineering (PhD), including applied mechanics option, civil engineering option. *Program availability:* Part-time. *Degree requirements:* For master's, comprehensive exam, thesis (for some programs); for doctorate, comprehensive exam, thesis/dissertation. *Entrance requirements:* For master's and doctorate, GRE General Test. Additional exam requirements/recommendations for international students: required—TOEFL (minimum score 550 paper-based). Electronic applications accepted.

Ohio University, Graduate College, Russ College of Engineering and Technology, Department of Civil Engineering, Athens, OH 45701-2979. Offers civil engineering (PhD); construction engineering and management (MS); environmental (MS); geoenvironmental (MS); geotechnical (MS); mechanics (MS); structures (MS); transportation (MS); water resources (MS). *Program availability:* Part-time. *Degree requirements:* For master's, comprehensive exam (for some programs), thesis or alternative; for doctorate, comprehensive exam, thesis/dissertation. *Entrance requirements:* For master's, GRE General Test, minimum GPA of 3.0, 3 letters of recommendation; for doctorate, GRE General Test. Additional exam requirements/recommendations for international students: required—TOEFL (minimum score 550 paper-based; 80 iBT) or IELTS (minimum score 6.5). Electronic applications accepted.

Oregon State University, College of Engineering, Program in Civil Engineering, Corvallis, OR 97331. Offers civil engineering (M Eng, MS, PhD); coastal and ocean engineering (M Eng, MS, PhD); construction engineering management (M Eng, MS, PhD); engineering education (M Eng, MS, PhD); geomatics (M Eng, MS, PhD); geotechnical engineering (M Eng, MS, PhD); infrastructure materials (M Eng, MS, PhD); structural engineering (M Eng, MS, PhD); transportation engineering (M Eng). *Entrance requirements:* For master's and doctorate, GRE. Additional exam requirements/recommendations for international students: required—TOEFL (minimum score 80 iBT), IELTS (minimum score 6.5). *Expenses:* Contact institution.

Pittsburg State University, Graduate School, College of Technology, School of Construction, Pittsburg, KS 66762. Offers construction engineering technology (MET); construction management (MS). *Program availability:* Part-time, 100% online, blended/hybrid learning. *Degree requirements:* For master's, thesis or alternative. *Entrance requirements:* Additional exam requirements/recommendations for international students: required—TOEFL (minimum score 550 paper-based; 79 iBT), IELTS (minimum score 6.5), PTE (minimum score 53). Electronic applications accepted. *Expenses:* Contact institution.

Stanford University, School of Engineering, Department of Civil and Environmental Engineering, Stanford, CA 94305-2004. Offers atmosphere and energy (MS, PhD); construction (MS), including construction engineering and management, design-construction integration, sustainable design and construction; environmental engineering and science (MS, PhD); environmental fluid mechanics and hydrology (PhD); structural engineering (MS). *Expenses: Tuition:* Full-time $52,479; part-time $34,110 per unit. *Required fees:* $672; $224 per quarter. Tuition and fees vary according to program and student level.
Website: http://www-ce.stanford.edu/

Stevens Institute of Technology, Graduate School, Charles V. Schaefer Jr. School of Engineering and Science, Department of Civil, Environmental, and Ocean Engineering, Program in Construction Engineering and Management, Hoboken, NJ 07030. Offers construction management (MS, Certificate), including construction accounting/estimating (Certificate), construction engineering (Certificate), construction law/disputes (Certificate), construction/quality management (Certificate). *Program availability:* Part-time, evening/weekend. *Faculty:* 23 full-time (8 women), 21 part-time/adjunct (2 women). *Students:* 98 full-time (9 women), 22 part-time (6 women); includes 8 minority (4 Black or African American, non-Hispanic/Latino; 4 Asian, non-Hispanic/Latino), 95 international. Average age 25. In 2019, 77 master's awarded. Terminal master's awarded for partial completion of doctoral program. *Degree requirements:* For master's, thesis optional, minimum B average in major field and overall; for Certificate, minimum B average. *Entrance requirements:* For master's, International applicants must submit TOEFL/IELTS scores and fulfill the English Language Proficiency Requirement. Applicants to full-time programs who do not qualify for a score waiver are required to submit GRE/GMAT scores. Additional exam requirements/recommendations for international students: required—TOEFL (minimum score 74 iBT), IELTS (minimum score 6). *Application deadline:* For fall admission, 4/15 for domestic and international students; for spring admission, 11/1 for domestic and international students; for summer admission, 5/1 for domestic students. Applications are processed on a rolling basis.

Application fee: $60. Electronic applications accepted. *Expenses: Tuition:* Full-time $52,134. *Required fees:* $1880. Tuition and fees vary according to course load. *Financial support:* Fellowships, research assistantships, teaching assistantships, career-related internships or fieldwork, Federal Work-Study, scholarships/grants, and unspecified assistantships available. Financial award application deadline: 2/15; financial award applicants required to submit FAFSA. *Unit head:* Dr. Jean Zu, Dean of SES, 201-216.8233, Fax: 201-216.8372, E-mail: Jean.Zu@stevens.edu. *Application contact:* Graduate Admission, 888-783-8367, Fax: 888-511-1306, E-mail: graduate@stevens.edu.

The University of Alabama, Graduate School, College of Engineering, Department of Civil, Construction and Environmental Engineering, Tuscaloosa, AL 35487-0205. Offers civil engineering (MSCE, PhD); environmental engineering (MS). *Program availability:* Part-time. *Faculty:* 18 full-time (1 woman). *Students:* 64 full-time (23 women), 5 part-time (2 women); includes 4 minority (2 Asian, non-Hispanic/Latino; 2 Hispanic/Latino), 41 international. Average age 29. 116 applicants, 63% accepted, 17 enrolled. In 2019, 22 master's, 4 doctorates awarded. Terminal master's awarded for partial completion of doctoral program. *Degree requirements:* For master's, thesis or alternative; for doctorate, comprehensive exam, thesis/dissertation. *Entrance requirements:* For master's and doctorate, GRE General Test (minimum combined score of 300), minimum overall GPA of 3.0 in last hours of course work. Additional exam requirements/recommendations for international students: required—TOEFL (minimum score 550 paper-based; 79 iBT), IELTS (minimum score 6.5), PTE (minimum score 59). *Application deadline:* Applications are processed on a rolling basis. Application fee: $50 ($60 for international students). Electronic applications accepted. *Expenses: Tuition, area resident:* Full-time $10,780; part-time $440 per credit hour. Tuition, nonresident: full-time $30,250; part-time $1550 per credit hour. *Financial support:* In 2019–20, 36 students received support. Fellowships with full tuition reimbursements available, research assistantships with full tuition reimbursements available, teaching assistantships with full tuition reimbursements available, scholarships/grants, tuition waivers (partial), and unspecified assistantships available. Financial award application deadline: 1/5. *Unit head:* Dr. W. Edward Back, Head/Professor, 205-348-6550, Fax: 205-348-0783, E-mail: eback@eng.ua.edu. *Application contact:* Dr. Andrew Graettinger, Professor and Graduate Program Director, 205-348-1707, Fax: 205-348-0783, E-mail: andrewg@eng.ua.edu.
Website: http://cce.eng.ua.edu/

The University of Alabama at Birmingham, School of Engineering, Professional Engineering Degrees, Birmingham, AL 35294. Offers advanced safety engineering and management (M Eng); construction engineering management (M Eng); design and commercialization (M Eng); information engineering management (M Eng); structural engineering (M Eng); sustainable smart cities (M Eng). *Program availability:* Part-time, evening/weekend, online only, 100% online. *Faculty:* 5 full-time (1 woman), 15 part-time/adjunct (3 women). *Students:* 13 full-time (4 women), 315 part-time (70 women); includes 83 minority (64 Black or African American, non-Hispanic/Latino; 3 American Indian or Alaska Native, non-Hispanic/Latino; 9 Asian, non-Hispanic/Latino; 7 Hispanic/Latino), 8 international. 126 applicants, 84% accepted, 90 enrolled. In 2019, 123 master's awarded. *Entrance requirements:* For master's, 3.0 GPA on 4.0 scale, undergraduate degree from a nationally accredited school. Additional exam requirements/recommendations for international students: required—TOEFL (minimum score 80 iBT); recommended—IELTS (minimum score 6.5). *Application deadline:* For fall admission, 8/1 for domestic and international students; for spring admission, 12/1 for domestic and international students; for summer admission, 5/1 for domestic and international students. Applications are processed on a rolling basis. Application fee: $50 ($60 for international students). Electronic applications accepted. *Expenses:* Contact institution. *Unit head:* Dr. Gregg Janowski, Associate Dean for Graduate Programs and Assessment, E-mail: janowski@uab.edu. *Application contact:* Jesse Kepply, Director of Student and Academic Services, 205-996-5696, E-mail: gradschool@uab.edu.

University of Alberta, Faculty of Graduate Studies and Research, Department of Civil and Environmental Engineering, Edmonton, AB T6G 2E1, Canada. Offers construction engineering and management (M Eng, M Sc, PhD); environmental engineering (M Eng, M Sc, PhD); environmental science (M Sc, PhD); geoenvironmental engineering (M Eng, M Sc, PhD); geotechnical engineering (M Eng, M Sc, PhD); mining engineering (M Eng, M Sc, PhD); petroleum engineering (M Eng, M Sc, PhD); structural engineering (M Eng, M Sc, PhD); water resources (M Eng, M Sc, PhD). *Program availability:* Part-time, online learning. *Degree requirements:* For master's, thesis (for some programs); for doctorate, thesis/dissertation. *Entrance requirements:* For master's, minimum GPA of 3.0 in last 2 years of undergraduate studies; for doctorate, minimum GPA of 3.0. Additional exam requirements/recommendations for international students: required—TOEFL (minimum score 550 paper-based). Electronic applications accepted.

University of Michigan, College of Engineering, Department of Civil and Environmental Engineering, Ann Arbor, MI 48109. Offers civil engineering (MSE, PhD, CE); construction engineering and management (M Eng, MSE); environmental engineering (MSE, PhD); structural engineering (M Eng); MBA/MSE. *Program availability:* Part-time. Terminal master's awarded for partial completion of doctoral program. *Degree requirements:* For master's, thesis optional; for doctorate, comprehensive exam, thesis/dissertation, oral defense of dissertation, preliminary and written exams. *Entrance requirements:* For master's and doctorate, GRE General Test. Additional exam requirements/recommendations for international students: required—TOEFL. Electronic applications accepted.

University of Missouri–Kansas City, School of Computing and Engineering, Kansas City, MO 64110-2499. Offers civil engineering (MS); computer and electrical engineering (PhD); computer science (MS), including bioinformatics, software engineering, telecommunications networking; computer science and informatics (PhD); computing (PhD); electrical engineering (MS); engineering (PhD); engineering and construction management (Graduate Certificate); mechanical engineering (MS); telecommunications and computer networking (PhD). *Program availability:* Part-time. *Degree requirements:* For doctorate, thesis/dissertation. *Entrance requirements:* For master's, GRE General Test, minimum GPA of 3.0, 3 letters of recommendation from professors; for doctorate, GRE General Test, minimum GPA of 3.5. Additional exam requirements/recommendations for international students: required—TOEFL (minimum score 550 paper-based; 80 iBT).

University of New Brunswick Fredericton, School of Graduate Studies, Faculty of Engineering, Department of Civil Engineering, Fredericton, NB E3B 5A3, Canada. Offers construction engineering and management (M Eng, M Sc E, PhD); environmental engineering (M Eng, M Sc E, PhD); environmental studies (M Eng); geotechnical engineering (M Eng, M Sc E, PhD); groundwater/hydrology (M Eng, M Sc E, PhD); materials (M Eng, M Sc E, PhD); pavements (M Eng, M Sc E, PhD); structures (M Eng,

M Sc E, PhD); transportation (M Eng, M Sc E, PhD). *Program availability:* Part-time. *Faculty:* 17 full-time (2 women). *Students:* 31 full-time (6 women), 10 part-time (0 women), 12 international. Average age 27. In 2019, 11 master's awarded. *Degree requirements:* For master's, thesis; for doctorate, comprehensive exam, thesis/dissertation, qualifying exam; 27 credit hours of courses. *Entrance requirements:* For master's, minimum GPA of 3.0; B Sc E in civil engineering or related engineering degree; for doctorate, minimum GPA of 3.0; graduate degree in engineering or applied science. Additional exam requirements/recommendations for international students: required—IELTS (minimum score 7.5), TWE (minimum score 4), Michigan English Language Assessment Battery (minimum score 85) or CanTest (minimum score 4.5); recommended—TOEFL (minimum score 580 paper-based). *Application deadline:* For fall admission, 5/1 for domestic students; for winter admission, 11/1 for domestic students. Applications are processed on a rolling basis. Application fee: $50 Canadian dollars. Electronic applications accepted. *Expenses: Tuition, area resident:* Full-time $6975 Canadian dollars; part-time $3423 Canadian dollars per year. Tuition, state resident: full-time $6975 Canadian dollars; part-time $3423 Canadian dollars per year. Tuition, Canadian resident: full-time $6975 Canadian dollars; part-time $3423 Canadian dollars per year. *International tuition:* $12,435 Canadian dollars full-time. *Required fees:* $92.25 Canadian dollars per term. Full-time tuition and fees vary according to degree level, campus/location, program, reciprocity agreements and student level. *Financial support:* Fellowships, research assistantships, teaching assistantships, career-related internships or fieldwork, and scholarships/grants available. Financial award application deadline: 1/15. *Unit head:* Dr. Jeff Rankin, Chair, 506-453-4618, Fax: 506-453-3568, E-mail: ktm@unb.ca. *Application contact:* MaryBeth Nicholson, Graduate Secretary, 506-452-6127, Fax: 506-453-3568, E-mail: mbnich@unb.ca.
Website: http://go.unb.ca/gradprograms

University of Puerto Rico at Mayagüez, Graduate Studies, College of Engineering, Department of Civil Engineering and Surveying, Mayagüez, PR 00681-9000. Offers civil engineering (ME, MS, PhD), including construction engineering and management (ME, MS), environmental engineering, geotechnical engineering (ME, MS), structural engineering, transportation engineering. *Program availability:* Part-time. Terminal master's awarded for partial completion of doctoral program. *Degree requirements:* For master's, one foreign language, thesis; for doctorate, one foreign language, comprehensive exam, thesis/dissertation, qualifying exams. *Entrance requirements:* For master's, proficiency in English and Spanish; BS in civil engineering or its equivalent; for doctorate, proficiency in English and Spanish. Electronic applications accepted.

University of Virginia, School of Architecture, Program in the Constructed Environment, Charlottesville, VA 22903. Offers PhD. *Degree requirements:* For doctorate, thesis/dissertation. *Entrance requirements:* For doctorate, GRE, master's degree or equivalent, official transcripts, sample of academic writing, three letters of recommendation, resume or curriculum vitae, graphic portfolio. Additional exam requirements/recommendations for international students: required—TOEFL.

University of Washington, Graduate School, College of Engineering, Department of Civil and Environmental Engineering, Seattle, WA 98195-2700. Offers construction engineering (MSCE, PhD); environmental engineering (MSCE, PhD); geotechnical engineering (MSCE, PhD); hydrology and hydrodynamics (MSCE, PhD); structural engineering and mechanics (MSCE, PhD); transportation engineering (MSCE, PhD). *Program availability:* Part-time, 100% online. *Students:* 248 full-time (97 women), 174 part-time (63 women); includes 90 minority (8 Black or African American, non-Hispanic/Latino; 2 American Indian or Alaska Native, non-Hispanic/Latino; 46 Asian, non-Hispanic/Latino; 18 Hispanic/Latino; 16 Two or more races, non-Hispanic/Latino), 118 international. Average age 28. 756 applicants, 59% accepted, 164 enrolled. In 2019, 133 master's, 21 doctorates awarded. Terminal master's awarded for partial completion of doctoral program. *Degree requirements:* For master's, thesis optional; for doctorate, comprehensive exam, thesis/dissertation, qualifying, general and final exams; completion of degree within 10 years. *Entrance requirements:* For master's, GRE General Test, minimum GPA of 3.0, statement of purpose, letters of recommendation, transcripts; for doctorate, GRE General Test, minimum GPA of 3.5, statement of purpose, letters of recommendation, transcripts, resume. Additional exam requirements/recommendations for international students: required—TOEFL (minimum score 580 paper-based; 92 iBT). *Application deadline:* For fall admission, 12/15 for domestic and international students. Applications are processed on a rolling basis. Application fee: $85. Electronic applications accepted. *Expenses:* Contact institution. *Financial support:* In 2019–20, 21 fellowships with full tuition reimbursements (averaging $30,600 per year), 76 research assistantships with full tuition reimbursements (averaging $30,600 per year), 27 teaching assistantships with full tuition reimbursements (averaging $30,120 per year) were awarded; Federal Work-Study, institutionally sponsored loans, scholarships/grants, health care benefits, tuition waivers, and unspecified assistantships also available. Support available to part-time students. Financial award application deadline: 12/15. *Unit head:* Dr. Laura Lowes, Professor/Chair, 206-685-2563, Fax: 206-543-1543, E-mail: lowes@uw.edu. *Application contact:* Bryan Crockett, Director of Academic Services, 206-616-1891, Fax: 206-543-1543, E-mail: ceginfo@u.washington.edu.
Website: http://www.ce.washington.edu/

University of Wisconsin–Madison, Graduate School, College of Engineering, Department of Civil and Environmental Engineering, Madison, WI 53706-1380. Offers construction engineering and management (MS); environmental science and engineering (MS); geological/geotechnical engineering (MS); structural engineering (MS); transportation engineering (MS); water resources engineering (MS). *Program availability:* Part-time. Terminal master's awarded for partial completion of doctoral program. *Degree requirements:* For master's, thesis (for some programs), minimum of 30 credits; minimum overall GPA of 3.0. *Entrance requirements:* For master's, GRE General Test, bachelor's degree; minimum GPA of 3.0 for last 60 credits of course work. Additional exam requirements/recommendations for international students: required—TOEFL (minimum score 580 paper-based; 92 iBT). Electronic applications accepted. *Expenses:* Contact institution.

Wentworth Institute of Technology, Master of Engineering in Civil Engineering Program, Boston, MA 02115-5998. Offers construction engineering (M Eng); infrastructure engineering (M Eng). *Program availability:* Part-time-only, evening/weekend. *Degree requirements:* For master's, thesis optional, capstone course. *Entrance requirements:* For master's, resume, statement of purpose, official transcripts, two professional recommendations, bachelor's degree, minimum GPA of 3.0, one year of professional experience in a technical role and/or technical organization. Additional exam requirements/recommendations for international students: recommended—TOEFL (minimum score 550 paper-based). Electronic applications accepted. *Expenses:* Contact institution.

Environmental Engineering

Air Force Institute of Technology, Graduate School of Engineering and Management, Department of Systems and Engineering Management, Dayton, OH 45433-7765. Offers cost analysis (MS); environmental and engineering management (MS); environmental engineering science (MS); information resource/systems management (MS). *Accreditation:* ABET. *Program availability:* Part-time. *Degree requirements:* For master's, thesis. *Entrance requirements:* For master's, GRE, GMAT, minimum GPA of 3.0.

The American University in Cairo, School of Sciences and Engineering, Cairo, Egypt. Offers biotechnology (MS); chemistry (MS); computer science (MS); computing (M Comp); construction engineering (M Eng, MS); electronics and communications engineering (M Eng); environmental engineering (MS); environmental system design (M Eng); mechanical engineering (M Eng, MS); nanotechnology (MS); physics (MS); robotics, control and smart systems (MS); sciences and engineering (PhD); sustainable development (MS, Graduate Diploma). *Program availability:* Part-time, evening/weekend. *Degree requirements:* For master's, comprehensive exam (for some programs), thesis (for some programs); for doctorate, comprehensive exam (for some programs), thesis/dissertation. *Entrance requirements:* Additional exam requirements/recommendations for international students: required—TOEFL (minimum score 450 paper-based; 45 iBT), IELTS (minimum score 5). Electronic applications accepted.

Arizona State University at Tempe, Ira A. Fulton Schools of Engineering, School of Sustainable Engineering and the Built Environment, Tempe, AZ 85287-5306. Offers civil, environmental and sustainable engineering (MS, MSE, PhD); construction engineering (MSE); construction management (MS, PhD). *Program availability:* Part-time, evening/weekend, online learning. Terminal master's awarded for partial completion of doctoral program. *Degree requirements:* For master's, thesis optional, comprehensive exams (MSE); interactive Program of Study (iPOS) submitted before completing 50 percent of required credit hours; for doctorate, comprehensive exam, thesis/dissertation, interactive Program of Study (iPOS) submitted before completing 50 percent of required credit hours. *Entrance requirements:* For master's, GRE, minimum GPA of 3.0 or equivalent in last 2 years of work leading to bachelor's degree; for doctorate, GRE, minimum GPA of 3.0 in last 2 years of work leading to bachelor's degree, 3.2 in all graduate-level coursework with master's degree; 3 letters of recommendation; resume/curriculum vitae; letter of intent; thesis (if applicable); statement of research interests. Additional exam requirements/recommendations for international students: required—TOEFL, IELTS, or PTE. Electronic applications accepted. *Expenses:* Contact institution.

California Institute of Technology, Division of Engineering and Applied Science, Option in Environmental Science and Engineering, Pasadena, CA 91125-0001. Offers MS, PhD. *Degree requirements:* For doctorate, thesis/dissertation. Electronic applications accepted.

California Institute of Technology, Division of Geological and Planetary Sciences, Pasadena, CA 91125-0001. Offers environmental science and engineering (MS, PhD); geobiology (MS, PhD); geochemistry (MS, PhD); geology (MS, PhD); geophysics (MS, PhD); planetary science (MS, PhD). *Degree requirements:* For doctorate, thesis/dissertation. *Entrance requirements:* For doctorate, GRE General Test. Additional exam requirements/recommendations for international students: required—TOEFL; recommended—IELTS, TWE. Electronic applications accepted.

California Polytechnic State University, San Luis Obispo, College of Engineering, Department of Civil and Environmental Engineering, San Luis Obispo, CA 93407. Offers MS. *Program availability:* Part-time. *Faculty:* 11 full-time (1 woman), 1 part-time/adjunct (0 women). *Students:* 45 full-time (21 women), 4 part-time (0 women); includes 21 minority (9 Asian, non-Hispanic/Latino; 6 Hispanic/Latino; 6 Two or more races, non-Hispanic/Latino), 5 international. Average age 23. 79 applicants, 78% accepted, 38 enrolled. In 2019, 34 master's awarded. *Degree requirements:* For master's, comprehensive exam (for some programs), thesis (for some programs). *Entrance requirements:* For master's, GRE. Additional exam requirements/recommendations for international students: required—TOEFL (minimum score 80 iBT). *Application deadline:* For fall admission, 1/1 for domestic students, 3/1 priority date for international students. Applications are processed on a rolling basis. Application fee: $55. Electronic applications accepted. *Expenses:* Tuition, state resident: full-time $7176; part-time $4164 per year. Tuition, nonresident: full-time $18,690; part-time $8916 per year. *Required fees:* $4206; $3185 per unit. $1061 per term. *Financial support:* Fellowships, research assistantships, teaching assistantships, career-related internships or fieldwork, and scholarships/grants available. Financial award application deadline: 3/2; financial award applicants required to submit FAFSA. *Unit head:* Dr. Robb Moss, Graduate Coordinator, 805-756-6427, E-mail: rmoss@calpoly.edu. *Application contact:* Dr. Robb Moss, Graduate Coordinator, 805-756-6427, E-mail: rmoss@calpoly.edu.
Website: http://ceenve.calpoly.edu

California State University, Fullerton, Graduate Studies, College of Engineering and Computer Science, Department of Civil and Environmental Engineering, Fullerton, CA 92831-3599. Offers civil engineering (MS), including architectural engineering, environmental engineering. *Program availability:* Part-time. *Degree requirements:* For master's, comprehensive exam, project or thesis. *Entrance requirements:* For master's, minimum undergraduate GPA of 2.5.

Carleton University, Faculty of Graduate Studies, Faculty of Engineering and Design, Department of Civil and Environmental Engineering, Ottawa, ON K1S 5B6, Canada. Offers M Eng, MA Sc, PhD. *Degree requirements:* For master's, thesis optional; for doctorate, thesis/dissertation. *Entrance requirements:* For master's, honors degree; for doctorate, MA Sc or M Eng. Additional exam requirements/recommendations for international students: required—TOEFL.

Carnegie Mellon University, Carnegie Institute of Technology, Department of Civil and Environmental Engineering, Pittsburgh, PA 15213. Offers advanced infrastructure systems (MS, PhD); advanced infrastructure systems technology development and application (MS); air quality engineering and science (MS); civil and environmental engineering (MS, PhD); civil and environmental engineering/engineering and public policy (PhD); civil engineering (MS, PhD); computational mechanics (MS, PhD); computational modeling and monitoring for resilient structural and material systems (MS); energy infrastructure systems (MS); environmental engineering (MS, PhD); environmental management and science (MS, PhD); IT-based sustainable global infrastructure and construction management (MS); sustainability and green design (MS); water quality engineering and science (MS). *Program availability:* Part-time. *Faculty:* 23 full-time (5 women), 12 part-time/adjunct (3 women). *Students:* 261 full-time (109 women); includes 19 minority (7 Black or African American, non-Hispanic/Latino; 8 Asian, non-Hispanic/Latino; 4 Hispanic/Latino), 214 international. Average age 25. 649 applicants, 57% accepted, 106 enrolled. In 2019, 80 master's, 12 doctorates awarded. Terminal master's awarded for partial completion of doctoral program. *Degree requirements:* For master's, thesis optional; for doctorate, comprehensive exam, thesis/dissertation, two-part qualifying exam, public defense of dissertation. *Entrance requirements:* For master's, GRE General Test, BS in engineering, science, or mathematics; for doctorate, GRE General Test, BS or MS in engineering, science, or mathematics. Additional exam requirements/recommendations for international students: required—TOEFL (minimum score 84 iBT), TOEFL (minimum score 84 iBT) or IELTS (7.0). *Application deadline:* For fall admission, 1/5 priority date for domestic and international students; for spring admission, 9/15 priority date for domestic and international students. Applications are processed on a rolling basis. Application fee: $75. Electronic applications accepted. *Financial support:* In 2019–20, 113 students received support. Fellowships with tuition reimbursements available, research assistantships with tuition reimbursements available, teaching assistantships, scholarships/grants, health care benefits, tuition waivers (full and partial), and unspecified assistantships available. Financial award application deadline: 1/5. *Unit head:* Dr. David A. Dzombak, Professor and Department Head, 412-268-2941, Fax: 412-268-7813, E-mail: dzombak@cmu.edu. *Application contact:* David A. Vey, Director of Graduate Programs, 412-268-2292, Fax: 412-268-7813, E-mail: dvey@andrew.cmu.edu.
Website: http://www.cmu.edu/cee/

Carnegie Mellon University, Tepper School of Business, Pittsburgh, PA 15213-3891. Offers accounting (PhD); business management and software engineering (MBMSE); business technologies (PhD); civil engineering and industrial management (MS); computational finance (MSCF); economics (PhD); environmental engineering and management (MEEM); financial economics (PhD); industrial administration (MBA), including administration and public management; marketing (PhD); mathematical finance (PhD); operations management (PhD); operations research (PhD); organizational behavior and theory (PhD); production and operations management (PhD); public policy and management (MS, MSED); software engineering and business management (MS); JD/MS; JD/MSIA; M Div/MS; MOM/MSIA; MSCF/MSIA. *Program availability:* Part-time. Terminal master's awarded for partial completion of doctoral program. *Degree requirements:* For doctorate, thesis/dissertation. *Entrance requirements:* For master's, GMAT. Additional exam requirements/recommendations for international students: required—TOEFL. *Expenses:* Contact institution.

The Catholic University of America, School of Engineering, Department of Mechanical Engineering, Washington, DC 20064. Offers energy and environment (MME); general (MME); mechanical engineering (MSE, PhD). *Program availability:* Part-time. *Faculty:* 10 full-time (0 women), 6 part-time/adjunct (4 women). *Students:* 7 full-time (1 woman), 35 part-time (13 women); includes 7 minority (1 Black or African American, non-Hispanic/Latino; 2 Asian, non-Hispanic/Latino; 1 Hispanic/Latino; 3 Two or more races, non-Hispanic/Latino), 8 international. Average age 31. 26 applicants, 73% accepted, 8 enrolled. In 2019, 9 master's, 3 doctorates awarded. Terminal master's awarded for partial completion of doctoral program. *Degree requirements:* For master's, thesis (for some programs); for doctorate, comprehensive exam, thesis/dissertation. *Entrance requirements:* For master's and doctorate, statement of purpose, official copies of academic transcripts, three letters of recommendation. Additional exam requirements/recommendations for international students: required—TOEFL (minimum score 550 paper-based; 80 iBT). *Application deadline:* For fall admission, 7/15 priority date for domestic students, 7/1 for international students; for spring admission, 11/15 priority date for domestic students, 11/1 for international students. Applications are processed on a rolling basis. Application fee: $55. Electronic applications accepted. *Expenses:* Contact institution. *Financial support:* Fellowships, research assistantships, teaching assistantships, Federal Work-Study, scholarships/grants, tuition waivers (full and partial), and unspecified assistantships available. Financial award application deadline: 2/1; financial award applicants required to submit FAFSA. *Unit head:* Dr. Sen Nieh, Chair, 202-319-5170, Fax: 202-319-5173, E-mail: nieh@cua.edu. *Application contact:* Dr. Steven Brown, Director of Graduate Admissions, 202-319-5057, Fax: 202-319-6533, E-mail: cua-admissions@cua.edu.
Website: https://engineering.catholic.edu/mechanical/index.html

Clarkson University, Institute for a Sustainable Environment, Program in Environmental Science and Engineering, Potsdam, NY 13699. Offers MS, PhD. *Program availability:* Part-time. *Students:* 18 full-time (10 women); includes 1 minority (Hispanic/Latino), 7 international. 23 applicants, 39% accepted, 5 enrolled. In 2019, 5 master's, 1 doctorate awarded. *Degree requirements:* For master's, thesis; for doctorate, comprehensive exam, thesis/dissertation. *Entrance requirements:* For master's and doctorate, GRE. Additional exam requirements/recommendations for international students: required—TOEFL (minimum score 550 paper-based, 80 iBT) or IELTS (6.5). *Application deadline:* Applications are processed on a rolling basis. Application fee: $50. Electronic applications accepted. *Expenses: Tuition:* Full-time $24,984; part-time $1388. *Required fees:* $225. Tuition and fees vary according to campus/location and program. *Financial support:* Scholarships/grants and unspecified assistantships available. *Unit head:* Dr. Susan Powers, Director of the Institute for a Sustainable Environment/Associate Director of Sustainability, 315-268-6542, E-mail: spowers@clarkson.edu. *Application contact:* Dan Capogna, Director of Graduate Admissions & Recruitment, 518-631-9910, E-mail: graduate@clarkson.edu.
Website: https://www.clarkson.edu/academics/graduate

Clarkson University, Wallace H. Coulter School of Engineering, Department of Civil and Environmental Engineering, Potsdam, NY 13699. Offers ME, MS, PhD. *Faculty:* 19 full-time (2 women), 6 part-time/adjunct (1 woman). *Students:* 17 full-time (8 women), 2 part-time (both women); includes 1 minority (Black or African American, non-Hispanic/Latino), 13 international. 69 applicants, 61% accepted, 3 enrolled. In 2019, 8 master's, 5 doctorates awarded. *Degree requirements:* For master's, thesis (for MS); project (for ME); for doctorate, comprehensive exam, thesis/dissertation. *Entrance requirements:* For master's and doctorate, GRE. Additional exam requirements/recommendations for international students: required—TOEFL (minimum score 550 paper-based, 80 iBT) or IELTS (6.5). *Application deadline:* Applications are processed on a rolling basis. Application fee: $50. Electronic applications accepted. *Expenses: Tuition:* Full-time $24,984; part-time $1388. *Required fees:* $225. Tuition and fees vary according to campus/location and program. *Financial support:* Scholarships/grants and unspecified assistantships available. *Unit head:* Dr. John Dempsey, Chair of Civil and Environmental Engineering, 315-268-6529, E-mail: jdempsey@clarkson.edu. *Application contact:* Daniel Capogna, Director of Graduate Admissions & Recruitment, 518-631-9910, E-mail: graduate@clarkson.edu.
Website: https://www.clarkson.edu/academics/graduate

Clemson University, Graduate School, College of Engineering, Computing and Applied Sciences, Department of Environmental Engineering and Earth Sciences, Anderson, SC 29625. Offers biosystems engineering (MS, PhD); environmental engineering and science (MS, PhD); environmental health physics (MS); hydrogeology (MS). *Program availability:* Part-time. *Faculty:* 30 full-time (9 women), 2 part-time/adjunct (1 woman). *Students:* 80 full-time (31 women), 12 part-time (4 women); includes 5 minority (1 Black

or African American, non-Hispanic/Latino; 1 Hispanic/Latino; 1 Native Hawaiian or other Pacific Islander, non-Hispanic/Latino; 2 Two or more races, non-Hispanic/Latino), 34 international. Average age 25. 108 applicants, 65% accepted, 30 enrolled. In 2019, 21 master's, 5 doctorates awarded. *Degree requirements:* For master's, thesis or alternative; for doctorate, comprehensive exam, thesis/dissertation. *Entrance requirements:* For master's and doctorate, GRE General Test, unofficial transcripts, letters of recommendation. Additional exam requirements/recommendations for international students: required—TOEFL (minimum score 80 paper-based; 80 iBT); recommended—IELTS (minimum score 6.5), TSE (minimum score 54). *Application deadline:* For fall admission, 2/15 for domestic and international students. Applications are processed on a rolling basis. Application fee: $80 ($90 for international students). Electronic applications accepted. *Expenses: Tuition, area resident:* Full-time $10,600; part-time $8688 per semester. Tuition, state resident: full-time $10,600; part-time $8688 per semester. Tuition, nonresident: full-time $22,050; part-time $17,412 per semester. *International tuition:* $22,050 full-time. *Required fees:* $1196; $617 per semester. $617 per semester. Tuition and fees vary according to course load, degree level, campus/location and program. *Financial support:* In 2019–20, 47 students received support, including 3 fellowships with full and partial tuition reimbursements available (averaging $16,000 per year), 15 research assistantships with full and partial tuition reimbursements available (averaging $22,327 per year), 24 teaching assistantships with full and partial tuition reimbursements available (averaging $21,681 per year); career-related internships or fieldwork and unspecified assistantships also available. Financial award application deadline: 2/15. *Unit head:* Dr. David Freedman, Department Chair, 864-656-5566, E-mail: dfreedm@clemson.edu. *Application contact:* Dr. Mark Schlautman, Graduate Program Coordinator, 864-656-4059, E-mail: mschlau@clemson.edu.
Website: https://www.clemson.edu/cecas/departments/eees/

Cleveland State University, College of Graduate Studies, Fenn College of Engineering, Department of Civil and Environmental Engineering, Cleveland, OH 44115. Offers MS, D Eng. *Program availability:* Part-time, evening/weekend. *Entrance requirements:* For master's, GRE General Test, GRE Subject Test, minimum GPA of 2.75; for doctorate, GRE General Test, GRE Subject Test, minimum GPA of 3.25. Additional exam requirements/recommendations for international students: required—TOEFL (minimum score 550 paper-based; 78 iBT). Electronic applications accepted. *Expenses:* Tuition, state resident: full-time $10,215; part-time $6810 per credit hour. Tuition, nonresident: full-time $17,496; part-time $11,664 per credit hour. *International tuition:* $19,316 full-time. Tuition and fees vary according to degree level and program.

Colorado School of Mines, Office of Graduate Studies, Department of Civil and Environmental Engineering, Golden, CO 80401. Offers civil and environmental engineering (MS, PhD); environmental engineering science (MS, PhD); hydrologic science and engineering (MS, PhD); underground construction and tunneling (MS, PhD). *Program availability:* Part-time. *Degree requirements:* For master's, thesis (for some programs); for doctorate, comprehensive exam, thesis/dissertation. *Entrance requirements:* For master's and doctorate, GRE General Test. Additional exam requirements/recommendations for international students: required—TOEFL (minimum score 550 paper-based; 79 iBT). Electronic applications accepted. *Expenses:* Tuition, state resident: full-time $16,650; part-time $925 per credit hour. Tuition, nonresident: full-time $37,350; part-time $2075 per credit hour. *International tuition:* $37,350 full-time. *Required fees:* $2412.

Columbia University, Fu Foundation School of Engineering and Applied Science, Department of Earth and Environmental Engineering, New York, NY 10027. Offers earth and environmental engineering (Eng Sc D, PhD); earth resources engineering (MS); MS/PhD. *Program availability:* Part-time, online learning. Terminal master's awarded for partial completion of doctoral program. *Degree requirements:* For master's, thesis; for doctorate, thesis/dissertation, qualifying exam. *Entrance requirements:* For master's and doctorate, GRE General Test. Additional exam requirements/recommendations for international students: required—TOEFL, IELTS, PTE. Electronic applications accepted. *Expenses: Tuition:* Full-time $47,600; part-time $1880 per credit. One-time fee: $105.

Concordia University, School of Graduate Studies, Faculty of Engineering and Computer Science, Department of Building, Civil and Environmental Engineering, Montréal, QC H3G 1M8, Canada. Offers building engineering (M Eng, MA Sc, PhD, Certificate); civil engineering (M Eng, MA Sc, PhD); environmental engineering (Certificate). *Degree requirements:* For master's, thesis or alternative; for doctorate, comprehensive exam, thesis/dissertation.

Cornell University, Graduate School, Graduate Fields of Engineering, Field of Civil and Environmental Engineering, Ithaca, NY 14853. Offers engineering management (M Eng, MS, PhD); environmental engineering (M Eng, MS, PhD); environmental fluid mechanics and hydrology (M Eng, MS, PhD); environmental systems engineering (M Eng, MS, PhD); geotechnical engineering (M Eng, MS, PhD); remote sensing (M Eng, MS, PhD); structural engineering (M Eng, MS, PhD); structural mechanics (M Eng, MS); transportation engineering (MS, PhD); transportation systems engineering (M Eng); water resource systems (M Eng, MS, PhD). Terminal master's awarded for partial completion of doctoral program. *Degree requirements:* For master's, thesis (MS); for doctorate, comprehensive exam, thesis/dissertation. *Entrance requirements:* For master's and doctorate, GRE General Test (recommended), 2 letters of recommendation. Additional exam requirements/recommendations for international students: required—TOEFL (minimum score 600 paper-based; 77 iBT). Electronic applications accepted.

Dalhousie University, Faculty of Engineering, Department of Civil and Resource Engineering, Halifax, NS B3J 2X4, Canada. Offers civil engineering (M Eng, MA Sc, PhD); environmental engineering (M Eng, MA Sc); mineral resource engineering (M Eng, MA Sc, PhD). *Degree requirements:* For master's, thesis; for doctorate, thesis/dissertation. *Entrance requirements:* Additional exam requirements/recommendations for international students: required—TOEFL, IELTS, CANTEST, CAEL, or Michigan English Language Assessment Battery. Electronic applications accepted.

Drexel University, College of Engineering, Department of Civil, Architectural, and Environmental Engineering, Program in Environmental Engineering, Philadelphia, PA 19104-2875. Offers MS, PhD. *Program availability:* Part-time, evening/weekend. Terminal master's awarded for partial completion of doctoral program. *Degree requirements:* For master's, thesis optional; for doctorate, thesis/dissertation. Electronic applications accepted.

Drexel University, College of Engineering, Department of Civil, Architectural, and Environmental Engineering, Program in Geotechnical, Geoenvironmental and Geosynthetics Engineering, Philadelphia, PA 19104-2875. Offers MS, PhD.

Duke University, Graduate School, Pratt School of Engineering, Department of Civil and Environmental Engineering, Durham, NC 27708. Offers civil and environmental engineering (MS, PhD); civil engineering (M Eng); computational mechanics and scientific computing (M Eng); environmental engineering (M Eng, MS, PhD); risk engineering (M Eng). Terminal master's awarded for partial completion of doctoral program. *Degree requirements:* For doctorate, thesis/dissertation. *Entrance requirements:* For master's and doctorate, GRE General Test. Additional exam requirements/recommendations for international students: required—TOEFL (minimum

score 550 paper-based; 90 iBT), IELTS (minimum score 7). Electronic applications accepted.

Duke University, Graduate School, Pratt School of Engineering, Master of Engineering Program, Durham, NC 27708-0271. Offers biomedical engineering (M Eng); civil engineering (M Eng); computational mechanics and scientific computing (M Eng); electrical and computer engineering (M Eng); environmental engineering (M Eng); materials science and engineering (M Eng); mechanical engineering (M Eng); photonics and optical sciences (M Eng); risk engineering (M Eng). *Program availability:* Part-time. *Entrance requirements:* For master's, GRE General Test, resume, 3 letters of recommendation, statement of purpose, transcripts. Additional exam requirements/recommendations for international students: required—TOEFL. Electronic applications accepted.

Florida Atlantic University, College of Engineering and Computer Science, Department of Civil, Environmental and Geomatics Engineering, Boca Raton, FL 33431-0991. Offers civil engineering (MS); environmental engineering (MS). *Program availability:* Part-time, evening/weekend. *Faculty:* 11 full-time (0 women). *Students:* 22 full-time (9 women), 15 part-time (11 women); includes 10 minority (2 Black or African American, non-Hispanic/Latino; 3 Asian, non-Hispanic/Latino; 4 Hispanic/Latino; 1 Two or more races, non-Hispanic/Latino), 18 international. Average age 28. 43 applicants, 42% accepted, 15 enrolled. In 2019, 26 master's awarded. *Entrance requirements:* For master's, GRE General Test, minimum GPA of 3.0 in last 60 hours of undergraduate course work. Additional exam requirements/recommendations for international students: required—TOEFL (minimum score 550 paper-based; 61 iBT), IELTS (minimum score 6). *Application deadline:* For fall admission, 7/1 priority date for domestic students, 2/15 for international students; for spring admission, 11/1 for domestic students, 7/15 for international students. Applications are processed on a rolling basis. Application fee: $30. *Expenses: Tuition:* Full-time $20,536; part-time $371.82 per credit hour. Tuition and fees vary according to program. *Financial support:* Research assistantships with full tuition reimbursements, teaching assistantships with full tuition reimbursements, career-related internships or fieldwork, Federal Work-Study, scholarships/grants, and unspecified assistantships available. Financial award applicants required to submit FAFSA. *Unit head:* Dr. Yan Yong, Chair, 561-297-3445, Fax: 561-297-0493, E-mail: cege@fau.edu. *Application contact:* Dr. Frederick Bloetscher, Associate Dean and Professor, 561-297-0744, E-mail: fbloetsch@fau.edu.
Website: http://www.cege.fau.edu/

Florida International University, College of Engineering and Computing, Department of Civil and Environmental Engineering, Miami, FL 33175. Offers civil engineering (MS, PhD); environmental engineering (MS). *Program availability:* Part-time, evening/weekend, online learning. *Faculty:* 25 full-time (7 women), 15 part-time/adjunct (2 women). *Students:* 87 full-time (27 women), 32 part-time (8 women); includes 31 minority (3 Black or African American, non-Hispanic/Latino; 1 Asian, non-Hispanic/Latino; 26 Hispanic/Latino; 1 Two or more races, non-Hispanic/Latino), 81 international. Average age 30. 132 applicants, 48% accepted, 30 enrolled. In 2019, 20 master's, 8 doctorates awarded. Terminal master's awarded for partial completion of doctoral program. *Degree requirements:* For master's, thesis or alternative; for doctorate, comprehensive exam, thesis/dissertation. *Entrance requirements:* For master's, bachelor's degree in related field, 3 letters of recommendation, minimum GPA of 3.0; for doctorate, GRE General Test, minimum graduate GPA of 3.3, 3 letters of recommendation, master's degree, resume, statement of purpose. Additional exam requirements/recommendations for international students: required—TOEFL (minimum score 550 paper-based; 80 iBT). *Application deadline:* For fall admission, 6/1 for domestic students, 4/1 for international students; for spring admission, 10/1 for domestic students, 9/1 for international students. Applications are processed on a rolling basis. Application fee: $30. Electronic applications accepted. *Expenses: Tuition, area resident:* Full-time $8912; part-time $446 per credit hour. Tuition, state resident: full-time $8912; part-time $446 per credit hour. Tuition, nonresident: full-time $21,393; part-time $992 per credit hour. *Required fees:* $2194. *Financial support:* Federal Work-Study, institutionally sponsored loans, scholarships/grants, health care benefits, and unspecified assistantships available. Financial award application deadline: 3/1; financial award applicants required to submit FAFSA. *Unit head:* Dr. Atorod Azizinamini, Chair, 305-348-2824, Fax: 305-348-2802, E-mail: aazizina@fiu.edu. *Application contact:* Nanett Rojas, Manager, Admissions Operations, 305-348-7464, Fax: 305-348-7441, E-mail: gradadm@fiu.edu.
Website: http://cec.fiu.edu

Florida State University, The Graduate School, FAMU-FSU College of Engineering, Department of Civil and Environmental Engineering, Tallahassee, FL 32306. Offers M Eng, MS, PhD. *Program availability:* Part-time. *Faculty:* 17 full-time (2 women), 3 part-time/adjunct (0 women). *Students:* 63 full-time (20 women); includes 10 minority (6 Black or African American, non-Hispanic/Latino; 2 Asian, non-Hispanic/Latino; 2 Hispanic/Latino), 41 international. Average age 23. 182 applicants, 41% accepted, 20 enrolled. In 2019, 10 master's, 4 doctorates awarded. *Degree requirements:* For master's, comprehensive exam, thesis optional; for doctorate, thesis/dissertation. *Entrance requirements:* For master's, GRE General Test (minimum score 1000 in old version), BS in engineering or related field, minimum GPA of 3.0; for doctorate, GRE General Test, master's degree in engineering or related field, minimum GPA of 3.0. Additional exam requirements/recommendations for international students: required—TOEFL (minimum score 550 paper-based; 80 iBT); recommended—IELTS (minimum score 6.5). *Application deadline:* For fall admission, 7/1 for domestic and international students; for spring admission, 11/1 for domestic and international students; for summer admission, 3/1 for domestic and international students. Applications are processed on a rolling basis. Application fee: $30. Electronic applications accepted. *Financial support:* In 2019–20, 55 students received support, including 24 research assistantships with full tuition reimbursements available, 20 teaching assistantships with full tuition reimbursements available; fellowships with full tuition reimbursements available, Federal Work-Study, scholarships/grants, tuition waivers (full), and unspecified assistantships also available. Financial award application deadline: 3/1; financial award applicants required to submit FAFSA. *Unit head:* Dr. Lisa Spainhour, Chair and Professor, 850-410-6143, Fax: 850-410-6142, E-mail: spainhou@eng.famu.fsu.edu. *Application contact:* Mable Johnson, Office Manager, 850-410-6139, Fax: 850-410-6292, E-mail: mjohnson5@eng.famu.fsu.edu.
Website: http://www.eng.famu.fsu.edu/cee/

Gannon University, School of Graduate Studies, College of Engineering and Business, School of Engineering and Computer Science, Program in Environmental Science and Engineering, Erie, PA 16541-0001. Offers environmental health (MSEH); environmental health and engineering (MS). *Program availability:* Part-time, evening/weekend. *Degree requirements:* For master's, thesis (for some programs), research paper or project (for some programs). *Entrance requirements:* For master's, GRE, bachelor's degree in science or engineering from an accredited college or university. Additional exam requirements/recommendations for international students: required—TOEFL (minimum score 79 iBT), GRE. Electronic applications accepted. Application fee is waived when completed online.

The George Washington University, School of Engineering and Applied Science, Department of Civil and Environmental Engineering, Washington, DC 20052. Offers MS,

PhD, App Sc, Engr, Graduate Certificate. *Program availability:* Part-time, evening/weekend. *Degree requirements:* For master's, thesis optional; for doctorate, thesis/dissertation, final and qualifying exams. *Entrance requirements:* For master's, appropriate bachelor's degree, minimum GPA of 3.0; for doctorate, GRE (if highest earned degree is BS), appropriate bachelor's or master's degree, minimum GPA of 3.4; for other advanced degree, appropriate master's degree, minimum GPA of 3.0. Additional exam requirements/recommendations for international students: required—TOEFL or The George Washington University English as a Foreign Language Test.

Georgia Institute of Technology, Graduate Studies, College of Engineering, School of Civil and Environmental Engineering, Atlanta, GA 30332. Offers civil engineering (MS, PhD); engineering science and mechanics (MS, PhD); environmental engineering (MS, PhD). *Program availability:* Part-time. *Faculty:* 50 full-time (13 women), 3 part-time/adjunct (0 women). *Students:* 350 full-time (117 women), 46 part-time (16 women); includes 48 minority (8 Black or African American, non-Hispanic/Latino; 22 Asian, non-Hispanic/Latino; 16 Hispanic/Latino; 2 Two or more races, non-Hispanic/Latino), 260 international. Average age 26. 758 applicants, 55% accepted, 123 enrolled. In 2019, 150 master's, 32 doctorates awarded. Terminal master's awarded for partial completion of doctoral program. *Degree requirements:* For master's, thesis optional; for doctorate, comprehensive exam, thesis/dissertation. *Entrance requirements:* For master's and doctorate, GRE. Additional exam requirements/recommendations for international students: required—TOEFL (minimum score 577 paper-based; 90 iBT), IELTS (minimum score 7), TOEFL is the preferred method with the requirements shown on the programs. *Application deadline:* For fall admission, 12/15 for domestic and international students; for spring admission, 8/31 for domestic and international students; for summer admission, 12/15 for domestic and international students. Applications are processed on a rolling basis. Application fee: $75 ($85 for international students). Electronic applications accepted. *Expenses: Tuition, area resident:* Full-time $14,064; part-time $586 per credit hour. Tuition, state resident: full-time $14,064; part-time $586 per credit hour. Tuition, nonresident: full-time $29,140; part-time $1215 per credit hour. *International tuition:* $29,140 full-time. *Required fees:* $2024; $840 per semester. $2096. Tuition and fees vary according to course load. *Financial support:* In 2019–20, 16 fellowships, 166 research assistantships, 26 teaching assistantships were awarded; career-related internships or fieldwork, Federal Work-Study, institutionally sponsored loans, tuition waivers (full and partial), and unspecified assistantships also available. Support available to part-time students. Financial award application deadline: 7/1; financial award applicants required to submit FAFSA. *Unit head:* Donald Webster, School Chair, 404-894-2201, Fax: 404-894-2278, E-mail: dwebster@ce.gatech.edu. *Application contact:* Marla Bruner, Director of Graduate Studies, 404-894-1610, Fax: 404-894-1609, E-mail: gradinfo@mail.gatech.edu.
Website: https://ce.gatech.edu/

Harvard University, Graduate School of Arts and Sciences, Harvard John A. Paulson School of Engineering and Applied Sciences, Cambridge, MA 02138. Offers applied mathematics (PhD); applied physics (PhD); computational science and engineering (ME, SM); computer science (PhD); data science (SM); design engineering (MDE); engineering science (ME), including electrical engineering (ME, SM, PhD); engineering sciences (SM, PhD), including bioengineering (PhD), electrical engineering (ME, SM, PhD), environmental science and engineering (PhD), materials science and mechanical engineering (PhD). *Program availability:* Part-time. Terminal master's awarded for partial completion of doctoral program. *Degree requirements:* For master's, thesis (for ME); for doctorate, comprehensive exam, thesis/dissertation. *Entrance requirements:* For master's and doctorate, GRE General Test, GRE Subject Test (recommended), 3 letters of recommendation. Additional exam requirements/recommendations for international students: required—TOEFL (minimum score 80 iBT). Electronic applications accepted. *Expenses:* Contact institution.

Idaho State University, Graduate School, College of Science and Engineering, Department of Civil and Environmental Engineering, Pocatello, ID 83209-8060. Offers civil engineering (MS); environmental engineering (MS); environmental science and management (MS). *Program availability:* Part-time. *Degree requirements:* For master's, comprehensive exam (for some programs), thesis optional, thesis project, 2 semesters of seminar. *Entrance requirements:* For master's, GRE. Additional exam requirements/recommendations for international students: required—TOEFL (minimum score 550 paper-based; 80 iBT). Electronic applications accepted.

Illinois Institute of Technology, Graduate College, Armour College of Engineering, Department of Civil, Architectural and Environmental Engineering, Chicago, IL 60616. Offers architectural engineering (M Arch E); civil engineering (MS, PhD), including architectural engineering (MS), construction engineering and management (MS), geoenvironmental engineering (MS), geotechnical engineering (MS), structural engineering (MS), transportation engineering (MS); construction engineering and management (MCEM); environmental engineering (M Env E, MS, PhD); geoenvironmental engineering (M Geoenv E); geotechnical engineering (MGE); infrastructure engineering and management (MPW); structural engineering (MSE); transportation engineering (M Trans E). *Program availability:* Part-time, evening/weekend, online learning. Terminal master's awarded for partial completion of doctoral program. *Degree requirements:* For master's, thesis (for some programs); for doctorate, comprehensive exam, thesis/dissertation. *Entrance requirements:* For master's, GRE General Test (minimum score 900 Quantitative and Verbal, 2.5 Analytical Writing), minimum undergraduate GPA of 3.0; for doctorate, GRE General Test (minimum score 1000 Quantitative and Verbal, 3.0 Analytical Writing), minimum undergraduate GPA of 3.0. Additional exam requirements/recommendations for international students: required—TOEFL (minimum score 550 paper-based; 80 iBT). Electronic applications accepted.

Instituto Tecnologico de Santo Domingo, Graduate School, Area of Engineering, Santo Domingo, Dominican Republic. Offers construction administration (MS, Certificate); data telecommunications (M Eng, MS, Certificate); industrial engineering (M Eng, Certificate); industrial management (M Mgmt); information technology (Certificate); maintenance engineering (M Eng); occupational hazard prevention (M Mgmt); production management (Certificate); quantitative methods (Certificate); sanitary and environmental engineering (M Eng); structural engineering (M Eng); systems engineering and electronic data processing (Certificate); transportation (Certificate).

Instituto Tecnológico y de Estudios Superiores de Monterrey, Campus Ciudad de México, Virtual University Division, Ciudad de Mexico, Mexico. Offers administration of information technologies (MA); computer sciences (MA); education (MA, PhD); educational technology (MA); environmental engineering (MA); environmental systems (MA); humanistic studies (MA); industrial engineering (MA); international business for Latin America (MA); quality systems (MA); quality systems and productivity (MA). *Program availability:* Part-time, evening/weekend, online learning. *Entrance requirements:* For master's and doctorate, Instituto entrance exam. Additional exam requirements/recommendations for international students: required—TOEFL.

Instituto Tecnológico y de Estudios Superiores de Monterrey, Campus Monterrey, Graduate and Research Division, Programs in Engineering, Monterrey, Mexico. Offers applied statistics (M Eng); artificial intelligence (PhD); automation engineering (M Eng); chemical engineering (M Eng); civil engineering (M Eng); electrical engineering (M Eng); electronic engineering (M Eng); environmental engineering (M Eng); industrial engineering (M Eng, PhD); manufacturing engineering (M Eng); mechanical engineering (M Eng); systems and quality engineering (M Eng). *Program availability:* Part-time, evening/weekend. Terminal master's awarded for partial completion of doctoral program. *Degree requirements:* For master's, one foreign language, thesis; for doctorate, one foreign language, thesis/dissertation. *Entrance requirements:* For master's, EXADEP; for doctorate, GRE, master's degree in related field. Additional exam requirements/recommendations for international students: required—TOEFL.

Iowa State University of Science and Technology, Department of Civil and Construction Engineering, Ames, IA 50011. Offers civil engineering (MS, PhD), including civil engineering materials, construction engineering and management, environmental engineering, geotechnical engineering, structural engineering, transportation engineering. *Degree requirements:* For master's, thesis or alternative; for doctorate, thesis/dissertation. *Entrance requirements:* For master's and doctorate, GRE General Test. Additional exam requirements/recommendations for international students: required—TOEFL (minimum score 550 paper-based; 82 iBT), IELTS (minimum score 6.5). Electronic applications accepted.

Jackson State University, Graduate School, College of Science, Engineering and Technology, Department of Civil and Environmental Engineering and Industrial Systems and Technology, Jackson, MS 39217. Offers civil engineering (MS, PhD); coastal engineering (MS, PhD); environmental engineering (MS, PhD); hazardous materials management (MS); technology education (MS Ed). *Program availability:* Part-time, evening/weekend. *Degree requirements:* For master's, comprehensive exam, thesis or alternative. *Entrance requirements:* For master's, GRE General Test. Additional exam requirements/recommendations for international students: required—TOEFL (minimum score 520 paper-based; 67 iBT).

Johns Hopkins University, Engineering Program for Professionals, Part-time Program in Environmental Engineering, Baltimore, MD 21218. Offers MS, Graduate Certificate, Post-Master's Certificate. *Program availability:* Part-time, evening/weekend, online only, 100% online. *Entrance requirements:* Additional exam requirements/recommendations for international students: required—TOEFL (minimum score 600 paper-based; 100 iBT).

Johns Hopkins University, Engineering Program for Professionals, Part-time Program in Environmental Engineering and Science, Baltimore, MD 21218. Offers MEE, MS, Graduate Certificate, Post-Master's Certificate. *Program availability:* Part-time, evening/weekend, online only, 100% online. *Entrance requirements:* Additional exam requirements/recommendations for international students: required—TOEFL (minimum score 600 paper-based; 100 iBT). Electronic applications accepted.

Johns Hopkins University, G. W. C. Whiting School of Engineering, Department of Environmental Health and Engineering, Baltimore, MD 21218. Offers MA, MS, MSE, PhD. Terminal master's awarded for partial completion of doctoral program. *Degree requirements:* For master's, thesis optional, 1-year full-time residency; for doctorate, comprehensive exam, thesis/dissertation, oral exam, 2-year full-time residency. *Entrance requirements:* For master's and doctorate, GRE General Test, 3 letters of recommendation, statement of purpose, transcripts. Additional exam requirements/recommendations for international students: required—TOEFL (minimum score 600 paper-based, 100 iBT) or IELTS (7). Electronic applications accepted.

Kansas State University, Graduate School, College of Engineering, Department of Civil Engineering, Manhattan, KS 66506. Offers civil engineering (MS, PhD); environmental engineering (MS, PhD); geotechnical engineering (MS, PhD); structural engineering (MS, PhD); transportation engineering (MS, PhD); water resources engineering (MS, PhD). *Program availability:* Part-time, evening/weekend, online learning. *Degree requirements:* For master's, thesis or alternative; for doctorate, thesis/dissertation. *Entrance requirements:* For master's, GRE General Test, bachelor's degree or course work in related engineering fields; for doctorate, GRE General Test. Additional exam requirements/recommendations for international students: required—TOEFL (minimum score 550 paper-based; 79 iBT). Electronic applications accepted.

Kennesaw State University, Southern Polytechnic College of Engineering and Engineering Technology, Program in Civil Engineering, Kennesaw, GA 30144. Offers environmental engineering (MS); geotechnical engineering (MS); structural engineering (MS); transportation and pavement engineering (MS); water resources engineering (MS). *Program availability:* Online learning. *Students:* 9 full-time (2 women), 30 part-time (4 women); includes 20 minority (9 Black or African American, non-Hispanic/Latino; 5 Asian, non-Hispanic/Latino; 5 Hispanic/Latino; 1 Two or more races, non-Hispanic/Latino), 3 international. Average age 34. 12 applicants, 92% accepted, 8 enrolled. In 2019, 12 master's awarded. *Degree requirements:* For master's, thesis optional. *Entrance requirements:* Additional exam requirements/recommendations for international students: required—TOEFL (minimum score 80 iBT), IELTS (minimum score 6.5). *Application deadline:* For fall admission, 11/1 for domestic and international students; for spring admission, 4/1 for domestic and international students. Applications are processed on a rolling basis. Application fee: $60. Electronic applications accepted. *Expenses: Tuition, area resident:* Full-time $7104; part-time $296 per credit hour. Tuition, state resident: full-time $7104; part-time $296 per credit hour. Tuition, nonresident: full-time $25,584; part-time $1066 per credit hour. *International tuition:* $25,584 full-time. *Required fees:* $2006; $1706 per unit. $853 per semester. *Unit head:* Metin Oguzmert, Coordinator, 470-578-5083, E-mail: moguzmer@kennesaw.edu. *Application contact:* Admissions Counselor, 470-578-4377, E-mail: ksugrad@kennesaw.edu.
Website: http://engineering.kennesaw.edu/civil-construction/degrees/ms-civil-engineering.php

Lakehead University, Graduate Studies, Faculty of Engineering, Thunder Bay, ON P7B 5E1, Canada. Offers control engineering (M Sc Engr); electrical/computer engineering (M Sc Engr); environmental engineering (M Sc Engr). *Program availability:* Part-time. *Degree requirements:* For master's, thesis. *Entrance requirements:* For master's, bachelor's degree in chemical, electrical or mechanical engineering, minimum B average. Additional exam requirements/recommendations for international students: required—TOEFL.

Lehigh University, P.C. Rossin College of Engineering and Applied Science, Department of Civil and Environmental Engineering, Bethlehem, PA 18015. Offers M Eng, MS, PhD. *Program availability:* Part-time, blended/hybrid learning. *Faculty:* 19 full-time (3 women). *Students:* 60 full-time (15 women), 10 part-time (3 women); includes 5 minority (1 Asian, non-Hispanic/Latino; 4 Hispanic/Latino), 47 international. Average age 28. 141 applicants, 46% accepted, 11 enrolled. In 2019, 28 master's, 8 doctorates awarded. *Degree requirements:* For master's, thesis (for some programs); for doctorate, comprehensive exam, thesis/dissertation. *Entrance requirements:* For master's and doctorate, GRE. Additional exam requirements/recommendations for international students: required—TOEFL (minimum score 550 paper-based; 79 iBT), IELTS (minimum score 6.5). *Application deadline:* For fall admission, 7/15 priority date for domestic and international students; for spring admission, 12/1 priority date for domestic and international students; for summer admission, 5/30 priority date for domestic and international students. Application fee: $75. Electronic applications accepted. Application fee is waived when completed online. *Financial support:* In 2019–20, 30

students received support, including 3 fellowships with full tuition reimbursements available (averaging $22,050 per year), 20 research assistantships with full and partial tuition reimbursements available (averaging $29,400 per year), 7 teaching assistantships with full tuition reimbursements available (averaging $22,050 per year); unspecified assistantships also available. Financial award application deadline: 1/15; financial award applicants required to submit FAFSA. *Unit head:* Shamin Pakzad, Chair, 610-758-3566, E-mail: snp208@lehigh.edu. *Application contact:* Renee Keiderling, Graduate Coordinator, 610-758-3530, E-mail: rmk419@lehigh.edu.
Website: http://www.lehigh.edu/~incee/

Louisiana State University and Agricultural & Mechanical College, Graduate School, College of Engineering, Department of Civil and Environmental Engineering, Baton Rouge, LA 70803. Offers environmental engineering (MSCE, PhD); geotechnical engineering (MSCE, PhD); structural engineering and mechanics (MSCE, PhD); transportation engineering (MSCE, PhD); water resources (MSCE, PhD).

Manhattan College, Graduate Programs, School of Engineering, Program in Environmental Engineering, Riverdale, NY 10471. Offers ME, MS. *Program availability:* Part-time, evening/weekend. *Degree requirements:* For master's, thesis optional, 30 credits, minimum GPA of 3.0. *Entrance requirements:* For master's, GRE (recommended), minimum GPA of 3.0. Additional exam requirements/recommendations for international students: required—TOEFL (minimum score 550 paper-based; 80 iBT), IELTS (minimum score 6).

Marquette University, Graduate School, College of Engineering, Department of Civil and Environmental Engineering, Milwaukee, WI 53201-1881. Offers construction engineering and management (MS, PhD, Certificate); environmental engineering (MS, PhD); structural design (Certificate); structural engineering and structural mechanics (MS, PhD); transportation (Certificate); transportation engineering and materials (MS, PhD); waste and wastewater treatment processes (Certificate); water resources engineering (Certificate). *Program availability:* Part-time, evening/weekend. Terminal master's awarded for partial completion of doctoral program. *Degree requirements:* For master's, comprehensive exam (for some programs), thesis or alternative; for doctorate, thesis/dissertation. *Entrance requirements:* For master's, GRE General Test (recommended), minimum GPA of 3.0, official transcripts from all current and previous colleges/universities except Marquette, three letters of recommendation; for doctorate, GRE General Test, minimum GPA of 3.0, official transcripts from all current and previous colleges/universities except Marquette, three letters of recommendation, brief statement of purpose, submission of any English language publications authored by applicant (strongly recommended). Additional exam requirements/recommendations for international students: required—TOEFL (minimum score 530 paper-based). Electronic applications accepted.

Marshall University, Academic Affairs Division, College of Information Technology and Engineering, Program in Engineering, Huntington, WV 25755. Offers engineering management (MSE); environmental engineering (MSE); transportation and infrastructure engineering (MSE). *Program availability:* Part-time, evening/weekend. *Degree requirements:* For master's, final project, oral exam. *Entrance requirements:* For master's, GMAT or GRE General Test, minimum undergraduate GPA of 2.75.

Massachusetts Institute of Technology, School of Engineering, Department of Civil and Environmental Engineering, Cambridge, MA 02139. Offers biological oceanography (PhD, Sc D); chemical oceanography (PhD, Sc D); civil and environmental engineering (M Eng, SM, PhD, Sc D); civil and environmental systems (PhD, Sc D); civil engineering (PhD, Sc D, CE); civil engineering and computation (PhD); coastal engineering (PhD, Sc D); construction engineering and management (PhD, Sc D); environmental biology (PhD, Sc D); environmental chemistry (PhD, Sc D); environmental engineering (PhD, Sc D); environmental engineering and computation (PhD); environmental fluid mechanics (PhD, Sc D); geotechnical and geoenvironmental engineering (PhD, Sc D); hydrology (PhD, Sc D); information technology (PhD, Sc D); oceanographic engineering (PhD, Sc D); structures and materials (PhD, Sc D); transportation (PhD, Sc D); SM/MBA. *Degree requirements:* For master's, thesis; for doctorate, comprehensive exam, thesis/dissertation; for CE, comprehensive exam, thesis. *Entrance requirements:* For master's, doctorate, and CE, GRE General Test. Additional exam requirements/recommendations for international students: required—TOEFL, IELTS. Electronic applications accepted.

McGill University, Faculty of Graduate and Postdoctoral Studies, Faculty of Engineering, Department of Chemical Engineering, Montréal, QC H3A 2T5, Canada. Offers chemical engineering (M Eng, PhD); environmental engineering (M Eng).

McGill University, Faculty of Graduate and Postdoctoral Studies, Faculty of Engineering, Department of Civil Engineering and Applied Mechanics, Montréal, QC H3A 2T5, Canada. Offers environmental engineering (M Eng, M Sc, PhD); fluid mechanics (M Sc); fluid mechanics and hydraulic engineering (M Eng, PhD); materials engineering (M Eng, PhD); rehabilitation of urban infrastructure (M Eng, PhD); soil behavior (M Eng, PhD); soil mechanics and foundations (M Eng, PhD); structures and structural mechanics (M Eng, PhD); water resources (M Sc); water resources engineering (M Eng, PhD).

Memorial University of Newfoundland, School of Graduate Studies, Interdisciplinary Program in Environmental Systems Engineering and Management, St. John's, NL A1C 5S7, Canada. Offers MA Sc. *Degree requirements:* For master's, project course. *Entrance requirements:* For master's, 2nd class engineering degree. *Expenses:* Contact institution.

Mercer University, Graduate Studies, Macon Campus, School of Engineering, Macon, GA 31207. Offers biomedical engineering (MSE); computer engineering (MSE); electrical engineering (MSE); engineering management (MSE); environmental engineering (MSE); environmental systems (MS); mechanical engineering (MSE); software engineering (MSE); software systems (MS); technical communications management (MS); technical management (MS). *Program availability:* Part-time-only, evening/weekend, online learning. *Faculty:* 27 full-time (9 women), 2 part-time/adjunct (0 women). *Students:* 38 full-time (10 women), 51 part-time (20 women); includes 22 minority (5 Black or African American, non-Hispanic/Latino; 11 Asian, non-Hispanic/Latino; 4 Hispanic/Latino; 2 Two or more races, non-Hispanic/Latino), 2 international. Average age 26. In 2019, 70 master's awarded. *Degree requirements:* For master's, thesis or alternative. *Entrance requirements:* For master's, GRE (minimum score 300), minimum undergraduate GPA of 3.0. Additional exam requirements/recommendations for international students: required—TOEFL (minimum score 550 paper-based; 80 iBT). *Application deadline:* For fall admission, 4/1 priority date for domestic and international students; for spring admission, 11/1 priority date for domestic and international students. Applications are processed on a rolling basis. Application fee: $75. *Expenses:* Tuition: $938.00 ($700.00 for Technical Communication Management program) per credit hour; Facility and Technology Fee: $17.00 per credit hour. *Financial support:* Federal Work-Study available. Financial award applicants required to submit FAFSA. *Unit head:* Dr. Laura W. Lackey, Dean, 478-301-4106, Fax: 478-301-5593, E-mail: lackey_l@mercer.edu. *Application contact:* Dr. Sinjae Hyun, Program Director, 478-301-2214, Fax: 478-301-5593, E-mail: hyun_s@mercer.edu.
Website: http://engineering.mercer.edu/

Michigan State University, The Graduate School, College of Engineering, Department of Civil and Environmental Engineering, East Lansing, MI 48824. Offers civil engineering (MS, PhD); environmental engineering (MS, PhD); environmental engineering-environmental toxicology (PhD). *Program availability:* Part-time. *Entrance requirements:* Additional exam requirements/recommendations for international students: required—TOEFL. Electronic applications accepted.

Michigan Technological University, Graduate School, College of Engineering, Department of Civil and Environmental Engineering, Houghton, MI 49931. Offers civil engineering (MS, PhD); environmental engineering (MS, PhD); environmental engineering science (MS). *Program availability:* Part-time, 100% online. *Faculty:* 37 full-time, 14 part-time/adjunct (4 women). *Students:* 48 full-time (23 women), 22 part-time (7 women); includes 5 minority (2 Black or African American, non-Hispanic/Latino; 1 Hispanic/Latino; 2 Two or more races, non-Hispanic/Latino), 29 international. Average age 28. 297 applicants, 36% accepted, 23 enrolled. In 2019, 37 master's, 3 doctorates awarded. *Degree requirements:* For master's, comprehensive exam (for some programs), thesis (for some programs); for doctorate, comprehensive exam, thesis/dissertation. *Entrance requirements:* For master's and doctorate, GRE (Michigan Tech students exempt), statement of purpose, personal statement, official transcripts, 2 letters of recommendation. Additional exam requirements/recommendations for international students: required—TOEFL (minimum score 100 iBT), IELTS (minimum score 7), TOEFL (recommended minimum score 100 iBT) or IELTS (recommended minimum score of 7.0). *Application deadline:* For fall admission, 1/15 priority date for domestic and international students; for spring admission, 9/15 priority date for domestic and international students; for summer admission, 2/15 priority date for domestic and international students. Applications are processed on a rolling basis. Application fee: $0. Electronic applications accepted. *Expenses:* $1,212 per credit. *Financial support:* In 2019–20, 47 students received support, including 7 fellowships with tuition reimbursements available (averaging $16,590 per year), 16 research assistantships with tuition reimbursements available (averaging $16,590 per year), 5 teaching assistantships with tuition reimbursements available (averaging $16,590 per year); career-related internships or fieldwork, Federal Work-Study, scholarships/grants, health care benefits, unspecified assistantships, and cooperative program also available. Financial award applicants required to submit FAFSA. *Unit head:* Dr. Audra N. Morse, Chair, 906-487-3240, Fax: 906-487-2943, E-mail: anmorse@mtu.edu. *Application contact:* Angela Keranen, Administrative Aide, 906-487-2474, Fax: 906-487-2943, E-mail: amkerane@mtu.edu.
Website: http://www.mtu.edu/cee/

Missouri University of Science and Technology, Department of Civil, Architectural, and Environmental Engineering, Rolla, MO 65401. Offers civil engineering (MS, DE, PhD); environmental engineering (MS). *Program availability:* Part-time, evening/weekend. Terminal master's awarded for partial completion of doctoral program. *Degree requirements:* For master's, thesis optional; for doctorate, comprehensive exam, thesis/dissertation. *Entrance requirements:* For master's, GRE General Test (minimum combined score 1100), minimum GPA of 3.0; for doctorate, GRE General Test (minimum score: verbal and quantitative 400, writing 3.5), minimum GPA of 3.0. Additional exam requirements/recommendations for international students: required—TOEFL (minimum score 550 paper-based). Electronic applications accepted. *Expenses:* Tuition, state resident: full-time $7839; part-time $435.50 per credit hour. Tuition, nonresident: full-time $22,169; part-time $1231.60 per credit hour. *International tuition:* $18,156.60 full-time. *Required fees:* $649.76. One-time fee: $119. Tuition and fees vary according to course load and program.

Montana State University, The Graduate School, College of Engineering, Department of Chemical and Biological Engineering, Bozeman, MT 59717. Offers chemical engineering (MS); engineering (PhD), including chemical engineering option, environmental engineering option; environmental engineering (MS). *Program availability:* Part-time. *Degree requirements:* For master's, comprehensive exam, thesis (for some programs); for doctorate, comprehensive exam, thesis/dissertation. *Entrance requirements:* For master's and doctorate, GRE General Test. Additional exam requirements/recommendations for international students: required—TOEFL (minimum score 550 paper-based). Electronic applications accepted.

Montana Technological University, Department of Environmental Engineering, Butte, MT 59701-8997. Offers MS. *Program availability:* Part-time. *Faculty:* 7 full-time (2 women). *Students:* 8 full-time (2 women); includes 1 minority (Black or African American, non-Hispanic/Latino). Average age 26. 4 applicants, 100% accepted, 4 enrolled. In 2019, 3 master's awarded. *Degree requirements:* For master's, thesis. *Entrance requirements:* For master's, GRE General Test, minimum GPA of 3.0. Additional exam requirements/recommendations for international students: required—TOEFL (minimum score 525 paper-based; 78 iBT), IELTS (minimum score 6.5). *Application deadline:* For fall admission, 4/1 priority date for domestic students, 3/1 priority date for international students; for spring admission, 10/1 priority date for domestic students, 6/1 priority date for international students. Applications are processed on a rolling basis. Application fee: $50. Electronic applications accepted. *Financial support:* In 2019–20, 3 students received support, including 4 teaching assistantships with partial tuition reimbursements available (averaging $4,000 per year); research assistantships with full tuition reimbursements available, career-related internships or fieldwork, tuition waivers (full and partial), and unspecified assistantships also available. Financial award application deadline: 4/1; financial award applicants required to submit FAFSA. *Unit head:* Dr. Kumar Ganesan, Head, 406-496-4239, Fax: 406-496-4650, E-mail: kganesan@mtech.edu. *Application contact:* Daniel Stirling, Administrator, Graduate School, 406-496-4304, Fax: 406-496-4710, E-mail: gradschool@mtech.edu.
Website: http://www.mtech.edu/academics/gradschool/degreeprograms/degrees-environmental-engineering.htm

New Jersey Institute of Technology, Newark College of Engineering, Newark, NJ 07102. Offers biomedical engineering (MS, PhD); biopharmaceutical engineering (MS); chemical engineering (MS, PhD); civil engineering (MS, PhD); computer engineering (MS); critical infrastructure systems (MS); electrical engineering (MS, PhD); engineering management (MS); engineering science (MS); environmental engineering (MS, PhD); healthcare systems management (MS); industrial engineering (MS, PhD); internet engineering (MS); manufacturing systems engineering (MS); materials science & engineering (PhD); materials science and engineering (MS); mechanical engineering (MS, PhD); occupational safety and health engineering (MS). *Program availability:* Part-time, evening/weekend. *Faculty:* 151 full-time (29 women), 135 part-time/adjunct (15 women). *Students:* 576 full-time (161 women), 528 part-time (111 women); includes 366 minority (61 Black or African American, non-Hispanic/Latino; 1 American Indian or Alaska Native, non-Hispanic/Latino; 166 Asian, non-Hispanic/Latino; 115 Hispanic/Latino; 23 Two or more races, non-Hispanic/Latino), 450 international. Average age 28. 2,053 applicants, 67% accepted, 338 enrolled. In 2019, 474 master's, 30 doctorates awarded. Terminal master's awarded for partial completion of doctoral program. *Degree requirements:* For master's, thesis (for some programs); for doctorate, thesis/dissertation. *Entrance requirements:* For master's, GRE General Test, minimum GPA 2.8, personal statement, 1 letter of recommendation, transcripts; for doctorate, GRE General Test, minimum GPA of 3.5, personal statement, 3 letters of recommendation,

transcripts. Additional exam requirements/recommendations for international students: required—TOEFL (minimum score 550 paper-based; 79 iBT), IELTS (minimum score 6.5). *Application deadline:* For fall admission, 6/1 priority date for domestic students, 5/1 priority date for international students; for spring admission, 11/15 priority date for domestic and international students. Applications are processed on a rolling basis. Application fee: $75. Electronic applications accepted. *Expenses:* $23,828 per year (in-state), $33,744 per year (out-of-state). *Financial support:* In 2019–20, 352 students received support, including 33 fellowships with full tuition reimbursements available (averaging $24,000 per year), 89 research assistantships with full tuition reimbursements available (averaging $24,000 per year), 112 teaching assistantships with full tuition reimbursements available (averaging $24,000 per year); career-related internships or fieldwork, Federal Work-Study, scholarships/grants, and unspecified assistantships also available. Financial award application deadline: 1/15. *Unit head:* Dr. Moshe Kam, Dean, 973-596-5534, Fax: 973-596-2316, E-mail: moshe.kam@njit.edu. *Application contact:* Stephen Eck, Executive Director of University Admissions, 973-596-3300, Fax: 973-596-3461, E-mail: admissions@njit.edu.
Website: http://engineering.njit.edu/

New Mexico Institute of Mining and Technology, Center for Graduate Studies, Department of Civil and Environmental Engineering, Socorro, NM 87801. Offers environmental engineering (MS), including air quality engineering and science, hazardous waste engineering, water quality engineering and science. *Degree requirements:* For master's, thesis, thesis or independent study. *Entrance requirements:* Additional exam requirements/recommendations for international students: required—TOEFL (minimum score 540 paper-based).

New Mexico State University, College of Engineering, Department of Civil and Geological Engineering, Las Cruces, NM 88003-8001. Offers civil and geological engineering (PhD); master of science (MS Env E, MSCE). *Program availability:* Part-time. *Faculty:* 16 full-time (3 women). *Students:* 44 full-time (15 women), 12 part-time (3 women); includes 18 minority (1 Black or African American, non-Hispanic/Latino; 1 American Indian or Alaska Native, non-Hispanic/Latino; 2 Asian, non-Hispanic/Latino; 12 Hispanic/Latino; 2 Two or more races, non-Hispanic/Latino), 30 international. Average age 30. 53 applicants, 43% accepted, 6 enrolled. In 2019, 20 master's, 4 doctorates awarded. *Degree requirements:* For master's, thesis optional; for doctorate, comprehensive exam, thesis/dissertation, qualifying exam. *Entrance requirements:* For master's and doctorate, BS in engineering, minimum GPA of 3.0. Additional exam requirements/recommendations for international students: required—TOEFL (minimum score 550 paper-based; 79 iBT), IELTS (minimum score 6.5). *Application deadline:* For fall admission, 4/1 priority date for domestic and international students; for spring admission, 9/1 priority date for domestic and international students. Applications are processed on a rolling basis. Application fee: $40 ($50 for international students). Electronic applications accepted. *Financial support:* In 2019–20, 52 students received support, including 9 fellowships (averaging $3,267 per year), 25 research assistantships (averaging $15,281 per year), 18 teaching assistantships (averaging $10,630 per year); career-related internships or fieldwork, Federal Work-Study, scholarships/grants, traineeships, health care benefits, and unspecified assistantships also available. Support available to part-time students. Financial award application deadline: 3/1. *Unit head:* Dr. David Jauregui, Department Head, 575-646-3801, Fax: 575-646-6049, E-mail: jauregui@nmsu.edu. *Application contact:* Dr. David Jauregui, Department Head, 575-646-3801, Fax: 575-646-6049, E-mail: jauregui@nmsu.edu.
Website: http://ce.nmsu.edu

New York Institute of Technology, College of Engineering and Computing Sciences, Department of Environmental Technology and Sustainability, Old Westbury, NY 11568. Offers MS. *Program availability:* Part-time. *Faculty:* 3 full-time (1 woman), 1 part-time/adjunct (0 women). *Students:* 25 full-time (11 women), 7 part-time (2 women); includes 8 minority (3 Black or African American, non-Hispanic/Latino; 2 Asian, non-Hispanic/Latino; 1 Hispanic/Latino; 2 Two or more races, non-Hispanic/Latino), 19 international. Average age 29. 84 applicants, 75% accepted, 15 enrolled. In 2019, 18 master's awarded. *Entrance requirements:* For master's, Graduates of foreign universities are required to take the GRE and submit their scores. Applicants with a GPA below 2.85 may, at the discretion of the dean, be asked to take the GRE or other diagnostic tests., bachelor's degree or equivalent in engineering, technology, the sciences, or related areas; minimum undergraduate GPA of 2.85; copies of transcripts from all schools attended and proof of degree. Additional exam requirements/recommendations for international students: required—TOEFL (minimum score 79 iBT), IELTS (minimum score 6), PTE (minimum score 53), Duolingo English Test. *Application deadline:* For fall admission, 7/1 for domestic students, 6/1 for international students; for spring admission, 12/1 for domestic and international students. Applications are processed on a rolling basis. Application fee: $50. Electronic applications accepted. *Expenses: Tuition:* Full-time $23,760; part-time $1320 per credit. *Required fees:* $260; $220 per unit. Full-time tuition and fees vary according to degree level and program. Part-time tuition and fees vary according to course load and program. *Financial support:* In 2019–20, 21 students received support. Fellowships, research assistantships, teaching assistantships, Federal Work-Study, scholarships/grants, and unspecified assistantships available. Support available to part-time students. Financial award application deadline: 2/15; financial award applicants required to submit FAFSA. *Unit head:* Dr. David Nadler, Department Chair, 516-686-1373, Fax: 516-686-7919, E-mail: dnadler@nyit.edu. *Application contact:* Alice Dolitsky, Director, Graduate Admissions, 800-345-6948, Fax: 516-686-1116, E-mail: grad@nyit.edu.
Website: https://www.nyit.edu/departments/environmental_technology_and_sustainability

New York University, Tandon School of Engineering, Department of Civil and Urban Engineering, Major in Environmental Engineering, New York, NY 10012-1019. Offers environmental engineering (MS). *Program availability:* Part-time, evening/weekend. *Entrance requirements:* Additional exam requirements/recommendations for international students: recommended—TOEFL (minimum score 550 paper-based; 90 iBT), IELTS (minimum score 7). Electronic applications accepted.

North Dakota State University, College of Graduate and Interdisciplinary Studies, College of Engineering, Department of Civil and Environmental Engineering, Fargo, ND 58102. Offers civil engineering (MS, PhD); environmental engineering (MS). *Program availability:* Part-time, online learning. *Degree requirements:* For master's, thesis; for doctorate, comprehensive exam, thesis/dissertation. *Entrance requirements:* Additional exam requirements/recommendations for international students: required—TOEFL (minimum score 525 paper-based; 71 iBT). Electronic applications accepted. Tuition and fees vary according to program and reciprocity agreements.

Northeastern University, College of Engineering, Boston, MA 02115-5096. Offers bioengineering (MS, PhD); chemical engineering (MS, PhD); civil engineering (MS, PhD); computer engineering (PhD); computer systems engineering (MS); electrical and computer engineering (MS); electrical and computer engineering leadership (MS); electrical engineering (PhD); energy systems (MS); engineering and public policy (MS); engineering management (MS, Certificate); environmental engineering (MS); industrial engineering (MS, PhD); information assurance (PhD); information systems (MS); interdisciplinary engineering (PhD); mechanical engineering (PhD); operations research (MS); telecommunication systems management (MS). *Program availability:* Part-time, online learning. Electronic applications accepted. *Expenses:* Contact institution.

Northwestern University, McCormick School of Engineering and Applied Science, Department of Civil and Environmental Engineering, Evanston, IL 60208-3109. Offers environmental engineering and science (MS, PhD); geotechnical engineering (MS, PhD); mechanics of materials and solids (MS, PhD); project management (MS); structural engineering and materials (MS, PhD); transportation systems analysis and planning (MS, PhD). *Program availability:* Part-time. Terminal master's awarded for partial completion of doctoral program. *Degree requirements:* For master's, comprehensive exam (for some programs), thesis (for some programs); for doctorate, comprehensive exam, thesis/dissertation. *Entrance requirements:* For master's and doctorate, GRE General Test, minimum 2 letters of recommendation, transcripts from all academic institutions attended. Additional exam requirements/recommendations for international students: required—TOEFL (minimum score 577 paper-based; 90 iBT), IELTS (minimum score 7). Electronic applications accepted.

Norwich University, College of Graduate and Continuing Studies, Master of Civil Engineering Program, Northfield, VT 05663. Offers construction management (MCE); environmental (MCE); geotechnical (MCE); structural (MCE). *Program availability:* Evening/weekend, online only, mostly all online with a week-long residency requirement. *Degree requirements:* For master's, capstone. *Entrance requirements:* For master's, minimum undergraduate GPA of 2.75. Additional exam requirements/recommendations for international students: required—TOEFL (minimum score 550 paper-based; 80 iBT), IELTS (minimum score 6.5). Electronic applications accepted. *Expenses:* Contact institution.

Ohio University, Graduate College, Russ College of Engineering and Technology, Department of Civil Engineering, Athens, OH 45701-2979. Offers civil engineering (PhD); construction engineering and management (MS); environmental (MS); geoenvironmental (MS); geotechnical (MS); mechanics (MS); structures (MS); transportation (MS); water resources (MS). *Program availability:* Part-time. *Degree requirements:* For master's, comprehensive exam (for some programs), thesis or alternative; for doctorate, comprehensive exam, thesis/dissertation. *Entrance requirements:* For master's, GRE General Test, minimum GPA of 3.0, 3 letters of recommendation; for doctorate, GRE General Test. Additional exam requirements/recommendations for international students: required—TOEFL (minimum score 550 paper-based; 80 iBT) or IELTS (minimum score 6.5). Electronic applications accepted.

Oklahoma State University, College of Agricultural Science and Natural Resources, Department of Biosystems and Agricultural Engineering, Stillwater, OK 74078. Offers biosystems engineering (MS, PhD); environmental and natural resources (MS, PhD). *Faculty:* 17 full-time (6 women). *Students:* 8 full-time (3 women), 12 part-time (4 women); includes 1 minority (Black or African American, non-Hispanic/Latino), 13 international. Average age 32. 12 applicants, 25% accepted, 2 enrolled. In 2019, 6 master's, 8 doctorates awarded. *Entrance requirements:* For master's and doctorate, GRE or GMAT. Additional exam requirements/recommendations for international students: required—TOEFL (minimum score 550 paper-based; 79 iBT). *Application deadline:* For fall admission, 3/1 priority date for international students; for spring admission, 8/1 priority date for international students. Applications are processed on a rolling basis. Application fee: $50 ($75 for international students). Electronic applications accepted. *Expenses: Tuition, area resident:* Full-time $4148.10; part-time $2765.40. Tuition, state resident: full-time $4148.10; part-time $2765.40. Tuition, nonresident: full-time $15,775; part-time $10,516.80. *International tuition:* $15,775.20 full-time. *Required fees:* $2196.90; $122.05 per credit hour. Tuition and fees vary according to course load, campus/location and program. *Financial support:* In 2019–20, 19 research assistantships (averaging $1,661 per year), 1 teaching assistantship (averaging $1,000 per year) were awarded; career-related internships or fieldwork, Federal Work-Study, scholarships/grants, health care benefits, tuition waivers (partial), and unspecified assistantships also available. Support available to part-time students. Financial award application deadline: 3/1; financial award applicants required to submit FAFSA. *Unit head:* Dr. John Veenstra, Department Head, 405-744-5431, Fax: 405-744-6059, E-mail: jveenst@okstate.edu. *Application contact:* Dr. Ning Wang, Professor/Graduate Coordinator, 405-744-2877, E-mail: ning.wang@okstate.edu.
Website: http://bae.okstate.edu/

Oklahoma State University, College of Engineering, Architecture and Technology, School of Civil and Environmental Engineering, Stillwater, OK 74078. Offers civil engineering (MS, PhD). *Faculty:* 16 full-time (1 woman), 1 (woman) part-time/adjunct. *Students:* 30 full-time (7 women), 40 part-time (10 women); includes 5 minority (3 American Indian or Alaska Native, non-Hispanic/Latino; 2 Two or more races, non-Hispanic/Latino), 40 international. Average age 28. 47 applicants, 49% accepted, 18 enrolled. In 2019, 11 master's, 6 doctorates awarded. *Entrance requirements:* For master's and doctorate, GRE or GMAT. Additional exam requirements/recommendations for international students: required—TOEFL (minimum score 550 paper-based; 79 iBT). *Application deadline:* For fall admission, 3/1 priority date for international students; for spring admission, 8/1 priority date for international students. Applications are processed on a rolling basis. Application fee: $50 ($75 for international students). Electronic applications accepted. *Expenses: Tuition, area resident:* Full-time $4148.10; part-time $2765.40. Tuition, state resident: full-time $4148.10; part-time $2765.40. Tuition, nonresident: full-time $15,775; part-time $10,516.80. *International tuition:* $15,775.20 full-time. *Required fees:* $2196.90; $122.05 per credit hour. Tuition and fees vary according to course load, campus/location and program. *Financial support:* In 2019–20, 51 research assistantships (averaging $1,915 per year), 1 teaching assistantship (averaging $2,000 per year) were awarded; career-related internships or fieldwork, Federal Work-Study, scholarships/grants, health care benefits, tuition waivers (partial), and unspecified assistantships also available. Support available to part-time students. Financial award application deadline: 3/1; financial award applicants required to submit FAFSA. *Unit head:* Dr. Norb Delatte, Department Head, 405-744-5190, Fax: 405-744-7554, E-mail: norb.delatte@okstate.edu. *Application contact:* Dr. Sheryl Tucker, Dean, 405-744-6368, Fax: 405-744-0355, E-mail: gradi@okstate.edu.
Website: http://cive.okstate.edu

Old Dominion University, Frank Batten College of Engineering and Technology, Program in Civil and Environmental Engineering, Norfolk, VA 23529. Offers D Eng, PhD. *Program availability:* Part-time, evening/weekend, blended/hybrid learning. *Degree requirements:* For doctorate, comprehensive exam, thesis/dissertation, candidacy exam. *Entrance requirements:* For doctorate, GRE, minimum GPA of 3.5. Electronic applications accepted. *Expenses:* Contact institution.

Old Dominion University, Frank Batten College of Engineering and Technology, Program in Environmental Engineering, Norfolk, VA 23529. Offers ME, MS. *Program availability:* Part-time, evening/weekend, blended/hybrid learning. *Degree requirements:* For master's, comprehensive exam, thesis optional. *Entrance requirements:* For master's, GRE, minimum GPA of 3.0. Additional exam requirements/recommendations for international students: required—TOEFL (minimum score 550 paper-based, 80 iBT) or IELTS (6.5). Electronic applications accepted. *Expenses:* Contact institution.

Oregon Health & Science University, School of Medicine, Graduate Programs in Medicine, Department of Environmental and Biomolecular Systems, Portland, OR 97239-3098. Offers biochemistry and molecular biology (MS, PhD); environmental science and engineering (MS, PhD). *Program availability:* Part-time. Terminal master's awarded for partial completion of doctoral program. *Degree requirements:* For master's, thesis (for some programs); for doctorate, comprehensive exam, thesis/dissertation, qualifying exam. *Entrance requirements:* For master's and doctorate, GRE General Test (minimum scores: 153 Verbal/148 Quantitative/4.5 Analytical) or MCAT (for some programs). Electronic applications accepted.

Oregon State University, College of Engineering, Program in Environmental Engineering, Corvallis, OR 97331. Offers bioremediation (M Eng, MS, PhD). *Entrance requirements:* For master's and doctorate, GRE. Additional exam requirements/recommendations for international students: required—TOEFL (minimum score 92 iBT). Electronic applications accepted. *Expenses:* Contact institution.

Penn State Harrisburg, Graduate School, School of Science, Engineering and Technology, Middletown, PA 17057. Offers civil engineering (MS); computer science (MS); electrical engineering (M Eng, MS); engineering management (MPS); engineering science (M Eng); environmental engineering (M Eng); environmental pollution control (MEPC, MS); mechanical engineering (MS); structural engineering (Certificate). *Program availability:* Part-time, evening/weekend.

Penn State University Park, Graduate School, College of Engineering, Department of Civil and Environmental Engineering, University Park, PA 16802. Offers civil engineering (M Eng, MS, PhD); environmental engineering (M Eng, MS, PhD).

Polytechnic University of Puerto Rico, Miami Campus, Graduate School, Miami, FL 33166. Offers accounting (MBA); business administration (MBA); construction management (MEM); environmental management (MEM); finance (MBA); human resources management (MBA); logistics and supply chain management (MBA); management of international enterprises (MBA); manufacturing management (MEM); marketing management (MBA); project management (MBA). *Program availability:* Part-time, evening/weekend, online learning. *Entrance requirements:* For master's, minimum GPA of 3.0. Electronic applications accepted.

Polytechnic University of Puerto Rico, Orlando Campus, Graduate School, Orlando, FL 32825. Offers accounting (MBA); business administration (MBA); construction management (MEM); engineering management (MEM); environmental management (MEM); finance (MBA); human resources management (MBA); management of international enterprises (MBA); management of technology (MBA); manufacturing management (MEM). *Program availability:* Part-time, evening/weekend, online learning. *Entrance requirements:* For master's, minimum GPA of 3.0. Additional exam requirements/recommendations for international students: recommended—TOEFL. Electronic applications accepted.

Polytechnique Montréal, Graduate Programs, Department of Civil, Geological and Mining Engineering, Montréal, QC H3C 3A7, Canada. Offers civil, geological and mining engineering (DESS); environmental engineering (M Eng, M Sc A, PhD); geotechnical engineering (M Eng, M Sc A, PhD); hydraulics engineering (M Eng, M Sc A, PhD); structural engineering (M Eng, M Sc A, PhD); transportation engineering (M Eng, M Sc A, PhD). *Program availability:* Part-time. *Degree requirements:* For master's, one foreign language, thesis; for doctorate, one foreign language, thesis/dissertation. *Entrance requirements:* For master's, minimum GPA of 2.75; for doctorate, minimum GPA of 3.0.

Portland State University, Graduate Studies, Maseeh College of Engineering and Computer Science, Department of Civil and Environmental Engineering, Portland, OR 97207-0751. Offers civil and environmental engineering (M Eng, MS, PhD). *Program availability:* Part-time, evening/weekend. *Faculty:* 21 full-time (5 women), 3 part-time/adjunct (0 women). *Students:* 36 full-time (11 women), 35 part-time (12 women); includes 12 minority (2 Black or African American, non-Hispanic/Latino; 3 Asian, non-Hispanic/Latino; 3 Hispanic/Latino; 4 Two or more races, non-Hispanic/Latino), 22 international. Average age 32. 45 applicants, 47% accepted, 9 enrolled. In 2019, 33 master's, 3 doctorates awarded. *Degree requirements:* For master's, comprehensive exam (for some programs), thesis (for some programs); for doctorate, one foreign language, comprehensive exam, thesis/dissertation, oral and written exams. *Entrance requirements:* For master's, BS in an engineering field, science, or closely-related area with minimum GPA of 3.0; for doctorate, MS in an engineering field, science, or closely-related area. Additional exam requirements/recommendations for international students: required—TOEFL (minimum score 550 paper-based). *Application deadline:* For fall admission, 1/4 priority date for domestic and international students; for winter admission, 9/1 for domestic and international students; for spring admission, 11/1 for domestic and international students. Applications are processed on a rolling basis. Application fee: $65. *Expenses:* Contact institution. *Financial support:* In 2019–20, 41 students received support, including 11 research assistantships with tuition reimbursements available (averaging $15,789 per year), 12 teaching assistantships with tuition reimbursements available (averaging $12,750 per year); career-related internships or fieldwork, Federal Work-Study, scholarships/grants, and unspecified assistantships also available. Support available to part-time students. Financial award application deadline: 3/1; financial award applicants required to submit FAFSA. *Unit head:* Dr. Chris Monsere, Chair, 503-725-9746, Fax: 503-725-4298, E-mail: monserec@cecs.pdx.edu. *Application contact:* Sarah Phillips, Department Manager, 503-725-4244, Fax: 503-725-4298, E-mail: sap23@pdx.edu.
Website: http://www.pdx.edu/cee/

Princeton University, Graduate School, School of Engineering and Applied Science, Department of Civil and Environmental Engineering, Princeton, NJ 08544-1019. Offers M Eng, MSE, PhD. Terminal master's awarded for partial completion of doctoral program. *Degree requirements:* For master's, thesis (MSE); for doctorate, thesis/dissertation, general exam. *Entrance requirements:* For master's, GRE General Test, 3 letters of recommendation; for doctorate, GRE General Test, official transcript(s), 3 letters of recommendation, personal statement. Additional exam requirements/recommendations for international students: required—TOEFL. Electronic applications accepted.

Purdue University, College of Engineering, Division of Environmental and Ecological Engineering, West Lafayette, IN 47907. Offers MS, PhD. *Faculty:* 1. *Students:* 54. *Degree requirements:* For master's, thesis optional; for doctorate, thesis/dissertation. *Application deadline:* For fall admission, 12/15 for domestic and international students; for spring admission, 9/15 for domestic and international students. Application fee: $60 ($75 for international students). *Financial support:* Fellowships with full and partial tuition reimbursements, research assistantships with full and partial tuition reimbursements, teaching assistantships with full and partial tuition reimbursements, career-related internships or fieldwork, scholarships/grants, health care benefits, and unspecified assistantships available. *Unit head:* Dr. John W. Sutherland, Professor/Head of Environmental and Ecological Engineering, 765-496-9697, E-mail: jwsuther@purdue.edu. *Application contact:* Cresta Cates, Graduate Administrative Assistant, 765-496-0545, E-mail: eeegrad@purdue.edu.
Website: https://engineering.purdue.edu/EEE

Rensselaer Polytechnic Institute, Graduate School, School of Engineering, Program in Environmental Engineering, Troy, NY 12180-3590. Offers M Eng, MS, PhD. *Faculty:* 17 full-time (3 women), 3 part-time/adjunct (0 women). *Students:* 3 full-time (0 women), 2 international. Average age 25. 37 applicants, 5% accepted, 1 enrolled. In 2019, 2 master's awarded. Terminal master's awarded for partial completion of doctoral program. *Degree requirements:* For master's, thesis (for some programs); for doctorate, thesis/dissertation. *Entrance requirements:* For master's and doctorate, GRE. Additional exam requirements/recommendations for international students: required—TOEFL (minimum score 570 paper-based; 88 iBT), IELTS (minimum score 6.5), PTE (minimum score 60). *Application deadline:* For fall admission, 1/1 priority date for domestic students, 1/1 for international students; for spring admission, 8/15 for domestic and international students. Applications are processed on a rolling basis. Application fee: $75. Electronic applications accepted. *Financial support:* In 2019–20, research assistantships (averaging $23,000 per year), teaching assistantships with full tuition reimbursements (averaging $23,000 per year) were awarded; fellowships also available. Financial award application deadline: 1/1. *Unit head:* Dr. Marianne Nyman, Graduate Program Director, 518-276-2268, E-mail: nymanm@rpi.edu. *Application contact:* Jarron Decker, Director of Graduate Admissions, 518-276-6216, Fax: 518-276-4072, E-mail: gradadmissions@rpi.edu.
Website: http://cee.rpi.edu/graduate

Rice University, Graduate Programs, George R. Brown School of Engineering, Department of Civil and Environmental Engineering, Houston, TX 77251-1892. Offers civil engineering (MCE, MS, PhD); environmental engineering (MEE, MES, MS, PhD); environmental science (MEE, MES, MS, PhD). *Program availability:* Part-time. *Degree requirements:* For master's, thesis (for some programs); for doctorate, thesis/dissertation. *Entrance requirements:* For master's and doctorate, GRE General Test, GRE Subject Test, minimum GPA of 3.25. Additional exam requirements/recommendations for international students: required—TOEFL (minimum score 600 paper-based; 90 iBT). Electronic applications accepted.

Rose-Hulman Institute of Technology, Graduate Studies, Department of Civil and Environmental Engineering, Terre Haute, IN 47803-3999. Offers civil engineering (MS); environmental engineering (MS). *Program availability:* Part-time. *Faculty:* 8 full-time (2 women). *Students:* 2 full-time (1 woman), 1 part-time (0 women). Average age 25. 3 applicants, 100% accepted, 2 enrolled. In 2019, 2 master's awarded. *Degree requirements:* For master's, thesis (for some programs). *Entrance requirements:* For master's, GRE, minimum GPA of 3.0. Additional exam requirements/recommendations for international students: required—TOEFL (minimum score 580 paper-based; 94 iBT), IELTS (minimum score 7). *Application deadline:* For fall admission, 2/1 priority date for domestic and international students; for winter admission, 10/1 for domestic students, 4/1 for international students; for spring admission, 1/15 for domestic students, 11/1 for international students. Applications are processed on a rolling basis. Application fee: $75. Electronic applications accepted. *Financial support:* In 2019–20, 2 students received support. Fellowships with tuition reimbursements available, research assistantships with tuition reimbursements available, institutionally sponsored loans, scholarships/grants, tuition waivers (full and partial), and unspecified assistantships available. *Unit head:* Dr. Kevin Sutterer, Department Head, 812-877-8959, E-mail: sutterer@rose-hulman.edu. *Application contact:* Dr. Craig Downing, Associate Dean of Lifelong Learning, 812-877-8822, E-mail: downing@rose-hulman.edu.
Website: https://www.rose-hulman.edu/academics/academic-departments/civil-and-environmental-engineering/index.html

Rutgers University - New Brunswick, Graduate School-New Brunswick, Department of Civil and Environmental Engineering, Piscataway, NJ 08854-8097. Offers MS, PhD. *Program availability:* Part-time, evening/weekend. Terminal master's awarded for partial completion of doctoral program. *Degree requirements:* For master's, comprehensive exam, thesis or alternative; for doctorate, comprehensive exam, thesis/dissertation. *Entrance requirements:* For master's and doctorate, GRE General Test. Additional exam requirements/recommendations for international students: required—TOEFL (minimum score 580 paper-based). Electronic applications accepted.

Southern Illinois University Carbondale, Graduate School, College of Engineering, Program in Engineering Science, Carbondale, IL 62901-4701. Offers engineering science (PhD), including civil and environmental engineering, electrical and computer engineering, mechanical engineering and energy processes, mining and mineral resources engineering. *Degree requirements:* For doctorate, thesis/dissertation. *Entrance requirements:* For doctorate, GRE General Test, minimum GPA of 3.5. Additional exam requirements/recommendations for international students: required—TOEFL.

Southern Illinois University Edwardsville, Graduate School, School of Engineering, Department of Civil Engineering, Program in Environmental Engineering, Edwardsville, IL 62026. Offers MS. *Program availability:* Part-time, evening/weekend. *Degree requirements:* For master's, thesis (for some programs), research paper. *Entrance requirements:* For master's, minimum undergraduate GPA of 2.75 in science, math, and engineering courses. Additional exam requirements/recommendations for international students: required—TOEFL (minimum score 550 paper-based, 79 iBT), IELTS (minimum score 6.5), Michigan Test of English Language Proficiency or PTE. Electronic applications accepted.

Southern Methodist University, Lyle School of Engineering, Department of Civil and Environmental Engineering, Dallas, TX 75275-0340. Offers civil and environmental engineering (PhD); civil engineering (MS), including geotechnical engineering, structural engineering, transportation systems; environmental engineering (MS); sustainability and development (MA). *Program availability:* Part-time, evening/weekend, online learning. Terminal master's awarded for partial completion of doctoral program. *Degree requirements:* For master's, thesis optional; for doctorate, thesis/dissertation, oral and written qualifying exams. *Entrance requirements:* For master's, GRE General Test, minimum GPA of 3.0 in last 2 years; bachelor's degree in engineering, mathematics, or sciences; for doctorate, GRE, BS and MS in related field, minimum GPA of 3.3. Additional exam requirements/recommendations for international students: required—TOEFL. Electronic applications accepted.

State University of New York College of Environmental Science and Forestry, Department of Environmental Resources Engineering, Syracuse, NY 13210-2779. Offers ecological engineering (MPS, MS, PhD); environmental management (MPS); environmental resources engineering (MPS, MS, PhD); geospatial information science and engineering (MPS, MS, PhD); water resources engineering (MPS, MS, PhD). *Program availability:* Part-time. *Faculty:* 9 full-time (1 woman), 3 part-time/adjunct (0 women). *Students:* 22 full-time (13 women), 4 part-time (1 woman); includes 1 minority (Asian, non-Hispanic/Latino), 15 international. Average age 31. 32 applicants, 31% accepted, 7 enrolled. In 2019, 3 master's, 2 doctorates awarded. Terminal master's awarded for partial completion of doctoral program. *Degree requirements:* For master's, thesis (for some programs); for doctorate, comprehensive exam, thesis/dissertation. *Entrance requirements:* For master's and doctorate, GRE General Test, minimum GPA of 3.0. Additional exam requirements/recommendations for international students: required—TOEFL (minimum score 550 paper-based; 80 iBT), IELTS (minimum score 6). *Application deadline:* For fall admission, 1/15 priority date for domestic and international students; for spring admission, 11/1 priority date for domestic and international students.

Applications are processed on a rolling basis. Application fee: $60. Electronic applications accepted. *Expenses:* Tuition, state resident: full-time $11,310; part-time $472 per credit hour. Tuition, nonresident: full-time $23,100; part-time $963 per credit hour. *Required fees:* $1890; $95.21 per credit hour. *Financial support:* In 2019–20, 8 students received support. Unspecified assistantships available. Financial award application deadline: 6/30; financial award applicants required to submit FAFSA. *Unit head:* Dr. Lindi Quackenbush, Chair, 315-470-4727, Fax: 315-470-4710, E-mail: ljquackc@esf.edu. *Application contact:* Laura Payne, Administrative Assistant, Office of Instruction & Graduate Studies, 315-470-6599, Fax: 315-470-6978, E-mail: esfgrad@esf.edu.
Website: http://www.esf.edu/ere

Stevens Institute of Technology, Graduate School, Charles V. Schaefer Jr. School of Engineering and Science, Department of Civil, Environmental, and Ocean Engineering, Program in Environmental Engineering, Hoboken, NJ 07030. Offers environmental engineering (PhD, Certificate), including environmental compatibility in engineering (Certificate), environmental hydrology (Certificate), environmental processes (Certificate), hydraulics (Certificate), soil and groundwater pollution control (Certificate), water quality control (Certificate); environmental processes (M Eng); inland and coastal environmental hydrodynamics (M Eng); modeling of environmental systems (M Eng); soil and groundwater pollution control (M Eng). *Program availability:* Part-time, evening/weekend. *Faculty:* 23 full-time (8 women), 21 part-time/adjunct (2 women). *Students:* 46 full-time (18 women), 14 part-time (6 women); includes 7 minority (2 Black or African American, non-Hispanic/Latino; 4 Asian, non-Hispanic/Latino; 1 Hispanic/Latino), 35 international. Average age 28. In 2019, 31 master's, 2 doctorates, 10 other advanced degrees awarded. Terminal master's awarded for partial completion of doctoral program. *Degree requirements:* For master's, thesis optional, minimum B average in major field and overall; for doctorate, comprehensive exam (for some programs), thesis/dissertation; for Certificate, minimum B average. *Entrance requirements:* For master's, International applicants must submit TOEFL/IELTS scores and fulfill the English Language Proficiency Requirement. Applicants to full-time programs who do not qualify for a score waiver are required to submit GRE/GMAT scores. Additional exam requirements/recommendations for international students: required—TOEFL (minimum score 74 iBT), IELTS (minimum score 6). *Application deadline:* For fall admission, 4/15 for domestic and international students; for spring admission, 11/1 for domestic and international students; for summer admission, 5/1 for domestic students. Applications are processed on a rolling basis. Application fee: $60. Electronic applications accepted. *Expenses: Tuition:* Full-time $52,134. *Required fees:* $1880. Tuition and fees vary according to course load. *Financial support:* Fellowships, research assistantships, teaching assistantships, career-related internships or fieldwork, Federal Work-Study, scholarships/grants, and unspecified assistantships available. Financial award application deadline: 2/15; financial award applicants required to submit FAFSA. *Unit head:* Dr. Jean Zu, Dean of SES, 201-216.8233, Fax: 201-216.8372, E-mail: Jean.Zu@stevens.edu. *Application contact:* Graduate Admission, 888-783-8367, Fax: 888-511-1306, E-mail: graduate@stevens.edu.

Syracuse University, College of Engineering and Computer Science, MS Program in Environmental Engineering, Syracuse, NY 13244. Offers MS. *Program availability:* Part-time. *Degree requirements:* For master's, thesis optional. *Entrance requirements:* For master's, GRE General Test, three letters of recommendation, personal statement, resume, official transcripts. Additional exam requirements/recommendations for international students: required—TOEFL (minimum score 100 iBT). Electronic applications accepted.

Syracuse University, College of Engineering and Computer Science, MS Program in Environmental Engineering Science, Syracuse, NY 13244. Offers MS. *Program availability:* Part-time. *Entrance requirements:* For master's, GRE General Test, three letters of recommendation, personal statement, resume, official transcripts. Additional exam requirements/recommendations for international students: required—TOEFL (minimum score 100 iBT). Electronic applications accepted.

Temple University, College of Engineering, Department of Civil and Environmental Engineering, Philadelphia, PA 19122-6096. Offers civil engineering (MSCE); environmental engineering (MS Env E); storm water management (Graduate Certificate). *Program availability:* Part-time, evening/weekend. *Faculty:* 16 full-time (2 women), 18 part-time/adjunct (4 women). *Students:* 40 full-time (15 women), 7 part-time (1 woman); includes 6 minority (3 Black or African American, non-Hispanic/Latino; 2 Asian, non-Hispanic/Latino; 1 Two or more races, non-Hispanic/Latino), 30 international. 68 applicants, 56% accepted, 14 enrolled. In 2019, 9 master's awarded. Terminal master's awarded for partial completion of doctoral program. *Degree requirements:* For master's, thesis optional. *Entrance requirements:* For master's, GRE General Test. Waivers are considered on a case by case basis for master's applicants. Additional exam requirements/recommendations for international students: required—TOEFL (minimum score 79 iBT), IELTS (minimum score 6.5). *Application deadline:* For fall admission, 6/1 priority date for domestic students, 3/1 priority date for international students; for spring admission, 11/1 priority date for domestic students, 8/1 priority date for international students. Applications are processed on a rolling basis. Application fee: $60. Electronic applications accepted. *Expenses:* 1,135 per credit hour in-state resident; 1,490 per credit hour out-of state resident. *Financial support:* In 2019–20, 16 research assistantships with full tuition reimbursements (averaging $19,739 per year), 18 teaching assistantships with full tuition reimbursements (averaging $19,739 per year) were awarded. Financial award applicants required to submit FAFSA. *Unit head:* Dr. Rominder Suri, Chair, Department of Civil and Environmental Engineering, 215-204-2378, Fax: 215-204-6936, E-mail: rominder.suri@temple.edu. *Application contact:* Colleen Baillie, Director of Enrollment Management, 215-204-7800, Fax: 215-204-6936, E-mail: gradengr@temple.edu.
Website: http://engineering.temple.edu/department/civil-environmental-engineering

Tennessee State University, The School of Graduate Studies and Research, College of Engineering, Nashville, TN 37209-1561. Offers biomedical engineering (ME); civil engineering (ME); computer and information systems engineering (MS, PhD); electrical engineering (ME); environmental engineering (ME); manufacturing engineering (ME); mathematical sciences (MS); mechanical engineering (ME). *Program availability:* Part-time, evening/weekend. *Degree requirements:* For master's, project; for doctorate, comprehensive exam, thesis/dissertation. *Entrance requirements:* For doctorate, minimum GPA of 3.3.

Texas A&M University–Kingsville, College of Graduate Studies, Frank H. Dotterweich College of Engineering, Department of Environmental Engineering, Kingsville, TX 78363. Offers ME, MS, PhD. *Degree requirements:* For master's, variable foreign language requirement, comprehensive exam, thesis (for some programs); for doctorate, variable foreign language requirement, comprehensive exam, thesis/dissertation (for some programs). *Entrance requirements:* For master's, GRE (minimum quantitative and verbal score of 294), MAT, GMAT, minimum undergraduate GPA of 2.8; for doctorate, GRE, MAT, GMAT. Additional exam requirements/recommendations for international students: required—TOEFL (minimum score 550 paper-based; 79 iBT). Electronic applications accepted.

Tufts University, School of Engineering, Department of Civil and Environmental Engineering, Medford, MA 02155. Offers bioengineering (MS), including environmental biotechnology; civil and environmental engineering (MS, PhD), including applied data science, environmental and water resources engineering, environmental health, geosystems engineering, structural engineering and mechanics; PhD/PhD. *Program availability:* Part-time. Terminal master's awarded for partial completion of doctoral program. *Degree requirements:* For master's, thesis (for some programs); for doctorate, thesis/dissertation. *Entrance requirements:* For master's and doctorate, GRE General Test. Additional exam requirements/recommendations for international students: required—TOEFL (minimum score 550 paper-based; 80 iBT), IELTS (minimum score 6.5). Electronic applications accepted. Full-time tuition and fees vary according to degree level, program and student level. Part-time tuition and fees vary according to course load.

Universidad Central del Este, Graduate School, San Pedro de Macoris, Dominican Republic. Offers environmental engineering (ME); financial management (M Ad); higher education (M Ed), including higher education management, higher education pedagogy; human resources (M Ad). *Entrance requirements:* For master's, letters of recommendation.

Universidad Nacional Pedro Henriquez Urena, Graduate School, Santo Domingo, Dominican Republic. Offers agricultural diversity (MS), including horticultural/fruit production, tropical animal production; conservation of monuments and cultural assets (M Arch); ecology and environment (MS); environmental engineering (MEE); international relations (MA); natural resource management (MS); political science (MA); project optimization (MPM); project feasibility (MPM); project management (MPM); sanitation engineering (ME); science for teachers (MS); tropical Caribbean architecture (M Arch).

Université de Sherbrooke, Faculty of Engineering, Program in the Environment, Sherbrooke, QC J1K 2R1, Canada. Offers M Env. *Degree requirements:* For master's, thesis.

University at Buffalo, the State University of New York, Graduate School, School of Engineering and Applied Sciences, Department of Civil, Structural, and Environmental Engineering, Buffalo, NY 14260. Offers civil engineering (MS, PhD); engineering science (MS), including data sciences, green energy, Internet of Things, nanoelectronics; environmental and water resources engineering (MS). *Program availability:* Part-time, online learning. Terminal master's awarded for partial completion of doctoral program. *Degree requirements:* For master's, project, thesis, or comprehensive exam; for doctorate, thesis/dissertation. *Entrance requirements:* For master's and doctorate, GRE General Test, letters of reference. Additional exam requirements/recommendations for international students: required—TOEFL (minimum score 550 paper-based; 79 iBT). Electronic applications accepted. *Expenses: Tuition, area resident:* Full-time $11,310; part-time $471 per credit hour. Tuition, state resident: full-time $11,310; part-time $471 per credit hour. Tuition, nonresident: full-time $23,100; part-time $963 per credit hour. *International tuition:* $23,100 full-time. *Required fees:* $2820.

The University of Alabama, Graduate School, College of Engineering, Department of Civil, Construction and Environmental Engineering, Tuscaloosa, AL 35487-0205. Offers civil engineering (MSCE, PhD); environmental engineering (MS). *Program availability:* Part-time. *Faculty:* 18 full-time (1 woman). *Students:* 64 full-time (23 women), 5 part-time (2 women); includes 4 minority (2 Asian, non-Hispanic/Latino; 2 Hispanic/Latino), 41 international. Average age 29. 116 applicants, 63% accepted, 17 enrolled. In 2019, 22 master's, 4 doctorates awarded. Terminal master's awarded for partial completion of doctoral program. *Degree requirements:* For master's, thesis or alternative; for doctorate, comprehensive exam, thesis/dissertation. *Entrance requirements:* For master's and doctorate, GRE General Test (minimum combined score of 300), minimum overall GPA of 3.0 in last hours of course work. Additional exam requirements/recommendations for international students: required—TOEFL (minimum score 550 paper-based; 79 iBT), IELTS (minimum score 6.5), PTE (minimum score 59). *Application deadline:* Applications are processed on a rolling basis. Application fee: $50 ($60 for international students). Electronic applications accepted. *Expenses: Tuition, area resident:* Full-time $10,780; part-time $440 per credit hour. Tuition, nonresident: full-time $30,250; part-time $1550 per credit hour. *Financial support:* In 2019–20, 36 students received support. Fellowships with full tuition reimbursements available, research assistantships with full tuition reimbursements available, teaching assistantships with full tuition reimbursements available, scholarships/grants, tuition waivers (partial), and unspecified assistantships available. Financial award application deadline: 1/5. *Unit head:* Dr. W. Edward Back, Head/Professor, 205-348-6550, Fax: 205-348-0783, E-mail: eback@eng.ua.edu. *Application contact:* Dr. Andrew Graettinger, Professor and Graduate Program Director, 205-348-1707, Fax: 205-348-0783, E-mail: andrewg@eng.ua.edu.
Website: http://cce.eng.ua.edu/

The University of Alabama in Huntsville, School of Graduate Studies, College of Engineering, Department of Civil and Environmental Engineering, Huntsville, AL 35899. Offers civil and environmental engineering (PhD); civil engineering (MSE), including civil engineering. *Program availability:* Part-time. *Degree requirements:* For master's, comprehensive exam, thesis or alternative, oral and written exams; for doctorate, comprehensive exam, thesis/dissertation, oral and written exams. *Entrance requirements:* For master's, GRE General Test, BSE, minimum GPA of 3.0; for doctorate, GRE General Test, minimum GPA of 3.0. Additional exam requirements/recommendations for international students: required—TOEFL (minimum score 500 paper-based; 80 iBT), IELTS (minimum score 6.5). Electronic applications accepted.

University of Alaska Fairbanks, College of Engineering and Mines, Department of Civil and Environmental Engineering, Fairbanks, AK 99775-5900. Offers civil engineering (MS); design and construction management (Graduate Certificate); environmental engineering (PhD). *Program availability:* Part-time. *Degree requirements:* For master's, comprehensive exam, thesis (for some programs), oral defense of project or thesis; for doctorate, comprehensive exam, thesis/dissertation. *Entrance requirements:* For master's, bachelor's degree from accredited institution with minimum cumulative undergraduate and major GPA of 3.0. Additional exam requirements/recommendations for international students: required—TOEFL (minimum score 550 paper-based; 79 iBT), IELTS (minimum score 6.5). Electronic applications accepted. *Expenses:* Contact institution.

University of Alberta, Faculty of Graduate Studies and Research, Department of Civil and Environmental Engineering, Edmonton, AB T6G 2E1, Canada. Offers construction engineering and management (M Eng, M Sc, PhD); environmental engineering (M Eng, M Sc, PhD); environmental science (M Sc, PhD); geoenvironmental engineering (M Eng, M Sc, PhD); geotechnical engineering (M Eng, M Sc, PhD); mining engineering (M Eng, M Sc, PhD); petroleum engineering (M Eng, M Sc, PhD); structural engineering (M Eng, M Sc, PhD); water resources (M Eng, M Sc, PhD). *Program availability:* Part-time, online learning. *Degree requirements:* For master's, thesis (for some programs); for doctorate, thesis/dissertation. *Entrance requirements:* For master's, minimum GPA of 3.0 in last 2 years of undergraduate studies; for doctorate, minimum GPA of 3.0. Additional exam requirements/recommendations for international students: required—TOEFL (minimum score 550 paper-based). Electronic applications accepted.

The University of Arizona, College of Engineering, Department of Chemical and Environmental Engineering, Tucson, AZ 85721-0011. Offers chemical engineering (MS, PhD); environmental engineering (MS, PhD). *Program availability:* Part-time. *Degree requirements:* For master's, thesis; for doctorate, comprehensive exam, thesis/dissertation, departmental qualifying exams. *Entrance requirements:* For master's and doctorate, GRE General Test, 3 letters of recommendation, resume, statement of purpose. Additional exam requirements/recommendations for international students: required—TOEFL (minimum score 550 paper-based; 79 iBT). Electronic applications accepted.

University of Arkansas, Graduate School, College of Engineering, Department of Civil Engineering, Program in Environmental Engineering, Fayetteville, AR 72701. Offers MS En E, MSE. *Application deadline:* For fall admission, 8/1 for domestic students, 4/1 for international students; for spring admission, 12/1 for domestic students, 10/1 for international students; for summer admission, 4/15 for domestic students, 3/1 for international students. Applications are processed on a rolling basis. Application fee: $60. Electronic applications accepted. *Financial support:* Fellowships, research assistantships, teaching assistantships, career-related internships or fieldwork, and Federal Work-Study available. Support available to part-time students. Financial award application deadline: 4/1; financial award applicants required to submit FAFSA. *Unit head:* Dr. Micah Hale, Department Chair, 479-575-6348, E-mail: micah@uark.edu. *Application contact:* Dr. Julian Fairey, Graduate Coordinator, 479-575-4023, E-mail: julianf@uark.edu.
Website: https://civil-engineering.uark.edu/research/environmental-engineering.php

University of Arkansas, Graduate School, Interdisciplinary Program in Environmental Dynamics, Fayetteville, AR 72701. Offers PhD. *Students:* 15 full-time (7 women), 10 part-time (5 women); includes 3 minority (2 Black or African American, non-Hispanic/Latino; 1 Asian, non-Hispanic/Latino), 8 international. 6 applicants, 100% accepted. In 2019, 2 doctorates awarded. *Application deadline:* For fall admission, 8/1 for domestic students, 4/1 for international students; for spring admission, 12/1 for domestic students, 10/1 for international students; for summer admission, 4/15 for domestic students, 3/1 for international students. Applications are processed on a rolling basis. Application fee: $60. Electronic applications accepted. *Financial support:* In 2019–20, 5 research assistantships, 9 teaching assistantships were awarded; fellowships with tuition reimbursements also available. Financial award application deadline: 4/1. *Unit head:* Dr. Peter S. Ungar, Director, 479-575-6361, Fax: 479-575-3469, E-mail: pungar@uark.edu. *Application contact:* JoAnn Kvamme, Assistant Director, 479-575-6603, Fax: 479-575-3469, E-mail: jkvamme@uark.edu.
Website: https://environmental-dynamics.uark.edu

University of Calgary, Faculty of Graduate Studies, Schulich School of Engineering, Program in Chemical and Petroleum Engineering, Calgary, AB T2N 1N4, Canada. Offers chemical engineering (M Eng, M Sc, PhD); energy and environment engineering (M Eng, M Sc, PhD); energy and environmental systems (M Eng, M Sc, PhD); environmental engineering (M Eng, M Sc, PhD); petroleum engineering (M Eng, M Sc, PhD); reservoir characterization (M Eng, M Sc). *Program availability:* Part-time. *Degree requirements:* For master's, thesis (for some programs); for doctorate, comprehensive exam, thesis/dissertation, candidacy exam. *Entrance requirements:* For master's, minimum GPA of 3.0 or equivalent; for doctorate, minimum GPA of 3.5 or equivalent. Additional exam requirements/recommendations for international students: required—TOEFL (minimum score 550 paper-based; 80 iBT), IELTS (minimum score 7). Electronic applications accepted.

University of Calgary, Faculty of Graduate Studies, Schulich School of Engineering, Program in Civil Engineering, Calgary, AB T2N 1N4, Canada. Offers avalanche mechanics (M Sc, PhD); civil engineering (M Eng, M Sc, PhD); energy and environment engineering (M Eng, M Sc, PhD); environmental engineering (M Eng, M Sc, PhD); geotechnical engineering (M Eng, M Sc, PhD); materials science (M Eng, M Sc, PhD); project management (M Eng, M Sc, PhD); structures and solid mechanics (M Eng, M Sc, PhD); transportation engineering (M Eng, M Sc, PhD); water resources (M Eng, M Sc, PhD). *Program availability:* Part-time. *Degree requirements:* For master's, thesis; for doctorate, thesis/dissertation, written and oral candidacy exam. *Entrance requirements:* For master's, minimum GPA of 3.0; for doctorate, minimum GPA of 3.5. Additional exam requirements/recommendations for international students: required—TOEFL (minimum score 580 paper-based; 93 iBT), IELTS (minimum score 7). Electronic applications accepted.

University of California, Berkeley, Graduate Division, College of Engineering, Department of Civil and Environmental Engineering, Berkeley, CA 94720. Offers engineering and project management (M Eng, MS, PhD); environmental engineering (M Eng, MS, PhD); geoengineering (M Eng, MS, PhD); structural engineering, mechanics and materials (M Eng, MS, PhD); transportation engineering (M Eng, MS, PhD); M Arch/MS; MCP/MS; MPP/MS. Terminal master's awarded for partial completion of doctoral program. *Degree requirements:* For master's, comprehensive exam (for some programs), thesis (for some programs), comprehensive exam or thesis (MS); for doctorate, thesis/dissertation, qualifying exam. *Entrance requirements:* For master's, GRE General Test, minimum GPA of 3.0, 3 letters of recommendation; for doctorate, GRE General Test, minimum GPA of 3.5, 3 letters of recommendation. Additional exam requirements/recommendations for international students: required—TOEFL (minimum score 570 paper-based; 90 iBT). Electronic applications accepted.

University of California, Davis, College of Engineering, Program in Civil and Environmental Engineering, Davis, CA 95616. Offers M Engr, MS, D Engr, PhD, Certificate, M Engr/MBA. *Degree requirements:* For master's, comprehensive exam (for some programs), thesis (for some programs); for doctorate, thesis/dissertation. *Entrance requirements:* For master's, GRE General Test, minimum GPA of 3.0; for doctorate, GRE, minimum graduate GPA of 3.5. Additional exam requirements/recommendations for international students: required—TOEFL (minimum score 550 paper-based). Electronic applications accepted.

University of California, Irvine, Samueli School of Engineering, Department of Civil and Environmental Engineering, Irvine, CA 92697. Offers MS, PhD. *Program availability:* Part-time. *Students:* 132 full-time (57 women), 7 part-time (2 women); includes 25 minority (2 Black or African American, non-Hispanic/Latino; 16 Asian, non-Hispanic/Latino; 6 Hispanic/Latino; 1 Two or more races, non-Hispanic/Latino), 79 international. Average age 27. 434 applicants, 47% accepted, 37 enrolled. In 2019, 49 master's, 16 doctorates awarded. Terminal master's awarded for partial completion of doctoral program. *Entrance requirements:* For master's and doctorate, GRE General Test, minimum GPA of 3.0, 3 letters of recommendation. Additional exam requirements/recommendations for international students: required—TOEFL (minimum score 550 paper-based). *Application deadline:* For fall admission, 1/15 priority date for domestic students, 1/15 for international students. Applications are processed on a rolling basis. Application fee: $120 ($140 for international students). Electronic applications accepted. *Financial support:* Fellowships, research assistantships with full tuition reimbursements, teaching assistantships, institutionally sponsored loans, traineeships, health care benefits, and unspecified assistantships available. Financial award application deadline: 3/1; financial award applicants required to submit FAFSA. *Unit head:* Prof. Brett F. Sanders, Chair and Professor, 949-824-4327, Fax: 949-824-3672, E-mail: bsanders@uci.edu. *Application contact:* Connie Cheng, Assistant Director, 949-824-3562, Fax: 949-824-8200, E-mail: connie.cheng@uci.edu.
Website: http://www.eng.uci.edu/dept/cee

University of California, Los Angeles, Graduate Division, Fielding School of Public Health, Department of Environmental Health Sciences, Los Angeles, CA 90095. Offers environmental health sciences (MS, PhD); environmental science and engineering (D Env); molecular toxicology (PhD); JD/MPH. *Accreditation:* ABET (one or more programs are accredited); CEPH. *Degree requirements:* For master's, comprehensive exam or thesis; for doctorate, thesis/dissertation, oral and written qualifying exams. *Entrance requirements:* For master's, GRE General Test, minimum GPA of 3.0; for doctorate, GRE General Test, minimum undergraduate GPA of 3.0. Electronic applications accepted.

University of California, Los Angeles, Graduate Division, Henry Samueli School of Engineering and Applied Science, Department of Civil and Environmental Engineering, Los Angeles, CA 90095-1593. Offers MS, PhD. *Degree requirements:* For master's, comprehensive exam or thesis; for doctorate, thesis/dissertation, qualifying exams. *Entrance requirements:* For master's, GRE General Test, minimum GPA of 3.0; for doctorate, GRE General Test, minimum GPA of 3.25. Additional exam requirements/recommendations for international students: required—TOEFL (minimum score 560 paper-based; 87 iBT), IELTS (minimum score 7). Electronic applications accepted.

University of California, Los Angeles, Graduate Division, Institute of the Environment and Sustainability, Los Angeles, CA 90095-1496. Offers environmental science and engineering (D Env). *Degree requirements:* For doctorate, thesis/dissertation, oral and written qualifying exams. *Entrance requirements:* For doctorate, GRE General Test, minimum undergraduate GPA of 3.0, master's degree or equivalent in a natural science, engineering, or public health.

University of California, Merced, Graduate Division, School of Engineering, Merced, CA 95343. Offers biological engineering and small scale technologies (MS, PhD); electrical engineering and computer science (MS, PhD); environmental systems (MS, PhD); management of innovation, sustainability, and technology (MM); mechanical engineering (MS, PhD). *Faculty:* 60 full-time (16 women). *Students:* 244 full-time (83 women), 1 (woman) part-time; includes 56 minority (2 Black or African American, non-Hispanic/Latino; 20 Asian, non-Hispanic/Latino; 30 Hispanic/Latino; 1 Native Hawaiian or other Pacific Islander, non-Hispanic/Latino; 3 Two or more races, non-Hispanic/Latino), 153 international. Average age 28. 330 applicants, 32% accepted, 67 enrolled. In 2019, 30 master's, 17 doctorates awarded. Terminal master's awarded for partial completion of doctoral program. *Degree requirements:* For master's, variable foreign language requirement, comprehensive exam, thesis or alternative, oral defense; for doctorate, variable foreign language requirement, comprehensive exam, thesis/dissertation, oral defense. *Entrance requirements:* For master's and doctorate, GRE. Additional exam requirements/recommendations for international students: required—TOEFL (minimum score 550 paper-based; 80 iBT); recommended—IELTS (minimum score 6.5). *Application deadline:* For fall admission, 1/15 for domestic and international students. Application fee: $105 ($125 for international students). Electronic applications accepted. *Expenses: Tuition, area resident:* Full-time $11,442; part-time $5721. Tuition, state resident: full-time $11,442; part-time $5721. Tuition, nonresident: full-time $26,544; part-time $13,272. *International tuition:* $26,544 full-time. *Required fees:* $564 per semester. *Financial support:* In 2019–20, 205 students received support, including 6 fellowships with full tuition reimbursements available (averaging $22,005 per year), 76 research assistantships with full tuition reimbursements available (averaging $21,420 per year), 123 teaching assistantships with full tuition reimbursements available (averaging $21,911 per year); scholarships/grants, traineeships, and health care benefits also available. *Unit head:* Dr. Mark Matsumoto, Dean, 209-228-4047, Fax: 209-228-4047, E-mail: mmatsumoto@ucmerced.edu. *Application contact:* Tsu Ya, Director of Admissions and Academic Services, 209-228-4521, Fax: 209-228-6906, E-mail: tya@ucmerced.edu.

University of California, Riverside, Graduate Division, Department of Chemical and Environmental Engineering, Riverside, CA 92521-0102. Offers MS, PhD. *Program availability:* Part-time. Terminal master's awarded for partial completion of doctoral program. *Degree requirements:* For master's, thesis (for some programs); for doctorate, comprehensive exam, thesis/dissertation. *Entrance requirements:* For master's and doctorate, GRE General Test, minimum GPA of 3.0. Additional exam requirements/recommendations for international students: required—TOEFL (minimum score 550 paper-based; 80 iBT). Electronic applications accepted.

University of Central Florida, College of Engineering and Computer Science, Department of Civil, Environmental, and Construction Engineering, Program in Environmental Engineering, Orlando, FL 32816. Offers MS, MS Env E, PhD. *Program availability:* Part-time, evening/weekend. *Students:* 26 full-time (14 women), 19 part-time (6 women); includes 12 minority (2 Asian, non-Hispanic/Latino; 10 Hispanic/Latino), 13 international. Average age 29. 44 applicants, 50% accepted, 15 enrolled. In 2019, 8 master's, 5 doctorates awarded. *Degree requirements:* For master's, thesis or alternative; for doctorate, thesis/dissertation, departmental qualifying exam, candidacy exam. *Entrance requirements:* For master's, minimum GPA of 3.0 in last 60 hours of course work, letters of recommendation, goal statement, resume; for doctorate, GRE General Test, minimum GPA of 3.0 in last 60 hours of course work, letters of recommendation, goal statement, resume. Additional exam requirements/recommendations for international students: required—TOEFL. *Application deadline:* For fall admission, 7/15 for domestic students; for spring admission, 12/1 for domestic students. Application fee: $30. Electronic applications accepted. *Financial support:* In 2019–20, 17 students received support, including 3 fellowships with partial tuition reimbursements available (averaging $17,000 per year), 14 research assistantships with partial tuition reimbursements available (averaging $6,954 per year), 3 teaching assistantships with partial tuition reimbursements available (averaging $7,875 per year); career-related internships or fieldwork, Federal Work-Study, institutionally sponsored loans, health care benefits, tuition waivers (partial), and unspecified assistantships also available. Financial award application deadline: 3/1; financial award applicants required to submit FAFSA. *Unit head:* Dr. Andrew Randall, Graduate Director, 407-823-2841, E-mail: andrew.randall@ucf.edu. *Application contact:* Associate Director, Graduate Admissions, 407-823-2766, Fax: 407-823-6442, E-mail: gradadmissions@ucf.edu.
Website: http://cece.ucf.edu/

University of Cincinnati, Graduate School, College of Engineering and Applied Science, Department of Biomedical, Chemical and Environmental Engineering, Program in Environmental Engineering, Cincinnati, OH 45221. Offers MS, PhD. *Program availability:* Part-time. *Degree requirements:* For master's, project or thesis; for doctorate, one foreign language, thesis/dissertation. *Entrance requirements:* For master's and doctorate, GRE General Test. Additional exam requirements/recommendations for international students: required—TOEFL (minimum score 580 paper-based; 92 iBT). Electronic applications accepted.

University of Colorado Boulder, Graduate School, College of Engineering and Applied Science, Department of Civil, Environmental, and Architectural Engineering, Boulder, CO 80309. Offers MS, PhD. Terminal master's awarded for partial completion of doctoral program. *Degree requirements:* For master's, comprehensive exam, thesis or alternative; for doctorate, thesis/dissertation. *Entrance requirements:* For master's, GRE

General Test, minimum undergraduate GPA of 3.0. Electronic applications accepted. Application fee is waived when completed online.

University of Colorado Denver, College of Engineering, Design and Computing, Department of Civil Engineering, Denver, CO 80217. Offers civil engineering (EASPh D); civil engineering systems (PhD); environmental and sustainability engineering (MS, PhD); geographic information systems (MS); geotechnical engineering (MS, PhD); hydrology and hydraulics (MS, PhD); structural engineering (MS, PhD); transportation engineering (MS, PhD). *Program availability:* Part-time, evening/weekend. *Degree requirements:* For master's, comprehensive exam, 30 credit hours, project or thesis; for doctorate, comprehensive exam, thesis/dissertation, 60 credit hours (30 of which are dissertation research). *Entrance requirements:* For master's, GRE, statement of purpose, transcripts, three references; for doctorate, GRE, statement of purpose, transcripts, references, letter of support from faculty stating willingness to serve as dissertation advisor and outlining plan for financial support. Additional exam requirements/recommendations for international students: required—TOEFL (minimum score 537 paper-based; 75 iBT); recommended—IELTS (minimum score 6.5). Electronic applications accepted. Tuition and fees vary according to course load, program and reciprocity agreements.

University of Connecticut, Graduate School, School of Engineering, Department of Civil and Environmental Engineering, Field of Environmental Engineering, Storrs, CT 06269. Offers MS, PhD. *Degree requirements:* For master's, comprehensive exam; for doctorate, thesis/dissertation. *Entrance requirements:* For master's and doctorate, GRE General Test. Additional exam requirements/recommendations for international students: required—TOEFL (minimum score 550 paper-based). Electronic applications accepted.

University of Dayton, Department of Civil and Environmental Engineering and Engineering Mechanics, Dayton, OH 45469. Offers engineering mechanics (MSEM); environmental engineering (MSCE); geotechnical engineering (MSCE); structural engineering (MSCE); transportation engineering (MSCE); water resources engineering (MSCE). *Program availability:* Part-time, blended/hybrid learning. *Degree requirements:* For master's, thesis or alternative. *Entrance requirements:* For master's, minimum GPA of 3.0 in undergraduate work. Additional exam requirements/recommendations for international students: required—TOEFL (minimum score 550 paper-based; 80 iBT); recommended—IELTS (minimum score 6.5), TSE (minimum score 60). Electronic applications accepted.

University of Delaware, College of Engineering, Department of Civil and Environmental Engineering, Newark, DE 19716. Offers environmental engineering (MAS, MCE, PhD); geotechnical engineering (MAS, MCE, PhD); ocean engineering (MAS, MCE, PhD); structural engineering (MAS, MCE, PhD); transportation engineering (MAS, MCE, PhD); water resource engineering (MAS, MCE, PhD). *Program availability:* Part-time. Terminal master's awarded for partial completion of doctoral program. *Degree requirements:* For master's, thesis; for doctorate, thesis/dissertation. *Entrance requirements:* For master's and doctorate, GRE General Test. Additional exam requirements/recommendations for international students: required—TOEFL. Electronic applications accepted.

University of Detroit Mercy, College of Engineering and Science, Detroit, MI 48221. Offers chemistry (MS); civil and environmental engineering (DE); electrical and computer engineering (ME); electrical engineering (DE); engineering management (M Eng Mgt); environmental engineering (MEE); mechanical engineering (MME, DE); product development (MS); software engineering (MSSE); teaching of mathematics (MATM). *Program availability:* Part-time, evening/weekend. *Degree requirements:* For doctorate, thesis/dissertation. Electronic applications accepted. Application fee is waived when completed online. *Expenses:* Contact institution.

University of Florida, Graduate School, Herbert Wertheim College of Engineering, Department of Environmental Engineering Sciences, Gainesville, FL 32611. Offers environmental engineering sciences (ME, MS, PhD, Engr); geographic information systems (ME, MS, PhD); hydrologic sciences (ME, MS, PhD); wetland sciences (ME, MS, PhD); JD/MS. *Program availability:* Part-time, evening/weekend, online learning. Terminal master's awarded for partial completion of doctoral program. *Degree requirements:* For master's, comprehensive exam (for some programs), thesis (for some programs), project, thesis or coursework; for doctorate, comprehensive exam, thesis/dissertation; for Engr, project or thesis. *Entrance requirements:* For master's and doctorate, minimum GPA of 3.0; for Engr, GRE General Test. Additional exam requirements/recommendations for international students: required—TOEFL (minimum score 550 paper-based; 80 iBT), IELTS (minimum score 6). Electronic applications accepted.

University of Georgia, College of Engineering, Athens, GA 30602. Offers MS.

University of Guelph, Office of Graduate and Postdoctoral Studies, College of Physical and Engineering Science, School of Engineering, Guelph, ON N1G 2W1, Canada. Offers biological engineering (M Eng, M Sc, MA Sc, PhD); engineering systems and computing (M Eng, M Sc, MA Sc, PhD); environmental engineering (M Eng, M Sc, MA Sc, PhD); water resources engineering (M Eng, M Sc, MA Sc, PhD). *Program availability:* Part-time. *Degree requirements:* For master's, thesis (for some programs); for doctorate, comprehensive exam, thesis/dissertation. *Entrance requirements:* For master's, minimum B- average during previous 2 years of course work; for doctorate, minimum B average. Additional exam requirements/recommendations for international students: required—TOEFL (minimum score 550 paper-based; 89 iBT), IELTS (minimum score 6.5). Electronic applications accepted.

University of Hawaii at Manoa, Office of Graduate Education, College of Engineering, Department of Civil and Environmental Engineering, Honolulu, HI 96822. Offers MS, PhD. *Program availability:* Part-time. *Degree requirements:* For master's, comprehensive exam, thesis; for doctorate, comprehensive exam, thesis/dissertation. *Entrance requirements:* For master's and doctorate, GRE General Test or EIT Exam. Additional exam requirements/recommendations for international students: required—TOEFL (minimum score 540 paper-based; 76 iBT), IELTS (minimum score 5).

University of Illinois at Urbana-Champaign, Graduate College, College of Engineering, Department of Civil and Environmental Engineering, Champaign, IL 61820. Offers civil engineering (MS, PhD); environmental engineering in civil engineering (MS, PhD); M Arch/MS; MBA/MS. *Program availability:* Part-time, evening/weekend, online learning.

The University of Iowa, Graduate College, College of Engineering, Department of Civil and Environmental Engineering, Iowa City, IA 52242-1316. Offers environmental engineering and science (MS, PhD); hydraulics and water resources (MS, PhD); structures, mechanics and materials (MS, PhD); sustainable water development (MS, PhD); transportation engineering (MS, PhD). *Program availability:* Part-time. Terminal master's awarded for partial completion of doctoral program. *Degree requirements:* For master's, thesis optional, exam; for doctorate, comprehensive exam, thesis/dissertation, exam. *Entrance requirements:* For master's, GRE (minimum combined score of 301 on verbal and quantitative), minimum undergraduate GPA of 3.0; for doctorate, GRE (minimum combined score of 301 on verbal and quantitative), minimum graduate GPA of 3.0. Additional exam requirements/recommendations for international students: required—TOEFL (minimum score 550 paper-based; 81 iBT), IELTS (minimum score 7). Electronic applications accepted.

The University of Kansas, Graduate Studies, School of Engineering, Program in Environmental Engineering, Lawrence, KS 66045. Offers MS, PhD. *Program availability:* Part-time. *Students:* 11 full-time (3 women), 4 part-time (3 women); includes 4 minority (1 Black or African American, non-Hispanic/Latino; 2 Asian, non-Hispanic/Latino; 1 Two or more races, non-Hispanic/Latino), 10 international. Average age 29. 11 applicants, 55% accepted, 2 enrolled. In 2019, 5 master's, 1 doctorate awarded. *Entrance requirements:* For master's and doctorate, GRE, BS in engineering, recommendations, resume, statement of purpose. Additional exam requirements/recommendations for international students: required—TOEFL, IELTS. *Application deadline:* For fall admission, 12/15 priority date for domestic and international students; for spring admission, 9/15 priority date for domestic and international students. Application fee: $65 ($85 for international students). Electronic applications accepted. *Expenses:* Tuition, state resident: full-time $9989. Tuition, nonresident: full-time $23,950. *International tuition:* $23,950 full-time. *Required fees:* $984; $81.99 per credit hour. Tuition and fees vary according to course load, campus/location and program. *Financial support:* Fellowships, research assistantships, teaching assistantships, career-related internships or fieldwork, and scholarships/grants available. Financial award application deadline: 12/15. *Unit head:* David Darwin, Chair, 785-864-3827, E-mail: daved@ku.edu. *Application contact:* Susan Scott, Administrative Assistant, 785-864-3826, E-mail: s523s307@ku.edu.
Website: http://ceae.ku.edu/overview-3

The University of Manchester, School of Mechanical, Aerospace and Civil Engineering, Manchester, United Kingdom. Offers advanced manufacturing technology (M Ent); aerospace engineering (M Phil, M Sc, PhD); civil engineering (M Phil, M Sc, PhD); environmental engineering (M Phil, PhD); management of projects (M Phil, M Sc, PhD); mechanical engineering (M Phil, M Sc, PhD); mechanical engineering design (M Ent); nuclear engineering (M Phil, D Eng, PhD).

University of Maryland, Baltimore County, The Graduate School, College of Engineering and Information Technology, Department of Chemical, Biochemical, and Environmental Engineering, Program in Environmental Engineering, Baltimore, MD 21250. Offers MS, PhD. *Program availability:* Part-time. *Faculty:* 6 full-time (2 women). *Students:* 11 full-time (3 women), 2 part-time (1 woman); includes 2 minority (1 Black or African American, non-Hispanic/Latino; 1 Asian, non-Hispanic/Latino), 8 international. Average age 30. 24 applicants, 21% accepted, 3 enrolled. In 2019, 1 master's, 1 doctorate awarded. *Degree requirements:* For master's, comprehensive exam (for some programs), thesis (for some programs); for doctorate, comprehensive exam, thesis/dissertation, qualifying exam. *Entrance requirements:* For master's and doctorate, GRE General Test, BS in environmental engineering or related field of engineering. Additional exam requirements/recommendations for international students: required—TOEFL (minimum score 550 paper-based; 80 iBT). *Application deadline:* For fall admission, 6/1 for domestic students, 1/1 for international students; for spring admission, 11/1 for domestic students, 6/1 for international students. Applications are processed on a rolling basis. Application fee: $70. Electronic applications accepted. *Expenses:* $14,382 per year. *Financial support:* In 2019–20, 9 students received support, including 1 fellowship, 6 research assistantships with full tuition reimbursements available, 2 teaching assistantships with full tuition reimbursements available; career-related internships or fieldwork, Federal Work-Study, scholarships/grants, health care benefits, tuition waivers (partial), and unspecified assistantships also available. Support available to part-time students. Financial award application deadline: 6/30; financial award applicants required to submit FAFSA. *Unit head:* Dr. Mark Marten, Professor and Interim Chair, 410-455-3400, Fax: 410-455-1049, E-mail: reedb@umbc.edu. *Application contact:* Dr. Jennie Leach, Professor and Graduate Program Director, 410-455-8152, Fax: 410-455-6500, E-mail: mariajose@umbc.edu.
Website: https://cbee.umbc.edu/

University of Maryland, College Park, Academic Affairs, A. James Clark School of Engineering, Department of Civil and Environmental Engineering, College Park, MD 20742. Offers M Eng, MS, PhD. *Program availability:* Part-time, evening/weekend, online learning. *Degree requirements:* For master's, thesis optional; for doctorate, thesis/dissertation, qualifying exam. *Entrance requirements:* For master's and doctorate, GRE General Test, 3 letters of recommendation. Electronic applications accepted.

University of Massachusetts Amherst, Graduate School, College of Engineering, Department of Civil and Environmental Engineering, Amherst, MA 01003. Offers civil engineering (MSCE, PhD); environmental and water resources engineering (MSCE); geotechnical engineering (MSCE); structural engineering and mechanics (MSCE); transportation engineering (MSCE). *Program availability:* Part-time. Terminal master's awarded for partial completion of doctoral program. *Degree requirements:* For master's, thesis or alternative; for doctorate, comprehensive exam, thesis/dissertation. *Entrance requirements:* For master's and doctorate, GRE General Test. Additional exam requirements/recommendations for international students: required—TOEFL (minimum score 550 paper-based; 80 iBT), IELTS (minimum score 6.5). Electronic applications accepted.

University of Massachusetts Lowell, Francis College of Engineering, Department of Civil and Environmental Engineering and College of Sciences, Program in Environmental Studies, Lowell, MA 01854. Offers MS, PhD. *Program availability:* Part-time. *Degree requirements:* For master's, thesis optional. *Entrance requirements:* For master's, GRE General Test.

University of Memphis, Graduate School, Herff College of Engineering, Department of Civil Engineering, Memphis, TN 38152. Offers civil engineering (PhD); engineering seismology (MS); environmental engineering (MS); freight transportation (Graduate Certificate); geotechnical engineering (MS); structural engineering (MS); transportation engineering (MS); water resources engineering (MS). *Students:* 15 full-time (4 women), 8 part-time (1 woman); includes 1 minority (Black or African American, non-Hispanic/Latino), 12 international. Average age 27. 26 applicants, 38% accepted, 5 enrolled. In 2019, 11 master's awarded. Terminal master's awarded for partial completion of doctoral program. *Degree requirements:* For master's, comprehensive exam, thesis optional; for doctorate, comprehensive exam, thesis/dissertation. *Entrance requirements:* For master's, GRE General Test, minimum undergraduate GPA of 2.5; bachelor's degree in engineering or a related science or mathematics program; three letters of reference; for doctorate, GRE General Test, bachelor's degree in engineering or engineering science; three letters of reference; for Graduate Certificate, minimum undergraduate GPA of 2.75; bachelor's degree in engineering or engineering science. Additional exam requirements/recommendations for international students: required—TOEFL (minimum score 550 paper-based; 79 iBT). *Application deadline:* For fall admission, 8/1 for domestic students; for spring admission, 12/1 for domestic students. Application fee: $35 ($60 for international students). Electronic applications accepted. *Expenses: Tuition, area resident:* Full-time $9216; part-time $512 per credit hour. Tuition, state resident: full-time $9216; part-time $512 per credit hour. Tuition, nonresident: full-time $12,672; part-time $704 per credit hour. *International tuition:* $16,128 full-time. *Required fees:* $1530; $85 per credit hour. Tuition and fees vary according to program. *Financial support:* Fellowships with full tuition reimbursements, research assistantships with full tuition reimbursements, career-related internships or

fieldwork, Federal Work-Study, scholarships/grants, and unspecified assistantships available. Financial award application deadline: 2/1; financial award applicants required to submit FAFSA. *Unit head:* Dr. Shahram Pezeshk, Chair, 901-678-2746, Fax: 901-678-3026, E-mail: spezeshk@memphis.edu. *Application contact:* Dr. Roger Meier, Graduate Coordinator, 901-678-3284, E-mail: rwmeier@memphis.edu.
Website: https://www.memphis.edu/ce

University of Michigan, College of Engineering, Department of Civil and Environmental Engineering, Ann Arbor, MI 48109. Offers civil engineering (MSE, PhD, CE); construction engineering and management (M Eng, MSE); environmental engineering (MSE, PhD); structural engineering (M Eng); MBA/MSE. *Program availability:* Part-time. Terminal master's awarded for partial completion of doctoral program. *Degree requirements:* For master's, thesis optional; for doctorate, comprehensive exam, thesis/dissertation, oral defense of dissertation, preliminary and written exams. *Entrance requirements:* For master's and doctorate, GRE General Test. Additional exam requirements/recommendations for international students: required—TOEFL. Electronic applications accepted.

University of Mississippi, Graduate School, School of Engineering, University, MS 38677. Offers aeroacoustics (MS, PhD); chemical engineering (MS, PhD); civil engineering (MS, PhD); computational hydroscience (MS, PhD); computer science (MS, PhD); electrical engineering (MS, PhD); electromagnetics (MS, PhD); environmental engineering (MS, PhD); geology and geological engineering (MS, PhD); hydrology (MS); material science (MS); mechanical engineering (MS, PhD); telecommunications (MS). *Students:* 104 full-time (23 women), 19 part-time (5 women); includes 10 minority (3 Black or African American, non-Hispanic/Latino; 6 Asian, non-Hispanic/Latino; 1 Hispanic/Latino), 72 international. Average age 30. In 2019, 36 master's, 17 doctorates awarded. *Expenses:* Tuition, state resident: full-time $8718; part-time $484.25 per credit hour. Tuition, nonresident: full-time $24,990; part-time $1388.25 per credit hour. *Required fees:* $100; $4.16 per credit hour. *Unit head:* Dr. David Puleo, Dean, 662-915-5780, Fax: 662-915-5387, E-mail: engineer@olemiss.edu. *Application contact:* Temeka Smith, Graduate Activities Specialist for Admissions, 662-915-7474, Fax: 662-915-7577, E-mail: gschool@olemiss.edu.

University of Missouri, Office of Research and Graduate Studies, College of Engineering, Department of Civil and Environmental Engineering, Columbia, MO 65211. Offers civil engineering (MS, PhD). *Degree requirements:* For master's, report or thesis. *Entrance requirements:* For master's and doctorate, GRE General Test. Additional exam requirements/recommendations for international students: required—TOEFL (minimum score 550 paper-based; 80 iBT).

University of Nebraska–Lincoln, Graduate College, College of Engineering, Interdepartmental Area of Environmental Engineering, Lincoln, NE 68588. Offers MS, PhD. *Degree requirements:* For master's, thesis optional; for doctorate, comprehensive exam, thesis/dissertation. *Entrance requirements:* For master's and doctorate, GRE General Test. Additional exam requirements/recommendations for international students: required—TOEFL (minimum score 550 paper-based). Electronic applications accepted.

University of New Brunswick Fredericton, School of Graduate Studies, Faculty of Engineering, Department of Civil Engineering, Fredericton, NB E3B 5A3, Canada. Offers construction engineering and management (M Eng, M Sc E, PhD); environmental engineering (M Eng, M Sc E, PhD); environmental studies (M Eng); geotechnical engineering (M Eng, M Sc E, PhD); groundwater/hydrology (M Eng, M Sc E, PhD); materials (M Eng, M Sc E, PhD); pavements (M Eng, M Sc E, PhD); structures (M Eng, M Sc E, PhD); transportation (M Eng, M Sc E, PhD). *Program availability:* Part-time. *Faculty:* 17 full-time (2 women). *Students:* 31 full-time (6 women), 10 part-time (0 women), 12 international. Average age 27. In 2019, 11 master's awarded. *Degree requirements:* For master's, thesis; for doctorate, comprehensive exam, thesis/dissertation, qualifying exam; 27 credit hours of courses. *Entrance requirements:* For master's, minimum GPA of 3.0; B Sc E in civil engineering or related engineering degree; for doctorate, minimum GPA of 3.0; graduate degree in engineering or applied science. Additional exam requirements/recommendations for international students: required—IELTS (minimum score 7.5), TWE (minimum score 4), Michigan English Language Assessment Battery (minimum score 85) or CanTest (minimum score 4.5); recommended—TOEFL (minimum score 580 paper-based). *Application deadline:* For fall admission, 5/1 for domestic students; for winter admission, 11/1 for domestic students. Applications are processed on a rolling basis. Application fee: $50 Canadian dollars. Electronic applications accepted. *Expenses: Tuition, area resident:* Full-time $6975 Canadian dollars; part-time $3423 Canadian dollars per year. Tuition, state resident: full-time $6975 Canadian dollars; part-time $3423 Canadian dollars per year. Tuition, Canadian resident: full-time $6975 Canadian dollars; part-time $3423 Canadian dollars per year. *International tuition:* $12,435 Canadian dollars full-time. *Required fees:* $92.25 Canadian dollars per term. Full-time tuition and fees vary according to degree level, campus/location, program, reciprocity agreements and student level. *Financial support:* Fellowships, research assistantships, teaching assistantships, career-related internships or fieldwork, and scholarships/grants available. Financial award application deadline: 1/15. *Unit head:* Dr. Jeff Rankin, Chair, 506-453-4618, Fax: 506-453-3568, E-mail: ktm@unb.ca. *Application contact:* MaryBeth Nicholson, Graduate Secretary, 506-452-6127, Fax: 506-453-3568, E-mail: mbnich@unb.ca.
Website: http://go.unb.ca/gradprograms

University of New Hampshire, Graduate School, College of Engineering and Physical Sciences, Department of Civil and Environmental Engineering, Durham, NH 03824. Offers M Engr, MS, PhD. *Program availability:* Part-time. *Students:* 30 full-time (16 women), 16 part-time (6 women); includes 2 minority (both Hispanic/Latino), 14 international. Average age 25. 59 applicants, 69% accepted, 21 enrolled. In 2019, 3 master's, 1 doctorate awarded. *Entrance requirements:* For master's and doctorate, GRE. Additional exam requirements/recommendations for international students: required—TOEFL (minimum score 550 paper-based; 80 iBT), IELTS (minimum score 6.5), PTE. *Application deadline:* For fall admission, 7/1 for domestic students, 4/1 for international students; for spring admission, 12/1 for domestic students. Application fee: $65. Electronic applications accepted. *Financial support:* In 2019–20, 30 students received support, including 2 fellowships, 7 research assistantships, 21 teaching assistantships; Federal Work-Study, scholarships/grants, and tuition waivers (full and partial) also available. Support available to part-time students. Financial award application deadline: 2/15. *Unit head:* Dr. Erin Bell, Chair, 603-862-3850. *Application contact:* Kristen Parenteau, Administrative Assistant, 603-862-1440, E-mail: cee.graduate@unh.edu.
Website: http://www.ceps.unh.edu/cee

University of New Haven, Graduate School, Tagliatela College of Engineering, Program in Environmental Engineering, West Haven, CT 06516. Offers environmental engineering (MS); industrial and hazardous waste (MS); water and wastewater treatment (MS); water resources (MS). *Program availability:* Part-time, evening/weekend, 100% online. *Students:* 15 full-time (7 women), 32 part-time (13 women); includes 7 minority (2 Black or African American, non-Hispanic/Latino; 2 Asian, non-Hispanic/Latino; 3 Hispanic/Latino), 17 international. Average age 30. 67 applicants, 97% accepted, 11 enrolled. In 2019, 15 master's awarded. *Degree requirements:* For master's, thesis or alternative, research project. *Entrance requirements:* For master's, bachelor's degree in engineering. Additional exam requirements/recommendations for international students: required—TOEFL (minimum score 75 iBT), IELTS, PTE (minimum score 50). *Application deadline:* Applications are processed on a rolling basis. Application fee: $50. Electronic applications accepted. Application fee is waived when completed online. *Financial support:* Research assistantships with partial tuition reimbursements, teaching assistantships with partial tuition reimbursements, career-related internships or fieldwork, Federal Work-Study, scholarships/grants, and unspecified assistantships available. Support available to part-time students. Financial award application deadline: 5/1; financial award applicants required to submit FAFSA. *Unit head:* Dr. Emese Hadnagy, Associate Professor, 203-932-1232, E-mail: EHadnagy@newhaven.edu. *Application contact:* Selina O'Toole, Senior Associate Director of Graduate Admissions, 203-932-7337, E-mail: sotoole@newhaven.edu.
Website: https://www.newhaven.edu/engineering/graduate-programs/environmental-engineering/

The University of North Carolina at Chapel Hill, Graduate School, Gillings School of Global Public Health, Department of Environmental Sciences and Engineering, Chapel Hill, NC 27599. Offers environmental engineering (MPH, MS, MSEE, MSPH); environmental health sciences (MPH, MS, MSPH, PhD); MPH/MCRP; MS/MCRP; MSPH/MCRP. *Faculty:* 26 full-time (10 women), 38 part-time/adjunct (10 women). *Students:* 87 full-time (53 women); includes 10 minority (2 Black or African American, non-Hispanic/Latino; 3 Asian, non-Hispanic/Latino; 1 Hispanic/Latino; 4 Two or more races, non-Hispanic/Latino), 19 international. Average age 28. 101 applicants, 47% accepted, 19 enrolled. In 2019, 20 master's, 16 doctorates awarded. Terminal master's awarded for partial completion of doctoral program. *Degree requirements:* For master's, comprehensive exam, thesis (for some programs), research paper; for doctorate, comprehensive exam, thesis/dissertation. *Entrance requirements:* For master's and doctorate, GRE General Test, 3 letters of recommendation (academic and/or professional; at least one academic). Additional exam requirements/recommendations for international students: required—TOEFL (minimum score 90 iBT), IELTS (minimum score 7). *Application deadline:* For fall admission, 4/9 for domestic and international students. Application fee: $90. Electronic applications accepted. *Financial support:* Fellowships with tuition reimbursements, research assistantships with tuition reimbursements, teaching assistantships with tuition reimbursements, career-related internships or fieldwork, Federal Work-Study, scholarships/grants, traineeships, health care benefits, and unspecified assistantships available. Support available to part-time students. Financial award application deadline: 12/10; financial award applicants required to submit FAFSA. *Unit head:* Dr. Barbara J. Turpin, Professor and Chair, 919-966-1024, Fax: 919-966-7911, E-mail: esechair@unc.edu. *Application contact:* Adia Ware, Academic Coordinator, 919-966-3844, Fax: 919-966-7911, E-mail: aware@unc.edu.
Website: https://sph.unc.edu/envr/environmental-sciences-and-engineering-home/

The University of North Carolina at Charlotte, William States Lee College of Engineering, Department of Civil and Environmental Engineering, Charlotte, NC 28223-0001. Offers civil engineering (MSCE), including environmental & water resources, geo-environmental, geo technical, structural, and transportation; infrastructure and environmental systems (PhD), including infrastructure and environmental systems design. *Program availability:* Part-time, evening/weekend. *Faculty:* 24 full-time (6 women), 5 part-time/adjunct (2 women). *Students:* 63 full-time (23 women), 45 part-time (11 women); includes 13 minority (1 Black or African American, non-Hispanic/Latino; 7 Asian, non-Hispanic/Latino; 4 Hispanic/Latino; 1 Two or more races, non-Hispanic/Latino), 53 international. Average age 30. 82 applicants, 67% accepted, 29 enrolled. In 2019, 28 master's, 7 doctorates awarded. *Degree requirements:* For master's, thesis optional; for doctorate, thesis/dissertation. *Entrance requirements:* For master's, GRE, undergraduate degree in civil and environmental engineering or a closely-related field; minimum undergraduate GPA of 3.0; for doctorate, GRE General Test, equivalent to U.S. baccalaureate or master's degree from regionally-accredited college or university in engineering, earth science and geology, chemical and biological sciences or a related field with minimum undergraduate GPA of 3.2, graduate 3.5. Additional exam requirements/recommendations for international students: required—TOEFL (minimum score 557 paper-based; 83 iBT), IELTS (minimum score 6.5), TOEFL (minimum score 557 paper-based, 83 iBT) or IELTS (6.5). *Application deadline:* Applications are processed on a rolling basis. Application fee: $75. Electronic applications accepted. *Expenses:* Contact institution. *Financial support:* In 2019–20, 24 students received support, including 2 fellowships (averaging $44,382 per year), 22 research assistantships (averaging $10,081 per year); teaching assistantships, career-related internships or fieldwork, institutionally sponsored loans, scholarships/grants, and unspecified assistantships also available. Support available to part-time students. Financial award application deadline: 3/1; financial award applicants required to submit FAFSA. *Unit head:* Dr. John L. Daniels, Professor, Department Chair, 704-687-1219, E-mail: jodaniel@uncc.edu. *Application contact:* Kathy B. Giddings, Director of Graduate Admissions, 704-687-5503, Fax: 704-687-1668, E-mail: gradadm@uncc.edu.
Website: http://cee.uncc.edu/

University of North Dakota, Graduate School, School of Engineering and Mines, Department of Environmental Engineering, Grand Forks, ND 58202. Offers M Engr, MS, PhD. *Degree requirements:* For master's, thesis. *Entrance requirements:* For master's, GRE General Test, minimum GPA of 3.0. Additional exam requirements/recommendations for international students: required—TOEFL (minimum score 550 paper-based; 79 iBT), IELTS (minimum score 6.5). Electronic applications accepted.

University of Notre Dame, The Graduate School, College of Engineering, Department of Civil and Environmental Engineering and Earth Sciences, Notre Dame, IN 46556. Offers bioengineering (MS Bio E); civil engineering (MSCE); civil engineering and geological sciences (PhD); earth sciences (MS); environmental engineering (MS Env E). Terminal master's awarded for partial completion of doctoral program. *Degree requirements:* For master's, comprehensive exam; for doctorate, thesis/dissertation, candidacy exam. *Entrance requirements:* For master's and doctorate, GRE General Test. Additional exam requirements/recommendations for international students: required—TOEFL (minimum score 600 paper-based; 80 iBT). Electronic applications accepted.

University of Oklahoma, Gallogly College of Engineering, School of Civil Engineering and Environmental Science, Norman, OK 73019-0390. Offers civil engineering (MS, PhD), including civil engineering; environmental engineering (MS, PhD); environmental science (M Env Sc, PhD), including environmental science. *Program availability:* Part-time. Terminal master's awarded for partial completion of doctoral program. *Degree requirements:* For master's, thesis; for doctorate, comprehensive exam, thesis/dissertation, general exam. *Entrance requirements:* For master's and doctorate, GRE. Additional exam requirements/recommendations for international students: required—TOEFL (minimum score 79 iBT) or IELTS (minimum score 6.5). Electronic applications accepted. *Expenses:* Tuition, state resident: full-time $6583.20; part-time $274.30 per credit hour. Tuition, nonresident: full-time $21,242; part-time $885.10 per credit hour. *International tuition:* $21,242.40 full-time. *Required fees:* $1994.20; $72.55 per credit hour. $126.50 per semester. Tuition and fees vary according to course load and degree level.

Environmental Engineering

University of Pittsburgh, Swanson School of Engineering, Department of Civil and Environmental Engineering, Pittsburgh, PA 15260. Offers MSCEE, PhD. *Program availability:* Part-time, 100% online. Terminal master's awarded for partial completion of doctoral program. *Degree requirements:* For doctorate, comprehensive exam, thesis/dissertation, final oral exams. *Entrance requirements:* For master's and doctorate, minimum GPA of 3.0. Additional exam requirements/recommendations for international students: required—TOEFL (minimum score 550 paper-based; 80 iBT). Electronic applications accepted. *Expenses:* Contact institution.

University of Puerto Rico at Mayagüez, Graduate Studies, College of Engineering, Department of Civil Engineering and Surveying, Mayagüez, PR 00681-9000. Offers civil engineering (ME, MS, PhD), including construction engineering and management (ME, MS), environmental engineering, geotechnical engineering (ME, MS), structural engineering, transportation engineering. *Program availability:* Part-time. Terminal master's awarded for partial completion of doctoral program. *Degree requirements:* For master's, one foreign language, thesis; for doctorate, one foreign language, comprehensive exam, thesis/dissertation, qualifying exams. *Entrance requirements:* For master's, proficiency in English and Spanish; BS in civil engineering or its equivalent; for doctorate, proficiency in English and Spanish. Electronic applications accepted.

University of Regina, Faculty of Graduate Studies and Research, Faculty of Engineering and Applied Science, Program in Environmental Systems Engineering, Regina, SK S4S 0A2, Canada. Offers environmental systems (M Eng, MA Sc, PhD). *Program availability:* Part-time. *Faculty:* 9 full-time (2 women), 2 part-time/adjunct (0 women). *Students:* 64 full-time (31 women), 8 part-time (3 women). Average age 30. 94 applicants, 17% accepted. In 2019, 12 master's, 1 doctorate awarded. *Degree requirements:* For master's, thesis, project, report, co-op; for doctorate, comprehensive exam, thesis/dissertation. *Entrance requirements:* For master's, 4 years bachelor degree, at least 70 per cent from a four-year baccalaureate degree (or equivalent). Additional exam requirements/recommendations for international students: required—TOEFL (minimum score 580 paper-based; 80 iBT), IELTS (minimum score 6.5), PTE (minimum score 59), other options are CAEL, MELAB, Cantest and U of R ESL. *Application deadline:* For fall admission, 1/31 for domestic and international students; for winter admission, 7/31 for domestic and international students. Application fee: $100. Electronic applications accepted. *Expenses:* 11,036.50 -This amount is based on three semesters tuition, registered in 6 credit hours per semester. Plus one year student fees and books. There is additional 438.75 if student is in Co-op route. *Financial support:* Fellowships, research assistantships, teaching assistantships, career-related internships or fieldwork, Federal Work-Study, scholarships/grants, unspecified assistantships, and travel award and Graduate Scholarship base funds available. Support available to part-time students. Financial award application deadline: 9/30. *Unit head:* Dr. Yee-Chung Jin, Program Chair, 306-585-4567, Fax: 306-585-4855, E-mail: Yee-chung.Jin@uregina.ca. *Application contact:* Dr. Kelvin Ng, Graduate Coordinator, 306-585-8487, Fax: 306-585-4855, E-mail: kelvin.ng@uregina.ca. Website: http://www.uregina.ca/engineering/

University of Rhode Island, Graduate School, College of Engineering, Department of Civil and Environmental Engineering, Kingston, RI 02881. Offers civil and environmental engineering (MS, PhD), including environmental engineering, geotechnical engineering, structural engineering, transportation engineering. *Program availability:* Part-time. *Faculty:* 12 full-time (3 women). *Students:* 23 full-time (7 women), 11 part-time (3 women); includes 3 minority (2 Asian, non-Hispanic/Latino; 1 Hispanic/Latino), 16 international. 26 applicants, 65% accepted, 10 enrolled. In 2019, 9 master's, 3 doctorates awarded. *Entrance requirements:* Additional exam requirements/recommendations for international students: required—TOEFL. *Application deadline:* For fall admission, 7/15 for domestic students, 2/1 for international students; for spring admission, 11/15 for domestic students, 7/15 for international students. Application fee: $65. Electronic applications accepted. *Expenses: Tuition, area resident:* Full-time $13,734; part-time $763 per credit. Tuition, state resident: full-time $13,734; part-time $763 per credit. Tuition, nonresident: full-time $26,512; part-time $1473 per credit. *International tuition:* $26,512 full-time. *Required fees:* $1780; $52 per credit. $35 per term. One-time fee: $165. *Financial support:* In 2019–20, 8 research assistantships with tuition reimbursements (averaging $11,061 per year), 5 teaching assistantships with tuition reimbursements (averaging $14,558 per year) were awarded. Financial award application deadline: 2/1; financial award applicants required to submit FAFSA. *Unit head:* Dr. Leon Thiem, Chair, 401-874-2693, Fax: 401-874-2786, E-mail: leonthiem@uri.edu. *Application contact:* Dr. Ali Akanda, Graduate Program Director, 401-874-7050, E-mail: akanda@uri.edu. Website: http://www.uri.edu/cve/

University of South Alabama, College of Engineering, Department of Civil, Coastal, and Environmental Engineering, Mobile, AL 36688-0002. Offers MSCE. *Faculty:* 3 full-time (0 women). *Students:* 12 full-time (6 women), 1 part-time (0 women), 5 international. Average age 25. 18 applicants, 72% accepted, 5 enrolled. In 2019, 6 master's awarded. *Degree requirements:* For master's, comprehensive exam, thesis optional. *Entrance requirements:* For master's, GRE. Additional exam requirements/recommendations for international students: required—TOEFL (minimum score 550 paper-based; 79 iBT), IELTS (minimum score 6.5). *Application deadline:* For fall admission, 7/1 priority date for domestic students, 6/15 priority date for international students; for spring admission, 12/1 priority date for domestic students, 11/1 priority date for international students; for summer admission, 5/1 priority date for domestic students, 4/1 priority date for international students. Applications are processed on a rolling basis. Application fee: $35. Electronic applications accepted. *Expenses:* Contact institution. *Financial support:* Fellowships, research assistantships, teaching assistantships, career-related internships or fieldwork, Federal Work-Study, institutionally sponsored loans, scholarships/grants, and unspecified assistantships available. Support available to part-time students. Financial award application deadline: 3/31; financial award applicants required to submit FAFSA. *Unit head:* Dr. Kevin White, Chair, Professor, Department of Civil, Coastal, and Environmental Engineering, College of Engineering, 251-460-6174, Fax: 251-461-1400, E-mail: kwhite@southalabama.edu. *Application contact:* Brenda Poole, Academic Records Specialist, 251-460-6140, Fax: 251-460-6343, E-mail: engineering@alabama.edu. Website: https://www.southalabama.edu/colleges/engineering/ce/

University of Southern California, Graduate School, Viterbi School of Engineering, Sonny Astani Department of Civil and Environmental Engineering, Los Angeles, CA 90089. Offers applied mechanics (MS); civil engineering (MS, PhD); computer-aided engineering (ME, Graduate Certificate); construction management (MCM); engineering technology commercialization (Graduate Certificate); environmental engineering (MS, PhD); environmental quality management (ME); structural design (ME); sustainable cities (Graduate Certificate); transportation systems (MS, Graduate Certificate); water and waste management (MS). *Program availability:* Part-time, evening/weekend. Terminal master's awarded for partial completion of doctoral program. *Degree requirements:* For master's, thesis optional; for doctorate, thesis/dissertation. *Entrance requirements:* For master's and doctorate, GRE General Test. Additional exam requirements/recommendations for international students: recommended—TOEFL. Electronic applications accepted.

University of South Florida, College of Engineering, Department of Civil and Environmental Engineering, Tampa, FL 33620-9951. Offers civil engineering (MCE, MSCE), including geotechnical engineering, materials science and engineering, structures engineering, transportation engineering, water resources; environmental engineering (MEVE, MSEV, PhD), including engineering for international development (MSEV). *Program availability:* Part-time. *Faculty:* 19 full-time (5 women). *Students:* 144 full-time (46 women), 76 part-time (22 women); includes 35 minority (8 Black or African American, non-Hispanic/Latino; 5 Asian, non-Hispanic/Latino; 18 Hispanic/Latino; 4 Two or more races, non-Hispanic/Latino), 123 international. Average age 28. 220 applicants, 65% accepted, 59 enrolled. In 2019, 82 master's, 15 doctorates awarded. Terminal master's awarded for partial completion of doctoral program. *Degree requirements:* For master's, comprehensive exam, thesis (for some programs); for doctorate, comprehensive exam, thesis/dissertation. *Entrance requirements:* For master's, GRE required, bachelor's degree in appropriate field, minimum GPA of 3.0 in major, letters of reference, statement of purpose, resume, intake form; for doctorate, GRE with V (45th percentile), Q (75th percentile), and AW (55th percentile), letters of recommendation, statement of purpose, resume, intake form. Additional exam requirements/recommendations for international students: required—TOEFL, TOEFL (minimum score 550 paper-based; 79 iBT) or IELTS (minimum score 6.5). *Application deadline:* For fall admission, 2/15 for domestic students, 2/15 priority date for international students; for spring admission, 10/15 for domestic students, 9/15 priority date for international students. Application fee: $30. Electronic applications accepted. *Financial support:* In 2019–20, 45 students received support, including 44 research assistantships (averaging $14,123 per year), 21 teaching assistantships with tuition reimbursements available (averaging $15,329 per year). *Unit head:* Dr. Manjriker Gunaratne, Professor and Department Chair, 813-974-5818, Fax: 813-974-2957, E-mail: gunaratn@usf.edu. *Application contact:* Dr. Sarina J. Ergas, Professor and Graduate Program Coordinator, 813-974-1119, Fax: 813-974-2957, E-mail: sergas@usf.edu. Website: http://www.usf.edu/engineering/cee/

The University of Tennessee, Graduate School, Tickle College of Engineering, Department of Civil and Environmental Engineering, Program in Environmental Engineering, Knoxville, TN 37996-2010. Offers MS, MS/MBA. *Program availability:* Part-time, online learning. *Faculty:* 11 full-time (2 women). *Students:* 20 full-time (5 women), 6 part-time (2 women); includes 2 minority (1 Hispanic/Latino; 1 Two or more races, non-Hispanic/Latino), 2 international. Average age 27. 18 applicants, 78% accepted, 10 enrolled. In 2019, 4 master's awarded. *Degree requirements:* For master's, thesis or alternative. *Entrance requirements:* For master's, GRE General Test (for MS students pursuing research thesis), minimum GPA of 2.7 (for U.S. degree holders), 3.0 (for international degree holders); 3 references; statement of purpose; resume. Additional exam requirements/recommendations for international students: required—TOEFL (minimum score 550 paper-based; 80 iBT), IELTS (minimum score 6.5). *Application deadline:* For fall admission, 2/1 priority date for domestic and international students; for spring admission, 6/15 for domestic and international students; for summer admission, 10/15 for domestic and international students. Applications are processed on a rolling basis. Application fee: $60. Electronic applications accepted. *Financial support:* In 2019–20, 15 students received support, including 10 research assistantships with full tuition reimbursements available (averaging $21,036 per year), 5 teaching assistantships with full tuition reimbursements available (averaging $19,400 per year); career-related internships or fieldwork, Federal Work-Study, institutionally sponsored loans, health care benefits, and unspecified assistantships also available. Financial award application deadline: 2/1; financial award applicants required to submit FAFSA. *Unit head:* Dr. Chris Cox, Head, 865-974-2503, Fax: 865-974-2669, E-mail: gdreed@utk.edu. *Application contact:* Dr. Khalid Alshibli, Associate Head, 865-974-7728, Fax: 865-974-2669, E-mail: alshibli@utk.edu. Website: http://www.engr.utk.edu/civil/

The University of Texas at Austin, Graduate School, Cockrell School of Engineering, Department of Civil, Architectural and Environmental Engineering, Program in Environmental and Water Resources Engineering, Austin, TX 78712-1111. Offers MS, PhD. *Program availability:* Part-time. *Degree requirements:* For master's, thesis or alternative. *Entrance requirements:* For master's, GRE General Test. Additional exam requirements/recommendations for international students: required—TOEFL. Electronic applications accepted.

The University of Texas at El Paso, Graduate School, College of Engineering, Department of Civil Engineering, El Paso, TX 79968-0001. Offers civil engineering (MS, PhD); construction management (MS, Certificate); environmental engineering (MEENE, MSENE). *Program availability:* Part-time, evening/weekend. *Degree requirements:* For master's, comprehensive exam, thesis optional; for doctorate, comprehensive exam, thesis/dissertation. *Entrance requirements:* For master's, GRE, minimum GPA of 3.0; for doctorate, GRE. Additional exam requirements/recommendations for international students: required—TOEFL. Electronic applications accepted.

The University of Texas at El Paso, Graduate School, College of Engineering, Department of Mechanical Engineering, El Paso, TX 79968-0001. Offers environmental science and engineering (PhD); mechanical engineering (MS). *Program availability:* Part-time. *Degree requirements:* For master's, thesis optional; for doctorate, thesis/dissertation. *Entrance requirements:* For master's, GRE, minimum GPA of 3.0, letter of reference; for doctorate, GRE, minimum GPA of 3.5, letters of reference, BS or equivalent. Additional exam requirements/recommendations for international students: required—TOEFL; recommended—IELTS. Electronic applications accepted.

The University of Texas at San Antonio, College of Engineering, Department of Civil and Environmental Engineering, San Antonio, TX 78249-0617. Offers civil engineering (MCE, MSCE); environmental science and engineering (PhD). *Program availability:* Part-time. *Degree requirements:* For master's, comprehensive exam, thesis (for some programs); for doctorate, comprehensive exam, thesis/dissertation, written qualifying exam, dissertation proposal. *Entrance requirements:* For master's, GRE General Test, BS in civil engineering or related field from accredited institution, statement of research/specialization interest, recommendation by the Civil Engineering Master's Program Admissions Committee; for doctorate, GRE, BS and MS from accredited institution, minimum GPA of 3.0 in upper-division and graduate courses, three letters of recommendation, letter of research interest, resume/curriculum vitae. Additional exam requirements/recommendations for international students: required—TOEFL (minimum score 550 paper-based; 79 iBT), IELTS (minimum score 6.5). Electronic applications accepted. *Expenses:* Contact institution.

The University of Texas at Tyler, College of Engineering, Department of Civil Engineering, Tyler, TX 75799-0001. Offers environmental engineering (MS); industrial safety (MS); structural engineering (MS); transportation engineering (MS); water resources engineering (MS). *Program availability:* Part-time, evening/weekend. *Faculty:* 5 full-time. *Students:* 7 full-time (0 women), 8 part-time (6 women); includes 4 minority (1 Asian, non-Hispanic/Latino; 3 Hispanic/Latino), 4 international. Average age 28. 14 applicants, 79% accepted, 4 enrolled. In 2019, 6 master's awarded. *Entrance requirements:* For master's, GRE General Test, bachelor's degree in engineering, associated science degree. Additional exam requirements/recommendations for international students: required—TOEFL. *Application deadline:* For fall admission, 8/17 priority date for domestic students, 7/1 priority date for international students; for spring admission, 12/21 priority date for domestic students, 11/1 priority date for international students. Application fee: $25 ($50 for international students). *Financial support:* Application deadline: 7/1. *Unit head:* Dr. Torey Nalbone, Chair, 903-565-5520, E-mail: tnalbone@uttyler.edu. *Application contact:* Dr. Torey Nalbone, Chair, 903-565-5520, E-mail: tnalbone@uttyler.edu. Website: https://www.uttyler.edu/ce/

University of Utah, Graduate School, College of Engineering, Department of Civil and Environmental Engineering, Salt Lake City, UT 84112. Offers civil and environmental engineering (MS, PhD); nuclear engineering (MS, PhD). *Faculty:* 22 full-time (5 women), 2 part-time/adjunct (1 woman). *Students:* 75 full-time (18 women), 38 part-time (3 women); includes 18 minority (1 Black or African American, non-Hispanic/Latino; 8 Asian, non-Hispanic/Latino; 6 Hispanic/Latino; 3 Two or more races, non-Hispanic/Latino), 44 international. Average age 29. 104 applicants, 36% accepted, 21 enrolled. In 2019, 26 master's, 12 doctorates awarded. Terminal master's awarded for partial completion of doctoral program. *Degree requirements:* For master's, comprehensive exam (for some programs), thesis (for some programs); for doctorate, comprehensive exam, thesis/dissertation. *Entrance requirements:* For master's and doctorate, GRE, Online application completed through ApplyYourself portal, GPA of 3.0+ on 4.0 scale, CV, personal statement, unofficial transcripts, three letters of reference, proof of English proficiency. Additional exam requirements/recommendations for international students: required—TOEFL (minimum score 80 iBT), IELTS (minimum score 6.5), Either IELTS or TOEFL required, not both. *Application deadline:* For fall admission, 1/1 priority date for domestic and international students; for spring admission, 10/1 for domestic and international students. Applications are processed on a rolling basis. Application fee: $0 ($30 for international students). Electronic applications accepted. *Expenses:* $58.29 per credit hour. *Financial support:* In 2019–20, 1 student received support, including 8 fellowships with full tuition reimbursements available (averaging $28,375 per year), 48 research assistantships with full tuition reimbursements available (averaging $24,000 per year), 15 teaching assistantships with full tuition reimbursements available (averaging $24,000 per year); health care benefits and unspecified assistantships also available. Financial award application deadline: 1/1. *Unit head:* Dr. Michael E. Barber, Chair, 801-581-6931, Fax: 801-585-5477, E-mail: barber@civil.utah.edu. *Application contact:* Courtney Phillips, Academic Advisor, 801-581-6678, Fax: 801-585-5477, E-mail: cveen-graduate@utah.edu. Website: http://www.civil.utah.edu

University of Vermont, Graduate College, College of Engineering and Mathematical Sciences, Department of Civil and Environmental Engineering, Burlington, VT 05405. Offers MS, PhD. *Degree requirements:* For master's, thesis or alternative; for doctorate, thesis/dissertation. *Entrance requirements:* For master's and doctorate, GRE General Test. Additional exam requirements/recommendations for international students: required—TOEFL (minimum score 550 paper-based, 90 iBT) or IELTS (6.5). Electronic applications accepted.

University of Washington, Graduate School, College of Engineering, Department of Civil and Environmental Engineering, Seattle, WA 98195-2700. Offers construction engineering (MSCE, PhD); environmental engineering (MSCE, PhD); geotechnical engineering (MSCE, PhD); hydrology and hydrodynamics (MSCE, PhD); structural engineering and mechanics (MSCE, PhD); transportation engineering (MSCE, PhD). *Program availability:* Part-time, 100% online. *Students:* 248 full-time (97 women), 174 part-time (63 women); includes 90 minority (8 Black or African American, non-Hispanic/Latino; 2 American Indian or Alaska Native, non-Hispanic/Latino; 46 Asian, non-Hispanic/Latino; 18 Hispanic/Latino; 16 Two or more races, non-Hispanic/Latino), 118 international. Average age 28. 756 applicants, 59% accepted, 164 enrolled. In 2019, 133 master's, 21 doctorates awarded. Terminal master's awarded for partial completion of doctoral program. *Degree requirements:* For master's, thesis optional; for doctorate, comprehensive exam, thesis/dissertation, qualifying, general and final exams; completion of degree within 10 years. *Entrance requirements:* For master's, GRE General Test, minimum GPA of 3.0, statement of purpose, letters of recommendation, transcripts; for doctorate, GRE General Test, minimum GPA of 3.5, statement of purpose, letters of recommendation, transcripts, resume. Additional exam requirements/recommendations for international students: required—TOEFL (minimum score 580 paper-based; 92 iBT). *Application deadline:* For fall admission, 12/15 for domestic and international students. Applications are processed on a rolling basis. Application fee: $85. Electronic applications accepted. *Expenses:* Contact institution. *Financial support:* In 2019–20, 21 fellowships with full tuition reimbursements (averaging $30,600 per year), 76 research assistantships with full tuition reimbursements (averaging $30,600 per year), 27 teaching assistantships with full tuition reimbursements (averaging $30,120 per year) were awarded; Federal Work-Study, institutionally sponsored loans, scholarships/grants, health care benefits, tuition waivers, and unspecified assistantships also available. Support available to part-time students. Financial award application deadline: 12/15. *Unit head:* Dr. Laura Lowes, Professor/Chair, 206-685-2563, Fax: 206-543-1543, E-mail: lowes@uw.edu. *Application contact:* Bryan Crockett, Director of Academic Services, 206-616-1891, Fax: 206-543-1543, E-mail: ceginfo@u.washington.edu. Website: http://www.ce.washington.edu/

University of Waterloo, Graduate Studies and Postdoctoral Affairs, Faculty of Engineering, Department of Civil and Environmental Engineering, Waterloo, ON N2L 3G1, Canada. Offers M Eng, MA Sc, PhD. *Program availability:* Part-time. *Degree requirements:* For master's, research paper or thesis; for doctorate, comprehensive exam, thesis/dissertation. *Entrance requirements:* For master's, honors degree, minimum B average; for doctorate, master's degree, minimum A- average. Additional exam requirements/recommendations for international students: required—TOEFL, IELTS, PTE. Electronic applications accepted.

The University of Western Ontario, School of Graduate and Postdoctoral Studies, Physical Sciences Division, Faculty of Engineering, London, ON N6A 3K7, Canada. Offers chemical and biochemical engineering (ME Sc, PhD); civil and environmental engineering (M Eng, ME Sc, PhD); electrical and computer engineering (M Eng, ME Sc, PhD); mechanical and materials engineering (M Eng, ME Sc, PhD). *Program availability:* Part-time. Terminal master's awarded for partial completion of doctoral program. *Degree requirements:* For master's, thesis; for doctorate, thesis/dissertation. *Entrance requirements:* For master's, minimum B average; for doctorate, minimum B+ average.

University of Windsor, Faculty of Graduate Studies, Faculty of Engineering, Department of Civil and Environmental Engineering, Windsor, ON N9B 3P4, Canada. Offers civil engineering (M Eng, MA Sc, PhD); environmental engineering (M Eng, MA Sc, PhD). *Program availability:* Part-time. *Degree requirements:* For master's, thesis; for doctorate, comprehensive exam, thesis/dissertation. *Entrance requirements:* For master's, minimum B average; for doctorate, master's degree, minimum A average. Additional exam requirements/recommendations for international students: required—TOEFL (minimum score 580 paper-based). Electronic applications accepted.

University of Wisconsin–Madison, Graduate School, College of Engineering, Department of Civil and Environmental Engineering, Madison, WI 53706-1380. Offers construction engineering and management (MS); environmental science and engineering (MS); geological/geotechnical engineering (MS); structural engineering (MS); transportation engineering (MS); water resources engineering (MS). *Program*

availability: Part-time. Terminal master's awarded for partial completion of doctoral program. *Degree requirements:* For master's, thesis (for some programs), minimum of 30 credits; minimum overall GPA of 3.0. *Entrance requirements:* For master's, GRE General Test, bachelor's degree; minimum GPA of 3.0 for last 60 credits of course work. Additional exam requirements/recommendations for international students: required—TOEFL (minimum score 580 paper-based; 92 iBT). Electronic applications accepted. *Expenses:* Contact institution.

University of Wyoming, College of Engineering and Applied Science, Department of Chemical Engineering, Program in Environmental Engineering, Laramie, WY 82071. Offers MS. *Program availability:* Part-time. *Degree requirements:* For master's, thesis optional. *Entrance requirements:* For master's, GRE General Test, minimum GPA of 3.0. Additional exam requirements/recommendations for international students: required—TOEFL (minimum score 550 paper-based). Electronic applications accepted.

Université Laval, Faculty of Sciences and Engineering, Department of Civil Engineering, Programs in Civil Engineering, Québec, QC G1K 7P4, Canada. Offers civil engineering (M Sc, PhD); environmental technology (M Sc). Terminal master's awarded for partial completion of doctoral program. *Degree requirements:* For master's, thesis (for some programs); for doctorate, comprehensive exam, thesis/dissertation. *Entrance requirements:* For master's and doctorate, knowledge of French and English. Electronic applications accepted.

Utah State University, School of Graduate Studies, College of Engineering, Department of Civil and Environmental Engineering, Logan, UT 84322. Offers ME, MS, PhD, CE. *Degree requirements:* For master's, thesis (for some programs); for doctorate, thesis/dissertation. *Entrance requirements:* For master's and doctorate, GRE General Test, minimum GPA of 3.0. Additional exam requirements/recommendations for international students: required—TOEFL. Electronic applications accepted.

Vanderbilt University, School of Engineering, Department of Civil and Environmental Engineering, Program in Environmental Engineering, Nashville, TN 37240-1001. Offers environmental engineering (M Eng); environmental management (MS, PhD). *Program availability:* Part-time. Terminal master's awarded for partial completion of doctoral program. *Degree requirements:* For master's, thesis or alternative; for doctorate, thesis/dissertation. *Entrance requirements:* For master's and doctorate, GRE General Test. Additional exam requirements/recommendations for international students: required—TOEFL. Electronic applications accepted. *Expenses: Tuition:* Full-time $51,018; part-time $2087 per hour. *Required fees:* $542. Tuition and fees vary according to program.

Villanova University, College of Engineering, Department of Civil and Environmental Engineering, Program in Water Resources and Environmental Engineering, Villanova, PA 19085-1699. Offers urban water resources design (Certificate); water resources and environmental engineering (MSWREE). *Program availability:* Part-time, evening/weekend, online learning. *Degree requirements:* For master's, thesis optional. *Entrance requirements:* For master's, GRE General Test (for applicants with degrees from foreign universities), BCE or bachelor's degree in science or related engineering field, minimum GPA of 3.0. Additional exam requirements/recommendations for international students: required—TOEFL (minimum score 600 paper-based; 100 iBT). Electronic applications accepted.

Virginia Polytechnic Institute and State University, VT Online, Blacksburg, VA 24061. Offers advanced transportation systems (Certificate); aerospace engineering (MS); agricultural and life sciences (MSLFS); business information systems (Graduate Certificate); career and technical education (MS); civil engineering (MS); computer engineering (M Eng, MS); decision support systems (Graduate Certificate); eLearning leadership (MA); electrical engineering (M Eng, MS); engineering administration (MEA); environmental engineering (Certificate); environmental politics and policy (Graduate Certificate); environmental sciences and engineering (MS); foundations of political analysis (Graduate Certificate); health product risk management (Graduate Certificate); industrial and systems engineering (MS); information policy and society (Graduate Certificate); information security (Graduate Certificate); information technology (MIT); instructional technology (MA); integrative STEM education (MA Ed); liberal arts (Graduate Certificate); life sciences: health product risk management (MS); natural resources (MNR, Graduate Certificate); networking (Graduate Certificate); nonprofit and nongovernmental organization management (Graduate Certificate); ocean engineering (MS); political science (MA); security studies (Graduate Certificate); software development (Graduate Certificate). *Expenses:* Tuition, state resident: full-time $13,700; part-time $761.25 per credit hour. Tuition, nonresident: full-time $27,614; part-time $1534 per credit hour. *Required fees:* $886.50 per term. Tuition and fees vary according to campus/location and program.

Washington State University, Voiland College of Engineering and Architecture, Department of Civil and Environmental Engineering, Pullman, WA 99164-2910. Offers civil engineering (MS, PhD); environmental engineering (MS). *Program availability:* Part-time. Terminal master's awarded for partial completion of doctoral program. *Degree requirements:* For master's, comprehensive exam (for some programs), thesis (for some programs), oral exam; for doctorate, comprehensive exam, thesis/dissertation, oral exam, written exam. *Entrance requirements:* For master's, minimum GPA of 3.0, 3 letters of recommendation, statement of purpose; for doctorate, minimum GPA of 3.4, 3 letters of recommendation, statement of purpose. Additional exam requirements/recommendations for international students: required—TOEFL (minimum score 550 paper-based), IELTS. Electronic applications accepted.

Washington University in St. Louis, School of Engineering and Applied Science, Department of Energy, Environmental and Chemical Engineering, St. Louis, MO 63130-4899. Offers chemical engineering (MS, D Sc); environmental engineering (MS, D Sc). *Program availability:* Part-time. Terminal master's awarded for partial completion of doctoral program. *Degree requirements:* For master's, thesis optional; for doctorate, thesis/dissertation, preliminary exam, qualifying exam. *Entrance requirements:* For master's and doctorate, GRE, minimum B average during final 2 years of course work. Additional exam requirements/recommendations for international students: required—TOEFL, TWE. Electronic applications accepted.

Worcester Polytechnic Institute, Graduate Admissions, Department of Civil and Environmental Engineering, Worcester, MA 01609-2280. Offers civil engineering (MS); construction project management (Graduate Certificate). *Program availability:* Part-time, evening/weekend, 100% online, blended/hybrid learning. *Degree requirements:* For master's, thesis optional; for doctorate, comprehensive exam, thesis/dissertation. *Entrance requirements:* For master's, required for all international applicants; recommended for all others, 3 letters of recommendation; for doctorate, required for all international applicants; recommended for all others, 3 letters of recommendation, statement of purpose. Additional exam requirements/recommendations for international students: required—TOEFL (minimum score 563 paper-based; 84 iBT), IELTS (minimum score 7). Electronic applications accepted.

Yale University, Graduate School of Arts and Sciences, School of Engineering and Applied Science, Program in Environmental Engineering, New Haven, CT 06520. Offers MS, PhD.

Youngstown State University, College of Graduate Studies, College of Science, Technology, Engineering and Mathematics, Department of Civil/Environmental and

Chemical Engineering, Youngstown, OH 44555-0001. Offers civil and environmental engineering (MSE). *Program availability:* Part-time, evening/weekend. *Degree requirements:* For master's, thesis optional. *Entrance requirements:* For master's, minimum GPA of 2.75 in field. Additional exam requirements/recommendations for international students: required—TOEFL.

Fire Protection Engineering

Oklahoma State University, College of Arts and Sciences, Department of Political Science, Stillwater, OK 74078. Offers fire and emergency management administration (MS, PhD); political science (MA). *Faculty:* 9 full-time (5 women). *Students:* 9 full-time (1 woman), 4 part-time (3 women); includes 3 minority (2 Black or African American, non-Hispanic/Latino; 1 Asian, non-Hispanic/Latino), 1 international. Average age 25. 12 applicants, 67% accepted, 6 enrolled. In 2019, 11 master's awarded. *Entrance requirements:* For master's and doctorate, GRE. Additional exam requirements/recommendations for international students: required—TOEFL (minimum score 550 paper-based; 79 iBT). *Application deadline:* For fall admission, 3/1 priority date for international students; for spring admission, 8/1 priority date for international students. Applications are processed on a rolling basis. Application fee: $50 ($75 for international students). Electronic applications accepted. *Expenses: Tuition, area resident:* Full-time $4148.10; part-time $2765.40. Tuition, state resident: full-time $4148.10; part-time $2765.40. Tuition, nonresident: full-time $15,775; part-time $10,516.80. *International tuition:* $15,775.20 full-time. *Required fees:* $2196.90; $122.05 per credit hour. Tuition and fees vary according to course load, campus/location and program. *Financial support:* In 2019–20, 9 teaching assistantships (averaging $1,625 per year) were awarded; research assistantships, career-related internships or fieldwork, Federal Work-Study, scholarships/grants, health care benefits, tuition waivers (partial), and unspecified assistantships also available. Support available to part-time students. Financial award application deadline: 3/1; financial award applicants required to submit FAFSA. *Unit head:* Dr. Rebekah Herrick, Interim Department Head, 405-744-8437, E-mail: rebekah.herrick@okstate.edu. *Application contact:* Dr. Sheryl Tucker, Dean, 405-744-6368, Fax: 405-744-0355, E-mail: gradi@okstate.edu.
Website: http://polsci.okstate.edu

University of Maryland, College Park, Academic Affairs, A. James Clark School of Engineering, Department of Fire Protection Engineering, College Park, MD 20742. Offers M Eng, MS. *Program availability:* Part-time, evening/weekend. *Degree requirements:* For master's, thesis optional. *Entrance requirements:* For master's, GRE General Test, minimum GPA of 3.0, BS in any engineering or physical science area, 3 letters of recommendation. Electronic applications accepted.

University of New Haven, Graduate School, Henry C. Lee College of Criminal Justice and Forensic Sciences, Fire and Explosion Investigation, West Haven, CT 06516. Offers fire science (MS); fire/arson investigation (MS, Graduate Certificate); forensic science (Graduate Certificate); public safety management (MS). *Program availability:* Part-time, evening/weekend. *Students:* Average age 30. 12 applicants, 100% accepted, 5 enrolled. In 2019, 8 master's awarded. *Degree requirements:* For master's, thesis or alternative, research project or internship. *Entrance requirements:* Additional exam requirements/recommendations for international students: required—TOEFL (minimum score 80 iBT), IELTS, PTE (minimum score 53). *Application deadline:* Applications are processed on a rolling basis. Application fee: $50. Electronic applications accepted. Application fee is waived when completed online. *Financial support:* Research assistantships with partial tuition reimbursements, teaching assistantships with partial tuition reimbursements, Federal Work-Study, scholarships/grants, and unspecified assistantships available. Support available to part-time students. Financial award applicants required to submit FAFSA. *Unit head:* Dr. Sorin Iliescu, Assistant Professor, 203-932-7239, E-mail: siliescu@newhaven.edu. *Application contact:* Selina O'Toole, Senior Associate Director of Graduate Admissions, 203-932-7337, E-mail: SOToole@newhaven.edu.
Website: https://www.newhaven.edu/lee-college/graduate-programs/fire-science/

The University of North Carolina at Charlotte, William States Lee College of Engineering, Department of Engineering Technology and Construction Management, Charlotte, NC 28223-0001. Offers applied energy (Graduate Certificate); applied energy & electromechanical systems (MS); construction and facilities management (MS); fire protection and safety management (MS), including fire protection, fire administration. *Program availability:* Part-time. *Faculty:* 25 full-time (8 women), 1 part-time/adjunct (0 women). *Students:* 36 full-time (9 women), 23 part-time (4 women); includes 7 minority (2 Black or African American, non-Hispanic/Latino; 1 Asian, non-Hispanic/Latino; 2 Hispanic/Latino; 2 Two or more races, non-Hispanic/Latino), 27 international. Average age 28. 68 applicants, 76% accepted, 12 enrolled. In 2019, 41 master's awarded. *Degree requirements:* For master's, thesis optional. *Entrance requirements:* For master's, GRE, minimum undergraduate GPA of 3.0, recommendations, statistics; integral and differential calculus (for students pursuing fire protection concentration or applied energy and electromechanical systems program); for Graduate Certificate, bachelor's degree in engineering, engineering technology, construction management or a closely-related technical or scientific field; undergraduate coursework of at least 3 semesters in engineering analysis or calculus; minimum GPA of 3.0. Additional exam requirements/recommendations for international students: required—TOEFL (minimum score 557 paper-based; 83 iBT), IELTS (minimum score 6.5), TOEFL (minimum score 557 paper-based, 83 iBT) or IELTS (6.5). *Application deadline:* Applications are processed on a rolling basis. Application fee: $75. Electronic applications accepted. *Expenses:* Contact institution. *Financial support:* In 2019–20, 22 students received support, including 22 research assistantships (averaging $6,115 per year); career-related internships or fieldwork, institutionally sponsored loans, scholarships/grants, and unspecified assistantships also available. Support available to part-time students. Financial award applicants required to submit FAFSA. *Unit head:* Dr. Anthony Brizendine, Chair, 704-687-5032, E-mail: albrizen@uncc.edu. *Application contact:* Kathy B. Giddings, Director of Graduate Admissions, 704-687-5503, Fax: 704-687-1668, E-mail: gradadm@uncc.edu.
Website: http://et.uncc.edu/

Worcester Polytechnic Institute, Graduate Admissions, Department of Fire Protection Engineering, Worcester, MA 01609-2280. Offers MS, PhD, Advanced Certificate, Graduate Certificate. *Program availability:* Part-time, evening/weekend, 100% online, blended/hybrid learning. Terminal master's awarded for partial completion of doctoral program. *Degree requirements:* For master's, thesis optional; for doctorate, comprehensive exam, thesis/dissertation. *Entrance requirements:* For master's, BS in engineering or physical sciences, 3 letters of recommendation, General GRE for international applicants; for doctorate, General GRE, 3 letters of recommendation, statement of purpose. Additional exam requirements/recommendations for international students: required—TOEFL (minimum score 563 paper-based; 84 iBT), IELTS (minimum score 7), GRE. Electronic applications accepted.

Geotechnical Engineering

The Citadel, The Military College of South Carolina, Citadel Graduate College, School of Engineering, Department of Civil and Environmental Engineering, Charleston, SC 29409. Offers built environment and public health (Graduate Certificate); civil engineering (MS); geotechnical engineering (Graduate Certificate); structural engineering (Graduate Certificate); transportation engineering (Graduate Certificate). *Program availability:* Part-time, evening/weekend. *Degree requirements:* For master's, plan of study outlining intended areas of interest and top four corresponding courses of interest. *Entrance requirements:* For master's, official transcript of baccalaureate degree from ABET-accredited engineering program or approved alternative; 2 letters of recommendation; for Graduate Certificate, official transcript of baccalaureate degree directly from an accredited college or university. Additional exam requirements/recommendations for international students: required—TOEFL (minimum score 550 paper-based; 79 iBT). Electronic applications accepted.

Clemson University, Graduate School, College of Engineering, Computing and Applied Sciences, Glenn Department of Civil Engineering, Clemson, SC 29634. Offers civil engineering (MS, PhD), including construction engineering and management, construction materials, geotechnical engineering, structural engineering, transportation engineering, water resources engineering. *Program availability:* Part-time, 100% online. *Faculty:* 24 full-time (4 women), 3 part-time/adjunct (2 women). *Students:* 101 full-time (20 women), 44 part-time (9 women); includes 9 minority (3 Black or African American, non-Hispanic/Latino; 1 Asian, non-Hispanic/Latino; 2 Hispanic/Latino; 3 Two or more races, non-Hispanic/Latino), 97 international. Average age 29. 248 applicants, 62% accepted, 61 enrolled. In 2019, 43 master's, 11 doctorates awarded. *Degree requirements:* For master's, thesis or alternative, oral exam, seminar; for doctorate, comprehensive exam, thesis/dissertation, oral exam, seminar. *Entrance requirements:* For master's and doctorate, GRE General Test, unofficial transcripts, letters of recommendation, statement of purpose. Additional exam requirements/recommendations for international students: required—TOEFL (minimum score 80 paper-based; 80 iBT), PTE (minimum score 54); recommended—IELTS (minimum score 6.5). *Application deadline:* For fall admission, 4/15 for domestic and international students; for spring admission, 9/15 for domestic and international students. Applications are processed on a rolling basis. Application fee: $80 ($90 for international students). Electronic applications accepted. *Expenses: Tuition, area resident:* Full-time $10,600; part-time $8688 per semester. Tuition, state resident: full-time $10,600; part-time $8688 per semester. Tuition, nonresident: full-time $22,050; part-time $17,412 per semester. *International tuition:* $22,050 full-time. *Required fees:* $1196; $617 per semester. $617 per semester. Tuition and fees vary according to course load, degree level, campus/location and program. *Financial support:* In 2019–20, 101 students received support, including 2 fellowships with full and partial tuition reimbursements available (averaging $34,000 per year), 61 research assistantships with full and partial tuition reimbursements available (averaging $18,222 per year), 4 teaching assistantships with full and partial tuition reimbursements available (averaging $20,567 per year); career-related internships or fieldwork and unspecified assistantships also available. Financial award application deadline: 4/15. *Unit head:* Dr. Jesus M de la Garza, Department Chair, 864-656-3001, E-mail: jdelaga@clemson.edu. *Application contact:* Dr. Abdul Khan, Graduate Program Coordinator, 864-656-3327, E-mail: abdkhan@clemson.edu.
Website: https://www.clemson.edu/cecas/departments/ce/

Cornell University, Graduate School, Graduate Fields of Engineering, Field of Civil and Environmental Engineering, Ithaca, NY 14853. Offers engineering management (M Eng, MS, PhD); environmental engineering (M Eng, MS, PhD); environmental fluid mechanics and hydrology (M Eng, MS, PhD); environmental systems engineering (M Eng, MS, PhD); geotechnical engineering (M Eng, MS, PhD); remote sensing (M Eng, MS, PhD); structural engineering (M Eng, MS, PhD); structural mechanics (M Eng, MS); transportation engineering (MS, PhD); transportation systems engineering (M Eng); water resource systems (M Eng, MS, PhD). Terminal master's awarded for partial completion of doctoral program. *Degree requirements:* For master's, thesis (MS); for doctorate, comprehensive exam, thesis/dissertation. *Entrance requirements:* For master's and doctorate, GRE General Test (recommended), 2 letters of recommendation. Additional exam requirements/recommendations for international students: required—TOEFL (minimum score 600 paper-based; 77 iBT). Electronic applications accepted.

Drexel University, College of Engineering, Department of Civil, Architectural, and Environmental Engineering, Program in Geotechnical, Geoenvironmental and Geosynthetics Engineering, Philadelphia, PA 19104-2875. Offers MS, PhD.

Illinois Institute of Technology, Graduate College, Armour College of Engineering, Department of Civil, Architectural and Environmental Engineering, Chicago, IL 60616. Offers architectural engineering (M Arch E); civil engineering (MS, PhD), including architectural engineering (MS), construction engineering and management (MS), geoenvironmental engineering (MS), geotechnical engineering (MS), structural engineering (MS), transportation engineering (MS); construction engineering and management (MCEM); environmental engineering (M Env E, MS, PhD); geoenvironmental engineering (M Geoenv E); geotechnical engineering (MGE); infrastructure engineering and management (MPW); structural engineering (MSE); transportation engineering (M Trans E). *Program availability:* Part-time, evening/weekend, online learning. Terminal master's awarded for partial completion of doctoral program. *Degree requirements:* For master's, thesis (for some programs); for doctorate, comprehensive exam, thesis/dissertation. *Entrance requirements:* For master's, GRE

General Test (minimum score 900 Quantitative and Verbal, 2.5 Analytical Writing), minimum undergraduate GPA of 3.0; for doctorate, GRE General Test (minimum score 1000 Quantitative and Verbal, 3.0 Analytical Writing), minimum undergraduate GPA of 3.0. Additional exam requirements/recommendations for international students: required—TOEFL (minimum score 550 paper-based; 80 iBT). Electronic applications accepted.

Iowa State University of Science and Technology, Department of Civil and Construction Engineering, Ames, IA 50011. Offers civil engineering (MS, PhD), including civil engineering materials, construction engineering and management, environmental engineering, geotechnical engineering, structural engineering, transportation engineering. *Degree requirements:* For master's, thesis or alternative; for doctorate, thesis/dissertation. *Entrance requirements:* For master's and doctorate, GRE General Test. Additional exam requirements/recommendations for international students: required—TOEFL (minimum score 550 paper-based; 82 iBT), IELTS (minimum score 6.5). Electronic applications accepted.

Kansas State University, Graduate School, College of Engineering, Department of Civil Engineering, Manhattan, KS 66506. Offers civil engineering (MS, PhD); environmental engineering (MS, PhD); geotechnical engineering (MS, PhD); structural engineering (MS, PhD); transportation engineering (MS, PhD); water resources engineering (MS, PhD). *Program availability:* Part-time, evening/weekend, online learning. *Degree requirements:* For master's, thesis or alternative; for doctorate, thesis/ dissertation. *Entrance requirements:* For master's, GRE General Test, bachelor's degree or course work in related engineering fields; for doctorate, GRE General Test. Additional exam requirements/recommendations for international students: required—TOEFL (minimum score 550 paper-based; 79 iBT). Electronic applications accepted.

Kennesaw State University, Southern Polytechnic College of Engineering and Engineering Technology, Program in Civil Engineering, Kennesaw, GA 30144. Offers environmental engineering (MS); geotechnical engineering (MS); structural engineering (MS); transportation and pavement engineering (MS); water resources engineering (MS). *Program availability:* Online learning. *Students:* 9 full-time (2 women), 30 part-time (4 women); includes 20 minority (9 Black or African American, non-Hispanic/Latino; 5 Asian, non-Hispanic/Latino; 5 Hispanic/Latino; 1 Two or more races, non-Hispanic/Latino), 3 international. Average age 34. 12 applicants, 92% accepted, 8 enrolled. In 2019, 12 master's awarded. *Degree requirements:* For master's, thesis optional. *Entrance requirements:* Additional exam requirements/recommendations for international students: required—TOEFL (minimum score 80 iBT), IELTS (minimum score 6.5). *Application deadline:* For fall admission, 11/1 for domestic and international students; for spring admission, 4/1 for domestic and international students. Applications are processed on a rolling basis. Application fee: $60. Electronic applications accepted. *Expenses: Tuition, area resident:* Full-time $7104; part-time $296 per credit hour. Tuition, state resident: full-time $7104; part-time $296 per credit hour. Tuition, nonresident: full-time $25,584; part-time $1066 per credit hour. *International tuition:* $25,584 full-time. *Required fees:* $2006; $1706 per unit. $853 per semester. *Unit head:* Metin Oguzmert, Coordinator, 470-578-5083, E-mail: moguzmer@kennesaw.edu. *Application contact:* Admissions Counselor, 470-578-4377, E-mail: ksugrad@kennesaw.edu.
Website: http://engineering.kennesaw.edu/civil-construction/degrees/ms-civil-engineering.php

Louisiana State University and Agricultural & Mechanical College, Graduate School, College of Engineering, Department of Civil and Environmental Engineering, Baton Rouge, LA 70803. Offers environmental engineering (MSCE, PhD); geotechnical engineering (MSCE, PhD); structural engineering and mechanics (MSCE, PhD); transportation engineering (MSCE, PhD); water resources (MSCE, PhD).

Massachusetts Institute of Technology, School of Engineering, Department of Civil and Environmental Engineering, Cambridge, MA 02139. Offers biological oceanography (PhD, Sc D); chemical oceanography (PhD, Sc D); civil and environmental engineering (M Eng, SM, PhD, Sc D); civil and environmental systems (PhD, Sc D); civil engineering (PhD, Sc D, CE); civil engineering and computation (PhD); coastal engineering (PhD, Sc D); construction engineering and management (PhD, Sc D); environmental biology (PhD, Sc D); environmental chemistry (PhD, Sc D); environmental engineering (PhD, Sc D); environmental engineering and computation (PhD); environmental fluid mechanics (PhD, Sc D); geotechnical and geoenvironmental engineering (PhD, Sc D); hydrology (PhD, Sc D); information technology (PhD, Sc D); oceanographic engineering (PhD, Sc D); structures and materials (PhD, Sc D); transportation (PhD, Sc D); SM/MBA. *Degree requirements:* For master's, thesis; for doctorate, comprehensive exam, thesis/dissertation; for CE, comprehensive exam, thesis. *Entrance requirements:* For master's, doctorate, and CE, GRE General Test. Additional exam requirements/recommendations for international students: required—TOEFL, IELTS. Electronic applications accepted.

McGill University, Faculty of Graduate and Postdoctoral Studies, Faculty of Engineering, Department of Civil Engineering and Applied Mechanics, Montréal, QC H3A 2T5, Canada. Offers environmental engineering (M Eng, M Sc, PhD); fluid mechanics (M Sc); fluid mechanics and hydraulic engineering (M Eng, PhD); materials engineering (M Eng, PhD); rehabilitation of urban infrastructure (M Eng, PhD); soil behavior (M Eng, PhD); soil mechanics and foundations (M Eng, PhD); structures and structural mechanics (M Eng, PhD); water resources (M Sc); water resources engineering (M Eng, PhD).

Missouri University of Science and Technology, Program in Geotechnics, Rolla, MO 65409. Offers ME. *Expenses:* Tuition, state resident: full-time $7839; part-time $435.50 per credit hour. Tuition, nonresident: full-time $22,169; part-time $1231.60 per credit hour. *International tuition:* $18,156.60 full-time. *Required fees:* $649.76. One-time fee: $119. Tuition and fees vary according to course load and program.

Northwestern University, McCormick School of Engineering and Applied Science, Department of Civil and Environmental Engineering, Evanston, IL 60208-3109. Offers environmental engineering and science (MS, PhD); geotechnical engineering (MS, PhD); mechanics of materials and solids (MS, PhD); project management (MS); structural engineering and materials (MS, PhD); transportation systems analysis and planning (MS, PhD). *Program availability:* Part-time. Terminal master's awarded for partial completion of doctoral program. *Degree requirements:* For master's, comprehensive exam (for some programs), thesis (for some programs); for doctorate, comprehensive exam, thesis/dissertation. *Entrance requirements:* For master's and doctorate, GRE General Test, minimum 2 letters of recommendation, transcripts from all academic institutions attended. Additional exam requirements/recommendations for international students: required—TOEFL (minimum score 577 paper-based; 90 iBT), IELTS (minimum score 7). Electronic applications accepted.

Norwich University, College of Graduate and Continuing Studies, Master of Civil Engineering Program, Northfield, VT 05663. Offers construction management (MCE); environmental (MCE); geotechnical (MCE); structural (MCE). *Program availability:* Evening/weekend, online only, mostly all online with a week-long residency requirement. *Degree requirements:* For master's, capstone. *Entrance requirements:* For master's, minimum undergraduate GPA of 2.75. Additional exam requirements/recommendations for international students: required—TOEFL (minimum score 550 paper-based; 80 iBT),

IELTS (minimum score 6.5). Electronic applications accepted. *Expenses:* Contact institution.

Ohio University, Graduate College, Russ College of Engineering and Technology, Department of Civil Engineering, Athens, OH 45701-2979. Offers civil engineering (PhD); construction engineering and management (MS); environmental (MS); geoenvironmental (MS); geotechnical (MS); mechanics (MS); structures (MS); transportation (MS); water resources (MS). *Program availability:* Part-time. *Degree requirements:* For master's, comprehensive exam (for some programs), thesis or alternative; for doctorate, comprehensive exam, thesis/dissertation. *Entrance requirements:* For master's, GRE General Test, minimum GPA of 3.0, 3 letters of recommendation; for doctorate, GRE General Test. Additional exam requirements/recommendations for international students: required—TOEFL (minimum score 550 paper-based; 80 iBT) or IELTS (minimum score 6.5). Electronic applications accepted.

Old Dominion University, Frank Batten College of Engineering and Technology, Program in Civil Engineering, Norfolk, VA 23529. Offers civil engineering (ME, MS), including coastal engineering, geotechnical engineering, hydraulics and water resources, structural engineering, transportation engineering. *Program availability:* Part-time, evening/weekend, blended/hybrid learning. *Degree requirements:* For master's, comprehensive exam, thesis optional. *Entrance requirements:* For master's, GRE, minimum GPA of 3.0. Additional exam requirements/recommendations for international students: required—TOEFL (minimum score 550 paper-based, 80 iBT) or IELTS (6.5). Electronic applications accepted. *Expenses:* Contact institution.

Oregon State University, College of Engineering, Program in Civil Engineering, Corvallis, OR 97331. Offers civil engineering (M Eng, MS, PhD); coastal and ocean engineering (M Eng, MS, PhD); construction engineering management (M Eng, MS, PhD); engineering education (M Eng, MS, PhD); geomatics (M Eng, MS, PhD); geotechnical engineering (M Eng, MS, PhD); infrastructure materials (M Eng, MS, PhD); structural engineering (M Eng, MS, PhD); transportation engineering (M Eng). *Entrance requirements:* For master's and doctorate, GRE. Additional exam requirements/recommendations for international students: required—TOEFL (minimum score 80 iBT), IELTS (minimum score 6.5). *Expenses:* Contact institution.

Penn State University Park, Graduate School, College of Earth and Mineral Sciences, John and Willie Leone Family Department of Energy and Mineral Engineering, University Park, PA 16802. Offers MS, PhD.

Polytechnique Montréal, Graduate Programs, Department of Civil, Geological and Mining Engineering, Montréal, QC H3C 3A7, Canada. Offers civil, geological and mining engineering (DESS); environmental engineering (M Eng, M Sc A, PhD); geotechnical engineering (M Eng, M Sc A, PhD); hydraulics engineering (M Eng, M Sc A, PhD); structural engineering (M Eng, M Sc A, PhD); transportation engineering (M Eng, M Sc A, PhD). *Program availability:* Part-time. *Degree requirements:* For master's, one foreign language, thesis; for doctorate, one foreign language, thesis/dissertation. *Entrance requirements:* For master's, minimum GPA of 2.75; for doctorate, minimum GPA of 3.0.

Southern Illinois University Edwardsville, Graduate School, School of Engineering, Department of Civil Engineering, Program in Geotechnical Engineering, Edwardsville, IL 62026. Offers MS. *Program availability:* Part-time, evening/weekend. *Degree requirements:* For master's, thesis (for some programs), research paper. *Entrance requirements:* For master's, minimum undergraduate GPA of 2.75 in science, math, and engineering courses. Additional exam requirements/recommendations for international students: required—TOEFL (minimum score 550 paper-based, 79 iBT), IELTS (minimum score 6.5), Michigan Test of English Language Proficiency or PTE. Electronic applications accepted.

Southern Methodist University, Lyle School of Engineering, Department of Civil and Environmental Engineering, Dallas, TX 75275-0340. Offers civil and environmental engineering (PhD); civil engineering (MS), including geotechnical engineering, structural engineering, transportation systems; environmental engineering (MS); sustainability and development (MA). *Program availability:* Part-time, evening/weekend, online learning. Terminal master's awarded for partial completion of doctoral program. *Degree requirements:* For master's, thesis optional; for doctorate, thesis/dissertation, oral and written qualifying exams. *Entrance requirements:* For master's, GRE General Test, minimum GPA of 3.0 in last 2 years; bachelor's degree in engineering, mathematics, or sciences; for doctorate, GRE, BS and MS in related field, minimum GPA of 3.3. Additional exam requirements/recommendations for international students: required—TOEFL. Electronic applications accepted.

Tufts University, School of Engineering, Department of Civil and Environmental Engineering, Medford, MA 02155. Offers bioengineering (MS), including environmental biotechnology; civil and environmental engineering (MS, PhD), including applied data science, environmental and water resources engineering, environmental health, geosystems engineering, structural engineering and mechanics; PhD/PhD. *Program availability:* Part-time. Terminal master's awarded for partial completion of doctoral program. *Degree requirements:* For master's, thesis (for some programs); for doctorate, thesis/dissertation. *Entrance requirements:* For master's and doctorate, GRE General Test. Additional exam requirements/recommendations for international students: required—TOEFL (minimum score 550 paper-based; 80 iBT), IELTS (minimum score 6.5). Electronic applications accepted. Full-time tuition and fees vary according to degree level, program and student level. Part-time tuition and fees vary according to course load.

University of Alberta, Faculty of Graduate Studies and Research, Department of Civil and Environmental Engineering, Edmonton, AB T6G 2E1, Canada. Offers construction engineering and management (M Eng, M Sc, PhD); environmental engineering (M Eng, M Sc, PhD); environmental science (M Sc, PhD); geoenvironmental engineering (M Eng, M Sc, PhD); geotechnical engineering (M Eng, M Sc, PhD); mining engineering (M Eng, M Sc, PhD); petroleum engineering (M Eng, M Sc, PhD); structural engineering (M Eng, M Sc, PhD); water resources (M Eng, M Sc, PhD). *Program availability:* Part-time, online learning. *Degree requirements:* For master's, thesis (for some programs); for doctorate, thesis/dissertation. *Entrance requirements:* For master's, minimum GPA of 3.0 in last 2 years of undergraduate studies; for doctorate, minimum GPA of 3.0. Additional exam requirements/recommendations for international students: required—TOEFL (minimum score 550 paper-based). Electronic applications accepted.

University of Calgary, Faculty of Graduate Studies, Schulich School of Engineering, Program in Civil Engineering, Calgary, AB T2N 1N4, Canada. Offers avalanche mechanics (M Sc, PhD); civil engineering (M Eng, M Sc, PhD); energy and environment engineering (M Eng, M Sc, PhD); environmental engineering (M Eng, M Sc, PhD); geotechnical engineering (M Eng, M Sc, PhD); materials science (M Eng, M Sc, PhD); project management (M Eng, M Sc, PhD); structures and solid mechanics (M Eng, M Sc, PhD); transportation engineering (M Eng, M Sc, PhD); water resources (M Eng, M Sc, PhD). *Program availability:* Part-time. *Degree requirements:* For master's, thesis; for doctorate, thesis/dissertation, written and oral candidacy exam. *Entrance requirements:* For master's, minimum GPA of 3.0; for doctorate, minimum GPA of 3.5. Additional exam requirements/recommendations for international students: required—TOEFL (minimum score 580 paper-based; 93 iBT), IELTS (minimum score 7). Electronic applications accepted.

Geotechnical Engineering

University of Calgary, Faculty of Graduate Studies, Schulich School of Engineering, Program in Geomatics Engineering, Calgary, AB T2N 1N4, Canada. Offers M Eng, M Sc, PhD. *Program availability:* Part-time. *Degree requirements:* For master's, thesis (for some programs), minimum of 4 half-courses, completion of seminar course; for doctorate, comprehensive exam, thesis/dissertation, minimum of 3 half-courses, completion of two seminar courses, candidacy exam. *Entrance requirements:* For master's, B Sc or equivalent with minimum GPA of 3.0; for doctorate, M Sc or transfer from M Sc program with minimum GPA of 3.5. Additional exam requirements/recommendations for international students: required—TOEFL (minimum score 550 paper-based; 80 iBT) or IELTS (minimum score 7). Electronic applications accepted.

University of California, Berkeley, Graduate Division, College of Engineering, Department of Civil and Environmental Engineering, Berkeley, CA 94720. Offers engineering and project management (M Eng, MS, PhD); environmental engineering (M Eng, MS, PhD); geoengineering (M Eng, MS, PhD); structural engineering, mechanics and materials (M Eng, MS, PhD); transportation engineering (M Eng, MS, PhD); M Arch/MS; MCP/MS; MPP/MS. Terminal master's awarded for partial completion of doctoral program. *Degree requirements:* For master's, comprehensive exam (for some programs), thesis (for some programs), comprehensive exam or thesis (MS); for doctorate, thesis/dissertation, qualifying exam. *Entrance requirements:* For master's, GRE General Test, minimum GPA of 3.0, 3 letters of recommendation; for doctorate, GRE General Test, minimum GPA of 3.5, 3 letters of recommendation. Additional exam requirements/recommendations for international students: required—TOEFL (minimum score 570 paper-based; 90 iBT). Electronic applications accepted.

University of Colorado Denver, College of Engineering, Design and Computing, Department of Civil Engineering, Denver, CO 80217. Offers civil engineering (EASPhD); civil engineering systems (PhD); environmental and sustainability engineering (MS, PhD); geographic information systems (MS); geotechnical engineering (MS, PhD); hydrology and hydraulics (MS, PhD); structural engineering (MS, PhD); transportation engineering (MS, PhD). *Program availability:* Part-time, evening/weekend. *Degree requirements:* For master's, comprehensive exam, 30 credit hours, project or thesis; for doctorate, comprehensive exam, thesis/dissertation, 60 credit hours (30 of which are dissertation research). *Entrance requirements:* For master's, GRE, statement of purpose, transcripts, three references; for doctorate, GRE, statement of purpose, transcripts, references, letter of support from faculty stating willingness to serve as dissertation advisor and outlining plan for financial support. Additional exam requirements/recommendations for international students: required—TOEFL (minimum score 537 paper-based; 75 iBT); recommended—IELTS (minimum score 6.5). Electronic applications accepted. Tuition and fees vary according to course load, program and reciprocity agreements.

University of Dayton, Department of Civil and Environmental Engineering and Engineering Mechanics, Dayton, OH 45469. Offers engineering mechanics (MSEM); environmental engineering (MSCE); geotechnical engineering (MSCE); structural engineering (MSCE); transportation engineering (MSCE); water resources engineering (MSCE). *Program availability:* Part-time, blended/hybrid learning. *Degree requirements:* For master's, thesis or alternative. *Entrance requirements:* For master's, minimum GPA of 3.0 in undergraduate work. Additional exam requirements/recommendations for international students: required—TOEFL (minimum score 550 paper-based; 80 iBT); recommended—IELTS (minimum score 6.5), TSE (minimum score 60). Electronic applications accepted.

University of Delaware, College of Engineering, Department of Civil and Environmental Engineering, Newark, DE 19716. Offers environmental engineering (MAS, MCE, PhD); geotechnical engineering (MAS, MCE, PhD); ocean engineering (MAS, MCE, PhD); structural engineering (MAS, MCE, PhD); transportation engineering (MAS, MCE, PhD); water resource engineering (MAS, MCE, PhD). *Program availability:* Part-time. Terminal master's awarded for partial completion of doctoral program. *Degree requirements:* For master's, thesis; for doctorate, thesis/dissertation. *Entrance requirements:* For master's and doctorate, GRE General Test. Additional exam requirements/recommendations for international students: required—TOEFL. Electronic applications accepted.

University of Massachusetts Amherst, Graduate School, College of Engineering, Department of Civil and Environmental Engineering, Amherst, MA 01003. Offers civil engineering (MSCE, PhD); environmental and water resources engineering (MSCE); geotechnical engineering (MSCE); structural engineering and mechanics (MSCE); transportation engineering (MSCE). *Program availability:* Part-time. Terminal master's awarded for partial completion of doctoral program. *Degree requirements:* For master's, thesis or alternative; for doctorate, comprehensive exam, thesis/dissertation. *Entrance requirements:* For master's and doctorate, GRE General Test. Additional exam requirements/recommendations for international students: required—TOEFL (minimum score 550 paper-based; 80 iBT), IELTS (minimum score 6.5). Electronic applications accepted.

University of Memphis, Graduate School, Herff College of Engineering, Department of Civil Engineering, Memphis, TN 38152. Offers civil engineering (PhD); engineering seismology (MS); environmental engineering (MS); freight transportation (Graduate Certificate); geotechnical engineering (MS); structural engineering (MS); transportation engineering (MS); water resources engineering (MS). *Students:* 15 full-time (4 women), 8 part-time (1 woman); includes 1 minority (Black or African American, non-Hispanic/Latino; 12 international. Average age 27. 26 applicants, 38% accepted, 5 enrolled. In 2019, 11 master's awarded. Terminal master's awarded for partial completion of doctoral program. *Degree requirements:* For master's, comprehensive exam, thesis optional; for doctorate, comprehensive exam, thesis/dissertation. *Entrance requirements:* For master's, GRE General Test, minimum undergraduate GPA of 2.5; bachelor's degree in engineering or a related science or mathematics program; three letters of reference; for doctorate, GRE General Test, bachelor's degree in engineering or engineering science; three letters of reference; for Graduate Certificate, minimum undergraduate GPA of 2.75; bachelor's degree in engineering or engineering science. Additional exam requirements/recommendations for international students: required—TOEFL (minimum score 550 paper-based; 79 iBT). *Application deadline:* For fall admission, 8/1 for domestic students; for spring admission, 12/1 for domestic students. Application fee: $35 ($60 for international students). Electronic applications accepted. *Expenses: Tuition, area resident:* Full-time $9216; part-time $512 per credit hour. Tuition, state resident: full-time $9216; part-time $512 per credit hour. Tuition, nonresident: full-time $12,672; part-time $704 per credit hour. *International tuition:* $16,128 full-time. *Required fees:* $1530; $85 per credit hour. Tuition and fees vary according to program. *Financial support:* Fellowships with full tuition reimbursements, research assistantships with full tuition reimbursements, career-related internships or fieldwork, Federal Work-Study, scholarships/grants, and unspecified assistantships available. Financial award application deadline: 2/1; financial award applicants required to submit FAFSA. *Unit head:* Dr. Shahram Pezeshk, Chair, 901-678-2746, Fax: 901-678-3026, E-mail: spezeshk@memphis.edu. *Application contact:* Dr. Roger Meier, Graduate Coordinator, 901-678-3284, E-mail: rwmeier@memphis.edu. Website: https://www.memphis.edu/ce

University of New Brunswick Fredericton, School of Graduate Studies, Faculty of Engineering, Department of Civil Engineering, Fredericton, NB E3B 5A3, Canada. Offers construction engineering and management (M Eng, M Sc E, PhD); environmental

engineering (M Eng, M Sc E, PhD); environmental studies (M Eng); geotechnical engineering (M Eng, M Sc E, PhD); groundwater/hydrology (M Eng, M Sc E, PhD); materials (M Eng, M Sc E, PhD); pavements (M Eng, M Sc E, PhD); structures (M Eng, M Sc E, PhD); transportation (M Eng, M Sc E, PhD). *Program availability:* Part-time. *Faculty:* 17 full-time (2 women). *Students:* 31 full-time (6 women), 10 part-time (0 women), 12 international. Average age 27. In 2019, 11 master's awarded. *Degree requirements:* For master's, thesis; for doctorate, comprehensive exam, thesis/dissertation, qualifying exam; 27 credit hours of courses. *Entrance requirements:* For master's, minimum GPA of 3.0; B Sc E in civil engineering or related engineering degree; for doctorate, minimum GPA of 3.0; graduate degree in engineering or applied science. Additional exam requirements/recommendations for international students: required—IELTS (minimum score 7.5), TWE (minimum score 4), Michigan English Language Assessment Battery (minimum score 85) or CanTest (minimum score 4.5); recommended—TOEFL (minimum score 580 paper-based). *Application deadline:* For fall admission, 5/1 for domestic students; for winter admission, 11/1 for domestic students. Applications are processed on a rolling basis. Application fee: $50 Canadian dollars. Electronic applications accepted. *Expenses: Tuition, area resident:* Full-time $6975 Canadian dollars; part-time $3423 Canadian dollars per year. Tuition, state resident: full-time $6975 Canadian dollars; part-time $3423 Canadian dollars per year. Tuition, Canadian resident: full-time $6975 Canadian dollars; part-time $3423 Canadian dollars per year. *International tuition:* $12,435 Canadian dollars full-time. *Required fees:* $92.25 Canadian dollars per term. Full-time tuition and fees vary according to degree level, campus/location, program, reciprocity agreements and student level. *Financial support:* Fellowships, research assistantships, teaching assistantships, career-related internships or fieldwork, and scholarships/grants available. Financial award application deadline: 1/15. *Unit head:* Dr. Jeff Rankin, Chair, 506-453-4618, Fax: 506-453-3568, E-mail: ktm@unb.ca. *Application contact:* MaryBeth Nicholson, Graduate Secretary, 506-452-6127, Fax: 506-453-3568, E-mail: mbnich@unb.ca. Website: http://go.unb.ca/gradprograms

University of Puerto Rico at Mayagüez, Graduate Studies, College of Engineering, Department of Civil Engineering and Surveying, Mayagüez, PR 00681-9000. Offers civil engineering (ME, MS, PhD), including construction engineering and management (ME, MS), environmental engineering, geotechnical engineering (ME, MS), structural engineering, transportation engineering. *Program availability:* Part-time. Terminal master's awarded for partial completion of doctoral program. *Degree requirements:* For master's, one foreign language, thesis; for doctorate, one foreign language, comprehensive exam, thesis/dissertation, qualifying exams. *Entrance requirements:* For master's, proficiency in English and Spanish; BS in civil engineering or its equivalent; for doctorate, proficiency in English and Spanish. Electronic applications accepted.

University of Rhode Island, Graduate School, College of Engineering, Department of Ocean Engineering, Narragansett, RI 02882. Offers ocean engineering (MS, PhD), including acoustics, geomechanics (MS), hydrodynamics (MS), ocean instrumentation (MS), offshore energy (MS), offshore structures (MS), water wave mechanics (MS). *Program availability:* Part-time. *Faculty:* 9 full-time (1 woman). *Students:* 19 full-time (6 women), 16 part-time (5 women); includes 2 minority (1 Asian, non-Hispanic/Latino; 1 Two or more races, non-Hispanic/Latino), 9 international. 27 applicants, 89% accepted, 11 enrolled. In 2019, 18 master's, 4 doctorates awarded. *Entrance requirements:* Additional exam requirements/recommendations for international students: required—TOEFL. *Application deadline:* For fall admission, 7/15 for domestic students, 2/1 for international students; for spring admission, 11/15 for domestic students, 7/15 for international students; for summer admission, 4/15 for domestic students. Application fee: $65. Electronic applications accepted. *Expenses: Tuition, area resident:* Full-time $13,734; part-time $763 per credit. Tuition, state resident: full-time $13,734; part-time $763 per credit. Tuition, nonresident: full-time $26,512; part-time $1473 per credit. *International tuition:* $26,512 full-time. *Required fees:* $1780; $52 per credit. $35 per term. One-time fee: $165. *Financial support:* In 2019–20, 9 research assistantships with tuition reimbursements (averaging $8,915 per year), 3 teaching assistantships with tuition reimbursements (averaging $14,330 per year) were awarded. Financial award application deadline: 2/1; financial award applicants required to submit FAFSA. *Unit head:* Dr. Stephen Grilli, Chairman, 401-874-6636, E-mail: grilli@uri.edu. *Application contact:* Christopher Baxter, Graduate Program Director, 401-874-6575, E-mail: cbaxter@uri.edu. Website: http://www.oce.uri.edu/

University of Southern California, Graduate School, Viterbi School of Engineering, Mork Family Department of Chemical Engineering and Materials Science, Los Angeles, CA 90089. Offers chemical engineering (MS, PhD, Engr); geoscience technologies (MS); materials engineering (MS); materials science (MS, PhD, Engr); petroleum engineering (MS, PhD, Engr); smart oilfield technologies (MS, Graduate Certificate). Terminal master's awarded for partial completion of doctoral program. *Degree requirements:* For master's, thesis optional; for doctorate, thesis/dissertation. *Entrance requirements:* For master's and doctorate, GRE General Test. Additional exam requirements/recommendations for international students: recommended—TOEFL. Electronic applications accepted. *Expenses:* Contact institution.

University of South Florida, College of Engineering, Department of Civil and Environmental Engineering, Tampa, FL 33620-9951. Offers civil engineering (MCE, MSCE), including geotechnical engineering, materials science and engineering, structures engineering, transportation engineering, water resources; environmental engineering (MEVE, MSEV, PhD), including engineering for international development (MSEV). *Program availability:* Part-time. *Faculty:* 19 full-time (5 women). *Students:* 144 full-time (46 women), 76 part-time (22 women); includes 35 minority (8 Black or African American, non-Hispanic/Latino; 5 Asian, non-Hispanic/Latino; 18 Hispanic/Latino; 4 Two or more races, non-Hispanic/Latino), 123 international. Average age 28. 220 applicants, 65% accepted, 59 enrolled. In 2019, 82 master's, 15 doctorates awarded. Terminal master's awarded for partial completion of doctoral program. *Degree requirements:* For master's, comprehensive exam, thesis (for some programs); for doctorate, comprehensive exam, thesis/dissertation. *Entrance requirements:* For master's, GRE required, bachelor's degree in appropriate field, minimum GPA of 3.0 in major, letters of reference, statement of purpose, resume, intake form; for doctorate, GRE with V (45th percentile), Q (75th percentile), and AW (55th percentile), letters of recommendation, statement of purpose, resume, intake form. Additional exam requirements/recommendations for international students: required—TOEFL, TOEFL (minimum score 550 paper-based; 79 iBT) or IELTS (minimum score 6.5). *Application deadline:* For fall admission, 2/15 for domestic students, 2/15 priority date for international students; for spring admission, 10/15 for domestic students, 9/15 priority date for international students. Application fee: $30. Electronic applications accepted. *Financial support:* In 2019–20, 45 students received support, including 44 research assistantships (averaging $14,123 per year), 21 teaching assistantships with tuition reimbursements available (averaging $15,329 per year). *Unit head:* Dr. Manjriker Gunaratne, Professor and Department Chair, 813-974-5818, Fax: 813-974-2957, E-mail: gunaratn@usf.edu. *Application contact:* Dr. Sarina J. Ergas, Professor and Graduate Program Coordinator, 813-974-1119, Fax: 813-974-2957, E-mail: sergas@usf.edu. Website: http://www.usf.edu/engineering/cee/

The University of Texas at Austin, Graduate School, Cockrell School of Engineering, Department of Petroleum and Geosystems Engineering, Austin, TX 78712-1111. Offers energy and earth resources (MA); petroleum engineering (MS, PhD). *Program availability:* Evening/weekend, online learning. *Entrance requirements:* For master's and doctorate, GRE General Test. Electronic applications accepted.

University of Washington, Graduate School, College of Engineering, Department of Civil and Environmental Engineering, Seattle, WA 98195-2700. Offers construction engineering (MSCE, PhD); environmental engineering (MSCE, PhD); geotechnical engineering (MSCE, PhD); hydrology and hydrodynamics (MSCE, PhD); structural engineering and mechanics (MSCE, PhD); transportation engineering (MSCE, PhD). *Program availability:* Part-time, 100% online. *Students:* 248 full-time (97 women), 174 part-time (63 women); includes 90 minority (8 Black or African American, non-Hispanic/Latino; 2 American Indian or Alaska Native, non-Hispanic/Latino; 46 Asian, non-Hispanic/Latino; 18 Hispanic/Latino; 16 Two or more races, non-Hispanic/Latino), 118 international. Average age 28. 756 applicants, 59% accepted, 164 enrolled. In 2019, 133 master's, 21 doctorates awarded. Terminal master's awarded for partial completion of doctoral program. *Degree requirements:* For master's, thesis optional; for doctorate, comprehensive exam, thesis/dissertation, qualifying, general and final exams; completion of degree within 10 years. *Entrance requirements:* For master's, GRE General Test, minimum GPA of 3.0, statement of purpose, letters of recommendation, transcripts; for doctorate, GRE General Test, minimum GPA of 3.5, statement of purpose, letters of recommendation, transcripts, resume. Additional exam requirements/recommendations for international students: required—TOEFL (minimum score 580 paper-based; 92 iBT). *Application deadline:* For fall admission, 12/15 for domestic and international students. Applications are processed on a rolling basis. Application fee:

$85. Electronic applications accepted. *Expenses:* Contact institution. *Financial support:* In 2019–20, 21 fellowships with full tuition reimbursements (averaging $30,600 per year), 76 research assistantships with full tuition reimbursements (averaging $30,600 per year), 27 teaching assistantships with full tuition reimbursements (averaging $30,120 per year) were awarded; Federal Work-Study, institutionally sponsored loans, scholarships/grants, health care benefits, tuition waivers, and unspecified assistantships also available. Support available to part-time students. Financial award application deadline: 12/15. *Unit head:* Dr. Laura Lowes, Professor/Chair, 206-685-2563, Fax: 206-543-1543, E-mail: lowes@uw.edu. *Application contact:* Bryan Crockett, Director of Academic Services, 206-616-1891, Fax: 206-543-1543, E-mail: ceginfo@u.washington.edu.
Website: http://www.ce.washington.edu/

University of Wisconsin–Madison, Graduate School, College of Engineering, Department of Civil and Environmental Engineering, Madison, WI 53706-1380. Offers construction engineering and management (MS); environmental science and engineering (MS); geological/geotechnical engineering (MS); structural engineering (MS); transportation engineering (MS); water resources engineering (MS). *Program availability:* Part-time. Terminal master's awarded for partial completion of doctoral program. *Degree requirements:* For master's, thesis (for some programs), minimum of 30 credits; minimum overall GPA of 3.0. *Entrance requirements:* For master's, GRE General Test, bachelor's degree; minimum GPA of 3.0 for last 60 credits of course work. Additional exam requirements/recommendations for international students: required—TOEFL (minimum score 580 paper-based; 92 iBT). Electronic applications accepted. *Expenses:* Contact institution.

Hazardous Materials Management

Humboldt State University, Academic Programs, College of Natural Resources and Sciences, Programs in Natural Resources, Arcata, CA 95521-8299. Offers natural resources (MS), including fisheries, forestry, natural resources planning and interpretation, rangeland resources and wildland soils, wastewater utilization, watershed management, wildlife. *Program availability:* Part-time. Faculty: 21 full-time (5 women), 16 part-time/adjunct (4 women). *Students:* 44 full-time (22 women), 41 part-time (19 women); includes 21 minority (3 American Indian or Alaska Native, non-Hispanic/Latino; 10 Hispanic/Latino; 8 Two or more races, non-Hispanic/Latino), 3 international. Average age 30. 42 applicants, 50% accepted, 20 enrolled. In 2019, 26 master's awarded. *Degree requirements:* For master's, thesis or alternative. *Entrance requirements:* For master's, GRE, appropriate bachelor's degree, minimum GPA of 2.5, 3 letters of recommendation, resume. Additional exam requirements/recommendations for international students: required—TOEFL (minimum score 500 paper-based). *Application deadline:* For fall admission, 2/1 for domestic and international students; for spring admission, 9/30 for domestic and international students. Applications are processed on a rolling basis. Application fee: $55. *Expenses:* Tuition, state resident: full-time $7176; part-time $4164 per term. *Required fees:* $2120; $1672 per term. *Financial support:* Fellowships, career-related internships or fieldwork, and Federal Work-Study available. Support available to part-time students. Financial award application deadline: 3/1; financial award applicants required to submit FAFSA. *Unit head:* Dr. Erin Kelly, Graduate Program Coordinator, 707-826-5805, E-mail: eck107@humboldt.edu. *Application contact:* Dr. Erin Kelly, Graduate Program Coordinator, 707-826-5805, E-mail: eck107@humboldt.edu.
Website: http://www.humboldt.edu/cnrs/graduate_programs

Indiana University Bloomington, School of Public and Environmental Affairs, Environmental Science Programs, Bloomington, IN 47405. Offers applied ecology (MSES); energy (MSES); environmental chemistry, toxicology, and risk assessment (MSES); environmental science (PhD); hazardous materials management (Certificate); specialized environmental science (MSES); water resources (MSES); JD/MSES; MSES/MA; MSES/MPA; MSES/MS. *Program availability:* Part-time. Terminal master's awarded for partial completion of doctoral program. *Degree requirements:* For master's, capstone or thesis; internship; for doctorate, comprehensive exam, thesis/dissertation. *Entrance requirements:* For master's, GRE General Test or GMAT, official transcripts, 3 letters of recommendation, resume, personal statement; for doctorate, GRE General Test or LSAT, official transcripts, 3 letters of recommendation, resume or curriculum vitae, statement of purpose. Additional exam requirements/recommendations for international students: required—TOEFL (minimum score 600 paper-based; 96 iBT); recommended—IELTS (minimum score 7). Electronic applications accepted.

Jackson State University, Graduate School, College of Science, Engineering and Technology, Department of Civil and Environmental Engineering and Industrial Systems and Technology, Jackson, MS 39217. Offers civil engineering (MS, PhD); coastal engineering (MS, PhD); environmental engineering (MS, PhD); hazardous materials management (MS); technology education (MS Ed). *Program availability:* Part-time, evening/weekend. *Degree requirements:* For master's, comprehensive exam, thesis or alternative. *Entrance requirements:* For master's, GRE General Test. Additional exam requirements/recommendations for international students: required—TOEFL (minimum score 520 paper-based; 67 iBT).

Marquette University, Graduate School, College of Engineering, Department of Civil and Environmental Engineering, Milwaukee, WI 53201-1881. Offers construction engineering and management (MS, PhD, Certificate); environmental engineering (MS, PhD); structural design (Certificate); structural engineering and structural mechanics (MS, PhD); transportation (Certificate); transportation engineering and materials (MS, PhD); waste and wastewater treatment processes (Certificate); water resources engineering (Certificate). *Program availability:* Part-time, evening/weekend. Terminal master's awarded for partial completion of doctoral program. *Degree requirements:* For master's, comprehensive exam (for some programs), thesis or alternative; for doctorate, thesis/dissertation. *Entrance requirements:* For master's, GRE General Test (recommended), minimum GPA of 3.0, official transcripts from all current and previous colleges/universities except Marquette, three letters of recommendation; for doctorate, GRE General Test, minimum GPA of 3.0, official transcripts from all current and previous colleges/universities except Marquette, three letters of recommendation, brief statement of purpose, submission of any English language publications authored by applicant (strongly recommended). Additional exam requirements/recommendations for international students: required—TOEFL (minimum score 530 paper-based). Electronic applications accepted.

New Mexico Institute of Mining and Technology, Center for Graduate Studies, Department of Civil and Environmental Engineering, Socorro, NM 87801. Offers environmental engineering (MS), including air quality engineering and science, hazardous waste engineering, water quality engineering and science. *Degree requirements:* For master's, thesis, thesis or independent study. *Entrance requirements:*

Additional exam requirements/recommendations for international students: required—TOEFL (minimum score 540 paper-based).

Rutgers University - New Brunswick, Graduate School-New Brunswick, Department of Environmental Sciences, Piscataway, NJ 08854-8097. Offers air pollution and resources (MS, PhD); aquatic biology (MS, PhD); aquatic chemistry (MS, PhD); atmospheric science (MS, PhD); chemistry and physics of aerosol and hydrosol systems (MS, PhD); environmental chemistry (MS, PhD); environmental microbiology (MS, PhD); environmental toxicology (PhD); exposure assessment (PhD); fate and effects of pollutants (MS, PhD); pollution prevention and control (MS, PhD); water and wastewater treatment (MS, PhD); water resources (MS, PhD). Terminal master's awarded for partial completion of doctoral program. *Degree requirements:* For master's, comprehensive exam, thesis or alternative, oral final exam; for doctorate, comprehensive exam, thesis/dissertation, thesis defense, qualifying exam. *Entrance requirements:* For master's and doctorate, GRE General Test. Additional exam requirements/recommendations for international students: required—TOEFL. Electronic applications accepted.

University of Colorado Denver, College of Liberal Arts and Sciences, Department of Geography and Environmental Sciences, Denver, CO 80217. Offers environmental sciences (MS), including air quality, ecosystems, environmental health, geospatial analysis, hazardous waste, water quality. *Program availability:* Part-time, evening/weekend. *Degree requirements:* For master's, thesis or alternative, 30 credits including 21 of core requirements and 9 of environmental science electives. *Entrance requirements:* For master's, GRE General Test, BA in one of the natural/physical sciences or engineering (or equivalent background); prerequisite coursework in calculus and physics (one semester each); general chemistry with lab and general biology with lab (two semesters each); three letters of recommendation. Additional exam requirements/recommendations for international students: required—TOEFL (minimum score 537 paper-based; 75 iBT); recommended—IELTS (minimum score 6.5). Electronic applications accepted. Tuition and fees vary according to course load, program and reciprocity agreements.

The University of Manchester, School of Materials, Manchester, United Kingdom. Offers advanced aerospace materials engineering (M Sc); advanced metallic systems (PhD); biomedical materials (M Phil, M Sc, PhD); ceramics and glass (M Phil, M Sc, PhD); composite materials (M Sc, PhD); corrosion and protection (M Phil, M Sc, PhD); materials (M Phil, PhD); metallic materials (M Phil, M Sc, PhD); nanostructural materials (M Phil, M Sc, PhD); paper science (M Phil, M Sc, PhD); polymer science and engineering (M Phil, M Sc, PhD); technical textiles (M Sc); textile design, fashion and management (M Phil, M Sc, PhD); textile science and technology (M Phil, M Sc, PhD); textiles (M Phil, PhD); textiles and fashion (M Ent).

University of New Haven, Graduate School, Tagliatela College of Engineering, Program in Environmental Engineering, West Haven, CT 06516. Offers environmental engineering (MS); industrial and hazardous waste (MS); water and wastewater treatment (MS); water resources (MS). *Program availability:* Part-time, evening/weekend, 100% online. *Students:* 15 full-time (7 women), 32 part-time (13 women); includes 7 minority (2 Black or African American, non-Hispanic/Latino; 2 Asian, non-Hispanic/Latino; 3 Hispanic/Latino), 17 international. Average age 30. 67 applicants, 97% accepted, 11 enrolled. In 2019, 15 master's awarded. *Degree requirements:* For master's, thesis or alternative, research project. *Entrance requirements:* For master's, bachelor's degree in engineering. Additional exam requirements/recommendations for international students: required—TOEFL (minimum score 75 iBT), IELTS, PTE (minimum score 50). *Application deadline:* Applications are processed on a rolling basis. Application fee: $50. Electronic applications accepted. Application fee is waived when completed online. *Financial support:* Research assistantships with partial tuition reimbursements, teaching assistantships with partial tuition reimbursements, career-related internships or fieldwork, Federal Work-Study, scholarships/grants, and unspecified assistantships available. Support available to part-time students. Financial award application deadline: 5/1; financial award applicants required to submit FAFSA. *Unit head:* Dr. Emese Hadnagy, Associate Professor, 203-932-1232, E-mail: EHadnagy@newhaven.edu. *Application contact:* Selina O'Toole, Senior Associate Director of Graduate Admissions, 203-932-7337, E-mail: sotoole@newhaven.edu.
Website: https://www.newhaven.edu/engineering/graduate-programs/environmental-engineering/

University of South Carolina, The Graduate School, Arnold School of Public Health, Department of Environmental Health Sciences, Program in Hazardous Materials Management, Columbia, SC 29208. Offers MPH, MSPH, PhD. *Degree requirements:* For master's, comprehensive exam, thesis (for some programs), practicum (MPH); for doctorate, one foreign language, comprehensive exam, thesis/dissertation. *Entrance requirements:* Additional exam requirements/recommendations for international students: required—TOEFL (minimum score 570 paper-based). Electronic applications accepted.

Hazardous Materials Management

University of Southern California, Graduate School, Viterbi School of Engineering, Sonny Astani Department of Civil and Environmental Engineering, Los Angeles, CA 90089. Offers applied mechanics (MS); civil engineering (MS, PhD); computer-aided engineering (ME, Graduate Certificate); construction management (MCM); engineering technology commercialization (Graduate Certificate); environmental engineering (MS, PhD); environmental quality management (ME); structural design (ME); sustainable cities (Graduate Certificate); transportation systems (MS, Graduate Certificate); water and waste management (MS). *Program availability:* Part-time, evening/weekend. Terminal master's awarded for partial completion of doctoral program. *Degree requirements:* For master's, thesis optional; for doctorate, thesis/dissertation. *Entrance requirements:* For master's and doctorate, GRE General Test. Additional exam requirements/recommendations for international students: recommended—TOEFL. Electronic applications accepted.

Hydraulics

Drexel University, College of Engineering, Department of Civil, Architectural, and Environmental Engineering, Philadelphia, PA 19104-2875. Offers architectural/building systems engineering (MS, PhD); civil engineering (MS, PhD); environmental engineering (MS, PhD); geotechnical, geoenvironmental and geosynthetics engineering (MS, PhD); hydraulics, hydrology and water resources engineering (MS, PhD); structures (MS). *Program availability:* Part-time, evening/weekend. *Degree requirements:* For master's, thesis optional; for doctorate, thesis/dissertation. *Entrance requirements:* For master's, minimum GPA of 3.0; for doctorate, minimum GPA of 3.5, MS in civil engineering. Additional exam requirements/recommendations for international students: required—TOEFL. Electronic applications accepted.

McGill University, Faculty of Graduate and Postdoctoral Studies, Faculty of Engineering, Department of Civil Engineering and Applied Mechanics, Montréal, QC H3A 2T5, Canada. Offers environmental engineering (M Eng, M Sc, PhD); fluid mechanics (M Sc); fluid mechanics and hydraulic engineering (M Eng, PhD); materials engineering (M Eng, PhD); rehabilitation of urban infrastructure (M Eng, PhD); soil behavior (M Eng, PhD); soil mechanics and foundations (M Eng, PhD); structures and structural mechanics (M Eng, PhD); water resources (M Sc); water resources engineering (M Eng, PhD).

Old Dominion University, Frank Batten College of Engineering and Technology, Program in Civil Engineering, Norfolk, VA 23529. Offers civil engineering (ME, MS), including coastal engineering, geotechnical engineering, hydraulics and water resources, structural engineering, transportation engineering. *Program availability:* Part-time, evening/weekend, blended/hybrid learning. *Degree requirements:* For master's, comprehensive exam, thesis optional. *Entrance requirements:* For master's, GRE, minimum GPA of 3.0. Additional exam requirements/recommendations for international students: required—TOEFL (minimum score 550 paper-based, 80 iBT) or IELTS (6.5). Electronic applications accepted. *Expenses:* Contact institution.

Polytechnique Montréal, Graduate Programs, Department of Civil, Geological and Mining Engineering, Montréal, QC H3C 3A7, Canada. Offers civil, geological and mining engineering (DESS); environmental engineering (M Eng, M Sc A, PhD); geotechnical engineering (M Eng, M Sc A, PhD); hydraulics engineering (M Eng, M Sc A, PhD); structural engineering (M Eng, M Sc A, PhD); transportation engineering (M Eng, M Sc A, PhD). *Program availability:* Part-time. *Degree requirements:* For master's, one foreign language, thesis; for doctorate, one foreign language, thesis/dissertation. *Entrance requirements:* For master's, minimum GPA of 2.75; for doctorate, minimum GPA of 3.0.

Stevens Institute of Technology, Graduate School, Charles V. Schaefer Jr. School of Engineering and Science, Department of Civil, Environmental, and Ocean Engineering, Program in Environmental Engineering, Hoboken, NJ 07030. Offers environmental engineering (PhD, Certificate), including environmental compatibility in engineering (Certificate), environmental hydrology (Certificate), environmental processes (Certificate), hydraulics (Certificate), soil and groundwater pollution control (Certificate), water quality control (Certificate); environmental processes (M Eng); inland and coastal environmental hydrodynamics (M Eng); modeling of environmental systems (M Eng); soil and groundwater pollution control (M Eng). *Program availability:* Part-time, evening/weekend. *Faculty:* 23 full-time (8 women), 21 part-time/adjunct (2 women). *Students:* 46 full-time (18 women), 14 part-time (6 women); includes 7 minority (2 Black or African American, non-Hispanic/Latino; 4 Asian, non-Hispanic/Latino; 1 Hispanic/Latino), 35 international. Average age 28. In 2019, 31 master's, 2 doctorates, 10 other advanced degrees awarded. Terminal master's awarded for partial completion of doctoral program. *Degree requirements:* For master's, thesis optional, minimum B average in major field and overall; for doctorate, comprehensive exam (for some programs), thesis/dissertation; for Certificate, minimum B average. *Entrance requirements:* For master's, International applicants must submit TOEFL/IELTS scores and fulfill the English Language Proficiency Requirement. Applicants to full-time programs who do not qualify for a score waiver are required to submit GRE/GMAT scores. Additional exam requirements/recommendations for international students: required—TOEFL (minimum score 74 iBT), IELTS (minimum score 6). *Application deadline:* For fall admission, 4/15 for domestic and international students; for spring admission, 11/1 for domestic and international students; for summer admission, 5/1 for domestic students. Applications are processed on a rolling basis. Application fee: $60. Electronic applications accepted. *Expenses: Tuition:* Full-time $52,134. *Required fees:* $1880. Tuition and fees vary according to course load. *Financial support:* Fellowships, research assistantships, teaching assistantships, career-related internships or fieldwork, Federal Work-Study, scholarships/grants, and unspecified assistantships available. Financial award application deadline: 2/15; financial award applicants required to submit FAFSA. *Unit head:* Dr. Jean Zu, Dean of SES, 201-216.8233, Fax: 201-216.8372, E-mail: Jean.Zu@stevens.edu. *Application contact:* Graduate Admission, 888-783-8367, Fax: 888-511-1306, E-mail: graduate@stevens.edu.

University of Colorado Denver, College of Engineering, Design and Computing, Department of Civil Engineering, Denver, CO 80217. Offers civil engineering (EASPh D); civil engineering systems (PhD); environmental and sustainability engineering (MS, PhD); geographic information systems (MS); geotechnical engineering (MS, PhD); hydrology and hydraulics (MS, PhD); structural engineering (MS, PhD); transportation engineering (MS, PhD). *Program availability:* Part-time, evening/weekend. *Degree requirements:* For master's, comprehensive exam, 30 credit hours, project or thesis; for doctorate, comprehensive exam, thesis/dissertation, 60 credit hours (30 of which are dissertation research). *Entrance requirements:* For master's, GRE, statement of purpose, transcripts, three references; for doctorate, GRE, statement of purpose, transcripts, references, letter of support from faculty stating willingness to serve as dissertation advisor and outlining plan for financial support. Additional exam requirements/recommendations for international students: required—TOEFL (minimum score 537 paper-based; 75 iBT); recommended—IELTS (minimum score 6.5). Electronic applications accepted. Tuition and fees vary according to course load, program and reciprocity agreements.

The University of Iowa, Graduate College, College of Engineering, Department of Civil and Environmental Engineering, Iowa City, IA 52242-1316. Offers environmental engineering and science (MS, PhD); hydraulics and water resources (MS, PhD); structures, mechanics and materials (MS, PhD); sustainable water development (MS, PhD); transportation engineering (MS, PhD). *Program availability:* Part-time. Terminal master's awarded for partial completion of doctoral program. *Degree requirements:* For master's, thesis optional, exam; for doctorate, comprehensive exam, thesis/dissertation, exam. *Entrance requirements:* For master's, GRE (minimum combined score of 301 on verbal and quantitative), minimum undergraduate GPA of 3.0; for doctorate, GRE (minimum combined score of 301 on verbal and quantitative), minimum graduate GPA of 3.0. Additional exam requirements/recommendations for international students: required—TOEFL (minimum score 550 paper-based; 81 iBT), IELTS (minimum score 7). Electronic applications accepted.

Structural Engineering

California State University, Northridge, Graduate Studies, College of Engineering and Computer Science, Department of Civil Engineering and Construction Management, Northridge, CA 91330. Offers engineering (MS), including structural engineering. *Program availability:* Part-time, evening/weekend. *Degree requirements:* For master's, thesis. *Entrance requirements:* Additional exam requirements/recommendations for international students: required—TOEFL.

The Citadel, The Military College of South Carolina, Citadel Graduate College, School of Engineering, Department of Civil and Environmental Engineering, Charleston, SC 29409. Offers built environment and public health (Graduate Certificate); civil engineering (MS); geotechnical engineering (Graduate Certificate); structural engineering (Graduate Certificate); transportation engineering (Graduate Certificate). *Program availability:* Part-time, evening/weekend. *Degree requirements:* For master's, plan of study outlining intended areas of interest and top four corresponding courses of interest. *Entrance requirements:* For master's, official transcript of baccalaureate degree from ABET-accredited engineering program or approved alternative; 2 letters of recommendation; for Graduate Certificate, official transcript of baccalaureate degree directly from an accredited college or university. Additional exam requirements/recommendations for international students: required—TOEFL (minimum score 550 paper-based; 79 iBT). Electronic applications accepted.

Clemson University, Graduate School, College of Engineering, Computing and Applied Sciences, Glenn Department of Civil Engineering, Clemson, SC 29634. Offers civil engineering (MS, PhD), including construction engineering and management, construction materials, geotechnical engineering, structural engineering, transportation engineering, water resources engineering. *Program availability:* Part-time, 100% online. *Faculty:* 24 full-time (4 women), 3 part-time/adjunct (2 women). *Students:* 101 full-time (20 women), 44 part-time (9 women); includes 9 minority (3 Black or African American, non-Hispanic/Latino; 1 Asian, non-Hispanic/Latino; 2 Hispanic/Latino; 3 Two or more races, non-Hispanic/Latino), 97 international. Average age 29. 248 applicants, 62% accepted, 61 enrolled. In 2019, 43 master's, 11 doctorates awarded. *Degree requirements:* For master's, thesis or alternative, oral exam, seminar; for doctorate, comprehensive exam, thesis/dissertation, oral exam, seminar. *Entrance requirements:* For master's and doctorate, GRE General Test, unofficial transcripts, letters of recommendation, statement of purpose. Additional exam requirements/recommendations for international students: required—TOEFL (minimum score 80 paper-based; 80 iBT), PTE (minimum score 54); recommended—IELTS (minimum score 6.5). *Application deadline:* For fall admission, 4/15 for domestic and international students; for spring admission, 9/15 for domestic and international students. Applications are processed on a rolling basis. Application fee: $80 ($90 for international students). Electronic applications accepted. *Expenses: Tuition, area resident:* Full-time $10,600; part-time $8688 per semester. Tuition, state resident: full-time $10,600; part-time $8688 per semester. Tuition, nonresident: full-time $22,050; part-time $17,412 per semester. *International tuition:* $22,050 full-time. *Required fees:* $1196; $617 per semester. $617 per semester. Tuition and fees vary according to course load, degree level, campus/location and program. *Financial support:* In 2019–20, 101 students received support, including 2 fellowships with full and partial tuition reimbursements available (averaging $34,000 per year), 61 research assistantships with full and partial tuition reimbursements available (averaging $18,222 per year), 4 teaching assistantships with full and partial tuition reimbursements available (averaging $20,567 per year); career-related internships or fieldwork and unspecified assistantships also available. Financial award application deadline: 4/15. *Unit head:* Dr. Jesus M de la Garza, Department Chair, 864-656-3001, E-mail: jdelaga@clemson.edu. *Application contact:* Dr. Abdul Khan, Graduate Program Coordinator, 864-656-3327, E-mail: abdkhan@clemson.edu.
Website: https://www.clemson.edu/cecas/departments/ce/

Cornell University, Graduate School, Graduate Fields of Engineering, Field of Civil and Environmental Engineering, Ithaca, NY 14853. Offers engineering management (M Eng, MS, PhD); environmental engineering (M Eng, MS, PhD); environmental fluid mechanics and hydrology (M Eng, MS, PhD); environmental systems engineering (M Eng, MS, PhD); geotechnical engineering (M Eng, MS, PhD); remote sensing (M Eng, MS, PhD); structural engineering (M Eng, MS, PhD); structural mechanics (M Eng, MS); transportation engineering (MS, PhD); transportation systems engineering (M Eng);

water resource systems (M Eng, MS, PhD). Terminal master's awarded for partial completion of doctoral program. *Degree requirements:* For master's, thesis (MS); for doctorate, comprehensive exam, thesis/dissertation. *Entrance requirements:* For master's and doctorate, GRE General Test (recommended), 2 letters of recommendation. Additional exam requirements/recommendations for international students: required—TOEFL (minimum score 600 paper-based; 77 iBT). Electronic applications accepted.

Drexel University, College of Engineering, Department of Civil, Architectural, and Environmental Engineering, Philadelphia, PA 19104-2875. Offers architectural/building systems engineering (MS, PhD); civil engineering (MS, PhD); environmental engineering (MS, PhD); geotechnical, geoenvironmental and geosynthetics engineering (MS, PhD); hydraulics, hydrology and water resources engineering (MS, PhD); structures (MS). *Program availability:* Part-time, evening/weekend. *Degree requirements:* For master's, thesis optional; for doctorate, thesis/dissertation. *Entrance requirements:* For master's, minimum GPA of 3.0; for doctorate, minimum GPA of 3.5, MS in civil engineering. Additional exam requirements/recommendations for international students: required—TOEFL. Electronic applications accepted.

Illinois Institute of Technology, Graduate College, Armour College of Engineering, Department of Civil, Architectural and Environmental Engineering, Chicago, IL 60616. Offers architectural engineering (M Arch E); civil engineering (MS, PhD), including architectural engineering (MS), construction engineering and management (MS), geoenvironmental engineering (MS), geotechnical engineering (MS), structural engineering (MS), transportation engineering (MS); construction engineering and management (MCEM); environmental engineering (M Env E, MS, PhD); geoenvironmental engineering (M Geoenv E); geotechnical engineering (MGE); infrastructure engineering and management (MPW); structural engineering (MSE); transportation engineering (M Trans E). *Program availability:* Part-time, evening/weekend, online learning. Terminal master's awarded for partial completion of doctoral program. *Degree requirements:* For master's, thesis (for some programs); for doctorate, comprehensive exam, thesis/dissertation. *Entrance requirements:* For master's, GRE General Test (minimum score 900 Quantitative and Verbal, 2.5 Analytical Writing), minimum undergraduate GPA of 3.0; for doctorate, GRE General Test (minimum score 1000 Quantitative and Verbal, 3.0 Analytical Writing), minimum undergraduate GPA of 3.0. Additional exam requirements/recommendations for international students: required—TOEFL (minimum score 550 paper-based; 80 iBT). Electronic applications accepted.

Instituto Tecnologico de Santo Domingo, Graduate School, Area of Engineering, Santo Domingo, Dominican Republic. Offers construction administration (MS, Certificate); data telecommunications (M Eng, MS, Certificate); industrial engineering (M Eng, Certificate); industrial management (M Mgmt); information technology (Certificate); maintenance engineering (M Eng); occupational hazard prevention (M Mgmt); production management (Certificate); quantitative methods (Certificate); sanitary and environmental engineering (M Eng); structural engineering (M Eng); systems engineering and electronic data processing (Certificate); transportation (Certificate).

Iowa State University of Science and Technology, Department of Civil and Construction Engineering, Ames, IA 50011. Offers civil engineering (MS, PhD), including civil engineering materials, construction engineering and management, environmental engineering, geotechnical engineering, structural engineering, transportation engineering. *Degree requirements:* For master's, thesis or alternative; for doctorate, thesis/dissertation. *Entrance requirements:* For master's and doctorate, GRE General Test. Additional exam requirements/recommendations for international students: required—TOEFL (minimum score 550 paper-based; 82 iBT), IELTS (minimum score 6.5). Electronic applications accepted.

Kansas State University, Graduate School, College of Engineering, Department of Civil Engineering, Manhattan, KS 66506. Offers civil engineering (MS, PhD); environmental engineering (MS, PhD); geotechnical engineering (MS, PhD); structural engineering (MS, PhD); transportation engineering (MS, PhD); water resources engineering (MS, PhD). *Program availability:* Part-time, evening/weekend, online learning. *Degree requirements:* For master's, thesis or alternative; for doctorate, thesis/dissertation. *Entrance requirements:* For master's, GRE General Test, bachelor's degree or course work in related engineering fields; for doctorate, GRE General Test. Additional exam requirements/recommendations for international students: required—TOEFL (minimum score 550 paper-based; 79 iBT). Electronic applications accepted.

Kennesaw State University, Southern Polytechnic College of Engineering and Engineering Technology, Program in Civil Engineering, Kennesaw, GA 30144. Offers environmental engineering (MS); geotechnical engineering (MS); structural engineering (MS); transportation and pavement engineering (MS); water resources engineering (MS). *Program availability:* Online learning. *Students:* 9 full-time (2 women), 30 part-time (4 women); includes 20 minority (9 Black or African American, non-Hispanic/Latino; 5 Asian, non-Hispanic/Latino; 5 Hispanic/Latino; 1 Two or more races, non-Hispanic/Latino), 3 international. Average age 34. 12 applicants, 92% accepted, 8 enrolled. In 2019, 12 master's awarded. *Degree requirements:* For master's, thesis optional. *Entrance requirements:* Additional exam requirements/recommendations for international students: required—TOEFL (minimum score 80 iBT), IELTS (minimum score 6.5). *Application deadline:* For fall admission, 11/1 for domestic and international students; for spring admission, 4/1 for domestic and international students. Applications are processed on a rolling basis. Application fee: $60. Electronic applications accepted. *Expenses: Tuition, area resident:* Full-time $7104; part-time $296 per credit hour. Tuition, state resident: full-time $7104; part-time $296 per credit hour. Tuition, nonresident: full-time $25,584; part-time $1066 per credit hour. *International tuition:* $25,584 full-time. *Required fees:* $2006; $1706 per unit. $853 per semester. *Unit head:* Metin Oguzmert, Coordinator, 470-578-5083, E-mail: moguzmer@kennesaw.edu. *Application contact:* Admissions Counselor, 470-578-4377, E-mail: ksugrad@kennesaw.edu.
Website: http://engineering.kennesaw.edu/civil-construction/degrees/ms-civil-engineering.php

Louisiana State University and Agricultural & Mechanical College, Graduate School, College of Engineering, Department of Civil and Environmental Engineering, Baton Rouge, LA 70803. Offers environmental engineering (MSCE, PhD); geotechnical engineering (MSCE, PhD); structural engineering and mechanics (MSCE, PhD); transportation engineering (MSCE, PhD); water resources (MSCE, PhD).

Marquette University, Graduate School, College of Engineering, Department of Civil and Environmental Engineering, Milwaukee, WI 53201-1881. Offers construction engineering and management (MS, PhD, Certificate); environmental engineering (MS, PhD); structural design (Certificate); structural engineering and structural mechanics (MS, PhD); transportation (Certificate); transportation engineering and materials (MS, PhD); waste and wastewater treatment processes (Certificate); water resources engineering (Certificate). *Program availability:* Part-time, evening/weekend. Terminal master's awarded for partial completion of doctoral program. *Degree requirements:* For master's, comprehensive exam (for some programs), thesis or alternative; for doctorate, thesis/dissertation. *Entrance requirements:* For master's, GRE General Test (recommended), minimum GPA of 3.0, official transcripts from all current and previous colleges/universities except Marquette, three letters of recommendation; for doctorate, GRE General Test, minimum GPA of 3.0, official transcripts from all current and previous colleges/universities except Marquette, three letters of recommendation, brief statement of purpose, submission of any English language publications authored by applicant (strongly recommended). Additional exam requirements/recommendations for international students: required—TOEFL (minimum score 530 paper-based). Electronic applications accepted.

Massachusetts Institute of Technology, School of Engineering, Department of Civil and Environmental Engineering, Cambridge, MA 02139. Offers biological oceanography (PhD, Sc D); chemical oceanography (PhD, Sc D); civil and environmental engineering (M Eng, SM, PhD, Sc D); civil and environmental systems (PhD, Sc D); civil engineering (PhD, Sc D, CE); civil engineering and computation (PhD); coastal engineering (PhD, Sc D); construction engineering and management (PhD, Sc D); environmental biology (PhD, Sc D); environmental chemistry (PhD, Sc D); environmental engineering (PhD, Sc D); environmental engineering and computation (PhD); environmental fluid mechanics (PhD, Sc D); geotechnical and geoenvironmental engineering (PhD, Sc D); hydrology (PhD, Sc D); information technology (PhD, Sc D); oceanographic engineering (PhD, Sc D); structures and materials (PhD, Sc D); transportation (PhD, Sc D); SM/MBA. *Degree requirements:* For master's, thesis; for doctorate, comprehensive exam, thesis/dissertation; for CE, comprehensive exam, thesis. *Entrance requirements:* For master's, doctorate, and CE, GRE General Test. Additional exam requirements/recommendations for international students: required—TOEFL, IELTS. Electronic applications accepted.

McGill University, Faculty of Graduate and Postdoctoral Studies, Faculty of Engineering, Department of Civil Engineering and Applied Mechanics, Montréal, QC H3A 2T5, Canada. Offers environmental engineering (M Eng, M Sc, PhD); fluid mechanics (M Sc); fluid mechanics and hydraulic engineering (M Eng, PhD); materials engineering (M Eng, PhD); rehabilitation of urban infrastructure (M Eng, PhD); soil behavior (M Eng, PhD); soil mechanics and foundations (M Eng, PhD); structures and structural mechanics (M Eng, PhD); water resources (M Sc); water resources engineering (M Eng, PhD).

Northwestern University, McCormick School of Engineering and Applied Science, Department of Civil and Environmental Engineering, Evanston, IL 60208-3109. Offers environmental engineering and science (MS, PhD); geotechnical engineering (MS, PhD); mechanics of materials and solids (MS, PhD); project management (MS); structural engineering and materials (MS, PhD); transportation systems analysis and planning (MS, PhD). *Program availability:* Part-time. Terminal master's awarded for partial completion of doctoral program. *Degree requirements:* For master's, comprehensive exam (for some programs), thesis (for some programs); for doctorate, comprehensive exam, thesis/dissertation. *Entrance requirements:* For master's and doctorate, GRE General Test, minimum 2 letters of recommendation, transcripts from all academic institutions attended. Additional exam requirements/recommendations for international students: required—TOEFL (minimum score 577 paper-based; 90 iBT), IELTS (minimum score 7). Electronic applications accepted.

Norwich University, College of Graduate and Continuing Studies, Master of Civil Engineering Program, Northfield, VT 05663. Offers construction management (MCE); environmental (MCE); geotechnical (MCE); structural (MCE). *Program availability:* Evening/weekend, online only, mostly all online with a week-long residency requirement. *Degree requirements:* For master's, capstone. *Entrance requirements:* For master's, minimum undergraduate GPA of 2.75. Additional exam requirements/recommendations for international students: required—TOEFL (minimum score 550 paper-based; 80 iBT), IELTS (minimum score 6.5). Electronic applications accepted. *Expenses:* Contact institution.

Ohio University, Graduate College, Russ College of Engineering and Technology, Department of Civil Engineering, Athens, OH 45701-2979. Offers civil engineering (PhD); construction engineering and management (MS); environmental (MS); geoenvironmental (MS); geotechnical (MS); mechanics (MS); structures (MS); transportation (MS); water resources (MS). *Program availability:* Part-time. *Degree requirements:* For master's, comprehensive exam (for some programs), thesis or alternative; for doctorate, comprehensive exam, thesis/dissertation. *Entrance requirements:* For master's, GRE General Test, minimum GPA of 3.0, 3 letters of recommendation; for doctorate, GRE General Test. Additional exam requirements/recommendations for international students: required—TOEFL (minimum score 550 paper-based; 80 iBT) or IELTS (minimum score 6.5). Electronic applications accepted.

Old Dominion University, Frank Batten College of Engineering and Technology, Program in Civil Engineering, Norfolk, VA 23529. Offers civil engineering (ME, MS), including coastal engineering, geotechnical engineering, hydraulics and water resources, structural engineering, transportation engineering. *Program availability:* Part-time, evening/weekend, blended/hybrid learning. *Degree requirements:* For master's, comprehensive exam, thesis optional. *Entrance requirements:* For master's, GRE, minimum GPA of 3.0. Additional exam requirements/recommendations for international students: required—TOEFL (minimum score 550 paper-based, 80 iBT) or IELTS (6.5). Electronic applications accepted. *Expenses:* Contact institution.

Oregon State University, College of Engineering, Program in Civil Engineering, Corvallis, OR 97331. Offers civil engineering (M Eng, MS, PhD); coastal and ocean engineering (M Eng, MS, PhD); construction engineering management (M Eng, MS, PhD); engineering education (M Eng, MS, PhD); geomatics (M Eng, MS, PhD); geotechnical engineering (M Eng, MS, PhD); infrastructure materials (M Eng, MS, PhD); structural engineering (M Eng, MS, PhD); transportation engineering (M Eng). *Entrance requirements:* For master's and doctorate, GRE. Additional exam requirements/recommendations for international students: required—TOEFL (minimum score 80 iBT), IELTS (minimum score 6.5). *Expenses:* Contact institution.

Penn State Harrisburg, Graduate School, School of Science, Engineering and Technology, Middletown, PA 17057. Offers civil engineering (MS); computer science (MS); electrical engineering (M Eng, MS); engineering management (MPS); engineering science (M Eng); environmental engineering (M Eng); environmental pollution control (MEPC, MS); mechanical engineering (MS); structural engineering (Certificate). *Program availability:* Part-time, evening/weekend.

Polytechnique Montréal, Graduate Programs, Department of Civil, Geological and Mining Engineering, Montréal, QC H3C 3A7, Canada. Offers civil, geological and mining engineering (DESS); environmental engineering (M Eng, M Sc A, PhD); geotechnical engineering (M Eng, M Sc A, PhD); hydraulics engineering (M Eng, M Sc A, PhD); structural engineering (M Eng, M Sc A, PhD); transportation engineering (M Eng, M Sc A, PhD). *Program availability:* Part-time. *Degree requirements:* For master's, one foreign language, thesis; for doctorate, one foreign language, thesis/dissertation. *Entrance requirements:* For master's, minimum GPA of 2.75; for doctorate, minimum GPA of 3.0.

Pontificia Universidad Catolica Madre y Maestra, Graduate School, Faculty of Engineering Sciences, Santiago, Dominican Republic. Offers earthquake engineering (ME); logistics management (ME).

Structural Engineering

Southern Illinois University Edwardsville, Graduate School, School of Engineering, Department of Civil Engineering, Program in Structural Engineering, Edwardsville, IL 62026. Offers MS. *Program availability:* Part-time, evening/weekend. *Degree requirements:* For master's, thesis (for some programs), research paper. *Entrance requirements:* For master's, minimum undergraduate GPA of 2.75 in science, math, and engineering courses. Additional exam requirements/recommendations for international students: required—TOEFL (minimum score 550 paper-based, 79 iBT), IELTS (minimum score 6.5), Michigan Test of English Language Proficiency or PTE. Electronic applications accepted.

Southern Methodist University, Lyle School of Engineering, Department of Civil and Environmental Engineering, Dallas, TX 75275-0340. Offers civil and environmental engineering (PhD); civil engineering (MS), including geotechnical engineering, structural engineering, transportation systems; environmental engineering (MS); sustainability and development (MA). *Program availability:* Part-time, evening/weekend, online learning. Terminal master's awarded for partial completion of doctoral program. *Degree requirements:* For master's, thesis optional; for doctorate, thesis/dissertation, oral and written qualifying exams. *Entrance requirements:* For master's, GRE General Test, minimum GPA of 3.0 in last 2 years; bachelor's degree in engineering, mathematics, or sciences; for doctorate, GRE, BS and MS in related field, minimum GPA of 3.3. Additional exam requirements/recommendations for international students: required—TOEFL. Electronic applications accepted.

Stanford University, School of Engineering, Department of Civil and Environmental Engineering, Stanford, CA 94305-2004. Offers atmosphere and energy (MS, PhD); construction (MS), including construction engineering and management, design-construction integration, sustainable design and construction; environmental engineering and science (MS, PhD); environmental fluid mechanics and hydrology (PhD); structural engineering (MS). *Expenses: Tuition:* Full-time $52,479; part-time $34,110 per unit. *Required fees:* $672; $224 per quarter. Tuition and fees vary according to program and student level.
Website: http://www-ce.stanford.edu/

Stevens Institute of Technology, Graduate School, Charles V. Schaefer Jr. School of Engineering and Science, Department of Civil, Environmental, and Ocean Engineering, Program in Civil Engineering, Hoboken, NJ 07030. Offers civil engineering (PhD, Certificate), including geotechnical engineering (Certificate); geotechnical/geoenvironmental engineering (M Eng, Engr); hydrologic modeling (M Eng); stormwater management (M Eng); structural engineering (M Eng, Engr); transportation engineering (M Eng); water resources engineering (M Eng). *Program availability:* Part-time, evening/weekend. *Faculty:* 23 full-time (8 women), 21 part-time/adjunct (2 women). *Students:* 38 full-time (6 women), 19 part-time (6 women); includes 11 minority (2 Black or African American, non-Hispanic/Latino; 1 American Indian or Alaska Native, non-Hispanic/Latino; 8 Asian, non-Hispanic/Latino), 29 international. Average age 25. In 2019, 38 master's, 2 doctorates awarded. Terminal master's awarded for partial completion of doctoral program. *Degree requirements:* For master's, thesis optional, minimum B average in major field and overall; for doctorate, comprehensive exam (for some programs), thesis/dissertation; for other advanced degree, minimum B average. *Entrance requirements:* For master's, International applicants must submit TOEFL/IELTS scores and fulfill the English Language Proficiency Requirement. Applicants to full-time programs who do not qualify for a score waiver are required to submit GRE/GMAT scores. Additional exam requirements/recommendations for international students: required—TOEFL (minimum score 74 iBT), IELTS (minimum score 6). *Application deadline:* For fall admission, 4/15 for domestic and international students; for spring admission, 11/1 for domestic and international students; for summer admission, 5/1 for domestic students. Applications are processed on a rolling basis. Application fee: $60. Electronic applications accepted. *Expenses: Tuition:* Full-time $52,134. *Required fees:* $1880. Tuition and fees vary according to course load. *Financial support:* Fellowships, research assistantships, teaching assistantships, career-related internships or fieldwork, Federal Work-Study, scholarships/grants, and unspecified assistantships available. Financial award application deadline: 2/15; financial award applicants required to submit FAFSA. *Unit head:* Dr. Jean Zu, Dean of SES, 201-216.8233, Fax: 201-216.8372, E-mail: Jean.Zu@stevens.edu. *Application contact:* Graduate Admission, 888-783-8367, Fax: 888-511-1306, E-mail: graduate@stevens.edu.

Tufts University, School of Engineering, Department of Civil and Environmental Engineering, Medford, MA 02155. Offers bioengineering (MS), including environmental biotechnology; civil and environmental engineering (MS, PhD), including applied data science, environmental and water resources engineering, environmental health, geosystems engineering, structural engineering and mechanics; PhD/PhD. *Program availability:* Part-time. Terminal master's awarded for partial completion of doctoral program. *Degree requirements:* For master's, thesis (for some programs); for doctorate, thesis/dissertation. *Entrance requirements:* For master's and doctorate, GRE General Test. Additional exam requirements/recommendations for international students: required—TOEFL (minimum score 550 paper-based; 80 iBT), IELTS (minimum score 6.5). Electronic applications accepted. Full-time tuition and fees vary according to degree level, program and student level. Part-time tuition and fees vary according to course load.

University at Buffalo, the State University of New York, Graduate School, School of Engineering and Applied Sciences, Department of Civil, Structural, and Environmental Engineering, Buffalo, NY 14260. Offers civil engineering (MS, PhD); engineering science (MS), including data sciences, green energy, Internet of Things, nanoelectronics; environmental and water resources engineering (MS). *Program availability:* Part-time, online learning. Terminal master's awarded for partial completion of doctoral program. *Degree requirements:* For master's, project, thesis, or comprehensive exam; for doctorate, thesis/dissertation. *Entrance requirements:* For master's and doctorate, GRE General Test, letters of reference. Additional exam requirements/recommendations for international students: required—TOEFL (minimum score 550 paper-based; 79 iBT). Electronic applications accepted. *Expenses: Tuition, area resident:* Full-time $11,310; part-time $471 per credit hour. Tuition, state resident: full-time $11,310; part-time $471 per credit hour. Tuition, nonresident: full-time $23,100; part-time $963 per credit hour. *International tuition:* $23,100 full-time. *Required fees:* $2820.

The University of Alabama at Birmingham, School of Engineering, Professional Engineering Degrees, Birmingham, AL 35294. Offers advanced safety engineering and management (M Eng); construction engineering management (M Eng); design and commercialization (M Eng); information engineering management (M Eng); structural engineering (M Eng); sustainable smart cities (M Eng). *Program availability:* Part-time, evening/weekend, online only, 100% online. *Faculty:* 5 full-time (1 woman), 15 part-time/adjunct (3 women). *Students:* 13 full-time (4 women), 315 part-time (70 women); includes 83 minority (64 Black or African American, non-Hispanic/Latino; 3 American Indian or Alaska Native, non-Hispanic/Latino; 9 Asian, non-Hispanic/Latino; 7 Hispanic/Latino), 8 international. 126 applicants, 84% accepted, 90 enrolled. In 2019, 123 master's awarded. *Entrance requirements:* For master's, 3.0 GPA on 4.0 scale, undergraduate degree from a nationally accredited school. Additional exam requirements/recommendations for international students: required—TOEFL (minimum score 80 iBT); recommended—IELTS (minimum score 6.5). *Application deadline:* For fall admission, 8/1 for domestic and international students; for spring admission, 12/1 for domestic and international students; for summer admission, 5/1 for domestic and international students. Applications are processed on a rolling basis. Application fee: $50 ($60 for international students). Electronic applications accepted. *Expenses:* Contact institution. *Unit head:* Dr. Gregg Janowski, Associate Dean for Graduate Programs and Assessment, E-mail: janowski@uab.edu. *Application contact:* Jesse Kepply, Director of Student and Academic Services, 205-996-5696, E-mail: gradschool@uab.edu.

University of Alberta, Faculty of Graduate Studies and Research, Department of Civil and Environmental Engineering, Edmonton, AB T6G 2E1, Canada. Offers construction engineering and management (M Eng, M Sc, PhD); environmental engineering (M Eng, M Sc, PhD); environmental science (M Sc, PhD); geoenvironmental engineering (M Eng, M Sc, PhD); geotechnical engineering (M Eng, M Sc, PhD); mining engineering (M Eng, M Sc, PhD); petroleum engineering (M Eng, M Sc, PhD); structural engineering (M Eng, M Sc, PhD); water resources (M Eng, M Sc, PhD). *Program availability:* Part-time, online learning. *Degree requirements:* For master's, thesis (for some programs); for doctorate, thesis/dissertation. *Entrance requirements:* For master's, minimum GPA of 3.0 in last 2 years of undergraduate studies; for doctorate, minimum GPA of 3.0. Additional exam requirements/recommendations for international students: required—TOEFL (minimum score 550 paper-based). Electronic applications accepted.

University of Calgary, Faculty of Graduate Studies, Schulich School of Engineering, Program in Civil Engineering, Calgary, AB T2N 1N4, Canada. Offers avalanche mechanics (M Sc, PhD); civil engineering (M Eng, M Sc, PhD); energy and environment engineering (M Eng, M Sc, PhD); environmental engineering (M Eng, M Sc, PhD); geotechnical engineering (M Eng, M Sc, PhD); materials science (M Eng, M Sc, PhD); project management (M Eng, M Sc, PhD); structures and solid mechanics (M Eng, M Sc, PhD); transportation engineering (M Eng, M Sc, PhD); water resources (M Eng, M Sc, PhD). *Program availability:* Part-time. *Degree requirements:* For master's, thesis; for doctorate, thesis/dissertation, written and oral candidacy exam. *Entrance requirements:* For master's, minimum GPA of 3.0; for doctorate, minimum GPA of 3.5. Additional exam requirements/recommendations for international students: required—TOEFL (minimum score 580 paper-based; 93 iBT), IELTS (minimum score 7). Electronic applications accepted.

University of California, Berkeley, Graduate Division, College of Engineering, Department of Civil and Environmental Engineering, Berkeley, CA 94720. Offers engineering and project management (M Eng, MS, PhD); environmental engineering (M Eng, MS, PhD); geoengineering (M Eng, MS, PhD); structural engineering, mechanics and materials (M Eng, MS, PhD); transportation engineering (M Eng, MS, PhD); M Arch/MS; MCP/MS; MPP/MS. Terminal master's awarded for partial completion of doctoral program. *Degree requirements:* For master's, comprehensive exam (for some programs), thesis (for some programs), comprehensive exam or thesis (MS); for doctorate, thesis/dissertation, qualifying exam. *Entrance requirements:* For master's, GRE General Test, minimum GPA of 3.0, 3 letters of recommendation; for doctorate, GRE General Test, minimum GPA of 3.5, 3 letters of recommendation. Additional exam requirements/recommendations for international students: required—TOEFL (minimum score 570 paper-based; 90 iBT). Electronic applications accepted.

University of California, San Diego, Graduate Division, Department of Structural Engineering, La Jolla, CA 92093. Offers structural engineering (MS, PhD); structural health monitoring, prognosis, and validated simulations (MS). *Students:* 164 full-time (40 women), 20 part-time (6 women). 386 applicants, 57% accepted, 72 enrolled. In 2019, 65 master's, 12 doctorates awarded. *Degree requirements:* For master's, comprehensive exam (for some programs), thesis (for some programs); for doctorate, comprehensive exam, thesis/dissertation, 1-quarter teaching assistantship. *Entrance requirements:* For master's and doctorate, GRE General Test. Additional exam requirements/recommendations for international students: required—TOEFL (minimum score 550 paper-based; 80 iBT), IELTS (minimum score 7). *Application deadline:* For fall admission, 1/29 for domestic students. Application fee: $105 ($125 for international students). Electronic applications accepted. *Financial support:* Fellowships, research assistantships, teaching assistantships, scholarships/grants, and readerships available. Financial award applicants required to submit FAFSA. *Unit head:* John McCartney, Chair, 858-534-9630, E-mail: mccartney@eng.ucsd.edu. *Application contact:* Joana Halnez, Graduate Coordinator, 858-534-4185, E-mail: se-info@ucsd.edu.
Website: http://www.structures.ucsd.edu/

University of Central Florida, College of Engineering and Computer Science, Department of Civil, Environmental, and Construction Engineering, Orlando, FL 32816. Offers civil engineering (PhD, Certificate), including civil engineering (PhD), structural engineering (Certificate), transportation engineering (Certificate); environmental engineering (MS, PhD). *Program availability:* Part-time, evening/weekend. *Students:* 110 full-time (38 women), 81 part-time (23 women); includes 38 minority (5 Black or African American, non-Hispanic/Latino; 7 Asian, non-Hispanic/Latino; 25 Hispanic/Latino; 1 Two or more races, non-Hispanic/Latino), 87 international. Average age 30. 162 applicants, 46% accepted, 41 enrolled. In 2019, 30 master's, 19 doctorates, 3 other advanced degrees awarded. *Degree requirements:* For master's, thesis or alternative; for doctorate, comprehensive exam, thesis/dissertation, departmental qualifying exam, candidacy exam. *Entrance requirements:* For master's, letters of recommendation, resume, goal statement; for doctorate, GRE General Test, letters of recommendation, resume, goal statement. Additional exam requirements/recommendations for international students: required—TOEFL. *Application deadline:* For fall admission, 7/15 priority date for domestic students; for spring admission, 12/1 priority date for domestic students. Application fee: $30. Electronic applications accepted. *Financial support:* In 2019–20, 76 students received support, including 22 fellowships with partial tuition reimbursements available (averaging $13,082 per year), 55 research assistantships with partial tuition reimbursements available (averaging $7,773 per year), 17 teaching assistantships with partial tuition reimbursements available (averaging $6,990 per year); career-related internships or fieldwork, Federal Work-Study, institutionally sponsored loans, health care benefits, tuition waivers (partial), and unspecified assistantships also available. Financial award application deadline: 3/1; financial award applicants required to submit FAFSA. *Unit head:* Dr. Mohamed Abdel-Aty, Chair, 407-823-2841, E-mail: m.aty@ucf.edu. *Application contact:* Associate Director, Graduate Admissions, 407-823-2766, Fax: 407-823-6442, E-mail: gradadmissions@ucf.edu.
Website: http://cece.ucf.edu/

University of Colorado Denver, College of Engineering, Design and Computing, Department of Civil Engineering, Denver, CO 80217. Offers civil engineering (EASPh D); civil engineering systems (PhD); environmental and sustainability engineering (MS, PhD); geographic information systems (MS); geotechnical engineering (MS, PhD); hydrology and hydraulics (MS, PhD); structural engineering (MS, PhD); transportation engineering (MS, PhD). *Program availability:* Part-time, evening/weekend. *Degree requirements:* For master's, comprehensive exam, 30 credit hours, project or thesis; for doctorate, comprehensive exam, thesis/dissertation, 60 credit hours (30 of which are dissertation research). *Entrance requirements:* For master's, GRE, statement of purpose, transcripts, three references; for doctorate, GRE, statement of purpose, transcripts, references, letter of support from faculty stating willingness to serve as dissertation advisor and outlining plan for financial support. Additional exam requirements/recommendations for international students: required—TOEFL (minimum score 537 paper-based; 75 iBT); recommended—IELTS (minimum score 6.5). Electronic applications accepted. Tuition and fees vary according to course load, program and reciprocity agreements.

University of Dayton, Department of Civil and Environmental Engineering and Engineering Mechanics, Dayton, OH 45469. Offers engineering mechanics (MSEM); environmental engineering (MSCE); geotechnical engineering (MSCE); structural engineering (MSCE); transportation engineering (MSCE); water resources engineering (MSCE). *Program availability:* Part-time, blended/hybrid learning. *Degree requirements:* For master's, thesis or alternative. *Entrance requirements:* For master's, minimum GPA of 3.0 in undergraduate work. Additional exam requirements/recommendations for international students: required—TOEFL (minimum score 550 paper-based; 80 iBT); recommended—IELTS (minimum score 6.5), TSE (minimum score 60). Electronic applications accepted.

University of Delaware, College of Engineering, Department of Civil and Environmental Engineering, Newark, DE 19716. Offers environmental engineering (MAS, MCE, PhD); geotechnical engineering (MAS, MCE, PhD); ocean engineering (MAS, MCE, PhD); structural engineering (MAS, MCE, PhD); transportation engineering (MAS, MCE, PhD); water resource engineering (MAS, MCE, PhD). *Program availability:* Part-time. Terminal master's awarded for partial completion of doctoral program. *Degree requirements:* For master's, thesis; for doctorate, thesis/dissertation. *Entrance requirements:* For master's and doctorate, GRE General Test. Additional exam requirements/recommendations for international students: required—TOEFL. Electronic applications accepted.

The University of Manchester, School of Materials, Manchester, United Kingdom. Offers advanced aerospace materials engineering (M Sc); advanced metallic systems (PhD); biomedical materials (M Phil, M Sc, PhD); ceramics and glass (M Phil, M Sc, PhD); composite materials (M Sc, PhD); corrosion and protection (M Phil, M Sc, PhD); materials (M Phil, PhD); metallic materials (M Phil, M Sc, PhD); nanostructural materials (M Phil, M Sc, PhD); paper science (M Phil, M Sc, PhD); polymer science and engineering (M Phil, M Sc, PhD); technical textiles (M Sc); textile design, fashion and management (M Phil, M Sc, PhD); textile science and technology (M Phil, M Sc, PhD); textiles (M Phil, PhD); textiles and fashion (M Ent).

University of Massachusetts Amherst, Graduate School, College of Engineering, Department of Civil and Environmental Engineering, Amherst, MA 01003. Offers civil engineering (MSCE, PhD); environmental and water resources engineering (MSCE); geotechnical engineering (MSCE); structural engineering and mechanics (MSCE); transportation engineering (MSCE). *Program availability:* Part-time. Terminal master's awarded for partial completion of doctoral program. *Degree requirements:* For master's, thesis or alternative; for doctorate, comprehensive exam, thesis/dissertation. *Entrance requirements:* For master's and doctorate, GRE General Test. Additional exam requirements/recommendations for international students: required—TOEFL (minimum score 550 paper-based; 80 iBT), IELTS (minimum score 6.5). Electronic applications accepted.

University of Memphis, Graduate School, Herff College of Engineering, Department of Civil Engineering, Memphis, TN 38152. Offers civil engineering (PhD); engineering seismology (MS); environmental engineering (MS); freight transportation (Graduate Certificate); geotechnical engineering (MS); structural engineering (MS); transportation engineering (MS); water resources engineering (MS). *Students:* 15 full-time (4 women), 8 part-time (1 woman); includes 1 minority (Black or African American, non-Hispanic/Latino), 12 international. Average age 27. 26 applicants, 38% accepted, 5 enrolled. In 2019, 11 master's awarded. Terminal master's awarded for partial completion of doctoral program. *Degree requirements:* For master's, comprehensive exam, thesis optional; for doctorate, comprehensive exam, thesis/dissertation. *Entrance requirements:* For master's, GRE General Test, minimum undergraduate GPA of 2.5; bachelor's degree in engineering or a related science or mathematics program; three letters of reference; for doctorate, GRE General Test, bachelor's degree in engineering or engineering science; three letters of reference; for Graduate Certificate, minimum undergraduate GPA of 2.75; bachelor's degree in engineering or engineering science. Additional exam requirements/recommendations for international students: required—TOEFL (minimum score 550 paper-based; 79 iBT). *Application deadline:* For fall admission, 8/1 for domestic students; for spring admission, 12/1 for domestic students. Application fee: $35 ($60 for international students). Electronic applications accepted. *Expenses: Tuition, area resident:* Full-time $9216; part-time $512 per credit hour. Tuition, state resident: full-time $9216; part-time $512 per credit hour. Tuition, nonresident: full-time $12,672; part-time $704 per credit hour. *International tuition:* $16,128 full-time. *Required fees:* $1530; $85 per credit hour. Tuition and fees vary according to program. *Financial support:* Fellowships with full tuition reimbursements, research assistantships with full tuition reimbursements, career-related internships or fieldwork, Federal Work-Study, scholarships/grants, and unspecified assistantships available. Financial award application deadline: 2/1; financial award applicants required to submit FAFSA. *Unit head:* Dr. Shahram Pezeshk, Chair, 901-678-2746, Fax: 901-678-3026, E-mail: spezeshk@memphis.edu. *Application contact:* Dr. Roger Meier, Graduate Coordinator, 901-678-3284, E-mail: rwmeier@memphis.edu.
Website: https://www.memphis.edu/ce

University of Michigan, College of Engineering, Department of Civil and Environmental Engineering, Ann Arbor, MI 48109. Offers civil engineering (MSE, PhD, CE); construction engineering and management (M Eng, MSE); environmental engineering (MSE, PhD); structural engineering (M Eng); MBA/MSE. *Program availability:* Part-time. Terminal master's awarded for partial completion of doctoral program. *Degree requirements:* For master's, thesis optional; for doctorate, comprehensive exam, thesis/dissertation, oral defense of dissertation, preliminary and written exams. *Entrance requirements:* For master's and doctorate, GRE General Test. Additional exam requirements/recommendations for international students: required—TOEFL. Electronic applications accepted.

University of New Brunswick Fredericton, School of Graduate Studies, Faculty of Engineering, Department of Civil Engineering, Fredericton, NB E3B 5A3, Canada. Offers construction engineering and management (M Eng, M Sc E, PhD); environmental engineering (M Eng, M Sc E, PhD); environmental studies (M Eng); geotechnical engineering (M Eng, M Sc E, PhD); groundwater/hydrology (M Eng, M Sc E, PhD); materials (M Eng, M Sc E, PhD); pavements (M Eng, M Sc E, PhD); structures (M Eng, M Sc E, PhD); transportation (M Eng, M Sc E, PhD). *Program availability:* Part-time. *Faculty:* 17 full-time (2 women). *Students:* 31 full-time (6 women), 10 part-time (0 women), 12 international. Average age 27. In 2019, 11 master's awarded. *Degree requirements:* For master's, thesis; for doctorate, comprehensive exam, thesis/dissertation, qualifying exam; 27 credit hours of courses. *Entrance requirements:* For master's, minimum GPA of 3.0; B Sc E in civil engineering or related engineering degree; for doctorate, minimum GPA of 3.0; graduate degree in engineering or applied science. Additional exam requirements/recommendations for international students: required—IELTS (minimum score 7.5), TWE (minimum score 4), Michigan English Language Assessment Battery (minimum score 85) or CanTest (minimum score 4.5); recommended—TOEFL (minimum score 580 paper-based). *Application deadline:* For fall admission, 5/1 for domestic students; for winter admission, 11/1 for domestic students. Applications are processed on a rolling basis. Application fee: $50 Canadian dollars. Electronic applications accepted. *Expenses: Tuition, area resident:* Full-time $6975 Canadian dollars; part-time $3423 Canadian dollars per year. Tuition, state resident: full-time $6975 Canadian dollars; part-time $3423 Canadian dollars per year. Tuition, Canadian resident: full-time $6975 Canadian dollars; part-time $3423 Canadian dollars per year. *International tuition:* $12,435 Canadian dollars full-time. *Required fees:* $92.25 Canadian dollars per term. Full-time tuition and fees vary according to degree level, campus/location, program, reciprocity agreements and student level. *Financial support:* Fellowships, research assistantships, teaching assistantships, career-related internships or fieldwork, and scholarships/grants available. Financial award application deadline: 1/15. *Unit head:* Dr. Jeff Rankin, Chair, 506-453-4618, Fax: 506-453-3568, E-mail: ktm@unb.ca. *Application contact:* MaryBeth Nicholson, Graduate Secretary, 506-452-6127, Fax: 506-453-3568, E-mail: mbnich@unb.ca.
Website: http://go.unb.ca/gradprograms

University of Puerto Rico at Mayagüez, Graduate Studies, College of Engineering, Department of Civil Engineering and Surveying, Mayagüez, PR 00681-9000. Offers civil engineering (ME, MS, PhD), including construction engineering and management (ME, MS), environmental engineering, geotechnical engineering (ME, MS), structural engineering, transportation engineering. *Program availability:* Part-time. Terminal master's awarded for partial completion of doctoral program. *Degree requirements:* For master's, one foreign language, thesis; for doctorate, one foreign language, comprehensive exam, thesis/dissertation, qualifying exams. *Entrance requirements:* For master's, proficiency in English and Spanish; BS in civil engineering or its equivalent; for doctorate, proficiency in English and Spanish. Electronic applications accepted.

University of South Florida, College of Engineering, Department of Civil and Environmental Engineering, Tampa, FL 33620-9951. Offers civil engineering (MCE, MSCE), including geotechnical engineering, materials science and engineering, structures engineering, transportation engineering, water resources; environmental engineering (MEVE, MSEV, PhD), including engineering for international development (MSEV). *Program availability:* Part-time. *Faculty:* 19 full-time (5 women). *Students:* 144 full-time (46 women), 76 part-time (22 women); includes 35 minority (8 Black or African American, non-Hispanic/Latino; 5 Asian, non-Hispanic/Latino; 18 Hispanic/Latino; 4 Two or more races, non-Hispanic/Latino), 123 international. Average age 28. 220 applicants, 65% accepted, 59 enrolled. In 2019, 82 master's, 15 doctorates awarded. Terminal master's awarded for partial completion of doctoral program. *Degree requirements:* For master's, comprehensive exam, thesis (for some programs); for doctorate, comprehensive exam, thesis/dissertation. *Entrance requirements:* For master's, GRE required, bachelor's degree in appropriate field, minimum GPA of 3.0 in major, letters of reference, statement of purpose, resume, intake form; for doctorate, GRE with V (45th percentile), Q (75th percentile), and AW (55th percentile), letters of recommendation, statement of purpose, resume, intake form. Additional exam requirements/recommendations for international students: required—TOEFL, TOEFL (minimum score 550 paper-based; 79 iBT) or IELTS (minimum score 6.5). *Application deadline:* For fall admission, 2/15 for domestic students, 2/15 priority date for international students; for spring admission, 10/15 for domestic students, 9/15 priority date for international students. Application fee: $30. Electronic applications accepted. *Financial support:* In 2019–20, 45 students received support, including 44 research assistantships (averaging $14,123 per year), 21 teaching assistantships with tuition reimbursements available (averaging $15,329 per year). *Unit head:* Dr. Manjriker Gunaratne, Professor and Department Chair, 813-974-5818, Fax: 813-974-2957, E-mail: gunaratn@usf.edu. *Application contact:* Dr. Sarina J. Ergas, Professor and Graduate Program Coordinator, 813-974-1119, Fax: 813-974-2957, E-mail: sergas@usf.edu.
Website: http://www.usf.edu/engineering/cee/

The University of Texas at Tyler, College of Engineering, Department of Civil Engineering, Tyler, TX 75799-0001. Offers environmental engineering (MS); industrial safety (MS); structural engineering (MS); transportation engineering (MS); water resources engineering (MS). *Program availability:* Part-time, evening/weekend. *Faculty:* 5 full-time. *Students:* 7 full-time (0 women), 8 part-time (6 women); includes 4 minority (1 Asian, non-Hispanic/Latino; 3 Hispanic/Latino), 4 international. Average age 28. 14 applicants, 79% accepted, 4 enrolled. In 2019, 6 master's awarded. *Entrance requirements:* For master's, GRE General Test, bachelor's degree in engineering, associated science degree. Additional exam requirements/recommendations for international students: required—TOEFL. *Application deadline:* For fall admission, 8/17 priority date for domestic students, 7/1 priority date for international students; for spring admission, 12/21 priority date for domestic students, 11/1 priority date for international students. Application fee: $25 ($50 for international students). *Financial support:* Application deadline: 7/1. *Unit head:* Dr. Torey Nalbone, Chair, 903-565-5520, E-mail: tnalbone@uttyler.edu. *Application contact:* Dr. Torey Nalbone, Chair, 903-565-5520, E-mail: tnalbone@uttyler.edu.
Website: https://www.uttyler.edu/ce/

University of Washington, Graduate School, College of Engineering, Department of Civil and Environmental Engineering, Seattle, WA 98195-2700. Offers construction engineering (MSCE, PhD); environmental engineering (MSCE, PhD); geotechnical engineering (MSCE, PhD); hydrology and hydrodynamics (MSCE, PhD); structural engineering and mechanics (MSCE, PhD); transportation engineering (MSCE, PhD). *Program availability:* Part-time, 100% online. *Students:* 248 full-time (97 women), 174 part-time (63 women); includes 90 minority (8 Black or African American, non-Hispanic/Latino; 2 American Indian or Alaska Native, non-Hispanic/Latino; 46 Asian, non-Hispanic/Latino; 18 Hispanic/Latino; 16 Two or more races, non-Hispanic/Latino), 118 international. Average age 28. 756 applicants, 59% accepted, 164 enrolled. In 2019, 133 master's, 21 doctorates awarded. Terminal master's awarded for partial completion of doctoral program. *Degree requirements:* For master's, thesis optional; for doctorate, comprehensive exam, thesis/dissertation, qualifying, general and final exams; completion of degree within 10 years. *Entrance requirements:* For master's, GRE General Test, minimum GPA of 3.0, statement of purpose, letters of recommendation, transcripts; for doctorate, GRE General Test, minimum GPA of 3.5, statement of purpose, letters of recommendation, transcripts, resume. Additional exam requirements/recommendations for international students: required—TOEFL (minimum score 580 paper-based; 92 iBT). *Application deadline:* For fall admission, 12/15 for domestic and international students. Applications are processed on a rolling basis. Application fee: $85. Electronic applications accepted. *Expenses:* Contact institution. *Financial support:* In 2019–20, 21 fellowships with full tuition reimbursements (averaging $30,600 per year), 76 research assistantships with full tuition reimbursements (averaging $30,600 per year), 27 teaching assistantships with full tuition reimbursements (averaging $30,120 per year) were awarded; Federal Work-Study, institutionally sponsored loans, scholarships/grants, health care benefits, tuition waivers, and unspecified assistantships also available. Support available to part-time students. Financial award application deadline: 12/15. *Unit head:* Dr. Laura Lowes, Professor/Chair, 206-685-2563, Fax: 206-543-1543, E-mail: lowes@uw.edu. *Application contact:* Bryan Crockett, Director of Academic Services, 206-616-1891, Fax: 206-543-1543, E-mail: ceginfo@u.washington.edu.
Website: http://www.ce.washington.edu/

University of Wisconsin–Madison, Graduate School, College of Engineering, Department of Civil and Environmental Engineering, Madison, WI 53706-1380. Offers construction engineering and management (MS); environmental science and engineering (MS); geological/geotechnical engineering (MS); structural engineering (MS); transportation engineering (MS); water resources engineering (MS). *Program availability:* Part-time. Terminal master's awarded for partial completion of doctoral program. *Degree requirements:* For master's, thesis (for some programs), minimum of 30 credits; minimum overall GPA of 3.0. *Entrance requirements:* For master's, GRE General Test, bachelor's degree; minimum GPA of 3.0 for last 60 credits of course work. Additional exam requirements/recommendations for international students: required—TOEFL (minimum score 580 paper-based; 92 iBT). Electronic applications accepted. *Expenses:* Contact institution.

Surveying Science and Engineering

University of New Brunswick Fredericton, School of Graduate Studies, Faculty of Engineering, Department of Geodesy and Geomatics Engineering, Fredericton, NB E3B 5A3, Canada. Offers M Eng, M Sc E, PhD. *Faculty:* 9 full-time (2 women), 2 part-time/adjunct (0 women). *Students:* 33 full-time (9 women), 5 part-time (0 women), 26 international. Average age 30. In 2019, 3 master's, 2 doctorates awarded. *Degree requirements:* For master's, thesis; for doctorate, comprehensive exam, thesis/dissertation, qualifying exam. *Entrance requirements:* For master's and doctorate, minimum GPA of 3.0. Additional exam requirements/recommendations for international students: required—TOEFL (minimum score 550 paper-based; 80 iBT), IELTS (minimum score 7), TWE (minimum score 4), Michigan English Language Assessment Battery (minimum score 85) or CanTest (minimum score 4.5). *Application deadline:* For fall admission, 3/1 for domestic students. Applications are processed on a rolling basis. Application fee: $50 Canadian dollars. Electronic applications accepted. *Expenses: Tuition, area resident:* Full-time $6975 Canadian dollars; part-time $3423 Canadian dollars per year. Tuition, state resident: full-time $6975 Canadian dollars; part-time $3423 Canadian dollars per year. Tuition, Canadian resident: full-time $6975 Canadian dollars; part-time $3423 Canadian dollars per year. *International tuition:* $12,435 Canadian dollars full-time. *Required fees:* $92.25 Canadian dollars per term. Full-time tuition and fees vary according to degree level, campus/location, program, reciprocity agreements and student level. *Financial support:* Fellowships, research assistantships, and teaching assistantships available. Financial award application deadline: 1/15. *Unit head:* Dr. Monica Wachowicz, Director of Graduate Studies, 506-447-8113, Fax: 506-453-4943, E-mail: monicaw@unb.ca. *Application contact:* Alicia Farnham, Graduate Secretary, 506-458-7085, Fax: 506-453-4943, E-mail: afarnham@unb.ca.
Website: http://go.unb.ca/gradprograms

Transportation and Highway Engineering

Arizona State University at Tempe, College of Liberal Arts and Sciences, School of Geographical Sciences and Urban Planning, Tempe, AZ 85287-5302. Offers geographic information systems (MAS); geographical information science (Graduate Certificate); geography (MA, PhD); transportation systems (Graduate Certificate); urban and environmental planning (MUEP); urban planning (PhD). *Accreditation:* ACSP. Terminal master's awarded for partial completion of doctoral program. *Degree requirements:* For master's, thesis, interactive Program of Study (iPOS) submitted before completing 50 percent of required credit hours; for doctorate, comprehensive exam, thesis/dissertation, interactive Program of Study (iPOS) submitted before completing 50 percent of required credit hours. *Entrance requirements:* For master's and doctorate, GRE, minimum GPA of 3.0 or equivalent in last 2 years of work leading to bachelor's degree. Additional exam requirements/recommendations for international students: required—TOEFL, IELTS, or PTE. Electronic applications accepted. *Expenses:* Contact institution.

ArtCenter College of Design, Graduate Transportation Systems and Design Program, Pasadena, CA 91103. Offers transportation systems (MS).

The Catholic University of America, School of Engineering, Department of Civil Engineering, Washington, DC 20064. Offers civil engineering (MS, PhD); transportation and infrastructure systems (Certificate). *Program availability:* Part-time. *Faculty:* 6 full-time (1 woman), 3 part-time/adjunct (1 woman). *Students:* 13 full-time (4 women), 22 part-time (5 women); includes 12 minority (7 Black or African American, non-Hispanic/Latino; 5 Two or more races, non-Hispanic/Latino), 23 international. Average age 32. 43 applicants, 58% accepted, 10 enrolled. In 2019, 15 master's, 1 doctorate awarded. *Degree requirements:* For master's, thesis optional; for doctorate, comprehensive exam, thesis/dissertation. *Entrance requirements:* For master's and doctorate, GRE General Test, statement of purpose, official copies of academic transcripts, three letters of recommendation. Additional exam requirements/recommendations for international students: required—TOEFL (minimum score 550 paper-based; 80 iBT). *Application deadline:* For fall admission, 7/15 priority date for domestic students, 7/1 for international students; for spring admission, 11/15 priority date for domestic students, 11/1 for international students. Applications are processed on a rolling basis. Application fee: $55. Electronic applications accepted. *Expenses:* Contact institution. *Financial support:* Fellowships, research assistantships, teaching assistantships, Federal Work-Study, scholarships/grants, tuition waivers (full and partial), and unspecified assistantships available. Financial award application deadline: 2/1; financial award applicants required to submit FAFSA. *Unit head:* Dr. Arash Massoudieh, Chair, 202-319-5671, Fax: 202-319-6677, E-mail: massoudieh@cua.edu. *Application contact:* Dr. Steven Brown, Director of Graduate Admissions, 202-319-5057, Fax: 202-319-6533, E-mail: cua-admissions@cua.edu.
Website: https://engineering.catholic.edu/civil/index.html

The Citadel, The Military College of South Carolina, Citadel Graduate College, School of Engineering, Department of Civil and Environmental Engineering, Charleston, SC 29409. Offers built environment and public health (Graduate Certificate); civil engineering (MS); geotechnical engineering (Graduate Certificate); structural engineering (Graduate Certificate); transportation engineering (Graduate Certificate). *Program availability:* Part-time, evening/weekend. *Degree requirements:* For master's, plan of study outlining intended areas of interest and top four corresponding courses of interest. *Entrance requirements:* For master's, official transcript of baccalaureate degree from ABET-accredited engineering program or approved alternative; 2 letters of recommendation; for Graduate Certificate, official transcript of baccalaureate degree directly from an accredited college or university. Additional exam requirements/recommendations for international students: required—TOEFL (minimum score 550 paper-based; 79 iBT). Electronic applications accepted.

Clemson University, Graduate School, College of Engineering, Computing and Applied Sciences, Glenn Department of Civil Engineering, Clemson, SC 29634. Offers civil engineering (MS, PhD), including construction engineering and management, construction materials, geotechnical engineering, structural engineering, transportation engineering, water resources engineering. *Program availability:* Part-time, 100% online. *Faculty:* 24 full-time (4 women), 3 part-time/adjunct (2 women). *Students:* 101 full-time (20 women), 44 part-time (9 women); includes 9 minority (3 Black or African American, non-Hispanic/Latino; 1 Asian, non-Hispanic/Latino; 2 Hispanic/Latino; 3 Two or more races, non-Hispanic/Latino), 97 international. Average age 29. 248 applicants, 62% accepted, 61 enrolled. In 2019, 43 master's, 11 doctorates awarded. *Degree requirements:* For master's, thesis or alternative, oral exam, seminar; for doctorate, comprehensive exam, thesis/dissertation, oral exam, seminar. *Entrance requirements:* For master's and doctorate, GRE General Test, unofficial transcripts, letters of recommendation, statement of purpose. Additional exam requirements/recommendations for international students: required—TOEFL (minimum score 80 paper-based; 80 iBT), PTE (minimum score 54); recommended—IELTS (minimum score 6.5). *Application deadline:* For fall admission, 4/15 for domestic and international students; for spring admission, 9/15 for domestic and international students. Applications are processed on a rolling basis. Application fee: $80 ($90 for international students). Electronic applications accepted. *Expenses: Tuition, area resident:* Full-time $10,600; part-time $8688 per semester. Tuition, state resident: full-time $10,600; part-time $8688 per semester. Tuition, nonresident: full-time $22,050; part-time $17,412 per semester. *International tuition:* $22,050 full-time. *Required fees:* $1196; $617 per semester. $617 per semester. Tuition and fees vary according to course load, degree level, campus/location and program. *Financial support:* In 2019–20, 101 students received support, including 2 fellowships with full and partial tuition reimbursements available (averaging $34,000 per year), 61 research assistantships with full and partial tuition reimbursements available (averaging $18,222 per year), 4 teaching assistantships with full and partial tuition reimbursements available (averaging $20,567 per year); career-related internships or fieldwork and unspecified assistantships also available. Financial award application deadline: 4/15. *Unit head:* Dr. Jesus M de la Garza, Department Chair, 864-656-3001, E-mail: jdelaga@clemson.edu. *Application contact:* Dr. Abdul Khan, Graduate Program Coordinator, 864-656-3327, E-mail: abdkhan@clemson.edu.
Website: https://www.clemson.edu/cecas/departments/ce/

College for Creative Studies, Graduate Programs, Detroit, MI 48202-4034. Offers color and materials design (MFA); integrated design (MFA); interaction design (MFA); transportation design (MFA). *Accreditation:* NASAD.

Cornell University, Graduate School, Graduate Fields of Engineering, Field of Civil and Environmental Engineering, Ithaca, NY 14853. Offers engineering management (M Eng, MS, PhD); environmental engineering (M Eng, MS, PhD); environmental fluid mechanics and hydrology (M Eng, MS, PhD); environmental systems engineering (M Eng, MS, PhD); geotechnical engineering (M Eng, MS, PhD); remote sensing (M Eng, MS, PhD); structural engineering (M Eng, MS, PhD); structural mechanics (M Eng, MS); transportation engineering (MS, PhD); transportation systems engineering (M Eng); water resource systems (M Eng, MS, PhD). Terminal master's awarded for partial completion of doctoral program. *Degree requirements:* For master's, thesis (MS); for doctorate, comprehensive exam, thesis/dissertation. *Entrance requirements:* For master's and doctorate, GRE General Test (recommended), 2 letters of recommendation. Additional exam requirements/recommendations for international students: required—TOEFL (minimum score 600 paper-based; 77 iBT). Electronic applications accepted.

George Mason University, Volgenau School of Engineering, Sid and Reva Dewberry Department of Civil, Environmental, and Infrastructure Engineering, Fairfax, VA 22030. Offers construction project management (MS); transportation engineering (PhD). *Degree requirements:* For master's, thesis (for some programs), 30 credits, departmental seminars; for doctorate, thesis/dissertation, qualifying exams. *Entrance requirements:* For master's, GRE, photocopy of passport; 2 official college transcripts; resume; official bank statement; proof of financial support; expanded goals statement; self-evaluation form; BS in engineering or other related science; 3 letters of recommendation; for doctorate, GRE (for those who received degree outside of the U.S.), photocopy of passport; 2 official college transcripts; resume; official bank statement; proof of financial support; expanded goals statement; self-evaluation form; baccalaureate degree in engineering or related science; master's degree (preferred); 3 letters of recommendation. Additional exam requirements/recommendations for international students: required—TOEFL (minimum score 575 paper-based; 88 iBT), IELTS (minimum score 6.5), PTE (minimum score 59). Electronic applications accepted. *Expenses:* Contact institution.

Illinois Institute of Technology, Graduate College, Armour College of Engineering, Department of Civil, Architectural and Environmental Engineering, Chicago, IL 60616. Offers architectural engineering (M Arch E); civil engineering (MS, PhD), including architectural engineering (MS), construction engineering and management (MS), geoenvironmental engineering (MS), geotechnical engineering (MS), structural engineering (MS), transportation engineering (MS); construction engineering and management (MCEM); environmental engineering (M Env E, MS, PhD); geoenvironmental engineering (M Geoenv E); geotechnical engineering (MGE); infrastructure engineering and management (MPW); structural engineering (MSE); transportation engineering (M Trans E). *Program availability:* Part-time, evening/weekend, online learning. Terminal master's awarded for partial completion of doctoral program. *Degree requirements:* For master's, thesis (for some programs); for doctorate, comprehensive exam, thesis/dissertation. *Entrance requirements:* For master's, GRE General Test (minimum score 900 Quantitative and Verbal, 2.5 Analytical Writing), minimum undergraduate GPA of 3.0; for doctorate, GRE General Test (minimum score 1000 Quantitative and Verbal, 3.0 Analytical Writing), minimum undergraduate GPA of

3.0. Additional exam requirements/recommendations for international students: required—TOEFL (minimum score 550 paper-based; 80 iBT). Electronic applications accepted.

Iowa State University of Science and Technology, Department of Civil and Construction Engineering, Ames, IA 50011. Offers civil engineering (MS, PhD), including civil engineering materials, construction engineering and management, environmental engineering, geotechnical engineering, structural engineering, transportation engineering. *Degree requirements:* For master's, thesis or alternative; for doctorate, thesis/dissertation. *Entrance requirements:* For master's and doctorate, GRE General Test. Additional exam requirements/recommendations for international students: required—TOEFL (minimum score 550 paper-based; 82 iBT), IELTS (minimum score 6.5). Electronic applications accepted.

Kansas State University, Graduate School, College of Engineering, Department of Civil Engineering, Manhattan, KS 66506. Offers civil engineering (MS, PhD); environmental engineering (MS, PhD); geotechnical engineering (MS, PhD); structural engineering (MS, PhD); transportation engineering (MS, PhD); water resources engineering (MS, PhD). *Program availability:* Part-time, evening/weekend, online learning. *Degree requirements:* For master's, thesis or alternative; for doctorate, thesis/dissertation. *Entrance requirements:* For master's, GRE General Test, bachelor's degree or course work in related engineering fields; for doctorate, GRE General Test. Additional exam requirements/recommendations for international students: required—TOEFL (minimum score 550 paper-based; 79 iBT). Electronic applications accepted.

Kennesaw State University, Southern Polytechnic College of Engineering and Engineering Technology, Program in Civil Engineering, Kennesaw, GA 30144. Offers environmental engineering (MS); geotechnical engineering (MS); structural engineering (MS); transportation and pavement engineering (MS); water resources engineering (MS). *Program availability:* Online learning. *Students:* 9 full-time (2 women), 30 part-time (4 women); includes 20 minority (9 Black or African American, non-Hispanic/Latino; 5 Asian, non-Hispanic/Latino; 5 Hispanic/Latino; 1 Two or more races, non-Hispanic/Latino), 3 international. Average age 34. 12 applicants, 92% accepted, 8 enrolled. In 2019, 12 master's awarded. *Degree requirements:* For master's, thesis optional. *Entrance requirements:* Additional exam requirements/recommendations for international students: required—TOEFL (minimum score 80 iBT), IELTS (minimum score 6.5). *Application deadline:* For fall admission, 11/1 for domestic and international students; for spring admission, 4/1 for domestic and international students. Applications are processed on a rolling basis. Application fee: $60. Electronic applications accepted. *Expenses: Tuition, area resident:* Full-time $7104; part-time $296 per credit hour. Tuition, state resident: full-time $7104; part-time $296 per credit hour. Tuition, nonresident: full-time $25,584; part-time $1066 per credit hour. *International tuition:* $25,584 full-time. *Required fees:* $2006; $1706 per unit. $853 per semester. *Unit head:* Metin Oguzmert, Coordinator, 470-578-5083, E-mail: moguzmer@kennesaw.edu. *Application contact:* Admissions Counselor, 470-578-4377, E-mail: ksugrad@kennesaw.edu.
Website: http://engineering.kennesaw.edu/civil-construction/degrees/ms-civil-engineering.php

Louisiana State University and Agricultural & Mechanical College, Graduate School, College of Engineering, Department of Civil and Environmental Engineering, Baton Rouge, LA 70803. Offers environmental engineering (MSCE, PhD); geotechnical engineering (MSCE, PhD); structural engineering and mechanics (MSCE, PhD); transportation engineering (MSCE, PhD); water resources (MSCE, PhD).

Marquette University, Graduate School, College of Engineering, Department of Civil and Environmental Engineering, Milwaukee, WI 53201-1881. Offers construction engineering and management (MS, PhD, Certificate); environmental engineering (MS, PhD); structural design (Certificate); structural engineering and structural mechanics (MS, PhD); transportation (Certificate); transportation engineering and materials (MS, PhD); waste and wastewater treatment processes (Certificate); water resources engineering (Certificate). *Program availability:* Part-time, evening/weekend. Terminal master's awarded for partial completion of doctoral program. *Degree requirements:* For master's, comprehensive exam (for some programs), thesis or alternative; for doctorate, thesis/dissertation. *Entrance requirements:* For master's, GRE General Test (recommended), minimum GPA of 3.0, official transcripts from all current and previous colleges/universities except Marquette, three letters of recommendation; for doctorate, GRE General Test, minimum GPA of 3.0, official transcripts from all current and previous colleges/universities except Marquette, three letters of recommendation, brief statement of purpose, submission of any English language publications authored by applicant (strongly recommended). Additional exam requirements/recommendations for international students: required—TOEFL (minimum score 530 paper-based). Electronic applications accepted.

Marshall University, Academic Affairs Division, College of Information Technology and Engineering, Program in Engineering, Huntington, WV 25755. Offers engineering management (MSE); environmental engineering (MSE); transportation and infrastructure engineering (MSE). *Program availability:* Part-time, evening/weekend. *Degree requirements:* For master's, final project, oral exam. *Entrance requirements:* For master's, GMAT or GRE General Test, minimum undergraduate GPA of 2.75.

Massachusetts Institute of Technology, School of Engineering, Department of Civil and Environmental Engineering, Cambridge, MA 02139. Offers biological oceanography (PhD, Sc D); chemical oceanography (PhD, Sc D); civil and environmental engineering (M Eng, SM, PhD, Sc D); civil and environmental systems (PhD, Sc D); civil engineering (PhD, Sc D, CE); civil engineering and computation (PhD); coastal engineering (PhD, Sc D); construction engineering and management (PhD, Sc D); environmental biology (PhD, Sc D); environmental chemistry (PhD, Sc D); environmental engineering (PhD, Sc D); environmental engineering and computation (PhD); environmental fluid mechanics (PhD, Sc D); geotechnical and geoenvironmental engineering (PhD, Sc D); hydrology (PhD, Sc D); information technology (PhD, Sc D); oceanographic engineering (PhD, Sc D); structures and materials (PhD, Sc D); transportation (PhD, Sc D); SM/MBA. *Degree requirements:* For master's, thesis; for doctorate, comprehensive exam, thesis/dissertation; for CE, comprehensive exam, thesis. *Entrance requirements:* For master's, doctorate, and CE, GRE General Test. Additional exam requirements/recommendations for international students: required—TOEFL, IELTS. Electronic applications accepted.

Morgan State University, School of Graduate Studies, Clarence M. Mitchell, Jr. School of Engineering, Department of Transportation and Urban Infrastructure Studies, Baltimore, MD 21251. Offers transportation (MS, PhD, Postbaccalaureate Certificate). *Program availability:* Part-time, evening/weekend. *Faculty:* 4 full-time (2 women), 3 part-time/adjunct (1 woman). *Students:* 15 full-time (3 women), 3 part-time (0 women); includes 9 minority (7 Black or African American, non-Hispanic/Latino; 2 Asian, non-Hispanic/Latino), 8 international. Average age 37. 11 applicants, 91% accepted, 3 enrolled. In 2019, 4 master's, 2 doctorates awarded. *Degree requirements:* For master's, thesis optional, comprehensive exam or equivalent; for doctorate, thesis/dissertation optional, omprehensive exam or equivalent. *Entrance requirements:* For master's, minimum undergraduate GPA of 2.5. Additional exam requirements/recommendations for international students: required—TOEFL (minimum score 550 paper-based). *Application deadline:* For fall admission, 5/1 for domestic students, 4/1 for international students; for spring admission, 11/15 for domestic students, 10/1 for international students. Applications are processed on a rolling basis. Application fee: $50 ($70 for international students). Electronic applications accepted. *Expenses:* Tuition, state resident: full-time $455; part-time $455 per credit hour. Tuition, nonresident: full-time $894; part-time $894 per credit hour. *Required fees:* $82; $82 per credit hour. *Financial support:* In 2019–20, 4 students received support. Fellowships with full and partial tuition reimbursements available, research assistantships with full and partial tuition reimbursements available, teaching assistantships with full and partial tuition reimbursements available, career-related internships or fieldwork, scholarships/grants, tuition waivers (full and partial), and unspecified assistantships available. Support available to part-time students. Financial award application deadline: 2/1. *Unit head:* Dr. Anthony A. Saka, Department Chair, 443-885-5067, Fax: 443-885-8324, E-mail: anthony.saka@morgan.edu. *Application contact:* Dr. Jahmaine Smith, Director of Admission, 443-885-3185, Fax: 443-885-8226, E-mail: gradapply@morgan.edu.
Website: https://www.morgan.edu/soe/transportation

New Jersey Institute of Technology, Newark College of Engineering, Newark, NJ 07102. Offers biomedical engineering (MS, PhD); biopharmaceutical engineering (MS); chemical engineering (MS, PhD); civil engineering (MS, PhD); computer engineering (MS); critical infrastructure systems (MS); electrical engineering (MS, PhD); engineering management (MS); engineering science (MS); environmental engineering (MS, PhD); healthcare systems management (MS); industrial engineering (MS, PhD); internet engineering (MS); manufacturing systems engineering (MS); materials science & engineering (PhD); materials science and engineering (MS); mechanical engineering (MS, PhD); occupational safety and health engineering (MS). *Program availability:* Part-time, evening/weekend. *Faculty:* 151 full-time (29 women), 135 part-time/adjunct (15 women). *Students:* 576 full-time (161 women), 528 part-time (111 women); includes 366 minority (61 Black or African American, non-Hispanic/Latino; 1 American Indian or Alaska Native, non-Hispanic/Latino; 166 Asian, non-Hispanic/Latino; 115 Hispanic/Latino; 23 Two or more races, non-Hispanic/Latino), 450 international. Average age 28. 2,053 applicants, 67% accepted, 338 enrolled. In 2019, 474 master's, 30 doctorates awarded. Terminal master's awarded for partial completion of doctoral program. *Degree requirements:* For master's, thesis (for some programs); for doctorate, thesis/dissertation. *Entrance requirements:* For master's, GRE General Test, minimum GPA 2.8, personal statement, 1 letter of recommendation, transcripts; for doctorate, GRE General Test, minimum GPA of 3.5, personal statement, 3 letters of recommendation, transcripts. Additional exam requirements/recommendations for international students: required—TOEFL (minimum score 550 paper-based; 79 iBT), IELTS (minimum score 6.5). *Application deadline:* For fall admission, 6/1 priority date for domestic students, 5/1 priority date for international students; for spring admission, 11/15 priority date for domestic and international students. Applications are processed on a rolling basis. Application fee: $75. Electronic applications accepted. *Expenses:* $23,828 per year (in-state), $33,744 per year (out-of-state). *Financial support:* In 2019–20, 352 students received support, including 33 fellowships with full tuition reimbursements available (averaging $24,000 per year), 89 research assistantships with full tuition reimbursements available (averaging $24,000 per year), 112 teaching assistantships with full tuition reimbursements available (averaging $24,000 per year); career-related internships or fieldwork, Federal Work-Study, scholarships/grants, and unspecified assistantships also available. Financial award application deadline: 1/15. *Unit head:* Dr. Moshe Kam, Dean, 973-596-5534, Fax: 973-596-2316, E-mail: moshe.kam@njit.edu. *Application contact:* Stephen Eck, Executive Director of University Admissions, 973-596-3300, Fax: 973-596-3461, E-mail: admissions@njit.edu.
Website: http://engineering.njit.edu/

New York University, Tandon School of Engineering, Department of Civil and Urban Engineering, Major in Transportation Planning and Engineering, New York, NY 10012-1019. Offers transportation planning and engineering (PhD); transportation planning and engineering (MS). *Program availability:* Part-time, evening/weekend. *Entrance requirements:* Additional exam requirements/recommendations for international students: required—TOEFL (minimum score 550 paper-based; 90 iBT); recommended—IELTS (minimum score 7). Electronic applications accepted.

North Dakota State University, College of Graduate and Interdisciplinary Studies, College of Engineering, Doctoral Program in Engineering, Fargo, ND 58102. Offers environmental and conservation science (PhD); materials and nanotechnology (PhD); natural resource management (PhD); STEM education (PhD); transportation and logistics (PhD). *Degree requirements:* For doctorate, comprehensive exam, thesis/dissertation. *Entrance requirements:* For doctorate, bachelor's degree in engineering, minimum GPA of 3.0. Additional exam requirements/recommendations for international students: required—TOEFL. Electronic applications accepted. *Expenses:* Contact institution.

Northwestern University, McCormick School of Engineering and Applied Science, Department of Civil and Environmental Engineering, Evanston, IL 60208-3109. Offers environmental engineering and science (MS, PhD); geotechnical engineering (MS, PhD); mechanics of materials and solids (MS, PhD); project management (MS); structural engineering and materials (MS, PhD); transportation systems analysis and planning (MS, PhD). *Program availability:* Part-time. Terminal master's awarded for partial completion of doctoral program. *Degree requirements:* For master's, comprehensive exam (for some programs), thesis (for some programs); for doctorate, comprehensive exam, thesis/dissertation. *Entrance requirements:* For master's and doctorate, GRE General Test, minimum 2 letters of recommendation, transcripts from all academic institutions attended. Additional exam requirements/recommendations for international students: required—TOEFL (minimum score 577 paper-based; 90 iBT), IELTS (minimum score 7). Electronic applications accepted.

Ohio University, Graduate College, Russ College of Engineering and Technology, Department of Civil Engineering, Athens, OH 45701-2979. Offers civil engineering (PhD); construction engineering and management (MS); environmental (MS); geoenvironmental (MS); geotechnical (MS); mechanics (MS); structures (MS); transportation (MS); water resources (MS). *Program availability:* Part-time. *Degree requirements:* For master's, comprehensive exam (for some programs), thesis or alternative; for doctorate, comprehensive exam, thesis/dissertation. *Entrance requirements:* For master's, GRE General Test, minimum GPA of 3.0, 3 letters of recommendation; for doctorate, GRE General Test. Additional exam requirements/recommendations for international students: required—TOEFL (minimum score 550 paper-based; 80 iBT) or IELTS (minimum score 6.5). Electronic applications accepted.

Old Dominion University, Frank Batten College of Engineering and Technology, Program in Civil Engineering, Norfolk, VA 23529. Offers civil engineering (ME, MS), including coastal engineering, geotechnical engineering, hydraulics and water resources, structural engineering, transportation engineering. *Program availability:* Part-time, evening/weekend, blended/hybrid learning. *Degree requirements:* For master's, comprehensive exam, thesis optional. *Entrance requirements:* For master's, GRE, minimum GPA of 3.0. Additional exam requirements/recommendations for international students: required—TOEFL (minimum score 550 paper-based, 80 iBT) or IELTS (6.5). Electronic applications accepted. *Expenses:* Contact institution.

Transportation and Highway Engineering

Oregon State University, College of Engineering, Program in Civil Engineering, Corvallis, OR 97331. Offers civil engineering (M Eng, MS, PhD); coastal and ocean engineering (M Eng, MS, PhD); construction engineering management (M Eng, MS, PhD); engineering education (M Eng, MS, PhD); geomatics (M Eng, MS, PhD); geotechnical engineering (M Eng, MS, PhD); infrastructure materials (M Eng, MS, PhD); structural engineering (M Eng, MS, PhD); transportation engineering (M Eng). *Entrance requirements:* For master's and doctorate, GRE. Additional exam requirements/recommendations for international students: required—TOEFL (minimum score 80 iBT), IELTS (minimum score 6.5). *Expenses:* Contact institution.

Polytechnique Montréal, Graduate Programs, Department of Civil, Geological and Mining Engineering, Montréal, QC H3C 3A7, Canada. Offers civil, geological and mining engineering (DESS); environmental engineering (M Eng, M Sc A, PhD); geotechnical engineering (M Eng, M Sc A, PhD); hydraulics engineering (M Eng, M Sc A, PhD); structural engineering (M Eng, M Sc A, PhD); transportation engineering (M Eng, M Sc A, PhD). *Program availability:* Part-time. *Degree requirements:* For master's, one foreign language, thesis; for doctorate, one foreign language, thesis/dissertation. *Entrance requirements:* For master's, minimum GPA of 2.75; for doctorate, minimum GPA of 3.0.

Rensselaer Polytechnic Institute, Graduate School, School of Engineering, Program in Transportation Engineering, Troy, NY 12180-3590. Offers M Eng, MS, PhD. *Faculty:* 18 full-time (3 women), 4 part-time/adjunct (0 women). *Students:* 12 full-time (7 women); includes 1 minority (Asian, non-Hispanic/Latino), 10 international. Average age 29. 9 applicants, 22% accepted, 2 enrolled. Terminal master's awarded for partial completion of doctoral program. *Degree requirements:* For master's, thesis (for some programs); for doctorate, thesis/dissertation. *Entrance requirements:* For master's and doctorate, GRE. Additional exam requirements/recommendations for international students: required—TOEFL (minimum score 570 paper-based; 88 iBT), IELTS (minimum score 6.5), PTE (minimum score 60). *Application deadline:* For fall admission, 1/1 priority date for domestic and international students; for spring admission, 8/15 priority date for domestic and international students. Applications are processed on a rolling basis. Application fee: $75. Electronic applications accepted. *Financial support:* In 2019–20, research assistantships (averaging $23,000 per year), teaching assistantships (averaging $23,000 per year) were awarded; fellowships also available. Financial award application deadline: 1/1. *Unit head:* Dr. Michael O'Rourke, Graduate Program Director, 518-276-6933, E-mail: orourm@rpi.edu. *Application contact:* Jarron Decker, Director of Graduate Admissions, 518-276-6216, Fax: 518-276-4072, E-mail: gradadmissions@rpi.edu.
Website: http://cee.rpi.edu/graduate

South Carolina State University, College of Graduate and Professional Studies, Department of Civil and Mechanical Engineering Technology, Orangeburg, SC 29117-0001. Offers transportation (MS). *Program availability:* Part-time, evening/weekend. *Degree requirements:* For master's, comprehensive exam, thesis, departmental qualifying exam. *Entrance requirements:* For master's, GRE. Additional exam requirements/recommendations for international students: recommended—TOEFL. Electronic applications accepted.

Southern Illinois University Edwardsville, Graduate School, School of Engineering, Department of Civil Engineering, Program in Transportation Engineering, Edwardsville, IL 62026. Offers MS. *Program availability:* Part-time, evening/weekend. *Degree requirements:* For master's, thesis (for some programs), research paper. *Entrance requirements:* For master's, minimum undergraduate GPA of 2.75 in science, math, and engineering courses. Additional exam requirements/recommendations for international students: required—TOEFL (minimum score 550 paper-based, 79 iBT), IELTS (minimum score 6.5), Michigan Test of English Language Proficiency or PTE. Electronic applications accepted.

Southern Methodist University, Lyle School of Engineering, Department of Civil and Environmental Engineering, Dallas, TX 75275-0340. Offers civil and environmental engineering (PhD); civil engineering (MS), including geotechnical engineering, structural engineering, transportation systems; environmental engineering (MS); sustainability and development (MA). *Program availability:* Part-time, evening/weekend, online learning. Terminal master's awarded for partial completion of doctoral program. *Degree requirements:* For master's, thesis optional; for doctorate, thesis/dissertation, oral and written qualifying exams. *Entrance requirements:* For master's, GRE General Test, minimum GPA of 3.0 in last 2 years; bachelor's degree in engineering, mathematics, or sciences; for doctorate, GRE, BS and MS in related field, minimum GPA of 3.3. Additional exam requirements/recommendations for international students: required—TOEFL. Electronic applications accepted.

Stevens Institute of Technology, Graduate School, Charles V. Schaefer Jr. School of Engineering and Science, Department of Civil, Environmental, and Ocean Engineering, Program in Civil Engineering, Hoboken, NJ 07030. Offers civil engineering (PhD, Certificate), including geotechnical engineering (Certificate); geotechnical/geoenvironmental engineering (M Eng, Engr); hydrologic modeling (M Eng); stormwater management (M Eng); structural engineering (M Eng, Engr); transportation engineering (M Eng); water resources engineering (M Eng). *Program availability:* Part-time, evening/weekend. *Faculty:* 23 full-time (8 women), 21 part-time/adjunct (2 women). *Students:* 38 full-time (6 women), 19 part-time (6 women); includes 11 minority (2 Black or African American, non-Hispanic/Latino; 1 American Indian or Alaska Native, non-Hispanic/Latino; 8 Asian, non-Hispanic/Latino), 29 international. Average age 25. In 2019, 38 master's, 2 doctorates awarded. Terminal master's awarded for partial completion of doctoral program. *Degree requirements:* For master's, thesis optional, minimum B average in major field and overall; for doctorate, comprehensive exam (for some programs), thesis/dissertation; for other advanced degree, minimum B average. *Entrance requirements:* For master's, International applicants must submit TOEFL/IELTS scores and fulfill the English Language Proficiency Requirement. Applicants to full-time programs who do not qualify for a score waiver are required to submit GRE/GMAT scores. Additional exam requirements/recommendations for international students: required—TOEFL (minimum score 74 iBT), IELTS (minimum score 6). *Application deadline:* For fall admission, 4/15 for domestic and international students; for spring admission, 11/1 for domestic and international students; for summer admission, 5/1 for domestic students. Applications are processed on a rolling basis. Application fee: $60. Electronic applications accepted. *Expenses: Tuition:* Full-time $52,134. *Required fees:* $1880. Tuition and fees vary according to course load. *Financial support:* Fellowships, research assistantships, teaching assistantships, career-related internships or fieldwork, Federal Work-Study, scholarships/grants, and unspecified assistantships available. Financial award application deadline: 2/15; financial award applicants required to submit FAFSA. *Unit head:* Dr. Jean Zu, Dean of SES, 201-216.8233, Fax: 201-216.8372, E-mail: Jean.Zu@stevens.edu. *Application contact:* Graduate Admission, 888-783-8367, Fax: 888-511-1306, E-mail: graduate@stevens.edu.

Texas Southern University, School of Science and Technology, Program in Transportation, Planning and Management, Houston, TX 77004-4584. Offers MS. *Program availability:* Part-time, evening/weekend. *Degree requirements:* For master's, comprehensive exam, thesis optional. *Entrance requirements:* For master's, GRE General Test, minimum GPA of 2.5. Additional exam requirements/recommendations for international students: required—TOEFL. Electronic applications accepted.

University of Arkansas, Graduate School, College of Engineering, Department of Civil Engineering, Fayetteville, AR 72701. Offers civil engineering (MSCE, MSE, PhD); environmental engineering (MS En E, MSE); transportation engineering (MSE, MSTE). *Students:* 42 full-time (16 women), 11 part-time (2 women); includes 5 minority (1 Black or African American, non-Hispanic/Latino; 3 Hispanic/Latino; 1 Two or more races, non-Hispanic/Latino), 30 international. 25 applicants, 72% accepted. In 2019, 16 master's, 3 doctorates awarded. *Degree requirements:* For master's, thesis optional; for doctorate, one foreign language, thesis/dissertation. *Application deadline:* For fall admission, 8/1 for domestic students, 4/1 for international students; for spring admission, 12/1 for domestic students, 10/1 for international students; for summer admission, 4/15 for domestic students, 3/1 for international students. Applications are processed on a rolling basis. Application fee: $60. Electronic applications accepted. *Financial support:* In 2019–20, 37 research assistantships, 1 teaching assistantship were awarded; fellowships with tuition reimbursements, career-related internships or fieldwork, and Federal Work-Study also available. Support available to part-time students. Financial award application deadline: 4/1; financial award applicants required to submit FAFSA. *Unit head:* Dr. Micah Hale, Department Head, 479-575-6348, E-mail: micah@uark.edu. *Application contact:* Dr. Julian Fairey, Graduate Coordinator, 479-575-4023, E-mail: julianf@uark.edu.
Website: https://civil-engineering.uark.edu/

University of Calgary, Faculty of Graduate Studies, Schulich School of Engineering, Program in Civil Engineering, Calgary, AB T2N 1N4, Canada. Offers avalanche mechanics (M Sc, PhD); civil engineering (M Eng, M Sc, PhD); energy and environment engineering (M Eng, M Sc, PhD); environmental engineering (M Eng, M Sc, PhD); geotechnical engineering (M Eng, M Sc, PhD); materials science (M Eng, M Sc, PhD); project management (M Eng, M Sc, PhD); structures and solid mechanics (M Eng, M Sc, PhD); transportation engineering (M Eng, M Sc, PhD); water resources (M Eng, M Sc, PhD). *Program availability:* Part-time. *Degree requirements:* For master's, thesis; for doctorate, thesis/dissertation, written and oral candidacy exam. *Entrance requirements:* For master's, minimum GPA of 3.0; for doctorate, minimum GPA of 3.5. Additional exam requirements/recommendations for international students: required—TOEFL (minimum score 580 paper-based; 93 iBT), IELTS (minimum score 7). Electronic applications accepted.

University of California, Berkeley, Graduate Division, College of Engineering, Department of Civil and Environmental Engineering, Berkeley, CA 94720. Offers engineering and project management (M Eng, MS, PhD); environmental engineering (M Eng, MS, PhD); geoengineering (M Eng, MS, PhD); structural engineering, mechanics and materials (M Eng, MS, PhD); transportation engineering (M Eng, MS, PhD); M Arch/MS; MCP/MS; MPP/MS. Terminal master's awarded for partial completion of doctoral program. *Degree requirements:* For master's, comprehensive exam (for some programs), thesis (for some programs), comprehensive exam or thesis (MS); for doctorate, thesis/dissertation, qualifying exam. *Entrance requirements:* For master's, GRE General Test, minimum GPA of 3.0, 3 letters of recommendation; for doctorate, GRE General Test, minimum GPA of 3.5, 3 letters of recommendation. Additional exam requirements/recommendations for international students: required—TOEFL (minimum score 570 paper-based; 90 iBT). Electronic applications accepted.

University of California, Davis, College of Engineering, Graduate Group in Transportation Technology and Policy, Davis, CA 95616. Offers MS, PhD. Terminal master's awarded for partial completion of doctoral program. *Degree requirements:* For master's, comprehensive exam (for some programs), thesis (for some programs); for doctorate, thesis/dissertation. *Entrance requirements:* For master's, GRE General Test, minimum GPA of 3.0; for doctorate, GRE General Test, minimum GPA of 3.5. Additional exam requirements/recommendations for international students: required—TOEFL (minimum score 550 paper-based). Electronic applications accepted.

University of California, Irvine, Institute of Transportation Studies, Irvine, CA 92697. Offers MA, PhD. *Students:* 8 full-time (3 women), 1 part-time (0 women); includes 1 minority (Asian, non-Hispanic/Latino), 7 international. Average age 33. In 2019, 2 master's, 1 doctorate awarded. *Entrance requirements:* For master's and doctorate, GRE General Test, minimum GPA of 3.0. *Application deadline:* For fall admission, 1/15 for domestic and international students. Application fee: $120 ($140 for international students). *Financial support:* Fellowships, research assistantships with full tuition reimbursements, teaching assistantships, institutionally sponsored loans, traineeships, health care benefits, and unspecified assistantships available. Financial award application deadline: 3/1. *Unit head:* Stephen G. Ritchie, Director, 949-824-4214, E-mail: sritchie@uci.edu. *Application contact:* Amelia Regan, Director, Transportation Science Program, 949-824-2611, E-mail: aregan@uci.edu.
Website: http://www.its.uci.edu/

University of Central Florida, College of Engineering and Computer Science, Department of Civil, Environmental, and Construction Engineering, Orlando, FL 32816. Offers civil engineering (PhD, Certificate), including civil engineering (PhD), structural engineering (Certificate), transportation engineering (Certificate); environmental engineering (MS, PhD). *Program availability:* Part-time, evening/weekend. *Students:* 110 full-time (38 women), 81 part-time (23 women); includes 38 minority (5 Black or African American, non-Hispanic/Latino; 7 Asian, non-Hispanic/Latino; 25 Hispanic/Latino; 1 Two or more races, non-Hispanic/Latino), 87 international. Average age 30. 162 applicants, 46% accepted, 41 enrolled. In 2019, 30 master's, 19 doctorates, 3 other advanced degrees awarded. *Degree requirements:* For master's, thesis or alternative; for doctorate, comprehensive exam, thesis/dissertation, departmental qualifying exam, candidacy exam. *Entrance requirements:* For master's, letters of recommendation, resume, goal statement; for doctorate, GRE General Test, letters of recommendation, resume, goal statement. Additional exam requirements/recommendations for international students: required—TOEFL. *Application deadline:* For fall admission, 7/15 priority date for domestic students; for spring admission, 12/1 priority date for domestic students. Application fee: $30. Electronic applications accepted. *Financial support:* In 2019–20, 76 students received support, including 22 fellowships with partial tuition reimbursements available (averaging $13,082 per year), 55 research assistantships with partial tuition reimbursements available (averaging $7,773 per year), 17 teaching assistantships with partial tuition reimbursements available (averaging $6,990 per year); career-related internships or fieldwork, Federal Work-Study, institutionally sponsored loans, health care benefits, tuition waivers (partial), and unspecified assistantships also available. Financial award application deadline: 3/1; financial award applicants required to submit FAFSA. *Unit head:* Dr. Mohamed Abdel-Aty, Chair, 407-823-2841, E-mail: m.aty@ucf.edu. *Application contact:* Associate Director, Graduate Admissions, 407-823-2766, Fax: 407-823-6442, E-mail: gradadmissions@ucf.edu.
Website: http://cece.ucf.edu/

University of Colorado Denver, College of Engineering, Design and Computing, Department of Civil Engineering, Denver, CO 80217. Offers civil engineering (EASPh D); civil engineering systems (PhD); environmental and sustainability engineering (MS, PhD); geographic information systems (MS); geotechnical engineering (MS, PhD); hydrology and hydraulics (MS, PhD); structural engineering (MS, PhD); transportation engineering (MS, PhD). *Program availability:* Part-time, evening/weekend. *Degree requirements:* For master's, comprehensive exam, 30 credit hours, project or thesis; for doctorate, comprehensive exam, thesis/dissertation, 60 credit hours

(30 of which are dissertation research). *Entrance requirements:* For master's, GRE, statement of purpose, transcripts, three references; for doctorate, GRE, statement of purpose, transcripts, references, letter of support from faculty stating willingness to serve as dissertation advisor and outlining plan for financial support. Additional exam requirements/recommendations for international students: required—TOEFL (minimum score 537 paper-based; 75 iBT); recommended—IELTS (minimum score 6.5). Electronic applications accepted. Tuition and fees vary according to course load, program and reciprocity agreements.

University of Colorado Denver, College of Engineering, Design and Computing, Master of Engineering Program, Denver, CO 80217-3364. Offers civil engineering (M Eng), including civil engineering, geographic information systems, transportation systems; electrical engineering (M Eng); mechanical engineering (M Eng). *Program availability:* Part-time. *Entrance requirements:* For master's, GRE (for those with GPA below 2.75), transcripts, references, statement of purpose. Tuition and fees vary according to course load, program and reciprocity agreements.

University of Dayton, Department of Civil and Environmental Engineering and Engineering Mechanics, Dayton, OH 45469. Offers engineering mechanics (MSEM); environmental engineering (MSCE); geotechnical engineering (MSCE); structural engineering (MSCE); transportation engineering (MSCE); water resources engineering (MSCE). *Program availability:* Part-time, blended/hybrid learning. *Degree requirements:* For master's, thesis or alternative. *Entrance requirements:* For master's, minimum GPA of 3.0 in undergraduate work. Additional exam requirements/recommendations for international students: required—TOEFL (minimum score 550 paper-based; 80 iBT); recommended—IELTS (minimum score 6.5), TSE (minimum score 60). Electronic applications accepted.

University of Delaware, College of Engineering, Department of Civil and Environmental Engineering, Newark, DE 19716. Offers environmental engineering (MAS, MCE, PhD); geotechnical engineering (MAS, MCE, PhD); ocean engineering (MAS, MCE, PhD); structural engineering (MAS, MCE, PhD); transportation engineering (MAS, MCE, PhD); water resource engineering (MAS, MCE, PhD). *Program availability:* Part-time. Terminal master's awarded for partial completion of doctoral program. *Degree requirements:* For master's, thesis; for doctorate, thesis/dissertation. *Entrance requirements:* For master's and doctorate, GRE General Test. Additional exam requirements/recommendations for international students: required—TOEFL. Electronic applications accepted.

The University of Iowa, Graduate College, College of Engineering, Department of Civil and Environmental Engineering, Iowa City, IA 52242-1316. Offers environmental engineering and science (MS, PhD); hydraulics and water resources (MS, PhD); structures, mechanics and materials (MS, PhD); sustainable water development (MS, PhD); transportation engineering (MS, PhD). *Program availability:* Part-time. Terminal master's awarded for partial completion of doctoral program. *Degree requirements:* For master's, thesis optional, exam; for doctorate, comprehensive exam, thesis/dissertation, exam. *Entrance requirements:* For master's, GRE (minimum combined score of 301 on verbal and quantitative), minimum undergraduate GPA of 3.0; for doctorate, GRE (minimum combined score of 301 on verbal and quantitative), minimum graduate GPA of 3.0. Additional exam requirements/recommendations for international students: required—TOEFL (minimum score 550 paper-based; 81 iBT), IELTS (minimum score 7). Electronic applications accepted.

University of Massachusetts Amherst, Graduate School, College of Engineering, Department of Civil and Environmental Engineering, Amherst, MA 01003. Offers civil engineering (MSCE, PhD); environmental and water resources engineering (MSCE); geotechnical engineering (MSCE); structural engineering and mechanics (MSCE); transportation engineering (MSCE). *Program availability:* Part-time. Terminal master's awarded for partial completion of doctoral program. *Degree requirements:* For master's, thesis or alternative; for doctorate, comprehensive exam, thesis/dissertation. *Entrance requirements:* For master's and doctorate, GRE General Test. Additional exam requirements/recommendations for international students: required—TOEFL (minimum score 550 paper-based; 80 iBT), IELTS (minimum score 6.5). Electronic applications accepted.

University of Memphis, Graduate School, Herff College of Engineering, Department of Civil Engineering, Memphis, TN 38152. Offers civil engineering (PhD); engineering seismology (MS); environmental engineering (MS); freight transportation (Graduate Certificate); geotechnical engineering (MS); structural engineering (MS); transportation engineering (MS); water resources engineering (MS). *Students:* 15 full-time (4 women), 8 part-time (1 woman); includes 1 minority (Black or African American, non-Hispanic/Latino), 12 international. Average age 27. 26 applicants, 38% accepted, 5 enrolled. In 2019, 11 master's awarded. Terminal master's awarded for partial completion of doctoral program. *Degree requirements:* For master's, comprehensive exam, thesis optional; for doctorate, comprehensive exam, thesis/dissertation. *Entrance requirements:* For master's, GRE General Test, minimum undergraduate GPA of 2.5; bachelor's degree in engineering or a related science or mathematics program; three letters of reference; for doctorate, GRE General Test, bachelor's degree in engineering or engineering science; three letters of reference; for Graduate Certificate, minimum undergraduate GPA of 2.75; bachelor's degree in engineering or engineering science. Additional exam requirements/recommendations for international students: required—TOEFL (minimum score 550 paper-based; 79 iBT). *Application deadline:* For fall admission, 8/1 for domestic students; for spring admission, 12/1 for domestic students. Application fee: $35 ($60 for international students). Electronic applications accepted. *Expenses: Tuition, area resident:* Full-time $9216; part-time $512 per credit hour. Tuition, state resident: full-time $9216; part-time $512 per credit hour. Tuition, nonresident: full-time 12,672; part-time $704 per credit hour. *International tuition:* $16,128 full-time. *Required fees:* $1530; $85 per credit hour. Tuition and fees vary according to program. *Financial support:* Fellowships with full tuition reimbursements, research assistantships with full tuition reimbursements, career-related internships or fieldwork, Federal Work-Study, scholarships/grants, and unspecified assistantships available. Financial award application deadline: 2/1; financial award applicants required to submit FAFSA. *Unit head:* Dr. Shahram Pezeshk, Chair, 901-678-2746, Fax: 901-678-3026, E-mail: spezeshk@memphis.edu. *Application contact:* Dr. Roger Meier, Graduate Coordinator, 901-678-3284, E-mail: rwmeier@memphis.edu. Website: https://www.memphis.edu/ce

University of Nevada, Las Vegas, Graduate College, Howard R. Hughes College of Engineering, Department of Civil and Environmental Engineering and Construction, Las Vegas, NV 89154-4015. Offers civil and environmental engineering (MS, PhD); civil and environmental engineering /transportation (MS). *Program availability:* Part-time. *Faculty:* 16 full-time (3 women). *Students:* 43 full-time (15 women), 32 part-time (7 women); includes 19 minority (1 Black or African American, non-Hispanic/Latino; 4 Asian, non-Hispanic/Latino; 8 Hispanic/Latino; 6 Two or more races, non-Hispanic/Latino), 39 international. Average age 29. 49 applicants, 71% accepted, 19 enrolled. In 2019, 25 master's, 3 doctorates awarded. *Degree requirements:* For master's, thesis (for some programs); for doctorate, comprehensive exam, thesis/dissertation, preliminary exam. *Entrance requirements:* For master's, GRE General Test, bachelor's degree with minimum GPA of 3.0; statement of purpose; letter of recommendation; for doctorate, GRE General Test, master's degree; statement of purpose; 3 letters of recommendation. Additional exam requirements/recommendations for international students: required—

TOEFL (minimum score 550 paper-based; 80 iBT), IELTS (minimum score 7). *Application deadline:* For fall admission, 6/15 for domestic students, 3/15 for international students; for spring admission, 11/15 for domestic students, 8/30 for international students. Application fee: $60 ($95 for international students). Electronic applications accepted. *Expenses:* Contact institution. *Financial support:* In 2019–20, 38 students received support, including 13 research assistantships with full tuition reimbursements available (averaging $16,231 per year), 25 teaching assistantships with full tuition reimbursements available (averaging $16,629 per year); institutionally sponsored loans, scholarships/grants, health care benefits, and unspecified assistantships also available. Financial award application deadline: 3/15; financial award applicants required to submit FAFSA. *Unit head:* Dr. Sajjad Ahmad, Chair/Professor, 702-895-5456, Fax: 702-895-3936, E-mail: ceec.chair@unlv.edu. *Application contact:* Dr. Pramen P. Shrestha, Graduate Coordinator, 702-895-3841, Fax: 702-895-3936, E-mail: ceec.gradcoord@unlv.edu. Website: http://www.unlv.edu/ceec

University of New Brunswick Fredericton, School of Graduate Studies, Faculty of Engineering, Department of Civil Engineering, Fredericton, NB E3B 5A3, Canada. Offers construction engineering and management (M Eng, M Sc E, PhD); environmental engineering (M Eng, M Sc E, PhD); environmental studies (M Eng); geotechnical engineering (M Eng, M Sc E, PhD); groundwater/hydrology (M Eng, M Sc E, PhD); materials (M Eng, M Sc E, PhD); pavements (M Eng, M Sc E, PhD); structures (M Eng, M Sc E, PhD); transportation (M Eng, M Sc E, PhD). *Program availability:* Part-time. *Faculty:* 17 full-time (2 women). *Students:* 31 full-time (6 women), 10 part-time (0 women), 12 international. Average age 27. In 2019, 11 master's awarded. *Degree requirements:* For master's, thesis; for doctorate, comprehensive exam, thesis/dissertation, qualifying exam; 27 credit hours of courses. *Entrance requirements:* For master's, minimum GPA of 3.0; B Sc E in civil engineering or related engineering degree; for doctorate, minimum GPA of 3.0; graduate degree in engineering or applied science. Additional exam requirements/recommendations for international students: required—IELTS (minimum score 7.5), TWE (minimum score 4), Michigan English Language Assessment Battery (minimum score 85) or CanTest (minimum score 4.5); recommended—TOEFL (minimum score 580 paper-based). *Application deadline:* For fall admission, 5/1 for domestic students; for winter admission, 11/1 for domestic students. Applications are processed on a rolling basis. Application fee: $50 Canadian dollars. Electronic applications accepted. *Expenses: Tuition, area resident:* Full-time $6975 Canadian dollars; part-time $3423 Canadian dollars per year. Tuition, state resident: full-time $6975 Canadian dollars; part-time $3423 Canadian dollars per year. Tuition, Canadian resident: full-time $6975 Canadian dollars; part-time $3423 Canadian dollars per year. *International tuition:* $12,435 Canadian dollars full-time. *Required fees:* $92.25 Canadian dollars per term. Full-time tuition and fees vary according to degree level, campus/location, program, reciprocity agreements and student level. *Financial support:* Fellowships, research assistantships, teaching assistantships, career-related internships or fieldwork, and scholarships/grants available. Financial award application deadline: 1/15. *Unit head:* Dr. Jeff Rankin, Chair, 506-453-4618, Fax: 506-453-3568, E-mail: ktm@unb.ca. *Application contact:* MaryBeth Nicholson, Graduate Secretary, 506-452-6127, Fax: 506-453-3568, E-mail: mbnich@unb.ca. Website: http://go.unb.ca/gradprograms

University of Puerto Rico at Mayagüez, Graduate Studies, College of Engineering, Department of Civil Engineering and Surveying, Mayagüez, PR 00681-9000. Offers civil engineering (ME, MS, PhD), including construction engineering and management (ME, MS), environmental engineering, geotechnical engineering (ME, MS), structural engineering, transportation engineering. *Program availability:* Part-time. Terminal master's awarded for partial completion of doctoral program. *Degree requirements:* For master's, one foreign language, thesis; for doctorate, one foreign language, comprehensive exam, thesis/dissertation, qualifying exams. *Entrance requirements:* For master's, proficiency in English and Spanish; BS in civil engineering or its equivalent; for doctorate, proficiency in English and Spanish. Electronic applications accepted.

University of Southern California, Graduate School, Sol Price School of Public Policy, Master of Planning Program, Los Angeles, CA 90089. Offers sustainable cities (Graduate Certificate); transportation systems (Graduate Certificate); urban planning (M Pl); M Arch/M Pl; M Pl/MA; M Pl/MPP; M Pl/MRED; M Pl/MS; M Pl/MSW; MBA/M Pl; ML Arch/M Pl; MPA/M Pl. *Accreditation:* ACSP. *Program availability:* Part-time. *Degree requirements:* For master's, comprehensive exam, internship. *Entrance requirements:* For master's, GRE, GMAT. Additional exam requirements/recommendations for international students: required—TOEFL (minimum score 600 paper-based; 100 iBT). Electronic applications accepted.

University of Southern California, Graduate School, Viterbi School of Engineering, Daniel J. Epstein Department of Industrial and Systems Engineering, Los Angeles, CA 90089. Offers digital supply chain management (MS); engineering management (MS); engineering technology communication (Graduate Certificate); health systems operations (Graduate Certificate); industrial and systems engineering (MS, PhD, Engr); manufacturing engineering (MS); operations research engineering (MS); optimization and supply chain management (Graduate Certificate); product development engineering (MS); safety systems and security (MS); systems architecting and engineering (MS, Graduate Certificate); systems safety and security (Graduate Certificate); transportation systems (Graduate Certificate); MS/MBA. *Program availability:* Part-time, evening/weekend, online learning. Terminal master's awarded for partial completion of doctoral program. *Degree requirements:* For master's, thesis optional; for doctorate, thesis/dissertation. *Entrance requirements:* For master's and doctorate, GRE General Test. Additional exam requirements/recommendations for international students: recommended—TOEFL. Electronic applications accepted.

University of Southern California, Graduate School, Viterbi School of Engineering, Sonny Astani Department of Civil and Environmental Engineering, Los Angeles, CA 90089. Offers applied mechanics (MS); civil engineering (MS, PhD); computer-aided engineering (ME, Graduate Certificate); construction management (MCM); engineering technology commercialization (Graduate Certificate); environmental engineering (MS, PhD); environmental quality management (ME); structural design (ME); sustainable cities (Graduate Certificate); transportation systems (MS, Graduate Certificate); water and waste management (MS). *Program availability:* Part-time, evening/weekend. Terminal master's awarded for partial completion of doctoral program. *Degree requirements:* For master's, thesis optional; for doctorate, thesis/dissertation. *Entrance requirements:* For master's and doctorate, GRE General Test. Additional exam requirements/recommendations for international students: recommended—TOEFL. Electronic applications accepted.

University of South Florida, College of Engineering, Department of Civil and Environmental Engineering, Tampa, FL 33620-9951. Offers civil engineering (MCE, MSCE), including geotechnical engineering, materials science and engineering, structures engineering, transportation engineering, water resources; environmental engineering (MEVE, MSEV, PhD), including engineering for international development (MSEV). *Program availability:* Part-time. *Faculty:* 19 full-time (5 women). *Students:* 144 full-time (46 women), 76 part-time (22 women); includes 35 minority (8 Black or African American, non-Hispanic/Latino; 5 Asian, non-Hispanic/Latino; 18 Hispanic/Latino; 4 Two or more races, non-Hispanic/Latino), 123 international. Average age 28. 220 applicants,

65% accepted, 59 enrolled. In 2019, 82 master's, 15 doctorates awarded. Terminal master's awarded for partial completion of doctoral program. *Degree requirements:* For master's, comprehensive exam, thesis (for some programs); for doctorate, comprehensive exam, thesis/dissertation. *Entrance requirements:* For master's, GRE required, bachelor's degree in appropriate field, minimum GPA of 3.0 in major, letters of reference, statement of purpose, resume, intake form; for doctorate, GRE with V (45th percentile), Q (75th percentile), and AW (55th percentile), letters of recommendation, statement of purpose, resume, intake form. Additional exam requirements/recommendations for international students: required—TOEFL, TOEFL (minimum score 550 paper-based; 79 iBT) or IELTS (minimum score 6.5). *Application deadline:* For fall admission, 2/15 for domestic students, 2/15 priority date for international students; for spring admission, 10/15 for domestic students, 9/15 priority date for international students. Application fee: $30. Electronic applications accepted. *Financial support:* In 2019–20, 45 students received support, including 44 research assistantships (averaging $14,123 per year), 21 teaching assistantships with tuition reimbursements available (averaging $15,329 per year). *Unit head:* Dr. Manjriker Gunaratne, Professor and Department Chair, 813-974-5818, Fax: 813-974-2957, E-mail: gunaratn@usf.edu. *Application contact:* Dr. Sarina J. Ergas, Professor and Graduate Program Coordinator, 813-974-1119, Fax: 813-974-2957, E-mail: sergas@usf.edu.
Website: http://www.usf.edu/engineering/cee/

University of South Florida, Innovative Education, Tampa, FL 33620-9951. Offers adult, career and higher education (Graduate Certificate), including college teaching, leadership in developing human resources, leadership in higher education; Africana studies (Graduate Certificate), including diasporas and health disparities, genocide and human rights; aging studies (Graduate Certificate), including gerontology; art research (Graduate Certificate), including museum studies; business foundations (Graduate Certificate); chemical and biomedical engineering (Graduate Certificate), including materials science and engineering, water, health and sustainability; child and family studies (Graduate Certificate), including positive behavior support; civil and industrial engineering (Graduate Certificate), including transportation systems analysis; community and family health (Graduate Certificate), including maternal and child health, social marketing and public health, violence and injury: prevention and intervention, women's health; criminology (Graduate Certificate), including criminal justice administration; data science for public administration (Graduate Certificate); digital humanities (Graduate Certificate); educational measurement and research (Graduate Certificate), including evaluation; English (Graduate Certificate), including comparative literary studies, creative writing, professional and technical communication; entrepreneurship (Graduate Certificate); environmental health (Graduate Certificate), including safety management; epidemiology and biostatistics (Graduate Certificate), including applied biostatistics, biostatistics, concepts and tools of epidemiology, epidemiology, epidemiology of infectious diseases; geography, environment and planning (Graduate Certificate), including community development, environmental policy and management, geographical information systems; geology (Graduate Certificate), including hydrogeology; global health (Graduate Certificate), including disaster management, global health and Latin American and Caribbean studies, global health practice, humanitarian assistance, infection control; government and international affairs (Graduate Certificate), including Cuban studies, globalization studies; health policy and management (Graduate Certificate), including health management and leadership, public health policy and programs; hearing specialist: early intervention (Graduate Certificate); industrial and management systems engineering (Graduate Certificate), including systems engineering, technology management; information studies (Graduate Certificate), including school library media specialist; information systems/decision sciences (Graduate Certificate), including analytics and business intelligence; instructional technology (Graduate Certificate), including distance education, Florida digital/virtual educator, instructional design, multimedia design, Web design; internal medicine, bioethics and medical humanities (Graduate Certificate), including biomedical ethics; Latin American and Caribbean studies (Graduate Certificate); leadership for coastal resiliency planning (Graduate Certificate); mass communications (Graduate Certificate), including multimedia journalism; mathematics and statistics (Graduate Certificate), including mathematics; medicine (Graduate Certificate), including aging and neuroscience, bioinformatics, biotechnology, brain fitness and memory management, clinical investigation, hand and upper limb rehabilitation, health informatics, health sciences, integrative weight management, intellectual property, medicine and gender, metabolic and nutritional medicine, metabolic cardiology, pharmacy sciences; national and competitive intelligence (Graduate Certificate); nursing (Graduate Certificate), including simulation based academic fellowship in advanced pain management; psychological and social foundations (Graduate Certificate), including career counseling, college teaching, diversity in education, mental health counseling, school counseling; public affairs (Graduate Certificate), including nonprofit management, public management, research administration; public health (Graduate Certificate), including assessing chemical toxicity and public health risks, health equity, pharmacoepidemiology, public health generalist, toxicology, translational research in adolescent behavioral health; public health practices (Graduate Certificate), including planning for healthy communities; rehabilitation and mental health counseling (Graduate Certificate), including integrative mental health care, marriage and family therapy, rehabilitation technology; secondary education (Graduate Certificate), including ESOL, foreign language education: culture and content, foreign language education: professional; social work (Graduate Certificate), including geriatric social work/clinical gerontology; special education (Graduate Certificate), including autism spectrum disorder, disabilities education: severe/profound; world languages (Graduate Certificate), including teaching English as a second language (TESL) or foreign language. *Unit head:* Dr. Cynthia DeLuca, Associate Vice President and Assistant Vice Provost, 813-974-3077, Fax: 813-974-7061, E-mail: deluca@usf.edu. *Application contact:* Owen Hooper, Director, Summer and Alternative Calendar Programs, 813-974-6917, E-mail: hooper@usf.edu.
Website: http://www.usf.edu/innovative-education/

The University of Texas at Tyler, College of Engineering, Department of Civil Engineering, Tyler, TX 75799-0001. Offers environmental engineering (MS); industrial safety (MS); structural engineering (MS); transportation engineering (MS); water resources engineering (MS). *Program availability:* Part-time, evening/weekend. *Faculty:* 5 full-time. *Students:* 7 full-time (0 women), 8 part-time (6 women); includes 4 minority (1 Asian, non-Hispanic/Latino; 3 Hispanic/Latino), 4 international. Average age 28. 14 applicants, 79% accepted, 4 enrolled. In 2019, 6 master's awarded. *Entrance requirements:* For master's, GRE General Test, bachelor's degree in engineering, associated science degree. Additional exam requirements/recommendations for international students: required—TOEFL. *Application deadline:* For fall admission, 8/17 priority date for domestic students, 7/1 priority date for international students; for spring admission, 12/21 priority date for domestic students, 11/1 priority date for international students. Application fee: $25 ($50 for international students). *Financial support:* Application deadline: 7/1. *Unit head:* Dr. Torey Nalbone, Chair, 903-565-5520, E-mail: tnalbone@uttyler.edu. *Application contact:* Dr. Torey Nalbone, Chair, 903-565-5520, E-mail: tnalbone@uttyler.edu.
Website: https://www.uttyler.edu/ce/

University of Washington, Graduate School, College of Engineering, Department of Civil and Environmental Engineering, Seattle, WA 98195-2700. Offers construction engineering (MSCE, PhD); environmental engineering (MSCE, PhD); geotechnical engineering (MSCE, PhD); hydrology and hydrodynamics (MSCE, PhD); structural engineering and mechanics (MSCE, PhD); transportation engineering (MSCE, PhD). *Program availability:* Part-time, 100% online. *Students:* 248 full-time (97 women), 174 part-time (63 women); includes 90 minority (8 Black or African American, non-Hispanic/Latino; 2 American Indian or Alaska Native, non-Hispanic/Latino; 46 Asian, non-Hispanic/Latino; 18 Hispanic/Latino; 16 Two or more races, non-Hispanic/Latino), 118 international. Average age 28. 756 applicants, 59% accepted, 164 enrolled. In 2019, 133 master's, 21 doctorates awarded. Terminal master's awarded for partial completion of doctoral program. *Degree requirements:* For master's, thesis optional; for doctorate, comprehensive exam, thesis/dissertation, qualifying, general and final exams; completion of degree within 10 years. *Entrance requirements:* For master's, GRE General Test, minimum GPA of 3.0, statement of purpose, letters of recommendation, transcripts; for doctorate, GRE General Test, minimum GPA of 3.5, statement of purpose, letters of recommendation, transcripts, resume. Additional exam requirements/recommendations for international students: required—TOEFL (minimum score 580 paper-based; 92 iBT). *Application deadline:* For fall admission, 12/15 for domestic and international students. Applications are processed on a rolling basis. Application fee: $85. Electronic applications accepted. *Expenses:* Contact institution. *Financial support:* In 2019–20, 21 fellowships with full tuition reimbursements (averaging $30,600 per year), 76 research assistantships with full tuition reimbursements (averaging $30,600 per year), 27 teaching assistantships with full tuition reimbursements (averaging $30,120 per year) were awarded; Federal Work-Study, institutionally sponsored loans, scholarships/grants, health care benefits, tuition waivers, and unspecified assistantships also available. Support available to part-time students. Financial award application deadline: 12/15. *Unit head:* Dr. Laura Lowes, Professor/Chair, 206-685-2563, Fax: 206-543-1543, E-mail: lowes@uw.edu. *Application contact:* Bryan Crockett, Director of Academic Services, 206-616-1891, Fax: 206-543-1543, E-mail: ceginfo@u.washington.edu.
Website: http://www.ce.washington.edu/

University of Wisconsin–Madison, Graduate School, College of Engineering, Department of Civil and Environmental Engineering, Madison, WI 53706-1380. Offers construction engineering and management (MS); environmental science and engineering (MS); geological/geotechnical engineering (MS); structural engineering (MS); transportation engineering (MS); water resources engineering (MS). *Program availability:* Part-time. Terminal master's awarded for partial completion of doctoral program. *Degree requirements:* For master's, thesis (for some programs), minimum of 30 credits; minimum overall GPA of 3.0. *Entrance requirements:* For master's, GRE General Test, bachelor's degree; minimum GPA of 3.0 for last 60 credits of course work. Additional exam requirements/recommendations for international students: required—TOEFL (minimum score 580 paper-based; 92 iBT). Electronic applications accepted. *Expenses:* Contact institution.

Virginia Polytechnic Institute and State University, VT Online, Blacksburg, VA 24061. Offers advanced transportation systems (Certificate); aerospace engineering (MS); agricultural and life sciences (MSLFS); business information systems (Graduate Certificate); career and technical education (MS); civil engineering (MS); computer engineering (M Eng, MS); decision support systems (Graduate Certificate); eLearning leadership (MA); electrical engineering (M Eng, MS); engineering administration (MEA); environmental engineering (Certificate); environmental politics and policy (Graduate Certificate); environmental sciences and engineering (MS); foundations of political analysis (Graduate Certificate); health product risk management (Graduate Certificate); industrial and systems engineering (MS); information policy and society (Graduate Certificate); information security (Graduate Certificate); information technology (MIT); instructional technology (MA); integrative STEM education (MA Ed); liberal arts (Graduate Certificate); life sciences: health product risk management (MS); natural resources (MNR, Graduate Certificate); networking (Graduate Certificate); nonprofit and nongovernmental organization management (Graduate Certificate); ocean engineering (MS); political science (MA); security studies (Graduate Certificate); software development (Graduate Certificate). *Expenses:* Tuition, state resident: full-time $13,700; part-time $761.25 per credit hour. Tuition, nonresident: full-time $27,614; part-time $1534 per credit hour. *Required fees:* $886.50 per term. Tuition and fees vary according to campus/location and program.

Wentworth Institute of Technology, Master of Engineering in Civil Engineering Program, Boston, MA 02115-5998. Offers construction engineering (M Eng); infrastructure engineering (M Eng). *Program availability:* Part-time-only, evening/weekend. *Degree requirements:* For master's, thesis optional, capstone course. *Entrance requirements:* For master's, resume, statement of purpose, official transcripts, two professional recommendations, bachelor's degree, minimum GPA of 3.0, one year of professional experience in a technical role and/or technical organization. Additional exam requirements/recommendations for international students: recommended—TOEFL (minimum score 550 paper-based). Electronic applications accepted. *Expenses:* Contact institution.

Water Resources Engineering

Carnegie Mellon University, Carnegie Institute of Technology, Department of Civil and Environmental Engineering, Pittsburgh, PA 15213. Offers advanced infrastructure systems (MS, PhD); advanced infrastructure systems technology development and application (MS); air quality engineering and science (MS); civil and environmental engineering (MS, PhD); civil and environmental engineering/engineering and public policy (PhD); civil engineering (MS, PhD); computational mechanics (MS, PhD); computational modeling and monitoring for resilient structural and material systems (MS); energy infrastructure systems (MS); environmental engineering (MS, PhD); environmental management and science (MS, PhD); IT-based sustainable global infrastructure and construction management (MS); sustainability and green design (MS); water quality engineering and science (MS). *Program availability:* Part-time. *Faculty:* 23 full-time (5 women), 12 part-time/adjunct (3 women). *Students:* 261 full-time (109 women); includes 19 minority (7 Black or African American, non-Hispanic/Latino; 8 Asian, non-Hispanic/Latino; 4 Hispanic/Latino), 214 international. Average age 25. 649

applicants, 57% accepted, 106 enrolled. In 2019, 80 master's, 12 doctorates awarded. Terminal master's awarded for partial completion of doctoral program. *Degree requirements:* For master's, thesis optional; for doctorate, comprehensive exam, thesis/dissertation, two-part qualifying exam, public defense of dissertation. *Entrance requirements:* For master's, GRE General Test, BS in engineering, science, or mathematics; for doctorate, GRE General Test, BS or MS in engineering, science, or mathematics. Additional exam requirements/recommendations for international students: required—TOEFL (minimum score 84 iBT), TOEFL (minimum score 84 iBT) or IELTS (7.0). *Application deadline:* For fall admission, 1/5 priority date for domestic and international students; for spring admission, 9/15 priority date for domestic and international students. Applications are processed on a rolling basis. Application fee: $75. Electronic applications accepted. *Financial support:* In 2019–20, 113 students received support. Fellowships with tuition reimbursements available, research assistantships with tuition reimbursements available, teaching assistantships, scholarships/grants, health care benefits, tuition waivers (full and partial), and unspecified assistantships available. Financial award application deadline: 1/5. *Unit head:* Dr. David A. Dzombak, Professor and Department Head, 412-268-2941, Fax: 412-268-7813, E-mail: dzombak@cmu.edu. *Application contact:* David A. Vey, Director of Graduate Programs, 412-268-2292, Fax: 412-268-7813, E-mail: dvey@andrew.cmu.edu.
Website: http://www.cmu.edu/cee/

Clemson University, Graduate School, College of Engineering, Computing and Applied Sciences, Glenn Department of Civil Engineering, Clemson, SC 29634. Offers civil engineering (MS, PhD), including construction engineering and management, construction materials, geotechnical engineering, structural engineering, transportation engineering, water resources engineering. *Program availability:* Part-time, 100% online. *Faculty:* 24 full-time (4 women), 3 part-time/adjunct (2 women). *Students:* 101 full-time (20 women), 44 part-time (9 women); includes 9 minority (3 Black or African American, non-Hispanic/Latino; 1 Asian, non-Hispanic/Latino; 2 Hispanic/Latino; 3 Two or more races, non-Hispanic/Latino), 97 international. Average age 29. 248 applicants, 62% accepted, 61 enrolled. In 2019, 43 master's, 11 doctorates awarded. *Degree requirements:* For master's, thesis or alternative, oral exam, seminar; for doctorate, comprehensive exam, thesis/dissertation, oral exam, seminar. *Entrance requirements:* For master's and doctorate, GRE General Test, unofficial transcripts, letters of recommendation, statement of purpose. Additional exam requirements/recommendations for international students: required—TOEFL (minimum score 80 paper-based; 80 iBT), PTE (minimum score 54); recommended—IELTS (minimum score 6.5). *Application deadline:* For fall admission, 4/15 for domestic and international students; for spring admission, 9/15 for domestic and international students. Applications are processed on a rolling basis. Application fee: $80 ($90 for international students). Electronic applications accepted. *Expenses: Tuition, area resident:* Full-time $10,600; part-time $8688 per semester. Tuition, state resident: full-time $10,600; part-time $8688 per semester. Tuition, nonresident: full-time $22,050; part-time $17,412 per semester. *International tuition:* $22,050 full-time. *Required fees:* $1196; $617 per semester. $617 per semester. Tuition and fees vary according to course load, degree level, campus/location and program. *Financial support:* In 2019–20, 101 students received support, including 2 fellowships with full and partial tuition reimbursements available (averaging $34,000 per year), 61 research assistantships with full and partial tuition reimbursements available (averaging $18,222 per year), 4 teaching assistantships with full and partial tuition reimbursements available (averaging $20,567 per year); career-related internships or fieldwork and unspecified assistantships also available. Financial award application deadline: 4/15. *Unit head:* Dr. Jesus M de la Garza, Department Chair, 864-656-3001, E-mail: jdelaga@clemson.edu. *Application contact:* Dr. Abdul Khan, Graduate Program Coordinator, 864-656-3327, E-mail: abdkhan@clemson.edu.
Website: https://www.clemson.edu/cecas/departments/ce/

Cornell University, Graduate School, Graduate Fields of Engineering, Field of Civil and Environmental Engineering, Ithaca, NY 14853. Offers engineering management (M Eng, MS, PhD); environmental engineering (M Eng, MS, PhD); environmental fluid mechanics and hydrology (M Eng, MS, PhD); environmental systems engineering (M Eng, MS, PhD); geotechnical engineering (M Eng, MS, PhD); remote sensing (M Eng, MS, PhD); structural engineering (M Eng, MS, PhD); structural mechanics (M Eng, MS); transportation engineering (MS, PhD); transportation systems engineering (M Eng); water resource systems (M Eng, MS, PhD). Terminal master's awarded for partial completion of doctoral program. *Degree requirements:* For master's, thesis (MS); for doctorate, comprehensive exam, thesis/dissertation. *Entrance requirements:* For master's and doctorate, GRE General Test (recommended), 2 letters of recommendation. Additional exam requirements/recommendations for international students: required—TOEFL (minimum score 600 paper-based; 77 iBT). Electronic applications accepted.

Indiana University Bloomington, School of Public and Environmental Affairs, Environmental Science Programs, Bloomington, IN 47405. Offers applied ecology (MSES); energy (MSES); environmental chemistry, toxicology, and risk assessment (MSES); environmental science (PhD); hazardous materials management (Certificate); specialized environmental science (MSES); water resources (MSES); JD/MSES; MSES/MA; MSES/MPA; MSES/MS. *Program availability:* Part-time. Terminal master's awarded for partial completion of doctoral program. *Degree requirements:* For master's, capstone or thesis; internship; for doctorate, comprehensive exam, thesis/dissertation. *Entrance requirements:* For master's, GRE General Test or GMAT, official transcripts, 3 letters of recommendation, resume, personal statement; for doctorate, GRE General Test or LSAT, official transcripts, 3 letters of recommendation, resume or curriculum vitae, statement of purpose. Additional exam requirements/recommendations for international students: required—TOEFL (minimum score 600 paper-based; 96 iBT); recommended—IELTS (minimum score 7). Electronic applications accepted.

Kansas State University, Graduate School, College of Engineering, Department of Civil Engineering, Manhattan, KS 66506. Offers civil engineering (MS, PhD); environmental engineering (MS, PhD); geotechnical engineering (MS, PhD); structural engineering (MS, PhD); transportation engineering (MS, PhD); water resources engineering (MS, PhD). *Program availability:* Part-time, evening/weekend, online learning. *Degree requirements:* For master's, thesis or alternative; for doctorate, thesis/dissertation. *Entrance requirements:* For master's, GRE General Test, bachelor's degree or course work in related engineering fields; for doctorate, GRE General Test. Additional exam requirements/recommendations for international students: required—TOEFL (minimum score 550 paper-based; 79 iBT). Electronic applications accepted.

Kennesaw State University, Southern Polytechnic College of Engineering and Engineering Technology, Program in Civil Engineering, Kennesaw, GA 30144. Offers environmental engineering (MS); geotechnical engineering (MS); structural engineering (MS); transportation and pavement engineering (MS); water resources engineering (MS). *Program availability:* Online learning. *Students:* 9 full-time (2 women), 30 part-time (4 women); includes 20 minority (9 Black or African American, non-Hispanic/Latino; 5 Asian, non-Hispanic/Latino; 5 Hispanic/Latino; 1 Two or more races, non-Hispanic/Latino), 3 international. Average age 34. 12 applicants, 92% accepted, 8 enrolled. In 2019, 12 master's awarded. *Degree requirements:* For master's, thesis optional. *Entrance requirements:* Additional exam requirements/recommendations for international students: required—TOEFL (minimum score 80 iBT), IELTS (minimum score 6.5). *Application deadline:* For fall admission, 11/1 for domestic and international students; for spring admission, 4/1 for domestic and international students. Applications are processed on a rolling basis. Application fee: $60. Electronic applications accepted. *Expenses: Tuition, area resident:* Full-time $7104; part-time $296 per credit hour. Tuition, state resident: full-time $7104; part-time $296 per credit hour. Tuition, nonresident: full-time $25,584; part-time $1066 per credit hour. *International tuition:* $25,584 full-time. *Required fees:* $2006; $1706 per unit. $853 per semester. *Unit head:* Metin Oguzmert, Coordinator, 470-578-5083, E-mail: moguzmer@kennesaw.edu. *Application contact:* Admissions Counselor, 470-578-4377, E-mail: ksugrad@kennesaw.edu.
Website: http://engineering.kennesaw.edu/civil-construction/degrees/ms-civil-engineering.php

Lawrence Technological University, College of Engineering, Southfield, MI 48075-1058. Offers architectural engineering (MS); automotive engineering (MS); biomedical engineering (MS); civil engineering (MA, MS, PhD), including environmental engineering (MS), geotechnical engineering (MS), structural engineering (MS), transportation engineering (MS), water resource engineering (MS); construction engineering management (MA); electrical and computer engineering (MS); engineering management (MEM); engineering technology (MS); fire engineering (MS); industrial engineering (MS), including healthcare systems; manufacturing systems (ME); mechanical engineering (MS, DE, PhD), including automotive engineering (MS), energy engineering (MS), manufacturing (DE), solid mechanics (MS), thermal/fluid systems (MS); mechatronic systems engineering (MS). *Program availability:* Part-time, evening/weekend. *Faculty:* 23 full-time (2 women), 20 part-time/adjunct (1 woman). *Students:* 14 full-time (5 women), 286 part-time (54 women); includes 26 minority (13 Black or African American, non-Hispanic/Latino; 8 Asian, non-Hispanic/Latino; 3 Hispanic/Latino; 2 Two or more races, non-Hispanic/Latino), 150 international. Average age 29. 384 applicants, 58% accepted, 74 enrolled. In 2019, 223 master's, 7 doctorates awarded. Terminal master's awarded for partial completion of doctoral program. *Degree requirements:* For master's, thesis optional; for doctorate, comprehensive exam, thesis/dissertation optional. *Entrance requirements:* Additional exam requirements/recommendations for international students: required—TOEFL (minimum score 550 paper-based; 79 iBT), IELTS (minimum score 6.5). *Application deadline:* For fall admission, 5/24 for international students; for spring admission, 10/13 for international students; for summer admission, 2/18 for international students. Applications are processed on a rolling basis. Application fee: $50. Electronic applications accepted. *Expenses: Tuition:* Full-time $16,618; part-time $8309 per year. *Required fees:* $600; $600. *Financial support:* In 2019–20, 21 students received support. Unspecified assistantships available. Financial award application deadline: 4/1; financial award applicants required to submit FAFSA. *Unit head:* Dr. Nabil Grace, Dean, 248-204-2500, Fax: 248-204-2509, E-mail: engrdean@ltu.edu. *Application contact:* Jane Rohrback, Director of Admissions, 248-204-3160, Fax: 248-204-2228, E-mail: admissions@ltu.edu.
Website: http://www.ltu.edu/engineering/index.asp

Louisiana State University and Agricultural & Mechanical College, Graduate School, College of Engineering, Department of Civil and Environmental Engineering, Baton Rouge, LA 70803. Offers environmental engineering (MSCE, PhD); geotechnical engineering (MSCE, PhD); structural engineering and mechanics (MSCE, PhD); transportation engineering (MSCE, PhD); water resources (MSCE, PhD).

Marquette University, Graduate School, College of Engineering, Department of Civil and Environmental Engineering, Milwaukee, WI 53201-1881. Offers construction engineering and management (MS, PhD, Certificate); environmental engineering (MS, PhD); structural design (Certificate); structural engineering and structural mechanics (MS, PhD); transportation (Certificate); transportation engineering and materials (MS, PhD); waste and wastewater treatment processes (Certificate); water resources engineering (Certificate). *Program availability:* Part-time, evening/weekend. Terminal master's awarded for partial completion of doctoral program. *Degree requirements:* For master's, comprehensive exam (for some programs), thesis or alternative; for doctorate, thesis/dissertation. *Entrance requirements:* For master's, GRE General Test (recommended), minimum GPA of 3.0, official transcripts from all current and previous colleges/universities except Marquette, three letters of recommendation; for doctorate, GRE General Test, minimum GPA of 3.0, official transcripts from all current and previous colleges/universities except Marquette, three letters of recommendation, brief statement of purpose, submission of any English language publications authored by applicant (strongly recommended). Additional exam requirements/recommendations for international students: required—TOEFL (minimum score 530 paper-based). Electronic applications accepted.

McGill University, Faculty of Graduate and Postdoctoral Studies, Faculty of Engineering, Department of Civil Engineering and Applied Mechanics, Montréal, QC H3A 2T5, Canada. Offers environmental engineering (M Eng, M Sc, PhD); fluid mechanics (M Sc); fluid mechanics and hydraulic engineering (M Eng, PhD); materials engineering (M Eng, PhD); rehabilitation of urban infrastructure (M Eng, PhD); soil behavior (M Eng, PhD); soil mechanics and foundations (M Eng, PhD); structures and structural mechanics (M Eng, PhD); water resources (M Sc); water resources engineering (M Eng, PhD).

New Mexico Institute of Mining and Technology, Center for Graduate Studies, Department of Civil and Environmental Engineering, Socorro, NM 87801. Offers environmental engineering (MS), including air quality engineering and science, hazardous waste engineering, water quality engineering and science. *Degree requirements:* For master's, thesis, thesis or independent study. *Entrance requirements:* Additional exam requirements/recommendations for international students: required—TOEFL (minimum score 540 paper-based).

Ohio University, Graduate College, Russ College of Engineering and Technology, Department of Civil Engineering, Athens, OH 45701-2979. Offers civil engineering (PhD); construction engineering and management (MS); environmental (MS); geoenvironmental (MS); geotechnical (MS); mechanics (MS); structures (MS); transportation (MS); water resources (MS). *Program availability:* Part-time. *Degree requirements:* For master's, comprehensive exam (for some programs), thesis or alternative; for doctorate, comprehensive exam, thesis/dissertation. *Entrance requirements:* For master's, GRE General Test, minimum GPA of 3.0, 3 letters of recommendation; for doctorate, GRE General Test. Additional exam requirements/recommendations for international students: required—TOEFL (minimum score 550 paper-based; 80 iBT) or IELTS (minimum score 6.5). Electronic applications accepted.

Oregon State University, College of Engineering, Program in Biological and Ecological Engineering, Corvallis, OR 97331. Offers bio-based products and fuels (M Eng, MS, PhD); biological systems analysis (M Eng, MS, PhD); bioprocessing (M Eng, MS, PhD); ecosystems analysis and modeling (M Eng, MS, PhD); water quality (M Eng, MS, PhD); water resources (M Eng, MS, PhD). Terminal master's awarded for partial completion of doctoral program. *Entrance requirements:* For master's and doctorate, GRE, minimum GPA of 3.0 in last 90 hours. Additional exam requirements/recommendations for international students: required—TOEFL (minimum score 80 iBT), IELTS (minimum score 6.5). *Expenses:* Contact institution.

Water Resources Engineering

Oregon State University, Interdisciplinary/Institutional Programs, Program in Water Resources Engineering, Corvallis, OR 97331. Offers MS, PhD, JD/MS. *Entrance requirements:* For master's and doctorate, GRE. Additional exam requirements/recommendations for international students: required—TOEFL (minimum score 80 iBT), IELTS (minimum score 6.5).

State University of New York College of Environmental Science and Forestry, Department of Environmental Resources Engineering, Syracuse, NY 13210-2779. Offers ecological engineering (MPS, MS, PhD); environmental management (MPS); environmental resources engineering (MPS, MS, PhD); geospatial information science and engineering (MPS, MS, PhD); water resources engineering (MPS, MS, PhD). *Program availability:* Part-time. *Faculty:* 9 full-time (1 woman), 3 part-time/adjunct (0 women). *Students:* 22 full-time (13 women), 4 part-time (1 woman); includes 1 minority (Asian, non-Hispanic/Latino), 15 international. Average age 31. 32 applicants, 31% accepted, 7 enrolled. In 2019, 3 master's, 2 doctorates awarded. Terminal master's awarded for partial completion of doctoral program. *Degree requirements:* For master's, thesis (for some programs); for doctorate, comprehensive exam, thesis/dissertation. *Entrance requirements:* For master's and doctorate, GRE General Test, minimum GPA of 3.0. Additional exam requirements/recommendations for international students: required—TOEFL (minimum score 550 paper-based; 80 iBT), IELTS (minimum score 6). *Application deadline:* For fall admission, 1/15 priority date for domestic and international students; for spring admission, 11/1 priority date for domestic and international students. Applications are processed on a rolling basis. Application fee: $60. Electronic applications accepted. *Expenses:* Tuition, state resident: full-time $11,310; part-time $472 per credit hour. Tuition, nonresident: full-time $23,100; part-time $963 per credit hour. *Required fees:* $1890; $95.21 per credit hour. *Financial support:* In 2019–20, 8 students received support. Unspecified assistantships available. Financial award application deadline: 6/30; financial award applicants required to submit FAFSA. *Unit head:* Dr. Lindi Quackenbush, Chair, 315-470-4727, Fax: 315-470-4710, E-mail: ljquackc@esf.edu. *Application contact:* Laura Payne, Administrative Assistant, Office of Instruction & Graduate Studies, 315-470-6599, Fax: 315-470-6978, E-mail: esfgrad@esf.edu.
Website: http://www.esf.edu/ere

Stevens Institute of Technology, Graduate School, Charles V. Schaefer Jr. School of Engineering and Science, Department of Civil, Environmental, and Ocean Engineering, Program in Civil Engineering, Hoboken, NJ 07030. Offers civil engineering (PhD, Certificate), including geotechnical engineering (Certificate); geotechnical/geoenvironmental engineering (M Eng, Engr); hydrologic modeling (M Eng); stormwater management (M Eng); structural engineering (M Eng, Engr); transportation engineering (M Eng); water resources engineering (M Eng). *Program availability:* Part-time, evening/weekend. *Faculty:* 23 full-time (8 women), 21 part-time/adjunct (2 women). *Students:* 38 full-time (6 women), 19 part-time (6 women); includes 11 minority (2 Black or African American, non-Hispanic/Latino; 1 American Indian or Alaska Native, non-Hispanic/Latino; 8 Asian, non-Hispanic/Latino), 29 international. Average age 25. In 2019, 38 master's, 2 doctorates awarded. Terminal master's awarded for partial completion of doctoral program. *Degree requirements:* For master's, thesis optional, minimum B average in major field and overall; for doctorate, comprehensive exam (for some programs), thesis/dissertation; for other advanced degree, minimum B average. *Entrance requirements:* For master's, International applicants must submit TOEFL/IELTS scores and fulfill the English Language Proficiency Requirement. Applicants to full-time programs who do not qualify for a score waiver are required to submit GRE/GMAT scores. Additional exam requirements/recommendations for international students: required—TOEFL (minimum score 74 iBT), IELTS (minimum score 6). *Application deadline:* For fall admission, 4/15 for domestic and international students; for spring admission, 11/1 for domestic and international students; for summer admission, 5/1 for domestic students. Applications are processed on a rolling basis. Application fee: $60. Electronic applications accepted. *Expenses: Tuition:* Full-time $52,134. *Required fees:* $1880. Tuition and fees vary according to course load. *Financial support:* Fellowships, research assistantships, teaching assistantships, career-related internships or fieldwork, Federal Work-Study, scholarships/grants, and unspecified assistantships available. Financial award application deadline: 2/15; financial award applicants required to submit FAFSA. *Unit head:* Dr. Jean Zu, Dean of SES, 201-216.8233, Fax: 201-216.8372, E-mail: Jean.Zu@stevens.edu. *Application contact:* Graduate Admission, 888-783-8367, Fax: 888-511-1306, E-mail: graduate@stevens.edu.

Tufts University, School of Engineering, Department of Civil and Environmental Engineering, Medford, MA 02155. Offers bioengineering (MS), including environmental biotechnology; civil and environmental engineering (MS, PhD), including applied data science, environmental and water resources engineering, environmental health, geosystems engineering, structural engineering and mechanics; PhD/PhD. *Program availability:* Part-time. Terminal master's awarded for partial completion of doctoral program. *Degree requirements:* For master's, thesis (for some programs); for doctorate, thesis/dissertation. *Entrance requirements:* For master's and doctorate, GRE General Test. Additional exam requirements/recommendations for international students: required—TOEFL (minimum score 550 paper-based; 80 iBT), IELTS (minimum score 6.5). Electronic applications accepted. Full-time tuition and fees vary according to degree level, program and student level. Part-time tuition and fees vary according to course load.

University at Buffalo, the State University of New York, Graduate School, School of Engineering and Applied Sciences, Department of Civil, Structural, and Environmental Engineering, Buffalo, NY 14260. Offers civil engineering (MS, PhD); engineering science (MS), including data sciences, green energy, Internet of Things, nanoelectronics; environmental and water resources engineering (MS). *Program availability:* Part-time, online learning. Terminal master's awarded for partial completion of doctoral program. *Degree requirements:* For master's, project, thesis, or comprehensive exam; for doctorate, thesis/dissertation. *Entrance requirements:* For master's and doctorate, GRE General Test, letters of reference. Additional exam requirements/recommendations for international students: required—TOEFL (minimum score 550 paper-based; 79 iBT). Electronic applications accepted. *Expenses: Tuition, area resident:* Full-time $11,310; part-time $471 per credit hour. Tuition, state resident: full-time $11,310; part-time $471 per credit hour. Tuition, nonresident: full-time $23,100; part-time $963 per credit hour. *International tuition:* $23,100 full-time. *Required fees:* $2820.

University of Alberta, Faculty of Graduate Studies and Research, Department of Civil and Environmental Engineering, Edmonton, AB T6G 2E1, Canada. Offers construction engineering and management (M Eng, M Sc, PhD); environmental engineering (M Eng, M Sc, PhD); environmental science (M Sc, PhD); geoenvironmental engineering (M Eng, M Sc, PhD); geotechnical engineering (M Eng, M Sc, PhD); mining engineering (M Eng, M Sc, PhD); petroleum engineering (M Eng, M Sc, PhD); structural engineering (M Eng, M Sc, PhD); water resources (M Eng, M Sc, PhD). *Program availability:* Part-time, online learning. *Degree requirements:* For master's, thesis (for some programs); for doctorate, thesis/dissertation. *Entrance requirements:* For master's, minimum GPA of 3.0 in last 2 years of undergraduate studies; for doctorate, minimum GPA of 3.0.

Additional exam requirements/recommendations for international students: required—TOEFL (minimum score 550 paper-based). Electronic applications accepted.

University of California, Berkeley, Graduate Division, College of Engineering, Department of Civil and Environmental Engineering, Berkeley, CA 94720. Offers engineering and project management (M Eng, MS, PhD); environmental engineering (M Eng, MS, PhD); geoengineering (M Eng, MS, PhD); structural engineering, mechanics and materials (M Eng, MS, PhD); transportation engineering (M Eng, MS, PhD); M Arch/MS; MCP/MS; MPP/MS. Terminal master's awarded for partial completion of doctoral program. *Degree requirements:* For master's, comprehensive exam (for some programs), thesis (for some programs), comprehensive exam or thesis (MS); for doctorate, thesis/dissertation, qualifying exam. *Entrance requirements:* For master's, GRE General Test, minimum GPA of 3.0, 3 letters of recommendation; for doctorate, GRE General Test, minimum GPA of 3.5, 3 letters of recommendation. Additional exam requirements/recommendations for international students: required—TOEFL (minimum score 570 paper-based; 90 iBT). Electronic applications accepted.

University of Dayton, Department of Civil and Environmental Engineering and Engineering Mechanics, Dayton, OH 45469. Offers engineering mechanics (MSEM); environmental engineering (MSCE); geotechnical engineering (MSCE); structural engineering (MSCE); transportation engineering (MSCE); water resources engineering (MSCE). *Program availability:* Part-time, blended/hybrid learning. *Degree requirements:* For master's, thesis or alternative. *Entrance requirements:* For master's, minimum GPA of 3.0 in undergraduate work. Additional exam requirements/recommendations for international students: required—TOEFL (minimum score 550 paper-based; 80 iBT); recommended—IELTS (minimum score 6.5), TSE (minimum score 60). Electronic applications accepted.

University of Delaware, College of Engineering, Department of Civil and Environmental Engineering, Newark, DE 19716. Offers environmental engineering (MAS, MCE, PhD); geotechnical engineering (MAS, MCE, PhD); ocean engineering (MAS, MCE, PhD); structural engineering (MAS, MCE, PhD); transportation engineering (MAS, MCE, PhD); water resource engineering (MAS, MCE, PhD). *Program availability:* Part-time. Terminal master's awarded for partial completion of doctoral program. *Degree requirements:* For master's, thesis; for doctorate, thesis/dissertation. *Entrance requirements:* For master's and doctorate, GRE General Test. Additional exam requirements/recommendations for international students: required—TOEFL. Electronic applications accepted.

University of Guelph, Office of Graduate and Postdoctoral Studies, College of Physical and Engineering Science, School of Engineering, Guelph, ON N1G 2W1, Canada. Offers biological engineering (M Eng, M Sc, MA Sc, PhD); engineering systems and computing (M Eng, M Sc, MA Sc, PhD); environmental engineering (M Eng, M Sc, MA Sc, PhD); water resources engineering (M Eng, M Sc, MA Sc, PhD). *Program availability:* Part-time. *Degree requirements:* For master's, thesis (for some programs); for doctorate, comprehensive exam, thesis/dissertation. *Entrance requirements:* For master's, minimum B- average during previous 2 years of course work; for doctorate, minimum B average. Additional exam requirements/recommendations for international students: required—TOEFL (minimum score 550 paper-based; 89 iBT), IELTS (minimum score 6.5). Electronic applications accepted.

University of Idaho, College of Graduate Studies, College of Agricultural and Life Sciences, Water Resources Program, Moscow, ID 83844-2282. Offers engineering and science (MS, PhD); law, management and policy (MS, PhD); science and management (MS, PhD). *Faculty:* 20 full-time (6 women). *Students:* 16 full-time, 11 part-time. Average age 32. In 2019, 7 master's, 2 doctorates awarded. *Entrance requirements:* For master's, minimum GPA of 3.0. Additional exam requirements/recommendations for international students: required—TOEFL (minimum score 550 paper-based; 79 iBT), IELTS (minimum score 6.5), Michigan English Language Assessment Battery (minimum score of 77). *Application deadline:* For fall admission, 7/30 for domestic students; for spring admission, 12/1 for domestic students. Applications are processed on a rolling basis. Application fee: $60. Electronic applications accepted. *Expenses:* Tuition, state resident: full-time $7753.80; part-time $502 per credit hour. Tuition, nonresident: full-time $26,990; part-time $1571 per credit hour. *Required fees:* $2122.20; $47 per credit hour. *Financial support:* Applicants required to submit FAFSA.
Website: https://www.uidaho.edu/cals/water-resources

The University of Iowa, Graduate College, College of Engineering, Department of Civil and Environmental Engineering, Iowa City, IA 52242-1316. Offers environmental engineering and science (MS, PhD); hydraulics and water resources (MS, PhD); structures, mechanics and materials (MS, PhD); sustainable water development (MS, PhD); transportation engineering (MS, PhD). *Program availability:* Part-time. Terminal master's awarded for partial completion of doctoral program. *Degree requirements:* For master's, thesis optional, exam; for doctorate, comprehensive exam, thesis/dissertation, exam. *Entrance requirements:* For master's, GRE (minimum combined score of 301 on verbal and quantitative), minimum undergraduate GPA of 3.0; for doctorate, GRE (minimum combined score of 301 on verbal and quantitative), minimum graduate GPA of 3.0. Additional exam requirements/recommendations for international students: required—TOEFL (minimum score 550 paper-based; 81 iBT), IELTS (minimum score 7). Electronic applications accepted.

University of Massachusetts Amherst, Graduate School, College of Engineering, Department of Civil and Environmental Engineering, Amherst, MA 01003. Offers civil engineering (MSCE, PhD); environmental and water resources engineering (MSCE); geotechnical engineering (MSCE); structural engineering and mechanics (MSCE); transportation engineering (MSCE). *Program availability:* Part-time. Terminal master's awarded for partial completion of doctoral program. *Degree requirements:* For master's, thesis or alternative; for doctorate, comprehensive exam, thesis/dissertation. *Entrance requirements:* For master's and doctorate, GRE General Test. Additional exam requirements/recommendations for international students: required—TOEFL (minimum score 550 paper-based; 80 iBT), IELTS (minimum score 6.5). Electronic applications accepted.

University of Memphis, Graduate School, Herff College of Engineering, Department of Civil Engineering, Memphis, TN 38152. Offers civil engineering (PhD); engineering seismology (MS); environmental engineering (MS); freight transportation (Graduate Certificate); geotechnical engineering (MS); structural engineering (MS); transportation engineering (MS); water resources engineering (MS). *Students:* 15 full-time (4 women), 8 part-time (1 woman); includes 1 minority (Black or African American, non-Hispanic/Latino), 12 international. Average age 27. 26 applicants, 38% accepted, 5 enrolled. In 2019, 11 master's awarded. Terminal master's awarded for partial completion of doctoral program. *Degree requirements:* For master's, comprehensive exam, thesis optional; for doctorate, comprehensive exam, thesis/dissertation. *Entrance requirements:* For master's, GRE General Test, minimum undergraduate GPA of 2.5; bachelor's degree in engineering or a related science or mathematics program; three letters of reference; for doctorate, GRE General Test, bachelor's degree in engineering or engineering science; three letters of reference; for Graduate Certificate, minimum undergraduate GPA of 2.75; bachelor's degree in engineering or engineering science. Additional exam requirements/recommendations for international students: required—TOEFL (minimum score 550 paper-based; 79 iBT). *Application deadline:* For fall admission, 8/1 for domestic students; for spring admission, 12/1 for domestic students.

Application fee: $35 ($60 for international students). Electronic applications accepted. *Expenses: Tuition, area resident:* Full-time $9216; part-time $512 per credit hour. Tuition, state resident: full-time $9216; part-time $512 per credit hour. Tuition, nonresident: full-time $12,672; part-time $704 per credit hour. *International tuition:* $16,128 full-time. *Required fees:* $1530; $85 per credit hour. Tuition and fees vary according to program. *Financial support:* Fellowships with full tuition reimbursements, research assistantships with full tuition reimbursements, career-related internships or fieldwork, Federal Work-Study, scholarships/grants, and unspecified assistantships available. Financial award application deadline: 2/1; financial award applicants required to submit FAFSA. *Unit head:* Dr. Shahram Pezeshk, Chair, 901-678-2746, Fax: 901-678-3026, E-mail: spezeshk@memphis.edu. *Application contact:* Dr. Roger Meier, Graduate Coordinator, 901-678-3284, E-mail: rwmeier@memphis.edu. Website: https://www.memphis.edu/ce

University of New Haven, Graduate School, Tagliatela College of Engineering, Program in Environmental Engineering, West Haven, CT 06516. Offers environmental engineering (MS); industrial and hazardous waste (MS); water and wastewater treatment (MS); water resources (MS). *Program availability:* Part-time, evening/weekend, 100% online. *Students:* 15 full-time (7 women), 32 part-time (13 women); includes 7 minority (2 Black or African American, non-Hispanic/Latino; 2 Asian, non-Hispanic/Latino; 3 Hispanic/Latino), 17 international. Average age 30. 67 applicants, 97% accepted, 11 enrolled. In 2019, 15 master's awarded. *Degree requirements:* For master's, thesis or alternative, research project. *Entrance requirements:* For master's, bachelor's degree in engineering. Additional exam requirements/recommendations for international students: required—TOEFL (minimum score 75 iBT), IELTS, PTE (minimum score 50). *Application deadline:* Applications are processed on a rolling basis. Application fee: $50. Electronic applications accepted. Application fee is waived when completed online. *Financial support:* Research assistantships with partial tuition reimbursements, teaching assistantships with partial tuition reimbursements, career-related internships or fieldwork, Federal Work-Study, scholarships/grants, and unspecified assistantships available. Support available to part-time students. Financial award application deadline: 5/1; financial award applicants required to submit FAFSA. *Unit head:* Dr. Emese Hadnagy, Associate Professor, 203-932-1232, E-mail: EHadnagy@newhaven.edu. *Application contact:* Selina O'Toole, Senior Associate Director of Graduate Admissions, 203-932-7337, E-mail: sotoole@newhaven.edu. Website: https://www.newhaven.edu/engineering/graduate-programs/environmental-engineering/

University of South Florida, College of Engineering, Department of Civil and Environmental Engineering, Tampa, FL 33620-9951. Offers civil engineering (MCE, MSCE), including geotechnical engineering, materials science and engineering, structures engineering, transportation engineering, water resources; environmental engineering (MEVE, MSEV, PhD), including engineering for international development (MSEV). *Program availability:* Part-time. *Faculty:* 19 full-time (5 women). *Students:* 144 full-time (46 women), 76 part-time (22 women); includes 35 minority (8 Black or African American, non-Hispanic/Latino; 5 Asian, non-Hispanic/Latino; 18 Hispanic/Latino; 4 Two or more races, non-Hispanic/Latino), 123 international. Average age 28. 220 applicants, 65% accepted, 59 enrolled. In 2019, 82 master's, 15 doctorates awarded. Terminal master's awarded for partial completion of doctoral program. *Degree requirements:* For master's, comprehensive exam, thesis (for some programs); for doctorate, comprehensive exam, thesis/dissertation. *Entrance requirements:* For master's, GRE required, bachelor's degree in appropriate field, minimum GPA of 3.0 in major, letters of reference, statement of purpose, resume, intake form; for doctorate, GRE with V (45th percentile), Q (75th percentile), and AW (55th percentile), letters of recommendation, statement of purpose, resume, intake form. Additional exam requirements/recommendations for international students: required—TOEFL, TOEFL (minimum score 550 paper-based; 79 iBT) or IELTS (minimum score 6.5). *Application deadline:* For fall admission, 2/15 for domestic students, 2/15 priority date for international students; for spring admission, 10/15 for domestic students, 9/15 priority date for international students. Application fee: $30. Electronic applications accepted. *Financial support:* In 2019–20, 45 students received support, including 44 research assistantships (averaging $14,123 per year), 21 teaching assistantships with tuition reimbursements available (averaging $15,329 per year). *Unit head:* Dr. Manjriker Gunaratne, Professor and Department Chair, 813-974-5818, Fax: 813-974-2957, E-mail: gunaratn@usf.edu. *Application contact:* Dr. Sarina J. Ergas, Professor and Graduate Program Coordinator, 813-974-1119, Fax: 813-974-2957, E-mail: sergas@usf.edu. Website: http://www.usf.edu/engineering/cee/

University of South Florida, Innovative Education, Tampa, FL 33620-9951. Offers adult, career and higher education (Graduate Certificate), including college teaching, leadership in developing human resources, leadership in higher education; Africana studies (Graduate Certificate), including diasporas and health disparities, genocide and human rights; aging studies (Graduate Certificate), including gerontology; art research (Graduate Certificate), including museum studies; business foundations (Graduate Certificate); chemical and biomedical engineering (Graduate Certificate), including materials science and engineering, water, health and sustainability; child and family studies (Graduate Certificate), including positive behavior support; civil and industrial engineering (Graduate Certificate), including transportation systems analysis; community and family health (Graduate Certificate), including maternal and child health, social marketing and public health, violence and injury: prevention and intervention, women's health; criminology (Graduate Certificate), including criminal justice administration; data science for public administration (Graduate Certificate); digital humanities (Graduate Certificate); educational measurement and research (Graduate Certificate), including evaluation; English (Graduate Certificate), including comparative literary studies, creative writing, professional and technical communication; entrepreneurship (Graduate Certificate); environmental health (Graduate Certificate), including safety management; epidemiology and biostatistics (Graduate Certificate), including applied biostatistics, biostatistics, concepts and tools of epidemiology, epidemiology, epidemiology of infectious diseases; geography, environment and planning (Graduate Certificate), including community development, environmental policy and management, geographical information systems; geology (Graduate Certificate), including hydrogeology; global health (Graduate Certificate), including disaster management, global health and Latin American and Caribbean studies, global health practice, humanitarian assistance, infection control; government and international affairs (Graduate Certificate), including Cuban studies, globalization studies; health policy and management (Graduate Certificate), including health management and leadership, public health policy and programs; hearing specialist: early intervention (Graduate Certificate); industrial and management systems engineering (Graduate Certificate), including systems engineering, technology management; information studies (Graduate Certificate), including school library media specialist; information systems/decision sciences (Graduate Certificate), including analytics and business intelligence; instructional technology (Graduate Certificate), including distance education, Florida digital/virtual educator, instructional design, multimedia design, Web design; internal medicine, bioethics and medical humanities (Graduate Certificate), including biomedical

ethics; Latin American and Caribbean studies (Graduate Certificate); leadership for coastal resiliency planning (Graduate Certificate); mass communications (Graduate Certificate), including multimedia journalism; mathematics and statistics (Graduate Certificate), including mathematics; medicine (Graduate Certificate), including aging and neuroscience, bioinformatics, biotechnology, brain fitness and memory management, clinical investigation, hand and upper limb rehabilitation, health informatics, health sciences, integrative weight management, intellectual property, medicine and gender, metabolic and nutritional medicine, metabolic cardiology, pharmacy sciences; national and competitive intelligence (Graduate Certificate); nursing (Graduate Certificate), including simulation based academic fellowship in advanced pain management; psychological and social foundations (Graduate Certificate), including career counseling, college teaching, diversity in education, mental health counseling, school counseling; public affairs (Graduate Certificate), including nonprofit management, public management, research administration; public health (Graduate Certificate), including assessing chemical toxicity and public health risks, health equity, pharmacoepidemiology, public health generalist, toxicology, translational research in adolescent behavioral health; public health practices (Graduate Certificate), including planning for healthy communities; rehabilitation and mental health counseling (Graduate Certificate), including integrative mental health care, marriage and family therapy, rehabilitation technology; secondary education (Graduate Certificate), including ESOL, foreign language education: culture and content, foreign language education: professional; social work (Graduate Certificate), including geriatric social work/clinical gerontology; special education (Graduate Certificate), including autism spectrum disorder, disabilities education: severe/profound; world languages (Graduate Certificate), including teaching English as a second language (TESL) or foreign language. *Unit head:* Dr. Cynthia DeLuca, Associate Vice President and Assistant Vice Provost, 813-974-3077, Fax: 813-974-7061, E-mail: deluca@usf.edu. *Application contact:* Owen Hooper, Director, Summer and Alternative Calendar Programs, 813-974-6917, E-mail: hooper@usf.edu. Website: http://www.usf.edu/innovative-education/

University of South Florida, Patel College of Global Sustainability, Tampa, FL 33620-9951. Offers energy, global, water and sustainable tourism (Graduate Certificate); global sustainability (MA), including building sustainable enterprise, climate change and sustainability, coastal sustainability, entrepreneurship, food sustainability and security, sustainability policy, sustainable energy, sustainable tourism, water. *Faculty:* 1 full-time (0 women). *Students:* 82 full-time (56 women), 75 part-time (49 women); includes 34 minority (8 Black or African American, non-Hispanic/Latino; 4 Asian, non-Hispanic/Latino; 17 Hispanic/Latino; 5 Two or more races, non-Hispanic/Latino), 43 international. Average age 29. 121 applicants, 79% accepted, 65 enrolled. In 2019, 93 master's awarded. *Degree requirements:* For master's, comprehensive exam (for some programs), thesis or alternative, internship. *Entrance requirements:* For master's, GPA of at least 3.25 or greater; alternatively a GPA of at least 3.00 along with a GRE Verbal score of 153 (61 percentile) or higher, Quantitative of 153 (51 percentile) or higher and Analytical Writing of 3.5 or higher, all taken within 5 years of application; at least 2 letters of recommendation from professors or supervisors. Additional exam requirements/recommendations for international students: required—TOEFL (minimum score 550 paper-based; 79 iBT). *Application deadline:* For fall admission, 6/1 for domestic students, 5/1 for international students; for spring admission, 10/15 for domestic students, 9/15 for international students. Electronic applications accepted. *Financial support:* In 2019–20, 35 students received support. *Unit head:* Dr. Govindan Parayil, Dean, 813-974-9694, E-mail: gparayil@usf.edu. *Application contact:* Dr. Govindan Parayil, Dean, 813-974-9694, E-mail: gparayil@usf.edu. Website: http://psgs.usf.edu/

The University of Texas at Austin, Graduate School, Cockrell School of Engineering, Department of Civil, Architectural and Environmental Engineering, Program in Environmental and Water Resources Engineering, Austin, TX 78712-1111. Offers MS, PhD. *Program availability:* Part-time. *Degree requirements:* For master's, thesis or alternative. *Entrance requirements:* For master's, GRE General Test. Additional exam requirements/recommendations for international students: required—TOEFL. Electronic applications accepted.

The University of Texas at Tyler, College of Engineering, Department of Civil Engineering, Tyler, TX 75799-0001. Offers environmental engineering (MS); industrial safety (MS); structural engineering (MS); transportation engineering (MS); water resources engineering (MS). *Program availability:* Part-time, evening/weekend. *Faculty:* 5 full-time. *Students:* 7 full-time (0 women), 8 part-time (6 women); includes 4 minority (1 Asian, non-Hispanic/Latino; 3 Hispanic/Latino), 4 international. Average age 28. 14 applicants, 79% accepted, 4 enrolled. In 2019, 6 master's awarded. *Entrance requirements:* For master's, GRE General Test, bachelor's degree in engineering, associated science degree. Additional exam requirements/recommendations for international students: required—TOEFL. *Application deadline:* For fall admission, 8/17 priority date for domestic students, 7/1 priority date for international students; for spring admission, 12/21 priority date for domestic students, 11/1 priority date for international students. Application fee: $25 ($50 for international students). *Financial support:* Application deadline: 7/1. *Unit head:* Dr. Torey Nalbone, Chair, 903-565-5520, E-mail: tnalbone@uttyler.edu. *Application contact:* Dr. Torey Nalbone, Chair, 903-565-5520, E-mail: tnalbone@uttyler.edu. Website: https://www.uttyler.edu/ce/

University of Wisconsin–Madison, Graduate School, College of Engineering, Department of Civil and Environmental Engineering, Madison, WI 53706-1380. Offers construction engineering and management (MS); environmental science and engineering (MS); geological/geotechnical engineering (MS); structural engineering (MS); transportation engineering (MS); water resources engineering (MS). *Program availability:* Part-time. Terminal master's awarded for partial completion of doctoral program. *Degree requirements:* For master's, thesis (for some programs), minimum of 30 credits; minimum overall GPA of 3.0. *Entrance requirements:* For master's, GRE General Test, bachelor's degree; minimum GPA of 3.0 for last 60 credits of course work. Additional exam requirements/recommendations for international students: required—TOEFL (minimum score 580 paper-based; 92 iBT). Electronic applications accepted. *Expenses:* Contact institution.

Villanova University, College of Engineering, Department of Civil and Environmental Engineering, Program in Water Resources and Environmental Engineering, Villanova, PA 19085-1699. Offers urban water resources design (Certificate); water resources and environmental engineering (MSWREE). *Program availability:* Part-time, evening/weekend, online learning. *Degree requirements:* For master's, thesis optional. *Entrance requirements:* For master's, GRE General Test (for applicants with degrees from foreign universities), BCE or bachelor's degree in science or related engineering field, minimum GPA of 3.0. Additional exam requirements/recommendations for international students: required—TOEFL (minimum score 600 paper-based; 100 iBT). Electronic applications accepted.

Section 8
Computer Science and Information Technology

This section contains a directory of institutions offering graduate work in computer science and information technology, followed by in-depth entries submitted by institutions that chose to prepare detailed program descriptions. Additional information about programs listed in the directory but not augmented by an in-depth entry may be obtained by writing directly to the dean of a graduate school or chair of a department at the address given in the directory.

For programs offering related work, see also in this book *Electrical and Computer Engineering, Engineering and Applied Sciences,* and *Industrial Engineering.* In the other guides in this series:

Graduate Programs in the Humanities, Arts & Social Sciences
See *Communication and Media*
Graduate Programs in the Biological/Biomedical Sciences & Health-Related Medical Professions
See *Allied Health*
Graduate Programs in the Physical Sciences, Mathematics, Agricultural Sciences, the Environment & Natural Resources
See *Mathematical Sciences*
Graduate Programs in Business, Education, Information Studies, Law & Social Work
See *Business Administration and Management* and *Library and Information Studies*

CONTENTS

Artificial Intelligence/Robotics

The American University in Cairo, School of Sciences and Engineering, Cairo, Egypt. Offers biotechnology (MS); chemistry (MS); computer science (MS); computing (M Comp); construction engineering (M Eng, MS); electronics and communications engineering (M Eng); environmental engineering (MS); environmental system design (M Eng); mechanical engineering (M Eng, MS); nanotechnology (MS); physics (MS); robotics, control and smart systems (MS); sciences and engineering (PhD); sustainable development (MS, Graduate Diploma). *Program availability:* Part-time, evening/weekend. *Degree requirements:* For master's, comprehensive exam (for some programs), thesis (for some programs); for doctorate, comprehensive exam (for some programs), thesis/dissertation. *Entrance requirements:* Additional exam requirements/recommendations for international students: required—TOEFL (minimum score 450 paper-based; 45 iBT), IELTS (minimum score 5). Electronic applications accepted.

Brandeis University, Rabb School of Continuing Studies, Division of Graduate Professional Studies, Master of Science in Robotic Software Engineering Program, Waltham, MA 02454-9110. Offers MS. *Program availability:* Part-time-only. *Entrance requirements:* For master's, bachelor's degree in computer science or software engineering, or 2-3 years of experience in software engineering and undergraduate courses in linear algebra, calculus, and probability/statistics, official transcripts, resume, statement of goals, letter of recommendation. Additional exam requirements/ recommendations for international students: required—TOEFL (minimum score 600 paper-based; 100 iBT), IELTS (minimum score 7), TWE (minimum score 4.5), PTE (minimum score 68). Electronic applications accepted. *Expenses:* Contact institution.

California State University, Northridge, Graduate Studies, College of Engineering and Computer Science, Department of Manufacturing Systems Engineering and Management, Northridge, CA 91330. Offers engineering automation (MS); engineering management (MS); manufacturing systems engineering (MS); materials engineering (MS). *Program availability:* Online learning. *Entrance requirements:* For master's, GRE (if cumulative undergraduate GPA less than 3.0).

Carnegie Mellon University, Dietrich College of Humanities and Social Sciences, Department of Statistics, Pittsburgh, PA 15213-3891. Offers machine learning and statistics (PhD); mathematical finance (PhD); statistics (MS, PhD), including applied statistics (PhD), computational statistics (PhD), theoretical statistics (PhD); statistics and public policy (PhD). Terminal master's awarded for partial completion of doctoral program. *Degree requirements:* For doctorate, comprehensive exam, thesis/ dissertation. *Entrance requirements:* For master's and doctorate, GRE General Test. Additional exam requirements/recommendations for international students: required— TOEFL.

Carnegie Mellon University, School of Computer Science, Department of Machine Learning, Pittsburgh, PA 15213-3891. Offers MS, PhD.

Carnegie Mellon University, School of Computer Science, Program in Automated Science: Biological Experimentation, Pittsburgh, PA 15213-3891. Offers MS.

Carnegie Mellon University, School of Computer Science, Robotics Institute, Pittsburgh, PA 15213-3891. Offers computer vision (MS); robotic systems development (MS); robotics (MS, PhD); robotics technology (MS). *Degree requirements:* For doctorate, thesis/dissertation. *Entrance requirements:* For doctorate, GRE General Test, GRE Subject Test. Additional exam requirements/recommendations for international students: required—TOEFL.

College of Staten Island of the City University of New York, Graduate Programs, Division of Science and Technology, Program in Computer Science, Staten Island, NY 10314-6600. Offers computer science (MS), including artificial intelligence and data analytics, cloud computing and software engineering, cybersecurity and networks. *Program availability:* Part-time, evening/weekend. *Faculty:* 6. *Students:* 42. 48 applicants, 67% accepted, 15 enrolled. In 2019, 10 master's awarded. *Degree requirements:* For master's, thesis optional, a program of 10 courses (30 credits) with at least a 3.0 (B) average. Exceptional students may be permitted to satisfy six credits of the total credit requirement with a master's thesis. *Entrance requirements:* For master's, GRE General Test, BS in Computer Science or related area with a B average (3.0 out of 4.0) overall and in the major, a resume, and demonstratable knowledge in several areas. Additional exam requirements/recommendations for international students: required— TOEFL (minimum score 550 paper-based; 79 iBT), IELTS (minimum score 6.5). *Application deadline:* For fall admission, 7/20 priority date for domestic students, 4/25 for international students; for spring admission, 11/2 priority date for domestic students, 11/2 for international students. Applications are processed on a rolling basis. Application fee: $75. Electronic applications accepted. *Expenses: Tuition, area resident:* Full-time $11,090; part-time $470 per credit. Tuition, state resident: full-time $11,090; part-time $470 per credit. Tuition, nonresident: full-time $20,520; part-time $855 per credit. *International tuition:* $20,520 full-time. *Required fees:* $559; $181 per semester. Tuition and fees vary according to program. *Unit head:* Dr. Xiaowen Zhang, Associate Professor, 718-982-3262, E-mail: xiaowen.zhang@csi.cuny.edu. *Application contact:* Sasha Spence, Associate Director for Graduate Admissions, 718-982-2019, Fax: 718-982-2500, E-mail: sasha.spence@csi.cuny.edu.
Website: https://www.csi.cuny.edu/academics-and-research/departments-programs/computer-science

Cornell University, Graduate School, Graduate Fields of Engineering, Field of Computer Science, Ithaca, NY 14853. Offers algorithms (M Eng, PhD); applied logic and automated reasoning (M Eng, PhD); artificial intelligence (M Eng, PhD); computer graphics (M Eng, PhD); computer science (M Eng, PhD); computer vision (M Eng, PhD); concurrency and distributed computing (M Eng, PhD); information organization and retrieval (M Eng, PhD); operating systems (M Eng, PhD); parallel computing (M Eng, PhD); programming environments (M Eng, PhD); programming languages and methodology (M Eng, PhD); robotics (M Eng, PhD); scientific computing (M Eng, PhD); theory of computation (M Eng, PhD). *Degree requirements:* For doctorate, comprehensive exam, thesis/dissertation. *Entrance requirements:* For master's, GRE General Test, 2 letters of recommendation; for doctorate, GRE General Test, GRE Subject Test (computer science or mathematics), 3 letters of recommendation. Additional exam requirements/recommendations for international students: required— TOEFL (minimum score 505 paper-based; 77 iBT). Electronic applications accepted.

Illinois Institute of Technology, Graduate College, College of Science, Department of Computer Science, Chicago, IL 60616. Offers business (MCS); computational intelligence (MCS); computer science (MCS, MS, PhD); cyber-physical systems (MCS); data analytics (MCS); data science (MAS); database systems (MCS); distributed and cloud computing (MCS); education (MCS); finance (MCS); information security and assurance (MCS); networking and communications (MCS); software engineering (MCS); telecommunications and software engineering (MAS); MS/MAS. *Program availability:* Part-time, evening/weekend, online learning. Terminal master's awarded for partial completion of doctoral program. *Degree requirements:* For master's, thesis optional; for doctorate, comprehensive exam, thesis/dissertation. *Entrance*

requirements: For master's, GRE General Test with minimum scores of 298 Quantitative and Verbal, 3.0 Analytical Writing (for MS); GRE General Test with minimum scores of 292 Quantitative and Verbal, 2.5 Analytical Writing (for MAS), minimum undergraduate GPA of 3.0; for doctorate, GRE General Test (minimum scores: 304 Quantitative and Verbal, 3.5 Analytical Writing), minimum undergraduate GPA of 3.0. Additional exam requirements/recommendations for international students: required—TOEFL (minimum score 523 paper-based; 70 iBT). Electronic applications accepted.

Indiana University Bloomington, School of Informatics, Computing, and Engineering, Program in Intelligent Systems Engineering, Bloomington, IN 47405-7000. Offers PhD. *Program availability:* Part-time. *Degree requirements:* For doctorate, thesis/dissertation, qualifying exam. *Entrance requirements:* For doctorate, GRE, statement of purpose, curriculum vitae, 3 letters of recommendation, transcripts. Additional exam requirements/recommendations for international students: required—TOEFL. Electronic applications accepted.

Instituto Tecnológico y de Estudios Superiores de Monterrey, Campus Monterrey, Graduate and Research Division, Program in Computer Science, Monterrey, Mexico. Offers artificial intelligence (PhD); computer science (MS); information systems (MS); information technology (MS). *Program availability:* Part-time. *Degree requirements:* For master's, one foreign language, thesis; for doctorate, one foreign language, thesis/dissertation. *Entrance requirements:* For master's, EXADEP; for doctorate, master's degree in related field. Additional exam requirements/recommendations for international students: required—TOEFL.

Instituto Tecnológico y de Estudios Superiores de Monterrey, Campus Monterrey, Graduate and Research Division, Programs in Engineering, Monterrey, Mexico. Offers applied statistics (M Eng); artificial intelligence (PhD); automation engineering (M Eng); chemical engineering (M Eng); civil engineering (M Eng); electrical engineering (M Eng); electronic engineering (M Eng); environmental engineering (M Eng); industrial engineering (M Eng, PhD); manufacturing engineering (M Eng); mechanical engineering (M Eng); systems and quality engineering (M Eng). *Program availability:* Part-time, evening/weekend. Terminal master's awarded for partial completion of doctoral program. *Degree requirements:* For master's, one foreign language, thesis; for doctorate, one foreign language, thesis/dissertation. *Entrance requirements:* For master's, EXADEP; for doctorate, GRE, master's degree in related field. Additional exam requirements/recommendations for international students: required—TOEFL.

Johns Hopkins University, G. W. C. Whiting School of Engineering, Master of Science in Engineering in Robotics Program, Baltimore, MD 21218. Offers robotics (MSE). *Degree requirements:* For master's, thesis optional, 10 courses or 8 courses and an essay. *Entrance requirements:* For master's, GRE, proficiencies in multivariable integral and differential calculus, linear algebra, ordinary differential equations, physics, probability and statistics, basic numerical methods using existing programming environments, and standard programming languages (C++, Java, or MATLAB); 3 letters of recommendation; statement of purpose; transcripts. Additional exam requirements/recommendations for international students: required—IELTS preferred (minimum score 7) or TOEFL (minimum score 600 paper-based, 100 iBT). Electronic applications accepted.

Lawrence Technological University, College of Arts and Sciences, Southfield, MI 48075-1058. Offers bioinformatics (Graduate Certificate); computer science (MS), including data science, big data, and data mining, intelligent systems; educational technology (MA), including robotics; instructional design, communication, and presentation (Graduate Certificate); integrated science (MA); science education (MA); technical and professional communication (MS, Graduate Certificate); writing for the digital age (Graduate Certificate). *Program availability:* Part-time, evening/weekend. *Faculty:* 5 full-time (2 women), 2 part-time/adjunct (1 woman). *Students:* 1 (woman) full-time, 25 part-time (15 women); includes 6 minority (3 Black or African American, non-Hispanic/Latino; 2 Asian, non-Hispanic/Latino; 1 Hispanic/Latino), 6 international. Average age 34. 50 applicants, 68% accepted, 3 enrolled. In 2019, 14 master's, 4 other advanced degrees awarded. *Degree requirements:* For master's, thesis (for some programs). *Entrance requirements:* Additional exam requirements/recommendations for international students: required—TOEFL (minimum score 550 paper-based; 79 iBT), IELTS (minimum score 6.5). *Application deadline:* For fall admission, 5/24 for international students; for spring admission, 10/13 for international students; for summer admission, 2/18 for international students. Applications are processed on a rolling basis. Application fee: $50. Electronic applications accepted. *Expenses: Tuition:* Full-time $16,618; part-time $8309 per year. *Required fees:* $600; $600. *Financial support:* In 2019–20, 4 students received support. Scholarships/grants and tuition reduction available. Financial award application deadline: 4/1; financial award applicants required to submit FAFSA. *Unit head:* Glen Bauer, Interim Dean, 248-204-3532, Fax: 248-204-3518, E-mail: scidean@ltu.edu. *Application contact:* Jane Rohrback, Director of Admissions, 248-204-3160, Fax: 248-204-2228, E-mail: admissions@ltu.edu.

New York University, Tandon School of Engineering, Department of Mechanical and Aerospace Engineering, Major in Mechatronics and Robotics, New York, NY 10012-1019. Offers mechatronics and robotics (MS). *Program availability:* Part-time, evening/weekend. *Degree requirements:* For master's, comprehensive exam (for some programs), thesis (for some programs). *Entrance requirements:* Additional exam requirements/recommendations for international students: required—TOEFL (minimum score 550 paper-based; 90 iBT); recommended—IELTS (minimum score 7). Electronic applications accepted.

Northwestern University, McCormick School of Engineering and Applied Science, Department of Mechanical Engineering, MS in Robotics Program, Evanston, IL 60208. Offers MS. *Entrance requirements:* For master's, GRE General Test (recommended). Additional exam requirements/recommendations for international students: required— TOEFL (minimum score 100 iBT), IELTS (minimum score 7). Electronic applications accepted.

Oregon State University, College of Engineering, Program in Robotics, Corvallis, OR 97331. Offers M Eng, MS, PhD. *Entrance requirements:* For master's and doctorate, GRE. *Expenses:* Contact institution.

Portland State University, Graduate Studies, College of Liberal Arts and Sciences, Systems Science Program, Portland, OR 97207-0751. Offers computational intelligence (Certificate); computer modeling and simulation (Certificate); systems science (MS); systems science/anthropology (PhD); systems science/business administration (PhD); systems science/civil engineering (PhD); systems science/economics (PhD); systems science/engineering management (PhD); systems science/general (PhD); systems science/mathematical sciences (PhD); systems science/mechanical engineering (PhD); systems science/psychology (PhD); systems science/sociology (PhD). *Program availability:* Part-time. *Faculty:* 2 full-time (0 women), 6 part-time/adjunct (1 woman). *Students:* 6 full-time (3 women), 25 part-time (8 women); includes 7 minority (2 Asian, non-Hispanic/Latino; 4 Hispanic/Latino; 1 Two or more races, non-Hispanic/Latino), 2

international. Average age 39. 25 applicants, 80% accepted, 15 enrolled. In 2019, 7 master's, 2 doctorates awarded. Terminal master's awarded for partial completion of doctoral program. *Degree requirements:* For master's, comprehensive exam (for some programs), thesis optional; for doctorate, variable foreign language requirement, comprehensive exam (for some programs), thesis/dissertation. *Entrance requirements:* For master's, GRE/GMAT (recommended), minimum GPA of 3.0 on undergraduate or graduate work, 2 letters of recommendation, statement of interest; for doctorate, GRE required, minimum GPA of 3.0 undergraduate, 3.25 graduate; 3 letters of recommendation; statement of interest. Additional exam requirements/recommendations for international students: required—TOEFL (minimum score 550 paper-based; 80 iBT). *Application deadline:* For fall admission, 3/15 priority date for domestic and international students. Application fee: $65. Electronic applications accepted. *Expenses: Tuition, area resident:* Full-time $13,020; part-time $6510 per year. Tuition, state resident: full-time $13,020; part-time $6510 per year. Tuition, nonresident: full-time $19,830; part-time $9915 per year. *International tuition:* $19,830 full-time. *Required fees:* $1226. One-time fee: $350. Tuition and fees vary according to course load, program and reciprocity agreements. *Financial support:* Research assistantships, teaching assistantships, career-related internships or fieldwork, Federal Work-Study, scholarships/grants, and unspecified assistantships available. Support available to part-time students. Financial award application deadline: 3/1; financial award applicants required to submit FAFSA. *Unit head:* Dr. Wayne Wakeland, Chair, 503-725-4975, E-mail: wakeland@pdx.edu. *Application contact:* Dr. Wayne Wakeland, Chair, 503-725-4975, E-mail: wakeland@pdx.edu.
Website: http://www.pdx.edu/sysc/

Queen's University at Kingston, Smith School of Business, Master of Management in Artificial Intelligence Program, Kingston, ON K7L 3N6, Canada. Offers MM.

South Dakota School of Mines and Technology, Graduate Division, Program in Computational Sciences and Robotics, Rapid City, SD 57701-3995. Offers MS. *Program availability:* Part-time. *Entrance requirements:* Additional exam requirements/recommendations for international students: required—TOEFL (minimum score 520 paper-based; 68 iBT), TWE. Electronic applications accepted.

Stevens Institute of Technology, Graduate School, Charles V. Schaefer Jr. School of Engineering and Science, Department of Electrical and Computer Engineering, Program in Electrical Engineering, Hoboken, NJ 07030. Offers autonomous robotics (Certificate); electrical engineering (M Eng, PhD, Certificate), including computer architecture and digital systems (M Eng), microelectronics and photonics science and technology (M Eng), signal processing for communications (M Eng), telecommunications systems engineering (M Eng), wireless communications (M Eng, Certificate). *Program availability:* Part-time, evening/weekend. *Faculty:* 20 full-time (6 women), 2 part-time/adjunct. *Students:* 137 full-time (21 women), 23 part-time (5 women); includes 6 minority (2 Black or African American, non-Hispanic/Latino; 4 Asian, non-Hispanic/Latino), 134 international. Average age 25. In 2019, 82 master's, 5 doctorates, 1 other advanced degree awarded. Terminal master's awarded for partial completion of doctoral program. *Degree requirements:* For master's, thesis optional, minimum B average in major field and overall; for doctorate, comprehensive exam (for some programs), thesis/dissertation; for Certificate, minimum B average. *Entrance requirements:* For master's, International applicants must submit TOEFL/IELTS scores and fulfill the English Language Proficiency Requirement. Applicants to full-time programs who do not qualify for a score waiver are required to submit GRE/GMAT scores. Additional exam requirements/recommendations for international students: required—TOEFL (minimum score 74 iBT), IELTS (minimum score 6). *Application deadline:* For fall admission, 4/15 for domestic and international students; for spring admission, 11/1 for domestic and international students; for summer admission, 5/1 for domestic students. Applications are processed on a rolling basis. Application fee: $60. Electronic applications accepted. *Expenses:* Tuition: Full-time $52,134. *Required fees:* $1880. Tuition and fees vary according to course load. *Financial support:* Fellowships, research assistantships, teaching assistantships, career-related internships or fieldwork, Federal Work-Study, scholarships/grants, and unspecified assistantships available. Financial award application deadline: 2/15; financial award applicants required to submit FAFSA. *Unit head:* Dr. Jean Zu, Dean of SES, 201-216.8233, Fax: 201-216.8372, E-mail: Jean.Zu@stevens.edu. *Application contact:* Graduate Admissions, 888-783-8367, Fax: 888-511-1306, E-mail: graduate@stevens.edu.

Temple University, College of Science and Technology, Department of Computer and Information Sciences, Philadelphia, PA 19122-6096. Offers computational data science (MS); computer and information sciences (PhD), including artificial intelligence, computer and network systems, information systems, software systems; computer science (MS); cyber defense and information assurance (PSM); information science and technology (MS). *Program availability:* Part-time, evening/weekend, online learning. *Faculty:* 39 full-time (9 women), 8 part-time/adjunct (1 woman). *Students:* 97 full-time (28 women), 22 part-time (11 women); includes 14 minority (3 Black or African American, non-Hispanic/Latino; 8 Asian, non-Hispanic/Latino; 3 Hispanic/Latino), 83 international. 133 applicants, 56% accepted, 35 enrolled. In 2019, 15 master's, 7 doctorates awarded. *Degree requirements:* For doctorate, thesis/dissertation. *Entrance requirements:* For master's, GRE, 3 letters of recommendation, statement of goals; for doctorate, GRE, 3 letters of recommendation, bachelor's degree in related field, statement of goals, resume. Additional exam requirements/recommendations for international students: required—TOEFL (minimum score 85 iBT), IELTS (minimum score 6.5), PTE (minimum score 58), one of three is required. *Application deadline:* Applications are processed on a rolling basis. Application fee: $60. Electronic applications accepted. *Expenses:* Contact institution. *Financial support:* Research assistantships, teaching assistantships, health care benefits, and unspecified assistantships available. Financial award applicants required to submit FAFSA. *Unit head:* Jamie Payton, Department Chairperson, 215-204-8245, E-mail: Jamie.payton@temple.edu. *Application contact:* Eduard Dragut, Graduate Chair, 215-204-0521, E-mail: cisadmit@temple.edu.
Website: https://cis.temple.edu/

Tufts University, School of Engineering, Department of Computer Science, Medford, MA 02155. Offers bioengineering (MS), including bioinformatics; cognitive science/computer science (PhD); computer science (MS, PhD); soft material robotics (PhD). *Program availability:* Part-time. Terminal master's awarded for partial completion of doctoral program. *Entrance requirements:* For master's and doctorate, GRE General Test. Additional exam requirements/recommendations for international students: required—TOEFL (minimum score 550 paper-based; 80 iBT), IELTS (minimum score 6.5). Electronic applications accepted. Full-time tuition and fees vary according to degree level, program and student level. Part-time tuition and fees vary according to course load.

University of California, Riverside, Graduate Division, Department of Electrical Engineering, Riverside, CA 92521-0102. Offers electrical engineering (MS, PhD), including computer engineering (MS), control and robotics (PhD). Terminal master's awarded for partial completion of doctoral program. *Degree requirements:* For master's, thesis optional; for doctorate, thesis/dissertation, qualifying exams. *Entrance requirements:* For master's and doctorate, GRE General Test, minimum GPA of 3.25.

Additional exam requirements/recommendations for international students: required—TOEFL (minimum score 550 paper-based; 80 iBT). Electronic applications accepted.

University of California, San Diego, Graduate Division, Department of Electrical and Computer Engineering, La Jolla, CA 92093. Offers applied ocean science (MS, PhD); applied physics (MS, PhD); communication theory and systems (MS, PhD); computer engineering (MS, PhD); electronic circuits and systems (MS, PhD); intelligent systems, robotics and control (MS, PhD); medical devices and systems (MS, PhD); nanoscale devices and systems (MS, PhD); photonics (MS, PhD); signal and image processing (MS, PhD). *Students:* 983 full-time (216 women), 80 part-time (15 women). 3,675 applicants, 33% accepted, 430 enrolled. In 2019, 287 master's, 50 doctorates awarded. Terminal master's awarded for partial completion of doctoral program. *Degree requirements:* For master's, comprehensive exam (for some programs), thesis (for some programs); for doctorate, comprehensive exam, thesis/dissertation. *Entrance requirements:* For master's and doctorate, GRE General Test, minimum GPA of 3.0, resume or curriculum vitae (recommended). Additional exam requirements/recommendations for international students: required—TOEFL (minimum score 550 paper-based; 80 iBT), IELTS (minimum score 7), PTE (minimum score 65). *Application deadline:* For fall admission, 12/18 for domestic students. Application fee: $105 ($125 for international students). Electronic applications accepted. *Financial support:* Fellowships, research assistantships, teaching assistantships, scholarships/grants, traineeships, and unspecified assistantships available. Financial award applicants required to submit FAFSA. *Unit head:* Bill Lin, Chair, 858-822-1383, E-mail: billin@ucsd.edu. *Application contact:* Sean Jones, Graduate Admissions Coordinator, 858-534-3213, E-mail: ecegradapps@ece.ucsd.edu.
Website: http://ece.ucsd.edu/

University of Georgia, Franklin College of Arts and Sciences, Artificial Intelligence Center, Athens, GA 30602. Offers MS. *Degree requirements:* For master's, thesis. *Entrance requirements:* For master's, GRE General Test. Electronic applications accepted.

University of Michigan, College of Engineering, Department of Integrative Systems and Design, Ann Arbor, MI 48109. Offers automotive engineering (M Eng); design science (MS, PhD); energy systems engineering (M Eng, MS); global automotive and manufacturing engineering (M Eng); manufacturing engineering (M Eng, D Eng); pharmaceutical engineering (M Eng); robotics and autonomous vehicles (M Eng); systems engineering and design (M Eng); MBA/M Eng; MSE/MS. *Program availability:* Part-time, online learning. Terminal master's awarded for partial completion of doctoral program. *Degree requirements:* For master's, capstone project; for doctorate, thesis/dissertation. *Entrance requirements:* For master's and doctorate, GRE. Additional exam requirements/recommendations for international students: required—TOEFL. Electronic applications accepted.

University of Michigan, College of Engineering, Program in Robotics, Ann Arbor, MI 48109. Offers MS, PhD. *Entrance requirements:* For master's and doctorate, GRE General Test. Additional exam requirements/recommendations for international students: required—TOEFL.

University of Nebraska at Omaha, Graduate Studies, College of Information Science and Technology, Department of Computer Science, Omaha, NE 68182. Offers artificial intelligence (Certificate); communication networks (Certificate); computer science (MA, MS); computer science education (MS, Certificate); software engineering (Certificate); system and architecture (Certificate). *Program availability:* Part-time, evening/weekend. *Degree requirements:* For master's, comprehensive exam, thesis (for some programs). *Entrance requirements:* For master's, GRE General Test, minimum GPA of 3.0, prior course work in computer science, official transcripts, resume, 2 letters of recommendation; for Certificate, minimum GPA of 3.0, resume. Additional exam requirements/recommendations for international students: required—TOEFL, IELTS, PTE. Electronic applications accepted.

University of Pennsylvania, School of Engineering and Applied Science, Program in Robotics, Philadelphia, PA 19104. Offers MSE. *Program availability:* Part-time. *Students:* 88 full-time (22 women), 16 part-time (4 women); includes 21 minority (15 Asian, non-Hispanic/Latino; 1 Hispanic/Latino; 5 Two or more races, non-Hispanic/Latino), 58 international. Average age 24. 600 applicants, 16% accepted, 36 enrolled. In 2019, 82 master's awarded. *Degree requirements:* For master's, comprehensive exam, thesis optional. *Entrance requirements:* For master's, GRE, bachelor's degree, letters of recommendation, resume, personal statement. Additional exam requirements/recommendations for international students: required—TOEFL (minimum score 100 iBT), IELTS (minimum score 7). *Application deadline:* For fall admission, 2/1 priority date for domestic and international students. Application fee: $80. Electronic applications accepted. *Expenses:* Contact institution. *Application contact:* Associate Director of Graduate Admissions, 215-898-4542, Fax: 215-573-5577, E-mail: admissions1@seas.upenn.edu.
Website: http://www.grasp.upenn.edu

University of Pittsburgh, School of Computing and Information, Intelligent Systems Program, Pittsburgh, PA 15260. Offers MS, PhD. *Program availability:* Part-time, evening/weekend. *Degree requirements:* For master's, research project; for doctorate, comprehensive exam, thesis/dissertation. *Entrance requirements:* For master's, GRE General Test, BS, relevant experience; for doctorate, GRE General Test. Additional exam requirements/recommendations for international students: required—TOEFL (minimum score 90 iBT), IELTS (minimum score 7). Electronic applications accepted. *Expenses:* Contact institution.

University of Rochester, Hajim School of Engineering and Applied Sciences, Department of Computer Science, Rochester, NY 14627. Offers algorithms and complexity (MS); artificial intelligence and machine learning (MS); computer architecture (MS); computer science (PhD); human computer interaction (MS); natural language processing (MS); programming languages and computer systems (MS). *Faculty:* 19 full-time (3 women). *Students:* 124 full-time (23 women), 1 (woman) part-time; includes 6 minority (2 Black or African American, non-Hispanic/Latino; 3 Asian, non-Hispanic/Latino; 1 Two or more races, non-Hispanic/Latino), 98 international. Average age 26. 925 applicants, 16% accepted, 37 enrolled. In 2019, 42 master's, 4 doctorates awarded. Terminal master's awarded for partial completion of doctoral program. *Degree requirements:* For master's, comprehensive exam (for some programs), thesis (for some programs); for doctorate, comprehensive exam, thesis/dissertation, qualifying exam. *Entrance requirements:* For master's and doctorate, GRE General Test, personal statement, transcripts, three letters of recommendation. Additional exam requirements/recommendations for international students: required—TOEFL (minimum score 100 iBT), IELTS. *Application deadline:* For fall admission, 12/15 for domestic and international students. Application fee: $60. Electronic applications accepted. *Financial support:* In 2019–20, 74 students received support, including 4 fellowships with full tuition reimbursements available (averaging $33,708 per year), 40 research assistantships with full tuition reimbursements available (averaging $31,200 per year), 30 teaching assistantships with full tuition reimbursements available (averaging $31,200 per year); scholarships/grants, traineeships, health care benefits, and tuition waivers (full and partial) also available. Financial award application deadline: 12/15. *Unit head:* Michael Scott, Professor and Chair, 585-275-7745, E-mail: scott@cs.rochester.edu.

Application contact: Emily Tevens, Graduate Coordinator, 585-275-7737, E-mail: etevens@cs.rochester.edu.
Website: https://www.cs.rochester.edu/graduate/index.html

University of Southern California, Graduate School, Viterbi School of Engineering, Department of Computer Science, Los Angeles, CA 90089. Offers computer networks (MS); computer science (MS, PhD); computer security (MS); game development (MS); high performance computing and simulations (MS); human language technology (MS); intelligent robotics (MS); multimedia and creative technologies (MS); software engineering (MS). *Program availability:* Part-time, evening/weekend, online learning. *Entrance requirements:* For master's and doctorate, GRE General Test. Additional exam requirements/recommendations for international students: required—TOEFL. Electronic applications accepted.

Villanova University, College of Engineering, Department of Electrical and Computer Engineering, Program in Computer Engineering, Villanova, PA 19085-1699. Offers computer architectures (Certificate); computer engineering (MSCPE); intelligent control systems (Certificate). *Program availability:* Part-time, evening/weekend. *Degree requirements:* For master's, thesis optional. *Entrance requirements:* For master's, GRE General Test (for applicants with degrees from foreign universities), BEE, minimum GPA of 3.0. Additional exam requirements/recommendations for international students: required—TOEFL (minimum score 600 paper-based; 100 iBT). Electronic applications accepted.

Villanova University, College of Engineering, Department of Electrical and Computer Engineering, Program in Electrical Engineering, Villanova, PA 19085-1699. Offers electric power systems (Certificate); electrical engineering (MSEE); electro mechanical systems (Certificate); high frequency systems (Certificate); intelligent control systems (Certificate); wireless and digital communications (Certificate). *Program availability:* Part-time, evening/weekend. *Degree requirements:* For master's, thesis optional. *Entrance requirements:* For master's, GRE General Test (for applicants with degrees from foreign universities), BEE, minimum GPA of 3.0. Additional exam requirements/recommendations for international students: required—TOEFL (minimum score 600 paper-based; 100 iBT).

Worcester Polytechnic Institute, Graduate Admissions, Program in Robotics Engineering, Worcester, MA 01609-2280. Offers robotics engineering (MS). *Program availability:* Part-time, evening/weekend, 100% online, blended/hybrid learning. Terminal master's awarded for partial completion of doctoral program. *Degree requirements:* For master's, thesis or capstone design project; for doctorate, thesis/dissertation. *Entrance requirements:* For master's and doctorate, GRE, 3 letters of recommendation, statement of purpose. Additional exam requirements/recommendations for international students: required—TOEFL (minimum score 563 paper-based; 84 iBT), IELTS (minimum score 7). Electronic applications accepted.

Bioinformatics

Arizona State University at Tempe, College of Health Solutions, Department of Biomedical Informatics, Phoenix, AZ 85004. Offers MS, PhD. Terminal master's awarded for partial completion of doctoral program. *Degree requirements:* For master's, interactive Program of Study (iPOS) submitted before completing 50 percent of required credit hours; for doctorate, comprehensive exam, thesis/dissertation, interactive Program of Study (iPOS) submitted before completing 50 percent of required credit hours. *Entrance requirements:* For master's, GRE or MCAT, bachelor's degree with minimum GPA of 3.25 in computer science, biology, physiology, nursing, statistics, engineering, related fields, or unrelated fields with appropriate academic backgrounds; resume/curriculum vitae; statement of purpose; 3 letters of recommendation; all official transcripts; for doctorate, GRE or MCAT, bachelor's degree with minimum GPA of 3.5 in computer science, biology, physiology, nursing, statistics, engineering, related fields, or unrelated fields with appropriate academic backgrounds; resume/curriculum vitae; statement of purpose; 3 letters of recommendation; all official transcripts. Additional exam requirements/recommendations for international students: required—TOEFL (minimum score 550 paper-based; 83 iBT), IELTS (minimum score 6.5). Electronic applications accepted.

Boston University, Graduate School of Arts and Sciences and College of Engineering, Intercollegiate Program in Bioinformatics, Boston, MA 02215. Offers MS, PhD. *Students:* 71 full-time (31 women), 16 part-time (8 women); includes 10 minority (2 Black or African American, non-Hispanic/Latino; 5 Asian, non-Hispanic/Latino; 3 Hispanic/Latino), 42 international. Average age 25. 302 applicants, 33% accepted, 31 enrolled. Terminal master's awarded for partial completion of doctoral program. *Degree requirements:* For master's, thesis or alternative, internship; for doctorate, comprehensive exam, thesis/dissertation. *Entrance requirements:* For master's and doctorate, 3 letters of recommendation, transcripts, personal statement, resume. Additional exam requirements/recommendations for international students: required—TOEFL (minimum score 550 paper-based; 84 iBT). *Application deadline:* For fall admission, 12/1 for domestic and international students; for spring admission, 12/15 for domestic and international students. Application fee: $95. Electronic applications accepted. *Financial support:* In 2019–20, 45 students received support, including 6 fellowships with full tuition reimbursements available (averaging $23,340 per year), 30 research assistantships with full tuition reimbursements available (averaging $23,340 per year); career-related internships or fieldwork, Federal Work-Study, scholarships/grants, traineeships, and health care benefits also available. Financial award application deadline: 12/1. *Unit head:* Tom Tullius, Director, 617-353-2482, E-mail: tullius@bu.edu. *Application contact:* David King, Administrator, 617-358-0751, Fax: 617-353-5929, E-mail: dking@bu.edu.
Website: http://www.bu.edu/bioinformatics

Brandeis University, Rabb School of Continuing Studies, Division of Graduate Professional Studies, Master of Science in Bioinformatics Program, Waltham, MA 02454-9110. Offers MS. *Program availability:* Part-time-only. *Entrance requirements:* For master's, undergraduate-level coursework in molecular biology, organic chemistry, and programming in Java, C++ or C; four-year bachelor's degree from regionally-accredited U.S. institution or equivalent; official transcript(s) from every college or university attended; resume or curriculum vitae; statement of goals; letter of recommendation. Additional exam requirements/recommendations for international students: required—TWE (minimum score 4.5), TOEFL (minimum scores: 600 paper-based, 100 iBT), IELTS (7), or PTE (68). Electronic applications accepted. *Expenses:* Contact institution.

California State University, Dominguez Hills, College of Natural and Behavioral Sciences, Department of Biology, Carson, CA 90747-0001. Offers MS. *Program availability:* Part-time, evening/weekend. *Degree requirements:* For master's, thesis. *Entrance requirements:* For master's, minimum GPA of 2.75. Additional exam requirements/recommendations for international students: required—TOEFL (minimum score 550 paper-based). Electronic applications accepted.

Clemson University, Graduate School, College of Behavioral, Social and Health Sciences, Department of Public Health Sciences, Clemson, SC 29634. Offers applied health research and evaluation (MS, PhD); biomedical data science and informatics (PhD); clinical and translational research (Certificate). *Faculty:* 23 full-time (13 women). *Students:* 20 full-time (13 women), 41 part-time (31 women); includes 11 minority (2 Black or African American, non-Hispanic/Latino; 6 Asian, non-Hispanic/Latino; 2 Hispanic/Latino; 1 Two or more races, non-Hispanic/Latino), 3 international. Average age 32. 50 applicants, 84% accepted, 36 enrolled. In 2019, 11 master's, 3 other advanced degrees awarded. *Expenses:* Full-Time Student per Semester: Tuition: $6225 (in-state), $13425 (out-of-state), Fees: $598; Graduate Assistant Per Semester: $1144; Part-Time Student Per Credit Hour: $833 (in-state), $1731 (out-of-state), Fees: $617; other fees apply depending on program, credit hours, campus & residency. Doctoral Base Fee per Semester: $4938 (in-state), $10405 (out-of-state). *Financial support:* In 2019–20, 24 students received support, including 2 fellowships with full and partial tuition reimbursements available (averaging $5,000 per year), 9 research assistantships with full and partial tuition reimbursements available (averaging $18,428 per year), 7 teaching assistantships with full and partial tuition reimbursements available (averaging $17,325 per year); career-related internships or fieldwork and unspecified assistantships also available. *Application contact:* Dr. Sarah Griffin, Graduate Program Director, 864-656-1622, E-mail: sgriffi@clemson.edu.
Website: http://www.clemson.edu/cbshs/departments/public-health/index.html

Dalhousie University, Faculty of Computer Science, Halifax, NS B3H 1W5, Canada. Offers computational biology and bioinformatics (M Sc); computer science (MA Sc, MC Sc, PhD); electronic commerce (MEC); health informatics (MHI). *Degree requirements:* For master's, thesis (for some programs); for doctorate, thesis/dissertation. *Entrance requirements:* Additional exam requirements/recommendations for international students: required—1 of 5 approved tests: TOEFL, IELTS, CANTEST, CAEL, Michigan English Language Assessment Battery. Electronic applications accepted.

Duke University, Graduate School, Department of Computational Biology and Bioinformatics, Durham, NC 27708. Offers PhD, Certificate. *Degree requirements:* For doctorate, thesis/dissertation. *Entrance requirements:* For doctorate, GRE General Test. Additional exam requirements/recommendations for international students: required—TOEFL (minimum score 577 paper-based; 90 iBT) or IELTS (minimum score 7). Electronic applications accepted.

Emory University, Rollins School of Public Health, Department of Biostatistics and Bioinformatics, Atlanta, GA 30322-1100. Offers bioinformatics (PhD); biostatistics (MPH, MSPH); public health informatics (MSPH). *Program availability:* Part-time. *Degree requirements:* For master's, thesis, practicum. *Entrance requirements:* For master's, GRE General Test. Additional exam requirements/recommendations for international students: required—TOEFL (minimum score 550 paper-based; 80 iBT). Electronic applications accepted.

George Mason University, College of Science, School of Systems Biology, Manassas, VA 22030. Offers bioinformatics and computational biology (MS, PhD, Certificate); bioinformatics management (MS); biology (MS); biosciences (PhD). *Degree requirements:* For master's, comprehensive exam (for some programs), research project or thesis; for doctorate, comprehensive exam, thesis/dissertation. *Entrance requirements:* For master's, GRE, resume; 3 letters of recommendation; expanded goals statement; 2 copies of official transcripts; bachelor's degree in related field with minimum GPA of 3.0 in last 60 hours; for doctorate, GRE, self-assessment form; resume; 3 letters of recommendation; expanded goals statement; 2 copies of official transcripts; bachelor's degree in related field with minimum GPA of 3.0 in last 60 hours; for Certificate, resume; 2 copies of official transcripts. Additional exam requirements/recommendations for international students: required—TOEFL (minimum score 575 paper-based; 88 iBT), IELTS (minimum score 6.5), PTE (minimum score 59). Electronic applications accepted.

Georgetown University, Graduate School of Arts and Sciences, Department of Biostatistics, Bioinformatics and Biomathematics, Washington, DC 20057-1484. Offers biostatistics (MS, Certificate), including bioinformatics (MS), epidemiology (MS); epidemiology (Certificate). *Entrance requirements:* For master's, GRE General Test. Additional exam requirements/recommendations for international students: required—TOEFL.

Georgia State University, College of Arts and Sciences, Department of Biology, Program in Applied and Environmental Microbiology, Atlanta, GA 30302-3083. Offers applied and environmental microbiology (MS, PhD); bioinformatics (MS). *Program availability:* Part-time. Terminal master's awarded for partial completion of doctoral program. *Degree requirements:* For master's, comprehensive exam (for some programs), thesis optional; for doctorate, comprehensive exam, thesis/dissertation. *Entrance requirements:* For master's and doctorate, GRE. *Application deadline:* For fall admission, 7/1 priority date for domestic students, 6/1 priority date for international students; for spring admission, 11/15 priority date for domestic students, 10/15 priority date for international students. Applications are processed on a rolling basis. Application fee: $50. Electronic applications accepted. *Expenses: Tuition, area resident:* Full-time $7164; part-time $398 per credit hour. Tuition, state resident: full-time $7164; part-time $398 per credit hour. Tuition, nonresident: full-time $22,662; part-time $1259 per credit hour. *International tuition:* $22,662 full-time. *Required fees:* $2128; $312 per credit hour. Tuition and fees vary according to course load and program. *Financial support:* In 2019–20, fellowships with full tuition reimbursements (averaging $22,000 per year), research assistantships with full tuition reimbursements (averaging $20,000 per year) were awarded. Financial award application deadline: 12/3. *Unit head:* Dr. Charles Derby, Director of Graduate Studies, 404-413-5393, Fax: 404-413-5446, E-mail: cderby@gsu.edu. *Application contact:* Dr. Charles Derby, Director of Graduate Studies, 404-413-5393, Fax: 404-413-5446, E-mail: cderby@gsu.edu.
Website: http://biology.gsu.edu/

Georgia State University, College of Arts and Sciences, Department of Biology, Program in Cellular and Molecular Biology and Physiology, Atlanta, GA 30302-3083. Offers bioinformatics (MS); cellular and molecular biology and physiology (MS, PhD). *Program availability:* Part-time. Terminal master's awarded for partial completion of doctoral program. *Entrance requirements:* For master's and doctorate, GRE. *Application deadline:* Applications are processed on a rolling basis. Application fee: $50. Electronic applications accepted. *Expenses: Tuition, area resident:* Full-time $7164; part-time $398 per credit hour. Tuition, state resident: full-time $7164; part-time $398 per credit hour. Tuition, nonresident: full-time $22,662; part-time $1259 per credit hour. *International tuition:* $22,662 full-time. *Required fees:* $2128; $312 per credit hour. Tuition and fees vary according to course load and program. *Financial support:* Fellowships and research assistantships available. Financial award application deadline: 12/3. *Unit head:* Dr. Charles Derby, Director of Graduate Studies, 404-413-5393, Fax: 404-413-5446, E-mail: cderby@gsu.edu. *Application contact:* Dr. Charles Derby, Director of Graduate Studies, 404-413-5393, Fax: 404-413-5446, E-mail: cderby@gsu.edu. Website: http://biology.gsu.edu/

Georgia State University, College of Arts and Sciences, Department of Biology, Program in Molecular Genetics and Biochemistry, Atlanta, GA 30302-3083. Offers bioinformatics (MS); molecular genetics and biochemistry (MS, PhD). *Program availability:* Part-time. Terminal master's awarded for partial completion of doctoral program. *Entrance requirements:* For master's and doctorate, GRE. *Application deadline:* Applications are processed on a rolling basis. Application fee: $50. Electronic applications accepted. *Expenses: Tuition, area resident:* Full-time $7164; part-time $398 per credit hour. Tuition, state resident: full-time $7164; part-time $398 per credit hour. Tuition, nonresident: full-time $22,662; part-time $1259 per credit hour. *International tuition:* $22,662 full-time. *Required fees:* $2128; $312 per credit hour. Tuition and fees vary according to course load and program. *Financial support:* Fellowships and research assistantships available. Financial award application deadline: 12/3. *Unit head:* Dr. Geert de Vries, Chair, 404-413-5658, Fax: 404-413-3518, E-mail: devries@gsu.edu. *Application contact:* Dr. Geert de Vries, Chair, 404-413-5658, Fax: 404-413-3518, E-mail: devries@gsu.edu. Website: http://biology.gsu.edu/

Georgia State University, College of Arts and Sciences, Department of Biology, Program in Neurobiology and Behavior, Atlanta, GA 30302-3083. Offers bioinformatics (MS); neurobiology and behavior (MS, PhD). *Program availability:* Part-time. Terminal master's awarded for partial completion of doctoral program. *Entrance requirements:* For master's and doctorate, GRE. *Application deadline:* Applications are processed on a rolling basis. Application fee: $50. Electronic applications accepted. *Expenses: Tuition, area resident:* Full-time $7164; part-time $398 per credit hour. Tuition, state resident: full-time $7164; part-time $398 per credit hour. Tuition, nonresident: full-time $22,662; part-time $1259 per credit hour. *International tuition:* $22,662 full-time. *Required fees:* $2128; $312 per credit hour. Tuition and fees vary according to course load and program. *Financial support:* Fellowships and research assistantships available. Financial award application deadline: 12/3. *Unit head:* Dr. Geert de Vries, Chair, 404-413-5658, Fax: 404-413-3518, E-mail: devries@gsu.edu. *Application contact:* Dr. Geert de Vries, Chair, 404-413-5658, Fax: 404-413-3518, E-mail: devries@gsu.edu. Website: http://biology.gsu.edu/

Georgia State University, College of Arts and Sciences, Department of Chemistry, Atlanta, GA 30302-3083. Offers analytical chemistry (MS, PhD); biochemistry (MS, PhD); bioinformatics (MS, PhD); biophysical chemistry (PhD); computational chemistry (MS, PhD); geochemistry (PhD); organic/medicinal chemistry (MS, PhD); physical chemistry (MS). *Program availability:* Part-time. *Faculty:* 24 full-time (5 women), 1 part-time/adjunct (0 women). *Students:* 141 full-time (57 women), 6 part-time (1 woman); includes 36 minority (19 Black or African American, non-Hispanic/Latino; 9 Asian, non-Hispanic/Latino; 5 Hispanic/Latino; 3 Two or more races, non-Hispanic/Latino), 76 international. Average age 29. 111 applicants, 38% accepted, 34 enrolled. In 2019, 28 master's, 24 doctorates awarded. Terminal master's awarded for partial completion of doctoral program. *Degree requirements:* For master's, one foreign language, comprehensive exam (for some programs); thesis (for some programs); for doctorate, one foreign language, comprehensive exam, thesis/dissertation. *Entrance requirements:* For master's and doctorate, GRE. *Application deadline:* For fall admission, 7/1 priority date for domestic and international students; for winter admission, 11/15 priority date for domestic and international students; for spring admission, 4/15 priority date for domestic and international students. Applications are processed on a rolling basis. Application fee: $50. Electronic applications accepted. *Expenses: Tuition, area resident:* Full-time $7164; part-time $398 per credit hour. Tuition, state resident: full-time $7164; part-time $398 per credit hour. Tuition, nonresident: full-time $22,662; part-time $1259 per credit hour. *International tuition:* $22,662 full-time. *Required fees:* $2128; $312 per credit hour. Tuition and fees vary according to course load and program. *Financial support:* Fellowships with full tuition reimbursements, research assistantships with full tuition reimbursements, and teaching assistantships with full tuition reimbursements available. Financial award applicants required to submit FAFSA. *Unit head:* Dr. Donald Hamelberg, Professor; Chair, 404-413-5564, Fax: 404-413-5505, E-mail: dhamelberg@gsu.edu. *Application contact:* Dr. Donald Hamelberg, Professor; Chair, 404-413-5564, Fax: 404-413-5505, E-mail: dhamelberg@gsu.edu. Website: http://chemistry.gsu.edu/

Georgia State University, College of Arts and Sciences, Department of Computer Science, Atlanta, GA 30302-3083. Offers bioinformatics (MS, PhD); computer science (MS, PhD). *Program availability:* Part-time. *Faculty:* 29 full-time (6 women), 4 part-time/adjunct (1 woman). *Students:* 179 full-time (64 women), 23 part-time (7 women); includes 27 minority (7 Black or African American, non-Hispanic/Latino; 12 Asian, non-Hispanic/Latino; 4 Hispanic/Latino; 4 Two or more races, non-Hispanic/Latino), 160 international. Average age 29. 311 applicants, 43% accepted, 39 enrolled. In 2019, 52 master's, 9 doctorates awarded. Terminal master's awarded for partial completion of doctoral program. *Entrance requirements:* For master's and doctorate, GRE General Test. Additional exam requirements/recommendations for international students: required—TOEFL (minimum score 550 paper-based; 80 iBT). *Application deadline:* For fall admission, 3/15 for domestic and international students; for spring admission, 10/15 for domestic and international students. Application fee: $50. Electronic applications accepted. *Expenses: Tuition, area resident:* Full-time $7164; part-time $398 per credit hour. Tuition, state resident: full-time $7164; part-time $398 per credit hour. Tuition, nonresident: full-time $22,662; part-time $1259 per credit hour. *International tuition:* $22,662 full-time. *Required fees:* $2128; $312 per credit hour. Tuition and fees vary according to course load and program. *Financial support:* In 2019–20, fellowships with full tuition reimbursements (averaging $22,000 per year), research assistantships with full tuition reimbursements (averaging $16,000 per year), teaching assistantships with full tuition reimbursements (averaging $16,000 per year) were awarded; institutionally sponsored loans, health care benefits, and unspecified assistantships also available. Financial award application deadline: 2/15; financial award applicants required to submit FAFSA. *Unit head:* Dr. Yi Pan, Regents Professor and Chair, 404-413-5342, Fax: 404-413-5717, E-mail: yipan@gsu.edu. *Application contact:* Dr. Yi Pan, Regents Professor and Chair, 404-413-5342, Fax: 404-413-5717, E-mail: yipan@gsu.edu. Website: http://www.cs.gsu.edu/

Georgia State University, College of Arts and Sciences, Department of Mathematics and Statistics, Atlanta, GA 30302-3083. Offers bioinformatics (MS, PhD); biostatistics (MS, PhD); discrete mathematics (MS); mathematics (MS, PhD); scientific computing (MS); statistics (MS). *Program availability:* Part-time. *Faculty:* 25 full-time (8 women). *Students:* 91 full-time (44 women), 15 part-time (5 women); includes 29 minority (9 Black or African American, non-Hispanic/Latino; 14 Asian, non-Hispanic/Latino; 4 Hispanic/Latino; 2 Two or more races, non-Hispanic/Latino), 57 international. Average age 32.

128 applicants, 49% accepted, 30 enrolled. In 2019, 26 master's, 4 doctorates awarded. Terminal master's awarded for partial completion of doctoral program. *Entrance requirements:* For master's and doctorate, GRE. Additional exam requirements/recommendations for international students: required—TOEFL (minimum score 550 paper-based; 80 iBT). *Application deadline:* For fall admission, 7/1 priority date for domestic and international students; for spring admission, 11/15 priority date for domestic and international students. Application fee: $50. Electronic applications accepted. *Expenses: Tuition, area resident:* Full-time $7164; part-time $398 per credit hour. Tuition, state resident: full-time $7164; part-time $398 per credit hour. Tuition, nonresident: full-time $22,662; part-time $1259 per credit hour. *International tuition:* $22,662 full-time. *Required fees:* $2128; $312 per credit hour. Tuition and fees vary according to course load and program. *Financial support:* In 2019–20, fellowships with full tuition reimbursements (averaging $22,000 per year), research assistantships with full tuition reimbursements (averaging $9,000 per year), teaching assistantships with full tuition reimbursements (averaging $9,000 per year) were awarded; institutionally sponsored loans, scholarships/grants, health care benefits, and unspecified assistantships also available. Financial award application deadline: 2/1. *Unit head:* Dr. Guantao Chen, Chair, 404-413-6436, Fax: 404-413-6403, E-mail: gchen@gsu.edu. *Application contact:* Dr. Guantao Chen, Chair, 404-413-6436, Fax: 404-413-6403, E-mail: gchen@gsu.edu. Website: https://www.mathstat.gsu.edu/

Grand Valley State University, Padnos College of Engineering and Computing, Health Informatics and Bioinformatics Program, Allendale, MI 49401-9403. Offers MS. *Program availability:* Part-time, evening/weekend. *Students:* 11 full-time (8 women), 17 part-time (9 women), 17 international. Average age 26. 22 applicants, 91% accepted, 6 enrolled. In 2019, 10 master's awarded. *Degree requirements:* For master's, capstone course. *Entrance requirements:* For master's, GRE or GMAT if undergraduate GPA is less than 3.0, minimum GPA of 3.0, resume, personal statement, minimum of 2 letters of recommendation, previous academic study or work experience. Additional exam requirements/recommendations for international students: required—TOEFL (minimum iBT score of 80), IELTS (6.5), or Michigan English Language Assessment Battery (77). *Application deadline:* For fall admission, 2/1 priority date for domestic students. Applications are processed on a rolling basis. Application fee: $30. Electronic applications accepted. *Expenses:* $733 per credit hour, 36 credit hours. *Financial support:* In 2019–20, 7 students received support, including 2 fellowships, 5 research assistantships with full and partial tuition reimbursements available (averaging $8,000 per year); career-related internships or fieldwork, tuition waivers (full and partial), and unspecified assistantships also available. *Unit head:* Dr. Paul Leidig, Director, 616-331-2060, Fax: 616-331-2144, E-mail: leidigp@gvsu.edu. *Application contact:* Dr. Guenter Tusch, Graduate Program Director, 616-331-2046, Fax: 616-331-2144, E-mail: tuschg@gvsu.edu. Website: https://www.gvsu.edu/grad/bioinfo/

Hood College, Graduate School, Program in Bioinformatics, Frederick, MD 21701-8575. Offers MS, Certificate. *Program availability:* Part-time-only, evening/weekend. *Degree requirements:* For master's, capstone project. *Entrance requirements:* For master's, bachelor's degree in life science or computer science field, minimum GPA of 2.75, written statement of intent (250 words). Additional exam requirements/recommendations for international students: required—TOEFL (minimum score 575 paper-based; 89 iBT), IELTS (minimum score 6.5). Electronic applications accepted. *Expenses:* Contact institution.

Hunter College of the City University of New York, Graduate School, School of Arts and Sciences, Department of Mathematics and Statistics, New York, NY 10065-5085. Offers adolescent mathematics education (MA); applied mathematics (MA); bioinformatics (MA); pure mathematics (MA); statistics (MA). *Program availability:* Part-time, evening/weekend. *Degree requirements:* For master's, one foreign language, comprehensive exam, thesis (for some programs). *Entrance requirements:* For master's, GRE General Test, 24 credits in mathematics. Additional exam requirements/recommendations for international students: required—TOEFL.

Indiana University Bloomington, School of Informatics, Computing, and Engineering, Department of Computer Science, Bloomington, IN 47405. Offers bioinformatics (MS); computer science (MS, PhD); cybersecurity risk management (MS); secure computing (MS, Graduate Certificate). Terminal master's awarded for partial completion of doctoral program. *Degree requirements:* For master's, thesis optional; for doctorate, comprehensive exam, thesis/dissertation, oral and written exams. *Entrance requirements:* For master's and doctorate, GRE General Test, statement of purpose, bachelor's degree. Additional exam requirements/recommendations for international students: required—TOEFL. Electronic applications accepted.

Indiana University Bloomington, School of Informatics, Computing, and Engineering, Program in Informatics, Bloomington, IN 47405. Offers informatics (MS, PhD), including bioinformatics (PhD), complex systems (PhD), computing, culture and society (PhD), health informatics (PhD), human-computer interaction (MS), human-computer interaction design (PhD), music informatics (PhD), security informatics (PhD); visual heritage (PhD). *Program availability:* Part-time. Terminal master's awarded for partial completion of doctoral program. *Degree requirements:* For master's, thesis, capstone project; for doctorate, variable foreign language requirement, comprehensive exam, thesis/dissertation. *Entrance requirements:* For master's and doctorate, GRE, resume/curriculum vitae, transcripts, 3 letters of recommendation. Additional exam requirements/recommendations for international students: required—TOEFL (minimum score 600 paper-based; 100 iBT). Electronic applications accepted.

Indiana University-Purdue University Indianapolis, School of Informatics and Computing, Department of BioHealth Informatics, Indianapolis, IN 46202. Offers bioinformatics (MS, PhD); health informatics (MS, PhD).

Iowa State University of Science and Technology, Bioinformatics and Computational Biology Program, Ames, IA 50011. Offers MS, PhD. *Degree requirements:* For doctorate, thesis/dissertation. *Entrance requirements:* For master's and doctorate, GRE General Test. Additional exam requirements/recommendations for international students: recommended—TOEFL, IELTS. Electronic applications accepted.

Johns Hopkins University, Advanced Academic Programs, Program in Bioinformatics, Washington, DC 21218. Offers MS. *Program availability:* Part-time, evening/weekend, 100% online. *Entrance requirements:* For master's, minimum GPA of 3.0; coursework in programming and data structures, biology, and chemistry. Additional exam requirements/recommendations for international students: required—TOEFL (minimum score 100 iBT). Electronic applications accepted.

Lawrence Technological University, College of Arts and Sciences, Southfield, MI 48075-1058. Offers bioinformatics (Graduate Certificate); computer science (MS), including data science, big data, and data mining; intelligent systems; educational technology (MA), including robotics; instructional design, communication, and presentation (Graduate Certificate); integrated science (MA); science education (MA); technical and professional communication (MS, Graduate Certificate); writing for the digital age (Graduate Certificate). *Program availability:* Part-time, evening/weekend. *Faculty:* 5 full-time (2 women), 2 part-time/adjunct (1 woman). *Students:* 1 (woman) full-time, 25 part-time (15 women); includes 6 minority (3 Black or African American, non-

Hispanic/Latino; 2 Asian, non-Hispanic/Latino; 1 Hispanic/Latino), 6 international. Average age 34. 50 applicants, 68% accepted, 3 enrolled. In 2019, 14 master's, 4 other advanced degrees awarded. *Degree requirements:* For master's, thesis (for some programs). *Entrance requirements:* Additional exam requirements/recommendations for international students: required—TOEFL (minimum score 550 paper-based; 79 iBT), IELTS (minimum score 6.5). *Application deadline:* For fall admission, 5/24 for international students; for spring admission, 10/13 for international students; for summer admission, 2/18 for international students. Applications are processed on a rolling basis. Application fee: $50. Electronic applications accepted. *Expenses: Tuition:* Full-time $16,618; part-time $8309 per year. *Required fees:* $600; $600. *Financial support:* In 2019–20, 4 students received support. Scholarships/grants and tuition reduction available. Financial award application deadline: 4/1; financial award applicants required to submit FAFSA. *Unit head:* Glen Bauer, Interim Dean, 248-204-3532, Fax: 248-204-3518, E-mail: scidean@ltu.edu. *Application contact:* Jane Rohrback, Director of Admissions, 248-204-3160, Fax: 248-204-2228, E-mail: admissions@ltu.edu.

Lewis University, College of Aviation, Science and Technology, Program in Data Science, Romeoville, IL 60446. Offers computational biology and bioinformatics (MS); computer science (MS). *Program availability:* Part-time, evening/weekend, 100% online, blended/hybrid learning. *Students:* 22 full-time (6 women), 95 part-time (35 women); includes 33 minority (5 Black or African American, non-Hispanic/Latino; 11 Asian, non-Hispanic/Latino; 9 Hispanic/Latino; 2 Native Hawaiian or other Pacific Islander, non-Hispanic/Latino; 6 Two or more races, non-Hispanic/Latino), 10 international. Average age 33. *Entrance requirements:* For master's, bachelor's degree, undergraduate coursework in calculus, minimum undergraduate GPA of 3.0, resume, statement of purpose, two letters of recommendation. Additional exam requirements/recommendations for international students: required—TOEFL (minimum score 550 paper-based; 79 iBT), IELTS (minimum score 6). *Application deadline:* For fall admission, 5/1 priority date for international students; for winter admission, 11/1 priority date for international students. Applications are processed on a rolling basis. Application fee: $40. Electronic applications accepted. *Financial support:* Federal Work-Study and unspecified assistantships available. Financial award application deadline: 5/1; financial award applicants required to submit FAFSA. *Unit head:* Dr. Piotr Szczurek, Program Director. *Application contact:* Sheri Vilcek, Graduate Admissions Counselor, 815-836-5610, E-mail: grad@lewisu.edu.
Website: http://www.lewisu.edu/academics/data-science/index.htm

Loyola University Chicago, Graduate School, Program in Bioinformatics, Chicago, IL 60660. Offers thesis (MS). *Program availability:* Part-time. *Faculty:* 31 full-time (7 women). *Students:* 8 full-time (4 women), 3 part-time (0 women); includes 2 minority (both Asian, non-Hispanic/Latino), 1 international. Average age 25. 24 applicants, 54% accepted, 2 enrolled. In 2019, 2 master's awarded. *Degree requirements:* For master's, thesis (for some programs). *Entrance requirements:* For master's, official college transcripts, 2 letters of recommendation, a current resume/CV, brief (500-1000 words) statement of purpose. Additional exam requirements/recommendations for international students: required—TOEFL (minimum score 79 paper-based; 550 iBT), IELTS (minimum score 6.5), TOEFL or IELTS. *Application deadline:* For fall admission, 3/15 for domestic and international students; for spring admission, 10/15 for domestic and international students. Application fee: $0. Electronic applications accepted. *Expenses: Tuition:* Full-time $18,540; part-time $1033 per credit hour. *Required fees:* $904; $230 per credit hour. *Financial support:* In 2019–20, 5 students received support, including 3 research assistantships with full tuition reimbursements available (averaging $18,000 per year), 2 teaching assistantships with partial tuition reimbursements available (averaging $9,000 per year); Federal Work-Study, scholarships/grants, and health care benefits also available. Financial award application deadline: 2/1. *Unit head:* Dr. Catherine Putonti, Program Director, 773-508-3277, Fax: 773-508-3646, E-mail: cputonti@luc.edu. *Application contact:* Jill Schur, Director of Graduate Enrollment Management, 312-915-8902, E-mail: gradinfo@luc.edu.
Website: https://www.luc.edu/bioinformatics/msinbioinformatics/

Marquette University, Graduate School, College of Arts and Sciences, Department of Mathematical and Statistical Sciences, Milwaukee, WI 53201-1881. Offers bioinformatics (MS); computational sciences (MS, PhD); computing (MS); mathematics education (MS). *Program availability:* Part-time, evening/weekend, online learning. Terminal master's awarded for partial completion of doctoral program. *Degree requirements:* For master's, thesis (for some programs), essay with oral presentation; for doctorate, comprehensive exam, thesis/dissertation, qualifying examination. *Entrance requirements:* For master's, official transcripts from all current and previous colleges/universities except Marquette, three letters of recommendation; for doctorate, GRE General Test, official transcripts from all current and previous colleges/universities except Marquette, three letters of recommendation. Additional exam requirements/recommendations for international students: required—TOEFL (minimum score 530 paper-based). Electronic applications accepted.

Marquette University, Graduate School, College of Arts and Sciences, Program in Bioinformatics, Milwaukee, WI 53201-1881. Offers MS. *Program availability:* Part-time, evening/weekend, online learning. *Degree requirements:* For master's, research practicum or thesis. *Entrance requirements:* For master's, GRE (strongly recommended), official transcripts from all current and previous colleges/universities except Marquette; essay outlining relevant work experience or education, career goals, possible areas of interest, and reasons for seeking admission; three letters of reference. Additional exam requirements/recommendations for international students: required—TOEFL (minimum score 530 paper-based). Electronic applications accepted.

Massachusetts Institute of Technology, School of Engineering, Harvard-MIT Health Sciences and Technology Program, Cambridge, MA 02139. Offers health sciences and technology (SM, PhD, Sc D), including bioastronautics (PhD, Sc D), bioinformatics and integrative genomics (PhD, Sc D), medical engineering and medical physics (PhD, Sc D), speech and hearing bioscience and technology (PhD, Sc D). Terminal master's awarded for partial completion of doctoral program. *Degree requirements:* For doctorate, comprehensive exam, thesis/dissertation. *Entrance requirements:* For doctorate, GRE General Test. Additional exam requirements/recommendations for international students: required—TOEFL, IELTS. Electronic applications accepted.

McGill University, Faculty of Graduate and Postdoctoral Studies, Faculty of Science, Department of Biology, Montréal, QC H3A 2T5, Canada. Offers bioinformatics (M Sc, PhD); environment (M Sc, PhD); neo-tropical environment (M Sc, PhD).

Morgan State University, School of Graduate Studies, School of Computer, Mathematical, and Natural Sciences, Department of Computer Science, Baltimore, MD 21251. Offers bioinformatics (MS); computer science (MS). *Program availability:* Part-time, evening/weekend. *Faculty:* 11 full-time (2 women), 3 part-time/adjunct (1 woman). *Students:* 5 full-time (4 women), 1 part-time (0 women); includes 2 minority (both Black or African American, non-Hispanic/Latino), 2 international. Average age 36. 9 applicants, 100% accepted, 3 enrolled. In 2019, 1 master's awarded. *Degree requirements:* For master's, comprehensive exam, thesis. *Entrance requirements:* For master's, Minimum GPA 3.0. Additional exam requirements/recommendations for international students: required—TOEFL (minimum score 550 paper-based; 70 iBT). *Application deadline:* For fall admission, 2/1 priority date for domestic students, 4/1 for international students; for spring admission, 10/1 priority date for domestic students, 10/1 for international students. Applications are processed on a rolling basis. Application fee: $50 ($70 for international students). Electronic applications accepted. *Expenses:* Tuition, state resident: full-time $455; part-time $455 per credit hour. Tuition, nonresident: full-time $894; part-time $894 per credit hour. *Required fees:* $82; $82 per credit hour. *Financial support:* In 2019–20, 3 students received support. Fellowships with tuition reimbursements available, research assistantships with full and partial tuition reimbursements available, teaching assistantships with full and partial tuition reimbursements available, scholarships/grants, tuition waivers (full and partial), and unspecified assistantships available. Support available to part-time students. Financial award application deadline: 2/1. *Unit head:* Dr. Shuangbao (Paul) Wang, Chair, 443-885-3962, E-mail: Shuangbao.Wang@morgan.edu. *Application contact:* Dr. Jahmaine Smith, Director of Admissions, 443-885-3185, Fax: 443-885-8226, E-mail: gradapply@morgan.edu.
Website: https://www.morgan.edu/physics

New Mexico State University, College of Arts and Sciences, Department of Computer Science, Las Cruces, NM 88003-8001. Offers bioinformatics (MS); computer science (MS, PhD). *Program availability:* Part-time. *Faculty:* 13 full-time (3 women). *Students:* 80 full-time (24 women), 16 part-time (1 woman); includes 24 minority (4 Black or African American, non-Hispanic/Latino; 12 Asian, non-Hispanic/Latino; 7 Hispanic/Latino; 1 Two or more races, non-Hispanic/Latino), 60 international. Average age 30. 118 applicants, 81% accepted, 27 enrolled. In 2019, 21 master's, 7 doctorates awarded. Terminal master's awarded for partial completion of doctoral program. *Degree requirements:* For master's, comprehensive exam, thesis or alternative; for doctorate, comprehensive exam, thesis/dissertation, qualifying exam, thesis proposal. *Entrance requirements:* For master's and doctorate, BS in computer science. Additional exam requirements/recommendations for international students: required—TOEFL (minimum score 550 paper-based; 79 iBT), IELTS (minimum score 6.5). *Application deadline:* For fall admission, 3/1 priority date for domestic and international students; for spring admission, 11/1 priority date for domestic and international students. Applications are processed on a rolling basis. Application fee: $40 ($50 for international students). Electronic applications accepted. *Financial support:* In 2019–20, 73 students received support, including 1 fellowship (averaging $4,844 per year), 30 research assistantships (averaging $14,577 per year), 22 teaching assistantships (averaging $10,198 per year); career-related internships or fieldwork, Federal Work-Study, scholarships/grants, traineeships, health care benefits, and unspecified assistantships also available. Support available to part-time students. Financial award application deadline: 3/1. *Unit head:* Dr. Son Tran, Department Head, 575-646-3723, Fax: 575-646-1002, E-mail: stran@cs.nmsu.edu. *Application contact:* Dr. Joe Song, Associate Professor, 575-646-3723, Fax: 575-646-1002, E-mail: gradcs@cs.nmsu.edu.
Website: http://www.cs.nmsu.edu/

New York University, Tandon School of Engineering, Department of Computer Science and Engineering, Major in Bioinformatics, New York, NY 10012-1019. Offers bioinformatics (MS). *Program availability:* Part-time, online learning. *Degree requirements:* For master's, comprehensive exam (for some programs), thesis (for some programs). *Entrance requirements:* Additional exam requirements/recommendations for international students: required—TOEFL (minimum score 550 paper-based; 90 iBT); recommended—IELTS (minimum score 7). Electronic applications accepted.

North Dakota State University, College of Graduate and Interdisciplinary Studies, Interdisciplinary Program in Genomics and Bioinformatics, Fargo, ND 58102. Offers MS, PhD. *Program availability:* Part-time. *Degree requirements:* For master's, thesis; for doctorate, comprehensive exam, thesis/dissertation. *Entrance requirements:* For master's and doctorate, minimum GPA of 3.0. Additional exam requirements/recommendations for international students: required—TOEFL. Electronic applications accepted. Tuition and fees vary according to program and reciprocity agreements.

Northeastern University, College of Science, Boston, MA 02115-5096. Offers applied mathematics (MS); bioinformatics (MS); biology (PhD); biotechnology (MS); chemistry and chemical biology (MS, PhD); environmental science and policy (MS); marine and environmental sciences (PhD); marine biology (MS); mathematics (MS, PhD); operations research (MSOR); physics (MS, PhD); psychology (PhD). *Program availability:* Part-time. Terminal master's awarded for partial completion of doctoral program. *Degree requirements:* For master's, comprehensive exam (for some programs), thesis; for doctorate, comprehensive exam (for some programs), thesis/dissertation. *Entrance requirements:* For master's, GRE General Test. Electronic applications accepted. *Expenses:* Contact institution.

Nova Southeastern University, Dr. Kiran C. Patel College of Osteopathic Medicine, Fort Lauderdale, FL 33314-7796. Offers biomedical informatics (MS, Graduate Certificate), including biomedical informatics (MS), clinical informatics (Graduate Certificate), public health informatics (Graduate Certificate); disaster and emergency management (MS); medical education (MS); nutrition (MS, Graduate Certificate), including functional nutrition and herbal therapy (Graduate Certificate); osteopathic medicine (DO); public health (MPH, Graduate Certificate), including health education (Graduate Certificate); social medicine (Graduate Certificate); DO/DMD. *Accreditation:* AOsA; CEPH. *Program availability:* Part-time, 100% online, blended/hybrid learning. *Faculty:* 73 full-time (43 women), 35 part-time/adjunct (14 women). *Students:* 1,410 full-time (740 women), 182 part-time (118 women); includes 895 minority (126 Black or African American, non-Hispanic/Latino; 1 American Indian or Alaska Native, non-Hispanic/Latino; 416 Asian, non-Hispanic/Latino; 309 Hispanic/Latino; 1 Native Hawaiian or other Pacific Islander, non-Hispanic/Latino; 42 Two or more races, non-Hispanic/Latino), 70 international. Average age 26. 5,078 applicants, 10% accepted, 495 enrolled. In 2019, 117 master's, 233 doctorates, 3 other advanced degrees awarded. *Degree requirements:* For master's, comprehensive exam (for MPH); field/special projects; for doctorate, comprehensive exam, COMLEX Board Exams; for Graduate Certificate, thesis or alternative. *Entrance requirements:* For master's, GRE; for doctorate, MCAT, coursework in biology, chemistry, organic chemistry, physics (all with labs), biochemistry, and English. *Application deadline:* For fall admission, 1/15 for domestic students. Applications are processed on a rolling basis. Application fee: $50. Electronic applications accepted. *Expenses:* Contact institution. *Financial support:* In 2019–20, 83 students received support, including 24 fellowships with tuition reimbursements available; Federal Work-Study and scholarships/grants also available. Financial award application deadline: 6/1; financial award applicants required to submit FAFSA. *Unit head:* Elaine M. Wallace, Dean, 954-262-1457, Fax: 954-262-2250, E-mail: ewallace@nova.edu. *Application contact:* HPD Admissions, 877-640-0218, E-mail: hpdinfo@nova.edu.
Website: https://www.osteopathic.nova.edu/

Oregon Health & Science University, School of Medicine, Graduate Programs in Medicine, Department of Medical Informatics and Clinical Epidemiology, Portland, OR 97239-3098. Offers bioinformatics and computational biology (MS, PhD); clinical informatics (MBI, MS, PhD, Certificate); health information management (Certificate). *Program availability:* Part-time, online learning. Terminal master's awarded for partial completion of doctoral program. *Degree requirements:* For master's, thesis or capstone project; for doctorate, comprehensive exam, thesis/dissertation, qualifying exam. *Entrance requirements:* For master's and doctorate, GRE General Test (minimum scores: 153 Verbal/148 Quantitative/4.5 Analytical), coursework in computer programming, human anatomy and physiology. Electronic applications accepted. *Expenses:* Contact institution.

Oregon State University, Interdisciplinary/Institutional Programs, Program in Molecular and Cellular Biology, Corvallis, OR 97331. Offers bioinformatics (PhD); biotechnology (PhD); genome biology (PhD); molecular virology (PhD); plant molecular biology (PhD). *Degree requirements:* For doctorate, thesis/dissertation, oral and written qualifying exams. *Entrance requirements:* For doctorate, GRE. Additional exam requirements/recommendations for international students: required—TOEFL (minimum score 80 iBT), IELTS (minimum score 6.5).

Penn State Hershey Medical Center, College of Medicine, Graduate School Programs in the Biomedical Sciences, Huck Institutes of the Life Sciences, Intercollege Graduate Program in Bioinformatics and Genomics, Hershey, PA 17033-2360. Offers MS, PhD.

Rice University, Graduate Programs, George R. Brown School of Engineering, Department of Statistics, Houston, TX 77251-1892. Offers bioinformatics (PhD); biostatistics (PhD); computational finance (PhD); general statistics (PhD); statistics (M Stat, MA); MBA/M Stat. *Program availability:* Part-time. *Degree requirements:* For master's, comprehensive exam; for doctorate, comprehensive exam, thesis/dissertation. *Entrance requirements:* For master's and doctorate, GRE General Test, minimum GPA of 3.0. Additional exam requirements/recommendations for international students: required—TOEFL (minimum score 630 paper-based; 90 iBT). Electronic applications accepted.

Rochester Institute of Technology, Graduate Enrollment Services, College of Science, School of Life Sciences, MS Program in Bioinformatics, Rochester, NY 14623-5603. Offers MS. *Program availability:* Part-time. *Degree requirements:* For master's, thesis. *Entrance requirements:* For master's, GRE, minimum GPA of 3.2 (recommended), two letters of recommendation. Additional exam requirements/recommendations for international students: required—TOEFL (minimum score 570 paper-based; 79 iBT), IELTS (minimum score 6.5), PTE (minimum score 58). Electronic applications accepted.

Rowan University, Graduate School, College of Science and Mathematics, Program in Bioinformatics, Glassboro, NJ 08028-1701. Offers MS. *Entrance requirements:* For master's, GRE, BS in biology, biochemistry, chemistry, computer science, or related field with minimum GPA of 2.5. Additional exam requirements/recommendations for international students: required—TOEFL. Electronic applications accepted. *Expenses: Tuition, area resident:* Part-time $715.50 per semester hour. Tuition, state resident: part-time $715.50 per semester hour. Tuition, nonresident: part-time $715.50 per semester hour. *Required fees:* $161.55 per semester hour.

Rutgers University - Newark, School of Health Related Professions, Department of Health Informatics, Program in Biomedical Informatics, Newark, NJ 07102. Offers MS, PhD, DMD/MS, MD/MS. *Program availability:* Part-time, evening/weekend, online learning. *Degree requirements:* For master's, thesis; for doctorate, comprehensive exam, thesis/dissertation. *Entrance requirements:* For master's, BS, transcript of highest degree, statement of research interests, curriculum vitae, basic understanding of database concepts and calculus, 3 reference letters; for doctorate, master's degree, transcripts of highest degree, statement of research interests, curriculum vitae, basic understanding of database concepts and calculus, 3 reference letters. Additional exam requirements/recommendations for international students: required—TOEFL. Electronic applications accepted.

Saint Louis University, Graduate Programs, College of Arts and Sciences, Department of Computer Science, St. Louis, MO 63103. Offers bioinformatics and computational biology (MS); computer science (MS); software engineering (MS).

Simon Fraser University, Office of Graduate Studies and Postdoctoral Fellows, Faculty of Science, Department of Biological Sciences, Burnaby, BC V5A 1S6, Canada. Offers bioinformatics (Graduate Diploma); biological sciences (M Sc, PhD); environmental toxicology (MET); pest management (MPM). *Degree requirements:* For master's, thesis; for doctorate, thesis/dissertation, candidacy exam; for Graduate Diploma, practicum. *Entrance requirements:* For master's, minimum GPA of 3.0 (on scale of 4.33) or 3.33 based on last 60 credits of undergraduate courses; for doctorate, minimum GPA of 3.5 (on scale of 4.33); for Graduate Diploma, minimum GPA of 2.5 (on scale of 4.33) or 2.67 based on last 60 credits of undergraduate courses. Additional exam requirements/recommendations for international students: recommended—TOEFL (minimum score 580 paper-based; 93 iBT), IELTS (minimum score 7), TWE (minimum score 5). Electronic applications accepted.

Simon Fraser University, Office of Graduate Studies and Postdoctoral Fellows, Faculty of Science, Department of Molecular Biology and Biochemistry, Burnaby, BC V5A 1S6, Canada. Offers bioinformatics (Graduate Diploma); molecular biology and biochemistry (M Sc, PhD). *Degree requirements:* For master's, thesis; for doctorate, thesis/dissertation; for Graduate Diploma, practicum. *Entrance requirements:* For master's, minimum GPA of 3.0 (on scale of 4.33) or 3.33 based on last 60 credits of undergraduate courses; for doctorate, minimum GPA of 3.5; for Graduate Diploma, minimum GPA of 2.5 (on scale of 4.33) or 2.67 based on last 60 credits of undergraduate courses. Additional exam requirements/recommendations for international students: recommended—TOEFL (minimum score 580 paper-based; 100 iBT), IELTS (minimum score 7.5), TWE (minimum score 5). Electronic applications accepted.

State University of New York at Oswego, Graduate Studies, Program in Biomedical and Health Informatics, Oswego, NY 13126. Offers health informatics professional (MS); health informatics: intelligent health systems (MS); health information management: health data science (MS). *Program availability:* Online learning. *Students:* 49. In 2019, 3 master's awarded. *Entrance requirements:* For master's, GRE (recommended), official transcripts, statement of purpose, resume, two letters of recommendation. Additional exam requirements/recommendations for international students: required—TOEFL. *Application deadline:* Applications are processed on a rolling basis. Application fee: $65. Electronic applications accepted. *Financial support:* Fellowships, research assistantships, teaching assistantships, institutionally sponsored loans, scholarships/grants, and unspecified assistantships available. Financial award applicants required to submit FAFSA. *Unit head:* Dr. Isabelle Bichindaritz, Director, 315-312-3152, E-mail: ibichind@oswego.edu. *Application contact:* Dr. Isabelle Bichindaritz, Director, 315-312-3152, E-mail: ibichind@oswego.edu.
Website: http://oswego.edu/bhi

Stony Brook University, State University of New York, Graduate School, College of Engineering and Applied Sciences, Department of Biomedical Informatics, Stony Brook, NY 11794. Offers MS, PhD, AGC. *Faculty:* 4 full-time (0 women). *Students:* 8 full-time (5 women), 5 part-time (1 woman); includes 3 minority (1 Black or African American, non-Hispanic/Latino; 1 Asian, non-Hispanic/Latino; 1 Hispanic/Latino), 6 international. Average age 28. 34 applicants, 41% accepted, 6 enrolled. In 2019, 1 master's, 1 doctorate, 1 other advanced degree awarded. *Degree requirements:* For doctorate, thesis/dissertation, qualifying examination, teaching requirement. *Entrance requirements:* For master's, GRE, minimum B average or equivalent, two letters of recommendation; for doctorate, GRE; for AGC, minimum B average or equivalent, statement of purpose, three letters of recommendation. Additional exam requirements/recommendations for international students: required—TOEFL. *Application deadline:* For fall admission, 1/15 for domestic students; for spring admission, 10/1 for domestic students. *Expenses:* Contact institution. *Financial support:* In 2019–20, 3 fellowships, 3 research assistantships, 1 teaching assistantship were awarded. *Unit head:* Dr. Joel H. Saltz, Professor/Founding Chair, 631-638-1420, Fax: 631-638-1323, E-mail: joel.saltz@stonybrook.edu. *Application contact:* Craig Stewart, Senior Staff Assistant, 631-638-2864, Fax: 631-638-1323, E-mail: craig.stewart@stonybrookmedicine.edu.
Website: http://bmi.stonybrookmedicine.edu/

Tufts University, School of Engineering, Department of Computer Science, Medford, MA 02155. Offers bioengineering (MS), including bioinformatics; cognitive science/computer science (PhD); computer science (MS, PhD); soft material robotics (PhD). *Program availability:* Part-time. Terminal master's awarded for partial completion of doctoral program. *Entrance requirements:* For master's and doctorate, GRE General Test. Additional exam requirements/recommendations for international students: required—TOEFL (minimum score 550 paper-based; 80 iBT), IELTS (minimum score 6.5). Electronic applications accepted. Full-time tuition and fees vary according to degree level, program and student level. Part-time tuition and fees vary according to course load.

Université de Montréal, Faculty of Medicine, Biochemistry Department, Montréal, QC H3C 3J7, Canada. Offers M Sc, PhD. Electronic applications accepted.

Université de Montréal, Faculty of Medicine, Program in Bioinformatics, Montréal, QC H3C 3J7, Canada. Offers M Sc, PhD.

University at Buffalo, the State University of New York, Graduate School, Jacobs School of Medicine and Biomedical Sciences, Graduate Programs in Medicine and Biomedical Sciences, Program in Genetics, Genomics and Bioinformatics, Buffalo, NY 14203. Offers MS, PhD, MD/PhD. *Faculty:* 59 full-time (16 women). *Students:* 12 full-time (6 women); includes 5 minority (all Asian, non-Hispanic/Latino). Average age 25. 9 applicants, 89% accepted, 3 enrolled. In 2019, 6 master's awarded. Terminal master's awarded for partial completion of doctoral program. *Degree requirements:* For master's, thesis or alternative; for doctorate, thesis/dissertation. *Entrance requirements:* For master's and doctorate, GRE. Additional exam requirements/recommendations for international students: required—TOEFL (minimum score 100 iBT); recommended—IELTS (minimum score 6.5). *Application deadline:* For fall admission, 3/1 for domestic and international students. Application fee: $85. Electronic applications accepted. *Expenses: Tuition, area resident:* Full-time $11,310; part-time $471 per credit hour. Tuition, state resident: full-time $11,310; part-time $471 per credit hour. Tuition, nonresident: full-time $23,100; part-time $963 per credit hour. *International tuition:* $23,100 full-time. *Required fees:* $2820. *Unit head:* Dr. Richard Gronostajski, Director, 716-829-3471, Fax: 716-849-6655, E-mail: rgron@buffalo.edu. *Application contact:* M. Sara Thomas, Program Administrator, 716-829-3890, E-mail: msthomas@buffalo.edu.
Website: http://medicine.buffalo.edu/education/ggb.html

The University of Alabama at Birmingham, Joint Health Sciences, Genetics, Genomics, and Bioinformatics Theme, Birmingham, AL 35294. Offers PhD. *Students:* Average age 27. 39 applicants, 18% accepted, 4 enrolled. In 2019, 4 doctorates awarded. *Degree requirements:* For doctorate, comprehensive exam, thesis/dissertation. *Entrance requirements:* For doctorate, personal statement, resume or curriculum vitae, letters of recommendation, research experience, interview. Additional exam requirements/recommendations for international students: required—TOEFL (minimum score 80 iBT), IELTS (minimum score 6.5). *Application deadline:* For fall admission, 12/31 for domestic and international students. Applications are processed on a rolling basis. Electronic applications accepted. *Financial support:* In 2019–20, fellowships with full tuition reimbursements (averaging $30,000 per year), research assistantships with full tuition reimbursements (averaging $31,000 per year) were awarded; health care benefits also available. *Unit head:* Dr. Kevin Dybvig, Theme Director, 205-934-9327, E-mail: dybvig@uab.edu. *Application contact:* Alyssa Zasada, Admissions Manager for Graduate Biomedical Sciences, 205-934-3857, E-mail: grad-gbs@uab.edu.
Website: http://www.uab.edu/gbs/home/themes/ggb

University of Arkansas at Little Rock, Graduate School, George W. Donaghey College of Engineering and Information Technology, Program in Bioinformatics, Little Rock, AR 72204-1099. Offers MS, PhD. *Entrance requirements:* For doctorate, MS in bioinformatics. Additional exam requirements/recommendations for international students: required—TOEFL.

University of Arkansas for Medical Sciences, Graduate School, Little Rock, AR 72205. Offers biochemistry and molecular biology (MS, PhD); bioinformatics (MS, PhD); cellular physiology and molecular biophysics (MS, PhD); clinical nutrition (MS); interdisciplinary biomedical sciences (MS, PhD, Certificate); interdisciplinary toxicology (MS); microbiology and immunology (PhD); neurobiology and developmental sciences (PhD); pharmacology (PhD); MD/PhD. *Program availability:* Part-time. Terminal master's awarded for partial completion of doctoral program. *Degree requirements:* For master's, comprehensive exam (for some programs), thesis (for some programs); for doctorate, thesis/dissertation. *Entrance requirements:* For master's and doctorate, GRE. Additional exam requirements/recommendations for international students: required—TOEFL. Electronic applications accepted. *Expenses:* Contact institution.

The University of British Columbia, Faculty of Medicine, Department of Cellular and Physiological Sciences, Vancouver, BC V6T 1Z3, Canada. Offers bioinformatics (M Sc, PhD); cell and developmental biology (M Sc, PhD); genome science and technology (M Sc, PhD); neuroscience (M Sc, PhD). *Degree requirements:* For master's, thesis, oral defense; for doctorate, comprehensive exam, thesis/dissertation, oral defense. *Entrance requirements:* For master's, minimum overall B+ average in third- and fourth-year courses; for doctorate, minimum overall B+ average in master's degree (or equivalent) from approved institution with clear evidence of research ability or potential. Additional exam requirements/recommendations for international students: required—TOEFL, IELTS. *Expenses:* Contact institution.

University of California, Los Angeles, Graduate Division, College of Letters and Science, Interdepartmental Program in Bioinformatics, Los Angeles, CA 90095. Offers MS, PhD. Terminal master's awarded for partial completion of doctoral program. *Degree requirements:* For master's, comprehensive exam, thesis, one quarter of teaching experience; for doctorate, thesis/dissertation, oral and written qualifying exams; one quarter of teaching experience. *Entrance requirements:* For doctorate, GRE General Test, bachelor's degree; minimum undergraduate GPA of 3.0 (or its equivalent if letter grade system not used). Additional exam requirements/recommendations for international students: required—TOEFL. Electronic applications accepted.

University of California, Riverside, Graduate Division, Graduate Program in Genetics, Genomics, and Bioinformatics, Riverside, CA 92521-0102. Offers PhD. *Degree requirements:* For doctorate, thesis/dissertation, qualifying exams, teaching experience. *Entrance requirements:* For doctorate, GRE General Test, minimum GPA of 3.2. Additional exam requirements/recommendations for international students: required—TOEFL (minimum score 550 paper-based, 80 iBT) or IELTS. Electronic applications accepted.

Bioinformatics

University of California, San Diego, Graduate Division, Program in Bioinformatics and Systems Biology, La Jolla, CA 92093. Offers PhD. *Students:* 67 full-time (23 women), 1 part-time (0 women). 296 applicants, 10% accepted, 13 enrolled. In 2019, 10 doctorates awarded. *Degree requirements:* For doctorate, comprehensive exam, thesis/dissertation, two quarters as teaching assistant. *Entrance requirements:* For doctorate, GRE General Test. Additional exam requirements/recommendations for international students: required—TOEFL (minimum score 550 paper-based; 80 iBT), IELTS (minimum score 7). *Application deadline:* For fall admission, 12/10 for domestic students. Application fee: $105 ($125 for international students). Electronic applications accepted. *Financial support:* Fellowships, research assistantships, teaching assistantships, scholarships/grants, and traineeships available. Financial award applicants required to submit FAFSA. *Unit head:* Trey Ideker, Director, 858-822-4558, E-mail: tideker@ucsd.edu. *Application contact:* Savannah Orosco, Graduate Coordinator, 858-822-0831, E-mail: bioinfo@ucsd.edu.
Website: http://bioinformatics.ucsd.edu/

University of California, San Diego, School of Medicine and Graduate Division, Graduate Studies in Biomedical Sciences, La Jolla, CA 92093-0685. Offers anthropogeny (PhD); bioinformatics (PhD); biomedical science (PhD); multi-scale biology (PhD). *Students:* 171 full-time (96 women). 702 applicants, 14% accepted, 34 enrolled. In 2019, 24 doctorates awarded. *Degree requirements:* For doctorate, comprehensive exam, thesis/dissertation, 1-quarter teaching assistantship. *Entrance requirements:* For doctorate, As of 2018, applicants are no longer required to submit scores for either the GRE General or Subject Tests. Applicants can optionally submit scores for the GRE General Test (verbal, quantitative, and analytical sections) and/or an applicable GRE Subject Test (Biology, Biochemistry (discontinued December 2016), or Chemistry). Additional exam requirements/recommendations for international students: required—TOEFL (minimum score 550 paper-based; 80 iBT), IELTS (minimum score 7). *Application deadline:* For fall admission, 11/27 for domestic students. Application fee: $105 ($125 for international students). Electronic applications accepted. *Financial support:* Fellowships, research assistantships, teaching assistantships, scholarships/grants, traineeships, unspecified assistantships, and stipends available. Financial award applicants required to submit FAFSA. *Unit head:* Asa Gustafsson, Chair, 858-822-5569, E-mail: abgustafsson@ucsd.edu. *Application contact:* Leanne Nordeman, Graduate Coordinator, 858-534-3982, E-mail: biomedsci@ucsd.edu.
Website: http://biomedsci.ucsd.edu

University of California, San Francisco, School of Pharmacy and Graduate Division, Program in Bioinformatics, San Francisco, CA 94158-2517. Offers PhD. Terminal master's awarded for partial completion of doctoral program. *Degree requirements:* For doctorate, thesis/dissertation, cumulative qualifying exams, proposal defense. *Entrance requirements:* For doctorate, GRE General Test, minimum GPA of 3.0, bachelor's degree. Additional exam requirements/recommendations for international students: required—TOEFL (minimum score 550 paper-based; 80 iBT).

University of California, Santa Cruz, Jack Baskin School of Engineering, Department of Biomolecular Engineering, Santa Cruz, CA 95064. Offers MS, PhD. *Faculty:* 13 full-time (3 women), 3 part-time/adjunct (2 women). *Students:* 70 full-time (27 women), 2 part-time (1 woman); includes 19 minority (2 Black or African American, non-Hispanic/Latino; 2 American Indian or Alaska Native, non-Hispanic/Latino; 11 Asian, non-Hispanic/Latino; 4 Hispanic/Latino), 12 international. 108 applicants, 31% accepted, 14 enrolled. In 2019, 5 master's, 9 doctorates awarded. Terminal master's awarded for partial completion of doctoral program. *Degree requirements:* For master's, thesis, Research project with written report; for doctorate, thesis/dissertation. *Entrance requirements:* Additional exam requirements/recommendations for international students: required—TOEFL (minimum score 570 paper-based; 89 iBT), IELTS (minimum score 8), Non-native English speakers must submit either TOEFL or IELTS scores. *Application deadline:* For fall admission, 12/1 for domestic and international students. Application fee: $120 ($140 for international students). Electronic applications accepted. *Financial support:* In 2019–20, 70 students received support, including 17 fellowships (averaging $25,377 per year), 45 research assistantships (averaging $26,136 per year), 27 teaching assistantships (averaging $21,909 per year); institutionally sponsored loans, scholarships/grants, and tuition waivers (full and partial) also available. Financial award application deadline: 12/1; financial award applicants required to submit FAFSA. *Unit head:* Dr. Josh Stuart, Professor and Department Chair, E-mail: jstuart@ucsc.edu. *Application contact:* Theo-Alyce Gordon, Graduate Student Advisor, 831-459-2438, E-mail: bsoe-ga@rt.ucsc.edu.
Website: http://grad.soe.ucsc.edu/bmeb

University of Chicago, Graham School of Continuing Liberal and Professional Studies, Master of Science Program in Biomedical Informatics, Chicago, IL 60637-1513. Offers M Sc. *Program availability:* Part-time, evening/weekend. *Entrance requirements:* For master's, 3 letters of recommendation, statement of purpose, transcripts, resume or curriculum vitae. Additional exam requirements/recommendations for international students: required—TOEFL (minimum score 104 iBT), IELTS (minimum score 7). Electronic applications accepted.

University of Cincinnati, Graduate School, College of Medicine, Graduate Programs in Biomedical Sciences, Department of Biomedical Informatics, Cincinnati, OH 45221. Offers PhD, Graduate Certificate. *Program availability:* Part-time. *Degree requirements:* For doctorate, comprehensive exam, thesis/dissertation. *Entrance requirements:* For doctorate and Graduate Certificate, GRE. Additional exam requirements/recommendations for international students: required—TOEFL (minimum score 520 paper-based; 80 iBT), IELTS (minimum score 6.5). Electronic applications accepted. *Expenses:* Contact institution.

University of Colorado Denver, School of Medicine, Program in Pharmacology, Aurora, CO 80206. Offers bioinformatics (PhD); biomolecular structure (PhD). *Degree requirements:* For doctorate, comprehensive exam, thesis/dissertation, major seminar, 3 research rotations in the first year, 30 hours each of course work and thesis. *Entrance requirements:* For doctorate, GRE General Test, three letters of recommendation, personal statement. Additional exam requirements/recommendations for international students: required—TOEFL (minimum score 550 paper-based; 80 iBT). Electronic applications accepted. Tuition and fees vary according to course load, program and reciprocity agreements.

University of Georgia, Institute of Bioinformatics, Athens, GA 30602. Offers MS, PhD.

University of Idaho, College of Graduate Studies, College of Science, Department of Bioinformatics and Computational Biology, Moscow, ID 83844-2282. Offers MS, PhD. *Faculty:* 15. *Students:* 18. Average age 29. In 2019, 3 master's, 4 doctorates awarded. *Degree requirements:* For master's, thesis; for doctorate, thesis/dissertation. *Entrance requirements:* For master's, GRE, minimum GPA of 3.0. Additional exam requirements/recommendations for international students: required—TOEFL (minimum score 100 iBT). *Application deadline:* For fall admission, 1/6 for domestic students; for spring admission, 9/1 for domestic students. Applications are processed on a rolling basis. Application fee: $60. Electronic applications accepted. *Expenses:* Tuition, state resident: full-time $7753.80; part-time $502 per credit hour. Tuition, nonresident: full-time $26,990; part-time $1571 per credit hour. *Required fees:* $2122.20; $47 per credit hour. *Financial support:* Applicants required to submit FAFSA. *Unit head:* Dr. David Tank, Director, 208-885-6010, E-mail: bcb@uidaho.edu. *Application contact:* Dr. David Tank, Director, 208-885-6010, E-mail: bcb@uidaho.edu.
Website: https://www.uidaho.edu/sci/bcb

University of Illinois at Chicago, College of Engineering, Department of Bioengineering, Chicago, IL 60607-7128. Offers MS, PhD. Terminal master's awarded for partial completion of doctoral program. *Degree requirements:* For master's, thesis; for doctorate, thesis/dissertation. *Entrance requirements:* For master's and doctorate, GRE Subject Test, minimum GPA of 3.0. Additional exam requirements/recommendations for international students: required—TOEFL. Electronic applications accepted. *Expenses:* Contact institution.

University of Illinois at Urbana-Champaign, Graduate College, College of Agricultural, Consumer and Environmental Sciences, Department of Crop Sciences, Champaign, IL 61820. Offers bioinformatics: crop sciences (MS); crop sciences (MS, PhD). *Program availability:* Online learning.

University of Illinois at Urbana-Champaign, Graduate College, College of Engineering, Department of Computer Science, Champaign, IL 61820. Offers bioinformatics (MS); computer science (MCS, MS, PhD); MCS/JD; MCS/M Arch; MCS/MBA. *Program availability:* Part-time, evening/weekend, online learning.

University of Illinois at Urbana-Champaign, Graduate College, School of Information Sciences, Champaign, IL 61820. Offers bioinformatics (MS); digital libraries (CAS); information management (MS); library and information science (MS, PhD, CAS). *Accreditation:* ALA (one or more programs are accredited). *Program availability:* Part-time, online learning. *Entrance requirements:* For degree, master's degree in library and information science or related field with minimum GPA of 3.0.

The University of Iowa, Graduate College, Program in Informatics, Iowa City, IA 52242-1316. Offers bioinformatics (MS, PhD); bioinformatics and computational biology (Certificate); geoinformatics (MS, PhD, Certificate); health informatics (MS, PhD, Certificate); information science (MS, PhD, Certificate). *Degree requirements:* For master's, thesis optional; for doctorate, comprehensive exam, thesis/dissertation. *Entrance requirements:* For master's and doctorate, GRE General Test, minimum GPA of 3.0. Additional exam requirements/recommendations for international students: required—TOEFL (minimum score 550 paper-based; 81 iBT). Electronic applications accepted.

University of Louisville, School of Interdisciplinary and Graduate Studies, Louisville, KY 40292. Offers interdisciplinary studies (MA, MS, PhD), including bioethics and medical humanities (MA), bioinformatics (PhD), sustainability (MA, MS), translational bioengineering (PhD), translational neuroscience (PhD). *Program availability:* Part-time. *Students:* 36 full-time (21 women), 14 part-time (5 women); includes 5 minority (1 Black or African American, non-Hispanic/Latino; 3 Hispanic/Latino; 1 Two or more races, non-Hispanic/Latino), 10 international. Average age 32. 27 applicants, 70% accepted, 14 enrolled. In 2019, 3 master's, 1 doctorate awarded. *Degree requirements:* For master's, variable foreign language requirement, comprehensive exam (for some programs), thesis (for some programs); for doctorate, variable foreign language requirement, comprehensive exam, thesis/dissertation. *Entrance requirements:* For master's and doctorate, GRE General Test, Application fee, two letters of recommendation, transcripts from previous post-secondary educational institutions. Additional exam requirements/recommendations for international students: required—TOEFL (minimum score 550 paper-based; 79 iBT), IELTS (minimum score 6.5). *Application deadline:* For fall admission, 7/1 priority date for domestic students, 5/1 priority date for international students; for winter admission, 7/1 priority date for domestic students, 5/1 for international students; for spring admission, 12/1 priority date for domestic students, 11/1 for international students; for summer admission, 4/1 priority date for domestic students, 4/1 for international students. Applications are processed on a rolling basis. Application fee: $65. Electronic applications accepted. *Expenses: Tuition, area resident:* Full-time $13,000; part-time $723 per credit hour. Tuition, state resident: full-time $13,000; part-time $723 per credit hour. Tuition, nonresident: full-time $27,114; part-time $1507 per credit hour. *International tuition:* $27,114 full-time. *Required fees:* $196. Tuition and fees vary according to program and reciprocity agreements. *Financial support:* In 2019–20, 35 students received support, including 120 fellowships with full tuition reimbursements available (averaging $20,000 per year); scholarships/grants, health care benefits, unspecified assistantships, and Diversity scholarships also available. Financial award application deadline: 1/1; financial award applicants required to submit FAFSA. *Unit head:* Dr. Paul J. DeMarco, Acting Vice Provost for Graduate Affairs, Acting Dean of the Graduate School, 502-852-0788, Fax: 502-852-2365, E-mail: paul.demarco@louisville.edu. *Application contact:* Dr. Barbara Clark, Acting Associate Dean of the Graduate School, 502-852-6498, Fax: 502-852-3111, E-mail: gradadm@louisville.edu.
Website: http://www.graduate.louisville.edu

University of Maine, Graduate School, Graduate School of Biomedical Science and Engineering, Orono, ME 04469. Offers bioinformatics (PSM); biomedical engineering (PhD); biomedical science (PhD). *Faculty:* 182 full-time (60 women). *Students:* 47 full-time (26 women), 1 part-time (0 women); includes 2 minority (1 Hispanic/Latino; 1 Two or more races, non-Hispanic/Latino), 9 international. Average age 30. 111 applicants, 17% accepted, 15 enrolled. In 2019, 7 doctorates awarded. *Degree requirements:* For doctorate, comprehensive exam, thesis/dissertation. *Entrance requirements:* For doctorate, GRE General Test, master's degree. Additional exam requirements/recommendations for international students: required—TOEFL (minimum score 80 iBT), IELTS (minimum score 6.5), PTE (minimum score 60). *Application deadline:* For fall admission, 1/1 priority date for domestic and international students. Applications are processed on a rolling basis. Application fee: $65. Electronic applications accepted. *Expenses: Tuition, area resident:* Full-time $8100; part-time $450 per credit hour. Tuition, state resident: full-time $8100; part-time $450 per credit hour. Tuition, nonresident: full-time $26,388; part-time $1466 per credit hour. *International tuition:* $26,388 full-time. *Required fees:* $1257; $278 per semester. Tuition and fees vary according to course load. *Financial support:* In 2019–20, 47 students received support, including 1 fellowship with tuition reimbursement available (averaging $34,000 per year), 41 research assistantships with full tuition reimbursements available (averaging $20,000 per year), 5 teaching assistantships with full tuition reimbursements available (averaging $15,825 per year); career-related internships or fieldwork, scholarships/grants, and unspecified assistantships also available. Financial award application deadline: 3/1; financial award applicants required to submit FAFSA. *Unit head:* Scott G Delcourt, Assistant Vice President for Graduate Studies and Senior Associate Dean, 207-581-3291, Fax: 207-581-3232, E-mail: graduate@maine.edu. *Application contact:* Scott G Delcourt, Assistant Vice President for Graduate Studies and Senior Associate Dean, 207-581-3291, Fax: 207-581-3232, E-mail: graduate@maine.edu.
Website: http://gsbse.umaine.edu/

The University of Manchester, School of Biological Sciences, Manchester, United Kingdom. Offers adaptive organismal biology (M Phil, PhD); animal biology (M Phil, PhD); biochemistry (M Phil, PhD); bioinformatics (M Phil, PhD); biomolecular sciences (M Phil, PhD); biotechnology (M Phil, PhD); cell biology (M Phil, PhD); cell matrix research (M Phil, PhD); channels and transporters (M Phil, PhD); developmental biology (M Phil, PhD); environmental biology (M Phil, PhD); evolutionary biology (M Phil, PhD);

gene expression (M Phil, PhD); genetics (M Phil, PhD); history of science, technology and medicine (M Phil, PhD); immunology (M Phil, PhD); integrative neurobiology and behavior (M Phil, PhD); membrane trafficking (M Phil, PhD); microbiology (M Phil, PhD); molecular and cellular neuroscience (M Phil, PhD); molecular biology (M Phil, PhD); molecular cancer studies (M Phil, PhD); neuroscience (M Phil, PhD); ophthalmology (M Phil, PhD); optometry (M Phil, PhD); organelle function (M Phil, PhD); pharmacology (M Phil, PhD); physiology (M Phil, PhD); plant sciences (M Phil, PhD); stem cell research (M Phil, PhD); structural biology (M Phil, PhD); systems neuroscience (M Phil, PhD); toxicology (M Phil, PhD).

University of Maryland, College Park, Academic Affairs, College of Computer, Mathematical and Natural Sciences, Department of Biology, PhD Program in Biological Sciences, College Park, MD 20742. Offers behavior, ecology, evolution, and systematics (PhD); computational biology, bioinformatics, and genomics (PhD); molecular and cellular biology (PhD); physiological systems (PhD). *Degree requirements:* For doctorate, comprehensive exam, thesis/dissertation, thesis work presentation in seminar. *Entrance requirements:* For doctorate, GRE General Test; GRE Subject Test in biology (recommended), academic transcripts, statement of purpose/research interests, 3 letters of recommendation. Additional exam requirements/recommendations for international students: required—TOEFL. Electronic applications accepted.

University of Massachusetts Medical School, Graduate School of Biomedical Sciences, Worcester, MA 01655. Offers biomedical sciences (PhD), including biochemistry and molecular pharmacology, bioinformatics and computational biology, cancer biology, immunology and microbiology, interdisciplinary, neuroscience, translational science; biomedical sciences (millennium program) (PhD); clinical and population health research (PhD); clinical investigation (MS). *Faculty:* 1,258 full-time (525 women), 372 part-time/adjunct (238 women). *Students:* 344 full-time (198 women), 1 (woman) part-time; includes 73 minority (12 Black or African American, non-Hispanic/Latino; 1 American Indian or Alaska Native, non-Hispanic/Latino; 45 Asian, non-Hispanic/Latino; 15 Hispanic/Latino), 120 international. Average age 29. 581 applicants, 23% accepted, 56 enrolled. In 2019, 6 master's, 49 doctorates awarded. Terminal master's awarded for partial completion of doctoral program. *Degree requirements:* For master's, comprehensive exam, thesis; for doctorate, comprehensive exam, thesis/dissertation. *Entrance requirements:* For master's, MD, PhD, DVM, or PharmD; for doctorate, bachelor's degree. Additional exam requirements/recommendations for international students: required—TOEFL, IELTS, TOEFL (minimum score 100 IBT) or IELTS (minimum score 7.0). *Application deadline:* For fall admission, 12/1 for domestic and international students. Applications are processed on a rolling basis. Application fee: $80. Electronic applications accepted. Application fee is waived when completed online. *Expenses:* Contact institution. *Financial support:* In 2019–20, 22 fellowships with full tuition reimbursements (averaging $33,061 per year), 322 research assistantships with full tuition reimbursements (averaging $32,850 per year) were awarded; institutionally sponsored loans and scholarships/grants also available. Financial award application deadline: 5/15. *Unit head:* Dr. Mary Ellen Lane, Dean, 508-856-4018, E-mail: maryellen.lane@umassmed.edu. *Application contact:* Dr. Kendall Knight, Assistant Vice Provost for Admissions, 508-856-5628, Fax: 508-856-3659, E-mail: kendall.knight@umassmed.edu.
Website: http://www.umassmed.edu/gsbs/

University of Memphis, Graduate School, College of Arts and Sciences, Department of Computer Science, Memphis, TN 38152. Offers bioinformatics (MS); computer science (MS, PhD). *Students:* 80 full-time (29 women), 32 part-time (5 women); includes 19 minority (7 Black or African American, non-Hispanic/Latino; 10 Asian, non-Hispanic/Latino; 2 Hispanic/Latino), 73 international. Average age 30. 112 applicants, 70% accepted, 23 enrolled. In 2019, 7 master's, 5 doctorates awarded. Terminal master's awarded for partial completion of doctoral program. *Degree requirements:* For master's, comprehensive exam, thesis; for doctorate, comprehensive exam, thesis/dissertation, qualifying exam, final exam. *Entrance requirements:* For master's and doctorate, GRE, letters of recommendation. Additional exam requirements/recommendations for international students: required—TOEFL (minimum score 550 paper-based; 79 iBT). *Application deadline:* Applications are processed on a rolling basis. Application fee: $35 ($60 for international students). *Expenses: Tuition, area resident:* Full-time $9216; part-time $512 per credit hour. Tuition, state resident: full-time $9216; part-time $512 per credit hour. Tuition, nonresident: full-time $12,672; part-time $704 per credit hour. *International tuition:* $16,128 full-time. *Required fees:* $1530; $85 per credit hour. Tuition and fees vary according to program. *Financial support:* Fellowships, research assistantships with full tuition reimbursements, teaching assistantships with full tuition reimbursements, Federal Work-Study, scholarships/grants, and unspecified assistantships available. Financial award application deadline: 2/1; financial award applicants required to submit FAFSA. *Unit head:* Dr. Lan Wang, Chair, 901-678-1643, Fax: 901-678-1506, E-mail: lanwang@memphis.edu. *Application contact:* Dr. Scott Fleming, Graduate Coordinator, 901-678-3142, E-mail: info@cs.memphis.edu.
Website: https://www.memphis.edu/cs/

University of Michigan, Rackham Graduate School, Program in Biomedical Sciences (PIBS) and Rackham Graduate School, Program in Bioinformatics, Ann Arbor, MI 48109. Offers MS, PhD. *Program availability:* Part-time. Terminal master's awarded for partial completion of doctoral program. *Degree requirements:* For master's, thesis optional, summer internship or rotation; for doctorate, thesis/dissertation, oral defense of dissertation, preliminary exam, two rotations. *Entrance requirements:* For master's and doctorate, GRE or MCAT. Additional exam requirements/recommendations for international students: required—TOEFL (minimum score 100 iBT). Electronic applications accepted.

University of Minnesota Rochester, Graduate Programs, Rochester, MN 55904. Offers bioinformatics and computational biology (MS, PhD); business administration (MBA); occupational therapy (MOT). *Accreditation:* AOTA.

University of Missouri, Office of Research and Graduate Studies, Informatics Institute, Columbia, MO 65211. Offers MS. *Entrance requirements:* Additional exam requirements/recommendations for international students: required—TOEFL, IELTS. Electronic applications accepted.

University of Missouri–Kansas City, School of Computing and Engineering, Kansas City, MO 64110-2499. Offers civil engineering (MS); computer and electrical engineering (PhD); computer science (MS), including bioinformatics, software engineering, telecommunications networking; computer science and informatics (PhD); computing (PhD); electrical engineering (MS); engineering (PhD); engineering and construction management (Graduate Certificate); mechanical engineering (MS); telecommunications and computer networking (PhD). *Program availability:* Part-time. *Degree requirements:* For doctorate, thesis/dissertation. *Entrance requirements:* For master's, GRE General Test, minimum GPA of 3.0, 3 letters of recommendation from professors; for doctorate, GRE General Test, minimum GPA of 3.5. Additional exam requirements/recommendations for international students: required—TOEFL (minimum score 550 paper-based; 80 iBT).

University of Nebraska at Omaha, Graduate Studies, College of Information Science and Technology, School of Interdisciplinary Informatics, Omaha, NE 68182. Offers biomedical informatics (MS, PhD); information assurance (MS). *Program availability:* Part-time, evening/weekend. *Degree requirements:* For master's, comprehensive exam, thesis (for some programs); for doctorate, comprehensive exam, thesis/dissertation. *Entrance requirements:* For master's and doctorate, GRE General Test, letters of recommendation, resume, transcripts. Additional exam requirements/recommendations for international students: required—TOEFL, IELTS, PTE.

University of Nebraska–Lincoln, Graduate College, College of Arts and Sciences and College of Engineering, Department of Computer Science and Engineering, Lincoln, NE 68588. Offers bioinformatics (MS, PhD); computer engineering (MS, PhD); computer science (MS, PhD); information technology (PhD). *Degree requirements:* For master's, thesis optional; for doctorate, comprehensive exam, thesis/dissertation. *Entrance requirements:* For master's and doctorate, GRE General Test. Additional exam requirements/recommendations for international students: required—TOEFL (minimum score 600 paper-based). Electronic applications accepted.

University of Nebraska Medical Center, Program in Biomedical Informatics, Omaha, NE 68198. Offers MS, PhD. *Program availability:* Part-time. *Degree requirements:* For master's, comprehensive exam, thesis; for doctorate, comprehensive exam, thesis/dissertation. *Entrance requirements:* For master's and doctorate, GRE, clinical training and experience (medicine, nursing, dentistry, or allied health degree). Additional exam requirements/recommendations for international students: required—TOEFL (minimum score 550 paper-based; 80 iBT), IELTS. Electronic applications accepted. *Expenses:* Contact institution.

The University of North Carolina at Chapel Hill, School of Medicine and Graduate School, Biological and Biomedical Sciences Program, Curriculum in Bioinformatics and Computational Biology, Chapel Hill, NC 27599. Offers PhD. *Faculty:* 40 full-time (6 women). *Students:* 11 full-time (6 women); includes 2 minority (1 Black or African American, non-Hispanic/Latino; 1 Asian, non-Hispanic/Latino), 3 international. Average age 27. In 2019, 6 doctorates awarded. *Degree requirements:* For doctorate, comprehensive exam, thesis/dissertation. *Entrance requirements:* Additional exam requirements/recommendations for international students: required—TOEFL. *Application deadline:* For fall admission, 12/3 for domestic and international students. Applications are processed on a rolling basis. Application fee: $77. Electronic applications accepted. *Financial support:* In 2019–20, 2 fellowships with full tuition reimbursements (averaging $32,000 per year), 9 research assistantships with full tuition reimbursements (averaging $32,000 per year) were awarded; career-related internships or fieldwork, health care benefits, and tuition waivers (full) also available. *Unit head:* Dr. Will Valdar, Director, 919-843-2833, E-mail: william.valdar@unc.edu. *Application contact:* Jeffrey Steinbach, Assistant Director of Admissions, 919-843-7129, E-mail: jsteinba@email.unc.edu.
Website: http://bcb.unc.edu/

The University of North Carolina at Charlotte, College of Computing and Informatics, Program in Computing and Information Systems, Charlotte, NC 28223-0001. Offers computing and information systems (PhD), including bioinformatics, business information systems and operations management, computer science, interdisciplinary, software and information systems. *Students:* 97 full-time (26 women), 26 part-time (6 women); includes 5 minority (2 Black or African American, non-Hispanic/Latino; 1 Asian, non-Hispanic/Latino; 1 Hispanic/Latino; 1 Two or more races, non-Hispanic/Latino), 95 international. Average age 30. 65 applicants, 48% accepted, 24 enrolled. In 2019, 20 doctorates awarded. *Degree requirements:* For doctorate, thesis/dissertation, Qualifying Exam. *Entrance requirements:* For doctorate, GRE or GMAT, baccalaureate degree, minimum GPA of 3.0 on courses related to the chosen field of PhD study, one-page essay, three reference letters. Additional exam requirements/recommendations for international students: required—TOEFL (minimum score 557 paper-based; 83 iBT), IELTS (minimum score 6.5), TOEFL (minimum score 557 paper-based, 83 iBT) or IELTS (6.5). *Application deadline:* For fall admission, 2/1 priority date for domestic students; for spring admission, 9/1 priority date for domestic students. Applications are processed on a rolling basis. Application fee: $75. Electronic applications accepted. *Expenses:* Tuition, state resident: full-time $4337. Tuition, nonresident: full-time $17,771. *Required fees:* $3093. Tuition and fees vary according to course load, degree level and program. *Financial support:* Career-related internships or fieldwork, institutionally sponsored loans, scholarships/grants, health care benefits, and unspecified assistantships available. Support available to part-time students. Financial award applicants required to submit FAFSA. *Unit head:* Dr. Fatma Mili, Dean, 704-687-8450. *Application contact:* Kathy B. Giddings, Director of Graduate Admissions, 704-687-5503, Fax: 704-687-1668, E-mail: gradadm@uncc.edu.

University of Pittsburgh, School of Medicine, Graduate Programs in Medicine, Biomedical Informatics Programs, Pittsburgh, PA 15260. Offers MS, PhD, Certificate. Terminal master's awarded for partial completion of doctoral program. *Degree requirements:* For master's, comprehensive exam, thesis; for doctorate, comprehensive exam, thesis/dissertation. *Entrance requirements:* For master's and doctorate, GRE, transcripts, letters of recommendation. Additional exam requirements/recommendations for international students: required—TOEFL (minimum score 600 paper-based; 100 iBT), IELTS (minimum score 7). Electronic applications accepted. *Expenses:* Contact institution.

University of Rochester, School of Medicine and Dentistry, Graduate Programs in Medicine and Dentistry, Department of Biostatistics and Computational Biology, Programs in Statistics, Rochester, NY 14642. Offers bioinformatics and computational biology (PhD).

University of Southern California, Graduate School, Dana and David Dornsife College of Letters, Arts and Sciences, Department of Biological Sciences, Program in Molecular and Computational Biology, Los Angeles, CA 90089. Offers computational biology and bioinformatics (PhD); molecular biology (PhD). *Degree requirements:* For doctorate, comprehensive exam, thesis/dissertation, qualifying examination, dissertation defense. *Entrance requirements:* For doctorate, GRE, 3 letters of recommendation, personal statement, resume, minimum GPA of 3.0. Additional exam requirements/recommendations for international students: required—TOEFL (minimum score 600 paper-based; 100 iBT). Electronic applications accepted.

University of South Florida, Innovative Education, Tampa, FL 33620-9951. Offers adult, career and higher education (Graduate Certificate), including college teaching, leadership in developing human resources, leadership in higher education; Africana studies (Graduate Certificate), including diasporas and health disparities, genocide and human rights; aging studies (Graduate Certificate), including gerontology; art research (Graduate Certificate), including museum studies; business foundations (Graduate Certificate); chemical and biomedical engineering (Graduate Certificate), including materials science and engineering, water, health and sustainability; child and family studies (Graduate Certificate), including positive behavior support; civil and industrial engineering (Graduate Certificate), including transportation systems analysis; community and family health (Graduate Certificate), including maternal and child health, social marketing and public health, violence and injury: prevention and intervention, women's health; criminology (Graduate Certificate), including criminal justice administration; data science for public administration (Graduate Certificate); digital humanities (Graduate Certificate); educational measurement and research (Graduate

Certificate), including evaluation; English (Graduate Certificate), including comparative literary studies, creative writing, professional and technical communication; entrepreneurship (Graduate Certificate); environmental health (Graduate Certificate), including safety management; epidemiology and biostatistics (Graduate Certificate), including applied biostatistics, biostatistics, concepts and tools of epidemiology, epidemiology, epidemiology of infectious diseases; geography, environment and planning (Graduate Certificate), including community development, environmental policy and management, geographical information systems; geology (Graduate Certificate), including hydrogeology; global health (Graduate Certificate), including disaster management, global health and Latin American and Caribbean studies, global health practice, humanitarian assistance, infection control; government and international affairs (Graduate Certificate), including Cuban studies, globalization studies; health policy and management (Graduate Certificate), including health management and leadership, public health policy and programs; hearing specialist: early intervention (Graduate Certificate); industrial and management systems engineering (Graduate Certificate), including systems engineering, technology management; information studies (Graduate Certificate), including school library media specialist; information systems/decision sciences (Graduate Certificate), including analytics and business intelligence; instructional technology (Graduate Certificate), including distance education, Florida digital/virtual educator, instructional design, multimedia design, Web design; internal medicine, bioethics and medical humanities (Graduate Certificate), including biomedical ethics; Latin American and Caribbean studies (Graduate Certificate); leadership for coastal resiliency planning (Graduate Certificate); mass communications (Graduate Certificate), including multimedia journalism; mathematics and statistics (Graduate Certificate), including mathematics; medicine (Graduate Certificate), including aging and neuroscience, bioinformatics, biotechnology, brain fitness and memory management, clinical investigation, hand and upper limb rehabilitation, health informatics, health sciences, integrative weight management, intellectual property, medicine and gender, metabolic and nutritional medicine, metabolic cardiology, pharmacy sciences; national and competitive intelligence (Graduate Certificate); nursing (Graduate Certificate), including simulation based academic fellowship in advanced pain management; psychological and social foundations (Graduate Certificate), including career counseling, college teaching, diversity in education, mental health counseling, school counseling; public affairs (Graduate Certificate), including nonprofit management, public management, research administration; public health (Graduate Certificate), including assessing chemical toxicity and public health risks, health equity, pharmacoepidemiology, public health generalist, toxicology, translational research in adolescent behavioral health; public health practices (Graduate Certificate), including planning for healthy communities; rehabilitation and mental health counseling (Graduate Certificate), including integrative mental health care, marriage and family therapy, rehabilitation technology; secondary education (Graduate Certificate), including ESOL, foreign language education: culture and content, foreign language education: professional; social work (Graduate Certificate), including geriatric social work/clinical gerontology; special education (Graduate Certificate), including autism spectrum disorder, disabilities education: severe/profound; world languages (Graduate Certificate), including teaching English as a second language (TESL) or foreign language. *Unit head:* Dr. Cynthia DeLuca, Associate Vice President and Assistant Vice Provost, 813-974-3077, Fax: 813-974-7061, E-mail: deluca@usf.edu. *Application contact:* Owen Hooper, Director, Summer and Alternative Calendar Programs, 813-974-6917, E-mail: hooper@usf.edu.
Website: http://www.usf.edu/innovative-education/

University of South Florida, Morsani College of Medicine and College of Graduate Studies, Graduate Programs in Medical Sciences, Tampa, FL 33620-9951. Offers bioinformatics and computational biology (MSBCB). *Faculty:* 1 (woman) full-time. *Students:* 355 full-time (207 women), 229 part-time (145 women); includes 283 minority (71 Black or African American, non-Hispanic/Latino; 2 American Indian or Alaska Native, non-Hispanic/Latino; 89 Asian, non-Hispanic/Latino; 103 Hispanic/Latino; 2 Native Hawaiian or other Pacific Islander, non-Hispanic/Latino; 16 Two or more races, non-Hispanic/Latino), 48 international. Average age 28. 898 applicants, 57% accepted, 323 enrolled. In 2019, 227 master's, 13 doctorates awarded. Terminal master's awarded for partial completion of doctoral program. *Degree requirements:* For master's, comprehensive exam, thesis; for doctorate, comprehensive exam, thesis/dissertation. *Entrance requirements:* For master's, GRE General Test or GMAT, bachelor's degree or equivalent from regionally-accredited university with minimum GPA of 3.0 in upper-division sciences coursework; prerequisites in general biology, general chemistry, general physics, organic chemistry, quantitative analysis, and integral and differential calculus; for doctorate, GRE General Test, bachelor's degree from regionally-accredited university with minimum GPA of 3.0 in upper-division sciences coursework; 3 letters of recommendation; personal interview; 1-2 page personal statement; prerequisites in biology, chemistry, physics, organic chemistry, quantitative analysis, and integral/differential calculus. Additional exam requirements/recommendations for international students: required—TOEFL (minimum score 550 paper-based; 79 iBT) or IELTS (minimum score 6.5). *Application deadline:* For fall admission, 2/1 priority date for domestic students, 2/1 for international students. Application fee: $30. Electronic applications accepted. *Expenses:* Contact institution. *Financial support:* In 2019–20, 106 students received support. *Unit head:* Dr. Michael Barber, Professor/Associate Dean for Graduate and Postdoctoral Affairs, 813-974-9908, Fax: 813-974-4317, E-mail: mbarber@health.usf.edu. *Application contact:* Dr. Eric Bennett, Graduate Director, PhD Program in Medical Sciences, 813-974-1545, Fax: 813-974-4317, E-mail: esbennet@health.usf.edu.
Website: http://health.usf.edu/nocms/medicine/graduatestudies/

The University of Tennessee at Chattanooga, Program in Computer Science, Chattanooga, TN 37403. Offers biomedical informatics (Post Master's Certificate); computer science (MS). *Program availability:* Part-time, 100% online. *Students:* 27 full-time (7 women), 31 part-time (10 women); includes 16 minority (4 Black or African American, non-Hispanic/Latino; 2 Asian, non-Hispanic/Latino; 6 Hispanic/Latino; 4 Two or more races, non-Hispanic/Latino), 6 international. Average age 29. 35 applicants, 71% accepted, 16 enrolled. In 2019, 18 master's awarded. *Degree requirements:* For master's, thesis or alternative, project in lieu of thesis. *Entrance requirements:* For master's, GRE General Test, minimum cumulative undergraduate GPA of 2.7 or 3.0 in senior year. Additional exam requirements/recommendations for international students: required—TOEFL (minimum score 550 paper-based; 79 iBT), IELTS (minimum score 6). *Application deadline:* For fall admission, 6/15 priority date for domestic students, 7/1 for international students; for spring admission, 11/1 priority date for domestic students, 11/1 for international students. Applications are processed on a rolling basis. Application fee: $35 ($40 for international students). Electronic applications accepted. *Financial support:* Research assistantships, teaching assistantships, career-related internships or fieldwork, scholarships/grants, health care benefits, and unspecified assistantships available. Support available to part-time students. Financial award application deadline: 7/1; financial award applicants required to submit FAFSA. *Unit head:* Dr. Luay Wahsheh, Department Head, 423-425-4361, Fax: 423-425-5311, E-mail: luay-a-wahsheh@utc.edu. *Application contact:* Dr. Joanne Romagni, Dean of the Graduate School, 423-425-4478, Fax: 423-425-5223, E-mail: joanne-romagni@utc.edu.
Website: https://www.utc.edu/college-engineering-computer-science/programs/computer-science-engineering/grad/masters-programs.php

The University of Texas at El Paso, Graduate School, College of Science, Department of Biological Sciences, El Paso, TX 79968-0001. Offers bioinformatics (MS); biological sciences (MS, PhD). *Program availability:* Part-time, evening/weekend. *Degree requirements:* For master's, thesis; for doctorate, thesis/dissertation. *Entrance requirements:* For master's, GRE, minimum GPA of 3.0, letters of recommendation; for doctorate, GRE, statement of purpose, letters of recommendation. Additional exam requirements/recommendations for international students: required—TOEFL; recommended—IELTS. Electronic applications accepted.

The University of Texas Health Science Center at Houston, School of Biomedical Informatics, Houston, TX 77030. Offers applied biomedical informatics (MS, Certificate); biomedical informatics (MS, PhD, Certificate); health data science (Certificate); public health informatics (Certificate); MPH/MS; MPH/PhD. *Program availability:* Part-time, 100% online, blended/hybrid learning. *Faculty:* 39 full-time (15 women), 4 part-time/adjunct (0 women). *Students:* 53 full-time (32 women), 227 part-time (107 women); includes 135 minority (34 Black or African American, non-Hispanic/Latino; 1 American Indian or Alaska Native, non-Hispanic/Latino; 53 Asian, non-Hispanic/Latino; 41 Hispanic/Latino; 1 Native Hawaiian or other Pacific Islander, non-Hispanic/Latino; 5 Two or more races, non-Hispanic/Latino), 54 international. Average age 31. 163 applicants, 80% accepted, 86 enrolled. In 2019, 44 master's, 2 doctorates awarded. *Degree requirements:* For master's, thesis or alternative, practicum with capstone report; for doctorate, comprehensive exam, thesis/dissertation, Ph.D.: Qualifying Exam and Dissertation; DHI: Qualifying Exam and Translational Research Project. *Entrance requirements:* For master's, official transcripts from all colleges and universities, WES or ECE course by course evaluation for international transcripts, resume and/or CV, 3 letters of reference from educators and employers, goal statement; for doctorate, Ph.D. program: Graduate Record Exam (GRE), other items apply to both PhD and DHI doctoral degrees, official transcripts, WES and ECE course-by-course evaluation for international students, resume and/or CV, 3 letters of reference from educators and employer, goal statement; for the DHI only: Letter of Support to facilitate translational practice project; for certificate, official transcripts from all colleges and universities, WES or ECE course by course evaluation for international transcripts, resume and/or CV, 1 letter of reference, goal statement. Additional exam requirements/recommendations for international students: required—TOEFL (minimum score 87 iBT), IELTS (minimum score 7). *Application deadline:* For fall admission, 7/1 for domestic and international students; for winter admission, 12/1 for domestic and international students; for spring admission, 11/1 for domestic and international students; for summer admission, 3/1 for domestic and international students. Applications are processed on a rolling basis. Application fee: $60. Electronic applications accepted. *Expenses:* Approximate total costs to complete each program offered. Certificates online: $6,693 state resident full-time, $7,913 state resident part-time, $15,828 nonresident full-time, $17,048 nonresident part-time (subtract $110 for classroom); aLL MS online: $18,398.50 state resident, $42,149.50 nonresident; classroom $15,868.50 state resident, $39,619.50 nonresident; PhD: $32,963 state resident, $80,259 nonresident; DHI: $25,113 state resident, $63,669 nonresident. *Financial support:* In 2019–20, 102 students received support, including 58 research assistantships (averaging $20,191 per year), 7 teaching assistantships (averaging $3,568 per year); career-related internships or fieldwork, institutionally sponsored loans, scholarships/grants, health care benefits, and unspecified assistantships also available. Support available to part-time students. Financial award application deadline: 5/1; financial award applicants required to submit FAFSA. *Unit head:* Dr. Jiajie Zhang, Dean/Chair in Informatics Excellence, 713-500-3922, E-mail: jiajie.zhang@uth.tmc.edu. *Application contact:* Jaime N Hargrave, Director, Student Affairs, 713-500-3920, Fax: 713-500-0360, E-mail: jaime.n.hargrave@uth.tmc.edu.
Website: https://sbmi.uth.edu/

The University of Texas Health Science Center at Houston, School of Public Health, Houston, TX 77030. Offers behavioral science (PhD); biostatistics (MPH, MS, PhD); environmental health (MPH); epidemiology (MPH, MS, PhD); general public health (Certificate); genomics and bioinformatics (Certificate); health disparities (Certificate); health promotion/health education (MPH, Dr PH); healthcare management (Certificate); management, policy and community health (MPH, Dr PH, PhD); maternal and child health (Certificate); public health informatics (Certificate); DDS/MPH; JD/MPH; MBA/MPH; MD/MPH; MGPS/MPH; MP Aff/MPH; MS/MPH; MSN/MPH; MSW/MPH; PhD/MPH. *Accreditation:* CAHME; CEPH. *Program availability:* Part-time. *Degree requirements:* For master's, thesis (for some programs); for doctorate, comprehensive exam, thesis/dissertation. *Entrance requirements:* For master's and doctorate, GRE General Test. Additional exam requirements/recommendations for international students: required—TOEFL (minimum score 600 paper-based, 100 iBT) or IELTS (7.5). Electronic applications accepted. *Expenses:* Contact institution.

The University of Texas Medical Branch, Graduate School of Biomedical Sciences, Program in Biochemistry and Molecular Biology, Galveston, TX 77555. Offers biochemistry (PhD); bioinformatics (PhD); biophysics (PhD); cell biology (PhD); computational biology (PhD); structural biology (PhD). *Degree requirements:* For doctorate, thesis/dissertation. *Entrance requirements:* Additional exam requirements/recommendations for international students: required—TOEFL (minimum score 550 paper-based). Electronic applications accepted.

University of the Sciences, Program in Bioinformatics, Philadelphia, PA 19104-4495. Offers MS. *Program availability:* Part-time, evening/weekend. *Entrance requirements:* Additional exam requirements/recommendations for international students: required—TOEFL, TWE. *Expenses:* Contact institution.

The University of Toledo, College of Graduate Studies, College of Medicine and Life Sciences, Interdepartmental Programs, Toledo, OH 43606-3390. Offers bioinformatics and proteomics/genomics (MSBS); biomarkers and bioinformatics (Certificate); biomarkers and diagnostics (PSM); human donation sciences (MSBS); medical sciences (MSBS); MD/MSBS. *Degree requirements:* For master's, thesis or alternative. *Entrance requirements:* For master's, GRE, minimum undergraduate GPA of 3.0, three letters of recommendation, statement of purpose, transcripts from all prior institutions attended, resume; for Certificate, minimum undergraduate GPA of 3.0, three letters of recommendation, statement of purpose, transcripts from all prior institutions attended, resume. Additional exam requirements/recommendations for international students: required—TOEFL (minimum score 550 paper-based; 80 iBT). Electronic applications accepted.

University of Utah, School of Medicine and Graduate School, Graduate Programs in Medicine, Department of Biomedical Informatics, Salt Lake City, UT 84112-1107. Offers MS, PhD, Certificate. *Program availability:* Part-time, online learning. *Degree requirements:* For master's, comprehensive exam, thesis; for doctorate, comprehensive exam, thesis/dissertation, qualifying exam. *Entrance requirements:* For master's and doctorate, GRE General Test (minimum 60th percentile), minimum GPA of 3.3. Additional exam requirements/recommendations for international students: required—TOEFL (minimum score 600 paper-based). Electronic applications accepted. *Expenses:* Tuition, state resident: full-time $7085; part-time $272.51 per credit hour. Tuition, nonresident: full-time $24,937; part-time $959.12 per credit hour. *Required fees:*

$880.52; $880.52 per semester. Tuition and fees vary according to degree level, program and student level.

University of Washington, Graduate School, School of Medicine, Graduate Programs in Medicine, Department of Medical Education and Biomedical Informatics, Division of Biomedical and Health Informatics, Seattle, WA 98195. Offers MS, PhD. *Entrance requirements:* For master's and doctorate, GRE General Test, minimum GPA of 3.0; previous undergraduate course work in biology, computer programming, and mathematics. Additional exam requirements/recommendations for international students: required—TOEFL (minimum score 580 paper-based; 70 iBT). Electronic applications accepted.

University of Wisconsin–Madison, School of Medicine and Public Health, Biomedical Data Science Graduate Program, Madison, WI 53706-1380. Offers MS, PhD.

Vanderbilt University, Department of Biomedical Informatics, Nashville, TN 37240-1001. Offers MS, PhD. *Program availability:* Part-time. *Faculty:* 28 full-time (6 women). *Students:* 22 full-time (9 women), 1 (woman) part-time; includes 8 minority (1 Black or African American, non-Hispanic/Latino; 5 Asian, non-Hispanic/Latino; 1 Hispanic/Latino; 1 Two or more races, non-Hispanic/Latino). Average age 31. 57 applicants, 25% accepted, 7 enrolled. In 2019, 6 master's, 2 doctorates awarded. Terminal master's awarded for partial completion of doctoral program. *Degree requirements:* For master's, thesis; for doctorate, thesis/dissertation, final and qualifying exams. *Entrance requirements:* For master's and doctorate, GRE General Test. Additional exam requirements/recommendations for international students: required—TOEFL (minimum score 570 paper-based; 88 iBT). *Application deadline:* For fall admission, 1/15 for domestic and international students. Electronic applications accepted. *Expenses: Tuition:* Full-time $51,018; part-time $2087 per hour. *Required fees:* $542. Tuition and fees vary according to program. *Financial support:* Fellowships with tuition reimbursements, research assistantships with tuition reimbursements, teaching assistantships with tuition reimbursements, Federal Work-Study, institutionally sponsored loans, scholarships/grants, traineeships, and health care benefits available. Financial award application deadline: 1/15; financial award applicants required to submit CSS PROFILE or FAFSA. *Unit head:* Dr. Kevin Johnson, Chair, 615-936-1423, Fax: 615-936-1427, E-mail: kevin.johnson@vanderbilt.edu. *Application contact:* Cynthia Gadd, Director of Graduate Studies, 615-936-1050, Fax: 615-936-1427, E-mail: cindy.gadd@vanderbilt.edu.
Website: https://medschool.vanderbilt.edu/dbmi/

Virginia Polytechnic Institute and State University, Graduate School, Intercollege, Blacksburg, VA 24061. Offers genetics, bioinformatics, and computational biology (PhD); information technology (MIT); macromolecular science and engineering (MS, PhD); translational biology, medicine, and health (PhD). *Students:* 203 full-time (86 women), 745 part-time (218 women); includes 278 minority (64 Black or African American, non-Hispanic/Latino; 119 Asian, non-Hispanic/Latino; 59 Hispanic/Latino; 1 Native Hawaiian or other Pacific Islander, non-Hispanic/Latino; 35 Two or more races, non-Hispanic/Latino), 93 international. Average age 33. 603 applicants, 78% accepted, 327 enrolled. In 2019, 138 master's, 20 doctorates awarded. *Degree requirements:* For master's, comprehensive exam (for some programs), thesis (for some programs); for doctorate, comprehensive exam (for some programs), thesis/dissertation (for some programs). *Entrance requirements:* For master's and doctorate, GRE/GMAT. Additional exam requirements/recommendations for international students: required—TOEFL (minimum score 90 iBT). *Application deadline:* For fall admission, 8/1 for domestic students, 4/1 for international students; for spring admission, 1/1 for domestic students, 9/1 for international students. Applications are processed on a rolling basis. Application fee: $75. Electronic applications accepted. *Expenses:* Tuition, state resident: full-time $13,700; part-time $761.25 per credit hour. Tuition, nonresident: full-time $27,614; part-time $1534 per credit hour. *Required fees:* $886.50 per term. Tuition and fees vary according to campus/location and program. *Financial support:* In 2019–20, 4 fellowships with full and partial tuition reimbursements (averaging $17,088 per year), 153 research assistantships with full tuition reimbursements (averaging $23,076 per year), 27 teaching assistantships with full tuition reimbursements (averaging $19,900 per year) were awarded; scholarships/grants also available. Financial award application

deadline: 3/1; financial award applicants required to submit FAFSA. *Unit head:* Dr. Karen P. DePauw, Vice President and Dean for Graduate Education, 540-231-7581, Fax: 540-231-1670, E-mail: kpdepauw@vt.edu. *Application contact:* Dr. Janice Austin, 540-231-6691, E-mail: grads@vt.edu.

Wayne State University, College of Engineering, Department of Computer Science, Detroit, MI 48202. Offers computer science (MS, PhD), including bioinformatics and computational biology (PhD); data science and business analytics (MS). *Faculty:* 23. *Students:* 97 full-time (41 women), 42 part-time (10 women); includes 15 minority (3 Black or African American, non-Hispanic/Latino; 9 Asian, non-Hispanic/Latino; 2 Hispanic/Latino; 1 Two or more races, non-Hispanic/Latino), 94 international. Average age 30. 276 applicants, 31% accepted, 30 enrolled. In 2019, 42 master's, 10 doctorates awarded. *Degree requirements:* For master's, thesis (for some programs), practicum (for MS in data science and business analytics); for doctorate, thesis/dissertation. *Entrance requirements:* For master's, GRE only for Data Science and Business Analytics degree, minimum GPA of 3.0, three letters of recommendation, adequate preparation in computer science and mathematics courses, personal statement, resume (for MS in data science and business analytics); for doctorate, GRE, bachelor's or master's degree in computer science or related field; minimum GPA of 3.3 in most recent degree; three letters of recommendation; personal statement; adequate preparation in computer science and mathematics courses. Additional exam requirements/recommendations for international students: required—TOEFL (minimum score 550 paper-based; 79 iBT), TWE (minimum score 5.5); recommended—IELTS (minimum score 6.5). *Application deadline:* For fall admission, 6/1 priority date for domestic students, 5/1 priority date for international students; for winter admission, 10/1 priority date for domestic students, 9/1 priority date for international students; for spring admission, 2/1 priority date for domestic students, 1/2 priority date for international students. Applications are processed on a rolling basis. Application fee: $50. Electronic applications accepted. *Expenses:* $790 per credit hour in-state tuition, $1579 per credit hour out-of-state tuition. MS degree is 30 credits; PhD degree is 90 credits. *Financial support:* In 2019–20, 92 students received support, including 4 fellowships with tuition reimbursements available (averaging $20,000 per year), 18 research assistantships with tuition reimbursements available (averaging $20,693 per year), 32 teaching assistantships with tuition reimbursements available (averaging $20,760 per year); scholarships/grants, health care benefits, and unspecified assistantships also available. Financial award application deadline: 2/17; financial award applicants required to submit FAFSA. *Unit head:* Dr. Loren Schwiebert, Chair, 313-577-5474, E-mail: loren@wayne.edu. *Application contact:* Robert Reynolds, Graduate Program Director, 313-577-0726, E-mail: csgradadvisor@cs.wayne.edu.
Website: http://engineering.wayne.edu/cs/

Wesleyan University, Graduate Studies, Department of Biology, Middletown, CT 06459. Offers cell and developmental biology (PhD); evolution and ecology (PhD); genetics and genomics (PhD), including bioinformatics; neurobiology and behavior (PhD). Terminal master's awarded for partial completion of doctoral program. *Degree requirements:* For doctorate, comprehensive exam, thesis/dissertation, public seminar. *Entrance requirements:* For doctorate, GRE, official transcripts, three recommendation letters, essay. Additional exam requirements/recommendations for international students: required—TOEFL. Electronic applications accepted.

Worcester Polytechnic Institute, Graduate Admissions, Program in Bioinformatics and Computational Biology, Worcester, MA 01609-2280. Offers bioinformatics & computational biology (PhD). *Program availability:* Evening/weekend. *Entrance requirements:* For master's and doctorate, GRE, 3 letters of recommendation, statement of purpose. Additional exam requirements/recommendations for international students: required—TOEFL (minimum score 563 paper-based; 84 iBT), IELTS (minimum score 7). Electronic applications accepted.

Yale University, Yale School of Medicine and Graduate School of Arts and Sciences, Combined Program in Biological and Biomedical Sciences (BBS), Computational Biology and Bioinformatics Track, New Haven, CT 06520. Offers PhD, MD/PhD. *Entrance requirements:* Additional exam requirements/recommendations for international students: required—TOEFL.

Computer and Information Systems Security

American InterContinental University Online, Program in Information Technology, Schaumburg, IL 60173. Offers Internet security (MIT); IT project management (MIT). *Program availability:* Evening/weekend, online learning. *Entrance requirements:* Additional exam requirements/recommendations for international students: required—TOEFL (minimum score 550 paper-based). Electronic applications accepted.

American Public University System, AMU/APU Graduate Programs, Charles Town, WV 25414. Offers accounting (MS); applied business analytics (MS); business administration (MBA); criminal justice (MA); cybersecurity studies (MS); educational leadership (M Ed); environmental policy and management (MS); global security (DGS); health information management (MS); history (MA), including American military history, American Revolution, civil war, war since 1945, World War II; information technology (MS); international relations and conflict resolution (MA), including American politics and government, comparative government and development, general, international relations, public policy; national security studies (MA); nursing (MSN); political science (MA); public policy (MPP); reverse logistics management (MA), including comparative and security issues, conflict resolution, international and transnational security issues, peacekeeping; space studies (MS); sports management (MS); strategic intelligence (DSI); teaching (M Ed), including secondary social studies; transportation and logistics management (MA). *Program availability:* Part-time, evening/weekend, online only, 100% online. *Students:* 461 full-time (193 women), 7,322 part-time (3,127 women); includes 3,089 minority (1,404 Black or African American, non-Hispanic/Latino; 30 American Indian or Alaska Native, non-Hispanic/Latino; 210 Asian, non-Hispanic/Latino; 753 Hispanic/Latino; 445 Native Hawaiian or other Pacific Islander, non-Hispanic/Latino; 247 Two or more races, non-Hispanic/Latino), 117 international. Average age 37. In 2019, 2,681 master's awarded. *Degree requirements:* For master's, comprehensive exam or practicum; for doctorate, practicum. *Entrance requirements:* For master's, official transcript showing earned bachelor's degree from institution accredited by recognized accrediting body. Additional exam requirements/recommendations for international students: required—TOEFL (minimum score 550 paper-based), IELTS (minimum score 6.5). *Application deadline:* Applications are processed on a rolling basis. Application fee: $0. Electronic applications accepted. *Financial support:* Scholarships/grants available. Financial award applicants required to submit FAFSA. *Unit head:* Dr. Wallace Boston, President, 877-468-6268, Fax: 304-728-2348, E-mail: president@apus.edu. *Application contact:* Yoci Deal, Associate Vice President, Graduate and International Admissions, 877-468-6268, Fax: 304-724-3764, E-mail: info@apus.edu.
Website: http://www.apus.edu

Augusta University, Hull College of Business, Augusta, GA 30912. Offers business administration (MBA); information security management (MS). *Accreditation:* AACSB. *Program availability:* Part-time, evening/weekend. *Entrance requirements:* For master's, GMAT.

Austin Peay State University, College of Graduate Studies, College of Science, Technology, Engineering and Mathematics, Professional Science Master's Program, Clarksville, TN 37044. Offers data management and analysis (MS, PSM); information assurance and security (MS, PSM); mathematical finance (MS, PSM); mathematics instruction (MS); predictive analytics (MS, PSM). *Program availability:* Part-time, online learning. *Faculty:* 15 full-time (0 women), 3 part-time/adjunct (0 women). *Students:* 71 full-time (20 women), 82 part-time (31 women); includes 30 minority (17 Black or African American, non-Hispanic/Latino; 3 Asian, non-Hispanic/Latino; 3 Hispanic/Latino; 7 Two or more races, non-Hispanic/Latino), 59 international. Average age 27. 109 applicants, 91% accepted, 53 enrolled. In 2019, 36 master's awarded. *Entrance requirements:* For master's, GRE, minimum undergraduate GPA of 2.5. Additional exam requirements/recommendations for international students: required—TOEFL (minimum score 500 paper-based). *Application deadline:* For fall admission, 8/5 priority date for domestic students. Applications are processed on a rolling basis. Application fee: $45 ($55 for international students). Electronic applications accepted. *Financial support:* Research assistantships with full tuition reimbursements, career-related internships or fieldwork, Federal Work-Study, institutionally sponsored loans, scholarships/grants, and unspecified assistantships available. Support available to part-time students. Financial award application deadline: 7/1; financial award applicants required to submit FAFSA. *Unit head:* Dr. Matt Jones, Graduate Coordinator, 931-221-7814, E-mail: gradpsm@apsu.edu. *Application contact:* Megan Mitchell, Coordinator of Graduate Admissions, 800-859-4723, Fax: 931-221-7641, E-mail: gradadmissions@apsu.edu.
Website: http://www.apsu.edu/csci/masters_degrees/index.php

Bay Path University, Program in Cybersecurity Management, Longmeadow, MA 01106-2292. Offers MS. *Program availability:* Part-time, evening/weekend, online only, 100% online. *Entrance requirements:* For master's, completed application; official undergraduate and graduate transcripts (a GPA of 3.0 or higher is preferred); original essay of at least 250 words on the topic: "Why the MS in Cybersecurity Management is important to my personal and professional goals"; current resume; 2 recommendations. Electronic applications accepted. Application fee is waived when completed online. *Expenses:* Contact institution.

Computer and Information Systems Security

Benedictine University, Graduate Programs, Program in Business Administration, Lisle, IL 60532. Offers accounting (MBA); entrepreneurship and managing innovation (MBA); financial management (MBA); health administration (MBA); human resource management (MBA); information systems security (MBA); international business (MBA); management consulting (MBA); management information systems (MBA); marketing management (MBA); operations management and logistics (MBA); organizational leadership (MBA). *Program availability:* Part-time, evening/weekend, 100% online, blended/hybrid learning. *Entrance requirements:* For master's, GMAT or GRE test scores or completed test waiver form, official transcripts; 2 letters of reference from individuals familiar with the applicant's professional or academic work, excluding family or personal friends; a 1-2 page essay addressing educational and career goals; current résumé listing chronological work history; personal interview may be required prior to an admission decision. Additional exam requirements/recommendations for international students: required—TOEFL (minimum score 550 paper-based; 79 iBT), IELTS (minimum score 6.5). Electronic applications accepted.

Boston University, Graduate School of Arts and Sciences, Department of Computer Science, Boston, MA 02215. Offers computer science (MS, PhD); cyber security (MS); data-centric computing (MS). *Students:* 227 full-time (52 women), 48 part-time (14 women); includes 9 minority (8 Asian, non-Hispanic/Latino; 1 Hispanic/Latino), 236 international. Average age 24. 2,102 applicants, 25% accepted, 117 enrolled. In 2019, 87 master's, 10 doctorates awarded. Terminal master's awarded for partial completion of doctoral program. *Degree requirements:* For master's, thesis optional, project; for doctorate, comprehensive exam, thesis/dissertation. *Entrance requirements:* For master's and doctorate, GRE General Test, 3 letters of recommendation, transcripts, personal statement. Additional exam requirements/recommendations for international students: required—TOEFL (minimum score 550 paper-based; 84 iBT). *Application deadline:* For fall admission, 12/15 for domestic and international students. Applications are processed on a rolling basis. Application fee: $95. Electronic applications accepted. *Financial support:* In 2019–20, 112 students received support, including 4 fellowships with full tuition reimbursements available (averaging $23,340 per year), 53 research assistantships with full tuition reimbursements available (averaging $23,340 per year), 43 teaching assistantships with full tuition reimbursements available (averaging $23,340 per year); Federal Work-Study, scholarships/grants, and health care benefits also available. Support available to part-time students. Financial award application deadline: 12/15. *Unit head:* Abraham Matta, Chair, 617-353-8919, Fax: 617-353-6457, E-mail: matta@bu.edu. *Application contact:* Kori MacDonald, Program Coordinator, 617-353-8919, Fax: 617-353-6457, E-mail: korimac@bu.edu.
Website: http://www.bu.edu/cs

Boston University, Metropolitan College, Department of Computer Science, Boston, MA 02215. Offers computer information systems (MS), including computer networks, data analytics, database management and business intelligence, health informatics, IT project management, security, Web application development; computer networks (Certificate); computer science (MS); data analytics (Certificate); digital forensics (Certificate); health informatics (Certificate); information technology project management (Certificate); software development (MS); software engineering in health care systems (Certificate); telecommunications (MS), including security. *Program availability:* Part-time, evening/weekend, online learning. *Faculty:* 16 full-time (3 women), 52 part-time/adjunct (5 women). *Students:* 253 full-time (80 women), 856 part-time (243 women); includes 246 minority (53 Black or African American, non-Hispanic/Latino; 1 American Indian or Alaska Native, non-Hispanic/Latino; 129 Asian, non-Hispanic/Latino; 48 Hispanic/Latino; 15 Two or more races, non-Hispanic/Latino), 418 international. Average age 30. 1,079 applicants, 72% accepted, 297 enrolled. In 2019, 513 master's awarded. *Entrance requirements:* For master's and Certificate, official transcripts from regionally-accredited bachelor's degree program, 3 letters of recommendation, professional resume, personal statement. Additional exam requirements/recommendations for international students: required—TOEFL (minimum score 84 iBT), IELTS. *Application deadline:* For fall admission, 8/1 priority date for domestic students, 6/1 priority date for international students; for spring admission, 12/1 priority date for domestic students, 11/15 priority date for international students; for summer admission, 4/1 priority date for domestic students, 3/1 priority date for international students. Applications are processed on a rolling basis. Application fee: $85. Electronic applications accepted. *Expenses:* Contact institution. *Financial support:* In 2019–20, 11 research assistantships (averaging $8,400 per year), 23 teaching assistantships (averaging $3,400 per year) were awarded; unspecified assistantships also available. Support available to part-time students. Financial award applicants required to submit FAFSA. *Unit head:* Dr. Anatoly Temkin, Chair, 617-353-2566, Fax: 617-353-2367, E-mail: csinfo@bu.edu. *Application contact:* Enrollment Services, 617-353-6004, E-mail: met@bu.edu.
Website: http://www.bu.edu/csmet/

Boston University, Metropolitan College, Program in Criminal Justice, Boston, MA 02215. Offers cybercrime investigation and cybersecurity (MCJ); strategic management (MCJ). *Program availability:* Part-time, evening/weekend, online learning. *Faculty:* 6 full-time (2 women), 2 part-time/adjunct (0 women). *Students:* 9 full-time (6 women), 130 part-time (75 women); includes 50 minority (17 Black or African American, non-Hispanic/Latino; 1 American Indian or Alaska Native, non-Hispanic/Latino; 12 Asian, non-Hispanic/Latino; 18 Hispanic/Latino; 2 Two or more races, non-Hispanic/Latino), 8 international. Average age 31. In 2019, 142 master's awarded. *Degree requirements:* For master's, comprehensive examination (for on-campus program only). *Entrance requirements:* Additional exam requirements/recommendations for international students: required—TOEFL (minimum score 84 iBT). *Application deadline:* For fall admission, 8/1 priority date for domestic students, 6/1 priority date for international students; for spring admission, 12/1 priority date for domestic students, 11/15 priority date for international students; for summer admission, 4/1 priority date for domestic students, 3/1 priority date for international students. Applications are processed on a rolling basis. Application fee: $85. Electronic applications accepted. *Expenses:* Contact institution. *Financial support:* In 2019–20, 9 research assistantships (averaging $4,200 per year) were awarded; scholarships/grants and unspecified assistantships also available. Support available to part-time students. Financial award applicants required to submit FAFSA. *Unit head:* Dr. Mary Ellen Mastrorilli, Associate Professor of the Practice and Chair, 617-353-3025, Fax: 617-358-3595, E-mail: memastro@bu.edu. *Application contact:* Enrollment Services, 617-353-9185, E-mail: met@bu.edu.
Website: http://www.bu.edu/met/cj/

Brandeis University, Rabb School of Continuing Studies, Division of Graduate Professional Studies, Master of Science in Information Security Leadership Program, Waltham, MA 02454-9110. Offers MS. *Program availability:* Part-time-only. *Entrance requirements:* For master's, undergraduate degree with work experience and/or coursework in networking, computer science, and computer security; 4-year bachelor's degree from regionally-accredited U.S. institution or equivalent; official transcript(s) from every college/university attended; resume or curriculum vitae; statement of goals; letter of recommendation. Additional exam requirements/recommendations for international students: required—TWE (minimum score 4.5), TOEFL (minimum scores: 600 paper-based, 100 iBT), IELTS (7), or PTE (68). Electronic applications accepted. *Expenses:* Contact institution.

California State University, San Bernardino, Graduate Studies, College of Business and Public Administration, Program in Business Administration, San Bernardino, CA 92407. Offers accounting (MBA); entrepreneurship (MBA); finance (MBA); global business (MBA); information management (MBA); information security (MBA); management (MBA); supply chain management (MBA). *Accreditation:* AACSB. *Program availability:* Part-time, evening/weekend, online learning. *Faculty:* 4 full-time (2 women), 7 part-time/adjunct (4 women). *Students:* 42 full-time (22 women), 207 part-time (87 women); includes 130 minority (13 Black or African American, non-Hispanic/Latino; 29 Asian, non-Hispanic/Latino; 82 Hispanic/Latino; 6 Two or more races, non-Hispanic/Latino), 55 international. Average age 31. 298 applicants, 61% accepted, 75 enrolled. In 2019, 113 master's awarded. *Degree requirements:* For master's, comprehensive exam, thesis. *Entrance requirements:* Additional exam requirements/recommendations for international students: required—TOEFL. *Application deadline:* For fall admission, 7/16 for domestic students, 7/20 for international students; for winter admission, 10/23 for domestic students, 10/20 for international students; for spring admission, 1/22 for domestic students, 1/20 for international students. Application fee: $55. *Expenses:* Contact institution. *Financial support:* Application deadline: 3/1. *Unit head:* Dr. Lawrence C. Rose, Dean, 909-537-3703, Fax: 909-537-7026, E-mail: lrose@csusb.edu. *Application contact:* Ernest Silvers, MBA Program Director, 909-537-5703, E-mail: esilvers@csusb.edu.
Website: http://mba.csusb.edu/

California State University, San Bernardino, Graduate Studies, College of Social and Behavioral Sciences, Program in National Cyber Security Studies, San Bernardino, CA 92407. Offers MA. *Students:* 5 full-time (2 women), 5 part-time (1 woman); includes 6 minority (2 Black or African American, non-Hispanic/Latino; 1 Asian, non-Hispanic/Latino; 3 Hispanic/Latino). Average age 27. 8 applicants, 25% accepted, 1 enrolled. In 2019, 7 master's awarded. *Entrance requirements:* Additional exam requirements/recommendations for international students: required—TOEFL. *Application deadline:* For fall admission, 4/15 for domestic students; for winter admission, 10/16 for domestic students; for spring admission, 1/22 for domestic students. Application fee: $55. *Financial support:* Unspecified assistantships available. *Unit head:* Dr. Mark Clark, Director, 909-537-5491, E-mail: mtclark@csusb.edu. *Application contact:* Dr. Dorota Huizinga, Dean, 909-537-3064, E-mail: dorota.huizinga@csusb.edu.

California State University, San Marcos, College of Science and Mathematics, Program in Computer Science, San Marcos, CA 92096-0001. Offers computer science (MS); cybersecurity (MS). *Program availability:* Part-time. *Entrance requirements:* For master's, GRE General Test, statement of purpose, letters of recommendation. Additional exam requirements/recommendations for international students: required—TOEFL (minimum score 550 paper-based; 80 iBT). *Application deadline:* For fall admission, 5/30 for domestic students; for spring admission, 8/30 for domestic students, 11/1 for international students. Application fee: $55. *Expenses: Tuition, area resident:* Full-time $7176. Tuition, state resident: full-time $7176. Tuition, nonresident: full-time $18,640. *International tuition:* $18,640 full-time. *Required fees:* $1960. *Financial support:* Fellowships, research assistantships, teaching assistantships, and tuition waivers available. *Unit head:* Ali Ahmadinia, Professor, 760-750-8502, E-mail: aahmadinia@csusm.edu. *Application contact:* Dr. Charles De Leone, Interim Dean of Office of Graduate Studies and Research, 760-750-8045, Fax: 760-750-8045, E-mail: apply@csusm.edu.

California University of Pennsylvania, School of Graduate Studies and Research, Eberly College of Science and Technology, Program in Cybersecurity, California, PA 15419-1394. Offers PSM. *Expenses: Tuition, area resident:* Full-time $9288; part-time $516 per credit. Tuition, state resident: full-time $9288; part-time $516 per credit. Tuition, nonresident: full-time $13,932; part-time $774 per credit. *Required fees:* $3631; $291.13 per credit. Part-time tuition and fees vary according to course load.

Capella University, School of Business and Technology, Doctoral Programs in Technology, Minneapolis, MN 55402. Offers general information technology (PhD); global operations and supply chain management (DBA); information assurance and security (PhD); information technology education (PhD); information technology management (DBA, PhD).

Capella University, School of Business and Technology, Master's Programs in Technology, Minneapolis, MN 55402. Offers enterprise software architecture (MS); general information systems and technology management (MS); global operations and supply chain management (MBA); information assurance and security (MS); information technology management (MBA); network management (MS).

Capitol Technology University, Graduate Programs, Laurel, MD 20708-9759. Offers business administration (MBA); computer science (MS); electrical engineering (MS); information and telecommunications systems management (MS); information architecture (MS); network security (MS). *Program availability:* Part-time, evening/weekend, online learning. *Entrance requirements:* For master's, minimum GPA of 3.0. Electronic applications accepted.

Cardinal Stritch University, College of Business and Management, Milwaukee, WI 53217-3985. Offers cyber security (MBA); healthcare management (MBA); justice administration (MBA); marketing (MBA). *Accreditation:* ACBSP. *Program availability:* Part-time, evening/weekend, 100% online, blended/hybrid learning. *Degree requirements:* For master's, thesis. *Entrance requirements:* For master's, 3 years of management or related experience, minimum GPA of 2.5. Additional exam requirements/recommendations for international students: required—TOEFL (minimum score 79 iBT), IELTS (minimum score 6.5). Electronic applications accepted. *Expenses:* Contact institution.

Carnegie Mellon University, Carnegie Institute of Technology, Information Networking Institute, Pittsburgh, PA 15213. Offers information networking (MS); information security (MS); information technology - information security (MS); information technology - mobility (MS); information technology - software management (MS). *Degree requirements:* For master's, thesis optional. *Entrance requirements:* For master's, GRE General Test, bachelor's degree in computer science, computer engineering, or electrical engineering, or related technology degree; programming skills (C/C++ fluency for some programs). Additional exam requirements/recommendations for international students: required—TOEFL.

Carnegie Mellon University, Heinz College, School of Information Systems and Management, Master of Science in Information Security Policy and Management Program, Pittsburgh, PA 15213-3891. Offers MSISPM. *Entrance requirements:* For master's, GRE or GMAT, college-level course in advanced algebra/pre-calculus; college-level courses in economics and statistics (recommended). Additional exam requirements/recommendations for international students: required—TOEFL or IELTS.

Central Michigan University, Central Michigan University Global Campus, Program in Cybersecurity, Mount Pleasant, MI 48859. Offers Certificate. *Program availability:* Part-time, evening/weekend. Electronic applications accepted. *Expenses: Tuition, area resident:* Full-time $12,267; part-time $8178 per year. Tuition, state resident: full-time $12,267; part-time $8178 per year. Tuition, nonresident: full-time $12,267; part-time $8178 per year. *International tuition:* $16,110 full-time. *Required fees:* $225 per semester. Tuition and fees vary according to degree level and program.

Champlain College, Graduate Studies, Burlington, VT 05402-0670. Offers business (MBA); digital forensic science (MS); early childhood education (M Ed); emergent media (MFA, MS); executive leadership (MS); health care administration (MS); information security operations (MS); law (MS); mediation and applied conflict studies (MS). *Program availability:* Part-time, online learning. *Degree requirements:* For master's, capstone project. *Entrance requirements:* Additional exam requirements/recommendations for international students: required—TOEFL (minimum score 550 paper-based; 80 iBT). Electronic applications accepted.

City University of Seattle, Graduate Division, School of Management, Seattle, WA 98121. Offers accounting (Certificate); change leadership (MBA, Certificate); computer systems (MS); finance (Certificate); financial management (MBA); general management (MBA); general management-Europe (MBA); global marketing (MBA); human resources management (Certificate); individualized study (MBA); information security (MS); information systems (MBA); leadership (MA); marketing (MBA, Certificate); project management (MBA, MS, Certificate); sustainable business (Certificate); technology management (MBA, Certificate). *Program availability:* Part-time, evening/weekend, online learning. *Degree requirements:* For master's, comprehensive exam (for some programs), thesis (for some programs). *Entrance requirements:* For master's, baccalaureate degree or equivalent from an accredited or otherwise recognized institution. Additional exam requirements/recommendations for international students: required—TOEFL (minimum score 567 paper-based; 87 iBT); recommended—IELTS. Electronic applications accepted.

Claremont Graduate University, Graduate Programs, Center for Information Systems and Technology, Claremont, CA 91711-6160. Offers cybersecurity and networking (MS); data science and analytics (MS); electronic commerce (PhD); geographic information systems (MS); health informatics (MS); information systems (Certificate); IT strategy and innovation (MS); knowledge management (PhD); systems development (PhD); telecommunications and networking (PhD); MBA/MS. *Program availability:* Part-time. *Degree requirements:* For doctorate, comprehensive exam, thesis/dissertation, portfolio. *Entrance requirements:* For master's and doctorate, GMAT, GRE General Test. Additional exam requirements/recommendations for international students: required—TOEFL (minimum score 75 iBT). Electronic applications accepted.

College of Saint Elizabeth, Program in Justice Administration and Public Service, Morristown, NJ 07960-6989. Offers counter terrorism (Certificate); cyber security investigation (Certificate); justice administration and public service (MA); leadership in community policing (Certificate). *Program availability:* Part-time, 100% online, blended/hybrid learning. *Degree requirements:* For master's, thesis. *Entrance requirements:* Additional exam requirements/recommendations for international students: required—TOEFL (minimum score 550 paper-based; 79 iBT), IELTS (minimum score 6.5). Electronic applications accepted. Application fee is waived when completed online. *Expenses:* Contact institution.

College of Staten Island of the City University of New York, Graduate Programs, Division of Science and Technology, Program in Computer Science, Staten Island, NY 10314-6600. Offers computer science (MS), including artificial intelligence and data analytics, cloud computing and software engineering, cybersecurity and networks. *Program availability:* Part-time, evening/weekend. *Faculty:* 6. *Students:* 42. 48 applicants, 67% accepted, 15 enrolled. In 2019, 10 master's awarded. *Degree requirements:* For master's, thesis optional, a program of 10 courses (30 credits) with at least a 3.0 (B) average. Exceptional students may be permitted to satisfy six credits of the total credit requirement with a master's thesis. *Entrance requirements:* For master's, GRE General Test, BS in Computer Science or related area with a B average (3.0 out of 4.0) overall and in the major, a resume, and demonstrable knowledge in several areas. Additional exam requirements/recommendations for international students: required—TOEFL (minimum score 550 paper-based; 79 iBT), IELTS (minimum score 6.5). *Application deadline:* For fall admission, 7/20 priority date for domestic students, 4/25 for international students; for spring admission, 11/2 priority date for domestic students, 11/2 for international students. Applications are processed on a rolling basis. Application fee: $75. Electronic applications accepted. *Expenses: Tuition, area resident:* Full-time $11,090; part-time $470 per credit. Tuition, state resident: full-time $11,090; part-time $470 per credit. Tuition, nonresident: full-time $20,520; part-time $855 per credit. *International tuition:* $20,520 full-time. *Required fees:* $559; $181 per semester. Tuition and fees vary according to program. *Unit head:* Dr. Xiaowen Zhang, Associate Professor, 718-982-3262, E-mail: xiaowen.zhang@csi.cuny.edu. *Application contact:* Sasha Spence, Associate Director for Graduate Admissions, 718-982-2019, Fax: 718-982-2500, E-mail: sasha.spence@csi.cuny.edu.
Website: https://www.csi.cuny.edu/academics-and-research/departments-programs/computer-science

Colorado Christian University, Program in Business Administration, Lakewood, CO 80226. Offers corporate training (MBA); information security (MA); leadership (MBA); project management (MBA). *Program availability:* Part-time, evening/weekend, online learning. *Degree requirements:* For master's, thesis optional. *Entrance requirements:* For master's, GMAT, 2 letters of recommendation, resume. Additional exam requirements/recommendations for international students: required—TOEFL. Electronic applications accepted. *Expenses:* Contact institution.

Colorado Technical University Aurora, Program in Computer Science, Aurora, CO 80014. Offers computer systems security (MSCS); database systems (MSCS); software engineering (MSCS). *Program availability:* Part-time, evening/weekend. *Degree requirements:* For master's, thesis or alternative. *Entrance requirements:* For master's, minimum undergraduate GPA of 3.0, resume.

Colorado Technical University Aurora, Program in Information Science, Aurora, CO 80014. Offers information systems security (MSM).

Colorado Technical University Colorado Springs, Graduate Studies, Program in Computer Science, Colorado Springs, CO 80907. Offers computer science (DCS); computer systems security (MSCS); database systems (MSCS); software engineering (MSCS). *Program availability:* Part-time, evening/weekend, online learning. *Degree requirements:* For master's, thesis or alternative; for doctorate, thesis/dissertation. *Entrance requirements:* For doctorate, minimum graduate GPA of 3.0, 5 years of related work experience.

Colorado Technical University Colorado Springs, Graduate Studies, Program in Information Science, Colorado Springs, CO 80907. Offers information systems security (MSM). *Program availability:* Online learning.

Columbus State University, Graduate Studies, Turner College of Business, Columbus, GA 31907-5645. Offers applied computer science (MS), including informational assurance, modeling and simulation, software development; business administration (MBA); cyber security (MS); human resource management (Certificate); information systems security (Certificate); modeling and simulation (Certificate); organizational leadership (MS), including human resource management, leader development, servant leadership; servant leadership (Certificate). *Accreditation:* AACSB. *Program availability:* Part-time, evening/weekend, 100% online, blended/hybrid learning. *Entrance requirements:* For master's, GMAT, GRE, minimum undergraduate GPA of 2.75, letters of recommendation. Additional exam requirements/recommendations for international students: required—TOEFL (minimum score 550 paper-based; 79 iBT). Electronic applications accepted. *Expenses:* Contact institution.

Concordia University, School of Graduate Studies, Faculty of Engineering and Computer Science, Concordia Institute for Information Systems Engineering (CIISE), Montréal, QC H3G 1M8, Canada. Offers 3D graphics and game development (Certificate); information and systems engineering (PhD); information systems security (M Eng, MA Sc); quality systems engineering (M Eng, MA Sc); service engineering and network management (Certificate).

Concordia University, Nebraska, Program in Computer Science, Seward, NE 68434. Offers cyber operations (MS). *Program availability:* Online learning.

Concordia University of Edmonton, Program in Information Systems Security Management, Edmonton, AB T5B 4E4, Canada. Offers MA.

Concordia University, St. Paul, College of Business and Technology, St. Paul, MN 55104-5494. Offers business administration (MBA), including cyber-security leadership; health care management (MBA); human resource management (MA); information technology (MBA); leadership and management (MA); strategic communication management (MA). *Accreditation:* ACBSP. *Program availability:* Part-time, evening/weekend, 100% online, blended/hybrid learning. *Degree requirements:* For master's, thesis (for some programs). *Entrance requirements:* For master's, official transcripts from regionally-accredited institution stating the conferral of a bachelor's degree with minimum cumulative GPA of 3.0; personal statement; professional resume. Additional exam requirements/recommendations for international students: recommended—TOEFL (minimum score 547 paper-based; 78 iBT), IELTS (minimum score 6). Electronic applications accepted. *Expenses:* Contact institution.

Davenport University, Sneden Graduate School, Grand Rapids, MI 49512. Offers accounting (MBA); business administration (EMBA); finance (MBA); health care management (MBA); human resources (MBA); information assurance (MS); occupational therapy (MSOT); public health (MPH); strategic management (MBA). *Program availability:* Evening/weekend. *Entrance requirements:* For master's, GMAT, minimum undergraduate GPA of 2.75. Additional exam requirements/recommendations for international students: required—TOEFL. Electronic applications accepted.

DePaul University, College of Computing and Digital Media, Chicago, IL 60604. Offers animation (MA, MFA); applied technology (MS); business information technology (MS); computational finance (MS); computer and information sciences (PhD); computer science (MS); creative producing (MFA); cybersecurity (MS); data science (MS); digital communication and media arts (MA); documentary (MFA); e-commerce technology (MS); experience design (MA); film and television (MS); film and television directing (MFA); game design (MFA); game programming (MS); health informatics (MS); human centered design (PhD); human-computer interaction (MS); information systems (MS); network engineering and security (MS); product innovation and computing (MS); screenwriting (MFA); software engineering (MS); JD/MS. *Program availability:* Part-time, evening/weekend, online learning. *Degree requirements:* For master's, thesis (for some programs); for doctorate, comprehensive exam, thesis/dissertation. *Entrance requirements:* For master's, GRE or GMAT (for MS in computational finance only), bachelor's degree, resume (MS in predictive analytics only), IT experience (MS in information technology project management only), portfolio review (all MFA programs and MA in animation); for doctorate, GRE, master's degree in computer science. Additional exam requirements/recommendations for international students: required—TOEFL (minimum score 590 paper-based; 80 iBT), IELTS (minimum score 6.5), PTE (minimum score 53). Electronic applications accepted. *Expenses:* Contact institution.

DeSales University, Division of Science and Mathematics, Center Valley, PA 18034-9568. Offers cyber security (Postbaccalaureate Certificate); data analytics (Postbaccalaureate Certificate); information systems (MS), including cyber security, digital forensics, healthcare information management, project management. *Program availability:* Part-time, evening/weekend, 100% online, blended/hybrid learning. *Faculty:* 2 full-time (both women), 5 part-time/adjunct (1 woman). *Students:* 2 full-time (0 women), 17 part-time (4 women); includes 3 minority (2 Asian, non-Hispanic/Latino; 1 Two or more races, non-Hispanic/Latino). Average age 36. 15 applicants, 60% accepted, 9 enrolled. In 2019, 6 master's awarded. *Entrance requirements:* For master's, GRE or GMAT, bachelor's degree in computer-related discipline from accredited college or university, minimum undergraduate GPA of 3.0, personal statement, three letters of recommendation. Additional exam requirements/recommendations for international students: required—TOEFL. *Application deadline:* Applications are processed on a rolling basis. Application fee: $50. Electronic applications accepted. *Expenses:* Contact institution. *Financial support:* Applicants required to submit FAFSA. *Unit head:* Dr. Ronald Nordone, Dean of Graduate Studies, 610-282-1100 Ext. 1289, E-mail: Ronald.Nordone@desale.edu. *Application contact:* Julia Ferraro, Director of Graduate Admissions, 610-282-1100 Ext. 1768, E-mail: gradadmissions@desales.edu.
Website: http://www.desales.edu/home/academics/graduate-studies/programs-of-study/msis---master-of-science-in-information-systems

Drury University, Cybersecurity Leadership Certificate Program, Springfield, MO 65802. Offers Certificate. *Program availability:* Part-time, evening/weekend, blended/hybrid learning. *Faculty:* 1 full-time (0 women), 2 part-time/adjunct (1 woman). *Students:* 3 full-time (2 women); includes 1 minority (American Indian or Alaska Native, non-Hispanic/Latino). Average age 44. 3 applicants, 100% accepted, 3 enrolled. *Entrance requirements:* For degree, bachelor's degree, minimum GPA of 3.0. Additional exam requirements/recommendations for international students: recommended—TOEFL (minimum score 80 iBT), IELTS (minimum score 6.5). *Application deadline:* For fall admission, 8/10 priority date for domestic and international students; for spring admission, 1/8 priority date for domestic and international students; for summer admission, 5/26 priority date for domestic and international students. Applications are processed on a rolling basis. Application fee: $25. Electronic applications accepted. *Expenses:* Contact institution. *Financial support:* Career-related internships or fieldwork available. Financial award application deadline: 6/30; financial award applicants required to submit FAFSA. *Unit head:* Dr. Robin Soster, Director, 417-873-7612, E-mail: rsoster@drury.edu. *Application contact:* Dr. Robin Soster, Director, 417-873-7612, E-mail: rsoster@drury.edu.
Website: http://www.drury.edu/cybersecurity

East Carolina University, Graduate School, College of Engineering and Technology, Department of Technology Systems, Greenville, NC 27858-4353. Offers computer network professional (Certificate); cyber security professional (Certificate); information assurance (Certificate); Lean Six Sigma Black Belt (Certificate); network technology (MS), including computer networking management, digital communications technology, information security, Web technologies; occupational safety (MS); technology management (MS, PhD), including industrial distribution and logistics (MS); Website developer (Certificate). *Application deadline:* For fall admission, 6/1 priority date for domestic students. *Expenses: Tuition, area resident:* Full-time $4749; part-time $185 per credit hour. Tuition, state resident: full-time $4749; part-time $185 per credit hour. Tuition, nonresident: full-time $17,898; part-time $864 per credit hour. *International tuition:* $17,898 full-time. *Required fees:* $2787. *Financial support:* Application deadline: 6/1. *Unit head:* Dr. Tijjani Mohammed, Chair, 252-328-9668, E-mail: mohammedt@

ecu.edu. *Application contact:* Graduate School Admissions, 252-328-6012, Fax: 252-328-6071, E-mail: gradschool@ecu.edu.
Website: https://cet.ecu.edu/techsystems/

Eastern Illinois University, Graduate School, Lumpkin College of Business and Technology, School of Technology, Program in Cybersecurity, Charleston, IL 61920. Offers MS.

Eastern Michigan University, Graduate School, College of Engineering and Technology, School of Information Security and Applied Computing, Program in Cybersecurity, Ypsilanti, MI 48197. Offers Graduate Certificate. *Students:* 1 (woman) full-time, 8 part-time (1 woman); includes 2 minority (1 Black or African American, non-Hispanic/Latino; 1 Hispanic/Latino). Average age 32. 25 applicants, 60% accepted, 8 enrolled. Application fee: $45. *Application contact:* Dr. Munther Abualkibash, Program Coordinator, 734-487-2490, Fax: 734-483-8755, E-mail: pc_sisac@emich.edu.

EC-Council University, Master of Science in Cyber Security Program, Albuquerque, NM 87109. Offers information assurance management (MSCS). *Program availability:* Part-time, online only, 100% online. *Degree requirements:* For master's, capstone. *Entrance requirements:* Additional exam requirements/recommendations for international students: required—TOEFL (minimum score 500 paper-based; 71 iBT), IELTS (minimum score 6.1). Electronic applications accepted.

ECPI University, Graduate Programs, Virginia Beach, VA 23462. Offers business administration (MBA), including management, information technology management; cybersecurity (MS), including cyber operations, cybersecurity policy; information systems (MS). *Program availability:* Part-time, evening/weekend, 100% online, blended/hybrid learning. *Faculty:* 17 full-time (8 women), 25 part-time/adjunct (7 women). *Students:* 345 full-time (173 women); includes 157 minority (91 Black or African American, non-Hispanic/Latino; 5 American Indian or Alaska Native, non-Hispanic/Latino; 24 Asian, non-Hispanic/Latino; 25 Hispanic/Latino; 2 Native Hawaiian or other Pacific Islander, non-Hispanic/Latino; 10 Two or more races, non-Hispanic/Latino), 11 international. Average age 35. In 2019, 128 master's awarded. *Entrance requirements:* Additional exam requirements/recommendations for international students: required—TOEFL (minimum score 550 paper-based; 79 iBT), IELTS (minimum score 6.5), PTE (minimum score 54). *Expenses: Tuition:* Full-time $12,960; part-time $6480 per semester. Full-time tuition and fees vary according to program. *Financial support:* In 2019–20, 155 students received support. Career-related internships or fieldwork, Federal Work-Study, institutionally sponsored loans, and scholarships/grants available. Financial award applicants required to submit FAFSA.

Embry-Riddle Aeronautical University–Daytona, Department of Electrical, Computer, Software and Systems Engineering, Daytona Beach, FL 32114-3900. Offers cybersecurity engineering (MS); electrical and computer engineering (MSECE); software engineering (MSSE); systems engineering (MS). *Degree requirements:* For master's, thesis optional. *Entrance requirements:* For master's, GRE (for some programs). Additional exam requirements/recommendations for international students: required—TOEFL (minimum score 550 paper-based, 79 iBT) or IELTS (6). Electronic applications accepted.

Embry-Riddle Aeronautical University–Worldwide, Department of Security and Emergency Services, Daytona Beach, FL 32114-3900. Offers cybersecurity management and policy (MSCMP); human security and resilience (MSHSR). *Program availability:* Part-time, evening/weekend, EagleVision Classroom (between classrooms), EagleVision Home (faculty and students at home), and a blend of Classroom or Home. *Degree requirements:* For master's, capstone project (for MSHSR). *Entrance requirements:* Additional exam requirements/recommendations for international students: required—TOEFL (minimum score 550 paper-based; 79 iBT), IELTS (minimum score 6). Electronic applications accepted.

Endicott College, Endicott College School of Arts and Sciences, Program in Homeland Security, Beverly, MA 01915. Offers cybersecurity (MS, Postbaccalaureate Certificate); emergency management (MS). *Program availability:* Part-time, evening/weekend, 100% online. *Faculty:* 2 full-time (1 woman), 17 part-time/adjunct (4 women). *Students:* 16 full-time (7 women), 14 part-time (4 women); includes 5 minority (3 Black or African American, non-Hispanic/Latino; 2 Hispanic/Latino). Average age 29. 23 applicants, 74% accepted, 14 enrolled. In 2019, 18 master's, 2 other advanced degrees awarded. *Degree requirements:* For master's, Capstone project. *Entrance requirements:* For master's, Updated resume; Official transcript of all post-secondary academic work; 250-500 word essay on specified topic; 2 letters of recommendation; Interview with program director; for Postbaccalaureate Certificate, Same as Master's. Additional exam requirements/recommendations for international students: required—TOEFL. *Application deadline:* Applications are processed on a rolling basis. Application fee: $50. Electronic applications accepted. *Expenses:* Tuition varies by program. *Financial support:* Applicants required to submit FAFSA. *Unit head:* Dr. Joshua McCabe, Assistant Dean, Social Sciences, 978-232-2380, E-mail: gwong@endicott.edu. *Application contact:* Ian Menchini, Director, Graduate Enrollment and Advising, 978-232-5292, Fax: 978-232-3000, E-mail: imenchin@endicott.edu.
Website: https://www.endicott.edu/academics/schools/arts-sciences/graduate-programs/homeland-security-studies-program

Fairfield University, School of Engineering, Fairfield, CT 06824. Offers database management (CAS); electrical and computer engineering (MS); information security (CAS); management of technology (MS); mechanical engineering (MS); network technology (CAS); software engineering (MS); Web application development (CAS). *Program availability:* Part-time, evening/weekend. *Faculty:* 10 full-time (2 women), 15 part-time/adjunct (1 woman). *Students:* 46 full-time (24 women), 57 part-time (10 women); includes 23 minority (5 Black or African American, non-Hispanic/Latino; 9 Asian, non-Hispanic/Latino; 9 Hispanic/Latino), 33 international. Average age 29. 68 applicants, 62% accepted, 30 enrolled. In 2019, 100 master's awarded. *Degree requirements:* For master's, capstone course. *Entrance requirements:* For master's, resume, 2 recommendations. Additional exam requirements/recommendations for international students: required—TOEFL (minimum score 550 paper-based; 80 iBT), IELTS (minimum score 6.5), TOEFL (minimum score 550 paper-based; 80 iBT) or IELTS (minimum score 6.5). *Application deadline:* For fall admission, 5/15 for international students; for spring admission, 10/15 for international students. Applications are processed on a rolling basis. Application fee: $60. Electronic applications accepted. *Expenses:* Tuition $900/credit hour; Registration Fee $50/semester; Graduate Student Activity Fee (Fall and Spring) $65/semester. *Financial support:* In 2019–20, 20 students received support. Scholarships/grants and unspecified assistantships available. Financial award applicants required to submit FAFSA. *Unit head:* Richard Heist, Dean, 203-254-4147, Fax: 203-254-4013, E-mail: rheist@fairfield.edu. *Application contact:* Melanie Rogers, Director of Graduate Admission, 203-254-4184, Fax: 203-254-4073, E-mail: gradadmis@fairfield.edu.
Website: http://www.fairfield.edu/soe

Florida Institute of Technology, College of Engineering and Science, Program in Information Assurance and Cybersecurity, Melbourne, FL 32901-6975. Offers MS. *Program availability:* Part-time, evening/weekend, 100% online. *Degree requirements:* For master's, comprehensive exam (for some programs), thesis optional, minimum of 33 credit hours, capstone project or thesis. *Entrance requirements:* For master's, GRE General Test, transcripts. Additional exam requirements/recommendations for international students: required—TOEFL (minimum score 550 paper-based; 79 iBT). Electronic applications accepted.

Florida International University, College of Engineering and Computing, School of Computing and Information Sciences, Miami, FL 33199. Offers computer science (MS, PhD); cybersecurity (MS); data science (MS); information technology (MS); telecommunications and networking (MS). *Program availability:* Part-time, evening/weekend. *Faculty:* 53 full-time (14 women), 33 part-time/adjunct (9 women). *Students:* 162 full-time (39 women), 140 part-time (26 women); includes 160 minority (11 Black or African American, non-Hispanic/Latino; 1 American Indian or Alaska Native, non-Hispanic/Latino; 9 Asian, non-Hispanic/Latino; 132 Hispanic/Latino; 7 Two or more races, non-Hispanic/Latino), 120 international. Average age 30. 360 applicants, 49% accepted, 73 enrolled. In 2019, 89 master's, 13 doctorates awarded. *Degree requirements:* For master's, thesis or alternative; for doctorate, comprehensive exam, thesis/dissertation. *Entrance requirements:* For master's and doctorate, GRE General Test, 3 letters of recommendation, minimum GPA of 3.0. Additional exam requirements/recommendations for international students: required—TOEFL (minimum score 550 paper-based; 80 iBT). *Application deadline:* For fall admission, 6/1 for domestic students, 4/1 for international students; for spring admission, 10/1 for domestic students, 9/1 for international students. Applications are processed on a rolling basis. Application fee: $30. Electronic applications accepted. *Expenses: Tuition, area resident:* Full-time $8912; part-time $446 per credit hour. Tuition, state resident: full-time $8912; part-time $446 per credit hour. Tuition, nonresident: full-time $21,393; part-time $992 per credit hour. *Required fees:* $2194. *Financial support:* Research assistantships, teaching assistantships, institutionally sponsored loans, scholarships/grants, and unspecified assistantships available. Financial award application deadline: 3/1; financial award applicants required to submit FAFSA. *Unit head:* Dr. Sundararaj S. Iyengar, Director, 305-348-3947, Fax: 305-348-3549, E-mail: sundararaj.iyengar@fiu.edu. *Application contact:* Nanett Rojas, Manager, Admissions Operations, 305-348-7464, Fax: 305-348-7441, E-mail: gradadm@fiu.edu.

Florida State University, The Graduate School, Department of Anthropology, Department of Computer Science, Tallahassee, FL 32306. Offers computer network and system administration (MS); computer science (MS, PhD); cyber criminology (MS); cyber security (MS). *Program availability:* Part-time. *Faculty:* 33 full-time (6 women), 2 part-time/adjunct (0 women). *Students:* 129 full-time (28 women), 10 part-time (3 women); includes 13 minority (1 Black or African American, non-Hispanic/Latino; 3 Asian, non-Hispanic/Latino; 3 Hispanic/Latino; 6 Two or more races, non-Hispanic/Latino), 93 international. Average age 29. 270 applicants, 56% accepted, 37 enrolled. In 2019, 48 master's, 7 doctorates awarded. Terminal master's awarded for partial completion of doctoral program. *Degree requirements:* For master's, comprehensive exam (for some programs), thesis (for some programs); for doctorate, comprehensive exam, thesis/dissertation, qualifying exam, preliminary exam, prospectus defense. *Entrance requirements:* For master's, GRE General Test, minimum undergraduate GPA of 3.0; for doctorate, GRE General Test, minimum GPA of 3.0. Additional exam requirements/recommendations for international students: required—TOEFL (minimum score 550 paper-based; 80 iBT), IELTS (minimum score 6.5). *Application deadline:* For fall admission, 6/1 for domestic students, 1/15 priority date for international students; for spring admission, 11/1 for domestic students, 9/1 priority date for international students. Applications are processed on a rolling basis. Application fee: $30. Electronic applications accepted. *Financial support:* In 2019–20, 117 students received support, including 13 fellowships with full tuition reimbursements available (averaging $36,000 per year), 39 research assistantships with full tuition reimbursements available (averaging $23,900 per year), 62 teaching assistantships with full tuition reimbursements available (averaging $19,375 per year); scholarships/grants, health care benefits, tuition waivers (full), and unspecified assistantships also available. Financial award application deadline: 1/15; financial award applicants required to submit FAFSA. *Unit head:* Dr. Xin Yuan, Chairman, 850-644-9133, Fax: 850-644-0058, E-mail: xyuan@cs.fsu.edu. *Application contact:* Daniel B. Clawson, Graduate Coordinator, 850-645-4975, Fax: 850-644-0058, E-mail: clawson@cs.fsu.edu.
Website: http://www.cs.fsu.edu/

George Mason University, School of Business, Program in Management of Secure Information Systems, Fairfax, VA 22030. Offers MS. *Degree requirements:* For master's, thesis, capstone project. *Entrance requirements:* For master's, current resume; official copies of transcripts from all colleges or universities attended; two professional letters of recommendation; goal statement; interview. Additional exam requirements/recommendations for international students: required—TOEFL (minimum score 650 paper-based; 93 iBT), IELTS, PTE. Electronic applications accepted. *Expenses:* Contact institution.

The George Washington University, School of Engineering and Applied Science, Department of Computer Science, Washington, DC 20052. Offers computer science (MS, D Sc); cybersecurity (MS). *Program availability:* Part-time, evening/weekend. *Degree requirements:* For master's, thesis optional; for doctorate, thesis/dissertation, dissertation defense, qualifying exam. *Entrance requirements:* For master's, appropriate bachelor's degree, minimum GPA of 3.0; for doctorate, GRE (if highest earned degree is BS), appropriate bachelor's or master's degree, minimum GPA of 3.3; for other advanced degree, appropriate master's degree, minimum GPA of 3.4. Additional exam requirements/recommendations for international students: required—TOEFL or The George Washington University English as a Foreign Language Test.

Georgia Southern University, Jack N. Averitt College of Graduate Studies, College of Behavioral and Social Sciences, Program in Criminal Justice and Criminology, Statesboro, GA 30458. Offers criminal justice (MS); cyber crime (Certificate). *Program availability:* Part-time, evening/weekend, 100% online. *Faculty:* 13 full-time (9 women). *Students:* 20 full-time (10 women), 10 part-time (6 women); includes 14 minority (12 Black or African American, non-Hispanic/Latino; 2 Hispanic/Latino). Average age 28. 14 applicants, 93% accepted, 10 enrolled. In 2019, 9 master's awarded. *Degree requirements:* For master's, comprehensive exam, field practicum or thesis. *Entrance requirements:* For master's, GRE General Test (minimum score 150 on verbal, 141 on quantitative, or 4 on analytical section) or MAT, minimum GPA of 2.5, 2 letters of recommendation, letter of intent (500-1000 words). Additional exam requirements/recommendations for international students: required—TOEFL (minimum score 523 paper-based; 70 iBT). *Application deadline:* For fall admission, 6/1 priority date for domestic students, 5/1 priority date for international students; for spring admission, 11/15 priority date for domestic students, 9/15 priority date for international students; for summer admission, 4/15 priority date for domestic students, 9/15 for international students. Applications are processed on a rolling basis. Application fee: $30. Electronic applications accepted. *Expenses: Tuition, area resident:* Full-time $4986; part-time $277 per credit hour. Tuition, nonresident: full-time $19,890; part-time $1105 per credit hour. *International tuition:* $19,890 full-time. *Required fees:* $2114; $1057 per semester. $1057 per semester. Tuition and fees vary according to course load, campus/location and program. *Financial support:* In 2019–20, 13 students received support, including 5 research assistantships with full tuition reimbursements available (averaging $8,000 per year); teaching assistantships, career-related internships or fieldwork, Federal Work-Study, scholarships/grants, and unspecified assistantships also available. Support

available to part-time students. Financial award application deadline: 3/15; financial award applicants required to submit FAFSA. *Unit head:* Dr. Daniel Skidmore-Hess, Department Head, 912-344-2532, Fax: 912-344-3438, E-mail: daniel.skidmore-hess@armstrong.edu. *Application contact:* McKenzie Peterman, Graduate Admissions Specialist, 912-478-5678, Fax: 912-478-0740, E-mail: mpeterman@georgiasouthern.edu.
Website: https://www.armstrong.edu/academic-departments/cjsps-master-of-science-in-criminal-justice

Hampton University, School of Science, Department of Computer Science, Program in Information Assurance, Hampton, VA 23668. Offers MS. *Students:* 3 full-time (2 women); all minorities (all Black or African American, non-Hispanic/Latino). Average age 23. 1 applicant, 100% accepted. In 2019, 3 master's awarded. Application fee: $35. *Unit head:* Dr. Chutima Boonthum-Denecke, Director, 757-727-5082. *Application contact:* Dr. Chutima Boonthum-Denecke, Director, 757-727-5082.

Harrisburg University of Science and Technology, Program in Information Systems Engineering and Management, Harrisburg, PA 17101. Offers analytics (MS); digital government (MS); digital health (MS); entrepreneurship (MS); information security (MS); software engineering and systems development (MS). *Program availability:* Part-time, evening/weekend. *Degree requirements:* For master's, thesis optional. *Entrance requirements:* For master's, baccalaureate degree. Additional exam requirements/recommendations for international students: required—TOEFL (minimum score 520 paper-based; 80 iBT); recommended—IELTS (minimum score 6). Electronic applications accepted. *Expenses: Tuition:* Full-time $15,900; part-time $7950 per credit hour.

Hofstra University, Fred DeMatteis School of Engineering and Applied Sciences, Hempstead, NY 11549. Offers computer science (MS). *Program availability:* Part-time, evening/weekend, blended/hybrid learning. *Faculty:* 8 full-time (2 women), 6 part-time/adjunct (0 women). *Students:* 26 full-time (7 women), 34 part-time (7 women); includes 19 minority (3 Black or African American, non-Hispanic/Latino; 1 American Indian or Alaska Native, non-Hispanic/Latino; 6 Asian, non-Hispanic/Latino; 8 Hispanic/Latino; 1 Native Hawaiian or other Pacific Islander, non-Hispanic/Latino), 19 international. Average age 28. 107 applicants, 63% accepted, 26 enrolled. In 2019, 17 master's awarded. *Degree requirements:* For master's, thesis optional, 30 credits, minimum GPA of 3.0. *Entrance requirements:* For master's, GRE, minimum GPA of 3.0. Additional exam requirements/recommendations for international students: required—TOEFL (minimum score 550 paper-based; 80 iBT); recommended—IELTS (minimum score 6.5). *Application deadline:* Applications are processed on a rolling basis. Application fee: $75. Electronic applications accepted. *Expenses: Tuition:* Full-time $25,164; part-time $1398 per credit. *Required fees:* $580; $165 per semester. Tuition and fees vary according to course load, degree level and program. *Financial support:* In 2019–20, 29 students received support, including 22 fellowships with full and partial tuition reimbursements available (averaging $3,686 per year), 2 research assistantships with full and partial tuition reimbursements available (averaging $6,675 per year); career-related internships or fieldwork, Federal Work-Study, institutionally sponsored loans, scholarships/grants, tuition waivers (full and partial), unspecified assistantships, and scholarships and endowed scholarships also available. Support available to part-time students. Financial award applicants required to submit FAFSA. *Unit head:* Dr. Sina Rabbany, Dean, 516-463-6672, E-mail: sina.y.rabbany@hofstra.edu. *Application contact:* Sunil Samuel, Assistant Vice President of Admissions, 516-463-4723, Fax: 516-463-4664, E-mail: graduateadmission@hofstra.edu.
Website: http://www.hofstra.edu/academics/colleges/seas/

Hood College, Graduate School, Programs in Computer and Information Sciences, Frederick, MD 21701-8575. Offers computer science (MS); cybersecurity (MS, Certificate); information technology (MS). *Program availability:* Part-time, evening/weekend, 100% online. *Degree requirements:* For master's, thesis optional, capstone (S). *Entrance requirements:* For master's, minimum GPA of 2.75, essay, resume. Additional exam requirements/recommendations for international students: required—TOEFL (minimum score 575 paper-based; 89 iBT), IELTS (minimum score 6.5). Electronic applications accepted. *Expenses:* Contact institution.

Illinois Institute of Technology, Graduate College, College of Science, Department of Computer Science, Chicago, IL 60616. Offers business (MCS); computational intelligence (MCS); computer science (MCS, MS, PhD); cyber-physical systems (MCS); data analytics (MCS); data science (MAS); database systems (MCS); distributed and cloud computing (MCS); education (MCS); finance (MCS); information security and assurance (MCS); networking and communications (MCS); software engineering (MCS); telecommunications and software engineering (MAS); MS/MAS. *Program availability:* Part-time, evening/weekend, online learning. Terminal master's awarded for partial completion of doctoral program. *Degree requirements:* For master's, thesis optional; for doctorate, comprehensive exam, thesis/dissertation. *Entrance requirements:* For master's, GRE General Test with minimum scores of 298 Quantitative and Verbal, 3.0 Analytical Writing (for MS); GRE General Test with minimum scores of 292 Quantitative and Verbal, 2.5 Analytical Writing (for MAS), minimum undergraduate GPA of 3.0; for doctorate, GRE General Test (minimum scores: 304 Quantitative and Verbal, 3.5 Analytical Writing), minimum undergraduate GPA of 3.0. Additional exam requirements/recommendations for international students: required—TOEFL (minimum score 523 paper-based; 70 iBT). Electronic applications accepted.

Illinois Institute of Technology, Graduate College, School of Applied Technology, Department of Information Technology and Management, Wheaton, IL 60189. Offers cyber forensics and security (MAS); information technology and management (MAS). *Program availability:* Part-time, evening/weekend, online learning. *Entrance requirements:* For master's, GRE (minimum score 300 Quantitative and Verbal, 2.5 Analytical Writing), bachelor's degree with minimum cumulative undergraduate GPA of 3.0 (or its equivalent) from accredited institution. Additional exam requirements/recommendations for international students: required—TOEFL (minimum score 523 paper-based; 70 iBT); recommended—IELTS (minimum score 5.5). Electronic applications accepted.

Indiana University Bloomington, School of Informatics, Computing, and Engineering, Program in Informatics, Bloomington, IN 47405. Offers informatics (MS, PhD), including bioinformatics (PhD), complex systems (PhD), computing, culture and society (PhD), health informatics (PhD), human-computer interaction (MS), human-computer interaction design (PhD), music informatics (PhD), security informatics (PhD); visual heritage (PhD). *Program availability:* Part-time. Terminal master's awarded for partial completion of doctoral program. *Degree requirements:* For master's, thesis, capstone project; for doctorate, variable foreign language requirement, comprehensive exam, thesis/dissertation. *Entrance requirements:* For master's and doctorate, GRE, resume/curriculum vitae, transcripts, 3 letters of recommendation. Additional exam requirements/recommendations for international students: required—TOEFL (minimum score 600 paper-based; 100 iBT). Electronic applications accepted.

Indiana University-Purdue University Indianapolis, School of Engineering and Technology, MS in Technology Program, Indianapolis, IN 46202. Offers applied data management and analytics (MS); facilities management (MS); information security and assurance (MS); motorsports (MS); organizational leadership (MS); technical communication (MS). *Program availability:* Online learning.

Indiana University-Purdue University Indianapolis, School of Science, Department of Computer and Information Science, Indianapolis, IN 46202-5132. Offers biocomputing (Graduate Certificate); biometrics (Graduate Certificate); computer science (MS, PhD); computer security (Graduate Certificate); databases and data mining (Graduate Certificate); software engineering (Graduate Certificate). *Program availability:* Part-time. Terminal master's awarded for partial completion of doctoral program. *Degree requirements:* For master's and Graduate Certificate, thesis optional; for doctorate, thesis/dissertation. *Entrance requirements:* For master's and doctorate, GRE, BS in computer science or the equivalent with a minimum GPA of 3.0 (or equivalent); for Graduate Certificate, BS in computer science or the equivalent with a minimum GPA of 3.0 (or equivalent). Additional exam requirements/recommendations for international students: required—PTE (minimum score 58), TOEFL (minimum score 550 paper-based, 79 iBT) or IELTS (6.5).

The Institute of World Politics, Graduate Programs in National Security, Intelligence, and International Affairs, Washington, DC 20036. Offers American foreign policy (Certificate); comparative political culture (Certificate); conflict prevention (Certificate); counterintelligence (Certificate); counterterrorism (Certificate); cyber statecraft (Certificate); economic statecraft (Certificate); homeland security (Certificate); intelligence (Certificate); international politics (Certificate); national security affairs (Executive MA, Certificate); nonviolent conflict (Certificate); peace building, stabilization, and humanitarian affairs (Certificate); public diplomacy and strategic influence (Certificate); statecraft and international affairs (MA); statecraft and national security (MA, DSNS); strategic communication (Certificate); strategic intelligence studies (MA, Professional MA); strategic soft power (Certificate). *Program availability:* Part-time, evening/weekend. *Degree requirements:* For master's, 52 credit hours, comprehensive written and oral exam (for MA); proficiency in critical language (for MA in statecraft and international affairs); 28 credit hours (for Executive MA); 36 credit hours (for Professional MA); for doctorate, comprehensive exam, thesis/dissertation; for Certificate, 20 credit hours. *Entrance requirements:* For master's, resume, personal statement, 3 references, essay; 7-10 years of professional experience (for Executive MA); 5-7 years of professional experience (for Professional MA); for doctorate, MA. Additional exam requirements/recommendations for international students: required—TOEFL. Electronic applications accepted.

Inter American University of Puerto Rico, Guayama Campus, Department of Natural and Applied Sciences, Guayama, PR 00785. Offers computer security and networks (MS); networking and security (MCS).

Iona College, School of Arts and Science, Department of Computer Science, New Rochelle, NY 10801-1890. Offers computer science (MS); cyber security (MS); game development (MS). *Program availability:* Part-time, evening/weekend. *Faculty:* 9 full-time (4 women), 1 (woman) part-time/adjunct. *Students:* 2 full-time (0 women), 10 part-time (2 women); includes 4 minority (2 Black or African American, non-Hispanic/Latino; 1 Asian, non-Hispanic/Latino; 1 Hispanic/Latino), 1 international. Average age 26. 16 applicants, 100% accepted, 6 enrolled. In 2019, 6 master's awarded. *Degree requirements:* For master's, thesis optional. *Entrance requirements:* For master's, minimum GPA of 3.0. Additional exam requirements/recommendations for international students: required—TOEFL (minimum score 550 paper-based; 80 iBT), IELTS (minimum score 6.5). *Application deadline:* For fall admission, 8/1 priority date for domestic students, 5/1 priority date for international students; for spring admission, 1/1 priority date for domestic students, 9/1 priority date for international students. Applications are processed on a rolling basis. Electronic applications accepted. *Financial support:* In 2019–20, 5 students received support, including 2 research assistantships with full and partial tuition reimbursements available (averaging $5,072 per year); scholarships/grants, tuition waivers (partial), and unspecified assistantships also available. Support available to part-time students. Financial award application deadline: 4/15; financial award applicants required to submit FAFSA. *Unit head:* Frances Bailie, PhD, Chair, 914-633-2335, E-mail: fbailie@iona.edu. *Application contact:* Christopher Kash, Assistant Director, Graduate Admissions, 914-633-2403, Fax: 914-633-2277, E-mail: ckash@iona.edu.
Website: http://www.iona.edu/Academics/School-of-Arts-Science/Departments/Computer-Science/Graduate-Programs.aspx

Iona College, School of Arts and Science, Department of Criminal Justice, New Rochelle, NY 10801-1890. Offers criminal justice (MS); cybercrime and security (AC); forensic criminology and criminal justice systems (Certificate). *Program availability:* Part-time, evening/weekend. *Faculty:* 4 full-time (1 woman), 5 part-time/adjunct (1 woman). *Students:* 17 full-time (12 women), 8 part-time (3 women); includes 15 minority (4 Black or African American, non-Hispanic/Latino; 1 Asian, non-Hispanic/Latino; 10 Hispanic/Latino). Average age 26. 20 applicants, 70% accepted, 9 enrolled. In 2019, 13 master's, 5 other advanced degrees awarded. *Degree requirements:* For master's, thesis (for some programs), thesis or literature review. *Entrance requirements:* For master's, minimum GPA of 3.0. Additional exam requirements/recommendations for international students: required—TOEFL (minimum score 550 paper-based; 80 iBT), IELTS (minimum score 6.5). *Application deadline:* For fall admission, 8/1 priority date for domestic students, 5/1 priority date for international students; for spring admission, 1/1 priority date for domestic students, 9/1 priority date for international students. Applications are processed on a rolling basis. Electronic applications accepted. *Financial support:* In 2019–20, 17 students received support. Scholarships/grants and unspecified assistantships available. Financial award application deadline: 4/15; financial award applicants required to submit FAFSA. *Unit head:* Marcus Aldredge, PhD, Chair, 914-633-2594, E-mail: maldredge@iona.edu. *Application contact:* Christopher Kash, Assistant Director of Graduate Admissions, 914-633-2403, Fax: 914-633-2277, E-mail: ckash@iona.edu.
Website: http://www.iona.edu/Academics/School-of-Arts-Science/Departments/Criminal-Justice/Graduate-Programs.aspx

James Madison University, The Graduate School, College of Integrated Science and Engineering, Program in Computer Science, Harrisonburg, VA 22807. Offers digital forensics (MS); information security (MS). *Program availability:* Online learning. *Students:* 3 full-time (1 woman), 55 part-time (11 women); includes 14 minority (8 Black or African American, non-Hispanic/Latino; 3 Asian, non-Hispanic/Latino; 3 Hispanic/Latino), 3 international. Average age 30. In 2019, 2 master's awarded. Application fee: $60. Electronic applications accepted. *Financial support:* In 2019–20, 2 students received support. Fellowships, Federal Work-Study, and assistantships (averaging $7911) available. Financial award application deadline: 3/1; financial award applicants required to submit FAFSA. *Unit head:* Dr. Sharon J. Simmons, Department Head, 540-568-4196, E-mail: simmonsj@jmu.edu. *Application contact:* Lynette D. Michael, Director of Graduate Admissions, 540-568-6131 Ext. 6395, Fax: 540-568-7860, E-mail: michaeld@jmu.edu.
Website: http://www.jmu.edu/cs/

Johns Hopkins University, Engineering Program for Professionals, Part-time Program in Cybersecurity, Baltimore, MD 21218. Offers MS, Post-Master's Certificate. *Program availability:* Part-time, evening/weekend, 100% online, blended/hybrid learning. *Entrance requirements:* Additional exam requirements/recommendations for international students: required—TOEFL (minimum score 600 paper-based; 100 iBT). Electronic applications accepted.

Johns Hopkins University, G. W. C. Whiting School of Engineering, Master of Science in Security Informatics Program, Baltimore, MD 21218. Offers MSSI. *Degree requirements:* For master's, 10 courses, capstone project. *Entrance requirements:* For master's, GRE, minimum GPA of 3.0, 2 letters of recommendation, statement of purpose, transcripts. Additional exam requirements/recommendations for international students: required—TOEFL (minimum score 600 paper-based, 100 iBT) or IELTS (7). Electronic applications accepted.

Johnson & Wales University, Graduate Studies, MBA Program, Providence, RI 02903-3703. Offers accounting (MBA); business administration (MBA); finance (MBA); global fashion merchandising and management (MBA); hospitality (MBA); human resource management (MBA); information security/assurance (MBA); information technology (MBA); nonprofit management (MBA); operations and supply chain management (MBA); organizational leadership (MBA); organizational psychology (MBA); sport leadership (MBA). *Program availability:* Part-time, online learning. *Entrance requirements:* For master's, minimum GPA of 2.75. Additional exam requirements/recommendations for international students: required—TOEFL (minimum score 550 paper-based); recommended—IELTS, TWE.

Johnson & Wales University, Graduate Studies, MS Program in Information Security/ Assurance, Providence, RI 02903-3703. Offers MS. *Program availability:* Online learning.

Keiser University, MS in Information Security Program, Fort Lauderdale, FL 33309. Offers MS.

Kennesaw State University, College of Computing and Software Engineering, Program in Information Technology, Kennesaw, GA 30144. Offers data management and analytics (Graduate Certificate); health information technology (Postbaccalaureate Certificate); information technology (MSIT); information technology foundations (Postbaccalaureate Certificate); information technology security (Graduate Certificate). *Program availability:* Part-time, evening/weekend, blended/hybrid learning. *Students:* 73 full-time (38 women), 142 part-time (52 women); includes 101 minority (56 Black or African American, non-Hispanic/Latino; 31 Asian, non-Hispanic/Latino; 10 Hispanic/ Latino; 4 Two or more races, non-Hispanic/Latino), 37 international. Average age 32. 52 applicants, 85% accepted, 34 enrolled. In 2019, 95 master's awarded. *Degree requirements:* For master's, thesis optional. *Entrance requirements:* For master's, minimum GPA of 2.75; for other advanced degree, bachelor's degree. Additional exam requirements/recommendations for international students: required—TOEFL (minimum score 80 iBT), IELTS (minimum score 6.5). *Application deadline:* For fall admission, 7/1 priority date for domestic students, 5/1 priority date for international students; for spring admission, 11/1 priority date for domestic students, 9/1 priority date for international students; for summer admission, 4/1 priority date for domestic students, 3/1 priority date for international students. Applications are processed on a rolling basis. Application fee: $60. Electronic applications accepted. *Expenses: Tuition, area resident:* Full-time $7104; part-time $296 per credit hour. Tuition, state resident: full-time $7104; part-time $296 per credit hour. Tuition, nonresident: full-time $25,584; part-time $1066 per credit hour. *International tuition:* $25,584 full-time. *Required fees:* $2006; $1706 per unit. $853 per semester. *Financial support:* Applicants required to submit FAFSA. *Application contact:* Admission Counselor, 470-578-4377, Fax: 470-578-9172, E-mail: ksugrad@kennesaw.edu.
Website: http://ccse.kennesaw.edu/it/

Kent State University, College of Communication and Information, School of Emerging Media and Technology, Kent, OH 44242-0001. Offers digital sciences (MDS), including data sciences; digital systems management (MDS); digital systems software development (MDS); digital systems telecommunication network (MDS); digital systems training technology (MDS); enterprise architecture (MDS). *Program availability:* Part-time, 100% online. *Faculty:* 1 (woman) full-time, 5 part-time/adjunct (2 women). *Students:* 7 full-time (5 women), 20 part-time (4 women); includes 5 minority (1 Black or African American, non-Hispanic/Latino; 1 Asian, non-Hispanic/Latino; 1 Hispanic/Latino; 2 Two or more races, non-Hispanic/Latino), 6 international. Average age 35. 35 applicants, 77% accepted, 8 enrolled. In 2019, 35 master's awarded. *Degree requirements:* For master's, thesis, capstone or thesis. *Entrance requirements:* For master's, GRE, minimum GPA of 3.0, transcripts, goal statement, resume, 3 letters of recommendation. may have GRE waived if applicant has 36 months of relevant work experience. Additional exam requirements/recommendations for international students: required—TOEFL (minimum score 79 iBT), IELTS (minimum score 6.5), PTE (minimum score 58), Michigan English Language Assessment Battery (minimum score 77). *Application deadline:* For fall admission, 7/1 for domestic students, 5/15 for international students; for spring admission, 11/15 for domestic students, 10/1 for international students; for summer admission, 4/15 for domestic students, 3/15 for international students. Applications are processed on a rolling basis. Application fee: $45 ($70 for international students). Electronic applications accepted. *Financial support:* Career-related internships or fieldwork and scholarships/grants available. *Unit head:* Dr. Amy Reynolds, Ph.D., Dean, 330-672-2950, E-mail: areyno24@kent.edu. *Application contact:* Tang Tang, Professor/Graduate Coordinator, 330-672-1132, E-mail: ttang2@kent.edu.
Website: http://www.kent.edu/emat

Lawrence Technological University, College of Management, Southfield, MI 48075-1058. Offers business administration (MBA, DBA), including business analytics (MBA, MS), cybersecurity (MBA, MS), finance (MBA), information systems (MBA), information technology (MBA), marketing (MBA), project management (MBA, MS); cybersecurity (Graduate Certificate); health IT management (Graduate Certificate); information assurance management (Graduate Certificate); information systems (MS), including enterprise resource planning, enterprise security management, project management (MBA, MS); information technology (MS, DM), including business analytics (MBA, MS), cybersecurity (MBA, MS), information assurance (MS), project management (MBA, MS); management (PhD); nonprofit management and leadership (Graduate Certificate); operations management (MS), including manufacturing operations, service operations; project management (Graduate Certificate). *Accreditation:* ACBSP. *Program availability:* Part-time, evening/weekend, 100% online. *Faculty:* 9 full-time (3 women), 12 part-time/ adjunct (3 women). *Students:* 5 full-time (1 woman), 226 part-time (92 women); includes 51 minority (28 Black or African American, non-Hispanic/Latino; 1 American Indian or Alaska Native, non-Hispanic/Latino; 11 Asian, non-Hispanic/Latino; 6 Hispanic/Latino; 1 Native Hawaiian or other Pacific Islander, non-Hispanic/Latino; 4 Two or more races, non-Hispanic/Latino), 45 international. Average age 33. 123 applicants, 58% accepted, 49 enrolled. In 2019, 96 master's, 3 doctorates, 9 other advanced degrees awarded. Terminal master's awarded for partial completion of doctoral program. *Degree requirements:* For master's, thesis (for some programs); for doctorate, comprehensive exam, thesis/dissertation. *Entrance requirements:* Additional exam requirements/ recommendations for international students: required—TOEFL (minimum score 550 paper-based; 79 iBT), IELTS (minimum score 6.5). *Application deadline:* For fall admission, 5/24 for international students; for spring admission, 10/13 for international students; for summer admission, 2/18 for international students. Applications are processed on a rolling basis. Application fee: $50. Electronic applications accepted. *Expenses: Tuition:* Full-time $16,618; part-time $8309 per year. *Required fees:* $600; $600. *Financial support:* In 2019–20, 25 students received support, including 8 research assistantships with partial tuition reimbursements available (averaging $3,360 per year); career-related internships or fieldwork, unspecified assistantships, and corporate tuition incentives also available. Financial award application deadline: 4/1; financial award applicants required to submit FAFSA. *Unit head:* Dr. Bahman Mirshab, Dean, 248-204-3050, E-mail: mgtdean@ltu.edu. *Application contact:* Jane Rohrback, Director of Admissions, 248-204-3160, Fax: 248-204-2228, E-mail: admissions@ltu.edu.
Website: http://www.ltu.edu/management/index.asp

Lewis University, College of Aviation, Science and Technology, Program in Computer Science, Romeoville, IL 60446. Offers cyber security (MS); intelligent systems (MS); software engineering (MS). *Program availability:* Part-time, evening/weekend, 100% online, blended/hybrid learning. *Students:* 32 full-time (11 women), 92 part-time (23 women); includes 36 minority (9 Black or African American, non-Hispanic/Latino; 11 Asian, non-Hispanic/Latino; 11 Hispanic/Latino; 1 Native Hawaiian or other Pacific Islander, non-Hispanic/Latino; 4 Two or more races, non-Hispanic/Latino), 13 international. Average age 32. *Entrance requirements:* For master's, bachelor's degree; minimum undergraduate GPA of 3.0; resume; statement of purpose; two letters of recommendation; undergraduate coursework in discrete mathematics, programming or algorithms. Additional exam requirements/recommendations for international students: required—TOEFL (minimum score 550 paper-based; 79 iBT), IELTS (minimum score 6). *Application deadline:* For fall admission, 5/1 for international students; for winter admission, 11/15 for international students. Applications are processed on a rolling basis. Application fee: $40. Electronic applications accepted. *Financial support:* Federal Work-Study and unspecified assistantships available. Financial award application deadline: 5/1; financial award applicants required to submit FAFSA. *Unit head:* Dr. Khaled Alzoubi, Program Director. *Application contact:* Sheri Vilcek, Graduate Admissions Counselor, 815-836-5610, E-mail: grad@lewisu.edu.
Website: http://www.lewisu.edu/academics/mscomputerscience/index.htm

Lewis University, College of Business, Program in Information Security - Management, Romeoville, IL 60446. Offers MS. *Students:* 4 full-time (1 woman), 14 part-time (3 women); includes 12 minority (6 Black or African American, non-Hispanic/Latino; 2 Asian, non-Hispanic/Latino; 1 Hispanic/Latino; 3 Two or more races, non-Hispanic/ Latino). Average age 36. *Financial support:* Federal Work-Study and unspecified assistantships available. *Unit head:* Dr. Ryan Butt, Dean. *Application contact:* Linda Campbell, Graduate Admission Counselor, 815-836-5610, E-mail: grad@lewisu.edu.

Liberty University, School of Business, Lynchburg, VA 24515. Offers accounting (MBA, MS), including audit and financial reporting (MS), business (MS), financial services (MS), forensic accounting (MS), leadership (MS), taxation (MS); cyber security (MS); executive leadership (MA); international business (DBA); leadership (DBA); marketing (MBA, MS, DBA), including digital marketing and advertising (MS), project management (MS), public relations (MS), sports marketing and media (MS); project management (MBA, DBA); public relations (MBA). *Program availability:* Part-time, online learning. *Students:* 3,187 full-time (1,641 women), 4,818 part-time (2,180 women); includes 2,429 minority (1,588 Black or African American, non-Hispanic/Latino; 36 American Indian or Alaska Native, non-Hispanic/Latino; 176 Asian, non-Hispanic/Latino; 397 Hispanic/Latino; 21 Native Hawaiian or other Pacific Islander, non-Hispanic/Latino; 211 Two or more races, non-Hispanic/Latino), 171 international. Average age 36. 8,665 applicants, 42% accepted, 1,753 enrolled. In 2019, 2,008 master's, 28 doctorates awarded. *Entrance requirements:* For master's, minimum undergraduate GPA of 3.0, 15 hours of upper-level business courses. Additional exam requirements/recommendations for international students: required—TOEFL (minimum score 600 paper-based; 100 iBT). *Application deadline:* Applications are processed on a rolling basis. Application fee: $50. Electronic applications accepted. *Expenses:* Contact institution. *Financial support:* In 2019–20, 990 students received support. Teaching assistantships and Federal Work-Study available. Financial award applicants required to submit FAFSA. *Unit head:* Dr. Dave Bratt, Dean, 434-592-7321, E-mail: dabrat@liberty.edu. *Application contact:* Jay Bridge, Director of Graduate Admissions, 800-424-9595, Fax: 800-628-7977, E-mail: gradadmissions@liberty.edu.
Website: https://www.liberty.edu/business/

Lindenwood University, Graduate Programs, School of Accelerated Degree Programs, St. Charles, MO 63301-1695. Offers administration (MSA), including management, marketing, project management; business administration (MBA); communications (MA), including digital and multimedia, media management, promotions, training and development; criminal justice and administration (MS); healthcare administration (MS); human resource management (MS); information technology (Certificate); managing information security (MS); managing information technology (MS); managing virtualization and cloud computing (MS); writing (MFA). *Program availability:* Part-time, evening/weekend, 100% online. *Faculty:* 11 full-time (6 women), 66 part-time/adjunct (23 women). *Students:* 408 full-time (262 women), 60 part-time (40 women); includes 149 minority (111 Black or African American, non-Hispanic/ Latino; 2 American Indian or Alaska Native, non-Hispanic/Latino; 2 Asian, non-Hispanic/ Latino; 18 Hispanic/Latino; 1 Native Hawaiian or other Pacific Islander, non-Hispanic/ Latino; 15 Two or more races, non-Hispanic/Latino), 33 international. Average age 39. 268 applicants, 46% accepted, 99 enrolled. In 2019, 347 master's awarded. *Degree requirements:* For master's, thesis (for some programs), minimum cumulative GPA of 3.0; for Certificate, minimum cumulative GPA of 3.0. *Entrance requirements:* For master's, resume, personal statement, official undergraduate transcript, minimum undergraduate cumulative GPA of 3.0. Additional exam requirements/recommendations for international students: required—TOEFL (minimum score 553 paper-based; 81 iBT); recommended—IELTS (minimum score 6.5). *Application deadline:* For fall admission, 9/ 30 priority date for domestic and international students; for winter admission, 1/6 priority date for domestic and international students; for spring admission, 4/6 priority date for domestic and international students; for summer admission, 7/8 priority date for domestic and international students. Applications are processed on a rolling basis. Application fee: $0 ($100 for international students). Electronic applications accepted. *Expenses:* Contact institution. *Financial support:* In 2019–20, 145 students received support. Career-related internships or fieldwork, institutionally sponsored loans, scholarships/grants, tuition waivers (partial), and unspecified assistantships available. Financial award application deadline: 6/30; financial award applicants required to submit FAFSA. *Unit head:* Dr. Gina Ganahl, Dean, Accelerated Degree Programs, 636-949-4501, Fax: 636-949-4505, E-mail: gganahl@lindenwood.edu. *Application contact:* Kara Schilli, Assistant Vice President, University Admissions, 636-949-4349, Fax: 636-949-4109, E-mail: adultadmissions@lindenwood.edu.
Website: https://www.lindenwood.edu/academics/academic-schools/school-of-accelerated-degree-programs/

Lipscomb University, College of Computing and Technology, Nashville, TN 37204-3951. Offers data science (MS, Certificate); information technology (MS, Certificate), including data science (MS), information security (MS), information technology management (MS), software engineering (MS); software engineering (MS, Certificate). *Program availability:* Part-time, evening/weekend. *Degree requirements:* For master's, capstone project. *Entrance requirements:* For master's, GRE, 2 references, transcripts, resume, personal statement. Additional exam requirements/recommendations for international students: required—TOEFL (minimum score 570 paper-based; 80 iBT). Electronic applications accepted. *Expenses:* Contact institution.

London Metropolitan University, Graduate Programs, London, United Kingdom. Offers applied psychology (M Sc); architecture (MA); biomedical science (M Sc); blood science (M Sc); cancer pharmacology (M Sc); computer networking and cyber security (M Sc); computing and information systems (M Sc); conference interpreting (MA); counter-terrorism studies (M Sc); creative, digital and professional writing (MA); crime, violence and prevention (M Sc); criminology (M Sc); curating contemporary art (MA); data analytics (M Sc); digital media (MA); early childhood studies (MA); education (MA, Ed D); financial services law, regulation and compliance (LL M); food science (M Sc); forensic psychology (M Sc); health and social care management and policy (M Sc); human nutrition (M Sc); human resource management (MA); human rights and international conflict (MA); information technology (M Sc); intelligence and security studies (M Sc); international oil, gas and energy law (LL M); international relations (MA); interpreting (MA); learning and teaching in higher education (MA); legal practice (LL M); media and entertainment law (LL M); organizational and consumer psychology (M Sc); psychological therapy (M Sc); psychology of mental health (M Sc); public health (M Sc); public policy and management (MPA); security studies (M Sc); social work (M Sc); spatial planning and urban design (MA); sports therapy (M Sc); supporting older children and young people with dyslexia (MA); teaching languages (MA), including Arabic, English; translation (MA); woman and child abuse (MA).

Long Island University - Riverhead, Graduate Programs, Riverhead, NY 11901. Offers applied behavior analysis (Advanced Certificate); childhood education (MS), including grades 1-6; cybersecurity policy (Advanced Certificate); homeland security management (MS, Advanced Certificate); literacy education (MS); literacy education B-6 (MS); teaching students with disabilities (MS), including grades 1-6; TESOL (Advanced Certificate). *Accreditation:* TEAC. *Program availability:* Part-time. *Entrance requirements:* Additional exam requirements/recommendations for international students: required—TOEFL or IELTS. Electronic applications accepted. *Expenses:* Contact institution.

Louisiana Tech University, Graduate School, College of Business, Ruston, LA 71272. Offers accounting (M Acc, DBA); computer information systems (DBA); finance (MBA, DBA); information assurance (MBA); innovation (MBA); management (DBA); marketing (MBA, DBA). *Accreditation:* AACSB. *Program availability:* Part-time, evening/weekend, 100% online, blended/hybrid learning. *Degree requirements:* For doctorate, thesis/dissertation. *Entrance requirements:* For master's and doctorate, GMAT, transcript with bachelor's degree awarded. Additional exam requirements/recommendations for international students: required—TOEFL (minimum score 550 paper-based; 80 iBT), IELTS (minimum score 6.5). Electronic applications accepted. *Expenses: Tuition, area resident:* Full-time $6592; part-time $400 per credit. Tuition, state resident: full-time $6592; part-time $400 per credit. Tuition, nonresident: full-time $13,333; part-time $681 per credit. *International tuition:* $13,333 full-time. *Required fees:* $3011; $3011 per unit.

Marymount University, School of Business and Technology, Program in Cybersecurity, Arlington, VA 22207-4299. Offers cybersecurity (MS, D Sc), including data science (MS), digital health (MS); cybersecurity with information technology (MS/MS); MS/MS. *Program availability:* Part-time, evening/weekend, 100% online, blended/hybrid learning. *Faculty:* 5 full-time (4 women), 7 part-time/adjunct (0 women). *Students:* 41 full-time (15 women), 108 part-time (35 women); includes 85 minority (40 Black or African American, non-Hispanic/Latino; 27 Asian, non-Hispanic/Latino; 14 Hispanic/Latino; 4 Two or more races, non-Hispanic/Latino), 23 international. Average age 36. 111 applicants, 97% accepted, 50 enrolled. In 2019, 30 master's, 2 other advanced degrees awarded. *Degree requirements:* For master's, thesis, A minimum grade of B- is needed to receive credit for a course in the program. Must maintain a minimum cumulative GPA of 3.0.; for doctorate, thesis/dissertation, Residency requirements (or pass a comprehensive exam), professional paper presentation at a professional event, service commitments in field, dissertation committee formation, and successful defense of dissertation; for Certificate, A minimum grade of B- is needed to receive credit for a course in the program. All coursework must be completed at Marymount University within three years of matriculation. *Entrance requirements:* For master's, resume, certification or demonstrated work experience in computer networking; for doctorate, resume, interview, three writing samples demonstrating research on a topic in technology, research statement and personal statement outlining personal goals and research focuses for the program. Additional exam requirements/recommendations for international students: required—TOEFL (minimum score 600 paper-based; 96 iBT), IELTS (minimum score 6.5), PTE (minimum score 58). *Application deadline:* For fall admission, 7/16 priority date for domestic and international students; for spring admission, 11/16 priority date for domestic and international students; for summer admission, 4/16 priority date for domestic and international students. Applications are processed on a rolling basis. Application fee: $40. Electronic applications accepted. *Expenses:* $1,060 per credit. *Financial support:* In 2019–20, 16 students received support. Research assistantships, teaching assistantships, career-related internships or fieldwork, scholarships/grants, and unspecified assistantships available. Support available to part-time students. Financial award application deadline: 3/1; financial award applicants required to submit FAFSA. *Unit head:* Dr. Diane Murphy, Chair/Director, Information Technology, Management Sciences and Cybersecurity, 703-284-5958, E-mail: diane.murphy@marymount.edu. *Application contact:* Fiona McDonnell, Administrative Assistant, 703-284-5901, E-mail: gadmissi@marymount.edu.
Website: https://www.marymount.edu/Academics/School-of-Business-and-Technology/Graduate-Programs

Marymount University, School of Business and Technology, Program in Information Technology, Arlington, VA 22207-4299. Offers health care informatics (Certificate); information technology (MS, Certificate), including cybersecurity (MS), health care informatics (MS), project management (MS), software engineering (MS); information technology project management and technology leadership (Certificate); information technology with business administration (MS/MBA); information technology with health care management (MS/MS); MS/MBA; MS/MS. *Program availability:* Part-time, evening/weekend. *Faculty:* 5 full-time (3 women), 7 part-time/adjunct (2 women). *Students:* 46 full-time (22 women), 30 part-time (15 women); includes 30 minority (16 Black or African American, non-Hispanic/Latino; 7 Asian, non-Hispanic/Latino; 7 Hispanic/Latino), 27 international. Average age 31. 61 applicants, 95% accepted, 27 enrolled. In 2019, 29 master's, 2 other advanced degrees awarded. *Degree requirements:* For master's, thesis or alternative, A minimum grade of B- is needed to receive credit for a course in the program. Must maintain a minimum cumulative GPA of 3.0. *Entrance requirements:* For master's, Resume, bachelor's degree in computer-related field or degree in another subject with a certificate in a computer-related field or related work experience. Software Engineering Track: bachelor's degree in Computer Science or work in software development. Project Mgmt/Tech Leadership Track: minimum 2 years of IT experience. Additional exam requirements/recommendations for international students: required—TOEFL (minimum score 600 paper-based; 96 iBT), IELTS (minimum score 6.5), PTE (minimum score 58). *Application deadline:* For fall admission, 7/16 priority date for domestic and international students; for spring admission, 11/16 priority date for domestic and international students; for summer admission, 4/16 priority date for domestic and international students. Applications are processed on a rolling basis.

Application fee: $40. Electronic applications accepted. *Expenses:* $1,060 per credit. *Financial support:* In 2019–20, 12 students received support. Research assistantships, teaching assistantships, career-related internships or fieldwork, scholarships/grants, and unspecified assistantships available. Support available to part-time students. Financial award application deadline: 3/1; financial award applicants required to submit FAFSA. *Unit head:* Dr. Diane Murphy, Chair/Director, Information Technology, Management Sciences and Cybersecurity, 703-284-5958, E-mail: diane.murphy@marymount.edu. *Application contact:* Fiona McDonnell, Administrative Assistant, 703-284-5901, E-mail: gadmissi@marymount.edu.
Website: https://www.marymount.edu/Academics/School-of-Business-and-Technology/Graduate-Programs/Information-Technology-(M-S-)

Maryville University of Saint Louis, The John E. Simon School of Business, St. Louis, MO 63141-7299. Offers accounting (MBA, MS, Certificate); business studies (Certificate); cybersecurity (MBA, MS, Certificate); financial services (MBA, Certificate); health administration (MBA); healthcare administration (Certificate); human resource management (MBA); human resources management (Certificate); information technology (MBA); information technology management (Certificate); management (MBA, Certificate); management and leadership (MA); marketing (MBA, Certificate); project management (MBA, Certificate); sport business management (MBA); supply chain management (Certificate); supply chain management/logistics (MBA). *Accreditation:* ACBSP. *Program availability:* Part-time, 100% online, blended/hybrid learning. *Faculty:* 3 full-time (0 women), 107 part-time/adjunct (28 women). *Students:* 315 full-time (155 women), 738 part-time (344 women); includes 329 minority (186 Black or African American, non-Hispanic/Latino; 5 American Indian or Alaska Native, non-Hispanic/Latino; 48 Asian, non-Hispanic/Latino; 60 Hispanic/Latino; 30 Two or more races, non-Hispanic/Latino), 38 international. Average age 34. In 2019, 388 master's awarded. *Degree requirements:* For master's, capstone course (for MBA). *Entrance requirements:* Additional exam requirements/recommendations for international students: required—TOEFL (minimum score 563 paper-based; 85 iBT). *Application deadline:* Applications are processed on a rolling basis. Electronic applications accepted. *Expenses:* Contact institution. *Financial support:* Career-related internships or fieldwork, Federal Work-Study, tuition waivers (partial), and campus employment available. Financial award application deadline: 4/1; financial award applicants required to submit FAFSA. *Unit head:* Tammy Gocial, Associate Academic Vice President/Interim Dean, 314-529-9401, Fax: 314-529-9975, E-mail: tgocial@maryville.edu. *Application contact:* Chris Gourdine, Assistant Dean Business Administration, 314-529-6861, Fax: 314-529-9975, E-mail: cgourdine@maryville.edu.
Website: http://www.maryville.edu/bu/business-administration-masters/

Marywood University, Academic Affairs, Munley College of Liberal Arts and Sciences, Department of Mathematics and Computer Science, Scranton, PA 18509-1598. Offers information security (MS).

Mercy College, School of Liberal Arts, Program in Cybersecurity, Dobbs Ferry, NY 10522-1189. Offers MS. *Program availability:* Part-time, evening/weekend, 100% online, blended/hybrid learning. *Students:* 16 full-time (3 women), 25 part-time (3 women); includes 25 minority (11 Black or African American, non-Hispanic/Latino; 4 Asian, non-Hispanic/Latino; 9 Hispanic/Latino; 1 Two or more races, non-Hispanic/Latino), 2 international. Average age 30. 32 applicants, 56% accepted, 14 enrolled. In 2019, 16 master's awarded. *Degree requirements:* For master's, thesis optional, thesis or capstone project required. *Entrance requirements:* For master's, transcript(s); letter of recommendation; CV; plan of study and research; interview may be required. Additional exam requirements/recommendations for international students: required—TOEFL (minimum score 80 iBT), IELTS (minimum score 6.5). *Application deadline:* Applications are processed on a rolling basis. Application fee: $40. Electronic applications accepted. *Expenses:* Contact institution. *Financial support:* Career-related internships or fieldwork, Federal Work-Study, scholarships/grants, and unspecified assistantships available. Support available to part-time students. Financial award applicants required to submit FAFSA. *Unit head:* Dr. Peter West, Dean, School of Liberal Arts, 914-674-3033, E-mail: pwest@mercy.edu. *Application contact:* Allison Gurdineer, Executive Director of Admissions, 877-637-2946, Fax: 914-674-7382, E-mail: admissions@mercy.edu.
Website: https://www.mercy.edu/degrees-programs/ms-cybersecurity

Mercyhurst University, Graduate Studies, Program in Data Science, Erie, PA 16546. Offers MS. Electronic applications accepted.

Metropolitan State University, College of Management, St. Paul, MN 55106-5000. Offers business administration (MBA, DBA); business analytics (Graduate Certificate); database administration (Graduate Certificate); global supply chain management (Graduate Certificate); information assurance security (Graduate Certificate); management information systems (MMIS); MIS generalist (Graduate Certificate); MIS systems analysis and design (Graduate Certificate); project management (Graduate Certificate). *Program availability:* Part-time, evening/weekend. *Degree requirements:* For master's, thesis optional, computer language (MMIS). *Entrance requirements:* For master's, GMAT (for MBA), resume. Additional exam requirements/recommendations for international students: required—TOEFL (minimum score 550 paper-based). Electronic applications accepted.

Middle Georgia State University, Office of Graduate Studies, Macon, GA 31206. Offers adult/gerontology acute care nurse practitioner (MSN); information technology (MS), including health informatics, information security and digital forensics, software development. *Entrance requirements:* For master's, GRE. Additional exam requirements/recommendations for international students: required—TOEFL (minimum score 523 paper-based; 69 iBT). *Expenses:* Contact institution.

Mississippi College, Graduate School, College of Arts and Sciences, School of Science and Mathematics, Department of Engineering, Computer Science, and Physics, Clinton, MS 39058. Offers computer science (M Ed, MS); cybersecurity and information assurance (MS). *Program availability:* Part-time. *Degree requirements:* For master's, comprehensive exam, thesis or alternative. *Entrance requirements:* For master's, GRE. Additional exam requirements/recommendations for international students: recommended—TOEFL, IELTS.

Missouri Western State University, CyberSecurity, St. Joseph, MO 64507-2294. Offers MS. *Program availability:* Part-time. *Students:* 4 full-time (1 woman), 1 part-time (0 women); includes 1 minority (Asian, non-Hispanic/Latino), 4 international. Average age 26. 11 applicants, 9% accepted, 1 enrolled. In 2019, 6 master's awarded. *Entrance requirements:* For master's, Completion of an undergraduate degree in computer science, computer information system, engineering or a closely related discipline from an accredited undergraduate institution; minimum GPA of 3.0. Additional exam requirements/recommendations for international students: recommended—TOEFL (minimum score 79 iBT), IELTS (minimum score 6). *Application deadline:* For fall admission, 7/15 for domestic and international students; for spring admission, 11/1 for domestic and international students; for summer admission, 4/29 for domestic and international students. Applications are processed on a rolling basis. Application fee: $45 ($50 for international students). Electronic applications accepted. *Expenses:* Tuition, state resident: full-time $6469.02; part-time $359.39 per credit hour. Tuition, nonresident: full-time $11,581; part-time $643.39 per credit hour. *Required fees:* $345.20; $99.10 per credit hour. Tuition and fees vary according to course load,

campus/location and program. *Financial support:* Scholarships/grants and unspecified assistantships available. Support available to part-time students. *Unit head:* Dr. Yipkei Kwok, Assistant Professor, 816-271-4523, E-mail: ykwok@missouriwestern.edu. *Application contact:* Dr. Susan Bashinski, Dean of the Graduate School, 816-271-4394, Fax: 816-271-4525, E-mail: graduate@missouriwestern.edu.
Website: https://www.missouriwestern.edu/csmp/cybersecurity/

National University, School of Engineering and Computing, La Jolla, CA 92037-1011. Offers computer science (MS), including advanced computing; cyber security and information assurance (MS); data analytics (MS); electrical engineering (MS); engineering management (MS); information technology management (MS); management information systems (MS); sustainability management (MS). *Program availability:* Part-time, evening/weekend, 100% online, blended/hybrid learning. *Degree requirements:* For master's, thesis (for some programs). *Entrance requirements:* For master's, interview, minimum GPA of 2.5. Additional exam requirements/recommendations for international students: required—TOEFL (minimum score 550 paper-based; 79 iBT), IELTS (minimum score 6). Electronic applications accepted. *Expenses: Tuition:* Full-time $442; part-time $442 per unit.

Naval Postgraduate School, Departments and Academic Groups, Department of Computer Science, Monterey, CA 93943. Offers computer science (MS, PhD); identity management and cyber security (MA); modeling of virtual environments and simulations (MS, PhD); software engineering (MS, PhD). *Program availability:* Part-time, online learning. *Degree requirements:* For master's, thesis; for doctorate, thesis/dissertation.

New Jersey City University, College of Professional Studies, Program in National Security Studies, Jersey City, NJ 07305-1597. Offers civil security leadership (D Sc); national security studies (MS, Certificate). *Program availability:* Part-time. *Entrance requirements:* Additional exam requirements/recommendations for international students: required—TOEFL (minimum score 79 iBT).

New Jersey Institute of Technology, Ying Wu College of Computing, Newark, NJ 07102. Offers big data management and mining (Certificate); business and information systems (Certificate); computer science (PhD); computing and business (MS); data mining (Certificate); data science (MS); information security (Certificate); information systems (PhD); information technology administration and security (MS); IT administration (Certificate); network security and information assurance (Certificate); software engineering (MS), including information systems; software engineering analysis/design (Certificate); Web systems development (Certificate). *Program availability:* Part-time, evening/weekend. *Faculty:* 78 full-time (16 women), 63 part-time/adjunct (10 women). *Students:* 668 full-time (210 women), 290 part-time (81 women); includes 277 minority (46 Black or African American, non-Hispanic/Latino; 1 American Indian or Alaska Native, non-Hispanic/Latino; 161 Asian, non-Hispanic/Latino; 53 Hispanic/Latino; 16 Two or more races, non-Hispanic/Latino), 565 international. Average age 27. 2,671 applicants, 62% accepted, 360 enrolled. In 2019, 407 master's, 5 doctorates, 12 other advanced degrees awarded. Terminal master's awarded for partial completion of doctoral program. *Degree requirements:* For master's, thesis optional; for doctorate, thesis/dissertation. *Entrance requirements:* For master's, GRE General Test; for doctorate, GRE General Test, minimum graduate GPA of 3.5. Additional exam requirements/recommendations for international students: required—TOEFL (minimum score 550 paper-based; 79 iBT), IELTS (minimum score 6.5). *Application deadline:* For fall admission, 6/1 priority date for domestic students, 5/1 priority date for international students; for spring admission, 11/15 priority date for domestic and international students. Applications are processed on a rolling basis. Application fee: $75. Electronic applications accepted. *Expenses:* $23,828 per year (in-state), $33,744 per year (out-of-state). *Financial support:* In 2019–20, 383 students received support, including 8 fellowships with full tuition reimbursements available, 34 research assistantships with full tuition reimbursements available (averaging $24,000 per year), 57 teaching assistantships with full tuition reimbursements available (averaging $24,000 per year); career-related internships or fieldwork, Federal Work-Study, scholarships/grants, and unspecified assistantships also available. Financial award application deadline: 1/15. *Unit head:* Dr. Craig Gotsman, Dean, 973-596-3366, Fax: 973-596-5777, E-mail: craig.gotsman@njit.edu. *Application contact:* Stephen Eck, Executive Director of University Admissions, 973-596-3300, Fax: 973-596-3461, E-mail: admissions@njit.edu.
Website: http://computing.njit.edu/

New York Institute of Technology, College of Engineering and Computing Sciences, Department of Computer Science, Old Westbury, NY 11568. Offers computer science (MS); information, network, and computer security (MS). *Program availability:* Part-time. *Faculty:* 13 full-time (6 women), 24 part-time/adjunct (2 women). *Students:* 173 full-time (61 women), 53 part-time (11 women); includes 69 minority (13 Black or African American, non-Hispanic/Latino; 40 Asian, non-Hispanic/Latino; 10 Hispanic/Latino; 1 Native Hawaiian or other Pacific Islander, non-Hispanic/Latino; 5 Two or more races, non-Hispanic/Latino), 135 international. Average age 26. 1,292 applicants, 51% accepted, 96 enrolled. In 2019, 184 master's awarded. *Degree requirements:* For master's, thesis or alternative. *Entrance requirements:* For master's, Graduates of foreign universities are required to take the GRE and submit their scores. Applicants with a GPA below 2.85 may, at the discretion of the dean, be asked to take the GRE or other diagnostic tests, bachelor's degree in computer science, engineering, management, math, information technology, or related area; minimum undergraduate GPA of 2.85; transcripts from all schools attended and proof of degree. Additional exam requirements/recommendations for international students: required—TOEFL (minimum score 79 iBT), IELTS (minimum score 6), PTE (minimum score 53), Duolingo English Test. *Application deadline:* Applications are processed on a rolling basis. Application fee: $50. Electronic applications accepted. *Expenses: Tuition:* Full-time $23,760; part-time $1320 per credit. *Required fees:* $260; $220 per unit. Full-time tuition and fees vary according to degree level and program. Part-time tuition and fees vary according to course load and program. *Financial support:* In 2019–20, 143 students received support. Fellowships, research assistantships, teaching assistantships, Federal Work-Study, scholarships/grants, and unspecified assistantships available. Support available to part-time students. Financial award application deadline: 2/15; financial award applicants required to submit FAFSA. *Unit head:* Dr. Frank Lee, Department Chair, 516-686-7456, Fax: 516-686-7439, E-mail: fli@nyit.edu. *Application contact:* Alice Dolitsky, Director, Graduate Admissions, 800-345-6948, E-mail: grad@nyit.edu.
Website: https://www.nyit.edu/departments/computer_science

New York University, Tandon School of Engineering, Department of Computer Science and Engineering, Major in Cyber Security, New York, NY 10012-1019. Offers cyber security (MS). *Program availability:* Online learning. *Degree requirements:* For master's, comprehensive exam (for some programs), thesis (for some programs). *Entrance requirements:* Additional exam requirements/recommendations for international students: required—TOEFL (minimum score 550 paper-based; 90 iBT); recommended—IELTS (minimum score 7). Electronic applications accepted.

New York University, Tandon School of Engineering, Department of Computer Science and Engineering, Major in Cybersecurity Risk and Strategy, New York, NY 10012-1019. Offers MS. *Program availability:* Part-time, online learning. *Degree requirements:* For master's, comprehensive exam (for some programs), thesis (for some programs). *Entrance requirements:* Additional exam requirements/recommendations for international students: required—TOEFL (minimum score 550 paper-based; 90 iBT); recommended—IELTS (minimum score 7). Electronic applications accepted.

Niagara University, Graduate Division of Arts and Sciences, Program in Information Security and Digital Forensics, Niagara University, NY 14109. Offers MS. *Program availability:* Part-time. *Entrance requirements:* For master's, GRE. Additional exam requirements/recommendations for international students: required—TOEFL (minimum score 550 paper-based; 79 iBT), IELTS (minimum score 6).

Northcentral University, Graduate Studies, San Diego, CA 92106. Offers business (MBA, DBA, PhD, Postbaccalaureate Certificate); education (M Ed, Ed D, PhD, Ed S, Post-Master's Certificate, Postbaccalaureate Certificate); marriage and family therapy (MA, DMFT, PhD, Post-Master's Certificate, Postbaccalaureate Certificate); psychology (MA, PhD, Post-Master's Certificate, Postbaccalaureate Certificate); technology (MS, PhD), including computer science, cybersecurity (MS), data science, technology and innovation management (PhD). *Program availability:* Part-time, evening/weekend, online only, 100% online. *Degree requirements:* For doctorate, comprehensive exam, thesis/dissertation. *Entrance requirements:* For master's, bachelor's degree from regionally- or nationally-accredited institution, current resume or curriculum vitae, statement of intent, interview, and background check (for marriage and family therapy); for doctorate, post-baccalaureate master's degree and/or doctoral degree from nationally- or regionally-accredited academic institution; for other advanced degree, bachelor's-level or higher degree from accredited institution or university (for Post-Baccalaureate Certificate); master's and/or doctoral degree from regionally- or nationally-accredited academic institution (for Post-Master's Certificate). Additional exam requirements/recommendations for international students: required—TOEFL (minimum score 550 paper-based; 79 iBT), IELTS (minimum score 6.5), PTE (minimum score 53). Electronic applications accepted. *Expenses: Tuition:* Part-time $1053 per credit. *Required fees:* $95 per course. Full-time tuition and fees vary according to degree level and program.

Northeastern University, College of Engineering, Boston, MA 02115-5096. Offers bioengineering (MS, PhD); chemical engineering (MS, PhD); civil engineering (MS, PhD); computer engineering (PhD); computer systems engineering (MS); electrical and computer engineering (MS); electrical and computer engineering leadership (MS); electrical engineering (PhD); energy systems (MS); engineering and public policy (MS); engineering management (MS, Certificate); environmental engineering (MS); industrial engineering (MS, PhD); information assurance (PhD); information systems (MS); interdisciplinary engineering (PhD); mechanical engineering (PhD); operations research (MS); telecommunication systems management (MS). *Program availability:* Part-time, online learning. Electronic applications accepted. *Expenses:* Contact institution.

Northern Kentucky University, Office of Graduate Programs, College of Informatics, Department of Business Informatics, Highland Heights, KY 41099. Offers business informatics (MS, Certificate); corporate information security (Certificate); enterprise resource planning (Certificate). *Program availability:* Part-time, evening/weekend. *Entrance requirements:* For master's, GRE or GMAT. Additional exam requirements/recommendations for international students: required—TOEFL (minimum score 79 iBT); recommended—IELTS (minimum score 6.5). Electronic applications accepted.

Northwestern University, School of Professional Studies, Program in Information Systems, Evanston, IL 60208. Offers analytics and business intelligence (MS); database and Internet technologies (MS); information systems (MS); information systems management (MS); information systems security (MS); medical informatics (MS); software project management and development (MS). *Program availability:* Part-time, evening/weekend.

Norwich University, College of Graduate and Continuing Studies, Master of Science in Information Security and Assurance Program, Northfield, VT 05663. Offers information security and assurance (MS), including computer forensic investigation/incident response team management, critical infrastructure protection and cyber crime, cyber law and international perspectives on cyberspace, project management, vulnerability management. *Program availability:* Evening/weekend, online only, mostly all online with a week-long residency requirement. *Entrance requirements:* For master's, minimum undergraduate GPA of 2.75. Additional exam requirements/recommendations for international students: required—TOEFL (minimum score 550 paper-based; 80 iBT), IELTS (minimum score 6.5). Electronic applications accepted. *Expenses:* Contact institution.

Nova Southeastern University, College of Engineering and Computing, Fort Lauderdale, FL 33314-7796. Offers computer science (MS, PhD); information assurance (PhD); information assurance and cybersecurity (MS); information systems (PhD); information technology (MS); management information systems (MS). *Program availability:* Part-time, evening/weekend, blended/hybrid learning. *Faculty:* 18 full-time (6 women), 20 part-time/adjunct (4 women). *Students:* 206 full-time (67 women), 244 part-time (71 women); includes 229 minority (93 Black or African American, non-Hispanic/Latino; 1 American Indian or Alaska Native, non-Hispanic/Latino; 36 Asian, non-Hispanic/Latino; 84 Hispanic/Latino; 1 Native Hawaiian or other Pacific Islander, non-Hispanic/Latino; 14 Two or more races, non-Hispanic/Latino), 80 international. Average age 40. 212 applicants, 58% accepted, 63 enrolled. In 2019, 142 master's, 41 doctorates awarded. Terminal master's awarded for partial completion of doctoral program. *Degree requirements:* For master's, thesis optional; for doctorate, thesis/dissertation. *Entrance requirements:* For master's, minimum undergraduate GPA of 2.5; for doctorate, master's degree, minimum graduate GPA of 3.25. Additional exam requirements/recommendations for international students: required—TOEFL (minimum score 80 iBT), IELTS (minimum score 6), PTE (minimum score 54). *Application deadline:* Applications are processed on a rolling basis. Application fee: $50. Electronic applications accepted. *Expenses:* Contact institution. *Financial support:* Federal Work-Study, scholarships/grants, and corporate financial support available. Financial award application deadline: 4/15; financial award applicants required to submit FAFSA. *Unit head:* Dr. Meline Kevorkian, Associate Provost, Dean of Computing and Engineering, 954-262-2063, Fax: 954-262-2752, E-mail: melinek@nova.edu. *Application contact:* Nancy Azoulay, Director, Admissions, 954-262-2026, Fax: 954-262-2752, E-mail: azoulayn@nova.edu.
Website: http://scis.nova.edu

Our Lady of the Lake University, School of Business and Leadership, Program in Information Systems and Security, San Antonio, TX 78207-4689. Offers MS. *Program availability:* Part-time, online only, 100% online. *Entrance requirements:* For master's, GRE or GMAT, official transcripts showing baccalaureate degree from regionally-accredited institution in technical discipline and minimum GPA of 3.0 for cumulative undergraduate work or 3.2 in the major field (technical discipline) of study. Additional exam requirements/recommendations for international students: required—TOEFL. Electronic applications accepted. Application fee is waived when completed online.

Pace University, Seidenberg School of Computer Science and Information Systems, New York, NY 10038. Offers chief information security officer (APC); computer science (MS, PhD); enterprise analytics (MS); information and communication technology strategy and innovation (APC); information systems (MS, APC); information technology (MS); professional studies in computing (DPS); secure software and information engineering (APC); security and information assurance (Certificate); software development and engineering (MS, Certificate); telecommunications systems and networks (MS, Certificate). *Program availability:* Part-time, evening/weekend, online only, 100% online, blended/hybrid learning. *Degree requirements:* For master's, thesis or alternative, capstone course; for doctorate, comprehensive exam (for some programs), thesis/dissertation. *Entrance requirements:* Additional exam requirements/recommendations for international students: required—TOEFL (minimum score 78 iBT), IELTS (minimum score 6.5) or PTE (minimum score 52). Electronic applications accepted. *Expenses:* Contact institution.

Penn State Great Valley, Graduate Studies, Management Division, Malvern, PA 19355-1488. Offers business administration (MBA); cyber security (Certificate); data analytics (MPS, MS, Certificate); distributed energy and grid modernization (Certificate); finance (M Fin); health sector management (Certificate); human resource management (Certificate); information science (MSIS); leadership development (MLD); new ventures and entrepreneurship (Certificate); sustainable management practices (Certificate). *Accreditation:* AACSB.

Portland State University, Graduate Studies, Maseeh College of Engineering and Computer Science, Department of Computer Science, Portland, OR 97207-0751. Offers computer science (MS, PhD); computer security (Certificate). *Program availability:* Part-time. *Faculty:* 28 full-time (9 women), 5 part-time/adjunct (0 women). *Students:* 120 full-time (39 women), 98 part-time (26 women); includes 45 minority (28 Asian, non-Hispanic/Latino; 9 Hispanic/Latino; 1 Native Hawaiian or other Pacific Islander, non-Hispanic/Latino; 7 Two or more races, non-Hispanic/Latino), 72 international. Average age 31. 186 applicants, 55% accepted, 52 enrolled. In 2019, 82 master's, 1 doctorate awarded. *Degree requirements:* For master's, thesis or alternative; for doctorate, comprehensive exam, thesis/dissertation. *Entrance requirements:* For master's, GRE (minimum scores 60th percentile in Quantitative and 25th percentile in Verbal), BS in engineering field, science or closely-related area; minimum GPA of 3.0 or equivalent; 2 letters of recommendation; personal statement; for doctorate, GRE (minimum scores 60th percentile in Quantitative and 25th percentile in Verbal), MS in computer science or allied field. Additional exam requirements/recommendations for international students: required—TOEFL (minimum score 550 paper-based). *Application deadline:* For fall admission, 3/1 for domestic and international students; for winter admission, 5/15 for domestic and international students; for spring admission, 11/1 for domestic students, 10/1 for international students. Applications are processed on a rolling basis. Application fee: $65. *Expenses:* Contact institution. *Financial support:* In 2019–20, 37 students received support, including 8 research assistantships with full and partial tuition reimbursements available (averaging $20,325 per year), 26 teaching assistantships with full and partial tuition reimbursements available (averaging $14,081 per year); career-related internships or fieldwork, Federal Work-Study, scholarships/grants, tuition waivers (full and partial), and unspecified assistantships also available. Support available to part-time students. Financial award application deadline: 3/1; financial award applicants required to submit FAFSA. *Unit head:* Dr. Mark Jones, Chair, 503-725-3206, Fax: 503-725-3211, E-mail: mpj@pdx.edu. *Application contact:* Krys Sarreal, Department Manager, 503-725-4255, Fax: 503-725-3211, E-mail: sarreal@pdx.edu.
Website: http://www.pdx.edu/computer-science/

Purdue University, Graduate School, Interdisciplinary Program in Information Security, West Lafayette, IN 47907. Offers MS. *Students:* 4 full-time (1 woman), 1 part-time (0 women), 4 international. Average age 31. 23 applicants, 35% accepted, 3 enrolled. *Entrance requirements:* For master's, GRE, minimum undergraduate GPA of 3.0 or equivalent. Additional exam requirements/recommendations for international students: required—TOEFL (minimum score 550 paper-based; 100 iBT); recommended—TWE. *Application deadline:* For fall admission, 4/1 priority date for domestic and international students; for spring admission, 10/1 priority date for domestic and international students. Applications are processed on a rolling basis. Application fee: $60 ($75 for international students). Electronic applications accepted. *Unit head:* Dr. Eugene Spafford, Head of the Graduate Program, 765-454-7825, E-mail: advising@cerias.purdue.edu. *Application contact:* Dr. Eugene Spafford, Head of the Graduate Program, 765-454-7825, E-mail: advising@cerias.purdue.edu.
Website: http://www.cerias.purdue.edu/site/education/graduate_program/

Purdue University Global, School of Information Technology, Davenport, IA 52807. Offers decision support systems (MS); information security and assurance (MS). *Program availability:* Part-time, evening/weekend, online learning. *Entrance requirements:* Additional exam requirements/recommendations for international students: required—TOEFL (minimum score 550 paper-based; 80 iBT).

Quinnipiac University, School of Engineering, Hamden, CT 06518-1940. Offers cybersecurity (MS). *Expenses: Tuition:* Part-time $1055 per credit. *Required fees:* $945 per semester. Tuition and fees vary according to course load and program.

Regent University, Graduate School, Robertson School of Government, Virginia Beach, VA 23464. Offers government (MA), including American government, healthcare policy and ethics (MA, MPA), international relations, law and public policy, national security studies, political communication, political theory, religion and politics; national security studies (MA), including cybersecurity, homeland security, international security, Middle East politics; public administration (MPA), including emergency management and homeland security, federal government, general public administration, healthcare policy and ethics (MA, MPA), law, nonprofit administration and faith-based organizations, public leadership and management, servant leadership. *Program availability:* Part-time, evening/weekend, 100% online, blended/hybrid learning. *Faculty:* 5 full-time (1 woman), 19 part-time/adjunct (2 women). *Students:* 36 full-time (22 women), 159 part-time (89 women); includes 82 minority (52 Black or African American, non-Hispanic/Latino; 2 American Indian or Alaska Native, non-Hispanic/Latino; 2 Asian, non-Hispanic/Latino; 23 Hispanic/Latino; 3 Two or more races, non-Hispanic/Latino), 4 international. Average age 36. 181 applicants, 70% accepted, 75 enrolled. In 2019, 58 master's awarded. *Degree requirements:* For master's, thesis optional, internship. *Entrance requirements:* For master's, GRE General Test or LSAT, personal essay, writing sample, resume, college transcripts. Additional exam requirements/recommendations for international students: required—TOEFL (minimum score 577 paper-based). *Application deadline:* For fall admission, 5/1 priority date for domestic students; for spring admission, 11/1 priority date for domestic students. Applications are processed on a rolling basis. Application fee: $50. Electronic applications accepted. *Expenses:* Contact institution. *Financial support:* In 2019–20, 132 students received support. Career-related internships or fieldwork, scholarships/grants, and unspecified assistantships available. Support available to part-time students. Financial award applicants required to submit FAFSA. *Unit head:* Dr. Stephen Perry, Interim Dean, 757-352-4082, E-mail: sperry@regent.edu. *Application contact:* Heidi Cece, Assistant Vice President for Enrollment Management, 800-373-5504, Fax: 757-352-4381, E-mail: admissions@regent.edu.
Website: https://www.regent.edu/robertson-school-of-government/

Regis University, College of Computer and Information Sciences, Denver, CO 80221-1099. Offers agile technologies (Certificate); cybersecurity (Certificate); data science (M Sc); database administration with Oracle (Certificate); database development (Certificate); database technologies (M Sc); enterprise Java software development (Certificate); enterprise resource planning (Certificate); executive information technology (Certificate); health care informatics (Certificate); health care informatics and information management (M Sc); information assurance (M Sc); information assurance policy management (Certificate); information technology management (M Sc); mobile software development (Certificate); software engineering (M Sc, Certificate); software engineering and database technology (M Sc); storage area networks (Certificate); systems engineering (M Sc, Certificate). *Program availability:* Part-time, evening/weekend, 100% online, blended/hybrid learning. *Degree requirements:* For master's, thesis (for some programs), final research project. *Entrance requirements:* For master's, official transcript reflecting baccalaureate degree awarded from regionally-accredited college or university, 2 years of related experience, resume, interview. Additional exam requirements/recommendations for international students: required—TOEFL (minimum score 550 paper-based; 82 iBT). Electronic applications accepted. *Expenses:* Contact institution.

Robert Morris University, School of Informatics, Humanities and Social Sciences, Moon Township, PA 15108. Offers communication and information systems (MS); cyber security (MS); data analytics (MS); information security and assurance (MS); information systems and communications (D Sc); information systems management (MS); information technology project management (MS); Internet information systems (MS); organizational leadership (MS). *Program availability:* Part-time-only, evening/weekend, 100% online. *Faculty:* 23 full-time (9 women), 11 part-time/adjunct (0 women). *Students:* 224 part-time (90 women); includes 46 minority (28 Black or African American, non-Hispanic/Latino; 5 Asian, non-Hispanic/Latino; 9 Hispanic/Latino; 4 Two or more races, non-Hispanic/Latino), 31 international. Average age 35. In 2019, 118 master's, 14 doctorates awarded. *Degree requirements:* For master's, Completion of 30 credits; for doctorate, thesis/dissertation, Completion of 63 credits. *Entrance requirements:* For doctorate, employer letter of endorsement, interview. Additional exam requirements/recommendations for international students: required—TOEFL (minimum score 550 paper-based; 79 iBT). *Application deadline:* For fall admission, 7/1 priority date for domestic and international students; for spring admission, 11/1 priority date for domestic and international students. Applications are processed on a rolling basis. Application fee: $35. Electronic applications accepted. Application fee is waived when completed online. *Expenses:* $960 per credit tuition plus $85 per credit fees (for master's); $32,940 per year tuition and fees (for doctorate). *Financial support:* Institutionally sponsored loans available. Support available to part-time students. Financial award application deadline: 5/1; financial award applicants required to submit FAFSA. *Unit head:* Dr. Amjad Ali, Dean, School of Informatics, Humanities and Social Sciences, 412-397-3000. *Application contact:* Kellie Laurenzi, Associate Vice President, Enrollment Management, 412-397-5200, E-mail: graduateadmissions@rmu.edu.
Website: https://www.rmu.edu/academics/schools/sihss

Robert Morris University Illinois, Morris Graduate School of Management, Chicago, IL 60605. Offers accounting (MBA); accounting/finance (MBA); business analytics (MIS); health care administration (MM); higher education administration (MM); human performance (MS); human resource management (MBA); information security (MIS); information systems management (MIS); law enforcement administration (MM); management (MBA); management/finance (MBA); management/human resource management (MBA); sports administration (MM). *Program availability:* Part-time, evening/weekend. *Entrance requirements:* For master's, official transcripts and letters of recommendation (for some programs); written personal statement. Additional exam requirements/recommendations for international students: required—TOEFL (minimum score 550 paper-based). Electronic applications accepted.

Rochester Institute of Technology, Graduate Enrollment Services, Golisano College of Computing and Information Sciences, Computing Security Department, Advanced Certificate Program in Cybersecurity, Rochester, NY 14623-5603. Offers Advanced Certificate. *Program availability:* Part-time, 100% online. *Entrance requirements:* For degree, GRE required for international students only. However, for students from US universities with a GPA that is lower than required, GRE scores can strengthen their application., minimum GPA of 3.0 (recommended), Have knowledge of computing networking and system administration, and introductory knowledge of computing security. Additional exam requirements/recommendations for international students: required—TOEFL (minimum score 570 paper-based; 88 iBT), IELTS (minimum score 6.5), PTE (minimum score 61). Electronic applications accepted.

Rochester Institute of Technology, Graduate Enrollment Services, Golisano College of Computing and Information Sciences, Computing Security Department, MS Program in Computing Security, Rochester, NY 14623-5603. Offers MS. *Program availability:* Part-time, 100% online. *Degree requirements:* For master's, thesis or alternative, Thesis, Project, and Capstone options. *Entrance requirements:* For master's, GRE required for individuals with degrees from international universities., minimum GPA of 3.0 (recommended), Hold a relevant baccalaureate degree, two letters of recommendation. Additional exam requirements/recommendations for international students: required—TOEFL (minimum score 570 paper-based; 88 iBT), IELTS (minimum score 6.5), PTE (minimum score 61). Electronic applications accepted.

Roger Williams University, School of Justice Studies, Bristol, RI 02809. Offers criminal justice (MS); cybersecurity (MS); leadership (MS), including health care administration (MPA, MS), public management (MPA, MS); public administration (MPA), including health care administration (MPA, MS), public management (MPA, MS); MS/JD. *Program availability:* Part-time, evening/weekend, 100% online, blended/hybrid learning. *Faculty:* 1 (woman) full-time, 5 part-time/adjunct (0 women). *Students:* 24 full-time (15 women), 109 part-time (59 women); includes 31 minority (9 Black or African American, non-Hispanic/Latino; 1 Asian, non-Hispanic/Latino; 17 Hispanic/Latino; 4 Two or more races, non-Hispanic/Latino), 2 international. Average age 34. 94 applicants, 83% accepted, 46 enrolled. In 2019, 46 master's awarded. *Degree requirements:* For master's, thesis. *Entrance requirements:* For master's, No, Letter of intent, transcripts, two letters of recommendation, resume, background check (cybersecurity). Additional exam requirements/recommendations for international students: required—TOEFL (minimum score 85 paper-based), IELTS (minimum score 6.5). *Application deadline:* Applications are processed on a rolling basis. Application fee: $50. Electronic applications accepted. Application fee is waived when completed online. *Expenses: Tuition:* Full-time $15,768. *Required fees:* $900; $450. *Financial support:* In 2019–20, 8 students received support. Scholarships/grants and unspecified assistantships available. Financial award application deadline: 3/15; financial award applicants required to submit FAFSA. *Unit head:* Dr. Eric Bronson, Dean and Professor of Criminal Justice, 401-254-3336, E-mail: ebronson@rwu.edu. *Application contact:* Marcus Hanscom, Director of Graduate Admission, 401-254-3345, Fax: 401-254-3557, E-mail: gradadmit@rwu.edu.
Website: http://www.rwu.edu/academics/departments/criminaljustice.htm#graduate

Rowan University, Graduate School, College of Science and Mathematics, Networks Certificate of Graduate Study Program, Glassboro, NJ 08028-1701. Offers CGS. Electronic applications accepted. *Expenses: Tuition, area resident:* Part-time $715.50 per semester hour. Tuition, state resident: part-time $715.50 per semester hour. Tuition, nonresident: part-time $715.50 per semester hour. *Required fees:* $161.55 per semester hour.

Sacred Heart University, Graduate Programs, College of Arts and Sciences, Department of Computing, Fairfield, CT 06825. Offers computer science (MS); computer science gaming (MS); cybersecurity (MS); information technology (MS). *Program availability:* Part-time, evening/weekend. *Degree requirements:* For master's, thesis or alternative. *Entrance requirements:* For master's, bachelor's degree, minimum GPA of

3.0. Additional exam requirements/recommendations for international students: required—TOEFL (minimum score 570 paper-based, 80 iBT), TWE, or IELTS (6.5). Electronic applications accepted. *Expenses:* Contact institution.

Saginaw Valley State University, College of Science, Engineering, and Technology, University Center, MI 48710. Offers computer science and information systems (MS); energy and materials (MS). *Program availability:* Part-time, evening/weekend. *Faculty:* 6 full-time (1 woman), 1 part-time/adjunct (0 women). *Students:* 7 full-time (2 women), 11 part-time (1 woman); includes 2 minority (both Asian, non-Hispanic/Latino), 4 international. Average age 32. 29 applicants, 62% accepted, 4 enrolled. In 2019, 4 master's awarded. *Degree requirements:* For master's, field project or thesis work. *Entrance requirements:* For master's, minimum GPA of 3.0. Additional exam requirements/recommendations for international students: required—TOEFL (minimum score 550 paper-based; 79 iBT). *Application deadline:* For fall admission, 7/15 for international students; for winter admission, 11/15 for international students; for spring admission, 4/15 for international students. Applications are processed on a rolling basis. Application fee: $30 ($90 for international students). Electronic applications accepted. *Expenses: Tuition, area resident:* Full-time $11,212; part-time $622.90 per credit hour. Tuition, state resident: full-time $11,212; part-time $622.90 per credit hour. Tuition, nonresident: full-time $11,212; part-time $1253 per credit hour. *Required fees:* $263; $14.60 per credit hour. Tuition and fees vary according to course load, degree level and program. *Financial support:* Federal Work-Study and scholarships/grants available. Support available to part-time students. Financial award application deadline: 4/1; financial award applicants required to submit FAFSA. *Unit head:* Dr. Robert Tuttle, Program Coordinator, 989-964-4144, Fax: 989-964-2717. *Application contact:* Jenna Briggs, Director, Graduate and International Admissions, 989-964-6096, Fax: 989-964-2788, E-mail: gradadm@svsu.edu.
Website: http://www.svsu.edu/collegeofscienceengineeringtechnology/

St. Cloud State University, School of Graduate Studies, College of Science and Engineering, Program in Information Assurance, St. Cloud, MN 56301-4498. Offers MS. *Program availability:* Part-time. *Degree requirements:* For master's, 30 to 33 credits of coursework. *Entrance requirements:* For master's, minimum overall GPA of 2.75 in previous undergraduate and graduate records or in last half of undergraduate work. Electronic applications accepted.

St. Cloud State University, School of Graduate Studies, Herberger Business School, St. Cloud, MN 56301-4498. Offers business administration (MBA); information assurance (MS). *Accreditation:* AACSB. *Program availability:* Part-time, evening/weekend. *Degree requirements:* For master's, thesis or alternative. *Entrance requirements:* For master's, GMAT, minimum GPA of 2.75. Additional exam requirements/recommendations for international students: required—Michigan English Language Assessment Battery; recommended—TOEFL (minimum score 550 paper-based), IELTS (minimum score 6.5). Electronic applications accepted. *Expenses:* Contact institution.

Saint Leo University, Graduate Studies in Business, Saint Leo, FL 33574-6665. Offers accounting (M Acc); cybersecurity management (MBA); health care management (MBA); human resource management (MBA); marketing (MBA); marketing research and social media analytics (MBA); software engineering (MS). *Accreditation:* ACBSP. *Program availability:* Part-time, evening/weekend, 100% online, blended/hybrid learning. *Faculty:* 51 full-time (15 women), 45 part-time/adjunct (18 women). *Students:* 8 full-time (2 women), 1,963 part-time (1,176 women); includes 1,147 minority (580 Black or African American, non-Hispanic/Latino; 8 American Indian or Alaska Native, non-Hispanic/Latino; 43 Asian, non-Hispanic/Latino; 250 Hispanic/Latino; 4 Native Hawaiian or other Pacific Islander, non-Hispanic/Latino; 262 Two or more races, non-Hispanic/Latino), 96 international. Average age 37. 818 applicants, 78% accepted, 424 enrolled. In 2019, 766 master's, 14 doctorates awarded. *Degree requirements:* For doctorate, comprehensive exam, thesis/dissertation. *Entrance requirements:* For master's, GMAT with minimum score 500 (for M Acc), official transcripts, current resume, 2 professional recommendations, personal statement, bachelor's degree from regionally-accredited university; undergraduate degree in accounting and minimum undergraduate GPA of 3.0 (for M Acc); minimum undergraduate GPA of 3.0 in final 2 years of undergraduate study and 2 years' work experience (for MBA); for doctorate, GMAT (minimum score of 550) if master's GPA is under 3.25, official transcripts, current resume, 2 professional recommendations, personal statement, master's degree from regionally-accredited university with minimum GPA of 3.25, 3 years' work experience, interview. Additional exam requirements/recommendations for international students: required—TOEFL (minimum score 550 paper-based; 78 iBT). *Application deadline:* For fall admission, 7/1 priority date for domestic and international students; for spring admission, 11/12 priority date for domestic students, 11/1 for international students. Applications are processed on a rolling basis. Electronic applications accepted. *Expenses:* DBA $16,350 per FT yr., MS Cybersecurity $14,010 per FT yr. *Financial support:* In 2019–20, 1,510 students received support. Scholarships/grants, unspecified assistantships, and tuition remission for Saint Leo employees and their dependents available. Financial award application deadline: 3/1; financial award applicants required to submit FAFSA. *Unit head:* Dr. Robyn Parker, Dean, School of Business, 352-588-8599, Fax: 352-588-8912, E-mail: mbaslu@saintleo.edu. *Application contact:* Saint Leo University Office of Graduate Admissions, 800-707-8846, Fax: 352-588-7873, E-mail: grad.admissions@saintleo.edu.
Website: https://www.saintleo.edu/college-of-business

St. Mary's University, School of Science, Engineering and Technology, Program in Cybersecurity, San Antonio, TX 78228. Offers MS, Certificate. *Program availability:* Part-time, evening/weekend. *Degree requirements:* For master's, project or thesis. *Entrance requirements:* For master's, GRE (minimum quantitative score 152), minimum GPA of 3.0, written statement of purpose indicating applicant's interests and objectives, two letters of recommendation concerning applicant's potential for succeeding in graduate program, official transcripts of all college-level work. Additional exam requirements/recommendations for international students: required—TOEFL (minimum score 550 paper-based; 80 iBT), IELTS (minimum score 6). Electronic applications accepted.

Saint Mary's University of Minnesota, Schools of Graduate and Professional Programs, Graduate School of Business and Technology, Cybersecurity Program, Winona, MN 55987-1399. Offers MS. *Unit head:* Don Heier, Director, 507-457-1575, E-mail: dheier@smumn.edu. *Application contact:* Laurie Roy, Director of Admissions of Schools of Graduate and Professional Programs, 507-457-8606, Fax: 612-728-5121, E-mail: lroy@smumn.edu.
Website: https://onlineprograms.smumn.edu/mscs/masters-cybersecurity?_ga-2.250083014.1736907137.1523547391-1359115499.1515170921

Salem International University, School of Business, Salem, WV 26426-0500. Offers information security (MBA); international business (MBA). *Program availability:* Part-time, online learning. *Entrance requirements:* For master's, minimum undergraduate GPA of 2.5, course work in business, resume. Additional exam requirements/recommendations for international students: recommended—TOEFL (minimum score 550 paper-based), IELTS (minimum score 6.5). Electronic applications accepted. *Expenses:* Contact institution.

Salve Regina University, Program in Administration of Justice and Homeland Security, Newport, RI 02840. Offers administration of justice and homeland security (MS); cybersecurity and intelligence (CGS); digital forensics (CGS); leadership in justice (CGS). *Program availability:* Part-time, evening/weekend, some in-person. *Entrance requirements:* For master's, none. Additional exam requirements/recommendations for international students: required—TOEFL (minimum score 600 paper-based; 100 iBT). *Application deadline:* For fall admission, 7/1 priority date for domestic students, 3/15 priority date for international students; for spring admission, 11/1 priority date for domestic students, 9/5 priority date for international students. Applications are processed on a rolling basis. Application fee: $0. Electronic applications accepted. *Financial support:* Application deadline: 3/1; applicants required to submit FAFSA. *Unit head:* Jeffrey Mace, Director, 401-341-2338, E-mail: jeffrey.mac@salve.edu. *Application contact:* Laurie Reilly, Graduate Admissions Manager, 401-341-2153, Fax: 401-341-2973, E-mail: laurie.reilly@salve.edu.
Website: http://www.salve.edu/graduate-studies/administration-of-justice-and-homeland-security

Salve Regina University, Program in Business Administration, Newport, RI 02840-4192. Offers cybersecurity issues in business (MBA); entrepreneurial enterprise (MBA); health care administration and management (MBA); nonprofit management (MBA); social ventures (MBA). *Program availability:* Part-time, evening/weekend, online learning. *Entrance requirements:* For master's, GMAT, GRE General Test, or MAT, 6 undergraduate credits each in accounting, economics, quantitative analysis and calculus or statistics. Additional exam requirements/recommendations for international students: required—TOEFL (minimum score 600 paper-based; 100 iBT) or IELTS. Electronic applications accepted.

Sam Houston State University, College of Sciences, Department of Computer Science, Huntsville, TX 77341. Offers computing and information science (MS); digital forensics (MS); information assurance and security (MS). *Program availability:* Part-time. *Degree requirements:* For master's, comprehensive exam, thesis optional, internship; for doctorate, comprehensive exam, thesis/dissertation. *Entrance requirements:* For master's, GRE General Test, letters of recommendation. Additional exam requirements/recommendations for international students: required—TOEFL (minimum score 550 paper-based; 79 iBT), IELTS (minimum score 6.5). Electronic applications accepted.

The SANS Technology Institute, Programs in Information Security, Bethesda, MD 20814. Offers information security engineering (MS); information security management (MS).

Seattle Pacific University, Master of Arts in Management Program, Seattle, WA 98119-1997. Offers business intelligence and data analytics (MA); cybersecurity (MA); faith and business (MA); human resources (MA); social and sustainable management (MA). *Entrance requirements:* For master's, GMAT scores above 500 (25 verbal; 30 quantitative; 4.4 analytical writing) are preferred, bachelor's degree from accredited college or university, resume, essay, official transcript. *Application deadline:* For fall admission, 8/1 for domestic students, 6/1 for international students; for winter admission, 11/1 for domestic students, 9/1 for international students; for spring admission, 2/1 for domestic students, 12/1 for international students; for summer admission, 5/1 for domestic students. Application fee: $50.
Website: http://spu.edu/academics/school-of-business-and-economics/graduate-programs/ma-management

Southern Arkansas University–Magnolia, School of Graduate Studies, Magnolia, AR 71753. Offers agriculture (MS); business administration (MBA), including agribusiness, social entrepreneurship, supply chain management; clinical and mental health counseling (MS); computer and information sciences (MS), including cyber security and privacy, data science, information technology; gifted and talented (M Ed), including curriculum and instruction, educational administration and supervision, gifted and talented P-8/7-12, instructional specialist P-4; higher, adult and lifelong education (M Ed); kinesiology (M Ed), including coaching; library media and information specialist (M Ed); public administration (MPA); school counseling K-12 (M Ed); student affairs and college counseling (M Ed); teaching (MAT). *Accreditation:* NCATE. *Program availability:* Part-time, 100% online, blended/hybrid learning. *Faculty:* 33 full-time (18 women), 29 part-time/adjunct (17 women). *Students:* 134 full-time (80 women), 704 part-time (471 women); includes 223 minority (158 Black or African American, non-Hispanic/Latino; 5 American Indian or Alaska Native, non-Hispanic/Latino; 19 Asian, non-Hispanic/Latino; 6 Hispanic/Latino; 1 Native Hawaiian or other Pacific Islander, non-Hispanic/Latino; 34 Two or more races, non-Hispanic/Latino), 135 international. Average age 28. 290 applicants, 99% accepted, 149 enrolled. In 2019, 177 master's awarded. *Degree requirements:* For master's, comprehensive exam (for some programs), thesis optional. *Entrance requirements:* For master's, GRE, MAT or GMAT, minimum GPA of 2.5. Additional exam requirements/recommendations for international students: required—TOEFL (minimum score 550 paper-based), IELTS (minimum score 6). *Application deadline:* For fall admission, 8/1 for domestic and international students; for spring admission, 12/1 for domestic students, 11/15 for international students; for summer admission, 5/1 for domestic students, 5/10 for international students. Applications are processed on a rolling basis. Application fee: $25 ($90 for international students). Electronic applications accepted. *Expenses: Tuition, area resident:* Full-time $6720; part-time $3360 per semester. Tuition, state resident: full-time $6720; part-time $3360 per semester. Tuition, nonresident: full-time $10,560; part-time $5280 per semester. *International tuition:* $10,560 full-time. *Required fees:* $2046; $1023 $267. One-time fee: $25. Tuition and fees vary according to course load. *Financial support:* Career-related internships or fieldwork, Federal Work-Study, scholarships/grants, tuition waivers (full), and unspecified assistantships available. Financial award applicants required to submit FAFSA. *Unit head:* Dr. Kim Bloss, Dean, School of Graduate Studies, 870-235-4150, Fax: 870-235-5227, E-mail: kkbloss@saumag.edu. *Application contact:* Talia Jett, Admissions Coordinator, 870-2355450, Fax: 870-235-5227, E-mail: taliajett@saumag.edu.
Website: http://www.saumag.edu/graduate

Southern New Hampshire University, School of Arts and Sciences, Manchester, NH 03106-1045. Offers clinical mental health counseling (MS); creative writing (MA); criminal justice (MS); cyber security (MS); English (MA); fiction and nonfiction (MFA); history (MA); political science (MS); psychology (MS). *Program availability:* Part-time, evening/weekend. *Degree requirements:* For master's, one foreign language, thesis. *Entrance requirements:* For master's, minimum GPA of 3.0 (for MFA). Additional exam requirements/recommendations for international students: required—TOEFL (minimum score 550 paper-based; 79 iBT), IELTS (minimum score 6.5), TWE (minimum score 5). Electronic applications accepted. *Expenses:* Contact institution.

Southern Utah University, Program in Cyber Security and Information Assurance, Cedar City, UT 84720-2498. Offers cyber and web security (MS). *Program availability:* Part-time, online only, 100% online. *Degree requirements:* For master's, thesis, if students choose not to work on a capstone project/thesis for their CSIA graduate degree, they can take any two (2) additional courses (6 credits) from either emphasis (Cyber and Web Security or GRC and IS Controls). *Entrance requirements:* For master's, GRE (minimum score of 300), qualifying entrance exam. Additional exam requirements/recommendations for international students: required—TOEFL (minimum score 550 paper-based; 80 iBT), IELTS (minimum score 6). Electronic applications accepted. *Expenses:* Contact institution.

State University of New York Polytechnic Institute, Program in Network and Computer Security, Utica, NY 13502. Offers MS. *Program availability:* Part-time. *Degree requirements:* For master's, thesis or project. *Entrance requirements:* For master's, GRE or approved GRE waiver, undergraduate prereq in math and computer science. Additional exam requirements/recommendations for international students: required—TOEFL (minimum score 79 iBT), IELTS (minimum score 6.5), PTE (minimum score 53), TOEFL, IELTS, or PTE; GRE. Electronic applications accepted.

Stephen F. Austin State University, Graduate School, College of Sciences and Mathematics, Department of Computer Science, Nacogdoches, TX 75962. Offers cyber security (MS). *Program availability:* Part-time. *Degree requirements:* For master's, comprehensive exam, thesis optional. *Entrance requirements:* For master's, GRE General Test. Additional exam requirements/recommendations for international students: required—TOEFL.

Stevens Institute of Technology, Graduate School, School of Business, Program in Information Systems, Hoboken, NJ 07030. Offers computer science (MS); e-commerce (MS); enterprise systems (MS); entrepreneurial information technology (MS); information architecture (MS); information management (MS, Certificate); information security (MS); information technology in financial services industry (MS); information technology in the pharmaceutical industry (MS); information technology outsourcing management (MS); project management (MS, Certificate); software engineering (MS); telecommunications (MS). *Program availability:* Part-time, evening/weekend. *Faculty:* 59 full-time (11 women), 30 part-time/adjunct (5 women). *Students:* 221 full-time (80 women), 52 part-time (18 women); includes 24 minority (8 Black or African American, non-Hispanic/Latino; 16 Asian, non-Hispanic/Latino), 225 international. Average age 27. In 2019, 188 master's awarded. Terminal master's awarded for partial completion of doctoral program. *Degree requirements:* For master's, thesis optional, minimum B average in major field and overall; for Certificate, minimum B average. *Entrance requirements:* For master's, International applicants must submit TOEFL/IELTS scores and fulfill the English Language Proficiency Requirement. Applicants to full-time programs who do not qualify for a score waiver are required to submit GRE/GMAT scores. Additional exam requirements/recommendations for international students: required—TOEFL (minimum score 74 iBT), IELTS (minimum score 6). *Application deadline:* For fall admission, 4/1 for domestic and international students; for spring admission, 11/1 for domestic and international students; for summer admission, 5/1 for domestic students. Applications are processed on a rolling basis. Application fee: $60. Electronic applications accepted. *Expenses: Tuition:* Full-time $52,134. *Required fees:* $1880. Tuition and fees vary according to course load. *Financial support:* Fellowships, research assistantships, teaching assistantships, career-related internships or fieldwork, Federal Work-Study, scholarships/grants, and unspecified assistantships available. Financial award application deadline: 2/15; financial award applicants required to submit FAFSA. *Unit head:* Dr. Gregory Prastacos, Dean of SB, 201-216-8366, E-mail: gprastac@stevens.edu. *Application contact:* Graduate Admissions, 888-783-8367, Fax: 888-511-1306, E-mail: graduate@stevens.edu. Website: https://www.stevens.edu/school-business/masters-programs/information-systems

Stevenson University, Program in Cybersecurity and Digital Forensics, Stevenson, MD 21153. Offers MS. *Program availability:* Part-time, 100% online. *Faculty:* 3 part-time/adjunct (2 women). *Students:* 3 full-time (0 women), 21 part-time (7 women); includes 8 minority (4 Black or African American, non-Hispanic/Latino; 2 Hispanic/Latino; 2 Two or more races, non-Hispanic/Latino). Average age 31. 26 applicants, 50% accepted, 6 enrolled. In 2019, 11 master's awarded. *Degree requirements:* For master's, capstone. *Entrance requirements:* For master's, personal statement (3-5 paragraphs), bachelor's degree in a technical or quantitative field of study OR related professional work experience (highly recommended), official college transcript from your degree-granting institution, minimum cumulative GPA of 3.0 on a 4.0 scale in past academic work. *Application deadline:* For fall admission, 8/9 priority date for domestic students; for spring admission, 1/11 priority date for domestic students; for summer admission, 5/1 priority date for domestic students. Applications are processed on a rolling basis. Application fee: $0. Electronic applications accepted. *Expenses:* $695 per credit. *Financial support:* Unspecified assistantships available. Financial award applicants required to submit FAFSA. *Unit head:* Steven R. Engorn, Graduate Program Director, 443-352-4074, E-mail: CHJOHNSON@stevenson.edu. *Application contact:* Amanda Millar, Director, Admissions, 443-334-3334, Fax: 443-394-0538, E-mail: amillar@stevenson.edu. Website: https://www.stevenson.edu/online/academics/online-graduate-programs/cybersecurity-digital-forensics/index.html

Stratford University, School of Graduate Studies, Falls Church, VA 22043. Offers accounting (MS); business administration (MBA, DBA); cyber security (MS); cyber security leadership and policy (MS); digital forensics (MS); healthcare administration (MS); information systems (MS); information technology (DIT); networking and telecommunications (MS); software engineering (MS). *Program availability:* Part-time, evening/weekend, 100% online, blended/hybrid learning. *Degree requirements:* For master's, comprehensive exam, capstone project. *Entrance requirements:* For master's, GRE or GMAT, baccalaureate degree. Additional exam requirements/recommendations for international students: required—TOEFL (minimum score 79 iBT), IELTS (minimum score 6.5), PTE (minimum score 5). Electronic applications accepted.

Strayer University, Graduate Studies, Washington, DC 20005-2603. Offers accounting (MS); acquisition (MBA); business administration (MBA); communications technology (MS); educational management (M Ed); finance (MBA); health services administration (MHSA); hospitality and tourism management (MBA); human resource management (MBA); information systems (MS), including computer security management, decision support system management, enterprise resource management, network management, software engineering management, systems development management; management (MBA); management information systems (MS); marketing (MBA); professional accounting (MS), including accounting information systems, controllership, taxation; public administration (MPA); supply chain management (MBA); technology in education (M Ed). *Accreditation:* ACBSP. *Program availability:* Part-time, evening/weekend, online learning. *Degree requirements:* For master's, thesis. *Entrance requirements:* For master's, GMAT, GRE General Test, bachelor's degree from an accredited college or university, minimum undergraduate GPA of 2.75. Electronic applications accepted.

Syracuse University, College of Engineering and Computer Science, Programs in Cybersecurity, Syracuse, NY 13244. Offers MS, CAS. *Program availability:* Part-time, evening/weekend. *Entrance requirements:* For master's, GRE, three letters of recommendation, personal statement, resume, official transcripts. Additional exam requirements/recommendations for international students: required—TOEFL (minimum score 100 iBT). Electronic applications accepted.

Syracuse University, School of Information Studies, CAS Program in Information Security Management, Syracuse, NY 13244. Offers CAS. *Program availability:* Part-time, evening/weekend, online learning. *Entrance requirements:* For degree, resume, personal statement, official transcripts. Additional exam requirements/recommendations

for international students: required—TOEFL (minimum score 100 iBT). Electronic applications accepted.

Temple University, College of Science and Technology, Department of Computer and Information Sciences, Philadelphia, PA 19122-6096. Offers computational data science (MS); computer and information sciences (PhD), including artificial intelligence, computer and network systems, information systems, software systems; computer science (MS); cyber defense and information assurance (PSM); information science and technology (MS). *Program availability:* Part-time, evening/weekend, online learning. *Faculty:* 39 full-time (9 women), 8 part-time/adjunct (1 woman). *Students:* 97 full-time (28 women), 22 part-time (11 women); includes 14 minority (3 Black or African American, non-Hispanic/Latino; 8 Asian, non-Hispanic/Latino; 3 Hispanic/Latino), 83 international. 133 applicants, 56% accepted, 35 enrolled. In 2019, 15 master's, 7 doctorates awarded. *Degree requirements:* For doctorate, thesis/dissertation. *Entrance requirements:* For master's, GRE, 3 letters of recommendation, statement of goals; for doctorate, GRE, 3 letters of recommendation, bachelor's degree in related field, statement of goals, resume. Additional exam requirements/recommendations for international students: required—TOEFL (minimum score 85 iBT), IELTS (minimum score 6.5), PTE (minimum score 58), one of three is required. *Application deadline:* Applications are processed on a rolling basis. Application fee: $60. Electronic applications accepted. *Expenses:* Contact institution. *Financial support:* Research assistantships, teaching assistantships, health care benefits, and unspecified assistantships available. Financial award applicants required to submit FAFSA. *Unit head:* Jamie Payton, Department Chairperson, 215-204-8245, E-mail: Jamie.payton@temple.edu. *Application contact:* Eduard Dragut, Graduate Chair, 215-204-0521, E-mail: cisadmit@temple.edu. Website: https://cis.temple.edu/

Thomas Edison State University, School of Applied Science and Technology, Trenton, NJ 08608. Offers clinical trials management (MS); cybersecurity (Graduate Certificate); information technology (MS); nuclear energy technology management (MS); technical studies (MS). *Program availability:* Part-time, online learning. *Degree requirements:* For master's, project. *Entrance requirements:* Additional exam requirements/recommendations for international students: required—TOEFL (minimum score 550 paper-based; 79 iBT). Electronic applications accepted.

Trident University International, College of Business Administration, Program in Business Administration, Cypress, CA 90630. Offers business administration (PhD); conflict and negotiation management (MBA); criminal justice administration (MBA); entrepreneurship (MBA); finance (MBA); general management (MBA); government accounting (MBA); human resource management (MBA); information security and digital assurance management (MBA); information technology management (MBA); international business (MBA); logistics management (MBA); marketing (MBA); project management (MBA); public management (MBA); quality management (MBA); strategic leadership (MBA). *Program availability:* Part-time, evening/weekend, online learning. *Degree requirements:* For doctorate, comprehensive exam, thesis/dissertation, defense of dissertation. *Entrance requirements:* For master's, minimum GPA of 2.5 (students with GPA 3.0 or greater may transfer up to 30% of graduate level credits); for doctorate, minimum GPA of 3.4, curriculum vitae, course work in research methods or statistics. Additional exam requirements/recommendations for international students: required—TOEFL. Electronic applications accepted.

Tuskegee University, Graduate Programs, Andrew F. Brimmer College of Business and Information Science, Tuskegee, AL 36088. Offers information systems and security management (MS). *Degree requirements:* For master's, thesis. *Entrance requirements:* For master's, GRE or GMAT, baccalaureate degree in computer science, management information systems, accounting, finance, management, information technology, or a closely-related field.

Universidad del Este, Graduate School, Carolina, PR 00984. Offers accounting (MBA); adult education (M Ed); agribusiness (MBA); criminal justice and criminology (MA); curriculum and instruction - early education (M Ed); curriculum and instruction - elementary (M Ed); curriculum and instruction - English (M Ed); curriculum and instruction - Spanish (M Ed); human resources (MBA); information security management (MBA); information technology and Web business development (MBA); management (MBA); public policy (MPA); social work (MA), including clinical social work; special education (M Ed); strategic leadership (MBA).

Université de Sherbrooke, Faculty of Administration, Program in Governance, Audit and Security of Information Technology, Longueuil, QC J4K0A8, Canada. Offers M Adm. *Program availability:* Part-time, evening/weekend, online learning. *Degree requirements:* For master's, thesis. *Entrance requirements:* For master's, bachelor's degree, related work experience. Electronic applications accepted.

University at Albany, State University of New York, College of Emergency Preparedness, Homeland Security and Cybersecurity, Albany, NY 12222-0001. Offers cybersecurity (Certificate); emergency preparedness (Certificate); homeland security (Certificate); information science (MS, PhD). *Program availability:* 100% online, blended/hybrid learning. *Faculty:* 25 full-time (9 women), 35 part-time/adjunct (11 women). *Students:* 63 full-time (44 women), 127 part-time (93 women); includes 31 minority (9 Black or African American, non-Hispanic/Latino; 3 Asian, non-Hispanic/Latino; 18 Hispanic/Latino; 1 Two or more races, non-Hispanic/Latino), 22 international. Average age 27. 173 applicants, 77% accepted, 76 enrolled. In 2019, 35 master's, 2 doctorates, 24 other advanced degrees awarded. *Degree requirements:* For doctorate, thesis/dissertation optional. *Entrance requirements:* For master's and doctorate, GRE, transcripts from all schools attended, 3 letters of recommendation, resume, personal statement. Additional exam requirements/recommendations for international students: required—TOEFL (minimum score 550 paper-based). *Application deadline:* For fall admission, 1/15 for domestic students; for spring admission, 11/15 for domestic students. Application fee: $75. Electronic applications accepted. *Expenses: Tuition, area resident:* Full-time $11,530; part-time $480 per credit hour. Tuition, nonresident: full-time $23,530; part-time $980 per credit hour. *International tuition:* $23,530 full-time. *Required fees:* $2185; $96 per credit hour. Part-time tuition and fees vary according to course load and program. *Financial support:* Research assistantships, teaching assistantships, career-related internships or fieldwork, traineeships, and unspecified assistantships available. *Unit head:* Dr. Robert Griffin, Dean, 518-442-5258, E-mail: rpgriffin@albany.edu. *Application contact:* Jennifer J Goodall, Vice Dean, 518-949-3283, E-mail: jgoodall@albany.edu. Website: http://www.albany.edu/cehc/

University at Albany, State University of New York, School of Business, MBA Programs, Albany, NY 12222-0001. Offers business administration (MBA); cyber security (MBA); entrepreneurship (MBA); finance (MBA); human resource information systems (MBA); information systems and business analytics (MBA); marketing (MBA); JD/MBA. *Program availability:* Part-time, evening/weekend. *Faculty:* 29 full-time (13 women), 9 part-time/adjunct (2 women). *Students:* 101 full-time (33 women), 140 part-time (91 women); includes 70 minority (23 Black or African American, non-Hispanic/Latino; 1 American Indian or Alaska Native, non-Hispanic/Latino; 25 Asian, non-Hispanic/Latino; 21 Hispanic/Latino), 22 international. Average age 25. 144 applicants, 68% accepted, 83 enrolled. In 2019, 103 master's awarded. *Degree requirements:* For

master's, thesis (for some programs), field or research project. *Entrance requirements:* For master's, GMAT, resume, statement of goals, 3 letters of recommendation, official undergraduate transcripts. Additional exam requirements/recommendations for international students: required—TOEFL (minimum score 100 paper-based; 90 iBT), IELTS (minimum score 7). *Application deadline:* For fall admission, 5/15 priority date for domestic students, 5/15 for international students; for spring admission, 12/15 for domestic students; for summer admission, 4/19 for domestic students. Applications are processed on a rolling basis. Application fee: $75. Electronic applications accepted. *Expenses:* FT-MBA: 17,153 / Evening-MBA: 735.13 per credit hour. *Financial support:* In 2019–20, 21 students received support, including 1 fellowship with partial tuition reimbursement available, 4 research assistantships with partial tuition reimbursements available (averaging $6,000 per year), 20 teaching assistantships with partial tuition reimbursements available (averaging $7,141 per year); tuition waivers (partial) also available. Financial award application deadline: 4/15; financial award applicants required to submit FAFSA. *Unit head:* Dr. Nilanjan Sen, Dean, 518-956-8370, Fax: 518-442-3273, E-mail: nsen@albany.edu. *Application contact:* Zina Mega Lawrence, Assistant Dean of Graduate Student Services, 518-956-8320, Fax: 518-442-4042, E-mail: zlawrence@albany.edu.
Website: https://graduatebusiness.albany.edu/

University of Advancing Technology, Master of Science Program in Technology, Tempe, AZ 85283-1042. Offers advancing computer science (MS); emerging technologies (MS); game production and management (MS); information assurance (MS); technology leadership (MS). *Degree requirements:* For master's, project or thesis. *Entrance requirements:* Additional exam requirements/recommendations for international students: required—TOEFL (minimum score 550 paper-based). Electronic applications accepted.

The University of Alabama at Birmingham, Collat School of Business, Program in Management Information Systems, Birmingham, AL 35294. Offers management information systems (MS), including cybersecurity management, information technology management. *Program availability:* Part-time, evening/weekend, online only, 100% online. *Faculty:* 7 full-time (1 woman), 4 part-time/adjunct (2 women). *Students:* 2 full-time (1 woman), 82 part-time (35 women); includes 36 minority (24 Black or African American, non-Hispanic/Latino; 5 Asian, non-Hispanic/Latino; 4 Hispanic/Latino; 3 Two or more races, non-Hispanic/Latino). Average age 36. 21 applicants, 86% accepted, 15 enrolled. In 2019, 35 master's awarded. *Entrance requirements:* For master's, GMAT or GRE. Additional exam requirements/recommendations for international students: required—TOEFL (minimum score 80 iBT), IELTS (minimum score 6.5). *Application deadline:* For fall admission, 8/1 for domestic and international students; for spring admission, 12/1 for domestic and international students; for summer admission, 5/1 for domestic and international students. Applications are processed on a rolling basis. Application fee: $70 ($85 for international students). Electronic applications accepted. *Unit head:* Dr. Jack Howard, Department Chair, 205-934-8846, Fax: 205-934-8886, E-mail: jlhoward@uab.edu. *Application contact:* Wendy England, Online Program Coordinator, 205-934-8813, Fax: 205-975-4429.
Website: https://businessdegrees.uab.edu/mis-degree-masters/

The University of Alabama at Birmingham, College of Arts and Sciences, Program in Computer Forensics and Security Management, Birmingham, AL 35294. Offers MS. *Students:* 4 full-time (1 woman), 6 part-time (2 women); includes 2 minority (1 Black or African American, non-Hispanic/Latino; 1 Hispanic/Latino), 3 international. Average age 34. In 2019, 3 master's awarded. *Degree requirements:* For master's, field practicum (internship). *Entrance requirements:* For master's, GRE General Test (minimum combined score of 320) or GMAT (minimum total score of 550), minimum GPA of 3.0. *Application deadline:* For fall admission, 3/1 for domestic students. Application fee: $45 ($60 for international students). Electronic applications accepted. *Unit head:* Dr. Anthony Skjellum, Program Co-Director, Computer and Information Sciences, 205-934-2213, Fax: 205-934-5473, E-mail: tony@cis.uab.edu. *Application contact:* Dr. John J. Sloan, III, Program Co-Director, Justice Sciences, 205-934-2069, E-mail: prof@uab.edu.
Website: http://www.uab.edu/cas/justice-sciences/graduate-programs/master-of-science-in-computer-forensics-and-security-management-mscfsm

The University of Alabama in Huntsville, School of Graduate Studies, College of Business Administration, Programs in Information Systems, Huntsville, AL 35899. Offers cybersecurity (MS, Certificate); enterprise resource planning (Certificate); information systems (MSIS); supply chain and logistics management (MS); supply chain management (Certificate). *Program availability:* Part-time. *Degree requirements:* For master's, comprehensive exam, thesis or alternative. *Entrance requirements:* For master's, GMAT (minimum score 500), minimum AACSB index of 1080. Additional exam requirements/recommendations for international students: required—TOEFL (minimum score 550 paper-based; 80 iBT), IELTS (minimum score 6.5). Electronic applications accepted.

The University of Alabama in Huntsville, School of Graduate Studies, College of Science, Department of Computer Science, Huntsville, AL 35899. Offers computer science (MS, PhD); cybersecurity (MS); modeling and simulation (MS, PhD, Certificate); software engineering (MSSE, Certificate). *Program availability:* Part-time. *Degree requirements:* For master's, comprehensive exam, thesis or alternative, oral and written exams; for doctorate, comprehensive exam, thesis/dissertation, oral and written exams. *Entrance requirements:* For master's, doctorate, and Certificate, GRE General Test, minimum GPA of 3.0. Additional exam requirements/recommendations for international students: required—TOEFL (minimum score 550 paper-based; 80 iBT), IELTS (minimum score 6.5). Electronic applications accepted.

University of Colorado Colorado Springs, College of Engineering and Applied Science, Program in General Engineering, Colorado Springs, CO 80918. Offers computer science (PhD); cybersecurity (ME); energy engineering (ME); engineering management (ME); engineering systems (ME); software engineering (ME); space operations (ME). *Program availability:* Part-time, evening/weekend, blended/hybrid learning. *Faculty:* 1 full-time (0 women), 12 part-time/adjunct (3 women). *Students:* 2 full-time (1 woman), 88 part-time (22 women); includes 23 minority (3 Black or African American, non-Hispanic/Latino; 6 Asian, non-Hispanic/Latino; 9 Hispanic/Latino; 5 Two or more races, non-Hispanic/Latino), 7 international. Average age 32. 36 applicants, 53% accepted, 15 enrolled. In 2019, 28 master's awarded. *Degree requirements:* For master's, thesis, portfolio, or project. *Entrance requirements:* For master's, GRE may be required based on past academic performance., Professional recommendation letters are required for all applicants.; for doctorate, GRE (minimum score of 148 new grading scale on the quantitative portion if the applicant has not graduated from a program of recognized standing), minimum GPA of 3.3 in the bachelor's or master's degree program attempted. Additional exam requirements/recommendations for international students: required—TOEFL (minimum score 80 iBT), IELTS (minimum score 6). *Application deadline:* For fall admission, 7/1 for domestic and international students; for spring admission, 11/1 for domestic and international students. Applications are processed on a rolling basis. Application fee: $60 ($100 for international students). Electronic applications accepted. *Expenses:* Contact institution. *Financial support:* In 2019–20, 5 students received support. Career-related internships or fieldwork, Federal Work-Study, scholarships/grants, traineeships, health care benefits, and unspecified assistantships available. Support available to part-time students. Financial award application deadline: 3/1; financial award applicants required to submit FAFSA. *Unit head:* Dr. Donald Rabern, Dean of Engineering and Applied Science, 719-255-3543, E-mail: drabern@uccs.edu. *Application contact:* Dawn House, Extended Studies Coordinator, 719-255-3246, E-mail: dhouse@uccs.edu.
Website: https://www.uccs.edu/easonline/degree-programs/engineering-management-degree

University of Dallas, Satish and Yasmin Gupta College of Business, Irving, TX 75062. Offers accounting (MBA, MS); business administration (DBA); business analytics (MS); business management (MBA); corporate finance (MBA); cybersecurity (MS); finance (MS); financial services (MBA); global business (MBA, MS); health services management (MBA); human resource management (MBA); information and technology management (MS); information assurance (MBA); information technology (MBA); information technology service management (MBA); marketing management (MBA); organization development (MBA); project management (MBA); sports and entertainment management (MBA); strategic leadership (MBA); supply chain management (MBA). *Accreditation:* AACSB. *Program availability:* Part-time, evening/weekend, 100% online, blended/hybrid learning. *Students:* 120 full-time (53 women), 531 part-time (203 women); includes 353 minority (173 Black or African American, non-Hispanic/Latino; 1 American Indian or Alaska Native, non-Hispanic/Latino; 78 Asian, non-Hispanic/Latino; 92 Hispanic/Latino; 2 Native Hawaiian or other Pacific Islander, non-Hispanic/Latino; 7 Two or more races, non-Hispanic/Latino), 96 international. Average age 33. 291 applicants, 96% accepted, 141 enrolled. In 2019, 302 master's, 4 doctorates awarded. *Degree requirements:* For doctorate, thesis/dissertation. *Entrance requirements:* For master's and doctorate, U.S. bachelor's degree with a minimum cumulative GPA of 2.0 from a regionally accredited college or university (or comparable foreign degree); minimum 3.0 GPA in any graduate-level coursework completed; good academic standing with all colleges attended. Additional exam requirements/recommendations for international students: required—TOEFL (minimum score 80 iBT), IELTS (minimum score 6.5), PTE (minimum score 67). *Application deadline:* Applications are processed on a rolling basis. Application fee: $50. Electronic applications accepted. *Expenses:* $1,250 / Credit Hour, $160 Matriculation Fee, $100 Graduation Fee. *Financial support:* Research assistantships, teaching assistantships, scholarships/grants, and unspecified assistantships available. Support available to part-time students. Financial award application deadline: 2/15; financial award applicants required to submit FAFSA. *Unit head:* Brett J.L. Landry, Dean, 972-721-5356, E-mail: blandry@udallas.edu. *Application contact:* Breonna Collins, Director, Graduate Admissions, 972-7215304, E-mail: bcollins@udallas.edu.
Website: http://www.udallas.edu/cob/

University of Dayton, School of Business Administration, Dayton, OH 45469. Offers accounting (MBA); cyber security (MBA); finance (MBA); marketing (MBA); JD/MBA. *Accreditation:* AACSB. *Program availability:* Part-time, evening/weekend, blended/hybrid learning. *Entrance requirements:* For master's, GMAT (minimum score of 500 total, 19 verbal); GRE (minimum score of 149 verbal, 146 quantitative), minimum GPA of 3.0, current resume. Additional exam requirements/recommendations for international students: required—TOEFL (minimum score 550 paper-based; 80 iBT); recommended—IELTS (minimum score 6.5). Electronic applications accepted. *Expenses:* Contact institution.

University of Denver, Daniel Felix Ritchie School of Engineering and Computer Science, Department of Computer Science, Denver, CO 80208. Offers computer science (MS, PhD); cybersecurity (MS); data science (MS). *Program availability:* Part-time, evening/weekend. *Faculty:* 18 full-time (3 women), 3 part-time/adjunct (1 woman). *Students:* 25 full-time (10 women), 135 part-time (39 women); includes 36 minority (4 Black or African American, non-Hispanic/Latino; 9 Asian, non-Hispanic/Latino; 16 Hispanic/Latino; 7 Two or more races, non-Hispanic/Latino), 50 international. Average age 30. 315 applicants, 69% accepted, 90 enrolled. In 2019, 44 master's awarded. *Degree requirements:* For doctorate, variable foreign language requirement, comprehensive exam, thesis/dissertation, reading competency in two languages, modern typesetting system, or additional coursework. *Entrance requirements:* For master's and doctorate, GRE General Test, bachelor's degree, transcripts, personal statement, resume or curriculum vitae, three letters of recommendation. Additional exam requirements/recommendations for international students: required—TOEFL (minimum score 550 paper-based; 80 iBT). *Application deadline:* For fall admission, 1/15 priority date for domestic and international students; for winter admission, 10/25 for domestic and international students; for spring admission, 2/7 for domestic and international students; for summer admission, 4/24 for domestic and international students. Applications are processed on a rolling basis. Application fee: $65. Electronic applications accepted. *Financial support:* In 2019–20, 78 students received support, including 1 research assistantship with tuition reimbursement available (averaging $6,900 per year), 17 teaching assistantships with tuition reimbursements available (averaging $17,487 per year); career-related internships or fieldwork, Federal Work-Study, institutionally sponsored loans, scholarships/grants, and unspecified assistantships also available. Financial award application deadline: 2/15; financial award applicants required to submit FAFSA. *Unit head:* Dr. Chris GauthierDickey, Professor and Chair, 303-871-3318, E-mail: Chris.GauthierDickey@du.edu. *Application contact:* Information Contact, 303-871-2458, E-mail: info@cs.du.edu.
Website: http://ritchieschool.du.edu/departments/computer-science/

University of Detroit Mercy, College of Liberal Arts and Education, Detroit, MI 48221. Offers addiction counseling (MA); addiction studies (Certificate); clinical mental health counseling (MA); clinical psychology (MA, PhD); computer and information systems (MS); criminal justice (MA); curriculum and instruction (MA); economics (MA); educational administration (MA); financial economics (MA); industrial/organizational psychology (MA); information assurance (MS); intelligence analysis (MA); liberal studies (MALS); religious studies (MA); school counseling (MA, Certificate); school psychology (Spec); security administration (MS); special education: emotionally impaired/behaviorally disordered (MA); special education: learning disabilities (MA). *Program availability:* Part-time, evening/weekend. *Degree requirements:* For doctorate, departmental qualifying exam.

University of Fairfax, Graduate Programs, Vienna, VA 22182. Offers business administration (DBA); computer science (MCS); cybersecurity (MBA, MS); general business administration (MBA); information technology (MBA); project management (MBA).

University of Houston, College of Technology, Department of Information and Logistics Technology, Houston, TX 77204. Offers information security (MS); supply chain and logistics technology (MS); technology project management (MS). *Program availability:* Part-time. *Degree requirements:* For master's, project or thesis (most programs). *Entrance requirements:* For master's, GMAT. Additional exam requirements/recommendations for international students: required—TOEFL (minimum score 550 paper-based; 79 iBT). Electronic applications accepted.

University of Louisville, J. B. Speed School of Engineering, Department of Computer Engineering and Computer Science, Louisville, KY 40292-0001. Offers computer engineering and computer science (M Eng); computer science (MS, PhD); cybersecurity (Certificate); data science (Certificate). *Accreditation:* ABET (one or more programs are accredited). *Program availability:* Part-time, 100% online, blended/hybrid learning.

Faculty: 16 full-time (1 woman), 4 part-time/adjunct (3 women). *Students:* 82 full-time (28 women), 120 part-time (29 women); includes 35 minority (10 Black or African American, non-Hispanic/Latino; 15 Asian, non-Hispanic/Latino; 4 Hispanic/Latino; 6 Two or more races, non-Hispanic/Latino), 58 international. Average age 32. 90 applicants, 50% accepted, 32 enrolled. In 2019, 47 master's, 5 doctorates, 25 other advanced degrees awarded. Terminal master's awarded for partial completion of doctoral program. *Degree requirements:* For master's, thesis optional; for doctorate, comprehensive exam, thesis/dissertation. *Entrance requirements:* For master's, Two letters of recommendation, official final transcripts; for doctorate, GRE, Two letters of recommendation, personal statement, official final transcripts. Additional exam requirements/recommendations for international students: required—TOEFL (minimum score 550 paper-based; 80 iBT), IELTS (minimum score 6.5). *Application deadline:* For fall admission, 5/1 priority date for domestic and international students; for spring admission, 11/1 priority date for domestic and international students; for summer admission, 3/1 priority date for domestic and international students. Applications are processed on a rolling basis. Application fee: $65. Electronic applications accepted. *Expenses: Tuition, area resident:* Full-time $13,000; part-time $723 per credit hour. Tuition, state resident: full-time $13,000; part-time $723 per credit hour. Tuition, nonresident: full-time $27,114; part-time $1507 per credit hour. *International tuition:* $27,114 full-time. *Required fees:* $196. Tuition and fees vary according to program and reciprocity agreements. *Financial support:* In 2019–20, 70 students received support, including 1 fellowship with full tuition reimbursement available (averaging $22,000 per year), 14 teaching assistantships with full tuition reimbursements available (averaging $22,000 per year); research assistantships, scholarships/grants, health care benefits, and tuition waivers (full) also available. Financial award application deadline: 1/1. *Unit head:* Dr. Wei Zhang, Chair, Computer Science and Engineering, 502-852-0715, E-mail: wei.zhang@louisville.edu. *Application contact:* Dr. Mehmed Kantardzic, Director of Graduate Studies, 502-852-3703, E-mail: mehmed.kantardzic@louisville.edu.
Website: http://louisville.edu/speed/computer

University of Maryland, Baltimore County, The Graduate School, College of Engineering and Information Technology, Department of Computer Science and Electrical Engineering, Program in Cybersecurity, Baltimore, MD 21250. Offers cybersecurity (MPS); cybersecurity operations (Postbaccalaureate Certificate); cybersecurity strategy and policy (Postbaccalaureate Certificate). *Program availability:* Part-time. *Students:* 33 full-time (7 women), 128 part-time (35 women); includes 77 minority (28 Black or African American, non-Hispanic/Latino; 29 Asian, non-Hispanic/Latino; 16 Hispanic/Latino; 4 Two or more races, non-Hispanic/Latino), 10 international. Average age 37. 161 applicants, 63% accepted, 55 enrolled. In 2019, 59 master's, 32 other advanced degrees awarded. *Degree requirements:* For master's, comprehensive exam (for some programs). *Entrance requirements:* For master's, bachelor's degree in computer science, computer engineering, engineering, math, or information systems, or in other field with relevant work experience; curriculum vitae and two letters of recommendation (for international students). *Application deadline:* For fall admission, 8/1 for domestic and international students; for spring admission, 11/1 for international students. Applications are processed on a rolling basis. Application fee: $70. Electronic applications accepted. *Expenses:* $14,382 per year. *Financial support:* In 2019–20, 5 students received support, including 1 fellowship, 3 research assistantships, 1 teaching assistantship; career-related internships or fieldwork, Federal Work-Study, health care benefits, and unspecified assistantships also available. Support available to part-time students. Financial award application deadline: 6/30; financial award applicants required to submit FAFSA. *Unit head:* Dr. Anupam Joshi, Professor and Chair, 410-455-3500, E-mail: joshi@cs.umbc.edu. *Application contact:* Dr. Richard Forno, Lecturer and Graduate Program Director, 410-455-3788, Fax: 410-455-3969, E-mail: richard.forno@umbc.edu.
Website: http://cyber.umbc.edu/

University of Maryland Global Campus, University of Maryland Global Campus, Cloud Computing Architecture, Adelphi, MD 20783. Offers MS. *Program availability:* Part-time, evening/weekend, online learning. *Students:* 222 part-time (62 women); includes 132 minority (94 Black or African American, non-Hispanic/Latino; 1 American Indian or Alaska Native, non-Hispanic/Latino; 20 Asian, non-Hispanic/Latino; 14 Hispanic/Latino; 1 Native Hawaiian or other Pacific Islander, non-Hispanic/Latino; 2 Two or more races, non-Hispanic/Latino), 20 international. Average age 37. 143 applicants, 100% accepted, 50 enrolled. In 2019, 29 master's awarded. *Application deadline:* Applications are processed on a rolling basis. Application fee: $50. Electronic applications accepted. *Financial support:* Scholarships/grants available. Support available to part-time students. Financial award application deadline: 6/1; financial award applicants required to submit FAFSA. *Unit head:* Patrick Appiah-Kubi, Program Director, 240-684-2400, E-mail: patrick.AppiahKubi@umgc.edu. *Application contact:* Admissions, 800-888-8682, E-mail: studentsfirst@umuc.edu.
Website: https://www.umgc.edu/academic-programs/masters-degrees/cloud-computing-architecture.cfm

University of Maryland Global Campus, University of Maryland Global Campus, Cybersecurity Management and Policy, Adelphi, MD 20783. Offers MS, Certificate. *Program availability:* Part-time, evening/weekend, online learning. *Students:* 517 part-time (193 women); includes 287 minority (201 Black or African American, non-Hispanic/Latino; 4 American Indian or Alaska Native, non-Hispanic/Latino; 34 Asian, non-Hispanic/Latino; 32 Hispanic/Latino; 2 Native Hawaiian or other Pacific Islander, non-Hispanic/Latino; 14 Two or more races, non-Hispanic/Latino), 7 international. Average age 37. 313 applicants, 100% accepted, 121 enrolled. In 2019, 178 master's, 42 other advanced degrees awarded. *Degree requirements:* For master's, thesis or alternative, capstone course. *Application deadline:* Applications are processed on a rolling basis. Application fee: $50. Electronic applications accepted. *Financial support:* Scholarships/grants available. Support available to part-time students. Financial award application deadline: 6/1; financial award applicants required to submit FAFSA. *Unit head:* Bruce deGrazia, Program Chair, 240-684-2400, E-mail: bruce.degrazia@umgc.edu. *Application contact:* Admissions, 800-888-8682, E-mail: studentsfirst@umuc.edu.
Website: https://www.umgc.edu/academic-programs/masters-degrees/cybersecurity-management-policy-ms.cfm

University of Maryland Global Campus, University of Maryland Global Campus, Cybersecurity Technology, Adelphi, MD 20783. Offers MS, Certificate. *Program availability:* Part-time, evening/weekend, online learning. *Students:* 1,040 part-time (305 women); includes 608 minority (413 Black or African American, non-Hispanic/Latino; 5 American Indian or Alaska Native, non-Hispanic/Latino; 66 Asian, non-Hispanic/Latino; 86 Hispanic/Latino; 3 Native Hawaiian or other Pacific Islander, non-Hispanic/Latino; 35 Two or more races, non-Hispanic/Latino), 11 international. Average age 36. 604 applicants, 100% accepted, 214 enrolled. In 2019, 667 master's, 125 other advanced degrees awarded. *Degree requirements:* For master's, thesis or alternative, capstone course. *Application deadline:* Applications are processed on a rolling basis. Application fee: $50. Electronic applications accepted. *Financial support:* Scholarships/grants available. Support available to part-time students. Financial award application deadline: 6/1; financial award applicants required to submit FAFSA. *Unit head:* Mansur Hasib, Program Chair, 240-684-2400, E-mail: Mansur.Hasib@umgc.edu. *Application contact:* Admissions, 800-888-8682, E-mail: studentsfirst@umuc.edu.
Website: https://www.umgc.edu/academic-programs/masters-degrees/cybersecurity-technology-ms.cfm

University of Maryland Global Campus, University of Maryland Global Campus, Digital Forensics and Cyber Investigation, Adelphi, MD 20783. Offers MS, Certificate. *Program availability:* Part-time, evening/weekend, online learning. *Students:* 257 part-time (141 women); includes 143 minority (98 Black or African American, non-Hispanic/Latino; 1 American Indian or Alaska Native, non-Hispanic/Latino; 9 Asian, non-Hispanic/Latino; 21 Hispanic/Latino; 1 Native Hawaiian or other Pacific Islander, non-Hispanic/Latino; 13 Two or more races, non-Hispanic/Latino), 2 international. Average age 35. 177 applicants, 100% accepted, 72 enrolled. In 2019, 125 master's, 2 other advanced degrees awarded. *Degree requirements:* For master's, thesis or alternative, capstone course. *Application deadline:* Applications are processed on a rolling basis. Application fee: $50. Electronic applications accepted. *Financial support:* Scholarships/grants available. Support available to part-time students. Financial award application deadline: 6/1; financial award applicants required to submit FAFSA. *Unit head:* Patrick O'Guinn, 240-684-2400, E-mail: patrick.oguinn@umgc.edu. *Application contact:* Admissions, 800-888-8682, E-mail: studentfirst@umgc.edu.
Website: https://www.umgc.edu/academic-programs/masters-degrees/digital-forensics-cyber-investigation-ms.cfm

University of Michigan–Dearborn, College of Engineering and Computer Science, PhD Program in Computer and Information Science, Dearborn, MI 48128. Offers data management (PhD); data science (PhD); software engineering (PhD); systems and security (PhD). *Faculty:* 19 full-time (1 woman), 5 part-time/adjunct (0 women). *Students:* 8 full-time (5 women), 6 part-time (1 woman); includes 1 minority (Asian, non-Hispanic/Latino), 11 international. Average age 28. 17 applicants, 24% accepted, 3 enrolled. In 2019, 1 doctorate awarded. *Degree requirements:* For doctorate, comprehensive exam, thesis/dissertation. *Entrance requirements:* For doctorate, GRE, bachelor's or master's degree in computer science or closely-related field. Additional exam requirements/recommendations for international students: required—TOEFL (minimum score 560 paper-based; 84 iBT), IELTS (minimum score 6.5). *Application deadline:* For fall admission, 2/1 for domestic and international students. Application fee: $60. Electronic applications accepted. *Financial support:* Research assistantships with full tuition reimbursements, teaching assistantships with full tuition reimbursements, scholarships/grants, health care benefits, and unspecified assistantships available. Financial award application deadline: 2/1; financial award applicants required to submit FAFSA. *Unit head:* Dr. Di Ma, Director, 313-583-6737, E-mail: dmadma@umich.edu. *Application contact:* Office of Graduate Studies, 313-583-6321, E-mail: umd-graduatestudies@umich.edu.
Website: https://umdearborn.edu/cecs/departments/computer-and-information-science/graduate-programs/phd-computer-and-information-science

University of Minnesota, Twin Cities Campus, College of Science and Engineering, Technological Leadership Institute, Program in Security Technologies, Minneapolis, MN 55455-0213. Offers MSST. *Program availability:* Part-time. *Degree requirements:* For master's, capstone project. *Entrance requirements:* Additional exam requirements/recommendations for international students: required—TOEFL (minimum score 580 paper-based; 90 iBT). Electronic applications accepted.

University of Missouri–St. Louis, College of Business Administration, St. Louis, MO 63121. Offers accounting (M Acc); business administration (MBA, DBA, PhD, Certificate), including logistics and supply chain management (PhD); business intelligence (Certificate); cybersecurity (Certificate); digital and social media marketing (Certificate); human resources management (Certificate); information systems (MS); logistics and supply chain management (Certificate); marketing management (Certificate). *Program availability:* Part-time, evening/weekend. *Degree requirements:* For doctorate, thesis/dissertation. *Entrance requirements:* For master's, GMAT, 2 letters of recommendation; for doctorate, GMAT or GRE, 3 letters of recommendation. Additional exam requirements/recommendations for international students: recommended—TOEFL (minimum score 550 paper-based; 79 iBT), IELTS (minimum score 6.5). Electronic applications accepted. *Expenses: Tuition, area resident:* Full-time $9005.40; part-time $6003.60 per credit hour. Tuition, state resident: full-time $9005.40; part-time $6003.60 per credit hour. Tuition, nonresident: full-time $22,108; part-time $14,738.40 per credit hour. *International tuition:* $22,107.60 full-time. Tuition and fees vary according to course load.

University of Nebraska at Omaha, Graduate Studies, College of Information Science and Technology, Department of Information Systems and Quantitative Analysis, Omaha, NE 68182. Offers data analytics (Certificate); information assurance (Certificate); information technology (MIT, PhD); management information systems (MS); project management (Certificate); systems analysis and design (Certificate). *Program availability:* Part-time, evening/weekend. *Degree requirements:* For master's, comprehensive exam, thesis (for some programs); for doctorate, comprehensive exam, thesis/dissertation. *Entrance requirements:* For master's, GRE General Test, minimum GPA of 3.0, 3 letters of recommendation, writing sample, resume, official transcripts; for doctorate, GMAT or GRE General Test, minimum GPA of 3.0, 3 letters of recommendation, writing sample, resume, official transcripts; for Certificate, minimum GPA of 3.0, official transcripts. Additional exam requirements/recommendations for international students: required—TOEFL, IELTS, PTE. Electronic applications accepted.

University of Nebraska at Omaha, Graduate Studies, College of Information Science and Technology, School of Interdisciplinary Informatics, Omaha, NE 68182. Offers biomedical informatics (MS, PhD); information assurance (MS). *Program availability:* Part-time, evening/weekend. *Degree requirements:* For master's, comprehensive exam, thesis (for some programs); for doctorate, comprehensive exam, thesis/dissertation. *Entrance requirements:* For master's and doctorate, GRE General Test, letters of recommendation, resume, transcripts. Additional exam requirements/recommendations for international students: required—TOEFL, IELTS, PTE.

University of Nevada, Las Vegas, Graduate College, Greenspun College of Urban Affairs, School of Public Policy and Leadership, Las Vegas, NV 89154-4030. Offers crisis and emergency management (MS); emergency crisis management cybersecurity (Certificate); environmental science (MS, PhD); non-profit management (Certificate); public administration (MPA); public affairs (PhD); public management (Certificate); urban leadership (MA). *Program availability:* Part-time. *Faculty:* 12 full-time (5 women), 6 part-time/adjunct (1 woman). *Students:* 106 full-time (61 women), 96 part-time (71 women); includes 118 minority (34 Black or African American, non-Hispanic/Latino; 1 American Indian or Alaska Native, non-Hispanic/Latino; 11 Asian, non-Hispanic/Latino; 49 Hispanic/Latino; 2 Native Hawaiian or other Pacific Islander, non-Hispanic/Latino; 21 Two or more races, non-Hispanic/Latino), 5 international. Average age 36. 115 applicants, 77% accepted, 73 enrolled. In 2019, 49 master's, 13 doctorates, 16 other advanced degrees awarded. *Degree requirements:* For master's, comprehensive exam (for some programs), thesis (for some programs), oral exam; for doctorate, comprehensive exam, thesis/dissertation; for Certificate, portfolio. *Entrance requirements:* For master's, GRE General Test or GMAT, bachelor's degree with minimum GPA 2.75; statement of purpose; 3 letters of recommendation; for doctorate, GRE General Test, master's degree with minimum GPA of 3.5; 3 letters of recommendation; statement of purpose; writing sample; personal interview; for Certificate, bachelor's degree; 2 letters of recommendation; writing sample. Additional

exam requirements/recommendations for international students: required—TOEFL (minimum score 550 paper-based; 80 iBT), IELTS (minimum score 7). *Application deadline:* For fall admission, 6/1 for domestic and international students; for spring admission, 11/1 for domestic and international students; for summer admission, 3/1 for domestic students. Application fee: $60 ($95 for international students). Electronic applications accepted. *Expenses:* Contact institution. *Financial support:* In 2019–20, 25 students received support, including 15 research assistantships with full tuition reimbursements available (averaging $15,700 per year), 10 teaching assistantships with full tuition reimbursements available (averaging $16,625 per year); institutionally sponsored loans, scholarships/grants, health care benefits, and unspecified assistantships also available. Financial award application deadline: 3/15; financial award applicants required to submit FAFSA. *Unit head:* Dr. Christopher Stream, Director, 702-895-5120, Fax: 702-895-4436, E-mail: sppl.chair@unlv.edu. *Application contact:* Dr. Jayce Farmer, Graduate Coordinator, 702-895-4828, E-mail: sppl.gradcoord@unlv.edu.
Website: https://www.unlv.edu/publicpolicy

University of New Hampshire, Graduate School Manchester Campus, Manchester, NH 03101. Offers business administration (MBA); cybersecurity policy and risk management (MS); educational administration and supervision (Ed S); educational studies (M Ed); elementary education (M Ed); information technology (MS); public administration (MPA); public health (MPH, Certificate); secondary education (M Ed, MAT); social work (MSW); substance use disorders (Certificate). *Program availability:* Part-time, evening/weekend. *Students:* 118 full-time (56 women), 110 part-time (47 women); includes 23 minority (4 Black or African American, non-Hispanic/Latino; 5 Asian, non-Hispanic/Latino; 13 Hispanic/Latino; 1 Two or more races, non-Hispanic/Latino), 39 international. Average age 32. 231 applicants, 78% accepted, 64 enrolled. In 2019, 47 master's, 3 other advanced degrees awarded. *Entrance requirements:* Additional exam requirements/recommendations for international students: required—TOEFL (minimum score 550 paper-based; 80 iBT), IELTS, PTE. *Application deadline:* For fall admission, 6/1 for domestic students, 4/1 for international students; for spring admission, 12/1 for domestic students. Application fee: $65. Electronic applications accepted. *Financial support:* In 2019–20, 11 students received support, including 1 teaching assistantship; fellowships, research assistantships, Federal Work-Study, scholarships/grants, health care benefits, and unspecified assistantships also available. Support available to part-time students. Financial award application deadline: 2/15; financial award applicants required to submit FAFSA. *Unit head:* Candice Morey, Educational Programs Coordinator, 603-641-4313, E-mail: unhm.gradcenter@unh.edu. *Application contact:* Candice Morey, Educational Programs Coordinator, 603-641-4313, E-mail: unhm.gradcenter@unh.edu.
Website: http://www.gradschool.unh.edu/manchester/

University of New Haven, Graduate School, Tagliatela College of Engineering, Program in Cybersecurity and Networks, West Haven, CT 06516. Offers MS. *Students:* 41 full-time (14 women), 15 part-time (4 women); includes 4 minority (1 Black or African American, non-Hispanic/Latino; 1 Asian, non-Hispanic/Latino; 2 Hispanic/Latino), 35 international. Average age 26. 84 applicants, 73% accepted, 20 enrolled. In 2019, 5 master's awarded. *Application deadline:* Applications are processed on a rolling basis. Application fee: $50. *Financial support:* Applicants required to submit FAFSA. *Unit head:* Dr. Barun Chandra, Associate Professor, 203-932-7089, E-mail: bchandra@newhaven.edu. *Application contact:* Selina O'Toole, Senior Associate Director of Graduate Admissions, 203-932-7337, E-mail: sotoole@newhaven.edu.
Website: http://www.newhaven.edu/engineering/graduate-programs/cybersecurity-networks/

University of New Mexico, Anderson School of Management, Department of Accounting, Albuquerque, NM 87131. Offers accounting (MBA); advanced accounting (M Acct); information assurance (M Acct); professional accounting (M Acct); tax accounting (M Acct); JD/M Acct. *Accreditation:* AACSB. *Program availability:* Part-time, evening/weekend. *Faculty:* 15 full-time (9 women), 5 part-time/adjunct (2 women). *Students:* 82 part-time (50 women); includes 47 minority (2 Black or African American, non-Hispanic/Latino; 4 American Indian or Alaska Native, non-Hispanic/Latino; 8 Asian, non-Hispanic/Latino; 32 Hispanic/Latino; 1 Two or more races, non-Hispanic/Latino), 8 international. Average age 31. 45 applicants, 51% accepted, 20 enrolled. In 2019, 53 master's awarded. *Entrance requirements:* For master's, GMAT of 500 or higher, GRE conversion to GMAT of 500 or higher, LSAT of 155 or higher, PCAT or MCAT of 55 composite or higher, Minimum GPA of 3.0 in last 60 hours of coursework. We offer exam waivers for applicants with 3.25 gpa in upper division coursework. Additional exam requirements/recommendations for international students: required—TOEFL (minimum score 550 paper-based; 79 iBT), IELTS (minimum score 6.5). *Application deadline:* For fall admission, 4/1 priority date for domestic students, 5/1 priority date for international students; for spring admission, 10/1 priority date for domestic and international students; for summer admission, 2/1 priority date for domestic students, 2/1 for international students. Applications are processed on a rolling basis. Application fee: $100 ($70 for international students). Electronic applications accepted. *Expenses:* $542.36 is cost per credit hour, $6508.32 is cost per semester for full time study. *Financial support:* In 2019–20, 21 students received support, including 14 fellowships (averaging $16,744 per year), research assistantships with partial tuition reimbursements available (averaging $15,345 per year); career-related internships or fieldwork, Federal Work-Study, scholarships/grants, and unspecified assistantships also available. Support available to part-time students. Financial award application deadline: 6/1; financial award applicants required to submit FAFSA. *Unit head:* Dr. Richard Brody, Department Chair, 505-277-6471, E-mail: tmarmijo@unm.edu. *Application contact:* Dr. Richard Brody, Department Chair, 505-277-6471, E-mail: tmarmijo@unm.edu.
Website: https://www.mgt.unm.edu/acct/default.asp?mm-faculty

University of New Mexico, Anderson School of Management, Department of Marketing, Information Systems, Information Assurance, and Operations Management, Albuquerque, NM 87131. Offers information assurance (MBA); information systems and assurance (MS); management information systems (MBA); marketing management (MBA); operations management (MBA). *Program availability:* Part-time. *Faculty:* 17 full-time (6 women), 12 part-time/adjunct (5 women). *Students:* 68 part-time (28 women); includes 34 minority (1 Black or African American, non-Hispanic/Latino; 2 American Indian or Alaska Native, non-Hispanic/Latino; 6 Asian, non-Hispanic/Latino; 23 Hispanic/Latino; 2 Two or more races, non-Hispanic/Latino), 15 international. Average age 28. In 2019, 44 master's awarded. *Degree requirements:* For master's, comprehensive exam. *Entrance requirements:* For master's, GMAT of 500 or higher, GRE conversion to GMAT of 500 or higher, LSAT of 155 or higher, PCAT or MCAT of 55 composite or higher, Minimum GPA of 3.0 in last 60 hours of coursework. We offer exam waivers for applicants with 3.5 gpa in upper division coursework from AACSB-Accredited bachelor's degree. Additional exam requirements/recommendations for international students: required—TOEFL (minimum score 550 paper-based; 79 iBT), IELTS (minimum score 6.5). *Application deadline:* For fall admission, 4/1 priority date for domestic and international students; for spring admission, 10/1 priority date for domestic and international students; for summer admission, 2/1 priority date for domestic and international students. Applications are processed on a rolling basis. Application fee: $100 ($70 for international students). Electronic applications accepted. *Expenses:* $542.36 per credit hour, $6508.32 per semester for full time study. *Financial support:* In 2019–20, 11 students received support, including 16 fellowships (averaging $16,320 per year), 5 research assistantships with partial tuition reimbursements available (averaging $15,180 per year); career-related internships or fieldwork, Federal Work-Study, scholarships/grants, and unspecified assistantships also available. Support available to part-time students. Financial award application deadline: 6/1; financial award applicants required to submit FAFSA. *Unit head:* Dr. Mary Margaret Rogers, Chair, 505-277-6471, E-mail: mmrogers@unm.edu. *Application contact:* Lisa Beauchene-Lawson, Supervisor, Graduate Admissions & Advisement, 505-277-3290, E-mail: andersongrad@unm.edu.
Website: https://www.mgt.unm.edu/mids/default.asp?mm-faculty

The University of North Carolina at Charlotte, College of Computing and Informatics, Department of Software and Information Systems, Charlotte, NC 28223-0001. Offers advanced databases and knowledge discovery (Graduate Certificate); game design and development (Graduate Certificate); information security and privacy (Graduate Certificate); information technology (MS); management of information technology (Graduate Certificate); network security (Graduate Certificate); secure software development (Graduate Certificate). *Program availability:* Part-time, evening/weekend. *Faculty:* 21 full-time (8 women), 5 part-time/adjunct (0 women). *Students:* 138 full-time (64 women), 98 part-time (38 women); includes 47 minority (25 Black or African American, non-Hispanic/Latino; 9 Asian, non-Hispanic/Latino; 10 Hispanic/Latino; 1 Native Hawaiian or other Pacific Islander, non-Hispanic/Latino; 2 Two or more races, non-Hispanic/Latino), 136 international. Average age 28. 298 applicants, 75% accepted, 78 enrolled. In 2019, 107 master's, 20 other advanced degrees awarded. *Degree requirements:* For master's, thesis optional, internship project or project report. *Entrance requirements:* For master's, GRE or GMAT, undergraduate or equivalent course work in data structures, object-oriented programming in C++, C#, or Java with minimum GPA of 3.0, undergraduate GPA of at least 3.0 and a junior/senior GPA of at least 3.0, statement of purpose, 3 letters of recommendation from academic and/or professional references; for Graduate Certificate, bachelor's degree from accredited institution in computing, mathematical, engineering or business discipline with minimum overall GPA of 2.8, junior/senior 3.0; substantial knowledge of data structures and object-oriented programming in C++, C# or Java. Additional exam requirements/recommendations for international students: required—TOEFL (minimum score 557 paper-based; 83 iBT), IELTS (minimum score 6.5), TOEFL (minimum score 557 paper-based, 83 iBT) or IELTS (6.5). *Application deadline:* Applications are processed on a rolling basis. Application fee: $75. Electronic applications accepted. *Expenses:* Contact institution. *Financial support:* In 2019–20, 65 students received support, including 2 fellowships (averaging $51,459 per year), 21 research assistantships (averaging $14,084 per year), 42 teaching assistantships (averaging $7,186 per year); career-related internships or fieldwork, institutionally sponsored loans, scholarships/grants, and unspecified assistantships also available. Support available to part-time students. Financial award application deadline: 3/1; financial award applicants required to submit FAFSA. *Unit head:* Dr. Mary Lou Maher, Chair, 704-687-1940, E-mail: m.maher@uncc.edu. *Application contact:* Kathy B. Giddings, Director of Graduate Admissions, 704-687-5503, Fax: 704-687-1668, E-mail: gradadm@uncc.edu.
Website: http://sis.uncc.edu/

University of Rhode Island, Graduate School, College of Arts and Sciences, Department of Computer Science and Statistics, Kingston, RI 02881. Offers computer science (MS, PhD); cyber security (PSM, Graduate Certificate); digital forensics (Graduate Certificate). *Program availability:* Part-time, evening/weekend, 100% online, blended/hybrid learning. *Faculty:* 20 full-time (6 women). *Students:* 29 full-time (13 women), 88 part-time (19 women); includes 16 minority (5 Black or African American, non-Hispanic/Latino; 5 Asian, non-Hispanic/Latino; 5 Hispanic/Latino; 1 Two or more races, non-Hispanic/Latino), 13 international. 77 applicants, 82% accepted, 39 enrolled. In 2019, 47 master's, 3 doctorates, 25 other advanced degrees awarded. Terminal master's awarded for partial completion of doctoral program. *Entrance requirements:* Additional exam requirements/recommendations for international students: required—TOEFL. *Application deadline:* For fall admission, 7/15 for domestic students, 2/1 for international students; for spring admission, 11/15 for domestic students, 7/15 for international students. Application fee: $65. Electronic applications accepted. *Expenses: Tuition, area resident:* Full-time $13,734; part-time $763 per credit. Tuition, state resident: full-time $13,734; part-time $763 per credit. Tuition, nonresident: full-time $26,512; part-time $1473 per credit. *International tuition:* $26,512 full-time. *Required fees:* $1780; $52 per credit. $35 per term. One-time fee: $165. *Financial support:* In 2019–20, 3 research assistantships with tuition reimbursements (averaging $9,645 per year), 15 teaching assistantships with tuition reimbursements (averaging $13,546 per year) were awarded; unspecified assistantships also available. Financial award application deadline: 2/1; financial award applicants required to submit FAFSA. *Unit head:* Dr. Lisa DiPippo, Chair, 401-874-2701, Fax: 401-874-4617, E-mail: dipippo@cs.uri.edu. *Application contact:* Dr. Lutz Hamel, Graduate Program Director, 401-874-2701, E-mail: lutzhamel@uri.edu.
Website: http://www.cs.uri.edu/

University of San Diego, Division of Professional and Continuing Education, San Diego, CA 92110-2492. Offers cyber security operations and leadership (MS); law enforcement and public safety leadership (MS). *Program availability:* Part-time-only, evening/weekend, 100% online. *Faculty:* 2 full-time (1 woman), 17 part-time/adjunct (1 woman). *Students:* 329 part-time (82 women); includes 141 minority (28 Black or African American, non-Hispanic/Latino; 2 American Indian or Alaska Native, non-Hispanic/Latino; 20 Asian, non-Hispanic/Latino; 83 Hispanic/Latino; 2 Native Hawaiian or other Pacific Islander, non-Hispanic/Latino; 6 Two or more races, non-Hispanic/Latino). Average age 39. 265 applicants, 86% accepted, 130 enrolled. In 2019, 168 master's awarded. *Entrance requirements:* For master's, GMAT, GRE, or LSAT if GPA is under 2.75. Additional exam requirements/recommendations for international students: required—TOEFL (minimum score 115 iBT). *Application deadline:* For fall admission, 8/3 for domestic and international students; for spring admission, 12/2 for domestic and international students; for summer admission, 4/22 for domestic and international students. Applications are processed on a rolling basis. Application fee: $45. Electronic applications accepted. *Financial support:* Application deadline: 4/1; applicants required to submit FAFSA. *Unit head:* Dr. Chell Roberts, Assoc. Provost for Professional Education and Online Dev., 619-260-4585, Fax: 619-260-2961, E-mail: continuinged@sandiego.edu. *Application contact:* Erika Garwood, Associate Director of Graduate Admissions, 619-260-4524, Fax: 619-260-4158, E-mail: grads@sandiego.edu.
Website: http://pce.sandiego.edu/

University of San Diego, Shiley-Marcos School of Engineering, San Diego, CA 92110-2492. Offers cyber security engineering (MS). *Program availability:* Part-time, evening/weekend. *Faculty:* 2 full-time (0 women), 3 part-time/adjunct (0 women). *Students:* 67 part-time (10 women); includes 34 minority (5 Black or African American, non-Hispanic/Latino; 11 Asian, non-Hispanic/Latino; 15 Hispanic/Latino; 3 Two or more races, non-Hispanic/Latino), 2 international. Average age 34. 65 applicants, 86% accepted, 37 enrolled. In 2019, 30 master's awarded. *Degree requirements:* For master's, capstone course. *Entrance requirements:* For master's, GMAT, GRE, or LSAT if GPA is under 2.75. Additional exam requirements/recommendations for international students: required—TOEFL (minimum score 120 iBT). *Application deadline:* For fall admission, 8/3 for domestic students; for spring admission, 12/2 for domestic students; for summer admission, 4/13 for domestic students. Applications are processed on a rolling basis. Application fee: $45. Electronic applications accepted. *Financial support:* In 2019–20, 5

students received support. Institutionally sponsored loans and scholarships/grants available. Financial award application deadline: 4/1; financial award applicants required to submit FAFSA. *Unit head:* Dr. Chell Roberts, Dean, 619-260-4627, E-mail: croberts@sandiego.edu. *Application contact:* Erika Garwood, Associate Director of Graduate Admissions, 619-260-4524, Fax: 619-260-4158, E-mail: grads@sandiego.edu.
Website: http://www.sandiego.edu/engineering/

University of Southern California, Graduate School, Viterbi School of Engineering, Department of Computer Science, Los Angeles, CA 90089. Offers computer networks (MS); computer science (MS, PhD); computer security (MS); game development (MS); high performance computing and simulations (MS); human language technology (MS); intelligent robotics (MS); multimedia and creative technologies (MS); software engineering (MS). *Program availability:* Part-time, evening/weekend, online learning. *Entrance requirements:* For master's and doctorate, GRE General Test. Additional exam requirements/recommendations for international students: required—TOEFL. Electronic applications accepted.

University of South Florida, College of Graduate Studies, Tampa, FL 33620-9951. Offers cybersecurity (MS), including computer security fundamentals, cyber intelligence, digital forensics, information assurance. *Program availability:* Part-time, evening/weekend, online learning. *Faculty:* 1 (woman) full-time. *Students:* 70 full-time (15 women), 161 part-time (32 women); includes 112 minority (32 Black or African American, non-Hispanic/Latino; 1 American Indian or Alaska Native, non-Hispanic/Latino; 24 Asian, non-Hispanic/Latino; 51 Hispanic/Latino; 4 Two or more races, non-Hispanic/Latino), 4 international. Average age 34. 101 applicants, 76% accepted, 54 enrolled. In 2019, 133 master's awarded. Terminal master's awarded for partial completion of doctoral program. *Degree requirements:* For master's, variable foreign language requirement, comprehensive exam, thesis (for some programs), practicum. *Entrance requirements:* For master's, GRE General Test, 250-500 word essay in which student describes academic and professional background, reasons for pursuing degree, and professional goals pertaining to cybersecurity; 2 letters of recommendation; current resume or CV. Video or phone interview may be required. Additional exam requirements/recommendations for international students: required—TOEFL, TOEFL (minimum score 550 paper-based; 79 iBT) or IELTS (minimum score 6.5). *Application deadline:* For fall admission, 2/15 for domestic and international students; for spring admission, 10/15 for domestic students, 9/15 for international students; for summer admission, 2/15 for domestic and international students. Application fee: $30. Electronic applications accepted. *Financial support:* In 2019–20, 20 students received support. Teaching assistantships available. Financial award application deadline: 2/1; financial award applicants required to submit FAFSA. *Unit head:* Dr. Dwayne Smith, Senior Vice Provost and Dean of the Office of Graduate Studies, 813-974-7359, Fax: 813-974-5762, E-mail: mdsmith8@usf.edu. *Application contact:* Paul Crawford, Associate Director for Graduate Admissions, 813-974-8800, E-mail: pjcrawford@usf.edu.
Website: https://www.usf.edu/graduate-studies/

The University of Tampa, Sykes College of Business, Tampa, FL 33606-1490. Offers accounting (MS); business analytics (MBA); cybersecurity (MBA, MS); entrepreneurship (MBA, MS); finance (MBA, MS); information systems management (MBA); innovation management (MBA); international business (MBA); marketing (MBA, MS); nonprofit management (MBA, Certificate). *Accreditation:* AACSB. *Program availability:* Part-time, evening/weekend. *Degree requirements:* For master's, capstone. *Entrance requirements:* For master's, GMAT or GRE, official transcripts from all colleges and/or universities previously attended, resume, personal statement, letters of recommendation. Additional exam requirements/recommendations for international students: required—TOEFL (minimum score 577 paper-based; 90 iBT), IELTS (minimum score 7.5). Electronic applications accepted. *Expenses:* Contact institution.

The University of Texas at Austin, Graduate School, School of Information, Austin, TX 78712-1111. Offers identity management and security (MSIMS); information (PhD); information studies (MSIS); MSIS/MA. *Accreditation:* ALA (one or more programs are accredited). *Program availability:* Part-time. *Degree requirements:* For doctorate, 2 foreign languages, thesis/dissertation. *Entrance requirements:* For master's and doctorate, GRE General Test. Electronic applications accepted.

The University of Texas at El Paso, Graduate School, College of Engineering, Department of Computer Science, El Paso, TX 79968-0001. Offers computer science (MS, PhD); cyber security (Graduate Certificate); information technology (MSIT); software engineering (MS). *Program availability:* Part-time, evening/weekend. *Degree requirements:* For master's, thesis optional; for doctorate, thesis/dissertation. *Entrance requirements:* For master's, GRE, minimum GPA of 3.0; for doctorate, GRE, statement of purpose, letters of reference. Additional exam requirements/recommendations for international students: required—TOEFL; recommended—IELTS. Electronic applications accepted.

The University of Texas at San Antonio, College of Business, Department of Information Systems and Cyber Security, San Antonio, TX 78249-0617. Offers cyber security (MSIT); information technology (MS, PhD); management of technology (MBA); technology entrepreneurship and management (Certificate). *Program availability:* Part-time, evening/weekend. *Degree requirements:* For master's, comprehensive exam (for some programs), thesis optional; for doctorate, comprehensive exam, thesis/dissertation. *Entrance requirements:* For master's and doctorate, GMAT/GRE, official transcripts, statement of purpose, letters of recommendation. Additional exam requirements/recommendations for international students: required—TOEFL (minimum score 550 paper-based; 79 iBT), IELTS (minimum score 6.5). Electronic applications accepted. *Expenses:* Contact institution.

The University of Texas at Tyler, Soules College of Business, Department of Management and Marketing, Tyler, TX 75799-0001. Offers cyber security (MBA); engineering management (MBA); general management (MBA); healthcare management (MBA); internal assurance and consulting (MBA); marketing (MBA); oil, gas and energy (MBA); organizational development (MBA); quality management (MBA). *Accreditation:* AACSB. *Program availability:* Part-time, online learning. *Faculty:* 13 full-time (5 women). *Students:* Average age 29. *Entrance requirements:* Additional exam requirements/recommendations for international students: required—TOEFL (minimum score 550 paper-based). *Application deadline:* For fall admission, 8/17 priority date for domestic students, 7/1 priority date for international students; for spring admission, 12/21 priority date for domestic students, 11/1 priority date for international students. Application fee: $25 ($50 for international students). *Unit head:* Dr. Krist Swimberghe, Chair, 903-565-5803, E-mail: kswimberghe@uttyler.edu. *Application contact:* Dr. Krist Swimberghe, Chair, 903-565-5803, E-mail: kswimberghe@uttyler.edu.
Website: https://www.uttyler.edu/cbt/manamark/

The University of Tulsa, Graduate School, College of Engineering and Natural Sciences, Tandy School of Computer Science, Tulsa, OK 74104-3189. Offers computer science (MS, PhD); cyber security (MS); JD/MS; MBA/MS. *Program availability:* Part-time. Terminal master's awarded for partial completion of doctoral program. *Degree requirements:* For master's, thesis (for some programs); for doctorate, comprehensive exam, thesis/dissertation. *Entrance requirements:* For master's and doctorate, GRE General Test. Additional exam requirements/recommendations for international students: required—TOEFL (minimum score 550 paper-based; 80 iBT), IELTS (minimum score 6). Electronic applications accepted. *Expenses: Tuition:* Full-time $22,896; part-time $1272 per credit hour. *Required fees:* $6 per credit hour. Tuition and fees vary according to course load and program.

University of Utah, Graduate School, David Eccles School of Business, Master of Science in Information Systems Program, Salt Lake City, UT 84112. Offers information systems (MS, Graduate Certificate), including business intelligence and analytics, IT security, product and process management, software and systems architecture. *Program availability:* Part-time, evening/weekend, 100% online, blended/hybrid learning. *Students:* 141 full-time (34 women), 95 part-time (24 women); includes 39 minority (2 Black or African American, non-Hispanic/Latino; 10 Asian, non-Hispanic/Latino; 19 Hispanic/Latino; 8 Two or more races, non-Hispanic/Latino), 65 international. Average age 31. In 2019, 153 master's awarded. *Entrance requirements:* For master's, GMAT/GRE, minimum undergraduate GPA of 3.0, 2 letters of recommendation, personal statement, professional resume. Additional exam requirements/recommendations for international students: required—TOEFL (minimum score 550 paper-based; 80 iBT), IELTS (minimum score 6.5). *Application deadline:* For fall admission, 7/27 for domestic students, 3/30 for international students; for spring admission, 12/7 for domestic students, 9/7 priority date for international students; for summer admission, 4/12 for domestic students, 1/11 for international students. Applications are processed on a rolling basis. Application fee: $55 ($65 for international students). Electronic applications accepted. *Expenses:* Contact institution. *Financial support:* Fellowships with partial tuition reimbursements, teaching assistantships, tuition waivers (partial), and unspecified assistantships available. Financial award application deadline: 6/1; financial award applicants required to submit FAFSA. *Unit head:* Dr. Mark Parker, Associate Dean, Specialized Masters Program, 801-585-5177, Fax: 801-581-3666, E-mail: mark.parker@eccles.utah.edu. *Application contact:* Kaylee Miller, Admissions Coordinator, 801-587-5878, Fax: 801-581-3666, E-mail: kaylee.miller@eccles.utah.edu.
Website: http://msis.eccles.utah.edu

University of Washington, Graduate School, Information School, Seattle, WA 98195. Offers information management (MSIM), including business intelligence, data science, information architecture, information consulting, information security, user experience; information science (PhD); library and information science (MLIS). *Accreditation:* ALA (one or more programs are accredited). *Program availability:* Part-time, evening/weekend, 100% online coursework with required attendance at on-campus orientation at start of program. *Faculty:* 49 full-time (30 women), 33 part-time/adjunct (19 women). *Students:* 394 full-time (249 women), 283 part-time (198 women); includes 154 minority (33 Black or African American, non-Hispanic/Latino; 8 American Indian or Alaska Native, non-Hispanic/Latino; 71 Asian, non-Hispanic/Latino; 38 Hispanic/Latino; 4 Native Hawaiian or other Pacific Islander, non-Hispanic/Latino), 184 international. Average age 30. 1,205 applicants, 47% accepted, 307 enrolled. In 2019, 234 master's, 5 doctorates awarded. Terminal master's awarded for partial completion of doctoral program. *Degree requirements:* For master's, thesis or alternative, capstone or culminating project; for doctorate, comprehensive exam, thesis/dissertation. *Entrance requirements:* For master's, GRE General Test, GMAT Requirements vary for degree programs as test scores may be optional for some applicants.; for doctorate, GRE General Test May not be required for all applicants. Additional exam requirements/recommendations for international students: required—TOEFL (minimum score 590 paper-based; 100 iBT). *Application deadline:* For fall admission, 12/1 priority date for domestic and international students. Application fee: $85. Electronic applications accepted. *Expenses:* Graduate degrees: $845 per credit plus approximately $200 in quarterly fees (for MLIS), $896 per credit plus approximately $200 in quarterly fees (for MSIM); PhD: $5798 per quarter in-state full-time, $10,098 per quarter out-of-state full-time. *Financial support:* In 2019–20, 73 students received support, including 14 fellowships with full tuition reimbursements available (averaging $46,977 per year), 90 research assistantships with full tuition reimbursements available (averaging $22,137 per year), 70 teaching assistantships with full tuition reimbursements available (averaging $22,849 per year); Federal Work-Study, institutionally sponsored loans, scholarships/grants, health care benefits, tuition waivers (full and partial), and unspecified assistantships also available. Support available to part-time students. Financial award application deadline: 10/1; financial award applicants required to submit FAFSA. *Unit head:* Dr. Anind Dey, Dean, E-mail: anind@uw.edu. *Application contact:* Kari Brothers, Admissions Counselor, 206-616-5541, Fax: 206-616-3152, E-mail: kari683@uw.edu.
Website: http://ischool.uw.edu/

University of West Florida, Hal Marcus College of Science and Engineering, Department of Computer Science, Pensacola, FL 32514-5750. Offers computer science (MS), including computer science, database systems, software engineering; information technology (MS), including cybersecurity, database management. *Program availability:* Part-time, evening/weekend. *Degree requirements:* For master's, thesis optional. *Entrance requirements:* For master's, GRE, MAT, or GMAT, official transcripts; minimum undergraduate GPA of 3.0; letter of intent; three letters of recommendation. Additional exam requirements/recommendations for international students: required—TOEFL (minimum score 550 paper-based).

University of Wisconsin–Madison, Graduate School, Wisconsin School of Business, Wisconsin Full-Time MBA Program, Madison, WI 53706-1380. Offers applied security analysis (MBA); arts administration (MBA); brand and product management (MBA); corporate finance and investment banking (MBA); marketing research (MBA); operations and technology management (MBA); real estate (MBA); risk management and insurance (MBA); strategic human resource management (MBA); supply chain management (MBA). *Faculty:* 131 full-time (35 women), 33 part-time/adjunct (11 women). *Students:* 146 full-time (51 women); includes 21 minority (2 Black or African American, non-Hispanic/Latino; 1 American Indian or Alaska Native, non-Hispanic/Latino; 6 Asian, non-Hispanic/Latino; 8 Hispanic/Latino; 4 Two or more races, non-Hispanic/Latino), 41 international. Average age 28. 314 applicants, 44% accepted, 67 enrolled. In 2019, 104 master's awarded. *Entrance requirements:* For master's, GMAT or GRE, U.S. active military, U.S. veterans, candidates with terminal degrees (JD, PhD) or those with 5 years of work experience can apply for a GMAT or GRE waiver, bachelor's degree, standardized test scores (GMAT or GRE), English proficiency test (TOEFL, IELTS, or PTE for applicants whose native language is not English or whose undergraduate instruction was not in English), 2 years of work experience preferred, 1 completed recommendation, resume, essays (one required, one recommended, one optional). Additional exam requirements/recommendations for international students: required—TOEFL (minimum score 100 iBT), IELTS (minimum score 7.5), TOEFL is not required for international students whose undergraduate training was in English. *Application deadline:* For fall admission, 11/1 for domestic and international students; for winter admission, 1/10 for domestic and international students; for spring admission, 3/1 for domestic and international students; for summer admission, 4/27 for domestic students, 4/27 priority date for international students. Applications are processed on a rolling basis. Application fee: $75 ($81 for international students). Electronic applications accepted. *Expenses:* $43,061 resident (includes tuition and fees for 2-year program), $82,214 non-resident (includes tuition and fees for the 2-year program). *Financial support:* Fellowships, research assistantships, teaching assistantships, scholarships/grants, health care benefits, tuition waivers (full and partial), and unspecified assistantships available. Financial award application deadline: 1/10. *Unit head:* Dr. Enno Siemsen, Associate Dean of the MBA and Masters Programs, 608-890-3130, E-mail:

esiemsen@wisc.edu. *Application contact:* Betsy Kacizak, Director of Admissions and Recruitment, Full-Time MBA and Masters Programs, 608-262-8948, E-mail: betsy.kacizak@wisc.edu.
Website: https://wsb.wisc.edu/

Utah Valley University, Program in Cybersecurity, Orem, UT 84058-5999. Offers Graduate Certificate. *Program availability:* Part-time. *Faculty:* 2 full-time. *Students:* 4 full-time (1 woman), 25 part-time (3 women); includes 6 minority (2 Black or African American, non-Hispanic/Latino; 1 Asian, non-Hispanic/Latino; 2 Hispanic/Latino; 1 Two or more races, non-Hispanic/Latino). Average age 35. 27 applicants, 41% accepted, 11 enrolled. *Entrance requirements:* For degree, bachelor's degree; 2 years of IT or IT security industry experience; undergraduate courses in data communication, programming, and servers. *Expenses:* 2 Semester Resident Tuition: 4,644; 2 Semester Resident Fees: 420; 2 Semester Non-resident Tuition: 12,036; 2 Semester Non-resident Fees: 420. *Financial support:* Applicants required to submit FAFSA. *Unit head:* Robert Jorgensen, Director, 801-863-5282, E-mail: robert.jorgensen@uvu.edu. *Application contact:* Shauna Reher, Administrative Assistant, 801-863-7348, E-mail: graduate_studies@uvu.edu.
Website: https://www.uvu.edu/cybersecurity/academics/index.html

Utica College, Program in Cybersecurity, Utica, NY 13502. Offers MPS, MS. *Program availability:* Part-time, evening/weekend, 100% online. *Faculty:* 5 full-time (0 women), 8 part-time/adjunct (0 women). *Students:* 280 full-time (75 women), 88 part-time (32 women); includes 97 minority (52 Black or African American, non-Hispanic/Latino; 1 American Indian or Alaska Native, non-Hispanic/Latino; 15 Asian, non-Hispanic/Latino; 23 Hispanic/Latino; 6 Two or more races, non-Hispanic/Latino). Average age 34. 232 applicants, 78% accepted, 148 enrolled. In 2019, 155 master's awarded. *Entrance requirements:* For master's, BS, minimum GPA of 3.0. Additional exam requirements/recommendations for international students: recommended—TOEFL (minimum score 525 paper-based). *Application deadline:* Applications are processed on a rolling basis. Electronic applications accepted. *Expenses:* Contact institution. *Financial support:* Application deadline: 3/15; applicants required to submit FAFSA. *Unit head:* Joseph Giordano, Chair, 315-792-2521. *Application contact:* John D. Rowe, Director of Graduate Admissions, 315-792-3824, Fax: 315-792-3003, E-mail: jrowe@utica.edu.
Website: http://programs.online.utica.edu/programs/masters-cybersecurity.asp

Valparaiso University, Graduate School and Continuing Education, Program in Cyber Security, Valparaiso, IN 46383. Offers MS. *Program availability:* Part-time, evening/weekend, online learning. *Degree requirements:* For master's, internship or research project. *Entrance requirements:* Additional exam requirements/recommendations for international students: required—TOEFL (minimum score 550 paper-based; 80 iBT), IELTS (minimum score 6). Electronic applications accepted.

Vanderbilt University, School of Engineering, Program in Cyber-Physical Systems, Nashville, TN 37240-1001. Offers M Eng. *Entrance requirements:* For master's, resume or curriculum vitae, three letters of recommendation, statement of purpose. Electronic applications accepted. *Expenses: Tuition:* Full-time $51,018; part-time $2087 per hour. *Required fees:* $542. Tuition and fees vary according to program.

Virginia International University, School of Computer Information Systems, Fairfax, VA 22030. Offers business intelligence (Graduate Certificate); business intelligence and data analytics (MIS); computer science (MS), including computer animation and gaming, cybersecurity, data management networking, intelligent systems, software applications development, software engineering; cybersecurity (MIS); data management (MIS); enterprise project management (MIS); health informatics (MIS); information assurance (MIS); information systems (Graduate Certificate); information systems management (MS, Graduate Certificate); information technology (MS); information technology audit and compliance (Graduate Certificate); knowledge management (MIS); software engineering (MS). *Program availability:* Part-time, online learning. *Entrance requirements:* For master's, bachelor's degree. Additional exam requirements/recommendations for international students: required—TOEFL (minimum score 550 paper-based; 80 iBT), IELTS. Electronic applications accepted.

Virginia Polytechnic Institute and State University, VT Online, Blacksburg, VA 24061. Offers advanced transportation systems (Certificate); aerospace engineering (MS); agricultural and life sciences (MSLFS); business information systems (Graduate Certificate); career and technical education (MS); civil engineering (MS); computer engineering (M Eng, MS); decision support systems (Graduate Certificate); eLearning leadership (MA); electrical engineering (M Eng, MS); engineering administration (MEA); environmental engineering (Certificate); environmental politics and policy (Graduate Certificate); environmental sciences and engineering (MS); foundations of political analysis (Graduate Certificate); health product risk management (Graduate Certificate); industrial and systems engineering (MS); information policy and society (Graduate Certificate); information security (Graduate Certificate); information technology (MIT); instructional technology (MA); integrative STEM education (MA Ed); liberal arts (Graduate Certificate); life sciences: health product risk management (MS); natural resources (MNR, Graduate Certificate); networking (Graduate Certificate); nonprofit and nongovernmental organization management (Graduate Certificate); ocean engineering (MS); political science (MA); security studies (Graduate Certificate); software development (Graduate Certificate). *Expenses:* Tuition, state resident: full-time $13,700; part-time $761.25 per credit hour. Tuition, nonresident: full-time $27,614; part-time $1534 per credit hour. *Required fees:* $886.50 per term. Tuition and fees vary according to campus/location and program.

Walden University, Graduate Programs, School of Information Systems and Technology, Minneapolis, MN 55401. Offers information systems (Graduate Certificate); information systems management (MISM); information technology (MS, DIT), including health informatics (MS), information assurance and cyber security (MS), information systems (MS), software engineering (MS). *Program availability:* Part-time, evening/weekend, online only, 100% online. *Degree requirements:* For doctorate, thesis/dissertation (for some programs), residency. *Entrance requirements:* For master's, bachelor's degree or higher; minimum GPA of 2.5; official transcripts; goal statement (for some programs); access to computer and Internet; for doctorate, master's degree or higher; three years of related professional or academic experience (preferred); minimum GPA of 3.0; goal statement and current resume (for select programs); official transcripts; access to computer and Internet; for Graduate Certificate, relevant work experience; access to computer and Internet. Additional exam requirements/recommendations for international students: required—TOEFL (minimum score 550 paper-based, 79 iBT), IELTS (minimum score 6.5), Michigan English Language Assessment Battery (minimum score 82), or PTE (minimum score 53). Electronic applications accepted.

Walsh College of Accountancy and Business Administration, Graduate Programs, Program in Information Technology, Troy, MI 48083. Offers chief information officer (MSIT); cybersecurity (MSIT); data science (MSIT); global project and program management (MSIT). *Program availability:* Part-time, evening/weekend. *Entrance requirements:* For master's, minimum overall cumulative GPA of 2.75 from all colleges previously attended. Additional exam requirements/recommendations for international students: required—TOEFL (minimum score 550 paper-based, 79-80 internet based), IELTS (6.5), Michigan Test of English Language Proficiency, or MTELP (80). Electronic applications accepted. *Expenses:* Contact institution.

Webster University, George Herbert Walker School of Business and Technology, Department of Mathematics and Computer Science, St. Louis, MO 63119-3194. Offers cybersecurity (MS). *Program availability:* Part-time, evening/weekend, online learning. *Entrance requirements:* For master's, 36 hours of graduate course work. Additional exam requirements/recommendations for international students: required—TOEFL.

Western Governors University, College of Information Technology, Salt Lake City, UT 84107. Offers cybersecurity and information assurance (MS); data analytics (MS); information technology management (MS). *Program availability:* Online learning. *Degree requirements:* For master's, capstone project. Application fee is waived when completed online.

West Virginia University, College of Business and Economics, Morgantown, WV 26506. Offers accountancy (M Acc); accounting (PhD); business administration (MBA); business cyber security management (MS); business data analytics (MS); economics (MA, PhD); finance (MS, PhD); forensic and fraud examination (MS); industrial relations (MS); management (PhD); marketing (PhD). *Program availability:* Part-time, online learning. Terminal master's awarded for partial completion of doctoral program. *Degree requirements:* For master's, thesis optional; for doctorate, comprehensive exam, thesis/dissertation. *Entrance requirements:* For doctorate, GRE General Test, minimum GPA of 3.0. Additional exam requirements/recommendations for international students: required—TOEFL (minimum score 550 paper-based; 92 iBT). Electronic applications accepted. *Expenses:* Contact institution.

Wilmington University, College of Technology, New Castle, DE 19720-6491. Offers cybersecurity (MS); information assurance (MS); information systems technologies (MS); management and management information systems (MS); technology project management (MS); Web design (MS). *Program availability:* Part-time, evening/weekend. *Entrance requirements:* Additional exam requirements/recommendations for international students: required—TOEFL (minimum score 500 paper-based). Electronic applications accepted.

Computer Science

Acadia University, Faculty of Pure and Applied Science, Jodrey School of Computer Science, Wolfville, NS B4P 2R6, Canada. Offers M Sc. *Entrance requirements:* For master's, honors degree in computer science. Additional exam requirements/recommendations for international students: required—TOEFL (minimum score 580 paper-based; 93 iBT), IELTS (minimum score 6.5).

Air Force Institute of Technology, Graduate School of Engineering and Management, Department of Electrical and Computer Engineering, Dayton, OH 45433-7765. Offers computer engineering (MS, PhD); computer systems/science (MS); electrical engineering (MS, PhD); electro-optics (MS, PhD). *Accreditation:* ABET (one or more programs are accredited). *Program availability:* Part-time. *Degree requirements:* For master's, thesis; for doctorate, thesis/dissertation. *Entrance requirements:* For master's and doctorate, GRE General Test, minimum GPA of 3.0, U.S. citizenship.

Alabama Agricultural and Mechanical University, School of Graduate Studies, College of Engineering, Technology, and Physical Sciences, Department of Electrical Engineering and Computer Science, Huntsville, AL 35811. Offers computer science (MS); material engineering (M Eng), including electrical engineering. *Program availability:* Evening/weekend. *Degree requirements:* For master's, comprehensive exam, thesis optional. *Entrance requirements:* For master's, GRE General Test. Additional exam requirements/recommendations for international students: required—TOEFL (minimum score 500 paper-based; 61 iBT). Electronic applications accepted.

Alcorn State University, School of Graduate Studies, School of Arts and Sciences, Department of Mathematics and Computer Science, Lorman, MS 39096-7500. Offers computer and information science (MS).

American Sentinel University, Graduate Programs, Aurora, CO 80014. Offers business administration (MBA); business intelligence (MS); computer science (MSCS); health information management (MS); healthcare (MBA); information systems (MSIS); nursing (MSN). *Program availability:* Part-time, evening/weekend, online learning. *Entrance requirements:* Additional exam requirements/recommendations for international students: required—TOEFL (minimum score 600 paper-based). Electronic applications accepted.

The American University in Cairo, School of Sciences and Engineering, Cairo, Egypt. Offers biotechnology (MS); chemistry (MS); computer science (MS); computing (M Comp); construction engineering (M Eng, MS); electronics and communications engineering (M Eng); environmental engineering (MS); environmental system design (M Eng); mechanical engineering (M Eng, MS); nanotechnology (MS); physics (MS); robotics, control and smart systems (MS); sciences and engineering (PhD); sustainable development (MS, Graduate Diploma). *Program availability:* Part-time, evening/weekend. *Degree requirements:* For master's, comprehensive exam (for some programs), thesis (for some programs); for doctorate, comprehensive exam (for some programs), thesis/dissertation. *Entrance requirements:* Additional exam requirements/recommendations for international students: required—TOEFL (minimum score 450 paper-based; 45 iBT), IELTS (minimum score 5). Electronic applications accepted.

American University of Armenia, Graduate Programs, Yerevan, Armenia. Offers business administration (MBA); computer and information science (MS), including business management, design and manufacturing, energy (ME, MS), industrial engineering and systems management; economics (MS); industrial engineering and systems management (ME), including business, computer aided design/manufacturing, energy (ME, MS), information technology; law (LL M); political science and international affairs (MPSIA); public health (MPH); teaching English as a foreign language (MA). *Program availability:* Part-time, evening/weekend. *Degree requirements:* For master's, thesis (for some programs), capstone/project. *Entrance requirements:* For master's, GRE, GMAT, or LSAT. Additional exam requirements/recommendations for international students: recommended—TOEFL (minimum score 79 iBT), IELTS (minimum score 6.5).

Appalachian State University, Cratis D. Williams School of Graduate Studies, Department of Computer Science, Boone, NC 28608. Offers MS. *Program availability:* Part-time. *Degree requirements:* For master's, comprehensive exam, thesis. *Entrance requirements:* For master's, GRE General Test, 3 letters of recommendation. Additional exam requirements/recommendations for international students: required—TOEFL (minimum score 570 paper-based; 79 iBT), IELTS (minimum score 6.5). Electronic applications accepted.

Arizona State University at Tempe, Ira A. Fulton Schools of Engineering, The Polytechnic School, Department of Engineering, Mesa, AZ 85212. Offers simulation, modeling, and applied cognitive science (PhD). *Program availability:* Part-time. *Degree requirements:* For doctorate, comprehensive exam, thesis/dissertation, interactive Program of Study (iPOS) submitted before completing 50 percent of required credit hours. *Entrance requirements:* For doctorate, GRE, master's degree in psychology, engineering, cognitive science, or computer science; 3 letters of recommendation; statement of research interests. Additional exam requirements/recommendations for international students: required—TOEFL, IELTS, or PTE. Electronic applications accepted.

Arizona State University at Tempe, Ira A. Fulton Schools of Engineering, School of Computing, Informatics, and Decision Systems Engineering, Tempe, AZ 85287-8809. Offers computer engineering (MS, PhD); computer science (MCS, MS, PhD); industrial engineering (MS, PhD); software engineering (MS). *Program availability:* Part-time, evening/weekend, online learning. Terminal master's awarded for partial completion of doctoral program. *Degree requirements:* For master's, comprehensive exam (for some programs), portfolio (MCS); interactive Program of Study (iPOS) submitted before completing 50 percent of required credit hours; for doctorate, comprehensive exam, thesis/dissertation, interactive Program of Study (iPOS) submitted before completing 50 percent of required credit hours. *Entrance requirements:* For master's, GRE, minimum GPA of 3.0 or equivalent in last 2 years of work leading to bachelor's degree; for doctorate, GRE, minimum GPA of 3.0 in last 2 years of work leading to bachelor's degree. Additional exam requirements/recommendations for international students: required—TOEFL, IELTS, or PTE. Electronic applications accepted. *Expenses:* Contact institution.

Arkansas State University, Graduate School, College of Sciences and Mathematics, Department of Computer Science, State University, AR 72467. Offers MS. *Program availability:* Part-time. *Degree requirements:* For master's, comprehensive exam, thesis or alternative. *Entrance requirements:* For master's, GRE General Test or MAT, appropriate bachelor's degree, official transcripts, immunization records. Additional exam requirements/recommendations for international students: required—TOEFL (minimum score 550 paper-based; 79 iBT), IELTS (minimum score 6), PTE (minimum score 56). Electronic applications accepted.

Auburn University, Graduate School, Samuel Ginn College of Engineering, Department of Computer Science and Software Engineering, Auburn University, AL 36849. Offers MS, MSWE, PhD. *Program availability:* Part-time. *Faculty:* 29 full-time (4 women), 1 (woman) part-time/adjunct. *Students:* 126 full-time (32 women), 67 part-time (20 women); includes 23 minority (9 Black or African American, non-Hispanic/Latino; 7 Asian, non-Hispanic/Latino; 5 Hispanic/Latino; 2 Two or more races, non-Hispanic/Latino), 118 international. Average age 30. 223 applicants, 57% accepted, 46 enrolled. In 2019, 48 master's, 4 doctorates awarded. *Degree requirements:* For master's, thesis (for some programs); for doctorate, thesis/dissertation. *Entrance requirements:* For master's and doctorate, GRE General Test, GRE Subject Test. Additional exam requirements/recommendations for international students: required—TOEFL (minimum score 550 paper-based; 79 iBT). *Application deadline:* For fall admission, 3/31 priority date for domestic and international students; for spring admission, 9/30 priority date for domestic and international students. Applications are processed on a rolling basis. Application fee: $60 ($70 for international students). Electronic applications accepted. *Expenses: Tuition, area resident:* Full-time $9828; part-time $546 per credit hour. Tuition, state resident: full-time $9828; part-time $546 per credit hour. Tuition, nonresident: full-time $29,484; part-time $1638 per credit hour. *International tuition:* $29,744 full-time. Tuition and fees vary according to course load, program and reciprocity agreements. *Financial support:* In 2019–20, 46 research assistantships (averaging $15,194 per year), 53 teaching assistantships (averaging $14,222 per year) were awarded; Federal Work-Study also available. Support available to part-time students. Financial award application deadline: 3/15; financial award applicants required to submit FAFSA. *Unit head:* Dr. Hari Narayanan, Chair, 334-844-63102, E-mail: naraynh@auburn.edu. *Application contact:* Dr. George Flowers, Dean of the Graduate School, 334-844-2125.
Website: http://www.eng.auburn.edu/cse/

Ball State University, Graduate School, College of Sciences and Humanities, Department of Computer Science, Muncie, IN 47306. Offers computer science (MA, MS). *Program availability:* Part-time. *Entrance requirements:* For master's, GRE General Test, minimum baccalaureate GPA of 2.75 or 3.0 in latter half of baccalaureate, goals statement, three letters of recommendation. Additional exam requirements/recommendations for international students: required—TOEFL (minimum score 550 paper-based; 79 iBT), IELTS (minimum score 6.5). Electronic applications accepted. *Expenses: Tuition, area resident:* Full-time $7506; part-time $417 per credit hour. Tuition, nonresident: full-time $20,610; part-time $1145 per credit hour. *Required fees:* $2126. Tuition and fees vary according to course load, campus/location and program.

Baylor University, Graduate School, School of Engineering and Computer Science, Department of Computer Science, Waco, TX 76798. Offers MS, PhD. *Program availability:* Part-time. Terminal master's awarded for partial completion of doctoral program. *Degree requirements:* For master's, thesis (for some programs); for doctorate, comprehensive exam, thesis/dissertation. *Entrance requirements:* For master's and doctorate, GRE, course training in computer science equivalent to BS in computer science from Baylor University. Additional exam requirements/recommendations for international students: required—TOEFL (minimum score 550 paper-based; 90 iBT). Electronic applications accepted.

Binghamton University, State University of New York, Graduate School, Thomas J. Watson School of Engineering and Applied Science, Department of Computer Science, Binghamton, NY 13902-6000. Offers MS, PhD. *Program availability:* Part-time, online learning. *Degree requirements:* For master's, comprehensive exam (for some programs), thesis or alternative; for doctorate, comprehensive exam, thesis/dissertation. *Entrance requirements:* For master's and doctorate, GRE General Test. Additional exam requirements/recommendations for international students: required—TOEFL (minimum score 550 paper-based; 80 iBT). Electronic applications accepted. *Expenses:* Contact institution.

Boise State University, College of Engineering, Department of Computer Science, Boise, ID 83725-0399. Offers computer science (MS); computer science teacher endorsement (Graduate Certificate); STEM education (MS), including computer science. *Program availability:* Part-time. *Students:* 31 full-time (6 women), 35 part-time (11 women); includes 8 minority (1 Black or African American, non-Hispanic/Latino; 1 Asian, non-Hispanic/Latino; 3 Hispanic/Latino; 3 Two or more races, non-Hispanic/Latino), 24 international. Average age 30. 57 applicants, 47% accepted, 16 enrolled. In 2019, 8 master's awarded. *Degree requirements:* For master's, comprehensive exam, thesis. *Entrance requirements:* For master's, GRE General Test, minimum GPA of 3.0. Additional exam requirements/recommendations for international students: required—TOEFL (minimum score 550 paper-based; 80 iBT), IELTS (minimum score 6).

Application fee: $65 ($95 for international students). Electronic applications accepted. *Expenses: Tuition, area resident:* Full-time $7110; part-time $470 per credit hour. Tuition, state resident: full-time $7110; part-time $470 per credit hour. Tuition, nonresident: full-time $24,030; part-time $827 per credit hour. *International tuition:* $827 full-time. *Required fees:* $2536. Tuition and fees vary according to course load and program. *Financial support:* Research assistantships, scholarships/grants, and unspecified assistantships available. Financial award applicants required to submit FAFSA. *Unit head:* Dr. Tim Andersen, Department Chair, 208-426-5768, E-mail: tim@cs.boisestate.edu. *Application contact:* Dr. Jerry Fails, Graduate Program Coordinator, 208-426-5783, E-mail: jerryfails@boisestate.edu.
Website: https://www.boisestate.edu/coen-cs/

Boston University, Graduate School of Arts and Sciences, Department of Computer Science, Boston, MA 02215. Offers computer science (MS, PhD); cyber security (MS); data-centric computing (MS). *Students:* 227 full-time (52 women), 48 part-time (14 women); includes 9 minority (8 Asian, non-Hispanic/Latino; 1 Hispanic/Latino), 236 international. Average age 24. 2,102 applicants, 25% accepted, 117 enrolled. In 2019, 87 master's, 10 doctorates awarded. Terminal master's awarded for partial completion of doctoral program. *Degree requirements:* For master's, thesis optional, project; for doctorate, comprehensive exam, thesis/dissertation. *Entrance requirements:* For master's and doctorate, GRE General Test, 3 letters of recommendation, transcripts, personal statement. Additional exam requirements/recommendations for international students: required—TOEFL (minimum score 550 paper-based; 84 iBT). *Application deadline:* For fall admission, 12/15 for domestic and international students. Applications are processed on a rolling basis. Application fee: $95. Electronic applications accepted. *Financial support:* In 2019–20, 112 students received support, including 4 fellowships with full tuition reimbursements available (averaging $23,340 per year), 53 research assistantships with full tuition reimbursements available (averaging $23,340 per year), 43 teaching assistantships with full tuition reimbursements available (averaging $23,340 per year); Federal Work-Study, scholarships/grants, and health care benefits also available. Support available to part-time students. Financial award application deadline: 12/15. *Unit head:* Abraham Matta, Chair, 617-353-8919, Fax: 617-353-6457, E-mail: matta@bu.edu. *Application contact:* Kori MacDonald, Program Coordinator, 617-353-8919, Fax: 617-353-6457, E-mail: korimac@bu.edu.
Website: http://www.bu.edu/cs

Boston University, Metropolitan College, Department of Computer Science, Boston, MA 02215. Offers computer information systems (MS), including computer networks, data analytics, database management and business intelligence, health informatics, IT project management, security, Web application development; computer networks (Certificate); computer science (MS); data analytics (Certificate); digital forensics (Certificate); health informatics (Certificate); information technology project management (Certificate); software development (MS); software engineering in health care systems (Certificate); telecommunications (MS), including security. *Program availability:* Part-time, evening/weekend, online learning. *Faculty:* 16 full-time (3 women), 52 part-time/adjunct (5 women). *Students:* 253 full-time (80 women), 856 part-time (243 women); includes 246 minority (53 Black or African American, non-Hispanic/Latino; 1 American Indian or Alaska Native, non-Hispanic/Latino; 129 Asian, non-Hispanic/Latino; 48 Hispanic/Latino; 15 Two or more races, non-Hispanic/Latino), 418 international. Average age 30. 1,079 applicants, 72% accepted, 297 enrolled. In 2019, 513 master's awarded. *Entrance requirements:* For master's and Certificate, official transcripts from regionally-accredited bachelor's degree program, 3 letters of recommendation, professional resume, personal statement. Additional exam requirements/recommendations for international students: required—TOEFL (minimum score 84 iBT), IELTS. *Application deadline:* For fall admission, 8/1 priority date for domestic students, 6/1 priority date for international students; for spring admission, 12/1 priority date for domestic students, 11/15 priority date for international students; for summer admission, 4/1 priority date for domestic students, 3/1 priority date for international students. Applications are processed on a rolling basis. Application fee: $85. Electronic applications accepted. *Expenses:* Contact institution. *Financial support:* In 2019–20, 11 research assistantships (averaging $8,400 per year), 23 teaching assistantships (averaging $3,400 per year) were awarded; unspecified assistantships also available. Support available to part-time students. Financial award applicants required to submit FAFSA. *Unit head:* Dr. Anatoly Temkin, Chair, 617-353-2566, Fax: 617-353-2367, E-mail: csinfo@bu.edu. *Application contact:* Enrollment Services, 617-353-6004, E-mail: met@bu.edu.
Website: http://www.bu.edu/csmet/

Bowie State University, Graduate Programs, Department of Computer Science, Bowie, MD 20715-9465. Offers MS. *Program availability:* Part-time, evening/weekend. *Degree requirements:* For master's, comprehensive exam, thesis optional, research paper. *Entrance requirements:* For master's, minimum undergraduate GPA of 2.5. Electronic applications accepted. *Expenses: Tuition, area resident:* Full-time $11,942. Tuition, state resident: full-time $11,942. Tuition, nonresident: full-time $18,806. *International tuition:* $18,806 full-time. *Required fees:* $1106; $1106 per semester. $553 per semester.

Bowie State University, Graduate Programs, Program in Computer Science, Bowie, MD 20715-9465. Offers App Sc D. *Program availability:* Part-time, evening/weekend. Electronic applications accepted. *Expenses: Tuition, area resident:* Full-time $11,942. Tuition, state resident: full-time $11,942. Tuition, nonresident: full-time $18,806. *International tuition:* $18,806 full-time. *Required fees:* $1106; $1106 per semester. $553 per semester.

Bowling Green State University, Graduate College, College of Arts and Sciences, Department of Computer Science, Bowling Green, OH 43403. Offers computer science (MS), including operations research, parallel and distributed computing, software engineering. *Program availability:* Part-time. *Degree requirements:* For master's, thesis or alternative. *Entrance requirements:* For master's, GRE General Test. Additional exam requirements/recommendations for international students: required—TOEFL. Electronic applications accepted.

Bradley University, The Graduate School, College of Liberal Arts and Sciences, Department of Computer Science and Information Systems, Peoria, IL 61625-0002. Offers computer information systems (MS); computer science (MS). *Program availability:* Part-time, evening/weekend. *Faculty:* 10 full-time (2 women), 1 part-time/adjunct. *Students:* 23 full-time (12 women), 4 part-time (2 women), 24 international. Average age 26. 76 applicants, 62% accepted, 14 enrolled. In 2019, 11 master's awarded. *Degree requirements:* For master's, comprehensive exam, thesis or alternative, programming test. *Entrance requirements:* For master's, GRE. Additional exam requirements/recommendations for international students: required—TOEFL (minimum score 550 paper-based; 79 iBT), IELTS (minimum score 6.5), PTE (minimum score 58). *Application deadline:* For fall admission, 5/15 priority date for domestic and international students; for spring admission, 10/15 priority date for domestic and international students. Applications are processed on a rolling basis. Application fee: $40 ($50 for international students). Electronic applications accepted. *Expenses: Tuition:* Part-time $930 per credit hour. *Financial support:* In 2019–20, 11 students received support, including 2 research assistantships with partial tuition reimbursements available (averaging $8,370 per year), 7 teaching assistantships with partial tuition

Computer Science

reimbursements available (averaging $4,185 per year); scholarships/grants, tuition waivers (partial), and unspecified assistantships also available. Support available to part-time students. Financial award application deadline: 4/1. *Unit head:* Dr. Steven Dolins, Chair, 309-677-3284, E-mail: sdolins@bradley.edu. *Application contact:* Rachel Webb, Director of On-Campus Graduate Admissions and International Student and Scholar Services, 309-677-2375, E-mail: rkwebb@bradley.edu. Website: http://www.bradley.edu/academic/departments/csis/

Brandeis University, Graduate School of Arts and Sciences, Department of Computer Science, Waltham, MA 02454-9110. Offers computer science (PhD). *Program availability:* Part-time. *Faculty:* 24 full-time (6 women), 3 part-time/adjunct (1 woman). *Students:* 145 full-time (61 women), 4 part-time (2 women); includes 9 minority (4 Asian, non-Hispanic/Latino; 2 Hispanic/Latino; 3 Two or more races, non-Hispanic/Latino), 104 international. Average age 26. 610 applicants, 39% accepted, 59 enrolled. In 2019, 38 master's, 4 doctorates awarded. Terminal master's awarded for partial completion of doctoral program. *Degree requirements:* For master's, thesis (for some programs), thesis, capstone project, or internship; for doctorate, thesis/dissertation. *Entrance requirements:* For master's and doctorate, GRE General, Transcripts, letters of recommendation, resume, and statement of purpose. Additional exam requirements/recommendations for international students: required—TOEFL, IELTS, PTE. *Application deadline:* For fall admission, 1/15 for domestic and international students. Applications are processed on a rolling basis. Application fee: $75. Electronic applications accepted. *Financial support:* In 2019–20, 38 teaching assistantships (averaging $3,550 per year) were awarded; fellowships, research assistantships, scholarships/grants, health care benefits, and tuition waivers also available. Support available to part-time students. *Unit head:* Dr. Nianwen Xue, Director of Graduate Studies, 781-736-2728, E-mail: xuen@brandeis.edu. *Application contact:* Anne Gudaitis, Administrator, 781-736-2723, E-mail: compsci@brandeis.edu. Website: http://www.brandeis.edu/gsas/programs/computer_science.html

Bridgewater State University, College of Graduate Studies, Bartlett College of Science and Mathematics, Department of Computer Science, Bridgewater, MA 02325. Offers MS.

Brigham Young University, Graduate Studies, College of Physical and Mathematical Sciences, Department of Computer Science, Provo, UT 84602-1001. Offers MS, PhD. *Faculty:* 24 full-time (1 woman). *Students:* 107 full-time (10 women); includes 17 minority (15 Asian, non-Hispanic/Latino; 2 Hispanic/Latino). Average age 29. 44 applicants, 68% accepted, 20 enrolled. In 2019, 29 master's, 6 doctorates awarded. Terminal master's awarded for partial completion of doctoral program. *Degree requirements:* For master's, thesis (for some programs); for doctorate, thesis/dissertation, residency. *Entrance requirements:* For master's, GRE General Test, minimum GPA of 3.25 in last 60 hours; for doctorate, GRE General Test, minimum GPA of 3.5 in last 60 hours, undergraduate degree in computer science. Additional exam requirements/recommendations for international students: required—TOEFL (minimum score 620 paper-based; 105 iBT). *Application deadline:* For fall admission, 12/15 for domestic and international students; for winter admission, 7/15 for domestic and international students. Application fee: $50. Electronic applications accepted. *Financial support:* In 2019–20, 31 students received support, including 73 research assistantships (averaging $18,017 per year), 28 teaching assistantships (averaging $8,116 per year); fellowships with full tuition reimbursements available and scholarships/grants also available. Financial award application deadline: 3/1. *Unit head:* Dr. Michael Jones, Chair, 801-422-2217, Fax: 801-422-0169, E-mail: jones@cs.byu.edu. *Application contact:* Dr. Jennifer Bonnett, Graduate Advisor, 801-422-2217, Fax: 801-422-0169, E-mail: jen@cs.byu.edu. Website: https://cs.byu.edu/

Brock University, Faculty of Graduate Studies, Faculty of Mathematics and Science, Program in Computer Science, St. Catharines, ON L2S 3A1, Canada. Offers M Sc. *Program availability:* Part-time. *Degree requirements:* For master's, thesis. *Entrance requirements:* For master's, honors degree. Additional exam requirements/recommendations for international students: required—TOEFL (minimum score 550 paper-based; 80 iBT), IELTS (minimum score 6.5), TWE (minimum score 4).

Brooklyn College of the City University of New York, School of Natural and Behavioral Sciences, Department of Computer and Information Science, Brooklyn, NY 11210-2889. Offers computer science (MA); health informatics (MS); information systems (MS); parallel and distributed computing (Advanced Certificate). *Program availability:* Part-time, evening/weekend. *Degree requirements:* For master's, comprehensive exam, thesis or alternative. *Entrance requirements:* For master's, previous course work in computer science, 2 letters of recommendation. Additional exam requirements/recommendations for international students: required—TOEFL (minimum score 525 paper-based; 70 iBT). Electronic applications accepted.

Brown University, Graduate School, Department of Computer Science, Providence, RI 02912. Offers Sc M, PhD. *Degree requirements:* For master's, thesis or alternative; for doctorate, one foreign language, comprehensive exam, thesis/dissertation. *Entrance requirements:* For master's and doctorate, GRE General Test, GRE Subject Test.

California Institute of Technology, Division of Engineering and Applied Science, Option in Computer Science, Pasadena, CA 91125-0001. Offers MS, PhD. *Degree requirements:* For master's, thesis; for doctorate, thesis/dissertation. Electronic applications accepted.

California Polytechnic State University, San Luis Obispo, College of Engineering, Department of Computer Science, San Luis Obispo, CA 93407. Offers MS. *Program availability:* Part-time. *Faculty:* 9 full-time (2 women), 1 part-time/adjunct (0 women). *Students:* 24 full-time (4 women), 6 part-time (2 women); includes 7 minority (3 Asian, non-Hispanic/Latino; 4 Two or more races, non-Hispanic/Latino), 4 international. Average age 24. 194 applicants, 18% accepted, 18 enrolled. In 2019, 26 master's awarded. *Entrance requirements:* For master's, GRE. Additional exam requirements/recommendations for international students: required—TOEFL (minimum score 80 iBT). *Application deadline:* For fall admission, 2/1 for domestic and international students. Applications are processed on a rolling basis. Application fee: $55. Electronic applications accepted. *Expenses:* Tuition, state resident: full-time $7176; part-time $4164 per year. Tuition, nonresident: full-time $18,690; part-time $8916 per year. *Required fees:* $4206; $3185 per unit. $1061 per term. *Financial support:* Fellowships, research assistantships, teaching assistantships, career-related internships or fieldwork, institutionally sponsored loans, scholarships/grants, and unspecified assistantships available. Financial award application deadline: 3/2; financial award applicants required to submit FAFSA. *Unit head:* Dr. Zoe Wood, Graduate Coordinator, 805-756-5540, E-mail: zwood@calpoly.edu. *Application contact:* Dr. Zoe Wood, Graduate Coordinator, 805-756-5540, E-mail: zwood@calpoly.edu. Website: http://www.csc.calpoly.edu/programs/ms-csc/

California State Polytechnic University, Pomona, Program in Computer Science, Pomona, CA 91768-2557. Offers computer science (MS). *Program availability:* Part-time, evening/weekend. *Degree requirements:* For master's, thesis. *Entrance requirements:* Additional exam requirements/recommendations for international students: required—TOEFL (minimum score 550 paper-based). Electronic applications accepted. *Expenses:* Contact institution.

California State University Channel Islands, Extended University and International Programs, MS Computer Science, Camarillo, CA 93012. Offers MS. *Program availability:* Part-time, evening/weekend. *Students:* 45 full-time (8 women); includes 15 minority (1 Black or African American, non-Hispanic/Latino; 6 Asian, non-Hispanic/Latino; 5 Hispanic/Latino; 3 Two or more races, non-Hispanic/Latino), 15 international. 17 applicants, 65% accepted, 11 enrolled. *Degree requirements:* For master's, thesis. *Entrance requirements:* Additional exam requirements/recommendations for international students: required—TOEFL (minimum score 550 paper-based; 80 iBT), IELTS (minimum score 6). *Application deadline:* For fall admission, 6/1 for domestic students, 5/1 for international students; for spring admission, 11/1 for domestic and international students. Application fee: $70. Electronic applications accepted. *Financial support:* Career-related internships or fieldwork and scholarships/grants available. Financial award applicants required to submit FAFSA. *Unit head:* Dr. Brian Thoms, Program Director for Computer Science, 805-437-3714, E-mail: Brian.Thoms@csuci.edu. *Application contact:* Andrew Conley, Graduate Programs Recruiter, 805-437-2652, E-mail: andrew.conley@csuci.edu. Website: https://ext.csuci.edu/

California State University, Chico, Office of Graduate Studies, College of Engineering, Computer Science, and Construction Management, Department of Computer Science, Chico, CA 95929-0722. Offers MS. *Program availability:* Online learning. *Degree requirements:* For master's, thesis or project and oral defense. *Entrance requirements:* For master's, GRE General Test (waived if graduated from ABET-accredited institution), fall admissions only; 2 letters of recommendation, statement of purpose, departmental letter of recommendation access waiver form. Additional exam requirements/recommendations for international students: required—TOEFL (minimum score 550 paper-based; 80 iBT), IELTS (minimum score 6.5). Electronic applications accepted.

California State University, Dominguez Hills, College of Natural and Behavioral Sciences, Department of Computer Science, Carson, CA 90747-0001. Offers MS. *Degree requirements:* For master's, comprehensive exam (for some programs), thesis (for some programs). *Entrance requirements:* For master's, GRE (minimum score 900), minimum GPA of 2.75. Additional exam requirements/recommendations for international students: required—TOEFL (minimum score 550 paper-based). Electronic applications accepted.

California State University, East Bay, Office of Graduate Studies, College of Science, Department of Computer Science, Hayward, CA 94542-3000. Offers computer networks (MS); computer science (MS). *Program availability:* Part-time. *Degree requirements:* For master's, thesis or capstone experience. *Entrance requirements:* For master's, GRE, minimum GPA of 3.0 in field, 2.75 overall; baccalaureate degree in computer science or related field. Additional exam requirements/recommendations for international students: required—TOEFL (minimum score 550 paper-based). Electronic applications accepted.

California State University, Fresno, Division of Research and Graduate Studies, College of Science and Mathematics, Department of Computer Science, Fresno, CA 93740-8027. Offers MS. *Program availability:* Part-time, evening/weekend. *Degree requirements:* For master's, thesis or alternative. *Entrance requirements:* For master's, GRE General Test, minimum GPA of 2.75. Additional exam requirements/recommendations for international students: required—TOEFL. Electronic applications accepted. *Expenses:* Tuition, state resident: full-time $4012; part-time $2506 per semester.

California State University, Fullerton, Graduate Studies, College of Engineering and Computer Science, Department of Computer Science, Fullerton, CA 92831-3599. Offers computer science (MS); software engineering (MS). *Program availability:* Part-time, online learning. *Degree requirements:* For master's, comprehensive exam, project or thesis. *Entrance requirements:* For master's, GRE General Test, minimum undergraduate GPA of 2.5.

California State University, Long Beach, Graduate Studies, College of Engineering, Department of Computer Engineering and Computer Science, Long Beach, CA 90840. Offers computer engineering (MSCS); computer science (MSCS). *Program availability:* Part-time. *Degree requirements:* For master's, thesis or alternative. *Entrance requirements:* Additional exam requirements/recommendations for international students: required—TOEFL. Electronic applications accepted.

California State University, Los Angeles, Graduate Studies, College of Engineering, Computer Science, and Technology, Department of Computer Science, Los Angeles, CA 90032-8530. Offers MS. *Entrance requirements:* Additional exam requirements/recommendations for international students: required—TOEFL (minimum score 550 paper-based). Electronic applications accepted. *Expenses: Tuition, area resident:* Full-time $7176; part-time $4164 per year. Tuition, state resident: full-time $7176; part-time $4164 per year. Tuition, nonresident: full-time $14,304; part-time $8916 per year. *International tuition:* $14,304 full-time. *Required fees:* $1037.76; $1037.76 per unit. Tuition and fees vary according to degree level and program.

California State University, Northridge, Graduate Studies, College of Engineering and Computer Science, Department of Computer Science, Northridge, CA 91330. Offers computer science (MS); software engineering (MS). *Program availability:* Part-time, evening/weekend. *Degree requirements:* For master's, thesis. *Entrance requirements:* For master's, GRE General Test, minimum GPA of 2.5. Additional exam requirements/recommendations for international students: required—TOEFL.

California State University, Sacramento, College of Engineering and Computer Science, Department of Computer Science, Sacramento, CA 95819. Offers computer science (MS); software engineering (MS). *Program availability:* Part-time, evening/weekend. *Students:* 130 full-time (55 women), 52 part-time (21 women); includes 18 minority (3 Black or African American, non-Hispanic/Latino; 13 Asian, non-Hispanic/Latino; 2 Hispanic/Latino), 149 international. Average age 26. 400 applicants, 31% accepted, 36 enrolled. In 2019, 41 master's awarded. *Degree requirements:* For master's, thesis, thesis, project or comprehensive exam; writing proficiency exam. *Entrance requirements:* For master's, GRE, minimum GPA of 3.0 in last 60 units attempted. Additional exam requirements/recommendations for international students: required—TOEFL (minimum score 550 paper-based; 80 iBT); recommended—IELTS (minimum score 7). *Application deadline:* For fall admission, 3/1 for domestic students, 2/1 for international students; for spring admission, 9/15 for domestic students, 8/15 for international students. Applications are processed on a rolling basis. Application fee: $70. Electronic applications accepted. *Expenses:* Contact institution. *Financial support:* Teaching assistantships, career-related internships or fieldwork, Federal Work-Study, and scholarships/grants available. Support available to part-time students. Financial award application deadline: 3/1; financial award applicants required to submit FAFSA. *Unit head:* Dr. Nik Faroughi, Chair, E-mail: faroughi@csus.edu. *Application contact:* Jose Martinez, Graduate Admissions Supervisor, 916-278-7871, E-mail: martinj@skymail.csus.edu. Website: http://www.ecs.csus.edu/csc

California State University, San Bernardino, Graduate Studies, College of Natural Sciences, Program in Computer Science, San Bernardino, CA 92407. Offers MS. *Faculty:* 3 full-time (0 women). *Students:* 7 full-time (0 women), 9 part-time (all women); includes 4 minority (2 Asian, non-Hispanic/Latino; 2 Hispanic/Latino), 10 international. Average age 26. 121 applicants, 27% accepted, 4 enrolled. In 2019, 9 master's awarded. *Entrance requirements:* Additional exam requirements/recommendations for international students: required—TOEFL. *Application deadline:* For fall admission, 7/16 for domestic students; for winter admission, 10/16 for domestic students; for spring admission, 1/22 for domestic students. Application fee: $55. *Unit head:* Dr. Haiyan Qiao, Director, 909-537-5415, Fax: 909-537-7004, E-mail: hqiao@csusb.edu. *Application contact:* Dr. Dorota Huizinga, Dean of Graduate Studies, 909-537-3064, E-mail: dorota.huizinga@csusb.edu.

California State University, San Marcos, College of Science and Mathematics, Program in Computer Science, San Marcos, CA 92096-0001. Offers computer science (MS); cybersecurity (MS). *Program availability:* Part-time. *Entrance requirements:* For master's, GRE General Test, statement of purpose, letters of recommendation. Additional exam requirements/recommendations for international students: required—TOEFL (minimum score 550 paper-based; 80 iBT). *Application deadline:* For fall admission, 5/30 for domestic students; for spring admission, 8/30 for domestic students, 11/1 for international students. Application fee: $55. *Expenses: Tuition, area resident:* Full-time $7176. Tuition, state resident: full-time $7176. Tuition, nonresident: full-time $18,640. *International tuition:* $18,640 full-time. *Required fees:* $1960. *Financial support:* Fellowships, research assistantships, teaching assistantships, and tuition waivers available. *Unit head:* Ali Ahmadinia, Professor, 760-750-8502, E-mail: aahmadinia@csusm.edu. *Application contact:* Dr. Charles De Leone, Interim Dean of Office of Graduate Studies and Research, 760-750-8045, Fax: 760-750-8045, E-mail: apply@csusm.edu.

Capitol Technology University, Graduate Programs, Laurel, MD 20708-9759. Offers business administration (MBA); computer science (MS); electrical engineering (MS); information and telecommunications systems management (MS); information architecture (MS); network security (MS). *Program availability:* Part-time, evening/weekend, online learning. *Entrance requirements:* For master's, minimum GPA of 3.0. Electronic applications accepted.

Carleton University, Faculty of Graduate Studies, Faculty of Science, School of Computer Science, Ottawa, ON K1S 5B6, Canada. Offers computer science (MCS, PhD); information and system science (M Sc). *Program availability:* Part-time. *Degree requirements:* For master's, thesis optional, project; for doctorate, comprehensive exam, thesis/dissertation. *Entrance requirements:* For master's, honors degree. Additional exam requirements/recommendations for international students: required—TOEFL.

Carnegie Mellon University, School of Computer Science, Department of Computer Science, Pittsburgh, PA 15213-3891. Offers algorithms, combinatorics, and optimization (PhD); computer science (MS, PhD); pure and applied logic (PhD). *Degree requirements:* For doctorate, thesis/dissertation. *Entrance requirements:* For doctorate, GRE General Test, GRE Subject Test, BS in computer science or equivalent. Additional exam requirements/recommendations for international students: required—TOEFL.

Carnegie Mellon University, School of Computer Science, Language Technologies Institute, Pittsburgh, PA 15213-3891. Offers MLT, MS, PhD. Terminal master's awarded for partial completion of doctoral program. *Degree requirements:* For doctorate, thesis/dissertation. *Entrance requirements:* For master's and doctorate, GRE General Test, GRE Subject Test. Additional exam requirements/recommendations for international students: required—TOEFL.

Case Western Reserve University, School of Graduate Studies, Case School of Engineering, Department of Computer and Data Sciences, Cleveland, OH 44106. Offers computer engineering (MS, PhD); computing and information sciences (MS, PhD); electrical engineering (MS, PhD); systems and control engineering (MS, PhD). *Program availability:* Part-time, evening/weekend, online only, 100% online. Terminal master's awarded for partial completion of doctoral program. *Degree requirements:* For master's, thesis; for doctorate, thesis/dissertation, qualifying exam, teaching experience. *Entrance requirements:* For master's and doctorate, GRE General Test. Additional exam requirements/recommendations for international students: required—TOEFL.

The Catholic University of America, School of Engineering, Department of Electrical Engineering and Computer Science, Washington, DC 20064. Offers computer science (MSCS, PhD); electrical engineering (MEE, PhD). *Program availability:* Part-time. *Faculty:* 10 full-time (1 woman), 9 part-time/adjunct (8 women). *Students:* 13 full-time (5 women), 71 part-time (26 women); includes 18 minority (8 Black or African American, non-Hispanic/Latino; 5 Asian, non-Hispanic/Latino; 2 Hispanic/Latino; 3 Two or more races, non-Hispanic/Latino), 40 international. Average age 34. 75 applicants, 83% accepted, 27 enrolled. In 2019, 20 master's, 8 doctorates awarded. *Degree requirements:* For master's, thesis or alternative; for doctorate, comprehensive exam, thesis/dissertation, oral exams. *Entrance requirements:* For master's and doctorate, statement of purpose, official copies of academic transcripts, three letters of recommendation. Additional exam requirements/recommendations for international students: required—TOEFL (minimum score 550 paper-based; 80 iBT). *Application deadline:* For fall admission, 7/15 priority date for domestic students, 7/1 for international students; for spring admission, 11/15 priority date for domestic students, 11/1 for international students. Applications are processed on a rolling basis. Application fee: $55. Electronic applications accepted. *Expenses:* Contact institution. *Financial support:* Fellowships, research assistantships, teaching assistantships, Federal Work-Study, scholarships/grants, tuition waivers (full and partial), and unspecified assistantships available. Financial award application deadline: 2/1; financial award applicants required to submit FAFSA. *Unit head:* Dr. Nader Namazi, Chair, 202-319-5193, E-mail: namazi@cua.edu. *Application contact:* Dr. Steven Brown, Director of Graduate Admissions, 202-319-5057, Fax: 202-319-6533, E-mail: cua-admissions@cua.edu.
Website: https://engineering.catholic.edu/eecs/index.html

Central Connecticut State University, School of Graduate Studies, School of Engineering, Science and Technology, Department of Computer Science, New Britain, CT 06050-4010. Offers computer information technology (MS). *Program availability:* Part-time, evening/weekend. *Degree requirements:* For master's, thesis or alternative, special project. *Entrance requirements:* For master's, minimum undergraduate GPA of 2.7, letters of recommendation, resume. Additional exam requirements/recommendations for international students: required—TOEFL (minimum score 550 paper-based; 79 iBT); recommended—IELTS (minimum score 6.5). Electronic applications accepted.

Central Connecticut State University, School of Graduate Studies, School of Engineering, Science and Technology, Department of Mathematical Sciences, New Britain, CT 06050-4010. Offers data mining (MS, Certificate); mathematics (MA, MS), including actuarial science (MA); computer science (MA), statistics (MA); mathematics education leadership (Sixth Year Certificate); mathematics for secondary education (Certificate). *Program availability:* Part-time, evening/weekend, 100% online. *Degree requirements:* For master's, comprehensive exam, thesis or alternative, special project; for other advanced degree, qualifying exam. *Entrance requirements:* For master's, minimum undergraduate GPA of 2.7; for other advanced degree, minimum undergraduate GPA of 3.0, essay, letters of recommendation. Additional exam requirements/recommendations for international students: required—TOEFL (minimum score 550 paper-based; 79 iBT); recommended—IELTS (minimum score 6.5). Electronic applications accepted.

Central Michigan University, College of Graduate Studies, College of Science and Engineering, Department of Computer Science, Mount Pleasant, MI 48859. Offers MS. *Program availability:* Part-time. *Degree requirements:* For master's, thesis or alternative. *Entrance requirements:* For master's, bachelor's degree from accredited institution with minimum GPA of 3.0 in last two years of study. Electronic applications accepted. *Expenses: Tuition, area resident:* Full-time $12,267; part-time $8178 per year. Tuition, state resident: full-time $12,267; part-time $8178 per year. Tuition, nonresident: full-time $12,267; part-time $8178 per year. *International tuition:* $16,110 full-time. *Required fees:* $225 per semester. Tuition and fees vary according to degree level and program.

Chicago State University, School of Graduate and Professional Studies, College of Arts and Sciences, Department of Mathematics and Computer Science, Chicago, IL 60628. Offers computer science (MS); mathematics (MS). *Degree requirements:* For master's, thesis optional, oral exam. *Entrance requirements:* For master's, minimum GPA of 2.75.

Christopher Newport University, Graduate Studies, Master of Science in Applied Physics and Computer Science, Newport News, VA 23606. Offers applied physics and computer science (MS). *Program availability:* Part-time. *Faculty:* 5 full-time (1 woman). *Students:* 7 full-time (2 women), 9 part-time (2 women); includes 3 minority (all Hispanic/Latino). Average age 24. 7 applicants, 43% accepted, 2 enrolled. In 2019, 6 master's awarded. *Entrance requirements:* For master's, GRE General Test, minimum GPA of 3.0. Additional exam requirements/recommendations for international students: required—TOEFL (minimum score 580 paper-based; 92 iBT), IELTS (minimum score 7). *Application deadline:* For fall admission, 7/15 priority date for domestic students, 3/1 for international students; for spring admission, 11/1 for domestic students, 10/1 for international students; for summer admission, 3/15 for domestic students, 3/1 for international students. Applications are processed on a rolling basis. Application fee: $65. Electronic applications accepted. *Expenses: Tuition, area resident:* Full-time $7578; part-time $421 per credit hour. Tuition, state resident: full-time $7578; part-time $421 per credit hour. Tuition, nonresident: full-time $16,686; part-time $927 per credit hour. *International tuition:* $16,686 full-time. *Required fees:* $4428; $246 per credit hour. Tuition and fees vary according to course load and program. *Financial support:* Application deadline: 3/1; applicants required to submit FAFSA. *Unit head:* Dr. Peter Monaghan, Graduate Program Director, 757-594-8293, E-mail: peter.monaghan@cnu.edu. *Application contact:* Dr. Peter Monaghan, Graduate Program Director, 757-594-8293, E-mail: peter.monaghan@cnu.edu.
Website: https://cnu.edu/admission/graduate/apcs/

City College of the City University of New York, Graduate School, Grove School of Engineering, Department of Computer Science, New York, NY 10031-9198. Offers computer science (MS, PhD); information systems (MIS). *Degree requirements:* For master's, thesis optional; for doctorate, one foreign language, comprehensive exam, thesis/dissertation. *Entrance requirements:* For master's and doctorate, GRE General Test. Additional exam requirements/recommendations for international students: required—TOEFL (minimum score 500 paper-based; 61 iBT).

City University of Seattle, Graduate Division, School of Management, Seattle, WA 98121. Offers accounting (Certificate); change leadership (MBA, Certificate); computer systems (MS); finance (Certificate); financial management (MBA); general management (MBA); general management-Europe (MBA); global marketing (MBA); human resources management (Certificate); individualized study (MBA); information security (MS); information systems (MBA); leadership (MA); marketing (MBA, Certificate); project management (MBA, MS, Certificate); sustainable business (Certificate); technology management (MBA, Certificate). *Program availability:* Part-time, evening/weekend, online learning. *Degree requirements:* For master's, comprehensive exam (for some programs), thesis (for some programs). *Entrance requirements:* For master's, baccalaureate degree or equivalent from an accredited or otherwise recognized institution. Additional exam requirements/recommendations for international students: required—TOEFL (minimum score 567 paper-based; 87 iBT); recommended—IELTS. Electronic applications accepted.

Clark Atlanta University, School of Arts and Sciences, Department of Computer and Information Science, Atlanta, GA 30314. Offers MS. *Program availability:* Part-time. *Degree requirements:* For master's, one foreign language, thesis. *Entrance requirements:* For master's, GRE General Test, minimum GPA of 2.5. Additional exam requirements/recommendations for international students: required—TOEFL (minimum score 500 paper-based; 61 iBT).

Clarkson University, School of Arts and Sciences, Department of Computer Science, Potsdam, NY 13699. Offers MS, PhD. *Faculty:* 6 full-time (2 women), 1 part-time/adjunct (0 women). *Students:* 21 full-time (4 women), 6 part-time (0 women); includes 2 minority (1 Asian, non-Hispanic/Latino; 1 Native Hawaiian or other Pacific Islander, non-Hispanic/Latino), 11 international. 69 applicants, 54% accepted, 12 enrolled. In 2019, 2 master's, 1 doctorate awarded. *Degree requirements:* For master's, thesis; for doctorate, comprehensive exam, thesis/dissertation. *Entrance requirements:* For master's and doctorate, GRE. Additional exam requirements/recommendations for international students: required—TOEFL (minimum score 550 paper-based; 80 iBT) or IELTS (6.5). *Application deadline:* Applications are processed on a rolling basis. Application fee: $50. Electronic applications accepted. *Expenses: Tuition:* Full-time $24,984; part-time $1388. *Required fees:* $225. Tuition and fees vary according to campus/location and program. *Financial support:* Scholarships/grants and unspecified assistantships available. *Unit head:* Dr. Christopher Lynch, Chair of Computer Science, 315-268-2334, E-mail: clynch@clarkson.edu. *Application contact:* Daniel Capogna, Director of Graduate Admissions & Recruitment, 518-631-9910, E-mail: graduate@clarkson.edu.
Website: https://www.clarkson.edu/academics/graduate

Clemson University, Graduate School, College of Engineering, Computing and Applied Sciences, School of Computing, Clemson, SC 29634. Offers computer science (MS, PhD); digital production arts (MFA); human centered computing (PhD). *Program availability:* Part-time. *Faculty:* 47 full-time (12 women), 2 part-time/adjunct (1 woman). *Students:* 244 full-time (69 women), 28 part-time (11 women); includes 22 minority (10 Black or African American, non-Hispanic/Latino; 4 Asian, non-Hispanic/Latino; 6 Hispanic/Latino; 2 Two or more races, non-Hispanic/Latino), 176 international. Average age 26. 493 applicants, 65% accepted, 128 enrolled. In 2019, 60 master's, 6 doctorates awarded. Terminal master's awarded for partial completion of doctoral program. *Degree requirements:* For master's, thesis (for some programs); for doctorate, comprehensive exam, thesis/dissertation. *Entrance requirements:* For master's and doctorate, GRE General Test, unofficial transcripts, letters of recommendation. Additional exam requirements/recommendations for international students: required—IELTS (minimum score 6.5); recommended—TOEFL (minimum score 550 paper-based; 80 iBT), TSE (minimum score 54). *Application deadline:* For fall admission, 5/15 priority date for domestic students, 4/15 priority date for international students; for spring admission, 10/15 priority date for domestic students, 9/15 priority date for international students. Applications are processed on a rolling basis. Application fee: $80 ($90 for international students). Electronic applications accepted. *Expenses: Tuition, area resident:* Full-time $10,600; part-time $8688 per semester. Tuition, state resident: full-time $10,600; part-time $8688 per semester. Tuition, nonresident: full-time $22,050; part-time $17,412 per semester. *International tuition:* $22,050 full-time. *Required fees:* $1196; $617 per

semester. $617 per semester. Tuition and fees vary according to course load, degree level, campus/location and program. *Financial support:* In 2019–20, 126 students received support, including 26 fellowships with full and partial tuition reimbursements available (averaging $7,469 per year), 45 research assistantships with full and partial tuition reimbursements available (averaging $18,213 per year), 48 teaching assistantships with full and partial tuition reimbursements available (averaging $19,078 per year); career-related internships or fieldwork, traineeships, and unspecified assistantships also available. Financial award application deadline: 1/1. *Unit head:* Dr. Amy Apon, Director, 864-656-5769, E-mail: aapon@clemson.edu. *Application contact:* Adam Rollins, Student Services Graduate Program Coordinator, 864-656-5853, E-mail: rollin7@clemson.edu.
Website: https://www.clemson.edu/cecas/departments/computing/index.html

Coastal Carolina University, Gupta College of Science, Conway, SC 29528-6054. Offers applied computing and information systems (Certificate); coastal marine and wetland studies (MS); information systems technology (MS); marine science (PhD); sport management (MS). *Program availability:* Part-time, evening/weekend, 100% online. *Faculty:* 29 full-time (10 women), 3 part-time/adjunct (1 woman). *Students:* 55 full-time (30 women), 35 part-time (13 women); includes 15 minority (10 Black or African American, non-Hispanic/Latino; 4 Hispanic/Latino; 1 Two or more races, non-Hispanic/Latino), 13 international. Average age 27. 88 applicants, 68% accepted, 35 enrolled. In 2019, 45 master's awarded. *Degree requirements:* For master's, comprehensive exam (for some programs), thesis optional, sport management: comprehensive exam; for doctorate, comprehensive exam, thesis/dissertation. *Entrance requirements:* For master's, GRE, GMAT, 3 letters of recommendation, resume, official transcripts, written statement of educational and career goals, Sport Management: writing sample; for doctorate, GRE, official transcripts; baccalaureate or master's degree; minimum GPA of 3.0 for all collegiate coursework; successful completion of at least two semesters of college-level calculus, physics, and chemistry; 3 letters of recommendation; written statement of educational and career goals; resume. Additional exam requirements/recommendations for international students: required—TOEFL (minimum score 550 paper-based; 79 iBT). *Application deadline:* For fall admission, 1/15 priority date for domestic and international students; for spring admission, 11/1 priority date for domestic and international students. Applications are processed on a rolling basis. Application fee: $45. Electronic applications accepted. *Expenses: Tuition, area resident:* Full-time $10,764; part-time $598 per credit hour. Tuition, state resident: full-time $10,764; part-time $598 per credit hour. Tuition, nonresident: full-time $19,836; part-time $1102 per credit hour. *International tuition:* $19,836 full-time. *Required fees:* $90; $5 per credit hour. *Financial support:* Fellowships, research assistantships, teaching assistantships, and tuition waivers available. Financial award application deadline: 3/1; financial award applicants required to submit FAFSA. *Unit head:* Dr. Michael H. Roberts, Dean/Vice President for Emerging Initiatives, 843-349-2282, Fax: 843-349-2545, E-mail: mroberts@coastal.edu. *Application contact:* Dr. Robert Young, Interim Dean, College of Graduate Studies and Research, 843-349-2277, Fax: 843-349-6444, E-mail: ryoung@coastal.edu.
Website: https://www.coastal.edu/science/

College of Charleston, Graduate School, School of Sciences and Mathematics, Program in Computer and Information Sciences, Charleston, SC 29424-0001. Offers MS. *Program availability:* Part-time, evening/weekend. *Degree requirements:* For master's, thesis optional. *Entrance requirements:* For master's, GRE. Additional exam requirements/recommendations for international students: required—TOEFL (minimum score 81 iBT). Electronic applications accepted.

The College of Saint Rose, Graduate Studies, School of Mathematics and Sciences, Program in Computer Information Systems, Albany, NY 12203-1419. Offers MS, Advanced Certificate. *Program availability:* Part-time, evening/weekend. *Students:* 19 full-time (9 women), 30 part-time (8 women); includes 10 minority (1 Black or African American, non-Hispanic/Latino; 7 Asian, non-Hispanic/Latino; 1 Hispanic/Latino; 1 Two or more races, non-Hispanic/Latino), 34 international. Average age 29. 52 applicants, 90% accepted, 12 enrolled. In 2019, 16 master's, 3 other advanced degrees awarded. *Degree requirements:* For master's, comprehensive exam, research component, project. *Entrance requirements:* For master's, minimum GPA of 3.0, 9 undergraduate credits in math. Additional exam requirements/recommendations for international students: required—TOEFL (minimum score 550 paper-based; 80 iBT), IELTS (minimum score 6), PTE (minimum score 56). *Application deadline:* For fall admission, 4/1 priority date for domestic and international students; for spring admission, 10/15 priority date for domestic and international students; for summer admission, 3/15 priority date for domestic and international students. Applications are processed on a rolling basis. Application fee: $40. Electronic applications accepted. *Expenses: Tuition:* Full-time $14,382; part-time $799 per credit hour. *Required fees:* $954; $698. Tuition and fees vary according to course load. *Financial support:* Career-related internships or fieldwork, scholarships/grants, tuition waivers (partial), and unspecified assistantships available. Support available to part-time students. Financial award application deadline: 4/15; financial award applicants required to submit FAFSA. *Unit head:* Dr. John Avitabile, Department Chair, 518-458-5317, E-mail: avitabij@strose.edu. *Application contact:* Daniel Gallagher, Assistant Vice President for Graduate Recruitment and Enrollment, 518-485-3390.
Website: https://www.strose.edu/computer-information-systems/

College of Staten Island of the City University of New York, Graduate Programs, Division of Science and Technology, Program in Computer Science, Staten Island, NY 10314-6600. Offers computer science (MS), including artificial intelligence and data analytics, cloud computing and software engineering, cybersecurity and networks. *Program availability:* Part-time, evening/weekend. *Faculty:* 6. *Students:* 42. 48 applicants, 67% accepted, 15 enrolled. In 2019, 10 master's awarded. *Degree requirements:* For master's, thesis optional, a program of 10 courses (30 credits) with at least a 3.0 (B) average. Exceptional students may be permitted to satisfy six credits of the total credit requirement with a master's thesis. *Entrance requirements:* For master's, GRE General Test, BS in Computer Science or related area with a B average (3.0 out of 4.0) overall and in the major, a resume, and demonstratable knowledge in several areas. Additional exam requirements/recommendations for international students: required—TOEFL (minimum score 550 paper-based; 79 iBT), IELTS (minimum score 6.5). *Application deadline:* For fall admission, 7/20 priority date for domestic students, 4/25 for international students; for spring admission, 11/2 priority date for domestic students, 11/2 for international students. Applications are processed on a rolling basis. Application fee: $75. Electronic applications accepted. *Expenses: Tuition, area resident:* Full-time $11,090; part-time $470 per credit. Tuition, state resident: full-time $11,090; part-time $470 per credit. Tuition, nonresident: full-time $20,520; part-time $855 per credit. *International tuition:* $20,520 full-time. *Required fees:* $559; $181 per semester. Tuition and fees vary according to program. *Unit head:* Dr. Xiaowen Zhang, Associate Professor, 718-982-3262, E-mail: xiaowen.zhang@csi.cuny.edu. *Application contact:* Sasha Spence, Associate Director for Graduate Admissions, 718-982-2019, Fax: 718-982-2500, E-mail: sasha.spence@csi.cuny.edu.
Website: https://www.csi.cuny.edu/academics-and-research/departments-programs/computer-science

Colorado School of Mines, Office of Graduate Studies, Department of Electrical Engineering and Computer Science, Golden, CO 80401-1887. Offers electrical engineering (MS, PhD). *Program availability:* Part-time. *Degree requirements:* For master's, thesis (for some programs); for doctorate, comprehensive exam, thesis/dissertation. *Entrance requirements:* For master's and doctorate, GRE General Test. Additional exam requirements/recommendations for international students: required—TOEFL (minimum score 550 paper-based; 79 iBT). Electronic applications accepted. *Expenses:* Tuition, state resident: full-time $16,650; part-time $925 per credit hour. Tuition, nonresident: full-time $37,350; part-time $2075 per credit hour. *International tuition:* $37,350 full-time. *Required fees:* $2412.

Colorado State University, College of Natural Sciences, Department of Computer Science, Fort Collins, CO 80523-1873. Offers MCS, MS, PhD. *Program availability:* Part-time, 100% online, blended/hybrid learning. *Faculty:* 17 full-time (3 women), 3 part-time/adjunct (0 women). *Students:* 79 full-time (25 women), 91 part-time (19 women); includes 15 minority (1 Black or African American, non-Hispanic/Latino; 6 Asian, non-Hispanic/Latino; 5 Hispanic/Latino; 3 Two or more races, non-Hispanic/Latino), 98 international. Average age 29. 636 applicants, 18% accepted, 69 enrolled. In 2019, 31 master's, 6 doctorates awarded. Terminal master's awarded for partial completion of doctoral program. *Degree requirements:* For master's, thesis (for some programs); for doctorate, thesis/dissertation. *Entrance requirements:* For master's, minimum GPA of 3.2, BS in computer science; for doctorate, minimum GPA of 3.2, BS/MS in computer science, research experience. Additional exam requirements/recommendations for international students: required—TOEFL (minimum score 580 paper-based; 92 iBT), IELTS (minimum score 6.5), PTE (minimum score 62), GRE (without degree from U.S. institution). *Application deadline:* For fall admission, 2/1 for domestic and international students; for spring admission, 8/15 for domestic and international students. Application fee: $60 ($70 for international students). Electronic applications accepted. *Expenses:* Contact institution. *Financial support:* In 2019–20, 1 fellowship (averaging $17,865 per year), 24 research assistantships (averaging $18,753 per year), 36 teaching assistantships (averaging $18,028 per year) were awarded; health care benefits and unspecified assistantships also available. *Unit head:* Dr. Craig Partridge, Professor and Chair, 970-491-6633, E-mail: craig.partridge@colostate.edu. *Application contact:* Graduate Processor, E-mail: gradinfo@cs.colostate.edu.
Website: https://compsci.colostate.edu

Colorado Technical University Aurora, Program in Computer Science, Aurora, CO 80014. Offers computer systems security (MSCS); database systems (MSCS); software engineering (MSCS). *Program availability:* Part-time, evening/weekend. *Degree requirements:* For master's, thesis or alternative. *Entrance requirements:* For master's, minimum undergraduate GPA of 3.0, resume.

Colorado Technical University Colorado Springs, Graduate Studies, Program in Computer Science, Colorado Springs, CO 80907. Offers computer science (DCS); computer systems security (MSCS); database systems (MSCS); software engineering (MSCS). *Program availability:* Part-time, evening/weekend, online learning. *Degree requirements:* For master's, thesis or alternative; for doctorate, thesis/dissertation. *Entrance requirements:* For doctorate, minimum graduate GPA of 3.0, 5 years of related work experience.

Columbia University, Fu Foundation School of Engineering and Applied Science, Department of Computer Science, New York, NY 10027. Offers computer science (MS, Eng Sc D, PhD). *Program availability:* Part-time, online learning. Terminal master's awarded for partial completion of doctoral program. *Degree requirements:* For master's, thesis optional; for doctorate, comprehensive exam, thesis/dissertation, candidacy exam. *Entrance requirements:* For master's and doctorate, GRE General Test. Additional exam requirements/recommendations for international students: required—TOEFL, IELTS, PTE. Electronic applications accepted. *Expenses: Tuition:* Full-time $47,600; part-time $1880 per credit. One-time fee: $105.

Columbus State University, Graduate Studies, Turner College of Business, Columbus, GA 31907-5645. Offers applied computer science (MS), including informational assurance, modeling and simulation, software development; business administration (MBA); cyber security (MS); human resource management (Certificate); information systems security (Certificate); modeling and simulation (Certificate); organizational leadership (MS), including human resource management, leader development, servant leadership; servant leadership (Certificate). *Accreditation:* AACSB. *Program availability:* Part-time, evening/weekend, 100% online, blended/hybrid learning. *Entrance requirements:* For master's, GMAT, GRE, minimum undergraduate GPA of 2.75, letters of recommendation. Additional exam requirements/recommendations for international students: required—TOEFL (minimum score 550 paper-based; 79 iBT). Electronic applications accepted. *Expenses:* Contact institution.

Concordia University, School of Graduate Studies, Faculty of Engineering and Computer Science, Department of Computer Science and Software Engineering, Montréal, QC H3G 1M8, Canada. Offers computer science (M App Comp Sc, M Comp Sc, PhD, Diploma); software engineering (M Eng, MA Sc). *Degree requirements:* For master's, one foreign language, thesis optional; for doctorate, one foreign language, comprehensive exam, thesis/dissertation.

Concordia University, Nebraska, Program in Computer Science, Seward, NE 68434. Offers cyber operations (MS). *Program availability:* Online learning.

Cornell University, Graduate School, Graduate Fields of Engineering, Field of Computer Science, Ithaca, NY 14853. Offers algorithms (M Eng, PhD); applied logic and automated reasoning (M Eng, PhD); artificial intelligence (M Eng, PhD); computer graphics (M Eng, PhD); computer science (M Eng, PhD); computer vision (M Eng, PhD); concurrency and distributed computing (M Eng, PhD); information organization and retrieval (M Eng, PhD); operating systems (M Eng, PhD); parallel computing (M Eng, PhD); programming environments (M Eng, PhD); programming languages and methodology (M Eng, PhD); robotics (M Eng, PhD); scientific computing (M Eng, PhD); theory of computation (M Eng, PhD). *Degree requirements:* For doctorate, comprehensive exam, thesis/dissertation. *Entrance requirements:* For master's, GRE General Test, 2 letters of recommendation; for doctorate, GRE General Test, GRE Subject Test (computer science or mathematics), 3 letters of recommendation. Additional exam requirements/recommendations for international students: required—TOEFL (minimum score 505 paper-based; 77 iBT). Electronic applications accepted.

Dakota State University, Beacom College of Computer and Cyber Sciences, Madison, SD 57042-1799. Offers applied computer science (MSACS); banking security (Graduate Certificate); cyber security (D Sc); ethical hacking (Graduate Certificate); information assurance and computer security (MSIA). *Program availability:* Part-time, evening/weekend, online learning. *Faculty:* 18 full-time (2 women), 1 part-time/adjunct (0 women). *Students:* 44 full-time (5 women), 127 part-time (26 women); includes 43 minority (17 Black or African American, non-Hispanic/Latino; 2 American Indian or Alaska Native, non-Hispanic/Latino; 11 Asian, non-Hispanic/Latino; 9 Hispanic/Latino; 2 Native Hawaiian or other Pacific Islander, non-Hispanic/Latino; 2 Two or more races, non-Hispanic/Latino), 9 international. Average age 35. 205 applicants, 30% accepted, 56 enrolled. In 2019, 19 master's, 7 doctorates, 5 other advanced degrees awarded. *Entrance requirements:* Additional exam requirements/recommendations for international students: required—PTE (minimum score 53), TOEFL (minimum score 550

paper-based, 79 iBT, or IELTS 6.5). *Application deadline:* For fall admission, 6/15 for domestic students, 4/15 for international students; for spring admission, 11/15 for domestic students, 9/15 priority date for international students; for summer admission, 4/15 for domestic and international students. Applications are processed on a rolling basis. Application fee: $35. *Expenses: Tuition, area resident:* Full-time $7919. Tuition, state resident: full-time $7919. Tuition, nonresident: full-time $14,784. *International tuition:* $14,784 full-time. *Required fees:* $961. *Financial support:* Fellowships, career-related internships or fieldwork, Federal Work-Study, scholarships/grants, unspecified assistantships, and Administrative Assistantships available. Support available to part-time students. Financial award applicants required to submit FAFSA. *Unit head:* Dr. Pat Engebretson, Dean, Beacom College of Computer and Cyber Science, 605-256-5798, E-mail: pat.engebretson@dsu.edu. *Application contact:* Erin Blankespoor, Senior Secretary, Office of Graduate Studies, 605-256-5799, E-mail: erin.blankespoor@dsu.edu.
Website: https://dsu.edu/academics/colleges/beacom-college-of-computer-and-cyber-sciences

Dalhousie University, Faculty of Computer Science, Halifax, NS B3H 1W5, Canada. Offers computational biology and bioinformatics (M Sc); computer science (MA Sc, MC Sc, PhD); electronic commerce (MEC); health informatics (MHI). *Degree requirements:* For master's, thesis (for some programs); for doctorate, thesis/dissertation. *Entrance requirements:* Additional exam requirements/recommendations for international students: required—1 of 5 approved tests: TOEFL, IELTS, CANTEST, CAEL, Michigan English Language Assessment Battery. Electronic applications accepted.

Dartmouth College, Guarini School of Graduate and Advanced Studies, Department of Computer Science, Hanover, NH 03755. Offers MS, PhD. Terminal master's awarded for partial completion of doctoral program. *Entrance requirements:* For master's and doctorate, GRE General Test, GRE Subject Test. Additional exam requirements/recommendations for international students: required—TOEFL. Electronic applications accepted.

DePaul University, College of Computing and Digital Media, Chicago, IL 60604. Offers animation (MA, MFA); applied technology (MS); business information technology (MS); computational finance (MS); computer and information sciences (PhD); computer science (MS); creative producing (MFA); cybersecurity (MS); data science (MS); digital communication and media arts (MA); documentary (MFA); e-commerce technology (MS); experience design (MA); film and television (MS); film and television directing (MFA); game design (MFA); game programming (MS); health informatics (MS); human centered design (PhD); human-computer interaction (MS); information systems (MS); network engineering and security (MS); product innovation and computing (MS); screenwriting (MFA); software engineering (MS); JD/MS. *Program availability:* Part-time, evening/weekend, online learning. *Degree requirements:* For master's, thesis (for some programs); for doctorate, comprehensive exam, thesis/dissertation. *Entrance requirements:* For master's, GRE or GMAT (for MS in computational finance only), bachelor's degree, resume (MS in predictive analytics only), IT experience (MS in information technology project management only), portfolio review (all MFA programs and MA in animation); for doctorate, GRE, master's degree in computer science. Additional exam requirements/recommendations for international students: required—TOEFL (minimum score 590 paper-based; 80 iBT), IELTS (minimum score 6.5), PTE (minimum score 53). Electronic applications accepted. *Expenses:* Contact institution.

DigiPen Institute of Technology, Graduate Programs, Redmond, WA 98052. Offers computer science (MS); digital art and animation (MFA). *Program availability:* Part-time. *Degree requirements:* For master's, comprehensive exam (for some programs), thesis (for some programs). *Entrance requirements:* For master's, GRE General Test (for MSCS), art portfolio (for MFA); official transcripts from all post-secondary education including final transcript indicating degree earned, statement of purpose, and 2 letters of recommendation. Additional exam requirements/recommendations for international students: required—TOEFL (minimum score 550 paper-based; 80 iBT). Electronic applications accepted. *Expenses:* Contact institution.

Drexel University, College of Computing and Informatics, Department of Computer Science, Philadelphia, PA 19104-2875. Offers computer science (MS, PhD, Postbaccalaureate Certificate); software engineering (MS). *Program availability:* Part-time, evening/weekend, 100% online. Terminal master's awarded for partial completion of doctoral program. *Degree requirements:* For doctorate, thesis/dissertation. *Entrance requirements:* For master's and doctorate, GRE General Test. Additional exam requirements/recommendations for international students: required—TOEFL (minimum score 90 iBT), IELTS (minimum score 6.5). Electronic applications accepted.

Duke University, Graduate School, Department of Computer Science, Durham, NC 27708. Offers MS, PhD. *Degree requirements:* For doctorate, thesis/dissertation. *Entrance requirements:* For master's, GRE General Test; for doctorate, GRE General Test, GRE Subject Test (recommended). Additional exam requirements/recommendations for international students: required—TOEFL (minimum score 577 paper-based; 90 iBT) or IELTS (minimum score 7). Electronic applications accepted.

East Carolina University, Graduate School, College of Engineering and Technology, Department of Computer Science, Greenville, NC 27858-4353. Offers computer science (MS); software engineering (MS). *Program availability:* Part-time, evening/weekend. *Application deadline:* For fall admission, 11/1 priority date for domestic students, 10/1 priority date for international students; for spring admission, 3/1 priority date for domestic and international students. *Expenses: Tuition, area resident:* Full-time $4749; part-time $185 per credit hour. Tuition, state resident: full-time $4749; part-time $185 per credit hour. Tuition, nonresident: full-time $17,898; part-time $864 per credit hour. *International tuition:* $17,898 full-time. *Required fees:* $2787. *Financial support:* Application deadline: 3/1. *Unit head:* Dr. Venkat Gudivada, Chair, 252-328-9693, E-mail: gudivadav15@ecu.edu. *Application contact:* Graduate School Admissions, 252-328-6012, Fax: 252-328-6071, E-mail: gradschool@ecu.edu.
Website: https://cet.ecu.edu/csci/

East Carolina University, Graduate School, College of Engineering and Technology, Department of Technology Systems, Greenville, NC 27858-4353. Offers computer network professional (Certificate); cyber security professional (Certificate); information assurance (Certificate); Lean Six Sigma Black Belt (Certificate); network technology (MS), including computer networking management, digital communications technology, information security, Web technologies; occupational safety (MS); technology management (MS, PhD), including industrial distribution and logistics (MS); Website developer (Certificate). *Application deadline:* For fall admission, 6/1 priority date for domestic students. *Expenses: Tuition, area resident:* Full-time $4749; part-time $185 per credit hour. Tuition, state resident: full-time $4749; part-time $185 per credit hour. Tuition, nonresident: full-time $17,898; part-time $864 per credit hour. *International tuition:* $17,898 full-time. *Required fees:* $2787. *Financial support:* Application deadline: 6/1. *Unit head:* Dr. Tijjani Mohammed, Chair, 252-328-9668, E-mail: mohammedt@ecu.edu. *Application contact:* Graduate School Admissions, 252-328-6012, Fax: 252-328-6071, E-mail: gradschool@ecu.edu.
Website: https://cet.ecu.edu/techsystems/

Eastern Illinois University, Graduate School, Lumpkin College of Business and Technology, School of Technology, Program in Technology, Charleston, IL 61920. Offers MS. *Program availability:* Part-time, evening/weekend. *Degree requirements:* For master's, comprehensive exam (for some programs), thesis (for some programs). *Entrance requirements:* For master's, GMAT or GRE. Additional exam requirements/recommendations for international students: required—TOEFL (minimum score 500 paper-based; 61 iBT), IELTS (minimum score 6). Electronic applications accepted.

Eastern Michigan University, Graduate School, College of Arts and Sciences, Department of Computer Science, Ypsilanti, MI 48197. Offers MS, Graduate Certificate. *Program availability:* Part-time, evening/weekend, online learning. *Faculty:* 14 full-time (5 women). *Students:* 25 full-time (13 women), 16 part-time (8 women); includes 6 minority (1 Black or African American, non-Hispanic/Latino; 4 Asian, non-Hispanic/Latino; 1 Hispanic/Latino), 22 international. Average age 28. 88 applicants, 39% accepted, 12 enrolled. In 2019, 17 master's awarded. *Entrance requirements:* For master's, at least 18 credit hours of computer science courses including data structures, programming languages like java, C or C++, computer organization; courses in discrete mathematics, probability and statistics, linear algebra and calculus; minimum GPA of 2.75 in computer science. Additional exam requirements/recommendations for international students: required—TOEFL. *Application deadline:* For fall admission, 8/1 for domestic students, 5/1 for international students; for winter admission, 12/1 for domestic students, 10/1 for international students; for spring admission, 4/1 for domestic students, 2/1 for international students. Application fee: $45. *Financial support:* Fellowships, research assistantships with full tuition reimbursements, teaching assistantships with full tuition reimbursements, career-related internships or fieldwork, Federal Work-Study, institutionally sponsored loans, scholarships/grants, tuition waivers (partial), and unspecified assistantships available. Support available to part-time students. Financial award applicants required to submit FAFSA. *Unit head:* Dr. Augstine C. Ikeji, Department Head, 734-487-0056, Fax: 734-487-6824, E-mail: aikeji@emich.edu. *Application contact:* Dr. Krish Narayanan, Graduate Coordinator, 734-487-1256, Fax: 734-487-6824, E-mail: knarayana@emich.edu.
Website: http://www.emich.edu/compsci

Eastern Washington University, Graduate Studies, College of Science, Technology, Engineering and Mathematics, Department of Computer Science, Cheney, WA 99004-2431. Offers computer science (MS). *Program availability:* Part-time. *Faculty:* 8 full-time (3 women). *Students:* 12 full-time (3 women), 9 part-time (4 women), 2 international. Average age 31. 16 applicants, 69% accepted, 9 enrolled. In 2019, 4 master's awarded. *Degree requirements:* For master's, comprehensive exam, thesis or alternative. *Entrance requirements:* For master's, minimum GPA of 3.0. Additional exam requirements/recommendations for international students: required—TOEFL (minimum score 580 paper-based; 92 iBT), IELTS (minimum score 7), PTE (minimum score 63). *Application deadline:* For fall admission, 4/1 priority date for domestic students; for spring admission, 1/15 for domestic students. Applications are processed on a rolling basis. Application fee: $75. Electronic applications accepted. *Financial support:* Teaching assistantships with partial tuition reimbursements, career-related internships or fieldwork, Federal Work-Study, institutionally sponsored loans, scholarships/grants, health care benefits, tuition waivers (partial), and unspecified assistantships available. Support available to part-time students. Financial award application deadline: 2/1. *Unit head:* Dr. Tony Tian, Director, 509-359-6162, E-mail: ytian@ewu.edu. *Application contact:* Dr. Tony Tian, Director, 509-359-6162, E-mail: ytian@ewu.edu.
Website: http://www.ewu.edu/cshe/programs/computer-science.xml

East Stroudsburg University of Pennsylvania, Graduate and Extended Studies, College of Arts and Sciences, Department of Computer Science, East Stroudsburg, PA 18301-2999. Offers MS. *Program availability:* Part-time, evening/weekend. *Degree requirements:* For master's, comprehensive exam, thesis or alternative. *Entrance requirements:* For master's, bachelor's degree in computer science or related field. Additional exam requirements/recommendations for international students: recommended—TOEFL (minimum score 560 paper-based; 83 iBT), IELTS. Electronic applications accepted.

East Tennessee State University, School of Graduate Studies, College of Business and Technology, Department of Computing, Johnson City, TN 37614. Offers applied computer science (MS); emerging technologies (Postbaccalaureate Certificate); information technology (MS). *Program availability:* Part-time, evening/weekend. *Degree requirements:* For master's, comprehensive exam, thesis optional, capstone, oral exam. *Entrance requirements:* For master's, GRE General Test, minimum GPA of 3.0, three letters of recommendation. Additional exam requirements/recommendations for international students: required—TOEFL (minimum score 550 paper-based; 79 iBT). Electronic applications accepted.

Elizabeth City State University, Department of Mathematics and Computer Science, Elizabeth City, NC 27909-7806. Offers mathematics (MS), including applied mathematics, community college teaching, mathematics education, remote sensing. *Program availability:* Part-time, evening/weekend. *Degree requirements:* For master's, thesis. *Entrance requirements:* Additional exam requirements/recommendations for international students: required—TOEFL. Electronic applications accepted.

Emory University, Laney Graduate School, Department of Mathematics and Computer Science, Atlanta, GA 30322-1100. Offers computer science (MS); computer science and informatics (PhD); mathematics (MS, PhD). Terminal master's awarded for partial completion of doctoral program. *Degree requirements:* For master's, thesis; for doctorate, one foreign language, comprehensive exam, thesis/dissertation. *Entrance requirements:* For master's and doctorate, GRE General Test. Additional exam requirements/recommendations for international students: recommended—TOEFL. Electronic applications accepted.

Fairleigh Dickinson University, Florham Campus, Maxwell Becton College of Arts and Sciences, Department of Computer Science, Madison, NJ 07940-1099. Offers MS.

Fairleigh Dickinson University, Metropolitan Campus, University College: Arts, Sciences, and Professional Studies, School of Computer Sciences and Engineering, Program in Computer Science, Teaneck, NJ 07666-1914. Offers MS.

Fitchburg State University, Division of Graduate and Continuing Education, Program in Computer Science, Fitchburg, MA 01420-2697. Offers computer science (MS); data science (MS). *Program availability:* Part-time, evening/weekend. *Entrance requirements:* Additional exam requirements/recommendations for international students: required—TOEFL (minimum score 550 paper-based; 79 iBT). Electronic applications accepted. *Expenses:* Contact institution.

Florida Atlantic University, College of Engineering and Computer Science, Department of Computer and Electrical Engineering and Computer Science, Boca Raton, FL 33431-0991. Offers bioengineering (MS); computer engineering (MS, PhD); computer science (MS, PhD); electrical engineering (MS, PhD). *Program availability:* Part-time, evening/weekend. *Faculty:* 39 full-time (8 women). *Students:* 112 full-time (26 women), 139 part-time (27 women); includes 104 minority (22 Black or African American, non-Hispanic/Latino; 22 Asian, non-Hispanic/Latino; 52 Hispanic/Latino; 8 Two or more races, non-Hispanic/Latino), 63 international. Average age 32. 231 applicants, 54% accepted, 91 enrolled. In 2019, 67 master's, 14 doctorates awarded. Terminal master's awarded for partial completion of doctoral program. *Degree*

requirements: For master's, thesis optional; for doctorate, thesis/dissertation, qualifying exam. *Entrance requirements:* For master's, GRE General Test, minimum GPA of 3.0; for doctorate, GRE General Test, master's degree, minimum GPA of 3.5. Additional exam requirements/recommendations for international students: required—TOEFL (minimum score 500 paper-based; 61 iBT), IELTS (minimum score 6). *Application deadline:* For fall admission, 7/1 priority date for domestic students, 2/15 for international students; for spring admission, 11/1 for domestic students, 7/15 for international students. Applications are processed on a rolling basis. Application fee: $30. *Expenses: Tuition:* Full-time $20,536; part-time $371.82 per credit hour. Tuition and fees vary according to program. *Financial support:* Fellowships, research assistantships with partial tuition reimbursements, teaching assistantships with full tuition reimbursements, career-related internships or fieldwork, and Federal Work-Study available. Support available to part-time students. Financial award application deadline: 4/1; financial award applicants required to submit FAFSA. *Unit head:* Jean Mangiaracina, Graduate Program Administrator, 561-297-6482, E-mail: jmangiar@fau.edu. *Application contact:* Jean Mangiaracina, Graduate Program Administrator, 561-297-6482, E-mail: jmangiar@fau.edu.
Website: http://www.ceecs.fau.edu/

Florida Institute of Technology, College of Engineering and Science, Program in Computer Science, Melbourne, FL 32901-6975. Offers MS, PhD. *Program availability:* Part-time. Terminal master's awarded for partial completion of doctoral program. *Degree requirements:* For master's, comprehensive exam (for some programs), thesis optional, minimum of 30 credits; for doctorate, comprehensive exam, thesis/dissertation, minimum of 72 credits beyond bachelor's degree, publications. *Entrance requirements:* For master's, GRE General Test, 3 letters of recommendation, transcript, 12 credits of advanced coursework in computer science; for doctorate, GRE General Test, GRE Subject Test in computer science (recommended), 3 letters of recommendation, minimum GPA of 3.5 in both bachelor's and master's degree in computer science, resume, statement of objectives. Additional exam requirements/recommendations for international students: required—TOEFL (minimum score 550 paper-based; 79 iBT). Electronic applications accepted.

Florida International University, College of Engineering and Computing, School of Computing and Information Sciences, Miami, FL 33199. Offers computer science (MS, PhD); cybersecurity (MS); data science (MS); information technology (MS); telecommunications and networking (MS). *Program availability:* Part-time, evening/weekend. *Faculty:* 53 full-time (14 women), 33 part-time/adjunct (9 women). *Students:* 162 full-time (39 women), 140 part-time (26 women); includes 160 minority (11 Black or African American, non-Hispanic/Latino; 1 American Indian or Alaska Native, non-Hispanic/Latino; 9 Asian, non-Hispanic/Latino; 132 Hispanic/Latino; 7 Two or more races, non-Hispanic/Latino), 120 international. Average age 30. 360 applicants, 49% accepted, 73 enrolled. In 2019, 89 master's, 13 doctorates awarded. *Degree requirements:* For master's, thesis or alternative; for doctorate, comprehensive exam, thesis/dissertation. *Entrance requirements:* For master's and doctorate, GRE General Test, 3 letters of recommendation, minimum GPA of 3.0. Additional exam requirements/recommendations for international students: required—TOEFL (minimum score 550 paper-based; 80 iBT). *Application deadline:* For fall admission, 6/1 for domestic students, 4/1 for international students; for spring admission, 10/1 for domestic students, 9/1 for international students. Applications are processed on a rolling basis. Application fee: $30. Electronic applications accepted. *Expenses: Tuition, area resident:* Full-time $8912; part-time $446 per credit hour. Tuition, state resident: full-time $8912; part-time $446 per credit hour. Tuition, nonresident: full-time $21,393; part-time $992 per credit hour. *Required fees:* $2194. *Financial support:* Research assistantships, teaching assistantships, institutionally sponsored loans, scholarships/grants, and unspecified assistantships available. Financial award application deadline: 3/1; financial award applicants required to submit FAFSA. *Unit head:* Dr. Sundararaj S. Iyengar, Director, 305-348-3947, Fax: 305-348-3549, E-mail: sundararaj.iyengar@fiu.edu. *Application contact:* Nanett Rojas, Manager, Admissions Operations, 305-348-7464, Fax: 305-348-7441, E-mail: gradadm@fiu.edu.

Florida Polytechnic University, Graduate Programs, Lakeland, FL 33805. Offers computer science (MS); engineering (MS).

Fontbonne University, Graduate Programs, St. Louis, MO 63105-3098. Offers accounting (MBA, MS); art (MA); art (K-12) (MAT); business (MBA); computer science (MS); deaf education (MA); early intervention in deaf education (MA); education (MA), including autism spectrum disorders, curriculum and instruction, diverse learners, early childhood education, reading, special education; elementary education (MAT); family and consumer sciences (MA), including multidisciplinary health communication studies; fine arts (MFA); instructional design and technology (MS); management and leadership (MM); middle school education (MAT); secondary education (MAT); special education (MAT); speech-language pathology (MS); supply chain management (MS); theatre (MA). *Accreditation:* ASHA. *Program availability:* Part-time, evening/weekend, online learning. *Degree requirements:* For master's, comprehensive exam (for some programs), thesis (for some programs). *Entrance requirements:* Additional exam requirements/recommendations for international students: required—TOEFL (minimum score 500 paper-based; 65 iBT). Electronic applications accepted. *Expenses: Tuition:* Full-time $6975; part-time $775 per credit hour. *Required fees:* $225; $25 per credit hour. Tuition and fees vary according to degree level and program.

Fordham University, Graduate School of Arts and Sciences, Department of Computer and Information Sciences, New York, NY 10458. Offers computer science (MS); data analytics (MS). *Program availability:* Part-time, evening/weekend. *Students:* Average age 31. 378 applicants, 71% accepted, 94 enrolled. In 2019, 62 master's awarded. *Entrance requirements:* For master's, GRE General Test. Additional exam requirements/recommendations for international students: required—TOEFL (minimum score 550 paper-based). *Application deadline:* For fall admission, 1/4 priority date for domestic students; for spring admission, 11/1 for domestic students. Application fee: $70. Electronic applications accepted. *Financial support:* In 2019–20, 5 students received support, including 3 research assistantships with tuition reimbursements available (averaging $15,000 per year); career-related internships or fieldwork, institutionally sponsored loans, tuition waivers (full and partial), and unspecified assistantships also available. Financial award application deadline: 1/4; financial award applicants required to submit CSS PROFILE or FAFSA. *Unit head:* Dr. Damian Lyons, Chair, 718-817-4485, Fax: 718-817-4488, E-mail: dlyons@fordham.edu. *Application contact:* Garrett Marino, Director of Graduate Admissions, 718-817-4419, Fax: 718-817-3566, E-mail: gmarino10@fordham.edu.

Franklin University, Computer Science Program, Columbus, OH 43215-5399. Offers MS. *Program availability:* Part-time, evening/weekend. *Entrance requirements:* For master's, minimum undergraduate GPA of 2.75. Additional exam requirements/recommendations for international students: required—TOEFL (minimum score 550 paper-based). Electronic applications accepted. *Expenses:* Contact institution.

Frostburg State University, College of Liberal Arts and Sciences, Department of Computer Science, Program in Applied Computer Science, Frostburg, MD 21532-1099. Offers MS. *Entrance requirements:* Additional exam requirements/recommendations for international students: required—TOEFL. Electronic applications accepted.

Gannon University, School of Graduate Studies, College of Engineering and Business, School of Engineering and Computer Science, Program in Computer and Information Science, Erie, PA 16541-0001. Offers information analytics (MSCIS); software engineering (MSCIS). *Program availability:* Part-time, evening/weekend. *Degree requirements:* For master's, thesis (for some programs), directed research. *Entrance requirements:* For master's, 3 letters of recommendation; resume; transcripts; baccalaureate degree in computer science, information systems, information science, software engineering, or related field from regionally-accredited institution with minimum GPA of 2.5. Additional exam requirements/recommendations for international students: required—TOEFL (minimum score 79 iBT). Electronic applications accepted. Application fee is waived when completed online.

George Mason University, Volgenau School of Engineering, Department of Computer Science, Fairfax, VA 22030. Offers MS, PhD, Certificate. *Degree requirements:* For master's, thesis optional, 30 credits (10 courses); for doctorate, comprehensive exam, thesis/dissertation, 72 credits (includes dissertation research and coursework); for Certificate, 12 credits (4 courses). *Entrance requirements:* For master's and Certificate, GRE (for applicants who have not earned bachelor's degree from U.S. institution), BS in computer science or related field; for doctorate, GRE, personal goals statement; 2 official copies of transcripts; self-evaluation form; 3 letters of recommendation; photocopy of passport; proof of financial support; official bank statement; resume; 4-year baccalaureate degree in computer science or related field. Additional exam requirements/recommendations for international students: required—TOEFL (minimum score 575 paper-based; 88 iBT), IELTS (minimum score 6.5), PTE (minimum score 59). Electronic applications accepted. *Expenses:* Contact institution.

Georgetown University, Graduate School of Arts and Sciences, Department of Computer Science, Washington, DC 20057. Offers MS, PhD. *Program availability:* Part-time, evening/weekend. *Degree requirements:* For master's, thesis optional. *Entrance requirements:* For master's, GRE, basic course work in data structures, advanced math, and programming; 3 letters of recommendation. Additional exam requirements/recommendations for international students: required—TOEFL. Electronic applications accepted.

The George Washington University, School of Engineering and Applied Science, Department of Computer Science, Washington, DC 20052. Offers computer science (MS, D Sc); cybersecurity (MS). *Program availability:* Part-time, evening/weekend. *Degree requirements:* For master's, thesis optional; for doctorate, thesis/dissertation, dissertation defense, qualifying exam. *Entrance requirements:* For master's, appropriate bachelor's degree, minimum GPA of 3.0; for doctorate, GRE (if highest earned degree is BS), appropriate bachelor's or master's degree, minimum GPA of 3.3; for other advanced degree, appropriate master's degree, minimum GPA of 3.4. Additional exam requirements/recommendations for international students: required—TOEFL or The George Washington University English as a Foreign Language Test.

Georgia Southwestern State University, Department of Computer Science, Americus, GA 31709. Offers computer information systems (Graduate Certificate); computer science (MS). *Program availability:* Part-time, online only, 100% online. *Faculty:* 4 full-time (0 women), 1 part-time/adjunct (0 women). *Students:* 4 full-time (1 woman), 17 part-time (5 women); includes 8 minority (5 Black or African American, non-Hispanic/Latino; 2 Asian, non-Hispanic/Latino; 1 Hispanic/Latino), 7 international. Average age 36. 34 applicants, 38% accepted, 11 enrolled. In 2019, 4 master's awarded. *Degree requirements:* For master's, thesis optional, minimum cumulative GPA of 3.0; maximum of 6 credit hours with C grade can be applied to the degree; no courses with D grade; degree must be completed within 7 calendar years from date of initial enrollment in graduate course work; for Graduate Certificate, minimum cumulative GPA of 3.0; maximum of 6 credit hours with C grade can be applied to the degree; no courses with D grade; degree must be completed within 7 calendar years from date of initial enrollment in graduate course work. *Entrance requirements:* For master's and Graduate Certificate, GRE, bachelor's degree from regionally-accredited college; minimum undergraduate GPA of 2.5 as reported on official final transcripts from all institutions attended; a minimum 3.0 GPA on all previous graduate work attempted; three letters of recommendation; completion of prerequisite undergraduate computer science courses. Additional exam requirements/recommendations for international students: required—TOEFL (minimum score 523 paper-based; 69 iBT), IELTS (minimum score 6.5). *Application deadline:* For fall admission, 6/30 for domestic students; for spring admission, 11/30 for domestic students; for summer admission, 4/30 for domestic students. Applications are processed on a rolling basis. Application fee: $25. Electronic applications accepted. *Expenses:* $257.00 per credit hour tuition, plus fees, which vary according to enrolled credit hours. *Financial support:* Application deadline: 6/1; applicants required to submit FAFSA. *Application contact:* Office of Graduate Admissions, 800-338-0082, Fax: 229-931-2983, E-mail: graduateadmissions@gsw.edu.
Website: https://www.gsw.edu/academics/schools-and-departments/college-of-business-and-computing/cobac-grad

Georgia State University, College of Arts and Sciences, Department of Computer Science, Atlanta, GA 30302-3083. Offers bioinformatics (MS, PhD); computer science (MS, PhD). *Program availability:* Part-time. *Faculty:* 29 full-time (6 women), 4 part-time/adjunct (1 woman). *Students:* 179 full-time (64 women), 23 part-time (7 women); includes 27 minority (7 Black or African American, non-Hispanic/Latino; 12 Asian, non-Hispanic/Latino; 4 Hispanic/Latino; 4 Two or more races, non-Hispanic/Latino), 160 international. Average age 29. 311 applicants, 43% accepted, 39 enrolled. In 2019, 52 master's, 9 doctorates awarded. Terminal master's awarded for partial completion of doctoral program. *Entrance requirements:* For master's and doctorate, GRE General Test. Additional exam requirements/recommendations for international students: required—TOEFL (minimum score 550 paper-based; 80 iBT). *Application deadline:* For fall admission, 3/15 for domestic and international students; for spring admission, 10/15 for domestic and international students. Application fee: $50. Electronic applications accepted. *Expenses: Tuition, area resident:* Full-time $7164; part-time $398 per credit hour. Tuition, state resident: full-time $7164; part-time $398 per credit hour. Tuition, nonresident: full-time $22,662; part-time $1259 per credit hour. *International tuition:* $22,662 full-time. *Required fees:* $2128; $312 per credit hour. Tuition and fees vary according to course load and program. *Financial support:* In 2019–20, fellowships with full tuition reimbursements (averaging $22,000 per year), research assistantships with full tuition reimbursements (averaging $16,000 per year), teaching assistantships with full tuition reimbursements (averaging $16,000 per year) were awarded; institutionally sponsored loans, health care benefits, and unspecified assistantships also available. Financial award application deadline: 2/15; financial award applicants required to submit FAFSA. *Unit head:* Dr. Yi Pan, Regents Professor and Chair, 404-413-5342, Fax: 404-413-5717, E-mail: yipan@gsu.edu. *Application contact:* Dr. Yi Pan, Regents Professor and Chair, 404-413-5342, Fax: 404-413-5717, E-mail: yipan@gsu.edu.
Website: http://www.cs.gsu.edu/

Georgia State University, College of Arts and Sciences, Department of Mathematics and Statistics, Atlanta, GA 30302-3083. Offers bioinformatics (MS, PhD); biostatistics (MS, PhD); discrete mathematics (MS); mathematics (MS, PhD); scientific computing (MS); statistics (MS). *Program availability:* Part-time. *Faculty:* 25 full-time (8 women). *Students:* 91 full-time (44 women), 15 part-time (5 women); includes 29 minority (9 Black or African American, non-Hispanic/Latino; 14 Asian, non-Hispanic/Latino; 4 Hispanic/

Latino; 2 Two or more races, non-Hispanic/Latino), 57 international. Average age 32. 128 applicants, 49% accepted, 30 enrolled. In 2019, 26 master's, 4 doctorates awarded. Terminal master's awarded for partial completion of doctoral program. *Entrance requirements:* For master's and doctorate, GRE. Additional exam requirements/recommendations for international students: required—TOEFL (minimum score 550 paper-based; 80 iBT). *Application deadline:* For fall admission, 7/1 priority date for domestic and international students; for spring admission, 11/15 priority date for domestic and international students. Application fee: $50. Electronic applications accepted. *Expenses: Tuition, area resident:* Full-time $7164; part-time $398 per credit hour. Tuition, state resident: full-time $7164; part-time $398 per credit hour. Tuition, nonresident: full-time $22,662; part-time $1259 per credit hour. *International tuition:* $22,662 full-time. *Required fees:* $2128; $312 per credit hour. Tuition and fees vary according to course load and program. *Financial support:* In 2019–20, fellowships with full tuition reimbursements (averaging $22,000 per year), research assistantships with full tuition reimbursements (averaging $9,000 per year), teaching assistantships with full tuition reimbursements (averaging $9,000 per year) were awarded; institutionally sponsored loans, scholarships/grants, health care benefits, and unspecified assistantships also available. Financial award application deadline: 2/1. *Unit head:* Dr. Guantao Chen, Chair, 404-413-6436, Fax: 404-413-6403, E-mail: gchen@gsu.edu. *Application contact:* Dr. Guantao Chen, Chair, 404-413-6436, Fax: 404-413-6403, E-mail: gchen@gsu.edu. Website: https://www.mathstat.gsu.edu/

Governors State University, College of Arts and Sciences, Program in Computer Science, University Park, IL 60484. Offers MS. *Program availability:* Part-time. *Faculty:* 39 full-time (14 women), 25 part-time/adjunct (12 women). *Students:* 65 full-time (18 women), 24 part-time (6 women); includes 14 minority (9 Black or African American, non-Hispanic/Latino; 5 Hispanic/Latino), 62 international. Average age 29. 347 applicants, 73% accepted, 31 enrolled. In 2019, 47 master's awarded. *Application deadline:* For fall admission, 4/1 for domestic students. Applications are processed on a rolling basis. Application fee: $50. Electronic applications accepted. *Expenses: Tuition, area resident:* full-time $8472; part-time $353 per credit hour. Tuition, state resident: full-time $8472; part-time $353 per credit hour. Tuition, nonresident: full-time $16,944; part-time $706 per credit hour. *International tuition:* $16,944 full-time. *Required fees:* $2520; $105 per credit hour. $38 per term. Tuition and fees vary according to course load, degree level and program. *Financial support:* Application deadline: 5/1; applicants required to submit FAFSA. *Unit head:* Mary Carrington, Chair, Division of Science, Mathematics, and Technology, 708-534-5000 Ext. 4532, E-mail: mcarrington@govst.edu. *Application contact:* Mary Carrington, Chair, Division of Science, Mathematics, and Technology, 708-534-5000 Ext. 4532, E-mail: mcarrington@govst.edu.

The Graduate Center, City University of New York, Graduate Studies, Program in Computer Science, New York, NY 10016-4039. Offers PhD. *Degree requirements:* For doctorate, one foreign language, thesis/dissertation. *Entrance requirements:* For doctorate, GRE General Test. Additional exam requirements/recommendations for international students: required—TOEFL. Electronic applications accepted.

Grand Valley State University, Padnos College of Engineering and Computing, School of Computing and Information Systems, Allendale, MI 49401-9403. Offers MS. *Program availability:* Part-time, evening/weekend. *Faculty:* 10 full-time (0 women). *Students:* 11 full-time (4 women), 52 part-time (9 women); includes 12 minority (2 Black or African American, non-Hispanic/Latino; 5 Asian, non-Hispanic/Latino; 4 Hispanic/Latino; 1 Two or more races, non-Hispanic/Latino), 12 international. Average age 30. 31 applicants, 58% accepted, 6 enrolled. In 2019, 23 master's awarded. *Degree requirements:* For master's, thesis optional, thesis, project, or capstone. *Entrance requirements:* For master's, GRE (recommended with GPA below 3.0), minimum GPA of 3.0; knowledge of a programming language; coursework or experience in: computer architecture and/or organization, data structures and algorithms, databases, discrete math, networking, operating systems, and software engineering; minimum of 2 letters of recommendation; resume; personal statement. Additional exam requirements/recommendations for international students: required—Michigan English Language Assessment Battery (minimum score 77), TOEFL (minimum iBT score of 80), or IELTS (6.5); GRE. *Application deadline:* For fall admission, 6/1 for international students; for winter admission, 9/1 for international students. Applications are processed on a rolling basis. Application fee: $30. Electronic applications accepted. *Expenses:* $733 per credit hour, 33 credit hours. *Financial support:* In 2019–20, 13 students received support, including 6 fellowships, 5 research assistantships with full and partial tuition reimbursements available (averaging $8,000 per year). *Unit head:* Dr. Paul Leidig, Director, 616-331-2060, Fax: 616-331-2144, E-mail: leidigp@gvsu.edu. *Application contact:* Dr. D. Robert Adams, Graduate Program Director, 616-331-3885, Fax: 616-331-2144, E-mail: adamsr@gvsu.edu. Website: http://www.cis.gvsu.edu/

Hampton University, School of Science, Department of Computer Science, Hampton, VA 23668. Offers computer science (MS); information assurance (MS). *Program availability:* Part-time, evening/weekend. *Students:* 2 part-time (1 woman); both minorities (1 Black or African American, non-Hispanic/Latino; 1 Asian, non-Hispanic/Latino). Average age 38. 1 applicant. In 2019, 1 master's awarded. *Degree requirements:* For master's, thesis or alternative. *Entrance requirements:* For master's, GRE General Test. Additional exam requirements/recommendations for international students: required—TOEFL (minimum score 525 paper-based) or IELTS (6.5). *Application deadline:* For fall admission, 6/1 priority date for domestic students, 4/1 priority date for international students; for spring admission, 11/1 priority date for domestic students, 9/1 priority date for international students; for summer admission, 4/1 priority date for domestic students, 2/1 priority date for international students. Applications are processed on a rolling basis. Application fee: $35. Electronic applications accepted. *Financial support:* In 2019–20, 5 fellowships (averaging $38,900 per year), 1 research assistantship were awarded; career-related internships or fieldwork, Federal Work-Study, and scholarships/grants also available. Support available to part-time students. Financial award application deadline: 6/30; financial award applicants required to submit FAFSA. *Unit head:* Dr. Jean Muhammad, Chair, 757-727-5552. *Application contact:* Dr. Jean Muhammad, Chair, 757-727-5552.

Harvard University, Graduate School of Arts and Sciences, Harvard John A. Paulson School of Engineering and Applied Sciences, Cambridge, MA 02138. Offers applied mathematics (PhD); applied physics (PhD); computational science and engineering (ME, SM); computer science (PhD); data science (SM); design engineering (MDE); engineering science (ME), including electrical engineering (ME, SM, PhD); engineering sciences (SM, PhD), including bioengineering (PhD), electrical engineering (ME, SM, PhD), environmental science and engineering (PhD), materials science and mechanical engineering (PhD). *Program availability:* Part-time. Terminal master's awarded for partial completion of doctoral program. *Degree requirements:* For master's, thesis (for ME); for doctorate, comprehensive exam, thesis/dissertation. *Entrance requirements:* For master's and doctorate, GRE General Test, GRE Subject Test (recommended), 3 letters of recommendation. Additional exam requirements/recommendations for international students: required—TOEFL (minimum score 80 iBT). Electronic applications accepted. *Expenses:* Contact institution.

Hood College, Graduate School, Programs in Computer and Information Sciences, Frederick, MD 21701-8575. Offers computer science (MS); cybersecurity (MS, Certificate); information technology (MS). *Program availability:* Part-time, evening/weekend, 100% online. *Degree requirements:* For master's, thesis optional, capstone (S). *Entrance requirements:* For master's, minimum GPA of 2.75, essay, resume. Additional exam requirements/recommendations for international students: required—TOEFL (minimum score 575 paper-based; 89 iBT), IELTS (minimum score 6.5). Electronic applications accepted. *Expenses:* Contact institution.

Howard University, College of Engineering, Architecture, and Computer Sciences, School of Engineering and Computer Science, Department of Systems and Computer Science, Washington, DC 20059-0002. Offers MCS. *Program availability:* Part-time. *Degree requirements:* For master's, thesis. *Entrance requirements:* For master's, GRE General Test, minimum GPA of 3.0. Additional exam requirements/recommendations for international students: required—TOEFL. Electronic applications accepted.

Illinois Institute of Technology, Graduate College, College of Science, Department of Computer Science, Chicago, IL 60616. Offers business (MCS); computational intelligence (MCS); computer science (MCS, MS, PhD); cyber-physical systems (MCS); data analytics (MCS); data science (MAS); database systems (MCS); distributed and cloud computing (MCS); education (MCS); finance (MCS); information security and assurance (MCS); networking and communications (MCS); software engineering (MCS); telecommunications and software engineering (MAS); MS/MAS. *Program availability:* Part-time, evening/weekend, online learning. Terminal master's awarded for partial completion of doctoral program. *Degree requirements:* For master's, thesis optional; for doctorate, comprehensive exam, thesis/dissertation. *Entrance requirements:* For master's, GRE General Test with minimum scores of 298 Quantitative and Verbal, 3.0 Analytical Writing (for MS); GRE General Test with minimum scores of 292 Quantitative and Verbal, 2.5 Analytical Writing (for MAS), minimum undergraduate GPA of 3.0; for doctorate, GRE General Test (minimum scores: 304 Quantitative and Verbal, 3.5 Analytical Writing), minimum undergraduate GPA of 3.0. Additional exam requirements/recommendations for international students: required—TOEFL (minimum score 523 paper-based; 70 iBT). Electronic applications accepted.

Indiana State University, College of Graduate and Professional Studies, College of Arts and Sciences, Department of Mathematics and Computer Science, Terre Haute, IN 47809. Offers computer science (MS); mathematics (MA, MS). *Program availability:* Part-time. *Degree requirements:* For master's, thesis or alternative. *Entrance requirements:* For master's, 24 semester hours of course work in undergraduate mathematics. Electronic applications accepted.

Indiana University Bloomington, School of Informatics, Computing, and Engineering, Department of Computer Science, Bloomington, IN 47405. Offers bioinformatics (MS); computer science (MS, PhD); cybersecurity risk management (MS); secure computing (MS, Graduate Certificate). Terminal master's awarded for partial completion of doctoral program. *Degree requirements:* For master's, thesis optional; for doctorate, comprehensive exam, thesis/dissertation, oral and written exams. *Entrance requirements:* For master's and doctorate, GRE General Test, statement of purpose, bachelor's degree. Additional exam requirements/recommendations for international students: required—TOEFL. Electronic applications accepted.

Indiana University Bloomington, School of Informatics, Computing, and Engineering, Program in Informatics, Bloomington, IN 47405. Offers informatics (MS, PhD), including bioinformatics (PhD), complex systems (PhD), computing, culture and society (PhD), health informatics (PhD), human-computer interaction (MS), human-computer interaction design (PhD), music informatics (PhD), security informatics (PhD), visual heritage (PhD). *Program availability:* Part-time. Terminal master's awarded for partial completion of doctoral program. *Degree requirements:* For master's, thesis, capstone project; for doctorate, variable foreign language requirement, comprehensive exam, thesis/dissertation. *Entrance requirements:* For master's and doctorate, GRE, resume/curriculum vitae, transcripts, 3 letters of recommendation. Additional exam requirements/recommendations for international students: required—TOEFL (minimum score 600 paper-based; 100 iBT). Electronic applications accepted.

Indiana University-Purdue University Indianapolis, School of Science, Department of Computer and Information Science, Indianapolis, IN 46202-5132. Offers biocomputing (Graduate Certificate); biometrics (Graduate Certificate); computer science (MS, PhD); computer security (Graduate Certificate); databases and data mining (Graduate Certificate); software engineering (Graduate Certificate). *Program availability:* Part-time. Terminal master's awarded for partial completion of doctoral program. *Degree requirements:* For master's and Graduate Certificate, thesis optional; for doctorate, thesis/dissertation. *Entrance requirements:* For master's and doctorate, GRE, BS in computer science or the equivalent with a minimum GPA of 3.0 (or equivalent); for Graduate Certificate, BS in computer science or the equivalent with a minimum GPA of 3.0 (or equivalent). Additional exam requirements/recommendations for international students: required—PTE (minimum score 58), TOEFL (minimum score 550 paper-based, 79 iBT) or IELTS (6.5).

Indiana University South Bend, College of Liberal Arts and Sciences, South Bend, IN 46615. Offers advanced computer programming (Graduate Certificate); applied informatics (Graduate Certificate); applied mathematics and computer science (MS); behavior modification (Graduate Certificate); computer applications (Graduate Certificate); computer programming (Graduate Certificate); correctional management and supervision (Graduate Certificate); English (MA); health systems management (Graduate Certificate); international studies (Graduate Certificate); liberal studies (MLS); nonprofit management (Graduate Certificate); paralegal studies (Graduate Certificate); professional writing (Graduate Certificate); public affairs (MPA); public management (Graduate Certificate); social and cultural diversity (Graduate Certificate); strategic sustainability leadership (Graduate Certificate); technology for administration (Graduate Certificate). *Program availability:* Part-time, evening/weekend. *Degree requirements:* For master's, variable foreign language requirement, thesis (for some programs). *Entrance requirements:* For master's, minimum GPA of 3.0. Additional exam requirements/recommendations for international students: required—TOEFL (minimum score 550 paper-based; 80 iBT). *Expenses:* Contact institution.

Instituto Tecnológico y de Estudios Superiores de Monterrey, Campus Central de Veracruz, Graduate Programs, Córdoba, Mexico. Offers administration (MA); administration of information technologies (MTI); computer sciences (MCC); education (MEE); educational institution administration (MAD); educational technology (MTE); electronic commerce (MCE); finance (MAF); humanistic studies (MEH); international business for Latin America (MNL); marketing (MMT); science (MCP). *Program availability:* Part-time, evening/weekend, online learning. *Degree requirements:* For master's, thesis (for some programs). *Entrance requirements:* For master's, PAEP College Board. Electronic applications accepted.

Instituto Tecnológico y de Estudios Superiores de Monterrey, Campus Ciudad de México, Virtual University Division, Ciudad de Mexico, Mexico. Offers administration of information technologies (MA); computer sciences (MA); education (MA, PhD); educational technology (MA); environmental engineering (MA); environmental systems (MA); humanistic studies (MA); industrial engineering (MA); international business for Latin America (MA); quality systems (MA); quality systems and productivity (MA).

Program availability: Part-time, evening/weekend, online learning. *Entrance requirements:* For master's and doctorate, Instituto entrance exam. Additional exam requirements/recommendations for international students: required—TOEFL.

Instituto Tecnológico y de Estudios Superiores de Monterrey, Campus Cuernavaca, Programs in Information Science, Temixco, Mexico. Offers administration of information technology (MATI); computer science (MCC, DCC); information technology (MTI).

Instituto Tecnológico y de Estudios Superiores de Monterrey, Campus Estado de México, Professional and Graduate Division, Estado de Mexico, Mexico. Offers administration of information technologies (MITA); architecture (M Arch); business administration (GMBA, MBA); computer sciences (MCS, PhD); education (M Ed); educational institution administration (MAD); educational technology and innovation (PhD); electronic commerce (MEC); environmental systems (MS); finance (MAF); humanistic studies (MHS); information sciences and knowledge management (MISKM); information systems (MS); manufacturing systems (MS); marketing (MEM); quality systems and productivity (MS); science and materials engineering (PhD); telecommunications management (MTM). *Program availability:* Part-time, online learning. *Degree requirements:* For master's, one foreign language, thesis (for some programs); for doctorate, one foreign language, thesis/dissertation. *Entrance requirements:* For master's, E-PAEP 500, interview; for doctorate, E-PAEP 500, research proposal. Additional exam requirements/recommendations for international students: required—TOEFL (minimum score 550 paper-based).

Instituto Tecnológico y de Estudios Superiores de Monterrey, Campus Irapuato, Graduate Programs, Irapuato, Mexico. Offers administration (MBA); administration of information technology (MAIT); administration of telecommunications (MAT); architecture (M Arch); computer science (MCS); education (M Ed); educational administration (MEA); educational innovation and technology (DEIT); educational technology (MET); electronic commerce (MBA); environmental administration and planning (MEAP); environmental systems (MES); finances (MBA); humanistic studies (MHS); international management for Latin American executives (MIMLAE); library and information science (MLIS); manufacturing quality management (MMQM); marketing research (MBA).

Instituto Tecnológico y de Estudios Superiores de Monterrey, Campus Monterrey, Graduate and Research Division, Program in Computer Science, Monterrey, Mexico. Offers artificial intelligence (PhD); computer science (MS); information systems (MS); information technology (MS). *Program availability:* Part-time. *Degree requirements:* For master's, one foreign language, thesis; for doctorate, one foreign language, thesis/dissertation. *Entrance requirements:* For master's, EXADEP; for doctorate, master's degree in related field. Additional exam requirements/recommendations for international students: required—TOEFL.

Inter American University of Puerto Rico, Fajardo Campus, Graduate Programs, Fajardo, PR 00738-7003. Offers computer science (MS); educational management and leadership (MA Ed); general business (MBA); human resources (MBA); management information systems (MBA); marketing (MBA); special education (MA Ed). *Program availability:* Online learning.

Inter American University of Puerto Rico, Guayama Campus, Department of Natural and Applied Sciences, Guayama, PR 00785. Offers computer security and networks (MS); networking and security (MCS).

Inter American University of Puerto Rico, Metropolitan Campus, Graduate Programs, Program in Open Information Systems, San Juan, PR 00919-1293. Offers MS. *Degree requirements:* For master's, 2 foreign languages.

Iona College, School of Arts and Science, Department of Computer Science, New Rochelle, NY 10801-1890. Offers computer science (MS); cyber security (MS); game development (MS). *Program availability:* Part-time, evening/weekend. *Faculty:* 9 full-time (4 women), 1 (woman) part-time/adjunct. *Students:* 2 full-time (0 women), 10 part-time (2 women); includes 4 minority (2 Black or African American, non-Hispanic/Latino; 1 Asian, non-Hispanic/Latino; 1 Hispanic/Latino), 1 international. Average age 26. 16 applicants, 100% accepted, 6 enrolled. In 2019, 6 master's awarded. *Degree requirements:* For master's, thesis optional. *Entrance requirements:* For master's, minimum GPA of 3.0. Additional exam requirements/recommendations for international students: required—TOEFL (minimum score 550 paper-based; 80 iBT), IELTS (minimum score 6.5). *Application deadline:* For fall admission, 8/1 priority date for domestic students, 5/1 priority date for international students; for spring admission, 1/1 priority date for domestic students, 9/1 priority date for international students. Applications are processed on a rolling basis. Electronic applications accepted. *Financial support:* In 2019–20, 5 students received support, including 2 research assistantships with full and partial tuition reimbursements available (averaging $5,072 per year); scholarships/grants, tuition waivers (partial), and unspecified assistantships also available. Support available to part-time students. Financial award application deadline: 4/15; financial award applicants required to submit FAFSA. *Unit head:* Frances Bailie, PhD, Chair, 914-633-2335, E-mail: fbailie@iona.edu. *Application contact:* Christopher Kash, Assistant Director, Graduate Admissions, 914-633-2403, Fax: 914-633-2277, E-mail: ckash@iona.edu.
Website: http://www.iona.edu/Academics/School-of-Arts-Science/Departments/Computer-Science/Graduate-Programs.aspx

Iowa State University of Science and Technology, Department of Computer Science, Ames, IA 50011. Offers MS, PhD. *Degree requirements:* For master's, thesis; for doctorate, thesis/dissertation. *Entrance requirements:* For master's and doctorate, GRE General Test. Additional exam requirements/recommendations for international students: recommended—TOEFL (minimum score 550 paper-based; 79 iBT), IELTS (minimum score 6.5). Electronic applications accepted.

Jackson State University, Graduate School, College of Science, Engineering and Technology, Department of Computer Science, Jackson, MS 39217. Offers MS. *Program availability:* Part-time, evening/weekend. *Degree requirements:* For master's, comprehensive exam, thesis. *Entrance requirements:* For master's, GRE General Test. Additional exam requirements/recommendations for international students: required—TOEFL (minimum score 520 paper-based; 67 iBT).

Jacksonville State University, Graduate Studies, School of Science, Program in Computer Systems and Software Design, Jacksonville, AL 36265-1602. Offers MS. *Program availability:* Part-time, evening/weekend. *Degree requirements:* For master's, comprehensive exam, thesis (for some programs). *Entrance requirements:* Additional exam requirements/recommendations for international students: required—TOEFL (minimum score 500 paper-based; 61 iBT). Electronic applications accepted.

James Madison University, The Graduate School, College of Integrated Science and Engineering, Program in Computer Science, Harrisonburg, VA 22807. Offers digital forensics (MS); information security (MS). *Program availability:* Online learning. *Students:* 3 full-time (1 woman), 55 part-time (11 women); includes 14 minority (8 Black or African American, non-Hispanic/Latino; 3 Asian, non-Hispanic/Latino; 3 Hispanic/Latino), 3 international. Average age 30. In 2019, 2 master's awarded. Application fee: $60. Electronic applications accepted. *Financial support:* In 2019–20, 2 students received support. Fellowships, Federal Work-Study, and assistantships (averaging $7911) available. Financial award application deadline: 3/1; financial award applicants required to submit FAFSA. *Unit head:* Dr. Sharon J. Simmons, Department Head, 540-568-4196, E-mail: simmonsj@jmu.edu. *Application contact:* Lynette D. Michael, Director of Graduate Admissions, 540-568-6131 Ext. 6395, Fax: 540-568-7860, E-mail: michaeld@jmu.edu.
Website: http://www.jmu.edu/cs/

Johns Hopkins University, Engineering Program for Professionals, Part-time Program in Computer Science, Baltimore, MD 21218. Offers communications and networking (MS); computer science (Post-Master's Certificate). *Program availability:* Part-time, evening/weekend, 100% online, blended/hybrid learning. *Entrance requirements:* Additional exam requirements/recommendations for international students: required—TOEFL (minimum score 600 paper-based; 100 iBT). Electronic applications accepted.

Johns Hopkins University, Engineering Program for Professionals, Part-time Program in Electrical and Computer Engineering, Baltimore, MD 21218. Offers communications and networking (MS); electrical and computer engineering (Graduate Certificate, Post-Master's Certificate); photonics (MS). *Program availability:* Part-time, evening/weekend, 100% online, blended/hybrid learning. *Entrance requirements:* Additional exam requirements/recommendations for international students: required—TOEFL (minimum score 600 paper-based; 100 iBT). Electronic applications accepted.

Johns Hopkins University, G. W. C. Whiting School of Engineering, Department of Computer Science, Baltimore, MD 21218. Offers MSE, MSSI, PhD. Terminal master's awarded for partial completion of doctoral program. *Degree requirements:* For master's, thesis optional; for doctorate, comprehensive exam, thesis/dissertation, oral exam. *Entrance requirements:* For master's, GRE General Test, 2 letters of recommendation, statement of purpose, transcripts; for doctorate, GRE General Test, 3 letters of recommendation, statement of purpose, transcripts. Additional exam requirements/recommendations for international students: required—TOEFL (minimum score 600 paper-based, 100 iBT) or IELTS (7). Electronic applications accepted.

Johns Hopkins University, G. W. C. Whiting School of Engineering, Master of Science in Engineering Management Program, Baltimore, MD 21218. Offers biomaterials (MSEM); civil engineering (MSEM); communications science (MSEM); computer science (MSEM); environmental systems analysis, economics and public policy (MSEM); fluid mechanics (MSEM); materials science and engineering (MSEM); mechanical engineering (MSEM); mechanics and materials (MSEM); nano-biotechnology (MSEM); nanomaterials and nanotechnology (MSEM); operations research (MSEM); probability and statistics (MSEM); smart product and device design (MSEM). *Entrance requirements:* For master's, GRE, 3 letters of recommendation, statement of purpose, transcripts. Additional exam requirements/recommendations for international students: required—TOEFL (minimum score 600 paper-based, 100 iBT) or IELTS (7). Electronic applications accepted.

Kansas State University, Graduate School, College of Engineering, Department of Computer Science, Manhattan, KS 66506. Offers MS, MSE, PhD. *Program availability:* Part-time, online learning. Terminal master's awarded for partial completion of doctoral program. *Degree requirements:* For master's, thesis or alternative; for doctorate, thesis/dissertation. *Entrance requirements:* For master's, GRE General Test, bachelor's degree in computer science, minimum GPA of 3.0; for doctorate, GRE General Test, master's degree in computer science or bachelor's degree and strong advanced computer knowledge. Additional exam requirements/recommendations for international students: required—TOEFL (minimum score 575 paper-based; 90 iBT), IELTS, or PTE. Electronic applications accepted.

Kennesaw State University, College of Computing and Software Engineering, Program in Computer Science, Kennesaw, GA 30144. Offers MS. *Program availability:* Part-time, evening/weekend, blended/hybrid learning. *Students:* 73 full-time (35 women), 39 part-time (10 women); includes 35 minority (12 Black or African American, non-Hispanic/Latino; 14 Asian, non-Hispanic/Latino; 5 Hispanic/Latino; 4 Two or more races, non-Hispanic/Latino), 52 international. Average age 29. 40 applicants, 90% accepted, 19 enrolled. In 2019, 33 master's awarded. *Degree requirements:* For master's, thesis optional. *Entrance requirements:* For master's, GMAT or GRE, minimum GPA of 2.75. Additional exam requirements/recommendations for international students: required—TOEFL (minimum score 80 iBT), IELTS (minimum score 6.5). *Application deadline:* For fall admission, 7/1 priority date for domestic students, 7/1 for international students; for spring admission, 11/1 priority date for domestic students, 11/1 for international students; for summer admission, 4/1 for domestic and international students. Applications are processed on a rolling basis. Application fee: $60. Electronic applications accepted. *Expenses: Tuition, area resident:* Full-time $7104; part-time $296 per credit hour. Tuition, state resident: full-time $7104; part-time $296 per credit hour. Tuition, nonresident: full-time $25,584; part-time $1066 per credit hour. *International tuition:* $25,584 full-time. *Required fees:* $2006; $1706 per unit. $853 per semester. *Financial support:* Applicants required to submit FAFSA. *Application contact:* Admissions Counselor, 470-578-4377, Fax: 470-578-9172, E-mail: ksugrad@kennesaw.edu.
Website: http://ccse.kennesaw.edu/cs/

Kent State University, College of Arts and Sciences, Department of Computer Science, Kent, OH 44242-0001. Offers MA, MS, PhD. *Program availability:* Part-time. *Faculty:* 20 full-time (2 women), 2 part-time/adjunct (0 women). *Students:* 97 full-time (31 women), 14 part-time (2 women); includes 4 minority (2 Asian, non-Hispanic/Latino; 1 Hispanic/Latino; 1 Two or more races, non-Hispanic/Latino), 85 international. Average age 27. 310 applicants, 58% accepted, 33 enrolled. In 2019, 29 master's, 8 doctorates awarded. *Degree requirements:* For master's, thesis optional, M.S. - Capstone Project and Graduate Internship for Thesis option; M.A. - Master's Seminar; for doctorate, comprehensive exam, thesis/dissertation, preliminary examination, two public presentations of project/research work. *Entrance requirements:* For master's, GRE, transcripts, goal statement, resume, 3 letters of recommendation, core components of an undergraduate computer science curriculum; for doctorate, GRE, pass Preliminary Examination within 12 months of entrance into the Doctoral program, transcript, goal statement, 3 letters of recommendation, master's degree in computer science (or closely related field). Additional exam requirements/recommendations for international students: required—TOEFL (minimum score 71 iBT), IELTS (minimum score 6), PTE (minimum score 48), Michigan English Language Assessment Battery (minimum score 74). *Application deadline:* For fall admission, 6/1 for domestic and international students; for spring admission, 10/10 for domestic and international students. Applications are processed on a rolling basis. Application fee: $45 ($70 for international students). Electronic applications accepted. *Financial support:* Fellowships with full tuition reimbursements, research assistantships with full tuition reimbursements, teaching assistantships with full tuition reimbursements, Federal Work-Study, and unspecified assistantships available. Financial award application deadline: 1/31. *Unit head:* Dr. Javed I Khan, Professor and Chair, 330-672-9055, E-mail: javed@kent.edu. *Application contact:* Dr. Cheng Chang Lu, Professor, Assistant Chair and Graduate Advisor, 330-672-9031, Fax: 330-672-0737, E-mail: clu@kent.edu.
Website: http://www.kent.edu/cs

Kutztown University of Pennsylvania, College of Liberal Arts and Sciences, Program in Computer Science, Kutztown, PA 19530-0730. Offers MS. *Program availability:* Part-

time, evening/weekend. *Faculty:* 6 full-time (2 women). *Students:* 14 full-time (6 women), 10 part-time (2 women); includes 4 minority (1 Asian, non-Hispanic/Latino; 2 Hispanic/Latino; 1 Two or more races, non-Hispanic/Latino), 1 international. Average age 28. 23 applicants, 87% accepted, 13 enrolled. In 2019, 6 master's awarded. *Entrance requirements:* For master's, GRE General Test, 3 letters of recommendation. Additional exam requirements/recommendations for international students: required—TOEFL (minimum score 550 paper-based, 79 iBT), IELTS (minimum score 6.5), or PTE (minimum score 53). *Application deadline:* For fall admission, 8/1 for domestic and international students; for spring admission, 12/1 for domestic and international students. Application fee: $35. Electronic applications accepted. *Expenses: Tuition, area resident:* Full-time $9288; part-time $515 per credit. Tuition, state resident: full-time $9288. Tuition, nonresident: full-time $13,932; part-time $774 per credit. *Required fees:* $1688; $94 per credit. *Financial support:* Career-related internships or fieldwork, Federal Work-Study, and unspecified assistantships available. Financial award application deadline: 3/1; financial award applicants required to submit FAFSA. *Unit head:* Dr. Lisa Frye, Chairperson, 610-683-4422, Fax: 610-683-4129, E-mail: frye@kutztown.edu. *Application contact:* Dr. Lisa Frye, Chairperson, 610-683-4422, Fax: 610-683-4129, E-mail: frye@kutztown.edu.
Website: https://www.kutztown.edu/academics/graduate-programs/computer-science.htm

Lakehead University, Graduate Studies, School of Mathematical Sciences, Thunder Bay, ON P7B 5E1, Canada. Offers computer science (M Sc); mathematical science (MA). *Program availability:* Part-time, evening/weekend. *Degree requirements:* For master's, thesis optional. *Entrance requirements:* For master's, minimum B average, honours degree in mathematics or computer science. Additional exam requirements/recommendations for international students: required—TOEFL.

Lamar University, College of Graduate Studies, College of Arts and Sciences, Department of Computer Science, Beaumont, TX 77710. Offers MS. *Program availability:* Part-time. *Faculty:* 13 full-time (3 women), 3 part-time/adjunct (1 woman). *Students:* 50 full-time (18 women), 19 part-time (8 women); includes 2 minority (both Asian, non-Hispanic/Latino), 63 international. Average age 27. 161 applicants, 83% accepted, 22 enrolled. In 2019, 41 master's awarded. *Degree requirements:* For master's, comprehensive exams and project or thesis. *Entrance requirements:* For master's, GRE General Test, minimum GPA of 3.3 in last 60 hours of undergraduate course work or 3.0 overall. Additional exam requirements/recommendations for international students: required—TOEFL (minimum score 527 paper-based; 71 iBT), IELTS (minimum score 6). *Application deadline:* Applications are processed on a rolling basis. Application fee: $25 ($50 for international students). *Expenses: Tuition, area resident:* Full-time $6324; part-time $351 per credit. Tuition, state resident: full-time $6324; part-time $351 per credit. Tuition, nonresident: full-time $13,920; part-time $773 per credit. *International tuition:* $13,920 full-time. *Required fees:* $2462; $327 per credit. Tuition and fees vary according to course load, campus/location and reciprocity agreements. *Financial support:* In 2019–20, 2 research assistantships with partial tuition reimbursements (averaging $6,000 per year), 4 teaching assistantships with partial tuition reimbursements (averaging $6,000 per year) were awarded; institutionally sponsored loans, scholarships/grants, and tuition waivers (partial) also available. Financial award applicants required to submit FAFSA. *Unit head:* Dr. Stefan Andrei, Chair, 409-880-8775, Fax: 409-880-2364. *Application contact:* Celeste Contreas, Director, Admissions and Academic Services, 409-880-8888, Fax: 409-880-7419, E-mail: gradmissions@lamar.edu.
Website: http://artssciences.lamar.edu/computer-science

La Salle University, School of Arts and Sciences, Program in Computer Information Science, Philadelphia, PA 19141-1199. Offers application development (Certificate); computer information science (MS). *Program availability:* Part-time, evening/weekend, online only, 100% online. *Degree requirements:* For master's, capstone project. *Entrance requirements:* For master's, GRE, MAT, or GMAT, minimum undergraduate GPA of 3.0; two letters of recommendation; resume; telephone or in-person interview. Additional exam requirements/recommendations for international students: required—TOEFL. Electronic applications accepted. Application fee is waived when completed online. *Expenses:* Contact institution.

Lawrence Technological University, College of Arts and Sciences, Southfield, MI 48075-1058. Offers bioinformatics (Graduate Certificate); computer science (MS), including data science, big data, and data mining, intelligent systems; educational technology (MA), including robotics; instructional design, communication, and presentation (Graduate Certificate); integrated science (MA); science education (MA); technical and professional communication (MS, Graduate Certificate); writing for the digital age (Graduate Certificate). *Program availability:* Part-time, evening/weekend. *Faculty:* 5 full-time (2 women), 2 part-time/adjunct (1 woman). *Students:* 1 (woman) full-time, 25 part-time (15 women); includes 6 minority (3 Black or African American, non-Hispanic/Latino; 2 Asian, non-Hispanic/Latino; 1 Hispanic/Latino), 6 international. Average age 34. 50 applicants, 68% accepted, 3 enrolled. In 2019, 14 master's, 4 other advanced degrees awarded. *Degree requirements:* For master's, thesis (for some programs). *Entrance requirements:* Additional exam requirements/recommendations for international students: required—TOEFL (minimum score 550 paper-based; 79 iBT), IELTS (minimum score 6.5). *Application deadline:* For fall admission, 5/24 for international students; for spring admission, 10/13 for international students; for summer admission, 2/18 for international students. Applications are processed on a rolling basis. Application fee: $50. Electronic applications accepted. *Expenses: Tuition:* Full-time $16,618; part-time $8309 per year. *Required fees:* $600; $600. *Financial support:* In 2019–20, 4 students received support. Scholarships/grants and tuition reduction available. Financial award application deadline: 4/1; financial award applicants required to submit FAFSA. *Unit head:* Glen Bauer, Interim Dean, 248-204-3532, Fax: 248-204-3518, E-mail: scidean@ltu.edu. *Application contact:* Jane Rohrback, Director of Admissions, 248-204-3160, Fax: 248-204-2228, E-mail: admissions@ltu.edu.

Lebanese American University, School of Arts and Sciences, Beirut, Lebanon. Offers computer science (MS); international affairs (MA).

Lehigh University, P.C. Rossin College of Engineering and Applied Science, Department of Computer Science and Engineering, Bethlehem, PA 18015. Offers computer engineering (M Eng, MS, PhD); computer science (M Eng, MS, PhD); MBA/E. *Program availability:* Part-time. *Faculty:* 16 full-time (2 women), 2 part-time/adjunct (1 woman). *Students:* 63 full-time (18 women), 2 part-time (0 women); includes 3 minority (1 Black or African American, non-Hispanic/Latino; 1 Asian, non-Hispanic/Latino; 1 Hispanic/Latino), 47 international. Average age 26. 282 applicants, 32% accepted, 25 enrolled. In 2019, 21 master's, 6 doctorates awarded. Terminal master's awarded for partial completion of doctoral program. *Degree requirements:* For master's, thesis optional, oral presentation of thesis; for doctorate, thesis/dissertation, qualifying, general, and oral exams. *Entrance requirements:* For master's, GRE General Test, minimum GPA of 3.0; for doctorate, GRE General Test, minimum GPA of 3.5. Additional exam requirements/recommendations for international students: required—TOEFL (minimum score 550 paper-based; 79 iBT), IELTS (minimum score 6.5). *Application deadline:* For fall admission, 4/1 for domestic and international students; for spring admission, 11/1 for domestic and international students. Application fee: $75. Electronic applications accepted. *Expenses:* 1500/credit hour. *Financial support:* In 2019–20, 14 students received support, including 2 fellowships with full tuition reimbursements available (averaging $23,025 per year), 6 research assistantships with full tuition reimbursements available (averaging $22,050 per year), 6 teaching assistantships with full tuition reimbursements available (averaging $22,050 per year). Financial award application deadline: 1/15. *Unit head:* Jeffrey C Trinkle, Chair, 610-758-4124, E-mail: jct519@lehigh.edu. *Application contact:* Heidi Wegrzyn, Graduate Coordinator, 610-758-3065, E-mail: hew207@lehigh.edu.
Website: http://www.cse.lehigh.edu/

Lehman College of the City University of New York, School of Natural and Social Sciences, Department of Mathematics and Computer Science, Program in Computer Science, Bronx, NY 10468-1589. Offers MS. *Degree requirements:* For master's, one foreign language, thesis or alternative. *Expenses: Tuition, area resident:* Full-time $5545; part-time $2820. *Required fees:* $240.

Lewis University, College of Aviation, Science and Technology, Program in Data Science, Romeoville, IL 60446. Offers computational biology and bioinformatics (MS); computer science (MS). *Program availability:* Part-time, evening/weekend, 100% online, blended/hybrid learning. *Students:* 22 full-time (6 women), 95 part-time (35 women); includes 33 minority (5 Black or African American, non-Hispanic/Latino; 11 Asian, non-Hispanic/Latino; 9 Hispanic/Latino; 2 Native Hawaiian or other Pacific Islander, non-Hispanic/Latino; 6 Two or more races, non-Hispanic/Latino), 10 international. Average age 33. *Entrance requirements:* For master's, bachelor's degree, undergraduate coursework in calculus, minimum undergraduate GPA of 3.0, resume, statement of purpose, two letters of recommendation. Additional exam requirements/recommendations for international students: required—TOEFL (minimum score 550 paper-based; 79 iBT), IELTS (minimum score 6). *Application deadline:* For fall admission, 5/1 priority date for international students; for winter admission, 11/1 priority date for international students. Applications are processed on a rolling basis. Application fee: $40. Electronic applications accepted. *Financial support:* Federal Work-Study and unspecified assistantships available. Financial award application deadline: 5/1; financial award applicants required to submit FAFSA. *Unit head:* Dr. Piotr Szczurek, Program Director. *Application contact:* Sheri Vilcek, Graduate Admissions Counselor, 815-836-5610, E-mail: grad@lewisu.edu.
Website: http://www.lewisu.edu/academics/data-science/index.htm

Long Island University - Brooklyn, School of Business, Public Administration and Information Sciences, Brooklyn, NY 11201-8423. Offers accounting (MBA); accounting (MS); business administration (MBA); computer science (MS); gerontology (Advanced Certificate); health administration (MPA); human resources management (MS); not-for-profit management (Advanced Certificate); public administration (MPA); taxation (MS). *Program availability:* Part-time, evening/weekend. *Entrance requirements:* Additional exam requirements/recommendations for international students: required—TOEFL (minimum score 550 paper-based; 75 iBT). Electronic applications accepted.

Louisiana State University and Agricultural & Mechanical College, Graduate School, College of Engineering, Division of Computer Science, Baton Rouge, LA 70803. Offers computer science (MSSS, PhD); systems science (MSSS).

Louisiana State University in Shreveport, College of Arts and Sciences, Program in Computer Systems Technology, Shreveport, LA 71115-2399. Offers MS. *Program availability:* Part-time, evening/weekend. *Degree requirements:* For master's, comprehensive exam (for some programs), thesis or alternative. *Entrance requirements:* For master's, GRE, programming course in high-level language, interview. Additional exam requirements/recommendations for international students: required—TOEFL (minimum score 550 paper-based; 80 iBT). Electronic applications accepted.

Louisiana Tech University, Graduate School, College of Engineering and Science, Ruston, LA 71272. Offers applied physics (MS); biomedical engineering (PhD); computer science (MS); engineering (MS, PhD), including cyberspace engineering (PhD), engineering education (PhD), engineering physics (PhD), materials and infrastructure systems (PhD), micro/nanoscale systems (PhD); engineering and technology management (MS); mathematics (MS); molecular science and nanotechnology (MS, PhD). *Program availability:* Part-time-only. Terminal master's awarded for partial completion of doctoral program. *Degree requirements:* For master's, thesis (for some programs); for doctorate, thesis/dissertation. *Entrance requirements:* For master's and Graduate Certificate, GRE General Test, minimum GPA of 3.0 in last 60 hours. Additional exam requirements/recommendations for international students: required—TOEFL (minimum score 550 paper-based; 80 iBT), IELTS (minimum score 6.5). Electronic applications accepted. *Expenses: Tuition, area resident:* Full-time $6592; part-time $400 per credit. Tuition, state resident: full-time $6592; part-time $400 per credit. Tuition, nonresident: full-time $13,333; part-time $681 per credit. *International tuition:* $13,333 full-time. *Required fees:* $3011; $3011 per unit.

Loyola University Chicago, Graduate School, Department of Computer Science, Chicago, IL 60660. Offers computer science (MS); information technology (MS); software engineering (MS). *Program availability:* Part-time, evening/weekend, online only, 100% online, blended/hybrid learning. *Faculty:* 16 full-time (3 women), 18 part-time/adjunct (2 women). *Students:* 34 full-time (12 women), 37 part-time (10 women); includes 26 minority (6 Black or African American, non-Hispanic/Latino; 16 Asian, non-Hispanic/Latino; 4 Hispanic/Latino), 20 international. Average age 33. 115 applicants, 41% accepted, 17 enrolled. In 2019, 45 master's awarded. *Degree requirements:* For master's, thesis optional, 30 credits/ten courses. *Entrance requirements:* For master's, statement of purpose, one letter of recommendation, transcripts, international transcript evaluation (if applicable). Additional exam requirements/recommendations for international students: required—TOEFL (minimum score 550 paper-based; 79 iBT), IELTS (minimum score 6.5), PTE (minimum score 53), Duolingo English Test. *Application deadline:* Applications are processed on a rolling basis. Application fee: $50. Electronic applications accepted. Application fee is waived when completed online. *Expenses:* $1033 per credit; $115-452 fees per semester. *Financial support:* In 2019–20, 16 students received support, including 2 fellowships with full tuition reimbursements available, 1 research assistantship with full tuition reimbursement available (averaging $18,000 per year), 13 teaching assistantships with partial tuition reimbursements available (averaging $9,925 per year); Federal Work-Study, health care benefits, and tuition waivers (full and partial) also available. Financial award application deadline: 4/1. *Unit head:* Dr. Chandra Sekharan, Chair, 773-508-8150, Fax: 773-508-3739, E-mail: info@cs.luc.edu. *Application contact:* Cecilia Murphy, Graduate Program Secretary, 773-508-8035, E-mail: gpd@cs.luc.edu.
Website: http://luc.edu/cs

Maharishi International University, Graduate Studies, Program in Computer Science, Fairfield, IA 52557. Offers MS. *Degree requirements:* For master's, thesis or alternative. *Entrance requirements:* For master's, GRE General Test, minimum GPA of 3.0. Additional exam requirements/recommendations for international students: required—TOEFL.

Marist College, Graduate Programs, School of Computer Science and Mathematics, Poughkeepsie, NY 12601-1387. Offers business analytics (Adv C); computer science/software development (MS); information systems (MS, Adv C). *Program availability:* Part-time, evening/weekend, online learning. *Entrance requirements:* For master's, resume. Additional exam requirements/recommendations for international students:

required—TOEFL (minimum score 550 paper-based; 80 iBT); recommended—IELTS (minimum score 6.5). Electronic applications accepted.

Marquette University, Graduate School, College of Arts and Sciences, Department of Mathematical and Statistical Sciences, Milwaukee, WI 53201-1881. Offers bioinformatics (MS); computational sciences (MS, PhD); computing (MS); mathematics education (MS). *Program availability:* Part-time, evening/weekend, online learning. Terminal master's awarded for partial completion of doctoral program. *Degree requirements:* For master's, thesis (for some programs), essay with oral presentation; for doctorate, comprehensive exam, thesis/dissertation, qualifying examination. *Entrance requirements:* For master's, official transcripts from all current and previous colleges/universities except Marquette, three letters of recommendation; for doctorate, GRE General Test, official transcripts from all current and previous colleges/universities except Marquette, three letters of recommendation. Additional exam requirements/recommendations for international students: required—TOEFL (minimum score 530 paper-based). Electronic applications accepted.

Marquette University, Graduate School, College of Arts and Sciences, Program in Computing, Milwaukee, WI 53201-1881. Offers MS. *Program availability:* Part-time, evening/weekend, online learning. *Degree requirements:* For master's, thesis optional, enrollment in the Professional Seminar in Computing each term. *Entrance requirements:* For master's, official transcripts from all current and previous colleges/universities except Marquette, essay, three letters of reference. Additional exam requirements/recommendations for international students: required—TOEFL (minimum score 530 paper-based). Electronic applications accepted.

Marshall University, Academic Affairs Division, College of Information Technology and Engineering, Program in Computer Science, Huntington, WV 25755. Offers MS. *Degree requirements:* For master's, thesis or project. *Entrance requirements:* Additional exam requirements/recommendations for international students: required—IELTS (minimum score 5.5).

Massachusetts Institute of Technology, School of Engineering, Department of Electrical Engineering and Computer Science, Cambridge, MA 02139. Offers computer science (PhD, Sc D, ECS); computer science and engineering (PhD, Sc D); computer science and molecular biology (M Eng); electrical engineering (PhD, Sc D, EE); electrical engineering and computer science (M Eng, SM, PhD, Sc D); SM/MBA. *Degree requirements:* For master's and other advanced degree, thesis; for doctorate, comprehensive exam, thesis/dissertation. *Entrance requirements:* Additional exam requirements/recommendations for international students: required—TOEFL, IELTS. Electronic applications accepted.

McGill University, Faculty of Graduate and Postdoctoral Studies, Faculty of Science, School of Computer Science, Montréal, QC H3A 2T5, Canada. Offers M Sc, PhD.

McMaster University, School of Graduate Studies, Faculty of Engineering, Department of Computing and Software, Hamilton, ON L8S 4M2, Canada. Offers computer science (M Sc, PhD); software engineering (M Eng, MA Sc, PhD). *Program availability:* Part-time. *Degree requirements:* For master's, thesis. *Entrance requirements:* Additional exam requirements/recommendations for international students: required—TOEFL (minimum score 550 paper-based).

McNeese State University, Doré School of Graduate Studies, College of Science and Agriculture, Department of Mathematical Sciences, Lake Charles, LA 70609. Offers computer science (MS); mathematics (MS); statistics (MS). *Program availability:* Evening/weekend. *Degree requirements:* For master's, comprehensive exam, thesis or alternative, written exam. *Entrance requirements:* For master's, GRE.

Memorial University of Newfoundland, School of Graduate Studies, Department of Computer Science, St. John's, NL A1C 5S7, Canada. Offers M Sc, PhD. *Program availability:* Part-time. *Degree requirements:* For master's, thesis; for doctorate, comprehensive exam, thesis/dissertation, oral thesis defense. *Entrance requirements:* For master's, GRE (strongly recommended), honors degree in computer science or related field; for doctorate, GRE (strongly recommended), master's degree in computer science. Electronic applications accepted.

Merrimack College, School of Science and Engineering, North Andover, MA 01845-5800. Offers civil engineering (MS); computer science (MS); data science (MS); engineering management (MS); mechanical engineering (MS), including engineering management. *Program availability:* Part-time, evening/weekend, 100% online. *Degree requirements:* For master's, comprehensive exam, thesis optional, internship or capstone (for some programs). *Entrance requirements:* For master's, official college transcripts, resume, personal statement, 2 recommendations. Additional exam requirements/recommendations for international students: required—TOEFL (minimum score 84 iBT), IELTS (minimum score 6.5), PTE (minimum score 56). Electronic applications accepted. Application fee is waived when completed online. *Expenses:* Contact institution.

Metropolitan State University, College of Sciences, St. Paul, MN 55106-5000. Offers computer science (MS, PSM).

Michigan State University, The Graduate School, College of Engineering, Department of Computer Science and Engineering, East Lansing, MI 48824. Offers computer science (MS, PhD). *Entrance requirements:* Additional exam requirements/recommendations for international students: required—TOEFL. Electronic applications accepted.

Middle Tennessee State University, College of Graduate Studies, College of Basic and Applied Sciences, Department of Computer Science, Murfreesboro, TN 37132. Offers MS. *Program availability:* Part-time, evening/weekend, online learning. *Degree requirements:* For master's, comprehensive exam, thesis. *Entrance requirements:* For master's, GRE. Additional exam requirements/recommendations for international students: required—TOEFL (minimum score 525 paper-based; 71 iBT) or IELTS (minimum score 6). Electronic applications accepted.

Midwestern State University, Billie Doris McAda Graduate School, College of Science and Mathematics, Department of Computer Science, Wichita Falls, TX 76308. Offers MS. *Program availability:* Part-time, evening/weekend. *Degree requirements:* For master's, comprehensive exam, thesis. *Entrance requirements:* For master's, GRE General Test. Additional exam requirements/recommendations for international students: required—TOEFL (minimum score 573 paper-based). Electronic applications accepted.

Mills College, Graduate Studies, Program in Computer Science, Oakland, CA 94613-1000. Offers computer science (Certificate); interdisciplinary computer science (MA). *Program availability:* Part-time. *Degree requirements:* For master's, thesis. *Entrance requirements:* For master's, three letters of recommendation. Additional exam requirements/recommendations for international students: required—TOEFL (minimum score 600 paper-based; 100 iBT) or IELTS (minimum score 7). Electronic applications accepted. *Expenses:* Contact institution.

Minnesota State University Mankato, College of Graduate Studies and Research, College of Science, Engineering and Technology, Department of Computer Information Science, Mankato, MN 56001. Offers information technology (MS). *Degree requirements:* For master's, comprehensive exam, thesis or alternative. *Entrance requirements:* For master's, GRE General Test, minimum GPA of 3.0 during previous 2 years. Additional exam requirements/recommendations for international students: required—TOEFL (minimum score 550 paper-based; 80 iBT). Electronic applications accepted.

Mississippi College, Graduate School, College of Arts and Sciences, School of Science and Mathematics, Department of Engineering, Computer Science, and Physics, Clinton, MS 39058. Offers computer science (M Ed, MS); cybersecurity and information assurance (MS). *Program availability:* Part-time. *Degree requirements:* For master's, comprehensive exam, thesis or alternative. *Entrance requirements:* For master's, GRE. Additional exam requirements/recommendations for international students: recommended—TOEFL, IELTS.

Mississippi State University, Bagley College of Engineering, Department of Computer Science and Engineering, Mississippi State, MS 39762. Offers MS, PhD. *Program availability:* Part-time, blended/hybrid learning. *Faculty:* 15 full-time (3 women), 2 part-time/adjunct (0 women). *Students:* 66 full-time (20 women), 20 part-time (1 woman); includes 15 minority (6 Black or African American, non-Hispanic/Latino; 5 Asian, non-Hispanic/Latino; 2 Hispanic/Latino; 2 Two or more races, non-Hispanic/Latino), 28 international. Average age 28. 127 applicants, 50% accepted, 26 enrolled. In 2019, 20 master's, 4 doctorates awarded. *Degree requirements:* For master's, thesis optional, comprehensive oral exam; for doctorate, thesis/dissertation, comprehensive oral or written exam. *Entrance requirements:* For master's, GRE, minimum GPA of 2.75; for doctorate, GRE. Additional exam requirements/recommendations for international students: required—TOEFL (minimum score 550 paper-based; 79 iBT); recommended—IELTS (minimum score 6.5). *Application deadline:* For fall admission, 7/1 for domestic students, 5/1 for international students; for spring admission, 11/1 for domestic students, 9/1 for international students. Applications are processed on a rolling basis. Application fee: $60 ($80 for international students). Electronic applications accepted. *Expenses: Tuition, area resident:* Full-time $8880; part-time $456 per credit hour. Tuition, state resident: full-time $8880. Tuition, nonresident: full-time $23,840; part-time $1236 per credit hour. *Required fees:* $110; $11.12 per credit hour. Tuition and fees vary according to course load. *Financial support:* In 2019–20, 13 research assistantships with full tuition reimbursements (averaging $16,912 per year), 17 teaching assistantships with full tuition reimbursements (averaging $14,169 per year) were awarded; Federal Work-Study, institutionally sponsored loans, and unspecified assistantships also available. Financial award application deadline: 4/1; financial award applicants required to submit FAFSA. *Unit head:* Dr. Shahram Rahimi, Department Head and Professor, 662-325-7450, Fax: 662-325-8997, E-mail: office@cse.msstate.edu. *Application contact:* Angie Campbell, Admissions and Enrollment Assistant, 662-325-9514, E-mail: acampbell@grad.msstate.edu.
Website: http://www.cse.msstate.edu/

Missouri State University, Graduate College, College of Natural and Applied Sciences, Department of Computer Science, Springfield, MO 65897. Offers natural and applied science (MNAS), including computer science. *Program availability:* Part-time. *Degree requirements:* For master's, comprehensive exam, thesis or alternative. *Entrance requirements:* For master's, GRE, minimum GPA of 3.0. Additional exam requirements/recommendations for international students: required—TOEFL (minimum score 550 paper-based; 79 iBT), IELTS (minimum score 6). Electronic applications accepted. *Expenses: Tuition, area resident:* Full-time $2600; part-time $1735 per credit hour. Tuition, nonresident: full-time $5240; part-time $3495 per credit hour. *International tuition:* $5240 full-time. *Required fees:* $530; $438 per credit hour. Tuition and fees vary according to class time, course level, course load, degree level, campus/location and program.

Missouri University of Science and Technology, Department of Computer Science, Rolla, MO 65401. Offers MS, PhD. *Program availability:* Part-time. Terminal master's awarded for partial completion of doctoral program. *Degree requirements:* For doctorate, thesis/dissertation, departmental qualifying exam. *Entrance requirements:* For master's, GRE General Test (minimum score 700 quantitative, 4 writing); for doctorate, GRE Subject Test (minimum score: quantitative 600, writing 3.5). Additional exam requirements/recommendations for international students: required—TOEFL (minimum score 550 paper-based). Electronic applications accepted. *Expenses:* Tuition, state resident: full-time $7839; part-time $435.50 per credit hour. Tuition, nonresident: full-time $22,169; part-time $1231.60 per credit hour. *International tuition:* $18,156.60 full-time. *Required fees:* $649.76. One-time fee: $119. Tuition and fees vary according to course load and program.

Monmouth University, Graduate Studies, Program in Computer Science, West Long Branch, NJ 07764-1898. Offers MS. *Program availability:* Part-time, evening/weekend. *Faculty:* 9 full-time (3 women), 6 part-time/adjunct (1 woman). *Students:* 26 full-time (11 women), 21 part-time (4 women); includes 8 minority (1 Black or African American, non-Hispanic/Latino; 4 Asian, non-Hispanic/Latino; 3 Hispanic/Latino), 23 international. Average age 28. In 2019, 18 master's awarded. *Degree requirements:* For master's, thesis (for some programs), practicum. *Entrance requirements:* For master's, minimum GPA of 3.0 in major, 2.75 overall; two letters of recommendation; calculus I and II with minimum C grade; two semesters of computer programming within past five years with minimum B grade; undergraduate degree in major that requires substantial component of software development and/or business administration. Additional exam requirements/recommendations for international students: required—TOEFL (minimum score 550 paper-based, 79 iBT), IELTS (minimum score 6), Michigan English Language Assessment Battery (minimum score 77) or Certificate of Advanced English (minimum score 160). *Application deadline:* For fall admission, 7/15 priority date for domestic students, 6/1 for international students; for spring admission, 12/1 priority date for domestic students, 11/1 for international students; for summer admission, 5/1 for domestic students. Applications are processed on a rolling basis. Application fee: $50. Electronic applications accepted. *Expenses: Tuition:* Full-time $22,194; part-time $14,796 per credit. *Required fees:* $712; $178 per semester. $178 per semester. Tuition and fees vary according to course load. *Financial support:* In 2019–20, 23 students received support. Research assistantships, teaching assistantships, scholarships/grants, and unspecified assistantships available. Support available to part-time students. Financial award applicants required to submit FAFSA. *Unit head:* Dr. Jiacun Wang, Program Director, 732-571-7501, Fax: 732-263-5202, E-mail: jwang@monmouth.edu. *Application contact:* Laurie Kuhn, Associate Director of Graduate Admission, 732-571-3452, Fax: 732-263-5123, E-mail: gradadm@monmouth.edu.
Website: https://www.monmouth.edu/graduate/ms-computer-science/

Monroe College, King Graduate School, Bronx, NY 10468. Offers accounting (MS); business administration (MBA), including entrepreneurship, finance, general business administration, healthcare management, human resources, information technology, marketing; computer science (MS); criminal justice (MS); hospitality management (MS); public health (MPH), including biostatistics and epidemiology, community health, health administration and leadership. *Program availability:* Online learning.

Montana State University, The Graduate School, College of Engineering, Department of Computer Science, Bozeman, MT 59717. Offers computer science (MS, PhD). *Program availability:* Part-time. *Degree requirements:* For master's, comprehensive exam; for doctorate, comprehensive exam, thesis/dissertation. *Entrance requirements:* For master's and doctorate, GRE. Additional exam requirements/recommendations for international students: required—TOEFL (minimum score 550 paper-based). Electronic applications accepted.

Montclair State University, The Graduate School, College of Science and Mathematics, CISCO Certificate Program, Montclair, NJ 07043-1624. Offers Certificate.

Montclair State University, The Graduate School, College of Science and Mathematics, MS Program in Computer Science, Montclair, NJ 07043-1624. Offers computer science (MS); information technology (MS). *Program availability:* Part-time, evening/weekend. *Degree requirements:* For master's, comprehensive exam, thesis or alternative. *Entrance requirements:* For master's, GRE General Test, 2 letters of recommendation, essay. Additional exam requirements/recommendations for international students: required—TOEFL (minimum score 83 iBT) or IELTS (minimum score 6.5). Electronic applications accepted.

Morgan State University, School of Graduate Studies, School of Computer, Mathematical, and Natural Sciences, Department of Computer Science, Baltimore, MD 21251. Offers bioinformatics (MS); computer science (MS). *Program availability:* Part-time, evening/weekend. *Faculty:* 11 full-time (2 women), 3 part-time/adjunct (1 woman). *Students:* 5 full-time (4 women), 1 part-time (0 women); includes 2 minority (both Black or African American, non-Hispanic/Latino), 2 international. Average age 36. 9 applicants, 100% accepted, 3 enrolled. In 2019, 1 master's awarded. *Degree requirements:* For master's, comprehensive exam, thesis. *Entrance requirements:* For master's, Minimum GPA 3.0. Additional exam requirements/recommendations for international students: required—TOEFL (minimum score 550 paper-based; 70 iBT). *Application deadline:* For fall admission, 2/1 priority date for domestic students, 4/1 for international students; for spring admission, 10/1 priority date for domestic students, 10/1 for international students. Applications are processed on a rolling basis. Application fee: $50 ($70 for international students). Electronic applications accepted. *Expenses:* Tuition, state resident: full-time $455; part-time $455 per credit hour. Tuition, nonresident: full-time $894; part-time $894 per credit hour. *Required fees:* $82; $82 per credit hour. *Financial support:* In 2019–20, 3 students received support. Fellowships with tuition reimbursements available, research assistantships with full and partial tuition reimbursements available, teaching assistantships with full and partial tuition reimbursements available, scholarships/grants, tuition waivers (full and partial), and unspecified assistantships available. Support available to part-time students. Financial award application deadline: 2/1. *Unit head:* Dr. Shuangbao (Paul) Wang, Chair, 443-885-3962, E-mail: Shuangbao.Wang@morgan.edu. *Application contact:* Dr. Jahmaine Smith, Director of Admissions, 443-885-3185, Fax: 443-885-8226, E-mail: gradapply@morgan.edu.
Website: https://www.morgan.edu/physics

Murray State University, Arthur J. Bauernfeind College of Business, Department of Computer Science and Information Systems, Murray, KY 42071. Offers MSIS. *Program availability:* Part-time, evening/weekend, 100% online, blended/hybrid learning. *Entrance requirements:* For master's, GRE or GMAT, minimum university GPA of 2.75. Additional exam requirements/recommendations for international students: required—TOEFL (minimum score 527 paper-based; 71 iBT). Electronic applications accepted.

National University, School of Engineering and Computing, La Jolla, CA 92037-1011. Offers computer science (MS), including advanced computing; cyber security and information assurance (MS); data analytics (MS); electrical engineering (MS); engineering management (MS); information technology management (MS); management information systems (MS); sustainability management (MS). *Program availability:* Part-time, evening/weekend, 100% online, blended/hybrid learning. *Degree requirements:* For master's, thesis (for some programs). *Entrance requirements:* For master's, interview, minimum GPA of 2.5. Additional exam requirements/recommendations for international students: required—TOEFL (minimum score 550 paper-based; 79 iBT), IELTS (minimum score 6). Electronic applications accepted. *Expenses: Tuition:* Full-time $442; part-time $442 per unit.

Naval Postgraduate School, Departments and Academic Groups, Department of Computer Science, Monterey, CA 93943. Offers computer science (MS, PhD); identity management and cyber security (MA); modeling of virtual environments and simulations (MS, PhD); software engineering (MS, PhD). *Program availability:* Part-time, online learning. *Degree requirements:* For master's, thesis; for doctorate, thesis/dissertation.

Naval Postgraduate School, Departments and Academic Groups, Space Systems Academic Group, Monterey, CA 93943. Offers applied physics (MS); astronautical engineering (MS); computer science (MS); electrical engineering (MS); mechanical engineering (MS); space systems (Engr); space systems operations (MS). *Program availability:* Part-time. *Degree requirements:* For master's and Engr, thesis; for doctorate, thesis/dissertation.

New Jersey Institute of Technology, Ying Wu College of Computing, Newark, NJ 07102. Offers big data management and mining (Certificate); business and information systems (Certificate); computer science (PhD); computing and business (MS); data mining (Certificate); data science (MS); information security (Certificate); information systems (PhD); information technology administration and security (MS); IT administration (Certificate); network security and information assurance (Certificate); software engineering (MS), including information systems; software engineering analysis/design (Certificate); Web systems development (Certificate). *Program availability:* Part-time, evening/weekend. *Faculty:* 78 full-time (16 women), 63 part-time/adjunct (10 women). *Students:* 668 full-time (210 women), 290 part-time (81 women); includes 277 minority (46 Black or African American, non-Hispanic/Latino; 1 American Indian or Alaska Native, non-Hispanic/Latino; 161 Asian, non-Hispanic/Latino; 53 Hispanic/Latino; 16 Two or more races, non-Hispanic/Latino), 565 international. Average age 27. 2,671 applicants, 62% accepted, 360 enrolled. In 2019, 407 master's, 5 doctorates, 12 other advanced degrees awarded. Terminal master's awarded for partial completion of doctoral program. *Degree requirements:* For master's, thesis optional; for doctorate, thesis/dissertation. *Entrance requirements:* For master's, GRE General Test; for doctorate, GRE General Test, minimum graduate GPA of 3.5. Additional exam requirements/recommendations for international students: required—TOEFL (minimum score 550 paper-based; 79 iBT), IELTS (minimum score 6.5). *Application deadline:* For fall admission, 6/1 priority date for domestic students, 5/1 priority date for international students; for spring admission, 11/15 priority date for domestic and international students. Applications are processed on a rolling basis. Application fee: $75. Electronic applications accepted. *Expenses:* $23,828 per year (in-state), $33,744 per year (out-of-state). *Financial support:* In 2019–20, 383 students received support, including 8 fellowships with full tuition reimbursements available, 34 research assistantships with full tuition reimbursements available (averaging $24,000 per year), 57 teaching assistantships with full tuition reimbursements available (averaging $24,000 per year); career-related internships or fieldwork, Federal Work-Study, scholarships/grants, and unspecified assistantships also available. Financial award application deadline: 1/15. *Unit head:* Dr. Craig Gotsman, Dean, 973-596-3366, Fax: 973-596-5777, E-mail: craig.gotsman@njit.edu. *Application contact:* Stephen Eck, Executive Director of University Admissions, 973-596-3300, Fax: 973-596-3461, E-mail: admissions@njit.edu.
Website: http://computing.njit.edu/

New Mexico Highlands University, Graduate Studies, College of Arts and Sciences, Department of Computer Sciences, Las Vegas, NM 87701. Offers media arts and computer science (MS), including computer science. *Degree requirements:* For master's, comprehensive exam, thesis. *Entrance requirements:* For master's, minimum undergraduate GPA of 3.0. Additional exam requirements/recommendations for international students: required—TOEFL (minimum score 540 paper-based).

New Mexico Institute of Mining and Technology, Center for Graduate Studies, Department of Computer Science and Engineering, Socorro, NM 87801. Offers computer science (MS, PhD). *Program availability:* Part-time. *Degree requirements:* For master's, thesis optional; for doctorate, thesis/dissertation. *Entrance requirements:* For master's, GRE General Test; for doctorate, GRE General Test, GRE Subject Test. Additional exam requirements/recommendations for international students: required—TOEFL. Electronic applications accepted.

New York Institute of Technology, College of Engineering and Computing Sciences, Department of Computer Science, Old Westbury, NY 11568. Offers computer science (MS); information, network, and computer security (MS). *Program availability:* Part-time. *Faculty:* 13 full-time (6 women), 24 part-time/adjunct (2 women). *Students:* 173 full-time (61 women), 53 part-time (11 women); includes 69 minority (13 Black or African American, non-Hispanic/Latino; 40 Asian, non-Hispanic/Latino; 10 Hispanic/Latino; 1 Native Hawaiian or other Pacific Islander, non-Hispanic/Latino; 5 Two or more races, non-Hispanic/Latino), 135 international. Average age 26. 1,292 applicants, 51% accepted, 96 enrolled. In 2019, 184 master's awarded. *Degree requirements:* For master's, thesis or alternative. *Entrance requirements:* For master's, Graduates of foreign universities are required to take the GRE and submit their scores. Applicants with a GPA below 2.85 may, at the discretion of the dean, be asked to take the GRE or other diagnostic tests, bachelor's degree in computer science, engineering, management, math, information technology, or related area; minimum undergraduate GPA of 2.85; transcripts from all schools attended and proof of degree. Additional exam requirements/recommendations for international students: required—TOEFL (minimum score 79 iBT), IELTS (minimum score 6), PTE (minimum score 53), Duolingo English Test. *Application deadline:* Applications are processed on a rolling basis. Application fee: $50. Electronic applications accepted. *Expenses: Tuition:* Full-time $23,760; part-time $1320 per credit. *Required fees:* $260; $220 per unit. Full-time tuition and fees vary according to degree level and program. Part-time tuition and fees vary according to course load and program. *Financial support:* In 2019–20, 143 students received support. Fellowships, research assistantships, teaching assistantships, Federal Work-Study, scholarships/grants, and unspecified assistantships available. Support available to part-time students. Financial award application deadline: 2/15; financial award applicants required to submit FAFSA. *Unit head:* Dr. Frank Lee, Department Chair, 516-686-7456, Fax: 516-686-7439, E-mail: fli@nyit.edu. *Application contact:* Alice Dolitsky, Director, Graduate Admissions, 800-345-6948, E-mail: grad@nyit.edu.
Website: https://www.nyit.edu/departments/computer_science

New York University, Graduate School of Arts and Science, Courant Institute of Mathematical Sciences, Department of Computer Science, New York, NY 10012-1019. Offers computer science (MS, PhD); information systems (MS); scientific computing (MS). *Program availability:* Part-time, evening/weekend. *Degree requirements:* For doctorate, thesis/dissertation, oral and written exams. *Entrance requirements:* For master's and doctorate, GRE General Test. Additional exam requirements/recommendations for international students: required—TOEFL, IELTS.

New York University, Tandon School of Engineering, Department of Computer Science and Engineering, Major in Computer Science, New York, NY 10012-1019. Offers computer science (PhD). *Program availability:* Part-time, evening/weekend. *Degree requirements:* For master's, comprehensive exam (for some programs), thesis (for some programs); for doctorate, comprehensive exam, thesis/dissertation, qualifying exam. *Entrance requirements:* For master's, BA or BS in computer science, mathematics, science, or engineering; working knowledge of a high-level program; for doctorate, GRE General Test, GRE Subject Test, BA or BS in science, engineering, or management; MS or 1 year of graduate course work. Additional exam requirements/recommendations for international students: required—TOEFL (minimum score 550 paper-based; 90 iBT); recommended—IELTS (minimum score 7). Electronic applications accepted.

Norfolk State University, School of Graduate Studies, School of Science and Technology, Department of Computer Science, Norfolk, VA 23504. Offers MS.

North Carolina Agricultural and Technical State University, The Graduate College, College of Engineering, Department of Computer Science, Greensboro, NC 27411. Offers MSCS, PhD. *Program availability:* Part-time. *Degree requirements:* For master's, thesis optional.

North Carolina State University, Graduate School, College of Engineering, Department of Computer Science, Raleigh, NC 27695. Offers MC Sc, MS, PhD. *Program availability:* Part-time, online learning. *Degree requirements:* For master's, thesis optional; for doctorate, thesis/dissertation. *Entrance requirements:* For master's, GRE General Test, GRE Subject Test, minimum GPA of 3.0; for doctorate, GRE General Test, GRE Subject Test (recommended), minimum GPA of 3.5. Additional exam requirements/recommendations for international students: required—TOEFL. Electronic applications accepted.

North Carolina State University, Graduate School, College of Engineering, Department of Electrical and Computer Engineering and Department of Computer Science, Program in Computer Networking, Raleigh, NC 27695. Offers MS. *Degree requirements:* For master's, thesis optional. *Entrance requirements:* For master's, GRE General Test, GRE Subject Test (recommended). Electronic applications accepted.

North Central College, School of Graduate and Professional Studies, Department of Computer Science, Naperville, IL 60566-7063. Offers MS. *Program availability:* Part-time, evening/weekend. *Degree requirements:* For master's, thesis optional, project. *Entrance requirements:* For master's, interview. Additional exam requirements/recommendations for international students: required—TOEFL (minimum score 550 paper-based; 80 iBT), IELTS (minimum score 6.5). Electronic applications accepted. Application fee is waived when completed online. *Expenses:* Contact institution.

Northcentral University, Graduate Studies, San Diego, CA 92106. Offers business (MBA, DBA, PhD, Postbaccalaureate Certificate); education (M Ed, Ed D, PhD, Ed S, Post-Master's Certificate, Postbaccalaureate Certificate); marriage and family therapy (MA, DMFT, PhD, Post-Master's Certificate, Postbaccalaureate Certificate); psychology (MA, PhD, Post-Master's Certificate, Postbaccalaureate Certificate); technology (MS, PhD), including computer science, cybersecurity (MS), data science, technology and innovation management (PhD). *Program availability:* Part-time, evening/weekend, online only, 100% online. *Degree requirements:* For doctorate, comprehensive exam, thesis/dissertation. *Entrance requirements:* For master's, bachelor's degree from regionally- or nationally-accredited institution, current resume or curriculum vitae, statement of intent, interview, and background check (for marriage and family therapy); for doctorate, post-baccalaureate master's degree and/or doctoral degree from nationally- or regionally-accredited academic institution; for other advanced degree, bachelor's-level or higher degree from accredited institution or university (for Post-Baccalaureate Certificate); master's and/or doctoral degree from regionally- or nationally-accredited academic institution (for Post-Master's Certificate). Additional exam requirements/

recommendations for international students: required—TOEFL (minimum score 550 paper-based; 79 iBT), IELTS (minimum score 6.5), PTE (minimum score 53). Electronic applications accepted. *Expenses: Tuition:* Part-time $1053 per credit. *Required fees:* $95 per course. Full-time tuition and fees vary according to degree level and program.

North Dakota State University, College of Graduate and Interdisciplinary Studies, College of Science and Mathematics, Department of Computer Science, Fargo, ND 58102. Offers computer science (MS, PhD); software engineering (MS, MSE, PhD, Certificate). *Program availability:* Part-time. *Degree requirements:* For master's, comprehensive exam, thesis optional; for doctorate, thesis/dissertation, qualifying exam. *Entrance requirements:* For master's, minimum GPA of 3.0, BS in computer science or related field; for doctorate, minimum GPA of 3.25, MS in computer science or related field. Additional exam requirements/recommendations for international students: required—TOEFL (minimum score 550 paper-based; 79 iBT). Electronic applications accepted. Tuition and fees vary according to program and reciprocity agreements.

Northeastern Illinois University, College of Graduate Studies and Research, College of Arts and Sciences, Program in Computer Science, Chicago, IL 60625. Offers MS. *Program availability:* Part-time, evening/weekend. *Degree requirements:* For master's, comprehensive exam, research project or thesis. *Entrance requirements:* For master's, minimum GPA of 2.75, proficiency in 2 higher-level computer languages, course in discrete mathematics. Additional exam requirements/recommendations for international students: required—TOEFL (minimum score 550 paper-based; 79 iBT). Electronic applications accepted.

Northeastern University, College of Computer and Information Science, Boston, MA 02115-5096. Offers computer science (MS, PhD); data science (MS); game science and design (MS); health informatics (MS); information assurance (MS); network science (PhD); personal health informatics (PhD). *Program availability:* Part-time, evening/weekend. Terminal master's awarded for partial completion of doctoral program. *Degree requirements:* For master's, thesis optional; for doctorate, comprehensive exam, thesis/dissertation. Electronic applications accepted. *Expenses:* Contact institution.

Northern Arizona University, College of Engineering, Informatics, and Applied Sciences, School of Informatics, Computing, and Cyber Systems, Flagstaff, AZ 86011. Offers engineering (M Eng), including computer science and engineering, electrical engineering; informatics and computing (PhD). *Program availability:* Part-time. *Degree requirements:* For master's, variable foreign language requirement, comprehensive exam (for some programs), thesis (for some programs); for doctorate, variable foreign language requirement, comprehensive exam (for some programs), thesis/dissertation (for some programs). *Entrance requirements:* Additional exam requirements/recommendations for international students: required—TOEFL (minimum score 80 iBT), IELTS (minimum score 6.5). Electronic applications accepted.

Northern Illinois University, Graduate School, College of Liberal Arts and Sciences, Department of Computer Science, De Kalb, IL 60115-2854. Offers MS. *Program availability:* Part-time, evening/weekend. *Faculty:* 14 full-time (3 women). *Students:* 65 full-time (19 women), 42 part-time (14 women); includes 4 minority (1 Black or African American, non-Hispanic/Latino; 1 Asian, non-Hispanic/Latino; 1 Hispanic/Latino; 1 Two or more races, non-Hispanic/Latino), 97 international. Average age 25. 201 applicants, 58% accepted, 28 enrolled. In 2019, 72 master's awarded. *Degree requirements:* For master's, comprehensive exam. *Entrance requirements:* For master's, GRE General Test, minimum GPA of 2.75. Additional exam requirements/recommendations for international students: required—TOEFL (minimum score 550 paper-based). *Application deadline:* For fall admission, 6/1 for domestic students, 5/1 for international students; for spring admission, 11/1 for domestic students, 10/1 for international students. Applications are processed on a rolling basis. Application fee: $40. Electronic applications accepted. *Financial support:* In 2019–20, 6 research assistantships with full tuition reimbursements, 28 teaching assistantships with full tuition reimbursements were awarded; fellowships with full tuition reimbursements, career-related internships or fieldwork, Federal Work-Study, scholarships/grants, tuition waivers (full), and unspecified assistantships also available. Support available to part-time students. Financial award applicants required to submit FAFSA. *Unit head:* Dr. Nicholas Karonis, Chair, 815-753-0349, Fax: 815-753-0342, E-mail: karonis@niu.edu. *Application contact:* Graduate School Office, 815-753-0395, E-mail: gradsch@niu.edu.
Website: http://www.cs.niu.edu/

Northern Kentucky University, Office of Graduate Programs, College of Informatics, Department of Computer Science, Highland Heights, KY 41099. Offers computer science (MSCS); geographic information systems (Certificate); secure software engineering (Certificate). *Program availability:* Part-time, evening/weekend. *Degree requirements:* For master's, thesis optional. *Entrance requirements:* For master's, GRE, minimum GPA of 3.0, at least 4 semesters of undergraduate study in computer science including intermediate computer programming and data structures, one year of calculus, one course in discrete mathematics. Additional exam requirements/recommendations for international students: required—TOEFL (minimum score 550 paper-based; 79 iBT); recommended—IELTS (minimum score 6.5). Electronic applications accepted.

Northwestern Polytechnic University, School of Engineering, Fremont, CA 94539-7482. Offers computer engineering (DCE); computer science (MS); computer systems engineering (MS); electrical engineering (MS). *Program availability:* Part-time, evening/weekend. *Degree requirements:* For master's, thesis optional; for doctorate, thesis/dissertation. *Entrance requirements:* For master's, minimum GPA of 3.0. Additional exam requirements/recommendations for international students: required—TOEFL (minimum score 550 paper-based; 79 iBT).

Northwestern University, McCormick School of Engineering and Applied Science, Department of Electrical Engineering and Computer Science, Evanston, IL 60208. Offers computer engineering (MS, PhD); computer science (MS, PhD); electrical engineering (MS, PhD); information technology (MS). *Program availability:* Part-time. Terminal master's awarded for partial completion of doctoral program. *Degree requirements:* For master's, comprehensive exam (for some programs), thesis optional; for doctorate, comprehensive exam, thesis/dissertation. *Entrance requirements:* For master's and doctorate, GRE General Test. Additional exam requirements/recommendations for international students: required—TOEFL (minimum score 577 paper-based; 90 iBT), IELTS (minimum score 7). Electronic applications accepted.

Northwest Missouri State University, Graduate School, School of Computer Science and Information Systems, Maryville, MO 64468-6001. Offers applied computer science (MS); information systems (MS); instructional technology (MS). *Program availability:* Part-time. *Faculty:* 15 full-time (5 women). *Students:* 204 full-time (77 women), 54 part-time (26 women), 257 international. Average age 24. 478 applicants, 72% accepted, 62 enrolled. In 2019, 129 master's awarded. *Degree requirements:* For master's, comprehensive exam. *Entrance requirements:* For master's, GRE General Test, minimum GPA of 3.0. Additional exam requirements/recommendations for international students: required—TOEFL (minimum score 550 paper-based; 71 iBT). *Application deadline:* Applications are processed on a rolling basis. Application fee: $0 ($75 for international students). Electronic applications accepted. *Expenses:* Contact institution. *Financial support:* Research assistantships, teaching assistantships with full tuition reimbursements, and unspecified assistantships available. Financial award application deadline: 4/1; financial award applicants required to submit FAFSA. *Unit head:* Dr. Douglas Hawley, Director of School of Computer Science and Information Systems, 660-562-1200, Fax: 660-562-1963, E-mail: hawley@nwmissouri.edu. *Application contact:* Dr. Gregory Haddock, Dean of Graduate School, 660-562-1145, Fax: 660-562-1096, E-mail: gradsch@nwmissouri.edu.
Website: http://www.nwmissouri.edu/csis/

Notre Dame College, Graduate Programs, South Euclid, OH 44121. Offers mild/moderate needs (M Ed); reading (M Ed); security policy studies (MA, Graduate Certificate); technology (M Ed). *Program availability:* Part-time, evening/weekend, online only, 100% online. *Faculty:* 11 full-time (8 women), 8 part-time/adjunct (5 women). *Students:* 20 full-time (17 women), 83 part-time (59 women); includes 28 minority (12 Black or African American, non-Hispanic/Latino; 2 Hispanic/Latino; 1 Native Hawaiian or other Pacific Islander, non-Hispanic/Latino; 13 Two or more races, non-Hispanic/Latino). Average age 35. In 2019, 5 master's awarded. *Degree requirements:* For master's, thesis. *Entrance requirements:* For master's, GRE General Test, MAT, minimum undergraduate GPA of 2.75, valid teaching certificate, bachelor's degree in an education-related field from accredited college or university, official transcripts of most recent college work. *Application deadline:* For fall admission, 8/1 priority date for domestic students; for spring admission, 1/1 for domestic students. Applications are processed on a rolling basis. Application fee: $40. *Expenses: Tuition:* Full-time $590; part-time $590 per credit hour. *Financial support:* Tuition waivers (full) available. Support available to part-time students. Financial award application deadline: 4/15; financial award applicants required to submit FAFSA. *Unit head:* Florentine Hoelker, Dean of Online and Graduate Programs, 215-373-6469, E-mail: fhoelker@ndc.edu. *Application contact:* Brandy Viol, Assistant Dean of Enrollment, 216-373-5350, Fax: 216-373-6330, E-mail: bviol@ndc.edu.
Website: https://online.notredamecollege.edu/online-degrees/#master

Nova Southeastern University, College of Engineering and Computing, Fort Lauderdale, FL 33314-7796. Offers computer science (MS, PhD); information assurance (PhD); information assurance and cybersecurity (MS); information systems (PhD); information technology (MS); management information systems (MS). *Program availability:* Part-time, evening/weekend, blended/hybrid learning. *Faculty:* 18 full-time (6 women), 20 part-time/adjunct (4 women). *Students:* 206 full-time (67 women), 244 part-time (71 women); includes 229 minority (93 Black or African American, non-Hispanic/Latino; 1 American Indian or Alaska Native, non-Hispanic/Latino; 36 Asian, non-Hispanic/Latino; 84 Hispanic/Latino; 1 Native Hawaiian or other Pacific Islander, non-Hispanic/Latino; 14 Two or more races, non-Hispanic/Latino), 80 international. Average age 40. 212 applicants, 58% accepted, 63 enrolled. In 2019, 142 master's, 41 doctorates awarded. Terminal master's awarded for partial completion of doctoral program. *Degree requirements:* For master's, thesis optional; for doctorate, thesis/dissertation. *Entrance requirements:* For master's, minimum undergraduate GPA of 2.5; for doctorate, master's degree, minimum graduate GPA of 3.25. Additional exam requirements/recommendations for international students: required—TOEFL (minimum score 80 iBT), IELTS (minimum score 6), PTE (minimum score 54). *Application deadline:* Applications are processed on a rolling basis. Application fee: $50. Electronic applications accepted. *Expenses:* Contact institution. *Financial support:* Federal Work-Study, scholarships/grants, and corporate financial support available. Financial award application deadline: 4/15; financial award applicants required to submit FAFSA. *Unit head:* Dr. Meline Kevorkian, Associate Provost, Dean of Computering and Engineering, 954-262-2063, Fax: 954-262-2752, E-mail: melinek@nova.edu. *Application contact:* Nancy Azoulay, Director, Admissions, 954-262-2026, Fax: 954-262-2752, E-mail: azoulayn@nova.edu.
Website: http://scis.nova.edu

Oakland University, Graduate Study and Lifelong Learning, School of Engineering and Computer Science, Department of Computer Science and Engineering, Rochester, MI 48309-4401. Offers computer science (MS); computer science and informatics (PhD); software engineering and information technology (MS). *Program availability:* Part-time, evening/weekend. *Entrance requirements:* For master's, minimum GPA of 3.0. Electronic applications accepted. *Expenses:* Contact institution.

The Ohio State University, Graduate School, College of Engineering, Department of Computer Science and Engineering, Columbus, OH 43210. Offers MS, PhD. *Entrance requirements:* For master's and doctorate, GRE (minimum score Quantitative 750 old, 159 new; Verbal 500 old, 155 new; Analytical Writing 3.0); GRE Subject Test in computer science (strongly recommended for those whose undergraduate degree is not in computer science). Additional exam requirements/recommendations for international students: required—TOEFL (minimum score 550 paper-based; 79 iBT), Michigan English Language Assessment Battery (minimum score 82); recommended—IELTS (minimum score 7). Electronic applications accepted.

Ohio University, Graduate College, Russ College of Engineering and Technology, School of Electrical Engineering and Computer Science, Athens, OH 45701-2979. Offers electrical engineering (MS); electrical engineering and computer science (PhD). *Degree requirements:* For master's, comprehensive exam (for some programs), thesis; for doctorate, comprehensive exam, thesis/dissertation, qualifying exams. *Entrance requirements:* For master's, GRE, BSEE or BSCS, minimum GPA of 3.0; for doctorate, GRE, MSEE or MSCS, minimum GPA of 3.0. Additional exam requirements/recommendations for international students: required—TOEFL (minimum score 550 paper-based; 80 iBT) or IELTS (minimum score 6.5). Electronic applications accepted.

Oklahoma Christian University, Graduate School of Engineering and Computer Science, Oklahoma City, OK 73136-1100. Offers electrical and computer engineering (MSE); engineering management (MSE); mechanical engineering (MSE); software engineering (MSCS, MSE). *Program availability:* Part-time. *Entrance requirements:* Additional exam requirements/recommendations for international students: required—TOEFL (minimum score 550 paper-based). Electronic applications accepted. *Expenses:* Contact institution.

Oklahoma City University, Meinders School of Business, Oklahoma City, OK 73106-1402. Offers business (MBA, MSA); computer science (MS); energy legal studies (MS); energy management (MS); JD/MBA. *Program availability:* Part-time, evening/weekend, 100% online. *Degree requirements:* For master's, practicum/capstone. *Entrance requirements:* For master's, undergraduate degree from accredited institution, minimum GPA of 3.0, essay, letters of recommendation. Additional exam requirements/recommendations for international students: required—TOEFL (minimum score 550 paper-based; 80 iBT). Electronic applications accepted. *Expenses:* Contact institution.

Oklahoma State University, College of Arts and Sciences, Department of Computer Science, Stillwater, OK 74078. Offers MS, PhD. *Faculty:* 14 full-time (2 women). *Students:* 24 full-time (9 women), 27 part-time (11 women); includes 4 minority (2 Asian, non-Hispanic/Latino; 2 Two or more races, non-Hispanic/Latino), 42 international. Average age 29. 120 applicants, 37% accepted, 22 enrolled. In 2019, 28 master's, 1 doctorate awarded. *Entrance requirements:* For master's, GRE; for doctorate, GRE General Test, GRE Subject Test in computer science (recommended), 3 letters of recommendation. Additional exam requirements/recommendations for international students: required—TOEFL (minimum score 550 paper-based; 79 iBT). *Application deadline:* For fall admission, 3/1 priority date for international students; for spring admission, 8/1 priority date for international students. Applications are processed on a

rolling basis. Application fee: $50 ($75 for international students). Electronic applications accepted. *Expenses: Tuition, area resident:* Full-time $4148.10; part-time $2765.40. Tuition, state resident: full-time $4148.10; part-time $2765.40. Tuition, nonresident: full-time $15,775; part-time $10,516.80. *International tuition:* $15,775.20 full-time. *Required fees:* $2196.90; $122.05 per credit hour. Tuition and fees vary according to course load, campus/location and program. *Financial support:* In 2019–20, 25 teaching assistantships (averaging $1,933 per year) were awarded; research assistantships, career-related internships or fieldwork, Federal Work-Study, scholarships/grants, health care benefits, tuition waivers (partial), and unspecified assistantships also available. Support available to part-time students. Financial award application deadline: 3/1; financial award applicants required to submit FAFSA. *Unit head:* Dr. K. M. George, Department Head, 405-744-5668, Fax: 405-774-9097, E-mail: kmg@cs.okstate.edu. *Application contact:* Dr. Sheryl Tucker, Dean, 405-744-6368, Fax: 405-744-0355, E-mail: gradi@okstate.edu.
Website: https://computerscience.okstate.edu/

Old Dominion University, College of Sciences, Program in Computer Science, Norfolk, VA 23529. Offers computer information systems (MS); computer science (MS, PhD). *Program availability:* Part-time, 100% online. Terminal master's awarded for partial completion of doctoral program. *Degree requirements:* For master's, comprehensive exam, thesis optional, 34 credit hours; for doctorate, comprehensive exam, thesis/dissertation, 48 credit hours beyond the MS. *Entrance requirements:* For master's, GRE General Test, minimum GPA of 3.0; for doctorate, GRE General Test, MS in computer science. Additional exam requirements/recommendations for international students: required—TOEFL (minimum score 550 paper-based; 79 iBT), IELTS (minimum score 6.5). Electronic applications accepted.

Oregon Health & Science University, School of Medicine, Graduate Programs in Medicine, Department of Computer Science and Electrical Engineering, Portland, OR 97239-3098. Offers computer science and engineering (MS, PhD); electrical engineering (MS, PhD). *Program availability:* Part-time. Terminal master's awarded for partial completion of doctoral program. *Degree requirements:* For master's, thesis (for some programs); for doctorate, comprehensive exam, thesis/dissertation, qualifying exam. *Entrance requirements:* For master's and doctorate, GRE General Test (minimum scores: 153 Verbal/148 Quantitative/4.5 Analytical). Electronic applications accepted.

Oregon State University, College of Engineering, Program in Computer Science, Corvallis, OR 97331. Offers algorithms and cryptography (M Eng, MS, PhD). *Entrance requirements:* For master's and doctorate, GRE. Additional exam requirements/recommendations for international students: required—TOEFL (minimum score 600 paper-based; 80 iBT), IELTS (minimum score 6.5). *Expenses:* Contact institution.

Pace University, Seidenberg School of Computer Science and Information Systems, New York, NY 10038. Offers chief information security officer (APC); computer science (MS, PhD); enterprise analytics (MS); information and communication technology strategy and innovation (APC); information systems (MS, APC); information technology (MS); professional studies in computing (DPS); secure software and information engineering (APC); security and information assurance (Certificate); software development and engineering (MS, Certificate); telecommunications systems and networks (MS, Certificate). *Program availability:* Part-time, evening/weekend, online only, 100% online, blended/hybrid learning. *Degree requirements:* For master's, thesis or alternative, capstone course; for doctorate, comprehensive exam (for some programs), thesis/dissertation. *Entrance requirements:* Additional exam requirements/recommendations for international students: required—TOEFL (minimum score 78 iBT), IELTS (minimum score 6.5) or PTE (minimum score 52). Electronic applications accepted. *Expenses:* Contact institution.

Pacific States University, College of Computer Science and Information Systems, Los Angeles, CA 90010. Offers computer science (MS); information systems (MS). *Program availability:* Part-time, evening/weekend. *Entrance requirements:* For master's, bachelor's degree in physics, engineering, computer science, information systems, or applied mathematics; minimum undergraduate GPA of 2.5 during last 90 quarter units of course work. Additional exam requirements/recommendations for international students: required—TOEFL (minimum score 500 paper-based; 61 iBT), IELTS (minimum score 5.5).

Penn State Harrisburg, Graduate School, School of Science, Engineering and Technology, Middletown, PA 17057. Offers civil engineering (MS); computer science (MS); electrical engineering (M Eng, MS); engineering management (MPS); engineering science (M Eng); environmental engineering (M Eng); environmental pollution control (MEPC, MS); mechanical engineering (MS); structural engineering (Certificate). *Program availability:* Part-time, evening/weekend.

Penn State University Park, Graduate School, College of Engineering, Department of Computer Science and Engineering, University Park, PA 16802. Offers M Eng, MS, PhD.

See Display below and Close-Up on page 275.

Polytechnic University of Puerto Rico, Graduate School, Hato Rey, PR 00918. Offers business administration (MBA), including computer information systems, general management, management of information systems, management of international enterprises; civil engineering (ME, MS); computer engineering (ME, MS); computer science (MCS, MS); electrical engineering (ME, MS); engineering management (MEM); environmental management (MEM); landscape architecture (M Land Arch); manufacturing competitiveness (MMC, MS); manufacturing engineering (ME, MS); mechanical engineering (M Mech E). *Accreditation:* ASLA. *Program availability:* Part-time, evening/weekend. *Entrance requirements:* For master's, 3 letters of recommendation.

Polytechnique Montréal, Graduate Programs, Department of Electrical and Computer Engineering, Montréal, QC H3C 3A7, Canada. Offers automation (M Eng, M Sc A, PhD); computer science (M Eng, M Sc A, PhD); electrical engineering (DESS); electrotechnology (M Eng, M Sc A, PhD); microelectronics (M Eng, M Sc A, PhD); microwave technology (M Eng, M Sc A, PhD). *Program availability:* Part-time, evening/weekend. *Degree requirements:* For master's, one foreign language, thesis; for doctorate, one foreign language, thesis/dissertation. *Entrance requirements:* For master's, minimum GPA of 2.75; for doctorate, minimum GPA of 3.0.

Portland State University, Graduate Studies, Maseeh College of Engineering and Computer Science, Department of Computer Science, Portland, OR 97207-0751. Offers computer science (MS, PhD); computer security (Certificate). *Program availability:* Part-time. *Faculty:* 28 full-time (9 women), 5 part-time/adjunct (0 women). *Students:* 120 full-time (39 women), 98 part-time (26 women); includes 45 minority (28 Asian, non-Hispanic/Latino; 9 Hispanic/Latino; 1 Native Hawaiian or other Pacific Islander, non-Hispanic/Latino; 7 Two or more races, non-Hispanic/Latino), 72 international. Average age 31. 186 applicants, 55% accepted, 52 enrolled. In 2019, 82 master's, 1 doctorate awarded. *Degree requirements:* For master's, thesis or alternative; for doctorate, comprehensive exam, thesis/dissertation. *Entrance requirements:* For master's, GRE (minimum scores 60th percentile in Quantitative and 25th percentile in Verbal), BS in engineering field, science or closely-related area; minimum GPA of 3.0 or equivalent; 2 letters of recommendation; personal statement; for doctorate, GRE (minimum scores 60th percentile in Quantitative and 25th percentile in Verbal), MS in computer science or allied field. Additional exam requirements/recommendations for international students: required—TOEFL (minimum score 550 paper-based). *Application deadline:* For fall admission, 3/1 for domestic and international students; for winter admission, 5/15 for

domestic and international students; for spring admission, 11/1 for domestic students, 10/1 for international students. Applications are processed on a rolling basis. Application fee: $65. *Expenses:* Contact institution. *Financial support:* In 2019–20, 37 students received support, including 8 research assistantships with full and partial tuition reimbursements available (averaging $20,325 per year), 26 teaching assistantships with full and partial tuition reimbursements available (averaging $14,081 per year); career-related internships or fieldwork, Federal Work-Study, scholarships/grants, tuition waivers (full and partial), and unspecified assistantships also available. Support available to part-time students. Financial award application deadline: 3/1; financial award applicants required to submit FAFSA. *Unit head:* Dr. Mark Jones, Chair, 503-725-3206, Fax: 503-725-3211, E-mail: mpj@pdx.edu. *Application contact:* Krys Sarreal, Department Manager, 503-725-4255, Fax: 503-725-3211, E-mail: sarreal@pdx.edu.
Website: http://www.pdx.edu/computer-science/

Prairie View A&M University, College of Engineering, Prairie View, TX 77446. Offers computer information systems (MSCIS); computer science (MSCS); electrical engineering (MSEE, PhDEE); general engineering (MS Engr). *Program availability:* Part-time, evening/weekend. *Faculty:* 30 full-time (8 women), 1 part-time/adjunct (0 women). *Students:* 121 full-time (38 women), 55 part-time (14 women); includes 82 minority (61 Black or African American, non-Hispanic/Latino; 14 Asian, non-Hispanic/Latino; 7 Hispanic/Latino), 77 international. Average age 32. 139 applicants, 84% accepted, 40 enrolled. In 2019, 78 master's, 2 doctorates awarded. *Degree requirements:* For master's, thesis optional; for doctorate, comprehensive exam, thesis/dissertation. *Entrance requirements:* For master's, GRE General Test (minimum score of 900), bachelor's degree in engineering from ABET-accredited institution; for doctorate, minimum GPA of 3.0. Additional exam requirements/recommendations for international students: required—TOEFL (minimum score 550 paper-based; 79 iBT). *Application deadline:* For fall admission, 5/1 priority date for domestic and international students; for spring admission, 10/1 priority date for domestic students, 9/1 priority date for international students; for summer admission, 3/1 priority date for domestic students, 2/1 priority date for international students. Applications are processed on a rolling basis. Application fee: $50. Electronic applications accepted. *Expenses: Tuition, area resident:* Full-time $5479.68. Tuition, state resident: full-time $5479.68. Tuition, nonresident: full-time $15,439. *International tuition:* $15,438.74 full-time. *Required fees:* $2149.32. *Financial support:* In 2019–20, 64 students received support, including 64 research assistantships (averaging $14,400 per year), 8 teaching assistantships (averaging $14,400 per year); career-related internships or fieldwork, institutionally sponsored loans, scholarships/grants, health care benefits, tuition waivers (full), and unspecified assistantships also available. Financial award application deadline: 4/1; financial award applicants required to submit FAFSA. *Unit head:* Dr. Pamela H Obiomon, Dean, 936-261-9890, Fax: 936-261-9868, E-mail: phobiomon@pvamu.edu. *Application contact:* Pauline Walker, Administrative Assistant II, Research and Graduate Studies, 936-261-3521, Fax: 936-261-3529, E-mail: gradadmissions@pvamu.edu.

Princeton University, Graduate School, School of Engineering and Applied Science, Department of Computer Science, Princeton, NJ 08544-1019. Offers MSE, PhD. Terminal master's awarded for partial completion of doctoral program. *Degree requirements:* For master's, thesis; for doctorate, thesis/dissertation, general exam. *Entrance requirements:* For master's, GRE General Test, GRE Subject Test (recommended), 3 letters of recommendation; for doctorate, GRE General Test, GRE Subject Test (recommended), official transcript(s), 3 letters of recommendation, personal statement. Additional exam requirements/recommendations for international students: required—TOEFL. Electronic applications accepted.

Purdue University, Graduate School, College of Science, Department of Computer Sciences, West Lafayette, IN 47907. Offers MS, PhD. *Program availability:* Part-time. *Faculty:* 55 full-time (8 women), 5 part-time/adjunct (3 women). *Students:* 220 full-time (38 women), 132 part-time (32 women); includes 29 minority (4 Black or African American, non-Hispanic/Latino; 17 Asian, non-Hispanic/Latino; 7 Hispanic/Latino; 1 Two or more races, non-Hispanic/Latino), 272 international. Average age 27. 1,997 applicants, 14% accepted, 92 enrolled. In 2019, 63 master's, 26 doctorates awarded. Terminal master's awarded for partial completion of doctoral program. *Degree requirements:* For master's, thesis optional; for doctorate, comprehensive exam, thesis/dissertation. *Entrance requirements:* For master's and doctorate, minimum GPA of 3.5. Additional exam requirements/recommendations for international students: required—TOEFL (minimum score 600 paper-based; 95 iBT), TWE (minimum score 5). *Application deadline:* For fall admission, 12/15 for domestic and international students; for spring admission, 10/1 for domestic and international students. Application fee: $60 ($75 for international students). Electronic applications accepted. *Financial support:* Fellowships with partial tuition reimbursements, research assistantships with partial tuition reimbursements, teaching assistantships with partial tuition reimbursements, health care benefits, and unspecified assistantships available. Financial award application deadline: 12/15. *Unit head:* Prof. Susan Hambrusch Hambrusch, Head, 765-494-6003, E-mail: seh@cs.purdue.edu. *Application contact:* Shelley Straley, Graduate Contact, 765-494-6004, E-mail: sstrale@purdue.edu.
Website: http://www.cs.purdue.edu/

Purdue University Fort Wayne, College of Engineering, Technology, and Computer Science, Department of Computer Science, Fort Wayne, IN 46805-1499. Offers applied computer science (MS). *Program availability:* Part-time. *Entrance requirements:* For master's, GRE General Test, minimum GPA of 3.0. Additional exam requirements/recommendations for international students: required—TOEFL (minimum score 550 paper-based; 79 iBT); recommended—TWE. Electronic applications accepted.

Purdue University Northwest, Graduate Studies Office, School of Engineering, Mathematics, and Science, Department of Mathematics, Computer Science, and Statistics, Hammond, IN 46323-2094. Offers computer science (MS); mathematics (MAT, MS). *Program availability:* Part-time. *Entrance requirements:* Additional exam requirements/recommendations for international students: required—TOEFL.

Queens College of the City University of New York, Mathematics and Natural Sciences Division, Department of Computer Science, Queens, NY 11367-1597. Offers MA. *Program availability:* Part-time, evening/weekend. *Degree requirements:* For master's, thesis optional. *Entrance requirements:* For master's, minimum GPA of 3.0. Additional exam requirements/recommendations for international students: required—TOEFL (minimum score 61 iBT), IELTS (minimum score 5). Electronic applications accepted.

Queen's University at Kingston, School of Graduate Studies, Faculty of Arts and Science, School of Computing, Kingston, ON K7L 3N6, Canada. Offers M Sc, PhD. *Degree requirements:* For master's, thesis; for doctorate, comprehensive exam, thesis/dissertation. *Entrance requirements:* For master's, honours B Sc in computer science; for doctorate, M Sc in computer science. Additional exam requirements/recommendations for international students: required—TOEFL, TWE.

Regis University, College of Computer and Information Sciences, Denver, CO 80221-1099. Offers agile technologies (Certificate); cybersecurity (Certificate); data science (M Sc); database administration with Oracle (Certificate); database development (Certificate); database technologies (M Sc); enterprise Java software development (Certificate); enterprise resource planning (Certificate); executive information technology (Certificate); health care informatics (Certificate); health care informatics and information management (M Sc); information assurance (M Sc); information assurance policy management (Certificate); information technology management (M Sc); mobile software development (Certificate); software engineering (M Sc, Certificate); software engineering and database technology (M Sc); storage area networks (Certificate); systems engineering (M Sc, Certificate). *Program availability:* Part-time, evening/weekend, 100% online, blended/hybrid learning. *Degree requirements:* For master's, thesis (for some programs), final research project. *Entrance requirements:* For master's, official transcript reflecting baccalaureate degree awarded from regionally-accredited college or university, 2 years of related experience, resume, interview. Additional exam requirements/recommendations for international students: required—TOEFL (minimum score 550 paper-based; 82 iBT). Electronic applications accepted. *Expenses:* Contact institution.

Rensselaer at Hartford, Department of Computer and Information Science, Hartford, CT 06120-2991. Offers computer science (MS); information technology (MS). *Program availability:* Part-time, evening/weekend. *Degree requirements:* For master's, thesis optional. *Entrance requirements:* For master's, GRE. Additional exam requirements/recommendations for international students: required—TOEFL (minimum score 600 paper-based; 100 iBT). Electronic applications accepted.

Rensselaer Polytechnic Institute, Graduate School, School of Science, Program in Computer Science, Troy, NY 12180-3590. Offers MS, PhD. *Program availability:* Part-time. *Faculty:* 32 full-time (8 women), 1 (woman) part-time/adjunct. *Students:* 87 full-time (20 women), 1 part-time (0 women); includes 19 minority (3 Black or African American, non-Hispanic/Latino; 10 Asian, non-Hispanic/Latino; 3 Hispanic/Latino; 3 Two or more races, non-Hispanic/Latino), 40 international. Average age 26. 263 applicants, 22% accepted, 24 enrolled. In 2019, 22 master's, 14 doctorates awarded. Terminal master's awarded for partial completion of doctoral program. *Degree requirements:* For master's, thesis; for doctorate, comprehensive exam, thesis/dissertation. *Entrance requirements:* For master's and doctorate, GRE. Additional exam requirements/recommendations for international students: required—TOEFL (minimum score 570 paper-based; 88 iBT), IELTS (minimum score 6.5), PTE (minimum score 60). *Application deadline:* For fall admission, 1/1 priority date for domestic and international students; for spring admission, 8/15 priority date for domestic and international students. Applications are processed on a rolling basis. Application fee: $75. Electronic applications accepted. *Financial support:* In 2019–20, research assistantships (averaging $23,000 per year), teaching assistantships (averaging $23,000 per year) were awarded; fellowships also available. Financial award application deadline: 1/1. *Unit head:* Dr. Mohammed Zaki, Graduate Program Director, 518-276-6340, E-mail: sibel@cs.rpi.edu. *Application contact:* Jarron Decker, Director of Graduate Admissions, 518-276-6216, Fax: 518-276-4072, E-mail: gradadmissions@rpi.edu.
Website: https://science.rpi.edu/computer-science

Rice University, Graduate Programs, George R. Brown School of Engineering, Department of Computer Science, Houston, TX 77251-1892. Offers MCS, MS, PhD. Terminal master's awarded for partial completion of doctoral program. *Degree requirements:* For master's, comprehensive exam; for doctorate, comprehensive exam, thesis/dissertation. *Entrance requirements:* For master's and doctorate, bachelor's degree. Additional exam requirements/recommendations for international students: required—TOEFL. Electronic applications accepted.

Rivier University, School of Graduate Studies, Department of Computer Science and Mathematics, Nashua, NH 03060. Offers computer science (MS); mathematics (MAT). *Program availability:* Part-time, evening/weekend. *Entrance requirements:* For master's, GRE Subject Test. Electronic applications accepted.

Rochester Institute of Technology, Graduate Enrollment Services, Golisano College of Computing and Information Sciences, Computer Science Department, MS Program in Computer Science, Rochester, NY 14623-5603. Offers MS. *Program availability:* Part-time. *Degree requirements:* For master's, thesis or alternative, Thesis or Project. *Entrance requirements:* For master's, GRE scores are required for students with degrees from international universities, recommended for all other applicants, minimum GPA of 3.0, personal statement, two letters of recommendation. Additional exam requirements/recommendations for international students: required—TOEFL (minimum score 570 paper-based; 88 iBT), IELTS (minimum score 6.5), PTE (minimum score 61). Electronic applications accepted.

Rochester Institute of Technology, Graduate Enrollment Services, Golisano College of Computing and Information Sciences, Computing and Information Sciences Department, PhD Program in Computing and Information Sciences, Rochester, NY 14623-5603. Offers PhD. *Program availability:* Part-time. *Degree requirements:* For doctorate, comprehensive exam, thesis/dissertation. *Entrance requirements:* For doctorate, GRE, minimum GPA of 3.0, statement of purpose, resume, two letters of recommendation, professional or research paper sample(s) (if available). Additional exam requirements/recommendations for international students: required—TOEFL (minimum score 570 paper-based; 88 iBT), IELTS (minimum score 6.5), PTE (minimum score 61). Electronic applications accepted. *Expenses:* Contact institution.

Rochester Institute of Technology, Graduate Enrollment Services, Golisano College of Computing and Information Sciences, Information Science and Technologies Department, MS Program in Networking and Systems Administration, Rochester, NY 14623-5603. Offers MS. *Program availability:* Part-time, 100% online. *Degree requirements:* For master's, thesis or alternative, Thesis or Project. *Entrance requirements:* For master's, GRE required for individuals with degrees from international universities. The GRE is recommended for students whose GPA is below 3.0., minimum GPA of 3.0, two letters of recommendation. Additional exam requirements/recommendations for international students: required—TOEFL (minimum score 570 paper-based; 88 iBT), IELTS (minimum score 6.5), PTE (minimum score 61). Electronic applications accepted. *Expenses:* Contact institution.

Roosevelt University, Graduate Division, College of Arts and Sciences, Department of Computer Science and Data Science, Chicago, IL 60605. Offers computer science (MS). *Program availability:* Part-time, evening/weekend. Electronic applications accepted.

Rowan University, Graduate School, College of Science and Mathematics, Program in Computer Science, Glassboro, NJ 08028-1701. Offers MS. *Degree requirements:* For master's, thesis optional. *Entrance requirements:* For master's, bachelor's degree (or its equivalent) in related field from accredited institution; official transcripts from all colleges attended; current professional resume; two letters of recommendation; statement of professional objectives; minimum undergraduate cumulative GPA of 3.0. Electronic applications accepted. *Expenses: Tuition, area resident:* Part-time $715.50 per semester hour. Tuition, state resident: part-time $715.50 per semester hour. Tuition, nonresident: part-time $715.50 per semester hour. *Required fees:* $161.55 per semester hour.

Royal Military College of Canada, Division of Graduate Studies, Faculty of Science, Department of Mathematics and Computer Science, Kingston, ON K7K 7B4, Canada. Offers computer science (M Sc); mathematics (M Sc). *Degree requirements:* For master's, thesis. *Entrance requirements:* For master's, honours degree with second-class standing. Electronic applications accepted.

Rutgers University - Camden, Graduate School of Arts and Sciences, Program in Computer Science, Camden, NJ 08102. Offers MS. *Program availability:* Part-time, evening/weekend. *Degree requirements:* For master's, comprehensive exam, thesis (for some programs), 30 credits. *Entrance requirements:* For master's, GRE, 3 letters of recommendation; statement of personal, professional, and academic goals; computer science undergraduate degree (preferred). Additional exam requirements/recommendations for international students: required—TOEFL, IELTS. Electronic applications accepted.

Rutgers University - New Brunswick, Graduate School-New Brunswick, Program in Computer Science, Piscataway, NJ 08854-8097. Offers MS, PhD. *Program availability:* Part-time. Terminal master's awarded for partial completion of doctoral program. *Degree requirements:* For master's, comprehensive exam, thesis; for doctorate, comprehensive exam, thesis/dissertation. *Entrance requirements:* For master's and doctorate, GRE General Test, GRE Subject Test. Additional exam requirements/recommendations for international students: required—TOEFL.

Sacred Heart University, Graduate Programs, College of Arts and Sciences, Department of Computing, Fairfield, CT 06825. Offers computer science (MS); computer science gaming (MS); cybersecurity (MS); information technology (MS). *Program availability:* Part-time, evening/weekend. *Degree requirements:* For master's, thesis or alternative. *Entrance requirements:* For master's, bachelor's degree, minimum GPA of 3.0. Additional exam requirements/recommendations for international students: required—TOEFL (minimum score 570 paper-based, 80 iBT), TWE, or IELTS (6.5). Electronic applications accepted. *Expenses:* Contact institution.

Saginaw Valley State University, College of Science, Engineering, and Technology, University Center, MI 48710. Offers computer science and information systems (MS); energy and materials (MS). *Program availability:* Part-time, evening/weekend. *Faculty:* 6 full-time (1 woman), 1 part-time/adjunct (0 women). *Students:* 7 full-time (2 women), 11 part-time (1 woman); includes 2 minority (both Asian, non-Hispanic/Latino), 4 international. Average age 32. 29 applicants, 62% accepted, 4 enrolled. In 2019, 4 master's awarded. *Degree requirements:* For master's, field project or thesis work. *Entrance requirements:* For master's, minimum GPA of 3.0. Additional exam requirements/recommendations for international students: required—TOEFL (minimum score 550 paper-based; 79 iBT). *Application deadline:* For fall admission, 7/15 for international students; for winter admission, 11/15 for international students; for spring admission, 4/15 for international students. Applications are processed on a rolling basis. Application fee: $30 ($90 for international students). Electronic applications accepted. *Expenses: Tuition, area resident:* Full-time $11,212; part-time $622.90 per credit hour. *Tuition, state resident:* full-time $11,212; part-time $622.90 per credit hour. *Tuition, nonresident:* full-time $11,212; part-time $1253 per credit hour. *Required fees:* $263; $14.60 per credit hour. Tuition and fees vary according to course load, degree level and program. *Financial support:* Federal Work-Study and scholarships/grants available. Support available to part-time students. Financial award application deadline: 4/1; financial award applicants required to submit FAFSA. *Unit head:* Dr. Robert Tuttle, Program Coordinator, 989-964-4144, Fax: 989-964-2717. *Application contact:* Jenna Briggs, Director, Graduate and International Admissions, 989-964-6096, Fax: 989-964-2788, E-mail: gradadm@svsu.edu.
Website: http://www.svsu.edu/collegeofscienceengineeringtechnology/

St. Cloud State University, School of Graduate Studies, College of Science and Engineering, Department of Computer Science and Information Technology, St. Cloud, MN 56301-4498. Offers computer science (MS); instructional technology (Graduate Certificate). *Degree requirements:* For master's, thesis or alternative. *Entrance requirements:* For master's, GRE General Test, minimum GPA of 2.75. Additional exam requirements/recommendations for international students: required—Michigan English Language Assessment Battery; recommended—TOEFL (minimum score 550 paper-based), IELTS (minimum score 6.5). Electronic applications accepted.

St. Francis Xavier University, Graduate Studies, Department of Mathematics, Statistics and Computer Science, Antigonish, NS B2G 2W5, Canada. Offers computer science (M Sc). *Degree requirements:* For master's, thesis. *Entrance requirements:* For master's, bachelor's degree or equivalent in computer science with minimum B average, 2 letters of recommendation. Additional exam requirements/recommendations for international students: required—TOEFL (minimum score 580 paper-based). *Expenses: Tuition, area resident:* Part-time $1731 Canadian dollars per course. *Tuition, state resident:* part-time $1731 Canadian dollars per course. *Tuition, nonresident:* part-time $1988 Canadian dollars per course. *International tuition:* $3976 Canadian dollars full-time. *Required fees:* $185 Canadian dollars per course. Tuition and fees vary according to course level, course load, degree level and program.

Saint Joseph's University, College of Arts and Sciences, Department of Computer Science, Philadelphia, PA 19131-1395. Offers computer science (MS); mathematics and computer science (Post-Master's Certificate). *Program availability:* Part-time, evening/weekend. *Entrance requirements:* For master's, 2 letters of recommendation, resume, personal statement, official transcripts. Additional exam requirements/recommendations for international students: required—TOEFL (minimum score 550 paper-based; 80 iBT), IELTS (minimum score 6.5). Electronic applications accepted. *Expenses:* Contact institution.

Saint Louis University, Graduate Programs, College of Arts and Sciences, Department of Computer Science, St. Louis, MO 63103. Offers bioinformatics and computational biology (MS); computer science (MS); software engineering (MS).

St. Mary's University, School of Science, Engineering and Technology, Program in Computer Information Systems, San Antonio, TX 78228. Offers MS. *Program availability:* Part-time, evening/weekend. *Degree requirements:* For master's, comprehensive exam, thesis optional. *Entrance requirements:* For master's, GMAT (minimum score of 334) or GRE General Test (minimum quantitative score of 148, analytical writing 2.5), minimum GPA of 3.0 in a bachelor's degree, written statement of purpose indicating interest and objective, two letters of recommendation, official transcripts of all college-level work. Additional exam requirements/recommendations for international students: required—TOEFL (minimum score 530 paper-based; 80 iBT), IELTS (minimum score 6). Electronic applications accepted.

St. Mary's University, School of Science, Engineering and Technology, Program in Computer Science, San Antonio, TX 78228. Offers MS. *Program availability:* Part-time, evening/weekend. *Degree requirements:* For master's, thesis or project. *Entrance requirements:* For master's, GRE (minimum quantitative score 148, analytical writing 2.5), GMAT (minimum score 334), written statement of purpose indicating interest and objective, two letters of recommendation, official transcripts of all college-level work, minimum GPA of 3.0 in a bachelor's degree. Additional exam requirements/recommendations for international students: required—TOEFL (minimum score 550 paper-based; 80 iBT), IELTS (minimum score 6). Electronic applications accepted.

Saint Xavier University, Graduate Studies, College of Arts and Sciences, Department of Computer Science, Chicago, IL 60655-3105. Offers MACS. *Degree requirements:* For master's, thesis optional.

Sam Houston State University, College of Sciences, Department of Computer Science, Huntsville, TX 77341. Offers computing and information science (MS); digital

forensics (MS); information assurance and security (MS). *Program availability:* Part-time. *Degree requirements:* For master's, comprehensive exam, thesis optional, internship; for doctorate, comprehensive exam, thesis/dissertation. *Entrance requirements:* For master's, GRE General Test, letters of recommendation. Additional exam requirements/recommendations for international students: required—TOEFL (minimum score 550 paper-based; 79 iBT), IELTS (minimum score 6.5). Electronic applications accepted.

San Diego State University, Graduate and Research Affairs, College of Sciences, Program in Computer Science, San Diego, CA 92182. Offers MS. *Program availability:* Part-time. *Degree requirements:* For master's, comprehensive exam or thesis. *Entrance requirements:* For master's, GRE General Test. Additional exam requirements/recommendations for international students: required—TOEFL. Electronic applications accepted.

San Francisco State University, Division of Graduate Studies, College of Science and Engineering, Department of Computer Science, San Francisco, CA 94132-1722. Offers MS. *Program availability:* Part-time. *Application deadline:* Applications are processed on a rolling basis. *Expenses: Tuition, area resident:* Full-time $7176; part-time $4164 per year. *Tuition, state resident:* full-time $7176; part-time $4164 per year. *Tuition, nonresident:* full-time $16,680; part-time $396 per unit. *International tuition:* $16,680 full-time. *Required fees:* $1524; $1524 per unit. $762 per semester. Tuition and fees vary according to degree level and program. *Unit head:* Dr. Arno Puder, Chair, 415-338-7688, Fax: 415-338-6826, E-mail: arno@sfsu.edu. *Application contact:* Prof. Hui Yang, Graduate Coordinator, 415-338-2221, Fax: 415-338-6826, E-mail: huiyang@sfsu.edu.
Website: https://cs.sfsu.edu/graduate-program/new-students

San Francisco State University, Division of Graduate Studies, College of Science and Engineering, School of Engineering, San Francisco, CA 94132-1722. Offers embedded electrical and computer systems (MS); energy systems (MS); structural/earthquake engineering (MS). *Program availability:* Part-time. *Application deadline:* Applications are processed on a rolling basis. Electronic applications accepted. *Expenses: Tuition, area resident:* Full-time $7176; part-time $4164 per year. *Tuition, state resident:* full-time $7176; part-time $4164 per year. *Tuition, nonresident:* full-time $16,680; part-time $396 per unit. *International tuition:* $16,680 full-time. *Required fees:* $1524; $1524 per unit. $762 per semester. Tuition and fees vary according to degree level and program. *Unit head:* Dr. Kwok-Siong Teh, Director, 415-338-1228, Fax: 415-338-0525, E-mail: ksteh@sfsu.edu. *Application contact:* Dr. Hamid Shahnasser, Graduate Coordinator, 415-338-2124, Fax: 415-338-0525, E-mail: hamid@sfsu.edu.
Website: http://engineering.sfsu.edu/

Santa Clara University, School of Engineering, Santa Clara, CA 95053. Offers applied mathematics (MS); bioengineering (MS); civil, environmental, and sustainable engineering (MS); computer science and engineering (MS, PhD, Engineer); electrical engineering (MS, PhD, Engineer); engineering management and leadership (MS); mechanical engineering (MS, PhD, Engineer); power systems and sustainable energy (MS); software engineering (MS). *Program availability:* Part-time. *Entrance requirements:* For master's, GRE, official transcript; for doctorate, GRE, Official transcript, 500 word statement of purpose, three letters of recommendation. Additional exam requirements/recommendations for international students: required—TOEFL (minimum score 79 iBT), IELTS (minimum score 6.5). Electronic applications accepted.

Seattle University, College of Science and Engineering, Program in Computer Science, Seattle, WA 98122-1090. Offers MSCS. *Faculty:* 17 full-time (5 women), 2 part-time/adjunct (0 women). *Students:* 81 full-time (35 women), 75 part-time (22 women); includes 31 minority (16 Asian, non-Hispanic/Latino; 10 Hispanic/Latino; 5 Two or more races, non-Hispanic/Latino), 67 international. Average age 28. 125 applicants, 56% accepted, 52 enrolled. In 2019, 7 master's awarded. *Entrance requirements:* For master's, GRE, bachelor's degree in computer science or related discipline from regionally-accredited institution; minimum GPA of 3.0; letter of intent; 2 academic or professional recommendations; official transcripts. Additional exam requirements/recommendations for international students: required—TOEFL (minimum score 580 paper-based; 92 iBT). *Application deadline:* For fall admission, 7/20 for domestic students, 4/1 for international students; for winter admission, 11/20 for domestic students, 9/1 for international students; for spring admission, 2/20 for domestic students, 12/1 for international students. *Financial support:* In 2019–20, 15 students received support. *Unit head:* Dr. Richard LeBlanc, Chair, 206-296-5510, Fax: 206-296-2071, E-mail: leblanc@seattleu.edu. *Application contact:* Janet Shandley, Director of Graduate Admissions, 206-296-5900, Fax: 206-298-5656, E-mail: grad_admissions@seattleu.edu.
Website: https://www.seattleu.edu/scieng/computer-science/graduate/mscs/

Shippensburg University of Pennsylvania, School of Graduate Studies, College of Arts and Sciences, Department of Computer Science and Engineering, Shippensburg, PA 17257-2299. Offers agile software engineering (Certificate); computer science (MS); IT leadership (Certificate). *Program availability:* Part-time, evening/weekend. *Faculty:* 4 full-time (2 women). *Students:* 8 full-time (3 women), 5 part-time (2 women); includes 4 minority (2 Black or African American, non-Hispanic/Latino; 2 Asian, non-Hispanic/Latino), 5 international. Average age 28. 39 applicants, 44% accepted, 6 enrolled. In 2019, 5 master's awarded. *Entrance requirements:* For master's, GRE (if GPA less than 2.75), professional resume. Additional exam requirements/recommendations for international students: required—TOEFL (minimum score 70 iBT), IELTS (minimum score 6), TOEFL (minimum score 70 iBT) or IELTS (minimum score 6). *Application deadline:* For fall admission, 4/30 for international students. Applications are processed on a rolling basis. Application fee: $45. Electronic applications accepted. *Expenses:* Tuition, state resident: part-time $516 per credit. Tuition, nonresident: part-time $774 per credit. *Required fees:* $149 per credit. *Financial support:* In 2019–20, 8 students received support. Career-related internships or fieldwork, scholarships/grants, unspecified assistantships, and resident hall director and student payroll positions available. Support available to part-time students. Financial award application deadline: 3/1; financial award applicants required to submit FAFSA. *Unit head:* Dr. Jeonghwa Lee, Professor and Director of Graduate Studies, 717-477-1178, Fax: 717-477-4002, E-mail: jlee@ship.edu. *Application contact:* Maya T. Mapp, Director of Admissions, 717-477-1231, Fax: 717-477-4016, E-mail: mtmapp@ship.edu.
Website: http://www.ship.edu/engineering/cs

Simon Fraser University, Office of Graduate Studies and Postdoctoral Fellows, Faculty of Applied Sciences, School of Computing Science, Burnaby, BC V5A 1S6, Canada. Offers M Sc, PhD, M Sc/MSE. *Degree requirements:* For master's, comprehensive exam, thesis or alternative; for doctorate, comprehensive exam, thesis/dissertation, qualifying exams. *Entrance requirements:* For master's, minimum GPA of 3.0 (on scale of 4.33) or 3.33 based on last 60 credits of undergraduate courses; for doctorate, minimum GPA of 3.5 (on scale of 4.33). Additional exam requirements/recommendations for international students: recommended—TOEFL (minimum score 580 paper-based; 93 iBT), IELTS (minimum score 7), TWE (minimum score 5). Electronic applications accepted.

Simon Fraser University, Office of Graduate Studies and Postdoctoral Fellows, Faculty of Communication, Art and Technology, School of Interactive Arts and Technology, Surrey, BC V3T 2W1, Canada. Offers M Sc, MA, PhD. *Degree requirements:* For master's, thesis, seminar presentation; for doctorate, comprehensive exam, thesis/dissertation, seminar presentations. *Entrance requirements:* For master's, minimum GPA of 3.0 (on scale of 4.33) or 3.33 based on last 60 credits of undergraduate courses; for doctorate, minimum GPA of 3.5 (on scale of 4.33). Additional exam requirements/recommendations for international students: required—TOEFL (minimum score 580 paper-based; 93 iBT), IELTS (minimum score 7), TWE (minimum score 5). Electronic applications accepted.

Sofia University, Residential Programs, Palo Alto, CA 94303. Offers clinical psychology (Psy D); computer science (MS); counseling psychology (MA); transpersonal psychology (MA, PhD). *Program availability:* Part-time, evening/weekend. Terminal master's awarded for partial completion of doctoral program. *Degree requirements:* For doctorate, thesis/dissertation. *Entrance requirements:* For master's, bachelor's degree; for doctorate, bachelor's degree; master's degree (for some programs). Electronic applications accepted.

Southern Adventist University, School of Computing, Collegedale, TN 37315-0370. Offers computer science (MS). *Program availability:* Part-time. *Degree requirements:* For master's, professional software development portfolio. *Entrance requirements:* For master's, minimum GPA of 3.0. Additional exam requirements/recommendations for international students: required—TOEFL (minimum score 80 iBT). Electronic applications accepted.

Southern Arkansas University–Magnolia, School of Graduate Studies, Magnolia, AR 71753. Offers agriculture (MS); business administration (MBA), including agribusiness, social entrepreneurship, supply chain management; clinical and mental health counseling (MS); computer and information sciences (MS), including cyber security and privacy, data science, information technology; gifted and talented (M Ed), including curriculum and instruction, educational administration and supervision, gifted and talented P-8/7-12, instructional specialist P-4; higher, adult and lifelong education (M Ed); kinesiology (M Ed), including coaching; library media and information specialist (M Ed); public administration (MPA); school counseling K-12 (M Ed); student affairs and college counseling (M Ed); teaching (MAT). *Accreditation:* NCATE. *Program availability:* Part-time, 100% online, blended/hybrid learning. *Faculty:* 33 full-time (18 women), 29 part-time/adjunct (17 women). *Students:* 134 full-time (80 women), 704 part-time (471 women); includes 223 minority (158 Black or African American, non-Hispanic/Latino; 5 American Indian or Alaska Native, non-Hispanic/Latino; 19 Asian, non-Hispanic/Latino; 6 Hispanic/Latino; 1 Native Hawaiian or other Pacific Islander, non-Hispanic/Latino; 34 Two or more races, non-Hispanic/Latino), 135 international. Average age 28. 290 applicants, 99% accepted, 149 enrolled. In 2019, 177 master's awarded. *Degree requirements:* For master's, comprehensive exam (for some programs), thesis optional. *Entrance requirements:* For master's, GRE, MAT or GMAT, minimum GPA of 2.5. Additional exam requirements/recommendations for international students: required—TOEFL (minimum score 550 paper-based), IELTS (minimum score 6). *Application deadline:* For fall admission, 8/1 for domestic and international students; for spring admission, 12/1 for domestic students, 11/15 for international students; for summer admission, 5/1 for domestic students, 5/10 for international students. Applications are processed on a rolling basis. Application fee: $25 ($90 for international students). Electronic applications accepted. *Expenses: Tuition, area resident:* Full-time $6720; part-time $3360 per semester. Tuition, state resident: full-time $6720; part-time $3360 per semester. Tuition, nonresident: full-time $10,560; part-time $5280 per semester. *International tuition:* $10,560 full-time. *Required fees:* $2046; $1023 $267. One-time fee: $25. Tuition and fees vary according to course load. *Financial support:* Career-related internships or fieldwork, Federal Work-Study, scholarships/grants, tuition waivers (full), and unspecified assistantships available. Financial award applicants required to submit FAFSA. *Unit head:* Dr. Kim Bloss, Dean, School of Graduate Studies, 870-235-4150, Fax: 870-235-5227, E-mail: kkbloss@saumag.edu. *Application contact:* Talia Jett, Admissions Coordinator, 870-2355450, Fax: 870-235-5227, E-mail: taliajett@saumag.edu.
Website: http://www.saumag.edu/graduate

Southern Connecticut State University, School of Graduate Studies, School of Arts and Sciences, Department of Computer Science, New Haven, CT 06515-1355. Offers MS. *Program availability:* Part-time, evening/weekend. *Entrance requirements:* For master's, GRE. Electronic applications accepted.

Southern Illinois University Carbondale, Graduate School, College of Science, Department of Computer Science, Carbondale, IL 62901-4701. Offers MS, PhD. *Degree requirements:* For master's, thesis; for doctorate, thesis/dissertation. *Entrance requirements:* For master's, previous undergraduate course work in computer science, minimum GPA of 2.7; for doctorate, GRE General Test, minimum GPA of 3.25. Additional exam requirements/recommendations for international students: required—TOEFL.

Southern Illinois University Edwardsville, Graduate School, School of Engineering, Department of Computer Science, Edwardsville, IL 62026. Offers MS. *Program availability:* Part-time, evening/weekend. *Degree requirements:* For master's, thesis (for some programs), final exam, final project. *Entrance requirements:* Additional exam requirements/recommendations for international students: required—TOEFL (minimum score 550 paper-based; 79 iBT), IELTS (minimum score 6.5). Electronic applications accepted.

Southern Methodist University, Lyle School of Engineering, Department of Computer Science and Engineering, Dallas, TX 75275-0122. Offers computer engineering (MS, PhD); computer science (MS, PhD); security engineering (MS); software engineering (MS, DE). *Program availability:* Part-time, evening/weekend, online learning. Terminal master's awarded for partial completion of doctoral program. *Degree requirements:* For master's, thesis optional; for doctorate, thesis/dissertation, oral and written qualifying exams, oral final exam (PhD). *Entrance requirements:* For master's, GRE General Test, minimum GPA of 3.0 in last 2 years; bachelor's degree in engineering, mathematics, or sciences; for doctorate, preliminary counseling exam (PhD), minimum GPA of 3.0, bachelor's degree in related field, MA (for DE). Additional exam requirements/recommendations for international students: required—TOEFL (minimum score 550 paper-based).

Southern Oregon University, Graduate Studies, Department of Computer Science, Ashland, OR 97520. Offers applied computer science (PSM). *Program availability:* Part-time, online learning. *Degree requirements:* For master's, thesis (for some programs). *Entrance requirements:* For master's, GRE General Test, minimum cumulative GPA of 3.0 in the last 90 quarter credits (60 semester credits) of undergraduate coursework. Additional exam requirements/recommendations for international students: required—TOEFL (minimum score 540 paper-based; 76 iBT), IELTS (minimum score 6), ELPT (minimum score 964) or ELS (minimum score 112). Electronic applications accepted.

Southern University and Agricultural and Mechanical College, Graduate School, College of Sciences and Engineering, Department of Computer Science, Baton Rouge, LA 70813. Offers information systems (MS); micro/minicomputer architecture (MS); operating systems (MS). *Program availability:* Part-time, online learning. *Degree requirements:* For master's, thesis. *Entrance requirements:* For master's, GRE General Test, minimum GPA of 3.0, bachelor's degree in computer science or related field. Additional exam requirements/recommendations for international students: required—TOEFL (minimum score 525 paper-based).

Stanford University, School of Engineering, Department of Computer Science, Stanford, CA 94305-2004. Offers MS, PhD. *Expenses: Tuition:* Full-time $52,479; part-time $34,110 per unit. *Required fees:* $672; $224 per quarter. Tuition and fees vary according to program and student level.
Website: http://www.cs.stanford.edu/

Stanford University, School of Engineering, Institute for Computational and Mathematical Engineering, Stanford, CA 94305-2004. Offers MS, PhD. *Expenses: Tuition:* Full-time $52,479; part-time $34,110 per unit. *Required fees:* $672; $224 per quarter. Tuition and fees vary according to program and student level.
Website: http://icme.stanford.edu/

State University of New York Polytechnic Institute, Program in Computer and Information Science, Utica, NY 13502. Offers MS. *Program availability:* Part-time. *Degree requirements:* For master's, thesis, thesis or project. *Entrance requirements:* For master's, GRE or approved GRE waiver, undergraduate prerequisite courses in math and computer science. Additional exam requirements/recommendations for international students: required—TOEFL (minimum score 79 iBT), IELTS (minimum score 6.5), PTE (minimum score 53), Only ONE of above. Electronic applications accepted.

Stevens Institute of Technology, Graduate School, Charles V. Schaefer Jr. School of Engineering and Science, Department of Computer Science, Program in Computer Science, Hoboken, NJ 07030. Offers MS, PhD, Certificate. *Program availability:* Part-time, evening/weekend. *Faculty:* 25 full-time (5 women), 12 part-time/adjunct (3 women). *Students:* 480 full-time (108 women), 62 part-time (10 women); includes 36 minority (9 Black or African American, non-Hispanic/Latino; 1 American Indian or Alaska Native, non-Hispanic/Latino; 26 Asian, non-Hispanic/Latino), 450 international. Average age 25. In 2019, 235 master's, 4 doctorates awarded. Terminal master's awarded for partial completion of doctoral program. *Degree requirements:* For master's, thesis optional, minimum B average in major field and overall; for doctorate, comprehensive exam (for some programs), thesis/dissertation; for Certificate, minimum B average. *Entrance requirements:* For master's, International applicants must submit TOEFL/IELTS scores and fulfill the English Language Proficiency Requirement. Applicants to full-time programs who do not qualify for a score waiver are required to submit GRE/GMAT scores. Additional exam requirements/recommendations for international students: required—TOEFL (minimum score 74 iBT), IELTS (minimum score 6). *Application deadline:* For fall admission, 4/15 for domestic and international students; for spring admission, 11/1 for domestic and international students; for summer admission, 5/1 for domestic students. Applications are processed on a rolling basis. Application fee: $60. Electronic applications accepted. *Expenses: Tuition:* Full-time $52,134. *Required fees:* $1880. Tuition and fees vary according to course load. *Financial support:* Fellowships, research assistantships, teaching assistantships, career-related internships or fieldwork, Federal Work-Study, scholarships/grants, and unspecified assistantships available. Financial award application deadline: 2/15; financial award applicants required to submit FAFSA. *Unit head:* Dr. Jean Zu, Dean of SES, 201-216.8233, Fax: 201-216.8372, E-mail: Jean.Zu@stevens.edu. *Application contact:* Graduate Admissions, 888-783-8367, Fax: 888-511-1306, E-mail: graduate@stevens.edu.

Stevens Institute of Technology, Graduate School, School of Business, Program in Information Systems, Hoboken, NJ 07030. Offers computer science (MS); e-commerce (MS); enterprise systems (MS); entrepreneurial information technology (MS); information architecture (MS); information management (MS, Certificate); information security (MS); information technology in financial services industry (MS); information technology in the pharmaceutical industry (MS); information technology outsourcing management (MS); project management (MS, Certificate); software engineering (MS); telecommunications (MS). *Program availability:* Part-time, evening/weekend. *Faculty:* 59 full-time (11 women), 30 part-time/adjunct (5 women). *Students:* 221 full-time (80 women), 52 part-time (18 women); includes 24 minority (8 Black or African American, non-Hispanic/Latino; 16 Asian, non-Hispanic/Latino), 225 international. Average age 27. In 2019, 188 master's awarded. Terminal master's awarded for partial completion of doctoral program. *Degree requirements:* For master's, thesis optional, minimum B average in major field and overall; for Certificate, minimum B average. *Entrance requirements:* For master's, International applicants must submit TOEFL/IELTS scores and fulfill the English Language Proficiency Requirement. Applicants to full-time programs who do not qualify for a score waiver are required to submit GRE/GMAT scores. Additional exam requirements/recommendations for international students: required—TOEFL (minimum score 74 iBT), IELTS (minimum score 6). *Application deadline:* For fall admission, 4/1 for domestic and international students; for spring admission, 11/1 for domestic and international students; for summer admission, 5/1 for domestic students. Applications are processed on a rolling basis. Application fee: $60. Electronic applications accepted. *Expenses: Tuition:* Full-time $52,134. *Required fees:* $1880. Tuition and fees vary according to course load. *Financial support:* Fellowships, research assistantships, teaching assistantships, career-related internships or fieldwork, Federal Work-Study, scholarships/grants, and unspecified assistantships available. Financial award application deadline: 2/15; financial award applicants required to submit FAFSA. *Unit head:* Dr. Gregory Prastacos, Dean of SB, 201-216-8366, E-mail: gprastac@stevens.edu. *Application contact:* Graduate Admissions, 888-783-8367, Fax: 888-511-1306, E-mail: graduate@stevens.edu.
Website: https://www.stevens.edu/school-business/masters-programs/information-systems

Stony Brook University, State University of New York, Graduate School, College of Engineering and Applied Sciences, Department of Computer Science, Stony Brook, NY 11794. Offers MS, PhD, Certificate. *Faculty:* 47 full-time (4 women), 4 part-time/adjunct (1 woman). *Students:* 567 full-time (129 women), 169 part-time (46 women); includes 29 minority (22 Asian, non-Hispanic/Latino; 6 Hispanic/Latino; 1 Two or more races, non-Hispanic/Latino), 680 international. Average age 25. 2,246 applicants, 35% accepted, 323 enrolled. In 2019, 299 master's, 19 doctorates awarded. Terminal master's awarded for partial completion of doctoral program. *Degree requirements:* For master's, thesis or alternative; for doctorate, comprehensive exam, thesis/dissertation. *Entrance requirements:* For master's and doctorate, GRE General Test. Additional exam requirements/recommendations for international students: required—TOEFL (minimum score 90 iBT). *Application deadline:* For fall admission, 1/15 for domestic students; for spring admission, 10/1 for domestic students. Application fee: $100. *Expenses:* Contact institution. *Financial support:* In 2019–20, 7 fellowships, 94 research assistantships, 119 teaching assistantships were awarded. *Unit head:* Prof. Samir Das, Chair, 631-632-1807, E-mail: samir@cs.stonybrook.edu. *Application contact:* Cynthia Scalzo, Coordinator, 631-632-1521, E-mail: cscalzo@cs.stonybrook.edu.
Website: http://www.cs.sunysb.edu/

Stratford University, School of Graduate Studies, Falls Church, VA 22043. Offers accounting (MS); business administration (MBA, DBA); cyber security (MS); cyber security leadership and policy (MS); digital forensics (MS); healthcare administration (MS); information systems (MS); information technology (DIT); networking and telecommunications (MS); software engineering (MS). *Program availability:* Part-time, evening/weekend, 100% online, blended/hybrid learning. *Degree requirements:* For master's, comprehensive exam, capstone project. *Entrance requirements:* For master's, GRE or GMAT, baccalaureate degree. Additional exam requirements/recommendations for international students: required—TOEFL (minimum score 79 iBT), IELTS (minimum score 6.5), PTE (minimum score 5). Electronic applications accepted.

Syracuse University, College of Engineering and Computer Science, MS Program in Computer Science, Syracuse, NY 13244. Offers MS. *Program availability:* Part-time. *Degree requirements:* For master's, comprehensive exam (for some programs), thesis (for some programs). *Entrance requirements:* For master's, GRE General Test, three letters of recommendation, resume, personal statement, official transcripts. Additional exam requirements/recommendations for international students: required—TOEFL (minimum score 100 iBT). Electronic applications accepted.

Temple University, College of Science and Technology, Department of Computer and Information Sciences, Philadelphia, PA 19122-6096. Offers computational data science (MS); computer and information sciences (PhD), including artificial intelligence, computer and network systems, information systems, software systems; computer science (MS); cyber defense and information assurance (PSM); information science and technology (MS). *Program availability:* Part-time, evening/weekend, online learning. *Faculty:* 39 full-time (9 women), 8 part-time/adjunct (1 woman). *Students:* 97 full-time (28 women), 22 part-time (11 women); includes 14 minority (3 Black or African American, non-Hispanic/Latino; 8 Asian, non-Hispanic/Latino; 3 Hispanic/Latino), 83 international. 133 applicants, 56% accepted, 35 enrolled. In 2019, 15 master's, 7 doctorates awarded. *Degree requirements:* For doctorate, thesis/dissertation. *Entrance requirements:* For master's, GRE, 3 letters of recommendation, statement of goals; for doctorate, GRE, 3 letters of recommendation, bachelor's degree in related field, statement of goals, resume. Additional exam requirements/recommendations for international students: required—TOEFL (minimum score 85 iBT), IELTS (minimum score 6.5), PTE (minimum score 58), one of three is required. *Application deadline:* Applications are processed on a rolling basis. Application fee: $60. Electronic applications accepted. *Expenses:* Contact institution. *Financial support:* Research assistantships, teaching assistantships, health care benefits, and unspecified assistantships available. Financial award applicants required to submit FAFSA. *Unit head:* Jamie Payton, Department Chairperson, 215-204-8245, E-mail: Jamie.payton@temple.edu. *Application contact:* Eduard Dragut, Graduate Chair, 215-204-0521, E-mail: cisadmit@temple.edu.
Website: https://cis.temple.edu/

Tennessee Technological University, College of Graduate Studies, College of Engineering, Department of Computer Science, Cookeville, TN 38505. Offers MS, PhD. *Program availability:* Part-time. *Students:* 11 full-time (1 woman), 18 part-time (4 women); includes 2 minority (both Black or African American, non-Hispanic/Latino), 7 international. 41 applicants, 71% accepted, 8 enrolled. *Degree requirements:* For master's, thesis or alternative. *Entrance requirements:* For master's, GRE. Additional exam requirements/recommendations for international students: required—TOEFL (minimum score 550 paper-based; 79 iBT), IELTS (minimum score 5.5), PTE (minimum score 53), or TOEIC (Test of English as an International Communication). *Application deadline:* For fall admission, 8/1 for domestic students, 5/1 for international students; for spring admission, 12/1 for domestic students, 10/1 for international students; for summer admission, 5/1 for domestic students, 2/1 for international students. Applications are processed on a rolling basis. Application fee: $35 ($40 for international students). Electronic applications accepted. *Expenses: Tuition, area resident:* Part-time $597 per credit hour. Tuition, state resident: part-time $597 per credit hour. Tuition, nonresident: part-time $1323 per credit hour. *Financial support:* Research assistantships and teaching assistantships available. Financial award application deadline: 4/1. *Unit head:* Dr. Jerry Gannod, Chairperson, 931-372-3691, Fax: 931-372-3686, E-mail: jgannod@tntech.edu. *Application contact:* Shelia K. Kendrick, Coordinator of Graduate Studies, 931-372-3808, Fax: 931-372-3497, E-mail: skendrick@tntech.edu.

Texas A&M University, College of Engineering, Department of Computer Science and Engineering, College Station, TX 77843. Offers computer engineering (M Eng, MS); computer science (MCS, MS, PhD). *Program availability:* Part-time. *Faculty:* 51. *Students:* 357 full-time (78 women), 50 part-time (5 women); includes 55 minority (5 Black or African American, non-Hispanic/Latino; 31 Asian, non-Hispanic/Latino; 15 Hispanic/Latino; 1 Native Hawaiian or other Pacific Islander, non-Hispanic/Latino; 3 Two or more races, non-Hispanic/Latino), 303 international. Average age 27. 2,303 applicants, 13% accepted, 124 enrolled. In 2019, 116 master's, 15 doctorates awarded. *Degree requirements:* For master's, comprehensive exam (for some programs), thesis (for some programs); for doctorate, comprehensive exam, thesis/dissertation. *Entrance requirements:* For master's and doctorate, GRE General Test, letters of recommendation. Additional exam requirements/recommendations for international students: required—TOEFL (minimum score 550 paper-based; 80 iBT), IELTS (minimum score 6), PTE (minimum score 53). *Application deadline:* For fall admission, 1/1 priority date for domestic and international students; for spring admission, 8/1 priority date for domestic and international students. Applications are processed on a rolling basis. Application fee: $65 ($90 for international students). Electronic applications accepted. *Expenses:* Contact institution. *Financial support:* In 2019–20, 353 students received support, including 8 fellowships with tuition reimbursements available (averaging $24,239 per year), 169 research assistantships with tuition reimbursements available (averaging $14,534 per year), 102 teaching assistantships with tuition reimbursements available (averaging $11,535 per year); career-related internships or fieldwork, institutionally sponsored loans, scholarships/grants, traineeships, health care benefits, tuition waivers (full and partial), and unspecified assistantships also available. Support available to part-time students. Financial award application deadline: 3/15; financial award applicants required to submit FAFSA. *Unit head:* Scott Schaefer, Department Head, 979-845-5820, E-mail: schaefer@cse.tamu.edu. *Application contact:* Dr. Duncan M. Walker, Professor and Graduate Advisor, 979-458-4087, E-mail: grad-advisor@cse.tamu.edu.
Website: http://engineering.tamu.edu/cse/

Texas A&M University–Corpus Christi, College of Graduate Studies, College of Science and Engineering, Program in Computer Science, Corpus Christi, TX 78412. Offers MS. *Program availability:* Part-time, evening/weekend. *Degree requirements:* For master's, comprehensive exam (for some programs), thesis (for some programs), thesis or project. *Entrance requirements:* For master's, GRE (taken within 5 years), essay (500-1,000 words). Additional exam requirements/recommendations for international students: required—TOEFL (minimum score 550 paper-based; 79 iBT), IELTS (minimum score 6.5). Electronic applications accepted.

Texas A&M University–Kingsville, College of Graduate Studies, Frank H. Dotterweich College of Engineering, Department of Electrical Engineering and Computer Science, Program in Computer Science, Kingsville, TX 78363. Offers MS. *Degree requirements:* For master's, variable foreign language requirement, comprehensive exam, thesis (for some programs). *Entrance requirements:* For master's, GRE (minimum Quantitative and Verbal score of 288), MAT, GMAT, minimum undergraduate GPA of 3.0. Additional exam requirements/recommendations for international students: required—TOEFL (minimum score 550 paper-based; 79 iBT). Electronic applications accepted.

Texas Southern University, School of Science and Technology, Department of Computer Science, Houston, TX 77004-4584. Offers MS. Electronic applications accepted.

Texas State University, The Graduate College, College of Science and Engineering, Doctoral Program in Computer Science, San Marcos, TX 78666. Offers PhD. *Program availability:* Part-time. *Degree requirements:* For doctorate, comprehensive exam, thesis/dissertation, qualifying exam; dissertation defense; demonstration of significant experience designing and implementing a substantial piece of software. *Entrance requirements:* For doctorate, official GRE (general test only) required with competitive scores in the verbal reasoning and quantitative reasoning sections, baccalaureate degree in computer science with minimum GPA of 3.0 in last 60 hours of undergraduate course work or master's degree in computer science with minimum GPA of 3.3; interview; resume; 3 letters of recommendation from those with knowledge of academic abilities. Additional exam requirements/recommendations for international students: required—TOEFL (minimum score 85 iBT), IELTS (minimum score 6.5). Electronic applications accepted.

Texas State University, The Graduate College, College of Science and Engineering, Master's Program in Computer Science, San Marcos, TX 78666. Offers MA, MS. *Program availability:* Part-time. *Degree requirements:* For master's, comprehensive exam, thesis (for some programs). *Entrance requirements:* For master's, official GRE (general test only) required with competitive scores in the verbal reasoning and quantitative reasoning sections, baccalaureate degree from regionally-accredited university with minimum GPA of 2.75 on last 60 undergraduate semester hours, a copy of an official transcript from each institution where course credit was granted, 3 letters of recommendation, academic vitae (resume), statement of purpose. Additional exam requirements/recommendations for international students: required—TOEFL (minimum score 550 paper-based; 78 iBT), IELTS (minimum score 6.5). Electronic applications accepted.

Towson University, Jess and Mildred Fisher College of Science and Mathematics, Program in Computer Science, Towson, MD 21252-0001. Offers MS. *Program availability:* Part-time, evening/weekend. *Students:* 53 full-time (19 women), 77 part-time (21 women); includes 63 minority (28 Black or African American, non-Hispanic/Latino; 25 Asian, non-Hispanic/Latino; 5 Hispanic/Latino; 5 Two or more races, non-Hispanic/Latino), 28 international. *Entrance requirements:* For master's, minimum GPA of 3.0, bachelor's degree in computer science or bachelor's degree in any other field and completion of 1-3 preparatory courses. *Application deadline:* For fall admission, 1/17 for domestic students, 5/15 for international students; for spring admission, 10/15 for domestic students, 12/1 for international students. Applications are processed on a rolling basis. Application fee: $45. Electronic applications accepted. *Expenses: Tuition, area resident:* Full-time $7920; part-time $439 per credit. Tuition, nonresident: full-time $16,344; part-time $908 per credit. *International tuition:* $16,344 full-time. *Required fees:* $2628; $146 per credit. $876 per term. *Financial support:* Application deadline: 4/1. *Unit head:* Dr. Subrata Acharya, Program Director, 410-704-2633, E-mail: sacharya@towson.edu. *Application contact:* Coverley Beidleman, Assistant Director of Graduate Admissions, 410-704-5630, Fax: 410-704-3030, E-mail: grads@towson.edu.
Website: https://www.towson.edu/fcsm/departments/computerinfosci/grad/computersci/

Toyota Technological Institute at Chicago, Program in Computer Science, Chicago, IL 60637. Offers PhD. *Degree requirements:* For doctorate, thesis/dissertation.

Trent University, Graduate Studies, Program in Applications of Modeling in the Natural and Social Sciences, Department of Computer Studies, Peterborough, ON K9J 7B8, Canada. Offers M Sc. *Degree requirements:* For master's, thesis. *Entrance requirements:* For master's, honours degree.

Troy University, Graduate School, College of Arts and Sciences, Program in Computer Science, Troy, AL 36082. Offers MS. *Program availability:* Part-time, evening/weekend. *Faculty:* 5 full-time (2 women), 1 part-time/adjunct (0 women). *Students:* 16 full-time (7 women), 9 part-time (2 women); includes 2 minority (1 Asian, non-Hispanic/Latino; 1 Hispanic/Latino), 18 international. Average age 30. 41 applicants, 68% accepted, 5 enrolled. In 2019, 21 master's awarded. *Degree requirements:* For master's, thesis or research paper and comprehensive exam; minimum GPA of 3.0; admission to candidacy. *Entrance requirements:* For master's, GRE (minimum score of 920 on old exam or 294 on new exam) (verbal plus quantitative), bachelor's degree; minimum undergraduate GPA of 2.5 or 3.0 on last 30 semester hours. Additional exam requirements/recommendations for international students: required—TOEFL (minimum score 523 paper-based; 70 iBT), IELTS (minimum score 6). *Application deadline:* For fall admission, 6/1 for international students; for spring admission, 10/15 for international students. Applications are processed on a rolling basis. Application fee: $50. Electronic applications accepted. *Expenses: Tuition, area resident:* Full-time $7650; part-time $2550 per semester hour. Tuition, state resident: full-time $7650; part-time $2550 per semester hour. Tuition, nonresident: full-time $15,300; part-time $5100 per semester hour. *International tuition:* $15,300 full-time. *Required fees:* $856; $352 per semester hour. $176 per semester. *Financial support:* In 2019–20, 15 students received support. Fellowships, research assistantships, teaching assistantships, career-related internships or fieldwork, Federal Work-Study, scholarships/grants, traineeships, tuition waivers, and unspecified assistantships available. Support available to part-time students. Financial award application deadline: 3/1; financial award applicants required to submit FAFSA. *Unit head:* Dr. Bill Zhong, Department Chairman/Professor, 334-670-3388, Fax: 334-670-3729, E-mail: jzhong@troy.edu. *Application contact:* Haley McKinnon, Director of Graduate Admissions, 334-670-3178, Fax: 334-670-3912, E-mail: hmckinnon@troy.edu.
Website: https://www.troy.edu/academics/academic-programs/computer-science.html

Tufts University, Graduate School of Arts and Sciences, Graduate Certificate Programs, Computer Science Program, Medford, MA 02155. Offers Certificate. *Program availability:* Part-time, evening/weekend. Electronic applications accepted. Full-time tuition and fees vary according to degree level, program and student level. Part-time tuition and fees vary according to course load.

Tufts University, Graduate School of Arts and Sciences, Graduate Certificate Programs, Post-Baccalaureate Minor Program in Computer Science, Medford, MA 02155. Offers Certificate. *Program availability:* Part-time, evening/weekend. Electronic applications accepted. Full-time tuition and fees vary according to degree level, program and student level. Part-time tuition and fees vary according to course load.

Tufts University, School of Engineering, Department of Computer Science, Medford, MA 02155. Offers bioengineering (MS), including bioinformatics; cognitive science/computer science (PhD); computer science (MS, PhD); soft material robotics (PhD). *Program availability:* Part-time. Terminal master's awarded for partial completion of doctoral program. *Entrance requirements:* For master's and doctorate, GRE General Test. Additional exam requirements/recommendations for international students: required—TOEFL (minimum score 550 paper-based; 80 iBT), IELTS (minimum score 6.5). Electronic applications accepted. Full-time tuition and fees vary according to degree level, program and student level. Part-time tuition and fees vary according to course load.

Universidad Autonoma de Guadalajara, Graduate Programs, Guadalajara, Mexico. Offers administrative law and justice (LL M); advertising and corporate communications

(MA); architecture (M Arch); business (MBA); computational science (MCC); education (Ed M, Ed D); English-Spanish translation (MA); entrepreneurship and management (MBA); integrated management of digital animation (MA); international business (MIB); international corporate law (LL M); Internet technologies (MS); manufacturing systems (MMS); occupational health (MS); philosophy (MA, PhD); power electronics (MS); quality systems (MQS); renewable energy (MS); social evaluation of projects (MBA); strategic market research (MBA); tax law (MA); teaching mathematics (MA).

Universidad de las Américas Puebla, Division of Graduate Studies, School of Engineering, Program in Computer Engineering, Puebla, Mexico. Offers computer science (MS). *Program availability:* Part-time, evening/weekend. *Degree requirements:* For master's, one foreign language, thesis.

Universidad de las Américas Puebla, Division of Graduate Studies, School of Engineering, Program in Computer Science, Puebla, Mexico. Offers PhD.

Université de Moncton, Faculty of Sciences, Information Technology Programs, Moncton, NB E1A 3E9, Canada. Offers M Sc, Certificate, Diploma. *Program availability:* Part-time. *Degree requirements:* For master's, thesis. Electronic applications accepted.

Université de Montréal, Faculty of Arts and Sciences, Department of Computer Science and Operational Research, Montréal, QC H3C 3J7, Canada. Offers computer systems (M Sc, PhD); electronic commerce (M Sc). *Program availability:* Part-time. Terminal master's awarded for partial completion of doctoral program. *Degree requirements:* For master's, one foreign language, thesis; for doctorate, one foreign language, thesis/dissertation, general exam. *Entrance requirements:* For master's, B Sc in related field; for doctorate, MA or M Sc in related field. Electronic applications accepted.

Université du Québec à Trois-Rivières, Graduate Programs, Program in Mathematics and Computer Science, Trois-Rivières, QC G9A 5H7, Canada. Offers M Sc.

Université du Québec en Outaouais, Graduate Programs, Program in Computer Network, Gatineau, QC J8X 3X7, Canada. Offers computer science (M Sc, PhD, DESS). *Program availability:* Part-time, evening/weekend. *Degree requirements:* For master's, thesis; for doctorate, thesis/dissertation.

University at Albany, State University of New York, College of Engineering and Applied Sciences, Department of Computer Science, Albany, NY 12222-0001. Offers MS, PhD. *Program availability:* Part-time, blended/hybrid learning. *Faculty:* 25 full-time (6 women), 7 part-time/adjunct (0 women). *Students:* 108 full-time (28 women), 47 part-time (10 women); includes 15 minority (2 Black or African American, non-Hispanic/Latino; 11 Asian, non-Hispanic/Latino; 1 Hispanic/Latino; 1 Two or more races, non-Hispanic/Latino), 120 international. Average age 26. 325 applicants, 49% accepted, 43 enrolled. In 2019, 145 master's, 3 doctorates awarded. *Degree requirements:* For master's, thesis optional, project or thesis; for doctorate, comprehensive exam, thesis/dissertation, area exams. *Entrance requirements:* For master's and doctorate, GRE General Test, transcripts from all schools attended, 3 letters of recommendation, resume, personal statement. Additional exam requirements/recommendations for international students: required—TOEFL (minimum score 550 paper-based). *Application deadline:* For fall admission, 8/1 for domestic students, 5/1 for international students; for spring admission, 11/1 for domestic and international students. Application fee: $75. Electronic applications accepted. *Expenses: Tuition, area resident:* Full-time $11,530; part-time $480 per credit hour. Tuition, nonresident: full-time $23,530; part-time $980 per credit hour. *International tuition:* $23,530 full-time. *Required fees:* $2185; $96 per credit hour. Part-time tuition and fees vary according to course load and program. *Financial support:* Fellowships, research assistantships, teaching assistantships, career-related internships or fieldwork, and Federal Work-Study available. Financial award application deadline: 3/1. *Unit head:* Randy Moulic, Chair, 518-956-8242, Fax: 518-442-5638, E-mail: jmoulic@albany.edu. *Application contact:* Randy Moulic, Chair, 518-956-8242, Fax: 518-442-5638, E-mail: jmoulic@albany.edu.
Website: http://www.cs.albany.edu/

University at Buffalo, the State University of New York, Graduate School, School of Engineering and Applied Sciences, Department of Computer Science and Engineering, Buffalo, NY 14260. Offers computer science and engineering (MS, PhD); information assurance (Certificate). *Program availability:* Part-time. Terminal master's awarded for partial completion of doctoral program. *Degree requirements:* For master's, thesis or alternative; for doctorate, thesis/dissertation, comprehensive qualifying exam. *Entrance requirements:* For master's and doctorate, GRE General Test. Additional exam requirements/recommendations for international students: required—TOEFL (minimum score 550 paper-based; 79 iBT). Electronic applications accepted. *Expenses: Tuition, area resident:* Full-time $11,310; part-time $471 per credit hour. Tuition, state resident: full-time $11,310; part-time $471 per credit hour. Tuition, nonresident: full-time $23,100; part-time $963 per credit hour. *International tuition:* $23,100 full-time. *Required fees:* $2820.

University of Advancing Technology, Master of Science Program in Technology, Tempe, AZ 85283-1042. Offers advancing computer science (MS); emerging technologies (MS); game production and management (MS); information assurance (MS); technology leadership (MS). *Degree requirements:* For master's, project or thesis. *Entrance requirements:* Additional exam requirements/recommendations for international students: required—TOEFL (minimum score 550 paper-based). Electronic applications accepted.

The University of Akron, Graduate School, Buchtel College of Arts and Sciences, Department of Computer Science, Akron, OH 44325. Offers MS. *Entrance requirements:* For master's, baccalaureate degree in computer science or a related field; three letters of recommendation; statement of purpose; resume; knowledge of one high-level programming language; mathematical maturity; proficiency in data structures, computer organization, and operating systems. Additional exam requirements/recommendations for international students: required—TOEFL (minimum score 79 iBT), IELTS (minimum score 6.5). Electronic applications accepted.

The University of Alabama, Graduate School, College of Engineering, Department of Computer Science, Tuscaloosa, AL 35487-0290. Offers MS, PhD. *Program availability:* Part-time. *Faculty:* 15 full-time (2 women). *Students:* 50 full-time (12 women), 2 part-time (0 women); includes 10 minority (5 Black or African American, non-Hispanic/Latino; 1 American Indian or Alaska Native, non-Hispanic/Latino; 2 Asian, non-Hispanic/Latino; 2 Hispanic/Latino), 31 international. Average age 29. 125 applicants, 65% accepted, 19 enrolled. In 2019, 8 master's, 3 doctorates awarded. Terminal master's awarded for partial completion of doctoral program. *Degree requirements:* For master's, comprehensive exam, thesis (for some programs); for doctorate, comprehensive exam, thesis/dissertation. *Entrance requirements:* For master's and doctorate, GRE. Additional exam requirements/recommendations for international students: required—TOEFL (minimum score 550 paper-based; 79 iBT). *Application deadline:* For fall admission, 6/1 priority date for domestic students, 3/1 for international students; for winter admission, 8/1 for international students; for spring admission, 11/1 priority date for domestic students, 8/1 for international students; for summer admission, 1/1 for international students. Applications are processed on a rolling basis. Application fee: $50 ($60 for international students). Electronic applications accepted. *Expenses: Tuition, area resident:* Full-time $10,780; part-time $440 per credit hour. Tuition, nonresident: full-time $30,250; part-time $1550 per credit hour. *Financial support:* In 2019–20, 17 students received support. Fellowships with full tuition reimbursements available, research assistantships with full tuition reimbursements available, teaching assistantships with full tuition reimbursements available, health care benefits, and unspecified assistantships available. Financial award application deadline: 3/15. *Unit head:* Dr. Susan Vrbsky, Associate Professor and Interim Department Head, 205-348-1671, E-mail: vrbsky@cs.ua.edu. *Application contact:* Dr. Jeffrey Carver, Professor, 205-348-9829, Fax: 205-348-0219, E-mail: carver@cs.ua.edu.
Website: http://cs.ua.edu/

The University of Alabama at Birmingham, College of Arts and Sciences, Program in Computer and Information Sciences, Birmingham, AL 35294. Offers MS, PhD. *Students:* 47 full-time (8 women), 11 part-time (2 women); includes 2 minority (1 Asian, non-Hispanic/Latino; 1 Hispanic/Latino), 34 international. Average age 29. 168 applicants, 54% accepted, 14 enrolled. In 2019, 15 master's, 1 doctorate awarded. Terminal master's awarded for partial completion of doctoral program. *Degree requirements:* For master's, thesis optional; for doctorate, thesis/dissertation. *Entrance requirements:* For master's, GRE General Test, minimum GPA of 3.0, letters of recommendation; for doctorate, GRE General Test, minimum GPA of 3.5 overall or on last 60 hours; letters of recommendation. Additional exam requirements/recommendations for international students: required—TOEFL, IELTS. *Application deadline:* For fall admission, 2/1 for domestic students; for spring admission, 9/1 for domestic students. Applications are processed on a rolling basis. Application fee: $45 ($60 for international students). Electronic applications accepted. *Financial support:* Fellowships with full tuition reimbursements, research assistantships with full tuition reimbursements, teaching assistantships with full tuition reimbursements, career-related internships or fieldwork, Federal Work-Study, institutionally sponsored loans, scholarships/grants, traineeships, health care benefits, and unspecified assistantships available. Support available to part-time students. Financial award application deadline: 3/10. *Unit head:* Dr. Chengcui Zhang, Graduate Program Director, 205-934-8606, Fax: 205-934-5473, E-mail: czhang02@uab.edu. *Application contact:* Susan Noblitt Banks, Director of Graduate School Operations, 205-934-8227, Fax: 205-934-8413, E-mail: gradschool@uab.edu.
Website: https://cis.uab.edu/academics/graduates/

The University of Alabama in Huntsville, School of Graduate Studies, College of Science, Department of Computer Science, Huntsville, AL 35899. Offers computer science (MS, PhD); cybersecurity (MS); modeling and simulation (MS, PhD, Certificate); software engineering (MSSE, Certificate). *Program availability:* Part-time. *Degree requirements:* For master's, comprehensive exam, thesis or alternative, oral and written exams; for doctorate, comprehensive exam, thesis/dissertation, oral and written exams. *Entrance requirements:* For master's, doctorate, and Certificate, GRE General Test, minimum GPA of 3.0. Additional exam requirements/recommendations for international students: required—TOEFL (minimum score 550 paper-based; 80 iBT), IELTS (minimum score 6.5). Electronic applications accepted.

University of Alaska Fairbanks, College of Engineering and Mines, Department of Computer Science, Fairbanks, AK 99775-6670. Offers MS. *Program availability:* Part-time. *Degree requirements:* For master's, comprehensive exam, oral defense of project or thesis. *Entrance requirements:* For master's, GRE General Test, GRE Subject Test (computer science), bachelor's degree from accredited institution with minimum cumulative undergraduate and major GPA of 3.0. Additional exam requirements/recommendations for international students: required—TOEFL (minimum score 600 paper-based). Electronic applications accepted. *Expenses:* Contact institution.

University of Alberta, Faculty of Graduate Studies and Research, Department of Computing Science, Edmonton, AB T6G 2E1, Canada. Offers M Sc, PhD. *Program availability:* Part-time. Terminal master's awarded for partial completion of doctoral program. *Degree requirements:* For master's, thesis (for some programs), oral exam, seminar; for doctorate, thesis/dissertation, oral exam, seminar. *Entrance requirements:* For master's and doctorate, GRE General Test. Additional exam requirements/recommendations for international students: required—TOEFL.

The University of Arizona, College of Science, Department of Computer Science, Tucson, AZ 85721. Offers MS, PhD. *Program availability:* Part-time. *Faculty:* 21 full-time (2 women). *Students:* 75 full-time (13 women), 4 part-time (3 women); includes 6 minority (1 Black or African American, non-Hispanic/Latino; 5 Asian, non-Hispanic/Latino), 48 international. Average age 28. 223 applicants, 21% accepted, 12 enrolled. In 2019, 10 master's, 3 doctorates awarded. Terminal master's awarded for partial completion of doctoral program. *Degree requirements:* For master's, thesis optional, 30-31 units of coursework, 3.0 cumulative GPA, 3.5 GPA in six core courses; for doctorate, comprehensive exam, thesis/dissertation, 3rd and 5th semester portfolios in place of pre-qualifying and qualifying exams, 37 units of major coursework (includes 12 units of research and a 1 unit colloquium course), 9 or more units of minor coursework, 18 units of dissertation, 3.33 cumulative GPA, 3.5 GPA in six core courses. *Entrance requirements:* For master's, GRE General Test, typical minimum undergraduate GPA is 3.2, must have at a minimum demonstrated advanced undergraduate studies in Systems (i.e. through an operating systems or compilers course) and Theory (i.e. through an algorithms or theory of computation course); for doctorate, GRE General Test, typical minimum undergraduate GPA is 3.5, graduate GPA is 3.7, must have at a minimum demonstrated advanced undergraduate studies in Systems (i.e. through an operating systems or compilers course) and Theory (i.e. through an algorithms or theory of computation course). Additional exam requirements/recommendations for international students: required—TOEFL (minimum score 60 paper-based; 79 iBT). *Application deadline:* For fall admission, 1/15 for domestic and international students. Application fee: $85 ($95 for international students). Electronic applications accepted. *Financial support:* In 2019–20, 79 students received support, including 5 fellowships (averaging $10,000 per year), 45 research assistantships with full tuition reimbursements available (averaging $18,400 per year), 24 teaching assistantships with full tuition reimbursements available (averaging $18,400 per year); scholarships/grants, health care benefits, and tuition waivers (full and partial) also available. Financial award application deadline: 1/15. *Unit head:* Dr. Todd Proebsting, Department Head, 520-621-4324, Fax: 520-621-0308, E-mail: depthead@cs.arizona.edu. *Application contact:* Chelsea Skotnicki, Graduate Program Coordinator, 520-626-8470, Fax: 520-621-0308, E-mail: gradadvising@cs.arizona.edu.
Website: https://www.cs.arizona.edu/

University of Arkansas, Graduate School, College of Engineering, Department of Computer Science and Computer Engineering, Program in Computer Science, Fayetteville, AR 72701. Offers MS, PhD. *Students:* 38 full-time (9 women), 15 part-time (3 women); includes 1 minority (Asian, non-Hispanic/Latino), 38 international. 37 applicants, 54% accepted. In 2019, 9 master's, 3 doctorates awarded. *Application deadline:* For fall admission, 8/1 for domestic students, 4/1 for international students; for spring admission, 12/1 for domestic students, 10/1 for international students; for summer admission, 4/15 for domestic students, 3/1 for international students. Applications are processed on a rolling basis. Application fee: $60. Electronic applications accepted. *Financial support:* In 2019–20, 16 research assistantships, 6 teaching assistantships were awarded; fellowships with tuition reimbursements, career-related internships or fieldwork, and Federal Work-Study also available. Support available to part-time students. Financial award application deadline: 4/1; financial award applicants required

to submit FAFSA. *Unit head:* Dr. Xiaoqing Liu, Department Head, 479-575-6197, Fax: 479-575-5339, E-mail: frankliu@uark.edu. *Application contact:* Dr. Brajendra Nath Panda, Professor, Associate Department Head for Graduate Program, 479-575-2067, Fax: 479-575-5339, E-mail: bpanda@uark.edu.
Website: https://computer-science-and-computer-engineering.uark.edu/index.php

University of Arkansas at Little Rock, Graduate School, George W. Donaghey College of Engineering and Information Technology, Department of Computer Science, Little Rock, AR 72204-1099. Offers MS, PhD. *Program availability:* Part-time, evening/weekend. *Degree requirements:* For master's, thesis optional. *Entrance requirements:* For master's, GRE General Test, minimum GPA of 3.0; bachelor's degree in computer science, mathematics, or appropriate alternative.

University of Bridgeport, School of Engineering, Departments of Computer Science and Computer Engineering, Bridgeport, CT 06604. Offers computer engineering (MS); computer science (MS); computer science and engineering (PhD). *Degree requirements:* For master's, thesis optional; for doctorate, comprehensive exam, thesis/dissertation. *Entrance requirements:* Additional exam requirements/recommendations for international students: recommended—TOEFL (minimum score 550 paper-based; 80 iBT), IELTS (minimum score 6.5). Electronic applications accepted. *Expenses:* Contact institution.

The University of British Columbia, Faculty of Science, Department of Computer Science, Vancouver, BC V6T 1Z4, Canada. Offers computer science (M Sc, PhD); data science (MDS). *Program availability:* Part-time. *Degree requirements:* For doctorate, comprehensive exam, thesis/dissertation. *Entrance requirements:* Additional exam requirements/recommendations for international students: required—TOEFL. Electronic applications accepted. *Expenses:* Contact institution.

University of Calgary, Faculty of Graduate Studies, Faculty of Science, Program in Computer Science, Calgary, AB T2N 1N4, Canada. Offers computer science (M Sc, PhD); software engineering (M Sc). *Program availability:* Part-time. *Degree requirements:* For master's, comprehensive exam (for some programs), thesis (for some programs); for doctorate, thesis/dissertation, oral and written departmental exam. *Entrance requirements:* For master's, bachelor's degree in computer science; for doctorate, M Sc in computer science. Additional exam requirements/recommendations for international students: required—TOEFL (minimum score 600 paper-based); recommended—TWE. Electronic applications accepted.

University of California, Berkeley, Graduate Division, College of Engineering, Department of Electrical Engineering and Computer Sciences, Berkeley, CA 94720. Offers computer science (MS, PhD); electrical engineering (M Eng, MS, PhD). Terminal master's awarded for partial completion of doctoral program. *Degree requirements:* For master's, comprehensive exam (for some programs), thesis (for some programs), comprehensive exam or thesis; for doctorate, thesis/dissertation, qualifying exam. *Entrance requirements:* For master's and doctorate, GRE General Test, minimum GPA of 3.0, 3 letters of recommendation. Additional exam requirements/recommendations for international students: required—TOEFL (minimum score 570 paper-based; 90 iBT). Electronic applications accepted.

University of California, Davis, College of Engineering, Graduate Group in Computer Science, Davis, CA 95616. Offers MS, PhD. Terminal master's awarded for partial completion of doctoral program. *Degree requirements:* For master's, comprehensive exam (for some programs), thesis optional; for doctorate, comprehensive exam, thesis/dissertation. *Entrance requirements:* For master's and doctorate, GRE General Test, GRE Subject Test, minimum GPA of 3.0. Additional exam requirements/recommendations for international students: required—TOEFL (minimum score 550 paper-based). Electronic applications accepted.

University of California, Irvine, Donald Bren School of Information and Computer Sciences, Department of Computer Science, Irvine, CA 92697. Offers MS, PhD. *Students:* 466 full-time (113 women), 15 part-time (6 women); includes 53 minority (2 Black or African American, non-Hispanic/Latino; 44 Asian, non-Hispanic/Latino; 4 Hispanic/Latino; 3 Two or more races, non-Hispanic/Latino), 338 international. Average age 26. 4,167 applicants, 14% accepted, 185 enrolled. In 2019, 169 master's, 24 doctorates awarded. Application fee: $120 ($140 for international students). *Unit head:* Alexandru Nicolau, Chair, 949-824-4079, E-mail: nicolau@ics.uci.edu. *Application contact:* Holly Byrnes, Department Manager, 949-824-6753, E-mail: hbyrnes@uci.edu. Website: http://www.cs.uci.edu/

University of California, Irvine, Donald Bren School of Information and Computer Sciences, Program in Networked Systems, Irvine, CA 92697. Offers MS, PhD. *Students:* 50 full-time (10 women), 2 part-time (1 woman); includes 2 minority (both Asian, non-Hispanic/Latino), 49 international. Average age 25. 201 applicants, 44% accepted, 22 enrolled. In 2019, 13 master's, 1 doctorate awarded. *Application deadline:* For fall admission, 1/15 for domestic students. Application fee: $120 ($140 for international students). *Financial support:* Fellowships, research assistantships, and teaching assistantships available. *Unit head:* Nalini Venkatasubramanian, Director, 949-824-5898, Fax: 949-824-4056, E-mail: nalini@uci.edu. *Application contact:* Athina Markopoulou, Co-Director, 949-824-0357, Fax: 949-824-3203, E-mail: athina@uci.edu. Website: http://www.networkedsystems.uci.edu/

University of California, Irvine, Samueli School of Engineering, Department of Electrical Engineering and Computer Science, Irvine, CA 92697. Offers electrical engineering and computer science (MS, PhD); networked systems (MS, PhD). *Program availability:* Part-time. *Students:* 274 full-time (65 women), 11 part-time (3 women); includes 24 minority (3 Black or African American, non-Hispanic/Latino; 15 Asian, non-Hispanic/Latino; 2 Hispanic/Latino; 1 Native Hawaiian or other Pacific Islander, non-Hispanic/Latino; 3 Two or more races, non-Hispanic/Latino), 226 international. Average age 27. 1,538 applicants, 27% accepted, 81 enrolled. In 2019, 88 master's, 26 doctorates awarded. Terminal master's awarded for partial completion of doctoral program. *Entrance requirements:* For master's and doctorate, GRE General Test, minimum GPA of 3.0, 3 letters of recommendation. Additional exam requirements/recommendations for international students: required—TOEFL (minimum score 550 paper-based). *Application deadline:* For fall admission, 1/15 priority date for domestic students, 1/15 for international students. Applications are processed on a rolling basis. Application fee: $120 ($140 for international students). Electronic applications accepted. *Financial support:* Fellowships, research assistantships with full tuition reimbursements, teaching assistantships, institutionally sponsored loans, traineeships, health care benefits, and unspecified assistantships available. Financial award application deadline: 3/1; financial award applicants required to submit FAFSA. *Unit head:* Prof. H. Kumar Wickramasinghe, Chair, 949-824-2213, E-mail: hkwick@uci.edu. *Application contact:* Jean Bennett, Director of Graduate Student Affairs, 949-824-6475, Fax: 949-824-8200, E-mail: jean.bennett@uci.edu.
Website: http://www.eng.uci.edu/dept/eecs

University of California, Los Angeles, Graduate Division, Henry Samueli School of Engineering and Applied Science, Department of Computer Science, Los Angeles, CA 90095-1596. Offers MS, PhD, MBA/MS. *Degree requirements:* For master's, comprehensive exam or thesis; for doctorate, thesis/dissertation, qualifying exams. *Entrance requirements:* For master's, GRE General Test, GRE Subject Test, minimum GPA of 3.0; for doctorate, GRE General Test, GRE Subject Test, minimum GPA of 3.25.

Additional exam requirements/recommendations for international students: required—TOEFL (minimum score 560 paper-based; 87 iBT), IELTS (minimum score 7). Electronic applications accepted.

University of California, Merced, Graduate Division, School of Engineering, Merced, CA 95343. Offers biological engineering and small scale technologies (MS, PhD); electrical engineering and computer science (MS, PhD); environmental systems (MS, PhD); management of innovation, sustainability, and technology (MM); mechanical engineering (MS, PhD). *Faculty:* 60 full-time (16 women). *Students:* 244 full-time (83 women), 1 (woman) part-time; includes 56 minority (2 Black or African American, non-Hispanic/Latino; 20 Asian, non-Hispanic/Latino; 30 Hispanic/Latino; 1 Native Hawaiian or other Pacific Islander, non-Hispanic/Latino; 3 Two or more races, non-Hispanic/Latino), 153 international. Average age 28. 330 applicants, 32% accepted, 67 enrolled. In 2019, 30 master's, 17 doctorates awarded. Terminal master's awarded for partial completion of doctoral program. *Degree requirements:* For master's, variable foreign language requirement, comprehensive exam, thesis or alternative, oral defense; for doctorate, variable foreign language requirement, comprehensive exam, thesis/dissertation, oral defense. *Entrance requirements:* For master's and doctorate, GRE. Additional exam requirements/recommendations for international students: required—TOEFL (minimum score 550 paper-based; 80 iBT); recommended—IELTS (minimum score 6.5). *Application deadline:* For fall admission, 1/15 for domestic and international students. Application fee: $105 ($125 for international students). Electronic applications accepted. *Expenses: Tuition,* area resident: Full-time $11,442; part-time $5721. Tuition, state resident: full-time $11,442; part-time $5721. Tuition, nonresident: full-time $26,544; part-time $13,272. International tuition: $26,544 full-time. Required fees: $564 per semester. *Financial support:* In 2019–20, 205 students received support, including 6 fellowships with full tuition reimbursements available (averaging $22,005 per year), 76 research assistantships with full tuition reimbursements available (averaging $21,420 per year), 123 teaching assistantships with full tuition reimbursements available (averaging $21,911 per year); scholarships/grants, traineeships, and health care benefits also available. *Unit head:* Dr. Mark Matsumoto, Dean, 209-228-4047, Fax: 209-228-4047, E-mail: mmatsumoto@ucmerced.edu. *Application contact:* Tsu Ya, Director of Admissions and Academic Services, 209-228-4521, Fax: 209-228-6906, E-mail: tya@ucmerced.edu.

University of California, Riverside, Graduate Division, Department of Computer Science and Engineering, Riverside, CA 92521. Offers computer engineering (MS); computer science (MS, PhD). Terminal master's awarded for partial completion of doctoral program. *Degree requirements:* For master's, comprehensive exam, project, or thesis; for doctorate, thesis/dissertation, written and oral qualifying exams, dissertation defense. *Entrance requirements:* For master's and doctorate, GRE General Test (minimum expected score of 300 verbal and quantitative combined), minimum GPA of 3.2 in junior/senior years of undergraduate study (last two years). Additional exam requirements/recommendations for international students: required—TOEFL (minimum score 550 paper-based, 80 iBT) or IELTS (7). Electronic applications accepted. *Expenses:* Contact institution.

University of California, San Diego, Graduate Division, Department of Computer Science and Engineering, La Jolla, CA 92093. Offers computer engineering (MS, PhD); computer science (MS, PhD). *Students:* 665 full-time (158 women), 187 part-time (39 women). 5,619 applicants, 15% accepted, 281 enrolled. In 2019, 333 master's, 25 doctorates awarded. Terminal master's awarded for partial completion of doctoral program. *Degree requirements:* For master's, comprehensive exam (for some programs), thesis (for some programs), comprehensive exam or thesis; for doctorate, comprehensive exam, thesis/dissertation, 1-quarter teaching assistantship. *Entrance requirements:* For master's and doctorate, GRE General Test. Additional exam requirements/recommendations for international students: required—TOEFL (minimum score 550 paper-based; 80 iBT), IELTS (minimum score 7). *Application deadline:* For fall admission, 12/17 for domestic students. Application fee: $105 ($125 for international students). Electronic applications accepted. *Financial support:* Fellowships, research assistantships, teaching assistantships, career-related internships or fieldwork, and scholarships/grants available. Financial award applicants required to submit FAFSA. *Unit head:* Sorin Lerner, Chair, 858-534-8883, E-mail: lerner@cs.ucsd.edu. *Application contact:* Julie Conner, Graduate Coordinator, 858-534-8872, E-mail: gradinfo@cs.ucsd.edu.
Website: http://cse.ucsd.edu

University of California, Santa Barbara, Graduate Division, College of Engineering, Department of Computer Science, Santa Barbara, CA 93106-5110. Offers computer science (MS, PhD), including cognitive science (PhD), computational science and engineering (PhD), technology and society (PhD). Terminal master's awarded for partial completion of doctoral program. *Degree requirements:* For master's, comprehensive exam (for some programs), thesis (for some programs), project (for some programs); for doctorate, thesis/dissertation. *Entrance requirements:* For master's and doctorate, GRE. Additional exam requirements/recommendations for international students: required—TOEFL (minimum score 600 paper-based; 100 iBT), IELTS (minimum score 7). Electronic applications accepted.

University of California, Santa Cruz, Jack Baskin School of Engineering, Department of Applied Mathematics, Santa Cruz, CA 95064. Offers scientific computing and applied mathematics (MS); statistics and applied mathematics (MS, PhD), including applied mathematics, statistics. *Program availability:* Part-time. *Faculty:* 9 full-time (2 women). *Students:* 46 full-time (15 women); includes 14 minority (1 American Indian or Alaska Native, non-Hispanic/Latino; 7 Asian, non-Hispanic/Latino; 5 Hispanic/Latino; 1 Native Hawaiian or other Pacific Islander, non-Hispanic/Latino), 14 international. 62 applicants, 34% accepted, 10 enrolled. In 2019, 12 master's, 4 doctorates awarded. Terminal master's awarded for partial completion of doctoral program. *Degree requirements:* For master's, thesis, seminar, capstone project; for doctorate, thesis/dissertation, seminar, first-year exam, qualifying exam. *Entrance requirements:* For master's and doctorate, GRE General Test (waived due to pandemic); GRE Subject Test in math (recommended). Additional exam requirements/recommendations for international students: required—TOEFL (minimum score 570 paper-based; 89 iBT); recommended—IELTS (minimum score 8). *Application deadline:* For fall admission, 1/10 for domestic and international students. Application fee: $105 ($125 for international students). Electronic applications accepted. *Expenses:* $18,365 Annually. *Financial support:* In 2019–20, 20 students received support, including 9 fellowships with full and partial tuition reimbursements available (averaging $24,000 per year), 20 research assistantships with full tuition reimbursements available (averaging $22,415 per year), 32 teaching assistantships with partial tuition reimbursements available (averaging $21,911 per year); health care benefits and tuition waivers (full and partial) also available. Financial award application deadline: 1/10; financial award applicants required to submit FAFSA. *Unit head:* Dr. Qi Gong, Professor and Department Chair, 831-459-3753, E-mail: qigong@soe.ucsc.edu. *Application contact:* Theo-Alyce Gordon, Graduate Student Advisor, 831-459-2438, E-mail: bsoe-ga@rt.ucsc.edu.
Website: https://www.soe.ucsc.edu/departments/applied-mathematics

University of California, Santa Cruz, Jack Baskin School of Engineering, Department of Computer Science and Engineering, Santa Cruz, CA 95064. Offers MS, PhD. *Program availability:* Part-time. *Faculty:* 44 full-time (9 women), 5 part-time/adjunct (1

woman). *Students:* 282 full-time (88 women), 29 part-time (6 women); includes 55 minority (7 Black or African American, non-Hispanic/Latino; 2 American Indian or Alaska Native, non-Hispanic/Latino; 30 Asian, non-Hispanic/Latino; 15 Hispanic/Latino; 1 Native Hawaiian or other Pacific Islander, non-Hispanic/Latino), 176 international. 1,313 applicants, 23% accepted, 131 enrolled. In 2019, 77 master's, 25 doctorates awarded. Terminal master's awarded for partial completion of doctoral program. *Degree requirements:* For master's, thesis (for some programs); for doctorate, thesis/dissertation, qualifying exam. *Entrance requirements:* For master's and doctorate, GRE General Test (temporarily waived due to pandemic). Additional exam requirements/recommendations for international students: required—TOEFL (minimum score 570 paper-based; 89 iBT); recommended—IELTS (minimum score 8). *Application deadline:* For fall admission, 1/10 for domestic and international students. Application fee: $105 ($125 for international students). Electronic applications accepted. *Financial support:* In 2019–20, 45 fellowships (averaging $21,000 per year), 295 research assistantships with full tuition reimbursements (averaging $22,415 per year), 324 teaching assistantships with full and partial tuition reimbursements (averaging $21,911 per year) were awarded; health care benefits and tuition waivers (full and partial) also available. Financial award application deadline: 1/10; financial award applicants required to submit FAFSA. *Unit head:* Dr. Martine Schlag, Professor and Department Chair, 831-459-3243, E-mail: martine@soe.ucsc.edu. *Application contact:* Graduate Student Advisor, E-mail: bsoe-ga@rt.ucsc.edu.
Website: https://grad.soe.ucsc.edu/cse

University of Central Arkansas, Graduate School, College of Natural Sciences and Math, Department of Applied Computing, Conway, AR 72035-0001. Offers MS. *Entrance requirements:* For master's, GRE, minimum GPA of 2.7. Additional exam requirements/recommendations for international students: required—TOEFL (minimum score 550 paper-based; 80 iBT). Electronic applications accepted.

University of Central Florida, College of Engineering and Computer Science, Department of Computer Science, Orlando, FL 32816. Offers computer science (MS, PhD). *Program availability:* Part-time, evening/weekend. *Students:* 352 full-time (92 women), 188 part-time (48 women); includes 115 minority (27 Black or African American, non-Hispanic/Latino; 1 American Indian or Alaska Native, non-Hispanic/Latino; 29 Asian, non-Hispanic/Latino; 55 Hispanic/Latino; 3 Two or more races, non-Hispanic/Latino), 261 international. Average age 29. 741 applicants, 78% accepted, 203 enrolled. In 2019, 129 master's, 21 doctorates awarded. *Degree requirements:* For master's, thesis or alternative; for doctorate, thesis/dissertation, candidacy exam, departmental qualifying exam. *Entrance requirements:* For master's, GRE General Test, GRE Subject Test, minimum GPA of 3.0 in last 60 hours, letters of recommendation, resume; for doctorate, GRE Subject Test, minimum GPA of 3.0 in last 60 hours, letters of recommendation, resume, goal statement. Additional exam requirements/recommendations for international students: required—TOEFL. *Application deadline:* For fall admission, 7/15 for domestic students; for spring admission, 12/1 for domestic students. Application fee: $30. Electronic applications accepted. *Financial support:* In 2019–20, 164 students received support, including 37 fellowships with partial tuition reimbursements available (averaging $8,903 per year), 123 research assistantships with partial tuition reimbursements available (averaging $9,332 per year), 37 teaching assistantships with partial tuition reimbursements available (averaging $9,389 per year); career-related internships or fieldwork, Federal Work-Study, institutionally sponsored loans, health care benefits, tuition waivers (partial), and unspecified assistantships also available. Financial award application deadline: 3/1; financial award applicants required to submit FAFSA. *Unit head:* Dr. Gary Leavens, Chair, 407-823-4758, Fax: 407-823-1488, E-mail: leavens@eecs.ucf.edu. *Application contact:* Associate Director, Graduate Admissions, 407-823-2766, Fax: 407-823-6442, E-mail: gradadmissions@ucf.edu.
Website: http://www.cs.ucf.edu/

University of Central Missouri, The Graduate School, Warrensburg, MO 64093. Offers accountancy (MA); accounting (MBA); applied mathematics (MS); aviation safety (MA); biology (MS); business administration (MBA); career and technology education (MS); college student personnel administration (MS); communication (MA); computer information systems and information technology (MS); computer science (MS); counseling (MS); criminal justice and criminology (MS); educational leadership (Ed S); educational leadership and policy analysis (Ed D); educational technology (MS, Ed S); elementary and early childhood education (MSE); English (MA); english language learners - teaching english as a second language (MA); environmental studies (MA); finance (MBA); history (MA); industrial hygiene (MS); industrial management (MS); information systems (MBA); kinesiology (MS); library science and information services (MS); literacy education (MSE); marketing (MBA); mathematics (MS); music (MA); occupational safety management (MS); professional leadership - adult, career, and technical education (Ed S); professional leadership - counseling (Ed S); psychology (MS); rural family nursing (MS); school administration (MSE); social gerontology (MS); sociology (MA); special education (MSE); speech language pathology (MS); teaching (MAT); technology (MS); technology management (PhD); theatre (MA). *Accreditation:* ASHA. *Program availability:* Part-time, 100% online, blended/hybrid learning. *Faculty:* 236 full-time (113 women), 97 part-time/adjunct (61 women). *Students:* 787 full-time (448 women), 1,459 part-time (997 women); includes 213 minority (72 Black or African American, non-Hispanic/Latino; 5 American Indian or Alaska Native, non-Hispanic/Latino; 27 Asian, non-Hispanic/Latino; 59 Hispanic/Latino; 50 Two or more races, non-Hispanic/Latino), 574 international. Average age 30. 1,477 applicants, 68% accepted, 664 enrolled. In 2019, 831 master's, 93 other advanced degrees awarded. *Degree requirements:* For master's and Ed S, comprehensive exam (for some programs), thesis (for some programs). *Entrance requirements:* For master's, A GRE or GMAT test score may be required by some of the programs, A minimum GPA, letters of recommendation, a statement of purpose may be required by some of the programs; for Ed S, A master's degree is required for the application of an Education Specialist's degree program. Additional exam requirements/recommendations for international students: required—TOEFL (minimum score 550 paper-based; 79 iBT). *Application deadline:* For fall admission, 6/1 priority date for domestic and international students; for spring admission, 10/15 priority date for domestic and international students; for summer admission, 4/1 priority date for domestic and international students. Applications are processed on a rolling basis. Application fee: $30 ($75 for international students). Electronic applications accepted. *Expenses: Tuition, area resident:* Full-time $7524; part-time $313.50 per credit hour. Tuition, state resident: full-time $7524; part-time $313.50 per credit hour. Tuition, nonresident: full-time $15,048; part-time $627 per credit hour. *International tuition:* $15,048 full-time. *Required fees:* $915; $30.50 per credit hour. *Financial support:* In 2019–20, 89 students received support. Research assistantships, teaching assistantships, career-related internships or fieldwork, Federal Work-Study, scholarships/grants, unspecified assistantships, and administrative and laboratory assistantships available. Support available to part-time students. Financial award application deadline: 4/1; financial award applicants required to submit FAFSA. *Unit head:* Shellie Hewitt, Director of Graduate and International Student Services, 660-543-4621, Fax: 660-543-4778, E-mail: hewitt@ucmo.edu. *Application contact:* Shellie Hewitt, Director of Graduate and International Student Services, 660-543-4621, Fax: 660-543-4778, E-mail: hewitt@ucmo.edu.
Website: http://www.ucmo.edu/graduate/

University of Central Oklahoma, The Jackson College of Graduate Studies, College of Mathematics and Science, Department of Mathematics and Statistics, Edmond, OK 73034-5209. Offers applied mathematical science (MS), including mathematics, statistics, teaching; applied mathematics and computer science (MS). *Program availability:* Part-time. *Degree requirements:* For master's, comprehensive exam (for some programs), thesis (for some programs). *Entrance requirements:* Additional exam requirements/recommendations for international students: required—TOEFL (minimum score 550 paper-based; 79 iBT), IELTS (minimum score 6.5). Electronic applications accepted.

University of Chicago, Division of the Physical Sciences, Master's Program in Computer Science, Chicago, IL 60637-1513. Offers MS. *Program availability:* Part-time, evening/weekend. *Entrance requirements:* For master's, GRE General Test, personal statement, 3 letters of recommendation, transcripts for all previous degrees and institutions attended. Additional exam requirements/recommendations for international students: required—TOEFL (minimum score 90 iBT), IELTS (minimum score 7). Electronic applications accepted.

University of Chicago, Division of the Physical Sciences, PhD Program in Computer Science, Chicago, IL 60637. Offers PhD. *Degree requirements:* For doctorate, thesis/dissertation. *Entrance requirements:* For doctorate, GRE General Test, 3 letters of recommendation, statement of purpose, transcripts, resume or curriculum vitae. Additional exam requirements/recommendations for international students: required—TOEFL (minimum score 104 iBT), IELTS (minimum score 7). Electronic applications accepted.

University of Cincinnati, Graduate School, College of Engineering and Applied Science, Department of Electrical Engineering and Computing Systems, Program in Computer Science, Cincinnati, OH 45221. Offers MS. *Degree requirements:* For master's, thesis. *Entrance requirements:* For master's, GRE General Test, GRE Subject Test or BS in computer science. Additional exam requirements/recommendations for international students: required—TOEFL (minimum score 550 paper-based).

University of Cincinnati, Graduate School, College of Engineering and Applied Science, Department of Electrical Engineering and Computing Systems, Program in Computer Science and Engineering, Cincinnati, OH 45221. Offers PhD. *Degree requirements:* For doctorate, thesis/dissertation. *Entrance requirements:* For doctorate, GRE General Test. Additional exam requirements/recommendations for international students: required—TOEFL.

University of Colorado Boulder, Graduate School, College of Engineering and Applied Science, Department of Computer Science, Boulder, CO 80309. Offers ME, MS, PhD. Terminal master's awarded for partial completion of doctoral program. *Degree requirements:* For master's, comprehensive exam, thesis or alternative; for doctorate, one foreign language, thesis/dissertation. *Entrance requirements:* For master's, minimum undergraduate GPA of 3.0. Electronic applications accepted. Application fee is waived when completed online.

University of Colorado Denver, Business School, Program in Computer Science and Information Systems, Denver, CO 80217. Offers PhD. *Degree requirements:* For doctorate, comprehensive exam, thesis/dissertation. *Entrance requirements:* For doctorate, GMAT or GRE General Test, letters of recommendation, portfolio, essay describing applicant's motivation and initial plan for doctoral study, resume. Additional exam requirements/recommendations for international students: required—TOEFL (minimum score 525 paper-based; 71 iBT); recommended—IELTS (minimum score 6.5). Electronic applications accepted. *Expenses:* Contact institution.

University of Colorado Denver, College of Engineering, Design and Computing, Department of Computer Science and Engineering, Denver, CO 80217. Offers computer science (MS); computer science and engineering (EASPh D); computer science and information systems (PhD). *Program availability:* Part-time, evening/weekend. *Degree requirements:* For master's, thesis or alternative, at least 30 semester hours of computer science courses while maintaining minimum GPA of 3.0; for doctorate, comprehensive exam, thesis/dissertation, at least 60 hours beyond the master's degree level, 30 of which are dissertation research. *Entrance requirements:* For master's, GRE, minimum GPA of 3.0, 10 semester hours of university-level calculus, at least one math course beyond calculus, statement of purpose, letters of recommendation; for doctorate, GRE or GMAT. Additional exam requirements/recommendations for international students: required—TOEFL (minimum score 537 paper-based; 75 iBT). Electronic applications accepted. Tuition and fees vary according to course load, program and reciprocity agreements.

University of Colorado Denver, College of Liberal Arts and Sciences, Program in Integrated Sciences, Denver, CO 80217. Offers applied science (MIS); computer science (MIS); mathematics (MIS). *Program availability:* Part-time, evening/weekend. *Entrance requirements:* For master's, GRE if undergraduate GPA is 3.0 or less, minimum of 40 semester hours in mathematics, computer science, physics, biology, chemistry and/or geology; essay; three letters of recommendation. Tuition and fees vary according to course load, program and reciprocity agreements.

University of Connecticut, Graduate School, School of Engineering, Department of Computer Science and Engineering, Storrs, CT 06269. Offers computer science (MS, PhD), including artificial intelligence, computer architecture, computer science, operating systems, robotics, software engineering. Terminal master's awarded for partial completion of doctoral program. *Degree requirements:* For master's, comprehensive exam, thesis or alternative; for doctorate, thesis/dissertation. *Entrance requirements:* For master's and doctorate, GRE General Test. Additional exam requirements/recommendations for international students: required—TOEFL (minimum score 550 paper-based). Electronic applications accepted.

University of Dayton, Department of Computer Science, Dayton, OH 45469. Offers MCS. *Program availability:* Part-time. *Degree requirements:* For master's, software project, additional coursework, or thesis. *Entrance requirements:* For master's, minimum GPA of 3.0, undergraduate degree in computer science or related field. Additional exam requirements/recommendations for international students: required—TOEFL (minimum score 550 paper-based; 80 iBT). Electronic applications accepted.

University of Delaware, College of Engineering, Department of Computer and Information Sciences, Newark, DE 19716. Offers MS, PhD. *Program availability:* Part-time. Terminal master's awarded for partial completion of doctoral program. *Degree requirements:* For master's, thesis optional; for doctorate, comprehensive exam, thesis/dissertation. *Entrance requirements:* For master's and doctorate, GRE General Test. Additional exam requirements/recommendations for international students: required—TOEFL (minimum score 550 paper-based). Electronic applications accepted.

University of Denver, Daniel Felix Ritchie School of Engineering and Computer Science, Department of Computer Science, Denver, CO 80208. Offers computer science (MS, PhD); cybersecurity (MS); data science (MS). *Program availability:* Part-time, evening/weekend. *Faculty:* 18 full-time (3 women), 3 part-time/adjunct (1 woman). *Students:* 25 full-time (10 women), 135 part-time (39 women); includes 36 minority (4 Black or African American, non-Hispanic/Latino; 9 Asian, non-Hispanic/Latino; 16 Hispanic/Latino; 7 Two or more races, non-Hispanic/Latino), 50 international. Average age 30. 315 applicants, 69% accepted, 90 enrolled. In 2019, 44 master's awarded.

Degree requirements: For doctorate, variable foreign language requirement, comprehensive exam, thesis/dissertation, reading competency in two languages, modern typesetting system, or additional coursework. *Entrance requirements:* For master's and doctorate, GRE General Test, bachelor's degree, transcripts, personal statement, resume or curriculum vitae, three letters of recommendation. Additional exam requirements/recommendations for international students: required—TOEFL (minimum score 550 paper-based; 80 iBT). *Application deadline:* For fall admission, 1/15 priority date for domestic and international students; for winter admission, 10/25 for domestic and international students; for spring admission, 2/7 for domestic and international students; for summer admission, 4/24 for domestic and international students. Applications are processed on a rolling basis. Application fee: $65. Electronic applications accepted. *Financial support:* In 2019–20, 78 students received support, including 1 research assistantship with tuition reimbursement available (averaging $6,900 per year), 17 teaching assistantships with tuition reimbursements available (averaging $17,487 per year); career-related internships or fieldwork, Federal Work-Study, institutionally sponsored loans, scholarships/grants, and unspecified assistantships also available. Financial award application deadline: 2/15; financial award applicants required to submit FAFSA. *Unit head:* Dr. Chris GauthierDickey, Professor and Chair, 303-871-3318, E-mail: Chris.GauthierDickey@du.edu. *Application contact:* Information Contact, 303-871-2458, E-mail: info@cs.du.edu.
Website: http://ritchieschool.du.edu/departments/computer-science/

University of Detroit Mercy, College of Liberal Arts and Education, Detroit, MI 48221. Offers addiction counseling (MA); addiction studies (Certificate); clinical mental health counseling (MA); clinical psychology (MA, PhD); computer and information systems (MS); criminal justice (MA); curriculum and instruction (MA); economics (MA); educational administration (MA); financial economics (MA); industrial/organizational psychology (MA); information assurance (MS); intelligence analysis (MA); liberal studies (MALS); religious studies (MA); school counseling (MA, Certificate); school psychology (Spec); security administration (MS); special education: emotionally impaired/behaviorally disordered (MA); special education: learning disabilities (MA). *Program availability:* Part-time, evening/weekend. *Degree requirements:* For doctorate, departmental qualifying exam.

University of Fairfax, Graduate Programs, Vienna, VA 22182. Offers business administration (DBA); computer science (MCS); cybersecurity (MBA, MS); general business administration (MBA); information technology (MBA); project management (MBA).

University of Florida, Graduate School, Herbert Wertheim College of Engineering, Department of Computer and Information Science and Engineering, Gainesville, FL 32611. Offers computer engineering (ME, MS, PhD); computer science (MS); digital arts and sciences (MS). *Program availability:* Part-time, online learning. Terminal master's awarded for partial completion of doctoral program. *Degree requirements:* For master's, comprehensive exam, thesis optional; for doctorate, comprehensive exam, thesis/dissertation. *Entrance requirements:* For master's and doctorate, minimum GPA of 3.0. Additional exam requirements/recommendations for international students: required—TOEFL (minimum score 550 paper-based; 80 iBT), IELTS (minimum score 6). Electronic applications accepted.

University of Georgia, Franklin College of Arts and Sciences, Department of Computer Science, Athens, GA 30602. Offers applied mathematical science (MAMS); computer science (MS, PhD). *Degree requirements:* For doctorate, thesis/dissertation. *Entrance requirements:* For master's and doctorate, GRE General Test. Electronic applications accepted.

University of Guelph, Office of Graduate and Postdoctoral Studies, College of Physical and Engineering Science, Department of Computing and Information Science, Guelph, ON N1G 2W1, Canada. Offers applied computer science (M Sc); computer science (PhD). *Degree requirements:* For master's, thesis; for doctorate, comprehensive exam, thesis/dissertation. *Entrance requirements:* For master's, major or minor in computer science, honors degree; for doctorate, M Sc in computer science or related discipline. Additional exam requirements/recommendations for international students: required—TOEFL (minimum score 600 paper-based; 89 iBT), IELTS (minimum score 6.5). Electronic applications accepted.

University of Hawaii at Manoa, Office of Graduate Education, College of Natural Sciences, Department of Information and Computer Sciences, Honolulu, HI 96822. Offers computer science (MS, PhD); library and information science (MLI Sc, Graduate Certificate, including advanced library and information science (Graduate Certificate), library and information science (MLI Sc). *Program availability:* Part-time. *Degree requirements:* For master's, thesis optional; for doctorate, comprehensive exam, thesis/dissertation. *Entrance requirements:* For master's and doctorate, GRE. Additional exam requirements/recommendations for international students: required—TOEFL (minimum score 580 paper-based; 92 iBT), IELTS (minimum score 5).

University of Houston, College of Natural Sciences and Mathematics, Department of Computer Science, Houston, TX 77204. Offers MA, PhD. *Program availability:* Part-time. Terminal master's awarded for partial completion of doctoral program. *Degree requirements:* For master's, thesis or alternative; for doctorate, comprehensive exam, thesis/dissertation. *Entrance requirements:* For master's and doctorate, GRE. Additional exam requirements/recommendations for international students: required—TOEFL (minimum score 550 paper-based; 79 iBT), IELTS (minimum score 6.5). Electronic applications accepted.

University of Houston–Clear Lake, School of Science and Computer Engineering, Program in Computer Science, Houston, TX 77058-1002. Offers MS. *Program availability:* Part-time, evening/weekend. *Entrance requirements:* For master's, GRE General Test. Additional exam requirements/recommendations for international students: required—TOEFL (minimum score 550 paper-based).

University of Houston–Victoria, School of Arts and Sciences, Department of Computer Science, Victoria, TX 77901-4450. Offers computer information systems (MS); computer science (MS). *Program availability:* Part-time, evening/weekend, online learning. *Degree requirements:* For master's, comprehensive exam (for some programs), thesis (for some programs). *Entrance requirements:* For master's, GRE. Additional exam requirements/recommendations for international students: required—TOEFL (minimum score 550 paper-based).

University of Idaho, College of Graduate Studies, College of Engineering, Department of Computer Science, Moscow, ID 83844-2282. Offers MS, PhD. *Faculty:* 15 full-time. *Students:* 70 full-time (13 women), 22 part-time (5 women). Average age 33. In 2019, 11 master's, 4 doctorates awarded. *Degree requirements:* For doctorate, thesis/dissertation. *Entrance requirements:* For master's and doctorate, minimum GPA of 3.0. Additional exam requirements/recommendations for international students: required—TOEFL (minimum score 79 iBT). *Application deadline:* For fall admission, 7/30 for domestic students; for spring admission, 12/1 for domestic students. Applications are processed on a rolling basis. Application fee: $60. Electronic applications accepted. *Expenses:* Tuition, state resident: full-time $7753.80; part-time $502 per credit hour. Tuition, nonresident: full-time $26,990; part-time $1571 per credit hour. *Required fees:* $2122.20; $47 per credit hour. *Financial support:* Research assistantships, teaching assistantships, and career-related internships or fieldwork available. Financial award

applicants required to submit FAFSA. *Unit head:* Dr. Terry Soule, Chair, 208-885-6592, E-mail: csinfo@uidaho.edu. *Application contact:* Dr. Terry Soule, Chair, 208-885-6592, E-mail: csinfo@uidaho.edu.
Website: https://www.uidaho.edu/engr/departments/cs

University of Illinois at Chicago, College of Engineering, Department of Computer Science, Chicago, IL 60607-7128. Offers MS, PhD. *Program availability:* Part-time. *Degree requirements:* For master's, thesis or alternative; for doctorate, thesis/dissertation, departmental qualifying exam. *Entrance requirements:* For master's, BS in related field, minimum GPA of 2.75; for doctorate, GRE General Test, minimum GPA of 2.75, MS in related field. Additional exam requirements/recommendations for international students: required—TOEFL. *Expenses:* Contact institution.

University of Illinois at Chicago, College of Liberal Arts and Sciences, Department of Mathematics, Statistics, and Computer Science, Chicago, IL 60607-7128. Offers mathematics (DA); probability and statistics (PhD); secondary school mathematics (MST); statistics (MS). *Program availability:* Part-time. *Degree requirements:* For master's, comprehensive exam; for doctorate, one foreign language, thesis/dissertation. *Entrance requirements:* For master's and doctorate, GRE General Test, minimum GPA of 3.0. Additional exam requirements/recommendations for international students: required—TOEFL (minimum score 100 iBT). Electronic applications accepted.

University of Illinois at Springfield, Graduate Programs, College of Liberal Arts and Sciences, Program in Computer Science, Springfield, IL 62703-5407. Offers MS. *Program availability:* Part-time, 100% online, blended/hybrid learning. *Faculty:* 18 full-time (4 women), 2 part-time/adjunct (1 woman). *Students:* 115 full-time (46 women), 204 part-time (49 women); includes 73 minority (12 Black or African American, non-Hispanic/Latino; 45 Asian, non-Hispanic/Latino; 11 Hispanic/Latino; 5 Two or more races, non-Hispanic/Latino), 132 international. Average age 30. 550 applicants, 59% accepted, 94 enrolled. In 2019, 189 master's awarded. *Degree requirements:* For master's, comprehensive closure exercise. *Entrance requirements:* For master's, minimum undergraduate GPA of 2.7; bachelor's degree in computer science or the equivalent. Additional exam requirements/recommendations for international students: required—TOEFL (minimum score 550 paper-based; 79 iBT). *Application deadline:* Applications are processed on a rolling basis. Application fee: $60 ($75 for international students). Electronic applications accepted. *Expenses:* $40.75 per credit hour for onground and online students (differential tuition on top of the $33.25 per credit hour online fee). *Financial support:* In 2019–20, research assistantships with full tuition reimbursements (averaging $10,562 per year), teaching assistantships with full tuition reimbursements (averaging $10,652 per year) were awarded; fellowships, career-related internships or fieldwork, Federal Work-Study, scholarships/grants, health care benefits, and unspecified assistantships also available. Support available to part-time students. Financial award application deadline: 11/15; financial award applicants required to submit FAFSA. *Unit head:* Dr. Sviatoslav Braynov, Program Administrator, 217-206-8245, Fax: 217-206-6217, E-mail: sbray2@uis.edu. *Application contact:* Dr. Sviatoslav Braynov, Program Administrator, 217-206-8245, Fax: 217-206-6217, E-mail: sbray2@uis.edu.
Website: csc@uis.edu

University of Illinois at Urbana-Champaign, Graduate College, College of Engineering, Department of Computer Science, Champaign, IL 61820. Offers bioinformatics (MS); computer science (MCS, MS, PhD); MCS/JD; MCS/M Arch; MCS/MBA. *Program availability:* Part-time, evening/weekend, online learning.

The University of Iowa, Graduate College, College of Liberal Arts and Sciences, Department of Computer Science, Iowa City, IA 52242-1316. Offers MCS, PhD. *Degree requirements:* For master's, thesis optional, exam; for doctorate, comprehensive exam, thesis/dissertation. *Entrance requirements:* For master's, minimum GPA of 3.0; for doctorate, GRE General Test, minimum GPA of 3.0. Additional exam requirements/recommendations for international students: required—TOEFL (minimum score 550 paper-based; 81 iBT). Electronic applications accepted.

The University of Kansas, Graduate Studies, School of Engineering, Program in Computer Science, Lawrence, KS 66045. Offers MS, PhD. *Program availability:* Part-time, evening/weekend. *Students:* 53 full-time (16 women), 13 part-time (2 women); includes 6 minority (2 Black or African American, non-Hispanic/Latino; 3 Asian, non-Hispanic/Latino; 1 Two or more races, non-Hispanic/Latino), 33 international. Average age 27. 96 applicants, 55% accepted, 21 enrolled. In 2019, 13 master's, 4 doctorates awarded. Terminal master's awarded for partial completion of doctoral program. *Entrance requirements:* For master's, GRE (minimum scores: 146 verbal and 155 quantitative), minimum GPA of 3.0, official transcript, three recommendations, statement of academic objectives, resume; for doctorate, GRE (minimum scores: 146 verbal and 155 quantitative), minimum GPA of 3.5, official transcript, three recommendations, statement of academic objectives, resume. Additional exam requirements/recommendations for international students: required—TOEFL, IELTS. *Application deadline:* For fall admission, 12/15 priority date for domestic and international students; for spring admission, 10/1 for domestic and international students. Application fee: $65 ($85 for international students). Electronic applications accepted. *Expenses:* Tuition, state resident: full-time $9989. Tuition, nonresident: full-time $23,950. International tuition: $23,950 full-time. *Required fees:* $984; $81.99 per credit hour. Tuition and fees vary according to course load, campus/location and program. *Financial support:* Fellowships, research assistantships, teaching assistantships, career-related internships or fieldwork, scholarships/grants, and unspecified assistantships available. Financial award application deadline: 12/15. *Unit head:* Erik Perrins, Chair, 785-864-4486, E-mail: perrins@ku.edu. *Application contact:* Joy Grisafe-Gross, Graduate Admissions Contact, 785-864-4487, E-mail: jgrisafe@ku.edu.

University of Kentucky, Graduate School, College of Engineering, Program in Computer Science, Lexington, KY 40506-0032. Offers MS, PhD. *Degree requirements:* For master's, comprehensive exam, thesis optional; for doctorate, one foreign language, comprehensive exam, thesis/dissertation. *Entrance requirements:* For master's, GRE General Test, minimum undergraduate GPA of 2.75; for doctorate, GRE General Test, minimum undergraduate GPA of 3.0. Additional exam requirements/recommendations for international students: required—TOEFL (minimum score 550 paper-based). Electronic applications accepted.

University of Lethbridge, School of Graduate Studies, Lethbridge, AB T1K 3M4, Canada. Offers addictions counseling (M Sc); agricultural biotechnology (M Sc); agricultural studies (M Sc, MA); anthropology (MA); archaeology (M Sc, MA); art (MA, MFA); biochemistry (M Sc); biological sciences (M Sc); biomolecular science (PhD); biosystems and biodiversity (PhD); Canadian studies (MA); chemistry (M Sc); computer science (M Sc); computer science and geographical information science (M Sc); counseling (MC); counseling psychology (M Ed); dramatic arts (MA); earth, space, and physical science (PhD); economics (MA); education (MA, PhD); educational leadership (M Ed); English (MA); environmental science (M Sc); evolution and behavior (PhD); exercise science (M Sc); French (MA); French/German (MA); French/Spanish (MA); general education (M Ed); geography (M Sc, MA); German (MA); health sciences (M Sc); individualized multidisciplinary (M Sc, MA); kinesiology (M Sc, MA); management (M Sc), including accounting, finance, human resource management and labor relations, information systems, international management, marketing, policy and strategy; mathematics (M Sc); music (M Mus, MA); Native American studies (MA); neuroscience (M Sc, PhD); new media (MA, MFA); nursing (M Sc, MN); philosophy (MA); physics (M Sc); political science (MA); psychology (M Sc, MA); religious studies (MA); sociology (MA); theatre and dramatic arts (MFA); theoretical and computational science (PhD); urban and regional studies (MA); women and gender studies (MA). *Program availability:* Part-time, evening/weekend. *Degree requirements:* For master's, thesis (for some programs); for doctorate, comprehensive exam, thesis/dissertation. *Entrance requirements:* For master's, GMAT (for M Sc in management), bachelor's degree in related field, minimum GPA of 3.0 during previous 20 graded semester courses, 2 years' teaching or related experience (M Ed); for doctorate, master's degree, minimum graduate GPA of 3.5. Additional exam requirements/recommendations for international students: required—TOEFL (minimum score 580 paper-based; 93 iBT). Electronic applications accepted.

University of Louisville, J. B. Speed School of Engineering, Department of Computer Engineering and Computer Science, Louisville, KY 40292-0001. Offers computer engineering and computer science (M Eng); computer science (MS, PhD); cybersecurity (Certificate); data science (Certificate). *Accreditation:* ABET (one or more programs are accredited). *Program availability:* Part-time, 100% online, blended/hybrid learning. *Faculty:* 16 full-time (1 woman), 4 part-time/adjunct (3 women). *Students:* 82 full-time (28 women), 120 part-time (29 women); includes 35 minority (10 Black or African American, non-Hispanic/Latino; 15 Asian, non-Hispanic/Latino; 4 Hispanic/Latino; 6 Two or more races, non-Hispanic/Latino), 58 international. Average age 32. 90 applicants, 50% accepted, 32 enrolled. In 2019, 47 master's, 5 doctorates, 25 other advanced degrees awarded. Terminal master's awarded for partial completion of doctoral program. *Degree requirements:* For master's, thesis optional; for doctorate, comprehensive exam, thesis/dissertation. *Entrance requirements:* For master's, Two letters of recommendation, official final transcripts; for doctorate, GRE, Two letters of recommendation, personal statement, official final transcripts. Additional exam requirements/recommendations for international students: required—TOEFL (minimum score 550 paper-based; 80 iBT), IELTS (minimum score 6.5). *Application deadline:* For fall admission, 5/1 priority date for domestic and international students; for spring admission, 11/1 priority date for domestic and international students; for summer admission, 3/1 priority date for domestic and international students. Applications are processed on a rolling basis. Application fee: $65. Electronic applications accepted. *Expenses: Tuition, area resident:* Full-time $13,000; part-time $723 per credit hour. Tuition, state resident: full-time $13,000; part-time $723 per credit hour. Tuition, nonresident: full-time $27,114; part-time $1507 per credit hour. *International tuition:* $27,114 full-time. *Required fees:* $196. Tuition and fees vary according to program and reciprocity agreements. *Financial support:* In 2019–20, 70 students received support, including 1 fellowship with full tuition reimbursement available (averaging $22,000 per year), 14 teaching assistantships with full tuition reimbursements available (averaging $22,000 per year); research assistantships, scholarships/grants, health care benefits, and tuition waivers (full) also available. Financial award application deadline: 1/1. *Unit head:* Dr. Wei Zhang, Chair, Computer Science and Engineering, 502-852-0715, E-mail: wei.zhang@louisville.edu. *Application contact:* Dr. Mehmed Kantardzic, Director of Graduate Studies, 502-852-3703, E-mail: mehmed.kantardzic@louisville.edu.
Website: http://louisville.edu/speed/computer

University of Maine, Graduate School, College of Liberal Arts and Sciences, School of Computing and Information Science, Orono, ME 04469. Offers MS, PhD, CGS. *Program availability:* Part-time. *Faculty:* 13 full-time (2 women), 2 part-time/adjunct (1 woman). *Students:* 37 full-time (12 women), 26 part-time (16 women); includes 7 minority (2 Black or African American, non-Hispanic/Latino; 1 American Indian or Alaska Native, non-Hispanic/Latino; 2 Asian, non-Hispanic/Latino; 2 Two or more races, non-Hispanic/Latino), 12 international. Average age 35. 83 applicants, 90% accepted, 49 enrolled. In 2019, 4 master's, 2 doctorates, 7 other advanced degrees awarded. *Degree requirements:* For master's, thesis (for some programs); for doctorate, comprehensive exam, thesis/dissertation. *Entrance requirements:* For master's and doctorate, GRE General Test, GRE Subject Test. Additional exam requirements/recommendations for international students: required—TOEFL (minimum score 550 paper-based; 80 iBT). *Application deadline:* Applications are processed on a rolling basis. Application fee: $65. Electronic applications accepted. *Expenses: Tuition, area resident:* Full-time $8100; part-time $450 per credit hour. Tuition, state resident: full-time $8100; part-time $450 per credit hour. Tuition, nonresident: full-time $26,388; part-time $1466 per credit hour. *International tuition:* $26,388 full-time. *Required fees:* $1257; $278 per semester. Tuition and fees vary according to course load. *Financial support:* In 2019–20, 14 students received support, including 1 fellowship with full tuition reimbursement available (averaging $17,850 per year), 11 research assistantships with full tuition reimbursements available (averaging $17,000 per year), 2 teaching assistantships with full tuition reimbursements available (averaging $15,825 per year); career-related internships or fieldwork, Federal Work-Study, institutionally sponsored loans, tuition waivers (full), and unspecified assistantships also available. Financial award application deadline: 3/1; financial award applicants required to submit FAFSA. *Unit head:* Dr. Max Egenhofer, Acting Director, 207-581-2114, Fax: 207-581-2206. *Application contact:* Scott G. Delcourt, Assistant Vice President for Graduate Studies and Senior Associate Dean, 207-581-3291, Fax: 207-581-3232, E-mail: graduate@maine.edu.
Website: http://umaine.edu/cis/

University of Management and Technology, Program in Computer Science, Arlington, VA 22209-1609. Offers computer science (MS); information technology (AC); project management (AC); software engineering (MS). *Program availability:* Part-time, evening/weekend, online learning. *Entrance requirements:* For master's, 3 recommendations, resume. Additional exam requirements/recommendations for international students: required—TOEFL (minimum score 530 paper-based; 71 iBT). Electronic applications accepted. *Expenses: Tuition:* Full-time $7020; part-time $390 per credit hour. *Required fees:* $90; $30 per semester.

The University of Manchester, School of Computer Science, Manchester, United Kingdom. Offers M Phil, PhD.

University of Manitoba, Faculty of Graduate Studies, Faculty of Science, Department of Computer Science, Winnipeg, MB R3T 2N2, Canada. Offers M Sc, PhD. *Degree requirements:* For master's, thesis or alternative; for doctorate, thesis/dissertation.

University of Maryland, Baltimore County, The Graduate School, College of Engineering and Information Technology, Department of Computer Science and Electrical Engineering, Program in Computer Science, Baltimore, MD 21250. Offers MS, PhD. *Program availability:* Part-time. *Faculty:* 34 full-time (7 women), 49 part-time/adjunct (10 women). *Students:* 191 full-time (62 women), 45 part-time (11 women); includes 19 minority (5 Black or African American, non-Hispanic/Latino; 12 Asian, non-Hispanic/Latino; 2 Hispanic/Latino), 174 international. Average age 27. 372 applicants, 53% accepted, 45 enrolled. In 2019, 62 master's, 9 doctorates awarded. *Degree requirements:* For master's, comprehensive exam (for some programs), thesis (for some programs); for doctorate, comprehensive exam, thesis/dissertation. *Entrance requirements:* For master's, GRE General Test, strong background in computer science and math courses; for doctorate, GRE General Test, MS in computer science (strongly recommended). Additional exam requirements/recommendations for international students: required—TOEFL (minimum score 550 paper-based; 80 iBT). *Application deadline:* For fall admission, 6/1 for domestic students, 1/1 for international students; for spring admission, 11/1 for domestic students, 6/1 for international students. Applications are processed on a rolling basis. Application fee: $70. Electronic applications accepted. *Expenses:* $14,382 per year. *Financial support:* In 2019–20, 107 students received support, including 1 fellowship with full tuition reimbursement available, 44 research assistantships with full tuition reimbursements available, 62 teaching assistantships with full tuition reimbursements available; career-related internships or fieldwork, Federal Work-Study, scholarships/grants, health care benefits, tuition waivers (partial), and unspecified assistantships also available. Support available to part-time students. Financial award application deadline: 6/30; financial award applicants required to submit FAFSA. *Unit head:* Dr. Anupam Joshi, Professor and Chair, 410-455-3500, Fax: 410-455-3969, E-mail: joshi@cs.umbc.edu. *Application contact:* Dr. Charles Nicholas, Professor and Interim Graduate Program Director, 410-455-3000, Fax: 410-455-3969, E-mail: nicholas@umbc.edu.
Website: http://www.csee.umbc.edu/

University of Maryland, Baltimore County, The Graduate School, College of Engineering and Information Technology, Department of Information Systems, Program in Human-Centered Computing, Baltimore, MD 21250. Offers MS, PhD. *Program availability:* Part-time, evening/weekend. *Students:* 36 full-time (21 women), 19 part-time (13 women); includes 14 minority (8 Black or African American, non-Hispanic/Latino; 5 Asian, non-Hispanic/Latino; 1 Two or more races, non-Hispanic/Latino), 25 international. Average age 31. 73 applicants, 56% accepted, 15 enrolled. In 2019, 14 master's, 2 doctorates awarded. Terminal master's awarded for partial completion of doctoral program. *Degree requirements:* For master's, comprehensive exam (for some programs), thesis optional; for doctorate, comprehensive exam, thesis/dissertation. *Entrance requirements:* For master's, minimum GPA of 3.0; for doctorate, GRE General Test or GMAT, competence in statistical analysis and experimental design. Additional exam requirements/recommendations for international students: required—TOEFL (minimum score 550 paper-based; 80 iBT). *Application deadline:* For fall admission, 6/1 for domestic students, 1/1 for international students; for spring admission, 11/1 for domestic students, 6/1 for international students. Applications are processed on a rolling basis. Application fee: $70. Electronic applications accepted. *Expenses:* $14,382 per year. *Financial support:* In 2019–20, 13 students received support, including 5 research assistantships with full tuition reimbursements available, 8 teaching assistantships with full tuition reimbursements available; fellowships with full tuition reimbursements available, career-related internships or fieldwork, Federal Work-Study, scholarships/grants, health care benefits, tuition waivers (partial), and unspecified assistantships also available. Support available to part-time students. Financial award application deadline: 6/30; financial award applicants required to submit FAFSA. *Unit head:* Dr. Arrya Gangopadhyay, Professor and Chair, 410-455-2620, Fax: 410-455-1217, E-mail: gangopad@umbc.edu. *Application contact:* Dr. Amy Hurst, Associate Professor and Graduate Program Director, 410-455-8146, Fax: 410-455-1217, E-mail: amyhurst@umbc.edu.
Website: https://informationsystems.umbc.edu/

University of Maryland, College Park, Academic Affairs, College of Computer, Mathematical and Natural Sciences, Department of Computer Science, College Park, MD 20742. Offers MS, PhD. *Program availability:* Part-time, evening/weekend. Terminal master's awarded for partial completion of doctoral program. *Degree requirements:* For master's, thesis or scholarly paper and exam; for doctorate, thesis/dissertation. *Entrance requirements:* For master's and doctorate, GRE General Test, GRE Subject Test (recommended), minimum GPA of 3.0, 3 letters of recommendation. Additional exam requirements/recommendations for international students: required—TOEFL; recommended—TWE. Electronic applications accepted.

University of Maryland Eastern Shore, Graduate Programs, Department of Mathematics and Computer Science, Princess Anne, MD 21853. Offers applied computer science (MS). *Program availability:* Part-time, evening/weekend. *Degree requirements:* For master's, thesis or alternative, research project. *Entrance requirements:* For master's, GRE General Test, minimum GPA of 3.0. Additional exam requirements/recommendations for international students: required—TOEFL (minimum score 80 iBT). Electronic applications accepted.

University of Massachusetts Amherst, Graduate School, College of Natural Sciences, School of Computer Science, Amherst, MA 01003. Offers MS, PhD. *Program availability:* Part-time. Terminal master's awarded for partial completion of doctoral program. *Degree requirements:* For master's, thesis or alternative; for doctorate, comprehensive exam, thesis/dissertation. *Entrance requirements:* For master's and doctorate, GRE General Test. Additional exam requirements/recommendations for international students: required—TOEFL (minimum score 550 paper-based; 80 iBT), IELTS (minimum score 6.5), TWE. Electronic applications accepted.

University of Massachusetts Boston, College of Science and Mathematics, Program in Computer Science, Boston, MA 02125-3393. Offers MS, PhD. *Program availability:* Part-time, evening/weekend. *Entrance requirements:* For master's and doctorate, GRE General Test, minimum GPA of 2.75. Additional exam requirements/recommendations for international students: required—TOEFL (minimum score 80 iBT).

University of Massachusetts Dartmouth, Graduate School, College of Engineering, Department of Computer Science, North Dartmouth, MA 02747-2300. Offers computer science (MS, Graduate Certificate); software development and design (Postbaccalaureate Certificate). *Program availability:* Part-time, 100% online, blended/hybrid learning. *Degree requirements:* For master's, thesis, thesis or project. *Entrance requirements:* For master's, GRE unless UMass Dartmouth graduate in computer science, statement of purpose (minimum of 300 words), resume, 3 letters of recommendation, official transcripts; for other advanced degree, statement of purpose (minimum of 300 words), resume, official transcripts. Additional exam requirements/recommendations for international students: required—TOEFL (minimum score 533 paper-based; 72 iBT), IELTS (minimum score 6). Electronic applications accepted.

University of Massachusetts Lowell, College of Sciences, Department of Computer Science, Lowell, MA 01854. Offers MS, PhD. *Program availability:* Part-time. *Degree requirements:* For master's, thesis optional; for doctorate, thesis/dissertation. *Entrance requirements:* For master's and doctorate, GRE General Test.

University of Memphis, Graduate School, College of Arts and Sciences, Department of Computer Science, Memphis, TN 38152. Offers bioinformatics (MS); computer science (MS, PhD). *Students:* 80 full-time (29 women), 32 part-time (5 women); includes 19 minority (7 Black or African American, non-Hispanic/Latino; 10 Asian, non-Hispanic/Latino; 2 Hispanic/Latino), 73 international. Average age 30. 112 applicants, 70% accepted, 23 enrolled. In 2019, 7 master's, 5 doctorates awarded. Terminal master's awarded for partial completion of doctoral program. *Degree requirements:* For master's, comprehensive exam, thesis; for doctorate, comprehensive exam, thesis/dissertation, qualifying exam, final exam. *Entrance requirements:* For master's and doctorate, GRE, letters of recommendation. Additional exam requirements/recommendations for international students: required—TOEFL (minimum score 550 paper-based; 79 iBT). *Application deadline:* Applications are processed on a rolling basis. Application fee: $35 ($60 for international students). *Expenses: Tuition, area resident:* Full-time $9216; part-time $512 per credit hour. Tuition, state resident: full-time $9216; part-time $512 per

credit hour. Tuition, nonresident: full-time $12,672; part-time $704 per credit hour. *International tuition:* $16,128 full-time. *Required fees:* $1530; $85 per credit hour. Tuition and fees vary according to program. *Financial support:* Fellowships, research assistantships with full tuition reimbursements, teaching assistantships with full tuition reimbursements, Federal Work-Study, scholarships/grants, and unspecified assistantships available. Financial award application deadline: 2/1; financial award applicants required to submit FAFSA. *Unit head:* Dr. Lan Wang, Chair, 901-678-1643, Fax: 901-678-1506, E-mail: lanwang@memphis.edu. *Application contact:* Dr. Scott Fleming, Graduate Coordinator, 901-678-3142, E-mail: info@cs.memphis.edu.
Website: https://www.memphis.edu/cs/

University of Miami, Graduate School, College of Arts and Sciences, Department of Computer Science, Coral Gables, FL 33124. Offers MS, PhD. *Program availability:* Part-time, online learning. *Degree requirements:* For master's, comprehensive exam (for some programs), thesis. *Entrance requirements:* For master's, GRE. Additional exam requirements/recommendations for international students: required—TOEFL. Electronic applications accepted.

University of Michigan, College of Engineering, Department of Computer Science and Engineering, Ann Arbor, MI 48109. Offers MS, MSE, PhD. *Program availability:* Part-time.

University of Michigan–Dearborn, College of Engineering and Computer Science, PhD Program in Computer and Information Science, Dearborn, MI 48128. Offers data management (PhD); data science (PhD); software engineering (PhD); systems and security (PhD). *Faculty:* 19 full-time (1 woman), 5 part-time/adjunct (0 women). *Students:* 8 full-time (5 women), 6 part-time (1 woman); includes 1 minority (Asian, non-Hispanic/Latino), 11 international. Average age 28. 17 applicants, 24% accepted, 3 enrolled. In 2019, 1 doctorate awarded. *Degree requirements:* For doctorate, comprehensive exam, thesis/dissertation. *Entrance requirements:* For doctorate, GRE, bachelor's or master's degree in computer science or closely-related field. Additional exam requirements/recommendations for international students: required—TOEFL (minimum score 560 paper-based; 84 iBT), IELTS (minimum score 6.5). *Application deadline:* For fall admission, 2/1 for domestic and international students. Application fee: $60. Electronic applications accepted. *Financial support:* Research assistantships with full tuition reimbursements, teaching assistantships with full tuition reimbursements, scholarships/grants, health care benefits, and unspecified assistantships available. Financial award application deadline: 2/1; financial award applicants required to submit FAFSA. *Unit head:* Dr. Di Ma, Director, 313-583-6737, E-mail: dmadma@umich.edu. *Application contact:* Office of Graduate Studies, 313-583-6321, E-mail: umd-graduatestudies@umich.edu.
Website: https://umdearborn.edu/cecs/departments/computer-and-information-science/graduate-programs/phd-computer-and-information-science

University of Michigan–Flint, College of Arts and Sciences, Program in Computer Science and Information Systems, Flint, MI 48502-1950. Offers computer science (MS); information systems (MS), including business information systems, health information systems. *Program availability:* Part-time, evening/weekend, 100% online. *Faculty:* 13 full-time (4 women), 9 part-time/adjunct (3 women). *Students:* 29 full-time (13 women), 49 part-time (11 women); includes 13 minority (5 Black or African American, non-Hispanic/Latino; 1 American Indian or Alaska Native, non-Hispanic/Latino; 2 Asian, non-Hispanic/Latino; 4 Hispanic/Latino; 1 Two or more races, non-Hispanic/Latino), 27 international. Average age 31. 196 applicants, 59% accepted, 15 enrolled. In 2019, 29 master's awarded. *Degree requirements:* For master's, thesis optional, Non Thesis option available. *Entrance requirements:* For master's, BS from regionally-accredited institution in computer science, computer information systems, or computer engineering (preferred); minimum overall undergraduate GPA of 3.0. Additional exam requirements/recommendations for international students: required—TOEFL (minimum score 84 iBT), IELTS (minimum score 6.5). *Application deadline:* For fall admission, 8/1 for domestic students, 5/1 for international students; for winter admission, 11/15 for domestic students, 10/1 for international students; for spring admission, 3/15 for domestic students, 1/1 for international students; for summer admission, 5/15 for domestic students. Applications are processed on a rolling basis. Application fee: $55. Electronic applications accepted. *Expenses:* Contact institution. *Financial support:* Federal Work-Study, scholarships/grants, and unspecified assistantships available. Financial award application deadline: 3/1; financial award applicants required to submit FAFSA. *Unit head:* Dr. Mark Allison, Department Chair, 810-424-5509, Fax: 810-766-6780, E-mail: markalli@umich.edu. *Application contact:* Matt Bohlen, Associate Director of Graduate Programs, 810-762-3171, Fax: 810-766-6789, E-mail: mbohlen@umflint.edu.
Website: http://www.umflint.edu/graduateprograms/computer-science-information-systems-ms

University of Minnesota, Duluth, Graduate School, Swenson College of Science and Engineering, Department of Computer Science, Duluth, MN 55812-2496. Offers MS. *Program availability:* Part-time. *Entrance requirements:* For master's, GRE General Test, minimum GPA of 3.0. Additional exam requirements/recommendations for international students: required—TOEFL (minimum score 550 paper-based). Electronic applications accepted.

University of Minnesota, Twin Cities Campus, College of Science and Engineering, Department of Computer Science and Engineering, Minneapolis, MN 55455-0213. Offers computer science (MCS, MS, PhD); data science (MS); software engineering (MSSE). *Program availability:* Part-time. Terminal master's awarded for partial completion of doctoral program. *Degree requirements:* For doctorate, thesis/dissertation. *Entrance requirements:* For master's and doctorate, GRE General Test. Additional exam requirements/recommendations for international students: required—TOEFL. Electronic applications accepted.

University of Minnesota, Twin Cities Campus, College of Science and Engineering, Scientific Computation Program, Minneapolis, MN 55455-0213. Offers MS, PhD. *Program availability:* Part-time. *Degree requirements:* For master's, thesis; for doctorate, thesis/dissertation. *Entrance requirements:* For master's and doctorate, GRE General Test. Additional exam requirements/recommendations for international students: required—TOEFL (minimum score 550 paper-based; 79 iBT), IELTS (minimum score 6.5). Electronic applications accepted.

University of Mississippi, Graduate School, School of Engineering, University, MS 38677. Offers aeroacoustics (MS, PhD); chemical engineering (MS, PhD); civil engineering (MS, PhD); computational hydroscience (MS, PhD); computer science (MS, PhD); electrical engineering (MS, PhD); electromagnetics (MS, PhD); environmental engineering (MS, PhD); geology and geological engineering (MS, PhD); hydrology (MS); material science (MS); mechanical engineering (MS, PhD); telecommunications (MS). *Students:* 104 full-time (23 women), 19 part-time (5 women); includes 10 minority (3 Black or African American, non-Hispanic/Latino; 6 Asian, non-Hispanic/Latino; 1 Hispanic/Latino), 72 international. Average age 30. In 2019, 36 master's, 17 doctorates awarded. *Expenses:* Tuition, state resident: full-time $8718; part-time $484.25 per credit hour. Tuition, nonresident: full-time $24,990; part-time $1388.25 per credit hour. *Required fees:* $100; $4.16 per credit hour. *Unit head:* Dr. David Puleo, Dean, 662-915-5780, Fax: 662-915-5387, E-mail: engineer@olemiss.edu. *Application contact:* Temeka Smith, Graduate Activities Specialist for Admissions, 662-915-7474, Fax: 662-915-7577, E-mail: gschool@olemiss.edu.

University of Missouri, Office of Research and Graduate Studies, College of Engineering, Department of Electrical Engineering and Computer Science, Columbia, MO 65211. Offers computer engineering (MSCE); computer science (MS, PhD); electrical and computer engineering (PhD); electrical engineering (MSEE). *Entrance requirements:* For master's, GRE General Test, minimum GPA of 3.0; for doctorate, GRE General Test, GRE Subject Test, minimum GPA of 3.0. Additional exam requirements/recommendations for international students: required—TOEFL.

University of Missouri–Kansas City, School of Computing and Engineering, Kansas City, MO 64110-2499. Offers civil engineering (MS); computer and electrical engineering (PhD); computer science (MS), including bioinformatics, software engineering, telecommunications networking; computer science and informatics (PhD); computing (PhD); electrical engineering (MS); engineering (PhD); engineering and construction management (Graduate Certificate); mechanical engineering (MS); telecommunications and computer networking (PhD). *Program availability:* Part-time. *Degree requirements:* For doctorate, thesis/dissertation. *Entrance requirements:* For master's, GRE General Test, minimum GPA of 3.0, 3 letters of recommendation from professors; for doctorate, GRE General Test, minimum GPA of 3.5. Additional exam requirements/recommendations for international students: required—TOEFL (minimum score 550 paper-based; 80 iBT).

University of Missouri–St. Louis, College of Arts and Sciences, Department of Mathematics and Computer Science, St. Louis, MO 63121. Offers computer science (MS); mathematical and computational sciences (PhD); mathematics (MA). *Program availability:* Part-time, evening/weekend. *Degree requirements:* For master's, thesis optional; for doctorate, thesis/dissertation. *Entrance requirements:* For master's, GRE (for teaching assistantships), 2 letters of recommendation; C programming, C++ or Java (for computer science); for doctorate, GRE General Test, 3 letters of recommendation. Additional exam requirements/recommendations for international students: required—TOEFL (minimum score 550 paper-based; 79 iBT), IELTS (minimum score 6.5). Electronic applications accepted. *Expenses: Tuition, area resident:* Full-time $9005.40; part-time $6003.60 per credit hour. Tuition, state resident: full-time $9005.40; part-time $6003.60 per credit hour. Tuition, nonresident: full-time $22,108; part-time $14,738.40 per credit hour. *International tuition:* $22,107.60 full-time. Tuition and fees vary according to course load.

University of Montana, Graduate School, College of Humanities and Sciences, Department of Computer Science, Missoula, MT 59812. Offers MS. *Program availability:* Part-time. *Degree requirements:* For master's, project or thesis. *Entrance requirements:* For master's, GRE General Test. Additional exam requirements/recommendations for international students: required—TOEFL (minimum score 525 paper-based).

University of Nebraska at Omaha, Graduate Studies, College of Information Science and Technology, Department of Computer Science, Omaha, NE 68182. Offers artificial intelligence (Certificate); communication networks (Certificate); computer science (MA, MS); computer science education (MS, Certificate); software engineering (Certificate); system and architecture (Certificate). *Program availability:* Part-time, evening/weekend. *Degree requirements:* For master's, comprehensive exam, thesis (for some programs). *Entrance requirements:* For master's, GRE General Test, minimum GPA of 3.0, prior course work in computer science, official transcripts, resume, 2 letters of recommendation; for Certificate, minimum GPA of 3.0, resume. Additional exam requirements/recommendations for international students: required—TOEFL, IELTS, PTE. Electronic applications accepted.

University of Nebraska–Lincoln, Graduate College, College of Arts and Sciences and College of Engineering, Department of Computer Science and Engineering, Lincoln, NE 68588. Offers bioinformatics (MS, PhD); computer engineering (MS, PhD); computer science (MS, PhD); information technology (PhD). *Degree requirements:* For master's, thesis optional; for doctorate, comprehensive exam, thesis/dissertation. *Entrance requirements:* For master's and doctorate, GRE General Test. Additional exam requirements/recommendations for international students: required—TOEFL (minimum score 600 paper-based). Electronic applications accepted.

University of Nevada, Reno, Graduate School, College of Engineering, Department of Computer Science and Engineering, Reno, NV 89557. Offers MS, PhD. Terminal master's awarded for partial completion of doctoral program. *Degree requirements:* For master's, thesis optional; for doctorate, thesis/dissertation. *Entrance requirements:* For master's, GRE General Test, minimum GPA of 2.75; for doctorate, GRE General Test, minimum GPA of 3.0. Additional exam requirements/recommendations for international students: required—TOEFL (minimum score 500 paper-based; 61 iBT), IELTS (minimum score 6). Electronic applications accepted.

University of New Hampshire, Graduate School, College of Engineering and Physical Sciences, Department of Computer Science, Durham, NH 03824. Offers MS, PhD. *Program availability:* Part-time, evening/weekend. *Students:* 64 full-time (12 women), 23 part-time (5 women); includes 1 minority (Asian, non-Hispanic/Latino), 58 international. Average age 28. 176 applicants, 64% accepted, 27 enrolled. In 2019, 16 master's, 1 doctorate awarded. *Entrance requirements:* For master's and doctorate, GRE General Test. Additional exam requirements/recommendations for international students: required—TOEFL (minimum score 550 paper-based; 80 iBT), IELTS (minimum score 6.5), PTE. *Application deadline:* For fall admission, 4/1 for domestic students; for spring admission, 12/1 for domestic students. Application fee: $65. Electronic applications accepted. *Financial support:* In 2019–20, 67 students received support, including 16 research assistantships, 16 teaching assistantships; fellowships, career-related internships or fieldwork, Federal Work-Study, scholarships/grants, and tuition waivers (full and partial) also available. Support available to part-time students. Financial award application deadline: 3/1. *Unit head:* Radim Bartos, Department Chair, 603-862-3792. *Application contact:* Rebecca Kibler, Department Coordinator, 603-862-3778, E-mail: rebecca.kibler@unh.edu.
Website: http://www.ceps.unh.edu/computer-science

University of New Haven, Graduate School, Tagliatela College of Engineering, Program in Computer Science, West Haven, CT 06516. Offers computer programming (Graduate Certificate); computer science (MS); network systems (MS); software development (MS). *Program availability:* Part-time, evening/weekend. *Students:* 107 full-time (36 women), 26 part-time (7 women); includes 11 minority (2 Black or African American, non-Hispanic/Latino; 7 Asian, non-Hispanic/Latino; 1 Hispanic/Latino; 1 Two or more races, non-Hispanic/Latino), 104 international. Average age 26. 560 applicants, 61% accepted, 26 enrolled. In 2019, 41 master's awarded. *Entrance requirements:* Additional exam requirements/recommendations for international students: required—TOEFL (minimum score 75 iBT), IELTS, PTE (minimum score 50). *Application deadline:* Applications are processed on a rolling basis. Application fee: $50. Electronic applications accepted. Application fee is waived when completed online. *Financial support:* Research assistantships with partial tuition reimbursements, teaching assistantships with partial tuition reimbursements, career-related internships or fieldwork, Federal Work-Study, scholarships/grants, and unspecified assistantships available. Support available to part-time students. Financial award applicants required to submit FAFSA. *Unit head:* Dr. Barun Chandra, Associate Professor, 203-932-7089,

E-mail: bchandra@newhaven.edu. *Application contact:* Selina O'Toole, Senior Associate Director of Graduate Admissions, 203-932-7337, E-mail: sotoole@newhaven.edu.
Website: https://www.newhaven.edu/engineering/graduate-programs/computer-science/

University of New Mexico, Graduate Studies, School of Engineering, Program in Computer Science, Albuquerque, NM 87131. Offers MS, PhD. *Program availability:* Part-time. *Faculty:* 15 full-time (4 women), 5 part-time/adjunct (0 women). *Students:* 56 full-time (16 women), 88 part-time (21 women); includes 32 minority (2 Black or African American, non-Hispanic/Latino; 10 Asian, non-Hispanic/Latino; 19 Hispanic/Latino; 1 Native Hawaiian or other Pacific Islander, non-Hispanic/Latino), 53 international. 129 applicants, 41% accepted, 25 enrolled. In 2019, 30 master's, 7 doctorates awarded. Terminal master's awarded for partial completion of doctoral program. *Entrance requirements:* For master's and doctorate, GRE General Test, minimum GPA of 3.0. Additional exam requirements/recommendations for international students: required—TOEFL (minimum score 550 paper-based; 80 iBT), IELTS (minimum score 6.5), IELTS or TOEFL, not both. *Application deadline:* For fall admission, 1/15 for domestic students, 3/1 for international students; for spring admission, 8/1 for domestic and international students. Applications are processed on a rolling basis. Application fee: $50. Electronic applications accepted. *Expenses:* Tuition, state resident: full-time $7633; part-time $972 per year. Tuition, nonresident: full-time $22,586; part-time $3840 per year. *International tuition:* $23,292 full-time. *Required fees:* $8608. Tuition and fees vary according to course level, course load, degree level, program and student level. *Financial support:* In 2019–20, 32 research assistantships with full tuition reimbursements, 13 teaching assistantships with full tuition reimbursements were awarded; fellowships with full tuition reimbursements, career-related internships or fieldwork, scholarships/grants, and health care benefits also available. Financial award application deadline: 1/15; financial award applicants required to submit FAFSA. *Unit head:* Dr. Darko Stefanovic, Chairperson, 505-277-3112, Fax: 505-277-6927, E-mail: darko@cs.unm.edu. *Application contact:* Lynn Conner, Sr. Academic Advisor, 505-277-3112, Fax: 505-277-6927, E-mail: ljconner@unm.edu.
Website: https://www.cs.unm.edu/programs-and-degrees/masters/index.html

University of New Orleans, Graduate School, College of Sciences, Department of Computer Science, New Orleans, LA 70148. Offers MS, PhD. *Entrance requirements:* For master's, GRE General Test. Additional exam requirements/recommendations for international students: required—TOEFL (minimum score 550 paper-based; 79 iBT), IELTS (minimum score 6.5). Electronic applications accepted.

The University of North Carolina at Chapel Hill, Graduate School, College of Arts and Sciences, Department of Computer Science, Chapel Hill, NC 27599. Offers MS, PhD. *Program availability:* Part-time, online learning. Terminal master's awarded for partial completion of doctoral program. *Degree requirements:* For master's, comprehensive exam, thesis or alternative, programming product; for doctorate, comprehensive exam, thesis/dissertation, programming product, teaching requirement. *Entrance requirements:* For master's and doctorate, GRE General Test, minimum GPA of 3.0. Additional exam requirements/recommendations for international students: required—TOEFL (minimum score 575 paper-based). Electronic applications accepted.

The University of North Carolina at Charlotte, College of Computing and Informatics, Program in Computing and Information Systems, Charlotte, NC 28223-0001. Offers computing and information systems (PhD), including bioinformatics, business information systems and operations management, computer science, interdisciplinary, software and information systems. *Students:* 97 full-time (26 women), 26 part-time (6 women); includes 5 minority (2 Black or African American, non-Hispanic/Latino; 1 Asian, non-Hispanic/Latino; 1 Hispanic/Latino; 1 Two or more races, non-Hispanic/Latino), 95 international. Average age 30. 65 applicants, 48% accepted, 24 enrolled. In 2019, 20 doctorates awarded. *Degree requirements:* For doctorate, thesis/dissertation, Qualifying Exam. *Entrance requirements:* For doctorate, GRE or GMAT, baccalaureate degree, minimum GPA of 3.0 on courses related to the chosen field of PhD study, one-page essay, three reference letters. Additional exam requirements/recommendations for international students: required—TOEFL (minimum score 557 paper-based; 83 iBT), IELTS (minimum score 6.5), TOEFL (minimum score 557 paper-based, 83 iBT) or IELTS (6.5). *Application deadline:* For fall admission, 2/1 priority date for domestic students; for spring admission, 9/1 priority date for domestic students. Applications are processed on a rolling basis. Application fee: $75. Electronic applications accepted. *Expenses:* Tuition, state resident: full-time $4337. Tuition, nonresident: full-time $17,771. *Required fees:* $3093. Tuition and fees vary according to course load, degree level and program. *Financial support:* Career-related internships or fieldwork, institutionally sponsored loans, scholarships/grants, health care benefits, and unspecified assistantships available. Support available to part-time students. Financial award applicants required to submit FAFSA. *Unit head:* Dr. Fatma Mili, Dean, 704-687-8450. *Application contact:* Kathy B. Giddings, Director of Graduate Admissions, 704-687-5503, Fax: 704-687-1668, E-mail: gradadm@uncc.edu.

The University of North Carolina at Greensboro, Graduate School, College of Arts and Sciences, Department of Computer Science, Greensboro, NC 27412-5001. Offers MS.

The University of North Carolina Wilmington, Interdisciplinary Program in Computer Science and Information Systems, Wilmington, NC 28403-3297. Offers computer science and information systems (MS); data science (MS). *Faculty:* 10 full-time (2 women). *Students:* 11 full-time (5 women), 13 part-time (2 women); includes 2 minority (1 Asian, non-Hispanic/Latino; 1 Two or more races, non-Hispanic/Latino), 10 international. Average age 30. 23 applicants, 52% accepted, 6 enrolled. In 2019, 8 master's awarded. *Degree requirements:* For master's, thesis or alternative, research project. *Entrance requirements:* For master's, GMAT or GRE, 3 letters of recommendation, resume, statement of interest. Additional exam requirements/recommendations for international students: required—TOEFL (minimum score 79 iBT), IELTS (minimum score 6.5). *Application deadline:* For fall admission, 6/1 for domestic students; for spring admission, 11/15 for domestic students. Applications are processed on a rolling basis. Application fee: $75. Electronic applications accepted. *Expenses:* $3,818.47 full-time in-state; $10,732.97 full-time out-of-state. *Financial support:* Scholarships/grants and unspecified assistantships available. Financial award application deadline: 1/1; financial award applicants required to submit FAFSA. *Unit head:* Dr. Clayton Ferner, Program Coordinator, 910-962-7552, E-mail: cferner@uncw.edu. *Application contact:* Candace Wilhelm, Graduate Coordinator, 910-962-3903, Fax: 910-962-7457, E-mail: wilhelmc@uncw.edu.
Website: http://csb.uncw.edu/mscsis/

University of North Dakota, Graduate School, John D. Odegard School of Aerospace Sciences, Department of Computer Science, Grand Forks, ND 58202. Offers MS. *Program availability:* Part-time. *Degree requirements:* For master's, comprehensive exam, thesis or alternative. *Entrance requirements:* For master's, GRE General Test, minimum GPA of 3.0. Additional exam requirements/recommendations for international students: required—TOEFL (minimum score 550 paper-based; 79 iBT), IELTS (minimum score 6.5). Electronic applications accepted.

University of Northern British Columbia, Office of Graduate Studies, Prince George, BC V2N 4Z9, Canada. Offers business administration (Diploma); community health science (M Sc); disability management (MA); education (M Ed); first nations studies (MA); gender studies (MA); history (MA); interdisciplinary studies (MA); international studies (MA); mathematical, computer and physical sciences (M Sc); natural resources and environmental studies (M Sc, MA, MNRES, PhD); political science (MA); psychology (M Sc, PhD); social work (MSW). *Program availability:* Part-time, evening/weekend, online learning. *Degree requirements:* For master's, thesis; for doctorate, thesis/dissertation. *Entrance requirements:* For master's, GRE, minimum B average in undergraduate course work; for doctorate, candidacy exam, minimum A average in graduate course work.

University of North Florida, College of Computing, Engineering, and Construction, School of Computing, Jacksonville, FL 32224. Offers computer science (MS); information systems (MS); software engineering (MS). *Program availability:* Part-time. *Degree requirements:* For master's, thesis. *Entrance requirements:* For master's, GRE General Test, minimum GPA of 3.0 in last 60 hours of course work. Additional exam requirements/recommendations for international students: required—TOEFL (minimum score 500 paper-based; 61 iBT). Electronic applications accepted.

University of North Texas, Toulouse Graduate School, Denton, TX 76203-5459. Offers accounting (MS); applied anthropology (MA, MS); applied behavior analysis (Certificate); applied geography (MA); applied technology and performance improvement (M Ed, MS); art education (MA); art history (MA); arts leadership (Certificate); audiology (Au D); behavior analysis (MS); behavioral science (PhD); biochemistry and molecular biology (MS); biology (MA, MS); biomedical engineering (MS); business analysis (MS); chemistry (MS); clinical health psychology (PhD); communication studies (MA, MS); computer engineering (MS); computer science (MS); counseling (M Ed, MS), including clinical mental health counseling (MS), college and university counseling, elementary school counseling, secondary school counseling; creative writing (MA); criminal justice (MS); curriculum and instruction (M Ed); decision sciences (MBA); design (MA, MFA), including fashion design (MFA), innovation studies, interior design (MFA); early childhood studies (MS); economics (MS); educational leadership (M Ed, Ed D); educational psychology (MS, PhD), including family studies (MS), gifted and talented (MS), human development (MS), learning and cognition (MS), research, measurement and evaluation (MS); electrical engineering (MS); emergency management (MPA); engineering technology (MS); English (MA); English as a second language (MA); environmental science (MS); finance (MBA, MS); financial management (MPA); French (MA); health services management (MBA); higher education (M Ed, Ed D); history (MA, MS); hospitality management (MS); human resources management (MPA); information science (MS); information systems (PhD); information technologies (MBA); interdisciplinary studies (MA, MS); international studies (MA); international sustainable tourism (MS); jazz studies (MM); journalism (MA, MJ, Graduate Certificate), including interactive and virtual digital communication (Graduate Certificate), narrative journalism (Graduate Certificate), public relations (Graduate Certificate); kinesiology (MS); linguistics (MA); local government management (MPA); logistics (PhD); logistics and supply chain management (MBA); long-term care, senior housing, and aging services (MA); management (PhD); marketing (MBA); mathematics (MA, MS); mechanical and energy engineering (MS, PhD); music (MA), including ethnomusicology, music theory, musicology, performance; music composition (PhD); music education (MM Ed, PhD); nonprofit management (MPA); operations and supply chain management (MBA); performance (MM, DMA); philosophy (MA); political science (MA); professional and technical communication (MA); radio, television and film (MA, MFA); rehabilitation counseling (Certificate); sociology (MA); Spanish (MA); special education (M Ed); speech-language pathology (MA); strategic management (MBA); studio art (MFA); teaching (M Ed); MBA/MS. *Program availability:* Part-time, evening/weekend, online learning. Terminal master's awarded for partial completion of doctoral program. *Degree requirements:* For master's, variable foreign language requirement, comprehensive exam (for some programs), thesis (for some programs); for doctorate, variable foreign language requirement, comprehensive exam (for some programs), thesis/dissertation; for other advanced degree, variable foreign language requirement, comprehensive exam (for some programs). *Entrance requirements:* For master's and doctorate, GRE, GMAT. Additional exam requirements/recommendations for international students: required—TOEFL (minimum score 550 paper-based; 79 iBT). Electronic applications accepted.

University of Notre Dame, The Graduate School, College of Engineering, Department of Computer Science and Engineering, Notre Dame, IN 46556. Offers MSCSE, PhD. Terminal master's awarded for partial completion of doctoral program. *Degree requirements:* For master's, comprehensive exam; for doctorate, thesis/dissertation, candidacy exam. *Entrance requirements:* For master's and doctorate, GRE General Test. Additional exam requirements/recommendations for international students: required—TOEFL (minimum score 600 paper-based; 80 iBT). Electronic applications accepted.

University of Oklahoma, Gallogly College of Engineering, School of Computer Science, Norman, OK 73019. Offers computer science (PhD), including bioinformatics, general/standard. *Program availability:* Part-time. *Degree requirements:* For master's, comprehensive exam (for some programs), thesis (for some programs), 5 seminars; for doctorate, comprehensive exam, thesis/dissertation, 5 seminars. *Entrance requirements:* For master's and doctorate, GRE, bachelor's degree, resume, 3 letters of recommendation, statement of purpose. Additional exam requirements/recommendations for international students: required—TOEFL (minimum score 79 iBT) or IELTS (minimum score 6.5). Electronic applications accepted. *Expenses:* Tuition, state resident: full-time $6583.20; part-time $274.30 per credit hour. Tuition, nonresident: full-time $21,242; part-time $885.10 per credit hour. *International tuition:* $21,242.40 full-time. *Required fees:* $1994.20; $72.55 per credit hour. $126.50 per semester. Tuition and fees vary according to course load and degree level.

University of Oregon, Graduate School, College of Arts and Sciences, Department of Computer and Information Science, Eugene, OR 97403. Offers MA, MS, PhD. *Program availability:* Part-time. Terminal master's awarded for partial completion of doctoral program. *Degree requirements:* For doctorate, thesis/dissertation. *Entrance requirements:* For master's and doctorate, GRE General Test, minimum GPA of 3.0. Additional exam requirements/recommendations for international students: required—TOEFL.

University of Ottawa, Faculty of Graduate and Postdoctoral Studies, Faculty of Engineering, Ottawa-Carleton Institute for Computer Science, Ottawa, ON K1N 6N5, Canada. Offers MCS, PhD. *Degree requirements:* For master's, thesis or alternative; for doctorate, comprehensive exam, thesis/dissertation, two seminars. *Entrance requirements:* For master's, honors degree or equivalent, minimum B average; for doctorate, minimum B+ average. Electronic applications accepted.

University of Pennsylvania, School of Engineering and Applied Science, Department of Computer and Information Science, Philadelphia, PA 19104. Offers computer and information science (MSE, PhD); computer and information technology (MCIT); computer graphics and game technology (MSE). *Program availability:* Part-time. *Faculty:* 61 full-time (9 women), 9 part-time/adjunct (0 women). *Students:* 250 full-time (63 women), 23 part-time (2 women); includes 36 minority (6 Black or African American,

non-Hispanic/Latino; 27 Asian, non-Hispanic/Latino; 2 Hispanic/Latino; 1 Two or more races, non-Hispanic/Latino), 173 international. Average age 26. 2,124 applicants, 12% accepted, 103 enrolled. In 2019, 87 master's, 18 doctorates awarded. Terminal master's awarded for partial completion of doctoral program. *Degree requirements:* For master's, comprehensive exam, thesis optional; for doctorate, comprehensive exam, thesis/dissertation. *Entrance requirements:* For master's and doctorate, GRE, bachelor's degree, letters of recommendation, resume, personal statement. Additional exam requirements/recommendations for international students: required—TOEFL (minimum score 100 iBT), IELTS (minimum score 7). *Application deadline:* For fall admission, 12/15 priority date for domestic and international students. Application fee: $80. Electronic applications accepted. *Expenses:* Contact institution. *Application contact:* Associate Director of Graduate Admissions, 215-898-4542, Fax: 215-573-5577, E-mail: admissions2@upenn.edu.
Website: http://www.cis.upenn.edu/prospective-students/graduate/

University of Pittsburgh, School of Computing and Information, Department of Computer Science, Pittsburgh, PA 15260. Offers MS, PhD. *Program availability:* Part-time, online learning. *Faculty:* 21 full-time (5 women), 1 part-time/adjunct (0 women). *Students:* 95 full-time (23 women), 8 part-time (2 women); includes 8 minority (5 Asian, non-Hispanic/Latino; 1 Hispanic/Latino; 2 Two or more races, non-Hispanic/Latino), 75 international. Average age 28. 521 applicants, 14% accepted, 27 enrolled. In 2019, 13 master's, 6 doctorates awarded. Terminal master's awarded for partial completion of doctoral program. *Degree requirements:* For master's, thesis optional; for doctorate, comprehensive exam, thesis/dissertation. *Entrance requirements:* For master's, GRE, BS degree, GPA of at least 3.0, Applicants must have completed courses in areas of Computer Science and Mathematics; for doctorate, GRE. Additional exam requirements/recommendations for international students: required—TOEFL (minimum score 90 iBT). *Application deadline:* For fall admission, 1/15 priority date for domestic and international students; for spring admission, 9/15 for domestic students, 6/15 for international students. Applications are processed on a rolling basis. Application fee: $50. Electronic applications accepted. *Expenses:* Fall & spring: $24,74 in-state, $41,952 out-of-state, $950 mandatory fees. *Financial support:* In 2019–20, 67 students received support, including 7 fellowships with full and partial tuition reimbursements available (averaging $23,846 per year), 26 research assistantships with full and partial tuition reimbursements available (averaging $19,950 per year), 34 teaching assistantships with full and partial tuition reimbursements available (averaging $19,585 per year); institutionally sponsored loans, scholarships/grants, health care benefits, tuition waivers, and unspecified assistantships also available. Financial award application deadline: 1/15; financial award applicants required to submit FAFSA. *Unit head:* Dr. Alexandros Labrinidis, Chair and Professor, 412-624-8843, Fax: 412-624-5249, E-mail: labrinid@cs.pitt.edu. *Application contact:* Keena M. Walker, Department and Graduate Support Administrator, 412-624-8495, Fax: 412-624-5249, E-mail: keena@cs.pitt.edu.
Website: http://www.cs.pitt.edu/

University of Portland, Shiley School of Engineering, Portland, OR 97203-5798. Offers biomedical engineering (MBME); civil engineering (ME); computer science (ME); electrical engineering (ME); mechanical engineering (ME). *Program availability:* Part-time, evening/weekend. *Degree requirements:* For master's, thesis optional. *Entrance requirements:* For master's, GRE General Test, minimum GPA of 3.0, 2 letters of recommendation, resume, statement of goals, official transcripts. Additional exam requirements/recommendations for international students: required—TOEFL (minimum score 80 iBT), IELTS (minimum score 7). Electronic applications accepted. *Expenses:* Contact institution.

University of Puerto Rico at Mayagüez, Graduate Studies, College of Engineering, Computer Science and Engineering Program, Mayagüez, PR 00681-9000. Offers PhD. *Program availability:* Part-time. *Degree requirements:* For doctorate, one foreign language, comprehensive exam, thesis/dissertation. *Entrance requirements:* For doctorate, GRE General Test, BS in engineering or science; undergraduate courses in data structures, programming language, calculus III and linear algebra, or the equivalent. Electronic applications accepted.

University of Puerto Rico at Mayagüez, Graduate Studies, College of Engineering, Department of Electrical and Computer Engineering, Mayagüez, PR 00681-9000. Offers computer engineering (ME, MS); computing and information sciences and engineering (PhD); electrical engineering (ME, MS). *Program availability:* Part-time. Terminal master's awarded for partial completion of doctoral program. *Degree requirements:* For master's, one foreign language, comprehensive exam, thesis; for doctorate, one foreign language, comprehensive exam, thesis/dissertation. *Entrance requirements:* For master's and doctorate, proficiency in English and Spanish; BS in electrical or computer engineering, or equivalent; minimum GPA of 3.0. Electronic applications accepted.

University of Regina, Faculty of Graduate Studies and Research, Faculty of Science, Department of Computer Science, Regina, SK S4S 0A2, Canada. Offers M Sc, PhD. *Program availability:* Part-time. *Faculty:* 18 full-time (5 women), 11 part-time/adjunct (0 women). *Students:* 143 full-time (50 women), 9 part-time (3 women). Average age 25. 391 applicants, 8% accepted. In 2019, 33 master's, 2 doctorates awarded. *Degree requirements:* For master's, thesis (for some programs), project or report; for doctorate, thesis/dissertation. *Entrance requirements:* For master's, 4 years bachelor degree in Computer science or related program; for doctorate, applicants must have obtained a thesis-based master's degree in the discipline to qualify as a doctoral student. Applicants must have academic credentials consistent with being fully-qualified to undertake graduate work at the doctoral level. Additional exam requirements/recommendations for international students: required—TOEFL (minimum score 580 paper-based; 80 iBT), IELTS (minimum score 6.5), PTE (minimum score 59), options are CAEL, MELAB, Cantest and U of R ESL. *Application deadline:* For fall admission, 3/15 for domestic and international students; for winter admission, 7/15 for domestic and international students; for spring admission, 11/15 for domestic and international students. Application fee: $100. Electronic applications accepted. *Expenses:* Tuition: Full-time $6684 Canadian dollars. *Required fees:* $100 Canadian dollars; $3351.45 Canadian dollars per trimester. $1117.15 Canadian dollars per semester. Tuition and fees vary according to course level, course load, degree level and program. *Financial support:* Fellowships, research assistantships, teaching assistantships, career-related internships or fieldwork, Federal Work-Study, scholarships/grants, unspecified assistantships, and travel award and Graduate Scholarship Base Funds available. Financial award application deadline: 9/30. *Unit head:* Dr. David Gerhard, Department Head, 306-585-5227, Fax: 306-585-4745, E-mail: gerhard@cs.uregina.ca. *Application contact:* Dr. Orland Hoeber, Graduate Program Coordinator, 306-585-4598, Fax: 306-585-4745, E-mail: gscoord@cs.uregina.ca.
Website: http://www.cs.uregina.ca

University of Rhode Island, Graduate School, College of Arts and Sciences, Department of Computer Science and Statistics, Kingston, RI 02881. Offers computer science (MS, PhD); cyber security (PSM, Graduate Certificate); digital forensics (Graduate Certificate). *Program availability:* Part-time, evening/weekend, 100% online, blended/hybrid learning. *Faculty:* 20 full-time (6 women). *Students:* 29 full-time (13 women), 88 part-time (19 women); includes 16 minority (5 Black or African American, non-Hispanic/Latino; 5 Asian, non-Hispanic/Latino; 5 Hispanic/Latino; 1 Two or more races, non-Hispanic/Latino), 13 international. 77 applicants, 82% accepted, 39 enrolled.

In 2019, 47 master's, 3 doctorates, 25 other advanced degrees awarded. Terminal master's awarded for partial completion of doctoral program. *Entrance requirements:* Additional exam requirements/recommendations for international students: required—TOEFL. *Application deadline:* For fall admission, 7/15 for domestic students, 2/1 for international students; for spring admission, 11/15 for domestic students, 7/15 for international students. Application fee: $65. Electronic applications accepted. *Expenses: Tuition, area resident:* Full-time $13,734; part-time $763 per credit. Tuition, state resident: Full-time $13,734; part-time $763 per credit. Tuition, nonresident: Full-time $26,512; part-time $1473 per credit. *International tuition:* $26,512 full-time. *Required fees:* $1780; $52 per credit. $35 per term. One-time fee: $165. *Financial support:* In 2019–20, 3 research assistantships with tuition reimbursements (averaging $9,645 per year), 15 teaching assistantships with tuition reimbursements (averaging $13,546 per year) were awarded; unspecified assistantships also available. Financial award application deadline: 2/1; financial award applicants required to submit FAFSA. *Unit head:* Dr. Lisa DiPippo, Chair, 401-874-2701, Fax: 401-874-4617, E-mail: dipippo@cs.uri.edu. *Application contact:* Dr. Lutz Hamel, Graduate Program Director, 401-874-2701, E-mail: lutzhamel@uri.edu.
Website: http://www.cs.uri.edu/

University of Rochester, Hajim School of Engineering and Applied Sciences, Department of Computer Science, Rochester, NY 14627. Offers algorithms and complexity (MS); artificial intelligence and machine learning (MS); computer architecture (MS); computer science (PhD); human computer interaction (MS); natural language processing (MS); programming languages and computer systems (MS). *Faculty:* 19 full-time (3 women). *Students:* 124 full-time (23 women), 1 (woman) part-time; includes 6 minority (2 Black or African American, non-Hispanic/Latino; 3 Asian, non-Hispanic/Latino; 1 Two or more races, non-Hispanic/Latino), 98 international. Average age 26. 925 applicants, 16% accepted, 37 enrolled. In 2019, 42 master's, 4 doctorates awarded. Terminal master's awarded for partial completion of doctoral program. *Degree requirements:* For master's, comprehensive exam (for some programs), thesis (for some programs); for doctorate, comprehensive exam, thesis/dissertation, qualifying exam. *Entrance requirements:* For master's and doctorate, GRE General Test, personal statement, transcripts, three letters of recommendation. Additional exam requirements/recommendations for international students: required—TOEFL (minimum score 100 iBT), IELTS. *Application deadline:* For fall admission, 12/15 for domestic and international students. Application fee: $60. Electronic applications accepted. *Financial support:* In 2019–20, 74 students received support, including 4 fellowships with full tuition reimbursements available (averaging $33,708 per year), 40 research assistantships with full tuition reimbursements available (averaging $31,200 per year), 30 teaching assistantships with full tuition reimbursements available (averaging $31,200 per year); scholarships/grants, traineeships, health care benefits, and tuition waivers (full and partial) also available. Financial award application deadline: 12/15. *Unit head:* Michael Scott, Professor and Chair, 585-275-7745, E-mail: scott@cs.rochester.edu. *Application contact:* Emily Tevens, Graduate Coordinator, 585-275-7737, E-mail: etevens@cs.rochester.edu.
Website: https://www.cs.rochester.edu/graduate/index.html

University of San Francisco, College of Arts and Sciences, Computer Science Program, San Francisco, CA 94117. Offers MS. *Program availability:* Part-time. *Faculty:* 7 full-time (2 women), 3 part-time/adjunct (0 women). *Students:* 114 full-time (43 women), 2 part-time (1 woman); includes 15 minority (13 Asian, non-Hispanic/Latino; 2 Hispanic/Latino), 90 international. Average age 27. 512 applicants, 35% accepted, 54 enrolled. In 2019, 32 master's awarded. *Degree requirements:* For master's, thesis optional. *Entrance requirements:* For master's, GRE General Test, GRE Subject Test, BS in computer science or related field. Additional exam requirements/recommendations for international students: required—TOEFL (minimum score 79 iBT), IELTS (minimum score 6.5), PTE (minimum score 53). *Application deadline:* For fall admission, 3/1 for domestic and international students. Applications are processed on a rolling basis. Application fee: $55. Electronic applications accepted. Application fee is waived when completed online. *Financial support:* Fellowships with partial tuition reimbursements, teaching assistantships, career-related internships or fieldwork, and scholarships/grants available. Financial award applicants required to submit FAFSA. *Unit head:* Gian Bruno, Graduate Director, 415-422-5247, E-mail: gbruno@usfca.edu. *Application contact:* Information Contact, 415-422-5101, E-mail: asgraduate@usfca.edu.
Website: https://www.usfca.edu/arts-sciences/graduate-programs/computer-science

University of Saskatchewan, College of Graduate and Postdoctoral Studies, College of Arts and Science, Department of Computer Science, Saskatoon, SK S7N 5A2, Canada. Offers M Sc, PhD. *Degree requirements:* For master's, thesis; for doctorate, comprehensive exam (for some programs), thesis/dissertation. *Entrance requirements:* For master's and doctorate, GRE. Additional exam requirements/recommendations for international students: required—TOEFL (minimum score 80 iBT); recommended—IELTS (minimum score 6.5). Electronic applications accepted.

University of South Alabama, School of Computing, Mobile, AL 36688-0002. Offers computer science (MS); information systems (MS). *Program availability:* Part-time, evening/weekend. *Faculty:* 18 full-time (3 women). *Students:* 83 full-time (26 women), 18 part-time (5 women); includes 22 minority (13 Black or African American, non-Hispanic/Latino; 1 American Indian or Alaska Native, non-Hispanic/Latino; 3 Asian, non-Hispanic/Latino; 1 Hispanic/Latino; 1 Native Hawaiian or other Pacific Islander, non-Hispanic/Latino; 3 Two or more races, non-Hispanic/Latino), 28 international. Average age 32. 61 applicants, 82% accepted, 25 enrolled. In 2019, 29 master's, 2 doctorates awarded. *Degree requirements:* For master's, comprehensive exam; for doctorate, comprehensive exam, thesis/dissertation. *Entrance requirements:* For master's and doctorate, GRE. Additional exam requirements/recommendations for international students: required—TOEFL (minimum score 525 paper-based; 71 iBT), IELTS (minimum score 6), TOEFL or IELTS required. *Application deadline:* For fall admission, 7/15 priority date for domestic students, 6/15 priority date for international students; for spring admission, 12/1 priority date for domestic students, 11/1 priority date for international students; for summer admission, 5/1 priority date for domestic students, 4/1 priority date for international students. Applications are processed on a rolling basis. Application fee: $45. Electronic applications accepted. *Expenses:* Contact institution. *Financial support:* Fellowships, research assistantships, teaching assistantships, Federal Work-Study, institutionally sponsored loans, scholarships/grants, and unspecified assistantships available. Support available to part-time students. Financial award application deadline: 3/31; financial award applicants required to submit FAFSA. *Unit head:* Dr. Alec Yasinsac, Dean, Professor, School of Computing, 251-460-6390, Fax: 251-460-7274, E-mail: yasinsac@southalabama.edu. *Application contact:* Dr. Debra Chapman, Director of Graduate Studies, Assistant Professor, School of Computing, 251-460-1599, Fax: 251-460-7274, E-mail: dchapman@southalabama.edu.
Website: http://www.southalabama.edu/colleges/soc/

University of South Carolina, The Graduate School, College of Engineering and Computing, Department of Computer Science and Engineering, Columbia, SC 29208. Offers computer science and engineering (ME, MS, PhD); software engineering (MS). *Program availability:* Part-time, evening/weekend, online learning. *Degree requirements:* For master's, comprehensive exam, thesis (for some programs); for doctorate, comprehensive exam, thesis/dissertation. *Entrance requirements:* For master's and doctorate, GRE General Test. Additional exam requirements/recommendations for international students: required—TOEFL (minimum score 570 paper-based). Electronic applications accepted.

University of South Dakota, Graduate School, College of Arts and Sciences, Department of Computer Science, Vermillion, SD 57069. Offers MS. *Program availability:* Part-time. *Degree requirements:* For master's, thesis optional. *Entrance requirements:* For master's, GRE General Test, GRE Subject Test (recommended), minimum GPA of 2.7. Additional exam requirements/recommendations for international students: required—TOEFL (minimum score 550 paper-based; 79 iBT). Electronic applications accepted.

University of Southern California, Graduate School, Viterbi School of Engineering, Department of Computer Science, Los Angeles, CA 90089. Offers computer networks (MS); computer science (MS, PhD); computer security (MS); game development (MS); high performance computing and simulations (MS); human language technology (MS); intelligent robotics (MS); multimedia and creative technologies (MS); software engineering (MS). *Program availability:* Part-time, evening/weekend, online learning. *Entrance requirements:* For master's and doctorate, GRE General Test. Additional exam requirements/recommendations for international students: required—TOEFL. Electronic applications accepted.

University of Southern Maine, College of Science, Technology, and Health, Department of Computer Science, Portland, ME 04103. Offers computer science (MS); software systems (CGS). *Program availability:* Part-time. *Degree requirements:* For master's, thesis. *Entrance requirements:* For master's, GRE General Test, minimum GPA of 3.0. Additional exam requirements/recommendations for international students: required—TOEFL. Electronic applications accepted. *Expenses: Tuition, area resident:* Full-time $864; part-time $432 per credit hour. Tuition, state resident: full-time $864; part-time $432 per credit hour. Tuition, nonresident: full-time $2372; part-time $1186 per credit hour. *Required fees:* $141; $108 per credit hour. Tuition and fees vary according to course load.

University of Southern Mississippi, College of Arts and Sciences, School of Computing Sciences and Computer Engineering, Hattiesburg, MS 39406-0001. Offers computational science (MS, PhD); computer science (MS). *Students:* 31 full-time (6 women), 8 part-time (2 women); includes 11 minority (1 Black or African American, non-Hispanic/Latino; 8 Asian, non-Hispanic/Latino; 1 Hispanic/Latino; 1 Two or more races, non-Hispanic/Latino), 22 international. 68 applicants, 37% accepted, 11 enrolled. In 2019, 19 master's awarded. *Degree requirements:* For master's, comprehensive exam, thesis; for doctorate, comprehensive exam, thesis/dissertation. *Entrance requirements:* For master's, GRE General Test, minimum GPA of 2.75 in last 60 hours; for doctorate, GRE General Test, minimum GPA of 3.5. Additional exam requirements/recommendations for international students: required—TOEFL, IELTS. *Application deadline:* Applications are processed on a rolling basis. Application fee: $60. Electronic applications accepted. *Expenses: Tuition, area resident:* Full-time $4393; part-time $488 per credit hour. Tuition, nonresident: full-time $5393; part-time $600 per credit hour. *Required fees:* $6 per semester. *Financial support:* Research assistantships with full tuition reimbursements, teaching assistantships with full tuition reimbursements, Federal Work-Study, institutionally sponsored loans, scholarships/grants, health care benefits, and unspecified assistantships available. Financial award application deadline: 3/15; financial award applicants required to submit FAFSA. *Unit head:* Andrew H. Sung, Director, 601-266-4949, Fax: 601-266-5829. *Application contact:* Andrew H. Sung, Director, 601-266-4949, Fax: 601-266-5829.
Website: https://www.usm.edu/computing-sciences-computer-engineering/index.php

University of South Florida, College of Engineering, Department of Computer Science and Engineering, Tampa, FL 33620-9951. Offers computer engineering (MSCP); computer science and engineering (PhD). *Program availability:* Part-time. *Faculty:* 33 full-time (6 women). *Students:* 177 full-time (57 women), 36 part-time (10 women); includes 30 minority (7 Black or African American, non-Hispanic/Latino; 9 Asian, non-Hispanic/Latino; 13 Hispanic/Latino; 1 Two or more races, non-Hispanic/Latino), 161 international. Average age 27. 595 applicants, 35% accepted, 64 enrolled. In 2019, 56 master's, 11 doctorates awarded. Terminal master's awarded for partial completion of doctoral program. *Degree requirements:* For master's, comprehensive exam, thesis or alternative; for doctorate, comprehensive exam, thesis/dissertation, teaching of at least one undergraduate computer science and engineering course. *Entrance requirements:* For master's, GRE General Test, minimum GPA of 3.0, three letters of recommendation, statement of purpose, mathematical preparation; for the MSIT, evidence of completion of a defined subset of the required core courses of the USF BSIT; for doctorate, GRE General Test, minimum GPA of 3.0, three letters of recommendation, statement of purpose that includes three areas of research interest, mathematical preparation. Additional exam requirements/recommendations for international students: required—TOEFL, TOEFL (minimum score 550 paper-based; 79 iBT) or IELTS (minimum score 6.5). *Application deadline:* For fall admission, 2/15 for domestic and international students; for spring admission, 10/15 for domestic students, 9/15 for international students. Application fee: $30. Electronic applications accepted. *Financial support:* In 2019–20, 25 students received support, including 30 research assistantships with tuition reimbursements available (averaging $14,942 per year), 35 teaching assistantships with tuition reimbursements available (averaging $14,003 per year); unspecified assistantships also available. Financial award application deadline: 1/1; financial award applicants required to submit FAFSA. *Unit head:* Dr. Lawrence Hall, Professor and Department Chair, 813-974-4195, Fax: 813-974-5094, E-mail: hall@cse.usf.edu. *Application contact:* Dr. Yu Sun, Graduate Program Director, 813-974-7508, E-mail: yusun@usf.edu.
Website: http://www.cse.usf.edu/

The University of Tennessee, Graduate School, College of Arts and Sciences, Department of Computer Science, Knoxville, TN 37996. Offers MS, PhD. *Program availability:* Part-time. *Degree requirements:* For master's, thesis or alternative; for doctorate, thesis/dissertation. *Entrance requirements:* For master's and doctorate, GRE General Test, minimum GPA of 2.7. Additional exam requirements/recommendations for international students: required—TOEFL. Electronic applications accepted.

The University of Tennessee, Graduate School, Tickle College of Engineering, Min H. Kao Department of Electrical Engineering and Computer Science, Program in Computer Science, Knoxville, TN 37996-2250. Offers MS, PhD. *Program availability:* Part-time. *Faculty:* 25 full-time (4 women). *Students:* 84 full-time (10 women), 10 part-time (3 women); includes 14 minority (2 Black or African American, non-Hispanic/Latino; 9 Asian, non-Hispanic/Latino; 1 Hispanic/Latino; 2 Two or more races, non-Hispanic/Latino), 21 international. Average age 29. 155 applicants, 25% accepted, 27 enrolled. In 2019, 22 master's, 7 doctorates awarded. *Degree requirements:* For master's, thesis or alternative; for doctorate, comprehensive exam, thesis/dissertation. *Entrance requirements:* For master's, GRE General Test (for MS students pursuing research thesis), minimum GPA of 2.7 (for U.S. degree holders), 3.0 (for international degree holders); 3 references; personal statement; for doctorate, GRE General Test, minimum GPA of 3.0 on previous graduate coursework; 3 references; personal statement. Additional exam requirements/recommendations for international students: required—TOEFL (minimum score 550 paper-based; 80 iBT), IELTS (minimum score 6.5). *Application deadline:* For fall admission, 2/1 priority date for domestic and international students; for spring admission, 6/15 for domestic and international students; for summer admission, 10/15 for domestic and international students. Applications are processed on a rolling basis. Application fee: $60. Electronic applications accepted. *Financial support:* In 2019–20, 46 students received support, including 18 fellowships with full tuition reimbursements available (averaging $28,488 per year), 18 research assistantships with full tuition reimbursements available (averaging $22,876 per year), 10 teaching assistantships with full tuition reimbursements available (averaging $18,061 per year); career-related internships or fieldwork, Federal Work-Study, institutionally sponsored loans, health care benefits, and unspecified assistantships also available. Financial award application deadline: 2/1; financial award applicants required to submit FAFSA. *Unit head:* Dr. Gregory Peterson, PhD, Head, 865-974-3461, Fax: 865-974-5483, E-mail: gdp@utk.edu. *Application contact:* Dr. Jens Gregor, PhD, Associate Head, 865-974-4399, Fax: 865-974-5483, E-mail: jgregor@utk.edu.
Website: http://www.eecs.utk.edu

The University of Tennessee at Chattanooga, Program in Computer Science, Chattanooga, TN 37403. Offers biomedical informatics (Post Master's Certificate); computer science (MS). *Program availability:* Part-time, 100% online. *Students:* 27 full-time (7 women), 31 part-time (10 women); includes 16 minority (4 Black or African American, non-Hispanic/Latino; 2 Asian, non-Hispanic/Latino; 6 Hispanic/Latino; 4 Two or more races, non-Hispanic/Latino), 6 international. Average age 29. 35 applicants, 71% accepted, 16 enrolled. In 2019, 18 master's awarded. *Degree requirements:* For master's, thesis or alternative, project in lieu of thesis. *Entrance requirements:* For master's, GRE General Test, minimum cumulative undergraduate GPA of 2.7 or 3.0 in senior year. Additional exam requirements/recommendations for international students: required—TOEFL (minimum score 550 paper-based; 79 iBT), IELTS (minimum score 6). *Application deadline:* For fall admission, 6/15 priority date for domestic students, 7/1 for international students; for spring admission, 11/1 priority date for domestic students, 11/1 for international students. Applications are processed on a rolling basis. Application fee: $35 ($40 for international students). Electronic applications accepted. *Financial support:* Research assistantships, teaching assistantships, career-related internships or fieldwork, scholarships/grants, health care benefits, and unspecified assistantships available. Support available to part-time students. Financial award application deadline: 7/1; financial award applicants required to submit FAFSA. *Unit head:* Dr. Luay Wahsheh, Department Head, 423-425-4361, Fax: 423-425-5311, E-mail: luay-a-wahsheh@utc.edu. *Application contact:* Dr. Joanne Romagni, Dean of the Graduate School, 423-425-4478, Fax: 423-425-5223, E-mail: joanne-romagni@utc.edu.
Website: https://www.utc.edu/college-engineering-computer-science/programs/computer-science-engineering/grad/masters-programs.php

The University of Texas at Arlington, Graduate School, College of Engineering, Department of Computer Science and Engineering, Arlington, TX 76019. Offers computer engineering (MS, PhD); computer science (MS, PhD); software engineering (MS). *Program availability:* Part-time, online learning. Terminal master's awarded for partial completion of doctoral program. *Degree requirements:* For master's, comprehensive exam (for some programs), thesis; for doctorate, comprehensive exam, thesis/dissertation. *Entrance requirements:* For master's, GRE General Test, minimum GPA of 3.0 (3.2 in computer science-related classes); for doctorate, GRE General Test, minimum GPA of 3.5. Additional exam requirements/recommendations for international students: required—TOEFL (minimum score 550 paper-based; 92 iBT), IELTS (minimum score 6.5).

The University of Texas at Austin, Graduate School, College of Natural Sciences, Department of Computer Science, Austin, TX 78712-1111. Offers MSCS, PhD. *Program availability:* Online learning. *Degree requirements:* For master's, thesis optional; for doctorate, thesis/dissertation, oral proposal, final defense. *Entrance requirements:* For master's and doctorate, GRE General Test, GRE Subject Test, bachelor's degree in computer sciences (preferred). Additional exam requirements/recommendations for international students: required—TOEFL. Electronic applications accepted.

The University of Texas at Dallas, Erik Jonsson School of Engineering and Computer Science, Department of Computer Science, Richardson, TX 75080. Offers computer science (MSCS, PhD); software engineering (MS, PhD). *Program availability:* Part-time, evening/weekend. *Faculty:* 49 full-time (6 women), 21 part-time/adjunct (5 women). *Students:* 977 full-time (277 women), 297 part-time (80 women); includes 119 minority (12 Black or African American, non-Hispanic/Latino; 76 Asian, non-Hispanic/Latino; 24 Hispanic/Latino; 7 Two or more races, non-Hispanic/Latino), 1,034 international. Average age 27. 4,176 applicants, 21% accepted, 411 enrolled. In 2019, 456 master's, 21 doctorates awarded. *Degree requirements:* For master's, thesis optional; for doctorate, comprehensive exam, thesis/dissertation. *Entrance requirements:* For master's, GRE General Test, minimum GPA of 3.0 in undergraduate course work, 3.3 in quantitative course work; for doctorate, GRE General Test, minimum GPA of 3.5. Additional exam requirements/recommendations for international students: required—TOEFL (minimum score 550 paper-based). *Application deadline:* For fall admission, 7/15 for domestic students, 5/1 priority date for international students; for spring admission, 11/15 for domestic students, 9/1 priority date for international students. Applications are processed on a rolling basis. Application fee: $50 ($100 for international students). Electronic applications accepted. *Expenses: Tuition, area resident:* Full-time $16,504. Tuition, state resident: full-time $16,504. Tuition, nonresident: full-time $34,266. Tuition and fees vary according to course load. *Financial support:* In 2019–20, 167 students received support, including 7 fellowships (averaging $3,024 per year), 63 research assistantships with partial tuition reimbursements available (averaging $23,525 per year), 89 teaching assistantships with partial tuition reimbursements available (averaging $17,157 per year); career-related internships or fieldwork, Federal Work-Study, institutionally sponsored loans, and scholarships/grants also available. Support available to part-time students. Financial award application deadline: 4/30; financial award applicants required to submit FAFSA. *Unit head:* Dr. Gopal Gupta, Department Head, 972-883-4107, Fax: 972-883-2399, E-mail: gupta@utdallas.edu. *Application contact:* Dr. Ovidiu Daescu, Associate Department Head, 972-883-4196, E-mail: daescu@utdallas.edu.
Website: http://cs.utdallas.edu/

The University of Texas at El Paso, Graduate School, College of Engineering, Department of Computer Science, El Paso, TX 79968-0001. Offers computer science (MS, PhD); cyber security (Graduate Certificate); information technology (MSIT); software engineering (MS). *Program availability:* Part-time, evening/weekend. *Degree requirements:* For master's, thesis optional; for doctorate, thesis/dissertation. *Entrance requirements:* For master's, GRE, minimum GPA of 3.0; for doctorate, GRE, statement of purpose, letters of reference. Additional exam requirements/recommendations for international students: required—TOEFL; recommended—IELTS. Electronic applications accepted.

The University of Texas at San Antonio, College of Sciences, Department of Computer Science, San Antonio, TX 78249-0617. Offers MS, PhD. *Program availability:* Part-time. Terminal master's awarded for partial completion of doctoral program. *Degree requirements:* For master's, 36 credits of coursework; thesis or comprehensive exam within 6 years; minimum GPA of 3.0; for doctorate, comprehensive exam, thesis/dissertation, continuous enrollment until time of graduation; admission to candidacy; oral examination; 90 credits of coursework and research; minimum GPA of 3.0 on all coursework. *Entrance requirements:* For master's and doctorate, GRE General Test, bachelor's degree in computer science offered by UTSA or an equivalent academic preparation from an accredited college or university in the United States or a comparable foreign institution; minimum GPA of 3.0; at least 24 semester credit hours in the area (12 of which must be at the upper-division level). Additional exam requirements/recommendations for international students: required—TOEFL (minimum score 550 paper-based; 79 iBT), IELTS (minimum score 6.5). Electronic applications accepted. *Expenses:* Contact institution.

The University of Texas at Tyler, Soules College of Business, Department of Computer Science, Tyler, TX 75799-0001. Offers MS. *Faculty:* 6 full-time (1 woman), 1 part-time/adjunct (0 women). *Students:* 11 full-time (0 women), 4 part-time (2 women); includes 1 minority (Hispanic/Latino), 7 international. Average age 27. 25 applicants, 56% accepted, 5 enrolled. In 2019, 14 master's awarded. *Degree requirements:* For master's, comprehensive exam, thesis optional. *Entrance requirements:* For master's, GRE General Test, previous course work in data structures and computer organization, 6 hours of course work in calculus and statistics. Additional exam requirements/recommendations for international students: required—TOEFL. *Application deadline:* For fall admission, 6/15 priority date for domestic students, 7/1 priority date for international students; for spring admission, 10/15 priority date for domestic students, 11/1 priority date for international students. Applications are processed on a rolling basis. Application fee: $25 ($50 for international students). Electronic applications accepted. *Financial support:* In 2019–20, 5 research assistantships (averaging $2,590 per year), 5 teaching assistantships (averaging $3,090 per year) were awarded; scholarships/grants also available. Financial award application deadline: 7/1; financial award applicants required to submit FAFSA. *Unit head:* Dr. Stephen Rainwater, Chair, 903-566-7403, E-mail: srainwater@uttyler.edu. *Application contact:* Dr. Stephen Rainwater, Chair, 903-566-7403, E-mail: srainwater@uttyler.edu.
Website: https://www.uttyler.edu/cs

The University of Texas of the Permian Basin, Office of Graduate Studies, College of Arts and Sciences, Department of Math and Computer Science, Odessa, TX 79762-0001. Offers computer science (MS). *Program availability:* Part-time, evening/weekend. *Degree requirements:* For master's, comprehensive exam, thesis or alternative. *Entrance requirements:* For master's, GRE General Test. Additional exam requirements/recommendations for international students: required—TOEFL (minimum score 550 paper-based).

The University of Texas Rio Grande Valley, College of Engineering and Computer Science, Department of Computer Science, Edinburg, TX 78539. Offers computer science (MS); information technology (MS). *Faculty:* 11 full-time (3 women). *Students:* 45 full-time (9 women), 49 part-time (5 women); includes 70 minority (5 Asian, non-Hispanic/Latino; 65 Hispanic/Latino), 19 international. Average age 28. 53 applicants, 79% accepted, 25 enrolled. In 2019, 22 master's awarded. *Expenses: Tuition, area resident:* Full-time $5959; part-time $440 per credit hour. Tuition, state resident: full-time $5959. Tuition, nonresident: full-time $5959. *International tuition:* $13,321 full-time. *Required fees:* $1169; $185 per credit hour.
Website: utrgv.edu/csci/

University of the District of Columbia, School of Engineering and Applied Sciences, Program in Computer Science, Washington, DC 20008-1175. Offers MS, MSCS. *Degree requirements:* For master's, thesis optional.

The University of Toledo, College of Graduate Studies, College of Engineering, Department of Electrical Engineering and Computer Science, Toledo, OH 43606-3390. Offers computer science (MS, PhD); electrical engineering (MS, PhD). *Program availability:* Part-time, evening/weekend. *Degree requirements:* For master's, thesis or alternative; for doctorate, thesis/dissertation, qualifying exam. *Entrance requirements:* For master's, GRE General Test, minimum GPA of 3.0; for doctorate, GRE General Test, minimum GPA of 3.3. Additional exam requirements/recommendations for international students: required—TOEFL (minimum score 550 paper-based; 80 iBT). Electronic applications accepted.

University of Toronto, School of Graduate Studies, Faculty of Arts and Science, Department of Computer Science, Toronto, ON M5S 1A1, Canada. Offers applied computing (M Sc AC); computer science (M Sc, PhD). *Program availability:* Part-time. *Degree requirements:* For master's, thesis; for doctorate, thesis/dissertation, thesis defense/oral exam. *Entrance requirements:* For master's, GRE (recommended), minimum B+ average overall and in final year; resume; 3 letters of reference; background in computer science and mathematics (preferred); for doctorate, minimum B+ average overall and in final year; resume; 3 letters of reference; background in computer science and mathematics (preferred). Additional exam requirements/recommendations for international students: required—TOEFL (minimum score 580 paper-based), TWE (minimum score 5). Electronic applications accepted.

The University of Tulsa, Graduate School, College of Engineering and Natural Sciences, Tandy School of Computer Science, Tulsa, OK 74104-3189. Offers computer science (MS, PhD); cyber security (MS); JD/MS; MBA/MS. *Program availability:* Part-time. Terminal master's awarded for partial completion of doctoral program. *Degree requirements:* For master's, thesis (for some programs); for doctorate, comprehensive exam, thesis/dissertation. *Entrance requirements:* For master's and doctorate, GRE General Test. Additional exam requirements/recommendations for international students: required—TOEFL (minimum score 550 paper-based; 80 iBT), IELTS (minimum score 6). Electronic applications accepted. *Expenses: Tuition:* Full-time $22,896; part-time $1272 per credit hour. *Required fees:* $6 per credit hour. Tuition and fees vary according to course load and program.

University of Utah, Graduate School, College of Engineering, School of Computing, Salt Lake City, UT 84112-9205. Offers computer science (MS, PhD); computing (MS, PhD); software development (MS); MS/MBA. Terminal master's awarded for partial completion of doctoral program. *Degree requirements:* For master's, comprehensive exam (for some programs), thesis optional; for doctorate, comprehensive exam, thesis/dissertation. *Entrance requirements:* For master's and doctorate, GRE General Test, minimum GPA of 3.0. Additional exam requirements/recommendations for international students: required—TOEFL (minimum score 500 paper-based; 61 iBT), IELTS (minimum score 6.5). Electronic applications accepted. *Expenses:* Contact institution.

University of Vermont, Graduate College, College of Engineering and Mathematical Sciences, Department of Computer Science, Burlington, VT 05405. Offers MS, PhD. *Degree requirements:* For master's, thesis or alternative. *Entrance requirements:* For master's and doctorate, GRE General Test. Additional exam requirements/recommendations for international students: required—TOEFL (minimum score 550 paper-based, 90 iBT) or IELTS (6.5). Electronic applications accepted.

University of Victoria, Faculty of Graduate Studies, Faculty of Engineering, Department of Computer Science, Victoria, BC V8W 2Y2, Canada. Offers M Sc, PhD. *Program availability:* Part-time. Terminal master's awarded for partial completion of doctoral program. *Degree requirements:* For master's, thesis or alternative; for doctorate, thesis/dissertation, candidacy exam. *Entrance requirements:* For master's, GRE (recommended), B Sc in computer science/software engineering or the equivalent or bachelor's degree in mathematics with emphasis on computer science

(recommended); for doctorate, GRE (recommended), MS in computer science or equivalent (recommended). Additional exam requirements/recommendations for international students: required—TOEFL (minimum score 575 paper-based), IELTS (minimum score 7). Electronic applications accepted.

University of Virginia, School of Engineering and Applied Science, Department of Computer Science, Charlottesville, VA 22903. Offers MCS, MS, PhD. *Degree requirements:* For master's, thesis (for some programs); for doctorate, comprehensive exam, thesis/dissertation. *Entrance requirements:* For master's, GRE General Test, 3 letters of recommendation; for doctorate, GRE General Test, 3 letters of recommendation; essay. Additional exam requirements/recommendations for international students: required—TOEFL (minimum score 650 paper-based; 90 iBT), IELTS (minimum score 7). Electronic applications accepted.

University of Washington, Graduate School, College of Engineering, Paul G. Allen School of Computer Science and Engineering, Seattle, WA 98195-2350. Offers MS, PhD. *Program availability:* Part-time, evening/weekend. *Students:* 332 full-time (99 women), 174 part-time (30 women); includes 112 minority (5 Black or African American, non-Hispanic/Latino; 75 Asian, non-Hispanic/Latino; 11 Hispanic/Latino; 21 Two or more races, non-Hispanic/Latino), 217 international. Average age 27. 2,248 applicants, 9% accepted, 96 enrolled. In 2019, 128 master's, 36 doctorates awarded. *Degree requirements:* For doctorate, thesis/dissertation, independent project. *Entrance requirements:* For master's, GRE General Test; for doctorate, GRE General Test, minimum GPA of 3.0, statement of purpose, curriculum vitae, letters of recommendation, transcript. Additional exam requirements/recommendations for international students: required—TOEFL (minimum score 580 paper-based; 92 iBT). *Application deadline:* For fall admission, 12/15 for domestic and international students. Applications are processed on a rolling basis. Application fee: $85. Electronic applications accepted. *Expenses:* Contact institution. *Financial support:* In 2019–20, 33 fellowships with full tuition reimbursements (averaging $36,840 per year), 234 research assistantships with full tuition reimbursements (averaging $36,840 per year), 102 teaching assistantships with full tuition reimbursements (averaging $36,000 per year) were awarded; Federal Work-Study, institutionally sponsored loans, scholarships/grants, health care benefits, tuition waivers (full), and unspecified assistantships also available. Support available to part-time students. Financial award application deadline: 12/15. *Unit head:* Magda Balazinska, Director/Chair, 206-616-1069, Fax: 206-543-2969, E-mail: magda@cs.washington.edu. *Application contact:* Elise DeGoede Dorough, Graduate Admissions Information Contact, 206-543-1695, Fax: 206-543-2969, E-mail: elised@cs.washington.edu.
Website: http://www.cs.washington.edu/

University of Waterloo, Graduate Studies and Postdoctoral Affairs, Faculty of Mathematics, David R. Cheriton School of Computer Science, Waterloo, ON N2L 3G1, Canada. Offers computer science (M Math, PhD); software engineering (M Math); statistics and computing (M Math). *Program availability:* Part-time. *Degree requirements:* For master's, research paper or thesis; for doctorate, comprehensive exam, thesis/dissertation. *Entrance requirements:* For master's, honors degree in field, minimum B+ average; for doctorate, master's degree, minimum B+ average. Additional exam requirements/recommendations for international students: required—TOEFL, IELTS, PTE. Electronic applications accepted.

The University of Western Ontario, School of Graduate and Postdoctoral Studies, Faculty of Science, Department of Computer Science, London, ON N6A 3K7, Canada. Offers M Sc, PhD. *Program availability:* Part-time. *Degree requirements:* For master's, thesis, project, or course work; for doctorate, thesis/dissertation. *Entrance requirements:* For master's, B Sc in computer science or comparable academic qualifications; for doctorate, M Sc in computer science or comparable academic qualifications. Additional exam requirements/recommendations for international students: required—TOEFL.

University of West Florida, Hal Marcus College of Science and Engineering, Department of Computer Science, Pensacola, FL 32514-5750. Offers computer science (MS), including computer science, database systems, software engineering; information technology (MS), including cybersecurity, database management. *Program availability:* Part-time, evening/weekend. *Degree requirements:* For master's, thesis optional. *Entrance requirements:* For master's, GRE, MAT, or GMAT, official transcripts; minimum undergraduate GPA of 3.0; letter of intent; three letters of recommendation. Additional exam requirements/recommendations for international students: required—TOEFL (minimum score 550 paper-based).

University of Windsor, Faculty of Graduate Studies, Faculty of Science, School of Computer Science, Windsor, ON N9B 3P4, Canada. Offers M Sc, PhD. *Program availability:* Part-time. *Degree requirements:* For master's, thesis; for doctorate, comprehensive exam, thesis/dissertation. *Entrance requirements:* For master's, GRE, minimum B average; for doctorate, master's degree in computer science, minimum B+ average. Additional exam requirements/recommendations for international students: required—TOEFL (minimum score 580 paper-based). Electronic applications accepted.

University of Wisconsin–Madison, Graduate School, College of Letters and Science, Department of Computer Sciences, Madison, WI 53706-1380. Offers MS, PhD. *Program availability:* Part-time. Terminal master's awarded for partial completion of doctoral program. *Degree requirements:* For doctorate, thesis/dissertation. *Entrance requirements:* For master's and doctorate, GRE General Test, GRE Subject Test. Electronic applications accepted.

University of Wisconsin–Milwaukee, Graduate School, College of Engineering and Applied Science, Computer Science Program, Milwaukee, WI 53201-0413. Offers MS. *Program availability:* Part-time. *Degree requirements:* For master's, comprehensive exam (for some programs), thesis or alternative. *Entrance requirements:* For master's, GRE, minimum GPA of 2.75. Additional exam requirements/recommendations for international students: required—TOEFL (minimum score 550 paper-based; 79 iBT), IELTS (minimum score 6.5). Electronic applications accepted.

University of Wisconsin–Milwaukee, Graduate School, College of Engineering and Applied Science, Program in Engineering, Milwaukee, WI 53201-0413. Offers biomedical engineering (MS); civil engineering (MS, PhD); computer science (PhD); electrical and computer engineering (MS); electrical engineering (PhD); engineering mechanics (MS); industrial and management engineering (MS); industrial engineering (PhD); manufacturing engineering (MS); materials (PhD); materials engineering (MS); mechanical engineering (MS). *Program availability:* Part-time. *Degree requirements:* For master's, comprehensive exam (for some programs), thesis or alternative; for doctorate, comprehensive exam, thesis/dissertation, internship. *Entrance requirements:* For master's, GRE, minimum GPA of 2.75; for doctorate, GRE, minimum GPA of 3.5. Additional exam requirements/recommendations for international students: required—TOEFL (minimum score 550 paper-based; 79 iBT), IELTS (minimum score 6.5).

University of Wisconsin–Parkside, College of Business, Economics, and Computing, Program in Computer and Information Systems, Kenosha, WI 53141-2000. Offers MSCIS. *Entrance requirements:* For master's, GRE General Test or GMAT, 3 letters of recommendation, minimum GPA of 3.0. *Expenses: Tuition, area resident:* Full-time $9173; part-time $509.64 per credit. Tuition, state resident: full-time $9173; part-time $509.64 per credit. Tuition, nonresident: full-time $18,767; part-time $1042.64 per credit. *International tuition:* $18,767 full-time. *Required fees:* $1123.20; $63.64 per credit. Tuition and fees vary according to campus/location, program and reciprocity agreements.

University of Wisconsin–Platteville, School of Graduate Studies, College of Engineering, Mathematics and Science, Program in Computer Science, Platteville, WI 53818-3099. Offers MS. *Program availability:* Part-time. *Degree requirements:* For master's, comprehensive exam, thesis or alternative. *Entrance requirements:* Additional exam requirements/recommendations for international students: required—TOEFL (minimum score 550 paper-based; 79 iBT), IELTS (minimum score 6.5). Electronic applications accepted.

University of Wyoming, College of Engineering and Applied Science, Department of Computer Science, Laramie, WY 82071. Offers MS, PhD. *Program availability:* Part-time. Terminal master's awarded for partial completion of doctoral program. *Degree requirements:* For master's, thesis; for doctorate, thesis/dissertation. *Entrance requirements:* For master's and doctorate, GRE General Test, minimum GPA of 3.0. Additional exam requirements/recommendations for international students: required—TOEFL (minimum score 550 paper-based), IELTS (minimum score 6). Electronic applications accepted.

Université Laval, Faculty of Sciences and Engineering, Department of Computer Science, Programs in Computer Science, Québec, QC G1K 7P4, Canada. Offers M Sc, PhD. Terminal master's awarded for partial completion of doctoral program. *Degree requirements:* For master's, thesis; for doctorate, thesis/dissertation. *Entrance requirements:* For master's and doctorate, knowledge of French and English. Electronic applications accepted.

Université TÉLUQ, Graduate Programs, Québec, QC G1K 9H5, Canada. Offers computer science (PhD); corporate finance (MS); distance learning (MS). *Program availability:* Part-time.

Utah State University, School of Graduate Studies, College of Engineering, Department of Computer Science, Logan, UT 84322. Offers MCS, MS, PhD. *Program availability:* Part-time, evening/weekend, online learning. *Degree requirements:* For master's, thesis (for some programs), research project; for doctorate, thesis/dissertation. *Entrance requirements:* For master's, GRE General Test, GRE Subject Test, minimum GPA of 3.25, prerequisite coursework in math, 3 recommendation letters; for doctorate, GRE General Test, minimum GPA of 3.25, BS or MS. Additional exam requirements/recommendations for international students: required—TOEFL. Electronic applications accepted.

Vanderbilt University, School of Engineering, Department of Electrical Engineering and Computer Science, Program in Computer Science, Nashville, TN 37240-1001. Offers M Eng, MS, PhD. *Program availability:* Part-time. Terminal master's awarded for partial completion of doctoral program. *Degree requirements:* For master's, thesis (for some programs); for doctorate, comprehensive exam, thesis/dissertation. *Entrance requirements:* For master's and doctorate, GRE General Test, 3 letters of recommendation. Additional exam requirements/recommendations for international students: required—TOEFL. Electronic applications accepted. *Expenses: Tuition:* Full-time $51,018; part-time $2087 per hour. *Required fees:* $542. Tuition and fees vary according to program.

Villanova University, College of Engineering, Department of Electrical and Computer Engineering, Program in Computer Engineering, Villanova, PA 19085-1699. Offers computer architectures (Certificate); computer engineering (MSCPE); intelligent control systems (Certificate). *Program availability:* Part-time, evening/weekend. *Degree requirements:* For master's, thesis optional. *Entrance requirements:* For master's, GRE General Test (for applicants with degrees from foreign universities), BEE, minimum GPA of 3.0. Additional exam requirements/recommendations for international students: required—TOEFL (minimum score 600 paper-based; 100 iBT). Electronic applications accepted.

Villanova University, Graduate School of Liberal Arts and Sciences, Department of Computing Sciences, Villanova, PA 19085-1699. Offers computer science (MS). *Program availability:* Part-time, evening/weekend. *Degree requirements:* For master's, thesis optional, independent study project. *Entrance requirements:* For master's, GRE, minimum GPA of 3.0, 3 recommendation letters. Additional exam requirements/recommendations for international students: required—TOEFL. Electronic applications accepted.

Virginia Commonwealth University, Graduate School, School of Engineering, Department of Computer Science, Richmond, VA 23284-9005. Offers computer science (MS). *Degree requirements:* For master's, thesis optional. *Entrance requirements:* For master's, GRE General Test; for doctorate, GRE. Additional exam requirements/recommendations for international students: required—TOEFL (minimum score 600 paper-based; 100 iBT). Electronic applications accepted.

Virginia International University, School of Computer Information Systems, Fairfax, VA 22030. Offers business intelligence (Graduate Certificate); business intelligence and data analytics (MIS); computer science (MS), including computer animation and gaming, cybersecurity, data management networking, intelligent systems, software applications development, software engineering; cybersecurity (MIS); data management (MIS); enterprise project management (MIS); health informatics (MIS); information assurance (MIS); information systems (Graduate Certificate); information systems management (MS, Graduate Certificate); information technology (MS); information technology audit and compliance (Graduate Certificate); knowledge management (MIS); software engineering (MS). *Program availability:* Part-time, online learning. *Entrance requirements:* For master's, bachelor's degree. Additional exam requirements/recommendations for international students: required—TOEFL (minimum score 550 paper-based; 80 iBT), IELTS. Electronic applications accepted.

Virginia Polytechnic Institute and State University, Graduate School, College of Engineering, Blacksburg, VA 24061. Offers aerospace engineering (PhD, M Eng/MS); biological systems engineering (PhD); biomedical engineering (MS, PhD); chemical engineering (PhD); civil engineering (PhD); computer engineering (PhD); computer science and applications (MS); electrical engineering (PhD); engineering education (PhD); M Eng/MS. *Faculty:* 447 full-time (90 women), 6 part-time/adjunct (2 women). *Students:* 1,881 full-time (495 women), 326 part-time (70 women); includes 264 minority (51 Black or African American, non-Hispanic/Latino; 2 American Indian or Alaska Native, non-Hispanic/Latino; 96 Asian, non-Hispanic/Latino; 69 Hispanic/Latino; 46 Two or more races, non-Hispanic/Latino), 1,247 international. Average age 27. 4,014 applicants, 44% accepted, 658 enrolled. In 2019, 489 master's, 200 doctorates awarded. *Degree requirements:* For master's, comprehensive exam (for some programs), thesis (for some programs); for doctorate, comprehensive exam (for some programs), thesis/dissertation (for some programs). *Entrance requirements:* For master's and doctorate, GRE/GMAT. Additional exam requirements/recommendations for international students: required—TOEFL (minimum score 90 iBT). *Application deadline:* For fall admission, 8/1 for domestic students, 4/1 for international students; for spring admission, 1/1 for domestic students, 9/1 for international students. Applications are processed on a rolling basis. Application fee: $75. Electronic applications accepted. *Expenses:* Tuition, state resident: full-time $13,700; part-time $761.25 per credit hour. Tuition, nonresident: full-time $27,614; part-time $1534 per credit hour. *Required fees:* $886.50 per term. Tuition and fees vary according to campus/location and program. *Financial support:* In 2019–20, 47 fellowships with full tuition reimbursements (averaging $19,703 per year), 1,163 research assistantships with full tuition reimbursements (averaging $20,602 per year), 554 teaching assistantships with full tuition reimbursements (averaging $16,333 per year) were awarded; scholarships/grants and unspecified assistantships also available. Financial award application deadline: 3/1; financial award applicants required to submit FAFSA. *Unit head:* Dr. Julia Ross, Dean, 540-231-9752, Fax: 540-231-3031, E-mail: rjulie@vt.edu. *Application contact:* Linda Perkins, Executive Assistant, 540-231-9752, Fax: 540-231-3031, E-mail: lperkins@vt.edu.
Website: http://www.eng.vt.edu/

Virginia Polytechnic Institute and State University, VT Online, Blacksburg, VA 24061. Offers advanced transportation systems (Certificate); aerospace engineering (MS); agricultural and life sciences (MSLFS); business information systems (Graduate Certificate); career and technical education (MS); civil engineering (MS); computer engineering (M Eng, MS); decision support systems (Graduate Certificate); eLearning leadership (MA); electrical engineering (M Eng, MS); engineering administration (MEA); environmental engineering (Certificate); environmental politics and policy (Graduate Certificate); environmental sciences and engineering (MS); foundations of political analysis (Graduate Certificate); health product risk management (Graduate Certificate); industrial and systems engineering (MS); information policy and society (Graduate Certificate); information security (Graduate Certificate); information technology (MIT); instructional technology (MA); integrative STEM education (MA Ed); liberal arts (Graduate Certificate); life sciences: health product risk management (MS); natural resources (MNR, Graduate Certificate); networking (Graduate Certificate); nonprofit and nongovernmental organization management (Graduate Certificate); ocean engineering (MS); political science (MA); security studies (Graduate Certificate); software development (Graduate Certificate). *Expenses:* Tuition, state resident: full-time $13,700; part-time $761.25 per credit hour. Tuition, nonresident: full-time $27,614; part-time $1534 per credit hour. *Required fees:* $886.50 per term. Tuition and fees vary according to campus/location and program.

Wake Forest University, Graduate School of Arts and Sciences, Department of Computer Science, Winston-Salem, NC 27109. Offers MS. *Program availability:* Part-time. *Degree requirements:* For master's, one foreign language, thesis optional. *Entrance requirements:* For master's, GRE General Test. Additional exam requirements/recommendations for international students: required—TOEFL (minimum score 79 iBT). Electronic applications accepted.

Washington State University, Voiland College of Engineering and Architecture, Engineering and Computer Science Programs, Vancouver Campus, Pullman, WA 99164. Offers MS. *Degree requirements:* For master's, comprehensive exam, thesis optional. *Entrance requirements:* For master's, official transcripts from all colleges and universities attended; one-page statement of purpose; three letters of recommendation. Additional exam requirements/recommendations for international students: required—TOEFL; recommended—IELTS. Electronic applications accepted.

Washington State University, Voiland College of Engineering and Architecture, School of Electrical Engineering and Computer Science, Pullman, WA 99164-2752. Offers computer engineering (MS); computer science (MS); electrical engineering (MS); electrical engineering and computer science (PhD); electrical power engineering (MS). *Program availability:* Part-time. *Degree requirements:* For master's, comprehensive exam (for some programs), thesis or alternative; for doctorate, comprehensive exam, thesis/dissertation. *Entrance requirements:* For master's and doctorate, GRE General Test, minimum GPA of 3.0, 3 letters of recommendation, statement of purpose, transcripts. Additional exam requirements/recommendations for international students: required—TOEFL (minimum score 580 paper-based).

Washington University in St. Louis, School of Engineering and Applied Science, Department of Computer Science and Engineering, St. Louis, MO 63130-4899. Offers computer engineering (MS, PhD); computer science (MS, PhD); computer science and engineering (M Eng). *Program availability:* Part-time. Terminal master's awarded for partial completion of doctoral program. *Degree requirements:* For master's, thesis optional; for doctorate, thesis/dissertation. *Entrance requirements:* For doctorate, GRE General Test. Additional exam requirements/recommendations for international students: required—TOEFL. Electronic applications accepted.

Wayne State University, College of Engineering, Department of Computer Science, Detroit, MI 48202. Offers computer science (MS, PhD), including bioinformatics and computational biology (PhD); data science and business analytics (MS). *Faculty:* 23. *Students:* 97 full-time (41 women), 42 part-time (10 women); includes 15 minority (3 Black or African American, non-Hispanic/Latino; 9 Asian, non-Hispanic/Latino; 2 Hispanic/Latino; 1 Two or more races, non-Hispanic/Latino), 94 international. Average age 30. 276 applicants, 31% accepted, 30 enrolled. In 2019, 42 master's, 10 doctorates awarded. *Degree requirements:* For master's, thesis (for some programs), practicum (for MS in data science and business analytics); for doctorate, thesis/dissertation. *Entrance requirements:* For master's, GRE only for Data Science and Business Analytics degree, minimum GPA of 3.0, three letters of recommendation, adequate preparation in computer science and mathematics courses, personal statement, resume (for MS in data science and business analytics); for doctorate, GRE, bachelor's or master's degree in computer science or related field; minimum GPA of 3.3 in most recent degree; three letters of recommendation; personal statement; adequate preparation in computer science and mathematics courses. Additional exam requirements/recommendations for international students: required—TOEFL (minimum score 550 paper-based; 79 iBT), TWE (minimum score 5.5); recommended—IELTS (minimum score 6.5). *Application deadline:* For fall admission, 6/1 priority date for domestic students, 5/1 priority date for international students; for winter admission, 10/1 priority date for domestic students, 9/1 priority date for international students; for spring admission, 2/1 priority date for domestic students, 1/2 priority date for international students. Applications are processed on a rolling basis. Application fee: $50. Electronic applications accepted. *Expenses:* $790 per credit hour in-state tuition, $1579 per credit hour out-of-state tuition. MS degree is 30 credits; PhD degree is 90 credits. *Financial support:* In 2019–20, 92 students received support, including 4 fellowships with tuition reimbursements available (averaging $20,000 per year), 18 research assistantships with tuition reimbursements available (averaging $20,693 per year), 32 teaching assistantships with tuition reimbursements available (averaging $20,760 per year); scholarships/grants, health care benefits, and unspecified assistantships also available. Financial award application deadline: 2/17; financial award applicants required to submit FAFSA. *Unit head:* Dr. Loren Schwiebert, Chair, 313-577-5474, E-mail: loren@wayne.edu. *Application contact:* Robert Reynolds, Graduate Program Director, 313-577-0726, E-mail: csgradadvisor@cs.wayne.edu.
Website: http://engineering.wayne.edu/cs/

Webster University, George Herbert Walker School of Business and Technology, Department of Mathematics and Computer Science, St. Louis, MO 63119-3194. Offers cybersecurity (MS). *Program availability:* Part-time, evening/weekend, online learning. *Entrance requirements:* For master's, 36 hours of graduate course work. Additional exam requirements/recommendations for international students: required—TOEFL.

Wentworth Institute of Technology, Master of Science in Applied Computer Science Program, Boston, MA 02115-5998. Offers MS. *Program availability:* Part-time, online only, 100% online. *Entrance requirements:* Additional exam requirements/recommendations for international students: recommended—TOEFL (minimum score 550 paper-based). Electronic applications accepted. *Expenses:* Contact institution.

Wesleyan University, Graduate Studies, Department of Mathematics and Computer Science, Middletown, CT 06459. Offers computer science (MA); mathematics (MA, PhD). Terminal master's awarded for partial completion of doctoral program. *Degree requirements:* For master's, one foreign language, thesis; for doctorate, 2 foreign languages, comprehensive exam (for some programs), thesis/dissertation. *Entrance requirements:* For master's, GRE General Test, GRE Subject Test; for doctorate, GRE Subject Test. Additional exam requirements/recommendations for international students: recommended—TOEFL. Electronic applications accepted.

Western Illinois University, School of Graduate Studies, College of Business and Technology, School of Computer Science, Macomb, IL 61455-1390. Offers MS. *Program availability:* Part-time. *Entrance requirements:* For master's, proficiency in Java. Additional exam requirements/recommendations for international students: required—TOEFL (minimum score 550 paper-based; 80 iBT). Electronic applications accepted.

Western Kentucky University, Graduate School, Ogden College of Science and Engineering, The School of Engineering and Applied Sciences, Bowling Green, KY 42101. Offers computer science (MS); engineering technology management (MS).

Western Michigan University, Graduate College, College of Engineering and Applied Sciences, Department of Computer Science, Kalamazoo, MI 49008. Offers MS, PhD. *Degree requirements:* For master's, thesis optional; for doctorate, 2 foreign languages, thesis/dissertation.

Western Washington University, Graduate School, College of Sciences and Technology, Department of Computer Science, Bellingham, WA 98225-5996. Offers MS. *Program availability:* Part-time. *Degree requirements:* For master's, thesis optional, project. *Entrance requirements:* For master's, GRE General Test, minimum GPA of 3.0 in last 60 semester hours or last 90 quarter hours. Additional exam requirements/recommendations for international students: required—TOEFL (minimum score 567 paper-based). Electronic applications accepted.

West Virginia University, Statler College of Engineering and Mineral Resources, Morgantown, WV 26506. Offers aerospace engineering (MSAE, PhD); chemical engineering (MS Ch E, PhD); civil engineering (MSCE, PhD); computer engineering (PhD); computer science (MSCS, PhD); electrical engineering (MSEE, PhD); energy systems engineering (MSESE); engineering (MSE); industrial engineering (MSIE, PhD); industrial hygiene (MS); material science and engineering (MSMSE, PhD); mechanical engineering (MSME, PhD); mining engineering (MS Min E, PhD); petroleum and natural gas engineering (MSPNGE, PhD); safety management (MS); software engineering (MSSE). *Program availability:* Part-time. Terminal master's awarded for partial completion of doctoral program. *Degree requirements:* For master's, thesis optional; for doctorate, comprehensive exam, thesis/dissertation. *Entrance requirements:* Additional exam requirements/recommendations for international students: required—TOEFL (minimum score 550 paper-based). Electronic applications accepted. *Expenses:* Contact institution.

Wichita State University, Graduate School, College of Engineering, Department of Electrical Engineering and Computer Science, Wichita, KS 67260. Offers computer networking (MS); computer science (MS); electrical and computer engineering (MS); electrical engineering and computer science (PhD). *Program availability:* Part-time, evening/weekend.

Winston-Salem State University, Program in Computer Science and Information Technology, Winston-Salem, NC 27110-0003. Offers MS. *Program availability:* Part-time. *Degree requirements:* For master's, thesis optional. *Entrance requirements:* For master's, GRE, resume. Electronic applications accepted.

Worcester Polytechnic Institute, Graduate Admissions, Department of Computer Science, Worcester, MA 01609-2280. Offers computer science (MS, PhD, Advanced Certificate, Graduate Certificate). *Program availability:* Part-time, evening/weekend. Terminal master's awarded for partial completion of doctoral program. *Degree requirements:* For master's, thesis optional; for doctorate, comprehensive exam, thesis/dissertation. *Entrance requirements:* For master's and doctorate, GRE General Test recommended for students seeking funding, 3 letters of recommendation, statement of purpose. Additional exam requirements/recommendations for international students: required—TOEFL (minimum score 563 paper-based; 84 iBT), IELTS (minimum score 7). Electronic applications accepted.

Wright State University, Graduate School, College of Engineering and Computer Science, Department of Computer Science and Engineering, Computer Science Program, Dayton, OH 45435. Offers MS. *Degree requirements:* For master's, thesis optional. *Entrance requirements:* For master's, GRE General Test, minimum GPA of 3.0 in major, 2.7 overall. Additional exam requirements/recommendations for international students: required—TOEFL.

Wright State University, Graduate School, College of Engineering and Computer Science, Department of Computer Science and Engineering, Program in Computer Science and Engineering, Dayton, OH 45435. Offers PhD. *Degree requirements:* For doctorate, thesis/dissertation, candidacy and general exams. *Entrance requirements:* For doctorate, GRE General Test, minimum GPA of 3.3. Additional exam requirements/recommendations for international students: required—TOEFL.

Yale University, Graduate School of Arts and Sciences, Department of Computer Science, New Haven, CT 06520. Offers MS, PhD. *Degree requirements:* For doctorate, thesis/dissertation. *Entrance requirements:* For doctorate, GRE General Test, GRE Subject Test.

York University, Faculty of Graduate Studies, Lassonde School of Engineering, Program in Computer Science, Toronto, ON M3J 1P3, Canada. Offers M Sc, PhD. *Degree requirements:* For master's, thesis or alternative; for doctorate, comprehensive exam, thesis/dissertation, internship or practicum. Electronic applications accepted.

Youngstown State University, College of Graduate Studies, College of Science, Technology, Engineering and Mathematics, Department of Computer Science and Information Systems, Youngstown, OH 44555-0001. Offers computing and information systems (MCIS). *Program availability:* Part-time. *Degree requirements:* For master's, thesis or capstone project. *Entrance requirements:* For master's, GRE or GMAT. Additional exam requirements/recommendations for international students: required—TOEFL (minimum score 550 paper-based).

Youngstown State University, College of Graduate Studies, College of Science, Technology, Engineering and Mathematics, Department of Mathematics and Statistics, Youngstown, OH 44555-0001. Offers actuarial science (MS); applied mathematics (MS); computer science (MS); mathematics (MS); secondary/community college mathematics (MS); statistics (MS). *Program availability:* Part-time. *Degree requirements:* For master's, comprehensive exam, thesis optional. *Entrance requirements:* For master's, minimum GPA of 2.7 in computer science and mathematics. Additional exam requirements/recommendations for international students: required—TOEFL.

Data Science/Data Analytics

American University, College of Arts and Sciences, Department of Mathematics and Statistics, Washington, DC 22016-8050. Offers applied statistics (Certificate); biostatistics (MS); data science (Certificate); mathematics (MA); professional science: quantitative analysis (MS); statistics (MS). *Program availability:* Part-time, evening/weekend. *Degree requirements:* For master's, comprehensive exam, thesis or alternative. *Entrance requirements:* For master's, GRE; please see website: https://www.american.edu/cas/mathstat/, statement of purpose, transcripts, 2 letters of recommendation, resume; for Certificate, bachelor's degree, statement of purpose, transcripts, resume. Additional exam requirements/recommendations for international students: required—TOEFL (minimum score 600 paper-based; 100 iBT). *Expenses:* Contact institution.

Austin Peay State University, College of Graduate Studies, College of Science, Technology, Engineering and Mathematics, Professional Science Master's Program, Clarksville, TN 37044. Offers data management and analysis (MS, PSM); information assurance and security (MS, PSM); mathematical finance (MS, PSM); mathematics instruction (MS); predictive analytics (MS, PSM). *Program availability:* Part-time, online learning. *Faculty:* 15 full-time (0 women), 3 part-time/adjunct (0 women). *Students:* 71 full-time (20 women), 82 part-time (31 women); includes 30 minority (17 Black or African American, non-Hispanic/Latino; 3 Asian, non-Hispanic/Latino; 3 Hispanic/Latino; 7 Two or more races, non-Hispanic/Latino), 59 international. Average age 27. 109 applicants, 91% accepted, 53 enrolled. In 2019, 36 master's awarded. *Entrance requirements:* For master's, GRE, minimum undergraduate GPA of 2.5. Additional exam requirements/recommendations for international students: required—TOEFL (minimum score 500 paper-based). *Application deadline:* For fall admission, 8/5 priority date for domestic students. Applications are processed on a rolling basis. Application fee: $45 ($55 for international students). Electronic applications accepted. *Financial support:* Research assistantships with full tuition reimbursements, career-related internships or fieldwork, Federal Work-Study, institutionally sponsored loans, scholarships/grants, and unspecified assistantships available. Support available to part-time students. Financial award application deadline: 7/1; financial award applicants required to submit FAFSA. *Unit head:* Dr. Matt Jones, Graduate Coordinator, 931-221-7814, E-mail: gradpsm@apsu.edu. *Application contact:* Megan Mitchell, Coordinator of Graduate Admissions, 800-859-4723, Fax: 931-221-7641, E-mail: gradadmissions@apsu.edu.
Website: http://www.apsu.edu/csci/masters_degrees/index.php

Azusa Pacific University, School of Behavioral and Applied Sciences, Department of Psychology, Azusa, CA 91702-7000. Offers child life (MS); research psychology and data analytics (MS).

Boston University, Metropolitan College, Department of Computer Science, Boston, MA 02215. Offers computer information systems (MS), including computer networks, data analytics, database management and business intelligence, health informatics, IT project management, security, Web application development; computer networks (Certificate); computer science (MS); data analytics (Certificate); digital forensics (Certificate); health informatics (Certificate); information technology project management (Certificate); software development (MS); software engineering in health care systems (Certificate); telecommunications (MS), including security. *Program availability:* Part-time, evening/weekend, online learning. *Faculty:* 16 full-time (3 women), 52 part-time/adjunct (5 women). *Students:* 253 full-time (80 women), 856 part-time (243 women); includes 246 minority (53 Black or African American, non-Hispanic/Latino; 1 American Indian or Alaska Native, non-Hispanic/Latino; 129 Asian, non-Hispanic/Latino; 48 Hispanic/Latino; 15 Two or more races, non-Hispanic/Latino), 418 international. Average age 30. 1,079 applicants, 72% accepted, 297 enrolled. In 2019, 513 master's awarded. *Entrance requirements:* For master's and Certificate, official transcripts from regionally-accredited bachelor's degree program, 3 letters of recommendation, professional resume, personal statement. Additional exam requirements/recommendations for international students: required—TOEFL (minimum score 84 iBT), IELTS. *Application deadline:* For fall admission, 8/1 priority date for domestic students, 6/1 priority date for international students; for spring admission, 12/1 priority date for domestic students, 11/15 priority date for international students; for summer admission, 4/1 priority date for domestic students, 3/1 priority date for international students. Applications are processed on a rolling basis. Application fee: $85. Electronic applications accepted. *Expenses:* Contact institution. *Financial support:* In 2019–20, 11 research assistantships (averaging $8,400 per year), 23 teaching assistantships (averaging $3,400 per year) were awarded; unspecified assistantships also available. Support available to part-time students. Financial award applicants required to submit FAFSA. *Unit head:* Dr. Anatoly Temkin, Chair, 617-353-2566, Fax: 617-353-2367, E-mail: csinfo@bu.edu. *Application contact:* Enrollment Services, 617-353-6004, E-mail: met@bu.edu.
Website: http://www.bu.edu/csmet/

Brandman University, School of Business and Professional Studies, Irvine, CA 92618. Offers accounting (MBA); business administration (MBA); business intelligence and data analytics (MBA); e-business strategic management (MBA); entrepreneurship (MBA); finance (MBA); health administration (MBA); human resources (MBA, MS); international business (MBA); marketing (MBA); organizational leadership (MA, MBA, MPA); public administration (MPA).

Buffalo State College, State University of New York, The Graduate School, Program in Multidisciplinary Studies, Buffalo, NY 14222-1095. Offers data science and analytics (MS); individualized studies (MA, MS); nutrition (MS). *Program availability:* Part-time, evening/weekend. *Degree requirements:* For master's, thesis or project. *Entrance requirements:* For master's, minimum GPA of 2.5. Additional exam requirements/recommendations for international students: required—TOEFL (minimum score 550 paper-based).

Central European University, Center for Network Science, 1051, Hungary. Offers PhD. *Degree requirements:* For doctorate, comprehensive exam, thesis/dissertation. *Entrance requirements:* For doctorate, master's degree in physics, mathematics, computer science, sociology, political science, economics, or equivalent; two references. Additional exam requirements/recommendations for international students: required—TOEFL. Electronic applications accepted.

Claremont Graduate University, Graduate Programs, Center for Information Systems and Technology, Claremont, CA 91711-6160. Offers cybersecurity and networking (MS); data science and analytics (MS); electronic commerce (PhD); geographic information systems (MS); health informatics (MS); information systems (Certificate); IT strategy and innovation (MS); knowledge management (PhD); systems development (PhD); telecommunications and networking (PhD); MBA/MS. *Program availability:* Part-time. *Degree requirements:* For doctorate, comprehensive exam, thesis/dissertation, portfolio. *Entrance requirements:* For master's and doctorate, GMAT, GRE General Test. Additional exam requirements/recommendations for international students: required—TOEFL (minimum score 75 iBT). Electronic applications accepted.

College of Saint Elizabeth, Program in Data Analytics, Morristown, NJ 07960-6989. Offers MS. *Program availability:* Part-time. *Degree requirements:* For master's, thesis. *Entrance requirements:* Additional exam requirements/recommendations for international students: required—TOEFL (minimum score 550 paper-based; 79 iBT), IELTS (minimum score 6.5). Electronic applications accepted. Application fee is waived when completed online.

College of Staten Island of the City University of New York, Graduate Programs, Division of Science and Technology, Program in Computer Science, Staten Island, NY 10314-6600. Offers computer science (MS), including artificial intelligence and data analytics, cloud computing and software engineering, cybersecurity and networks. *Program availability:* Part-time, evening/weekend. *Faculty:* 6. *Students:* 42. 48 applicants, 67% accepted, 15 enrolled. In 2019, 10 master's awarded. *Degree requirements:* For master's, thesis optional, a program of 10 courses (30 credits) with at least a 3.0 (B) average. Exceptional students may be permitted to satisfy six credits of the total credit requirement with a master's thesis. *Entrance requirements:* For master's, GRE General Test, BS in Computer Science or related area with a B average (3.0 out of 4.0) overall and in the major, a resume, and demonstratable knowledge in several areas. Additional exam requirements/recommendations for international students: required—TOEFL (minimum score 550 paper-based; 79 iBT), IELTS (minimum score 6.5). *Application deadline:* For fall admission, 7/20 priority date for domestic students, 4/25 for international students; for spring admission, 11/2 priority date for domestic students, 11/2 for international students. Applications are processed on a rolling basis. Application fee: $75. Electronic applications accepted. *Expenses: Tuition, area resident:* Full-time $11,090; part-time $470 per credit. Tuition, state resident: full-time $11,090; part-time $470 per credit. Tuition, nonresident: full-time $20,520; part-time $855 per credit. *International tuition:* $20,520 full-time. *Required fees:* $559; $181 per semester. Tuition and fees vary according to program. *Unit head:* Dr. Xiaowen Zhang, Associate Professor, 718-982-3262, E-mail: xiaowen.zhang@csi.cuny.edu. *Application contact:* Sasha Spence, Associate Director for Graduate Admissions, 718-982-2019, Fax: 718-982-2500, E-mail: sasha.spence@csi.cuny.edu.
Website: https://www.csi.cuny.edu/academics-and-research/departments-programs/computer-science

College of Staten Island of the City University of New York, Graduate Programs, Lucille and Jay Chazanoff School of Business, Program in Business Analytics of Large-Scale Data, Staten Island, NY 10314-6600. Offers Advanced Certificate. *Program availability:* Part-time, evening/weekend. *Degree requirements:* For Advanced Certificate, Students must maintain a GPA of 3.0 to be rewarded the certificate. Students below 3.0 may continue the program but may not be rewarded the certificate. If a grade of 2.0-3.0 is received in a course, s/he will be encouraged to retake the course. minimum GPA of 3.0. *Entrance requirements:* For degree, assessment test in statistical methods, bachelor's degree in business, economics, or a related field, or be in a graduate student program with a GPA of 3.0; 2 letters of recommendation; resume; cover letter of the applicants experience. Additional exam requirements/recommendations for international students: required—TOEFL (minimum score 550 paper-based; 79 iBT), IELTS (minimum score 6.5). *Application deadline:* For fall admission, 4/25 priority date for domestic students, 4/25 for international students; for spring admission, 11/25 priority date for domestic students, 11/25 for international students. Applications are processed on a rolling basis. Application fee: $75. Electronic applications accepted. *Expenses: Tuition, area resident:* Full-time $11,090; part-time $470 per credit. Tuition, state resident: full-time $11,090; part-time $470 per credit. Tuition, nonresident: full-time $20,520; part-time $855 per credit. *International tuition:* $20,520 full-time. *Required fees:* $559; $181 per semester. Tuition and fees vary according to program. *Unit head:* Prof. Hyoung Suk Shim, Graduate Program Coordinator, 718-982-3309, E-mail: hyoungsuk.shim@csi.cuny.edu. *Application contact:* Sasha Spence, Associate Director for Graduate Admissions, 718-982-2019, Fax: 718-982-2500, E-mail: sasha.spence@csi.cuny.edu.
Website: https://www.csi.cuny.edu/admissions/graduate-admissions/graduate-programs-and-requirements/business-analytics-large-scale-data

Colorado Technical University Aurora, Program in Computer Science, Aurora, CO 80014. Offers computer systems security (MSCS); database systems (MSCS); software engineering (MSCS). *Program availability:* Part-time, evening/weekend. *Degree requirements:* For master's, thesis or alternative. *Entrance requirements:* For master's, minimum undergraduate GPA of 3.0, resume.

Colorado Technical University Colorado Springs, Graduate Studies, Program in Computer Science, Colorado Springs, CO 80907. Offers computer science (DCS); computer systems security (MSCS); database systems (MSCS); software engineering (MSCS). *Program availability:* Part-time, evening/weekend, online learning. *Degree requirements:* For master's, thesis or alternative; for doctorate, thesis/dissertation. *Entrance requirements:* For doctorate, minimum graduate GPA of 3.0, 5 years of related work experience.

Columbia University, Fu Foundation School of Engineering and Applied Science, Data Science Institute, New York, NY 10027. Offers MS. *Program availability:* Part-time. *Entrance requirements:* For master's, GRE General Test. Additional exam requirements/recommendations for international students: required—TOEFL, IELTS, PTE. *Expenses:* Contact institution.

DePaul University, College of Computing and Digital Media, Chicago, IL 60604. Offers animation (MA, MFA); applied technology (MS); business information technology (MS); computational finance (MS); computer and information sciences (PhD); computer science (MS); creative producing (MFA); cybersecurity (MS); data science (MS); digital communication and media arts (MA); documentary (MFA); e-commerce technology (MS); experience design (MA); film and television (MS); film and television directing (MFA); game design (MFA); game programming (MS); health informatics (MS); human centered design (PhD); human-computer interaction (MS); information systems (MS); network engineering and security (MS); product innovation and computing (MS); screenwriting (MFA); software engineering (MS); JD/MS. *Program availability:* Part-time, evening/weekend, online learning. *Degree requirements:* For master's, thesis (for some programs); for doctorate, comprehensive exam, thesis/dissertation. *Entrance requirements:* For master's, GRE or GMAT (for MS in computational finance only), bachelor's degree, resume (MS in predictive analytics only), IT experience (MS in information technology project management only), portfolio review (all MFA programs and MA in animation); for doctorate, GRE, master's degree in computer science. Additional exam requirements/recommendations for international students: required—TOEFL (minimum score 590 paper-based; 80 iBT), IELTS (minimum score 6.5), PTE (minimum score 53). Electronic applications accepted. *Expenses:* Contact institution.

DeSales University, Division of Science and Mathematics, Center Valley, PA 18034-9568. Offers cyber security (Postbaccalaureate Certificate); data analytics (Postbaccalaureate Certificate); information systems (MS), including cyber security, digital forensics, healthcare information management, project management. *Program availability:* Part-time, evening/weekend, 100% online, blended/hybrid learning. *Faculty:* 2 full-time (both women), 5 part-time/adjunct (1 woman). *Students:* 2 full-time (0 women), 17 part-time (4 women); includes 3 minority (2 Asian, non-Hispanic/Latino; 1 Two or more races, non-Hispanic/Latino). Average age 36. 15 applicants, 60% accepted, 9 enrolled. In 2019, 6 master's awarded. *Entrance requirements:* For master's, GRE or GMAT, bachelor's degree in computer-related discipline from accredited college or university, minimum undergraduate GPA of 3.0, personal statement, three letters of recommendation. Additional exam requirements/recommendations for international students: required—TOEFL. *Application deadline:* Applications are processed on a rolling basis. Application fee: $50. Electronic applications accepted. *Expenses:* Contact institution. *Financial support:* Applicants required to submit FAFSA. *Unit head:* Dr. Ronald Nordone, Dean of Graduate Studies, 610-282-1100 Ext. 1289, E-mail: Ronald.Nordone@desale.edu. *Application contact:* Julia Ferraro, Director of Graduate Admissions, 610-282-1100 Ext. 1768, E-mail: gradadmissions@desales.edu.
Website: http://www.desales.edu/home/academics/graduate-studies/programs-of-study/msis—-master-of-science-in-information-systems

Elmhurst University, Graduate Programs, Program in Data Science, Elmhurst, IL 60126-3296. Offers MS. *Program availability:* Part-time, evening/weekend, 100% online. *Faculty:* 2 full-time (0 women), 1 part-time/adjunct (0 women). *Students:* 2 full-time (1 woman), 50 part-time (14 women); includes 17 minority (4 Black or African American, non-Hispanic/Latino; 7 Asian, non-Hispanic/Latino; 5 Hispanic/Latino; 1 Two or more races, non-Hispanic/Latino). Average age 33. 45 applicants, 36% accepted, 16 enrolled. In 2019, 15 master's awarded. *Entrance requirements:* For master's, 3 recommendations, resume, statement of purpose, interview. Additional exam requirements/recommendations for international students: required—TOEFL (minimum score 550 paper-based; 79 iBT). *Application deadline:* Applications are processed on a rolling basis. Application fee: $0. Electronic applications accepted. *Expenses:* $870 per semester hour. *Financial support:* In 2019–20, 16 students received support. Scholarships/grants available. Support available to part-time students. Financial award applicants required to submit FAFSA. *Unit head:* Dr. Jim Kulich, Director, 630-617-3575, E-mail: jimk@elmhurst.edu. *Application contact:* Timothy J. Panfil, Senior Director of Graduate Admission and Enrollment Management, 630-617-3300 Ext. 3256, E-mail: panfilt@elmhurst.edu.
Website: http://www.elmhurst.edu/data_science

Fairfield University, School of Engineering, Fairfield, CT 06824. Offers database management (CAS); electrical and computer engineering (MS); information security (CAS); management of technology (MS); mechanical engineering (MS); network technology (CAS); software engineering (MS); Web application development (CAS). *Program availability:* Part-time, evening/weekend. *Faculty:* 10 full-time (2 women), 15 part-time/adjunct (1 woman). *Students:* 46 full-time (24 women), 57 part-time (10 women); includes 23 minority (5 Black or African American, non-Hispanic/Latino; 9 Asian, non-Hispanic/Latino; 9 Hispanic/Latino), 33 international. Average age 29. 68 applicants, 62% accepted, 30 enrolled. In 2019, 100 master's awarded. *Degree requirements:* For master's, capstone course. *Entrance requirements:* For master's, resume, 2 recommendations. Additional exam requirements/recommendations for international students: required—TOEFL (minimum score 550 paper-based; 80 iBT), IELTS (minimum score 6.5), TOEFL (minimum score 550 paper-based; 80 iBT) or IELTS (minimum score 6.5). *Application deadline:* For fall admission, 5/15 for international students; for spring admission, 10/15 for international students. Applications are processed on a rolling basis. Application fee: $60. Electronic applications accepted. *Expenses:* Tuition $900/credit hour; Registration Fee $50/semester; Graduate Student Activity Fee (Fall and Spring) $65/semester. *Financial support:* In 2019–20, 20 students received support. Scholarships/grants and unspecified assistantships available. Financial award applicants required to submit FAFSA. *Unit head:* Richard Heist, Dean, 203-254-4147, Fax: 203-254-4013, E-mail: rheist@fairfield.edu. *Application contact:* Melanie Rogers, Director of Graduate Admission, 203-254-4184, Fax: 203-254-4073, E-mail: gradadmis@fairfield.edu.
Website: http://www.fairfield.edu/soe

Fitchburg State University, Division of Graduate and Continuing Education, Program in Computer Science, Fitchburg, MA 01420-2697. Offers computer science (MS); data science (MS). *Program availability:* Part-time, evening/weekend. *Entrance requirements:* Additional exam requirements/recommendations for international students: required—TOEFL (minimum score 550 paper-based; 79 iBT). Electronic applications accepted. *Expenses:* Contact institution.

Florida International University, College of Engineering and Computing, School of Computing and Information Sciences, Miami, FL 33199. Offers computer science (MS, PhD); cybersecurity (MS); data science (MS); information technology (MS); telecommunications and networking (MS). *Program availability:* Part-time, evening/weekend. *Faculty:* 53 full-time (14 women), 33 part-time/adjunct (9 women). *Students:* 162 full-time (39 women), 140 part-time (26 women); includes 160 minority (11 Black or African American, non-Hispanic/Latino; 1 American Indian or Alaska Native, non-Hispanic/Latino; 9 Asian, non-Hispanic/Latino; 132 Hispanic/Latino; 7 Two or more races, non-Hispanic/Latino), 120 international. Average age 30. 360 applicants, 49% accepted, 73 enrolled. In 2019, 89 master's, 13 doctorates awarded. *Degree requirements:* For master's, thesis or alternative; for doctorate, comprehensive exam, thesis/dissertation. *Entrance requirements:* For master's and doctorate, GRE General Test, 3 letters of recommendation, minimum GPA of 3.0. Additional exam requirements/recommendations for international students: required—TOEFL (minimum score 550 paper-based; 80 iBT). *Application deadline:* For fall admission, 6/1 for domestic students, 4/1 for international students; for spring admission, 10/1 for domestic students, 9/1 for international students. Applications are processed on a rolling basis. Application fee: $30. Electronic applications accepted. *Expenses: Tuition, area resident:* Full-time $8912; part-time $446 per credit hour. Tuition, state resident: full-time $8912; part-time $446 per credit hour. Tuition, nonresident: full-time $21,393; part-time $992 per credit hour. *Required fees:* $2194. *Financial support:* Research assistantships, teaching assistantships, institutionally sponsored loans, scholarships/grants, and unspecified assistantships available. Financial award application deadline: 3/1; financial award applicants required to submit FAFSA. *Unit head:* Dr. Sundararaj S. Iyengar, Director, 305-348-3947, Fax: 305-348-3549, E-mail: sundararaj.iyengar@fiu.edu. *Application contact:* Nanett Rojas, Manager, Admissions Operations, 305-348-7464, Fax: 305-348-7441, E-mail: gradadm@fiu.edu.

Fordham University, Graduate School of Arts and Sciences, Department of Computer and Information Sciences, New York, NY 10458. Offers computer science (MS); data analytics (MS). *Program availability:* Part-time, evening/weekend. *Students:* Average

age 31. 378 applicants, 71% accepted, 94 enrolled. In 2019, 62 master's awarded. *Entrance requirements:* For master's, GRE General Test. Additional exam requirements/recommendations for international students: required—TOEFL (minimum score 550 paper-based). *Application deadline:* For fall admission, 1/4 priority date for domestic students; for spring admission, 11/1 for domestic students. Application fee: $70. Electronic applications accepted. *Financial support:* In 2019–20, 5 students received support, including 3 research assistantships with tuition reimbursements available (averaging $15,000 per year); career-related internships or fieldwork, institutionally sponsored loans, tuition waivers (full and partial), and unspecified assistantships also available. Financial award application deadline: 1/4; financial award applicants required to submit CSS PROFILE or FAFSA. *Unit head:* Dr. Damian Lyons, Chair, 718-817-4485, Fax: 718-817-4488, E-mail: dlyons@fordham.edu. *Application contact:* Garrett Marino, Director of Graduate Admissions, 718-817-4419, Fax: 718-817-3566, E-mail: gmarino10@fordham.edu.

George Mason University, College of Health and Human Services, Department of Health Administration and Policy, Fairfax, VA 22030. Offers health and medical policy (MS); health informatics (MS); health informatics and data analytics (Certificate); health services research (PhD); health systems management (MHA); quality improvement and outcomes management in health care systems (Certificate). *Accreditation:* CAHME. *Program availability:* Part-time, evening/weekend, 100% online. *Degree requirements:* For master's, comprehensive exam, internship; for doctorate, thesis/dissertation. *Entrance requirements:* For master's, GRE recommended if undergraduate GPA is below 3.0 (for MS in health and medical policy), 2 official transcripts; expanded goals statement; 3 letters of recommendation; resume; 1 year of work experience (for MHA in health systems management); minimum GPA of 3.25 preferred (for MS in health informatics); for doctorate, GRE, professional and volunteer experience, evidence of ability to write and conduct research at the doctoral level, master's degree or equivalent; for Certificate, 2 official transcripts; expanded goals statement; 3 letters of recommendation; resume. Additional exam requirements/recommendations for international students: required—TOEFL (minimum score 575 paper-based; 88 iBT), IELTS (minimum score 6.5), PTE (minimum score 59). Electronic applications accepted. *Expenses:* Contact institution.

George Mason University, College of Science, Department of Computational and Data Sciences, Fairfax, VA 22030. Offers computational science (MS); computational sciences and informatics (PhD); computational social science (PhD, Certificate); data science (Certificate). *Degree requirements:* For master's, comprehensive exam (for some programs), thesis optional; for doctorate, comprehensive exam, thesis/dissertation. *Entrance requirements:* For master's, GRE General Test and TOEFL for students with degrees outside US, minimum GPA of 3.0 in last 60 credits of undergraduate study, minimum of 1 course in differential equations, proficiency in using a high-level computer programming language; for doctorate, GRE and TOEFL for students with degrees outside US, minimum GPA of 3.0 in last 60 credits of undergraduate study, minimum 1 course in differential equations, knowledge of a computer programming language such as C, C++, Fortran, Python; for Certificate, TOEFL for students with degrees outside US, minimum GPA of 3.0 in last 60 credits of undergraduate study, minimum 1 course in differential equations, knowledge of a computer programming language such as C, C++, Fortran, Python. Additional exam requirements/recommendations for international students: required—TOEFL.

George Mason University, Volgenau School of Engineering, Department of Information Sciences and Technology, Program in Data Analytics Engineering, Fairfax, VA 22030. Offers MS. *Entrance requirements:* For master's, three letters of recommendation; detailed statement of career goals and professional aspiration; self-evaluation form. Additional exam requirements/recommendations for international students: required—TOEFL (minimum score 575 paper-based; 88 iBT), IELTS (minimum score 6.5), PTE (minimum score 59). Electronic applications accepted. *Expenses:* Contact institution.

The Graduate Center, City University of New York, Graduate Studies, Program in Data Analysis and Visualization, New York, NY 10016-4039. Offers data analysis (MS); data studies (MS); data visualization (MS).

The Graduate Center, City University of New York, Graduate Studies, Program in Data Science, New York, NY 10016-4039. Offers MS.

Grand Canyon University, College of Doctoral Studies, Phoenix, AZ 85017-1097. Offers data analytics (DBA); general psychology (PhD), including cognition and instruction, industrial and organizational psychology, integrating technology, learning, and psychology, performance psychology; management (DBA); marketing (DBA); organizational leadership (Ed D), including behavioral health, Christian ministry, health care administration, organizational development. *Degree requirements:* For doctorate, comprehensive exam, thesis/dissertation. *Entrance requirements:* For doctorate, minimum GPA of 3.4 on earned advanced degree from regionally-accredited institution; transcripts; goals statement.

HEC Montreal, School of Business Administration, Doctoral Program in Administration, Montréal, QC H3T 2A7, Canada. Offers accounting (PhD); applied economics (PhD); data science (PhD); finance (PhD); financial engineering (PhD); information technology (PhD); international business (PhD); logistics and operations management (PhD); management science (PhD); management, strategy and organizations (PhD); marketing (PhD); organizational behaviour and human resources (PhD). *Accreditation:* AACSB. *Entrance requirements:* For doctorate, TAGE MAGE, GMAT, or GRE, master's degree in administration or related field. Electronic applications accepted.

IGlobal University, Graduate Programs, Vienna, VA 22182. Offers accounting (MBA); data management and analytics (MSIT); entrepreneurship (MBA); finance (MBA); global business management (MBA); health care management (MBA); hospitality and tourism management (MBA); human resources management (MBA); information technology (MBA); information technology systems and management (MSIT); leadership and management (MBA); project management (MBA); public service and administration (MBA); software design and management (MSIT).

Illinois Institute of Technology, Graduate College, College of Science, Department of Applied Mathematics, Chicago, IL 60616. Offers applied mathematics (MS, PhD); data science (MAS); mathematical finance (MAS). Terminal master's awarded for partial completion of doctoral program. *Degree requirements:* For master's, comprehensive exam, thesis; for doctorate, comprehensive exam, thesis/dissertation. *Entrance requirements:* For master's, GRE General Test (minimum scores: 304 Quantitative and Verbal, 2.5 Analytical Writing), minimum undergraduate GPA of 3.0; three letters of recommendation; for doctorate, GRE General Test (minimum scores: 304 Quantitative and Verbal, 3.0 Analytical Writing), minimum undergraduate GPA of 3.5; three letters of recommendation. Additional exam requirements/recommendations for international students: required—TOEFL (minimum score 550 paper-based; 80 iBT). Electronic applications accepted.

Illinois Institute of Technology, Graduate College, College of Science, Department of Computer Science, Chicago, IL 60616. Offers business (MCS); computational intelligence (MCS); computer science (MCS, MS, PhD); cyber-physical systems (MCS); data analytics (MCS); data science (MAS); database systems (MCS); distributed and cloud computing (MCS); education (MCS); finance (MCS); information security and assurance (MCS); networking and communications (MCS); software engineering

(MCS); telecommunications and software engineering (MAS); MS/MAS. *Program availability:* Part-time, evening/weekend, online learning. Terminal master's awarded for partial completion of doctoral program. *Degree requirements:* For master's, thesis optional; for doctorate, comprehensive exam, thesis/dissertation. *Entrance requirements:* For master's, GRE General Test with minimum scores of 298 Quantitative and Verbal, 3.0 Analytical Writing (for MS); GRE General Test with minimum scores of 292 Quantitative and Verbal, 2.5 Analytical Writing (for MAS), minimum undergraduate GPA of 3.0; for doctorate, GRE General Test (minimum scores: 304 Quantitative and Verbal, 3.5 Analytical Writing), minimum undergraduate GPA of 3.0. Additional exam requirements/recommendations for international students: required—TOEFL (minimum score 523 paper-based; 70 iBT). Electronic applications accepted.

Indiana University Bloomington, School of Informatics, Computing, and Engineering, Program in Data Science, Bloomington, IN 47408. Offers MS, Graduate Certificate. *Program availability:* Part-time, evening/weekend, 100% online, blended/hybrid learning. *Entrance requirements:* For master's, GRE, statement of purpose, 3 recommendation letters, transcripts. Additional exam requirements/recommendations for international students: required—TOEFL (minimum score 100 iBT). Electronic applications accepted. *Expenses:* Contact institution.

Indiana University-Purdue University Indianapolis, School of Informatics and Computing, Department of Human-Centered Computing, Indianapolis, IN 46202. Offers human-computer interaction (MS, PhD); informatics (MS), including data analytics; media arts and science (MS).

Indiana University-Purdue University Indianapolis, School of Science, Department of Computer and Information Science, Indianapolis, IN 46202-5132. Offers biocomputing (Graduate Certificate); biometrics (Graduate Certificate); computer science (MS, PhD); computer security (Graduate Certificate); databases and data mining (Graduate Certificate); software engineering (Graduate Certificate). *Program availability:* Part-time. Terminal master's awarded for partial completion of doctoral program. *Degree requirements:* For master's and Graduate Certificate, thesis optional; for doctorate, thesis/dissertation. *Entrance requirements:* For master's and doctorate, GRE, BS in computer science or the equivalent with a minimum GPA of 3.0 (or equivalent); for Graduate Certificate, BS in computer science or the equivalent with a minimum GPA of 3.0 (or equivalent). Additional exam requirements/recommendations for international students: required—PTE (minimum score 58), TOEFL (minimum score 550 paper-based, 79 iBT) or IELTS (6.5).

Johnson & Wales University, Graduate Studies, MS Program in Data Analytics, Providence, RI 02903-3703. Offers MS. *Program availability:* Online learning.

Kansas State University, Graduate School, College of Business, Program in Business Administration, Manhattan, KS 66506. Offers data analytics (MBA); finance (MBA); management (MBA); marketing (MBA); technology entrepreneurship (MBA). *Accreditation:* AACSB. *Program availability:* Part-time, 100% online. *Entrance requirements:* For master's, GMAT (minimum score of 500), minimum undergraduate GPA of 3.0. Additional exam requirements/recommendations for international students: required—TOEFL (minimum score 550 paper-based; 79 iBT); recommended—IELTS (minimum score 7). Electronic applications accepted. *Expenses:* Contact institution.

Keck Graduate Institute, Minerva Schools at KGI, San Francisco, CA 94103. Offers MDS. *Program availability:* Part-time-only. In 2019, 3 master's awarded. *Degree requirements:* For master's, thesis. *Entrance requirements:* Additional exam requirements/recommendations for international students: required—No standardized tests or exams required. *Application deadline:* For fall admission, 10/1 for domestic and international students; for winter admission, 2/1 for domestic and international students; for spring admission, 4/1 for domestic and international students; for summer admission, 5/15 for domestic and international students. Applications are processed on a rolling basis. Application fee: $0. Electronic applications accepted. *Unit head:* Dr. Joshua Fost, Dean of Graduate Studies, E-mail: jfost@minerva.kgi.edu. *Application contact:* Samantha Maskey, Admissions Program Manager, E-mail: samantha@minervaproject.com.
Website: https://www.minerva.kgi.edu/

Kennesaw State University, Analytics and Data Science Institute, Kennesaw, GA 30144. Offers PhD. *Students:* 20 full-time (10 women), 3 part-time (0 women); includes 3 minority (1 Black or African American, non-Hispanic/Latino; 2 Asian, non-Hispanic/Latino), 12 international. Average age 33. 49 applicants, 16% accepted, 6 enrolled. In 2019, 3 doctorates awarded. *Degree requirements:* For doctorate, comprehensive exam, thesis/dissertation. *Entrance requirements:* For doctorate, GRE, Resume, Statement, Letters of Recommendation, Base SAS Certification, Math through Calculus II. Additional exam requirements/recommendations for international students: required—TOEFL (minimum score 80 iBT), IELTS (minimum score 6.5). *Application deadline:* For fall admission, 2/1 for domestic and international students. Application fee: $60. Electronic applications accepted. *Expenses: Tuition, area resident:* Full-time $7104; part-time $296 per credit hour. Tuition, state resident: full-time $7104; part-time $296 per credit hour. Tuition, nonresident: full-time $25,584; part-time $1066 per credit hour. *International tuition:* $25,584 full-time. *Required fees:* $2006; $1706 per unit. $853 per semester. *Financial support:* In 2019–20, 5 research assistantships with full and partial tuition reimbursements (averaging $36,000 per year) were awarded. *Unit head:* Sherrill Hayes, Program Director, 470-578-6499, E-mail: shayes32@kennesaw.edu. *Application contact:* Admissions Counselor, 470-578-4377, Fax: 470-578-9172, E-mail: ksugrad@kennesaw.edu.
Website: http://datascience.kennesaw.edu/

Kennesaw State University, College of Computing and Software Engineering, Program in Information Technology, Kennesaw, GA 30144. Offers data management and analytics (Graduate Certificate); health information technology (Postbaccalaureate Certificate); information technology (MSIT); information technology foundations (Postbaccalaureate Certificate); information technology security (Graduate Certificate). *Program availability:* Part-time, evening/weekend, blended/hybrid learning. *Students:* 73 full-time (38 women), 142 part-time (52 women); includes 101 minority (56 Black or African American, non-Hispanic/Latino; 31 Asian, non-Hispanic/Latino; 10 Hispanic/Latino; 4 Two or more races, non-Hispanic/Latino), 37 international. Average age 32. 52 applicants, 85% accepted, 34 enrolled. In 2019, 95 master's awarded. *Degree requirements:* For master's, thesis optional. *Entrance requirements:* For master's, minimum GPA of 2.75; for other advanced degree, bachelor's degree. Additional exam requirements/recommendations for international students: required—TOEFL (minimum score 80 iBT), IELTS (minimum score 6.5). *Application deadline:* For fall admission, 7/1 priority date for domestic students, 5/1 priority date for international students; for spring admission, 11/1 priority date for domestic students, 9/1 priority date for international students; for summer admission, 4/1 priority date for domestic students, 3/1 priority date for international students. Applications are processed on a rolling basis. Application fee: $60. Electronic applications accepted. *Expenses: Tuition, area resident:* Full-time $7104; part-time $296 per credit hour. Tuition, state resident: full-time $7104; part-time $296 per credit hour. Tuition, nonresident: full-time $25,584; part-time $1066 per credit hour. *International tuition:* $25,584 full-time. *Required fees:* $2006; $1706 per unit. $853 per semester. *Financial support:* Applicants required to submit FAFSA. *Application contact:* Admission Counselor, 470-578-4377, Fax: 470-578-9172, E-mail: ksugrad@

kennesaw.edu.
Website: http://ccse.kennesaw.edu/it/

Lawrence Technological University, College of Arts and Sciences, Southfield, MI 48075-1058. Offers bioinformatics (Graduate Certificate); computer science (MS), including data science, big data, and data mining, intelligent systems; educational technology (MA), including robotics; instructional design, communication, and presentation (Graduate Certificate); integrated science (MA); science education (MA); technical and professional communication (MS, Graduate Certificate); writing for the digital age (Graduate Certificate). *Program availability:* Part-time, evening/weekend. *Faculty:* 5 full-time (2 women), 2 part-time/adjunct (1 woman). *Students:* 1 (woman) full-time, 25 part-time (15 women); includes 6 minority (3 Black or African American, non-Hispanic/Latino; 2 Asian, non-Hispanic/Latino; 1 Hispanic/Latino), 6 international. Average age 34. 50 applicants, 68% accepted, 3 enrolled. In 2019, 14 master's, 4 other advanced degrees awarded. *Degree requirements:* For master's, thesis (for some programs). *Entrance requirements:* Additional exam requirements/recommendations for international students: required—TOEFL (minimum score 550 paper-based; 79 iBT), IELTS (minimum score 6.5). *Application deadline:* For fall admission, 5/24 for international students; for spring admission, 10/13 for international students; for summer admission, 2/18 for international students. Applications are processed on a rolling basis. Application fee: $50. Electronic applications accepted. *Expenses: Tuition:* Full-time $16,618; part-time $8309 per year. *Required fees:* $600; $600. *Financial support:* In 2019–20, 4 students received support. Scholarships/grants and tuition reduction available. Financial award application deadline: 4/1; financial award applicants required to submit FAFSA. *Unit head:* Glen Bauer, Interim Dean, 248-204-3532, Fax: 248-204-3518, E-mail: scidean@ltu.edu. *Application contact:* Jane Rohrback, Director of Admissions, 248-204-3160, Fax: 248-204-2228, E-mail: admissions@ltu.edu.

Lipscomb University, College of Computing and Technology, Nashville, TN 37204-3951. Offers data science (MS, Certificate); information technology (MS, Certificate), including data science (MS), information security (MS), information technology management (MS), software engineering (MS); software engineering (MS, Certificate). *Program availability:* Part-time, evening/weekend. *Degree requirements:* For master's, capstone project. *Entrance requirements:* For master's, GRE, 2 references, transcripts, resume, personal statement. Additional exam requirements/recommendations for international students: required—TOEFL (minimum score 570 paper-based; 80 iBT). Electronic applications accepted. *Expenses:* Contact institution.

London Metropolitan University, Graduate Programs, London, United Kingdom. Offers applied psychology (M Sc); architecture (MA); biomedical science (M Sc); blood science (M Sc); cancer pharmacology (M Sc); computer networking and cyber security (M Sc); computing and information systems (M Sc); conference interpreting (MA); counter-terrorism studies (M Sc); creative, digital and professional writing (MA); crime, violence and prevention (M Sc); criminology (M Sc); curating contemporary art (MA); data analytics (M Sc); digital media (MA); early childhood studies (MA); education (MA, Ed D); financial services law, regulation and compliance (LL M); food science (M Sc); forensic psychology (M Sc); health and social care management and policy (M Sc); human nutrition (M Sc); human resource management (MA); human rights and international conflict (MA); information technology (M Sc); intelligence and security studies (M Sc); international oil, gas and energy law (LL M); international relations (MA); interpreting (MA); learning and teaching in higher education (MA); legal practice (LL M); media and entertainment law (LL M); organizational and consumer psychology (M Sc); psychological therapy (M Sc); psychology of mental health (M Sc); public health (M Sc); public policy and management (MPA); security studies (M Sc); social work (M Sc); spatial planning and urban design (MA); sports therapy (M Sc); supporting older children and young people with dyslexia (MA); teaching languages (MA), including Arabic, English; translation (MA); woman and child abuse (MA).

Manhattan College, Graduate Programs, School of Science, Program in Applied Mathematics - Data Analytics, Riverdale, NY 10471. Offers MS. *Program availability:* Part-time, evening/weekend. *Faculty:* 10 full-time (4 women). *Students:* 10 full-time (1 woman), 4 part-time (1 woman); includes 4 minority (1 Black or African American, non-Hispanic/Latino; 3 Hispanic/Latino), 1 international. Average age 24. 15 applicants, 13% accepted, 5 enrolled. In 2019, 2 master's awarded. *Degree requirements:* For master's, comprehensive exam. *Entrance requirements:* Additional exam requirements/recommendations for international students: required—TOEFL (minimum score 550 paper-based; 80 iBT), IELTS (minimum score 6.5), TOEFL or IELTS is required. *Application deadline:* Applications are processed on a rolling basis. Application fee: $75. Electronic applications accepted. *Financial support:* In 2019–20, 2 students received support. Unspecified assistantships available. *Unit head:* Dr. Janet McShane, Interim Dean of Science, 718-862-7368, E-mail: janet.mcshane@manhattan.edu. *Application contact:* Kevin Taylor, Director of Admissions for Graduate and Professional Studies, 718-862-7825, E-mail: ktaylor02@manhattan.edu.
Website: https://manhattan.edu/academics/5-year-programs/applied-mathematics-data-analytics.php

Maryville University of Saint Louis, College of Arts and Sciences, St. Louis, MO 63141-7299. Offers actuarial science (MS); data science (MS); strategic communication and leadership (MA). *Program availability:* Part-time. *Faculty:* 10 full-time (5 women), 14 part-time/adjunct (6 women). *Students:* 48 full-time (30 women), 79 part-time (52 women); includes 33 minority (11 Black or African American, non-Hispanic/Latino; 9 Asian, non-Hispanic/Latino; 10 Hispanic/Latino; 3 Two or more races, non-Hispanic/Latino), 45 international. Average age 32. In 2019, 55 master's awarded. *Entrance requirements:* For master's, strong mathematics background, 2 letters of recommendation, and personal statement (MS). Additional exam requirements/recommendations for international students: required—TOEFL (minimum score 550 paper-based; 80 iBT). *Application deadline:* Applications are processed on a rolling basis. Electronic applications accepted. *Expenses:* Contact institution. *Financial support:* Application deadline: 4/1; applicants required to submit FAFSA. *Unit head:* Jennifer Yukna, Dean, 314-529-6858, Fax: 314-529-9965, E-mail: jyukna@maryville.edu. *Application contact:* Shani Lenore-Jenkins, Vice President of Enrollment, 314-529-9359, E-mail: slenore@maryville.edu.
Website: https://www.maryville.edu/as/

Merrimack College, School of Science and Engineering, North Andover, MA 01845-5800. Offers civil engineering (MS); computer science (MS); data science (MS); engineering management (MS); mechanical engineering (MS), including engineering management. *Program availability:* Part-time, evening/weekend, 100% online. *Degree requirements:* For master's, comprehensive exam, thesis optional, internship or capstone (for some programs). *Entrance requirements:* For master's, official college transcripts, resume, personal statement, 2 recommendations. Additional exam requirements/recommendations for international students: required—TOEFL (minimum score 84 iBT), IELTS (minimum score 6.5), PTE (minimum score 56). Electronic applications accepted. Application fee is waived when completed online. *Expenses:* Contact institution.

Metropolitan State University, College of Management, St. Paul, MN 55106-5000. Offers business administration (MBA, DBA); business analytics (Graduate Certificate); database administration (Graduate Certificate); global supply chain management (Graduate Certificate); information assurance security (Graduate Certificate); management information systems (MMIS); MIS generalist (Graduate Certificate); MIS systems analysis and design (Graduate Certificate); project management (Graduate Certificate). *Program availability:* Part-time, evening/weekend. *Degree requirements:* For master's, thesis optional, computer language (MMIS). *Entrance requirements:* For master's, GMAT (for MBA), resume. Additional exam requirements/recommendations for international students: required—TOEFL (minimum score 550 paper-based). Electronic applications accepted.

Michigan Technological University, Graduate School, Interdisciplinary Programs, Houghton, MI 49931. Offers automotive systems and controls (Graduate Certificate); biochemistry and molecular biology (PhD); computational science and engineering (PhD); data science (Graduate Certificate); sustainability (Graduate Certificate). *Program availability:* Part-time. *Faculty:* 132 full-time, 6 part-time/adjunct. *Students:* 57 full-time (20 women), 19 part-time; includes 7 minority (3 Black or African American, non-Hispanic/Latino; 1 American Indian or Alaska Native, non-Hispanic/Latino; 1 Asian, non-Hispanic/Latino; 2 Two or more races, non-Hispanic/Latino), 42 international. Average age 30. 475 applicants, 29% accepted, 25 enrolled. In 2019, 23 master's, 10 doctorates, 36 other advanced degrees awarded. Terminal master's awarded for partial completion of doctoral program. *Degree requirements:* For master's, comprehensive exam (for some programs), thesis (for some programs); for doctorate, comprehensive exam, thesis/dissertation. *Entrance requirements:* For master's, doctorate, and Graduate Certificate, GRE, statement of purpose, personal statement, official transcripts, 2-3 letters of recommendation. Additional exam requirements/recommendations for international students: required—TOEFL or IELTS. *Application deadline:* Applications are processed on a rolling basis. Application fee: $0. Electronic applications accepted. *Expenses: Tuition, area resident:* Full-time $19,206; part-time $1067 per credit. Tuition, state resident: full-time $19,206; part-time $1067 per credit. Tuition, nonresident: full-time $19,206; part-time $1067 per credit. *International tuition:* $19,206 full-time. *Required fees:* $248; $248 per unit. $124 per semester. Tuition and fees vary according to course load and program. *Financial support:* In 2019–20, 54 students received support, including 9 fellowships with tuition reimbursements available (averaging $16,590 per year), 14 research assistantships with tuition reimbursements available (averaging $16,590 per year), 10 teaching assistantships with tuition reimbursements available (averaging $16,590 per year); career-related internships or fieldwork, Federal Work-Study, scholarships/grants, health care benefits, unspecified assistantships, and cooperative program also available. Financial award applicants required to submit FAFSA. *Unit head:* Dr. Will H Cantrell, Dean of the Graduate School, 906-487-3007, Fax: 906-487-2284, E-mail: cantrell@mtu.edu. *Application contact:* Ashli Wells, Assistant Director of Graduate Enrollment Services, 906-487-3513, Fax: 906-487-2284, E-mail: aesniego@mtu.edu.

Montclair State University, The Graduate School, College of Humanities and Social Sciences, Data Collection and Management Certificate Program, Montclair, NJ 07043-1624. Offers Certificate.

National University, School of Engineering and Computing, La Jolla, CA 92037-1011. Offers computer science (MS), including advanced computing; cyber security and information assurance (MS); data analytics (MS); electrical engineering (MS); engineering management (MS); information technology management (MS); management information systems (MS); sustainability management (MS). *Program availability:* Part-time, evening/weekend, 100% online, blended/hybrid learning. *Degree requirements:* For master's, thesis (for some programs). *Entrance requirements:* For master's, interview, minimum GPA of 2.5. Additional exam requirements/recommendations for international students: required—TOEFL (minimum score 550 paper-based; 79 iBT), IELTS (minimum score 6). Electronic applications accepted. *Expenses: Tuition:* Full-time $442; part-time $442 per unit.

New College of Florida, Program in Data Science, Sarasota, FL 34243. Offers MDS. *Entrance requirements:* For master's, bachelor's degree, course in linear algebra, programming proficiency. Additional exam requirements/recommendations for international students: required—TOEFL (minimum score 560 paper-based; 83 iBT), IELTS (minimum score 6.5).

New Jersey Institute of Technology, Ying Wu College of Computing, Newark, NJ 07102. Offers big data management and mining (Certificate); business and information systems (Certificate); computer science (PhD); computing and business (MS); data mining (Certificate); data science (MS); information security (Certificate); information systems (PhD); information technology administration and security (MS); IT administration (Certificate); network security and information assurance (Certificate); software engineering (MS), including information systems; software engineering analysis/design (Certificate); Web systems development (Certificate). *Program availability:* Part-time, evening/weekend. *Faculty:* 78 full-time (16 women), 63 part-time/adjunct (10 women). *Students:* 668 full-time (210 women), 290 part-time (81 women); includes 277 minority (46 Black or African American, non-Hispanic/Latino; 1 American Indian or Alaska Native, non-Hispanic/Latino; 161 Asian, non-Hispanic/Latino; 53 Hispanic/Latino; 16 Two or more races, non-Hispanic/Latino), 565 international. Average age 27. 2,671 applicants, 62% accepted, 360 enrolled. In 2019, 407 master's, 5 doctorates, 12 other advanced degrees awarded. Terminal master's awarded for partial completion of doctoral program. *Degree requirements:* For master's, thesis optional; for doctorate, thesis/dissertation. *Entrance requirements:* For master's, GRE General Test; for doctorate, GRE General Test, minimum graduate GPA of 3.5. Additional exam requirements/recommendations for international students: required—TOEFL (minimum score 550 paper-based; 79 iBT), IELTS (minimum score 6.5). *Application deadline:* For fall admission, 6/1 priority date for domestic students, 5/1 priority date for international students; for spring admission, 11/15 priority date for domestic and international students. Applications are processed on a rolling basis. Application fee: $75. Electronic applications accepted. *Expenses:* $23,828 per year (in-state), $33,744 per year (out-of-state). *Financial support:* In 2019–20, 383 students received support, including 8 fellowships with full tuition reimbursements available, 34 research assistantships with full tuition reimbursements available (averaging $24,000 per year), 57 teaching assistantships with full tuition reimbursements available (averaging $24,000 per year); career-related internships or fieldwork, Federal Work-Study, scholarships/grants, and unspecified assistantships also available. Financial award application deadline: 1/15. *Unit head:* Dr. Craig Gotsman, Dean, 973-596-3366, Fax: 973-596-5777, E-mail: craig.gotsman@njit.edu. *Application contact:* Stephen Eck, Executive Director of University Admissions, 973-596-3300, Fax: 973-596-3461, E-mail: admissions@njit.edu.
Website: http://computing.njit.edu/

The New School, Parsons School of Design, Program in Data Visualization, New York, NY 10011. Offers MS. *Program availability:* Part-time. *Faculty:* 3 full-time (0 women), 4 part-time/adjunct (1 woman). *Students:* 21 full-time (10 women), 9 part-time (4 women); includes 6 minority (1 Black or African American, non-Hispanic/Latino; 3 Asian, non-Hispanic/Latino; 1 Hispanic/Latino; 1 Two or more races, non-Hispanic/Latino), 15 international. Average age 31. 65 applicants, 52% accepted, 20 enrolled. In 2019, 19 master's awarded. *Degree requirements:* For master's, thesis or alternative. *Entrance requirements:* For master's, transcripts, resume, statement of purpose, recommendation letters, portfolio, programming sample and/or writing sample, interview. Additional exam requirements/recommendations for international students: required—TOEFL (minimum

score 92 iBT), IELTS (minimum score 7), PTE (minimum score 63). *Application deadline:* For fall admission, 1/1 priority date for domestic and international students; for summer admission, 1/1 priority date for domestic and international students. Applications are processed on a rolling basis. Application fee: $50. Electronic applications accepted. *Expenses:* 1810 per credit. *Financial support:* In 2019–20, 23 students received support, including 3 research assistantships (averaging $2,764 per year), 2 teaching assistantships (averaging $2,341 per year); Federal Work-Study, scholarships/grants, and unspecified assistantships also available. Support available to part-time students. Financial award application deadline: 2/1; financial award applicants required to submit FAFSA. *Unit head:* Daniel Sauter, Program Director, 212-229-8908 Ext. 4876, E-mail: sauterd@newschool.edu. *Application contact:* Simone Varadian, Senior Director, 212-229-5150 Ext. 4117, E-mail: varadias@newschool.edu.
Website: http://www.newschool.edu/parsons/ms-data-visualization/

New York University, Graduate School of Arts and Science, Department of Data Science, New York, NY 10012-1019. Offers MS. *Entrance requirements:* For master's, GRE or GMAT. Additional exam requirements/recommendations for international students: required—TOEFL, IELTS. Electronic applications accepted.

New York University, School of Professional Studies, Division of Programs in Business, Program in Management and Systems, New York, NY 10012-1019. Offers management and systems (MS), including database technologies, enterprise risk management, strategy and leadership, systems management. *Program availability:* Part-time, evening/weekend, 100% online, blended/hybrid learning. *Degree requirements:* For master's, thesis, capstone project. *Entrance requirements:* For master's, GRE or GMAT (only upon request), bachelor's degree, resume with relevant professional work, internship or volunteer experience, 2 letters of recommendation, personal statement. Additional exam requirements/recommendations for international students: required—TOEFL (minimum score 600 paper-based; 100 iBT), IELTS (minimum score 7). Electronic applications accepted. *Expenses:* Contact institution.

Northcentral University, Graduate Studies, San Diego, CA 92106. Offers business (MBA, DBA, PhD, Postbaccalaureate Certificate); education (M Ed, Ed D, PhD, Ed S, Post-Master's Certificate, Postbaccalaureate Certificate); marriage and family therapy (MA, DMFT, PhD, Post-Master's Certificate, Postbaccalaureate Certificate); psychology (MA, PhD, Post-Master's Certificate, Postbaccalaureate Certificate); technology (MS, PhD), including computer science, cybersecurity (MS), data science, technology and innovation management (PhD). *Program availability:* Part-time, evening/weekend, online only, 100% online. *Degree requirements:* For doctorate, comprehensive exam, thesis/dissertation. *Entrance requirements:* For master's, bachelor's degree from regionally- or nationally-accredited institution, current resume or curriculum vitae, statement of intent, interview, and background check (for marriage and family therapy); for doctorate, post-baccalaureate master's degree and/or doctoral degree from nationally- or regionally-accredited academic institution; for other advanced degree, bachelor's-level or higher degree from accredited institution or university (for Post-Baccalaureate Certificate); master's and/or doctoral degree from regionally- or nationally-accredited academic institution (for Post-Master's Certificate). Additional exam requirements/recommendations for international students: required—TOEFL (minimum score 550 paper-based; 79 iBT), IELTS (minimum score 6.5), PTE (minimum score 53). Electronic applications accepted. *Expenses: Tuition:* Part-time $1053 per credit. *Required fees:* $95 per course. Full-time tuition and fees vary according to degree level and program.

Northeastern University, College of Computer and Information Science, Boston, MA 02115-5096. Offers computer science (MS, PhD); data science (MS); game science and design (MS); health informatics (MS); information assurance (MS); network science (PhD); personal health informatics (PhD). *Program availability:* Part-time, evening/weekend. Terminal master's awarded for partial completion of doctoral program. *Degree requirements:* For master's, thesis optional; for doctorate, comprehensive exam, thesis/dissertation. Electronic applications accepted. *Expenses:* Contact institution.

Northwestern University, School of Professional Studies, Program in Data Science, Evanston, IL 60208. Offers computer-based data mining (MS); marketing analytics (MS); predictive modeling (MS); risk analytics (MS); Web analytics (MS). *Program availability:* Online learning. *Entrance requirements:* For master's, official transcripts, two letters of recommendation, statement of purpose, current resume or curriculum vitae. Additional exam requirements/recommendations for international students: required—TOEFL (minimum score 600 paper-based; 100 iBT) or IELTS (minimum score 7).

Northwestern University, School of Professional Studies, Program in Information Systems, Evanston, IL 60208. Offers analytics and business intelligence (MS); database and Internet technologies (MS); information systems (MS); information systems management (MS); information systems security (MS); medical informatics (MS); software project management and development (MS). *Program availability:* Part-time, evening/weekend.

Ohio Dominican University, Division of Business, Program in Business Administration, Columbus, OH 43219-2099. Offers accounting (MBA); data analytics (MBA); finance (MBA); leadership (MBA); risk management (MBA); sport management (MBA). *Program availability:* Part-time, evening/weekend, 100% online, blended/hybrid learning. *Faculty:* 9 full-time (3 women), 9 part-time/adjunct (0 women). *Students:* 46 full-time (26 women), 83 part-time (41 women); includes 30 minority (16 Black or African American, non-Hispanic/Latino; 2 American Indian or Alaska Native, non-Hispanic/Latino; 4 Asian, non-Hispanic/Latino; 3 Hispanic/Latino; 5 Two or more races, non-Hispanic/Latino), 12 international. Average age 30. 75 applicants, 96% accepted, 55 enrolled. In 2019, 56 master's awarded. *Entrance requirements:* For master's, minimum overall GPA of 3.0 in undergraduate degree from regionally-accredited institution or 2.75 in last 60 semester hours of bachelor's degree. Additional exam requirements/recommendations for international students: required—TOEFL (minimum score 550 paper-based), IELTS (minimum score 6.5). *Application deadline:* For fall admission, 8/15 for domestic students, 6/10 for international students; for spring admission, 1/4 for domestic students, 11/2 for international students; for summer admission, 5/30 for domestic students. Applications are processed on a rolling basis. Application fee: $25. Electronic applications accepted. *Expenses: Tuition:* Full-time $10,800; part-time $600 per credit hour. *Required fees:* $225 per semester. Tuition and fees vary according to program. *Financial support:* Applicants required to submit FAFSA. *Unit head:* Dr. Thomas Eveland, Director of Graduate Programs in Business, 614-251-4569, E-mail: evelandt@ohiodominican.edu. *Application contact:* John W. Naughton, Vice President for Enrollment and Student Success, 614-251-4721, Fax: 614-251-6654, E-mail: grad@ohiodominican.edu.
Website: http://www.ohiodominican.edu/academics/graduate/mba

Oregon State University, College of Science, Program in Data Analytics, Corvallis, OR 97331. Offers MS. *Program availability:* Part-time, online only, 100% online. *Expenses:* Contact institution.

Penn State Great Valley, Graduate Studies, Management Division, Malvern, PA 19355-1488. Offers business administration (MBA); cyber security (Certificate); data analytics (MPS, MS, Certificate); distributed energy and grid modernization (Certificate); finance (M Fin); health sector management (Certificate); human resource management (Certificate); information science (MSIS); leadership development (MLD); new ventures and entrepreneurship (Certificate); sustainable management practices (Certificate). *Accreditation:* AACSB.

Queens College of the City University of New York, School of Social Sciences, Department of Sociology, Queens, NY 11367-1597. Offers data analytics and applied social research (MA). *Program availability:* Part-time, evening/weekend. *Entrance requirements:* For master's, minimum GPA of 3.0. Additional exam requirements/recommendations for international students: required—TOEFL (minimum score 100 iBT), IELTS (minimum score 7). Electronic applications accepted.

Radford University, College of Graduate Studies and Research, Data and Information Management, MS, Radford, VA 24142. Offers MS. *Program availability:* Part-time. *Entrance requirements:* For master's, GRE (minimum scores of 152 on quantitative portion and 148 on verbal portion, or 650 and 420, respectively, under old scoring system), minimum GPA of 3.0 overall from accredited educational institution, three letters of reference from faculty members familiar with academic performance in major coursework or from colleagues or supervisors familiar with work. Additional exam requirements/recommendations for international students: required—TOEFL (minimum score 567 paper-based). Electronic applications accepted.

Regis University, College of Computer and Information Sciences, Denver, CO 80221-1099. Offers agile technologies (Certificate); cybersecurity (Certificate); data science (M Sc); database administration with Oracle (Certificate); database development (Certificate); database technologies (M Sc); enterprise Java software development (Certificate); enterprise resource planning (Certificate); executive information technology (Certificate); health care informatics (Certificate); health care informatics and information management (M Sc); information assurance (M Sc); information assurance policy management (Certificate); information technology management (M Sc); mobile software development (Certificate); software engineering (M Sc, Certificate); software engineering and database technology (M Sc); storage area networks (Certificate); systems engineering (M Sc, Certificate). *Program availability:* Part-time, evening/weekend, 100% online, blended/hybrid learning. *Degree requirements:* For master's, thesis (for some programs), final research project. *Entrance requirements:* For master's, official transcript reflecting baccalaureate degree awarded from regionally-accredited college or university, 2 years of related experience, resume, interview. Additional exam requirements/recommendations for international students: required—TOEFL (minimum score 550 paper-based; 82 iBT). Electronic applications accepted. *Expenses:* Contact institution.

Robert Morris University, School of Informatics, Humanities and Social Sciences, Moon Township, PA 15108. Offers communication and information systems (MS); cyber security (MS); data analytics (MS); information security and assurance (MS); information systems and communications (D Sc); information systems management (MS); information technology project management (MS); Internet information systems (MS); organizational leadership (MS). *Program availability:* Part-time-only, evening/weekend, 100% online. *Faculty:* 23 full-time (9 women), 11 part-time/adjunct (0 women). *Students:* 224 part-time (90 women); includes 46 minority (28 Black or African American, non-Hispanic/Latino; 5 Asian, non-Hispanic/Latino; 9 Hispanic/Latino; 4 Two or more races, non-Hispanic/Latino), 31 international. Average age 35. In 2019, 118 master's, 14 doctorates awarded. *Degree requirements:* For master's, Completion of 30 credits; for doctorate, thesis/dissertation, Completion of 63 credits. *Entrance requirements:* For doctorate, employer letter of endorsement, interview. Additional exam requirements/recommendations for international students: required—TOEFL (minimum score 550 paper-based; 79 iBT). *Application deadline:* For fall admission, 7/1 priority date for domestic and international students; for spring admission, 11/1 priority date for domestic and international students. Applications are processed on a rolling basis. Application fee: $35. Electronic applications accepted. Application fee is waived when completed online. *Expenses:* $960 per credit tuition plus $85 per credit fees (for master's); $32,940 per year tuition and fees (for doctorate). *Financial support:* Institutionally sponsored loans available. Support available to part-time students. Financial award application deadline: 5/1; financial award applicants required to submit FAFSA. *Unit head:* Dr. Amjad Ali, Dean, School of Informatics, Humanities and Social Sciences, 412-397-3000. *Application contact:* Kellie Laurenzi, Associate Vice President, Enrollment Management, 412-397-5200, E-mail: graduateadmissions@rmu.edu.
Website: https://www.rmu.edu/academics/schools/sihss

Rochester Institute of Technology, Graduate Enrollment Services, Golisano College of Computing and Information Sciences, Computer Science Department, Advanced Certificate Program in Big Data Analytics, Rochester, NY 14623-5603. Offers Advanced Certificate. *Program availability:* Part-time, 100% online. *Entrance requirements:* For degree, GRE for applicants with degrees from foreign universities, personal statement, 2 letters of recommendation, minimum cumulative GPA of 3.0 (or equivalent). Additional exam requirements/recommendations for international students: required—TOEFL (minimum score 550 paper-based; 79 iBT), IELTS (minimum score 6.5), PTE (minimum score 58). Electronic applications accepted. *Expenses:* Contact institution.

Rockhurst University, Helzberg School of Management, Kansas City, MO 64110-2561. Offers accounting (MBA); business intelligence (MBA, Certificate); business intelligence and analytics (MS); data science (MBA, Certificate); entrepreneurship (MBA); finance (MBA); fundraising leadership (MBA, Certificate); healthcare management (MBA, Certificate); human capital (Certificate); international business (Certificate); management (MA, MBA, Certificate); nonprofit administration (Certificate); organizational development (Certificate); science leadership (Certificate). *Accreditation:* AACSB. *Program availability:* Part-time, evening/weekend. *Entrance requirements:* For master's, GMAT or GRE. Additional exam requirements/recommendations for international students: required—TOEFL (minimum score 550 paper-based; 79 iBT). Electronic applications accepted.

St. John's University, College of Professional Studies, Department of Computer Science, Mathematics and Science, Queens, NY 11439. Offers data mining and predictive analytics (MS). *Entrance requirements:* For master's, letters of recommendation, transcripts, resume, personal statement, prerequisites: calculus, probability and statistics. Additional exam requirements/recommendations for international students: required—TOEFL (minimum score 80 iBT), IELTS (minimum score 6.5). Electronic applications accepted.

Saint Mary's University of Minnesota, Schools of Graduate and Professional Programs, Graduate School of Business and Technology, Business Intelligence and Data Analytics Program, Winona, MN 55987-1399. Offers MS. *Unit head:* Michael Ratajczyk, Director, 507-457-1698, E-mail: mratajcz@smumn.edu. *Application contact:* Laurie Roy, Director of Admission of Schools of Graduate and Professional Programs, 507-457-8606, Fax: 612-728-5121, E-mail: lroy@smumn.edu.
Website: https://onlineprograms.smumn.edu/msbida/masters-in-business-intelligence-and-analytics?_ga-2.146577908.1736907137.1523547391-1359115499.1515170921

Saint Peter's University, Graduate Business Programs, Program in Data Science, Jersey City, NJ 07306-5997. Offers business analytics (MS). *Program availability:* Part-time. *Entrance requirements:* Additional exam requirements/recommendations for international students: required—TOEFL (minimum score 550 paper-based; 79 iBT), IELTS (minimum score 6.5).

Data Science/Data Analytics

Seattle Pacific University, Master of Arts in Management Program, Seattle, WA 98119-1997. Offers business intelligence and data analytics (MA); cybersecurity (MA); faith and business (MA); human resources (MA); social and sustainable management (MA). *Entrance requirements:* For master's, GMAT scores above 500 (25 verbal; 30 quantitative; 4.4 analytical writing) are preferred, bachelor's degree from accredited college or university, resume, essay, official transcript. *Application deadline:* For fall admission, 8/1 for domestic students, 6/1 for international students; for winter admission, 11/1 for domestic students, 9/1 for international students; for spring admission, 2/1 for domestic students, 12/1 for international students; for summer admission, 5/1 for domestic students. Application fee: $50.
Website: http://spu.edu/academics/school-of-business-and-economics/graduate-programs/ma-management

Slippery Rock University of Pennsylvania, Graduate Studies (Recruitment), College of Health, Engineering, and Science, Department of Mathematics and Statistics, Slippery Rock, PA 16057-1383. Offers data analytics (MS). *Program availability:* Part-time, blended/hybrid learning. *Faculty:* 3 full-time (1 woman). *Students:* 6 full-time (3 women), 22 part-time (10 women); includes 2 minority (1 Asian, non-Hispanic/Latino; 1 Hispanic/Latino). Average age 32. 36 applicants, 83% accepted, 19 enrolled. In 2019, 13 master's awarded. *Entrance requirements:* For master's, official transcripts; minimum GPA of 3.0; completion of following prerequisite courses with minimum C grade: differential calculus, integral calculus, probability/inferential statistics, and a programming language (C, C++, C#, Java, Python); familiarity with multivariable calculus, linear algebra, and math statistics. Additional exam requirements/recommendations for international students: required—TOEFL (minimum score 550 paper-based; 80 iBT). *Application deadline:* For fall admission, 5/1 priority date for domestic students, 3/1 priority date for international students; for spring admission, 10/1 priority date for domestic students, 9/1 priority date for international students. Applications are processed on a rolling basis. Application fee: $25 ($30 for international students). Electronic applications accepted. *Expenses:* $516 per credit in-state tuition; $173.61 per credit in-state fees; $774 per credit out-of-state tuition; $224.31 per credit out-of-state fees; $516 per credit in-state tuition, $105.40 per credit in-state fees (for distance education); $526 per credit out-of-state tuition; $118.90 per credit out-of-state fees (for distance education). *Financial support:* In 2019–20, 3 students received support. Career-related internships or fieldwork, Federal Work-Study, institutionally sponsored loans, scholarships/grants, tuition waivers (partial), and unspecified assistantships available. Support available to part-time students. Financial award application deadline: 5/1; financial award applicants required to submit FAFSA. *Unit head:* Dr. Dil Singhabahu, Graduate Coordinator, 724-738-2521, Fax: 724-738-4807, E-mail: dil.singhabahu@sru.edu. *Application contact:* Brandi Weber-Mortimer, Director of Graduate Admissions, 724-738-4340, E-mail: graduate.admissions@sru.edu.
Website: http://www.sru.edu/academics/colleges-and-departments/ches/departments/mathematics-and-statistics

Southern Arkansas University–Magnolia, School of Graduate Studies, Magnolia, AR 71753. Offers agriculture (MS); business administration (MBA), including agribusiness, social entrepreneurship, supply chain management; clinical and mental health counseling (MS); computer and information sciences (MS), including cyber security and privacy, data science, information technology; gifted and talented (M Ed), including curriculum and instruction, educational administration and supervision, gifted and talented P-8/7-12, instructional specialist P-4; higher, adult and lifelong education (M Ed); kinesiology (M Ed), including coaching; library media and information specialist (M Ed); public administration (MPA); school counseling K-12 (M Ed); student affairs and college counseling (M Ed); teaching (MAT). *Accreditation:* NCATE. *Program availability:* Part-time, 100% online, blended/hybrid learning. *Faculty:* 33 full-time (18 women), 29 part-time/adjunct (17 women). *Students:* 134 full-time (80 women), 704 part-time (471 women); includes 223 minority (158 Black or African American, non-Hispanic/Latino; 5 American Indian or Alaska Native, non-Hispanic/Latino; 19 Asian, non-Hispanic/Latino; 6 Hispanic/Latino; 1 Native Hawaiian or other Pacific Islander, non-Hispanic/Latino; 34 Two or more races, non-Hispanic/Latino), 135 international. Average age 28. 290 applicants, 99% accepted, 149 enrolled. In 2019, 177 master's awarded. *Degree requirements:* For master's, comprehensive exam (for some programs), thesis optional. *Entrance requirements:* For master's, GRE, MAT or GMAT, minimum GPA of 2.5. Additional exam requirements/recommendations for international students: required—TOEFL (minimum score 550 paper-based), IELTS (minimum score 6). *Application deadline:* For fall admission, 8/1 for domestic and international students; for spring admission, 12/1 for domestic students, 11/15 for international students; for summer admission, 5/1 for domestic students, 5/10 for international students. Applications are processed on a rolling basis. Application fee: $25 ($90 for international students). Electronic applications accepted. *Expenses:* Tuition, area resident: Full-time $6720; part-time $3360 per semester. Tuition, state resident: full-time $6720; part-time $3360 per semester. Tuition, nonresident: full-time $10,560; part-time $5280 per semester. International tuition: $10,560 full-time. Required fees: $2046; $1023 $267. One-time fee: $25. Tuition and fees vary according to course load. *Financial support:* Career-related internships or fieldwork, Federal Work-Study, scholarships/grants, tuition waivers (full), and unspecified assistantships available. Financial award applicants required to submit FAFSA. *Unit head:* Dr. Kim Bloss, Dean, School of Graduate Studies, 870-235-4150, Fax: 870-235-5227, E-mail: kkbloss@saumag.edu. *Application contact:* Talia Jett, Admissions Coordinator, 870-2355450, Fax: 870-235-5227, E-mail: taliajett@saumag.edu.
Website: http://www.saumag.edu/graduate

Southern Methodist University, Dedman College of Humanities and Sciences, Department of Statistical Science, Dallas, TX 75275-0332. Offers applied statistics and data analytics (MS); biostatistics (PhD); statistical science (PhD). *Program availability:* Part-time. *Degree requirements:* For master's, thesis, oral and written exams; for doctorate, thesis/dissertation, oral and written exams. *Entrance requirements:* For master's, GRE General Test, 12 hours of advanced math courses; for doctorate, GRE General Test, minimum GPA of 3.0. Additional exam requirements/recommendations for international students: required—TOEFL. Electronic applications accepted.

Southern Methodist University, Lyle School of Engineering, Department of Multidisciplinary Studies, Dallas, TX 75275. Offers data science (MS), including business analytics, machine learning; datacenter systems engineering (MS); design and innovation (MA). *Program availability:* Part-time, online learning. *Entrance requirements:* For master's, BS in one of the engineering disciplines, computer science, one of the quantitative sciences or mathematics; minimum of two years of college-level mathematics including one year of college-level calculus.

Southern New Hampshire University, School of Business, Manchester, NH 03106-1045. Offers accounting (MBA, Graduate Certificate); accounting finance (MS); accounting/auditing (MS); accounting/forensic accounting (MS); accounting/management accounting (MS); accounting/taxation (MS); applied economics (MS); athletic administration (MBA, Graduate Certificate); business administration (IMBA, Certificate), including business information systems (Certificate), human resource management (Certificate); business analytics (MBA); business intelligence (MBA); communication (MA), including new media and marketing, public relations; community economic development (MBA); criminal justice (MBA); data analytics (MS); economics

(MBA); engineering management (MBA); entrepreneurship (MBA); finance (MBA, MS, Graduate Certificate); finance/corporate finance (MS); finance/investments (MS); forensic accounting (MBA); forensic accounting and fraud examination (Graduate Certificate); healthcare informatics (MBA); healthcare management (MBA); human resource management (MS); human resources (MBA); information technology (MS); information technology management (MBA); international business (PhD); Internet marketing (MBA); leadership (MBA); leadership of nonprofit organizations (Graduate Certificate); management (MS); marketing (MBA, MS, Graduate Certificate); music business (MBA); operations and project management (MS); operations and supply chain management (MBA, Graduate Certificate); organizational leadership (MS); project management (MBA, Graduate Certificate); public administration (MBA, Graduate Certificate); quantitative analysis (MBA); Six Sigma (Graduate Certificate); Six Sigma quality (MBA); social media marketing (MBA, Graduate Certificate); sport management (MBA, MS, Graduate Certificate); sustainability and environmental compliance (MBA); MBA/Certificate. *Accreditation:* ACBSP. *Program availability:* Part-time, evening/weekend, online learning. Terminal master's awarded for partial completion of doctoral program. *Degree requirements:* For master's, one foreign language, comprehensive exam (for some programs), thesis or alternative; for doctorate, one foreign language, comprehensive exam, thesis/dissertation. *Entrance requirements:* For master's, minimum GPA of 2.5; for doctorate, GMAT. Additional exam requirements/recommendations for international students: required—TOEFL (minimum score 500 paper-based). Electronic applications accepted.

Stockton University, Office of Graduate Studies, Program in Data Science and Strategic Analytics, Galloway, NJ 08205-9441. Offers MS. *Program availability:* Part-time, online learning. *Faculty:* 5 full-time (2 women), 2 part-time/adjunct (0 women). *Students:* 31 part-time (12 women); includes 7 minority (1 Black or African American, non-Hispanic/Latino; 3 Asian, non-Hispanic/Latino; 1 Hispanic/Latino; 2 Two or more races, non-Hispanic/Latino), 1 international. Average age 30. 38 applicants, 82% accepted, 25 enrolled. In 2019, 11 master's awarded. *Entrance requirements:* For master's, GRE. *Application deadline:* For fall admission, 7/1 for domestic and international students; for spring admission, 9/1 for domestic and international students. Applications are processed on a rolling basis. Application fee: $50. Electronic applications accepted. *Expenses: Tuition, area resident:* Full-time $750.92; part-time $78.58 per credit hour. Tuition, state resident: full-time $750.92; part-time $78.58 per credit hour. Tuition, nonresident: full-time $846; part-time $78.58 per credit hour. *International tuition:* $1195.96 full-time. *Required fees:* $1464; $78.58 per credit hour. One-time fee: $50 full-time. *Financial support:* Fellowships, research assistantships, career-related internships or fieldwork, Federal Work-Study, and scholarships/grants available. Support available to part-time students. Financial award application deadline: 3/1; financial award applicants required to submit FAFSA. *Unit head:* Dr. J. Russell Manson, Director, 609-652-4354. *Application contact:* Tara Williams, Assistant Director of Graduate Enrollment, 609-626-3640, Fax: 609-626-6050, E-mail: gradschool@stockton.edu.
Website: https://stockton.edu/graduate/data-science_strategic-analytics.html

Suffolk University, Sawyer Business School, Department of Public Administration, Boston, MA 02108-2770. Offers community health (MPA); information systems, performance management, and big data analytics (MPA); nonprofit management (MPA); state and local government (MPA); JD/MPA; MPA/MS; MPA/MSCJ; MPA/MSMHC; MPA/MSPS. *Accreditation:* NASPAA (one or more programs are accredited). *Program availability:* Part-time, evening/weekend. *Faculty:* 12 full-time (7 women), 4 part-time/adjunct (3 women). *Students:* 13 full-time (5 women), 72 part-time (55 women); includes 35 minority (21 Black or African American, non-Hispanic/Latino; 3 Asian, non-Hispanic/Latino; 9 Hispanic/Latino; 2 Two or more races, non-Hispanic/Latino), 2 international. Average age 35. 89 applicants, 85% accepted, 30 enrolled. In 2019, 40 master's awarded. *Entrance requirements:* Additional exam requirements/recommendations for international students: required—TOEFL (minimum score 550 paper-based; 80 iBT). *Application deadline:* For fall admission, 3/15 priority date for domestic and international students; for spring admission, 10/15 priority date for domestic and international students. Applications are processed on a rolling basis. Application fee: $50. Electronic applications accepted. *Expenses:* Contact institution. *Financial support:* In 2019–20, 47 students received support, including 2 fellowships (averaging $2,657 per year); career-related internships or fieldwork, Federal Work-Study, institutionally sponsored loans, and scholarships/grants also available. Support available to part-time students. Financial award application deadline: 4/1; financial award applicants required to submit FAFSA. *Unit head:* Brenda Bond, Director/Department Chair, 617-305-1768, E-mail: bbond@suffolk.edu. *Application contact:* Mara Marzocchi, Associate Director of Graduate Admissions, 617-573-8302, Fax: 617-305-1733, E-mail: grad.admission@suffolk.edu.
Website: http://www.suffolk.edu/mpa

Syracuse University, School of Information Studies, CAS Program in Data Science, Syracuse, NY 13244. Offers CAS. *Program availability:* Part-time, evening/weekend, online learning. *Entrance requirements:* For degree, resume, personal statement. Additional exam requirements/recommendations for international students: required—TOEFL (minimum score 100 iBT). Electronic applications accepted.

Syracuse University, School of Information Studies, MS Program in Applied Data Science, Syracuse, NY 13244. Offers MS, MS/CAS. *Program availability:* Part-time, evening/weekend, online learning. *Entrance requirements:* For master's, GRE General Test, resume. Additional exam requirements/recommendations for international students: required—TOEFL (minimum score 100 iBT). Electronic applications accepted.

Texas Tech University, Rawls College of Business Administration, Lubbock, TX 79409-2101. Offers accounting (MSA, PhD), including audit/financial reporting (MSA), taxation (MSA); data science (MS); finance (PhD); general business (MBA); healthcare management (MS); information systems and operations management (PhD); management (PhD); marketing (PhD); STEM (MBA); JD/MBA; JD/MSA; MBA/M Arch; MBA/MD; MBA/MS; MBA/Pharm D. *Accreditation:* AACSB. *Program availability:* Part-time, evening/weekend, 100% online, blended/hybrid learning. *Faculty:* 90 full-time (20 women). *Students:* 505 full-time (209 women), 251 part-time (87 women); includes 239 minority (50 Black or African American, non-Hispanic/Latino; 2 American Indian or Alaska Native, non-Hispanic/Latino; 39 Asian, non-Hispanic/Latino; 112 Hispanic/Latino; 36 Two or more races, non-Hispanic/Latino), 96 international. Average age 28. 534 applicants, 57% accepted, 229 enrolled. In 2019, 415 master's, 10 doctorates awarded. *Degree requirements:* For master's, thesis (for MS); capstone course; for doctorate, comprehensive exam, thesis/dissertation, qualifying exams. *Entrance requirements:* For master's, GMAT, GRE, MCAT, PCAT, LSAT, or DAT, holistic review of academic credentials, resume, essay, letters of recommendation; for doctorate, GMAT, GRE, holistic review of academic credentials, resume, statement of purpose, letters of recommendation. Additional exam requirements/recommendations for international students: required—TOEFL (minimum score 550 paper-based; 79 iBT), IELTS (minimum score 6.5), PTE (minimum score 60). *Application deadline:* For fall admission, 7/1 priority date for domestic students, 1/15 for international students; for spring admission, 12/1 priority date for domestic students, 6/15 for international students; for summer admission, 5/1 priority date for domestic students, 1/15 for international students. Applications are processed on a rolling basis. Application fee: $60. Electronic

applications accepted. *Expenses:* Tuition, state resident: full-time $7944; part-time $331 per credit hour. Tuition, nonresident: full-time $17,904; part-time $746 per credit hour. *Required fees:* $2556; $55.50 per credit hour. $612 per semester. Tuition and fees vary according to program. *Financial support:* In 2019–20, 373 students received support, including 1 fellowship with full tuition reimbursement available (averaging $34,000 per year), 2 research assistantships with full tuition reimbursements available (averaging $21,742 per year), 57 teaching assistantships with full tuition reimbursements available (averaging $22,750 per year); career-related internships or fieldwork, Federal Work-Study, scholarships/grants, traineeships, health care benefits, and unspecified assistantships also available. Financial award application deadline: 3/1; financial award applicants required to submit FAFSA. *Unit head:* Dr. Margaret Williams, Dean, 806-834-2839, Fax: 806-742-1092, E-mail: margaret.l.williams@ttu.edu. *Application contact:* Elisa Dunman, Lead Administrator, Graduate and Professional Programs, 806-834-7772, E-mail: rawlsgrad@ttu.edu.
Website: http://www.depts.ttu.edu/rawlsbusiness/graduate/

Tufts University, School of Engineering, Department of Civil and Environmental Engineering, Medford, MA 02155. Offers bioengineering (MS), including environmental biotechnology; civil and environmental engineering (MS, PhD), including applied data science, environmental and water resources engineering, environmental health, geosystems engineering, structural engineering and mechanics; PhD/PhD. *Program availability:* Part-time. Terminal master's awarded for partial completion of doctoral program. *Degree requirements:* For master's, thesis (for some programs); for doctorate, thesis/dissertation. *Entrance requirements:* For master's and doctorate, GRE General Test. Additional exam requirements/recommendations for international students: required—TOEFL (minimum score 550 paper-based; 80 iBT), IELTS (minimum score 6.5). Electronic applications accepted. Full-time tuition and fees vary according to degree level, program and student level. Part-time tuition and fees vary according to course load.

University at Buffalo, the State University of New York, Graduate School, School of Engineering and Applied Sciences, Department of Civil, Structural, and Environmental Engineering, Buffalo, NY 14260. Offers civil engineering (MS, PhD); engineering science (MS), including data sciences, green energy, Internet of Things, nanoelectronics; environmental and water resources engineering (MS). *Program availability:* Part-time, online learning. Terminal master's awarded for partial completion of doctoral program. *Degree requirements:* For master's, project, thesis, or comprehensive exam; for doctorate, thesis/dissertation. *Entrance requirements:* For master's and doctorate, GRE General Test, letters of reference. Additional exam requirements/recommendations for international students: required—TOEFL (minimum score 550 paper-based; 79 iBT). Electronic applications accepted. *Expenses:* Tuition, area resident: Full-time $11,310; part-time $471 per credit hour. Tuition, state resident: full-time $11,310; part-time $471 per credit hour. Tuition, nonresident: full-time $23,100; part-time $963 per credit hour. *International tuition:* $23,100 full-time. *Required fees:* $2820.

The University of Arizona, College of Agriculture and Life Sciences, Department of Agricultural and Resource Economics, Tucson, AZ 85721. Offers applied econometrics and data analytics (MS); applied economics and policy analysis (MS). *Program availability:* Part-time. *Degree requirements:* For master's, thesis or alternative. *Entrance requirements:* For master's, GRE General Test, 3 letters of recommendation, minimum GPA of 3.0. Additional exam requirements/recommendations for international students: required—TOEFL (minimum score 550 paper-based; 79 iBT). Electronic applications accepted.

University of California, Berkeley, Graduate Division, School of Information, Program in Information and Data Science, Berkeley, CA 94720. Offers MIDS. *Program availability:* Online only, 100% online. *Degree requirements:* For master's, capstone project. Electronic applications accepted.

University of California, San Diego, Graduate Division, Program in Data Science and Engineering, La Jolla, CA 92093. Offers MAS. *Program availability:* Part-time. *Students:* 66 part-time (15 women). 97 applicants, 42% accepted, 31 enrolled. In 2019, 26 master's awarded. *Degree requirements:* For master's, capstone team project. *Entrance requirements:* For master's, 2 letters of recommendation, statement of purpose, resume/curriculum vitae. Additional exam requirements/recommendations for international students: required—TOEFL (minimum score 550 paper-based; 80 iBT), IELTS (minimum score 7). *Application deadline:* For fall admission, 7/1 for domestic students. Application fee: $105 ($125 for international students). Electronic applications accepted. *Expenses:* Contact institution. *Financial support:* Applicants required to submit FAFSA. *Unit head:* Dr. Alin Deutsch, Co-Director, 858-822-2276, E-mail: datasciencemas@eng.ucsd.edu. *Application contact:* Yvonne Wu, Program Coordinator, 858-246-1463, E-mail: yvwu@ucsd.edu.
Website: http://jacobsschool.ucsd.edu/mas/dse/

University of Colorado Denver, Business School, Program in Marketing, Denver, CO 80217. Offers advanced market analytics in a big data world (MS); brand communication in the digital era (MS); global marketing (MS); high-tech and entrepreneurial marketing (MS); marketing and global sustainability (MS); marketing intelligence and strategy in the 21st century (MS); sports and entertainment business (MS). *Program availability:* Part-time, evening/weekend. *Degree requirements:* For master's, 30 semester hours (21 of marketing core courses, 9 of marketing electives). *Entrance requirements:* For master's, GMAT, resume, essay, two letters of recommendation, financial statements (for international applicants). Additional exam requirements/recommendations for international students: required—TOEFL (minimum score 525 paper-based; 71 iBT); recommended—IELTS (minimum score 6.5). Electronic applications accepted. *Expenses:* Contact institution.

University of Denver, Daniel Felix Ritchie School of Engineering and Computer Science, Department of Computer Science, Denver, CO 80208. Offers computer science (MS, PhD); cybersecurity (MS); data science (MS). *Program availability:* Part-time, evening/weekend. *Faculty:* 18 full-time (3 women), 3 part-time/adjunct (1 woman). *Students:* 25 full-time (10 women), 135 part-time (39 women); includes 36 minority (4 Black or African American, non-Hispanic/Latino; 9 Asian, non-Hispanic/Latino; 16 Hispanic/Latino; 7 Two or more races, non-Hispanic/Latino); 50 international. Average age 30. 315 applicants, 69% accepted, 90 enrolled. In 2019, 44 master's awarded. *Degree requirements:* For doctorate, variable foreign language requirement, comprehensive exam, thesis/dissertation, reading competency in two languages, modern typesetting system, or additional coursework. *Entrance requirements:* For master's and doctorate, GRE General Test, bachelor's degree, transcripts, personal statement, resume or curriculum vitae, three letters of recommendation. Additional exam requirements/recommendations for international students: required—TOEFL (minimum score 550 paper-based; 80 iBT). *Application deadline:* For fall admission, 1/15 priority date for domestic and international students; for winter admission, 10/25 for domestic and international students; for spring admission, 2/7 for domestic and international students; for summer admission, 4/24 for domestic and international students. Applications are processed on a rolling basis. Application fee: $65. Electronic applications accepted. *Financial support:* In 2019–20, 78 students received support, including 1 research assistantship with tuition reimbursement available (averaging $6,900 per year), 17 teaching assistantships with tuition reimbursements available (averaging $17,487 per year); career-related internships or fieldwork, Federal Work-Study, institutionally sponsored loans, scholarships/grants, and unspecified assistantships also available. Financial award application deadline: 2/15; financial award applicants required to submit FAFSA. *Unit head:* Dr. Chris GauthierDickey, Professor and Chair, 303-871-3318, E-mail: Chris.GauthierDickey@du.edu. *Application contact:* Information Contact, 303-871-2458, E-mail: info@cs.du.edu.
Website: http://ritchieschool.du.edu/departments/computer-science/

University of Houston - Downtown, College of Sciences and Technology, Houston, TX 77002. Offers data analytics (MS). *Program availability:* Part-time, evening/weekend. *Faculty:* 14 full-time (7 women). *Students:* 62 full-time (25 women), 95 part-time (41 women); includes 88 minority (23 Black or African American, non-Hispanic/Latino; 36 Asian, non-Hispanic/Latino; 27 Hispanic/Latino; 2 Two or more races, non-Hispanic/Latino), 28 international. Average age 33. 67 applicants, 88% accepted, 40 enrolled. In 2019, 51 master's awarded. *Degree requirements:* For master's, capstone course, internship course or approved directed study. *Entrance requirements:* For master's, resume, transcripts. Additional exam requirements/recommendations for international students: required—TOEFL (minimum score 553 paper-based; 81 iBT). *Application deadline:* For fall admission, 8/9 for domestic students, 5/1 for international students; for spring admission, 12/2 for domestic students; for summer admission, 6/1 for domestic students, 4/1 for international students. Application fee: $35 ($80 for international students). Electronic applications accepted. *Expenses:* $386 in-state resident; $758 non-resident, per credit. *Financial support:* Federal Work-Study and scholarships/grants available. Financial award application deadline: 4/1; financial award applicants required to submit FAFSA. *Unit head:* Dr. J. Akif Uzman, Dean, 713-221-8019, E-mail: st_dean@uhd.edu. *Application contact:* Ceshia Love, Director of Admissions, 713-221-8093, Fax: 713-221-8658, E-mail: gradadmissions@uhd.edu.
Website: https://www.uhd.edu/academics/sciences/pages/master-in-data-analytics.aspx

University of Illinois at Springfield, Graduate Programs, College of Liberal Arts and Sciences, Program in Data Analytics, Springfield, IL 62703-5407. Offers MS. *Program availability:* Part-time, 100% online, blended/hybrid learning. *Faculty:* 7 full-time (3 women). *Students:* 20 full-time (8 women), 38 part-time (16 women); includes 15 minority (1 Black or African American, non-Hispanic/Latino; 8 Asian, non-Hispanic/Latino; 6 Hispanic/Latino), 19 international. Average age 33. 144 applicants, 38% accepted, 11 enrolled. In 2019, 9 master's awarded. *Degree requirements:* For master's, thesis or alternative, capstone course. *Entrance requirements:* For master's, bachelor's degree or equivalent with minimum undergraduate GPA of 3.0; completion of all prerequisite courses with minimum grade of B-; written evidence of ability to perform at a high academic level by submitting a personal and academic statement; completed a course in data structures and algorithms. Additional exam requirements/recommendations for international students: required—TOEFL (minimum score 500 paper-based; 61 iBT). *Application deadline:* Applications are processed on a rolling basis. Application fee: $60 ($75 for international students). Electronic applications accepted. *Expenses:* $33.25 per credit hour (online fee). *Financial support:* In 2019–20, research assistantships with full tuition reimbursements (averaging $10,562 per year), teaching assistantships with full tuition reimbursements (averaging $10,652 per year) were awarded; fellowships, career-related internships or fieldwork, Federal Work-Study, scholarships/grants, health care benefits, and unspecified assistantships also available. Support available to part-time students. Financial award application deadline: 11/15; financial award applicants required to submit FAFSA. *Unit head:* Dr. Hei-Chi Chan, Program Administrator, 217-206-7331, E-mail: hchan1@uis.edu. *Application contact:* Dr. Hei-Chi Chan, Program Administrator, 217-206-7331, E-mail: hchan1@uis.edu.
Website: http://www.uis.edu/dataanalytics/

University of Louisville, J. B. Speed School of Engineering, Department of Computer Engineering and Computer Science, Louisville, KY 40292-0001. Offers computer engineering and computer science (M Eng); computer science (MS, PhD); cybersecurity (Certificate); data science (Certificate). *Accreditation:* ABET (one or more programs are accredited). *Program availability:* Part-time, 100% online, blended/hybrid learning. *Faculty:* 16 full-time (1 woman), 4 part-time/adjunct (3 women). *Students:* 82 full-time (28 women), 120 part-time (29 women); includes 35 minority (10 Black or African American, non-Hispanic/Latino; 15 Asian, non-Hispanic/Latino; 4 Hispanic/Latino; 6 Two or more races, non-Hispanic/Latino), 58 international. Average age 32. 90 applicants, 50% accepted, 32 enrolled. In 2019, 47 master's, 5 doctorates, 25 other advanced degrees awarded. Terminal master's awarded for partial completion of doctoral program. *Degree requirements:* For master's, thesis optional; for doctorate, comprehensive exam, thesis/dissertation. *Entrance requirements:* For master's, Two letters of recommendation, official final transcripts; for doctorate, GRE, Two letters of recommendation, personal statement, official final transcripts. Additional exam requirements/recommendations for international students: required—TOEFL (minimum score 550 paper-based; 80 iBT), IELTS (minimum score 6.5). *Application deadline:* For fall admission, 5/1 priority date for domestic and international students; for spring admission, 11/1 priority date for domestic and international students; for summer admission, 3/1 priority date for domestic and international students. Applications are processed on a rolling basis. Application fee: $65. Electronic applications accepted. *Expenses:* Tuition, area resident: Full-time $13,000; part-time $723 per credit hour. Tuition, state resident: full-time $13,000; part-time $723 per credit hour. Tuition, nonresident: full-time $27,114; part-time $1507 per credit hour. *International tuition:* $27,114 full-time. *Required fees:* $196. Tuition and fees vary according to program and reciprocity agreements. *Financial support:* In 2019–20, 70 students received support, including 1 fellowship with full tuition reimbursement available (averaging $22,000 per year), 14 teaching assistantships with full tuition reimbursements available (averaging $22,000 per year); research assistantships, scholarships/grants, health care benefits, and tuition waivers (full) also available. Financial award application deadline: 1/1. *Unit head:* Dr. Wei Zhang, Chair, Computer Science and Engineering, 502-852-0715, E-mail: wei.zhang@louisville.edu. *Application contact:* Dr. Mehmed Kantardzic, Director of Graduate Studies, 502-852-3703, E-mail: mehmed.kantardzic@louisville.edu.
Website: http://louisville.edu/speed/computer

University of Maryland, Baltimore County, The Graduate School, College of Engineering and Information Technology, Department of Computer Science and Electrical Engineering, Program in Data Science, Baltimore, MD 21250. Offers MPS. *Program availability:* Part-time. *Students:* 65 full-time (23 women), 78 part-time (26 women); includes 41 minority (14 Black or African American, non-Hispanic/Latino; 16 Asian, non-Hispanic/Latino; 8 Hispanic/Latino; 3 Two or more races, non-Hispanic/Latino), 55 international. Average age 29. 301 applicants, 54% accepted, 76 enrolled. In 2019, 7 master's awarded. *Entrance requirements:* For master's, one semester of statistics, calculus I or II (depending upon track), academic or professional experience equivalent to basic programming courses. Additional exam requirements/recommendations for international students: required—TOEFL (minimum score 550 paper-based; 80 iBT). *Application deadline:* For fall admission, 8/1 for domestic and international students; for spring admission, 11/1 for domestic and international students. Applications are processed on a rolling basis. Application fee: $70. Electronic applications accepted. *Expenses:* Tuition, area resident: Full-time $659. Tuition, state resident: full-time $659. Tuition, nonresident: full-time $1132. *International tuition:* $1132 full-time. *Required fees:* $140; $140 per credit hour. *Financial support:* In 2019–20, 5 students received support, including 4 research assistantships, 1 teaching

assistantship; fellowships, career-related internships or fieldwork, Federal Work-Study, health care benefits, and unspecified assistantships also available. Support available to part-time students. Financial award application deadline: 6/30; financial award applicants required to submit FAFSA. *Unit head:* Dr. Abhijit Dutt, Director, E-mail: adutt@umbc.edu. *Application contact:* Keara Fliggins, Program Management Specialist, 410-455-3000, Fax: 410-455-3969, E-mail: fliggins@umbc.edu.
Website: http://datascience.umbc.edu/

University of Maryland Global Campus, University of Maryland Global Campus, Data Analytics, Adelphi, MD 20783. Offers MS, Certificate. *Program availability:* Part-time, evening/weekend, online learning. *Students:* 318 part-time (123 women); includes 161 minority (89 Black or African American, non-Hispanic/Latino; 41 Asian, non-Hispanic/Latino; 19 Hispanic/Latino; 12 Two or more races, non-Hispanic/Latino), 20 international. Average age 37. 281 applicants, 100% accepted, 68 enrolled. In 2019, 115 master's, 22 other advanced degrees awarded. *Application deadline:* Applications are processed on a rolling basis. Application fee: $50. Electronic applications accepted. *Financial support:* Scholarships/grants available. Support available to part-time students. Financial award application deadline: 6/1; financial award applicants required to submit FAFSA. *Unit head:* Elena Gortcheva, Program Director, 240-684-2400, E-mail: elena.gortcheva@umgc.edu. *Application contact:* Admissions, 800-888-8682, E-mail: studentsfirst@umuc.edu.
Website: https://www.umgc.edu/academic-programs/masters-degrees/data-analytics.cfm

University of Massachusetts Dartmouth, Graduate School, Program in Data Science, North Dartmouth, MA 02747-2300. Offers MS. *Program availability:* Part-time, online learning. *Degree requirements:* For master's, thesis, practicum. *Entrance requirements:* For master's, GRE, statement of purpose (minimum 300 words), resume, official transcripts, 3 letters of recommendation. Additional exam requirements/recommendations for international students: required—TOEFL (minimum score 533 paper-based; 72 iBT), IELTS (minimum score 6). Electronic applications accepted.

University of Michigan, Rackham Graduate School, College of Literature, Science, and the Arts, Department of Statistics, Ann Arbor, MI 48109. Offers applied statistics (MS); data science (MS); statistics (AM, PhD). Terminal master's awarded for partial completion of doctoral program. *Degree requirements:* For doctorate, comprehensive exam, thesis/dissertation, oral defense of dissertation, preliminary exams. *Entrance requirements:* For master's and doctorate, GRE General Test. Additional exam requirements/recommendations for international students: required—TOEFL (minimum score 560 paper-based; 84 iBT), IELTS (minimum score 6.5). Electronic applications accepted.

University of Michigan, Rackham Graduate School, Program in Survey Methodology, Ann Arbor, MI 48109. Offers data science (MS, PhD); social and psychological (MS, PhD); statistical (MS, PhD); survey methodology (Certificate). *Program availability:* Part-time. Terminal master's awarded for partial completion of doctoral program. *Degree requirements:* For master's, internships; for doctorate, comprehensive exam, thesis/dissertation. *Entrance requirements:* For master's and doctorate, GRE, 3 letters of recommendation, academic statement of purpose, personal statement, resume or curriculum vitae, academic transcripts; for Certificate, 3 letters of recommendation, academic statement of purpose, personal statement, resume or curriculum vitae, academic transcripts. Additional exam requirements/recommendations for international students: required—TOEFL (minimum score 560 paper-based; 84 iBT). Electronic applications accepted. *Expenses:* Contact institution.

University of Michigan–Dearborn, College of Engineering and Computer Science, Master of Science in Data Science Program, Dearborn, MI 48128. Offers MS. *Program availability:* Part-time, evening/weekend. *Faculty:* 19 full-time (1 woman), 5 part-time/adjunct (0 women). *Students:* 37 full-time (19 women), 36 part-time (17 women); includes 6 minority (1 Black or African American, non-Hispanic/Latino; 5 Asian, non-Hispanic/Latino), 50 international. Average age 29. 178 applicants, 55% accepted, 25 enrolled. In 2019, 3 master's awarded. *Entrance requirements:* Additional exam requirements/recommendations for international students: required—TOEFL (minimum score 560 paper-based; 84 iBT), IELTS (minimum score 6.5). *Application deadline:* For fall admission, 8/1 for domestic students, 5/1 for international students; for winter admission, 12/1 for domestic students, 9/1 for international students; for spring admission, 4/1 for domestic students, 1/1 for international students. Applications are processed on a rolling basis. Application fee: $60. Electronic applications accepted. *Financial support:* Scholarships/grants, unspecified assistantships, and non-resident tuition scholarships available. Support available to part-time students. Financial award application deadline: 3/1; financial award applicants required to submit FAFSA. *Unit head:* Dr. William Grosky, Director, 313-583-6424, E-mail: wgrosky@umich.edu. *Application contact:* Office of Graduate Studies, 313-583-6321, E-mail: umd-graduatestudies@umich.edu.
Website: https://umdearborn.edu/cecs/departments/computer-and-information-science/graduate-programs/ms-data-science

University of Michigan–Dearborn, College of Engineering and Computer Science, PhD Program in Computer and Information Science, Dearborn, MI 48128. Offers data management (PhD); data science (PhD); software engineering (PhD); systems and security (PhD). *Faculty:* 19 full-time (1 woman), 5 part-time/adjunct (0 women). *Students:* 8 full-time (5 women), 6 part-time (1 woman); includes 1 minority (Asian, non-Hispanic/Latino), 11 international. Average age 28. 17 applicants, 24% accepted, 3 enrolled. In 2019, 1 doctorate awarded. *Degree requirements:* For doctorate, comprehensive exam, thesis/dissertation. *Entrance requirements:* For doctorate, GRE, bachelor's or master's degree in computer science or closely-related field. Additional exam requirements/recommendations for international students: required—TOEFL (minimum score 560 paper-based; 84 iBT), IELTS (minimum score 6.5). *Application deadline:* For fall admission, 2/1 for domestic and international students. Application fee: $60. Electronic applications accepted. *Financial support:* Research assistantships with full tuition reimbursements, teaching assistantships with full tuition reimbursements, scholarships/grants, health care benefits, and unspecified assistantships available. Financial award application deadline: 2/1; financial award applicants required to submit FAFSA. *Unit head:* Dr. Di Ma, Director, 313-583-6737, E-mail: dmadma@umich.edu. *Application contact:* Office of Graduate Studies, 313-583-6321, E-mail: umd-graduatestudies@umich.edu.
Website: https://umdearborn.edu/cecs/departments/computer-and-information-science/graduate-programs/phd-computer-and-information-science

University of Minnesota, Twin Cities Campus, College of Science and Engineering, Department of Computer Science and Engineering, Program in Data Science, Minneapolis, MN 55455-0213. Offers MS. *Entrance requirements:* For master's, GRE. Additional exam requirements/recommendations for international students: required—TOEFL. Electronic applications accepted.

University of Mississippi, Graduate School, School of Accountancy, University, MS 38677. Offers accountancy (M Acc, PhD); accounting and data analytics (MA); taxation accounting (M Tax). *Accreditation:* AACSB. *Students:* 229 full-time (105 women), 12 part-time (4 women); includes 33 minority (9 Black or African American, non-Hispanic/Latino; 3 American Indian or Alaska Native, non-Hispanic/Latino; 1 Asian, non-Hispanic/Latino; 12 Hispanic/Latino; 8 Native Hawaiian or other Pacific Islander, non-Hispanic/Latino), 7 international. Average age 23. *Expenses:* Tuition, state resident: full-time $8718; part-time $484.25 per credit hour. Tuition, nonresident: full-time $24,990; part-time $1388.25 per credit hour. *Required fees:* $100; $4.16 per credit hour. *Unit head:* Dr. W. Mark Wilder, Dean, School of Accountancy, 662-915-7468, Fax: 662-915-7483, E-mail: umaccy@olemiss.edu. *Application contact:* Tameka Smith, Graduate Activities Specialist for Admissions, 662-915-7474, Fax: 662-915-7577, E-mail: gschool@olemiss.edu.
Website: https://www.olemiss.edu

University of Nebraska at Omaha, Graduate Studies, College of Information Science and Technology, Department of Information Systems and Quantitative Analysis, Omaha, NE 68182. Offers data analytics (Certificate); information assurance (Certificate); information technology (MIT, PhD); management information systems (MS); project management (Certificate); systems analysis and design (Certificate). *Program availability:* Part-time, evening/weekend. *Degree requirements:* For master's, comprehensive exam, thesis (for some programs); for doctorate, comprehensive exam, thesis/dissertation. *Entrance requirements:* For master's, GRE General Test, minimum GPA of 3.0, 3 letters of recommendation, writing sample, resume, official transcripts; for doctorate, GMAT or GRE General Test, minimum GPA of 3.0, 3 letters of recommendation, writing sample, resume, official transcripts; for Certificate, minimum GPA of 3.0, official transcripts. Additional exam requirements/recommendations for international students: required—TOEFL, IELTS, PTE. Electronic applications accepted.

University of Nevada, Las Vegas, Graduate College, Lee Business School, Department of Management, Entrepreneurship and Technology, Las Vegas, NV 89154-6034. Offers data analytics (Certificate); data analytics and applied economics (MS); hotel administration/management information systems (MS/MS); management (Certificate); management information systems (MS, Certificate); new venture management (Certificate); MS/MS. *Program availability:* Part-time, evening/weekend. *Faculty:* 9 full-time (1 woman), 2 part-time/adjunct (0 women). *Students:* 70 full-time (27 women), 51 part-time (20 women); includes 46 minority (6 Black or African American, non-Hispanic/Latino; 19 Asian, non-Hispanic/Latino; 15 Hispanic/Latino; 6 Two or more races, non-Hispanic/Latino), 39 international. Average age 31. 80 applicants, 83% accepted, 39 enrolled. In 2019, 28 master's, 8 other advanced degrees awarded. *Entrance requirements:* For master's, GMAT or GRE, bachelor's degree with minimum GPA 3.0; 2 letters of recommendation; for Certificate, GMAT or GRE. Additional exam requirements/recommendations for international students: required—TOEFL (minimum score 550 paper-based; 80 iBT), IELTS (minimum score 7). *Application deadline:* For fall admission, 8/1 for domestic students, 5/1 for international students; for spring admission, 11/15 for domestic students, 10/1 for international students. Application fee: $60 ($95 for international students). Electronic applications accepted. *Expenses:* Contact institution. *Financial support:* In 2019–20, 37 students received support, including 24 research assistantships with full tuition reimbursements available (averaging $11,458 per year), 13 teaching assistantships with full tuition reimbursements available (averaging $11,250 per year); institutionally sponsored loans, scholarships/grants, health care benefits, and unspecified assistantships also available. Financial award application deadline: 3/15; financial award applicants required to submit FAFSA. *Unit head:* Dr. Rajiv Kishore, Chair/ Professor, 702-895-1709, Fax: 702-895-4370, E-mail: met.chair@unlv.edu. *Application contact:* Dr. Han-fen Hu, Graduate Coordinator, 702-895-1365, Fax: 702-895-4370, E-mail: met.gradcoord@unlv.edu.
Website: https://www.unlv.edu/met

The University of North Carolina Wilmington, Interdisciplinary Program in Computer Science and Information Systems, Wilmington, NC 28403-3297. Offers computer science and information systems (MS); data science (MS). *Faculty:* 10 full-time (2 women). *Students:* 11 full-time (5 women), 13 part-time (2 women); includes 2 minority (1 Asian, non-Hispanic/Latino; 1 Two or more races, non-Hispanic/Latino), 10 international. Average age 30. 23 applicants, 52% accepted, 6 enrolled. In 2019, 8 master's awarded. *Degree requirements:* For master's, thesis or alternative, research project. *Entrance requirements:* For master's, GMAT or GRE, 3 letters of recommendation, resume, statement of interest. Additional exam requirements/recommendations for international students: required—TOEFL (minimum score 79 iBT), IELTS (minimum score 6.5). *Application deadline:* For fall admission, 6/1 for domestic students; for spring admission, 11/15 for domestic students. Applications are processed on a rolling basis. Application fee: $75. Electronic applications accepted. *Expenses:* $3,818.47 full-time in-state; $10,732.97 full-time out-of-state. *Financial support:* Scholarships/grants and unspecified assistantships available. Financial award application deadline: 1/1; financial award applicants required to submit FAFSA. *Unit head:* Dr. Clayton Ferner, Program Coordinator, 910-962-7552, E-mail: cferner@uncw.edu. *Application contact:* Candace Wilhelm, Graduate Coordinator, 910-962-3903, Fax: 910-962-7457, E-mail: wilhelmc@uncw.edu.
Website: http://csb.uncw.edu/mscsis/

University of Pennsylvania, School of Engineering and Applied Science, Program in Data Science, Philadelphia, PA 19104. Offers MSE. *Program availability:* Part-time. *Students:* 62 full-time (25 women), 5 part-time (3 women); includes 5 minority (3 Asian, non-Hispanic/Latino; 2 Two or more races, non-Hispanic/Latino), 57 international. Average age 24. 1,107 applicants, 9% accepted, 26 enrolled. In 2019, 37 master's awarded. *Degree requirements:* For master's, comprehensive exam, thesis optional. *Entrance requirements:* For master's, GRE, bachelor's degree, letters of recommendation, resume, personal statement. Additional exam requirements/recommendations for international students: required—TOEFL (minimum score 100 iBT), IELTS (minimum score 7). *Application deadline:* For fall admission, 3/15 priority date for domestic and international students. Application fee: $80. *Expenses:* Contact institution. *Application contact:* Associate Director of Graduate Admissions, 215-898-4542, Fax: 215-573-5577, E-mail: admissions2@seas.upenn.edu.
Website: https://dats.seas.upenn.edu/

University of Pittsburgh, School of Computing and Information, Department of Informatics and Networked Systems, Pittsburgh, PA 15260. Offers big data analytics (Certificate); information science (MSIS, PhD, Certificate), including telecommunications (PhD); security assurance/information systems (Certificate); telecommunications (MST, Certificate). *Program availability:* Part-time, evening/weekend. *Faculty:* 23 full-time (7 women), 19 part-time/adjunct (7 women). *Students:* 332 full-time (110 women), 54 part-time (25 women); includes 15 minority (4 Black or African American, non-Hispanic/Latino; 7 Asian, non-Hispanic/Latino; 1 Hispanic/Latino; 3 Two or more races, non-Hispanic/Latino), 331 international. Average age 26. 725 applicants, 73% accepted, 108 enrolled. In 2019, 192 master's, 5 doctorates awarded. *Degree requirements:* For master's, thesis optional; for doctorate, comprehensive exam, thesis/dissertation. *Entrance requirements:* For master's, GRE, GMAT, bachelor's degree with min GPA of 3.0, course-work in structured programming language, statistics, mathematics, probability; for doctorate, GRE, GMAT, Master's degree, min GPA of 3.3, course-work in statistics or mathematics, programming, cognitive psychology, systems analysis and design, data structures; for Certificate, Master's degree in Information Science, Telecommunications or related field. Additional exam requirements/recommendations for international students: required—TOEFL (minimum score 550 paper-based; 80 iBT), IELTS (minimum score 6.5). *Application deadline:* For fall admission, 1/15 priority date

for domestic and international students; for winter admission, 11/1 priority date for domestic students, 6/15 priority date for international students; for spring admission, 11/1 priority date for domestic students, 6/15 priority date for international students; for summer admission, 3/15 priority date for domestic students, 12/15 priority date for international students. Applications are processed on a rolling basis. Application fee: $50. Electronic applications accepted. *Expenses:* Fall & spring: $24,742 in-state, $41,952 out-of-state, $950 mandatory fees *Financial support:* In 2019–20, 58 students received support, including 1 fellowship with full and partial tuition reimbursement available (averaging $24,456 per year), 26 research assistantships with full and partial tuition reimbursements available (averaging $19,480 per year), 31 teaching assistantships with full and partial tuition reimbursements available (averaging $19,480 per year); institutionally sponsored loans, scholarships/grants, health care benefits, and unspecified assistantships also available. Financial award application deadline: 1/15; financial award applicants required to submit FAFSA. *Unit head:* Dr. Prashant Krishnamurthy, Chair and Professor, 412-624-5144, Fax: 412-624-5231, E-mail: prashk@pitt.edu. *Application contact:* Shabana Reza, Enrollment Manager, 412-624-3988, Fax: 412-624-5231, E-mail: shabana.reza@pitt.edu.
Website: http://www.dins.pitt.edu/

University of Rochester, School of Arts and Sciences, Goergen Institute for Data Science, Rochester, NY 14627. Offers business and social science (MS); computational and statistical methods (MS); health and biomedical sciences (MS). *Students:* 66 full-time (29 women), 6 part-time (2 women); includes 9 minority (1 Black or African American, non-Hispanic/Latino; 5 Asian, non-Hispanic/Latino; 2 Hispanic/Latino; 1 Two or more races, non-Hispanic/Latino), 52 international. Average age 26. 544 applicants, 33% accepted, 39 enrolled. In 2019, 22 master's awarded. *Degree requirements:* For master's, oral exam. *Entrance requirements:* For master's, transcripts, three letters of recommendation, statement of purpose, resume/curriculum vitae. Additional exam requirements/recommendations for international students: required—TOEFL (minimum score 100 iBT), IELTS (minimum score 7). *Application deadline:* For fall admission, 4/15 priority date for domestic and international students. Application fee: $60. Electronic applications accepted. *Financial support:* In 2019–20, 4 students received support, including 4 teaching assistantships (averaging $1,500 per year); tuition waivers (partial) also available. *Unit head:* Mujdat Cetin, Director, 585-276-5061, E-mail: mujdat.cetin@rochester.edu. *Application contact:* Lisa Altman, Education Program Coordinator, 585-275-5288, E-mail: lisa.altman@rochester.edu.
Website: http://www.sas.rochester.edu/dsc/graduate/index.html

University of St. Thomas, School of Engineering, St. Paul, MN 55105. Offers data science (MS); electrical engineering (MS); information technology (MS); manufacturing engineering (MS); manufacturing systems (Certificate); mechanical engineering (MS); medical device development (Certificate); regulatory science (MS); software engineering (MS); software management (MS); systems engineering (MS); technology leadership (Certificate); technology management (MS). *Program availability:* Part-time, evening/weekend. *Entrance requirements:* For master's, resume, official transcripts. Additional exam requirements/recommendations for international students: required—TOEFL (minimum score 80 iBT), IELTS (minimum score 6.5). Electronic applications accepted. *Expenses:* Contact institution.

University of San Francisco, College of Arts and Sciences, Data Science Program, San Francisco, CA 94117. Offers MS. *Faculty:* 7 full-time (3 women). *Students:* 86 full-time (39 women); includes 19 minority (12 Asian, non-Hispanic/Latino; 3 Hispanic/Latino; 4 Two or more races, non-Hispanic/Latino), 52 international. Average age 25. 821 applicants, 22% accepted, 86 enrolled. In 2019, 81 master's awarded. *Entrance requirements:* For master's, GRE or GMAT, prerequisite courses in inferential statistics, linear algebra, computer programming (Java, Mathematica, Matlab, Python or C++), and a social science course. Additional exam requirements/recommendations for international students: required—TOEFL (minimum score 90 iBT), IELTS (minimum score 6.5), PTE (minimum score 61). *Application deadline:* For summer admission, 3/1 for domestic and international students. Applications are processed on a rolling basis. Application fee: $55. Electronic applications accepted. Application fee is waived when completed online. *Financial support:* Career-related internships or fieldwork and scholarships/grants available. Financial award applicants required to submit FAFSA. *Unit head:* Kirsten Keihl, Graduate Director, 415-422-2966, E-mail: info@datascience.usfca.edu. *Application contact:* Information Contact, 415-422-5101, Fax: 415-422-2217, E-mail: asgraduate@usfca.edu.
Website: https://www.usfca.edu/arts-sciences/graduate-programs/data-science

University of Southern Indiana, Graduate Studies, Romain College of Business, Program in Business Administration, Evansville, IN 47712-3590. Offers accounting (MBA); data analytics (MBA); engineering management (MBA); general business administration (MBA); healthcare administration (MBA); human resource management (MBA). *Accreditation:* AACSB. *Program availability:* Part-time, evening/weekend, 100% online, blended/hybrid learning. *Entrance requirements:* For master's, GMAT or GRE, minimum GPA of 2.5, resume, 3 professional references. Additional exam requirements/recommendations for international students: required—TOEFL (minimum score 550 paper-based; 79 iBT), IELTS (minimum score 6). Electronic applications accepted.

University of South Florida, Innovative Education, Tampa, FL 33620-9951. Offers adult, career and higher education (Graduate Certificate), including college teaching, leadership in developing human resources, leadership in higher education; Africana studies (Graduate Certificate), including diasporas and health disparities, genocide and human rights; aging studies (Graduate Certificate), including gerontology; art research (Graduate Certificate), including museum studies; business foundations (Graduate Certificate); chemical and biomedical engineering (Graduate Certificate), including materials science and engineering, water, health and sustainability; child and family studies (Graduate Certificate), including positive behavior support; civil and industrial engineering (Graduate Certificate), including transportation systems analysis; community and family health (Graduate Certificate), including maternal and child health, social marketing and public health, violence and injury: prevention and intervention, women's health; criminology (Graduate Certificate), including criminal justice administration; data science for public administration (Graduate Certificate); digital humanities (Graduate Certificate); educational measurement and research (Graduate Certificate), including evaluation; English (Graduate Certificate), including comparative literary studies, creative writing, professional and technical communication; entrepreneurship (Graduate Certificate); environmental health (Graduate Certificate), including safety management; epidemiology and biostatistics (Graduate Certificate), including applied biostatistics, biostatistics, concepts and tools of epidemiology, epidemiology, epidemiology of infectious diseases; geography, environment and planning (Graduate Certificate), including community development, environmental policy and management, geographical information systems; geology (Graduate Certificate), including hydrogeology; global health (Graduate Certificate), including disaster management, global health and Latin American and Caribbean studies, global health practice, humanitarian assistance, infection control; government and international affairs (Graduate Certificate), including Cuban studies, globalization studies; health policy and management (Graduate Certificate), including health management and leadership, public health policy and programs; hearing specialist: early intervention (Graduate Certificate); industrial and management systems engineering (Graduate Certificate),

including systems engineering, technology management; information studies (Graduate Certificate), including school library media specialist; information systems/decision sciences (Graduate Certificate), including analytics and business intelligence; instructional technology (Graduate Certificate), including distance education, Florida digital/virtual educator, instructional design, multimedia design, Web design; internal medicine, bioethics and medical humanities (Graduate Certificate), including biomedical ethics; Latin American and Caribbean studies (Graduate Certificate); leadership for coastal resiliency planning (Graduate Certificate); mass communications (Graduate Certificate), including multimedia journalism; mathematics and statistics (Graduate Certificate), including mathematics; medicine (Graduate Certificate), including aging and neuroscience, bioinformatics, biotechnology, brain fitness and memory management, clinical investigation, hand and upper limb rehabilitation, health informatics, health sciences, integrative weight management, intellectual property, medicine and gender, metabolic and nutritional medicine, metabolic cardiology, pharmacy sciences; national and competitive intelligence (Graduate Certificate); nursing (Graduate Certificate), including simulation based academic fellowship in advanced pain management; psychological and social foundations (Graduate Certificate), including career counseling, college teaching, diversity in education, mental health counseling, school counseling; public affairs (Graduate Certificate), including nonprofit management, public management, research administration; public health (Graduate Certificate), including assessing chemical toxicity and public health risks, health equity, pharmacoepidemiology, public health generalist, toxicology, translational research in adolescent behavioral health; public health practices (Graduate Certificate), including planning for healthy communities; rehabilitation and mental health counseling (Graduate Certificate), including integrative mental health care, marriage and family therapy, rehabilitation technology; secondary education (Graduate Certificate), including ESOL, foreign language education: culture and content, foreign language education: professional; social work (Graduate Certificate), including geriatric social work/clinical gerontology; special education (Graduate Certificate), including autism spectrum disorder, disabilities education: severe/profound; world languages (Graduate Certificate), including teaching English as a second language (TESL) or foreign language. *Unit head:* Dr. Cynthia DeLuca, Associate Vice President and Assistant Vice Provost, 813-974-3077, Fax: 813-974-7061, E-mail: deluca@usf.edu. *Application contact:* Owen Hooper, Director, Summer and Alternative Calendar Programs, 813-974-6917, E-mail: hooper@usf.edu.
Website: http://www.usf.edu/innovative-education/

The University of Tennessee, Graduate School, Tickle College of Engineering, Bredesen Center for Interdisciplinary Research and Graduate Education, Knoxville, TN 37996. Offers data science and engineering (PhD); energy science and engineering (PhD). *Students:* 76 full-time (25 women); includes 12 minority (3 Black or African American, non-Hispanic/Latino; 3 Asian, non-Hispanic/Latino; 4 Hispanic/Latino; 2 Two or more races, non-Hispanic/Latino), 24 international. Average age 30. 83 applicants, 24% accepted, 20 enrolled. In 2019, 12 doctorates awarded. *Degree requirements:* For doctorate, comprehensive exam, thesis/dissertation, qualifying examination. *Entrance requirements:* For doctorate, GRE General Test, research interest letter, resume/curriculum vitae, 3 letters of recommendation. Additional exam requirements/recommendations for international students: required—TOEFL (minimum score 550 paper-based; 80 iBT), IELTS (minimum score 6.5). *Application deadline:* For fall admission, 1/31 for domestic and international students. Applications are processed on a rolling basis. Application fee: $60. Electronic applications accepted. *Financial support:* In 2019–20, 76 students received support, including 76 fellowships with full tuition reimbursements available (averaging $28,000 per year); health care benefits also available. Financial award application deadline: 1/31. *Unit head:* Dr. Sudarsanam Babu, Director, 865-974-7999, Fax: 865-974-9482, E-mail: sbabu@utk.edu. *Application contact:* Dr. Sudarsanam Babu, Director, 865-974-7999, Fax: 865-974-9482, E-mail: sbabu@utk.edu.
Website: http://bredesencenter.utk.edu/

The University of Texas at Dallas, School of Natural Sciences and Mathematics, Department of Mathematical Sciences, Richardson, TX 75080. Offers actuarial science (MS); mathematics (MS, PhD), including applied mathematics, data science (MS), engineering mathematics (MS), mathematics (MS); statistics (MS, PhD). *Program availability:* Part-time, evening/weekend. *Faculty:* 29 full-time (6 women), 5 part-time/adjunct (0 women). *Students:* 146 full-time (49 women), 40 part-time (23 women); includes 40 minority (2 Black or African American, non-Hispanic/Latino; 24 Asian, non-Hispanic/Latino; 8 Hispanic/Latino; 6 Two or more races, non-Hispanic/Latino), 102 international. Average age 32. 298 applicants, 34% accepted, 54 enrolled. In 2019, 50 master's, 12 doctorates awarded. *Degree requirements:* For master's, thesis optional; for doctorate, thesis/dissertation. *Entrance requirements:* For master's, GRE General Test, minimum GPA of 3.0 in upper-level course work in field; for doctorate, GRE General Test, minimum GPA of 3.5 in upper-level course work in field. Additional exam requirements/recommendations for international students: required—TOEFL (minimum score 550 paper-based). *Application deadline:* For fall admission, 7/15 for domestic students, 5/1 priority date for international students; for spring admission, 11/15 for domestic students, 9/1 priority date for international students. Applications are processed on a rolling basis. Application fee: $50 ($100 for international students). Electronic applications accepted. *Expenses:* Tuition, area resident: Full-time $16,504. Tuition, state resident: full-time $16,504. Tuition, nonresident: full-time $34,266. Tuition and fees vary according to course load. *Financial support:* In 2019–20, 104 students received support, including 1 fellowship (averaging $1,000 per year), 7 research assistantships (averaging $25,714 per year), 91 teaching assistantships with partial tuition reimbursements available (averaging $18,096 per year); career-related internships or fieldwork, Federal Work-Study, institutionally sponsored loans, scholarships/grants, and unspecified assistantships also available. Support available to part-time students. Financial award application deadline: 4/30; financial award applicants required to submit FAFSA. *Unit head:* Dr. Vladimir Dragovic, Department Head, 972-883-2161, Fax: 972-883-6622, E-mail: utdmath@utdallas.edu. *Application contact:* Evangelina Bustamante, Graduate Student Coordinator, 972-883-2163, Fax: 972-883-6622, E-mail: utdmath@utdallas.edu.
Website: http://www.utdallas.edu/math

The University of Texas Health Science Center at Houston, School of Biomedical Informatics, Houston, TX 77030. Offers applied biomedical informatics (MS, Certificate); biomedical informatics (MS, PhD, Certificate); health data science (Certificate); public health informatics (Certificate); MPH/MS; MPH/PhD. *Program availability:* Part-time, 100% online, blended/hybrid learning. *Faculty:* 39 full-time (15 women), 4 part-time/adjunct (0 women). *Students:* 53 full-time (32 women), 227 part-time (107 women); includes 135 minority (34 Black or African American, non-Hispanic/Latino; 1 American Indian or Alaska Native, non-Hispanic/Latino; 53 Asian, non-Hispanic/Latino; 41 Hispanic/Latino; 1 Native Hawaiian or other Pacific Islander, non-Hispanic/Latino; 5 Two or more races, non-Hispanic/Latino), 54 international. Average age 31. 163 applicants, 80% accepted, 86 enrolled. In 2019, 44 master's, 2 doctorates awarded. *Degree requirements:* For master's, thesis or alternative, practicum with capstone report; for doctorate, comprehensive exam, thesis/dissertation, Ph.D.: Qualifying Exam and Dissertation; DHI: Qualifying Exam and Translational Research Project. *Entrance requirements:* For master's, official transcripts from all colleges and universities, WES or

ECE course by course evaluation for international transcripts, resume and/or curriculum vitae, 3 letters of reference from educators and employers, goal statement; for doctorate, Ph.D. program: Graduate Record Exam (GRE), other items apply to both PhD and DHI doctoral degrees, official transcripts, WES and ECE course-by-course evaluation for international students, resume and/or curriculum vitae, 3 letters of reference from educators and employer, goal statement; for the DHI only: Letter of Support to facilitate translational practice project; for Certificate: official transcripts from all colleges and universities, WES or ECE course by course evaluation for international transcripts, resume and/or curriculum vitae, 1 letter of reference, goal statement. Additional exam requirements/recommendations for international students: required—TOEFL (minimum score 87 iBT), IELTS (minimum score 7). *Application deadline:* For fall admission, 7/1 for domestic and international students; for winter admission, 12/1 for domestic and international students; for spring admission, 11/1 for domestic and international students; for summer admission, 3/1 for domestic and international students. Applications are processed on a rolling basis. Application fee: $60. Electronic applications accepted. *Expenses:* Approximate total costs to complete each program offered. Certificates online: $6,693 state resident full-time, $7,913 state resident part-time, $15,828 nonresident full-time, $17,048 nonresident part-time (subtract $110 for classroom); aLL MS online: $18,398.50 state resident, $42,149.50 nonresident; classroom $15,868.50 state resident, $39,619.50 nonresident; PhD: $32,963 state resident, $80,259 nonresident; DHI: $25,113 state resident, $63,669 nonresident. *Financial support:* In 2019–20, 102 students received support, including 58 research assistantships (averaging $20,191 per year), 7 teaching assistantships (averaging $3,568 per year); career-related internships or fieldwork, institutionally sponsored loans, scholarships/grants, health care benefits, and unspecified assistantships also available. Support available to part-time students. Financial award application deadline: 5/1; financial award applicants required to submit FAFSA. *Unit head:* Dr. Jiajie Zhang, Dean/Chair in Informatics Excellence, 713-500-3922, E-mail: jiajie.zhang@uth.tmc.edu. *Application contact:* Jaime N Hargrave, Director, Student Affairs, 713-500-3920, Fax: 713-500-0360, E-mail: jaime.n.hargrave@uth.tmc.edu.
Website: https://sbmi.uth.edu/

University of Vermont, Graduate College, College of Engineering and Mathematical Sciences, Program in Complex Systems and Data Science, Burlington, VT 05405. Offers MS, PhD. *Entrance requirements:* Additional exam requirements/recommendations for international students: required—TOEFL (minimum iBT score of 90) or IELTS (6.5). Electronic applications accepted.

University of Virginia, Data Science Institute, Charlottesville, VA 22903. Offers MS, MBA/MSDS. *Entrance requirements:* For master's, GRE or GMAT, undergraduate degree, personal statement, official transcripts, two letters of recommendation. Additional exam requirements/recommendations for international students: required—TOEFL or IELTS. *Expenses:* Contact institution.

University of Washington, Graduate School, Information School, Seattle, WA 98195. Offers information management (MSIM), including business intelligence, data science, information architecture, information consulting, information security, user experience; information science (PhD); library and information science (MLIS). *Accreditation:* ALA (one or more programs are accredited). *Program availability:* Part-time, evening/weekend, 100% online coursework with required attendance at on-campus orientation at start of program. *Faculty:* 49 full-time (30 women), 33 part-time/adjunct (19 women). *Students:* 394 full-time (249 women), 283 part-time (198 women); includes 154 minority (33 Black or African American, non-Hispanic/Latino; 8 American Indian or Alaska Native, non-Hispanic/Latino; 71 Asian, non-Hispanic/Latino; 38 Hispanic/Latino; 4 Native Hawaiian or other Pacific Islander, non-Hispanic/Latino), 184 international. Average age 30. 1,205 applicants, 47% accepted, 307 enrolled. In 2019, 234 master's, 5 doctorates awarded. Terminal master's awarded for partial completion of doctoral program. *Degree requirements:* For master's, thesis or alternative, capstone or culminating project; for doctorate, comprehensive exam, thesis/dissertation. *Entrance requirements:* For master's, GRE General Test, GMAT (requirements vary for degree programs as test scores may be optional for some applicants); for doctorate, GRE General Test (may not be required for all applicants). Additional exam requirements/recommendations for international students: required—TOEFL (minimum score 590 paper-based; 100 iBT). *Application deadline:* For fall admission, 12/1 priority date for domestic and international students. Application fee: $85. Electronic applications accepted. *Expenses:* Graduate degrees: $845 per credit plus approximately $200 in quartlerly fees (for MLIS); $896 per credit plus approximately $200 in quartlerly fees (for MSIM); PhD: $5798 per quarter in-state full-time, $10,098 per quarter out-of-state full-time. *Financial support:* In 2019–20, 73 students received support, including 14 fellowships with full tuition reimbursements available (averaging $46,977 per year), 90 research assistantships with full tuition reimbursements available (averaging $22,137 per year), 70 teaching assistantships with full tuition reimbursements available (averaging $22,849 per year); Federal Work-Study, institutionally sponsored loans, scholarships/grants, health care benefits, tuition waivers (full and partial), and unspecified assistantships also available. Support available to part-time students. Financial award application deadline: 10/1; financial award applicants required to submit FAFSA. *Unit head:* Dr. Anind Dey, Dean, E-mail: anind@uw.edu. *Application contact:* Kari Brothers, Admissions Counselor, 206-616-5541, Fax: 206-616-3152, E-mail: kari683@uw.edu.
Website: http://ischool.uw.edu/

University of West Florida, Hal Marcus College of Science and Engineering, Department of Computer Science, Pensacola, FL 32514-5750. Offers computer science (MS), including computer science, database systems, software engineering; information technology (MS), including cybersecurity, database management. *Program availability:* Part-time, evening/weekend. *Degree requirements:* For master's, thesis optional. *Entrance requirements:* For master's, GRE, MAT, or GMAT, official transcripts; minimum undergraduate GPA of 3.0; letter of intent; three letters of recommendation. Additional exam requirements/recommendations for international students: required—TOEFL (minimum score 550 paper-based).

University of Wisconsin–La Crosse, College of Science and Health, Department of Mathematics and Statistics, La Crosse, WI 54601-3742. Offers data science (MS). *Program availability:* Part-time, online learning. *Faculty:* 7 full-time (1 woman). *Students:* 10 full-time (4 women), 113 part-time (22 women); includes 21 minority (2 Black or African American, non-Hispanic/Latino; 1 American Indian or Alaska Native, non-Hispanic/Latino; 11 Asian, non-Hispanic/Latino; 6 Hispanic/Latino; 1 Two or more races, non-Hispanic/Latino), 14 international. Average age 37. 42 applicants, 100% accepted, 31 enrolled. In 2019, 10 master's awarded. Application fee: $56. Electronic applications accepted. *Unit head:* Dr. Robert Allen, Department Chair, 608-785-8383, E-mail: rallen@uwlax.edu. *Application contact:* Jennifer Weber, Senior Student Service Coordinator Graduate Admissions, 608-785-8939, E-mail: admissions@uwlax.edu.
Website: http://www.uwlax.edu/mathematics/

University of Wisconsin–Stevens Point, College of Letters and Science, Department of Computing and New Media Technologies, Stevens Point, WI 54481-3897. Offers data science (MS).

Virginia International University, School of Computer Information Systems, Fairfax, VA 22030. Offers business intelligence (Graduate Certificate); business intelligence and data analytics (MIS); computer science (MS), including computer animation and gaming, cybersecurity, data management networking, intelligent systems, software applications development, software engineering; cybersecurity (MIS); data management (MIS); enterprise project management (MIS); health informatics (MIS); information assurance (MIS); information systems (Graduate Certificate); information systems management (MS, Graduate Certificate); information technology (MS); information technology audit and compliance (Graduate Certificate); knowledge management (MIS); software engineering (MS). *Program availability:* Part-time, online learning. *Entrance requirements:* For master's, bachelor's degree. Additional exam requirements/recommendations for international students: required—TOEFL (minimum score 550 paper-based; 80 iBT), IELTS. Electronic applications accepted.

Walsh College of Accountancy and Business Administration, Graduate Programs, Program in Information Technology, Troy, MI 48083. Offers chief information officer (MSIT); cybersecurity (MSIT); data science (MSIT); global project and program management (MSIT). *Program availability:* Part-time, evening/weekend. *Entrance requirements:* For master's, minimum overall cumulative GPA of 2.75 from all colleges previously attended. Additional exam requirements/recommendations for international students: required—TOEFL (minimum score 550 paper-based, 79-80 internet based), IELTS (6.5), Michigan Test of English Language Proficiency, or MTELP (80). Electronic applications accepted. *Expenses:* Contact institution.

Washington University in St. Louis, Olin Business School, Business Analytics, St. Louis, MO 63130. Offers MS. *Program availability:* Part-time. *Faculty:* 85 full-time (16 women), 46 part-time/adjunct (13 women). *Students:* 159 full-time (105 women); includes 3 minority (1 Black or African American, non-Hispanic/Latino; 2 Asian, non-Hispanic/Latino), 150 international. Average age 23. 508 applicants, 23% accepted, 48 enrolled. In 2019, 44 master's awarded. *Degree requirements:* For master's, 39 credit hours. *Entrance requirements:* For master's, GMAT or GRE, U.S. bachelor's degree or equivalent, one letter of recommendation. Additional exam requirements/recommendations for international students: required—TOEFL, IELTS. *Application deadline:* For fall admission, 10/10 for domestic and international students; for winter admission, 1/15 for domestic students, 1/15 priority date for international students; for spring admission, 3/18 for domestic and international students. Applications are processed on a rolling basis. Application fee: $100. Electronic applications accepted. *Financial support:* Institutionally sponsored loans and scholarships/grants available. Financial award applicants required to submit FAFSA. *Unit head:* Dr. Ashley Macrander, Asst. Dean & Dir., Grad Prog Student Services, 314-935-9144, Fax: 314-935-9095, E-mail: malter@wustl.edu. *Application contact:* Ruthie Pyles, Asst Dean and Dir of Grad Admissions & Fin Aid, 314-935-7301, Fax: 314-935-4464, E-mail: olingradadmissions@wustl.edu.
Website: https://olin.wustl.edu/EN-US/academic-programs/specialized-masters-programs/ms-in-business-analytics/Pages/default.aspx

Wayne State University, College of Engineering, Department of Computer Science, Detroit, MI 48202. Offers computer science (MS, PhD), including bioinformatics and computational biology (PhD); data science and business analytics (MS). *Faculty:* 23. *Students:* 97 full-time (41 women), 42 part-time (10 women); includes 15 minority (3 Black or African American, non-Hispanic/Latino; 9 Asian, non-Hispanic/Latino; 2 Hispanic/Latino; 1 Two or more races, non-Hispanic/Latino), 94 international. Average age 30. 276 applicants, 31% accepted, 30 enrolled. In 2019, 42 master's, 10 doctorates awarded. *Degree requirements:* For master's, thesis (for some programs), practicum (for MS in data science and business analytics); for doctorate, thesis/dissertation. *Entrance requirements:* For master's, GRE only for Data Science and Business Analytics degree, minimum GPA of 3.0, three letters of recommendation, adequate preparation in computer science and mathematics courses, personal statement, resume (for MS in data science and business analytics); for doctorate, GRE, bachelor's or master's degree in computer science or related field; minimum GPA of 3.3 in most recent degree; three letters of recommendation; personal statement; adequate preparation in computer science and mathematics courses. Additional exam requirements/recommendations for international students: required—TOEFL (minimum score 550 paper-based; 79 iBT), TWE (minimum score 5.5); recommended—IELTS (minimum score 6.5). *Application deadline:* For fall admission, 6/1 priority date for domestic students, 5/1 priority date for international students; for winter admission, 10/1 priority date for domestic students, 9/1 priority date for international students; for spring admission, 2/1 priority date for domestic students, 1/2 priority date for international students. Applications are processed on a rolling basis. Application fee: $50. Electronic applications accepted. *Expenses:* $790 per credit hour in-state tuition, $1579 per credit hour out-of-state tuition. MS degree is 30 credits; PhD degree is 90 credits. *Financial support:* In 2019–20, 92 students received support, including 4 fellowships with tuition reimbursements available (averaging $20,000 per year), 18 research assistantships with tuition reimbursements available (averaging $20,693 per year), 32 teaching assistantships with tuition reimbursements available (averaging $20,760 per year); scholarships/grants, health care benefits, and unspecified assistantships also available. Financial award application deadline: 2/17; financial award applicants required to submit FAFSA. *Unit head:* Dr. Loren Schwiebert, Chair, 313-577-5474, E-mail: loren@wayne.edu. *Application contact:* Robert Reynolds, Graduate Program Director, 313-577-0726, E-mail: csgradadvisor@cs.wayne.edu.
Website: http://engineering.wayne.edu/cs/

Wayne State University, College of Engineering, Department of Industrial and Systems Engineering, Detroit, MI 48202. Offers data science and business analytics (MS); engineering management (MS); industrial engineering (MS, PhD); manufacturing engineering (MS); systems engineering (Certificate). *Program availability:* Online learning. *Faculty:* 12. *Students:* 126 full-time (31 women), 105 part-time (28 women); includes 42 minority (23 Black or African American, non-Hispanic/Latino; 12 Asian, non-Hispanic/Latino; 4 Hispanic/Latino; 3 Two or more races, non-Hispanic/Latino), 124 international. Average age 30. 407 applicants, 36% accepted, 39 enrolled. In 2019, 123 master's, 8 doctorates awarded. *Degree requirements:* For master's, thesis optional; for doctorate, thesis/dissertation. *Entrance requirements:* For master's, GRE or GMAT (for applicants to MS in data science and business analytics), BS from ABET-accredited institution; for doctorate, GRE, graduate degree in engineering or related discipline with minimum graduate GPA of 3.5, statement of purpose, resume/curriculum vitae, three letters of recommendation; for Certificate, GRE (for applicants from non-ABET institutions), BS in engineering or other technical field from ABET-accredited institution with minimum GPA of 3.0 in upper-division course work, at least one year of full-time work experience as practicing engineer or technical leader. Additional exam requirements/recommendations for international students: required—TOEFL (minimum score 550 paper-based; 79 iBT), TWE (minimum score 5.5), Michigan English Language Assessment Battery (minimum score 85); GRE; recommended—IELTS (minimum score 6.5). *Application deadline:* Applications are processed on a rolling basis. Application fee: $50. Electronic applications accepted. *Expenses:* $790 per credit hour in-state tuition, $1579 per credit hour out-of-state tuition. MS programs 30 credits hours; PhD 90 credit hours. *Financial support:* In 2019–20, 125 students received support, including 2 fellowships with tuition reimbursements available (averaging $20,000 per year), 6 research assistantships with tuition reimbursements available (averaging $22,879 per year), 9 teaching assistantships with tuition reimbursements available (averaging $20,792 per year); scholarships/grants, tuition waivers (full), and unspecified assistantships also available. Financial award applicants required to submit FAFSA. *Unit head:* Dr. Ratna Babu Chinnam, Professor and Interim Chair, 313-577-4846, Fax: 313-

577-8833; E-mail: ratna.chinnam@wayne.edu. *Application contact:* Eric Scimeca, Graduate Program Coordinator, 313-577-0412, E-mail: eric.scimeca@wayne.edu. Website: http://engineering.wayne.edu/ise/

Wayne State University, Mike Ilitch School of Business, Detroit, MI 48201. Offers accounting (MS, MSA, Postbaccalaureate Certificate); business (EMS, Graduate Certificate); business administration (MBA, PhD); data science (MS), including business analytics; entrepreneurship and innovation (Postbaccalaureate Certificate); finance (MS); information systems management (Postbaccalaureate Certificate); taxation (MST); JD/MBA. *Accreditation:* AACSB. *Program availability:* Part-time, evening/weekend. *Faculty:* 29. *Students:* 259 full-time (146 women), 1,156 part-time (521 women); includes 413 minority (233 Black or African American, non-Hispanic/Latino; 1 American Indian or Alaska Native, non-Hispanic/Latino; 79 Asian, non-Hispanic/Latino; 58 Hispanic/Latino; 42 Two or more races, non-Hispanic/Latino), 74 international. Average age 30. 1,106 applicants, 40% accepted, 272 enrolled. In 2019, 386 master's, 3 doctorates, 50 other advanced degrees awarded. *Degree requirements:* For doctorate, thesis/dissertation. *Entrance requirements:* For master's, GMAT, GRE, LSAT, MCAT, at least three years of relevant work experience that shows increased responsibility, or minimum GPA of 3.0 from AACSB-accredited program or 3.2 from regionally-accredited program, undergraduate degree from accredited institution; undergraduate degree in accounting, business administration, or area of business administration (for MS); for doctorate, GMAT (minimum score of 600), minimum undergraduate GPA of 3.0, 3.5 upper-division or graduate; three letters of recommendation; brief essay; undergraduate degree from accredited institution; personal statement; for other advanced degree, bachelor's degree from accredited institution. Additional exam requirements/recommendations for international students: required—TOEFL (minimum score 550 paper-based; 79 iBT), Michigan English Language Assessment Battery (minimum score 85); recommended—IELTS (minimum score 6.5), TWE (minimum score 5.5). *Application deadline:* For fall admission, 7/1 for domestic students, 5/1 priority date for international students; for winter admission, 11/1 for domestic students, 9/1 priority date for international students; for spring admission, 3/1 for domestic students, 1/1 priority date for international students. Applications are processed on a rolling basis. Application fee: $50. Electronic applications accepted. *Expenses:* Cost per credit, registration fee, student services fee. *Financial support:* In 2019–20, 199 students received support, including 1 fellowship with tuition reimbursement available (averaging $20,000 per year),

7 research assistantships with tuition reimbursements available (averaging $22,129 per year), 2 teaching assistantships with tuition reimbursements available (averaging $19,967 per year); scholarships/grants, health care benefits, and unspecified assistantships also available. Support available to part-time students. Financial award applicants required to submit FAFSA. *Unit head:* Dr. Robert Forsythe, Dean, School of Business Administration, 313-577-4501, E-mail: robert.forsythe@wayne.edu. *Application contact:* Kiantee N. Rupert-Jones, Assistant Dean, 313-577-4511, E-mail: ag2233@wayne.edu. Website: http://ilitchbusiness.wayne.edu/

Weill Cornell Medicine, Weill Cornell Graduate School of Medical Sciences, Program in Healthcare Policy and Research, New York, NY 10065. Offers biostatistics and data science (MS); health informatics (MS); health policy and economics (MS). *Program availability:* Part-time. *Degree requirements:* For master's, thesis. *Entrance requirements:* For master's, GRE, MCAT, or GMAT (recommended), official transcripts, resume, personal statement, 3 letters of reference. Additional exam requirements/recommendations for international students: required—TOEFL. *Expenses:* Contact institution.

Western Governors University, College of Information Technology, Salt Lake City, UT 84107. Offers cybersecurity and information assurance (MS); data analytics (MS); information technology management (MS). *Program availability:* Online learning. *Degree requirements:* For master's, capstone project. Application fee is waived when completed online.

Worcester Polytechnic Institute, Graduate Admissions, Program in Data Science, Worcester, MA 01609-2280. Offers data science (Graduate Certificate). *Program availability:* Part-time, evening/weekend, 100% online, blended/hybrid learning. *Entrance requirements:* For master's and doctorate, GRE or GMAT required for all international applicants, recommended for US students; 3 letters of recommendation; statement of purpose. Additional exam requirements/recommendations for international students: required—TOEFL (minimum score 563 paper-based; 84 iBT), IELTS, GRE or GMAT. Electronic applications accepted.

Yeshiva University, The Katz School, Program in Data Analytics and Visualization, New York, NY 10033-3201. Offers MS. *Program availability:* Part-time, online learning.

Financial Engineering

Baruch College of the City University of New York, Weissman School of Arts and Sciences, Program in Financial Engineering, New York, NY 10010-5585. Offers MS. *Program availability:* Part-time, evening/weekend. *Entrance requirements:* For master's, 3 recommendations. Electronic applications accepted.

Claremont Graduate University, Graduate Programs, Financial Engineering Program, Claremont, CA 91711-6160. Offers MSFE, MS/EMBA, MS/MBA, MS/PhD. *Entrance requirements:* For master's, GRE General Test or GMAT. Additional exam requirements/recommendations for international students: required—TOEFL (minimum score 75 iBT). Electronic applications accepted.

Columbia University, Fu Foundation School of Engineering and Applied Science, Department of Industrial Engineering and Operations Research, New York, NY 10027. Offers financial engineering (MS); industrial engineering (MS); industrial engineering and operations research (PhD); management science and engineering (MS); operations research (MS); MS/MBA. *Program availability:* Part-time, evening/weekend, online learning. *Degree requirements:* For doctorate, thesis/dissertation, oral and written qualifying exams. *Entrance requirements:* For master's and doctorate, GRE General Test. Additional exam requirements/recommendations for international students: required—TOEFL, IELTS, PTE. Electronic applications accepted. *Expenses:* Tuition: Full-time $47,600; part-time $1880 per credit. One-time fee: $105.

HEC Montreal, School of Business Administration, Doctoral Program in Administration, Montréal, QC H3T 2A7, Canada. Offers accounting (PhD); applied economics (PhD); data science (PhD); finance (PhD); financial engineering (PhD); information technology (PhD); international business (PhD); logistics and operations management (PhD); management science (PhD); management, strategy and organizations (PhD); marketing (PhD); organizational behaviour and human resources (PhD). *Accreditation:* AACSB. *Entrance requirements:* For doctorate, TAGE MAGE, GMAT, or GRE, master's degree in administration or related field. Electronic applications accepted.

HEC Montreal, School of Business Administration, Master of Science Programs in Administration, Program in Financial Engineering, Montréal, QC H3T 2A7, Canada. Offers M Sc. *Entrance requirements:* For master's, BBA, undergraduate degree in another field, degree deemed equivalent by program director and minimum GPA of 3.0 on 4.3 scale. Additional exam requirements/recommendations for international students: required—TAGE MAGE (minimum recommended score of 300), GMAT (minimum recommended score of 630), or GRE. Electronic applications accepted.

The International University of Monaco, Graduate Programs, Monte Carlo, Monaco. Offers entrepreneurship (EMBA, MBA); financial engineering (M Sc); hedge fund and private equity (M Sc); international marketing (EMBA, MBA); international wealth management (M Sc); luxury goods and services (EMBA, M Sc, MBA); wealth and asset management (EMBA, MBA). *Program availability:* Part-time. *Degree requirements:* For master's, comprehensive exam (for some programs), applied research project. *Entrance requirements:* Additional exam requirements/recommendations for international students: required—TOEFL (minimum score 550 paper-based), IELTS. Electronic applications accepted.

New York University, Tandon School of Engineering, Department of Finance and Risk Engineering, New York, NY 10012-1019. Offers financial engineering (MS), including capital markets, computational finance, financial technology. *Program availability:* Part-time, evening/weekend. *Degree requirements:* For master's, comprehensive exam (for some programs), thesis (for some programs). *Entrance requirements:* For master's, GMAT, minimum B average in undergraduate course work. Additional exam requirements/recommendations for international students: required—TOEFL (minimum score 550 paper-based; 90 iBT); recommended—IELTS (minimum score 7). Electronic applications accepted. *Expenses:* Contact institution.

North Carolina State University, Graduate School, College of Agriculture and Life Sciences and College of Engineering and College of Sciences, Program in Financial Mathematics, Raleigh, NC 27695. Offers MFM. *Program availability:* Part-time. *Degree requirements:* For master's, thesis optional, project/internship. *Entrance requirements:* For master's, GRE General Test. Additional exam requirements/recommendations for international students: required—TOEFL (minimum score 550 paper-based). Electronic applications accepted.

Princeton University, Graduate School, School of Engineering and Applied Science, Department of Operations Research and Financial Engineering, Princeton, NJ 08544-1019. Offers M Eng, MSE, PhD. Terminal master's awarded for partial completion of doctoral program. *Degree requirements:* For master's, thesis (MSE); for doctorate, thesis/dissertation, general exam. *Entrance requirements:* For master's and doctorate, GRE General Test, official transcript(s), 3 letters of recommendation, personal statement. Additional exam requirements/recommendations for international students: required—TOEFL. Electronic applications accepted.

Rensselaer Polytechnic Institute, Graduate School, Lally School of Management, Program in Quantitative Finance and Risk Analytics, Troy, NY 12180-3590. Offers MS, MS/MBA. *Program availability:* Part-time. *Faculty:* 36 full-time (9 women), 5 part-time/adjunct (0 women). *Students:* 40 full-time (18 women), 43 part-time (19 women); includes 3 minority (2 Asian, non-Hispanic/Latino; 1 Hispanic/Latino), 76 international. Average age 24. 329 applicants, 53% accepted, 24 enrolled. In 2019, 44 master's awarded. *Entrance requirements:* For master's, GMAT or GRE, personal statement. Additional exam requirements/recommendations for international students: required—TOEFL (minimum score 570 paper-based; 88 iBT), IELTS (minimum score 6.5), PTE (minimum score 60). *Application deadline:* For fall admission, 1/1 for domestic and international students. Applications are processed on a rolling basis. Application fee: $75. Electronic applications accepted. *Financial support:* Scholarships/grants available. Financial award application deadline: 1/1. *Unit head:* Dr. Qiang Wu, Graduate Program Director, 518-276-3338, E-mail: wuq2@rpi.edu. *Application contact:* Jarron Decker, Director of Graduate Admissions, 518-276-6216, Fax: 518-276-4072, E-mail: gradadmissions@rpi.edu. Website: https://lallyschool.rpi.edu/graduate-programs/ms-qfra

Stevens Institute of Technology, Graduate School, School of Business, Program in Financial Engineering, Hoboken, NJ 07030. Offers MS, PhD, Certificate. *Program availability:* Part-time, evening/weekend. *Faculty:* 59 full-time (11 women), 30 part-time/adjunct (5 women). *Students:* 167 full-time (41 women), 40 part-time (12 women); includes 19 minority (1 Black or African American, non-Hispanic/Latino; 2 American Indian or Alaska Native, non-Hispanic/Latino; 15 Asian, non-Hispanic/Latino; 1 Two or more races, non-Hispanic/Latino), 159 international. Average age 27. In 2019, 91 master's, 5 doctorates, 4 other advanced degrees awarded. Terminal master's awarded for partial completion of doctoral program. *Degree requirements:* For master's, thesis optional, minimum B average in major field and overall; for doctorate, comprehensive exam (for some programs), thesis/dissertation; for Certificate, minimum B average. *Entrance requirements:* For master's, International applicants must submit TOEFL/IELTS scores and fulfill the English Language Proficiency Requirement. Applicants to full-time programs who do not qualify for a score waiver are required to submit GRE/GMAT scores. Additional exam requirements/recommendations for international students: required—TOEFL (minimum score 74 iBT), IELTS (minimum score 6). *Application deadline:* For fall admission, 4/1 for domestic and international students; for spring admission, 11/1 for domestic and international students; for summer admission, 5/1 for domestic students. Applications are processed on a rolling basis. Application fee: $60. Electronic applications accepted. *Expenses: Tuition:* Full-time $52,134. *Required fees:* $1880. Tuition and fees vary according to course load. *Financial support:* Fellowships, research assistantships, teaching assistantships, career-related internships or fieldwork, Federal Work-Study, scholarships/grants, and unspecified assistantships available. Financial award application deadline: 2/15; financial award applicants required to submit FAFSA. *Unit head:* Dr. Gregory Prastacos, Dean of SB, 201-216-8366, E-mail: gprastac@stevens.edu. *Application contact:* Graduate Admissions, 888-783-8367, Fax: 888-511-1306, E-mail: graduate@stevens.edu. Website: https://www.stevens.edu/school-systems-enterprises/masters-degree-programs/financial-engineering

Temple University, Fox School of Business, Specialized Master's Programs, Philadelphia, PA 19122-6096. Offers accountancy (MS); actuarial science (MS); finance (MS); financial engineering (MS); human resource management (MS); innovation management and entrepreneurship (MS); marketing (MS); statistics (MS). *Accreditation:* AACSB. *Program availability:* Part-time. *Entrance requirements:* For master's, GRE General Test or GMAT, minimum undergraduate GPA of 3.0. Additional exam requirements/recommendations for international students: required—TOEFL (minimum score 600 paper-based; 100 iBT), IELTS (minimum score 7.5).

University of California, Berkeley, Graduate Division, Haas School of Business, Master of Financial Engineering Program, Berkeley, CA 94720. Offers MFE. *Degree requirements:* For master's, comprehensive exam, internship/applied finance project. *Entrance requirements:* For master's, GMAT or GRE (waived if candidate holds PhD), bachelor's degree with minimum GPA of 3.0 or equivalent; two recommendation letters; proficiency in math, statistics, computer science, and economics/finance. Additional exam requirements/recommendations for international students: required—TOEFL (minimum score 570 paper-based, 90 iBT) or IELTS (minimum score 7). Electronic applications accepted. *Expenses:* Contact institution.

University of California, Los Angeles, Graduate Division, UCLA Anderson School of Management, Los Angeles, CA 90095-1481. Offers accounting (PhD); behavioral decision making (PhD); business administration (EMBA, MBA); business administration/computer science (MBA/MSCS); business administration/latin american studies (MBA/MLAS); business administration/law (MBA/JD); business administration/library science (MBA/MLIS); business administration/medicine (MBA/MD); business administration/nursing (MBA/MN); business administration/public health (MBA/MPH); business administration/public policy (MBA/MPP); business administration/urban and regional planning (MBA/MURP); business analytics (MSBA); decisions, operations, and technology management (PhD); finance (PhD); financial engineering (MFE); global economics and management (PhD); management and organizations (PhD); marketing (PhD); strategy and policy (PhD); DDS/MBA; MBA/JD; MBA/MD; MBA/MLAS; MBA/MLIS; MBA/MN; MBA/MPH; MBA/MPP; MBA/MSCS; MBA/MURP. *Accreditation:* AACSB. *Program availability:* Part-time, evening/weekend. *Faculty:* 81 full-time (21 women), 110 part-time/adjunct (21 women). *Students:* 1,033 full-time (377 women), 1,162 part-time (391 women); includes 768 minority (47 Black or African American, non-Hispanic/Latino; 3 American Indian or Alaska Native, non-Hispanic/Latino; 533 Asian, non-Hispanic/Latino; 105 Hispanic/Latino; 2 Native Hawaiian or other Pacific Islander, non-Hispanic/Latino; 78 Two or more races, non-Hispanic/Latino), 575 international. Average age 31. 6,394 applicants, 29% accepted, 932 enrolled. In 2019, 991 master's, 9 doctorates awarded. Terminal master's awarded for partial completion of doctoral program. *Degree requirements:* For master's, comprehensive exam, field consulting project (for MBA, FEMBA, EMBA, UCLA-NUS EMBA, MFE, and MSBA); internship (for MBA only); for doctorate, comprehensive exam, thesis/dissertation, oral and written qualifying exams. *Entrance requirements:* For master's, GMAT or GRE required (for MBA, MFE, MSBA); Executive Assessment (EA) also accepted for EMBA, UCLA-NUS EMBA, and FEMBA (only for candidates with 10+ years of work experience); STEM Master's degree, JD, MD, CPA, or extensive quantitative experience can waive exam requirement for EMBA, 4-year bachelor's degree or equivalent; 2 letters of recommendation; interview (invitation only); 1 essay (for MBA & FEMBA); 2 essays (for EMBA, MFE, MSBA); average 4-8 years of full-time work experience (for FEMBA); minimum 8 years of work experience with at least 5 years at management level (for EMBA & UCLA-NUS EMBA); for doctorate, GMAT or GRE, bachelor's degree from college or university of full-recognized standing with 3.0 minimum GPA, 3 letters of recommendation; statement of purpose. Additional exam requirements/recommendations for international students: required—TOEFL (minimum score 560 paper-based; 87 iBT), IELTS (minimum score 7), TOEFL with minimum iBT score of 100 (for MSBA program). *Application deadline:* For fall admission, 10/2 for domestic and international students; for winter admission, 1/8 for domestic and international students; for spring admission, 4/16 for domestic and international students. Applications are processed on a rolling basis. Application fee: $200. Electronic applications accepted. *Expenses:* $65,114 per year for MBA; $78,470 per year for MFE; $66,710 per year for MSBA; $32,474 per year for PhD; $83,996 per year for EMBA; $62,500 per year for UCLA-NUS EMBA (UC portion only); $42,853 per year for FEMBA. *Financial support:* Fellowships, research assistantships with partial tuition reimbursements, teaching assistantships with partial tuition reimbursements, career-related internships or fieldwork, institutionally sponsored loans, and scholarships/grants available. Support available to part-time students. *Unit head:* Dr. Antonio Bernardo, Dean and John E. Anderson Chair in Management, 310-825-7982, Fax: 310-206-2073, E-mail: a.bernardo@anderson.ucla.edu. *Application contact:* Alex Lawrence, Assistant Dean and Director of MBA Admissions, 310-825-6944, Fax: 310-825-8582, E-mail: mba.admissions@anderson.ucla.edu. Website: http://www.anderson.ucla.edu/

University of Illinois at Urbana-Champaign, Graduate College, College of Engineering, Joint Program in Financial Engineering, Champaign, IL 61820. Offers MS. *Degree requirements:* For master's, thesis or alternative.

Game Design and Development

Academy of Art University, Graduate Programs, School of Game Development, San Francisco, CA 94105-3410. Offers MA, MFA. *Program availability:* Part-time, 100% online. *Faculty:* 10 full-time (0 women), 28 part-time/adjunct (8 women). *Students:* 134 full-time (54 women), 67 part-time (22 women); includes 31 minority (4 Black or African American, non-Hispanic/Latino; 12 Asian, non-Hispanic/Latino; 8 Hispanic/Latino; 7 Two or more races, non-Hispanic/Latino), 100 international. Average age 29. 71 applicants, 100% accepted, 57 enrolled. In 2019, 41 master's awarded. *Degree requirements:* For master's, final review. *Entrance requirements:* For master's, statement of intent; resume; portfolio/reel; official college transcripts. *Application deadline:* Applications are processed on a rolling basis. Application fee: $50. Electronic applications accepted. *Expenses:* Tuition: Full-time $1083; part-time $1083 per credit hour. *Required fees:* $860; $860 per unit. $430 per term. One-time fee: $145. Tuition and fees vary according to program. *Financial support:* Career-related internships or fieldwork, Federal Work-Study, and scholarships/grants available. Financial award application deadline: 8/10; financial award applicants required to submit FAFSA. Website: http://www.academyart.edu/academics/game-development

Concordia University, School of Graduate Studies, Faculty of Engineering and Computer Science, Concordia Institute for Information Systems Engineering (CIISE), Montréal, QC H3G 1M8, Canada. Offers 3D graphics and game development (Certificate); information and systems engineering (PhD); information systems security (M Eng, MA Sc); quality systems engineering (M Eng, MA Sc); service engineering and network management (Certificate).

DePaul University, College of Computing and Digital Media, Chicago, IL 60604. Offers animation (MA, MFA); applied technology (MS); business information technology (MS); computational finance (MS); computer and information sciences (PhD); computer science (MS); creative producing (MFA); cybersecurity (MS); data science (MS); digital communication and media arts (MA); documentary (MFA); e-commerce technology (MS); experience design (MA); film and television (MS); film and television directing (MFA); game design (MFA); game programming (MS); health informatics (MS); human centered design (PhD); human-computer interaction (MS); information systems (MS); network engineering and security (MS); product innovation and computing (MS); screenwriting (MFA); software engineering (MS); JD/MS. *Program availability:* Part-time, evening/weekend, online learning. *Degree requirements:* For master's, thesis (for some programs); for doctorate, comprehensive exam, thesis/dissertation. *Entrance requirements:* For master's, GRE or GMAT (for MS in computational finance only), bachelor's degree, resume (MS in predictive analytics only), IT experience (MS in information technology project management only), portfolio review (all MFA programs and MA in animation); for doctorate, GRE, master's degree in computer science. Additional exam requirements/recommendations for international students: required—TOEFL (minimum score 590 paper-based; 80 iBT), IELTS (minimum score 6.5), PTE (minimum score 53). Electronic applications accepted. *Expenses:* Contact institution.

Full Sail University, Game Design Master of Science Program - Campus, Winter Park, FL 32792-7437. Offers MS.

Iona College, School of Arts and Science, Department of Computer Science, New Rochelle, NY 10801-1890. Offers computer science (MS); cyber security (MS); game development (MS). *Program availability:* Part-time, evening/weekend. *Faculty:* 9 full-time (4 women), 1 (woman) part-time/adjunct. *Students:* 2 full-time (0 women), 10 part-time (2 women); includes 4 minority (2 Black or African American, non-Hispanic/Latino; 1 Asian, non-Hispanic/Latino; 1 Hispanic/Latino), 1 international. Average age 26. 16 applicants, 100% accepted, 6 enrolled. In 2019, 6 master's awarded. *Degree requirements:* For master's, thesis optional. *Entrance requirements:* For master's, minimum GPA of 3.0. Additional exam requirements/recommendations for international students: required—TOEFL (minimum score 550 paper-based; 80 iBT), IELTS (minimum score 6.5). *Application deadline:* For fall admission, 8/1 priority date for domestic students, 5/1 priority date for international students; for spring admission, 1/1 priority date for domestic students, 9/1 priority date for international students. Applications are processed on a rolling basis. Electronic applications accepted. *Financial support:* In 2019–20, 5 students received support, including 2 research assistantships with full and partial tuition reimbursements available (averaging $5,072 per year); scholarships/grants, tuition waivers (partial), and unspecified assistantships also available. Support available to part-time students. Financial award application deadline: 4/15; financial award applicants required to submit FAFSA. *Unit head:* Frances Bailie, PhD, Chair, 914-633-2335, E-mail: fbailie@iona.edu. *Application contact:* Christopher Kash, Assistant Director, Graduate Admissions, 914-633-2403, Fax: 914-633-2277, E-mail: ckash@iona.edu. Website: http://www.iona.edu/Academics/School-of-Arts-Science/Departments/Computer-Science/Graduate-Programs.aspx

Long Island University - Post, College of Arts, Communications and Design, Brookville, NY 11548-1300. Offers art (MA); clinical art therapy (MA); clinical art therapy and counseling (MA); digital game design and development (MA); fine arts and design (MFA); interactive multimedia arts (MA); museum studies (MA); music (MA); theatre (MFA). *Degree requirements:* For master's, variable foreign language requirement, comprehensive exam (for some programs), thesis. *Entrance requirements:* For master's, performance audition or portfolio. Additional exam requirements/recommendations for international students: required—TOEFL (minimum score 550 paper-based; 79 iBT). Electronic applications accepted.

Michigan State University, The Graduate School, College of Communication Arts and Sciences, Department of Media and Information, East Lansing, MI 48824. Offers media and information management (MA); serious game design (MA). *Entrance requirements:* Additional exam requirements/recommendations for international students: required—TOEFL. Electronic applications accepted.

New York University, Tisch School of the Arts, Game Center, Brooklyn, NY 11201. Offers game design (MFA). *Degree requirements:* For master's, thesis. *Entrance requirements:* Additional exam requirements/recommendations for international students: required—TOEFL (minimum score 100 paper-based; 100 iBT), IELTS (minimum score 7.5). Electronic applications accepted.

Rochester Institute of Technology, Graduate Enrollment Services, Golisano College of Computing and Information Sciences, Interactive Games and Media School, MS Program in Game Design and Development, Rochester, NY 14623-5603. Offers MS. *Degree requirements:* For master's, thesis or alternative, capstone experience. *Entrance requirements:* For master's, GRE required for individuals with degrees from international universities., portfolio, minimum GPA of 3.0 (recommended). Additional exam requirements/recommendations for international students: required—TOEFL (minimum score 570 paper-based; 88 iBT), IELTS (minimum score 6.5), PTE (minimum score 61). Electronic applications accepted.

Sacred Heart University, Graduate Programs, College of Arts and Sciences, Department of Computing, Fairfield, CT 06825. Offers computer science (MS); computer science gaming (MS); cybersecurity (MS); information technology (MS). *Program availability:* Part-time, evening/weekend. *Degree requirements:* For master's, thesis or alternative. *Entrance requirements:* For master's, bachelor's degree, minimum GPA of 3.0. Additional exam requirements/recommendations for international students: required—TOEFL (minimum score 570 paper-based, 80 iBT), TWE, or IELTS (6.5). Electronic applications accepted. *Expenses:* Contact institution.

Savannah College of Art and Design, Program in Interactive Design and Game Development, Savannah, GA 31402-3146. Offers MA, MFA. *Program availability:* Part-time, 100% online. *Degree requirements:* For master's, final project (for MA); thesis (for MFA). *Entrance requirements:* For master's, GRE (recommended), portfolio (submitted in digital format), audition or writing submission, resume, statement of purpose, two letters of recommendation. Additional exam requirements/recommendations for international students: recommended—TOEFL (minimum score 550 paper-based; 85 iBT), IELTS (minimum score 6.5). Electronic applications accepted.

University of Advancing Technology, Master of Science Program in Technology, Tempe, AZ 85283-1042. Offers advancing computer science (MS); emerging technologies (MS); game production and management (MS); information assurance (MS); technology leadership (MS). *Degree requirements:* For master's, project or thesis. *Entrance requirements:* Additional exam requirements/recommendations for international students: required—TOEFL (minimum score 550 paper-based). Electronic applications accepted.

University of California, Santa Cruz, Jack Baskin School of Engineering, Department of Computational Media, Santa Cruz, CA 95064. Offers computational media (MS, PhD);

games and playable media (MS). *Faculty:* 14 full-time (4 women), 5 part-time/adjunct (1 woman). *Students:* 108 full-time (35 women); includes 24 minority (2 Black or African American, non-Hispanic/Latino; 17 Asian, non-Hispanic/Latino; 4 Hispanic/Latino; 1 Native Hawaiian or other Pacific Islander, non-Hispanic/Latino, 57 international. 180 applicants, 67% accepted, 56 enrolled. In 2019, 8 master's, 1 doctorate awarded. Terminal master's awarded for partial completion of doctoral program. *Degree requirements:* For master's, thesis, Capstone project or research project with written report; for doctorate, thesis/dissertation. *Entrance requirements:* Additional exam requirements/recommendations for international students: required—TOEFL (minimum score 570 paper-based; 89 iBT), IELTS (minimum score 8), Non-native speakers must submit either TOEFL or IELTS scores. *Application deadline:* For fall admission, 1/10 for domestic and international students. Application fee: $120 ($140 for international students). Electronic applications accepted. *Financial support:* In 2019–20, 64 students received support, including 23 fellowships (averaging $12,023 per year), 15 research assistantships (averaging $8,092 per year), 47 teaching assistantships (averaging $21,909 per year); institutionally sponsored loans also available. Financial award application deadline: 1/10; financial award applicants required to submit FAFSA. *Unit head:* Dr. Sri Kurniawan, Professor and Department Chair, E-mail: skurnia@ucsc.edu. *Application contact:* Emily Jackson, Graduate Advisor, 831-459-3531, E-mail: bsoe-ga@rt.ucsc.edu.
Website: https://grad.soe.ucsc.edu/computational-media

The University of North Carolina at Charlotte, College of Computing and Informatics, Department of Software and Information Systems, Charlotte, NC 28223-0001. Offers advanced databases and knowledge discovery (Graduate Certificate); game design and development (Graduate Certificate); information security and privacy (Graduate Certificate); information technology (MS); management of information technology (Graduate Certificate); network security (Graduate Certificate); secure software development (Graduate Certificate). *Program availability:* Part-time, evening/weekend. *Faculty:* 21 full-time (8 women), 5 part-time/adjunct (0 women). *Students:* 138 full-time (64 women), 98 part-time (38 women); includes 47 minority (25 Black or African American, non-Hispanic/Latino; 9 Asian, non-Hispanic/Latino; 10 Hispanic/Latino; 1 Native Hawaiian or other Pacific Islander, non-Hispanic/Latino; 2 Two or more races, non-Hispanic/Latino), 136 international. Average age 28. 298 applicants, 75% accepted, 78 enrolled. In 2019, 107 master's, 20 other advanced degrees awarded. *Degree requirements:* For master's, thesis optional, internship project or project report. *Entrance requirements:* For master's, GRE or GMAT, undergraduate or equivalent course work in data structures, object-oriented programming in C++, C#, or Java with minimum GPA of 3.0, undergraduate GPA of at least 3.0 and a junior/senior GPA of at least 3.0, statement of purpose, 3 letters of recommendation from academic and/or professional references; for Graduate Certificate, bachelor's degree from accredited institution in computing, mathematical, engineering or business discipline with minimum overall GPA of 2.8, junior/senior 3.0; substantial knowledge of data structures and object-oriented programming in C++, C# or Java. Additional exam requirements/recommendations for international students: required—TOEFL (minimum score 557 paper-based; 83 iBT), IELTS (minimum score 6.5), TOEFL (minimum score 557 paper-based, 83 iBT) or IELTS (6.5). *Application deadline:* Applications are processed on a rolling basis. Application fee: $75. Electronic applications accepted. *Expenses:* Contact institution. *Financial support:* In 2019–20, 65 students received support, including 2 fellowships (averaging $51,459 per year), 21 research assistantships (averaging $14,084 per year), 42 teaching assistantships (averaging $7,186 per year); career-related internships or fieldwork, institutionally sponsored loans, scholarships/grants, and unspecified assistantships also available. Support available to part-time students. Financial award application deadline: 3/1; financial award applicants required to submit FAFSA. *Unit head:* Dr. Mary Lou Maher, Chair, 704-687-1940, E-mail: m.maher@uncc.edu. *Application contact:* Kathy B. Giddings, Director of Graduate Admissions, 704-687-5503, Fax: 704-687-1668, E-mail: gradadm@uncc.edu.
Website: http://sis.uncc.edu/

University of Pennsylvania, School of Engineering and Applied Science, Department of Computer and Information Science, Philadelphia, PA 19104. Offers computer and information science (MSE, PhD); computer and information technology (MCIT); computer graphics and game technology (MSE). *Program availability:* Part-time. *Faculty:* 61 full-time (9 women), 9 part-time/adjunct (0 women). *Students:* 250 full-time (63 women), 23 part-time (2 women); includes 36 minority (6 Black or African American, non-Hispanic/Latino; 27 Asian, non-Hispanic/Latino; 2 Hispanic/Latino; 1 Two or more races, non-Hispanic/Latino), 173 international. Average age 26. 2,124 applicants, 12% accepted, 103 enrolled. In 2019, 87 master's, 18 doctorates awarded. Terminal master's awarded for partial completion of doctoral program. *Degree requirements:* For master's, comprehensive exam, thesis optional; for doctorate, comprehensive exam, thesis/dissertation. *Entrance requirements:* For master's and doctorate, GRE, bachelor's degree, letters of recommendation, resume, personal statement. Additional exam requirements/recommendations for international students: required—TOEFL (minimum score 100 iBT), IELTS (minimum score 7). *Application deadline:* For fall admission, 12/15 priority date for domestic and international students. Application fee: $80. Electronic applications accepted. *Expenses:* Contact institution. *Application contact:* Associate Director of Graduate Admissions, 215-898-4542, Fax: 215-573-5577, E-mail: admissions2@upenn.edu.
Website: http://www.cis.upenn.edu/prospective-students/graduate/

University of Southern California, Graduate School, School of Cinematic Arts, Interactive Media and Games Division, Los Angeles, CA 90089. Offers interactive media (MFA). *Degree requirements:* For master's, thesis, thesis project. *Entrance requirements:* Additional exam requirements/recommendations for international students: required—TOEFL (minimum score 600 paper-based; 100 iBT). Electronic applications accepted. *Expenses:* Contact institution.

University of Southern California, Graduate School, Viterbi School of Engineering, Department of Computer Science, Los Angeles, CA 90089. Offers computer networks (MS); computer science (MS, PhD); computer security (MS); game development (MS); high performance computing and simulations (MS); human language technology (MS); intelligent robotics (MS); multimedia and creative technologies (MS); software engineering (MS). *Program availability:* Part-time, evening/weekend, online learning. *Entrance requirements:* For master's and doctorate, GRE General Test. Additional exam requirements/recommendations for international students: required—TOEFL. Electronic applications accepted.

University of Utah, Graduate School, College of Engineering, Department of Entertainment Arts and Engineering, Salt Lake City, UT 84112. Offers game art (MEAE); game engineering (MEAE); game production (MEAE); technical art (MEAE). *Faculty:* 11 full-time (2 women), 23 part-time/adjunct (3 women). *Students:* 129 full-time (34 women); includes 71 minority (1 Black or African American, non-Hispanic/Latino; 63 Asian, non-Hispanic/Latino; 7 Hispanic/Latino), 57 international. Average age 25. 221 applicants, 49% accepted, 75 enrolled. In 2019, 58 master's awarded. *Degree requirements:* For master's, Thesis Game Project. *Entrance requirements:* For master's, n/a, Portfolio submission, Code Sample Submission, Letters of Recommendation. Additional exam requirements/recommendations for international students: required—TOEFL (minimum score 100 iBT), IELTS (minimum score 7), GRE. *Application deadline:* For fall admission, 2/28 for domestic and international students. Application fee: $55. Electronic applications accepted. Application fee is waived when completed online. *Expenses:* Https://fbs.admin.utah.edu/download/income/Graduate/EAEngRes.pdf. *Financial support:* In 2019–20, 83 students received support, including 26 research assistantships with partial tuition reimbursements available (averaging $15,900 per year), 53 teaching assistantships with partial tuition reimbursements available (averaging $15,900 per year); scholarships/grants, health care benefits, and unspecified assistantships also available. Financial award application deadline: 2/28; financial award applicants required to submit FAFSA. *Unit head:* Hallie Huber, Academic Program Manager, 801-581-5460, E-mail: hallie.huber@utah.edu. *Application contact:* CJ Lederman, Graduate Student Advisor, 801-587-1299, E-mail: cj@eae.utah.edu.
Website: http://eae.utah.edu/

Virginia International University, School of Computer Information Systems, Fairfax, VA 22030. Offers business intelligence (Graduate Certificate); business intelligence and data analytics (MIS); computer science (MS), including computer animation and gaming, cybersecurity, data management networking, intelligent systems, software applications development, software engineering; cybersecurity (MIS); data management (MIS); enterprise project management (MIS); health informatics (MIS); information assurance (MIS); information systems (Graduate Certificate); information systems management (MS, Graduate Certificate); information technology (MS); information technology audit and compliance (Graduate Certificate); knowledge management (MIS); software engineering (MS). *Program availability:* Part-time, online learning. *Entrance requirements:* For master's, bachelor's degree. Additional exam requirements/recommendations for international students: required—TOEFL (minimum score 550 paper-based; 80 iBT), IELTS. Electronic applications accepted.

Worcester Polytechnic Institute, Graduate Admissions, Program in Interactive Media and Game Development, Worcester, MA 01609-2280. Offers interactive media & game development (MS). *Program availability:* Part-time, evening/weekend. *Entrance requirements:* For master's, GRE (recommended), 3 letters of recommendation, statement of purpose, portfolio (recommended). Additional exam requirements/recommendations for international students: required—TOEFL (minimum score 563 paper-based; 84 iBT), IELTS (minimum score 7). Electronic applications accepted.

Health Informatics

Adelphi University, College of Nursing and Public Health, Program in Health Information Technology, Garden City, NY 11530-0701. Offers MS, Advanced Certificate. *Entrance requirements:* Additional exam requirements/recommendations for international students: required—TOEFL (minimum score 550 paper-based; 80 iBT), IELTS (minimum score 6.5). *Expenses:* Contact institution.

American Public University System, AMU/APU Graduate Programs, Charles Town, WV 25414. Offers accounting (MS); applied business analytics (MS); business administration (MBA); criminal justice (MA); cybersecurity studies (MS); educational leadership (M Ed); environmental policy and management (MS); global security (DGS); health information management (MS); history (MA), including American military history, American Revolution, civil war, war since 1945, World War II; information technology (MS); international relations and conflict resolution (MA), including American politics and government, comparative government and development, general, international relations, public policy; national security studies (MA); nursing (MSN); political science (MA); public policy (MPP); reverse logistics management (MA), including comparative and security issues, conflict resolution, international and transnational security issues, peacekeeping; space studies (MS); sports management (MS); strategic intelligence (DSI); teaching (M Ed), including secondary social studies; transportation and logistics management (MA). *Program availability:* Part-time, evening/weekend, online only, 100% online. *Students:* 461 full-time (193 women), 7,322 part-time (3,127 women); includes 3,089 minority (1,404 Black or African American, non-Hispanic/Latino; 30 American Indian or Alaska Native, non-Hispanic/Latino; 210 Asian, non-Hispanic/Latino; 753 Hispanic/Latino; 445 Native Hawaiian or other Pacific Islander, non-Hispanic/Latino; 247 Two or more races, non-Hispanic/Latino), 117 international. Average age 37. In 2019, 2,681 master's awarded. *Degree requirements:* For master's, comprehensive exam or practicum; for doctorate, practicum. *Entrance requirements:* For master's, official transcript showing earned bachelor's degree from institution accredited by recognized accrediting body. Additional exam requirements/recommendations for international students: required—TOEFL (minimum score 550 paper-based), IELTS (minimum score 6.5). *Application deadline:* Applications are processed on a rolling basis. Application fee: $0. Electronic applications accepted. *Financial support:* Scholarships/grants available. Financial award applicants required to submit FAFSA. *Unit head:* Dr. Wallace Boston, President, 877-468-6268, Fax: 304-728-2348, E-mail: president@apus.edu. *Application contact:* Yoci Deal, Associate Vice President, Graduate and International Admissions, 877-468-6268, Fax: 304-724-3764, E-mail: info@apus.edu.
Website: http://www.apus.edu

American Sentinel University, Graduate Programs, Aurora, CO 80014. Offers business administration (MBA); business intelligence (MS); computer science (MSCS); health information management (MS); healthcare (MBA); information systems (MSIS); nursing (MSN). *Program availability:* Part-time, evening/weekend, online learning. *Entrance requirements:* Additional exam requirements/recommendations for international students: required—TOEFL (minimum score 600 paper-based). Electronic applications accepted.

Arkansas Tech University, College of Natural and Health Sciences, Russellville, AR 72801. Offers fisheries and wildlife biology (MS); health informatics (MS); nursing (MSN). *Program availability:* Part-time, evening/weekend, 100% online, blended/hybrid learning. *Students:* 6 full-time (2 women), 53 part-time (37 women); includes 7 minority (5 Black or African American, non-Hispanic/Latino; 1 Asian, non-Hispanic/Latino; 1 Hispanic/Latino). Average age 35. In 2019, 15 master's awarded. *Degree requirements:* For master's, thesis (for some programs), project. *Entrance requirements:* Additional exam requirements/recommendations for international students: required—TOEFL (minimum score 550 paper-based; 79 iBT), IELTS (minimum score 6.5), PTE (minimum score 58). *Application deadline:* For fall admission, 3/1 priority date for domestic students, 5/1 priority date for international students; for spring admission, 10/1 priority date for domestic and international students. Applications are processed on a rolling

basis. Application fee: $40 ($90 for international students). Electronic applications accepted. *Expenses: Tuition, area resident:* Full-time $7008; part-time $292 per credit hour. Tuition, state resident: full-time $7008; part-time $292 per credit hour. Tuition, nonresident: full-time $14,016; part-time $584 per credit hour. *International tuition:* $14,016 full-time. *Required fees:* $343 per term. *Financial support:* In 2019–20, research assistantships with full and partial tuition reimbursements (averaging $4,800 per year), teaching assistantships with full and partial tuition reimbursements (averaging $4,800 per year) were awarded; career-related internships or fieldwork, Federal Work-Study, scholarships/grants, health care benefits, and unspecified assistantships also available. Support available to part-time students. Financial award application deadline: 4/15; financial award applicants required to submit FAFSA. *Unit head:* Dr. Jeff Robertson, Dean, 479-968-0498, E-mail: jrobertson@atu.edu. *Application contact:* Dr. Richard Schoephoerster, Dean of Graduate College and Research, 479-968-0398, Fax: 479-964-0542, E-mail: gradcollege@atu.edu.
Website: http://www.atu.edu/nhs/

Augusta University, College of Allied Health Sciences, Program in Public Health, Augusta, GA 30912. Offers environmental health (MPH); health informatics (MPH); health management (MPH); social and behavioral sciences (MPH). *Accreditation:* CEPH. *Program availability:* Part-time. *Degree requirements:* For master's, thesis (for some programs). *Entrance requirements:* For master's, GRE General Test, three letters of recommendation. Additional exam requirements/recommendations for international students: required—TOEFL. Electronic applications accepted.

Barry University, College of Health Sciences, Graduate Certificate Programs, Miami Shores, FL 33161-6695. Offers health care leadership (Certificate); health care planning and informatics (Certificate); histotechnology (Certificate); long term care management (Certificate); medical group practice management (Certificate); quality improvement and outcomes management (Certificate).

Bay Path University, Program in Healthcare Management, Longmeadow, MA 01106-2292. Offers health informatics (MS); organizational excellence (MS). *Program availability:* Part-time, online only, 100% online. *Entrance requirements:* For master's, completed application; official undergraduate and graduate transcripts (a GPA of 3.0 or higher is preferred); original essay of at least 250 words on the topic: "Why the MS in Healthcare Management is important to my personal and professional goals"; current resume; 2 recommendations. Electronic applications accepted. Application fee is waived when completed online.

Belmont University, College of Pharmacy, Nashville, TN 37212. Offers advanced pharmacotherapy (Pharm D); health care informatics (Pharm D); management (Pharm D); missions/public health (Pharm D); Pharm D/MBA. *Accreditation:* ACPE. *Faculty:* 29 full-time (16 women), 4 part-time/adjunct (2 women). *Students:* 354 full-time (242 women); includes 120 minority (50 Black or African American, non-Hispanic/Latino; 1 American Indian or Alaska Native, non-Hispanic/Latino; 41 Asian, non-Hispanic/Latino; 18 Hispanic/Latino; 10 Two or more races, non-Hispanic/Latino), 3 international. Average age 25. In 2019, 67 doctorates awarded. *Degree requirements:* For doctorate, comprehensive exam. *Entrance requirements:* For doctorate, PCAT. Additional exam requirements/recommendations for international students: required—TOEFL. *Application deadline:* For fall admission, 8/31 priority date for domestic students; for spring admission, 3/1 for domestic students. Applications are processed on a rolling basis. Application fee: $50. Electronic applications accepted. *Expenses:* Contact institution. *Financial support:* In 2019–20, 112 students received support. Career-related internships or fieldwork and scholarships/grants available. Financial award application deadline: 12/1; financial award applicants required to submit FAFSA. *Unit head:* Dr. David Gregory, Dean, 615-460-6746, Fax: 615-460-6741, E-mail: david.gregory@belmont.edu. *Application contact:* Dr. David Gregory, Dean, 615-460-6746, Fax: 615-460-6741, E-mail: david.gregory@belmont.edu.
Website: http://www.belmont.edu/pharmacy/index.html

Benedictine University, Graduate Programs, Program in Public Health, Lisle, IL 60532. Offers administration of health care institutions (MPH); dietetics (MPH); disaster management (MPH); health education (MPH); health information systems (MPH); management information systems (MPH/MS); MBA/MPH; MPH/MS. *Accreditation:* CEPH. *Program availability:* Part-time, evening/weekend, 100% online. *Entrance requirements:* For master's, GRE, MAT, GMAT, LSAT, DAT or other graduate professional exams, official transcript; 2 letters of recommendation from individuals familiar with the applicant's professional or academic work, excluding family or personal friends; essay describing the candidate's career path. Additional exam requirements/recommendations for international students: required—TOEFL (minimum score 600 paper-based; 79 iBT), IELTS (minimum score 6.5). Electronic applications accepted.

Boston University, Metropolitan College, Department of Computer Science, Boston, MA 02215. Offers computer information systems (MS), including computer networks, data analytics, database management and business intelligence, health informatics, IT project management, security, Web application development; computer networks (Certificate); computer science (MS); data analytics (Certificate); digital forensics (Certificate); health informatics (Certificate); information technology project management (Certificate); software development (MS); software engineering in health care systems (Certificate); telecommunications (MS), including security. *Program availability:* Part-time, evening/weekend, online learning. *Faculty:* 16 full-time (3 women), 52 part-time/adjunct (5 women). *Students:* 253 full-time (80 women), 856 part-time (243 women); includes 246 minority (53 Black or African American, non-Hispanic/Latino; 1 American Indian or Alaska Native, non-Hispanic/Latino; 129 Asian, non-Hispanic/Latino; 48 Hispanic/Latino; 15 Two or more races, non-Hispanic/Latino), 418 international. Average age 30. 1,079 applicants, 72% accepted, 297 enrolled. In 2019, 513 master's awarded. *Entrance requirements:* For master's and Certificate, official transcripts from regionally-accredited bachelor's degree program, 3 letters of recommendation, professional resume, personal statement. Additional exam requirements/recommendations for international students: required—TOEFL (minimum score 84 iBT), IELTS. *Application deadline:* For fall admission, 8/1 priority date for domestic students, 6/1 priority date for international students; for spring admission, 12/1 priority date for domestic students, 11/15 priority date for international students; for summer admission, 4/1 priority date for domestic students, 3/1 priority date for international students. Applications are processed on a rolling basis. Application fee: $85. Electronic applications accepted. *Expenses:* Contact institution. *Financial support:* In 2019–20, 11 research assistantships (averaging $8,400 per year), 23 teaching assistantships (averaging $3,400 per year) were awarded; unspecified assistantships also available. Support available to part-time students. Financial award applicants required to submit FAFSA. *Unit head:* Dr. Anatoly Temkin, Chair, 617-353-2566, Fax: 617-353-2367, E-mail: csinfo@bu.edu. *Application contact:* Enrollment Services, 617-353-6004, E-mail: met@bu.edu.
Website: http://www.bu.edu/csmet/

Brandeis University, Rabb School of Continuing Studies, Division of Graduate Professional Studies, Master of Science in Health and Medical Informatics Program, Waltham, MA 02454-9110. Offers MS. *Program availability:* Part-time-only. *Entrance requirements:* For master's, four-year bachelor's degree from regionally-accredited U.S. institution or equivalent; official transcript(s) from every college or university attended; resume or curriculum vitae; statement of goals; letter of recommendation. Additional exam requirements/recommendations for international students: required—TWE (minimum score 4.5), TOEFL (minimum scores: 600 paper-based, 100 iBT), IELTS (7), or PTE (68). Electronic applications accepted. *Expenses:* Contact institution.

Brooklyn College of the City University of New York, School of Natural and Behavioral Sciences, Department of Computer and Information Science, Brooklyn, NY 11210-2889. Offers computer science (MA); health informatics (MS); information systems (MS); parallel and distributed computing (Advanced Certificate). *Program availability:* Part-time, evening/weekend. *Degree requirements:* For master's, comprehensive exam, thesis or alternative. *Entrance requirements:* For master's, previous course work in computer science, 2 letters of recommendation. Additional exam requirements/recommendations for international students: required—TOEFL (minimum score 525 paper-based; 70 iBT). Electronic applications accepted.

Canisius College, Graduate Division, School of Education and Human Services, Office of Professional Studies, Buffalo, NY 14208-1098. Offers applied nutrition (MS, Certificate); community and school health (MS); health and human performance (MS); health information technology (MS); respiratory care (MS). *Program availability:* Part-time, evening/weekend, 100% online, blended/hybrid learning. *Faculty:* 1 full-time (0 women), 20 part-time/adjunct (11 women). *Students:* 12 full-time (8 women), 28 part-time (17 women); includes 9 minority (3 Black or African American, non-Hispanic/Latino; 1 Asian, non-Hispanic/Latino; 3 Hispanic/Latino; 2 Two or more races, non-Hispanic/Latino). Average age 33. 24 applicants, 88% accepted, 11 enrolled. In 2019, 27 master's awarded. *Degree requirements:* For master's, thesis (for some programs), Programs require Thesis/Project or Internship. *Entrance requirements:* For master's, GRE recommended, bachelor's degree transcript, two letters of recommendation, current licensure (for applied nutrition), minimum GPA of 2.7, current resume. Additional exam requirements/recommendations for international students: required—TOEFL (550+ PBT or 79+ IBT), IELTS (6.5+), or CAEL (70+). *Application deadline:* Applications are processed on a rolling basis. Application fee: $0. Electronic applications accepted. *Expenses: Tuition:* Part-time $900 per credit. *Required fees:* $25 per credit hour. $65 per term. Part-time tuition and fees vary according to course load and program. *Financial support:* Career-related internships or fieldwork, Federal Work-Study, scholarships/grants, tuition waivers (partial), and unspecified assistantships available. Support available to part-time students. Financial award application deadline: 4/30; financial award applicants required to submit FAFSA. *Unit head:* Dennis W. Koch, Director, Office of Professional Studies, 716-888-8292, E-mail: koch5@canisius.edu. *Application contact:* Dennis W. Koch, Director, Office of Professional Studies, 716-888-8292, E-mail: koch5@canisius.edu.
Website: http://www.canisius.edu/graduate/

Capella University, School of Public Service Leadership, Master's Programs in Nursing, Minneapolis, MN 55402. Offers diabetes nursing (MSN); general nursing (MSN); gerontology nursing (MSN); health information management (MS); nurse educator (MSN); nursing leadership and administration (MSN). *Accreditation:* AACN.

Chatham University, Program in Healthcare Informatics, Pittsburgh, PA 15232-2826. Offers MHI. *Program availability:* Online learning. *Entrance requirements:* Additional exam requirements/recommendations for international students: required—TOEFL (minimum score 600 paper-based; 100 iBT), IELTS, TWE. Application fee is waived when completed online. *Expenses: Tuition:* Part-time $1017 per credit. *Required fees:* $30 per credit. Tuition and fees vary according to program.

Claremont Graduate University, Graduate Programs, Center for Information Systems and Technology, Claremont, CA 91711-6160. Offers cybersecurity and networking (MS); data science and analytics (MS); electronic commerce (PhD); geographic information systems (MS); health informatics (MS); information systems (Certificate); IT strategy and innovation (MS); knowledge management (PhD); systems development (PhD); telecommunications and networking (PhD); MBA/MS. *Program availability:* Part-time. *Degree requirements:* For doctorate, comprehensive exam, thesis/dissertation, portfolio. *Entrance requirements:* For master's and doctorate, GMAT, GRE General Test. Additional exam requirements/recommendations for international students: required—TOEFL (minimum score 75 iBT). Electronic applications accepted.

Clarkson University, Program in Data Analytics, Potsdam, NY 13699. Offers MS. *Program availability:* Part-time, evening/weekend, 100% online. *Students:* 25 full-time (4 women), 17 part-time (9 women); includes 6 minority (4 Asian, non-Hispanic/Latino; 1 Hispanic/Latino; 1 Two or more races, non-Hispanic/Latino), 15 international. 83 applicants, 77% accepted, 15 enrolled. In 2019, 12 master's awarded. *Entrance requirements:* For master's, GMAT or GRE. Additional exam requirements/recommendations for international students: required—TOEFL (minimum score 550 paper-based, 80 iBT) or IELTS (6.5). *Application deadline:* Applications are processed on a rolling basis. Application fee: $50. Electronic applications accepted. *Expenses:* Contact institution. *Financial support:* Scholarships/grants and unspecified assistantships available. *Unit head:* Boris Jukic, Professor of Operations & Information Systems / Director of Business Analytics, 315-268-3884, E-mail: bjukic@clarkson.edu. *Application contact:* Daniel Capogna, Director of Graduate Admissions, 518-631-9910, E-mail: graduate@clarkson.edu.
Website: https://www.clarkson.edu/academics/graduate

The College of St. Scholastica, Graduate Studies, Department of Health Information Management, Duluth, MN 55811-4199. Offers MA, Certificate. *Program availability:* Part-time. *Degree requirements:* For master's, thesis. *Entrance requirements:* Additional exam requirements/recommendations for international students: required—TOEFL (minimum score 550 paper-based; 79 iBT). Electronic applications accepted. *Expenses:* Contact institution.

Colorado Mesa University, Department of Health Sciences, Grand Junction, CO 81501-3122. Offers advanced nursing practice (MSN); family nurse practitioner (DNP); health information technology systems (Graduate Certificate); nursing education (MSN). *Accreditation:* AACN. *Program availability:* Part-time, evening/weekend, 100% online, blended/hybrid learning. *Degree requirements:* For master's and doctorate, capstone. *Entrance requirements:* For master's and doctorate, minimum GPA of 3.0 in BSN program. Additional exam requirements/recommendations for international students: required—TOEFL (minimum score 550 paper-based). Electronic applications accepted.

Dakota State University, College of Business and Information Systems, Madison, SD 57042. Offers analytics (MSA); business analytics (Graduate Certificate); general management (MBA); health informatics and information management (MSHI); information systems (MSIS, D Sc IS); information technology (Graduate Certificate). *Accreditation:* ACBSP. *Program availability:* Part-time, evening/weekend, 100% online, blended/hybrid learning. *Faculty:* 23 full-time (8 women), 1 (woman) part-time/adjunct. *Students:* 35 full-time (8 women), 177 part-time (51 women); includes 58 minority (23 Black or African American, non-Hispanic/Latino; 6 American Indian or Alaska Native, non-Hispanic/Latino; 18 Asian, non-Hispanic/Latino; 10 Hispanic/Latino; 1 Two or more races, non-Hispanic/Latino), 45 international. Average age 38. 230 applicants, 34% accepted, 70 enrolled. In 2019, 49 master's, 2 doctorates, 13 other advanced degrees awarded. *Degree requirements:* For master's, comprehensive exam, thesis optional, Examination, integrative project; for doctorate, comprehensive exam, thesis/dissertation, portfolio. *Entrance requirements:* For master's, GRE General Test, Demonstration of information systems skills, minimum GPA of 2.7; for doctorate, GRE General Test,

Demonstration of information systems skills; for Graduate Certificate, GMAT. Additional exam requirements/recommendations for international students: required—PTE (minimum score 53), TOEFL (minimum score 550 paper-based, 79 iBT, or IELTS 6.5). *Application deadline:* For fall admission, 6/15 for domestic students, 4/15 for international students; for spring admission, 11/15 for domestic students, 9/15 priority date for international students; for summer admission, 4/15 for domestic and international students. Applications are processed on a rolling basis. Application fee: $35. *Expenses: Tuition, area resident:* Full-time $7919. Tuition, state resident: full-time $7919. Tuition, nonresident: full-time $14,784. *International tuition:* $14,784 full-time. *Required fees:* $961. *Financial support:* Fellowships, career-related internships or fieldwork, Federal Work-Study, scholarships/grants, unspecified assistantships, and Administrative Assistantships available. Support available to part-time students. Financial award applicants required to submit FAFSA. *Unit head:* Dr. Dorine Bennett, Dean of College of Business and Information Systems, 605-256-5176, E-mail: dorine.bennett@dsu.edu. *Application contact:* Erin Blankespoor, Senior Secretary, Office of Graduate Studies, 605-256-5799, E-mail: erin.blankespoor@dsu.edu. Website: http://dsu.edu/academics/colleges/college-of-business-and-information-systems

Dartmouth College, Guarini School of Graduate and Advanced Studies, Institute for Quantitative Biomedical Sciences, Hanover, NH 03755. Offers epidemiology (MS); health data science (MS); quantitative biomedical sciences (PhD). *Entrance requirements:* For doctorate, GRE (minimum scores: 1200 old scoring, 308 new scoring verbal and quantitative; analytical writing 4.5; verbal 500 old scoring, 153 new scoring). Electronic applications accepted.

DePaul University, College of Computing and Digital Media, Chicago, IL 60604. Offers animation (MA, MFA); applied technology (MS); business information technology (MS); computational finance (MS); computer and information sciences (PhD); computer science (MS); creative producing (MFA); cybersecurity (MS); data science (MS); digital communication and media arts (MA); documentary (MFA); e-commerce technology (MS); experience design (MA); film and television (MS); film and television directing (MFA); game design (MFA); game programming (MS); health informatics (MS); human centered design (PhD); human-computer interaction (MS); information systems (MS); network engineering and security (MS); product innovation and computing (MS); screenwriting (MFA); software engineering (MS); JD/MS. *Program availability:* Part-time, evening/weekend, online learning. *Degree requirements:* For master's, thesis (for some programs); for doctorate, comprehensive exam, thesis/dissertation. *Entrance requirements:* For master's, GRE or GMAT (for MS in computational finance only), bachelor's degree, resume (MS in predictive analytics only), IT experience (MS in information technology project management only), portfolio review (all MFA programs and MA in animation); for doctorate, GRE, master's degree in computer science. Additional exam requirements/recommendations for international students: required—TOEFL (minimum score 590 paper-based; 80 iBT), IELTS (minimum score 6.5), PTE (minimum score 53). Electronic applications accepted. *Expenses:* Contact institution.

DeSales University, Division of Science and Mathematics, Center Valley, PA 18034-9568. Offers cyber security (Postbaccalaureate Certificate); data analytics (Postbaccalaureate Certificate); information systems (MS), including cyber security, digital forensics, healthcare information management, project management. *Program availability:* Part-time, evening/weekend, 100% online, blended/hybrid learning. *Faculty:* 2 full-time (both women), 5 part-time/adjunct (1 woman). *Students:* 2 full-time (0 women), 17 part-time (4 women); includes 3 minority (2 Asian, non-Hispanic/Latino; 1 Two or more races, non-Hispanic/Latino). Average age 36. 15 applicants, 60% accepted, 9 enrolled. In 2019, 6 master's awarded. *Entrance requirements:* For master's, GRE or GMAT, bachelor's degree in computer-related discipline from accredited college or university, minimum undergraduate GPA of 3.0, personal statement, three letters of recommendation. Additional exam requirements/recommendations for international students: required—TOEFL. *Application deadline:* Applications are processed on a rolling basis. Application fee: $50. Electronic applications accepted. *Expenses:* Contact institution. *Financial support:* Applicants required to submit FAFSA. *Unit head:* Dr. Ronald Nordone, Dean of Graduate Studies, 610-282-1100 Ext. 1289, E-mail: Ronald.Nordone@desale.edu. *Application contact:* Julia Ferraro, Director of Graduate Admissions, 610-282-1100 Ext. 1768, E-mail: gradadmissions@desales.edu. Website: http://www.desales.edu/home/academics/graduate-studies/programs-of-study/msis----master-of-science-in-information-systems

Duke University, School of Medicine, Program in Clinical Informatics, Durham, NC 27710. Offers MS. *Program availability:* Part-time, evening/weekend. *Entrance requirements:* For master's, essay, two letters of recommendation (one addressing work or educational experience and conveying ability to work at the level of a master's program and one addressing interpersonal skills, values, or character); interview with the program director. Additional exam requirements/recommendations for international students: required—TOEFL, GRE. Electronic applications accepted.

East Carolina University, Graduate School, College of Allied Health Sciences, Department of Health Services and Information Management, Greenville, NC 27858-4353. Offers health care administration (Certificate); health care management (Certificate); health informatics (Certificate); health informatics and information management (MS); health information management (Certificate). *Program availability:* Part-time, evening/weekend, online learning. *Degree requirements:* For master's, comprehensive exam, thesis optional. *Entrance requirements:* For master's, GRE General Test or GMAT. Additional exam requirements/recommendations for international students: recommended—TOEFL, IELTS. *Application deadline:* For fall admission, 5/1 priority date for domestic students; for spring admission, 10/15 priority date for domestic students. Applications are processed on a rolling basis. Electronic applications accepted. *Expenses: Tuition, area resident:* Full-time $4749; part-time $185 per credit hour. Tuition, state resident: full-time $4749; part-time $185 per credit hour. Tuition, nonresident: full-time $17,898; part-time $864 per credit hour. *International tuition:* $17,898 full-time. *Required fees:* $2787. *Unit head:* Dr. Leigh W Cellucci, Chair. *Application contact:* Graduate School Admissions, 252-328-6012, Fax: 252-328-6071, E-mail: gradschool@ecu.edu. Website: http://www.ecu.edu/cs-dhs/hsim/index.cfm

Emory University, Rollins School of Public Health, Department of Biostatistics and Bioinformatics, Atlanta, GA 30322-1100. Offers bioinformatics (PhD); biostatistics (MPH, MSPH); public health informatics (MSPH). *Program availability:* Part-time. *Degree requirements:* For master's, thesis, practicum. *Entrance requirements:* For master's, GRE General Test. Additional exam requirements/recommendations for international students: required—TOEFL (minimum score 550 paper-based; 80 iBT). Electronic applications accepted.

Emory University, Rollins School of Public Health, Online Program in Public Health, Atlanta, GA 30322-1100. Offers applied epidemiology (MPH); applied public health informatics (MPH); prevention science (MPH). *Program availability:* Part-time, evening/weekend, online learning. *Degree requirements:* For master's, thesis, practicum. *Entrance requirements:* For master's, GRE. Additional exam requirements/recommendations for international students: required—TOEFL (minimum score 550 paper-based; 80 iBT). Electronic applications accepted.

George Mason University, College of Health and Human Services, Department of Health Administration and Policy, Fairfax, VA 22030. Offers health and medical policy (MS); health informatics (MS); health informatics and data analytics (Certificate); health services research (PhD); health systems management (MHA); quality improvement and outcomes management in health care systems (Certificate). *Accreditation:* CAHME. *Program availability:* Part-time, evening/weekend, 100% online. *Degree requirements:* For master's, comprehensive exam, internship; for doctorate, thesis/dissertation. *Entrance requirements:* For master's, GRE recommended if undergraduate GPA is below 3.0 (for MS in health and medical policy), 2 official transcripts; expanded goals statement; 3 letters of recommendation; resume; 1 year of work experience (for MHA in health systems management); minimum GPA of 3.25 preferred (for MS in health informatics); for doctorate, GRE, professional and volunteer experience, evidence of ability to write and conduct research at the doctoral level, master's degree or equivalent; for Certificate, 2 official transcripts; expanded goals statement; 3 letters of recommendation; resume. Additional exam requirements/recommendations for international students: required—TOEFL (minimum score 575 paper-based; 88 iBT), IELTS (minimum score 6.5), PTE (minimum score 59). Electronic applications accepted. *Expenses:* Contact institution.

Georgia Southwestern State University, College of Nursing and Health Sciences, Americus, GA 31709-4693. Offers family nurse practitioner (MSN); health informatics (Postbaccalaureate Certificate); nurse educator (Post Master's Certificate); nursing educator (MSN); nursing informatics (MSN); nursing leadership (MSN). *Program availability:* Part-time, online only, all theory courses are offered online. *Faculty:* 9 full-time (all women), 5 part-time/adjunct (all women). *Students:* 18 full-time (14 women), 104 part-time (91 women); includes 45 minority (31 Black or African American, non-Hispanic/Latino; 1 American Indian or Alaska Native, non-Hispanic/Latino; 4 Asian, non-Hispanic/Latino; 3 Hispanic/Latino; 6 Two or more races, non-Hispanic/Latino). Average age 36. 96 applicants, 45% accepted, 24 enrolled. In 2019, 53 master's awarded. *Degree requirements:* For master's, thesis (for some programs), minimum cumulative GPA of 3.0; maximum of 6 credit hours with C grade and no D grades; degree completed within 7 calendar years from initial enrollment date in graduate courses; for other advanced degree, minimum cumulative GPA of 3.0; maximum of 6 credit hours with C grade and no D grades; degree completed within 7 calendar years from initial enrollment date in graduate courses. *Entrance requirements:* For master's, baccalaureate degree in nursing from regionally-accredited institution and nationally-accredited nursing program with minimum GPA of 3.0; three completed recommendation forms from professional peer or clinical supervisor; current unencumbered RN license in state where clinical course requirements will be met; proof of immunizations; for other advanced degree, baccalaureate or masters degree (depending upon certificate) in nursing from regionally-accredited institution and nationally-accredited nursing program with minimum GPA of 3.0; three completed recommendation forms from professional peer or clinical supervisor; current unencumbered RN license in state where clinical course requirements will be met;. Application fee: $25. Electronic applications accepted. *Expenses:* $385.00 per credit hour tuition, plus fees, which vary according to enrolled credit hours. *Financial support:* Application deadline: 6/1; applicants required to submit FAFSA. *Unit head:* Dr. Sandra Daniel, Dean, 229-931-2275. *Application contact:* Office of Graduate Admissions, 800-338-0082, Fax: 229-931-2983, E-mail: graduateadmissions@gsw.edu. Website: https://www.gsw.edu/academics/schools-and-departments/college-of-nursing-and-health-sciences/school-of-nursing/nursing-programs/graduate

Georgia State University, J. Mack Robinson College of Business, Department of Computer Information Systems, Atlanta, GA 30302-3083. Offers computer information systems (PhD); health informatics (MBA, MS); information systems (MSIS, Certificate); information systems development and project management (MBA); information systems management (MBA); managing information technology (Exec MS); the wireless organization (MBA). *Program availability:* Part-time, evening/weekend. *Faculty:* 14 full-time (1 woman), 3 part-time/adjunct (1 woman). *Students:* 130 full-time (66 women), 7 part-time (2 women); includes 25 minority (15 Black or African American, non-Hispanic/Latino; 7 Asian, non-Hispanic/Latino; 3 Two or more races, non-Hispanic/Latino), 99 international. Average age 29. 368 applicants, 58% accepted, 84 enrolled. In 2019, 102 master's, 3 doctorates, 1 other advanced degree awarded. *Entrance requirements:* For master's, GRE or GMAT, transcripts from all institutions attended, resume, essays; for doctorate, GRE or GMAT, three letters of recommendation, personal statement, transcripts from all institutions attended, resume. Additional exam requirements/recommendations for international students: required—TOEFL (minimum score 610 paper-based; 101 iBT), IELTS (minimum score 7). *Application deadline:* For fall admission, 5/1 priority date for domestic students, 2/1 priority date for international students; for spring admission, 9/15 priority date for domestic students, 4/1 priority date for international students. Applications are processed on a rolling basis. Application fee: $50. Electronic applications accepted. *Expenses: Tuition, area resident:* Full-time $7164; part-time $398 per credit hour. Tuition, state resident: full-time $7164; part-time $398 per credit hour. Tuition, nonresident: full-time $22,662; part-time $1259 per credit hour. *International tuition:* $22,662 full-time. *Required fees:* $2128; $312 per credit hour. Tuition and fees vary according to course load and program. *Financial support:* Research assistantships, teaching assistantships, scholarships/grants, tuition waivers, and unspecified assistantships available. Financial award applicants required to submit FAFSA. *Unit head:* Dr. Ephraim R. McLean, Professor/Chair, 404-413-7360, Fax: 404-413-7394. *Application contact:* Toby McChesney, Assistant Dean for Graduate Recruiting and Student Services, 404-413-7167, Fax: 404-413-7167, E-mail: rcbgradadmissions@gsu.edu. Website: http://cis.robinson.gsu.edu/

Georgia State University, J. Mack Robinson College of Business, Institute of Health Administration, Atlanta, GA 30302-3083. Offers health administration (MBA, MSHA); health informatics (MBA, MSCIS); MBA/MHA; PMBA/MHA. *Accreditation:* CAHME. *Program availability:* Part-time, evening/weekend. *Faculty:* 4 full-time (1 woman). *Students:* 37 full-time (18 women), 38 part-time (25 women); includes 37 minority (18 Black or African American, non-Hispanic/Latino; 11 Asian, non-Hispanic/Latino; 4 Hispanic/Latino; 4 Two or more races, non-Hispanic/Latino), 11 international. Average age 31. 57 applicants, 47% accepted, 19 enrolled. In 2019, 26 master's awarded. *Entrance requirements:* For master's, GRE or GMAT, transcripts from all institutions attended, resume, essays. Additional exam requirements/recommendations for international students: required—TOEFL (minimum score 610 paper-based; 101 iBT), IELTS (minimum score 7). *Application deadline:* For fall admission, 5/1 priority date for domestic students, 2/1 priority date for international students; for spring admission, 9/15 priority date for domestic students, 4/1 priority date for international students. Applications are processed on a rolling basis. Application fee: $50. Electronic applications accepted. *Expenses: Tuition, area resident:* Full-time $7164; part-time $398 per credit hour. Tuition, state resident: full-time $7164; part-time $398 per credit hour. Tuition, nonresident: full-time $22,662; part-time $1259 per credit hour. *International tuition:* $22,662 full-time. *Required fees:* $2128; $312 per credit hour. Tuition and fees vary according to course load and program. *Financial support:* Research assistantships, teaching assistantships, scholarships/grants, tuition waivers, and unspecified assistantships available. *Unit head:* Dr. Andrew T. Sumner, Chair in Health Administration/Director of the Institute of Health, 404-413-7630, Fax: 404-413-7631.

Health Informatics

Application contact: Toby McChesney, Assistant Dean for Graduate Recruiting and Student Services, 404-413-7167, Fax: 404-413-7162, E-mail: rcbgradadmissions@gsu.edu.
Website: https://robinson.gsu.edu/academic-departments/health-administration/

Grand Canyon University, College of Nursing and Health Care Professions, Phoenix, AZ 85017-1097. Offers acute care nurse practitioner (MSN, PMC); family nurse practitioner (MSN, PMC); health care administration (MS); health care informatics (MS, MSN); leadership in health care systems (MSN); nursing (DNP); nursing education (MSN, PMC); public health (MPH, MSN); MBA/MSN. *Accreditation:* AACN. *Program availability:* Part-time, evening/weekend, online learning. *Degree requirements:* For master's and PMC, comprehensive exam (for some programs). *Entrance requirements:* For master's, minimum cumulative and science course undergraduate GPA of 3.0. Additional exam requirements/recommendations for international students: required—TOEFL (minimum score 575 paper-based; 90 iBT), IELTS (minimum score 7).

Hofstra University, School of Health Professions and Human Services, Programs in Health, Hempstead, NY 11549. Offers foundations of public health (Advanced Certificate); health administration (MHA); health informatics (MS); occupational therapy (MS); public health (MPH); security and privacy in health information systems (Advanced Certificate); sports science (MS); teacher of students with speech-language disabilities (Advanced Certificate). *Program availability:* Part-time, evening/weekend. *Students:* 291 full-time (220 women), 128 part-time (88 women); includes 192 minority (69 Black or African American, non-Hispanic/Latino; 3 American Indian or Alaska Native, non-Hispanic/Latino; 72 Asian, non-Hispanic/Latino; 37 Hispanic/Latino; 4 Native Hawaiian or other Pacific Islander, non-Hispanic/Latino; 7 Two or more races, non-Hispanic/Latino), 25 international. Average age 29. 676 applicants, 52% accepted, 132 enrolled. In 2019, 170 master's, 1 other advanced degree awarded. *Degree requirements:* For master's, internship, minimum GPA of 3.0. *Entrance requirements:* For master's, interview, 2 letters of recommendation, essay, resume. Additional exam requirements/recommendations for international students: required—TOEFL (minimum score 550 paper-based; 80 iBT); recommended—IELTS (minimum score 6.5). *Application deadline:* Applications are processed on a rolling basis. Application fee: $75. Electronic applications accepted. *Expenses: Tuition:* Full-time $25,164; part-time $1398 per credit. *Required fees:* $580; $165 per semester. Tuition and fees vary according to course load, degree level and program. *Financial support:* In 2019–20, 181 students received support, including 104 fellowships with full and partial tuition reimbursements available (averaging $3,465 per year), 5 research assistantships with full and partial tuition reimbursements available (averaging $7,172 per year); career-related internships or fieldwork, Federal Work-Study, institutionally sponsored loans, scholarships/grants, traineeships, tuition waivers (full and partial), unspecified assistantships, and scholarships and endowed scholarships also available. Support available to part-time students. Financial award applicants required to submit FAFSA. *Unit head:* Dr. Corinne Kyriacou, Chairperson, 516-463-4553, E-mail: corinne.m.kyriacou@hofstra.edu. *Application contact:* Sunil Samuel, Assistant Vice President of Admissions, 516-463-4723, Fax: 516-463-4664, E-mail: graduateadmission@hofstra.edu.
Website: http://www.hofstra.edu/academics/colleges/healthscienceshumanservices/

Indiana University Bloomington, School of Informatics, Computing, and Engineering, Program in Informatics, Bloomington, IN 47405. Offers informatics (MS, PhD), including bioinformatics (PhD), complex systems (PhD), computing, culture and society (PhD), health informatics (PhD), human-computer interaction (MS), human-computer interaction design (PhD), music informatics (PhD), security informatics (PhD); visual heritage (PhD). *Program availability:* Part-time. Terminal master's awarded for partial completion of doctoral program. *Degree requirements:* For master's, thesis, capstone project; for doctorate, variable foreign language requirement, comprehensive exam, thesis/dissertation. *Entrance requirements:* For master's and doctorate, GRE, resume/curriculum vitae, transcripts, 3 letters of recommendation. Additional exam requirements/recommendations for international students: required—TOEFL (minimum score 600 paper-based; 100 iBT). Electronic applications accepted.

Indiana University-Purdue University Indianapolis, School of Informatics and Computing, Department of BioHealth Informatics, Indianapolis, IN 46202. Offers bioinformatics (MS, PhD); health informatics (MS, PhD).

Jacksonville University, Brooks Rehabilitation College of Healthcare Sciences, School of Applied Health Sciences, Program in Health Informatics, Jacksonville, FL 32211. Offers MS. *Program availability:* Part-time, 100% online, blended/hybrid learning. *Students:* 3 full-time (2 women), 28 part-time (19 women); includes 19 minority (8 Black or African American, non-Hispanic/Latino; 1 American Indian or Alaska Native, non-Hispanic/Latino; 4 Asian, non-Hispanic/Latino; 5 Hispanic/Latino; 1 Two or more races, non-Hispanic/Latino). Average age 40. 36 applicants, 39% accepted, 14 enrolled. In 2019, 28 master's awarded. *Entrance requirements:* For master's, baccalaureate degree in any discipline from regionally-accredited institution with minimum GPA of 3.0; official transcripts; evidence of undergraduate course completion in statistics and college algebra; resume or curriculum vitae demonstrating healthcare experience. Additional exam requirements/recommendations for international students: required—TOEFL (minimum score 540 paper-based; 76 iBT), IELTS (minimum score 6). *Application deadline:* Applications are processed on a rolling basis. Application fee: $50. Electronic applications accepted. *Expenses:* Contact institution. *Financial support:* Federal Work-Study, institutionally sponsored loans, scholarships/grants, and health care benefits available. Financial award application deadline: 3/15; financial award applicants required to submit FAFSA. *Unit head:* Dr. Teresa MacGregor, Executive Director of Graduate and Professional Studies, 904-256-7980, E-mail: tmacgre@ju.edu. *Application contact:* Antonio Starke, Assistant Director of Graduate Admissions, 904-256-7472, E-mail: astarke2@ju.edu.
Website: https://www.ju.edu/healthinformatics/

Johns Hopkins University, School of Medicine, Graduate Programs in Medicine, Department of Health Sciences Informatics, Baltimore, MD 21218. Offers applied health sciences informatics (MS); clinical informatics (Certificate); health sciences informatics (PhD); health sciences informatics research (MS). *Degree requirements:* For master's, thesis, publications, practica. *Entrance requirements:* Additional exam requirements/recommendations for international students: recommended—TOEFL. Electronic applications accepted.

Kennesaw State University, Coles College of Business, Program in Health Management and Informatics, Kennesaw, GA 30144. Offers MS. *Program availability:* Part-time-only, evening/weekend, online only, blended/hybrid learning. *Students:* 7 full-time (5 women), 73 part-time (55 women); includes 51 minority (33 Black or African American, non-Hispanic/Latino; 1 American Indian or Alaska Native, non-Hispanic/Latino; 9 Asian, non-Hispanic/Latino; 5 Hispanic/Latino; 3 Two or more races, non-Hispanic/Latino), 9 international. Average age 35. 39 applicants, 87% accepted, 34 enrolled. In 2019, 3 master's awarded. *Entrance requirements:* Additional exam requirements/recommendations for international students: required—TOEFL (minimum score 80 iBT), IELTS (minimum score 6.5). *Application deadline:* For fall admission, 7/1 for domestic and international students. Applications are processed on a rolling basis. Application fee: $60. Electronic applications accepted. *Expenses:* Contact institution. *Unit head:* Dr. Sweta Sneha, Director, 470-578-2436, E-mail: ssneha@kennesaw.edu. *Application contact:* Admissions Counselor, 470-578-4377, Fax: 470-578-9172, E-mail: ksugrad@kennesaw.edu.
Website: http://coles.kennesaw.edu/mshmi/

Kennesaw State University, College of Computing and Software Engineering, Program in Information Technology, Kennesaw, GA 30144. Offers data management and analytics (Graduate Certificate); health information technology (Postbaccalaureate Certificate); information technology (MSIT); information technology foundations (Postbaccalaureate Certificate); information technology security (Graduate Certificate). *Program availability:* Part-time, evening/weekend, blended/hybrid learning. *Students:* 73 full-time (38 women), 142 part-time (52 women); includes 101 minority (56 Black or African American, non-Hispanic/Latino; 31 Asian, non-Hispanic/Latino; 10 Hispanic/Latino; 4 Two or more races, non-Hispanic/Latino), 37 international. Average age 32. 52 applicants, 85% accepted, 34 enrolled. In 2019, 95 master's awarded. *Degree requirements:* For master's, thesis optional. *Entrance requirements:* For master's, minimum GPA of 2.75; for other advanced degree, bachelor's degree. Additional exam requirements/recommendations for international students: required—TOEFL (minimum score 80 iBT), IELTS (minimum score 6.5). *Application deadline:* For fall admission, 7/1 priority date for domestic students, 5/1 priority date for international students; for spring admission, 11/1 priority date for domestic students, 9/1 priority date for international students; for summer admission, 4/1 priority date for domestic students, 3/1 priority date for international students. Applications are processed on a rolling basis. Application fee: $60. Electronic applications accepted. *Expenses: Tuition, area resident:* Full-time $7104; part-time $296 per credit hour. Tuition, state resident: full-time $7104; part-time $296 per credit hour. Tuition, nonresident: full-time $25,584; part-time $1066 per credit hour. *International tuition:* $25,584 full-time. *Required fees:* $2006; $1706 per unit. $853 per semester. *Financial support:* Applicants required to submit FAFSA. *Application contact:* Admission Counselor, 470-578-4377, Fax: 470-578-9172, E-mail: ksugrad@kennesaw.edu.
Website: http://ccse.kennesaw.edu/it/

Kent State University, College of Communication and Information, School of Information, Kent, OH 44242-0001. Offers health informatics (MS), including health informatics, knowledge management, user experience design; library and information science (MLIS), including K-12 school library media; M Ed/MLIS; MBA/MLIS; MLIS/MS. *Accreditation:* ALA (one or more programs are accredited). *Program availability:* Part-time, 100% online. *Faculty:* 16 full-time (13 women), 26 part-time/adjunct (12 women). *Students:* 148 full-time (120 women), 372 part-time (274 women); includes 89 minority (34 Black or African American, non-Hispanic/Latino; 16 Asian, non-Hispanic/Latino; 26 Hispanic/Latino; 13 Two or more races, non-Hispanic/Latino), 2 international. Average age 32. 211 applicants, 100% accepted, 142 enrolled. In 2019, 32 master's awarded. *Degree requirements:* For master's, thesis, portfolio (MLIS); internship, project, paper, or thesis. *Entrance requirements:* For master's, GRE if total GPA is below 3.0 in highest completed degree, minimum GPA of 3.0, statement of purpose, 3 letters of recommendation, curriculum vitae/resume, transcripts, writing sample, personal interview, application essay, student profile form. Additional exam requirements/recommendations for international students: required—TOEFL (minimum score 94 iBT), IELTS (minimum score 7), PTE (minimum score 65), Michigan English Language Assessment Battery (minimum score 82). *Application deadline:* For fall admission, 3/15 priority date for domestic students, 3/15 for international students; for spring admission, 9/15 priority date for domestic students, 9/15 for international students; for summer admission, 1/15 priority date for domestic students, 1/15 for international students. Applications are processed on a rolling basis. Application fee: $45 ($70 for international students). Electronic applications accepted. *Financial support:* Fellowships with full tuition reimbursements, research assistantships with full tuition reimbursements, teaching assistantships with full tuition reimbursements, scholarships/grants, and unspecified assistantships available. Financial award application deadline: 3/1. *Unit head:* Dr. Kendra Albright, Ph.D., Director and Professor, 330-672-8535, E-mail: kalbrig7@kent.edu. *Application contact:* Dr. Kendra Albright, Ph.D., Director and Professor, 330-672-8535, E-mail: kalbrig7@kent.edu.
Website: https://www.kent.edu/iSchool

Liberty University, School of Health Sciences, Lynchburg, VA 24515. Offers anatomy and cell biology (PhD); biomedical sciences (MS); epidemiology (MPH); exercise science (MS), including clinical, community physical activity, human performance, nutrition; global health (MPH); health promotion (MPH); medical sciences (MA), including biopsychology, business management, health informatics, molecular medicine, public health; nutrition (MPH). *Program availability:* Part-time, online learning. *Students:* 820 full-time (588 women), 889 part-time (612 women); includes 611 minority (402 Black or African American, non-Hispanic/Latino; 10 American Indian or Alaska Native, non-Hispanic/Latino; 43 Asian, non-Hispanic/Latino; 85 Hispanic/Latino; 1 Native Hawaiian or other Pacific Islander, non-Hispanic/Latino; 70 Two or more races, non-Hispanic/Latino), 67 international. Average age 32. 2,610 applicants, 33% accepted, 406 enrolled. In 2019, 445 master's awarded. *Degree requirements:* For master's, thesis (for some programs); for doctorate, thesis/dissertation. *Entrance requirements:* For doctorate, MAT or GRE, minimum GPA of 3.25 in master's program, 2-3 recommendations, writing samples (for some programs), letter of intent, professional vitae. Additional exam requirements/recommendations for international students: required—TOEFL (minimum score 600 paper-based; 100 iBT). Application fee: $50. *Expenses: Tuition:* Full-time $545; part-time $410 per credit hour. One-time fee: $50. *Financial support:* In 2019–20, 918 students received support. Federal Work-Study available. Financial award applicants required to submit FAFSA. *Unit head:* Dr. Ralph Linstra, Dean. *Application contact:* Jay Bridge, Director of Admissions, 800-424-9595, Fax: 800-628-7977, E-mail: gradadmissions@liberty.edu.
Website: https://www.liberty.edu/health-sciences/

Lipscomb University, College of Pharmacy, Nashville, TN 37204-3951. Offers healthcare informatics (MS); pharmacy (Pharm D); Pharm D/MM; Pharm D/MS. *Accreditation:* ACPE. *Degree requirements:* For master's, capstone project; for doctorate, comprehensive exam. *Entrance requirements:* For master's, GRE, 2 references, transcripts, resume, personal statement, eligibility documentation (degree and/or experience in related area); for doctorate, PCAT (minimum 45th percentile), 66 pre-professional semester hours, minimum GPA of 2.5, interview, PharmCAS application (for international students). Additional exam requirements/recommendations for international students: required—TOEFL (minimum score 550 paper-based; 80 iBT). Electronic applications accepted. *Expenses:* Contact institution.

Logan University, College of Health Sciences, Chesterfield, MO 63017. Offers health informatics (MS); health professions education (DHPE); nutrition and human performance (MS); sports science and rehabilitation (MS). *Program availability:* Part-time, online only, 100% online. *Entrance requirements:* For master's, minimum GPA of 2.5; 6 hours of biology and physical science; bachelor's degree and 9 hours of business health administration (for health informatics). Additional exam requirements/recommendations for international students: required—TOEFL (minimum score 500 paper-based; 79 iBT); recommended—IELTS (minimum score 6.5). Electronic applications accepted. *Expenses:* Contact institution.

Louisiana Tech University, Graduate School, College of Applied and Natural Sciences, Ruston, LA 71272. Offers biology (MS); dietetics (Graduate Certificate); health informatics (MHI); molecular science and nanotechnology (MS, PhD). *Program* *availability:* Part-time. *Degree requirements:* For master's, comprehensive exam (for some programs), thesis (for some programs); for doctorate, comprehensive exam, thesis/dissertation. *Entrance requirements:* For master's and doctorate, GRE General Test, transcript with bachelor's degree awarded; for Graduate Certificate, transcript with bachelor's degree awarded. Additional exam requirements/recommendations for international students: required—TOEFL (minimum score 550 paper-based; 80 iBT), IELTS (minimum score 6.5). Electronic applications accepted. *Expenses: Tuition, area resident:* Full-time $6592; part-time $400 per credit. Tuition, state resident: full-time $6592; part-time $400 per credit. Tuition, nonresident: full-time $13,333; part-time $681 per credit. *International tuition:* $13,333 full-time. *Required fees:* $3011; $3011 per unit.

Marshall University, Academic Affairs Division, College of Health Professions, Department of Health Informatics, Huntington, WV 25755. Offers MS.

Marymount University, School of Business and Technology, Program in Information Technology, Arlington, VA 22207-4299. Offers health care informatics (Certificate); information technology (MS, Certificate), including cybersecurity (MS), health care informatics (MS), project management (MS), software engineering (MS); information technology project management and technology leadership (Certificate); information technology with business administration (MS/MBA); information technology with health care management (MS/MS); MS/MBA; MS/MS. *Program availability:* Part-time, evening/weekend. *Faculty:* 5 full-time (3 women), 7 part-time/adjunct (2 women). *Students:* 46 full-time (22 women), 30 part-time (15 women); includes 30 minority (16 Black or African American, non-Hispanic/Latino; 7 Asian, non-Hispanic/Latino; 7 Hispanic/Latino), 27 international. Average age 31. 61 applicants, 95% accepted, 27 enrolled. In 2019, 29 master's, 2 other advanced degrees awarded. *Degree requirements:* For master's, thesis or alternative, A minimum grade of B- is needed to receive credit for a course in the program. Must maintain a minimum cumulative GPA of 3.0. *Entrance requirements:* For master's, Resume, bachelor's degree in computer-related field or degree in another subject with a certificate in a computer-related field or related work experience. Software Engineering Track: bachelor's degree in Computer Science or work in software development. Project Mgmt/Tech Leadership Track: minimum 2 years of IT experience. Additional exam requirements/recommendations for international students: required— TOEFL (minimum score 600 paper-based; 96 iBT), IELTS (minimum score 6.5), PTE (minimum score 58). *Application deadline:* For fall admission, 7/16 priority date for domestic and international students; for spring admission, 11/16 priority date for domestic and international students; for summer admission, 4/16 priority date for domestic and international students. Applications are processed on a rolling basis. Application fee: $40. Electronic applications accepted. *Expenses:* $1,060 per credit. *Financial support:* In 2019–20, 12 students received support. Research assistantships, teaching assistantships, career-related internships or fieldwork, scholarships/grants, and unspecified assistantships available. Support available to part-time students. Financial award application deadline: 3/1; financial award applicants required to submit FAFSA. *Unit head:* Dr. Diane Murphy, Chair/Director, Information Technology, Management Sciences and Cybersecurity, 703-284-5958, E-mail: diane.murphy@marymount.edu. *Application contact:* Fiona McDonnell, Administrative Assistant, 703-284-5901, E-mail: gadmissi@marymount.edu.
Website: https://www.marymount.edu/Academics/School-of-Business-and-Technology/Graduate-Programs/Information-Technology-(M-S-)

Mercer University, Graduate Studies, Cecil B. Day Campus, College of Professional Advancement, Atlanta, GA 31207. Offers certified rehabilitation counseling (MS); clinical mental health (MS); counselor education and supervision (PhD); criminal justice and public safety leadership (MS); health informatics (MS); human services (MS), including child and adolescent services, gerontology services; organizational leadership (MS), including leadership for the health care professional, leadership for the nonprofit organization, organizational development and change; school counseling (MS). *Program availability:* Part-time, evening/weekend, 100% online, blended/hybrid learning. *Faculty:* 19 full-time (11 women), 34 part-time/adjunct (30 women). *Students:* 193 full-time (156 women), 277 part-time (225 women); includes 260 minority (211 Black or African American, non-Hispanic/Latino; 2 American Indian or Alaska Native, non-Hispanic/Latino; 23 Asian, non-Hispanic/Latino; 19 Hispanic/Latino; 5 Two or more races, non-Hispanic/Latino), 3 international. Average age 32. 300 applicants, 45% accepted, 114 enrolled. In 2019, 183 master's, 7 doctorates awarded. *Degree requirements:* For master's, comprehensive exam (for some programs), thesis (for some programs); for doctorate, thesis/dissertation. *Entrance requirements:* For master's, GRE or MAT, Georgia Professional Standards Commission (GPSC) Certification at the SC-5 level; for doctorate, GRE or MAT. Additional exam requirements/recommendations for international students: recommended—TOEFL (minimum score 550 paper-based; 80 iBT), IELTS (minimum score 6.5). *Application deadline:* For fall admission, 7/1 priority date for domestic and international students; for spring admission, 11/1 priority date for domestic and international students; for summer admission, 4/1 priority date for domestic and international students. Application fee: $35. Electronic applications accepted. Application fee is waived when completed online. *Expenses:* Contact institution. *Financial support:* In 2019–20, 32 students received support. Federal Work-Study, scholarships/grants, and unspecified assistantships available. Financial award applicants required to submit FAFSA. *Unit head:* Dr. Priscilla R. Danheiser, Dean, 678-547-6028, Fax: 678-547-6008, E-mail: danheiser_p@mercer.edu. *Application contact:* Theatis Anderson, Asst VP for Enrollment Management, 678-547-6421, E-mail: anderson_t@mercer.edu.
Website: https://professionaladvancement.mercer.edu/

Middle Georgia State University, Office of Graduate Studies, Macon, GA 31206. Offers adult/gerontology acute care nurse practitioner (MSN); information technology (MS), including health informatics, information security and digital forensics, software development. *Entrance requirements:* For master's, GRE. Additional exam requirements/recommendations for international students: required—TOEFL (minimum score 523 paper-based; 69 iBT). *Expenses:* Contact institution.

Midwestern State University, Billie Doris McAda Graduate School, Robert D. and Carol Gunn College of Health Sciences and Human Services, Department of Criminal Justice and Health Services Administration, Wichita Falls, TX 76308. Offers criminal justice (MA); health information management (MHA); health services administration (Graduate Certificate); medical practice management (MHA); public and community sector health care management (MHA); rural and urban hospital management (MHA). *Program availability:* Part-time, evening/weekend. *Degree requirements:* For master's, comprehensive exam, thesis. *Entrance requirements:* For master's, GRE. Additional exam requirements/recommendations for international students: required—TOEFL (minimum score 550 paper-based). Electronic applications accepted.

Millennia Atlantic University, Graduate Programs, Doral, FL 33178. Offers accounting (MBA); business administration (MBA); health information management (MS); human resource management (MA). *Program availability:* Online learning.

Montana Technological University, Health Care Informatics Program, Butte, MT 59701-8997. Offers Certificate. *Program availability:* Part-time, evening/weekend, online learning. *Faculty:* 4 full-time (2 women). *Students:* 1 part-time (0 women). Average age 42. In 2019, 3 Certificates awarded. *Entrance requirements:* Additional exam requirements/recommendations for international students: required—TOEFL (minimum score 545 paper-based; 78 iBT), IELTS (minimum score 6.5). *Application deadline:* For

fall admission, 4/1 priority date for domestic students, 3/1 priority date for international students; for spring admission, 10/1 priority date for domestic students, 6/1 priority date for international students. Applications are processed on a rolling basis. Application fee: $50. Electronic applications accepted. *Financial support:* Scholarships/grants available. Financial award application deadline: 4/1; financial award applicants required to submit FAFSA. *Unit head:* Dr. Charie Faught, Department Head, 406-496-4884, Fax: 406-496-4435, E-mail: cfaught@mtech.edu. *Application contact:* Daniel Stirling, Administrator, Graduate School, 406-496-4304, Fax: 406-496-4710, E-mail: gradschool@mtech.edu. Website: http://www.mtech.edu/academics/gradschool/distancelearning/distancelearning-hci.htm

National University, School of Health and Human Services, La Jolla, CA 92037-1011. Offers clinical affairs (MS); clinical regulatory affairs (MS); complementary and integrative healthcare (MS); family nurse practitioner (MSN); health and life science analytics (MS); health informatics (MS, Certificate); healthcare administration (MHA); nurse anesthesia (MSNA); nursing administration (MSN); nursing informatics (MSN); psychiatric-mental health nurse practitioner (MSN); public health (MPH), including health promotion, healthcare administration, mental health. *Accreditation:* CEPH. *Program availability:* Part-time, evening/weekend, 100% online, blended/hybrid learning. *Degree requirements:* For master's, thesis (for some programs). *Entrance requirements:* For master's, interview, minimum GPA of 2.5. Additional exam requirements/recommendations for international students: required—TOEFL (minimum score 550 paper-based; 79 iBT), IELTS (minimum score 6). Electronic applications accepted. *Expenses: Tuition:* Full-time $442; part-time $442 per unit.

Northeastern University, College of Computer and Information Science, Boston, MA 02115-5096. Offers computer science (MS, PhD); data science (MS); game science and design (MS); health informatics (MS); information assurance (MS); network science (PhD); personal health informatics (PhD). *Program availability:* Part-time, evening/weekend. Terminal master's awarded for partial completion of doctoral program. *Degree requirements:* For master's, thesis optional; for doctorate, comprehensive exam, thesis/dissertation. Electronic applications accepted. *Expenses:* Contact institution.

Northern Kentucky University, Office of Graduate Programs, College of Informatics, Program in Health Informatics, Highland Heights, KY 41099. Offers MS, Certificate. *Program availability:* Part-time, evening/weekend, online learning. *Degree requirements:* For master's, capstone, electronic portfolio. *Entrance requirements:* For master's, MAT, GRE, or GMAT, official transcripts from accredited college or university, minimum GPA of 3.0, letter of career goals and background, statement addressing computer proficiencies; references (recommended). Additional exam requirements/ recommendations for international students: required—TOEFL (minimum score 79 iBT); recommended—IELTS (minimum score 6.5). Electronic applications accepted.

Northwestern University, Feinberg School of Medicine, Driskill Graduate Program in Life Sciences, Chicago, IL 60611. Offers biostatistics (PhD); epidemiology (PhD); health and biomedical informatics (PhD); health services and outcomes research (PhD); healthcare quality and patient safety (PhD); translational outcomes in science (PhD). *Degree requirements:* For doctorate, comprehensive exam, thesis/dissertation, written and oral qualifying exams. *Entrance requirements:* For doctorate, GRE General Test. Additional exam requirements/recommendations for international students: required— TOEFL (minimum score 600 paper-based). Electronic applications accepted.

Northwestern University, School of Professional Studies, Program in Health Informatics, Evanston, IL 60208. Offers MS. *Program availability:* Online learning.

Nova Southeastern University, Dr. Kiran C. Patel College of Osteopathic Medicine, Fort Lauderdale, FL 33314-7796. Offers biomedical informatics (MS, Graduate Certificate), including biomedical informatics (MS), clinical informatics (Graduate Certificate), public health informatics (Graduate Certificate); disaster and emergency management (MS); medical education (MS); nutrition (MS, Graduate Certificate), including functional nutrition and herbal therapy (Graduate Certificate); osteopathic medicine (DO); public health (MPH, Graduate Certificate), including health education (Graduate Certificate); social medicine (Graduate Certificate); DO/DMD. *Accreditation:* AOsA; CEPH. *Program availability:* Part-time, 100% online, blended/hybrid learning. *Faculty:* 73 full-time (43 women), 35 part-time/adjunct (14 women). *Students:* 1,410 full-time (740 women), 182 part-time (118 women); includes 895 minority (126 Black or African American, non-Hispanic/Latino; 1 American Indian or Alaska Native, non-Hispanic/Latino; 416 Asian, non-Hispanic/Latino; 309 Hispanic/Latino; 1 Native Hawaiian or other Pacific Islander, non-Hispanic/Latino; 42 Two or more races, non-Hispanic/Latino), 70 international. Average age 26. 5,078 applicants, 10% accepted, 495 enrolled. In 2019, 117 master's, 233 doctorates, 3 other advanced degrees awarded. *Degree requirements:* For master's, comprehensive exam (for MPH); field/special projects; for doctorate, comprehensive exam, COMLEX Board Exams; for Graduate Certificate, thesis or alternative. *Entrance requirements:* For master's, GRE; for doctorate, MCAT, coursework in biology, chemistry, organic chemistry, physics (all with labs), biochemistry, and English. *Application deadline:* For fall admission, 1/15 for domestic students. Applications are processed on a rolling basis. Application fee: $50. Electronic applications accepted. *Expenses:* Contact institution. *Financial support:* In 2019–20, 83 students received support, including 24 fellowships with tuition reimbursements available; Federal Work-Study and scholarships/grants also available. Financial award application deadline: 6/1; financial award applicants required to submit FAFSA. *Unit head:* Elaine M. Wallace, Dean, 954-262-1457, Fax: 954-262-2250, E-mail: ewallace@nova.edu. *Application contact:* HPD Admissions, 877-640-0218, E-mail: hpdinfo@nova.edu.
Website: https://www.osteopathic.nova.edu/

Oregon Health & Science University, School of Medicine, Graduate Programs in Medicine, Department of Medical Informatics and Clinical Epidemiology, Portland, OR 97239-3098. Offers bioinformatics and computational biology (MS, PhD); clinical informatics (MBI, MS, PhD, Certificate); health information management (Certificate). *Program availability:* Part-time, online learning. Terminal master's awarded for partial completion of doctoral program. *Degree requirements:* For master's, thesis or capstone project; for doctorate, comprehensive exam, thesis/dissertation, qualifying exam. *Entrance requirements:* For master's and doctorate, GRE General Test (minimum scores: 153 Verbal/148 Quantitative/4.5 Analytical), coursework in computer programming, human anatomy and physiology. Electronic applications accepted. *Expenses:* Contact institution.

Regis University, College of Computer and Information Sciences, Denver, CO 80221-1099. Offers agile technologies (Certificate); cybersecurity (Certificate); data science (M Sc); database administration with Oracle (Certificate); database development (Certificate); database technologies (M Sc); enterprise Java software development (Certificate); enterprise resource planning (Certificate); executive information technology (Certificate); health care informatics (Certificate); health care informatics and information management (M Sc); information assurance (M Sc); information assurance policy management (Certificate); information technology management (M Sc); mobile software development (Certificate); software engineering (M Sc, Certificate); software engineering and database technology (M Sc); storage area networks (Certificate); systems engineering (M Sc, Certificate). *Program availability:* Part-time, evening/weekend, 100% online, blended/hybrid learning. *Degree requirements:* For master's, thesis (for some programs), final research project. *Entrance requirements:* For master's, official transcript reflecting baccalaureate degree awarded from regionally-accredited college or university, 2 years of related experience, resume, interview. Additional exam requirements/recommendations for international students: required—TOEFL (minimum score 550 paper-based; 82 iBT). Electronic applications accepted. *Expenses:* Contact institution.

Roberts Wesleyan College, Health Administration Programs, Rochester, NY 14624-1997. Offers health administration (MS); healthcare informatics administration (MS). *Program availability:* Evening/weekend, online learning. *Degree requirements:* For master's, thesis or alternative. *Entrance requirements:* For master's, minimum GPA of 3.0, verifiable work experience or recommendation.

Rochester Institute of Technology, Graduate Enrollment Services, Golisano College of Computing and Information Sciences, Information Science and Technologies Department, MS Program in Health Informatics, Rochester, NY 14623-5603. Offers MS. *Program availability:* Part-time, evening/weekend, online only, 100% online. *Degree requirements:* For master's, Capstone. *Entrance requirements:* For master's, minimum GPA of 3.0 (preferred), 2 letters of recommendation, resume, minimum of 3 years experience in a relevant field recommended, interview may be required, GRE required for international students. Additional exam requirements/recommendations for international students: required—TOEFL (minimum score 88 iBT), IELTS (minimum score 6.5). Electronic applications accepted. *Expenses:* Contact institution.

Rutgers University - New Brunswick, Edward J. Bloustein School of Planning and Public Policy, Program in Public Informatics, Piscataway, NJ 08854-8097. Offers MPI.

Sacred Heart University, Graduate Programs, College of Health Professions, Department of Health Science, Fairfield, CT 06825. Offers healthcare informatics (MS). *Program availability:* Part-time, evening/weekend. *Degree requirements:* For master's, comprehensive exam (for some programs). *Entrance requirements:* For master's, bachelor's degree, minimum cumulative undergraduate GPA of 3.0, personal essay, two letters of recommendation, resume. Additional exam requirements/recommendations for international students: required—TOEFL (minimum score 570 paper-based, 80 iBT), TWE, or IELTS (6.5). Electronic applications accepted. *Expenses:* Contact institution.

St. Catherine University, Graduate Programs, Program in Health Informatics, St. Paul, MN 55105. Offers MHI. *Program availability:* Online learning. *Expenses:* Contact institution.

St. Joseph's College, Long Island Campus, Programs in Health Care Administration, Field in Health Care Management - Health Information Systems, Patchogue, NY 11772-2399. Offers MBA. *Program availability:* Part-time, evening/weekend, 100% online, blended/hybrid learning. *Faculty:* 10 full-time (4 women), 18 part-time/adjunct (7 women). *Students:* 2 full-time (1 woman), 17 part-time (12 women); includes 7 minority (1 Black or African American, non-Hispanic/Latino; 1 Asian, non-Hispanic/Latino; 5 Hispanic/Latino). Average age 38. 15 applicants, 27% accepted, 3 enrolled. In 2019, 11 master's awarded. *Entrance requirements:* For master's, Application, $25 application fee, official transcripts, two letters of recommendation, current resume, 250 word written statement. Additional exam requirements/recommendations for international students: required—TOEFL (minimum score 80 iBT). *Application deadline:* Applications are processed on a rolling basis. Application fee: $25. Electronic applications accepted. *Expenses: Tuition:* Full-time $19,350; part-time $1075 per credit. *Required fees:* $410. *Financial support:* In 2019–20, 6 students received support. *Unit head:* John Sardelis, Associate Chair and Professor, 631-687-1493, E-mail: jsardelis@sjcny.edu. *Application contact:* John Sardelis, Associate Chair and Professor, 631-687-1493, E-mail: jsardelis@sjcny.edu.
Website: https://www.sjcny.edu/long-island/academics/graduate/degree/health-care-management-health-information-systems-concentration

St. Joseph's College, New York, Programs in Health Care Administration, Field in Health Care Management - Health Information Systems, Brooklyn, NY 11205-3688. Offers MBA. *Program availability:* Part-time, evening/weekend, 100% online, blended/hybrid learning. *Faculty:* 6 full-time (3 women), 11 part-time/adjunct (7 women). *Students:* 7 part-time (6 women); includes 5 minority (3 Black or African American, non-Hispanic/Latino; 1 Asian, non-Hispanic/Latino; 1 Hispanic/Latino). Average age 37. 2 applicants, 50% accepted. In 2019, 5 master's awarded. *Entrance requirements:* For master's, Application, $25 application fee, two letters of recommendation, current resume, 250 word essay, official transcripts. Additional exam requirements/recommendations for international students: required—TOEFL (minimum score 80 iBT). *Application deadline:* Applications are processed on a rolling basis. Application fee: $25. Electronic applications accepted. *Expenses: Tuition:* Full-time $19,350; part-time $1075 per credit. *Required fees:* $400. *Financial support:* In 2019–20, 1 student received support. *Unit head:* Dr. Lauren Pete, Chair, 718-940-5890, E-mail: lpete@sjcny.edu. *Application contact:* Dr. Lauren Pete, Chair, 718-940-5890, E-mail: lpete@sjcny.edu.
Website: https://www.sjcny.edu/brooklyn/academics/graduate/graduate-degrees/health-care-management-health-info-sys-concentration

Saint Joseph's University, School of Health Studies and Education, Department of Health Services, Philadelphia, PA 19131-1395. Offers health administration (MS); health informatics (MS); organizations development and leadership (MS). *Program availability:* Part-time, evening/weekend. *Entrance requirements:* For master's, GRE (if GPA less than 2.75), 2 letters of recommendation, resume, personal statement, official transcripts. Additional exam requirements/recommendations for international students: required—TOEFL (minimum score 550 paper-based; 80 iBT), IELTS (minimum score 6.5). Electronic applications accepted. *Expenses:* Contact institution.

Samford University, School of Public Health, Birmingham, AL 35229. Offers health informatics (MSHI); healthcare administration (MHA); nutrition (MS); public health (MPH); social work (MSW). *Accreditation:* CSWE. *Program availability:* Part-time, online only, 100% online. *Faculty:* 16 full-time (9 women), 5 part-time/adjunct (4 women). *Students:* 76 full-time (71 women), 16 part-time (14 women); includes 19 minority (14 Black or African American, non-Hispanic/Latino; 1 Asian, non-Hispanic/Latino; 1 Hispanic/Latino; 3 Two or more races, non-Hispanic/Latino). Average age 28. 74 applicants, 78% accepted, 39 enrolled. In 2019, 51 master's awarded. *Degree requirements:* For master's, capstone course. *Entrance requirements:* For master's, GRE, MAT, recommendations, resume, personal statement, transcripts, application. Additional exam requirements/recommendations for international students: required—TOEFL (minimum score 590 paper-based; 90 iBT), IELTS (minimum score 6.5). *Application deadline:* For fall admission, 10/1 for domestic students; for winter admission, 12/1 for domestic students; for spring admission, 5/1 for domestic students. Applications are processed on a rolling basis. Application fee: $75. Electronic applications accepted. *Expenses: Tuition:* Full-time $17,754; part-time $862 per credit hour. *Required fees:* $550; $550 per unit. Full-time tuition and fees vary according to course load, program and student level. *Financial support:* In 2019–20, 30 students received support. Scholarships/grants available. Financial award application deadline: 5/1; financial award applicants required to submit FAFSA. *Unit head:* Dr. Keith Elder, Ph.D., Dean, School of Public Health, 205-726-4655, E-mail: kelder@samford.edu. *Application contact:* Dr. Marian Carter, Ed.D, Assistant Dean of Enrollment Management, 205-726-2611, E-mail: mwcarter@samford.edu.
Website: http://www.samford.edu/publichealth

Slippery Rock University of Pennsylvania, Graduate Studies (Recruitment), College of Health, Engineering, and Science, Department of Computer Science, Slippery Rock, PA 16057-1383. Offers health informatics (MS). *Program availability:* Part-time, evening/weekend, online only, 100% online. *Students:* 6 full-time (1 woman), 14 part-time (7 women); includes 2 minority (both Black or African American, non-Hispanic/Latino), 1 international. Average age 31. 22 applicants, 77% accepted, 13 enrolled. In 2019, 8 master's awarded. *Entrance requirements:* For master's, minimum GPA of 3.0. Additional exam requirements/recommendations for international students: required—TOEFL (minimum score 550 paper-based; 80 iBT). *Application deadline:* For fall admission, 5/1 priority date for domestic students, 3/1 priority date for international students; for spring admission, 10/1 priority date for domestic students, 9/1 priority date for international students. Applications are processed on a rolling basis. Application fee: $25 ($30 for international students). Electronic applications accepted. *Expenses:* Contact institution. *Financial support:* In 2019–20, 2 students received support. Career-related internships or fieldwork, Federal Work-Study, institutionally sponsored loans, scholarships/grants, tuition waivers (partial), and unspecified assistantships available. Support available to part-time students. Financial award application deadline: 5/1; financial award applicants required to submit FAFSA. *Unit head:* Dr. Sam Thangiah, Department Chair, 724-738-2141, Fax: 724-738-4513, E-mail: sam.thangiah@sru.edu. *Application contact:* Brandi Weber-Mortimer, Director of Graduate Admissions, 724-738-2051, Fax: 724-738-2146, E-mail: graduate.admissions@sru.edu.
Website: http://www.sru.edu/academics/colleges-and-departments/ches/departments/computer-science

Southern Illinois University Edwardsville, Graduate School, Program in Healthcare Informatics, Edwardsville, IL 62026. Offers MS. *Program availability:* Part-time, evening/weekend. *Degree requirements:* For master's, comprehensive exam. *Entrance requirements:* For master's, baccalaureate degree with minimum GPA of 2.75. Additional exam requirements/recommendations for international students: required—TOEFL (minimum score 550 paper-based; 79 iBT), IELTS (minimum score 6.5). Electronic applications accepted.

Southern New Hampshire University, School of Business, Manchester, NH 03106-1045. Offers accounting (MBA, Graduate Certificate); accounting finance (MS); accounting/auditing (MS); accounting/forensic accounting (MS); accounting/management accounting (MS); accounting/taxation (MS); applied economics (MS); athletic administration (MBA, Graduate Certificate); business administration (IMBA, Certificate), including business information systems (Certificate), human resource management (Certificate); business analytics (MBA); business intelligence (MBA); communication (MA), including new media and marketing, public relations; community economic development (MBA); criminal justice (MBA); data analytics (MS); economics (MBA); engineering management (MBA); entrepreneurship (MBA); finance (MBA, MS, Graduate Certificate); finance/corporate finance (MS); finance/investments (MS); forensic accounting (MBA); forensic accounting and fraud examination (Graduate Certificate); healthcare informatics (MBA); healthcare management (MBA); human resource management (MS); human resources (MBA); information technology (MS); information technology management (MBA); international business (PhD); Internet marketing (MBA); leadership (MBA); leadership of nonprofit organizations (Graduate Certificate); management (MS); marketing (MBA, MS, Graduate Certificate); music business (MBA); operations and project management (MS); operations and supply chain management (MBA, Graduate Certificate); organizational leadership (MS); project management (MBA, Graduate Certificate); public administration (MBA, Graduate Certificate); quantitative analysis (MBA); Six Sigma (Graduate Certificate); Six Sigma quality (MBA); social media marketing (MBA, Graduate Certificate); sport management (MBA, MS, Graduate Certificate); sustainability and environmental compliance (MBA); MBA/Certificate. *Accreditation:* ACBSP. *Program availability:* Part-time, evening/weekend, online learning. Terminal master's awarded for partial completion of doctoral program. *Degree requirements:* For master's, one foreign language, comprehensive exam (for some programs), thesis or alternative; for doctorate, one foreign language, comprehensive exam, thesis/dissertation. *Entrance requirements:* For master's, minimum GPA of 2.5; for doctorate, GMAT. Additional exam requirements/recommendations for international students: required—TOEFL (minimum score 500 paper-based). Electronic applications accepted.

State University of New York at Oswego, Graduate Studies, Program in Biomedical and Health Informatics, Oswego, NY 13126. Offers health informatics professional (MS); health informatics: intelligent health systems (MS); health information management: health data science (MS). *Program availability:* Online learning. *Students:* 49. In 2019, 3 master's awarded. *Entrance requirements:* For master's, GRE (recommended), official transcripts, statement of purpose, resume, two letters of recommendation. Additional exam requirements/recommendations for international students: required—TOEFL. *Application deadline:* Applications are processed on a rolling basis. Application fee: $65. Electronic applications accepted. *Financial support:* Fellowships, research assistantships, teaching assistantships, institutionally sponsored loans, scholarships/grants, and unspecified assistantships available. Financial award applicants required to submit FAFSA. *Unit head:* Dr. Isabelle Bichindaritz, Director, 315-312-3152, E-mail: ibichind@oswego.edu. *Application contact:* Dr. Isabelle Bichindaritz, Director, 315-312-3152, E-mail: ibichind@oswego.edu.
Website: http://oswego.edu/bhi

Stephens College, Division of Graduate and Continuing Studies, Columbia, MO 65215-0002. Offers counseling (M Ed), including addictions counseling, clinical mental health counseling, school counseling; health information administration (Postbaccalaureate Certificate); physician assistant studies (MPAS); TV and screenwriting (MFA). *Program availability:* Part-time, evening/weekend, online learning. *Entrance requirements:* For master's, minimum GPA of 3.0 in last 60 hours. Additional exam requirements/recommendations for international students: required—TOEFL (minimum score 79 iBT). Electronic applications accepted.

Stony Brook University, State University of New York, Stony Brook Medicine, School of Health Technology and Management, Stony Brook, NY 11794. Offers applied health informatics (MS); disability studies (Certificate); health administration (MHA); health and rehabilitation sciences (PhD); health care management (Advanced Certificate); health care policy and management (MS); occupational therapy (MS); physical therapy (DPT); physician assistant (MS). *Accreditation:* AOTA; APTA. *Faculty:* 53 full-time (37 women), 54 part-time/adjunct (34 women). *Students:* 605 full-time (417 women), 65 part-time (43 women); includes 225 minority (28 Black or African American, non-Hispanic/Latino; 110 Asian, non-Hispanic/Latino; 73 Hispanic/Latino; 1 Native Hawaiian or other Pacific Islander, non-Hispanic/Latino; 13 Two or more races, non-Hispanic/Latino), 9 international. Average age 26. 1,816 applicants, 21% accepted, 293 enrolled. In 2019, 152 master's, 86 doctorates, 21 other advanced degrees awarded. *Entrance requirements:* For master's, GRE General Test, minimum GPA of 3.0, work experience in field, references; for doctorate, GRE, three references, essay. Additional exam requirements/recommendations for international students: required—TOEFL (minimum score 550 paper-based). *Application deadline:* For fall admission, 1/15 for domestic students; for spring admission, 10/1 for domestic students. Application fee: $100. *Expenses:* Contact institution. *Financial support:* Fellowships, research assistantships, teaching assistantships, career-related internships or fieldwork, Federal Work-Study,

and institutionally sponsored loans available. Financial award application deadline: 3/15. *Unit head:* Dr. Stacy Jafee Gropack, Dean and Professor, 631-444-2252, Fax: 631-444-7621, E-mail: stacy.jaffeegropack@stonybrook.edu. *Application contact:* Jessica M Rotolo, Executive Assistant to the Dean, 631-444-2252, Fax: 631-444-7621, E-mail: jessica.rotolo@stonybrook.edu.
Website: http://healthtechnology.stonybrookmedicine.edu/

Temple University, College of Public Health, Department of Health Services Administration and Policy, Philadelphia, PA 19122-6096. Offers health informatics (MS); health policy (PhD); health policy and management (MPH). *Program availability:* Part-time, evening/weekend, online learning. *Faculty:* 8 full-time (5 women), 3 part-time/adjunct (all women). *Students:* 28 full-time (21 women), 72 part-time (58 women); includes 48 minority (21 Black or African American, non-Hispanic/Latino; 14 Asian, non-Hispanic/Latino; 12 Hispanic/Latino; 1 Two or more races, non-Hispanic/Latino), 8 international. 173 applicants, 71% accepted, 55 enrolled. In 2019, 18 master's awarded. *Degree requirements:* For doctorate, comprehensive exam, thesis/dissertation, area paper, oral presentation, article critique. *Entrance requirements:* For master's, GRE, 3 letters of reference, statement of goals, resume, clearances for clinical/field education (M.P.H. only); for doctorate, GRE, 3 letters of reference, statement of goals, resume, writing sample. Additional exam requirements/recommendations for international students: required—TOEFL (minimum score 79 iBT), IELTS (minimum score 6.5), PTE (minimum score 53), one of three is required. Application fee: $60. Electronic applications accepted. *Expenses:* Contact institution. *Financial support:* Fellowships, research assistantships, teaching assistantships, Federal Work-Study, scholarships/grants, and health care benefits available. Financial award applicants required to submit FAFSA. *Unit head:* Stephen Lepore, Interim Department Chair, 215-204-9422, E-mail: slepore@temple.edu. *Application contact:* Annemarie Szambelak, Assistant Director of Admissions, 215-204-4526, E-mail: aszambelak@temple.edu.
Website: https://cph.temple.edu/healthadminpolicy/

Texas State University, The Graduate College, College of Health Professions, Program in Health Information Management, San Marcos, TX 78666. Offers MHIIM. *Program availability:* Part-time, evening/weekend. *Degree requirements:* For master's, comprehensive exam, thesis optional, committee review. *Entrance requirements:* For master's, baccalaureate degree from regionally-accredited institution with minimum GPA of 2.75 on last 60 hours of undergraduate work, 3 letters of reference, written statement of purpose, current resume, background course work in statistics and computer information systems. Additional exam requirements/recommendations for international students: required—TOEFL (minimum score 550 paper-based; 78 iBT), IELTS (minimum score 6). Electronic applications accepted.

Trident University International, College of Health Sciences, Program in Health Sciences, Cypress, CA 90630. Offers clinical research administration (MS, Certificate); emergency and disaster management (MS, Certificate); environmental health science (Certificate); health care administration (PhD); health care management (MS), including health informatics; health education (MS, Certificate); health informatics (Certificate); health sciences (PhD); international health (MS); international health: educator or researcher option (PhD); international health: practitioner option (PhD); law and expert witness studies (MS, Certificate); public health (MS); quality assurance (Certificate). *Program availability:* Part-time, evening/weekend, online learning. *Degree requirements:* For doctorate, comprehensive exam, thesis/dissertation, defense of dissertation. *Entrance requirements:* For master's, minimum GPA of 2.5 (students with GPA 3.0 or greater may transfer up to 30% of graduate level credits); for doctorate, minimum GPA of 3.4, curriculum vitae, course work in research methods or statistics. Additional exam requirements/recommendations for international students: required—TOEFL. Electronic applications accepted.

The University of Alabama at Birmingham, School of Health Professions, Graduate Programs in Health Informatics, Birmingham, AL 35294. Offers data analytics user experience (MSHI). *Program availability:* Fall and Spring Residential Visit. *Faculty:* 7 full-time (5 women), 3 part-time/adjunct (1 woman). *Students:* 48 full-time (22 women); includes 22 minority (16 Black or African American, non-Hispanic/Latino; 6 Asian, non-Hispanic/Latino). Average age 32. 52 applicants, 63% accepted, 30 enrolled. In 2019, 30 master's awarded. *Degree requirements:* For master's, Applied capstone project. *Entrance requirements:* For master's, minimum undergraduate GPA of 3.0, letters of recommendation, interview. Additional exam requirements/recommendations for international students: required—TOEFL, IELTS. *Application deadline:* For fall admission, 5/31 for domestic students. Application fee: $45 ($60 for international students). Electronic applications accepted. *Financial support:* Career-related internships or fieldwork, Federal Work-Study, and Employee tuition assistance available. Financial award applicants required to submit FAFSA. *Unit head:* Dr. Sue S Feldman, Program Director, 205-9750809. *Application contact:* Misty Altiparmak, Director of Operations, 205-934-3509, E-mail: maltima@uab.edu.
Website: http://www.uab.edu/hi

University of Central Florida, College of Community Innovation and Education, Department of Health Management and Informatics, Orlando, FL 32816. Offers health administration (MHA); health care informatics (MS); health information administration (Certificate). *Accreditation:* CAHME. *Program availability:* Part-time, evening/weekend. *Students:* 169 full-time (106 women), 233 part-time (159 women); includes 247 minority (87 Black or African American, non-Hispanic/Latino; 61 Asian, non-Hispanic/Latino; 82 Hispanic/Latino; 17 Two or more races, non-Hispanic/Latino), 4 international. Average age 30. 316 applicants, 80% accepted, 165 enrolled. In 2019, 135 master's awarded. *Degree requirements:* For master's, comprehensive exam, thesis or alternative, research report. *Entrance requirements:* For master's, letters of recommendation, resume, goal statement. Additional exam requirements/recommendations for international students: required—TOEFL. *Application deadline:* For fall admission, 7/15 for domestic students; for spring admission, 12/1 for domestic students. Application fee: $30. Electronic applications accepted. *Financial support:* In 2019–20, 3 students received support, including 1 fellowship (averaging $10,000 per year), 1 research assistantship with partial tuition reimbursement available (averaging $4,704 per year), 1 teaching assistantship (averaging $9,074 per year); career-related internships or fieldwork, Federal Work-Study, institutionally sponsored loans, and unspecified assistantships also available. Financial award application deadline: 3/1; financial award applicants required to submit FAFSA. *Unit head:* Dr. Reid Oetjen, Interim Chair, 407-823-5668, E-mail: reid.oetjen@ucf.edu. *Application contact:* Associate Director, Graduate Admissions, 407-823-2766, Fax: 407-823-6442, E-mail: gradadmissions@ucf.edu.
Website: https://www.cohpa.ucf.edu/hmi/

University of Cincinnati, Graduate School, College of Allied Health Sciences, Department of Clinical and Health Information Sciences, Cincinnati, OH 45221. Offers health informatics (MHI). *Program availability:* Part-time, online learning.

University of Colorado Denver, Business School, Program in Information Systems, Denver, CO 80217. Offers accounting and information systems audit and control (MS); business intelligence systems (MS); digital health entrepreneurship (MS); enterprise risk management (MS); enterprise technology management (MS); geographic information systems (MS); health information technology (MS); technology innovation and entrepreneurship (MS); Web and mobile computing (MS). *Program availability:* Part-time, evening/weekend, online learning. *Degree requirements:* For master's, 30 credit hours. *Entrance requirements:* For master's, GMAT, resume, essay, two letters of recommendation, financial statements (for international applicants). Additional exam requirements/recommendations for international students: required—TOEFL (minimum score 525 paper-based; 71 iBT); recommended—IELTS (minimum score 6.5). Electronic applications accepted. *Expenses:* Contact institution.

The University of Findlay, Office of Graduate Admissions, Findlay, OH 45840. Offers applied security and analytics (MSAS); athletic training (MAT); business (MBA), including certified management accountant, certified public accountant, health care management, hospitality management; education (MA Ed, Ed D), including children's literature (MA Ed), curriculum and teaching (MA Ed), education (MA Ed), educational administration (MA Ed), human resource development (MA Ed), mathematics (MA Ed), reading (MA Ed), science education (MA Ed), superintendent (Ed D), teaching (Ed D), technology (MA Ed); environmental, safety, and health management (MSEM); health informatics (MS); occupational therapy (MOT); pharmacy (Pharm D); physical therapy (DPT); physician assistant (MPA); rhetoric and writing (MA); teaching English to speakers of other languages (TESOL) and applied linguistics (MA). *Program availability:* Part-time, evening/weekend, 100% online, blended/hybrid learning. *Students:* 688 full-time (430 women), 553 part-time (308 women), 170 international. Average age 28. 865 applicants, 31% accepted, 235 enrolled. In 2019, 363 master's, 141 doctorates awarded. *Degree requirements:* For master's, comprehensive exam (for some programs), thesis (for some programs), cumulative project, capstone project; for doctorate, thesis/dissertation (for some programs). *Entrance requirements:* For master's, GRE/GMAT, bachelor's degree from accredited institution, minimum undergraduate GPA of 2.5 in last 64 hours of course work; for doctorate, GRE, MAT, minimum cumulative GPA of 3.0. Additional exam requirements/recommendations for international students: required—TOEFL (minimum score 79 iBT), IELTS (minimum score 7), PTE (minimum score 61). *Application deadline:* Applications are processed on a rolling basis. Electronic applications accepted. *Financial support:* In 2019–20, 10 research assistantships with partial tuition reimbursements (averaging $7,200 per year), 35 teaching assistantships with partial tuition reimbursements (averaging $7,200 per year) were awarded; Federal Work-Study, institutionally sponsored loans, and unspecified assistantships also available. Financial award applicants required to submit FAFSA. *Unit head:* Dave M. Emsweller, Director of Admissions, Interim, 419-434-4578, E-mail: emsweller@findlay.edu. *Application contact:* Amber Feehan, Graduate Admissions Counselor, 419-434-6933, Fax: 419-434-4898, E-mail: feehan@findlay.edu.
Website: http://www.findlay.edu/admissions/graduate/Pages/default.aspx

University of Illinois at Chicago, College of Applied Health Sciences, Program in Health Informatics, Chicago, IL 60607-7128. Offers health informatics (MS, CAS); health information management (Certificate). *Program availability:* Part-time, online learning. *Expenses:* Contact institution.

University of Illinois at Urbana-Champaign, Graduate College, School of Information Sciences, Champaign, IL 61820. Offers bioinformatics (MS); digital libraries (CAS); information management (MS); library and information science (MS, PhD, CAS). *Accreditation:* ALA (one or more programs are accredited). *Program availability:* Part-time, online learning. *Entrance requirements:* For degree, master's degree in library and information science or related field with minimum GPA of 3.0.

The University of Iowa, Graduate College, Program in Informatics, Iowa City, IA 52242-1316. Offers bioinformatics (MS, PhD); bioinformatics and computational biology (Certificate); geoinformatics (MS, PhD, Certificate); health informatics (MS, PhD, Certificate); information science (MS, PhD, Certificate). *Degree requirements:* For master's, thesis optional; for doctorate, comprehensive exam, thesis/dissertation. *Entrance requirements:* For master's and doctorate, GRE General Test, minimum GPA of 3.0. Additional exam requirements/recommendations for international students: required—TOEFL (minimum score 550 paper-based; 81 iBT). Electronic applications accepted.

The University of Kansas, University of Kansas Medical Center, Interprofessional Program in Health Informatics, Kansas City, KS 66045. Offers MS, Post Master's Certificate. *Program availability:* Part-time, evening/weekend, 100% online, blended/hybrid learning. *Faculty:* 4 full-time. *Students:* 11 part-time (5 women); includes 5 minority (2 Black or African American, non-Hispanic/Latino; 1 Asian, non-Hispanic/Latino; 1 Hispanic/Latino; 1 Two or more races, non-Hispanic/Latino), 1 international. Average age 36. In 2019, 1 other advanced degree awarded. *Degree requirements:* For master's, comprehensive exam, research paper, minimum GPA of 3.0; for Post Master's Certificate, minimum GPA of 3.0. *Entrance requirements:* For master's, minimum GPA of 3.0, official copies of transcripts, 3 references, resume, personal statement; for Post Master's Certificate, minimum cumulative GPA of 3.0, official copies of transcripts, 3 references, resume, personal statement. Additional exam requirements/recommendations for international students: required—TOEFL or IELTS. *Application deadline:* For fall admission, 4/1 for domestic and international students; for spring admission, 9/1 for domestic and international students. Application fee: $60. Electronic applications accepted. *Expenses:* Tuition, state resident: full-time $9989. Tuition, nonresident: full-time $23,950. *International tuition:* $23,950 full-time. *Required fees:* $984; $81.99 per credit hour. Tuition and fees vary according to course load, campus/location and program. *Financial support:* Application deadline: 3/1; applicants required to submit FAFSA. *Unit head:* Dr. E. LaVerne Manos, Director, Center for Interprofessional Health Informatics, 913-588-1671, Fax: 913-588-1660, E-mail: lmanos@kumc.edu. *Application contact:* Teresa Stenner, Program Manager, 913-588-3362, Fax: 913-588-1660, E-mail: healthinformatics@kumc.edu.
Website: http://www.kumc.edu/health-informatics.html

University of Lynchburg, Graduate Studies, Program in Health Informatics Management, Lynchburg, VA 24501-3199. Offers Certificate. *Program availability:* Part-time. *Entrance requirements:* For degree, official transcripts from each college attended indicating all college coursework completed. Additional exam requirements/recommendations for international students: required—TOEFL (minimum score 550 paper-based; 80 iBT), IELTS (minimum score 6). Electronic applications accepted. Application fee is waived when completed online. *Expenses:* Contact institution.

University of Maryland, Baltimore County, The Graduate School, College of Engineering and Information Technology, Department of Information Systems, Program in Health Information Technology, Baltimore, MD 21250. Offers MPS. *Program availability:* Part-time. *Students:* 18 full-time (14 women), 36 part-time (28 women); includes 33 minority (12 Black or African American, non-Hispanic/Latino; 21 Asian, non-Hispanic/Latino), 8 international. Average age 30. 36 applicants, 83% accepted, 18 enrolled. In 2019, 21 master's awarded. *Entrance requirements:* For master's, minimum undergraduate GPA of 3.0. Additional exam requirements/recommendations for international students: required—TOEFL (minimum score 550 paper-based; 80 iBT), GRE. *Application deadline:* For fall admission, 8/1 for domestic and international students; for spring admission, 11/1 for domestic and international students. Applications are processed on a rolling basis. Application fee: $70. Electronic applications accepted. *Expenses:* $14,382 per year. *Financial support:* In 2019–20, 1 student received support, including 1 research assistantship (averaging $18,000 per year), teaching assistantships (averaging $18,000 per year); fellowships, career-related internships or fieldwork, Federal Work-Study, health care benefits, and unspecified assistantships also available. Support available to part-time students. Financial award application deadline: 6/30; financial award applicants required to submit FAFSA. *Unit head:* Dr. Vandana Janejq, Professor and Chair, 410-455-6238, Fax: 410-455-1217, E-mail: vjaneja@umbc.edu. *Application contact:* Dr. Vandana Janejq, Professor and Chair, 410-455-6238, Fax: 410-455-1217, E-mail: vjaneja@umbc.edu. Website: http://healthtech.umbc.edu/

University of Maryland Global Campus, University of Maryland Global Campus, Health Informatics Administration, Adelphi, MD 20783. Offers MS. *Program availability:* Part-time, evening/weekend, online learning. *Students:* 5 full-time (all women), 415 part-time (296 women); includes 288 minority (204 Black or African American, non-Hispanic/Latino; 1 American Indian or Alaska Native, non-Hispanic/Latino; 46 Asian, non-Hispanic/Latino; 27 Hispanic/Latino; 1 Native Hawaiian or other Pacific Islander, non-Hispanic/Latino; 9 Two or more races, non-Hispanic/Latino, 13 international. Average age 36. 172 applicants, 100% accepted, 75 enrolled. In 2019, 103 master's awarded. *Degree requirements:* For master's, thesis or alternative, capstone course. *Application deadline:* Applications are processed on a rolling basis. Application fee: $50. Electronic applications accepted. *Financial support:* Scholarships/grants available. Support available to part-time students. Financial award application deadline: 6/1; financial award applicants required to submit FAFSA. *Unit head:* Liliya Roberts, Program Director, 240-684-2400, E-mail: Liliya.Roberts@umgc.edu. *Application contact:* Admissions, 800-888-8682, E-mail: studentsfirst@umuc.edu. Website: https://www.umgc.edu/academic-programs/masters-degrees/health-informatics-administration.cfm

University of Michigan, School of Information, Ann Arbor, MI 48109-1285. Offers health informatics (MHI); information (MSI, PhD). *Accreditation:* ALA (one or more programs are accredited). *Program availability:* Part-time. Terminal master's awarded for partial completion of doctoral program. *Degree requirements:* For master's, thesis optional, internship; for doctorate, thesis/dissertation. *Entrance requirements:* For master's and doctorate, GRE General Test. Additional exam requirements/recommendations for international students: required—TOEFL (minimum score 100 iBT). Electronic applications accepted. *Expenses:* Contact institution.

University of Michigan–Dearborn, College of Education, Health, and Human Services, Master of Science Program in Health Information Technology, Dearborn, MI 48128. Offers MS. *Program availability:* Part-time, evening/weekend. *Faculty:* 2 part-time/adjunct (both women). *Students:* 4 full-time (all women), 23 part-time (18 women); includes 8 minority (3 Black or African American, non-Hispanic/Latino; 3 Asian, non-Hispanic/Latino; 1 Hispanic/Latino; 1 Two or more races, non-Hispanic/Latino), 5 international. Average age 32. 21 applicants, 71% accepted, 10 enrolled. In 2019, 8 master's awarded. *Entrance requirements:* Additional exam requirements/recommendations for international students: required—TOEFL (minimum score 560 paper-based; 84 iBT), IELTS (minimum score 6.5). *Application deadline:* For fall admission, 3/15 for domestic and international students. Application fee: $60. Electronic applications accepted. *Financial support:* Career-related internships or fieldwork and scholarships/grants available. Financial award application deadline: 3/1; financial award applicants required to submit FAFSA. *Unit head:* Dr. Paul Fossum, Director, Master's Programs, 313-593-0982, E-mail: pfossum@umich.edu. *Application contact:* Office of Graduate Studies, 313-583-6321, E-mail: umd-graduatestudies@umich.edu. Website: http://umdearborn.edu/cehhs/cehhs_m_hit/

University of Michigan–Flint, College of Arts and Sciences, Program in Computer Science and Information Systems, Flint, MI 48502-1950. Offers computer science (MS); information systems (MS), including business information systems, health information systems. *Program availability:* Part-time, evening/weekend, 100% online. *Faculty:* 13 full-time (4 women), 9 part-time/adjunct (3 women). *Students:* 29 full-time (13 women), 49 part-time (11 women); includes 13 minority (5 Black or African American, non-Hispanic/Latino; 1 American Indian or Alaska Native, non-Hispanic/Latino; 2 Asian, non-Hispanic/Latino; 4 Hispanic/Latino; 1 Two or more races, non-Hispanic/Latino), 27 international. Average age 31. 196 applicants, 59% accepted, 15 enrolled. In 2019, 29 master's awarded. *Degree requirements:* For master's, thesis optional, Non Thesis option available. *Entrance requirements:* For master's, BS from regionally-accredited institution in computer science, computer information systems, or computer engineering (preferred); minimum overall undergraduate GPA of 3.0. Additional exam requirements/recommendations for international students: required—TOEFL (minimum score 84 iBT), IELTS (minimum score 6.5). *Application deadline:* For fall admission, 8/1 for domestic students, 5/1 for international students; for winter admission, 11/15 for domestic students, 10/1 for international students; for spring admission, 3/15 for domestic students, 1/1 for international students; for summer admission, 5/15 for domestic students. Applications are processed on a rolling basis. Application fee: $55. Electronic applications accepted. *Expenses:* Contact institution. *Financial support:* Federal Work-Study, scholarships/grants, and unspecified assistantships available. Financial award application deadline: 3/1; financial award applicants required to submit FAFSA. *Unit head:* Dr. Mark Allison, Department Chair, 810-424-5509, Fax: 810-766-6780, E-mail: markalli@umich.edu. *Application contact:* Matt Bohlen, Associate Director of Graduate Programs, 810-762-3171, Fax: 810-766-6789, E-mail: mbohlen@umflint.edu. Website: http://www.umflint.edu/graduateprograms/computer-science-information-systems-ms

University of Minnesota, Twin Cities Campus, Graduate School, Program in Health Informatics, Minneapolis, MN 55455-0213. Offers MHI, MS, PhD, MD/MHI. *Program availability:* Part-time. *Degree requirements:* For master's, thesis or alternative; for doctorate, thesis/dissertation. *Entrance requirements:* For master's and doctorate, GRE General Test, previous course work in life sciences, programming, calculus. Additional exam requirements/recommendations for international students: required—TOEFL (minimum score 550 paper-based). Electronic applications accepted.

University of Missouri, School of Medicine and Office of Research and Graduate Studies, Graduate Programs in Medicine, Department of Health Management and Informatics, Columbia, MO 65211. Offers health administration (MHA); health informatics (MS, Certificate). *Accreditation:* CAHME. *Program availability:* Part-time. *Entrance requirements:* For master's, GRE General Test or GMAT, minimum GPA of 3.0. Additional exam requirements/recommendations for international students: required—TOEFL (minimum score 550 paper-based; 80 iBT), IELTS (minimum score 6.5). Electronic applications accepted.

University of New England, College of Graduate and Professional Studies, Portland, ME 04005-9526. Offers advanced educational leadership (CAGS); applied nutrition (MS); career and technical education (MS Ed); curriculum and instruction (MS Ed); education (CAGS, Post-Master's Certificate); educational leadership (MS Ed, Ed D); generalist (MS Ed); health informatics (MS, Graduate Certificate); inclusion education (MS Ed); literacy K-12 (MS Ed); medical education leadership (MMEL); public health (MPH, Graduate Certificate); reading specialist (MS Ed); social work (MSW). *Program availability:* Part-time, evening/weekend, online only, 100% online. *Faculty:* 2 full-time (1 woman), 63 part-time/adjunct (44 women). *Students:* 1,001 full-time (795 women), 470 part-time (378 women); includes 306 minority (211 Black or African American, non-Hispanic/Latino; 12 American Indian or Alaska Native, non-Hispanic/Latino; 61 Asian, non-Hispanic/Latino; 14 Hispanic/Latino; 4 Native Hawaiian or other Pacific Islander, non-Hispanic/Latino; 4 Two or more races, non-Hispanic/Latino). Average age 36. In

2019, 614 master's, 85 doctorates, 79 other advanced degrees awarded. *Application deadline:* Applications are processed on a rolling basis. Electronic applications accepted. *Financial support:* Application deadline: 5/1; applicants required to submit FAFSA. *Unit head:* Dr. Martha Wilson, Dean of the College of Graduate and Professional Studies, 207-221-4985, E-mail: mwilson13@une.edu. *Application contact:* Nicole Lindsay, Director of Online Admissions, 207-221-4966, E-mail: nlindsay1@une.edu. Website: http://online.une.edu

University of Phoenix–Online Campus, College of Health Sciences and Nursing, Phoenix, AZ 85034-7209. Offers family nurse practitioner (Certificate); health care (Certificate); health care education (Certificate); health care informatics (Certificate); informatics (MSN); nursing (MSN); nursing and health care education (MSN); MSN/MBA; MSN/MHA. *Accreditation:* AACN. *Program availability:* Evening/weekend, online learning. *Entrance requirements:* Additional exam requirements/recommendations for international students: required—TOEFL, TOEIC (Test of English as an International Communication), Berlitz Online English Proficiency Exam, PTE, or IELTS. Electronic applications accepted. *Expenses:* Contact institution.

University of Pittsburgh, School of Health and Rehabilitation Sciences, Department of Health Information Management, Pittsburgh, PA 15260. Offers health and rehabilitation sciences (MS), including health information systems, healthcare supervision and management. *Accreditation:* APTA. *Program availability:* Part-time, 100% online. *Faculty:* 7 full-time (4 women), 1 (woman) part-time/adjunct. *Students:* 17 full-time (9 women), 14 part-time (10 women); includes 7 minority (4 Black or African American, non-Hispanic/Latino; 1 Asian, non-Hispanic/Latino; 2 Hispanic/Latino), 8 international. Average age 29. 59 applicants, 78% accepted, 17 enrolled. In 2019, 17 master's awarded. *Entrance requirements:* Additional exam requirements/recommendations for international students: required—International applicants may provide Duolingo English Test, IELTS or TOEFL scores to verify English language proficiency. *Application deadline:* Applications are processed on a rolling basis. Application fee: $50. Electronic applications accepted. *Financial support:* In 2019–20, 3 students received support, including 3 research assistantships with full tuition reimbursements available (averaging $30,000 per year). *Unit head:* Dr. Bambang Parmanto, Professor and Chair, Department of Health Information Management, 412-383-6649, E-mail: parmanto@pitt.edu. *Application contact:* Jessica Maguire, Director of Admissions, 412-383-6557, Fax: 412-383-6535, E-mail: maguire@pitt.edu. Website: http://www.shrs.pitt.edu/him

University of Puerto Rico - Medical Sciences Campus, School of Health Professions, Program in Health Information Administration, San Juan, PR 00936-5067. Offers MS. *Program availability:* Part-time. *Degree requirements:* For master's, one foreign language, thesis or alternative, internship. *Entrance requirements:* For master's, EXADEP or GRE General Test, minimum GPA of 2.5, interview, fluency in Spanish.

University of St. Augustine for Health Sciences, Graduate Programs, Master of Health Science Program, San Marcos, CA 92069. Offers athletic training (MHS); executive leadership (MHS); informatics (MHS); teaching and learning (MHS). *Program availability:* Online learning. *Degree requirements:* For master's, comprehensive project.

University of San Diego, Hahn School of Nursing and Health Science, San Diego, CA 92110-2492. Offers adult-gerontology clinical nurse specialist (MSN); adult-gerontology nurse practitioner/family nurse practitioner (MSN); clinical nurse leader (MSN); executive nurse leader (MSN); family nurse practitioner (MSN); healthcare informatics (MS); master's entry program in clinical nursing (for non-rns) (MSN); nursing (PhD); nursing informatics (MSN); nursing practice (DNP); psychiatric-mental health nurse practitioner (MSN). *Accreditation:* AACN. *Program availability:* Part-time, evening/weekend. *Faculty:* 28 full-time (23 women), 43 part-time/adjunct (32 women). *Students:* 252 full-time (202 women), 288 part-time (227 women); includes 261 minority (53 Black or African American, non-Hispanic/Latino; 2 American Indian or Alaska Native, non-Hispanic/Latino; 106 Asian, non-Hispanic/Latino; 76 Hispanic/Latino; 24 Two or more races, non-Hispanic/Latino), 24 international. Average age 34. In 2019, 174 master's, 47 doctorates awarded. *Degree requirements:* For doctorate, thesis/dissertation (for some programs), residency (DNP). *Entrance requirements:* For master's, GRE General Test (for entry-level nursing), BSN, current California RN licensure (except for entry-level nursing), minimum GPA of 3.0; for doctorate, minimum GPA of 3.5, MSN, current California RN licensure. Additional exam requirements/recommendations for international students: required—TOEFL (minimum score 580 paper-based; 83 iBT), TWE. *Application deadline:* Applications are processed on a rolling basis. Application fee: $55. Electronic applications accepted. *Financial support:* In 2019–20, 284 students received support. Institutionally sponsored loans, scholarships/grants, and traineeships available. Support available to part-time students. Financial award application deadline: 4/1; financial award applicants required to submit FAFSA. *Unit head:* Dr. Jane Georges, Dean, Hahn School of Nursing and Health Science, 619-260-4550, Fax: 619-260-6814, E-mail: nursing@sandiego.edu. *Application contact:* Erika Garwood, Associate Director of Graduate Admissions, 619-260-4524, Fax: 619-260-4158, E-mail: grads@sandiego.edu. Website: http://www.sandiego.edu/nursing/

University of San Francisco, School of Nursing and Health Professions, Program in Health Informatics, San Francisco, CA 94117. Offers MS. *Program availability:* Part-time, evening/weekend. *Students:* 23 full-time (19 women), 13 part-time (8 women); includes 12 minority (1 Black or African American, non-Hispanic/Latino; 7 Asian, non-Hispanic/Latino; 3 Hispanic/Latino; 1 Two or more races, non-Hispanic/Latino), 16 international. Average age 30. 66 applicants, 58% accepted, 16 enrolled. In 2019, 24 master's awarded. *Entrance requirements:* Additional exam requirements/recommendations for international students: required—TOEFL (minimum score 600 paper-based; 90 iBT), IELTS, PTE (minimum score 68). *Application deadline:* For fall admission, 5/15 for domestic students; for spring admission, 11/15 for domestic students. Applications are processed on a rolling basis. Application fee: $55. Electronic applications accepted. *Financial support:* Scholarships/grants available. *Unit head:* Dr. Andrew Nguyen, Program Director, 415-422-6681, E-mail: nursing@usfca.edu. *Application contact:* Carolyn Arroyo, Graduate Enrollment Manager, 415-422-2807, E-mail: carroyo2@usfca.edu. Website: https://www.usfca.edu/nursing/programs/masters/health-informatics

University of South Carolina Upstate, Graduate Programs, Spartanburg, SC 29303-4999. Offers early childhood education (M Ed); elementary education (M Ed); informatics (MS); special education: visual impairment (M Ed). *Accreditation:* NCATE. *Program availability:* Part-time, evening/weekend. *Faculty:* 15 full-time (11 women), 6 part-time/adjunct (4 women). *Students:* 23 full-time (15 women), 432 part-time (375 women); includes 68 minority (42 Black or African American, non-Hispanic/Latino; 6 Asian, non-Hispanic/Latino; 12 Hispanic/Latino; 8 Two or more races, non-Hispanic/Latino), 3 international. Average age 24. In 2019, 11 master's awarded. *Degree requirements:* For master's, variable foreign language requirement, comprehensive exam (for some programs), thesis or alternative, professional portfolio. *Entrance requirements:* For master's, GRE General Test or MAT, interview, minimum undergraduate GPA of 2.5, teaching certificate, 2 letters of recommendation. *Application deadline:* Applications are processed on a rolling basis. Application fee: $50. Electronic applications accepted. *Expenses:* Tuition, area resident: Full-time $6867; part-time

$572.25 per semester. Tuition, nonresident: full-time $14,880; part-time $1240 per semester hour. *Required fees:* $35; $35 per term. $25.50 per term. Tuition and fees vary according to course load and program. *Financial support:* Institutionally sponsored loans and institutional work-study available. Financial award application deadline: 7/15; financial award applicants required to submit FAFSA. *Unit head:* Dr. Tina Herzberg, Director of Graduate Programs, 864-503-5572, Fax: 864-503-5573, E-mail: therzberg@uscupstate.edu. *Application contact:* Donette Stewart, Associate Vice Chancellor for Enrollment Services, 864-503-5280, E-mail: dstewart@uscupstate.edu.
Website: http://www.uscupstate.edu/graduate/

University of South Florida, Innovative Education, Tampa, FL 33620-9951. Offers adult, career and higher education (Graduate Certificate), including college teaching, leadership in developing human resources, leadership in higher education; Africana studies (Graduate Certificate), including diasporas and health disparities, genocide and human rights; aging studies (Graduate Certificate), including gerontology; art research (Graduate Certificate), including museum studies; business foundations (Graduate Certificate); chemical and biomedical engineering (Graduate Certificate), including materials science and engineering, water, health and sustainability; child and family studies (Graduate Certificate), including positive behavior support; civil and industrial engineering (Graduate Certificate), including transportation systems analysis; community and family health (Graduate Certificate), including maternal and child health, social marketing and public health, violence and injury: prevention and intervention, women's health; criminology (Graduate Certificate), including criminal justice' administration; data science for public administration (Graduate Certificate); digital humanities (Graduate Certificate); educational measurement and research (Graduate Certificate), including evaluation; English (Graduate Certificate), including comparative literary studies, creative writing, professional and technical communication; entrepreneurship (Graduate Certificate); environmental health (Graduate Certificate), including safety management; epidemiology and biostatistics (Graduate Certificate), including applied biostatistics, biostatistics, concepts and tools of epidemiology, epidemiology, epidemiology of infectious diseases; geography, environment and planning (Graduate Certificate), including community development, environmental policy and management, geographical information systems; geology (Graduate Certificate), including hydrogeology; global health (Graduate Certificate), including disaster management, global health and Latin American and Caribbean studies, global health practice, humanitarian assistance, infection control; government and international affairs (Graduate Certificate), including Cuban studies, globalization studies; health policy and management (Graduate Certificate), including health management and leadership, public health policy and programs; hearing specialist: early intervention (Graduate Certificate); industrial and management systems engineering (Graduate Certificate), including systems engineering, technology management; information studies (Graduate Certificate), including school library media specialist; information systems/decision sciences (Graduate Certificate), including analytics and business intelligence; instructional technology (Graduate Certificate), including distance education, Florida digital/virtual educator, instructional design, multimedia design, Web design; internal medicine, bioethics and medical humanities (Graduate Certificate), including biomedical ethics; Latin American and Caribbean studies (Graduate Certificate); leadership for coastal resiliency planning (Graduate Certificate); mass communications (Graduate Certificate), including multimedia journalism; mathematics and statistics (Graduate Certificate), including mathematics; medicine (Graduate Certificate), including aging and neuroscience, bioinformatics, biotechnology, brain fitness and memory management, clinical investigation, hand and upper limb rehabilitation, health informatics, health sciences, integrative weight management, intellectual property, medicine and gender, metabolic and nutritional medicine, metabolic cardiology, pharmacy sciences; national and competitive intelligence (Graduate Certificate); nursing (Graduate Certificate), including simulation based academic fellowship in advanced pain management; psychological and social foundations (Graduate Certificate), including career counseling, college teaching, diversity in education, mental health counseling, school counseling; public affairs (Graduate Certificate), including nonprofit management, public management, research administration; public health (Graduate Certificate), including assessing chemical toxicity and public health risks, health equity, pharmacoepidemiology, public health generalist, toxicology, translational research in adolescent behavioral health; public health practices (Graduate Certificate), including planning for healthy communities; rehabilitation and mental health counseling (Graduate Certificate), including integrative mental health care, marriage and family therapy, rehabilitation technology; secondary education (Graduate Certificate), including ESOL, foreign language education: culture and content, foreign language education: professional; social work (Graduate Certificate), including geriatric social work/clinical gerontology; special education (Graduate Certificate), including autism spectrum disorder, disabilities education: severe/profound; world languages (Graduate Certificate), including teaching English as a second language (TESL) or foreign language. *Unit head:* Dr. Cynthia DeLuca, Associate Vice President and Assistant Vice Provost, 813-974-3077, Fax: 813-974-7061, E-mail: deluca@usf.edu. *Application contact:* Owen Hooper, Director, Summer and Alternative Calendar Programs, 813-974-6917, E-mail: hooper@usf.edu.
Website: http://www.usf.edu/innovative-education/

The University of Tennessee Health Science Center, College of Health Professions, Memphis, TN 38163-0002. Offers audiology (MS, Au D); clinical laboratory science (MSCLS); cytopathology practice (MCP); health informatics and information management (MHIIM); occupational therapy (MOT); physical therapy (DPT, ScDPT); physician assistant (MMS); speech-language pathology (MS). *Accreditation:* AOTA; APTA. *Program availability:* Part-time, evening/weekend, online learning. Terminal master's awarded for partial completion of doctoral program. *Degree requirements:* For master's, comprehensive exam, thesis; for doctorate, comprehensive exam, residency. *Entrance requirements:* For master's, GRE (MOT, MSCLS), minimum GPA of 3.0, 3 letters of reference, national accreditation (MSCLS), GRE if GPA is less than 3.0 (MCP); for doctorate, GRE. Additional exam requirements/recommendations for international students: required—TOEFL (minimum score 550 paper-based; 80 iBT). Electronic applications accepted. *Expenses:* Contact institution.

The University of Texas Health Science Center at Houston, School of Public Health, Houston, TX 77030. Offers behavioral science (PhD); biostatistics (MPH, MS, PhD); environmental health (MPH); epidemiology (MPH, MS, PhD); general public health (Certificate); genomics and bioinformatics (Certificate); health disparities (Certificate); health promotion/health education (MPH, Dr PH); healthcare management (Certificate); management, policy and community health (MPH, Dr PH, PhD); maternal and child health (Certificate); public health informatics (Certificate); DDS/MPH; JD/MPH; MBA/MPH; MD/MPH; MGPS/MPH; MP Aff/MPH; MS/MPH; MSN/MPH; MSW/MPH; PhD/MPH. *Accreditation:* CAHME; CEPH. *Program availability:* Part-time. *Degree requirements:* For master's, thesis (for some programs); for doctorate, comprehensive exam, thesis/dissertation. *Entrance requirements:* For master's and doctorate, GRE General Test. Additional exam requirements/recommendations for international students: required—TOEFL (minimum score 600 paper-based, 100 iBT) or IELTS (7.5). Electronic applications accepted. *Expenses:* Contact institution.

University of Toronto, Faculty of Medicine, Institute of Health Policy, Management and Evaluation, Program in Health Informatics, Toronto, ON M5S 1A1, Canada. Offers MHI.

Entrance requirements: For master's, minimum B average in last academic year. Additional exam requirements/recommendations for international students: required—TOEFL (minimum score 580 paper-based; 93 iBT), TWE (minimum score 5). Electronic applications accepted.

University of Victoria, Faculty of Graduate Studies, Faculty of Human and Social Development, School of Health Information Science, Victoria, BC V8W 2Y2, Canada. Offers M Sc. *Degree requirements:* For master's, thesis or research project. *Entrance requirements:* Additional exam requirements/recommendations for international students: required—TOEFL (minimum score 575 paper-based).

University of Virginia, School of Medicine, Department of Public Health Sciences, Program in Clinical Research, Charlottesville, VA 22903. Offers clinical investigation and patient-oriented research (MS); informatics in medicine (MS). *Program availability:* Part-time. *Degree requirements:* For master's, thesis (for some programs). *Entrance requirements:* For master's, 2 letters of recommendation. Additional exam requirements/recommendations for international students: required—TOEFL (minimum score 600 paper-based; 90 iBT). Electronic applications accepted.

University of Washington, Graduate School, School of Medicine, Graduate Programs in Medicine, Department of Medical Education and Biomedical Informatics, Division of Biomedical and Health Informatics, Seattle, WA 98195. Offers MS, PhD. *Entrance requirements:* For master's and doctorate, GRE General Test, minimum GPA of 3.0; previous undergraduate course work in biology, computer programming, and mathematics. Additional exam requirements/recommendations for international students: required—TOEFL (minimum score 580 paper-based; 70 iBT). Electronic applications accepted.

University of Washington, Graduate School, School of Public Health, Program in Health Informatics and Health Information Management, Seattle, WA 98195. Offers MHIHIM. *Students:* 30 part-time (20 women); includes 24 minority (8 Black or African American, non-Hispanic/Latino; 1 American Indian or Alaska Native, non-Hispanic/Latino; 13 Asian, non-Hispanic/Latino; 2 Hispanic/Latino). Average age 32. 24 applicants, 83% accepted, 20 enrolled. In 2019, 18 master's awarded. *Degree requirements:* For master's, capstone project. Electronic applications accepted. *Expenses:* $48,330. *Financial support:* Applicants required to submit FAFSA.
Website: http://www.health-informatics.uw.edu/

University of Waterloo, Graduate Studies and Postdoctoral Affairs, Faculty of Applied Health Sciences, School of Public Health and Health Systems, Waterloo, ON N2L 3G1, Canada. Offers health evaluation (MHE); health informatics (MHI); health studies and gerontology (M Sc, PhD); public health (MPH). *Program availability:* Part-time. *Degree requirements:* For master's, thesis; for doctorate, comprehensive exam, thesis/dissertation. *Entrance requirements:* For master's, honors degree, minimum B average, resume, writing sample; for doctorate, GRE (recommended), master's degree, minimum B average, resume, writing sample. Additional exam requirements/recommendations for international students: required—TOEFL, IELTS, PTE. Electronic applications accepted.

University of Wisconsin–Milwaukee, Graduate School, College of Engineering and Applied Science, Biomedical and Health Informatics Program, Milwaukee, WI 53201-0413. Offers health information systems (PhD); health services management and policy (PhD); knowledge based systems (PhD); medical imaging and instrumentation (PhD); public health informatics (PhD). *Degree requirements:* For doctorate, comprehensive exam, thesis/dissertation. *Entrance requirements:* For doctorate, GRE, GMAT or MCAT. Additional exam requirements/recommendations for international students: required—TOEFL (minimum score 600 paper-based; 79 iBT), IELTS (minimum score 6.5). Electronic applications accepted.

University of Wisconsin–Milwaukee, Graduate School, College of Health Sciences, Department of Health Informatics and Administration, Milwaukee, WI 53201-0413. Offers health care informatics (MS); healthcare administration (MHA). *Degree requirements:* For master's, comprehensive exam, thesis optional. *Entrance requirements:* For master's, GRE General Test. Additional exam requirements/recommendations for international students: required—TOEFL (minimum score 550 paper-based; 79 iBT), IELTS (minimum score 6.5).

Virginia International University, School of Computer Information Systems, Fairfax, VA 22030. Offers business intelligence (Graduate Certificate); business intelligence and data analytics (MIS); computer science (MS), including computer animation and gaming, cybersecurity, data management networking, intelligent systems, software applications development, software engineering; cybersecurity (MIS); data management (MIS); enterprise project management (MIS); health informatics (MIS); information assurance (MIS); information systems (Graduate Certificate); information systems management (MS, Graduate Certificate); information technology (MS); information technology audit and compliance (Graduate Certificate); knowledge management (MIS); software engineering (MS). *Program availability:* Part-time, online learning. *Entrance requirements:* For master's, bachelor's degree. Additional exam requirements/recommendations for international students: required—TOEFL (minimum score 550 paper-based; 80 iBT), IELTS. Electronic applications accepted.

Walden University, Graduate Programs, School of Health Sciences, Minneapolis, MN 55401. Offers clinical research administration (MS, Graduate Certificate); health education and promotion (MS, PhD), including behavioral health (PhD); disease surveillance (PhD); emergency preparedness (MS), general (MHA, MS), global health (PhD), health policy (PhD), health policy and advocacy (MS), population health (PhD); health informatics (MS); health services (PhD), including community health, healthcare administration, leadership, public health policy, self-designed; healthcare administration (MHA, DHA), including general (MHA, MS); leadership and organizational development (MHA); public health (MPH, Dr PH, PhD, Graduate Certificate), including community health education (PhD), epidemiology (PhD); systems policy (MHA). *Program availability:* Part-time, evening/weekend, online only, 100% online. *Degree requirements:* For doctorate, thesis/dissertation, residency. *Entrance requirements:* For master's, bachelor's degree or higher; minimum GPA of 2.5; official transcripts; goal statement (for some programs); access to computer and Internet; for doctorate, master's degree or higher; three years of related professional or academic experience (preferred); minimum GPA of 3.0; goal statement and current resume (for select programs); official transcripts; access to computer and Internet; for Graduate Certificate, relevant work experience; access to computer and Internet. Additional exam requirements/recommendations for international students: required—TOEFL (minimum score 550 paper-based, 79 iBT), IELTS (minimum score 6.5), Michigan English Language Assessment Battery (minimum score 82), or PTE (minimum score 53). Electronic applications accepted.

Walden University, Graduate Programs, School of Information Systems and Technology, Minneapolis, MN 55401. Offers information systems (Graduate Certificate); information systems management (MISM); information technology (MS, DIT), including health informatics (MS), information assurance and cyber security (MS), information systems (MS), software engineering (MS). *Program availability:* Part-time, evening/weekend, online only, 100% online. *Degree requirements:* For doctorate, thesis/dissertation (for some programs), residency. *Entrance requirements:* For master's, bachelor's degree or higher; minimum GPA of 2.5; official transcripts; goal statement (for some programs); access to computer and Internet; for doctorate, master's degree or higher; three years of related professional or academic experience (preferred); minimum GPA of 3.0; goal statement and current resume (for select programs); official transcripts; access to computer and Internet; for Graduate Certificate, relevant work experience; access to computer and Internet. Additional exam requirements/recommendations for international students: required—TOEFL (minimum score 550 paper-based, 79 iBT), IELTS (minimum score 6.5), Michigan English Language Assessment Battery (minimum score 82), or PTE (minimum score 53). Electronic applications accepted.

Weill Cornell Medicine, Weill Cornell Graduate School of Medical Sciences, Program in Healthcare Policy and Research, New York, NY 10065. Offers biostatistics and data science (MS); health informatics (MS); health policy and economics (MS). *Program availability:* Part-time. *Degree requirements:* For master's, thesis. *Entrance requirements:* For master's, GRE, MCAT, or GMAT (recommended), official transcripts, resume, personal statement, 3 letters of reference. Additional exam requirements/recommendations for international students: required—TOEFL. *Expenses:* Contact institution.

Human-Computer Interaction

Brandeis University, Rabb School of Continuing Studies, Division of Graduate Professional Studies, Master of Science in User-Centered Design Program, Waltham, MA 02454-9110. Offers MS. *Program availability:* Part-time-only. *Degree requirements:* For master's, capstone. *Entrance requirements:* For master's, four-year bachelor's degree from regionally-accredited U.S. institution or equivalent; official transcript(s) from every college or university attended; resume or curriculum vitae; statement of goals; letter of recommendation. Additional exam requirements/recommendations for international students: required—TWE (minimum score 4.5), TOEFL (minimum scores: 600 paper-based, 100 iBT), IELTS (7), or PTE (68). Electronic applications accepted. *Expenses:* Contact institution.

Carnegie Mellon University, School of Computer Science, Department of Human-Computer Interaction, Pittsburgh, PA 15213-3891. Offers MHCI, PhD. *Entrance requirements:* For master's, GRE General Test, GRE Subject Test.

Cornell University, Graduate School, Graduate Fields of Agriculture and Life Sciences, Field of Communication, Ithaca, NY 14853. Offers communication (MS, PhD); human-computer interaction (MS, PhD); language and communication (MS, PhD); media communication and society (MS, PhD); organizational communication (MS, PhD); science, environment and health communication (MS, PhD); social psychology of communication (MS, PhD). *Degree requirements:* For master's, thesis (MS); for doctorate, comprehensive exam, thesis/dissertation. *Entrance requirements:* For master's and doctorate, GRE General Test, 3 letters of recommendation. Additional exam requirements/recommendations for international students: required—TOEFL (minimum score 600 paper-based; 100 iBT). Electronic applications accepted.

Cornell University, Graduate School, Graduate Fields of Arts and Sciences, Field of Information Science, Ithaca, NY 14853. Offers cognition (PhD); human computer interaction (PhD); information science (PhD); information systems (PhD); social aspects of information (PhD). *Degree requirements:* For doctorate, comprehensive exam, thesis/dissertation. *Entrance requirements:* For doctorate, GRE General Test, 3 letters of recommendation. Additional exam requirements/recommendations for international students: required—TOEFL (minimum score 550 paper-based; 77 iBT). Electronic applications accepted.

Dalhousie University, Faculty of Engineering, Department of Engineering Mathematics and Internetworking, Halifax, NS B3J 2X4, Canada. Offers engineering mathematics (M Sc, PhD); internetworking (M Eng). *Degree requirements:* For master's, thesis; for doctorate, thesis/dissertation. *Entrance requirements:* Additional exam requirements/recommendations for international students: required—TOEFL, IELTS, CANTEST, CAEL, or Michigan English Language Assessment Battery. Electronic applications accepted.

DePaul University, College of Computing and Digital Media, Chicago, IL 60604. Offers animation (MA, MFA); applied technology (MS); business information technology (MS); computational finance (MS); computer and information sciences (PhD); computer science (MS); creative producing (MFA); cybersecurity (MS); data science (MS); digital communication and media arts (MA); documentary (MFA); e-commerce technology (MS); experience design (MA); film and television (MS); film and television directing (MFA); game design (MFA); game programming (MS); health informatics (MS); human centered design (PhD); human-computer interaction (MS); information systems (MS); network engineering and security (MS); product innovation and computing (MS); screenwriting (MFA); software engineering (MS); JD/MS. *Program availability:* Part-time, evening/weekend, online learning. *Degree requirements:* For master's, thesis (for some programs); for doctorate, comprehensive exam, thesis/dissertation. *Entrance requirements:* For master's, GRE or GMAT (for MS in computational finance only), bachelor's degree, resume (MS in predictive analytics only), IT experience (MS in information technology project management only), portfolio review (all MFA programs and MA in animation); for doctorate, GRE, master's degree in computer science. Additional exam requirements/recommendations for international students: required—TOEFL (minimum score 590 paper-based; 80 iBT), IELTS (minimum score 6.5), PTE (minimum score 53). Electronic applications accepted. *Expenses:* Contact institution.

Florida Institute of Technology, College of Aeronautics, Program in Aviation Human Factors, Melbourne, FL 32901-6975. Offers aviation human factors (MS). *Program availability:* Part-time. *Degree requirements:* For master's, comprehensive exam (for some programs), thesis optional, minimum of 36 credit hours. *Entrance requirements:* For master's, GRE General Test, 3 letters of recommendation, statement of objectives, resume. Additional exam requirements/recommendations for international students: required—TOEFL (minimum score 550 paper-based; 79 iBT). Electronic applications accepted.

Harrisburg University of Science and Technology, Program in Human-Centered Interaction Design, Philadelphia, PA 19130. Offers MS. *Expenses: Tuition:* Full-time $15,900; part-time $7950 per credit hour.

Indiana University Bloomington, School of Informatics, Computing, and Engineering, Program in Informatics, Bloomington, IN 47405. Offers informatics (MS, PhD), including bioinformatics (PhD), complex systems (PhD), computing, culture and society (PhD), health informatics (PhD), human-computer interaction (MS), human-computer interaction design (PhD), music informatics (PhD), security informatics (PhD), visual heritage (PhD). *Program availability:* Part-time. Terminal master's awarded for partial completion of doctoral program. *Degree requirements:* For master's, thesis, capstone project; for doctorate, variable foreign language requirement, comprehensive exam, thesis/dissertation. *Entrance requirements:* For master's and doctorate, GRE, resume/curriculum vitae, transcripts, 3 letters of recommendation. Additional exam requirements/recommendations for international students: required—TOEFL (minimum score 600 paper-based; 100 iBT). Electronic applications accepted.

Indiana University-Purdue University Indianapolis, School of Informatics and Computing, Department of Human-Centered Computing, Indianapolis, IN 46202. Offers human-computer interaction (MS, PhD); informatics (MS), including data analytics; media arts and science (MS).

Iowa State University of Science and Technology, Program in Human-Computer Interaction, Ames, IA 50011. Offers MS, PhD. *Degree requirements:* For master's, thesis; for doctorate, thesis/dissertation. *Entrance requirements:* For master's, GRE General Test; for doctorate, GRE General Test, e-portfolio of research. Additional exam requirements/recommendations for international students: required—TOEFL (minimum score 580 paper-based; 95 iBT), IELTS (minimum score 7). Electronic applications accepted.

Rochester Institute of Technology, Graduate Enrollment Services, Golisano College of Computing and Information Sciences, Information Science and Technologies Department, MS Program in Human Computer Interaction, Rochester, NY 14623-5603. Offers MS. *Program availability:* Part-time, evening/weekend, 100% online. *Degree requirements:* For master's, thesis or alternative, Thesis or Capstone. *Entrance requirements:* For master's, GRE required for individuals with degrees from international universities., minimum GPA of 3.0 (if you have less than a 3.0, you are required to submit GRE scores), resume, 2 letters of recommendation. Additional exam requirements/recommendations for international students: required—TOEFL (minimum score 570 paper-based; 88 iBT), IELTS (minimum score 6.5), PTE (minimum score 61). Electronic applications accepted.

State University of New York at Oswego, Graduate Studies, College of Liberal Arts and Sciences, Human-Computer Interaction, Oswego, NY 13126. Offers MA. *Program availability:* Part-time. *Students:* 33. In 2019, 17 master's awarded. *Entrance requirements:* For master's, GRE, minimum GPA of 3.0. Additional exam requirements/recommendations for international students: required—TOEFL (minimum score 560 paper-based). *Application deadline:* For fall admission, 4/1 for domestic and international students; for spring admission, 10/1 for domestic and international students. Applications are processed on a rolling basis. Application fee: $65. *Financial support:* Fellowships with full tuition reimbursements and teaching assistantships with partial tuition reimbursements available. Financial award application deadline: 4/1. *Unit head:* Dr. Damian Schofield, Director, 315-312-4628, E-mail: schofield@cs.oswego.edu. *Application contact:* Dr. Kristen Eichhorn, Dean of Graduate Studies, 315-312-3692, E-mail: kristen.eichhorn@oswego.edu.

Tufts University, Graduate School of Arts and Sciences, Graduate Certificate Programs, Human-Computer Interaction Program, Medford, MA 02155. Offers Certificate. *Program availability:* Part-time, evening/weekend. Electronic applications accepted. Full-time tuition and fees vary according to degree level, program and student level. Part-time tuition and fees vary according to course load.

University of Baltimore, Graduate School, Yale Gordon College of Arts and Sciences, Program in Interaction Design and Information Architecture, Baltimore, MD 21201-5779. Offers MS. *Program availability:* Part-time, evening/weekend. *Degree requirements:* For master's, project or thesis. *Entrance requirements:* For master's, GRE General Test or Miller Analogy Test, undergraduate GPA of 3.0.

University of Illinois at Urbana-Champaign, Graduate College, School of Information Sciences, Champaign, IL 61820. Offers bioinformatics (MS); digital libraries (CAS); information management (MS); library and information science (MS, PhD, CAS). *Accreditation:* ALA (one or more programs are accredited). *Program availability:* Part-time, online learning. *Entrance requirements:* For degree, master's degree in library and information science or related field with minimum GPA of 3.0.

University of Rochester, Hajim School of Engineering and Applied Sciences, Department of Computer Science, Rochester, NY 14627. Offers algorithms and complexity (MS); artificial intelligence and machine learning (MS); computer architecture (MS); computer science (PhD); human computer interaction (MS); natural language processing (MS); programming languages and computer systems (MS). *Faculty:* 19 full-time (3 women). *Students:* 124 full-time (23 women), 1 (woman) part-time; includes 6 minority (2 Black or African American, non-Hispanic/Latino; 3 Asian, non-Hispanic/Latino; 1 Two or more races, non-Hispanic/Latino), 98 international. Average age 26. 925 applicants, 16% accepted, 37 enrolled. In 2019, 42 master's, 4 doctorates awarded. Terminal master's awarded for partial completion of doctoral program. *Degree requirements:* For master's, comprehensive exam (for some programs), thesis (for some programs); for doctorate, comprehensive exam, thesis/dissertation, qualifying exam. *Entrance requirements:* For master's and doctorate, GRE General Test, personal statement, transcripts, three letters of recommendation. Additional exam requirements/recommendations for international students: required—TOEFL (minimum score 100 iBT), IELTS. *Application deadline:* For fall admission, 12/15 for domestic and international students. Application fee: $60. Electronic applications accepted. *Financial support:* In 2019–20, 74 students received support, including 4 fellowships with full tuition reimbursements available (averaging $33,708 per year), 40 research assistantships with full tuition reimbursements available (averaging $31,200 per year), 30 teaching assistantships with full tuition reimbursements available (averaging $31,200 per year); scholarships/grants, traineeships, health care benefits, and tuition waivers (full and partial) also available. Financial award application deadline: 12/15. *Unit head:* Michael Scott, Professor and Chair, 585-275-7745, E-mail: scott@cs.rochester.edu. *Application contact:* Emily Tevens, Graduate Coordinator, 585-275-7737, E-mail: etevens@cs.rochester.edu.
Website: https://www.cs.rochester.edu/graduate/index.html

University of Washington, Graduate School, College of Engineering, Department of Human Centered Design and Engineering, Seattle, WA 98195-2315. Offers human centered design and engineering (MS, PhD); user centered design (Certificate). *Program availability:* Part-time, evening/weekend. *Students:* 149 full-time (109 women), 188 part-time (123 women); includes 102 minority (9 Black or African American, non-Hispanic/Latino; 53 Asian, non-Hispanic/Latino; 23 Hispanic/Latino; 17 Two or more races, non-Hispanic/Latino), 96 international. Average age 29. 814 applicants, 27% accepted, 138 enrolled. In 2019, 76 master's, 6 doctorates awarded. Terminal master's awarded for partial completion of doctoral program. *Degree requirements:* For master's, thesis or alternative; for doctorate, comprehensive exam, thesis/dissertation, preliminary, general, and final exams. *Entrance requirements:* For master's, minimum GPA of 3.0, transcripts, 3 letters of recommendation, curriculum vitae, personal statement of objectives; for doctorate, GRE General Test, minimum GPA of 3.0, transcripts, 3 letters of recommendation, curriculum vitae, personal statement of objectives. Additional exam requirements/recommendations for international students: required—TOEFL (minimum score 623 paper-based; 106 iBT). *Application deadline:* For fall admission, 12/2 for domestic and international students. Application fee: $85. Electronic applications accepted. *Expenses:* Contact institution. *Financial support:* In 2019–20, 1 fellowship with full tuition reimbursement (averaging $32,640 per year), 30 research assistantships with full tuition reimbursements (averaging $32,640 per year),

17 teaching assistantships with full tuition reimbursements (averaging $33,240 per year) were awarded; Federal Work-Study, institutionally sponsored loans, scholarships/grants, health care benefits, tuition waivers (full), and unspecified assistantships also available. Support available to part-time students. Financial award application deadline: 12/2. *Unit head:* Dr. Julie Kientz, Professor/Chair, 206-543-2567, Fax: 206-543-8858, E-mail: hcdechr@uw.edu. *Application contact:* Pat Reilly, Academic Services Manager, 206-543-1798, Fax: 206-543-8858, E-mail: preilly@uw.edu. Website: http://www.hcde.washington.edu/

Information Science

Alcorn State University, School of Graduate Studies, School of Arts and Sciences, Department of Mathematics and Computer Science, Lorman, MS 39096-7500. Offers computer and information science (MS).

American InterContinental University Atlanta, Program in Information Technology, Atlanta, GA 30328. Offers MIT. *Program availability:* Part-time, evening/weekend. *Degree requirements:* For master's, technical proficiency demonstration. *Entrance requirements:* For master's, Computer Programmer Aptitude Battery Exam, interview. Electronic applications accepted.

American InterContinental University Online, Program in Information Technology, Schaumburg, IL 60173. Offers Internet security (MIT); IT project management (MIT). *Program availability:* Evening/weekend, online learning. *Entrance requirements:* Additional exam requirements/recommendations for international students: required—TOEFL (minimum score 550 paper-based). Electronic applications accepted.

American University of Armenia, Graduate Programs, Yerevan, Armenia. Offers business administration (MBA); computer and information science (MS), including business management, design and manufacturing, energy (ME, MS), industrial engineering and systems management; economics (MS); industrial engineering and systems management (ME), including business, computer aided design/manufacturing, energy (ME, MS), information technology; law (LL M); political science and international affairs (MPSIA); public health (MPH); teaching English as a foreign language (MA). *Program availability:* Part-time, evening/weekend. *Degree requirements:* For master's, thesis (for some programs), capstone/project. *Entrance requirements:* For master's, GRE, GMAT, or LSAT. Additional exam requirements/recommendations for international students: recommended—TOEFL (minimum score 79 iBT), IELTS (minimum score 6.5).

Arizona State University at Tempe, Ira A. Fulton Schools of Engineering, The Polytechnic School, Programs in Technology Management, Mesa, AZ 85212. Offers aviation management and human factors (MS); environmental technology management (MS); global technology and development (MS); graphic information technology (MS); management of technology (MS). *Program availability:* Part-time, evening/weekend, online learning. *Degree requirements:* For master's, thesis or applied project and oral defense; interactive Program of Study (iPOS) submitted before completing 50 percent of required credit hours. *Entrance requirements:* For master's, GRE, minimum GPA of 3.0 or equivalent in last 2 years of work leading to bachelor's degree. Additional exam requirements/recommendations for international students: required—TOEFL, IELTS, or PTE. Electronic applications accepted.

Arkansas Tech University, College of Engineering and Applied Sciences, Russellville, AR 72801. Offers electrical engineering (M Engr); emergency management (MS); information technology (MS); mechanical engineering (M Engr). *Program availability:* Part-time, evening/weekend, 100% online, blended/hybrid learning. *Students:* 38 full-time (11 women), 45 part-time (22 women); includes 13 minority (10 Black or African American, non-Hispanic/Latino; 1 Asian, non-Hispanic/Latino; 1 Hispanic/Latino; 1 Two or more races, non-Hispanic/Latino), 24 international. Average age 32. In 2019, 26 master's awarded. *Degree requirements:* For master's, comprehensive exam (for some programs), thesis (for some programs). *Entrance requirements:* Additional exam requirements/recommendations for international students: required—TOEFL (minimum score 550 paper-based; 79 iBT), IELTS (minimum score 6.5), PTE (minimum score 58). *Application deadline:* For fall admission, 3/1 priority date for domestic students, 5/1 priority date for international students; for spring admission, 10/1 priority date for domestic and international students. Applications are processed on a rolling basis. Application fee: $40 ($90 for international students). Electronic applications accepted. *Expenses: Tuition, area resident:* Full-time $7008; part-time $292 per credit hour. Tuition, state resident: Full-time $7008; part-time $292 per credit hour. Tuition, nonresident: full-time $14,016; part-time $584 per credit hour. *International tuition:* $14,016 full-time. *Required fees:* $343 per term. *Financial support:* In 2019–20, research assistantships with full and partial tuition reimbursements (averaging $4,800 per year), teaching assistantships with full and partial tuition reimbursements (averaging $4,800 per year) were awarded; career-related internships or fieldwork, Federal Work-Study, scholarships/grants, health care benefits, and unspecified assistantships also available. Support available to part-time students. Financial award application deadline: 4/15; financial award applicants required to submit FAFSA. *Unit head:* Dr. Judy Cezeaux, Dean, 479-968-0353, E-mail: jcezeaux@atu.edu. *Application contact:* Dr. Richard Schoephoerster, Dean of Graduate College and Research, 479-968-0398, Fax: 479-964-0542, E-mail: gradcollege@atu.edu. Website: http://www.atu.edu/appliedsci/

Aspen University, Program in Information Technology, Denver, CO 80246-1930. Offers MS, Certificate. *Program availability:* Part-time, evening/weekend, online only, 100% online. *Degree requirements:* For master's, comprehensive exam. *Entrance requirements:* For master's and Certificate, www.aspen.edu, www.aspen.edu. Electronic applications accepted.

Ball State University, Graduate School, College of Communication, Information, and Media, Center for Information and Communication Sciences, Muncie, IN 47306. Offers information and communication sciences (MS); information and communication technologies (Certificate). *Program availability:* Part-time, 100% online. *Entrance requirements:* For master's, minimum baccalaureate GPA of 2.75 or 3.0 in latter half of baccalaureate, statement of goals. Additional exam requirements/recommendations for international students: required—TOEFL (minimum score 550 paper-based; 79 iBT), IELTS (minimum score 6.5). Electronic applications accepted. *Expenses: Tuition, area resident:* Full-time $7506; part-time $417 per credit hour. Tuition, nonresident: full-time $20,610; part-time $1145 per credit hour. *Required fees:* $2126. Tuition and fees vary according to course load, campus/location and program.

Barry University, School of Adult and Continuing Education, Program in Information Technology, Miami Shores, FL 33161-6695. Offers MS. *Program availability:* Part-time, evening/weekend. *Entrance requirements:* For master's, GMAT, GRE or MAT, bachelor's degree in information technology, related area or professional experience. Electronic applications accepted.

Bellevue University, Graduate School, College of Information Technology, Bellevue, NE 68005-3098. Offers computer information systems (MS); cybersecurity (MS); management of information systems (MS); project management (MPM).

Bentley University, McCallum Graduate School of Business, Masters in Digital Innovation, Waltham, MA 02452-4705. Offers MSIT. *Program availability:* Part-time, evening/weekend, blended/hybrid learning. *Faculty:* 105 full-time (40 women), 17 part-time/adjunct (5 women). *Students:* 15 full-time (9 women), 24 part-time (10 women); includes 6 minority (2 Black or African American, non-Hispanic/Latino; 1 American Indian or Alaska Native, non-Hispanic/Latino; 2 Asian, non-Hispanic/Latino; 1 Hispanic/Latino), 20 international. Average age 29. 47 applicants, 60% accepted, 16 enrolled. In 2019, 37 master's awarded. *Entrance requirements:* For master's, GMAT or GRE General Test (may be waived for qualified students), Transcripts; Resume; Two essays; Two letters of recommendation; Interview (may be requested by Bentley). Additional exam requirements/recommendations for international students: required—TOEFL-Paper (minimum score 72) or TOEFL-IBT (minimum score 100) or IELTS (minimum score 7). *Application deadline:* For fall admission, 8/1 for domestic students, 7/1 for international students; for spring admission, 12/15 for domestic students, 11/1 for international students. Applications are processed on a rolling basis. Application fee: $150. Electronic applications accepted. *Financial support:* In 2019–20, 16 students received support. Scholarships/grants and unspecified assistantships available. Financial award application deadline: 6/1; financial award applicants required to submit FAFSA. *Unit head:* Akram Ahmed, Senior Lecturer and MSDI Program Director, 781-891-2713, E-mail: aahmed@bentley.edu. *Application contact:* Office of Graduate Admissions, 781-891-2108, E-mail: applygrad@bentley.edu. Website: https://www.bentley.edu/academics/graduate-programs/masters-digital-innovation

Bradley University, The Graduate School, College of Liberal Arts and Sciences, Department of Computer Science and Information Systems, Peoria, IL 61625-0002. Offers computer information systems (MS); computer science (MS). *Program availability:* Part-time, evening/weekend. *Faculty:* 10 full-time (2 women), 1 part-time/adjunct. *Students:* 23 full-time (12 women), 4 part-time (2 women), 24 international. Average age 26. 76 applicants, 62% accepted, 14 enrolled. In 2019, 11 master's awarded. *Degree requirements:* For master's, comprehensive exam, thesis or alternative, programming test. *Entrance requirements:* For master's, GRE. Additional exam requirements/recommendations for international students: required—TOEFL (minimum score 550 paper-based; 79 iBT), IELTS (minimum score 6.5), PTE (minimum score 58). *Application deadline:* For fall admission, 5/15 priority date for domestic and international students; for spring admission, 10/15 priority date for domestic and international students. Applications are processed on a rolling basis. Application fee: $40 ($50 for international students). Electronic applications accepted. *Expenses: Tuition:* Part-time $930 per credit hour. *Financial support:* In 2019–20, 11 students received support, including 2 research assistantships with partial tuition reimbursements available (averaging $8,370 per year), 7 teaching assistantships with partial tuition reimbursements available (averaging $4,185 per year); scholarships/grants, tuition waivers (partial), and unspecified assistantships also available. Support available to part-time students. Financial award application deadline: 4/1. *Unit head:* Dr. Steven Dolins, Chair, 309-677-3284, E-mail: sdolins@bradley.edu. *Application contact:* Rachel Webb, Director of On-Campus Graduate Admissions and International Student and Scholar Services, 309-677-2375, E-mail: rkwebb@bradley.edu. Website: http://www.bradley.edu/academic/departments/csis/

Brigham Young University, Graduate Studies, Ira A. Fulton College of Engineering, School of Technology, Provo, UT 84602-1001. Offers construction management (MS); information technology (MS); manufacturing engineering technology (MS); technology and engineering education (MS). *Faculty:* 16 full-time (1 woman). *Students:* 14 full-time (2 women); includes 3 minority (1 Hispanic/Latino; 2 Two or more races, non-Hispanic/Latino), 3 international. Average age 28. 15 applicants, 73% accepted, 11 enrolled. In 2019, 7 master's awarded. *Degree requirements:* For master's, thesis. *Entrance requirements:* For master's, GRE General Test; GMAT or GRE (for construction management emphasis), BS degree in information technology, manufacturing engineering technology, construction management, technology and engineering education, or related field; basic sciences background, along with engineering mathematics, computers or electronics, management, architecture, and manufacturing methods. Additional exam requirements/recommendations for international students: required—TOEFL (minimum score 580 paper-based; 85 iBT). *Application deadline:* For fall admission, 2/15 for domestic and international students; for winter admission, 9/10 for domestic and international students; for spring admission, 2/15 for domestic and international students; for summer admission, 2/15 for domestic and international students. Application fee: $50. Electronic applications accepted. *Financial support:* In 2019–20, 10 students received support, including 5 research assistantships with full and partial tuition reimbursements available (averaging $27,617 per year), 5 teaching assistantships with full and partial tuition reimbursements available (averaging $11,446 per year); scholarships/grants also available. Financial award application deadline: 1/15; financial award applicants required to submit FAFSA. *Unit head:* Dr. Barry M. Lunt, Director, 801-422-6300, Fax: 801-422-0490, E-mail: blunt@byu.edu. *Application contact:* Samuel Cardenas, Academic Advisor, 801-422-1819, Fax: 801-422-0490, E-mail: samuel_cardenas@byu.edu. Website: http://www.et.byu.edu/sot/

Brooklyn College of the City University of New York, School of Natural and Behavioral Sciences, Department of Computer and Information Science, Brooklyn, NY 11210-2889. Offers computer science (MA); health informatics (MS); information systems (MS); parallel and distributed computing (Advanced Certificate). *Program availability:* Part-time, evening/weekend. *Degree requirements:* For master's, comprehensive exam, thesis or alternative. *Entrance requirements:* For master's, previous course work in computer science, 2 letters of recommendation. Additional exam requirements/recommendations for international students: required—TOEFL (minimum score 525 paper-based; 70 iBT). Electronic applications accepted.

Information Science

California State University, Fullerton, Graduate Studies, College of Business and Economics, Department of Information Systems and Decision Sciences, Fullerton, CA 92831-3599. Offers decision science (MBA); information systems (MBA, MS); information systems and decision sciences (MS); information systems and e-commerce (MS); information technology (MS). *Program availability:* Part-time. *Entrance requirements:* For master's, GMAT, minimum AACSB index of 950.

Capitol Technology University, Graduate Programs, Laurel, MD 20708-9759. Offers business administration (MBA); computer science (MS); electrical engineering (MS); information and telecommunications systems management (MS); information architecture (MS); network security (MS). *Program availability:* Part-time, evening/weekend, online learning. *Entrance requirements:* For master's, minimum GPA of 3.0. Electronic applications accepted.

Carleton University, Faculty of Graduate Studies, Faculty of Engineering and Design, Ottawa-Carleton Institute for Electrical Engineering, Department of Systems and Computer Engineering, Program in Information and Systems Science, Ottawa, ON K1S 5B6, Canada. Offers M Sc.

Carleton University, Faculty of Graduate Studies, Faculty of Science, Information and Systems Science Program, Ottawa, ON K1S 5B6, Canada. Offers M Sc. *Degree requirements:* For master's, thesis optional. *Entrance requirements:* For master's, honors degree. Additional exam requirements/recommendations for international students: required—TOEFL.

Carleton University, Faculty of Graduate Studies, Faculty of Science, School of Computer Science, Ottawa, ON K1S 5B6, Canada. Offers computer science (MCS, PhD); information and system science (M Sc). *Program availability:* Part-time. *Degree requirements:* For master's, thesis optional, project; for doctorate, comprehensive exam, thesis/dissertation. *Entrance requirements:* For master's, honors degree. Additional exam requirements/recommendations for international students: required—TOEFL.

Carnegie Mellon University, Heinz College Australia, Master of Science in Information Technology Program (Adelaide, South Australia), Adelaide SA 5000, Australia. Offers MSIT. *Entrance requirements:* For master's, GRE or GMAT, college-level course in advanced algebra/pre-calculus; college-level courses in economics and statistics (recommended). Additional exam requirements/recommendations for international students: required—TOEFL or IELTS.

Carnegie Mellon University, Heinz College, School of Information Systems and Management, Master of Information Systems Management Program, Pittsburgh, PA 15213-3891. Offers MISM. *Entrance requirements:* For master's, GRE or GMAT, college-level course in advanced algebra/pre-calculus; college-level courses in economics and statistics (recommended). Additional exam requirements/recommendations for international students: required—TOEFL or IELTS.

Carnegie Mellon University, School of Computer Science, Language Technologies Institute, Pittsburgh, PA 15213-3891. Offers MLT, MS, PhD. Terminal master's awarded for partial completion of doctoral program. *Degree requirements:* For doctorate, thesis/dissertation. *Entrance requirements:* For master's and doctorate, GRE General Test, GRE Subject Test. Additional exam requirements/recommendations for international students: required—TOEFL.

Case Western Reserve University, School of Graduate Studies, Case School of Engineering, Department of Computer and Data Sciences, Cleveland, OH 44106. Offers computer engineering (MS, PhD); computing and information sciences (MS, PhD); electrical engineering (MS, PhD); systems and control engineering (MS, PhD). *Program availability:* Part-time, evening/weekend, online only, 100% online. Terminal master's awarded for partial completion of doctoral program. *Degree requirements:* For master's, thesis; for doctorate, thesis/dissertation, qualifying exam, teaching experience. *Entrance requirements:* For master's and doctorate, GRE General Test. Additional exam requirements/recommendations for international students: required—TOEFL.

The Citadel, The Military College of South Carolina, Citadel Graduate College, School of Science and Mathematics, Department of Mathematics and Computer Science, Charleston, SC 29409. Offers computer and information sciences (MS). *Accreditation:* NCATE (one or more programs are accredited). *Program availability:* Part-time, evening/weekend. *Degree requirements:* For master's, comprehensive exam (for some programs), thesis (for some programs). *Entrance requirements:* For master's, GRE General Test (minimum combined score of 300 on the verbal and quantitative sections, 1000 under the old grading system, 4.0 on the writing assessment for MS); MAT with minimum raw score of 396 (for MA Ed), minimum undergraduate GPA of 3.0 and competency demonstrated through coursework, approved work experience, or a program-administrated competency exam, in the areas of basic computer architecture, object-oriented programming, discrete mathematics, and data structures (for MS). Additional exam requirements/recommendations for international students: required—TOEFL (minimum score 550 paper-based; 79 iBT). Electronic applications accepted.

Claremont Graduate University, Graduate Programs, Center for Information Systems and Technology, Claremont, CA 91711-6160. Offers cybersecurity and networking (MS); data science and analytics (MS); electronic commerce (PhD); geographic information systems (MS); health informatics (MS); information systems (Certificate); IT strategy and innovation (MS); knowledge management (PhD); systems development (PhD); telecommunications and networking (PhD); MBA/MS. *Program availability:* Part-time. *Degree requirements:* For doctorate, comprehensive exam, thesis/dissertation, portfolio. *Entrance requirements:* For master's and doctorate, GMAT, GRE General Test. Additional exam requirements/recommendations for international students: required—TOEFL (minimum score 75 iBT). Electronic applications accepted.

Clark Atlanta University, School of Arts and Sciences, Department of Computer and Information Science, Atlanta, GA 30314. Offers MS. *Program availability:* Part-time. *Degree requirements:* For master's, one foreign language, thesis. *Entrance requirements:* For master's, GRE General Test, minimum GPA of 2.5. Additional exam requirements/recommendations for international students: required—TOEFL (minimum score 500 paper-based; 61 iBT).

Clark University, Graduate School, School of Professional Studies, Program in Information Technology, Worcester, MA 01610-1477. Offers MSIT. *Program availability:* Part-time, evening/weekend. *Degree requirements:* For master's, thesis or alternative. *Entrance requirements:* For master's, 2 references, resume or curriculum vitae, personal statement. Additional exam requirements/recommendations for international students: required—TOEFL (minimum score 575 paper-based; 90 iBT), IELTS (minimum score 6.5). Electronic applications accepted. *Expenses:* Contact institution.

The College of Saint Rose, Graduate Studies, School of Mathematics and Sciences, Program in Computer Information Systems, Albany, NY 12203-1419. Offers MS, Advanced Certificate. *Program availability:* Part-time, evening/weekend. *Students:* 19 full-time (9 women), 30 part-time (8 women); includes 10 minority (1 Black or African American, non-Hispanic/Latino; 7 Asian, non-Hispanic/Latino; 1 Hispanic/Latino; 1 Two or more races, non-Hispanic/Latino), 34 international. Average age 29. 52 applicants, 90% accepted, 12 enrolled. In 2019, 16 master's, 3 other advanced degrees awarded. *Degree requirements:* For master's, comprehensive exam, research component, project. *Entrance requirements:* For master's, minimum GPA of 3.0, 9 undergraduate credits in math. Additional exam requirements/recommendations for international students: required—TOEFL (minimum score 550 paper-based; 80 iBT), IELTS (minimum score 6), PTE (minimum score 56). *Application deadline:* For fall admission, 4/1 priority date for domestic and international students; for spring admission, 10/15 priority date for domestic and international students; for summer admission, 3/15 priority date for domestic and international students. Applications are processed on a rolling basis. Application fee: $40. Electronic applications accepted. *Expenses: Tuition:* Full-time $14,382; part-time $799 per credit hour. *Required fees:* $954; $698. Tuition and fees vary according to course load. *Financial support:* Career-related internships or fieldwork, scholarships/grants, tuition waivers (partial), and unspecified assistantships available. Support available to part-time students. Financial award application deadline: 4/15; financial award applicants required to submit FAFSA. *Unit head:* Dr. John Avitabile, Department Chair, 518-458-5317, E-mail: avitabij@strose.edu. *Application contact:* Daniel Gallagher, Assistant Vice President for Graduate Recruitment and Enrollment, 518-485-3390.
Website: https://www.strose.edu/computer-information-systems/

Cornell University, Graduate School, Graduate Fields of Arts and Sciences, Field of Information Science, Ithaca, NY 14853. Offers cognition (PhD); human computer interaction (PhD); information science (PhD); information systems (PhD); social aspects of information (PhD). *Degree requirements:* For doctorate, comprehensive exam, thesis/dissertation. *Entrance requirements:* For doctorate, GRE General Test, 3 letters of recommendation. Additional exam requirements/recommendations for international students: required—TOEFL (minimum score 550 paper-based; 77 iBT). Electronic applications accepted.

Dakota State University, College of Business and Information Systems, Madison, SD 57042. Offers analytics (MSA); business analytics (Graduate Certificate); general management (MBA); health informatics and information management (MSHI); information systems (MSIS, D Sc IS); information technology (Graduate Certificate). *Accreditation:* ACBSP. *Program availability:* Part-time, evening/weekend, 100% online, blended/hybrid learning. *Faculty:* 23 full-time (8 women), 1 (woman) part-time/adjunct. *Students:* 35 full-time (8 women), 177 part-time (51 women); includes 58 minority (23 Black or African American, non-Hispanic/Latino; 6 American Indian or Alaska Native, non-Hispanic/Latino; 18 Asian, non-Hispanic/Latino; 10 Hispanic/Latino; 1 Two or more races, non-Hispanic/Latino), 45 international. Average age 38. 230 applicants, 34% accepted, 70 enrolled. In 2019, 49 master's, 2 doctorates, 13 other advanced degrees awarded. *Degree requirements:* For master's, comprehensive exam, thesis optional, Examination, integrative project; for doctorate, comprehensive exam, thesis/dissertation, portfolio. *Entrance requirements:* For master's, GRE General Test, Demonstration of information systems skills, minimum GPA of 2.7; for doctorate, GRE General Test, Demonstration of information systems skills; for Graduate Certificate, GMAT. Additional exam requirements/recommendations for international students: required—PTE (minimum score 53), TOEFL (minimum score 550 paper-based, 79 iBT, or IELTS 6.5). *Application deadline:* For fall admission, 6/15 for domestic students, 4/15 for international students; for spring admission, 11/15 for domestic students, 9/15 priority date for international students; for summer admission, 4/15 for domestic and international students. Applications are processed on a rolling basis. Application fee: $35. *Expenses: Tuition, area resident:* Full-time $7919. Tuition, state resident: full-time $7919. Tuition, nonresident: full-time $14,784. *International tuition:* $14,784 full-time. *Required fees:* $961. *Financial support:* Fellowships, career-related internships or fieldwork, Federal Work-Study, scholarships/grants, unspecified assistantships, and Administrative Assistantships available. Support available to part-time students. Financial award applicants required to submit FAFSA. *Unit head:* Dr. Dorine Bennett, Dean of College of Business and Information Systems, 605-256-5176, E-mail: dorine.bennett@dsu.edu. *Application contact:* Erin Blankespoor, Senior Secretary, Office of Graduate Studies, 605-256-5799, E-mail: erin.blankespoor@dsu.edu.
Website: http://dsu.edu/academics/colleges/college-of-business-and-information-systems

DePaul University, College of Computing and Digital Media, Chicago, IL 60604. Offers animation (MA, MFA); applied technology (MS); business information technology (MS); computational finance (MS); computer and information sciences (PhD); computer science (MS); creative producing (MFA); cybersecurity (MS); data science (MS); digital communication and media arts (MA); documentary (MFA); e-commerce technology (MS); experience design (MA); film and television (MS); film and television directing (MFA); game design (MFA); game programming (MS); health informatics (MS); human centered design (PhD); human-computer interaction (MS); information systems (MS); network engineering and security (MS); product innovation and computing (MS); screenwriting (MFA); software engineering (MS); JD/MS. *Program availability:* Part-time, evening/weekend, online learning. *Degree requirements:* For master's, thesis (for some programs); for doctorate, comprehensive exam, thesis/dissertation. *Entrance requirements:* For master's, GRE or GMAT (for MS in computational finance only), bachelor's degree, resume (MS in predictive analytics only), IT experience (MS in information technology project management only), portfolio review (all MFA programs and MA in animation); for doctorate, GRE, master's degree in computer science. Additional exam requirements/recommendations for international students: required—TOEFL (minimum score 590 paper-based; 80 iBT), IELTS (minimum score 6.5), PTE (minimum score 53). Electronic applications accepted. *Expenses:* Contact institution.

Drexel University, College of Computing and Informatics, Department of Information Science, Philadelphia, PA 19104-2875. Offers health informatics (MS); information science (PhD, Post-Master's Certificate, Postbaccalaureate Certificate); information systems (MS); library and information science (MS). *Accreditation:* ALA. *Program availability:* Part-time, evening/weekend, 100% online. *Degree requirements:* For doctorate, thesis/dissertation. *Entrance requirements:* For master's and doctorate, GRE General Test. Additional exam requirements/recommendations for international students: required—TOEFL (minimum score 90 iBT), IELTS (minimum score 6.5). Electronic applications accepted.

East Tennessee State University, School of Graduate Studies, College of Business and Technology, Department of Computing, Johnson City, TN 37614. Offers applied computer science (MS); emerging technologies (Postbaccalaureate Certificate); information technology (MS). *Program availability:* Part-time, evening/weekend. *Degree requirements:* For master's, comprehensive exam, thesis optional, capstone, oral exam. *Entrance requirements:* For master's, GRE General Test, minimum GPA of 3.0, three letters of recommendation. Additional exam requirements/recommendations for international students: required—TOEFL (minimum score 550 paper-based; 79 iBT). Electronic applications accepted.

Florida Institute of Technology, College of Engineering and Science, Program in Computer Information Systems, Melbourne, FL 32901-6975. Offers MS. *Program availability:* Part-time. *Degree requirements:* For master's, comprehensive exam (for some programs), thesis optional, minimum of 30 credits. *Entrance requirements:* For master's, 3 letters of recommendation, resume, mathematical proficiency, GRE recommended. Additional exam requirements/recommendations for international students: required—TOEFL (minimum score 550 paper-based; 79 iBT). Electronic applications accepted.

Florida International University, College of Engineering and Computing, School of Computing and Information Sciences, Miami, FL 33199. Offers computer science (MS,

PhD); cybersecurity (MS); data science (MS); information technology (MS); telecommunications and networking (MS). *Program availability:* Part-time, evening/weekend. *Faculty:* 53 full-time (14 women), 33 part-time/adjunct (9 women). *Students:* 162 full-time (39 women), 140 part-time (26 women); includes 160 minority (11 Black or African American, non-Hispanic/Latino; 1 American Indian or Alaska Native, non-Hispanic/Latino; 9 Asian, non-Hispanic/Latino; 132 Hispanic/Latino; 7 Two or more races, non-Hispanic/Latino), 120 international. Average age 30. 360 applicants, 49% accepted, 73 enrolled. In 2019, 89 master's, 13 doctorates awarded. *Degree requirements:* For master's, thesis or alternative; for doctorate, comprehensive exam, thesis/dissertation. *Entrance requirements:* For master's and doctorate, GRE General Test, 3 letters of recommendation, minimum GPA of 3.0. Additional exam requirements/recommendations for international students: required—TOEFL (minimum score 550 paper-based; 80 iBT). *Application deadline:* For fall admission, 6/1 for domestic students, 4/1 for international students; for spring admission, 10/1 for domestic students, 9/1 for international students. Applications are processed on a rolling basis. Application fee: $30. Electronic applications accepted. *Expenses: Tuition, area resident:* Full-time $8912; part-time $446 per credit hour. Tuition, state resident: full-time $8912; part-time $446 per credit hour. Tuition, nonresident: full-time $21,393; part-time $992 per credit hour. *Required fees:* $2194. *Financial support:* Research assistantships, teaching assistantships, institutionally sponsored loans, scholarships/grants, and unspecified assistantships available. Financial award application deadline: 3/1; financial award applicants required to submit FAFSA. *Unit head:* Dr. Sundararaj S. Iyengar, Director, 305-348-3947, Fax: 305-348-3549, E-mail: sundararaj.iyengar@fiu.edu. *Application contact:* Nanett Rojas, Manager, Admissions Operations, 305-348-7464, Fax: 305-348-7441, E-mail: gradadm@fiu.edu.

Gannon University, School of Graduate Studies, College of Engineering and Business, School of Engineering and Computer Science, Program in Computer and Information Science, Erie, PA 16541-0001. Offers information analytics (MSCIS); software engineering (MSCIS). *Program availability:* Part-time, evening/weekend. *Degree requirements:* For master's, thesis (for some programs), directed research. *Entrance requirements:* For master's, 3 letters of recommendation; resume; transcripts; baccalaureate degree in computer science, information systems, information science, software engineering, or related field from regionally-accredited institution with minimum GPA of 2.5. Additional exam requirements/recommendations for international students: required—TOEFL (minimum score 79 iBT). Electronic applications accepted. Application fee is waived when completed online.

Gannon University, School of Graduate Studies, College of Engineering and Business, School of Engineering and Computer Science, Program in Information Analytics, Erie, PA 16541-0001. Offers MSCIS. *Program availability:* Part-time, evening/weekend. *Entrance requirements:* For master's, baccalaureate degree in computer science, information systems, information science, software engineering, or a related field from regionally-accredited institution with minimum GPA of 2.5; resume; transcripts; 3 letters of recommendation. Additional exam requirements/recommendations for international students: required—TOEFL (minimum score 79 iBT). Electronic applications accepted. Application fee is waived when completed online.

George Mason University, Volgenau School of Engineering, Department of Information Sciences and Technology, Fairfax, VA 22030. Offers applied information technology (MS); data analytics engineering (MS); information sciences and technology (Certificate). *Program availability:* Evening/weekend, 100% online. *Entrance requirements:* For master's, GRE/GMAT, personal goals statement; 2 copies of official transcripts; 3 letters of recommendation; resume; official bank statement; proof of financial support; photocopy of passport; baccalaureate degree from an accredited program with minimum B average in last 60 credit hours. Additional exam requirements/recommendations for international students: required—TOEFL (minimum score 575 paper-based; 88 iBT), IELTS (minimum score 6.5), PTE (minimum score 59). Electronic applications accepted. *Expenses:* Contact institution.

George Mason University, Volgenau School of Engineering, Program in Information Technology, Fairfax, VA 22030. Offers PhD. *Degree requirements:* For doctorate, comprehensive exam, thesis/dissertation, 18 credits of courses beyond MS; qualifying exams. *Entrance requirements:* For doctorate, GRE, MS and BS in a related field; 2 official copies of transcripts; 3 letters of recommendation; resume; expanded goals statement. Additional exam requirements/recommendations for international students: required—TOEFL (minimum score 575 paper-based; 88 iBT), IELTS (minimum score 6.5), PTE (minimum score 59). Electronic applications accepted. *Expenses:* Contact institution.

Georgia State University, J. Mack Robinson College of Business, Department of Computer Information Systems, Atlanta, GA 30302-3083. Offers computer information systems (PhD); health informatics (MBA, MS); information systems (MSIS, Certificate); information systems development and project management (MBA); information systems management (MBA); managing information technology (Exec MS); the wireless organization (MBA). *Program availability:* Part-time, evening/weekend. *Faculty:* 14 full-time (1 woman), 3 part-time/adjunct (1 woman). *Students:* 130 full-time (66 women), 7 part-time (2 women); includes 25 minority (15 Black or African American, non-Hispanic/Latino; 7 Asian, non-Hispanic/Latino; 3 Two or more races, non-Hispanic/Latino), 99 international. Average age 29. 368 applicants, 58% accepted, 84 enrolled. In 2019, 102 master's, 3 doctorates, 1 other advanced degree awarded. *Entrance requirements:* For master's, GRE or GMAT, transcripts from all institutions attended, resume, essays; for doctorate, GRE or GMAT, three letters of recommendation, personal statement, transcripts from all institutions attended, resume. Additional exam requirements/recommendations for international students: required—TOEFL (minimum score 610 paper-based; 101 iBT), IELTS (minimum score 7). *Application deadline:* For fall admission, 5/1 priority date for domestic students, 2/1 priority date for international students; for spring admission, 9/15 priority date for domestic students, 4/1 priority date for international students. Applications are processed on a rolling basis. Application fee: $50. Electronic applications accepted. *Expenses: Tuition, area resident:* Full-time $7164; part-time $398 per credit hour. Tuition, state resident: full-time $7164; part-time $398 per credit hour. Tuition, nonresident: full-time $22,662; part-time $1259 per credit hour. *International tuition:* $22,662 full-time. *Required fees:* $2128; $312 per credit hour. Tuition and fees vary according to course load and program. *Financial support:* Research assistantships, teaching assistantships, scholarships/grants, tuition waivers, and unspecified assistantships available. Financial award applicants required to submit FAFSA. *Unit head:* Dr. Ephraim R. McLean, Professor/Chair, 404-413-7360, Fax: 404-413-7394. *Application contact:* Toby McChesney, Assistant Dean for Graduate Recruiting and Student Services, 404-413-7167, Fax: 404-413-7167, E-mail: rcbgradadmissions@gsu.edu.
Website: http://cis.robinson.gsu.edu/

Grand Valley State University, Padnos College of Engineering and Computing, School of Computing and Information Systems, Allendale, MI 49401-9403. Offers MS. *Program availability:* Part-time, evening/weekend. *Faculty:* 10 full-time (0 women). *Students:* 11 full-time (4 women), 52 part-time (9 women); includes 12 minority (2 Black or African American, non-Hispanic/Latino; 5 Asian, non-Hispanic/Latino; 4 Hispanic/Latino; 1 Two or more races, non-Hispanic/Latino), 12 international. Average age 30. 31 applicants, 58% accepted, 6 enrolled. In 2019, 23 master's awarded. *Degree requirements:* For

master's, thesis optional, thesis, project, or capstone. *Entrance requirements:* For master's, GRE (recommended with GPA below 3.0), minimum GPA of 3.0; knowledge of a programming language; coursework or experience in: computer architecture and/or organization, data structures and algorithms, databases, discrete math, networking, operating systems, and software engineering; minimum of 2 letters of recommendation; resume; personal statement. Additional exam requirements/recommendations for international students: required—Michigan English Language Assessment Battery (minimum score 77), TOEFL (minimum iBT score of 80), or IELTS (6.5); GRE. *Application deadline:* For fall admission, 6/1 for international students; for winter admission, 9/1 for international students. Applications are processed on a rolling basis. Application fee: $30. Electronic applications accepted. *Expenses:* $733 per credit hour, 33 credit hours. *Financial support:* In 2019–20, 13 students received support, including 6 fellowships, 5 research assistantships with full and partial tuition reimbursements available (averaging $8,000 per year). *Unit head:* Dr. Paul Leidig, Director, 616-331-2060, Fax: 616-331-2144, E-mail: leidigp@gvsu.edu. *Application contact:* Dr. D. Robert Adams, Graduate Program Director, 616-331-3885, Fax: 616-331-2144, E-mail: adamsr@gvsu.edu.
Website: http://www.cis.gvsu.edu/

Hardin-Simmons University, Graduate School, Kelley College of Business, Abilene, TX 79698-0001. Offers business administration (MBA); information science (MS); sports management (MBA). *Accreditation:* ACBSP. *Program availability:* Part-time. *Degree requirements:* For master's, thesis or alternative. *Entrance requirements:* For master's, GMAT, minimum GPA of 3.0 in upper-level course work, resume, interview. Additional exam requirements/recommendations for international students: required—TOEFL (minimum score 550 paper-based; 79 iBT). Electronic applications accepted.

Harvard University, Extension School, Cambridge, MA 02138-3722. Offers applied sciences (CAS); biotechnology (ALM); educational technologies (ALM); educational technology (CET); English for graduate and professional studies (DGP); environmental management (ALM, CEM); information technology (ALM); journalism (ALM); liberal arts (ALM); management (ALM, CM); mathematics for teaching (ALM); museum studies (ALM); premedical studies (Diploma); publication and communication (CPC). *Program availability:* Part-time, evening/weekend. *Degree requirements:* For master's, thesis. *Entrance requirements:* For master's, 3 completed graduate courses with grade of B or higher. Additional exam requirements/recommendations for international students: required—TOEFL (minimum score 600 paper-based), TWE (minimum score 5). *Expenses:* Contact institution.

Harvard University, Graduate School of Arts and Sciences, Program in Information, Technology and Management, Cambridge, MA 02138. Offers PhD.

Hood College, Graduate School, Program in Management Information Systems, Frederick, MD 21701-8575. Offers MS. *Program availability:* Part-time, evening/weekend. *Entrance requirements:* For master's, minimum GPA of 2.75, essay, resume. Additional exam requirements/recommendations for international students: required—TOEFL (minimum score 575 paper-based; 89 iBT), IELTS (minimum score 6.5). Electronic applications accepted. *Expenses:* Contact institution.

Hood College, Graduate School, Programs in Computer and Information Sciences, Frederick, MD 21701-8575. Offers computer science (MS); cybersecurity (MS, Certificate); information technology (MS). *Program availability:* Part-time, evening/weekend, 100% online. *Degree requirements:* For master's, thesis optional, capstone (S). *Entrance requirements:* For master's, minimum GPA of 2.75, essay, resume. Additional exam requirements/recommendations for international students: required—TOEFL (minimum score 575 paper-based; 89 iBT), IELTS (minimum score 6.5). Electronic applications accepted. *Expenses:* Contact institution.

Indiana University Bloomington, School of Informatics, Computing, and Engineering, Department of Information and Library Science, Bloomington, IN 47405-3907. Offers information architecture (Graduate Certificate); information science (MIS, PhD); library and information science (Sp LIS); library science (MLS); JD/MLS; MIS/MA; MLS/MA; MPA/MIS; MPA/MLS. *Accreditation:* ALA (one or more programs are accredited). *Program availability:* Part-time. Terminal master's awarded for partial completion of doctoral program. *Degree requirements:* For master's, internship; for doctorate, comprehensive exam, thesis/dissertation. *Entrance requirements:* For master's, GRE General Test (for applicants whose previous undergraduate degree GPA was below 3.0 or previous graduate degree GPA was below 3.2), 3 letters of reference, resume, personal statement (500 words minimum), transcripts; for doctorate, GRE General Test, resume, personal statement (800-1000 words), writing sample, transcripts, 3 letters of reference. Additional exam requirements/recommendations for international students: required—TOEFL (minimum score 600 paper-based; 100 iBT), IELTS. Electronic applications accepted. *Expenses:* Contact institution.

Indiana University Bloomington, School of Informatics, Computing, and Engineering, Program in Informatics, Bloomington, IN 47405. Offers informatics (MS, PhD), including bioinformatics (PhD), complex systems (PhD), computing, culture and society (PhD), health informatics (PhD), human-computer interaction (MS), human-computer interaction design (PhD), music informatics (PhD), security informatics (PhD); visual heritage (PhD). *Program availability:* Part-time. Terminal master's awarded for partial completion of doctoral program. *Degree requirements:* For master's, thesis, capstone project; for doctorate, variable foreign language requirement, comprehensive exam, thesis/dissertation. *Entrance requirements:* For master's and doctorate, GRE, resume/curriculum vitae, transcripts, 3 letters of recommendation. Additional exam requirements/recommendations for international students: required—TOEFL (minimum score 600 paper-based; 100 iBT). Electronic applications accepted.

Indiana University-Purdue University Indianapolis, School of Informatics and Computing, Department of Library and Information Science, Indianapolis, IN 46202. Offers MLS. *Accreditation:* ALA. *Program availability:* Part-time, evening/weekend, 100% online. *Entrance requirements:* For master's, GRE General Test. Additional exam requirements/recommendations for international students: required—TOEFL (minimum score 600 paper-based).

Instituto Tecnologico de Santo Domingo, Graduate School, Area of Engineering, Santo Domingo, Dominican Republic. Offers construction administration (MS, Certificate); data telecommunications (M Eng, MS, Certificate); industrial engineering (M Eng, Certificate); industrial management (M Mgmt); information technology (Certificate); maintenance engineering (M Eng); occupational hazard prevention (M Mgmt); production management (Certificate); quantitative methods (Certificate); sanitary and environmental engineering (M Eng); structural engineering (M Eng); systems engineering and electronic data processing (Certificate); transportation (Certificate).

Instituto Tecnológico y de Estudios Superiores de Monterrey, Campus Cuernavaca, Programs in Information Science, Temixco, Mexico. Offers administration of information technology (MATI); computer science (MCC, DCC); information technology (MTI).

Instituto Tecnológico y de Estudios Superiores de Monterrey, Campus Estado de México, Professional and Graduate Division, Estado de Mexico, Mexico. Offers administration of information technologies (MITA); architecture (M Arch); business administration (GMBA, MBA); computer sciences (MCS, PhD); education (M Ed); educational institution administration (MAD); educational technology and innovation (PhD); electronic commerce (MEC); environmental systems (MS); finance (MAF); humanistic studies (MHS); information sciences and knowledge management (MISKM); information systems (MS); manufacturing systems (MS); marketing (MEM); quality systems and productivity (MS); science and materials engineering (PhD); telecommunications management (MTM). *Program availability:* Part-time, online learning. *Degree requirements:* For master's, one foreign language, thesis (for some programs); for doctorate, one foreign language, thesis/dissertation. *Entrance requirements:* For master's, E-PAEP 500, interview; for doctorate, E-PAEP 500, research proposal. Additional exam requirements/recommendations for international students: required—TOEFL (minimum score 550 paper-based).

Instituto Tecnológico y de Estudios Superiores de Monterrey, Campus Irapuato, Graduate Programs, Irapuato, Mexico. Offers administration (MBA); administration of information technology (MAIT); administration of telecommunications (MAT); architecture (M Arch); computer science (MCS); education (M Ed); educational administration (MEA); educational innovation and technology (DEIT); educational technology (MET); electronic commerce (MBA); environmental administration and planning (MEAP); environmental systems (MES); finances (MBA); humanistic studies (MHS); international management for Latin American executives (MIMLAE); library and information science (MLIS); manufacturing quality management (MMQM); marketing research (MBA).

Instituto Tecnológico y de Estudios Superiores de Monterrey, Campus Monterrey, Graduate and Research Division, Program in Computer Science, Monterrey, Mexico. Offers artificial intelligence (PhD); computer science (MS); information systems (MS); information technology (MS). *Program availability:* Part-time. *Degree requirements:* For master's, one foreign language, thesis; for doctorate, one foreign language, thesis/dissertation. *Entrance requirements:* For master's, EXADEP; for doctorate, master's degree in related field. Additional exam requirements/recommendations for international students: required—TOEFL.

Instituto Tecnológico y de Estudios Superiores de Monterrey, Campus Monterrey, Graduate and Research Division, Program in Informatics, Monterrey, Mexico. Offers PhD. *Program availability:* Part-time. *Degree requirements:* For doctorate, one foreign language, thesis/dissertation, technological project, arbitrated publication of articles. *Entrance requirements:* For doctorate, GRE General Test, GRE Subject Test, master's degree in related field. Additional exam requirements/recommendations for international students: required—TOEFL.

Instituto Tecnológico y de Estudios Superiores de Monterrey, Campus Sonora Norte, Program in Technological Information Management, Hermosillo, Mexico. Offers MA.

Iowa State University of Science and Technology, Program in Information Assurance, Ames, IA 50011. Offers M Eng, MS. *Degree requirements:* For master's, thesis or alternative. *Entrance requirements:* For master's, GRE General Test. Additional exam requirements/recommendations for international students: required—TOEFL (minimum score 570 paper-based; 79 iBT), IELTS (minimum score 6.5). Electronic applications accepted.

Kennesaw State University, Coles College of Business, Program in Information Systems, Kennesaw, GA 30144. Offers MSIS. *Program availability:* Part-time. *Students:* 3 full-time (all women), 24 part-time (16 women); includes 13 minority (6 Black or African American, non-Hispanic/Latino; 6 Asian, non-Hispanic/Latino; 1 Two or more races, non-Hispanic/Latino), 2 international. Average age 38. 18 applicants, 56% accepted, 7 enrolled. In 2019, 17 master's awarded. *Entrance requirements:* For master's, GMAT or GRE General Test, minimum GPA of 2.75. Additional exam requirements/recommendations for international students: required—TOEFL (minimum score 80 iBT), IELTS (minimum score 6.5). *Application deadline:* For fall admission, 7/1 for domestic and international students; for spring admission, 11/1 for domestic and international students; for summer admission, 4/1 for domestic and international students. Applications are processed on a rolling basis. Application fee: $60. Electronic applications accepted. *Expenses: Tuition, area resident:* Full-time $7104; part-time $296 per credit hour. Tuition, state resident: full-time $7104; part-time $296 per credit hour. Tuition, nonresident: full-time $25,584; part-time $1066 per credit hour. *International tuition:* $25,584 full-time. *Required fees:* $2006; $1706 per unit. $853 per semester. *Financial support:* Application deadline: 4/1; applicants required to submit FAFSA. *Unit head:* Dr. Tridib Bandyopadhyay, Director, 470-578-2144, E-mail: tbandyop@kennesaw.edu. *Application contact:* Admissions Counselor, 470-578-4377, Fax: 770-578-9172, E-mail: ksugrad@kennesaw.edu.
Website: http://coles.kennesaw.edu/msis/

Kennesaw State University, College of Computing and Software Engineering, Program in Information Technology, Kennesaw, GA 30144. Offers data management and analytics (Graduate Certificate); health information technology (Postbaccalaureate Certificate); information technology (MSIT); information technology foundations (Postbaccalaureate Certificate); information technology security (Graduate Certificate). *Program availability:* Part-time, evening/weekend, blended/hybrid learning. *Students:* 73 full-time (38 women), 142 part-time (52 women); includes 101 minority (56 Black or African American, non-Hispanic/Latino; 31 Asian, non-Hispanic/Latino; 10 Hispanic/Latino; 4 Two or more races, non-Hispanic/Latino), 37 international. Average age 32. 52 applicants, 85% accepted, 34 enrolled. In 2019, 95 master's awarded. *Degree requirements:* For master's, thesis optional. *Entrance requirements:* For master's, minimum GPA of 2.75; for other advanced degree, bachelor's degree. Additional exam requirements/recommendations for international students: required—TOEFL (minimum score 80 iBT), IELTS (minimum score 6.5). *Application deadline:* For fall admission, 7/1 priority date for domestic students, 5/1 priority date for international students; for spring admission, 11/1 priority date for domestic students, 9/1 priority date for international students; for summer admission, 4/1 priority date for domestic students, 3/1 priority date for international students. Applications are processed on a rolling basis. Application fee: $60. Electronic applications accepted. *Expenses: Tuition, area resident:* Full-time $7104; part-time $296 per credit hour. Tuition, state resident: full-time $7104; part-time $296 per credit hour. Tuition, nonresident: full-time $25,584; part-time $1066 per credit hour. *International tuition:* $25,584 full-time. *Required fees:* $2006; $1706 per unit. $853 per semester. *Financial support:* Applicants required to submit FAFSA. *Application contact:* Admission Counselor, 470-578-4377, Fax: 470-578-9172, E-mail: ksugrad@kennesaw.edu.
Website: http://ccse.kennesaw.edu/it/

Kent State University, College of Communication and Information, School of Information, Kent, OH 44242-0001. Offers health informatics (MS), including health informatics, knowledge management, user experience design; library and information science (MLIS), including K-12 school library media; M Ed/MLIS; MBA/MLIS; MLIS/MS. *Accreditation:* ALA (one or more programs are accredited). *Program availability:* Part-time, 100% online. *Faculty:* 16 full-time (13 women), 26 part-time/adjunct (12 women). *Students:* 148 full-time (120 women), 372 part-time (274 women); includes 89 minority (34 Black or African American, non-Hispanic/Latino; 16 Asian, non-Hispanic/Latino; 26 Hispanic/Latino; 13 Two or more races, non-Hispanic/Latino), 2 international. Average age 32. 211 applicants, 100% accepted, 142 enrolled. In 2019, 32 master's awarded. *Degree requirements:* For master's, thesis, portfolio (MLIS); internship, project, paper, or thesis. *Entrance requirements:* For master's, GRE if total GPA is below 3.0 in highest completed degree, minimum GPA of 3.0, statement of purpose, 3 letters of recommendation, curriculum vitae/resume, transcripts, writing sample, personal interview, application essay, student profile form. Additional exam requirements/recommendations for international students: required—TOEFL (minimum score 94 iBT), IELTS (minimum score 7), PTE (minimum score 65), Michigan English Language Assessment Battery (minimum score 82). *Application deadline:* For fall admission, 3/15 priority date for domestic students, 3/15 for international students; for spring admission, 9/15 priority date for domestic students, 9/15 for international students; for summer admission, 1/15 priority date for domestic students, 1/15 for international students. Applications are processed on a rolling basis. Application fee: $45 ($70 for international students). Electronic applications accepted. *Financial support:* Fellowships with full tuition reimbursements, research assistantships with full tuition reimbursements, teaching assistantships with full tuition reimbursements, scholarships/grants, and unspecified assistantships available. Financial award application deadline: 3/1. *Unit head:* Dr. Kendra Albright, Ph.D., Director and Professor, 330-672-8535, E-mail: kalbrig7@kent.edu. *Application contact:* Dr. Kendra Albright, Ph.D., Director and Professor, 330-672-8535, E-mail: kalbrig7@kent.edu.
Website: https://www.kent.edu/iSchool

Lawrence Technological University, College of Management, Southfield, MI 48075-1058. Offers business administration (MBA, DBA), including business analytics (MBA, MS), cybersecurity (MBA, MS), finance (MBA), information systems (MBA), information technology (MBA), marketing (MBA), project management (MBA, MS); cybersecurity (Graduate Certificate); health IT management (Graduate Certificate); information assurance management (Graduate Certificate); information systems (MS), including enterprise resource planning, enterprise security management, project management (MBA, MS); information technology (MS, DM), including business analytics (MBA, MS), cybersecurity (MBA, MS), information assurance (MS), project management (MBA, MS); management (PhD); nonprofit management and leadership (Graduate Certificate); operations management (MS), including manufacturing operations, service operations; project management (Graduate Certificate). *Accreditation:* ACBSP. *Program availability:* Part-time, evening/weekend, 100% online. *Faculty:* 9 full-time (3 women), 12 part-time/adjunct (3 women). *Students:* 5 full-time (1 woman), 226 part-time (92 women); includes 51 minority (28 Black or African American, non-Hispanic/Latino; 1 American Indian or Alaska Native, non-Hispanic/Latino; 11 Asian, non-Hispanic/Latino; 6 Hispanic/Latino; 1 Native Hawaiian or other Pacific Islander, non-Hispanic/Latino; 4 Two or more races, non-Hispanic/Latino), 45 international. Average age 33. 123 applicants, 58% accepted, 49 enrolled. In 2019, 96 master's, 3 doctorates, 9 other advanced degrees awarded. Terminal master's awarded for partial completion of doctoral program. *Degree requirements:* For master's, thesis (for some programs); for doctorate, comprehensive exam, thesis/dissertation. *Entrance requirements:* Additional exam requirements/recommendations for international students: required—TOEFL (minimum score 550 paper-based; 79 iBT), IELTS (minimum score 6.5). *Application deadline:* For fall admission, 5/24 for international students; for spring admission, 10/13 for international students; for summer admission, 2/18 for international students. Applications are processed on a rolling basis. Application fee: $50. Electronic applications accepted. *Expenses: Tuition:* Full-time $16,618; part-time $8309 per year. *Required fees:* $600; $600. *Financial support:* In 2019–20, 25 students received support, including 8 research assistantships with partial tuition reimbursements available (averaging $3,360 per year); career-related internships or fieldwork, unspecified assistantships, and corporate tuition incentives also available. Financial award application deadline: 4/1; financial award applicants required to submit FAFSA. *Unit head:* Dr. Bahman Mirshab, Dean, 248-204-3050, E-mail: mgtdean@ltu.edu. *Application contact:* Jane Rohrback, Director of Admissions, 248-204-3160, Fax: 248-204-2228, E-mail: admissions@ltu.edu.
Website: http://www.ltu.edu/management/index.asp

Lehigh University, College of Business, Department of Accounting, Bethlehem, PA 18015. Offers accounting and information analysis (MS). *Accreditation:* AACSB. *Program availability:* Part-time. *Faculty:* 9 full-time (1 woman). *Students:* 13 full-time (10 women); includes 1 minority (Hispanic/Latino), 8 international. Average age 24. 38 applicants, 61% accepted, 10 enrolled. In 2019, 24 master's awarded. *Entrance requirements:* For master's, GMAT. Additional exam requirements/recommendations for international students: required—TOEFL (minimum score 105 iBT). *Application deadline:* For fall admission, 4/15 for domestic and international students. Application fee: $75. *Expenses:* Contact institution. *Financial support:* In 2019–20, 19 students received support. Fellowships and scholarships/grants available. Financial award application deadline: 1/15. *Unit head:* Dr. C. Bryan Cloyd, Chairman, 610-758-2816, Fax: 610-758-6429, E-mail: cbc215@lehigh.edu. *Application contact:* Mary Theresa Taglang, Director of Recruitment and Admissions, 610-758-4386, Fax: 610-758-5283, E-mail: mtt4@lehigh.edu.
Website: https://cbe.lehigh.edu/academics/graduate/master-accounting-and-information-analysis

Loyola University Chicago, Graduate School, Department of Computer Science, Chicago, IL 60660. Offers computer science (MS); information technology (MS); software engineering (MS). *Program availability:* Part-time, evening/weekend, online only, 100% online, blended/hybrid learning. *Faculty:* 16 full-time (3 women), 18 part-time/adjunct (2 women). *Students:* 34 full-time (12 women), 37 part-time (10 women); includes 26 minority (6 Black or African American, non-Hispanic/Latino; 16 Asian, non-Hispanic/Latino; 4 Hispanic/Latino), 20 international. Average age 33. 115 applicants, 41% accepted, 17 enrolled. In 2019, 45 master's awarded. *Degree requirements:* For master's, thesis optional, 30 credits/ten courses. *Entrance requirements:* For master's, statement of purpose, one letter of recommendation, transcripts, international transcript evaluation (if applicable). Additional exam requirements/recommendations for international students: required—TOEFL (minimum score 550 paper-based; 79 iBT), IELTS (minimum score 6.5), PTE (minimum score 53), Duolingo English Test. *Application deadline:* Applications are processed on a rolling basis. Application fee: $50. Electronic applications accepted. Application fee is waived when completed online. *Expenses:* $1033 per credit; $115-452 fees per sememster. *Financial support:* In 2019–20, 16 students received support, including 2 fellowships with full tuition reimbursements available, 1 research assistantship with full tuition reimbursement available (averaging $18,000 per year), 13 teaching assistantships with partial tuition reimbursements available (averaging $9,925 per year); Federal Work-Study, health care benefits, and tuition waivers (full and partial) also available. Financial award application deadline: 4/1. *Unit head:* Dr. Chandra Sekharan, Chair, 773-508-8150, Fax: 773-508-3739, E-mail: info@cs.luc.edu. *Application contact:* Cecilia Murphy, Graduate Program Secretary, 773-508-8035, E-mail: gpd@cs.luc.edu.
Website: http://luc.edu/cs

Marshall University, Academic Affairs Division, College of Information Technology and Engineering, Program in Information Systems, Huntington, WV 25755. Offers MS. *Program availability:* Part-time, evening/weekend. *Degree requirements:* For master's, final project, oral exam. *Entrance requirements:* For master's, GRE General Test or MAT, minimum undergraduate GPA of 2.5.

Maryville University of Saint Louis, The John E. Simon School of Business, St. Louis, MO 63141-7299. Offers accounting (MBA, MS, Certificate); business studies (Certificate); cybersecurity (MBA, MS, Certificate); financial services (MBA, Certificate); health administration (MBA); healthcare administration (Certificate); human resource management (MBA); human resources management (Certificate); information technology (MBA); information technology management (Certificate); management (MBA, Certificate); management and leadership (MA); marketing (MBA, Certificate); project management (MBA, Certificate); sport business management (MBA); supply chain management (Certificate); supply chain management/logistics (MBA). *Accreditation:* ACBSP. *Program availability:* Part-time, 100% online, blended/hybrid learning. *Faculty:* 3 full-time (0 women), 107 part-time/adjunct (28 women). *Students:* 315 full-time (155 women), 738 part-time (344 women); includes 329 minority (186 Black or African American, non-Hispanic/Latino; 5 American Indian or Alaska Native, non-Hispanic/Latino; 48 Asian, non-Hispanic/Latino; 60 Hispanic/Latino; 30 Two or more races, non-Hispanic/Latino), 38 international. Average age 34. In 2019, 388 master's awarded. *Degree requirements:* For master's, capstone course (for MBA). *Entrance requirements:* Additional exam requirements/recommendations for international students: required—TOEFL (minimum score 563 paper-based; 85 iBT). *Application deadline:* Applications are processed on a rolling basis. Electronic applications accepted. *Expenses:* Contact institution. *Financial support:* Career-related internships or fieldwork, Federal Work-Study, tuition waivers (partial), and campus employment available. Financial award application deadline: 4/1; financial award applicants required to submit FAFSA. *Unit head:* Tammy Gocial, Associate Academic Vice President/Interim Dean, 314-529-9401, Fax: 314-529-9975, E-mail: tgocial@maryville.edu. *Application contact:* Chris Gourdine, Assistant Dean Business Administration, 314-529-6861, Fax: 314-529-9975, E-mail: cgourdine@maryville.edu.
Website: http://www.maryville.edu/bu/business-administration-masters/

Massachusetts Institute of Technology, School of Engineering, Department of Civil and Environmental Engineering, Cambridge, MA 02139. Offers biological oceanography (PhD, Sc D); chemical oceanography (PhD, Sc D); civil and environmental engineering (M Eng, SM, PhD, Sc D); civil and environmental systems (PhD, Sc D); civil engineering (PhD, Sc D, CE); civil engineering and computation (PhD); coastal engineering (PhD, Sc D); construction engineering and management (PhD, Sc D); environmental biology (PhD, Sc D); environmental chemistry (PhD, Sc D); environmental engineering (PhD, Sc D); environmental engineering and computation (PhD); environmental fluid mechanics (PhD, Sc D); geotechnical and geoenvironmental engineering (PhD, Sc D); hydrology (PhD, Sc D); information technology (PhD, Sc D); oceanographic engineering (PhD, Sc D); structures and materials (PhD, Sc D); transportation (PhD, Sc D); SM/MBA. *Degree requirements:* For master's, thesis; for doctorate, comprehensive exam, thesis/dissertation; for CE, comprehensive exam, thesis. *Entrance requirements:* For master's, doctorate, and CE, GRE General Test. Additional exam requirements/recommendations for international students: required—TOEFL, IELTS. Electronic applications accepted.

Minnesota State University Mankato, College of Graduate Studies and Research, College of Science, Engineering and Technology, Department of Computer Information Science, Mankato, MN 56001. Offers information technology (MS). *Degree requirements:* For master's, comprehensive exam, thesis or alternative. *Entrance requirements:* For master's, GRE General Test, minimum GPA of 3.0 during previous 2 years. Additional exam requirements/recommendations for international students: required—TOEFL (minimum score 550 paper-based; 80 iBT). Electronic applications accepted.

Missouri University of Science and Technology, Department of Business and Information Technology, Rolla, MO 65401. Offers business administration (MBA); information science and technology (MS). *Degree requirements:* For master's, thesis or alternative. *Entrance requirements:* Additional exam requirements/recommendations for international students: required—TOEFL (minimum score 600 paper-based); recommended—IELTS. Electronic applications accepted. *Expenses:* Tuition, state resident: full-time $7839; part-time $435.50 per credit hour. Tuition, nonresident: full-time $22,169; part-time $1231.60 per credit hour. *International tuition:* $18,156.60 full-time. *Required fees:* $649.76. One-time fee: $119. Tuition and fees vary according to course load and program.

Monroe College, King Graduate School, Bronx, NY 10468. Offers accounting (MS); business administration (MBA), including entrepreneurship, finance, general business administration, healthcare management, human resources, information technology, marketing; computer science (MS); criminal justice (MS); hospitality management (MS); public health (MPH), including biostatistics and epidemiology, community health, health administration and leadership. *Program availability:* Online learning.

Naval Postgraduate School, Departments and Academic Groups, Department of Information Sciences, Monterey, CA 93943. Offers electronic warfare systems engineering (MS); information sciences (PhD); information systems and operations (MS); information technology management (MS); information warfare systems engineering (MS); knowledge superiority (Certificate); remote sensing intelligence (MS); system technology (command, control and communications) (MS). *Program availability:* Part-time. *Degree requirements:* For master's, thesis (for some programs); for doctorate, thesis/dissertation.

New Jersey Institute of Technology, Ying Wu College of Computing, Newark, NJ 07102. Offers big data management and mining (Certificate); business and information systems (Certificate); computer science (PhD); computing and business (MS); data mining (Certificate); data science (MS); information security (Certificate); information systems (PhD); information technology administration and security (MS); IT administration (Certificate); network security and information assurance (Certificate); software engineering (MS), including information systems; software engineering analysis/design (Certificate); Web systems development (Certificate). *Program availability:* Part-time, evening/weekend. *Faculty:* 78 full-time (16 women), 63 part-time/adjunct (10 women). *Students:* 668 full-time (210 women), 290 part-time (81 women); includes 277 minority (46 Black or African American, non-Hispanic/Latino; 1 American Indian or Alaska Native, non-Hispanic/Latino; 161 Asian, non-Hispanic/Latino; 53 Hispanic/Latino; 16 Two or more races, non-Hispanic/Latino), 565 international. Average age 27. 2,671 applicants, 62% accepted, 360 enrolled. In 2019, 407 master's, 5 doctorates, 12 other advanced degrees awarded. Terminal master's awarded for partial completion of doctoral program. *Degree requirements:* For master's, thesis optional; for doctorate, thesis/dissertation. *Entrance requirements:* For master's, GRE General Test; for doctorate, GRE General Test, minimum graduate GPA of 3.5. Additional exam requirements/recommendations for international students: required—TOEFL (minimum score 550 paper-based; 79 iBT), IELTS (minimum score 6.5). *Application deadline:* For fall admission, 6/1 priority date for domestic students, 5/1 priority date for international students; for spring admission, 11/15 priority date for domestic and international students. Applications are processed on a rolling basis. Application fee: $75. Electronic applications accepted. *Expenses:* $23,828 per year (in-state), $33,744 per year (out-of-state). *Financial support:* In 2019–20, 383 students received support, including 8 fellowships with full tuition reimbursements available, 34 research assistantships with full tuition reimbursements available (averaging $24,000 per year), 57 teaching assistantships with full tuition reimbursements available (averaging $24,000 per year); career-related internships or fieldwork, Federal Work-Study, scholarships/grants, and unspecified assistantships also available. Financial award application deadline: 1/15. *Unit head:* Dr. Craig Gotsman, Dean, 973-596-3366, Fax: 973-596-5777, E-mail: craig.gotsman@njit.edu. *Application contact:* Stephen Eck, Executive Director of University Admissions, 973-596-3300, Fax: 973-596-3461, E-mail: admissions@njit.edu.
Website: http://computing.njit.edu/

Northern Kentucky University, Office of Graduate Programs, College of Informatics, Department of Business Informatics, Highland Heights, KY 41099. Offers business informatics (MS, Certificate); corporate information security (Certificate); enterprise resource planning (Certificate). *Program availability:* Part-time, evening/weekend. *Entrance requirements:* For master's, GRE or GMAT. Additional exam requirements/recommendations for international students: required—TOEFL (minimum score 79 iBT); recommended—IELTS (minimum score 6.5). Electronic applications accepted.

Northwestern University, McCormick School of Engineering and Applied Science, Department of Electrical Engineering and Computer Science, MS in Information Technology Program, Evanston, IL 60208. Offers MS. *Program availability:* Part-time, evening/weekend. *Entrance requirements:* For master's, GRE (recommended), work experience in an IT-related position. Additional exam requirements/recommendations for international students: required—TOEFL (minimum score 80 iBT), IELTS (minimum score 7). Electronic applications accepted.

Northwestern University, School of Professional Studies, Program in Information Design and Strategy, Evanston, IL 60208. Offers MS.

Nova Southeastern University, College of Engineering and Computing, Fort Lauderdale, FL 33314-7796. Offers computer science (MS, PhD); information assurance (PhD); information assurance and cybersecurity (MS); information systems (PhD); information technology (MS); management information systems (MS). *Program availability:* Part-time, evening/weekend, blended/hybrid learning. *Faculty:* 18 full-time (6 women), 20 part-time/adjunct (4 women). *Students:* 206 full-time (67 women), 244 part-time (71 women); includes 229 minority (93 Black or African American, non-Hispanic/Latino; 1 American Indian or Alaska Native, non-Hispanic/Latino; 36 Asian, non-Hispanic/Latino; 84 Hispanic/Latino; 1 Native Hawaiian or other Pacific Islander, non-Hispanic/Latino; 14 Two or more races, non-Hispanic/Latino), 80 international. Average age 40. 212 applicants, 58% accepted, 63 enrolled. In 2019, 142 master's, 41 doctorates awarded. Terminal master's awarded for partial completion of doctoral program. *Degree requirements:* For master's, thesis optional; for doctorate, thesis/dissertation. *Entrance requirements:* For master's, minimum undergraduate GPA of 2.5; for doctorate, master's degree, minimum graduate GPA of 3.25. Additional exam requirements/recommendations for international students: required—TOEFL (minimum score 80 iBT), IELTS (minimum score 6), PTE (minimum score 54). *Application deadline:* Applications are processed on a rolling basis. Application fee: $50. Electronic applications accepted. *Expenses:* Contact institution. *Financial support:* Federal Work-Study, scholarships/grants, and corporate financial support available. Financial award application deadline: 4/15; financial award applicants required to submit FAFSA. *Unit head:* Dr. Meline Kevorkian, Associate Provost, Dean of Computering and Engineering, 954-262-2063, Fax: 954-262-2752, E-mail: melinek@nova.edu. *Application contact:* Nancy Azoulay, Director, Admissions, 954-262-2026, Fax: 954-262-2752, E-mail: azoulayn@nova.edu.
Website: http://scis.nova.edu

Oklahoma State University, Spears School of Business, Department of Management Science and Information Systems, Stillwater, OK 74078. Offers management information systems (MS); management science and information systems (PhD); telecommunications management (MS). *Program availability:* Part-time, online learning. *Faculty:* 12 full-time (2 women), 2 part-time/adjunct (0 women). *Students:* 31 full-time (16 women), 60 part-time (15 women); includes 11 minority (2 Black or African American, non-Hispanic/Latino; 3 American Indian or Alaska Native, non-Hispanic/Latino; 3 Asian, non-Hispanic/Latino; 1 Hispanic/Latino; 2 Two or more races, non-Hispanic/Latino), 43 international. Average age 30. 109 applicants, 61% accepted, 23 enrolled. In 2019, 58 master's, 1 doctorate awarded. *Entrance requirements:* For master's and doctorate, GRE or GMAT. Additional exam requirements/recommendations for international students: required—TOEFL (minimum score 550 paper-based; 79 iBT). *Application deadline:* For fall admission, 3/1 priority date for international students; for spring admission, 8/1 priority date for international students. Applications are processed on a rolling basis. Application fee: $50 ($75 for international students). Electronic applications accepted. *Expenses: Tuition, area resident:* Full-time $4148.10; part-time $2765.40. Tuition, state resident: full-time $4148.10; part-time $2765.40. Tuition, nonresident: full-time $15,775; part-time $10,516.80. *International tuition:* $15,775.20 full-time. *Required fees:* $2196.90; $122.05 per credit hour. Tuition and fees vary according to course load, campus/location and program. *Financial support:* In 2019–20, 10 research assistantships (averaging $2,000 per year), 11 teaching assistantships (averaging $1,198 per year) were awarded; career-related internships or fieldwork, Federal Work-Study, scholarships/grants, health care benefits, tuition waivers (partial), and unspecified assistantships also available. Support available to part-time students. Financial award application deadline: 3/1; financial award applicants required to submit FAFSA. *Unit head:* Dr. Rick Wilson, Department Head, 405-744-3551, Fax: 405-744-5180, E-mail: rick.wilson@okstate.edu. *Application contact:* Dr. Sheryl Tucker, Vice Prov/Dean/Prof, 405-744-6368, E-mail: gradi@okstate.edu.
Website: https://business.okstate.edu/departments_programs/msis/index.html

Old Dominion University, Strome College of Business, Doctoral Program in Business Administration, Norfolk, VA 23529. Offers business administration (PhD), including finance, IT and supply chain management, marketing, strategic management. *Accreditation:* AACSB. *Degree requirements:* For doctorate, comprehensive exam, thesis/dissertation. *Entrance requirements:* For doctorate, GMAT or GRE. Additional exam requirements/recommendations for international students: required—TOEFL (minimum score 550 paper-based; 79 iBT). Electronic applications accepted.

Pace University, Seidenberg School of Computer Science and Information Systems, New York, NY 10038. Offers chief information security officer (APC); computer science (MS, PhD); enterprise analytics (MS); information and communication technology strategy and innovation (APC); information systems (MS, APC); information technology (MS); professional studies in computing (DPS); secure software and information engineering (APC); security and information assurance (Certificate); software development and engineering (MS, Certificate); telecommunications systems and networks (MS, Certificate). *Program availability:* Part-time, evening/weekend, online only, 100% online, blended/hybrid learning. *Degree requirements:* For master's, thesis or alternative, capstone course; for doctorate, comprehensive exam (for some programs), thesis/dissertation. *Entrance requirements:* Additional exam requirements/recommendations for international students: required—TOEFL (minimum score 78 iBT), IELTS (minimum score 6.5) or PTE (minimum score 52). Electronic applications accepted. *Expenses:* Contact institution.

Penn State Great Valley, Graduate Studies, Management Division, Malvern, PA 19355-1488. Offers business administration (MBA); cyber security (Certificate); data analytics (MPS, MS, Certificate); distributed energy and grid modernization (Certificate); finance (M Fin); health sector management (Certificate); human resource management (Certificate); information science (MSIS); leadership development (MLD); new ventures and entrepreneurship (Certificate); sustainable management practices (Certificate). *Accreditation:* AACSB.

Penn State University Park, Graduate School, College of Information Sciences and Technology, University Park, PA 16802. Offers information sciences (MPS); information sciences and technology (MS, PhD). *Program availability:* Part-time, evening/weekend. *Entrance requirements:* Additional exam requirements/recommendations for international students: required—TOEFL (minimum score 550 paper-based; 80 iBT), IELTS. Electronic applications accepted. *Expenses:* Contact institution.

Purdue University Fort Wayne, College of Engineering, Technology, and Computer Science, Program in Technology, Fort Wayne, IN 46805-1499. Offers facilities/construction management (MS); industrial technology/manufacturing (MS); information technology/advanced computer applications (MS). *Program availability:* Part-time. *Entrance requirements:* For master's, minimum GPA of 3.0. Additional exam requirements/recommendations for international students: required—TOEFL (minimum score 550 paper-based; 79 iBT), TWE. Electronic applications accepted.

Regis University, College of Computer and Information Sciences, Denver, CO 80221-1099. Offers agile technologies (Certificate); cybersecurity (Certificate); data science (M Sc); database administration with Oracle (Certificate); database development (Certificate); database technologies (M Sc); enterprise Java software development (Certificate); enterprise resource planning (Certificate); executive information technology (Certificate); health care informatics (Certificate); health care informatics and information management (M Sc); information assurance (M Sc); information assurance policy management (Certificate); information technology management (M Sc); mobile software development (Certificate); software engineering (M Sc, Certificate); software engineering and database technology (M Sc); storage area networks (Certificate); systems engineering (M Sc, Certificate). *Program availability:* Part-time, evening/weekend, 100% online, blended/hybrid learning. *Degree requirements:* For master's, thesis (for some programs), final research project. *Entrance requirements:* For master's, official transcript reflecting baccalaureate degree awarded from regionally-accredited college or university, 2 years of related experience, resume, interview. Additional exam requirements/recommendations for international students: required—TOEFL (minimum score 550 paper-based; 82 iBT). Electronic applications accepted. *Expenses:* Contact institution.

Rensselaer at Hartford, Department of Computer and Information Science, Program in Information Technology, Hartford, CT 06120-2991. Offers MS. *Program availability:* Part-time, evening/weekend. *Entrance requirements:* For master's, GRE. Additional exam requirements/recommendations for international students: required—TOEFL (minimum score 600 paper-based; 100 iBT). Electronic applications accepted.

Rensselaer Polytechnic Institute, Graduate School, School of Science, Program in Information Technology, Troy, NY 12180-3590. Offers MS. *Program availability:* Part-time. *Faculty:* 5 part-time/adjunct (2 women). *Students:* 55 full-time (23 women), 5 part-time (2 women); includes 4 minority (1 Asian, non-Hispanic/Latino; 3 Hispanic/Latino), 47 international. Average age 24. 176 applicants, 69% accepted, 37 enrolled. In 2019, 19 master's awarded. *Entrance requirements:* For master's, GRE, IT Background Evaluation Form. Additional exam requirements/recommendations for international students: required—TOEFL (minimum score 570 paper-based; 88 iBT), IELTS (minimum score 6.5), PTE (minimum score 60). *Application deadline:* For fall admission, 1/1 priority date for domestic and international students; for spring admission, 8/15 priority date for domestic and international students. Applications are processed on a rolling basis. Application fee: $75. Electronic applications accepted. *Financial support:* In 2019–20, teaching assistantships with full tuition reimbursements (averaging $23,000 per year) were awarded. Financial award application deadline: 1/1. *Unit head:* Dr. Peter Fox, Graduate Program Director, 518-276-4862, E-mail: pfox@cs.rpi.edu. *Application contact:* Jarron Decker, Director of Graduate Admissions, 518-276-6216, Fax: 518-276-4072, E-mail: gradadmissions@rpi.edu.
Website: https://science.rpi.edu/itws

Robert Morris University, School of Informatics, Humanities and Social Sciences, Moon Township, PA 15108. Offers communication and information systems (MS); cyber security (MS); data analytics (MS); information security and assurance (MS); information systems and communications (D Sc); information systems management (MS); information technology project management (MS); Internet information systems (MS); organizational leadership (MS). *Program availability:* Part-time-only, evening/weekend, 100% online. *Faculty:* 23 full-time (9 women), 11 part-time/adjunct (0 women). *Students:* 224 part-time (90 women); includes 46 minority (28 Black or African American, non-Hispanic/Latino; 5 Asian, non-Hispanic/Latino; 9 Hispanic/Latino; 4 Two or more races, non-Hispanic/Latino), 31 international. Average age 35. In 2019, 118 master's, 14 doctorates awarded. *Degree requirements:* For master's, Completion of 30 credits; for doctorate, thesis/dissertation, Completion of 63 credits. *Entrance requirements:* For doctorate, employer letter of endorsement, interview. Additional exam requirements/recommendations for international students: required—TOEFL (minimum score 550 paper-based; 79 iBT). *Application deadline:* For fall admission, 7/1 priority date for domestic and international students; for spring admission, 11/1 priority date for domestic and international students. Applications are processed on a rolling basis. Application fee: $35. Electronic applications accepted. Application fee is waived when completed online. *Expenses:* $960 per credit tuition plus $85 per credit fees (for master's); $32,940 per year tuition and fees (for doctorate). *Financial support:* Institutionally sponsored loans available. Support available to part-time students. Financial award application deadline: 5/1; financial award applicants required to submit FAFSA. *Unit head:* Dr. Amjad Ali, Dean, School of Informatics, Humanities and Social Sciences, 412-397-3000. *Application contact:* Kellie Laurenzi, Associate Vice President, Enrollment Management, 412-397-5200, E-mail: graduateadmissions@rmu.edu.
Website: https://www.rmu.edu/academics/schools/sihss

Rochester Institute of Technology, Graduate Enrollment Services, Golisano College of Computing and Information Sciences, Computing and Information Sciences Department, PhD Program in Computing and Information Sciences, Rochester, NY 14623-5603. Offers PhD. *Program availability:* Part-time. *Degree requirements:* For doctorate, comprehensive exam, thesis/dissertation. *Entrance requirements:* For doctorate, GRE, minimum GPA of 3.0, statement of purpose, resume, 2 letters of recommendation, professional or research paper sample(s) (if available). Additional exam requirements/recommendations for international students: required—TOEFL (minimum score 570 paper-based; 88 iBT), IELTS (minimum score 6.5), PTE (minimum score 61). Electronic applications accepted. *Expenses:* Contact institution.

Rochester Institute of Technology, Graduate Enrollment Services, Golisano College of Computing and Information Sciences, Information Science and Technologies Department, MS Program in Information Sciences and Technologies, Rochester, NY 14623-5603. Offers MS. *Program availability:* Part-time, online learning. *Degree requirements:* For master's, thesis or alternative, Thesis or Project. *Entrance requirements:* For master's, GRE required for individuals with degrees from international universities. GRE scores are strongly recommended for students whose GPA is below 3.0., minimum GPA of 3.0, resume, two letters of recommendation. Additional exam requirements/recommendations for international students: required—TOEFL (minimum score 570 paper-based; 88 iBT), IELTS (minimum score 6.5), PTE (minimum score 61). Electronic applications accepted.

Rutgers University - New Brunswick, School of Communication and Information, Master of Information, New Brunswick, NJ 08901. Offers MI. *Accreditation:* ALA. *Program availability:* Part-time, online learning. *Entrance requirements:* For master's, GRE General Test. Additional exam requirements/recommendations for international students: required—TOEFL. Electronic applications accepted.

Sacred Heart University, Graduate Programs, College of Arts and Sciences, Department of Computing, Fairfield, CT 06825. Offers computer science (MS); computer science gaming (MS); cybersecurity (MS); information technology (MS). *Program availability:* Part-time, evening/weekend. *Degree requirements:* For master's, thesis or alternative. *Entrance requirements:* For master's, bachelor's degree, minimum GPA of 3.0. Additional exam requirements/recommendations for international students: required—TOEFL (minimum score 570 paper-based, 80 iBT), TWE, or IELTS (6.5). Electronic applications accepted. *Expenses:* Contact institution.

St. John's University, St. John's College of Liberal Arts and Sciences, Department of Government and Politics and Division of Library and Information Science, Program in Government and Library and Information Science, Queens, NY 11439. Offers MA/MS. *Program availability:* Part-time, evening/weekend. *Entrance requirements:* Additional exam requirements/recommendations for international students: required—TOEFL (minimum score 80 iBT), IELTS (minimum score 6.5). Electronic applications accepted.

St. Mary's University, School of Science, Engineering and Technology, Program in Computer Information Systems, San Antonio, TX 78228. Offers MS. *Program availability:* Part-time, evening/weekend. *Degree requirements:* For master's, comprehensive exam, thesis optional. *Entrance requirements:* For master's, GMAT (minimum score of 334) or GRE General Test (minimum quantitative score of 148, analytical writing 2.5), minimum GPA of 3.0 in a bachelor's degree, written statement of purpose indicating interest and objective, two letters of recommendation, official transcripts of all college-level work. Additional exam requirements/recommendations for international students: required—TOEFL (minimum score 530 paper-based; 80 iBT), IELTS (minimum score 6). Electronic applications accepted.

Sam Houston State University, College of Sciences, Department of Computer Science, Huntsville, TX 77341. Offers computing and information science (MS); digital forensics (MS); information assurance and security (MS). *Program availability:* Part-time. *Degree requirements:* For master's, comprehensive exam, thesis optional, internship; for doctorate, comprehensive exam, thesis/dissertation. *Entrance requirements:* For master's, GRE General Test, letters of recommendation. Additional exam requirements/recommendations for international students: required—TOEFL (minimum score 550 paper-based; 79 iBT), IELTS (minimum score 6.5). Electronic applications accepted.

Shippensburg University of Pennsylvania, School of Graduate Studies, College of Arts and Sciences, Department of Computer Science and Engineering, Shippensburg, PA 17257-2299. Offers agile software engineering (Certificate); computer science (MS); IT leadership (Certificate). *Program availability:* Part-time, evening/weekend. *Faculty:* 4 full-time (2 women). *Students:* 8 full-time (3 women), 5 part-time (2 women); includes 4 minority (2 Black or African American, non-Hispanic/Latino; 2 Asian, non-Hispanic/Latino), 5 international. Average age 28. 39 applicants, 44% accepted, 6 enrolled. In 2019, 5 master's awarded. *Entrance requirements:* For master's, GRE (if GPA less than 2.75), professional resume. Additional exam requirements/recommendations for international students: required—TOEFL (minimum score 70 iBT), IELTS (minimum score 6), TOEFL (minimum score 70 iBT) or IELTS (minimum score 6). *Application deadline:* For fall admission, 4/30 for international students. Applications are processed on a rolling basis. Application fee: $45. Electronic applications accepted. *Expenses:* Tuition, state resident: part-time $516 per credit. Tuition, nonresident: part-time $774 per credit. *Required fees:* $149 per credit. *Financial support:* In 2019–20, 8 students received support. Career-related internships or fieldwork, scholarships/grants, unspecified assistantships, and resident hall director and student payroll positions available. Support available to part-time students. Financial award application deadline: 3/1; financial award applicants required to submit FAFSA. *Unit head:* Dr. Jeonghwa Lee, Professor and Director of Graduate Studies, 717-477-1178, Fax: 717-477-4002, E-mail: jlee@ship.edu. *Application contact:* Maya T. Mapp, Director of Admissions, 717-477-1231, Fax: 717-477-4016, E-mail: mtmapp@ship.edu.
Website: http://www.ship.edu/engineering/cs

Southern Methodist University, Lyle School of Engineering, Department of Engineering Management, Information, and Systems, Dallas, TX 75275. Offers engineering entrepreneurship (MS); engineering management (MS, DE); information engineering and management (MSIEM); operations research (MS, PhD); systems engineering (MS). *Program availability:* Part-time, evening/weekend, online learning. Terminal master's awarded for partial completion of doctoral program. *Degree requirements:* For master's, thesis optional; for doctorate, thesis/dissertation, oral and written qualifying exams. *Entrance requirements:* For master's, minimum GPA of 3.0 in last 2 years; bachelor's degree in engineering, mathematics, sciences, or technical area; for doctorate, GRE General Test (operations research, engineering management), bachelor's degree in related field. Additional exam requirements/recommendations for international students: required—TOEFL.

Southern States University, Graduate Programs, San Diego, CA 92110. Offers business administration (MBA); information technology (MSIT).

State University of New York Polytechnic Institute, Program in Computer and Information Science, Utica, NY 13502. Offers MS. *Program availability:* Part-time. *Degree requirements:* For master's, thesis, thesis or project. *Entrance requirements:* For master's, GRE or approved GRE waiver, undergraduate prerequisite courses in math and computer science. Additional exam requirements/recommendations for international students: required—TOEFL (minimum score 79 iBT), IELTS (minimum score 6.5), PTE (minimum score 53), Only ONE of above. Electronic applications accepted.

State University of New York Polytechnic Institute, Program in Information Design and Technology, Utica, NY 13502. Offers MS. *Program availability:* Part-time. *Degree requirements:* For master's, project or thesis. Electronic applications accepted.

Stevens Institute of Technology, Graduate School, School of Business, Program in Information Systems, Hoboken, NJ 07030. Offers computer science (MS); e-commerce (MS); enterprise systems (MS); entrepreneurial information technology (MS); information architecture (MS); information management (MS, Certificate); information security (MS); information technology in financial services industry (MS); information technology in the pharmaceutical industry (MS); information technology outsourcing management (MS); project management (MS, Certificate); software engineering (MS); telecommunications (MS). *Program availability:* Part-time, evening/weekend. *Faculty:* 59 full-time (11 women), 30 part-time/adjunct (5 women). *Students:* 221 full-time (80 women), 52 part-time (18 women); includes 24 minority (8 Black or African American, non-Hispanic/Latino; 16 Asian, non-Hispanic/Latino), 225 international. Average age 27. In 2019, 188 master's awarded. Terminal master's awarded for partial completion of

doctoral program. *Degree requirements:* For master's, thesis optional, minimum B average in major field and overall; for Certificate, minimum B average. *Entrance requirements:* For master's, International applicants must submit TOEFL/IELTS scores and fulfill the English Language Proficiency Requirement. Applicants to full-time programs who do not qualify for a score waiver are required to submit GRE/GMAT scores. Additional exam requirements/recommendations for international students: required—TOEFL (minimum score 74 iBT), IELTS (minimum score 6). *Application deadline:* For fall admission, 4/1 for domestic and international students; for spring admission, 11/1 for domestic and international students; for summer admission, 5/1 for domestic students. Applications are processed on a rolling basis. Application fee: $60. Electronic applications accepted. *Expenses: Tuition:* Full-time $52,134. *Required fees:* $1880. Tuition and fees vary according to course load. *Financial support:* Fellowships, research assistantships, teaching assistantships, career-related internships or fieldwork, Federal Work-Study, scholarships/grants, and unspecified assistantships available. Financial award application deadline: 2/15; financial award applicants required to submit FAFSA. *Unit head:* Dr. Gregory Prastacos, Dean of SB, 201-216-8366, E-mail: gprastac@stevens.edu. *Application contact:* Graduate Admissions, 888-783-8367, Fax: 888-511-1306, E-mail: graduate@stevens.edu.
Website: https://www.stevens.edu/school-business/masters-programs/information-systems

Strayer University, Graduate Studies, Washington, DC 20005-2603. Offers accounting (MS); acquisition (MBA); business administration (MBA); communications technology (MS); educational management (M Ed); finance (MBA); health services administration (MHSA); hospitality and tourism management (MBA); human resource management (MBA); information systems (MS), including computer security management, decision support system management, enterprise resource management, network management, software engineering management, systems development management; management (MBA); management information systems (MS); marketing (MBA); professional accounting (MS), including accounting information systems, controllership, taxation; public administration (MPA); supply chain management (MBA); technology in education (M Ed). *Accreditation:* ACBSP. *Program availability:* Part-time, evening/weekend, online learning. *Degree requirements:* For master's, thesis. *Entrance requirements:* For master's, GMAT, GRE General Test, bachelor's degree from an accredited college or university, minimum undergraduate GPA of 2.75. Electronic applications accepted.

Syracuse University, College of Engineering and Computer Science, PhD Program in Computer and Information Science and Engineering, Syracuse, NY 13244. Offers PhD. *Program availability:* Part-time. *Degree requirements:* For doctorate, comprehensive exam, thesis/dissertation. *Entrance requirements:* For doctorate, GRE General Test, GRE Subject Test (computer science), three letters of recommendation, personal statement, official transcripts, resume. Additional exam requirements/recommendations for international students: required—TOEFL (minimum score 100 iBT). Electronic applications accepted.

Syracuse University, School of Information Studies, MS Program in Library and Information Science, Syracuse, NY 13244. Offers MS. *Accreditation:* ALA. *Program availability:* Part-time, evening/weekend, online learning. *Entrance requirements:* For master's, GRE General Test, two letters of recommendation, personal statement, resume. Additional exam requirements/recommendations for international students: required—TOEFL (minimum score 100 iBT). Electronic applications accepted.

Syracuse University, School of Information Studies, PhD Program in Information Science and Technology, Syracuse, NY 13244. Offers PhD. *Degree requirements:* For doctorate, comprehensive exam, thesis/dissertation. *Entrance requirements:* For doctorate, GRE General Test, writing sample, personal statement, three letters of recommendation, official transcripts. Additional exam requirements/recommendations for international students: required—TOEFL (minimum score 100 iBT). Electronic applications accepted.

Temple University, College of Science and Technology, Department of Computer and Information Sciences, Philadelphia, PA 19122-6096. Offers computational data science (MS); computer and information sciences (PhD), including artificial intelligence, computer and network systems, information systems, software systems; computer science (MS); cyber defense and information assurance (PSM); information science and technology (MS). *Program availability:* Part-time, evening/weekend, online learning. *Faculty:* 39 full-time (9 women), 8 part-time/adjunct (1 woman). *Students:* 97 full-time (28 women), 22 part-time (11 women); includes 14 minority (3 Black or African American, non-Hispanic/Latino; 8 Asian, non-Hispanic/Latino; 3 Hispanic/Latino), 83 international. 133 applicants, 56% accepted, 35 enrolled. In 2019, 15 master's, 7 doctorates awarded. *Degree requirements:* For doctorate, thesis/dissertation. *Entrance requirements:* For master's, GRE, 3 letters of recommendation, statement of goals; for doctorate, GRE, 3 letters of recommendation, bachelor's degree in related field, statement of goals, resume. Additional exam requirements/recommendations for international students: required—TOEFL (minimum score 85 iBT), IELTS (minimum score 6.5), PTE (minimum score 58), one of three is required. *Application deadline:* Applications are processed on a rolling basis. Application fee: $60. Electronic applications accepted. *Expenses:* Contact institution. *Financial support:* Research assistantships, teaching assistantships, health care benefits, and unspecified assistantships available. Financial award applicants required to submit FAFSA. *Unit head:* Jamie Payton, Department Chairperson, 215-204-8245, E-mail: Jamie.payton@temple.edu. *Application contact:* Eduard Dragut, Graduate Chair, 215-204-0521, E-mail: cisadmit@temple.edu.
Website: https://cis.temple.edu/

Texas Woman's University, Graduate School, College of Arts and Sciences, Department of Mathematics and Computer Science, Denton, TX 76204. Offers emphasis in mathematics or computer science (MAT); informatics (MS); mathematics (MS); mathematics teaching (MS). *Program availability:* Part-time, evening/weekend, blended/hybrid learning. *Faculty:* 10 full-time (7 women), 1 part-time/adjunct (0 women). *Students:* 28 full-time (21 women), 70 part-time (54 women); includes 63 minority (26 Black or African American, non-Hispanic/Latino; 19 Asian, non-Hispanic/Latino; 15 Hispanic/Latino; 3 Two or more races, non-Hispanic/Latino), 4 international. Average age 35. 38 applicants, 92% accepted, 24 enrolled. In 2019, 20 master's awarded. *Degree requirements:* For master's, comprehensive exam, thesis or alternative, professional paper, capstone or thesis (depending on degree). *Entrance requirements:* For master's, minimum GPA of 3.0 in last 60 undergraduate credit hours, 2 semesters of calculus, 2 additional advanced math courses, 2 letters of reference (for MS in mathematics, mathematics teaching); minimum GPA of 3.0, statement of intent, resume, 2 letters of recommendation (for MS in informatics). Additional exam requirements/recommendations for international students: required—TOEFL (minimum score 79 iBT); recommended—IELTS (minimum score 6.5), TSE (minimum score 53). *Application deadline:* For fall admission, 3/1 priority date for domestic and international students; for spring admission, 11/1 priority date for domestic students, 7/1 priority date for international students; for summer admission, 5/1 priority date for domestic students, 2/1 priority date for international students. Applications are processed on a rolling basis. Application fee: $50 ($75 for international students). Electronic applications accepted. *Expenses: Tuition, area resident:* Full-time $4973.40; part-time $276.30 per semester hour. Tuition, state resident: full-time $4973.40; part-time $276.30 per semester hour. Tuition, nonresident: full-time $12,569; part-time $698.30 per semester hour. *International tuition:* $12,569.40 full-time. *Required fees:* $2524.30. Tuition and fees vary according to course level, course load, degree level and program. *Financial support:* In 2019–20, 30 students received support, including 13 teaching assistantships (averaging $13,259 per year); career-related internships or fieldwork, scholarships/grants, health care benefits, and unspecified assistantships also available. Support available to part-time students. Financial award application deadline: 3/1; financial award applicants required to submit FAFSA. *Unit head:* Dr. Marie-Anne Demuynck, Interim Chair, 940-898-2166, Fax: 940-898-2179, E-mail: mathcs@twu.edu. *Application contact:* Korie Hawkins, Associate Director of Admissions, Graduate Recruitment, 940-898-3188, Fax: 940-898-3081, E-mail: admissions@twu.edu.
Website: http://www.twu.edu/math-computer-science/

Thomas Edison State University, School of Applied Science and Technology, Trenton, NJ 08608. Offers clinical trials management (MS); cybersecurity (Graduate Certificate); information technology (MS); nuclear energy technology management (MS); technical studies (MS). *Program availability:* Part-time, online learning. *Degree requirements:* For master's, project. *Entrance requirements:* Additional exam requirements/recommendations for international students: required—TOEFL (minimum score 550 paper-based; 79 iBT). Electronic applications accepted.

Towson University, Jess and Mildred Fisher College of Science and Mathematics, Program in Applied Information Technology, Towson, MD 21252-0001. Offers applied information technology (MS); Internet application development (Postbaccalaureate Certificate). *Students:* 79 full-time (33 women), 126 part-time (43 women); includes 113 minority (77 Black or African American, non-Hispanic/Latino; 23 Asian, non-Hispanic/Latino; 5 Hispanic/Latino; 8 Two or more races, non-Hispanic/Latino), 36 international. *Entrance requirements:* For master's and Postbaccalaureate Certificate, bachelor's degree, minimum GPA of 3.0. Additional exam requirements/recommendations for international students: required—TOEFL. *Application deadline:* For fall admission, 1/17 for domestic students, 5/15 for international students; for spring admission, 10/15 for domestic students, 12/1 for international students. Applications are processed on a rolling basis. Application fee: $45. Electronic applications accepted. *Expenses: Tuition, area resident:* Full-time $7920; part-time $439 per credit. Tuition, nonresident: full-time $16,344; part-time $908 per credit. *International tuition:* $16,344 full-time. *Required fees:* $2628; $146 per credit. $876 per term. *Unit head:* Dr. Suranjan Charkraborty, Graduate Program Director, 410-704-4769, E-mail: ait@towson.edu. *Application contact:* Coverley Beidleman, Assistant Director of Graduate Admissions, 410-704-5630, Fax: 410-704-3030, E-mail: cbeidleman@towson.edu.
Website: https://www.towson.edu/fcsm/departments/emergingtech/

Towson University, Jess and Mildred Fisher College of Science and Mathematics, Program in Information Technology, Towson, MD 21252-0001. Offers D Sc. *Students:* 48 full-time (17 women), 14 part-time (2 women); includes 14 minority (10 Black or African American, non-Hispanic/Latino; 3 Asian, non-Hispanic/Latino; 1 Two or more races, non-Hispanic/Latino), 37 international. 42 applicants, 98% accepted, 25 enrolled. In 2019, 1 doctorate awarded. *Entrance requirements:* For doctorate, minimum GPA of 3.0, letter of intent, resume, 2 letters of recommendation, personal assessment forms, official transcripts. Additional exam requirements/recommendations for international students: required—TOEFL (minimum score 550 paper-based). *Application deadline:* For fall admission, 1/17 for domestic students, 5/15 for international students; for spring admission, 10/15 for domestic students, 12/1 for international students. Applications are processed on a rolling basis. Application fee: $45. Electronic applications accepted. *Expenses: Tuition, area resident:* Full-time $7920; part-time $439 per credit. Tuition, nonresident: full-time $16,344; part-time $908 per credit. *International tuition:* $16,344 full-time. *Required fees:* $2628; $146 per credit. $876 per term. *Financial support:* Application deadline: 4/1. *Unit head:* Dr. Chao Lu, Graduate Program Director, 410-704-3950, E-mail: clu@towson.edu. *Application contact:* Coverley Beidleman, Assistant Director of Graduate Admissions, 410-704-5630, Fax: 410-704-3030, E-mail: grads@towson.edu.
Website: https://www.towson.edu/fcsm/departments/computerinfosci/grad/infotech/

Trevecca Nazarene University, Graduate Education Program, Nashville, TN 37210-2877. Offers accountability and instructional leadership (Ed S); curriculum and instruction for Christian school educators (M Ed); curriculum and instruction K-12 (M Ed); educational leadership (M Ed); English second language (M Ed); library and information science (MLI Sc); special education: visual impairments (M Ed); teaching (MAT), including teaching 6-12, teaching K-5. *Accreditation:* NCATE. *Program availability:* Part-time, evening/weekend, online learning. *Degree requirements:* For master's, comprehensive exam, exit assessment/e-portfolio. *Entrance requirements:* For master's, GRE or MAT; PRAXIS (for MAT), minimum GPA of 3.0, official transcript from regionally-accredited institution, references, interview, writing sample, at least 3 years' successful teaching experience (for M Ed in educational leadership); for Ed S, GRE or MAT, master's degree with minimum GPA of 3.0, official transcript from regionally accredited institution, at least 3 years' successful teaching experience, interview, writing sample, background and fingerprinting check, recommendations. Additional exam requirements/recommendations for international students: required—TOEFL (minimum score 550 paper-based). Electronic applications accepted. *Expenses:* Contact institution.

Université de Sherbrooke, Faculty of Sciences, Department of Informatics, Sherbrooke, QC J1K 2R1, Canada. Offers M Sc, PhD. *Degree requirements:* For master's, thesis. Electronic applications accepted.

University at Albany, State University of New York, College of Emergency Preparedness, Homeland Security and Cybersecurity, Informatics, Albany, NY 12222. Offers PhD. *Program availability:* Part-time, blended/hybrid learning. *Faculty:* 4 full-time (1 woman), 14 part-time/adjunct (4 women). *Students:* 11 full-time (8 women), 22 part-time (8 women); includes 7 minority (3 Black or African American, non-Hispanic/Latino; 1 Asian, non-Hispanic/Latino; 3 Hispanic/Latino), 15 international. Average age 27. 35 applicants, 60% accepted, 18 enrolled. In 2019, 2 doctorates awarded. *Degree requirements:* For doctorate, comprehensive exam. *Entrance requirements:* For doctorate, GRE, transcripts from all schools attended, 3 letters of recommendation, resume, personal statement. Additional exam requirements/recommendations for international students: required—TOEFL (minimum score 550 paper-based). *Application deadline:* For fall admission, 1/15 for domestic students; for spring admission, 11/15 for domestic students. Application fee: $75. Electronic applications accepted. *Expenses: Tuition, area resident:* Full-time $11,530; part-time $480 per credit hour. Tuition, nonresident: full-time $23,530; part-time $980 per credit hour. *International tuition:* $23,530 full-time. *Required fees:* $2185; $96 per credit hour. Part-time tuition and fees vary according to course load and program. *Financial support:* Research assistantships, teaching assistantships, and career-related internships or fieldwork available. *Unit head:* Peter Bloniarz, Chair, 518-956-8240, E-mail: p.blonairz@albany.edu. *Application contact:* Peter Bloniarz, Chair, 518-956-8240, E-mail: p.blonairz@albany.edu.

University at Albany, State University of New York, College of Emergency Preparedness, Homeland Security and Cybersecurity, MS Program in Information Science, Albany, NY 12222-0001. Offers MS. *Accreditation:* ALA. *Program availability:* Blended/hybrid learning. *Faculty:* 21 full-time (8 women), 21 part-time/adjunct (7 women). *Students:* 51 full-time (36 women), 105 part-time (85 women); includes 24

minority (6 Black or African American, non-Hispanic/Latino; 2 Asian, non-Hispanic/ Latino; 15 Hispanic/Latino; 1 Two or more races, non-Hispanic/Latino), 7 international. Average age 27. 138 applicants, 83% accepted, 38 enrolled. In 2019, 35 master's awarded. *Degree requirements:* For master's, thesis optional, Internship of 150 hours. *Entrance requirements:* For master's, GRE, transcripts from all schools attended, 3 letters of recommendation, resume, personal statement. Additional exam requirements/ recommendations for international students: required—TOEFL (minimum score 550 paper-based). *Application deadline:* For fall admission, 1/15 for domestic students; for spring admission, 11/15 for domestic students. Application fee: $75. Electronic applications accepted. *Expenses: Tuition, area resident:* Full-time $11,530; part-time $480 per credit hour. Tuition, nonresident: full-time $23,530; part-time $980 per credit hour. *International tuition:* $23,530 full-time. *Required fees:* $2185; $96 per credit hour. Part-time tuition and fees vary according to course load and program. *Financial support:* Research assistantships, teaching assistantships, career-related internships or fieldwork, and unspecified assistantships available. Financial award applicants required to submit FAFSA. *Unit head:* Robert P Griffin, Dean, 518-442-5258, E-mail: rpgriffin@albany.edu. *Application contact:* Robert P Griffin, Dean, 518-442-5258, E-mail: rpgriffin@albany.edu.
Website: http://www.albany.edu/informationstudies/

The University of Alabama at Birmingham, College of Arts and Sciences, Program in Computer and Information Sciences, Birmingham, AL 35294. Offers MS, PhD. *Students:* 47 full-time (8 women), 11 part-time (2 women); includes 2 minority (1 Asian, non-Hispanic/Latino; 1 Hispanic/Latino), 34 international. Average age 29. 168 applicants, 54% accepted, 14 enrolled. In 2019, 15 master's, 1 doctorate awarded. Terminal master's awarded for partial completion of doctoral program. *Degree requirements:* For master's, thesis optional; for doctorate, thesis/dissertation. *Entrance requirements:* For master's, GRE General Test, minimum GPA of 3.0, letters of recommendation; for doctorate, GRE General Test, minimum GPA of 3.5 overall or on last 60 hours; letters of recommendation. Additional exam requirements/recommendations for international students: required—TOEFL, IELTS. *Application deadline:* For fall admission, 2/1 for domestic students; for spring admission, 9/1 for domestic students. Applications are processed on a rolling basis. Application fee: $45 ($60 for international students). Electronic applications accepted. *Financial support:* Fellowships with full tuition reimbursements, research assistantships with full tuition reimbursements, teaching assistantships with full tuition reimbursements, career-related internships or fieldwork, Federal Work-Study, institutionally sponsored loans, scholarships/grants, traineeships, health care benefits, and unspecified assistantships available. Support available to part-time students. Financial award application deadline: 3/10. *Unit head:* Dr. Chengcui Zhang, Graduate Program Director, 205-934-8606, Fax: 205-934-5473, E-mail: czhang02@uab.edu. *Application contact:* Susan Noblitt Banks, Director of Graduate School Operations, 205-934-8227, Fax: 205-934-8413, E-mail: gradschool@uab.edu.
Website: https://cis.uab.edu/academics/graduates/

University of Arkansas at Little Rock, Graduate School, George W. Donaghey College of Engineering and Information Technology, Program in Information Quality, Little Rock, AR 72204-1099. Offers MS, PhD, Graduate Certificate.

University of California, Irvine, Donald Bren School of Information and Computer Sciences, Department of Informatics, Irvine, CA 92697. Offers information and computer science (MS, PhD). *Students:* 180 full-time (84 women), 4 part-time (1 woman); includes 50 minority (8 Black or African American, non-Hispanic/Latino; 33 Asian, non-Hispanic/ Latino; 7 Hispanic/Latino; 2 Two or more races, non-Hispanic/Latino), 87 international. Average age 28. 741 applicants, 33% accepted, 102 enrolled. In 2019, 52 master's, 8 doctorates awarded. Application fee: $120 ($140 for international students). *Unit head:* Andre van der Hoek, Chair, 949-824-6326, Fax: 949-824-4056, E-mail: andre@uci.edu. *Application contact:* Melissa Mazmanian, Vice Chair for Graduate Affairs, 949-824-9284, Fax: 949-824-2056, E-mail: m.mazmani@ics.uci.edu.
Website: http://www.informatics.uci.edu/

University of California, Merced, Graduate Division, School of Social Sciences, Humanities and Arts, Merced, CA 95343. Offers cognitive and information sciences (PhD); interdisciplinary humanities (MA, PhD); psychological sciences (MA, PhD); social sciences (MA, PhD); sociology (MA, PhD). *Faculty:* 113 full-time (57 women), 2 part-time/adjunct (0 women). *Students:* 194 full-time (128 women), 1 (woman) part-time; includes 81 minority (5 Black or African American, non-Hispanic/Latino; 18 Asian, non-Hispanic/Latino; 54 Hispanic/Latino; 4 Two or more races, non-Hispanic/Latino), 39 international. Average age 31. 218 applicants, 48% accepted, 36 enrolled. In 2019, 12 master's, 23 doctorates awarded. Terminal master's awarded for partial completion of doctoral program. *Degree requirements:* For master's, variable foreign language requirement, comprehensive exam, thesis or alternative, oral defense; for doctorate, variable foreign language requirement, comprehensive exam, thesis/dissertation, oral defense. *Entrance requirements:* For master's and doctorate, GRE. Additional exam requirements/recommendations for international students: required—TOEFL (minimum score 550 paper-based; 80 iBT); recommended—IELTS (minimum score 6.5). *Application deadline:* For fall admission, 1/15 for domestic and international students. Application fee: $105 ($125 for international students). Electronic applications accepted. *Expenses: Tuition, area resident:* Full-time $11,442; part-time $5721. Tuition, state resident: full-time $11,442; part-time $5721. Tuition, nonresident: full-time $26,544; part-time $13,272. *International tuition:* $26,544 full-time. *Required fees:* $564 per semester. *Financial support:* In 2019–20, 183 students received support, including 7 fellowships with full tuition reimbursements available (averaging $22,005 per year), 5 research assistantships with full tuition reimbursements available (averaging $21,420 per year), 171 teaching assistantships with full tuition reimbursements available (averaging $21,911 per year); scholarships/grants, traineeships, and health care benefits also available. *Unit head:* Dr. Jeffrey Gilger, Dean, 209-228-4343, E-mail: jgilger@ucmerced.edu. *Application contact:* Tsu Ya, Director of Admissions and Academic Services, 209-228-4521, Fax: 209-228-6906, E-mail: tya@ucmerced.edu.

University of Central Missouri, The Graduate School, Warrensburg, MO 64093. Offers accountancy (MA); accounting (MBA); applied mathematics (MS); aviation safety (MA); biology (MS); business administration (MBA); career and technology education (MS); college student personnel administration (MS); communication (MA); computer information systems and information technology (MS); computer science (MS); counseling (MS); criminal justice and criminology (MS); educational leadership (Ed S); educational leadership and policy analysis (Ed D); educational technology (MS, Ed S); elementary and early childhood education (MSE); English (MA); english language learners - teaching english as a second language (MA); environmental studies (MA); finance (MBA); history (MA); industrial hygiene (MS); industrial management (MS); information systems (MBA); kinesiology (MS); library science and information services (MS); literacy education (MSE); marketing (MBA); mathematics (MS); music (MA); occupational safety management (MS); professional leadership - adult, career, and technical education (Ed S); professional leadership - counseling (Ed S); psychology (MS); rural family nursing (MS); school administration (MSE); social gerontology (MS); sociology (MA); special education (MSE); speech language pathology (MS); teaching (MAT); technology (MS); technology management (PhD); theatre (MA). *Accreditation:* ASHA. *Program availability:* Part-time, 100% online, blended/hybrid learning. *Faculty:* 236 full-time (113 women), 97 part-time/adjunct (61 women). *Students:* 787 full-time (448 women), 1,459 part-time (997 women); includes 213 minority (72 Black or African American, non-Hispanic/Latino; 5 American Indian or Alaska Native, non-Hispanic/ Latino; 27 Asian, non-Hispanic/Latino; 59 Hispanic/Latino; 50 Two or more races, non-Hispanic/Latino), 574 international. Average age 30. 1,477 applicants, 68% accepted, 664 enrolled. In 2019, 831 master's, 93 other advanced degrees awarded. *Degree requirements:* For master's and Ed S, comprehensive exam (for some programs), thesis (for some programs). *Entrance requirements:* For master's, A GRE or GMAT test score may be required by some of the programs, A minimum GPA, letters of recommendation, a statement of purpose may be required by some of the programs; for Ed S, A master's degree is required for the application of an Education Specialist's degree program. Additional exam requirements/recommendations for international students: required—TOEFL (minimum score 550 paper-based; 79 iBT). *Application deadline:* For fall admission, 6/1 priority date for domestic and international students; for spring admission, 10/15 priority date for domestic and international students; for summer admission, 4/1 priority date for domestic and international students. Applications are processed on a rolling basis. Application fee: $30 ($75 for international students). Electronic applications accepted. *Expenses: Tuition, area resident:* Full-time $7524; part-time $313.50 per credit hour. Tuition, state resident: full-time $7524; part-time $313.50 per credit hour. Tuition, nonresident: full-time $15,048; part-time $627 per credit hour. *International tuition:* $15,048 full-time. *Required fees:* $915; $30.50 per credit hour. *Financial support:* In 2019–20, 89 students received support. Research assistantships, teaching assistantships, career-related internships or fieldwork, Federal Work-Study, scholarships/grants, unspecified assistantships, and administrative and laboratory assistantships available. Support available to part-time students. Financial award application deadline: 4/1; financial award applicants required to submit FAFSA. *Unit head:* Shellie Hewitt, Director of Graduate and International Student Services, 660-543-4621, Fax: 660-543-4778, E-mail: hewitt@ucmo.edu. *Application contact:* Shellie Hewitt, Director of Graduate and International Student Services, 660-543-4621, Fax: 660-543-4778, E-mail: hewitt@ucmo.edu.
Website: http://www.ucmo.edu/graduate/

University of Cincinnati, Graduate School, College of Education, Criminal Justice, and Human Services, School of Information Technology, Cincinnati, OH 45221. Offers MS, Graduate Certificate. *Program availability:* Part-time, 100% online, blended/hybrid learning.

University of Colorado Boulder, Graduate School, College of Media, Communication and Information, Department of Information Science, Boulder, CO 80309. Offers PhD. Electronic applications accepted.

University of Colorado Denver, College of Engineering, Design and Computing, Department of Computer Science and Engineering, Denver, CO 80217. Offers computer science (MS); computer science and engineering (EASPh D); computer science and information systems (PhD). *Program availability:* Part-time, evening/weekend. *Degree requirements:* For master's, thesis or alternative, at least 30 semester hours of computer science courses while maintaining minimum GPA of 3.0; for doctorate, comprehensive exam, thesis/dissertation, at least 60 hours beyond the master's degree level, 30 of which are dissertation research. *Entrance requirements:* For master's, GRE, minimum GPA of 3.0, 10 semester hours of university-level calculus, at least one math course beyond calculus, statement of purpose, letters of recommendation; for doctorate, GRE or GMAT. Additional exam requirements/recommendations for international students: required—TOEFL (minimum score 537 paper-based; 75 iBT). Electronic applications accepted. Tuition and fees vary according to course load, program and reciprocity agreements.

University of Delaware, College of Engineering, Department of Computer and Information Sciences, Newark, DE 19716. Offers MS, PhD. *Program availability:* Part-time. Terminal master's awarded for partial completion of doctoral program. *Degree requirements:* For master's, thesis optional; for doctorate, comprehensive exam, thesis/ dissertation. *Entrance requirements:* For master's and doctorate, GRE General Test. Additional exam requirements/recommendations for international students: required—TOEFL (minimum score 550 paper-based). Electronic applications accepted.

University of Denver, University College, Denver, CO 80208. Offers arts and culture (MA, Certificate); communication management (MS, Certificate), including translation studies (Certificate), world history and culture (Certificate); environmental policy and management (MS); geographic information systems (MS); global affairs (MA, Certificate), including human capital in organizations (Certificate), philanthropic leadership (Certificate), project management (Certificate), strategic innovation and change (Certificate); healthcare leadership (MS); information communications and technology (MS); leadership and organizations (MS); professional creative writing (MA, Certificate), including emergency planning and response (Certificate), organizational security (Certificate); security management (MS, Certificate); strategic human resources (Certificate). *Program availability:* Part-time, evening/weekend, 100% online, blended/ hybrid learning. *Faculty:* 104 part-time/adjunct (52 women). *Students:* 59 full-time (33 women), 1,893 part-time (1,210 women); includes 545 minority (133 Black or African American, non-Hispanic/Latino; 16 American Indian or Alaska Native, non-Hispanic/ Latino; 64 Asian, non-Hispanic/Latino; 252 Hispanic/Latino; 4 Native Hawaiian or other Pacific Islander, non-Hispanic/Latino; 76 Two or more races, non-Hispanic/Latino), 78 international. Average age 32. 1,290 applicants, 91% accepted, 752 enrolled. In 2019, 457 master's, 181 other advanced degrees awarded. *Degree requirements:* For master's, capstone project. *Entrance requirements:* For master's, baccalaureate degree, transcripts, two letters of recommendation, personal statement, resume, writing sample (Master of Arts in Professional Creative Writing). Additional exam requirements/ recommendations for international students: required—TOEFL (minimum score 550 paper-based; 80 iBT). *Application deadline:* For fall admission, 6/19 priority date for domestic students, 6/14 priority date for international students; for winter admission, 10/ 25 priority date for domestic students, 9/27 priority date for international students; for spring admission, 2/7 priority date for domestic students, 1/10 priority date for international students; for summer admission, 4/24 priority date for domestic students, 3/ 27 priority date for international students. Applications are processed on a rolling basis. Application fee: $75. Electronic applications accepted. *Expenses:* Contact institution. *Financial support:* In 2019–20, 56 students received support. Teaching assistantships available. Financial award applicants required to submit FAFSA. *Unit head:* Dr. Michael McGuire, Dean, 303-871-3518, E-mail: michael.mcguire@du.edu. *Application contact:* Admission Team, 303-871-2291, E-mail: ucoladm@du.edu.
Website: http://universitycollege.du.edu/

University of Fairfax, Graduate Programs, Vienna, VA 22182. Offers business administration (DBA); computer science (MCS); cybersecurity (MBA, MS); general business administration (MBA); information technology (MBA); project management (MBA).

University of Florida, Graduate School, Herbert Wertheim College of Engineering, Department of Computer and Information Science and Engineering, Gainesville, FL 32611. Offers computer engineering (ME, MS, PhD); computer science (MS); digital arts and sciences (MS). *Program availability:* Part-time, online learning. Terminal master's awarded for partial completion of doctoral program. *Degree requirements:* For master's, comprehensive exam, thesis optional; for doctorate, comprehensive exam, thesis/ dissertation. *Entrance requirements:* For master's and doctorate, minimum GPA of 3.0.

Additional exam requirements/recommendations for international students: required—TOEFL (minimum score 550 paper-based; 80 iBT), IELTS (minimum score 6). Electronic applications accepted.

University of Hawaii at Manoa, Office of Graduate Education, Interdisciplinary Program in Communication and Information Sciences, Honolulu, HI 96822. Offers PhD. *Program availability:* Part-time. *Degree requirements:* For doctorate, comprehensive exam, thesis/dissertation. *Entrance requirements:* For doctorate, GRE or GMAT. Additional exam requirements/recommendations for international students: required—TOEFL (minimum score 600 paper-based; 100 iBT), IELTS (minimum score 7).

University of Hawaii at Manoa, Office of Graduate Education, Shidler College of Business, Program in Business Administration, Honolulu, HI 96822. Offers Asian business studies (MBA); Chinese business studies (MBA); decision sciences (MBA); entrepreneurship (MBA); finance (MBA); finance and banking (MBA); human resources management (MBA); information management (MBA); information technology (MBA); international business (MBA); Japanese business studies (MBA); marketing (MBA); organizational behavior (MBA); organizational management (MBA); real estate (MBA); student-designed track (MBA). *Accreditation:* AACSB. *Program availability:* Part-time, evening/weekend. *Degree requirements:* For master's, thesis optional. *Entrance requirements:* For master's, GMAT, minimum GPA of 3.0. Additional exam requirements/recommendations for international students: required—TOEFL (minimum score 600 paper-based; 100 iBT), IELTS (minimum score 7). *Expenses:* Contact institution.

University of Houston, Bauer College of Business, Decision and Information Sciences Program, Houston, TX 77204. Offers PhD. *Program availability:* Evening/weekend.

University of Houston, College of Technology, Department of Information and Logistics Technology, Houston, TX 77204. Offers information security (MS); supply chain and logistics technology (MS); technology project management (MS). *Program availability:* Part-time. *Degree requirements:* For master's, project or thesis (most programs). *Entrance requirements:* For master's, GMAT. Additional exam requirements/recommendations for international students: required—TOEFL (minimum score 550 paper-based; 79 iBT). Electronic applications accepted.

University of Houston–Clear Lake, School of Science and Computer Engineering, Program in Computer Information Systems, Houston, TX 77058-1002. Offers MS. *Program availability:* Part-time, evening/weekend. *Entrance requirements:* For master's, GRE General Test. Additional exam requirements/recommendations for international students: required—TOEFL (minimum score 550 paper-based).

University of Illinois at Urbana-Champaign, Graduate College, School of Information Sciences, Champaign, IL 61820. Offers bioinformatics (MS); digital libraries (CAS); information management (MS); library and information science (MS, PhD, CAS). *Accreditation:* ALA (one or more programs are accredited). *Program availability:* Part-time, online learning. *Entrance requirements:* For degree, master's degree in library and information science or related field with minimum GPA of 3.0.

University of Illinois at Urbana-Champaign, Illinois Informatics Institute, Champaign, IL 61820. Offers PhD. *Degree requirements:* For doctorate, thesis/dissertation.

The University of Iowa, Graduate College, Program in Informatics, Iowa City, IA 52242-1316. Offers bioinformatics (MS, PhD); bioinformatics and computational biology (Certificate); geoinformatics (MS, PhD, Certificate); health informatics (MS, PhD, Certificate); information science (MS, PhD, Certificate). *Degree requirements:* For master's, thesis optional; for doctorate, comprehensive exam, thesis/dissertation. *Entrance requirements:* For master's and doctorate, GRE General Test, minimum GPA of 3.0. Additional exam requirements/recommendations for international students: required—TOEFL (minimum score 550 paper-based; 81 iBT). Electronic applications accepted.

University of Kentucky, Graduate School, College of Communication and Information, Program in Information Communication Technology, Lexington, KY 40506-0032. Offers MA, PhD. *Degree requirements:* For master's, comprehensive exam, thesis optional; for doctorate, comprehensive exam, thesis/dissertation. *Entrance requirements:* For master's, GRE General Test, minimum undergraduate GPA of 2.75; for doctorate, GRE General Test, minimum graduate GPA of 3.0, undergraduate 2.75. Additional exam requirements/recommendations for international students: required—TOEFL (minimum score 550 paper-based). Electronic applications accepted.

University of Maine, Graduate School, College of Liberal Arts and Sciences, School of Computing and Information Science, Orono, ME 04469. Offers MS, PhD, CGS. *Program availability:* Part-time. *Faculty:* 13 full-time (2 women), 2 part-time/adjunct (1 woman). *Students:* 37 full-time (12 women), 26 part-time (16 women); includes 7 minority (2 Black or African American, non-Hispanic/Latino; 1 American Indian or Alaska Native, non-Hispanic/Latino; 2 Asian, non-Hispanic/Latino; 2 Two or more races, non-Hispanic/Latino), 12 international. Average age 35. 83 applicants, 90% accepted, 49 enrolled. In 2019, 4 master's, 2 doctorates, 7 other advanced degrees awarded. *Degree requirements:* For master's, thesis (for some programs); for doctorate, comprehensive exam, thesis/dissertation. *Entrance requirements:* For master's and doctorate, GRE General Test, GRE Subject Test. Additional exam requirements/recommendations for international students: required—TOEFL (minimum score 550 paper-based; 80 iBT). *Application deadline:* Applications are processed on a rolling basis. Application fee: $65. Electronic applications accepted. *Expenses: Tuition, area resident:* Full-time $8100; part-time $450 per credit hour. Tuition, state resident: full-time $8100; part-time $450 per credit hour. Tuition, nonresident: full-time $26,388; part-time $1466 per credit hour. *International tuition:* $26,388 full-time. *Required fees:* $1257; $278 per semester. Tuition and fees vary according to course load. *Financial support:* In 2019–20, 14 students received support, including 1 fellowship with full tuition reimbursement available (averaging $17,850 per year), 11 research assistantships with full tuition reimbursements available (averaging $17,000 per year), 2 teaching assistantships with full tuition reimbursements available (averaging $15,825 per year); career-related internships or fieldwork, Federal Work-Study, institutionally sponsored loans, tuition waivers (full), and unspecified assistantships also available. Financial award application deadline: 3/1; financial award applicants required to submit FAFSA. *Unit head:* Dr. Max Egenhofer, Acting Director, 207-581-2114, Fax: 207-581-2206. *Application contact:* Scott G. Delcourt, Assistant Vice President for Graduate Studies and Senior Associate Dean, 207-581-3291, Fax: 207-581-3232, E-mail: graduate@maine.edu. Website: http://umaine.edu/cis/

University of Maryland, Baltimore County, The Graduate School, College of Engineering and Information Technology, Department of Information Systems, Program in Information Systems, Baltimore, MD 21250. Offers MS, PhD. *Program availability:* Part-time, 100% online. *Students:* 167 full-time (77 women), 183 part-time (67 women); includes 94 minority (36 Black or African American, non-Hispanic/Latino; 2 American Indian or Alaska Native, non-Hispanic/Latino; 42 Asian, non-Hispanic/Latino; 6 Hispanic/Latino; 8 Two or more races, non-Hispanic/Latino), 172 international. Average age 31. 367 applicants, 78% accepted, 136 enrolled. In 2019, 110 master's, 7 doctorates awarded. *Degree requirements:* For master's, comprehensive exam (for some programs), thesis optional; for doctorate, comprehensive exam, thesis/dissertation. *Entrance requirements:* For master's, minimum GPA of 3.0; for doctorate, GRE General

Test or GMAT, competence in statistical analysis, experimental design, programming, databases, and computer networks. Additional exam requirements/recommendations for international students: required—TOEFL (minimum score 550 paper-based; 80 iBT). *Application deadline:* For fall admission, 6/1 for domestic students, 1/1 for international students; for spring admission, 11/1 for domestic students, 6/1 for international students. Applications are processed on a rolling basis. Application fee: $70. Electronic applications accepted. *Expenses:* $14,382 per year. *Financial support:* In 2019–20, 50 students received support, including 1 fellowship with full tuition reimbursement available, 28 research assistantships with full tuition reimbursements available, 21 teaching assistantships with full tuition reimbursements available; career-related internships or fieldwork, Federal Work-Study, scholarships/grants, health care benefits, tuition waivers (partial), and unspecified assistantships also available. Support available to part-time students. Financial award application deadline: 6/30; financial award applicants required to submit FAFSA. *Unit head:* Dr. Arrya Gangopadhyay, Professor and Chair, 410-455-2620, Fax: 410-455-1217, E-mail: gangopad@umbc.edu. *Application contact:* Dr. Zhiyuan Chen, Associate Professor and Graduate Program Director, 410-455-8833, Fax: 410-455-1217, E-mail: zhchen@umbc.edu. Website: https://informationsystems.umbc.edu/

University of Maryland Global Campus, University of Maryland Global Campus, Information Technology, Adelphi, MD 20783. Offers MS. *Program availability:* Part-time, evening/weekend, online learning. *Students:* 17 full-time (5 women), 1,247 part-time (451 women); includes 701 minority (493 Black or African American, non-Hispanic/Latino; 4 American Indian or Alaska Native, non-Hispanic/Latino; 86 Asian, non-Hispanic/Latino; 83 Hispanic/Latino; 4 Native Hawaiian or other Pacific Islander, non-Hispanic/Latino; 31 Two or more races, non-Hispanic/Latino), 55 international. Average age 36. 480 applicants, 100% accepted, 215 enrolled. In 2019, 389 master's awarded. *Degree requirements:* For master's, thesis or alternative, capstone course. *Application deadline:* Applications are processed on a rolling basis. Application fee: $50. Electronic applications accepted. *Financial support:* Scholarships/grants available. Support available to part-time students. Financial award application deadline: 6/1; financial award applicants required to submit FAFSA. *Unit head:* Daniel Mintz, Department Chair, 240-684-2400, E-mail: daniel.mintz@umgc.edu. *Application contact:* Admissions, 800-888-8682, E-mail: studentsfirst@umgc.edu. Website: https://www.umgc.edu/academic-programs/masters-degrees/information-technology/index.cfm

University of Michigan, School of Information, Ann Arbor, MI 48109-1285. Offers health informatics (MHI); information (MSI, PhD). *Accreditation:* ALA (one or more programs are accredited). *Program availability:* Part-time. Terminal master's awarded for partial completion of doctoral program. *Degree requirements:* For master's, thesis optional, internship; for doctorate, thesis/dissertation. *Entrance requirements:* For master's and doctorate, GRE General Test. Additional exam requirements/recommendations for international students: required—TOEFL (minimum score 100 iBT). Electronic applications accepted. *Expenses:* Contact institution.

University of Michigan–Dearborn, College of Engineering and Computer Science, Master of Science Program in Computer and Information Science, Dearborn, MI 48128. Offers MS. *Program availability:* Part-time, evening/weekend, 100% online. *Faculty:* 19 full-time (1 woman), 5 part-time/adjunct (0 women). *Students:* 36 full-time (22 women), 43 part-time (14 women); includes 12 minority (2 Black or African American, non-Hispanic/Latino; 7 Asian, non-Hispanic/Latino; 1 Hispanic/Latino; 2 Two or more races, non-Hispanic/Latino), 47 international. Average age 28. 173 applicants, 47% accepted, 25 enrolled. In 2019, 27 master's awarded. *Degree requirements:* For master's, thesis optional. *Entrance requirements:* For master's, bachelor's degree with minimum GPA of 3.0. Additional exam requirements/recommendations for international students: required—TOEFL (minimum score 560 paper-based; 84 iBT), IELTS (minimum score 6.5). *Application deadline:* For fall admission, 8/1 priority date for domestic students, 5/1 for international students; for winter admission, 12/1 priority date for domestic students, 9/1 for international students; for spring admission, 4/1 priority date for domestic students, 1/1 for international students. Applications are processed on a rolling basis. Application fee: $60. Electronic applications accepted. *Financial support:* Research assistantships with full tuition reimbursements, teaching assistantships with full tuition reimbursements, career-related internships or fieldwork, scholarships/grants, unspecified assistantships, and non-resident tuition scholarships available. Support available to part-time students. Financial award application deadline: 3/1; financial award applicants required to submit FAFSA. *Unit head:* Dr. David Yoon, Director, 313-436-9146, E-mail: dhyoon@umich.edu. *Application contact:* Office of Graduate Studies, 313-583-6321, E-mail: umd-graduatestudies@umich.edu. Website: https://umdearborn.edu/cecs/departments/computer-and-information-science/graduate-programs/masters-computer-and-information-science

University of Michigan–Dearborn, College of Engineering and Computer Science, PhD Program in Computer and Information Science, Dearborn, MI 48128. Offers data management (PhD); data science (PhD); software engineering (PhD); systems and security (PhD). *Faculty:* 19 full-time (1 woman), 5 part-time/adjunct (0 women). *Students:* 8 full-time (5 women), 6 part-time (1 woman); includes 1 minority (Asian, non-Hispanic/Latino), 11 international. Average age 28. 17 applicants, 24% accepted, 3 enrolled. In 2019, 1 doctorate awarded. *Degree requirements:* For doctorate, comprehensive exam, thesis/dissertation. *Entrance requirements:* For doctorate, GRE, bachelor's or master's degree in computer science or closely-related field. Additional exam requirements/recommendations for international students: required—TOEFL (minimum score 560 paper-based; 84 iBT), IELTS (minimum score 6.5). *Application deadline:* For fall admission, 2/1 for domestic and international students. Application fee: $60. Electronic applications accepted. *Financial support:* Research assistantships with full tuition reimbursements, teaching assistantships with full tuition reimbursements, scholarships/grants, health care benefits, and unspecified assistantships available. Financial award application deadline: 2/1; financial award applicants required to submit FAFSA. *Unit head:* Dr. Di Ma, Director, 313-583-6737, E-mail: dmadma@umich.edu. *Application contact:* Office of Graduate Studies, 313-583-6321, E-mail: umd-graduatestudies@umich.edu. Website: https://umdearborn.edu/cecs/departments/computer-and-information-science/graduate-programs/phd-computer-and-information-science

University of Michigan–Flint, College of Arts and Sciences, Program in Computer Science and Information Systems, Flint, MI 48502-1950. Offers computer science (MS); information systems (MS), including business information systems, health information systems. *Program availability:* Part-time, evening/weekend, 100% online. *Faculty:* 13 full-time (4 women), 9 part-time/adjunct (3 women). *Students:* 29 full-time (13 women), 49 part-time (11 women); includes 13 minority (5 Black or African American, non-Hispanic/Latino; 1 American Indian or Alaska Native, non-Hispanic/Latino; 2 Asian, non-Hispanic/Latino; 4 Hispanic/Latino; 1 Two or more races, non-Hispanic/Latino), 27 international. Average age 31. 196 applicants, 59% accepted, 15 enrolled. In 2019, 29 master's awarded. *Degree requirements:* For master's, thesis optional, Non Thesis option available. *Entrance requirements:* For master's, BS from regionally-accredited institution in computer science, computer information systems, or computer engineering (preferred); minimum overall undergraduate GPA of 3.0. Additional exam requirements/recommendations for international students: required—TOEFL (minimum score 84 iBT),

IELTS (minimum score 6.5). *Application deadline:* For fall admission, 8/1 for domestic students, 5/1 for international students; for winter admission, 11/15 for domestic students, 10/1 for international students; for spring admission, 3/15 for domestic students, 1/1 for international students; for summer admission, 5/15 for domestic students. Applications are processed on a rolling basis. Application fee: $55. Electronic applications accepted. *Expenses:* Contact institution. *Financial support:* Federal Work-Study, scholarships/grants, and unspecified assistantships available. Financial award application deadline: 3/1; financial award applicants required to submit FAFSA. *Unit head:* Dr. Mark Allison, Department Chair, 810-424-5509, Fax: 810-766-6780, E-mail: markalli@umich.edu. *Application contact:* Matt Bohlen, Associate Director of Graduate Programs, 810-762-3171, Fax: 810-766-6789, E-mail: mbohlen@umflint.edu.
Website: http://www.umflint.edu/graduateprograms/computer-science-information-systems-ms

University of Nebraska at Omaha, Graduate Studies, College of Information Science and Technology, Department of Information Systems and Quantitative Analysis, Omaha, NE 68182. Offers data analytics (Certificate); information assurance (Certificate); information technology (MIT, PhD); management information systems (MS); project management (Certificate); systems analysis and design (Certificate). *Program availability:* Part-time, evening/weekend. *Degree requirements:* For master's, comprehensive exam, thesis (for some programs); for doctorate, comprehensive exam, thesis/dissertation. *Entrance requirements:* For master's, GRE General Test, minimum GPA of 3.0, 3 letters of recommendation, writing sample, resume, official transcripts; for doctorate, GMAT or GRE General Test, minimum GPA of 3.0, 3 letters of recommendation, writing sample, resume, official transcripts; for Certificate, minimum GPA of 3.0, official transcripts. Additional exam requirements/recommendations for international students: required—TOEFL, IELTS, PTE. Electronic applications accepted.

University of Nebraska–Lincoln, Graduate College, College of Arts and Sciences and College of Engineering, Department of Computer Science and Engineering, Lincoln, NE 68588. Offers bioinformatics (MS, PhD); computer engineering (MS, PhD); computer science (MS, PhD); information technology (PhD). *Degree requirements:* For master's, thesis optional; for doctorate, comprehensive exam, thesis/dissertation. *Entrance requirements:* For master's and doctorate, GRE General Test. Additional exam requirements/recommendations for international students: required—TOEFL (minimum score 600 paper-based). Electronic applications accepted.

University of North Alabama, College of Arts and Sciences, Department of Interdisciplinary and Professional Studies, Florence, AL 35632-0001. Offers professional studies (MPS), including community development, higher education administration, information technology, security and safety leadership. *Program availability:* Part-time, 100% online. *Degree requirements:* For master's, thesis optional. *Entrance requirements:* For master's, ETS PPI, personal statement; three letters of recommendation. Additional exam requirements/recommendations for international students: required—TOEFL (minimum score 79 iBT), IELTS (minimum score 6), PTE (minimum score 54). Electronic applications accepted.

The University of North Carolina at Charlotte, College of Computing and Informatics, Department of Software and Information Systems, Charlotte, NC 28223-0001. Offers advanced databases and knowledge discovery (Graduate Certificate); game design and development (Graduate Certificate); information security and privacy (Graduate Certificate); information technology (MS); management of information technology (Graduate Certificate); network security (Graduate Certificate); secure software development (Graduate Certificate). *Program availability:* Part-time, evening/weekend. *Faculty:* 21 full-time (8 women), 5 part-time/adjunct (0 women). *Students:* 138 full-time (64 women), 98 part-time (38 women); includes 47 minority (25 Black or African American, non-Hispanic/Latino; 9 Asian, non-Hispanic/Latino; 10 Hispanic/Latino; 1 Native Hawaiian or other Pacific Islander, non-Hispanic/Latino; 2 Two or more races, non-Hispanic/Latino), 136 international. Average age 28. 298 applicants, 75% accepted, 78 enrolled. In 2019, 107 master's, 20 other advanced degrees awarded. *Degree requirements:* For master's, thesis optional, internship project or project report. *Entrance requirements:* For master's, GRE or GMAT, undergraduate or equivalent course work in data structures, object-oriented programming in C++, C#, or Java with minimum GPA of 3.0, undergraduate GPA of at least 3.0 and a junior/senior GPA of at least 3.0, statement of purpose, 3 letters of recommendation from academic and/or professional references; for Graduate Certificate, bachelor's degree from accredited institution in computing, mathematical, engineering or business discipline with minimum overall GPA of 2.8, junior/senior 3.0; substantial knowledge of data structures and object-oriented programming in C++, C# or Java. Additional exam requirements/recommendations for international students: required—TOEFL (minimum score 557 paper-based; 83 iBT), IELTS (minimum score 6.5), TOEFL (minimum score 557 paper-based, 83 iBT) or IELTS (6.5). *Application deadline:* Applications are processed on a rolling basis. Application fee: $75. Electronic applications accepted. *Expenses:* Contact institution. *Financial support:* In 2019–20, 65 students received support, including 2 fellowships (averaging $51,459 per year), 21 research assistantships (averaging $14,084 per year), 42 teaching assistantships (averaging $7,186 per year); career-related internships or fieldwork, institutionally sponsored loans, scholarships/grants, and unspecified assistantships also available. Support available to part-time students. Financial award application deadline: 3/1; financial award applicants required to submit FAFSA. *Unit head:* Dr. Mary Lou Maher, Chair, 704-687-1940, E-mail: m.maher@uncc.edu. *Application contact:* Kathy B. Giddings, Director of Graduate Admissions, 704-687-5503, Fax: 704-687-1668, E-mail: gradadm@uncc.edu.
Website: http://sis.uncc.edu/

University of North Texas, Toulouse Graduate School, Denton, TX 76203-5459. Offers accounting (MS); applied anthropology (MA, MS); applied behavior analysis (Certificate); applied geography (MA); applied technology and performance improvement (M Ed, MS); art education (MA); art history (MA); arts leadership (Certificate); audiology (Au D); behavior analysis (MS); behavioral science (PhD); biochemistry and molecular biology (MS); biology (MA, MS); biomedical engineering (MS); business analysis (MS); chemistry (MS); clinical health psychology (PhD); communication studies (MA, MS); computer engineering (MS); computer science (MS); counseling (M Ed, MS), including clinical mental health counseling (MS), college and university counseling, elementary school counseling, secondary school counseling; creative writing (MA); criminal justice (MS); curriculum and instruction (M Ed); decision sciences (MBA); design (MA, MFA), including fashion design (MFA), innovation studies, interior design (MFA); early childhood studies (MS); economics (MS); educational leadership (M Ed, Ed D); educational psychology (MS, PhD), including family studies (MS), gifted and talented (MS), human development (MS), learning and cognition (MS), research, measurement and evaluation (MS); electrical engineering (MS); emergency management (MPA); engineering technology (MS); English (MA); English as a second language (MA); environmental science (MS); finance (MBA, MS); financial management (MPA); French (MA); health services management (MBA); higher education (M Ed, Ed D); history (MA, MS); hospitality management (MS); human resources management (MPA); information science (MS); information systems (PhD); information technologies (MBA); interdisciplinary studies (MA, MS); international studies (MA); international sustainable tourism (MS); jazz studies (MM); journalism (MA, MJ, Graduate Certificate), including interactive and virtual digital communication (Graduate Certificate), narrative journalism (Graduate Certificate), public relations (Graduate Certificate); kinesiology (MS); linguistics (MA); local government management (MPA); logistics (PhD); logistics and supply chain management (MBA); long-term care, senior housing, and aging services (MA); management (PhD); marketing (MBA); mathematics (MA, MS); mechanical and energy engineering (MS, PhD); music (MA), including ethnomusicology, music theory, musicology, performance; music composition (PhD); music education (MM Ed, PhD); nonprofit management (MPA); operations and supply chain management (MBA); performance (MM, DMA); philosophy (MA); political science (MA); professional and technical communication (MA); radio, television and film (MA, MFA); rehabilitation counseling (Certificate); sociology (MA); Spanish (MA); special education (M Ed); speech-language pathology (MA); strategic management (MBA); studio art (MFA); teaching (M Ed); MBA/MS. *Program availability:* Part-time, evening/weekend, online learning. Terminal master's awarded for partial completion of doctoral program. *Degree requirements:* For master's, variable foreign language requirement, comprehensive exam (for some programs), thesis (for some programs); for doctorate, variable foreign language requirement, comprehensive exam (for some programs), thesis/dissertation; for other advanced degree, variable foreign language requirement, comprehensive exam (for some programs). *Entrance requirements:* For master's and doctorate, GRE, GMAT. Additional exam requirements/recommendations for international students: required—TOEFL (minimum score 550 paper-based; 79 iBT). Electronic applications accepted.

University of Oregon, Graduate School, College of Arts and Sciences, Department of Computer and Information Science, Eugene, OR 97403. Offers MA, MS, PhD. *Program availability:* Part-time. Terminal master's awarded for partial completion of doctoral program. *Degree requirements:* For doctorate, thesis/dissertation. *Entrance requirements:* For master's and doctorate, GRE General Test, minimum GPA of 3.0. Additional exam requirements/recommendations for international students: required—TOEFL.

University of Ottawa, Faculty of Graduate and Postdoctoral Studies, Faculty of Engineering, Engineering Management Program, Ottawa, ON K1N 6N5, Canada. Offers engineering management (M Eng); information technology (Certificate); project management (Certificate). *Degree requirements:* For master's, thesis or alternative. *Entrance requirements:* For master's and Certificate, honors degree or equivalent, minimum B average. Electronic applications accepted.

University of Pennsylvania, School of Engineering and Applied Science, Department of Computer and Information Science, Philadelphia, PA 19104. Offers computer and information science (MSE, PhD); computer and information technology (MCIT); computer graphics and game technology (MSE). *Program availability:* Part-time. *Faculty:* 61 full-time (9 women), 9 part-time/adjunct (0 women). *Students:* 250 full-time (63 women), 23 part-time (2 women); includes 36 minority (6 Black or African American, non-Hispanic/Latino; 27 Asian, non-Hispanic/Latino; 2 Hispanic/Latino; 1 Two or more races, non-Hispanic/Latino), 173 international. Average age 26. 2,124 applicants, 12% accepted, 103 enrolled. In 2019, 87 master's, 18 doctorates awarded. Terminal master's awarded for partial completion of doctoral program. *Degree requirements:* For master's, comprehensive exam, thesis optional; for doctorate, comprehensive exam, thesis/dissertation. *Entrance requirements:* For master's and doctorate, GRE, bachelor's degree, letters of recommendation, resume, personal statement. Additional exam requirements/recommendations for international students: required—TOEFL (minimum score 100 iBT), IELTS (minimum score 7). *Application deadline:* For fall admission, 12/15 priority date for domestic and international students. Application fee: $80. Electronic applications accepted. *Expenses:* Contact institution. *Application contact:* Associate Director of Graduate Admissions, 215-898-4542, Fax: 215-573-5577, E-mail: admissions2@upenn.edu.
Website: http://www.cis.upenn.edu/prospective-students/graduate/

University of Pittsburgh, School of Computing and Information, Department of Informatics and Networked Systems, Pittsburgh, PA 15260. Offers big data analytics (Certificate); information science (MSIS, PhD, Certificate), including telecommunications (PhD); security assurance/information systems (Certificate); telecommunications (MST, Certificate). *Program availability:* Part-time, evening/weekend. *Faculty:* 23 full-time (7 women), 19 part-time/adjunct (7 women). *Students:* 332 full-time (110 women), 54 part-time (25 women); includes 15 minority (4 Black or African American, non-Hispanic/Latino; 7 Asian, non-Hispanic/Latino; 1 Hispanic/Latino; 3 Two or more races, non-Hispanic/Latino), 331 international. Average age 26. 725 applicants, 73% accepted, 108 enrolled. In 2019, 192 master's, 5 doctorates awarded. *Degree requirements:* For master's, thesis optional; for doctorate, comprehensive exam, thesis/dissertation. *Entrance requirements:* For master's, GRE, GMAT, bachelor's degree with min GPA of 3.0, course-work in structured programming language, statistics, mathematics, probability; for doctorate, GRE, GMAT, Master's degree, min GPA of 3.3, course-work in statistics or mathematics, programming, cognitive psychology, systems analysis and design, data structures; for Certificate, Master's degree in Information Science, Telecommunications or related field. Additional exam requirements/recommendations for international students: required—TOEFL (minimum score 550 paper-based; 80 iBT), IELTS (minimum score 6.5). *Application deadline:* For fall admission, 1/15 priority date for domestic and international students; for winter admission, 11/1 priority date for domestic students, 6/15 priority date for international students; for spring admission, 11/1 priority date for domestic students, 6/15 priority date for international students; for summer admission, 3/15 priority date for domestic students, 12/15 priority date for international students. Applications are processed on a rolling basis. Application fee: $50. Electronic applications accepted. *Expenses:* Fall & spring: $24,742 in-state, $41,952 out-of-state, $950 mandatory fees. *Financial support:* In 2019–20, 58 students received support, including 1 fellowship with full and partial tuition reimbursement available (averaging $24,456 per year), 26 research assistantships with full and partial tuition reimbursements available (averaging $19,480 per year), 31 teaching assistantships with full and partial tuition reimbursements available (averaging $19,480 per year); institutionally sponsored loans, scholarships/grants, health care benefits, and unspecified assistantships also available. Financial award application deadline: 1/15; financial award applicants required to submit FAFSA. *Unit head:* Dr. Prashant Krishnamurthy, Chair and Professor, 412-624-5144, Fax: 412-624-5231, E-mail: prashk@pitt.edu. *Application contact:* Shabana Reza, Enrollment Manager, 412-624-3988, Fax: 412-624-5231, E-mail: shabana.reza@pitt.edu.
Website: http://www.dins.pitt.edu/

University of Pittsburgh, School of Computing and Information, Department of Information Culture and Data Stewardship, Pittsburgh, PA Informatio. Offers library and information science (MLIS, PhD). *Accreditation:* ALA. *Program availability:* Part-time, 100% online, blended/hybrid learning. *Faculty:* 9 full-time (5 women). *Students:* 40 full-time (27 women), 36 part-time (32 women); includes 9 minority (1 Black or African American, non-Hispanic/Latino; 3 Asian, non-Hispanic/Latino; 1 Hispanic/Latino; 4 Two or more races, non-Hispanic/Latino), 8 international. Average age 30. 135 applicants, 85% accepted, 58 enrolled. In 2019, 32 master's, 1 doctorate awarded. *Degree requirements:* For master's, thesis optional; for doctorate, comprehensive exam, thesis/dissertation. *Entrance requirements:* For master's, bachelor's degree from accredited university. Min GPA 3.0; for doctorate, GRE, GRE. Additional exam requirements/recommendations for international students: required—TOEFL (minimum score 550

paper-based; 80 iBT). *Application deadline:* For fall admission, 1/15 priority date for domestic and international students. Applications are processed on a rolling basis. Application fee: $50. Electronic applications accepted. *Expenses:* Fall & spring: $36,814 in-state, $62,640 out-of-state on-campus, $36,814 online, $950 mandatory fees. *Financial support:* In 2019–20, 16 students received support, including 3 research assistantships with full and partial tuition reimbursements available (averaging $19,480 per year), 7 teaching assistantships with full and partial tuition reimbursements available (averaging $19,480 per year); career-related internships or fieldwork, institutionally sponsored loans, scholarships/grants, health care benefits, and unspecified assistantships also available. Financial award application deadline: 1/15; financial award applicants required to submit FAFSA. *Unit head:* Dr. Bruce R. Childers, Chair, 412-624-8421, Fax: 421-624-5231, E-mail: childers@cs.pitt.edu. *Application contact:* Shabana Reza, Enrollment Manager, 412-624-3988, Fax: 412-624-5231, E-mail: shabana.reza@pitt.edu.
Website: http://www.icds.pitt.edu/

University of Puerto Rico at Mayagüez, Graduate Studies, College of Engineering, Department of Electrical and Computer Engineering, Mayagüez, PR 00681-9000. Offers computer engineering (ME, MS); computing and information sciences and engineering (PhD); electrical engineering (ME, MS). *Program availability:* Part-time. Terminal master's awarded for partial completion of doctoral program. *Degree requirements:* For master's, one foreign language, comprehensive exam, thesis; for doctorate, one foreign language, comprehensive exam, thesis/dissertation. *Entrance requirements:* For master's and doctorate, proficiency in English and Spanish; BS in electrical or computer engineering, or equivalent; minimum GPA of 3.0. Electronic applications accepted.

University of Puerto Rico at Rio Piedras, Graduate School of Information Sciences and Technologies, San Juan, PR 00931-3300. Offers administration of academic libraries (PMC); administration of public libraries (PMC); administration of special libraries (PMC); consultant in information services (PMC); documents and files administration (Post-Graduate Certificate); electronic information resources analyst (Post-Graduate Certificate); information science (MIS); librarianship and information services (MLS); school librarian (Post-Graduate Certificate); school librarian distance education mode (Post-Graduate Certificate); specialist in legal information (PMC). *Accreditation:* ALA. *Program availability:* Part-time. *Degree requirements:* For master's, comprehensive exam, thesis, portfolio. *Entrance requirements:* For master's, PAEG, GRE, interview, minimum GPA of 3.0, 3 letters of recommendation; for other advanced degree, PAEG, GRE, minimum GPA of 3.0, IST master's degree.

University of St. Thomas, School of Engineering, St. Paul, MN 55105. Offers data science (MS); electrical engineering (MS); information technology (MS); manufacturing engineering (MS); manufacturing systems (Certificate); mechanical engineering (MS); medical device development (Certificate); regulatory science (MS); software engineering (MS); software management (MS); systems engineering (MS); technology leadership (Certificate); technology management (MS). *Program availability:* Part-time, evening/weekend. *Entrance requirements:* For master's, resume, official transcripts. Additional exam requirements/recommendations for international students: required—TOEFL (minimum score 80 iBT), IELTS (minimum score 6.5). Electronic applications accepted. *Expenses:* Contact institution.

University of South Africa, College of Human Sciences, Pretoria, South Africa. Offers adult education (M Ed); African languages (MA, PhD); African politics (MA, PhD); Afrikaans (MA, PhD); ancient history (MA, PhD); ancient Near Eastern studies (MA, PhD); anthropology (MA, PhD); applied linguistics (MA); Arabic (MA, PhD); archaeology (MA); art history (MA); Biblical archaeology (MA); Biblical studies (M Th, D Th, PhD); Christian spirituality (M Th, D Th); church history (M Th, D Th); classical studies (MA, PhD); clinical psychology (MA); communication (MA, PhD); comparative education (M Ed, Ed D); consulting psychology (D Admin, D Com, PhD); curriculum studies (M Ed, Ed D); development studies (M Admin, MA, D Admin, PhD); didactics (M Ed, Ed D); education (M Tech); education management (M Ed, Ed D); educational psychology (M Ed); English (MA); environmental education (M Ed); French (MA, PhD); German (MA, PhD); Greek (MA); guidance and counseling (M Ed); health studies (MA, PhD), including health sciences education (MA), health services management (MA), medical and surgical nursing science (critical care general) (MA), midwifery and neonatal nursing science (MA), trauma and emergency care (MA); history (MA, PhD); history of education (Ed D); inclusive education (M Ed, Ed D); information and communications technology policy and regulation (MA); information science (MA, MIS, PhD); international politics (MA, PhD); Islamic studies (MA, PhD); Italian (MA, PhD); Judaica (MA, PhD); linguistics (MA, PhD); mathematical education (M Ed); mathematics education (MA); missiology (M Th, D Th); modern Hebrew (MA, PhD); musicology (MA, MMus, D Mus, PhD); natural science education (M Ed); New Testament (M Th, D Th); Old Testament (D Th); pastoral therapy (M Th, D Th); philosophy (MA); philosophy of education (M Ed, Ed D); politics (MA, PhD); Portuguese (MA, PhD); practical theology (M Th, D Th); psychology (MA, MS, PhD); psychology of education (M Ed, Ed D); public health (MA); religious studies (MA, D Th, PhD); Romance languages (MA); Russian (MA, PhD); Semitic languages (MA, PhD); social behavior studies in HIV/AIDS (MA); social science (mental health) (MA); social science in development studies (MA); social science in psychology (MA); social science in social work (MA); social science in sociology (MA); social work (MSW, DSW, PhD); socio-education (M Ed, Ed D); sociolinguistics (MA); sociology (MA, PhD); Spanish (MA, PhD); systematic theology (M Th, D Th); TESOL (teaching English to speakers of other languages) (MA); theological ethics (M Th, D Th); theory of literature (MA, PhD); urban ministries (D Th); urban ministry (M Th).

University of South Carolina Upstate, Graduate Programs, Spartanburg, SC 29303-4999. Offers early childhood education (M Ed); elementary education (M Ed); informatics (MS); special education: visual impairment (M Ed). *Accreditation:* NCATE. *Program availability:* Part-time, evening/weekend. *Faculty:* 15 full-time (11 women), 6 part-time/adjunct (4 women). *Students:* 23 full-time (15 women), 432 part-time (375 women); includes 68 minority (42 Black or African American, non-Hispanic/Latino; 6 Asian, non-Hispanic/Latino; 12 Hispanic/Latino; 8 Two or more races, non-Hispanic/Latino), 3 international. Average age 24. In 2019, 11 master's awarded. *Degree requirements:* For master's, variable foreign language requirement, comprehensive exam (for some programs), thesis or alternative, professional portfolio. *Entrance requirements:* For master's, GRE General Test or MAT, interview, minimum undergraduate GPA of 2.5, teaching certificate, 2 letters of recommendation. *Application deadline:* Applications are processed on a rolling basis. Application fee: $50. Electronic applications accepted. *Expenses: Tuition, area resident:* Full-time $6867; part-time $572.25 per semester. Tuition, nonresident: full-time $14,880; part-time $1240 per semester hour. *Required fees:* $35; $35 per term. $25.50 per term. Tuition and fees vary according to course load and program. *Financial support:* Institutionally sponsored loans and institutional work-study available. Financial award application deadline: 7/15; financial award applicants required to submit FAFSA. *Unit head:* Dr. Tina Herzberg, Director of Graduate Programs, 864-503-5572, Fax: 864-503-5573, E-mail: therzberg@uscupstate.edu. *Application contact:* Donette Stewart, Associate Vice Chancellor for Enrollment Services, 864-503-5280, E-mail: dstewart@uscupstate.edu.
Website: http://www.uscupstate.edu/graduate/

University of Southern Mississippi, College of Education and Human Sciences, School of Library and Information Science, Hattiesburg, MS 39406-0001. Offers library and information science (MLIS); youth services and literature (Graduate Certificate). *Accreditation:* ALA (one or more programs are accredited). *Program availability:* Part-time, evening/weekend, online learning. *Students:* 56 full-time (48 women), 123 part-time (102 women); includes 39 minority (34 Black or African American, non-Hispanic/Latino; 4 Hispanic/Latino; 1 Two or more races, non-Hispanic/Latino), 3 international. 107 applicants, 51% accepted, 46 enrolled. In 2019, 53 master's awarded. *Degree requirements:* For master's, comprehensive exam, thesis. *Entrance requirements:* For master's, GRE General Test, minimum GPA of 3.0. Additional exam requirements/recommendations for international students: required—TOEFL, IELTS. *Application deadline:* For fall admission, 3/15 priority date for domestic students, 3/15 for international students; for spring admission, 1/10 priority date for domestic and international students. Applications are processed on a rolling basis. Application fee: $60. Electronic applications accepted. *Expenses: Tuition, area resident:* Full-time $4393; part-time $488 per credit hour. Tuition, nonresident: full-time $5393; part-time $600 per credit hour. *Required fees:* $6 per semester. *Financial support:* Fellowships with tuition reimbursements, research assistantships with full tuition reimbursements, teaching assistantships with full tuition reimbursements, career-related internships or fieldwork, Federal Work-Study, institutionally sponsored loans, scholarships/grants, health care benefits, and unspecified assistantships available. Financial award application deadline: 3/15; financial award applicants required to submit FAFSA. *Unit head:* Dr. Theresa Welsh, Director, 601-266-4236, Fax: 601-266-5774. *Application contact:* Dr. Theresa Welsh, Director, 601-266-4236, Fax: 601-266-5774.
Website: https://www.usm.edu/library-information-science

University of South Florida, College of Arts and Sciences, School of Information, Tampa, FL 33620-9951. Offers library and information science (MA). *Accreditation:* ALA (one or more programs are accredited). *Program availability:* Part-time, evening/weekend, online learning. *Faculty:* 15 full-time (7 women). *Students:* 108 full-time (77 women), 182 part-time (137 women); includes 83 minority (23 Black or African American, non-Hispanic/Latino; 7 Asian, non-Hispanic/Latino; 49 Hispanic/Latino; 4 Two or more races, non-Hispanic/Latino). Average age 32. 141 applicants, 86% accepted, 71 enrolled. In 2019, 128 master's awarded. *Degree requirements:* For master's, comprehensive exam, thesis (for some programs). *Entrance requirements:* For master's, GRE not required for Intelligence Studies; GRE required for Library and Information Science with preferred minimum scores of 734d percentile (156v), 10th percentile (141Q). May be waived under certain criteria, goals statement, resume or CV, some programs need understanding of programming/coding, computational problem solving and operating systems (for Intelligence Studies); GRE, writing sample, 3 letters of recommendation, resume, statement of purpose (for Library and Information Science). Additional exam requirements/recommendations for international students: required—TOEFL, TOEFL (minimum score 550 paper-based; 79 iBT) or IELTS (minimum score 6.5). *Application deadline:* For fall admission, 6/1 priority date for domestic students, 5/1 for international students; for spring admission, 10/15 priority date for domestic students, 9/15 for international students. Applications are processed on a rolling basis. Application fee: $30. Electronic applications accepted. *Financial support:* In 2019–20, 62 students received support. Unspecified assistantships available. Financial award application deadline: 6/30. *Unit head:* Dr. Jim Andrews, Director and Associate Professor, 813-974-2108, Fax: 813-974-6840, E-mail: jimandrews@usf.edu. *Application contact:* Dr. Randy Borum, Graduate Program Director, 813-974-3520, Fax: 813-974-6840, E-mail: wborum@usf.edu.
Website: http://si.usf.edu/

The University of Tennessee, Graduate School, College of Communication and Information, School of Information Sciences, Knoxville, TN 37996. Offers MS, PhD. *Accreditation:* ALA (one or more programs are accredited). *Program availability:* Part-time, evening/weekend, online learning. *Degree requirements:* For master's, 42 semester hours; written comprehensive exam, online e-portfolio, or thesis; for doctorate, thesis/dissertation or alternative. *Entrance requirements:* For master's, GRE General Test, minimum GPA of 2.7; for doctorate, GRE General Test (minimum scores at or above the 50th percentile on the 3 components, taken within the past five years), master's degree; minimum undergraduate GPA of 3.0, graduate 3.5; recommendation letters from at least three former instructors or professional supervisors; personal statement; interview. Additional exam requirements/recommendations for international students: required—TOEFL. Electronic applications accepted.

The University of Texas at El Paso, Graduate School, College of Engineering, Department of Computer Science, El Paso, TX 79968-0001. Offers computer science (MS, PhD); cyber security (Graduate Certificate); information technology (MSIT); software engineering (MS). *Program availability:* Part-time, evening/weekend. *Degree requirements:* For master's, thesis optional; for doctorate, thesis/dissertation. *Entrance requirements:* For master's, GRE, minimum GPA of 3.0; for doctorate, GRE, statement of purpose, letters of reference. Additional exam requirements/recommendations for international students: required—TOEFL; recommended—IELTS. Electronic applications accepted.

The University of Texas at San Antonio, College of Business, Department of Information Systems and Cyber Security, San Antonio, TX 78249-0617. Offers cyber security (MSIT); information technology (MS, PhD); management of technology (MBA); technology entrepreneurship and management (Certificate). *Program availability:* Part-time, evening/weekend. *Degree requirements:* For master's, comprehensive exam (for some programs), thesis optional; for doctorate, comprehensive exam, thesis/dissertation. *Entrance requirements:* For master's and doctorate, GMAT/GRE, official transcripts, statement of purpose, letters of recommendation. Additional exam requirements/recommendations for international students: required—TOEFL (minimum score 550 paper-based; 79 iBT), IELTS (minimum score 6.5). Electronic applications accepted. *Expenses:* Contact institution.

University of the Sacred Heart, Graduate Programs, Department of Business Administration, Program in Information Technology, San Juan, PR 00914-0383. Offers Certificate.

University of Washington, Graduate School, Information School, Seattle, WA 98195. Offers information management (MSIM), including business intelligence, data science, information architecture, information consulting, information security, user experience; information science (PhD); library and information science (MLIS). *Accreditation:* ALA (one or more programs are accredited). *Program availability:* Part-time, evening/weekend, 100% online coursework with required attendance at on-campus orientation at start of program. *Faculty:* 49 full-time (30 women), 33 part-time/adjunct (19 women). *Students:* 394 full-time (249 women), 283 part-time (198 women); includes 154 minority (33 Black or African American, non-Hispanic/Latino; 8 American Indian or Alaska Native, non-Hispanic/Latino; 71 Asian, non-Hispanic/Latino; 38 Hispanic/Latino; 4 Native Hawaiian or other Pacific Islander, non-Hispanic/Latino), 184 international. Average age 30. 1,205 applicants, 47% accepted, 307 enrolled. In 2019, 234 master's, 5 doctorates awarded. Terminal master's awarded for partial completion of doctoral program. *Degree requirements:* For master's, thesis or alternative, capstone or culminating project; for doctorate, comprehensive exam, thesis/dissertation. *Entrance requirements:* For master's, GRE General Test, GMAT Requirements vary for degree programs as test scores may be optional for some applicants.; for doctorate, GRE General Test May not be required for all applicants. Additional exam requirements/recommendations for

international students: required—TOEFL (minimum score 590 paper-based; 100 iBT). *Application deadline:* For fall admission, 12/1 priority date for domestic and international students. Application fee: $85. Electronic applications accepted. *Expenses:* Graduate degrees: $845 per credit plus approximately $200 in quarterly fees (for MLIS), $896 per credit plus approximately $200 in quarterly fees (for MSIM); PhD: $5798 per quarter in-state full-time, $10,098 per quarter out-of-state full-time. *Financial support:* In 2019–20, 73 students received support, including 14 fellowships with full tuition reimbursements available (averaging $46,977 per year), 90 research assistantships with full tuition reimbursements available (averaging $22,137 per year), 70 teaching assistantships with full tuition reimbursements available (averaging $22,849 per year); Federal Work-Study, institutionally sponsored loans, scholarships/grants, health care benefits, tuition waivers (full and partial), and unspecified assistantships also available. Support available to part-time students. Financial award application deadline: 10/1; financial award applicants required to submit FAFSA. *Unit head:* Dr. Anind Dey, Dean, E-mail: anind@uw.edu. *Application contact:* Kari Brothers, Admissions Counselor, 206-616-5541, Fax: 206-616-3152, E-mail: kari683@uw.edu.
Website: http://ischool.uw.edu/

University of Waterloo, Graduate Studies and Postdoctoral Affairs, Faculty of Engineering, Department of Management Sciences, Waterloo, ON N2L 3G1, Canada. Offers applied operations research (MA Sc, MMS, PhD); information systems (MA Sc, MMS, PhD); management of technology (MA Sc, MMS, PhD). *Program availability:* Part-time, online learning. *Degree requirements:* For master's, research paper or thesis; for doctorate, comprehensive exam, thesis/dissertation. *Entrance requirements:* For master's, GMAT or GRE, honors degree, minimum B average, resume; for doctorate, GMAT or GRE, master's degree, minimum A- average, resume. Additional exam requirements/recommendations for international students: required—TOEFL, IELTS, PTE. Electronic applications accepted.

University of Wisconsin–Parkside, College of Business, Economics, and Computing, Program in Computer and Information Systems, Kenosha, WI 53141-2000. Offers MSCIS. *Entrance requirements:* For master's, GRE General Test or GMAT, 3 letters of recommendation, minimum GPA of 3.0. *Expenses: Tuition, area resident:* Full-time $9173; part-time $509.64 per credit. Tuition, state resident: full-time $9173; part-time $509.64 per credit. Tuition, nonresident: full-time $18,767; part-time $1042.64 per credit. *International tuition:* $18,767 full-time. *Required fees:* $1123.20; $63.64 per credit. Tuition and fees vary according to campus/location, program and reciprocity agreements.

University of Wisconsin–Stout, Graduate School, College of Science, Technology, Engineering and Mathematics, Program in Information and Communication Technologies, Menomonie, WI 54751. Offers MS. *Program availability:* Part-time, online learning. *Degree requirements:* For master's, thesis. *Entrance requirements:* For master's, minimum GPA of 2.75. Additional exam requirements/recommendations for international students: required—TOEFL (minimum score 500 paper-based; 61 iBT). Electronic applications accepted.

Western Governors University, College of Information Technology, Salt Lake City, UT 84107. Offers cybersecurity and information assurance (MS); data analytics (MS); information technology management (MS). *Program availability:* Online learning. *Degree requirements:* For master's, capstone project. Application fee is waived when completed online.

Youngstown State University, College of Graduate Studies, College of Science, Technology, Engineering and Mathematics, Department of Computer Science and Information Systems, Youngstown, OH 44555-0001. Offers computing and information systems (MCIS). *Program availability:* Part-time. *Degree requirements:* For master's, thesis or capstone project. *Entrance requirements:* For master's, GRE or GMAT. Additional exam requirements/recommendations for international students: required—TOEFL (minimum score 550 paper-based).

Internet Engineering

Dalhousie University, Faculty of Engineering, Department of Engineering Mathematics and Internetworking, Halifax, NS B3J 2X4, Canada. Offers engineering mathematics (M Sc, PhD); internetworking (M Eng). *Degree requirements:* For master's, thesis; for doctorate, thesis/dissertation. *Entrance requirements:* Additional exam requirements/recommendations for international students: required—TOEFL, IELTS, CANTEST, CAEL, or Michigan English Language Assessment Battery. Electronic applications accepted.

New Jersey Institute of Technology, Newark College of Engineering, Newark, NJ 07102. Offers biomedical engineering (MS, PhD); biopharmaceutical engineering (MS); chemical engineering (MS, PhD); civil engineering (MS, PhD); computer engineering (MS); critical infrastructure systems (MS); electrical engineering (MS, PhD); engineering management (MS); engineering science (MS); environmental engineering (MS, PhD); healthcare systems management (MS); industrial engineering (MS, PhD); internet engineering (MS); manufacturing systems engineering (MS); materials science & engineering (PhD); materials science and engineering (MS); mechanical engineering (MS, PhD); occupational safety and health engineering (MS). *Program availability:* Part-time, evening/weekend. *Faculty:* 151 full-time (29 women), 135 part-time/adjunct (15 women). *Students:* 576 full-time (161 women), 528 part-time (111 women); includes 366 minority (61 Black or African American, non-Hispanic/Latino; 1 American Indian or Alaska Native, non-Hispanic/Latino; 166 Asian, non-Hispanic/Latino; 115 Hispanic/Latino; 23 Two or more races, non-Hispanic/Latino), 450 international. Average age 28. 2,053 applicants, 67% accepted, 338 enrolled. In 2019, 474 master's, 30 doctorates awarded. Terminal master's awarded for partial completion of doctoral program. *Degree requirements:* For master's, thesis (for some programs); for doctorate, thesis/dissertation. *Entrance requirements:* For master's, GRE General Test, minimum GPA 2.8, personal statement, 1 letter of recommendation, transcripts; for doctorate, GRE General Test, minimum GPA of 3.5, personal statement, 3 letters of recommendation, transcripts. Additional exam requirements/recommendations for international students: required—TOEFL (minimum score 550 paper-based; 79 iBT), IELTS (minimum score 6.5). *Application deadline:* For fall admission, 6/1 priority date for domestic students, 5/1 priority date for international students; for spring admission, 11/15 priority date for domestic and international students. Applications are processed on a rolling basis. Application fee: $75. Electronic applications accepted. *Expenses:* $23,828 per year (in-state), $33,744 per year (out-of-state). *Financial support:* In 2019–20, 352 students received support, including 33 fellowships with full tuition reimbursements available (averaging $24,000 per year), 89 research assistantships with full tuition reimbursements available (averaging $24,000 per year), 112 teaching assistantships with full tuition reimbursements available (averaging $24,000 per year); career-related internships or fieldwork, Federal Work-Study, scholarships/grants, and unspecified assistantships also available. Financial award application deadline: 1/15. *Unit head:* Dr. Moshe Kam, Dean, 973-596-5534, Fax: 973-596-2316, E-mail: moshe.kam@njit.edu. *Application contact:* Stephen Eck, Executive Director of University Admissions, 973-596-3300, Fax: 973-596-3461, E-mail: admissions@njit.edu.
Website: http://engineering.njit.edu/

Wilmington University, College of Technology, New Castle, DE 19720-6491. Offers cybersecurity (MS); information assurance (MS); information systems technologies (MS); management and management information systems (MS); technology project management (MS); Web design (MS). *Program availability:* Part-time, evening/weekend. *Entrance requirements:* Additional exam requirements/recommendations for international students: required—TOEFL (minimum score 500 paper-based). Electronic applications accepted.

Medical Informatics

Arizona State University at Tempe, College of Health Solutions, Department of Biomedical Informatics, Phoenix, AZ 85004. Offers MS, PhD. Terminal master's awarded for partial completion of doctoral program. *Degree requirements:* For master's, interactive Program of Study (iPOS) submitted before completing 50 percent of required credit hours; for doctorate, comprehensive exam, thesis/dissertation, interactive Program of Study (iPOS) submitted before completing 50 percent of required credit hours. *Entrance requirements:* For master's, GRE or MCAT, bachelor's degree with minimum GPA of 3.25 in computer science, biology, physiology, nursing, statistics, engineering, related fields, or unrelated fields with appropriate academic backgrounds; resume/curriculum vitae; statement of purpose; 3 letters of recommendation; all official transcripts; for doctorate, GRE or MCAT, bachelor's degree with minimum GPA of 3.5 in computer science, biology, physiology, nursing, statistics, engineering, related fields, or unrelated fields with appropriate academic backgrounds; resume/curriculum vitae; statement of purpose; 3 letters of recommendation; all official transcripts. Additional exam requirements/recommendations for international students: required—TOEFL (minimum score 550 paper-based; 83 iBT), IELTS (minimum score 6.5). Electronic applications accepted.

Brandeis University, Rabb School of Continuing Studies, Division of Graduate Professional Studies, Master of Science in Health and Medical Informatics Program, Waltham, MA 02454-9110. Offers MS. *Program availability:* Part-time-only. *Entrance requirements:* For master's, four-year bachelor's degree from regionally-accredited U.S. institution or equivalent; official transcript(s) from every college or university attended; resume or curriculum vitae; statement of goals; letter of recommendation. Additional exam requirements/recommendations for international students: required—TWE (minimum score 4.5), TOEFL (minimum scores: 600 paper-based, 100 iBT), IELTS (7), or PTE (68). Electronic applications accepted. *Expenses:* Contact institution.

Columbia University, College of Dental Medicine and Graduate School of Arts and Sciences, Programs in Dental Specialties, New York, NY 10027. Offers advanced education in general dentistry (Certificate); biomedical informatics (MA, PhD); endodontics (Certificate); orthodontics (MS, Certificate); periodontics (MS, Certificate); prosthodontics (MS, Certificate); science education (MA). *Degree requirements:* For master's, thesis, presentation of seminar. *Entrance requirements:* For master's, GRE General Test, DDS or equivalent. *Expenses:* Contact institution.

Columbia University, College of Physicians and Surgeons, Department of Biomedical Informatics, New York, NY 10032. Offers M Phil, MA, PhD, MD/PhD. *Degree requirements:* For doctorate, thesis/dissertation. *Entrance requirements:* For master's and doctorate, GRE General Test, knowledge of computational techniques. Additional exam requirements/recommendations for international students: required—TOEFL. Electronic applications accepted. *Expenses: Tuition:* Full-time $47,600; part-time $1880 per credit. One-time fee: $105.

Dalhousie University, Faculty of Computer Science, Halifax, NS B3H 1W5, Canada. Offers computational biology and bioinformatics (M Sc); computer science (MA Sc, MC Sc, PhD); electronic commerce (MEC); health informatics (MHI). *Degree requirements:* For master's, thesis (for some programs); for doctorate, thesis/dissertation. *Entrance requirements:* Additional exam requirements/recommendations for international students: required—1 of 5 approved tests: TOEFL, IELTS, CANTEST, CAEL, Michigan English Language Assessment Battery. Electronic applications accepted.

Grand Valley State University, Padnos College of Engineering and Computing, Health Informatics and Bioinformatics Program, Allendale, MI 49401-9403. Offers MS. *Program availability:* Part-time, evening/weekend. *Students:* 11 full-time (8 women), 17 part-time (9 women), 17 international. Average age 26. 22 applicants, 91% accepted, 6 enrolled. In 2019, 10 master's awarded. *Degree requirements:* For master's, capstone course. *Entrance requirements:* For master's, GRE or GMAT if undergraduate GPA is less than 3.0, minimum GPA of 3.0, resume, personal statement, minimum of 2 letters of recommendation, previous academic study or work experience. Additional exam requirements/recommendations for international students: required—TOEFL (minimum iBT score of 80), IELTS (6.5), or Michigan English Language Assessment Battery (77). *Application deadline:* For fall admission, 2/1 priority date for domestic students. Applications are processed on a rolling basis. Application fee: $30. Electronic applications accepted. *Expenses:* $733 per credit hour, 36 credit hours. *Financial support:* In 2019–20, 7 students received support, including 2 fellowships, 5 research assistantships with full and partial tuition reimbursements available (averaging $8,000

per year); career-related internships or fieldwork, tuition waivers (full and partial), and unspecified assistantships also available. *Unit head:* Dr. Paul Leidig, Director, 616-331-2060, Fax: 616-331-2144, E-mail: leidigp@gvsu.edu. *Application contact:* Dr. Guenter Tusch, Graduate Program Director, 616-331-2046, Fax: 616-331-2144, E-mail: tuschg@gvsu.edu.
Website: https://www.gvsu.edu/grad/bioinfo/

Johns Hopkins University, School of Medicine, Graduate Programs in Medicine, Department of Health Sciences Informatics, Baltimore, MD 21218. Offers applied health sciences informatics (MS); clinical informatics (Certificate); health sciences informatics (PhD); health sciences informatics research (MS). *Degree requirements:* For master's, thesis, publications, practica. *Entrance requirements:* Additional exam requirements/recommendations for international students: recommended—TOEFL. Electronic applications accepted.

Middle Tennessee State University, College of Graduate Studies, College of Basic and Applied Sciences, Program in Professional Science, Murfreesboro, TN 37132. Offers actuarial sciences (MS); biostatistics (MS); biotechnology (MS); engineering management (MS); health care informatics (MS). *Program availability:* Part-time, evening/weekend, online learning. *Degree requirements:* For master's, comprehensive exam. *Entrance requirements:* For master's, GRE. Additional exam requirements/recommendations for international students: required—TOEFL (minimum score 525 paper-based; 71 iBT) or IELTS (minimum score 6).

Northwestern University, Feinberg School of Medicine, Driskill Graduate Program in Life Sciences, Chicago, IL 60611. Offers biostatistics (PhD); epidemiology (PhD); health and biomedical informatics (PhD); health services and outcomes research (PhD); healthcare quality and patient safety (PhD); translational outcomes in science (PhD). *Degree requirements:* For doctorate, comprehensive exam, thesis/dissertation, written and oral qualifying exams. *Entrance requirements:* For doctorate, GRE General Test. Additional exam requirements/recommendations for international students: required—TOEFL (minimum score 600 paper-based). Electronic applications accepted.

Northwestern University, School of Professional Studies, Program in Information Systems, Evanston, IL 60208. Offers analytics and business intelligence (MS); database and Internet technologies (MS); information systems (MS); information systems management (MS); information systems security (MS); medical informatics (MS); software project management and development (MS). *Program availability:* Part-time, evening/weekend.

Nova Southeastern University, Dr. Kiran C. Patel College of Osteopathic Medicine, Fort Lauderdale, FL 33314-7796. Offers biomedical informatics (MS, Graduate Certificate), including biomedical informatics (MS), clinical informatics (Graduate Certificate), public health informatics (Graduate Certificate); disaster and emergency management (MS); medical education (MS); nutrition (MS, Graduate Certificate), including functional nutrition and herbal therapy (Graduate Certificate); osteopathic medicine (DO); public health (MPH, Graduate Certificate), including health education (Graduate Certificate); social medicine (Graduate Certificate); DO/DMD. *Accreditation:* AOsA; CEPH. *Program availability:* Part-time, 100% online, blended/hybrid learning. *Faculty:* 73 full-time (43 women), 35 part-time/adjunct (14 women). *Students:* 1,410 full-time (740 women), 182 part-time (118 women); includes 895 minority (126 Black or African American, non-Hispanic/Latino; 1 American Indian or Alaska Native, non-Hispanic/Latino; 416 Asian, non-Hispanic/Latino; 309 Hispanic/Latino; 1 Native Hawaiian or other Pacific Islander, non-Hispanic/Latino; 42 Two or more races, non-Hispanic/Latino), 70 international. Average age 26. 5,078 applicants, 10% accepted, 495 enrolled. In 2019, 117 master's, 233 doctorates, 3 other advanced degrees awarded. *Degree requirements:* For master's, comprehensive exam (for MPH); field/special projects; for doctorate, comprehensive exam, COMLEX Board Exams; for Graduate Certificate, thesis or alternative. *Entrance requirements:* For master's, GRE; for doctorate, MCAT, coursework in biology, chemistry, organic chemistry, physics (all with labs), biochemistry, and English. *Application deadline:* For fall admission, 1/15 for domestic students. Applications are processed on a rolling basis. Application fee: $50. Electronic applications accepted. *Expenses:* Contact institution. *Financial support:* In 2019–20, 83 students received support, including 24 fellowships with tuition reimbursements available; Federal Work-Study and scholarships/grants also available. Financial award application deadline: 6/1; financial award applicants required to submit FAFSA. *Unit head:* Elaine M. Wallace, Dean, 954-262-1457, Fax: 954-262-2250, E-mail: ewallace@nova.edu. *Application contact:* HPD Admissions, 877-640-0218, E-mail: hpdinfo@nova.edu.
Website: https://www.osteopathic.nova.edu/

Oregon Health & Science University, School of Medicine, Graduate Programs in Medicine, Department of Medical Informatics and Clinical Epidemiology, Portland, OR 97239-3098. Offers bioinformatics and computational biology (MS, PhD); clinical informatics (MBI, MS, PhD, Certificate); health information management (Certificate). *Program availability:* Part-time, online learning. Terminal master's awarded for partial completion of doctoral program. *Degree requirements:* For master's, thesis or capstone project; for doctorate, comprehensive exam, thesis/dissertation, qualifying exam. *Entrance requirements:* For master's and doctorate, GRE General Test (minimum scores: 153 Verbal/148 Quantitative/4.5 Analytical), coursework in computer programming, human anatomy and physiology. Electronic applications accepted. *Expenses:* Contact institution.

Regis University, College of Computer and Information Sciences, Denver, CO 80221-1099. Offers agile technologies (Certificate); cybersecurity (Certificate); data science (M Sc); database administration with Oracle (Certificate); database development (Certificate); database technologies (M Sc); enterprise Java software development (Certificate); enterprise resource planning (Certificate); executive information technology (Certificate); health care informatics (Certificate); health care informatics and information management (M Sc); information assurance (M Sc); information assurance policy management (Certificate); information technology management (M Sc); mobile software development (Certificate); software engineering (M Sc, Certificate); software engineering and database technology (M Sc); storage area networks (Certificate); systems engineering (M Sc, Certificate). *Program availability:* Part-time, evening/weekend, 100% online, blended/hybrid learning. *Degree requirements:* For master's, thesis (for some programs), final research project. *Entrance requirements:* For master's, official transcript reflecting baccalaureate degree awarded from regionally-accredited college or university, 2 years of related experience, resume, interview. Additional exam requirements/recommendations for international students: required—TOEFL (minimum score 550 paper-based; 82 iBT). Electronic applications accepted. *Expenses:* Contact institution.

Rutgers University - Newark, School of Health Related Professions, Department of Health Informatics, Program in Biomedical Informatics, Newark, NJ 07102. Offers MS, PhD, DMD/MS, MD/MS. *Program availability:* Part-time, evening/weekend, online learning. *Degree requirements:* For master's, thesis; for doctorate, comprehensive exam, thesis/dissertation. *Entrance requirements:* For master's, BS, transcript of highest degree, statement of research interests, curriculum vitae, basic understanding of database concepts and calculus, 3 reference letters; for doctorate, master's degree, transcripts of highest degree, statement of research interests, curriculum vitae, basic understanding of database concepts and calculus, 3 reference letters. Additional exam requirements/recommendations for international students: required—TOEFL. Electronic applications accepted.

Rutgers University - Newark, School of Health Related Professions, Department of Health Informatics, Program in Health Care Informatics, Newark, NJ 07102. Offers Certificate. *Program availability:* Part-time, evening/weekend, online learning. *Entrance requirements:* For degree, all transcripts, basic proficiency in programming language, BS, 3 reference letters. Additional exam requirements/recommendations for international students: required—TOEFL (minimum score 500 paper-based; 79 iBT). Electronic applications accepted.

Stanford University, School of Medicine, Stanford Center for Biomedical Informatics Research, Stanford, CA 94305-2004. Offers MS, PhD. *Expenses: Tuition:* Full-time $52,479; part-time $34,110 per unit. *Required fees:* $672; $224 per quarter. Tuition and fees vary according to program and student level.
Website: http://bmir.stanford.edu/

University at Buffalo, the State University of New York, Graduate School, Jacobs School of Medicine and Biomedical Sciences, Graduate Programs in Medicine and Biomedical Sciences, Department of Biomedical Informatics, Buffalo, NY 14260. Offers bioinformatics and translational research informatics (PhD); biomedical informatics (MS); biomedical ontology (PhD); clinical informatics and decision support (PhD). *Program availability:* Part-time. *Faculty:* 5 full-time (1 woman), 1 part-time/adjunct (0 women). *Students:* 12 full-time (7 women), 10 part-time (3 women); includes 11 minority (1 Black or African American, non-Hispanic/Latino; 8 Asian, non-Hispanic/Latino; 2 Hispanic/Latino). Average age 32. 37 applicants, 35% accepted, 4 enrolled. In 2019, 2 master's awarded. Terminal master's awarded for partial completion of doctoral program. *Degree requirements:* For master's, thesis or alternative; for doctorate, variable foreign language requirement, comprehensive exam (for some programs), thesis/dissertation. *Entrance requirements:* For master's, 3 letters of recommendation; for doctorate, GRE, MCAT, 3 letters of recommendation. Additional exam requirements/recommendations for international students: required—TOEFL (minimum score 600 paper-based; 100 iBT), IELTS (minimum score 7.5). *Application deadline:* Applications are processed on a rolling basis. Application fee: $85. Electronic applications accepted. *Expenses: Tuition, area resident:* Full-time $11,310; part-time $471 per credit hour. Tuition, state resident: full-time $11,310; part-time $471 per credit hour. Tuition, nonresident: full-time $23,100; part-time $963 per credit hour. *International tuition:* $23,100 full-time. *Required fees:* $2820. *Financial support:* In 2019–20, 9 students received support, including 3 fellowships with full and partial tuition reimbursements available (averaging $50,000 per year), 7 research assistantships with full and partial tuition reimbursements available (averaging $28,000 per year); traineeships, health care benefits, and unspecified assistantships also available. *Unit head:* Dr. Peter L. Elkin, MD, Professor and Chair, 716-816-7292, Fax: 716-842-4170, E-mail: elkinp@buffalo.edu. *Application contact:* Winanne Conway, Assistant to the Chair, 716-888-4858, Fax: 716-842-4170, E-mail: wwconway@buffalo.edu.
Website: http://medicine.buffalo.edu/departments/biomedical-informatics.html

The University of Arizona, College of Nursing, Tucson, AZ 85721. Offers health care informatics (Certificate); nurse practitioner (MS); nursing (DNP, PhD). *Accreditation:* AACN; AANA/CANAEP. *Program availability:* Part-time, online learning. Terminal master's awarded for partial completion of doctoral program. *Degree requirements:* For master's, thesis optional; for doctorate, comprehensive exam, thesis/dissertation. *Entrance requirements:* For master's, BSN, eligibility for RN license; for doctorate, BSN; for Certificate, GRE General Test, Arizona RN license, BSN, minimum GPA of 3.0. Additional exam requirements/recommendations for international students: required—TOEFL (minimum score 550 paper-based; 79 iBT). Electronic applications accepted. *Expenses:* Contact institution.

University of California, Davis, Graduate Studies, Graduate Group in Health Informatics, Davis, CA 95616. Offers MS. *Entrance requirements:* Additional exam requirements/recommendations for international students: required—TOEFL (minimum score 550 paper-based).

University of Colorado Denver, College of Nursing, Aurora, CO 80045. Offers adult clinical nurse specialist (MS); adult nurse practitioner (MS); family nurse practitioner (MS); family psychiatric mental health nurse practitioner (MS); health care informatics (MS); nurse-midwifery (MS); nursing (DNP, PhD); nursing leadership and health care systems (MS); pediatric nurse practitioner (MS); women's health (MS); MS/PhD. *Accreditation:* ACNM/ACME (one or more programs are accredited). *Program availability:* Part-time, evening/weekend, online learning. Terminal master's awarded for partial completion of doctoral program. *Degree requirements:* For master's, thesis optional; for doctorate, comprehensive exam, thesis/dissertation, 42 credits of coursework. *Entrance requirements:* For master's, GRE if cumulative undergraduate GPA is less than 3.0, undergraduate nursing degree from ACEN- or CCNE-accredited school or university; completion of research and statistics courses with minimum grade of C; copy of current and unencumbered nursing license; for doctorate, GRE, bachelor's and/or master's degrees in nursing from ACEN- or CCNE-accredited institution; portfolio; minimum undergraduate GPA of 3.0, graduate 3.5; graduate-level intermediate statistics and master's-level nursing theory courses with minimum B grade; interview. Additional exam requirements/recommendations for international students: required—TOEFL (minimum score 560 paper-based; 83 iBT). Electronic applications accepted. *Expenses:* Contact institution.

University of Illinois at Urbana-Champaign, Graduate College, School of Information Sciences, Champaign, IL 61820. Offers bioinformatics (MS); digital libraries (CAS); information management (MS); library and information science (MS, PhD, CAS). *Accreditation:* ALA (one or more programs are accredited). *Program availability:* Part-time, online learning. *Entrance requirements:* For degree, master's degree in library and information science or related field with minimum GPA of 3.0.

The University of Kansas, University of Kansas Medical Center, School of Nursing, Kansas City, KS 66045. Offers adult/gerontological clinical nurse specialist (PMC); adult/gerontological nurse practitioner (PMC); health care informatics (PMC); health professions educator (PMC); nurse midwife (PMC); nursing (MS, DNP, PhD); organizational leadership (PMC); psychiatric/mental health nurse practitioner (PMC); public health nursing (PMC). *Accreditation:* AACN; ACNM/ACME. *Program availability:* Part-time, 100% online, blended/hybrid learning. *Faculty:* 65. *Students:* 57 full-time (53 women), 267 part-time (242 women); includes 65 minority (14 Black or African American, non-Hispanic/Latino; 2 American Indian or Alaska Native, non-Hispanic/Latino; 21 Asian, non-Hispanic/Latino; 9 Hispanic/Latino; 1 Native Hawaiian or other Pacific Islander, non-Hispanic/Latino; 18 Two or more races, non-Hispanic/Latino), 2 international. Average age 35. In 2019, 26 master's, 48 doctorates, 5 other advanced degrees awarded. Terminal master's awarded for partial completion of doctoral program. *Degree requirements:* For master's, comprehensive exam, thesis (for some programs), general oral exam; for doctorate, thesis/dissertation or alternative, comprehensive oral exam (for DNP); comprehensive written and oral exam, or three publications (for PhD). *Entrance requirements:* For master's, bachelor's degree in nursing, minimum GPA of 3.0, 1 year of clinical experience, RN license in KS and MO; for doctorate, GRE General Test (for PhD only), bachelor's degree in nursing, minimum

GPA of 3.5, RN license in KS and MO. Additional exam requirements/recommendations for international students: required—TOEFL. *Application deadline:* For fall admission, 4/1 for domestic and international students; for spring admission, 9/1 for domestic and international students. Application fee: $75. Electronic applications accepted. *Expenses:* Contact institution. *Financial support:* Research assistantships with tuition reimbursements, teaching assistantships with tuition reimbursements, scholarships/grants, and traineeships available. Financial award application deadline: 3/1; financial award applicants required to submit FAFSA. *Unit head:* Dr. Sally Maliski, Professor and Dean, 913-588-1601, Fax: 913-588-1660, E-mail: smaliski@kumc.edu. *Application contact:* Dr. Pamela K. Barnes, Associate Dean, Student Affairs and Enrollment Management, 913-588-1619, Fax: 913-588-1615, E-mail: pbarnes2@kumc.edu.
Website: http://nursing.kumc.edu

University of Phoenix - Phoenix Campus, College of Health Sciences and Nursing, Tempe, AZ 85282-2371. Offers family nurse practitioner (MSN, Certificate); gerontology health care (Certificate); health care education (MSN, Certificate); health care informatics (Certificate); informatics (MSN); nursing (MSN); MSN/MHA. *Program availability:* Evening/weekend, online learning. *Entrance requirements:* Additional exam requirements/recommendations for international students: required—TOEFL, TOEIC (Test of English as an International Communication), Berlitz Online English Proficiency Exam, PTE, or IELTS. Electronic applications accepted. *Expenses:* Contact institution.

University of Washington, Graduate School, School of Medicine, Graduate Programs in Medicine, Department of Medical Education and Biomedical Informatics, Division of Biomedical and Health Informatics, Seattle, WA 98195. Offers MS, PhD. *Entrance requirements:* For master's and doctorate, GRE General Test, minimum GPA of 3.0; previous undergraduate course work in biology, computer programming, and mathematics. Additional exam requirements/recommendations for international students: required—TOEFL (minimum score 580 paper-based; 70 iBT). Electronic applications accepted.

University of Wisconsin–Milwaukee, Graduate School, College of Health Sciences, Department of Health Informatics and Administration, Milwaukee, WI 53201-0413. Offers health care informatics (MS); healthcare administration (MHA). *Degree requirements:* For master's, comprehensive exam, thesis optional. *Entrance requirements:* For master's, GRE General Test. Additional exam requirements/recommendations for international students: required—TOEFL (minimum score 550 paper-based; 79 iBT), IELTS (minimum score 6.5).

Modeling and Simulation

Arizona State University at Tempe, Ira A. Fulton Schools of Engineering, ASU Engineering Online Programs, Tempe, AZ 85287. Offers construction (MS); embedded systems (M Eng); enterprise systems innovation and management (MSE); modeling and simulation (M Eng); quality and reliability engineering (M Eng); software engineering (MSE); systems engineering (M Eng).

Arizona State University at Tempe, Ira A. Fulton Schools of Engineering, The Polytechnic School, Department of Engineering, Mesa, AZ 85212. Offers simulation, modeling, and applied cognitive science (PhD). *Program availability:* Part-time. *Degree requirements:* For doctorate, comprehensive exam, thesis/dissertation, interactive Program of Study (iPOS) submitted before completing 50 percent of required credit hours. *Entrance requirements:* For doctorate, GRE, master's degree in psychology, engineering, cognitive science, or computer science; 3 letters of recommendation; statement of research interests. Additional exam requirements/recommendations for international students: required—TOEFL, IELTS, or PTE. Electronic applications accepted.

Carnegie Mellon University, Carnegie Institute of Technology, Department of Civil and Environmental Engineering, Pittsburgh, PA 15213. Offers advanced infrastructure systems (MS, PhD); advanced infrastructure systems technology development and application (MS); air quality engineering and science (MS); civil and environmental engineering (MS, PhD); civil and environmental engineering/engineering and public policy (PhD); civil engineering (MS, PhD); computational mechanics (MS, PhD); computational modeling and monitoring for resilient structural and material systems (MS); energy infrastructure systems (MS); environmental engineering (MS, PhD); environmental management and science (MS, PhD); IT-based sustainable global infrastructure and construction management (MS); sustainability and green design (MS); water quality engineering and science (MS). *Program availability:* Part-time. *Faculty:* 23 full-time (5 women), 12 part-time/adjunct (3 women). *Students:* 261 full-time (109 women); includes 19 minority (7 Black or African American, non-Hispanic/Latino; 8 Asian, non-Hispanic/Latino; 4 Hispanic/Latino), 214 international. Average age 25. 649 applicants, 57% accepted, 106 enrolled. In 2019, 80 master's, 12 doctorates awarded. Terminal master's awarded for partial completion of doctoral program. *Degree requirements:* For master's, thesis optional; for doctorate, comprehensive exam, thesis/dissertation, two-part qualifying exam, public defense of dissertation. *Entrance requirements:* For master's, GRE General Test, BS in engineering, science, or mathematics; for doctorate, GRE General Test, BS or MS in engineering, science, or mathematics. Additional exam requirements/recommendations for international students: required—TOEFL (minimum score 84 iBT), TOEFL (minimum score 84 iBT) or IELTS (7.0). *Application deadline:* For fall admission, 1/5 priority date for domestic and international students; for spring admission, 9/15 priority date for domestic and international students. Applications are processed on a rolling basis. Application fee: $75. Electronic applications accepted. *Financial support:* In 2019–20, 113 students received support. Fellowships with tuition reimbursements available, research assistantships with tuition reimbursements available, teaching assistantships, scholarships/grants, health care benefits, tuition waivers (full and partial), and unspecified assistantships available. Financial award application deadline: 1/5. *Unit head:* Dr. David A. Dzombak, Professor and Department Head, 412-268-2941, Fax: 412-268-7813, E-mail: dzombak@cmu.edu. *Application contact:* David A. Vey, Director of Graduate Programs, 412-268-2292, Fax: 412-268-7813, E-mail: dvey@andrew.cmu.edu.
Website: http://www.cmu.edu/cee/

Columbus State University, Graduate Studies, Turner College of Business, Columbus, GA 31907-5645. Offers applied computer science (MS), including informational assurance, modeling and simulation, software development; business administration (MBA); cyber security (MS); human resource management (Certificate); information systems security (Certificate); modeling and simulation (Certificate); organizational leadership (MS), including human resource management, leader development, servant leadership; servant leadership (Certificate). *Accreditation:* AACSB. *Program availability:* Part-time, evening/weekend, 100% online, blended/hybrid learning. *Entrance requirements:* For master's, GMAT, GRE, minimum undergraduate GPA of 2.75, letters of recommendation. Additional exam requirements/recommendations for international students: required—TOEFL (minimum score 550 paper-based; 79 iBT). Electronic applications accepted. *Expenses:* Contact institution.

Naval Postgraduate School, Departments and Academic Groups, Department of Computer Science, Monterey, CA 93943. Offers computer science (MS, PhD); identity management and cyber security (MA); modeling of virtual environments and simulations (MS, PhD); software engineering (MS, PhD). *Program availability:* Part-time, online learning. *Degree requirements:* For master's, thesis; for doctorate, thesis/dissertation.

Old Dominion University, College of Arts and Letters, Graduate Program in International Studies, Norfolk, VA 23529. Offers conflict and cooperation (MA, PhD); interdependence and transnationalism (MA, PhD); international cultural studies (MA, PhD); international political economy and development (MA, PhD); modeling and simulation (MA, PhD); U.S. foreign policy and international relations (MA, PhD). *Program availability:* Part-time. Terminal master's awarded for partial completion of doctoral program. *Degree requirements:* For master's, one foreign language, comprehensive exam, thesis optional; for doctorate, one foreign language, comprehensive exam, thesis/dissertation. *Entrance requirements:* For master's, GRE General Test, sample of written work, 2 letters of recommendation; for doctorate, GRE General Test, sample of written work, 3 letters of recommendation. Additional exam requirements/recommendations for international students: required—TOEFL (minimum score 570 paper-based). Electronic applications accepted. *Expenses:* Contact institution.

Old Dominion University, Frank Batten College of Engineering and Technology, Program in Modeling and Simulation, Norfolk, VA 23529. Offers ME, MS, D Eng, PhD. *Program availability:* Part-time, evening/weekend, 100% online, blended/hybrid learning. Terminal master's awarded for partial completion of doctoral program. *Degree requirements:* For master's, comprehensive exam (for some programs), thesis (for some programs); for doctorate, comprehensive exam, thesis/dissertation, candidacy exam. *Entrance requirements:* For master's, GRE, proficiency in calculus, calculus-based statistics, and computer science; for doctorate, GRE, graduate-level proficiency in calculus, calculus-based statistics, and computer science. Additional exam requirements/recommendations for international students: required—TOEFL (minimum score 550 paper-based; 79 iBT). Electronic applications accepted.

Portland State University, Graduate Studies, College of Liberal Arts and Sciences, Systems Science Program, Portland, OR 97207-0751. Offers computational intelligence (Certificate); computer modeling and simulation (Certificate); systems science (MS); systems science/anthropology (PhD); systems science/business administration (PhD); systems science/civil engineering (PhD); systems science/economics (PhD); systems science/engineering management (PhD); systems science/general (PhD); systems science/mathematical sciences (PhD); systems science/mechanical engineering (PhD); systems science/psychology (PhD); systems science/sociology (PhD). *Program availability:* Part-time. *Faculty:* 2 full-time (0 women), 6 part-time/adjunct (1 woman). *Students:* 6 full-time (3 women), 25 part-time (8 women); includes 7 minority (2 Asian, non-Hispanic/Latino; 4 Hispanic/Latino; 1 Two or more races, non-Hispanic/Latino), 2 international. Average age 39. 25 applicants, 80% accepted, 15 enrolled. In 2019, 7 master's, 2 doctorates awarded. Terminal master's awarded for partial completion of doctoral program. *Degree requirements:* For master's, comprehensive exam (for some programs), thesis optional; for doctorate, variable foreign language requirement, comprehensive exam (for some programs), thesis/dissertation. *Entrance requirements:* For master's, GRE/GMAT (recommended), minimum GPA of 3.0 on undergraduate or graduate work, 2 letters of recommendation, statement of interest; for doctorate, GRE required, minimum GPA of 3.0 undergraduate, 3.25 graduate; 3 letters of recommendation; statement of interest. Additional exam requirements/recommendations for international students: required—TOEFL (minimum score 550 paper-based; 80 iBT). *Application deadline:* For fall admission, 3/15 priority date for domestic and international students. Application fee: $65. Electronic applications accepted. *Expenses: Tuition, area resident:* Full-time $13,020; part-time $6510 per year. Tuition, state resident: full-time $13,020; part-time $6510 per year. Tuition, nonresident: full-time $19,830; part-time $9915 per year. *International tuition:* $19,830 full-time. *Required fees:* $1226. One-time fee: $350. Tuition and fees vary according to course load, program and reciprocity agreements. *Financial support:* Research assistantships, teaching assistantships, career-related internships or fieldwork, Federal Work-Study, scholarships/grants, and unspecified assistantships available. Support available to part-time students. Financial award application deadline: 3/1; financial award applicants required to submit FAFSA. *Unit head:* Dr. Wayne Wakeland, Chair, 503-725-4975, E-mail: wakeland@pdx.edu. *Application contact:* Dr. Wayne Wakeland, Chair, 503-725-4975, E-mail: wakeland@pdx.edu.
Website: http://www.pdx.edu/sysc/

Rochester Institute of Technology, Graduate Enrollment Services, College of Science, School of Mathematical Sciences, PhD Program in Mathematical Modeling, Rochester, NY 14623-5603. Offers PhD. *Degree requirements:* For doctorate, thesis/dissertation. *Entrance requirements:* For doctorate, GRE, official transcripts, minimum GPA of 3.0 in primary field of study, previous mathematical coursework beyond calculus, two letters of recommendation, personal statement. Additional exam requirements/recommendations for international students: required—TOEFL (minimum score 100 iBT), IELTS (minimum score 7), PTE (minimum score 68). Electronic applications accepted. *Expenses:* Contact institution.

Stevens Institute of Technology, Graduate School, Charles V. Schaefer Jr. School of Engineering and Science, Department of Civil, Environmental, and Ocean Engineering, Program in Civil Engineering, Hoboken, NJ 07030. Offers civil engineering (PhD, Certificate), including geotechnical engineering (Certificate); geotechnical/geoenvironmental engineering (M Eng, Engr); hydrologic modeling (M Eng); stormwater management (M Eng); structural engineering (M Eng, Engr); transportation engineering (M Eng); water resources engineering (M Eng). *Program availability:* Part-time, evening/weekend. *Faculty:* 23 full-time (8 women), 21 part-time/adjunct (2 women). *Students:* 38 full-time (6 women), 19 part-time (6 women); includes 11 minority (2 Black or African American, non-Hispanic/Latino; 1 American Indian or Alaska Native, non-Hispanic/Latino; 8 Asian, non-Hispanic/Latino), 29 international. Average age 25. In 2019, 38 master's, 2 doctorates awarded. Terminal master's awarded for partial completion of doctoral program. *Degree requirements:* For master's, thesis optional, minimum B average in major field and overall; for doctorate, comprehensive exam (for some programs), thesis/dissertation; for other advanced degree, minimum B average. *Entrance requirements:* For master's, International applicants must submit TOEFL/IELTS scores and fulfill the English Language Proficiency Requirement. Applicants to full-time programs who do not qualify for a score waiver are required to submit GRE/

GMAT scores. Additional exam requirements/recommendations for international students: required—TOEFL (minimum score 74 iBT), IELTS (minimum score 6). *Application deadline:* For fall admission, 4/15 for domestic and international students; for spring admission, 11/1 for domestic and international students; for summer admission, 5/1 for domestic students. Applications are processed on a rolling basis. Application fee: $60. Electronic applications accepted. *Expenses: Tuition:* Full-time $52,134. *Required fees:* $1880. Tuition and fees vary according to course load. *Financial support:* Fellowships, research assistantships, teaching assistantships, career-related internships or fieldwork, Federal Work-Study, scholarships/grants, and unspecified assistantships available. Financial award application deadline: 2/15; financial award applicants required to submit FAFSA. *Unit head:* Dr. Jean Zu, Dean of SES, 201-216.8233, Fax: 201-216.8372, E-mail: Jean.Zu@stevens.edu. *Application contact:* Graduate Admission, 888-783-8367, Fax: 888-511-1306, E-mail: graduate@stevens.edu.

Trent University, Graduate Studies, Program in Applications of Modeling in the Natural and Social Sciences, Peterborough, ON K9J 7B8, Canada. Offers applications of modeling in the natural and social sciences (MA); biology (M Sc, PhD); chemistry (M Sc); computer studies (M Sc); geography (M Sc, PhD); physics (M Sc). *Program availability:* Part-time. *Degree requirements:* For master's, thesis. *Entrance requirements:* For master's, honours degree.

University at Buffalo, the State University of New York, Graduate School, College of Arts and Sciences, Department of Geography, N Tonawanda, NY 14261. Offers earth systems science (MA, MS); economic geography and business geographics (MS); environmental modeling and analysis (MA); geographic information science (MA, MS); geography (MA, PhD); health geography (MS); international trade (MA); urban and regional analysis (MA). *Program availability:* Part-time. *Faculty:* 22 full-time (9 women), 3 part-time/adjunct (1 woman). *Students:* 61 full-time (26 women); includes 37 minority (2 Black or African American, non-Hispanic/Latino; 34 Asian, non-Hispanic/Latino; 1 Hispanic/Latino). Average age 28. 120 applicants, 62% accepted, 12 enrolled. In 2019, 23 master's, 3 doctorates awarded. Terminal master's awarded for partial completion of doctoral program. *Degree requirements:* For master's, thesis (for some programs), project or portfolio; for doctorate, thesis/dissertation, dissertation/thesis. *Entrance requirements:* For master's, GRE General Test, minimum GPA of 2.9; for doctorate, GRE General Test, minimum GPA of 3.0. Additional exam requirements/recommendations for international students: required—TOEFL (minimum score 550 paper-based; 79 iBT). *Application deadline:* For fall admission, 5/1 priority date for domestic students, 3/10 priority date for international students; for spring admission, 11/1 priority date for domestic students, 9/1 priority date for international students. Applications are processed on a rolling basis. Application fee: $75. Electronic applications accepted. *Expenses:* Contact institution. *Financial support:* In 2019–20, 15 students received support, including 9 fellowships with full tuition reimbursements available (averaging $4,500 per year), 7 research assistantships with full tuition reimbursements available (averaging $14,000 per year), 13 teaching assistantships with full tuition reimbursements available (averaging $14,080 per year); career-related internships or fieldwork, Federal Work-Study, institutionally sponsored loans, traineeships, health care benefits, and unspecified assistantships also available. Financial award application deadline: 1/10. *Unit head:* Dr. Chris Larsen, Interim Chair, 716-645-0488, Fax: 716-645-2329, E-mail: larsen@buffalo.edu. *Application contact:* Wendy Zitzka, Graduate Secretary, 716-645-0471, Fax: 716-645-2329, E-mail: wzitzka@buffalo.edu.
Website: http://www.geog.buffalo.edu/

The University of Alabama in Huntsville, School of Graduate Studies, College of Science, Department of Computer Science, Huntsville, AL 35899. Offers computer science (MS, PhD); cybersecurity (MS); modeling and simulation (MS, PhD, Certificate); software engineering (MSSE, Certificate). *Program availability:* Part-time. *Degree requirements:* For master's, comprehensive exam, thesis or alternative, oral and written exams; for doctorate, comprehensive exam, thesis/dissertation, oral and written exams. *Entrance requirements:* For master's, doctorate, and Certificate, GRE General Test, minimum GPA of 3.0. Additional exam requirements/recommendations for international students: required—TOEFL (minimum score 550 paper-based; 80 iBT), IELTS (minimum score 6.5). Electronic applications accepted.

University of California, San Diego, Graduate Division, Department of Structural Engineering, La Jolla, CA 92093. Offers structural engineering (MS, PhD); structural health monitoring, prognosis, and validated simulations (MS). *Students:* 164 full-time (40 women), 20 part-time (6 women). 386 applicants, 57% accepted, 72 enrolled. In 2019, 65 master's, 12 doctorates awarded. *Degree requirements:* For master's, comprehensive exam (for some programs), thesis (for some programs); for doctorate, comprehensive exam, thesis/dissertation, 1-quarter teaching assistantship. *Entrance requirements:* For master's and doctorate, GRE General Test. Additional exam requirements/recommendations for international students: required—TOEFL (minimum score 550 paper-based; 80 iBT), IELTS (minimum score 7). *Application deadline:* For fall admission, 1/29 for domestic students. Application fee: $105 ($125 for international students). Electronic applications accepted. *Financial support:* Fellowships, research assistantships, teaching assistantships, scholarships/grants, and readerships available. Financial award applicants required to submit FAFSA. *Unit head:* John McCartney, Chair, 858-534-9630, E-mail: mccartney@eng.ucsd.edu. *Application contact:* Joana Halnez, Graduate Coordinator, 858-534-4185, E-mail: se-info@ucsd.edu.
Website: http://www.structures.ucsd.edu/

University of Central Florida, College of Community Innovation and Education, Department of Learning Science and Educational Research, Education Doctoral Programs, Orlando, FL 32816. Offers applied learning and instruction (MA); curriculum and instruction (M Ed); instructional design and technology (MA, Certificate), including e-learning (Certificate), educational technology (Certificate), instructional design (Certificate), instructional design and technology (MA), instructional design for simulations (Certificate); sport and exercise science (MS), including applied exercise physiology. *Program availability:* Part-time, evening/weekend. *Students:* 1 full-time (0 women), 2 part-time (1 woman); includes 1 minority (Black or African American, non-Hispanic/Latino). Average age 41. *Entrance requirements:* Additional exam requirements/recommendations for international students: required—TOEFL. Application fee: $30. Electronic applications accepted. *Financial support:* Scholarships/grants, health care benefits, and unspecified assistantships available. Financial award application deadline: 3/1; financial award applicants required to submit FAFSA. *Unit head:* Dr. Jeffrey Stout, Chair, 407-823-0211, E-mail: jeffrey.stout@ucf.edu. *Application contact:* Associate Director, Graduate Admissions, 407-823-2766, Fax: 407-823-6442, E-mail: gradadmissions@ucf.edu.
Website: https://ccie.ucf.edu/lser/

University of Central Florida, College of Community Innovation and Education, Department of Learning Science and Educational Research, Program in Instructional Design and Technology, Orlando, FL 32816. Offers e-learning (Certificate); educational technology (Certificate); instructional design (Certificate); instructional design and technology (MA), including e-learning, educational technology, instructional systems; instructional design for simulations (Certificate). *Program availability:* Part-time. *Students:* 24 full-time (21 women), 128 part-time (96 women); includes 60 minority (18 Black or African American, non-Hispanic/Latino; 1 American Indian or Alaska Native, non-Hispanic/Latino; 5 Asian, non-Hispanic/Latino; 33 Hispanic/Latino; 3 Two or more races, non-Hispanic/Latino), 1 international. Average age 37. 80 applicants, 93% accepted, 47 enrolled. In 2019, 40 master's, 16 other advanced degrees awarded. *Entrance requirements:* For master's, letters of recommendation, resume. Additional exam requirements/recommendations for international students: required—TOEFL. *Application deadline:* For fall admission, 7/15 for domestic students; for spring admission, 12/1 for domestic students. Application fee: $30. Electronic applications accepted. *Financial support:* In 2019–20, 7 students received support, including 2 fellowships (averaging $1,000 per year), 5 research assistantships with partial tuition reimbursements available (averaging $7,060 per year), 4 teaching assistantships (averaging $4,779 per year); health care benefits also available. Financial award application deadline: 3/1; financial award applicants required to submit FAFSA. *Unit head:* Dr. Richard Hartshorne, Program Coordinator, 407-823-1861, E-mail: richard.hartshorne@ucf.edu. *Application contact:* Associate Director, Graduate Admissions, 407-823-2766, Fax: 407-823-6442, E-mail: gradadmissions@ucf.edu.
Website: https://edcollege.ucf.edu/insttech/

University of Central Florida, College of Graduate Studies, Program in Modeling and Simulation, Orlando, FL 32816. Offers modeling and simulation (MS, PhD); modeling and simulation of behavioral cybersecurity (Certificate); modeling and simulation of technical systems (Certificate). *Students:* 21 full-time (10 women), 30 part-time (12 women); includes 13 minority (3 Black or African American, non-Hispanic/Latino; 4 Asian, non-Hispanic/Latino; 6 Hispanic/Latino), 3 international. Average age 36. 45 applicants, 69% accepted, 28 enrolled. In 2019, 4 other advanced degrees awarded. *Degree requirements:* For master's, thesis or alternative; for doctorate, comprehensive exam, thesis/dissertation. *Entrance requirements:* For master's, letters of recommendation, resume, goal statement; for doctorate, GRE, letters of recommendation, resume, goal statement. Additional exam requirements/recommendations for international students: required—TOEFL. *Application deadline:* For fall admission, 7/15 for domestic students; for spring admission, 12/1 for domestic students. Application fee: $30. Electronic applications accepted. *Financial support:* In 2019–20, 11 students received support, including 4 fellowships with partial tuition reimbursements available (averaging $12,250 per year), 8 research assistantships with partial tuition reimbursements available (averaging $7,900 per year), 3 teaching assistantships (averaging $10,251 per year). Financial award application deadline: 3/1; financial award applicants required to submit FAFSA. *Unit head:* Dr. Joseph LaViola, Jr., Program Director, 407-882-2285, E-mail: jjl@eecs.ucf.edu. *Application contact:* Associate Director, Graduate Admissions, 407-823-2766, Fax: 407-823-6442, E-mail: gradadmissions@ucf.edu.
Website: http://www.ist.ucf.edu/

The University of Manchester, School of Chemical Engineering and Analytical Science, Manchester, United Kingdom. Offers biocatalysis (M Phil, PhD); chemical engineering (M Phil, PhD); chemical engineering and analytical science (M Phil, D Eng, PhD); colloids, crystals, interfaces and materials (M Phil, PhD); environment and sustainable technology (M Phil, PhD); instrumentation (M Phil, PhD); multi-scale modeling (M Phil, PhD); process integration (M Phil, PhD); systems biology (M Phil, PhD).

University of Southern California, Graduate School, Viterbi School of Engineering, Department of Computer Science, Los Angeles, CA 90089. Offers computer networks (MS); computer science (MS, PhD); computer security (MS); game development (MS); high performance computing and simulations (MS); human language technology (MS); intelligent robotics (MS); multimedia and creative technologies (MS); software engineering (MS). *Program availability:* Part-time, evening/weekend, online learning. *Entrance requirements:* For master's and doctorate, GRE General Test. Additional exam requirements/recommendations for international students: required—TOEFL. Electronic applications accepted.

Université Laval, Faculty of Administrative Sciences, Programs in Business Administration, Québec, QC G1K 7P4, Canada. Offers accounting (MBA); agri-food management (MBA); electronic business (MBA, Diploma); factory management and logistics (MBA); finance (MBA); firm management (MBA); geomatic management (MBA); information technology management (MBA); international management (MBA); management (MBA); management accounting (MBA, Diploma); marketing (MBA); modeling and organizational decision (MBA); occupational health and safety management (MBA); pharmacy management (MBA); social and environmental responsibility (MBA); technological entrepreneurship (Diploma). *Accreditation:* AACSB. *Program availability:* Part-time, evening/weekend, online learning. *Entrance requirements:* For master's and Diploma, knowledge of French and English. Electronic applications accepted.

Worcester Polytechnic Institute, Graduate Admissions, Programs in Interdisciplinary Studies, Worcester, MA 01609-2280. Offers bioscience administration (MS); nuclear science and engineering (Graduate Certificate); power systems management (MS); social science (PhD); system dynamics and innovation management (MS, Graduate Certificate); systems modeling (MS). *Program availability:* Part-time, evening/weekend, 100% online. Terminal master's awarded for partial completion of doctoral program. *Degree requirements:* For master's, thesis; for doctorate, comprehensive exam, thesis/dissertation. *Entrance requirements:* For master's and doctorate, 3 letters of recommendation. Additional exam requirements/recommendations for international students: required—TOEFL (minimum score 563 paper-based; 84 iBT), IELTS (minimum score 7). Electronic applications accepted.

Software Engineering

Arizona State University at Tempe, Ira A. Fulton Schools of Engineering, ASU Engineering Online Programs, Tempe, AZ 85287. Offers construction (MS); embedded systems (M Eng); enterprise systems innovation and management (MSE); modeling and simulation (M Eng); quality and reliability engineering (M Eng); software engineering (MSE); systems engineering (M Eng).

Software Engineering

Arizona State University at Tempe, Ira A. Fulton Schools of Engineering, School of Computing, Informatics, and Decision Systems Engineering, Tempe, AZ 85287-8809. Offers computer engineering (MS, PhD); computer science (MCS, MS, PhD); industrial engineering (MS, PhD); software engineering (MS). *Program availability:* Part-time, evening/weekend, online learning. Terminal master's awarded for partial completion of doctoral program. *Degree requirements:* For master's, comprehensive exam (for some programs), portfolio (MCS); interactive Program of Study (iPOS) submitted before completing 50 percent of required credit hours; for doctorate, comprehensive exam, thesis/dissertation, interactive Program of Study (iPOS) submitted before completing 50 percent of required credit hours. *Entrance requirements:* For master's, GRE, minimum GPA of 3.0 or equivalent in last 2 years of work leading to bachelor's degree; for doctorate, GRE, minimum GPA of 3.0 in last 2 years of work leading to bachelor's degree. Additional exam requirements/recommendations for international students: required—TOEFL, IELTS, or PTE. Electronic applications accepted. *Expenses:* Contact institution.

Auburn University, Graduate School, Samuel Ginn College of Engineering, Department of Computer Science and Software Engineering, Auburn University, AL 36849. Offers MS, MSWE, PhD. *Program availability:* Part-time. *Faculty:* 29 full-time (4 women), 1 (woman) part-time/adjunct. *Students:* 126 full-time (32 women), 67 part-time (20 women); includes 23 minority (9 Black or African American, non-Hispanic/Latino; 7 Asian, non-Hispanic/Latino; 5 Hispanic/Latino; 2 Two or more races, non-Hispanic/Latino), 118 international. Average age 30. 223 applicants, 57% accepted, 46 enrolled. In 2019, 48 master's, 4 doctorates awarded. *Degree requirements:* For master's, thesis (for some programs); for doctorate, thesis/dissertation. *Entrance requirements:* For master's and doctorate, GRE General Test, GRE Subject Test. Additional exam requirements/recommendations for international students: required—TOEFL (minimum score 550 paper-based; 79 iBT). *Application deadline:* For fall admission, 3/31 priority date for domestic and international students; for spring admission, 9/30 priority date for domestic and international students. Applications are processed on a rolling basis. Application fee: $60 ($70 for international students). Electronic applications accepted. *Expenses:* Tuition, area resident: Full-time $9828; part-time $546 per credit hour. Tuition, state resident: full-time $9828; part-time $546 per credit hour. Tuition, nonresident: full-time $29,484; part-time $1638 per credit hour. *International tuition:* $29,744 full-time. Tuition and fees vary according to course load, program and reciprocity agreements. *Financial support:* In 2019–20, 46 research assistantships (averaging $15,194 per year), 53 teaching assistantships (averaging $14,222 per year) were awarded; Federal Work-Study also available. Support available to part-time students. Financial award application deadline: 3/15; financial award applicants required to submit FAFSA. *Unit head:* Dr. Hari Narayanan, Chair, 334-844-63102, E-mail: naraynh@auburn.edu. *Application contact:* Dr. George Flowers, Dean of the Graduate School, 334-844-2125.
Website: http://www.eng.auburn.edu/cse/

Boston University, Metropolitan College, Department of Computer Science, Boston, MA 02215. Offers computer information systems (MS), including computer networks, data analytics, database management and business intelligence, health informatics, IT project management, security, Web application development; computer networks (Certificate); computer science (MS); data analytics (Certificate); digital forensics (Certificate); health informatics (Certificate); information technology project management (Certificate); software development (MS); software engineering in health care systems (Certificate); telecommunications (MS), including security. *Program availability:* Part-time, evening/weekend, online learning. *Faculty:* 16 full-time (3 women), 52 part-time/adjunct (5 women). *Students:* 253 full-time (80 women), 856 part-time (243 women); includes 246 minority (53 Black or African American, non-Hispanic/Latino; 1 American Indian or Alaska Native, non-Hispanic/Latino; 129 Asian, non-Hispanic/Latino; 48 Hispanic/Latino; 15 Two or more races, non-Hispanic/Latino), 418 international. Average age 30. 1,079 applicants, 72% accepted, 297 enrolled. In 2019, 513 master's awarded. *Entrance requirements:* For master's and Certificate, official transcripts from regionally-accredited bachelor's degree program, 3 letters of recommendation, professional resume, personal statement. Additional exam requirements/recommendations for international students: required—TOEFL (minimum score 84 iBT), IELTS. *Application deadline:* For fall admission, 8/1 priority date for domestic students, 6/1 priority date for international students; for spring admission, 12/1 priority date for domestic students, 11/15 priority date for international students; for summer admission, 4/1 priority date for domestic students, 3/1 priority date for international students. Applications are processed on a rolling basis. Application fee: $85. Electronic applications accepted. *Expenses:* Contact institution. *Financial support:* In 2019–20, 11 research assistantships (averaging $8,400 per year), 23 teaching assistantships (averaging $3,400 per year) were awarded; unspecified assistantships also available. Support available to part-time students. Financial award applicants required to submit FAFSA. *Unit head:* Dr. Anatoly Temkin, Chair, 617-353-2566, Fax: 617-353-2367, E-mail: csinfo@bu.edu. *Application contact:* Enrollment Services, 617-353-6004, E-mail: met@bu.edu.
Website: http://www.bu.edu/csmet/

Bowling Green State University, Graduate College, College of Arts and Sciences, Department of Computer Science, Bowling Green, OH 43403. Offers computer science (MS), including operations research, parallel and distributed computing, software engineering. *Program availability:* Part-time. *Degree requirements:* For master's, thesis or alternative. *Entrance requirements:* For master's, GRE General Test. Additional exam requirements/recommendations for international students: required—TOEFL. Electronic applications accepted.

Brandeis University, Rabb School of Continuing Studies, Division of Graduate Professional Studies, Master of Science in Robotic Software Engineering Program, Waltham, MA 02454-9110. Offers MS. *Program availability:* Part-time-only. *Entrance requirements:* For master's, bachelor's degree in computer science or software engineering, or 2-3 years of experience in software engineering and undergraduate courses in linear algebra, calculus, and probability/statistics, official transcripts, resume, statement of goals, letter of recommendation. Additional exam requirements/recommendations for international students: required—TOEFL (minimum score 600 paper-based; 100 iBT), IELTS (minimum score 7), TWE (minimum score 4.5), PTE (minimum score 68). Electronic applications accepted. *Expenses:* Contact institution.

Brandeis University, Rabb School of Continuing Studies, Division of Graduate Professional Studies, Master of Software Engineering Program, Waltham, MA 02454-9110. Offers MSE. *Program availability:* Part-time-only. *Entrance requirements:* For master's, programming language (Java, C++, C), software engineering, and data structures, or equivalent work experience; 4-year bachelor's degree from regionally-accredited U.S. institution or equivalent; official transcript(s) from every college/university attended; resume or curriculum vitae; statement of goals; letter of recommendation. Additional exam requirements/recommendations for international students: required—TWE (minimum score 4.5), TOEFL (minimum scores: 600 paper-based, 100 iBT), IELTS (7), or PTE (68). Electronic applications accepted. *Expenses:* Contact institution.

California State University, Fullerton, Graduate Studies, College of Engineering and Computer Science, Department of Computer Science, Fullerton, CA 92831-3599. Offers computer science (MS); software engineering (MS). *Program availability:* Part-time, online learning. *Degree requirements:* For master's, comprehensive exam, project or thesis. *Entrance requirements:* For master's, GRE General Test, minimum undergraduate GPA of 2.5.

California State University, Northridge, Graduate Studies, College of Engineering and Computer Science, Department of Computer Science, Northridge, CA 91330. Offers computer science (MS); software engineering (MS). *Program availability:* Part-time, evening/weekend. *Degree requirements:* For master's, thesis. *Entrance requirements:* For master's, GRE General Test, minimum GPA of 2.5. Additional exam requirements/recommendations for international students: required—TOEFL.

California State University, Sacramento, College of Engineering and Computer Science, Department of Computer Science, Sacramento, CA 95819. Offers computer science (MS); software engineering (MS). *Program availability:* Part-time, evening/weekend. *Students:* 130 full-time (55 women), 52 part-time (21 women); includes 18 minority (3 Black or African American, non-Hispanic/Latino; 13 Asian, non-Hispanic/Latino; 2 Hispanic/Latino), 149 international. Average age 26. 400 applicants, 31% accepted, 36 enrolled. In 2019, 41 master's awarded. *Degree requirements:* For master's, thesis, thesis, project or comprehensive exam; writing proficiency exam. *Entrance requirements:* For master's, GRE, minimum GPA of 3.0 in last 60 units attempted. Additional exam requirements/recommendations for international students: required—TOEFL (minimum score 550 paper-based; 80 iBT); recommended—IELTS (minimum score 7). *Application deadline:* For fall admission, 3/1 for domestic students, 2/1 for international students; for spring admission, 9/15 for domestic students, 8/15 for international students. Applications are processed on a rolling basis. Application fee: $70. Electronic applications accepted. *Expenses:* Contact institution. *Financial support:* Teaching assistantships, career-related internships or fieldwork, Federal Work-Study, and scholarships/grants available. Support available to part-time students. Financial award application deadline: 3/1; financial award applicants required to submit FAFSA. *Unit head:* Dr. Nik Faroughi, Chair, E-mail: faroughi@csus.edu. *Application contact:* Jose Martinez, Graduate Admissions Supervisor, 916-278-7871, E-mail: martinj@skymail.csus.edu.
Website: http://www.ecs.csus.edu/csc

Carnegie Mellon University, Carnegie Institute of Technology, Information Networking Institute, Pittsburgh, PA 15213. Offers information networking (MS); information security (MS); information technology - information security (MS); information technology - mobility (MS); information technology - software management (MS). *Degree requirements:* For master's, thesis optional. *Entrance requirements:* For master's, GRE General Test, bachelor's degree in computer science, computer engineering, or electrical engineering, or related technology degree; programming skills (C/C++ fluency for some programs). Additional exam requirements/recommendations for international students: required—TOEFL.

Carnegie Mellon University, School of Computer Science, Software Engineering Program, Pittsburgh, PA 15213-3891. Offers MSE, PhD. *Entrance requirements:* For master's, GRE General Test, GRE Subject Test (computer science), 2 years of experience in large-scale software development project.

Carnegie Mellon University, Tepper School of Business, Pittsburgh, PA 15213-3891. Offers accounting (PhD); business management and software engineering (MBMSE); business technologies (PhD); civil engineering and industrial management (MS); computational finance (MSCF); economics (PhD); environmental engineering and management (MEEM); financial economics (PhD); industrial administration (MBA), including administration and public management; marketing (PhD); mathematical finance (PhD); operations management (PhD); operations research (PhD); organizational behavior and theory (PhD); production and operations management (PhD); public policy and management (MS, MSED); software engineering and business management (MS); JD/MS; JD/MSIA; M Div/MS; MOM/MSIA; MSCF/MSIA. *Program availability:* Part-time. Terminal master's awarded for partial completion of doctoral program. *Degree requirements:* For doctorate, thesis/dissertation. *Entrance requirements:* For master's, GMAT. Additional exam requirements/recommendations for international students: required—TOEFL. *Expenses:* Contact institution.

Carroll University, Program in Software Engineering, Waukesha, WI 53186-5593. Offers MSE. *Program availability:* Part-time, evening/weekend. *Degree requirements:* For master's, professional experience, capstone project. *Entrance requirements:* For master's, BA or BS, 2 years of professional experience. Additional exam requirements/recommendations for international students: required—TOEFL. Electronic applications accepted.

Cleveland State University, College of Graduate Studies, Fenn College of Engineering, Department of Electrical and Computer Engineering, Cleveland, OH 44115. Offers electrical engineering (MS, D Eng); software engineering (MS). *Program availability:* Part-time, evening/weekend. *Faculty:* 15 full-time (2 women), 1 part-time/adjunct (0 women). *Students:* 90 full-time (29 women), 52 part-time (11 women); includes 10 minority (1 Black or African American, non-Hispanic/Latino; 8 Asian, non-Hispanic/Latino; 1 Hispanic/Latino), 95 international. Average age 26. 1,083 applicants, 44% accepted, 89 enrolled. In 2019, 76 master's awarded. Terminal master's awarded for partial completion of doctoral program. *Entrance requirements:* For master's, GRE General Test (minimum score 650 quantitative), minimum GPA of 2.75; for doctorate, GRE General Test (minimum quantitative score in 80th percentile), minimum GPA of 3.25. *Application deadline:* Applications are processed on a rolling basis. Application fee: $40. Electronic applications accepted. *Expenses:* Contact institution. *Financial support:* In 2019–20, 31 students received support, including 10 research assistantships with tuition reimbursements available (averaging $8,300 per year), 12 teaching assistantships with tuition reimbursements available (averaging $9,500 per year); career-related internships or fieldwork, scholarships/grants, and unspecified assistantships also available. Financial award applicants required to submit FAFSA. *Unit head:* Dr. Chansu Yu, Chairperson, 216-687-2584, Fax: 216-687-5405, E-mail: f.xiong@csuohio.edu. *Application contact:* Deborah L. Brown, Interim Assistant Director, Graduate Admissions, 216-523-7572, Fax: 216-687-9214, E-mail: d.l.brown@csuohio.edu.
Website: http://www.csuohio.edu/ece

College of Staten Island of the City University of New York, Graduate Programs, Division of Science and Technology, Program in Computer Science, Staten Island, NY 10314-6600. Offers computer science (MS), including artificial intelligence and data analytics, cloud computing and software engineering, cybersecurity and networks. *Program availability:* Part-time, evening/weekend. *Faculty:* 6. *Students:* 42. 48 applicants, 67% accepted, 15 enrolled. In 2019, 10 master's awarded. *Degree requirements:* For master's, thesis optional, a program of 10 courses (30 credits) with at least a 3.0 (B) average. Exceptional students may be permitted to satisfy six credits of the total credit requirement with a master's thesis. *Entrance requirements:* For master's, GRE General Test, BS in Computer Science or related area with a B average (3.0 out of 4.0) overall and in the major, a resume, and demonstrable knowledge in several areas. Additional exam requirements/recommendations for international students: required—TOEFL (minimum score 550 paper-based; 79 iBT), IELTS (minimum score 6.5). *Application deadline:* For fall admission, 7/20 priority date for domestic students, 4/25 for

international students; for spring admission, 11/2 priority date for domestic students, 11/2 for international students. Applications are processed on a rolling basis. Application fee: $75. Electronic applications accepted. *Expenses: Tuition, area resident:* Full-time $11,090; part-time $470 per credit. Tuition, state resident: full-time $11,090; part-time $470 per credit. Tuition, nonresident: full-time $20,520; part-time $855 per credit. *International tuition:* $20,520 full-time. *Required fees:* $559; $181 per semester. Tuition and fees vary according to program. *Unit head:* Dr. Xiaowen Zhang, Associate Professor, 718-982-3262, E-mail: xiaowen.zhang@csi.cuny.edu. *Application contact:* Sasha Spence, Associate Director for Graduate Admissions, 718-982-2019, Fax: 718-982-2500, E-mail: sasha.spence@csi.cuny.edu.
Website: https://www.csi.cuny.edu/academics-and-research/departments-programs/computer-science

Colorado Technical University Aurora, Program in Computer Science, Aurora, CO 80014. Offers computer systems security (MSCS); database systems (MSCS); software engineering (MSCS). *Program availability:* Part-time, evening/weekend. *Degree requirements:* For master's, thesis or alternative. *Entrance requirements:* For master's, minimum undergraduate GPA of 3.0, resume.

Colorado Technical University Colorado Springs, Graduate Studies, Program in Computer Science, Colorado Springs, CO 80907. Offers computer science (DCS); computer systems security (MSCS); database systems (MSCS); software engineering (MSCS). *Program availability:* Part-time, evening/weekend, online learning. *Degree requirements:* For master's, thesis or alternative; for doctorate, thesis/dissertation. *Entrance requirements:* For doctorate, minimum graduate GPA of 3.0, 5 years of related work experience.

Concordia University, School of Graduate Studies, Faculty of Engineering and Computer Science, Department of Computer Science and Software Engineering, Montréal, QC H3G 1M8, Canada. Offers computer science (M App Comp Sc, M Comp Sc, PhD, Diploma); software engineering (M Eng, MA Sc). *Degree requirements:* For master's, one foreign language, thesis optional; for doctorate, one foreign language, comprehensive exam, thesis/dissertation.

DePaul University, College of Computing and Digital Media, Chicago, IL 60604. Offers animation (MA, MFA); applied technology (MS); business information technology (MS); computational finance (MS); computer and information sciences (PhD); computer science (MS); creative producing (MFA); cybersecurity (MS); data science (MS); digital communication and media arts (MA); documentary (MFA); e-commerce technology (MS); experience design (MA); film and television (MS); film and television directing (MFA); game design (MFA); game programming (MS); health informatics (MS); human centered design (PhD); human-computer interaction (MS); information systems (MS); network engineering and security (MS); product innovation and computing (MS); screenwriting (MFA); software engineering (MS); JD/MS. *Program availability:* Part-time, evening/weekend, online learning. *Degree requirements:* For master's, thesis (for some programs); for doctorate, comprehensive exam, thesis/dissertation. *Entrance requirements:* For master's, GRE or GMAT (for MS in computational finance only), bachelor's degree, resume (MS in predictive analytics only), IT experience (MS in information technology project management only), portfolio review (all MFA programs and MA in animation); for doctorate, GRE, master's degree in computer science. Additional exam requirements/recommendations for international students: required—TOEFL (minimum score 590 paper-based; 80 iBT), IELTS (minimum score 6.5), PTE (minimum score 53). Electronic applications accepted. *Expenses:* Contact institution.

Drexel University, College of Computing and Informatics, Department of Computer Science, Philadelphia, PA 19104-2875. Offers computer science (MS, PhD, Postbaccalaureate Certificate); software engineering (MS). *Program availability:* Part-time, evening/weekend, 100% online. Terminal master's awarded for partial completion of doctoral program. *Degree requirements:* For doctorate, thesis/dissertation. *Entrance requirements:* For master's and doctorate, GRE General Test. Additional exam requirements/recommendations for international students: required—TOEFL (minimum score 90 iBT), IELTS (minimum score 6.5). Electronic applications accepted.

Drexel University, College of Engineering, Department of Electrical and Computer Engineering, Program in Software Engineering, Philadelphia, PA 19104-2875. Offers MSSE. *Entrance requirements:* For master's, GRE. Additional exam requirements/recommendations for international students: required—TOEFL. Electronic applications accepted.

East Carolina University, Graduate School, College of Engineering and Technology, Department of Computer Science, Greenville, NC 27858-4353. Offers computer science (MS); software engineering (MS). *Program availability:* Part-time, evening/weekend. *Application deadline:* For fall admission, 11/1 priority date for domestic students, 10/1 priority date for international students; for spring admission, 3/1 priority date for domestic and international students. *Expenses: Tuition, area resident:* Full-time $4749; part-time $185 per credit hour. Tuition, state resident: full-time $4749; part-time $185 per credit hour. Tuition, nonresident: full-time $17,898; part-time $864 per credit hour. *International tuition:* $17,898 full-time. *Required fees:* $2787. *Financial support:* Application deadline: 3/1. *Unit head:* Dr. Venkat Gudivada, Chair, 252-328-9693, E-mail: gudivadav15@ecu.edu. *Application contact:* Graduate School Admissions, 252-328-6012, Fax: 252-328-6071, E-mail: gradschool@ecu.edu.
Website: https://cet.ecu.edu/csci/

Embry-Riddle Aeronautical University–Daytona, Department of Electrical, Computer, Software and Systems Engineering, Daytona Beach, FL 32114-3900. Offers cybersecurity engineering (MS); electrical and computer engineering (MSECE); software engineering (MSSE); systems engineering (MS). *Degree requirements:* For master's, thesis optional. *Entrance requirements:* For master's, GRE (for some programs). Additional exam requirements/recommendations for international students: required—TOEFL (minimum score 550 paper-based, 79 iBT) or IELTS (6). Electronic applications accepted.

Fairfield University, School of Engineering, Fairfield, CT 06824. Offers database management (CAS); electrical and computer engineering (MS); information security (CAS); management of technology (MS); mechanical engineering (MS); network technology (CAS); software engineering (MS); Web application development (CAS). *Program availability:* Part-time, evening/weekend. *Faculty:* 10 full-time (2 women), 15 part-time/adjunct (1 woman). *Students:* 46 full-time (24 women), 57 part-time (10 women); includes 23 minority (5 Black or African American, non-Hispanic/Latino; 9 Asian, non-Hispanic/Latino; 9 Hispanic/Latino), 33 international. Average age 29. 68 applicants, 62% accepted, 30 enrolled. In 2019, 100 master's awarded. *Degree requirements:* For master's, capstone course. *Entrance requirements:* For master's, resume, 2 recommendations. Additional exam requirements/recommendations for international students: required—TOEFL (minimum score 550 paper-based; 80 iBT), IELTS (minimum score 6.5), TOEFL (minimum score 550 paper-based; 80 iBT) or IELTS (minimum score 6.5). *Application deadline:* For fall admission, 5/15 for international students; for spring admission, 10/15 for international students. Applications are processed on a rolling basis. Application fee: $60. Electronic applications accepted. *Expenses:* Tuition $900/credit hour; Registration Fee $50/semester; Graduate Student Activity Fee (Fall and Spring) $65/semester. *Financial support:* In 2019–20, 20 students received support. Scholarships/grants and

unspecified assistantships available. Financial award applicants required to submit FAFSA. *Unit head:* Richard Heist, Dean, 203-254-4147, Fax: 203-254-4013, E-mail: rheist@fairfield.edu. *Application contact:* Melanie Rogers, Director of Graduate Admission, 203-254-4184, Fax: 203-254-4073, E-mail: gradadmis@fairfield.edu.
Website: http://www.fairfield.edu/soe

Florida Agricultural and Mechanical University, Division of Graduate Studies, Research, and Continuing Education, College of Science and Technology, Department of Computer Information Sciences, Tallahassee, FL 32307-3200. Offers software engineering (MS). *Entrance requirements:* Additional exam requirements/recommendations for international students: required—TOEFL.

Florida Institute of Technology, College of Engineering and Science, Program in Software Engineering, Melbourne, FL 32901-6975. Offers MS. *Program availability:* Part-time. *Degree requirements:* For master's, comprehensive exam (for some programs), thesis or alternative, internship, minimum of 30 credit hours. *Entrance requirements:* For master's, GRE General Test, 3 letters of recommendation, specific courses in mathematical studies. Additional exam requirements/recommendations for international students: required—TOEFL (minimum score 550 paper-based; 79 iBT). Electronic applications accepted.

Gannon University, School of Graduate Studies, College of Engineering and Business, School of Engineering and Computer Science, Program in Computer and Information Science, Erie, PA 16541-0001. Offers information analytics (MSCIS); software engineering (MSCIS). *Program availability:* Part-time, evening/weekend. *Degree requirements:* For master's, thesis (for some programs), directed research. *Entrance requirements:* For master's, 3 letters of recommendation; resume; transcripts; baccalaureate degree in computer science, information systems, information science, software engineering, or related field from regionally-accredited institution with minimum GPA of 2.5. Additional exam requirements/recommendations for international students: required—TOEFL (minimum score 79 iBT). Electronic applications accepted. Application fee is waived when completed online.

Gannon University, School of Graduate Studies, College of Engineering and Business, School of Engineering and Computer Science, Program in Electrical and Computer Engineering, Erie, PA 16541-0001. Offers MSEE, MSES. *Program availability:* Part-time, evening/weekend. *Degree requirements:* For master's, thesis (for some programs), oral exam (for some programs), design project (for some programs). *Entrance requirements:* For master's, bachelor's degree in electrical or computer engineering from an ABET-accredited program or its equivalent with minimum GPA of 2.5, transcripts, 3 letters of recommendation. Additional exam requirements/recommendations for international students: required—TOEFL (minimum score 79 iBT). Electronic applications accepted. Application fee is waived when completed online.

Gannon University, School of Graduate Studies, College of Engineering and Business, School of Engineering and Computer Science, Program in Software Engineering, Erie, PA 16541-0001. Offers MSCIS. *Program availability:* Part-time, evening/weekend. *Entrance requirements:* For master's, baccalaureate degree in computer science, information systems, information science, software engineering, or a related field from regionally-accredited institution with minimum GPA of 2.5; resume; transcripts; 3 letters of recommendation. Additional exam requirements/recommendations for international students: required—TOEFL (minimum score 79 iBT). Electronic applications accepted. Application fee is waived when completed online.

Harrisburg University of Science and Technology, Program in Information Systems Engineering and Management, Harrisburg, PA 17101. Offers analytics (MS); digital government (MS); digital health (MS); entrepreneurship (MS); information security (MS); software engineering and systems development (MS). *Program availability:* Part-time, evening/weekend. *Degree requirements:* For master's, thesis optional. *Entrance requirements:* For master's, baccalaureate degree. Additional exam requirements/recommendations for international students: required—TOEFL (minimum score 520 paper-based; 80 iBT); recommended—IELTS (minimum score 6). Electronic applications accepted. *Expenses: Tuition:* Full-time $15,900; part-time $7950 per credit hour.

Illinois Institute of Technology, Graduate College, Armour College of Engineering, Department of Electrical and Computer Engineering, Chicago, IL 60616. Offers biomedical imaging and signals (MAS); computer engineering (MS, PhD); electrical engineering (MS, PhD); electricity markets (MAS); network engineering (MAS); power engineering (MAS); telecommunications and software engineering (MAS); VLSI and microelectronics (MAS); MS/MS. *Program availability:* Part-time, evening/weekend, online learning. Terminal master's awarded for partial completion of doctoral program. *Degree requirements:* For master's, comprehensive exam (for some programs), thesis (for some programs); for doctorate, comprehensive exam, thesis/dissertation. *Entrance requirements:* For master's and doctorate, GRE General Test (minimum score 1100 Quantitative and Verbal, 3.5 Analytical Writing), minimum undergraduate GPA of 3.0. Additional exam requirements/recommendations for international students: required—TOEFL (minimum score 550 paper-based; 80 iBT); recommended—IELTS (minimum score 5.5). Electronic applications accepted.

Illinois Institute of Technology, Graduate College, College of Science, Department of Computer Science, Chicago, IL 60616. Offers business (MCS); computational intelligence (MCS); computer science (MCS, MS, PhD); cyber-physical systems (MCS); data analytics (MCS); data science (MAS); database systems (MCS); distributed and cloud computing (MCS); education (MCS); finance (MCS); information security and assurance (MCS); networking and communications (MCS); software engineering (MCS); telecommunications and software engineering (MAS); MS/MAS. *Program availability:* Part-time, evening/weekend, online learning. Terminal master's awarded for partial completion of doctoral program. *Degree requirements:* For master's, thesis optional; for doctorate, comprehensive exam, thesis/dissertation. *Entrance requirements:* For master's, GRE General Test with minimum scores of 298 Quantitative and Verbal, 3.0 Analytical Writing (for MS); GRE General Test with minimum scores of 292 Quantitative and Verbal, 2.5 Analytical Writing (for MAS), minimum undergraduate GPA of 3.0; for doctorate, GRE General Test (minimum scores: 304 Quantitative and Verbal, 3.5 Analytical Writing), minimum undergraduate GPA of 3.0. Additional exam requirements/recommendations for international students: required—TOEFL (minimum score 523 paper-based; 70 iBT). Electronic applications accepted.

Indiana University-Purdue University Indianapolis, School of Science, Department of Computer and Information Science, Indianapolis, IN 46202-5132. Offers biocomputing (Graduate Certificate); biometrics (Graduate Certificate); computer science (MS, PhD); computer security (Graduate Certificate); databases and data mining (Graduate Certificate); software engineering (Graduate Certificate). *Program availability:* Part-time. Terminal master's awarded for partial completion of doctoral program. *Degree requirements:* For master's and Graduate Certificate, thesis optional; for doctorate, thesis/dissertation. *Entrance requirements:* For master's and doctorate, GRE, BS in computer science or the equivalent with a minimum GPA of 3.0 (or equivalent); for Graduate Certificate, BS in computer science or the equivalent with a minimum GPA of 3.0 (or equivalent). Additional exam requirements/recommendations for international students: required—PTE (minimum score 58), TOEFL (minimum score 550 paper-based, 79 iBT) or IELTS (6.5).

Software Engineering

Instituto Tecnologico de Santo Domingo, Graduate School, Area of Engineering, Santo Domingo, Dominican Republic. Offers construction administration (MS, Certificate); data telecommunications (M Eng, MS, Certificate); industrial engineering (M Eng, Certificate); industrial management (M Mgmt); information technology (Certificate); maintenance engineering (M Eng); occupational hazard prevention (M Mgmt); production management (Certificate); quantitative methods (Certificate); sanitary and environmental engineering (M Eng); structural engineering (M Eng); systems engineering and electronic data processing (Certificate); transportation (Certificate).

International Technological University, Program in Software Engineering, San Jose, CA 95134. Offers MSSE. *Program availability:* Part-time, evening/weekend. *Degree requirements:* For master's, thesis or alternative, capstone project. *Entrance requirements:* Additional exam requirements/recommendations for international students: required—TOEFL, IELTS. Electronic applications accepted.

Jacksonville State University, Graduate Studies, School of Science, Program in Computer Systems and Software Design, Jacksonville, AL 36265-1602. Offers MS. *Program availability:* Part-time, evening/weekend. *Degree requirements:* For master's, comprehensive exam, thesis (for some programs). *Entrance requirements:* Additional exam requirements/recommendations for international students: required—TOEFL (minimum score 500 paper-based; 61 iBT). Electronic applications accepted.

Kennesaw State University, College of Computing and Software Engineering, Program in Software Engineering, Kennesaw, GA 30144. Offers software engineering (MSSWE, Graduate Certificate); software engineering foundations (Graduate Certificate). *Program availability:* Part-time, evening/weekend, blended/hybrid learning. *Students:* 25 full-time (12 women), 59 part-time (10 women); includes 44 minority (21 Black or African American, non-Hispanic/Latino; 1 American Indian or Alaska Native, non-Hispanic/Latino; 14 Asian, non-Hispanic/Latino; 6 Hispanic/Latino; 2 Two or more races, non-Hispanic/Latino), 13 international. Average age 32. 25 applicants, 92% accepted, 18 enrolled. In 2019, 22 master's awarded. *Degree requirements:* For master's, thesis optional, capstone. *Entrance requirements:* For master's, GRE (recommended). Additional exam requirements/recommendations for international students: required—TOEFL (minimum score 80 iBT), IELTS (minimum score 6.5). *Application deadline:* For fall admission, 7/1 priority date for domestic students, 6/1 priority date for international students; for spring admission, 11/1 priority date for domestic students, 9/1 priority date for international students; for summer admission, 4/1 priority date for domestic students, 3/1 priority date for international students. Applications are processed on a rolling basis. Application fee: $60. Electronic applications accepted. *Expenses: Tuition, area resident:* Full-time $7104; part-time $296 per credit hour. Tuition, state resident: full-time $7104; part-time $296 per credit hour. Tuition, nonresident: full-time $25,584; part-time $1066 per credit hour. *International tuition:* $25,584 full-time. *Required fees:* $2006; $1706 per unit. $853 per semester. *Financial support:* Applicants required to submit FAFSA. *Application contact:* Admission Counselor, 470-578-4377, Fax: 470-578-9172, E-mail: ksugrad@kennesaw.edu.
Website: http://ccse.kennesaw.edu/swegd/

Lewis University, College of Aviation, Science and Technology, Program in Computer Science, Romeoville, IL 60446. Offers cyber security (MS); intelligent systems (MS); software engineering (MS). *Program availability:* Part-time, evening/weekend, 100% online, blended/hybrid learning. *Students:* 32 full-time (11 women), 92 part-time (23 women); includes 36 minority (9 Black or African American, non-Hispanic/Latino; 11 Asian, non-Hispanic/Latino; 11 Hispanic/Latino; 1 Native Hawaiian or other Pacific Islander, non-Hispanic/Latino; 4 Two or more races, non-Hispanic/Latino), 13 international. Average age 32. *Entrance requirements:* For master's, bachelor's degree; minimum undergraduate GPA of 3.0; resume; statement of purpose; two letters of recommendation; undergraduate coursework in discrete mathematics, programming or algorithms. Additional exam requirements/recommendations for international students: required—TOEFL (minimum score 550 paper-based; 79 iBT), IELTS (minimum score 6). *Application deadline:* For fall admission, 5/1 for international students; for winter admission, 11/15 for international students. Applications are processed on a rolling basis. Application fee: $40. Electronic applications accepted. *Financial support:* Federal Work-Study and unspecified assistantships available. Financial award application deadline: 5/1; financial award applicants required to submit FAFSA. *Unit head:* Dr. Khaled Alzoubi, Program Director. *Application contact:* Sheri Vilcek, Graduate Admissions Counselor, 815-836-5610, E-mail: grad@lewisu.edu.
Website: http://www.lewisu.edu/academics/mscomputerscience/index.htm

Lipscomb University, College of Computing and Technology, Nashville, TN 37204-3951. Offers data science (MS, Certificate); information technology (MS, Certificate), including data science (MS), information security (MS), information technology management (MS), software engineering (MS); software engineering (MS, Certificate). *Program availability:* Part-time, evening/weekend. *Degree requirements:* For master's, capstone project. *Entrance requirements:* For master's, GRE, 2 references, transcripts, resume, personal statement. Additional exam requirements/recommendations for international students: required—TOEFL (minimum score 570 paper-based; 80 iBT). Electronic applications accepted. *Expenses:* Contact institution.

Loyola University Chicago, Graduate School, Department of Computer Science, Chicago, IL 60660. Offers computer science (MS); information technology (MS); software engineering (MS). *Program availability:* Part-time, evening/weekend, online only, 100% online, blended/hybrid learning. *Faculty:* 16 full-time (3 women), 18 part-time/adjunct (2 women). *Students:* 34 full-time (12 women), 37 part-time (10 women); includes 26 minority (6 Black or African American, non-Hispanic/Latino; 16 Asian, non-Hispanic/Latino; 4 Hispanic/Latino), 20 international. Average age 33. 115 applicants, 41% accepted, 17 enrolled. In 2019, 45 master's awarded. *Degree requirements:* For master's, thesis optional, 30 credits/ten courses. *Entrance requirements:* For master's, statement of purpose, one letter of recommendation, transcripts, international transcript evaluation (if applicable). Additional exam requirements/recommendations for international students: required—TOEFL (minimum score 550 paper-based; 79 iBT), IELTS (minimum score 6.5), PTE (minimum score 53), Duolingo English Test. *Application deadline:* Applications are processed on a rolling basis. Application fee: $50. Electronic applications accepted. Application fee is waived when completed online. *Expenses:* $1033 per credit; $115-452 fees per sememster. *Financial support:* In 2019–20, 16 students received support, including 2 fellowships with full tuition reimbursements available, 1 research assistantship with full tuition reimbursement available (averaging $18,000 per year), 13 teaching assistantships with partial tuition reimbursements available (averaging $9,925 per year); Federal Work-Study, health care benefits, and tuition waivers (full and partial) also available. Financial award application deadline: 4/1. *Unit head:* Dr. Chandra Sekharan, Chair, 773-508-8150, Fax: 773-508-3739, E-mail: info@cs.luc.edu. *Application contact:* Cecilia Murphy, Graduate Program Secretary, 773-508-8035, E-mail: gpd@cs.luc.edu.
Website: http://luc.edu/cs

Marist College, Graduate Programs, School of Computer Science and Mathematics, Poughkeepsie, NY 12601-1387. Offers business analytics (Adv C); computer science/software development (MS); information systems (MS, Adv C). *Program availability:* Part-time, evening/weekend, online learning. *Entrance requirements:* For master's, resume. Additional exam requirements/recommendations for international students: required—TOEFL (minimum score 550 paper-based; 80 iBT); recommended—IELTS (minimum score 6.5). Electronic applications accepted.

Marymount University, School of Business and Technology, Program in Information Technology, Arlington, VA 22207-4299. Offers health care informatics (Certificate); information technology (MS, Certificate), including cybersecurity (MS), health care informatics (MS), project management (MS), software engineering (MS); information technology project management and technology leadership (Certificate); information technology with business administration (MS/MBA); information technology with health care management (MS/MS); MS/MBA; MS/MS. *Program availability:* Part-time, evening/weekend. *Faculty:* 5 full-time (3 women), 7 part-time/adjunct (2 women). *Students:* 46 full-time (22 women), 30 part-time (15 women); includes 30 minority (16 Black or African American, non-Hispanic/Latino; 7 Asian, non-Hispanic/Latino; 7 Hispanic/Latino), 27 international. Average age 31. 61 applicants, 95% accepted, 27 enrolled. In 2019, 29 master's, 2 other advanced degrees awarded. *Degree requirements:* For master's, thesis or alternative, A minimum grade of B- is needed to receive credit for a course in the program. Must maintain a minimum cumulative GPA of 3.0. *Entrance requirements:* For master's, Resume, bachelor's degree in computer-related field or degree in another subject with a certificate in a computer-related field or related work experience. Software Engineering Track: bachelor's degree in Computer Science or work in software development. Project Mgmt/Tech Leadership Track: minimum 2 years of IT experience. Additional exam requirements/recommendations for international students: required—TOEFL (minimum score 600 paper-based; 96 iBT), IELTS (minimum score 6.5), PTE (minimum score 58). *Application deadline:* For fall admission, 7/16 priority date for domestic and international students; for spring admission, 11/16 priority date for domestic and international students; for summer admission, 4/16 priority date for domestic and international students. Applications are processed on a rolling basis. Application fee: $40. Electronic applications accepted. *Expenses:* $1,060 per credit. *Financial support:* In 2019–20, 12 students received support. Research assistantships, teaching assistantships, career-related internships or fieldwork, scholarships/grants, and unspecified assistantships available. Support available to part-time students. Financial award application deadline: 3/1; financial award applicants required to submit FAFSA. *Unit head:* Dr. Diane Murphy, Chair/Director, Information Technology, Management Sciences and Cybersecurity, 703-284-5958, E-mail: diane.murphy@marymount.edu. *Application contact:* Fiona McDonnell, Administrative Assistant, 703-284-5901, E-mail: gadmissi@marymount.edu.
Website: https://www.marymount.edu/Academics/School-of-Business-and-Technology/Graduate-Programs/Information-Technology-(M-S-)

McMaster University, School of Graduate Studies, Faculty of Engineering, Department of Computing and Software, Hamilton, ON L8S 4M2, Canada. Offers computer science (M Sc, PhD); software engineering (M Eng, MA Sc, PhD). *Program availability:* Part-time. *Degree requirements:* For master's, thesis. *Entrance requirements:* Additional exam requirements/recommendations for international students: required—TOEFL (minimum score 550 paper-based).

Mercer University, Graduate Studies, Macon Campus, School of Engineering, Macon, GA 31207. Offers biomedical engineering (MSE); computer engineering (MSE); electrical engineering (MSE); engineering management (MSE); environmental engineering (MSE); environmental systems (MS); mechanical engineering (MSE); software engineering (MSE); software systems (MS); technical communications management (MS); technical management (MS). *Program availability:* Part-time-only, evening/weekend, online learning. *Faculty:* 27 full-time (9 women), 2 part-time/adjunct (0 women). *Students:* 38 full-time (10 women), 51 part-time (20 women); includes 22 minority (5 Black or African American, non-Hispanic/Latino; 11 Asian, non-Hispanic/Latino; 4 Hispanic/Latino; 2 Two or more races, non-Hispanic/Latino), 2 international. Average age 26. In 2019, 70 master's awarded. *Degree requirements:* For master's, thesis or alternative. *Entrance requirements:* For master's, GRE (minimum score 300), minimum undergraduate GPA of 3.0. Additional exam requirements/recommendations for international students: required—TOEFL (minimum score 550 paper-based; 80 iBT). *Application deadline:* For fall admission, 4/1 priority date for domestic and international students; for spring admission, 11/1 priority date for domestic and international students. Applications are processed on a rolling basis. Application fee: $75. *Expenses:* Tuition: $938.00 ($700.00 for Technical Communication Management program) per credit hour; Facility and Technology Fee: $17.00 per credit hour. *Financial support:* Federal Work-Study available. Financial award applicants required to submit FAFSA. *Unit head:* Dr. Laura W. Lackey, Dean, 478-301-4106, Fax: 478-301-5593, E-mail: lackey_l@mercer.edu. *Application contact:* Dr. Sinjae Hyun, Program Director, 478-301-2214, Fax: 478-301-5593, E-mail: hyun_s@mercer.edu.
Website: http://engineering.mercer.edu/

Monmouth University, Graduate Studies, Program in Software Engineering, West Long Branch, NJ 07764-1898. Offers MS, Certificate. *Program availability:* Part-time, evening/weekend, online learning. *Faculty:* 9 full-time (3 women), 6 part-time/adjunct (1 woman). *Students:* 12 full-time (1 woman), 11 part-time (2 women); includes 5 minority (2 Black or African American, non-Hispanic/Latino; 1 Asian, non-Hispanic/Latino; 2 Hispanic/Latino), 15 international. Average age 26. In 2019, 16 master's awarded. *Degree requirements:* For master's, thesis optional, practicum. *Entrance requirements:* For master's and Certificate, bachelor's degree in software engineering, computer science, computer engineering or other engineering-related discipline; minimum GPA of 3.0 in major, 2.5 overall; completed course work in computer programming, data structures and algorithms, and software engineering. Additional exam requirements/recommendations for international students: required—TOEFL (minimum score 550 paper-based, 79 iBT), IELTS (minimum score 6), Michigan English Language Assessment Battery (minimum score 77) or Certificate of Advanced English (minimum score 160). *Application deadline:* For fall admission, 7/15 priority date for domestic students, 6/1 for international students; for spring admission, 12/1 priority date for domestic students, 11/1 for international students; for summer admission, 5/1 for domestic students. Applications are processed on a rolling basis. Application fee: $50. Electronic applications accepted. *Expenses:* $1,233 per credit. *Financial support:* In 2019–20, 19 students received support. Research assistantships, teaching assistantships, scholarships/grants, and unspecified assistantships available. Support available to part-time students. Financial award applicants required to submit FAFSA. *Unit head:* Dr. Jiacun Wang, Program Director, 732-571-7501, Fax: 732-263-5253, E-mail: jwang@monmouth.edu. *Application contact:* Laurie Kuhn, Associate Director of Graduate Admission, 732-571-3452, Fax: 732-263-5123, E-mail: gradadm@monmouth.edu.
Website: http://www.monmouth.edu/graduate_se

Naval Postgraduate School, Departments and Academic Groups, Department of Computer Science, Monterey, CA 93943. Offers computer science (MS, PhD); identity management and cyber security (MA); modeling of virtual environments and simulations (MS, PhD); software engineering (MS, PhD). *Program availability:* Part-time, online learning. *Degree requirements:* For master's, thesis; for doctorate, thesis/dissertation.

New Jersey Institute of Technology, Ying Wu College of Computing, Newark, NJ 07102. Offers big data management and mining (Certificate); business and information systems (Certificate); computer science (PhD); computing and business (MS); data mining (Certificate); data science (MS); information security (Certificate); information

systems (PhD); information technology administration and security (MS); IT administration (Certificate); network security and information assurance (Certificate); software engineering (MS), including information systems; software engineering analysis/design (Certificate); Web systems development (Certificate). *Program availability:* Part-time, evening/weekend. *Faculty:* 78 full-time (16 women), 63 part-time/adjunct (10 women). *Students:* 668 full-time (210 women), 290 part-time (81 women); includes 277 minority (46 Black or African American, non-Hispanic/Latino; 1 American Indian or Alaska Native, non-Hispanic/Latino; 161 Asian, non-Hispanic/Latino; 53 Hispanic/Latino; 16 Two or more races, non-Hispanic/Latino), 565 international. Average age 27. 2,671 applicants, 62% accepted, 360 enrolled. In 2019, 407 master's, 5 doctorates, 12 other advanced degrees awarded. Terminal master's awarded for partial completion of doctoral program. *Degree requirements:* For master's, thesis optional; for doctorate, thesis/dissertation. *Entrance requirements:* For master's, GRE General Test; for doctorate, GRE General Test, minimum graduate GPA of 3.5. Additional exam requirements/recommendations for international students: required—TOEFL (minimum score 550 paper-based; 79 iBT), IELTS (minimum score 6.5). *Application deadline:* For fall admission, 6/1 priority date for domestic students, 5/1 priority date for international students; for spring admission, 11/15 priority date for domestic and international students. Applications are processed on a rolling basis. Application fee: $75. Electronic applications accepted. *Expenses:* $23,828 per year (in-state), $33,744 per year (out-of-state). *Financial support:* In 2019–20, 383 students received support, including 8 fellowships with full tuition reimbursements available, 34 research assistantships with full tuition reimbursements available (averaging $24,000 per year), 57 teaching assistantships with full tuition reimbursements available (averaging $24,000 per year); career-related internships or fieldwork, Federal Work-Study, scholarships/grants, and unspecified assistantships also available. Financial award application deadline: 1/15. *Unit head:* Dr. Craig Gotsman, Dean, 973-596-3366, Fax: 973-596-5777, E-mail: craig.gotsman@njit.edu. *Application contact:* Stephen Eck, Executive Director of University Admissions, 973-596-3300, Fax: 973-596-3461, E-mail: admissions@njit.edu.
Website: http://computing.njit.edu/

New York University, Tandon School of Engineering, Department of Computer Science and Engineering, Major in Software Engineering, New York, NY 10012-1019. Offers Graduate Certificate. Electronic applications accepted.

North Dakota State University, College of Graduate and Interdisciplinary Studies, College of Science and Mathematics, Department of Computer Science, Program in Software Engineering, Fargo, ND 58102. Offers MS, MSE, PhD, Certificate. *Program availability:* Part-time, online learning. Terminal master's awarded for partial completion of doctoral program. *Entrance requirements:* Additional exam requirements/recommendations for international students: required—TOEFL. Electronic applications accepted. Tuition and fees vary according to program and reciprocity agreements.

Northern Kentucky University, Office of Graduate Programs, College of Informatics, Department of Computer Science, Highland Heights, KY 41099. Offers computer science (MSCS); geographic information systems (Certificate); secure software engineering (Certificate). *Program availability:* Part-time, evening/weekend. *Degree requirements:* For master's, thesis optional. *Entrance requirements:* For master's, GRE, minimum GPA of 3.0, at least 4 semesters of undergraduate study in computer science including intermediate computer programming and data structures, one year of calculus, one course in discrete mathematics. Additional exam requirements/recommendations for international students: required—TOEFL (minimum score 550 paper-based; 79 iBT); recommended—IELTS (minimum score 6.5). Electronic applications accepted.

Northwestern University, School of Professional Studies, Program in Information Systems, Evanston, IL 60208. Offers analytics and business intelligence (MS); database and Internet technologies (MS); information systems (MS); information systems management (MS); information systems security (MS); medical informatics (MS); software project management and development (MS). *Program availability:* Part-time, evening/weekend.

Oakland University, Graduate Study and Lifelong Learning, School of Engineering and Computer Science, Department of Computer Science and Engineering, Rochester, MI 48309-4401. Offers computer science (MS); computer science and informatics (PhD); software engineering and information technology (MS). *Program availability:* Part-time, evening/weekend. *Entrance requirements:* For master's, minimum GPA of 3.0. Electronic applications accepted. *Expenses:* Contact institution.

Oklahoma Christian University, Graduate School of Engineering and Computer Science, Oklahoma City, OK 73136-1100. Offers electrical and computer engineering (MSE); engineering management (MSE); mechanical engineering (MSE); software engineering (MSCS, MSE). *Program availability:* Part-time. *Entrance requirements:* Additional exam requirements/recommendations for international students: required—TOEFL (minimum score 550 paper-based). Electronic applications accepted. *Expenses:* Contact institution.

Pace University, Seidenberg School of Computer Science and Information Systems, New York, NY 10038. Offers chief information security officer (APC); computer science (MS, PhD); enterprise analytics (MS); information and communication technology strategy and innovation (APC); information systems (MS, APC); information technology (MS); professional studies in computing (DPS); secure software and information engineering (APC); security and information assurance (Certificate); software development and engineering (MS, Certificate); telecommunications systems and networks (MS, Certificate). *Program availability:* Part-time, evening/weekend, online only, 100% online, blended/hybrid learning. *Degree requirements:* For master's, thesis or alternative, capstone course; for doctorate, comprehensive exam (for some programs), thesis/dissertation. *Entrance requirements:* Additional exam requirements/recommendations for international students: required—TOEFL (minimum score 78 iBT), IELTS (minimum score 6.5) or PTE (minimum score 52). Electronic applications accepted. *Expenses:* Contact institution.

Penn State Great Valley, Graduate Studies, Engineering Division, Malvern, PA 19355-1488. Offers engineering management (MEM); software engineering (MSE); systems engineering (M Eng, Certificate).

Regis University, College of Computer and Information Sciences, Denver, CO 80221-1099. Offers agile technologies (Certificate); cybersecurity (Certificate); data science (M Sc); database administration with Oracle (Certificate); database development (Certificate); database technologies (M Sc); enterprise Java software development (Certificate); enterprise resource planning (Certificate); executive information technology (Certificate); health care informatics (Certificate); health care informatics and information management (M Sc); information assurance (M Sc); information assurance policy management (Certificate); information technology management (M Sc); mobile software development (Certificate); software engineering (M Sc, Certificate); software engineering and database technology (M Sc); storage area networks (Certificate); systems engineering (M Sc, Certificate). *Program availability:* Part-time, evening/weekend, 100% online, blended/hybrid learning. *Degree requirements:* For master's, thesis (for some programs), final research project. *Entrance requirements:* For master's, official transcript reflecting baccalaureate degree awarded from regionally-accredited college or university, 2 years of related experience, resume, interview. Additional exam requirements/recommendations for international students: required—TOEFL (minimum score 550 paper-based; 82 iBT). Electronic applications accepted. *Expenses:* Contact institution.

Rochester Institute of Technology, Graduate Enrollment Services, Golisano College of Computing and Information Sciences, Software Engineering Department, MS Program in Software Engineering, Rochester, NY 14623-5603. Offers MS. *Program availability:* Part-time. *Degree requirements:* For master's, thesis or alternative, Thesis or Capstone. *Entrance requirements:* For master's, GRE required for individuals with degrees from international universities., minimum GPA of 3.0 (recommended), professional essay (1-4 pages), resume, two letters of recommendation. Additional exam requirements/recommendations for international students: required—TOEFL (minimum score 570 paper-based; 88 iBT), IELTS (minimum score 6.5), PTE (minimum score 61). Electronic applications accepted.

Royal Military College of Canada, Division of Graduate Studies, Faculty of Engineering, Department of Electrical and Computer Engineering, Kingston, ON K7K 7B4, Canada. Offers computer engineering (M Eng, PhD); electrical engineering (M Eng, PhD); software engineering (M Eng, PhD). *Degree requirements:* For master's, thesis; for doctorate, comprehensive exam, thesis/dissertation. *Entrance requirements:* For master's, honours degree with second-class standing in the appropriate field; for doctorate, master's degree. Electronic applications accepted.

Saint Louis University, Graduate Programs, College of Arts and Sciences, Department of Computer Science, St. Louis, MO 63103. Offers bioinformatics and computational biology (MS); computer science (MS); software engineering (MS).

St. Mary's University, School of Science, Engineering and Technology, Program in Software Engineering, San Antonio, TX 78228. Offers MS, Certificate. *Program availability:* Part-time. *Degree requirements:* For master's, thesis (for some programs), thesis or project. *Entrance requirements:* For master's, GRE (minimum quantitative score of 148), bachelor's degree in software engineering, computer science, computer engineering or closely-related discipline; minimum GPA of 3.0. Additional exam requirements/recommendations for international students: required—TOEFL (minimum score 550 paper-based; 80 iBT), IELTS (minimum score 6.5). Electronic applications accepted.

San Jose State University, Program in Computer Engineering, San Jose, CA 95192-0180. Offers computer engineering (MS); software engineering (MS). *Faculty:* 14 full-time (5 women), 28 part-time/adjunct (4 women). *Students:* 833 full-time (352 women), 352 part-time (101 women); includes 186 minority (7 Black or African American, non-Hispanic/Latino; 160 Asian, non-Hispanic/Latino; 19 Hispanic/Latino), 922 international. Average age 27. 1,637 applicants, 23% accepted, 224 enrolled. In 2019, 515 master's awarded. *Entrance requirements:* For master's, GRE General Test. *Application deadline:* For fall admission, 7/1 for domestic students, 5/1 for international students; for spring admission, 12/1 for domestic students, 11/1 for international students. Applications are processed on a rolling basis. Application fee: $70. Electronic applications accepted. *Expenses: Tuition, area resident:* Full-time $7176; part-time $4164. Tuition, state resident: full-time $7176; part-time $4164. Tuition, nonresident: full-time $7176; part-time $4165 per credit hour. *International tuition:* $7176 full-time. *Required fees:* $2110; $2110. *Financial support:* In 2019–20, 30 students received support. Scholarships/grants available. Financial award applicants required to submit FAFSA. *Unit head:* Xiao Su, Department Chair, 408-924-7366, E-mail: xiao.su@sjsu.edu. *Application contact:* David Bruck, MS Computer Engineering Advisor, E-mail: David.bruck@sjsu.edu.
Website: https://cmpe.sjsu.edu/

Santa Clara University, School of Engineering, Santa Clara, CA 95053. Offers applied mathematics (MS); bioengineering (MS); civil, environmental, and sustainable engineering (MS); computer science and engineering (MS, PhD, Engineer); electrical engineering (MS, PhD, Engineer); engineering management and leadership (MS); mechanical engineering (MS, PhD, Engineer); power systems and sustainable energy (MS); software engineering (MS). *Program availability:* Part-time. *Entrance requirements:* For master's, GRE, official transcript; for doctorate, GRE, Official transcript, 500 word statement of purpose, three letters of recommendation. Additional exam requirements/recommendations for international students: required—TOEFL (minimum score 79 iBT), IELTS (minimum score 6.5). Electronic applications accepted.

Shippensburg University of Pennsylvania, School of Graduate Studies, College of Arts and Sciences, Department of Computer Science and Engineering, Shippensburg, PA 17257-2299. Offers agile software engineering (Certificate); computer science (MS); IT leadership (Certificate). *Program availability:* Part-time, evening/weekend. *Faculty:* 4 full-time (2 women). *Students:* 8 full-time (3 women), 5 part-time (2 women); includes 4 minority (2 Black or African American, non-Hispanic/Latino; 2 Asian, non-Hispanic/Latino), 5 international. Average age 28. 39 applicants, 44% accepted, 6 enrolled. In 2019, 5 master's awarded. *Entrance requirements:* For master's, GRE (if GPA less than 2.75), professional resume. Additional exam requirements/recommendations for international students: required—TOEFL (minimum score 70 iBT), IELTS (minimum score 6), TOEFL (minimum score 70 iBT) or IELTS (minimum score 6). *Application deadline:* For fall admission, 4/30 for international students. Applications are processed on a rolling basis. Application fee: $45. Electronic applications accepted. *Expenses:* Tuition, state resident: part-time $516 per credit. Tuition, nonresident: part-time $774 per credit. *Required fees:* $149 per credit. *Financial support:* In 2019–20, 8 students received support. Career-related internships or fieldwork, scholarships/grants, unspecified assistantships, and resident hall director and student payroll positions available. Support available to part-time students. Financial award application deadline: 3/1; financial award applicants required to submit FAFSA. *Unit head:* Dr. Jeonghwa Lee, Professor and Director of Graduate Studies, 717-477-1178, Fax: 717-477-4002, E-mail: jlee@ship.edu. *Application contact:* Maya T. Mapp, Director of Admissions, 717-477-1231, Fax: 717-477-4016, E-mail: mtmapp@ship.edu.
Website: http://www.ship.edu/engineering/cs

Southern Methodist University, Lyle School of Engineering, Department of Computer Science and Engineering, Dallas, TX 75275-0122. Offers computer engineering (MS, PhD); computer science (MS, PhD); security engineering (MS); software engineering (MS, DE). *Program availability:* Part-time, evening/weekend, online learning. Terminal master's awarded for partial completion of doctoral program. *Degree requirements:* For master's, thesis optional; for doctorate, thesis/dissertation, oral and written qualifying exams, oral final exam (PhD). *Entrance requirements:* For master's, GRE General Test, minimum GPA of 3.0 in last 2 years; bachelor's degree in engineering, mathematics, or sciences; for doctorate, preliminary counseling exam (PhD), minimum GPA of 3.0, bachelor's degree in related field, MA (for DE). Additional exam requirements/recommendations for international students: required—TOEFL (minimum score 550 paper-based).

Stevens Institute of Technology, Graduate School, School of Systems and Enterprises, Program in Software Engineering, Hoboken, NJ 07030. Offers MS, Certificate. *Program availability:* Part-time, evening/weekend. *Faculty:* 22 full-time (8 women), 15 part-time/adjunct (3 women). *Students:* 98 full-time (20 women), 23 part-time (8 women); includes 13 minority (7 Black or African American, non-Hispanic/Latino; 5 Asian, non-Hispanic/Latino; 1 Hispanic/Latino), 92 international. Average age 26. In

2019, 27 master's, 22 other advanced degrees awarded. Terminal master's awarded for partial completion of doctoral program. *Degree requirements:* For master's, thesis optional, minimum B average in major field and overall; for Certificate, minimum B average. *Entrance requirements:* For master's, International applicants must submit TOEFL/IELTS scores and fulfill the English Language Proficiency Requirement. Applicants to full-time programs who do not qualify for a score waiver are required to submit GRE/GMAT scores. Additional exam requirements/recommendations for international students: required—TOEFL (minimum score 74 iBT), IELTS (minimum score 6). *Application deadline:* For fall admission, 4/15 for domestic and international students; for spring admission, 11/1 for domestic and international students; for summer admission, 5/1 for domestic students. Applications are processed on a rolling basis. Application fee: $60. Electronic applications accepted. *Expenses: Tuition:* Full-time $52,134. *Required fees:* $1880. Tuition and fees vary according to course load. *Financial support:* Fellowships, research assistantships, teaching assistantships, career-related internships or fieldwork, Federal Work-Study, scholarships/grants, and unspecified assistantships available. Financial award application deadline: 2/15; financial award applicants required to submit FAFSA. *Unit head:* Dr. Yehia Massoud, Dean of SSE, 201-216.8025, E-mail: yehia.massoud@stevens.edu. *Application contact:* Graduate Admissions, 888-783-8367, Fax: 888-511-1306, E-mail: graduate@stevens.edu.

Stratford University, School of Graduate Studies, Falls Church, VA 22043. Offers accounting (MS); business administration (MBA, DBA); cyber security (MS); cyber security leadership and policy (MS); digital forensics (MS); healthcare administration (MS); information systems (MS); information technology (DIT); networking and telecommunications (MS); software engineering (MS). *Program availability:* Part-time, evening/weekend, 100% online, blended/hybrid learning. *Degree requirements:* For master's, comprehensive exam, capstone project. *Entrance requirements:* For master's, GRE or GMAT, baccalaureate degree. Additional exam requirements/recommendations for international students: required—TOEFL (minimum score 79 iBT), IELTS (minimum score 6.5), PTE (minimum score 5). Electronic applications accepted.

Strayer University, Graduate Studies, Washington, DC 20005-2603. Offers accounting (MS); acquisition (MBA); business administration (MBA); communications technology (MS); educational management (M Ed); finance (MBA); health services administration (MHSA); hospitality and tourism management (MBA); human resource management (MBA); information systems (MS), including computer security management, decision support system management, enterprise resource management, network management, software engineering management, systems development management; management (MBA); management information systems (MS); marketing (MBA); professional accounting (MS), including accounting information systems, controllership, taxation; public administration (MPA); supply chain management (MBA); technology in education (M Ed). *Accreditation:* ACBSP. *Program availability:* Part-time, evening/weekend, online learning. *Degree requirements:* For master's, thesis. *Entrance requirements:* For master's, GMAT, GRE General Test, bachelor's degree from an accredited college or university, minimum undergraduate GPA of 2.75. Electronic applications accepted.

Texas State University, The Graduate College, College of Science and Engineering, Program in Software Engineering, San Marcos, TX 78666. Offers MS. *Program availability:* Part-time. *Degree requirements:* For master's, comprehensive exam, thesis optional. *Entrance requirements:* For master's, official GRE (general test only) required with competitive scores in the verbal reasoning and quantitative reasoning sections, baccalaureate degree from regionally-accredited university with minimum GPA of 2.75 on last 60 undergraduate semester hours, 3 letters of reference, academic vitae (resume), statement of purpose. Additional exam requirements/recommendations for international students: required—TOEFL (minimum score 550 paper-based; 78 iBT), IELTS (minimum score 6.5). Electronic applications accepted.

Texas Tech University, Graduate School, Edward E. Whitacre Jr. College of Engineering, Department of Computer Science, Lubbock, TX 79409-3104. Offers computer science (MS, PhD); software engineering (MS). *Program availability:* Part-time, blended/hybrid learning. *Faculty:* 18 full-time (3 women). *Students:* 106 full-time (40 women), 34 part-time (5 women); includes 13 minority (5 Asian, non-Hispanic/Latino; 5 Hispanic/Latino; 3 Two or more races, non-Hispanic/Latino), 109 international. Average age 28. 265 applicants, 59% accepted, 55 enrolled. In 2019, 24 master's, 5 doctorates awarded. Terminal master's awarded for partial completion of doctoral program. *Degree requirements:* For master's, comprehensive exam (for some programs), thesis (for some programs); for doctorate, comprehensive exam, thesis/dissertation. *Entrance requirements:* For master's and doctorate, GRE (Verbal and Quantitative). Additional exam requirements/recommendations for international students: required—TOEFL (minimum score 550 paper-based; 79 iBT). *Application deadline:* For fall admission, 6/1 priority date for domestic students, 1/15 priority date for international students; for spring admission, 9/1 priority date for domestic students, 6/15 priority date for international students. Applications are processed on a rolling basis. Application fee: $65. Electronic applications accepted. *Expenses:* Contact institution. *Financial support:* In 2019–20, 106 students received support, including 91 fellowships (averaging $3,838 per year), 27 research assistantships (averaging $19,522 per year), 15 teaching assistantships (averaging $22,166 per year); scholarships/grants, tuition waivers (partial), and unspecified assistantships also available. Financial award application deadline: 4/15; financial award applicants required to submit FAFSA. *Unit head:* Dr. Rattikorn Hewett, Department Chair and Professor, 806-742-3527, Fax: 806-742-3519, E-mail: rattikorn.hewett@ttu.edu. *Application contact:* Jeremy Herrera, Staff Graduate Advisor, 806-742-3527, Fax: 806-742-3519, E-mail: jeremy.herrera@ttu.edu.
Website: www.cs.ttu.edu/

The University of Alabama in Huntsville, School of Graduate Studies, College of Engineering, Department of Electrical and Computer Engineering, Huntsville, AL 35899. Offers computer engineering (MSE, PhD); electrical engineering (MSE, PhD), including optics and photonics technology (MSE); optical science and engineering (PhD); software engineering (MSSE). *Program availability:* Part-time. *Degree requirements:* For master's, comprehensive exam, thesis or alternative, oral and written exams; for doctorate, comprehensive exam, thesis/dissertation, oral and written exams. *Entrance requirements:* For master's, GRE General Test, appropriate bachelor's degree, minimum GPA of 3.0; for doctorate, GRE General Test, minimum GPA of 3.0. Additional exam requirements/recommendations for international students: required—TOEFL (minimum score 500 paper-based; 80 iBT), IELTS (minimum score 6.5). Electronic applications accepted.

The University of Alabama in Huntsville, School of Graduate Studies, College of Science, Department of Computer Science, Huntsville, AL 35899. Offers computer science (MS, PhD); cybersecurity (MS); modeling and simulation (MS, PhD, Certificate); software engineering (MSSE, Certificate). *Program availability:* Part-time. *Degree requirements:* For master's, comprehensive exam, thesis or alternative, oral and written exams; for doctorate, comprehensive exam, thesis/dissertation, oral and written exams. *Entrance requirements:* For master's, doctorate, and Certificate, GRE General Test, minimum GPA of 3.0. Additional exam requirements/recommendations for international students: required—TOEFL (minimum score 550 paper-based; 80 iBT), IELTS (minimum score 6.5). Electronic applications accepted.

University of Calgary, Faculty of Graduate Studies, Faculty of Science, Program in Computer Science, Calgary, AB T2N 1N4, Canada. Offers computer science (M Sc, PhD); software engineering (M Sc). *Program availability:* Part-time. *Degree requirements:* For master's, comprehensive exam (for some programs), thesis (for some programs); for doctorate, thesis/dissertation, oral and written departmental exam. *Entrance requirements:* For master's, bachelor's degree in computer science; for doctorate, M Sc in computer science. Additional exam requirements/recommendations for international students: required—TOEFL (minimum score 600 paper-based); recommended—TWE. Electronic applications accepted.

University of Colorado Colorado Springs, College of Engineering and Applied Science, Program in General Engineering, Colorado Springs, CO 80918. Offers computer science (PhD); cybersecurity (ME); energy engineering (ME); engineering management (ME); engineering systems (ME); software engineering (ME); space operations (ME). *Program availability:* Part-time, evening/weekend, blended/hybrid learning. *Faculty:* 1 full-time (0 women), 12 part-time/adjunct (3 women). *Students:* 2 full-time (1 woman), 88 part-time (22 women); includes 23 minority (3 Black or African American, non-Hispanic/Latino; 6 Asian, non-Hispanic/Latino; 9 Hispanic/Latino; 5 Two or more races, non-Hispanic/Latino), 7 international. Average age 32. 36 applicants, 53% accepted, 15 enrolled. In 2019, 28 master's awarded. *Degree requirements:* For master's, thesis, portfolio, or project. *Entrance requirements:* For master's, GRE may be required based on past academic performance., Professional recommendation letters are required for all applicants.; for doctorate, GRE (minimum score of 148 new grading scale on the quantitative portion if the applicant has not graduated from a program of recognized standing), minimum GPA of 3.3 in the bachelor's or master's degree program attempted. Additional exam requirements/recommendations for international students: required—TOEFL (minimum score 80 iBT), IELTS (minimum score 6). *Application deadline:* For fall admission, 7/1 for domestic and international students; for spring admission, 11/1 for domestic and international students. Applications are processed on a rolling basis. Application fee: $60 ($100 for international students). Electronic applications accepted. *Expenses:* Contact institution. *Financial support:* In 2019–20, 5 students received support. Career-related internships or fieldwork, Federal Work-Study, scholarships/grants, traineeships, health care benefits, and unspecified assistantships available. Support available to part-time students. Financial award application deadline: 3/1; financial award applicants required to submit FAFSA. *Unit head:* Dr. Donald Rabern, Dean of Engineering and Applied Science, 719-255-3543, E-mail: drabern@uccs.edu. *Application contact:* Dawn House, Extended Studies Coordinator, 719-255-3246, E-mail: dhouse@uccs.edu.
Website: https://www.uccs.edu/easonline/degree-programs/engineering-management-degree

University of Connecticut, Graduate School, School of Engineering, Department of Computer Science and Engineering, Storrs, CT 06269. Offers computer science (MS, PhD), including artificial intelligence, computer architecture, computer science, operating systems, robotics, software engineering. Terminal master's awarded for partial completion of doctoral program. *Degree requirements:* For master's, comprehensive exam, thesis or alternative; for doctorate, thesis/dissertation. *Entrance requirements:* For master's and doctorate, GRE General Test. Additional exam requirements/recommendations for international students: required—TOEFL (minimum score 550 paper-based). Electronic applications accepted.

University of Detroit Mercy, College of Engineering and Science, Detroit, MI 48221. Offers chemistry (MS); civil and environmental engineering (DE); electrical and computer engineering (ME); electrical engineering (DE); engineering management (M Eng Mgt); environmental engineering (MEE); mechanical engineering (MME, DE); product development (MS); software engineering (MSSE); teaching of mathematics (MATM). *Program availability:* Part-time, evening/weekend. *Degree requirements:* For doctorate, thesis/dissertation. Electronic applications accepted. Application fee is waived when completed online. *Expenses:* Contact institution.

University of Houston–Clear Lake, School of Science and Computer Engineering, Program in Software Engineering, Houston, TX 77058-1002. Offers MS. *Program availability:* Part-time, evening/weekend. *Entrance requirements:* For master's, GRE General Test. Additional exam requirements/recommendations for international students: required—TOEFL (minimum score 550 paper-based).

University of Management and Technology, Program in Computer Science, Arlington, VA 22209-1609. Offers computer science (MS); information technology (AC); project management (AC); software engineering (MS). *Program availability:* Part-time, evening/weekend, online learning. *Entrance requirements:* For master's, 3 recommendations, resume. Additional exam requirements/recommendations for international students: required—TOEFL (minimum score 530 paper-based; 71 iBT). Electronic applications accepted. *Expenses: Tuition:* Full-time $7020; part-time $390 per credit hour. *Required fees:* $90; $30 per semester.

University of Massachusetts Dartmouth, Graduate School, College of Engineering, Department of Computer Science, North Dartmouth, MA 02747-2300. Offers computer science (MS, Graduate Certificate); software development and design (Postbaccalaureate Certificate). *Program availability:* Part-time, 100% online, blended/hybrid learning. *Degree requirements:* For master's, thesis, thesis or project. *Entrance requirements:* For master's, GRE unless UMass Dartmouth graduate in computer science, statement of purpose (minimum of 300 words), resume, 3 letters of recommendation, official transcripts; for other advanced degree, statement of purpose (minimum of 300 words), resume, official transcripts. Additional exam requirements/recommendations for international students: required—TOEFL (minimum score 533 paper-based; 72 iBT), IELTS (minimum score 6). Electronic applications accepted.

University of Michigan–Dearborn, College of Engineering and Computer Science, Master of Science in Software Engineering Program, Dearborn, MI 48128. Offers MS. *Program availability:* Part-time, evening/weekend, 100% online. *Faculty:* 19 full-time (1 woman), 5 part-time/adjunct (0 women). *Students:* 7 full-time (2 women), 42 part-time (8 women); includes 14 minority (1 Black or African American, non-Hispanic/Latino; 10 Asian, non-Hispanic/Latino; 2 Hispanic/Latino; 1 Two or more races, non-Hispanic/Latino), 7 international. Average age 29. 47 applicants, 57% accepted, 18 enrolled. In 2019, 11 master's awarded. *Degree requirements:* For master's, thesis optional. *Entrance requirements:* For master's, bachelor's degree in mathematics, computer science or engineering; minimum GPA of 3.0. Additional exam requirements/recommendations for international students: required—TOEFL (minimum score 560 paper-based; 84 iBT), IELTS (minimum score 6.5). *Application deadline:* For fall admission, 8/1 priority date for domestic students, 5/1 priority date for international students; for winter admission, 12/1 priority date for domestic students, 9/1 priority date for international students; for spring admission, 4/1 priority date for domestic students, 1/1 priority date for international students. Applications are processed on a rolling basis. Application fee: $60. Electronic applications accepted. *Financial support:* Research assistantships with full tuition reimbursements, teaching assistantships with full tuition reimbursements, scholarships/grants, health care benefits, and non-resident tuition scholarships available. Support available to part-time students. Financial award application deadline: 3/1; financial award applicants required to submit FAFSA. *Unit head:* Dr. Zhiwei Xu, Chair, 313-583-6436, E-mail: zwxu@umich.edu. *Application contact:* Office of Graduate Studies, 313-583-6321, E-mail: umd-graduatestudies@

umich.edu.
Website: https://umdearborn.edu/cecs/departments/computer-and-information-science/graduate-programs/ms-software-engineering

University of Michigan–Dearborn, College of Engineering and Computer Science, PhD Program in Computer and Information Science, Dearborn, MI 48128. Offers data management (PhD); data science (PhD); software engineering (PhD); systems and security (PhD). *Faculty:* 19 full-time (1 woman), 5 part-time/adjunct (0 women). *Students:* 8 full-time (5 women), 6 part-time (1 woman); includes 1 minority (Asian, non-Hispanic/Latino), 11 international. Average age 28. 17 applicants, 24% accepted, 3 enrolled. In 2019, 1 doctorate awarded. *Degree requirements:* For doctorate, comprehensive exam, thesis/dissertation. *Entrance requirements:* For doctorate, GRE, bachelor's or master's degree in computer science or closely-related field. Additional exam requirements/recommendations for international students: required—TOEFL (minimum score 560 paper-based; 84 iBT), IELTS (minimum score 6.5). *Application deadline:* For fall admission, 2/1 for domestic and international students. Application fee: $60. Electronic applications accepted. *Financial support:* Research assistantships with full tuition reimbursements, teaching assistantships with full tuition reimbursements, scholarships/grants, health care benefits, and unspecified assistantships available. Financial award application deadline: 2/1; financial award applicants required to submit FAFSA. *Unit head:* Dr. Di Ma, Director, 313-583-6737, E-mail: dmadma@umich.edu. *Application contact:* Office of Graduate Studies, 313-583-6321, E-mail: umd-graduatestudies@umich.edu.
Website: https://umdearborn.edu/cecs/departments/computer-and-information-science/graduate-programs/phd-computer-and-information-science

University of Minnesota, Twin Cities Campus, College of Science and Engineering, Department of Computer Science and Engineering, Program in Software Engineering, Minneapolis, MN 55455-0213. Offers MSSE. *Program availability:* Part-time, evening/weekend. *Degree requirements:* For master's, thesis optional, capstone project. *Entrance requirements:* For master's, 1 year of work experience in software field; minimum undergraduate GPA of 3.0. Additional exam requirements/recommendations for international students: required—TOEFL. Electronic applications accepted.

University of Missouri–Kansas City, School of Computing and Engineering, Kansas City, MO 64110-2499. Offers civil engineering (MS); computer and electrical engineering (PhD); computer science (MS), including bioinformatics, software engineering, telecommunications networking; computer science and informatics (PhD); computing (PhD); electrical engineering (MS); engineering (PhD); engineering and construction management (Graduate Certificate); mechanical engineering (MS); telecommunications and computer networking (PhD). *Program availability:* Part-time. *Degree requirements:* For doctorate, thesis/dissertation. *Entrance requirements:* For master's, GRE General Test, minimum GPA of 3.0, 3 letters of recommendation from professors; for doctorate, GRE General Test, minimum GPA of 3.5. Additional exam requirements/recommendations for international students: required—TOEFL (minimum score 550 paper-based; 80 iBT).

University of Nebraska at Omaha, Graduate Studies, College of Information Science and Technology, Department of Computer Science, Omaha, NE 68182. Offers artificial intelligence (Certificate); communication networks (Certificate); computer science (MA, MS); computer science education (MS, Certificate); software engineering (Certificate); system and architecture (Certificate). *Program availability:* Part-time, evening/weekend. *Degree requirements:* For master's, comprehensive exam, thesis (for some programs). *Entrance requirements:* For master's, GRE General Test, minimum GPA of 3.0, prior course work in computer science, official transcripts, resume, 2 letters of recommendation; for Certificate, minimum GPA of 3.0, resume. Additional exam requirements/recommendations for international students: required—TOEFL, IELTS, PTE. Electronic applications accepted.

University of New Haven, Graduate School, Tagliatela College of Engineering, Program in Computer Science, West Haven, CT 06516. Offers computer programming (Graduate Certificate); computer science (MS); network systems (MS); software development (MS). *Program availability:* Part-time, evening/weekend. *Students:* 107 full-time (36 women), 26 part-time (7 women); includes 11 minority (2 Black or African American, non-Hispanic/Latino; 7 Asian, non-Hispanic/Latino; 1 Hispanic/Latino; 1 Two or more races, non-Hispanic/Latino), 104 international. Average age 26. 560 applicants, 61% accepted, 26 enrolled. In 2019, 41 master's awarded. *Entrance requirements:* Additional exam requirements/recommendations for international students: required—TOEFL (minimum score 75 iBT), IELTS, PTE (minimum score 50). *Application deadline:* Applications are processed on a rolling basis. Application fee: $50. Electronic applications accepted. Application fee is waived when completed online. *Financial support:* Research assistantships with partial tuition reimbursements, teaching assistantships with partial tuition reimbursements, career-related internships or fieldwork, Federal Work-Study, scholarships/grants, and unspecified assistantships available. Support available to part-time students. Financial award applicants required to submit FAFSA. *Unit head:* Dr. Barun Chandra, Associate Professor, 203-932-7089, E-mail: bchandra@newhaven.edu. *Application contact:* Selina O'Toole, Senior Associate Director of Graduate Admissions, 203-932-7337, E-mail: sotoole@newhaven.edu.
Website: https://www.newhaven.edu/engineering/graduate-programs/computer-science/

University of North Florida, College of Computing, Engineering, and Construction, School of Computing, Jacksonville, FL 32224. Offers computer science (MS); information systems (MS); software engineering (MS). *Program availability:* Part-time. *Degree requirements:* For master's, thesis. *Entrance requirements:* For master's, GRE General Test, minimum GPA of 3.0 in last 60 hours of course work. Additional exam requirements/recommendations for international students: required—TOEFL (minimum score 500 paper-based; 61 iBT). Electronic applications accepted.

University of Regina, Faculty of Graduate Studies and Research, Faculty of Engineering and Applied Science, Program in Software Systems Engineering, Regina, SK S4S 0A2, Canada. Offers software systems (M Eng, MA Sc, PhD). *Program availability:* Part-time. *Faculty:* 6 full-time (1 woman), 2 part-time/adjunct (0 women). *Students:* 12 full-time (4 women), 7 part-time (2 women). Average age 30. 105 applicants, 11% accepted. In 2019, 5 master's, 1 doctorate awarded. *Degree requirements:* For master's, thesis (for some programs), project, report. coop placement; for doctorate, comprehensive exam, thesis/dissertation. *Entrance requirements:* For master's, minimum graduating average of 70 percent from four-year baccalaureate degree (or equivalent); for doctorate, completion of thesis-based master's degree in engineering or closely-related field. Additional exam requirements/recommendations for international students: required—TOEFL (minimum score 580 paper-based; 80 iBT), IELTS (minimum score 6.5), PTE (minimum score 59), other options are CAEL, MELAB, Cantest and U of R ESL. *Application deadline:* For fall admission, 1/31 for domestic and international students; for winter admission, 7/31 for domestic and international students. Applications are processed on a rolling basis. Application fee: $100 Canadian dollars. Electronic applications accepted. *Expenses:* 11,036.50 -This amount is based on three semesters tuition, registered in 6 credit hours per semester. Plus one year student fees and books. There is additional 438.75 if student is in Co-op route. *Financial support:* Fellowships, research assistantships, teaching assistantships, career-related internships or fieldwork, Federal Work-Study, scholarships/grants, unspecified assistantships, and Travel award and Graduate Scholarship Base funds available. Financial award application deadline: 9/30. *Unit head:* Craig Gelowitz, Program Chair/coordinator, Software Systems Engineering, 306-585-4733, Fax: 306-585-4855, E-mail: craig.gelowitz@uregina.ca. *Application contact:* Dr. Christine Chan, Graduate Coordinator, 306-585-5225, E-mail: christine.chan@uregina.ca.
Website: http://www.uregina.ca/engineering/

University of St. Thomas, School of Engineering, St. Paul, MN 55105. Offers data science (MS); electrical engineering (MS); information technology (MS); manufacturing engineering (MS); manufacturing systems (Certificate); mechanical engineering (MS); medical device development (Certificate); regulatory science (MS); software engineering (MS); software management (MS); systems engineering (MS); technology leadership (Certificate); technology management (MS). *Program availability:* Part-time, evening/weekend. *Entrance requirements:* For master's, resume, official transcripts. Additional exam requirements/recommendations for international students: required—TOEFL (minimum score 80 iBT), IELTS (minimum score 6.5). Electronic applications accepted. *Expenses:* Contact institution.

The University of Scranton, Kania School of Management, Program in Software Engineering, Scranton, PA 18510. Offers MS. *Program availability:* Part-time, evening/weekend. *Degree requirements:* For master's, comprehensive exam (for some programs), thesis (for some programs), capstone experience. *Entrance requirements:* For master's, minimum GPA of 3.0, three letters of reference. Additional exam requirements/recommendations for international students: required—TOEFL (minimum score 500 paper-based; 80 iBT), IELTS (minimum score 6.5). Electronic applications accepted.

University of South Carolina, The Graduate School, College of Engineering and Computing, Department of Computer Science and Engineering, Columbia, SC 29208. Offers computer science and engineering (ME, MS, PhD); software engineering (MS). *Program availability:* Part-time, evening/weekend, online learning. *Degree requirements:* For master's, comprehensive exam, thesis (for some programs); for doctorate, comprehensive exam, thesis/dissertation. *Entrance requirements:* For master's and doctorate, GRE General Test. Additional exam requirements/recommendations for international students: required—TOEFL (minimum score 570 paper-based). Electronic applications accepted.

University of Southern California, Graduate School, Viterbi School of Engineering, Department of Computer Science, Los Angeles, CA 90089. Offers computer networks (MS); computer science (MS, PhD); computer security (MS); game development (MS); high performance computing and simulations (MS); human language technology (MS); intelligent robotics (MS); multimedia and creative technologies (MS); software engineering (MS). *Program availability:* Part-time, evening/weekend, online learning. *Entrance requirements:* For master's and doctorate, GRE General Test. Additional exam requirements/recommendations for international students: required—TOEFL. Electronic applications accepted.

University of Southern Maine, College of Science, Technology, and Health, Department of Computer Science, Portland, ME 04103. Offers computer science (MS); software systems (CGS). *Program availability:* Part-time. *Degree requirements:* For master's, thesis. *Entrance requirements:* For master's, GRE General Test, minimum GPA of 3.0. Additional exam requirements/recommendations for international students: required—TOEFL. Electronic applications accepted. *Expenses: Tuition, area resident:* Full-time $864; part-time $432 per credit hour. *Tuition, state resident:* full-time $864; part-time $432 per credit hour. *Tuition, nonresident:* full-time $2372; part-time $1186 per credit hour. *Required fees:* $141; $108 per credit hour. Tuition and fees vary according to course load.

The University of Texas at Arlington, Graduate School, College of Engineering, Department of Computer Science and Engineering, Arlington, TX 76019. Offers computer engineering (MS, PhD); computer science (MS, PhD); software engineering (MS). *Program availability:* Part-time, online learning. Terminal master's awarded for partial completion of doctoral program. *Degree requirements:* For master's, comprehensive exam (for some programs), thesis; for doctorate, comprehensive exam, thesis/dissertation. *Entrance requirements:* For master's, GRE General Test, minimum GPA of 3.0 (3.2 in computer science-related classes); for doctorate, GRE General Test, minimum GPA of 3.5. Additional exam requirements/recommendations for international students: required—TOEFL (minimum score 550 paper-based; 92 iBT), IELTS (minimum score 6.5).

The University of Texas at Dallas, Erik Jonsson School of Engineering and Computer Science, Department of Computer Science, Richardson, TX 75080. Offers computer science (MSCS, PhD); software engineering (MS, PhD). *Program availability:* Part-time, evening/weekend. *Faculty:* 49 full-time (6 women), 21 part-time/adjunct (5 women). *Students:* 977 full-time (277 women), 297 part-time (80 women); includes 119 minority (12 Black or African American, non-Hispanic/Latino; 76 Asian, non-Hispanic/Latino; 24 Hispanic/Latino; 7 Two or more races, non-Hispanic/Latino), 1,034 international. Average age 27. 4,176 applicants, 21% accepted, 411 enrolled. In 2019, 456 master's, 21 doctorates awarded. *Degree requirements:* For master's, thesis optional; for doctorate, comprehensive exam, thesis/dissertation. *Entrance requirements:* For master's, GRE General Test, minimum GPA of 3.0 in undergraduate course work, 3.3 in quantitative course work; for doctorate, GRE General Test, minimum GPA of 3.5. Additional exam requirements/recommendations for international students: required—TOEFL (minimum score 550 paper-based). *Application deadline:* For fall admission, 7/15 for domestic students, 5/1 priority date for international students; for spring admission, 11/15 for domestic students, 9/1 priority date for international students. Applications are processed on a rolling basis. Application fee: $50 ($100 for international students). Electronic applications accepted. *Expenses: Tuition, area resident:* Full-time $16,504. *Tuition, state resident:* full-time $16,504. *Tuition, nonresident:* full-time $34,266. Tuition and fees vary according to course load. *Financial support:* In 2019–20, 167 students received support, including 7 fellowships (averaging $3,024 per year), 63 research assistantships with partial tuition reimbursements available (averaging $23,525 per year), 89 teaching assistantships with partial tuition reimbursements available (averaging $17,157 per year); career-related internships or fieldwork, Federal Work-Study, institutionally sponsored loans, and scholarships/grants also available. Support available to part-time students. Financial award application deadline: 4/30; financial award applicants required to submit FAFSA. *Unit head:* Dr. Gopal Gupta, Department Head, 972-883-4107, Fax: 972-883-2399, E-mail: gupta@utdallas.edu. *Application contact:* Dr. Ovidiu Daescu, Associate Department Head, 972-883-4196, E-mail: daescu@utdallas.edu.
Website: http://cs.utdallas.edu/

The University of Texas at El Paso, Graduate School, College of Engineering, Department of Computer Science, El Paso, TX 79968-0001. Offers computer science (MS, PhD); cyber security (Graduate Certificate); information technology (MSIT); software engineering (MS). *Program availability:* Part-time, evening/weekend. *Degree requirements:* For master's, thesis optional; for doctorate, thesis/dissertation. *Entrance requirements:* For master's, GRE, minimum GPA of 3.0; for doctorate, GRE, statement of purpose, letters of reference. Additional exam requirements/recommendations for international students: required—TOEFL; recommended—IELTS. Electronic applications accepted.

University of Utah, Graduate School, College of Engineering, School of Computing, Salt Lake City, UT 84112-9205. Offers computer science (MS, PhD); computing (MS, PhD); software development (MS); MS/MBA. Terminal master's awarded for partial completion of doctoral program. *Degree requirements:* For master's, comprehensive exam (for some programs), thesis optional; for doctorate, comprehensive exam, thesis/dissertation. *Entrance requirements:* For master's and doctorate, GRE General Test, minimum GPA of 3.0. Additional exam requirements/recommendations for international students: required—TOEFL (minimum score 500 paper-based; 61 iBT), IELTS (minimum score 6.5). Electronic applications accepted. *Expenses:* Contact institution.

University of Utah, Graduate School, David Eccles School of Business, Master of Science in Information Systems Program, Salt Lake City, UT 84112. Offers information systems (MS, Graduate Certificate), including business intelligence and analytics, IT security, product and process management, software and systems architecture. *Program availability:* Part-time, evening/weekend, 100% online, blended/hybrid learning. *Students:* 141 full-time (34 women), 95 part-time (24 women); includes 39 minority (2 Black or African American, non-Hispanic/Latino; 10 Asian, non-Hispanic/Latino; 19 Hispanic/Latino; 8 Two or more races, non-Hispanic/Latino), 65 international. Average age 31. In 2019, 153 master's awarded. *Entrance requirements:* For master's, GMAT/GRE, minimum undergraduate GPA of 3.0, 2 letters of recommendation, personal statement, professional resume. Additional exam requirements/recommendations for international students: required—TOEFL (minimum score 550 paper-based; 80 iBT), IELTS (minimum score 6.5). *Application deadline:* For fall admission, 7/27 for domestic students, 3/30 for international students; for spring admission, 12/7 for domestic students, 9/7 priority date for international students; for summer admission, 4/12 for domestic students, 1/11 for international students. Applications are processed on a rolling basis. Application fee: $55 ($65 for international students). Electronic applications accepted. *Expenses:* Contact institution. *Financial support:* Fellowships with partial tuition reimbursements, teaching assistantships, tuition waivers (partial), and unspecified assistantships available. Financial award application deadline: 6/1; financial award applicants required to submit FAFSA. *Unit head:* Dr. Mark Parker, Associate Dean, Specialized Masters Program, 801-585-5177, Fax: 801-581-3666, E-mail: mark.parker@eccles.utah.edu. *Application contact:* Kaylee Miller, Admissions Coordinator, 801-587-5878, Fax: 801-581-3666, E-mail: kaylee.miller@eccles.utah.edu. Website: http://msis.eccles.utah.edu

University of Washington, Bothell, Program in Computing and Software Systems, Bothell, WA 98011. Offers MS. *Program availability:* Part-time, evening/weekend. *Degree requirements:* For master's, comprehensive exam (for some programs), thesis optional. *Entrance requirements:* For master's, GRE. Additional exam requirements/recommendations for international students: required—TOEFL (minimum score 580 paper-based; 92 iBT) or IELTS (minimum score 7). Electronic applications accepted. *Expenses:* Contact institution.

University of Washington, Tacoma, Graduate Programs, Program in Computing and Software Systems, Tacoma, WA 98402-3100. Offers MS. *Program availability:* Part-time. *Degree requirements:* For master's, capstone project/thesis or 15 credits elective coursework. *Entrance requirements:* For master's, GRE, personal statement, resume, transcripts, 3 recommendations. Additional exam requirements/recommendations for international students: required—TOEFL (minimum score 580 paper-based; 92 iBT), IELTS (minimum score 7). Electronic applications accepted.

University of Waterloo, Graduate Studies and Postdoctoral Affairs, Faculty of Mathematics, David R. Cheriton School of Computer Science, Waterloo, ON N2L 3G1, Canada. Offers computer science (M Math, PhD); software engineering (M Math); statistics and computing (M Math). *Program availability:* Part-time. *Degree requirements:* For master's, research paper or thesis; for doctorate, comprehensive exam, thesis/dissertation. *Entrance requirements:* For master's, honors degree in field, minimum B+ average; for doctorate, master's degree, minimum B+ average. Additional exam requirements/recommendations for international students: required—TOEFL, IELTS, PTE. Electronic applications accepted.

University of West Florida, Hal Marcus College of Science and Engineering, Department of Computer Science, Pensacola, FL 32514-5750. Offers computer science (MS), including computer science, database systems, software engineering; information technology (MS), including cybersecurity, database management. *Program availability:* Part-time, evening/weekend. *Degree requirements:* For master's, thesis optional. *Entrance requirements:* For master's, GRE, MAT, or GMAT, official transcripts; minimum undergraduate GPA of 3.0; letter of intent; three letters of recommendation. Additional exam requirements/recommendations for international students: required—TOEFL (minimum score 550 paper-based).

University of Wisconsin–La Crosse, College of Science and Health, Department of Computer Science, La Crosse, WI 54601. Offers software engineering (MSE). *Program availability:* Part-time. *Faculty:* 9 full-time (2 women). *Students:* 29 full-time (3 women), 7 part-time (0 women), 23 international. Average age 24. 19 applicants, 95% accepted, 17 enrolled. In 2019, 13 master's awarded. *Degree requirements:* For master's, thesis. *Entrance requirements:* Additional exam requirements/recommendations for international students: recommended—TOEFL (minimum score 550 paper-based; 79 iBT), IELTS (minimum score 6). *Application deadline:* For fall admission, 5/1 priority date for domestic and international students; for spring admission, 11/1 priority date for domestic and international students. Applications are processed on a rolling basis. Electronic applications accepted. *Financial support:* Research assistantships with partial tuition reimbursements, Federal Work-Study, scholarships/grants, health care benefits, and tuition waivers (partial) available. Support available to part-time students. *Unit head:* Dr. Kenny Hunt, Department Chair, 608-785-6822, E-mail: hunt@cs.uwlax.edu. *Application contact:* Jennifer Weber, Senior Student Services Coordinator Graduate Admissions, 608-785-8939, E-mail: admissions@uwlax.edu. Website: http://www.cs.uwlax.edu/

Université Laval, Faculty of Sciences and Engineering, Program in Software Engineering, Québec, QC G1K 7P4, Canada. Offers Diploma. *Program availability:* Part-time. *Entrance requirements:* For degree, knowledge of French. Electronic applications accepted.

Vermont Technical College, Program in Computer Software Engineering, Randolph Center, VT 05061-0500. Offers MS.

Virginia International University, School of Computer Information Systems, Fairfax, VA 22030. Offers business intelligence (Graduate Certificate); business intelligence and data analytics (MIS); computer science (MS), including computer animation and gaming, cybersecurity, data management networking, intelligent systems, software applications development, software engineering; cybersecurity (MIS); data management (MIS); enterprise project management (MIS); health informatics (MIS); information assurance (MIS); information systems (Graduate Certificate); information systems management (MS, Graduate Certificate); information technology (MS); information technology audit and compliance (Graduate Certificate); knowledge management (MIS); software engineering (MS). *Program availability:* Part-time, online learning. *Entrance requirements:* For master's, bachelor's degree. Additional exam requirements/recommendations for international students: required—TOEFL (minimum score 550 paper-based; 80 iBT), IELTS. Electronic applications accepted.

Virginia Polytechnic Institute and State University, VT Online, Blacksburg, VA 24061. Offers advanced transportation systems (Certificate); aerospace engineering (MS); agricultural and life sciences (MSLFS); business information systems (Graduate Certificate); career and technical education (MS); civil engineering (MS); computer engineering (M Eng, MS); decision support systems (Graduate Certificate); eLearning leadership (MA); electrical engineering (M Eng, MS); engineering administration (MEA); environmental engineering (Certificate); environmental politics and policy (Graduate Certificate); environmental sciences and engineering (MS); foundations of political analysis (Graduate Certificate); health product risk management (Graduate Certificate); industrial and systems engineering (MS); information policy and society (Graduate Certificate); information security (Graduate Certificate); information technology (MIT); instructional technology (MA); integrative STEM education (MA Ed); liberal arts (Graduate Certificate); life sciences: health product risk management (MS); natural resources (MNR, Graduate Certificate); networking (Graduate Certificate); nonprofit and nongovernmental organization management (Graduate Certificate); ocean engineering (MS); political science (MA); security studies (Graduate Certificate); software development (Graduate Certificate). *Expenses:* Tuition, state resident: full-time $13,700; part-time $761.25 per credit hour. Tuition, nonresident: full-time $27,614; part-time $1534 per credit hour. *Required fees:* $886.50 per term. Tuition and fees vary according to campus/location and program.

West Virginia University, Statler College of Engineering and Mineral Resources, Morgantown, WV 26506. Offers aerospace engineering (MSAE, PhD); chemical engineering (MS Ch E, PhD); civil engineering (MSCE, PhD); computer engineering (PhD); computer science (MSCS, PhD); electrical engineering (MSEE, PhD); energy systems engineering (MSESE); engineering (MSE); industrial engineering (MSIE, PhD); industrial hygiene (MS); material science and engineering (MSMSE, PhD); mechanical engineering (MSME, PhD); mining engineering (MS Min E, PhD); petroleum and natural gas engineering (MSPNGE, PhD); safety management (MS); software engineering (MSSE). *Program availability:* Part-time. Terminal master's awarded for partial completion of doctoral program. *Degree requirements:* For master's, thesis optional; for doctorate, comprehensive exam, thesis/dissertation. *Entrance requirements:* Additional exam requirements/recommendations for international students: required—TOEFL (minimum score 550 paper-based). Electronic applications accepted. *Expenses:* Contact institution.

Systems Science

Arizona State University at Tempe, College of Liberal Arts and Sciences, School of Life Sciences, Tempe, AZ 85287-4601. Offers animal behavior (PhD); applied ethics (biomedical and health ethics) (MA); biology (MS, PhD), including biology, biology and society, complex adaptive systems science (PhD), plant biology and conservation (MS); environmental life sciences (PhD); evolutionary biology (PhD); history and philosophy of science (PhD); human and social dimensions of science and technology (PhD); microbiology (PhD); molecular and cellular biology (PhD); neuroscience (PhD). Terminal master's awarded for partial completion of doctoral program. *Degree requirements:* For master's, thesis (for some programs), interactive Program of Study (iPOS) submitted before completing 50 percent of required credit hours; for doctorate, variable foreign language requirement, comprehensive exam, thesis/dissertation, interactive Program of Study (iPOS) submitted before completing 50 percent of required credit hours. *Entrance requirements:* For master's and doctorate, GRE, minimum GPA of 3.0 or equivalent in last 2 years of work leading to bachelor's degree. Additional exam requirements/recommendations for international students: required—TOEFL (minimum score 600 paper-based; 100 iBT). Electronic applications accepted.

Arizona State University at Tempe, Ira A. Fulton Schools of Engineering, ASU Engineering Online Programs, Tempe, AZ 85287. Offers construction (MS); embedded systems (M Eng); enterprise systems innovation and management (MSE); modeling and simulation (M Eng); quality and reliability engineering (M Eng); software engineering (MSE); systems engineering (M Eng).

Binghamton University, State University of New York, Graduate School, Thomas J. Watson School of Engineering and Applied Science, Department of Systems Science and Industrial Engineering, Binghamton, NY 13902-6000. Offers executive health systems (MS); industrial and systems engineering (M Eng); systems science and industrial engineering (MS, PhD). *Program availability:* Part-time, evening/weekend, online learning. *Degree requirements:* For master's, thesis; for doctorate, thesis/dissertation. *Entrance requirements:* For master's and doctorate, GRE General Test. Additional exam requirements/recommendations for international students: required—TOEFL (minimum score 550 paper-based; 80 iBT). Electronic applications accepted. *Expenses:* Contact institution.

Carleton University, Faculty of Graduate Studies, Faculty of Engineering and Design, Ottawa-Carleton Institute for Electrical Engineering, Department of Systems and Computer Engineering, Program in Information and Systems Science, Ottawa, ON K1S 5B6, Canada. Offers M Sc.

Carleton University, Faculty of Graduate Studies, Faculty of Science, Information and Systems Science Program, Ottawa, ON K1S 5B6, Canada. Offers M Sc. *Degree requirements:* For master's, thesis optional. *Entrance requirements:* For master's, honors degree. Additional exam requirements/recommendations for international students: required—TOEFL.

Carleton University, Faculty of Graduate Studies, Faculty of Science, School of Computer Science, Ottawa, ON K1S 5B6, Canada. Offers computer science (MCS, PhD); information and system science (M Sc). *Program availability:* Part-time. *Degree requirements:* For master's, thesis optional, project; for doctorate, comprehensive exam, thesis/dissertation. *Entrance requirements:* For master's, honors degree. Additional exam requirements/recommendations for international students: required—TOEFL.

Claremont Graduate University, Graduate Programs, Center for Information Systems and Technology, Claremont, CA 91711-6160. Offers cybersecurity and networking (MS);

data science and analytics (MS); electronic commerce (PhD); geographic information systems (MS); health informatics (MS); information systems (Certificate); IT strategy and innovation (MS); knowledge management (PhD); systems development (PhD); telecommunications and networking (PhD); MBA/MS. *Program availability:* Part-time. *Degree requirements:* For doctorate, comprehensive exam, thesis/dissertation, portfolio. *Entrance requirements:* For master's and doctorate, GMAT, GRE General Test. Additional exam requirements/recommendations for international students: required—TOEFL (minimum score 75 iBT). Electronic applications accepted.

Eastern Illinois University, Graduate School, Lumpkin College of Business and Technology, School of Technology, Charleston, IL 61920. Offers computer technology (Certificate); cybersecurity (MS); quality systems (Certificate); sustainable energy (MS); technology (MS); technology security (Certificate); work performance improvement (Certificate); MS/MBA; MS/MS. *Program availability:* Part-time, evening/weekend.

Fairleigh Dickinson University, Metropolitan Campus, University College: Arts, Sciences, and Professional Studies, Program in Systems Science, Teaneck, NJ 07666-1914. Offers MS. *Entrance requirements:* For master's, GRE General Test.

Harrisburg University of Science and Technology, Program in Information Systems Engineering and Management, Harrisburg, PA 17101. Offers analytics (MS); digital government (MS); digital health (MS); entrepreneurship (MS); information security (MS); software engineering and systems development (MS). *Program availability:* Part-time, evening/weekend. *Degree requirements:* For master's, thesis optional. *Entrance requirements:* For master's, baccalaureate degree. Additional exam requirements/recommendations for international students: required—TOEFL (minimum score 520 paper-based; 80 iBT); recommended—IELTS (minimum score 6). Electronic applications accepted. *Expenses: Tuition:* Full-time $15,900; part-time $7950 per credit hour.

Hood College, Graduate School, Program in Management Information Systems, Frederick, MD 21701-8575. Offers MS. *Program availability:* Part-time, evening/weekend. *Entrance requirements:* For master's, minimum GPA of 2.75, essay, resume. Additional exam requirements/recommendations for international students: required—TOEFL (minimum score 575 paper-based; 89 iBT), IELTS (minimum score 6.5). Electronic applications accepted. *Expenses:* Contact institution.

Louisiana State University and Agricultural & Mechanical College, Graduate School, College of Engineering, Division of Computer Science, Baton Rouge, LA 70803. Offers computer science (MSSS, PhD); systems science (MSSS).

Louisiana State University in Shreveport, College of Arts and Sciences, Program in Computer Systems Technology, Shreveport, LA 71115-2399. Offers MS. *Program availability:* Part-time, evening/weekend. *Degree requirements:* For master's, comprehensive exam (for some programs), thesis or alternative. *Entrance requirements:* For master's, GRE, programming course in high-level language, interview. Additional exam requirements/recommendations for international students: required—TOEFL (minimum score 550 paper-based; 80 iBT). Electronic applications accepted.

Miami University, College of Engineering and Computing, Department of Computer Science and Software Engineering, Oxford, OH 45056. Offers computer science (MCS).

Oakland University, Graduate Study and Lifelong Learning, School of Engineering and Computer Science, Department of Electrical and Computer Engineering, Rochester, MI 48309-4401. Offers electrical and computer engineering (MS, PhD); embedded systems (MS); mechatronics (MS). *Program availability:* Part-time, evening/weekend. *Entrance requirements:* For master's, minimum GPA of 3.0. Additional exam requirements/recommendations for international students: required—TOEFL (minimum score 550 paper-based). Electronic applications accepted. *Expenses:* Contact institution.

Portland State University, Graduate Studies, College of Liberal Arts and Sciences, Systems Science Program, Portland, OR 97207-0751. Offers computational intelligence (Certificate); computer modeling and simulation (Certificate); systems science (MS); systems science/anthropology (PhD); systems science/business administration (PhD); systems science/civil engineering (PhD); systems science/economics (PhD); systems science/engineering management (PhD); systems science/general (PhD); systems science/mathematical sciences (PhD); systems science/mechanical engineering (PhD); systems science/psychology (PhD); systems science/sociology (PhD). *Program availability:* Part-time. *Faculty:* 2 full-time (0 women), 6 part-time/adjunct (1 woman). *Students:* 6 full-time (3 women), 25 part-time (8 women); includes 7 minority (2 Asian, non-Hispanic/Latino; 4 Hispanic/Latino; 1 Two or more races, non-Hispanic/Latino), 2 international. Average age 39. 25 applicants, 80% accepted, 15 enrolled. In 2019, 7 master's, 2 doctorates awarded. Terminal master's awarded for partial completion of doctoral program. *Degree requirements:* For master's, comprehensive exam (for some programs), thesis optional; for doctorate, variable foreign language requirement, comprehensive exam (for some programs), thesis/dissertation. *Entrance requirements:* For master's, GRE/GMAT (recommended), minimum GPA of 3.0 on undergraduate or graduate work, 2 letters of recommendation, statement of interest; for doctorate, GRE required, minimum GPA of 3.0 undergraduate, 3.25 graduate; 3 letters of recommendation; statement of interest. Additional exam requirements/recommendations for international students: required—TOEFL (minimum score 550 paper-based; 80 iBT). *Application deadline:* For fall admission, 3/15 priority date for domestic and international students. Application fee: $65. Electronic applications accepted. *Expenses: Tuition, area resident:* Full-time $13,020; part-time $6510 per year. Tuition, state resident: full-time $13,020; part-time $6510 per year. Tuition, nonresident: full-time $19,830; part-time $9915 per year. *International tuition:* $19,830 full-time. *Required fees:* $1226. One-time fee: $350. Tuition and fees vary according to course load, program and reciprocity agreements. *Financial support:* Research assistantships, teaching assistantships, career-related internships or fieldwork, Federal Work-Study, scholarships/grants, and unspecified assistantships available. Support available to part-time students. Financial award application deadline: 3/1; financial award applicants required to submit FAFSA. *Unit head:* Dr. Wayne Wakeland, Chair, 503-725-4975, E-mail: wakeland@pdx.edu. *Application contact:* Dr. Wayne Wakeland, Chair, 503-725-4975, E-mail: wakeland@pdx.edu. Website: http://www.pdx.edu/sysc/

Rensselaer at Hartford, Department of Engineering, Program in Computer and Systems Engineering, Hartford, CT 06120-2991. Offers ME. *Entrance requirements:* For master's, GRE.

Stevens Institute of Technology, Graduate School, Charles V. Schaefer Jr. School of Engineering and Science, Department of Mechanical Engineering, Program in Integrated Product Development, Hoboken, NJ 07030. Offers armament engineering (M Eng); computer and electrical engineering (M Eng); manufacturing technologies (M Eng); systems reliability and design (M Eng). *Program availability:* Part-time, evening/weekend. *Faculty:* 29 full-time (3 women), 11 part-time/adjunct (0 women). *Degree requirements:* For master's, thesis optional, minimum B average in major field

and overall. *Entrance requirements:* For master's, International applicants must submit TOEFL/IELTS scores and fulfill the English Language Proficiency Requirement. Applicants to full-time programs who do not qualify for a score waiver are required to submit GRE/GMAT scores. Additional exam requirements/recommendations for international students: required—TOEFL (minimum score 74 iBT), IELTS (minimum score 6). *Application deadline:* For fall admission, 4/15 for domestic and international students; for spring admission, 11/1 for domestic and international students; for summer admission, 5/1 for domestic students. Applications are processed on a rolling basis. Application fee: $60. Electronic applications accepted. *Expenses: Tuition:* Full-time $52,134. *Required fees:* $1880. Tuition and fees vary according to course load. *Financial support:* Fellowships, research assistantships, teaching assistantships, career-related internships or fieldwork, Federal Work-Study, scholarships/grants, and unspecified assistantships available. Financial award application deadline: 2/15; financial award applicants required to submit FAFSA. *Unit head:* Dr. Jean Zu, Dean of SES, 201-216.8233, Fax: 201-216.8372, E-mail: Jean.Zu@stevens.edu. *Application contact:* Graduate Admissions, 888-783-8367, Fax: 888-511-1306, E-mail: graduate@stevens.edu.

Stevens Institute of Technology, Graduate School, School of Systems and Enterprises, Program in Socio-Technical Systems, Hoboken, NJ 07030. Offers MS, PhD. *Program availability:* Part-time, evening/weekend. *Faculty:* 22 full-time (8 women), 15 part-time/adjunct (3 women). *Students:* 1 (woman) part-time. Average age 32. *Degree requirements:* For master's, thesis optional, minimum B average in major field and overall; for doctorate, comprehensive exam (for some programs), thesis/dissertation. *Entrance requirements:* For master's, International applicants must submit TOEFL/IELTS scores and fulfill the English Language Proficiency Requirement. Applicants to full-time programs who do not qualify for a score waiver are required to submit GRE/GMAT scores. Additional exam requirements/recommendations for international students: required—TOEFL (minimum score 74 iBT), IELTS (minimum score 6). *Application deadline:* For fall admission, 4/15 for domestic and international students; for spring admission, 11/1 for domestic and international students; for summer admission, 5/1 for domestic students. Applications are processed on a rolling basis. Application fee: $60. Electronic applications accepted. *Expenses: Tuition:* Full-time $52,134. *Required fees:* $1880. Tuition and fees vary according to course load. *Financial support:* Fellowships, research assistantships, teaching assistantships, career-related internships or fieldwork, Federal Work-Study, scholarships/grants, and unspecified assistantships available. Financial award application deadline: 2/15; financial award applicants required to submit FAFSA. *Unit head:* Dr. Yehia Massoud, Dean of SSE, 201-216.8025, E-mail: yehia.massoud@stevens.edu. *Application contact:* Graduate Admissions, 888-783-8367, Fax: 888-511-1306, E-mail: graduate@stevens.edu.

Strayer University, Graduate Studies, Washington, DC 20005-2603. Offers accounting (MS); acquisition (MBA); business administration (MBA); communications technology (MS); educational management (M Ed); finance (MBA); health services administration (MHSA); hospitality and tourism management (MBA); human resource management (MBA); information systems (MS), including computer security management, decision support system management, enterprise resource management, network management, software engineering management, systems development management; management (MBA); management information systems (MS); marketing (MBA); professional accounting (MS), including accounting information systems, controllership, taxation; public administration (MPA); supply chain management (MBA); technology in education (M Ed). *Accreditation:* ACBSP. *Program availability:* Part-time, evening/weekend, online learning. *Degree requirements:* For master's, thesis. *Entrance requirements:* For master's, GMAT, GRE General Test, bachelor's degree from an accredited college or university, minimum undergraduate GPA of 2.75. Electronic applications accepted.

Universidad Autonoma de Guadalajara, Graduate Programs, Guadalajara, Mexico. Offers administrative law and justice (LL M); advertising and corporate communications (MA); architecture (M Arch); business (MBA); computational science (MCC); education (Ed M, Ed D); English-Spanish translation (MA); entrepreneurship and management (MBA); integrated management of digital animation (MA); international business (MIB); international corporate law (LL M); Internet technologies (MS); manufacturing systems (MMS); occupational health (MS); philosophy (MA, PhD); power electronics (MS); quality systems (MQS); renewable energy (MS); social evaluation of projects (MBA); strategic market research (MBA); tax law (MA); teaching mathematics (MA).

University of Michigan, College of Engineering, Department of Integrative Systems and Design, Ann Arbor, MI 48109. Offers automotive engineering (M Eng); design science (MS, PhD); energy systems engineering (M Eng, MS); global automotive and manufacturing engineering (M Eng); manufacturing engineering (M Eng, D Eng); pharmaceutical engineering (M Eng); robotics and autonomous vehicles (M Eng); systems engineering and design (M Eng); MBA/M Eng; MSE/MS. *Program availability:* Part-time, online learning. Terminal master's awarded for partial completion of doctoral program. *Degree requirements:* For master's, capstone project; for doctorate, thesis/dissertation. *Entrance requirements:* For master's and doctorate, GRE. Additional exam requirements/recommendations for international students: required—TOEFL. Electronic applications accepted.

University of Ottawa, Faculty of Graduate and Postdoctoral Studies, Interdisciplinary Programs, Ottawa, ON K1N 6N5, Canada. Offers e-business (Certificate); e-commerce (Certificate); finance (Certificate); health services and policies research (Diploma); population health (PhD); population health risk assessment and management (Certificate); public management and governance (Certificate); systems science (Certificate).

University of Ottawa, Faculty of Graduate and Postdoctoral Studies, Systems Science Program, Ottawa, ON K1N 6N5, Canada. Offers M Sc, M Sys Sc, Certificate. *Program availability:* Part-time, evening/weekend. *Degree requirements:* For master's and Certificate, thesis optional. *Entrance requirements:* For master's, bachelor's degree or equivalent, minimum B average; for Certificate, honors degree or equivalent, minimum B average. Additional exam requirements/recommendations for international students: recommended—TOEFL. Electronic applications accepted.

Worcester Polytechnic Institute, Graduate Admissions, Department of Social Science and Policy Studies, Worcester, MA 01609-2280. Offers interdisciplinary social science (PhD); system dynamics (MS, Graduate Certificate). *Program availability:* Part-time, evening/weekend, 100% online. *Entrance requirements:* For master's and doctorate, GRE General Test, 3 letters of recommendation, statement of purpose. Additional exam requirements/recommendations for international students: required—TOEFL (minimum score 563 paper-based; 84 iBT), IELTS (minimum score 7). Electronic applications accepted.

PENN STATE UNIVERSITY PARK

Department of Computer Science and Engineering within the School of Electrical Engineering and Computer Science

PennState College of Engineering | ELECTRICAL ENGINEERING AND COMPUTER SCIENCE

Programs of Study

The Pennsylvania State University (Penn State), founded in 1855, is the Commonwealth of Pennsylvania's sole land-grant institution and its largest public university.

The mission of the Department of Computer Science and Engineering (CSE), which is housed in the School of Electrical Engineering and Computer Science, is to educate computer scientists and computer engineers of the highest caliber, and to discover and disseminate new findings from rigorous research that advances and improves the overall quality of life.

The department offers three graduate programs. Students may start in a master's program and then continue in the Ph.D. program.

Master of Engineering (M.E.) in Computer Science and Engineering: This one-year intensive master's degree program is meant to prepare students for work in industry. As such, there is no thesis required, although a final paper is required during the last semester of the program. The program requires the completion of 30 credits.

Master of Science (M.S.) in Computer Science and Engineering: This program requires the completion of 30 credits. Students interested in an M.S. in CSE should have already successfully completed Operating Systems Design and Construction, Introduction to Computer Architecture, Programming Language Concepts, Data Structures and Algorithms, and Logical Design of Digital Systems or Introduction to the Theory of Computation.

Ph.D. in Computer Science and Engineering: Students who do not have a degree in CE or CS must take a minimum of 33 credits. Students who have a degree in CE or CS must take a minimum of 21 credits. All students in the Ph.D. program are required to pass a written candidacy examination within the first three regular semesters, offered at the beginning of each fall and spring semester. The examination tests the student's background preparation and problem-solving ability.

Research

Graduate students at Penn State enjoy a supportive research environment that provides modern facilities and sufficient funding to make groundbreaking discoveries. According to National Science Foundation data for 2017, Penn State's computer science and engineering program ranked 23rd for research and development expenditures, making research a priority.

The School of Electrical Engineering and Computer Science was created in the spring of 2015 to allow greater access to courses offered by both CSE and Electrical Engineering departments and to foster collaborative re-search. Some of the areas of research within the school, specifically related to CSE, include:

- Communications, information theory, and coding over networked systems
- Computational science
- Computer architecture
- Computer networks and mobile systems
- Computer vision and image processing
- Data science and artificial intelligence
- Electronic materials and devices
- Integrated circuits and systems
- Operating systems and cloud computing
- Programming languages and compilers
- Security and privacy
- Theoretical computer science

The Department hosts prominent large-scale research programs including the Collaborative Research Alliance for the Science of Security, a Collaborative Technology Alliance for Network Science, multiple DARPA awards, and both the prestigious NSF Expedition and an NSF Frontier awards. In addition, most of the faculty are well funded through various grants from several federal and industrial sources. State-of-the-art research labs provide a conducive environment work in many areas such as computer architecture and systems, computer vision and robotics, embedded system design and VLSI, networking and security, high performance computing, bioinformatics and machine learning/data science.

Financial Aid

Graduate students at Penn State often receive research assistantships and teaching assistantships to help fund their education. Approximately 4,000 assistantships are awarded each year. Many research assistantships are 48-week appointments, covering the 36-week period of the academic year and an additional 12 weeks for the two summer session terms.

The majority of CSE Ph.D. students receive research and/or teaching assistantships during their studies.

In addition, paid positions are often available in the department.

Cost of Study

The tuition rate for the 2020–21 academic year is $23,928 per year for Pennsylvania residents and $39,720 per year for non-Pennsylvania residents.

Living and Housing Costs

On-campus housing is available. University Park offers graduate and family housing ranging from single unfurnished apartments up to three-bedroom family apartments. Ample off-campus housing is also popular with graduate students.

Location

The University is located in the beautiful town of State College, which is considered one of the best college towns in the United States. The area has 130,000 residents and offers a wide variety of cultural and outdoor recreational activities, as well as outstanding University events, from collegiate sports to fine arts productions.

The University

Penn State is in the top 1% of universities worldwide and consistently ranks near top nationally in annual spending on science and engineering research. It also has the largest alumni network in the nation. The College of Engineering is exceptionally strong, as it was ranked fourth in the latest National Science Foundation rankings of Higher Education Research and Development (HERD) research expenditures. The college's total funding in 2019-2020 was $117 million, helping to enable cutting-edge research to take place.

Faculty

Research plays an important role in CSE graduate education. The 52 faculty members work on some of the most leading-edge research areas in bioinformatics, computer vision, databases, embedded and hardware systems, enterprise computing and IT infrastructure management, network and security, numerical analysis, and scientific computer and theoretical computer science.

Penn State University Park

A full listing of CSE faculty and their areas of research is available at https://www.eecs.psu.edu/departments/cse-faculty-list.aspx.

Applying

Admission to the CSE department is extremely competitive. Applicants are expected to have a B.S. degree in computer science and engineering, computer engineering, computer science, or a closely related degree. Exceptional candidates from related fields are also welcomed to apply. Only well-prepared and highly competitive candidates should apply to enter the Ph.D. program directly from the B.S. program, because they will be required to take the candidacy examinations within one year after entry into the program.

Applicants are required to complete the University's application form. They must provide formal transcripts, letters of reference, and a personal statement of technical interests, goals, and experience.

For consideration as a teaching assistant, an international student whose first language is not English must submit a TOEFL score with a minimum of 80 and a Test of Spoken English (TSE) speaking score of 19 or more. It should be noted that students admitted to the graduate program who do not demonstrate satisfactory proficiency in English will be required to take additional English and/or Speech Communication courses.

Students who intend to continue from the M.S. into the Ph.D. program should apply to resume study at least one semester prior to the transition. An updated personal statement and a letter of reference from a professor should accompany that request. Standards for entry to the Ph.D. program are generally more rigorous than for the M.S. program. Satisfactory completion of the M.S. program does not guarantee admission to the Ph.D. program.

Additional information regarding the application process is available at https://www.eecs.psu.edu/students/graduate/EECS-How-to-apply-CSE .aspx.

Correspondence and Information

Jennifer Houser
School of Electrical Engineering and Computer Science
The Pennsylvania State University
W209K Westgate Building
University Park, Pennsylvania 16802
United States
Phone: 814-865-9505
Fax: 814-865-7647
E-mail: jjh2@psu.edu
Website: https://www.eecs.psu.edu/students/graduate/Graduate-Degree-
Programs-CSE.aspx

Section 9
Electrical and Computer Engineering

This section contains a directory of institutions offering graduate work in electrical and computer engineering, followed by in-depth entries submitted by institutions that chose to prepare detailed program descriptions. Additional information about programs listed in the directory but not augmented by an in-depth entry may be obtained by writing directly to the dean of a graduate school or chair of a department at the address given in the directory.

For programs offering related work, see also in this book *Computer Science and Information Technology, Energy and Power Engineering, Engineering and Applied Sciences, Industrial Engineering,* and *Mechanical Engineering and Mechanics.* In another guide in this series:

Graduate Programs in the Physical Sciences, Mathematics, Agricultural Sciences, the Environment & Natural Resources
See *Mathematical Sciences* and *Physics*

CONTENTS

Program Directories

Featured School: Display and Close-Up

See:

Computer Engineering

Air Force Institute of Technology, Graduate School of Engineering and Management, Department of Electrical and Computer Engineering, Dayton, OH 45433-7765. Offers computer engineering (MS, PhD); computer systems/science (MS); electrical engineering (MS, PhD); electro-optics (MS, PhD). *Accreditation:* ABET (one or more programs are accredited). *Program availability:* Part-time. *Degree requirements:* For master's, thesis; for doctorate, thesis/dissertation. *Entrance requirements:* For master's and doctorate, GRE General Test, minimum GPA of 3.0, U.S. citizenship.

American University of Sharjah, Graduate Programs, Sharjah, United Arab Emirates. Offers accounting (MS); biomedical engineering (MSBME); business administration (MBA); chemical engineering (MS Ch E); civil engineering (MSCE); computer engineering (MS); electrical engineering (MSEE); engineering systems management (MS, PhD); mathematics (MS); mechanical engineering (MSME); mechatronics engineering (MS); teaching English to speakers of other languages (MA); translation and interpreting (MA); urban planning (MUP). *Program availability:* Part-time, evening/weekend. *Degree requirements:* For master's, thesis (for some programs). *Entrance requirements:* For master's, GMAT (for MBA). Additional exam requirements/recommendations for international students: required—TOEFL (minimum score 550 paper-based; 80 iBT), TWE (minimum score 5); recommended—IELTS (minimum score 6.5). Electronic applications accepted.

Arizona State University at Tempe, Ira A. Fulton Schools of Engineering, School of Computing, Informatics, and Decision Systems Engineering, Tempe, AZ 85287-8809. Offers computer engineering (MS, PhD); computer science (MCS, MS, PhD); industrial engineering (MS, PhD); software engineering (MS). *Program availability:* Part-time, evening/weekend, online learning. Terminal master's awarded for partial completion of doctoral program. *Degree requirements:* For master's, comprehensive exam (for some programs), portfolio (MCS); interactive Program of Study (iPOS) submitted before completing 50 percent of required credit hours; for doctorate, comprehensive exam, thesis/dissertation, interactive Program of Study (iPOS) submitted before completing 50 percent of required credit hours. *Entrance requirements:* For master's, GRE, minimum GPA of 3.0 or equivalent in last 2 years of work leading to bachelor's degree; for doctorate, GRE, minimum GPA of 3.0 in last 2 years of work leading to bachelor's degree. Additional exam requirements/recommendations for international students: required—TOEFL, IELTS, or PTE. Electronic applications accepted. *Expenses:* Contact institution.

Atlantis University, School of Engineering, Miami, FL 33132. Offers computer engineering (MS).

Auburn University, Graduate School, Samuel Ginn College of Engineering, Department of Electrical and Computer Engineering, Auburn University, AL 36849. Offers MEE, MS, PhD. *Program availability:* Part-time. *Faculty:* 32 full-time (1 woman), 4 part-time/adjunct (1 woman). *Students:* 72 full-time (14 women), 40 part-time (4 women); includes 9 minority (3 Black or African American, non-Hispanic/Latino; 4 Asian, non-Hispanic/Latino; 2 Hispanic/Latino), 69 international. Average age 29. 126 applicants, 52% accepted, 25 enrolled. In 2019, 25 master's, 11 doctorates awarded. *Degree requirements:* For master's, comprehensive exam, thesis (for some programs); for doctorate, thesis/dissertation. *Entrance requirements:* For master's and doctorate, GRE General Test, GRE Subject Test. Additional exam requirements/recommendations for international students: required—TOEFL (minimum score 550 paper-based; 79 iBT). *Application deadline:* For fall admission, 3/31 priority date for domestic and international students; for spring admission, 9/30 priority date for domestic and international students. Applications are processed on a rolling basis. Application fee: $60 ($70 for international students). Electronic applications accepted. *Expenses: Tuition, area resident:* Full-time $9828; part-time $546 per credit hour. Tuition, state resident: full-time $9828; part-time $546 per credit hour. Tuition, nonresident: full-time $29,484; part-time $1638 per credit hour. *International tuition:* $29,744 full-time. Tuition and fees vary according to course load, program and reciprocity agreements. *Financial support:* In 2019–20, 12 fellowships (averaging $44,000 per year), 64 research assistantships (averaging $14,895 per year), 15 teaching assistantships (averaging $16,396 per year) were awarded; Federal Work-Study also available. Support available to part-time students. Financial award application deadline: 3/15; financial award applicants required to submit FAFSA. *Unit head:* Dr. Mark Nelms, Head, 334-844-1830, E-mail: nelmsrm@auburn.edu. *Application contact:* Dr. George Flowers, Dean of the Graduate School, 334-844-2125.
Website: http://www.eng.auburn.edu/ee/

Baylor University, Graduate School, School of Engineering and Computer Science, Department of Electrical and Computer Engineering, Waco, TX 76798. Offers MS, PhD. *Faculty:* 19 full-time (2 women). *Students:* 45 full-time (8 women), 3 part-time (0 women); includes 10 minority (1 Black or African American, non-Hispanic/Latino; 1 American Indian or Alaska Native, non-Hispanic/Latino; 3 Asian, non-Hispanic/Latino; 3 Hispanic/Latino; 2 Two or more races, non-Hispanic/Latino), 17 international. 48 applicants, 27% accepted, 6 enrolled. In 2019, 8 master's, 3 doctorates awarded. *Degree requirements:* For master's, thesis (for some programs); for doctorate, comprehensive exam, thesis/dissertation. *Entrance requirements:* For master's and doctorate, GRE. Additional exam requirements/recommendations for international students: required—TOEFL (minimum score 550 paper-based; 100 iBT). *Application deadline:* For fall admission, 2/15 for domestic and international students; for spring admission, 12/1 for domestic and international students. Applications are processed on a rolling basis. Application fee: $50. Electronic applications accepted. *Expenses:* Contact institution. *Financial support:* In 2019–20, 19 students received support, including 17 research assistantships with full tuition reimbursements available (averaging $18,750 per year), 19 teaching assistantships with full tuition reimbursements available (averaging $16,000 per year); fellowships, scholarships/grants, health care benefits, tuition waivers (full), and unspecified assistantships also available. Financial award application deadline: 4/15. *Unit head:* Dr. Kwang Y. Lee, Chair, 254-710-4817, Fax: 254-710-3010, E-mail: kwang_y_lee@baylor.edu. *Application contact:* Dr. Ian Gravagne, Electrical and Computer Engineering Graduate Director, 254-710-7303, Fax: 254-710-3010, E-mail: ian_gravagne@baylor.edu.
Website: http://www.ecs.baylor.edu/ece/

Baylor University, Graduate School, School of Engineering and Computer Science, Department of Engineering, Waco, TX 76798. Offers biomedical engineering (MSBME); electrical and computer engineering (MSECE, PhD); engineering (ME); mechanical engineering (MSME).

Boise State University, College of Engineering, Department of Electrical and Computer Engineering, Boise, ID 83725-0399. Offers M Engr, MS, PhD. *Program availability:* Part-time. *Students:* 38 full-time (9 women), 16 part-time (2 women); includes 5 minority (2 Asian, non-Hispanic/Latino; 2 Hispanic/Latino; 1 Two or more races, non-Hispanic/Latino), 33 international. Terminal master's awarded for partial completion of doctoral program. *Degree requirements:* For master's, comprehensive exam, thesis (for some programs); for doctorate, thesis/dissertation. *Entrance requirements:* For master's, GRE General Test, minimum GPA of 3.0. Additional exam requirements/recommendations for international students: required—TOEFL, IELTS. Electronic applications accepted. *Expenses: Tuition, area resident:* Full-time $7110; part-time $470 per credit hour. Tuition, state resident: full-time $7110; part-time $470 per credit hour. Tuition, nonresident: full-time $24,030; part-time $827 per credit hour. *International tuition:* $827 full-time. *Required fees:* $2536. Tuition and fees vary according to course load and program. *Financial support:* Research assistantships, scholarships/grants, and unspecified assistantships available. Financial award applicants required to submit FAFSA. *Unit head:* Dr. Browning Jim, Department Chair, 208-426-2470, E-mail: jimbrowning@boisestate.edu. *Application contact:* Hao Chen, Graduate Program Coordinator, 208-426-1020, E-mail: haochen@boisestate.edu.
Website: https://www.boisestate.edu/coen-ece/

Boston University, College of Engineering, Department of Electrical and Computer Engineering, Boston, MA 02215. Offers computer engineering (M Eng, MS, PhD). *Program availability:* Part-time. *Students:* 272 full-time (84 women), 68 part-time (13 women); includes 23 minority (2 Black or African American, non-Hispanic/Latino; 16 Asian, non-Hispanic/Latino; 2 Hispanic/Latino; 3 Two or more races, non-Hispanic/Latino), 258 international. Average age 24. 1,686 applicants, 32% accepted, 127 enrolled. In 2019, 118 master's, 12 doctorates awarded. Terminal master's awarded for partial completion of doctoral program. *Degree requirements:* For master's, thesis (for some programs); for doctorate, comprehensive exam, thesis/dissertation. *Entrance requirements:* For master's and doctorate, GRE General Test. Additional exam requirements/recommendations for international students: required—TOEFL (minimum score 90 iBT), IELTS (minimum score 7). Application fee: $95. Application fee is waived when completed online. *Financial support:* Application deadline: 1/15. *Unit head:* Dr. William C. Karl, Interim Chairman, 617-353-9880, Fax: 617-353-6440, E-mail: wckarl@bu.edu. *Application contact:* Dr. William C. Karl, Interim Chairman, 617-353-9880, Fax: 617-353-6440, E-mail: wckarl@bu.edu.
Website: http://www.bu.edu/ece/

Boston University, Metropolitan College, Department of Computer Science, Boston, MA 02215. Offers computer information systems (MS), including computer networks, data analytics, database management and business intelligence, health informatics, IT project management, security, Web application development; computer networks (Certificate); computer science (MS); data analytics (Certificate); digital forensics (Certificate); health informatics (Certificate); information technology project management (Certificate); software development (MS); software engineering in health care systems (Certificate); telecommunications (MS), including security. *Program availability:* Part-time, evening/weekend, online learning. *Faculty:* 16 full-time (3 women), 52 part-time/adjunct (5 women). *Students:* 253 full-time (80 women), 856 part-time (243 women); includes 246 minority (53 Black or African American, non-Hispanic/Latino; 1 American Indian or Alaska Native, non-Hispanic/Latino; 129 Asian, non-Hispanic/Latino; 48 Hispanic/Latino; 15 Two or more races, non-Hispanic/Latino), 418 international. Average age 30. 1,079 applicants, 72% accepted, 297 enrolled. In 2019, 513 master's awarded. *Entrance requirements:* For master's and Certificate, official transcripts from regionally-accredited bachelor's degree program, 3 letters of recommendation, professional resume, personal statement. Additional exam requirements/recommendations for international students: required—TOEFL (minimum score 84 iBT), IELTS. *Application deadline:* For fall admission, 8/1 priority date for domestic students, 6/1 priority date for international students; for spring admission, 12/1 priority date for domestic students, 11/15 priority date for international students; for summer admission, 4/1 priority date for domestic students, 3/1 priority date for international students. Applications are processed on a rolling basis. Application fee: $85. Electronic applications accepted. *Expenses:* Contact institution. *Financial support:* In 2019–20, 11 research assistantships (averaging $8,400 per year), 23 teaching assistantships (averaging $3,400 per year) were awarded; unspecified assistantships also available. Support available to part-time students. Financial award applicants required to submit FAFSA. *Unit head:* Dr. Anatoly Temkin, Chair, 617-353-2566, Fax: 617-353-2367, E-mail: csinfo@bu.edu. *Application contact:* Enrollment Services, 617-353-6004, E-mail: met@bu.edu.
Website: http://www.bu.edu/csmet/

Brigham Young University, Graduate Studies, Ira A. Fulton College of Engineering, Department of Electrical and Computer Engineering, Provo, UT 84602. Offers electrical & computer engineering (PhD). *Faculty:* 21 full-time (1 woman), 2 part-time/adjunct (1 woman). *Students:* 91 full-time (4 women); includes 5 minority (1 Asian, non-Hispanic/Latino; 4 Two or more races, non-Hispanic/Latino), 13 international. Average age 26. 59 applicants, 42% accepted, 25 enrolled. In 2019, 16 master's, 6 doctorates awarded. *Degree requirements:* For master's, thesis optional. *Entrance requirements:* For master's and doctorate, GRE General Test, Minimum GPA of 3.2 in last 60 hours of course work. Additional exam requirements/recommendations for international students: required—TOEFL (minimum score 580 paper-based; 85 iBT), IELTS (minimum score 7). *Application deadline:* For fall admission, 1/15 for domestic and international students; for winter admission, 8/15 for domestic and international students. Application fee: $50. Electronic applications accepted. *Financial support:* In 2019–20, 66 students received support, including 4 fellowships with full and partial tuition reimbursements available (averaging $21,240 per year), 71 research assistantships with full and partial tuition reimbursements available (averaging $15,600 per year), 13 teaching assistantships with full and partial tuition reimbursements available (averaging $17,028 per year); scholarships/grants also available. Financial award application deadline: 12/15; financial award applicants required to submit FAFSA. *Unit head:* Dr. Aaron Hawkins, Department Chair, 801-422-4012, Fax: 801-422-0201, E-mail: hawkins@ee.byu.edu. *Application contact:* Ashley Johansen, Graduate Secretary, 801-422-1160, Fax: 801-422-0201, E-mail: ashley_johansen@byu.edu.
Website: http://www.ee.byu.edu/

Brown University, Graduate School, School of Engineering, Program in Electrical Sciences and Computer Engineering, Providence, RI 02912. Offers Sc M, PhD. *Degree requirements:* For doctorate, thesis/dissertation, preliminary exam.

Bucknell University, Graduate Studies, College of Engineering, Department of Electrical and Computer Engineering, Lewisburg, PA 17837. Offers MSEE. *Program availability:* Part-time. *Degree requirements:* For master's, thesis. *Entrance requirements:* For master's, GRE General Test, minimum GPA of 3.0. Additional exam requirements/recommendations for international students: required—TOEFL (minimum score 600 paper-based).

California State University, Chico, Office of Graduate Studies, College of Engineering, Computer Science, and Construction Management, Electrical and Computer Engineering Department, Option in Computer Engineering, Chico, CA 95929-0722. Offers MS. *Degree requirements:* For master's, comprehensive exam, thesis or project plan. *Entrance requirements:* For master's, GRE General Test, Fall Admissions only. 2

letters of recommendation, statement of purpose, departmental letter of recommendation access waiver form. Additional exam requirements/recommendations for international students: required—TOEFL (minimum score 550 paper-based; 80 iBT), IELTS (minimum score 6.8), PTE (minimum score 59). Electronic applications accepted.

California State University, Fresno, Division of Research and Graduate Studies, Lyles College of Engineering, Department of Electrical and Computer Engineering, Fresno, CA 93740-8027. Offers computer engineering (MSE); electrical engineering (MSE). *Program availability:* Part-time, evening/weekend. *Degree requirements:* For master's, thesis or alternative. *Entrance requirements:* For master's, GRE General Test, minimum GPA of 2.7. Additional exam requirements/recommendations for international students: required—TOEFL. Electronic applications accepted. *Expenses:* Tuition, state resident: full-time $4012; part-time $2506 per semester.

California State University, Fullerton, Graduate Studies, College of Engineering and Computer Science, Program in Computer Engineering, Fullerton, CA 92831-3599. Offers MS.

California State University, Long Beach, Graduate Studies, College of Engineering, Department of Computer Engineering and Computer Science, Long Beach, CA 90840. Offers computer engineering (MSCS); computer science (MSCS). *Program availability:* Part-time. *Degree requirements:* For master's, thesis or alternative. *Entrance requirements:* Additional exam requirements/recommendations for international students: required—TOEFL. Electronic applications accepted.

Carnegie Mellon University, Carnegie Institute of Technology, Department of Electrical and Computer Engineering, Pittsburgh, PA 15213-3891. Offers MS, PhD. *Program availability:* Part-time. *Degree requirements:* For master's, thesis; for doctorate, thesis/dissertation, qualifying exam, teaching experience. *Entrance requirements:* For master's and doctorate, GRE General Test. Additional exam requirements/recommendations for international students: required—TOEFL.

Case Western Reserve University, School of Graduate Studies, Case School of Engineering, Department of Computer and Data Sciences, Cleveland, OH 44106. Offers computer engineering (MS, PhD); computing and information sciences (MS, PhD); electrical engineering (MS, PhD); systems and control engineering (MS, PhD). *Program availability:* Part-time, evening/weekend, online only, 100% online. Terminal master's awarded for partial completion of doctoral program. *Degree requirements:* For master's, thesis; for doctorate, thesis/dissertation, qualifying exam, teaching experience. *Entrance requirements:* For master's and doctorate, GRE General Test. Additional exam requirements/recommendations for international students: required—TOEFL.

The Citadel, The Military College of South Carolina, Citadel Graduate College, School of Engineering, Department of Electrical and Computer Engineering, Charleston, SC 29409. Offers computer engineering (Graduate Certificate); electrical engineering (MS). *Program availability:* Part-time, evening/weekend. *Degree requirements:* For master's, 30 hours of coursework with minimum GPA of 3.0 on hours earned at The Citadel. *Entrance requirements:* For master's, GRE, 2 letters of recommendation; official transcript of baccalaureate degree from an ABET accredited engineering program or approved alternative. Additional exam requirements/recommendations for international students: required—TOEFL (minimum score 550 paper-based; 79 iBT). Electronic applications accepted.

Clemson University, Graduate School, College of Engineering, Computing and Applied Sciences, Holcombe Department of Electrical and Computer Engineering, Clemson, SC 29634. Offers computer engineering (MS, PhD); electrical engineering (M Engr, MS, PhD). *Program availability:* Part-time, evening/weekend, 100% online, blended/hybrid learning. *Faculty:* 37 full-time (3 women). *Students:* 154 full-time (34 women), 26 part-time (4 women); includes 13 minority (5 Black or African American, non-Hispanic/Latino; 1 American Indian or Alaska Native, non-Hispanic/Latino; 4 Asian, non-Hispanic/Latino; 1 Hispanic/Latino; 2 Two or more races, non-Hispanic/Latino), 103 international. Average age 27. 348 applicants, 48% accepted, 60 enrolled. In 2019, 36 master's, 11 doctorates awarded. *Degree requirements:* For master's, comprehensive exam (for some programs), thesis (for some programs); for doctorate, comprehensive exam, thesis/dissertation, departmental qualifying exam. *Entrance requirements:* For master's and doctorate, GRE General Test, unofficial transcripts, letters of recommendation. Additional exam requirements/recommendations for international students: required—TOEFL (minimum score 80 paper-based; 95 iBT); recommended—IELTS (minimum score 7), TSE (minimum score 54). *Application deadline:* For fall admission, 1/15 priority date for domestic students, 4/15 for international students; for spring admission, 9/15 priority date for domestic students, 9/15 for international students. Applications are processed on a rolling basis. Application fee: $80 ($90 for international students). Electronic applications accepted. *Expenses:* Full-Time Student per Semester: Tuition: $5300 (in-state), $11025 (out-of-state), Fees: $598; Graduate Assistant Per Semester: $1144; Part-Time Student Per Credit Hour: $724 (in-state), $1451 (out-of-state), Fees: $617; other fees apply depending on program, credit hours, campus & residency. Doctoral Base Fee per Semester: $4938 (in-state), $10405 (out-of-state). *Financial support:* In 2019–20, 178 students received support, including 33 fellowships with full and partial tuition reimbursements available (averaging $7,853 per year), 91 research assistantships with full and partial tuition reimbursements available (averaging $22,951 per year), 41 teaching assistantships with full and partial tuition reimbursements available (averaging $16,328 per year); career-related internships or fieldwork and unspecified assistantships also available. Financial award application deadline: 1/15. *Unit head:* Dr. Hai Xiao, Interim Department Chair, 864-656-5912, E-mail: haix@clemson.edu. *Application contact:* Dr. Harlan Russell, Graduate Program Coordinator, 864-656-7214, E-mail: harlanr@clemson.edu.
Website: http://www.clemson.edu/cecas/departments/ece/index.html

Colorado Technical University Aurora, Program in Computer Engineering, Aurora, CO 80014. Offers MS.

Colorado Technical University Colorado Springs, Graduate Studies, Program in Computer Engineering, Colorado Springs, CO 80907. Offers MSCE. *Program availability:* Part-time, evening/weekend, online learning. *Degree requirements:* For master's, thesis or alternative.

Columbia University, Fu Foundation School of Engineering and Applied Science, Department of Electrical Engineering, New York, NY 10027. Offers computer engineering (MS); electrical engineering (MS, PhD). *Program availability:* Part-time, online learning. *Degree requirements:* For doctorate, thesis/dissertation, qualifying exam. *Entrance requirements:* For master's and doctorate, GRE General Test. Additional exam requirements/recommendations for international students: required—TOEFL, IELTS, PTE. Electronic applications accepted. *Expenses:* Tuition: Full-time $47,600; part-time $1880 per credit. One-time fee: $105.

Concordia University, School of Graduate Studies, Faculty of Engineering and Computer Science, Department of Electrical and Computer Engineering, Montréal, QC H3G 1M8, Canada. Offers M Eng, MA Sc, PhD. *Degree requirements:* For master's, thesis optional; for doctorate, comprehensive exam, thesis/dissertation.

Cornell University, Graduate School, Graduate Fields of Engineering, Field of Electrical and Computer Engineering, Ithaca, NY 14853. Offers computer engineering (M Eng, PhD); electrical engineering (M Eng, PhD); electrical systems (M Eng, PhD);

electrophysics (M Eng, PhD). *Degree requirements:* For doctorate, comprehensive exam, thesis/dissertation. *Entrance requirements:* For master's, GRE General Test, 2 letters of recommendation; for doctorate, GRE General Test, 3 letters of recommendation. Additional exam requirements/recommendations for international students: required—TOEFL (minimum score 600 paper-based; 77 iBT). Electronic applications accepted.

Dalhousie University, Faculty of Engineering, Department of Electrical and Computer Engineering, Halifax, NS B3J 1Z1, Canada. Offers M Eng, MA Sc, PhD. *Degree requirements:* For master's, thesis; for doctorate, thesis/dissertation. *Entrance requirements:* Additional exam requirements/recommendations for international students: required—TOEFL, IELTS, CANTEST, CAEL, or Michigan English Language Assessment Battery. Electronic applications accepted.

Dartmouth College, Dartmouth Engineering - Thayer School of Engineering, Program in Electrical Engineering, Hanover, NH 03755. Offers MS, PhD. Terminal master's awarded for partial completion of doctoral program. *Degree requirements:* For master's, thesis (for some programs); for doctorate, thesis/dissertation. *Entrance requirements:* For master's and doctorate, GRE General Test. Additional exam requirements/recommendations for international students: required—TOEFL, IELTS. *Application deadline:* For fall admission, 1/1 priority date for domestic students, 1/1 for international students. Applications are processed on a rolling basis. Application fee: $45. Electronic applications accepted. *Financial support:* Fellowships, research assistantships, teaching assistantships, career-related internships or fieldwork, institutionally sponsored loans, scholarships/grants, and tuition waivers (full and partial) available. Financial award application deadline: 2/15; financial award applicants required to submit CSS PROFILE. *Unit head:* Dr. George Cybenko, Dorothy and Walter Gramm Professor of Engineering, 603-646-3843, E-mail: george.cybenko@dartmouth.edu. *Application contact:* Candace S. Potter, Graduate Admissions & Financial Aid Administrator, 603-646-3844, Fax: 603-646-1620, E-mail: candace.s.potter@dartmouth.edu.
Website: http://engineering.dartmouth.edu/

Drexel University, College of Engineering, Department of Electrical and Computer Engineering, Program in Computer Engineering, Philadelphia, PA 19104-2875. Offers MS. *Program availability:* Part-time, evening/weekend. *Degree requirements:* For master's, thesis (for some programs). Electronic applications accepted.

Duke University, Graduate School, Pratt School of Engineering, Department of Electrical and Computer Engineering, Durham, NC 27708. Offers M Eng, MS, PhD, JD/MS. Terminal master's awarded for partial completion of doctoral program. *Degree requirements:* For doctorate, thesis/dissertation. *Entrance requirements:* For master's and doctorate, GRE General Test. Additional exam requirements/recommendations for international students: required—TOEFL (minimum score 90 iBT), IELTS (minimum score 7). Electronic applications accepted.

Duke University, Graduate School, Pratt School of Engineering, Master of Engineering Program, Durham, NC 27708-0271. Offers biomedical engineering (M Eng); civil engineering (M Eng); computational mechanics and scientific computing (M Eng); electrical and computer engineering (M Eng); environmental engineering (M Eng); materials science and engineering (M Eng); mechanical engineering (M Eng); photonics and optical sciences (M Eng); risk engineering (M Eng). *Program availability:* Part-time. *Entrance requirements:* For master's, GRE General Test, resume, 3 letters of recommendation, statement of purpose, transcripts. Additional exam requirements/recommendations for international students: required—TOEFL. Electronic applications accepted.

East Carolina University, Graduate School, College of Engineering and Technology, Greenville, NC 27858-4353. Offers MCM, MS, PhD, Certificate. *Program availability:* Part-time, evening/weekend, online learning. *Application deadline:* For fall admission, 6/1 priority date for domestic students. *Expenses:* Tuition, area resident: Full-time $4749; part-time $185 per credit hour. Tuition, state resident: full-time $4749; part-time $185 per credit hour. Tuition, nonresident: full-time $17,898; part-time $864 per credit hour. *International tuition:* $17,898 full-time. *Required fees:* $2787. *Financial support:* Application deadline: 6/1. *Unit head:* Dr. Harry Ploehn, Dean, 252-328-9600, E-mail: ploehnh17@ecu.edu. *Application contact:* Graduate School Admissions, 252-328-6012, Fax: 252-328-6071, E-mail: gradschool@ecu.edu.
Website: https://cet.ecu.edu/

Fairfield University, School of Engineering, Fairfield, CT 06824. Offers database management (CAS); electrical and computer engineering (MS); information security (CAS); management of technology (MS); mechanical engineering (MS); network technology (CAS); software engineering (MS); Web application development (CAS). *Program availability:* Part-time, evening/weekend. *Faculty:* 10 full-time (2 women), 15 part-time/adjunct (1 woman). *Students:* 46 full-time (24 women), 57 part-time (10 women); includes 23 minority (5 Black or African American, non-Hispanic/Latino; 9 Asian, non-Hispanic/Latino; 9 Hispanic/Latino), 33 international. Average age 29. 68 applicants, 62% accepted, 30 enrolled. In 2019, 100 master's awarded. *Degree requirements:* For master's, capstone course. *Entrance requirements:* For master's, resume, 2 recommendations. Additional exam requirements/recommendations for international students: required—TOEFL (minimum score 550 paper-based; 80 iBT), IELTS (minimum score 6.5), TOEFL (minimum score 550 paper-based; 80 iBT) or IELTS (minimum score 6.5). *Application deadline:* For fall admission, 5/15 for international students; for spring admission, 10/15 for international students. Applications are processed on a rolling basis. Application fee: $60. Electronic applications accepted. *Expenses:* Tuition $900/credit hour; Registration Fee $50/semester; Graduate Student Activity Fee (Fall and Spring) $65/semester. *Financial support:* In 2019–20, 20 students received support. Scholarships/grants and unspecified assistantships available. Financial award applicants required to submit FAFSA. *Unit head:* Richard Heist, Dean, 203-254-4147, Fax: 203-254-4013, E-mail: rheist@fairfield.edu. *Application contact:* Melanie Rogers, Director of Graduate Admission, 203-254-4184, Fax: 203-254-4073, E-mail: gradadmis@fairfield.edu.
Website: http://www.fairfield.edu/soe

Fairleigh Dickinson University, Metropolitan Campus, University College: Arts, Sciences, and Professional Studies, School of Computer Sciences and Engineering, Program in Computer Engineering, Teaneck, NJ 07666-1914. Offers MS.

Florida Atlantic University, College of Engineering and Computer Science, Department of Computer and Electrical Engineering and Computer Science, Boca Raton, FL 33431-0991. Offers bioengineering (MS); computer engineering (MS, PhD); computer science (MS, PhD); electrical engineering (MS, PhD). *Program availability:* Part-time, evening/weekend. *Faculty:* 39 full-time (8 women). *Students:* 112 full-time (26 women), 139 part-time (27 women); includes 104 minority (22 Black or African American, non-Hispanic/Latino; 22 Asian, non-Hispanic/Latino; 52 Hispanic/Latino; 8 Two or more races, non-Hispanic/Latino), 63 international. Average age 32. 231 applicants, 54% accepted, 91 enrolled. In 2019, 67 master's, 14 doctorates awarded. Terminal master's awarded for partial completion of doctoral program. *Degree requirements:* For master's, thesis optional; for doctorate, thesis/dissertation, qualifying exam. *Entrance requirements:* For master's, GRE General Test, minimum GPA of 3.0; for doctorate, GRE General Test, master's degree, minimum GPA of 3.5. Additional exam requirements/recommendations for international students: required—TOEFL

(minimum score 500 paper-based; 61 iBT), IELTS (minimum score 6). *Application deadline:* For fall admission, 7/1 priority date for domestic students, 2/15 for international students; for spring admission, 11/1 for domestic students, 7/15 for international students. Applications are processed on a rolling basis. Application fee: $30. *Expenses: Tuition:* Full-time $20,536; part-time $371.82 per credit hour. Tuition and fees vary according to program. *Financial support:* Fellowships, research assistantships with partial tuition reimbursements, teaching assistantships with full tuition reimbursements, career-related internships or fieldwork, and Federal Work-Study available. Support available to part-time students. Financial award application deadline: 4/1; financial award applicants required to submit FAFSA. *Unit head:* Jean Mangiaracina, Graduate Program Administrator, 561-297-6482, E-mail: jmangiar@fau.edu. *Application contact:* Jean Mangiaracina, Graduate Program Administrator, 561-297-6482, E-mail: jmangiar@fau.edu.
Website: http://www.ceecs.fau.edu/

Florida Institute of Technology, College of Engineering and Science, Program in Computer Engineering, Melbourne, FL 32901-6975. Offers MS, PhD. *Program availability:* Part-time. Terminal master's awarded for partial completion of doctoral program. *Degree requirements:* For master's, comprehensive exam (for some programs), thesis optional, thesis or final examination, 30 credit hours; for doctorate, thesis/dissertation, 24 credit hours of coursework, 24 credit hours of dissertation, yearly seminar demonstrating progress. *Entrance requirements:* For master's, GRE; for doctorate, GRE, 3 letters of recommendation, resume, statement of objectives. Additional exam requirements/recommendations for international students: required—TOEFL (minimum score 550 paper-based; 79 iBT). Electronic applications accepted.

Florida International University, College of Engineering and Computing, Department of Electrical and Computer Engineering, Miami, FL 33175. Offers computer engineering (MS); electrical engineering (MS, PhD). *Program availability:* Part-time, evening/weekend. *Faculty:* 34 full-time (2 women), 12 part-time/adjunct (2 women). *Students:* 162 full-time (27 women), 52 part-time (13 women); includes 81 minority (13 Black or African American, non-Hispanic/Latino; 7 Asian, non-Hispanic/Latino; 59 Hispanic/Latino; 2 Two or more races, non-Hispanic/Latino), 120 international. Average age 28. 213 applicants, 48% accepted, 66 enrolled. In 2019, 33 master's, 17 doctorates awarded. Terminal master's awarded for partial completion of doctoral program. *Degree requirements:* For master's, thesis optional; for doctorate, comprehensive exam, thesis/dissertation. *Entrance requirements:* For master's, minimum undergraduate GPA of 3.0 in upper-level coursework, resume, letters of recommendation, letter of intent; for doctorate, GRE General Test, minimum graduate GPA of 3.3, resume, letters of recommendation, letter of intent. Additional exam requirements/recommendations for international students: required—TOEFL (minimum score 550 paper-based; 80 iBT). *Application deadline:* For fall admission, 6/1 for domestic students, 4/1 for international students; for spring admission, 10/1 for domestic students, 9/1 for international students. Applications are processed on a rolling basis. Application fee: $30. Electronic applications accepted. *Expenses: Tuition, area resident:* Full-time $8912; part-time $446 per credit hour. Tuition, state resident: full-time $8912; part-time $446 per credit hour. Tuition, nonresident: full-time $21,393; part-time $992 per credit hour. *Required fees:* $2194. *Financial support:* Institutionally sponsored loans, scholarships/grants, and unspecified assistantships available. Financial award application deadline: 3/1; financial award applicants required to submit FAFSA. *Unit head:* Dr. Shekhar Bhansali, Chair, 305-348-4439, Fax: 305-348-3747, E-mail: sbhansa@fiu.edu. *Application contact:* Nanett Rojas, Manager, Admissions Operations, 305-348-7464, Fax: 305-348-7441, E-mail: gradadm@fiu.edu.
Website: http://cec.fiu.edu

George Mason University, Volgenau School of Engineering, Department of Electrical and Computer Engineering, Fairfax, VA 22030. Offers computer engineering (MS); electrical and computer engineering (PhD, Certificate). *Degree requirements:* For master's, thesis optional; for doctorate, comprehensive exam, thesis or scholarly paper. *Entrance requirements:* For master's, GRE, personal goals statement; 2 official copies of transcripts; self-evaluation form; 3 letters of recommendation; resume; official bank statement; photocopy of passport; proof of financial support; for doctorate, GRE (waived for GMU electrical and computer engineering master's graduates with minimum GPA of 3.0), personal goals statement; 2 official copies of transcripts; self-evaluation form; 3 letters of recommendation; resume; official bank statement; photocopy of passport; proof of financial support. Additional exam requirements/recommendations for international students: required—TOEFL (minimum score 575 paper-based; 88 iBT), IELTS (minimum score 6.5), PTE (minimum score 59). Electronic applications accepted. *Expenses:* Contact institution.

The George Washington University, School of Engineering and Applied Science, Department of Electrical and Computer Engineering, Washington, DC 20052. Offers electrical engineering (MS, PhD); telecommunication and computers (MS). *Program availability:* Part-time, evening/weekend. *Degree requirements:* For master's, thesis optional; for doctorate, comprehensive exam, thesis/dissertation, dissertation defense, qualifying exam. *Entrance requirements:* For master's, appropriate bachelor's degree, minimum GPA of 3.0; for doctorate, GRE (if highest earned degree is BS), appropriate bachelor's or master's degree, minimum GPA of 3.3; for other advanced degree, appropriate master's degree, minimum GPA of 3.0. Additional exam requirements/recommendations for international students: required—TOEFL or The George Washington University English as a Foreign Language Test.

Georgia Institute of Technology, Graduate Studies, College of Engineering, School of Electrical and Computer Engineering, Atlanta, GA 30332. Offers MS, PhD. *Program availability:* Part-time, 100% online. *Faculty:* 91 full-time (11 women), 1 part-time/adjunct (0 women). *Students:* 955 full-time (177 women), 198 part-time (34 women); includes 208 minority (22 Black or African American, non-Hispanic/Latino; 128 Asian, non-Hispanic/Latino; 43 Hispanic/Latino; 15 Two or more races, non-Hispanic/Latino), 706 international. Average age 26. 2,329 applicants, 31% accepted, 334 enrolled. In 2019, 349 master's, 84 doctorates awarded. Terminal master's awarded for partial completion of doctoral program. *Degree requirements:* For master's, thesis optional; for doctorate, comprehensive exam, thesis/dissertation. *Entrance requirements:* For master's and doctorate, GRE General Test, Three (3) Letters of Recommendation. Additional exam requirements/recommendations for international students: required—TOEFL (minimum score 577 paper-based; 90 iBT), IELTS (minimum score 7), TOEFL is the preferred method with the requirements shown on the programs. *Application deadline:* For fall admission, 12/16 for domestic students, 12/1 for international students. Applications are processed on a rolling basis. Application fee: $75 ($85 for international students). Electronic applications accepted. *Expenses: Tuition, area resident:* Full-time $14,064; part-time $586 per credit hour. Tuition, state resident: full-time $14,064; part-time $586 per credit hour. Tuition, nonresident: full-time $29,140; part-time $1215 per credit hour. *International tuition:* $29,140 full-time. *Required fees:* $2024; $840 per semester. $2096. Tuition and fees vary according to course load. *Financial support:* In 2019–20, 34 fellowships, 460 research assistantships, 143 teaching assistantships were awarded; career-related internships or fieldwork, Federal Work-Study, institutionally sponsored loans, tuition waivers (full and partial), and unspecified assistantships also available. Support available to part-time students. Financial award application deadline: 7/1; financial award applicants required to submit FAFSA. *Unit head:* Magnus Egerstedt, School Chair, 404-894-2901, Fax: 404-894-4641, E-mail: magnus.egerstedt@ece.gatech.edu. *Application contact:* Marla Bruner, Director of Graduate Studies, 404-894-1610, Fax: 404-894-1609, E-mail: gradinfo@mail.gatech.edu.
Website: http://www.ece.gatech.edu

Grand Valley State University, Padnos College of Engineering and Computing, School of Engineering, Allendale, MI 49401-9403. Offers electrical and computer engineering (MSE); mechanical engineering (MSE); product design and manufacturing engineering (MSE). *Program availability:* Part-time, evening/weekend. *Faculty:* 22 full-time (6 women), 1 part-time/adjunct (0 women). *Students:* 23 full-time (2 women), 35 part-time (5 women); includes 4 minority (2 Asian, non-Hispanic/Latino; 1 Hispanic/Latino; 1 Two or more races, non-Hispanic/Latino), 25 international. Average age 27. 46 applicants, 78% accepted, 10 enrolled. In 2019, 32 master's awarded. *Degree requirements:* For master's, capstone experience. *Entrance requirements:* For master's, engineering degree, minimum GPA of 3.0, resume, 3 confidential letters of recommendation, 1-2 page essay, base of underlying relevant knowledge/evidence from academic records or relevant wok experience. Additional exam requirements/recommendations for international students: required—Michigan English Language Assessment Battery (minimum score 77), TOEFL (minimum iBT score of 80), or IELTS (6.5); GRE. *Application deadline:* Applications are processed on a rolling basis. Application fee: $30. Electronic applications accepted. *Expenses:* $733 per credit hour, 33 credit hours. *Financial support:* In 2019–20, 40 students received support, including 8 fellowships, 34 research assistantships with full and partial tuition reimbursements available (averaging $4,000 per year); career-related internships or fieldwork, Federal Work-Study, institutionally sponsored loans, scholarships/grants, and unspecified assistantships also available. *Unit head:* Dr. Wael Mokhtar, Director, 616-331-6015, Fax: 616-331-7215, E-mail: mokhtarw@gvsu.edu. *Application contact:* Dr. Shabbir Choudhuri, Graduate Program Director, 616-331-6845, Fax: 616-331-7215, E-mail: choudhus@gvsu.edu.
Website: http://www.engineer.gvsu.edu/

Illinois Institute of Technology, Graduate College, Armour College of Engineering, Department of Electrical and Computer Engineering, Chicago, IL 60616. Offers biomedical imaging and signals (MAS); computer engineering (MS, PhD); electrical engineering (MS, PhD); electricity markets (MAS); network engineering (MAS); power engineering (MAS); telecommunications and software engineering (MAS); VLSI and microelectronics (MAS); MS/MS. *Program availability:* Part-time, evening/weekend, online learning. Terminal master's awarded for partial completion of doctoral program. *Degree requirements:* For master's, comprehensive exam (for some programs), thesis (for some programs); for doctorate, comprehensive exam, thesis/dissertation. *Entrance requirements:* For master's and doctorate, GRE General Test (minimum score 1100 Quantitative and Verbal, 3.5 Analytical Writing), minimum undergraduate GPA of 3.0. Additional exam requirements/recommendations for international students: required—TOEFL (minimum score 550 paper-based; 80 iBT); recommended—IELTS (minimum score 5.5). Electronic applications accepted.

Indiana State University, College of Graduate and Professional Studies, College of Technology, Department of Electronics and Computer Engineering Technology, Terre Haute, IN 47809. Offers electronics and computer technology (MS). *Degree requirements:* For master's, thesis or alternative. *Entrance requirements:* For master's, bachelor's degree in industrial technology or related field. Additional exam requirements/recommendations for international students: required—TOEFL. Electronic applications accepted.

Indiana University-Purdue University Indianapolis, School of Engineering and Technology, Department of Electrical and Computer Engineering, Indianapolis, IN 46202. Offers electrical and computer engineering (MS, PhD); engineering (MSE). *Degree requirements:* For master's, thesis optional; for doctorate, thesis/dissertation. *Entrance requirements:* For master's, GRE, minimum GPA of 3.0, three recommendation letters, statement of purpose/intent; for doctorate, GRE, minimum GPA of 3.0, three recommendation letters, statement of purpose/intent, curriculum vitae. Additional exam requirements/recommendations for international students: required—TOEFL; recommended—IELTS, TSE. Electronic applications accepted. *Expenses:* Contact institution.

Instituto Tecnológico y de Estudios Superiores de Monterrey, Campus Chihuahua, Graduate Programs, Chihuahua, Mexico. Offers computer systems engineering (Ingeniero); electrical engineering (Ingeniero); electromechanical engineering (Ingeniero); electronic engineering (Ingeniero); engineering administration (MEA); industrial engineering (MIE, Ingeniero); international trade (MIT); mechanical engineering (Ingeniero).

International Technological University, Program in Computer Engineering, San Jose, CA 95134. Offers MSCE. *Program availability:* Part-time, evening/weekend. *Degree requirements:* For master's, thesis or alternative, capstone project. *Entrance requirements:* Additional exam requirements/recommendations for international students: required—TOEFL, IELTS. Electronic applications accepted.

Iowa State University of Science and Technology, Department of Electrical and Computer Engineering, Ames, IA 50011. Offers computer engineering (M Eng, MS, PhD); electrical engineering (M Eng, MS, PhD). *Degree requirements:* For master's, thesis or alternative; for doctorate, thesis/dissertation. *Entrance requirements:* For master's and doctorate, GRE General Test. Additional exam requirements/recommendations for international students: required—TOEFL (minimum score 570 paper-based; 79 iBT), IELTS (minimum score 6.5). Electronic applications accepted.

Iowa State University of Science and Technology, Program in Computer Engineering, Ames, IA 50011. Offers M Eng, MS, PhD. *Entrance requirements:* For master's and doctorate, GRE. Additional exam requirements/recommendations for international students: required—TOEFL (minimum score 570 paper-based; 79 iBT), IELTS (minimum score 6.5). Electronic applications accepted.

Johns Hopkins University, Engineering Program for Professionals, Part-time Program in Electrical and Computer Engineering, Baltimore, MD 21218. Offers communications and networking (MS); electrical and computer engineering (Graduate Certificate, Post-Master's Certificate); photonics (MS). *Program availability:* Part-time, evening/weekend, 100% online, blended/hybrid learning. *Entrance requirements:* Additional exam requirements/recommendations for international students: required—TOEFL (minimum score 600 paper-based; 100 iBT). Electronic applications accepted.

Johns Hopkins University, G. W. C. Whiting School of Engineering, Department of Electrical and Computer Engineering, Baltimore, MD 21218. Offers MSE, PhD. Terminal master's awarded for partial completion of doctoral program. *Degree requirements:* For master's, thesis optional; for doctorate, thesis/dissertation, qualifying and oral exams, seminar. *Entrance requirements:* For master's and doctorate, GRE General Test, transcripts, 3 letters of recommendation, statement of purpose. Additional exam requirements/recommendations for international students: required—TOEFL (minimum score 600 paper-based, 100 iBT) or IELTS (7). Electronic applications accepted.

Kansas State University, Graduate School, College of Engineering, Department of Electrical and Computer Engineering, Manhattan, KS 66506. Offers electrical engineering (MS), including bioengineering, communication systems, design of computer systems, electrical engineering, energy and power systems, integrated circuits and devices, real time embedded systems, renewable energy, signal processing. *Program availability:* Part-time, evening/weekend, online learning. *Degree requirements:* For master's, thesis or alternative, final exam; for doctorate, thesis/dissertation, final exam, preliminary exams. *Entrance requirements:* For master's, GRE General Test, bachelor's degree in electrical engineering or computer science, minimum GPA of 3.0; for doctorate, GRE General Test. Additional exam requirements/recommendations for international students: required—TOEFL (minimum score 600 paper-based; 85 iBT). Electronic applications accepted.

Lakehead University, Graduate Studies, Faculty of Engineering, Thunder Bay, ON P7B 5E1, Canada. Offers control engineering (M Sc Engr); electrical/computer engineering (M Sc Engr); environmental engineering (M Sc Engr). *Program availability:* Part-time. *Degree requirements:* For master's, thesis. *Entrance requirements:* For master's, bachelor's degree in chemical, electrical or mechanical engineering, minimum B average. Additional exam requirements/recommendations for international students: required—TOEFL.

Lawrence Technological University, College of Engineering, Southfield, MI 48075-1058. Offers architectural engineering (MS); automotive engineering (MS); biomedical engineering (MS); civil engineering (MA, MS, PhD), including environmental engineering (MS), geotechnical engineering (MS), structural engineering (MS), transportation engineering (MS), water resource engineering (MS); construction engineering management (MA); electrical and computer engineering (MS); engineering management (MEM); engineering technology (MS); fire engineering (MS); industrial engineering (MS), including healthcare systems; manufacturing systems (ME); mechanical engineering (MS, DE, PhD), including automotive engineering (MS), energy engineering (MS), manufacturing (DE), solid mechanics (MS), thermal/fluid systems (MS); mechatronic systems engineering (MS). *Program availability:* Part-time, evening/weekend. *Faculty:* 23 full-time (2 women), 20 part-time/adjunct (1 woman). *Students:* 14 full-time (5 women), 286 part-time (54 women); includes 26 minority (13 Black or African American, non-Hispanic/Latino; 8 Asian, non-Hispanic/Latino; 3 Hispanic/Latino; 2 Two or more races, non-Hispanic/Latino), 150 international. Average age 29. 384 applicants, 58% accepted, 74 enrolled. In 2019, 223 master's, 7 doctorates awarded. Terminal master's awarded for partial completion of doctoral program. *Degree requirements:* For master's, thesis optional; for doctorate, comprehensive exam, thesis/dissertation optional. *Entrance requirements:* Additional exam requirements/recommendations for international students: required—TOEFL (minimum score 550 paper-based; 79 iBT), IELTS (minimum score 6.5). *Application deadline:* For fall admission, 5/24 for international students; for spring admission, 10/13 for international students; for summer admission, 2/18 for international students. Applications are processed on a rolling basis. Application fee: $50. Electronic applications accepted. *Expenses: Tuition:* Full-time $16,618; part-time $8309 per year. *Required fees:* $600; $600. *Financial support:* In 2019–20, 21 students received support. Unspecified assistantships available. Financial award application deadline: 4/1; financial award applicants required to submit FAFSA. *Unit head:* Dr. Nabil Grace, Dean, 248-204-2500, Fax: 248-204-2509, E-mail: engrdean@ltu.edu. *Application contact:* Jane Rohrback, Director of Admissions, 248-204-3160, Fax: 248-204-2228, E-mail: admissions@ltu.edu. Website: http://www.ltu.edu/engineering/index.asp

Lehigh University, P.C. Rossin College of Engineering and Applied Science, Department of Computer Science and Engineering, Bethlehem, PA 18015. Offers computer engineering (M Eng, MS, PhD); computer science (M Eng, MS, PhD); MBA/E. *Program availability:* Part-time. *Faculty:* 16 full-time (2 women), 2 part-time/adjunct (1 woman). *Students:* 63 full-time (18 women), 2 part-time (0 women); includes 3 minority (1 Black or African American, non-Hispanic/Latino; 1 Asian, non-Hispanic/Latino; 1 Hispanic/Latino), 47 international. Average age 26. 282 applicants, 32% accepted, 25 enrolled. In 2019, 21 master's, 6 doctorates awarded. Terminal master's awarded for partial completion of doctoral program. *Degree requirements:* For master's, thesis optional, oral presentation of thesis; for doctorate, thesis/dissertation, qualifying, general, and oral exams. *Entrance requirements:* For master's, GRE General Test, minimum GPA of 3.0; for doctorate, GRE General Test, minimum GPA of 3.5. Additional exam requirements/recommendations for international students: required—TOEFL (minimum score 550 paper-based; 79 iBT), IELTS (minimum score 6.5). *Application deadline:* For fall admission, 4/1 for domestic and international students; for spring admission, 11/1 for domestic and international students. Application fee: $75. Electronic applications accepted. *Expenses:* 1500/credit hour. *Financial support:* In 2019–20, 14 students received support, including 2 fellowships with full tuition reimbursements available (averaging $23,025 per year), 6 research assistantships with full tuition reimbursements available (averaging $22,050 per year), 6 teaching assistantships with full tuition reimbursements available (averaging $22,050 per year). Financial award application deadline: 1/15. *Unit head:* Jeffrey C Trinkle, Chair, 610-758-4124, E-mail: jct519@lehigh.edu. *Application contact:* Heidi Wegrzyn, Graduate Coordinator, 610-758-3065, E-mail: hew207@lehigh.edu. Website: http://www.cse.lehigh.edu/

Lehigh University, P.C. Rossin College of Engineering and Applied Science, Department of Electrical and Computer Engineering, Bethlehem, PA 18015. Offers electrical engineering (M Eng, MS, PhD); photonics (MS). *Program availability:* Part-time. *Faculty:* 15 full-time (4 women). *Students:* 66 full-time (6 women), 3 part-time (0 women); includes 1 minority (Black or African American, non-Hispanic/Latino), 61 international. Average age 26. 264 applicants, 13% accepted, 16 enrolled. In 2019, 18 master's, 8 doctorates awarded. Terminal master's awarded for partial completion of doctoral program. *Degree requirements:* For master's, thesis optional; for doctorate, thesis/dissertation, qualifying or comprehensive exam for all 1st year PhD's; general exam 7 months or more prior to completion/dissertation defense. *Entrance requirements:* For master's and doctorate, GRE General Test, BS in field or related field. Additional exam requirements/recommendations for international students: required—TOEFL (minimum score 79 iBT), IELTS (minimum score 6.5), TOEFL or IELTS. *Application deadline:* For fall admission, 4/1 for domestic and international students; for spring admission, 11/1 for domestic and international students. Application fee: $75. Electronic applications accepted. *Financial support:* In 2019–20, 48 students received support, including 8 fellowships with full tuition reimbursements available (averaging $29,400 per year), 32 research assistantships with full tuition reimbursements available (averaging $29,400 per year), 8 teaching assistantships with full tuition reimbursements available (averaging $29,400 per year). Financial award application deadline: 1/15. *Unit head:* Dr. Chengshan Xiao, Chair, 610-758-4069, Fax: 610-758-6279, E-mail: chx417@lehigh.edu. *Application contact:* Ruby Scott, Graduate Coordinator, 610-758-4070, Fax: 610-758-6279, E-mail: rls304@lehigh.edu. Website: http://www.ece.lehigh.edu/

Louisiana State University and Agricultural & Mechanical College, Graduate School, College of Engineering, Division of Electrical and Computer Engineering, Baton Rouge, LA 70803. Offers MSEE, PhD.

Manhattan College, Graduate Programs, School of Engineering, Program in Computer Engineering, Riverdale, NY 10471. Offers MS. *Program availability:* Part-time, evening/weekend. *Degree requirements:* For master's, thesis or alternative. *Entrance requirements:* For master's, GRE (recommended), minimum GPA of 3.0. Additional

exam requirements/recommendations for international students: required—TOEFL (minimum score 550 paper-based; 80 iBT), IELTS (minimum score 6).

Marquette University, Graduate School, College of Engineering, Department of Electrical and Computer Engineering, Milwaukee, WI 53201-1881. Offers digital signal processing (Certificate); electric machines, drives, and controls (Certificate); electrical and computer engineering (MS, PhD); microwaves and antennas (Certificate); sensors and smart systems (Certificate). *Program availability:* Part-time, evening/weekend. Terminal master's awarded for partial completion of doctoral program. *Degree requirements:* For master's, comprehensive exam (for some programs), thesis optional; for doctorate, thesis/dissertation, dissertation defense, qualifying exam. *Entrance requirements:* For master's, GRE General Test (recommended), official transcripts from all current and previous colleges/universities except Marquette, three letters of recommendation; for doctorate, GRE General Test, minimum GPA of 3.0, official transcripts from all current and previous colleges/universities except Marquette, three letters of recommendation, statement of purpose, submission of any English language publications authored by applicant (strongly recommended). Additional exam requirements/recommendations for international students: required—TOEFL (minimum score 530 paper-based). Electronic applications accepted.

Marshall University, Academic Affairs Division, College of Information Technology and Engineering, Program in Electrical and Computer Engineering, Huntington, WV 25755. Offers MSEE.

Massachusetts Institute of Technology, School of Engineering, Department of Electrical Engineering and Computer Science, Cambridge, MA 02139. Offers computer science (PhD, Sc D, ECS); computer science and engineering (PhD, Sc D); computer science and molecular biology (M Eng); electrical engineering (PhD, Sc D, EE); electrical engineering and computer science (M Eng, SM, PhD, Sc D); SM/MBA. *Degree requirements:* For master's and other advanced degree, thesis; for doctorate, comprehensive exam, thesis/dissertation. *Entrance requirements:* Additional exam requirements/recommendations for international students: required—TOEFL, IELTS. Electronic applications accepted.

McGill University, Faculty of Graduate and Postdoctoral Studies, Faculty of Engineering, Department of Electrical and Computer Engineering, Montréal, QC H3A 2T5, Canada. Offers M Eng, PhD.

Memorial University of Newfoundland, School of Graduate Studies, Faculty of Engineering and Applied Science, St. John's, NL A1C 5S7, Canada. Offers civil engineering (M Eng, PhD); electrical and computer engineering (M Eng, PhD); mechanical engineering (M Eng, PhD); ocean and naval architecture engineering (M Eng, PhD). *Program availability:* Part-time. *Degree requirements:* For master's, thesis; for doctorate, comprehensive exam, thesis/dissertation, oral thesis defense. *Entrance requirements:* For master's, 2nd class degree; for doctorate, master's degree in engineering. Electronic applications accepted.

Memorial University of Newfoundland, School of Graduate Studies, Interdisciplinary Program in Computer Engineering, St. John's, NL A1C 5S7, Canada. Offers MA Sc. *Degree requirements:* For master's, project course. *Entrance requirements:* For master's, 2nd class engineering degree. Electronic applications accepted. *Expenses:* Contact institution.

Mercer University, Graduate Studies, Macon Campus, School of Engineering, Macon, GA 31207. Offers biomedical engineering (MSE); computer engineering (MSE); electrical engineering (MSE); engineering management (MSE); environmental engineering (MSE); environmental systems (MS); mechanical engineering (MSE); software engineering (MSE); software systems (MS); technical communications management (MS); technical management (MS). *Program availability:* Part-time-only, evening/weekend, online learning. *Faculty:* 27 full-time (9 women), 2 part-time/adjunct (0 women). *Students:* 38 full-time (10 women), 51 part-time (20 women); includes 22 minority (5 Black or African American, non-Hispanic/Latino; 11 Asian, non-Hispanic/Latino; 4 Hispanic/Latino; 2 Two or more races, non-Hispanic/Latino), 2 international. Average age 26. In 2019, 70 master's awarded. *Degree requirements:* For master's, thesis or alternative. *Entrance requirements:* For master's, GRE (minimum score 300), minimum undergraduate GPA of 3.0. Additional exam requirements/recommendations for international students: required—TOEFL (minimum score 550 paper-based; 80 iBT). *Application deadline:* For fall admission, 4/1 priority date for domestic and international students; for spring admission, 11/1 priority date for domestic and international students. Applications are processed on a rolling basis. Application fee: $75. *Expenses:* Tuition: $938.00 ($700.00 for Technical Communication Management program) per credit hour; Facility and Technology Fee: $17.00 per credit hour. *Financial support:* Federal Work-Study available. Financial award applicants required to submit FAFSA. *Unit head:* Dr. Laura W. Lackey, Dean, 478-301-4106, Fax: 478-301-5593, E-mail: lackey_l@mercer.edu. *Application contact:* Dr. Sinjae Hyun, Program Director, 478-301-2214, Fax: 478-301-5593, E-mail: hyun_s@mercer.edu. Website: http://engineering.mercer.edu/

Miami University, College of Engineering and Computing, Department of Electrical and Computer Engineering, Oxford, OH 45056. Offers MS.

Michigan Technological University, Graduate School, College of Engineering, Department of Electrical and Computer Engineering, Houghton, MI 49931. Offers advanced electric power engineering (Graduate Certificate); electrical engineering (PhD). *Program availability:* Part-time, evening/weekend, 100% online, blended/hybrid learning. *Faculty:* 40 full-time, 7 part-time/adjunct. *Students:* 102 full-time (22 women), 33 part-time; includes 3 minority (1 Black or African American, non-Hispanic/Latino; 2 Asian, non-Hispanic/Latino), 90 international. Average age 28. 567 applicants, 38% accepted, 50 enrolled. In 2019, 71 master's, 15 doctorates, 20 other advanced degrees awarded. Terminal master's awarded for partial completion of doctoral program. *Degree requirements:* For master's, comprehensive exam (for some programs), thesis (for some programs); for doctorate, comprehensive exam, thesis/dissertation. *Entrance requirements:* For master's, statement of purpose, personal statement, official transcripts, 2 letters of recommendation; for doctorate, GRE, statement of purpose, personal statement, official transcripts, 2 letters of recommendation; for Graduate Certificate, statement of purpose, personal statement, official transcripts. Additional exam requirements/recommendations for international students: required—TOEFL (minimum score 79 iBT), IELTS (minimum score 6.5). *Application deadline:* For fall admission, 2/15 priority date for domestic and international students; for spring admission, 8/15 priority date for domestic and international students. Applications are processed on a rolling basis. Application fee: $0. Electronic applications accepted. *Expenses:* $1,212 per credit. *Financial support:* In 2019–20, 88 students received support, including 7 fellowships with tuition reimbursements available (averaging $16,590 per year), 15 research assistantships with tuition reimbursements available (averaging $16,590 per year), 19 teaching assistantships with tuition reimbursements available (averaging $16,590 per year); career-related internships or fieldwork, Federal Work-Study, scholarships/grants, health care benefits, unspecified assistantships, and cooperative program also available. Financial award application deadline: 2/15; financial award applicants required to submit FAFSA. *Unit head:* Dr. Glen E. Archer, Interim Chair and Principal Lecturer, 906-487-2550, Fax: 906-487-2949, E-mail: gearcher@mtu.edu. *Application contact:* Alexandra Holmstrom, Graduate Program Coordinator, 906-487-

1995, Fax: 906-487-2949, E-mail: aholmstr@mtu.edu.
Website: http://www.mtu.edu/ece/

Michigan Technological University, Graduate School, Interdisciplinary Programs, Houghton, MI 49931. Offers automotive systems and controls (Graduate Certificate); biochemistry and molecular biology (PhD); computational science and engineering (PhD); data science (Graduate Certificate); sustainability (Graduate Certificate). *Program availability:* Part-time. *Faculty:* 132 full-time, 6 part-time/adjunct. *Students:* 57 full-time (20 women), 19 part-time; includes 7 minority (3 Black or African American, non-Hispanic/Latino; 1 American Indian or Alaska Native, non-Hispanic/Latino; 1 Asian, non-Hispanic/Latino; 2 Two or more races, non-Hispanic/Latino), 42 international. Average age 30. 475 applicants, 29% accepted, 25 enrolled. In 2019, 23 master's, 10 doctorates, 36 other advanced degrees awarded. Terminal master's awarded for partial completion of doctoral program. *Degree requirements:* For master's, comprehensive exam (for some programs), thesis (for some programs); for doctorate, comprehensive exam, thesis/dissertation. *Entrance requirements:* For master's, doctorate, and Graduate Certificate, GRE, statement of purpose, personal statement, official transcripts, 2-3 letters of recommendation. Additional exam requirements/recommendations for international students: required—TOEFL or IELTS. *Application deadline:* Applications are processed on a rolling basis. Application fee: $0. Electronic applications accepted. *Expenses: Tuition, area resident:* Full-time $19,206; part-time $1067 per credit. Tuition, state resident: full-time $19,206; part-time $1067 per credit. Tuition, nonresident: full-time $19,206; part-time $1067 per credit. *International tuition:* $19,206 full-time. *Required fees:* $248; $248 per unit. $124 per semester. Tuition and fees vary according to course load and program. *Financial support:* In 2019–20, 54 students received support, including 9 fellowships with tuition reimbursements available (averaging $16,590 per year), 14 research assistantships with tuition reimbursements available (averaging $16,590 per year), 10 teaching assistantships with tuition reimbursements available (averaging $16,590 per year); career-related internships or fieldwork, Federal Work-Study, scholarships/grants, health care benefits, unspecified assistantships, and cooperative program also available. Financial award applicants required to submit FAFSA. *Unit head:* Dr. Will H Cantrell, Dean of the Graduate School, 906-487-3007, Fax: 906-487-2284, E-mail: cantrell@mtu.edu. *Application contact:* Ashli Wells, Assistant Director of Graduate Enrollment Services, 906-487-3513, Fax: 906-487-2284, E-mail: aesniego@mtu.edu.

Mississippi State University, Bagley College of Engineering, Department of Electrical and Computer Engineering, Mississippi State, MS 39762. Offers MS, PhD. *Program availability:* Part-time, blended/hybrid learning. *Faculty:* 15 full-time (2 women), 1 part-time/adjunct (0 women). *Students:* 56 full-time (10 women), 54 part-time (7 women); includes 10 minority (3 Black or African American, non-Hispanic/Latino; 4 Asian, non-Hispanic/Latino; 3 Hispanic/Latino), 47 international. Average age 32. 92 applicants, 68% accepted, 19 enrolled. In 2019, 8 master's, 7 doctorates awarded. Terminal master's awarded for partial completion of doctoral program. *Degree requirements:* For master's, comprehensive exam, thesis optional; for doctorate, comprehensive exam, thesis/dissertation, written exam, oral preliminary exam. *Entrance requirements:* For master's, GRE (for graduates from program not accredited by EAC/ABET), minimum GPA of 3.0 on BS; for doctorate, GRE (for graduates from program not accredited by EAC/ABET), minimum GPA of 3.5 on BS or MS. Additional exam requirements/recommendations for international students: required—TOEFL (minimum score 550 paper-based; 79 iBT); recommended—IELTS (minimum score 6.5). *Application deadline:* For fall admission, 7/1 for domestic students, 5/1 for international students; for spring admission, 11/1 for domestic students, 9/1 for international students. Applications are processed on a rolling basis. Application fee: $60 ($80 for international students). Electronic applications accepted. *Expenses: Tuition, area resident:* Full-time $8880; part-time $456 per credit hour. Tuition, state resident: full-time $8880. Tuition, nonresident: full-time $23,840; part-time $1236 per credit hour. *Required fees:* $110; $11.12 per credit hour. Tuition and fees vary according to course load. *Financial support:* In 2019–20, 17 research assistantships with full tuition reimbursements (averaging $17,722 per year), 23 teaching assistantships with full tuition reimbursements (averaging $16,748 per year) were awarded; Federal Work-Study, institutionally sponsored loans, scholarships/grants, and unspecified assistantships also available. Financial award application deadline: 4/1; financial award applicants required to submit FAFSA. *Unit head:* Dr. James E. Fowler, Jr., Professor/Interim Department Head, 662-325-3912, Fax: 662-325-2298, E-mail: ece-head@ece.msstate.edu. *Application contact:* Angie Campbell, Admissions and Enrollment Assistant, 662-325-9514, E-mail: acampbell@grad.msstate.edu.
Website: http://www.ece.msstate.edu/

Missouri University of Science and Technology, Department of Electrical and Computer Engineering, Rolla, MO 65401. Offers computer engineering (MS, DE, PhD); electrical engineering (MS, DE, PhD). *Program availability:* Part-time, evening/weekend. Terminal master's awarded for partial completion of doctoral program. *Degree requirements:* For master's, thesis optional; for doctorate, comprehensive exam, thesis/dissertation, departmental qualifying exam. *Entrance requirements:* For master's, GRE General Test (minimum score 1100 verbal and quantitative, writing 4.5); for doctorate, GRE General Test (minimum score: verbal and quantitative 1100, writing 3.5). Additional exam requirements/recommendations for international students: required—TOEFL (minimum score 550 paper-based). Electronic applications accepted. *Expenses:* Tuition, state resident: full-time $7839; part-time $435.50 per credit hour. Tuition, nonresident: full-time $22,169; part-time $1231.60 per credit hour. *International tuition:* $18,156.60 full-time. *Required fees:* $649.76. One-time fee: $119. Tuition and fees vary according to course load and program.

Montana State University, The Graduate School, College of Engineering, Department of Electrical and Computer Engineering, Bozeman, MT 59717. Offers electrical engineering (MS); engineering (PhD), including electrical and computer engineering option. *Program availability:* Part-time. *Degree requirements:* For master's, comprehensive exam, thesis (for some programs); for doctorate, comprehensive exam, thesis/dissertation. *Entrance requirements:* For master's, GRE, BS in electrical or computer engineering or related field; for doctorate, GRE, MS in electrical or computer engineering or related field. Additional exam requirements/recommendations for international students: required—TOEFL (minimum score 550 paper-based). Electronic applications accepted.

Naval Postgraduate School, Departments and Academic Groups, Department of Electrical and Computer Engineering, Monterey, CA 93943-5216. Offers computer engineering (MS); electrical engineer (EE); electrical engineering (PhD); engineering acoustics (MS); engineering science (MS). *Program availability:* Part-time, online learning. *Degree requirements:* For master's and EE, thesis (for some programs), capstone project or research/dissertation paper (for some programs); for doctorate, thesis/dissertation.

New Jersey Institute of Technology, Newark College of Engineering, Newark, NJ 07102. Offers biomedical engineering (MS, PhD); biopharmaceutical engineering (MS); chemical engineering (MS, PhD); civil engineering (MS, PhD); computer engineering (MS); critical infrastructure systems (MS); electrical engineering (MS, PhD); engineering management (MS); engineering science (MS); environmental engineering (MS, PhD); healthcare systems management (MS); industrial engineering (MS, PhD); internet engineering (MS); manufacturing systems engineering (MS); materials science & engineering (PhD); materials science and engineering (MS); mechanical engineering (MS, PhD); occupational safety and health engineering (MS). *Program availability:* Part-time, evening/weekend. *Faculty:* 151 full-time (29 women), 135 part-time/adjunct (15 women). *Students:* 576 full-time (161 women), 528 part-time (111 women); includes 366 minority (61 Black or African American, non-Hispanic/Latino; 1 American Indian or Alaska Native, non-Hispanic/Latino; 166 Asian, non-Hispanic/Latino; 115 Hispanic/Latino; 23 Two or more races, non-Hispanic/Latino), 450 international. Average age 28. 2,053 applicants, 67% accepted, 338 enrolled. In 2019, 474 master's, 30 doctorates awarded. Terminal master's awarded for partial completion of doctoral program. *Degree requirements:* For master's, thesis (for some programs); for doctorate, thesis/dissertation. *Entrance requirements:* For master's, GRE General Test, minimum GPA 2.8, personal statement, 1 letter of recommendation, transcripts; for doctorate, GRE General Test, minimum GPA of 3.5, personal statement, 3 letters of recommendation, transcripts. Additional exam requirements/recommendations for international students: required—TOEFL (minimum score 550 paper-based; 79 iBT), IELTS (minimum score 6.5). *Application deadline:* For fall admission, 6/1 priority date for domestic students, 5/1 priority date for international students; for spring admission, 11/15 priority date for domestic and international students. Applications are processed on a rolling basis. Application fee: $75. Electronic applications accepted. *Expenses:* $23,828 per year (in-state), $33,744 per year (out-of-state). *Financial support:* In 2019–20, 352 students received support, including 33 fellowships with full tuition reimbursements available (averaging $24,000 per year), 89 research assistantships with full tuition reimbursements available (averaging $24,000 per year), 112 teaching assistantships with full tuition reimbursements available (averaging $24,000 per year); career-related internships or fieldwork, Federal Work-Study, scholarships/grants, and unspecified assistantships also available. Financial award application deadline: 1/15. *Unit head:* Dr. Moshe Kam, Dean, 973-596-5534, Fax: 973-596-2316, E-mail: moshe.kam@njit.edu. *Application contact:* Stephen Eck, Executive Director of University Admissions, 973-596-3300, Fax: 973-596-3461, E-mail: admissions@njit.edu.
Website: http://engineering.njit.edu/

New York Institute of Technology, College of Engineering and Computing Sciences, Department of Electrical and Computer Engineering, Old Westbury, NY 11568. Offers MS. *Program availability:* Part-time. *Faculty:* 17 full-time (4 women), 9 part-time/adjunct (1 woman). *Students:* 46 full-time (10 women), 38 part-time (12 women); includes 27 minority (5 Black or African American, non-Hispanic/Latino; 17 Asian, non-Hispanic/Latino; 5 Hispanic/Latino), 41 international. Average age 26. 273 applicants, 47% accepted, 26 enrolled. In 2019, 46 master's awarded. *Degree requirements:* For master's, thesis or alternative. *Entrance requirements:* For master's, Graduates of foreign universities are required to take the GRE and submit their scores. Applicants with a GPA below 2.85 may, at the discretion of the dean, be asked to take the GRE or other diagnostic tests, For Bioengineering - bachelor's degree or its equivalent in computer science, life sciences, electrical engineering, physics, or related areas; for Electrical and Computer Engineering - bachelor's degree or equivalent in electrical or computer engineering or a closely related field with appropriate undergraduate courses; minimum undergraduate GPA o. Additional exam requirements/recommendations for international students: required—TOEFL (minimum score 79 iBT), IELTS (minimum score 6), PTE (minimum score 53), Duolingo English Test. *Application deadline:* For fall admission, 7/1 for domestic students, 6/1 for international students; for spring admission, 12/1 for domestic and international students. Applications are processed on a rolling basis. Application fee: $50. Electronic applications accepted. *Expenses: Tuition:* Full-time $23,760; part-time $1320 per credit. *Required fees:* $260; $220 per unit. Full-time tuition and fees vary according to degree level and program. Part-time tuition and fees vary according to course load and program. *Financial support:* In 2019–20, 46 students received support. Fellowships, research assistantships, teaching assistantships, Federal Work-Study, scholarships/grants, and unspecified assistantships available. Support available to part-time students. Financial award application deadline: 2/15; financial award applicants required to submit FAFSA. *Unit head:* Dr. Aydin Farajidavar, Department Chairperson, 516-686-4014, Fax: 516-686-7439, E-mail: afarajid@nyit.edu. *Application contact:* Alice Dolitsky, Director, Graduate Admissions, 800-345-6948, Fax: 516-686-1116, E-mail: admissions@nyit.edu.
Website: https://www.nyit.edu/departments/electrical_and_computer_engineering

New York University, Tandon School of Engineering, Department of Electrical and Computer Engineering, Major in Computer Engineering, New York, NY 10012-1019. Offers computer engineering (MS). *Program availability:* Online learning. *Degree requirements:* For master's, comprehensive exam (for some programs), thesis (for some programs). *Entrance requirements:* For master's, BS in electrical engineering. Additional exam requirements/recommendations for international students: required—TOEFL (minimum score 550 paper-based; 90 iBT); recommended—IELTS (minimum score 7). Electronic applications accepted.

Norfolk State University, School of Graduate Studies, School of Science and Technology, Program in Electronics Engineering, Norfolk, VA 23504. Offers MS.

North Carolina Agricultural and Technical State University, The Graduate College, College of Engineering, Department of Electrical and Computer Engineering, Greensboro, NC 27411. Offers electrical engineering (MSEE, PhD), including communications and signal processing, computer engineering, electronic and optical materials and devices, power systems and control. *Program availability:* Part-time. *Degree requirements:* For master's, project, thesis defense; for doctorate, thesis/dissertation. *Entrance requirements:* For master's, GRE General Test, GRE Subject Test, minimum GPA of 2.8; for doctorate, GRE General Test, minimum GPA of 3.0.

North Carolina State University, Graduate School, College of Engineering, Department of Electrical and Computer Engineering, Program in Computer Engineering, Raleigh, NC 27695. Offers MS, PhD. *Degree requirements:* For master's, thesis (for some programs); for doctorate, thesis/dissertation. *Entrance requirements:* For master's and doctorate, GRE. Additional exam requirements/recommendations for international students: required—TOEFL (minimum score 575 paper-based). Electronic applications accepted.

North Dakota State University, College of Graduate and Interdisciplinary Studies, College of Engineering, Department of Electrical and Computer Engineering, Fargo, ND 58102. Offers M Eng, MS, PhD. *Program availability:* Part-time. Terminal master's awarded for partial completion of doctoral program. *Degree requirements:* For master's, comprehensive exam, thesis; for doctorate, comprehensive exam, thesis/dissertation. *Entrance requirements:* Additional exam requirements/recommendations for international students: required—TOEFL (minimum score 525 paper-based; 71 iBT). Electronic applications accepted. Tuition and fees vary according to program and reciprocity agreements.

Northeastern University, College of Engineering, Boston, MA 02115-5096. Offers bioengineering (MS, PhD); chemical engineering (MS, PhD); civil engineering (MS, PhD); computer engineering (PhD); computer systems engineering (MS); electrical and computer engineering (MS); electrical and computer engineering leadership (MS); electrical engineering (PhD); energy systems (MS); engineering and public policy (MS); engineering management (MS, Certificate); environmental engineering (MS); industrial engineering (MS, PhD); information assurance (PhD); information systems (MS);

interdisciplinary engineering (PhD); mechanical engineering (PhD); operations research (MS); telecommunication systems management (MS). *Program availability:* Part-time, online learning. Electronic applications accepted. *Expenses:* Contact institution.

Northern Arizona University, College of Engineering, Informatics, and Applied Sciences, School of Informatics, Computing, and Cyber Systems, Flagstaff, AZ 86011. Offers engineering (M Eng), including computer science and engineering, electrical engineering; informatics and computing (PhD). *Program availability:* Part-time. *Degree requirements:* For master's, variable foreign language requirement, comprehensive exam (for some programs), thesis (for some programs); for doctorate, variable foreign language requirement, comprehensive exam (for some programs), thesis/dissertation (for some programs). *Entrance requirements:* Additional exam requirements/recommendations for international students: required—TOEFL (minimum score 80 iBT), IELTS (minimum score 6.5). Electronic applications accepted.

Northwestern Polytechnic University, School of Engineering, Fremont, CA 94539-7482. Offers computer engineering (DCE); computer science (MS); computer systems engineering (MS); electrical engineering (MS). *Program availability:* Part-time, evening/weekend. *Degree requirements:* For master's, thesis optional; for doctorate, thesis/dissertation. *Entrance requirements:* For master's, minimum GPA of 3.0. Additional exam requirements/recommendations for international students: required—TOEFL (minimum score 550 paper-based; 79 iBT).

Northwestern University, McCormick School of Engineering and Applied Science, Department of Electrical Engineering and Computer Science, Evanston, IL 60208. Offers computer engineering (MS, PhD); computer science (MS, PhD); electrical engineering (MS, PhD); information technology (MS). *Program availability:* Part-time. Terminal master's awarded for partial completion of doctoral program. *Degree requirements:* For master's, comprehensive exam (for some programs), thesis optional; for doctorate, comprehensive exam, thesis/dissertation. *Entrance requirements:* For master's and doctorate, GRE General Test. Additional exam requirements/recommendations for international students: required—TOEFL (minimum score 577 paper-based; 90 iBT), IELTS (minimum score 7). Electronic applications accepted.

Oakland University, Graduate Study and Lifelong Learning, School of Engineering and Computer Science, Department of Computer Science and Engineering, Rochester, MI 48309-4401. Offers computer science (MS); computer science and informatics (PhD); software engineering and information technology (MS). *Program availability:* Part-time, evening/weekend. *Entrance requirements:* For master's, minimum GPA of 3.0. Electronic applications accepted. *Expenses:* Contact institution.

Oakland University, Graduate Study and Lifelong Learning, School of Engineering and Computer Science, Department of Electrical and Computer Engineering, Rochester, MI 48309-4401. Offers electrical and computer engineering (MS, PhD); embedded systems (MS); mechatronics (MS). *Program availability:* Part-time, evening/weekend. *Entrance requirements:* For master's, minimum GPA of 3.0. Additional exam requirements/recommendations for international students: required—TOEFL (minimum score 550 paper-based). Electronic applications accepted. *Expenses:* Contact institution.

The Ohio State University, Graduate School, College of Engineering, Department of Computer Science and Engineering, Columbus, OH 43210. Offers MS, PhD. *Entrance requirements:* For master's and doctorate, GRE (minimum score Quantitative 750 old, 159 new; Verbal 500 old, 155 new; Analytical Writing 3.0); GRE Subject Test in computer science (strongly recommended for those whose undergraduate degree is not in computer science). Additional exam requirements/recommendations for international students: required—TOEFL (minimum score 550 paper-based; 79 iBT), Michigan English Language Assessment Battery (minimum score 82); recommended—IELTS (minimum score 7). Electronic applications accepted.

The Ohio State University, Graduate School, College of Engineering, Department of Electrical and Computer Engineering, Columbus, OH 43210. Offers electrical and computer engineering (MS, PhD); electrical engineering (MS, PhD). *Program availability:* Part-time. Terminal master's awarded for partial completion of doctoral program. *Entrance requirements:* For master's, GRE General Test (for all graduates of foreign universities and for applicants if undergraduate GPA below 3.2); for doctorate, GRE General Test (for all graduates of foreign universities and for applicants if graduate work GPA is below 3.5). Additional exam requirements/recommendations for international students: required—TOEFL (minimum score 580 paper-based; 92 iBT); recommended—IELTS (minimum score 7.5). Electronic applications accepted.

Oklahoma Christian University, Graduate School of Engineering and Computer Science, Oklahoma City, OK 73136-1100. Offers electrical and computer engineering (MSE); engineering management (MSE); mechanical engineering (MSE); software engineering (MSCS, MSE). *Program availability:* Part-time. *Entrance requirements:* Additional exam requirements/recommendations for international students: required—TOEFL (minimum score 550 paper-based). Electronic applications accepted. *Expenses:* Contact institution.

Oklahoma State University, College of Engineering, Architecture and Technology, School of Electrical and Computer Engineering, Stillwater, OK 74078. Offers MS, PhD. *Program availability:* Online learning. *Faculty:* 17 full-time (1 woman). *Students:* 15 full-time (0 women), 30 part-time (7 women); includes 5 minority (1 Asian, non-Hispanic/Latino; 2 Hispanic/Latino; 2 Two or more races, non-Hispanic/Latino), 27 international. Average age 29. 81 applicants, 31% accepted, 15 enrolled. In 2019, 17 master's, 9 doctorates awarded. *Entrance requirements:* For master's and doctorate, GRE or GMAT. Additional exam requirements/recommendations for international students: required—TOEFL (minimum score 550 paper-based; 79 iBT). *Application deadline:* For fall admission, 3/1 priority date for international students; for spring admission, 8/1 priority date for international students. Applications are processed on a rolling basis. Application fee: $50 ($75 for international students). Electronic applications accepted. *Expenses: Tuition, area resident:* Full-time $4148.10; part-time $2765.40. Tuition, state resident: full-time $4148.10; part-time $2765.40. Tuition, nonresident: full-time $15,775; part-time $10,516.80. *International tuition:* $15,775.20 full-time. *Required fees:* $2196.90; $122.05 per credit hour. Tuition and fees vary according to course load, campus/location and program. *Financial support:* In 2019–20, 9 research assistantships (averaging $2,382 per year), 21 teaching assistantships (averaging $1,860 per year) were awarded; career-related internships or fieldwork, Federal Work-Study, scholarships/grants, health care benefits, tuition waivers (partial), and unspecified assistantships also available. Support available to part-time students. Financial award application deadline: 3/1; financial award applicants required to submit FAFSA. *Unit head:* Dr. Jeffrey Young, Department Head, 405-744-5151, Fax: 405-744-9198, E-mail: jl.young@okstate.edu. *Application contact:* Dr. Sheryl Tucker, Vice Prov/Dean/Prof, 405-744-6368, E-mail: igrad@okstate.edu.
Website: http://ece.okstate.edu

Old Dominion University, Frank Batten College of Engineering and Technology, Graduate Program in Electrical and Computer Engineering, Norfolk, VA 23529. Offers ME, MS, D Eng, PhD. *Program availability:* Part-time, online learning. *Degree requirements:* For master's, comprehensive exam (for some programs), thesis (for some programs); for doctorate, thesis/dissertation, candidacy exam, diagnostic exam, proposal defense. *Entrance requirements:* For master's, GRE, two letters of recommendation, resume, personal statement of objectives; for doctorate, GRE, three letters of recommendation, resume, personal statement of objectives. Additional exam requirements/recommendations for international students: required—TOEFL (minimum score 550 paper-based; 79 iBT), IELTS (minimum score 6.5). Electronic applications accepted. *Expenses:* Contact institution.

Oregon Health & Science University, School of Medicine, Graduate Programs in Medicine, Department of Computer Science and Electrical Engineering, Portland, OR 97239-3098. Offers computer science and engineering (MS, PhD); electrical engineering (MS, PhD). *Program availability:* Part-time. Terminal master's awarded for partial completion of doctoral program. *Degree requirements:* For master's, thesis (for some programs); for doctorate, comprehensive exam, thesis/dissertation, qualifying exam. *Entrance requirements:* For master's and doctorate, GRE General Test (minimum scores: 153 Verbal/148 Quantitative/4.5 Analytical). Electronic applications accepted.

Oregon State University, College of Engineering, Program in Electrical and Computer Engineering, Corvallis, OR 97331. Offers M Eng, MS, PhD. *Entrance requirements:* For master's and doctorate, GRE. Additional exam requirements/recommendations for international students: required—TOEFL (minimum score 600 paper-based; 80 iBT), IELTS (minimum score 7). *Expenses:* Contact institution.

Oregon State University, College of Engineering, Program in Materials Science, Corvallis, OR 97331. Offers chemical engineering (MS, PhD); chemistry (MS, PhD); civil engineering (MS, PhD); electrical and computer engineering (MS, PhD); forest products (MS, PhD); mathematics (MS, PhD); mechanical engineering (MS, PhD); nuclear engineering (MS); physics (MS, PhD). *Entrance requirements:* For master's and doctorate, GRE. Additional exam requirements/recommendations for international students: required—TOEFL (minimum score 80 iBT), IELTS (minimum score 6.5). *Expenses:* Contact institution.

Penn State University Park, Graduate School, College of Engineering, Department of Computer Science and Engineering, University Park, PA 16802. Offers M Eng, MS, PhD.

See Display on page 213 and Close-Up on page 275.

Polytechnic University of Puerto Rico, Graduate School, Hato Rey, PR 00918. Offers business administration (MBA), including computer information systems, general management, management of information systems, management of international enterprises; civil engineering (ME, MS); computer engineering (ME, MS); computer science (MCS, MS); electrical engineering (ME, MS); engineering management (MEM); environmental management (MEM); landscape architecture (M Land Arch); manufacturing competitiveness (MMC, MS); manufacturing engineering (ME, MS); mechanical engineering (M Mech E). *Accreditation:* ASLA. *Program availability:* Part-time, evening/weekend. *Entrance requirements:* For master's, 3 letters of recommendation.

Polytechnique Montréal, Graduate Programs, Department of Electrical and Computer Engineering, Montréal, QC H3C 3A7, Canada. Offers automation (M Eng, M Sc A, PhD); computer science (M Eng, M Sc A, PhD); electrical engineering (DESS); electrotechnology (M Eng, M Sc A, PhD); microelectronics (M Eng, M Sc A, PhD); microwave technology (M Eng, M Sc A, PhD). *Program availability:* Part-time, evening/weekend. *Degree requirements:* For master's, one foreign language, thesis; for doctorate, one foreign language, thesis/dissertation. *Entrance requirements:* For master's, minimum GPA of 2.75; for doctorate, minimum GPA of 3.0.

Portland State University, Graduate Studies, Maseeh College of Engineering and Computer Science, Department of Electrical and Computer Engineering, Portland, OR 97207-0751. Offers MS, PhD. *Program availability:* Part-time, evening/weekend. *Faculty:* 19 full-time (2 women), 10 part-time/adjunct (1 woman). *Students:* 154 full-time (44 women), 99 part-time (27 women); includes 37 minority (8 Black or African American, non-Hispanic/Latino; 20 Asian, non-Hispanic/Latino; 5 Hispanic/Latino; 4 Two or more races, non-Hispanic/Latino), 159 international. Average age 29. 255 applicants, 82% accepted, 83 enrolled. In 2019, 134 master's, 5 doctorates awarded. *Degree requirements:* For master's, variable foreign language requirement, oral exam; for doctorate, one foreign language, comprehensive exam, thesis/dissertation, oral and written exams. *Entrance requirements:* For master's, GRE, minimum GPA of 2.75; for doctorate, GRE General Test, GRE Subject Test, master's degree in electrical engineering or related field, 3 reference letters, statement of purpose, writing sample. Additional exam requirements/recommendations for international students: required—TOEFL (minimum score 550 paper-based; 80 iBT). *Application deadline:* For fall admission, 2/1 for domestic and international students; for winter admission, 8/15 for domestic and international students; for spring admission, 11/1 for domestic and international students. Application fee: $65. *Expenses:* Contact institution. *Financial support:* In 2019–20, 50 students received support, including 15 research assistantships with full and partial tuition reimbursements available (averaging $18,156 per year), 12 teaching assistantships with full and partial tuition reimbursements available (averaging $14,324 per year); career-related internships or fieldwork, Federal Work-Study, scholarships/grants, and unspecified assistantships also available. Support available to part-time students. Financial award application deadline: 3/1; financial award applicants required to submit FAFSA. *Unit head:* Dr. James McNames, Chair, 503-725-5390, Fax: 503-725-3807, E-mail: mcnames@ece.pdx.edu. *Application contact:* Rachelle Braido, Graduate Coordinator, 503-725-2835, Fax: 503-725-3807, E-mail: braido@pdx.edu.
Website: http://www.pdx.edu/ece/

Purdue University, College of Engineering, School of Electrical and Computer Engineering, West Lafayette, IN 47907-2035. Offers MSECE, PhD. *Program availability:* Part-time, online learning. *Faculty:* 98. *Students:* 668. Terminal master's awarded for partial completion of doctoral program. *Degree requirements:* For master's, thesis optional; for doctorate, thesis/dissertation. *Application deadline:* For fall admission, 12/15 priority date for domestic and international students; for spring admission, 5/1 for domestic and international students. Application fee: $60 ($75 for international students). Electronic applications accepted. *Financial support:* Fellowships with full and partial tuition reimbursements, research assistantships with full and partial tuition reimbursements, teaching assistantships with full and partial tuition reimbursements, career-related internships or fieldwork, scholarships/grants, health care benefits, and unspecified assistantships available. *Unit head:* Dimitrios Peroulis, Department Head, E-mail: dperouli@purdue.edu. *Application contact:* Debra Bowman, Graduate Admissions, 765-494-3392, E-mail: dbowman1@purdue.edu.
Website: https://engineering.purdue.edu/ECE

Purdue University Fort Wayne, College of Engineering, Technology, and Computer Science, Department of Electrical and Computer Engineering, Fort Wayne, IN 46805-1499. Offers computer engineering (MSE); electrical engineering (MSE); systems engineering (MSE). *Program availability:* Part-time. *Entrance requirements:* For master's, minimum GPA of 3.0, bachelor's degree in engineering discipline. Additional exam requirements/recommendations for international students: required—TOEFL (minimum score 550 paper-based; 79 iBT); recommended—TWE. Electronic applications accepted.

Purdue University Northwest, Graduate Studies Office, School of Engineering, Mathematics, and Science, Department of Engineering, Hammond, IN 46323-2094.

Offers computer engineering (MSE); electrical engineering (MSE); engineering (MS); mechanical engineering (MSE). *Program availability:* Evening/weekend. *Entrance requirements:* Additional exam requirements/recommendations for international students: required—TOEFL.

Queen's University at Kingston, School of Graduate Studies, Faculty of Engineering and Applied Science, Department of Electrical and Computer Engineering, Kingston, ON K7L 3N6, Canada. Offers M Eng, M Sc, M Sc Eng, PhD. *Program availability:* Part-time. *Degree requirements:* For master's, thesis optional; for doctorate, comprehensive exam, thesis/dissertation. *Entrance requirements:* Additional exam requirements/ recommendations for international students: required—TOEFL (minimum score 580 paper-based).

Rensselaer at Hartford, Department of Engineering, Program in Computer and Systems Engineering, Hartford, CT 06120-2991. Offers ME. *Entrance requirements:* For master's, GRE.

Rensselaer Polytechnic Institute, Graduate School, School of Engineering, Program in Computer and Systems Engineering, Troy, NY 12180-3590. Offers M Eng, MS, PhD. *Faculty:* 40 full-time (6 women), 1 part-time/adjunct (0 women). *Students:* 18 full-time (2 women), 2 part-time (0 women); includes 2 minority (1 Asian, non-Hispanic/Latino; 1 Hispanic/Latino), 14 international. Average age 25. 71 applicants, 54% accepted, 10 enrolled. In 2019, 7 master's, 2 doctorates awarded. Terminal master's awarded for partial completion of doctoral program. *Degree requirements:* For master's, thesis (for some programs); for doctorate, thesis/dissertation. *Entrance requirements:* For master's and doctorate, GRE. Additional exam requirements/recommendations for international students: required—TOEFL (minimum score 570 paper-based; 88 iBT), IELTS (minimum score 6.5), PTE (minimum score 60). *Application deadline:* For fall admission, 1/1 priority date for domestic and international students; for spring admission, 8/15 priority date for domestic and international students; for summer admission, 1/1 priority date for domestic and international students. Applications are processed on a rolling basis. Application fee: $75. Electronic applications accepted. *Financial support:* In 2019–20, research assistantships (averaging $23,000 per year), teaching assistantships (averaging $23,000 per year) were awarded; fellowships also available. Financial award application deadline: 1/1. *Unit head:* Dr. Hussein Abouzeid, Graduate Program Director, 518-576-6534, E-mail: abouzeid@ecse.rpi.edu. *Application contact:* Jarron Decker, Director of Graduate Admissions, 518-276-6216, Fax: 518-276-4072, E-mail: gradadmissions@rpi.edu.
Website: https://ecse.rpi.edu/

Rice University, Graduate Programs, George R. Brown School of Engineering, Department of Electrical and Computer Engineering, Houston, TX 77251-1892. Offers bioengineering (MS, PhD); circuits, controls, and communication systems (MS, PhD); computer science and engineering (MS, PhD); electrical engineering (MEE); lasers, microwaves, and solid-state electronics (MS, PhD); MBA/MEE. *Program availability:* Part-time. *Degree requirements:* For master's, thesis (for some programs); for doctorate, thesis/dissertation. *Entrance requirements:* For master's and doctorate, GRE General Test, GRE Subject Test, minimum GPA of 3.0. Additional exam requirements/ recommendations for international students: required—TOEFL (minimum score 600 paper-based; 90 iBT). Electronic applications accepted.

Rice University, Graduate Programs, George R. Brown School of Engineering, Program in Computational Science and Engineering, Houston, TX 77251-1892. Offers MCSE.

Rochester Institute of Technology, Graduate Enrollment Services, Kate Gleason College of Engineering, Computer Engineering Department, MS Program in Computer Engineering, Rochester, NY 14623-5603. Offers MS. *Program availability:* Part-time. *Degree requirements:* For master's, thesis or alternative, Thesis or Project. *Entrance requirements:* For master's, GRE, minimum GPA of 3.0 (recommended), two letters of recommendation. Additional exam requirements/recommendations for international students: required—TOEFL (minimum score 550 paper-based; 79 iBT), IELTS (minimum score 6.5), PTE (minimum score 58). Electronic applications accepted.

Rose-Hulman Institute of Technology, Graduate Studies, Department of Electrical and Computer Engineering, Terre Haute, IN 47803-3999. Offers electrical and computer engineering (M Eng); electrical engineering (MS); systems engineering and management (MS). *Program availability:* Part-time. *Faculty:* 19 full-time (2 women), 1 (woman) part-time/adjunct. *Students:* 2 full-time (0 women), 3 part-time (0 women), 2 international. Average age 27. 7 applicants, 71% accepted. In 2019, 5 master's awarded. *Degree requirements:* For master's, thesis (for some programs). *Entrance requirements:* For master's, GRE, minimum GPA of 3.0. Additional exam requirements/ recommendations for international students: required—TOEFL (minimum score 580 paper-based; 94 iBT), IELTS (minimum score 7). *Application deadline:* For fall admission, 2/1 priority date for domestic and international students; for winter admission, 10/1 for domestic students, 4/1 for international students; for spring admission, 1/15 for domestic students, 11/1 for international students. Applications are processed on a rolling basis. Application fee: $75. Electronic applications accepted. *Financial support:* In 2019–20, 5 students received support. Fellowships with tuition reimbursements available, research assistantships with tuition reimbursements available, institutionally sponsored loans, scholarships/grants, tuition waivers (full and partial), and unspecified assistantships available. *Unit head:* Dr. Mario Simoni, Department Head, 812-877-8341, Fax: 812-877-8895, E-mail: simoni@rose-hulman.edu. *Application contact:* Dr. Craig Downing, Associate Dean of the Faculty, 812-877-8822, E-mail: downing@rose-hulman.edu.
Website: https://www.rose-hulman.edu/academics/academic-departments/electrical-computer-engineering/index.html

Royal Military College of Canada, Division of Graduate Studies, Faculty of Engineering, Department of Electrical and Computer Engineering, Kingston, ON K7K 7B4, Canada. Offers computer engineering (M Eng, PhD); electrical engineering (M Eng, PhD); software engineering (M Eng, PhD). *Degree requirements:* For master's, thesis; for doctorate, comprehensive exam, thesis/dissertation. *Entrance requirements:* For master's, honours degree with second-class standing in the appropriate field; for doctorate, master's degree. Electronic applications accepted.

Rutgers University - New Brunswick, Graduate School-New Brunswick, Department of Electrical and Computer Engineering, Piscataway, NJ 08854-8097. Offers communications and solid-state electronics (MS, PhD); computer engineering (MS, PhD); control systems (MS, PhD); digital signal processing (MS, PhD). *Program availability:* Part-time. Terminal master's awarded for partial completion of doctoral program. *Degree requirements:* For master's, thesis or alternative; for doctorate, thesis/ dissertation. *Entrance requirements:* For master's and doctorate, GRE General Test. Additional exam requirements/recommendations for international students: required—TOEFL. Electronic applications accepted.

St. Mary's University, School of Science, Engineering and Technology, Program in Computer Engineering, San Antonio, TX 78228. Offers MS. *Program availability:* Part-time. *Degree requirements:* For master's, thesis or project. *Entrance requirements:* For master's, GRE (minimum quantitative score of 148), bachelor's degree in computer engineering, electrical engineering or a closely-related discipline; minimum GPA of 3.0; written statement of purpose; two letters of recommendation; official transcripts.

Additional exam requirements/recommendations for international students: required—TOEFL (minimum score 550 paper-based; 80 iBT), IELTS (minimum score 6.5). Electronic applications accepted.

San Jose State University, Program in Computer Engineering, San Jose, CA 95192-0180. Offers computer engineering (MS); software engineering (MS). *Faculty:* 14 full-time (5 women), 28 part-time/adjunct (4 women). *Students:* 833 full-time (352 women), 352 part-time (101 women); includes 186 minority (7 Black or African American, non-Hispanic/Latino; 160 Asian, non-Hispanic/Latino; 19 Hispanic/Latino), 922 international. Average age 27. 1,637 applicants, 23% accepted, 224 enrolled. In 2019, 515 master's awarded. *Entrance requirements:* For master's, GRE General Test. *Application deadline:* For fall admission, 7/1 for domestic students, 5/1 for international students; for spring admission, 12/1 for domestic students, 11/1 for international students. Applications are processed on a rolling basis. Application fee: $70. Electronic applications accepted. *Expenses: Tuition, area resident:* Full-time $7176; part-time $4164. Tuition, state resident: full-time $7176; part-time $4164. Tuition, nonresident: full-time $7176; part-time $4165 per credit hour. *International tuition:* $7176 full-time. *Required fees:* $2110; $2110. *Financial support:* In 2019–20, 30 students received support. Scholarships/grants available. Financial award applicants required to submit FAFSA. *Unit head:* Xiao Su, Department Chair, 408-924-7366, E-mail: xiao.su@sjsu.edu. *Application contact:* David Bruck, MS Computer Engineering Advisor, E-mail: David.bruck@sjsu.edu.
Website: https://cmpe.sjsu.edu/

Santa Clara University, School of Engineering, Santa Clara, CA 95053. Offers applied mathematics (MS); bioengineering (MS); civil, environmental, and sustainable engineering (MS); computer science and engineering (MS, PhD, Engineer); electrical engineering (MS, PhD, Engineer); engineering management and leadership (MS); mechanical engineering (MS, PhD, Engineer); power systems and sustainable energy (MS); software engineering (MS). *Program availability:* Part-time. *Entrance requirements:* For master's, GRE, official transcript; for doctorate, GRE, Official transcript, 500 word statement of purpose, three letters of recommendation. Additional exam requirements/recommendations for international students: required—TOEFL (minimum score 79 iBT), IELTS (minimum score 6.5). Electronic applications accepted.

Southern Illinois University Carbondale, Graduate School, College of Engineering, Department of Electrical and Computer Engineering, Carbondale, IL 62901-4701. Offers MS, PhD, JD/MS. *Degree requirements:* For master's, comprehensive exam, thesis. *Entrance requirements:* For master's, GRE, minimum GPA of 2.7; for doctorate, GRE, minimum GPA of 3.25. Additional exam requirements/recommendations for international students: required—TOEFL.

Southern Illinois University Carbondale, Graduate School, College of Engineering, Program in Engineering Science, Carbondale, IL 62901-4701. Offers engineering science (PhD), including civil and environmental engineering, electrical and computer engineering, mechanical engineering and energy processes, mining and mineral resources engineering. *Degree requirements:* For doctorate, thesis/dissertation. *Entrance requirements:* For doctorate, GRE General Test, minimum GPA of 3.5. Additional exam requirements/recommendations for international students: required—TOEFL.

Southern Methodist University, Lyle School of Engineering, Department of Computer Science and Engineering, Dallas, TX 75275-0122. Offers computer engineering (MS, PhD); computer science (MS, PhD); security engineering (MS); software engineering (MS, DE). *Program availability:* Part-time, evening/weekend, online learning. Terminal master's awarded for partial completion of doctoral program. *Degree requirements:* For master's, thesis optional; for doctorate, thesis/dissertation, oral and written qualifying exams, oral final exam (PhD). *Entrance requirements:* For master's, GRE General Test, minimum GPA of 3.0 in last 2 years; bachelor's degree in engineering, mathematics, or sciences; for doctorate, preliminary counseling exam (PhD), minimum GPA of 3.0, bachelor's degree in related field, MA (for DE). Additional exam requirements/ recommendations for international students: required—TOEFL (minimum score 550 paper-based).

Stevens Institute of Technology, Graduate School, Charles V. Schaefer Jr. School of Engineering and Science, Department of Electrical and Computer Engineering, Program in Computer Engineering, Hoboken, NJ 07030. Offers computer engineering (PhD, Certificate), including digital signal processing (Certificate), digital systems and VLSI design (Certificate), multimedia technology (Certificate), networked information systems (Certificate), real-time and embedded systems (Certificate), secure network systems design (Certificate); computer systems (M Eng); data communications and networks (M Eng); digital systems design (M Eng); engineered software systems (M Eng); image processing and multimedia (M Eng); information system security (M Eng); information systems (M Eng). *Program availability:* Part-time, evening/weekend. *Faculty:* 20 full-time (6 women), 2 part-time/adjunct. *Students:* 92 full-time (14 women), 19 part-time (1 woman); includes 10 minority (1 Black or African American, non-Hispanic/Latino; 8 Asian, non-Hispanic/Latino; 1 Hispanic/Latino), 83 international. Average age 25. In 2019, 45 master's, 3 doctorates, 27 other advanced degrees awarded. Terminal master's awarded for partial completion of doctoral program. *Degree requirements:* For master's, thesis optional, minimum B average in major field and overall; for doctorate, comprehensive exam (for some programs), thesis/dissertation; for Certificate, minimum B average. *Entrance requirements:* For master's, International applicants must submit TOEFL/IELTS scores and fulfill the English Language Proficiency Requirement. Applicants to full-time programs who do not qualify for a score waiver are required to submit GRE/GMAT scores. Additional exam requirements/recommendations for international students: required—TOEFL (minimum score 74 iBT), IELTS (minimum score 6). *Application deadline:* For fall admission, 4/15 for domestic and international students; for spring admission, 11/1 for domestic and international students; for summer admission, 5/1 for domestic students. Applications are processed on a rolling basis. Application fee: $60. Electronic applications accepted. *Expenses: Tuition:* Full-time $52,134. *Required fees:* $1880. Tuition and fees vary according to course load. *Financial support:* Fellowships, research assistantships, teaching assistantships, career-related internships or fieldwork, Federal Work-Study, scholarships/grants, and unspecified assistantships available. Financial award application deadline: 2/15; financial award applicants required to submit FAFSA. *Unit head:* Dr. Jean Zu, Dean of SES, 201-216.8233, Fax: 201-216.8372, E-mail: Jean.Zu@stevens.edu. *Application contact:* Graduate Admissions, 888-783-8367, Fax: 888-511-1306, E-mail: graduate@stevens.edu.

Stevens Institute of Technology, Graduate School, Charles V. Schaefer Jr. School of Engineering and Science, Department of Mechanical Engineering, Program in Integrated Product Development, Hoboken, NJ 07030. Offers armament engineering (M Eng); computer and electrical engineering (M Eng); manufacturing technologies (M Eng); systems reliability and design (M Eng). *Program availability:* Part-time, evening/weekend. *Faculty:* 29 full-time (3 women), 11 part-time/adjunct (0 women). *Degree requirements:* For master's, thesis optional, minimum B average in major field and overall. *Entrance requirements:* For master's, International applicants must submit TOEFL/IELTS scores and fulfill the English Language Proficiency Requirement. Applicants to full-time programs who do not qualify for a score waiver are required to submit GRE/GMAT scores. Additional exam requirements/recommendations for international students: required—TOEFL (minimum score 74 iBT), IELTS (minimum score 6). *Application deadline:* For fall admission, 4/15 for domestic and international students; for spring admission, 11/1 for domestic and international students; for summer admission, 5/1 for domestic students. Applications are processed on a rolling basis. Application fee: $60. Electronic applications accepted. *Expenses: Tuition:* Full-time $52,134. *Required fees:* $1880. Tuition and fees vary according to course load. *Financial support:* Fellowships, research assistantships, teaching assistantships, career-related internships or fieldwork, Federal Work-Study, scholarships/grants, and unspecified assistantships available. Financial award application deadline: 2/15; financial award applicants required to submit FAFSA. *Unit head:* Dr. Jean Zu, Dean of SES, 201-216.8233, Fax: 201-216.8372, E-mail: Jean.Zu@stevens.edu. *Application contact:* Graduate Admissions, 888-783-8367, Fax: 888-511-1306, E-mail: graduate@stevens.edu.

Stony Brook University, State University of New York, Graduate School, College of Engineering and Applied Sciences, Department of Electrical and Computer Engineering, Program in Computer Engineering, Stony Brook, NY 11794. Offers MS, PhD. *Students:* 50 full-time (4 women), 20 part-time (3 women); includes 14 minority (11 Asian, non-Hispanic/Latino; 2 Hispanic/Latino; 1 Two or more races, non-Hispanic/Latino), 51 international. Average age 25. 142 applicants, 93% accepted, 27 enrolled. In 2019, 56 master's, 2 doctorates awarded. *Entrance requirements:* For master's, GRE; for doctorate, GRE, statement of purpose, resume, three recommendation letters. Additional exam requirements/recommendations for international students: required—TOEFL (minimum score 90 iBT). *Application deadline:* For fall admission, 1/15 for domestic students; for spring admission, 10/1 for domestic students. Application fee: $100. *Expenses:* Contact institution. *Financial support:* Research assistantships and teaching assistantships available. *Unit head:* Prof. Petar M. Djuric, Chair, 631-632-8420, Fax: 631-632-8494, E-mail: petar.djuric@stonybrook.edu. *Application contact:* Nicole Zinerco, Graduate Coordinator, 631-632-8401, Fax: 631-632-8494, E-mail: ecegradcoordinator@stonybrook.edu.

Syracuse University, College of Engineering and Computer Science, MS Program in Computer Engineering, Syracuse, NY 13244. Offers MS. *Program availability:* Part-time. *Degree requirements:* For master's, comprehensive exam (for some programs), thesis (for some programs). *Entrance requirements:* For master's, GRE General Test, three letters of recommendation, personal statement, resume, official transcripts. Additional exam requirements/recommendations for international students: required—TOEFL (minimum score 100 iBT). Electronic applications accepted.

Syracuse University, College of Engineering and Computer Science, PhD Program in Electrical and Computer Engineering, Syracuse, NY 13244. Offers PhD. *Program availability:* Part-time. *Degree requirements:* For doctorate, comprehensive exam, thesis/dissertation. *Entrance requirements:* For doctorate, GRE General Test, three letters of recommendation, personal statement, resume, official transcripts. Additional exam requirements/recommendations for international students: required—TOEFL (minimum score 100 iBT). Electronic applications accepted.

Tennessee State University, The School of Graduate Studies and Research, College of Engineering, Nashville, TN 37209-1561. Offers biomedical engineering (ME); civil engineering (ME); computer and information systems engineering (MS, PhD); electrical engineering (ME); environmental engineering (ME); manufacturing engineering (ME); mathematical sciences (MS); mechanical engineering (ME). *Program availability:* Part-time, evening/weekend. *Degree requirements:* For master's, project; for doctorate, comprehensive exam, thesis/dissertation. *Entrance requirements:* For doctorate, minimum GPA of 3.3.

Texas A&M University, College of Engineering, Department of Electrical and Computer Engineering, College Station, TX 77843. Offers computer engineering (M Eng, PhD); electrical engineering (M Eng). *Faculty:* 75. *Students:* 605 full-time (132 women), 130 part-time (25 women); includes 35 minority (1 Black or African American, non-Hispanic/Latino; 21 Asian, non-Hispanic/Latino; 11 Hispanic/Latino; 2 Two or more races, non-Hispanic/Latino), 643 international. Average age 26. 1,318 applicants, 50% accepted, 243 enrolled. In 2019, 218 master's, 52 doctorates awarded. *Degree requirements:* For master's, comprehensive exam (for some programs), thesis (for some programs); for doctorate, comprehensive exam, thesis/dissertation. *Entrance requirements:* For master's and doctorate, GRE General Test, letters of recommendation. Additional exam requirements/recommendations for international students: required—TOEFL (minimum score 550 paper-based; 80 iBT), IELTS (minimum score 6), PTE (minimum score 53). *Application deadline:* For fall admission, 5/1 for domestic students, 2/1 for international students; for spring admission, 10/1 for domestic students, 7/1 for international students. Application fee: $65 ($90 for international students). Electronic applications accepted. *Expenses:* Contact institution. *Financial support:* In 2019–20, 506 students received support, including 42 fellowships with tuition reimbursements available (averaging $10,572 per year), 204 research assistantships with tuition reimbursements available (averaging $14,937 per year), 128 teaching assistantships with tuition reimbursements available (averaging $12,615 per year); career-related internships or fieldwork, institutionally sponsored loans, scholarships/grants, traineeships, health care benefits, tuition waivers (full and partial), and unspecified assistantships also available. Support available to part-time students. Financial award application deadline: 3/15; financial award applicants required to submit FAFSA. *Unit head:* Dr. Miroslav M. Begovic, Department Head, 979-862-1553, E-mail: begovic@tamu.edu. *Application contact:* Katie Bryan, Academic Advisor IV - Graduate Program, 979-845-7467, E-mail: k.bryan@tamu.edu.
Website: http://engineering.tamu.edu/electrical/

Universidad del Turabo, Graduate Programs, School of Engineering, Gurabo, PR 00778-3030. Offers computer engineering (M Eng); electrical engineering (M Eng); mechanical engineering (M Eng); telecommunications and network systems administration (M Eng). *Entrance requirements:* For master's, GRE, EXADEP or GMAT, interview, essay, official transcript, recommendation letters. Electronic applications accepted.

The University of Akron, Graduate School, College of Engineering, Department of Electrical and Computer Engineering, Akron, OH 44325. Offers computer engineering (MS, PhD); electrical engineering (MS). *Program availability:* Evening/weekend. *Degree requirements:* For master's, oral comprehensive exam or thesis; for doctorate, one foreign language, thesis/dissertation, candidacy exam, qualifying exam. *Entrance requirements:* For master's, GRE, minimum GPA of 2.75, three letters of recommendation, statement of purpose; for doctorate, GRE, minimum GPA of 3.0 with bachelor's degree, 3.5 with master's degree; three letters of recommendation; statement of purpose; resume. Additional exam requirements/recommendations for international students: required—TOEFL (minimum score 79 iBT), IELTS (minimum score 6.5). Electronic applications accepted.

The University of Alabama, Graduate School, College of Engineering, Department of Electrical and Computer Engineering, Tuscaloosa, AL 35487-0286. Offers electrical engineering (MS, PhD). *Program availability:* Part-time, online learning. *Faculty:* 24 full-time (3 women). *Students:* 62 full-time (10 women), 5 part-time (1 woman); includes 1 minority (Black or African American, non-Hispanic/Latino), 48 international. Average age 28. 103 applicants, 71% accepted, 12 enrolled. In 2019, 4 master's, 7 doctorates awarded. *Degree requirements:* For master's, thesis or alternative; for doctorate, one foreign language, comprehensive exam, thesis/dissertation. *Entrance requirements:* For master's, GRE (for students from non ABET-accredited schools), minimum GPA of 3.0 in last 60 hours of course work or overall; for doctorate, GRE (for students from non ABET-accredited schools), minimum GPA of 3.0 overall. Additional exam requirements/recommendations for international students: required—TOEFL (minimum score 550 paper-based). *Application deadline:* For fall admission, 7/1 priority date for domestic students, 1/15 priority date for international students; for spring admission, 11/1 priority date for domestic students, 6/1 priority date for international students. Applications are processed on a rolling basis. Application fee: $50 ($60 for international students). Electronic applications accepted. *Expenses: Tuition, area resident:* Full-time $10,780; part-time $440 per credit hour. Tuition, nonresident: full-time $30,250; part-time $1550 per credit hour. *Financial support:* In 2019–20, 38 students received support. Fellowships with full tuition reimbursements available, research assistantships with full tuition reimbursements available, teaching assistantships with full tuition reimbursements available, health care benefits, and unspecified assistantships available. *Unit head:* Dr. Tim Haskew, Department Head, 205-348-1766, Fax: 205-348-6959, E-mail: thaskew@eng.ua.edu. *Application contact:* Dr. Steve Shepard, Graduate Program Coordinator/Associate Professor, 205-348-1650, Fax: 205-348-6419, E-mail: sshepard@eng.ua.edu.
Website: http://ece.eng.ua.edu

The University of Alabama at Birmingham, School of Engineering, Program in Electrical Engineering, Birmingham, AL 35294. Offers computer engineering (PhD); electrical and computer engineering (MSEE). *Program availability:* Part-time. *Faculty:* 8 full-time (0 women), 3 part-time/adjunct (0 women). *Students:* 35 full-time (9 women), 33 part-time (6 women); includes 7 minority (1 Black or African American, non-Hispanic/Latino; 2 Asian, non-Hispanic/Latino; 2 Hispanic/Latino; 2 Two or more races, non-Hispanic/Latino), 44 international. 73 applicants, 56% accepted, 7 enrolled. In 2019, 19 master's, 4 doctorates awarded. *Degree requirements:* For master's, comprehensive exam, thesis (for some programs); for doctorate, comprehensive exam, thesis/dissertation. *Entrance requirements:* For master's, GRE general test is required for all applicants who did not receive a BS degree from a program accredited by the Engineering Accreditation Committee of ABET http://www.abet.org, or from other programs with reciprocal agreement under the Washington Accord http://www.ieagreements.org/accords/washington/., A 3.0 on a 4.0 scale or better GPA in all junior and senior electrical and computer engineering and mathematics courses attempted;; for doctorate, GRE, An overall GPA of at least 3.0 on a 4.0 point scale, or at least 3.0 for the last 60 semester hours completed; and. Additional exam requirements/recommendations for international students: required—TOEFL (minimum score 80 iBT), IELTS (minimum score 6.5). *Application deadline:* For fall admission, 8/1 for domestic and international students; for spring admission, 12/1 for domestic and international students; for summer admission, 5/1 for domestic and international students. Applications are processed on a rolling basis. Application fee: $50 ($60 for international students). Electronic applications accepted. *Financial support:* In 2019–20, 12 students received support, including 4 fellowships with full tuition reimbursements available (averaging $29,748 per year), 7 research assistantships with full and partial tuition reimbursements available (averaging $19,748 per year), 1 teaching assistantship; unspecified assistantships also available. *Unit head:* Dr. J Iwan Alexander, Interim Chair, 205-934-8440, E-mail: ialex@uab.edu. *Application contact:* Jesse Keppley, Director of Student and Academic Services, 205-996-5696, E-mail: gradschool@uab.edu.
Website: https://www.uab.edu/engineering/home/graduate#msee

The University of Alabama in Huntsville, School of Graduate Studies, College of Engineering, Department of Electrical and Computer Engineering, Huntsville, AL 35899. Offers computer engineering (MSE, PhD); electrical engineering (MSE, PhD), including optics and photonics technology (MSE); optical science and engineering (PhD); software engineering (MSSE). *Program availability:* Part-time. *Degree requirements:* For master's, comprehensive exam, thesis or alternative, oral and written exams; for doctorate, comprehensive exam, thesis/dissertation, oral and written exams. *Entrance requirements:* For master's, GRE General Test, appropriate bachelor's degree, minimum GPA of 3.0; for doctorate, GRE General Test, minimum GPA of 3.0. Additional exam requirements/recommendations for international students: required—TOEFL (minimum score 500 paper-based; 80 iBT), IELTS (minimum score 6.5). Electronic applications accepted.

University of Alberta, Faculty of Graduate Studies and Research, Department of Electrical and Computer Engineering, Edmonton, AB T6G 2E1, Canada. Offers communications (M Eng, M Sc, PhD); computer engineering (M Eng, M Sc, PhD); electromagnetics (M Eng, M Sc, PhD); nanotechnology and microdevices (M Eng, M Sc, PhD); power/power electronics (M Eng, M Sc, PhD); systems (M Eng, M Sc, PhD). Terminal master's awarded for partial completion of doctoral program. *Degree requirements:* For master's, thesis; for doctorate, thesis/dissertation. *Entrance requirements:* Additional exam requirements/recommendations for international students: required—TOEFL. Electronic applications accepted.

The University of Arizona, College of Engineering, Department of Electrical and Computer Engineering, Tucson, AZ 85721. Offers MS, PhD. *Program availability:* Part-time. *Degree requirements:* For master's, thesis (for some programs); for doctorate, thesis/dissertation. *Entrance requirements:* For master's, GRE General Test, 3 letters of recommendation, statement of purpose; for doctorate, GRE General Test, master's degree in related field, 3 letters of recommendation, statement of purpose. Additional exam requirements/recommendations for international students: required—TOEFL (minimum score 550 paper-based; 79 iBT). Electronic applications accepted.

University of Arkansas, Graduate School, College of Engineering, Department of Computer Science and Computer Engineering, Program in Computer Engineering, Fayetteville, AR 72701. Offers MS Cmp E, MSE, PhD. *Students:* 7 full-time (2 women), 18 part-time (2 women); includes 5 minority (1 Black or African American, non-Hispanic/Latino; 1 American Indian or Alaska Native, non-Hispanic/Latino; 1 Asian, non-Hispanic/Latino; 2 Two or more races, non-Hispanic/Latino), 11 international. 6 applicants, 83% accepted. In 2019, 5 master's, 3 doctorates awarded. *Degree requirements:* For master's, thesis optional; for doctorate, one foreign language, thesis/dissertation. *Application deadline:* For fall admission, 8/1 for domestic students, 4/1 for international students; for spring admission, 12/1 for domestic students, 10/1 for international students; for summer admission, 4/15 for domestic students, 3/1 for international students. Applications are processed on a rolling basis. Application fee: $60. Electronic applications accepted. *Financial support:* In 2019–20, 8 research assistantships, 2 teaching assistantships were awarded; fellowships with tuition reimbursements, career-related internships or fieldwork, and Federal Work-Study also available. Support available to part-time students. Financial award application deadline: 4/1; financial award applicants required to submit FAFSA. *Unit head:* Dr. Xiaoqing Liu, Department Head, 479-575-6254, Fax: 479-575-5339, E-mail: frankliu@uark.edu. *Application contact:* Dr. Brajendra Nath Panda, Professor, Associate Depart. Head of Grad. Program, 479-575-2067, E-mail: bpanda@uark.edu.
Website: https://computer-science-and-computer-engineering.uark.edu/index.php

Computer Engineering

University of Bridgeport, School of Engineering, Departments of Computer Science and Computer Engineering, Bridgeport, CT 06604. Offers computer engineering (MS); computer science (MS); computer science and engineering (PhD). *Degree requirements:* For master's, thesis optional; for doctorate, comprehensive exam, thesis/dissertation. *Entrance requirements:* Additional exam requirements/recommendations for international students: recommended—TOEFL (minimum score 550 paper-based; 80 iBT), IELTS (minimum score 6.5). Electronic applications accepted. *Expenses:* Contact institution.

The University of British Columbia, Faculty of Applied Science, Department of Electrical and Computer Engineering, Vancouver, BC V6T 1Z4, Canada. Offers M Eng, MA Sc, PhD. *Program availability:* Part-time. *Degree requirements:* For master's, thesis (for some programs); for doctorate, thesis/dissertation. *Entrance requirements:* Additional exam requirements/recommendations for international students: required—TOEFL, IELTS. Electronic applications accepted. *Expenses:* Contact institution.

University of Calgary, Faculty of Graduate Studies, Schulich School of Engineering, Program in Electrical and Computer Engineering, Calgary, AB T2N 1N4, Canada. Offers M Eng, M Sc, PhD. *Program availability:* Part-time. *Degree requirements:* For master's, thesis (for M Sc); for doctorate, thesis/dissertation, candidacy exam. *Entrance requirements:* For master's, minimum GPA of 3.0; for doctorate, minimum GPA of 3.5. Additional exam requirements/recommendations for international students: required—TOEFL (minimum score 550 paper-based; 80 iBT) or IELTS (minimum score 7). Electronic applications accepted.

University of California, Davis, College of Engineering, Program in Electrical and Computer Engineering, Davis, CA 95616. Offers MS, PhD. Terminal master's awarded for partial completion of doctoral program. *Degree requirements:* For master's, comprehensive exam (for some programs), thesis (for some programs); for doctorate, thesis/dissertation, preliminary and qualifying exams, thesis defense. *Entrance requirements:* For master's, GRE General Test, minimum GPA of 3.2; for doctorate, GRE, minimum graduate GPA of 3.5. Additional exam requirements/recommendations for international students: required—TOEFL (minimum score 550 paper-based). Electronic applications accepted.

University of California, Los Angeles, Graduate Division, Henry Samueli School of Engineering and Applied Science, Department of Electrical and Computer Engineering, Los Angeles, CA 90095-1594. Offers MS, PhD. *Degree requirements:* For master's, comprehensive exam or thesis; for doctorate, thesis/dissertation, qualifying exams. *Entrance requirements:* For master's, GRE General Test, minimum GPA of 3.0; for doctorate, GRE General Test, minimum GPA of 3.25. Additional exam requirements/recommendations for international students: required—TOEFL (minimum score 560 paper-based; 87 iBT), IELTS (minimum score 7). Electronic applications accepted.

University of California, Riverside, Graduate Division, Department of Computer Science and Engineering, Computer Engineering Program, Riverside, CA 92521. Offers MS. *Degree requirements:* For master's, comprehensive exam, project, or thesis. *Entrance requirements:* For master's, GRE General Test (minimum expected score of 300 verbal and quantitative combined), minimum GPA of 3.2 in junior/senior years of undergraduate study (last two years). Additional exam requirements/recommendations for international students: required—TOEFL (minimum score 550 paper-based, 80 iBT) or IELTS (7). Electronic applications accepted. *Expenses:* Contact institution.

University of California, San Diego, Graduate Division, Department of Computer Science and Engineering, La Jolla, CA 92093. Offers computer engineering (MS, PhD); computer science (MS, PhD). *Students:* 665 full-time (158 women), 187 part-time (39 women). 5,619 applicants, 15% accepted, 281 enrolled. In 2019, 333 master's, 25 doctorates awarded. Terminal master's awarded for partial completion of doctoral program. *Degree requirements:* For master's, comprehensive exam (for some programs), thesis (for some programs), comprehensive exam or thesis; for doctorate, comprehensive exam, thesis/dissertation, 1-quarter teaching assistantship. *Entrance requirements:* For master's and doctorate, GRE General Test. Additional exam requirements/recommendations for international students: required—TOEFL (minimum score 550 paper-based; 80 iBT), IELTS (minimum score 7). *Application deadline:* For fall admission, 12/17 for domestic students. Application fee: $105 ($125 for international students). Electronic applications accepted. *Financial support:* Fellowships, research assistantships, teaching assistantships, career-related internships or fieldwork, and scholarships/grants available. Financial award applicants required to submit FAFSA. *Unit head:* Sorin Lerner, Chair, 858-534-8883, E-mail: lerner@cs.ucsd.edu. *Application contact:* Julie Conner, Graduate Coordinator, 858-534-8872, E-mail: gradinfo@cs.ucsd.edu.
Website: http://cse.ucsd.edu

University of California, San Diego, Graduate Division, Department of Electrical and Computer Engineering, La Jolla, CA 92093. Offers applied ocean science (MS, PhD); applied physics (MS, PhD); communication theory and systems (MS, PhD); computer engineering (MS, PhD); electronic circuits and systems (MS, PhD); intelligent systems, robotics and control (MS, PhD); medical devices and systems (MS, PhD); nanoscale devices and systems (MS, PhD); photonics (MS, PhD); signal and image processing (MS, PhD). *Students:* 983 full-time (216 women), 80 part-time (15 women). 3,675 applicants, 33% accepted, 430 enrolled. In 2019, 287 master's, 50 doctorates awarded. Terminal master's awarded for partial completion of doctoral program. *Degree requirements:* For master's, comprehensive exam (for some programs), thesis (for some programs); for doctorate, comprehensive exam, thesis/dissertation. *Entrance requirements:* For master's and doctorate, GRE General Test, minimum GPA of 3.0, resume or curriculum vitae (recommended). Additional exam requirements/recommendations for international students: required—TOEFL (minimum score 550 paper-based; 80 iBT), IELTS (minimum score 7), PTE (minimum score 65). *Application deadline:* For fall admission, 12/18 for domestic students. Application fee: $105 ($125 for international students). Electronic applications accepted. *Financial support:* Fellowships, research assistantships, teaching assistantships, scholarships/grants, traineeships, and unspecified assistantships available. Financial award applicants required to submit FAFSA. *Unit head:* Bill Lin, Chair, 858-822-1383, E-mail: billin@ucsd.edu. *Application contact:* Sean Jones, Graduate Admissions Coordinator, 858-534-3213, E-mail: ecegradapps@ece.ucsd.edu.
Website: http://ece.ucsd.edu/

University of California, Santa Barbara, Graduate Division, College of Engineering, Department of Computer Science, Santa Barbara, CA 93106-5110. Offers computer science (MS, PhD), including cognitive science (PhD); computational science and engineering (PhD); technology and society (PhD). Terminal master's awarded for partial completion of doctoral program. *Degree requirements:* For master's, comprehensive exam (for some programs), thesis (for some programs), project (for some programs); for doctorate, thesis/dissertation. *Entrance requirements:* For master's and doctorate, GRE. Additional exam requirements/recommendations for international students: required—TOEFL (minimum score 600 paper-based; 100 iBT), IELTS (minimum score 7). Electronic applications accepted.

University of California, Santa Barbara, Graduate Division, College of Engineering, Department of Electrical and Computer Engineering, Santa Barbara, CA 93106-2014. Offers communications, control and signal processing (MS, PhD); computer engineering (MS, PhD); electronics and photonics (MS, PhD); MS/PhD. *Degree requirements:* For master's, comprehensive exam, thesis; for doctorate, thesis/dissertation. *Entrance requirements:* For master's and doctorate, GRE General Test. Additional exam requirements/recommendations for international students: required—TOEFL (minimum score 550 paper-based; 80 iBT), IELTS (minimum score 7). Electronic applications accepted.

University of Central Florida, College of Engineering and Computer Science, Department of Electrical and Computer Engineering, Program in Computer Engineering, Orlando, FL 32816. Offers MS Cp E, PhD. *Program availability:* Part-time, evening/weekend. *Students:* 58 full-time (10 women), 25 part-time (4 women); includes 17 minority (3 Black or African American, non-Hispanic/Latino; 8 Asian, non-Hispanic/Latino; 6 Hispanic/Latino), 54 international. Average age 30. 68 applicants, 74% accepted, 21 enrolled. In 2019, 20 master's, 9 doctorates awarded. *Degree requirements:* For master's, thesis or alternative; for doctorate, thesis/dissertation, departmental qualifying exam, candidacy exam. *Entrance requirements:* For master's and doctorate, GRE General Test, minimum GPA of 3.0 in last 60 hours, letters of recommendation, resume, goal statement. Additional exam requirements/recommendations for international students: required—TOEFL. *Application deadline:* For fall admission, 7/15 for domestic students; for spring admission, 12/1 for domestic students. Application fee: $30. Electronic applications accepted. *Financial support:* In 2019–20, 41 students received support, including 11 fellowships with partial tuition reimbursements available (averaging $11,964 per year), 35 research assistantships with partial tuition reimbursements available (averaging $6,232 per year), 16 teaching assistantships with partial tuition reimbursements available (averaging $7,547 per year); tuition waivers (partial) also available. Financial award application deadline: 3/1; financial award applicants required to submit FAFSA. *Unit head:* Dr. Kalpathy Sundaram, Graduate Coordinator, 407-823-5326, Fax: 407-823-5835, E-mail: sundaram@eecs.ucf.edu. *Application contact:* Associate Director, Graduate Admissions, 407-823-2766, Fax: 407-823-6442, E-mail: gradadmissions@ucf.edu.
Website: http://www.ece.ucf.edu/

University of Cincinnati, Graduate School, College of Engineering and Applied Science, Department of Electrical Engineering and Computing Systems, Program in Computer Engineering, Cincinnati, OH 45221. Offers MS. *Degree requirements:* For master's, thesis. *Entrance requirements:* For master's, GRE General Test. Additional exam requirements/recommendations for international students: required—TOEFL (minimum score 550 paper-based). Electronic applications accepted.

University of Cincinnati, Graduate School, College of Engineering and Applied Science, Department of Electrical Engineering and Computing Systems, Program in Computer Science and Engineering, Cincinnati, OH 45221. Offers PhD. *Degree requirements:* For doctorate, thesis/dissertation. *Entrance requirements:* For doctorate, GRE General Test. Additional exam requirements/recommendations for international students: required—TOEFL.

University of Colorado Boulder, Graduate School, College of Engineering and Applied Science, Department of Electrical, Computer and Energy Engineering, Boulder, CO 80309. Offers ME, MS, PhD. Terminal master's awarded for partial completion of doctoral program. *Degree requirements:* For master's, thesis or alternative; for doctorate, one foreign language, thesis/dissertation, departmental qualifying exam. *Entrance requirements:* For master's, GRE General Test, minimum undergraduate GPA of 3.0; for doctorate, GRE General Test, minimum undergraduate GPA of 3.5. Electronic applications accepted. Application fee is waived when completed online.

University of Connecticut, Graduate School, School of Engineering, Department of Electrical and Computer Engineering, Storrs, CT 06269. Offers MS, PhD. Terminal master's awarded for partial completion of doctoral program. *Degree requirements:* For master's, comprehensive exam, thesis or alternative; for doctorate, thesis/dissertation. *Entrance requirements:* For master's and doctorate, GRE General Test. Additional exam requirements/recommendations for international students: required—TOEFL (minimum score 550 paper-based). Electronic applications accepted.

University of Dayton, Department of Electrical and Computer Engineering, Dayton, OH 45469. Offers computer engineering (MS); electrical engineering (MSEE, PhD). *Program availability:* Part-time, blended/hybrid learning. *Degree requirements:* For master's, thesis optional; for doctorate, variable foreign language requirement, thesis/dissertation. *Entrance requirements:* For master's, minimum GPA of 3.2, 3 letters of recommendation, bachelor's degree, transcripts; for doctorate, minimum GPA of 3.2, master's degree, transcripts, 3 letters of recommendation. Additional exam requirements/recommendations for international students: required—TOEFL (minimum score 550 paper-based; 80 iBT). Electronic applications accepted.

University of Delaware, College of Engineering, Department of Electrical and Computer Engineering, Newark, DE 19716. Offers MSECE, PhD. *Program availability:* Part-time, online learning. Terminal master's awarded for partial completion of doctoral program. *Degree requirements:* For master's, thesis optional; for doctorate, thesis/dissertation. *Entrance requirements:* For master's, GRE General Test; for doctorate, GRE General Test, qualifying exam. Additional exam requirements/recommendations for international students: required—TOEFL. Electronic applications accepted.

University of Denver, Daniel Felix Ritchie School of Engineering and Computer Science, Department of Electrical and Computer Engineering, Denver, CO 80208. Offers computer engineering (MS); electrical and computer engineering (PhD); electrical engineering (MS); engineering (MS); mechatronic systems engineering (MS, PhD). *Program availability:* Part-time, evening/weekend. *Faculty:* 12 full-time (2 women), 1 part-time/adjunct (0 women). *Students:* 2 full-time (0 women), 75 part-time (14 women); includes 19 minority (3 Black or African American, non-Hispanic/Latino; 4 Asian, non-Hispanic/Latino; 9 Hispanic/Latino; 3 Two or more races, non-Hispanic/Latino), 11 international. Average age 29. 83 applicants, 71% accepted, 40 enrolled. In 2019, 25 master's, 10 doctorates awarded. Terminal master's awarded for partial completion of doctoral program. *Degree requirements:* For master's, thesis optional; for doctorate, comprehensive exam, thesis/dissertation. *Entrance requirements:* For master's, GRE General Test, bachelor of science degree in computer engineering, electrical engineering, or closely related field, transcripts, personal statement, resume or curriculum vitae, three letters of recommendation; for doctorate, GRE General Test, master of science degree in computer engineering, management science and engineering, electrical engineering, mechanical engineering, or closely related areas, transcripts, personal statement, resume or curriculum vitae, three letters of recommendation. Additional exam requirements/recommendations for international students: required—TOEFL (minimum score 570 paper-based; 80 iBT). *Application deadline:* For fall admission, 1/15 priority date for domestic and international students; for winter admission, 10/25 for domestic and international students; for spring admission, 2/7 for domestic and international students; for summer admission, 4/24 for domestic and international students. Applications are processed on a rolling basis. Application fee: $65. Electronic applications accepted. *Financial support:* In 2019–20, 36 students received support, including 4 research assistantships with tuition reimbursements available (averaging $14,837 per year), 3 teaching assistantships with tuition reimbursements available (averaging $19,589 per year); Federal Work-Study, scholarships/grants, and unspecified assistantships also available. Financial award application deadline: 2/15; financial award applicants required to submit FAFSA. *Unit head:* Dr. Haluk Ogmen, Professor, Interim Chair and Senior Associate Dean, 303-871-2621, E-mail: Haluk.Ogmen@du.edu. *Application contact:* Druselle May, Assistant to the Chair, 303-871-6618, E-mail: Druselle.May@du.edu. Website: http://ritchieschool.du.edu/departments/ece/

University of Detroit Mercy, College of Engineering and Science, Detroit, MI 48221. Offers chemistry (MS); civil and environmental engineering (DE); electrical and computer engineering (ME); electrical engineering (DE); engineering management (M Eng Mgt); environmental engineering (MEE); mechanical engineering (MME, DE); product development (MS); software engineering (MSSE); teaching of mathematics (MATM). *Program availability:* Part-time, evening/weekend. *Degree requirements:* For doctorate, thesis/dissertation. Electronic applications accepted. Application fee is waived when completed online. *Expenses:* Contact institution.

University of Florida, Graduate School, Herbert Wertheim College of Engineering, Department of Computer and Information Science and Engineering, Gainesville, FL 32611. Offers computer engineering (ME, MS, PhD); computer science (MS); digital arts and sciences (MS). *Program availability:* Part-time, online learning. Terminal master's awarded for partial completion of doctoral program. *Degree requirements:* For master's, comprehensive exam, thesis optional; for doctorate, comprehensive exam, thesis/dissertation. *Entrance requirements:* For master's and doctorate, minimum GPA of 3.0. Additional exam requirements/recommendations for international students: required—TOEFL (minimum score 550 paper-based; 80 iBT), IELTS (minimum score 6). Electronic applications accepted.

University of Florida, Graduate School, Herbert Wertheim College of Engineering, Department of Electrical and Computer Engineering, Gainesville, FL 32611. Offers ME, MS, PhD, JD/MS, MSM/MS. *Program availability:* Part-time, online learning. Terminal master's awarded for partial completion of doctoral program. *Degree requirements:* For master's, comprehensive exam (for some programs), thesis (for some programs); for doctorate, comprehensive exam, thesis/dissertation. *Entrance requirements:* For master's, minimum GPA of 3.0; for doctorate, minimum GPA of 3.5. Additional exam requirements/recommendations for international students: required—TOEFL (minimum score 550 paper-based; 80 iBT), IELTS (minimum score 6). Electronic applications accepted.

University of Houston–Clear Lake, School of Science and Computer Engineering, Program in Computer Engineering, Houston, TX 77058-1002. Offers MS. *Program availability:* Part-time, evening/weekend. *Entrance requirements:* For master's, GRE General Test. Additional exam requirements/recommendations for international students: required—TOEFL (minimum score 550 paper-based).

University of Illinois at Chicago, College of Engineering, Department of Electrical and Computer Engineering, Chicago, IL 60607-7128. Offers MS, PhD. *Program availability:* Part-time. *Degree requirements:* For master's, thesis or alternative; for doctorate, thesis/dissertation, departmental qualifying exam. *Entrance requirements:* For master's, minimum GPA of 2.75, BS in related field; for doctorate, GRE General Test, minimum GPA of 2.75, MS in related field. Additional exam requirements/recommendations for international students: required—TOEFL. Electronic applications accepted. *Expenses:* Contact institution.

University of Illinois at Urbana-Champaign, Graduate College, College of Engineering, Department of Electrical and Computer Engineering, Champaign, IL 61820. Offers MS, PhD, MS/MBA.

The University of Iowa, Graduate College, College of Engineering, Department of Electrical and Computer Engineering, Iowa City, IA 52242-1316. Offers MS, PhD. *Program availability:* Part-time. *Degree requirements:* For master's, comprehensive exam, thesis optional; for doctorate, comprehensive exam, thesis/dissertation, qualifying exam. *Entrance requirements:* For master's and doctorate, GRE. Additional exam requirements/recommendations for international students: required—TOEFL (minimum score 550 paper-based; 81 iBT), IELTS (minimum score 7). Electronic applications accepted.

The University of Kansas, Graduate Studies, School of Engineering, Program in Computer Engineering, Lawrence, KS 66045. Offers MS. *Program availability:* Part-time. *Students:* 6 full-time (0 women), 3 part-time (1 woman), 4 international. Average age 27. 8 applicants, 63% accepted. In 2019, 3 master's awarded. *Entrance requirements:* For master's, GRE, minimum GPA of 3.0, official transcript, three recommendations, statement of academic objectives, resume. Additional exam requirements/recommendations for international students: required—TOEFL, IELTS. *Application deadline:* For fall admission, 12/15 priority date for domestic and international students; for spring admission, 10/1 for domestic and international students. Application fee $65 ($85 for international students). Electronic applications accepted. *Expenses:* Tuition, state resident: full-time $9989. Tuition, nonresident: full-time $23,950. *International tuition:* $23,950 full-time. *Required fees:* $984; $81.99 per credit hour. Tuition and fees vary according to course load, campus/location and program. *Financial support:* Fellowships, research assistantships, teaching assistantships, career-related internships or fieldwork, scholarships/grants, and unspecified assistantships available. Financial award application deadline: 12/15. *Unit head:* Erik Perrins, Chair, 785-864-4486, E-mail: perrins@ku.edu. *Application contact:* Joy Grisafe-Gross, Graduate Admissions Contact, 785-864-4487, E-mail: jgrisafe@ku.edu. Website: http://www.eecs.ku.edu/

University of Louisville, J. B. Speed School of Engineering, Department of Computer Engineering and Computer Science, Louisville, KY 40292-0001. Offers computer engineering and computer science (M Eng); computer science (MS, PhD); cybersecurity (Certificate); data science (Certificate). *Accreditation:* ABET (one or more programs are accredited). *Program availability:* Part-time, 100% online, blended/hybrid learning. *Faculty:* 16 full-time (1 woman), 4 part-time/adjunct (3 women). *Students:* 82 full-time (28 women), 120 part-time (29 women); includes 35 minority (10 Black or African American, non-Hispanic/Latino; 15 Asian, non-Hispanic/Latino; 4 Hispanic/Latino; 6 Two or more races, non-Hispanic/Latino), 58 international. Average age 32. 90 applicants, 50% accepted, 32 enrolled. In 2019, 47 master's, 5 doctorates, 25 other advanced degrees awarded. Terminal master's awarded for partial completion of doctoral program. *Degree requirements:* For master's, thesis optional; for doctorate, comprehensive exam, thesis/dissertation. *Entrance requirements:* For master's, Two letters of recommendation, official final transcripts; for doctorate, GRE, Two letters of recommendation, personal statement, official final transcripts. Additional exam requirements/recommendations for international students: required—TOEFL (minimum score 550 paper-based; 80 iBT), IELTS (minimum score 6.5). *Application deadline:* For fall admission, 5/1 priority date for domestic and international students; for spring admission, 11/1 priority date for domestic and international students; for summer admission, 3/1 priority date for domestic and international students. Applications are processed on a rolling basis. Application fee: $65. Electronic applications accepted. *Expenses: Tuition, area resident:* Full-time $13,000; part-time $723 per credit hour. Tuition, state resident: full-time $13,000; part-time $723 per credit hour. Tuition, nonresident: full-time $27,114; part-time $1507 per credit hour. *International tuition:* $27,114 full-time. *Required fees:* $196. Tuition and fees vary according to program and reciprocity agreements. *Financial support:* In 2019–20, 70 students received support,

including 1 fellowship with full tuition reimbursement available (averaging $22,000 per year), 14 teaching assistantships with full tuition reimbursements available (averaging $22,000 per year); research assistantships, scholarships/grants, health care benefits, and tuition waivers (full) also available. Financial award application deadline: 1/1. *Unit head:* Dr. Wei Zhang, Chair, Computer Science and Engineering, 502-852-0715, E-mail: wei.zhang@louisville.edu. *Application contact:* Dr. Mehmed Kantardzic, Director of Graduate Studies, 502-852-3703, E-mail: mehmed.kantardzic@louisville.edu. Website: http://louisville.edu/speed/computer

University of Louisville, J. B. Speed School of Engineering, Department of Electrical and Computer Engineering, Louisville, KY 40292-0001. Offers M Eng, MS, PhD. *Accreditation:* ABET (one or more programs are accredited). *Faculty:* 14 full-time (2 women), 4 part-time/adjunct (0 women). *Students:* 42 full-time (7 women), 31 part-time (7 women); includes 8 minority (3 Asian, non-Hispanic/Latino; 3 Hispanic/Latino; 2 Two or more races, non-Hispanic/Latino), 20 international. Average age 28. 27 applicants, 63% accepted, 12 enrolled. In 2019, 24 master's, 5 doctorates awarded. Terminal master's awarded for partial completion of doctoral program. *Degree requirements:* For master's, thesis optional; for doctorate, comprehensive exam, thesis/dissertation. *Entrance requirements:* For master's, 2 letters of recommendation, official transcripts; for doctorate, GRE, 2 letters of recommendation, official transcripts. Additional exam requirements/recommendations for international students: required—TOEFL (minimum score 550 paper-based; 80 iBT), IELTS (minimum score 6.5). *Application deadline:* For fall admission, 5/1 priority date for domestic and international students; for spring admission, 11/1 priority date for domestic and international students; for summer admission, 3/1 priority date for domestic and international students. Applications are processed on a rolling basis. Application fee: $65. Electronic applications accepted. *Expenses: Tuition, area resident:* Full-time $13,000; part-time $723 per credit hour. Tuition, state resident: full-time $13,000; part-time $723 per credit hour. Tuition, nonresident: full-time $27,114; part-time $1507 per credit hour. *International tuition:* $27,114 full-time. *Required fees:* $196. Tuition and fees vary according to program and reciprocity agreements. *Financial support:* In 2019–20, 42 students received support. Fellowships, research assistantships, teaching assistantships, scholarships/grants, health care benefits, and tuition waivers (full) available. Financial award application deadline: 1/1; financial award applicants required to submit FAFSA. *Unit head:* Bruce Alpenhaar, Chair, Electrical and Computer Engineering Department, 502-852-1554, E-mail: bruce.alphenaar@louisville.edu. *Application contact:* John Naber, Director of Graduate Studies, 502-852-7910, E-mail: john.naber@louisville.edu. Website: http://www.louisville.edu/speed/electrical/

University of Maine, Graduate School, College of Engineering, Department of Electrical and Computer Engineering, Orono, ME 04469. Offers computer engineering (MS); electrical engineering (MS, PhD). *Program availability:* Part-time. *Faculty:* 12 full-time (1 woman), 1 part-time/adjunct (0 women). *Students:* 13 full-time (4 women), 1 part-time (0 women); includes 2 minority (1 Asian, non-Hispanic/Latino; 1 Hispanic/Latino), 5 international. Average age 27. 9 applicants, 100% accepted, 6 enrolled. In 2019, 4 master's awarded. Terminal master's awarded for partial completion of doctoral program. *Degree requirements:* For master's, thesis (for some programs); for doctorate, comprehensive exam, thesis/dissertation. *Entrance requirements:* For master's and doctorate, GRE General Test. Additional exam requirements/recommendations for international students: required—TOEFL. *Application deadline:* For fall admission, 2/1 priority date for domestic students. Applications are processed on a rolling basis. Application fee: $65. Electronic applications accepted. *Expenses: Tuition, area resident:* Full-time $8100; part-time $450 per credit hour. Tuition, state resident: full-time $8100; part-time $450 per credit hour. Tuition, nonresident: full-time $26,388; part-time $1466 per credit hour. *International tuition:* $26,388 full-time. *Required fees:* $1257; $278 per semester. Tuition and fees vary according to course load. *Financial support:* In 2019–20, 10 students received support, including 12 research assistantships with full tuition reimbursements available (averaging $12,100 per year), 10 teaching assistantships with full tuition reimbursements available (averaging $14,300 per year); fellowships, Federal Work-Study, institutionally sponsored loans, and tuition waivers (full and partial) also available. Financial award application deadline: 3/1; financial award applicants required to submit FAFSA. *Unit head:* Dr. Donald Hummels, Chair, 207-581-2244. *Application contact:* Scott G. Delcourt, Assistant Vice President for Graduate Studies and Senior Associate Dean, 207-581-3291, Fax: 207-581-3232, E-mail: graduate@maine.edu. Website: http://www.ece.umaine.edu/

University of Manitoba, Faculty of Graduate Studies, Faculty of Engineering, Department of Electrical and Computer Engineering, Winnipeg, MB R3T 2N2, Canada. Offers M Eng, M Sc, PhD. *Degree requirements:* For master's, thesis; for doctorate, thesis/dissertation.

University of Maryland, Baltimore County, The Graduate School, College of Engineering and Information Technology, Department of Computer Science and Electrical Engineering, Program in Computer Engineering, Baltimore, MD 21250. Offers MS, PhD. *Program availability:* Part-time. *Faculty:* 17 full-time (3 women), 7 part-time/adjunct (0 women). *Students:* 29 full-time (6 women), 13 part-time (0 women); includes 4 minority (1 Black or African American, non-Hispanic/Latino; 3 Asian, non-Hispanic/Latino), 27 international. Average age 28. 53 applicants, 70% accepted, 14 enrolled. In 2019, 12 master's, 1 doctorate awarded. *Degree requirements:* For master's, comprehensive exam (for some programs), thesis or alternative; for doctorate, comprehensive exam, thesis/dissertation. *Entrance requirements:* For master's, GRE General Test, strong background in computer engineering, computer science, and math courses; for doctorate, GRE General Test, MS in computer science (strongly recommended); strong background in computer engineering, computer science, and mathematics courses. Additional exam requirements/recommendations for international students: required—TOEFL (minimum score 550 paper-based; 80 iBT). *Application deadline:* For fall admission, 6/1 for domestic students, 1/1 for international students; for spring admission, 11/1 for domestic students, 6/1 for international students. Applications are processed on a rolling basis. Application fee: $70. Electronic applications accepted. *Expenses:* $14,382 per year. *Financial support:* In 2019–20, 18 students received support, including 12 research assistantships with full tuition reimbursements available, 6 teaching assistantships with full tuition reimbursements available; fellowships, career-related internships or fieldwork, Federal Work-Study, scholarships/grants, health care benefits, tuition waivers (partial), and unspecified assistantships also available. Support available to part-time students. Financial award application deadline: 6/30; financial award applicants required to submit FAFSA. *Unit head:* Dr. Anupam Joshi, Professor and Chair, 410-455-3500, Fax: 410-455-3969, E-mail: joshi@cs.umbc.edu. *Application contact:* Dr. Chintan Patel, Professor and Graduate Program Director, 410-455-3963, Fax: 410-455-3969, E-mail: cpatel2@umbc.edu. Website: https://www.csee.umbc.edu/

University of Maryland, College Park, Academic Affairs, A. James Clark School of Engineering, Department of Electrical and Computer Engineering, College Park, MD 20742. Offers electrical and computer engineering (M Eng, MS, PhD); electrical engineering (MS, PhD); telecommunications (MS). *Program availability:* Part-time, evening/weekend, online learning. *Degree requirements:* For master's, thesis optional; for doctorate, thesis/dissertation, oral exam, qualifying exam. *Entrance requirements:*

For master's and doctorate, GRE General Test, 3 letters of recommendation. Electronic applications accepted.

University of Massachusetts Amherst, Graduate School, College of Engineering, Department of Electrical and Computer Engineering, Amherst, MA 01003. Offers MSECE, PhD. *Program availability:* Part-time. Terminal master's awarded for partial completion of doctoral program. *Degree requirements:* For master's, thesis or alternative; for doctorate, comprehensive exam, thesis/dissertation. *Entrance requirements:* For master's and doctorate, GRE General Test. Additional exam requirements/recommendations for international students: required—TOEFL (minimum score 550 paper-based; 80 iBT), IELTS (minimum score 6.5). Electronic applications accepted.

University of Massachusetts Dartmouth, Graduate School, College of Engineering, Department of Electrical and Computer Engineering, North Dartmouth, MA 02747-2300. Offers communications (Postbaccalaureate Certificate); computing infrastructure security (Postbaccalaureate Certificate); digital signal processing (Postbaccalaureate Certificate); electrical engineering (MS, PhD); electrical engineering systems (Postbaccalaureate Certificate). *Program availability:* Part-time. Terminal master's awarded for partial completion of doctoral program. *Degree requirements:* For master's, thesis, thesis or project; for doctorate, comprehensive exam, thesis/dissertation. *Entrance requirements:* For master's, GRE unless UMass Dartmouth graduate in computer engineering or electrical engineering, statement of purpose (minimum of 300 words), resume, 3 letters of recommendation, official transcripts; for doctorate, GRE unless UMass Dartmouth graduate in college of engineering major or about to receive electrical graduate certificate, statement of purpose (minimum of 300 words), resume, 3 letters of recommendation, official transcripts; for Postbaccalaureate Certificate, statement of purpose (minimum of 300 words), resume, official transcripts. Additional exam requirements/recommendations for international students: required—TOEFL (minimum score 550 paper-based; 79 iBT), IELTS (minimum score 6.5). Electronic applications accepted.

University of Massachusetts Lowell, Francis College of Engineering, Department of Electrical and Computer Engineering, Program in Computer Engineering, Lowell, MA 01854. Offers MS Eng, PhD. *Degree requirements:* For master's, thesis optional.

University of Memphis, Graduate School, Herff College of Engineering, Department of Electrical and Computer Engineering, Memphis, TN 38152. Offers computer engineering (MS, PhD); electrical engineering (MS, PhD); imaging and signal processing (Graduate Certificate). *Students:* 13 full-time (3 women), 8 part-time (3 women); includes 6 minority (4 Asian, non-Hispanic/Latino; 2 Hispanic/Latino), 9 international. Average age 27. 16 applicants, 88% accepted, 6 enrolled. In 2019, 7 master's awarded. *Degree requirements:* For master's, comprehensive exam, thesis or alternative; for doctorate, comprehensive exam, thesis/dissertation. *Entrance requirements:* For master's and doctorate, GRE General Test, MAT, or GMAT, three letters of recommendation. Additional exam requirements/recommendations for international students: required—TOEFL (minimum score 550 paper-based; 79 iBT). *Application deadline:* For fall admission, 8/1 for domestic students; for spring admission, 12/1 for domestic students. Application fee: $35 ($60 for international students). Electronic applications accepted. *Expenses: Tuition, area resident:* Full-time $9216; part-time $512 per credit hour. Tuition, state resident: full-time $9216; part-time $512 per credit hour. Tuition, nonresident: full-time $12,672; part-time $704 per credit hour. *International tuition:* $16,128 full-time. *Required fees:* $1530; $85 per credit hour. Tuition and fees vary according to program. *Financial support:* Fellowships, research assistantships, teaching assistantships, career-related internships or fieldwork, Federal Work-Study, scholarships/grants, and unspecified assistantships available. Financial award application deadline: 2/1; financial award applicants required to submit FAFSA. *Unit head:* Dr. Chrysanthe Preza, Chair, 901-678-2175, Fax: 901-678-5469, E-mail: cpreza@memphis.edu. *Application contact:* Dr. Aaron Robinson, Coordinator of Graduate Studies, 901-678-4996, Fax: 901-678-4996, E-mail: alrobins@memphis.edu.
Website: http://www.memphis.edu/eece/

University of Miami, Graduate School, College of Engineering, Department of Electrical and Computer Engineering, Coral Gables, FL 33124. Offers MSECE, PhD. *Program availability:* Part-time. *Degree requirements:* For master's, thesis (for some programs); for doctorate, comprehensive exam, thesis/dissertation, dissertation proposal defense. *Entrance requirements:* For master's, GRE General Test, minimum GPA of 3.0; for doctorate, GRE General Test, minimum undergraduate GPA of 3.3, graduate 3.5. Additional exam requirements/recommendations for international students: required—TOEFL (minimum score 550 paper-based; 59 iBT), IELTS (minimum score 7). Electronic applications accepted.

University of Michigan, College of Engineering, Department of Computer Science and Engineering, Ann Arbor, MI 48109. Offers MS, MSE, PhD. *Program availability:* Part-time.

University of Michigan, College of Engineering, Department of Electrical and Computer Engineering, Ann Arbor, MI 48109. Offers MS, MSE, PhD. *Program availability:* Part-time.

University of Michigan–Dearborn, College of Engineering and Computer Science, MSE Program in Computer Engineering, Dearborn, MI 48128. Offers MSE. *Program availability:* Part-time, evening/weekend, 100% online. *Faculty:* 22 full-time (2 women), 15 part-time/adjunct (0 women). *Students:* 9 full-time (4 women), 43 part-time (5 women); includes 6 minority (1 Black or African American, non-Hispanic/Latino; 1 Asian, non-Hispanic/Latino; 3 Hispanic/Latino; 1 Two or more races, non-Hispanic/Latino), 20 international. Average age 27. 69 applicants, 55% accepted, 15 enrolled. In 2019, 11 master's awarded. *Degree requirements:* For master's, thesis optional. *Entrance requirements:* For master's, bachelor's degree in electrical and/or computer engineering with minimum overall GPA of 3.0. Additional exam requirements/recommendations for international students: required—TOEFL (minimum score 560 paper-based; 84 iBT), IELTS (minimum score 6.5). *Application deadline:* For fall admission, 8/1 for domestic students, 5/1 for international students; for winter admission, 12/1 for domestic students, 9/1 for international students; for spring admission, 4/1 for domestic students, 1/1 for international students. Applications are processed on a rolling basis. Application fee: $60. Electronic applications accepted. *Financial support:* Research assistantships with full tuition reimbursements, teaching assistantships with full tuition reimbursements, scholarships/grants, unspecified assistantships, and non-resident tuition scholarships available. Financial award application deadline: 3/1; financial award applicants required to submit FAFSA. *Unit head:* Dr. Paul Richardson, Chair, 313-593-5420, E-mail: richarpc@umich.edu. *Application contact:* Office of Graduate Studies, 313-583-6321, E-mail: umd-graduatestudies@umich.edu.
Website: https://umdearborn.edu/cecs/departments/electrical-and-computer-engineering/graduate-programs/mse-computer-engineering

University of Michigan–Dearborn, College of Engineering and Computer Science, PhD Program Electrical, Electronics, and Computer Engineering, Dearborn, MI 48128. Offers PhD. *Faculty:* 22 full-time (2 women), 15 part-time/adjunct (0 women). *Students:* 1 full-time (0 women), 6 part-time (0 women), all international. Average age 25. 32 applicants, 16% accepted, 4 enrolled. *Degree requirements:* For doctorate, thesis/dissertation. *Entrance requirements:* For doctorate, GRE, bachelor's or master's degree in electrical/computer engineering, computer science, physical science, or mathematical science with minimum GPA of 3.2. Additional exam requirements/recommendations for international students: required—TOEFL (minimum score 560 paper-based; 84 iBT), IELTS (minimum score 6.5). *Application deadline:* For fall admission, 2/1 for domestic and international students. Application fee: $60. Electronic applications accepted. *Financial support:* Research assistantships with full tuition reimbursements, teaching assistantships with full tuition reimbursements, scholarships/grants, health care benefits, and unspecified assistantships available. Financial award application deadline: 2/1; financial award applicants required to submit FAFSA. *Unit head:* Dr. Ya Sha Yi, 313-583-6318, E-mail: yashayi@umich.edu. *Application contact:* Office of Graduate Studies, 313-583-6321, E-mail: umd-graduatestudies@umich.edu.
Website: https://umdearborn.edu/cecs/departments/electrical-and-computer-engineering/graduate-programs/phd-electrical-and-computer-engineering

University of Minnesota, Duluth, Graduate School, Swenson College of Science and Engineering, Department of Electrical and Computer Engineering, Duluth, MN 55812-2496. Offers MSECE. *Program availability:* Part-time. *Degree requirements:* For master's, thesis. *Entrance requirements:* Additional exam requirements/recommendations for international students: recommended—TOEFL, IELTS, TWE.

University of Minnesota, Twin Cities Campus, College of Science and Engineering, Department of Computer Science and Engineering, Minneapolis, MN 55455-0213. Offers computer science (MCS, MS, PhD); data science (MS); software engineering (MSSE). *Program availability:* Part-time. Terminal master's awarded for partial completion of doctoral program. *Degree requirements:* For doctorate, thesis/dissertation. *Entrance requirements:* For master's and doctorate, GRE General Test. Additional exam requirements/recommendations for international students: required—TOEFL. Electronic applications accepted.

University of Minnesota, Twin Cities Campus, College of Science and Engineering, Department of Electrical and Computer Engineering, Minneapolis, MN 55455-0213. Offers MSEE, PhD. *Program availability:* Part-time. *Degree requirements:* For master's, thesis or alternative; for doctorate, thesis/dissertation. *Entrance requirements:* Additional exam requirements/recommendations for international students: required—TOEFL (minimum score 550 paper-based). Electronic applications accepted.

University of Missouri, Office of Research and Graduate Studies, College of Engineering, Department of Electrical Engineering and Computer Science, Columbia, MO 65211. Offers computer engineering (MSCE); computer science (MS, PhD); electrical and computer engineering (PhD); electrical engineering (MSEE). *Entrance requirements:* For master's, GRE General Test, minimum GPA of 3.0; for doctorate, GRE General Test, GRE Subject Test, minimum GPA of 3.0. Additional exam requirements/recommendations for international students: required—TOEFL.

University of Missouri–Kansas City, School of Computing and Engineering, Kansas City, MO 64110-2499. Offers civil engineering (MS); computer and electrical engineering (PhD); computer science (MS), including bioinformatics, software engineering, telecommunications networking; computer science and informatics (PhD); computing (PhD); electrical engineering (MS); engineering (PhD); engineering and construction management (Graduate Certificate); mechanical engineering (MS); telecommunications and computer networking (PhD). *Program availability:* Part-time. *Degree requirements:* For doctorate, thesis/dissertation. *Entrance requirements:* For master's, GRE General Test, minimum GPA of 3.0, 3 letters of recommendation from professors; for doctorate, GRE General Test, minimum GPA of 3.5. Additional exam requirements/recommendations for international students: required—TOEFL (minimum score 550 paper-based; 80 iBT).

University of Nebraska–Lincoln, Graduate College, College of Arts and Sciences and College of Engineering, Department of Computer Science and Engineering, Lincoln, NE 68588. Offers bioinformatics (MS, PhD); computer engineering (MS, PhD); computer science (MS, PhD); information technology (PhD). *Degree requirements:* For master's, thesis optional; for doctorate, comprehensive exam, thesis/dissertation. *Entrance requirements:* For master's and doctorate, GRE General Test. Additional exam requirements/recommendations for international students: required—TOEFL (minimum score 600 paper-based). Electronic applications accepted.

University of Nevada, Reno, Graduate School, College of Engineering, Department of Computer Science and Engineering, Reno, NV 89557. Offers MS, PhD. Terminal master's awarded for partial completion of doctoral program. *Degree requirements:* For master's, thesis optional; for doctorate, thesis/dissertation. *Entrance requirements:* For master's, GRE General Test, minimum GPA of 2.75; for doctorate, GRE General Test, minimum GPA of 3.0. Additional exam requirements/recommendations for international students: required—TOEFL (minimum score 500 paper-based; 61 iBT), IELTS (minimum score 6). Electronic applications accepted.

University of New Brunswick Fredericton, School of Graduate Studies, Faculty of Engineering, Department of Electrical and Computer Engineering, Fredericton, NB E3B 5A3, Canada. Offers M Eng, M Sc E, PhD. *Program availability:* Part-time. *Faculty:* 18 full-time (3 women), 3 part-time/adjunct (0 women). *Students:* 50 full-time (9 women), 5 part-time (0 women), 31 international. Average age 27. In 2019, 8 master's, 1 doctorate awarded. *Degree requirements:* For master's, thesis, research proposal; 10 courses (for M Eng); for doctorate, comprehensive exam, thesis/dissertation, research proposal. *Entrance requirements:* For master's, minimum GPA of 3.3; references; for doctorate, M Sc; minimum GPA of 3.3; previous transcripts; references. Additional exam requirements/recommendations for international students: required—TOEFL (minimum score 580 paper-based; 93 iBT), IELTS (minimum score 7), TWE (minimum score 4). *Application deadline:* Applications are processed on a rolling basis. Application fee: $50 Canadian dollars. Electronic applications accepted. *Expenses: Tuition, area resident:* Full-time $6975 Canadian dollars; part-time $3423 Canadian dollars per year. Tuition, state resident: full-time $6975 Canadian dollars; part-time $3423 Canadian dollars per year. Tuition, Canadian resident: full-time $6975 Canadian dollars; part-time $3423 Canadian dollars per year. *International tuition:* $12,435 Canadian dollars full-time. *Required fees:* $92.25 Canadian dollars per term. Full-time tuition and fees vary according to degree level, campus/location, program, reciprocity agreements and student level. *Financial support:* Fellowships, research assistantships, and teaching assistantships available. Financial award application deadline: 1/15. *Unit head:* Dr. Bruce Colpitts, Chair, 504-447-3139, Fax: 504-453-3589, E-mail: colpitts@unb.ca. *Application contact:* Shelley Cormier, Graduate Secretary, 506-452-6142, Fax: 506-453-3589, E-mail: scormier@unb.ca.
Website: http://go.unb.ca/gradprograms

University of New Haven, Graduate School, Tagliatela College of Engineering, Program in Electrical Engineering, West Haven, CT 06516. Offers computer engineering (MS); control systems (MS); digital signal processing and communication (MS); electrical engineering (MS). *Program availability:* Part-time, evening/weekend. *Students:* 46 full-time (17 women), 8 part-time (1 woman); includes 4 minority (1 Black or African American, non-Hispanic/Latino; 1 Asian, non-Hispanic/Latino; 2 Hispanic/Latino), 46 international. Average age 24. 135 applicants, 76% accepted, 10 enrolled. In 2019, 20 master's awarded. *Entrance requirements:* For master's, bachelor's degree in electrical engineering. Additional exam requirements/recommendations for international students: required—TOEFL (minimum score 75 iBT), IELTS, PTE (minimum score 50).

Application deadline: Applications are processed on a rolling basis. Application fee: $50. Electronic applications accepted. Application fee is waived when completed online. *Financial support:* Research assistantships with partial tuition reimbursements, teaching assistantships with partial tuition reimbursements, career-related internships or fieldwork, Federal Work-Study, scholarships/grants, and unspecified assistantships available. Support available to part-time students. Financial award applicants required to submit FAFSA. *Unit head:* Dr. Junhui Zhao, Associate Professor, 203-932-1241, E-mail: JZhao@newhaven.edu. *Application contact:* Selina O'Toole, Senior Associate Director of Graduate Admissions, 203-932-7337, E-mail: sotoole@newhaven.edu.
Website: https://www.newhaven.edu/engineering/graduate-programs/electrical-engineering/

University of New Mexico, Graduate Studies, School of Engineering, Programs in Computer Engineering, Albuquerque, NM 87131. Offers MS, PhD. *Program availability:* Part-time, evening/weekend, online learning. *Faculty:* 9 full-time (1 woman), 3 part-time/adjunct (0 women). *Students:* 32 full-time (3 women), 37 part-time (6 women); includes 21 minority (4 Black or African American, non-Hispanic/Latino; 5 Asian, non-Hispanic/Latino; 11 Hispanic/Latino; 1 Two or more races, non-Hispanic/Latino), 29 international. 133 applicants, 72% accepted, 43 enrolled. In 2019, 17 master's, 2 doctorates awarded. Terminal master's awarded for partial completion of doctoral program. *Degree requirements:* For master's, thesis; for doctorate, comprehensive exam, thesis/dissertation. *Entrance requirements:* For master's, GRE General Test, minimum GPA of 3.0; for doctorate, GRE General Test, minimum GPA of 3.5. Additional exam requirements/recommendations for international students: required—TOEFL (minimum score 550 paper-based; 80 iBT), IELTS (minimum score 6.5), TOEFL or IELTS, not both. *Application deadline:* For fall admission, 6/15 for domestic students, 2/15 for international students; for spring admission, 11/1 for domestic students, 6/15 for international students. Application fee: $50. Electronic applications accepted. *Expenses:* Tuition, state resident: full-time $7633; part-time $972 per year. Tuition, nonresident: full-time $22,586; part-time $3840 per year. *International tuition:* $23,292 full-time. *Required fees:* $8608. Tuition and fees vary according to course level, course load, degree level, program and student level. *Financial support:* In 2019–20, 64 research assistantships, 22 teaching assistantships were awarded; fellowships, scholarships/grants, health care benefits, unspecified assistantships, and Project and Graduate Assistants also available. Financial award application deadline: 2/15; financial award applicants required to submit FAFSA. *Unit head:* Dr. Michael Devetsikiotis, Chair, 505-277-2436, Fax: 505-277-8298, E-mail: mdevets@unm.edu. *Application contact:* Yvone Nelson, Sr. Academic Advisor, 505-277-2600, Fax: 505-277-8298, E-mail: nelsony@unm.edu.
Website: http://www.ece.unm.edu/

University of New Mexico, Graduate Studies, School of Engineering, Programs in Electrical and Computer Engineering, Albuquerque, NM 87131. Offers MS, PhD. *Program availability:* Part-time, evening/weekend, online learning. *Faculty:* 19 full-time (4 women), 7 part-time/adjunct (1 woman). *Students:* 65 full-time (10 women), 77 part-time (12 women); includes 37 minority (1 Black or African American, non-Hispanic/Latino; 1 American Indian or Alaska Native, non-Hispanic/Latino; 6 Asian, non-Hispanic/Latino; 26 Hispanic/Latino; 3 Two or more races, non-Hispanic/Latino), 48 international. 133 applicants, 72% accepted, 43 enrolled. In 2019, 40 master's, 13 doctorates awarded. Terminal master's awarded for partial completion of doctoral program. *Degree requirements:* For master's, thesis; for doctorate, comprehensive exam, thesis/dissertation. *Entrance requirements:* For master's, GRE General Test, minimum GPA of 3.0; for doctorate, GRE General Test, minimum GPA of 3.5. Additional exam requirements/recommendations for international students: required—TOEFL (minimum score 550 paper-based; 80 iBT), IELTS (minimum score 6.5), TOEFL or IELTS, not both. *Application deadline:* For fall admission, 6/15 for domestic students, 2/15 for international students; for spring admission, 11/1 for domestic students, 6/15 for international students. Application fee: $50. Electronic applications accepted. *Expenses:* Tuition, state resident: full-time $7633; part-time $972 per year. Tuition, nonresident: full-time $22,586; part-time $3840 per year. *International tuition:* $23,292 full-time. *Required fees:* $8608. Tuition and fees vary according to course level, course load, degree level, program and student level. *Financial support:* In 2019–20, 64 research assistantships, 21 teaching assistantships were awarded; fellowships, scholarships/grants, health care benefits, unspecified assistantships, and Graduate and Project Assistantships also available. Financial award applicants required to submit FAFSA. *Unit head:* Dr. Michael Devetsikiotis, Chair, 505-277-2436, Fax: 505-277-8298, E-mail: mdevets@unm.edu. *Application contact:* Yvone Nelson, Sr. Academic Advisor, 505-277-2600, Fax: 505-277-8298, E-mail: nelsony@unm.edu.
Website: http://www.ece.unm.edu/

University of North Texas, Toulouse Graduate School, Denton, TX 76203-5459. Offers accounting (MS); applied anthropology (MA, MS); applied behavior analysis (Certificate); applied geography (MA); applied technology and performance improvement (M Ed, MS); art education (MA); art history (MA); arts leadership (Certificate); audiology (Au D); behavior analysis (MS); behavioral science (PhD); biochemistry and molecular biology (MS); biology (MA, MS); biomedical engineering (MS); business analysis (MS); chemistry (MS); clinical health psychology (PhD); communication studies (MA, MS); computer engineering (MS); computer science (MS); counseling (M Ed, MS), including clinical mental health counseling (MS), college and university counseling, elementary school counseling, secondary school counseling; creative writing (MA); criminal justice (MS); curriculum and instruction (M Ed); decision sciences (MBA); design (MA, MFA), including fashion design (MFA), innovation studies, interior design (MFA); early childhood studies (MS); economics (MS); educational leadership (M Ed, Ed D); educational psychology (MS, PhD), including family studies (MS), gifted and talented (MS), human development (MS), learning and cognition (MS), research, measurement and evaluation (MS); electrical engineering (MS); emergency management (MPA); engineering technology (MS); English (MA); English as a second language (MA); environmental science (MS); finance (MBA, MS); financial management (MPA); French (MA); health services management (MBA); higher education (M Ed, Ed D); history (MA, MS); hospitality management (MS); human resources management (MPA); information science (MS); information systems (PhD); information technologies (MBA); interdisciplinary studies (MA, MS); international studies (MA); international sustainable tourism (MS); jazz studies (MM); journalism (MA, MJ, Graduate Certificate), including interactive and virtual digital communication (Graduate Certificate), narrative journalism (Graduate Certificate), public relations (Graduate Certificate); kinesiology (MS); linguistics (MA); local government management (MPA); logistics (PhD); logistics and supply chain management (MBA); long-term care, senior housing, and aging services (MA); management (PhD); marketing (MBA); mathematics (MA, MS); mechanical and energy engineering (MS, PhD); music (MA), including ethnomusicology, music theory, musicology, performance; music composition (PhD); music education (MM Ed, PhD); nonprofit management (MPA); operations and supply chain management (MBA); performance (MM, DMA); philosophy (MA); political science (MA); professional and technical communication (MA); radio, television and film (MA, MFA); rehabilitation counseling (Certificate); sociology (MA); Spanish (MA); special education (M Ed); speech-language pathology (MA); strategic management (MBA); studio art (MFA); teaching (M Ed); MBA/MS. *Program availability:* Part-time, evening/weekend, online learning. Terminal master's awarded for partial completion of doctoral program. *Degree requirements:* For master's, variable foreign language requirement, comprehensive exam (for some programs), thesis (for some programs); for doctorate, variable foreign language requirement, comprehensive exam (for some programs), thesis/dissertation; for other advanced degree, variable foreign language requirement, comprehensive exam (for some programs). *Entrance requirements:* For master's and doctorate, GRE, GMAT. Additional exam requirements/recommendations for international students: required—TOEFL (minimum score 550 paper-based; 79 iBT). Electronic applications accepted.

University of Notre Dame, The Graduate School, College of Engineering, Department of Computer Science and Engineering, Notre Dame, IN 46556. Offers MSCSE, PhD. Terminal master's awarded for partial completion of doctoral program. *Degree requirements:* For master's, comprehensive exam; for doctorate, thesis/dissertation, candidacy exam. *Entrance requirements:* For master's and doctorate, GRE General Test. Additional exam requirements/recommendations for international students: required—TOEFL (minimum score 600 paper-based; 80 iBT). Electronic applications accepted.

University of Oklahoma, Gallogly College of Engineering, School of Electrical and Computer Engineering, Norman, OK 73019. Offers electrical and computer engineering (MS, PhD); telecommunications engineering (MS). *Program availability:* Part-time. Terminal master's awarded for partial completion of doctoral program. *Degree requirements:* For master's, comprehensive exam (for some programs), thesis (for some programs); for doctorate, thesis/dissertation, general exam. *Entrance requirements:* For master's and doctorate, GRE, minimum GPA of 3.0. Additional exam requirements/recommendations for international students: required—TOEFL (minimum score 79 iBT) or IELTS (minimum score 6.5). Electronic applications accepted. *Expenses:* Tuition, state resident: full-time $6583.20; part-time $274.30 per credit hour. Tuition, nonresident: full-time $21,242; part-time $885.10 per credit hour. *International tuition:* $21,242.40 full-time. *Required fees:* $1994.20; $72.55 per credit hour. $126.50 per semester. Tuition and fees vary according to course load and degree level.

University of Ottawa, Faculty of Graduate and Postdoctoral Studies, Faculty of Engineering, Ottawa-Carleton Institute for Electrical and Computer Engineering, Ottawa, ON K1N 6N5, Canada. Offers M Eng, MA Sc, PhD. *Degree requirements:* For master's, thesis or alternative, project; for doctorate, comprehensive exam, thesis/dissertation. *Entrance requirements:* For master's, honors degree or equivalent, minimum B average; for doctorate, minimum A- average. Electronic applications accepted.

University of Pittsburgh, Swanson School of Engineering, Department of Electrical and Computer Engineering, Pittsburgh, PA 15260. Offers electrical and computer engineering (MS, PhD). *Program availability:* Part-time, 100% online. Terminal master's awarded for partial completion of doctoral program. *Degree requirements:* For doctorate, comprehensive exam, thesis/dissertation, final oral exams. *Entrance requirements:* For master's and doctorate, GRE General Test, minimum GPA of 3.0. Additional exam requirements/recommendations for international students: required—TOEFL (minimum score 550 paper-based; 80 iBT). Electronic applications accepted. *Expenses:* Contact institution.

University of Puerto Rico at Mayagüez, Graduate Studies, College of Engineering, Computer Science and Engineering Program, Mayagüez, PR 00681-9000. Offers PhD. *Program availability:* Part-time. *Degree requirements:* For doctorate, one foreign language, comprehensive exam, thesis/dissertation. *Entrance requirements:* For doctorate, GRE General Test, BS in engineering or science; undergraduate courses in data structures, programming language, calculus III and linear algebra, or the equivalent. Electronic applications accepted.

University of Puerto Rico at Mayagüez, Graduate Studies, College of Engineering, Department of Electrical and Computer Engineering, Mayagüez, PR 00681-9000. Offers computer engineering (ME, MS); computing and information sciences and engineering (PhD); electrical engineering (ME, MS). *Program availability:* Part-time. Terminal master's awarded for partial completion of doctoral program. *Degree requirements:* For master's, one foreign language, comprehensive exam, thesis; for doctorate, one foreign language, comprehensive exam, thesis/dissertation. *Entrance requirements:* For master's and doctorate, proficiency in English and Spanish; BS in electrical or computer engineering, or equivalent; minimum GPA of 3.0. Electronic applications accepted.

University of Regina, Faculty of Graduate Studies and Research, Faculty of Engineering and Applied Science, Program in Electronic Systems Engineering, Regina, SK S4S 0A2, Canada. Offers electronic systems (M Eng, MA Sc, PhD). *Program availability:* Part-time. *Faculty:* 6 full-time (1 woman), 3 part-time/adjunct (0 women). *Students:* 32 full-time (7 women), 12 part-time (5 women). Average age 30. 162 applicants, 12% accepted. In 2019, 14 master's awarded. *Degree requirements:* For master's, thesis, project, report; for doctorate, comprehensive exam, thesis/dissertation. *Entrance requirements:* For master's, 4 years bachelor degree, at least 70 percent from a four-year baccalaureate degree (or equivalent). Additional exam requirements/recommendations for international students: required—TOEFL (minimum score 580 paper-based; 80 iBT), IELTS (minimum score 6.5), PTE (minimum score 59), other options are CAEL, MELAB, Cantest and U of R ESL. *Application deadline:* For fall admission, 3/31 for domestic students, 1/31 for international students; for winter admission, 7/31 for domestic and international students; for spring admission, 11/30 for domestic students. Application fee: $100. Electronic applications accepted. *Expenses:* 11,036.50 -This amount is based on three semesters tuition, registered in 6 credit hours per semester. Plus one year student fees and books. There is additional 438.75 if student is in Co-op route. *Financial support:* Fellowships, research assistantships, teaching assistantships, career-related internships or fieldwork, Federal Work-Study, scholarships/grants, unspecified assistantships, and travel award and Graduate Scholarship Base funds available. Financial award application deadline: 9/30. *Unit head:* Dr. Paul Laforge, Program Chair, 306-585-5305, Fax: 306-585-4855, E-mail: paul.laforge@uregina.ca. *Application contact:* Dr. Irfan Al-Anbaqi, Graduate Coordinator, 306-585-4703, Fax: 306-585-4855, E-mail: Irfan.Al-Anbagi@uregina.ca.
Website: http://www.uregina.ca/engineering/

University of Rhode Island, Graduate School, College of Engineering, Department of Electrical, Computer and Biomedical Engineering, Kingston, RI 02881. Offers acoustics and underwater acoustics (MS, PhD); biomedical engineering (MS, PhD); circuits and devices (MS); communication theory (MS, PhD); computer architectures and digital systems (MS, PhD); computer networks (MS, PhD); digital signal processing (MS); embedded systems and computer applications (MS, PhD); fault-tolerant computing (MS, PhD); materials and optics (MS, PhD); systems theory (MS, PhD). *Program availability:* Part-time. *Faculty:* 20 full-time (4 women), 1 part-time/adjunct (0 women). *Students:* 39 full-time (7 women), 14 part-time (1 woman); includes 7 minority (3 Black or African American, non-Hispanic/Latino; 1 American Indian or Alaska Native, non-Hispanic/Latino; 2 Asian, non-Hispanic/Latino; 1 Hispanic/Latino), 23 international. 31 applicants, 74% accepted, 13 enrolled. In 2019, 13 master's, 3 doctorates awarded. *Entrance requirements:* Additional exam requirements/recommendations for international students: required—TOEFL. *Application deadline:* For fall admission, 7/15 for domestic students, 2/1 for international students; for spring admission, 11/15 for domestic students, 7/15 for international students; for summer admission, 4/15 for domestic students. Application fee: $65. Electronic applications accepted. *Expenses: Tuition, area*

resident: Full-time $13,734; part-time $763 per credit. Tuition, state resident: full-time $13,734; part-time $763 per credit. Tuition, nonresident: full-time $26,512; part-time $1473 per credit. *International tuition:* $26,512 full-time. *Required fees:* $1780; $52 per credit. $35 per term. One-time fee: $165. *Financial support:* In 2019–20, 19 research assistantships with tuition reimbursements (averaging $10,247 per year), 9 teaching assistantships with tuition reimbursements (averaging $9,097 per year) were awarded. Financial award application deadline: 2/1; financial award applicants required to submit FAFSA. *Unit head:* Dr. Haibo He, Chair, 401-874-5844, E-mail: he@ele.uri.edu. *Application contact:* Dr. Frederick J. Vetter, Graduate Director, 401-874-5141, E-mail: vetter@ele.uri.edu.
Website: http://www.ele.uri.edu/

University of Rochester, Hajim School of Engineering and Applied Sciences, Department of Electrical and Computer Engineering, Rochester, NY 14627. Offers biomedical ultrasound and biomedical engineering (MS); integrated electronics and computer engineering (PhD); musical acoustics and signal processing (MS); physical electronics, electron magnetism, and acoustics (PhD); signal and image processing and communications (MS); signal processing and communications (PhD). *Faculty:* 20 full-time (1 woman). *Students:* 124 full-time (20 women); includes 5 minority (2 Black or African American, non-Hispanic/Latino; 2 Asian, non-Hispanic/Latino; 1 Hispanic/Latino), 96 international. Average age 27. 454 applicants, 43% accepted, 40 enrolled. In 2019, 39 master's, 7 doctorates awarded. Terminal master's awarded for partial completion of doctoral program. *Degree requirements:* For master's, thesis optional; for doctorate, comprehensive exam, thesis/dissertation, teaching assistant (two semesters), qualifying exam. *Entrance requirements:* For master's and doctorate, personal statement, three letters of recommendation, official transcripts. Additional exam requirements/recommendations for international students: required—TOEFL (minimum score 90 paper-based; 90 iBT), IELTS (minimum score 6.5). *Application deadline:* For fall admission, 1/15 for domestic and international students. Applications are processed on a rolling basis. Application fee: $60. Electronic applications accepted. *Financial support:* In 2019–20, 125 students received support, including 4 fellowships with full tuition reimbursements available (averaging $31,995 per year), 52 research assistantships with full tuition reimbursements available (averaging $29,510 per year), 69 teaching assistantships with full and partial tuition reimbursements available (averaging $15,000 per year); scholarships/grants, tuition waivers (full and partial), and unspecified assistantships also available. *Unit head:* Marvin Doyley, Professor and Chair, 585-275-3774, E-mail: m.doyley@rochester.edu. *Application contact:* Michele Foster, Graduate Program Coordinator, 585-275-4054, E-mail: michele.foster@rochester.edu.
Website: http://www.hajim.rochester.edu/ece/graduate/index.html

University of San Diego, Shiley-Marcos School of Engineering, San Diego, CA 92110-2492. Offers cyber security engineering (MS). *Program availability:* Part-time, evening/weekend. *Faculty:* 2 full-time (0 women), 3 part-time/adjunct (0 women). *Students:* 67 part-time (10 women); includes 34 minority (5 Black or African American, non-Hispanic/Latino; 11 Asian, non-Hispanic/Latino; 15 Hispanic/Latino; 3 Two or more races, non-Hispanic/Latino), 2 international. Average age 34. 65 applicants, 86% accepted, 37 enrolled. In 2019, 30 master's awarded. *Degree requirements:* For master's, capstone course. *Entrance requirements:* For master's, GMAT, GRE, or LSAT if GPA is under 2.75. Additional exam requirements/recommendations for international students: required—TOEFL (minimum score 120 iBT). *Application deadline:* For fall admission, 8/3 for domestic students; for spring admission, 12/2 for domestic students; for summer admission, 4/13 for domestic students. Applications are processed on a rolling basis. Application fee: $45. Electronic applications accepted. *Financial support:* In 2019–20, 5 students received support. Institutionally sponsored loans and scholarships/grants available. Financial award application deadline: 4/1; financial award applicants required to submit FAFSA. *Unit head:* Dr. Chell Roberts, Dean, 619-260-4627, E-mail: croberts@sandiego.edu. *Application contact:* Erika Garwood, Associate Director of Graduate Admissions, 619-260-4524, Fax: 619-260-4158, E-mail: grads@sandiego.edu.
Website: http://www.sandiego.edu/engineering/

University of South Alabama, College of Engineering, Department of Electrical and Computer Engineering, Mobile, AL 36688-0002. Offers computer engineering (MSEE); electrical engineering (MSEE). *Program availability:* Part-time. *Faculty:* 5 full-time (1 woman). *Students:* 9 full-time (0 women), 4 part-time (2 women); includes 1 minority (Black or African American, non-Hispanic/Latino), 4 international. Average age 28. 17 applicants, 71% accepted, 5 enrolled. In 2019, 7 master's awarded. *Degree requirements:* For master's, comprehensive exam, thesis optional. *Entrance requirements:* For master's, GRE. Additional exam requirements/recommendations for international students: required—TOEFL (minimum score 550 paper-based; 79 iBT), IELTS (minimum score 6.5). *Application deadline:* For fall admission, 7/1 priority date for domestic students, 6/15 priority date for international students; for spring admission, 12/1 priority date for domestic students, 11/1 priority date for international students; for summer admission, 5/1 priority date for domestic students, 4/1 priority date for international students. Applications are processed on a rolling basis. Application fee: $35. Electronic applications accepted. *Expenses:* Contact institution. *Financial support:* Fellowships, research assistantships, teaching assistantships, career-related internships or fieldwork, institutionally sponsored loans, scholarships/grants, and unspecified assistantships available. Support available to part-time students. Financial award application deadline: 3/31; financial award applicants required to submit FAFSA. *Unit head:* Dr. Hulya Kirkici, Chair, Professor, Department of Electrical and Computer Engineering, College of Engineering, 251-460-6117, Fax: 251-460-6028, E-mail: hkirkici@southalabama.edu. *Application contact:* Brenda Poole, Academic Records Specialist, 251-460-6140, Fax: 251-460-6343, E-mail: engineering@southalabama.edu.
Website: https://www.southalabama.edu/colleges/engineering/ece/

University of South Carolina, The Graduate School, College of Engineering and Computing, Department of Computer Science and Engineering, Columbia, SC 29208. Offers computer science and engineering (ME, MS, PhD); software engineering (MS). *Program availability:* Part-time, evening/weekend, online learning. *Degree requirements:* For master's, comprehensive exam, thesis (for some programs); for doctorate, comprehensive exam, thesis/dissertation. *Entrance requirements:* For master's and doctorate, GRE General Test. Additional exam requirements/recommendations for international students: required—TOEFL (minimum score 570 paper-based). Electronic applications accepted.

University of Southern California, Graduate School, Viterbi School of Engineering, Department of Computer Science, Los Angeles, CA 90089. Offers computer networks (MS); computer science (MS, PhD); computer security (MS); game development (MS); high performance computing and simulations (MS); human language technology (MS); intelligent robotics (MS); multimedia and creative technologies (MS); software engineering (MS). *Program availability:* Part-time, evening/weekend, online learning. *Entrance requirements:* For master's and doctorate, GRE General Test. Additional exam requirements/recommendations for international students: required—TOEFL. Electronic applications accepted.

University of Southern California, Graduate School, Viterbi School of Engineering, Ming Hsieh Department of Electrical Engineering, Los Angeles, CA 90089. Offers computer engineering (MS, PhD); electric power (MS); electrical engineering (MS, PhD, Engr); engineering technology commercialization (Graduate Certificate); multimedia and creative technologies (MS); telecommunications (MS); VLSI design (MS); wireless health technology (MS). *Program availability:* Part-time, online learning. Terminal master's awarded for partial completion of doctoral program. *Degree requirements:* For master's, thesis optional; for doctorate, thesis/dissertation. *Entrance requirements:* For master's and doctorate, GRE General Test. Additional exam requirements/recommendations for international students: recommended—TOEFL. Electronic applications accepted.

University of South Florida, College of Engineering, Department of Computer Science and Engineering, Tampa, FL 33620-9951. Offers computer engineering (MSCP); computer science and engineering (PhD). *Program availability:* Part-time. *Faculty:* 33 full-time (6 women). *Students:* 177 full-time (57 women), 36 part-time (10 women); includes 30 minority (7 Black or African American, non-Hispanic/Latino; 9 Asian, non-Hispanic/Latino; 13 Hispanic/Latino; 1 Two or more races, non-Hispanic/Latino), 161 international. Average age 27. 595 applicants, 35% accepted, 64 enrolled. In 2019, 56 master's, 11 doctorates awarded. Terminal master's awarded for partial completion of doctoral program. *Degree requirements:* For master's, comprehensive exam, thesis or alternative; for doctorate, comprehensive exam, thesis/dissertation, teaching of at least one undergraduate computer science and engineering course. *Entrance requirements:* For master's, GRE General Test, minimum GPA of 3.0, three letters of recommendation, statement of purpose, mathematical preparation; for the MSIT, evidence of completion of a defined subset of the required core courses of the USF BSIT; for doctorate, GRE General Test, minimum GPA of 3.0, three letters of recommendation, statement of purpose that includes three areas of research interest, mathematical preparation. Additional exam requirements/recommendations for international students: required—TOEFL, TOEFL (minimum score 550 paper-based; 79 iBT) or IELTS (minimum score 6.5). *Application deadline:* For fall admission, 2/15 for domestic and international students; for spring admission, 10/15 for domestic students, 9/15 for international students. Application fee: $30. Electronic applications accepted. *Financial support:* In 2019–20, 25 students received support, including 30 research assistantships with tuition reimbursements available (averaging $14,942 per year), 35 teaching assistantships with tuition reimbursements available (averaging $14,003 per year); unspecified assistantships also available. Financial award application deadline: 1/1; financial award applicants required to submit FAFSA. *Unit head:* Dr. Lawrence Hall, Professor and Department Chair, 813-974-4195, Fax: 813-974-5094, E-mail: hall@cse.usf.edu. *Application contact:* Dr. Yu Sun, Graduate Program Director, 813-974-7508, E-mail: yusun@usf.edu.
Website: http://www.cse.usf.edu/

The University of Tennessee, Graduate School, Tickle College of Engineering, Min H. Kao Department of Electrical Engineering and Computer Science, Program in Computer Engineering, Knoxville, TN 37996. Offers MS, PhD. *Program availability:* Part-time. *Faculty:* 8 full-time (0 women). *Students:* 27 full-time (5 women), 7 part-time (2 women); includes 5 minority (1 Black or African American, non-Hispanic/Latino; 3 Asian, non-Hispanic/Latino; 1 Hispanic/Latino), 15 international. Average age 28. 32 applicants, 41% accepted, 8 enrolled. In 2019, 5 master's, 3 doctorates awarded. *Degree requirements:* For master's, thesis or alternative; for doctorate, comprehensive exam, thesis/dissertation. *Entrance requirements:* For master's, GRE General Test (for MS students pursuing research thesis), minimum GPA of 2.7 (for U.S. degree holders), 3.0 (for international degree holders); 3 references; personal statement; for doctorate, GRE General Test, minimum GPA of 3.0 on previous graduate course work; 3 references; personal statement. Additional exam requirements/recommendations for international students: required—TOEFL (minimum score 550 paper-based; 80 iBT), IELTS (minimum score 6.5). *Application deadline:* For fall admission, 2/1 priority date for domestic and international students; for spring admission, 6/15 for domestic and international students; for summer admission, 10/15 for domestic and international students. Applications are processed on a rolling basis. Application fee: $60. Electronic applications accepted. *Financial support:* In 2019–20, 15 students received support, including 1 fellowship with full tuition reimbursement available (averaging $28,488 per year), 10 research assistantships with full tuition reimbursements available (averaging $22,458 per year), 4 teaching assistantships with full tuition reimbursements available (averaging $18,871 per year); career-related internships or fieldwork, Federal Work-Study, institutionally sponsored loans, health care benefits, and unspecified assistantships also available. Financial award application deadline: 2/1; financial award applicants required to submit FAFSA. *Unit head:* Dr. Gregory Peterson, PhD, Head, 865-974-3461, Fax: 865-974-5483, E-mail: gdp@utk.edu. *Application contact:* Dr. Jens Gregor, PhD, Associate Head, 865-974-4399, Fax: 865-974-5483, E-mail: jgregor@utk.edu.
Website: http://www.eecs.utk.edu

The University of Texas at Arlington, Graduate School, College of Engineering, Department of Computer Science and Engineering, Arlington, TX 76019. Offers computer engineering (MS, PhD); computer science (MS, PhD); software engineering (MS). *Program availability:* Part-time, online learning. Terminal master's awarded for partial completion of doctoral program. *Degree requirements:* For master's, comprehensive exam (for some programs), thesis; for doctorate, comprehensive exam, thesis/dissertation. *Entrance requirements:* For master's, GRE General Test, minimum GPA of 3.0 (3.2 in computer science-related classes); for doctorate, GRE General Test, minimum GPA of 3.5. Additional exam requirements/recommendations for international students: required—TOEFL (minimum score 550 paper-based; 92 iBT), IELTS (minimum score 6.5).

The University of Texas at Austin, Graduate School, Cockrell School of Engineering, Department of Electrical and Computer Engineering, Austin, TX 78712-1111. Offers MS, PhD. *Program availability:* Part-time. *Entrance requirements:* For master's, GRE General Test, minimum GPA of 3.3 in upper-division course work; for doctorate, GRE General Test. Electronic applications accepted.

The University of Texas at Dallas, Erik Jonsson School of Engineering and Computer Science, Department of Electrical and Computer Engineering, Richardson, TX 75080. Offers computer engineering (MS, PhD); electrical engineering (MSEE, PhD); telecommunications engineering (MSTE, PhD). *Program availability:* Part-time, evening/weekend. *Faculty:* 41 full-time (3 women), 11 part-time/adjunct (2 women). *Students:* 383 full-time (96 women), 142 part-time (32 women); includes 46 minority (8 Black or African American, non-Hispanic/Latino; 28 Asian, non-Hispanic/Latino; 7 Hispanic/Latino; 3 Two or more races, non-Hispanic/Latino), 423 international. Average age 28. 1,343 applicants, 25% accepted, 125 enrolled. In 2019, 184 master's, 44 doctorates awarded. *Degree requirements:* For master's, thesis or major design project; for doctorate, thesis/dissertation. *Entrance requirements:* For master's, GRE General Test, minimum GPA of 3.0 in related bachelor's degree; for doctorate, GRE General Test, minimum GPA of 3.5. Additional exam requirements/recommendations for international students: required—TOEFL (minimum score 550 paper-based). *Application deadline:* For fall admission, 7/15 for domestic students, 5/1 priority date for international students; for spring admission, 11/15 for domestic students, 9/1 priority date for international students. Applications are processed on a rolling basis. Application fee: $50 ($100 for international students). Electronic applications accepted. *Expenses: Tuition, area resident:* Full-time $16,504. Tuition, state resident: full-time $16,504. Tuition, nonresident: full-time $34,266. Tuition and fees vary according to course load. *Financial support:* In 2019–20, 208 students received support, including 14 fellowships (averaging $4,096 per year), 140 research assistantships with partial tuition reimbursements available (averaging $22,844 per year), 70 teaching assistantships with partial tuition reimbursements available (averaging $16,888 per year); Federal Work-Study, institutionally sponsored loans, scholarships/grants, unspecified assistantships, and cooperative positions also available. Support available to part-time students. Financial award application deadline: 4/30; financial award applicants required to submit FAFSA. *Unit head:* Dr. Lawrence Overzet, Department Head, 972-883-2154, Fax: 972-883-2710, E-mail: overzet@utdallas.edu. *Application contact:* Dr. Aria Nosratinia, Associate Department Head, 972-883-2894, E-mail: aria@utdallas.edu. Website: http://ece.utdallas.edu

The University of Texas at El Paso, Graduate School, College of Engineering, Department of Electrical and Computer Engineering, El Paso, TX 79968-0001. Offers computer engineering (MS); electric power and energy systems (Graduate Certificate); electrical and computer engineering (PhD); electrical engineering (MS). *Program availability:* Part-time, evening/weekend. Terminal master's awarded for partial completion of doctoral program. *Degree requirements:* For master's, thesis optional; for doctorate, thesis/dissertation. *Entrance requirements:* For master's, GRE General Test, minimum GPA of 3.0; for doctorate, GRE General Test, minimum graduate GPA of 3.0. Additional exam requirements/recommendations for international students: required— TOEFL. Electronic applications accepted.

The University of Texas at San Antonio, College of Engineering, Department of Electrical and Computer Engineering, San Antonio, TX 78249-0617. Offers advanced materials engineering (MS); computer engineering (MS); electrical engineering (MSEE, PhD). *Program availability:* Part-time. Terminal master's awarded for partial completion of doctoral program. *Degree requirements:* For master's, comprehensive exam, thesis (for some programs); for doctorate, comprehensive exam, thesis/dissertation. *Entrance requirements:* For master's, GRE General Test, bachelor's degree in electrical or computer engineering from ABET-accredited institution of higher education or related field; minimum GPA of 3.0 on the last 60 semester credit hours of undergraduate studies; for doctorate, GRE General Test, master's degree or minimum GPA of 3.3 in last 60 semester credit hours of undergraduate level coursework in electrical engineering; statement of purpose. Additional exam requirements/recommendations for international students: required—TOEFL (minimum score 550 paper-based; 79 iBT), IELTS (minimum score 6.5). Electronic applications accepted.

University of Toronto, School of Graduate Studies, Faculty of Applied Science and Engineering, Department of Electrical and Computer Engineering, Toronto, ON M5S 1A1, Canada. Offers M Eng, MA Sc, PhD. *Program availability:* Part-time. *Degree requirements:* For master's, thesis (for some programs), oral thesis defense (MA Sc); for doctorate, thesis/dissertation, qualifying exam, thesis defense. *Entrance requirements:* For master's, four-year degree in electrical or computer engineering, minimum B average, 2 letters of reference; for doctorate, minimum B+ average, MA Sc in electrical or computer engineering, 2 letters of reference. Additional exam requirements/recommendations for international students: required—TOEFL (minimum score 580 paper-based; 93 iBT). Electronic applications accepted.

University of Utah, Graduate School, College of Engineering, Department of Electrical and Computer Engineering, Salt Lake City, UT 84112. Offers electrical and computer engineering (MS, PhD); electrical engineering (ME); MS/MBA. *Program availability:* Part-time, evening/weekend, 100% online, blended/hybrid learning. *Faculty:* 32 full-time (4 women). *Students:* 125 full-time (20 women), 58 part-time (4 women); includes 19 minority (8 Asian, non-Hispanic/Latino; 9 Hispanic/Latino; 1 Native Hawaiian or other Pacific Islander, non-Hispanic/Latino; 1 Two or more races, non-Hispanic/Latino), 106 international. Average age 29. 210 applicants, 35% accepted, 55 enrolled. In 2019, 31 master's, 18 doctorates awarded. Terminal master's awarded for partial completion of doctoral program. *Degree requirements:* For master's, comprehensive exam, thesis optional; for doctorate, comprehensive exam, thesis/dissertation. *Entrance requirements:* For master's, The GRE is required, however this requirement may be waived if a student graduated from an ABET Accredited Engineering program. International students are required to take the TOEFL or IELTS exam, 3.2 GPA; for doctorate, The GRE is required, however this requirement may be waived if a student graduated from an ABET Accredited Engineering program. International students are required to take the TOEFL or IELTS exam, 3.5 GPA. Additional exam requirements/recommendations for international students: required—TOEFL (minimum score 80 paper-based; 80 iBT), IELTS (minimum score 6.5), GRE. *Application deadline:* For fall admission, 7/15 for domestic students, 1/15 for international students; for winter admission, 11/30 for domestic students, 9/30 for international students; for spring admission, 11/30 for domestic students, 9/30 for international students. Applications are processed on a rolling basis. Application fee: $30 ($45 for international students). Electronic applications accepted. *Expenses:* $17,170.88 to complete 32 credits for a degree state resident; $4,661.65 state resident full-time, $2,448.07 state resident part-time, $13,096.79 non-resident full time, $6763.55 non-resident part time *Financial support:* In 2019–20, 2 students received support, including 1 fellowship (averaging $13,000 per year), 86 research assistantships (averaging $13,151 per year), 21 teaching assistantships (averaging $12,952 per year); unspecified assistantships also available. Financial award application deadline: 1/15. *Unit head:* Prof. Florian Solzbacher, Professor and Chair, 801-581-6942, Fax: 801-581-5281, E-mail: florian.solzbacher@utah.edu. *Application contact:* John Bolke, Graduate Coordinator, 801-581-6943, Fax: 801-581-5281, E-mail: john.bolke@utah.edu. Website: http://www.ece.utah.edu/

University of Victoria, Faculty of Graduate Studies, Faculty of Engineering, Department of Electrical and Computer Engineering, Victoria, BC V8W 2Y2, Canada. Offers M Eng, MA Sc, PhD. *Degree requirements:* For master's, thesis; for doctorate, thesis/dissertation, candidacy exam. *Entrance requirements:* For master's, GRE (recommended), bachelor's degree in engineering; for doctorate, GRE (recommended), master's degree. Additional exam requirements/recommendations for international students: required—TOEFL (minimum score 575 paper-based), IELTS (minimum score 7). Electronic applications accepted.

University of Virginia, School of Engineering and Applied Science, Department of Electrical and Computer Engineering, Program in Computer Engineering, Charlottesville, VA 22903. Offers ME, MS, PhD. *Program availability:* Online learning. Terminal master's awarded for partial completion of doctoral program. *Degree requirements:* For master's, thesis (for some programs); for doctorate, comprehensive exam, thesis/dissertation. *Entrance requirements:* For master's, GRE General Test, 3 letters of recommendation; for doctorate, GRE General Test, 3 letters of recommendation; essay. Additional exam requirements/recommendations for international students: required—TOEFL (minimum score 650 paper-based; 90 iBT), IELTS (minimum score 7). Electronic applications accepted.

University of Washington, Graduate School, College of Engineering, Paul G. Allen School of Computer Science and Engineering, Seattle, WA 98195-2350. Offers MS, PhD. *Program availability:* Part-time, evening/weekend. *Students:* 332 full-time (99 women), 174 part-time (30 women); includes 112 minority (5 Black or African American, non-Hispanic/Latino; 75 Asian, non-Hispanic/Latino; 11 Hispanic/Latino; 21 Two or more

races, non-Hispanic/Latino), 217 international. Average age 27. 2,248 applicants, 9% accepted, 96 enrolled. In 2019, 128 master's, 36 doctorates awarded. *Degree requirements:* For doctorate, thesis/dissertation, independent project. *Entrance requirements:* For master's, GRE General Test; for doctorate, GRE General Test, minimum GPA of 3.0, statement of purpose, curriculum vitae, letters of recommendation, transcript. Additional exam requirements/recommendations for international students: required—TOEFL (minimum score 580 paper-based; 92 iBT). *Application deadline:* For fall admission, 12/15 for domestic and international students. Applications are processed on a rolling basis. Application fee: $85. Electronic applications accepted. *Expenses:* Contact institution. *Financial support:* In 2019–20, 33 fellowships with full tuition reimbursements (averaging $36,840 per year), 234 research assistantships with full tuition reimbursements (averaging $36,840 per year), 102 teaching assistantships with full tuition reimbursements (averaging $36,000 per year) were awarded; Federal Work-Study, institutionally sponsored loans, scholarships/grants, health care benefits, tuition waivers (full), and unspecified assistantships also available. Support available to part-time students. Financial award application deadline: 12/15. *Unit head:* Magda Balazinska, Director/Chair, 206-616-1069, Fax: 206-543-2969, E-mail: magda@cs.washington.edu. *Application contact:* Elise DeGoede Dorough, Graduate Admissions Information Contact, 206-543-1695, Fax: 206-543-2969, E-mail: elised@cs.washington.edu. Website: http://www.cs.washington.edu/

University of Washington, Bothell, Program in Computing and Software Systems, Bothell, WA 98011. Offers MS. *Program availability:* Part-time, evening/weekend. *Degree requirements:* For master's, comprehensive exam (for some programs), thesis optional. *Entrance requirements:* For master's, GRE. Additional exam requirements/recommendations for international students: required—TOEFL (minimum score 580 paper-based; 92 iBT) or IELTS (minimum score 7). Electronic applications accepted. *Expenses:* Contact institution.

University of Washington, Tacoma, Graduate Programs, Program in Computing and Software Systems, Tacoma, WA 98402-3100. Offers MS. *Program availability:* Part-time. *Degree requirements:* For master's, capstone project/thesis or 15 credits elective coursework. *Entrance requirements:* For master's, GRE, personal statement, resume, transcripts, 3 recommendations. Additional exam requirements/recommendations for international students: required—TOEFL (minimum score 580 paper-based; 92 iBT), IELTS (minimum score 7). Electronic applications accepted.

University of Waterloo, Graduate Studies and Postdoctoral Affairs, Faculty of Engineering, Department of Electrical and Computer Engineering, Waterloo, ON N2L 3G1, Canada. Offers M Eng, MA Sc, PhD. *Program availability:* Part-time. *Degree requirements:* For master's, research paper or thesis; for doctorate, comprehensive exam, thesis/dissertation. *Entrance requirements:* For master's, honors degree, minimum B+ average; for doctorate, master's degree, minimum A- average. Additional exam requirements/recommendations for international students: required—TOEFL, IELTS, PTE. Electronic applications accepted.

The University of Western Ontario, School of Graduate and Postdoctoral Studies, Physical Sciences Division, Faculty of Engineering, London, ON N6A 3K7, Canada. Offers chemical and biochemical engineering (ME Sc, PhD); civil and environmental engineering (M Eng, ME Sc, PhD); electrical and computer engineering (M Eng, ME Sc, PhD); mechanical and materials engineering (M Eng, ME Sc, PhD). *Program availability:* Part-time. Terminal master's awarded for partial completion of doctoral program. *Degree requirements:* For master's, thesis; for doctorate, thesis/dissertation. *Entrance requirements:* For master's, minimum B average; for doctorate, minimum B+ average.

University of Wisconsin–Milwaukee, Graduate School, College of Engineering and Applied Science, Program in Engineering, Milwaukee, WI 53201-0413. Offers biomedical engineering (MS); civil engineering (MS, PhD); computer science (PhD); electrical and computer engineering (MS); electrical engineering (PhD); engineering mechanics (MS); industrial and management engineering (MS); industrial engineering (PhD); manufacturing engineering (MS); materials (PhD); materials engineering (MS); mechanical engineering (MS). *Program availability:* Part-time. *Degree requirements:* For master's, comprehensive exam (for some programs), thesis or alternative; for doctorate, comprehensive exam, thesis/dissertation, internship. *Entrance requirements:* For master's, GRE, minimum GPA of 2.75; for doctorate, GRE, minimum GPA of 3.5. Additional exam requirements/recommendations for international students: required—TOEFL (minimum score 550 paper-based; 79 iBT), IELTS (minimum score 6.5).

Villanova University, College of Engineering, Department of Electrical and Computer Engineering, Program in Computer Engineering, Villanova, PA 19085-1699. Offers computer architectures (Certificate); computer engineering (MSCPE); intelligent control systems (Certificate). *Program availability:* Part-time, evening/weekend. *Degree requirements:* For master's, thesis optional. *Entrance requirements:* For master's, GRE General Test (for applicants with degrees from foreign universities), BEE, minimum GPA of 3.0. Additional exam requirements/recommendations for international students: required—TOEFL (minimum score 600 paper-based; 100 iBT). Electronic applications accepted.

Virginia Polytechnic Institute and State University, Graduate School, College of Engineering, Blacksburg, VA 24061. Offers aerospace engineering (PhD, M Eng/MS); biological systems engineering (PhD); biomedical engineering (MS, PhD); chemical engineering (PhD); civil engineering (PhD); computer engineering (PhD); computer science and applications (MS); electrical engineering (PhD); engineering education (PhD); M Eng/MS. *Faculty:* 447 full-time (90 women), 6 part-time/adjunct (2 women). *Students:* 1,881 full-time (495 women), 326 part-time (70 women); includes 264 minority (51 Black or African American, non-Hispanic/Latino; 2 American Indian or Alaska Native, non-Hispanic/Latino; 96 Asian, non-Hispanic/Latino; 69 Hispanic/Latino; 46 Two or more races, non-Hispanic/Latino), 1,247 international. Average age 27. 4,014 applicants, 44% accepted, 658 enrolled. In 2019, 489 master's, 200 doctorates awarded. *Degree requirements:* For master's, comprehensive exam (for some programs), thesis (for some programs); for doctorate, comprehensive exam (for some programs), thesis/dissertation (for some programs). *Entrance requirements:* For master's and doctorate, GRE/GMAT. Additional exam requirements/recommendations for international students: required—TOEFL (minimum score 90 iBT). *Application deadline:* For fall admission, 8/1 for domestic students, 4/1 for international students; for spring admission, 1/1 for domestic students, 9/1 for international students. Applications are processed on a rolling basis. Application fee: $75. Electronic applications accepted. *Expenses:* Tuition, state resident: full-time $13,700; part-time $761.25 per credit hour. Tuition, nonresident: full-time $27,614; part-time $1534 per credit hour. *Required fees:* $886.50 per term. Tuition and fees vary according to campus/location and program. *Financial support:* In 2019–20, 47 fellowships with full tuition reimbursements (averaging $19,703 per year), 1,163 research assistantships with full tuition reimbursements (averaging $20,602 per year), 554 teaching assistantships with full tuition reimbursements (averaging $16,333 per year) were awarded; scholarships/grants and unspecified assistantships also available. Financial award application deadline: 3/1; financial award applicants required to submit FAFSA. *Unit head:* Dr. Julia Ross, Dean, 540-231-9752, Fax: 540-231-3031, E-mail: rjulie@vt.edu. *Application contact:* Linda Perkins, Executive Assistant, 540-231-9752, Fax: 540-231-3031, E-mail: lperkins@vt.edu. Website: http://www.eng.vt.edu/

Computer Engineering

Virginia Polytechnic Institute and State University, VT Online, Blacksburg, VA 24061. Offers advanced transportation systems (Certificate); aerospace engineering (MS); agricultural and life sciences (MSLFS); business information systems (Graduate Certificate); career and technical education (MS); civil engineering (MS); computer engineering (M Eng, MS); decision support systems (Graduate Certificate); eLearning leadership (MA); electrical engineering (M Eng, MS); engineering administration (MEA); environmental engineering (Certificate); environmental politics and policy (Graduate Certificate); environmental sciences and engineering (MS); foundations of political analysis (Graduate Certificate); health product risk management (Graduate Certificate); industrial and systems engineering (MS); information policy and society (Graduate Certificate); information security (Graduate Certificate); information technology (MIT); instructional technology (MA); integrative STEM education (MA Ed); liberal arts (Graduate Certificate); life sciences: health product risk management (MS); natural resources (MNR, Graduate Certificate); networking (Graduate Certificate); nonprofit and nongovernmental organization management (Graduate Certificate); ocean engineering (MS); political science (MA); security studies (Graduate Certificate); software development (Graduate Certificate). *Expenses:* Tuition, state resident: full-time $13,700; part-time $761.25 per credit hour. Tuition, nonresident: full-time $27,614; part-time $1534 per credit hour. *Required fees:* $886.50 per term. Tuition and fees vary according to campus/location and program.

Washington State University, Voiland College of Engineering and Architecture, School of Electrical Engineering and Computer Science, Pullman, WA 99164-2752. Offers computer engineering (MS); computer science (MS); electrical engineering (MS); electrical engineering and computer science (PhD); electrical power engineering (MS). *Program availability:* Part-time. *Degree requirements:* For master's, comprehensive exam (for some programs), thesis or alternative; for doctorate, comprehensive exam, thesis/dissertation. *Entrance requirements:* For master's and doctorate, GRE General Test, minimum GPA of 3.0, 3 letters of recommendation, statement of purpose, transcripts. Additional exam requirements/recommendations for international students: required—TOEFL (minimum score 580 paper-based).

Washington University in St. Louis, School of Engineering and Applied Science, Department of Computer Science and Engineering, St. Louis, MO 63130-4899. Offers computer engineering (MS, PhD); computer science (MS, PhD); computer science and engineering (M Eng). *Program availability:* Part-time. Terminal master's awarded for partial completion of doctoral program. *Degree requirements:* For master's, thesis optional; for doctorate, thesis/dissertation. *Entrance requirements:* For doctorate, GRE General Test. Additional exam requirements/recommendations for international students: required—TOEFL. Electronic applications accepted.

Wayne State University, College of Engineering, Department of Electrical and Computer Engineering, Detroit, MI 48202. Offers computer engineering (MS, PhD); electrical engineering (MS, PhD). *Faculty:* 19. *Students:* 84 full-time (29 women), 47 part-time (8 women); includes 11 minority (3 Black or African American, non-Hispanic/Latino; 6 Asian, non-Hispanic/Latino; 1 Hispanic/Latino; 1 Two or more races, non-Hispanic/Latino), 76 international. Average age 29. 249 applicants, 35% accepted, 27 enrolled. In 2019, 52 master's, 9 doctorates awarded. *Degree requirements:* For master's, thesis optional; for doctorate, thesis/dissertation. *Entrance requirements:* For master's, GRE (recommended if BS is not from ABET-accredited university), BS from ABET-accredited university; for doctorate, GRE, minimum undergraduate GPA of 3.5 with major or substantial specialized work in proposed doctoral major field, or master's degree in electrical and computer engineering with minimum master's GPA of 3.6. Additional exam requirements/recommendations for international students: required—TOEFL (minimum score 550 paper-based; 79 iBT), TWE (minimum score 5.5), Michigan English Language Assessment Battery (minimum score 85); recommended—IELTS (minimum score 6.5). *Application deadline:* For fall admission, 6/1 priority date for domestic students, 5/1 priority date for international students; for winter admission, 10/1 priority date for domestic students, 9/1 priority date for international students; for spring admission, 2/1 priority date for domestic students, 1/1 priority date for international students. Applications are processed on a rolling basis. Application fee: $50. Electronic applications accepted. *Expenses:* $790 per credit hour in-state tuition, $1579 per credit hour out-of-state tuition. MS is a 30 credit hour program; PhD is a 90 credit hour program. *Financial support:* In 2019–20, 53 students received support, including 3 fellowships with tuition reimbursements available (averaging $20,000 per year), 10 research assistantships with tuition reimbursements available (averaging $18,526 per year), 10 teaching assistantships with tuition reimbursements available (averaging $20,792 per year); scholarships/grants, health care benefits, and unspecified assistantships also available. Support available to part-time students. Financial award applicants required to submit FAFSA. *Unit head:* Dr. Mohammed Ismail Elnaggar, Department Chair, 734-284-3100, E-mail: gd8686@wayne.edu. *Application contact:* Eric Scimeca, Graduate Program Coordinator, 313-577-0412, E-mail: eric.scimeca@wayne.edu.
Website: http://engineering.wayne.edu/ece/

Weber State University, Masters of Electrical Engineering, Ogden, UT 84408-1001. Offers computer engineering (MS). *Program availability:* Part-time. *Faculty:* 4 full-time (0

women). *Students:* 4 full-time (0 women), 3 part-time (0 women), 1 international. Average age 27. *Degree requirements:* For master's, thesis optional. *Entrance requirements:* Additional exam requirements/recommendations for international students: required—TOEFL (minimum score 79 iBT), IELTS (minimum score 6.5). *Application deadline:* For fall admission, 5/7 for domestic and international students; for spring admission, 11/7 for domestic and international students. Application fee: $60 ($65 for international students). Electronic applications accepted. *Expenses: Tuition, area resident:* Full-time $7197; part-time $4981. Tuition, state resident: full-time $7197; part-time $4981. Tuition, nonresident: full-time $16,560; part-time $11,589. *Required fees:* $643 per semester. One-time fee: $60. Tuition and fees vary according to course load and program. *Financial support:* In 2019–20, 2 students received support. *Unit head:* Dr. Justin B. Jackson, Department Chair, 801-626-6078, E-mail: justinjackson@weber.edu. *Application contact:* Scott Teichert, Director of Admissions, 801-626-7670, Fax: 801-626-6045, E-mail: scottteichert@weber.edu.
Website: http://www.weber.edu/east

Western Michigan University, Graduate College, College of Engineering and Applied Sciences, Department of Electrical and Computer Engineering, Kalamazoo, MI 49008. Offers computer engineering (MSE); electrical and computer engineering (PhD); electrical engineering (MSE). *Program availability:* Part-time. *Degree requirements:* For master's, thesis optional.

West Virginia University, Statler College of Engineering and Mineral Resources, Morgantown, WV 26506. Offers aerospace engineering (MSAE, PhD); chemical engineering (MS Ch E, PhD); civil engineering (MSCE, PhD); computer engineering (PhD); computer science (MSCS, PhD); electrical engineering (MSEE, PhD); energy systems engineering (MSESE); engineering (MSE); industrial engineering (MSIE, PhD); industrial hygiene (MS); material science and engineering (MSMSE, PhD); mechanical engineering (MSME, PhD); mining engineering (MS Min E, PhD); petroleum and natural gas engineering (MSPNGE, PhD); safety management (MS); software engineering (MSSE). *Program availability:* Part-time. Terminal master's awarded for partial completion of doctoral program. *Degree requirements:* For master's, thesis optional; for doctorate, comprehensive exam, thesis/dissertation. *Entrance requirements:* Additional exam requirements/recommendations for international students: required—TOEFL (minimum score 550 paper-based). Electronic applications accepted. *Expenses:* Contact institution.

Wichita State University, Graduate School, College of Engineering, Department of Electrical Engineering and Computer Science, Wichita, KS 67260. Offers computer networking (MS); computer science (MS); electrical and computer engineering (MS); electrical engineering and computer science (PhD). *Program availability:* Part-time, evening/weekend.

Worcester Polytechnic Institute, Graduate Admissions, Department of Electrical and Computer Engineering, Worcester, MA 01609-2280. Offers electrical and computer engineering (Advanced Certificate, Graduate Certificate); electrical engineering (M Eng, MS, PhD); power systems engineering (MS). *Program availability:* Part-time, evening/weekend, 100% online, blended/hybrid learning. Terminal master's awarded for partial completion of doctoral program. *Degree requirements:* For master's, thesis optional; for doctorate, comprehensive exam, thesis/dissertation. *Entrance requirements:* For master's, GRE (recommended), 3 letters of recommendation; for doctorate, GRE (recommended), 3 letters of recommendation, statement of purpose. Additional exam requirements/recommendations for international students: required—TOEFL (minimum score 563 paper-based; 84 iBT), IELTS (minimum score 7), GRE. Electronic applications accepted.

Wright State University, Graduate School, College of Engineering and Computer Science, Department of Computer Science and Engineering, Computer Engineering Program, Dayton, OH 45435. Offers MS. *Degree requirements:* For master's, thesis optional. *Entrance requirements:* For master's, GRE General Test, minimum GPA of 3.0 in major, 2.7 overall. Additional exam requirements/recommendations for international students: required—TOEFL.

Wright State University, Graduate School, College of Engineering and Computer Science, Department of Computer Science and Engineering, Program in Computer Science and Engineering, Dayton, OH 45435. Offers PhD. *Degree requirements:* For doctorate, thesis/dissertation, candidacy and general exams. *Entrance requirements:* For doctorate, GRE General Test, minimum GPA of 3.3. Additional exam requirements/recommendations for international students: required—TOEFL.

Youngstown State University, College of Graduate Studies, College of Science, Technology, Engineering and Mathematics, Department of Electrical and Computer Engineering, Youngstown, OH 44555-0001. Offers computer engineering (MSE); electrical engineering (MSE). *Program availability:* Part-time, evening/weekend. *Degree requirements:* For master's, thesis optional. *Entrance requirements:* For master's, minimum GPA of 2.75 in field. Additional exam requirements/recommendations for international students: required—TOEFL.

Electrical Engineering

Air Force Institute of Technology, Graduate School of Engineering and Management, Department of Electrical and Computer Engineering, Dayton, OH 45433-7765. Offers computer engineering (MS, PhD); computer systems/science (MS); electrical engineering (MS, PhD); electro-optics (MS, PhD). *Accreditation:* ABET (one or more programs are accredited). *Program availability:* Part-time. *Degree requirements:* For master's, thesis; for doctorate, thesis/dissertation. *Entrance requirements:* For master's and doctorate, GRE General Test, minimum GPA of 3.0, U.S. citizenship.

Alfred University, Graduate School, College of Ceramics, Inamori School of Engineering, Alfred, NY 14802-1205. Offers biomaterials engineering (MS); ceramic engineering (MS, PhD); electrical engineering (MS); glass science (MS, PhD); materials science and engineering (MS, PhD); mechanical engineering (MS). *Program availability:* Part-time. *Faculty:* 27 full-time (4 women), 2 part-time/adjunct (both women). *Students:* 30 full-time (11 women), 15 part-time (5 women); includes 2 minority (both Asian, non-Hispanic/Latino), 12 international. Average age 28. 24 applicants, 83% accepted, 18 enrolled. In 2019, 8 master's, 5 doctorates awarded. *Degree requirements:* For master's, comprehensive exam, thesis; for doctorate, comprehensive exam, thesis/dissertation. *Entrance requirements:* Additional exam requirements/recommendations for international students: required—TOEFL (minimum score 590 paper-based; 90 iBT), IELTS (minimum score 6.5). *Application deadline:* For fall admission, 3/1 priority date for domestic students, 3/15 for international students; for spring admission, 10/1 priority date for domestic students, 10/1 for international students. Applications are processed on a rolling basis. Application fee: $60. Electronic applications accepted. Application fee

is waived when completed online. *Expenses:* $23,530 per year. *Financial support:* In 2019–20, 31 students received support. Fellowships with full tuition reimbursements available, research assistantships with full tuition reimbursements available, teaching assistantships with full tuition reimbursements available, tuition waivers (full and partial), and unspecified assistantships available. Financial award application deadline: 3/15; financial award applicants required to submit FAFSA. *Unit head:* Dr. Gabrielle Gaustad, Dean, 607-871-2953, E-mail: gaustad@alfred.edu. *Application contact:* Lindsey Gertin, Assistant Director of Graduate Admissions, 607-871-2017, Fax: 607-871-2198, E-mail: gradinquiry@alfred.edu.
Website: http://engineering.alfred.edu/grad/

The American University in Cairo, School of Sciences and Engineering, Cairo, Egypt. Offers biotechnology (MS); chemistry (MS); computer science (MS); computing (M Comp); construction engineering (M Eng, MS); electronics and communications engineering (M Eng); environmental engineering (MS); environmental system design (M Eng); mechanical engineering (M Eng, MS); nanotechnology (MS); physics (MS); robotics, control and smart systems (MS); sciences and engineering (PhD); sustainable development (MS, Graduate Diploma). *Program availability:* Part-time, evening/weekend. *Degree requirements:* For master's, comprehensive exam (for some programs), thesis (for some programs); for doctorate, comprehensive exam (for some programs), thesis/dissertation. *Entrance requirements:* Additional exam requirements/recommendations for international students: required—TOEFL (minimum score 450 paper-based; 45 iBT), IELTS (minimum score 5). Electronic applications accepted.

American University of Sharjah, Graduate Programs, Sharjah, United Arab Emirates. Offers accounting (MS); biomedical engineering (MSBME); business administration (MBA); chemical engineering (MS Ch E); civil engineering (MSCE); computer engineering (MS); electrical engineering (MSEE); engineering systems management (MS, PhD); mathematics (MS); mechanical engineering (MSME); mechatronics engineering (MS); teaching English to speakers of other languages (MA); translation and interpreting (MA); urban planning (MUP). *Program availability:* Part-time, evening/weekend. *Degree requirements:* For master's, thesis (for some programs). *Entrance requirements:* For master's, GMAT (for MBA). Additional exam requirements/recommendations for international students: required—TOEFL (minimum score 550 paper-based; 80 iBT), TWE (minimum score 5); recommended—IELTS (minimum score 6.5). Electronic applications accepted.

Arizona State University at Tempe, Ira A. Fulton Schools of Engineering, School of Electrical, Computer and Energy Engineering, Tempe, AZ 85287-5706. Offers electrical engineering (MS, MSE, PhD); nuclear power generation (Graduate Certificate). *Program availability:* Part-time, evening/weekend, online learning. Terminal master's awarded for partial completion of doctoral program. *Degree requirements:* For master's, thesis and defense (MS); comprehensive exams (MSE); interactive Program of Study (iPOS) submitted before completing 50 percent of required credit hours; for doctorate, comprehensive exam, thesis/dissertation, interactive Program of Study (iPOS) submitted before completing 50 percent of required credit hours. *Entrance requirements:* For master's, GRE, minimum GPA of 3.0 in last 2 years of work leading to bachelor's degree, 3.5 if from non-ABET accredited school; for doctorate, GRE, master's degree with minimum GPA of 3.5 or 3.6 in last 2 years of ABET-accredited undergraduate program. Additional exam requirements/recommendations for international students: required—TOEFL, IELTS, or PTE. Electronic applications accepted. *Expenses:* Contact institution.

Arkansas Tech University, College of Engineering and Applied Sciences, Russellville, AR 72801. Offers electrical engineering (M Engr); emergency management (MS); information technology (MS); mechanical engineering (M Engr). *Program availability:* Part-time, evening/weekend, 100% online, blended/hybrid learning. *Students:* 38 full-time (11 women), 45 part-time (22 women); includes 13 minority (10 Black or African American, non-Hispanic/Latino; 1 Asian, non-Hispanic/Latino; 1 Hispanic/Latino; 1 Two or more races, non-Hispanic/Latino), 24 international. Average age 32. In 2019, 26 master's awarded. *Degree requirements:* For master's, comprehensive exam (for some programs), thesis (for some programs). *Entrance requirements:* Additional exam requirements/recommendations for international students: required—TOEFL (minimum score 550 paper-based; 79 iBT), IELTS (minimum score 6.5), PTE (minimum score 58). *Application deadline:* For fall admission, 3/1 priority date for domestic students, 5/1 priority date for international students; for spring admission, 10/1 priority date for domestic and international students. Applications are processed on a rolling basis. Application fee: $40 ($90 for international students). Electronic applications accepted. *Expenses: Tuition, area resident:* Full-time $7008; part-time $292 per credit hour. Tuition, state resident: full-time $7008; part-time $292 per credit hour. Tuition, nonresident: full-time $14,016; part-time $584 per credit hour. *International tuition:* $14,016 full-time. *Required fees:* $343 per term. *Financial support:* In 2019–20, research assistantships with full and partial tuition reimbursements (averaging $4,800 per year), teaching assistantships with full and partial tuition reimbursements (averaging $4,800 per year) were awarded; career-related internships or fieldwork, Federal Work-Study, scholarships/grants, health care benefits, and unspecified assistantships also available. Support available to part-time students. Financial award application deadline: 4/15; financial award applicants required to submit FAFSA. *Unit head:* Dr. Judy Cezeaux, Dean, 479-968-0353, E-mail: jcezeaux@atu.edu. *Application contact:* Dr. Richard Schoephoerster, Dean of Graduate College and Research, 479-968-0398, Fax: 479-964-0542, E-mail: gradcollege@atu.edu.
Website: http://www.atu.edu/appliedsci/

Auburn University, Graduate School, Samuel Ginn College of Engineering, Department of Electrical and Computer Engineering, Auburn University, AL 36849. Offers MEE, MS, PhD. *Program availability:* Part-time. *Faculty:* 32 full-time (1 woman), 4 part-time/adjunct (1 woman). *Students:* 72 full-time (14 women), 40 part-time (4 women); includes 9 minority (3 Black or African American, non-Hispanic/Latino; 4 Asian, non-Hispanic/Latino; 2 Hispanic/Latino), 69 international. Average age 29. 126 applicants, 52% accepted, 25 enrolled. In 2019, 25 master's, 11 doctorates awarded. *Degree requirements:* For master's, comprehensive exam, thesis (for some programs); for doctorate, thesis/dissertation. *Entrance requirements:* For master's and doctorate, GRE General Test, GRE Subject Test. Additional exam requirements/recommendations for international students: required—TOEFL (minimum score 550 paper-based; 79 iBT). *Application deadline:* For fall admission, 3/31 priority date for domestic and international students; for spring admission, 9/30 priority date for domestic and international students. Applications are processed on a rolling basis. Application fee: $60 ($70 for international students). Electronic applications accepted. *Expenses: Tuition, area resident:* Full-time $9828; part-time $546 per credit hour. Tuition, state resident: full-time $9828; part-time $546 per credit hour. Tuition, nonresident: full-time $29,484; part-time $1638 per credit hour. *International tuition:* $29,744 full-time. Tuition and fees vary according to course load, program and reciprocity agreements. *Financial support:* In 2019–20, 12 fellowships (averaging $44,000 per year), 64 research assistantships (averaging $14,895 per year), 15 teaching assistantships (averaging $16,396 per year) were awarded; Federal Work-Study also available. Support available to part-time students. Financial award application deadline: 3/15; financial award applicants required to submit FAFSA. *Unit head:* Dr. Mark Nelms, Head, 334-844-1830, E-mail: nelmsrm@auburn.edu. *Application contact:* Dr. George Flowers, Dean of the Graduate School, 334-844-2125.
Website: http://www.eng.auburn.edu/ee/

Baylor University, Graduate School, School of Engineering and Computer Science, Department of Electrical and Computer Engineering, Waco, TX 76798. Offers MS, PhD. *Faculty:* 19 full-time (2 women). *Students:* 45 full-time (8 women), 3 part-time (0 women); includes 10 minority (1 Black or African American, non-Hispanic/Latino; 1 American Indian or Alaska Native, non-Hispanic/Latino; 3 Asian, non-Hispanic/Latino; 3 Hispanic/Latino; 2 Two or more races, non-Hispanic/Latino), 17 international. 48 applicants, 27% accepted, 6 enrolled. In 2019, 8 master's, 3 doctorates awarded. *Degree requirements:* For master's, thesis (for some programs); for doctorate, comprehensive exam, thesis/dissertation. *Entrance requirements:* For master's and doctorate, GRE. Additional exam requirements/recommendations for international students: required—TOEFL (minimum score 550 paper-based; 100 iBT). *Application deadline:* For fall admission, 2/15 for domestic and international students; for spring admission, 12/1 for domestic and international students. Applications are processed on a rolling basis. Application fee: $50. Electronic applications accepted. *Expenses:* Contact institution. *Financial support:* In 2019–20, 19 students received support, including 17 research assistantships with full tuition reimbursements available (averaging $18,750 per year), 19 teaching assistantships with full tuition reimbursements available (averaging $16,000 per year); fellowships, scholarships/grants, health care benefits, tuition waivers (full), and unspecified assistantships also available. Financial award application deadline: 4/15. *Unit head:* Dr. Kwang Y. Lee, Chair, 254-710-4817, Fax: 254-710-3010, E-mail: kwang_y_lee@baylor.edu.

Application contact: Dr. Ian Gravagne, Electrical and Computer Engineering Graduate Director, 254-710-7303, Fax: 254-710-3010, E-mail: ian_gravagne@baylor.edu.
Website: http://www.ecs.baylor.edu/ece/

Baylor University, Graduate School, School of Engineering and Computer Science, Department of Engineering, Waco, TX 76798. Offers biomedical engineering (MSBME); electrical and computer engineering (MSECE, PhD); engineering (ME); mechanical engineering (MSME).

Binghamton University, State University of New York, Graduate School, Thomas J. Watson School of Engineering and Applied Science, Department of Electrical and Computer Engineering, Binghamton, NY 13902-6000. Offers MS, PhD. *Program availability:* Part-time, evening/weekend, online learning. *Degree requirements:* For master's, thesis (for some programs); for doctorate, comprehensive exam, thesis/dissertation. *Entrance requirements:* For master's and doctorate, GRE General Test. Additional exam requirements/recommendations for international students: required—TOEFL (minimum score 550 paper-based; 80 iBT). Electronic applications accepted. *Expenses:* Contact institution.

Boise State University, College of Engineering, Department of Electrical and Computer Engineering, Boise, ID 83725-0399. Offers M Engr, MS, PhD. *Program availability:* Part-time. *Students:* 38 full-time (9 women), 16 part-time (2 women); includes 5 minority (2 Asian, non-Hispanic/Latino; 2 Hispanic/Latino; 1 Two or more races, non-Hispanic/Latino), 33 international. Terminal master's awarded for partial completion of doctoral program. *Degree requirements:* For master's, comprehensive exam, thesis (for some programs); for doctorate, thesis/dissertation. *Entrance requirements:* For master's, GRE General Test, minimum GPA of 3.0. Additional exam requirements/recommendations for international students: required—TOEFL, IELTS. Electronic applications accepted. *Expenses: Tuition, area resident:* Full-time $7110; part-time $470 per credit hour. Tuition, state resident: full-time $7110; part-time $470 per credit hour. Tuition, nonresident: full-time $24,030; part-time $827 per credit hour. *International tuition:* $827 full-time. *Required fees:* $2536. Tuition and fees vary according to course load and program. *Financial support:* Research assistantships, scholarships/grants, and unspecified assistantships available. Financial award applicants required to submit FAFSA. *Unit head:* Dr. Browning Jim, Department Chair, 208-426-2470, E-mail: jimbrowning@boisestate.edu. *Application contact:* Hao Chen, Graduate Program Coordinator, 208-426-1020, E-mail: haochen@boisestate.edu.
Website: https://www.boisestate.edu/coen-ece/

Boston University, College of Engineering, Department of Electrical and Computer Engineering, Boston, MA 02215. Offers computer engineering (M Eng, MS, PhD). *Program availability:* Part-time. *Students:* 272 full-time (84 women), 68 part-time (13 women); includes 23 minority (2 Black or African American, non-Hispanic/Latino; 16 Asian, non-Hispanic/Latino; 2 Hispanic/Latino; 3 Two or more races, non-Hispanic/Latino), 258 international. Average age 24. 1,686 applicants, 32% accepted, 127 enrolled. In 2019, 118 master's, 12 doctorates awarded. Terminal master's awarded for partial completion of doctoral program. *Degree requirements:* For master's, thesis (for some programs); for doctorate, comprehensive exam, thesis/dissertation. *Entrance requirements:* For master's and doctorate, GRE General Test. Additional exam requirements/recommendations for international students: required—TOEFL (minimum score 90 iBT), IELTS (minimum score 7). Application fee: $95. Application fee is waived when completed online. *Financial support:* Application deadline: 1/15. *Unit head:* Dr. William C. Karl, Interim Chairman, 617-353-9880, Fax: 617-353-6440, E-mail: wckarl@bu.edu. *Application contact:* Dr. William C. Karl, Interim Chairman, 617-353-9880, Fax: 617-353-6440, E-mail: wckarl@bu.edu.
Website: http://www.bu.edu/ece/

Bradley University, The Graduate School, Caterpillar College of Engineering and Technology, Department of Electrical and Computer Engineering, Peoria, IL 61625-0002. Offers MSEE. *Program availability:* Part-time, evening/weekend. *Faculty:* 9 full-time. *Students:* 2 full-time (both women), 1 (woman) part-time, all international. Average age 25. 25 applicants, 56% accepted, 2 enrolled. In 2019, 4 master's awarded. *Degree requirements:* For master's, comprehensive exam, thesis or alternative. *Entrance requirements:* For master's, GRE, minimum GPA of 3.0, Essays, Recommendation letters, Transcripts. Additional exam requirements/recommendations for international students: required—TOEFL (minimum score 550 paper-based; 79 iBT), IELTS (minimum score 6.5), PTE (minimum score 58). *Application deadline:* For fall admission, 5/15 priority date for domestic and international students; for spring admission, 10/15 priority date for domestic and international students. Applications are processed on a rolling basis. Application fee: $40 ($50 for international students). Electronic applications accepted. *Expenses:* Tuition: Part-time $930 per credit hour. *Financial support:* In 2019–20, 2 students received support. Research assistantships, teaching assistantships, scholarships/grants, tuition waivers (partial), and unspecified assistantships available. Support available to part-time students. Financial award application deadline: 4/1. *Unit head:* Yufeng Lu, Interim Department Chair & Associate Professor, 309-677-3564, E-mail: ylu2@bradley.edu. *Application contact:* Rachel Webb, Director of On-Campus Graduate Admissions and International Student and Scholar Services, 309-677-2375, E-mail: rkwebb@bradley.edu.
Website: http://www.bradley.edu/academic/departments/electrical/

Brigham Young University, Graduate Studies, Ira A. Fulton College of Engineering, Department of Electrical and Computer Engineering, Provo, UT 84602. Offers electrical & computer engineering (PhD). *Faculty:* 21 full-time (1 woman), 2 part-time/adjunct (1 woman). *Students:* 91 full-time (4 women); includes 5 minority (1 Asian, non-Hispanic/Latino; 4 Two or more races, non-Hispanic/Latino), 13 international. Average age 26. 59 applicants, 42% accepted, 25 enrolled. In 2019, 16 master's, 6 doctorates awarded. *Degree requirements:* For master's, thesis optional. *Entrance requirements:* For master's and doctorate, GRE General Test, Minimum GPA of 3.2 in last 60 hours of course work. Additional exam requirements/recommendations for international students: required—TOEFL (minimum score 580 paper-based; 85 iBT), IELTS (minimum score 7). *Application deadline:* For fall admission, 1/15 for domestic and international students; for winter admission, 8/15 for domestic and international students. Application fee: $50. Electronic applications accepted. *Financial support:* In 2019–20, 66 students received support, including 4 fellowships with full and partial tuition reimbursements available (averaging $21,240 per year), 71 research assistantships with full and partial tuition reimbursements available (averaging $15,600 per year), 13 teaching assistantships with full and partial tuition reimbursements available (averaging $17,028 per year); scholarships/grants also available. Financial award application deadline: 12/15; financial award applicants required to submit FAFSA. *Unit head:* Dr. Aaron Hawkins, Department Chair, 801-422-4012, Fax: 801-422-0201, E-mail: hawkins@ee.byu.edu. *Application contact:* Ashley Johansen, Graduate Secretary, 801-422-1160, Fax: 801-422-0201, E-mail: ashley_johansen@byu.edu.
Website: http://www.ee.byu.edu/

Brown University, Graduate School, School of Engineering, Program in Electrical Sciences and Computer Engineering, Providence, RI 02912. Offers Sc M, PhD. *Degree requirements:* For doctorate, thesis/dissertation, preliminary exam.

Bucknell University, Graduate Studies, College of Engineering, Department of Electrical and Computer Engineering, Lewisburg, PA 17837. Offers MSEE. *Program* *availability:* Part-time. *Degree requirements:* For master's, thesis. *Entrance requirements:* For master's, GRE General Test, minimum GPA of 3.0. Additional exam requirements/recommendations for international students: required—TOEFL (minimum score 600 paper-based).

California Institute of Technology, Division of Engineering and Applied Science, Option in Electrical Engineering, Pasadena, CA 91125-0001. Offers MS, PhD, Engr. *Degree requirements:* For doctorate, thesis/dissertation. Electronic applications accepted.

California Polytechnic State University, San Luis Obispo, College of Engineering, Department of Electrical Engineering, San Luis Obispo, CA 93407. Offers MS. *Program availability:* Part-time. *Faculty:* 9 full-time (3 women). *Students:* 24 full-time (5 women), 3 part-time (0 women); includes 18 minority (15 Asian, non-Hispanic/Latino; 2 Hispanic/Latino; 1 Two or more races, non-Hispanic/Latino), 3 international. Average age 24. 60 applicants, 52% accepted, 15 enrolled. In 2019, 21 master's awarded. *Degree requirements:* For master's, comprehensive exam (for some programs), thesis (for some programs). *Entrance requirements:* For master's, GRE. Additional exam requirements/recommendations for international students: required—TOEFL (minimum score 80 iBT). *Application deadline:* For fall admission, 3/1 for domestic and international students. Applications are processed on a rolling basis. Application fee: $55. Electronic applications accepted. *Expenses:* Tuition, state resident: full-time $7176; part-time $4164 per year. Tuition, nonresident: full-time $18,690; part-time $8916 per year. *Required fees:* $4206; $3185 per unit. $1061 per term. *Financial support:* Fellowships, research assistantships, teaching assistantships, career-related internships or fieldwork, scholarships/grants, and unspecified assistantships available. Financial award application deadline: 3/2; financial award applicants required to submit FAFSA. *Unit head:* Dr. Jane Zhang, Graduate Coordinator, 805-756-7528, E-mail: jzhang@calpoly.edu. *Application contact:* Dr. Jane Zhang, Graduate Coordinator, 805-756-7528, E-mail: jzhang@calpoly.edu.
Website: http://www.ee.calpoly.edu/

California State Polytechnic University, Pomona, Program in Electrical Engineering, Pomona, CA 91768-2557. Offers communication systems (MSEE). *Program availability:* Part-time, evening/weekend. *Entrance requirements:* Additional exam requirements/recommendations for international students: required—TOEFL (minimum score 550 paper-based). Electronic applications accepted. *Expenses:* Contact institution.

California State University, Chico, Office of Graduate Studies, College of Engineering, Computer Science, and Construction Management, Electrical and Computer Engineering Department, Option in Electronics Engineering, Chico, CA 95929-0722. Offers electronic engineering (MS). *Degree requirements:* For master's, thesis or project plan. *Entrance requirements:* For master's, GRE General Test, Fall Admissions only. Two letters of recommendation, statement of purpose, departmental letter of recommendation access waiver form. Additional exam requirements/recommendations for international students: required—TOEFL (minimum score 550 paper-based; 80 iBT), IELTS (minimum score 6.5), PTE (minimum score 59). Electronic applications accepted.

California State University, Fresno, Division of Research and Graduate Studies, Lyles College of Engineering, Department of Electrical and Computer Engineering, Fresno, CA 93740-8027. Offers computer engineering (MSE); electrical engineering (MSE). *Program availability:* Part-time, evening/weekend. *Degree requirements:* For master's, thesis or alternative. *Entrance requirements:* For master's, GRE General Test, minimum GPA of 2.7. Additional exam requirements/recommendations for international students: required—TOEFL. Electronic applications accepted. *Expenses:* Tuition, state resident: full-time $4012; part-time $2506 per semester.

California State University, Fullerton, Graduate Studies, College of Engineering and Computer Science, Department of Electrical Engineering, Fullerton, CA 92831-3599. Offers electrical engineering (MS); systems engineering (MS). *Program availability:* Part-time. *Degree requirements:* For master's, comprehensive exam, project or thesis. *Entrance requirements:* For master's, GRE General Test, GRE Subject Test, minimum undergraduate GPA of 2.5, 3.0 graduate.

California State University, Long Beach, Graduate Studies, College of Engineering, Department of Electrical Engineering, Long Beach, CA 90840. Offers MSEE. *Program availability:* Part-time. *Degree requirements:* For master's, comprehensive exam or thesis. *Entrance requirements:* Additional exam requirements/recommendations for international students: required—TOEFL. Electronic applications accepted.

California State University, Los Angeles, Graduate Studies, College of Engineering, Computer Science, and Technology, Department of Electrical and Computer Engineering, Los Angeles, CA 90032-8530. Offers electrical engineering (MS). *Program availability:* Part-time, evening/weekend. *Degree requirements:* For master's, comprehensive exam or thesis. *Entrance requirements:* For master's, GRE General Test, GRE Subject Test. Additional exam requirements/recommendations for international students: required—TOEFL (minimum score 550 paper-based). Electronic applications accepted. *Expenses: Tuition, area resident:* Full-time $7176; part-time $4164 per year. Tuition, state resident: full-time $7176; part-time $4164 per year. Tuition, nonresident: full-time $14,304; part-time $8916 per year. *International tuition:* $14,304 full-time. *Required fees:* $1037.76; $1037.76 per unit. Tuition and fees vary according to degree level and program.

California State University, Northridge, Graduate Studies, College of Engineering and Computer Science, Department of Electrical and Computer Engineering, Northridge, CA 91330. Offers electrical engineering (MS). *Program availability:* Part-time, evening/weekend. *Degree requirements:* For master's, thesis or alternative. *Entrance requirements:* For master's, GRE General Test, minimum GPA of 2.75. Additional exam requirements/recommendations for international students: required—TOEFL.

California State University, Sacramento, College of Engineering and Computer Science, Department of Electrical and Electronic Engineering, Sacramento, CA 95819. Offers MS. *Program availability:* Part-time, evening/weekend. *Students:* 56 full-time (20 women), 44 part-time (16 women); includes 29 minority (6 Black or African American, non-Hispanic/Latino; 17 Asian, non-Hispanic/Latino; 4 Hispanic/Latino; 2 Native Hawaiian or other Pacific Islander, non-Hispanic/Latino), 55 international. Average age 28. 133 applicants, 66% accepted, 25 enrolled. In 2019, 36 master's awarded. *Degree requirements:* For master's, comprehensive exam (for some programs), thesis (for some programs), thesis or comprehensive exam, writing proficiency exam. *Entrance requirements:* For master's, minimum GPA of 3.0 in last 60 units of the BS in electrical and electronic engineering or equivalent, 3.25 in electrical and electronic engineering major or equivalent major. Additional exam requirements/recommendations for international students: required—TOEFL (minimum score 550 paper-based; 80 iBT); recommended—IELTS (minimum score 7). *Application deadline:* For fall admission, 3/1 for domestic students, 2/1 for international students; for spring admission, 9/15 for domestic students, 8/15 for international students. Applications are processed on a rolling basis. Application fee: $70. Electronic applications accepted. *Expenses:* Contact institution. *Financial support:* Teaching assistantships, career-related internships or fieldwork, Federal Work-Study, and scholarships/grants available. Support available to part-time students. Financial award application deadline: 3/1; financial award applicants required to submit FAFSA. *Unit head:* Dr. Fethi Belkhouche, Chair, 916-278-6873, E-mail: fbeklhou@csus.edu. *Application contact:* Jose Martinez, Graduate Admissions Supervisor, 916-278-7871, E-mail: martinj@skymail.csus.edu.
Website: http://www.ecs.csus.edu/eee

Capitol Technology University, Graduate Programs, Laurel, MD 20708-9759. Offers business administration (MBA); computer science (MS); electrical engineering (MS); information and telecommunications systems management (MS); information architecture (MS); network security (MS). *Program availability:* Part-time, evening/weekend, online learning. *Entrance requirements:* For master's, minimum GPA of 3.0. Electronic applications accepted.

Carleton University, Faculty of Graduate Studies, Faculty of Engineering and Design, Ottawa-Carleton Institute for Electrical Engineering, Department of Electronics, Ottawa, ON K1S 5B6, Canada. Offers electrical engineering (M Eng, MA Sc, PhD). *Degree requirements:* For master's, thesis optional; for doctorate, comprehensive exam, thesis/dissertation. *Entrance requirements:* For master's, honors degree; for doctorate, MA Sc or M Eng. Additional exam requirements/recommendations for international students: required—TOEFL.

Carleton University, Faculty of Graduate Studies, Faculty of Engineering and Design, Ottawa-Carleton Institute for Electrical Engineering, Department of Systems and Computer Engineering, Ottawa, ON K1S 5B6, Canada. Offers electrical engineering (MA Sc, PhD); information and systems science (M Sc); technology innovation management (M Eng, MA Sc). *Degree requirements:* For master's, thesis optional. *Entrance requirements:* For master's, honors degree. Additional exam requirements/recommendations for international students: required—TOEFL.

Carnegie Mellon University, Carnegie Institute of Technology, Department of Electrical and Computer Engineering, Pittsburgh, PA 15213-3891. Offers MS, PhD. *Program availability:* Part-time. *Degree requirements:* For master's, thesis; for doctorate, thesis/dissertation, qualifying exam, teaching experience. *Entrance requirements:* For master's and doctorate, GRE General Test. Additional exam requirements/recommendations for international students: required—TOEFL.

Case Western Reserve University, School of Graduate Studies, Case School of Engineering, Department of Computer and Data Sciences, Cleveland, OH 44106. Offers computer engineering (MS, PhD); computing and information sciences (MS, PhD); electrical engineering (MS, PhD); systems and control engineering (MS, PhD). *Program availability:* Part-time, evening/weekend, online only, 100% online. Terminal master's awarded for partial completion of doctoral program. *Degree requirements:* For master's, thesis; for doctorate, thesis/dissertation, qualifying exam, teaching experience. *Entrance requirements:* For master's and doctorate, GRE General Test. Additional exam requirements/recommendations for international students: required—TOEFL.

The Catholic University of America, School of Engineering, Department of Electrical Engineering and Computer Science, Washington, DC 20064. Offers computer science (MSCS, PhD); electrical engineering (MEE, PhD). *Program availability:* Part-time. *Faculty:* 10 full-time (1 woman), 9 part-time/adjunct (8 women). *Students:* 13 full-time (5 women), 71 part-time (26 women); includes 18 minority (8 Black or African American, non-Hispanic/Latino; 5 Asian, non-Hispanic/Latino; 2 Hispanic/Latino; 3 Two or more races, non-Hispanic/Latino), 40 international. Average age 34. 75 applicants, 83% accepted, 27 enrolled. In 2019, 20 master's, 8 doctorates awarded. *Degree requirements:* For master's, thesis or alternative; for doctorate, comprehensive exam, thesis/dissertation, oral exams. *Entrance requirements:* For master's and doctorate, statement of purpose, official copies of academic transcripts, three letters of recommendation. Additional exam requirements/recommendations for international students: required—TOEFL (minimum score 550 paper-based; 80 iBT). *Application deadline:* For fall admission, 7/15 priority date for domestic students, 7/1 for international students; for spring admission, 11/15 priority date for domestic students, 11/1 for international students. Applications are processed on a rolling basis. Application fee: $55. Electronic applications accepted. *Expenses:* Contact institution. *Financial support:* Fellowships, research assistantships, teaching assistantships, Federal Work-Study, scholarships/grants, tuition waivers (full and partial), and unspecified assistantships available. Financial award application deadline: 2/1; financial award applicants required to submit FAFSA. *Unit head:* Dr. Nader Namazi, Chair, 202-319-5193, E-mail: namazi@cua.edu. *Application contact:* Dr. Steven Brown, Director of Graduate Admissions, 202-319-5057, Fax: 202-319-6533, E-mail: cua-admissions@cua.edu.
Website: https://engineering.catholic.edu/eecs/index.html

The Citadel, The Military College of South Carolina, Citadel Graduate College, School of Engineering, Department of Electrical and Computer Engineering, Charleston, SC 29409. Offers computer engineering (Graduate Certificate); electrical engineering (MS). *Program availability:* Part-time, evening/weekend. *Degree requirements:* For master's, 30 hours of coursework with minimum GPA of 3.0 on hours earned at The Citadel. *Entrance requirements:* For master's, GRE, 2 letters of recommendation; official transcript of baccalaureate degree from an ABET accredited engineering program or approved alternative. Additional exam requirements/recommendations for international students: required—TOEFL (minimum score 550 paper-based; 79 iBT). Electronic applications accepted.

City College of the City University of New York, Graduate School, Grove School of Engineering, Department of Electrical Engineering, New York, NY 10031-9198. Offers ME, MS, PhD. *Program availability:* Part-time. *Degree requirements:* For master's, thesis optional; for doctorate, one foreign language, comprehensive exam, thesis/dissertation. *Entrance requirements:* For master's and doctorate, GRE General Test. Additional exam requirements/recommendations for international students: required—TOEFL (minimum score 500 paper-based; 61 iBT).

Clarkson University, Wallace H. Coulter School of Engineering, Master's Programs in Energy Systems, Schenectady, NY 13699. Offers electrical engineering (ME), including power engineering; energy systems (MS). *Program availability:* Part-time, evening/weekend. *Students:* 1 (woman) full-time, 3 part-time (1 woman); includes 1 minority (Hispanic/Latino). 14 applicants, 71% accepted, 1 enrolled. *Degree requirements:* For master's, project. *Entrance requirements:* Additional exam requirements/recommendations for international students: required—TOEFL (minimum score 550 paper-based, 80 iBT) or IELTS (6.5). *Application deadline:* Applications are processed on a rolling basis. Application fee: $50. Electronic applications accepted. *Expenses: Tuition:* Full-time $24,984; part-time $1388. *Required fees:* $225. Tuition and fees vary according to campus/location and program. *Financial support:* Scholarships/grants available. *Unit head:* Hugo Irizarry-Quinones, Associate Dean of Engineering, 518-631-9881, E-mail: hirizarr@clarkson.edu. *Application contact:* Daniel Capogna, Director of Graduate Admissions & Recruitment, 518-631-9910, E-mail: graduate@clarkson.edu.
Website: https://www.clarkson.edu/academics/graduate

Clemson University, Graduate School, College of Engineering, Computing and Applied Sciences, Holcombe Department of Electrical and Computer Engineering, Clemson, SC 29634. Offers computer engineering (MS, PhD); electrical engineering (M Engr, MS, PhD). *Program availability:* Part-time, evening/weekend, 100% online, blended/hybrid learning. *Faculty:* 37 full-time (3 women). *Students:* 154 full-time (34 women), 26 part-time (4 women); includes 13 minority (5 Black or African American, non-Hispanic/Latino; 1 American Indian or Alaska Native, non-Hispanic/Latino; 4 Asian, non-Hispanic/Latino; 1 Hispanic/Latino; 2 Two or more races, non-Hispanic/Latino), 103 international. Average age 27. 348 applicants, 48% accepted, 60 enrolled. In 2019, 36 master's, 11 doctorates awarded. *Degree requirements:* For master's, comprehensive exam (for some programs), thesis (for some programs); for doctorate, comprehensive exam, thesis/dissertation, departmental qualifying exam. *Entrance requirements:* For master's and doctorate, GRE General Test, unofficial transcripts, letters of recommendation. Additional exam requirements/recommendations for international students: required—TOEFL (minimum score 80 paper-based; 95 iBT); recommended—IELTS (minimum score 7), TSE (minimum score 54). *Application deadline:* For fall admission, 1/15 priority date for domestic students, 4/15 for international students; for spring admission, 9/15 priority date for domestic students, 9/15 for international students. Applications are processed on a rolling basis. Application fee: $80 ($90 for international students). Electronic applications accepted. *Expenses:* Full-Time Student per Semester: Tuition: $5300 (in-state), $11025 (out-of-state), Fees: $598; Graduate Assistant Per Semester: $1144; Part-Time Student Per Credit Hour: $724 (in-state), $1451 (out-of-state), Fees: $617; other fees apply depending on program, credit hours, campus & residency. Doctoral Base Fee per Semester: $4938 (in-state), $10405 (out-of-state). *Financial support:* In 2019–20, 178 students received support, including 33 fellowships with full and partial tuition reimbursements available (averaging $7,853 per year), 91 research assistantships with full and partial tuition reimbursements available (averaging $22,951 per year), 41 teaching assistantships with full and partial tuition reimbursements available (averaging $16,328 per year); career-related internships or fieldwork and unspecified assistantships also available. Financial award application deadline: 1/15. *Unit head:* Dr. Hai Xiao, Interim Department Chair, 864-656-5912, E-mail: haix@clemson.edu. *Application contact:* Dr. Harlan Russell, Graduate Program Coordinator, 864-656-7214, E-mail: harlanr@clemson.edu. Website: http://www.clemson.edu/cecas/departments/ece/index.html

Cleveland State University, College of Graduate Studies, Fenn College of Engineering, Department of Electrical and Computer Engineering, Cleveland, OH 44115. Offers electrical engineering (MS, D Eng); software engineering (MS). *Program availability:* Part-time, evening/weekend. *Faculty:* 15 full-time (2 women), 1 part-time/adjunct (0 women). *Students:* 90 full-time (29 women), 52 part-time (11 women); includes 10 minority (1 Black or African American, non-Hispanic/Latino; 8 Asian, non-Hispanic/Latino; 1 Hispanic/Latino), 95 international. Average age 26. 1,083 applicants, 44% accepted, 89 enrolled. In 2019, 76 master's awarded. Terminal master's awarded for partial completion of doctoral program. *Entrance requirements:* For master's, GRE General Test (minimum score 650 quantitative), minimum GPA of 2.75; for doctorate, GRE General Test (minimum quantitative score in 80th percentile), minimum GPA of 3.25. *Application deadline:* Applications are processed on a rolling basis. Application fee: $40. Electronic applications accepted. *Expenses:* Contact institution. *Financial support:* In 2019–20, 31 students received support, including 10 research assistantships with tuition reimbursements available (averaging $8,300 per year), 12 teaching assistantships with tuition reimbursements available (averaging $9,500 per year); career-related internships or fieldwork, scholarships/grants, and unspecified assistantships also available. Financial award applicants required to submit FAFSA. *Unit head:* Dr. Chansu Yu, Chairperson, 216-687-2584, Fax: 216-687-5405, E-mail: f.xiong@csuohio.edu. *Application contact:* Deborah L. Brown, Interim Assistant Director, Graduate Admissions, 216-523-7572, Fax: 216-687-9214, E-mail: d.l.brown@csuohio.edu. Website: http://www.csuohio.edu/ece

College of Staten Island of the City University of New York, Graduate Programs, Division of Science and Technology, Program in Electrical Engineering, Staten Island, NY 10314-6600. Offers ME. *Program availability:* Part-time, evening/weekend. *Faculty:* 3. *Students:* 8. 15 applicants, 33% accepted, 1 enrolled. In 2019, 2 master's awarded. *Degree requirements:* For master's, thesis or alternative, 30 credits and a study project, research project or comprehensive exam. *Entrance requirements:* For master's, The General Aptitude Test (GRE) is recommended but not required of applicants., BS in Electrical Engineering from an accredited institution (students with a baccalaureate degree in a related field such as Physics, Mathematics, or Computer Science may be accepted). Two letters of recommendation. Applicants must provide a one page personal statement which expresses their goals and philosophy for studying and practicing electrica. Additional exam requirements/recommendations for international students: required—TOEFL (minimum score 73 iBT), IELTS (minimum score 6). *Application deadline:* For fall admission, 6/30 priority date for domestic students, 6/30 for international students; for spring admission, 11/25 priority date for domestic students, 11/25 for international students. Applications are processed on a rolling basis. Application fee: $75. Electronic applications accepted. *Expenses:* $6,485 per semester full-time tuition for resident, $945 per credit full-time for non-resident; $550 per credit part-time for resident; $945 per credit part-time for non-resident; $559 fees per academic year for full-time; $280 fees per semester for part-time. *Unit head:* Prof. Mark D. Feuer, Coordinator, 718-982-2808, E-mail: mark.feuer@csi.cuny.edu. *Application contact:* Sasha Spence, Associate Director for Graduate Admissions, 718-982-2019, Fax: 718-982-2500, E-mail: sasha.spence@csi.cuny.edu. Website: https://www.csi.cuny.edu/academics-and-research/departments-programs/engineering-and-environmental-science/me-electrical-engineering

Colorado School of Mines, Office of Graduate Studies, Department of Electrical Engineering and Computer Science, Golden, CO 80401-1887. Offers electrical engineering (MS, PhD). *Program availability:* Part-time. *Degree requirements:* For master's, thesis (for some programs); for doctorate, comprehensive exam, thesis/dissertation. *Entrance requirements:* For master's and doctorate, GRE General Test. Additional exam requirements/recommendations for international students: required—TOEFL (minimum score 550 paper-based; 79 iBT). Electronic applications accepted. *Expenses:* Tuition, state resident: full-time $16,650; part-time $925 per credit hour. Tuition, nonresident: full-time $37,350; part-time $2075 per credit hour. *International tuition:* $37,350 full-time. *Required fees:* $2412.

Colorado State University, Walter Scott, Jr. College of Engineering, Department of Electrical and Computer Engineering, Fort Collins, CO 80523-1373. Offers computer engineering (ME, PhD); electrical engineering (MS). *Program availability:* Part-time, online learning. Terminal master's awarded for partial completion of doctoral program. *Degree requirements:* For master's, thesis (for some programs); for doctorate, comprehensive exam, thesis/dissertation. *Entrance requirements:* For master's and doctorate, GRE, minimum GPA of 3.0; transcripts; resume; 3 letters of reference. Additional exam requirements/recommendations for international students: required—TOEFL (minimum score 80 iBT), IELTS (minimum score 6.5). Electronic applications accepted. *Expenses:* Contact institution.

Colorado Technical University Aurora, Program in Electrical Engineering, Aurora, CO 80014. Offers MS.

Colorado Technical University Colorado Springs, Graduate Studies, Program in Electrical Engineering, Colorado Springs, CO 80907. Offers MSEE. *Program availability:* Part-time, evening/weekend, online learning. *Degree requirements:* For master's, thesis or alternative.

Columbia University, Fu Foundation School of Engineering and Applied Science, Department of Electrical Engineering, New York, NY 10027. Offers computer engineering (MS); electrical engineering (MS, PhD). *Program availability:* Part-time, online learning. *Degree requirements:* For doctorate, thesis/dissertation, qualifying

exam. *Entrance requirements:* For master's and doctorate, GRE General Test. Additional exam requirements/recommendations for international students: required—TOEFL, IELTS, PTE. Electronic applications accepted. *Expenses: Tuition:* Full-time $47,600; part-time $1880 per credit. One-time fee: $105.

Concordia University, School of Graduate Studies, Faculty of Engineering and Computer Science, Department of Electrical and Computer Engineering, Montréal, QC H3G 1M8, Canada. Offers M Eng, MA Sc, PhD. *Degree requirements:* For master's, thesis optional; for doctorate, comprehensive exam, thesis/dissertation.

Cooper Union for the Advancement of Science and Art, Albert Nerken School of Engineering, New York, NY 10003. Offers chemical engineering (ME); civil engineering (ME); electrical engineering (ME); mechanical engineering (ME). *Program availability:* Part-time. *Degree requirements:* For master's, thesis (for some programs), thesis or special project. *Entrance requirements:* For master's, BE or BS in an engineering discipline; official copies of school transcripts including secondary (high school), college and university work; two letters of recommendation; resume. Additional exam requirements/recommendations for international students: required—TOEFL (minimum score 600 paper-based; 100 iBT). Electronic applications accepted.

Cornell University, Graduate School, Graduate Fields of Engineering, Field of Electrical and Computer Engineering, Ithaca, NY 14853. Offers computer engineering (M Eng, PhD); electrical engineering (M Eng, PhD); electrical systems (M Eng, PhD); electrophysics (M Eng, PhD). *Degree requirements:* For doctorate, comprehensive exam, thesis/dissertation. *Entrance requirements:* For master's, GRE General Test, 2 letters of recommendation; for doctorate, GRE General Test, 3 letters of recommendation. Additional exam requirements/recommendations for international students: required—TOEFL (minimum score 600 paper-based; 77 iBT). Electronic applications accepted.

Dalhousie University, Faculty of Engineering, Department of Electrical and Computer Engineering, Halifax, NS B3J 1Z1, Canada. Offers M Eng, MA Sc, PhD. *Degree requirements:* For master's, thesis; for doctorate, thesis/dissertation. *Entrance requirements:* Additional exam requirements/recommendations for international students: required—TOEFL, IELTS, CANTEST, CAEL, or Michigan English Language Assessment Battery. Electronic applications accepted.

Dartmouth College, Dartmouth Engineering - Thayer School of Engineering, Program in Electrical Engineering, Hanover, NH 03755. Offers MS, PhD. Terminal master's awarded for partial completion of doctoral program. *Degree requirements:* For master's, thesis (for some programs); for doctorate, thesis/dissertation. *Entrance requirements:* For master's and doctorate, GRE General Test. Additional exam requirements/recommendations for international students: required—TOEFL, IELTS. *Application deadline:* For fall admission, 1/1 priority date for domestic students, 1/1 for international students. Applications are processed on a rolling basis. Application fee: $45. Electronic applications accepted. *Financial support:* Fellowships, research assistantships, teaching assistantships, career-related internships or fieldwork, institutionally sponsored loans, scholarships/grants, and tuition waivers (full and partial) available. Financial award application deadline: 2/15; financial award applicants required to submit CSS PROFILE. *Unit head:* Dr. George Cybenko, Dorothy and Walter Gramm Professor of Engineering, 603-646-3843, E-mail: george.cybenko@dartmouth.edu. *Application contact:* Candace S. Potter, Graduate Admissions & Financial Aid Administrator, 603-646-3844, Fax: 603-646-1620, E-mail: candace.s.potter@dartmouth.edu. Website: http://engineering.dartmouth.edu/

Drexel University, College of Engineering, Department of Electrical and Computer Engineering, Program in Electrical Engineering, Philadelphia, PA 19104-2875. Offers MSEE. *Program availability:* Part-time, evening/weekend. Terminal master's awarded for partial completion of doctoral program. *Degree requirements:* For master's, thesis (for some programs). Electronic applications accepted.

Duke University, Graduate School, Pratt School of Engineering, Department of Electrical and Computer Engineering, Durham, NC 27708. Offers M Eng, MS, PhD, JD/MS. Terminal master's awarded for partial completion of doctoral program. *Degree requirements:* For doctorate, thesis/dissertation. *Entrance requirements:* For master's and doctorate, GRE General Test. Additional exam requirements/recommendations for international students: required—TOEFL (minimum score 90 iBT), IELTS (minimum score 7). Electronic applications accepted.

Duke University, Graduate School, Pratt School of Engineering, Master of Engineering Program, Durham, NC 27708-0271. Offers biomedical engineering (M Eng); civil engineering (M Eng); computational mechanics and scientific computing (M Eng); electrical and computer engineering (M Eng); environmental engineering (M Eng); materials science and engineering (M Eng); mechanical engineering (M Eng); photonics and optical sciences (M Eng); risk engineering (M Eng). *Program availability:* Part-time. *Entrance requirements:* For master's, GRE General Test, resume, 3 letters of recommendation, statement of purpose, transcripts. Additional exam requirements/recommendations for international students: required—TOEFL. Electronic applications accepted.

Embry-Riddle Aeronautical University–Daytona, Department of Electrical, Computer, Software and Systems Engineering, Daytona Beach, FL 32114-3900. Offers cybersecurity engineering (MS); electrical and computer engineering (MSECE); software engineering (MSSE); systems engineering (MS). *Degree requirements:* For master's, thesis optional. *Entrance requirements:* For master's, GRE (for some programs). Additional exam requirements/recommendations for international students: required—TOEFL (minimum score 550 paper-based, 79 iBT) or IELTS (6). Electronic applications accepted.

Fairfield University, School of Engineering, Fairfield, CT 06824. Offers database management (CAS); electrical and computer engineering (MS); information security (CAS); management of technology (MS); mechanical engineering (MS); network technology (CAS); software engineering (MS); Web application development (CAS). *Program availability:* Part-time, evening/weekend. *Faculty:* 10 full-time (2 women), 15 part-time/adjunct (1 woman). *Students:* 46 full-time (24 women), 57 part-time (10 women); includes 23 minority (5 Black or African American, non-Hispanic/Latino; 9 Asian, non-Hispanic/Latino; 9 Hispanic/Latino), 33 international. Average age 29. 68 applicants, 62% accepted, 30 enrolled. In 2019, 100 master's awarded. *Degree requirements:* For master's, capstone course. *Entrance requirements:* For master's, resume, 2 recommendations. Additional exam requirements/recommendations for international students: required—TOEFL (minimum score 550 paper-based; 80 iBT), IELTS (minimum score 6.5), TOEFL (minimum score 550 paper-based; 80 iBT) or IELTS (minimum score 6.5). *Application deadline:* For fall admission, 5/15 for international students; for spring admission, 10/15 for international students. Applications are processed on a rolling basis. Application fee: $60. Electronic applications accepted. *Expenses:* Tuition $900/credit hour; Registration Fee $50/semester; Graduate Student Activity Fee (Fall and Spring) $65/semester. *Financial support:* In 2019–20, 20 students received support. Scholarships/grants and unspecified assistantships available. Financial award applicants required to submit FAFSA. *Unit head:* Richard Heist, Dean, 203-254-4147, Fax: 203-254-4013, E-mail: rheist@fairfield.edu. *Application contact:* Melanie Rogers, Director of Graduate

Admission, 203-254-4184, Fax: 203-254-4073, E-mail: gradadmis@fairfield.edu. Website: http://www.fairfield.edu/soe

Fairleigh Dickinson University, Metropolitan Campus, University College: Arts, Sciences, and Professional Studies, School of Computer Sciences and Engineering, Program in Electrical Engineering, Teaneck, NJ 07666-1914. Offers MSEE. *Entrance requirements:* For master's, GRE General Test.

Farmingdale State College, Program in Technology Management, Farmingdale, NY 11735. Offers construction management (MS); electrical and mechanical engineering (MS). *Degree requirements:* For master's, project or thesis.

Florida Agricultural and Mechanical University, Division of Graduate Studies, Research, and Continuing Education, FAMU-FSU College of Engineering, Department of Electrical and Computer Engineering, Tallahassee, FL 32307-3200. Offers electrical engineering (MS, PhD). *Degree requirements:* For master's, comprehensive exam, thesis, conference paper; for doctorate, comprehensive exam, thesis/dissertation, publishable paper. *Entrance requirements:* For master's, GRE General Test, minimum GPA of 3.0; for doctorate, minimum GPA of 3.3. Additional exam requirements/recommendations for international students: required—TOEFL (minimum score 550 paper-based).

Florida Atlantic University, College of Engineering and Computer Science, Department of Computer and Electrical Engineering and Computer Science, Boca Raton, FL 33431-0991. Offers bioengineering (MS); computer engineering (MS, PhD); computer science (MS, PhD); electrical engineering (MS, PhD). *Program availability:* Part-time, evening/weekend. *Faculty:* 39 full-time (8 women). *Students:* 112 full-time (26 women), 139 part-time (27 women); includes 104 minority (22 Black or African American, non-Hispanic/Latino; 22 Asian, non-Hispanic/Latino; 52 Hispanic/Latino; 8 Two or more races, non-Hispanic/Latino), 63 international. Average age 32. 231 applicants, 54% accepted, 91 enrolled. In 2019, 67 master's, 14 doctorates awarded. Terminal master's awarded for partial completion of doctoral program. *Degree requirements:* For master's, thesis optional; for doctorate, thesis/dissertation, qualifying exam. *Entrance requirements:* For master's, GRE General Test, minimum GPA of 3.0; for doctorate, GRE General Test, master's degree, minimum GPA of 3.5. Additional exam requirements/recommendations for international students: required—TOEFL (minimum score 500 paper-based; 61 iBT), IELTS (minimum score 6). *Application deadline:* For fall admission, 7/1 priority date for domestic students, 2/15 for international students; for spring admission, 11/1 for domestic students, 7/15 for international students. Applications are processed on a rolling basis. Application fee: $30. *Expenses: Tuition:* Full-time $20,536; part-time $371.82 per credit hour. Tuition and fees vary according to program. *Financial support:* Fellowships, research assistantships with partial tuition reimbursements, teaching assistantships with full tuition reimbursements, career-related internships or fieldwork, and Federal Work-Study available. Support available to part-time students. Financial award application deadline: 4/1; financial award applicants required to submit FAFSA. *Unit head:* Jean Mangiaracina, Graduate Program Administrator, 561-297-6482, E-mail: jmangiar@fau.edu. *Application contact:* Jean Mangiaracina, Graduate Program Administrator, 561-297-6482, E-mail: jmangiar@fau.edu.
Website: http://www.ceecs.fau.edu/

Florida Institute of Technology, College of Engineering and Science, Program in Electrical Engineering, Melbourne, FL 32901-6975. Offers MS, PhD. *Program availability:* Part-time. *Degree requirements:* For master's, comprehensive exam (for some programs), thesis optional, 30 credit hours; for doctorate, comprehensive exam, thesis/dissertation, significant original research, publication in professional journal of conference proceedings, minimum of 48 credit hours after master's degree. *Entrance requirements:* For master's, GRE, bachelor's degree from ABET-accredited program; for doctorate, GRE, 3 letters of recommendation, resume, statement of objectives, on-campus interview (highly recommended). Additional exam requirements/recommendations for international students: required—TOEFL (minimum score 550 paper-based; 79 iBT). Electronic applications accepted.

Florida International University, College of Engineering and Computing, Department of Electrical and Computer Engineering, Miami, FL 33175. Offers computer engineering (MS); electrical engineering (MS, PhD). *Program availability:* Part-time, evening/weekend. *Faculty:* 34 full-time (2 women), 12 part-time/adjunct (2 women). *Students:* 162 full-time (27 women), 52 part-time (13 women); includes 81 minority (13 Black or African American, non-Hispanic/Latino; 7 Asian, non-Hispanic/Latino; 59 Hispanic/Latino; 2 Two or more races, non-Hispanic/Latino), 120 international. Average age 28. 213 applicants, 48% accepted, 66 enrolled. In 2019, 33 master's, 17 doctorates awarded. Terminal master's awarded for partial completion of doctoral program. *Degree requirements:* For master's, thesis optional; for doctorate, comprehensive exam, thesis/dissertation. *Entrance requirements:* For master's, minimum undergraduate GPA of 3.0 in upper-level coursework, resume, letters of recommendation, letter of intent; for doctorate, GRE General Test, minimum graduate GPA of 3.3, resume, letters of recommendation, letter of intent. Additional exam requirements/recommendations for international students: required—TOEFL (minimum score 550 paper-based; 80 iBT). *Application deadline:* For fall admission, 6/1 for domestic students, 4/1 for international students; for spring admission, 10/1 for domestic students, 9/1 for international students. Applications are processed on a rolling basis. Application fee: $30. Electronic applications accepted. *Expenses: Tuition, area resident:* Full-time $8912; part-time $446 per credit hour. Tuition, state resident: full-time $8912; part-time $446 per credit hour. Tuition, nonresident: full-time $21,393; part-time $992 per credit hour. *Required fees:* $2194. *Financial support:* Institutionally sponsored loans, scholarships/grants, and unspecified assistantships available. Financial award application deadline: 3/1; financial award applicants required to submit FAFSA. *Unit head:* Dr. Shekhar Bhansali, Chair, 305-348-4439, Fax: 305-348-3747, E-mail: sbhansa@fiu.edu. *Application contact:* Nanett Rojas, Manager, Admissions Operations, 305-348-7464, Fax: 305-348-7441, E-mail: gradadm@fiu.edu.
Website: http://cec.fiu.edu

Florida State University, The Graduate School, FAMU-FSU College of Engineering, Department of Electrical and Computer Engineering, Tallahassee, FL 32306. Offers electrical engineering (MS, PhD). *Program availability:* Part-time. *Faculty:* 21 full-time (3 women). *Students:* 85 full-time (15 women); includes 14 minority (8 Black or African American, non-Hispanic/Latino; 1 Asian, non-Hispanic/Latino; 3 Hispanic/Latino; 2 Two or more races, non-Hispanic/Latino), 55 international. Average age 26. 111 applicants, 42% accepted, 20 enrolled. In 2019, 21 master's, 8 doctorates awarded. *Degree requirements:* For master's, comprehensive exam (for some programs), thesis (for some programs); for doctorate, thesis/dissertation, preliminary exam, qualifying exam. *Entrance requirements:* For master's, GRE General Test, minimum GPA of 3.0, BS in electrical engineering; for doctorate, GRE General Test, minimum graduate GPA of 3.3, MS in electrical engineering. Additional exam requirements/recommendations for international students: required—TOEFL (minimum score 550 paper-based; 80 iBT); recommended—IELTS. *Application deadline:* For fall admission, 3/1 for domestic and international students; for spring admission, 11/1 for domestic and international students; for summer admission, 3/1 for domestic and international students. Applications are processed on a rolling basis. Application fee: $30. Electronic applications accepted. *Financial support:* In 2019–20, 48 students received support, including 1 fellowship with full tuition reimbursement available, 27 research assistantships with full tuition reimbursements available, 32 teaching assistantships with full tuition reimbursements available; career-related internships or fieldwork, institutionally sponsored loans, scholarships/grants, tuition waivers (full), and unspecified assistantships also available. Financial award application deadline: 3/1; financial award applicants required to submit FAFSA. *Unit head:* Dr. Simon Foo, Chair and Professor, 850-410-6474, Fax: 850-410-6479, E-mail: foo@eng.famu.fsu.edu. *Application contact:* Melissa Jackson, Graduate Program Coordinator, 850-410-6454, Fax: 850-410-6479, E-mail: ecegrad@eng.famu.fsu.edu.
Website: http://www.eng.famu.fsu.edu/ece/

Gannon University, School of Graduate Studies, College of Engineering and Business, School of Engineering and Computer Science, Program in Electrical and Computer Engineering, Erie, PA 16541-0001. Offers MSEE, MSES. *Program availability:* Part-time, evening/weekend. *Degree requirements:* For master's, thesis (for some programs), oral exam (for some programs), design project (for some programs). *Entrance requirements:* For master's, bachelor's degree in electrical or computer engineering from an ABET-accredited program or its equivalent with minimum GPA of 2.5, transcripts, 3 letters of recommendation. Additional exam requirements/recommendations for international students: required—TOEFL (minimum score 79 iBT). Electronic applications accepted. Application fee is waived when completed online.

George Mason University, Volgenau School of Engineering, Department of Electrical and Computer Engineering, Fairfax, VA 22030. Offers computer engineering (MS); electrical and computer engineering (PhD, Certificate). *Degree requirements:* For master's, thesis optional; for doctorate, comprehensive exam, thesis or scholarly paper. *Entrance requirements:* For master's, GRE, personal goals statement; 2 official copies of transcripts; self-evaluation form; 3 letters of recommendation; resume; official bank statement; photocopy of passport; proof of financial support; for doctorate, GRE (waived for GMU electrical and computer engineering master's graduates with minimum GPA of 3.0), personal goals statement; 2 official copies of transcripts; self-evaluation form; 3 letters of recommendation; resume; official bank statement; photocopy of passport; proof of financial support. Additional exam requirements/recommendations for international students: required—TOEFL (minimum score 575 paper-based; 88 iBT), IELTS (minimum score 6.5), PTE (minimum score 59). Electronic applications accepted. *Expenses:* Contact institution.

The George Washington University, School of Engineering and Applied Science, Department of Electrical and Computer Engineering, Washington, DC 20052. Offers electrical engineering (MS, PhD); telecommunication and computers (MS). *Program availability:* Part-time, evening/weekend. *Degree requirements:* For master's, thesis optional; for doctorate, comprehensive exam, thesis/dissertation, dissertation defense, qualifying exam. *Entrance requirements:* For master's, appropriate bachelor's degree, minimum GPA of 3.0; for doctorate, GRE (if highest earned degree is BS), appropriate bachelor's or master's degree, minimum GPA of 3.3; for other advanced degree, appropriate master's degree, minimum GPA of 3.0. Additional exam requirements/recommendations for international students: required—TOEFL or The George Washington University English as a Foreign Language Test.

Georgia Institute of Technology, Graduate Studies, College of Engineering, School of Electrical and Computer Engineering, Atlanta, GA 30332. Offers MS, PhD. *Program availability:* Part-time, 100% online. *Faculty:* 91 full-time (11 women), 1 part-time/adjunct (0 women). *Students:* 955 full-time (177 women), 198 part-time (34 women); includes 208 minority (22 Black or African American, non-Hispanic/Latino; 128 Asian, non-Hispanic/Latino; 43 Hispanic/Latino; 15 Two or more races, non-Hispanic/Latino), 706 international. Average age 26. 2,329 applicants, 31% accepted, 334 enrolled. In 2019, 349 master's, 84 doctorates awarded. Terminal master's awarded for partial completion of doctoral program. *Degree requirements:* For master's, thesis optional; for doctorate, comprehensive exam, thesis/dissertation. *Entrance requirements:* For master's and doctorate, GRE General Test, Three (3) Letters of Recommendation. Additional exam requirements/recommendations for international students: required—TOEFL (minimum score 577 paper-based; 90 iBT), IELTS (minimum score 7), TOEFL is the preferred method with the requirements shown on the programs. *Application deadline:* For fall admission, 12/16 for domestic students, 12/1 for international students. Applications are processed on a rolling basis. Application fee: $75 ($85 for international students). Electronic applications accepted. *Expenses: Tuition, area resident:* Full-time $14,064; part-time $586 per credit hour. Tuition, state resident: full-time $14,064; part-time $586 per credit hour. Tuition, nonresident: full-time $29,140; part-time $1215 per credit hour. *International tuition:* $29,140 full-time. *Required fees:* $2024; $840 per semester. $2096. Tuition and fees vary according to course load. *Financial support:* In 2019–20, 34 fellowships, 460 research assistantships, 143 teaching assistantships were awarded; career-related internships or fieldwork, Federal Work-Study, institutionally sponsored loans, tuition waivers (full and partial), and unspecified assistantships also available. Support available to part-time students. Financial award application deadline: 7/1; financial award applicants required to submit FAFSA. *Unit head:* Magnus Egerstedt, School Chair, 404-894-2901, Fax: 404-894-4641, E-mail: magnus.egerstedt@ece.gatech.edu. *Application contact:* Marla Bruner, Director of Graduate Studies, 404-894-1610, Fax: 404-894-1609, E-mail: gradinfo@mail.gatech.edu.
Website: http://www.ece.gatech.edu

Georgia Southern University, Jack N. Averitt College of Graduate Studies, Allen E. Paulson College of Engineering and Computing, Department of Electrical and Computer Engineering, Statesboro, GA 30458. Offers MSAE. *Faculty:* 14 full-time (1 woman), 1 part-time/adjunct (0 women). *Students:* 17 full-time (0 women), 7 part-time (0 women); includes 3 minority (2 Black or African American, non-Hispanic/Latino; 1 Hispanic/Latino), 12 international. Average age 28. 37 applicants, 78% accepted, 5 enrolled. In 2019, 8 master's awarded. *Degree requirements:* For master's, thesis optional. *Entrance requirements:* For master's, GRE, minimum GPA of 2.75. Additional exam requirements/recommendations for international students: required—TOEFL (minimum score 550 paper-based; 80 iBT), IELTS (minimum score 6). *Application deadline:* For fall admission, 3/1 priority date for domestic students, 6/1 for international students; for spring admission, 10/1 priority date for domestic students, 10/1 for international students. Applications are processed on a rolling basis. Application fee: $50. Electronic applications accepted. *Expenses: Tuition, area resident:* Full-time $4986; part-time $277 per credit hour. Tuition, nonresident: full-time $19,890; part-time $1105 per credit hour. *International tuition:* $19,890 full-time. *Required fees:* $2114; $1057 per semester. $1057 per semester. Tuition and fees vary according to course load, campus/location and program. *Financial support:* In 2019–20, 20 students received support. Unspecified assistantships available. Financial award application deadline: 4/20; financial award applicants required to submit FAFSA. *Unit head:* Dr. Sungkyun Lim, Program Coordinator, 912-478-2266, E-mail: sklim@georgiasouthern.edu. *Application contact:* Dr. Sungkyun Lim, Program Coordinator, 912-478-2266, E-mail: sklim@georgiasouthern.edu.

Grand Valley State University, Padnos College of Engineering and Computing, School of Engineering, Allendale, MI 49401-9403. Offers electrical and computer engineering (MSE); mechanical engineering (MSE); product design and manufacturing engineering (MSE). *Program availability:* Part-time, evening/weekend. *Faculty:* 22 full-time (6 women), 1 part-time/adjunct (0 women). *Students:* 23 full-time (2 women), 35 part-time

(5 women); includes 4 minority (2 Asian, non-Hispanic/Latino; 1 Hispanic/Latino; 1 Two or more races, non-Hispanic/Latino), 25 international. Average age 27. 46 applicants, 78% accepted, 10 enrolled. In 2019, 32 master's awarded. *Degree requirements:* For master's, capstone experience. *Entrance requirements:* For master's, engineering degree, minimum GPA of 3.0, resume, 3 confidential letters of recommendation, 1-2 page essay, base of underlying relevant knowledge/evidence from academic records or relevant wok experience. Additional exam requirements/recommendations for international students: required—Michigan English Language Assessment Battery (minimum score 77), TOEFL (minimum iBT score of 80), or IELTS (6.5); GRE. *Application deadline:* Applications are processed on a rolling basis. Application fee: $30. Electronic applications accepted. *Expenses:* $733 per credit hour, 33 credit hours. *Financial support:* In 2019–20, 40 students received support, including 8 fellowships, 34 research assistantships with full and partial tuition reimbursements available (averaging $4,000 per year); career-related internships or fieldwork, Federal Work-Study, institutionally sponsored loans, scholarships/grants, and unspecified assistantships also available. *Unit head:* Dr. Wael Mokhtar, Director, 616-331-6015, Fax: 616-331-7215, E-mail: mokhtarw@gvsu.edu. *Application contact:* Dr. Shabbir Choudhuri, Graduate Program Director, 616-331-6845, Fax: 616-331-7215, E-mail: choudhus@gvsu.edu. Website: http://www.engineer.gvsu.edu/

Harvard University, Graduate School of Arts and Sciences, Harvard John A. Paulson School of Engineering and Applied Sciences, Cambridge, MA 02138. Offers applied mathematics (PhD); applied physics (PhD); computational science and engineering (ME, SM); computer science (PhD); data science (SM); design engineering (MDE); engineering science (ME), including electrical engineering (ME, SM, PhD); engineering sciences (SM, PhD), including bioengineering (PhD), electrical engineering (ME, SM, PhD), environmental science and engineering (PhD), materials science and mechanical engineering (PhD). *Program availability:* Part-time. Terminal master's awarded for partial completion of doctoral program. *Degree requirements:* For master's, thesis (for ME); for doctorate, comprehensive exam, thesis/dissertation. *Entrance requirements:* For master's and doctorate, GRE General Test, GRE Subject Test (recommended), 3 letters of recommendation. Additional exam requirements/recommendations for international students: required—TOEFL (minimum score 80 iBT). Electronic applications accepted. *Expenses:* Contact institution.

Howard University, College of Engineering, Architecture, and Computer Sciences, School of Engineering and Computer Science, Department of Electrical Engineering, Washington, DC 20059-0002. Offers M Eng, PhD. *Program availability:* Part-time. *Degree requirements:* For master's, thesis (for some programs), qualifying exam; for doctorate, thesis/dissertation, preliminary exam. *Entrance requirements:* For master's, GRE General Test, bachelor's degree in electrical engineering, minimum GPA of 3.0; for doctorate, GRE General Test, minimum GPA of 3.0. Additional exam requirements/recommendations for international students: required—TOEFL. Electronic applications accepted.

Illinois Institute of Technology, Graduate College, Armour College of Engineering, Department of Electrical and Computer Engineering, Chicago, IL 60616. Offers biomedical imaging and signals (MAS); computer engineering (MS, PhD); electrical engineering (MS, PhD); electricity markets (MAS); network engineering (MAS); power engineering (MAS); telecommunications and software engineering (MAS); VLSI and microelectronics (MAS); MS/MS. *Program availability:* Part-time, evening/weekend, online learning. Terminal master's awarded for partial completion of doctoral program. *Degree requirements:* For master's, comprehensive exam (for some programs), thesis (for some programs); for doctorate, comprehensive exam, thesis/dissertation. *Entrance requirements:* For master's and doctorate, GRE General Test (minimum score 1100 Quantitative and Verbal, 3.5 Analytical Writing), minimum undergraduate GPA of 3.0. Additional exam requirements/recommendations for international students: required—TOEFL (minimum score 550 paper-based; 80 iBT); recommended—IELTS (minimum score 5.5). Electronic applications accepted.

Indiana University-Purdue University Indianapolis, School of Engineering and Technology, Department of Electrical and Computer Engineering, Indianapolis, IN 46202. Offers electrical and computer engineering (MS, PhD); engineering (MSE). *Degree requirements:* For master's, thesis optional; for doctorate, thesis/dissertation. *Entrance requirements:* For master's, GRE, minimum GPA of 3.0, three recommendation letters, statement of purpose/intent; for doctorate, GRE, minimum GPA of 3.0, three recommendation letters, statement of purpose/intent, curriculum vitae. Additional exam requirements/recommendations for international students: required—TOEFL; recommended—IELTS, TSE. Electronic applications accepted. *Expenses:* Contact institution.

Instituto Tecnológico y de Estudios Superiores de Monterrey, Campus Chihuahua, Graduate Programs, Chihuahua, Mexico. Offers computer systems engineering (Ingeniero); electrical engineering (Ingeniero); electromechanical engineering (Ingeniero); electronic engineering (Ingeniero); engineering administration (MEA); industrial engineering (MIE, Ingeniero); international trade (MIT); mechanical engineering (Ingeniero).

Instituto Tecnológico y de Estudios Superiores de Monterrey, Campus Monterrey, Graduate and Research Division, Programs in Engineering, Monterrey, Mexico. Offers applied statistics (M Eng); artificial intelligence (PhD); automation engineering (M Eng); chemical engineering (M Eng); civil engineering (M Eng); electrical engineering (M Eng); electronic engineering (M Eng); environmental engineering (M Eng); industrial engineering (M Eng, PhD); manufacturing engineering (M Eng); mechanical engineering (M Eng); systems and quality engineering (M Eng). *Program availability:* Part-time, evening/weekend. Terminal master's awarded for partial completion of doctoral program. *Degree requirements:* For master's, one foreign language, thesis; for doctorate, one foreign language, thesis/dissertation. *Entrance requirements:* For master's, EXADEP; for doctorate, GRE, master's degree in related field. Additional exam requirements/recommendations for international students: required—TOEFL.

Inter American University of Puerto Rico, Bayamón Campus, Graduate School, Bayamón, PR 00957. Offers biology (MS), including environmental sciences and ecology, molecular biotechnology; electrical engineering (ME), including control system, potence system; human resources (MBA); mechanical engineering (ME, MS), including aerospace, energy. *Program availability:* Part-time, evening/weekend. *Degree requirements:* For master's, comprehensive exam, research project. *Entrance requirements:* For master's, EXADEP, GRE General Test, letters of recommendation. *Expenses:* Tuition: Full-time $3870; part-time $1935 per year. *Required fees:* $735; $642 per unit.

International Technological University, Program in Electrical Engineering, San Jose, CA 95134. Offers MSEE, PhD. *Program availability:* Part-time, evening/weekend. *Degree requirements:* For master's, thesis or capstone project; for doctorate, comprehensive exam, thesis/dissertation. *Entrance requirements:* For master's, 3 semesters of calculus, minimum GPA of 2.5. Additional exam requirements/recommendations for international students: required—TOEFL, IELTS. Electronic applications accepted.

Iowa State University of Science and Technology, Department of Electrical and Computer Engineering, Ames, IA 50011. Offers computer engineering (M Eng, MS,

PhD); electrical engineering (M Eng, MS, PhD). *Degree requirements:* For master's, thesis or alternative; for doctorate, thesis/dissertation. *Entrance requirements:* For master's and doctorate, GRE General Test. Additional exam requirements/recommendations for international students: required—TOEFL (minimum score 570 paper-based; 79 iBT), IELTS (minimum score 6.5). Electronic applications accepted.

Johns Hopkins University, Engineering Program for Professionals, Part-time Program in Electrical and Computer Engineering, Baltimore, MD 21218. Offers communications and networking (MS); electrical and computer engineering (Graduate Certificate, Post-Master's Certificate); photonics (MS). *Program availability:* Part-time, evening/weekend, 100% online, blended/hybrid learning. *Entrance requirements:* Additional exam requirements/recommendations for international students: required—TOEFL (minimum score 600 paper-based; 100 iBT). Electronic applications accepted.

Johns Hopkins University, G. W. C. Whiting School of Engineering, Department of Electrical and Computer Engineering, Baltimore, MD 21218. Offers MSE, PhD. Terminal master's awarded for partial completion of doctoral program. *Degree requirements:* For master's, thesis optional; for doctorate, thesis/dissertation, qualifying and oral exams, seminar. *Entrance requirements:* For master's and doctorate, GRE General Test, transcripts, 3 letters of recommendation, statement of purpose. Additional exam requirements/recommendations for international students: required—TOEFL (minimum score 600 paper-based, 100 iBT) or IELTS (7). Electronic applications accepted.

Kansas State University, Graduate School, College of Engineering, Department of Electrical and Computer Engineering, Manhattan, KS 66506. Offers electrical engineering (MS), including bioengineering, communication systems, design of computer systems, electrical engineering, energy and power systems, integrated circuits and devices, real time embedded systems, renewable energy, signal processing. *Program availability:* Part-time, evening/weekend, online learning. *Degree requirements:* For master's, thesis or alternative, final exam; for doctorate, thesis/dissertation, final exam, preliminary exams. *Entrance requirements:* For master's, GRE General Test, bachelor's degree in electrical engineering or computer science, minimum GPA of 3.0; for doctorate, GRE General Test. Additional exam requirements/recommendations for international students: required—TOEFL (minimum score 600 paper-based; 85 iBT). Electronic applications accepted.

Kennesaw State University, Southern Polytechnic College of Engineering and Engineering Technology, Program in Applied Engineering, Kennesaw, GA 30144. Offers electrical engineering (MS). *Program availability:* Part-time, evening/weekend. *Students:* 2 full-time (1 woman), 17 part-time (4 women); includes 8 minority (3 Black or African American, non-Hispanic/Latino; 2 Asian, non-Hispanic/Latino; 3 Hispanic/Latino). Average age 33. 7 applicants, 86% accepted, 6 enrolled. In 2019, 7 master's awarded. *Degree requirements:* For master's, thesis. *Entrance requirements:* For master's, GRE (minimum scores: 147 Verbal, 147 Quantitative, 3.5 Analytical), minimum GPA of 2.7. Additional exam requirements/recommendations for international students: required—TOEFL (minimum score 80 iBT), IELTS (minimum score 6.5). *Application deadline:* For fall admission, 7/1 priority date for domestic students, 5/1 priority date for international students; for spring admission, 11/1 priority date for domestic students, 9/1 priority date for international students. Applications are processed on a rolling basis. Application fee: $60. Electronic applications accepted. *Expenses: Tuition, area resident:* Full-time $7104; part-time $296 per credit hour. Tuition, state resident: full-time $7104; part-time $296 per credit hour. Tuition, nonresident: full-time $25,584; part-time $1066 per credit hour. *International tuition:* $25,584 full-time. *Required fees:* $2006; $1706 per unit. $853 per semester. *Financial support:* Applicants required to submit FAFSA. *Application contact:* Admissions Counselor, 470-578-4377, E-mail: ksugrad@kennesaw.edu. Website: http://engineering.kennesaw.edu/electrical/degrees/ms-applied-engineering.php

Kettering University, Graduate School, Electrical and Computer Engineering Department, Flint, MI 48504. Offers engineering (MS). *Program availability:* Part-time, evening/weekend, online learning. *Degree requirements:* For master's, thesis optional. *Entrance requirements:* Additional exam requirements/recommendations for international students: required—TOEFL (minimum score 550 paper-based; 79 iBT). Electronic applications accepted.

Lakehead University, Graduate Studies, Faculty of Engineering, Thunder Bay, ON P7B 5E1, Canada. Offers control engineering (M Sc Engr); electrical/computer engineering (M Sc Engr); environmental engineering (M Sc Engr). *Program availability:* Part-time. *Degree requirements:* For master's, thesis. *Entrance requirements:* For master's, bachelor's degree in chemical, electrical or mechanical engineering, minimum B average. Additional exam requirements/recommendations for international students: required—TOEFL.

Lamar University, College of Graduate Studies, College of Engineering, Phillip M. Drayer Department of Electrical Engineering, Beaumont, TX 77710. Offers ME, MES, DE. *Program availability:* Part-time. *Faculty:* 12 full-time (2 women). *Students:* 16 full-time (3 women), 17 part-time (1 woman); includes 2 minority (1 Asian, non-Hispanic/Latino; 1 Two or more races, non-Hispanic/Latino), 29 international. Average age 29. 59 applicants, 88% accepted, 7 enrolled. In 2019, 24 master's, 3 doctorates awarded. *Degree requirements:* For master's, thesis (for some programs); for doctorate, thesis/dissertation. *Entrance requirements:* For master's and doctorate, GRE General Test. Additional exam requirements/recommendations for international students: required—TOEFL (minimum score 550 paper-based; 79 iBT), IELTS (minimum score 6.5). *Application deadline:* Applications are processed on a rolling basis. Application fee: $25 ($50 for international students). Electronic applications accepted. *Expenses: Tuition, area resident:* Full-time $6324; part-time $351 per credit. Tuition, state resident: full-time $6324; part-time $351 per credit. Tuition, nonresident: full-time $13,920; part-time $773 per credit. *International tuition:* $13,920 full-time. *Required fees:* $2462; $327 per credit. Tuition and fees vary according to course load, campus/location and reciprocity agreements. *Financial support:* In 2019–20, 2 students received support. Fellowships with partial tuition reimbursements available, research assistantships with partial tuition reimbursements available, teaching assistantships with partial tuition reimbursements available, and tuition waivers (partial) available. Financial award applicants required to submit FAFSA. *Unit head:* Dr. Harley Ross Myler, Chair, 409-880-8746, Fax: 409-880-8121. *Application contact:* Celeste Contreas, Director, Admissions and Academic Services, 409-880-8888, Fax: 409-880-7419, E-mail: gradmissions@lamar.edu. Website: http://engineering.lamar.edu/electrical

Lawrence Technological University, College of Engineering, Southfield, MI 48075-1058. Offers architectural engineering (MS); automotive engineering (MS); biomedical engineering (MS); civil engineering (MA, MS, PhD), including environmental engineering (MS), geotechnical engineering (MS), structural engineering (MS), transportation engineering (MS), water resource engineering (MS); construction engineering management (MA); electrical and computer engineering (MS); engineering management (MEM); engineering technology (MS); fire engineering (MS); industrial engineering (MS), including healthcare systems; manufacturing systems (ME); mechanical engineering (MS, DE, PhD), including automotive engineering (MS), energy engineering (MS), manufacturing (DE), solid mechanics (MS), thermal/fluid systems (MS); mechatronic systems engineering (MS). *Program availability:* Part-time, evening/weekend. *Faculty:* 23 full-time (2 women), 20 part-time/adjunct (1 woman). *Students:* 14 full-time (5

women), 286 part-time (54 women); includes 26 minority (13 Black or African American, non-Hispanic/Latino; 8 Asian, non-Hispanic/Latino; 3 Hispanic/Latino; 2 Two or more races, non-Hispanic/Latino), 150 international. Average age 29. 384 applicants, 58% accepted, 74 enrolled. In 2019, 223 master's, 7 doctorates awarded. Terminal master's awarded for partial completion of doctoral program. *Degree requirements:* For master's, thesis optional; for doctorate, comprehensive exam, thesis/dissertation optional. *Entrance requirements:* Additional exam requirements/recommendations for international students: required—TOEFL (minimum score 550 paper-based; 79 iBT), IELTS (minimum score 6.5). *Application deadline:* For fall admission, 5/24 for international students; for spring admission, 10/13 for international students; for summer admission, 2/18 for international students. Applications are processed on a rolling basis. Application fee: $50. Electronic applications accepted. *Expenses: Tuition:* Full-time $16,618; part-time $8309 per year. *Required fees:* $600; $600. *Financial support:* In 2019–20, 21 students received support. Unspecified assistantships available. Financial award application deadline: 4/1; financial award applicants required to submit FAFSA. *Unit head:* Dr. Nabil Grace, Dean, 248-204-2500, Fax: 248-204-2509, E-mail: engrdean@ltu.edu. *Application contact:* Jane Rohrback, Director of Admissions, 248-204-3160, Fax: 248-204-2228, E-mail: admissions@ltu.edu.
Website: http://www.ltu.edu/engineering/index.asp

Lehigh University, P.C. Rossin College of Engineering and Applied Science, Department of Electrical and Computer Engineering, Bethlehem, PA 18015. Offers electrical engineering (M Eng, MS, PhD); photonics (MS). *Program availability:* Part-time. *Faculty:* 15 full-time (4 women). *Students:* 66 full-time (6 women), 3 part-time (0 women); includes 1 minority (Black or African American, non-Hispanic/Latino), 61 international. Average age 26. 264 applicants, 13% accepted, 16 enrolled. In 2019, 18 master's, 8 doctorates awarded. Terminal master's awarded for partial completion of doctoral program. *Degree requirements:* For master's, thesis optional; for doctorate, thesis/dissertation, qualifying or comprehensive exam for all 1st year PhD's; general exam 7 months or more prior to completion/dissertation defense. *Entrance requirements:* For master's and doctorate, GRE General Test, BS in field or related field. Additional exam requirements/recommendations for international students: required—TOEFL (minimum score 79 iBT), IELTS (minimum score 6.5), TOEFL or IELTS. *Application deadline:* For fall admission, 4/1 for domestic and international students; for spring admission, 11/1 for domestic and international students. Application fee: $75. Electronic applications accepted. *Financial support:* In 2019–20, 48 students received support, including 8 fellowships with full tuition reimbursements available (averaging $29,400 per year), 32 research assistantships with full tuition reimbursements available (averaging $29,400 per year), 8 teaching assistantships with full tuition reimbursements available (averaging $29,400 per year). Financial award application deadline: 1/15. *Unit head:* Dr. Chengshan Xiao, Chair, 610-758-4069, Fax: 610-758-6279, E-mail: chx417@lehigh.edu. *Application contact:* Ruby Scott, Graduate Coordinator, 610-758-4070, Fax: 610-758-6279, E-mail: rls304@lehigh.edu.
Website: http://www.ece.lehigh.edu/

Louisiana State University and Agricultural & Mechanical College, Graduate School, College of Engineering, Division of Electrical and Computer Engineering, Baton Rouge, LA 70803. Offers MSEE, PhD.

Loyola Marymount University, Frank R. Seaver College of Science and Engineering, Program in Electrical Engineering, Los Angeles, CA 90045. Offers electrical engineering (MS). *Program availability:* Part-time, evening/weekend. *Students:* 4 full-time (1 woman); includes 1 minority (Hispanic/Latino), 1 international. Average age 25. 25 applicants, 24% accepted, 4 enrolled. In 2019, 7 master's awarded. *Entrance requirements:* For master's, bachelor's degree in electrical engineering, computer science or similar; graduate admissions application; $50 application fee; letter of intent; 2 letters of reference (optional); undergrad GPA of at least 3.0; college calculus, circuits, electronics, signals linear systems, logic design. *Application deadline:* Applications are processed on a rolling basis. Application fee: $50. Electronic applications accepted. *Financial support:* Research assistantships, teaching assistantships, Federal Work-Study, scholarships/grants, and unspecified assistantships available. Financial award applicants required to submit FAFSA. *Unit head:* Dr. Gustavo Vejarano, Graduate Program Director, Electrical Engineering, 310-338-5761, E-mail: gustavo.vejarano@lmu.edu. *Application contact:* Ammar Dalal, Assistant Vice Provost for Graduate Enrollment, 310-338-2721, Fax: 310-338-6086, E-mail: graduateadmission@lmu.edu.
Website: http://cse.lmu.edu/graduateprograms/ese

Manhattan College, Graduate Programs, School of Engineering, Program in Electrical Engineering, Riverdale, NY 10471. Offers MS. *Program availability:* Part-time, evening/weekend. *Degree requirements:* For master's, thesis or alternative. *Entrance requirements:* For master's, GRE (recommended), minimum GPA of 3.0. Additional exam requirements/recommendations for international students: required—TOEFL (minimum score 550 paper-based; 80 iBT), IELTS (minimum score 6).

Marquette University, Graduate School, College of Engineering, Department of Electrical and Computer Engineering, Milwaukee, WI 53201-1881. Offers digital signal processing (Certificate); electric machines, drives, and controls (Certificate); electrical and computer engineering (MS, PhD); microwaves and antennas (Certificate); sensors and smart systems (Certificate). *Program availability:* Part-time, evening/weekend. Terminal master's awarded for partial completion of doctoral program. *Degree requirements:* For master's, comprehensive exam (for some programs), thesis optional; for doctorate, thesis/dissertation, dissertation defense, qualifying exam. *Entrance requirements:* For master's, GRE General Test (recommended), official transcripts from all current and previous colleges/universities except Marquette, three letters of recommendation; for doctorate, GRE General Test, minimum GPA of 3.0, official transcripts from all current and previous colleges/universities except Marquette, three letters of recommendation, statement of purpose, submission of any English language publications authored by applicant (strongly recommended). Additional exam requirements/recommendations for international students: required—TOEFL (minimum score 530 paper-based). Electronic applications accepted.

Marshall University, Academic Affairs Division, College of Information Technology and Engineering, Program in Electrical and Computer Engineering, Huntington, WV 25755. Offers MSEE.

Massachusetts Institute of Technology, School of Engineering, Department of Electrical Engineering and Computer Science, Cambridge, MA 02139. Offers computer science (PhD, Sc D, ECS); computer science and engineering (PhD, Sc D); computer science and molecular biology (M Eng); electrical engineering (PhD, Sc D, EE); electrical engineering and computer science (M Eng, SM, PhD, Sc D); SM/MBA. *Degree requirements:* For master's and other advanced degree, thesis; for doctorate, comprehensive exam, thesis/dissertation. *Entrance requirements:* Additional exam requirements/recommendations for international students: required—TOEFL, IELTS. Electronic applications accepted.

McGill University, Faculty of Graduate and Postdoctoral Studies, Faculty of Engineering, Department of Electrical and Computer Engineering, Montréal, QC H3A 2T5, Canada. Offers M Eng, PhD.

McMaster University, School of Graduate Studies, Faculty of Engineering, Department of Electrical and Computer Engineering, Hamilton, ON L8S 4M2, Canada. Offers electrical engineering (M Eng, MA Sc, PhD). *Degree requirements:* For master's, thesis; for doctorate, comprehensive exam, thesis/dissertation. *Entrance requirements:* Additional exam requirements/recommendations for international students: required—TOEFL (minimum score 550 paper-based).

McNeese State University, Doré School of Graduate Studies, College of Engineering and Computer Science, Master of Engineering Program, Lake Charles, LA 70609. Offers chemical engineering (M Eng); civil engineering (M Eng); electrical engineering (M Eng); engineering management (M Eng); mechanical engineering (M Eng). *Program availability:* Part-time, evening/weekend. *Entrance requirements:* For master's, GRE, baccalaureate degree, minimum overall GPA of 3.0. Additional exam requirements/recommendations for international students: required—TOEFL (minimum score 560 paper-based; 83 iBT).

Memorial University of Newfoundland, School of Graduate Studies, Faculty of Engineering and Applied Science, St. John's, NL A1C 5S7, Canada. Offers civil engineering (M Eng, PhD); electrical and computer engineering (M Eng, PhD); mechanical engineering (M Eng, PhD); ocean and naval architecture engineering (M Eng, PhD). *Program availability:* Part-time. *Degree requirements:* For master's, thesis; for doctorate, comprehensive exam, thesis/dissertation, oral thesis defense. *Entrance requirements:* For master's, 2nd class degree; for doctorate, master's degree in engineering. Electronic applications accepted.

Mercer University, Graduate Studies, Macon Campus, School of Engineering, Macon, GA 31207. Offers biomedical engineering (MSE); computer engineering (MSE); electrical engineering (MSE); engineering management (MSE); environmental engineering (MSE); environmental systems (MS); mechanical engineering (MSE); software engineering (MSE); software systems (MS); technical communications management (MS); technical management (MS). *Program availability:* Part-time-only, evening/weekend, online learning. *Faculty:* 27 full-time (9 women), 2 part-time/adjunct (0 women). *Students:* 38 full-time (10 women), 51 part-time (20 women); includes 22 minority (5 Black or African American, non-Hispanic/Latino; 11 Asian, non-Hispanic/Latino; 4 Hispanic/Latino; 2 Two or more races, non-Hispanic/Latino), 2 international. Average age 26. In 2019, 70 master's awarded. *Degree requirements:* For master's, thesis or alternative. *Entrance requirements:* For master's, GRE (minimum score 300), minimum undergraduate GPA of 3.0. Additional exam requirements/recommendations for international students: required—TOEFL (minimum score 550 paper-based; 80 iBT). *Application deadline:* For fall admission, 4/1 priority date for domestic and international students; for spring admission, 11/1 priority date for domestic and international students. Applications are processed on a rolling basis. Application fee: $75. *Expenses:* Tuition: $938.00 ($700.00 for Technical Communication Management program) per credit hour; Facility and Technology Fee: $17.00 per credit hour. *Financial support:* Federal Work-Study available. Financial award applicants required to submit FAFSA. *Unit head:* Dr. Laura W. Lackey, Dean, 478-301-4106, Fax: 478-301-5593, E-mail: lackey_l@mercer.edu. *Application contact:* Dr. Sinjae Hyun, Program Director, 478-301-2214, Fax: 478-301-5593, E-mail: hyun_s@mercer.edu.
Website: http://engineering.mercer.edu/

Miami University, College of Engineering and Computing, Department of Electrical and Computer Engineering, Oxford, OH 45056. Offers MS.

Michigan State University, The Graduate School, College of Engineering, Department of Electrical and Computer Engineering, East Lansing, MI 48824. Offers electrical engineering (MS, PhD). *Entrance requirements:* Additional exam requirements/recommendations for international students: required—TOEFL. Electronic applications accepted.

Michigan Technological University, Graduate School, College of Engineering, Department of Electrical and Computer Engineering, Houghton, MI 49931. Offers advanced electric power engineering (Graduate Certificate); electrical engineering (PhD). *Program availability:* Part-time, evening/weekend, 100% online, blended/hybrid learning. *Faculty:* 40 full-time, 7 part-time/adjunct. *Students:* 102 full-time (22 women), 33 part-time; includes 3 minority (1 Black or African American, non-Hispanic/Latino; 2 Asian, non-Hispanic/Latino), 90 international. Average age 28. 567 applicants, 38% accepted, 50 enrolled. In 2019, 71 master's, 15 doctorates, 20 other advanced degrees awarded. Terminal master's awarded for partial completion of doctoral program. *Degree requirements:* For master's, comprehensive exam (for some programs), thesis (for some programs); for doctorate, comprehensive exam, thesis/dissertation. *Entrance requirements:* For master's, statement of purpose, personal statement, official transcripts, 2 letters of recommendation; for doctorate, GRE, statement of purpose, personal statement, official transcripts, 2 letters of recommendation; for Graduate Certificate, statement of purpose, personal statement, official transcripts. Additional exam requirements/recommendations for international students: required—TOEFL (minimum score 79 iBT), IELTS (minimum score 6.5). *Application deadline:* For fall admission, 2/15 priority date for domestic and international students; for spring admission, 8/15 priority date for domestic and international students. Applications are processed on a rolling basis. Application fee: $0. Electronic applications accepted. *Expenses:* $1,212 per credit. *Financial support:* In 2019–20, 88 students received support, including 7 fellowships with tuition reimbursements available (averaging $16,590 per year), 15 research assistantships with tuition reimbursements available (averaging $16,590 per year), 19 teaching assistantships with tuition reimbursements available (averaging $16,590 per year); career-related internships or fieldwork, Federal Work-Study, scholarships/grants, health care benefits, unspecified assistantships, and cooperative program also available. Financial award application deadline: 2/15; financial award applicants required to submit FAFSA. *Unit head:* Dr. Glen E. Archer, Interim Chair and Principal Lecturer, 906-487-2550, Fax: 906-487-2949, E-mail: gearcher@mtu.edu. *Application contact:* Alexandra Holmstrom, Graduate Program Coordinator, 906-487-1995, Fax: 906-487-2949, E-mail: aholmstr@mtu.edu.
Website: http://www.mtu.edu/ece/

Mississippi State University, Bagley College of Engineering, Department of Electrical and Computer Engineering, Mississippi State, MS 39762. Offers MS, PhD. *Program availability:* Part-time, blended/hybrid learning. *Faculty:* 15 full-time (2 women), 1 part-time/adjunct (0 women). *Students:* 56 full-time (10 women), 54 part-time (7 women); includes 10 minority (3 Black or African American, non-Hispanic/Latino; 4 Asian, non-Hispanic/Latino; 3 Hispanic/Latino), 47 international. Average age 32. 92 applicants, 68% accepted, 19 enrolled. In 2019, 8 master's, 7 doctorates awarded. Terminal master's awarded for partial completion of doctoral program. *Degree requirements:* For master's, comprehensive exam, thesis optional; for doctorate, comprehensive exam, thesis/dissertation, written exam, oral preliminary exam. *Entrance requirements:* For master's, GRE (for graduates from program not accredited by EAC/ABET), minimum GPA of 3.0 on BS; for doctorate, GRE (for graduates from program not accredited by EAC/ABET), minimum GPA of 3.5 on BS or MS. Additional exam requirements/recommendations for international students: required—TOEFL (minimum score 550 paper-based; 79 iBT); recommended—IELTS (minimum score 6.5). *Application deadline:* For fall admission, 7/1 for domestic students, 5/1 for international students; for spring admission, 11/1 for domestic students, 9/1 for international students. Applications are processed on a rolling basis. Application fee: $60 ($80 for international students). Electronic applications accepted. *Expenses: Tuition, area resident:* Full-time $8880; part-time $456 per credit hour. Tuition, state resident: full-time $8880. Tuition,

nonresident: full-time $23,840; part-time $1236 per credit hour. *Required fees:* $110; $11.12 per credit hour. Tuition and fees vary according to course load. *Financial support:* In 2019–20, 17 research assistantships with full tuition reimbursements (averaging $17,722 per year), 23 teaching assistantships with full tuition reimbursements (averaging $16,748 per year) were awarded; Federal Work-Study, institutionally sponsored loans, scholarships/grants, and unspecified assistantships also available. Financial award application deadline: 4/1; financial award applicants required to submit FAFSA. *Unit head:* Dr. James E. Fowler, Jr., Professor/Interim Department Head, 662-325-3912, Fax: 662-325-2298, E-mail: ece-head@ece.msstate.edu. *Application contact:* Angie Campbell, Admissions and Enrollment Assistant, 662-325-9514, E-mail: acampbell@grad.msstate.edu.
Website: http://www.ece.msstate.edu/

Missouri University of Science and Technology, Department of Electrical and Computer Engineering, Rolla, MO 65401. Offers computer engineering (MS, DE, PhD); electrical engineering (MS, DE, PhD). *Program availability:* Part-time, evening/weekend. Terminal master's awarded for partial completion of doctoral program. *Degree requirements:* For master's, thesis optional; for doctorate, comprehensive exam, thesis/dissertation, departmental qualifying exam. *Entrance requirements:* For master's, GRE General Test (minimum score 1100 verbal and quantitative, writing 4.5); for doctorate, GRE General Test (minimum score: verbal and quantitative 1100, writing 3.5). Additional exam requirements/recommendations for international students: required—TOEFL (minimum score 550 paper-based). Electronic applications accepted. *Expenses:* Tuition, state resident: full-time $7839; part-time $435.50 per credit hour. Tuition, nonresident: full-time $22,169; part-time $1231.60 per credit hour. *International tuition:* $18,156.60 full-time. *Required fees:* $649.76. One-time fee: $119. Tuition and fees vary according to course load and program.

Montana State University, The Graduate School, College of Engineering, Department of Electrical and Computer Engineering, Bozeman, MT 59717. Offers electrical engineering (MS); engineering (PhD), including electrical and computer engineering option. *Program availability:* Part-time. *Degree requirements:* For master's, comprehensive exam, thesis (for some programs); for doctorate, comprehensive exam, thesis/dissertation. *Entrance requirements:* For master's, GRE, BS in electrical or computer engineering or related field; for doctorate, GRE, MS in electrical or computer engineering or related field. Additional exam requirements/recommendations for international students: required—TOEFL (minimum score 550 paper-based). Electronic applications accepted.

Montana Technological University, Electrical Engineering Program, Butte, MT 59701-8997. Offers MS. *Program availability:* Part-time. *Faculty:* 4 full-time (0 women). *Students:* 4 full-time (0 women), 3 part-time (0 women), 2 international. Average age 28. 5 applicants, 60% accepted, 2 enrolled. In 2019, 4 master's awarded. *Degree requirements:* For master's, comprehensive exam (for some programs), thesis optional. *Entrance requirements:* For master's, minimum GPA of 3.0. Additional exam requirements/recommendations for international students: required—TOEFL (minimum score 545 paper-based; 78 iBT), IELTS (minimum score 6.5). *Application deadline:* For fall admission, 4/1 priority date for domestic students, 3/1 priority date for international students; for spring admission, 10/1 priority date for domestic students, 6/1 priority date for international students. Applications are processed on a rolling basis. Application fee: $50. Electronic applications accepted. *Financial support:* In 2019–20, 3 students received support, including 5 teaching assistantships with partial tuition reimbursements available (averaging $4,000 per year); research assistantships with full tuition reimbursements available, career-related internships or fieldwork, tuition waivers (full and partial), and unspecified assistantships also available. Financial award application deadline: 4/1. *Unit head:* Dr. Matthew Donnelly, Professor, 406-496-4846, Fax: 406-496-4849, E-mail: mdonnelly@mtech.edu. *Application contact:* Daniel Stirling, Administrator, Graduate School, 406-496-4304, Fax: 406-496-4710, E-mail: gradschool@mtech.edu. Website: http://www.mtech.edu/academics/gradschool/degreeprograms/degrees-electrical-engineering.htm

Morgan State University, School of Graduate Studies, Clarence M. Mitchell, Jr. School of Engineering, Baltimore, MD 21251. Offers civil engineering (M Eng, D Eng); electrical and computer engineering (M Eng, MS, D Eng); industrial and systems engineering (M Eng, D Eng); transportation and urban infrastructure studies (MS, PhD, Postbaccalaureate Certificate), including transportation. *Program availability:* Part-time, evening/weekend. *Faculty:* 35 full-time (8 women), 19 part-time/adjunct (4 women). *Students:* 113 full-time (34 women), 24 part-time (4 women); includes 88 minority (75 Black or African American, non-Hispanic/Latino; 8 Asian, non-Hispanic/Latino; 2 Hispanic/Latino; 3 Two or more races, non-Hispanic/Latino), 36 international. Average age 35. 78 applicants, 83% accepted, 26 enrolled. In 2019, 23 master's, 11 doctorates awarded. *Degree requirements:* For master's, thesis optional, comprehensive exam or equivalent; for doctorate, thesis/dissertation, comprehensive exam or equivalent. *Entrance requirements:* For master's, GRE, minimum undergraduate GPA of 2.5; for doctorate, GRE, minimum GPA of 3.0. Additional exam requirements/recommendations for international students: required—TOEFL (minimum score 550 paper-based). *Application deadline:* For fall admission, 2/1 priority date for domestic students; for spring admission, 10/1 priority date for domestic students. Applications are processed on a rolling basis. Application fee: $50 ($70 for international students). Electronic applications accepted. *Expenses:* Tuition, state resident: full-time $455; part-time $455 per credit hour. Tuition, nonresident: full-time $894; part-time $894 per credit hour. *Required fees:* $82; $82 per credit hour. *Financial support:* In 2019–20, 35 students received support. Fellowships with full and partial tuition reimbursements available, research assistantships with full and partial tuition reimbursements available, teaching assistantships with full and partial tuition reimbursements available, career-related internships or fieldwork, scholarships/grants, and unspecified assistantships available. Financial award application deadline: 2/1. *Unit head:* Dr. Craig Scott, Interim Dean, 443-885-3231, E-mail: craig.scott@morgan.edu. *Application contact:* Dr. Jahmaine Smith, Director of Admissions, 443-885-3185, Fax: 443-885-8226, E-mail: gradapply@morgan.edu.
Website: https://morgan.edu/soe

National University, School of Engineering and Computing, La Jolla, CA 92037-1011. Offers computer science (MS), including advanced computing; cyber security and information assurance (MS); data analytics (MS); electrical engineering (MS); engineering management (MS); information technology management (MS); management information systems (MS); sustainability management (MS). *Program availability:* Part-time, evening/weekend, 100% online, blended/hybrid learning. *Degree requirements:* For master's, thesis (for some programs). *Entrance requirements:* For master's, interview, minimum GPA of 2.5. Additional exam requirements/recommendations for international students: required—TOEFL (minimum score 550 paper-based; 79 iBT), IELTS (minimum score 6). Electronic applications accepted. *Expenses: Tuition:* Full-time $442; part-time $442 per unit.

Naval Postgraduate School, Departments and Academic Groups, Department of Electrical and Computer Engineering, Monterey, CA 93943-5216. Offers computer engineering (MS); electrical engineer (EE); electrical engineering (PhD); engineering acoustics (MS); engineering science (MS). *Program availability:* Part-time, online learning. *Degree requirements:* For master's and EE, thesis (for some programs), capstone project or research/dissertation paper (for some programs); for doctorate, thesis/dissertation.

Naval Postgraduate School, Departments and Academic Groups, Space Systems Academic Group, Monterey, CA 93943. Offers applied physics (MS); astronautical engineering (MS); computer science (MS); electrical engineering (MS); mechanical engineering (MS); space systems (Engr); space systems operations (MS). *Program availability:* Part-time. *Degree requirements:* For master's and Engr, thesis; for doctorate, thesis/dissertation.

Naval Postgraduate School, Departments and Academic Groups, Undersea Warfare Academic Group, Monterey, CA 93943. Offers applied mathematics (MS); applied physics (MS); applied science (MS), including acoustics, operations research, physical oceanography, signal processing; electrical engineering (MS); engineering acoustics (MS, PhD); engineering science (MS), including electrical engineering, mechanical engineering; mechanical engineer (ME); mechanical engineering (MS, MSME); meteorology (MS); operations research (MS); physical oceanography (MS). *Program availability:* Part-time. *Degree requirements:* For master's, thesis.

New Jersey Institute of Technology, Newark College of Engineering, Newark, NJ 07102. Offers biomedical engineering (MS, PhD); biopharmaceutical engineering (MS); chemical engineering (MS, PhD); civil engineering (MS, PhD); computer engineering (MS); critical infrastructure systems (MS); electrical engineering (MS, PhD); engineering management (MS); engineering science (MS); environmental engineering (MS, PhD); healthcare systems management (MS); industrial engineering (MS, PhD); internet engineering (MS); manufacturing systems engineering (MS); materials science & engineering (PhD); materials science and engineering (MS); mechanical engineering (MS, PhD); occupational safety and health engineering (MS). *Program availability:* Part-time, evening/weekend. *Faculty:* 151 full-time (29 women), 135 part-time/adjunct (15 women). *Students:* 576 full-time (161 women), 528 part-time (111 women); includes 366 minority (61 Black or African American, non-Hispanic/Latino; 1 American Indian or Alaska Native, non-Hispanic/Latino; 166 Asian, non-Hispanic/Latino; 115 Hispanic/Latino; 23 Two or more races, non-Hispanic/Latino), 450 international. Average age 28. 2,053 applicants, 67% accepted, 338 enrolled. In 2019, 474 master's, 30 doctorates awarded. Terminal master's awarded for partial completion of doctoral program. *Degree requirements:* For master's, thesis (for some programs); for doctorate, thesis/dissertation. *Entrance requirements:* For master's, GRE General Test, minimum GPA 2.8, personal statement, 1 letter of recommendation, transcripts; for doctorate, GRE General Test, minimum GPA of 3.5, personal statement, 3 letters of recommendation, transcripts. Additional exam requirements/recommendations for international students: required—TOEFL (minimum score 550 paper-based; 79 iBT), IELTS (minimum score 6.5). *Application deadline:* For fall admission, 6/1 priority date for domestic students, 5/1 priority date for international students; for spring admission, 11/15 priority date for domestic and international students. Applications are processed on a rolling basis. Application fee: $75. Electronic applications accepted. *Expenses:* $23,828 per year (in-state), $33,744 per year (out-of-state). *Financial support:* In 2019–20, 352 students received support, including 33 fellowships with full tuition reimbursements available (averaging $24,000 per year), 89 research assistantships with full tuition reimbursements available (averaging $24,000 per year), 112 teaching assistantships with full tuition reimbursements available (averaging $24,000 per year); career-related internships or fieldwork, Federal Work-Study, scholarships/grants, and unspecified assistantships also available. Financial award application deadline: 1/15. *Unit head:* Dr. Moshe Kam, Dean, 973-596-5534, Fax: 973-596-2316, E-mail: moshe.kam@njit.edu. *Application contact:* Stephen Eck, Executive Director of University Admissions, 973-596-3300, Fax: 973-596-3461, E-mail: admissions@njit.edu.
Website: http://engineering.njit.edu/

New Mexico Institute of Mining and Technology, Center for Graduate Studies, Department of Electrical Engineering, Socorro, NM 87801. Offers MS. *Entrance requirements:* Additional exam requirements/recommendations for international students: required—TOEFL (minimum score 540 paper-based). Electronic applications accepted.

New York Institute of Technology, College of Engineering and Computing Sciences, Department of Electrical and Computer Engineering, Old Westbury, NY 11568. Offers MS. *Program availability:* Part-time. *Faculty:* 17 full-time (4 women), 9 part-time/adjunct (1 woman). *Students:* 46 full-time (10 women), 38 part-time (12 women); includes 27 minority (5 Black or African American, non-Hispanic/Latino; 17 Asian, non-Hispanic/Latino; 5 Hispanic/Latino), 41 international. Average age 26. 273 applicants, 47% accepted, 26 enrolled. In 2019, 46 master's awarded. *Degree requirements:* For master's, thesis or alternative. *Entrance requirements:* For master's, Graduates of foreign universities are required to take the GRE and submit their scores. Applicants with a GPA below 2.85 may, at the discretion of the dean, be asked to take the GRE or other diagnostic tests, For Bioengineering - bachelor's degree or its equivalent in computer science, life sciences, electrical engineering, physics, or related areas; for Electrical and Computer Engineering - bachelor's degree or equivalent in electrical or computer engineering or a closely related field with appropriate undergraduate courses; minimum undergraduate GPA o. Additional exam requirements/recommendations for international students: required—TOEFL (minimum score 79 iBT), IELTS (minimum score 6), PTE (minimum score 53), Duolingo English Test. *Application deadline:* For fall admission, 7/1 for domestic students, 6/1 for international students; for spring admission, 12/1 for domestic and international students. Applications are processed on a rolling basis. Application fee: $50. Electronic applications accepted. *Expenses: Tuition:* Full-time $23,760; part-time $1320 per credit. *Required fees:* $260; $220 per unit. Full-time tuition and fees vary according to degree level and program. Part-time tuition and fees vary according to course load and program. *Financial support:* In 2019–20, 46 students received support. Fellowships, research assistantships, teaching assistantships, Federal Work-Study, scholarships/grants, and unspecified assistantships available. Support available to part-time students. Financial award application deadline: 2/15; financial award applicants required to submit FAFSA. *Unit head:* Dr. Aydin Farajidavar, Department Chairperson, 516-686-4014, Fax: 516-686-7439, E-mail: afarajid@nyit.edu. *Application contact:* Alice Dolitsky, Director, Graduate Admissions, 800-345-6948, Fax: 516-686-1116, E-mail: admissions@nyit.edu.
Website: https://www.nyit.edu/departments/electrical_and_computer_engineering

New York University, Tandon School of Engineering, Department of Electrical and Computer Engineering, Major in Electrical Engineering, New York, NY 10012-1019. Offers electrical engineering (PhD). *Program availability:* Part-time, evening/weekend, online learning. *Degree requirements:* For master's, comprehensive exam (for some programs), thesis (for some programs); for doctorate, comprehensive exam, thesis/dissertation, qualifying exam. *Entrance requirements:* For master's, BS in electrical engineering; for doctorate, MS in electrical engineering. Additional exam requirements/recommendations for international students: required—TOEFL (minimum score 550 paper-based; 90 iBT); recommended—IELTS (minimum score 7). Electronic applications accepted.

Norfolk State University, School of Graduate Studies, School of Science and Technology, Program in Electronics Engineering, Norfolk, VA 23504. Offers MS.

Electrical Engineering

North Carolina Agricultural and Technical State University, The Graduate College, College of Engineering, Department of Electrical and Computer Engineering, Greensboro, NC 27411. Offers electrical engineering (MSEE, PhD), including communications and signal processing, computer engineering, electronic and optical materials and devices, power systems and control. *Program availability:* Part-time. *Degree requirements:* For master's, project, thesis defense; for doctorate, thesis/dissertation. *Entrance requirements:* For master's, GRE General Test, GRE Subject Test, minimum GPA of 2.8; for doctorate, GRE General Test, minimum GPA of 3.0.

North Carolina State University, Graduate School, College of Engineering, Department of Electrical and Computer Engineering, Program in Electrical Engineering, Raleigh, NC 27695. Offers MS, PhD. *Degree requirements:* For master's, thesis (for some programs); for doctorate, thesis/dissertation. *Entrance requirements:* For master's and doctorate, GRE. Additional exam requirements/recommendations for international students: required—TOEFL (minimum score 575 paper-based). Electronic applications accepted.

North Dakota State University, College of Graduate and Interdisciplinary Studies, College of Engineering, Department of Electrical and Computer Engineering, Fargo, ND 58102. Offers M Eng, MS, PhD. *Program availability:* Part-time. Terminal master's awarded for partial completion of doctoral program. *Degree requirements:* For master's, comprehensive exam, thesis; for doctorate, comprehensive exam, thesis/dissertation. *Entrance requirements:* Additional exam requirements/recommendations for international students: required—TOEFL (minimum score 525 paper-based; 71 iBT). Electronic applications accepted. Tuition and fees vary according to program and reciprocity agreements.

Northeastern University, College of Engineering, Boston, MA 02115-5096. Offers bioengineering (MS, PhD); chemical engineering (MS, PhD); civil engineering (MS, PhD); computer engineering (PhD); computer systems engineering (MS); electrical and computer engineering (MS); electrical and computer engineering leadership (MS); electrical engineering (PhD); energy systems (MS); engineering and public policy (MS); engineering management (MS, Certificate); environmental engineering (MS); industrial engineering (MS, PhD); information assurance (PhD); information systems (MS); interdisciplinary engineering (PhD); mechanical engineering (PhD); operations research (MS); telecommunication systems management (MS). *Program availability:* Part-time, online learning. Electronic applications accepted. *Expenses:* Contact institution.

Northern Arizona University, College of Engineering, Informatics, and Applied Sciences, School of Informatics, Computing, and Cyber Systems, Flagstaff, AZ 86011. Offers engineering (M Eng), including computer science and engineering, electrical engineering; informatics and computing (PhD). *Program availability:* Part-time. *Degree requirements:* For master's, variable foreign language requirement, comprehensive exam (for some programs), thesis (for some programs); for doctorate, variable foreign language requirement, comprehensive exam (for some programs), thesis/dissertation (for some programs). *Entrance requirements:* Additional exam requirements/recommendations for international students: required—TOEFL (minimum score 80 iBT), IELTS (minimum score 6.5). Electronic applications accepted.

Northern Illinois University, Graduate School, College of Engineering and Engineering Technology, Department of Electrical Engineering, De Kalb, IL 60115-2854. Offers MS. *Program availability:* Part-time, evening/weekend. *Faculty:* 9 full-time (0 women). *Students:* 24 full-time (6 women), 15 part-time (4 women); includes 4 minority (all Asian, non-Hispanic/Latino), 26 international. Average age 26. 51 applicants, 63% accepted, 14 enrolled. In 2019, 18 master's awarded. *Degree requirements:* For master's, comprehensive exam, thesis optional. *Entrance requirements:* For master's, GRE General Test, minimum GPA of 2.75. Additional exam requirements/recommendations for international students: required—TOEFL (minimum score 550 paper-based). *Application deadline:* For fall admission, 6/1 for domestic students, 5/1 for international students; for spring admission, 11/1 for domestic students, 10/1 for international students. Applications are processed on a rolling basis. Application fee: $40. Electronic applications accepted. *Financial support:* In 2019–20, 4 research assistantships with full tuition reimbursements, 25 teaching assistantships with full tuition reimbursements were awarded; fellowships with full tuition reimbursements, career-related internships or fieldwork, Federal Work-Study, scholarships/grants, tuition waivers (full), and staff assistantships also available. Support available to part-time students. Financial award applicants required to submit FAFSA. *Unit head:* Dr. Mansoor Alam, Chair, 815-753-1290, Fax: 815-753-1289, E-mail: mtaherne@niu.edu. *Application contact:* Graduate School Office, 815-753-0395, E-mail: gradsch@niu.edu.
Website: http://www.niu.edu/ee/

Northwestern Polytechnic University, School of Engineering, Fremont, CA 94539-7482. Offers computer engineering (DCE); computer science (MS); computer systems engineering (MS); electrical engineering (MS). *Program availability:* Part-time, evening/weekend. *Degree requirements:* For master's, thesis optional; for doctorate, thesis/dissertation. *Entrance requirements:* For master's, minimum GPA of 3.0. Additional exam requirements/recommendations for international students: required—TOEFL (minimum score 550 paper-based; 79 iBT).

Northwestern University, McCormick School of Engineering and Applied Science, Department of Electrical Engineering and Computer Science, Evanston, IL 60208. Offers computer engineering (MS, PhD); computer science (MS, PhD); electrical engineering (MS, PhD); information technology (MS). *Program availability:* Part-time. Terminal master's awarded for partial completion of doctoral program. *Degree requirements:* For master's, comprehensive exam (for some programs), thesis optional; for doctorate, comprehensive exam, thesis/dissertation. *Entrance requirements:* For master's and doctorate, GRE General Test. Additional exam requirements/recommendations for international students: required—TOEFL (minimum score 577 paper-based; 90 iBT), IELTS (minimum score 7). Electronic applications accepted.

Oakland University, Graduate Study and Lifelong Learning, School of Engineering and Computer Science, Department of Electrical and Computer Engineering, Rochester, MI 48309-4401. Offers electrical and computer engineering (MS, PhD); embedded systems (MS); mechatronics (MS). *Program availability:* Part-time, evening/weekend. *Entrance requirements:* For master's, minimum GPA of 3.0. Additional exam requirements/recommendations for international students: required—TOEFL (minimum score 550 paper-based). Electronic applications accepted. *Expenses:* Contact institution.

The Ohio State University, Graduate School, College of Engineering, Department of Electrical and Computer Engineering, Columbus, OH 43210. Offers electrical and computer engineering (MS, PhD); electrical engineering (MS, PhD). *Program availability:* Part-time. Terminal master's awarded for partial completion of doctoral program. *Entrance requirements:* For master's, GRE General Test (for all graduates of foreign universities and for applicants if undergraduate GPA below 3.2); for doctorate, GRE General Test (for all graduates of foreign universities and for applicants if graduate work GPA is below 3.5). Additional exam requirements/recommendations for international students: required—TOEFL (minimum score 580 paper-based; 92 iBT); recommended—IELTS (minimum score 7.5). Electronic applications accepted.

Ohio University, Graduate College, Russ College of Engineering and Technology, School of Electrical Engineering and Computer Science, Athens, OH 45701-2979. Offers electrical engineering (MS); electrical engineering and computer science (PhD). *Degree requirements:* For master's, comprehensive exam (for some programs), thesis; for doctorate, comprehensive exam, thesis/dissertation, qualifying exams. *Entrance requirements:* For master's, GRE, BSEE or BSCS, minimum GPA of 3.0; for doctorate, GRE, MSEE or MSCS, minimum GPA of 3.0. Additional exam requirements/recommendations for international students: required—TOEFL (minimum score 550 paper-based; 80 iBT) or IELTS (minimum score 6.5). Electronic applications accepted.

Oklahoma Christian University, Graduate School of Engineering and Computer Science, Oklahoma City, OK 73136-1100. Offers electrical and computer engineering (MSE); engineering management (MSE); mechanical engineering (MSE); software engineering (MSCS, MSE). *Program availability:* Part-time. *Entrance requirements:* Additional exam requirements/recommendations for international students: required—TOEFL (minimum score 550 paper-based). Electronic applications accepted. *Expenses:* Contact institution.

Oklahoma State University, College of Engineering, Architecture and Technology, School of Electrical and Computer Engineering, Stillwater, OK 74078. Offers MS, PhD. *Program availability:* Online learning. *Faculty:* 17 full-time (1 woman). *Students:* 15 full-time (0 women), 30 part-time (7 women); includes 5 minority (1 Asian, non-Hispanic/Latino; 2 Hispanic/Latino; 2 Two or more races, non-Hispanic/Latino), 27 international. Average age 29. 81 applicants, 31% accepted, 15 enrolled. In 2019, 17 master's, 9 doctorates awarded. *Entrance requirements:* For master's and doctorate, GRE or GMAT. Additional exam requirements/recommendations for international students: required—TOEFL (minimum score 550 paper-based; 79 iBT). *Application deadline:* For fall admission, 3/1 priority date for international students; for spring admission, 8/1 priority date for international students. Applications are processed on a rolling basis. Application fee: $50 ($75 for international students). Electronic applications accepted. *Expenses: Tuition, area resident:* Full-time $4148.10; part-time $2765.40. Tuition, state resident: full-time $4148.10; part-time $2765.40. Tuition, nonresident: full-time $15,775; part-time $10,516.80. *International tuition:* $15,775.20 full-time. *Required fees:* $2196.90; $122.05 per credit hour. Tuition and fees vary according to course load, campus/location and program. *Financial support:* In 2019–20, 9 research assistantships (averaging $2,382 per year), 21 teaching assistantships (averaging $1,860 per year) were awarded; career-related internships or fieldwork, Federal Work-Study, scholarships/grants, health care benefits, tuition waivers (partial), and unspecified assistantships also available. Support available to part-time students. Financial award application deadline: 3/1; financial award applicants required to submit FAFSA. *Unit head:* Dr. Jeffrey Young, Department Head, 405-744-5151, Fax: 405-744-9198, E-mail: jl.young@okstate.edu. *Application contact:* Dr. Sheryl Tucker, Vice Prov/Dean/Prof, 405-744-6368, E-mail: igrad@okstate.edu.
Website: http://ece.okstate.edu

Old Dominion University, Frank Batten College of Engineering and Technology, Graduate Program in Electrical and Computer Engineering, Norfolk, VA 23529. Offers ME, MS, D Eng, PhD. *Program availability:* Part-time, online learning. *Degree requirements:* For master's, comprehensive exam (for some programs), thesis (for some programs); for doctorate, thesis/dissertation, candidacy exam, diagnostic exam, proposal defense. *Entrance requirements:* For master's, GRE, two letters of recommendation, resume, personal statement of objectives; for doctorate, GRE, three letters of recommendation, resume, personal statement of objectives. Additional exam requirements/recommendations for international students: required—TOEFL (minimum score 550 paper-based; 79 iBT), IELTS (minimum score 6.5). Electronic applications accepted. *Expenses:* Contact institution.

Oregon Health & Science University, School of Medicine, Graduate Programs in Medicine, Department of Computer Science and Electrical Engineering, Portland, OR 97239-3098. Offers computer science and engineering (MS, PhD); electrical engineering (MS, PhD). *Program availability:* Part-time. Terminal master's awarded for partial completion of doctoral program. *Degree requirements:* For master's, thesis (for some programs); for doctorate, comprehensive exam, thesis/dissertation, qualifying exam. *Entrance requirements:* For master's and doctorate, GRE General Test (minimum scores: 153 Verbal/148 Quantitative/4.5 Analytical). Electronic applications accepted.

Oregon State University, College of Engineering, Program in Electrical and Computer Engineering, Corvallis, OR 97331. Offers M Eng, MS, PhD. *Entrance requirements:* For master's and doctorate, GRE. Additional exam requirements/recommendations for international students: required—TOEFL (minimum score 600 paper-based; 80 iBT), IELTS (minimum score 7). *Expenses:* Contact institution.

Oregon State University, College of Engineering, Program in Materials Science, Corvallis, OR 97331. Offers chemical engineering (MS, PhD); chemistry (MS, PhD); civil engineering (MS, PhD); electrical and computer engineering (MS, PhD); forest products (MS, PhD); mathematics (MS, PhD); mechanical engineering (MS, PhD); nuclear engineering (MS); physics (MS, PhD). *Entrance requirements:* For master's and doctorate, GRE. Additional exam requirements/recommendations for international students: required—TOEFL (minimum score 80 iBT), IELTS (minimum score 6.5). *Expenses:* Contact institution.

Penn State Harrisburg, Graduate School, School of Science, Engineering and Technology, Middletown, PA 17057. Offers civil engineering (MS); computer science (MS); electrical engineering (M Eng, MS); engineering management (MPS); engineering science (M Eng); environmental engineering (M Eng); environmental pollution control (MEPC, MS); mechanical engineering (MS); structural engineering (Certificate). *Program availability:* Part-time, evening/weekend.

Penn State University Park, Graduate School, College of Engineering, Department of Electrical Engineering, University Park, PA 16802. Offers MS, PhD.

Pittsburg State University, Graduate School, College of Technology, Department of Engineering Technology, Pittsburg, KS 66762. Offers electrical engineering technology (MET); general engineering technology (MET); manufacturing engineering technology (MET); mechanical engineering technology (MET); plastics engineering technology (MET). *Program availability:* Part-time, 100% online, blended/hybrid learning. *Degree requirements:* For master's, thesis optional. *Entrance requirements:* Additional exam requirements/recommendations for international students: required—TOEFL (minimum score 550 paper-based; 79 iBT), IELTS (minimum score 6.5), PTE (minimum score 51). Electronic applications accepted. *Expenses:* Contact institution.

Polytechnic University of Puerto Rico, Graduate School, Hato Rey, PR 00918. Offers business administration (MBA), including computer information systems, general management, management of information systems, management of international enterprises; civil engineering (ME, MS); computer engineering (ME, MS); computer science (MCS, MS); electrical engineering (ME, MS); engineering management (MEM); environmental management (MEM); landscape architecture (M Land Arch); manufacturing competitiveness (MMC, MS); manufacturing engineering (ME, MS); mechanical engineering (M Mech E). *Accreditation:* ASLA. *Program availability:* Part-time, evening/weekend. *Entrance requirements:* For master's, 3 letters of recommendation.

Polytechnique Montréal, Graduate Programs, Department of Electrical and Computer Engineering, Montréal, QC H3C 3A7, Canada. Offers automation (M Eng, M Sc A, PhD); computer science (M Eng, M Sc A, PhD); electrical engineering (DESS);

electrotechnology (M Eng, M Sc A, PhD); microelectronics (M Eng, M Sc A, PhD); microwave technology (M Eng, M Sc A, PhD). *Program availability:* Part-time, evening/weekend. *Degree requirements:* For master's, one foreign language, thesis; for doctorate, one foreign language, thesis/dissertation. *Entrance requirements:* For master's, minimum GPA of 2.75; for doctorate, minimum GPA of 3.0.

Portland State University, Graduate Studies, Maseeh College of Engineering and Computer Science, Department of Electrical and Computer Engineering, Portland, OR 97207-0751. Offers MS, PhD. *Program availability:* Part-time, evening/weekend. *Faculty:* 19 full-time (2 women), 10 part-time/adjunct (1 woman). *Students:* 154 full-time (44 women), 99 part-time (27 women); includes 37 minority (8 Black or African American, non-Hispanic/Latino; 20 Asian, non-Hispanic/Latino; 5 Hispanic/Latino; 4 Two or more races, non-Hispanic/Latino), 159 international. Average age 29. 255 applicants, 82% accepted, 83 enrolled. In 2019, 134 master's, 5 doctorates awarded. *Degree requirements:* For master's, variable foreign language requirement, oral exam; for doctorate, one foreign language, comprehensive exam, thesis/dissertation, oral and written exams. *Entrance requirements:* For master's, GRE, minimum GPA of 2.75; for doctorate, GRE General Test, GRE Subject Test, master's degree in electrical engineering or related field, 3 reference letters, statement of purpose, writing sample. Additional exam requirements/recommendations for international students: required—TOEFL (minimum score 550 paper-based; 80 iBT). *Application deadline:* For fall admission, 2/1 for domestic and international students; for winter admission, 8/15 for domestic and international students; for spring admission, 11/1 for domestic and international students. Application fee: $65. *Expenses:* Contact institution. *Financial support:* In 2019–20, 50 students received support, including 15 research assistantships with full and partial tuition reimbursements available (averaging $18,156 per year), 12 teaching assistantships with full and partial tuition reimbursements available (averaging $14,324 per year); career-related internships or fieldwork, Federal Work-Study, scholarships/grants, and unspecified assistantships also available. Support available to part-time students. Financial award application deadline: 3/1; financial award applicants required to submit FAFSA. *Unit head:* Dr. James McNames, Chair, 503-725-5390, Fax: 503-725-3807, E-mail: mcnames@ece.pdx.edu. *Application contact:* Rachelle Braido, Graduate Coordinator, 503-725-2835, Fax: 503-725-3807, E-mail: braido@pdx.edu.
Website: http://www.pdx.edu/ece/

Prairie View A&M University, College of Engineering, Prairie View, TX 77446. Offers computer information systems (MSCIS); computer science (MSCS); electrical engineering (MSEE, PhDEE); general engineering (MS Engr). *Program availability:* Part-time, evening/weekend. *Faculty:* 30 full-time (8 women), 1 part-time/adjunct (0 women). *Students:* 121 full-time (38 women), 55 part-time (14 women); includes 82 minority (61 Black or African American, non-Hispanic/Latino; 14 Asian, non-Hispanic/Latino; 7 Hispanic/Latino), 77 international. Average age 32. 139 applicants, 84% accepted, 40 enrolled. In 2019, 78 master's, 2 doctorates awarded. *Degree requirements:* For master's, thesis optional; for doctorate, comprehensive exam, thesis/dissertation. *Entrance requirements:* For master's, GRE General Test (minimum score of 900), bachelor's degree in engineering from ABET-accredited institution; for doctorate, minimum GPA of 3.0. Additional exam requirements/recommendations for international students: required—TOEFL (minimum score 550 paper-based; 79 iBT). *Application deadline:* For fall admission, 5/1 priority date for domestic and international students; for spring admission, 10/1 priority date for domestic students, 9/1 priority date for international students; for summer admission, 3/1 priority date for domestic students, 2/1 priority date for international students. Applications are processed on a rolling basis. Application fee: $50. Electronic applications accepted. *Expenses: Tuition, area resident:* Full-time $5479.68. Tuition, state resident: full-time $5479.68. Tuition, nonresident: full-time $15,439. *International tuition:* $15,438.74 full-time. *Required fees:* $2149.32. *Financial support:* In 2019–20, 64 students received support, including 64 research assistantships (averaging $14,400 per year), 8 teaching assistantships (averaging $14,400 per year); career-related internships or fieldwork, institutionally sponsored loans, scholarships/grants, health care benefits, tuition waivers (full), and unspecified assistantships also available. Financial award application deadline: 4/1; financial award applicants required to submit FAFSA. *Unit head:* Dr. Pamela H Obiomon, Dean, 936-261-9890, Fax: 936-261-9868, E-mail: phobiomon@pvamu.edu. *Application contact:* Pauline Walker, Administrative Assistant II, Research and Graduate Studies, 936-261-3521, Fax: 936-261-3529, E-mail: gradadmissions@pvamu.edu.

Princeton University, Graduate School, School of Engineering and Applied Science, Department of Electrical Engineering, Princeton, NJ 08544-1019. Offers M Eng, PhD. Terminal master's awarded for partial completion of doctoral program. *Degree requirements:* For doctorate, thesis/dissertation, general exam. *Entrance requirements:* For master's, GRE General Test, 3 letters of recommendation; for doctorate, GRE General Test, official transcript(s), 3 letters of recommendation, personal statement. Additional exam requirements/recommendations for international students: required—TOEFL. Electronic applications accepted.

Purdue University, College of Engineering, School of Electrical and Computer Engineering, West Lafayette, IN 47907-2035. Offers MSECE, PhD. *Program availability:* Part-time, online learning. *Faculty:* 98. *Students:* 668. Terminal master's awarded for partial completion of doctoral program. *Degree requirements:* For master's, thesis optional; for doctorate, thesis/dissertation. *Application deadline:* For fall admission, 12/15 priority date for domestic and international students; for spring admission, 5/1 for domestic and international students. Application fee: $60 ($75 for international students). Electronic applications accepted. *Financial support:* Fellowships with full and partial tuition reimbursements, research assistantships with full and partial tuition reimbursements, teaching assistantships with full and partial tuition reimbursements, career-related internships or fieldwork, scholarships/grants, health care benefits, and unspecified assistantships available. *Unit head:* Dimitrios Peroulis, Department Head, E-mail: dperouli@purdue.edu. *Application contact:* Debra Bowman, Graduate Admissions, 765-494-3392, E-mail: dbowman1@purdue.edu.
Website: https://engineering.purdue.edu/ECE

Purdue University Fort Wayne, College of Engineering, Technology, and Computer Science, Department of Electrical and Computer Engineering, Fort Wayne, IN 46805-1499. Offers computer engineering (MSE); electrical engineering (MSE); systems engineering (MSE). *Program availability:* Part-time. *Entrance requirements:* For master's, minimum GPA of 3.0, bachelor's degree in engineering discipline. Additional exam requirements/recommendations for international students: required—TOEFL (minimum score 550 paper-based; 79 iBT); recommended—TWE. Electronic applications accepted.

Purdue University Northwest, Graduate Studies Office, School of Engineering, Mathematics, and Science, Department of Engineering, Hammond, IN 46323-2094. Offers computer engineering (MSE); electrical engineering (MSE); engineering (MS); mechanical engineering (MSE). *Program availability:* Evening/weekend. *Entrance requirements:* Additional exam requirements/recommendations for international students: required—TOEFL.

Queen's University at Kingston, School of Graduate Studies, Faculty of Engineering and Applied Science, Department of Electrical and Computer Engineering, Kingston, ON K7L 3N6, Canada. Offers M Eng, M Sc, M Sc Eng, PhD. *Program availability:* Part-time. *Degree requirements:* For master's, thesis optional; for doctorate, comprehensive exam, thesis/dissertation. *Entrance requirements:* Additional exam requirements/recommendations for international students: required—TOEFL (minimum score 580 paper-based).

Rensselaer at Hartford, Department of Engineering, Program in Electrical Engineering, Hartford, CT 06120-2991. Offers ME, MS. *Program availability:* Part-time, evening/weekend. *Degree requirements:* For master's, thesis optional. *Entrance requirements:* For master's, GRE. Additional exam requirements/recommendations for international students: required—TOEFL (minimum score 600 paper-based; 100 iBT).

Rensselaer Polytechnic Institute, Graduate School, School of Engineering, Program in Electrical Engineering, Troy, NY 12180-3590. Offers M Eng, MS, PhD. *Faculty:* 40 full-time (7 women), 1 part-time/adjunct (0 women). *Students:* 100 full-time (23 women), 3 part-time (0 women); includes 10 minority (2 Black or African American, non-Hispanic/Latino; 3 Asian, non-Hispanic/Latino; 1 Hispanic/Latino; 4 Two or more races, non-Hispanic/Latino), 75 international. Average age 25. 282 applicants, 56% accepted, 46 enrolled. In 2019, 22 master's, 11 doctorates awarded. Terminal master's awarded for partial completion of doctoral program. *Degree requirements:* For master's, thesis (for some programs); for doctorate, thesis/dissertation. *Entrance requirements:* For master's and doctorate, GRE. Additional exam requirements/recommendations for international students: required—TOEFL (minimum score 570 paper-based; 88 iBT), IELTS (minimum score 6.5), PTE (minimum score 60). *Application deadline:* For fall admission, 1/1 priority date for domestic and international students; for spring admission, 8/15 priority date for domestic and international students. Applications are processed on a rolling basis. Application fee: $75. Electronic applications accepted. *Financial support:* In 2019–20, research assistantships (averaging $23,000 per year), teaching assistantships (averaging $23,000 per year) were awarded; fellowships also available. Financial award application deadline: 1/1. *Unit head:* Dr. Hussein Abouzeid, Graduate Program Director, 518-276-6534, E-mail: gpd@ecse.rpi.edu. *Application contact:* Jarron Decker, Director of Graduate Admissions, 518-276-6216, Fax: 518-276-4072, E-mail: gradadmissions@rpi.edu.
Website: http://www.ecse.rpi.edu/

Rice University, Graduate Programs, George R. Brown School of Engineering, Department of Electrical and Computer Engineering, Houston, TX 77251-1892. Offers bioengineering (MS, PhD); circuits, controls, and communication systems (MS, PhD); computer science and engineering (MS, PhD); electrical engineering (MEE); lasers, microwaves, and solid-state electronics (MS, PhD); MBA/MEE. *Program availability:* Part-time. *Degree requirements:* For master's, thesis (for some programs); for doctorate, thesis/dissertation. *Entrance requirements:* For master's and doctorate, GRE General Test, GRE Subject Test, minimum GPA of 3.0. Additional exam requirements/recommendations for international students: required—TOEFL (minimum score 600 paper-based; 90 iBT). Electronic applications accepted.

Rochester Institute of Technology, Graduate Enrollment Services, Kate Gleason College of Engineering, Electrical and Microelectronic Engineering Department, MS Program in Electrical Engineering, Rochester, NY 14623-5603. Offers MS. *Program availability:* Part-time, evening/weekend. *Entrance requirements:* For master's, GRE, baccalaureate degree from accredited university in engineering or related field, official transcripts, minimum GPA of 3.0, two letters of reference. Additional exam requirements/recommendations for international students: required—TOEFL (minimum score 550 paper-based; 79 iBT), IELTS (minimum score 6.5), PTE (minimum score 58). Electronic applications accepted.

Rochester Institute of Technology, Graduate Enrollment Services, Kate Gleason College of Engineering, Electrical and Microelectronic Engineering Department, MS Program in Microelectronic Engineering, Rochester, NY 14623-5603. Offers MS. *Program availability:* Part-time. *Degree requirements:* For master's, thesis. *Entrance requirements:* For master's, GRE, minimum GPA of 3.0 (recommended), two letters of recommendation. Additional exam requirements/recommendations for international students: required—TOEFL (minimum score 550 paper-based; 79 iBT), IELTS (minimum score 6.5), PTE (minimum score 58). Electronic applications accepted. *Expenses:* Contact institution.

Rose-Hulman Institute of Technology, Graduate Studies, Department of Electrical and Computer Engineering, Terre Haute, IN 47803-3999. Offers electrical and computer engineering (M Eng); electrical engineering (MS); systems engineering and management (MS). *Program availability:* Part-time. *Faculty:* 19 full-time (2 women), 1 (woman) part-time/adjunct. *Students:* 2 full-time (0 women), 3 part-time (0 women), 2 international. Average age 27. 7 applicants, 71% accepted. In 2019, 5 master's awarded. *Degree requirements:* For master's, thesis (for some programs). *Entrance requirements:* For master's, GRE, minimum GPA of 3.0. Additional exam requirements/recommendations for international students: required—TOEFL (minimum score 580 paper-based; 94 iBT), IELTS (minimum score 7). *Application deadline:* For fall admission, 2/1 priority date for domestic and international students; for winter admission, 10/1 for domestic students, 4/1 for international students; for spring admission, 1/15 for domestic students, 11/1 for international students. Applications are processed on a rolling basis. Application fee: $75. Electronic applications accepted. *Financial support:* In 2019–20, 5 students received support. Fellowships with tuition reimbursements available, research assistantships with tuition reimbursements available, institutionally sponsored loans, scholarships/grants, tuition waivers (full and partial), and unspecified assistantships available. *Unit head:* Dr. Mario Simoni, Department Head, 812-877-8341, Fax: 812-877-8895, E-mail: simoni@rose-hulman.edu. *Application contact:* Dr. Craig Downing, Associate Dean of the Faculty, 812-877-8822, E-mail: downing@rose-hulman.edu.
Website: https://www.rose-hulman.edu/academics/academic-departments/electrical-computer-engineering/index.html

Rowan University, Graduate School, College of Engineering, Department of Electrical Engineering, Glassboro, NJ 08028-1701. Offers MS. Electronic applications accepted. *Expenses: Tuition, area resident:* Part-time $715.50 per semester hour. Tuition, state resident: part-time $715.50 per semester hour. Tuition, nonresident: part-time $715.50 per semester hour. *Required fees:* $161.55 per semester hour.

Royal Military College of Canada, Division of Graduate Studies, Faculty of Engineering, Department of Electrical and Computer Engineering, Kingston, ON K7K 7B4, Canada. Offers computer engineering (M Eng, PhD); electrical engineering (M Eng, PhD); software engineering (M Eng, PhD). *Degree requirements:* For master's, thesis; for doctorate, comprehensive exam, thesis/dissertation. *Entrance requirements:* For master's, honours degree with second-class standing in the appropriate field; for doctorate, master's degree. Electronic applications accepted.

Rutgers University - New Brunswick, Graduate School-New Brunswick, Department of Electrical and Computer Engineering, Piscataway, NJ 08854-8097. Offers communications and solid-state electronics (MS, PhD); computer engineering (MS, PhD); control systems (MS, PhD); digital signal processing (MS, PhD). *Program availability:* Part-time. Terminal master's awarded for partial completion of doctoral program. *Degree requirements:* For master's, thesis or alternative; for doctorate, thesis/dissertation. *Entrance requirements:* For master's and doctorate, GRE General Test.

Additional exam requirements/recommendations for international students: required—TOEFL. Electronic applications accepted.

St. Cloud State University, School of Graduate Studies, College of Science and Engineering, Department of Electrical and Computer Engineering, St. Cloud, MN 56301-4498. Offers electrical engineering (MS). *Degree requirements:* For master's, thesis or alternative. *Entrance requirements:* For master's, GRE General Test, minimum GPA of 2.75. Additional exam requirements/recommendations for international students: required—Michigan English Language Assessment Battery; recommended—TOEFL (minimum score 550 paper-based), IELTS (minimum score 6.5). Electronic applications accepted.

St. Mary's University, School of Science, Engineering and Technology, Program in Electrical Engineering, San Antonio, TX 78228. Offers MS. *Program availability:* Part-time, evening/weekend. *Degree requirements:* For master's, thesis or project. *Entrance requirements:* For master's, GRE (minimum quantitative score of 148), bachelor's degree in electrical engineering, computer engineering or closely-related discipline; minimum undergraduate GPA of 3.0; written statement of purpose; two letters of recommendation; official transcripts. Additional exam requirements/recommendations for international students: required—TOEFL (minimum score 550 paper-based; 80 iBT), IELTS (minimum score 6.5). Electronic applications accepted.

San Diego State University, Graduate and Research Affairs, College of Engineering, Department of Electrical and Computer Engineering, San Diego, CA 92182. Offers electrical engineering (MS). *Program availability:* Evening/weekend. *Entrance requirements:* For master's, GRE General Test. Additional exam requirements/recommendations for international students: required—TOEFL. Electronic applications accepted.

San Francisco State University, Division of Graduate Studies, College of Science and Engineering, School of Engineering, San Francisco, CA 94132-1722. Offers embedded electrical and computer systems (MS); energy systems (MS); structural/earthquake engineering (MS). *Program availability:* Part-time. *Application deadline:* Applications are processed on a rolling basis. Electronic applications accepted. *Expenses: Tuition, area resident:* Full-time $7176; part-time $4164 per year. Tuition, state resident: full-time $7176; part-time $4164 per year. Tuition, nonresident: full-time $16,680; part-time $396 per unit. *International tuition:* $16,680 full-time. *Required fees:* $1524; $1524 per unit. $762 per semester. Tuition and fees vary according to degree level and program. *Unit head:* Dr. Kwok-Siong Teh, Director, 415-338-1228, Fax: 415-338-0525, E-mail: ksteh@sfsu.edu. *Application contact:* Dr. Hamid Shahnasser, Graduate Coordinator, 415-338-2124, Fax: 415-338-0525, E-mail: hamid@sfsu.edu.
Website: http://engineering.sfsu.edu/

San Jose State University, Program in Electrical Engineering, San Jose, CA 95192-0001. Offers MS. *Degree requirements:* For master's, thesis. *Entrance requirements:* For master's, GRE General Test. Electronic applications accepted. *Expenses: Tuition, area resident:* Full-time $7176; part-time $4164. Tuition, state resident: full-time $7176; part-time $4164. Tuition, nonresident: full-time $7176; part-time $4165 per credit hour. *International tuition:* $7176 full-time. *Required fees:* $2110; $2110.

Santa Clara University, School of Engineering, Santa Clara, CA 95053. Offers applied mathematics (MS); bioengineering (MS); civil, environmental, and sustainable engineering (MS); computer science and engineering (MS, PhD, Engineer); electrical engineering (MS, PhD, Engineer); engineering management and leadership (MS); mechanical engineering (MS, PhD, Engineer); power systems and sustainable energy (MS); software engineering (MS). *Program availability:* Part-time. *Entrance requirements:* For master's, GRE, official transcript; for doctorate, GRE, Official transcript, 500 word statement of purpose, three letters of recommendation. Additional exam requirements/recommendations for international students: required—TOEFL (minimum score 79 iBT), IELTS (minimum score 6.5). Electronic applications accepted.

South Dakota School of Mines and Technology, Graduate Division, Program in Electrical Engineering, Rapid City, SD 57701-3995. Offers MS. *Program availability:* Part-time. *Degree requirements:* For master's, thesis. *Entrance requirements:* Additional exam requirements/recommendations for international students: required—TOEFL (minimum score 520 paper-based; 68 iBT), TWE. Electronic applications accepted.

South Dakota State University, Graduate School, Jerome J. Lohr College of Engineering, Department of Electrical Engineering and Computer Science, Brookings, SD 57007. Offers electrical engineering (PhD); engineering (MS). *Program availability:* Part-time. *Degree requirements:* For master's, thesis (for some programs), oral exam; for doctorate, comprehensive exam, thesis/dissertation, oral exam. *Entrance requirements:* For master's and doctorate, GRE. Additional exam requirements/recommendations for international students: required—TOEFL (minimum score 575 paper-based).

Southern Illinois University Carbondale, Graduate School, College of Engineering, Department of Electrical and Computer Engineering, Carbondale, IL 62901-4701. Offers MS, PhD, JD/MS. *Degree requirements:* For master's, comprehensive exam, thesis. *Entrance requirements:* For master's, GRE, minimum GPA of 2.7; for doctorate, GRE, minimum GPA of 3.25. Additional exam requirements/recommendations for international students: required—TOEFL.

Southern Illinois University Carbondale, Graduate School, College of Engineering, Program in Engineering Science, Carbondale, IL 62901-4701. Offers engineering science (PhD), including civil and environmental engineering, electrical and computer engineering, mechanical engineering and energy processes, mining and mineral resources engineering. *Degree requirements:* For doctorate, thesis/dissertation. *Entrance requirements:* For doctorate, GRE General Test, minimum GPA of 3.5. Additional exam requirements/recommendations for international students: required—TOEFL.

Southern Illinois University Edwardsville, Graduate School, School of Engineering, Department of Electrical and Computer Engineering, Edwardsville, IL 62026. Offers electrical engineering (MS). *Program availability:* Part-time, evening/weekend. *Degree requirements:* For master's, thesis (for some programs), research paper, final exam. *Entrance requirements:* For master's, minimum undergraduate GPA of 2.75 in engineering, mathematics, and science courses. Additional exam requirements/recommendations for international students: required—TOEFL (minimum score 550 paper-based; 79 iBT), IELTS (minimum score 6.5). Electronic applications accepted.

Southern Methodist University, Lyle School of Engineering, Department of Electrical Engineering, Dallas, TX 75275-0338. Offers electrical engineering (MS, PhD); telecommunications and network engineering (MS). *Program availability:* Part-time, evening/weekend, online learning. Terminal master's awarded for partial completion of doctoral program. *Degree requirements:* For master's, thesis optional; for doctorate, thesis/dissertation, oral and written qualifying exams, oral final exam. *Entrance requirements:* For master's, GRE General Test, minimum GPA of 3.0 in last 2 years; bachelor's degree in engineering, mathematics, or sciences; for doctorate, preliminary counseling exam, minimum GPA of 3.0, bachelor's degree in related field. Additional exam requirements/recommendations for international students: required—TOEFL. Electronic applications accepted.

Stanford University, School of Engineering, Department of Electrical Engineering, Stanford, CA 94305-2004. Offers MS, PhD. *Expenses: Tuition:* Full-time $52,479; part-time $34,110 per unit. *Required fees:* $672; $224 per quarter. Tuition and fees vary according to program and student level.
Website: http://ee.stanford.edu/

Stevens Institute of Technology, Graduate School, Charles V. Schaefer Jr. School of Engineering and Science, Department of Electrical and Computer Engineering, Program in Electrical Engineering, Hoboken, NJ 07030. Offers autonomous robotics (Certificate); electrical engineering (M Eng, PhD, Certificate), including computer architecture and digital systems (M Eng), microelectronics and photonics science and technology (M Eng), signal processing for communications (M Eng), telecommunications systems engineering (M Eng), wireless communications (M Eng, Certificate). *Program availability:* Part-time, evening/weekend. *Faculty:* 20 full-time (6 women), 2 part-time/adjunct. *Students:* 137 full-time (21 women), 23 part-time (5 women); includes 6 minority (2 Black or African American, non-Hispanic/Latino; 4 Asian, non-Hispanic/Latino), 134 international. Average age 25. In 2019, 82 master's, 5 doctorates, 1 other advanced degree awarded. Terminal master's awarded for partial completion of doctoral program. *Degree requirements:* For master's, thesis optional, minimum B average in major field and overall; for doctorate, comprehensive exam (for some programs), thesis/dissertation; for Certificate, minimum B average. *Entrance requirements:* For master's, International applicants must submit TOEFL/IELTS scores and fulfill the English Language Proficiency Requirement. Applicants to full-time programs who do not qualify for a score waiver are required to submit GRE/GMAT scores. Additional exam requirements/recommendations for international students: required—TOEFL (minimum score 74 iBT), IELTS (minimum score 6). *Application deadline:* For fall admission, 4/15 for domestic and international students; for spring admission, 11/1 for domestic and international students; for summer admission, 5/1 for domestic students. Applications are processed on a rolling basis. Application fee: $60. Electronic applications accepted. *Expenses: Tuition:* Full-time $52,134. *Required fees:* $1880. Tuition and fees vary according to course load. *Financial support:* Fellowships, research assistantships, teaching assistantships, career-related internships or fieldwork, Federal Work-Study, scholarships/grants, and unspecified assistantships available. Financial award application deadline: 2/15; financial award applicants required to submit FAFSA. *Unit head:* Dr. Jean Zu, Dean of SES, 201-216.8233, Fax: 201-216.8372, E-mail: Jean.Zu@stevens.edu. *Application contact:* Graduate Admissions, 888-783-8367, Fax: 888-511-1306, E-mail: graduate@stevens.edu.

Stevens Institute of Technology, Graduate School, Charles V. Schaefer Jr. School of Engineering and Science, Department of Mechanical Engineering, Program in Integrated Product Development, Hoboken, NJ 07030. Offers armament engineering (M Eng); computer and electrical engineering (M Eng); manufacturing technologies (M Eng); systems reliability and design (M Eng). *Program availability:* Part-time, evening/weekend. *Faculty:* 29 full-time (3 women), 11 part-time/adjunct (0 women). *Degree requirements:* For master's, thesis optional, minimum B average in major field and overall. *Entrance requirements:* For master's, International applicants must submit TOEFL/IELTS scores and fulfill the English Language Proficiency Requirement. Applicants to full-time programs who do not qualify for a score waiver are required to submit GRE/GMAT scores. Additional exam requirements/recommendations for international students: required—TOEFL (minimum score 74 iBT), IELTS (minimum score 6). *Application deadline:* For fall admission, 4/15 for domestic and international students; for spring admission, 11/1 for domestic and international students; for summer admission, 5/1 for domestic students. Applications are processed on a rolling basis. Application fee: $60. Electronic applications accepted. *Expenses: Tuition:* Full-time $52,134. *Required fees:* $1880. Tuition and fees vary according to course load. *Financial support:* Fellowships, research assistantships, teaching assistantships, career-related internships or fieldwork, Federal Work-Study, scholarships/grants, and unspecified assistantships available. Financial award application deadline: 2/15; financial award applicants required to submit FAFSA. *Unit head:* Dr. Jean Zu, Dean of SES, 201-216.8233, Fax: 201-216.8372, E-mail: Jean.Zu@stevens.edu. *Application contact:* Graduate Admissions, 888-783-8367, Fax: 888-511-1306, E-mail: graduate@stevens.edu.

Stony Brook University, State University of New York, Graduate School, College of Engineering and Applied Sciences, Department of Electrical and Computer Engineering, Program in Electrical Engineering, Stony Brook, NY 11794. Offers MS, PhD. *Faculty:* 29 full-time (6 women), 7 part-time/adjunct (2 women). *Students:* 107 full-time (21 women), 31 part-time (6 women); includes 15 minority (3 Black or African American, non-Hispanic/Latino; 8 Asian, non-Hispanic/Latino; 3 Hispanic/Latino; 1 Two or more races, non-Hispanic/Latino), 106 international. 204 applicants, 87% accepted, 54 enrolled. In 2019, 66 master's, 11 doctorates awarded. *Entrance requirements:* For doctorate, GRE, two official transcripts, letters of recommendation. Additional exam requirements/recommendations for international students: required—TOEFL (minimum score 90 iBT). *Application deadline:* For fall admission, 1/15 for domestic students; for spring admission, 10/1 for domestic students. Application fee: $100. *Expenses:* Contact institution. *Financial support:* Fellowships, research assistantships, and teaching assistantships available. *Unit head:* Prof. Petar M. Djuric, Chair, 631-632-8420, Fax: 631-632-8494, E-mail: petar.djuric@stonybrook.edu. *Application contact:* Nicole Zinerco, Graduate Coordinator, 631-632-8401, Fax: 631-632-8494, E-mail: ecegradcoordinator@stonybrook.edu.

Syracuse University, College of Engineering and Computer Science, MS Program in Electrical Engineering, Syracuse, NY 13244. Offers MS. *Program availability:* Part-time. *Entrance requirements:* For master's, GRE General Test, three letters of recommendation, personal statement, resume, official transcripts. Additional exam requirements/recommendations for international students: required—TOEFL (minimum score 100 iBT). Electronic applications accepted.

Syracuse University, College of Engineering and Computer Science, PhD Program in Electrical and Computer Engineering, Syracuse, NY 13244. Offers PhD. *Program availability:* Part-time. *Degree requirements:* For doctorate, comprehensive exam, thesis/dissertation. *Entrance requirements:* For doctorate, GRE General Test, three letters of recommendation, personal statement, resume, official transcripts. Additional exam requirements/recommendations for international students: required—TOEFL (minimum score 100 iBT). Electronic applications accepted.

Temple University, College of Engineering, Department of Electrical and Computer Engineering, Philadelphia, PA 19122. Offers electrical and computer engineering (PhD); electrical engineering (MSEE). *Program availability:* Part-time, evening/weekend. *Faculty:* 18 full-time (3 women), 21 part-time/adjunct (2 women). *Students:* 41 full-time (14 women), 10 part-time (2 women); includes 7 minority (3 Asian, non-Hispanic/Latino; 3 Hispanic/Latino; 1 Two or more races, non-Hispanic/Latino), 32 international. 58 applicants, 52% accepted, 10 enrolled. In 2019, 14 master's, 2 doctorates awarded. Terminal master's awarded for partial completion of doctoral program. *Degree requirements:* For master's, thesis optional; for doctorate, thesis/dissertation, preliminary exam, dissertation proposal and defense. *Entrance requirements:* For master's, GRE General Test. Waivers are considered on a case by case basis for master's applicants., Competitive applicants to the master's programs should have an undergraduate GPA of at least 3.0 and GREs of at least the 50th percentile in each

section. Applicants should also possess an undergraduate degree in engineering from an ABET accredited or equivalent institution. Also required: letters of rec, resume, personal statement.; for doctorate, GRE General Test. Additional exam requirements/recommendations for international students: required—TOEFL (minimum score 79 iBT), IELTS (minimum score 6.5). *Application deadline:* For fall admission, 6/1 priority date for domestic students, 3/1 priority date for international students; for spring admission, 11/1 priority date for domestic students, 8/1 priority date for international students. Applications are processed on a rolling basis. Application fee: $60. Electronic applications accepted. *Expenses:* 1,135 per credit hour in-state resident; 1,490 per credit hour out-of-state resident. *Financial support:* In 2019–20, 1 fellowship with full tuition reimbursement (averaging $30,000 per year), 14 research assistantships with full tuition reimbursements (averaging $19,739 per year), 23 teaching assistantships with full tuition reimbursements (averaging $19,739 per year) were awarded. Financial award applicants required to submit FAFSA. *Unit head:* Dr. Li Bai, Chair, 215-204-6616, Fax: 215-204-6936, E-mail: lbai@temple.edu. *Application contact:* Colleen Baillie, Director of Enrollment Management, 215-204-7800, Fax: 215-204-6936, E-mail: gradengr@temple.edu.
Website: http://engineering.temple.edu/department/electrical-computer-engineering

Tennessee State University, The School of Graduate Studies and Research, College of Engineering, Nashville, TN 37209-1561. Offers biomedical engineering (ME); civil engineering (ME); computer and information systems engineering (MS, PhD); electrical engineering (ME); environmental engineering (ME); manufacturing engineering (ME); mathematical sciences (MS); mechanical engineering (ME). *Program availability:* Part-time, evening/weekend. *Degree requirements:* For master's, project; for doctorate, comprehensive exam, thesis/dissertation. *Entrance requirements:* For doctorate, minimum GPA of 3.3.

Tennessee Technological University, College of Graduate Studies, College of Engineering, Department of Electrical and Computer Engineering, Cookeville, TN 38505. Offers MS. *Program availability:* Part-time. *Faculty:* 19 full-time (0 women). *Students:* 1 full-time (0 women), 13 part-time (4 women), 5 international. 31 applicants, 61% accepted, 4 enrolled. In 2019, 7 master's awarded. *Degree requirements:* For master's, thesis. *Entrance requirements:* For master's, GRE. Additional exam requirements/recommendations for international students: required—TOEFL (minimum score 550 paper-based; 79 iBT), IELTS (minimum score 5.5), PTE (minimum score 53), or TOEIC (Test of English as an International Communication). *Application deadline:* For fall admission, 8/1 for domestic students, 5/1 for international students; for spring admission, 12/1 for domestic students, 10/1 for international students; for summer admission, 5/1 for domestic students, 2/1 for international students. Applications are processed on a rolling basis. Application fee: $35 ($40 for international students). Electronic applications accepted. *Expenses:* Tuition, area resident: Part-time $597 per credit hour. Tuition, state resident: part-time $597 per credit hour. Tuition, nonresident: part-time $1323 per credit hour. *Financial support:* Fellowships, research assistantships, teaching assistantships, and career-related internships or fieldwork available. Financial award application deadline: 4/1. *Unit head:* Dr. Allen MacKenzie, Chairperson, 931-372-3397, Fax: 931-372-3436, E-mail: amackenzie@tntech.edu. *Application contact:* Shelia K. Kendrick, Coordinator of Graduate Studies, 931-372-3808, Fax: 931-372-3497, E-mail: skendrick@tntech.edu.

Texas A&M University, College of Engineering, Department of Electrical and Computer Engineering, College Station, TX 77843. Offers computer engineering (M Eng, PhD); electrical engineering (M Eng). *Faculty:* 75. *Students:* 605 full-time (132 women), 130 part-time (25 women); includes 35 minority (1 Black or African American, non-Hispanic/Latino; 21 Asian, non-Hispanic/Latino; 11 Hispanic/Latino; 2 Two or more races, non-Hispanic/Latino), 643 international. Average age 26. 1,318 applicants, 50% accepted, 243 enrolled. In 2019, 218 master's, 52 doctorates awarded. *Degree requirements:* For master's, comprehensive exam (for some programs), thesis (for some programs); for doctorate, comprehensive exam, thesis/dissertation. *Entrance requirements:* For master's and doctorate, GRE General Test, letters of recommendation. Additional exam requirements/recommendations for international students: required—TOEFL (minimum score 550 paper-based; 80 iBT), IELTS (minimum score 6), PTE (minimum score 53). *Application deadline:* For fall admission, 5/1 for domestic students, 2/1 for international students; for spring admission, 10/1 for domestic students, 7/1 for international students. Application fee: $65 ($90 for international students). Electronic applications accepted. *Expenses:* Contact institution. *Financial support:* In 2019–20, 506 students received support, including 42 fellowships with tuition reimbursements available (averaging $10,572 per year), 204 research assistantships with tuition reimbursements available (averaging $14,937 per year), 128 teaching assistantships with tuition reimbursements available (averaging $12,615 per year); career-related internships or fieldwork, institutionally sponsored loans, scholarships/grants, traineeships, health care benefits, tuition waivers (full and partial), and unspecified assistantships also available. Support available to part-time students. Financial award application deadline: 3/15; financial award applicants required to submit FAFSA. *Unit head:* Dr. Miroslav M. Begovic, Department Head, 979-862-1553, E-mail: begovic@tamu.edu. *Application contact:* Katie Bryan, Academic Advisor IV - Graduate Program, 979-845-7467, E-mail: k.bryan@tamu.edu.
Website: http://engineering.tamu.edu/electrical/

Texas A&M University–Kingsville, College of Graduate Studies, Frank H. Dotterweich College of Engineering, Department of Electrical Engineering and Computer Science, Program in Electrical Engineering, Kingsville, TX 78363. Offers ME, MS. *Degree requirements:* For master's, variable foreign language requirement, comprehensive exam, thesis (for some programs). *Entrance requirements:* For master's, GRE (minimum score of 145 quantitative revised score, 800 quantitative and verbal old score), MAT, GMAT. Additional exam requirements/recommendations for international students: required—TOEFL (minimum score 550 paper-based; 79 iBT). Electronic applications accepted.

Texas State University, The Graduate College, College of Science and Engineering, Program in Engineering, San Marcos, TX 78666. Offers civil engineering (MS); electrical engineering (MS); industrial engineering (MS); mechanical and manufacturing engineering (MS). *Program availability:* Part-time. *Degree requirements:* For master's, comprehensive exam, thesis (for some programs), thesis or research project. *Entrance requirements:* For master's, official GRE (general test only) required with competitive scores in the verbal reasoning and quantitative reasoning sections, baccalaureate degree from regionally-accredited university in engineering, computer science, physics, technology, or closely-related field with minimum GPA of 3.0 on last 60 undergraduate semester hours; resume or curriculum vitae; 2 letters of recommendation; statement of purpose conveying research interest and professional aspirations. Additional exam requirements/recommendations for international students: required—TOEFL (minimum score 550 paper-based; 78 iBT), IELTS (minimum score 6.5). Electronic applications accepted.

Tufts University, Graduate School of Arts and Sciences, Graduate Certificate Programs, Microwave and Wireless Engineering Program, Medford, MA 02155. Offers Certificate. *Program availability:* Part-time, evening/weekend. Electronic applications accepted. Full-time tuition and fees vary according to degree level, program and student level. Part-time tuition and fees vary according to course load.

Tufts University, School of Engineering, Department of Electrical and Computer Engineering, Medford, MA 02155. Offers bioengineering (MS), including signals and systems; electrical engineering (MS, PhD); PhD/PhD. *Program availability:* Part-time. Terminal master's awarded for partial completion of doctoral program. *Degree requirements:* For master's, thesis or alternative; for doctorate, thesis/dissertation. *Entrance requirements:* For master's and doctorate, GRE General Test. Additional exam requirements/recommendations for international students: required—TOEFL (minimum score 550 paper-based; 80 iBT), IELTS (minimum score 6.5). Electronic applications accepted. Full-time tuition and fees vary according to degree level, program and student level. Part-time tuition and fees vary according to course load.

Tuskegee University, Graduate Programs, College of Engineering, Department of Electrical Engineering, Tuskegee, AL 36088. Offers MSEE. *Degree requirements:* For master's, thesis or alternative. *Entrance requirements:* For master's, GRE General Test, GRE Subject Test. Additional exam requirements/recommendations for international students: required—TOEFL (minimum score 500 paper-based).

Universidad de las Américas Puebla, Division of Graduate Studies, School of Engineering, Program in Electronic Engineering, Puebla, Mexico. Offers MS. *Program availability:* Part-time, evening/weekend.

Universidad del Turabo, Graduate Programs, School of Engineering, Gurabo, PR 00778-3030. Offers computer engineering (M Eng); electrical engineering (M Eng); mechanical engineering (M Eng); telecommunications and network systems administration (M Eng). *Entrance requirements:* For master's, GRE, EXADEP or GMAT, interview, essay, official transcript, recommendation letters. Electronic applications accepted.

Université de Moncton, Faculty of Engineering, Program in Electrical Engineering, Moncton, NB E1A 3E9, Canada. Offers M Sc A. *Degree requirements:* For master's, thesis, proficiency in French.

Université de Sherbrooke, Faculty of Engineering, Department of Electrical Engineering and Computer Engineering, Sherbrooke, QC J1K 2R1, Canada. Offers electrical engineering (M Sc A, PhD). *Degree requirements:* For master's, one foreign language, thesis; for doctorate, comprehensive exam, thesis/dissertation. *Entrance requirements:* For master's, bachelor's degree in engineering or equivalent. Electronic applications accepted.

Université du Québec à Trois-Rivières, Graduate Programs, Program in Electrical Engineering, Trois-Rivières, QC G9A 5H7, Canada. Offers M Sc A, PhD. *Program availability:* Part-time. *Degree requirements:* For master's, thesis; for doctorate, thesis/dissertation. *Entrance requirements:* For master's, appropriate bachelor's degree, proficiency in French; for doctorate, appropriate master's degree, proficiency in French.

University at Buffalo, the State University of New York, Graduate School, School of Engineering and Applied Sciences, Department of Electrical Engineering, Buffalo, NY 14260. Offers ME, MS, PhD. *Program availability:* Part-time. Terminal master's awarded for partial completion of doctoral program. *Degree requirements:* For master's, comprehensive exam (for some programs), thesis or exam; for doctorate, comprehensive exam, thesis/dissertation. *Entrance requirements:* For master's and doctorate, GRE General Test. Additional exam requirements/recommendations for international students: required—TOEFL (minimum score 550 paper-based; 79 iBT). Electronic applications accepted. *Expenses:* Tuition, area resident: Full-time $11,310; part-time $471 per credit hour. Tuition, state resident: full-time $11,310; part-time $471 per credit hour. Tuition, nonresident: full-time $23,100; part-time $963 per credit hour. *International tuition:* $23,100 full-time. *Required fees:* $2820.

The University of Akron, Graduate School, College of Engineering, Department of Electrical and Computer Engineering, Akron, OH 44325. Offers computer engineering (MS, PhD); electrical engineering (MS). *Program availability:* Evening/weekend. *Degree requirements:* For master's, oral comprehensive exam or thesis; for doctorate, one foreign language, thesis/dissertation, candidacy exam, qualifying exam. *Entrance requirements:* For master's, GRE, minimum GPA of 2.75, three letters of recommendation, statement of purpose; for doctorate, GRE, minimum GPA of 3.0 with bachelor's degree, 3.5 with master's degree; three letters of recommendation; statement of purpose; resume. Additional exam requirements/recommendations for international students: required—TOEFL (minimum score 79 iBT), IELTS (minimum score 6.5). Electronic applications accepted.

The University of Alabama, Graduate School, College of Engineering, Department of Electrical and Computer Engineering, Tuscaloosa, AL 35487-0286. Offers electrical engineering (MS, PhD). *Program availability:* Part-time, online learning. *Faculty:* 24 full-time (3 women). *Students:* 62 full-time (10 women), 5 part-time (1 woman); includes 1 minority (Black or African American, non-Hispanic/Latino), 48 international. Average age 28. 103 applicants, 71% accepted, 12 enrolled. In 2019, 4 master's, 7 doctorates awarded. *Degree requirements:* For master's, thesis or alternative; for doctorate, one foreign language, comprehensive exam, thesis/dissertation. *Entrance requirements:* For master's, GRE (for students from non ABET-accredited schools), minimum GPA of 3.0 in last 60 hours of course work or overall; for doctorate, GRE (for students from non ABET-accredited schools), minimum GPA of 3.0 overall. Additional exam requirements/recommendations for international students: required—TOEFL (minimum score 550 paper-based). *Application deadline:* For fall admission, 7/1 priority date for domestic students, 1/15 priority date for international students; for spring admission, 11/1 priority date for domestic students, 6/1 priority date for international students. Applications are processed on a rolling basis. Application fee: $50 ($60 for international students). Electronic applications accepted. *Expenses:* Tuition, area resident: Full-time $10,780; part-time $440 per credit hour. Tuition, nonresident: full-time $30,250; part-time $1550 per credit hour. *Financial support:* In 2019–20, 38 students received support. Fellowships with full tuition reimbursements available, research assistantships with full tuition reimbursements available, teaching assistantships with full tuition reimbursements available, health care benefits, and unspecified assistantships available. *Unit head:* Dr. Tim Haskew, Department Head, 205-348-1766, Fax: 205-348-6959, E-mail: thaskew@eng.ua.edu. *Application contact:* Dr. Steve Shepard, Graduate Program Coordinator/Associate Professor, 205-348-1650, Fax: 205-348-6419, E-mail: sshepard@eng.ua.edu.
Website: http://ece.eng.ua.edu

The University of Alabama at Birmingham, School of Engineering, Program in Electrical Engineering, Birmingham, AL 35294. Offers computer engineering (PhD); electrical and computer engineering (MSEE). *Program availability:* Part-time. *Faculty:* 8 full-time (0 women), 3 part-time/adjunct (0 women). *Students:* 35 full-time (9 women), 33 part-time (6 women); includes 7 minority (1 Black or African American, non-Hispanic/Latino; 2 Asian, non-Hispanic/Latino; 2 Hispanic/Latino; 2 Two or more races, non-Hispanic/Latino), 44 international. 73 applicants, 56% accepted, 7 enrolled. In 2019, 19 master's, 4 doctorates awarded. *Degree requirements:* For master's, comprehensive exam, thesis (for some programs); for doctorate, comprehensive exam, thesis/dissertation. *Entrance requirements:* For master's, GRE general test is required for all applicants who did not receive a BS degree from a program accredited by the Engineering Accreditation Committee of ABET http://www.abet.org, or from other programs with reciprocal agreement under the Washington Accord http://www.ieagreements.org/accords/washington/., A 3.0 on a 4.0 scale or better GPA in all

junior and senior electrical and computer engineering and mathematics courses attempted;; for doctorate, GRE, An overall GPA of at least 3.0 on a 4.0 point scale, or at least 3.0 for the last 60 semester hours completed; and. Additional exam requirements/recommendations for international students: required—TOEFL (minimum score 80 iBT), IELTS (minimum score 6.5). *Application deadline:* For fall admission, 8/1 for domestic and international students; for spring admission, 12/1 for domestic and international students; for summer admission, 5/1 for domestic and international students. Applications are processed on a rolling basis. Application fee: $50 ($60 for international students). Electronic applications accepted. *Financial support:* In 2019–20, 12 students received support, including 4 fellowships with full tuition reimbursements available (averaging $29,748 per year), 7 research assistantships with full and partial tuition reimbursements available (averaging $19,748 per year), 1 teaching assistantship; unspecified assistantships also available. *Unit head:* Dr. J Iwan Alexander, Interim Chair, 205-934-8440, E-mail: ialex@uab.edu. *Application contact:* Jesse Keppley, Director of Student and Academic Services, 205-996-5696, E-mail: gradschool@uab.edu.
Website: https://www.uab.edu/engineering/home/graduate#msee

The University of Alabama in Huntsville, School of Graduate Studies, College of Engineering, Department of Electrical and Computer Engineering, Huntsville, AL 35899. Offers computer engineering (MSE, PhD); electrical engineering (MSE, PhD), including optics and photonics technology (MSE); optical science and engineering (PhD); software engineering (MSSE). *Program availability:* Part-time. *Degree requirements:* For master's, comprehensive exam, thesis or alternative, oral and written exams; for doctorate, comprehensive exam, thesis/dissertation, oral and written exams. *Entrance requirements:* For master's, GRE General Test, appropriate bachelor's degree, minimum GPA of 3.0; for doctorate, GRE General Test, minimum GPA of 3.0. Additional exam requirements/recommendations for international students: required—TOEFL (minimum score 500 paper-based; 80 iBT), IELTS (minimum score 6.5). Electronic applications accepted.

University of Alaska Fairbanks, College of Engineering and Mines, Department of Electrical and Computer Engineering, Fairbanks, AK 99775-5915. Offers electrical engineering (MEE, MS). *Program availability:* Part-time. *Degree requirements:* For master's, comprehensive exam. *Entrance requirements:* For master's, GRE General Test, bachelor's degree from accredited institution with minimum cumulative undergraduate and major GPA of 3.0. Additional exam requirements/recommendations for international students: required—TOEFL (minimum score 550 paper-based; 79 iBT), IELTS (minimum score 6.5). Electronic applications accepted. *Expenses:* Contact institution.

University of Alberta, Faculty of Graduate Studies and Research, Department of Electrical and Computer Engineering, Edmonton, AB T6G 2E1, Canada. Offers communications (M Eng, M Sc, PhD); computer engineering (M Eng, M Sc, PhD); electromagnetics (M Eng, M Sc, PhD); nanotechnology and microdevices (M Eng, M Sc, PhD); power/power electronics (M Eng, M Sc, PhD); systems (M Eng, M Sc, PhD). Terminal master's awarded for partial completion of doctoral program. *Degree requirements:* For master's, thesis; for doctorate, thesis/dissertation. *Entrance requirements:* Additional exam requirements/recommendations for international students: required—TOEFL. Electronic applications accepted.

The University of Arizona, College of Engineering, Department of Electrical and Computer Engineering, Tucson, AZ 85721. Offers MS, PhD. *Program availability:* Part-time. *Degree requirements:* For master's, thesis (for some programs); for doctorate, thesis/dissertation. *Entrance requirements:* For master's, GRE General Test, 3 letters of recommendation, statement of purpose; for doctorate, GRE General Test, master's degree in related field, 3 letters of recommendation, statement of purpose. Additional exam requirements/recommendations for international students: required—TOEFL (minimum score 550 paper-based; 79 iBT). Electronic applications accepted.

University of Arkansas, Graduate School, College of Engineering, Department of Electrical Engineering, Fayetteville, AR 72701. Offers electrical engineering (MSEE, PhD); telecommunications engineering (MS Tc E). *Students:* 48 full-time (12 women), 100 part-time (13 women); includes 20 minority (4 Black or African American, non-Hispanic/Latino; 8 Asian, non-Hispanic/Latino; 7 Hispanic/Latino; 1 Two or more races, non-Hispanic/Latino), 77 international. 27 applicants, 74% accepted. In 2019, 25 master's, 6 doctorates awarded. *Degree requirements:* For master's, thesis optional; for doctorate, one foreign language, thesis/dissertation. *Entrance requirements:* For master's and doctorate, GRE General Test. *Application deadline:* For fall admission, 8/1 for domestic students, 4/1 for international students; for spring admission, 12/1 for domestic students, 10/1 for international students; for summer admission, 4/15 for domestic students, 3/1 for international students. Applications are processed on a rolling basis. Application fee: $60. Electronic applications accepted. *Financial support:* In 2019–20, 48 research assistantships, 8 teaching assistantships were awarded; fellowships with tuition reimbursements, career-related internships or fieldwork, and Federal Work-Study also available. Support available to part-time students. Financial award application deadline: 4/1; financial award applicants required to submit FAFSA. *Unit head:* Dr. Juan Carlos Balda, Department Head, 479-575-3005, Fax: 479-575-7967, E-mail: jbalda@uark.edu. *Application contact:* Dr. Hameed Naseem, Graduate Coordinator, 479-575-6052, Fax: 479-575-7967, E-mail: hnaseem@uark.edu.
Website: https://electrical-engineering.uark.edu/index.php

University of Bridgeport, School of Engineering, Department of Electrical Engineering, Bridgeport, CT 06604. Offers MS. *Program availability:* Part-time, evening/weekend. Terminal master's awarded for partial completion of doctoral program. *Degree requirements:* For master's, thesis optional. *Entrance requirements:* Additional exam requirements/recommendations for international students: recommended—TOEFL (minimum score 550 paper-based; 80 iBT), IELTS (minimum score 6.5). Electronic applications accepted. *Expenses:* Contact institution.

The University of British Columbia, Faculty of Applied Science, Department of Electrical and Computer Engineering, Vancouver, BC V6T 1Z4, Canada. Offers M Eng, MA Sc, PhD. *Program availability:* Part-time. *Degree requirements:* For master's, thesis (for some programs); for doctorate, thesis/dissertation. *Entrance requirements:* Additional exam requirements/recommendations for international students: required—TOEFL, IELTS. Electronic applications accepted. *Expenses:* Contact institution.

University of Calgary, Faculty of Graduate Studies, Schulich School of Engineering, Program in Electrical and Computer Engineering, Calgary, AB T2N 1N4, Canada. Offers M Eng, M Sc, PhD. *Program availability:* Part-time. *Degree requirements:* For master's, thesis (for M Sc); for doctorate, thesis/dissertation, candidacy exam. *Entrance requirements:* For master's, minimum GPA of 3.0; for doctorate, minimum GPA of 3.5. Additional exam requirements/recommendations for international students: required—TOEFL (minimum score 550 paper-based; 80 iBT) or IELTS (minimum score 7). Electronic applications accepted.

University of California, Berkeley, Graduate Division, College of Engineering, Department of Electrical Engineering and Computer Sciences, Berkeley, CA 94720. Offers computer science (MS, PhD); electrical engineering (M Eng, MS, PhD). Terminal master's awarded for partial completion of doctoral program. *Degree requirements:* For master's, comprehensive exam (for some programs), thesis (for some programs), comprehensive exam or thesis; for doctorate, thesis/dissertation, qualifying exam. *Entrance requirements:* For master's and doctorate, GRE General Test, minimum GPA of 3.0, 3 letters of recommendation. Additional exam requirements/recommendations for international students: required—TOEFL (minimum score 570 paper-based; 90 iBT). Electronic applications accepted.

University of California, Davis, College of Engineering, Program in Electrical and Computer Engineering, Davis, CA 95616. Offers MS, PhD. Terminal master's awarded for partial completion of doctoral program. *Degree requirements:* For master's, comprehensive exam (for some programs), thesis (for some programs); for doctorate, thesis/dissertation, preliminary and qualifying exams, thesis defense. *Entrance requirements:* For master's, GRE General Test, minimum GPA of 3.2; for doctorate, GRE, minimum graduate GPA of 3.5. Additional exam requirements/recommendations for international students: required—TOEFL (minimum score 550 paper-based). Electronic applications accepted.

University of California, Irvine, Samueli School of Engineering, Department of Electrical Engineering and Computer Science, Irvine, CA 92697. Offers electrical engineering and computer science (MS, PhD); networked systems (MS, PhD). *Program availability:* Part-time. *Students:* 274 full-time (65 women), 11 part-time (3 women); includes 24 minority (3 Black or African American, non-Hispanic/Latino; 15 Asian, non-Hispanic/Latino; 2 Hispanic/Latino; 1 Native Hawaiian or other Pacific Islander, non-Hispanic/Latino; 3 Two or more races, non-Hispanic/Latino), 226 international. Average age 27. 1,538 applicants, 27% accepted, 81 enrolled. In 2019, 88 master's, 26 doctorates awarded. Terminal master's awarded for partial completion of doctoral program. *Entrance requirements:* For master's and doctorate, GRE General Test, minimum GPA of 3.0, 3 letters of recommendation. Additional exam requirements/recommendations for international students: required—TOEFL (minimum score 550 paper-based). *Application deadline:* For fall admission, 1/15 priority date for domestic students, 1/15 for international students. Applications are processed on a rolling basis. Application fee: $120 ($140 for international students). Electronic applications accepted. *Financial support:* Fellowships, research assistantships with full tuition reimbursements, teaching assistantships, institutionally sponsored loans, traineeships, health care benefits, and unspecified assistantships available. Financial award application deadline: 3/1; financial award applicants required to submit FAFSA. *Unit head:* Prof. H. Kumar Wickramasinghe, Chair, 949-824-2213, E-mail: hkwick@uci.edu. *Application contact:* Jean Bennett, Director of Graduate Student Affairs, 949-824-6475, Fax: 949-824-8200, E-mail: jean.bennett@uci.edu.
Website: http://www.eng.uci.edu/dept/eecs

University of California, Los Angeles, Graduate Division, Henry Samueli School of Engineering and Applied Science, Department of Electrical and Computer Engineering, Los Angeles, CA 90095-1594. Offers MS, PhD. *Degree requirements:* For master's, comprehensive exam or thesis; for doctorate, thesis/dissertation, qualifying exams. *Entrance requirements:* For master's, GRE General Test, minimum GPA of 3.0; for doctorate, GRE General Test, minimum GPA of 3.25. Additional exam requirements/recommendations for international students: required—TOEFL (minimum score 560 paper-based; 87 iBT), IELTS (minimum score 7). Electronic applications accepted.

University of California, Merced, Graduate Division, School of Engineering, Merced, CA 95343. Offers biological engineering and small scale technologies (MS, PhD); electrical engineering and computer science (MS, PhD); environmental systems (MS, PhD); management of innovation, sustainability, and technology (MM); mechanical engineering (MS, PhD). *Faculty:* 60 full-time (16 women). *Students:* 244 full-time (83 women), 1 (woman) part-time; includes 56 minority (2 Black or African American, non-Hispanic/Latino; 20 Asian, non-Hispanic/Latino; 30 Hispanic/Latino; 1 Native Hawaiian or other Pacific Islander, non-Hispanic/Latino; 3 Two or more races, non-Hispanic/Latino), 153 international. Average age 28. 330 applicants, 32% accepted, 67 enrolled. In 2019, 30 master's, 17 doctorates awarded. Terminal master's awarded for partial completion of doctoral program. *Degree requirements:* For master's, variable foreign language requirement, comprehensive exam, thesis or alternative, oral defense; for doctorate, variable foreign language requirement, comprehensive exam, thesis/dissertation, oral defense. *Entrance requirements:* For master's and doctorate, GRE. Additional exam requirements/recommendations for international students: required—TOEFL (minimum score 550 paper-based; 80 iBT); recommended—IELTS (minimum score 6.5). *Application deadline:* For fall admission, 1/15 for domestic and international students. Application fee: $105 ($125 for international students). Electronic applications accepted. *Expenses: Tuition, area resident:* Full-time $11,442; part-time $5721. Tuition, state resident: full-time $11,442; part-time $5721. Tuition, nonresident: full-time $26,544; part-time $13,272. *International tuition:* $26,544 full-time. *Required fees:* $564 per semester. *Financial support:* In 2019–20, 205 students received support, including 6 fellowships with full tuition reimbursements available (averaging $22,005 per year), 76 research assistantships with full tuition reimbursements available (averaging $21,420 per year), 123 teaching assistantships with full tuition reimbursements available (averaging $21,911 per year); scholarships/grants, traineeships, and health care benefits also available. *Unit head:* Dr. Mark Matsumoto, Dean, 209-228-4047, Fax: 209-228-4047, E-mail: mmatsumoto@ucmerced.edu. *Application contact:* Tsu Ya, Director of Admissions and Academic Services, 209-228-4521, Fax: 209-228-6906, E-mail: tya@ucmerced.edu.

University of California, Riverside, Graduate Division, Department of Electrical Engineering, Riverside, CA 92521-0102. Offers electrical engineering (MS, PhD), including computer engineering (MS), control and robotics (PhD). Terminal master's awarded for partial completion of doctoral program. *Degree requirements:* For master's, thesis optional; for doctorate, thesis/dissertation, qualifying exams. *Entrance requirements:* For master's and doctorate, GRE General Test, minimum GPA of 3.25. Additional exam requirements/recommendations for international students: required—TOEFL (minimum score 550 paper-based; 80 iBT). Electronic applications accepted.

University of California, San Diego, Graduate Division, Department of Electrical and Computer Engineering, La Jolla, CA 92093. Offers applied ocean science (MS, PhD); applied physics (MS, PhD); communication theory and systems (MS, PhD); computer engineering (MS, PhD); electronic circuits and systems (MS, PhD); intelligent systems, robotics and control (MS, PhD); medical devices and systems (MS, PhD); nanoscale devices and systems (MS, PhD); photonics (MS, PhD); signal and image processing (MS, PhD). *Students:* 983 full-time (216 women), 80 part-time (15 women). 3,675 applicants, 33% accepted, 430 enrolled. In 2019, 287 master's, 50 doctorates awarded. Terminal master's awarded for partial completion of doctoral program. *Degree requirements:* For master's, comprehensive exam (for some programs), thesis (for some programs); for doctorate, comprehensive exam, thesis/dissertation. *Entrance requirements:* For master's and doctorate, GRE General Test, minimum GPA of 3.0, resume or curriculum vitae (recommended). Additional exam requirements/recommendations for international students: required—TOEFL (minimum score 550 paper-based; 80 iBT), IELTS (minimum score 7), PTE (minimum score 65). *Application deadline:* For fall admission, 12/18 for domestic students. Application fee: $105 ($125 for international students). Electronic applications accepted. *Financial support:* Fellowships, research assistantships, teaching assistantships, scholarships/grants, traineeships, and unspecified assistantships available. Financial award applicants required to submit FAFSA. *Unit head:* Bill Lin, Chair, 858-822-1383, E-mail: billin@

ucsd.edu. *Application contact:* Sean Jones, Graduate Admissions Coordinator, 858-534-3213, E-mail: ecegradapps@ece.ucsd.edu. Website: http://ece.ucsd.edu/

University of California, Santa Barbara, Graduate Division, College of Engineering, Department of Electrical and Computer Engineering, Santa Barbara, CA 93106-2014. Offers communications, control and signal processing (MS, PhD); computer engineering (MS, PhD); electronics and photonics (MS, PhD); MS/PhD. *Degree requirements:* For master's, comprehensive exam, thesis; for doctorate, thesis/dissertation. *Entrance requirements:* For master's and doctorate, GRE General Test. Additional exam requirements/recommendations for international students: required—TOEFL (minimum score 550 paper-based; 80 iBT), IELTS (minimum score 7). Electronic applications accepted.

University of California, Santa Cruz, Jack Baskin School of Engineering, Program in Electrical and Computer Engineering, Santa Cruz, CA 95064. Offers MS, PhD. *Faculty:* 21 full-time (3 women), 3 part-time/adjunct (0 women). *Students:* 91 full-time (24 women); includes 14 minority (1 Black or African American, non-Hispanic/Latino; 5 Asian, non-Hispanic/Latino; 6 Hispanic/Latino; 2 Native Hawaiian or other Pacific Islander, non-Hispanic/Latino, 57 international. 281 applicants, 49% accepted, 47 enrolled. In 2019, 42 master's, 6 doctorates awarded. Terminal master's awarded for partial completion of doctoral program. *Degree requirements:* For master's, comprehensive exam, thesis, thesis or comprehensive exam; for doctorate, thesis/dissertation, preliminary exam and qualifying exam. *Entrance requirements:* For master's and doctorate, GRE General Test (temporarily waived due to pandemic). Additional exam requirements/recommendations for international students: required—TOEFL (minimum score 570 paper-based; 89 iBT); recommended—IELTS (minimum score 8). *Application deadline:* For fall admission, 1/10 for domestic and international students. Application fee: $105 ($125 for international students). Electronic applications accepted. *Financial support:* In 2019–20, 57 students received support, including 38 fellowships with full and partial tuition reimbursements available (averaging $24,000 per year), 86 research assistantships with full tuition reimbursements available (averaging $22,415 per year), 54 teaching assistantships with partial tuition reimbursements available (averaging $21,911 per year); health care benefits and tuition waivers (full and partial) also available. Financial award application deadline: 1/10; financial award applicants required to submit FAFSA. *Unit head:* Dr. Ricardo Sanfelice, Professor and Graduate Director, 831-459-1016, E-mail: ricardo@ucsc.edu. *Application contact:* Jennifer Cornwell, Graduate Student Advisor, E-mail: bsoe-ga@rt.ucsc.edu. Website: https://grad.soe.ucsc.edu/ece

University of Central Florida, College of Engineering and Computer Science, Department of Electrical and Computer Engineering, Program in Electrical Engineering, Orlando, FL 32816. Offers MSEE, PhD. *Program availability:* Part-time, evening/weekend. *Students:* 111 full-time (18 women), 39 part-time (3 women); includes 30 minority (5 Black or African American, non-Hispanic/Latino; 8 Asian, non-Hispanic/Latino; 17 Hispanic/Latino), 91 international. Average age 31. 151 applicants, 74% accepted, 28 enrolled. In 2019, 26 master's, 14 doctorates awarded. *Degree requirements:* For master's, thesis or alternative; for doctorate, thesis/dissertation, departmental qualifying exam, candidacy exam. *Entrance requirements:* For master's, GRE General Test, minimum GPA of 3.0 in last 60 hours, letters of recommendation, resume, goal statement; for doctorate, GRE General Test, minimum GPA of 3.5 in last 60 hours, letters of recommendation, resume, goal statement. Additional exam requirements/recommendations for international students: required—TOEFL. *Application deadline:* For fall admission, 7/15 for domestic students; for spring admission, 12/1 for domestic students. Application fee: $30. Electronic applications accepted. *Financial support:* In 2019–20, 92 students received support, including 27 fellowships with partial tuition reimbursements available (averaging $11,407 per year), 64 research assistantships with partial tuition reimbursements available (averaging $7,703 per year), 32 teaching assistantships with partial tuition reimbursements available (averaging $8,158 per year); health care benefits and tuition waivers (partial) also available. Financial award application deadline: 3/1; financial award applicants required to submit FAFSA. *Unit head:* Dr. Zhihua Qu, Chair, 407-823-5976, Fax: 407-823-5835, E-mail: qu@ucf.edu. *Application contact:* Assistant Director, Graduate Admissions, 407-823-2766, Fax: 407-823-6442, E-mail: gradadmissions@ucf.edu. Website: http://web.eecs.ucf.edu/

University of Central Oklahoma, The Jackson College of Graduate Studies, College of Mathematics and Science, Department of Engineering and Physics, Edmond, OK 73034-5209. Offers engineering physics (MS), including biomedical engineering, electrical engineering, mechanical systems, physics. *Program availability:* Part-time. *Degree requirements:* For master's, thesis optional. *Entrance requirements:* For master's, GRE, 24 hours of course work in physics or equivalent, mathematics through differential equations, minimum GPA of 2.75 overall and 3.0 in last 60 hours attempted, two letters of recommendation. Additional exam requirements/recommendations for international students: required—TOEFL (minimum score 550 paper-based; 79 iBT), IELTS (minimum score 6.5). Electronic applications accepted.

University of Cincinnati, Graduate School, College of Engineering and Applied Science, Department of Electrical Engineering and Computing Systems, Program in Electrical Engineering, Cincinnati, OH 45221. Offers MS, PhD. *Degree requirements:* For master's, thesis; for doctorate, thesis/dissertation. *Entrance requirements:* For master's and doctorate, GRE General Test. Additional exam requirements/recommendations for international students: required—TOEFL (minimum score 550 paper-based).

University of Colorado Boulder, Graduate School, College of Engineering and Applied Science, Department of Electrical, Computer and Energy Engineering, Boulder, CO 80309. Offers ME, MS, PhD. Terminal master's awarded for partial completion of doctoral program. *Degree requirements:* For master's, thesis or alternative; for doctorate, one foreign language, thesis/dissertation, departmental qualifying exam. *Entrance requirements:* For master's, GRE General Test, minimum undergraduate GPA of 3.0; for doctorate, GRE General Test, minimum undergraduate GPA of 3.5. Electronic applications accepted. Application fee is waived when completed online.

University of Colorado Denver, College of Engineering, Design and Computing, Department of Electrical Engineering, Denver, CO 80217. Offers MS, EASPh D. *Program availability:* Part-time, evening/weekend. *Degree requirements:* For master's, thesis or project, 30 credit hours; for doctorate, thesis/dissertation, 60 credit hours beyond master's work (30 of which are for dissertation research). *Entrance requirements:* For master's and doctorate, GRE, three letters of recommendation, personal statement. Additional exam requirements/recommendations for international students: required—TOEFL (minimum score 550 paper-based; 80 iBT), TOEFL (minimum score 600 paper-based) for EAS PhD; recommended—IELTS (minimum score 6.8). Electronic applications accepted. Tuition and fees vary according to course load, program and reciprocity agreements.

University of Colorado Denver, College of Engineering, Design and Computing, Master of Engineering Program, Denver, CO 80217-3364. Offers civil engineering (M Eng), including civil engineering, geographic information systems, transportation systems; electrical engineering (M Eng); mechanical engineering (M Eng). *Program*

availability: Part-time. *Entrance requirements:* For master's, GRE (for those with GPA below 2.75), transcripts, references, statement of purpose. Tuition and fees vary according to course load, program and reciprocity agreements.

University of Connecticut, Graduate School, School of Engineering, Department of Electrical and Computer Engineering, Storrs, CT 06269. Offers MS, PhD. Terminal master's awarded for partial completion of doctoral program. *Degree requirements:* For master's, comprehensive exam, thesis or alternative; for doctorate, thesis/dissertation. *Entrance requirements:* For master's and doctorate, GRE General Test. Additional exam requirements/recommendations for international students: required—TOEFL (minimum score 550 paper-based). Electronic applications accepted.

University of Dayton, Department of Electrical and Computer Engineering, Dayton, OH 45469. Offers computer engineering (MS); electrical engineering (MSEE, PhD). *Program availability:* Part-time, blended/hybrid learning. *Degree requirements:* For master's, thesis optional; for doctorate, variable foreign language requirement, thesis/dissertation. *Entrance requirements:* For master's, minimum GPA of 3.2, 3 letters of recommendation, bachelor's degree, transcripts; for doctorate, minimum GPA of 3.2, master's degree, transcripts, 3 letters of recommendation. Additional exam requirements/recommendations for international students: required—TOEFL (minimum score 550 paper-based; 80 iBT). Electronic applications accepted.

University of Delaware, College of Engineering, Department of Electrical and Computer Engineering, Newark, DE 19716. Offers MSECE, PhD. *Program availability:* Part-time, online learning. Terminal master's awarded for partial completion of doctoral program. *Degree requirements:* For master's, thesis optional; for doctorate, thesis/dissertation. *Entrance requirements:* For master's, GRE General Test; for doctorate, GRE General Test, qualifying exam. Additional exam requirements/recommendations for international students: required—TOEFL. Electronic applications accepted.

University of Denver, Daniel Felix Ritchie School of Engineering and Computer Science, Department of Electrical and Computer Engineering, Denver, CO 80208. Offers computer engineering (MS); electrical and computer engineering (PhD); electrical engineering (MS); engineering (MS); mechatronic systems engineering (MS, PhD). *Program availability:* Part-time, evening/weekend. *Faculty:* 12 full-time (2 women), 1 part-time/adjunct (0 women). *Students:* 2 full-time (0 women), 75 part-time (14 women); includes 19 minority (3 Black or African American, non-Hispanic/Latino; 4 Asian, non-Hispanic/Latino; 9 Hispanic/Latino; 3 Two or more races, non-Hispanic/Latino), 11 international. Average age 29. 83 applicants, 71% accepted, 40 enrolled. In 2019, 25 master's, 10 doctorates awarded. Terminal master's awarded for partial completion of doctoral program. *Degree requirements:* For master's, thesis optional; for doctorate, comprehensive exam, thesis/dissertation. *Entrance requirements:* For master's, GRE General Test, bachelor of science degree in computer engineering, electrical engineering, or closely related field, transcripts, personal statement, resume or curriculum vitae, three letters of recommendation; for doctorate, GRE General Test, master of science degree in computer engineering, management science and engineering, electrical engineering, mechanical engineering, or closely related areas, transcripts, personal statement, resume or curriculum vitae, three letters of recommendation. Additional exam requirements/recommendations for international students: required—TOEFL (minimum score 570 paper-based; 80 iBT). *Application deadline:* For fall admission, 1/15 priority date for domestic and international students; for winter admission, 10/25 for domestic and international students; for spring admission, 2/7 for domestic and international students; for summer admission, 4/24 for domestic and international students. Applications are processed on a rolling basis. Application fee: $65. Electronic applications accepted. *Financial support:* In 2019–20, 36 students received support, including 4 research assistantships with tuition reimbursements available (averaging $14,837 per year), 3 teaching assistantships with tuition reimbursements available (averaging $19,589 per year); Federal Work-Study, scholarships/grants, and unspecified assistantships also available. Financial award application deadline: 2/15; financial award applicants required to submit FAFSA. *Unit head:* Dr. Haluk Ogmen, Professor, Interim Chair and Senior Associate Dean, 303-871-2621, E-mail: Haluk.Ogmen@du.edu. *Application contact:* Druselle May, Assistant to the Chair, 303-871-6618, E-mail: Druselle.May@du.edu. Website: http://ritchieschool.du.edu/departments/ece/

University of Detroit Mercy, College of Engineering and Science, Detroit, MI 48221. Offers chemistry (MS); civil and environmental engineering (DE); electrical and computer engineering (ME); electrical engineering (DE); engineering management (M Eng Mgt); environmental engineering (MEE); mechanical engineering (MME, DE); product development (MS); software engineering (MSSE); teaching of mathematics (MATM). *Program availability:* Part-time, evening/weekend. *Degree requirements:* For doctorate, thesis/dissertation. Electronic applications accepted. Application fee is waived when completed online. *Expenses:* Contact institution.

University of Florida, Graduate School, Herbert Wertheim College of Engineering, Department of Electrical and Computer Engineering, Gainesville, FL 32611. Offers ME, MS, PhD, JD/MS, MSM/MS. *Program availability:* Part-time, online learning. Terminal master's awarded for partial completion of doctoral program. *Degree requirements:* For master's, comprehensive exam (for some programs), thesis (for some programs); for doctorate, comprehensive exam, thesis/dissertation. *Entrance requirements:* For master's, minimum GPA of 3.0; for doctorate, minimum GPA of 3.5. Additional exam requirements/recommendations for international students: required—TOEFL (minimum score 550 paper-based; 80 iBT), IELTS (minimum score 6). Electronic applications accepted.

University of Hawaii at Manoa, Office of Graduate Education, College of Engineering, Department of Electrical Engineering, Honolulu, HI 96822. Offers MS, PhD. *Program availability:* Part-time. *Degree requirements:* For master's, comprehensive exam, thesis; for doctorate, comprehensive exam, thesis/dissertation. *Entrance requirements:* For master's and doctorate, GRE General Test. Additional exam requirements/recommendations for international students: required—TOEFL (minimum score 540 paper-based; 76 iBT), IELTS (minimum score 5).

University of Houston, Cullen College of Engineering, Department of Electrical and Computer Engineering, Houston, TX 77204. Offers electrical engineering (MEE, MSEE, PhD). *Program availability:* Part-time. Terminal master's awarded for partial completion of doctoral program. *Degree requirements:* For master's, thesis (for some programs); for doctorate, comprehensive exam, thesis/dissertation. *Entrance requirements:* For master's and doctorate, GRE General Test. Additional exam requirements/recommendations for international students: required—TOEFL (minimum score 580 paper-based; 92 iBT). Electronic applications accepted.

University of Idaho, College of Graduate Studies, College of Engineering, Department of Electrical and Computer Engineering, Moscow, ID 83844-2282. Offers electrical and computer engineering (MS, PhD); electrical engineering (M Engr). *Faculty:* 14. *Students:* 40 full-time (5 women), 47 part-time (5 women). Average age 32. In 2019, 15 master's, 2 doctorates awarded. *Entrance requirements:* For master's and doctorate, minimum GPA of 3.0. Additional exam requirements/recommendations for international students: required—TOEFL (minimum score 79 iBT). *Application deadline:* For fall admission, 7/30 for domestic students; for spring admission, 12/1 for domestic students. Applications are processed on a rolling basis. Application fee: $60. Electronic applications accepted.

Expenses: Tuition, state resident: full-time $7753.80; part-time $502 per credit hour. Tuition, nonresident: full-time $26,990; part-time $1571 per credit hour. *Required fees:* $2122.20; $47 per credit hour. *Financial support:* Fellowships, research assistantships, teaching assistantships, career-related internships or fieldwork, and Federal Work-Study available. Financial award applicants required to submit FAFSA. *Unit head:* Dr. Joe Law, Chair, 208-885-6554, E-mail: ece-info@uidaho.edu. *Application contact:* Dr. Joe Law, Chair, 208-885-6554, E-mail: ece-info@uidaho.edu.
Website: https://www.uidaho.edu/engr/departments/ece

University of Illinois at Chicago, College of Engineering, Department of Electrical and Computer Engineering, Chicago, IL 60607-7128. Offers MS, PhD. *Program availability:* Part-time. *Degree requirements:* For master's, thesis or alternative; for doctorate, thesis/dissertation, departmental qualifying exam. *Entrance requirements:* For master's, minimum GPA of 2.75, BS in related field; for doctorate, GRE General Test, minimum GPA of 2.75, MS in related field. Additional exam requirements/recommendations for international students: required—TOEFL. Electronic applications accepted. *Expenses:* Contact institution.

University of Illinois at Urbana-Champaign, Graduate College, College of Engineering, Department of Electrical and Computer Engineering, Champaign, IL 61820. Offers MS, PhD, MS/MBA.

The University of Iowa, Graduate College, College of Engineering, Department of Electrical and Computer Engineering, Iowa City, IA 52242-1316. Offers MS, PhD. *Program availability:* Part-time. *Degree requirements:* For master's, comprehensive exam, thesis optional; for doctorate, comprehensive exam, thesis/dissertation, qualifying exam. *Entrance requirements:* For master's and doctorate, GRE. Additional exam requirements/recommendations for international students: required—TOEFL (minimum score 550 paper-based; 81 iBT), IELTS (minimum score 7). Electronic applications accepted.

The University of Kansas, Graduate Studies, School of Engineering, Program in Electrical Engineering, Lawrence, KS 66045. Offers MS, PhD. *Program availability:* Part-time. *Students:* 51 full-time (6 women), 7 part-time (1 woman); includes 9 minority (1 Black or African American, non-Hispanic/Latino; 3 Asian, non-Hispanic/Latino; 5 Hispanic/Latino), 32 international. Average age 29. 43 applicants, 77% accepted, 13 enrolled. In 2019, 13 master's, 8 doctorates awarded. Terminal master's awarded for partial completion of doctoral program. *Entrance requirements:* For master's, GRE, minimum GPA of 3.0, official transcript, three recommendations, statement of academic objectives, resume; for doctorate, GRE, minimum GPA of 3.5, official transcript, three recommendations, statement of academic objectives, resume. Additional exam requirements/recommendations for international students: required—TOEFL, IELTS. *Application deadline:* For fall admission, 12/15 priority date for domestic and international students; for spring admission, 10/1 for domestic and international students. Application fee: $65 ($85 for international students). Electronic applications accepted. *Expenses:* Tuition, state resident: full-time $9989. Tuition, nonresident: full-time $23,950. *International tuition:* $23,950 full-time. *Required fees:* $984; $81.99 per credit hour. Tuition and fees vary according to course load, campus/location and program. *Financial support:* Fellowships, research assistantships, teaching assistantships, career-related internships or fieldwork, scholarships/grants, and unspecified assistantships available. Financial award application deadline: 12/15. *Unit head:* Erik Perrins, Chair, 785-864-4486, E-mail: perrins@ku.edu. *Application contact:* Joy Grisafe-Gross, Graduate Admissions Contact, 785-864-4487, E-mail: jgrisafe@ku.edu.

University of Kentucky, Graduate School, College of Engineering, Program in Electrical Engineering, Lexington, KY 40506-0032. Offers MSEE, PhD. *Degree requirements:* For master's, comprehensive exam, thesis optional; for doctorate, one foreign language, comprehensive exam, thesis/dissertation. *Entrance requirements:* For master's, GRE General Test, minimum undergraduate GPA of 2.75; for doctorate, GRE General Test, minimum undergraduate GPA of 3.0. Additional exam requirements/recommendations for international students: required—TOEFL (minimum score 550 paper-based). Electronic applications accepted.

University of Louisiana at Lafayette, College of Engineering, Department of Electrical and Computer Engineering, Lafayette, LA 70504. Offers electrical engineering (MS); systems engineering (PhD). *Degree requirements:* For master's, thesis or alternative; for doctorate, comprehensive exam, thesis/dissertation, final oral exam. *Entrance requirements:* For master's, GRE General Test, minimum GPA of 2.75. Additional exam requirements/recommendations for international students: required—TOEFL (minimum score 550 paper-based). Electronic applications accepted. *Expenses: Tuition, area resident:* Full-time $5511. Tuition, state resident: full-time $5511. Tuition, nonresident: full-time $19,239. *Required fees:* $46,637.

University of Louisville, J. B. Speed School of Engineering, Department of Electrical and Computer Engineering, Louisville, KY 40292-0001. Offers M Eng, MS, PhD. *Accreditation:* ABET (one or more programs are accredited). *Faculty:* 14 full-time (2 women), 4 part-time/adjunct (0 women). *Students:* 42 full-time (7 women), 31 part-time (7 women); includes 8 minority (3 Asian, non-Hispanic/Latino; 3 Hispanic/Latino; 2 Two or more races, non-Hispanic/Latino), 20 international. Average age 28. 27 applicants, 63% accepted, 12 enrolled. In 2019, 24 master's, 5 doctorates awarded. Terminal master's awarded for partial completion of doctoral program. *Degree requirements:* For master's, thesis optional; for doctorate, comprehensive exam, thesis/dissertation. *Entrance requirements:* For master's, 2 letters of recommendation, official transcripts; for doctorate, GRE, 2 letters of recommendation, official transcripts. Additional exam requirements/recommendations for international students: required—TOEFL (minimum score 550 paper-based; 80 iBT), IELTS (minimum score 6.5). *Application deadline:* For fall admission, 5/1 priority date for domestic and international students; for spring admission, 11/1 priority date for domestic and international students; for summer admission, 3/1 priority date for domestic and international students. Applications are processed on a rolling basis. Application fee: $65. Electronic applications accepted. *Expenses: Tuition, area resident:* Full-time $13,000; part-time $723 per credit hour. Tuition, state resident: full-time $13,000; part-time $723 per credit hour. Tuition, nonresident: full-time $27,114; part-time $1507 per credit hour. *International tuition:* $27,114 full-time. *Required fees:* $196. Tuition and fees vary according to program and reciprocity agreements. *Financial support:* In 2019–20, 42 students received support. Fellowships, research assistantships, teaching assistantships, scholarships/grants, health care benefits, and tuition waivers (full) available. Financial award application deadline: 1/1; financial award applicants required to submit FAFSA. *Unit head:* Bruce Alpenhaar, Chair, Electrical and Computer Engineering Department, 502-852-1554, E-mail: bruce.alphenaar@louisville.edu. *Application contact:* John Naber, Director of Graduate Studies, 502-852-7910, E-mail: john.naber@louisville.edu.
Website: http://www.louisville.edu/speed/electrical/

University of Maine, Graduate School, College of Engineering, Department of Electrical and Computer Engineering, Orono, ME 04469. Offers computer engineering (MS); electrical engineering (MS, PhD). *Program availability:* Part-time. *Faculty:* 12 full-time (1 woman), 1 part-time/adjunct (0 women). *Students:* 13 full-time (4 women), 1 part-time (0 women); includes 2 minority (1 Asian, non-Hispanic/Latino; 1 Hispanic/Latino), 5 international. Average age 27. 9 applicants, 100% accepted, 6 enrolled. In 2019, 4 master's awarded. Terminal master's awarded for partial completion of doctoral program. *Degree requirements:* For master's, thesis (for some programs); for doctorate, comprehensive exam, thesis/dissertation. *Entrance requirements:* For master's and doctorate, GRE General Test. Additional exam requirements/recommendations for international students: required—TOEFL. *Application deadline:* For fall admission, 2/1 priority date for domestic students. Applications are processed on a rolling basis. Application fee: $65. Electronic applications accepted. *Expenses: Tuition, area resident:* Full-time $8100; part-time $450 per credit hour. Tuition, state resident: full-time $8100; part-time $450 per credit hour. Tuition, nonresident: full-time $26,388; part-time $1466 per credit hour. *International tuition:* $26,388 full-time. *Required fees:* $1257; $278 per semester. Tuition and fees vary according to course load. *Financial support:* In 2019–20, 10 students received support, including 12 research assistantships with full tuition reimbursements available (averaging $12,100 per year), 10 teaching assistantships with full tuition reimbursements available (averaging $14,300 per year); fellowships, Federal Work-Study, institutionally sponsored loans, and tuition waivers (full and partial) also available. Financial award application deadline: 3/1; financial award applicants required to submit FAFSA. *Unit head:* Dr. Donald Hummels, Chair, 207-581-2244. *Application contact:* Scott G. Delcourt, Assistant Vice President for Graduate Studies and Senior Associate Dean, 207-581-3291, Fax: 207-581-3232, E-mail: graduate@maine.edu.
Website: http://www.ece.umaine.edu/

The University of Manchester, School of Electrical and Electronic Engineering, Manchester, United Kingdom. Offers M Phil, PhD.

University of Manitoba, Faculty of Graduate Studies, Faculty of Engineering, Department of Electrical and Computer Engineering, Winnipeg, MB R3T 2N2, Canada. Offers M Eng, M Sc, PhD. *Degree requirements:* For master's, thesis; for doctorate, thesis/dissertation.

University of Maryland, Baltimore County, The Graduate School, College of Engineering and Information Technology, Department of Computer Science and Electrical Engineering, Program in Electrical Engineering, Baltimore, MD 21250. Offers MS, PhD. *Program availability:* Part-time. *Students:* 48 full-time (14 women), 22 part-time (2 women); includes 18 minority (8 Black or African American, non-Hispanic/Latino; 6 Asian, non-Hispanic/Latino; 2 Hispanic/Latino; 1 Native Hawaiian or other Pacific Islander, non-Hispanic/Latino; 1 Two or more races, non-Hispanic/Latino), 38 international. Average age 32. 62 applicants, 74% accepted, 12 enrolled. In 2019, 8 master's, 5 doctorates awarded. *Degree requirements:* For master's, comprehensive exam (for some programs), thesis optional; for doctorate, comprehensive exam, thesis/dissertation. *Entrance requirements:* For master's and doctorate, GRE General Test, BS from ABET-accredited undergraduate program in electrical engineering or strong background in computer science, mathematics, physics, or other areas of engineering or science. Additional exam requirements/recommendations for international students: required—TOEFL (minimum score 550 paper-based; 80 iBT). *Application deadline:* For fall admission, 6/1 for domestic students, 1/1 for international students; for spring admission, 11/1 for domestic students, 6/1 for international students. Applications are processed on a rolling basis. Application fee: $70. Electronic applications accepted. *Expenses:* $14,382 per year. *Financial support:* In 2019–20, 32 students received support, including 1 fellowship with full tuition reimbursement available, 22 research assistantships with full tuition reimbursements available, 9 teaching assistantships with full tuition reimbursements available; career-related internships or fieldwork, Federal Work-Study, scholarships/grants, health care benefits, tuition waivers (partial), and unspecified assistantships also available. Support available to part-time students. Financial award application deadline: 6/30; financial award applicants required to submit FAFSA. *Unit head:* Dr. Anupam Joshi, Professor and Chair, 410-455-3500, Fax: 410-455-3969, E-mail: joshi@cs.umbc.edu. *Application contact:* Dr. Chintan Patel, Graduate Program Director, 410-455-3963, Fax: 410-455-3969, E-mail: cpatel12@cs.umbc.edu.
Website: https://www.csee.umbc.edu/

University of Maryland, College Park, Academic Affairs, A. James Clark School of Engineering, Department of Electrical and Computer Engineering, Electrical Engineering Program, College Park, MD 20742. Offers MS, PhD. *Degree requirements:* For master's, thesis or alternative; for doctorate, thesis/dissertation, oral exam, qualifying exam. *Entrance requirements:* For master's and doctorate, GRE General Test, minimum GPA of 3.0. Electronic applications accepted.

University of Massachusetts Amherst, Graduate School, College of Engineering, Department of Electrical and Computer Engineering, Amherst, MA 01003. Offers MSECE, PhD. *Program availability:* Part-time. Terminal master's awarded for partial completion of doctoral program. *Degree requirements:* For master's, thesis or alternative; for doctorate, comprehensive exam, thesis/dissertation. *Entrance requirements:* For master's and doctorate, GRE General Test. Additional exam requirements/recommendations for international students: required—TOEFL (minimum score 550 paper-based; 80 iBT), IELTS (minimum score 6.5). Electronic applications accepted.

University of Massachusetts Dartmouth, Graduate School, College of Engineering, Department of Electrical and Computer Engineering, North Dartmouth, MA 02747-2300. Offers communications (Postbaccalaureate Certificate); computing infrastructure security (Postbaccalaureate Certificate); digital signal processing (Postbaccalaureate Certificate); electrical engineering (MS, PhD); electrical engineering systems (Postbaccalaureate Certificate). *Program availability:* Part-time. Terminal master's awarded for partial completion of doctoral program. *Degree requirements:* For master's, thesis, thesis or project; for doctorate, comprehensive exam, thesis/dissertation. *Entrance requirements:* For master's, GRE unless UMass Dartmouth graduate in computer engineering or electrical engineering, statement of purpose (minimum of 300 words), resume, 3 letters of recommendation, official transcripts; for doctorate, GRE unless UMass Dartmouth graduate in college of engineering major or about to receive electrical graduate certificate, statement of purpose (minimum of 300 words), resume, 3 letters of recommendation, official transcripts; for Postbaccalaureate Certificate, statement of purpose (minimum of 300 words), resume, official transcripts. Additional exam requirements/recommendations for international students: required—TOEFL (minimum score 550 paper-based; 79 iBT), IELTS (minimum score 6.5). Electronic applications accepted.

University of Massachusetts Lowell, Francis College of Engineering, Department of Electrical and Computer Engineering, Program in Electrical Engineering, Lowell, MA 01854. Offers MS Eng, PhD. *Program availability:* Part-time, evening/weekend. Terminal master's awarded for partial completion of doctoral program. *Degree requirements:* For master's, thesis; for doctorate, 2 foreign languages, thesis/dissertation. *Entrance requirements:* For master's and doctorate, GRE General Test.

University of Memphis, Graduate School, Herff College of Engineering, Department of Electrical and Computer Engineering, Memphis, TN 38152. Offers computer engineering (MS, PhD); electrical engineering (MS, PhD); imaging and signal processing (Graduate Certificate). *Students:* 13 full-time (3 women), 8 part-time (3 women); includes 6 minority (4 Asian, non-Hispanic/Latino; 2 Hispanic/Latino), 9 international. Average age 27. 16 applicants, 88% accepted, 6 enrolled. In 2019, 7 master's awarded. *Degree requirements:* For master's, comprehensive exam, thesis or alternative; for doctorate, comprehensive exam, thesis/dissertation. *Entrance requirements:* For master's and doctorate, GRE General Test, MAT, or GMAT, three letters of recommendation. Additional exam requirements/recommendations for international students: required—TOEFL (minimum score 550 paper-based; 79 iBT). *Application deadline:* For fall admission, 8/1 for domestic students; for spring admission, 12/1 for domestic students. Application fee: $35 ($60 for international students). Electronic applications accepted. *Expenses: Tuition, area resident:* Full-time $9216; part-time $512 per credit hour. Tuition, state resident: full-time $9216; part-time $512 per credit hour. Tuition, nonresident: full-time $12,672; part-time $704 per credit hour. *International tuition:* $16,128 full-time. *Required fees:* $1530; $85 per credit hour. Tuition and fees vary according to program. *Financial support:* Fellowships, research assistantships, teaching assistantships, career-related internships or fieldwork, Federal Work-Study, scholarships/grants, and unspecified assistantships available. Financial award application deadline: 2/1; financial award applicants required to submit FAFSA. *Unit head:* Dr. Chrysanthe Preza, Chair, 901-678-2175, Fax: 901-678-5469, E-mail: cpreza@memphis.edu. *Application contact:* Dr. Aaron Robinson, Coordinator of Graduate Studies, 901-678-4996, Fax: 901-678-4996, E-mail: alrobins@memphis.edu. Website: http://www.memphis.edu/eece/

University of Miami, Graduate School, College of Engineering, Department of Electrical and Computer Engineering, Coral Gables, FL 33124. Offers MSECE, PhD. *Program availability:* Part-time. *Degree requirements:* For master's, thesis (for some programs); for doctorate, comprehensive exam, thesis/dissertation, dissertation proposal defense. *Entrance requirements:* For master's, GRE General Test, minimum GPA of 3.0; for doctorate, GRE General Test, minimum undergraduate GPA of 3.3, graduate 3.5. Additional exam requirements/recommendations for international students: required—TOEFL (minimum score 550 paper-based; 59 iBT), IELTS (minimum score 7). Electronic applications accepted.

University of Michigan, College of Engineering, Department of Electrical and Computer Engineering, Ann Arbor, MI 48109. Offers MS, MSE, PhD. *Program availability:* Part-time.

University of Michigan–Dearborn, College of Engineering and Computer Science, MSE Program in Electrical Engineering, Dearborn, MI 48128. Offers MSE. *Program availability:* Part-time, evening/weekend, 100% online. *Faculty:* 22 full-time (2 women), 15 part-time/adjunct (0 women). *Students:* 24 full-time (5 women), 142 part-time (31 women); includes 27 minority (6 Black or African American, non-Hispanic/Latino; 1 American Indian or Alaska Native, non-Hispanic/Latino; 16 Asian, non-Hispanic/Latino; 4 Hispanic/Latino), 37 international. Average age 27. 121 applicants, 57% accepted, 47 enrolled. In 2019, 68 master's awarded. *Degree requirements:* For master's, thesis optional. *Entrance requirements:* For master's, bachelor's degree in electrical and/or computer engineering with minimum overall GPA of 3.0. Additional exam requirements/recommendations for international students: required—TOEFL (minimum score 560 paper-based; 84 iBT), IELTS (minimum score 6.5). *Application deadline:* For fall admission, 8/1 for domestic students, 5/1 for international students; for winter admission, 12/1 for domestic students, 9/1 for international students; for spring admission, 4/1 for domestic students, 1/1 for international students. Applications are processed on a rolling basis. Application fee: $60. Electronic applications accepted. *Financial support:* Research assistantships with full tuition reimbursements, teaching assistantships with full tuition reimbursements, scholarships/grants, unspecified assistantships, and non-resident tuition scholarships available. Support available to part-time students. Financial award application deadline: 3/1; financial award applicants required to submit FAFSA. *Unit head:* Dr. Paul Richardson, Chair, 313-593-5420, E-mail: richarpc@umich.edu. *Application contact:* Office of Graduate Studies, 313-583-6321, E-mail: umd-graduatestudies@umich.edu. Website: https://umdearborn.edu/cecs/departments/electrical-and-computer-engineering/graduate-programs/mse-electrical-engineering

University of Michigan–Dearborn, College of Engineering and Computer Science, PhD Program Electrical, Electronics, and Computer Engineering, Dearborn, MI 48128. Offers PhD. *Faculty:* 22 full-time (2 women), 15 part-time/adjunct (0 women). *Students:* 1 full-time (0 women), 6 part-time (0 women), all international. Average age 25. 32 applicants, 16% accepted, 4 enrolled. *Degree requirements:* For doctorate, thesis/dissertation. *Entrance requirements:* For doctorate, GRE, bachelor's or master's degree in electrical/computer engineering, computer science, physical science, or mathematical science with minimum GPA of 3.2. Additional exam requirements/recommendations for international students: required—TOEFL (minimum score 560 paper-based; 84 iBT), IELTS (minimum score 6.5). *Application deadline:* For fall admission, 2/1 for domestic and international students. Application fee: $60. Electronic applications accepted. *Financial support:* Research assistantships with full tuition reimbursements, teaching assistantships with full tuition reimbursements, scholarships/grants, health care benefits, and unspecified assistantships available. Financial award application deadline: 2/1; financial award applicants required to submit FAFSA. *Unit head:* Dr. Ya Sha Yi, 313-583-6318, E-mail: yashayi@umich.edu. *Application contact:* Office of Graduate Studies, 313-583-6321, E-mail: umd-graduatestudies@umich.edu. Website: https://umdearborn.edu/cecs/departments/electrical-and-computer-engineering/graduate-programs/phd-electrical-and-computer-engineering

University of Minnesota, Duluth, Graduate School, Swenson College of Science and Engineering, Department of Electrical and Computer Engineering, Duluth, MN 55812-2496. Offers MSECE. *Program availability:* Part-time. *Degree requirements:* For master's, thesis. *Entrance requirements:* Additional exam requirements/recommendations for international students: recommended—TOEFL, IELTS, TWE.

University of Minnesota, Twin Cities Campus, College of Science and Engineering, Department of Electrical and Computer Engineering, Minneapolis, MN 55455-0213. Offers MSEE, PhD. *Program availability:* Part-time. *Degree requirements:* For master's, thesis or alternative; for doctorate, thesis/dissertation. *Entrance requirements:* Additional exam requirements/recommendations for international students: required—TOEFL (minimum score 550 paper-based). Electronic applications accepted.

University of Mississippi, Graduate School, School of Engineering, University, MS 38677. Offers aeroacoustics (MS, PhD); chemical engineering (MS, PhD); civil engineering (MS, PhD); computational hydroscience (MS, PhD); computer science (MS, PhD); electrical engineering (MS, PhD); electromagnetics (MS, PhD); environmental engineering (MS, PhD); geology and geological engineering (MS, PhD); hydrology (MS); material science (MS); mechanical engineering (MS, PhD); telecommunications (MS). *Students:* 104 full-time (23 women), 19 part-time (5 women); includes 10 minority (3 Black or African American, non-Hispanic/Latino; 6 Asian, non-Hispanic/Latino; 1 Hispanic/Latino), 72 international. Average age 30. In 2019, 36 master's, 17 doctorates awarded. *Expenses:* Tuition, state resident: full-time $8718; part-time $484.25 per credit hour. Tuition, nonresident: full-time $24,990; part-time $1388.25 per credit hour. *Required fees:* $100; $4.16 per credit hour. *Unit head:* Dr. David Puleo, Dean, 662-915-5780, Fax: 662-915-5387, E-mail: engineer@olemiss.edu. *Application contact:* Temeka Smith, Graduate Activities Specialist for Admissions, 662-915-7474, Fax: 662-915-7577, E-mail: gschool@olemiss.edu.

University of Missouri, Office of Research and Graduate Studies, College of Engineering, Department of Electrical Engineering and Computer Science, Columbia, MO 65211. Offers computer engineering (MSCE); computer science (MS, PhD);

electrical and computer engineering (PhD); electrical engineering (MSEE). *Entrance requirements:* For master's, GRE General Test, minimum GPA of 3.0; for doctorate, GRE General Test, GRE Subject Test, minimum GPA of 3.0. Additional exam requirements/recommendations for international students: required—TOEFL.

University of Missouri–Kansas City, School of Computing and Engineering, Kansas City, MO 64110-2499. Offers civil engineering (MS); computer and electrical engineering (PhD); computer science (MS), including bioinformatics, software engineering, telecommunications networking; computer science and informatics (PhD); computing (PhD); electrical engineering (MS); engineering (PhD); engineering and construction management (Graduate Certificate); mechanical engineering (MS); telecommunications and computer networking (PhD). *Program availability:* Part-time. *Degree requirements:* For doctorate, thesis/dissertation. *Entrance requirements:* For master's, GRE General Test, minimum GPA of 3.0, 3 letters of recommendation from professors; for doctorate, GRE General Test, minimum GPA of 3.5. Additional exam requirements/recommendations for international students: required—TOEFL (minimum score 550 paper-based; 80 iBT).

University of Nebraska–Lincoln, Graduate College, College of Engineering, Department of Electrical Engineering, Lincoln, NE 68588. Offers MS, PhD. *Degree requirements:* For master's, thesis optional; for doctorate, comprehensive exam, thesis/dissertation. *Entrance requirements:* For master's and doctorate, GRE General Test. Additional exam requirements/recommendations for international students: required—TOEFL (minimum score 550 paper-based). Electronic applications accepted.

University of Nevada, Reno, Graduate School, College of Engineering, Department of Electrical and Biomedical Engineering, Reno, NV 89557. Offers MS, PhD. Terminal master's awarded for partial completion of doctoral program. *Degree requirements:* For master's, thesis optional; for doctorate, thesis/dissertation. *Entrance requirements:* For master's, GRE General Test, minimum GPA of 2.75; for doctorate, GRE General Test, minimum GPA of 3.0. Additional exam requirements/recommendations for international students: required—TOEFL (minimum score 500 paper-based; 61 iBT), IELTS (minimum score 6). Electronic applications accepted.

University of New Brunswick Fredericton, School of Graduate Studies, Faculty of Engineering, Department of Electrical and Computer Engineering, Fredericton, NB E3B 5A3, Canada. Offers M Eng, M Sc E, PhD. *Program availability:* Part-time. *Faculty:* 18 full-time (3 women), 3 part-time/adjunct (0 women). *Students:* 50 full-time (9 women), 5 part-time (0 women), 31 international. Average age 27. In 2019, 8 master's, 1 doctorate awarded. *Degree requirements:* For master's, thesis, research proposal; 10 courses (for M Eng); for doctorate, comprehensive exam, thesis/dissertation, research proposal. *Entrance requirements:* For master's, minimum GPA of 3.3; references; for doctorate, M Sc; minimum GPA of 3.3; previous transcripts; references. Additional exam requirements/recommendations for international students: required—TOEFL (minimum score 580 paper-based; 93 iBT), IELTS (minimum score 7), TWE (minimum score 4). *Application deadline:* Applications are processed on a rolling basis. Application fee: $50 Canadian dollars. Electronic applications accepted. *Expenses: Tuition, area resident:* Full-time $6975 Canadian dollars; part-time $3423 Canadian dollars per year. Tuition, state resident: full-time $6975 Canadian dollars; part-time $3423 Canadian dollars per year. Tuition, Canadian resident: full-time $6975 Canadian dollars; part-time $3423 Canadian dollars per year. *International tuition:* $12,435 Canadian dollars full-time. *Required fees:* $92.25 Canadian dollars per term. Full-time tuition and fees vary according to degree level, campus/location, program, reciprocity agreements and student level. *Financial support:* Fellowships, research assistantships, and teaching assistantships available. Financial award application deadline: 1/15. *Unit head:* Dr. Bruce Colpitts, Chair, 504-447-3139, Fax: 504-453-3589, E-mail: colpitts@unb.ca. *Application contact:* Shelley Cormier, Graduate Secretary, 506-452-6142, Fax: 506-453-3589, E-mail: scormier@unb.ca. Website: http://go.unb.ca/gradprograms

University of New Hampshire, Graduate School, College of Engineering and Physical Sciences, Department of Electrical and Computer Engineering, Durham, NH 03824. Offers electrical and computer engineering (MS); electrical engineering (M Engr, PhD); ubiquitous computing (Certificate); wireless communication systems (Certificate). *Program availability:* Part-time, evening/weekend. *Students:* 26 full-time (5 women), 18 part-time (4 women); includes 2 minority (1 Black or African American, non-Hispanic/Latino; 1 Two or more races, non-Hispanic/Latino), 26 international. Average age 30. 51 applicants, 65% accepted, 10 enrolled. In 2019, 17 master's, 3 doctorates, 1 other advanced degree awarded. *Entrance requirements:* For master's and doctorate, GRE (for non-U.S. university bachelor's degree holders). Additional exam requirements/recommendations for international students: required—TOEFL (minimum score 550 paper-based; 80 iBT), IELTS, PTE. *Application deadline:* For fall admission, 7/1 for domestic students, 4/1 for international students; for spring admission, 12/1 for domestic students. Application fee: $65. Electronic applications accepted. *Financial support:* In 2019–20, 16 students received support, including 1 fellowship, 3 research assistantships, 12 teaching assistantships; Federal Work-Study, scholarships/grants, and tuition waivers (full and partial) also available. Support available to part-time students. Financial award application deadline: 2/15. *Unit head:* Kent Chamberlin, Chair, 603-862-3766. *Application contact:* Lauren Foxall, Administrative Assistant, 603-862-1358, E-mail: lauren.foxall@unh.edu. Website: http://www.ceps.unh.edu/ece

University of New Haven, Graduate School, Tagliatela College of Engineering, Program in Electrical Engineering, West Haven, CT 06516. Offers computer engineering (MS); control systems (MS); digital signal processing and communication (MS); electrical engineering (MS). *Program availability:* Part-time, evening/weekend. *Students:* 46 full-time (17 women), 8 part-time (1 woman); includes 4 minority (1 Black or African American, non-Hispanic/Latino; 1 Asian, non-Hispanic/Latino; 2 Hispanic/Latino), 46 international. Average age 24. 135 applicants, 76% accepted, 10 enrolled. In 2019, 20 master's awarded. *Entrance requirements:* For master's, bachelor's degree in electrical engineering. Additional exam requirements/recommendations for international students: required—TOEFL (minimum score 75 iBT), IELTS, PTE (minimum score 50). *Application deadline:* Applications are processed on a rolling basis. Application fee: $50. Electronic applications accepted. Application fee is waived when completed online. *Financial support:* Research assistantships with partial tuition reimbursements, teaching assistantships with partial tuition reimbursements, career-related internships or fieldwork, Federal Work-Study, scholarships/grants, and unspecified assistantships available. Support available to part-time students. Financial award applicants required to submit FAFSA. *Unit head:* Dr. Junhui Zhao, Associate Professor, 203-932-1241, E-mail: JZhao@newhaven.edu. *Application contact:* Selina O'Toole, Senior Associate Director of Graduate Admissions, 203-932-7337, E-mail: sotoole@newhaven.edu. Website: https://www.newhaven.edu/engineering/graduate-programs/electrical-engineering/

University of New Mexico, Graduate Studies, School of Engineering, Programs in Electrical and Computer Engineering, Albuquerque, NM 87131. Offers MS, PhD. *Program availability:* Part-time, evening/weekend, online learning. *Faculty:* 19 full-time (4 women), 7 part-time/adjunct (1 woman). *Students:* 65 full-time (10 women), 77 part-time (12 women); includes 37 minority (1 Black or African American, non-Hispanic/Latino; 1 American Indian or Alaska Native, non-Hispanic/Latino; 6 Asian, non-Hispanic/

Latino; 26 Hispanic/Latino; 3 Two or more races, non-Hispanic/Latino), 48 international. 133 applicants, 72% accepted, 43 enrolled. In 2019, 40 master's, 13 doctorates awarded. Terminal master's awarded for partial completion of doctoral program. *Degree requirements:* For master's, thesis; for doctorate, comprehensive exam, thesis/dissertation. *Entrance requirements:* For master's, GRE General Test, minimum GPA of 3.0; for doctorate, GRE General Test, minimum GPA of 3.5. Additional exam requirements/recommendations for international students: required—TOEFL (minimum score 550 paper-based; 80 iBT), IELTS (minimum score 6.5), TOEFL or IELTS, not both. *Application deadline:* For fall admission, 6/15 for domestic students, 2/15 for international students; for spring admission, 11/1 for domestic students, 6/15 for international students. Application fee: $50. Electronic applications accepted. *Expenses:* Tuition, state resident: full-time $7633; part-time $972 per year. Tuition, nonresident: full-time $22,586; part-time $3840 per year. *International tuition:* $23,292 full-time. *Required fees:* $8608. Tuition and fees vary according to course level, course load, degree level, program and student level. *Financial support:* In 2019–20, 64 research assistantships, 21 teaching assistantships were awarded; fellowships, scholarships/grants, health care benefits, unspecified assistantships, and Graduate and Project Assistantships also available. Financial award applicants required to submit FAFSA. *Unit head:* Dr. Michael Devetsikiotis, Chair, 505-277-2436, Fax: 505-277-8298, E-mail: mdevets@unm.edu. *Application contact:* Yvone Nelson, Sr. Academic Advisor, 505-277-2600, Fax: 505-277-8298, E-mail: nelsony@unm.edu.
Website: http://www.ece.unm.edu/

University of New Orleans, Graduate School, College of Engineering, Program in Engineering, New Orleans, LA 70148. Offers civil engineering (MS); electrical engineering (MS); mechanical engineering (MS); naval architecture and marine engineering (MS). *Degree requirements:* For master's, thesis optional. *Entrance requirements:* For master's, GRE General Test, minimum GPA of 3.0. Additional exam requirements/recommendations for international students: required—TOEFL (minimum score 550 paper-based; 79 iBT). Electronic applications accepted.

University of North Dakota, Graduate School, School of Engineering and Mines, Department of Electrical Engineering, Grand Forks, ND 58202. Offers M Engr, MS, PhD. *Program availability:* Part-time. *Degree requirements:* For master's, comprehensive exam, thesis or alternative. *Entrance requirements:* For master's, GRE General Test, minimum GPA of 3.0 (MS), 2.5 (M Engr). Additional exam requirements/recommendations for international students: required—TOEFL (minimum score 550 paper-based; 79 iBT), IELTS (minimum score 6.5). Electronic applications accepted.

University of North Florida, College of Computing, Engineering, and Construction, School of Engineering, Jacksonville, FL 32224. Offers MSCE, MSEE, MSME. *Program availability:* Part-time.

University of North Texas, Toulouse Graduate School, Denton, TX 76203-5459. Offers accounting (MS); applied anthropology (MA, MS); applied behavior analysis (Certificate); applied geography (MA); applied technology and performance improvement (M Ed, MS); art education (MA); art history (MA); arts leadership (Certificate); audiology (Au D); behavior analysis (MS); behavioral science (PhD); biochemistry and molecular biology (MS); biology (MA, MS); biomedical engineering (MS); business analysis (MS); chemistry (MS); clinical health psychology (PhD); communication studies (MA, MS); computer engineering (MS); computer science (MS); counseling (M Ed, MS), including clinical mental health counseling (MS), college and university counseling, elementary school counseling, secondary school counseling; creative writing (MA); criminal justice (MS); curriculum and instruction (M Ed); decision sciences (MBA); design (MA, MFA), including fashion design (MFA), innovation studies, interior design (MFA); early childhood studies (MS); economics (MS); educational leadership (M Ed, Ed D); educational psychology (MS, PhD), including family studies (MS), gifted and talented (MS), human development (MS), learning and cognition (MS), research, measurement and evaluation (MS); electrical engineering (MS); emergency management (MPA); engineering technology (MS); English (MA); English as a second language (MA); environmental science (MS); finance (MBA, MS); financial management (MPA); French (MA); health services management (MBA); higher education (M Ed, Ed D); history (MA, MS); hospitality management (MS); human resources management (MPA); information science (MS); information systems (PhD); information technologies (MBA); interdisciplinary studies (MA, MS); international studies (MA); international sustainable tourism (MS); jazz studies (MM); journalism (MA, MJ, Graduate Certificate), including interactive and virtual digital communication (Graduate Certificate), narrative journalism (Graduate Certificate), public relations (Graduate Certificate); kinesiology (MS); linguistics (MA); local government management (MPA); logistics (PhD); logistics and supply chain management (MBA); long-term care, senior housing, and aging services (MA); management (PhD); marketing (MBA); mathematics (MA, MS); mechanical and energy engineering (MS, PhD); music (MA), including ethnomusicology, music theory, musicology, performance; music composition (PhD); music education (MM Ed, PhD); nonprofit management (MPA); operations and supply chain management (MBA); performance (MM, DMA); philosophy (MA); political science (MA); professional and technical communication (MA); radio, television and film (MA, MFA); rehabilitation counseling (Certificate); sociology (MA); Spanish (MA); special education (M Ed); speech-language pathology (MA); strategic management (MBA); studio art (MFA); teaching (M Ed); MBA/MS. *Program availability:* Part-time, evening/weekend, online learning. Terminal master's awarded for partial completion of doctoral program. *Degree requirements:* For master's, variable foreign language requirement, comprehensive exam (for some programs), thesis (for some programs); for doctorate, variable foreign language requirement, comprehensive exam (for some programs), thesis/dissertation; for other advanced degree, variable foreign language requirement, comprehensive exam (for some programs). *Entrance requirements:* For master's and doctorate, GRE, GMAT. Additional exam requirements/recommendations for international students: required—TOEFL (minimum score 550 paper-based; 79 iBT). Electronic applications accepted.

University of Notre Dame, The Graduate School, College of Engineering, Department of Electrical Engineering, Notre Dame, IN 46556. Offers MSEE, PhD. Terminal master's awarded for partial completion of doctoral program. *Degree requirements:* For master's, comprehensive exam; for doctorate, thesis/dissertation, candidacy exam. *Entrance requirements:* For master's and doctorate, GRE General Test. Additional exam requirements/recommendations for international students: required—TOEFL (minimum score 600 paper-based; 80 iBT). Electronic applications accepted.

University of Oklahoma, Gallogly College of Engineering, School of Electrical and Computer Engineering, Norman, OK 73019. Offers electrical and computer engineering (MS, PhD); telecommunications engineering (MS). *Program availability:* Part-time. Terminal master's awarded for partial completion of doctoral program. *Degree requirements:* For master's, comprehensive exam (for some programs), thesis (for some programs); for doctorate, thesis/dissertation, general exam. *Entrance requirements:* For master's and doctorate, GRE, minimum GPA of 3.0. Additional exam requirements/recommendations for international students: required—TOEFL (minimum score 79 iBT) or IELTS (minimum score 6.5). Electronic applications accepted. *Expenses:* Tuition, state resident: full-time $6583.20; part-time $274.30 per credit hour. Tuition, nonresident: full-time $21,242; part-time $885.10 per credit hour. *International tuition:* $21,242.40 full-time. *Required fees:* $1994.20; $72.55 per credit hour. $126.50 per semester. Tuition and fees vary according to course load and degree level.

University of Ottawa, Faculty of Graduate and Postdoctoral Studies, Faculty of Engineering, Ottawa-Carleton Institute for Electrical and Computer Engineering, Ottawa, ON K1N 6N5, Canada. Offers M Eng, MA Sc, PhD. *Degree requirements:* For master's, thesis or alternative, project; for doctorate, comprehensive exam, thesis/dissertation. *Entrance requirements:* For master's, honors degree or equivalent, minimum B average; for doctorate, minimum A- average. Electronic applications accepted.

University of Pennsylvania, School of Engineering and Applied Science, Department of Electrical and Systems Engineering, Philadelphia, PA 19104. Offers MSE, PhD. *Program availability:* Part-time. *Faculty:* 34 full-time (5 women), 12 part-time/adjunct (2 women). *Students:* 311 full-time (101 women), 28 part-time (12 women); includes 21 minority (4 Black or African American, non-Hispanic/Latino; 14 Asian, non-Hispanic/Latino; 1 Hispanic/Latino; 2 Two or more races, non-Hispanic/Latino), 279 international. Average age 25. 1,257 applicants, 38% accepted, 118 enrolled. In 2019, 120 master's, 8 doctorates awarded. Terminal master's awarded for partial completion of doctoral program. *Degree requirements:* For master's, comprehensive exam, thesis optional; for doctorate, comprehensive exam, thesis/dissertation. *Entrance requirements:* For master's and doctorate, GRE, bachelor's degree, letters of recommendation, resume, personal statement. Additional exam requirements/recommendations for international students: required—TOEFL (minimum score 100 iBT), IELTS (minimum score 7). *Application deadline:* For fall admission, 12/15 priority date for domestic and international students. Application fee: $80. Electronic applications accepted. *Expenses:* Contact institution. *Application contact:* Associate Director of Graduate Admissions, 215-898-4542, Fax: 215-573-5577, E-mail: admissions1@seas.upenn.edu.

University of Pittsburgh, Swanson School of Engineering, Department of Electrical and Computer Engineering, Pittsburgh, PA 15260. Offers electrical and computer engineering (MS, PhD). *Program availability:* Part-time, 100% online. Terminal master's awarded for partial completion of doctoral program. *Degree requirements:* For doctorate, comprehensive exam, thesis/dissertation, final oral exams. *Entrance requirements:* For master's and doctorate, GRE General Test, minimum GPA of 3.0. Additional exam requirements/recommendations for international students: required—TOEFL (minimum score 550 paper-based; 80 iBT). Electronic applications accepted. *Expenses:* Contact institution.

University of Portland, Shiley School of Engineering, Portland, OR 97203-5798. Offers biomedical engineering (MBME); civil engineering (ME); computer science (ME); electrical engineering (ME); mechanical engineering (ME). *Program availability:* Part-time, evening/weekend. *Degree requirements:* For master's, thesis optional. *Entrance requirements:* For master's, GRE General Test, minimum GPA of 3.0, 2 letters of recommendation, resume, statement of goals, official transcripts. Additional exam requirements/recommendations for international students: required—TOEFL (minimum score 80 iBT), IELTS (minimum score 7). Electronic applications accepted. *Expenses:* Contact institution.

University of Puerto Rico at Mayagüez, Graduate Studies, College of Engineering, Department of Electrical and Computer Engineering, Mayagüez, PR 00681-9000. Offers computer engineering (ME, MS); computing and information sciences and engineering (PhD); electrical engineering (ME, MS). *Program availability:* Part-time. Terminal master's awarded for partial completion of doctoral program. *Degree requirements:* For master's, one foreign language, comprehensive exam, thesis; for doctorate, one foreign language, comprehensive exam, thesis/dissertation. *Entrance requirements:* For master's and doctorate, proficiency in English and Spanish; BS in electrical or computer engineering, or equivalent; minimum GPA of 3.0. Electronic applications accepted.

University of Rhode Island, Graduate School, College of Engineering, Department of Electrical, Computer and Biomedical Engineering, Kingston, RI 02881. Offers acoustics and underwater acoustics (MS, PhD); biomedical engineering (MS, PhD); circuits and devices (MS); communication theory (MS, PhD); computer architectures and digital systems (MS, PhD); computer networks (MS, PhD); digital signal processing (MS); embedded systems and computer applications (MS, PhD); fault-tolerant computing (MS, PhD); materials and optics (MS, PhD); systems theory (MS, PhD). *Program availability:* Part-time. *Faculty:* 20 full-time (4 women), 1 part-time/adjunct (0 women). *Students:* 39 full-time (7 women), 14 part-time (1 woman); includes 7 minority (3 Black or African American, non-Hispanic/Latino; 1 American Indian or Alaska Native, non-Hispanic/Latino; 2 Asian, non-Hispanic/Latino; 1 Hispanic/Latino), 23 international. 31 applicants, 74% accepted, 13 enrolled. In 2019, 13 master's, 3 doctorates awarded. *Entrance requirements:* Additional exam requirements/recommendations for international students: required—TOEFL. *Application deadline:* For fall admission, 7/15 for domestic students, 2/1 for international students; for spring admission, 11/15 for domestic students, 7/15 for international students; for summer admission, 4/15 for domestic students. Application fee: $65. Electronic applications accepted. *Expenses: Tuition, area resident:* Full-time $13,734; part-time $763 per credit. Tuition, state resident: full-time $13,734; part-time $763 per credit. Tuition, nonresident: full-time $26,512; part-time $1473 per credit. *International tuition:* $26,512 full-time. *Required fees:* $1780; $52 per credit. $35 per term. One-time fee: $165. *Financial support:* In 2019–20, 19 research assistantships with tuition reimbursements (averaging $10,247 per year), 9 teaching assistantships with tuition reimbursements (averaging $9,097 per year) were awarded. Financial award application deadline: 2/1; financial award applicants required to submit FAFSA. *Unit head:* Dr. Haibo He, Chair, 401-874-5844, E-mail: he@ele.uri.edu. *Application contact:* Dr. Frederick J. Vetter, Graduate Director, 401-874-5141, E-mail: vetter@ele.uri.edu.
Website: http://www.ele.uri.edu/

University of Rochester, Hajim School of Engineering and Applied Sciences, Department of Electrical and Computer Engineering, Rochester, NY 14627. Offers biomedical ultrasound and biomedical engineering (MS); integrated electronics and computer engineering (PhD); musical acoustics and signal processing (MS); physical electronics, electron magnetism, and acoustics (PhD); signal and image processing and communications (MS); signal processing and communications (PhD). *Faculty:* 20 full-time (1 woman). *Students:* 124 full-time (20 women); includes 5 minority (2 Black or African American, non-Hispanic/Latino; 2 Asian, non-Hispanic/Latino; 1 Hispanic/Latino), 96 international. Average age 27. 454 applicants, 43% accepted, 40 enrolled. In 2019, 39 master's, 7 doctorates awarded. Terminal master's awarded for partial completion of doctoral program. *Degree requirements:* For master's, thesis optional; for doctorate, comprehensive exam, thesis/dissertation, teaching assistant (two semesters), qualifying exam. *Entrance requirements:* For master's and doctorate, personal statement, three letters of recommendation, official transcripts. Additional exam requirements/recommendations for international students: required—TOEFL (minimum score 90 paper-based; 90 iBT), IELTS (minimum score 6.5). *Application deadline:* For fall admission, 1/15 for domestic and international students. Applications are processed on a rolling basis. Application fee: $60. Electronic applications accepted. *Financial support:* In 2019–20, 125 students received support, including 4 fellowships with full tuition reimbursements available (averaging $31,995 per year), 52 research assistantships with full tuition reimbursements available (averaging $29,510 per year), 69 teaching assistantships with full and partial tuition reimbursements available (averaging $15,000 per year); scholarships/grants, tuition waivers (full and partial), and

unspecified assistantships also available. *Unit head:* Marvin Doyley, Professor and Chair, 585-275-3774, E-mail: m.doyley@rochester.edu. *Application contact:* Michele Foster, Graduate Program Coordinator, 585-275-4054, E-mail: michele.foster@rochester.edu.
Website: http://www.hajim.rochester.edu/ece/graduate/index.html

University of St. Thomas, School of Engineering, St. Paul, MN 55105. Offers data science (MS); electrical engineering (MS); information technology (MS); manufacturing engineering (MS); manufacturing systems (Certificate); mechanical engineering (MS); medical device development (Certificate); regulatory science (MS); software engineering (MS); software management (MS); systems engineering (MS); technology leadership (Certificate); technology management (MS). *Program availability:* Part-time, evening/weekend. *Entrance requirements:* For master's, resume, official transcripts. Additional exam requirements/recommendations for international students: required—TOEFL (minimum score 80 iBT), IELTS (minimum score 6.5). Electronic applications accepted. *Expenses:* Contact institution.

University of Saskatchewan, College of Graduate and Postdoctoral Studies, College of Engineering, Electrical Engineering Program, Saskatoon, SK S7N 5E5, Canada. Offers M Eng, M Sc, PhD, PGD. *Program availability:* Part-time. *Degree requirements:* For master's, 30 credits (for M Eng); thesis and 12 credits (for MS); for doctorate, comprehensive exam, thesis/dissertation, qualifying exam, 18 credits; for PGD, 30 credits. *Entrance requirements:* For master's and doctorate, GRE. Additional exam requirements/recommendations for international students: required—TOEFL (minimum iBT score of 80), IELTS (6.5), CanTEST (4.5), or PTE (59). Electronic applications accepted.

University of South Alabama, College of Engineering, Department of Electrical and Computer Engineering, Mobile, AL 36688-0002. Offers computer engineering (MSEE); electrical engineering (MSEE). *Program availability:* Part-time. *Faculty:* 5 full-time (1 woman). *Students:* 9 full-time (0 women), 4 part-time (2 women); includes 1 minority (Black or African American, non-Hispanic/Latino), 4 international. Average age 28. 17 applicants, 71% accepted, 5 enrolled. In 2019, 7 master's awarded. *Degree requirements:* For master's, comprehensive exam, thesis optional. *Entrance requirements:* For master's, GRE. Additional exam requirements/recommendations for international students: required—TOEFL (minimum score 550 paper-based; 79 iBT), IELTS (minimum score 6.5). *Application deadline:* For fall admission, 7/1 priority date for domestic students, 6/15 priority date for international students; for spring admission, 12/1 priority date for domestic students, 11/1 priority date for international students; for summer admission, 5/1 priority date for domestic students, 4/1 priority date for international students. Applications are processed on a rolling basis. Application fee: $35. Electronic applications accepted. *Expenses:* Contact institution. *Financial support:* Fellowships, research assistantships, teaching assistantships, career-related internships or fieldwork, institutionally sponsored loans, scholarships/grants, and unspecified assistantships available. Support available to part-time students. Financial award application deadline: 3/31; financial award applicants required to submit FAFSA. *Unit head:* Dr. Hulya Kirkici, Chair, Professor, Department of Electrical and Computer Engineering, College of Engineering, 251-460-6117, Fax: 251-460-6028, E-mail: hkirkici@southalabama.edu. *Application contact:* Brenda Poole, Academic Records Specialist, 251-460-6140, Fax: 251-460-6343, E-mail: engineering@southalabama.edu. Website: https://www.southalabama.edu/colleges/engineering/ece/

University of South Carolina, The Graduate School, College of Engineering and Computing, Department of Electrical Engineering, Columbia, SC 29208. Offers ME, MS, PhD. *Program availability:* Part-time, evening/weekend, online learning. *Degree requirements:* For master's, comprehensive exam, thesis (for some programs); for doctorate, comprehensive exam, thesis/dissertation, qualifying exam. *Entrance requirements:* For master's and doctorate, GRE General Test. Additional exam requirements/recommendations for international students: required—TOEFL (minimum score 570 paper-based; 88 iBT). Electronic applications accepted.

University of Southern California, Graduate School, Viterbi School of Engineering, Ming Hsieh Department of Electrical Engineering, Los Angeles, CA 90089. Offers computer engineering (MS, PhD); electric power (MS); electrical engineering (MS, PhD, Engr); engineering technology commercialization (Graduate Certificate); multimedia and creative technologies (MS); telecommunications (MS); VLSI design (MS); wireless health technology (MS). *Program availability:* Part-time, online learning. Terminal master's awarded for partial completion of doctoral program. *Degree requirements:* For master's, thesis optional; for doctorate, thesis/dissertation. *Entrance requirements:* For master's and doctorate, GRE General Test. Additional exam requirements/recommendations for international students: recommended—TOEFL. Electronic applications accepted.

University of South Florida, College of Engineering, Department of Electrical Engineering, Tampa, FL 33620-9951. Offers MSEE, PhD. *Program availability:* Part-time, online learning. *Faculty:* 30 full-time (3 women), 1 part-time/adjunct (0 women). *Students:* 264 full-time (56 women), 71 part-time (7 women); includes 29 minority (8 Black or African American, non-Hispanic/Latino; 2 Asian, non-Hispanic/Latino; 18 Hispanic/Latino; 1 Two or more races, non-Hispanic/Latino), 270 international. Average age 27. 394 applicants, 65% accepted, 85 enrolled. In 2019, 121 master's, 16 doctorates awarded. Terminal master's awarded for partial completion of doctoral program. *Degree requirements:* For master's, comprehensive exam, thesis or alternative; for doctorate, comprehensive exam, thesis/dissertation. *Entrance requirements:* For master's, minimum GPA of 3.0, 3 letters of recommendation, resume, statement of purpose; for doctorate, GRE (with preferred minimum scores of Q> 155 (61%), V> 146 (28%)), minimum GPA of 3.0, 3 letters of recommendation, statement of purpose. Additional exam requirements/recommendations for international students: required—TOEFL, TOEFL (minimum score 550 paper-based; 79 iBT) or IELTS (minimum score 6.5). *Application deadline:* For fall admission, 2/15 for domestic and international students; for spring admission, 10/15 for domestic students, 9/15 for international students; for summer admission, 2/15 for domestic students, 1/15 for international students. Application fee: $30. Electronic applications accepted. *Financial support:* In 2019–20, 38 students received support, including 57 research assistantships (averaging $12,357 per year), 41 teaching assistantships with tuition reimbursements available (averaging $13,528 per year). Financial award applicants required to submit FAFSA. *Unit head:* Dr. Thomas Weller, Professor and Department Chair, 813-974-2740, E-mail: weller@usf.edu. *Application contact:* Dr. Andrew Hoff, Associate Professor and Graduate Program Director, 813-974-4958, Fax: 813-974-5250, E-mail: hoff@usf.edu.
Website: http://ee.eng.usf.edu/

The University of Tennessee, Graduate School, Tickle College of Engineering, Min H. Kao Department of Electrical Engineering and Computer Science, Program in Electrical Engineering, Knoxville, TN 37996-2250. Offers MS, PhD. *Program availability:* Part-time. *Faculty:* 28 full-time (5 women), 1 part-time/adjunct (0 women). *Students:* 118 full-time (24 women), 14 part-time (1 woman); includes 6 minority (2 Black or African American, non-Hispanic/Latino; 3 Asian, non-Hispanic/Latino; 1 Hispanic/Latino), 82 international. Average age 29. 155 applicants, 30% accepted, 25 enrolled. In 2019, 33 master's, 15 doctorates awarded. *Degree requirements:* For master's, thesis or alternative; for doctorate, comprehensive exam, thesis/dissertation. *Entrance*

requirements: For master's, GRE General Test (for MS students pursuing research thesis), minimum GPA of 2.7 (for U.S. degree holders), 3.0 (for international degree holders); 3 references; personal statement; for doctorate, GRE General Test, minimum GPA of 3.0 on previous graduate coursework; 3 references; personal statement. Additional exam requirements/recommendations for international students: required—TOEFL (minimum score 550 paper-based; 80 iBT), IELTS (minimum score 6.5). *Application deadline:* For fall admission, 2/1 priority date for domestic and international students; for spring admission, 6/15 for domestic and international students; for summer admission, 10/15 for domestic and international students. Applications are processed on a rolling basis. Application fee: $60. Electronic applications accepted. *Financial support:* In 2019–20, 71 students received support, including 24 fellowships with full tuition reimbursements available (averaging $28,488 per year), 34 research assistantships with full tuition reimbursements available (averaging $22,405 per year), 13 teaching assistantships with full tuition reimbursements available (averaging $20,522 per year); career-related internships or fieldwork, Federal Work-Study, institutionally sponsored loans, health care benefits, and unspecified assistantships also available. Financial award application deadline: 2/1; financial award applicants required to submit FAFSA. *Unit head:* Dr. Gregory Peterson, PhD, Head, 865-974-3461, Fax: 865-974-5483, E-mail: gdp@utk.edu. *Application contact:* Dr. Jens Gregor, PhD, Associate Head, 865-974-4399, Fax: 865-974-5483, E-mail: jgregor@utk.edu.
Website: http://www.eecs.utk.edu

The University of Tennessee at Chattanooga, Program in Engineering, Chattanooga, TN 37403. Offers automotive (MS Engr); chemical (MS Engr); civil (MS Engr); electrical (MS Engr); mechanical (MS Engr). *Program availability:* Part-time. *Students:* 29 full-time (4 women), 27 part-time (3 women); includes 9 minority (4 Black or African American, non-Hispanic/Latino; 2 Asian, non-Hispanic/Latino; 1 Hispanic/Latino; 1 Native Hawaiian or other Pacific Islander, non-Hispanic/Latino; 1 Two or more races, non-Hispanic/Latino), 19 international. Average age 29. 39 applicants, 74% accepted, 16 enrolled. In 2019, 22 master's awarded. *Degree requirements:* For master's, comprehensive exam, thesis or alternative, engineering project. *Entrance requirements:* For master's, GRE General Test, minimum undergraduate GPA of 2.7 or 3.0 in last two years of undergraduate coursework. Additional exam requirements/recommendations for international students: required—TOEFL (minimum score 550 paper-based; 79 iBT), IELTS (minimum score 6). *Application deadline:* For fall admission, 6/15 priority date for domestic students, 7/1 for international students; for spring admission, 11/1 priority date for domestic students, 11/1 for international students. Applications are processed on a rolling basis. Application fee: $35 ($40 for international students). Electronic applications accepted. *Financial support:* Research assistantships, teaching assistantships, career-related internships or fieldwork, scholarships/grants, health care benefits, and unspecified assistantships available. Support available to part-time students. Financial award application deadline: 7/1; financial award applicants required to submit FAFSA. *Unit head:* Dr. Daniel Pack, Dean, 423-425-2256, Fax: 423-425-5311, E-mail: daniel-pack@utc.edu. *Application contact:* Dr. Joanne Romagni, Dean of the Graduate School, 423-425-4478, Fax: 423-425-5223, E-mail: joanne-romagni@utc.edu.
Website: http://www.utc.edu/college-engineering-computer-science/graduate-programs/msengr.php

The University of Texas at Arlington, Graduate School, College of Engineering, Department of Electrical Engineering, Arlington, TX 76019. Offers M Engr, MS, PhD. *Program availability:* Part-time, evening/weekend, online learning. Terminal master's awarded for partial completion of doctoral program. *Degree requirements:* For master's, thesis optional; for doctorate, comprehensive exam, thesis/dissertation, written diagnostic exam. *Entrance requirements:* For master's, GRE General Test, minimum GPA of 3.25; for doctorate, GRE General Test, minimum GPA of 3.5. Additional exam requirements/recommendations for international students: required—TOEFL (minimum score 560 paper-based); recommended—TWE (minimum score 4).

The University of Texas at Austin, Graduate School, Cockrell School of Engineering, Department of Electrical and Computer Engineering, Austin, TX 78712-1111. Offers MS, PhD. *Program availability:* Part-time. *Entrance requirements:* For master's, GRE General Test, minimum GPA of 3.3 in upper-division course work; for doctorate, GRE General Test. Electronic applications accepted.

The University of Texas at Dallas, Erik Jonsson School of Engineering and Computer Science, Department of Electrical and Computer Engineering, Richardson, TX 75080. Offers computer engineering (MS, PhD); electrical engineering (MSEE, PhD); telecommunications engineering (MSTE, PhD). *Program availability:* Part-time, evening/weekend. *Faculty:* 41 full-time (3 women), 11 part-time/adjunct (2 women). *Students:* 383 full-time (96 women), 142 part-time (32 women); includes 46 minority (8 Black or African American, non-Hispanic/Latino; 28 Asian, non-Hispanic/Latino; 7 Hispanic/Latino; 3 Two or more races, non-Hispanic/Latino), 423 international. Average age 28. 1,343 applicants, 25% accepted, 125 enrolled. In 2019, 184 master's, 44 doctorates awarded. *Degree requirements:* For master's, thesis or major design project; for doctorate, thesis/dissertation. *Entrance requirements:* For master's, GRE General Test, minimum GPA of 3.0 in related bachelor's degree; for doctorate, GRE General Test, minimum GPA of 3.5. Additional exam requirements/recommendations for international students: required—TOEFL (minimum score 550 paper-based). *Application deadline:* For fall admission, 7/15 for domestic students, 5/1 priority date for international students; for spring admission, 11/15 for domestic students, 9/1 priority date for international students. Applications are processed on a rolling basis. Application fee: $50 ($100 for international students). Electronic applications accepted. *Expenses: Tuition, area resident:* Full-time $16,504. Tuition, state resident: full-time $16,504. Tuition, nonresident: full-time $34,266. Tuition and fees vary according to course load. *Financial support:* In 2019–20, 208 students received support, including 14 fellowships (averaging $4,096 per year), 140 research assistantships with partial tuition reimbursements available (averaging $22,844 per year), 70 teaching assistantships with partial tuition reimbursements available (averaging $16,888 per year); Federal Work-Study, institutionally sponsored loans, scholarships/grants, unspecified assistantships, and cooperative positions also available. Support available to part-time students. Financial award application deadline: 4/30; financial award applicants required to submit FAFSA. *Unit head:* Dr. Lawrence Overzet, Department Head, 972-883-2154, Fax: 972-883-2710, E-mail: overzet@utdallas.edu. *Application contact:* Dr. Aria Nosratinia, Associate Department Head, 972-883-2894, E-mail: aria@utdallas.edu.
Website: http://ece.utdallas.edu

The University of Texas at El Paso, Graduate School, College of Engineering, Department of Electrical and Computer Engineering, El Paso, TX 79968-0001. Offers computer engineering (MS); electric power and energy systems (Graduate Certificate); electrical and computer engineering (PhD); electrical engineering (MS). *Program availability:* Part-time, evening/weekend. Terminal master's awarded for partial completion of doctoral program. *Degree requirements:* For master's, thesis optional; for doctorate, thesis/dissertation. *Entrance requirements:* For master's, GRE General Test, minimum GPA of 3.0; for doctorate, GRE General Test, minimum graduate GPA of 3.0. Additional exam requirements/recommendations for international students: required—TOEFL. Electronic applications accepted.

The University of Texas at San Antonio, College of Engineering, Department of Electrical and Computer Engineering, San Antonio, TX 78249-0617. Offers advanced materials engineering (MS); computer engineering (MS); electrical engineering (MSEE, PhD). *Program availability:* Part-time. Terminal master's awarded for partial completion of doctoral program. *Degree requirements:* For master's, comprehensive exam, thesis (for some programs); for doctorate, comprehensive exam, thesis/dissertation. *Entrance requirements:* For master's, GRE General Test, bachelor's degree in electrical or computer engineering from ABET-accredited institution of higher education or related field; minimum GPA of 3.0 on the last 60 semester credit hours of undergraduate studies; for doctorate, GRE General Test, master's degree or minimum GPA of 3.3 in last 60 semester credit hours of undergraduate level coursework in electrical engineering; statement of purpose. Additional exam requirements/recommendations for international students: required—TOEFL (minimum score 550 paper-based; 79 iBT), IELTS (minimum score 6.5). Electronic applications accepted.

The University of Texas at Tyler, College of Engineering, Department of Electrical Engineering, Tyler, TX 75799-0001. Offers MS. *Program availability:* Part-time, evening/weekend. *Faculty:* 3 full-time (1 woman). *Students:* 4 full-time, 1 part-time; includes 2 minority (both Hispanic/Latino), 3 international. Average age 28. 8 applicants, 38% accepted, 1 enrolled. In 2019, 15 master's awarded. *Entrance requirements:* For master's, GRE General Test, bachelor's degree in electrical engineering. Additional exam requirements/recommendations for international students: required—TOEFL. *Application deadline:* For fall admission, 8/17 priority date for domestic students, 7/1 priority date for international students; for spring admission, 12/21 priority date for domestic students, 11/1 priority date for international students. Application fee: $25 ($50 for international students). *Financial support:* In 2019–20, 4 research assistantships (averaging $6,000 per year), 6 teaching assistantships (averaging $6,000 per year) were awarded. Financial award application deadline: 7/1. *Unit head:* Dr. Hassan El-Kishky, Chair, 903-565-5580, E-mail: helkishky@uttyler.edu. *Application contact:* Dr. Hassan El-Kishky, Chair, 903-565-5580, E-mail: helkishky@uttyler.edu.
Website: https://www.uttyler.edu/ee/

The University of Texas Rio Grande Valley, College of Engineering and Computer Science, Department of Electrical Engineering, Edinburg, TX 78539. Offers MSE. *Faculty:* 6 full-time. *Students:* 32 full-time (2 women), 17 part-time (2 women); includes 22 minority (1 Black or African American, non-Hispanic/Latino; 1 Asian, non-Hispanic/Latino; 20 Hispanic/Latino), 25 international. Average age 27. 54 applicants, 81% accepted, 19 enrolled. In 2019, 7 master's awarded. *Expenses: Tuition, area resident:* Full-time $5959; part-time $440 per credit hour. Tuition, state resident: full-time $5959. Tuition, nonresident: full-time $5959. *International tuition:* $13,321 full-time. *Required fees:* $1169; $185 per credit hour.
Website: utrgv.edu/ece/

University of the District of Columbia, School of Engineering and Applied Sciences, Program in Electrical Engineering, Washington, DC 20008-1175. Offers MSEE.

The University of Toledo, College of Graduate Studies, College of Engineering, Department of Electrical Engineering and Computer Science, Toledo, OH 43606-3390. Offers computer science (MS, PhD); electrical engineering (MS, PhD). *Program availability:* Part-time, evening/weekend. *Degree requirements:* For master's, thesis or alternative; for doctorate, thesis/dissertation, qualifying exam. *Entrance requirements:* For master's, GRE General Test, minimum GPA of 3.0; for doctorate, GRE General Test, minimum GPA of 3.3. Additional exam requirements/recommendations for international students: required—TOEFL (minimum score 550 paper-based; 80 iBT). Electronic applications accepted.

University of Toronto, School of Graduate Studies, Faculty of Applied Science and Engineering, Department of Electrical and Computer Engineering, Toronto, ON M5S 1A1, Canada. Offers M Eng, MA Sc, PhD. *Program availability:* Part-time. *Degree requirements:* For master's, thesis (for some programs), oral thesis defense (MA Sc); for doctorate, thesis/dissertation, qualifying exam, thesis defense. *Entrance requirements:* For master's, four-year degree in electrical or computer engineering, minimum B average, 2 letters of reference; for doctorate, minimum B+ average, MA Sc in electrical or computer engineering, 2 letters of reference. Additional exam requirements/recommendations for international students: required—TOEFL (minimum score 580 paper-based; 93 iBT). Electronic applications accepted.

The University of Tulsa, Graduate School, College of Engineering and Natural Sciences, Department of Electrical and Computer Engineering, Tulsa, OK 74104-3189. Offers computer engineering (ME, MSE, PhD); electrical engineering (ME, MSE). *Program availability:* Part-time. Terminal master's awarded for partial completion of doctoral program. *Degree requirements:* For master's, comprehensive exam (for some programs), design report (ME), thesis (MS); for doctorate, comprehensive exam, thesis/dissertation. *Entrance requirements:* For master's, GRE General Test. Additional exam requirements/recommendations for international students: required—TOEFL (minimum score 550 paper-based; 80 iBT), IELTS (minimum score 6). Electronic applications accepted. *Expenses: Tuition:* Full-time $22,896; part-time $1272 per credit hour. *Required fees:* $6 per credit hour. Tuition and fees vary according to course load and program.

University of Utah, Graduate School, College of Engineering, Department of Electrical and Computer Engineering, Salt Lake City, UT 84112. Offers electrical and computer engineering (MS, PhD); electrical engineering (ME); MS/MBA. *Program availability:* Part-time, evening/weekend, 100% online, blended/hybrid learning. *Faculty:* 32 full-time (4 women). *Students:* 125 full-time (20 women), 58 part-time (4 women); includes 19 minority (8 Asian, non-Hispanic/Latino; 9 Hispanic/Latino; 1 Native Hawaiian or other Pacific Islander, non-Hispanic/Latino; 1 Two or more races, non-Hispanic/Latino), 106 international. Average age 29. 210 applicants, 35% accepted, 55 enrolled. In 2019, 31 master's, 18 doctorates awarded. Terminal master's awarded for partial completion of doctoral program. *Degree requirements:* For master's, comprehensive exam, thesis optional; for doctorate, comprehensive exam, thesis/dissertation. *Entrance requirements:* For master's, The GRE is required, however this requirement may be waived if a student graduated from an ABET Accredited Engineering program. International students are required to take the TOEFL or IELTS exam, 3.2 GPA; for doctorate, The GRE is required, however this requirement may be waived if a student graduated from an ABET Accredited Engineering program. International students are required to take the TOEFL or IELTS exam, 3.5 GPA. Additional exam requirements/recommendations for international students: required—TOEFL (minimum score 80 paper-based; 80 iBT), IELTS (minimum score 6.5), GRE. *Application deadline:* For fall admission, 7/15 for domestic students, 1/15 for international students; for winter admission, 11/30 for domestic students, 9/30 for international students; for spring admission, 11/30 for domestic students, 9/30 for international students. Applications are processed on a rolling basis. Application fee: $30 ($45 for international students). Electronic applications accepted. *Expenses:* $17,170.88 to complete 32 credits for a degree state resident; $4,661.65 state resident full-time, $2,448.07 state resident part-time, $13,096.79 non-resident full time, $6763.55 non-resident part time *Financial support:* In 2019–20, 2 students received support, including 1 fellowship (averaging $13,000 per year), 86 research assistantships (averaging $13,151 per year), 21 teaching assistantships (averaging $12,952 per year); unspecified assistantships also available. Financial award application deadline: 1/15. *Unit head:* Prof. Florian Solzbacher, Professor and Chair, 801-581-6942, Fax: 801-581-5281, E-mail: florian.solzbacher@utah.edu. *Application contact:* John Bolke, Graduate Coordinator, 801-581-6943, Fax: 801-581-5281, E-mail: john.bolke@utah.edu.
Website: http://www.ece.utah.edu/

University of Vermont, Graduate College, College of Engineering and Mathematical Sciences, Program in Electrical Engineering, Burlington, VT 05405-0156. Offers MS, PhD. *Degree requirements:* For master's, thesis or alternative; for doctorate, thesis/dissertation. *Entrance requirements:* For master's, GRE General Test. Additional exam requirements/recommendations for international students: required—TOEFL (minimum score 550 paper-based, 90 iBT) or IELTS (6.5). Electronic applications accepted.

University of Victoria, Faculty of Graduate Studies, Faculty of Engineering, Department of Electrical and Computer Engineering, Victoria, BC V8W 2Y2, Canada. Offers M Eng, MA Sc, PhD. *Degree requirements:* For master's, thesis; for doctorate, thesis/dissertation, candidacy exam. *Entrance requirements:* For master's, GRE (recommended), bachelor's degree in engineering; for doctorate, GRE (recommended), master's degree. Additional exam requirements/recommendations for international students: required—TOEFL (minimum score 575 paper-based), IELTS (minimum score 7). Electronic applications accepted.

University of Virginia, School of Engineering and Applied Science, Department of Electrical and Computer Engineering, Program in Electrical Engineering, Charlottesville, VA 22903. Offers ME, MS, PhD. *Degree requirements:* For doctorate, thesis/dissertation. *Entrance requirements:* For master's, GRE General Test, 3 letters of recommendation; for doctorate, GRE General Test, 3 letters of recommendation; essay. Additional exam requirements/recommendations for international students: required—TOEFL (minimum score 650 paper-based; 100 iBT), IELTS (minimum score 7). Electronic applications accepted.

University of Washington, Graduate School, College of Engineering, Department of Electrical and Computer Engineering, Seattle, WA 98195-2500. Offers electrical engineering (MS, PhD); electrical engineering and nanotechnology (PhD). *Program availability:* Part-time, evening/weekend. *Students:* 282 full-time (62 women), 149 part-time (34 women); includes 85 minority (7 Black or African American, non-Hispanic/Latino; 56 Asian, non-Hispanic/Latino; 14 Hispanic/Latino; 8 Two or more races, non-Hispanic/Latino), 220 international. Average age 27. 1,356 applicants, 38% accepted, 164 enrolled. In 2019, 83 master's, 30 doctorates awarded. Terminal master's awarded for partial completion of doctoral program. *Degree requirements:* For master's, thesis optional; for doctorate, thesis/dissertation, qualifying, general, and final exams. *Entrance requirements:* For master's and doctorate, minimum GPA of 3.5 (recommended); resume or curriculum vitae, statement of purpose, 3 letters of recommendation, undergraduate and graduate transcripts. Additional exam requirements/recommendations for international students: required—TOEFL (minimum score 600 paper-based; 92 iBT). *Application deadline:* For fall admission, 12/15 for domestic and international students. Application fee: $85. Electronic applications accepted. *Expenses:* Contact institution. *Financial support:* In 2019–20, 5 fellowships with full tuition reimbursements (averaging $34,080 per year), 100 research assistantships with full tuition reimbursements (averaging $34,080 per year), 50 teaching assistantships with full tuition reimbursements (averaging $33,240 per year) were awarded; Federal Work-Study, institutionally sponsored loans, scholarships/grants, health care benefits, tuition waivers (full), and unspecified assistantships also available. Support available to part-time students. Financial award application deadline: 12/15. *Unit head:* Dr. Erik Klavins, Professor/Chair, 206-616-1743, Fax: 206-543-3842, E-mail: chair@ece.uw.edu. *Application contact:* Brenda Larson, Lead Academic Counselor, Graduate Programs, 206-616-1351, Fax: 206-543-3842, E-mail: grad@ece.uw.edu.
Website: http://www.ece.uw.edu

University of Waterloo, Graduate Studies and Postdoctoral Affairs, Faculty of Engineering, Department of Electrical and Computer Engineering, Waterloo, ON N2L 3G1, Canada. Offers M Eng, MA Sc, PhD. *Program availability:* Part-time. *Degree requirements:* For master's, research paper or thesis; for doctorate, comprehensive exam, thesis/dissertation. *Entrance requirements:* For master's, honors degree, minimum B+ average; for doctorate, master's degree, minimum A- average. Additional exam requirements/recommendations for international students: required—TOEFL, IELTS, PTE. Electronic applications accepted.

The University of Western Ontario, School of Graduate and Postdoctoral Studies, Physical Sciences Division, Faculty of Engineering, London, ON N6A 3K7, Canada. Offers chemical and biochemical engineering (ME Sc, PhD); civil and environmental engineering (M Eng, ME Sc, PhD); electrical and computer engineering (M Eng, ME Sc, PhD); mechanical and materials engineering (M Eng, ME Sc, PhD). *Program availability:* Part-time. Terminal master's awarded for partial completion of doctoral program. *Degree requirements:* For master's, thesis; for doctorate, thesis/dissertation. *Entrance requirements:* For master's, minimum B average; for doctorate, minimum B+ average.

University of Windsor, Faculty of Graduate Studies, Faculty of Engineering, Department of Electrical and Computer Engineering, Windsor, ON N9B 3P4, Canada. Offers electrical engineering (M Eng, MA Sc, PhD). *Program availability:* Part-time. *Degree requirements:* For master's, thesis; for doctorate, comprehensive exam, thesis/dissertation. *Entrance requirements:* For master's, minimum B average; for doctorate, master's degree, minimum B+ average. Additional exam requirements/recommendations for international students: required—TOEFL (minimum score 600 paper-based). Electronic applications accepted.

University of Wisconsin–Madison, Graduate School, College of Engineering, Department of Electrical and Computer Engineering, Madison, WI 53706-1380. Offers electrical engineering (MS, PhD); machine learning and signal processing (MS). *Program availability:* Blended/hybrid learning. Terminal master's awarded for partial completion of doctoral program. *Degree requirements:* For master's, thesis (for some programs), 30 semester hours of credit; 3.0 GPA; for doctorate, comprehensive exam, thesis/dissertation, 51 credits; qualifying and preliminary exams; 3.0 GPA. *Entrance requirements:* For master's and doctorate, GRE General Test, bachelor's degree; minimum GPA of 3.0 on last 60 semester hours. Additional exam requirements/recommendations for international students: required—TOEFL (minimum score 580 paper-based; 92 iBT), IELTS (minimum score 7). Electronic applications accepted. *Expenses:* Contact institution.

University of Wisconsin–Milwaukee, Graduate School, College of Engineering and Applied Science, Program in Engineering, Milwaukee, WI 53201-0413. Offers biomedical engineering (MS); civil engineering (MS, PhD); computer science (PhD); electrical and computer engineering (MS); electrical engineering (PhD); engineering mechanics (MS); industrial and management engineering (MS); industrial engineering (PhD); manufacturing engineering (MS); materials (PhD); materials engineering (MS); mechanical engineering (MS). *Program availability:* Part-time. *Degree requirements:* For master's, comprehensive exam (for some programs), thesis or alternative; for doctorate, comprehensive exam, thesis/dissertation, internship. *Entrance requirements:* For master's, GRE, minimum GPA of 2.75; for doctorate, GRE, minimum GPA of 3.5. Additional exam requirements/recommendations for international students: required—TOEFL (minimum score 550 paper-based; 79 iBT), IELTS (minimum score 6.5).

University of Wyoming, College of Engineering and Applied Science, Department of Electrical and Computer Engineering, Laramie, WY 82071. Offers electrical engineering (MS, PhD). *Program availability:* Part-time. *Degree requirements:* For master's, thesis (for some programs); for doctorate, comprehensive exam, thesis/dissertation, dissertation proposal/presentation. *Entrance requirements:* For master's, GRE General Test, minimum undergraduate GPA of 3.0; for doctorate, GRE General Test, minimum GPA of 3.0. Additional exam requirements/recommendations for international students: required—TOEFL (minimum score 550 paper-based; 79 iBT). Electronic applications accepted.

Université Laval, Faculty of Sciences and Engineering, Department of Electrical and Computer Engineering, Programs in Electrical Engineering, Québec, QC G1K 7P4, Canada. Offers M Sc, PhD. Terminal master's awarded for partial completion of doctoral program. *Degree requirements:* For master's, thesis (for some programs); for doctorate, thesis/dissertation. *Entrance requirements:* For master's and doctorate, knowledge of French and English. Electronic applications accepted.

Utah State University, School of Graduate Studies, College of Engineering, Department of Electrical and Computer Engineering, Logan, UT 84322. Offers electrical engineering (ME, MS, PhD). *Program availability:* Part-time. *Degree requirements:* For master's, thesis (for some programs); for doctorate, comprehensive exam, thesis/dissertation. *Entrance requirements:* For master's, GRE General Test, minimum GPA of 3.0, BS in electrical engineering, 3 recommendation letters; for doctorate, GRE General Test, minimum GPA of 3.0, MS in electrical engineering, 3 recommendation letters. Additional exam requirements/recommendations for international students: required—TOEFL. Electronic applications accepted.

Vanderbilt University, School of Engineering, Department of Electrical Engineering and Computer Science, Program in Electrical Engineering, Nashville, TN 37240-1001. Offers M Eng, MS, PhD. *Program availability:* Part-time. Terminal master's awarded for partial completion of doctoral program. *Degree requirements:* For master's, thesis; for doctorate, comprehensive exam, thesis/dissertation. *Entrance requirements:* For master's and doctorate, GRE General Test, 3 letters of recommendation. Additional exam requirements/recommendations for international students: required—TOEFL. Electronic applications accepted. *Expenses: Tuition:* Full-time $51,018; part-time $2087 per hour. *Required fees:* $542. Tuition and fees vary according to program.

Villanova University, College of Engineering, Department of Electrical and Computer Engineering, Program in Electrical Engineering, Villanova, PA 19085-1699. Offers electric power systems (Certificate); electrical engineering (MSEE); electro mechanical systems (Certificate); high frequency systems (Certificate); intelligent control systems (Certificate); wireless and digital communications (Certificate). *Program availability:* Part-time, evening/weekend. *Degree requirements:* For master's, thesis optional. *Entrance requirements:* For master's, GRE General Test (for applicants with degrees from foreign universities), BEE, minimum GPA of 3.0. Additional exam requirements/recommendations for international students: required—TOEFL (minimum score 600 paper-based; 100 iBT).

Virginia Polytechnic Institute and State University, Graduate School, College of Engineering, Blacksburg, VA 24061. Offers aerospace engineering (PhD, M Eng/MS); biological systems engineering (PhD); biomedical engineering (MS, PhD); chemical engineering (PhD); civil engineering (PhD); computer engineering (PhD); computer science and applications (MS); electrical engineering (PhD); engineering education (PhD); M Eng/MS. *Faculty:* 447 full-time (90 women), 6 part-time/adjunct (2 women). *Students:* 1,881 full-time (495 women), 326 part-time (70 women); includes 264 minority (51 Black or African American, non-Hispanic/Latino; 2 American Indian or Alaska Native, non-Hispanic/Latino; 96 Asian, non-Hispanic/Latino; 69 Hispanic/Latino; 46 Two or more races, non-Hispanic/Latino), 1,247 international. Average age 27. 4,014 applicants, 44% accepted, 658 enrolled. In 2019, 489 master's, 200 doctorates awarded. *Degree requirements:* For master's, comprehensive exam (for some programs), thesis (for some programs); for doctorate, comprehensive exam (for some programs), thesis/dissertation (for some programs). *Entrance requirements:* For master's and doctorate, GRE/GMAT. Additional exam requirements/recommendations for international students: required—TOEFL (minimum score 90 iBT). *Application deadline:* For fall admission, 8/1 for domestic students, 4/1 for international students; for spring admission, 1/1 for domestic students, 9/1 for international students. Applications are processed on a rolling basis. Application fee: $75. Electronic applications accepted. *Expenses:* Tuition, state resident: full-time $13,700; part-time $761.25 per credit hour. Tuition, nonresident: full-time $27,614; part-time $1534 per credit hour. *Required fees:* $886.50 per term. Tuition and fees vary according to campus/location and program. *Financial support:* In 2019–20, 47 fellowships with full tuition reimbursements (averaging $19,703 per year), 1,163 research assistantships with full tuition reimbursements (averaging $20,602 per year), 554 teaching assistantships with full tuition reimbursements (averaging $16,333 per year) were awarded; scholarships/grants and unspecified assistantships also available. Financial award application deadline: 3/1; financial award applicants required to submit FAFSA. *Unit head:* Dr. Julia Ross, Dean, 540-231-9752, Fax: 540-231-3031, E-mail: rjulie@vt.edu. *Application contact:* Linda Perkins, Executive Assistant, 540-231-9752, Fax: 540-231-3031, E-mail: lperkins@vt.edu.
Website: http://www.eng.vt.edu/

Virginia Polytechnic Institute and State University, VT Online, Blacksburg, VA 24061. Offers advanced transportation systems (Certificate); aerospace engineering (MS); agricultural and life sciences (MSLFS); business information systems (Graduate Certificate); career and technical education (MS); civil engineering (MS); computer engineering (M Eng, MS); decision support systems (Graduate Certificate); eLearning leadership (MA); electrical engineering (M Eng, MS); engineering administration (MEA); environmental engineering (Certificate); environmental politics and policy (Graduate Certificate); environmental sciences and engineering (MS); foundations of political analysis (Graduate Certificate); health product risk management (Graduate Certificate); industrial and systems engineering (MS); information policy and society (Graduate Certificate); information security (Graduate Certificate); information technology (MIT); instructional technology (MA); integrative STEM education (MA Ed); liberal arts (Graduate Certificate); life sciences: health product risk management (MS); natural resources (MNR, Graduate Certificate); networking (Graduate Certificate); nonprofit and nongovernmental organization management (Graduate Certificate); ocean engineering (MS); political science (MA); security studies (Graduate Certificate); software development (Graduate Certificate). *Expenses:* Tuition, state resident: full-time $13,700; part-time $761.25 per credit hour. Tuition, nonresident: full-time $27,614; part-time $1534 per credit hour. *Required fees:* $886.50 per term. Tuition and fees vary according to campus/location and program.

Washington State University, Voiland College of Engineering and Architecture, School of Electrical Engineering and Computer Science, Pullman, WA 99164-2752. Offers computer engineering (MS); computer science (MS); electrical engineering (MS); electrical engineering and computer science (PhD); electrical power engineering (MS). *Program availability:* Part-time. *Degree requirements:* For master's, comprehensive exam (for some programs), thesis or alternative; for doctorate, comprehensive exam, thesis/dissertation. *Entrance requirements:* For master's and doctorate, GRE General Test, minimum GPA of 3.0, 3 letters of recommendation, statement of purpose, transcripts. Additional exam requirements/recommendations for international students: required—TOEFL (minimum score 580 paper-based).

Wayne State University, College of Engineering, Department of Electrical and Computer Engineering, Detroit, MI 48202. Offers computer engineering (MS, PhD); electrical engineering (MS, PhD). *Faculty:* 19. *Students:* 84 full-time (29 women), 47 part-time (8 women); includes 11 minority (3 Black or African American, non-Hispanic/Latino; 6 Asian, non-Hispanic/Latino; 1 Hispanic/Latino; 1 Two or more races, non-Hispanic/Latino), 76 international. Average age 29. 249 applicants, 35% accepted, 27 enrolled. In 2019, 52 master's, 9 doctorates awarded. *Degree requirements:* For master's, thesis optional; for doctorate, thesis/dissertation. *Entrance requirements:* For master's, GRE (recommended if BS is not from ABET-accredited university), BS from ABET-accredited university; for doctorate, GRE, minimum undergraduate GPA of 3.5 with major or substantial specialized work in proposed doctoral major field, or master's degree in electrical and computer engineering with minimum master's GPA of 3.6. Additional exam requirements/recommendations for international students: required—TOEFL (minimum score 550 paper-based; 79 iBT), TWE (minimum score 5.5), Michigan English Language Assessment Battery (minimum score 85); recommended—IELTS (minimum score 6.5). *Application deadline:* For fall admission, 6/1 priority date for domestic students, 5/1 priority date for international students; for winter admission, 10/1 priority date for domestic students, 9/1 priority date for international students; for spring admission, 2/1 priority date for domestic students, 1/1 priority date for international students. Applications are processed on a rolling basis. Application fee: $50. Electronic applications accepted. *Expenses:* $790 per credit hour in-state tuition, $1579 per credit hour out-of-state tuition. MS is a 30 credit hour program; PhD is a 90 credit hour program. *Financial support:* In 2019–20, 53 students received support, including 3 fellowships with tuition reimbursements available (averaging $20,000 per year), 10 research assistantships with tuition reimbursements available (averaging $18,526 per year), 10 teaching assistantships with tuition reimbursements available (averaging $20,792 per year); scholarships/grants, health care benefits, and unspecified assistantships also available. Support available to part-time students. Financial award applicants required to submit FAFSA. *Unit head:* Dr. Mohammed Ismail Elnaggar, Department Chair, 734-284-3100, E-mail: gd8686@wayne.edu. *Application contact:* Eric Scimeca, Graduate Program Coordinator, 313-577-0412, E-mail: eric.scimeca@wayne.edu.
Website: http://engineering.wayne.edu/ece/

Western Michigan University, Graduate College, College of Engineering and Applied Sciences, Department of Electrical and Computer Engineering, Kalamazoo, MI 49008. Offers computer engineering (MSE); electrical and computer engineering (PhD); electrical engineering (MSE). *Program availability:* Part-time. *Degree requirements:* For master's, thesis optional.

Western New England University, College of Engineering, Department of Electrical Engineering, Springfield, MA 01119. Offers MSEE. *Program availability:* Part-time, evening/weekend. *Degree requirements:* For master's, comprehensive exam, thesis optional. *Entrance requirements:* For master's, official transcript, bachelor's degree in engineering or related field, two recommendations, resume. Additional exam requirements/recommendations for international students: required—TOEFL (minimum score 79 iBT). Electronic applications accepted. *Expenses:* Contact institution.

West Virginia University, Statler College of Engineering and Mineral Resources, Morgantown, WV 26506. Offers aerospace engineering (MSAE, PhD); chemical engineering (MS Ch E, PhD); civil engineering (MSCE, PhD); computer engineering (PhD); computer science (MSCS, PhD); electrical engineering (MSEE, PhD); energy systems engineering (MSESE); engineering (MSE); industrial engineering (MSIE, PhD); industrial hygiene (MS); material science and engineering (MSMSE, PhD); mechanical engineering (MSME, PhD); mining engineering (MS Min E, PhD); petroleum and natural gas engineering (MSPNGE, PhD); safety management (MS); software engineering (MSSE). *Program availability:* Part-time. Terminal master's awarded for partial completion of doctoral program. *Degree requirements:* For master's, thesis optional; for doctorate, comprehensive exam, thesis/dissertation. *Entrance requirements:* Additional exam requirements/recommendations for international students: required—TOEFL (minimum score 550 paper-based). Electronic applications accepted. *Expenses:* Contact institution.

Wichita State University, Graduate School, College of Engineering, Department of Electrical Engineering and Computer Science, Wichita, KS 67260. Offers computer networking (MS); computer science (MS); electrical and computer engineering (MS); electrical engineering and computer science (PhD). *Program availability:* Part-time, evening/weekend.

Widener University, Graduate Programs in Engineering, Program in Electrical Engineering, Chester, PA 19013. Offers M Eng. *Program availability:* Part-time, evening/weekend. *Degree requirements:* For master's, thesis optional. Electronic applications accepted. *Expenses: Tuition:* Full-time $48,750; part-time $917 per credit hour. Tuition and fees vary according to class time, degree level, campus/location and program.

Worcester Polytechnic Institute, Graduate Admissions, Department of Electrical and Computer Engineering, Worcester, MA 01609-2280. Offers electrical and computer engineering (Advanced Certificate, Graduate Certificate); electrical engineering (M Eng, MS, PhD); power systems engineering (MS). *Program availability:* Part-time, evening/weekend, 100% online, blended/hybrid learning. Terminal master's awarded for partial completion of doctoral program. *Degree requirements:* For master's, thesis optional; for doctorate, comprehensive exam, thesis/dissertation. *Entrance requirements:* For master's, GRE (recommended), 3 letters of recommendation; for doctorate, GRE (recommended), 3 letters of recommendation, statement of purpose. Additional exam requirements/recommendations for international students: required—TOEFL (minimum score 563 paper-based; 84 iBT), IELTS (minimum score 7), GRE. Electronic applications accepted.

Wright State University, Graduate School, College of Engineering and Computer Science, Department of Electrical Engineering, Dayton, OH 45435. Offers MS. *Program availability:* Part-time, evening/weekend. *Degree requirements:* For master's, thesis or course option alternative. *Entrance requirements:* Additional exam requirements/recommendations for international students: required—TOEFL.

Yale University, Graduate School of Arts and Sciences, School of Engineering and Applied Science, Department of Electrical Engineering, New Haven, CT 06520. Offers MS, PhD. Terminal master's awarded for partial completion of doctoral program. *Degree requirements:* For doctorate, thesis/dissertation, exam. *Entrance requirements:* For master's and doctorate, GRE General Test. Additional exam requirements/recommendations for international students: required—TOEFL.

Youngstown State University, College of Graduate Studies, College of Science, Technology, Engineering and Mathematics, Department of Electrical and Computer Engineering, Youngstown, OH 44555-0001. Offers computer engineering (MSE); electrical engineering (MSE). *Program availability:* Part-time, evening/weekend. *Degree requirements:* For master's, thesis optional. *Entrance requirements:* For master's, minimum GPA of 2.75 in field. Additional exam requirements/recommendations for international students: required—TOEFL.

Section 10
Energy and Power Engineering

This section contains a directory of institutions offering graduate work in energy and power engineering. Additional information about programs listed in the directory may be obtained by writing directly to the dean of a graduate school or chair of a department at the address given in the directory.

For programs offering related work, see also in this book *Computer Science and Information Technology, Engineering and Applied Sciences, Industrial Engineering,* and *Mechanical Engineering and Mechanics.* In another guide in this series:
Graduate Programs in the Physical Sciences, Mathematics, Agricultural Sciences, the Environment & Natural Resources

See *Physics* and *Mathematical Sciences*

CONTENTS

Program Directories

Energy and Power Engineering

Appalachian State University, Cratis D. Williams School of Graduate Studies, Department of Sustainable Technology and the Built Environment, Boone, NC 28608. Offers appropriate technology (MS); renewable energy engineering (MS). *Program availability:* Part-time. *Degree requirements:* For master's, comprehensive exam, thesis optional. *Entrance requirements:* For master's, GRE General Test, 3 letters of recommendation. Additional exam requirements/recommendations for international students: required—TOEFL (minimum score 550 paper-based; 79 iBT), IELTS (minimum score 6.5). Electronic applications accepted.

Arizona State University at Tempe, Ira A. Fulton Schools of Engineering, School for Engineering of Matter, Transport and Energy, Tempe, AZ 85281. Offers aerospace engineering (MS, PhD); chemical engineering (MS, PhD); materials science and engineering (MS, PhD); mechanical engineering (MS, PhD); solar energy engineering and commercialization (PSM). *Program availability:* Part-time, evening/weekend, online learning. Terminal master's awarded for partial completion of doctoral program. *Degree requirements:* For master's, thesis and oral defense (MS); applied project or comprehensive exam (MSE); interactive Program of Study (iPOS) submitted before completing 50 percent of required credit hours; for doctorate, comprehensive exam, thesis/dissertation, interactive Program of Study (iPOS) submitted before completing 50 percent of required credit hours. *Entrance requirements:* For master's, GRE, minimum GPA of 3.0 or equivalent in last 2 years of work leading to bachelor's degree; for doctorate, GRE, minimum GPA of 3.0 in last 2 years of work leading to bachelor's degree. Additional exam requirements/recommendations for international students: required—TOEFL, IELTS, or PTE. Electronic applications accepted. *Expenses:* Contact institution.

Carnegie Mellon University, Carnegie Institute of Technology, Department of Civil and Environmental Engineering, Pittsburgh, PA 15213. Offers advanced infrastructure systems (MS, PhD); advanced infrastructure systems technology development and application (MS); air quality engineering and science (MS); civil and environmental engineering (MS, PhD); civil and environmental engineering/engineering and public policy (PhD); civil engineering (MS, PhD); computational mechanics (MS, PhD); computational modeling and monitoring for resilient structural and material systems (MS); energy infrastructure systems (MS); environmental engineering (MS, PhD); environmental management and science (MS, PhD); IT-based sustainable global infrastructure and construction management (MS); sustainability and green design (MS); water quality engineering and science (MS). *Program availability:* Part-time. *Faculty:* 23 full-time (5 women), 12 part-time/adjunct (3 women). *Students:* 261 full-time (109 women); includes 19 minority (7 Black or African American, non-Hispanic/Latino; 8 Asian, non-Hispanic/Latino; 4 Hispanic/Latino), 214 international. Average age 25. 649 applicants, 57% accepted, 106 enrolled. In 2019, 80 master's, 12 doctorates awarded. Terminal master's awarded for partial completion of doctoral program. *Degree requirements:* For master's, thesis optional; for doctorate, comprehensive exam, thesis/dissertation, two-part qualifying exam, public defense of dissertation. *Entrance requirements:* For master's, GRE General Test, BS in engineering, science, or mathematics; for doctorate, GRE General Test, BS or MS in engineering, science, or mathematics. Additional exam requirements/recommendations for international students: required—TOEFL (minimum score 84 iBT), TOEFL (minimum score 84 iBT) or IELTS (7.0). *Application deadline:* For fall admission, 1/5 priority date for domestic and international students; for spring admission, 9/15 priority date for domestic and international students. Applications are processed on a rolling basis. Application fee: $75. Electronic applications accepted. *Financial support:* In 2019–20, 113 students received support. Fellowships with tuition reimbursements available, research assistantships with tuition reimbursements available, teaching assistantships, scholarships/grants, health care benefits, tuition waivers (full and partial), and unspecified assistantships available. Financial award application deadline: 1/5. *Unit head:* Dr. David A. Dzombak, Professor and Department Head, 412-268-2941, Fax: 412-268-7813, E-mail: dzombak@cmu.edu. *Application contact:* David A. Vey, Director of Graduate Programs, 412-268-2292, Fax: 412-268-7813, E-mail: dvey@andrew.cmu.edu.
Website: http://www.cmu.edu/cee/

Carnegie Mellon University, Mellon College of Science, Department of Chemistry, Pittsburgh, PA 15213-3891. Offers atmospheric chemistry (PhD); bioinorganic chemistry (PhD); bioorganic chemistry and chemical biology (PhD); biophysical chemistry (PhD); catalysis (PhD); green and environmental chemistry (PhD); materials and nanoscience (PhD); renewable energy (PhD); sensors, probes, and imaging (PhD); spectroscopy and single molecule analysis (PhD); theoretical and computational chemistry (PhD). *Program availability:* Part-time. Terminal master's awarded for partial completion of doctoral program. *Degree requirements:* For doctorate, thesis/dissertation, departmental qualifying and oral exams, teaching experience. *Entrance requirements:* For doctorate, GRE General Test, GRE Subject Test. Additional exam requirements/recommendations for international students: required—TOEFL. Electronic applications accepted.

The Catholic University of America, School of Engineering, Department of Mechanical Engineering, Washington, DC 20064. Offers energy and environment (MME); general (MME); mechanical engineering (MSE, PhD). *Program availability:* Part-time. *Faculty:* 10 full-time (0 women), 6 part-time/adjunct (4 women). *Students:* 7 full-time (1 woman), 35 part-time (13 women); includes 7 minority (1 Black or African American, non-Hispanic/Latino; 2 Asian, non-Hispanic/Latino; 1 Hispanic/Latino; 3 Two or more races, non-Hispanic/Latino), 8 international. Average age 31. 26 applicants, 73% accepted, 8 enrolled. In 2019, 9 master's, 3 doctorates awarded. Terminal master's awarded for partial completion of doctoral program. *Degree requirements:* For master's, thesis (for some programs); for doctorate, comprehensive exam, thesis/dissertation. *Entrance requirements:* For master's and doctorate, statement of purpose, official copies of academic transcripts, three letters of recommendation. Additional exam requirements/recommendations for international students: required—TOEFL (minimum score 550 paper-based; 80 iBT). *Application deadline:* For fall admission, 7/15 priority date for domestic students, 7/1 for international students; for spring admission, 11/15 priority date for domestic students, 11/1 for international students. Applications are processed on a rolling basis. Application fee: $55. Electronic applications accepted. *Expenses:* Contact institution. *Financial support:* Fellowships, research assistantships, teaching assistantships, Federal Work-Study, scholarships/grants, tuition waivers (full and partial), and unspecified assistantships available. Financial award application deadline: 2/1; financial award applicants required to submit FAFSA. *Unit head:* Dr. Sen Nieh, Chair, 202-319-5170, Fax: 202-319-5173, E-mail: nieh@cua.edu. *Application contact:* Dr. Steven Brown, Director of Graduate Admissions, 202-319-5057, Fax: 202-319-6533, E-mail: cua-admissions@cua.edu.
Website: https://engineering.catholic.edu/mechanical/index.html

Clarkson University, Wallace H. Coulter School of Engineering, Master's Programs in Energy Systems, Schenectady, NY 13699. Offers electrical engineering (ME), including power engineering; energy systems (MS). *Program availability:* Part-time, evening/weekend. *Students:* 1 (woman) full-time, 3 part-time (1 woman); includes 1 minority (Hispanic/Latino). 14 applicants, 71% accepted, 1 enrolled. *Degree requirements:* For master's, project. *Entrance requirements:* Additional exam requirements/recommendations for international students: required—TOEFL (minimum score 550 paper-based, 80 iBT) or IELTS (6.5). *Application deadline:* Applications are processed on a rolling basis. Application fee: $50. Electronic applications accepted. *Expenses:* Tuition: Full-time $24,984; part-time $1388. Required fees: $225. Tuition and fees vary according to campus/location and program. *Financial support:* Scholarships/grants available. *Unit head:* Hugo Irizarry-Quinones, Associate Dean of Engineering, 518-631-9881, E-mail: hirizarr@clarkson.edu. *Application contact:* Daniel Capogna, Director of Graduate Admissions & Recruitment, 518-631-9910, E-mail: graduate@clarkson.edu.
Website: https://www.clarkson.edu/academics/graduate

Cornell University, Graduate School, Graduate Fields of Agriculture and Life Sciences and Graduate Fields of Engineering, Field of Biological and Environmental Engineering, Ithaca, NY 14853. Offers bioenergy and integrated energy systems (M Eng, MPS, MS, PhD); biological engineering (M Eng, MPS, MS, PhD); bioprocess engineering (M Eng, MPS, MS, PhD); ecohydrology (M Eng, MPS, MS, PhD); environmental engineering (M Eng, MPS, MS, PhD); environmental management (MPS); food engineering (M Eng, MPS, MS, PhD); industrial biotechnology (M Eng, MPS, MS, PhD); nanobiotechnology (M Eng, MPS, MS, PhD); sustainable systems (M Eng, MPS, MS, PhD); synthetic biology (MS); synthetic biology (M Eng, MPS, PhD). Terminal master's awarded for partial completion of doctoral program. *Degree requirements:* For master's, thesis (MS); for doctorate, comprehensive exam, thesis/dissertation. *Entrance requirements:* For master's, letters of recommendation (3 for MS, 2 for M Eng and MPS); for doctorate, GRE General Test, 3 letters of recommendation. Additional exam requirements/recommendations for international students: required—TOEFL (minimum score 550 paper-based; 77 iBT). Electronic applications accepted.

Dartmouth College, Dartmouth Engineering - Thayer School of Engineering, Program in Energy Engineering, Hanover, NH 03755. Offers MS, PhD.

Florida State University, The Graduate School, FAMU-FSU College of Engineering, Department of Mechanical Engineering, Tallahassee, FL 32310-6046. Offers mechanical engineering (MS, PhD); sustainable energy (MS). *Program availability:* Part-time. *Faculty:* 25 full-time (3 women), 2 part-time/adjunct (1 woman). *Students:* 85 full-time (10 women); includes 20 minority (3 Black or African American, non-Hispanic/Latino; 6 Asian, non-Hispanic/Latino; 10 Hispanic/Latino; 1 Two or more races, non-Hispanic/Latino), 34 international. Average age 25. 145 applicants, 50% accepted, 24 enrolled. In 2019, 15 master's, 4 doctorates awarded. Terminal master's awarded for partial completion of doctoral program. *Degree requirements:* For master's, thesis optional, 30 credit hours (24 coursework, 6 research); for doctorate, thesis/dissertation, 45 credit hours (21 coursework, 24 research). *Entrance requirements:* For master's and doctorate, GRE General Test (minimum scores: Verbal 150, Quantitative 155), minimum GPA of 3.0, official transcripts, resume, personal statement, 3 letters of recommendation. Additional exam requirements/recommendations for international students: required—TOEFL (minimum score 550 paper-based; 80 iBT), IELTS (minimum score 6.5). *Application deadline:* For fall admission, 4/1 for domestic and international students; for spring admission, 11/1 for domestic and international students. Applications are processed on a rolling basis. Application fee: $30. Electronic applications accepted. *Financial support:* In 2019–20, 77 students received support, including 1 fellowship with full tuition reimbursement available, 75 research assistantships with full tuition reimbursements available, 34 teaching assistantships with full tuition reimbursements available (averaging $4,364 per year); career-related internships or fieldwork, institutionally sponsored loans, tuition waivers (full), and unspecified assistantships also available. Support available to part-time students. Financial award application deadline: 3/1; financial award applicants required to submit FAFSA. *Unit head:* Dr. Emmanuel Collins, Chair, 850-410-6373, Fax: 850-410-6337, E-mail: ecollins@eng.famu.fsu.edu. *Application contact:* Breda Arnell, Coordinator of Graduate Studies, 850-410-6196, Fax: 850-410-6337, E-mail: barnell@eng.famu.fsu.edu.
Website: http://www.eng.famu.fsu.edu/me/

Georgia Southern University, Jack N. Averitt College of Graduate Studies, Allen E. Paulson College of Engineering and Computing, Department of Mechanical Engineering, Program in Engineering/Energy Science, Statesboro, GA 30458. Offers MSAE. *Program availability:* Part-time. *Students:* 1 full-time (0 women), 1 (woman) part-time, both international. Average age 26. In 2019, 3 master's awarded. *Degree requirements:* For master's, comprehensive exam, thesis optional. *Entrance requirements:* For master's, undergraduate major or equivalent in proposed study area. Additional exam requirements/recommendations for international students: required—TOEFL (minimum score 550 paper-based; 80 iBT), IELTS (minimum score 6). *Application deadline:* For fall admission, 3/1 priority date for domestic and international students; for spring admission, 10/1 priority date for domestic students, 10/1 for international students. Applications are processed on a rolling basis. Application fee: $50. Electronic applications accepted. *Expenses: Tuition, area resident:* Full-time $4986; part-time $277 per credit hour. Tuition, nonresident: full-time $19,890; part-time $1105 per credit hour. *International tuition:* $19,890 full-time. *Required fees:* $2114; $1057 per semester. $1057 per semester. Tuition and fees vary according to course load, campus/location and program. *Financial support:* In 2019–20, 2 students received support. Unspecified assistantships available. Financial award application deadline: 4/20; financial award applicants required to submit FAFSA. *Unit head:* Dr. Biswanath Samanta, Program Coordinator, 912-478-0334, E-mail: bsamanta@georgiasouthern.edu. *Application contact:* Dr. Biswanath Samanta, Program Coordinator, 912-478-0334, E-mail: bsamanta@georgiasouthern.edu.

Instituto Tecnologico de Santo Domingo, Graduate School, Area of Basic And Environmental Sciences, Santo Domingo, Dominican Republic. Offers environmental science (M En S), including environmental education, environmental management, marine resources, natural resources management; mathematics (MS, PhD); renewable energy technology (MS, Certificate).

Inter American University of Puerto Rico, Bayamón Campus, Graduate School, Bayamón, PR 00957. Offers biology (MS), including environmental sciences and ecology, molecular biotechnology; electrical engineering (ME), including control system, potence system; human resources (MBA); mechanical engineering (ME, MS), including aerospace, energy. *Program availability:* Part-time, evening/weekend. *Degree requirements:* For master's, comprehensive exam, research project. *Entrance requirements:* For master's, EXADEP, GRE General Test, letters of recommendation. *Expenses: Tuition:* Full-time $3870; part-time $1935 per year. *Required fees:* $735; $642 per unit.

Kansas State University, Graduate School, College of Engineering, Department of Electrical and Computer Engineering, Manhattan, KS 66506. Offers electrical engineering (MS), including bioengineering, communication systems, design of computer systems, electrical engineering, energy and power systems, integrated circuits and devices, real time embedded systems, renewable energy, signal processing. *Program availability:* Part-time, evening/weekend, online learning. *Degree requirements:* For master's, thesis or alternative, final exam; for doctorate, thesis/dissertation, final exam, preliminary exams. *Entrance requirements:* For master's, GRE General Test, bachelor's degree in electrical engineering or computer science, minimum GPA of 3.0; for doctorate, GRE General Test. Additional exam requirements/recommendations for international students: required—TOEFL (minimum score 600 paper-based; 85 iBT). Electronic applications accepted.

Lawrence Technological University, College of Engineering, Southfield, MI 48075-1058. Offers architectural engineering (MS); automotive engineering (MS); biomedical engineering (MS); civil engineering (MA, MS, PhD), including environmental engineering (MS), geotechnical engineering (MS), structural engineering (MS), transportation engineering (MS), water resource engineering (MS); construction engineering management (MA); electrical and computer engineering (MS); engineering management (MEM); engineering technology (MS); fire engineering (MS); industrial engineering (MS), including healthcare systems; manufacturing systems (ME); mechanical engineering (MS, DE, PhD), including automotive engineering (MS), energy engineering (MS), manufacturing (DE), solid mechanics (MS), thermal/fluid systems (MS); mechatronic systems engineering (MS). *Program availability:* Part-time, evening/weekend. *Faculty:* 23 full-time (2 women), 20 part-time/adjunct (1 woman). *Students:* 14 full-time (5 women), 286 part-time (54 women); includes 26 minority (13 Black or African American, non-Hispanic/Latino; 8 Asian, non-Hispanic/Latino; 3 Hispanic/Latino; 2 Two or more races, non-Hispanic/Latino), 150 international. Average age 29. 384 applicants, 58% accepted, 74 enrolled. In 2019, 223 master's, 7 doctorates awarded. Terminal master's awarded for partial completion of doctoral program. *Degree requirements:* For master's, thesis optional; for doctorate, comprehensive exam, thesis/dissertation optional. *Entrance requirements:* Additional exam requirements/recommendations for international students: required—TOEFL (minimum score 550 paper-based; 79 iBT), IELTS (minimum score 6.5). *Application deadline:* For fall admission, 5/24 for international students; for spring admission, 10/13 for international students; for summer admission, 2/18 for international students. Applications are processed on a rolling basis. Application fee: $50. Electronic applications accepted. *Expenses: Tuition:* Full-time $16,618; part-time $8309 per year. *Required fees:* $600; $600. *Financial support:* In 2019–20, 21 students received support. Unspecified assistantships available. Financial award application deadline: 4/1; financial award applicants required to submit FAFSA. *Unit head:* Dr. Nabil Grace, Dean, 248-204-2500, Fax: 248-204-2509, E-mail: engrdean@ltu.edu. *Application contact:* Jane Rohrback, Director of Admissions, 248-204-3160, Fax: 248-204-2228, E-mail: admissions@ltu.edu.
Website: http://www.ltu.edu/engineering/index.asp

Lehigh University, P.C. Rossin College of Engineering and Applied Science, Program in Energy Systems Engineering, Bethlehem, PA 18015. Offers M Eng. *Program availability:* Part-time. *Faculty:* 1 full-time (0 women). *Students:* 7 full-time (0 women), 2 part-time (both women); includes 2 minority (1 Asian, non-Hispanic/Latino; 1 Hispanic/Latino), 2 international. Average age 25. 20 applicants, 95% accepted, 1 enrolled. In 2019, 9 master's awarded. *Entrance requirements:* For master's, GRE, bachelor's degree. Additional exam requirements/recommendations for international students: required—TOEFL (minimum score 79 iBT), IELTS (minimum score 6.5), TOEFL or IELTS required. *Application deadline:* For fall admission, 5/15 for domestic and international students. Application fee: $75. *Expenses:* Contact institution. *Financial support:* Application deadline: 1/15. *Unit head:* Prof. Ramesh Shankar, PhD, Director, 610-758-3529, E-mail: ras816@lehigh.edu. *Application contact:* Susan Kanarek, Graduate Coordinator, 610-758-3650, E-mail: sak319@lehigh.edu.
Website: https://engineering.lehigh.edu/ese

New Jersey Institute of Technology, Newark College of Engineering, Newark, NJ 07102. Offers biomedical engineering (MS, PhD); biopharmaceutical engineering (MS); chemical engineering (MS, PhD); civil engineering (MS, PhD); computer engineering (MS); critical infrastructure systems (MS); electrical engineering (MS, PhD); engineering management (MS); engineering science (MS); environmental engineering (MS, PhD); healthcare systems management (MS); industrial engineering (MS, PhD); internet engineering (MS); manufacturing systems engineering (MS); materials science & engineering (PhD); materials science and engineering (MS); mechanical engineering (MS, PhD); occupational safety and health engineering (MS). *Program availability:* Part-time, evening/weekend. *Faculty:* 151 full-time (29 women), 135 part-time/adjunct (15 women). *Students:* 576 full-time (161 women), 528 part-time (111 women); includes 366 minority (61 Black or African American, non-Hispanic/Latino; 1 American Indian or Alaska Native, non-Hispanic/Latino; 166 Asian, non-Hispanic/Latino; 115 Hispanic/Latino; 23 Two or more races, non-Hispanic/Latino), 450 international. Average age 28. 2,053 applicants, 67% accepted, 338 enrolled. In 2019, 474 master's, 30 doctorates awarded. Terminal master's awarded for partial completion of doctoral program. *Degree requirements:* For master's, thesis (for some programs); for doctorate, thesis/dissertation. *Entrance requirements:* For master's, GRE General Test, minimum GPA 2.8, personal statement, 1 letter of recommendation, transcripts; for doctorate, GRE General Test, minimum GPA of 3.5, personal statement, 3 letters of recommendation, transcripts. Additional exam requirements/recommendations for international students: required—TOEFL (minimum score 550 paper-based; 79 iBT), IELTS (minimum score 6.5). *Application deadline:* For fall admission, 6/1 priority date for domestic students, 5/1 priority date for international students; for spring admission, 11/15 priority date for domestic and international students. Applications are processed on a rolling basis. Application fee: $75. Electronic applications accepted. *Expenses:* $23,828 per year (in-state), $33,744 per year (out-of-state). *Financial support:* In 2019–20, 352 students received support, including 33 fellowships with full tuition reimbursements available (averaging $24,000 per year), 89 research assistantships with full tuition reimbursements available (averaging $24,000 per year), 112 teaching assistantships with full tuition reimbursements available (averaging $24,000 per year); career-related internships or fieldwork, Federal Work-Study, scholarships/grants, and unspecified assistantships also available. Financial award application deadline: 1/15. *Unit head:* Dr. Moshe Kam, Dean, 973-596-5534, Fax: 973-596-2316, E-mail: moshe.kam@njit.edu. *Application contact:* Stephen Eck, Executive Director of University Admissions, 973-596-3300, Fax: 973-596-3461, E-mail: admissions@njit.edu.
Website: http://engineering.njit.edu/

New York Institute of Technology, College of Engineering and Computing Sciences, Department of Energy Management, Old Westbury, NY 11568. Offers energy technology (Advanced Certificate); environmental management (Advanced Certificate); facilities management (Advanced Certificate); infrastructure security management (Advanced Certificate). *Program availability:* Part-time, evening/weekend, 100% online, blended/hybrid learning. *Faculty:* 3 full-time (1 woman), 6 part-time/adjunct (1 woman). *Students:* 33 full-time (4 women), 33 part-time (7 women); includes 18 minority (5 Black or African American, non-Hispanic/Latino; 5 Asian, non-Hispanic/Latino; 7 Hispanic/Latino; 1 Two or more races, non-Hispanic/Latino), 27 international. Average age 30. 114 applicants, 82% accepted, 24 enrolled. In 2019, 2 Advanced Certificates awarded. *Entrance requirements:* For degree, GRE is required for international students and for domestic students who do not meet the minimum GPA requirement, bachelor's degree or its equivalent from an accredited college or university; a background in engineering or management is desirable but not required. Copies of transcripts for all schools attended and proof of degree. Additional exam requirements/recommendations for international students: required—TOEFL (minimum score 79 iBT), IELTS (minimum score 6), PTE (minimum score 53), Duolingo English Test. *Application deadline:* For fall admission, 7/1 for domestic students, 6/1 for international students; for spring admission, 12/1 for domestic and international students. Applications are processed on a rolling basis. Application fee: $50. Electronic applications accepted. *Expenses: Tuition:* Full-time $23,760; part-time $1320 per credit. *Required fees:* $260; $220 per unit. Full-time tuition and fees vary according to degree level and program. Part-time tuition and fees vary according to course load and program. *Financial support:* In 2019–20, 18 students received support. Research assistantships, teaching assistantships, Federal Work-Study, scholarships/grants, and unspecified assistantships available. Support available to part-time students. Financial award application deadline: 2/15; financial award applicants required to submit FAFSA. *Unit head:* Dr. Robert Amundsen, Department Chair, 516-686-7578, E-mail: ramundse@nyit.edu. *Application contact:* Alice Dolitsky, Director, Graduate Admissions, 800-345-6948, Fax: 516-686-1116, E-mail: grad@nyit.edu.
Website: https://www.nyit.edu/departments/energy_management

North Carolina Agricultural and Technical State University, The Graduate College, College of Engineering, Department of Electrical and Computer Engineering, Greensboro, NC 27411. Offers electrical engineering (MSEE, PhD), including communications and signal processing, computer engineering, electronic and optical materials and devices, power systems and control. *Program availability:* Part-time. *Degree requirements:* For master's, project, thesis defense; for doctorate, thesis/dissertation. *Entrance requirements:* For master's, GRE General Test, GRE Subject Test, minimum GPA of 2.8; for doctorate, GRE General Test, minimum GPA of 3.0.

Northeastern University, College of Engineering, Boston, MA 02115-5096. Offers bioengineering (MS, PhD); chemical engineering (MS, PhD); civil engineering (MS, PhD); computer engineering (PhD); computer systems engineering (MS); electrical and computer engineering (MS); electrical and computer engineering leadership (MS); electrical engineering (PhD); energy systems (MS); engineering and public policy (MS); engineering management (MS, Certificate); environmental engineering (MS); industrial engineering (MS, PhD); information assurance (PhD); information systems (MS); interdisciplinary engineering (PhD); mechanical engineering (PhD); operations research (MS); telecommunication systems management (MS). *Program availability:* Part-time, online learning. Electronic applications accepted. *Expenses:* Contact institution.

Saginaw Valley State University, College of Science, Engineering, and Technology, University Center, MI 48710. Offers computer science and information systems (MS); energy and materials (MS). *Program availability:* Part-time, evening/weekend. *Faculty:* 6 full-time (1 woman), 1 part-time/adjunct (0 women). *Students:* 7 full-time (2 women), 11 part-time (1 woman); includes 2 minority (both Asian, non-Hispanic/Latino), 4 international. Average age 32. 29 applicants, 62% accepted, 4 enrolled. In 2019, 4 master's awarded. *Degree requirements:* For master's, field project or thesis work. *Entrance requirements:* For master's, minimum GPA of 3.0. Additional exam requirements/recommendations for international students: required—TOEFL (minimum score 550 paper-based; 79 iBT). *Application deadline:* For fall admission, 7/15 for international students; for winter admission, 11/15 for international students; for spring admission, 4/15 for international students. Applications are processed on a rolling basis. Application fee: $30 ($90 for international students). Electronic applications accepted. *Expenses: Tuition, area resident:* Full-time $11,212; part-time $622.90 per credit hour. Tuition, state resident: full-time $11,212; part-time $622.90 per credit hour. Tuition, nonresident: full-time $11,212; part-time $1253 per credit hour. *Required fees:* $263; $14.60 per credit hour. Tuition and fees vary according to course load, degree level and program. *Financial support:* Federal Work-Study and scholarships/grants available. Support available to part-time students. Financial award application deadline: 4/1; financial award applicants required to submit FAFSA. *Unit head:* Dr. Robert Tuttle, Program Coordinator, 989-964-4144, Fax: 989-964-2717. *Application contact:* Jenna Briggs, Director, Graduate and International Admissions, 989-964-6096, Fax: 989-964-2788, E-mail: gradadm@svsu.edu.
Website: http://www.svsu.edu/collegeofscienceengineeringtechnology/

San Francisco State University, Division of Graduate Studies, College of Science and Engineering, School of Engineering, San Francisco, CA 94132-1722. Offers embedded electrical and computer systems (MS); energy systems (MS); structural/earthquake engineering (MS). *Program availability:* Part-time. *Application deadline:* Applications are processed on a rolling basis. Electronic applications accepted. *Expenses: Tuition, area resident:* Full-time $7176; part-time $4164 per year. Tuition, state resident: full-time $7176; part-time $4164 per year. Tuition, nonresident: full-time $16,680; part-time $396 per unit. *International tuition:* $16,680 full-time. *Required fees:* $1524; $1524 per unit. $762 per semester. Tuition and fees vary according to degree level and program. *Unit head:* Dr. Kwok-Siong Teh, Director, 415-338-1228, Fax: 415-338-0525, E-mail: ksteh@sfsu.edu. *Application contact:* Dr. Hamid Shahnasser, Graduate Coordinator, 415-338-2124, Fax: 415-338-0525, E-mail: hamid@sfsu.edu.
Website: http://engineering.sfsu.edu/

Santa Clara University, School of Engineering, Santa Clara, CA 95053. Offers applied mathematics (MS); bioengineering (MS); civil, environmental, and sustainable engineering (MS); computer science and engineering (MS, PhD, Engineer); electrical engineering (MS, PhD, Engineer); engineering management and leadership (MS); mechanical engineering (MS, PhD, Engineer); power systems and sustainable energy (MS); software engineering (MS). *Program availability:* Part-time. *Entrance requirements:* For master's, GRE, official transcript; for doctorate, GRE, Official transcript, 500 word statement of purpose, three letters of recommendation. Additional exam requirements/recommendations for international students: required—TOEFL (minimum score 79 iBT), IELTS (minimum score 6.5). Electronic applications accepted.

Southern Illinois University Carbondale, Graduate School, College of Engineering, Program in Engineering Science, Carbondale, IL 62901-4701. Offers engineering science (PhD), including civil and environmental engineering, electrical and computer engineering, mechanical engineering and energy processes, mining and mineral resources engineering. *Degree requirements:* For doctorate, thesis/dissertation. *Entrance requirements:* For doctorate, GRE General Test, minimum GPA of 3.5. Additional exam requirements/recommendations for international students: required—TOEFL.

Stanford University, School of Earth, Energy and Environmental Sciences, Department of Energy Resources Engineering, Stanford, CA 94305-2004. Offers MS, PhD, Eng. *Expenses: Tuition:* Full-time $52,479; part-time $34,110 per unit. *Required fees:* $672; $224 per quarter. Tuition and fees vary according to program and student level.

Stanford University, School of Engineering, Department of Civil and Environmental Engineering, Stanford, CA 94305-2004. Offers atmosphere and energy (MS, PhD); construction (MS), including construction engineering and management, design-construction integration, sustainable design and construction; environmental engineering and science (MS, PhD); environmental fluid mechanics and hydrology (PhD); structural engineering (MS). *Expenses: Tuition:* Full-time $52,479; part-time

$34,110 per unit. *Required fees:* $672; $224 per quarter. Tuition and fees vary according to program and student level.
Website: http://www-ce.stanford.edu/

Texas A&M University–Kingsville, College of Graduate Studies, Frank H. Dotterweich College of Engineering, Program in Sustainable Energy Systems Engineering, Kingsville, TX 78363. Offers PhD. *Degree requirements:* For doctorate, variable foreign language requirement, comprehensive exam, thesis/dissertation (for some programs). *Entrance requirements:* For doctorate, GRE, MAT, GMAT, bachelor's or master's degree in engineering or science, curriculum vitae, official transcripts, statement of purpose, three letters of recommendation. Additional exam requirements/recommendations for international students: required—TOEFL (minimum score 550 paper-based; 79 iBT). Electronic applications accepted.

Texas Tech University, Graduate School, Interdisciplinary Programs, Lubbock, TX 79409-1030. Offers arid land studies (MS); biotechnology (MS); heritage and museum sciences (MA); interdisciplinary studies (MA, MS); wind science and engineering (PhD); JD/MS. *Program availability:* Part-time, 100% online, blended/hybrid learning. *Faculty:* 5 full-time (3 women). *Students:* 114 full-time (46 women), 94 part-time (59 women); includes 72 minority (30 Black or African American, non-Hispanic/Latino; 3 Asian, non-Hispanic/Latino; 31 Hispanic/Latino; 8 Two or more races, non-Hispanic/Latino), 34 international. Average age 31. 118 applicants, 85% accepted, 66 enrolled. In 2019, 57 master's, 4 doctorates awarded. Terminal master's awarded for partial completion of doctoral program. *Degree requirements:* For master's, comprehensive exam (for some programs), thesis (for some programs); for doctorate, comprehensive exam, thesis/dissertation (for some programs). *Entrance requirements:* Additional exam requirements/recommendations for international students: required—TOEFL (minimum score 550 paper-based; 79 iBT), IELTS (minimum score 6.5), PTE (minimum score 60), Cambridge Advanced (B), Cambridge Proficiency (C), ELS English for Academic Purposes (Level 112), Duolingo English Test (100). *Application deadline:* For fall admission, 6/1 priority date for domestic students, 1/15 priority date for international students; for spring admission, 9/1 priority date for domestic students, 6/15 priority date for international students. Applications are processed on a rolling basis. Application fee: $65. Electronic applications accepted. *Expenses:* Tuition, state resident: full-time $7944; part-time $331 per credit hour. Tuition, nonresident: full-time $17,904; part-time $746 per credit hour. *Required fees:* $2556; $55.50 per credit hour. $612 per semester. Tuition and fees vary according to program. *Financial support:* In 2019–20, 150 students received support, including 138 fellowships (averaging $5,639 per year), 26 research assistantships (averaging $18,634 per year), 16 teaching assistantships (averaging $13,404 per year); scholarships/grants and unspecified assistantships also available. Financial award application deadline: 4/15; financial award applicants required to submit FAFSA. *Unit head:* Dr. Mark A. Sheridan, Vice Provost for Graduate and Postdoctoral Affairs/Dean of the Graduate School, 806-834-5537, Fax: 806-742-1746, E-mail: mark.sheridan@ttu.edu. *Application contact:* Dr. David Doerfert, Associate Dean, 806-834-4477, Fax: 806-742-4038, E-mail: david.doerfert@ttu.edu.
Website: www.gradschool.ttu.edu

Universidad Autonoma de Guadalajara, Graduate Programs, Guadalajara, Mexico. Offers administrative law and justice (LL M); advertising and corporate communications (MA); architecture (M Arch); business (MBA); computational science (MCC); education (Ed M, Ed D); English-Spanish translation (MA); entrepreneurship and management (MBA); integrated management of digital animation (MA); international business (MIB); international corporate law (LL M); Internet technologies (MS); manufacturing systems (MMS); occupational health (MS); philosophy (MA, PhD); power electronics (MS); quality systems (MQS); renewable energy (MS); social evaluation of projects (MBA); strategic market research (MBA); tax law (MA); teaching mathematics (MA).

University at Buffalo, the State University of New York, Graduate School, School of Engineering and Applied Sciences, Department of Civil, Structural, and Environmental Engineering, Buffalo, NY 14260. Offers civil engineering (MS, PhD); engineering science (MS), including data sciences, green energy, Internet of Things, nanoelectronics; environmental and water resources engineering (MS). *Program availability:* Part-time, online learning. Terminal master's awarded for partial completion of doctoral program. *Degree requirements:* For master's, project, thesis, or comprehensive exam; for doctorate, thesis/dissertation. *Entrance requirements:* For master's and doctorate, GRE General Test, letters of reference. Additional exam requirements/recommendations for international students: required—TOEFL (minimum score 550 paper-based; 79 iBT). Electronic applications accepted. *Expenses: Tuition, area resident:* Full-time $11,310; part-time $471 per credit hour. Tuition, state resident: full-time $11,310; part-time $471 per credit hour. Tuition, nonresident: full-time $23,100; part-time $963 per credit hour. *International tuition:* $23,100 full-time. *Required fees:* $2820.

University of Alberta, Faculty of Graduate Studies and Research, Department of Electrical and Computer Engineering, Edmonton, AB T6G 2E1, Canada. Offers communications (M Eng, M Sc, PhD); computer engineering (M Eng, M Sc, PhD); electromagnetics (M Eng, M Sc, PhD); nanotechnology and microdevices (M Eng, M Sc, PhD); power/power electronics (M Eng, M Sc, PhD); systems (M Eng, M Sc, PhD). Terminal master's awarded for partial completion of doctoral program. *Degree requirements:* For master's, thesis; for doctorate, thesis/dissertation. *Entrance requirements:* Additional exam requirements/recommendations for international students: required—TOEFL. Electronic applications accepted.

The University of British Columbia, Faculty of Applied Science, Clean Energy Research Center, Vancouver, BC V6T 1Z1, Canada. Offers MEL. *Entrance requirements:* For master's, undergraduate degree in engineering or BS in environmental science; undergraduate thermodynamics course; three or more years of relevant work experience.

University of Calgary, Faculty of Graduate Studies, Schulich School of Engineering, Program in Chemical and Petroleum Engineering, Calgary, AB T2N 1N4, Canada. Offers chemical engineering (M Eng, M Sc, PhD); energy and environment engineering (M Eng, M Sc, PhD); energy and environmental systems (M Eng, M Sc, PhD); environmental engineering (M Eng, M Sc, PhD); petroleum engineering (M Eng, M Sc, PhD); reservoir characterization (M Eng, M Sc). *Program availability:* Part-time. *Degree requirements:* For master's, thesis (for some programs); for doctorate, comprehensive exam, thesis/dissertation, candidacy exam. *Entrance requirements:* For master's, minimum GPA of 3.0 or equivalent; for doctorate, minimum GPA of 3.5 or equivalent. Additional exam requirements/recommendations for international students: required—TOEFL (minimum score 550 paper-based; 80 iBT), IELTS (minimum score 7). Electronic applications accepted.

University of Calgary, Faculty of Graduate Studies, Schulich School of Engineering, Program in Civil Engineering, Calgary, AB T2N 1N4, Canada. Offers avalanche mechanics (M Sc, PhD); civil engineering (M Eng, M Sc, PhD); energy and environment engineering (M Eng, M Sc, PhD); environmental engineering (M Eng, M Sc, PhD); geotechnical engineering (M Eng, M Sc, PhD); materials science (M Eng, M Sc, PhD); project management (M Eng, M Sc, PhD); structures and solid mechanics (M Eng, M Sc, PhD); transportation engineering (M Eng, M Sc, PhD); water resources (M Eng, M Sc, PhD). *Program availability:* Part-time. *Degree requirements:* For master's, thesis; for doctorate, thesis/dissertation, written and oral candidacy exam. *Entrance requirements:* For master's, minimum GPA of 3.0; for doctorate, minimum GPA of 3.5. Additional exam requirements/recommendations for international students: required—TOEFL (minimum score 580 paper-based; 93 iBT), IELTS (minimum score 7). Electronic applications accepted.

University of Colorado Colorado Springs, College of Engineering and Applied Science, Program in General Engineering, Colorado Springs, CO 80918. Offers computer science (PhD); cybersecurity (ME); energy engineering (ME); engineering management (ME); engineering systems (ME); software engineering (ME); space operations (ME). *Program availability:* Part-time, evening/weekend, blended/hybrid learning. *Faculty:* 1 full-time (0 women), 12 part-time/adjunct (3 women). *Students:* 2 full-time (1 woman), 88 part-time (22 women); includes 23 minority (3 Black or African American, non-Hispanic/Latino; 6 Asian, non-Hispanic/Latino; 9 Hispanic/Latino; 5 Two or more races, non-Hispanic/Latino), 7 international. Average age 32. 36 applicants, 53% accepted, 15 enrolled. In 2019, 28 master's awarded. *Degree requirements:* For master's, thesis, portfolio, or project. *Entrance requirements:* For master's, GRE may be required based on past academic performance., Professional recommendation letters are required for all applicants.; for doctorate, GRE (minimum score of 148 new grading scale on the quantitative portion if the applicant has not graduated from a program of recognized standing), minimum GPA of 3.3 in the bachelor's or master's degree program attempted. Additional exam requirements/recommendations for international students: required—TOEFL (minimum score 80 iBT), IELTS (minimum score 6). *Application deadline:* For fall admission, 7/1 for domestic and international students; for spring admission, 11/1 for domestic and international students. Applications are processed on a rolling basis. Application fee: $60 ($100 for international students). Electronic applications accepted. *Expenses:* Contact institution. *Financial support:* In 2019–20, 5 students received support. Career-related internships or fieldwork, Federal Work-Study, scholarships/grants, traineeships, health care benefits, and unspecified assistantships available. Support available to part-time students. Financial award application deadline: 3/1; financial award applicants required to submit FAFSA. *Unit head:* Dr. Donald Rabern, Dean of Engineering and Applied Science, 719-255-3543, E-mail: drabern@uccs.edu. *Application contact:* Dawn House, Extended Studies Coordinator, 719-255-3246, E-mail: dhouse@uccs.edu.
Website: https://www.uccs.edu/easonline/degree-programs/engineering-management-degree

University of Illinois at Urbana-Champaign, Graduate College, College of Engineering, Department of Nuclear, Plasma, and Radiological Engineering, Urbana, IL 61801. Offers energy systems (M Eng); nuclear, plasma, and radiological engineering (MS, PhD). Terminal master's awarded for partial completion of doctoral program.

The University of Iowa, Graduate College, College of Engineering, Department of Mechanical Engineering, Iowa City, IA 52242-1316. Offers energy systems (MS, PhD); engineering design (MS, PhD); fluid dynamics (MS, PhD); materials and manufacturing (MS, PhD); wind energy (MS, PhD). Terminal master's awarded for partial completion of doctoral program. *Degree requirements:* For master's, oral exam or thesis; for doctorate, comprehensive exam, thesis/dissertation. *Entrance requirements:* For master's and doctorate, GRE (minimum Verbal score of 153, Quantitative 151), minimum undergraduate GPA of 3.0. Additional exam requirements/recommendations for international students: required—TOEFL (minimum score 600 paper-based; 100 iBT), IELTS (minimum score 7). Electronic applications accepted.

University of Massachusetts Lowell, Francis College of Engineering, Program in Energy Engineering, Lowell, MA 01854. Offers MS Eng, PhD. *Degree requirements:* For master's, thesis optional. *Entrance requirements:* For master's, GRE General Test. Additional exam requirements/recommendations for international students: required—TOEFL.

University of Memphis, Graduate School, Herff College of Engineering, Department of Mechanical Engineering, Memphis, TN 38152. Offers power systems (MS). *Program availability:* Part-time. *Students:* 4 full-time (1 woman), 4 part-time (0 women), 2 international. Average age 30. 9 applicants, 78% accepted, 3 enrolled. In 2019, 6 master's awarded. Terminal master's awarded for partial completion of doctoral program. *Degree requirements:* For master's, comprehensive exam, thesis or alternative; for doctorate, comprehensive exam, thesis/dissertation. *Entrance requirements:* For master's, GRE General Test, MAT, GMAT, BS in mechanical engineering, minimum undergraduate GPA of 3.0, three letters of recommendation; for doctorate, GRE, BS in mechanical engineering, minimum undergraduate GPA of 3.0, three letters of recommendation; for Graduate Certificate, letter of intent, two letters of recommendation. Additional exam requirements/recommendations for international students: required—TOEFL (minimum score 550 paper-based; 79 iBT). *Application deadline:* For fall admission, 8/1 for domestic students; for spring admission, 12/1 for domestic students. Application fee: $35 ($60 for international students). *Expenses: Tuition, area resident:* Full-time $9216; part-time $512 per credit hour. Tuition, state resident: full-time $9216; part-time $512 per credit hour. Tuition, nonresident: full-time $12,672; part-time $704 per credit hour. *International tuition:* $16,128 full-time. *Required fees:* $1530; $85 per credit hour. Tuition and fees vary according to program. *Financial support:* Fellowships with full tuition reimbursements, research assistantships with full tuition reimbursements, teaching assistantships with full tuition reimbursements, career-related internships or fieldwork, Federal Work-Study, scholarships/grants, and unspecified assistantships available. Financial award application deadline: 2/1; financial award applicants required to submit FAFSA. *Unit head:* Dr. Ali Fatemi, Chair, 901-678-2257, E-mail: afatemi@memphis.edu. *Application contact:* Dr. Teong Tan, Graduate Coordinator, 901-678-2701, Fax: 901-678-5459, E-mail: ttan@memphis.edu.
Website: http://www.memphis.edu/me/

University of Michigan, College of Engineering, Department of Integrative Systems and Design, Ann Arbor, MI 48109. Offers automotive engineering (M Eng); design science (MS, PhD); energy systems engineering (M Eng, MS); global automotive and manufacturing engineering (M Eng); manufacturing engineering (M Eng, D Eng); pharmaceutical engineering (M Eng); robotics and autonomous vehicles (M Eng); systems engineering and design (M Eng); MBA/M Eng; MSE/MS. *Program availability:* Part-time, online learning. Terminal master's awarded for partial completion of doctoral program. *Degree requirements:* For master's, capstone project; for doctorate, thesis/dissertation. *Entrance requirements:* For master's and doctorate, GRE. Additional exam requirements/recommendations for international students: required—TOEFL. Electronic applications accepted.

University of Michigan–Dearborn, College of Engineering and Computer Science, MSE Program in Energy Systems Engineering, Dearborn, MI 48128. Offers MSE. *Program availability:* Part-time, evening/weekend, 100% online. *Faculty:* 22 full-time (2 women), 15 part-time/adjunct (0 women). *Students:* 3 full-time (1 woman), 32 part-time (9 women); includes 4 minority (2 Asian, non-Hispanic/Latino; 1 Hispanic/Latino; 1 Two or more races, non-Hispanic/Latino), 5 international. Average age 28. 35 applicants, 57% accepted, 7 enrolled. In 2019, 11 master's awarded. *Entrance requirements:* Additional exam requirements/recommendations for international students: required—TOEFL (minimum score 560 paper-based; 84 iBT), IELTS (minimum score 6.5). *Application deadline:* For fall admission, 8/1 for domestic students, 5/1 for international students; for winter admission, 12/1 for domestic students, 9/1 for international students;

for spring admission, 4/1 for domestic students, 1/1 for international students. Applications are processed on a rolling basis. Application fee: $60. Electronic applications accepted. *Financial support:* Scholarships/grants, unspecified assistantships, and non-resident tuition scholarships available. Support available to part-time students. Financial award application deadline: 3/1; financial award applicants required to submit FAFSA. *Unit head:* Dr. Taehyung Kim, Director/Professor, 313-583-6736, E-mail: taehyung@umich.edu. *Application contact:* Office of Graduate Studies, 313-583-6321, E-mail: umd-graduatestudies@umich.edu.
Website: https://umdearborn.edu/cecs/departments/electrical-and-computer-engineering/graduate-programs/mse-energy-systems-engineering

The University of North Carolina at Charlotte, William States Lee College of Engineering, Department of Engineering Technology and Construction Management, Charlotte, NC 28223-0001. Offers applied energy (Graduate Certificate); applied energy & electromechanical systems (MS); construction and facilities management (MS); fire protection and safety management (MS), including fire protection, fire administration. *Program availability:* Part-time. *Faculty:* 25 full-time (8 women), 1 part-time/adjunct (0 women). *Students:* 36 full-time (9 women), 23 part-time (4 women); includes 7 minority (2 Black or African American, non-Hispanic/Latino; 1 Asian, non-Hispanic/Latino; 2 Hispanic/Latino; 2 Two or more races, non-Hispanic/Latino), 27 international. Average age 28. 68 applicants, 76% accepted, 12 enrolled. In 2019, 41 master's awarded. *Degree requirements:* For master's, thesis optional. *Entrance requirements:* For master's, GRE, minimum undergraduate GPA of 3.0, recommendations, statistics; integral and differential calculus (for students pursuing fire protection concentration or applied energy and electromechanical systems program); for Graduate Certificate, bachelor's degree in engineering, engineering technology, construction management or a closely-related technical or scientific field; undergraduate coursework of at least 3 semesters in engineering analysis or calculus; minimum GPA of 3.0. Additional exam requirements/recommendations for international students: required—TOEFL (minimum score 557 paper-based; 83 iBT), IELTS (minimum score 6.5), TOEFL (minimum score 557 paper-based, 83 iBT) or IELTS (6.5). *Application deadline:* Applications are processed on a rolling basis. Application fee: $75. Electronic applications accepted. *Expenses:* Contact institution. *Financial support:* In 2019–20, 22 students received support, including 22 research assistantships (averaging $6,115 per year); career-related internships or fieldwork, institutionally sponsored loans, scholarships/grants, and unspecified assistantships also available. Support available to part-time students. Financial award applicants required to submit FAFSA. *Unit head:* Dr. Anthony Brizendine, Chair, 704-687-5032, E-mail: albrizen@uncc.edu. *Application contact:* Kathy B. Giddings, Director of Graduate Admissions, 704-687-5503, Fax: 704-687-1668, E-mail: gradadm@uncc.edu.
Website: http://et.uncc.edu/

The University of North Carolina at Charlotte, William States Lee College of Engineering, Department of Systems Engineering and Engineering Management, Charlotte, NC 28223-0001. Offers energy analytics (Graduate Certificate); engineering management (MSEM); Lean Six Sigma (Graduate Certificate); logistics and supply chains (Graduate Certificate); systems and analytics (Graduate Certificate). *Program availability:* Part-time, evening/weekend, 100% online, blended/hybrid learning. *Faculty:* 9 full-time (2 women), 1 part-time/adjunct (0 women). *Students:* 24 full-time (7 women), 34 part-time (8 women); includes 16 minority (8 Black or African American, non-Hispanic/Latino; 2 American Indian or Alaska Native, non-Hispanic/Latino; 5 Asian, non-Hispanic/Latino; 1 Hispanic/Latino), 23 international. Average age 28. 104 applicants, 78% accepted, 25 enrolled. In 2019, 36 master's, 1 other advanced degree awarded. *Degree requirements:* For master's, thesis optional. *Entrance requirements:* For master's, GRE or MAT, bachelor's degree in engineering or a closely-related technical or scientific field, or in business, provided relevant technical course requirements have been met; undergraduate coursework in engineering economics, calculus, or statistics; minimum GPA of 3.0; statement of purpose; three letters of recommendation; for Graduate Certificate, bachelor's degree in engineering or closely-related technical or scientific field, or in business, provided relevant technical course requirements have been met; minimum GPA of 3.0; undergraduate coursework in engineering economics, calculus, and statistics; written description of work experience. Additional exam requirements/recommendations for international students: required—TOEFL (minimum score 557 paper-based; 83 iBT), IELTS (minimum score 6.5), TOEFL (minimum score 557 paper-based, 83 iBT) or IELTS (6.5). *Application deadline:* Applications are processed on a rolling basis. Application fee: $75. Electronic applications accepted. *Expenses:* Contact institution. *Financial support:* In 2019–20, 3 students received support, including 2 research assistantships (averaging $7,950 per year), 1 teaching assistantship (averaging $5,600 per year); career-related internships or fieldwork, institutionally sponsored loans, scholarships/grants, and unspecified assistantships also available. Support available to part-time students. Financial award applicants required to submit FAFSA. *Unit head:* Dr. Simon M. Hsiang, Professor and Deparment Chair, 704-687-1958, E-mail: shsiang1@uncc.edu. *Application contact:* Kathy B. Giddings, Director of Graduate Admissions, 704-687-5503, Fax: 704-687-1668, E-mail: gradadm@uncc.edu.
Website: http://seem.uncc.edu/

University of North Texas, Toulouse Graduate School, Denton, TX 76203-5459. Offers accounting (MS); applied anthropology (MA, MS); applied behavior analysis (Certificate); applied geography (MA); applied technology and performance improvement (M Ed, MS); art education (MA); art history (MA); arts leadership (Certificate); audiology (Au D); behavior analysis (MS); behavioral science (PhD); biochemistry and molecular biology (MS); biology (MA, MS); biomedical engineering (MS); business analysis (MS); chemistry (MS); clinical health psychology (PhD); communication studies (MA, MS); computer engineering (MS); computer science (MS); counseling (M Ed, MS), including clinical mental health counseling (MS), college and university counseling, elementary school counseling, secondary school counseling; creative writing (MA); criminal justice (MS); curriculum and instruction (M Ed); decision sciences (MBA); design (MA, MFA), including fashion design (MFA), innovation studies, interior design (MFA); early childhood studies (MS); economics (MS); educational leadership (M Ed, Ed D); educational psychology (MS, PhD), including family studies (MS), gifted and talented (MS), human development (MS), learning and cognition (MS), research, measurement and evaluation (MS); electrical engineering (MS); emergency management (MPA); engineering technology (MS); English (MA); English as a second language (MA); environmental science (MS); finance (MBA, MS); financial management (MPA); French (MA); health services management (MBA); higher education (M Ed, Ed D); history (MA, MS); hospitality management (MS); human resources management (MPA); information science (MS); information systems (PhD); information technologies (MBA); interdisciplinary studies (MA, MS); international studies (MA); international sustainable tourism (MS); jazz studies (MM); journalism (MA, MJ, Graduate Certificate), including interactive and virtual digital communication (Graduate Certificate), narrative journalism (Graduate Certificate), public relations (Graduate Certificate); kinesiology (MS); linguistics (MA); local government management (MPA); logistics (PhD); logistics and supply chain management (MBA); long-term care, senior housing, and aging services (MA); management (PhD); marketing (MBA); mathematics (MA, MS); mechanical and energy engineering (MS, PhD); music (MA), including ethnomusicology, music theory, musicology, performance; music composition (PhD); music education (MM Ed, PhD); nonprofit management (MPA); operations and supply chain management (MBA); performance (MM, DMA); philosophy (MA); political science (MA); professional and technical communication (MA); radio, television and film (MA, MFA); rehabilitation counseling (Certificate); sociology (MA); Spanish (MA); special education (M Ed); speech-language pathology (MA); strategic management (MBA); studio art (MFA); teaching (M Ed); MBA/MS. *Program availability:* Part-time, evening/weekend, online learning. Terminal master's awarded for partial completion of doctoral program. *Degree requirements:* For master's, variable foreign language requirement, comprehensive exam (for some programs), thesis (for some programs); for doctorate, variable foreign language requirement, comprehensive exam (for some programs), thesis/dissertation; for other advanced degree, variable foreign language requirement, comprehensive exam (for some programs). *Entrance requirements:* For master's and doctorate, GRE, GMAT. Additional exam requirements/recommendations for international students: required—TOEFL (minimum score 550 paper-based; 79 iBT). Electronic applications accepted.

University of Puerto Rico at Mayagüez, Graduate Studies, College of Engineering, Department of Mechanical Engineering, Mayagüez, PR 00681-9000. Offers mechanical engineering (ME, MS, PhD), including aerospace and unmanned vehicles (ME), automation/mechatronics, bioengineering, fluid mechanics, heat transfer/energy systems, manufacturing, mechanics of materials, micro and nano engineering. *Program availability:* Part-time. Terminal master's awarded for partial completion of doctoral program. *Degree requirements:* For master's, one foreign language, comprehensive exam, thesis; for doctorate, one foreign language, comprehensive exam, thesis/dissertation. *Entrance requirements:* For master's, BS in mechanical engineering or its equivalent; for doctorate, GRE, BS or MS in mechanical engineering or its equivalent; minimum GPA of 3.0. Additional exam requirements/recommendations for international students: required—TOEFL (minimum score 80 iBT). Electronic applications accepted.

The University of Tennessee, Graduate School, Tickle College of Engineering, Bredesen Center for Interdisciplinary Research and Graduate Education, Knoxville, TN 37996. Offers data science and engineering (PhD); energy science and engineering (PhD). *Students:* 76 full-time (25 women); includes 12 minority (3 Black or African American, non-Hispanic/Latino; 3 Asian, non-Hispanic/Latino; 4 Hispanic/Latino; 2 Two or more races, non-Hispanic/Latino), 24 international. Average age 30. 83 applicants, 24% accepted, 20 enrolled. In 2019, 12 doctorates awarded. *Degree requirements:* For doctorate, comprehensive exam, thesis/dissertation, qualifying examination. *Entrance requirements:* For doctorate, GRE General Test, research interest letter, resume/curriculum vitae, 3 letters of recommendation. Additional exam requirements/recommendations for international students: required—TOEFL (minimum score 550 paper-based; 80 iBT), IELTS (minimum score 6.5). *Application deadline:* For fall admission, 1/31 for domestic and international students. Applications are processed on a rolling basis. Application fee: $60. Electronic applications accepted. *Financial support:* In 2019–20, 76 students received support, including 76 fellowships with full tuition reimbursements available (averaging $28,000 per year); health care benefits also available. Financial award application deadline: 1/31. *Unit head:* Dr. Sudarsanam Babu, Director, 865-974-7999, Fax: 865-974-9482, E-mail: sbabu@utk.edu. *Application contact:* Dr. Sudarsanam Babu, Director, 865-974-7999, Fax: 865-974-9482, E-mail: sbabu@utk.edu.
Website: http://bredesencenter.utk.edu/

The University of Tennessee at Chattanooga, Engineering Management and Technology Program, Chattanooga, TN 37403. Offers construction management (Graduate Certificate); engineering management (MS); fundamentals of engineering management (Graduate Certificate); leadership and ethics (Graduate Certificate); logistics and supply chain management (Graduate Certificate); power systems management (Graduate Certificate); project and technology management (Graduate Certificate); quality management (Graduate Certificate). *Program availability:* 100% online, blended/hybrid learning. *Students:* 10 full-time (4 women), 44 part-time (6 women); includes 9 minority (4 Black or African American, non-Hispanic/Latino; 1 Asian, non-Hispanic/Latino; 2 Hispanic/Latino; 2 Two or more races, non-Hispanic/Latino), 9 international. Average age 33. 24 applicants, 88% accepted, 8 enrolled. In 2019, 21 master's, 1 other advanced degree awarded. *Degree requirements:* For master's, thesis or alternative, Project as alternative to thesis. *Entrance requirements:* For master's, GRE General Test, letters of recommendation; minimum undergraduate GPA of 2.7 overall or 3.0 in final two years; for Graduate Certificate, baccalaureate degree and professional experience or have already been admitted to engineering/engineering management graduate program. Additional exam requirements/recommendations for international students: required—TOEFL (minimum score 550 paper-based; 79 iBT), IELTS (minimum score 6). *Application deadline:* For fall admission, 6/15 priority date for domestic students, 7/1 for international students; for spring admission, 11/1 priority date for domestic students, 11/1 for international students. Applications are processed on a rolling basis. Application fee: $35 ($40 for international students). Electronic applications accepted. *Financial support:* Research assistantships, teaching assistantships, career-related internships or fieldwork, scholarships/grants, and unspecified assistantships available. Support available to part-time students. Financial award application deadline: 7/1; financial award applicants required to submit FAFSA. *Unit head:* Dr. Ahad Nasab, Department Head, 423-425-4032, Fax: 423-425-5818, E-mail: Ahad-Nasab@utc.edu. *Application contact:* Dr. Joanne Romagni, Dean of the Graduate School, 423-425-4478, Fax: 423-425-5223, E-mail: joanne-romagni@utc.edu.
Website: https://www.utc.edu/college-engineering-computer-science/programs/engineering-management-and-technology/index.php

The University of Texas at El Paso, Graduate School, College of Engineering, Department of Electrical and Computer Engineering, El Paso, TX 79968-0001. Offers computer engineering (MS); electric power and energy systems (Graduate Certificate); electrical and computer engineering (PhD); electrical engineering (MS). *Program availability:* Part-time, evening/weekend. Terminal master's awarded for partial completion of doctoral program. *Degree requirements:* For master's, thesis optional; for doctorate, thesis/dissertation. *Entrance requirements:* For master's, GRE General Test, minimum GPA of 3.0; for doctorate, GRE General Test, minimum graduate GPA of 3.0. Additional exam requirements/recommendations for international students: required—TOEFL. Electronic applications accepted.

Washington State University, Voiland College of Engineering and Architecture, School of Electrical Engineering and Computer Science, Pullman, WA 99164-2752. Offers computer engineering (MS); computer science (MS); electrical engineering (MS); electrical engineering and computer science (PhD); electrical power engineering (MS). *Program availability:* Part-time. *Degree requirements:* For master's, comprehensive exam (for some programs), thesis or alternative; for doctorate, comprehensive exam, thesis/dissertation. *Entrance requirements:* For master's and doctorate, GRE General Test, minimum GPA of 3.0, 3 letters of recommendation, statement of purpose, transcripts. Additional exam requirements/recommendations for international students: required—TOEFL (minimum score 580 paper-based).

Wayne State University, College of Engineering, Department of Engineering Dean, Detroit, MI 48202. Offers MS, Graduate Certificate. *Students:* 41 full-time (8 women), 49 part-time (19 women); includes 18 minority (3 Black or African American, non-Hispanic/Latino; 10 Asian, non-Hispanic/Latino; 3 Hispanic/Latino; 2 Two or more races, non-

Hispanic/Latino), 43 international. Average age 29. 214 applicants, 43% accepted, 37 enrolled. In 2019, 19 master's, 3 other advanced degrees awarded. *Degree requirements:* For master's, thesis optional. *Entrance requirements:* For master's, bachelor's degree in engineering; minimum GPA of 3.0 or significant relevant professional experience; for Graduate Certificate, bachelor's degree in engineering; minimum GPA of 2.7 or significant relevant professional experience. Additional exam requirements/recommendations for international students: required—TOEFL (minimum score 550 paper-based; 79 iBT); recommended—IELTS (minimum score 6.5). *Application deadline:* For fall admission, 6/1 priority date for domestic students, 5/1 priority date for international students; for winter admission, 10/1 priority date for domestic students, 9/1 priority date for international students; for spring admission, 2/1 priority date for domestic students, 1/1 priority date for international students; for summer admission, 2/1 priority date for domestic students, 1/1 priority date for international students. Applications are processed on a rolling basis. Application fee: $50. Electronic applications accepted. *Expenses:* $790 per credit hour in-state tuition, $1579 per credit hour out-of-state tuition. MS degree is 32 credit hours. *Financial support:* In 2019–20, 29 students received support, including 9 teaching assistantships (averaging $20,792 per year); fellowships and scholarships/grants also available. Support available to part-time students. Financial award applicants required to submit FAFSA. *Unit head:* Dr. Gene Y. Liao, Program Director, 313-577-8078, E-mail: geneliao@wayne.edu. *Application contact:* Rob Carlson, Graduate Program Coordinator, 313-577-9615, E-mail: rcarlson@wayne.edu.
Website: http://engineering.wayne.edu/aet/

West Virginia University, Statler College of Engineering and Mineral Resources, Morgantown, WV 26506. Offers aerospace engineering (MSAE, PhD); chemical engineering (MS Ch E, PhD); civil engineering (MSCE, PhD); computer engineering (PhD); computer science (MSCS, PhD); electrical engineering (MSEE, PhD); energy systems engineering (MSESE); engineering (MSE); industrial engineering (MSIE, PhD); industrial hygiene (MS); material science and engineering (MSMSE, PhD); mechanical engineering (MSME, PhD); mining engineering (MS Min E, PhD); petroleum and natural gas engineering (MSPNGE, PhD); safety management (MS); software engineering (MSSE). *Program availability:* Part-time. Terminal master's awarded for partial completion of doctoral program. *Degree requirements:* For master's, thesis optional; for doctorate, comprehensive exam, thesis/dissertation. *Entrance requirements:* Additional exam requirements/recommendations for international students: required—TOEFL (minimum score 550 paper-based). Electronic applications accepted. *Expenses:* Contact institution.

Worcester Polytechnic Institute, Graduate Admissions, Programs in Interdisciplinary Studies, Worcester, MA 01609-2280. Offers bioscience administration (MS); nuclear science and engineering (Graduate Certificate); power systems management (MS); social science (PhD); system dynamics and innovation management (MS, Graduate Certificate); systems modeling (MS). *Program availability:* Part-time, evening/weekend, 100% online. Terminal master's awarded for partial completion of doctoral program. *Degree requirements:* For master's, thesis; for doctorate, comprehensive exam, thesis/dissertation. *Entrance requirements:* For master's and doctorate, 3 letters of recommendation. Additional exam requirements/recommendations for international students: required—TOEFL (minimum score 563 paper-based; 84 iBT), IELTS (minimum score 7). Electronic applications accepted.

Nuclear Engineering

Air Force Institute of Technology, Graduate School of Engineering and Management, Department of Engineering Physics, Dayton, OH 45433-7765. Offers applied physics (MS, PhD); electro-optics (MS, PhD); materials science (PhD); nuclear engineering (MS, PhD); space physics (MS). *Program availability:* Part-time. *Degree requirements:* For master's, thesis; for doctorate, thesis/dissertation. *Entrance requirements:* For master's and doctorate, GRE General Test, minimum GPA of 3.0, U.S. citizenship.

Arizona State University at Tempe, Ira A. Fulton Schools of Engineering, School of Electrical, Computer and Energy Engineering, Tempe, AZ 85287-5706. Offers electrical engineering (MS, MSE, PhD); nuclear power generation (Graduate Certificate). *Program availability:* Part-time, evening/weekend, online learning. Terminal master's awarded for partial completion of doctoral program. *Degree requirements:* For master's, thesis and defense (MS); comprehensive exams (MSE); interactive Program of Study (iPOS) submitted before completing 50 percent of required credit hours; for doctorate, comprehensive exam, thesis/dissertation, interactive Program of Study (iPOS) submitted before completing 50 percent of required credit hours. *Entrance requirements:* For master's, GRE, minimum GPA of 3.0 in last 2 years of work leading to bachelor's degree, 3.5 if from non-ABET accredited school; for doctorate, GRE, master's degree with minimum GPA of 3.5 or 3.6 in last 2 years of ABET-accredited undergraduate program. Additional exam requirements/recommendations for international students: required—TOEFL, IELTS, or PTE. Electronic applications accepted. *Expenses:* Contact institution.

Colorado School of Mines, Office of Graduate Studies, Department of Physics, Golden, CO 80401. Offers applied physics (MS, PhD); materials science (MS, PhD); nuclear engineering (ME, MS, PhD). *Program availability:* Part-time. *Degree requirements:* For master's, thesis (for some programs); for doctorate, comprehensive exam, thesis/dissertation. *Entrance requirements:* For master's and doctorate, GRE General Test, GRE Subject Test. Additional exam requirements/recommendations for international students: required—TOEFL (minimum score 550 paper-based; 79 iBT). Electronic applications accepted. *Expenses:* Tuition, state resident: full-time $16,650; part-time $925 per credit hour. Tuition, nonresident: full-time $37,350; part-time $2075 per credit hour. *International tuition:* $37,350 full-time. *Required fees:* $2412.

Georgia Institute of Technology, Graduate Studies, College of Engineering, George W. Woodruff School of Mechanical Engineering, Atlanta, GA 30332-0405. Offers mechanical engineering (MS, MSME, PhD); nuclear and radiological engineering and medical physics (MS, MSMP, MSNE, PhD), including medical physics (MS, MSMP), nuclear and radiological engineering (PhD), nuclear engineering (MSNE). *Program availability:* Part-time, 100% online. *Faculty:* 100 full-time (13 women), 5 part-time/adjunct (1 woman). *Students:* 608 full-time (110 women), 200 part-time (43 women); includes 205 minority (19 Black or African American, non-Hispanic/Latino; 1 American Indian or Alaska Native, non-Hispanic/Latino; 107 Asian, non-Hispanic/Latino; 47 Hispanic/Latino; 31 Two or more races, non-Hispanic/Latino), 231 international. Average age 26. 1,352 applicants, 32% accepted, 200 enrolled. In 2019, 229 master's, 56 doctorates awarded. Terminal master's awarded for partial completion of doctoral program. *Degree requirements:* For master's, thesis; for doctorate, comprehensive exam, thesis/dissertation. *Entrance requirements:* For master's, GRE General Test, minimum 3.0 for the MSNRE and MSMP; for doctorate, GRE General Test, minimum GPA of 3.3. Additional exam requirements/recommendations for international students: required—TOEFL (minimum score 94 iBT), IELTS (minimum score 7), TOEFL is the preferred method with the requirements shown on the programs. *Application deadline:* For fall admission, 2/1 for domestic and international students; for spring admission, 11/1 for domestic students, 10/1 for international students. Applications are processed on a rolling basis. Application fee: $75 ($85 for international students). Electronic applications accepted. *Expenses: Tuition, area resident:* Full-time $14,064; part-time $586 per credit hour. Tuition, state resident: full-time $14,064; part-time $586 per credit hour. Tuition, nonresident: full-time $29,140; part-time $1215 per credit hour. *International tuition:* $29,140 full-time. *Required fees:* $2024; $840 per semester. $2096. Tuition and fees vary according to course load. *Financial support:* In 2019–20, 41 fellowships, 395 research assistantships, 8 teaching assistantships were awarded; career-related internships or fieldwork, Federal Work-Study, institutionally sponsored loans, tuition waivers (full and partial), and unspecified assistantships also available. Support available to part-time students. Financial award application deadline: 7/1; financial award applicants required to submit FAFSA. *Unit head:* Samuel Graham, School Chair, 404-894-3200, Fax: 404-894-1658, E-mail: sgraham@gatech.edu. *Application contact:* Marla Bruner, Director of Graduate Studies, 404-894-1610, Fax: 404-894-1609, E-mail: gradinfo@mail.gatech.edu.
Website: http://www.me.gatech.edu

Idaho State University, Graduate School, College of Science and Engineering, Department of Nuclear Engineering, Pocatello, ID 83209. Offers nuclear science and engineering (MS, PhD). *Program availability:* Part-time. *Degree requirements:* For master's, comprehensive exam (for some programs), thesis, seminar; for doctorate, comprehensive exam, thesis/dissertation, oral and written exams at the end of 1st year. *Entrance requirements:* For master's, GRE; for doctorate, master's degree in engineering, physics, geosciences, or math; 3 letters of recommendation. Additional exam requirements/recommendations for international students: required—TOEFL (minimum score 550 paper-based; 80 iBT). Electronic applications accepted.

Kansas State University, Graduate School, College of Engineering, Department of Mechanical and Nuclear Engineering, Manhattan, KS 66506. Offers mechanical engineering (MS); nuclear engineering (PhD). *Degree requirements:* For master's, thesis optional; for doctorate, comprehensive exam, thesis/dissertation. *Entrance requirements:* For master's, GRE General Test; for doctorate, GRE General Test, master's degree in mechanical engineering; minimum GPA of 3.0 overall or last 60 hours in calculus-based engineering or related program. Additional exam requirements/recommendations for international students: required—TOEFL (minimum score 550 paper-based; 79 iBT). Electronic applications accepted.

Massachusetts Institute of Technology, School of Engineering, Department of Nuclear Science and Engineering, Cambridge, MA 02139. Offers SM, PhD, Sc D, NE. *Degree requirements:* For master's and NE, thesis; for doctorate, comprehensive exam, thesis/dissertation. *Entrance requirements:* For master's, doctorate, and NE, GRE General Test. Additional exam requirements/recommendations for international students: required—TOEFL, IELTS. Electronic applications accepted.

McMaster University, School of Graduate Studies, Faculty of Engineering, Department of Engineering Physics, Hamilton, ON L8S 4M2, Canada. Offers engineering physics (M Eng, MA Sc, PhD); nuclear engineering (PhD). *Degree requirements:* For master's, thesis or alternative; for doctorate, comprehensive exam, thesis/dissertation. *Entrance requirements:* For master's, minimum B average in engineering, mathematics, or physical sciences. Additional exam requirements/recommendations for international students: required—TOEFL (minimum score 550 paper-based).

Missouri University of Science and Technology, Department of Mining and Nuclear Engineering, Rolla, MO 65401. Offers explosives engineering (MS, PhD); mining engineering (MS, DE, PhD); nuclear engineering (MS, DE, PhD). *Degree requirements:* For master's, thesis optional; for doctorate, comprehensive exam. *Entrance requirements:* For master's, GRE (minimum score 600 quantitative, 3 writing); for doctorate, GRE (minimum score: quantitative 600, writing 3.5). Additional exam requirements/recommendations for international students: required—TOEFL (minimum score 550 paper-based). Electronic applications accepted. *Expenses:* Tuition, state resident: full-time $7839; part-time $435.50 per credit hour. Tuition, nonresident: full-time $22,169; part-time $1231.60 per credit hour. *International tuition:* $18,156.60 full-time. *Required fees:* $649.76. One-time fee: $119. Tuition and fees vary according to course load and program.

North Carolina State University, Graduate School, College of Engineering, Department of Nuclear Engineering, Raleigh, NC 27695. Offers MNE, MS, PhD. *Degree requirements:* For master's, thesis (for some programs); for doctorate, thesis/dissertation. *Entrance requirements:* For master's, bachelor's degree in engineering or GRE; for doctorate, engineering degree or GRE. Electronic applications accepted.

The Ohio State University, Graduate School, College of Engineering, Department of Mechanical and Aerospace Engineering, Program in Nuclear Engineering, Columbus, OH 43210. Offers MS, PhD. *Entrance requirements:* For master's and doctorate, GRE. Additional exam requirements/recommendations for international students: required—TOEFL (minimum score 550 paper-based; 79 iBT), Michigan English Language Assessment Battery (minimum score 82); recommended—IELTS (minimum score 7). Electronic applications accepted.

Oregon State University, College of Engineering, Program in Nuclear Engineering, Corvallis, OR 97331. Offers application of nuclear techniques (M Eng, MS, PhD). *Entrance requirements:* For master's and doctorate, GRE. Additional exam requirements/recommendations for international students: required—TOEFL (minimum score 80 iBT), IELTS (minimum score 6.5). *Expenses:* Contact institution.

Penn State University Park, Graduate School, College of Engineering, Department of Mechanical and Nuclear Engineering, University Park, PA 16802. Offers additive manufacturing and design (MS); mechanical engineering (MS, PhD); nuclear engineering (M Eng, MS, PhD).

Polytechnique Montréal, Graduate Programs, Institute of Nuclear Engineering, Montréal, QC H3C 3A7, Canada. Offers nuclear engineering (M Eng, PhD, DESS); nuclear engineering, socio-economics of energy (M Sc A). *Degree requirements:* For master's, one foreign language, thesis; for doctorate, one foreign language, thesis/dissertation. *Entrance requirements:* For master's, minimum GPA of 2.75; for doctorate, minimum GPA of 3.0.

Purdue University, College of Engineering, School of Nuclear Engineering, West Lafayette, IN 47906. Offers MS, MSNE, PhD. *Program availability:* Part-time. *Faculty:*

19. *Students:* 49. Terminal master's awarded for partial completion of doctoral program. *Degree requirements:* For master's, thesis optional; for doctorate, thesis/dissertation. *Application deadline:* For fall admission, 5/1 priority date for domestic students, 3/1 priority date for international students; for spring admission, 8/15 for domestic and international students. Applications are processed on a rolling basis. Application fee: $60 ($75 for international students). Electronic applications accepted. *Financial support:* Fellowships with full and partial tuition reimbursements, research assistantships with full and partial tuition reimbursements, teaching assistantships with full and partial tuition reimbursements, career-related internships or fieldwork, scholarships/grants, and unspecified assistantships available. Support available to part-time students. *Unit head:* Dr. Seungjin Kim, Head of the School of Nuclear Engineering, 765-494-5742, E-mail: seungjin@purdue.edu. *Application contact:* Teresa Luse, Graduate Administrator, E-mail: nuclss@purdue.edu.
Website: https://engineering.purdue.edu/NE

Rensselaer Polytechnic Institute, Graduate School, School of Engineering, Program in Nuclear Engineering and Science, Troy, NY 12180-3590. Offers M Eng, MS, D Eng, PhD. *Faculty:* 55 full-time (6 women), 1 part-time/adjunct (0 women). *Students:* 26 full-time (4 women), 1 part-time (0 women); includes 5 minority (1 Asian, non-Hispanic/Latino; 2 Hispanic/Latino; 2 Two or more races, non-Hispanic/Latino), 11 international. Average age 28. 36 applicants, 39% accepted, 4 enrolled. In 2019, 3 master's, 6 doctorates awarded. Terminal master's awarded for partial completion of doctoral program. *Degree requirements:* For master's, thesis (for some programs); for doctorate, thesis/dissertation. *Entrance requirements:* For master's and doctorate, GRE. Additional exam requirements/recommendations for international students: required—TOEFL (minimum score 600 paper-based; 100 iBT), IELTS (minimum score 7), PTE (minimum score 68). *Application deadline:* For fall admission, 1/1 priority date for domestic and international students; for spring admission, 8/15 priority date for domestic and international students. Applications are processed on a rolling basis. Application fee: $75. Electronic applications accepted. *Financial support:* In 2019–20, research assistantships (averaging $23,000 per year), teaching assistantships (averaging $23,000 per year) were awarded; fellowships also available. Financial award application deadline: 1/1. *Unit head:* Dr. Theo Borca-Tasciuc, Graduate Program Director, 518-276-2627, E-mail: borcat@rpi.edu. *Application contact:* Jarron Decker, Director of Graduate Admissions, 518-276-6216, Fax: 518-276-4072, E-mail: gradadmissions@rpi.edu.
Website: http://mane.rpi.edu/

Texas A&M University, College of Engineering, Department of Nuclear Engineering, College Station, TX 77843. Offers nuclear engineering (M Eng, PhD). *Faculty:* 20. *Students:* 124 full-time (25 women), 29 part-time (7 women); includes 35 minority (3 Black or African American, non-Hispanic/Latino; 1 American Indian or Alaska Native, non-Hispanic/Latino; 5 Asian, non-Hispanic/Latino; 23 Hispanic/Latino; 3 Two or more races, non-Hispanic/Latino), 49 international. Average age 29. 83 applicants, 83% accepted, 39 enrolled. In 2019, 16 master's, 17 doctorates awarded. *Degree requirements:* For master's, comprehensive exam, thesis optional; for doctorate, comprehensive exam, thesis/dissertation. *Entrance requirements:* For master's and doctorate, GRE General Test, 3 letters of recommendation. Additional exam requirements/recommendations for international students: required—TOEFL (minimum score 550 paper-based; 80 iBT), IELTS (minimum score 6), PTE (minimum score 53). *Application deadline:* Applications are processed on a rolling basis. Application fee: $65 ($90 for international students). Electronic applications accepted. *Expenses:* Contact institution. *Financial support:* In 2019–20, 121 students received support, including 10 fellowships with tuition reimbursements available (averaging $27,561 per year), 86 research assistantships with tuition reimbursements available (averaging $17,574 per year), 25 teaching assistantships with tuition reimbursements available (averaging $14,165 per year); career-related internships or fieldwork, institutionally sponsored loans, scholarships/grants, traineeships, health care benefits, tuition waivers (full and partial), and unspecified assistantships also available. Support available to part-time students. Financial award application deadline: 3/15; financial award applicants required to submit FAFSA. *Unit head:* Dr. Michael Nastasi, Head, 979-862-2636, E-mail: nuen-dh@tamu.edu. *Application contact:* Tiffany Hector, Graduate Academic Advisor, 979-458-2072, E-mail: tiffany.alcala@tamu.edu.
Website: https://engineering.tamu.edu/nuclear

University of California, Berkeley, Graduate Division, College of Engineering, Department of Nuclear Engineering, Berkeley, CA 94720-1730. Offers M Eng, MS, PhD. Terminal master's awarded for partial completion of doctoral program. *Degree requirements:* For master's, comprehensive exam (for some programs), thesis (for some programs), project or thesis; for doctorate, thesis/dissertation, oral exam. *Entrance requirements:* For master's and doctorate, GRE General Test, minimum GPA of 3.0, 3 letters of recommendation. Additional exam requirements/recommendations for international students: required—TOEFL (minimum score 570 paper-based; 90 iBT). Electronic applications accepted.

University of Cincinnati, Graduate School, College of Engineering and Applied Science, Department of Mechanical and Materials Engineering, Cincinnati, OH 45221. Offers industrial engineering (PhD); mechanical engineering (MS, PhD); nuclear engineering (PhD); MBA/MS. *Program availability:* Part-time, evening/weekend. Terminal master's awarded for partial completion of doctoral program. *Degree requirements:* For doctorate, thesis/dissertation. *Entrance requirements:* For master's and doctorate, GRE General Test. Additional exam requirements/recommendations for international students: required—TOEFL (minimum score 575 paper-based). Electronic applications accepted.

University of Florida, Graduate School, Herbert Wertheim College of Engineering, Department of Materials Science and Engineering, Nuclear Engineering Program, Gainesville, FL 32611. Offers imaging science and technology (PhD); nuclear engineering sciences (ME, MS, PhD). *Program availability:* Part-time. Terminal master's awarded for partial completion of doctoral program. *Degree requirements:* For master's, comprehensive exam, thesis; for doctorate, comprehensive exam, thesis/dissertation. *Entrance requirements:* For master's and doctorate, minimum GPA of 3.0. Additional exam requirements/recommendations for international students: required—TOEFL (minimum score 550 paper-based; 80 iBT), IELTS (minimum score 6). Electronic applications accepted.

University of Idaho, College of Graduate Studies, College of Engineering, Program in Nuclear Engineering, Moscow, ID 83844-2282. Offers M Engr, MS, PhD. *Faculty:* 6. *Students:* 13 full-time, 13 part-time. Average age 35. In 2019, 6 master's awarded. *Entrance requirements:* For master's and doctorate, minimum GPA of 3.0. Additional exam requirements/recommendations for international students: required—TOEFL (minimum score 83 iBT). *Application deadline:* For fall admission, 7/30 for domestic students; for spring admission, 12/1 for domestic students. Applications are processed on a rolling basis. Application fee: $60. Electronic applications accepted. *Expenses:* Tuition, state resident: full-time $7753.80; part-time $502 per credit hour. Tuition, nonresident: full-time $26,990; part-time $1571 per credit hour. *Required fees:* $2122.20; $47 per credit hour. *Financial support:* Applicants required to submit FAFSA. *Unit head:* Dr. Richard Christensen, Chair, 208-282-6470, E-mail: engr-sss@uidaho.edu. *Application contact:* Dr. Richard Christensen, Chair, 208-282-6470, E-mail: engr-sss@uidaho.edu.

University of Illinois at Urbana-Champaign, Graduate College, College of Engineering, Department of Nuclear, Plasma, and Radiological Engineering, Urbana, IL 61801. Offers energy systems (M Eng); nuclear, plasma, and radiological engineering (MS, PhD). Terminal master's awarded for partial completion of doctoral program.

The University of Manchester, School of Mechanical, Aerospace and Civil Engineering, Manchester, United Kingdom. Offers advanced manufacturing technology (M Ent); aerospace engineering (M Phil, M Sc, PhD); civil engineering (M Phil, M Sc, PhD); environmental engineering (M Phil, PhD); management of projects (M Phil, M Sc, PhD); mechanical engineering (M Phil, M Sc, PhD); mechanical engineering design (M Ent); nuclear engineering (M Phil, D Eng, PhD).

University of Maryland, College Park, Academic Affairs, A. James Clark School of Engineering, Department of Materials Science and Engineering, Nuclear Engineering Program, College Park, MD 20742. Offers ME, MS, PhD. *Program availability:* Part-time, evening/weekend, online learning. *Degree requirements:* For master's, thesis optional; for doctorate, variable foreign language requirement, thesis/dissertation, oral exam. *Entrance requirements:* For master's and doctorate, GRE General Test, minimum GPA of 3.0. Additional exam requirements/recommendations for international students: required—TOEFL. Electronic applications accepted.

University of Massachusetts Lowell, Francis College of Engineering, Program in Energy Engineering, Lowell, MA 01854. Offers MS Eng, PhD. *Degree requirements:* For master's, thesis optional. *Entrance requirements:* For master's, GRE General Test. Additional exam requirements/recommendations for international students: required—TOEFL.

University of Michigan, College of Engineering, Department of Nuclear Engineering and Radiological Sciences, Ann Arbor, MI 48109. Offers nuclear engineering (Nuc E); nuclear engineering and radiological sciences (MSE, PhD); nuclear science (MS, PhD). Terminal master's awarded for partial completion of doctoral program. *Degree requirements:* For master's, thesis optional; for doctorate, thesis/dissertation, oral defense of dissertation, preliminary exams. *Entrance requirements:* For master's and doctorate, GRE General Test. Additional exam requirements/recommendations for international students: required—TOEFL. Electronic applications accepted.

University of Nevada, Las Vegas, Graduate College, Howard R. Hughes College of Engineering, Department of Mechanical Engineering, Las Vegas, NV 89154-4027. Offers aerospace engineering (MS); biomedical engineering (MS); materials and nuclear engineering (MS); mechanical engineering (MS, PhD); nuclear criticality safety engineering (Certificate); nuclear safeguards and security (Certificate). *Program availability:* Part-time. *Faculty:* 18 full-time (2 women), 1 (woman) part-time/adjunct. *Students:* 52 full-time (16 women), 26 part-time (7 women); includes 26 minority (5 Black or African American, non-Hispanic/Latino; 1 American Indian or Alaska Native, non-Hispanic/Latino; 7 Asian, non-Hispanic/Latino; 10 Hispanic/Latino; 3 Two or more races, non-Hispanic/Latino), 22 international. Average age 29. 45 applicants, 76% accepted, 14 enrolled. In 2019, 9 master's, 4 doctorates, 1 other advanced degree awarded. *Degree requirements:* For master's, thesis optional, design project; for doctorate, comprehensive exam, thesis/dissertation. *Entrance requirements:* For master's, GRE General Test, statement of purpose; 2 letters of recommendation; for doctorate, GRE General Test, 3 letters of recommendation; statement of purpose; bachelor's degree with minimum GPA of 3.5/master's degree with minimum GPA of 3.3. Additional exam requirements/recommendations for international students: required—TOEFL (minimum score 550 paper-based; 80 iBT), IELTS (minimum score 7). *Application deadline:* For fall admission, 8/1 for domestic students, 5/1 for international students; for spring admission, 12/1 for domestic students, 10/1 for international students. Application fee: $60 ($95 for international students). Electronic applications accepted. *Expenses:* Contact institution. *Financial support:* In 2019–20, 40 students received support, including 2 fellowships with full tuition reimbursements available (averaging $20,000 per year), 16 research assistantships with full tuition reimbursements available (averaging $16,738 per year), 26 teaching assistantships with full tuition reimbursements available (averaging $18,115 per year); institutionally sponsored loans, scholarships/grants, health care benefits, and unspecified assistantships also available. Financial award application deadline: 3/15; financial award applicants required to submit FAFSA. *Unit head:* Dr. Brendan O'Toole, Chair/Professor, 702-895-3885, Fax: 702-895-3936, E-mail: mechanical.chair@unlv.edu. *Application contact:* Dr. Hui Zhao, Graduate Coordinator, 702-895-1463, Fax: 702-895-3936, E-mail: mechanical.gradcoord@unlv.edu.
Website: http://me.unlv.edu/

University of New Mexico, Graduate Studies, School of Engineering, Program in Nuclear Engineering, Albuquerque, NM 87131. Offers MS, PhD. *Program availability:* Part-time, online learning. *Faculty:* 8 full-time (0 women), 2 part-time/adjunct (0 women). *Students:* 15 full-time (4 women), 27 part-time (4 women); includes 15 minority (3 Black or African American, non-Hispanic/Latino; 1 Asian, non-Hispanic/Latino; 9 Hispanic/Latino; 2 Two or more races, non-Hispanic/Latino), 6 international. 39 applicants, 79% accepted, 13 enrolled. In 2019, 10 master's, 4 doctorates awarded. Terminal master's awarded for partial completion of doctoral program. *Degree requirements:* For master's, thesis (for some programs); for doctorate, comprehensive exam, thesis/dissertation. *Entrance requirements:* For master's, GRE General Test, minimum GPA of 3.0, 3 letters of recommendation, letter of intent; for doctorate, GRE General Test, 3 letters of recommendation, letter of intent. Additional exam requirements/recommendations for international students: required—TOEFL (minimum score 550 paper-based; 80 iBT), IELTS (minimum score 6.5), TOEFL or IELTS, not both. *Application deadline:* For fall admission, 1/15 priority date for domestic students, 3/1 for international students; for spring admission, 7/15 priority date for domestic students, 8/1 for international students. Application fee: $50. Electronic applications accepted. *Expenses:* Tuition, state resident: full-time $7633; part-time $972 per year. Tuition, nonresident: full-time $22,586; part-time $3840 per year. *International tuition:* $23,292 full-time. *Required fees:* $8608. Tuition and fees vary according to course level, course load, degree level, program and student level. *Financial support:* Research assistantships, scholarships/grants, health care benefits, and tuition waivers (full) available. Financial award application deadline: 3/1; financial award applicants required to submit FAFSA. *Unit head:* Dr. Hyoung Lee, Chair, 505-277-5431, Fax: 505-277-5433, E-mail: leehk@unm.edu. *Application contact:* Krista Dominguez, Sr. Academic Advisor, 505-277-1004, Fax: 505-277-5431, E-mail: krisnava@unm.edu.
Website: https://ne.unm.edu/graduate/index.html

University of South Carolina, The Graduate School, College of Engineering and Computing, Department of Nuclear Engineering, Columbia, SC 29208. Offers ME, MS, PhD. *Program availability:* Part-time, evening/weekend, online learning. *Degree requirements:* For master's, thesis (for some programs); for doctorate, thesis/dissertation. *Entrance requirements:* For master's and doctorate, GRE General Test. Additional exam requirements/recommendations for international students: required—TOEFL (minimum score 600 paper-based; 100 iBT). Electronic applications accepted.

The University of Tennessee, Graduate School, Tickle College of Engineering, Department of Nuclear Engineering, Program in Nuclear Engineering, Knoxville, TN 37996-1410. Offers MS, PhD. *Program availability:* Part-time. *Faculty:* 15 full-time (1 woman), 4 part-time/adjunct (1 woman). *Students:* 101 full-time (16 women), 23 part-time (4 women); includes 12 minority (3 Asian, non-Hispanic/Latino; 6 Hispanic/Latino; 3

Two or more races, non-Hispanic/Latino), 16 international. Average age 29. 65 applicants, 55% accepted, 16 enrolled. In 2019, 24 master's, 8 doctorates awarded. *Degree requirements:* For master's, thesis or alternative; for doctorate, comprehensive exam, thesis/dissertation. *Entrance requirements:* For master's, GRE General Test (for MS students pursuing research thesis), minimum GPA of 2.7 (for U.S. degree holders), 3.0 (for international degree holders); for doctorate, GRE General Test, minimum GPA of 3.0 on previous graduate course work. Additional exam requirements/recommendations for international students: required—TOEFL (minimum score 550 paper-based; 80 iBT), IELTS (minimum score 6.5). *Application deadline:* For fall admission, 2/1 priority date for domestic and international students; for spring admission, 6/15 for domestic students, 5/15 for international students; for summer admission, 10/15 for domestic and international students. Applications are processed on a rolling basis. Application fee: $60. Electronic applications accepted. *Financial support:* In 2019–20, 121 students received support, including 32 fellowships with full tuition reimbursements available (averaging $13,128 per year), 72 research assistantships with full tuition reimbursements available (averaging $28,681 per year), 17 teaching assistantships with full tuition reimbursements available (averaging $24,759 per year); career-related internships or fieldwork, Federal Work-Study, institutionally sponsored loans, health care benefits, and unspecified assistantships also available. Financial award application deadline: 2/1; financial award applicants required to submit FAFSA. *Unit head:* Dr. J. Wesley Hines, Head, 865-974-2525, Fax: 865-974-0668, E-mail: jhines2@utk.edu. *Application contact:* Dr. Jason Hayward, PhD, Professor and Graduate Coordinator, 865-974-2525, E-mail: utne@utk.edu.

University of Utah, Graduate School, College of Engineering, Department of Civil and Environmental Engineering, Salt Lake City, UT 84112. Offers civil and environmental engineering (MS, PhD); nuclear engineering (MS, PhD). *Faculty:* 22 full-time (5 women), 2 part-time/adjunct (1 woman). *Students:* 75 full-time (18 women), 38 part-time (3 women); includes 18 minority (1 Black or African American, non-Hispanic/Latino; 8 Asian, non-Hispanic/Latino; 6 Hispanic/Latino; 3 Two or more races, non-Hispanic/Latino), 44 international. Average age 29. 104 applicants, 36% accepted, 21 enrolled. In 2019, 26 master's, 12 doctorates awarded. Terminal master's awarded for partial completion of doctoral program. *Degree requirements:* For master's, comprehensive exam (for some programs), thesis (for some programs); for doctorate, comprehensive exam, thesis/dissertation. *Entrance requirements:* For master's and doctorate, GRE, Online application completed through ApplyYourself portal, GPA of 3.0+ on 4.0 scale, CV, personal statement, unofficial transcripts, three letters of reference, proof of English proficiency. Additional exam requirements/recommendations for international students: required—TOEFL (minimum score 80 iBT), IELTS (minimum score 6.5), Either IELTS or TOEFL required, not both. *Application deadline:* For fall admission, 1/1 priority date for domestic and international students; for spring admission, 10/1 for domestic and international students. Applications are processed on a rolling basis. Application fee: $0 ($30 for international students). Electronic applications accepted. *Expenses:* $58.29 per credit hour. *Financial support:* In 2019–20, 1 student received support, including 8 fellowships with full tuition reimbursements available (averaging $28,375 per year), 48 research assistantships with full tuition reimbursements available (averaging $24,000 per year), 15 teaching assistantships with full tuition reimbursements available (averaging $24,000 per year); health care benefits and unspecified assistantships also available. Financial award application deadline: 1/1. *Unit head:* Dr. Michael E. Barber, Chair, 801-581-6931, Fax: 801-585-5477, E-mail: barber@civil.utah.edu. *Application contact:* Courtney Phillips, Academic Advisor, 801-581-6678, Fax: 801-585-5477, E-mail: cveen-graduate@utah.edu. Website: http://www.civil.utah.edu

University of Wisconsin–Madison, Graduate School, College of Engineering, Department of Engineering Physics, Madison, WI 53706-1380. Offers engineering mechanics (MS, PhD), including fundamentals of applied mechanics (MS); nuclear engineering and engineering physics (MS, PhD). *Program availability:* Part-time. Terminal master's awarded for partial completion of doctoral program. *Degree requirements:* For master's, thesis optional, 30 credits of technical courses; oral exam; minimum GPA of 3.0; for doctorate, comprehensive exam, thesis/dissertation, minimum of 60 credits; minimum GPA of 3.0. *Entrance requirements:* For master's and doctorate, GRE General Test, minimum GPA of 3.0 in last 60 hours, appropriate bachelor's degree. Additional exam requirements/recommendations for international students: required—TOEFL (minimum score 580 paper-based; 92 iBT), IELTS (minimum score 7). Electronic applications accepted.

Virginia Commonwealth University, Graduate School, School of Engineering, Department of Mechanical and Nuclear Engineering, Richmond, VA 23284-9005. Offers MS, PhD. *Entrance requirements:* For master's and doctorate, GRE. Additional exam requirements/recommendations for international students: required—TOEFL (minimum score 600 paper-based; 100 iBT). Electronic applications accepted.

Worcester Polytechnic Institute, Graduate Admissions, Programs in Interdisciplinary Studies, Worcester, MA 01609-2280. Offers bioscience administration (MS); nuclear science and engineering (Graduate Certificate); power systems management (MS); social science (PhD); system dynamics and innovation management (MS, Graduate Certificate); systems modeling (MS). *Program availability:* Part-time, evening/weekend, 100% online. Terminal master's awarded for partial completion of doctoral program. *Degree requirements:* For master's, thesis; for doctorate, comprehensive exam, thesis/dissertation. *Entrance requirements:* For master's and doctorate, 3 letters of recommendation. Additional exam requirements/recommendations for international students: required—TOEFL (minimum score 563 paper-based; 84 iBT), IELTS (minimum score 7). Electronic applications accepted.

Section 11
Engineering Design

This section contains a directory of institutions offering graduate work in engineering design. Additional information about programs listed in the directory may be obtained by writing directly to the dean of a graduate school or chair of a department at the address given in the directory.

For programs offering related work, see also in this book *Aerospace/Aeronautical Engineering; Agricultural Engineering and Bioengineering; Biomedical Engineering and Biotechnology; Computer Science and Information Technology; Electrical and Computer Engineering; Energy and Power Engineering; Engineering and Applied Sciences; Industrial Engineering; Management of Engineering and Technology;* and *Mechanical Engineering and Mechanics.* In another guide in this series:

Graduate Programs in the Biological/Biomedical Sciences & Health-Related Medical Professions
See *Biological and Biomedical Sciences*

CONTENTS

Program Directory

Engineering Design

Harvard University, Graduate School of Arts and Sciences, Harvard John A. Paulson School of Engineering and Applied Sciences, Cambridge, MA 02138. Offers applied mathematics (PhD); applied physics (PhD); computational science and engineering (ME, SM); computer science (PhD); data science (SM); design engineering (MDE); engineering science (ME), including electrical engineering (ME, SM, PhD); engineering sciences (SM, PhD), including bioengineering (PhD), electrical engineering (ME, SM, PhD), environmental science and engineering (PhD), materials science and mechanical engineering (PhD). *Program availability:* Part-time. Terminal master's awarded for partial completion of doctoral program. *Degree requirements:* For master's, thesis (for ME); for doctorate, comprehensive exam, thesis/dissertation. *Entrance requirements:* For master's and doctorate, GRE General Test, GRE Subject Test (recommended), 3 letters of recommendation. Additional exam requirements/recommendations for international students: required—TOEFL (minimum score 80 iBT). Electronic applications accepted. *Expenses:* Contact institution.

Northwestern University, McCormick School of Engineering and Applied Science, Department of Mechanical Engineering, MS in Product Design and Development Management Program, Evanston, IL 60208. Offers MS. *Program availability:* Part-time, evening/weekend. *Entrance requirements:* Additional exam requirements/ recommendations for international students: required—TOEFL (minimum score 100 iBT), IELTS (minimum score 7). Electronic applications accepted.

Northwestern University, McCormick School of Engineering and Applied Science, Segal Design Institute, MS in Engineering Design and Innovation Program, Evanston, IL 60208. Offers MS. *Entrance requirements:* For master's, GRE General Test, 2 letters of recommendation, portfolio, statement of purpose. Additional exam requirements/ recommendations for international students: required—TOEFL (minimum score 550 paper-based; 80 iBT) or IELTS (minimum score 7). Electronic applications accepted.

Ohio Dominican University, Division of Business, Columbus, OH 43219-2099. Offers business administration (MBA), including accounting, data analytics, finance, leadership, risk management, sport management; healthcare administration (MS); sport management (MS). *Accreditation:* ACBSP. *Program availability:* Part-time, evening/ weekend, 100% online, blended/hybrid learning. *Faculty:* 11 full-time (3 women), 13 part-time/adjunct (2 women). *Students:* 60 full-time (35 women), 104 part-time (52 women); includes 41 minority (25 Black or African American, non-Hispanic/Latino; 2 American Indian or Alaska Native, non-Hispanic/Latino; 5 Asian, non-Hispanic/Latino; 3 Hispanic/Latino; 6 Two or more races, non-Hispanic/Latino), 19 international. Average age 30. 103 applicants, 92% accepted, 75 enrolled. In 2019, 70 master's awarded. *Degree requirements:* For master's, thesis or alternative. *Entrance requirements:* Additional exam requirements/recommendations for international students: required— TOEFL (minimum score 550 paper-based), IELTS (minimum score 6.5). *Application deadline:* For fall admission, 8/15 for domestic students, 6/10 for international students; for spring admission, 1/4 for domestic students, 11/2 for international students. Applications are processed on a rolling basis. Application fee: $25. Electronic applications accepted. *Expenses: Tuition:* Full-time $10,800; part-time $600 per credit hour. *Required fees:* $225 per semester. Tuition and fees vary according to program. *Unit head:* Dr. Kenneth C. Fah, Chair, 614-251-4566, E-mail: fahk@ohiodominican.edu. *Application contact:* John W. Naughton, Vice President for Enrollment and Student Success, 614-251-4721, Fax: 614-251-6654, E-mail: grad@ohiodominican.edu. Website: http://www.ohiodominican.edu/academics/graduate/mba

Penn State University Park, Graduate School, College of Engineering, School of Engineering Design, Technology, and Professional Programs, University Park, PA 16802. Offers engineering design (M Eng, MS).

Rochester Institute of Technology, Graduate Enrollment Services, Kate Gleason College of Engineering, Design, Development and Manufacturing Department, Rochester, NY 14623-5603. Offers manufacturing leadership (MS); product development (MS). *Program availability:* Part-time-only, evening/weekend, 100% online, blended/hybrid learning. *Entrance requirements:* For master's, minimum GPA of 2.5, 2 years of related work experience. Electronic applications accepted. *Expenses:* Contact institution.

San Diego State University, Graduate and Research Affairs, College of Engineering, Department of Mechanical Engineering, San Diego, CA 92182. Offers engineering sciences and applied mechanics (PhD); manufacture and design (MS); mechanical engineering (MS). *Program availability:* Evening/weekend. *Degree requirements:* For master's, comprehensive exam (for some programs), thesis (for some programs); for doctorate, thesis/dissertation. *Entrance requirements:* For master's, GRE General Test; for doctorate, GRE, 3 letters of recommendation. Additional exam requirements/ recommendations for international students: required—TOEFL. Electronic applications accepted.

Stevens Institute of Technology, Graduate School, Charles V. Schaefer Jr. School of Engineering and Science, Department of Mechanical Engineering, Program in Product Architecture and Engineering, Hoboken, NJ 07030. Offers M Eng. *Program availability:* Part-time, evening/weekend. *Faculty:* 29 full-time (3 women), 11 part-time/adjunct (0 women). In 2019, 1 master's awarded. *Degree requirements:* For master's, thesis optional, minimum B average in major field and overall. *Entrance requirements:* For master's, International applicants must submit TOEFL/IELTS scores and fulfill the English Language Proficiency Requirement. Applicants to full-time programs who do not qualify for a score waiver are required to submit GRE/GMAT scores. Additional exam requirements/recommendations for international students: required—TOEFL (minimum score 74 iBT), IELTS (minimum score 6). *Application deadline:* For fall admission, 4/1 for domestic students, 4/15 for international students; for spring admission, 11/1 for domestic and international students; for summer admission, 5/1 for domestic students. Applications are processed on a rolling basis. *Expenses: Tuition:* Full-time $52,134. *Required fees:* $1880. Tuition and fees vary according to course load. *Financial support:* Fellowships, research assistantships, teaching assistantships, career-related internships or fieldwork, Federal Work-Study, scholarships/grants, and unspecified assistantships available. Financial award application deadline: 2/15; financial award applicants required to submit FAFSA. *Unit head:* Dr. Jean Zu, Dean of SES, 201-216.8233, Fax: 201-216.8372, E-mail: Jean.Zu@stevens.edu. *Application contact:* Graduate Admissions, 888-783-8367, Fax: 888-511-1306, E-mail: graduate@stevens.edu.

The University of Alabama at Birmingham, School of Engineering, Professional Engineering Degrees, Birmingham, AL 35294. Offers advanced safety engineering and management (M Eng); construction engineering management (M Eng); design and commercialization (M Eng); information engineering management (M Eng); structural engineering (M Eng); sustainable smart cities (M Eng). *Program availability:* Part-time, evening/weekend, online only, 100% online. *Faculty:* 5 full-time (1 woman), 15 part-time/ adjunct (3 women). *Students:* 13 full-time (4 women), 315 part-time (70 women); includes 83 minority (64 Black or African American, non-Hispanic/Latino; 3 American Indian or Alaska Native, non-Hispanic/Latino; 9 Asian, non-Hispanic/Latino; 7 Hispanic/ Latino), 8 international. 126 applicants, 84% accepted, 90 enrolled. In 2019, 123 master's awarded. *Entrance requirements:* For master's, 3.0 GPA on 4.0 scale, undergraduate degree from a nationally accredited school. Additional exam requirements/recommendations for international students: required—TOEFL (minimum score 80 iBT); recommended—IELTS (minimum score 6.5). *Application deadline:* For fall admission, 8/1 for domestic and international students; for spring admission, 12/1 for domestic and international students; for summer admission, 5/1 for domestic and international students. Applications are processed on a rolling basis. Application fee: $50 ($60 for international students). Electronic applications accepted. *Expenses:* Contact institution. *Unit head:* Dr. Gregg Janowski, Associate Dean for Graduate Programs and Assessment, E-mail: janowski@uab.edu. *Application contact:* Jesse Kepply, Director of Student and Academic Services, 205-996-5696, E-mail: gradschool@uab.edu.

University of Michigan, College of Engineering, Department of Integrative Systems and Design, Ann Arbor, MI 48109. Offers automotive engineering (M Eng); design science (MS, PhD); energy systems engineering (M Eng, MS); global automotive and manufacturing engineering (M Eng); manufacturing engineering (M Eng, D Eng); pharmaceutical engineering (M Eng); robotics and autonomous vehicles (M Eng); systems engineering and design (M Eng); MBA/M Eng; MSE/MS. *Program availability:* Part-time, online learning. Terminal master's awarded for partial completion of doctoral program. *Degree requirements:* For master's, capstone project; for doctorate, thesis/ dissertation. *Entrance requirements:* For master's and doctorate, GRE. Additional exam requirements/recommendations for international students: required—TOEFL. Electronic applications accepted.

Worcester Polytechnic Institute, Graduate Admissions, Foisie Business School, Worcester, MA 01609-2280. Offers business administration (PhD); information technology (MS), including information security management; management (MS, Graduate Certificate); marketing and innovation (MS); operations analytics and management (MS); supply chain management (MS). *Accreditation:* AACSB. *Program availability:* Part-time, evening/weekend, 100% online, blended/hybrid learning. *Degree requirements:* For master's, thesis optional. *Entrance requirements:* For master's and Graduate Certificate, GMAT or GRE General Test, 3 letters of recommendation, statement of purpose, resume. Additional exam requirements/recommendations for international students: required—TOEFL (minimum score 563 paper-based; 84 iBT), IELTS (minimum score 7). Electronic applications accepted.

Section 12
Engineering Physics

This section contains a directory of institutions offering graduate work in engineering physics. Additional information about programs listed in the directory may be obtained by writing directly to the dean of a graduate school or chair of a department at the address given in the directory.

For programs offering related work, see also in this book *Electrical and Computer Engineering, Energy and Power Engineering (Nuclear Engineering), Engineering and Applied Sciences,* and *Materials Sciences and Engineering.* In the other guides in this series:

Graduate Programs in the Biological/Biomedical Sciences & Health-Related Medical Professions
See *Biophysics* and *Health Sciences (Medical Physics)*

Graduate Programs in the Physical Sciences, Mathematics, Agricultural Sciences, the Environment & Natural Resources
See *Physics*

CONTENTS

Program Directory

Engineering Physics

Air Force Institute of Technology, Graduate School of Engineering and Management, Department of Engineering Physics, Dayton, OH 45433-7765. Offers applied physics (MS, PhD); electro-optics (MS, PhD); materials science (PhD); nuclear engineering (MS, PhD); space physics (MS). *Program availability:* Part-time. *Degree requirements:* For master's, thesis; for doctorate, thesis/dissertation. *Entrance requirements:* For master's and doctorate, GRE General Test, minimum GPA of 3.0, U.S. citizenship.

Cornell University, Graduate School, Graduate Fields of Engineering, Field of Applied Physics, Ithaca, NY 14853. Offers applied physics (PhD); engineering physics (M Eng). *Degree requirements:* For doctorate, comprehensive exam, thesis/dissertation, written exams. *Entrance requirements:* For master's, GRE General Test, 3 letters of recommendation; for doctorate, GRE General Test, GRE Subject Test (physics), GRE Writing Assessment, 3 letters of recommendation. Additional exam requirements/recommendations for international students: required—TOEFL (minimum score 600 paper-based; 77 iBT). Electronic applications accepted.

Embry-Riddle Aeronautical University–Daytona, Department of Physical Sciences, Daytona Beach, FL 32114-3900. Offers engineering physics (MS, PhD). *Degree requirements:* For master's, thesis or alternative; for doctorate, comprehensive exam, thesis/dissertation. *Entrance requirements:* For doctorate, GRE. Additional exam requirements/recommendations for international students: required—TOEFL (minimum score 550 paper-based, 79 iBT) or IELTS (6). Electronic applications accepted.

Louisiana Tech University, Graduate School, College of Engineering and Science, Ruston, LA 71272. Offers applied physics (MS); biomedical engineering (PhD); computer science (MS); engineering (MS, PhD), including cyberspace engineering (PhD), engineering education (PhD), engineering physics (PhD), materials and infrastructure systems (PhD), micro/nanoscale systems (PhD); engineering and technology management (MS); mathematics (MS); molecular science and nanotechnology (MS, PhD). *Program availability:* Part-time-only. Terminal master's awarded for partial completion of doctoral program. *Degree requirements:* For master's, thesis (for some programs); for doctorate, thesis/dissertation. *Entrance requirements:* For master's and Graduate Certificate, GRE General Test, minimum GPA of 3.0 in last 60 hours. Additional exam requirements/recommendations for international students: required—TOEFL (minimum score 550 paper-based; 80 iBT), IELTS (minimum score 6.5). Electronic applications accepted. *Expenses: Tuition, area resident:* Full-time $6592; part-time $400 per credit. Tuition, state resident: full-time $6592; part-time $400 per credit. Tuition, nonresident: full-time $13,333; part-time $681 per credit. *International tuition:* $13,333 full-time. *Required fees:* $3011; $3011 per unit.

McMaster University, School of Graduate Studies, Faculty of Engineering, Department of Engineering Physics, Hamilton, ON L8S 4M2, Canada. Offers engineering physics (M Eng, MA Sc, PhD); nuclear engineering (PhD). *Degree requirements:* For master's, thesis or alternative; for doctorate, comprehensive exam, thesis/dissertation. *Entrance requirements:* For master's, minimum B average in engineering, mathematics, or physical sciences. Additional exam requirements/recommendations for international students: required—TOEFL (minimum score 550 paper-based).

Polytechnique Montréal, Graduate Programs, Department of Engineering Physics, Montréal, QC H3C 3A7, Canada. Offers optical engineering (M Eng, M Sc A, PhD); solid-state physics and engineering (M Eng, M Sc A, PhD). *Program availability:* Part-time. *Degree requirements:* For master's, one foreign language, thesis; for doctorate, one foreign language, thesis/dissertation. *Entrance requirements:* For master's, minimum GPA of 2.75; for doctorate, minimum GPA of 3.0.

Queen's University at Kingston, School of Graduate Studies, Faculty of Arts and Science, Department of Physics, Engineering Physics and Astronomy, Kingston, ON K7L 3N6, Canada. Offers M Sc, M Sc Eng, PhD. *Program availability:* Part-time. *Degree requirements:* For master's, thesis; for doctorate, comprehensive exam, thesis/dissertation. *Entrance requirements:* For doctorate, M Sc or M Sc Eng. Additional exam requirements/recommendations for international students: required—TOEFL (minimum score 550 paper-based).

Rensselaer Polytechnic Institute, Graduate School, School of Engineering, Program in Engineering Physics, Troy, NY 12180-3590. Offers MS, PhD. *Program availability:* Part-time. *Faculty:* 48 full-time (7 women), 1 part-time/adjunct (0 women). *Students:* 1 applicant. Terminal master's awarded for partial completion of doctoral program. *Degree requirements:* For master's, thesis (for some programs); for doctorate, thesis/dissertation. *Entrance requirements:* For master's and doctorate, GRE. Additional exam requirements/recommendations for international students: required—TOEFL (minimum score 600 paper-based; 100 iBT), IELTS (minimum score 7), PTE (minimum score 68). *Application deadline:* For fall admission, 1/1 priority date for domestic and international students; for spring admission, 8/15 priority date for domestic and international students. Applications are processed on a rolling basis. Application fee: $75. Electronic applications accepted. *Financial support:* In 2019–20, 1 student received support, including research assistantships (averaging $23,000 per year), teaching assistantships (averaging $23,000 per year); fellowships also available. Financial award application deadline: 1/1. *Unit head:* Dr. Theo Borca-Tasciuc, Graduate Program Director, 518-276-2627, E-mail: borcat@rpi.edu. *Application contact:* Jarron Decker, Director of Graduate Admissions, 518-276-6216, Fax: 518-276-4072, E-mail: gradadmissions@rpi.edu.
Website: http://mane.rpi.edu/

Stanford University, School of Humanities and Sciences, Department of Applied Physics, Stanford, CA 94305-2004. Offers applied and engineering physics (MS). *Expenses: Tuition:* Full-time $52,479; part-time $34,110 per unit. *Required fees:* $672; $224 per quarter. Tuition and fees vary according to program and student level.
Website: http://www.stanford.edu/dept/app-physics/

University of California, San Diego, Graduate Division, Department of Mechanical and Aerospace Engineering, Program in Engineering Physics, La Jolla, CA 92093. Offers MS, PhD. *Students:* 22 full-time (5 women), 1 part-time (0 women). 23 applicants, 43% accepted, 6 enrolled. In 2019, 1 master's, 2 doctorates awarded. *Degree requirements:* For master's, comprehensive exam (for some programs), thesis (for some programs), comprehensive exam or thesis; for doctorate, comprehensive exam, thesis/dissertation. *Entrance requirements:* For master's and doctorate, GRE General Test, minimum GPA of 3.0. Additional exam requirements/recommendations for international students: required—TOEFL (minimum score 550 paper-based; 80 iBT), IELTS (minimum score 7). *Application deadline:* For fall admission, 12/18 for domestic students. Application fee: $105 ($125 for international students). Electronic applications accepted. *Financial support:* Fellowships, research assistantships, teaching assistantships, scholarships/grants, and unspecified assistantships available. Financial award applicants required to submit FAFSA. *Unit head:* Carlos Coimbra, Chair, 858-534-4285, E-mail: mae-chair-l@ucsd.edu. *Application contact:* Jackie Tam, Graduate Coordinator, 858-534-4387, E-mail: mae-gradadm-l@ucsd.edu.
Website: http://maeweb.ucsd.edu/

University of Central Oklahoma, The Jackson College of Graduate Studies, College of Mathematics and Science, Department of Engineering and Physics, Edmond, OK 73034-5209. Offers engineering physics (MS), including biomedical engineering, electrical engineering, mechanical systems, physics. *Program availability:* Part-time. *Degree requirements:* For master's, thesis optional. *Entrance requirements:* For master's, GRE, 24 hours of course work in physics or equivalent, mathematics through differential equations, minimum GPA of 2.75 overall and 3.0 in last 60 hours attempted, two letters of recommendation. Additional exam requirements/recommendations for international students: required—TOEFL (minimum score 550 paper-based; 79 iBT), IELTS (minimum score 6.5). Electronic applications accepted.

University of Oklahoma, College of Arts and Sciences, Homer L. Dodge Department of Physics and Astronomy, Norman, OK 73019. Offers engineering physics (MS); physics (MS, PhD). Terminal master's awarded for partial completion of doctoral program. *Degree requirements:* For master's, comprehensive exam, thesis (for some programs), thesis or qualifying exams; for doctorate, comprehensive exam, thesis/dissertation, qualifying exams. *Entrance requirements:* For master's and doctorate, GRE General Test and GRE Subject Test in physics (recommended), transcripts, statement of purpose, three letters of recommendation. Additional exam requirements/recommendations for international students: required—TOEFL (minimum score 79 iBT) or IELTS (minimum score 6.5). Electronic applications accepted. *Expenses:* Tuition, state resident: full-time $6583.20; part-time $274.30 per credit hour. Tuition, nonresident: full-time $21,242; part-time $885.10 per credit hour. *International tuition:* $21,242.40 full-time. *Required fees:* $1994.20; $72.55 per credit hour. $126.50 per semester. Tuition and fees vary according to course load and degree level.

University of Saskatchewan, College of Graduate and Postdoctoral Studies, College of Arts and Science, Department of Physics and Engineering Physics, Saskatoon, SK S7N 5A2, Canada. Offers M Sc, PhD. *Degree requirements:* For master's, thesis; for doctorate, comprehensive exam (for some programs), thesis/dissertation. *Entrance requirements:* Additional exam requirements/recommendations for international students: required—TOEFL (minimum score 80 iBT); recommended—IELTS (minimum score 6.5). Electronic applications accepted.

University of Virginia, School of Engineering and Applied Science, Program in Engineering Physics, Charlottesville, VA 22903. Offers ME, MS, PhD. *Program availability:* Online learning. *Degree requirements:* For master's, comprehensive exam; for doctorate, comprehensive exam, thesis/dissertation. *Entrance requirements:* For master's and doctorate, GRE General Test, 3 recommendations. Additional exam requirements/recommendations for international students: required—TOEFL. Electronic applications accepted.

University of Wisconsin–Madison, Graduate School, College of Engineering, Department of Engineering Physics, Madison, WI 53706-1380. Offers engineering mechanics (MS, PhD), including fundamentals of applied mechanics (MS); nuclear engineering and engineering physics (MS, PhD). *Program availability:* Part-time. Terminal master's awarded for partial completion of doctoral program. *Degree requirements:* For master's, thesis optional, 30 credits of technical courses; oral exam; minimum GPA of 3.0; for doctorate, comprehensive exam, thesis/dissertation, minimum of 60 credits; minimum GPA of 3.0. *Entrance requirements:* For master's and doctorate, GRE General Test, minimum GPA of 3.0 in last 60 hours, appropriate bachelor's degree. Additional exam requirements/recommendations for international students: required—TOEFL (minimum score 580 paper-based; 92 iBT), IELTS (minimum score 7). Electronic applications accepted.

Yale University, Graduate School of Arts and Sciences, School of Engineering and Applied Science, Department of Applied Physics, New Haven, CT 06520. Offers MS, PhD. Terminal master's awarded for partial completion of doctoral program. *Degree requirements:* For doctorate, thesis/dissertation, area exam. *Entrance requirements:* For master's and doctorate, GRE General Test. Additional exam requirements/recommendations for international students: required—TOEFL.

Section 13
Geological, Mineral/Mining, and Petroleum Engineering

This section contains a directory of institutions offering graduate work in geological, mineral/mining, and petroleum engineering. Additional information about programs listed in the directory may be obtained by writing directly to the dean of a graduate school or chair of a department at the address given in the directory.

For programs offering related work, see also in this book *Chemical Engineering, Civil and Environmental Engineering, Electrical and Computer Engineering, Energy and Power Engineering, Engineering and Applied Sciences, Management of Engineering and Technology,* and *Materials Sciences and Engineering.* In another guide in this series:

Graduate Programs in the Physical Sciences, Mathematics, Agricultural Sciences, the Environment & Natural Resources
See *Geosciences* and *Marine Sciences and Oceanography*

CONTENTS

Program Directories

Geological Engineering

Arizona State University at Tempe, College of Liberal Arts and Sciences, School of Earth and Space Exploration, Tempe, AZ 85287-1404. Offers astrophysics (MS, PhD); exploration systems design (PhD); geological sciences (MS, PhD). Terminal master's awarded for partial completion of doctoral program. *Degree requirements:* For master's, thesis, interactive Program of Study (iPOS) submitted before completing 50 percent of required credit hours; for doctorate, thesis/dissertation, interactive Program of Study (iPOS) submitted before completing 50 percent of required credit hours. *Entrance requirements:* For master's and doctorate, GRE, minimum GPA of 3.0 or equivalent in last 2 years of work leading to bachelor's degree. Additional exam requirements/recommendations for international students: required—TOEFL, IELTS, or PTE. Electronic applications accepted.

Colorado School of Mines, Office of Graduate Studies, Department of Geology and Geological Engineering, Golden, CO 80401. Offers environmental geochemistry (PMS); geochemistry (MS, PhD); geological engineering (ME, MS, PhD); geology (MS, PhD); hydrology (MS, PhD); mineral exploration (PMS); petroleum reservoir systems (PMS); underground construction and tunneling (MS). *Program availability:* Part-time. *Degree requirements:* For master's, thesis (for some programs); for doctorate, comprehensive exam, thesis/dissertation. *Entrance requirements:* For master's and doctorate, GRE General Test. Additional exam requirements/recommendations for international students: required—TOEFL (minimum score 550 paper-based; 79 iBT). Electronic applications accepted. *Expenses:* Tuition, state resident: full-time $16,650; part-time $925 per credit hour. Tuition, nonresident: full-time $37,350; part-time $2075 per credit hour. *International tuition:* $37,350 full-time. *Required fees:* $2412.

Colorado School of Mines, Office of Graduate Studies, Department of Geophysics, Golden, CO 80401. Offers geophysical engineering (ME, MS, PhD); geophysics (MS, PhD); hydrology (MS, PhD); mineral exploration and mining geosciences (PMS); petroleum reservoir systems (PMS). *Program availability:* Part-time. *Degree requirements:* For master's, thesis (for some programs); for doctorate, comprehensive exam, thesis/dissertation. *Entrance requirements:* For master's and doctorate, GRE General Test. Additional exam requirements/recommendations for international students: required—TOEFL (minimum score 550 paper-based; 79 iBT). Electronic applications accepted. *Expenses:* Tuition, state resident: full-time $16,650; part-time $925 per credit hour. Tuition, nonresident: full-time $37,350; part-time $2075 per credit hour. *International tuition:* $37,350 full-time. *Required fees:* $2412.

Missouri University of Science and Technology, Department of Geosciences and Geological and Petroleum Engineering, Rolla, MO 65401. Offers geological engineering (MS, DE, PhD); geology and geophysics (MS, PhD), including geochemistry, geology, geophysics, groundwater and environmental geology; petroleum engineering (MS, DE, PhD). *Program availability:* Part-time. *Degree requirements:* For master's, thesis optional; for doctorate, comprehensive exam, thesis/dissertation. *Entrance requirements:* For master's, GRE General Test (minimum score 600 quantitative, writing 3.5), minimum GPA of 3.0 in last 4 semesters; for doctorate, GRE General Test (minimum scores: Quantitative 600, Writing 3.5). Additional exam requirements/recommendations for international students: required—TOEFL (minimum score 550 paper-based). Electronic applications accepted. *Expenses:* Tuition, state resident: full-time $7839; part-time $435.50 per credit hour. Tuition, nonresident: full-time $22,169; part-time $1231.60 per credit hour. *International tuition:* $18,156.60 full-time. *Required fees:* $649.76. One-time fee: $119. Tuition and fees vary according to course load and program.

Montana Technological University, Geosciences Programs, Butte, MT 59701-8997. Offers geochemistry (MS); geological engineering (MS); geology (MS); geophysical engineering (MS); hydrogeological engineering (MS); hydrogeology (MS). *Program availability:* Part-time. *Faculty:* 18 full-time (5 women), 6 part-time/adjunct (2 women). *Students:* 24 full-time (6 women), 1 part-time (0 women); includes 1 minority (Hispanic/Latino), 2 international. Average age 28. 27 applicants, 52% accepted, 11 enrolled. In 2019, 13 master's awarded. *Degree requirements:* For master's, comprehensive exam (for some programs), thesis (for some programs). *Entrance requirements:* For master's, GRE General Test, minimum GPA of 3.0. Additional exam requirements/recommendations for international students: required—TOEFL (minimum score 545 paper-based; 78 iBT), IELTS (minimum score 6.5). *Application deadline:* For fall admission, 4/1 priority date for domestic students, 3/1 priority date for international students; for spring admission, 10/1 priority date for domestic students, 7/1 priority date for international students. Applications are processed on a rolling basis. Application fee: $50. Electronic applications accepted. *Financial support:* In 2019–20, 15 students received support, including 10 teaching assistantships with partial tuition reimbursements available (averaging $5,000 per year); research assistantships with partial tuition reimbursements available, career-related internships or fieldwork, tuition waivers (full and partial), and unspecified assistantships also available. Financial award application deadline: 4/1; financial award applicants required to submit FAFSA. *Unit head:* Dr. Glenn Shaw, Department Head, 406-496-4809, Fax: 406-496-4260, E-mail: gshaw@mtech.edu. *Application contact:* Daniel Stirling, Administrator, Graduate School, 406-496-4304, Fax: 406-496-4710, E-mail: gradschool@mtech.edu.
Website: http://www.mtech.edu/academics/gradschool/degreeprograms/degrees.htm

New Mexico Institute of Mining and Technology, Center for Graduate Studies, Department of Mineral Engineering, Socorro, NM 87801. Offers explosives engineering (MS); geotechnical engineering (MS); mining engineering (MS). *Degree requirements:* For master's, thesis. *Entrance requirements:* Additional exam requirements/recommendations for international students: required—TOEFL (minimum score 540 paper-based).

South Dakota School of Mines and Technology, Graduate Division, Department of Geology and Geological Engineering, Rapid City, SD 57701-3995. Offers geology and geological engineering (MS, PhD); paleontology (MS). *Program availability:* Part-time. *Degree requirements:* For master's, thesis; for doctorate, thesis/dissertation. *Entrance requirements:* For master's and doctorate, GRE General Test, GRE Subject Test. Additional exam requirements/recommendations for international students: required—TOEFL (minimum score 520 paper-based; 68 iBT), TWE. Electronic applications accepted.

The University of Akron, Graduate School, Buchtel College of Arts and Sciences, Department of Geosciences, Akron, OH 44325. Offers earth science (MS); engineering geology (MS); environmental geology (MS); geology (MS). *Program availability:* Part-time. *Entrance requirements:* For master's, minimum GPA of 2.75, three letters of recommendation, statement of purpose. Additional exam requirements/recommendations for international students: required—TOEFL (minimum score 79 iBT), IELTS (minimum score 6.5). Electronic applications accepted.

University of Alaska Fairbanks, College of Engineering and Mines, Department of Mining and Geological Engineering, Fairbanks, AK 99775-5800. Offers geological engineering (MS); mineral preparation engineering (MS); mining engineering (MS). *Program availability:* Part-time. *Degree requirements:* For master's, comprehensive exam, oral defense of project or thesis. *Entrance requirements:* For master's, GRE General Test (for geological engineering), bachelor's degree from accredited institution with minimum cumulative undergraduate and major GPA of 3.0. Additional exam requirements/recommendations for international students: required—TOEFL (minimum score 550 paper-based; 79 iBT), IELTS (minimum score 6.5). Electronic applications accepted. *Expenses:* Contact institution.

The University of Arizona, College of Engineering, Department of Mining and Geological Engineering, Tucson, AZ 85721. Offers mining and geological engineering (MS, PhD); mining engineering (Certificate), including mine health and safety, mine information and production technology, rock mechanics. *Program availability:* Part-time, online learning. *Degree requirements:* For master's, thesis; for doctorate, thesis/dissertation. *Entrance requirements:* For master's, GRE General Test, 3 letters of recommendation; for doctorate, GRE General Test, 3 letters of recommendation, statements of purpose. Additional exam requirements/recommendations for international students: required—TOEFL (minimum score 550 paper-based; 79 iBT). Electronic applications accepted.

The University of British Columbia, Faculty of Science, Department of Earth, Ocean and Atmospheric Sciences, Vancouver, BC V6T 1Z4, Canada. Offers atmospheric science (M Sc, PhD); geological engineering (M Eng, MA Sc, PhD); geological sciences (M Sc, PhD); geophysics (M Sc, MA Sc, PhD); oceanography (M Sc, PhD). *Degree requirements:* For master's, one foreign language, thesis (for some programs); for doctorate, one foreign language, comprehensive exam, thesis/dissertation. *Entrance requirements:* Additional exam requirements/recommendations for international students: required—TOEFL. *Expenses:* Contact institution.

University of Hawaii at Manoa, Office of Graduate Education, School of Ocean and Earth Science and Technology, Department of Geology and Geophysics, Honolulu, HI 96822. Offers high-pressure geophysics and geochemistry (MS, PhD); hydrogeology and engineering geology (MS, PhD); marine geology and geophysics (MS, PhD); planetary geosciences and remote sensing (MS, PhD); seismology and solid-earth geophysics (MS, PhD); volcanology, petrology, and geochemistry (MS, PhD). *Program availability:* Part-time. Terminal master's awarded for partial completion of doctoral program. *Degree requirements:* For master's, thesis optional; for doctorate, comprehensive exam, thesis/dissertation. *Entrance requirements:* For master's and doctorate, GRE General Test, minimum GPA of 3.0. Additional exam requirements/recommendations for international students: required—TOEFL (minimum score 580 paper-based; 92 iBT), IELTS (minimum score 5).

University of Idaho, College of Graduate Studies, College of Engineering, Department of Civil and Environmental Engineering, Moscow, ID 83844-2282. Offers civil and environmental engineering (M Engr, PhD); geological engineering (MS). *Faculty:* 11. *Students:* 23 full-time (5 women), 55 part-time (7 women). Average age 34. In 2019, 21 master's, 1 doctorate awarded. *Entrance requirements:* For master's and doctorate, minimum GPA of 3.0. Additional exam requirements/recommendations for international students: required—TOEFL (minimum score 550 paper-based; 79 iBT). *Application deadline:* For fall admission, 7/30 for domestic students; for spring admission, 12/1 for domestic students. Applications are processed on a rolling basis. Application fee: $60. Electronic applications accepted. *Expenses:* Tuition, state resident: full-time $7753.80; part-time $502 per credit hour. Tuition, nonresident: full-time $26,990; part-time $1571 per credit hour. *Required fees:* $2122.20; $47 per credit hour. *Financial support:* Fellowships, research assistantships, teaching assistantships, and career-related internships or fieldwork available. Financial award applicants required to submit FAFSA. *Unit head:* Patricia Colberg, Department Chair, 208-885-6782, E-mail: cee@uidaho.edu. *Application contact:* Patricia Colberg, Department Chair, 208-885-6782, E-mail: cee@uidaho.edu.
Website: http://www.uidaho.edu/engr/cee

University of Minnesota, Twin Cities Campus, College of Science and Engineering, Department of Civil, Environmental, and Geo-Engineering, Minneapolis, MN 55455-0213. Offers civil engineering (MCE, MS, PhD); geological engineering (M Geo E, MS); stream restoration science and engineering (Certificate). *Program availability:* Part-time. *Degree requirements:* For master's, thesis optional; for doctorate, thesis/dissertation. *Entrance requirements:* For master's and doctorate, GRE General Test. Additional exam requirements/recommendations for international students: required—TOEFL. Electronic applications accepted.

University of Mississippi, Graduate School, School of Engineering, University, MS 38677. Offers aeroacoustics (MS, PhD); chemical engineering (MS, PhD); civil engineering (MS, PhD); computational hydroscience (MS, PhD); computer science (MS, PhD); electrical engineering (MS, PhD); electromagnetics (MS, PhD); environmental engineering (MS, PhD); geology and geological engineering (MS, PhD); hydrology (MS); material science (MS); mechanical engineering (MS, PhD); telecommunications (MS). *Students:* 104 full-time (23 women), 19 part-time (5 women); includes 10 minority (3 Black or African American, non-Hispanic/Latino; 6 Asian, non-Hispanic/Latino; 1 Hispanic/Latino), 72 international. Average age 30. In 2019, 36 master's, 17 doctorates awarded. *Expenses:* Tuition, state resident: full-time $8718; part-time $484.25 per credit hour. Tuition, nonresident: full-time $24,990; part-time $1388.25 per credit hour. *Required fees:* $100; $4.16 per credit hour. *Unit head:* Dr. David Puleo, Dean, 662-915-5780, Fax: 662-915-5387, E-mail: engineer@olemiss.edu. *Application contact:* Temeka Smith, Graduate Activities Specialist for Admissions, 662-915-7474, Fax: 662-915-7577, E-mail: gschool@olemiss.edu.

University of Nevada, Reno, Graduate School, College of Science, Mackay School of Earth Sciences and Engineering, Department of Geological Sciences and Engineering, Program in Geological Engineering, Reno, NV 89557. Offers MS, PhD. Terminal master's awarded for partial completion of doctoral program. *Degree requirements:* For master's, thesis optional; for doctorate, thesis/dissertation. *Entrance requirements:* For master's and doctorate, GRE General Test, minimum GPA of 2.75. Additional exam requirements/recommendations for international students: required—TOEFL (minimum score 500 paper-based; 61 iBT), IELTS (minimum score 6). Electronic applications accepted.

University of North Dakota, Graduate School, School of Engineering and Mines, Department of Geological Engineering, Grand Forks, ND 58202. Offers MS, PhD. *Degree requirements:* For master's, thesis. *Entrance requirements:* For master's, GRE General Test. Additional exam requirements/recommendations for international students: required—TOEFL (minimum score 550 paper-based; 79 iBT), IELTS (minimum score 6.5). Electronic applications accepted.

University of Oklahoma, Mewbourne College of Earth and Energy, Mewbourne School of Petroleum and Geological Engineering, Norman, OK 73019. Offers geological engineering (MS, PhD); natural gas engineering and management (MS), including natural gas engineering and management; natural gas technology (Graduate

Certificate), including natural gas technology; petroleum engineering (MS, PhD). *Program availability:* Part-time, evening/weekend. *Degree requirements:* For master's, variable foreign language requirement, comprehensive exam (for some programs), thesis (for some programs); for doctorate, variable foreign language requirement, comprehensive exam, thesis/dissertation. *Entrance requirements:* For master's and doctorate, GRE, minimum GPA of 3.2, three letters of recommendation, statement of purpose, resume/curriculum vitae. Additional exam requirements/recommendations for international students: required—TOEFL (minimum score 79 iBT) or IELTS (minimum score 6.5). Electronic applications accepted. *Expenses:* Tuition, state resident: full-time $6583.20; part-time $274.30 per credit hour. Tuition, nonresident: full-time $21,242; part-time $885.10 per credit hour. *International tuition:* $21,242.40 full-time. *Required fees:* $1994.20; $72.55 per credit hour. $126.50 per semester. Tuition and fees vary according to course load and degree level.

University of Saskatchewan, College of Graduate and Postdoctoral Studies, College of Engineering, Civil and Geological Engineering Program, Saskatoon, SK S7N 5E5, Canada. Offers M Eng, M Sc, PhD. *Program availability:* Part-time. *Degree requirements:* For master's, 30 credits (for M Eng); thesis and 12 credits (for MS); for doctorate, comprehensive exam, thesis/dissertation, qualifying exam, 18 credits. *Entrance requirements:* For master's, GRE, minimum GPA of 5.0 on an 8.0 scale; for doctorate, GRE. Additional exam requirements/recommendations for international students: required—TOEFL (minimum iBT score of 80), IELTS (6.5), CanTEST (4.5), or PTE (59). Electronic applications accepted.

University of Utah, Graduate School, College of Mines and Earth Sciences, Department of Geology and Geophysics, Salt Lake City, UT 84112. Offers geological engineering (ME, MS, PhD); geology (MS, PhD); geophysics (MS, PhD). *Faculty:* 23 full-time (6 women). *Students:* 50 full-time (17 women), 24 part-time (18 women); includes 15 minority (7 Asian, non-Hispanic/Latino; 6 Hispanic/Latino; 2 Two or more races, non-Hispanic/Latino). Average age 31. 98 applicants, 12% accepted, 5 enrolled. In 2019, 10 master's, 10 doctorates awarded. *Degree requirements:* For master's, comprehensive exam, thesis, 30 credits of course work (10 of which are thesis research credit hours); for doctorate, comprehensive exam, thesis/dissertation. *Entrance requirements:* For master's and doctorate, GRE, Academic Transcripts, Letters of Reference, CV or Resume, Statement of Purpose. Additional exam requirements/recommendations for international students: required—TOEFL. *Application deadline:* For fall admission, 1/15 for domestic and international students; for spring admission, 9/15 for domestic and international students. Application fee: $55 ($65 for international students). Electronic applications accepted. *Expenses:* Tuition, state resident: full-time $7085; part-time $272.51 per credit hour. Tuition, nonresident: full-time $24,937; part-time $959.12 per credit hour. *Required fees:* $880.52; $880.52 per semester. Tuition and fees vary according to degree level, program and student level. *Financial support:* In 2019–20, 50 students received support, including 5 fellowships (averaging $21,800 per year), 22 research assistantships (averaging $11,318 per year), 12 teaching assistantships (averaging $16,333 per year); unspecified assistantships also available. Financial award application deadline: 1/15. *Unit head:* Thure Cerling, Department Chair, 801-585-6656, Fax: 801-581-7061, E-mail: thure.cerling@utah.edu. *Application contact:* Michelle Tuitupou, Academic Advisor, 801-585-6553, Fax: 801-581-7061, E-mail: michelle.tuitupou@utah.edu.
Website: http://www.earth.utah.edu/

University of Wisconsin–Madison, Graduate School, College of Engineering, Department of Civil and Environmental Engineering, Madison, WI 53706-1380. Offers construction engineering and management (MS); environmental science and engineering (MS); geological/geotechnical engineering (MS); structural engineering (MS); transportation engineering (MS); water resources engineering (MS). *Program availability:* Part-time. Terminal master's awarded for partial completion of doctoral program. *Degree requirements:* For master's, thesis (for some programs), minimum of 30 credits; minimum overall GPA of 3.0. *Entrance requirements:* For master's, GRE General Test, bachelor's degree; minimum GPA of 3.0 for last 60 credits of course work. Additional exam requirements/recommendations for international students: required—TOEFL (minimum score 580 paper-based; 92 iBT). Electronic applications accepted. *Expenses:* Contact institution.

University of Wisconsin–Madison, Graduate School, College of Engineering, Geological Engineering Program, Madison, WI 53706-1380. Offers geological engineering (MS). *Program availability:* Part-time. Terminal master's awarded for partial completion of doctoral program. *Degree requirements:* For master's, thesis optional, minimum of 30 credits; minimum GPA of 3.0; for doctorate, comprehensive exam, thesis/dissertation, minimum of 51 credits; minimum GPA of 3.0. *Entrance requirements:* For master's and doctorate, GRE, BS; minimum GPA of 3.0. Additional exam requirements/recommendations for international students: required—TOEFL (minimum score 580 paper-based; 92 iBT), IELTS (minimum score 7). Electronic applications accepted.

Mineral/Mining Engineering

Colorado School of Mines, Office of Graduate Studies, Department of Geology and Geological Engineering, Golden, CO 80401. Offers environmental geochemistry (PMS); geochemistry (MS, PhD); geological engineering (ME, MS, PhD); geology (MS, PhD); hydrology (MS, PhD); mineral exploration (PMS); petroleum reservoir systems (PMS); underground construction and tunneling (MS). *Program availability:* Part-time. *Degree requirements:* For master's, thesis (for some programs); for doctorate, comprehensive exam, thesis/dissertation. *Entrance requirements:* For master's and doctorate, GRE General Test. Additional exam requirements/recommendations for international students: required—TOEFL (minimum score 550 paper-based; 79 iBT). Electronic applications accepted. *Expenses:* Tuition, state resident: full-time $16,650; part-time $925 per credit hour. Tuition, nonresident: full-time $37,350; part-time $2075 per credit hour. *International tuition:* $37,350 full-time. *Required fees:* $2412.

Colorado School of Mines, Office of Graduate Studies, Department of Geophysics, Golden, CO 80401. Offers geophysical engineering (ME, MS, PhD); geophysics (MS, PhD); hydrology (MS, PhD); mineral exploration and mining geosciences (PMS); petroleum reservoir systems (PMS). *Program availability:* Part-time. *Degree requirements:* For master's, thesis (for some programs); for doctorate, comprehensive exam, thesis/dissertation. *Entrance requirements:* For master's and doctorate, GRE General Test. Additional exam requirements/recommendations for international students: required—TOEFL (minimum score 550 paper-based; 79 iBT). Electronic applications accepted. *Expenses:* Tuition, state resident: full-time $16,650; part-time $925 per credit hour. Tuition, nonresident: full-time $37,350; part-time $2075 per credit hour. *International tuition:* $37,350 full-time. *Required fees:* $2412.

Colorado School of Mines, Office of Graduate Studies, Department of Mining Engineering, Golden, CO 80401. Offers mining and earth systems engineering (MS); mining engineering (PhD); underground construction and tunneling (MS, PhD). *Program availability:* Part-time. *Degree requirements:* For master's, thesis (for some programs); for doctorate, comprehensive exam, thesis/dissertation. *Entrance requirements:* For master's and doctorate, GRE General Test. Additional exam requirements/recommendations for international students: required—TOEFL (minimum score 550 paper-based; 79 iBT). Electronic applications accepted. *Expenses:* Tuition, state resident: full-time $16,650; part-time $925 per credit hour. Tuition, nonresident: full-time $37,350; part-time $2075 per credit hour. *International tuition:* $37,350 full-time. *Required fees:* $2412.

Dalhousie University, Faculty of Engineering, Department of Civil and Resource Engineering, Halifax, NS B3J 2X4, Canada. Offers civil engineering (M Eng, MA Sc, PhD); environmental engineering (M Eng, MA Sc); mineral resource engineering (M Eng, MA Sc, PhD). *Degree requirements:* For master's, thesis; for doctorate, thesis/dissertation. *Entrance requirements:* Additional exam requirements/recommendations for international students: required—TOEFL, IELTS, CANTEST, CAEL, or Michigan English Language Assessment Battery. Electronic applications accepted.

Laurentian University, School of Graduate Studies and Research, Programme in Geology (Earth Sciences), Sudbury, ON P3E 2C6, Canada. Offers geology (M Sc); mineral deposits and precambrian geology (PhD); mineral exploration (M Sc). *Program availability:* Part-time. *Degree requirements:* For master's, thesis. *Entrance requirements:* For master's, honors degree with second class or better.

Laurentian University, School of Graduate Studies and Research, School of Engineering, Sudbury, ON P3E 2C6, Canada. Offers mineral resources engineering (M Eng, MA Sc); natural resources engineering (PhD). *Program availability:* Part-time.

McGill University, Faculty of Graduate and Postdoctoral Studies, Faculty of Engineering, Department of Mining and Materials Engineering, Montréal, QC H3A 2T5, Canada. Offers materials engineering (M Eng, PhD); mining engineering (M Eng, M Sc, PhD, Diploma).

Missouri University of Science and Technology, Department of Mining and Nuclear Engineering, Rolla, MO 65401. Offers explosives engineering (MS, PhD); mining engineering (MS, DE, PhD); nuclear engineering (MS, DE, PhD). *Degree requirements:* For master's, thesis optional; for doctorate, comprehensive exam. *Entrance requirements:* For master's, GRE (minimum score 600 quantitative, 3 writing); for doctorate, GRE (minimum score: quantitative 600, writing 3.5). Additional exam requirements/recommendations for international students: required—TOEFL (minimum score 550 paper-based). Electronic applications accepted. *Expenses:* Tuition, state resident: full-time $7839; part-time $435.50 per credit hour. Tuition, nonresident: full-time $22,169; part-time $1231.60 per credit hour. *International tuition:* $18,156.60 full-time. *Required fees:* $649.76. One-time fee: $119. Tuition and fees vary according to course load and program.

Montana Technological University, Department of Metallurgical/Mineral Processing Engineering, Butte, MT 59701-8997. Offers MS. *Program availability:* Part-time. *Faculty:* 6 full-time (0 women). *Students:* 7 full-time (1 woman), 3 international. Average age 27. 4 applicants, 75% accepted, 3 enrolled. In 2019, 2 master's awarded. *Degree requirements:* For master's, comprehensive exam (for some programs), thesis optional. *Entrance requirements:* For master's, GRE General Test, minimum GPA of 3.0. Additional exam requirements/recommendations for international students: required—TOEFL (minimum score 545 paper-based; 78 iBT), IELTS (minimum score 6.5). *Application deadline:* For fall admission, 4/1 priority date for domestic students, 3/1 priority date for international students; for spring admission, 10/1 priority date for domestic students, 6/1 priority date for international students. Applications are processed on a rolling basis. Application fee: $50. Electronic applications accepted. *Financial support:* In 2019–20, 4 students received support, including 2 teaching assistantships with partial tuition reimbursements available (averaging $5,000 per year); research assistantships with partial tuition reimbursements available, career-related internships or fieldwork, tuition waivers (full and partial), and unspecified assistantships also available. Financial award application deadline: 4/1; financial award applicants required to submit FAFSA. *Unit head:* Dr. Jerry Downey, Department Head, 406-496-4578, Fax: 406-496-4664, E-mail: jdowney@mtech.edu. *Application contact:* Daniel Stirling, Administrator, Graduate School, 406-496-4304, Fax: 406-496-4710, E-mail: gradschool@mtech.edu.
Website: http://www.mtech.edu/academics/gradschool/degreeprograms/degrees-metallurgical.htm

Montana Technological University, Mining Engineering Program, Butte, MT 59701-8997. Offers MS. *Program availability:* Part-time. *Faculty:* 4 full-time (0 women). *Students:* 5 full-time (3 women), 3 international. Average age 26. 8 applicants, 75% accepted, 3 enrolled. In 2019, 4 master's awarded. *Degree requirements:* For master's, thesis optional. *Entrance requirements:* For master's, minimum GPA of 3.0. Additional exam requirements/recommendations for international students: required—TOEFL (minimum score 545 paper-based; 78 iBT), IELTS (minimum score 6.5). *Application deadline:* For fall admission, 4/1 priority date for domestic students, 3/1 priority date for international students; for spring admission, 10/1 priority date for domestic students, 6/1 priority date for international students. Applications are processed on a rolling basis. Application fee: $50. Electronic applications accepted. *Financial support:* In 2019–20, 2 students received support, including 2 teaching assistantships with partial tuition reimbursements available (averaging $4,000 per year); research assistantships, career-related internships or fieldwork, tuition waivers (full and partial), and unspecified assistantships also available. Financial award application deadline: 4/1; financial award applicants required to submit FAFSA. *Unit head:* Dr. Scott Rosenthal, Department Head, 406-496-4867, Fax: 406-496-4260, E-mail: srosenthal@mtech.edu. *Application contact:* Daniel Stirling, Administrator, Graduate School, 406-496-4304, Fax: 406-496-4710, E-mail: gradschool@mtech.edu.
Website: http://www.mtech.edu/academics/gradschool/degreeprograms/degrees-mining-engineering.htm

New Mexico Institute of Mining and Technology, Center for Graduate Studies, Department of Mineral Engineering, Socorro, NM 87801. Offers explosives engineering (MS); geotechnical engineering (MS); mining engineering (MS). *Degree requirements:* For master's, thesis. *Entrance requirements:* Additional exam requirements/recommendations for international students: required—TOEFL (minimum score 540 paper-based).

Penn State University Park, Graduate School, College of Earth and Mineral Sciences, John and Willie Leone Family Department of Energy and Mineral Engineering, University Park, PA 16802. Offers MS, PhD.

Mineral/Mining Engineering

Queen's University at Kingston, School of Graduate Studies, Faculty of Engineering and Applied Science, The Robert M. Buchan Department of Mining, Kingston, ON K7L 3N6, Canada. Offers mining engineering (M Eng, M Sc, M Sc Eng, PhD). *Program availability:* Part-time. *Degree requirements:* For master's, thesis optional; for doctorate, comprehensive exam, thesis/dissertation. *Entrance requirements:* Additional exam requirements/recommendations for international students: required—TOEFL (minimum score 550 paper-based). Electronic applications accepted.

South Dakota School of Mines and Technology, Graduate Division, Department of Mining Engineering and Management, Rapid City, SD 57701-3995. Offers mining engineering (MS). *Program availability:* Part-time. *Entrance requirements:* For master's, GRE General Test. Additional exam requirements/recommendations for international students: required—TOEFL (minimum score 520 paper-based; 68 iBT), TWE. Electronic applications accepted.

Southern Illinois University Carbondale, Graduate School, College of Engineering, Department of Mining and Mineral Resources Engineering, Carbondale, IL 62901-4701. Offers mining engineering (MS). *Degree requirements:* For master's, comprehensive exam, thesis. *Entrance requirements:* For master's, GRE (recommended), minimum GPA of 2.7. Additional exam requirements/recommendations for international students: required—TOEFL.

Southern Illinois University Carbondale, Graduate School, College of Engineering, Program in Engineering Science, Carbondale, IL 62901-4701. Offers engineering science (PhD), including civil and environmental engineering, electrical and computer engineering, mechanical engineering and energy processes, mining and mineral resources engineering. *Degree requirements:* For doctorate, thesis/dissertation. *Entrance requirements:* For doctorate, GRE General Test, minimum GPA of 3.5. Additional exam requirements/recommendations for international students: required—TOEFL.

Université du Québec en Abitibi-Témiscamingue, Graduate Programs, Program in Engineering, Rouyn-Noranda, QC J9X 5E4, Canada. Offers engineering (ME); mineral engineering (ME); mining engineering (DESS).

University of Alaska Fairbanks, College of Engineering and Mines, Department of Mining and Geological Engineering, Fairbanks, AK 99775-5800. Offers geological engineering (MS); mineral preparation engineering (MS); mining engineering (MS). *Program availability:* Part-time. *Degree requirements:* For master's, comprehensive exam, oral defense of project or thesis. *Entrance requirements:* For master's, GRE General Test (for geological engineering), bachelor's degree from accredited institution with minimum cumulative undergraduate and major GPA of 3.0. Additional exam requirements/recommendations for international students: required—TOEFL (minimum score 550 paper-based; 79 iBT), IELTS (minimum score 6.5). Electronic applications accepted. *Expenses:* Contact institution.

University of Alberta, Faculty of Graduate Studies and Research, Department of Civil and Environmental Engineering, Edmonton, AB T6G 2E1, Canada. Offers construction engineering and management (M Eng, M Sc, PhD); environmental engineering (M Eng, M Sc, PhD); environmental science (M Sc, PhD); geoenvironmental engineering (M Eng, M Sc, PhD); geotechnical engineering (M Eng, M Sc, PhD); mining engineering (M Eng, M Sc, PhD); petroleum engineering (M Eng, M Sc, PhD); structural engineering (M Eng, M Sc, PhD); water resources (M Eng, M Sc, PhD). *Program availability:* Part-time, online learning. *Degree requirements:* For master's, thesis (for some programs); for doctorate, thesis/dissertation. *Entrance requirements:* For master's, minimum GPA of 3.0 in last 2 years of undergraduate studies; for doctorate, minimum GPA of 3.0. Additional exam requirements/recommendations for international students: required—TOEFL (minimum score 550 paper-based). Electronic applications accepted.

The University of Arizona, College of Engineering, Department of Mining and Geological Engineering, Tucson, AZ 85721. Offers mining and geological engineering (MS, PhD); mining engineering (Certificate), including mine health and safety, mine information and production technology, rock mechanics. *Program availability:* Part-time, online learning. *Degree requirements:* For master's, thesis; for doctorate, thesis/dissertation. *Entrance requirements:* For master's, GRE General Test, 3 letters of recommendation; for doctorate, GRE General Test, 3 letters of recommendation, statements of purpose. Additional exam requirements/recommendations for international students: required—TOEFL (minimum score 550 paper-based; 79 iBT). Electronic applications accepted.

The University of British Columbia, Faculty of Applied Science, Department of Mining Engineering, Vancouver, BC V6T 1Z4, Canada. Offers M Eng, MA Sc, PhD. *Degree requirements:* For master's, thesis; for doctorate, thesis/dissertation. *Entrance requirements:* Additional exam requirements/recommendations for international students: required—TOEFL, IELTS. Electronic applications accepted. *Expenses:* Contact institution.

University of Kentucky, Graduate School, College of Engineering, Program in Mining Engineering, Lexington, KY 40506-0032. Offers MME, MS Min, PhD. *Degree requirements:* For master's, comprehensive exam, thesis optional; for doctorate, one foreign language, comprehensive exam, thesis/dissertation. *Entrance requirements:* For master's, GRE General Test, minimum undergraduate GPA of 2.75; for doctorate, GRE General Test, minimum undergraduate GPA of 3.0. Additional exam requirements/recommendations for international students: required—TOEFL (minimum score 550 paper-based). Electronic applications accepted.

University of Nevada, Reno, Graduate School, College of Science, Mackay School of Earth Sciences and Engineering, Department of Mining and Metallurgical Engineering, Reno, NV 89557. Offers metallurgical engineering (MS); mining engineering (MS, PhD). *Degree requirements:* For master's, thesis optional. *Entrance requirements:* For master's, GRE, minimum GPA of 2.75. Additional exam requirements/recommendations for international students: required—TOEFL (minimum score 500 paper-based; 61 iBT), IELTS (minimum score 6). Electronic applications accepted.

The University of Texas at Austin, Graduate School, Cockrell School of Engineering, Department of Petroleum and Geosystems Engineering, Program in Energy and Earth Resources, Austin, TX 78712-1111. Offers MA. *Degree requirements:* For master's, thesis, seminar. *Entrance requirements:* For master's, GRE General Test. Additional exam requirements/recommendations for international students: required—TOEFL. Electronic applications accepted.

University of Utah, Graduate School, College of Mines and Earth Sciences, Department of Mining Engineering, Salt Lake City, UT 84112. Offers ME, MS, PhD. *Program availability:* Part-time. *Faculty:* 4 full-time (1 woman). *Students:* 12 full-time (4 women), 1 part-time (0 women), 7 international. Average age 32. 13 applicants, 46% accepted, 6 enrolled. In 2019, 2 master's, 1 doctorate awarded. Terminal master's awarded for partial completion of doctoral program. *Degree requirements:* For master's, thesis; for doctorate, one foreign language, comprehensive exam, thesis/dissertation. *Entrance requirements:* For master's, Statement of purpose, official transcript and three letters of recommendation; for doctorate, GRE exam is required for Ph.D. applicants and is optional for M.S. applicants., Statement of purpose, official transcript and three letters of recommendation. Additional exam requirements/recommendations for international students: required—TOEFL (minimum score 550 paper-based; 80 iBT), IELTS (minimum score 6.5). *Application deadline:* For fall admission, 4/1 for domestic and international students; for spring admission, 11/1 for domestic students, 8/1 for international students. Application fee: $55 ($65 for international students). Electronic applications accepted. *Expenses:* Tuition, state resident: full-time $7085; part-time $272.51 per credit hour. Tuition, nonresident: full-time $24,937; part-time $959.12 per credit hour. *Required fees:* $880.52; $880.52 per semester. Tuition and fees vary according to degree level, program and student level. *Financial support:* In 2019–20, 4 students received support, including 6 fellowships (averaging $19,667 per year), 9 research assistantships (averaging $11,778 per year), 1 teaching assistantship (averaging $4,000 per year); health care benefits also available. Financial award application deadline: 4/1. *Unit head:* Dr. Michael L. Free, DEPARTMENT HEAD, 801-585-3893, E-mail: mike.free@utah.edu. *Application contact:* Kitzia E. Casasola, ADMINISTRATIVE PROGRAM COORDINATOR, 801-585-5176, E-mail: kitzia.casasola@utah.edu.
Website: http://www.mining.utah.edu/

Université Laval, Faculty of Sciences and Engineering, Department of Mining, Metallurgical and Materials Engineering, Programs in Mining Engineering, Québec, QC G1K 7P4, Canada. Offers M Sc, PhD. Terminal master's awarded for partial completion of doctoral program. *Degree requirements:* For master's, thesis; for doctorate, comprehensive exam, thesis/dissertation. *Entrance requirements:* For master's and doctorate, knowledge of French and English. Electronic applications accepted.

West Virginia University, Statler College of Engineering and Mineral Resources, Morgantown, WV 26506. Offers aerospace engineering (MSAE, PhD); chemical engineering (MS Ch E, PhD); civil engineering (MSCE, PhD); computer engineering (PhD); computer science (MSCS, PhD); electrical engineering (MSEE, PhD); energy systems engineering (MSESE); engineering (MSE); industrial engineering (MSIE, PhD); industrial hygiene (MS); material science and engineering (MSMSE, PhD); mechanical engineering (MSME, PhD); mining engineering (MS Min E, PhD); petroleum and natural gas engineering (MSPNGE, PhD); safety management (MS); software engineering (MSSE). *Program availability:* Part-time. Terminal master's awarded for partial completion of doctoral program. *Degree requirements:* For master's, thesis optional; for doctorate, comprehensive exam, thesis/dissertation. *Entrance requirements:* Additional exam requirements/recommendations for international students: required—TOEFL (minimum score 550 paper-based). Electronic applications accepted. *Expenses:* Contact institution.

Petroleum Engineering

Colorado School of Mines, Office of Graduate Studies, Department of Petroleum Engineering, Golden, CO 80401. Offers petroleum engineering (ME, MS, PhD); petroleum reservoir systems (PMS). *Program availability:* Part-time. *Degree requirements:* For master's, thesis (for some programs); for doctorate, comprehensive exam, thesis/dissertation. *Entrance requirements:* For master's and doctorate, GRE General Test. Additional exam requirements/recommendations for international students: required—TOEFL (minimum score 550 paper-based; 79 iBT). Electronic applications accepted. *Expenses:* Tuition, state resident: full-time $16,650; part-time $925 per credit hour. Tuition, nonresident: full-time $37,350; part-time $2075 per credit hour. *International tuition:* $37,350 full-time. *Required fees:* $2412.

Louisiana State University and Agricultural & Mechanical College, Graduate School, College of Engineering, Department of Petroleum Engineering, Baton Rouge, LA 70803. Offers MS Pet E, PhD.

Missouri University of Science and Technology, Department of Geosciences and Geological and Petroleum Engineering, Rolla, MO 65401. Offers geological engineering (MS, DE, PhD); geology and geophysics (MS, PhD), including geochemistry, geology, geophysics, groundwater and environmental geology; petroleum engineering (MS, DE, PhD). *Program availability:* Part-time. *Degree requirements:* For master's, thesis optional; for doctorate, comprehensive exam, thesis/dissertation. *Entrance requirements:* For master's, GRE General Test (minimum score 600 quantitative, writing 3.5), minimum GPA of 3.0 in last 4 semesters; for doctorate, GRE General Test (minimum scores: Quantitative 600, Writing 3.5). Additional exam requirements/recommendations for international students: required—TOEFL (minimum score 550 paper-based). Electronic applications accepted. *Expenses:* Tuition, state resident: full-time $7839; part-time $435.50 per credit hour. Tuition, nonresident: full-time $22,169; part-time $1231.60 per credit hour. *International tuition:* $18,156.60 full-time. *Required fees:* $649.76. One-time fee: $119. Tuition and fees vary according to course load and program.

Montana Technological University, Department of Petroleum Engineering, Butte, MT 59701-8997. Offers MS. *Program availability:* Part-time, evening/weekend. *Faculty:* 5 full-time (1 woman), 1 part-time/adjunct (0 women). *Students:* 4 full-time (0 women), 1 international. Average age 26. 15 applicants, 20% accepted, 1 enrolled. In 2019, 3 master's awarded. *Degree requirements:* For master's, comprehensive exam, thesis optional. *Entrance requirements:* For master's, minimum GPA of 3.0. Additional exam requirements/recommendations for international students: required—TOEFL (minimum score 545 paper-based; 78 iBT), IELTS (minimum score 6.5). *Application deadline:* For fall admission, 4/1 priority date for domestic students, 3/1 priority date for international students; for spring admission, 10/1 priority date for domestic students, 6/1 priority date for international students. Applications are processed on a rolling basis. Application fee: $50. Electronic applications accepted. *Financial support:* In 2019–20, 6 students received support, including 5 teaching assistantships with partial tuition reimbursements available (averaging $4,800 per year); research assistantships, career-related internships or fieldwork, institutionally sponsored loans, tuition waivers (full and partial), and unspecified assistantships also available. Financial award application deadline: 4/1; financial award applicants required to submit FAFSA. *Unit head:* Dr. Todd Hoffman, Head, 406-496-4753, Fax: 406-496-4417, E-mail: thoffman@mtech.edu. *Application contact:* Daniel Stirling, Administrator, Graduate School, 406-496-4304, Fax: 406-496-4710, E-mail: gradschool@mtech.edu.
Website: http://www.mtech.edu/academics/gradschool/degreeprograms/degrees-petroleum-engineering.htm

New Mexico Institute of Mining and Technology, Center for Graduate Studies, Department of Petroleum and Natural Gas Engineering, Socorro, NM 87801. Offers petroleum engineering (MS, PhD). *Degree requirements:* For master's, thesis optional; for doctorate, thesis/dissertation. *Entrance requirements:* For master's, GRE General Test; for doctorate, GRE General Test, GRE Subject Test. Additional exam requirements/recommendations for international students: required—TOEFL (minimum score 540 paper-based).

Texas A&M University, College of Engineering, Harold Vance Department of Petroleum Engineering, College Station, TX 77843. Offers petroleum engineering (M Eng). *Program availability:* Part-time, online learning. *Faculty:* 29. *Students:* 148 full-time (29 women), 70 part-time (14 women); includes 36 minority (2 Black or African American, non-Hispanic/Latino; 18 Asian, non-Hispanic/Latino; 15 Hispanic/Latino; 1 Two or more races, non-Hispanic/Latino), 131 international. Average age 29. 159 applicants, 52% accepted, 43 enrolled. In 2019, 52 master's, 43 doctorates awarded. *Degree requirements:* For master's, comprehensive exam, thesis optional; for doctorate, comprehensive exam, thesis/dissertation. *Entrance requirements:* For master's and doctorate, GRE General Test. Additional exam requirements/recommendations for international students: required—TOEFL (minimum score 550 paper-based; 80 iBT), IELTS (minimum score 6), PTE (minimum score 53). *Application deadline:* For fall admission, 12/15 for domestic students; for spring admission, 9/1 for domestic students; for summer admission, 11/1 for domestic students. Applications are processed on a rolling basis. Application fee: $65 ($90 for international students). Electronic applications accepted. *Expenses:* Contact institution. *Financial support:* In 2019–20, 160 students received support, including 75 fellowships with tuition reimbursements available (averaging $5,810 per year), 104 research assistantships with tuition reimbursements available (averaging $15,374 per year), 32 teaching assistantships with tuition reimbursements available (averaging $13,206 per year); career-related internships or fieldwork, institutionally sponsored loans, scholarships/grants, traineeships, health care benefits, tuition waivers (full and partial), and unspecified assistantships also available. Support available to part-time students. Financial award application deadline: 3/15; financial award applicants required to submit FAFSA. *Unit head:* Dr. Jeff Spath, Department Head, 979-845-2278, E-mail: spath@tamu.edu. *Application contact:* Graduate Advisor, 979-847-9095, E-mail: pe-grad_info@tamu.edu.
Website: http://engineering.tamu.edu/petroleum

Texas A&M University–Kingsville, College of Graduate Studies, Frank H. Dotterweich College of Engineering, Wayne H. King Department of Chemical and Natural Gas Engineering, Program in Natural Gas Engineering, Kingsville, TX 78363. Offers ME, MS. *Degree requirements:* For master's, variable foreign language requirement, comprehensive exam, thesis (for some programs). *Entrance requirements:* For master's, GRE (minimum quantitative score of 150, verbal 145), MAT, GMAT, minimum GPA of 2.7. Additional exam requirements/recommendations for international students: required—TOEFL (minimum score 550 paper-based; 79 iBT). Electronic applications accepted.

University of Alaska Fairbanks, College of Engineering and Mines, Department of Petroleum Engineering, Fairbanks, AK 99775. Offers MS. *Program availability:* Part-time. *Degree requirements:* For master's, comprehensive exam, oral defense of project or thesis. *Entrance requirements:* For master's, bachelor's degree in engineering or the natural sciences with minimum cumulative undergraduate and major GPA of 3.0. Additional exam requirements/recommendations for international students: required—TOEFL (minimum score 550 paper-based; 79 iBT), IELTS (minimum score 6.5). Electronic applications accepted. *Expenses:* Contact institution.

University of Alberta, Faculty of Graduate Studies and Research, Department of Civil and Environmental Engineering, Edmonton, AB T6G 2E1, Canada. Offers construction engineering and management (M Eng, M Sc, PhD); environmental engineering (M Eng, M Sc, PhD); environmental science (M Sc, PhD); geoenvironmental engineering (M Eng, M Sc, PhD); geotechnical engineering (M Eng, M Sc, PhD); mining engineering (M Eng, M Sc, PhD); petroleum engineering (M Eng, M Sc, PhD); structural engineering (M Eng, M Sc, PhD); water resources (M Eng, M Sc, PhD). *Program availability:* Part-time, online learning. *Degree requirements:* For master's, thesis (for some programs); for doctorate, thesis/dissertation. *Entrance requirements:* For master's, minimum GPA of 3.0 in last 2 years of undergraduate studies; for doctorate, minimum GPA of 3.0. Additional exam requirements/recommendations for international students: required—TOEFL (minimum score 550 paper-based). Electronic applications accepted.

University of Calgary, Faculty of Graduate Studies, Schulich School of Engineering, Program in Chemical and Petroleum Engineering, Calgary, AB T2N 1N4, Canada. Offers chemical engineering (M Eng, M Sc, PhD); energy and environment engineering (M Eng, M Sc, PhD); energy and environmental systems (M Eng, M Sc, PhD); environmental engineering (M Eng, M Sc, PhD); petroleum engineering (M Eng, M Sc, PhD); reservoir characterization (M Eng, M Sc). *Program availability:* Part-time. *Degree requirements:* For master's, thesis (for some programs); for doctorate, comprehensive exam, thesis/dissertation, candidacy exam. *Entrance requirements:* For master's, minimum GPA of 3.0 or equivalent; for doctorate, minimum GPA of 3.5 or equivalent. Additional exam requirements/recommendations for international students: required—TOEFL (minimum score 550 paper-based; 80 iBT), IELTS (minimum score 7). Electronic applications accepted.

University of Houston, Cullen College of Engineering, Department of Chemical and Biomolecular Engineering, Houston, TX 77204. Offers chemical engineering (MCHE, PhD); petroleum engineering (M Pet E). *Program availability:* Part-time. Terminal master's awarded for partial completion of doctoral program. *Entrance requirements:* For master's and doctorate, GRE General Test. Additional exam requirements/recommendations for international students: required—TOEFL (minimum score 550 paper-based; 79 iBT), IELTS (minimum score 6.5).

The University of Kansas, Graduate Studies, School of Engineering, Program in Chemical and Petroleum Engineering, Lawrence, KS 66045. Offers chemical and petroleum engineering (PhD); chemical engineering (MS); petroleum engineering (MS); petroleum management (Certificate). *Program availability:* Part-time. *Students:* 44 full-time (14 women), 4 part-time (0 women), 26 international. Average age 28. 38 applicants, 61% accepted, 5 enrolled. In 2019, 10 master's awarded. *Entrance requirements:* For master's, GRE General Test, minimum GPA of 3.0, resume, personal statement, transcripts, three letters of recommendation; for doctorate, GRE General Test, minimum GPA of 3.5, resume, personal statement, transcripts, three letters of recommendation. Additional exam requirements/recommendations for international students: required—TOEFL, IELTS. *Application deadline:* For fall admission, 12/15 priority date for domestic and international students; for spring admission, 8/31 priority date for domestic and international students. Application fee: $65 ($85 for international students). Electronic applications accepted. *Expenses:* Tuition, state resident: full-time $9989. Tuition, nonresident: full-time $23,950. *International tuition:* $23,950 full-time. *Required fees:* $984; $81.99 per credit hour. Tuition and fees vary according to course load, campus/location and program. *Financial support:* Fellowships, research assistantships, teaching assistantships, career-related internships or fieldwork, Federal Work-Study, scholarships/grants, traineeships, and unspecified assistantships available. Financial award application deadline: 12/15; financial award applicants required to submit FAFSA. *Unit head:* Laurence R Weatherley, Chair, 785-864-3553, E-mail: lweather@ku.edu. *Application contact:* Martha Kehr, Graduate Admission Contact, 785-864-2900, E-mail: cpegrad@ku.edu.
Website: http://www.cpe.engr.ku.edu

The University of Kansas, Graduate Studies, School of Engineering, Program in Petroleum Engineering, Lawrence, KS 66045. Offers petroleum engineering (MS); petroleum management (Certificate). *Program availability:* Part-time. *Students:* 4 full-time (1 woman), 2 part-time (0 women), 4 international. Average age 26. 14 applicants, 29% accepted. In 2019, 1 master's, 4 other advanced degrees awarded. *Entrance requirements:* For master's, GRE, resume, personal statement, transcripts, three letters of recommendation. Additional exam requirements/recommendations for international students: required—TOEFL, IELTS. *Application deadline:* For fall admission, 12/15 priority date for domestic and international students; for spring admission, 8/31 priority date for domestic and international students. Application fee: $65 ($85 for international students). Electronic applications accepted. *Expenses:* Tuition, state resident: full-time $9989. Tuition, nonresident: full-time $23,950. *International tuition:* $23,950 full-time. *Required fees:* $984; $81.99 per credit hour. Tuition and fees vary according to course load, campus/location and program. *Financial support:* Research assistantships, teaching assistantships, Federal Work-Study, scholarships/grants, and unspecified assistantships available. Financial award application deadline: 12/15. *Unit head:* Laurence Weatherley, Chair, 785-864-3553, E-mail: lweather@ku.edu. *Application contact:* Martha Kehr, Graduate Admission Contact, 785-864-2900, E-mail: cpegrad@ku.edu.
Website: http://www.cpe.engr.ku.edu/

University of Louisiana at Lafayette, College of Engineering, Department of Petroleum Engineering, Lafayette, LA 70504. Offers MSE. *Program availability:* Evening/weekend. *Degree requirements:* For master's, comprehensive exam, thesis or alternative. *Entrance requirements:* For master's, GRE General Test, minimum GPA of 2.85. Electronic applications accepted. *Expenses: Tuition, area resident:* Full-time $5511. Tuition, state resident: full-time $5511. Tuition, nonresident: full-time $19,239. *Required fees:* $46,637.

University of Oklahoma, Mewbourne College of Earth and Energy, Mewbourne School of Petroleum and Geological Engineering, Norman, OK 73019. Offers geological engineering (MS, PhD); natural gas engineering and management (MS), including natural gas engineering and management; natural gas technology (Graduate Certificate), including natural gas technology; petroleum engineering (MS, PhD). *Program availability:* Part-time, evening/weekend. *Degree requirements:* For master's, variable foreign language requirement, comprehensive exam (for some programs), thesis (for some programs); for doctorate, variable foreign language requirement, comprehensive exam, thesis/dissertation. *Entrance requirements:* For master's and doctorate, GRE, minimum GPA of 3.2, three letters of recommendation, statement of purpose, resume/curriculum vitae. Additional exam requirements/recommendations for international students: required—TOEFL (minimum score 79 iBT) or IELTS (minimum score 6.5). Electronic applications accepted. *Expenses:* Tuition, state resident: full-time $6583.20; part-time $274.30 per credit hour. Tuition, nonresident: full-time $21,242; part-time $885.10 per credit hour. *International tuition:* $21,242.40 full-time. *Required fees:* $1994.20; $72.55 per credit hour. $126.50 per semester. Tuition and fees vary according to course load and degree level.

University of Pittsburgh, Swanson School of Engineering, Department of Chemical and Petroleum Engineering, Pittsburgh, PA 15260. Offers chemical engineering (MS Ch E, PhD); petroleum engineering (MSPE); MS Ch E/MSPE. *Program availability:* Part-time, 100% online. Terminal master's awarded for partial completion of doctoral program. *Degree requirements:* For doctorate, comprehensive exam, thesis/dissertation, final oral exams. *Entrance requirements:* For master's and doctorate, GRE General Test, minimum GPA of 3.0. Additional exam requirements/recommendations for international students: required—TOEFL (minimum score 550 paper-based; 80 iBT). Electronic applications accepted. *Expenses:* Contact institution.

University of Regina, Faculty of Graduate Studies and Research, Faculty of Engineering and Applied Science, Program in Petroleum Systems Engineering, Regina, SK S4S 0A2, Canada. Offers petroleum systems (M Eng, MA Sc, PhD). *Program availability:* Part-time. *Faculty:* 8 full-time (1 woman), 2 part-time/adjunct (0 women). *Students:* 50 full-time (13 women), 5 part-time (1 woman). Average age 30. 80 applicants, 18% accepted. In 2019, 15 master's, 5 doctorates awarded. *Degree requirements:* For master's, thesis (for some programs), project, report, co-op placement; for doctorate, comprehensive exam, thesis/dissertation. *Entrance requirements:* For master's, minimum graduating average of 70 percent from four-year baccalaureate degree (or equivalent); for doctorate, completion of thesis-based master's degree in engineering or closely-related field. Additional exam requirements/recommendations for international students: required—TOEFL (minimum score 580 paper-based; 80 iBT), IELTS (minimum score 6.5), PTE (minimum score 59), other options are CAEL, MELAB, Cantest and U of R ESL. *Application deadline:* For fall admission, 1/31 for domestic and international students; for winter admission, 7/31 for domestic and international students. Applications are processed on a rolling basis. Application fee: $100 Canadian dollars. Electronic applications accepted. *Expenses:* 11,036.50 -This amount is based on three semesters tuition, registered in 6 credit hours per semester. Plus one year student fees and books. There is additional 438.75 if student is in Co-op route. *Financial support:* Fellowships, research assistantships, teaching assistantships, career-related internships or fieldwork, Federal Work-Study, scholarships/grants, unspecified assistantships, and travel award and Graduate Scholarship Base funds available. Support available to part-time students. Financial award application deadline: 9/30. *Unit head:* Dr. Na jia, Program Chair, 306-337-3287, Fax: 306-585-4855, E-mail: Na.Jia@uregina.ca. *Application contact:* Dr. SD Jacob Muthu, Graduate Coordinator, 306-337-8125, Fax: 306-585-4855, E-mail: Jacob.Muthu@uregina.ca.
Website: http://www.uregina.ca/engineering/

University of Southern California, Graduate School, Viterbi School of Engineering, Mork Family Department of Chemical Engineering and Materials Science, Los Angeles, CA 90089. Offers chemical engineering (MS, PhD, Engr); geoscience technologies (MS); materials engineering (MS); materials science (MS, PhD, Engr); petroleum engineering (MS, PhD, Engr); smart oilfield technologies (MS, Graduate Certificate). Terminal master's awarded for partial completion of doctoral program. *Degree requirements:* For master's, thesis optional; for doctorate, thesis/dissertation. *Entrance requirements:* For master's and doctorate, GRE General Test. Additional exam requirements/recommendations for international students: recommended—TOEFL. Electronic applications accepted. *Expenses:* Contact institution.

The University of Texas at Austin, Graduate School, Cockrell School of Engineering, Department of Petroleum and Geosystems Engineering, Austin, TX 78712-1111. Offers energy and earth resources (MA); petroleum engineering (MS, PhD). *Program availability:* Evening/weekend, online learning. *Entrance requirements:* For master's and doctorate, GRE General Test. Electronic applications accepted.

The University of Tulsa, Graduate School, College of Engineering and Natural Sciences, McDougall School of Petroleum Engineering, Tulsa, OK 74104-3189. Offers ME, MSE, PhD. *Program availability:* Part-time. Terminal master's awarded for partial

Petroleum Engineering

completion of doctoral program. *Degree requirements:* For master's, thesis (MSE); for doctorate, comprehensive exam, thesis/dissertation. *Entrance requirements:* For master's and doctorate, GRE General Test. Additional exam requirements/recommendations for international students: required—TOEFL (minimum score 550 paper-based; 80 iBT), IELTS (minimum score 6). Electronic applications accepted. *Expenses: Tuition:* Full-time $22,896; part-time $1272 per credit hour. *Required fees:* $6 per credit hour. Tuition and fees vary according to course load and program.

University of Utah, Graduate School, College of Engineering, Department of Chemical Engineering, Salt Lake City, UT 84112. Offers chemical engineering (MS, PhD); petroleum engineering (MS); MS/MBA. *Program availability:* Part-time, blended/hybrid learning. *Faculty:* 19 full-time (2 women), 1 part-time/adjunct (0 women). *Students:* 58 full-time (12 women), 13 part-time (3 women); includes 5 minority (2 Asian, non-Hispanic/Latino; 2 Hispanic/Latino; 1 Two or more races, non-Hispanic/Latino), 41 international. Average age 28. 69 applicants, 48% accepted, 14 enrolled. In 2019, 25 master's, 11 doctorates awarded. *Degree requirements:* For master's, comprehensive exam (for some programs), thesis optional; for doctorate, comprehensive exam, thesis/dissertation, thesis proposal, thesis defense. *Entrance requirements:* For master's and doctorate, GRE, Toefl/IEITS, 3.0 minimum. Additional exam requirements/recommendations for international students: required—TOEFL (minimum score 80 paper-based), IELTS (minimum score 6.5), GRE. *Application deadline:* For fall admission, 1/1 priority date for domestic students, 12/15 priority date for international students; for spring admission, 10/1 priority date for domestic students. Application fee: $30 ($45 for international students). Electronic applications accepted. *Expenses:* 6,575.00 per semester. *Financial support:* In 2019–20, 3 students received support, including 11 fellowships (averaging $13,090 per year), 44 research assistantships with full tuition reimbursements available (averaging $16,227 per year); unspecified assistantships also available. Financial award application deadline: 1/15; financial award applicants required to submit FAFSA. *Unit head:* Dr. Eric G. Eddings, Chair, 801-581-3931, Fax: 801-585-9291, E-mail: eric.eddings@utah.edu. *Application contact:* Wanda Brown, Graduate Coordinator, 801-585-1181, Fax: 801-585-9291, E-mail: wanda.brown@chemeng.utah.edu. Website: http://www.che.utah.edu/

University of Wyoming, College of Engineering and Applied Science, Department of Petroleum Engineering, Laramie, WY 82071. Offers MS, PhD. *Program availability:* Part-time. Terminal master's awarded for partial completion of doctoral program. *Degree requirements:* For master's, thesis; for doctorate, thesis/dissertation. *Entrance requirements:* For master's and doctorate, GRE General Test, minimum GPA of 3.0. Additional exam requirements/recommendations for international students: required—TOEFL (minimum score 600 paper-based). Electronic applications accepted.

West Virginia University, Statler College of Engineering and Mineral Resources, Morgantown, WV 26506. Offers aerospace engineering (MSAE, PhD); chemical engineering (MS Ch E, PhD); civil engineering (MSCE, PhD); computer engineering (PhD); computer science (MSCS, PhD); electrical engineering (MSEE, PhD); energy systems engineering (MSESE); engineering (MSE); industrial engineering (MSIE, PhD); industrial hygiene (MS); material science and engineering (MSMSE, PhD); mechanical engineering (MSME, PhD); mining engineering (MS Min E, PhD); petroleum and natural gas engineering (MSPNGE, PhD); safety management (MS); software engineering (MSSE). *Program availability:* Part-time. Terminal master's awarded for partial completion of doctoral program. *Degree requirements:* For master's, thesis optional; for doctorate, comprehensive exam, thesis/dissertation. *Entrance requirements:* Additional exam requirements/recommendations for international students: required—TOEFL (minimum score 550 paper-based). Electronic applications accepted. *Expenses:* Contact institution.

Section 14
Industrial Engineering

This section contains a directory of institutions offering graduate work in industrial engineering. Additional information about programs listed in the directory may be obtained by writing directly to the dean of a graduate school or chair of a department at the address given in the directory.

For programs offering related work, see also in this book *Computer Science and Information Technology, Electrical and Computer Engineering, Energy and Power Engineering, Engineering and Applied Sciences,* and *Management of Engineering and Technology.* In the other guides in this series:

Graduate Programs in the Physical Sciences, Mathematics, Agricultural Sciences, the Environment & Natural Resources
See *Mathematical Sciences*
Graduate Programs in Business, Education, Information Studies, Law & Social Work

See *Business Administration and Management*

CONTENTS

Program Directories

Automotive Engineering

Clemson University, Graduate School, College of Engineering, Computing and Applied Sciences, Department of Automotive Engineering, Greenville, SC 29634. Offers MS, PhD, Certificate. *Faculty:* 16 full-time (1 woman), 4 part-time/adjunct (1 woman). *Students:* 221 full-time (19 women), 5 part-time (0 women); includes 6 minority (1 Black or African American, non-Hispanic/Latino; 3 Asian, non-Hispanic/Latino; 1 Hispanic/Latino; 1 Two or more races, non-Hispanic/Latino), 185 international. Average age 25. 319 applicants, 75% accepted, 136 enrolled. In 2019, 62 master's, 10 doctorates awarded. *Expenses:* Full-Time Student per Semester: Tuition: $6950 (in-state), $15500 (out-of-state), Fees: $598; Graduate Assistant Per Semester: $1144; Part-Time Student Per Credit Hour: $993 (in-state), $2215 (out-of-state), Fees: $46. *Financial support:* In 2019–20, 41 students received support, including 17 fellowships with full and partial tuition reimbursements available (averaging $11,947 per year), 22 research assistantships with full and partial tuition reimbursements available (averaging $22,144 per year), 1 teaching assistantship (averaging $20,000 per year); career-related internships or fieldwork and unspecified assistantships also available. *Unit head:* Dr. Zoran Filipi, Chair and Executive Director, 864-283-7222, E-mail: zfilipi@clemson.edu. *Application contact:* Dr. Beshah Ayalew, Graduate Coordinator, 864-283-7228, E-mail: beshah@clemson.edu.
Website: https://www.clemson.edu/cecas/departments/automotive-engineering/

College for Creative Studies, Graduate Programs, Detroit, MI 48202-4034. Offers color and materials design (MFA); integrated design (MFA); interaction design (MFA); transportation design (MFA). *Accreditation:* NASAD.

Lawrence Technological University, College of Engineering, Southfield, MI 48075-1058. Offers architectural engineering (MS); automotive engineering (MS); biomedical engineering (MS); civil engineering (MA, MS, PhD), including environmental engineering (MS), geotechnical engineering (MS), structural engineering (MS), transportation engineering (MS), water resource engineering (MS); construction engineering management (MA); electrical and computer engineering (MS); engineering management (MEM); engineering technology (MS); fire engineering (MS); industrial engineering (MS), including healthcare systems; manufacturing systems (ME); mechanical engineering (MS, DE, PhD), including automotive engineering (MS), energy engineering (MS), manufacturing (DE), solid mechanics (MS), thermal/fluid systems (MS); mechatronic systems engineering (MS). *Program availability:* Part-time, evening/weekend. *Faculty:* 23 full-time (2 women), 20 part-time/adjunct (1 woman). *Students:* 14 full-time (5 women), 286 part-time (54 women); includes 26 minority (13 Black or African American, non-Hispanic/Latino; 8 Asian, non-Hispanic/Latino; 3 Hispanic/Latino; 2 Two or more races, non-Hispanic/Latino), 150 international. Average age 29. 384 applicants, 58% accepted, 74 enrolled. In 2019, 223 master's, 7 doctorates awarded. Terminal master's awarded for partial completion of doctoral program. *Degree requirements:* For master's, thesis optional; for doctorate, comprehensive exam, thesis/dissertation optional. *Entrance requirements:* Additional exam requirements/recommendations for international students: required—TOEFL (minimum score 550 paper-based; 79 iBT), IELTS (minimum score 6.5). *Application deadline:* For fall admission, 5/24 for international students; for spring admission, 10/13 for international students; for summer admission, 2/18 for international students. Applications are processed on a rolling basis. Application fee: $50. Electronic applications accepted. *Expenses: Tuition:* Full-time $16,618; part-time $8309 per year. *Required fees:* $600; $600. *Financial support:* In 2019–20, 21 students received support. Unspecified assistantships available. Financial award application deadline: 4/1; financial award applicants required to submit FAFSA. *Unit head:* Dr. Nabil Grace, Dean, 248-204-2500, Fax: 248-204-2509, E-mail: engrdean@ltu.edu. *Application contact:* Jane Rohrback, Director of Admissions, 248-204-3160, Fax: 248-204-2228, E-mail: admissions@ltu.edu.
Website: http://www.ltu.edu/engineering/index.asp

Minnesota State University Mankato, College of Graduate Studies and Research, College of Science, Engineering and Technology, Department of Automotive and Manufacturing Engineering Technology, Mankato, MN 56001. Offers manufacturing engineering technology (MS). *Degree requirements:* For master's, comprehensive exam, thesis. *Entrance requirements:* For master's, minimum GPA of 2.75 during previous 2 years. Additional exam requirements/recommendations for international students: required—TOEFL (minimum score 525 paper-based). Electronic applications accepted.

University of Michigan, College of Engineering, Department of Integrative Systems and Design, Ann Arbor, MI 48109. Offers automotive engineering (M Eng); design science (MS, PhD); energy systems engineering (M Eng, MS); global automotive and manufacturing engineering (M Eng); manufacturing engineering (M Eng, D Eng); pharmaceutical engineering (M Eng); robotics and autonomous vehicles (M Eng); systems engineering and design (M Eng); MBA/M Eng; MSE/MS. *Program availability:* Part-time, online learning. Terminal master's awarded for partial completion of doctoral program. *Degree requirements:* For master's, capstone project; for doctorate, thesis/dissertation. *Entrance requirements:* For master's and doctorate, GRE. Additional exam requirements/recommendations for international students: required—TOEFL. Electronic applications accepted.

University of Michigan–Dearborn, College of Engineering and Computer Science, MSE Program in Automotive Systems Engineering, Dearborn, MI 48128. Offers MSE. *Program availability:* Part-time, evening/weekend, 100% online. *Faculty:* 24 full-time (4 women), 12 part-time/adjunct (2 women). *Students:* 58 full-time (1 woman), 109 part-time (9 women); includes 8 minority (1 Black or African American, non-Hispanic/Latino; 4 Asian, non-Hispanic/Latino; 3 Hispanic/Latino), 94 international. Average age 27. 271 applicants, 34% accepted, 36 enrolled. In 2019, 88 master's awarded. *Degree requirements:* For master's, thesis optional. *Entrance requirements:* For master's, BS or equivalent degree in engineering from ABET-accredited program with minimum cumulative GPA of 3.0. Additional exam requirements/recommendations for international students: required—TOEFL (minimum score 560 paper-based; 84 iBT), IELTS (minimum score 6.5). *Application deadline:* For fall admission, 8/1 priority date for domestic students, 5/1 for international students; for winter admission, 12/1 priority date for domestic students, 9/1 for international students; for spring admission, 4/1 priority date for domestic students, 1/1 for international students. Applications are processed on a rolling basis. Application fee: $60. Electronic applications accepted. *Financial support:* Research assistantships with full tuition reimbursements, scholarships/grants, unspecified assistantships, and non-resident tuition scholarships available. Financial award application deadline: 3/1; financial award applicants required to submit FAFSA. *Unit head:* Dr. Taehyun Shim, 313-5935127, E-mail: tshim@umich.edu. *Application contact:* Office of Graduate Studies, 313-583-6321, E-mail: umd-graduatestudies@umich.edu.
Website: https://umdearborn.edu/cecs/departments/mechanical-engineering/graduate-programs/mse-automotive-systems-engineering

The University of Tennessee at Chattanooga, Program in Engineering, Chattanooga, TN 37403. Offers automotive (MS Engr); chemical (MS Engr); civil (MS Engr); electrical (MS Engr); mechanical (MS Engr). *Program availability:* Part-time. *Students:* 29 full-time (4 women), 27 part-time (3 women); includes 9 minority (4 Black or African American, non-Hispanic/Latino; 2 Asian, non-Hispanic/Latino; 1 Hispanic/Latino; 1 Native Hawaiian or other Pacific Islander, non-Hispanic/Latino; 1 Two or more races, non-Hispanic/Latino), 19 international. Average age 29. 39 applicants, 74% accepted, 16 enrolled. In 2019, 22 master's awarded. *Degree requirements:* For master's, comprehensive exam, thesis or alternative, engineering project. *Entrance requirements:* For master's, GRE General Test, minimum undergraduate GPA of 2.7 or 3.0 in last two years of undergraduate coursework. Additional exam requirements/recommendations for international students: required—TOEFL (minimum score 550 paper-based; 79 iBT), IELTS (minimum score 6). *Application deadline:* For fall admission, 6/15 priority date for domestic students, 7/1 for international students; for spring admission, 11/1 priority date for domestic students, 11/1 for international students. Applications are processed on a rolling basis. Application fee: $35 ($40 for international students). Electronic applications accepted. *Financial support:* Research assistantships, teaching assistantships, career-related internships or fieldwork, scholarships/grants, health care benefits, and unspecified assistantships available. Support available to part-time students. Financial award application deadline: 7/1; financial award applicants required to submit FAFSA. *Unit head:* Dr. Daniel Pack, Dean, 423-425-2256, Fax: 423-425-5311, E-mail: daniel-pack@utc.edu. *Application contact:* Dr. Joanne Romagni, Dean of the Graduate School, 423-425-4478, Fax: 423-425-5223, E-mail: joanne-romagni@utc.edu.
Website: http://www.utc.edu/college-engineering-computer-science/graduate-programs/msengr.php

University of Wisconsin–Madison, Graduate School, College of Engineering, Department of Mechanical Engineering, Madison, WI 53706. Offers mechanical engineering (MS, PhD), including automotive engineering (MS), modeling and simulation (MS). *Program availability:* Part-time. Terminal master's awarded for partial completion of doctoral program. *Degree requirements:* For master's, thesis (for some programs), 30 credits; minimum GPA of 3.0; for doctorate, thesis/dissertation, qualifying exam, preliminary exam, final oral defense, 42 formal course credits, 18 thesis credits, minimum GPA of 3.25. *Entrance requirements:* For master's, GRE, BS in mechanical engineering or related field, minimum GPA of 3.2 in last 60 hours of course work; for doctorate, GRE, BS in mechanical engineering or related field, minimum undergraduate GPA of 3.2 in last 60 hours of course work. Additional exam requirements/recommendations for international students: required—TOEFL (minimum score 580 paper-based; 92 iBT), IELTS (minimum score 7). Electronic applications accepted.

Wayne State University, College of Engineering, Interdisciplinary, Detroit, MI 48202. Offers MS, Graduate Certificate. *Students:* 3 full-time (1 woman), 5 part-time (1 woman); includes 1 minority (Black or African American, non-Hispanic/Latino), 3 international. Average age 30. 18 applicants, 61% accepted, 2 enrolled. In 2019, 1 master's, 1 other advanced degree awarded. *Degree requirements:* For master's, thesis optional. *Entrance requirements:* For master's, bachelor's degree in engineering from accredited institution with minimum GPA of 3.0, significant professional experience, or enrollment in electric-drive vehicle engineering Graduate Certificate program; resume (optional); for Graduate Certificate, bachelor's degree in engineering from accredited institution with minimum GPA of 2.8 or significant professional experience. Additional exam requirements/recommendations for international students: required—TOEFL (minimum score 550 paper-based; 79 iBT, TWE (minimum score 5.5), Michigan English Language Assessment Battery (minimum score 85); recommended—IELTS (minimum score 6.5). *Application deadline:* For fall admission, 6/1 priority date for domestic students, 5/1 priority date for international students; for winter admission, 10/1 priority date for domestic students, 9/1 priority date for international students; for spring admission, 2/1 priority date for domestic students, 1/1 priority date for international students. Applications are processed on a rolling basis. Application fee: $50. Electronic applications accepted. *Expenses:* $790 per credit hour in-state tuition, $1579 per credit hour out-of-state tuition. MS is 32 credit hours. *Financial support:* In 2019–20, 2 students received support. Scholarships/grants and unspecified assistantships available. Financial award application deadline: 3/31; financial award applicants required to submit FAFSA. *Unit head:* Dr. Ece Yaprak, Division Chair, 313-577-8075, E-mail: yaprak@eng.wayne.edu. *Application contact:* Rob Carlson, Graduate Program Coordinator, 313-577-9615, E-mail: rcarlson@wayne.edu.
Website: http://engineering.wayne.edu/eve/index.php

Industrial/Management Engineering

American University of Armenia, Graduate Programs, Yerevan, Armenia. Offers business administration (MBA); computer and information science (MS), including business management, design and manufacturing, energy (ME, MS), industrial engineering and systems management; economics (MS); industrial engineering and systems management (ME), including business, computer aided design/manufacturing, energy (ME, MS), information technology; law (LL M); political science and international affairs (MPSIA); public health (MPH); teaching English as a foreign language (MA). *Program availability:* Part-time, evening/weekend. *Degree requirements:* For master's, thesis (for some programs), capstone/project. *Entrance requirements:* For master's, GRE, GMAT, or LSAT. Additional exam requirements/recommendations for international students: recommended—TOEFL (minimum score 79 iBT), IELTS (minimum score 6.5).

Arizona State University at Tempe, Ira A. Fulton Schools of Engineering, School of Computing, Informatics, and Decision Systems Engineering, Tempe, AZ 85287-8809. Offers computer engineering (MS, PhD); computer science (MCS, MS, PhD); industrial engineering (MS, PhD); software engineering (MS). *Program availability:* Part-time, evening/weekend, online learning. Terminal master's awarded for partial completion of doctoral program. *Degree requirements:* For master's, comprehensive exam (for some programs), portfolio (MCS); interactive Program of Study (iPOS) submitted before completing 50 percent of required credit hours; for doctorate, comprehensive exam, thesis/dissertation, interactive Program of Study (iPOS) submitted before completing 50 percent of required credit hours. *Entrance requirements:* For master's, GRE, minimum GPA of 3.0 or equivalent in last 2 years of work leading to bachelor's degree; for doctorate, GRE, minimum GPA of 3.0 in last 2 years of work leading to bachelor's degree. Additional exam requirements/recommendations for international students: required—TOEFL, IELTS, or PTE. Electronic applications accepted. *Expenses:* Contact institution.

Auburn University, Graduate School, Samuel Ginn College of Engineering, Department of Industrial and Systems Engineering, Auburn University, AL 36849. Offers MISE, MS, PhD, Graduate Certificate. *Program availability:* Part-time. *Faculty:* 18 full-time (2 women), 1 part-time/adjunct (0 women). *Students:* 68 full-time (20 women), 86 part-time (24 women); includes 22 minority (11 Black or African American, non-Hispanic/Latino; 4 Asian, non-Hispanic/Latino; 6 Hispanic/Latino; 1 Two or more races, non-Hispanic/Latino), 55 international. Average age 32. 174 applicants, 50% accepted, 33 enrolled. In 2019, 38 master's, 13 doctorates, 20 other advanced degrees awarded. *Degree requirements:* For master's, thesis, thesis (MS); for doctorate, thesis/dissertation. *Entrance requirements:* For master's and doctorate, GRE General Test. Additional exam requirements/recommendations for international students: required—TOEFL (minimum score 550 paper-based; 79 iBT). *Application deadline:* For fall admission, 3/31 priority date for domestic and international students; for spring admission, 9/30 priority date for domestic and international students. Applications are processed on a rolling basis. Application fee: $60 ($70 for international students). Electronic applications accepted. *Expenses: Tuition, area resident:* Full-time $9828; part-time $546 per credit hour. Tuition, state resident: full-time $9828; part-time $546 per credit hour. Tuition, nonresident: full-time $29,484; part-time $1638 per credit hour. *International tuition:* $29,744 full-time. Tuition and fees vary according to course load, program and reciprocity agreements. *Financial support:* In 2019–20, 66 fellowships, 35 research assistantships (averaging $12,812 per year), 30 teaching assistantships (averaging $13,793 per year) were awarded; Federal Work-Study also available. Support available to part-time students. Financial award application deadline: 3/15; financial award applicants required to submit FAFSA. *Unit head:* Dr. John Evans, Chair, 334-844-1418, E-mail: evansjl@auburn.edu. *Application contact:* Dr. George Flowers, Dean of the Graduate School, 334-844-2125.
Website: http://www.eng.auburn.edu/insy/

Binghamton University, State University of New York, Graduate School, Thomas J. Watson School of Engineering and Applied Science, Department of Systems Science and Industrial Engineering, Binghamton, NY 13902-6000. Offers executive health systems (MS); industrial and systems engineering (M Eng); systems science and industrial engineering (MS, PhD). *Program availability:* Part-time, evening/weekend, online learning. *Degree requirements:* For master's, thesis; for doctorate, thesis/dissertation. *Entrance requirements:* For master's and doctorate, GRE General Test. Additional exam requirements/recommendations for international students: required—TOEFL (minimum score 550 paper-based; 80 iBT). Electronic applications accepted. *Expenses:* Contact institution.

Bradley University, The Graduate School, Caterpillar College of Engineering and Technology, Department of Industrial and Manufacturing Engineering and Technology, Peoria, IL 61625-0002. Offers industrial engineering (MS); manufacturing engineering (MS). *Program availability:* Part-time, evening/weekend. *Faculty:* 10 full-time (1 woman). *Students:* 5 full-time (2 women), 5 part-time (1 woman), all international. Average age 28. 31 applicants, 48% accepted, 2 enrolled. In 2019, 11 master's awarded. *Degree requirements:* For master's, comprehensive exam, thesis or alternative, project. *Entrance requirements:* For master's, Minimum GPA of 2.5, Essays, Recommendation letters, Transcripts. Additional exam requirements/recommendations for international students: required—TOEFL (minimum score 550 paper-based; 79 iBT), IELTS (minimum score 6.5), PTE (minimum score 58). *Application deadline:* For fall admission, 5/15 priority date for domestic and international students; for spring admission, 10/15 priority date for domestic and international students. Applications are processed on a rolling basis. Application fee: $40 ($50 for international students). Electronic applications accepted. *Expenses: Tuition:* Part-time $930 per credit hour. *Financial support:* In 2019–20, 4 students received support. Research assistantships, teaching assistantships, scholarships/grants, tuition waivers (partial), and unspecified assistantships available. Support available to part-time students. Financial award application deadline: 4/1. *Unit head:* Dr. Joseph Chen, Chair, 309-677-2740, E-mail: jchen@bradley.edu. *Application contact:* Rachel Webb, Director of On-Campus Graduate Admissions and International Student and Scholar Services, 309-677-2375, E-mail: rkwebb@bradley.edu.
Website: http://www.bradley.edu/academic/departments/imet/

Buffalo State College, State University of New York, The Graduate School, School of the Professions, Department of Engineering Technology, Program in Industrial Technology, Buffalo, NY 14222-1095. Offers MS. *Degree requirements:* For master's, thesis or project. *Entrance requirements:* For master's, minimum GPA of 2.5. Additional exam requirements/recommendations for international students: required—TOEFL (minimum score 550 paper-based).

California Polytechnic State University, San Luis Obispo, College of Engineering, Department of Industrial Engineering, San Luis Obispo, CA 93407. Offers MS. *Program availability:* Part-time. *Faculty:* 5 full-time (1 woman), 1 (woman) part-time/adjunct. *Students:* 14 full-time (4 women), 2 part-time (0 women); includes 4 minority (2 Asian, non-Hispanic/Latino; 2 Two or more races, non-Hispanic/Latino), 4 international. Average age 23. 42 applicants, 60% accepted, 14 enrolled. In 2019, 6 master's awarded. *Entrance requirements:* For master's, GRE. Additional exam requirements/recommendations for international students: required—TOEFL (minimum score 80 iBT). *Application deadline:* For fall admission, 3/1 for domestic and international students. Applications are processed on a rolling basis. Application fee: $55. Electronic applications accepted. *Expenses:* Tuition, state resident: full-time $7176; part-time $4164 per year. Tuition, nonresident: full-time $18,690; part-time $8916 per year. *Required fees:* $4206; $3185 per unit. $1061 per term. *Financial support:* Fellowships, research assistantships, teaching assistantships, career-related internships or fieldwork, Federal Work-Study, institutionally sponsored loans, and scholarships/grants available. Support available to part-time students. Financial award application deadline: 3/2; financial award applicants required to submit FAFSA. *Unit head:* Dr. Tali Freed, Graduate Coordinator, 805-756-2544, E-mail: tfreed@calpoly.edu. *Application contact:* Dr. Tali Freed, Graduate Coordinator, 805-756-2544, E-mail: tfreed@calpoly.edu.
Website: http://www.ime.calpoly.edu/programs/graduate/

California State University, Fresno, Division of Research and Graduate Studies, Jordan College of Agricultural Sciences and Technology, Department of Industrial Technology, Fresno, CA 93740-8027. Offers MS. *Program availability:* Part-time, evening/weekend. *Degree requirements:* For master's, comprehensive exam (for some programs), thesis (for some programs). *Entrance requirements:* For master's, GRE General Test, minimum GPA of 2.5. Additional exam requirements/recommendations for international students: required—TOEFL. Electronic applications accepted. *Expenses:* Tuition, state resident: full-time $4012; part-time $2506 per semester.

California State University, Northridge, Graduate Studies, College of Engineering and Computer Science, Department of Manufacturing Systems Engineering and Management, Northridge, CA 91330. Offers engineering automation (MS); engineering management (MS); manufacturing systems engineering (MS); materials engineering (MS). *Program availability:* Online learning. *Entrance requirements:* For master's, GRE (if cumulative undergraduate GPA less than 3.0).

Clemson University, Graduate School, College of Engineering, Computing and Applied Sciences, Department of Industrial Engineering, Clemson, SC 29634. Offers M Engr, MS, PhD. *Program availability:* Part-time, 100% online. *Faculty:* 15 full-time (3 women). *Students:* 86 full-time (33 women), 126 part-time (29 women); includes 14 minority (4 Black or African American, non-Hispanic/Latino; 4 Asian, non-Hispanic/Latino; 4 Hispanic/Latino; 2 Two or more races, non-Hispanic/Latino), 126 international. Average age 29. 417 applicants, 38% accepted, 56 enrolled. In 2019, 58 master's, 3 doctorates awarded. Terminal master's awarded for partial completion of doctoral program. *Degree requirements:* For master's, thesis or alternative; for doctorate, comprehensive exam, thesis/dissertation. *Entrance requirements:* For master's and doctorate, GRE General Test, unofficial transcripts, letters of recommendation. Additional exam requirements/recommendations for international students: required—TOEFL (minimum score 80 paper-based; 80 iBT); recommended—IELTS (minimum score 6.5), TSE (minimum score 54). *Application deadline:* For fall admission, 4/1 for domestic students, 1/1 for international students. Applications are processed on a rolling basis. Application fee: $80 ($90 for international students). Electronic applications accepted. *Expenses: Tuition, area resident:* Full-time $10,600; part-time $8688 per semester. Tuition, state resident: full-time $10,600; part-time $8688 per semester. Tuition, nonresident: full-time $22,050; part-time $17,412 per semester. *International tuition:* $22,050 full-time. *Required fees:* $1196; $617 per semester. $617 per semester. Tuition and fees vary according to course load, degree level, campus/location and program. *Financial support:* In 2019–20, 53 students received support, including 2 fellowships with full and partial tuition reimbursements available (averaging $8,167 per year), 29 research assistantships with full and partial tuition reimbursements available (averaging $22,104 per year), 14 teaching assistantships with full and partial tuition reimbursements available (averaging $21,024 per year); career-related internships or fieldwork and unspecified assistantships also available. Financial award application deadline: 4/1. *Unit head:* Dr. Jeffrey Kharoufeh, Department Chair, 864-656-5540, E-mail: kharouf@clemson.edu. *Application contact:* Dr. Scott Mason, Graduate Coordinator, 864-656-5645, E-mail: mason@clemson.edu.
Website: https://www.clemson.edu/cecas/departments/ie/index.html

Colorado State University-Pueblo, College of Education, Engineering and Professional Studies, Department of Engineering, Pueblo, CO 81001-4901. Offers industrial and systems engineering (MS). *Degree requirements:* For master's, thesis optional. *Entrance requirements:* For master's, GRE General Test. Additional exam requirements/recommendations for international students: required—TOEFL (minimum score 500 paper-based).

Columbia University, Fu Foundation School of Engineering and Applied Science, Department of Industrial Engineering and Operations Research, New York, NY 10027. Offers financial engineering (MS); industrial engineering (MS); industrial engineering and operations research (PhD); management science and engineering (MS); operations research (MS); MS/MBA. *Program availability:* Part-time, evening/weekend, online learning. *Degree requirements:* For doctorate, thesis/dissertation, oral and written qualifying exams. *Entrance requirements:* For master's and doctorate, GRE General Test. Additional exam requirements/recommendations for international students: required—TOEFL, IELTS, PTE. Electronic applications accepted. *Expenses: Tuition:* Full-time $47,600; part-time $1880 per credit. One-time fee: $105.

Concordia University, School of Graduate Studies, Faculty of Engineering and Computer Science, Department of Mechanical and Industrial Engineering, Montréal, QC H3G 1M8, Canada. Offers industrial engineering (M Eng, MA Sc, PhD); mechanical engineering (M Eng, MA Sc, PhD, Certificate). *Degree requirements:* For master's, variable foreign language requirement, thesis or alternative; for doctorate, comprehensive exam, thesis/dissertation.

Cornell University, Graduate School, Graduate Fields of Agriculture and Life Sciences and Graduate Fields of Engineering, Field of Biological and Environmental Engineering, Ithaca, NY 14853. Offers bioenergy and integrated energy systems (M Eng, MPS, MS, PhD); biological engineering (M Eng, MPS, MS, PhD); bioprocess engineering (M Eng, MPS, MS, PhD); ecohydrology (M Eng, MPS, MS, PhD); environmental engineering (M Eng, MPS, MS, PhD); environmental management (MPS); food engineering (M Eng, MPS, MS, PhD); industrial biotechnology (M Eng, MPS, MS, PhD); nanobiotechnology (M Eng, MPS, MS, PhD); sustainable systems (M Eng, MPS, MS, PhD); synthetic biology (MS); syntheticbiology (M Eng, MPS, PhD). Terminal master's awarded for partial completion of doctoral program. *Degree requirements:* For master's, thesis (MS); for doctorate, comprehensive exam, thesis/dissertation. *Entrance requirements:* For master's, letters of recommendation (3 for MS, 2 for M Eng and MPS); for doctorate, GRE General Test, 3 letters of recommendation. Additional exam requirements/recommendations for international students: required—TOEFL (minimum score 550 paper-based; 77 iBT). Electronic applications accepted.

Cornell University, Graduate School, Graduate Fields of Engineering, Field of Operations Research and Information Engineering, Ithaca, NY 14853. Offers applied probability and statistics (PhD); manufacturing systems engineering (PhD); mathematical programming (PhD); operations research and industrial engineering (M Eng). *Degree requirements:* For doctorate, comprehensive exam, thesis/dissertation. *Entrance requirements:* For master's and doctorate, GRE General Test, 3 letters of recommendation. Additional exam requirements/recommendations for international students: required—TOEFL (minimum score 600 paper-based; 100 iBT). Electronic applications accepted.

Dalhousie University, Faculty of Engineering, Department of Industrial Engineering, Halifax, NS B3J 2X4, Canada. Offers M Eng, MA Sc, PhD. *Degree requirements:* For master's, thesis; for doctorate, thesis/dissertation. *Entrance requirements:* Additional exam requirements/recommendations for international students: required—TOEFL, IELTS, CANTEST, CAEL, or Michigan English Language Assessment Battery. Electronic applications accepted.

Eastern Kentucky University, The Graduate School, College of Business and Technology, Department of Technology, Program in Industrial Technology, Richmond, KY 40475-3102. Offers MS. *Program availability:* Part-time. *Entrance requirements:* For master's, GRE General Test, minimum GPA of 2.5.

Florida Agricultural and Mechanical University, Division of Graduate Studies, Research, and Continuing Education, FAMU-FSU College of Engineering, Department of Industrial and Manufacturing Engineering, Tallahassee, FL 32307-3200. Offers industrial engineering (MS, PhD). *Degree requirements:* For master's, thesis optional. *Entrance requirements:* For master's, GRE General Test, minimum GPA of 3.0. Additional exam requirements/recommendations for international students: required—TOEFL (minimum score 550 paper-based).

Florida State University, The Graduate School, FAMU-FSU College of Engineering, Department of Industrial and Manufacturing Engineering, Tallahassee, FL 32306. Offers

Industrial/Management Engineering

industrial engineering (MS, PhD). *Faculty:* 10 full-time (1 woman), 1 (woman) part-time/adjunct. *Students:* 45 full-time (17 women); includes 9 minority (6 Black or African American, non-Hispanic/Latino; 1 Asian, non-Hispanic/Latino; 2 Hispanic/Latino), 26 international. Average age 24. 129 applicants, 48% accepted, 18 enrolled. In 2019, 22 master's, 7 doctorates awarded. *Degree requirements:* For master's, thesis, proposal presentation, progress presentation, defense presentation; for doctorate, thesis/dissertation, preliminary exam, proposal exam, defense exam. *Entrance requirements:* For master's, GRE General Test (minimum new score of 146 Verbal and 155 Quantitative), minimum GPA of 3.0; for doctorate, GRE General Test (minimum new score of 146 Verbal and 155 Quantitative), minimum GPA of 3.0 (without MS in industrial engineering), 3.4 (with MS in industrial engineering). Additional exam requirements/recommendations for international students: required—TOEFL (minimum score 550 paper-based; 80 iBT); recommended—IELTS (minimum score 6.5). *Application deadline:* For fall admission, 3/1 for domestic and international students; for spring admission, 11/1 for domestic and international students; for summer admission, 1/1 for domestic and international students. Applications are processed on a rolling basis. Application fee: $30. Electronic applications accepted. *Financial support:* In 2019–20, 47 students received support, including 24 research assistantships with full tuition reimbursements available, 18 teaching assistantships with full tuition reimbursements available; fellowships with full tuition reimbursements available, scholarships/grants, tuition waivers (full), and unspecified assistantships also available. Financial award application deadline: 3/1; financial award applicants required to submit FAFSA. *Unit head:* Dr. Okenwa Okoli, Chair/Professor/Associate Director, 850-410-6352, Fax: 850-410-6342, E-mail: okoli@eng.famu.fsu.edu. *Application contact:* Shade' Ahmed, Graduate Studies Assistant, 850-410-6582, Fax: 850-410-6342, E-mail: saahmed@eng.famu.fsu.edu.
Website: http://www.eng.famu.fsu.edu/departments/industrial/

Georgia Institute of Technology, Graduate Studies, College of Engineering, H. Milton Stewart School of Industrial and Systems Engineering, Atlanta, GA 30332. Offers health systems (MS); industrial and systems engineering (MS, PhD), including industrial engineering; international logistics (MS); operations research (MS, PhD). *Program availability:* Part-time, 100% online. *Faculty:* 54 full-time (11 women), 3 part-time/adjunct. *Students:* 416 full-time (140 women), 86 part-time (32 women); includes 63 minority (5 Black or African American, non-Hispanic/Latino; 36 Asian, non-Hispanic/Latino; 15 Hispanic/Latino; 7 Two or more races, non-Hispanic/Latino), 359 international. Average age 25. 1,533 applicants, 29% accepted, 206 enrolled. In 2019, 203 master's, 21 doctorates awarded. Terminal master's awarded for partial completion of doctoral program. *Degree requirements:* For doctorate, comprehensive exam, thesis/dissertation. *Entrance requirements:* For master's, GRE General Test, Must have an undergraduate Bachelor of Science degree or the equivalent. MS Analytics applicants may substitute Graduate Management Admission Test (GMAT) scores as a substitute, although the GRE is preferred. Should describe any relevant work experience in the personal statement.; for doctorate, GRE General Test, Transcripts of prior academic work are required, as is evidence of an earned bachelor's degree. Also need a statement of purpose, resume, and three credible letters of reference. Additional exam requirements/recommendations for international students: required—TOEFL (minimum score 577 paper-based; 90 iBT), IELTS (minimum score 7), TOEFL is the preferred method with the requirements shown on the programs. *Application deadline:* For fall admission, 1/1 for domestic students, 12/15 for international students; for spring admission, 2/1 for domestic and international students. Applications are processed on a rolling basis. Application fee: $75 ($85 for international students). Electronic applications accepted. *Expenses:* Tuition, area resident: Full-time $14,064; part-time $586 per credit hour. Tuition, state resident: Full-time $14,064; part-time $586 per credit hour. Tuition, nonresident: full-time $29,140; part-time $1215 per credit hour. *International tuition:* $29,140 full-time. *Required fees:* $2024; $840 per semester. $2096. Tuition and fees vary according to course load. *Financial support:* In 2019–20, 10 fellowships, 140 research assistantships, 50 teaching assistantships were awarded; career-related internships or fieldwork, Federal Work-Study, institutionally sponsored loans, tuition waivers (full and partial), and unspecified assistantships also available. Support available to part-time students. Financial award application deadline: 7/1; financial award applicants required to submit FAFSA. *Unit head:* Edwin Romeijn, School Chair, 404-894-2300, Fax: 404-894-2301, E-mail: edwin.romeijn@isye.gatech.edu. *Application contact:* Marla Bruner, Director of Graduate Studies, 404-894-1610, Fax: 404-894-1609, E-mail: gradinfo@mail.gatech.edu.
Website: http://www.isye.gatech.edu

Illinois State University, Graduate School, College of Applied Science and Technology, Department of Technology, Normal, IL 61790. Offers MS. *Faculty:* 20 full-time (2 women), 18 part-time/adjunct (3 women). *Students:* 42 full-time (22 women), 53 part-time (27 women). Average age 31. 87 applicants, 85% accepted, 12 enrolled. In 2019, 51 master's awarded. *Degree requirements:* For master's, thesis or alternative. *Entrance requirements:* For master's, GRE General Test, minimum GPA of 2.8. *Application deadline:* Applications are processed on a rolling basis. Application fee: $50. *Expenses:* Tuition, area resident: Full-time $7956. Tuition, nonresident: full-time $9233. *Required fees:* $1797. *Financial support:* In 2019–20, 22 research assistantships were awarded; tuition waivers (full) and unspecified assistantships also available. Financial award application deadline: 4/1. *Unit head:* Dr. Ted Branoff, Department Chair, 309-438-3661, E-mail: tjbrano@IllinoisState.edu. *Application contact:* Dr. Klaus Scmidt, Graduate Coordinator, 309-438-3502, E-mail: kschmid@ilstu.edu.
Website: http://tec.illinoisstate.edu/

Instituto Tecnologico de Santo Domingo, Graduate School, Area of Engineering, Santo Domingo, Dominican Republic. Offers construction administration (MS, Certificate); data telecommunications (M Eng, MS, Certificate); industrial engineering (M Eng, Certificate); industrial management (M Mgmt); information technology (Certificate); maintenance engineering (M Eng); occupational hazard prevention (M Mgmt); production management (Certificate); quantitative methods (Certificate); sanitary and environmental engineering (M Eng); structural engineering (M Eng); systems engineering and electronic data processing (Certificate); transportation (Certificate).

Instituto Tecnológico y de Estudios Superiores de Monterrey, Campus Chihuahua, Graduate Programs, Chihuahua, Mexico. Offers computer systems engineering (Ingeniero); electrical engineering (Ingeniero); electromechanical engineering (Ingeniero); electronic engineering (Ingeniero); engineering administration (MEA); industrial engineering (MIE, Ingeniero); international trade (MIT); mechanical engineering (Ingeniero).

Instituto Tecnológico y de Estudios Superiores de Monterrey, Campus Ciudad de México, Virtual University Division, Ciudad de Mexico, Mexico. Offers administration of information technologies (MA); computer sciences (MA); education (MA, PhD); educational technology (MA); environmental engineering (MA); environmental systems (MA); humanistic studies (MA); industrial engineering (MA); international business for Latin America (MA); quality systems (MA); quality systems and productivity (MA). *Program availability:* Part-time, evening/weekend, online learning. *Entrance requirements:* For master's and doctorate, Instituto entrance exam. Additional exam requirements/recommendations for international students: required—TOEFL.

Instituto Tecnológico y de Estudios Superiores de Monterrey, Campus Laguna, Graduate School, Torreón, Mexico. Offers business administration (MBA); industrial engineering (MIE); management information systems (MS). *Program availability:* Part-time. *Entrance requirements:* For master's, GMAT.

Instituto Tecnológico y de Estudios Superiores de Monterrey, Campus Monterrey, Graduate and Research Division, Programs in Engineering, Monterrey, Mexico. Offers applied statistics (M Eng); artificial intelligence (PhD); automation engineering (M Eng); chemical engineering (M Eng); civil engineering (M Eng); electrical engineering (M Eng); electronic engineering (M Eng); environmental engineering (M Eng); industrial engineering (M Eng, PhD); manufacturing engineering (M Eng); mechanical engineering (M Eng); systems and quality engineering (M Eng). *Program availability:* Part-time, evening/weekend. Terminal master's awarded for partial completion of doctoral program. *Degree requirements:* For master's, one foreign language, thesis; for doctorate, one foreign language, thesis/dissertation. *Entrance requirements:* For master's, EXADEP; for doctorate, GRE, master's degree in related field. Additional exam requirements/recommendations for international students: required—TOEFL.

Iowa State University of Science and Technology, Department of Industrial and Manufacturing Systems Engineering, Ames, IA 50011. Offers industrial engineering (M Eng, MS, PhD); operations research (MS); systems engineering (M Eng). *Degree requirements:* For master's, thesis or alternative; for doctorate, thesis/dissertation. *Entrance requirements:* For master's and doctorate, GRE General Test. Additional exam requirements/recommendations for international students: required—TOEFL (minimum score 550 paper-based; 79 iBT), IELTS (minimum score 6.5). Electronic applications accepted.

Kansas State University, Graduate School, College of Engineering, Department of Industrial and Manufacturing Systems Engineering, Manhattan, KS 66506. Offers engineering management (MEM); industrial engineering (MS); operations research (MS). *Program availability:* Part-time, online learning. *Degree requirements:* For master's, thesis or alternative; for doctorate, thesis/dissertation. *Entrance requirements:* For master's, GRE General Test (minimum score of 750 old version, 159 new format on Quantitative portion of exam), bachelor's degree in engineering, mathematics, or physical science; for doctorate, GRE General Test (minimum score of 770 old version, 164 new format on Quantitative portion of exam), master's degree in engineering or industrial manufacturing. Additional exam requirements/recommendations for international students: required—PTE (minimum score 58), TOEFL (minimum score 550 paper-based; 79 iBT) or IELTS (minimum score 6.5). Electronic applications accepted.

Lawrence Technological University, College of Engineering, Southfield, MI 48075-1058. Offers architectural engineering (MS); automotive engineering (MS); biomedical engineering (MS); civil engineering (MA, MS, PhD), including environmental engineering (MS), geotechnical engineering (MS), structural engineering (MS), transportation engineering (MS), water resource engineering (MS); construction engineering management (MA); electrical and computer engineering (MS); engineering management (MEM); engineering technology (MS); fire engineering (MS); industrial engineering (MS), including healthcare systems; manufacturing systems (ME); mechanical engineering (MS, DE, PhD), including automotive engineering (MS), energy engineering (MS), manufacturing (DE), solid mechanics (MS), thermal/fluid systems (MS); mechatronic systems engineering (MS). *Program availability:* Part-time, evening/weekend. *Faculty:* 23 full-time (2 women), 20 part-time/adjunct (1 woman). *Students:* 14 full-time (5 women), 286 part-time (54 women); includes 26 minority (13 Black or African American, non-Hispanic/Latino; 8 Asian, non-Hispanic/Latino; 3 Hispanic/Latino; 2 Two or more races, non-Hispanic/Latino), 150 international. Average age 29. 384 applicants, 58% accepted, 74 enrolled. In 2019, 223 master's, 7 doctorates awarded. Terminal master's awarded for partial completion of doctoral program. *Degree requirements:* For master's, thesis optional; for doctorate, comprehensive exam, thesis/dissertation optional. *Entrance requirements:* Additional exam requirements/recommendations for international students: required—TOEFL (minimum score 550 paper-based; 79 iBT), IELTS (minimum score 6.5). *Application deadline:* For fall admission, 5/24 for international students; for spring admission, 10/13 for international students; for summer admission, 2/18 for international students. Applications are processed on a rolling basis. Application fee: $50. Electronic applications accepted. *Expenses:* Tuition: Full-time $16,618; part-time $8309 per year. *Required fees:* $600; $600. *Financial support:* In 2019–20, 21 students received support. Unspecified assistantships available. Financial award application deadline: 4/1; financial award applicants required to submit FAFSA. *Unit head:* Dr. Nabil Grace, Dean, 248-204-2500, Fax: 248-204-2509, E-mail: engrdean@ltu.edu. *Application contact:* Jane Rohrback, Director of Admissions, 248-204-3160, Fax: 248-204-2228, E-mail: admissions@ltu.edu.
Website: http://www.ltu.edu/engineering/index.asp

Lehigh University, P.C. Rossin College of Engineering and Applied Science, Department of Industrial and Systems Engineering, Bethlehem, PA 18015. Offers analytical finance (MS); healthcare systems engineering (M Eng, Certificate); industrial and systems engineering (M Eng, MS, PhD); management science and engineering (M Eng, MS); MBA/E. *Program availability:* Part-time, blended/hybrid learning. *Faculty:* 18 full-time (1 woman), 1 part-time/adjunct (0 women). *Students:* 71 full-time (16 women), 9 part-time (4 women); includes 2 minority (1 Asian, non-Hispanic/Latino; 1 Hispanic/Latino), 73 international. Average age 25. 290 applicants, 39% accepted, 26 enrolled. In 2019, 31 master's, 12 doctorates awarded. Terminal master's awarded for partial completion of doctoral program. *Degree requirements:* For master's, thesis (MS); project (M Eng); for doctorate, comprehensive exam, thesis/dissertation. *Entrance requirements:* For master's and doctorate, GRE General Test. Additional exam requirements/recommendations for international students: required—TOEFL (minimum score 550 paper-based; 79 iBT), IELTS (minimum score 6.5), TOEFL or IELTS required. *Application deadline:* For fall admission, 7/15 for domestic and international students; for spring admission, 12/1 for domestic and international students. Application fee: $75. *Financial support:* In 2019–20, 33 students received support, including 2 fellowships with full tuition reimbursements available (averaging $20,490 per year), 18 research assistantships with full tuition reimbursements available (averaging $20,490 per year), 11 teaching assistantships with full tuition reimbursements available (averaging $21,105 per year); health care benefits and unspecified assistantships also available. Financial award application deadline: 1/15. *Unit head:* Dr. Luis Nunes Vicente, Chairperson, 610-758-4050, Fax: 610-758-4886, E-mail: lnv@lehigh.edu. *Application contact:* Jennifer Vargas, Graduate Coordinator, 610-758-4050, Fax: 610-758-4886, E-mail: jav319@lehigh.edu.
Website: https://ise.lehigh.edu/

Mississippi State University, Bagley College of Engineering, Department of Industrial and Systems Engineering, Mississippi State, MS 39762. Offers human factors and ergonomics (MS); industrial and systems engineering (PhD); industrial systems (MS); management systems (MS); manufacturing systems (MS); operations research (MS). *Program availability:* Part-time, blended/hybrid learning. *Faculty:* 14 full-time (3 women). *Students:* 39 full-time (16 women), 64 part-time (18 women); includes 20 minority (7 Black or African American, non-Hispanic/Latino; 7 Asian, non-Hispanic/Latino; 5 Hispanic/Latino; 1 Two or more races, non-Hispanic/Latino), 28 international. Average age 36. 54 applicants, 44% accepted, 11 enrolled. In 2019, 14 master's, 6 doctorates awarded. *Degree requirements:* For master's, comprehensive exam (for some

programs), thesis optional, comprehensive oral or written exam; for doctorate, comprehensive exam, thesis/dissertation, candidacy exam. *Entrance requirements:* For master's, GRE (for graduates from program not accredited by EAC/ABET), minimum GPA of 3.0 on junior and senior years; for doctorate, GRE (for graduates from program not accredited by EAC/ABET), minimum GPA of 3.5 on master's degree and junior and senior years of BS. Additional exam requirements/recommendations for international students: required—TOEFL (minimum score 550 paper-based; 79 iBT); recommended—IELTS (minimum score 6.5). *Application deadline:* For fall admission, 7/1 for domestic students, 5/1 for international students; for spring admission, 11/1 for domestic students, 9/1 for international students. Applications are processed on a rolling basis. Application fee: $60 ($80 for international students). Electronic applications accepted. *Expenses: Tuition, area resident:* Full-time $8880; part-time $456 per credit hour. Tuition, state resident: full-time $8880. Tuition, nonresident: full-time $23,840; part-time $1236 per credit hour. *Required fees:* $110; $11.12 per credit hour. Tuition and fees vary according to course load. *Financial support:* In 2019–20, 21 research assistantships with full tuition reimbursements (averaging $17,482 per year), 4 teaching assistantships with full tuition reimbursements (averaging $15,706 per year) were awarded; Federal Work-Study, institutionally sponsored loans, and unspecified assistantships also available. Financial award application deadline: 4/1; financial award applicants required to submit FAFSA. *Unit head:* Dr. Kari Babski-Reeves, Professor, Department Head and Associate Dean for Research and Graduate Studies, 662-325-8430, Fax: 662-325-7618, E-mail: kari@ise.msstate.edu. *Application contact:* Ryan King, Admissions and Enrollment Assistant, 662-325-8951, E-mail: rjk101@grad.msstate.edu.
Website: http://www.ise.msstate.edu/

Montana State University, The Graduate School, College of Engineering, Department of Mechanical and Industrial Engineering, Bozeman, MT 59717. Offers engineering (PhD), including industrial engineering, mechanical engineering; industrial and management engineering (MS); mechanical engineering (MS). *Program availability:* Part-time. *Degree requirements:* For master's, comprehensive exam, thesis, oral exams; for doctorate, comprehensive exam, thesis/dissertation, qualifying exam. *Entrance requirements:* For master's, GRE, official transcript, minimum GPA of 3.0, demonstrated potential for success, statement of goals, three letters of recommendation, proof of funds affidavit; for doctorate, minimum undergraduate GPA of 3.0, 3.2 graduate; three letters of recommendation; statement of objectives. Additional exam requirements/recommendations for international students: required—TOEFL or IELTS. Electronic applications accepted.

Montana Technological University, Project Engineering and Management Program, Butte, MT 59701-8997. Offers MPEM. *Program availability:* Part-time, evening/weekend, online learning. *Faculty:* 1 full-time (0 women), 8 part-time/adjunct (2 women). *Students:* 5 part-time (1 woman). Average age 36. 6 applicants, 83% accepted, 4 enrolled. In 2019, 4 master's awarded. *Degree requirements:* For master's, comprehensive exam, final project presentation. *Entrance requirements:* For master's, minimum GPA of 3.0. Additional exam requirements/recommendations for international students: required—TOEFL (minimum score 550 paper-based; 80 iBT), IELTS (minimum score 7). *Application deadline:* For fall admission, 4/1 priority date for domestic students, 3/1 priority date for international students; for spring admission, 10/1 priority date for domestic students, 8/1 priority date for international students. Applications are processed on a rolling basis. Application fee: $50. Electronic applications accepted. *Financial support:* Application deadline: 4/1; applicants required to submit FAFSA. *Unit head:* Dr. Kumar Ganesan, Director, 406-496-4239, Fax: 406-496-4650, E-mail: kganesan@mtech.edu. *Application contact:* Daniel Stirling, Administrator, Graduate School, 406-496-4304, Fax: 406-496-4710, E-mail: gradschoo@mtech.edu.
Website: https://www.mtech.edu/academics/gradschool/distancelearning/distancelearning-pem.htm

Morgan State University, School of Graduate Studies, Clarence M. Mitchell, Jr. School of Engineering, Baltimore, MD 21251. Offers civil engineering (M Eng, D Eng); electrical and computer engineering (M Eng, MS, D Eng); industrial and systems engineering (M Eng, D Eng); transportation and urban infrastructure studies (MS, PhD, Postbaccalaureate Certificate), including transportation. *Program availability:* Part-time, evening/weekend. *Faculty:* 35 full-time (8 women), 19 part-time/adjunct (4 women). *Students:* 113 full-time (34 women), 24 part-time (4 women); includes 88 minority (75 Black or African American, non-Hispanic/Latino; 8 Asian, non-Hispanic/Latino; 2 Hispanic/Latino; 3 Two or more races, non-Hispanic/Latino), 36 international. Average age 35. 78 applicants, 83% accepted, 26 enrolled. In 2019, 23 master's, 11 doctorates awarded. *Degree requirements:* For master's, thesis optional, comprehensive exam or equivalent; for doctorate, thesis/dissertation, comprehensive exam or equivalent. *Entrance requirements:* For master's, GRE, minimum undergraduate GPA of 2.5; for doctorate, GRE, minimum GPA of 3.0. Additional exam requirements/recommendations for international students: required—TOEFL (minimum score 550 paper-based). *Application deadline:* For fall admission, 2/1 priority date for domestic students; for spring admission, 10/1 priority date for domestic students. Applications are processed on a rolling basis. Application fee: $50 ($70 for international students). Electronic applications accepted. *Expenses: Tuition, state resident:* full-time $455; part-time $455 per credit hour. Tuition, nonresident: full-time $894; part-time $894 per credit hour. *Required fees:* $82; $82 per credit hour. *Financial support:* In 2019–20, 35 students received support. Fellowships with full and partial tuition reimbursements available, research assistantships with full and partial tuition reimbursements available, teaching assistantships with full and partial tuition reimbursements available, career-related internships or fieldwork, scholarships/grants, and unspecified assistantships available. Financial award application deadline: 2/1. *Unit head:* Dr. Craig Scott, Interim Dean, 443-885-3231, E-mail: craig.scott@morgan.edu. *Application contact:* Dr. Jahmaine Smith, Director of Admissions, 443-885-3185, Fax: 443-885-8226, E-mail: gradapply@morgan.edu.
Website: https://morgan.edu/soe

New Jersey Institute of Technology, Newark College of Engineering, Newark, NJ 07102. Offers biomedical engineering (MS, PhD); biopharmaceutical engineering (MS); chemical engineering (MS, PhD); civil engineering (MS, PhD); computer engineering (MS); critical infrastructure systems (MS); electrical engineering (MS, PhD); engineering management (MS); engineering science (MS); environmental engineering (MS, PhD); healthcare systems management (MS); industrial engineering (MS, PhD); internet engineering (MS); manufacturing systems engineering (MS); materials science & engineering (PhD); materials science and engineering (MS); mechanical engineering (MS, PhD); occupational safety and health engineering (MS). *Program availability:* Part-time, evening/weekend. *Faculty:* 151 full-time (29 women), 135 part-time/adjunct (15 women). *Students:* 576 full-time (161 women), 528 part-time (111 women); includes 366 minority (61 Black or African American, non-Hispanic/Latino; 1 American Indian or Alaska Native, non-Hispanic/Latino; 166 Asian, non-Hispanic/Latino; 115 Hispanic/Latino; 23 Two or more races, non-Hispanic/Latino), 450 international. Average age 28. 2,053 applicants, 67% accepted, 338 enrolled. In 2019, 474 master's, 30 doctorates awarded. Terminal master's awarded for partial completion of doctoral program. *Degree requirements:* For master's, thesis (for some programs); for doctorate, thesis/dissertation. *Entrance requirements:* For master's, GRE General Test, minimum GPA 2.8, personal statement, 1 letter of recommendation, transcripts; for doctorate, GRE

General Test, minimum GPA of 3.5, personal statement, 3 letters of recommendation, transcripts. Additional exam requirements/recommendations for international students: required—TOEFL (minimum score 550 paper-based; 79 iBT), IELTS (minimum score 6.5). *Application deadline:* For fall admission, 6/1 priority date for domestic students, 5/1 priority date for international students; for spring admission, 11/15 priority date for domestic and international students. Applications are processed on a rolling basis. Application fee: $75. Electronic applications accepted. *Expenses:* $23,828 per year (in-state), $33,744 per year (out-of-state). *Financial support:* In 2019–20, 352 students received support, including 33 fellowships with full tuition reimbursements available (averaging $24,000 per year), 89 research assistantships with full tuition reimbursements available (averaging $24,000 per year), 112 teaching assistantships with full tuition reimbursements available (averaging $24,000 per year); career-related internships or fieldwork, Federal Work-Study, scholarships/grants, and unspecified assistantships also available. Financial award application deadline: 1/15. *Unit head:* Dr. Moshe Kam, Dean, 973-596-5534, Fax: 973-596-2316, E-mail: moshe.kam@njit.edu. *Application contact:* Stephen Eck, Executive Director of University Admissions, 973-596-3300, Fax: 973-596-3461, E-mail: admissions@njit.edu.
Website: http://engineering.njit.edu/

New York University, Tandon School of Engineering, Department of Technology Management, Major in Industrial Engineering, New York, NY 10012-1019. Offers MS. *Program availability:* Part-time, evening/weekend, online learning. *Entrance requirements:* For master's, BE or BS in engineering, physics, chemistry, mathematical sciences, or biological sciences, or MBA. Additional exam requirements/recommendations for international students: required—TOEFL (minimum score 550 paper-based; 90 iBT); recommended—IELTS (minimum score 7). Electronic applications accepted.

North Carolina Agricultural and Technical State University, The Graduate College, College of Engineering, Department of Industrial and Systems Engineering, Greensboro, NC 27411. Offers industrial and systems engineering (PhD); industrial engineering (MSIE). *Program availability:* Part-time. *Degree requirements:* For master's, thesis, project; for doctorate, thesis/dissertation. *Entrance requirements:* For master's, GRE General Test (recommended); for doctorate, GRE General Test, degree in engineering, BS in industrial engineering from ABET-accredited program with minimum cumulative credit point average of 3.7 or MS in discipline related to industrial engineering from college or university recognized by a regional or general accrediting agency with minimum cumulative GPA of 3.3. Additional exam requirements/recommendations for international students: required—TOEFL (minimum score 550 paper-based; 79 iBT).

North Carolina State University, Graduate School, College of Engineering, Edward P. Fitts Department of Industrial and Systems Engineering, Raleigh, NC 27695. Offers industrial engineering (MIE, MS, PhD). *Program availability:* Part-time. Terminal master's awarded for partial completion of doctoral program. *Entrance requirements:* For master's, GRE General Test, minimum GPA of 3.0; for doctorate, GRE General Test. Additional exam requirements/recommendations for international students: required—TOEFL. Electronic applications accepted.

North Dakota State University, College of Graduate and Interdisciplinary Studies, College of Engineering, Department of Industrial and Manufacturing Engineering, Fargo, ND 58102. Offers industrial and manufacturing engineering (MS, PhD); manufacturing engineering (MS). *Program availability:* Part-time. *Degree requirements:* For doctorate, comprehensive exam, thesis/dissertation. *Entrance requirements:* For master's, GRE General Test, bachelor's degree in engineering; for doctorate, GRE General Test, master's degree in engineering. Additional exam requirements/recommendations for international students: required—TOEFL (minimum score 550 paper-based; 79 iBT), TWE (minimum score 4). Electronic applications accepted. Tuition and fees vary according to program and reciprocity agreements.

Northeastern University, College of Engineering, Boston, MA 02115-5096. Offers bioengineering (MS, PhD); chemical engineering (MS, PhD); civil engineering (MS, PhD); computer engineering (PhD); computer systems engineering (MS); electrical and computer engineering (MS); electrical and computer engineering leadership (MS); electrical engineering (PhD); energy systems (MS); engineering and public policy (MS); engineering management (MS, Certificate); environmental engineering (MS); industrial engineering (MS, PhD); information assurance (PhD); information systems (MS); interdisciplinary engineering (PhD); mechanical engineering (PhD); operations research (MS); telecommunication systems management (MS). *Program availability:* Part-time, online learning. Electronic applications accepted. *Expenses:* Contact institution.

Northern Illinois University, Graduate School, College of Engineering and Engineering Technology, Department of Industrial Engineering, De Kalb, IL 60115-2854. Offers MS. *Program availability:* Part-time. *Faculty:* 4 full-time (1 woman), 1 part-time/adjunct (0 women). *Students:* 74 full-time (21 women), 63 part-time (12 women); includes 18 minority (2 Black or African American, non-Hispanic/Latino; 5 Asian, non-Hispanic/Latino; 7 Hispanic/Latino; 4 Two or more races, non-Hispanic/Latino), 93 international. Average age 27. 123 applicants, 76% accepted, 31 enrolled. In 2019, 58 master's awarded. *Degree requirements:* For master's, comprehensive exam, thesis optional. *Entrance requirements:* For master's, GRE General Test, minimum GPA of 2.75. Additional exam requirements/recommendations for international students: required—TOEFL (minimum score 550 paper-based). *Application deadline:* For fall admission, 6/1 for domestic students, 5/1 for international students; for spring admission, 11/1 for domestic students, 10/1 for international students. Applications are processed on a rolling basis. Application fee: $40. Electronic applications accepted. *Financial support:* In 2019–20, 21 research assistantships, 19 teaching assistantships were awarded; fellowships, Federal Work-Study, scholarships/grants, tuition waivers (full), and staff assistantships also available. Support available to part-time students. Financial award applicants required to submit FAFSA. *Unit head:* Dr. Purushothaman Damodaran, Chair, 815-753-1349, Fax: 815-753-0823. *Application contact:* Graduate School Office, 815-753-0395, E-mail: gradsch@niu.edu.
Website: http://www.niu.edu/isye

Northwestern University, McCormick School of Engineering and Applied Science, Department of Industrial Engineering and Management Sciences, Evanston, IL 60208. Offers analytics (MS); engineering management (MEM); industrial engineering and management science (MS, PhD). Terminal master's awarded for partial completion of doctoral program. *Degree requirements:* For master's, comprehensive exam; for doctorate, comprehensive exam, thesis/dissertation. *Entrance requirements:* For master's and doctorate, GRE General Test. Additional exam requirements/recommendations for international students: required—TOEFL (minimum score 577 paper-based; 90 iBT), IELTS (minimum score 7). Electronic applications accepted.

The Ohio State University, Graduate School, College of Engineering, Department of Integrated Systems Engineering, Columbus, OH 43210. Offers industrial and systems engineering (MS, PhD). *Entrance requirements:* For master's and doctorate, GRE General Test (desired minimum scores: Quantitative 166, Verbal 153, Analytical Writing 4.5). Additional exam requirements/recommendations for international students: required—TOEFL (minimum score 550 paper-based; 79 iBT), Michigan English

Language Assessment Battery (minimum score 82); recommended—IELTS (minimum score 7). Electronic applications accepted.

Ohio University, Graduate College, Russ College of Engineering and Technology, Department of Industrial and Systems Engineering, Athens, OH 45701-2979. Offers M Eng Mgt, MS. *Program availability:* Part-time, evening/weekend. *Degree requirements:* For master's, comprehensive exam (for some programs), thesis optional, research project. *Entrance requirements:* For master's, GRE General Test. Additional exam requirements/recommendations for international students: required—TOEFL (minimum score 550 paper-based; 80 iBT) or IELTS (minimum score 6.5). Electronic applications accepted.

Ohio University, Graduate College, Russ College of Engineering and Technology, Program in Mechanical and Systems Engineering, Athens, OH 45701-2979. Offers industrial and systems engineering (MS); mechanical and systems engineering (PhD). *Degree requirements:* For doctorate, comprehensive exam, thesis/dissertation. *Entrance requirements:* For doctorate, GRE General Test, MS in engineering or related field. Additional exam requirements/recommendations for international students: required—TOEFL (minimum score 550 paper-based; 80 iBT) or IELTS (minimum score 6.5). Electronic applications accepted.

Oklahoma State University, College of Engineering, Architecture and Technology, School of Industrial Engineering and Management, Stillwater, OK 74078. Offers MS, PhD. *Program availability:* Online learning. *Faculty:* 15 full-time (3 women). *Students:* 22 full-time (4 women), 108 part-time (17 women); includes 22 minority (5 Black or African American, non-Hispanic/Latino; 1 American Indian or Alaska Native, non-Hispanic/Latino; 5 Asian, non-Hispanic/Latino; 6 Hispanic/Latino; 5 Two or more races, non-Hispanic/Latino), 43 international. Average age 31. 132 applicants, 43% accepted, 35 enrolled. In 2019, 53 master's, 2 doctorates awarded. *Entrance requirements:* For master's and doctorate, GRE or GMAT. Additional exam requirements/recommendations for international students: required—TOEFL (minimum score 550 paper-based; 79 iBT). *Application deadline:* For fall admission, 3/1 priority date for international students; for spring admission, 8/1 priority date for international students. Applications are processed on a rolling basis. Application fee: $50 ($75 for international students). Electronic applications accepted. *Expenses: Tuition, area resident:* Full-time $4148.10; part-time $2765.40. Tuition, state resident: full-time $4148.10; part-time $2765.40. Tuition, nonresident: full-time $15,775; part-time $10,516.80. *International tuition:* $15,775.20 full-time. *Required fees:* $2196.90; $122.05 per credit hour. Tuition and fees vary according to course load, campus/location and program. *Financial support:* In 2019–20, 10 research assistantships (averaging $1,757 per year), 25 teaching assistantships (averaging $1,929 per year) were awarded; career-related internships or fieldwork, Federal Work-Study, scholarships/grants, health care benefits, tuition waivers (partial), and unspecified assistantships also available. Support available to part-time students. Financial award application deadline: 3/1; financial award applicants required to submit FAFSA. *Unit head:* Dr. Sunderesh Heragu, Head, 405-744-6055, Fax: 405-744-4654, E-mail: sunderesh.heragu@okstate.edu. *Application contact:* Dr. Sheryl Tucker, Vice Prov/Dean/Prof, 405-744-6368, E-mail: gradi@okstate.edu.
Website: http://iem.okstate.edu/

Oregon State University, College of Engineering, Program in Industrial Engineering, Corvallis, OR 97331. Offers advanced manufacturing (M Eng, MS, PhD); engineering management (M Eng); human systems engineering (M Eng, MS, PhD); information systems engineering (M Eng, MS, PhD); manufacturing systems engineering (M Eng, MS, PhD). *Program availability:* 100% online. *Entrance requirements:* For master's and doctorate, GRE. Additional exam requirements/recommendations for international students: required—TOEFL (minimum score 80 iBT), IELTS (minimum score 6.5). *Expenses:* Contact institution.

Penn State University Park, Graduate School, College of Engineering, Department of Industrial and Manufacturing Engineering, University Park, PA 16802. Offers industrial engineering (MS, PhD).

Polytechnique Montréal, Graduate Programs, Department of Mathematics and Industrial Engineering, Montréal, QC H3C 3A7, Canada. Offers ergonomy (M Eng, M Sc A, DESS); mathematical method in CA engineering (M Eng, M Sc A, PhD); operational research (M Eng, M Sc A, PhD); production (M Eng, M Sc A); technology management (M Eng, M Sc A). *Program availability:* Part-time. *Degree requirements:* For master's, one foreign language, thesis. *Entrance requirements:* For master's, minimum GPA of 2.75.

Purdue University, College of Engineering, School of Industrial Engineering, West Lafayette, IN 47907-2023. Offers MS, MSIE, PhD. *Program availability:* Part-time, online learning. *Faculty:* 30. *Students:* 276. Terminal master's awarded for partial completion of doctoral program. *Degree requirements:* For master's, thesis optional; for doctorate, thesis/dissertation. *Application deadline:* For fall admission, 1/5 for domestic and international students; for spring admission, 9/1 for domestic and international students. Applications are processed on a rolling basis. Application fee: $60 ($75 for international students). Electronic applications accepted. *Financial support:* Fellowships with full and partial tuition reimbursements, research assistantships with full and partial tuition reimbursements, teaching assistantships with full and partial tuition reimbursements, scholarships/grants, health care benefits, and unspecified assistantships available. *Unit head:* Dr. Abhijit Deshmukh, Head/Professor of Industrial Engineering, 765-496-6007, E-mail: abhi@purdue.edu. *Application contact:* Anita Park, Graduate Administrator, 765-494-5434, E-mail: apark@purdue.edu.
Website: https://engineering.purdue.edu/IE

Purdue University Fort Wayne, College of Engineering, Technology, and Computer Science, Program in Technology, Fort Wayne, IN 46805-1499. Offers facilities/construction management (MS); industrial technology/manufacturing (MS); information technology/advanced computer applications (MS). *Program availability:* Part-time. *Entrance requirements:* For master's, minimum GPA of 3.0. Additional exam requirements/recommendations for international students: required—TOEFL (minimum score 550 paper-based; 79 iBT), TWE. Electronic applications accepted.

Rensselaer Polytechnic Institute, Graduate School, School of Engineering, Program in Decision Sciences and Engineering Systems, Troy, NY 12180-3590. Offers PhD. *Faculty:* 3 full-time (2 women). *Students:* 15 full-time (2 women), 1 part-time (0 women), 11 international. Average age 30. 32 applicants, 25% accepted, 4 enrolled. In 2019, 3 doctorates awarded. Terminal master's awarded for partial completion of doctoral program. *Degree requirements:* For doctorate, thesis/dissertation. *Entrance requirements:* For doctorate, GRE. Additional exam requirements/recommendations for international students: required—TOEFL (minimum score 570 paper-based; 88 iBT), IELTS (minimum score 6.5), PTE (minimum score 60). *Application deadline:* For fall admission, 1/1 priority date for domestic students, 1/1 for international students. Applications are processed on a rolling basis. Application fee: $75. Electronic applications accepted. *Financial support:* In 2019–20, research assistantships (averaging $23,000 per year), teaching assistantships (averaging $23,000 per year) were awarded; fellowships also available. Financial award application deadline: 1/1. *Unit head:* Dr. Thomas Sharkey, Graduate Program Director, 518-276-2958, E-mail: sharkt@rpi.edu. *Application contact:* Jarron Decker, Director of Graduate Admissions, 518-276-6216, Fax: 518-276-4072, E-mail: gradadmissions@rpi.edu.
Website: http://ise.rpi.edu/

Rensselaer Polytechnic Institute, Graduate School, School of Engineering, Program in Industrial and Management Engineering, Troy, NY 12180-3590. Offers M Eng, MS. *Program availability:* Part-time. *Faculty:* 8 full-time (0 women). *Students:* 3 full-time (2 women); includes 1 minority (Black or African American, non-Hispanic/Latino), 1 international. Average age 25. 28 applicants, 32% accepted. In 2019, 5 master's awarded. *Degree requirements:* For master's, thesis (for some programs). *Entrance requirements:* For master's, GRE. Additional exam requirements/recommendations for international students: required—TOEFL (minimum score 570 paper-based; 88 iBT), IELTS (minimum score 6.5), PTE (minimum score 60). *Application deadline:* For fall admission, 1/1 priority date for domestic and international students; for spring admission, 8/15 priority date for domestic and international students. Applications are processed on a rolling basis. Application fee: $75. Electronic applications accepted. *Financial support:* In 2019–20, teaching assistantships (averaging $23,000 per year) were awarded. Financial award application deadline: 1/1. *Unit head:* Dr. Thomas Sharkey, Graduate Program Director, 518-276-2958, E-mail: sharkt@rpi.edu. *Application contact:* Jarron Decker, Director of Graduate Admissions, 518-276-6216, Fax: 518-276-4072, E-mail: gradadmissions@rpi.edu.
Website: http://ise.rpi.edu/

Rochester Institute of Technology, Graduate Enrollment Services, Kate Gleason College of Engineering, Industrial and Systems Engineering Department, ME Program in Industrial and Systems Engineering, Rochester, NY 14623-5603. Offers ME. *Program availability:* Part-time. *Degree requirements:* For master's, thesis or alternative, capstone project. *Entrance requirements:* For master's, GRE, minimum GPA of 3.0 (recommended), one-page statement of purpose, two letters of recommendation. Additional exam requirements/recommendations for international students: required—TOEFL (minimum score 580 paper-based; 90 iBT), IELTS (minimum score 6), PTE (minimum score 58). Electronic applications accepted.

Rochester Institute of Technology, Graduate Enrollment Services, Kate Gleason College of Engineering, Industrial and Systems Engineering Department, MS Program in Industrial and Systems Engineering, Rochester, NY 14623-5603. Offers MS. *Program availability:* Part-time. *Degree requirements:* For master's, thesis. *Entrance requirements:* For master's, GRE, minimum GPA of 3.0 (recommended), statement of purpose, 2 letters of recommendation. Additional exam requirements/recommendations for international students: required—TOEFL (minimum score 580 paper-based; 90 iBT), IELTS (minimum score 6.5), PTE (minimum score 58). Electronic applications accepted.

Rutgers University - New Brunswick, Graduate School-New Brunswick, Department of Industrial and Systems Engineering, Piscataway, NJ 08854-8097. Offers industrial and systems engineering (MS, PhD); information technology (MS); manufacturing systems engineering (MS); quality and reliability engineering (MS). *Program availability:* Part-time, evening/weekend. Terminal master's awarded for partial completion of doctoral program. *Degree requirements:* For master's, thesis or alternative, seminar; for doctorate, comprehensive exam, thesis/dissertation. *Entrance requirements:* For master's and doctorate, GRE General Test. Additional exam requirements/recommendations for international students: required—TOEFL.

St. Mary's University, School of Science, Engineering and Technology, Program in Industrial Engineering, San Antonio, TX 78228. Offers MS. *Program availability:* Part-time, evening/weekend. *Degree requirements:* For master's, project or thesis. *Entrance requirements:* For master's, GRE (minimum quantitative score of 148), BS in computer engineering, electrical engineering, or closely-related discipline; minimum GPA of 3.0; written statement of purpose indicating applicant's interests and objectives; two letters of recommendation. Additional exam requirements/recommendations for international students: required—TOEFL (minimum score 550 paper-based; 80 iBT), IELTS (minimum score 6). Electronic applications accepted.

San Jose State University, Program in Industrial and Systems Engineering, San Jose, CA 95192-0085. Offers MS. *Faculty:* 5 full-time (2 women), 9 part-time/adjunct (1 woman). *Students:* 196 full-time (112 women), 214 part-time (127 women); includes 85 minority (5 Black or African American, non-Hispanic/Latino; 61 Asian, non-Hispanic/Latino; 19 Hispanic/Latino), 262 international. Average age 27. 542 applicants, 39% accepted, 131 enrolled. In 2019, 141 master's awarded. *Application deadline:* For fall admission, 6/1 for domestic students, 5/1 for international students; for spring admission, 12/1 for domestic students, 11/1 for international students. Applications are processed on a rolling basis. Application fee: $70. Electronic applications accepted. *Expenses: Tuition, area resident:* Full-time $7176; part-time $4164. Tuition, state resident: full-time $7176; part-time $4164. Tuition, nonresident: full-time $7176; part-time $4165 per credit hour. *International tuition:* $7176 full-time. *Required fees:* $2110; $2110. *Financial support:* In 2019–20, 24 students received support. Scholarships/grants available. Financial award application deadline: 5/1; financial award applicants required to submit FAFSA. *Unit head:* Yasser Dessouky, Department Chair, 408-924-4133, E-mail: yasser.dessouky@sjsu.edu. *Application contact:* Yasser Dessouky, Department Chair, 408-924-4133, E-mail: yasser.dessouky@sjsu.edu.
Website: http://www.engr.sjsu.edu/ise/

Southern Illinois University Edwardsville, Graduate School, School of Engineering, Department of Mechanical and Industrial Engineering, Program in Industrial Engineering, Edwardsville, IL 62026. Offers MS. *Program availability:* Part-time, evening/weekend. *Degree requirements:* For master's, thesis (for some programs), final exam. *Entrance requirements:* For master's, GRE (for applicants whose degree is from non-ABET accredited institution). Additional exam requirements/recommendations for international students: required—TOEFL (minimum score 550 paper-based; 79 iBT), IELTS (minimum score 6.5). Electronic applications accepted.

Stanford University, School of Engineering, Department of Management Science and Engineering, Stanford, CA 94305-2004. Offers MS, PhD. *Expenses: Tuition:* Full-time $52,479; part-time $34,110 per unit. *Required fees:* $672; $224 per quarter. Tuition and fees vary according to program and student level.
Website: http://www.stanford.edu/dept/MSandE/

Texas A&M University, College of Engineering, Wm Michael Barnes '64 Department of Industrial and Systems Engineering, College Station, TX 77843. Offers engineering systems management (MS); industrial engineering (M Eng, MS, PhD). *Program availability:* Part-time, 100% online. *Faculty:* 39. *Students:* 241 full-time (52 women), 96 part-time (16 women); includes 20 minority (5 Black or African American, non-Hispanic/Latino; 6 Asian, non-Hispanic/Latino; 7 Hispanic/Latino; 2 Two or more races, non-Hispanic/Latino), 275 international. Average age 27. 551 applicants, 36% accepted, 81 enrolled. In 2019, 111 master's, 5 doctorates awarded. *Degree requirements:* For master's, comprehensive exam (for some programs), thesis optional; for doctorate, comprehensive exam, thesis/dissertation. *Entrance requirements:* For master's and doctorate, GRE General Test. Additional exam requirements/recommendations for international students: required—TOEFL (minimum score 550 paper-based; 80 iBT), IELTS (minimum score 6), PTE (minimum score 53). *Application deadline:* For fall admission, 8/14 for domestic students, 3/1 for international students; for spring admission, 12/1 for domestic students, 10/31 for international students. Applications are processed on a rolling basis. Application fee: $65 ($90 for international students).

Electronic applications accepted. *Expenses:* Contact institution. *Financial support:* In 2019–20, 237 students received support, including 8 fellowships with tuition reimbursements available (averaging $16,335 per year), 96 research assistantships with tuition reimbursements available (averaging $12,861 per year), 71 teaching assistantships with tuition reimbursements available (averaging $9,917 per year); career-related internships or fieldwork, institutionally sponsored loans, scholarships/grants, traineeships, health care benefits, tuition waivers (full and partial), and unspecified assistantships also available. Support available to part-time students. Financial award application deadline: 3/15; financial award applicants required to submit FAFSA. *Unit head:* Dr. Lewis Ntaimo, Interim Department Head, 979-845-5535, Fax: 979-458-4299, E-mail: ntaimo@tamu.edu. *Application contact:* Victoria Aregullin, Graduate Academic Advisor, 979-458-8403, E-mail: varegullin@tamu.edu. Website: http://engineering.tamu.edu/industrial

Texas A&M University–Kingsville, College of Graduate Studies, Frank H. Dotterweich College of Engineering, Department of Mechanical and Industrial Engineering, Program in Industrial Engineering, Kingsville, TX 78363. Offers ME, MS. *Degree requirements:* For master's, variable foreign language requirement, comprehensive exam, thesis (for some programs). *Entrance requirements:* For master's, GRE (minimum overall old score of 900-1000 depending on GPA), MAT, GMAT. Additional exam requirements/recommendations for international students: required—TOEFL (minimum score 550 paper-based; 79 iBT). Electronic applications accepted.

Texas Southern University, School of Science and Technology, Department of Industrial Technology, Houston, TX 77004-4584. Offers MS. *Degree requirements:* For master's, comprehensive exam. *Entrance requirements:* For master's, GRE General Test, minimum GPA of 2.5. Additional exam requirements/recommendations for international students: required—TOEFL. Electronic applications accepted.

Texas State University, The Graduate College, College of Science and Engineering, Program in Engineering, San Marcos, TX 78666. Offers civil engineering (MS); electrical engineering (MS); industrial engineering (MS); mechanical and manufacturing engineering (MS). *Program availability:* Part-time. *Degree requirements:* For master's, comprehensive exam, thesis (for some programs), thesis or research project. *Entrance requirements:* For master's, official GRE (general test only) required with competitive scores in the verbal reasoning and quantitative reasoning sections, baccalaureate degree from regionally-accredited university in engineering, computer science, physics, technology, or closely-related field with minimum GPA of 3.0 on last 60 undergraduate semester hours; resume or curriculum vitae; 2 letters of recommendation; statement of purpose conveying research interest and professional aspirations. Additional exam requirements/recommendations for international students: required—TOEFL (minimum score 550 paper-based; 78 iBT), IELTS (minimum score 6.5). Electronic applications accepted.

Universidad de las Américas Puebla, Division of Graduate Studies, School of Engineering, Program in Industrial Engineering, Puebla, Mexico. Offers industrial engineering (MS); production management (M Adm). *Program availability:* Part-time, evening/weekend. *Degree requirements:* For master's, one foreign language, thesis.

Université de Moncton, Faculty of Engineering, Program in Industrial Engineering, Moncton, NB E1A 3E9, Canada. Offers M Sc A. *Degree requirements:* For master's, thesis, proficiency in French.

Université du Québec à Trois-Rivières, Graduate Programs, Program in Industrial Engineering, Trois-Rivières, QC G9A 5H7, Canada. Offers M Sc, DESS. *Entrance requirements:* For degree, appropriate bachelor's degree, proficiency in French.

University at Buffalo, the State University of New York, Graduate School, School of Engineering and Applied Sciences, Department of Industrial and Systems Engineering, Buffalo, NY 14260. Offers advanced manufacturing (Certificate); industrial engineering (ME, MS, PhD), including data fusion (ME); engineering management (ME). *Program availability:* Part-time, online learning. Terminal master's awarded for partial completion of doctoral program. *Degree requirements:* For master's, comprehensive exam (for some programs), thesis or alternative; for doctorate, thesis/dissertation. *Entrance requirements:* For master's and doctorate, GRE General Test. Additional exam requirements/recommendations for international students: required—TOEFL (minimum score 550 paper-based; 79 iBT). Electronic applications accepted. *Expenses:* Tuition, area resident: Full-time $11,310; part-time $471 per credit hour. Tuition, state resident: full-time $11,310; part-time $471 per credit hour. Tuition, nonresident: full-time $23,100; part-time $963 per credit hour. *International tuition:* $23,100 full-time. *Required fees:* $2820.

The University of Alabama in Huntsville, School of Graduate Studies, College of Engineering, Department of Industrial and Systems Engineering and Engineering Management, Huntsville, AL 35899. Offers engineering management (MSE, PhD); industrial engineering (MSE, PhD); operations research (MSOR); systems engineering (MSE, PhD). *Program availability:* Part-time. *Degree requirements:* For master's, comprehensive exam, thesis or alternative, oral and written exams; for doctorate, comprehensive exam, thesis/dissertation, oral and written exams. *Entrance requirements:* For master's and doctorate, GRE General Test, minimum GPA of 3.0. Additional exam requirements/recommendations for international students: required—TOEFL (minimum score 500 paper-based; 80 iBT), IELTS (minimum score 6.5). Electronic applications accepted.

The University of Arizona, College of Engineering, Department of Systems and Industrial Engineering, Tucson, AZ 85721. Offers engineering management (Graduate Certificate); industrial engineering (MS); systems and industrial engineering (MS, PhD); systems engineering (MS, PhD, Graduate Certificate). *Program availability:* Part-time, online learning. *Degree requirements:* For doctorate, thesis/dissertation. *Entrance requirements:* For master's, GRE General Test (minimum score: 500 Verbal, 700 Quantitative), 3 letters of recommendation; for doctorate, GRE General Test (minimum score: 500 Verbal, 700 Quantitative), minimum GPA of 3.5, 3 letters of recommendation, letter of intent. Additional exam requirements/recommendations for international students: required—TOEFL (minimum score 575 paper-based; 80 iBT). Electronic applications accepted.

University of Arkansas, Graduate School, College of Engineering, Department of Industrial Engineering, Program in Industrial Engineering, Fayetteville, AR 72701. Offers MSE, MSIE, PhD. *Students:* 36 full-time (11 women), 13 part-time (4 women); includes 4 minority (2 Asian, non-Hispanic/Latino; 2 Hispanic/Latino), 31 international. 61 applicants, 59% accepted. In 2019, 10 master's, 5 doctorates awarded. *Degree requirements:* For master's, thesis optional; for doctorate, one foreign language, thesis/dissertation. *Application deadline:* For fall admission, 8/1 for domestic students, 4/1 for international students; for spring admission, 12/1 for domestic students, 10/1 for international students; for summer admission, 4/15 for domestic students, 3/1 for international students. Applications are processed on a rolling basis. Application fee: $60. Electronic applications accepted. *Financial support:* In 2019–20, 32 research assistantships were awarded; fellowships, teaching assistantships, career-related internships or fieldwork, and Federal Work-Study also available. Support available to part-time students. Financial award application deadline: 4/1; financial award applicants required to submit FAFSA. *Unit head:* Dr. Edward Pohl, Department Head, 479-575-6029, E-mail: epohl@uark.edu. *Application contact:* Dr. Haitao Liao, Graduate Coordinator, 479-575-6196, E-mail: liao@uark.edu. Website: https://industrial-engineering.uark.edu/

University of California, Berkeley, Graduate Division, College of Engineering, Department of Industrial Engineering and Operations Research, Berkeley, CA 94720. Offers decision analytics (M Eng); industrial engineering and operations research (M Eng, MS, PhD). *Program availability:* Part-time, evening/weekend. Terminal master's awarded for partial completion of doctoral program. *Degree requirements:* For master's, comprehensive exam (for some programs), thesis (for some programs), comprehensive exam or thesis (MS); for doctorate, thesis/dissertation, qualifying exam. *Entrance requirements:* For master's and doctorate, GRE General Test, minimum GPA of 3.0, 3 letters of recommendation. Additional exam requirements/recommendations for international students: required—TOEFL (minimum score 570 paper-based; 90 iBT). Electronic applications accepted.

University of Central Florida, College of Engineering and Computer Science, Department of Industrial Engineering and Management Systems, Orlando, FL 32816. Offers MS, MSEM, MSIE, PhD, Certificate. *Program availability:* Part-time, evening/weekend. *Students:* 104 full-time (36 women), 273 part-time (96 women); includes 126 minority (33 Black or African American, non-Hispanic/Latino; 1 American Indian or Alaska Native, non-Hispanic/Latino; 21 Asian, non-Hispanic/Latino; 65 Hispanic/Latino; 6 Two or more races, non-Hispanic/Latino), 62 international. Average age 32. 240 applicants, 67% accepted, 95 enrolled. In 2019, 102 master's, 19 doctorates, 22 other advanced degrees awarded. *Degree requirements:* For master's, thesis or alternative; for doctorate, thesis/dissertation, departmental qualifying exam, candidacy exam. *Entrance requirements:* For master's, minimum GPA of 3.0 in last 60 hours of course work, letters of recommendation, goal statement, resume; for doctorate, GRE, minimum GPA of 3.0 in last 60 hours of course work, letters of recommendation, goal statement, resume. Additional exam requirements/recommendations for international students: required—TOEFL. *Application deadline:* For fall admission, 7/15 for domestic students; for spring admission, 12/1 for domestic students. Application fee: $30. Electronic applications accepted. *Financial support:* In 2019–20, 45 students received support, including 19 fellowships with partial tuition reimbursements available (averaging $7,307 per year), 25 research assistantships with partial tuition reimbursements available (averaging $7,489 per year), 22 teaching assistantships with partial tuition reimbursements available (averaging $8,031 per year); career-related internships or fieldwork, Federal Work-Study, institutionally sponsored loans, health care benefits, tuition waivers (partial), and unspecified assistantships also available. Financial award application deadline: 3/1; financial award applicants required to submit FAFSA. *Unit head:* Dr. Waldemar Karwowski, Chair, 407-823-0042, E-mail: wkar@ucf.edu. *Application contact:* Associate Director, Graduate Admissions, 407-823-2766, Fax: 407-823-6442, E-mail: gradadmissions@ucf.edu. Website: http://iems.ucf.edu/

University of Cincinnati, Graduate School, College of Engineering and Applied Science, Department of Mechanical and Materials Engineering, Cincinnati, OH 45221. Offers industrial engineering (PhD); mechanical engineering (MS, PhD); nuclear engineering (PhD); MBA/MS. *Program availability:* Part-time, evening/weekend. Terminal master's awarded for partial completion of doctoral program. *Degree requirements:* For doctorate, thesis/dissertation. *Entrance requirements:* For master's and doctorate, GRE General Test. Additional exam requirements/recommendations for international students: required—TOEFL (minimum score 575 paper-based). Electronic applications accepted.

University of Florida, Graduate School, Herbert Wertheim College of Engineering, Department of Industrial and Systems Engineering, Gainesville, FL 32611. Offers industrial and systems engineering (ME, MS, PhD, Engr); quantitative finance (PhD). *Program availability:* Part-time, evening/weekend, online learning. Terminal master's awarded for partial completion of doctoral program. *Degree requirements:* For master's, thesis (for some programs); for doctorate, comprehensive exam (for some programs), thesis/dissertation (for some programs). *Entrance requirements:* For master's and doctorate, minimum GPA of 3.0; for Engr, GRE General Test. Additional exam requirements/recommendations for international students: required—TOEFL (minimum score 550 paper-based; 80 iBT), IELTS (minimum score 6). Electronic applications accepted.

University of Houston, Cullen College of Engineering, Department of Industrial Engineering, Houston, TX 77204. Offers MIE, PhD. *Program availability:* Part-time. Terminal master's awarded for partial completion of doctoral program. *Degree requirements:* For master's, thesis (for some programs); for doctorate, thesis/dissertation, departmental qualifying exam. *Entrance requirements:* For master's and doctorate, GRE General Test. Additional exam requirements/recommendations for international students: required—TOEFL; recommended—IELTS. Electronic applications accepted.

University of Illinois at Chicago, College of Engineering, Department of Mechanical and Industrial Engineering, Program in Industrial Engineering, Chicago, IL 60607-7128. Offers industrial engineering (MS); industrial engineering and operations research (PhD). *Program availability:* Part-time. *Degree requirements:* For doctorate, thesis/dissertation. *Entrance requirements:* For doctorate, GRE General Test, minimum GPA of 2.75. Additional exam requirements/recommendations for international students: required—TOEFL. Electronic applications accepted. *Expenses:* Contact institution.

University of Illinois at Urbana-Champaign, Graduate College, College of Engineering, Department of Industrial and Enterprise Systems Engineering, Urbana, IL 61801. Offers industrial engineering (MS, PhD); systems and entrepreneurial engineering (MS, PhD); MBA/MS.

University of Illinois at Urbana-Champaign, Graduate College, College of Engineering, Department of Mechanical Science and Engineering, Champaign, IL 61820. Offers mechanical engineering (MS, PhD); theoretical and applied mechanics (MS, PhD). Terminal master's awarded for partial completion of doctoral program. *Entrance requirements:* Additional exam requirements/recommendations for international students: required—TOEFL (minimum score 613 paper-based; 103 iBT), IELTS (minimum score 7).

The University of Iowa, Graduate College, College of Engineering, Department of Industrial Engineering, Iowa City, IA 52242-1316. Offers engineering design and manufacturing (MS, PhD); healthcare systems (MS, PhD); human factors (MS, PhD); information and engineering management (MS, PhD); operations research (MS, PhD); wind energy (MS, PhD). Terminal master's awarded for partial completion of doctoral program. *Degree requirements:* For master's, thesis optional, exam; for doctorate, comprehensive exam, thesis/dissertation, final defense exam. *Entrance requirements:* For master's and doctorate, GRE (minimum Verbal score of 153, Quantitative 151), minimum undergraduate GPA of 3.0. Additional exam requirements/recommendations for international students: required—TOEFL (minimum score 600 paper-based; 100 iBT), IELTS (minimum score 7). Electronic applications accepted.

University of Louisville, J. B. Speed School of Engineering, Department of Industrial Engineering, Louisville, KY 40292-0001. Offers engineering management (M Eng); industrial engineering (M Eng, MS, PhD); logistics and distribution (Certificate). *Accreditation:* ABET (one or more programs are accredited). *Program availability:* 100%

online. *Faculty:* 8 full-time (4 women), 8 part-time/adjunct (2 women). *Students:* 52 full-time (11 women), 117 part-time (41 women); includes 27 minority (11 Black or African American, non-Hispanic/Latino; 1 American Indian or Alaska Native, non-Hispanic/Latino; 8 Asian, non-Hispanic/Latino; 5 Hispanic/Latino; 2 Two or more races, non-Hispanic/Latino), 55 international. Average age 30. 97 applicants, 61% accepted, 46 enrolled. In 2019, 85 master's, 6 doctorates awarded. Terminal master's awarded for partial completion of doctoral program. *Degree requirements:* For master's and Certificate, thesis optional; for doctorate, comprehensive exam, thesis/dissertation. *Entrance requirements:* For master's, two letters of recommendation, official transcripts; for doctorate, GRE, two letters of recommendation, official transcripts. Additional exam requirements/recommendations for international students: required—TOEFL (minimum score 550 paper-based; 80 iBT), IELTS (minimum score 6.5). *Application deadline:* For fall admission, 5/1 priority date for domestic and international students; for spring admission, 11/1 priority date for domestic and international students; for summer admission, 3/1 priority date for domestic and international students. Applications are processed on a rolling basis. Application fee: $65. Electronic applications accepted. *Expenses: Tuition, area resident:* Full-time $13,000; part-time $723 per credit hour. Tuition, state resident: full-time $13,000; part-time $723 per credit hour. Tuition, nonresident: full-time $27,114; part-time $1507 per credit hour. *International tuition:* $27,114 full-time. *Required fees:* $196. Tuition and fees vary according to program and reciprocity agreements. *Financial support:* In 2019–20, 27 students received support. Fellowships, research assistantships, teaching assistantships, scholarships/grants, health care benefits, and tuition waivers (full) available. Financial award application deadline: 1/1. *Unit head:* Dr. Suraj M. Alexander, Chair, Industrial Engineering Department, 502-852-0082, E-mail: suraj.alexander@louisville.edu. *Application contact:* Lihui Bai, Director of Graduate Studies, 502-852-1416, E-mail: lihui.bai@louisville.edu.
Website: http://www.louisville.edu/speed/industrial/

University of Manitoba, Faculty of Graduate Studies, Faculty of Engineering, Department of Mechanical and Manufacturing Engineering, Winnipeg, MB R3T 2N2, Canada. Offers M Eng, M Sc, PhD. *Degree requirements:* For master's, thesis; for doctorate, thesis/dissertation.

University of Massachusetts Amherst, Graduate School, College of Engineering, Department of Mechanical and Industrial Engineering, Amherst, MA 01003. Offers industrial engineering and operations research (MS, PhD); mechanical engineering (MSME, PhD). *Program availability:* Part-time. Terminal master's awarded for partial completion of doctoral program. *Degree requirements:* For master's, thesis or alternative; for doctorate, comprehensive exam, thesis/dissertation. *Entrance requirements:* For master's and doctorate, GRE General Test. Additional exam requirements/recommendations for international students: required—TOEFL (minimum score 550 paper-based; 80 iBT), IELTS (minimum score 6.5). Electronic applications accepted.

University of Massachusetts Dartmouth, Graduate School, College of Engineering, Department of Mechanical Engineering, North Dartmouth, MA 02747-2300. Offers industrial and systems engineering (Postbaccalaureate Certificate); mechanical engineering (MS). *Program availability:* Part-time. *Degree requirements:* For master's, thesis, thesis or project. *Entrance requirements:* For master's, GRE unless UMass Dartmouth graduate in mechanical engineering, statement of purpose (minimum of 300 words), resume, 3 letters of recommendation, official transcripts; for Postbaccalaureate Certificate, statement of purpose (minimum of 300 words), resume, 3 letters of recommendation, official transcripts. Additional exam requirements/recommendations for international students: required—TOEFL (minimum score 533 paper-based; 72 iBT), IELTS (minimum score 6). Electronic applications accepted.

University of Massachusetts Lowell, College of Health Sciences, Department of Work Environment, Lowell, MA 01854. Offers cleaner production and pollution prevention (Sc D). *Program availability:* Part-time. Terminal master's awarded for partial completion of doctoral program. *Degree requirements:* For doctorate, thesis/dissertation. *Entrance requirements:* For doctorate, GRE General Test. Additional exam requirements/recommendations for international students: required—TOEFL.

University of Miami, Graduate School, College of Engineering, Department of Industrial Engineering, Coral Gables, FL 33124. Offers environmental health and safety (MS); ergonomics (PhD); industrial engineering (MSIE, PhD); management of technology (MS); occupational ergonomics and safety (MS, MSOES), including environmental health and safety (MS), occupational ergonomics and safety (MSOES); MBA/MSIE. *Program availability:* Part-time. *Degree requirements:* For master's, thesis (for some programs); for doctorate, comprehensive exam, thesis/dissertation. *Entrance requirements:* For master's and doctorate, GRE General Test, minimum GPA of 3.0. Additional exam requirements/recommendations for international students: required—TOEFL (minimum score 550 paper-based).

University of Michigan, College of Engineering, Department of Industrial and Operations Engineering, Ann Arbor, MI 48109. Offers MS, MSE, PhD, MBA/MS, MBA/MSE. *Program availability:* Part-time. Terminal master's awarded for partial completion of doctoral program. *Degree requirements:* For doctorate, oral defense of dissertation, preliminary exams, qualifying exam. *Entrance requirements:* For master's and doctorate, GRE General Test. Additional exam requirements/recommendations for international students: required—TOEFL. Electronic applications accepted.

University of Michigan–Dearborn, College of Engineering and Computer Science, MSE Program in Industrial and Systems Engineering, Dearborn, MI 48128. Offers MSE. *Program availability:* Part-time, evening/weekend, 100% online. *Faculty:* 17 full-time (4 women), 9 part-time/adjunct (1 woman). *Students:* 59 full-time (11 women), 62 part-time (24 women); includes 10 minority (3 Black or African American, non-Hispanic/Latino; 4 Asian, non-Hispanic/Latino; 3 Hispanic/Latino), 80 international. Average age 26. 236 applicants, 47% accepted, 26 enrolled. In 2019, 61 master's awarded. *Entrance requirements:* For master's, bachelor's degree in engineering, a physical science, computer science, or applied mathematics. Additional exam requirements/recommendations for international students: required—TOEFL (minimum score 560 paper-based; 84 iBT), IELTS (minimum score 6.5). *Application deadline:* For fall admission, 8/1 for domestic students, 5/1 for international students; for winter admission, 12/1 for domestic students, 9/1 for international students; for spring admission, 4/1 for domestic students, 1/1 for international students. Applications are processed on a rolling basis. Application fee: $60. Electronic applications accepted. *Financial support:* Research assistantships with full tuition reimbursements, teaching assistantships with full tuition reimbursements, scholarships/grants, and non-resident tuition scholarships available. Support available to part-time students. Financial award application deadline: 3/1; financial award applicants required to submit FAFSA. *Unit head:* Dr. Armen Zakarian, Chair, 313-593-5361, Fax: 313-593-3692, E-mail: zakarian@umich.edu. *Application contact:* Office of Graduate Studies, 313-583-6321, E-mail: umd-graduatestudies@umich.edu.
Website: https://umdearborn.edu/cecs/departments/industrial-and-manufacturing-systems-engineering/graduate-programs/mse-industrial-systems-engineering

University of Michigan–Dearborn, College of Engineering and Computer Science, PhD Program in Industrial and Systems Engineering, Dearborn, MI 48128. Offers PhD. *Faculty:* 17 full-time (4 women), 9 part-time/adjunct (1 woman). *Students:* 2 full-time (0 women), 11 part-time (5 women); includes 1 minority (Asian, non-Hispanic/Latino), 11 international. Average age 28. 22 applicants, 36% accepted, 5 enrolled. *Degree requirements:* For doctorate, thesis/dissertation, qualifying and preliminary examinations. *Entrance requirements:* For doctorate, GRE, master's degree in engineering, applied mathematics, computer science, or a physical science from accredited program. Additional exam requirements/recommendations for international students: required—TOEFL (minimum score 560 paper-based; 84 iBT), IELTS (minimum score 6.5). *Application deadline:* For fall admission, 2/1 for domestic and international students. Application fee: $60. Electronic applications accepted. *Financial support:* Research assistantships with full tuition reimbursements, teaching assistantships with full tuition reimbursements, scholarships/grants, health care benefits, and unspecified assistantships available. Financial award application deadline: 2/1; financial award applicants required to submit FAFSA. *Unit head:* Dr. Yubao Chen, Director, 313-593-5579, E-mail: yubao@umich.edu. *Application contact:* Office of Graduate Studies, 313-583-6321, E-mail: umd-graduatestudies@umich.edu.
Website: https://umdearborn.edu/cecs/departments/industrial-and-manufacturing-systems-engineering/graduate-programs/phd-industrial-and-systems-engineering

University of Minnesota, Twin Cities Campus, College of Science and Engineering, Department of Industrial and Systems Engineering, Minneapolis, MN 55455-0213. Offers MS, PhD. *Program availability:* Part-time. *Degree requirements:* For doctorate, thesis/dissertation. *Entrance requirements:* For master's, GRE General Test, minimum GPA of 3.0; for doctorate, GRE General Test. Additional exam requirements/recommendations for international students: required—TOEFL. Electronic applications accepted.

University of Missouri, Office of Research and Graduate Studies, College of Engineering, Department of Industrial and Manufacturing Systems Engineering, Columbia, MO 65211. Offers ME, MS, PhD, MS/MHA. *Degree requirements:* For master's, thesis or alternative; for doctorate, thesis/dissertation. *Entrance requirements:* For master's and doctorate, GRE General Test, minimum GPA of 3.0. Additional exam requirements/recommendations for international students: required—TOEFL.

University of Nebraska–Lincoln, Graduate College, College of Engineering, Department of Industrial and Management Systems Engineering, Lincoln, NE 68588. Offers engineering management (M Eng); industrial and management systems engineering (MS, PhD); manufacturing systems engineering (MS). *Program availability:* Online learning. *Degree requirements:* For master's, thesis optional; for doctorate, comprehensive exam, thesis/dissertation. *Entrance requirements:* For master's and doctorate, GRE. Additional exam requirements/recommendations for international students: required—TOEFL (minimum score 525 paper-based). Electronic applications accepted.

University of New Haven, Graduate School, Tagliatela College of Engineering, Program in Industrial Engineering, West Haven, CT 06516. Offers industrial engineering (MSIE); quality engineering (Graduate Certificate); MBA/MSIE. *Program availability:* Part-time, evening/weekend. *Students:* 59 full-time (9 women), 7 part-time (2 women); includes 3 minority (2 Black or African American, non-Hispanic/Latino; 1 Asian, non-Hispanic/Latino), 62 international. Average age 25. 179 applicants, 87% accepted, 23 enrolled. In 2019, 41 master's awarded. *Entrance requirements:* For master's, bachelor's degree in engineering. Additional exam requirements/recommendations for international students: required—TOEFL (minimum score 75 iBT), IELTS, PTE (minimum score 50). *Application deadline:* Applications are processed on a rolling basis. Application fee: $50. Electronic applications accepted. Application fee is waived when completed online. *Financial support:* Research assistantships with partial tuition reimbursements, teaching assistantships with partial tuition reimbursements, career-related internships or fieldwork, Federal Work-Study, scholarships/grants, and unspecified assistantships available. Support available to part-time students. Financial award applicants required to submit FAFSA. *Unit head:* Dr. Ali Montazer, Professor, 203-932-7050, E-mail: amontazer@newhaven.edu. *Application contact:* Selina O'Toole, Senior Associate Director of Graduate Admissions, 203-932-7337, E-mail: sotoole@newhaven.edu.
Website: https://www.newhaven.edu/engineering/graduate-programs/industrial-engineering/

University of Oklahoma, Gallogly College of Engineering, School of Industrial and Systems Engineering, Norman, OK 73019. Offers industrial and systems engineering (MS, PhD). *Degree requirements:* For master's, comprehensive exam, thesis or alternative, 30 units with thesis, 33 without thesis; for doctorate, comprehensive exam, thesis/dissertation, 90 units (30 units of credit given for approved master's degrees). *Entrance requirements:* For master's and doctorate, GRE, BS in engineering, mathematics or equivalent. Additional exam requirements/recommendations for international students: required—TOEFL (minimum score 79 iBT) or IELTS (minimum score 6.5). Electronic applications accepted. *Expenses:* Tuition, state resident: full-time $6583.20; part-time $274.30 per credit hour. Tuition, nonresident: full-time $21,242; part-time $885.10 per credit hour. *International tuition:* $21,242.40 full-time. *Required fees:* $1994.20; $72.55 per credit hour. $126.50 per semester. Tuition and fees vary according to course load and degree level.

University of Pittsburgh, Swanson School of Engineering, Department of Industrial Engineering, Pittsburgh, PA 15260. Offers MSIE, PhD. *Program availability:* Part-time, 100% online. Terminal master's awarded for partial completion of doctoral program. *Degree requirements:* For doctorate, comprehensive exam, thesis/dissertation, final oral exams. *Entrance requirements:* For master's and doctorate, GRE General Test, minimum GPA of 3.0. Additional exam requirements/recommendations for international students: required—TOEFL (minimum score 550 paper-based; 80 iBT). Electronic applications accepted. *Expenses:* Contact institution.

University of Puerto Rico at Mayagüez, Graduate Studies, College of Engineering, Department of Industrial Engineering, Mayagüez, PR 00681-9000. Offers ME, MS. *Program availability:* Part-time. *Degree requirements:* For master's, one foreign language, comprehensive exam, thesis, project. *Entrance requirements:* For master's, minimum GPA of 2.5; proficiency in English and Spanish; BS in engineering. Additional exam requirements/recommendations for international students: required—TOEFL (minimum score 80 iBT). Electronic applications accepted.

University of Regina, Faculty of Graduate Studies and Research, Faculty of Engineering and Applied Science, Program in Industrial Systems Engineering, Regina, SK S4S 0A2, Canada. Offers industrial systems (M Eng, MA Sc, PhD). *Program availability:* Part-time. *Faculty:* 12 full-time (1 woman), 2 part-time/adjunct (0 women). *Students:* 69 full-time (10 women), 6 part-time (1 woman). Average age 30. 215 applicants, 13% accepted. In 2019, 23 master's, 3 doctorates awarded. *Degree requirements:* For master's, thesis, project, report, co-op; for doctorate, comprehensive exam, thesis/dissertation. *Entrance requirements:* For master's, 4 years bachelor degree; at least 70 per cent from a four-year baccalaureate degree (or equivalent). Additional exam requirements/recommendations for international students: required—TOEFL (minimum score 580 paper-based; 80 iBT), IELTS (minimum score 6.5), PTE (minimum score 59), other options are CAEL, MELAB, Cantest and U of R ESL. *Application deadline:* For fall admission, 1/31 for domestic and international students; for winter admission, 7/31 for domestic and international students. Applications are

processed on a rolling basis. Application fee: $100. Electronic applications accepted. *Expenses:* 11,036.50 -This amount is based on three semesters tuition, registered in 6 credit hours per semester. Plus one year student fees and books. There is additional 438.75 if student is in Co-op route. *Financial support:* Fellowships, research assistantships, teaching assistantships, career-related internships or fieldwork, Federal Work-Study, scholarships/grants, unspecified assistantships, and travel award and Graduate Scholarship Base Funds available. Support available to part-time students. Financial award application deadline: 9/30. *Unit head:* Dr. Adisorn Aroonwilas, Program Chair, 306-337-2469, Fax: 306-585-4855, E-mail: Adisorn.Aroonwilas@uregina.ca. *Application contact:* Dr. Golam Kabir, Graduate Coordinator, 306-585-5271, Fax: 306-585-4855, E-mail: golam.kabir@uregina.ca.
Website: http://www.uregina.ca/engineering/

University of Rhode Island, Graduate School, College of Engineering, Department of Mechanical, Industrial and Systems Engineering, Kingston, RI 02881. Offers industrial and systems engineering (MS, PhD), including manufacturing systems, service and enterprise systems. *Program availability:* Part-time. *Faculty:* 17 full-time (4 women). *Students:* 32 full-time (9 women), 37 part-time (6 women); includes 7 minority (2 Black or African American, non-Hispanic/Latino; 1 Asian, non-Hispanic/Latino; 2 Hispanic/Latino; 2 Two or more races, non-Hispanic/Latino), 20 international. 38 applicants, 87% accepted, 25 enrolled. In 2019, 3 doctorates awarded. *Entrance requirements:* Additional exam requirements/recommendations for international students: required—TOEFL. *Application deadline:* For fall admission, 6/1 for domestic students, 2/1 for international students; for spring admission, 11/1 for domestic students, 7/1 for international students. Application fee: $65. Electronic applications accepted. *Expenses: Tuition, area resident:* Full-time $13,734; part-time $763 per credit. *Tuition, state resident:* full-time $13,734; part-time $763 per credit. *Tuition, nonresident:* full-time $26,512; part-time $1473 per credit. *International tuition:* $26,512 full-time. *Required fees:* $1780; $52 per credit. $35 per term. One-time fee: $165. *Financial support:* In 2019–20, 11 research assistantships with tuition reimbursements (averaging $9,584 per year), 11 teaching assistantships with tuition reimbursements (averaging $10,646 per year) were awarded. Financial award application deadline: 2/1; financial award applicants required to submit FAFSA. *Unit head:* Dr. Carl-Ernst Rousseau, Chair, 401-874-2542, E-mail: rousseau@uri.edu. *Application contact:* David Chelidze, Graduate Admissions, 401-874-2356, E-mail: chelidze@uri.edu.
Website: http://mcise.uri.edu/

University of Southern California, Graduate School, Viterbi School of Engineering, Daniel J. Epstein Department of Industrial and Systems Engineering, Los Angeles, CA 90089. Offers digital supply chain management (MS); engineering management (MS); engineering technology communication (Graduate Certificate); health systems operations (Graduate Certificate); industrial and systems engineering (MS, PhD, Engr); manufacturing engineering (MS); operations research engineering (MS); optimization and supply chain management (Graduate Certificate); product development engineering (MS); safety systems and security (MS); systems architecting and engineering (MS, Graduate Certificate); systems safety and security (Graduate Certificate); transportation systems (Graduate Certificate); MS/MBA. *Program availability:* Part-time, evening/weekend, online learning. Terminal master's awarded for partial completion of doctoral program. *Degree requirements:* For master's, thesis optional; for doctorate, thesis/dissertation. *Entrance requirements:* For master's and doctorate, GRE General Test. Additional exam requirements/recommendations for international students: recommended—TOEFL. Electronic applications accepted.

University of South Florida, College of Engineering, Department of Industrial and Management Systems Engineering, Tampa, FL 33620-9951. Offers MSEM, MSIE, MSIT, MSMSE, PhD. *Program availability:* Part-time, online learning. *Faculty:* 30 full-time (3 women), 1 part-time/adjunct (0 women). *Students:* 84 full-time (25 women), 60 part-time (15 women); includes 13 minority (2 Black or African American, non-Hispanic/Latino; 4 Asian, non-Hispanic/Latino; 7 Hispanic/Latino), 100 international. Average age 27. 280 applicants, 54% accepted, 37 enrolled. In 2019, 72 master's, 3 doctorates awarded. Terminal master's awarded for partial completion of doctoral program. *Degree requirements:* For master's, comprehensive exam, thesis (for some programs); for doctorate, comprehensive exam, thesis/dissertation, 2 tools of research as specified by dissertation committee. *Entrance requirements:* For master's, GRE General Test, BS in engineering (or equivalent), letters of recommendation, resume, two years professional experience or internship may be required; statement of purpose; for doctorate, GRE General Test, minimum GPA of 3.0, 3 letters of recommendation, statement of purpose, strong background in scientific and engineering principles. Ph.D. students must complete their total doctoral major as full-time Tampa campus students. Additional exam requirements/recommendations for international students: required—TOEFL, TOEFL (minimum score 550 paper-based; 79 iBT) or IELTS (minimum score 6.5). *Application deadline:* For fall admission, 2/15 for domestic and international students; for spring admission, 10/15 for domestic students, 9/15 for international students; for summer admission, 2/15 for domestic students, 1/15 for international students. Application fee: $30. Electronic applications accepted. *Financial support:* In 2019–20, 26 students received support, including 20 research assistantships with partial tuition reimbursements available (averaging $16,748 per year), 11 teaching assistantships with partial tuition reimbursements available (averaging $15,000 per year); tuition waivers (partial) also available. Financial award applicants required to submit FAFSA. *Unit head:* Dr. Tapas K. Das, Professor and Department Chair, 813-974-5585, Fax: 813-974-5953, E-mail: das@usf.edu. *Application contact:* Dr. Alex Savachkin, Associate Professor and Graduate Director, 813-974-5577, Fax: 813-974-5953, E-mail: alexs@usf.edu.
Website: http://imse.eng.usf.edu

University of South Florida, Innovative Education, Tampa, FL 33620-9951. Offers adult, career and higher education (Graduate Certificate), including college teaching, leadership in developing human resources, leadership in higher education; Africana studies (Graduate Certificate), including diasporas and health disparities, genocide and human rights; aging studies (Graduate Certificate), including gerontology; art research (Graduate Certificate), including museum studies; business foundations (Graduate Certificate); chemical and biomedical engineering (Graduate Certificate), including materials science and engineering, water, health and sustainability; child and family studies (Graduate Certificate), including positive behavior support; civil and industrial engineering (Graduate Certificate), including transportation systems analysis; community and family health (Graduate Certificate), including maternal and child health, social marketing and public health, violence and injury: prevention and intervention, women's health; criminology (Graduate Certificate), including criminal justice administration; data science for public administration (Graduate Certificate); digital humanities (Graduate Certificate); educational measurement and research (Graduate Certificate), including evaluation; English (Graduate Certificate), including comparative literary studies, creative writing, professional and technical communication; entrepreneurship (Graduate Certificate); environmental health (Graduate Certificate), including safety management; epidemiology and biostatistics (Graduate Certificate), including applied biostatistics, biostatistics, concepts and tools of epidemiology, epidemiology, epidemiology of infectious diseases; geography, environment and planning (Graduate Certificate), including community development, environmental policy and management, geographical information systems; geology (Graduate Certificate), including hydrogeology; global health (Graduate Certificate), including disaster management, global health and Latin American and Caribbean studies, global health practice, humanitarian assistance, infection control; government and international affairs (Graduate Certificate), including Cuban studies, globalization studies; health policy and management (Graduate Certificate), including health management and leadership, public health policy and programs; hearing specialist: early intervention (Graduate Certificate); industrial and management systems engineering (Graduate Certificate), including systems engineering, technology management; information studies (Graduate Certificate), including school library media specialist; information systems/decision sciences (Graduate Certificate), including analytics and business intelligence; instructional technology (Graduate Certificate), including distance education, Florida digital/virtual educator, instructional design, multimedia design, Web design; internal medicine, bioethics and medical humanities (Graduate Certificate), including biomedical ethics; Latin American and Caribbean studies (Graduate Certificate); leadership for coastal resiliency planning (Graduate Certificate); mass communications (Graduate Certificate), including multimedia journalism; mathematics and statistics (Graduate Certificate), including mathematics; medicine (Graduate Certificate), including aging and neuroscience, bioinformatics, biotechnology, brain fitness and memory management, clinical investigation, hand and upper limb rehabilitation, health informatics, health sciences, integrative weight management, intellectual property, medicine and gender, metabolic and nutritional medicine, metabolic cardiology, pharmacy sciences; national and competitive intelligence (Graduate Certificate); nursing (Graduate Certificate), including simulation based academic fellowship in advanced pain management; psychological and social foundations (Graduate Certificate), including career counseling, college teaching, diversity in education, mental health counseling, school counseling; public affairs (Graduate Certificate), including nonprofit management, public management, research administration; public health (Graduate Certificate), including assessing chemical toxicity and public health risks, health equity, pharmacoepidemiology, public health generalist, toxicology, translational research in adolescent behavioral health; public health practices (Graduate Certificate), including planning for healthy communities; rehabilitation and mental health counseling (Graduate Certificate), including integrative mental health care, marriage and family therapy, rehabilitation technology; secondary education (Graduate Certificate), including ESOL, foreign language education: culture and content, foreign language education: professional; social work (Graduate Certificate), including geriatric social work/clinical gerontology; special education (Graduate Certificate), including autism spectrum disorder, disabilities education: severe/profound; world languages (Graduate Certificate), including teaching English as a second language (TESL) or foreign language. *Unit head:* Dr. Cynthia DeLuca, Associate Vice President and Assistant Vice Provost, 813-974-3077, Fax: 813-974-7061, E-mail: deluca@usf.edu. *Application contact:* Owen Hooper, Director, Summer and Alternative Calendar Programs, 813-974-6917, E-mail: hooper@usf.edu.
Website: http://www.usf.edu/innovative-education/

The University of Tennessee, Graduate School, Tickle College of Engineering, Department of Industrial and Systems Engineering, Knoxville, TN 37966. Offers engineering management (MS); industrial engineering (MS, PhD); reliability and maintainability engineering (MS); MS/MBA. *Program availability:* Part-time, online learning. *Faculty:* 9 full-time (1 woman), 4 part-time/adjunct (1 woman). *Students:* 94 full-time (26 women), 51 part-time (15 women); includes 28 minority (13 Black or African American, non-Hispanic/Latino; 2 American Indian or Alaska Native, non-Hispanic/Latino; 5 Asian, non-Hispanic/Latino; 5 Hispanic/Latino; 3 Two or more races, non-Hispanic/Latino), 32 international. Average age 35. 77 applicants, 66% accepted, 28 enrolled. In 2019, 45 master's, 11 doctorates awarded. *Degree requirements:* For master's, thesis or alternative; for doctorate, comprehensive exam, thesis/dissertation. *Entrance requirements:* For master's, GRE General Test (for MS students pursuing research thesis), minimum GPA of 2.7 (for U.S. degree holders), 3.0 (for international degree holders); for doctorate, GRE General Test, minimum GPA of 3.0 on previous graduate course work. Additional exam requirements/recommendations for international students: required—TOEFL (minimum score 550 paper-based; 80 iBT), IELTS (minimum score 6.5). *Application deadline:* For fall admission, 2/1 priority date for domestic and international students; for spring admission, 6/15 for domestic and international students; for summer admission, 10/15 for domestic and international students. Applications are processed on a rolling basis. Application fee: $60. Electronic applications accepted. *Financial support:* In 2019–20, 61 students received support, including 9 fellowships with full tuition reimbursements available (averaging $22,671 per year), 36 research assistantships with full tuition reimbursements available (averaging $21,050 per year), 16 teaching assistantships with full tuition reimbursements available (averaging $19,219 per year); career-related internships or fieldwork, Federal Work-Study, institutionally sponsored loans, health care benefits, and unspecified assistantships also available. Financial award application deadline: 2/1; financial award applicants required to submit FAFSA. *Unit head:* Dr. John Kobza, Department Head, 865-974-3333, Fax: 865-974-0588, E-mail: jkobza@utk.edu. *Application contact:* Dr. Jim Ostrowski, Associate Professor and Director of Graduate Studies, 865-974-7657, E-mail: jostrows@utk.edu.
Website: http://www.engr.utk.edu/ie/

The University of Texas at Arlington, Graduate School, College of Engineering, Department of Industrial, Manufacturing, and Systems Engineering, Arlington, TX 76019. Offers engineering management (MS); industrial engineering (MS, PhD); logistics (MS); systems engineering (MS). *Program availability:* Part-time, evening/weekend, online learning. Terminal master's awarded for partial completion of doctoral program. *Degree requirements:* For master's, comprehensive exam, thesis optional; for doctorate, comprehensive exam, thesis/dissertation. *Entrance requirements:* For master's and doctorate, GRE General Test, minimum GPA of 3.0. Additional exam requirements/recommendations for international students: required—TOEFL (minimum score 550 paper-based).

The University of Texas at Austin, Graduate School, Cockrell School of Engineering, Department of Mechanical Engineering, Program in Operations Research and Industrial Engineering, Austin, TX 78712-1111. Offers MS, PhD. *Entrance requirements:* For master's and doctorate, GRE General Test. Additional exam requirements/recommendations for international students: required—TOEFL.

The University of Texas at El Paso, Graduate School, College of Engineering, Department of Industrial, Manufacturing and Systems Engineering, El Paso, TX 79968-0001. Offers industrial engineering (MS); manufacturing engineering (MS); systems engineering (MS). *Program availability:* Part-time, evening/weekend. *Degree requirements:* For master's, thesis optional. *Entrance requirements:* For master's, GRE General Test, minimum GPA of 3.0 in major. Additional exam requirements/recommendations for international students: required—TOEFL. Electronic applications accepted.

The University of Toledo, College of Graduate Studies, College of Engineering, Department of Mechanical, Industrial, and Manufacturing Engineering, Toledo, OH 43606-3390. Offers industrial engineering (MS, PhD); mechanical engineering (MS, PhD). *Program availability:* Part-time, online learning. *Degree requirements:* For master's, thesis optional; for doctorate, thesis/dissertation, qualifying exam. *Entrance requirements:* For master's, GRE General Test, minimum GPA of 3.0; for doctorate,

GRE General Test, minimum GPA of 3.3. Additional exam requirements/recommendations for international students: required—TOEFL (minimum score 550 paper-based; 80 iBT). Electronic applications accepted.

University of Toronto, School of Graduate Studies, Faculty of Applied Science and Engineering, Department of Mechanical and Industrial Engineering, Toronto, ON M5S 1A1, Canada. Offers M Eng, MA Sc, PhD. *Program availability:* Part-time. *Degree requirements:* For master's, thesis (for some programs), oral exam/thesis defense (MA Sc); for doctorate, thesis/dissertation, thesis defense, qualifying examination. *Entrance requirements:* For master's, GRE (recommended), minimum B+ average in last 2 years of undergraduate study, 2 letters of reference, resume, Canadian citizenship or permanent residency (M Eng); for doctorate, GRE (recommended), minimum B+ average, 2 letters of reference, resume. Additional exam requirements/recommendations for international students: required—TOEFL (minimum score 580 paper-based), Michigan English Language Assessment Battery (minimum score 85), IELTS (minimum score 7), or COPE (minimum score 4). Electronic applications accepted.

University of Washington, Graduate School, College of Engineering, Department of Industrial and Systems Engineering, Seattle, WA 98195-2650. Offers MISE, MS, PhD. *Program availability:* Part-time, online learning. *Students:* 50 full-time (19 women), 37 part-time (13 women); includes 17 minority (4 Black or African American, non-Hispanic/Latino; 6 Asian, non-Hispanic/Latino; 6 Hispanic/Latino; 1 Native Hawaiian or other Pacific Islander, non-Hispanic/Latino), 41 international. Average age 28. 220 applicants, 45% accepted, 35 enrolled. In 2019, 23 master's, 6 doctorates awarded. Terminal master's awarded for partial completion of doctoral program. *Degree requirements:* For master's, thesis optional; for doctorate, comprehensive exam, thesis/dissertation, qualifying, general, and final exams. *Entrance requirements:* For master's, GRE General Test, minimum GPA of 3.0; bachelor's degree in engineering, math, or science; transcripts; letters of recommendation; resume; statement of objectives; for doctorate, GRE General Test, minimum GPA of 3.0; master's degree in engineering, math, or science (preferred); transcripts; letters of recommendation; resume; statement of objectives. Additional exam requirements/recommendations for international students: required—TOEFL (minimum score 580 paper-based; 92 iBT). *Application deadline:* For fall admission, 1/2 priority date for domestic students, 1/2 for international students. Applications are processed on a rolling basis. Application fee: $85. Electronic applications accepted. *Expenses:* Contact institution. *Financial support:* In 2019–20, 1 fellowship with full tuition reimbursement (averaging $30,120 per year), 25 research assistantships with full tuition reimbursements (averaging $30,120 per year), 9 teaching assistantships with full tuition reimbursements (averaging $29,640 per year) were awarded; Federal Work-Study, institutionally sponsored loans, scholarships/grants, health care benefits, tuition waivers (full), and unspecified assistantships also available. Support available to part-time students. Financial award application deadline: 1/2. *Unit head:* Dr. Linda Ng Boyle, Professor/Chair, 206-543-1427, Fax: 206-685-3072, E-mail: linda@uw.edu. *Application contact:* Jennifer W. Tsai, Academic Counselor, 206-543-5041, Fax: 206-685-3072, E-mail: ieadvise@uw.edu.
Website: http://ise.washington.edu

University of Windsor, Faculty of Graduate Studies, Faculty of Engineering, Department of Industrial and Manufacturing Systems Engineering, Windsor, ON N9B 3P4, Canada. Offers industrial engineering (M Eng, MA Sc); manufacturing systems engineering (PhD). *Program availability:* Part-time. *Degree requirements:* For master's, thesis; for doctorate, comprehensive exam, thesis/dissertation. *Entrance requirements:* For master's, minimum B average; for doctorate, master's degree, minimum B average. Additional exam requirements/recommendations for international students: required—TOEFL (minimum score 560 paper-based). Electronic applications accepted.

University of Wisconsin–Madison, Graduate School, College of Engineering, Department of Industrial and Systems Engineering, Madison, WI 53706. Offers industrial engineering (MS, PhD), including human factors and health systems engineering (MS), systems engineering and analytics (MS). *Program availability:* Part-time. Terminal master's awarded for partial completion of doctoral program. *Degree requirements:* For master's, thesis optional, 30 credits; minimum GPA of 3.0; for doctorate, comprehensive exam, thesis/dissertation, minimum of 51 credits; minimum GPA of 3.0. *Entrance requirements:* For master's and doctorate, GRE General Test, minimum GPA of 3.0, BS in engineering or equivalent, course work in computer programming and statistics. Additional exam requirements/recommendations for international students: required—TOEFL (minimum score 580 paper-based; 92 iBT), IELTS (minimum score 7). Electronic applications accepted.

University of Wisconsin–Milwaukee, Graduate School, College of Engineering and Applied Science, Program in Engineering, Milwaukee, WI 53201-0413. Offers biomedical engineering (MS); civil engineering (MS, PhD); computer science (PhD); electrical and computer engineering (MS); electrical engineering (PhD); engineering mechanics (MS); industrial and management engineering (MS); industrial engineering (PhD); manufacturing engineering (MS); materials (PhD); materials engineering (MS); mechanical engineering (MS). *Program availability:* Part-time. *Degree requirements:* For master's, comprehensive exam (for some programs), thesis or alternative; for doctorate, comprehensive exam, thesis/dissertation, internship. *Entrance requirements:* For master's, GRE, minimum GPA of 2.75; for doctorate, GRE, minimum GPA of 3.5. Additional exam requirements/recommendations for international students: required—TOEFL (minimum score 550 paper-based; 79 iBT), IELTS (minimum score 6.5).

University of Wisconsin–Stout, Graduate School, College of Management, Program in Risk Control, Menomonie, WI 54751. Offers MS. *Program availability:* Part-time. *Degree requirements:* For master's, thesis. *Entrance requirements:* For master's, minimum GPA of 3.0. Additional exam requirements/recommendations for international students: required—TOEFL (minimum score 500 paper-based; 61 iBT). Electronic applications accepted.

Université Laval, Faculty of Sciences and Engineering, Programs in Industrial Engineering, Québec, QC G1K 7P4, Canada. Offers Diploma. *Program availability:* Part-time. *Entrance requirements:* For degree, knowledge of French. Electronic applications accepted.

Virginia Polytechnic Institute and State University, VT Online, Blacksburg, VA 24061. Offers advanced transportation systems (Certificate); aerospace engineering (MS); agricultural and life sciences (MSLFS); business information systems (Graduate Certificate); career and technical education (MS); civil engineering (MS); computer engineering (M Eng, MS); decision support systems (Graduate Certificate); eLearning leadership (MA); electrical engineering (M Eng, MS); engineering administration (MEA); environmental engineering (Certificate); environmental politics and policy (Graduate Certificate); environmental sciences and engineering (MS); foundations of political analysis (Graduate Certificate); health product risk management (Graduate Certificate); industrial and systems engineering (MS); information policy and society (Graduate Certificate); information security (Graduate Certificate); information technology (MIT); instructional technology (MA); integrative STEM education (MA Ed); liberal arts (Graduate Certificate); life sciences: health product risk management (MS); natural resources (MNR, Graduate Certificate); networking (Graduate Certificate); nonprofit and nongovernmental organization management (Graduate Certificate); ocean engineering (MS); political science (MA); security studies (Graduate Certificate); software development (Graduate Certificate). *Expenses:* Tuition, state resident: full-time $13,700; part-time $761.25 per credit hour. Tuition, nonresident: full-time $27,614; part-time $1534 per credit hour. *Required fees:* $886.50 per term. Tuition and fees vary according to campus/location and program.

Wayne State University, College of Engineering, Department of Industrial and Systems Engineering, Detroit, MI 48202. Offers data science and business analytics (MS); engineering management (MS); industrial engineering (MS, PhD); manufacturing engineering (MS); systems engineering (Certificate). *Program availability:* Online learning. *Faculty:* 12. *Students:* 126 full-time (31 women), 105 part-time (28 women); includes 42 minority (23 Black or African American, non-Hispanic/Latino; 12 Asian, non-Hispanic/Latino; 4 Hispanic/Latino; 3 Two or more races, non-Hispanic/Latino), 124 international. Average age 30. 407 applicants, 36% accepted, 39 enrolled. In 2019, 123 master's, 8 doctorates awarded. *Degree requirements:* For master's, thesis optional; for doctorate, thesis/dissertation. *Entrance requirements:* For master's, GRE or GMAT (for applicants to MS in data science and business analytics), BS from ABET-accredited institution; for doctorate, GRE, graduate degree in engineering or related discipline with minimum graduate GPA of 3.5, statement of purpose, resume/curriculum vitae, three letters of recommendation; for Certificate, GRE (for applicants from non-ABET institutions), BS in engineering or other technical field from ABET-accredited institution with minimum GPA of 3.0 in upper-division course work, at least one year of full-time work experience as practicing engineer or technical leader. Additional exam requirements/recommendations for international students: required—TOEFL (minimum score 550 paper-based; 79 iBT), TWE (minimum score 5.5), Michigan English Language Assessment Battery (minimum score 85); GRE; recommended—IELTS (minimum score 6.5). *Application deadline:* Applications are processed on a rolling basis. Application fee: $50. Electronic applications accepted. *Expenses:* $790 per credit hour in-state tuition, $1579 per credit hour out-of-state tuition. MS programs 30 credits hours; PhD 90 credit hours. *Financial support:* In 2019–20, 125 students received support, including 2 fellowships with tuition reimbursements available (averaging $20,000 per year), 6 research assistantships with tuition reimbursements available (averaging $22,879 per year), 9 teaching assistantships with tuition reimbursements available (averaging $20,792 per year); scholarships/grants, tuition waivers (full), and unspecified assistantships also available. Financial award applicants required to submit FAFSA. *Unit head:* Dr. Ratna Babu Chinnam, Professor and Interim Chair, 313-577-4846, Fax: 313-577-8833, E-mail: ratna.chinnam@wayne.edu. *Application contact:* Eric Scimeca, Graduate Program Coordinator, 313-577-0412, E-mail: eric.scimeca@wayne.edu.
Website: http://engineering.wayne.edu/ise/

Western Carolina University, Graduate School, College of Engineering and Technology, School of Engineering and Technology, Cullowhee, NC 28723. Offers technology (MS). *Program availability:* Part-time. *Degree requirements:* For master's, comprehensive exam. *Entrance requirements:* For master's, GRE, appropriate undergraduate degree with minimum GPA of 3.0, 3 letters of recommendation. Additional exam requirements/recommendations for international students: required—TOEFL (minimum score 550 paper-based; 79 iBT). *Expenses: Tuition, area resident:* Full-time $2217.50; part-time $1664 per semester. Tuition, state resident: full-time $2217.50; part-time $1664 per semester. Tuition, nonresident: full-time $7421; part-time $5566 per semester. *International tuition:* $7421 full-time. *Required fees:* $5598; $1954 per semester. Tuition and fees vary according to course load, campus/location and program.

Western Michigan University, Graduate College, College of Engineering and Applied Sciences, Department of Industrial and Entrepreneurial Engineering and Engineering Management, Kalamazoo, MI 49008. Offers engineering management (MS); industrial engineering (MSE, PhD). *Degree requirements:* For master's, thesis optional.

Western New England University, College of Engineering, Program in Industrial Engineering, Springfield, MA 01119. Offers MS. *Program availability:* Part-time, evening/weekend. *Degree requirements:* For master's, comprehensive exam, thesis optional. *Entrance requirements:* For master's, bachelor's degree in engineering or related field, two letters of recommendation, resume, transcript. Additional exam requirements/recommendations for international students: required—TOEFL (minimum score 79 iBT). Electronic applications accepted. *Expenses:* Contact institution.

West Virginia University, Statler College of Engineering and Mineral Resources, Morgantown, WV 26506. Offers aerospace engineering (MSAE, PhD); chemical engineering (MS Ch E, PhD); civil engineering (MSCE, PhD); computer engineering (PhD); computer science (MSCS, PhD); electrical engineering (MSEE, PhD); energy systems engineering (MSESE); engineering (MSE); industrial engineering (MSIE, PhD); industrial hygiene (MS); material science and engineering (MSMSE, PhD); mechanical engineering (MSME, PhD); mining engineering (MS Min E, PhD); petroleum and natural gas engineering (MSPNGE, PhD); safety management (MS); software engineering (MSSE). *Program availability:* Part-time. Terminal master's awarded for partial completion of doctoral program. *Degree requirements:* For master's, thesis optional; for doctorate, comprehensive exam, thesis/dissertation. *Entrance requirements:* Additional exam requirements/recommendations for international students: required—TOEFL (minimum score 550 paper-based). Electronic applications accepted. *Expenses:* Contact institution.

Wichita State University, Graduate School, College of Engineering, Department of Industrial and Manufacturing Engineering, Wichita, KS 67260. Offers engineering management (MEM); industrial engineering (MS, PhD). *Program availability:* Part-time. *Entrance requirements:* Additional exam requirements/recommendations for international students: required—TOEFL.

Wright State University, Graduate School, College of Engineering and Computer Science, Department of Biomedical, Industrial and Human Factors Engineering, Dayton, OH 45435. Offers biomedical engineering (MS); industrial and human factors engineering (MS). *Program availability:* Part-time. *Degree requirements:* For master's, thesis or course option alternative. *Entrance requirements:* Additional exam requirements/recommendations for international students: required—TOEFL.

Youngstown State University, College of Graduate Studies, College of Science, Technology, Engineering and Mathematics, Department of Mechanical, Industrial and Manufacturing Engineering, Youngstown, OH 44555-0001. Offers industrial and systems engineering (MSE); mechanical engineering (MSE). *Program availability:* Part-time, evening/weekend. *Degree requirements:* For master's, thesis optional. *Entrance requirements:* For master's, minimum GPA of 2.75 in field. Additional exam requirements/recommendations for international students: required—TOEFL.

Manufacturing Engineering

American University of Armenia, Graduate Programs, Yerevan, Armenia. Offers business administration (MBA); computer and information science (MS), including business management, design and manufacturing, energy (ME, MS), industrial engineering and systems management; economics (MS); industrial engineering and systems management (ME), including business, computer aided design/manufacturing, energy (ME, MS), information technology; law (LL M); political science and international affairs (MPSIA); public health (MPH); teaching English as a foreign language (MA). *Program availability:* Part-time, evening/weekend. *Degree requirements:* For master's, thesis (for some programs), capstone/project. *Entrance requirements:* For master's, GRE, GMAT, or LSAT. Additional exam requirements/recommendations for international students: recommended—TOEFL (minimum score 79 iBT), IELTS (minimum score 6.5).

Arizona State University at Tempe, Ira A. Fulton Schools of Engineering, The Polytechnic School, Program in Engineering Technology, Mesa, AZ 85212. Offers manufacturing engineering technology (MS). *Program availability:* Part-time, evening/weekend. *Degree requirements:* For master's, thesis or applied project and oral defense, final examination, interactive Program of Study (iPOS) submitted before completing 50 percent of required credit hours. *Entrance requirements:* For master's, bachelor's degree with minimum of 30 credit hours or equivalent in a technology area including course work applicable to the concentration being sought and minimum of 16 credit hours of math and science; industrial experience beyond bachelor's degree (recommended). Additional exam requirements/recommendations for international students: required—TOEFL, IELTS, or PTE. Electronic applications accepted.

Boston University, College of Engineering, Department of Mechanical Engineering, Boston, MA 02215. Offers manufacturing engineering (MS); mechanical engineering (PhD); MS/MBA. *Program availability:* Part-time, 100% online, blended/hybrid learning. *Students:* 174 full-time (43 women), 51 part-time (13 women); includes 39 minority (2 Black or African American, non-Hispanic/Latino; 14 Asian, non-Hispanic/Latino; 17 Hispanic/Latino; 6 Two or more races, non-Hispanic/Latino), 112 international. Average age 24. 773 applicants, 51% accepted, 78 enrolled. In 2019, 98 master's, 11 doctorates awarded. Terminal master's awarded for partial completion of doctoral program. *Degree requirements:* For master's, thesis (for some programs); for doctorate, comprehensive exam, thesis/dissertation. *Entrance requirements:* For master's and doctorate, GRE General Test. Additional exam requirements/recommendations for international students: required—TOEFL (minimum score 90 iBT), IELTS (minimum score 7). Application fee: $95. Application fee is waived when completed online. *Unit head:* Dr. Alice White, Chairperson, 617-353-2814, Fax: 617-353-5866, E-mail: aew1@bu.edu. *Application contact:* Dr. Alice White, Chairperson, 617-353-2814, Fax: 617-353-5866, E-mail: aew1@bu.edu.
Website: http://www.bu.edu/me/

Bradley University, The Graduate School, Caterpillar College of Engineering and Technology, Department of Industrial and Manufacturing Engineering and Technology, Peoria, IL 61625-0002. Offers industrial engineering (MS); manufacturing engineering (MS). *Program availability:* Part-time, evening/weekend. *Faculty:* 10 full-time (1 woman). *Students:* 5 full-time (2 women), 5 part-time (1 woman), all international. Average age 28. 31 applicants, 48% accepted, 2 enrolled. In 2019, 11 master's awarded. *Degree requirements:* For master's, comprehensive exam, thesis or alternative, project. *Entrance requirements:* For master's, Minimum GPA of 2.5, Essays, Recommendation letters, Transcripts. Additional exam requirements/recommendations for international students: required—TOEFL (minimum score 550 paper-based; 79 iBT), IELTS (minimum score 6.5), PTE (minimum score 58). *Application deadline:* For fall admission, 5/15 priority date for domestic and international students; for spring admission, 10/15 priority date for domestic and international students. Applications are processed on a rolling basis. Application fee: $40 ($50 for international students). Electronic applications accepted. *Expenses: Tuition:* Part-time $930 per credit hour. *Financial support:* In 2019–20, 4 students received support. Research assistantships, teaching assistantships, scholarships/grants, tuition waivers (partial), and unspecified assistantships available. Support available to part-time students. Financial award application deadline: 4/1. *Unit head:* Dr. Joseph Chen, Chair, 309-677-2740, E-mail: jchen@bradley.edu. *Application contact:* Rachel Webb, Director of On-Campus Graduate Admissions and International Student and Scholar Services, 309-677-2375, E-mail: rkwebb@bradley.edu.
Website: http://www.bradley.edu/academic/departments/imet/

Brigham Young University, Graduate Studies, Ira A. Fulton College of Engineering, School of Technology, Provo, UT 84602-1001. Offers construction management (MS); information technology (MS); manufacturing engineering technology (MS); technology and engineering education (MS). *Faculty:* 16 full-time (1 woman). *Students:* 14 full-time (2 women); includes 3 minority (1 Hispanic/Latino; 2 Two or more races, non-Hispanic/Latino), 3 international. Average age 28. 15 applicants, 73% accepted, 11 enrolled. In 2019, 7 master's awarded. *Degree requirements:* For master's, thesis. *Entrance requirements:* For master's, GRE General Test; GMAT or GRE (for construction management emphasis), BS degree in information technology, manufacturing engineering technology, construction management, technology and engineering education, or related field; basic sciences background, along with engineering mathematics, computers or electronics, management, architecture, and manufacturing methods. Additional exam requirements/recommendations for international students: required—TOEFL (minimum score 580 paper-based; 85 iBT). *Application deadline:* For fall admission, 2/15 for domestic and international students; for winter admission, 9/10 for domestic and international students; for spring admission, 2/15 for domestic and international students; for summer admission, 2/15 for domestic and international students. Application fee: $50. Electronic applications accepted. *Financial support:* In 2019–20, 10 students received support, including 5 research assistantships with full and partial tuition reimbursements available (averaging $27,617 per year), 5 teaching assistantships with full and partial tuition reimbursements available (averaging $11,446 per year); scholarships/grants also available. Financial award application deadline: 1/15; financial award applicants required to submit FAFSA. *Unit head:* Dr. Barry M. Lunt, Director, 801-422-6300, Fax: 801-422-0490, E-mail: blunt@byu.edu. *Application contact:* Samuel Cardenas, Academic Advisor, 801-422-1819, Fax: 801-422-0490, E-mail: samuel_cardenas@byu.edu.
Website: http://www.et.byu.edu/sot/

Buffalo State College, State University of New York, The Graduate School, School of the Professions, Department of Engineering Technology, Program in Mechanical and Manufacturing Technology, Buffalo, NY 14222-1095. Offers MS. *Accreditation:* NCATE. *Degree requirements:* For master's, thesis or project. *Entrance requirements:* For master's, minimum GPA of 2.5 in last 60 hours, New York teaching certificate. Additional exam requirements/recommendations for international students: required—TOEFL (minimum score 550 paper-based).

California State University, Northridge, Graduate Studies, College of Engineering and Computer Science, Department of Manufacturing Systems Engineering and Management, Northridge, CA 91330. Offers engineering automation (MS); engineering management (MS); manufacturing systems engineering (MS); materials engineering (MS). *Program availability:* Online learning. *Entrance requirements:* For master's, GRE (if cumulative undergraduate GPA less than 3.0).

The Citadel, The Military College of South Carolina, Citadel Graduate College, School of Engineering, Department of Mechanical Engineering, Charleston, SC 29409. Offers aeronautical engineering (Graduate Certificate); composites engineering (Graduate Certificate); manufacturing engineering (Graduate Certificate); mechanical engineering (MS); mechatronics engineering (Graduate Certificate); power and energy (Graduate Certificate). *Program availability:* Part-time, evening/weekend. *Degree requirements:* For master's, 30 hours of coursework with minimum GPA of 3.0 on hours earned at The Citadel. *Entrance requirements:* For master's, GRE, 2 letters of recommendation; official transcript of baccalaureate degree from an ABET accredited engineering program or approved alternative. Additional exam requirements/recommendations for international students: required—TOEFL (minimum score 550 paper-based; 79 iBT). Electronic applications accepted.

Cornell University, Graduate School, Graduate Fields of Engineering, Field of Operations Research and Information Engineering, Ithaca, NY 14853. Offers applied probability and statistics (PhD); manufacturing systems engineering (PhD); mathematical programming (PhD); operations research and industrial engineering (M Eng). *Degree requirements:* For doctorate, comprehensive exam, thesis/dissertation. *Entrance requirements:* For master's and doctorate, GRE General Test, 3 letters of recommendation. Additional exam requirements/recommendations for international students: required—TOEFL (minimum score 600 paper-based; 100 iBT). Electronic applications accepted.

Eastern Kentucky University, The Graduate School, College of Business and Technology, Department of Technology, Richmond, KY 40475-3102. Offers industrial education (MS), including occupational training and development, technical administration, technology education; industrial technology (MS). *Program availability:* Part-time, evening/weekend. *Entrance requirements:* For master's, GRE General Test, minimum GPA of 2.5.

East Tennessee State University, School of Graduate Studies, College of Business and Technology, Department of Engineering, Engineering Technology, and Surveying, Johnson City, TN 37614. Offers technology (MS). *Program availability:* Part-time. *Degree requirements:* For master's, comprehensive exam, thesis optional, capstone. *Entrance requirements:* For master's, bachelor's degree in technical or related area, minimum GPA of 3.0, undergraduate course in probability and statistics. Additional exam requirements/recommendations for international students: required—TOEFL (minimum score 550 paper-based; 79 iBT). Electronic applications accepted.

Florida State University, The Graduate School, FAMU-FSU College of Engineering, Department of Industrial and Manufacturing Engineering, Tallahassee, FL 32306. Offers industrial engineering (MS, PhD). *Faculty:* 10 full-time (1 woman), 1 (woman) part-time/adjunct. *Students:* 45 full-time (17 women); includes 9 minority (6 Black or African American, non-Hispanic/Latino; 1 Asian, non-Hispanic/Latino; 2 Hispanic/Latino), 26 international. Average age 24. 129 applicants, 48% accepted, 18 enrolled. In 2019, 22 master's, 7 doctorates awarded. *Degree requirements:* For master's, thesis, proposal presentation, progress presentation, defense presentation; for doctorate, thesis/dissertation, preliminary exam, proposal exam, defense exam. *Entrance requirements:* For master's, GRE General Test (minimum new score of 146 Verbal and 155 Quantitative), minimum GPA of 3.0; for doctorate, GRE General Test (minimum new score of 146 Verbal and 155 Quantitative), minimum GPA of 3.0 (without MS in industrial engineering), 3.4 (with MS in industrial engineering). Additional exam requirements/recommendations for international students: required—TOEFL (minimum score 550 paper-based; 80 iBT); recommended—IELTS (minimum score 6.5). *Application deadline:* For fall admission, 3/1 for domestic and international students; for spring admission, 11/1 for domestic and international students; for summer admission, 1/1 for domestic and international students. Applications are processed on a rolling basis. Application fee: $30. Electronic applications accepted. *Financial support:* In 2019–20, 47 students received support, including 24 research assistantships with full tuition reimbursements available, 18 teaching assistantships with full tuition reimbursements available; fellowships with full tuition reimbursements available, scholarships/grants, tuition waivers (full), and unspecified assistantships also available. Financial award application deadline: 3/1; financial award applicants required to submit FAFSA. *Unit head:* Dr. Okenwa Okoli, Chair/Professor/Associate Director, 850-410-6352, Fax: 850-410-6342, E-mail: okoli@eng.famu.fsu.edu. *Application contact:* Shade' Ahmed, Graduate Studies Assistant, 850-410-6582, Fax: 850-410-6342, E-mail: saahmed@eng.famu.fsu.edu.
Website: http://www.eng.famu.fsu.edu/departments/industrial/

Georgia Southern University, Jack N. Averitt College of Graduate Studies, Allen E. Paulson College of Engineering and Computing, Department of Mechanical Engineering, Statesboro, GA 30460. Offers engineering and information technology (MSAE), including engineering and information technology; engineering and manufacturing management (Graduate Certificate); engineering/energy science (MSAE); engineering/engineering management (MSAE); engineering/mechatronics (MSAE); occupational safety and environmental compliance (Graduate Certificate). *Program availability:* Part-time, evening/weekend. *Faculty:* 24 full-time (1 woman), 1 part-time/adjunct (0 women). *Students:* 13 full-time (0 women), 3 part-time (1 woman); includes 5 minority (1 Black or African American, non-Hispanic/Latino; 3 Asian, non-Hispanic/Latino; 1 Hispanic/Latino), 4 international. Average age 25. 24 applicants, 71% accepted, 11 enrolled. In 2019, 23 master's, 1 Graduate Certificate awarded. *Degree requirements:* For master's, comprehensive exam, thesis optional. *Entrance requirements:* For master's, GRE, undergraduate major or equivalent in proposed study area. Additional exam requirements/recommendations for international students: required—TOEFL (minimum score 550 paper-based; 80 iBT), IELTS (minimum score 6). *Application deadline:* For fall admission, 3/1 priority date for domestic and international students; for spring admission, 10/1 priority date for domestic students, 10/1 for international students. Applications are processed on a rolling basis. Application fee: $50. Electronic applications accepted. *Expenses: Tuition, area resident:* Full-time $4986; part-time $277 per credit hour. Tuition, nonresident: full-time $19,890; part-time $1105 per credit hour. *International tuition:* $19,890 full-time. *Required fees:* $2114; $1057 per semester. $1057 per semester. Tuition and fees vary according to course load, campus/location and program. *Financial support:* In 2019–20, 17 students received support, including 4 research assistantships with partial tuition reimbursements available (averaging $7,200 per year), teaching assistantships with partial tuition reimbursements available (averaging $7,200 per year); Federal Work-Study, scholarships/grants, tuition waivers (partial), and unspecified assistantships also available. Financial award application deadline: 4/15; financial award applicants required to submit FAFSA. *Unit head:* Dr. Brian Vlcek, Chair, 912-478-5761, Fax: 912-478-1455, E-mail: bvlcek@georgiasouthern.edu.

Grand Valley State University, Padnos College of Engineering and Computing, School of Engineering, Allendale, MI 49401-9403. Offers electrical and computer engineering (MSE); mechanical engineering (MSE); product design and manufacturing engineering (MSE). *Program availability:* Part-time, evening/weekend. *Faculty:* 22 full-time (6 women), 1 part-time/adjunct (0 women). *Students:* 23 full-time (2 women), 35 part-time (5 women); includes 4 minority (2 Asian, non-Hispanic/Latino; 1 Hispanic/Latino; 1 Two or more races, non-Hispanic/Latino), 25 international. Average age 27. 46 applicants, 78% accepted, 10 enrolled. In 2019, 32 master's awarded. *Degree requirements:* For master's, capstone experience. *Entrance requirements:* For master's, engineering degree, minimum GPA of 3.0, resume, 3 confidential letters of recommendation, 1-2 page essay, base of underlying relevant knowledge/evidence from academic records or relevant wok experience. Additional exam requirements/recommendations for international students: required—Michigan English Language Assessment Battery (minimum score 77), TOEFL (minimum iBT score of 80), or IELTS (6.5); GRE. *Application deadline:* Applications are processed on a rolling basis. Application fee: $30. Electronic applications accepted. *Expenses:* $733 per credit hour, 33 credit hours. *Financial support:* In 2019–20, 40 students received support, including 8 fellowships, 34 research assistantships with full and partial tuition reimbursements available (averaging $4,000 per year); career-related internships or fieldwork, Federal Work-Study, institutionally sponsored loans, scholarships/grants, and unspecified assistantships also available. *Unit head:* Dr. Wael Mokhtar, Director, 616-331-6015, Fax: 616-331-7215, E-mail: mokhtarw@gvsu.edu. *Application contact:* Dr. Shabbir Choudhuri, Graduate Program Director, 616-331-6845, Fax: 616-331-7215, E-mail: choudhus@gvsu.edu.
Website: http://www.engineer.gvsu.edu/

Illinois Institute of Technology, Graduate College, Armour College of Engineering, Department of Mechanical, Materials and Aerospace Engineering, Chicago, IL 60616. Offers manufacturing engineering (MAS, MS); materials science and engineering (MAS, MS, PhD); mechanical and aerospace engineering (MAS, MS, PhD), including economics (MS), energy (MS), environment (MS). *Program availability:* Part-time, evening/weekend, online learning. Terminal master's awarded for partial completion of doctoral program. *Degree requirements:* For master's, comprehensive exam (for some programs), thesis (for some programs); for doctorate, comprehensive exam, thesis/dissertation. *Entrance requirements:* For master's and doctorate, GRE General Test (minimum score 1000 Quantitative and Verbal, 3.0 Analytical Writing), minimum undergraduate GPA of 3.0. Additional exam requirements/recommendations for international students: required—TOEFL (minimum score 550 paper-based; 80 iBT). Electronic applications accepted.

Instituto Tecnológico y de Estudios Superiores de Monterrey, Campus Monterrey, Graduate and Research Division, Programs in Engineering, Monterrey, Mexico. Offers applied statistics (M Eng); artificial intelligence (PhD); automation engineering (M Eng); chemical engineering (M Eng); civil engineering (M Eng); electrical engineering (M Eng); electronic engineering (M Eng); environmental engineering (M Eng); industrial engineering (M Eng, PhD); manufacturing engineering (M Eng); mechanical engineering (M Eng); systems and quality engineering (M Eng). *Program availability:* Part-time, evening/weekend. Terminal master's awarded for partial completion of doctoral program. *Degree requirements:* For master's, one foreign language, thesis; for doctorate, one foreign language, thesis/dissertation. *Entrance requirements:* For master's, EXADEP; for doctorate, GRE, master's degree in related field. Additional exam requirements/recommendations for international students: required—TOEFL.

Kansas State University, Graduate School, College of Engineering, Department of Industrial and Manufacturing Systems Engineering, Manhattan, KS 66506. Offers engineering management (MEM); industrial engineering (MS); operations research (MS). *Program availability:* Part-time, online learning. *Degree requirements:* For master's, thesis or alternative; for doctorate, thesis/dissertation. *Entrance requirements:* For master's, GRE General Test (minimum score of 750 old version, 159 new format on Quantitative portion of exam), bachelor's degree in engineering, mathematics, or physical science; for doctorate, GRE General Test (minimum score of 770 old version, 164 new format on Quantitative portion of exam), master's degree in engineering or industrial manufacturing. Additional exam requirements/recommendations for international students: required—PTE (minimum score 58), TOEFL (minimum score 550 paper-based; 79 iBT) or IELTS (minimum score 6.5). Electronic applications accepted.

Kettering University, Graduate School, Department of Industrial and Manufacturing Engineering, Flint, MI 48504. Offers engineering (MS). *Program availability:* Part-time, evening/weekend, online learning. *Degree requirements:* For master's, thesis optional. *Entrance requirements:* Additional exam requirements/recommendations for international students: required—TOEFL (minimum score 550 paper-based; 79 iBT). Electronic applications accepted.

Lawrence Technological University, College of Engineering, Southfield, MI 48075-1058. Offers architectural engineering (MS); automotive engineering (MS); biomedical engineering (MS); civil engineering (MA, MS, PhD), including environmental engineering (MS), geotechnical engineering (MS), structural engineering (MS), transportation engineering (MS), water resource engineering (MS); construction engineering management (MA); electrical and computer engineering (MS); engineering management (MEM); engineering technology (MS); fire engineering (MS); industrial engineering (MS), including healthcare systems; manufacturing systems (ME); mechanical engineering (MS, DE, PhD), including automotive engineering (MS), energy engineering (MS), manufacturing (DE), solid mechanics (MS), thermal/fluid systems (MS); mechatronic systems engineering (MS). *Program availability:* Part-time, evening/weekend. *Faculty:* 23 full-time (2 women), 20 part-time/adjunct (1 woman). *Students:* 14 full-time (5 women), 286 part-time (54 women); includes 26 minority (13 Black or African American, non-Hispanic/Latino; 8 Asian, non-Hispanic/Latino; 3 Hispanic/Latino; 2 Two or more races, non-Hispanic/Latino), 150 international. Average age 29. 384 applicants, 58% accepted, 74 enrolled. In 2019, 223 master's, 7 doctorates awarded. Terminal master's awarded for partial completion of doctoral program. *Degree requirements:* For master's, thesis optional; for doctorate, comprehensive exam, thesis/dissertation optional. *Entrance requirements:* Additional exam requirements/recommendations for international students: required—TOEFL (minimum score 550 paper-based; 79 iBT), IELTS (minimum score 6.5). *Application deadline:* For fall admission, 5/24 for international students; for spring admission, 10/13 for international students; for summer admission, 2/18 for international students. Applications are processed on a rolling basis. Application fee: $50. Electronic applications accepted. *Expenses: Tuition:* Full-time $16,618; part-time $8309 per year. *Required fees:* $600; $600. *Financial support:* In 2019–20, 21 students received support. Unspecified assistantships available. Financial award application deadline: 4/1; financial award applicants required to submit FAFSA. *Unit head:* Dr. Nabil Grace, Dean, 248-204-2500, Fax: 248-204-2509, E-mail: engrdean@ltu.edu. *Application contact:* Jane Rohrback, Director of Admissions, 248-204-3160, Fax: 248-204-2228, E-mail: admissions@ltu.edu.
Website: http://www.ltu.edu/engineering/index.asp

Massachusetts Institute of Technology, School of Engineering, Department of Mechanical Engineering, Cambridge, MA 02139. Offers manufacturing (M Eng); mechanical engineering (SM, PhD, Sc D, Mech E); naval architecture and marine engineering (SM, PhD, Sc D); naval engineering (Naval E); ocean engineering (SM, PhD, Sc D); oceanographic engineering (SM, PhD, Sc D); SM/MBA. Terminal master's awarded for partial completion of doctoral program. *Degree requirements:* For master's, thesis; for doctorate, comprehensive exam, thesis/dissertation; for other advanced degree, comprehensive exam, thesis. *Entrance requirements:* For master's, doctorate, and other advanced degree, GRE General Test. Additional exam requirements/recommendations for international students: required—TOEFL, IELTS. Electronic applications accepted.

Michigan State University, The Graduate School, College of Agriculture and Natural Resources, School of Packaging, East Lansing, MI 48824. Offers MS, PhD. *Entrance requirements:* Additional exam requirements/recommendations for international students: required—TOEFL. Electronic applications accepted.

Minnesota State University Mankato, College of Graduate Studies and Research, College of Science, Engineering and Technology, Department of Automotive and Manufacturing Engineering Technology, Mankato, MN 56001. Offers manufacturing engineering technology (MS). *Degree requirements:* For master's, comprehensive exam, thesis. *Entrance requirements:* For master's, minimum GPA of 2.75 during previous 2 years. Additional exam requirements/recommendations for international students: required—TOEFL (minimum score 525 paper-based). Electronic applications accepted.

Missouri University of Science and Technology, Department of Mechanical and Aerospace Engineering, Rolla, MO 65401. Offers aerospace engineering (MS, PhD); manufacturing engineering (M Eng, MS); mechanical engineering (MS, PhD). *Program availability:* Part-time, evening/weekend. Terminal master's awarded for partial completion of doctoral program. *Degree requirements:* For master's, thesis optional; for doctorate, comprehensive exam, thesis/dissertation. *Entrance requirements:* For master's, GRE General Test (minimum score 1100 verbal and quantitative, writing 3.5), minimum GPA of 3.0; for doctorate, GRE General Test (minimum score: verbal and quantitative 1100, writing 3.5), minimum GPA of 3.5. Additional exam requirements/recommendations for international students: required—TOEFL (minimum score 550 paper-based). Electronic applications accepted. *Expenses:* Tuition, state resident: full-time $7839; part-time $435.50 per credit hour. Tuition, nonresident: full-time $22,169; part-time $1231.60 per credit hour. *International tuition:* $18,156.60 full-time. *Required fees:* $649.76. One-time fee: $119. Tuition and fees vary according to course load and program.

New Jersey Institute of Technology, Newark College of Engineering, Newark, NJ 07102. Offers biomedical engineering (MS, PhD); biopharmaceutical engineering (MS); chemical engineering (MS, PhD); civil engineering (MS, PhD); computer engineering (MS); critical infrastructure systems (MS); electrical engineering (MS, PhD); engineering management (MS); engineering science (MS); environmental engineering (MS, PhD); healthcare systems management (MS); industrial engineering (MS, PhD); internet engineering (MS); manufacturing systems engineering (MS); materials science & engineering (PhD); materials science and engineering (MS); mechanical engineering (MS, PhD); occupational safety and health engineering (MS). *Program availability:* Part-time, evening/weekend. *Faculty:* 151 full-time (29 women), 135 part-time/adjunct (15 women). *Students:* 576 full-time (161 women), 528 part-time (111 women); includes 366 minority (61 Black or African American, non-Hispanic/Latino; 1 American Indian or Alaska Native, non-Hispanic/Latino; 166 Asian, non-Hispanic/Latino; 115 Hispanic/Latino; 23 Two or more races, non-Hispanic/Latino), 450 international. Average age 28. 2,053 applicants, 67% accepted, 338 enrolled. In 2019, 474 master's, 30 doctorates awarded. Terminal master's awarded for partial completion of doctoral program. *Degree requirements:* For master's, thesis (for some programs); for doctorate, thesis/dissertation. *Entrance requirements:* For master's, GRE General Test, minimum GPA 2.8, personal statement, 1 letter of recommendation, transcripts; for doctorate, GRE General Test, minimum GPA of 3.5, personal statement, 3 letters of recommendation, transcripts. Additional exam requirements/recommendations for international students: required—TOEFL (minimum score 550 paper-based; 79 iBT), IELTS (minimum score 6.5). *Application deadline:* For fall admission, 6/1 priority date for domestic students, 5/1 priority date for international students; for spring admission, 11/15 priority date for domestic and international students. Applications are processed on a rolling basis. Application fee: $75. Electronic applications accepted. *Expenses:* $23,828 per year (in-state), $33,744 per year (out-of-state). *Financial support:* In 2019–20, 352 students received support, including 33 fellowships with full tuition reimbursements available (averaging $24,000 per year), 89 research assistantships with full tuition reimbursements available (averaging $24,000 per year), 112 teaching assistantships with full tuition reimbursements available (averaging $24,000 per year); career-related internships or fieldwork, Federal Work-Study, scholarships/grants, and unspecified assistantships also available. Financial award application deadline: 1/15. *Unit head:* Dr. Moshe Kam, Dean, 973-596-5534, Fax: 973-596-2316, E-mail: moshe.kam@njit.edu. *Application contact:* Stephen Eck, Executive Director of University Admissions, 973-596-3300, Fax: 973-596-3461, E-mail: admissions@njit.edu.
Website: http://engineering.njit.edu/

New York University, Tandon School of Engineering, Department of Technology Management, Major in Manufacturing Engineering, New York, NY 10012-1019. Offers manufacturing engineering (MS). *Program availability:* Part-time, evening/weekend, online learning. *Entrance requirements:* For master's, BE or BS in engineering, physics, chemistry, mathematical sciences, or biological sciences, or MBA. Additional exam requirements/recommendations for international students: required—TOEFL (minimum score 550 paper-based; 80 iBT); recommended—IELTS (minimum score 6.5). Electronic applications accepted.

North Carolina State University, Graduate School, College of Engineering, Integrated Manufacturing Systems Engineering Institute, Raleigh, NC 27695. Offers MIMS. *Program availability:* Part-time. *Degree requirements:* For master's, thesis optional. *Entrance requirements:* For master's, GRE. Additional exam requirements/recommendations for international students: required—TOEFL. Electronic applications accepted.

North Dakota State University, College of Graduate and Interdisciplinary Studies, College of Engineering, Department of Industrial and Manufacturing Engineering, Fargo, ND 58102. Offers industrial and manufacturing engineering (MS, PhD); manufacturing engineering (MS). *Program availability:* Part-time. *Degree requirements:* For doctorate, comprehensive exam, thesis/dissertation. *Entrance requirements:* For master's, GRE General Test, bachelor's degree in engineering; for doctorate, GRE General Test, master's degree in engineering. Additional exam requirements/recommendations for international students: required—TOEFL (minimum score 550 paper-based; 79 iBT), TWE (minimum score 4). Electronic applications accepted. Tuition and fees vary according to program and reciprocity agreements.

Oregon Institute of Technology, Program in Manufacturing Engineering Technology, Klamath Falls, OR 97601-8801. Offers MS. *Program availability:* Part-time, online learning. *Degree requirements:* For master's, one foreign language, project. *Entrance requirements:* For master's, GRE General Test. Electronic applications accepted.

Oregon State University, College of Engineering, Program in Industrial Engineering, Corvallis, OR 97331. Offers advanced manufacturing (M Eng, MS, PhD); engineering management (M Eng); human systems engineering (M Eng, MS, PhD); information systems engineering (M Eng, MS, PhD); manufacturing systems engineering (M Eng, MS, PhD). *Program availability:* 100% online. *Entrance requirements:* For master's and doctorate, GRE. Additional exam requirements/recommendations for international students: required—TOEFL (minimum score 80 iBT), IELTS (minimum score 6.5). *Expenses:* Contact institution.

Pittsburg State University, Graduate School, College of Technology, Department of Engineering Technology, Pittsburg, KS 66762. Offers electrical engineering technology (MET); general engineering technology (MET); manufacturing engineering technology (MET); mechanical engineering technology (MET); plastics engineering technology (MET). *Program availability:* Part-time, 100% online, blended/hybrid learning. *Degree requirements:* For master's, thesis optional. *Entrance requirements:* Additional exam requirements/recommendations for international students: required—TOEFL (minimum score 550 paper-based; 79 iBT), IELTS (minimum score 6.5), PTE (minimum score 51). Electronic applications accepted. *Expenses:* Contact institution.

Polytechnic University of Puerto Rico, Graduate School, Hato Rey, PR 00918. Offers business administration (MBA), including computer information systems, general management, management of information systems, management of international enterprises; civil engineering (ME, MS); computer engineering (ME, MS); computer science (MCS, MS); electrical engineering (ME, MS); engineering management (MEM); environmental management (MEM); landscape architecture (M Land Arch); manufacturing competitiveness (MMC, MS); manufacturing engineering (ME, MS); mechanical engineering (M Mech E). *Accreditation:* ASLA. *Program availability:* Part-time, evening/weekend. *Entrance requirements:* For master's, 3 letters of recommendation.

Rochester Institute of Technology, Graduate Enrollment Services, College of Applied Science and Technology, School of Engineering Technology, MS Program in Manufacturing and Mechanical Systems Integration, Rochester, NY 14623-5603. Offers MS. *Program availability:* Part-time, evening/weekend. *Degree requirements:* For master's, thesis (for some programs). *Entrance requirements:* For master's, GRE required for applicants with degrees from international universities, minimum GPA of 3.0 (recommended). Additional exam requirements/recommendations for international students: required—TOEFL (minimum score 550 paper-based; 80 iBT), IELTS (minimum score 6.5), PTE (minimum score 58). Electronic applications accepted.

Rochester Institute of Technology, Graduate Enrollment Services, College of Applied Science and Technology, School of Engineering Technology, MS Program in Packaging Science, Rochester, NY 14623-5603. Offers MS. *Program availability:* Part-time. *Degree requirements:* For master's, comprehensive exam (for some programs), thesis or alternative, thesis, project, or comprehensive exam. *Entrance requirements:* For master's, minimum GPA of 3.0 (recommended) in the final two years of graduate study. Additional exam requirements/recommendations for international students: required—TOEFL (minimum score 550 paper-based; 79 iBT), IELTS (minimum score 6.5), PTE (minimum score 58). Electronic applications accepted. *Expenses:* Contact institution.

Rochester Institute of Technology, Graduate Enrollment Services, Kate Gleason College of Engineering, Design, Development and Manufacturing Department, Rochester, NY 14623-5603. Offers manufacturing leadership (MS); product development (MS). *Program availability:* Part-time-only, evening/weekend, 100% online, blended/hybrid learning. *Entrance requirements:* For master's, minimum GPA of 2.5, 2 years of related work experience. Electronic applications accepted. *Expenses:* Contact institution.

Rochester Institute of Technology, Graduate Enrollment Services, Kate Gleason College of Engineering, Electrical and Microelectronic Engineering Department, ME Program in Microelectronic Manufacturing Engineering, Rochester, NY 14623-5603. Offers ME. *Program availability:* Part-time, evening/weekend, 100% online. *Degree requirements:* For master's, internship. *Entrance requirements:* For master's, minimum GPA of 3.0 (recommended), 2 letters of recommendation, hold a baccalaureate degree from an accredited institution in engineering or a related field. Additional exam requirements/recommendations for international students: required—TOEFL (minimum score 550 paper-based; 79 iBT), IELTS (minimum score 6.5), PTE (minimum score 28). Electronic applications accepted. *Expenses:* Contact institution.

Rochester Institute of Technology, Graduate Enrollment Services, Kate Gleason College of Engineering, Industrial and Systems Engineering Department, Rochester, NY 14623-5603. Offers engineering management (ME); industrial and systems engineering (ME, MS); sustainable engineering (ME, MS). *Program availability:* Part-time. *Entrance requirements:* For master's, GRE, minimum GPA of 3.0 (recommended). Electronic applications accepted. *Expenses:* Contact institution.

Southern Methodist University, Lyle School of Engineering, Department of Mechanical Engineering, Dallas, TX 75205. Offers manufacturing systems management (MS); mechanical engineering (MS, PhD). *Program availability:* Part-time, evening/weekend, online learning. Terminal master's awarded for partial completion of doctoral program. *Degree requirements:* For master's, thesis optional; for doctorate, thesis/dissertation, oral and written qualifying exams, oral final exam. *Entrance requirements:* For master's, GRE General Test, minimum GPA of 3.0 in last 2 years; bachelor's degree in engineering, mathematics, or sciences; for doctorate, preliminary counseling exam, minimum graduate GPA of 3.0, bachelor's degree in related field. Additional exam requirements/recommendations for international students: required—TOEFL.

Stevens Institute of Technology, Graduate School, Charles V. Schaefer Jr. School of Engineering and Science, Department of Mechanical Engineering, Program in Integrated Product Development, Hoboken, NJ 07030. Offers armament engineering (M Eng); computer and electrical engineering (M Eng); manufacturing technologies (M Eng); systems reliability and design (M Eng). *Program availability:* Part-time, evening/weekend. *Faculty:* 29 full-time (3 women), 11 part-time/adjunct (0 women). *Degree requirements:* For master's, thesis optional, minimum B average in major field and overall. *Entrance requirements:* For master's, International applicants must submit TOEFL/IELTS scores and fulfill the English Language Proficiency Requirement. Applicants to full-time programs who do not qualify for a score waiver are required to submit GRE/GMAT scores. Additional exam requirements/recommendations for international students: required—TOEFL (minimum score 74 iBT), IELTS (minimum score 6). *Application deadline:* For fall admission, 4/15 for domestic and international students; for spring admission, 11/1 for domestic and international students; for summer admission, 5/1 for domestic students. Applications are processed on a rolling basis. Application fee: $60. Electronic applications accepted. *Expenses: Tuition:* Full-time $52,134. *Required fees:* $1880. Tuition and fees vary according to course load. *Financial support:* Fellowships, research assistantships, teaching assistantships, career-related internships or fieldwork, Federal Work-Study, scholarships/grants, and unspecified assistantships available. Financial award application deadline: 2/15; financial award applicants required to submit FAFSA. *Unit head:* Dr. Jean Zu, Dean of SES, 201-216.8233, Fax: 201-216.8372, E-mail: Jean.Zu@stevens.edu. *Application contact:* Graduate Admissions, 888-783-8367, Fax: 888-511-1306, E-mail: graduate@stevens.edu.

Tennessee State University, The School of Graduate Studies and Research, College of Engineering, Nashville, TN 37209-1561. Offers biomedical engineering (ME); civil engineering (ME); computer and information systems engineering (MS, PhD); electrical engineering (ME); environmental engineering (ME); manufacturing engineering (ME); mathematical sciences (MS); mechanical engineering (ME). *Program availability:* Part-time, evening/weekend. *Degree requirements:* For master's, project; for doctorate, comprehensive exam, thesis/dissertation. *Entrance requirements:* For doctorate, minimum GPA of 3.3.

Texas A&M University, College of Engineering, Department of Engineering Technology and Industrial Distribution, College Station, TX 77843. Offers industrial distribution (MID); technical management (METM). *Faculty:* 43. *Students:* 192 full-time (59 women), 8 part-time (1 woman); includes 66 minority (16 Black or African American, non-Hispanic/Latino; 12 Asian, non-Hispanic/Latino; 35 Hispanic/Latino; 3 Two or more races, non-Hispanic/Latino), 3 international. Average age 37. 140 applicants, 84% accepted, 108 enrolled. In 2019, 45 master's awarded. *Degree requirements:* For master's, comprehensive exam (for some programs), thesis (for some programs). *Entrance requirements:* For master's, GRE, letters of recommendation. Additional exam requirements/recommendations for international students: required—TOEFL (minimum score 550 paper-based; 80 iBT), IELTS (minimum score 6), PTE (minimum score 53). *Application deadline:* For fall admission, 7/15 for domestic students, 4/15 for international students; for spring admission, 10/15 for domestic students, 9/15 for international students. Applications are processed on a rolling basis. Application fee: $65 ($90 for international students). Electronic applications accepted. *Expenses:* Contact institution. *Financial support:* In 2019–20, 84 students received support, including 1 fellowship with tuition reimbursement available (averaging $30,000 per year), 2 research assistantships with tuition reimbursements available (averaging $12,803 per year), 5 teaching assistantships with tuition reimbursements available (averaging $15,269 per year); career-related internships or fieldwork, institutionally sponsored loans, scholarships/grants, health care benefits, and tuition waivers (full and partial) also available. Support available to part-time students. Financial award application deadline: 3/15; financial award applicants required to submit FAFSA. *Unit head:* Dr. Reza Langari, Department Head, 979-862-4949, E-mail: rlangari@tamu.edu. *Application contact:* Haley Meyer, Academic Advisor Graduate Programs, E-mail: hmeyer@tamu.edu. Website: http://engineering.tamu.edu/etid

Texas State University, The Graduate College, College of Science and Engineering, Program in Engineering, San Marcos, TX 78666. Offers civil engineering (MS); electrical engineering (MS); industrial engineering (MS); mechanical and manufacturing engineering (MS). *Program availability:* Part-time. *Degree requirements:* For master's, comprehensive exam, thesis (for some programs), thesis or research project. *Entrance requirements:* For master's, official GRE (general test only) required with competitive scores in the verbal reasoning and quantitative reasoning sections, baccalaureate degree from regionally-accredited university in engineering, computer science, physics, technology, or closely-related field with minimum GPA of 3.0 on last 60 undergraduate semester hours; resume or curriculum vitae; 2 letters of recommendation; statement of purpose conveying research interest and professional aspirations. Additional exam requirements/recommendations for international students: required—TOEFL (minimum score 550 paper-based; 78 iBT), IELTS (minimum score 6.5). Electronic applications accepted.

Tufts University, Graduate School of Arts and Sciences, Graduate Certificate Programs, Manufacturing Engineering Program, Medford, MA 02155. Offers Certificate. *Program availability:* Part-time, evening/weekend. Electronic applications accepted. Full-time tuition and fees vary according to degree level, program and student level. Part-time tuition and fees vary according to course load.

Universidad Autonoma de Guadalajara, Graduate Programs, Guadalajara, Mexico. Offers administrative law and justice (LL M); advertising and corporate communications (MA); architecture (M Arch); business (MBA); computational science (MCC); education (Ed M, Ed D); English-Spanish translation (MA); entrepreneurship and management (MBA); integrated management of digital animation (MA); international business (MIB); international corporate law (LL M); Internet technologies (MS); manufacturing systems (MMS); occupational health (MS); philosophy (MA, PhD); power electronics (MS); quality systems (MQS); renewable energy (MS); social evaluation of projects (MBA); strategic market research (MBA); tax law (MA); teaching mathematics (MA).

Universidad de las Américas Puebla, Division of Graduate Studies, School of Engineering, Program in Manufacturing Administration, Puebla, Mexico. Offers MS.

University at Buffalo, the State University of New York, Graduate School, School of Engineering and Applied Sciences, Department of Industrial and Systems Engineering, Buffalo, NY 14260. Offers advanced manufacturing (Certificate); industrial engineering (ME, MS, PhD), including data fusion (ME); engineering management (ME). *Program availability:* Part-time, online learning. Terminal master's awarded for partial completion of doctoral program. *Degree requirements:* For master's, comprehensive exam (for some programs), thesis or alternative; for doctorate, thesis/dissertation. *Entrance requirements:* For master's and doctorate, GRE General Test. Additional exam requirements/recommendations for international students: required—TOEFL (minimum score 550 paper-based; 79 iBT). Electronic applications accepted. *Expenses: Tuition, area resident:* Full-time $11,310; part-time $471 per credit hour. Tuition, state resident: full-time $11,310; part-time $471 per credit hour. Tuition, nonresident: full-time $23,100; part-time $963 per credit hour. *International tuition:* $23,100 full-time. *Required fees:* $2820.

University of Calgary, Faculty of Graduate Studies, Schulich School of Engineering, Program in Mechanical and Manufacturing Engineering, Calgary, AB T2N 1N4, Canada. Offers M Eng, M Sc, PhD. *Program availability:* Part-time. *Degree requirements:* For master's, thesis (for some programs); for doctorate, thesis/dissertation, candidacy exam. *Entrance requirements:* For master's, minimum GPA of 3.0; for doctorate, minimum GPA of 3.3. Additional exam requirements/recommendations for international students: required—TOEFL (minimum score 550 paper-based; 80 iBT), IELTS (minimum score 7).

University of California, Irvine, Samueli School of Engineering, Program in Materials and Manufacturing Technology, Irvine, CA 92697. Offers engineering (MS, PhD). *Program availability:* Part-time. *Students:* 18 full-time (5 women), 4 part-time (2 women); includes 5 minority (3 Asian, non-Hispanic/Latino; 2 Hispanic/Latino), 13 international. Average age 28. 21 applicants, 48% accepted, 5 enrolled. In 2019, 5 master's, 2 doctorates awarded. *Entrance requirements:* For master's and doctorate, GRE General Test, 3 letters of recommendation, minimum GPA of 3.0. Additional exam requirements/recommendations for international students: required—TOEFL (minimum score 550 paper-based). *Application deadline:* For fall admission, 1/15 priority date for domestic students, 1/15 for international students. Applications are processed on a rolling basis. Application fee: $120 ($140 for international students). Electronic applications accepted. *Financial support:* Fellowships, research assistantships with full tuition reimbursements, teaching assistantships, institutionally sponsored loans, traineeships, health care benefits, and unspecified assistantships available. Financial award application deadline: 3/1; financial award applicants required to submit FAFSA. *Application contact:* Connie Cheng, Assistant Director of Graduate Student Affairs, 949-824-3562, Fax: 949-824-8200, E-mail: connie.cheng@uci.edu. Website: http://www.eng.uci.edu/

Manufacturing Engineering

University of California, Los Angeles, Graduate Division, Henry Samueli School of Engineering and Applied Science, Department of Mechanical and Aerospace Engineering, Program in Manufacturing Engineering, Los Angeles, CA 90095-1597. Offers MS. *Degree requirements:* For master's, comprehensive exam or thesis. *Entrance requirements:* For master's, GRE General Test, minimum GPA of 3.0. Additional exam requirements/recommendations for international students: required—TOEFL (minimum score 560 paper-based; 87 iBT), IELTS (minimum score 7). Electronic applications accepted.

The University of Iowa, Graduate College, College of Engineering, Department of Industrial Engineering, Iowa City, IA 52242-1316. Offers engineering design and manufacturing (MS, PhD); healthcare systems (MS, PhD); human factors (MS, PhD); information and engineering management (MS, PhD); operations research (MS, PhD); wind energy (MS, PhD). Terminal master's awarded for partial completion of doctoral program. *Degree requirements:* For master's, thesis optional, exam; for doctorate, comprehensive exam, thesis/dissertation, final defense exam. *Entrance requirements:* For master's and doctorate, GRE (minimum Verbal score of 153, Quantitative 151), minimum undergraduate GPA of 3.0. Additional exam requirements/recommendations for international students: required—TOEFL (minimum score 600 paper-based; 100 iBT), IELTS (minimum score 7). Electronic applications accepted.

The University of Iowa, Graduate College, College of Engineering, Department of Mechanical Engineering, Iowa City, IA 52242-1316. Offers energy systems (MS, PhD); engineering design (MS, PhD); fluid dynamics (MS, PhD); materials and manufacturing (MS, PhD); wind energy (MS, PhD). Terminal master's awarded for partial completion of doctoral program. *Degree requirements:* For master's, oral exam or thesis; for doctorate, comprehensive exam, thesis/dissertation. *Entrance requirements:* For master's and doctorate, GRE (minimum Verbal score of 153, Quantitative 151), minimum undergraduate GPA of 3.0. Additional exam requirements/recommendations for international students: required—TOEFL (minimum score 600 paper-based; 100 iBT), IELTS (minimum score 7). Electronic applications accepted.

University of Kentucky, Graduate School, College of Engineering, Program in Manufacturing Systems Engineering, Lexington, KY 40506-0032. Offers MSMSE. *Degree requirements:* For master's, comprehensive exam. *Entrance requirements:* For master's, GRE General Test, minimum undergraduate GPA of 2.75. Additional exam requirements/recommendations for international students: required—TOEFL (minimum score 550 paper-based). Electronic applications accepted.

University of Manitoba, Faculty of Graduate Studies, Faculty of Engineering, Department of Mechanical and Manufacturing Engineering, Winnipeg, MB R3T 2N2, Canada. Offers M Eng, M Sc, PhD. *Degree requirements:* For master's, thesis; for doctorate, thesis/dissertation.

University of Maryland, College Park, Academic Affairs, A. James Clark School of Engineering, Department of Mechanical Engineering, College Park, MD 20742. Offers electronic packaging and reliability (MS, PhD); manufacturing and design (MS, PhD); mechanics and materials (MS, PhD); reliability engineering (M Eng, MS, PhD); thermal and fluid sciences (MS, PhD). *Program availability:* Part-time, evening/weekend, online learning. *Degree requirements:* For master's, thesis optional; for doctorate, thesis/dissertation, qualifying exam. *Entrance requirements:* For master's, GRE General Test, 3 letters of recommendation; for doctorate, GRE General Test, minimum GPA of 3.0. Additional exam requirements/recommendations for international students: required—TOEFL. Electronic applications accepted.

University of Michigan, College of Engineering, Department of Integrative Systems and Design, Ann Arbor, MI 48109. Offers automotive engineering (M Eng); design science (MS, PhD); energy systems engineering (M Eng, MS); global automotive and manufacturing engineering (M Eng); manufacturing engineering (M Eng, D Eng); pharmaceutical engineering (M Eng); robotics and autonomous vehicles (M Eng); systems engineering and design (M Eng); MBA/M Eng; MSE/MS. *Program availability:* Part-time, online learning. Terminal master's awarded for partial completion of doctoral program. *Degree requirements:* For master's, capstone project; for doctorate, thesis/dissertation. *Entrance requirements:* For master's and doctorate, GRE. Additional exam requirements/recommendations for international students: required—TOEFL. Electronic applications accepted.

University of Michigan–Dearborn, College of Engineering and Computer Science, MSE Program in Manufacturing Systems Engineering, Dearborn, MI 48128. Offers MSE. *Program availability:* Part-time, evening/weekend, 100% online. *Faculty:* 17 full-time (4 women), 9 part-time/adjunct (1 woman). *Students:* 6 full-time (0 women), 10 part-time (2 women); includes 4 minority (2 Black or African American, non-Hispanic/Latino; 1 Asian, non-Hispanic/Latino; 1 Hispanic/Latino), 9 international. Average age 29. 18 applicants, 67% accepted, 4 enrolled. In 2019, 4 master's awarded. *Degree requirements:* For master's, thesis optional. *Entrance requirements:* For master's, BS in engineering or a physical science from accredited program with minimum B average. Additional exam requirements/recommendations for international students: required—TOEFL (minimum score 560 paper-based; 84 iBT), IELTS (minimum score 6.5). *Application deadline:* For fall admission, 8/1 priority date for domestic students, 5/1 priority date for international students; for winter admission, 12/1 priority date for domestic students, 9/1 priority date for international students; for spring admission, 4/1 priority date for domestic students, 1/1 priority date for international students. Applications are processed on a rolling basis. Application fee: $60. Electronic applications accepted. *Financial support:* Scholarships/grants, unspecified assistantships, and non-resident tuition scholarships available. Support available to part-time students. Financial award application deadline: 3/1; financial award applicants required to submit FAFSA. *Unit head:* Dr. Armen Zakarian, Chair, 313-593-5361, E-mail: zakarian@umich.edu. *Application contact:* Office of Graduate Studies, 313-583-6321, E-mail: umd-graduatestudies@umich.edu.
Website: https://umdearborn.edu/cecs/departments/industrial-and-manufacturing-systems-engineering/graduate-programs/mse-manufacturing-systems-engineering

University of Missouri, Office of Research and Graduate Studies, College of Engineering, Department of Industrial and Manufacturing Systems Engineering, Columbia, MO 65211. Offers ME, MS, PhD, MS/MHA. *Degree requirements:* For master's, thesis or alternative; for doctorate, thesis/dissertation. *Entrance requirements:* For master's and doctorate, GRE General Test, minimum GPA of 3.0. Additional exam requirements/recommendations for international students: required—TOEFL.

University of Nebraska–Lincoln, Graduate College, College of Engineering, Department of Industrial and Management Systems Engineering, Lincoln, NE 68588. Offers engineering management (M Eng); industrial and management systems engineering (MS, PhD); manufacturing systems engineering (MS). *Program availability:* Online learning. *Degree requirements:* For master's, thesis optional; for doctorate, comprehensive exam, thesis/dissertation. *Entrance requirements:* For master's and doctorate, GRE. Additional exam requirements/recommendations for international students: required—TOEFL (minimum score 525 paper-based). Electronic applications accepted.

University of New Mexico, Graduate Studies, School of Engineering, Manufacturing Engineering Program, Albuquerque, NM 87131-2039. Offers MEME, MBA/MEME. *Program availability:* Part-time. *Faculty:* 1 full-time (0 women). *Students:* 1 full-time (0 women); minority (Asian, non-Hispanic/Latino). In 2019, 2 master's awarded. *Degree requirements:* For master's, comprehensive exam (for some programs), thesis or alternative. *Entrance requirements:* For master's, GRE General Test (minimum combined score: 300), minimum GPA of 3.0. Additional exam requirements/recommendations for international students: required—TOEFL (minimum score 550 paper-based; 79 iBT), IELTS, PTE, Official English language proficiency results from either the TOEFL, IELTS, PTE-Academic, or Cambridge CPE or CAE. *Application deadline:* For fall admission, 7/30 priority date for domestic students, 3/1 for international students; for spring admission, 11/30 priority date for domestic students, 8/1 for international students. Application fee: $50. Electronic applications accepted. *Expenses:* Tuition, state resident: full-time $7633; part-time $972 per year. Tuition, nonresident: full-time $22,586; part-time $3840 per year. *International tuition:* $23,292 full-time. *Required fees:* $8608. Tuition and fees vary according to course level, course load, degree level, program and student level. *Financial support:* Research assistantships, teaching assistantships, career-related internships or fieldwork, health care benefits, and unspecified assistantships available. Support available to part-time students. Financial award application deadline: 3/1; financial award applicants required to submit FAFSA. *Unit head:* Dr. John E. Wood, Director, 505-272-7000, Fax: 505-272-7152, E-mail: jw@unm.edu. *Application contact:* Arden L. Ballantine, Information Contact, 505-272-7000, Fax: 505-272-7152, E-mail: aballant@unm.edu.
Website: http://www.mfg.unm.edu/

University of Puerto Rico at Mayagüez, Graduate Studies, College of Engineering, Department of Mechanical Engineering, Mayagüez, PR 00681-9000. Offers mechanical engineering (ME, MS, PhD), including aerospace and unmanned vehicles (ME), automation/mechatronics, bioengineering, fluid mechanics, heat transfer/energy systems, manufacturing, mechanics of materials, micro and nano engineering. *Program availability:* Part-time. Terminal master's awarded for partial completion of doctoral program. *Degree requirements:* For master's, one foreign language, comprehensive exam, thesis; for doctorate, one foreign language, comprehensive exam, thesis/dissertation. *Entrance requirements:* For master's, BS in mechanical engineering or its equivalent; for doctorate, GRE, BS or MS in mechanical engineering or its equivalent; minimum GPA of 3.0. Additional exam requirements/recommendations for international students: required—TOEFL (minimum score 80 iBT). Electronic applications accepted.

University of St. Thomas, School of Engineering, St. Paul, MN 55105. Offers data science (MS); electrical engineering (MS); information technology (MS); manufacturing engineering (MS); manufacturing systems (Certificate); mechanical engineering (MS); medical device development (Certificate); regulatory science (MS); software engineering (MS); software management (MS); systems engineering (MS); technology leadership (Certificate); technology management (MS). *Program availability:* Part-time, evening/weekend. *Entrance requirements:* For master's, resume, official transcripts. Additional exam requirements/recommendations for international students: required—TOEFL (minimum score 80 iBT), IELTS (minimum score 6.5). Electronic applications accepted. *Expenses:* Contact institution.

University of Southern California, Graduate School, Viterbi School of Engineering, Daniel J. Epstein Department of Industrial and Systems Engineering, Los Angeles, CA 90089. Offers digital supply chain management (MS); engineering management (MS); engineering technology communication (Graduate Certificate); health systems operations (Graduate Certificate); industrial and systems engineering (MS, PhD, Engr); manufacturing engineering (MS); operations research engineering (MS); optimization and supply chain management (Graduate Certificate); product development engineering (MS); safety systems and security (MS); systems architecting and engineering (MS, Graduate Certificate); systems safety and security (Graduate Certificate); transportation systems (Graduate Certificate); MS/MBA. *Program availability:* Part-time, evening/weekend, online learning. Terminal master's awarded for partial completion of doctoral program. *Degree requirements:* For master's, thesis optional; for doctorate, thesis/dissertation. *Entrance requirements:* For master's and doctorate, GRE General Test. Additional exam requirements/recommendations for international students: recommended—TOEFL. Electronic applications accepted.

The University of Texas at El Paso, Graduate School, College of Engineering, Department of Industrial, Manufacturing and Systems Engineering, El Paso, TX 79968-0001. Offers industrial engineering (MS); manufacturing engineering (MS); systems engineering (MS). *Program availability:* Part-time, evening/weekend. *Degree requirements:* For master's, thesis optional. *Entrance requirements:* For master's, GRE General Test, minimum GPA of 3.0 in major. Additional exam requirements/recommendations for international students: required—TOEFL. Electronic applications accepted.

The University of Texas at San Antonio, College of Engineering, Department of Mechanical Engineering, San Antonio, TX 78249-0617. Offers advanced manufacturing and enterprise engineering (MS); mechanical engineering (MS, PhD). *Program availability:* Part-time, evening/weekend. Terminal master's awarded for partial completion of doctoral program. *Degree requirements:* For master's, comprehensive exam, thesis; for doctorate, comprehensive exam, thesis/dissertation. *Entrance requirements:* For master's, GRE General Test, bachelor's degree in mechanical engineering or related field from accredited institution of higher education; for doctorate, GRE General Test, master's degree in mechanical engineering, or exceptionally outstanding undergraduate record in mechanical engineering or related field; minimum GPA of 3.33. Additional exam requirements/recommendations for international students: required—TOEFL (minimum score 550 paper-based; 79 iBT), IELTS (minimum score 6.5). Electronic applications accepted. *Expenses:* Contact institution.

The University of Texas Rio Grande Valley, College of Engineering and Computer Science, Department of Manufacturing and Industrial Engineering, Edinburg, TX 78539. Offers engineering management (MS); manufacturing engineering (MS), including systems engineering. *Faculty:* 5 full-time. *Students:* 26 full-time (8 women), 16 part-time (6 women); includes 22 minority (all Hispanic/Latino), 20 international. Average age 26. 21 applicants, 81% accepted, 9 enrolled. In 2019, 12 master's awarded. *Expenses:* Tuition, area resident: Full-time $5959; part-time $440 per credit hour. Tuition, state resident: full-time $5959. Tuition, nonresident: full-time $5959. *International tuition:* $13,321 full-time. *Required fees:* $1169; $185 per credit hour.
Website: utrgv.edu/maie/

University of Toronto, School of Graduate Studies, Advanced Design and Manufacturing Institute, Toronto, ON M5S 1A1, Canada. Offers M Eng. *Program availability:* Part-time. *Entrance requirements:* For master's, honours bachelor's degree in engineering with grades equivalent to a mid-B or better. Additional exam requirements/recommendations for international students: required—TOEFL (minimum score 580 paper-based; 93 iBT), TWE (minimum score 4). Electronic applications accepted.

University of Windsor, Faculty of Graduate Studies, Faculty of Engineering, Department of Industrial and Manufacturing Systems Engineering, Windsor, ON N9B 3P4, Canada. Offers industrial engineering (M Eng, MA Sc); manufacturing systems engineering (PhD). *Program availability:* Part-time. *Degree requirements:* For master's, thesis; for doctorate, comprehensive exam, thesis/dissertation. *Entrance requirements:* For master's, minimum B average; for doctorate, master's degree, minimum B average.

Additional exam requirements/recommendations for international students: required—TOEFL (minimum score 560 paper-based). Electronic applications accepted.

University of Wisconsin–Madison, Graduate School, College of Engineering, Manufacturing Systems Engineering Program, Madison, WI 53706. Offers MS. *Program availability:* Part-time. *Degree requirements:* For master's, thesis (for some programs), minimum of 30 credits; independent research projects; minimum GPA of 3.0. *Entrance requirements:* For master's, GRE General Test, BS in engineering or physical sciences coupled with industry experience; minimum GPA of 3.0; 2 years of relevant industry experience or project work. Additional exam requirements/recommendations for international students: required—TOEFL (minimum score 580 paper-based; 92 iBT), IELTS (minimum score 7). Electronic applications accepted. *Expenses:* Contact institution.

University of Wisconsin–Milwaukee, Graduate School, College of Engineering and Applied Science, Program in Engineering, Milwaukee, WI 53201-0413. Offers biomedical engineering (MS); civil engineering (MS, PhD); computer science (PhD); electrical and computer engineering (MS); electrical engineering (PhD); engineering mechanics (MS); industrial and management engineering (MS); industrial engineering (PhD); manufacturing engineering (MS); materials (PhD); materials engineering (MS); mechanical engineering (MS). *Program availability:* Part-time. *Degree requirements:* For master's, comprehensive exam (for some programs), thesis or alternative; for doctorate, comprehensive exam, thesis/dissertation, internship. *Entrance requirements:* For master's, GRE, minimum GPA of 2.75; for doctorate, GRE, minimum GPA of 3.5. Additional exam requirements/recommendations for international students: required—TOEFL (minimum score 550 paper-based; 79 iBT), IELTS (minimum score 6.5).

University of Wisconsin–Stout, Graduate School, College of Science, Technology, Engineering and Mathematics, Program in Manufacturing Engineering, Menomonie, WI 54751. Offers MS. *Program availability:* Online learning. *Degree requirements:* For master's, thesis. *Entrance requirements:* For master's, minimum GPA of 3.0. Additional exam requirements/recommendations for international students: required—TOEFL (minimum score 500 paper-based; 61 iBT). Electronic applications accepted.

Villanova University, College of Engineering, Department of Mechanical Engineering, Villanova, PA 19085-1699. Offers electro-mechanical systems (Certificate); machinery dynamics (Certificate); mechanical engineering (MSME); nonlinear dynamics and control (Certificate); thermofluid systems (Certificate). *Program availability:* Part-time, evening/weekend, online learning. *Degree requirements:* For master's, thesis optional. *Entrance requirements:* For master's, GRE General Test (for applicants with degrees from foreign universities), BME, minimum GPA of 3.0. Additional exam requirements/recommendations for international students: required—TOEFL (minimum score 600 paper-based; 100 iBT). Electronic applications accepted.

Wayne State University, College of Engineering, Department of Industrial and Systems Engineering, Detroit, MI 48202. Offers data science and business analytics (MS); engineering management (MS); industrial engineering (MS, PhD); manufacturing engineering (MS); systems engineering (Certificate). *Program availability:* Online learning. *Faculty:* 12. *Students:* 126 full-time (31 women), 105 part-time (28 women); includes 42 minority (23 Black or African American, non-Hispanic/Latino; 12 Asian, non-Hispanic/Latino; 4 Hispanic/Latino; 3 Two or more races, non-Hispanic/Latino), 124 international. Average age 30. 407 applicants, 36% accepted, 39 enrolled. In 2019, 123 master's, 8 doctorates awarded. *Degree requirements:* For master's, thesis optional; for doctorate, thesis/dissertation. *Entrance requirements:* For master's, GRE or GMAT (for applicants to MS in data science and business analytics), BS from ABET-accredited institution; for doctorate, GRE, graduate degree in engineering or related discipline with minimum graduate GPA of 3.5, statement of purpose, resume/curriculum vitae, three letters of recommendation; for Certificate, GRE (for applicants from non-ABET

institutions), BS in engineering or other technical field from ABET-accredited institution with minimum GPA of 3.0 in upper-division course work, at least one year of full-time work experience as practicing engineer or technical leader. Additional exam requirements/recommendations for international students: required—TOEFL (minimum score 550 paper-based; 79 iBT), TWE (minimum score 5.5), Michigan English Language Assessment Battery (minimum score 85); GRE; recommended—IELTS (minimum score 6.5). *Application deadline:* Applications are processed on a rolling basis. Application fee: $50. Electronic applications accepted. *Expenses:* $790 per credit hour in-state tuition, $1579 per credit hour out-of-state tuition. MS programs 30 credits hours; PhD 90 credit hours. *Financial support:* In 2019–20, 125 students received support, including 2 fellowships with tuition reimbursements available (averaging $20,000 per year), 6 research assistantships with tuition reimbursements available (averaging $22,879 per year), 9 teaching assistantships with tuition reimbursements available (averaging $20,792 per year); scholarships/grants, tuition waivers (full), and unspecified assistantships also available. Financial award applicants required to submit FAFSA. *Unit head:* Dr. Ratna Babu Chinnam, Professor and Interim Chair, 313-577-4846, Fax: 313-577-8833, E-mail: ratna.chinnam@wayne.edu. *Application contact:* Eric Scimeca, Graduate Program Coordinator, 313-577-0412, E-mail: eric.scimeca@wayne.edu. Website: http://engineering.wayne.edu/ise/

Western Illinois University, School of Graduate Studies, College of Business and Technology, Program in Engineering Technology Leadership, Macomb, IL 61455-1390. Offers MS. *Program availability:* Part-time. *Entrance requirements:* Additional exam requirements/recommendations for international students: required—TOEFL (minimum score 550 paper-based; 80 iBT). Electronic applications accepted.

Western Michigan University, Graduate College, College of Engineering and Applied Sciences, Department of Engineering Design, Manufacturing, and Management Systems, Kalamazoo, MI 49008. Offers MS.

Western New England University, College of Engineering, Master's Program in Engineering Management, Springfield, MA 01119. Offers business and engineering information systems (MSEM); general engineering management (MSEM); production and manufacturing systems (MSEM); quality engineering (MSEM); MSEM/MBA. *Program availability:* Part-time, evening/weekend, online learning. *Degree requirements:* For master's, thesis optional. *Entrance requirements:* For master's, official transcript, bachelor's degree in engineering or related field, two recommendations, resume. Additional exam requirements/recommendations for international students: required—TOEFL (minimum score 79 iBT). Electronic applications accepted. *Expenses:* Contact institution.

Wichita State University, Graduate School, College of Engineering, Department of Industrial and Manufacturing Engineering, Wichita, KS 67260. Offers engineering management (MEM); industrial engineering (MS, PhD). *Program availability:* Part-time. *Entrance requirements:* Additional exam requirements/recommendations for international students: required—TOEFL.

Worcester Polytechnic Institute, Graduate Admissions, Department of Mechanical Engineering, Program in Manufacturing Engineering, Worcester, MA 01609-2280. Offers manufacturing engineering (PhD). *Program availability:* Part-time, evening/weekend. Terminal master's awarded for partial completion of doctoral program. *Degree requirements:* For master's, thesis optional; for doctorate, comprehensive exam, thesis/dissertation, research proposal. *Entrance requirements:* For master's and doctorate, Required for international applicants; recommended for all others., 3 letters of recommendation. Additional exam requirements/recommendations for international students: required—TOEFL (minimum score 563 paper-based; 84 iBT), IELTS (minimum score 7), GRE. Electronic applications accepted.

Pharmaceutical Engineering

New Jersey Institute of Technology, Newark College of Engineering, Newark, NJ 07102. Offers biomedical engineering (MS, PhD); biopharmaceutical engineering (MS); chemical engineering (MS, PhD); civil engineering (MS, PhD); computer engineering (MS); critical infrastructure systems (MS); electrical engineering (MS, PhD); engineering management (MS); engineering science (MS); environmental engineering (MS, PhD); healthcare systems management (MS); industrial engineering (MS, PhD); internet engineering (MS); manufacturing systems engineering (MS); materials science & engineering (PhD); materials science and engineering (MS); mechanical engineering (MS, PhD); occupational safety and health engineering (MS). *Program availability:* Part-time, evening/weekend. *Faculty:* 151 full-time (29 women), 135 part-time/adjunct (15 women). *Students:* 576 full-time (161 women), 528 part-time (111 women); includes 366 minority (61 Black or African American, non-Hispanic/Latino; 1 American Indian or Alaska Native, non-Hispanic/Latino; 166 Asian, non-Hispanic/Latino; 115 Hispanic/Latino; 23 Two or more races, non-Hispanic/Latino), 450 international. Average age 28. 2,053 applicants, 67% accepted, 338 enrolled. In 2019, 474 master's, 30 doctorates awarded. Terminal master's awarded for partial completion of doctoral program. *Degree requirements:* For master's, thesis (for some programs); for doctorate, thesis/dissertation. *Entrance requirements:* For master's, GRE General Test, minimum GPA 2.8, personal statement, 1 letter of recommendation, transcripts; for doctorate, GRE General Test, minimum GPA of 3.5, personal statement, 3 letters of recommendation, transcripts. Additional exam requirements/recommendations for international students: required—TOEFL (minimum score 550 paper-based; 79 iBT), IELTS (minimum score 6.5). *Application deadline:* For fall admission, 6/1 priority date for domestic students, 5/1 priority date for international students; for spring admission, 11/15 priority date for domestic and international students. Applications are processed on a rolling basis.

Application fee: $75. Electronic applications accepted. *Expenses:* $23,828 per year (in-state), $33,744 per year (out-of-state). *Financial support:* In 2019–20, 352 students received support, including 33 fellowships with full tuition reimbursements available (averaging $24,000 per year), 89 research assistantships with full tuition reimbursements available (averaging $24,000 per year), 112 teaching assistantships with full tuition reimbursements available (averaging $24,000 per year); career-related internships or fieldwork, Federal Work-Study, scholarships/grants, and unspecified assistantships also available. Financial award application deadline: 1/15. *Unit head:* Dr. Moshe Kam, Dean, 973-596-5534, Fax: 973-596-2316, E-mail: moshe.kam@njit.edu. *Application contact:* Stephen Eck, Executive Director of University Admissions, 973-596-3300, Fax: 973-596-3461, E-mail: admissions@njit.edu. Website: http://engineering.njit.edu/

University of Michigan, College of Engineering, Department of Integrative Systems and Design, Ann Arbor, MI 48109. Offers automotive engineering (M Eng); design science (MS, PhD); energy systems engineering (M Eng, MS); global automotive and manufacturing engineering (M Eng); manufacturing engineering (M Eng, D Eng); pharmaceutical engineering (M Eng); robotics and autonomous vehicles (M Eng); systems engineering and design (M Eng); MBA/M Eng; MSE/MS. *Program availability:* Part-time, online learning. Terminal master's awarded for partial completion of doctoral program. *Degree requirements:* For master's, capstone project; for doctorate, thesis/dissertation. *Entrance requirements:* For master's and doctorate, GRE. Additional exam requirements/recommendations for international students: required—TOEFL. Electronic applications accepted.

Reliability Engineering

Arizona State University at Tempe, Ira A. Fulton Schools of Engineering, ASU Engineering Online Programs, Tempe, AZ 85287. Offers construction (MS); embedded systems (M Eng); enterprise systems innovation and management (MSE); modeling and simulation (M Eng); quality and reliability engineering (M Eng); software engineering (MSE); systems engineering (M Eng).

Rutgers University - New Brunswick, Graduate School-New Brunswick, Department of Industrial and Systems Engineering, Piscataway, NJ 08854-8097. Offers industrial and systems engineering (MS, PhD); information technology (MS); manufacturing

systems engineering (MS); quality and reliability engineering (MS). *Program availability:* Part-time, evening/weekend. Terminal master's awarded for partial completion of doctoral program. *Degree requirements:* For master's, thesis or alternative, seminar; for doctorate, comprehensive exam, thesis/dissertation. *Entrance requirements:* For master's and doctorate, GRE General Test. Additional exam requirements/recommendations for international students: required—TOEFL.

University of Maryland, College Park, Academic Affairs, A. James Clark School of Engineering, Department of Mechanical Engineering, Reliability Engineering Program,

College Park, MD 20742. Offers M Eng, MS, PhD. *Program availability:* Part-time, evening/weekend, online learning. *Degree requirements:* For master's, thesis optional; for doctorate, thesis/dissertation. *Entrance requirements:* For master's, GRE General Test, 3 letters of recommendation; for doctorate, GRE General Test, minimum GPA of 3.0. Additional exam requirements/recommendations for international students: required—TOEFL. Electronic applications accepted.

The University of Tennessee, Graduate School, Tickle College of Engineering, Department of Chemical and Biomolecular Engineering, Knoxville, TN 37996-2200. Offers chemical engineering (MS, PhD); reliability and maintainability engineering (MS); MS/MBA. *Program availability:* Part-time. *Faculty:* 18 full-time (1 woman). *Students:* 47 full-time (8 women), 3 part-time (0 women); includes 7 minority (2 Black or African American, non-Hispanic/Latino; 1 Asian, non-Hispanic/Latino; 4 Hispanic/Latino), 22 international. Average age 28. 57 applicants, 54% accepted, 11 enrolled. In 2019, 6 master's, 10 doctorates awarded. *Degree requirements:* For master's, thesis or alternative; for doctorate, comprehensive exam, thesis/dissertation. *Entrance requirements:* For master's, GRE General Test (for MS students pursuing research thesis), minimum GPA of 2.7 (for U.S. degree holders), 3.0 (for international degree holders); for doctorate, GRE General Test, minimum GPA of 3.0 on previous graduate course work. Additional exam requirements/recommendations for international students: required—TOEFL (minimum score 550 paper-based; 80 iBT), IELTS (minimum score 6.5). *Application deadline:* For fall admission, 2/1 priority date for domestic and international students; for spring admission, 6/15 for domestic and international students; for summer admission, 10/15 for domestic and international students. Applications are processed on a rolling basis. Application fee: $60. Electronic applications accepted. *Financial support:* In 2019–20, 69 students received support, including 13 fellowships (averaging $9,696 per year), 34 research assistantships with full tuition reimbursements available (averaging $26,620 per year), 22 teaching assistantships with full tuition reimbursements available (averaging $22,999 per year); career-related internships or fieldwork, Federal Work-Study, institutionally sponsored loans, health care benefits, and unspecified assistantships also available. Financial award application deadline: 2/1; financial award applicants required to submit FAFSA. *Unit head:* Dr. Bamin Khomami, Head, 865-974-2421, Fax: 865-974-7076, E-mail: bkhomami@utk.edu. *Application contact:* Dr. Cong Trinh, Graduate Recruiting Director, 865-974-2421, Fax: 865-974-7076, E-mail: ctrinh@utk.edu.
Website: http://www.engr.utk.edu/cbe/

The University of Tennessee, Graduate School, Tickle College of Engineering, Department of Industrial and Systems Engineering, Knoxville, TN 37966. Offers engineering management (MS); industrial engineering (MS, PhD); reliability and maintainability engineering (MS); MS/MBA. *Program availability:* Part-time, online learning. *Faculty:* 9 full-time (1 woman), 4 part-time/adjunct (1 woman). *Students:* 94 full-time (26 women), 51 part-time (15 women); includes 28 minority (13 Black or African American, non-Hispanic/Latino; 2 American Indian or Alaska Native, non-Hispanic/Latino; 5 Asian, non-Hispanic/Latino; 5 Hispanic/Latino; 3 Two or more races, non-Hispanic/Latino), 32 international. Average age 35. 77 applicants, 66% accepted, 28 enrolled. In 2019, 45 master's, 11 doctorates awarded. *Degree requirements:* For master's, thesis or alternative; for doctorate, comprehensive exam, thesis/dissertation. *Entrance requirements:* For master's, GRE General Test (for MS students pursuing research thesis), minimum GPA of 2.7 (for U.S. degree holders), 3.0 (for international degree holders); for doctorate, GRE General Test, minimum GPA of 3.0 on previous graduate course work. Additional exam requirements/recommendations for international students: required—TOEFL (minimum score 550 paper-based; 80 iBT), IELTS (minimum score 6.5). *Application deadline:* For fall admission, 2/1 priority date for domestic and international students; for spring admission, 6/15 for domestic and international students; for summer admission, 10/15 for domestic and international students. Applications are processed on a rolling basis. Application fee: $60. Electronic applications accepted. *Financial support:* In 2019–20, 61 students received support, including 9 fellowships with full tuition reimbursements available (averaging $22,671 per year), 36 research assistantships with full tuition reimbursements available (averaging $21,050 per year), 16 teaching assistantships with full tuition reimbursements available (averaging $19,219 per year); career-related internships or fieldwork, Federal Work-Study, institutionally sponsored loans, health care benefits, and unspecified assistantships also available. Financial award application deadline: 2/1; financial award applicants required to submit FAFSA. *Unit head:* Dr. John Kobza, Department Head, 865-974-3333, Fax: 865-974-0588, E-mail: jkobza@utk.edu. *Application contact:* Dr. Jim Ostrowski, Associate Professor and Director of Graduate Studies, 865-974-7657, E-mail: jostrows@utk.edu.
Website: http://www.engr.utk.edu/ie/

The University of Tennessee, Graduate School, Tickle College of Engineering, Department of Materials Science and Engineering, Knoxville, TN 37996-2200. Offers materials science and engineering (MS, PhD); reliability and maintainability engineering (MS); MS/MBA. *Program availability:* Part-time. *Faculty:* 26 full-time (5 women). *Students:* 78 full-time (28 women), 6 part-time (1 woman); includes 7 minority (2 Black or African American, non-Hispanic/Latino; 3 Asian, non-Hispanic/Latino; 2 Hispanic/Latino), 39 international. Average age 29. 85 applicants, 16% accepted, 11 enrolled. In 2019, 10 master's, 6 doctorates awarded. *Degree requirements:* For master's, thesis or alternative; for doctorate, comprehensive exam, thesis/dissertation. *Entrance requirements:* For master's, GRE General Test (for MS students pursuing research thesis), minimum GPA of 2.7 (for U.S. degree holders), 3.0 (for international degree holders); 3 references; for doctorate, GRE General Test, minimum GPA of 3.0 on previous graduate course work; 3 references. Additional exam requirements/recommendations for international students: required—TOEFL (minimum score 550 paper-based; 80 iBT), IELTS (minimum score 6.5). *Application deadline:* For fall admission, 2/1 priority date for domestic and international students; for spring admission, 6/15 for domestic and international students; for summer admission, 10/15 for domestic and international students. Applications are processed on a rolling basis. Application fee: $60. Electronic applications accepted. *Financial support:* In 2019–20, 103 students received support, including 17 fellowships with full tuition reimbursements available (averaging $11,364 per year), 65 research assistantships with full tuition reimbursements available (averaging $22,712 per year), 21 teaching assistantships with full tuition reimbursements available (averaging $21,410 per year); career-related internships or fieldwork, Federal Work-Study, institutionally sponsored loans, health care benefits, and unspecified assistantships also available. Financial award application deadline: 2/1; financial award applicants required to submit FAFSA. *Unit head:* Dr. Veerle Keppens, Head, 865-974-5336, Fax: 865-974-4115, E-mail: vkeppens@utk.edu. *Application contact:* Dr. Kurt Sickafus, Professor and Director of Graduate Studies, 865-974-4858, E-mail: kurt@utk.edu.
Website: http://www.engr.utk.edu/mse

The University of Tennessee, Graduate School, Tickle College of Engineering, Department of Nuclear Engineering, Program in Reliability and Maintainability Engineering, Knoxville, TN 37996. Offers MS. *Students:* 3 full-time (1 woman), 15 part-time (5 women); includes 3 minority (2 Asian, non-Hispanic/Latino; 1 Two or more races, non-Hispanic/Latino), 4 international. Average age 35. 9 applicants, 100% accepted, 7 enrolled. In 2019, 4 master's awarded. *Degree requirements:* For master's, thesis or alternative. *Entrance requirements:* For master's, GRE General Test (for MS students pursuing research thesis), minimum GPA of 2.7 (for U.S. degree holders), 3.0 (for international degree holders). Additional exam requirements/recommendations for international students: required—TOEFL (minimum score 550 paper-based; 80 iBT), IELTS (minimum score 6.5). *Application deadline:* For fall admission, 2/1 priority date for domestic and international students; for spring admission, 6/15 for domestic and international students; for summer admission, 10/15 for domestic and international students. Applications are processed on a rolling basis. Application fee: $60. Electronic applications accepted. *Financial support:* In 2019–20, 1 student received support, including 1 teaching assistantship with full tuition reimbursement available (averaging $20,000 per year); career-related internships or fieldwork, Federal Work-Study, institutionally sponsored loans, health care benefits, and unspecified assistantships also available. Financial award application deadline: 2/1; financial award applicants required to submit FAFSA. *Unit head:* Dr. J. Wesley Hines, PhD, Head, 865-974-2525, Fax: 865-974-0668, E-mail: jhines2@utk.edu. *Application contact:* Dr. Jason Hayward, PhD, Professor and Graduate Coordinator, 865-974-2525, E-mail: utne@utk.edu.
Website: http://www.engr.utk.edu/rme/

The University of Tennessee, Graduate School, Tickle College of Engineering, Min H. Kao Department of Electrical Engineering and Computer Science, Knoxville, TN 37996-2250. Offers computer engineering (MS, PhD); computer science (MS, PhD); electrical engineering (MS, PhD); reliability and maintainability engineering (MS); MS/MBA. *Program availability:* Part-time. *Faculty:* 61 full-time (9 women), 1 part-time/adjunct (0 women). *Students:* 229 full-time (39 women), 31 part-time (6 women); includes 25 minority (5 Black or African American, non-Hispanic/Latino; 15 Asian, non-Hispanic/Latino; 3 Hispanic/Latino; 2 Two or more races, non-Hispanic/Latino), 118 international. Average age 29. 342 applicants, 29% accepted, 60 enrolled. In 2019, 60 master's, 25 doctorates awarded. *Degree requirements:* For master's, thesis or alternative; for doctorate, comprehensive exam, thesis/dissertation. *Entrance requirements:* For master's, GRE General Test (for MS students pursuing research thesis), minimum GPA of 2.7 (for U.S. degree holders), 3.0 (for international degree holders); 3 references; personal statement; for doctorate, GRE General Test, minimum GPA of 3.0 on previous graduate course work; 3 references; personal statement. Additional exam requirements/recommendations for international students: required—TOEFL (minimum score 550 paper-based; 80 iBT), IELTS (minimum score 6.5). *Application deadline:* For fall admission, 2/1 priority date for domestic and international students; for spring admission, 6/15 for domestic and international students; for summer admission, 10/15 for domestic students, 10/16 for international students. Applications are processed on a rolling basis. Application fee: $60. Electronic applications accepted. *Financial support:* In 2019–20, 132 students received support, including 43 fellowships with full tuition reimbursements available (averaging $28,488 per year), 62 research assistantships with full tuition reimbursements available (averaging $22,550 per year), 27 teaching assistantships with full tuition reimbursements available (averaging $19,366 per year); career-related internships or fieldwork, Federal Work-Study, institutionally sponsored loans, health care benefits, and unspecified assistantships also available. Financial award application deadline: 2/1; financial award applicants required to submit FAFSA. *Unit head:* Dr. Gregory Peterson, PhD, Head, 865-974-3461, Fax: 865-974-5483, E-mail: gdp@utk.edu. *Application contact:* Dr. Jens Gregor, PhD, Associate Head, 865-974-4399, Fax: 865-974-5483, E-mail: jgregor@utk.edu.
Website: http://www.eecs.utk.edu

Safety Engineering

Embry-Riddle Aeronautical University–Prescott, Behavioral and Safety Sciences Department, Prescott, AZ 86301-3720. Offers aviation safety (MSSS). *Degree requirements:* For master's, research project, capstone, or thesis. *Entrance requirements:* For master's, transcripts, statement of goals, letters of recommendation, resume. Additional exam requirements/recommendations for international students: required—TOEFL (minimum score 550 paper-based; 79 iBT), IELTS (minimum score 6). Electronic applications accepted.

Florida Institute of Technology, College of Aeronautics, Program in Applied Aviation Safety, Melbourne, FL 32901-6975. Offers applied aviation safety (MSA). *Program availability:* Part-time. *Degree requirements:* For master's, comprehensive exam (for some programs), thesis optional, 36 credit hours. *Entrance requirements:* For master's, GRE, 3 letters of recommendation, resume, statement of objectives. Additional exam requirements/recommendations for international students: required—TOEFL (minimum score 550 paper-based; 79 iBT). Electronic applications accepted.

Indiana University Bloomington, School of Public Health, Department of Applied Health Science, Bloomington, IN 47405. Offers behavioral, social, and community health (MPH); family health (MPH); health behavior (PhD); nutrition science (MS); professional health education (MPH); public health administration (MPH); safety management (MS); school and college health education (MS). *Degree requirements:* For master's, thesis optional; for doctorate, comprehensive exam, thesis/dissertation. *Entrance requirements:* For master's, GRE (for MS in nutrition science), 3 recommendations; for doctorate, GRE, 3 recommendations. Additional exam requirements/recommendations for international students: required—TOEFL (minimum score 550 paper-based; 80 iBT). Electronic applications accepted.

Murray State University, Jesse D. Jones College of Science, Engineering and Technology, Department of Occupational Safety and Health, Murray, KY 42071. Offers environmental science (MS). *Program availability:* Part-time, evening/weekend, 100% online, blended/hybrid learning. *Entrance requirements:* For master's, GRE or GMAT, minimum university GPA of 2.75. Additional exam requirements/recommendations for international students: required—TOEFL (minimum score 527 paper-based; 71 iBT). Electronic applications accepted.

New Jersey Institute of Technology, Newark College of Engineering, Newark, NJ 07102. Offers biomedical engineering (MS, PhD); biopharmaceutical engineering (MS); chemical engineering (MS, PhD); civil engineering (MS, PhD); computer engineering (MS); critical infrastructure systems (MS); electrical engineering (MS, PhD); engineering management (MS); engineering science (MS); environmental engineering (MS, PhD); healthcare systems management (MS); industrial engineering (MS, PhD); internet engineering (MS); manufacturing systems engineering (MS); materials science &

engineering (PhD); materials science and engineering (MS); mechanical engineering (MS, PhD); occupational safety and health engineering (MS). *Program availability:* Part-time, evening/weekend. *Faculty:* 151 full-time (29 women), 135 part-time/adjunct (15 women). *Students:* 576 full-time (161 women), 528 part-time (111 women); includes 366 minority (61 Black or African American, non-Hispanic/Latino; 1 American Indian or Alaska Native, non-Hispanic/Latino; 166 Asian, non-Hispanic/Latino; 115 Hispanic/Latino; 23 Two or more races, non-Hispanic/Latino), 450 international. Average age 28. 2,053 applicants, 67% accepted, 338 enrolled. In 2019, 474 master's, 30 doctorates awarded. Terminal master's awarded for partial completion of doctoral program. *Degree requirements:* For master's, thesis (for some programs); for doctorate, thesis/dissertation. *Entrance requirements:* For master's, GRE General Test, minimum GPA 2.8, personal statement, 1 letter of recommendation, transcripts; for doctorate, GRE General Test, minimum GPA of 3.5, personal statement, 3 letters of recommendation, transcripts. Additional exam requirements/recommendations for international students: required—TOEFL (minimum score 550 paper-based; 79 iBT), IELTS (minimum score 6.5). *Application deadline:* For fall admission, 6/1 priority date for domestic students, 5/1 priority date for international students; for spring admission, 11/15 priority date for domestic and international students. Applications are processed on a rolling basis. Application fee: $75. Electronic applications accepted. *Expenses:* $23,828 per year (in-state), $33,744 per year (out-of-state). *Financial support:* In 2019–20, 352 students received support, including 33 fellowships with full tuition reimbursements available (averaging $24,000 per year), 89 research assistantships with full tuition reimbursements available (averaging $24,000 per year), 112 teaching assistantships with full tuition reimbursements available (averaging $24,000 per year); career-related internships or fieldwork, Federal Work-Study, scholarships/grants, and unspecified assistantships also available. Financial award application deadline: 1/15. *Unit head:* Dr. Moshe Kam, Dean, 973-596-5534, Fax: 973-596-2316, E-mail: moshe.kam@njit.edu. *Application contact:* Stephen Eck, Executive Director of University Admissions, 973-596-3300, Fax: 973-596-3461, E-mail: admissions@njit.edu.
Website: http://engineering.njit.edu/

Rochester Institute of Technology, Graduate Enrollment Services, College of Applied Science and Technology, School of Engineering Technology, MS Program in Environmental, Health and Safety Management, Rochester, NY 14623-5603. Offers MS. *Program availability:* Part-time, evening/weekend, 100% online, blended/hybrid learning. *Degree requirements:* For master's, thesis or alternative. *Entrance requirements:* For master's, minimum GPA of 3.0 (recommended). Additional exam requirements/recommendations for international students: required—TOEFL (minimum score 88 iBT), IELTS (minimum score 6.5), PTE (minimum score 61). Electronic applications accepted. *Expenses:* Contact institution.

The University of Alabama at Birmingham, School of Engineering, Professional Engineering Degrees, Birmingham, AL 35294. Offers advanced safety engineering and management (M Eng); construction engineering management (M Eng); design and commercialization (M Eng); information engineering management (M Eng); structural engineering (M Eng); sustainable smart cities (M Eng). *Program availability:* Part-time, evening/weekend, online only, 100% online. *Faculty:* 5 full-time (1 woman), 15 part-time/adjunct (3 women). *Students:* 13 full-time (4 women), 315 part-time (70 women); includes 83 minority (64 Black or African American, non-Hispanic/Latino; 3 American Indian or Alaska Native, non-Hispanic/Latino; 9 Asian, non-Hispanic/Latino; 7 Hispanic/Latino), 8 international. 126 applicants, 84% accepted, 90 enrolled. In 2019, 123 master's awarded. *Entrance requirements:* For master's, 3.0 GPA on 4.0 scale, undergraduate degree from a nationally accredited school. Additional exam requirements/recommendations for international students: required—TOEFL (minimum score 80 iBT); recommended—IELTS (minimum score 6.5). *Application deadline:* For fall admission, 8/1 for domestic and international students; for spring admission, 12/1 for domestic and international students; for summer admission, 5/1 for domestic and international students. Applications are processed on a rolling basis. Application fee: $50 ($60 for international students). Electronic applications accepted. *Expenses:* Contact institution. *Unit head:* Dr. Gregg Janowski, Associate Dean for Graduate Programs and Assessment, E-mail: janowski@uab.edu. *Application contact:* Jesse Kepply, Director of Student and Academic Services, 205-996-5696, E-mail: gradschool@uab.edu.

University of Minnesota, Duluth, Graduate School, Swenson College of Science and Engineering, Department of Mechanical and Industrial Engineering, Duluth, MN 55812-2496. Offers engineering management (MSEM); environmental health and safety (MEHS). *Program availability:* Part-time, evening/weekend, online learning. *Degree requirements:* For master's, comprehensive exam, thesis or alternative, capstone design project (MSEM), field project (MEHS). *Entrance requirements:* For master's, GRE (MEHS), interview (MEHS), letters of recommendation. Additional exam requirements/recommendations for international students: required—TOEFL (minimum score 550 paper-based).

University of Southern California, Graduate School, Viterbi School of Engineering, Daniel J. Epstein Department of Industrial and Systems Engineering, Los Angeles, CA 90089. Offers digital supply chain management (MS); engineering management (MS); engineering technology communication (Graduate Certificate); health systems operations (Graduate Certificate); industrial and systems engineering (MS, PhD, Engr); manufacturing engineering (MS); operations research engineering (MS); optimization and supply chain management (Graduate Certificate); product development engineering (MS); safety systems and security (MS); systems architecting and engineering (MS, Graduate Certificate); systems safety and security (Graduate Certificate); transportation systems (Graduate Certificate); MS/MBA. *Program availability:* Part-time, evening/weekend, online learning. Terminal master's awarded for partial completion of doctoral program. *Degree requirements:* For master's, thesis optional; for doctorate, thesis/dissertation. *Entrance requirements:* For master's and doctorate, GRE General Test. Additional exam requirements/recommendations for international students: recommended—TOEFL. Electronic applications accepted.

West Virginia University, Statler College of Engineering and Mineral Resources, Morgantown, WV 26506. Offers aerospace engineering (MSAE, PhD); chemical engineering (MS Ch E, PhD); civil engineering (MSCE, PhD); computer engineering (PhD); computer science (MSCS, PhD); electrical engineering (MSEE, PhD); energy systems engineering (MSESE); engineering (MSE); industrial engineering (MSIE, PhD); industrial hygiene (MS); material science and engineering (MSMSE, PhD); mechanical engineering (MSME, PhD); mining engineering (MS Min E, PhD); petroleum and natural gas engineering (MSPNGE, PhD); safety management (MS); software engineering (MSSE). *Program availability:* Part-time. Terminal master's awarded for partial completion of doctoral program. *Degree requirements:* For master's, thesis optional; for doctorate, comprehensive exam, thesis/dissertation. *Entrance requirements:* Additional exam requirements/recommendations for international students: required—TOEFL (minimum score 550 paper-based). Electronic applications accepted. *Expenses:* Contact institution.

Systems Engineering

Air Force Institute of Technology, Graduate School of Engineering and Management, Department of Aeronautics and Astronautics, Dayton, OH 45433-7765. Offers aeronautical engineering (MS, PhD); astronautical engineering (MS, PhD); materials science (MS, PhD); space operations (MS); systems engineering (MS, PhD). *Accreditation:* ABET (one or more programs are accredited). *Program availability:* Part-time. *Degree requirements:* For master's, thesis; for doctorate, thesis/dissertation. *Entrance requirements:* For master's and doctorate, GRE General Test, minimum GPA of 3.0, U.S. citizenship.

Arizona State University at Tempe, Ira A. Fulton Schools of Engineering, ASU Engineering Online Programs, Tempe, AZ 85287. Offers construction (MS); embedded systems (M Eng); enterprise systems innovation and management (MSE); modeling and simulation (M Eng); quality and reliability engineering (M Eng); software engineering (MSE); systems engineering (M Eng).

Auburn University, Graduate School, Samuel Ginn College of Engineering, Department of Industrial and Systems Engineering, Auburn University, AL 36849. Offers MISE, MS, PhD, Graduate Certificate. *Program availability:* Part-time. *Faculty:* 18 full-time (2 women), 1 part-time/adjunct (0 women). *Students:* 68 full-time (20 women), 86 part-time (24 women); includes 22 minority (11 Black or African American, non-Hispanic/Latino; 4 Asian, non-Hispanic/Latino; 6 Hispanic/Latino; 1 Two or more races, non-Hispanic/Latino), 55 international. Average age 32. 174 applicants, 50% accepted, 33 enrolled. In 2019, 38 master's, 13 doctorates, 20 other advanced degrees awarded. *Degree requirements:* For master's, thesis, thesis (MS); for doctorate, thesis/dissertation. *Entrance requirements:* For master's and doctorate, GRE General Test. Additional exam requirements/recommendations for international students: required—TOEFL (minimum score 550 paper-based; 79 iBT). *Application deadline:* For fall admission, 3/31 priority date for domestic and international students; for spring admission, 9/30 priority date for domestic and international students. Applications are processed on a rolling basis. Application fee: $60 ($70 for international students). Electronic applications accepted. *Expenses: Tuition, area resident:* Full-time $9828; part-time $546 per credit hour. Tuition, state resident: full-time $9828; part-time $546 per credit hour. Tuition, nonresident: full-time $29,484; part-time $1638 per credit hour. *International tuition:* $29,744 full-time. Tuition and fees vary according to course load, program and reciprocity agreements. *Financial support:* In 2019–20, 66 fellowships, 35 research assistantships (averaging $12,812 per year), 30 teaching assistantships (averaging $13,793 per year) were awarded; Federal Work-Study also available. Support available to part-time students. Financial award application deadline: 3/15; financial award applicants required to submit FAFSA. *Unit head:* Dr. John Evans, Chair, 334-844-1418, E-mail: evansjl@auburn.edu. *Application contact:* Dr. George Flowers, Dean of the Graduate School, 334-844-2125.
Website: http://www.eng.auburn.edu/insy/

Boston University, College of Engineering, Division of Systems Engineering, Brookline, MA 02215. Offers systems engineering (M Eng, MS, PhD), including engineering practice (M Eng). *Program availability:* Part-time. *Students:* 61 full-time (19 women), 7 part-time (1 woman); includes 2 minority (both Asian, non-Hispanic/Latino), 55 international. Average age 25. 273 applicants, 37% accepted, 24 enrolled. In 2019, 17 master's, 4 doctorates awarded. Terminal master's awarded for partial completion of doctoral program. *Degree requirements:* For master's, thesis (for some programs); for doctorate, comprehensive exam, thesis/dissertation. *Entrance requirements:* For master's and doctorate, GRE General Test. Additional exam requirements/recommendations for international students: required—TOEFL (minimum score 90 iBT), IELTS (minimum score 7). Application fee: $95. Application fee is waived when completed online. *Financial support:* Application deadline: 1/15. *Unit head:* Dr. Christos Cassandras, Division Head, 617-353-7154, Fax: 617-353-5548, E-mail: cgc@bu.edu. *Application contact:* Dr. Christos Cassandras, Division Head, 617-353-7154, Fax: 617-353-5548, E-mail: cgc@bu.edu.
Website: http://www.bu.edu/se/

California Institute of Technology, Division of Engineering and Applied Science, Option in Control and Dynamical Systems, Pasadena, CA 91125-0001. Offers MS, PhD. *Degree requirements:* For doctorate, thesis/dissertation.

California State Polytechnic University, Pomona, Program in Systems Engineering, Pomona, CA 91768-2557. Offers systems engineering (MS). *Program availability:* Part-time, evening/weekend. *Entrance requirements:* Additional exam requirements/recommendations for international students: required—TOEFL (minimum score 550 paper-based). Electronic applications accepted. *Expenses:* Contact institution.

California State University, Fullerton, Graduate Studies, College of Engineering and Computer Science, Department of Electrical Engineering, Fullerton, CA 92831-3599. Offers electrical engineering (MS); systems engineering (MS). *Program availability:* Part-time. *Degree requirements:* For master's, comprehensive exam, project or thesis. *Entrance requirements:* For master's, GRE General Test, GRE Subject Test, minimum undergraduate GPA of 2.5, 3.0 graduate.

California State University, Northridge, Graduate Studies, College of Engineering and Computer Science, Department of Manufacturing Systems Engineering and Management, Northridge, CA 91330. Offers engineering automation (MS); engineering management (MS); manufacturing systems engineering (MS); materials engineering (MS). *Program availability:* Online learning. *Entrance requirements:* For master's, GRE (if cumulative undergraduate GPA less than 3.0).

Carleton University, Faculty of Graduate Studies, Faculty of Engineering and Design, Ottawa-Carleton Institute for Electrical Engineering, Department of Systems and Computer Engineering, Ottawa, ON K1S 5B6, Canada. Offers electrical engineering (MA Sc, PhD); information and systems science (M Sc); technology innovation management (M Eng, MA Sc). *Degree requirements:* For master's, thesis optional. *Entrance requirements:* For master's, honors degree. Additional exam requirements/recommendations for international students: required—TOEFL.

Carnegie Mellon University, Carnegie Institute of Technology, Information Networking Institute, Pittsburgh, PA 15213. Offers information networking (MS); information security (MS); information technology - information security (MS); information technology - mobility (MS); information technology - software management (MS). *Degree requirements:* For master's, thesis optional. *Entrance requirements:* For master's, GRE General Test, bachelor's degree in computer science, computer engineering, or electrical engineering, or related technology degree; programming skills (C/C++ fluency for some programs). Additional exam requirements/recommendations for international students: required—TOEFL.

Case Western Reserve University, School of Graduate Studies, Case School of Engineering, Department of Computer and Data Sciences, Cleveland, OH 44106. Offers computer engineering (MS, PhD); computing and information sciences (MS, PhD); electrical engineering (MS, PhD); systems and control engineering (MS, PhD). *Program availability:* Part-time, evening/weekend, online only, 100% online. Terminal master's awarded for partial completion of doctoral program. *Degree requirements:* For master's, thesis; for doctorate, thesis/dissertation, qualifying exam, teaching experience. *Entrance requirements:* For master's and doctorate, GRE General Test. Additional exam requirements/recommendations for international students: required—TOEFL.

The Catholic University of America, School of Engineering, Program in Engineering Management, Washington, DC 20064. Offers engineering management (MSE, Certificate), including engineering management and organization (MSE), project and systems engineering management (MSE), technology management (MSE); program management (Certificate); systems engineering and management of information technology (Certificate). *Program availability:* Part-time. *Faculty:* 8 part-time/adjunct (4 women). *Students:* 18 full-time (2 women), 12 part-time (2 women); includes 5 minority (1 Asian, non-Hispanic/Latino; 4 Two or more races, non-Hispanic/Latino), 19 international. Average age 29. 40 applicants, 80% accepted, 14 enrolled. In 2019, 20 master's awarded. *Degree requirements:* For master's, minimum GPA of 3.0. *Entrance requirements:* For master's and Certificate, statement of purpose, official copies of academic transcripts, two letters of recommendation. Additional exam requirements/recommendations for international students: required—TOEFL (minimum score 550 paper-based; 80 iBT). *Application deadline:* For fall admission, 7/15 priority date for domestic students, 7/1 for international students; for spring admission, 11/15 priority date for domestic students, 11/1 for international students. Applications are processed on a rolling basis. Application fee: $55. Electronic applications accepted. *Expenses:* Contact institution. *Financial support:* Fellowships, research assistantships, teaching assistantships, Federal Work-Study, scholarships/grants, tuition waivers (full and partial), and unspecified assistantships available. Financial award application deadline: 2/1; financial award applicants required to submit FAFSA. *Unit head:* Melvin G. Williams, Jr., Director, 202-319-5191, Fax: 202-319-6860, E-mail: williamsme@cua.edu. *Application contact:* Dr. Steven Brown, Director of Graduate Admissions, 202-319-5057, Fax: 202-319-6533, E-mail: cua-admissions@cua.edu.
Website: https://engineering.catholic.edu/management/index.html

The Citadel, The Military College of South Carolina, Citadel Graduate College, School of Engineering, Department of Engineering Leadership and Program Management, Charleston, SC 29409. Offers project management (MS); systems engineering management (Graduate Certificate); technical program management (Graduate Certificate); technical project management (Graduate Certificate). *Program availability:* Part-time, evening/weekend. *Entrance requirements:* For master's, GRE or GMAT, minimum of one year of professional experience or permission from department head; two letters of reference; resume detailing previous work; for Graduate Certificate, one-page letter of intent; resume detailing previous work. Additional exam requirements/recommendations for international students: required—TOEFL (minimum score 550 paper-based; 79 iBT). Electronic applications accepted.

Colorado State University, Walter Scott, Jr. College of Engineering, Program in Engineering Science, Fort Collins, CO 80523. Offers engineering education (ME). *Program availability:* Part-time, evening/weekend, 100% online, blended/hybrid learning. Terminal master's awarded for partial completion of doctoral program. *Degree requirements:* For master's, comprehensive exam (for some programs), thesis (for some programs); for doctorate, comprehensive exam, thesis/dissertation. *Entrance requirements:* For master's and doctorate, GRE, relevant degree. Additional exam requirements/recommendations for international students: required—TOEFL (minimum score 550 paper-based; 80 iBT), IELTS (minimum score 6.5). Electronic applications accepted. *Expenses:* Contact institution.

Colorado State University-Pueblo, College of Education, Engineering and Professional Studies, Department of Engineering, Pueblo, CO 81001-4901. Offers industrial and systems engineering (MS). *Degree requirements:* For master's, thesis optional. *Entrance requirements:* For master's, GRE General Test. Additional exam requirements/recommendations for international students: required—TOEFL (minimum score 500 paper-based).

Colorado Technical University Aurora, Program in Systems Engineering, Aurora, CO 80014. Offers MS.

Colorado Technical University Colorado Springs, Graduate Studies, Program in Systems Engineering, Colorado Springs, CO 80907. Offers MS.

Concordia University, School of Graduate Studies, Faculty of Engineering and Computer Science, Concordia Institute for Information Systems Engineering (CIISE), Montréal, QC H3G 1M8, Canada. Offers 3D graphics and game development (Certificate); information and systems engineering (PhD); information systems security (M Eng, MA Sc); quality systems engineering (M Eng, MA Sc); service engineering and network management (Certificate).

Cornell University, Graduate School, Graduate Fields of Engineering, Field of Systems Engineering, Ithaca, NY 14853. Offers M Eng, PhD. *Degree requirements:* For master's, thesis. *Entrance requirements:* For master's, GRE General Test. Additional exam requirements/recommendations for international students: required—TOEFL (minimum score 600 paper-based; 77 iBT).

Dartmouth College, Dartmouth Engineering - Thayer School of Engineering, Program in Mechanical Engineering, Hanover, NH 03755. Offers MS, PhD. Terminal master's awarded for partial completion of doctoral program. *Degree requirements:* For master's, thesis (for some programs); for doctorate, thesis/dissertation. *Entrance requirements:* For master's and doctorate, GRE General Test. Additional exam requirements/recommendations for international students: required—TOEFL, IELTS. *Application deadline:* For fall admission, 1/1 priority date for domestic students, 1/1 for international students. Applications are processed on a rolling basis. Application fee: $45. Electronic applications accepted. *Financial support:* Fellowships, research assistantships, teaching assistantships, career-related internships or fieldwork, institutionally sponsored loans, scholarships/grants, and tuition waivers (full and partial) available. Financial award application deadline: 2/15; financial award applicants required to submit CSS PROFILE. *Unit head:* Dr. Laura Ray, Professor of Engineering, 603-646-1243, E-mail: laura.ray@dartmouth.edu. *Application contact:* Candace S. Potter, Graduate Admissions & Financial Aid Administrator, 603-646-3844, Fax: 603-646-1620, E-mail: candace.s.potter@dartmouth.edu.
Website: http://engineering.dartmouth.edu/

Embry-Riddle Aeronautical University–Daytona, Program in Unmanned and Autonomous Systems Engineering, Daytona Beach, FL 32114-3900. Offers systems engineering (MSUASE); technical (MSUASE); unmanned aircraft systems (MSUASE). *Degree requirements:* For master's, coursework, coursework plus two-semester capstone project, or thesis. *Entrance requirements:* Additional exam requirements/

recommendations for international students: required—TOEFL (minimum score 550 paper-based, 79 iBT) or IELTS (6). Electronic applications accepted.

Embry-Riddle Aeronautical University–Worldwide, Department of Decision Sciences, Daytona Beach, FL 32114-3900. Offers aviation and aerospace (MSPM); aviation/aerospace management (MSEM); financial management (MSEM, MSPM); general management (MSPM); global management (MSPM); human resources management (MSPM); information systems (MSPM); leadership (MSEM, MSPM); logistics and supply chain management (MSEM, MSLSCM, MSPM); management (MSEM, MSPM); project management (MSEM); systems engineering (MSEM, MSPM); technical management (MSPM). *Program availability:* Part-time, evening/weekend, EagleVision Classroom (between classrooms), EagleVision Home (faculty and students at home), and a blend of Classroom or Home. *Degree requirements:* For master's, comprehensive exam (for some programs), thesis (for some programs). *Entrance requirements:* Additional exam requirements/recommendations for international students: required—TOEFL (minimum score 550 paper-based; 79 iBT), IELTS (minimum score 6). Electronic applications accepted. *Expenses:* Contact institution.

Embry-Riddle Aeronautical University–Worldwide, Department of Engineering and Technology, Daytona Beach, FL 32114-3900. Offers aerospace engineering (MS); entrepreneurship in technology (MS); systems engineering (M Sys E), including engineering management, technical. *Program availability:* Part-time, evening/weekend, 100% online, blended/hybrid learning. *Entrance requirements:* For master's, GRE (for MS in aerospace engineering). Additional exam requirements/recommendations for international students: required—TOEFL (minimum score 550 paper-based; 79 iBT), IELTS (minimum score 6). Electronic applications accepted. *Expenses:* Contact institution.

Florida Institute of Technology, College of Engineering and Science, Program in Systems Engineering, Melbourne, FL 32901-6975. Offers MS, PhD. *Program availability:* Part-time. *Degree requirements:* For master's, comprehensive exam (for some programs), thesis optional, 30 credit hours; for doctorate, comprehensive exam, thesis/dissertation, 24 credit hours of coursework, 24 credit hours of research, technical paper in review for a peer reviewed journal and presented at recognized conference. *Entrance requirements:* For master's, GRE, minimum GPA of 3.0, 3 letters of recommendation, resume, bachelor's degree in engineering from ABET-accredited program, statement of objectives; for doctorate, GRE (minimum score of 315), minimum GPA of 3.5, 3 letters of recommendation, resume, statement of objectives. Additional exam requirements/recommendations for international students: required—TOEFL (minimum score 550 paper-based; 79 iBT). Electronic applications accepted.

George Mason University, Volgenau School of Engineering, Department of Systems Engineering and Operations Research, Fairfax, VA 22030. Offers operations research (MS); systems engineering and operations research (PhD, Certificate). *Program availability:* Evening/weekend, 100% online. *Degree requirements:* For master's, thesis optional; for doctorate, comprehensive exam, thesis/dissertation, qualifying exams. *Entrance requirements:* For master's, GRE General Test, BS in related field; minimum GPA of 3.0; 3 letters of recommendation; 2 official transcripts; expanded goals statement; proof of financial support; photocopy of passport; official bank statement; multivariable calculus, applied probability, statistics and a computer language course; self-evaluation form; for doctorate, GRE, MS with minimum GPA of 3.5; BS with minimum GPA of 3.0 in systems or operational research; 2 official transcripts; 3 letters of recommendation; resume; expanded goals statement; self evaluation form; photocopy of passport; official bank statement; proof of financial support; for Certificate, personal goals statement; 2 official transcripts; self-evaluation form; letter of recommendation; resume; official bank statement; photocopy of passport; proof of financial support; baccalaureate degree in related field. Additional exam requirements/recommendations for international students: required—TOEFL (minimum score 575 paper-based; 88 iBT), IELTS (minimum score 6.5), PTE (minimum score 59). Electronic applications accepted. *Expenses:* Contact institution.

Georgetown University, Graduate School of Arts and Sciences, School of Continuing Studies, Washington, DC 20057. Offers American studies (MALS); applied intelligence (MPS); Catholic studies (MALS); classical civilizations (MALS); emergency and disaster management (MPS); ethics and the professions (MALS); global strategic communications (MPS); hospitality management (MPS); human resources management (MPS); humanities (MALS); individualized study (MALS); integrated marketing communications (MPS); international affairs (MALS); Islam and Muslim-Christian relations (MALS); journalism (MPS); liberal studies (DLS); literature and society (MALS); medieval and early modern European studies (MALS); public relations and corporate communications (MPS); real estate (MPS); religious studies (MALS); social and public policy (MALS); sports industry management (MPS); systems engineering management (MPS); technology management (MPS); the theory and practice of American democracy (MALS); urban and regional planning (MPS); visual culture (MALS). *Entrance requirements:* Additional exam requirements/recommendations for international students: required—TOEFL.

The George Washington University, School of Engineering and Applied Science, Department of Engineering Management and Systems Engineering, Washington, DC 20052. Offers system engineering (PhD). *Program availability:* Part-time, evening/weekend. *Degree requirements:* For master's, thesis optional; for doctorate, one foreign language, thesis/dissertation, final and qualifying exams, submission of articles; for other advanced degree, professional project. *Entrance requirements:* For master's, appropriate bachelor's degree, minimum GPA of 2.7, second-semester calculus; for doctorate, appropriate master's degree, minimum GPA of 3.5, 2 letters of recommendation; for other advanced degree, appropriate master's degree, minimum GPA of 3.4. Additional exam requirements/recommendations for international students: required—TOEFL or The George Washington University English as a Foreign Language Test.

Georgia Southern University, Jack N. Averitt College of Graduate Studies, Allen E. Paulson College of Engineering and Computing, Department of Electrical and Computer Engineering, Statesboro, GA 30458. Offers MSAE. *Faculty:* 14 full-time (1 woman), 1 part-time/adjunct (0 women). *Students:* 17 full-time (0 women), 7 part-time (0 women); includes 3 minority (2 Black or African American, non-Hispanic/Latino; 1 Hispanic/Latino), 12 international. Average age 28. 37 applicants, 78% accepted, 5 enrolled. In 2019, 8 master's awarded. *Degree requirements:* For master's, thesis optional. *Entrance requirements:* For master's, GRE, minimum GPA of 2.75. Additional exam requirements/recommendations for international students: required—TOEFL (minimum score 550 paper-based; 80 iBT), IELTS (minimum score 6). *Application deadline:* For fall admission, 3/1 priority date for domestic students, 6/1 for international students; for spring admission, 10/1 priority date for domestic students, 10/1 for international students. Applications are processed on a rolling basis. Application fee: $50. Electronic applications accepted. *Expenses:* Tuition, area resident: Full-time $4986; part-time $277 per credit hour. Tuition, nonresident: full-time $19,890; part-time $1105 per credit hour. *International tuition:* $19,890 full-time. *Required fees:* $2114; $1057 per semester. $1057 per semester. Tuition and fees vary according to course load, campus/location and program. *Financial support:* In 2019–20, 20 students received support. Unspecified assistantships available. Financial award application deadline: 4/20; financial award applicants required to submit FAFSA. *Unit head:* Dr. Sungkyun Lim, Program

Coordinator, 912-478-2266, E-mail: sklim@georgiasouthern.edu. *Application contact:* Dr. Sungkyun Lim, Program Coordinator, 912-478-2266, E-mail: sklim@georgiasouthern.edu.

Harrisburg University of Science and Technology, Program in Information Systems Engineering and Management, Harrisburg, PA 17101. Offers analytics (MS); digital government (MS); digital health (MS); entrepreneurship (MS); information security (MS); software engineering and systems development (MS). *Program availability:* Part-time, evening/weekend. *Degree requirements:* For master's, thesis optional. *Entrance requirements:* For master's, baccalaureate degree. Additional exam requirements/recommendations for international students: required—TOEFL (minimum score 520 paper-based; 80 iBT); recommended—IELTS (minimum score 6). Electronic applications accepted. *Expenses: Tuition:* Full-time $15,900; part-time $7950 per credit hour.

Indiana University Bloomington, School of Informatics, Computing, and Engineering, Program in Intelligent Systems Engineering, Bloomington, IN 47405-7000. Offers PhD. *Program availability:* Part-time. *Degree requirements:* For doctorate, thesis/dissertation, qualifying exam. *Entrance requirements:* For doctorate, GRE, statement of purpose, curriculum vitae, 3 letters of recommendation, transcripts. Additional exam requirements/recommendations for international students: required—TOEFL. Electronic applications accepted.

Instituto Tecnológico y de Estudios Superiores de Monterrey, Campus Chihuahua, Graduate Programs, Chihuahua, Mexico. Offers computer systems engineering (Ingeniero); electrical engineering (Ingeniero); electromechanical engineering (Ingeniero); electronic engineering (Ingeniero); engineering administration (MEA); industrial engineering (MIE, Ingeniero); international trade (MIT); mechanical engineering (Ingeniero).

Instituto Tecnológico y de Estudios Superiores de Monterrey, Campus Monterrey, Graduate and Research Division, Programs in Engineering, Monterrey, Mexico. Offers applied statistics (M Eng); artificial intelligence (PhD); automation engineering (M Eng); chemical engineering (M Eng); civil engineering (M Eng); electrical engineering (M Eng); electronic engineering (M Eng); environmental engineering (M Eng); industrial engineering (M Eng, PhD); manufacturing engineering (M Eng); mechanical engineering (M Eng); systems and quality engineering (M Eng). *Program availability:* Part-time, evening/weekend. Terminal master's awarded for partial completion of doctoral program. *Degree requirements:* For master's, one foreign language, thesis; for doctorate, one foreign language, thesis/dissertation. *Entrance requirements:* For master's, EXADEP; for doctorate, GRE, master's degree in related field. Additional exam requirements/recommendations for international students: required—TOEFL.

Iowa State University of Science and Technology, Program in Systems Engineering, Ames, IA 50011. Offers M Eng. *Entrance requirements:* Additional exam requirements/recommendations for international students: required—TOEFL (minimum score 550 paper-based; 79 iBT), IELTS (minimum score 6.5). Electronic applications accepted.

Johns Hopkins University, Engineering Program for Professionals, Part-time Program in Systems Engineering, Baltimore, MD 21218. Offers MS, MSE, Graduate Certificate, Post-Master's Certificate. *Accreditation:* ABET. *Program availability:* Part-time, evening/weekend, 100% online, blended/hybrid learning. *Entrance requirements:* Additional exam requirements/recommendations for international students: required—TOEFL (minimum score 600 paper-based; 100 iBT). Electronic applications accepted.

Kennesaw State University, Southern Polytechnic College of Engineering and Engineering Technology, Program in Systems Engineering, Kennesaw, GA 30144. Offers systems engineering (MS). *Program availability:* Part-time, evening/weekend, online learning. *Students:* 2 full-time (1 woman), 38 part-time (5 women); includes 19 minority (8 Black or African American, non-Hispanic/Latino; 4 Asian, non-Hispanic/Latino; 5 Hispanic/Latino; 2 Two or more races, non-Hispanic/Latino), 1 international. Average age 34. 20 applicants, 85% accepted, 13 enrolled. In 2019, 6 master's awarded. *Degree requirements:* For master's, thesis optional. *Entrance requirements:* For master's, GRE. Additional exam requirements/recommendations for international students: required—TOEFL (minimum score 80 iBT), IELTS (minimum score 6.5). *Application deadline:* For fall admission, 7/1 priority date for domestic students, 5/1 for international students; for spring admission, 11/1 priority date for domestic students, 11/1 for international students. Applications are processed on a rolling basis. Application fee: $60. Electronic applications accepted. *Expenses: Tuition, area resident:* Full-time $7104; part-time $296 per credit hour. Tuition, state resident: full-time $7104; part-time $296 per credit hour. Tuition, nonresident: full-time $25,584; part-time $1066 per credit hour. *International tuition:* $25,584 full-time. *Required fees:* $2006; $1706 per unit. $853 per semester. *Financial support:* Applicants required to submit FAFSA. *Application contact:* Admissions Counselor, 470-578-4377, E-mail: ksugrad@kennesaw.edu. Website: http://engineering.kennesaw.edu/systems-industrial/degrees/ms-systems.php

Lehigh University, P.C. Rossin College of Engineering and Applied Science, Department of Industrial and Systems Engineering, Bethlehem, PA 18015. Offers analytical finance (MS); healthcare systems engineering (M Eng, Certificate); industrial and systems engineering (M Eng, MS, PhD); management science and engineering (M Eng, MS); MBA/E. *Program availability:* Part-time, blended/hybrid learning. *Faculty:* 18 full-time (1 woman), 1 part-time/adjunct (0 women). *Students:* 71 full-time (16 women), 9 part-time (4 women); includes 2 minority (1 Asian, non-Hispanic/Latino; 1 Hispanic/Latino), 73 international. Average age 25. 290 applicants, 39% accepted, 26 enrolled. In 2019, 31 master's, 12 doctorates awarded. Terminal master's awarded for partial completion of doctoral program. *Degree requirements:* For master's, thesis (MS); project (M Eng); for doctorate, comprehensive exam, thesis/dissertation. *Entrance requirements:* For master's and doctorate, GRE General Test. Additional exam requirements/recommendations for international students: required—TOEFL (minimum score 550 paper-based; 79 iBT), IELTS (minimum score 6.5), TOEFL or IELTS required. *Application deadline:* For fall admission, 7/15 for domestic and international students; for spring admission, 12/1 for domestic and international students. Application fee: $75. *Financial support:* In 2019–20, 33 students received support, including 2 fellowships with full tuition reimbursements available (averaging $20,490 per year), 18 research assistantships with full tuition reimbursements available (averaging $20,490 per year), 11 teaching assistantships with full tuition reimbursements available (averaging $21,105 per year); health care benefits and unspecified assistantships also available. Financial award application deadline: 1/15. *Unit head:* Dr. Luis Nunes Vicente, Chairperson, 610-758-4050, Fax: 610-758-4886, E-mail: lnv@lehigh.edu. *Application contact:* Jennifer Vargas, Graduate Coordinator, 610-758-4050, Fax: 610-758-4886, E-mail: jav319@lehigh.edu.
Website: https://ise.lehigh.edu/

Loyola Marymount University, Frank R. Seaver College of Science and Engineering, MBA/MS Program in Systems Engineering Leadership, Los Angeles, CA 90045-2659. Offers MBA/MS. *Entrance requirements:* Additional exam requirements/recommendations for international students: required—TOEFL, IELTS. Application fee: $50. Electronic applications accepted. *Financial support:* Research assistantships, teaching assistantships, Federal Work-Study, scholarships/grants, and unspecified assistantships available. Financial award applicants required to submit FAFSA. *Unit head:* Dr. Claire Leon, Systems Engineering Program Director, 310-338-7878, E-mail:

claire.leon@lmu.edu. *Application contact:* Ammar Dalal, Assistant Vice Provost for Graduate Enrollment, 310-338-2721, Fax: 310-338-6086, E-mail: graduateinfo@lmu.edu.

Loyola Marymount University, Frank R. Seaver College of Science and Engineering, Program in Healthcare Systems Engineering, Los Angeles, CA 90045. Offers MS. *Program availability:* Part-time, evening/weekend. *Students:* 23 full-time (13 women); includes 17 minority (5 Black or African American, non-Hispanic/Latino; 3 Asian, non-Hispanic/Latino; 6 Hispanic/Latino; 3 Two or more races, non-Hispanic/Latino), 2 international. Average age 26. 3 applicants, 100% accepted, 3 enrolled. In 2019, 14 master's awarded. *Entrance requirements:* For master's, graduate admissions application; undergrad GPA of at least 3.0; 2 letters of recommendation; essay demonstrating passion for career in healthcare. Additional exam requirements/recommendations for international students: required—TOEFL, IELTS. *Application deadline:* Applications are processed on a rolling basis. Application fee: $50. Electronic applications accepted. *Financial support:* Research assistantships, teaching assistantships, Federal Work-Study, scholarships/grants, and unspecified assistantships available. Financial award applicants required to submit FAFSA. *Unit head:* Dr. Bohdan W. Oppenheim, Associate Director for Healthcare Systems Engineering, 310-338-2825, E-mail: boppenheim@lmu.edu. *Application contact:* Ammar Dalal, Assistant Vice Provost for Graduate Enrollment, 310-338-2721, Fax: 310-338-6086, E-mail: graduateadmission@lmu.edu.
Website: http://cse.lmu.edu/graduateprograms/msinsystemsengineering/msdegreeprograminhealthcaresystemsengineering/

Loyola Marymount University, Frank R. Seaver College of Science and Engineering, Program in Systems Engineering, Los Angeles, CA 90045. Offers MS. *Program availability:* Part-time, evening/weekend. *Students:* 29 full-time (6 women); includes 19 minority (2 Black or African American, non-Hispanic/Latino; 3 Asian, non-Hispanic/Latino; 11 Hispanic/Latino; 1 Native Hawaiian or other Pacific Islander, non-Hispanic/Latino; 2 Two or more races, non-Hispanic/Latino), 6 international. Average age 31. 39 applicants, 33% accepted, 13 enrolled. In 2019, 15 master's awarded. *Entrance requirements:* For master's, graduate admissions application; undergrad GPA of at least 3.0; 2 letters of recommendation; essay demonstrating passion for systems engineering; resume; 2 year's related work experience (recommended). Additional exam requirements/recommendations for international students: required—TOEFL, IELTS. *Application deadline:* Applications are processed on a rolling basis. Application fee: $50. Electronic applications accepted. *Financial support:* Research assistantships, teaching assistantships, Federal Work-Study, scholarships/grants, and unspecified assistantships available. Financial award applicants required to submit FAFSA. *Unit head:* Dr. Claire Leon, Systems Engineering Program Director, 310-338-7878, E-mail: claire.leon@lmu.edu. *Application contact:* Ammar Dalal, Assistant Vice Provost for Graduate Enrollment, 310-338-2721, Fax: 310-338-6086, E-mail: graduateadmission@lmu.edu.
Website: http://cse.lmu.edu/graduateprograms/msinsystemsengineering

Massachusetts Institute of Technology, School of Engineering, Institute for Data, Systems, and Society, Cambridge, MA 02139. Offers social and engineering systems (PhD); technology and policy (SM). *Degree requirements:* For master's, thesis; for doctorate, comprehensive exam, thesis/dissertation. *Entrance requirements:* For doctorate, GRE General Test. Additional exam requirements/recommendations for international students: required—IELTS. Electronic applications accepted.

Massachusetts Institute of Technology, School of Engineering, System Design and Management Program, Cambridge, MA 02139-4307. Offers engineering and management (SM). *Degree requirements:* For master's, thesis.

Mississippi State University, Bagley College of Engineering, Department of Industrial and Systems Engineering, Mississippi State, MS 39762. Offers human factors and ergonomics (MS); industrial and systems engineering (PhD); industrial systems (MS); management systems (MS); manufacturing systems (MS); operations research (MS). *Program availability:* Part-time, blended/hybrid learning. *Faculty:* 14 full-time (3 women). *Students:* 39 full-time (16 women), 64 part-time (18 women); includes 20 minority (7 Black or African American, non-Hispanic/Latino; 7 Asian, non-Hispanic/Latino; 5 Hispanic/Latino; 1 Two or more races, non-Hispanic/Latino), 28 international. Average age 36. 54 applicants, 44% accepted, 11 enrolled. In 2019, 14 master's, 6 doctorates awarded. *Degree requirements:* For master's, comprehensive exam (for some programs), thesis optional, comprehensive oral or written exam; for doctorate, comprehensive exam, thesis/dissertation, candidacy exam. *Entrance requirements:* For master's, GRE (for graduates from program not accredited by EAC/ABET), minimum GPA of 3.0 on junior and senior years; for doctorate, GRE (for graduates from program not accredited by EAC/ABET), minimum GPA of 3.5 on master's degree and junior and senior years of BS. Additional exam requirements/recommendations for international students: required—TOEFL (minimum score 550 paper-based; 79 iBT); recommended—IELTS (minimum score 6.5). *Application deadline:* For fall admission, 7/1 for domestic students, 5/1 for international students; for spring admission, 11/1 for domestic students, 9/1 for international students. Applications are processed on a rolling basis. Application fee: $60 ($80 for international students). Electronic applications accepted. *Expenses: Tuition, area resident:* Full-time $8880; part-time $456 per credit hour. Tuition, state resident: full-time $8880. Tuition, nonresident: full-time $23,840; part-time $1236 per credit hour. *Required fees:* $110; $11.12 per credit hour. Tuition and fees vary according to course load. *Financial support:* In 2019–20, 21 research assistantships with full tuition reimbursements (averaging $17,482 per year), 4 teaching assistantships with full tuition reimbursements (averaging $15,706 per year) were awarded; Federal Work-Study, institutionally sponsored loans, and unspecified assistantships also available. Financial award application deadline: 4/1; financial award applicants required to submit FAFSA. *Unit head:* Dr. Kari Babski-Reeves, Professor, Department Head and Associate Dean for Research and Graduate Studies, 662-325-8430, Fax: 662-325-7618, E-mail: kari@ise.msstate.edu. *Application contact:* Ryan King, Admissions and Enrollment Assistant, 662-325-8951, E-mail: rjk101@grad.msstate.edu.
Website: http://www.ise.msstate.edu/

Missouri University of Science and Technology, Department of Engineering Management and Systems Engineering, Rolla, MO 65401. Offers engineering management (MS, PhD); systems engineering (MS, PhD). *Degree requirements:* For master's, thesis optional; for doctorate, comprehensive exam. *Entrance requirements:* For master's, GRE (minimum score 1150 verbal and quantitative, 4.5 writing); for doctorate, GRE (minimum score: 1100 verbal and quantitative, 3.5 writing). Additional exam requirements/recommendations for international students: required—TOEFL (minimum score 580 paper-based). Electronic applications accepted. *Expenses:* Tuition, state resident: full-time $7839; part-time $435.50 per credit hour. Tuition, nonresident: full-time $22,169; part-time $1231.60 per credit hour. *International tuition:* $18,156.60 full-time. *Required fees:* $649.76. One-time fee: $119. Tuition and fees vary according to course load and program.

Naval Postgraduate School, Departments and Academic Groups, Department of Systems Engineering, Monterey, CA 93943. Offers engineering systems (MS); product development (MS); systems engineering (MS, PhD, Certificate); systems engineering analysis (MS, PhD); systems engineering management (MS, PhD). *Program availability:*

Part-time. *Degree requirements:* For master's, thesis (for some programs), internal project, capstone project, or research/dissertation paper (for some programs); for doctorate, thesis/dissertation (for some programs), internal project, capstone project, or research/dissertation paper (for some programs).

New Mexico Institute of Mining and Technology, Center for Graduate Studies, Department of Mechanical Engineering, Socorro, NM 87801. Offers explosives engineering (MS); fluid and thermal sciences (MS); mechatronics systems engineering (MS); solid mechanics (MS). *Degree requirements:* For master's, thesis (for some programs). *Entrance requirements:* For master's, GRE General Test. Additional exam requirements/recommendations for international students: required—TOEFL (minimum score 540 paper-based).

New Mexico State University, College of Engineering, Department of Industrial Engineering, Las Cruces, NM 88003-8001. Offers industrial engineering (PhD); master of science (MSIE); systems engineering (Graduate Certificate). *Program availability:* Part-time-only, evening/weekend, 100% online. *Faculty:* 4 full-time (1 woman), 1 part-time/adjunct (0 women). *Students:* 28 full-time (5 women), 14 part-time (5 women); includes 13 minority (1 Black or African American, non-Hispanic/Latino; 1 Asian, non-Hispanic/Latino; 10 Hispanic/Latino; 1 Two or more races, non-Hispanic/Latino), 23 international. Average age 32. 44 applicants, 70% accepted, 11 enrolled. In 2019, 41 master's, 1 doctorate, 1 other advanced degree awarded. *Degree requirements:* For master's, thesis optional, only exit interview required for master of engineering program, no thesis required; master of science students have a thesis option or a project option, comprehensive exam is required of all MS students; for doctorate, comprehensive exam, thesis/dissertation, qualifying exam. *Entrance requirements:* Additional exam requirements/recommendations for international students: required—TOEFL (minimum score 550 paper-based; 79 iBT), IELTS (minimum score 6.5). *Application deadline:* For fall admission, 7/1 priority date for domestic students, 3/1 for international students; for spring admission, 11/1 for domestic students, 10/1 for international students. Applications are processed on a rolling basis. Application fee: $40 ($50 for international students). Electronic applications accepted. *Financial support:* In 2019–20, 27 students received support, including 2 fellowships (averaging $4,844 per year), 4 teaching assistantships (averaging $16,155 per year); career-related internships or fieldwork, Federal Work-Study, scholarships/grants, traineeships, health care benefits, and unspecified assistantships also available. Support available to part-time students. Financial award application deadline: 3/1. *Unit head:* Dr. Hansuk Sohn, Interim Department Head, 575-646-4923, Fax: 575-646-2976, E-mail: hsohn@nmsu.edu. *Application contact:* Dr. Hansuk Sohn, Interim Department Head, 575-646-4923, Fax: 575-646-2976, E-mail: hsohn@nmsu.edu.
Website: http://ie.nmsu.edu

North Carolina Agricultural and Technical State University, The Graduate College, College of Engineering, Department of Industrial and Systems Engineering, Greensboro, NC 27411. Offers industrial and systems engineering (PhD); industrial engineering (MSIE). *Program availability:* Part-time. *Degree requirements:* For master's, thesis, project; for doctorate, thesis/dissertation. *Entrance requirements:* For master's, GRE General Test (recommended); for doctorate, GRE General Test, degree in engineering, BS in industrial engineering from ABET-accredited program with minimum cumulative credit point average of 3.7 or MS in discipline related to industrial engineering from college or university recognized by a regional or general accrediting agency with minimum cumulative GPA of 3.3. Additional exam requirements/recommendations for international students: required—TOEFL (minimum score 550 paper-based; 79 iBT).

Northeastern University, College of Engineering, Boston, MA 02115-5096. Offers bioengineering (MS, PhD); chemical engineering (MS, PhD); civil engineering (MS, PhD); computer engineering (PhD); computer systems engineering (MS); electrical and computer engineering (MS); electrical and computer engineering leadership (MS); electrical engineering (PhD); energy systems (MS); engineering and public policy (MS); engineering management (MS, Certificate); environmental engineering (MS); industrial engineering (MS, PhD); information assurance (PhD); information systems (MS); interdisciplinary engineering (PhD); mechanical engineering (PhD); operations research (MS); telecommunication systems management (MS). *Program availability:* Part-time, online learning. Electronic applications accepted. *Expenses:* Contact institution.

Oakland University, Graduate Study and Lifelong Learning, School of Engineering and Computer Science, Department of Industrial and Systems Engineering, Program in Systems Engineering, Rochester, MI 48309-4401. Offers MS, PhD. *Degree requirements:* For doctorate, thesis/dissertation. *Entrance requirements:* For master's and doctorate, minimum GPA of 3.0. Additional exam requirements/recommendations for international students: required—TOEFL (minimum score 550 paper-based). Electronic applications accepted. *Expenses:* Contact institution.

The Ohio State University, Graduate School, College of Engineering, Department of Integrated Systems Engineering, Columbus, OH 43210. Offers industrial and systems engineering (MS, PhD). *Entrance requirements:* For master's and doctorate, GRE General Test (desired minimum scores: Quantitative 166, Verbal 153, Analytical Writing 4.5). Additional exam requirements/recommendations for international students: required—TOEFL (minimum score 550 paper-based; 79 iBT), Michigan English Language Assessment Battery (minimum score 82); recommended—IELTS (minimum score 7). Electronic applications accepted.

Ohio University, Graduate College, Russ College of Engineering and Technology, Department of Industrial and Systems Engineering, Athens, OH 45701-2979. Offers M Eng Mgt, MS. *Program availability:* Part-time, evening/weekend. *Degree requirements:* For master's, comprehensive exam (for some programs), thesis optional, research project. *Entrance requirements:* For master's, GRE General Test. Additional exam requirements/recommendations for international students: required—TOEFL (minimum score 550 paper-based; 80 iBT) or IELTS (minimum score 6.5). Electronic applications accepted.

Old Dominion University, Frank Batten College of Engineering and Technology, Program in Engineering Management and Systems Engineering, Norfolk, VA 23529. Offers D Eng, PhD. *Program availability:* Part-time, evening/weekend, 100% online, blended/hybrid learning. *Degree requirements:* For doctorate, thesis/dissertation, candidacy exam, project. *Entrance requirements:* For doctorate, GRE, resume, letters of recommendation, minimum GPA of 3.0, interview, essay outlining intended area of specialization. Additional exam requirements/recommendations for international students: required—TOEFL (minimum score 550 paper-based; 79 iBT). Electronic applications accepted.

Old Dominion University, Frank Batten College of Engineering and Technology, Program in Systems Engineering, Norfolk, VA 23529. Offers ME. *Program availability:* Part-time, evening/weekend, 100% online, blended/hybrid learning. *Degree requirements:* For master's, comprehensive exam, project. *Entrance requirements:* For master's, GRE, minimum GPA of 3.0. Additional exam requirements/recommendations for international students: required—TOEFL (minimum score 550 paper-based; 79 iBT). Electronic applications accepted. *Expenses:* Contact institution.

Oregon State University, College of Engineering, Program in Industrial Engineering, Corvallis, OR 97331. Offers advanced manufacturing (M Eng, MS, PhD); engineering management (M Eng); human systems engineering (M Eng, MS, PhD); information systems engineering (M Eng, MS, PhD); manufacturing systems engineering (M Eng, MS, PhD). *Program availability:* 100% online. *Entrance requirements:* For master's and doctorate, GRE. Additional exam requirements/recommendations for international students: required—TOEFL (minimum score 80 iBT), IELTS (minimum score 6.5). *Expenses:* Contact institution.

Penn State Great Valley, Graduate Studies, Engineering Division, Malvern, PA 19355-1488. Offers engineering management (MEM); software engineering (MSE); systems engineering (M Eng, Certificate).

Purdue University Fort Wayne, College of Engineering, Technology, and Computer Science, Department of Electrical and Computer Engineering, Fort Wayne, IN 46805-1499. Offers computer engineering (MSE); electrical engineering (MSE); systems engineering (MSE). *Program availability:* Part-time. *Entrance requirements:* For master's, minimum GPA of 3.0, bachelor's degree in engineering discipline. Additional exam requirements/recommendations for international students: required—TOEFL (minimum score 550 paper-based; 79 iBT); recommended—TWE. Electronic applications accepted.

Regis University, College of Computer and Information Sciences, Denver, CO 80221-1099. Offers agile technologies (Certificate); cybersecurity (Certificate); data science (M Sc); database administration with Oracle (Certificate); database development (Certificate); database technologies (M Sc); enterprise Java software development (Certificate); enterprise resource planning (Certificate); executive information technology (Certificate); health care informatics (Certificate); health care informatics and information management (M Sc); information assurance (M Sc); information assurance policy management (Certificate); information technology management (M Sc); mobile software development (Certificate); software engineering (M Sc, Certificate); software engineering and database technology (M Sc); storage area networks (Certificate); systems engineering (M Sc, Certificate). *Program availability:* Part-time, evening/weekend, 100% online, blended/hybrid learning. *Degree requirements:* For master's, thesis (for some programs), final research project. *Entrance requirements:* For master's, official transcript reflecting baccalaureate degree awarded from regionally-accredited college or university, 2 years of related experience, resume, interview. Additional exam requirements/recommendations for international students: required—TOEFL (minimum score 550 paper-based; 82 iBT). Electronic applications accepted. *Expenses:* Contact institution.

Rensselaer Polytechnic Institute, Graduate School, School of Engineering, Program in Computer and Systems Engineering, Troy, NY 12180-3590. Offers M Eng, MS, PhD. *Faculty:* 40 full-time (6 women), 1 part-time/adjunct (0 women). *Students:* 18 full-time (2 women), 2 part-time (0 women); includes 2 minority (1 Asian, non-Hispanic/Latino; 1 Hispanic/Latino), 14 international. Average age 25. 71 applicants, 54% accepted, 10 enrolled. In 2019, 7 master's, 2 doctorates awarded. Terminal master's awarded for partial completion of doctoral program. *Degree requirements:* For master's, thesis (for some programs); for doctorate, thesis/dissertation. *Entrance requirements:* For master's and doctorate, GRE. Additional exam requirements/recommendations for international students: required—TOEFL (minimum score 570 paper-based; 88 iBT), IELTS (minimum score 6.5), PTE (minimum score 60). *Application deadline:* For fall admission, 1/1 priority date for domestic and international students; for spring admission, 8/15 priority date for domestic and international students; for summer admission, 1/1 priority date for domestic and international students. Applications are processed on a rolling basis. Application fee: $75. Electronic applications accepted. *Financial support:* In 2019–20, research assistantships (averaging $23,000 per year), teaching assistantships (averaging $23,000 per year) were awarded; fellowships also available. Financial award application deadline: 1/1. *Unit head:* Dr. Hussein Abouzeid, Graduate Program Director, 518-576-6534, E-mail: abouzeid@ecse.rpi.edu. *Application contact:* Jarron Decker, Director of Graduate Admissions, 518-276-6216, Fax: 518-276-4072, E-mail: gradadmissions@rpi.edu.
Website: https://ecse.rpi.edu/

Rensselaer Polytechnic Institute, Graduate School, School of Engineering, Program in Decision Sciences and Engineering Systems, Troy, NY 12180-3590. Offers PhD. *Faculty:* 3 full-time (2 women). *Students:* 15 full-time (2 women), 1 part-time (0 women), 11 international. Average age 30. 32 applicants, 25% accepted, 4 enrolled. In 2019, 3 doctorates awarded. Terminal master's awarded for partial completion of doctoral program. *Degree requirements:* For doctorate, thesis/dissertation. *Entrance requirements:* For doctorate, GRE. Additional exam requirements/recommendations for international students: required—TOEFL (minimum score 570 paper-based; 88 iBT), IELTS (minimum score 6.5), PTE (minimum score 60). *Application deadline:* For fall admission, 1/1 priority date for domestic students, 1/1 for international students. Applications are processed on a rolling basis. Application fee: $75. Electronic applications accepted. *Financial support:* In 2019–20, research assistantships (averaging $23,000 per year), teaching assistantships (averaging $23,000 per year) were awarded; fellowships also available. Financial award application deadline: 1/1. *Unit head:* Dr. Thomas Sharkey, Graduate Program Director, 518-276-2958, E-mail: sharkt@rpi.edu. *Application contact:* Jarron Decker, Director of Graduate Admissions, 518-276-6216, Fax: 518-276-4072, E-mail: gradadmissions@rpi.edu.
Website: http://ise.rpi.edu/

Rensselaer Polytechnic Institute, Graduate School, School of Engineering, Program in Systems Engineering and Technology Management, Troy, NY 12180-3590. Offers M Eng. *Program availability:* Part-time, evening/weekend, online learning. *Faculty:* 8 full-time (0 women). *Students:* 6 full-time (3 women), 38 part-time (7 women); includes 10 minority (2 Black or African American, non-Hispanic/Latino; 1 American Indian or Alaska Native, non-Hispanic/Latino; 4 Asian, non-Hispanic/Latino; 3 Hispanic/Latino). Average age 30. 18 applicants, 61% accepted, 9 enrolled. In 2019, 5 master's awarded. *Degree requirements:* For master's, thesis (for some programs). *Entrance requirements:* For master's, GRE. Additional exam requirements/recommendations for international students: required—TOEFL (minimum score 570 paper-based; 88 iBT), IELTS (minimum score 6.5), PTE (minimum score 60). *Application deadline:* For fall admission, 1/1 priority date for domestic and international students; for spring admission, 8/15 priority date for domestic and international students. Applications are processed on a rolling basis. Application fee: $75. Electronic applications accepted. *Financial support:* Institutionally sponsored loans available. Financial award application deadline: 1/1. *Unit head:* Dr. Bill Foley, Graduate Program Director, 518-276-4009, E-mail: foleyw@rpi.edu. *Application contact:* Jarron Decker, Director of Graduate Admissions, 518-276-6216, Fax: 518-276-4072, E-mail: gradadmissions@rpi.edu.
Website: http://ise.rpi.edu/

Rochester Institute of Technology, Graduate Enrollment Services, Kate Gleason College of Engineering, Design, Development and Manufacturing Department, MS Program in Product Development, Rochester, NY 14623-5603. Offers MS. *Program availability:* Part-time, evening/weekend, 100% online, blended/hybrid learning. *Degree requirements:* For master's, capstone project. *Entrance requirements:* For master's, undergraduate degree in engineering or related field, minimum GPA of 3.0, 2 years of experience in product development, one professional recommendation, resume. Additional exam requirements/recommendations for international students: required—

TOEFL (minimum score 550 paper-based; 79 iBT), IELTS (minimum score 6.5), PTE (minimum score 58). Electronic applications accepted. *Expenses:* Contact institution.

Rochester Institute of Technology, Graduate Enrollment Services, Kate Gleason College of Engineering, Industrial and Systems Engineering Department, ME Program in Industrial and Systems Engineering, Rochester, NY 14623-5603. Offers ME. *Program availability:* Part-time. *Degree requirements:* For master's, thesis or alternative, capstone project. *Entrance requirements:* For master's, GRE, minimum GPA of 3.0 (recommended), one-page statement of purpose, two letters of recommendation. Additional exam requirements/recommendations for international students: required—TOEFL (minimum score 580 paper-based; 90 iBT), IELTS (minimum score 6), PTE (minimum score 58). Electronic applications accepted.

Rochester Institute of Technology, Graduate Enrollment Services, Kate Gleason College of Engineering, Industrial and Systems Engineering Department, MS Program in Industrial and Systems Engineering, Rochester, NY 14623-5603. Offers MS. *Program availability:* Part-time. *Degree requirements:* For master's, thesis. *Entrance requirements:* For master's, GRE, minimum GPA of 3.0 (recommended), statement of purpose, 2 letters of recommendation. Additional exam requirements/recommendations for international students: required—TOEFL (minimum score 580 paper-based; 90 iBT), IELTS (minimum score 6.5), PTE (minimum score 58). Electronic applications accepted.

Rochester Institute of Technology, Graduate Enrollment Services, Kate Gleason College of Engineering, Microsystems Engineering Department, PhD Program in Microsystems Engineering, Rochester, NY 14623-5603. Offers PhD. *Program availability:* Part-time. *Degree requirements:* For doctorate, comprehensive exam, thesis/dissertation. *Entrance requirements:* For doctorate, GRE, minimum GPA of 3.0 (recommended), resume, personal statement of educational and research objectives, minimum of 2 letters of recommendation. Additional exam requirements/recommendations for international students: required—TOEFL (minimum score 600 paper-based; 100 iBT), IELTS (minimum score 7), PTE (minimum score 68). Electronic applications accepted. *Expenses:* Contact institution.

Rose-Hulman Institute of Technology, Graduate Studies, Department of Electrical and Computer Engineering, Terre Haute, IN 47803-3999. Offers electrical and computer engineering (M Eng); electrical engineering (MS); systems engineering and management (MS). *Program availability:* Part-time. *Faculty:* 19 full-time (2 women), 1 (woman) part-time/adjunct. *Students:* 2 full-time (0 women), 3 part-time (0 women), 2 international. Average age 27. 7 applicants, 71% accepted. In 2019, 5 master's awarded. *Degree requirements:* For master's, thesis (for some programs). *Entrance requirements:* For master's, GRE, minimum GPA of 3.0. Additional exam requirements/recommendations for international students: required—TOEFL (minimum score 580 paper-based; 94 iBT), IELTS (minimum score 7). *Application deadline:* For fall admission, 2/1 priority date for domestic and international students; for winter admission, 10/1 for domestic students, 4/1 for international students; for spring admission, 1/15 for domestic students, 11/1 for international students. Applications are processed on a rolling basis. Application fee: $75. Electronic applications accepted. *Financial support:* In 2019–20, 5 students received support. Fellowships with tuition reimbursements available, research assistantships with tuition reimbursements available, institutionally sponsored loans, scholarships/grants, tuition waivers (full and partial), and unspecified assistantships available. *Unit head:* Dr. Mario Simoni, Department Head, 812-877-8341, Fax: 812-877-8895, E-mail: simoni@rose-hulman.edu. *Application contact:* Dr. Craig Downing, Associate Dean of the Faculty, 812-877-8822, E-mail: downing@rose-hulman.edu.
Website: https://www.rose-hulman.edu/academics/academic-departments/electrical-computer-engineering/index.html

Rutgers University - New Brunswick, Graduate School-New Brunswick, Department of Industrial and Systems Engineering, Piscataway, NJ 08854-8097. Offers industrial and systems engineering (MS, PhD); information technology (MS); manufacturing systems engineering (MS); quality and reliability engineering (MS). *Program availability:* Part-time, evening/weekend. Terminal master's awarded for partial completion of doctoral program. *Degree requirements:* For master's, thesis or alternative, seminar; for doctorate, comprehensive exam, thesis/dissertation. *Entrance requirements:* For master's and doctorate, GRE General Test. Additional exam requirements/recommendations for international students: required—TOEFL.

San Jose State University, Program in Industrial and Systems Engineering, San Jose, CA 95192-0085. Offers MS. *Faculty:* 5 full-time (2 women), 9 part-time/adjunct (1 woman). *Students:* 196 full-time (112 women), 214 part-time (127 women); includes 85 minority (5 Black or African American, non-Hispanic/Latino; 61 Asian, non-Hispanic/Latino; 19 Hispanic/Latino), 262 international. Average age 27. 542 applicants, 39% accepted, 131 enrolled. In 2019, 141 master's awarded. *Application deadline:* For fall admission, 6/1 for domestic students, 5/1 for international students; for spring admission, 12/1 for domestic students, 11/1 for international students. Applications are processed on a rolling basis. Application fee: $70. Electronic applications accepted. *Expenses: Tuition, area resident:* Full-time $7176; part-time $4164. *Tuition, state resident:* full-time $7176; part-time $4164. *Tuition, nonresident:* full-time $7176; part-time $4165 per credit hour. *International tuition:* $7176 full-time. *Required fees:* $2110; $2110. *Financial support:* In 2019–20, 24 students received support. Scholarships/grants available. Financial award application deadline: 5/1; financial award applicants required to submit FAFSA. *Unit head:* Yasser Dessouky, Department Chair, 408-924-4133, E-mail: yasser.dessouky@sjsu.edu. *Application contact:* Yasser Dessouky, Department Chair, 408-924-4133, E-mail: yasser.dessouky@sjsu.edu.
Website: http://www.engr.sjsu.edu/ise/

Simon Fraser University, Office of Graduate Studies and Postdoctoral Fellows, Faculty of Applied Sciences, School of Mechatronic Systems Engineering, Burnaby, BC V5A 1S6, Canada. Offers MA Sc, PhD. *Degree requirements:* For master's, one foreign language, thesis; for doctorate, one foreign language, comprehensive exam, thesis/dissertation. *Entrance requirements:* Additional exam requirements/recommendations for international students: required—TOEFL (minimum score 580 paper-based; 93 iBT), IELTS (minimum score 7), TWE (minimum score 5). Electronic applications accepted.

Southern Methodist University, Lyle School of Engineering, Department of Engineering Management, Information, and Systems, Dallas, TX 75275. Offers engineering entrepreneurship (MS); engineering management (MS, DE); information engineering and management (MSIEM); operations research (MS, PhD); systems engineering (MS). *Program availability:* Part-time, evening/weekend, online learning. Terminal master's awarded for partial completion of doctoral program. *Degree requirements:* For master's, thesis optional; for doctorate, thesis/dissertation, oral and written qualifying exams. *Entrance requirements:* For master's, minimum GPA of 3.0 in last 2 years; bachelor's degree in engineering, mathematics, sciences, or technical area; for doctorate, GRE General Test (operations research, engineering management), bachelor's degree in related field. Additional exam requirements/recommendations for international students: required—TOEFL.

Southern Methodist University, Lyle School of Engineering, Department of Multidisciplinary Studies, Dallas, TX 75275. Offers data science (MS), including business analytics, machine learning; datacenter systems engineering (MS); design and innovation (MA). *Program availability:* Part-time, online learning. *Entrance requirements:*

For master's, BS in one of the engineering disciplines, computer science, one of the quantitative sciences or mathematics; minimum of two years of college-level mathematics including one year of college-level calculus.

Stevens Institute of Technology, Graduate School, Charles V. Schaefer Jr. School of Engineering and Science, Department of Electrical and Computer Engineering, Program in Networked Information Systems, Hoboken, NJ 07030. Offers MS, Certificate. *Program availability:* Part-time, evening/weekend. *Faculty:* 20 full-time (6 women), 2 part-time/adjunct. *Students:* 1 part-time (0 women). Average age 48. In 2019, 2 master's, 1 other advanced degree awarded. Terminal master's awarded for partial completion of doctoral program. *Degree requirements:* For master's, thesis optional, minimum B average in major field and overall; for Certificate, minimum B average. *Entrance requirements:* For master's, International applicants must submit TOEFL/IELTS scores and fulfill the English Language Proficiency Requirement. Applicants to full-time programs who do not qualify for a score waiver are required to submit GRE/GMAT scores. Additional exam requirements/recommendations for international students: required—TOEFL (minimum score 74 iBT), IELTS (minimum score 6). *Application deadline:* For fall admission, 4/15 for domestic and international students; for spring admission, 11/1 for domestic and international students; for summer admission, 5/1 for domestic students. Applications are processed on a rolling basis. Application fee: $60. Electronic applications accepted. *Expenses: Tuition:* Full-time $52,134. *Required fees:* $1880. Tuition and fees vary according to course load. *Financial support:* Fellowships, research assistantships, teaching assistantships, career-related internships or fieldwork, Federal Work-Study, scholarships/grants, and unspecified assistantships available. Financial award application deadline: 2/15; financial award applicants required to submit FAFSA. *Unit head:* Dr. Jean Zu, Dean of SES, 201-216.8233, Fax: 201-216.8372, E-mail: Jean.Zu@stevens.edu. *Application contact:* Graduate Admissions, 888-783-8367, Fax: 201-511-1306, E-mail: graduate@stevens.edu.

Stevens Institute of Technology, Graduate School, School of Systems and Enterprises, Program in Systems Engineering, Hoboken, NJ 07030. Offers systems and supportability engineering (Certificate); systems engineering (M Eng, PhD); systems engineering and architecting (Certificate); systems engineering management (Certificate); systems engineering of embedded/cyber-physical systems (Certificate); systems engineering security (Certificate). *Program availability:* Part-time, evening/weekend. *Faculty:* 22 full-time (8 women), 15 part-time/adjunct (3 women). *Students:* 55 full-time (12 women), 164 part-time (42 women); includes 39 minority (9 Black or African American, non-Hispanic/Latino; 2 American Indian or Alaska Native, non-Hispanic/Latino; 24 Asian, non-Hispanic/Latino; 4 Hispanic/Latino), 36 international. Average age 31. In 2019, 126 master's, 7 doctorates, 159 other advanced degrees awarded. Terminal master's awarded for partial completion of doctoral program. *Degree requirements:* For master's, thesis optional, minimum B average in major field and overall; for doctorate, comprehensive exam (for some programs), thesis/dissertation; for Certificate, minimum B average. *Entrance requirements:* For master's, International applicants must submit TOEFL/IELTS scores and fulfill the English Language Proficiency Requirement. Applicants to full-time programs who do not qualify for a score waiver are required to submit GRE/GMAT scores. Additional exam requirements/recommendations for international students: required—TOEFL (minimum score 74 iBT), IELTS (minimum score 6). *Application deadline:* For fall admission, 4/15 for domestic and international students; for spring admission, 11/1 for domestic and international students; for summer admission, 5/1 for domestic students. Applications are processed on a rolling basis. Application fee: $60. Electronic applications accepted. *Expenses: Tuition:* Full-time $52,134. *Required fees:* $1880. Tuition and fees vary according to course load. *Financial support:* Fellowships, research assistantships, teaching assistantships, career-related internships or fieldwork, Federal Work-Study, scholarships/grants, and unspecified assistantships available. Financial award application deadline: 2/15; financial award applicants required to submit FAFSA. *Unit head:* Dr. Yehia Massoud, Dean of SSE, 201-216.8025, E-mail: yehia.massoud@stevens.edu. *Application contact:* Graduate Admissions, 888-783-8367, Fax: 888-511-1306, E-mail: graduate@stevens.edu.
Website: https://www.stevens.edu/school-systems-enterprises/masters-degree-programs/systems-engineering

Stony Brook University, State University of New York, Graduate School, College of Engineering and Applied Sciences, Department of Computer Science, Program in Information Systems Engineering, Stony Brook, NY 11794. Offers MS. *Entrance requirements:* Additional exam requirements/recommendations for international students: required—TOEFL. *Application deadline:* For fall admission, 1/15 for domestic students; for spring admission, 10/1 for domestic students. Application fee: $100. *Expenses:* Contact institution. *Unit head:* Prof. Samir Das, Chair, 631-632-1807, Fax: 631-632-8334, E-mail: samir@stonybrook.edu. *Application contact:* Prof. Samir Das, Chair, 631-632-1807, Fax: 631-632-8334, E-mail: samir@stonybrook.edu.

Tennessee State University, The School of Graduate Studies and Research, College of Engineering, Nashville, TN 37209-1561. Offers biomedical engineering (ME); civil engineering (ME); computer and information systems engineering (MS, PhD); electrical engineering (ME); environmental engineering (ME); manufacturing engineering (ME); mathematical sciences (MS); mechanical engineering (ME). *Program availability:* Part-time, evening/weekend. *Degree requirements:* For master's, project; for doctorate, comprehensive exam, thesis/dissertation. *Entrance requirements:* For doctorate, minimum GPA of 3.3.

Texas A&M University–Kingsville, College of Graduate Studies, Frank H. Dotterweich College of Engineering, Program in Sustainable Energy Systems Engineering, Kingsville, TX 78363. Offers PhD. *Degree requirements:* For doctorate, variable foreign language requirement, comprehensive exam, thesis/dissertation (for some programs). *Entrance requirements:* For doctorate, GRE, MAT, GMAT, bachelor's or master's degree in engineering or science, curriculum vitae, official transcripts, statement of purpose, three letters of recommendation. Additional exam requirements/recommendations for international students: required—TOEFL (minimum score 550 paper-based; 79 iBT). Electronic applications accepted.

The University of Alabama in Huntsville, School of Graduate Studies, College of Engineering, Department of Industrial and Systems Engineering and Engineering Management, Huntsville, AL 35899. Offers engineering management (MSE, PhD); industrial engineering (MSE, PhD); operations research (MSOR); systems engineering (MSE, PhD). *Program availability:* Part-time. *Degree requirements:* For master's, comprehensive exam, thesis or alternative, oral and written exams; for doctorate, comprehensive exam, thesis/dissertation, oral and written exams. *Entrance requirements:* For master's and doctorate, GRE General Test, minimum GPA of 3.0. Additional exam requirements/recommendations for international students: required—TOEFL (minimum score 500 paper-based; 80 iBT), IELTS (minimum score 6.5). Electronic applications accepted.

University of Alberta, Faculty of Graduate Studies and Research, Department of Electrical and Computer Engineering, Edmonton, AB T6G 2E1, Canada. Offers communications (M Eng, M Sc, PhD); computer engineering (M Eng, M Sc, PhD); electromagnetics (M Eng, M Sc, PhD); nanotechnology and microdevices (M Eng, M Sc, PhD); power/power electronics (M Eng, M Sc, PhD); systems (M Eng, M Sc, PhD).

Terminal master's awarded for partial completion of doctoral program. *Degree requirements:* For master's, thesis; for doctorate, thesis/dissertation. *Entrance requirements:* Additional exam requirements/recommendations for international students: required—TOEFL. Electronic applications accepted.

The University of Arizona, College of Engineering, Department of Systems and Industrial Engineering, Tucson, AZ 85721. Offers engineering management (Graduate Certificate); industrial engineering (MS); systems and industrial engineering (MS, PhD); systems engineering (MS, PhD, Graduate Certificate). *Program availability:* Part-time, online learning. *Degree requirements:* For doctorate, thesis/dissertation. *Entrance requirements:* For master's, GRE General Test (minimum score: 500 Verbal, 700 Quantitative), 3 letters of recommendation; for doctorate, GRE General Test (minimum score: 500 Verbal, 700 Quantitative), minimum GPA of 3.5, 3 letters of recommendation, letter of intent. Additional exam requirements/recommendations for international students: required—TOEFL (minimum score 575 paper-based; 80 iBT). Electronic applications accepted.

University of Arkansas at Little Rock, Graduate School, George W. Donaghey College of Engineering and Information Technology, Department of Systems Engineering, Little Rock, AR 72204-1099. Offers MS, PhD, Graduate Certificate.

University of California, Merced, Graduate Division, School of Engineering, Merced, CA 95343. Offers biological engineering and small scale technologies (MS, PhD); electrical engineering and computer science (MS, PhD); environmental systems (MS, PhD); management of innovation, sustainability, and technology (MM); mechanical engineering (MS, PhD). *Faculty:* 60 full-time (16 women). *Students:* 244 full-time (83 women), 1 (woman) part-time; includes 56 minority (2 Black or African American, non-Hispanic/Latino; 20 Asian, non-Hispanic/Latino; 30 Hispanic/Latino; 1 Native Hawaiian or other Pacific Islander, non-Hispanic/Latino; 3 Two or more races, non-Hispanic/Latino), 153 international. Average age 28. 330 applicants, 32% accepted, 67 enrolled. In 2019, 30 master's, 17 doctorates awarded. Terminal master's awarded for partial completion of doctoral program. *Degree requirements:* For master's, variable foreign language requirement, comprehensive exam, thesis or alternative, oral defense; for doctorate, variable foreign language requirement, comprehensive exam, thesis/dissertation, oral defense. *Entrance requirements:* For master's and doctorate, GRE. Additional exam requirements/recommendations for international students: required—TOEFL (minimum score 550 paper-based; 80 iBT); recommended—IELTS (minimum score 6.5). *Application deadline:* For fall admission, 1/15 for domestic and international students. Application fee: $105 ($125 for international students). Electronic applications accepted. *Expenses: Tuition, area resident:* Full-time $11,442; part-time $5721. Tuition, state resident: full-time $11,442; part-time $5721. Tuition, nonresident: full-time $26,544; part-time $13,272. *International tuition:* $26,544 full-time. *Required fees:* $564 per semester. *Financial support:* In 2019–20, 205 students received support, including 6 fellowships with full tuition reimbursements available (averaging $22,005 per year), 76 research assistantships with full tuition reimbursements available (averaging $21,420 per year), 123 teaching assistantships with full tuition reimbursements available (averaging $21,911 per year); scholarships/grants, traineeships, and health care benefits also available. *Unit head:* Dr. Mark Matsumoto, Dean, 209-228-4047, Fax: 209-228-4047, E-mail: mmatsumoto@ucmerced.edu. *Application contact:* Tsu Ya, Director of Admissions and Academic Services, 209-228-4521, Fax: 209-228-6906, E-mail: tya@ucmerced.edu.

University of Colorado Colorado Springs, College of Engineering and Applied Science, Program in General Engineering, Colorado Springs, CO 80918. Offers computer science (PhD); cybersecurity (ME); energy engineering (ME); engineering management (ME); engineering systems (ME); software engineering (ME); space operations (ME). *Program availability:* Part-time, evening/weekend, blended/hybrid learning. *Faculty:* 1 full-time (0 women), 12 part-time/adjunct (3 women). *Students:* 2 full-time (1 woman), 88 part-time (22 women); includes 23 minority (3 Black or African American, non-Hispanic/Latino; 6 Asian, non-Hispanic/Latino; 9 Hispanic/Latino; 5 Two or more races, non-Hispanic/Latino), 7 international. Average age 32. 36 applicants, 53% accepted, 15 enrolled. In 2019, 28 master's awarded. *Degree requirements:* For master's, thesis, portfolio, or project. *Entrance requirements:* For master's, GRE may be required based on past academic performance., Professional recommendation letters are required for all applicants.; for doctorate, GRE (minimum score of 148 new grading scale on the quantitative portion if the applicant has not graduated from a program of recognized standing), minimum GPA of 3.3 in the bachelor's or master's degree program attempted. Additional exam requirements/recommendations for international students: required—TOEFL (minimum score 80 iBT), IELTS (minimum score 6). *Application deadline:* For fall admission, 7/1 for domestic and international students; for spring admission, 11/1 for domestic and international students. Applications are processed on a rolling basis. Application fee: $60 ($100 for international students). Electronic applications accepted. *Expenses:* Contact institution. *Financial support:* In 2019–20, 5 students received support. Career-related internships or fieldwork, Federal Work-Study, scholarships/grants, traineeships, health care benefits, and unspecified assistantships available. Support available to part-time students. Financial award application deadline: 3/1; financial award applicants required to submit FAFSA. *Unit head:* Dr. Donald Rabern, Dean of Engineering and Applied Science, 719-255-3543, E-mail: drabern@uccs.edu. *Application contact:* Dawn House, Extended Studies Coordinator, 719-255-3246, E-mail: dhouse@uccs.edu.
Website: https://www.uccs.edu/easonline/degree-programs/engineering-management-degree

University of Florida, Graduate School, Herbert Wertheim College of Engineering, Department of Industrial and Systems Engineering, Gainesville, FL 32611. Offers industrial and systems engineering (ME, MS, PhD, Engr); quantitative finance (PhD). *Program availability:* Part-time, evening/weekend, online learning. Terminal master's awarded for partial completion of doctoral program. *Degree requirements:* For master's, thesis (for some programs); for doctorate, comprehensive exam (for some programs), thesis/dissertation (for some programs). *Entrance requirements:* For master's and doctorate, minimum GPA of 3.0; for Engr, GRE General Test. Additional exam requirements/recommendations for international students: required—TOEFL (minimum score 550 paper-based; 80 iBT), IELTS (minimum score 6). Electronic applications accepted.

University of Houston–Clear Lake, School of Science and Computer Engineering, Program in System Engineering, Houston, TX 77058-1002. Offers MS. *Entrance requirements:* Additional exam requirements/recommendations for international students: required—TOEFL (minimum score 550 paper-based).

University of Illinois at Urbana-Champaign, Graduate College, College of Engineering, Department of Industrial and Enterprise Systems Engineering, Urbana, IL 61801. Offers industrial engineering (MS, PhD); systems and entrepreneurial engineering (MS, PhD); MBA/MS.

University of Louisiana at Lafayette, College of Engineering, Department of Electrical and Computer Engineering, Lafayette, LA 70504. Offers electrical engineering (MS); systems engineering (PhD). *Degree requirements:* For master's, thesis or alternative; for doctorate, comprehensive exam, thesis/dissertation, final oral exam. *Entrance requirements:* For master's, GRE General Test, minimum GPA of 2.75. Additional exam requirements/recommendations for international students: required—TOEFL (minimum score 550 paper-based). Electronic applications accepted. *Expenses: Tuition, area resident:* Full-time $5511. Tuition, state resident: full-time $5511. Tuition, nonresident: full-time $19,239. *Required fees:* $46,637.

University of Maryland, Baltimore County, The Graduate School, Program in Systems Engineering, Baltimore, MD 21250. Offers MS, Postbaccalaureate Certificate. *Program availability:* Part-time. *Students:* 6 full-time (1 woman), 15 part-time (6 women); includes 11 minority (8 Black or African American, non-Hispanic/Latino; 1 Asian, non-Hispanic/Latino; 1 Hispanic/Latino; 1 Two or more races, non-Hispanic/Latino), 2 international. Average age 32. 25 applicants, 68% accepted, 9 enrolled. In 2019, 7 master's, 4 other advanced degrees awarded. *Degree requirements:* For master's, comprehensive exam (for some programs), thesis optional. *Entrance requirements:* For master's, undergraduate degree in engineering or information technology; minimum undergraduate GPA of 3.0. Additional exam requirements/recommendations for international students: required—TOEFL (minimum score 550 paper-based; 80 iBT), GRE General Test. *Application deadline:* For fall admission, 7/1 for domestic and international students; for spring admission, 12/1 for domestic and international students. Applications are processed on a rolling basis. Application fee: $70. Electronic applications accepted. *Expenses: Tuition, area resident:* Full-time $659. Tuition, state resident: full-time $659. Tuition, nonresident: full-time $1132. *International tuition:* $1132 full-time. *Required fees:* $140; $140 per credit hour. *Financial support:* Fellowships, research assistantships, teaching assistantships, career-related internships or fieldwork, Federal Work-Study, scholarships/grants, health care benefits, tuition waivers (partial), and unspecified assistantships available. Support available to part-time students. Financial award application deadline: 6/30; financial award applicants required to submit FAFSA. *Unit head:* Dr. Toby Gouker, Interim Graduate Program Director, 410-455-0616, Fax: 410-455-3969, E-mail: tgouker@umbc.edu. *Application contact:* Dr. Toby Gouker, Interim Graduate Program Director, 410-455-0616, E-mail: tgouker@umbc.edu.
Website: http://se.umbc.edu/

University of Maryland, College Park, Academic Affairs, A. James Clark School of Engineering, Systems Engineering Program, College Park, MD 20742. Offers M Eng, MS. *Program availability:* Part-time, evening/weekend. *Degree requirements:* For master's, thesis optional. *Entrance requirements:* For master's, GRE General Test, minimum GPA of 3.0. Electronic applications accepted.

University of Massachusetts Dartmouth, Graduate School, College of Engineering, Department of Mechanical Engineering, North Dartmouth, MA 02747-2300. Offers industrial and systems engineering (Postbaccalaureate Certificate); mechanical engineering (MS). *Program availability:* Part-time. *Degree requirements:* For master's, thesis, thesis or project. *Entrance requirements:* For master's, GRE unless UMass Dartmouth graduate in mechanical engineering, statement of purpose (minimum of 300 words), resume, 3 letters of recommendation, official transcripts; for Postbaccalaureate Certificate, statement of purpose (minimum of 300 words), resume, 3 letters of recommendation, official transcripts. Additional exam requirements/recommendations for international students: required—TOEFL (minimum score 533 paper-based; 72 iBT), IELTS (minimum score 6). Electronic applications accepted.

University of Michigan, College of Engineering, Department of Integrative Systems and Design, Ann Arbor, MI 48109. Offers automotive engineering (M Eng); design science (MS, PhD); energy systems engineering (M Eng, MS); global automotive and manufacturing engineering (M Eng); manufacturing engineering (M Eng, D Eng); pharmaceutical engineering (M Eng); robotics and autonomous vehicles (M Eng); systems engineering and design (M Eng); MBA/M Eng; MSE/MS. *Program availability:* Part-time, online learning. Terminal master's awarded for partial completion of doctoral program. *Degree requirements:* For master's, capstone project; for doctorate, thesis/dissertation. *Entrance requirements:* For master's and doctorate, GRE. Additional exam requirements/recommendations for international students: required—TOEFL. Electronic applications accepted.

University of Michigan–Dearborn, College of Engineering and Computer Science, MSE Program in Industrial and Systems Engineering, Dearborn, MI 48128. Offers MSE. *Program availability:* Part-time, evening/weekend, 100% online. *Faculty:* 17 full-time (4 women), 9 part-time/adjunct (1 woman). *Students:* 59 full-time (11 women), 62 part-time (24 women); includes 10 minority (3 Black or African American, non-Hispanic/Latino; 4 Asian, non-Hispanic/Latino; 3 Hispanic/Latino), 80 international. Average age 26. 236 applicants, 47% accepted, 26 enrolled. In 2019, 61 master's awarded. *Entrance requirements:* For master's, bachelor's degree in engineering, a physical science, computer science, or applied mathematics. Additional exam requirements/recommendations for international students: required—TOEFL (minimum score 560 paper-based; 84 iBT), IELTS (minimum score 6.5). *Application deadline:* For fall admission, 8/1 for domestic students, 5/1 for international students; for winter admission, 12/1 for domestic students, 9/1 for international students; for spring admission, 4/1 for domestic students, 1/1 for international students. Applications are processed on a rolling basis. Application fee: $60. Electronic applications accepted. *Financial support:* Research assistantships with full tuition reimbursements, teaching assistantships with full tuition reimbursements, scholarships/grants, and non-resident tuition scholarships available. Support available to part-time students. Financial award application deadline: 3/1; financial award applicants required to submit FAFSA. *Unit head:* Dr. Armen Zakarian, Chair, 313-593-5361, Fax: 313-593-3692, E-mail: zakarian@umich.edu. *Application contact:* Office of Graduate Studies, 313-583-6321, E-mail: umd-graduatestudies@umich.edu.
Website: https://umdearborn.edu/cecs/departments/industrial-and-manufacturing-systems-engineering/graduate-programs/mse-industrial-systems-engineering

University of Michigan–Dearborn, College of Engineering and Computer Science, PhD Program in Industrial and Systems Engineering, Dearborn, MI 48128. Offers PhD. *Faculty:* 17 full-time (4 women), 9 part-time/adjunct (1 woman). *Students:* 2 full-time (0 women), 11 part-time (5 women); includes 1 minority (Asian, non-Hispanic/Latino), 11 international. Average age 28. 22 applicants, 36% accepted, 5 enrolled. *Degree requirements:* For doctorate, thesis/dissertation, qualifying and preliminary examinations. *Entrance requirements:* For doctorate, GRE, master's degree in engineering, applied mathematics, computer science, or a physical science from accredited program. Additional exam requirements/recommendations for international students: required—TOEFL (minimum score 560 paper-based; 84 iBT), IELTS (minimum score 6.5). *Application deadline:* For fall admission, 2/1 for domestic and international students. Application fee: $60. Electronic applications accepted. *Financial support:* Research assistantships with full tuition reimbursements, teaching assistantships with full tuition reimbursements, scholarships/grants, health care benefits, and unspecified assistantships available. Financial award application deadline: 2/1; financial award applicants required to submit FAFSA. *Unit head:* Dr. Yubao Chen, Director, 313-593-5579, E-mail: yubao@umich.edu. *Application contact:* Office of Graduate Studies, 313-583-6321, E-mail: umd-graduatestudies@umich.edu.
Website: https://umdearborn.edu/cecs/departments/industrial-and-manufacturing-systems-engineering/graduate-programs/phd-industrial-and-systems-engineering

University of Nebraska at Omaha, Graduate Studies, College of Information Science and Technology, Department of Computer Science, Omaha, NE 68182. Offers artificial intelligence (Certificate); communication networks (Certificate); computer science (MA, MS); computer science education (MS, Certificate); software engineering (Certificate); system and architecture (Certificate). *Program availability:* Part-time, evening/weekend. *Degree requirements:* For master's, comprehensive exam, thesis (for some programs). *Entrance requirements:* For master's, GRE General Test, minimum GPA of 3.0, prior course work in computer science, official transcripts, resume, 2 letters of recommendation; for Certificate, minimum GPA of 3.0, resume. Additional exam requirements/recommendations for international students: required—TOEFL, IELTS, PTE. Electronic applications accepted.

University of New Mexico, Graduate Studies, School of Engineering, Program in Nanoscience and Microsystems Engineering, Albuquerque, NM 87131-2039. Offers MS, PhD. *Program availability:* Part-time. *Students:* 18 full-time (6 women), 24 part-time (2 women); includes 8 minority (3 Black or African American, non-Hispanic/Latino; 3 Asian, non-Hispanic/Latino; 2 Hispanic/Latino), 11 international. 11 applicants, 64% accepted, 4 enrolled. In 2019, 7 master's, 7 doctorates awarded. *Degree requirements:* For master's, comprehensive exam, thesis; for doctorate, comprehensive exam, thesis/dissertation. *Entrance requirements:* For master's and doctorate, GRE. Additional exam requirements/recommendations for international students: required—TOEFL (minimum score 550 paper-based; 80 iBT), IELTS (minimum score 6.5), TOEFL or IELTS, not both. *Application deadline:* For fall admission, 7/30 for domestic students, 2/1 for international students; for spring admission, 11/30 for domestic students, 6/1 for international students. Applications are processed on a rolling basis. Application fee: $50. Electronic applications accepted. *Expenses:* Tuition, state resident: full-time $7633; part-time $972 per year. Tuition, nonresident: full-time $22,586; part-time $3840 per year. *International tuition:* $23,292 full-time. *Required fees:* $8608. Tuition and fees vary according to course level, course load, degree level, program and student level. *Financial support:* Applicants required to submit FAFSA. *Unit head:* Dr. Sang M Han, Professor, 505-277-3118, Fax: 505-277-1979, E-mail: meister@unm.edu. *Application contact:* Linda Stewart, Graduate Programs Coordinator, 505-277-6824, Fax: 505-277-1979, E-mail: lbugge@unm.edu.
Website: http://nsme.unm.edu/

The University of North Carolina at Charlotte, William States Lee College of Engineering, Department of Civil and Environmental Engineering, Charlotte, NC 28223-0001. Offers civil engineering (MSCE), including environmental & water resources, geo-environmental, geo technical, structural, and transportation; infrastructure and environmental systems (PhD), including infrastructure and environmental systems design. *Program availability:* Part-time, evening/weekend. *Faculty:* 24 full-time (6 women), 5 part-time/adjunct (2 women). *Students:* 63 full-time (23 women), 45 part-time (11 women); includes 13 minority (1 Black or African American, non-Hispanic/Latino; 7 Asian, non-Hispanic/Latino; 4 Hispanic/Latino; 1 Two or more races, non-Hispanic/Latino), 53 international. Average age 30. 82 applicants, 67% accepted, 29 enrolled. In 2019, 28 master's, 7 doctorates awarded. *Degree requirements:* For master's, thesis optional; for doctorate, thesis/dissertation. *Entrance requirements:* For master's, GRE, undergraduate degree in civil and environmental engineering or a closely-related field; minimum undergraduate GPA of 3.0; for doctorate, GRE General Test, equivalent to U.S. baccalaureate or master's degree from regionally-accredited college or university in engineering, earth science and geology, chemical and biological sciences or a related field with minimum undergraduate GPA of 3.2, graduate 3.5. Additional exam requirements/recommendations for international students: required—TOEFL (minimum score 557 paper-based; 83 iBT), IELTS (minimum score 6.5), TOEFL (minimum score 557 paper-based, 83 iBT) or IELTS (6.5). *Application deadline:* Applications are processed on a rolling basis. Application fee: $75. Electronic applications accepted. *Expenses:* Contact institution. *Financial support:* In 2019–20, 24 students received support, including 2 fellowships (averaging $44,382 per year), 22 research assistantships (averaging $10,081 per year); teaching assistantships, career-related internships or fieldwork, institutionally sponsored loans, scholarships/grants, and unspecified assistantships also available. Support available to part-time students. Financial award application deadline: 3/1; financial award applicants required to submit FAFSA. *Unit head:* Dr. John L. Daniels, Professor, Department Chair, 704-687-1219, E-mail: jodaniel@uncc.edu. *Application contact:* Kathy B. Giddings, Director of Graduate Admissions, 704-687-5503, Fax: 704-687-1668, E-mail: gradadm@uncc.edu.
Website: http://cee.uncc.edu/

University of Pennsylvania, School of Engineering and Applied Science, Department of Electrical and Systems Engineering, Philadelphia, PA 19104. Offers MSE, PhD. *Program availability:* Part-time. *Faculty:* 34 full-time (5 women), 12 part-time/adjunct (2 women). *Students:* 311 full-time (101 women), 28 part-time (12 women); includes 21 minority (4 Black or African American, non-Hispanic/Latino; 14 Asian, non-Hispanic/Latino; 1 Hispanic/Latino; 2 Two or more races, non-Hispanic/Latino), 279 international. Average age 25. 1,257 applicants, 38% accepted, 118 enrolled. In 2019, 120 master's, 8 doctorates awarded. Terminal master's awarded for partial completion of doctoral program. *Degree requirements:* For master's, comprehensive exam, thesis optional; for doctorate, comprehensive exam, thesis/dissertation. *Entrance requirements:* For master's and doctorate, GRE, bachelor's degree, letters of recommendation, resume, personal statement. Additional exam requirements/recommendations for international students: required—TOEFL (minimum score 100 iBT), IELTS (minimum score 7). *Application deadline:* For fall admission, 12/15 priority date for domestic and international students. Application fee: $80. Electronic applications accepted. *Expenses:* Contact institution. *Application contact:* Associate Director of Graduate Admissions, 215-898-4542, Fax: 215-573-5577, E-mail: admissions1@seas.upenn.edu.

University of Pennsylvania, School of Engineering and Applied Science, Program in Embedded Systems, Philadelphia, PA 19104. Offers MSE. *Program availability:* Part-time. *Students:* 16 full-time (2 women), 5 part-time (1 woman); includes 3 minority (2 Asian, non-Hispanic/Latino; 1 Hispanic/Latino), 14 international. Average age 27. 144 applicants, 15% accepted, 7 enrolled. In 2019, 10 master's awarded. *Degree requirements:* For master's, comprehensive exam, thesis optional. *Entrance requirements:* For master's, GRE, bachelor's degree, letters of recommendation, resume, personal statement. Additional exam requirements/recommendations for international students: required—TOEFL (minimum score 100 iBT), IELTS (minimum score 7). *Application deadline:* For fall admission, 2/1 priority date for domestic and international students. Application fee: $80. Electronic applications accepted. *Expenses:* Contact institution. *Application contact:* Associate Director of Graduate Admissions, 215-898-4542, Fax: 215-573-5577, E-mail: admissions2@seas.upenn.edu.
Website: http://www.cis.upenn.edu/prospective-students/graduate/embs.php

University of Regina, Faculty of Graduate Studies and Research, Faculty of Engineering and Applied Science, Program in Industrial Systems Engineering, Regina, SK S4S 0A2, Canada. Offers industrial systems (M Eng, MA Sc, PhD). *Program availability:* Part-time. *Faculty:* 12 full-time (1 woman), 2 part-time/adjunct (0 women). *Students:* 69 full-time (10 women), 6 part-time (1 woman). Average age 30. 215 applicants, 13% accepted. In 2019, 23 master's, 3 doctorates awarded. *Degree requirements:* For master's, thesis, project, report, co-op; for doctorate, comprehensive exam, thesis/dissertation. *Entrance requirements:* For master's, 4 years bachelor degree; at least 70 per cent from a four-year baccalaureate degree (or equivalent). Additional exam requirements/recommendations for international students: required—

TOEFL (minimum score 580 paper-based; 80 iBT), IELTS (minimum score 6.5), PTE (minimum score 59), other options are CAEL, MELAB, Cantest and U of R ESL. *Application deadline:* For fall admission, 1/31 for domestic and international students; for winter admission, 7/31 for domestic and international students. Applications are processed on a rolling basis. Application fee: $100. Electronic applications accepted. *Expenses:* 11,036.50 -This amount is based on three semesters tuition, registered in 6 credit hours per semester. Plus one year student fees and books. There is additional 438.75 if student is in Co-op route. *Financial support:* Fellowships, research assistantships, teaching assistantships, career-related internships or fieldwork, Federal Work-Study, scholarships/grants, unspecified assistantships, and travel award and Graduate Scholarship Base Funds available. Support available to part-time students. Financial award application deadline: 9/30. *Unit head:* Dr. Adisorn Aroonwilas, Program Chair, 306-337-2469, Fax: 306-585-4855, E-mail: Adisorn.Aroonwilas@uregina.ca. *Application contact:* Dr. Golam Kabir, Graduate Coordinator, 306-585-5271, Fax: 306-585-4855, E-mail: golam.kabir@uregina.ca.
Website: http://www.uregina.ca/engineering/

University of Regina, Faculty of Graduate Studies and Research, Faculty of Engineering and Applied Science, Program in Petroleum Systems Engineering, Regina, SK S4S 0A2, Canada. Offers petroleum systems (M Eng, MA Sc, PhD). *Program availability:* Part-time. *Faculty:* 8 full-time (1 woman), 2 part-time/adjunct (0 women). *Students:* 50 full-time (13 women), 5 part-time (1 woman). Average age 30. 80 applicants, 18% accepted. In 2019, 15 master's, 5 doctorates awarded. *Degree requirements:* For master's, thesis (for some programs), project, report, co-op placement; for doctorate, comprehensive exam, thesis/dissertation. *Entrance requirements:* For master's, minimum graduating average of 70 percent from four-year baccalaureate degree (or equivalent); for doctorate, completion of thesis-based master's degree in engineering or closely-related field. Additional exam requirements/recommendations for international students: required—TOEFL (minimum score 580 paper-based; 80 iBT), IELTS (minimum score 6.5), PTE (minimum score 59), other options are CAEL, MELAB, Cantest and U of R ESL. *Application deadline:* For fall admission, 1/31 for domestic and international students; for winter admission, 7/31 for domestic and international students. Applications are processed on a rolling basis. Application fee: $100 Canadian dollars. Electronic applications accepted. *Expenses:* 11,036.50 -This amount is based on three semesters tuition, registered in 6 credit hours per semester. Plus one year student fees and books. There is additional 438.75 if student is in Co-op route. *Financial support:* Fellowships, research assistantships, teaching assistantships, career-related internships or fieldwork, Federal Work-Study, scholarships/grants, unspecified assistantships, and travel award and Graduate Scholarship Base funds available. Support available to part-time students. Financial award application deadline: 9/30. *Unit head:* Dr. Na jia, Program Chair, 306-337-3287, Fax: 306-585-4855, E-mail: Na.Jia@uregina.ca. *Application contact:* Dr. SD Jacob Muthu, Graduate Coordinator, 306-337-8125, Fax: 306-585-4855, E-mail: Jacob.Muthu@uregina.ca.
Website: http://www.uregina.ca/engineering/

University of Regina, Faculty of Graduate Studies and Research, Faculty of Engineering and Applied Science, Program in Process Systems Engineering, Regina, SK S4S 0A2, Canada. Offers process systems (M Eng, MA Sc, PhD). *Program availability:* Part-time. *Faculty:* 9 full-time (2 women). *Students:* 32 full-time (5 women), 3 part-time (0 women). Average age 30. 39 applicants, 21% accepted. In 2019, 11 master's, 2 doctorates awarded. *Degree requirements:* For master's, thesis (for some programs), project, report, co-op placement; for doctorate, comprehensive exam, thesis/dissertation. *Entrance requirements:* For master's, minimum graduating average of 70 percent from four-year baccalaureate degree (or equivalent); for doctorate, completion of thesis-based master's degree in engineering or closely-related field. Additional exam requirements/recommendations for international students: required—TOEFL (minimum score 580 paper-based; 80 iBT), IELTS (minimum score 6.5), PTE (minimum score 59), other options are CAEL, MELAB, Cantest and U of R ESL. *Application deadline:* For fall admission, 1/31 for domestic and international students; for winter admission, 7/31 for domestic and international students. Applications are processed on a rolling basis. Application fee: $100 Canadian dollars. Electronic applications accepted. *Expenses:* 11,036.50 -This amount is based on three semesters tuition, registered in 6 credit hours per semester. Plus one year student fees and books. There is additional 438.75 if student is in Co-op route. *Financial support:* Fellowships, research assistantships, teaching assistantships, career-related internships or fieldwork, Federal Work-Study, scholarships/grants, unspecified assistantships, and travel award and Graduate Scholarship Base Funds available. Support available to part-time students. Financial award application deadline: 9/30. *Unit head:* Dr. Raphael Idem, Program Chair, 306-585-4470, Fax: 306-585-4855, E-mail: Raphael.idem@uregina.ca. *Application contact:* Dr. Hussameldin Ibrahim, Graduate Coordinator, 306-337-3347, Fax: 306-585-4855, E-mail: hussameldin.ibrahim@uregina.ca.
Website: http://www.uregina.ca/engineering/

University of Rhode Island, Graduate School, College of Engineering, Department of Mechanical, Industrial and Systems Engineering, Kingston, RI 02881. Offers industrial and systems engineering (MS, PhD), including manufacturing systems, service and enterprise systems. *Program availability:* Part-time. *Faculty:* 17 full-time (4 women). *Students:* 32 full-time (9 women), 37 part-time (6 women); includes 7 minority (2 Black or African American, non-Hispanic/Latino; 1 Asian, non-Hispanic/Latino; 2 Hispanic/Latino; 2 Two or more races, non-Hispanic/Latino), 20 international. 38 applicants, 87% accepted, 25 enrolled. In 2019, 3 doctorates awarded. *Entrance requirements:* Additional exam requirements/recommendations for international students: required—TOEFL. *Application deadline:* For fall admission, 6/1 for domestic students, 2/1 for international students; for spring admission, 11/1 for domestic students, 7/1 for international students. Application fee: $65. Electronic applications accepted. *Expenses:* Tuition, area resident: Full-time $13,734; part-time $763 per credit. Tuition, state resident: full-time $13,734; part-time $763 per credit. Tuition, nonresident: full-time $26,512; part-time $1473 per credit. *International tuition:* $26,512 full-time. *Required fees:* $1780; $52 per credit. $35 per term. One-time fee: $165. *Financial support:* In 2019–20, 11 research assistantships with tuition reimbursements (averaging $9,584 per year), 11 teaching assistantships with tuition reimbursements (averaging $10,646 per year) were awarded. Financial award application deadline: 2/1; financial award applicants required to submit FAFSA. *Unit head:* Dr. Carl-Ernst Rousseau, Chair, 401-874-2542, E-mail: rousseau@uri.edu. *Application contact:* David Chelidze, Graduate Admissions, 401-874-2356, E-mail: chelidze@uri.edu.
Website: http://mcise.uri.edu/

University of St. Thomas, School of Engineering, St. Paul, MN 55105. Offers data science (MS); electrical engineering (MS); information technology (MS); manufacturing engineering (MS); manufacturing systems (Certificate); mechanical engineering (MS); medical device development (Certificate); regulatory science (MS); software engineering (MS); software management (MS); systems engineering (MS); technology leadership (Certificate); technology management (MS). *Program availability:* Part-time, evening/weekend. *Entrance requirements:* For master's, resume, official transcripts. Additional exam requirements/recommendations for international students: required—TOEFL (minimum score 80 iBT), IELTS (minimum score 6.5). Electronic applications accepted. *Expenses:* Contact institution.

Systems Engineering

University of South Alabama, College of Engineering, Program in Systems Engineering, Mobile, AL 36688-0002. Offers D Sc. *Faculty:* 6 full-time (0 women). *Students:* 11 full-time (4 women), 7 part-time (1 woman); includes 3 minority (2 Black or African American, non-Hispanic/Latino; 1 Hispanic/Latino), 6 international. Average age 36. 2 applicants, 100% accepted, 2 enrolled. In 2019, 4 doctorates awarded. *Degree requirements:* For doctorate, comprehensive exam, thesis/dissertation. *Entrance requirements:* For doctorate, GRE. Additional exam requirements/recommendations for international students: required—TOEFL (minimum score 550 paper-based; 79 iBT), IELTS (minimum score 6.5). *Application deadline:* For fall admission, 7/1 priority date for domestic students, 6/15 priority date for international students; for spring admission, 12/1 priority date for domestic students, 11/1 priority date for international students; for summer admission, 5/1 priority date for domestic students, 4/1 priority date for international students. Applications are processed on a rolling basis. Application fee: $35. Electronic applications accepted. *Expenses:* Contact institution. *Financial support:* Fellowships, research assistantships, teaching assistantships, career-related internships or fieldwork, Federal Work-Study, institutionally sponsored loans, scholarships/grants, and unspecified assistantships available. Support available to part-time students. Financial award application deadline: 3/31; financial award applicants required to submit FAFSA. *Unit head:* Dr. Robert Cloutier, Systems Engineering Chair, Professor, College of Engineering, 251-341-7993, Fax: 251-460-6343, E-mail: rcloutier@southalabama.edu. *Application contact:* Brenda Poole, Academic Records Specialist, 251-460-6140, Fax: 251-460-6343, E-mail: engineering@southalabama.edu. Website: https://www.southalabama.edu/colleges/engineering/se/

University of Southern California, Graduate School, Viterbi School of Engineering, Daniel J. Epstein Department of Industrial and Systems Engineering, Los Angeles, CA 90089. Offers digital supply chain management (MS); engineering management (MS); engineering technology communication (Graduate Certificate); health systems operations (Graduate Certificate); industrial and systems engineering (MS, PhD, Engr); manufacturing engineering (MS); operations research engineering (MS); optimization and supply chain management (Graduate Certificate); product development engineering (MS); safety systems and security (MS); systems architecting and engineering (MS, Graduate Certificate); systems safety and security (Graduate Certificate); transportation systems (Graduate Certificate); MS/MBA. *Program availability:* Part-time, evening/weekend, online learning. Terminal master's awarded for partial completion of doctoral program. *Degree requirements:* For master's, thesis optional; for doctorate, thesis/dissertation. *Entrance requirements:* For master's and doctorate, GRE General Test. Additional exam requirements/recommendations for international students: recommended—TOEFL. Electronic applications accepted.

University of South Florida, Innovative Education, Tampa, FL 33620-9951. Offers adult, career and higher education (Graduate Certificate), including college teaching, leadership in developing human resources, leadership in higher education; Africana studies (Graduate Certificate), including diasporas and health disparities, genocide and human rights; aging studies (Graduate Certificate), including gerontology; art research (Graduate Certificate), including museum studies; business foundations (Graduate Certificate); chemical and biomedical engineering (Graduate Certificate), including materials science and engineering, water, health and sustainability; child and family studies (Graduate Certificate), including positive behavior support; civil and industrial engineering (Graduate Certificate), including transportation systems / analysis; community and family health (Graduate Certificate), including maternal and child health, social marketing and public health, violence and injury: prevention and intervention, women's health; criminology (Graduate Certificate), including criminal justice administration; data science for public administration (Graduate Certificate); digital humanities (Graduate Certificate); educational measurement and research (Graduate Certificate), including evaluation; English (Graduate Certificate), including comparative literary studies, creative writing, professional and technical communication; entrepreneurship (Graduate Certificate); environmental health (Graduate Certificate), including safety management; epidemiology and biostatistics (Graduate Certificate), including applied biostatistics, biostatistics, concepts and tools of epidemiology, epidemiology, epidemiology of infectious diseases; geography, environment and planning (Graduate Certificate), including community development, environmental policy and management, geographical information systems; geology (Graduate Certificate), including hydrogeology; global health (Graduate Certificate), including disaster management, global health and Latin American and Caribbean studies, global health practice, humanitarian assistance, infection control; government and international affairs (Graduate Certificate), including Cuban studies, globalization studies; health policy and management (Graduate Certificate), including health management and leadership, public health policy and programs; hearing specialist: early intervention (Graduate Certificate); industrial and management systems engineering (Graduate Certificate), including systems engineering, technology management; information studies (Graduate Certificate), including school library media specialist; information systems/decision sciences (Graduate Certificate), including analytics and business intelligence; instructional technology (Graduate Certificate), including distance education, Florida digital/virtual educator, instructional design, multimedia design, Web design; internal medicine, bioethics and medical humanities (Graduate Certificate), including biomedical ethics; Latin American and Caribbean studies (Graduate Certificate); leadership for coastal resiliency planning (Graduate Certificate); mass communications (Graduate Certificate), including multimedia journalism; mathematics and statistics (Graduate Certificate), including mathematics; medicine (Graduate Certificate), including aging and neuroscience, bioinformatics, biotechnology, brain fitness and memory management, clinical investigation, hand and upper limb rehabilitation, health informatics, health sciences, integrative weight management, intellectual property, medicine and gender, metabolic and nutritional medicine, metabolic cardiology, pharmacy sciences; national and competitive intelligence (Graduate Certificate); nursing (Graduate Certificate), including simulation based academic fellowship in advanced pain management; psychological and social foundations (Graduate Certificate), including career counseling, college teaching, diversity in education, mental health counseling, school counseling; public affairs (Graduate Certificate), including nonprofit management, public management, research administration; public health (Graduate Certificate), including assessing chemical toxicity and public health risks, health equity, pharmacoepidemiology, public health generalist, toxicology, translational research in adolescent behavioral health; public health practices (Graduate Certificate), including planning for healthy communities; rehabilitation and mental health counseling (Graduate Certificate), including integrative mental health care, marriage and family therapy, rehabilitation technology; secondary education (Graduate Certificate), including ESOL, foreign language education: culture and content, foreign language education: professional; social work (Graduate Certificate), including geriatric social work/clinical gerontology; special education (Graduate Certificate), including autism spectrum disorder, disabilities education: severe/profound; world languages (Graduate Certificate), including teaching English as a second language (TESL) or foreign language. *Unit head:* Dr. Cynthia DeLuca, Associate Vice President and Assistant Vice Provost, 813-974-3077, Fax: 813-974-7061, E-mail: deluca@usf.edu. *Application contact:* Owen Hooper, Director, Summer and Alternative Calendar Programs, 813-974-6917, E-mail: hooper@usf.edu.
Website: http://www.usf.edu/innovative-education/

The University of Texas at Arlington, Graduate School, College of Engineering, Department of Industrial, Manufacturing, and Systems Engineering, Program in Systems Engineering, Arlington, TX 76019. Offers MS.

The University of Texas at Dallas, Erik Jonsson School of Engineering and Computer Science, Department of Systems Engineering, Richardson, TX 75080. Offers systems engineering and management (MS). *Program availability:* Part-time, evening/weekend. *Faculty:* 3 full-time (0 women), 2 part-time/adjunct (0 women). *Students:* 31 full-time (11 women), 53 part-time (17 women); includes 24 minority (9 Black or African American, non-Hispanic/Latino; 9 Asian, non-Hispanic/Latino; 6 Hispanic/Latino), 31 international. Average age 33. 123 applicants, 15% accepted, 16 enrolled. In 2019, 55 master's awarded. *Degree requirements:* For master's, thesis or major design project. *Entrance requirements:* For master's, GRE General Test, minimum GPA of 3.0 in related bachelor's degree. Additional exam requirements/recommendations for international students: required—TOEFL (minimum score 550 paper-based). *Application deadline:* For fall admission, 7/15 for domestic students, 5/1 priority date for international students; for spring admission, 11/15 for domestic students, 9/1 priority date for international students. Applications are processed on a rolling basis. Application fee: $50 ($100 for international students). Electronic applications accepted. *Expenses: Tuition, area resident:* Full-time $16,504. Tuition, state resident: full-time $16,504. Tuition, nonresident: full-time $34,266. Tuition and fees vary according to course load. *Financial support:* Fellowships, research assistantships with partial tuition reimbursements, teaching assistantships with partial tuition reimbursements, Federal Work-Study, institutionally sponsored loans, scholarships/grants, unspecified assistantships, and cooperative positions available. Support available to part-time students. Financial award application deadline: 4/30; financial award applicants required to submit FAFSA. *Unit head:* Dr. Stephen Yurkovich, Head, 972-883-2305, E-mail: yurkovich@utdallas.edu. *Application contact:* Dr. Stephen Yurkovich, Head, 972-883-2305, E-mail: yurkovich@utdallas.edu.
Website: https://syse.utdallas.edu/

The University of Texas at Dallas, Naveen Jindal School of Management, Program in Organizations, Strategy and International Management, Richardson, TX 75080. Offers business administration (MBA); executive business administration (EMBA); global leadership (EMBA); healthcare leadership and management (MS); healthcare management (EMBA); innovation and entrepreneurship (MS); international management studies (MS, PhD); management science (MS, PhD); project management (EMBA); systems engineering and management (MS); MS/MBA. *Program availability:* Part-time, evening/weekend. *Faculty:* 18 full-time (5 women), 30 part-time/adjunct (5 women). *Students:* 611 full-time (245 women), 768 part-time (372 women); includes 423 minority (86 Black or African American, non-Hispanic/Latino; 2 American Indian or Alaska Native, non-Hispanic/Latino; 210 Asian, non-Hispanic/Latino; 88 Hispanic/Latino; 37 Two or more races, non-Hispanic/Latino), 335 international. Average age 35. 1,456 applicants, 41% accepted, 403 enrolled. In 2019, 570 master's, 19 doctorates awarded. *Degree requirements:* For doctorate, thesis/dissertation. *Entrance requirements:* For master's and doctorate, GMAT. Additional exam requirements/recommendations for international students: required—TOEFL (minimum score 550 paper-based). *Application deadline:* For fall admission, 7/15 for domestic students, 5/1 priority date for international students; for spring admission, 11/15 for domestic students, 9/1 priority date for international students. Applications are processed on a rolling basis. Application fee: $50 ($100 for international students). Electronic applications accepted. *Expenses: Tuition, area resident:* Full-time $16,504. Tuition, state resident: full-time $16,504. Tuition, nonresident: full-time $34,266. Tuition and fees vary according to course load. *Financial support:* In 2019–20, 122 students received support, including 28 research assistantships with partial tuition reimbursements available (averaging $36,900 per year), 82 teaching assistantships with partial tuition reimbursements available (averaging $24,763 per year); Federal Work-Study, institutionally sponsored loans, scholarships/grants, and unspecified assistantships also available. Support available to part-time students. Financial award application deadline: 4/30; financial award applicants required to submit FAFSA. *Unit head:* Dr. Seung-Hyun Lee, Area Coordinator, 972-883-6267, Fax: 972-883-5977, E-mail: sxl029100@utdallas.edu. *Application contact:* Dr. Seung-Hyun Lee, Area Coordinator, 972-883-6267, Fax: 972-883-5977, E-mail: sxl029100@utdallas.edu.
Website: http://jindal.utdallas.edu/osim/

The University of Texas at El Paso, Graduate School, College of Engineering, Department of Industrial, Manufacturing and Systems Engineering, El Paso, TX 79968-0001. Offers industrial engineering (MS); manufacturing engineering (MS); systems engineering (MS). *Program availability:* Part-time, evening/weekend. *Degree requirements:* For master's, thesis optional. *Entrance requirements:* For master's, GRE General Test, minimum GPA of 3.0 in major. Additional exam requirements/recommendations for international students: required—TOEFL. Electronic applications accepted.

The University of Texas Rio Grande Valley, College of Engineering and Computer Science, Department of Manufacturing and Industrial Engineering, Edinburg, TX 78539. Offers engineering management (MS); manufacturing engineering (MS), including systems engineering. *Faculty:* 5 full-time. *Students:* 26 full-time (8 women), 16 part-time (6 women); includes 22 minority (all Hispanic/Latino), 20 international. Average age 26. 21 applicants, 81% accepted, 9 enrolled. In 2019, 12 master's awarded. *Expenses: Tuition, area resident:* Full-time $5959; part-time $440 per credit hour. Tuition, state resident: full-time $5959. Tuition, nonresident: full-time $5959. *International tuition:* $13,321 full-time. *Required fees:* $1169; $185 per credit hour.
Website: utrgv.edu/maie/

University of Utah, Graduate School, David Eccles School of Business, Master of Science in Information Systems Program, Salt Lake City, UT 84112. Offers information systems (MS, Graduate Certificate), including business intelligence and analytics, IT security, product and process management, software and systems architecture. *Program availability:* Part-time, evening/weekend, 100% online, blended/hybrid learning. *Students:* 141 full-time (34 women), 95 part-time (24 women); includes 39 minority (2 Black or African American, non-Hispanic/Latino; 10 Asian, non-Hispanic/Latino; 19 Hispanic/Latino; 8 Two or more races, non-Hispanic/Latino), 65 international. Average age 31. In 2019, 153 master's awarded. *Entrance requirements:* For master's, GMAT/GRE, minimum undergraduate GPA of 3.0, 2 letters of recommendation, personal statement, professional resume. Additional exam requirements/recommendations for international students: required—TOEFL (minimum score 550 paper-based; 80 iBT), IELTS (minimum score 6.5). *Application deadline:* For fall admission, 7/27 for domestic students, 3/30 for international students; for spring admission, 12/7 for domestic students, 9/7 priority date for international students; for summer admission, 4/12 for domestic students, 1/11 for international students. Applications are processed on a rolling basis. Application fee: $55 ($65 for international students). Electronic applications accepted. *Expenses:* Contact institution. *Financial support:* Fellowships with partial tuition reimbursements, teaching assistantships, tuition waivers (partial), and unspecified assistantships available. Financial award application deadline: 6/1; financial award applicants required to submit FAFSA. *Unit head:* Dr. Mark Parker, Associate Dean, Specialized Masters Program, 801-585-5177, Fax: 801-581-3666, E-mail: mark.parker@eccles.utah.edu. *Application contact:* Kaylee Miller, Admissions

Coordinator, 801-587-5878, Fax: 801-581-3666, E-mail: kaylee.miller@eccles.utah.edu. Website: http://msis.eccles.utah.edu

University of Virginia, School of Engineering and Applied Science, Department of Systems and Information Engineering, Charlottesville, VA 22903. Offers ME, MS, PhD, ME/MBA. *Program availability:* Online learning. *Degree requirements:* For master's, comprehensive exam (for some programs); for doctorate, comprehensive exam, thesis/dissertation. *Entrance requirements:* For master's, GRE General Test, 3 letters of recommendation; for doctorate, GRE General Test, 3 letters of recommendation; essay. Additional exam requirements/recommendations for international students: required—TOEFL (minimum score 650 paper-based; 90 iBT), IELTS (minimum score 7). Electronic applications accepted.

University of Washington, Graduate School, College of Engineering, Department of Industrial and Systems Engineering, Seattle, WA 98195-2650. Offers MISE, MS, PhD. *Program availability:* Part-time, online learning. *Students:* 50 full-time (19 women), 37 part-time (13 women); includes 17 minority (4 Black or African American, non-Hispanic/Latino; 6 Asian, non-Hispanic/Latino; 6 Hispanic/Latino; 1 Native Hawaiian or other Pacific Islander, non-Hispanic/Latino), 41 international. Average age 28. 220 applicants, 45% accepted, 35 enrolled. In 2019, 23 master's, 6 doctorates awarded. Terminal master's awarded for partial completion of doctoral program. *Degree requirements:* For master's, thesis optional; for doctorate, comprehensive exam, thesis/dissertation, qualifying, general, and final exams. *Entrance requirements:* For master's, GRE General Test, minimum GPA of 3.0; bachelor's degree in engineering, math, or science; transcripts; letters of recommendation; resume; statement of objectives; for doctorate, GRE General Test, minimum GPA of 3.0; master's degree in engineering, math, or science (preferred); transcripts; letters of recommendation; resume; statement of objectives. Additional exam requirements/recommendations for international students: required—TOEFL (minimum score 580 paper-based; 92 iBT). *Application deadline:* For fall admission, 1/2 priority date for domestic students, 1/2 for international students. Applications are processed on a rolling basis. Application fee: $85. Electronic applications accepted. *Expenses:* Contact institution. *Financial support:* In 2019–20, 1 fellowship with full tuition reimbursement (averaging $30,120 per year), 25 research assistantships with full tuition reimbursements (averaging $30,120 per year), 9 teaching assistantships with full tuition reimbursements (averaging $29,640 per year) were awarded; Federal Work-Study, institutionally sponsored loans, scholarships/grants, health care benefits, tuition waivers (full), and unspecified assistantships also available. Support available to part-time students. Financial award application deadline: 1/2. *Unit head:* Dr. Linda Ng Boyle, Professor/Chair, 206-543-1427, Fax: 206-685-3072, E-mail: linda@uw.edu. *Application contact:* Jennifer W. Tsai, Academic Counselor, 206-543-5041, Fax: 206-685-3072, E-mail: ieadvise@uw.edu. Website: http://ise.washington.edu

University of Waterloo, Graduate Studies and Postdoctoral Affairs, Faculty of Engineering, Department of Systems Design Engineering, Waterloo, ON N2L 3G1, Canada. Offers M Eng, MA Sc, PhD. *Program availability:* Part-time. *Degree requirements:* For master's, research project or thesis; for doctorate, comprehensive exam, thesis/dissertation. *Entrance requirements:* For master's, honors degree, minimum B average, resume; for doctorate, master's degree, minimum A- average. Additional exam requirements/recommendations for international students: required—TOEFL, IELTS, PTE. Electronic applications accepted.

University of Wisconsin–Madison, Graduate School, College of Engineering, Department of Industrial and Systems Engineering, Madison, WI 53706. Offers industrial engineering (MS, PhD), including human factors and health systems engineering (MS); systems engineering and analytics (MS). *Program availability:* Part-time. Terminal master's awarded for partial completion of doctoral program. *Degree requirements:* For master's, thesis optional, 30 credits; minimum GPA of 3.0; for doctorate, comprehensive exam, thesis/dissertation, minimum of 51 credits; minimum GPA of 3.0. *Entrance requirements:* For master's and doctorate, GRE General Test, minimum GPA of 3.0, BS in engineering or equivalent, course work in computer programming and statistics. Additional exam requirements/recommendations for international students: required—TOEFL (minimum score 580 paper-based; 92 iBT), IELTS (minimum score 7). Electronic applications accepted.

Virginia Polytechnic Institute and State University, VT Online, Blacksburg, VA 24061. Offers advanced transportation systems (Certificate); aerospace engineering (MS); agricultural and life sciences (MSLFS); business information systems (Graduate Certificate); career and technical education (MS); civil engineering (MS); computer engineering (M Eng, MS); decision support systems (Graduate Certificate); eLearning leadership (MA); electrical engineering (M Eng, MS); engineering administration (MEA); environmental engineering (Certificate); environmental politics and policy (Graduate Certificate); environmental sciences and engineering (MS); foundations of political analysis (Graduate Certificate); health product risk management (Graduate Certificate); industrial and systems engineering (MS); information policy and society (Graduate Certificate); information security (Graduate Certificate); information technology (MIT); instructional technology (MA); integrative STEM education (MA Ed); liberal arts (Graduate Certificate); life sciences: health product risk management (MS); natural resources (MNR, Graduate Certificate); networking (Graduate Certificate); nonprofit and nongovernmental organization management (Graduate Certificate); ocean engineering (MS); political science (MA); security studies (Graduate Certificate); software development (Graduate Certificate). *Expenses:* Tuition, state resident: full-time $13,700; part-time $761.25 per credit hour. Tuition, nonresident: full-time $27,614; part-time $1534 per credit hour. *Required fees:* $886.50 per term. Tuition and fees vary according to campus/location and program.

Wayne State University, College of Engineering, Department of Industrial and Systems Engineering, Detroit, MI 48202. Offers data science and business analytics (MS); engineering management (MS); industrial engineering (MS, PhD); manufacturing engineering (MS); systems engineering (Certificate). *Program availability:* Online learning. *Faculty:* 12. *Students:* 126 full-time (31 women), 105 part-time (28 women); includes 42 minority (23 Black or African American, non-Hispanic/Latino; 12 Asian, non-Hispanic/Latino; 4 Hispanic/Latino; 3 Two or more races, non-Hispanic/Latino), 124 international. Average age 30. 407 applicants, 36% accepted, 39 enrolled. In 2019, 123 master's, 8 doctorates awarded. *Degree requirements:* For master's, thesis optional; for doctorate, thesis/dissertation. *Entrance requirements:* For master's, GRE or GMAT (for applicants to MS in data science and business analytics), BS from ABET-accredited institution; for doctorate, GRE, graduate degree in engineering or related discipline with minimum graduate GPA of 3.5, statement of purpose, resume/curriculum vitae, three letters of recommendation; for Certificate, GRE (for applicants from non-ABET institutions), BS in engineering or other technical field from ABET-accredited institution with minimum GPA of 3.0 in upper-division course work, at least one year of full-time work experience as practicing engineer or technical leader. Additional exam requirements/recommendations for international students: required—TOEFL (minimum score 550 paper-based; 79 iBT), TWE (minimum score 5.5), Michigan English Language Assessment Battery (minimum score 85); GRE; recommended—IELTS (minimum score 6.5). *Application deadline:* Applications are processed on a rolling basis. Application fee: $50. Electronic applications accepted. *Expenses:* $790 per credit hour in-state tuition, $1579 per credit hour out-of-state tuition. MS programs 30 credits hours; PhD 90 credit hours. *Financial support:* In 2019–20, 125 students received support, including 2 fellowships with tuition reimbursements available (averaging $20,000 per year), 6 research assistantships with tuition reimbursements available (averaging $22,879 per year), 9 teaching assistantships with tuition reimbursements available (averaging $20,792 per year); scholarships/grants, tuition waivers (full), and unspecified assistantships also available. Financial award applicants required to submit FAFSA. *Unit head:* Dr. Ratna Babu Chinnam, Professor and Interim Chair, 313-577-4846, Fax: 313-577-8833, E-mail: ratna.chinnam@wayne.edu. *Application contact:* Eric Scimeca, Graduate Program Coordinator, 313-577-0412, E-mail: eric.scimeca@wayne.edu. Website: http://engineering.wayne.edu/ise/

Worcester Polytechnic Institute, Graduate Admissions, Program in Systems Engineering, Worcester, MA 01609-2280. Offers systems engineering (Graduate Certificate). *Program availability:* Part-time, evening/weekend, online only, 100% online. *Entrance requirements:* For master's, 3 letters of recommendation, statement of purpose. Additional exam requirements/recommendations for international students: required—TOEFL (minimum score 563 paper-based; 84 iBT), IELTS (minimum score 7). Electronic applications accepted.

Youngstown State University, College of Graduate Studies, College of Science, Technology, Engineering and Mathematics, Department of Mechanical, Industrial and Manufacturing Engineering, Youngstown, OH 44555-0001. Offers industrial and systems engineering (MSE); mechanical engineering (MSE). *Program availability:* Part-time, evening/weekend. *Degree requirements:* For master's, thesis optional. *Entrance requirements:* For master's, minimum GPA of 2.75 in field. Additional exam requirements/recommendations for international students: required—TOEFL.

Section 15
Management of Engineering and Technology

This section contains a directory of institutions offering graduate work in management of engineering and technology. Additional information about programs listed in the directory may be obtained by writing directly to the dean of a graduate school or chair of a department at the address given in the directory.

For programs offering related work, in the other guides in this series:

Graduate Programs in the Humanities, Arts & Social Sciences

See *Applied Arts and Design, Architecture, Economics,* and *Sociology, Anthropology, and Archaeology*

Graduate Programs in the Biological/Biomedical Sciences & Health-Related Medical Professions

See *Biophysics (Radiation Biology); Ecology, Environmental Biology, and Evolutionary Biology;* and *Health Services (Health Services Management and Hospital Administration)*

Graduate Programs in Business, Education, Information Studies, Law & Social Work

See *Business Administration and Management* and *Law*

CONTENTS

Program Directories

Construction Management

The American University in Dubai, Graduate Programs, Dubai, United Arab Emirates. Offers construction management (MS); education (M Ed); finance (MBA); generalist (MBA); marketing (MBA). *Program availability:* Part-time, evening/weekend. *Degree requirements:* For master's, thesis optional. *Entrance requirements:* For master's, GMAT (for MBA); GRE (for M Ed and MS), minimum undergraduate GPA of 3.0, official transcripts, two reference forms, curriculum vitae/resume, statement of career objectives, work experience. Additional exam requirements/recommendations for international students: required—TOEFL (minimum score 550 paper-based; 79 iBT). Electronic applications accepted.

Arizona State University at Tempe, Ira A. Fulton Schools of Engineering, ASU Engineering Online Programs, Tempe, AZ 85287. Offers construction (MS); embedded systems (M Eng); enterprise systems innovation and management (MSE); modeling and simulation (M Eng); quality and reliability engineering (M Eng); software engineering (MSE); systems engineering (M Eng).

Arizona State University at Tempe, Ira A. Fulton Schools of Engineering, School of Sustainable Engineering and the Built Environment, Tempe, AZ 85287-5306. Offers civil, environmental and sustainable engineering (MS, MSE, PhD); construction engineering (MSE); construction management (MS, PhD). *Program availability:* Part-time, evening/weekend, online learning. Terminal master's awarded for partial completion of doctoral program. *Degree requirements:* For master's, thesis optional, comprehensive exams (MSE); interactive Program of Study (iPOS) submitted before completing 50 percent of required credit hours; for doctorate, comprehensive exam, thesis/dissertation, interactive Program of Study (iPOS) submitted before completing 50 percent of required credit hours. *Entrance requirements:* For master's, GRE, minimum GPA of 3.0 or equivalent in last 2 years of work leading to bachelor's degree; for doctorate, GRE, minimum GPA of 3.0 in last 2 years of work leading to bachelor's degree, 3.2 in all graduate-level coursework with master's degree; 3 letters of recommendation; resume/curriculum vitae; letter of intent; thesis (if applicable); statement of research interests. Additional exam requirements/recommendations for international students: required—TOEFL, IELTS, or PTE. Electronic applications accepted. *Expenses:* Contact institution.

Brigham Young University, Graduate Studies, Ira A. Fulton College of Engineering, School of Technology, Provo, UT 84602-1001. Offers construction management (MS); information technology (MS); manufacturing engineering technology (MS); technology and engineering education (MS). *Faculty:* 16 full-time (1 woman). *Students:* 14 full-time (2 women); includes 3 minority (1 Hispanic/Latino; 2 Two or more races, non-Hispanic/Latino), 3 international. Average age 28. 15 applicants, 73% accepted, 11 enrolled. In 2019, 7 master's awarded. *Degree requirements:* For master's, thesis. *Entrance requirements:* For master's, GRE General Test; GMAT or GRE (for construction management emphasis), BS degree in information technology, manufacturing engineering technology, construction management, technology and engineering education, or related field; basic sciences background, along with engineering mathematics, computers or electronics, management, architecture, and manufacturing methods. Additional exam requirements/recommendations for international students: required—TOEFL (minimum score 580 paper-based; 85 iBT). *Application deadline:* For fall admission, 2/15 for domestic and international students; for winter admission, 9/10 for domestic and international students; for spring admission, 2/15 for domestic and international students; for summer admission, 2/15 for domestic and international students. Application fee: $50. Electronic applications accepted. *Financial support:* In 2019–20, 10 students received support, including 5 research assistantships with full and partial tuition reimbursements available (averaging $27,617 per year), 5 teaching assistantships with full and partial tuition reimbursements available (averaging $11,446 per year); scholarships/grants also available. Financial award application deadline: 1/15; financial award applicants required to submit FAFSA. *Unit head:* Dr. Barry M. Lunt, Director, 801-422-6300, Fax: 801-422-0490, E-mail: blunt@byu.edu. *Application contact:* Samuel Cardenas, Academic Advisor, 801-422-1819, Fax: 801-422-0490, E-mail: samuel_cardenas@byu.edu.
Website: http://www.et.byu.edu/sot/

California Baptist University, Program in Business Administration, Riverside, CA 92504-3206. Offers accounting (MBA); construction management (MBA); healthcare management (MBA); management (MBA). *Accreditation:* ACBSP. *Program availability:* Part-time, evening/weekend, 100% online, blended/hybrid learning. *Degree requirements:* For master's, thesis, Interdisciplinary Capstone Project. *Entrance requirements:* For master's, GMAT, minimum GPA of 2.5; two recommendations; comprehensive essay; resume; interview. Additional exam requirements/recommendations for international students: required—TOEFL (minimum score 80 iBT). Electronic applications accepted. *Expenses:* Contact institution.

California State University, Chico, Office of Graduate Studies, College of Engineering, Computer Science, and Construction Management, Chico, CA 95929-0722. Offers MS. *Program availability:* Part-time, online learning. *Degree requirements:* For master's, thesis or project or comprehensive exam. *Entrance requirements:* For master's, GRE, fall admissions only; 2 letters of recommendation, statement of purpose, departmental letter of recommendation access waiver form. Additional exam requirements/recommendations for international students: required—TOEFL (minimum score 550 paper-based; 80 iBT), IELTS (minimum score 6.5), PTE (minimum score 59). Electronic applications accepted.

California State University, East Bay, Office of Graduate Studies, College of Science, School of Engineering, Program in Construction Management, Hayward, CA 94542-3000. Offers MS. *Degree requirements:* For master's, comprehensive exam (for some programs), research project or exam. *Entrance requirements:* For master's, GRE or GMAT, baccalaureate degree from accredited university with minimum overall GPA of 2.5; relevant work experience; college algebra and trigonometry or equivalent level math courses; personal statement; resume; two letters of recommendation. Additional exam requirements/recommendations for international students: required—TOEFL (minimum score 550 paper-based; 79 iBT). Electronic applications accepted.

California State University, Northridge, Graduate Studies, College of Engineering and Computer Science, Department of Civil Engineering and Construction Management, Northridge, CA 91330. Offers engineering (MS), including structural engineering. *Program availability:* Part-time, evening/weekend. *Degree requirements:* For master's, thesis. *Entrance requirements:* Additional exam requirements/recommendations for international students: required—TOEFL.

Carnegie Mellon University, Carnegie Institute of Technology, Department of Civil and Environmental Engineering, Pittsburgh, PA 15213. Offers advanced infrastructure systems (MS, PhD); advanced infrastructure systems technology development and application (MS); air quality engineering and science (MS); civil and environmental engineering (MS, PhD); civil and environmental engineering/engineering and public policy (PhD); civil engineering (MS, PhD); computational mechanics (MS, PhD); computational modeling and monitoring for resilient structural and material systems (MS); energy infrastructure systems (MS); environmental engineering (MS, PhD); environmental management and science (MS, PhD); IT-based sustainable global infrastructure and construction management (MS); sustainability and green design (MS); water quality engineering and science (MS). *Program availability:* Part-time. *Faculty:* 23 full-time (5 women), 12 part-time/adjunct (3 women). *Students:* 261 full-time (109 women); includes 19 minority (7 Black or African American, non-Hispanic/Latino; 8 Asian, non-Hispanic/Latino; 4 Hispanic/Latino), 214 international. Average age 25. 649 applicants, 57% accepted, 106 enrolled. In 2019, 80 master's, 12 doctorates awarded. Terminal master's awarded for partial completion of doctoral program. *Degree requirements:* For master's, thesis optional; for doctorate, comprehensive exam, thesis/dissertation, two-part qualifying exam, public defense of dissertation. *Entrance requirements:* For master's, GRE General Test, BS in engineering, science, or mathematics; for doctorate, GRE General Test, BS or MS in engineering, science, or mathematics. Additional exam requirements/recommendations for international students: required—TOEFL (minimum score 84 iBT), TOEFL (minimum score 84 iBT) or IELTS (7.0). *Application deadline:* For fall admission, 1/5 priority date for domestic and international students; for spring admission, 9/15 priority date for domestic and international students. Applications are processed on a rolling basis. Application fee: $75. Electronic applications accepted. *Financial support:* In 2019–20, 113 students received support. Fellowships with tuition reimbursements available, research assistantships with tuition reimbursements available, teaching assistantships, scholarships/grants, health care benefits, tuition waivers (full and partial), and unspecified assistantships available. Financial award application deadline: 1/5. *Unit head:* Dr. David A. Dzombak, Professor and Department Head, 412-268-2941, Fax: 412-268-7813, E-mail: dzombak@cmu.edu. *Application contact:* David A. Vey, Director of Graduate Programs, 412-268-2292, Fax: 412-268-7813, E-mail: dvey@andrew.cmu.edu.
Website: http://www.cmu.edu/cee/

Carnegie Mellon University, College of Fine Arts, School of Architecture, Pittsburgh, PA 15213-3891. Offers architecture (MSA); architecture, engineering, and construction management (PhD); building performance and diagnostics (MS, PhD); computational design (MS, PhD); engineering construction management (MSA); tangible interaction design (MTID); urban design (MUD). Terminal master's awarded for partial completion of doctoral program. *Degree requirements:* For doctorate, thesis/dissertation. *Entrance requirements:* For master's and doctorate, GRE General Test. Additional exam requirements/recommendations for international students: required—TOEFL.

Central Connecticut State University, School of Graduate Studies, School of Engineering, Science and Technology, Department of Manufacturing and Construction Management, New Britain, CT 06050-4010. Offers construction management (MS, Certificate); lean manufacturing and Six Sigma (Certificate); supply chain and logistics (Certificate); technology management (MS). *Program availability:* Part-time, evening/weekend. *Degree requirements:* For master's, comprehensive exam, special project; for Certificate, qualifying exam. *Entrance requirements:* For master's, minimum undergraduate GPA of 2.7. Additional exam requirements/recommendations for international students: required—TOEFL (minimum score 550 paper-based; 79 iBT); recommended—IELTS (minimum score 6.5). Electronic applications accepted.

Clemson University, Graduate School, College of Architecture, Arts, and Humanities, Nieri Department of Construction Science and Management, Clemson, SC 29634. Offers MCSM. *Faculty:* 9 full-time (2 women), 3 part-time/adjunct (1 woman). *Students:* 14 full-time (2 women), 9 part-time (4 women); includes 4 minority (2 Black or African American, non-Hispanic/Latino; 1 American Indian or Alaska Native, non-Hispanic/Latino; 1 Hispanic/Latino), 9 international. Average age 31. 43 applicants, 91% accepted, 19 enrolled. In 2019, 9 master's awarded. *Expenses:* Tuition, area resident: Full-time $10,600; part-time $8688 per semester. Tuition, state resident: full-time $10,600; part-time $8688 per semester. Tuition, nonresident: full-time $22,050; part-time $17,412 per semester. International tuition: $22,050 full-time. Required fees: $1196; $617 per semester. $617 per semester. Tuition and fees vary according to course load, degree level, campus/location and program. *Financial support:* Career-related internships or fieldwork and unspecified assistantships available. *Unit head:* Dr. N. Mike Jackson, Department Chair, 864-656-3878, E-mail: nmjacks@clemson.edu. *Application contact:* Dr. Shima Clarke, Graduate Program Coordinator, 864-656-4498, E-mail: shimac@clemson.edu.
Website: http://www.clemson.edu/caah/csm/

Clemson University, Graduate School, College of Engineering, Computing and Applied Sciences, Glenn Department of Civil Engineering, Clemson, SC 29634. Offers civil engineering (MS, PhD), including construction engineering and management, construction materials, geotechnical engineering, structural engineering, transportation engineering, water resources engineering. *Program availability:* Part-time, 100% online. *Faculty:* 24 full-time (4 women), 3 part-time/adjunct (2 women). *Students:* 101 full-time (20 women), 44 part-time (9 women); includes 9 minority (3 Black or African American, non-Hispanic/Latino; 1 Asian, non-Hispanic/Latino; 2 Hispanic/Latino; 3 Two or more races, non-Hispanic/Latino), 97 international. Average age 29. 248 applicants, 62% accepted, 61 enrolled. In 2019, 43 master's, 11 doctorates awarded. *Degree requirements:* For master's, thesis or alternative, oral exam, seminar; for doctorate, comprehensive exam, thesis/dissertation, oral exam, seminar. *Entrance requirements:* For master's and doctorate, GRE General Test, unofficial transcripts, letters of recommendation, statement of purpose. Additional exam requirements/recommendations for international students: required—TOEFL (minimum score 80 paper-based; 80 iBT), PTE (minimum score 54); recommended—IELTS (minimum score 6.5). *Application deadline:* For fall admission, 4/15 for domestic and international students; for spring admission, 9/15 for domestic and international students. Applications are processed on a rolling basis. Application fee: $80 ($90 for international students). Electronic applications accepted. *Expenses:* Tuition, area resident: Full-time $10,600; part-time $8688 per semester. Tuition, state resident: full-time $10,600; part-time $8688 per semester. Tuition, nonresident: full-time $22,050; part-time $17,412 per semester. International tuition: $22,050 full-time. Required fees: $1196; $617 per semester. $617 per semester. Tuition and fees vary according to course load, degree level, campus/location and program. *Financial support:* In 2019–20, 101 students received support, including 2 fellowships with full and partial tuition reimbursements available (averaging $34,000 per year), 61 research assistantships with full and partial tuition reimbursements available (averaging $18,222 per year), 4 teaching assistantships with full and partial tuition reimbursements available (averaging $20,567 per year); career-related internships or fieldwork and unspecified assistantships also available. Financial award application deadline: 4/15. *Unit head:* Dr. Jesus M de la Garza, Department Chair, 864-656-3001, E-mail: jdelaga@clemson.edu. *Application contact:* Dr. Abdul Khan, Graduate Program Coordinator, 864-656-3327, E-mail:

abdkhan@clemson.edu. Website: https://www.clemson.edu/cecas/departments/ce/

Colorado State University, College of Health and Human Sciences, Department of Construction Management, Fort Collins, CO 80523-1584. Offers MS. *Program availability:* Part-time. *Faculty:* 6 full-time (1 woman). *Students:* 12 full-time (5 women), 1 part-time (0 women), 8 international. Average age 26. 64 applicants, 28% accepted, 4 enrolled. In 2019, 11 master's awarded. *Degree requirements:* For master's, thesis (for some programs), professional paper (for some programs); article submission for journal or proceedings with faculty advisor. *Entrance requirements:* For master's, GRE, official transcripts of all previously earned college credits from each institution attended, 3 letters of recommendation, complete resume describing all academic and work experience, statement of purpose with research interests. Additional exam requirements/recommendations for international students: required—TOEFL (minimum score 80 iBT), IELTS (minimum score 6.5), PTE, Requires at least one TOEFL, IELTS or PTE. *Application deadline:* For fall admission, 2/1 priority date for domestic and international students. Applications are processed on a rolling basis. Application fee: $60 ($70 for international students). Electronic applications accepted. *Expenses:* Tuition, state resident: full-time $10,520; part-time $5844 per credit hour. Tuition, nonresident: full-time $25,791; part-time $14,328 per credit hour. *International tuition:* $25,791 full-time. *Required fees:* $2512.80. Part-time tuition and fees vary according to course level, course load, degree level, program and student level. *Financial support:* In 2019–20, 9 students received support, including 2 research assistantships with full and partial tuition reimbursements available (averaging $15,210 per year), 9 teaching assistantships with full and partial tuition reimbursements available (averaging $17,100 per year); scholarships/grants and unspecified assistantships also available. Financial award application deadline: 2/1. *Unit head:* Dr. Paul Goodrum, Department Head, 970-491-6808, Fax: 970-491-2473, E-mail: paul.goodrum@colostate.edu. *Application contact:* Molly Weisshaar, Graduate Program Liaison, 970-491-7354, Fax: 970-491-2473, E-mail: cmgradadvising@colostate.edu. Website: http://www.cm.chhs.colostate.edu/

Columbia University, Fu Foundation School of Engineering and Applied Science, Department of Civil Engineering and Engineering Mechanics, New York, NY 10027. Offers civil engineering (MS, Eng Sc D, PhD); construction engineering and management (MS); engineering mechanics (MS, Eng Sc D, PhD). *Program availability:* Part-time, online learning. Terminal master's awarded for partial completion of doctoral program. *Degree requirements:* For doctorate, thesis/dissertation, qualifying exam. *Entrance requirements:* For master's and doctorate, GRE General Test. Additional exam requirements/recommendations for international students: required—TOEFL, IELTS, PTE. Electronic applications accepted. *Expenses: Tuition:* Full-time $47,600; part-time $1880 per credit. One-time fee: $105.

Columbia University, School of Professional Studies, Program in Construction Administration, New York, NY 10027. Offers MS. *Program availability:* Part-time, evening/weekend. *Degree requirements:* For master's, minimum GPA of 3.0 or internship. *Entrance requirements:* For master's, bachelor's degree, minimum GPA of 3.0. Additional exam requirements/recommendations for international students: recommended—TOEFL. Electronic applications accepted. *Expenses: Tuition:* Full-time $47,600; part-time $1880 per credit. One-time fee: $105.

Drexel University, Goodwin College of Professional Studies, School of Technology and Professional Studies, Philadelphia, PA 19104-2875. Offers construction management (MS); creativity and innovation (MS); engineering technology (MS); food science (MS); hospitality management (MS); professional studies: creativity studies (MS); professional studies: e-learning leadership (MS); professional studies: homeland security management (MS); project management (MS); property management (MS); sport management (MS). *Program availability:* Part-time, evening/weekend. *Entrance requirements:* Additional exam requirements/recommendations for international students: required—TOEFL, IELTS. Electronic applications accepted. Application fee is waived when completed online.

East Carolina University, Graduate School, College of Engineering and Technology, Department of Construction Management, Greenville, NC 27858-4353. Offers construction management (MCM); residential construction management (Certificate). *Expenses: Tuition,* area resident: Full-time $4749; part-time $185 per credit hour. Tuition, state resident: full-time $4749; part-time $185 per credit hour. Tuition, nonresident: full-time $17,898; part-time $864 per credit hour. *International tuition:* $17,898 full-time. *Required fees:* $2787. *Unit head:* Dr. George C Wang, Interim Chair, 252-737-1887, E-mail: wangg@ecu.edu. *Application contact:* Graduate School Admissions, 252-328-6012, Fax: 252-328-6071, E-mail: gradschool@ecu.edu. Website: https://cet.ecu.edu/construction/

Eastern Michigan University, Graduate School, College of Engineering and Technology, School of Visual and Built Environments, Programs in Construction Management, Ypsilanti, MI 48197. Offers construction (Certificate); construction management (MS); project leadership (Certificate); sustainable construction (Certificate). *Program availability:* Part-time, evening/weekend, online learning. *Students:* 12 full-time (4 women), 9 part-time (3 women); includes 5 minority (1 Black or African American, non-Hispanic/Latino; 2 Asian, non-Hispanic/Latino; 2 Two or more races, non-Hispanic/Latino), 9 international. Average age 31. 47 applicants, 38% accepted, 4 enrolled. In 2019, 13 master's awarded. *Entrance requirements:* Additional exam requirements/recommendations for international students: required—TOEFL. *Application deadline:* Applications are processed on a rolling basis. Application fee: $45. *Financial support:* Fellowships, research assistantships with full tuition reimbursements, teaching assistantships with full tuition reimbursements, career-related internships or fieldwork, Federal Work-Study, institutionally sponsored loans, scholarships/grants, tuition waivers (partial), and unspecified assistantships available. Support available to part-time students. Financial award applicants required to submit FAFSA. *Application contact:* Dr. Armagan Korkmaz, Advisor, 734-487-2492, Fax: 734-487-8755, E-mail: kkorkmaz@emich.edu.

Farmingdale State College, Program in Technology Management, Farmingdale, NY 11735. Offers construction management (MS); electrical and mechanical engineering (MS). *Degree requirements:* For master's, project or thesis.

Florida International University, College of Engineering and Computing, School of Construction, Miami, FL 33175. Offers construction management (MS, PMS). *Program availability:* Part-time, evening/weekend. *Students:* Average age 31. 102 applicants, 30% accepted, 11 enrolled. In 2019, 37 master's awarded. *Entrance requirements:* For master's, minimum GPA of 3.0 in upper-level course work. Additional exam requirements/recommendations for international students: required—TOEFL (minimum score 550 paper-based; 80 iBT). *Application deadline:* For fall admission, 6/1 for domestic students, 4/1 for international students; for spring admission, 10/1 for domestic students, 9/1 for international students. Applications are processed on a rolling basis. Application fee: $30. Electronic applications accepted. *Expenses: Tuition,* area resident: Full-time $8912; part-time $446 per credit hour. Tuition, state resident: full-time $8912; part-time $446 per credit hour. Tuition, nonresident: full-time $21,393; part-time $992 per credit hour. *Required fees:* $2194. *Financial support:* In 2019–20, 5 students received support. Institutionally sponsored loans, scholarships/grants, and unspecified assistantships available. Financial award application deadline: 3/1; financial award applicants required to submit FAFSA. *Unit head:* Dr. Irtishad Ahmad, Director, 305-348-3172, Fax: 305-348-6255, E-mail: ahmadi@fiu.edu. *Application contact:* Nanett Rojas, Manager, Admissions Operations, 305-348-7464, Fax: 305-348-7441, E-mail: gradadm@fiu.edu. Website: http://cec.fiu.edu

Georgia Southern University, Jack N. Averitt College of Graduate Studies, Allen E. Paulson College of Engineering and Computing, Department of Civil Engineering and Construction, Statesboro, GA 30458. Offers MSAE. *Faculty:* 17 full-time (2 women), 1 part-time/adjunct (0 women). *Students:* 8 full-time (1 woman), 6 part-time (3 women); includes 5 minority (3 Black or African American, non-Hispanic/Latino; 1 Hispanic/Latino; 1 Two or more races, non-Hispanic/Latino), 8 international. Average age 27. 12 applicants, 83% accepted, 6 enrolled. In 2019, 4 master's awarded. *Degree requirements:* For master's, comprehensive exam, thesis (for some programs). *Entrance requirements:* For master's, undergraduate major or equivalent in proposed study area. Additional exam requirements/recommendations for international students: required—TOEFL (minimum score 550 paper-based; 80 iBT), IELTS (minimum score 6). *Application deadline:* For fall admission, 3/1 priority date for domestic and international students; for spring admission, 10/1 priority date for domestic students, 10/1 for international students. Applications are processed on a rolling basis. Application fee: $50. Electronic applications accepted. *Expenses: Tuition,* area resident: Full-time $4986; part-time $277 per credit hour. Tuition, nonresident: full-time $19,890; part-time $1105 per credit hour. *International tuition:* $19,890 full-time. *Required fees:* $2114; $1057 per semester. $1057 per semester. Tuition and fees vary according to course load, campus/location and program. *Financial support:* In 2019–20, 11 students received support. Applicants required to submit FAFSA. *Unit head:* Dr. Francisco Cubas, Program Coordinator, 912-478-1894, E-mail: fcubassuazo@georgiasouthern.edu. *Application contact:* Dr. Francisco Cubas, Program Coordinator, 912-478-1894, E-mail: fcubassuazo@georgiasouthern.edu. Website: http://ceit.georgiasouthern.edu/cecm/

Illinois Institute of Technology, Graduate College, Armour College of Engineering, Department of Civil, Architectural and Environmental Engineering, Chicago, IL 60616. Offers architectural engineering (M Arch E); civil engineering (MS, PhD), including architectural engineering (MS), construction engineering and management (MS), geoenvironmental engineering (MS), geotechnical engineering (MS), structural engineering (MS), transportation engineering (MS); construction engineering and management (MCEM); environmental engineering (M Env E, MS, PhD); geoenvironmental engineering (M Geoenv E); geotechnical engineering (MGE); infrastructure engineering and management (MPW); structural engineering (MSE); transportation engineering (M Trans E). *Program availability:* Part-time, evening/weekend, online learning. Terminal master's awarded for partial completion of doctoral program. *Degree requirements:* For master's, thesis (for some programs); for doctorate, comprehensive exam, thesis/dissertation. *Entrance requirements:* For master's, GRE General Test (minimum score 900 Quantitative and Verbal, 2.5 Analytical Writing), minimum undergraduate GPA of 3.0; for doctorate, GRE General Test (minimum score 1000 Quantitative and Verbal, 3.0 Analytical Writing), minimum undergraduate GPA of 3.0. Additional exam requirements/recommendations for international students: required—TOEFL (minimum score 550 paper-based; 80 iBT). Electronic applications accepted.

Instituto Tecnologico de Santo Domingo, Graduate School, Area of Engineering, Santo Domingo, Dominican Republic. Offers construction administration (MS, Certificate); data telecommunications (M Eng, MS, Certificate); industrial engineering (M Eng, Certificate); industrial management (M Mgmt); information technology (Certificate); maintenance engineering (M Eng); occupational hazard prevention (M Mgmt); production management (Certificate); quantitative methods (Certificate); sanitary and environmental engineering (M Eng); structural engineering (M Eng); systems engineering and electronic data processing (Certificate); transportation (Certificate).

Kennesaw State University, College of Architecture and Construction Management, Program in Construction Management, Marietta, GA 30144. Offers MS. *Program availability:* Part-time, evening/weekend. *Students:* 6 full-time (2 women), 9 part-time (4 women); includes 9 minority (6 Black or African American, non-Hispanic/Latino; 2 Asian, non-Hispanic/Latino; 1 Hispanic/Latino), 2 international. Average age 35. 6 applicants, 67% accepted, 4 enrolled. In 2019, 5 master's awarded. *Degree requirements:* For master's, comprehensive exam, thesis or alternative. *Entrance requirements:* For master's, GMAT or GRE, 3 reference forms, minimum GPA of 2.75. Additional exam requirements/recommendations for international students: required—TOEFL (minimum score 80 iBT), IELTS (minimum score 6.5). *Application deadline:* For fall admission, 7/1 priority date for domestic students, 5/1 priority date for international students; for spring admission, 11/1 priority date for domestic students, 9/1 priority date for international students. Applications are processed on a rolling basis. Application fee: $60. Electronic applications accepted. *Expenses: Tuition,* area resident: Full-time $7104; part-time $296 per credit hour. Tuition, state resident: full-time $7104; part-time $296 per credit hour. Tuition, nonresident: full-time $25,584; part-time $1066 per credit hour. *International tuition:* $25,584 full-time. *Required fees:* $2006; $1706 per unit. $853 per semester. *Financial support:* Applicants required to submit FAFSA. *Unit head:* Dr. Khalid M. Siddiqi, Chair, 470-578-4216, E-mail: ksiddiqi@kennesaw.edu. *Application contact:* Admissions Counselor, 470-578-4377, Fax: 470-578-9172, E-mail: ksugrad@kennesaw.edu. Website: http://cacm.kennesaw.edu/constructionmanagement/

Louisiana State University and Agricultural & Mechanical College, Graduate School, College of Engineering, Department of Construction Management, Baton Rouge, LA 70803. Offers MS, PhD.

Manhattan College, Graduate Programs, School of Engineering, Program in Construction Management, Riverdale, NY 10471. Offers MS.

Marquette University, Graduate School, College of Engineering, Department of Civil and Environmental Engineering, Milwaukee, WI 53201-1881. Offers construction engineering and management (MS, PhD, Certificate); environmental engineering (MS, PhD); structural design (Certificate); structural engineering and structural mechanics (MS, PhD); transportation (Certificate); transportation engineering and materials (MS, PhD); waste and wastewater treatment processes (Certificate); water resources engineering (Certificate). *Program availability:* Part-time, evening/weekend. Terminal master's awarded for partial completion of doctoral program. *Degree requirements:* For master's, comprehensive exam (for some programs), thesis or alternative; for doctorate, thesis/dissertation. *Entrance requirements:* For master's, GRE General Test (recommended), minimum GPA of 3.0, official transcripts from all current and previous colleges/universities except Marquette, three letters of recommendation; for doctorate, GRE General Test, minimum GPA of 3.0, official transcripts from all current and previous colleges/universities except Marquette, three letters of recommendation, brief statement of purpose, submission of any English language publications authored by applicant (strongly recommended). Additional exam requirements/recommendations for international students: required—TOEFL (minimum score 530 paper-based). Electronic applications accepted.

Construction Management

Michigan State University, The Graduate School, College of Agriculture and Natural Resources and College of Social Science, School of Planning, Design and Construction, East Lansing, MI 48824. Offers construction management (MS, PhD); environmental design (MA); interior design and facilities management (MA); international planning studies (MIPS); urban and regional planning (MURP). *Degree requirements:* For master's, thesis or alternative. *Entrance requirements:* Additional exam requirements/recommendations for international students: required—TOEFL. Electronic applications accepted.

Missouri State University, Graduate College, College of Business, Department of Technology and Construction Management, Springfield, MO 65897. Offers project management (MS). *Program availability:* Part-time. *Degree requirements:* For master's, thesis or alternative. *Entrance requirements:* For master's, GRE or GMAT, minimum GPA of 2.75. Additional exam requirements/recommendations for international students: required—TOEFL (minimum score 550 paper-based; 79 iBT), IELTS (minimum score 6). Electronic applications accepted. *Expenses: Tuition, area resident:* Full-time $2600; part-time $1735 per credit hour. *Tuition, nonresident:* full-time $5240; part-time $3495 per credit hour. *International tuition:* $5240 full-time. *Required fees:* $530; $438 per credit hour. Tuition and fees vary according to class time, course level, course load, degree level, campus/location and program.

New England Institute of Technology, Program in Construction Management, East Greenwich, RI 02818. Offers MS. *Program availability:* Part-time, evening/weekend, online only, 100% online, blended/hybrid learning. *Faculty:* 2 part-time/adjunct (1 woman). *Students:* 22 full-time (8 women), 3 part-time (2 women); includes 7 minority (3 Black or African American, non-Hispanic/Latino; 1 American Indian or Alaska Native, non-Hispanic/Latino; 1 Asian, non-Hispanic/Latino; 2 Hispanic/Latino). Average age 32. In 2019, 8 master's awarded. *Entrance requirements:* For master's, Minimum GPA 2.5 awarded from a bachelor's degree in a related field from an accredited institution plus personal statement. Additional exam requirements/recommendations for international students: required—TOEFL. *Application deadline:* Applications are processed on a rolling basis. Application fee: $50. Electronic applications accepted. *Expenses:* Tuition is $595 per credit. For additional fee information, please visit https://www.neit.edu/Financial-Aid/Overview. *Unit head:* Dr. Douglas H. Sherman, Senior Vice President and Provost, 401-739-5000 Ext. 3481, Fax: 401-886-0859, E-mail: dsherman@neit.edu. *Application contact:* Tim Reardon, Vice President of Enrollment Management and Marketing, 401-739-5000, Fax: 401-886-0859, E-mail: treardon@neit.edu. Website: http://www.neit.edu/Programs/Masters-Degree-Programs/Construction-Management-Masters-Degree

NewSchool of Architecture and Design, Program in Construction Management, San Diego, CA 92101-6634. Offers MCM. *Program availability:* Part-time, online learning. *Degree requirements:* For master's, thesis. *Entrance requirements:* For master's, GRE/GMAT. Additional exam requirements/recommendations for international students: required—TOEFL, IELTS. Electronic applications accepted.

New York University, School of Professional Studies, Schack Institute of Real Estate, Program in Construction Management, New York, NY 10012-1019. Offers MS. *Program availability:* Part-time, evening/weekend. *Degree requirements:* For master's, thesis, capstone project. *Entrance requirements:* For master's, GRE or GMAT (only upon request), bachelor's degree, resume with relevant professional work, internship or volunteer experience, 2 letters of recommendation, personal statement. Additional exam requirements/recommendations for international students: required—TOEFL (minimum score 600 paper-based; 100 iBT), IELTS (minimum score 7). Electronic applications accepted. *Expenses:* Contact institution.

New York University, Tandon School of Engineering, Department of Civil and Urban Engineering, Major in Construction Management, New York, NY 10012-1019. Offers construction management (MS). *Entrance requirements:* Additional exam requirements/recommendations for international students: required—TOEFL (minimum score 550 paper-based; 90 iBT); recommended—IELTS (minimum score 7). Electronic applications accepted.

North Dakota State University, College of Graduate and Interdisciplinary Studies, College of Engineering, Department of Construction Management and Engineering, Fargo, ND 58102. Offers construction management (MCM, MS, Graduate Certificate). *Entrance requirements:* Additional exam requirements/recommendations for international students: required—TOEFL (minimum score 525 paper-based; 71 iBT). Electronic applications accepted. Tuition and fees vary according to program and reciprocity agreements.

Norwich University, College of Graduate and Continuing Studies, Master of Business Administration Program, Northfield, VT 05663. Offers construction management (MBA); energy management (MBA); finance (MBA); logistics (MBA); organizational leadership (MBA); project management (MBA); supply chain management (MBA). *Accreditation:* ACBSP. *Program availability:* Evening/weekend, online only, mostly all online with a week-long residency requirement. *Degree requirements:* For master's, comprehensive exam. *Entrance requirements:* For master's, minimum undergraduate GPA of 2.75. Additional exam requirements/recommendations for international students: required—TOEFL (minimum score 550 paper-based; 80 iBT), IELTS (minimum score 6.5). Electronic applications accepted. *Expenses:* Contact institution.

Norwich University, College of Graduate and Continuing Studies, Master of Civil Engineering Program, Northfield, VT 05663. Offers construction management (MCE); environmental (MCE); geotechnical (MCE); structural (MCE). *Program availability:* Evening/weekend, online only, mostly all online with a week-long residency requirement. *Degree requirements:* For master's, capstone. *Entrance requirements:* For master's, minimum undergraduate GPA of 2.75. Additional exam requirements/recommendations for international students: required—TOEFL (minimum score 550 paper-based; 80 iBT), IELTS (minimum score 6.5). Electronic applications accepted. *Expenses:* Contact institution.

Pittsburg State University, Graduate School, College of Technology, Department of Technology and Workforce Learning, Pittsburg, KS 66762. Offers career and technical education (MS); human resource development (MS); technology (MS), including automotive technology, construction management, graphic design, graphics management, information technology, innovation in technology, personnel development, technology management, workforce learning; workforce development and education (Ed S). *Program availability:* Part-time, evening/weekend, 100% online, blended/hybrid learning. *Degree requirements:* For master's, thesis or alternative; for Ed S, thesis optional. *Entrance requirements:* Additional exam requirements/recommendations for international students: required—TOEFL (minimum score 520 paper-based; 68 iBT), IELTS (minimum score 6), PTE (minimum score 47). Electronic applications accepted. *Expenses:* Contact institution.

Pittsburg State University, Graduate School, College of Technology, School of Construction, Pittsburg, KS 66762. Offers construction engineering technology (MET); construction management (MS). *Program availability:* Part-time, 100% online, blended/hybrid learning. *Degree requirements:* For master's, thesis or alternative. *Entrance requirements:* Additional exam requirements/recommendations for international students: required—TOEFL (minimum score 550 paper-based; 79 iBT), IELTS

(minimum score 6.5), PTE (minimum score 53). Electronic applications accepted. *Expenses:* Contact institution.

Polytechnic University of Puerto Rico, Miami Campus, Graduate School, Miami, FL 33166. Offers accounting (MBA); business administration (MBA); construction management (MEM); environmental management (MEM); finance (MBA); human resources management (MBA); logistics and supply chain management (MBA); management of international enterprises (MBA); manufacturing management (MEM); marketing management (MBA); project management (MBA). *Program availability:* Part-time, evening/weekend, online learning. *Entrance requirements:* For master's, minimum GPA of 3.0. Electronic applications accepted.

Polytechnic University of Puerto Rico, Orlando Campus, Graduate School, Orlando, FL 32825. Offers accounting (MBA); business administration (MBA); construction management (MEM); engineering management (MEM); environmental management (MEM); finance (MBA); human resources management (MBA); management of international enterprises (MBA); management of technology (MBA); manufacturing management (MEM). *Program availability:* Part-time, evening/weekend, online learning. *Entrance requirements:* For master's, minimum GPA of 3.0. Additional exam requirements/recommendations for international students: recommended—TOEFL. Electronic applications accepted.

Purdue University, Graduate School, Purdue Polytechnic Institute, Department of Building Construction Management, West Lafayette, IN 47907. Offers MS. *Program availability:* Online learning. *Faculty:* 15 full-time (3 women), 2 part-time/adjunct (0 women). *Students:* 34 full-time (10 women), 42 part-time (9 women); includes 8 minority (3 Black or African American, non-Hispanic/Latino; 3 Asian, non-Hispanic/Latino; 2 Hispanic/Latino), 41 international. Average age 29. 126 applicants, 45% accepted, 36 enrolled. In 2019, 21 master's awarded. *Entrance requirements:* For master's, GRE, BS/BA with minimum GPA of 3.0. Additional exam requirements/recommendations for international students: required—TOEFL (minimum score 550 paper-based; 77 iBT); recommended—TWE. *Application deadline:* For fall admission, 4/1 for domestic and international students; for spring admission, 10/1 for domestic students, 9/1 for international students; for summer admission, 4/1 for domestic students, 2/15 for international students. Application fee: $60 ($75 for international students). Electronic applications accepted. *Financial support:* Fellowships, research assistantships, and teaching assistantships available. *Unit head:* Zeljko Z Torbica, Head, 765-494-2465, E-mail: ztorbica@purdue.edu. *Application contact:* Brenda Sheets, Graduate Contact, 765-494-2465, E-mail: bhsheets@purdue.edu. Website: http://www.tech.purdue.edu/bcm/

Purdue University Fort Wayne, College of Engineering, Technology, and Computer Science, Program in Technology, Fort Wayne, IN 46805-1499. Offers facilities/construction management (MS); industrial technology/manufacturing (MS); information technology/advanced computer applications (MS). *Program availability:* Part-time. *Entrance requirements:* For master's, minimum GPA of 3.0. Additional exam requirements/recommendations for international students: required—TOEFL (minimum score 550 paper-based; 79 iBT), TWE. Electronic applications accepted.

South Dakota School of Mines and Technology, Graduate Division, Program in Construction Engineering Management, Rapid City, SD 57701-3995. Offers MS. *Program availability:* Part-time, evening/weekend, online learning. *Entrance requirements:* For master's, GRE General Test. Additional exam requirements/recommendations for international students: required—TOEFL (minimum score 520 paper-based; 68 iBT). Electronic applications accepted.

Stevens Institute of Technology, Graduate School, Charles V. Schaefer Jr. School of Engineering and Science, Department of Civil, Environmental, and Ocean Engineering, Program in Construction Engineering and Management, Hoboken, NJ 07030. Offers construction management (MS, Certificate), including construction accounting/estimating (Certificate), construction engineering (Certificate), construction law/disputes (Certificate), construction/quality management (Certificate). *Program availability:* Part-time, evening/weekend. *Faculty:* 23 full-time (8 women), 21 part-time/adjunct (2 women). *Students:* 98 full-time (9 women), 22 part-time (6 women); includes 8 minority (4 Black or African American, non-Hispanic/Latino; 4 Asian, non-Hispanic/Latino), 95 international. Average age 25. In 2019, 77 master's awarded. Terminal master's awarded for partial completion of doctoral program. *Degree requirements:* For master's, thesis optional, minimum B average in major field and overall; for Certificate, minimum B average. *Entrance requirements:* For master's, International applicants must submit TOEFL/IELTS scores and fulfill the English Language Proficiency Requirement. Applicants to full-time programs who do not qualify for a score waiver are required to submit GRE/GMAT scores. Additional exam requirements/recommendations for international students: required—TOEFL (minimum score 74 iBT), IELTS (minimum score 6). *Application deadline:* For fall admission, 4/15 for domestic and international students; for spring admission, 11/1 for domestic and international students; for summer admission, 5/1 for domestic students. Applications are processed on a rolling basis. Application fee: $60. Electronic applications accepted. *Expenses: Tuition:* Full-time $52,134. *Required fees:* $1880. Tuition and fees vary according to course load. *Financial support:* Fellowships, research assistantships, teaching assistantships, career-related internships or fieldwork, Federal Work-Study, scholarships/grants, and unspecified assistantships available. Financial award application deadline: 2/15; financial award applicants required to submit FAFSA. *Unit head:* Dr. Jean Zu, Dean of SES, 201-216.8233, Fax: 201-216.8372, E-mail: Jean.Zu@stevens.edu. *Application contact:* Graduate Admission, 888-783-8367, Fax: 888-511-1306, E-mail: graduate@stevens.edu.

Texas A&M University, College of Architecture, Department of Construction Science, College Station, TX 77843. Offers construction management (MS). *Faculty:* 18. *Students:* 45 full-time (17 women), 3 part-time (1 woman); includes 9 minority (2 Black or African American, non-Hispanic/Latino; 3 Asian, non-Hispanic/Latino; 4 Hispanic/Latino), 30 international. Average age 26. 45 applicants, 98% accepted, 27 enrolled. In 2019, 15 master's awarded. *Degree requirements:* For master's, comprehensive exam, thesis optional. *Entrance requirements:* For master's, GRE General Test, 3 recommendation letters, resume, statement of research interest, minimum undergraduate GPA of 3.0 in last 60 hours of applicant's undergraduate degree. Additional exam requirements/recommendations for international students: required—TOEFL (minimum score 550 paper-based; 80 iBT), IELTS (minimum score 6), PTE (minimum score 53). *Application deadline:* Applications are processed on a rolling basis. Application fee: $65 ($90 for international students). Electronic applications accepted. *Expenses:* Contact institution. *Financial support:* In 2019–20, 43 students received support, including 11 fellowships with tuition reimbursements available (averaging $1,273 per year), 5 research assistantships with tuition reimbursements available (averaging $11,132 per year), 8 teaching assistantships with tuition reimbursements available (averaging $8,446 per year); career-related internships or fieldwork, institutionally sponsored loans, scholarships/grants, traineeships, health care benefits, tuition waivers (full and partial), and unspecified assistantships also available. Support available to part-time students. Financial award application deadline: 3/15; financial award applicants required to submit FAFSA. *Unit head:* Prof. Patrick Suermann, Department Head, 979-458-3477. *Application contact:* Prof. Patrick Suermann,

Department Head, 979-458-3477. Website: http://cosc.arch.tamu.edu/

Thomas Jefferson University, College of Architecture and the Built Environment, Program in Construction Management, Philadelphia, PA 19107. Offers MS.

Universidad de las Américas Puebla, Division of Graduate Studies, School of Engineering, Program in Construction Management, Puebla, Mexico. Offers M Adm. *Program availability:* Part-time, evening/weekend. *Degree requirements:* For master's, one foreign language, thesis.

The University of Alabama at Birmingham, School of Engineering, Professional Engineering Degrees, Birmingham, AL 35294. Offers advanced safety engineering and management (M Eng); construction engineering management (M Eng); design and commercialization (M Eng); information engineering management (M Eng); structural engineering (M Eng); sustainable smart cities (M Eng). *Program availability:* Part-time, evening/weekend, online only, 100% online. *Faculty:* 5 full-time (1 woman), 15 part-time/adjunct (3 women). *Students:* 13 full-time (4 women), 315 part-time (70 women); includes 83 minority (64 Black or African American, non-Hispanic/Latino; 3 American Indian or Alaska Native, non-Hispanic/Latino; 9 Asian, non-Hispanic/Latino; 7 Hispanic/Latino), 8 international. 126 applicants, 84% accepted, 90 enrolled. In 2019, 123 master's awarded. *Entrance requirements:* For master's, 3.0 GPA on 4.0 scale, undergraduate degree from a nationally accredited school. Additional exam requirements/recommendations for international students: required—TOEFL (minimum score 80 iBT); recommended—IELTS (minimum score 6.5). *Application deadline:* For fall admission, 8/1 for domestic and international students; for spring admission, 12/1 for domestic and international students; for summer admission, 5/1 for domestic and international students. Applications are processed on a rolling basis. Application fee: $50 ($60 for international students). Electronic applications accepted. *Expenses:* Contact institution. *Unit head:* Dr. Gregg Janowski, Associate Dean for Graduate Programs and Assessment, E-mail: janowski@uab.edu. *Application contact:* Jesse Kepply, Director of Student and Academic Services, 205-996-5696, E-mail: gradschool@uab.edu.

University of Alaska Fairbanks, College of Engineering and Mines, Department of Civil and Environmental Engineering, Fairbanks, AK 99775-5900. Offers civil engineering (MS); design and construction management (Graduate Certificate); environmental engineering (PhD). *Program availability:* Part-time. *Degree requirements:* For master's, comprehensive exam, thesis (for some programs), oral defense of project or thesis; for doctorate, comprehensive exam, thesis/dissertation. *Entrance requirements:* For master's, bachelor's degree from accredited institution with minimum cumulative undergraduate and major GPA of 3.0. Additional exam requirements/recommendations for international students: required—TOEFL (minimum score 550 paper-based; 79 iBT), IELTS (minimum score 6.5). Electronic applications accepted. *Expenses:* Contact institution.

University of Arkansas at Little Rock, Graduate School, George W. Donaghey College of Engineering and Information Technology, Department of Construction Management and Civil and Construction Engineering, Little Rock, AR 72204-1099. Offers construction management (MS).

University of California, Berkeley, UC Berkeley Extension, Certificate Programs in Engineering, Construction and Facilities Management, Berkeley, CA 94720. Offers construction management (Certificate); HVAC (Certificate); integrated circuit design and techniques (online) (Certificate). *Program availability:* Online learning.

University of Denver, Daniels College of Business, Franklin L. Burns School of Real Estate and Construction Management, Denver, CO 80208. Offers real estate and the built environment (MBA, MS). *Program availability:* Part-time, evening/weekend. *Faculty:* 7 full-time (1 woman), 5 part-time/adjunct (1 woman). *Students:* 7 full-time (5 women), 40 part-time (11 women); includes 12 minority (3 Black or African American, non-Hispanic/Latino; 3 Asian, non-Hispanic/Latino; 4 Hispanic/Latino; 2 Two or more races, non-Hispanic/Latino). Average age 32. 46 applicants, 78% accepted, 24 enrolled. In 2019, 54 master's awarded. *Entrance requirements:* For master's, GRE General Test or GMAT, bachelor's degree, transcripts, essays, resume, interview. Additional exam requirements/recommendations for international students: required—TOEFL (minimum score 587 paper-based; 94 iBT), TWE. *Application deadline:* For fall admission, 10/15 priority date for domestic and international students; for spring admission, 9/15 priority date for domestic and international students. Applications are processed on a rolling basis. Application fee: $100. Electronic applications accepted. *Expenses:* Contact institution. *Financial support:* In 2019–20, 41 students received support. Teaching assistantships with tuition reimbursements available, Federal Work-Study, institutionally sponsored loans, scholarships/grants, and unspecified assistantships available. Support available to part-time students. Financial award application deadline: 2/15; financial award applicants required to submit FAFSA. *Unit head:* Dr. Barbara Jackson, Associate Professor and Director, 303-871-3470, E-mail: barbara.jackson@du.edu. *Application contact:* Ceci Smith, Assistant to the Director, 303-871-2145, E-mail: ceci.smith@du.edu.
Website: https://daniels.du.edu/burns-school/

University of Florida, Graduate School, College of Design, Construction and Planning, Doctoral Program in Design, Construction and Planning, Gainesville, FL 32611. Offers construction management (PhD); design, construction and planning (PhD); geographic information systems (PhD); historic preservation (PhD); interior design (PhD); landscape architecture (PhD); urban and regional planning (PhD). *Degree requirements:* For doctorate, thesis/dissertation. *Entrance requirements:* For doctorate, GRE General Test, minimum GPA of 3.0. Additional exam requirements/recommendations for international students: required—TOEFL (minimum score 550 paper-based; 80 iBT), IELTS (minimum score 6). Electronic applications accepted.

University of Florida, Graduate School, College of Design, Construction and Planning, M.E. Rinker, Sr. School of Construction Management, Gainesville, FL 32611. Offers construction management (MSCM); fire and emergency services (MFES); historic preservation (MSCM); international construction (MICM), including historic preservation; sustainable construction (MSCM); sustainable design (MSCM). *Program availability:* Part-time, online learning. *Degree requirements:* For master's, thesis. *Entrance requirements:* For master's, GRE General Test, minimum GPA of 3.0. Additional exam requirements/recommendations for international students: required—TOEFL (minimum score 550 paper-based; 80 iBT), IELTS (minimum score 6). Electronic applications accepted.

University of Houston, College of Technology, Department of Engineering Technology, Houston, TX 77204. Offers construction management (MS); engineering technology (MS); network communications (M Tech). *Program availability:* Part-time. *Degree requirements:* For master's, project or thesis (most programs). *Entrance requirements:* For master's, GRE. Additional exam requirements/recommendations for international students: required—TOEFL (minimum score 550 paper-based; 79 iBT). Electronic applications accepted.

The University of Kansas, Graduate Studies, School of Engineering, Program in Construction Management, Lawrence, KS 66045. Offers MCM. *Program availability:* Part-time, evening/weekend. *Students:* 2 full-time (both women), 4 part-time (2 women),

1 international. Average age 30. 20 applicants, 30% accepted, 3 enrolled. In 2019, 6 master's awarded. *Entrance requirements:* For master's, GRE, two letters of recommendation, statement of purpose, resume. Additional exam requirements/recommendations for international students: required—TOEFL, IELTS. *Application deadline:* For fall admission, 7/31 for domestic students, 5/15 for international students; for spring admission, 12/30 for domestic students, 10/15 for international students; for summer admission, 5/15 for domestic students. Application fee: $65 ($85 for international students). Electronic applications accepted. *Expenses:* Tuition, state resident: full-time $9989. Tuition, nonresident: full-time $23,950. *International tuition:* $23,950 full-time. *Required fees:* $984; $81.99 per credit hour. Tuition and fees vary according to course load, campus/location and program. *Financial support:* Career-related internships or fieldwork available. Financial award application deadline: 2/7. *Unit head:* David Darwin, Chair, 785-864-3827, Fax: 785-864-5631, E-mail: daved@ku.edu. *Application contact:* Susan Scott, Administrative Assistant, 785-864-3826, E-mail: s523s307@ku.edu.
Website: http://ceae.ku.edu/overview-6

University of New Mexico, Graduate Studies, School of Engineering, Program in Civil Engineering, Albuquerque, NM 87131-0001. Offers civil engineering (M Eng, MSCE); construction management (MCM); engineering (PhD). *Program availability:* Part-time. *Faculty:* 13 full-time (2 women), 4 part-time/adjunct (1 woman). *Students:* 12 full-time (5 women), 51 part-time (19 women); includes 11 minority (1 Black or African American, non-Hispanic/Latino; 9 Hispanic/Latino; 1 Two or more races, non-Hispanic/Latino), 26 international. 68 applicants, 53% accepted, 22 enrolled. In 2019, 27 master's, 5 doctorates awarded. Terminal master's awarded for partial completion of doctoral program. *Degree requirements:* For master's, comprehensive exam, thesis (for some programs); for doctorate, comprehensive exam, thesis/dissertation. *Entrance requirements:* For master's, GRE General Test (for MSCE and M Eng); GRE or GMAT (for MCM), minimum GPA of 3.0; for doctorate, GRE General Test, minimum GPA of 3.0. Additional exam requirements/recommendations for international students: required—TOEFL (minimum score 550 paper-based; 68 iBT), IELTS (minimum score 6), TOEFL or IELTS, not both. *Application deadline:* For fall admission, 7/15 for domestic students, 3/1 for international students; for spring admission, 11/10 for domestic students, 8/1 for international students. Applications are processed on a rolling basis. Application fee: $50. Electronic applications accepted. *Expenses:* Tuition, state resident: full-time $7633; part-time $972 per year. Tuition, nonresident: full-time $22,586; part-time $3840 per year. *International tuition:* $23,292 full-time. *Required fees:* $8608. Tuition and fees vary according to course level, course load, degree level, program and student level. *Financial support:* In 2019–20, 4 fellowships with full tuition reimbursements, 23 research assistantships with full tuition reimbursements, 5 teaching assistantships with full tuition reimbursements were awarded; scholarships/grants, health care benefits, and unspecified assistantships also available. Support available to part-time students. Financial award application deadline: 3/1; financial award applicants required to submit FAFSA. *Unit head:* Dr. Mahmoud R. Taha, Chair, 505-277-2722, Fax: 505-277-1988, E-mail: mrtaha@unm.edu. *Application contact:* Nicole Bingham, Sr. Academic Advisor, 505-277-2722, Fax: 505-277-1988, E-mail: civil@unm.edu.
Website: http://civil.unm.edu

University of North Florida, Coggin College of Business, MBA Program, Jacksonville, FL 32224. Offers accounting (MBA); construction management (MBA); e-commerce (MBA); economics (MBA); finance (MBA); human resource management (MBA); international business (MBA); logistics (MBA); management applications (MBA). *Accreditation:* AACSB. *Program availability:* Part-time, evening/weekend. *Entrance requirements:* For master's, GMAT or GRE, U.S. bachelor's degree from regionally-accredited university or equivalent foreign degree. Additional exam requirements/recommendations for international students: required—TOEFL (minimum score 550 paper-based; 79 iBT).

University of Oklahoma, Christopher C. Gibbs College of Architecture, Haskell and Irene Lemon Division of Construction Science, Norman, OK 73019-0390. Offers construction management (MS); construction science (MCM); planning, design, and construction (PhD), including construction. *Program availability:* Part-time. Terminal master's awarded for partial completion of doctoral program. *Degree requirements:* For master's, thesis optional, special project; for doctorate, thesis/dissertation. *Entrance requirements:* For master's, minimum GPA of 3.5. Additional exam requirements/recommendations for international students: required—TOEFL (minimum score 79 iBT) or IELTS (minimum score 6.5). Electronic applications accepted. *Expenses:* Tuition, state resident: full-time $6583.20; part-time $274.30 per credit hour. Tuition, nonresident: full-time $21,242; part-time $885.10 per credit hour. *International tuition:* $21,242.40 full-time. *Required fees:* $1994.20; $72.55 per credit hour. $126.50 per semester. Tuition and fees vary according to course load and degree level.

University of Southern California, Graduate School, Viterbi School of Engineering, Sonny Astani Department of Civil and Environmental Engineering, Los Angeles, CA 90089. Offers applied mechanics (MS); civil engineering (MS, PhD); computer-aided engineering (ME, Graduate Certificate); construction management (MCM); engineering technology commercialization (Graduate Certificate); environmental engineering (MS, PhD); environmental quality management (ME); structural design (ME); sustainable cities (Graduate Certificate); transportation systems (MS, Graduate Certificate); water and waste management (MS). *Program availability:* Part-time, evening/weekend. Terminal master's awarded for partial completion of doctoral program. *Degree requirements:* For master's, thesis optional; for doctorate, thesis/dissertation. *Entrance requirements:* For master's and doctorate, GRE General Test. Additional exam requirements/recommendations for international students: recommended—TOEFL. Electronic applications accepted.

The University of Tennessee at Chattanooga, Engineering Management and Technology Program, Chattanooga, TN 37403. Offers construction management (Graduate Certificate); engineering management (MS); fundamentals of engineering management (Graduate Certificate); leadership and ethics (Graduate Certificate); logistics and supply chain management (Graduate Certificate); power systems management (Graduate Certificate); project and technology management (Graduate Certificate); quality management (Graduate Certificate). *Program availability:* 100% online, blended/hybrid learning. *Students:* 10 full-time (4 women), 44 part-time (6 women); includes 9 minority (4 Black or African American, non-Hispanic/Latino; 1 Asian, non-Hispanic/Latino; 2 Hispanic/Latino; 2 Two or more races, non-Hispanic/Latino), 9 international. Average age 33. 24 applicants, 88% accepted, 8 enrolled. In 2019, 21 master's, 1 other advanced degree awarded. *Degree requirements:* For master's, thesis or alternative, Project as alternative to thesis. *Entrance requirements:* For master's, GRE General Test, letters of recommendation; minimum undergraduate GPA of 2.7 overall or 3.0 in final two years; for Graduate Certificate, baccalaureate degree and professional experience or have already been admitted to engineering/engineering management graduate program. Additional exam requirements/recommendations for international students: required—TOEFL (minimum score 550 paper-based; 79 iBT), IELTS (minimum score 6). *Application deadline:* For fall admission, 6/15 priority date for domestic students, 7/1 for international students; for spring admission, 11/1 priority date for domestic students, 11/1 for international students. Applications are processed on a rolling basis. Application fee: $35 ($40 for international students). Electronic applications

accepted. *Financial support:* Research assistantships, teaching assistantships, career-related internships or fieldwork, scholarships/grants, and unspecified assistantships available. Support available to part-time students. Financial award application deadline: 7/1; financial award applicants required to submit FAFSA. *Unit head:* Dr. Ahad Nasab, Department Head, 423-425-4032, Fax: 423-425-5818, E-mail: Ahad-Nasab@utc.edu. *Application contact:* Dr. Joanne Romagni, Dean of the Graduate School, 423-425-4478, Fax: 423-425-5223, E-mail: joanne-romagni@utc.edu.
Website: https://www.utc.edu/college-engineering-computer-science/programs/engineering-management-and-technology/index.php

The University of Texas at Arlington, Graduate School, College of Engineering, Department of Civil Engineering, Arlington, TX 76019. Offers civil engineering (M Engr, MS, PhD); construction management (MCM). *Program availability:* Part-time, evening/weekend, online learning. Terminal master's awarded for partial completion of doctoral program. *Degree requirements:* For master's, comprehensive exam, thesis (for some programs), oral and written exams; for doctorate, comprehensive exam, thesis/dissertation, oral and written defense of dissertation. *Entrance requirements:* For master's, GRE General Test, minimum GPA of 3.0 in last 60 hours of undergraduate course work; for doctorate, GRE General Test, minimum GPA of 3.5. Additional exam requirements/recommendations for international students: required—TOEFL. Electronic applications accepted.

The University of Texas at El Paso, Graduate School, College of Engineering, Department of Civil Engineering, El Paso, TX 79968-0001. Offers civil engineering (MS, PhD); construction management (MS, Certificate); environmental engineering (MEENE, MSENE). *Program availability:* Part-time, evening/weekend. *Degree requirements:* For master's, comprehensive exam, thesis optional; for doctorate, comprehensive exam, thesis/dissertation. *Entrance requirements:* For master's, GRE, minimum GPA of 3.0; for doctorate, GRE. Additional exam requirements/recommendations for international students: required—TOEFL. Electronic applications accepted.

University of Washington, Graduate School, College of Built Environments, Department of Construction Management, Seattle, WA 98195. Offers MSCM. *Program availability:* Part-time, evening/weekend. *Degree requirements:* For master's, thesis or alternative. *Entrance requirements:* For master's, GRE General Test, minimum GPA of 3.0. Additional exam requirements/recommendations for international students: required—TOEFL. Electronic applications accepted.

University of Wisconsin–Stout, Graduate School, College of Science, Technology, Engineering and Mathematics, Program in Construction Management, Menomonie, WI 54751. Offers MS. *Entrance requirements:* For master's, bachelor's degree in construction or a construction-related field from accredited institution, minimum GPA of 3.0, resume.

Wentworth Institute of Technology, Master of Science in Construction Management Program, Boston, MA 02115-5998. Offers MS. *Program availability:* Part-time-only, evening/weekend, 100% online, blended/hybrid learning. *Degree requirements:* For master's, thesis optional, capstone. *Entrance requirements:* For master's, two recommendations from employer; current resume; bachelor's degree in construction management or bachelor's degree with competencies in construction and statement of purpose; minimum GPA of 3.0. Additional exam requirements/recommendations for international students: recommended—TOEFL (minimum score 550 paper-based). Electronic applications accepted. *Expenses:* Contact institution.

Western Carolina University, Graduate School, College of Engineering and Technology, Kimmel School of Construction Management, Cullowhee, NC 28723. Offers MCM. *Program availability:* Part-time, evening/weekend, online learning. *Entrance requirements:* For master's, GRE or GMAT, appropriate undergraduate degree, resume, letters of recommendation, work experience. Additional exam requirements/recommendations for international students: required—TOEFL (minimum score 550 paper-based; 79 iBT). *Expenses: Tuition, area resident:* Full-time $2217.50; part-time $1664 per semester. Tuition, state resident: full-time $2217.50; part-time $1664 per semester. Tuition, nonresident: full-time $7421; part-time $5566 per semester. *International tuition:* $7421 full-time. *Required fees:* $5598; $1954 per semester. Tuition and fees vary according to course load, campus/location and program.

Energy Management and Policy

American College Dublin, Graduate Programs, Dublin, Ireland. Offers business administration (MBA); creative writing (MFA); international business (MBA); oil and gas management (MBA); performance (MFA).

American University of Armenia, Graduate Programs, Yerevan, Armenia. Offers business administration (MBA); computer and information science (MS), including business management, design and manufacturing, energy (ME, MS), industrial engineering and systems management; economics (MS); industrial engineering and systems management (ME), including business, computer aided design/manufacturing, energy (ME, MS), information technology; law (LL M); political science and international affairs (MPSIA); public health (MPH); teaching English as a foreign language (MA). *Program availability:* Part-time, evening/weekend. *Degree requirements:* For master's, thesis (for some programs), capstone/project. *Entrance requirements:* For master's, GRE, GMAT, or LSAT. Additional exam requirements/recommendations for international students: recommended—TOEFL (minimum score 79 iBT), IELTS (minimum score 6.5).

Boston University, Graduate School of Arts and Sciences, Department of Earth and Environment, Boston, MA 02215. Offers earth and environment (MA, PhD); energy and environment (MA); remote sensing and geospatial sciences (MA). *Students:* 68 full-time (37 women), 11 part-time (7 women); includes 5 minority (1 Asian, non-Hispanic/Latino; 4 Hispanic/Latino), 46 international. Average age 25. 194 applicants, 56% accepted, 31 enrolled. In 2019, 26 master's, 6 doctorates awarded. Terminal master's awarded for partial completion of doctoral program. *Degree requirements:* For master's, comprehensive exam (for some programs), thesis (for some programs); for doctorate, comprehensive exam, thesis/dissertation. *Entrance requirements:* For master's and doctorate, GRE General Test, 3 letters of recommendation, official transcripts, personal statement. Additional exam requirements/recommendations for international students: required—TOEFL (minimum score 550 paper-based; 84 iBT). *Application deadline:* For fall admission, 12/19 for domestic and international students; for winter admission, 11/1 for domestic and international students. Application fee: $95. Electronic applications accepted. *Financial support:* In 2019–20, 52 students received support, including 8 fellowships with full tuition reimbursements available (averaging $23,340 per year), 21 research assistantships with full tuition reimbursements available (averaging $23,340 per year), 17 teaching assistantships with full tuition reimbursements available (averaging $23,340 per year); Federal Work-Study, scholarships/grants, traineeships, and health care benefits also available. Financial award application deadline: 12/19. *Unit head:* Guido Salvucci, Interim Chair, 617-353-8344, E-mail: gdsalvuc@bu.edu. *Application contact:* Matt DiCintio, Graduate Program Coordinator, 617-353-2529, Fax: 617-353-8399, E-mail: dicintio@bu.edu.
Website: http://www.bu.edu/earth/

Clarkson University, Wallace H. Coulter School of Engineering, Master's Program in the Business of Energy, Schenectady, NY 13699. Offers MS, Advanced Certificate. *Program availability:* Part-time, evening/weekend. *Students:* 1 full-time (0 women), 9 part-time (2 women). 7 applicants, 86% accepted, 6 enrolled. In 2019, 7 other advanced degrees awarded. *Entrance requirements:* Additional exam requirements/recommendations for international students: required—TOEFL (minimum score 550 paper-based, 80 iBT) or IELTS (6.5). *Application deadline:* Applications are processed on a rolling basis. Application fee: $50. Electronic applications accepted. *Expenses: Tuition:* Full-time $24,984; part-time $1388. *Required fees:* $225. Tuition and fees vary according to campus/location and program. *Financial support:* Scholarships/grants available. *Unit head:* Hugo Irizarry-Quinones, Associate Dean of Engineering, 518-631-9881, E-mail: hirizarr@clarkson.edu. *Application contact:* Daniel Capogna, Director of Graduate Admissions & Recruitment, 518-631-9910, E-mail: graduate@clarkson.edu.
Website: https://www.clarkson.edu/academics/graduate

Colorado School of Mines, Office of Graduate Studies, Department of Economics and Business, Golden, CO 80401. Offers engineering and technology management (MS); mineral and energy economics (MS, PhD); operations research and engineering (PhD); petroleum economics and management with mineral and energy economics (MS). *Program availability:* Part-time. *Degree requirements:* For master's, thesis (for some programs); for doctorate, comprehensive exam, thesis/dissertation. *Entrance requirements:* For master's and doctorate, GRE General Test. Additional exam requirements/recommendations for international students: required—TOEFL (minimum score 550 paper-based; 79 iBT). Electronic applications accepted. *Expenses:* Tuition, state resident: full-time $16,650; part-time $925 per credit hour. Tuition, nonresident: full-time $37,350; part-time $2075 per credit hour. *International tuition:* $37,350 full-time. *Required fees:* $2412.

Colorado State University, Warner College of Natural Resources, Department of Ecosystem Science and Sustainability, Fort Collins, CO 80523-1476. Offers greenhouse gas management and accounting (MGMA); watershed science (MS). *Degree requirements:* For master's, thesis (for some programs). *Entrance requirements:* For master's, GRE (70th percentile or higher), minimum GPA of 3.0; resume; transcript; letters of recommendation; statement of purpose; undergraduate degree in a related field. Additional exam requirements/recommendations for international students: required—TOEFL (minimum score 550 paper-based; 80 iBT), IELTS (minimum score 6.5). Electronic applications accepted. *Expenses:* Contact institution.

Eastern Illinois University, Graduate School, Lumpkin College of Business and Technology, School of Technology, Program in Sustainable Energy, Charleston, IL 61920. Offers MS, MS/MBA, MS/MS. *Program availability:* Part-time, evening/weekend. *Degree requirements:* For master's, comprehensive exam. *Entrance requirements:* For master's, GMAT or GRE. Additional exam requirements/recommendations for international students: required—TOEFL (minimum score 500 paper-based; 61 iBT), IELTS (minimum score 6). Electronic applications accepted.

Franklin Pierce University, Graduate and Professional Studies, Rindge, NH 03461-0060. Offers curriculum and instruction (M Ed); elementary education (MS Ed); emerging network technologies (Graduate Certificate); energy and sustainability studies (MBA, Graduate Certificate); health administration (MBA, Graduate Certificate); human resource management (MBA, Graduate Certificate); information technology (MBA); leadership (MBA); nursing education (MS); nursing leadership (MS); physical therapy (DPT); physician assistant studies (MPAS); special education (M Ed); sports management (MBA). *Accreditation:* APTA. *Program availability:* Part-time, 100% online, blended/hybrid learning. *Degree requirements:* For master's, concentrated original research projects; student teaching; fieldwork and/or internship; leadership project; PRAXIS I and II (for M Ed); for doctorate, concentrated original research projects, clinical fieldwork and/or internship, leadership project. *Entrance requirements:* For master's, minimum GPA of 2.5, 3 letters of recommendation; competencies in accounting, economics, statistics, and computer skills through life experience or undergraduate coursework (for MBA); certification/e-portfolio, minimum C grade in all education courses (for M Ed); license to practice as RN (for MS); for doctorate, GRE, 80 hours of observation/work in PT settings; completion of anatomy, chemistry, physics, and statistics; minimum GPA of 3.0. Additional exam requirements/recommendations for international students: required—TOEFL (minimum score 550 paper-based; 61 iBT). Electronic applications accepted.

Indiana University Bloomington, School of Public and Environmental Affairs, Environmental Science Programs, Bloomington, IN 47405. Offers applied ecology (MSES); energy (MSES); environmental chemistry, toxicology, and risk assessment (MSES); environmental science (PhD); hazardous materials management (Certificate); specialized environmental science (MSES); water resources (MSES); JD/MSES; MSES/MA; MSES/MPA; MSES/MS. *Program availability:* Part-time. Terminal master's awarded for partial completion of doctoral program. *Degree requirements:* For master's, capstone or thesis; internship; for doctorate, comprehensive exam, thesis/dissertation. *Entrance requirements:* For master's, GRE General Test or GMAT, official transcripts, 3 letters of recommendation, resume, personal statement; for doctorate, GRE General Test or LSAT, official transcripts, 3 letters of recommendation, resume or curriculum vitae, statement of purpose. Additional exam requirements/recommendations for international students: required—TOEFL (minimum score 600 paper-based; 96 iBT); recommended—IELTS (minimum score 7). Electronic applications accepted.

Indiana University Bloomington, School of Public and Environmental Affairs, Public Affairs Programs, Bloomington, IN 47405. Offers economic development (MPA); energy (MPA); environmental policy (PhD); environmental policy and natural resource management (MPA); information systems (MPA); international development (MPA); local government management (MPA); nonprofit management (MPA, Certificate); policy analysis (MPA); public budgeting and financial management (Certificate); public finance (PhD); public financial administration (MPA); public management (MPA, PhD, Certificate); public policy analysis (PhD); social entrepreneurship (Certificate); specialized public affairs (MPA); sustainability and sustainable development (MPA); JD/MPA; MPA/MA; MPA/MIS; MPA/MLS; MSES/MPA. *Accreditation:* NASPAA (one or more programs are accredited). *Program availability:* Part-time. *Degree requirements:* For master's, capstone, internship; for doctorate, comprehensive exam, thesis/dissertation. *Entrance requirements:* For master's, GRE General Test or GMAT, official transcripts, 3 letters of recommendation, resume, personal statement; for doctorate,

GRE General Test, official transcripts, 3 letters of recommendation, statement of purpose. Additional exam requirements/recommendations for international students: required—TOEFL (minimum score 600 paper-based; 96 iBT); recommended—IELTS (minimum score 7). Electronic applications accepted.

Instituto Tecnologico de Santo Domingo, Graduate School, Area of Basic And Environmental Sciences, Santo Domingo, Dominican Republic. Offers environmental science (M En S), including environmental education, environmental management, marine resources, natural resources management; mathematics (MS, PhD); renewable energy technology (MS, Certificate).

Johns Hopkins University, Advanced Academic Programs, Program in Environmental Sciences and Policy, Washington, DC 21218. Offers energy policy and climate (MS); environmental sciences (MS); geographic information systems (MS, Certificate). *Program availability:* Part-time, evening/weekend, online learning. *Entrance requirements:* For master's, minimum GPA of 3.0, coursework in chemistry and calculus. Additional exam requirements/recommendations for international students: required—TOEFL (minimum score 100 iBT). Electronic applications accepted.

Kansas State University, Graduate School, College of Engineering, Department of Electrical and Computer Engineering, Manhattan, KS 66506. Offers electrical engineering (MS), including bioengineering, communication systems, design of computer systems, electrical engineering, energy and power systems, integrated circuits and devices, real time embedded systems, renewable energy, signal processing. *Program availability:* Part-time, evening/weekend, online learning. *Degree requirements:* For master's, thesis or alternative, final exam; for doctorate, thesis/dissertation, final exam, preliminary exams. *Entrance requirements:* For master's, GRE General Test, bachelor's degree in electrical engineering or computer science, minimum GPA of 3.0; for doctorate, GRE General Test. Additional exam requirements/recommendations for international students: required—TOEFL (minimum score 600 paper-based; 85 iBT). Electronic applications accepted.

New York Institute of Technology, College of Engineering and Computing Sciences, Department of Energy Management, Old Westbury, NY 11568. Offers energy technology (Advanced Certificate); environmental management (Advanced Certificate); facilities management (Advanced Certificate); infrastructure security management (Advanced Certificate). *Program availability:* Part-time, evening/weekend, 100% online, blended/hybrid learning. *Faculty:* 3 full-time (1 woman), 6 part-time/adjunct (1 woman). *Students:* 33 full-time (4 women), 33 part-time (7 women); includes 18 minority (5 Black or African American, non-Hispanic/Latino; 5 Asian, non-Hispanic/Latino; 7 Hispanic/Latino; 1 Two or more races, non-Hispanic/Latino), 27 international. Average age 30. 114 applicants, 82% accepted, 24 enrolled. In 2019, 2 Advanced Certificates awarded. *Entrance requirements:* For degree, GRE is required for international students and for domestic students who do not meet the minimum GPA requirement, bachelor's degree or its equivalent from an accredited college or university; a background in engineering or management is desirable but not required. Copies of transcripts for all schools attended and proof of degree. Additional exam requirements/recommendations for international students: required—TOEFL (minimum score 79 iBT), IELTS (minimum score 6), PTE (minimum score 53), Duolingo English Test. *Application deadline:* For fall admission, 7/1 for domestic students, 6/1 for international students; for spring admission, 12/1 for domestic and international students. Applications are processed on a rolling basis. Application fee: $50. Electronic applications accepted. *Expenses: Tuition:* Full-time $23,760; part-time $1320 per credit. *Required fees:* $260; $220 per unit. Full-time tuition and fees vary according to degree level and program. Part-time tuition and fees vary according to course load and program. *Financial support:* In 2019–20, 18 students received support. Research assistantships, teaching assistantships, Federal Work-Study, scholarships/grants, and unspecified assistantships available. Support available to part-time students. Financial award application deadline: 2/15; financial award applicants required to submit FAFSA. *Unit head:* Dr. Robert Amundsen, Department Chair, 516-686-7578, E-mail: ramundse@nyit.edu. *Application contact:* Alice Dolitsky, Director, Graduate Admissions, 800-345-6948, Fax: 516-686-1116, E-mail: grad@nyit.edu.
Website: https://www.nyit.edu/departments/energy_management

Norwich University, College of Graduate and Continuing Studies, Master of Business Administration Program, Northfield, VT 05663. Offers construction management (MBA); energy management (MBA); finance (MBA); logistics (MBA); organizational leadership (MBA); project management (MBA); supply chain management (MBA). *Accreditation:* ACBSP. *Program availability:* Evening/weekend, online only, mostly all online with a week-long residency requirement. *Degree requirements:* For master's, comprehensive exam. *Entrance requirements:* For master's, minimum undergraduate GPA of 2.75. Additional exam requirements/recommendations for international students: required—TOEFL (minimum score 550 paper-based; 80 iBT), IELTS (minimum score 6.5). Electronic applications accepted. *Expenses:* Contact institution.

Oklahoma Baptist University, Master of Business Administration in Transformational Leadership, Shawnee, OK 74804. Offers energy management (MBA); transformational leadership (MBA). *Accreditation:* ACBSP. *Program availability:* Part-time, evening/weekend, 100% online, blended/hybrid learning. *Degree requirements:* For master's, comprehensive exam. *Entrance requirements:* Additional exam requirements/recommendations for international students: recommended—TOEFL, IELTS. Electronic applications accepted.

Oklahoma City University, Meinders School of Business, Oklahoma City, OK 73106-1402. Offers business (MBA, MSA); computer science (MS); energy legal studies (MS); energy management (MS); JD/MBA. *Program availability:* Part-time, evening/weekend, 100% online. *Degree requirements:* For master's, practicum/capstone. *Entrance requirements:* For master's, undergraduate degree from accredited institution, minimum GPA of 3.0, essay, letters of recommendation. Additional exam requirements/recommendations for international students: required—TOEFL (minimum score 550 paper-based; 80 iBT). Electronic applications accepted. *Expenses:* Contact institution.

Portland State University, Graduate Studies, College of Urban and Public Affairs, Hatfield School of Government, Department of Public Administration, Portland, OR 97207-0751. Offers collaborative governance (Certificate); energy policy and management (Certificate); global management and leadership (MPA); health administration (MPA); human resource management (MPA); local government (MPA); natural resource policy and administration (MPA); nonprofit and public management (Certificate); nonprofit management (MPA); public administration (EMPA); public affairs and policy (PhD); sustainable food systems (Certificate). *Accreditation:* CAHME; NASPAA (one or more programs are accredited). *Program availability:* Part-time, evening/weekend. *Faculty:* 14 full-time (6 women), 9 part-time/adjunct (5 women). *Students:* 86 full-time (55 women), 119 part-time (73 women); includes 46 minority (3 Black or African American, non-Hispanic/Latino; 4 American Indian or Alaska Native, non-Hispanic/Latino; 8 Asian, non-Hispanic/Latino; 18 Hispanic/Latino; 2 Native Hawaiian or other Pacific Islander, non-Hispanic/Latino; 11 Two or more races, non-Hispanic/Latino), 17 international. Average age 35. 138 applicants, 82% accepted, 67 enrolled. In 2019, 64 master's, 2 doctorates awarded. *Degree requirements:* For master's, integrative field experience (MPA), practicum (MPH); for doctorate, comprehensive exam, thesis/dissertation. *Entrance requirements:* For master's, GRE (minimum scores: verbal 150, quantitative 149, and analytic writing 4.5), minimum GPA of 3.0, 3 recommendation letters, resume, 500-word statement of intent; for doctorate, GRE, 3 recommendation letters, resume, 500-word personal essay. Additional exam requirements/recommendations for international students: required—TOEFL (minimum score 550 paper-based; 80 iBT), IELTS (minimum score 7). *Application deadline:* For fall admission, 8/15 for domestic and international students; for winter admission, 10/31 for domestic and international students; for spring admission, 1/31 for domestic and international students. Applications are processed on a rolling basis. Application fee: $65. Electronic applications accepted. *Expenses: Tuition, area resident:* Full-time $13,020; part-time $6510 per year. Tuition, state resident: full-time $13,020; part-time $6510 per year. Tuition, nonresident: full-time $19,830; part-time $9915 per year. *International tuition:* $19,830 full-time. *Required fees:* $1226. One-time fee: $350. Tuition and fees vary according to course load, program and reciprocity agreements. *Financial support:* In 2019–20, 1 research assistantship with full and partial tuition reimbursement (averaging $8,500 per year), 3 teaching assistantships (averaging $7,840 per year) were awarded; career-related internships or fieldwork, Federal Work-Study, scholarships/grants, and unspecified assistantships also available. Support available to part-time students. Financial award application deadline: 3/1; financial award applicants required to submit FAFSA. *Unit head:* Dr. Masami Nishishiba, Chair, 503-725-5151, E-mail: nishism@pdx.edu. *Application contact:* Megan Heljeson, Office Coordinator, 503-725-3921, Fax: 503-725-8250, E-mail: publicad@pdx.edu.
Website: https://www.pdx.edu/hatfieldschool/public-administration

Portland State University, Graduate Studies, College of Urban and Public Affairs, Nohad A. Toulan School of Urban Studies and Planning, Portland, OR 97207-0751. Offers applied social demography (Certificate); energy policy and management (Certificate); real estate development (Certificate); sustainable food systems (Certificate); transportation (Certificate); urban design (Certificate); urban studies (PhD); urban studies and planning (MRED, MURP, MUS); urban studies: regional science (PhD). *Program availability:* Part-time, evening/weekend. *Faculty:* 16 full-time (9 women), 14 part-time/adjunct (6 women). *Students:* 92 full-time (51 women), 48 part-time (28 women); includes 28 minority (4 Black or African American, non-Hispanic/Latino; 6 Asian, non-Hispanic/Latino; 13 Hispanic/Latino; 5 Two or more races, non-Hispanic/Latino), 23 international. Average age 33. 196 applicants, 73% accepted, 53 enrolled. In 2019, 33 master's, 4 doctorates awarded. *Degree requirements:* For doctorate, comprehensive exam, thesis/dissertation. *Entrance requirements:* For doctorate, GRE General Test, minimum GPA of 2.75, statement of purpose, 3 letters of recommendation, resume/curriculum vitae. Additional exam requirements/recommendations for international students: required—TOEFL (minimum score 550 paper-based; 80 iBT). *Application deadline:* For fall admission, 1/15 for domestic and international students. Application fee: $65. Electronic applications accepted. *Expenses: Tuition, area resident:* Full-time $13,020; part-time $6510 per year. Tuition, state resident: full-time $13,020; part-time $6510 per year. Tuition, nonresident: full-time $19,830; part-time $9915 per year. *International tuition:* $19,830 full-time. *Required fees:* $1226. One-time fee: $350. Tuition and fees vary according to course load, program and reciprocity agreements. *Financial support:* In 2019–20, 29 research assistantships with full and partial tuition reimbursements (averaging $11,476 per year), 3 teaching assistantships with full and partial tuition reimbursements (averaging $9,752 per year) were awarded; career-related internships or fieldwork, Federal Work-Study, scholarships/grants, and unspecified assistantships also available. Support available to part-time students. Financial award application deadline: 3/1; financial award applicants required to submit FAFSA. *Unit head:* Dr. Aaron Golub, Director, 503-725-4069, E-mail: agolub@pdx.edu. *Application contact:* Erin Wennstrom, Office Coordinator, 503-725-4045, E-mail: epw@pdx.edu.
Website: https://www.pdx.edu/cupa/

Rice University, Graduate Programs, School of Social Sciences, Department of Economics, Houston, TX 77251-1892. Offers economics (PhD); energy economics (MEECON). *Degree requirements:* For doctorate, comprehensive exam, thesis/dissertation. *Entrance requirements:* For doctorate, GRE. Additional exam requirements/recommendations for international students: required—TOEFL (minimum score 600 paper-based; 90 iBT). Electronic applications accepted.

Samford University, Howard College of Arts and Sciences, Birmingham, AL 35229. Offers energy (MSEM); environmental management (MSEM); public health (MSEM); JD/MSEM. *Program availability:* Part-time-only, online only, 100% online. *Faculty:* 8 full-time (3 women), 1 part-time/adjunct (0 women). *Students:* 11 full-time (5 women); includes 3 minority (all Black or African American, non-Hispanic/Latino). Average age 29. 25 applicants, 20% accepted, 5 enrolled. In 2019, 5 master's awarded. Terminal master's awarded for partial completion of doctoral program. *Entrance requirements:* For master's, 2 letters of recommendation; minimum overall GPA of 3.0 (3 years or less since undergraduate degree); minimum overall GPA of 2.5 (after 3 years' relevant work experience). Additional exam requirements/recommendations for international students: required—TOEFL (minimum score 520 paper-based). *Application deadline:* Applications are processed on a rolling basis. Application fee: $35. Electronic applications accepted. *Expenses: Tuition:* Full-time $17,754; part-time $862 per credit hour. *Required fees:* $550; $550 per unit. Full-time tuition and fees vary according to course load, program and student level. *Financial support:* Career-related internships or fieldwork available. Financial award application deadline: 2/15; financial award applicants required to submit FAFSA. *Unit head:* Dr. Anthony Scott Overton, Professor and Chair, 205-726-2944, E-mail: aoverton@samford.edu. *Application contact:* David Frings, Assistant Graduate Director, 205-726-4537, E-mail: dmfrings@samford.edu.
Website: http://howard.samford.edu/

SIT Graduate Institute, Graduate Programs, Master's Program in Climate Change and Global Sustainability, Brattleboro, VT 05302-0676. Offers MA. *Expenses: Tuition:* Full-time $43,500; part-time $21,750 per credit.

Stony Brook University, State University of New York, Graduate School, College of Engineering and Applied Sciences, Department of Technology and Society, Program in Energy Technology and Policy, Stony Brook, NY 11794. Offers MS. *Program availability:* Part-time. *Degree requirements:* For master's, thesis, project. *Entrance requirements:* For master's, GRE. Additional exam requirements/recommendations for international students: required—TOEFL (minimum score 85 iBT), IELTS (minimum score 6.5). *Application deadline:* For fall admission, 7/2 for domestic students, 4/15 for international students; for spring admission, 12/3 for domestic students, 10/5 for international students; for summer admission, 4/15 for domestic students. Application fee: $100. Electronic applications accepted. *Expenses:* Contact institution. *Financial support:* Research assistantships, teaching assistantships, and career-related internships or fieldwork available. *Unit head:* Dr. Wolf Schafer, Chair, 631-632-7924, E-mail: wolf.schafer@stonybrook.edu. *Application contact:* Marypat Taveras, Coordinator, 631-632-8770, Fax: 631-632-7809, E-mail: marypat.taveras@stonybrook.edu.
Website: https://www.stonybrook.edu/commcms/est/masters/programs/msenergyenv.php

Tulane University, A. B. Freeman School of Business, New Orleans, LA 70118-5669. Offers accounting (M Acct); analytics (MBA); banking and financial services (M Fin); energy (M Fin, MBA); entrepreneurship (MBA); finance (MBA, PhD); financial accounting (PhD); international business (MBA); international management (MBA);

strategic management and leadership (MBA); JD/M Acct; JD/MBA; MBA/M Acc; MBA/MA; MBA/MD; MBA/ME; MBA/MPH. *Accreditation:* AACSB. *Program availability:* Part-time, evening/weekend. *Faculty:* 49 full-time (15 women), 53 part-time/adjunct (7 women). *Students:* 394 full-time (168 women), 379 part-time (162 women); includes 111 minority (41 Black or African American, non-Hispanic/Latino; 24 Asian, non-Hispanic/Latino; 38 Hispanic/Latino; 8 Two or more races, non-Hispanic/Latino), 427 international. Average age 28. 1,847 applicants, 72% accepted, 379 enrolled. In 2019, 791 master's awarded. Terminal master's awarded for partial completion of doctoral program. *Degree requirements:* For master's, one foreign language, comprehensive exam (for some programs); for doctorate, one foreign language, comprehensive exam, thesis/dissertation. *Entrance requirements:* For master's and doctorate, GMAT or GRE, interview. Additional exam requirements/recommendations for international students: required—TOEFL or IELTS. *Application deadline:* For fall admission, 11/1 priority date for domestic students, 11/1 for international students; for winter admission, 1/6 for domestic and international students; for spring admission, 3/1 priority date for domestic students, 3/1 for international students; for summer admission, 5/5 for domestic students. Applications are processed on a rolling basis. Application fee: $125. Electronic applications accepted. *Expenses:* Contact institution. *Financial support:* In 2019–20, 233 students received support. Fellowships with tuition reimbursements available, research assistantships, teaching assistantships, career-related internships or fieldwork, Federal Work-Study, tuition waivers (full and partial), and unspecified assistantships available. Support available to part-time students. Financial award application deadline: 4/15; financial award applicants required to submit FAFSA. *Unit head:* Ira Solomon, PhD, Dean, 504-865-5407, Fax: 504-865-5491, E-mail: businessdean@tulane.edu. *Application contact:* Melissa Booth, Assistant Dean for Graduate Admissions, 800-223-5402, E-mail: freeman.admissions@tulane.edu.
Website: http://www.freeman.tulane.edu

Université du Québec, Institut National de la Recherche Scientifique, Graduate Programs, Centre for Energie Materiaux Telecommunications, Varennes, QC J3X 1S2, Canada. Offers energy and materials science (M Sc, PhD); telecommunications (M Sc, PhD). *Program availability:* Part-time. *Faculty:* 38 full-time. *Students:* 208 full-time (61 women), 12 part-time (1 woman), 187 international. Average age 32. 36 applicants, 100% accepted, 29 enrolled. In 2019, 12 master's, 26 doctorates awarded. *Degree requirements:* For master's, thesis (for some programs); for doctorate, thesis/dissertation. *Entrance requirements:* For master's, appropriate bachelor's degree, proficiency in French; for doctorate, appropriate master's degree, proficiency in French. *Application deadline:* For fall admission, 3/30 for domestic and international students; for winter admission, 11/1 for domestic and international students; for spring admission, 3/1 for domestic and international students. Application fee: $45. Electronic applications accepted. *Financial support:* In 2019–20, fellowships (averaging $16,500 per year) were awarded; research assistantships and scholarships/grants also available. *Unit head:* Ana Tavares, Director, 514-228-6947, Fax: 450-929-8102, E-mail: ana.tavares@emt.inrs.ca. *Application contact:* Sean Otto, Registrar, 418-654-2518, Fax: 418-654-3858, E-mail: sean.otto@inrs.ca.
Website: http://www.emt.inrs.ca

University of Calgary, Faculty of Graduate Studies, Schulich School of Engineering, Program in Chemical and Petroleum Engineering, Calgary, AB T2N 1N4, Canada. Offers chemical engineering (M Eng, M Sc, PhD); energy and environment engineering (M Eng, M Sc, PhD); energy and environmental systems (M Eng, M Sc, PhD); environmental engineering (M Eng, M Sc, PhD); petroleum engineering (M Eng, M Sc, PhD); reservoir characterization (M Eng, M Sc). *Program availability:* Part-time. *Degree requirements:* For master's, thesis (for some programs); for doctorate, comprehensive exam, thesis/dissertation, candidacy exam. *Entrance requirements:* For master's, minimum GPA of 3.0 or equivalent; for doctorate, minimum GPA of 3.5 or equivalent. Additional exam requirements/recommendations for international students: required—TOEFL (minimum score 550 paper-based; 80 iBT), IELTS (minimum score 7). Electronic applications accepted.

University of California, Berkeley, Graduate Division, College of Natural Resources, Group in Energy and Resources, Berkeley, CA 94720. Offers MA, MS, PhD. *Degree requirements:* For master's, project or thesis; for doctorate, one foreign language, thesis/dissertation, qualifying exam. *Entrance requirements:* For master's and doctorate, GRE General Test, minimum GPA of 3.0, 3 letters of recommendation. Electronic applications accepted.

University of California, San Diego, Graduate Division, School of Global Policy and Strategy, Master of Public Policy Program, La Jolla, CA 92093. Offers American policy in global context (MPP); business, government and regulation (MPP); energy and environmental policy (MPP); health policy (MPP); program design and evaluation (MPP); security policy (MPP). *Entrance requirements:* For master's, GMAT or GRE General Test. Additional exam requirements/recommendations for international students: required—TOEFL (minimum score 90 iBT), IELTS (minimum score 7). Electronic applications accepted. *Expenses:* Contact institution.

University of Colorado Denver, Business School, Program in Global Energy Management, Denver, CO 80217. Offers MS. *Program availability:* Online learning. *Degree requirements:* For master's, 36 semester credit hours. *Entrance requirements:* For master's, GMAT if less than three years of experience in the energy industry (waived for students already holding a graduate degree), minimum of 5 years' experience in energy industry; resume; letters of recommendation; essays. Additional exam requirements/recommendations for international students: required—TOEFL (minimum score 525 paper-based; 71 iBT); recommended—IELTS (minimum score 6). Electronic applications accepted. *Expenses:* Contact institution.

University of Delaware, Center for Energy and Environmental Policy, Newark, DE 19716. Offers energy and environmental policy (MA, MEEP, PhD); urban affairs and public policy (PhD), including technology, environment, and society. *Degree requirements:* For master's, analytical paper or thesis; for doctorate, comprehensive exam, thesis/dissertation. *Entrance requirements:* For master's, GRE General Test, minimum GPA of 3.0; for doctorate, GRE General Test, minimum GPA of 3.5. Additional exam requirements/recommendations for international students: required—TOEFL. Electronic applications accepted.

University of Illinois at Urbana-Champaign, Graduate College, College of Agricultural, Consumer and Environmental Sciences, Program in Bioenergy, Champaign, IL 61820. Offers PSM.

University of Mary, Gary Tharaldson School of Business, Bismarck, ND 58504-9652. Offers business administration (MBA); energy management (MBA, MS); executive (MBA, MS); health care (MBA, MS); human resource management (MBA); project management (MBA, MPM); virtuous leadership (MBA, MPM, MS). *Program availability:* Part-time, evening/weekend. *Entrance requirements:* For master's, minimum GPA of 2.5. Additional exam requirements/recommendations for international students: required—TOEFL (minimum score 550 paper-based; 80 iBT). Electronic applications accepted.

University of Phoenix - Bay Area Campus, School of Business, San Jose, CA 95134-1805. Offers accountancy (MS); accounting (MBA); business administration (MBA, DBA); energy management (MBA); global management (MBA); health care management (MBA); human resource management (MBA); human resources management (MM); management (MM); marketing (MBA); organizational leadership (DM); project management (MBA); public administration (MPA); technology management (MBA). *Accreditation:* ACBSP. *Program availability:* Evening/weekend, online learning. *Degree requirements:* For master's, thesis (for some programs). *Entrance requirements:* For master's, minimum undergraduate GPA of 3.0, 3 years of work experience. Additional exam requirements/recommendations for international students: required—TOEFL (minimum score 550 paper-based; 79 iBT). Electronic applications accepted.

University of Phoenix–Online Campus, School of Business, Phoenix, AZ 85034-7209. Offers accountancy (MS); accounting (MBA, Certificate); business administration (MBA); energy management (MBA); global management (MBA); health care management (MBA); human resource management (MBA, Certificate); human resources management (MM); management (MM); marketing (MBA, Certificate); project management (MBA, Certificate); public administration (MBA, MM); technology management (MBA). *Program availability:* Evening/weekend, online learning. *Entrance requirements:* Additional exam requirements/recommendations for international students: required—TOEFL, TOEIC (Test of English as an International Communication), Berlitz Online English Proficiency Exam, PTE, or IELTS. Electronic applications accepted. *Expenses:* Contact institution.

University of Phoenix - Phoenix Campus, School of Business, Tempe, AZ 85282-2371. Offers accounting (MBA, MS, Certificate); business administration (MBA); energy management (MBA); global management (MBA); health care management (MBA); human resource management (MBA, Certificate); management (MM); marketing (MBA); project management (MBA); technology management (MBA). *Program availability:* Evening/weekend, online learning. *Entrance requirements:* Additional exam requirements/recommendations for international students: required—TOEFL, TOEIC (Test of English as an International Communication), Berlitz Online English Proficiency Exam, PTE, or IELTS. Electronic applications accepted. *Expenses:* Contact institution.

University of Pittsburgh, Graduate School of Public and International Affairs, Master of Public Administration Program, Pittsburgh, PA 15260. Offers energy and environment (MPA); governance and international public management (MPA); policy research and analysis (MPA); public and nonprofit management (MPA); urban affairs and planning (MPA); JD/MPA; MPH/MPA; MSIS/MPA; MSW/MPA. *Accreditation:* NASPAA. *Program availability:* Part-time, evening/weekend. *Faculty:* 33 full-time (11 women), 10 part-time/adjunct (5 women). *Students:* 76 full-time (51 women), 17 part-time (10 women); includes 9 minority (5 Black or African American, non-Hispanic/Latino; 1 Asian, non-Hispanic/Latino; 3 Hispanic/Latino), 37 international. Average age 26. 167 applicants, 91% accepted, 44 enrolled. In 2019, 49 master's awarded. *Degree requirements:* For master's, thesis optional, capstone seminar. *Entrance requirements:* For master's, Personal essay, resume, two letters of recommendation, transcripts. Additional exam requirements/recommendations for international students: required—TOEFL (minimum score 80 iBT), Duolingo English Test; recommended—IELTS (minimum score 6.5). *Application deadline:* For fall admission, 2/1 for domestic students, 1/15 priority date for international students; for spring admission, 11/1 for domestic students, 8/1 priority date for international students. Application fee: $50. Electronic applications accepted. *Expenses:* $24,480 in-state, $40,848 out-of-state. *Financial support:* In 2019–20, 30 students received support, including 2 fellowships with full tuition reimbursements available (averaging $16,060 per year); scholarships/grants also available. Financial award application deadline: 2/1; financial award applicants required to submit FAFSA. *Unit head:* Dr. John Keeler, Dean, 412-648-7605, Fax: 412-648-7601, E-mail: gspia@pitt.edu. *Application contact:* Dr. Michael Rizzi, Director of Student Services, 412-648-7643, Fax: 412-648-7641, E-mail: rizzim@pitt.edu.
Website: http://www.gspia.pitt.edu/

University of San Francisco, College of Arts and Sciences, Energy Systems Management Program, San Francisco, CA 94117. Offers MS. *Program availability:* Part-time, evening/weekend. *Faculty:* 2 full-time (1 woman), 1 part-time/adjunct (0 women). *Students:* 33 full-time (11 women); includes 8 minority (2 Black or African American, non-Hispanic/Latino; 2 Asian, non-Hispanic/Latino; 4 Hispanic/Latino), 17 international. Average age 29. 50 applicants, 72% accepted, 14 enrolled. In 2019, 16 master's awarded. *Entrance requirements:* Additional exam requirements/recommendations for international students: required—TOEFL (minimum score 90 iBT), IELTS (minimum score 6.5), PTE (minimum score 61). *Application deadline:* For fall admission, 2/15 priority date for domestic and international students. Applications are processed on a rolling basis. Application fee: $55. Electronic applications accepted. Application fee is waived when completed online. *Financial support:* Teaching assistantships with partial tuition reimbursements, career-related internships or fieldwork, and scholarships/grants available. Financial award applicants required to submit FAFSA. *Unit head:* Dr. Maggie Winslow, Graduate Director, 415-422-5101, E-mail: mwinslow@usfca.edu. *Application contact:* Dr. Maggie Winslow, Graduate Director, 415-422-5101, E-mail: mwinslow@usfca.edu.
Website: https://www.usfca.edu/arts-sciences/graduate-programs/energy-systems-management

The University of Texas at Tyler, Soules College of Business, Department of Management and Marketing, Tyler, TX 75799-0001. Offers cyber security (MBA); engineering management (MBA); general management (MBA); healthcare management (MBA); internal assurance and consulting (MBA); marketing (MBA); oil, gas and energy (MBA); organizational development (MBA); quality management (MBA). *Accreditation:* AACSB. *Program availability:* Part-time, online learning. *Faculty:* 13 full-time (5 women). *Students:* Average age 29. *Entrance requirements:* Additional exam requirements/recommendations for international students: required—TOEFL (minimum score 550 paper-based). *Application deadline:* For fall admission, 8/17 priority date for domestic students, 7/1 priority date for international students; for spring admission, 12/21 priority date for domestic students, 11/1 priority date for international students. Application fee: $25 ($50 for international students). *Unit head:* Dr. Krist Swimberghe, Chair, 903-565-5803, E-mail: kswimberghe@uttyler.edu. *Application contact:* Dr. Krist Swimberghe, Chair, 903-565-5803, E-mail: kswimberghe@uttyler.edu.
Website: https://www.uttyler.edu/cbt/manamark/

The University of Tulsa, Graduate School, Collins College of Business, Online Program in Energy Business, Tulsa, OK 74104-3189. Offers MEB. *Program availability:* Part-time, evening/weekend, online only, 100% online. *Degree requirements:* For master's, thesis optional. *Entrance requirements:* For master's, GMAT. Additional exam requirements/recommendations for international students: required—TOEFL (minimum score 577 paper-based; 91 iBT), IELTS (minimum score 6.5). Electronic applications accepted. *Expenses:* Contact institution.

Vermont Law School, Graduate and Professional Programs, Master's Programs, South Royalton, VT 05068-0096. Offers American legal studies (LL M); energy law (LL M); energy regulation and law (MERL); environmental law (LL M); environmental law and policy (MELP); food and agriculture law (LL M); food and agriculture law and policy (MFALP); JD/MELP; JD/MERL; JD/MFALP. *Program availability:* Part-time, 100% online, blended/hybrid learning. *Entrance requirements:* Additional exam requirements/recommendations for international students: required—TOEFL.

Waynesburg University, Graduate and Professional Studies, Canonsburg, PA 15370. Offers business (MBA), including energy management, finance, health systems, human resources, leadership, market development; counseling (MA), including addictions counseling, clinical mental health; counselor education and supervision (PhD); criminal investigation (MA); education (M Ed), including autism, curriculum and instruction, educational leadership, online teaching; nursing (MSN), including administration, education, informatics; nursing practice (DNP); special education (M Ed); technology (M Ed); MSN/MBA. *Accreditation:* AACN. *Program availability:* Part-time, evening/weekend. *Degree requirements:* For doctorate, thesis/dissertation. *Entrance requirements:* Additional exam requirements/recommendations for international students: required—TOEFL. Electronic applications accepted.

Engineering Management

Air Force Institute of Technology, Graduate School of Engineering and Management, Department of Systems and Engineering Management, Dayton, OH 45433-7765. Offers cost analysis (MS); environmental and engineering management (MS); environmental engineering science (MS); information resource/systems management (MS). *Accreditation:* ABET. *Program availability:* Part-time. *Degree requirements:* For master's, thesis. *Entrance requirements:* For master's, GRE, GMAT, minimum GPA of 3.0.

American University of Sharjah, Graduate Programs, Sharjah, United Arab Emirates. Offers accounting (MS); biomedical engineering (MSBME); business administration (MBA); chemical engineering (MS Ch E); civil engineering (MSCE); computer engineering (MS); electrical engineering (MSEE); engineering systems management (MS, PhD); mathematics (MS); mechanical engineering (MSME); mechatronics engineering (MS); teaching English to speakers of other languages (MA); translation and interpreting (MA); urban planning (MUP). *Program availability:* Part-time, evening/weekend. *Degree requirements:* For master's, thesis (for some programs). *Entrance requirements:* For master's, GMAT (for MBA). Additional exam requirements/recommendations for international students: required—TOEFL (minimum score 550 paper-based; 80 iBT), TWE (minimum score 5); recommended—IELTS (minimum score 6.5). Electronic applications accepted.

Arkansas State University, Graduate School, College of Engineering, State University, AR 72467. Offers engineering (MS Eng); engineering management (MEM). *Program availability:* Part-time. *Degree requirements:* For master's, comprehensive exam. *Entrance requirements:* For master's, GRE, appropriate bachelor's degree, official transcript, letters of recommendation, resume, immunization records. Additional exam requirements/recommendations for international students: required—TOEFL (minimum score 550 paper-based; 79 iBT), IELTS (minimum score 6), PTE (minimum score 56). Electronic applications accepted. *Expenses:* Contact institution.

California State Polytechnic University, Pomona, Program in Engineering Management, Pomona, CA 91768-2557. Offers MS. *Program availability:* Part-time, evening/weekend. *Entrance requirements:* Additional exam requirements/recommendations for international students: required—TOEFL (minimum score 550 paper-based). Electronic applications accepted. *Expenses:* Contact institution.

California State University, East Bay, Office of Graduate Studies, College of Science, School of Engineering, Program in Engineering Management, Hayward, CA 94542-3000. Offers MS. *Degree requirements:* For master's, comprehensive exam (for some programs), research project or exam. *Entrance requirements:* For master's, GRE or GMAT, minimum GPA of 2.5, personal statement, two letters of recommendation, resume, college algebra/trigonometry or equivalent. Additional exam requirements/recommendations for international students: required—TOEFL (minimum score 550 paper-based). Electronic applications accepted.

California State University, Long Beach, Graduate Studies, College of Engineering, Department of Mechanical and Aerospace Engineering, Long Beach, CA 90840. Offers aerospace engineering (MSAE); engineering and industrial applied mathematics (PhD); interdisciplinary engineering (MSE); management engineering (MSE); mechanical engineering (MSME). *Program availability:* Part-time. *Entrance requirements:* Additional exam requirements/recommendations for international students: required—TOEFL. Electronic applications accepted.

California State University Maritime Academy, Graduate Studies, Vallejo, CA 94590. Offers transportation and engineering management (MS), including engineering management, humanitarian disaster management, transportation. *Program availability:* Evening/weekend, online only, 100% online. *Degree requirements:* For master's, comprehensive exam (for some programs), thesis, Minimum GPA of 3.0 in 10 required courses including capstone course and project, demonstrated proficiency in graduate-level writing. *Entrance requirements:* For master's, GMAT/GRE (for applicants with fewer than five years of post-baccalaureate professional experience), Equivalent of four-year U.S. bachelor's degree with minimum GPA of 2.5 during last two years (60 semester units or 90 quarter units) of coursework in degree program. Additional exam requirements/recommendations for international students: required—TOEFL (minimum score 550 paper-based). Electronic applications accepted.

California State University, Northridge, Graduate Studies, College of Engineering and Computer Science, Department of Manufacturing Systems Engineering and Management, Northridge, CA 91330. Offers engineering automation (MS); engineering management (MS); manufacturing systems engineering (MS); materials engineering (MS). *Program availability:* Online learning. *Entrance requirements:* For master's, GRE (if cumulative undergraduate GPA less than 3.0).

Case Western Reserve University, School of Graduate Studies, Case School of Engineering, The Institute for Management and Engineering, Cleveland, OH 44106. Offers MEM. *Entrance requirements:* Additional exam requirements/recommendations for international students: required—TOEFL, IELTS (minimum score 7.5).

The Catholic University of America, School of Engineering, Program in Engineering Management, Washington, DC 20064. Offers engineering management (MSE, Certificate), including engineering management and organization (MSE), project and systems engineering management (MSE), technology management (MSE); program management (Certificate); systems engineering and management of information technology (Certificate). *Program availability:* Part-time. *Faculty:* 8 part-time/adjunct (4 women). *Students:* 18 full-time (2 women), 12 part-time (2 women); includes 5 minority (1 Asian, non-Hispanic/Latino; 4 Two or more races, non-Hispanic/Latino), 19 international. Average age 29. 40 applicants, 80% accepted, 14 enrolled. In 2019, 20 master's awarded. *Degree requirements:* For master's, minimum GPA of 3.0. *Entrance requirements:* For master's and Certificate, statement of purpose, official copies of academic transcripts, two letters of recommendation. Additional exam requirements/recommendations for international students: required—TOEFL (minimum score 550 paper-based; 80 iBT). *Application deadline:* For fall admission, 7/15 priority date for domestic students, 7/1 for international students; for spring admission, 11/15 priority date for domestic students, 11/1 for international students. Applications are processed on a rolling basis. Application fee: $55. Electronic applications accepted. *Expenses:* Contact institution. *Financial support:* Fellowships, research assistantships, teaching assistantships, Federal Work-Study, scholarships/grants, tuition waivers (full and partial), and unspecified assistantships available. Financial award application deadline: 2/1; financial award applicants required to submit FAFSA. *Unit head:* Melvin G. Williams, Jr., Director, 202-319-5191, Fax: 202-319-6860, E-mail: williamsme@cua.edu. *Application contact:* Dr. Steven Brown, Director of Graduate Admissions, 202-319-5057, Fax: 202-319-6533, E-mail: cua-admissions@cua.edu. Website: https://engineering.catholic.edu/management/index.html

Central Michigan University, Central Michigan University Global Campus, Program in Administration, Mount Pleasant, MI 48859. Offers acquisitions administration (MSA, Certificate); engineering management administration (MSA, Certificate); general administration (MSA, Certificate); health services administration (MSA, Certificate); human resources administration (MSA, Certificate); information resource management (MSA); information resource management administration (Certificate); international administration (MSA, Certificate); leadership (MSA, Certificate); philanthropy and fundraising administration (MSA, Certificate); public administration (MSA, Certificate); recreation and park administration (MSA); research administration (MSA, Certificate). *Program availability:* Part-time, evening/weekend, online learning. *Entrance requirements:* For master's, minimum GPA of 2.7 in major. Electronic applications accepted. *Expenses:* Tuition, area resident: Full-time $12,267; part-time $8178 per year. Tuition, state resident: full-time $12,267; part-time $8178 per year. Tuition, nonresident: full-time $12,267; part-time $8178 per year. International tuition: $16,110 full-time. *Required fees:* $225 per semester. Tuition and fees vary according to degree level and program.

The Citadel, The Military College of South Carolina, Citadel Graduate College, School of Engineering, Department of Engineering Leadership and Program Management, Charleston, SC 29409. Offers project management (MS); systems engineering management (Graduate Certificate); technical program management (Graduate Certificate); technical project management (Graduate Certificate). *Program availability:* Part-time, evening/weekend. *Entrance requirements:* For master's, GRE or GMAT, minimum of one year of professional experience or permission from department head; two letters of reference; resume detailing previous work; for Graduate Certificate, one-page letter of intent; resume detailing previous work. Additional exam requirements/recommendations for international students: required—TOEFL (minimum score 550 paper-based; 79 iBT). Electronic applications accepted.

Clarkson University, Program in Engineering Management, Potsdam, NY 13699. Offers MS. *Program availability:* Part-time-only, evening/weekend, blended/hybrid learning. *Faculty:* 7 part-time/adjunct (1 woman). *Students:* 211 part-time (54 women); includes 38 minority (8 Black or African American, non-Hispanic/Latino; 15 Asian, non-Hispanic/Latino; 11 Hispanic/Latino; 4 Two or more races, non-Hispanic/Latino), 19 international. 57 applicants, 98% accepted, 56 enrolled. In 2019, 62 master's awarded. *Degree requirements:* For master's, project. *Entrance requirements:* For master's, GRE or GMAT. Additional exam requirements/recommendations for international students: required—TOEFL (minimum score 550 paper-based, 80 iBT) or IELTS (6.5). *Application deadline:* Applications are processed on a rolling basis. Application fee: $50. Electronic applications accepted. *Expenses:* Contact institution. *Financial support:* Scholarships/grants available. *Unit head:* Hugo Irizarry-Quinones, Associate Dean of Engineering, 518-631-9881, E-mail: hirizarr@clarkson.edu. *Application contact:* Daniel Capogna, Director of Graduate Admissions & Recruitment, 518-631-9910, E-mail: graduate@clarkson.edu.
Website: https://www.clarkson.edu/academics/graduate

Colorado School of Mines, Office of Graduate Studies, Department of Economics and Business, Golden, CO 80401. Offers engineering and technology management (MS); mineral and energy economics (MS, PhD); operations research and engineering (PhD); petroleum economics and management with mineral and energy economics (MS). *Program availability:* Part-time. *Degree requirements:* For master's, thesis (for some programs); for doctorate, comprehensive exam, thesis/dissertation. *Entrance requirements:* For master's and doctorate, GRE General Test. Additional exam requirements/recommendations for international students: required—TOEFL (minimum score 550 paper-based; 79 iBT). Electronic applications accepted. *Expenses:* Tuition, state resident: full-time $16,650; part-time $925 per credit hour. Tuition, nonresident: full-time $37,350; part-time $2075 per credit hour. International tuition: $37,350 full-time. *Required fees:* $2412.

Cornell University, Graduate School, Graduate Fields of Engineering, Field of Civil and Environmental Engineering, Ithaca, NY 14853. Offers engineering management (M Eng, MS, PhD); environmental engineering (M Eng, MS, PhD); environmental fluid mechanics and hydrology (M Eng, MS, PhD); environmental systems engineering (M Eng, MS, PhD); geotechnical engineering (M Eng, MS, PhD); remote sensing (M Eng, MS, PhD); structural engineering (M Eng, MS, PhD); structural mechanics (M Eng, MS); transportation engineering (MS, PhD); transportation systems engineering (M Eng); water resource systems (M Eng, MS, PhD). Terminal master's awarded for partial completion of doctoral program. *Degree requirements:* For master's, thesis (MS); for doctorate, comprehensive exam, thesis/dissertation. *Entrance requirements:* For master's and doctorate, GRE General Test (recommended), 2 letters of recommendation. Additional exam requirements/recommendations for international students: required—TOEFL (minimum score 600 paper-based; 77 iBT). Electronic applications accepted.

Dartmouth College, Dartmouth Engineering - Thayer School of Engineering, Program in Engineering Management, Hanover, NH 03755. Offers MEM. In 2019, 59 master's awarded. *Degree requirements:* For master's, thesis or alternative. *Entrance requirements:* For master's, GRE General Test. Additional exam requirements/recommendations for international students: required—TOEFL, IELTS. *Application deadline:* For fall admission, 1/1 priority date for domestic students, 1/1 for international students. Applications are processed on a rolling basis. Application fee: $45. Electronic applications accepted. *Financial support:* Fellowships, teaching assistantships, career-related internships or fieldwork, institutionally sponsored loans, scholarships/grants, and tuition waivers (full and partial) available. Financial award application deadline: 2/15; financial award applicants required to submit CSS PROFILE. *Unit head:* Dr. Geoffrey G. Parker, Director, Professor of Engineering, 603-646-9075, Fax: 603-646-2580, E-mail: geoffrey.g.parker@dartmouth.edu. *Application contact:* Candace S. Potter, Graduate Admissions and Financial Aid Administrator, 603-646-3844, Fax: 603-646-1620, E-mail:

candace.s.potter@dartmouth.edu.
Website: https://mem.dartmouth.edu/

Drexel University, College of Engineering, Program in Engineering Management, Philadelphia, PA 19104-2875. Offers MS, Certificate. *Program availability:* Part-time, evening/weekend, online learning. *Degree requirements:* For master's, thesis optional. *Entrance requirements:* For master's, minimum GPA of 3.0. Additional exam requirements/recommendations for international students: required—TOEFL. Electronic applications accepted.

Duke University, Graduate School, Pratt School of Engineering, Distributed Master of Engineering Management Program (d-MEMP), Durham, NC 27708-0271. Offers MEM. *Program availability:* Part-time, evening/weekend, blended/hybrid learning. *Entrance requirements:* For master's, GRE General Test, resume, 3 letters of recommendation, statement of purpose, transcripts. Additional exam requirements/recommendations for international students: required—TOEFL. Electronic applications accepted. *Expenses:* Contact institution.

Duke University, Graduate School, Pratt School of Engineering, Master of Engineering Management Program, Durham, NC 27708-0271. Offers MEM. *Program availability:* Part-time, blended/hybrid learning. *Entrance requirements:* For master's, GRE General Test, resume, 3 letters of recommendation, statement of purpose, transcripts. Additional exam requirements/recommendations for international students: required—TOEFL. Electronic applications accepted. *Expenses:* Contact institution.

Eastern Michigan University, Graduate School, College of Engineering and Technology, School of Engineering, Program in Engineering Management, Ypsilanti, MI 48197. Offers MS. *Program availability:* Part-time, evening/weekend, online learning. *Students:* 5 full-time (1 woman), 60 part-time (14 women); includes 12 minority (5 Black or African American, non-Hispanic/Latino; 1 Asian, non-Hispanic/Latino; 2 Hispanic/Latino; 4 Two or more races, non-Hispanic/Latino), 7 international. Average age 34. 55 applicants, 36% accepted, 9 enrolled. In 2019, 27 master's awarded. *Entrance requirements:* Additional exam requirements/recommendations for international students: required—TOEFL. *Application deadline:* Applications are processed on a rolling basis. Application fee: $45. *Financial support:* Fellowships, research assistantships with full tuition reimbursements, teaching assistantships with full tuition reimbursements, career-related internships or fieldwork, Federal Work-Study, institutionally sponsored loans, scholarships/grants, tuition waivers (partial), and unspecified assistantships available. Support available to part-time students. Financial award applicants required to submit FAFSA. *Application contact:* Dr. Emad Y. H. Tanbour, Program Coordinator, 734-487-1865, Fax: 734-487-8755, E-mail: etanbour@emich.edu.

Embry-Riddle Aeronautical University–Worldwide, Department of Engineering and Technology, Daytona Beach, FL 32114-3900. Offers aerospace engineering (MS); entrepreneurship in technology (MS); systems engineering (M Sys E), including engineering management, technical. *Program availability:* Part-time, evening/weekend, 100% online, blended/hybrid learning. *Entrance requirements:* For master's, GRE (for MS in aerospace engineering). Additional exam requirements/recommendations for international students: required—TOEFL (minimum score 550 paper-based; 79 iBT), IELTS (minimum score 6). Electronic applications accepted. *Expenses:* Contact institution.

Florida Institute of Technology, College of Engineering and Science, Program in Engineering Management, Melbourne, FL 32901-6975. Offers MS. *Program availability:* Part-time. *Degree requirements:* For master's, comprehensive exam (for some programs), thesis optional, 30 credit hours. *Entrance requirements:* For master's, GRE (minimum score of 300), BS in engineering from ABET-accredited program, minimum GPA of 3.0, 3 letters of recommendation, resume, statement of objectives. Additional exam requirements/recommendations for international students: required—TOEFL (minimum score 550 paper-based; 79 iBT). Electronic applications accepted.

Florida International University, College of Engineering and Computing, Department of Engineering Management, Miami, FL 33199. Offers MS. *Accreditation:* CAHME. *Program availability:* Part-time, evening/weekend. *Faculty:* 3 full-time (1 woman), 4 part-time/adjunct (0 women). *Students:* 114 full-time (45 women), 95 part-time (31 women); includes 98 minority (23 Black or African American, non-Hispanic/Latino; 6 Asian, non-Hispanic/Latino; 65 Hispanic/Latino; 1 Native Hawaiian or other Pacific Islander, non-Hispanic/Latino; 3 Two or more races, non-Hispanic/Latino), 96 international. Average age 30. 150 applicants, 70% accepted, 69 enrolled. In 2019, 71 master's awarded. *Entrance requirements:* For master's, GRE, minimum GPA of 3.0. Additional exam requirements/recommendations for international students: required—TOEFL (minimum score 550 paper-based; 80 iBT). *Application deadline:* For fall admission, 6/1 for domestic students, 4/1 for international students; for spring admission, 10/1 for domestic students, 9/1 for international students. Applications are processed on a rolling basis. Application fee: $30. Electronic applications accepted. *Expenses: Tuition, area resident:* Full-time $8912; part-time $446 per credit hour. Tuition, state resident: full-time $8912; part-time $446 per credit hour. Tuition, nonresident: full-time $21,393; part-time $992 per credit hour. *Required fees:* $2194. *Financial support:* Institutionally sponsored loans and scholarships/grants available. Financial award application deadline: 3/1; financial award applicants required to submit FAFSA. *Unit head:* Dr. Chin-Sheng Chen, Director, 305-348-3753 Ext. 305, E-mail: chenc@fiu.edu. *Application contact:* Nanett Rojas, Manager, Admissions Operations, 305-348-7464, Fax: 305-348-7441, E-mail: gradadm@fiu.edu.

Gannon University, School of Graduate Studies, College of Engineering and Business, School of Engineering and Computer Science, Program in Engineering Management, Erie, PA 16541-0001. Offers MSEM. *Program availability:* Part-time, evening/weekend. *Entrance requirements:* For master's, bachelor's degree in engineering from an ABET-accredited program or its equivalent with minimum GPA of 2.5, transcripts, 3 letters of recommendation. Additional exam requirements/recommendations for international students: required—TOEFL (minimum score 79 iBT). Electronic applications accepted. Application fee is waived when completed online.

The George Washington University, School of Engineering and Applied Science, Department of Engineering Management and Systems Engineering, Washington, DC 20052. Offers system engineering (PhD). *Program availability:* Part-time, evening/weekend. *Degree requirements:* For master's, thesis optional; for doctorate, one foreign language, thesis/dissertation, final and qualifying exams, submission of articles; for other advanced degree, professional project. *Entrance requirements:* For master's, appropriate bachelor's degree, minimum GPA of 2.7, second-semester calculus; for doctorate, appropriate master's degree, minimum GPA of 3.5, 2 letters of recommendation; for other advanced degree, appropriate master's degree, minimum GPA of 3.4. Additional exam requirements/recommendations for international students: required—TOEFL or The George Washington University English as a Foreign Language Test.

Georgia Southern University, Jack N. Averitt College of Graduate Studies, Allen E. Paulson College of Engineering and Computing, Department of Mechanical Engineering, Statesboro, GA 30460. Offers engineering and information technology (MSAE), including engineering and information technology; engineering and manufacturing management (Graduate Certificate); engineering/energy science (MSAE); engineering/engineering management (MSAE); engineering/mechatronics (MSAE); occupational safety and environmental compliance (Graduate Certificate). *Program availability:* Part-time, evening/weekend. *Faculty:* 24 full-time (1 woman), 1 part-time/adjunct (0 women). *Students:* 13 full-time (0 women), 3 part-time (1 woman); includes 5 minority (1 Black or African American, non-Hispanic/Latino; 3 Asian, non-Hispanic/Latino; 1 Hispanic/Latino), 4 international. Average age 25. 24 applicants, 71% accepted, 11 enrolled. In 2019, 23 master's, 1 Graduate Certificate awarded. *Degree requirements:* For master's, comprehensive exam, thesis optional. *Entrance requirements:* For master's, GRE, undergraduate major or equivalent in proposed study area. Additional exam requirements/recommendations for international students: required—TOEFL (minimum score 550 paper-based; 80 iBT), IELTS (minimum score 6). *Application deadline:* For fall admission, 3/1 priority date for domestic and international students; for spring admission, 10/1 priority date for domestic students, 10/1 for international students. Applications are processed on a rolling basis. Application fee: $50. Electronic applications accepted. *Expenses: Tuition, area resident:* Full-time $4986; part-time $277 per credit hour. Tuition, nonresident: full-time $19,890; part-time $1105 per credit hour. *International tuition:* $19,890 full-time. *Required fees:* $2114; $1057 per semester. $1057 per semester. Tuition and fees vary according to course load, campus/location and program. *Financial support:* In 2019–20, 17 students received support, including 4 research assistantships with partial tuition reimbursements available (averaging $7,200 per year), teaching assistantships with partial tuition reimbursements available (averaging $7,200 per year); Federal Work-Study, scholarships/grants, tuition waivers (partial), and unspecified assistantships also available. Financial award application deadline: 4/15; financial award applicants required to submit FAFSA. *Unit head:* Dr. Brian Vlcek, Chair, 912-478-5761, Fax: 912-478-1455, E-mail: bvlcek@georgiasouthern.edu.

Indiana Tech, Program in Engineering Management, Fort Wayne, IN 46803-1297. Offers MSE. *Program availability:* Part-time, evening/weekend, online only, 100% online. *Entrance requirements:* For master's, BS in a technical field, minimum GPA of 2.5, one undergraduate course each in accounting and finance. Electronic applications accepted.

Instituto Tecnológico y de Estudios Superiores de Monterrey, Campus Chihuahua, Graduate Programs, Chihuahua, Mexico. Offers computer systems engineering (Ingeniero); electrical engineering (Ingeniero); electromechanical engineering (Ingeniero); electronic engineering (Ingeniero); engineering administration (MEA); industrial engineering (MIE, Ingeniero); international trade (MIT); mechanical engineering (Ingeniero).

International Technological University, Program in Engineering Management, San Jose, CA 95134. Offers MSEM. *Program availability:* Part-time, evening/weekend. *Degree requirements:* For master's, thesis or capstone project. *Entrance requirements:* Additional exam requirements/recommendations for international students: required—TOEFL, IELTS. Electronic applications accepted.

Johns Hopkins University, Engineering Program for Professionals, Part-time Program in Engineering Management, Baltimore, MD 21218. Offers MEM. *Program availability:* Part-time, evening/weekend, 100% online, blended/hybrid learning. *Entrance requirements:* Additional exam requirements/recommendations for international students: required—TOEFL (minimum score 600 paper-based; 100 iBT).

Johns Hopkins University, G. W. C. Whiting School of Engineering, Master of Science in Engineering Management Program, Baltimore, MD 21218. Offers biomaterials (MSEM); civil engineering (MSEM); communications science (MSEM); computer science (MSEM); environmental systems analysis, economics and public policy (MSEM); fluid mechanics (MSEM); materials science and engineering (MSEM); mechanical engineering (MSEM); mechanics and materials (MSEM); nano-biotechnology (MSEM); nanomaterials and nanotechnology (MSEM); operations research (MSEM); probability and statistics (MSEM); smart product and device design (MSEM). *Entrance requirements:* For master's, GRE, 3 letters of recommendation, statement of purpose, transcripts. Additional exam requirements/recommendations for international students: required—TOEFL (minimum score 600 paper-based, 100 iBT) or IELTS (7). Electronic applications accepted.

Kansas State University, Graduate School, College of Engineering, Department of Industrial and Manufacturing Systems Engineering, Manhattan, KS 66506. Offers engineering management (MEM); industrial engineering (MS); operations research (MS). *Program availability:* Part-time, online learning. *Degree requirements:* For master's, thesis or alternative; for doctorate, thesis/dissertation. *Entrance requirements:* For master's, GRE General Test (minimum score of 750 old version, 159 new format on Quantitative portion of exam), bachelor's degree in engineering, mathematics, or physical science; for doctorate, GRE General Test (minimum score of 770 old version, 164 new format on Quantitative portion of exam), master's degree in engineering or industrial manufacturing. Additional exam requirements/recommendations for international students: required—PTE (minimum score 58), TOEFL (minimum score 550 paper-based; 79 iBT) or IELTS (minimum score 6.5). Electronic applications accepted.

Kennesaw State University, Southern Polytechnic College of Engineering and Engineering Technology, Program in Engineering Management, Kennesaw, GA 30144. Offers MS. *Program availability:* 100% online. *Students:* 3 full-time (0 women), 46 part-time (13 women); includes 20 minority (10 Black or African American, non-Hispanic/Latino; 4 Asian, non-Hispanic/Latino; 6 Hispanic/Latino). Average age 35. 14 applicants, 93% accepted, 10 enrolled. In 2019, 11 master's awarded. *Entrance requirements:* Additional exam requirements/recommendations for international students: required—TOEFL (minimum score 80 iBT), IELTS (minimum score 6.5). *Application deadline:* For fall admission, 7/1 for domestic and international students; for spring admission, 11/1 for domestic and international students. Applications are processed on a rolling basis. Application fee: $60. Electronic applications accepted. *Expenses: Tuition, area resident:* Full-time $7104; part-time $296 per credit hour. Tuition, state resident: full-time $7104; part-time $296 per credit hour. Tuition, nonresident: full-time $25,584; part-time $1066 per credit hour. *International tuition:* $25,584 full-time. *Required fees:* $2006; $1706 per unit. $853 per semester. *Application contact:* Admissions Counselor, 470-578-4377, E-mail: ksugrad@kennesaw.ed.
Website: http://engineering.kennesaw.edu/systems-industrial/degrees/ms-engineering-management.php

Kettering University, Graduate School, Department of Business, Flint, MI 48504. Offers MBA, MS. *Accreditation:* ACBSP. *Program availability:* Part-time, evening/weekend, online learning. *Entrance requirements:* Additional exam requirements/recommendations for international students: required—TOEFL (minimum score 550 paper-based; 79 iBT). Electronic applications accepted.

Lawrence Technological University, College of Engineering, Southfield, MI 48075-1058. Offers architectural engineering (MS); automotive engineering (MS); biomedical engineering (MS); civil engineering (MA, MS, PhD), including environmental engineering (MS), geotechnical engineering (MS), structural engineering (MS), transportation engineering (MS), water resource engineering (MS); construction engineering management (MA); electrical and computer engineering (MS); engineering management (MEM); engineering technology (MS); fire engineering (MS); industrial engineering (MS), including healthcare systems; manufacturing systems (ME); mechanical engineering (MS, DE, PhD), including automotive engineering (MS), energy engineering (MS),

manufacturing (DE), solid mechanics (MS), thermal/fluid systems (MS); mechatronic systems engineering (MS). *Program availability:* Part-time, evening/weekend. *Faculty:* 23 full-time (2 women), 20 part-time/adjunct (1 woman). *Students:* 14 full-time (5 women), 286 part-time (54 women); includes 26 minority (13 Black or African American, non-Hispanic/Latino; 8 Asian, non-Hispanic/Latino; 3 Hispanic/Latino; 2 Two or more races, non-Hispanic/Latino), 150 international. Average age 29. 384 applicants, 58% accepted, 74 enrolled. In 2019, 223 master's, 7 doctorates awarded. Terminal master's awarded for partial completion of doctoral program. *Degree requirements:* For master's, thesis optional; for doctorate, comprehensive exam, thesis/dissertation optional. *Entrance requirements:* Additional exam requirements/recommendations for international students: required—TOEFL (minimum score 550 paper-based; 79 iBT), IELTS (minimum score 6.5). *Application deadline:* For fall admission, 5/24 for international students; for spring admission, 10/13 for international students; for summer admission, 2/18 for international students. Applications are processed on a rolling basis. Application fee: $50. Electronic applications accepted. *Expenses: Tuition:* Full-time $16,618; part-time $8309 per year. *Required fees:* $600; $600. *Financial support:* In 2019–20, 21 students received support. Unspecified assistantships available. Financial award application deadline: 4/1; financial award applicants required to submit FAFSA. *Unit head:* Dr. Nabil Grace, Dean, 248-204-2500, Fax: 248-204-2509, E-mail: engrdean@ltu.edu. *Application contact:* Jane Rohrback, Director of Admissions, 248-204-3160, Fax: 248-204-2228, E-mail: admissions@ltu.edu.
Website: http://www.ltu.edu/engineering/index.asp

Lehigh University, P.C. Rossin College of Engineering and Applied Science, Department of Industrial and Systems Engineering, Bethlehem, PA 18015. Offers analytical finance (MS); healthcare systems engineering (M Eng, Certificate); industrial and systems engineering (M Eng, MS, PhD); management science and engineering (M Eng, MS); MBA/E. *Program availability:* Part-time, blended/hybrid learning. *Faculty:* 18 full-time (1 woman), 1 part-time/adjunct (0 women). *Students:* 71 full-time (16 women), 9 part-time (4 women); includes 2 minority (1 Asian, non-Hispanic/Latino; 1 Hispanic/Latino), 73 international. Average age 25. 290 applicants, 39% accepted, 26 enrolled. In 2019, 31 master's, 12 doctorates awarded. Terminal master's awarded for partial completion of doctoral program. *Degree requirements:* For master's, thesis (MS); project (M Eng); for doctorate, comprehensive exam, thesis/dissertation. *Entrance requirements:* For master's and doctorate, GRE General Test. Additional exam requirements/recommendations for international students: required—TOEFL (minimum score 550 paper-based; 79 iBT), IELTS (minimum score 6.5), TOEFL or IELTS required. *Application deadline:* For fall admission, 7/15 for domestic and international students; for spring admission, 12/1 for domestic and international students. Application fee: $75. *Financial support:* In 2019–20, 33 students received support, including 2 fellowships with full tuition reimbursements available (averaging $20,490 per year), 18 research assistantships with full tuition reimbursements available (averaging $20,490 per year), 11 teaching assistantships with full tuition reimbursements available (averaging $21,105 per year); health care benefits and unspecified assistantships also available. Financial award application deadline: 1/15. *Unit head:* Dr. Luis Nunes Vicente, Chairperson, 610-758-4050, Fax: 610-758-4886, E-mail: lnv@lehigh.edu. *Application contact:* Jennifer Vargas, Graduate Coordinator, 610-758-4050, Fax: 610-758-4886, E-mail: jav319@lehigh.edu.
Website: https://ise.lehigh.edu/

LeTourneau University, Graduate Programs, Longview, TX 75607-7001. Offers business administration (MBA); counseling (MA); curriculum and instruction (M Ed); educational administration (M Ed); engineering (ME, MS); engineering management (MEM); health care administration (MS); marriage and family therapy (MA); psychology (MA); strategic leadership (MSL); teacher leadership (M Ed); teaching and learning (M Ed). *Program availability:* Part-time, 100% online, blended/hybrid learning. *Students:* 45 full-time (34 women), 243 part-time (186 women); includes 142 minority (89 Black or African American, non-Hispanic/Latino; 1 Asian, non-Hispanic/Latino; 26 Hispanic/Latino; 26 Two or more races, non-Hispanic/Latino), 2 international. Average age 37. In 2019, 143 master's awarded. *Entrance requirements:* Additional exam requirements/recommendations for international students: required—TOEFL (minimum score 525 paper-based; 80 iBT), IELTS (minimum score 6), Either a TOEFL or IELTS is required for graduate students. One or the other. *Application deadline:* Applications are processed on a rolling basis. Application fee: $0. Electronic applications accepted. *Financial support:* Unspecified assistantships and employee tuition waivers and institutionally sponsored loans available. Financial award applicants required to submit FAFSA.
Website: http://www.letu.edu

Long Island University - Post, College of Management, Brookville, NY 11548-1300. Offers accountancy (MS); finance (MBA); information systems (MS); international business (MBA); management (MBA); management engineering (MS); marketing (MBA); taxation (MS); technical project management (MS); JD/MBA. *Accreditation:* AACSB. *Program availability:* Part-time, evening/weekend, blended/hybrid learning. *Entrance requirements:* For master's, GMAT, GRE, or LSAT. Additional exam requirements/recommendations for international students: required—TOEFL (minimum score 550 paper-based, 75 iBT) or IELTS. Electronic applications accepted.

Louisiana Tech University, Graduate School, College of Engineering and Science, Ruston, LA 71272. Offers applied physics (MS); biomedical engineering (PhD); computer science (MS); engineering (MS, PhD), including cyberspace engineering (PhD), engineering education (PhD), engineering physics (PhD), materials and infrastructure systems (PhD), micro/nanoscale systems (PhD); engineering and technology management (MS); mathematics (MS); molecular science and nanotechnology (MS, PhD). *Program availability:* Part-time-only. Terminal master's awarded for partial completion of doctoral program. *Degree requirements:* For master's, thesis (for some programs); for doctorate, thesis/dissertation. *Entrance requirements:* For master's and Graduate Certificate, GRE General Test, minimum GPA of 3.0 in last 60 hours. Additional exam requirements/recommendations for international students: required—TOEFL (minimum score 550 paper-based; 80 iBT), IELTS (minimum score 6.5). Electronic applications accepted. *Expenses: Tuition, area resident:* Full-time $6592; part-time $400 per credit. Tuition, state resident: full-time $6592; part-time $400 per credit. Tuition, nonresident: full-time $13,333; part-time $681 per credit. *International tuition:* $13,333 full-time. *Required fees:* $3011; $3011 per unit.

Loyola Marymount University, Frank R. Seaver College of Science and Engineering, MBA/MS Program in Systems Engineering Leadership, Los Angeles, CA 90045-2659. Offers MBA/MS. *Entrance requirements:* Additional exam requirements/recommendations for international students: required—TOEFL, IELTS. Application fee: $50. Electronic applications accepted. *Financial support:* Research assistantships, teaching assistantships, Federal Work-Study, scholarships/grants, and unspecified assistantships available. Financial award applicants required to submit FAFSA. *Unit head:* Dr. Claire Leon, Systems Engineering Program Director, 310-338-7878, E-mail: claire.leon@lmu.edu. *Application contact:* Ammar Dalal, Assistant Vice Provost for Graduate Enrollment, 310-338-2721, Fax: 310-338-6086, E-mail: graduateinfo@lmu.edu.

Marquette University, Graduate School, College of Engineering, Department of Mechanical Engineering, Milwaukee, WI 53201-1881. Offers engineering innovation (Certificate); engineering management (MSEM); mechanical engineering (MS, PhD); new product and process development (Certificate). *Program availability:* Part-time, evening/weekend. Terminal master's awarded for partial completion of doctoral program. *Degree requirements:* For master's, comprehensive exam, thesis (for some programs); for doctorate, comprehensive exam, thesis/dissertation, qualifying exam. *Entrance requirements:* For master's, GRE General Test, minimum GPA of 3.0, official transcripts from all current and previous colleges/universities except Marquette, three letters of recommendation; for doctorate, GRE General Test, minimum GPA of 3.0, official transcripts from all current and previous colleges/universities except Marquette, three letters of recommendation, statement of purpose, copies of any published work. Additional exam requirements/recommendations for international students: required—TOEFL (minimum score 530 paper-based). Electronic applications accepted.

Marshall University, Academic Affairs Division, College of Information Technology and Engineering, Program in Engineering, Huntington, WV 25755. Offers engineering management (MSE); environmental engineering (MSE); transportation and infrastructure engineering (MSE). *Program availability:* Part-time, evening/weekend. *Degree requirements:* For master's, final project, oral exam. *Entrance requirements:* For master's, GMAT or GRE General Test, minimum undergraduate GPA of 2.75.

Massachusetts Institute of Technology, School of Engineering, System Design and Management Program, Cambridge, MA 02139-4307. Offers engineering and management (SM). *Degree requirements:* For master's, thesis.

McNeese State University, Doré School of Graduate Studies, College of Engineering and Computer Science, Master of Engineering Program, Lake Charles, LA 70609. Offers chemical engineering (M Eng); civil engineering (M Eng); electrical engineering (M Eng); engineering management (M Eng); mechanical engineering (M Eng). *Program availability:* Part-time, evening/weekend. *Entrance requirements:* For master's, GRE, baccalaureate degree, minimum overall GPA of 3.0. Additional exam requirements/recommendations for international students: required—TOEFL (minimum score 560 paper-based; 83 iBT).

Mercer University, Graduate Studies, Macon Campus, School of Engineering, Macon, GA 31207. Offers biomedical engineering (MSE); computer engineering (MSE); electrical engineering (MSE); engineering management (MSE); environmental engineering (MSE); environmental systems (MS); mechanical engineering (MSE); software engineering (MSE); software systems (MS); technical communications management (MS); technical management (MS). *Program availability:* Part-time-only, evening/weekend, online learning. *Faculty:* 27 full-time (9 women), 2 part-time/adjunct (0 women). *Students:* 38 full-time (10 women), 51 part-time (20 women); includes 22 minority (5 Black or African American, non-Hispanic/Latino; 11 Asian, non-Hispanic/Latino; 4 Hispanic/Latino; 2 Two or more races, non-Hispanic/Latino), 2 international. Average age 26. In 2019, 70 master's awarded. *Degree requirements:* For master's, thesis or alternative. *Entrance requirements:* For master's, GRE (minimum score 300), minimum undergraduate GPA of 3.0. Additional exam requirements/recommendations for international students: required—TOEFL (minimum score 550 paper-based; 80 iBT). *Application deadline:* For fall admission, 4/1 priority date for domestic and international students; for spring admission, 11/1 priority date for domestic and international students. Applications are processed on a rolling basis. Application fee: $75. *Expenses: Tuition:* $938.00 ($700.00 for Technical Communication Management program) per credit hour; Facility and Technology Fee: $17.00 per credit hour. *Financial support:* Federal Work-Study available. Financial award applicants required to submit FAFSA. *Unit head:* Dr. Laura W. Lackey, Dean, 478-301-4106, Fax: 478-301-5593, E-mail: lackey_l@mercer.edu. *Application contact:* Dr. Sinjae Hyun, Program Director, 478-301-2214, Fax: 478-301-5593, E-mail: hyun_s@mercer.edu.
Website: http://engineering.mercer.edu/

Merrimack College, School of Science and Engineering, North Andover, MA 01845-5800. Offers civil engineering (MS); computer science (MS); data science (MS); engineering management (MS); mechanical engineering (MS), including engineering management. *Program availability:* Part-time, evening/weekend, 100% online. *Degree requirements:* For master's, comprehensive exam, thesis optional, internship or capstone (for some programs). *Entrance requirements:* For master's, official college transcripts, resume, personal statement, 2 recommendations. Additional exam requirements/recommendations for international students: required—TOEFL (minimum score 84 iBT), IELTS (minimum score 6.5), PTE (minimum score 56). Electronic applications accepted. Application fee is waived when completed online. *Expenses:* Contact institution.

Middle Tennessee State University, College of Graduate Studies, College of Basic and Applied Sciences, Program in Professional Science, Murfreesboro, TN 37132. Offers actuarial sciences (MS); biostatistics (MS); biotechnology (MS); engineering management (MS); health care informatics (MS). *Program availability:* Part-time, evening/weekend, online learning. *Degree requirements:* For master's, comprehensive exam. *Entrance requirements:* For master's, GRE. Additional exam requirements/recommendations for international students: required—TOEFL (minimum score 525 paper-based; 71 iBT) or IELTS (minimum score 6).

Milwaukee School of Engineering, MBA in STEM Leadership Program, Milwaukee, WI 53202-3109. Offers MBA. *Program availability:* Part-time, evening/weekend. *Degree requirements:* For master's, thesis or alternative. *Entrance requirements:* For master's, GRE or GMAT if GPA is below 3.0, official transcripts, 2 letters of recommendation, personal essay, bachelor's degree from accredited university, 3 years work experience as teacher in a STEM field. Additional exam requirements/recommendations for international students: required—TOEFL (minimum score 90 iBT), IELTS (minimum score 7). Electronic applications accepted.

Milwaukee School of Engineering, MS Program in Engineering Management, Milwaukee, WI 53202-3109. Offers MS. *Program availability:* Part-time, evening/weekend. *Degree requirements:* For master's, thesis or alternative, thesis defense or capstone project. *Entrance requirements:* For master's, GRE General Test or GMAT if undergraduate GPA less than 2.8, bachelor's degree from accredited university; 2 letters of recommendation; work experience (strongly recommended). Additional exam requirements/recommendations for international students: required—TOEFL (minimum score 90 iBT), IELTS (minimum score 7). Electronic applications accepted.

Missouri University of Science and Technology, Department of Engineering Management and Systems Engineering, Rolla, MO 65401. Offers engineering management (MS, PhD); systems engineering (MS, PhD). *Degree requirements:* For master's, thesis optional; for doctorate, comprehensive exam. *Entrance requirements:* For master's, GRE (minimum score 1150 verbal and quantitative, 4.5 writing); for doctorate, GRE (minimum score: 1100 verbal and quantitative, 3.5 writing). Additional exam requirements/recommendations for international students: required—TOEFL (minimum score 580 paper-based). Electronic applications accepted. *Expenses:* Tuition, state resident: full-time $7839; part-time $435.50 per credit hour. Tuition, nonresident: full-time $22,169; part-time $1231.60 per credit hour. *International tuition:* $18,156.60 full-time. *Required fees:* $649.76. One-time fee: $119. Tuition and fees vary according to course load and program.

National University, School of Engineering and Computing, La Jolla, CA 92037-1011. Offers computer science (MS), including advanced computing; cyber security and information assurance (MS); data analytics (MS); electrical engineering (MS); engineering management (MS); information technology management (MS); management information systems (MS); sustainability management (MS). *Program availability:* Part-time, evening/weekend, 100% online, blended/hybrid learning. *Degree requirements:* For master's, thesis (for some programs). *Entrance requirements:* For master's, interview, minimum GPA of 2.5. Additional exam requirements/recommendations for international students: required—TOEFL (minimum score 550 paper-based; 79 iBT), IELTS (minimum score 6). Electronic applications accepted. *Expenses: Tuition:* Full-time $442; part-time $442 per unit.

Naval Postgraduate School, Departments and Academic Groups, Department of Systems Engineering, Monterey, CA 93943. Offers engineering systems (MS); product development (MS); systems engineering (MS, PhD, Certificate); systems engineering analysis (MS, PhD); systems engineering management (MS, PhD). *Program availability:* Part-time. *Degree requirements:* For master's, thesis (for some programs), internal project, capstone project, or research/dissertation paper (for some programs); for doctorate, thesis/dissertation (for some programs), internal project, capstone project, or research/dissertation paper (for some programs).

New England Institute of Technology, Program in Engineering Management, East Greenwich, RI 02818. Offers MSEM. *Program availability:* Part-time, evening/weekend, 100% online, blended/hybrid learning. *Students:* 6 full-time (0 women), 3 part-time (0 women); includes 4 minority (3 Black or African American, non-Hispanic/Latino; 1 Hispanic/Latino). Average age 30. In 2019, 6 master's awarded. *Entrance requirements:* For master's, Minimum GPA of 2.5 awarded bachelor's degree in related field from accredited institution plus personal statement. Additional exam requirements/recommendations for international students: required—TOEFL. *Application deadline:* Applications are processed on a rolling basis. Application fee: $50. Electronic applications accepted. *Unit head:* Dr. Douglas H. Sherman, Senior Vice President and Provost, 401-739-5000 Ext. 3481, Fax: 401-886-0859, E-mail: dsherman@neit.edu. *Application contact:* Tim Reardon, Vice President of Enrollment Management and Marketing, 401-739-5000, Fax: 401-886-0859, E-mail: treardon@neit.edu.
Website: https://www.neit.edu/Programs/Online-and-Hybrid-Degree-Programs/Engineering-Management-Masters-Degree

New Jersey Institute of Technology, Newark College of Engineering, Newark, NJ 07102. Offers biomedical engineering (MS, PhD); biopharmaceutical engineering (MS); chemical engineering (MS, PhD); civil engineering (MS, PhD); computer engineering (MS); critical infrastructure systems (MS); electrical engineering (MS, PhD); engineering management (MS); engineering science (MS); environmental engineering (MS, PhD); healthcare systems management (MS); industrial engineering (MS, PhD); internet engineering (MS); manufacturing systems engineering (MS); materials science & engineering (PhD); materials science and engineering (MS); mechanical engineering (MS, PhD); occupational safety and health engineering (MS). *Program availability:* Part-time, evening/weekend. *Faculty:* 151 full-time (29 women), 135 part-time/adjunct (15 women). *Students:* 576 full-time (161 women), 528 part-time (111 women); includes 366 minority (61 Black or African American, non-Hispanic/Latino; 1 American Indian or Alaska Native, non-Hispanic/Latino; 166 Asian, non-Hispanic/Latino; 115 Hispanic/Latino; 23 Two or more races, non-Hispanic/Latino), 450 international. Average age 28. 2,053 applicants, 67% accepted, 338 enrolled. In 2019, 474 master's, 30 doctorates awarded. Terminal master's awarded for partial completion of doctoral program. *Degree requirements:* For master's, thesis (for some programs); for doctorate, thesis/dissertation. *Entrance requirements:* For master's, GRE General Test, minimum GPA 2.8, personal statement, 1 letter of recommendation, transcripts; for doctorate, GRE General Test, minimum GPA of 3.5, personal statement, 3 letters of recommendation, transcripts. Additional exam requirements/recommendations for international students: required—TOEFL (minimum score 550 paper-based; 79 iBT), IELTS (minimum score 6.5). *Application deadline:* For fall admission, 6/1 priority date for domestic students, 5/1 priority date for international students; for spring admission, 11/15 priority date for domestic and international students. Applications are processed on a rolling basis. Application fee: $75. Electronic applications accepted. *Expenses:* $23,828 per year (in-state), $33,744 per year (out-of-state). *Financial support:* In 2019–20, 352 students received support, including 33 fellowships with full tuition reimbursements available (averaging $24,000 per year), 89 research assistantships with full tuition reimbursements available (averaging $24,000 per year), 112 teaching assistantships with full tuition reimbursements available (averaging $24,000 per year); career-related internships or fieldwork, Federal Work-Study, scholarships/grants, and unspecified assistantships also available. Financial award application deadline: 1/15. *Unit head:* Dr. Moshe Kam, Dean, 973-596-5534, Fax: 973-596-2316, E-mail: moshe.kam@njit.edu. *Application contact:* Stephen Eck, Executive Director of University Admissions, 973-596-3300, Fax: 973-596-3461, E-mail: admissions@njit.edu.
Website: http://engineering.njit.edu/

New Mexico Institute of Mining and Technology, Center for Graduate Studies, Department of Management, Socorro, NM 87801. Offers STEM education (MEM). *Program availability:* Part-time.

Northeastern University, College of Engineering, Boston, MA 02115-5096. Offers bioengineering (MS, PhD); chemical engineering (MS, PhD); civil engineering (MS, PhD); computer engineering (PhD); computer systems engineering (MS); electrical and computer engineering (MS); electrical and computer engineering leadership (MS); electrical engineering (PhD); energy systems (MS); engineering and public policy (MS); engineering management (MS, Certificate); environmental engineering (MS); industrial engineering (MS, PhD); information assurance (PhD); information systems (MS); interdisciplinary engineering (PhD); mechanical engineering (PhD); operations research (MS); telecommunication systems management (MS). *Program availability:* Part-time, online learning. Electronic applications accepted. *Expenses:* Contact institution.

Northwestern University, McCormick School of Engineering and Applied Science, Department of Industrial Engineering and Management Sciences, Master's in Engineering Management Program, Evanston, IL 60208. Offers MEM. *Program availability:* Part-time, evening/weekend. *Entrance requirements:* For master's, 3 years of work experience. Additional exam requirements/recommendations for international students: required—TOEFL (minimum score 100 iBT), IELTS (minimum score 7). Electronic applications accepted. *Expenses:* Contact institution.

Northwestern University, McCormick School of Engineering and Applied Science, MMM Program, Evanston, IL 60208. Offers design innovation (MBA, MS). *Entrance requirements:* For master's, GMAT or GRE, transcripts, two letters of recommendation, resume, evaluative interview report, work experience, two core essays, interest essay, video essay. Additional exam requirements/recommendations for international students: required—TOEFL, IELTS. *Expenses:* Contact institution.

Oakland University, Graduate Study and Lifelong Learning, School of Engineering and Computer Science, Department of Industrial and Systems Engineering, Program in Engineering Management, Rochester, MI 48309-4401. Offers MS. *Entrance requirements:* Additional exam requirements/recommendations for international students: required—TOEFL (minimum score 550 paper-based). Electronic applications accepted. *Expenses:* Contact institution.

Oklahoma Christian University, Graduate School of Engineering and Computer Science, Oklahoma City, OK 73136-1100. Offers electrical and computer engineering (MSE); engineering management (MSE); mechanical engineering (MSE); software engineering (MSCS, MSE). *Program availability:* Part-time. *Entrance requirements:* Additional exam requirements/recommendations for international students: required—TOEFL (minimum score 550 paper-based). Electronic applications accepted. *Expenses:* Contact institution.

Old Dominion University, Frank Batten College of Engineering and Technology, Program in Engineering Management, Norfolk, VA 23529. Offers MEM, MS. *Program availability:* Part-time, evening/weekend, 100% online, blended/hybrid learning, Portable Media. *Degree requirements:* For master's, comprehensive exam, thesis optional, project. *Entrance requirements:* For master's, GRE, minimum GPA of 3.0. Additional exam requirements/recommendations for international students: required—TOEFL (minimum score 550 paper-based; 79 iBT). Electronic applications accepted. *Expenses:* Contact institution.

Old Dominion University, Frank Batten College of Engineering and Technology, Program in Engineering Management and Systems Engineering, Norfolk, VA 23529. Offers D Eng, PhD. *Program availability:* Part-time, evening/weekend, 100% online, blended/hybrid learning. *Degree requirements:* For doctorate, thesis/dissertation, candidacy exam, project. *Entrance requirements:* For doctorate, GRE, resume, letters of recommendation, minimum GPA of 3.0, interview, essay outlining intended area of specialization. Additional exam requirements/recommendations for international students: required—TOEFL (minimum score 550 paper-based; 79 iBT). Electronic applications accepted.

Oregon State University, College of Engineering, Program in Industrial Engineering, Corvallis, OR 97331. Offers advanced manufacturing (M Eng, MS, PhD); engineering management (M Eng); human systems engineering (M Eng, MS, PhD); information systems engineering (M Eng, MS, PhD); manufacturing systems engineering (M Eng, MS, PhD). *Program availability:* 100% online. *Entrance requirements:* For master's and doctorate, GRE. Additional exam requirements/recommendations for international students: required—TOEFL (minimum score 80 iBT), IELTS (minimum score 6.5). *Expenses:* Contact institution.

Penn State Great Valley, Graduate Studies, Engineering Division, Malvern, PA 19355-1488. Offers engineering management (MEM); software engineering (MSE); systems engineering (M Eng, Certificate).

Penn State Harrisburg, Graduate School, School of Science, Engineering and Technology, Middletown, PA 17057. Offers civil engineering (MS); computer science (MS); electrical engineering (M Eng, MS); engineering management (MPS); engineering science (M Eng); environmental engineering (M Eng); environmental pollution control (MEPC, MS); mechanical engineering (MS); structural engineering (Certificate). *Program availability:* Part-time, evening/weekend.

Point Park University, School of Arts and Sciences, Department of Natural Sciences, Engineering and Technology, Pittsburgh, PA 15222-1984. Offers engineering management (MS); environmental studies (MS). *Program availability:* Part-time, evening/weekend. *Degree requirements:* For master's, comprehensive exam (for some programs), thesis or alternative. *Entrance requirements:* For master's, minimum QPA of 2.75, 2 letters of recommendation, minimum B average in engineering technology or a related field, official undergraduate transcript, statement of intent, resume. Additional exam requirements/recommendations for international students: required—TOEFL. Electronic applications accepted.

Polytechnic University of Puerto Rico, Graduate School, Hato Rey, PR 00918. Offers business administration (MBA), including computer information systems, general management, management of information systems, management of international enterprises; civil engineering (ME, MS); computer engineering (ME, MS); computer science (MCS, MS); electrical engineering (ME, MS); engineering management (MEM); environmental management (MEM); landscape architecture (M Land Arch); manufacturing competitiveness (MMC, MS); manufacturing engineering (ME, MS); mechanical engineering (M Mech E). *Accreditation:* ASLA. *Program availability:* Part-time, evening/weekend. *Entrance requirements:* For master's, 3 letters of recommendation.

Polytechnic University of Puerto Rico, Orlando Campus, Graduate School, Orlando, FL 32825. Offers accounting (MBA); business administration (MBA); construction management (MEM); engineering management (MEM); environmental management (MEM); finance (MBA); human resources management (MBA); management of international enterprises (MBA); management of technology (MBA); manufacturing management (MEM). *Program availability:* Part-time, evening/weekend, online learning. *Entrance requirements:* For master's, minimum GPA of 3.0. Additional exam requirements/recommendations for international students: recommended—TOEFL. Electronic applications accepted.

Portland State University, Graduate Studies, College of Liberal Arts and Sciences, Systems Science Program, Portland, OR 97207-0751. Offers computational intelligence (Certificate); computer modeling and simulation (Certificate); systems science (MS); systems science/anthropology (PhD); systems science/business administration (PhD); systems science/civil engineering (PhD); systems science/economics (PhD); systems science/engineering management (PhD); systems science/general (PhD); systems science/mathematical sciences (PhD); systems science/mechanical engineering (PhD); systems science/psychology (PhD); systems science/sociology (PhD). *Program availability:* Part-time. *Faculty:* 2 full-time (0 women), 6 part-time/adjunct (1 woman). *Students:* 6 full-time (3 women), 25 part-time (8 women); includes 7 minority (2 Asian, non-Hispanic/Latino; 4 Hispanic/Latino; 1 Two or more races, non-Hispanic/Latino), 2 international. Average age 39. 25 applicants, 80% accepted, 15 enrolled. In 2019, 7 master's, 2 doctorates awarded. Terminal master's awarded for partial completion of doctoral program. *Degree requirements:* For master's, comprehensive exam (for some programs), thesis optional; for doctorate, variable foreign language requirement, comprehensive exam (for some programs), thesis/dissertation. *Entrance requirements:* For master's, GRE/GMAT (recommended), minimum GPA of 3.0 on undergraduate or graduate work, 2 letters of recommendation, statement of interest; for doctorate, GRE required, minimum GPA of 3.0 undergraduate, 3.25 graduate; 3 letters of recommendation; statement of interest. Additional exam requirements/recommendations for international students: required—TOEFL (minimum score 550 paper-based; 80 iBT). *Application deadline:* For fall admission, 3/15 priority date for domestic and international students. Application fee: $65. Electronic applications accepted. *Expenses: Tuition, area resident:* Full-time $13,020; part-time $6510 per year. Tuition, state resident: full-time $13,020; part-time $6510 per year. Tuition, nonresident: full-time $19,830; part-time $9915 per year. *International tuition:* $19,830 full-time. *Required fees:* $1226. One-time fee: $350. Tuition and fees vary according to course load, program and reciprocity agreements. *Financial support:* Research assistantships, teaching assistantships, career-related internships or fieldwork, Federal Work-Study, scholarships/grants, and unspecified assistantships available. Support available to part-time students. Financial award application deadline: 3/1; financial award applicants required to submit FAFSA. *Unit head:* Dr. Wayne Wakeland, Chair, 503-725-4975, E-mail: wakeland@pdx.edu. *Application contact:* Dr. Wayne Wakeland, Chair, 503-725-

4975, E-mail: wakeland@pdx.edu.
Website: http://www.pdx.edu/sysc/

Portland State University, Graduate Studies, Maseeh College of Engineering and Computer Science, Department of Engineering and Technology Management, Portland, OR 97207-0751. Offers engineering and technology management (MS); technology management (PhD); MS/MBA; MS/MS. *Program availability:* Part-time, evening/weekend. *Faculty:* 4 full-time (1 woman), 6 part-time/adjunct (0 women). *Students:* 46 full-time (21 women), 68 part-time (18 women); includes 12 minority (2 Black or African American, non-Hispanic/Latino; 4 Asian, non-Hispanic/Latino; 5 Hispanic/Latino; 1 Two or more races, non-Hispanic/Latino), 62 international. Average age 36. 44 applicants, 80% accepted, 21 enrolled. In 2019, 33 master's, 4 doctorates awarded. *Degree requirements:* For master's, thesis or alternative, capstone; for doctorate, one foreign language, comprehensive exam, thesis/dissertation, oral and written exams. *Entrance requirements:* For master's, degree in engineering or related discipline; minimum GPA of 2.75 undergraduate or 3.0 graduate (at least 12 credits); minimum 4 years of experience in engineering or related discipline; 3 letters of recommendation; background in probability/statistics, differential equations, computer programming and linear algebra; for doctorate, GRE General Test (minimum combined score of 1100 for verbal and quantitative), minimum GPA of 3.0 undergraduate, 3.25 graduate. Additional exam requirements/recommendations for international students: required—TOEFL (minimum score 550 paper-based; 80 iBT). *Application deadline:* For fall admission, 4/1 for domestic students, 3/1 for international students; for winter admission, 9/1 for domestic students, 7/1 for international students; for spring admission, 11/1 for domestic students, 9/1 for international students; for summer admission, 2/1 for domestic students, 12/1 for international students. Application fee: $65. Electronic applications accepted. *Expenses:* Contact institution. *Financial support:* In 2019–20, 22 students received support, including 5 teaching assistantships with full and partial tuition reimbursements available (averaging $7,475 per year); research assistantships with full and partial tuition reimbursements available, career-related internships or fieldwork, Federal Work-Study, scholarships/grants, and unspecified assistantships also available. Support available to part-time students. Financial award application deadline: 3/1; financial award applicants required to submit FAFSA. *Unit head:* Dr. Timothy Anderson, Chair, 503-725-4668, Fax: 503-725-4667, E-mail: tim.anderson@pdx.edu. *Application contact:* Shawn Wall, Department Manager, E-mail: shawnw@pdx.edu.
Website: http://www.pdx.edu/engineering-technology-management/

Robert Morris University, School of Engineering, Mathematics and Science, Moon Township, PA 15108. Offers engineering management (MS). *Program availability:* Part-time-only, evening/weekend, 100% online. *Faculty:* 6 full-time (1 woman), 1 part-time/adjunct (0 women). *Students:* 20 part-time (8 women); includes 4 minority (1 Black or African American, non-Hispanic/Latino; 2 Asian, non-Hispanic/Latino; 1 Two or more races, non-Hispanic/Latino), 6 international. Average age 28. In 2019, 20 master's awarded. *Degree requirements:* For master's, Completion of 30 credits. *Entrance requirements:* For master's, letters of recommendation. Additional exam requirements/recommendations for international students: required—TOEFL (minimum score 550 paper-based; 79 iBT). *Application deadline:* For fall admission, 7/1 priority date for domestic and international students; for spring admission, 11/1 priority date for domestic and international students. Applications are processed on a rolling basis. Application fee: $35. Electronic applications accepted. *Expenses:* $1,020 per credit tuition plus $85 per credit fees. *Financial support:* Federal Work-Study, institutionally sponsored loans, and unspecified assistantships available. Financial award application deadline: 5/1; financial award applicants required to submit FAFSA. *Unit head:* Dr. Maria V. Kalevitch, Dean, 412-397-4020, E-mail: kalevitch@rmu.edu. *Application contact:* Kellie Laurenzi, Associate Vice President, Enrollment Management, 412-397-5200, E-mail: graduateadmissions@rmu.edu.
Website: https://www.rmu.edu/academics/schools/sems

Rochester Institute of Technology, Graduate Enrollment Services, Kate Gleason College of Engineering, Design, Development and Manufacturing Department, MS Program in Product Development, Rochester, NY 14623-5603. Offers MS. *Program availability:* Part-time, evening/weekend, 100% online, blended/hybrid learning. *Degree requirements:* For master's, capstone project. *Entrance requirements:* For master's, undergraduate degree in engineering or related field, minimum GPA of 3.0, 2 years of experience in product development, one professional recommendation, resume. Additional exam requirements/recommendations for international students: required—TOEFL (minimum score 550 paper-based; 79 iBT), IELTS (minimum score 6.5), PTE (minimum score 58). Electronic applications accepted. *Expenses:* Contact institution.

Rochester Institute of Technology, Graduate Enrollment Services, Kate Gleason College of Engineering, Industrial and Systems Engineering Department, ME Program in Engineering Management, Rochester, NY 14623-5603. Offers ME. *Program availability:* Part-time. *Degree requirements:* For master's, thesis or alternative, capstone. *Entrance requirements:* For master's, GRE, minimum GPA of 3.0 (recommended), letters of recommendation, 1-page statement of purpose. Additional exam requirements/recommendations for international students: required—TOEFL (minimum score 580 paper-based; 90 iBT), IELTS (minimum score 6.5), PTE (minimum score 58). Electronic applications accepted.

Rose-Hulman Institute of Technology, Graduate Studies, Department of Engineering Management, Terre Haute, IN 47803-3999. Offers M Eng, MS. *Program availability:* Part-time. *Faculty:* 5 full-time (2 women). *Students:* 8 full-time (2 women), 7 part-time (3 women); includes 3 minority (2 Asian, non-Hispanic/Latino; 1 Two or more races, non-Hispanic/Latino), 5 international. Average age 25. 11 applicants, 91% accepted, 6 enrolled. In 2019, 11 master's awarded. *Degree requirements:* For master's, integrated project. *Entrance requirements:* For master's, GRE, minimum GPA of 3.0. Additional exam requirements/recommendations for international students: required—TOEFL (minimum score 580 paper-based; 94 iBT), IELTS (minimum score 7). *Application deadline:* For fall admission, 2/1 priority date for domestic and international students; for winter admission, 10/1 for domestic students, 4/1 for international students; for spring admission, 1/15 for domestic students, 11/1 for international students. Applications are processed on a rolling basis. Application fee: $75. Electronic applications accepted. *Financial support:* In 2019–20, 13 students received support. Fellowships with tuition reimbursements available, research assistantships with tuition reimbursements available, institutionally sponsored loans, scholarships/grants, tuition waivers (full and partial), and unspecified assistantships available. *Unit head:* Dr. Craig Downing, Department Head, 812-877-8822, E-mail: downing@rose-hulman.edu. *Application contact:* Dr. Craig Downing, Department Head, 812-877-8822, E-mail: downing@rose-hulman.edu.
Website: https://www.rose-hulman.edu/academics/academic-departments/engineering-management/index.html

Saint Martin's University, Office of Graduate Studies, Program in Engineering Management, Lacey, WA 98503. Offers M Eng Mgt. *Program availability:* Part-time. *Students:* 5 full-time (3 women), 1 (woman) part-time; includes 3 minority (2 Hispanic/Latino; 1 Two or more races, non-Hispanic/Latino), 1 international. Average age 33. In 2019, 6 master's awarded. *Degree requirements:* For master's, comprehensive exam (for some programs), thesis optional. *Entrance requirements:* For master's, engineering license examination, minimum GPA of 2.8. Additional exam requirements/recommendations for international students: required—TOEFL (minimum score 550 paper-based; 79 iBT); recommended—IELTS (minimum score 6.5). *Application deadline:* For fall admission, 4/1 priority date for domestic and international students; for spring admission, 11/1 priority date for domestic and international students. Applications are processed on a rolling basis. Application fee: $50. Electronic applications accepted. *Expenses: Tuition:* Full-time $22,950; part-time $15,300 per year. Tuition and fees vary according to course level, course load, degree level, campus/location and program. *Financial support:* Fellowships, research assistantships, and Federal Work-Study available. Support available to part-time students. Financial award application deadline: 3/1; financial award applicants required to submit FAFSA. *Unit head:* Dr. David Olwell, Dean, Hal and Inge Marcus School of Engineering, 360-688-2731, Fax: 360-438-4522, E-mail: dolwell@stmartin.edu. *Application contact:* Timothy Greer, Graduate Admissions Recruiter, 360-412-6128, E-mail: tgreer@stmartin.edu.
Website: https://www.stmartin.edu

St. Mary's University, School of Science, Engineering and Technology, Program in Engineering Systems Management, San Antonio, TX 78228. Offers MS. *Program availability:* Part-time, evening/weekend, online learning. *Degree requirements:* For master's, thesis or project. *Entrance requirements:* For master's, GRE (minimum quantitative score of 148), BS in computer engineering, electrical engineering, or closely-related discipline; minimum GPA of 3.0; written statement of purpose indicating applicant's interests and objectives; two letters of recommendation. Additional exam requirements/recommendations for international students: required—TOEFL (minimum score 550 paper-based; 80 iBT), IELTS (minimum score 6). Electronic applications accepted.

Santa Clara University, School of Engineering, Santa Clara, CA 95053. Offers applied mathematics (MS); bioengineering (MS); civil, environmental, and sustainable engineering (MS); computer science and engineering (MS, PhD, Engineer); electrical engineering (MS, PhD, Engineer); engineering management and leadership (MS); mechanical engineering (MS, PhD, Engineer); power systems and sustainable energy (MS); software engineering (MS). *Program availability:* Part-time. *Entrance requirements:* For master's, GRE, official transcript; for doctorate, GRE, Official transcript, 500 word statement of purpose, three letters of recommendation. Additional exam requirements/recommendations for international students: required—TOEFL (minimum score 79 iBT), IELTS (minimum score 6.5). Electronic applications accepted.

South Dakota School of Mines and Technology, Graduate Division, Program in Construction Engineering Management, Rapid City, SD 57701-3995. Offers MS. *Program availability:* Part-time, evening/weekend, online learning. *Entrance requirements:* For master's, GRE General Test. Additional exam requirements/recommendations for international students: required—TOEFL (minimum score 520 paper-based; 68 iBT). Electronic applications accepted.

South Dakota School of Mines and Technology, Graduate Division, Program in Engineering Management, Rapid City, SD 57701-3995. Offers MS. *Program availability:* Part-time, online learning. *Entrance requirements:* For master's, GMAT. Additional exam requirements/recommendations for international students: required—TOEFL, TWE. Electronic applications accepted.

Southern Illinois University Carbondale, Graduate School, College of Engineering, Program in Quality Engineering Management, Carbondale, IL 62901-4701. Offers quality engineering and management (MS). *Degree requirements:* For master's, comprehensive exam, thesis. *Entrance requirements:* For master's, minimum GPA of 2.7. Additional exam requirements/recommendations for international students: required—TOEFL.

Southern Methodist University, Lyle School of Engineering, Department of Engineering Management, Information, and Systems, Dallas, TX 75275. Offers engineering entrepreneurship (MS); engineering management (MS, DE); information engineering and management (MSIEM); operations research (MS, PhD); systems engineering (MS). *Program availability:* Part-time, evening/weekend, online learning. Terminal master's awarded for partial completion of doctoral program. *Degree requirements:* For master's, thesis optional; for doctorate, thesis/dissertation, oral and written qualifying exams. *Entrance requirements:* For master's, minimum GPA of 3.0 in last 2 years; bachelor's degree in engineering, mathematics, sciences, or technical area; for doctorate, GRE General Test (operations research, engineering management), bachelor's degree in related field. Additional exam requirements/recommendations for international students: required—TOEFL.

Southern New Hampshire University, School of Business, Manchester, NH 03106-1045. Offers accounting (MBA, Graduate Certificate); accounting finance (MS); accounting/auditing (MS); accounting/forensic accounting (MS); accounting/management accounting (MS); accounting/taxation (MS); applied economics (MS); athletic administration (MBA, Graduate Certificate); business administration (IMBA, Certificate), including business information systems (Certificate), human resource management (Certificate); business analytics (MBA); business intelligence (MBA); communication (MA), including new media and marketing, public relations; community economic development (MBA); criminal justice (MBA); data analytics (MS); economics (MBA); engineering management (MBA); entrepreneurship (MBA); finance (MBA, MS, Graduate Certificate); finance/corporate finance (MS); finance/investments (MS); forensic accounting (MBA); forensic accounting and fraud examination (Graduate Certificate); healthcare informatics (MBA); healthcare management (MBA); human resource management (MS); human resources (MBA); information technology (MS); information technology management (MBA); international business (PhD); Internet marketing (MBA); leadership (MBA); leadership of nonprofit organizations (Graduate Certificate); management (MS); marketing (MBA, MS, Graduate Certificate); music business (MBA); operations and project management (MS); operations and supply chain management (MBA, Graduate Certificate); organizational leadership (MS); project management (MBA, Graduate Certificate); public administration (MBA, Graduate Certificate); quantitative analysis (MBA); Six Sigma (Graduate Certificate); Six Sigma quality (MBA); social media marketing (MBA, Graduate Certificate); sport management (MBA, MS, Graduate Certificate); sustainability and environmental compliance (MBA); MBA/Certificate. *Accreditation:* ACBSP. *Program availability:* Part-time, evening/weekend, online learning. Terminal master's awarded for partial completion of doctoral program. *Degree requirements:* For master's, one foreign language, comprehensive exam (for some programs), thesis or alternative; for doctorate, one foreign language, comprehensive exam, thesis/dissertation. *Entrance requirements:* For master's, minimum GPA of 2.5; for doctorate, GMAT. Additional exam requirements/recommendations for international students: required—TOEFL (minimum score 500 paper-based). Electronic applications accepted.

Stanford University, School of Engineering, Department of Management Science and Engineering, Stanford, CA 94305-2004. Offers MS, PhD. *Expenses: Tuition:* Full-time $52,479; part-time $34,110 per unit. *Required fees:* $672; $224 per quarter. Tuition and fees vary according to program and student level.
Website: http://www.stanford.edu/dept/MSandE/

Stevens Institute of Technology, Graduate School, School of Business, Program in Business Administration, Hoboken, NJ 07030. Offers business intelligence and analytics (MBA); engineering management (MBA); finance (MBA); information systems (MBA);

innovation and entrepreneurship (MBA); marketing (MBA); pharmaceutical management (MBA); project management (MBA, Certificate); technology management (MBA); telecommunications management (MBA). *Accreditation:* AACSB. *Program availability:* Part-time, evening/weekend. *Faculty:* 59 full-time (11 women), 30 part-time/adjunct (5 women). *Students:* 50 full-time (21 women), 242 part-time (112 women); includes 68 minority (13 Black or African American, non-Hispanic/Latino; 2 American Indian or Alaska Native, non-Hispanic/Latino; 51 Asian, non-Hispanic/Latino; 2 Hispanic/Latino), 55 international. Average age 36. In 2019, 60 master's awarded. Terminal master's awarded for partial completion of doctoral program. *Degree requirements:* For master's, thesis optional, minimum B average in major field and overall; for Certificate, minimum B average. *Entrance requirements:* For master's, International applicants must submit TOEFL/IELTS scores and fulfill the English Language Proficiency Requirement. Applicants to full-time programs who do not qualify for a score waiver are required to submit GRE/GMAT scores. Additional exam requirements/recommendations for international students: required—TOEFL (minimum score 74 iBT), IELTS (minimum score 6). *Application deadline:* For fall admission, 4/1 for domestic and international students; for spring admission, 11/1 for domestic and international students; for summer admission, 5/1 for domestic students. Applications are processed on a rolling basis. Application fee: $60. Electronic applications accepted. *Expenses: Tuition:* Full-time $52,134. *Required fees:* $1880. Tuition and fees vary according to course load. *Financial support:* Fellowships, research assistantships, teaching assistantships, career-related internships or fieldwork, Federal Work-Study, scholarships/grants, and unspecified assistantships available. Financial award application deadline: 2/15; financial award applicants required to submit FAFSA. *Unit head:* Dr. Gregory Prastacos, Dean, 201-216-8366, E-mail: gprastac@stevens.edu. *Application contact:* Graduate Admissions, 888-783-8367, Fax: 888-511-1306, E-mail: graduate@stevens.edu.
Website: https://www.stevens.edu/school-business/masters-programs/mbaemba

Stevens Institute of Technology, Graduate School, School of Systems and Enterprises, Program in Engineering Management, Hoboken, NJ 07030. Offers M Eng, PhD, Certificate. *Program availability:* Part-time, evening/weekend. *Faculty:* 22 full-time (8 women), 15 part-time/adjunct (3 women). *Students:* 120 full-time (37 women), 31 part-time (13 women); includes 9 minority (2 Black or African American, non-Hispanic/Latino; 1 American Indian or Alaska Native, non-Hispanic/Latino; 6 Asian, non-Hispanic/Latino), 111 international. Average age 25. In 2019, 77 master's, 36 other advanced degrees awarded. Terminal master's awarded for partial completion of doctoral program. *Degree requirements:* For master's, thesis optional, minimum B average in major field and overall; for doctorate, comprehensive exam (for some programs), thesis/dissertation; for Certificate, minimum B average. *Entrance requirements:* For master's, International applicants must submit TOEFL/IELTS scores and fulfill the English Language Proficiency Requirement. Applicants to full-time programs who do not qualify for a score waiver are required to submit GRE/GMAT scores. Additional exam requirements/recommendations for international students: required—TOEFL (minimum score 74 iBT), IELTS (minimum score 6). *Application deadline:* For fall admission, 4/15 for domestic and international students; for spring admission, 11/1 for domestic and international students; for summer admission, 5/1 for domestic students. Applications are processed on a rolling basis. Application fee: $60. Electronic applications accepted. *Expenses: Tuition:* Full-time $52,134. *Required fees:* $1880. Tuition and fees vary according to course load. *Financial support:* Fellowships, research assistantships, teaching assistantships, career-related internships or fieldwork, Federal Work-Study, scholarships/grants, and unspecified assistantships available. Financial award application deadline: 2/15; financial award applicants required to submit FAFSA. *Unit head:* Dr. Yehia Massoud, Dean of SSE, 201-216.8025, E-mail: yehia.massoud@stevens.edu. *Application contact:* Graduate Admissions, 888-783-8367, Fax: 888-511-1306, E-mail: graduate@stevens.edu.
Website: https://www.stevens.edu/school-systems-enterprises

Syracuse University, College of Engineering and Computer Science, MS Program in Engineering Management, Syracuse, NY 13244. Offers MS. *Program availability:* Part-time. *Entrance requirements:* For master's, GRE, three letters of recommendation, personal statement, resume, official transcripts. Additional exam requirements/recommendations for international students: required—TOEFL (minimum score 100 iBT). Electronic applications accepted.

Tarleton State University, College of Graduate Studies, College of Science and Technology, Department of Engineering Technology, Stephenville, TX 76402. Offers quality and engineering management (MS). *Program availability:* Part-time, evening/weekend, 100% online, blended/hybrid learning. *Faculty:* 2 full-time (1 woman), 1 part-time/adjunct (0 women). *Students:* 4 full-time (0 women), 46 part-time (7 women); includes 18 minority (9 Black or African American, non-Hispanic/Latino; 2 Asian, non-Hispanic/Latino; 5 Hispanic/Latino; 2 Two or more races, non-Hispanic/Latino). Average age 37. 23 applicants, 91% accepted, 17 enrolled. In 2019, 5 master's awarded. *Degree requirements:* For master's, comprehensive exam, thesis optional. *Entrance requirements:* For master's, GRE General Test, minimum GPA of 2.5. Additional exam requirements/recommendations for international students: required—TOEFL (minimum score 520 paper-based; 69 iBT); recommended—IELTS (minimum score 6), TSE (minimum score 50). *Application deadline:* For fall admission, 8/15 for domestic students; for spring admission, 1/7 for domestic students. Applications are processed on a rolling basis. Application fee: $50 ($130 for international students). Electronic applications accepted. *Expenses:* Tuition, state resident: part-time $221.73 per credit hour. Tuition, nonresident: part-time $636.73 per credit hour. *Required fees:* $198 per credit hour. $100 per semester. Tuition and fees vary according to degree level. *Financial support:* Application deadline: 5/1; applicants required to submit FAFSA. *Unit head:* Billy Gray, Department Head, 254-968-9374, E-mail: bgray@tarleton.edu. *Application contact:* Wendy Weiss, Graduate Admissions Coordinator, 254-968-9104, Fax: 254-968-9670, E-mail: weiss@tarleton.edu.
Website: https://www.tarleton.edu/engtech/index.html

Texas A&M University, College of Engineering, Wm Michael Barnes '64 Department of Industrial and Systems Engineering, College Station, TX 77843. Offers engineering systems management (MS); industrial engineering (M Eng, MS, PhD). *Program availability:* Part-time, 100% online. *Faculty:* 39. *Students:* 241 full-time (52 women), 96 part-time (16 women); includes 20 minority (5 Black or African American, non-Hispanic/Latino; 6 Asian, non-Hispanic/Latino; 7 Hispanic/Latino; 2 Two or more races, non-Hispanic/Latino), 275 international. Average age 27. 551 applicants, 36% accepted, 81 enrolled. In 2019, 111 master's, 5 doctorates awarded. *Degree requirements:* For master's, comprehensive exam (for some programs), thesis optional; for doctorate, comprehensive exam, thesis/dissertation. *Entrance requirements:* For master's and doctorate, GRE General Test. Additional exam requirements/recommendations for international students: required—TOEFL (minimum score 550 paper-based; 80 iBT), IELTS (minimum score 6), PTE (minimum score 53). *Application deadline:* For fall admission, 8/14 for domestic students, 3/1 for international students; for spring admission, 12/1 for domestic students, 10/31 for international students. Applications are processed on a rolling basis. Application fee: $65 ($90 for international students). Electronic applications accepted. *Expenses:* Contact institution. *Financial support:* In 2019–20, 237 students received support, including 8 fellowships with tuition reimbursements available (averaging $16,335 per year), 96 research assistantships with tuition reimbursements available (averaging $12,861 per year), 71 teaching assistantships with tuition reimbursements available (averaging $9,917 per year); career-related internships or fieldwork, institutionally sponsored loans, scholarships/grants, traineeships, health care benefits, tuition waivers (full and partial), and unspecified assistantships also available. Support available to part-time students. Financial award application deadline: 3/15; financial award applicants required to submit FAFSA. *Unit head:* Dr. Lewis Ntaimo, Interim Department Head, 979-845-5535, Fax: 979-458-4299, E-mail: ntaimo@tamu.edu. *Application contact:* Victoria Aregullin, Graduate Academic Advisor, 979-458-8403, E-mail: varegullin@tamu.edu.
Website: http://engineering.tamu.edu/industrial

Texas Tech University, Graduate School, Edward E. Whitacre Jr. College of Engineering, Department of Industrial, Manufacturing, and Systems Engineering, Lubbock, TX 79409-3061. Offers industrial engineering (MSIE, PhD); manufacturing engineering (MS); systems and engineering management (MSSEM). *Program availability:* Part-time, 100% online, blended/hybrid learning. *Faculty:* 20 full-time (3 women). *Students:* 59 full-time (8 women), 74 part-time (12 women); includes 22 minority (6 Black or African American, non-Hispanic/Latino; 3 Asian, non-Hispanic/Latino; 9 Hispanic/Latino; 4 Two or more races, non-Hispanic/Latino), 68 international. Average age 33. 209 applicants, 40% accepted, 28 enrolled. In 2019, 33 master's, 13 doctorates awarded. Terminal master's awarded for partial completion of doctoral program. *Degree requirements:* For master's, comprehensive exam, thesis optional; for doctorate, comprehensive exam, thesis/dissertation. *Entrance requirements:* For master's and doctorate, GRE (Verbal and Quantitative). Additional exam requirements/recommendations for international students: required—TOEFL (minimum score 550 paper-based; 79 iBT), Other English proficiency exams may be substituted for the TOEFL - see the TTU graduate school website. *Application deadline:* For fall admission, 6/1 priority date for domestic students, 1/15 priority date for international students; for spring admission, 9/1 priority date for domestic students, 6/15 priority date for international students. Applications are processed on a rolling basis. Application fee: $65. Electronic applications accepted. *Expenses:* Contact institution. *Financial support:* In 2019–20, 70 students received support, including 67 fellowships (averaging $2,668 per year), 19 research assistantships (averaging $23,015 per year), 13 teaching assistantships (averaging $20,383 per year); scholarships/grants, tuition waivers (partial), and unspecified assistantships also available. Financial award application deadline: 1/15; financial award applicants required to submit FAFSA. *Unit head:* Dr. Bryan A. Norman, Professor and Department Chair, 806-742-3543, E-mail: bryan.norman@ttu.edu. *Application contact:* Bianca Sasser, Academic Specialist, 806-742-3543, E-mail: grad.imse@ttu.edu.
Website: www.depts.ttu.edu/imse/

Trine University, Program in Engineering Management, Angola, IN 46703-1764. Offers MS.

Tufts University, School of Engineering, The Gordon Institute, Medford, MA 02155. Offers engineering management (MS); innovation and management (MS). *Program availability:* Part-time. *Entrance requirements:* Additional exam requirements/recommendations for international students: required—TOEFL (minimum score 550 paper-based; 80 iBT), IELTS (minimum score 6.5). Electronic applications accepted. *Expenses:* Contact institution.

Université de Sherbrooke, Faculty of Engineering, Programs in Engineering Management, Sherbrooke, QC J1K 2R1, Canada. Offers M Eng, Diploma. *Program availability:* Part-time, evening/weekend. *Entrance requirements:* For master's and Diploma, bachelor's degree in engineering, 1 year of practical experience. Electronic applications accepted.

University at Buffalo, the State University of New York, Graduate School, School of Engineering and Applied Sciences, Department of Industrial and Systems Engineering, Buffalo, NY 14260. Offers advanced manufacturing (Certificate); industrial engineering (ME, MS, PhD), including data fusion (ME), engineering management (ME). *Program availability:* Part-time, online learning. Terminal master's awarded for partial completion of doctoral program. *Degree requirements:* For master's, comprehensive exam (for some programs), thesis or alternative; for doctorate, thesis/dissertation. *Entrance requirements:* For master's and doctorate, GRE General Test. Additional exam requirements/recommendations for international students: required—TOEFL (minimum score 550 paper-based; 79 iBT). Electronic applications accepted. *Expenses: Tuition, area resident:* Full-time $11,310; part-time $471 per credit hour. Tuition, state resident: full-time $11,310; part-time $471 per credit hour. Tuition, nonresident: full-time $23,100; part-time $963 per credit hour. *International tuition:* $23,100 full-time. *Required fees:* $2820.

The University of Alabama at Birmingham, School of Engineering, Professional Engineering Degrees, Birmingham, AL 35294. Offers advanced safety engineering and management (M Eng); construction engineering management (M Eng); design and commercialization (M Eng); information engineering management (M Eng); structural engineering (M Eng); sustainable smart cities (M Eng). *Program availability:* Part-time, evening/weekend, online only, 100% online. *Faculty:* 5 full-time (1 woman), 15 part-time/adjunct (3 women). *Students:* 13 full-time (4 women), 315 part-time (70 women); includes 83 minority (64 Black or African American, non-Hispanic/Latino; 3 American Indian or Alaska Native, non-Hispanic/Latino; 9 Asian, non-Hispanic/Latino; 7 Hispanic/Latino), 8 international. 126 applicants, 84% accepted, 90 enrolled. In 2019, 123 master's awarded. *Entrance requirements:* For master's, 3.0 GPA on 4.0 scale, undergraduate degree from a nationally accredited school. Additional exam requirements/recommendations for international students: required—TOEFL (minimum score 80 iBT); recommended—IELTS (minimum score 6.5). *Application deadline:* For fall admission, 8/1 for domestic and international students; for spring admission, 12/1 for domestic and international students; for summer admission, 5/1 for domestic and international students. Applications are processed on a rolling basis. Application fee: $50 ($60 for international students). Electronic applications accepted. *Expenses:* Contact institution. *Unit head:* Dr. Gregg Janowski, Associate Dean for Graduate Programs and Assessment, E-mail: janowski@uab.edu. *Application contact:* Jesse Kepply, Director of Student and Academic Services, 205-996-5696, E-mail: gradschool@uab.edu.

University of Alberta, Faculty of Graduate Studies and Research, Department of Mechanical Engineering, Edmonton, AB T6G 2E1, Canada. Offers engineering management (M Eng); mechanical engineering (M Eng, M Sc, PhD); MBA/M Eng. *Program availability:* Part-time. *Degree requirements:* For master's, thesis; for doctorate, thesis/dissertation. *Entrance requirements:* For master's and doctorate, minimum GPA of 7.0 on a 9.0 scale. Additional exam requirements/recommendations for international students: required—TOEFL (minimum score 580 paper-based).

The University of Arizona, College of Engineering, Department of Systems and Industrial Engineering, Tucson, AZ 85721. Offers engineering management (Graduate Certificate); industrial engineering (MS); systems and industrial engineering (MS, PhD); systems engineering (MS, PhD, Graduate Certificate). *Program availability:* Part-time, online learning. *Degree requirements:* For doctorate, thesis/dissertation. *Entrance requirements:* For master's, GRE General Test (minimum score: 500 Verbal, 700 Quantitative), 3 letters of recommendation; for doctorate, GRE General Test (minimum score: 500 Verbal, 700 Quantitative), minimum GPA of 3.5, 3 letters of recommendation, letter of intent. Additional exam requirements/recommendations for international students: required—TOEFL (minimum score 575 paper-based; 80 iBT). Electronic applications accepted.

University of California, Berkeley, Graduate Division, College of Engineering, Department of Civil and Environmental Engineering, Berkeley, CA 94720. Offers engineering and project management (M Eng, MS, PhD); environmental engineering (M Eng, MS, PhD); geoengineering (M Eng, MS, PhD); structural engineering, mechanics and materials (M Eng, MS, PhD); transportation engineering (M Eng, MS, PhD); M Arch/MS; MCP/MS; MPP/MS. Terminal master's awarded for partial completion of doctoral program. *Degree requirements:* For master's, comprehensive exam (for some programs), thesis (for some programs), comprehensive exam or thesis (MS); for doctorate, thesis/dissertation, qualifying exam. *Entrance requirements:* For master's, GRE General Test, minimum GPA of 3.0, 3 letters of recommendation; for doctorate, GRE General Test, minimum GPA of 3.5, 3 letters of recommendation. Additional exam requirements/recommendations for international students: required—TOEFL (minimum score 570 paper-based; 90 iBT). Electronic applications accepted.

University of California, Irvine, Samueli School of Engineering, Program in Engineering Management, Irvine, CA 92697. Offers MS. *Students:* 11 full-time (9 women); includes 2 minority (both Hispanic/Latino), 6 international. Average age 26. 198 applicants, 20% accepted, 11 enrolled. In 2019, 17 master's awarded. *Application deadline:* For fall admission, 1/15 priority date for domestic students. Applications are processed on a rolling basis. Application fee: $120 ($140 for international students). *Application contact:* Jean Bennett, Director of Graduate Student Affairs, 949-824-6475, Fax: 949-824-8200, E-mail: jean.bennett@uci.edu.
Website: http://www.eng.uci.edu/admissions/graduate/programs-and-concentrations/engineering-management

University of Colorado Boulder, Graduate School, College of Engineering and Applied Science, Engineering Management Program, Boulder, CO 80309. Offers ME. *Entrance requirements:* For master's, minimum undergraduate GPA of 3.0. Electronic applications accepted. Application fee is waived when completed online.

University of Dayton, Department of Engineering Management, Systems and Technology, Dayton, OH 45469. Offers engineering management (MSEM); management science (MSMS). *Program availability:* Part-time, 100% online, blended/hybrid learning. *Degree requirements:* For master's, capstone project. *Entrance requirements:* For master's, bachelor's degree in engineering or other STEM discipline with minimum GPA of 3.0. Additional exam requirements/recommendations for international students: required—TOEFL (minimum score 550 paper-based; 80 iBT); recommended—IELTS. Electronic applications accepted.

University of Denver, Daniel Felix Ritchie School of Engineering and Computer Science, Department of Mechanical and Materials Engineering, Denver, CO 80208. Offers bioengineering (MS); engineering (MS, PhD), including management; materials science (MS, PhD); mechanical engineering (MS, PhD). *Program availability:* Part-time. *Faculty:* 12 full-time (2 women), 3 part-time/adjunct (1 woman). *Students:* 3 full-time (1 woman), 35 part-time (9 women); includes 3 minority (1 Black or African American, non-Hispanic/Latino; 1 Asian, non-Hispanic/Latino; 1 Hispanic/Latino), 16 international. Average age 27. 58 applicants, 81% accepted, 18 enrolled. In 2019, 16 master's, 4 doctorates awarded. Terminal master's awarded for partial completion of doctoral program. *Degree requirements:* For master's, thesis optional; for doctorate, comprehensive exam, thesis/dissertation. *Entrance requirements:* For master's, GRE General Test, bachelor's degree in engineering or closely related field, transcripts, personal statement, resume or curriculum vitae, two letters of recommendation; for doctorate, GRE General Test, master's degree in engineering or closely related field, transcripts, personal statement, resume or curriculum vitae, two letters of recommendation, recommended that applicants find a research advisor before submitting the application. Additional exam requirements/recommendations for international students: required—TOEFL (minimum score 550 paper-based; 80 iBT). *Application deadline:* For fall admission, 1/15 priority date for domestic and international students; for winter admission, 10/25 for domestic and international students; for spring admission, 2/7 for domestic and international students; for summer admission, 4/24 for domestic and international students. Applications are processed on a rolling basis. Application fee: $65. Electronic applications accepted. *Unit head:* Dr. Matt Gordon, Professor and Chair, 303-871-3580, E-mail: matthew.gordon@du.edu. *Application contact:* Chrissy Alexander, Assistant to the Chair, 303-871-3041, E-mail: Christine.Alexander@du.edu.
Website: http://ritchieschool.du.edu/departments/mme/

University of Detroit Mercy, College of Engineering and Science, Detroit, MI 48221. Offers chemistry (MS); civil and environmental engineering (DE); electrical and computer engineering (ME); electrical engineering (DE); engineering management (M Eng Mgt); environmental engineering (MEE); mechanical engineering (MME, DE); product development (MS); software engineering (MSSE); teaching of mathematics (MATM). *Program availability:* Part-time, evening/weekend. *Degree requirements:* For doctorate, thesis/dissertation. Electronic applications accepted. Application fee is waived when completed online. *Expenses:* Contact institution.

The University of Kansas, Graduate Studies, School of Engineering, Program in Engineering Management, Overland Park, KS 66213. Offers MS, Certificate. *Program availability:* Part-time, evening/weekend, online learning. *Students:* 5 full-time (0 women), 70 part-time (18 women); includes 17 minority (3 Black or African American, non-Hispanic/Latino; 1 American Indian or Alaska Native, non-Hispanic/Latino; 10 Asian, non-Hispanic/Latino; 3 Hispanic/Latino), 6 international. Average age 32. 22 applicants, 77% accepted, 14 enrolled. In 2019, 29 master's awarded. *Entrance requirements:* For master's, minimum GPA of 3.0, 2 years of industrial experience, BS in engineering or related science. Additional exam requirements/recommendations for international students: required—TOEFL, IELTS. Application fee: $65 ($85 for international students). Electronic applications accepted. *Expenses:* Tuition, state resident: full-time $9989. Tuition, nonresident: full-time $23,950. *International tuition:* $23,950 full-time. *Required fees:* $984; $81.99 per credit hour. Tuition and fees vary according to course load, campus/location and program. *Unit head:* Herbert R. Tuttle, Director, 913-897-8561, E-mail: htuttle@ku.edu. *Application contact:* Parveen Mozaffar, Program Advisor, 913-897-8560, E-mail: parveen@ku.edu.
Website: http://emgt.ku.edu/

University of Louisville, J. B. Speed School of Engineering, Department of Industrial Engineering, Louisville, KY 40292-0001. Offers engineering management (M Eng); industrial engineering (M Eng, MS, PhD); logistics and distribution (Certificate). *Accreditation:* ABET (one or more programs are accredited). *Program availability:* 100% online. *Faculty:* 8 full-time (4 women), 8 part-time/adjunct (2 women). *Students:* 52 full-time (11 women), 117 part-time (41 women); includes 27 minority (11 Black or African American, non-Hispanic/Latino; 1 American Indian or Alaska Native, non-Hispanic/Latino; 8 Asian, non-Hispanic/Latino; 5 Hispanic/Latino; 2 Two or more races, non-Hispanic/Latino), 55 international. Average age 30. 97 applicants, 61% accepted, 46 enrolled. In 2019, 85 master's, 6 doctorates awarded. Terminal master's awarded for partial completion of doctoral program. *Degree requirements:* For master's and Certificate, thesis optional; for doctorate, comprehensive exam, thesis/dissertation. *Entrance requirements:* For master's, two letters of recommendation, official transcripts; for doctorate, GRE, two letters of recommendation, official transcripts. Additional exam requirements/recommendations for international students: required—TOEFL (minimum score 550 paper-based; 80 iBT), IELTS (minimum score 6.5). *Application deadline:* For fall admission, 5/1 priority date for domestic and international students; for spring admission, 11/1 priority date for domestic and international students; for summer admission, 3/1 priority date for domestic and international students. Applications are processed on a rolling basis. Application fee: $65. Electronic applications accepted. *Expenses: Tuition, area resident:* Full-time $13,000; part-time $723 per credit hour. Tuition, state resident: full-time $13,000; part-time $723 per credit hour. Tuition, nonresident: full-time $27,114; part-time $1507 per credit hour. *International tuition:* $27,114 full-time. *Required fees:* $196. Tuition and fees vary according to program and reciprocity agreements. *Financial support:* In 2019–20, 27 students received support. Fellowships, research assistantships, teaching assistantships, scholarships/grants, health care benefits, and tuition waivers (full) available. Financial award application deadline: 1/1. *Unit head:* Dr. Suraj M. Alexander, Chair, Industrial Engineering Department, 502-852-0082, E-mail: suraj.alexander@louisville.edu. *Application contact:* Lihui Bai, Director of Graduate Studies, 502-852-1416, E-mail: lihui.bai@louisville.edu.
Website: http://www.louisville.edu/speed/industrial/

University of Management and Technology, Program in Engineering Management, Arlington, VA 22209-1609. Offers MS. *Expenses: Tuition:* Full-time $7020; part-time $390 per credit hour. *Required fees:* $90; $30 per semester.

The University of Manchester, School of Mechanical, Aerospace and Civil Engineering, Manchester, United Kingdom. Offers advanced manufacturing technology (M Ent); aerospace engineering (M Phil, M Sc, PhD); civil engineering (M Phil, M Sc, PhD); environmental engineering (M Phil, PhD); management of projects (M Phil, M Sc, PhD); mechanical engineering (M Phil, M Sc, PhD); mechanical engineering design (M Ent); nuclear engineering (M Phil, D Eng, PhD).

University of Maryland, Baltimore County, The Graduate School, Program in Engineering Management, Baltimore, MD 21250. Offers MS, Postbaccalaureate Certificate. *Program availability:* Part-time. *Faculty:* 2 full-time (0 women), 3 part-time/adjunct (0 women). *Students:* 26 full-time (10 women), 37 part-time (14 women); includes 19 minority (6 Black or African American, non-Hispanic/Latino; 9 Asian, non-Hispanic/Latino; 4 Hispanic/Latino), 25 international. Average age 28. 98 applicants, 56% accepted, 22 enrolled. In 2019, 32 master's, 3 other advanced degrees awarded. *Degree requirements:* For master's, comprehensive exam (for some programs), thesis optional. *Entrance requirements:* For master's, BS in engineering, computer science, mathematics, physics, chemistry, or other physical sciences; two letters of recommendation (for international students). Additional exam requirements/recommendations for international students: required—TOEFL (minimum score 550 paper-based; 80 iBT), GRE General Test. *Application deadline:* For fall admission, 7/1 for domestic and international students; for spring admission, 12/1 for domestic and international students. Applications are processed on a rolling basis. Application fee: $70. Electronic applications accepted. *Expenses: Tuition, area resident:* Full-time $659. Tuition, state resident: full-time $659. Tuition, nonresident: full-time $1132. *International tuition:* $1132 full-time. *Required fees:* $140; $140 per credit hour. *Financial support:* In 2019–20, 1 student received support, including 1 research assistantship; career-related internships or fieldwork, Federal Work-Study, scholarships/grants, health care benefits, and unspecified assistantships also available. Support available to part-time students. Financial award application deadline: 6/30; financial award applicants required to submit FAFSA. *Unit head:* Dr. Toby Gouker, Acting Graduate Program Director, 410-455-0616, Fax: 410-455-3969, E-mail: tgouker@umbc.edu. *Application contact:* Dr. Toby Gouker, Acting Graduate Program Director, 410-455-0616, Fax: 410-455-3969, E-mail: tgouker@umbc.edu.

University of Michigan–Dearborn, College of Engineering and Computer Science, MS Program in Engineering Management, Dearborn, MI 48128. Offers MS. *Program availability:* Part-time, evening/weekend, 100% online. *Faculty:* 17 full-time (4 women), 9 part-time/adjunct (1 woman). *Students:* 15 full-time (6 women), 166 part-time (34 women); includes 31 minority (11 Black or African American, non-Hispanic/Latino; 1 American Indian or Alaska Native, non-Hispanic/Latino; 12 Asian, non-Hispanic/Latino; 6 Hispanic/Latino; 1 Two or more races, non-Hispanic/Latino), 30 international. Average age 30. 109 applicants, 57% accepted, 33 enrolled. In 2019, 40 master's awarded. *Entrance requirements:* Additional exam requirements/recommendations for international students: required—TOEFL (minimum score 560 paper-based; 84 iBT), IELTS (minimum score 6.5). *Application deadline:* For fall admission, 8/1 for domestic students, 5/1 for international students; for winter admission, 12/1 for domestic students, 9/1 for international students; for spring admission, 4/1 for domestic students, 1/1 for international students. Applications are processed on a rolling basis. Application fee: $60. Electronic applications accepted. *Financial support:* Scholarships/grants, unspecified assistantships, and non-resident tuition scholarships available. Support available to part-time students. Financial award application deadline: 3/1; financial award applicants required to submit FAFSA. *Unit head:* Dr. Armen Zakarian, Chair, 313-593-5361, Fax: 313-593-3692, E-mail: zakarian@umich.edu. *Application contact:* Office of Graduate Studies, 313-583-6321, E-mail: umd-graduatestudies@umich.edu.
Website: https://umdearborn.edu/cecs/departments/industrial-and-manufacturing-systems-engineering/graduate-programs/ms-engineering-management

University of Minnesota, Duluth, Graduate School, Swenson College of Science and Engineering, Department of Mechanical and Industrial Engineering, Duluth, MN 55812-2496. Offers engineering management (MSEM); environmental health and safety (MEHS). *Program availability:* Part-time, evening/weekend, online learning. *Degree requirements:* For master's, comprehensive exam, thesis or alternative, capstone design project (MSEM), field project (MEHS). *Entrance requirements:* For master's, GRE (MEHS), interview (MEHS), letters of recommendation. Additional exam requirements/recommendations for international students: required—TOEFL (minimum score 550 paper-based).

University of Missouri–Kansas City, School of Computing and Engineering, Kansas City, MO 64110-2499. Offers civil engineering (MS); computer and electrical engineering (PhD); computer science (MS), including bioinformatics, software engineering, telecommunications networking; computer science and informatics (PhD); computing (PhD); electrical engineering (MS); engineering (PhD); engineering and construction management (Graduate Certificate); mechanical engineering (MS); telecommunications and computer networking (PhD). *Program availability:* Part-time. *Degree requirements:* For doctorate, thesis/dissertation. *Entrance requirements:* For master's, GRE General Test, minimum GPA of 3.0, 3 letters of recommendation from professors; for doctorate, GRE General Test, minimum GPA of 3.5. Additional exam requirements/recommendations for international students: required—TOEFL (minimum score 550 paper-based; 80 iBT).

University of Nebraska–Lincoln, Graduate College, College of Engineering, Department of Industrial and Management Systems Engineering, Lincoln, NE 68588. Offers engineering management (M Eng); industrial and management systems engineering (MS, PhD); manufacturing systems engineering (MS). *Program availability:* Online learning. *Degree requirements:* For master's, thesis optional; for doctorate, comprehensive exam, thesis/dissertation. *Entrance requirements:* For master's and doctorate, GRE. Additional exam requirements/recommendations for international students: required—TOEFL (minimum score 525 paper-based). Electronic applications accepted.

University of New Brunswick Fredericton, School of Graduate Studies, Faculty of Business Administration, Fredericton, NB E3B 5A3, Canada. Offers business administration (MBA); engineering management (MBA); entrepreneurship (MBA); sports and recreation management (MBA); MBA/LL B. *Program availability:* Part-time. *Faculty:* 32 full-time (11 women), 7 part-time/adjunct (3 women). *Students:* 73 full-time (27 women), 23 part-time (10 women), 40 international. Average age 32. In 2019, 31 master's awarded. *Degree requirements:* For master's, thesis optional. *Entrance requirements:* For master's, GMAT (minimum score 550), minimum GPA of 3.0; 3-5 years of work experience; 3 letters of reference with at least one academic reference. Additional exam requirements/recommendations for international students: required—TOEFL (minimum score 580 paper-based; 92 iBT), IELTS (minimum score 7), TOEFL (minimum score 580 paper-based; 92 iBT) or IELTS (minimum score 7). *Application deadline:* For fall admission, 10/31 priority date for domestic and international students; for spring admission, 3/31 priority date for domestic and international students. Application fee: $50 Canadian dollars. Electronic applications accepted. *Expenses: Tuition, area resident:* Full-time $6975 Canadian dollars; part-time $3423 Canadian dollars per year. Tuition, state resident: full-time $6975 Canadian dollars; part-time $3423 Canadian dollars per year. Tuition, Canadian resident: full-time $6975 Canadian dollars; part-time $3423 Canadian dollars per year. *International tuition:* $12,435 Canadian dollars full-time. *Required fees:* $92.25 Canadian dollars per term. Full-time tuition and fees vary according to degree level, campus/location, program, reciprocity agreements and student level. *Financial support:* Fellowships, research assistantships, and teaching assistantships available. Financial award application deadline: 1/15. *Unit head:* Dr. Donglei Du, Director of Graduate Studies, 506-458-7353, Fax: 506-453-3561, E-mail: ddu@unb.ca. *Application contact:* Marilyn Davis, Acting Graduate Secretary, 506-453-4766, Fax: 506-453-3561, E-mail: mbacontact@unb.ca.
Website: http://go.unb.ca/gradprograms

University of New Haven, Graduate School, Tagliatela College of Engineering, Program in Engineering and Operations Management, West Haven, CT 06516. Offers engineering and operations management (MS); engineering management (MS); Lean Six Sigma (Graduate Certificate). *Program availability:* Part-time. *Students:* 59 full-time (11 women), 25 part-time (3 women); includes 4 minority (2 Black or African American, non-Hispanic/Latino; 1 American Indian or Alaska Native, non-Hispanic/Latino; 1 Asian, non-Hispanic/Latino), 59 international. Average age 27. 288 applicants, 86% accepted, 26 enrolled. In 2019, 45 master's awarded. *Entrance requirements:* Additional exam requirements/recommendations for international students: required—TOEFL (minimum score 75 iBT), IELTS, PTE (minimum score 50). *Application deadline:* Applications are processed on a rolling basis. Application fee: $50. Electronic applications accepted. Application fee is waived when completed online. *Financial support:* Applicants required to submit FAFSA. *Unit head:* Dr. Ali Montazer, Professor, 203-932-7050, E-mail: amontazer@newhaven.edu. *Application contact:* Selina O'Toole, Senior Associate Director of Graduate Admissions, 203-932-7337, E-mail: sotoole@newhaven.edu.
Website: https://www.newhaven.edu/engineering/graduate-programs/operations-management/

University of New Orleans, Graduate School, College of Engineering, Program in Engineering Management, New Orleans, LA 70148. Offers MS. *Degree requirements:* For master's, thesis optional. *Entrance requirements:* For master's, GRE General Test, minimum GPA of 3.0. Additional exam requirements/recommendations for international students: required—TOEFL (minimum score 550 paper-based; 79 iBT). Electronic applications accepted.

University of Ottawa, Faculty of Graduate and Postdoctoral Studies, Faculty of Engineering, Engineering Management Program, Ottawa, ON K1N 6N5, Canada. Offers engineering management (M Eng); information technology (Certificate); project management (Certificate). *Degree requirements:* For master's, thesis or alternative. *Entrance requirements:* For master's and Certificate, honors degree or equivalent, minimum B average. Electronic applications accepted.

University of Puerto Rico at Mayagüez, Graduate Studies, College of Engineering, Department of Civil Engineering and Surveying, Mayagüez, PR 00681-9000. Offers civil engineering (ME, MS, PhD), including construction engineering and management (ME, MS), environmental engineering, geotechnical engineering (ME, MS), structural engineering, transportation engineering. *Program availability:* Part-time. Terminal master's awarded for partial completion of doctoral program. *Degree requirements:* For master's, one foreign language, thesis; for doctorate, one foreign language, comprehensive exam, thesis/dissertation, qualifying exams. *Entrance requirements:* For master's, proficiency in English and Spanish; BS in civil engineering or its equivalent; for doctorate, proficiency in English and Spanish. Electronic applications accepted.

University of Regina, Faculty of Graduate Studies and Research, Kenneth Levene Graduate School of Business, Program in Business Administration, Regina, SK S4S 0A2, Canada. Offers business foundations (PGD); engineering management (MBA); executive business administration (EMBA); international business (MBA); leadership (M Admin); organizational leadership (Master's Certificate); project management (Master's Certificate); public safety management (MBA). *Program availability:* Part-time, evening/weekend. *Students:* 10 full-time (5 women), 4 part-time (3 women). Average age 30. 57 applicants, 9% accepted. In 2019, 9 master's awarded. *Degree requirements:* For master's, project (for some programs). workplacement for Co-op concentration, and course work. *Entrance requirements:* For master's, GMAT, 3 years of relevant work experience, four-year undergraduate degree, post secondary transcript, 2 letters of recommendation; for other advanced degree, GMAT (for PGD), four-year undergraduate degree and 2 years of relevant work experience (for Master's Certificate); 3 years' work experience (for PGD). Additional exam requirements/recommendations for international students: required—TOEFL (minimum score 580 paper-based; 80 iBT), IELTS (minimum score 6.5), PTE (minimum score 59), other options are CAEL, MELAB, CANTEST or U of R ESl; GMAT is mandatory. *Application deadline:* For fall admission, 3/1 for domestic and international students; for winter admission, 7/1 for domestic and international students; for spring admission, 10/1 for domestic and international students; for summer admission, 10/1 for domestic and international students. Applications are processed on a rolling basis. Application fee: $100. Electronic applications accepted. *Expenses:* 22,876 - This amount is based on three semesters tuition and fees, registered in 6 credit hours per semester. Plus one year student fees and books. *Financial support:* Fellowships, research assistantships, teaching assistantships, career-related internships or fieldwork, Federal Work-Study, scholarships/grants, unspecified assistantships, and travel award and Graduate scholarship Base Funds available. Support available to part-time students. Financial award application deadline: 9/30. *Unit head:* Dr. Gina Grandy, Dean, 306-585-4435, Fax: 306-585-5361, E-mail: business.dean@uregina.ca. *Application contact:* Adrian Pitariu, Associate Dean, Research and Graduate Programs, 306-585-6294, Fax: 306-585-5361, E-mail: business.AD.levene@uregina.ca.
Website: http://www.uregina.ca/business/levene/

University of St. Thomas, School of Engineering, St. Paul, MN 55105. Offers data science (MS); electrical engineering (MS); information technology (MS); manufacturing engineering (MS); manufacturing systems (Certificate); mechanical engineering (MS); medical device development (Certificate); regulatory science (MS); software engineering (MS); software management (MS); systems engineering (MS); technology leadership (Certificate); technology management (MS). *Program availability:* Part-time, evening/weekend. *Entrance requirements:* For master's, resume, official transcripts. Additional exam requirements/recommendations for international students: required—TOEFL (minimum score 80 iBT), IELTS (minimum score 6.5). Electronic applications accepted. *Expenses:* Contact institution.

University of Southern California, Graduate School, Viterbi School of Engineering, Daniel J. Epstein Department of Industrial and Systems Engineering, Los Angeles, CA 90089. Offers digital supply chain management (MS); engineering management (MS); engineering technology communication (Graduate Certificate); health systems operations (Graduate Certificate); industrial and systems engineering (MS, PhD, Engr); manufacturing engineering (MS); operations research engineering (MS); optimization and supply chain management (Graduate Certificate); product development engineering (MS); safety systems and security (MS); systems architecting and engineering (MS, Graduate Certificate); systems safety and security (Graduate Certificate); transportation systems (Graduate Certificate); MS/MBA. *Program availability:* Part-time, evening/weekend, online learning. Terminal master's awarded for partial completion of doctoral program. *Degree requirements:* For master's, thesis optional; for doctorate, thesis/dissertation. *Entrance requirements:* For master's and doctorate, GRE General Test. Additional exam requirements/recommendations for international students: recommended—TOEFL. Electronic applications accepted.

University of Southern California, Graduate School, Viterbi School of Engineering, Department of Aerospace and Mechanical Engineering, Los Angeles, CA 90089. Offers aerospace and mechanical engineering: computational fluid and solid mechanics (MS); aerospace and mechanical engineering: dynamics and control (MS); aerospace engineering (MS, PhD, Engr), including aerospace engineering (PhD, Engr); green technologies (MS); mechanical engineering (MS, PhD, Engr), including energy conversion (MS), mechanical engineering (PhD, Engr), nuclear power (MS); product development engineering (MS). *Program availability:* Part-time, evening/weekend, online learning. Terminal master's awarded for partial completion of doctoral program. *Degree requirements:* For master's, thesis optional; for doctorate, thesis/dissertation. *Entrance requirements:* For master's, doctorate, and Engr, GRE General Test. Additional exam requirements/recommendations for international students: recommended—TOEFL. Electronic applications accepted.

University of Southern Indiana, Graduate Studies, Romain College of Business, Program in Business Administration, Evansville, IN 47712-3590. Offers accounting (MBA); data analytics (MBA); engineering management (MBA); general business administration (MBA); healthcare administration (MBA); human resource management (MBA). *Accreditation:* AACSB. *Program availability:* Part-time, evening/weekend, 100% online, blended/hybrid learning. *Entrance requirements:* For master's, GMAT or GRE, minimum GPA of 2.5, resume, 3 professional references. Additional exam requirements/recommendations for international students: required—TOEFL (minimum score 550 paper-based; 79 iBT), IELTS (minimum score 6). Electronic applications accepted.

University of South Florida, College of Engineering, Department of Industrial and Management Systems Engineering, Tampa, FL 33620-9951. Offers MSEM, MSIE, MSIT, MSMSE, PhD. *Program availability:* Part-time, online learning. *Faculty:* 30 full-time (3 women), 1 part-time/adjunct (0 women). *Students:* 84 full-time (25 women), 60 part-time (15 women); includes 13 minority (2 Black or African American, non-Hispanic/Latino; 4 Asian, non-Hispanic/Latino; 7 Hispanic/Latino), 100 international. Average age 27. 280 applicants, 54% accepted, 37 enrolled. In 2019, 72 master's, 3 doctorates awarded. Terminal master's awarded for partial completion of doctoral program. *Degree requirements:* For master's, comprehensive exam, thesis (for some programs); for doctorate, comprehensive exam, thesis/dissertation, 2 tools of research as specified by dissertation committee. *Entrance requirements:* For master's, GRE General Test, BS in engineering (or equivalent), letters of recommendation, resume, two years professional experience or internship may be required; statement of purpose; for doctorate, GRE General Test, minimum GPA of 3.0, 3 letters of recommendation, statement of purpose, strong background in scientific and engineering principles. Ph.D. students must complete their total doctoral major as full-time Tampa campus students. Additional exam requirements/recommendations for international students: required—TOEFL, TOEFL (minimum score 550 paper-based; 79 iBT) or IELTS (minimum score 6.5). *Application deadline:* For fall admission, 2/15 for domestic and international students; for spring admission, 10/15 for domestic students, 9/15 for international students; for summer admission, 2/15 for domestic students, 1/15 for international students. Application fee: $30. Electronic applications accepted. *Financial support:* In 2019–20, 26 students received support, including 20 research assistantships with partial tuition reimbursements available (averaging $16,748 per year), 11 teaching assistantships with partial tuition reimbursements available (averaging $15,000 per year); tuition waivers (partial) also available. Financial award applicants required to submit FAFSA. *Unit head:* Dr. Tapas K. Das, Professor and Department Chair, 813-974-5585, Fax: 813-974-5953, E-mail: das@usf.edu. *Application contact:* Dr. Alex Savachkin, Associate Professor and Graduate Director, 813-974-5577, Fax: 813-974-5953, E-mail: alexs@usf.edu.
Website: http://imse.eng.usf.edu

The University of Tennessee, Graduate School, Tickle College of Engineering, Department of Industrial and Systems Engineering, Knoxville, TN 37966. Offers engineering management (MS); industrial engineering (MS, PhD); reliability and maintainability engineering (MS); MS/MBA. *Program availability:* Part-time, online learning. *Faculty:* 9 full-time (1 woman), 4 part-time/adjunct (1 woman). *Students:* 94 full-time (26 women), 51 part-time (15 women); includes 28 minority (13 Black or African American, non-Hispanic/Latino; 2 American Indian or Alaska Native, non-Hispanic/Latino; 5 Asian, non-Hispanic/Latino; 5 Hispanic/Latino; 3 Two or more races, non-Hispanic/Latino), 32 international. Average age 35. 77 applicants, 66% accepted, 28 enrolled. In 2019, 45 master's, 11 doctorates awarded. *Degree requirements:* For master's, thesis or alternative; for doctorate, comprehensive exam, thesis/dissertation. *Entrance requirements:* For master's, GRE General Test (for MS students pursuing research thesis), minimum GPA of 2.7 (for U.S. degree holders), 3.0 (for international degree holders); for doctorate, GRE General Test, minimum GPA of 3.0 on previous graduate course work. Additional exam requirements/recommendations for international students: required—TOEFL (minimum score 550 paper-based; 80 iBT), IELTS (minimum score 6.5). *Application deadline:* For fall admission, 2/1 priority date for domestic and international students; for spring admission, 6/15 for domestic and international students; for summer admission, 10/15 for domestic and international students. Applications are processed on a rolling basis. Application fee: $60. Electronic applications accepted. *Financial support:* In 2019–20, 61 students received support, including 9 fellowships with full tuition reimbursements available (averaging $22,671 per year), 36 research assistantships with full tuition reimbursements available (averaging $21,050 per year), 16 teaching assistantships with full tuition reimbursements available (averaging $19,219 per year); career-related internships or fieldwork, Federal Work-Study, institutionally sponsored loans, health care benefits, and unspecified assistantships also available. Financial award application deadline: 2/1; financial award applicants required to submit FAFSA. *Unit head:* Dr. John Kobza, Department Head,

865-974-3333, Fax: 865-974-0588, E-mail: jkobza@utk.edu. *Application contact:* Dr. Jim Ostrowski, Associate Professor and Director of Graduate Studies, 865-974-7657, E-mail: jostrows@utk.edu.
Website: http://www.engr.utk.edu/ie/

The University of Tennessee at Chattanooga, Engineering Management and Technology Program, Chattanooga, TN 37403. Offers construction management (Graduate Certificate); engineering management (MS); fundamentals of engineering management (Graduate Certificate); leadership and ethics (Graduate Certificate); logistics and supply chain management (Graduate Certificate); power systems management (Graduate Certificate); project and technology management (Graduate Certificate); quality management (Graduate Certificate). *Program availability:* 100% online, blended/hybrid learning. *Students:* 10 full-time (4 women), 44 part-time (6 women); includes 9 minority (4 Black or African American, non-Hispanic/Latino; 1 Asian, non-Hispanic/Latino; 2 Hispanic/Latino; 2 Two or more races, non-Hispanic/Latino), 9 international. Average age 33. 24 applicants, 88% accepted, 8 enrolled. In 2019, 21 master's, 1 other advanced degree awarded. *Degree requirements:* For master's, thesis or alternative, Project as alternative to thesis. *Entrance requirements:* For master's, GRE General Test, letters of recommendation; minimum undergraduate GPA of 2.7 overall or 3.0 in final two years; for Graduate Certificate, baccalaureate degree and professional experience or have already been admitted to engineering/engineering management graduate program. Additional exam requirements/recommendations for international students: required—TOEFL (minimum score 550 paper-based; 79 iBT), IELTS (minimum score 6). *Application deadline:* For fall admission, 6/15 priority date for domestic students, 7/1 for international students; for spring admission, 11/1 priority date for domestic students, 11/1 for international students. Applications are processed on a rolling basis. Application fee: $35 ($40 for international students). Electronic applications accepted. *Financial support:* Research assistantships, teaching assistantships, career-related internships or fieldwork, scholarships/grants, and unspecified assistantships available. Support available to part-time students. Financial award application deadline: 7/1; financial award applicants required to submit FAFSA. *Unit head:* Dr. Ahad Nasab, Department Head, 423-425-4032, Fax: 423-425-5818, E-mail: Ahad-Nasab@utc.edu. *Application contact:* Dr. Joanne Romagni, Dean of the Graduate School, 423-425-4478, Fax: 423-425-5223, E-mail: joanne-romagni@utc.edu.
Website: https://www.utc.edu/college-engineering-computer-science/programs/engineering-management-and-technology/index.php

The University of Texas at Arlington, Graduate School, College of Engineering, Department of Industrial, Manufacturing, and Systems Engineering, Program in Engineering Management, Arlington, TX 76019. Offers MS. *Program availability:* Part-time, evening/weekend, online learning. *Degree requirements:* For master's, comprehensive exam, thesis optional. *Entrance requirements:* For master's, GRE, 3 years of full-time work experience, minimum GPA of 3.0. Additional exam requirements/recommendations for international students: required—TOEFL (minimum score 550 paper-based).

The University of Texas at Tyler, Soules College of Business, Department of Management and Marketing, Tyler, TX 75799-0001. Offers cyber security (MBA); engineering management (MBA); general management (MBA); healthcare management (MBA); internal assurance and consulting (MBA); marketing (MBA); oil, gas and energy (MBA); organizational development (MBA); quality management (MBA). *Accreditation:* AACSB. *Program availability:* Part-time, online learning. *Faculty:* 13 full-time (5 women). *Students:* Average age 29. *Entrance requirements:* Additional exam requirements/recommendations for international students: required—TOEFL (minimum score 550 paper-based). *Application deadline:* For fall admission, 8/17 priority date for domestic students, 7/1 priority date for international students; for spring admission, 12/21 priority date for domestic students, 11/1 priority date for international students. Application fee: $25 ($50 for international students). *Unit head:* Dr. Krist Swimberghe, Chair, 903-565-5803, E-mail: kswimberghe@uttyler.edu. *Application contact:* Dr. Krist Swimberghe, Chair, 903-565-5803, E-mail: kswimberghe@uttyler.edu.
Website: https://www.uttyler.edu/cbt/manamark/

The University of Texas Rio Grande Valley, College of Engineering and Computer Science, Department of Manufacturing and Industrial Engineering, Edinburg, TX 78539. Offers engineering management (MS); manufacturing engineering (MS), including systems engineering. *Faculty:* 5 full-time. *Students:* 26 full-time (8 women), 16 part-time (6 women); includes 22 minority (all Hispanic/Latino), 20 international. Average age 26. 21 applicants, 81% accepted, 9 enrolled. In 2019, 12 master's awarded. *Expenses:* Tuition, area resident: Full-time $5959; part-time $440 per credit hour. Tuition, state resident: full-time $5959. Tuition, nonresident: full-time $5959. International tuition: $13,321 full-time. *Required fees:* $1169; $185 per credit hour.
Website: utrgv.edu/maie/

University of Vermont, Graduate College, College of Engineering and Mathematical Sciences, Program in Engineering Management, Burlington, VT 05405. Offers MS. *Entrance requirements:* Additional exam requirements/recommendations for international students: required—TOEFL (minimum iBT score of 90) or IELTS (6.5).

University of Waterloo, Graduate Studies and Postdoctoral Affairs, Faculty of Engineering, Department of Management Sciences, Waterloo, ON N2L 3G1, Canada. Offers applied operations research (MA Sc, MMS, PhD); information systems (MA Sc, MMS, PhD); management of technology (MA Sc, MMS, PhD). *Program availability:* Part-time, online learning. *Degree requirements:* For master's, research paper or thesis; for doctorate, comprehensive exam, thesis/dissertation. *Entrance requirements:* For master's, GMAT or GRE, honors degree, minimum B average, resume; for doctorate, GMAT or GRE, master's degree, minimum A- average, resume. Additional exam requirements/recommendations for international students: required—TOEFL, IELTS, PTE. Electronic applications accepted.

Valparaiso University, Graduate School and Continuing Education, College of Business, Valparaiso, IN 46383. Offers business administration (MBA); business decision-making (Certificate); business intelligence (Certificate); engineering management (Certificate); finance (Certificate); general business (Certificate); leading the global enterprise (Certificate); management (Certificate); JD/MBA; MSN/MBA. *Accreditation:* AACSB. *Program availability:* Part-time, evening/weekend, online learning. *Entrance requirements:* For master's, GMAT, GRE, minimum GPA of 3.0. Additional exam requirements/recommendations for international students: required—TOEFL (minimum score 550 paper-based; 80 iBT), IELTS (minimum score 6). Electronic applications accepted. *Expenses:* Contact institution.

Virginia Polytechnic Institute and State University, VT Online, Blacksburg, VA 24061. Offers advanced transportation systems (Certificate); aerospace engineering (MS); agricultural and life sciences (MSLFS); business information systems (Graduate Certificate); career and technical education (MS); civil engineering (MS); computer engineering (M Eng, MS); decision support systems (Graduate Certificate); eLearning leadership (MA); electrical engineering (M Eng, MS); engineering administration (MEA); environmental engineering (Certificate); environmental politics and policy (Graduate Certificate); environmental sciences and engineering (MS); foundations of political analysis (Graduate Certificate); health product risk management (Graduate Certificate); industrial and systems engineering (MS); information policy and society (Graduate Certificate); information security (Graduate Certificate); information technology (MIT); instructional technology (MA); integrative STEM education (MA Ed); liberal arts (Graduate Certificate); life sciences: health product risk management (MS); natural resources (MNR, Graduate Certificate); networking (Graduate Certificate); nonprofit and nongovernmental organization management (Graduate Certificate); ocean engineering (MS); political science (MA); security studies (Graduate Certificate); software development (Graduate Certificate). *Expenses:* Tuition, state resident: full-time $13,700; part-time $761.25 per credit hour. Tuition, nonresident: full-time $27,614; part-time $1534 per credit hour. *Required fees:* $886.50 per term. Tuition and fees vary according to campus/location and program.

Washington State University, Voiland College of Engineering and Architecture, Program in Engineering and Technology Management, Pullman, WA 99164-2785. Offers METM, Certificate. *Program availability:* Part-time, evening/weekend, online learning. *Degree requirements:* For master's, one foreign language, comprehensive exam (for some programs). *Entrance requirements:* Additional exam requirements/recommendations for international students: required—TOEFL. Electronic applications accepted.

Wayne State University, College of Engineering, Department of Industrial and Systems Engineering, Detroit, MI 48202. Offers data science and business analytics (MS); engineering management (MS); industrial engineering (MS, PhD); manufacturing engineering (MS); systems engineering (Certificate). *Program availability:* Online learning. *Faculty:* 12. *Students:* 126 full-time (31 women), 105 part-time (28 women); includes 42 minority (23 Black or African American, non-Hispanic/Latino; 12 Asian, non-Hispanic/Latino; 4 Hispanic/Latino; 3 Two or more races, non-Hispanic/Latino), 124 international. Average age 30. 407 applicants, 36% accepted, 39 enrolled. In 2019, 123 master's, 8 doctorates awarded. *Degree requirements:* For master's, thesis optional; for doctorate, thesis/dissertation. *Entrance requirements:* For master's, GRE or GMAT (for applicants to MS in data science and business analytics), BS from ABET-accredited institution; for doctorate, GRE, graduate degree in engineering or related discipline with minimum graduate GPA of 3.5, statement of purpose, resume/curriculum vitae, three letters of recommendation; for Certificate, GRE (for applicants from non-ABET institutions), BS in engineering or other technical field from ABET-accredited institution with minimum GPA of 3.0 in upper-division course work, at least one year of full-time work experience as practicing engineer or technical leader. Additional exam requirements/recommendations for international students: required—TOEFL (minimum score 550 paper-based; 79 iBT), TWE (minimum score 5.5), Michigan English Language Assessment Battery (minimum score 85); GRE; recommended—IELTS (minimum score 6.5). *Application deadline:* Applications are processed on a rolling basis. Application fee: $50. Electronic applications accepted. *Expenses:* $790 per credit hour in-state tuition, $1579 per credit hour out-of-state tuition. MS programs 30 credits hours; PhD 90 credit hours. *Financial support:* In 2019–20, 125 students received support, including 2 fellowships with tuition reimbursements available (averaging $20,000 per year), 6 research assistantships with tuition reimbursements available (averaging $22,879 per year), 9 teaching assistantships with tuition reimbursements available (averaging $20,792 per year); scholarships/grants, tuition waivers (full), and unspecified assistantships also available. Financial award applicants required to submit FAFSA. *Unit head:* Dr. Ratna Babu Chinnam, Professor and Interim Chair, 313-577-4846, Fax: 313-577-8833, E-mail: ratna.chinnam@wayne.edu. *Application contact:* Eric Scimeca, Graduate Program Coordinator, 313-577-0412, E-mail: eric.scimeca@wayne.edu.
Website: http://engineering.wayne.edu/ise/

Western Michigan University, Graduate College, College of Engineering and Applied Sciences, Department of Industrial and Entrepreneurial Engineering and Engineering Management, Kalamazoo, MI 49008. Offers engineering management (MS); industrial engineering (MSE, PhD). *Degree requirements:* For master's, thesis optional.

Western New England University, College of Engineering, Master's Program in Engineering Management, Springfield, MA 01119. Offers business and engineering information systems (MSEM); general engineering management (MSEM); production and manufacturing systems (MSEM); quality engineering (MSEM); MSEM/MBA. *Program availability:* Part-time, evening/weekend, online learning. *Degree requirements:* For master's, thesis optional. *Entrance requirements:* For master's, official transcript, bachelor's degree in engineering or related field, two recommendations, resume. Additional exam requirements/recommendations for international students: required—TOEFL (minimum score 79 iBT). Electronic applications accepted. *Expenses:* Contact institution.

Western New England University, College of Engineering, PhD Program in Engineering Management, Springfield, MA 01119. Offers PhD. *Program availability:* Part-time, evening/weekend. *Degree requirements:* For doctorate, comprehensive exam, thesis/dissertation. *Entrance requirements:* For doctorate, GRE, official transcript, bachelor's or master's degree in engineering or related field, two letters of recommendation, minimum GPA of 3.5. Additional exam requirements/recommendations for international students: required—TOEFL (minimum score 550 paper-based; 79 iBT). Electronic applications accepted. *Expenses:* Contact institution.

Wichita State University, Graduate School, College of Engineering, Department of Industrial and Manufacturing Engineering, Wichita, KS 67260. Offers engineering management (MEM); industrial engineering (MS, PhD). *Program availability:* Part-time. *Entrance requirements:* Additional exam requirements/recommendations for international students: required—TOEFL.

Widener University, Graduate Programs in Engineering, Program in Engineering Management, Chester, PA 19013. Offers M Eng. *Program availability:* Part-time, evening/weekend. *Degree requirements:* For master's, thesis optional. Electronic applications accepted. *Expenses:* Tuition: Full-time $48,750; part-time $917 per credit hour. Tuition and fees vary according to class time, degree level, campus/location and program.

Ergonomics and Human Factors

Arizona State University at Tempe, Ira A. Fulton Schools of Engineering, The Polytechnic School, Programs in Technology Management, Mesa, AZ 85212. Offers aviation management and human factors (MS); environmental technology management (MS); global technology and development (MS); graphic information technology (MS); management of technology (MS). *Program availability:* Part-time, evening/weekend, online learning. *Degree requirements:* For master's, thesis or applied project and oral defense; interactive Program of Study (iPOS) submitted before completing 50 percent of required credit hours. *Entrance requirements:* For master's, GRE, minimum GPA of 3.0 or equivalent in last 2 years of work leading to bachelor's degree. Additional exam requirements/recommendations for international students: required—TOEFL, IELTS, or PTE. Electronic applications accepted.

Bentley University, McCallum Graduate School of Business, Masters in Human Factors in Information Design, Waltham, MA 02452-4705. Offers MSHFID. *Program availability:* Part-time, evening/weekend, 100% online, blended/hybrid learning. *Faculty:* 105 full-time (40 women), 17 part-time/adjunct (5 women). *Students:* 36 full-time (26 women), 72 part-time (46 women); includes 23 minority (1 Black or African American, non-Hispanic/Latino; 15 Asian, non-Hispanic/Latino; 3 Hispanic/Latino; 4 Two or more races, non-Hispanic/Latino), 20 international. Average age 32. 111 applicants, 63% accepted, 35 enrolled. In 2019, 43 master's awarded. *Entrance requirements:* For master's, GMAT or GRE General Test (may be waived for qualified applicants), Transcripts; Resume; Two essays; Two letters of recommendation; Interview (may be requested by Bentley). Additional exam requirements/recommendations for international students: required—TOEFL-Paper (minimum score 72) or TOEFL-IBT (minimum score 100) or IELTS (minimum score 7). *Application deadline:* For fall admission, 8/1 for domestic students, 7/1 for international students; for spring admission, 12/15 for domestic students, 11/1 for international students. Applications are processed on a rolling basis. Application fee: $150. Electronic applications accepted. *Financial support:* In 2019–20, 56 students received support. Scholarships/grants and unspecified assistantships available. Financial award application deadline: 6/1; financial award applicants required to submit FAFSA. *Unit head:* Dr. William M. Gribbons, Professor and MSHFID Director, 781-891-2926, E-mail: wgribbons@bentley.edu. *Application contact:* Office of Graduate Admissions, 781-891-2108, E-mail: applygrad@bentley.edu.
Website: https://www.bentley.edu/academics/graduate-programs/masters-human-factors

California State University, Long Beach, Graduate Studies, College of Liberal Arts, Department of Psychology, Long Beach, CA 90840. Offers human factors (MS); industrial/organizational psychology (MS); psychology (MA). *Program availability:* Part-time, evening/weekend. *Degree requirements:* For master's, comprehensive exam, thesis. *Entrance requirements:* For master's, GRE General Test, GRE Subject Test. Electronic applications accepted.

The Catholic University of America, School of Arts and Sciences, Department of Psychology, Washington, DC 20064. Offers applied experimental psychology (PhD); clinical psychology (PhD); general psychology (MA); human development psychology (PhD); human factors (MA); MA/JD. *Accreditation:* APA (one or more programs are accredited). *Program availability:* Part-time. *Faculty:* 9 full-time (5 women), 8 part-time/adjunct (all women). *Students:* 31 full-time (27 women), 40 part-time (33 women); includes 19 minority (3 Black or African American, non-Hispanic/Latino; 3 Asian, non-Hispanic/Latino; 5 Hispanic/Latino; 8 Two or more races, non-Hispanic/Latino), 6 international. Average age 28. 160 applicants, 25% accepted, 17 enrolled. In 2019, 19 master's, 8 doctorates awarded. *Degree requirements:* For master's, comprehensive exam, thesis (for some programs); for doctorate, comprehensive exam, thesis/dissertation. *Entrance requirements:* For master's, GRE General Test, statement of purpose, official copies of academic transcripts, three letters of recommendation; for doctorate, GRE General Test, GRE Subject Test, statement of purpose, official copies of academic transcripts, three letters of recommendation. Additional exam requirements/recommendations for international students: required—TOEFL (minimum score 550 paper-based; 80 iBT). *Application deadline:* For fall admission, 7/15 priority date for domestic students, 7/1 for international students; for spring admission, 11/15 priority date for domestic students, 11/1 for international students. Applications are processed on a rolling basis. Application fee: $55. Electronic applications accepted. *Expenses:* Contact institution. *Financial support:* Fellowships, research assistantships, teaching assistantships, Federal Work-Study, scholarships/grants, tuition waivers (full and partial), and unspecified assistantships available. Financial award application deadline: 2/1; financial award applicants required to submit FAFSA. *Unit head:* Dr. Brendan Rich, Chair, 202-319-5823, Fax: 202-319-6263, E-mail: richb@cua.edu. *Application contact:* Dr. Steven Brown, Director of Graduate Admissions, 202-319-5057, Fax: 202-319-6533, E-mail: cua-admissions@cua.edu.
Website: http://psychology.cua.edu/

Clemson University, Graduate School, College of Behavioral, Social and Health Sciences, Department of Psychology, Clemson, SC 29634. Offers applied psychology (MS); human factors psychology (PhD); industrial-organizational psychology (PhD). *Faculty:* 32 full-time (15 women). *Students:* 40 full-time (28 women), 4 part-time (2 women); includes 8 minority (2 Black or African American, non-Hispanic/Latino; 1 Asian, non-Hispanic/Latino; 5 Hispanic/Latino), 1 international. Average age 26. 168 applicants, 11% accepted, 14 enrolled. In 2019, 13 master's, 6 doctorates awarded. *Expenses:* Full-Time Student per Semester: Tuition: $6225 (in-state), $13425 (out-of-state), Fees: $598; Graduate Assistant Per Semester: $1144; Part-Time Student Per Credit Hour: $833 (in-state), $1731 (out-of-state), Fees: $617. Doctoral Base Fee per Semester: $4938 (in-state), $10405 (out-of-state). *Financial support:* In 2019–20, 43 students received support, including 5 fellowships with full and partial tuition reimbursements available (averaging $12,800 per year), 9 research assistantships with full and partial tuition reimbursements available (averaging $14,408 per year), 28 teaching assistantships with full and partial tuition reimbursements available (averaging $15,268 per year); career-related internships or fieldwork and unspecified assistantships also available. *Application contact:* Dr. Robert Sinclair, Graduate Program Coordinator, 864-656-3931, E-mail: RSINCLA@clemson.edu.
Website: http://www.clemson.edu/cbshs/departments/psychology/index.html

Cornell University, Graduate School, Graduate Fields of Human Ecology, Field of Design and Environmental Analysis, Ithaca, NY 14853. Offers applied research in human-environment relations (MS); facilities planning and management (MS); housing and design (MS); human factors and ergonomics (MS); human-environment relations (MS); interior design (MA, MPS). *Degree requirements:* For master's, thesis. *Entrance requirements:* For master's, GRE General Test, portfolio or slides of recent work; bachelor's degree in interior design, architecture or related design discipline; 2 letters of recommendation. Additional exam requirements/recommendations for international students: required—TOEFL (minimum score 600 paper-based; 105 iBT). Electronic applications accepted.

Embry-Riddle Aeronautical University–Daytona, Department of Human Factors and Behavioral Neurobiology, Daytona Beach, FL 32114-3900. Offers human factors (PhD). *Degree requirements:* For master's, thesis or alternative; for doctorate, comprehensive exam, thesis/dissertation. *Entrance requirements:* For doctorate, GRE. Additional exam requirements/recommendations for international students: required—TOEFL (minimum score 550 paper-based, 79 iBT) or IELTS (6). Electronic applications accepted.

Florida Institute of Technology, College of Aeronautics, Program in Aviation Human Factors, Melbourne, FL 32901-6975. Offers aviation human factors (MS). *Program availability:* Part-time. *Degree requirements:* For master's, comprehensive exam (for some programs), thesis optional, minimum of 36 credit hours. *Entrance requirements:* For master's, GRE General Test, 3 letters of recommendation, statement of objectives, resume. Additional exam requirements/recommendations for international students: required—TOEFL (minimum score 550 paper-based; 79 iBT). Electronic applications accepted.

Harvard University, Harvard T.H. Chan School of Public Health, Department of Environmental Health, Boston, MA 02115-6096. Offers environmental epidemiology (SM); environmental exposure assessment (SM); ergonomics and safety (SM); occupational health (SM); occupational hygiene (SM); population health sciences (PhD); risk and decision science (SM). *Program availability:* Part-time. *Faculty:* 42 full-time (13 women), 16 part-time/adjunct (4 women). *Students:* 39 full-time (29 women); includes 9 minority (3 Black or African American, non-Hispanic/Latino; 3 Asian, non-Hispanic/Latino; 1 Hispanic/Latino; 2 Two or more races, non-Hispanic/Latino), 20 international. Average age 29. 51 applicants, 55% accepted, 20 enrolled. In 2019, 10 master's, 8 doctorates awarded. *Degree requirements:* For doctorate, thesis/dissertation, qualifying exam. *Entrance requirements:* For master's, GRE, MCAT; for doctorate, GRE. Additional exam requirements/recommendations for international students: recommended—TOEFL (minimum score 600 paper-based; 100 iBT), IELTS (minimum score 7). *Application deadline:* For fall admission, 12/1 for domestic and international students. Application fee: $140. Electronic applications accepted. *Financial support:* Fellowships, research assistantships, teaching assistantships, career-related internships or fieldwork, Federal Work-Study, scholarships/grants, traineeships, and unspecified assistantships available. Support available to part-time students. Financial award application deadline: 2/15; financial award applicants required to submit FAFSA. *Unit head:* Dr. Russ Hauser, Chairman, 617-432-1270, Fax: 617-432-6913. *Application contact:* Vincent W. James, Director of Admissions, 617-432-1031, Fax: 617-432-7080, E-mail: admissions@hsph.harvard.edu.
Website: http://www.hsph.harvard.edu/environmental-health/

Indiana University Bloomington, School of Public Health, Department of Kinesiology, Bloomington, IN 47405. Offers applied sport science (MS); athletic administration/sport management (MS); athletic training (MS); biomechanics (MS); ergonomics (MS); exercise physiology (MS); human performance (PhD), including biomechanics, exercise physiology, motor learning/control, sport management; motor learning/control (MS); physical activity (MPH); physical activity, fitness and wellness (MS). *Program availability:* Part-time. Terminal master's awarded for partial completion of doctoral program. *Degree requirements:* For master's, thesis optional; for doctorate, variable foreign language requirement, comprehensive exam, thesis/dissertation. *Entrance requirements:* For master's, GRE General Test, minimum GPA of 2.8; for doctorate, GRE General Test, minimum graduate GPA of 3.5, undergraduate 3.0. Additional exam requirements/recommendations for international students: required—TOEFL (minimum score 80 iBT).

Michigan Technological University, Graduate School, College of Sciences and Arts, Department of Cognitive and Learning Sciences, Houghton, MI 49931. Offers applied cognitive science and human factors (MS, PhD); applied science education (MS); post-secondary STEM education (Graduate Certificate). *Program availability:* Part-time, blended/hybrid learning. *Faculty:* 25 full-time (12 women), 6 part-time/adjunct. *Students:* 12 full-time (8 women), 16 part-time (14 women); includes 3 minority (2 Black or African American, non-Hispanic/Latino; 1 Hispanic/Latino), 5 international. Average age 37. 47 applicants, 32% accepted, 4 enrolled. In 2019, 10 master's, 1 doctorate, 3 other advanced degrees awarded. Terminal master's awarded for partial completion of doctoral program. *Degree requirements:* For master's, comprehensive exam (for some programs), thesis (for some programs); for doctorate, comprehensive exam, thesis/dissertation, applied internship experience. *Entrance requirements:* For master's, GRE (for applied cognitive science and human factors program only), statement of purpose, personal statement, official transcripts, 3 letters of recommendation, resume/curriculum vitae; for doctorate, GRE, statement of purpose, personal statement, official transcripts, 3 letters of recommendation, resume/curriculum vitae. Additional exam requirements/recommendations for international students: required—TOEFL (minimum score 90 iBT), TOEFL (recommended minimum score 90 iBT) or IELTS. *Application deadline:* For fall admission, 2/1 priority date for domestic and international students. Applications are processed on a rolling basis. Application fee: $0. Electronic applications accepted. *Expenses: Tuition, area resident:* Full-time $19,206; part-time $1067 per credit. Tuition, state resident: full-time $19,206; part-time $1067 per credit. Tuition, nonresident: full-time $19,206; part-time $1067 per credit. *International tuition:* $19,206 full-time. *Required fees:* $248; $248 per unit. $124 per semester. Tuition and fees vary according to course load and program. *Financial support:* In 2019–20, 13 students received support, including 2 fellowships (averaging $16,590 per year), 5 research assistantships with tuition reimbursements available (averaging $16,590 per year), 4 teaching assistantships (averaging $16,590 per year); career-related internships or fieldwork, scholarships/grants, health care benefits, unspecified assistantships, and adjunct instructor positions also available. Financial award application deadline: 12/15; financial award applicants required to submit FAFSA. *Unit head:* Dr. Kelly S. Steelman, Interim Department Chair, 906-487-2792, Fax: 906-487-2468, E-mail: steelman@mtu.edu. *Application contact:* Dr. Kelly S. Steelman, Graduate Program Director, 906-487-2792, Fax: 906-487-2468, E-mail: steelman@mtu.edu.
Website: http://www.mtu.edu/cls/

Mississippi State University, Bagley College of Engineering, Department of Industrial and Systems Engineering, Mississippi State, MS 39762. Offers human factors and ergonomics (MS); industrial and systems engineering (PhD); industrial systems (MS); management systems (MS); manufacturing systems (MS); operations research (MS). *Program availability:* Part-time, blended/hybrid learning. *Faculty:* 14 full-time (3 women). *Students:* 39 full-time (16 women), 64 part-time (18 women); includes 20 minority (7 Black or African American, non-Hispanic/Latino; 7 Asian, non-Hispanic/Latino; 5 Hispanic/Latino; 1 Two or more races, non-Hispanic/Latino), 28 international. Average age 36. 54 applicants, 44% accepted, 11 enrolled. In 2019, 14 master's, 6 doctorates awarded. *Degree requirements:* For master's, comprehensive exam (for some programs), thesis optional, comprehensive oral or written exam; for doctorate, comprehensive exam, thesis/dissertation, candidacy exam. *Entrance requirements:* For master's, GRE (for graduates from program not accredited by EAC/ABET), minimum

GPA of 3.0 on junior and senior years; for doctorate, GRE (for graduates from program not accredited by EAC/ABET, minimum GPA of 3.5 on master's degree and junior and senior years of BS. Additional exam requirements/recommendations for international students: required—TOEFL (minimum score 550 paper-based; 79 iBT); recommended—IELTS (minimum score 6.5). *Application deadline:* For fall admission, 7/1 for domestic students, 5/1 for international students; for spring admission, 11/1 for domestic students, 9/1 for international students. Applications are processed on a rolling basis. Application fee: $60 ($80 for international students). Electronic applications accepted. *Expenses: Tuition, area resident:* Full-time $8880; part-time $456 per credit hour. Tuition, state resident: full-time $8880. Tuition, nonresident: full-time $23,840; part-time $1236 per credit hour. *Required fees:* $110; $11.12 per credit hour. Tuition and fees vary according to course load. *Financial support:* In 2019–20, 21 research assistantships with full tuition reimbursements (averaging $17,482 per year), 4 teaching assistantships with full tuition reimbursements (averaging $15,706 per year) were awarded; Federal Work-Study, institutionally sponsored loans, and unspecified assistantships also available. Financial award application deadline: 4/1; financial award applicants required to submit FAFSA. *Unit head:* Dr. Kari Babski-Reeves, Professor, Department Head and Associate Dean for Research and Graduate Studies, 662-325-8430, Fax: 662-325-7618, E-mail: kari@ise.msstate.edu. *Application contact:* Ryan King, Admissions and Enrollment Assistant, 662-325-8951, E-mail: rjk101@grad.msstate.edu.
Website: http://www.ise.msstate.edu/

North Carolina State University, Graduate School, College of Humanities and Social Sciences, Department of Psychology, Raleigh, NC 27695. Offers applied social and community psychology (PhD); human factors and applied cognition (PhD); industrial/organizational psychology (PhD); lifespan developmental psychology (PhD); school psychology (PhD). *Accreditation:* APA. *Degree requirements:* For doctorate, comprehensive exam, thesis/dissertation. *Entrance requirements:* For doctorate, GRE General Test, GRE Subject Test (industrial/organizational psychology), MAT (recommended), minimum GPA of 3.0 in major. Electronic applications accepted.

Old Dominion University, College of Sciences, Doctoral Program in Psychology, Norfolk, VA 23529. Offers applied psychological sciences (PhD); human factors psychology (PhD); industrial/organizational psychology (PhD). *Degree requirements:* For doctorate, comprehensive exam, thesis/dissertation, candidacy exam. *Entrance requirements:* For doctorate, GRE General Test, GRE Subject Test, 3 recommendation letters. Additional exam requirements/recommendations for international students: required—TOEFL. Electronic applications accepted. *Expenses:* Contact institution.

Purdue University, Graduate School, College of Health and Human Sciences, School of Health Sciences, West Lafayette, IN 47907. Offers health physics (MS, PhD); medical physics (MS, PhD); occupational and environmental health science (MS, PhD), including aerosol deposition and lung disease, ergonomics, exposure and risk assessment, indoor air quality and bioaerosols (PhD), liver/lung toxicology; radiological health (PhD); toxicology (PhD); MS/PhD. *Program availability:* Part-time. *Faculty:* 15 full-time (6 women), 1 part-time/adjunct (0 women). *Students:* 39 full-time (22 women), 6 part-time (3 women); includes 12 minority (2 Black or African American, non-Hispanic/Latino; 1 American Indian or Alaska Native, non-Hispanic/Latino; 3 Asian, non-Hispanic/Latino; 1 Hispanic/Latino; 5 Two or more races, non-Hispanic/Latino), 15 international. Average age 28. 61 applicants, 43% accepted, 14 enrolled. In 2019, 15 master's, 6 doctorates awarded. *Degree requirements:* For master's, thesis optional; for doctorate, one foreign language, thesis/dissertation. *Entrance requirements:* For master's and doctorate, GRE General Test, minimum undergraduate GPA of 3.0 or equivalent. Additional exam requirements/recommendations for international students: required—TOEFL (minimum score 550 paper-based; 77 iBT); recommended—TWE. *Application deadline:* For fall admission, 5/15 for domestic and international students; for spring admission, 10/15 for domestic and international students. Applications are processed on a rolling basis. Application fee: $60 ($75 for international students). Electronic applications accepted. *Financial support:* In 2019–20, fellowships with tuition reimbursements (averaging $14,400 per year), research assistantships with tuition reimbursements (averaging $12,000 per year), teaching assistantships with tuition reimbursements (averaging $12,000 per year) were awarded; career-related internships or fieldwork and traineeships also available. Support available to part-time students. Financial award applicants required to submit FAFSA. *Unit head:* Aaron Bowman, Head of the Graduate Program, 765-494-2684, E-mail: bowma117@purdue.edu. *Application contact:* Karen E. Walker, Graduate Contact, 765-494-1419, E-mail: kwalker@purdue.edu.
Website: https://www.purdue.edu/hhs/hsci/

Queen's University at Kingston, School of Graduate Studies, School of Kinesiology and Health Studies, Kingston, ON K7L 3N6, Canada. Offers biomechanics and ergonomics (M Sc, PhD); exercise physiology (M Sc, PhD); health promotion (M Sc, PhD); physical activity epidemiology (M Sc, PhD); sociocultural studies of sport, health and the body (MA, PhD); sport psychology (M Sc, PhD). *Program availability:* Part-time. *Degree requirements:* For master's, thesis (for some programs); for doctorate, comprehensive exam, thesis/dissertation. *Entrance requirements:* For master's and doctorate, minimum B+ average. Additional exam requirements/recommendations for international students: required—TOEFL. Electronic applications accepted.

Tufts University, School of Engineering, Department of Mechanical Engineering, Medford, MA 02155. Offers human factors (MS); mechanical engineering (MS, PhD); PhD/PhD. *Program availability:* Part-time. Terminal master's awarded for partial completion of doctoral program. *Degree requirements:* For master's, thesis; for doctorate, thesis/dissertation. *Entrance requirements:* For master's and doctorate, GRE General Test. Additional exam requirements/recommendations for international students: required—TOEFL (minimum score 550 paper-based; 80 iBT), IELTS (minimum score 6.5). Electronic applications accepted. Full-time tuition and fees vary according to degree level, program and student level. Part-time tuition and fees vary according to course load.

Université de Montréal, Faculty of Medicine, Programs in Ergonomics, Montréal, QC H3C 3J7, Canada. Offers occupational therapy (DESS).

Université du Québec à Montréal, Graduate Programs, Program in Ergonomics in Occupational Health and Safety, Montréal, QC H3C 3P8, Canada. Offers Diploma. *Program availability:* Part-time. *Entrance requirements:* For degree, appropriate bachelor's degree or equivalent, proficiency in French.

The University of Alabama, Graduate School, College of Human Environmental Sciences, Department of General Human Environmental Sciences, Tuscaloosa, AL

35487. Offers interactive technology (MS); quality management (MS); restaurant and meeting management (MS); rural community health (MS); sport management (MS). *Program availability:* Part-time, evening/weekend, online learning. *Faculty:* 2 full-time (both women). *Students:* 61 full-time (42 women), 108 part-time (54 women); includes 45 minority (26 Black or African American, non-Hispanic/Latino; 1 American Indian or Alaska Native, non-Hispanic/Latino; 2 Asian, non-Hispanic/Latino; 8 Hispanic/Latino; 8 Two or more races, non-Hispanic/Latino), 1 international. Average age 33. 89 applicants, 89% accepted, 61 enrolled. In 2019, 130 master's awarded. *Degree requirements:* For master's, comprehensive exam. *Entrance requirements:* For master's, GRE (for some specializations), minimum GPA of 3.0. Additional exam requirements/recommendations for international students: required—TOEFL. *Application deadline:* For fall admission, 7/1 for domestic students; for spring admission, 11/1 for domestic students; for summer admission, 4/15 for domestic students. Applications are processed on a rolling basis. Application fee: $50 ($60 for international students). Electronic applications accepted. *Expenses: Tuition, area resident:* Full-time $10,780; part-time $440 per credit hour. Tuition, nonresident: full-time $30,250; part-time $1550 per credit hour. *Financial support:* Teaching assistantships with full tuition reimbursements available. Financial award application deadline: 7/1. *Unit head:* Dr. Stuart L. Usdan, Dean, 205-348-6250, Fax: 205-348-3789, E-mail: susdan@ches.ua.edu. *Application contact:* Dr. Stuart Usdan, Associate Dean, 205-348-6150, Fax: 205-348-3789, E-mail: susdan@ches.ua.edu.
Website: http://www.ches.ua.edu/programs-of-study.html

University of Cincinnati, Graduate School, College of Medicine, Graduate Programs in Biomedical Sciences, Department of Environmental Health, Cincinnati, OH 45221. Offers environmental and industrial hygiene (MS, PhD); environmental and occupational medicine (MS); environmental genetics and molecular toxicology (MS, PhD); epidemiology and biostatistics (MS, PhD); occupational safety and ergonomics (MS, PhD). *Accreditation:* ABET (one or more programs are accredited); CEPH. Terminal master's awarded for partial completion of doctoral program. *Degree requirements:* For master's, thesis; for doctorate, thesis/dissertation, qualifying exam. *Entrance requirements:* For master's, GRE General Test, bachelor's degree in science; for doctorate, GRE General Test. Additional exam requirements/recommendations for international students: required—TOEFL (minimum score 600 paper-based; 100 iBT). Electronic applications accepted.

The University of Iowa, Graduate College, College of Engineering, Department of Industrial Engineering, Iowa City, IA 52242-1316. Offers engineering design and manufacturing (MS, PhD); healthcare systems (MS, PhD); human factors (MS, PhD); information and engineering management (MS, PhD); operations research (MS, PhD); wind energy (MS, PhD). Terminal master's awarded for partial completion of doctoral program. *Degree requirements:* For master's, thesis optional, exam; for doctorate, comprehensive exam, thesis/dissertation, final defense exam. *Entrance requirements:* For master's and doctorate, GRE (minimum Verbal score of 153, Quantitative 151), minimum undergraduate GPA of 3.0. Additional exam requirements/recommendations for international students: required—TOEFL (minimum score 600 paper-based; 100 iBT), IELTS (minimum score 7). Electronic applications accepted.

The University of Iowa, Graduate College, College of Public Health, Department of Occupational and Environmental Health, Iowa City, IA 52242-1316. Offers agricultural safety and health (MS, PhD); ergonomics (MPH); industrial hygiene (MS, PhD); occupational and environmental health (MPH, MS, PhD, Certificate); MS/MA; MS/MS. *Accreditation:* ABET (one or more programs are accredited). *Degree requirements:* For master's, thesis optional, exam; for doctorate, comprehensive exam, thesis/dissertation. *Entrance requirements:* For master's and doctorate, GRE General Test, minimum GPA of 3.0. Additional exam requirements/recommendations for international students: required—TOEFL (minimum score 600 paper-based; 100 iBT). Electronic applications accepted.

University of Miami, Graduate School, College of Engineering, Department of Industrial Engineering, Program in Occupational Ergonomics and Safety, Coral Gables, FL 33124. Offers environmental health and safety (MS); occupational ergonomics and safety (MSOES). *Program availability:* Part-time. *Degree requirements:* For master's, thesis optional. *Entrance requirements:* For master's, GRE General Test, minimum GPA of 3.0. Additional exam requirements/recommendations for international students: required—TOEFL (minimum score 550 paper-based). Electronic applications accepted.

University of Wisconsin–Madison, Graduate School, College of Engineering, Department of Industrial and Systems Engineering, Madison, WI 53706. Offers industrial engineering (MS, PhD), including human factors and health systems engineering (MS), systems engineering and analytics (MS). *Program availability:* Part-time. Terminal master's awarded for partial completion of doctoral program. *Degree requirements:* For master's, thesis optional, 30 credits; minimum GPA of 3.0; for doctorate, comprehensive exam, thesis/dissertation, minimum of 51 credits; minimum GPA of 3.0. *Entrance requirements:* For master's and doctorate, GRE General Test, minimum GPA of 3.0, BS in engineering or equivalent, course work in computer programming and statistics. Additional exam requirements/recommendations for international students: required—TOEFL (minimum score 580 paper-based; 92 iBT), IELTS (minimum score 7). Electronic applications accepted.

University of Wisconsin–Milwaukee, Graduate School, College of Health Sciences, Department of Occupational Science and Technology, Milwaukee, WI 53201-0413. Offers assistive technology and design (MS); disability and occupation (MS); ergonomics (MS); therapeutic recreation (MS). *Accreditation:* AOTA. *Entrance requirements:* Additional exam requirements/recommendations for international students: required—TOEFL (minimum score 550 paper-based; 79 iBT), IELTS (minimum score 6.5).

Wright State University, Graduate School, College of Engineering and Computer Science, Department of Biomedical, Industrial and Human Factors Engineering, Dayton, OH 45435. Offers biomedical engineering (MS); industrial and human factors engineering (MS). *Program availability:* Part-time. *Degree requirements:* For master's, thesis or course option alternative. *Entrance requirements:* Additional exam requirements/recommendations for international students: required—TOEFL.

Wright State University, Graduate School, College of Science and Mathematics, Department of Psychology, Program in Human Factors and Industrial/Organizational Psychology, Dayton, OH 45435. Offers MS, PhD. *Degree requirements:* For master's, thesis; for doctorate, thesis/dissertation.

Management of Technology

Air Force Institute of Technology, Graduate School of Engineering and Management, Department of Operational Sciences, Dayton, OH 45433-7765. Offers logistics management (MS); operations research (MS, PhD); space operations (MS). *Program availability:* Part-time. *Degree requirements:* For master's, thesis; for doctorate, thesis/

dissertation. *Entrance requirements:* For doctorate, GRE General Test, minimum GPA of 3.0, U.S. citizenship.

Arizona State University at Tempe, Ira A. Fulton Schools of Engineering, The Polytechnic School, Programs in Technology Management, Mesa, AZ 85212. Offers aviation management and human factors (MS); environmental technology management (MS); global technology and development (MS); graphic information technology (MS); management of technology (MS). *Program availability:* Part-time, evening/weekend, online learning. *Degree requirements:* For master's, thesis or applied project and oral defense; interactive Program of Study (iPOS) submitted before completing 50 percent of required credit hours. *Entrance requirements:* For master's, GRE, minimum GPA of 3.0 or equivalent in last 2 years of work leading to bachelor's degree. Additional exam requirements/recommendations for international students: required—TOEFL, IELTS, or PTE. Electronic applications accepted.

Athabasca University, Faculty of Business, Edmonton, AB T5L 4W1, Canada. Offers business administration (MBA); information technology management (MBA), including policing concentration; innovative management (DBA); management (GDM); project management (MBA, GDM). *Program availability:* Part-time, evening/weekend, online learning. *Degree requirements:* For master's, thesis or alternative, applied project. *Entrance requirements:* For master's, 3-8 years of managerial experience, 3 years with undergraduate degree, 5 years' managerial experience with professional designation, 8-10 years' management experience (on exception). Electronic applications accepted. *Expenses:* Contact institution.

Atlantis University, School of Computer Science and Information Technology, Miami, FL 33132. Offers information technology (MIT).

Boston University, Metropolitan College, Department of Administrative Sciences, Boston, MA 02215. Offers applied business analytics (MS); economic development and tourism management (MSAS); enterprise risk management (MS); financial management (MS); global marketing management (MS); innovation and technology (MSAS); insurance management (MS); project management (MS); supply chain management (MS). *Accreditation:* AACSB. *Program availability:* Part-time, evening/weekend, 100% online, blended/hybrid learning. *Faculty:* 25 full-time (5 women), 40 part-time/adjunct (6 women). *Students:* 596 full-time (316 women), 709 part-time (378 women); includes 175 minority (41 Black or African American, non-Hispanic/Latino; 1 American Indian or Alaska Native, non-Hispanic/Latino; 75 Asian, non-Hispanic/Latino; 52 Hispanic/Latino; 6 Two or more races, non-Hispanic/Latino), 862 international. Average age 27. 3,223 applicants, 61% accepted, 513 enrolled. In 2019, 517 master's awarded. *Degree requirements:* For master's, thesis optional. *Entrance requirements:* For master's, 1 year of work experience, minimum GPA of 3.0. Additional exam requirements/recommendations for international students: required—TOEFL (minimum score 84 iBT). *Application deadline:* For fall admission, 8/1 priority date for domestic students, 6/1 priority date for international students; for spring admission, 12/1 priority date for domestic students, 11/15 priority date for international students; for summer admission, 4/1 priority date for domestic students, 3/1 priority date for international students. Applications are processed on a rolling basis. Application fee: $85. Electronic applications accepted. *Expenses:* Contact institution. *Financial support:* In 2019–20, 15 students received support, including 23 research assistantships (averaging $8,400 per year), 47 teaching assistantships (averaging $4,200 per year); career-related internships or fieldwork, Federal Work-Study, and unspecified assistantships also available. Financial award applicants required to submit FAFSA. *Unit head:* Dr. John Sullivan, Chair, 617-353-3016, E-mail: adminsc@bu.edu. *Application contact:* Enrollment Services, 617-358-8162, E-mail: met@bu.edu.
Website: http://www.bu.edu/met/academic-community/departments/administrative-sciences/

California Lutheran University, Graduate Studies, School of Management, Thousand Oaks, CA 91360-2787. Offers business (IMBA); entrepreneurship (MBA, Certificate); finance (MBA, Certificate); financial planning (MBA, MS, Certificate); human capital management (MBA, Certificate); information technology (MS); information technology management (MBA, Certificate); international business (MBA, Certificate); management (MS); marketing (MBA, Certificate); public policy and administration (MPPA); quantitative economics (MS). *Program availability:* Part-time, evening/weekend, 100% online, blended/hybrid learning. *Degree requirements:* For master's, comprehensive exam (for some programs). *Entrance requirements:* For master's, GMAT, interview, minimum GPA of 3.0. Electronic applications accepted. *Expenses:* Contact institution.

California State University, Los Angeles, Graduate Studies, College of Engineering, Computer Science, and Technology, Department of Technology, Los Angeles, CA 90032-8530. Offers industrial and technical studies (MA). *Program availability:* Part-time, evening/weekend. *Entrance requirements:* For master's, minimum GPA of 2.5. Additional exam requirements/recommendations for international students: required—TOEFL (minimum score 550 paper-based). *Expenses: Tuition, area resident:* Full-time $7176; part-time $4164 per year. Tuition, state resident: full-time $7176; part-time $4164 per year. Tuition, nonresident: full-time $14,304; part-time $8916 per year. *International tuition:* $14,304 full-time. *Required fees:* $1037.76; $1037.76 per unit. Tuition and fees vary according to degree level and program.

Cambridge College, School of Management, Boston, MA 02129. Offers business administration (MBA); business negotiation and conflict resolution (M Mgt); general business (M Mgt); health care (MBA); health care management (M Mgt); small business development (M Mgt); technology management (M Mgt). *Program availability:* Part-time, evening/weekend, 100% online, blended/hybrid learning. *Degree requirements:* For master's, thesis, seminars. *Entrance requirements:* For master's, resume, 2 professional references. Additional exam requirements/recommendations for international students: required—TOEFL (minimum score 550 paper-based; 79 iBT), Michigan English Language Assessment Battery (minimum score 85); recommended—IELTS (minimum score 6). Electronic applications accepted. *Expenses:* Contact institution.

Campbellsville University, School of Business, Economics, and Technology, Campbellsville, KY 42718-2799. Offers business administration (MBA, Professional MBA); information technology management (MS); management (PhD); management and leadership (MML). *Program availability:* Part-time, evening/weekend, 100% online, blended/hybrid learning. *Degree requirements:* For master's, comprehensive exam (for some programs), thesis optional; for doctorate, comprehensive exam, thesis/dissertation. *Entrance requirements:* For master's, GRE or GMAT, letters of recommendation, college transcripts; for doctorate, GMAT, resume, official transcripts, references, personal essay, interview, completion of course in statistics and research methods. Additional exam requirements/recommendations for international students: required—TOEFL (minimum score 550 paper-based; 79 iBT); recommended—IELTS (minimum score 6). Electronic applications accepted. Application fee is waived when completed online. *Expenses:* Contact institution.

Capella University, School of Business and Technology, Doctoral Programs in Technology, Minneapolis, MN 55402. Offers general information technology (PhD); global operations and supply chain management (DBA); information assurance and security (PhD); information technology education (PhD); information technology management (DBA, PhD).

Capella University, School of Business and Technology, Master's Programs in Technology, Minneapolis, MN 55402. Offers enterprise software architecture (MS); general information systems and technology management (MS); global operations and supply chain management (MBA); information assurance and security (MS); information technology management (MBA); network management (MS).

Carleton University, Faculty of Graduate Studies, Faculty of Engineering and Design, Ottawa-Carleton Institute for Electrical Engineering, Department of Systems and Computer Engineering, Program in Technology Innovation Management, Ottawa, ON K1S 5B6, Canada. Offers M Eng, MA Sc. *Degree requirements:* For master's, thesis optional. *Entrance requirements:* For master's, honors degree. Additional exam requirements/recommendations for international students: required—TOEFL.

The Catholic University of America, School of Engineering, Program in Engineering Management, Washington, DC 20064. Offers engineering management (MSE, Certificate), including engineering management and organization (MSE), project and systems engineering management (MSE), technology management (MSE); program management (Certificate); systems engineering and management of information technology (Certificate). *Program availability:* Part-time. *Faculty:* 8 part-time/adjunct (4 women). *Students:* 18 full-time (2 women), 12 part-time (2 women); includes 5 minority (1 Asian, non-Hispanic/Latino; 4 Two or more races, non-Hispanic/Latino), 19 international. Average age 29. 40 applicants, 80% accepted, 14 enrolled. In 2019, 20 master's awarded. *Degree requirements:* For master's, minimum GPA of 3.0. *Entrance requirements:* For master's and Certificate, statement of purpose, official copies of academic transcripts, two letters of recommendation. Additional exam requirements/recommendations for international students: required—TOEFL (minimum score 550 paper-based; 80 iBT). *Application deadline:* For fall admission, 7/15 priority date for domestic students, 7/1 for international students; for spring admission, 11/15 priority date for domestic students, 11/1 for international students. Applications are processed on a rolling basis. Application fee: $55. Electronic applications accepted. *Expenses:* Contact institution. *Financial support:* Fellowships, research assistantships, teaching assistantships, Federal Work-Study, scholarships/grants, tuition waivers (full and partial), and unspecified assistantships available. Financial award application deadline: 2/1; financial award applicants required to submit FAFSA. *Unit head:* Melvin G. Williams, Jr., Director, 202-319-5191, Fax: 202-319-6860, E-mail: williamsme@cua.edu. *Application contact:* Dr. Steven Brown, Director of Graduate Admissions, 202-319-5057, Fax: 202-319-6533, E-mail: cua-admissions@cua.edu.
Website: https://engineering.catholic.edu/management/index.html

Central Connecticut State University, School of Graduate Studies, School of Engineering, Science and Technology, Department of Manufacturing and Construction Management, New Britain, CT 06050-4010. Offers construction management (MS, Certificate); lean manufacturing and Six Sigma (Certificate); supply chain and logistics (Certificate); technology management (MS). *Program availability:* Part-time, evening/weekend. *Degree requirements:* For master's, comprehensive exam, special project; for Certificate, qualifying exam. *Entrance requirements:* For master's, minimum undergraduate GPA of 2.7. Additional exam requirements/recommendations for international students: required—TOEFL (minimum score 550 paper-based; 79 iBT); recommended—IELTS (minimum score 6.5). Electronic applications accepted.

Central European University, Department of Economics, 1051, Hungary. Offers business administration (PhD); business analytics (M Sc); economic policy in global markets (MA); economics (MA, PhD); finance (MS); global economic relations (MA); technology management and innovation (MS). *Program availability:* Part-time. *Degree requirements:* For master's, one foreign language, thesis; for doctorate, one foreign language, comprehensive exam, thesis/dissertation. *Entrance requirements:* For master's and doctorate, interview. Additional exam requirements/recommendations for international students: required—TOEFL (minimum score 570 paper-based); recommended—IELTS (minimum score 6.5). Electronic applications accepted.

Champlain College, Graduate Studies, Burlington, VT 05402-0670. Offers business (MBA); digital forensic science (MS); early childhood education (M Ed); emergent media (MFA, MS); executive leadership (MS); health care administration (MS); information security operations (MS); law (MS); mediation and applied conflict studies (MS). *Program availability:* Part-time, online learning. *Degree requirements:* For master's, capstone project. *Entrance requirements:* Additional exam requirements/recommendations for international students: required—TOEFL (minimum score 550 paper-based; 80 iBT). Electronic applications accepted.

City University of Seattle, Graduate Division, School of Management, Seattle, WA 98121. Offers accounting (Certificate); change leadership (MBA, Certificate); computer systems (MS); finance (Certificate); financial management (MBA); general management (MBA); general management-Europe (MBA); global marketing (MBA); human resources management (Certificate); individualized study (MBA); information security (MS); information systems (MBA); leadership (MA); marketing (MBA, Certificate); project management (MBA, MS, Certificate); sustainable business (Certificate); technology management (MBA, Certificate). *Program availability:* Part-time, evening/weekend, online learning. *Degree requirements:* For master's, comprehensive exam (for some programs), thesis (for some programs). *Entrance requirements:* For master's, baccalaureate degree or equivalent from an accredited or otherwise recognized institution. Additional exam requirements/recommendations for international students: required—TOEFL (minimum score 567 paper-based; 87 iBT); recommended—IELTS. Electronic applications accepted.

Colorado School of Mines, Office of Graduate Studies, Department of Economics and Business, Golden, CO 80401. Offers engineering and technology management (MS); mineral and energy economics (MS, PhD); operations research and engineering (PhD); petroleum economics and management with mineral and energy economics (MS). *Program availability:* Part-time. *Degree requirements:* For master's, thesis (for some programs); for doctorate, comprehensive exam, thesis/dissertation. *Entrance requirements:* For master's and doctorate, GRE General Test. Additional exam requirements/recommendations for international students: required—TOEFL (minimum score 550 paper-based; 79 iBT). Electronic applications accepted. *Expenses:* Tuition, state resident: full-time $16,650; part-time $925 per credit hour. Tuition, nonresident: full-time $37,350; part-time $2075 per credit hour. *International tuition:* $37,350 full-time. *Required fees:* $2412.

Colorado Technical University Aurora, Programs in Business Administration and Management, Aurora, CO 80014. Offers accounting (MBA); business administration (MBA); business administration and management (EMBA); finance (MBA); human resource management (MBA); marketing (MBA); mediation and dispute resolution (MBA); operations management (MBA); project management (MBA); technology management (MBA). *Program availability:* Part-time, evening/weekend. *Degree requirements:* For master's, thesis or alternative. *Entrance requirements:* For master's, minimum undergraduate GPA of 3.0, resume.

Colorado Technical University Colorado Springs, Graduate Studies, Program in Management, Colorado Springs, CO 80907. Offers accounting (MBA, MSA); business administration (MBA); finance (MBA); human resources management (MBA); logistics/supply chain management (MBA); management (DM); marketing (MBA); mediation and dispute resolution (MBA); operations management (MBA); project management (MBA);

technology management (MBA). *Accreditation:* ACBSP. *Program availability:* Part-time, evening/weekend, online learning. *Degree requirements:* For master's, thesis or alternative; for doctorate, thesis/dissertation. *Entrance requirements:* For doctorate, minimum graduate GPA of 3.0, 5 years of related work experience.

Columbia University, School of Professional Studies, Program in Technology Management, New York, NY 10027. Offers Exec MS. *Program availability:* Part-time, evening/weekend. *Entrance requirements:* For master's, minimum undergraduate GPA of 3.0. Additional exam requirements/recommendations for international students: required—American Language Program placement test. Electronic applications accepted. *Expenses: Tuition:* Full-time $47,600; part-time $1880 per credit. One-time fee: $105.

East Carolina University, Graduate School, College of Engineering and Technology, Department of Technology Systems, Greenville, NC 27858-4353. Offers computer network professional (Certificate); cyber security professional (Certificate); information assurance (Certificate); Lean Six Sigma Black Belt (Certificate); network technology (MS), including computer networking management, digital communications technology, information security, Web technologies; occupational safety (MS); technology management (MS, PhD), including industrial distribution and logistics (MS); Website developer (Certificate). *Application deadline:* For fall admission, 6/1 priority date for domestic students. *Expenses: Tuition, area resident:* Full-time $4749; part-time $185 per credit hour. Tuition, state resident: full-time $4749; part-time $185 per credit hour. Tuition, nonresident: full-time $17,898; part-time $864 per credit hour. *International tuition:* $17,898 full-time. *Required fees:* $2787. *Financial support:* Application deadline: 6/1. *Unit head:* Dr. Tijjani Mohammed, Chair, 252-328-9668, E-mail: mohammedt@ecu.edu. *Application contact:* Graduate School Admissions, 252-328-6012, Fax: 252-328-6071, E-mail: gradschool@ecu.edu. Website: https://cet.ecu.edu/techsystems/

Eastern Michigan University, Graduate School, College of Engineering and Technology, Program in Technology, Ypsilanti, MI 48197. Offers PhD. *Program availability:* Part-time, evening/weekend. *Students:* 8 full-time (6 women), 25 part-time (11 women); includes 6 minority (5 Black or African American, non-Hispanic/Latino; 1 Asian, non-Hispanic/Latino), 14 international. Average age 41. 19 applicants, 11% accepted, 1 enrolled. In 2019, 8 doctorates awarded. *Degree requirements:* For doctorate, comprehensive exam, thesis/dissertation. *Entrance requirements:* For doctorate, GRE. Additional exam requirements/recommendations for international students: required—TOEFL. *Application deadline:* For fall admission, 5/15 priority date for domestic students, 2/15 priority date for international students; for winter admission, 10/15 priority date for domestic students, 9/1 priority date for international students; for summer admission, 3/15 priority date for domestic students, 3/1 priority date for international students. Applications are processed on a rolling basis. Application fee: $45. *Financial support:* Fellowships, research assistantships with tuition reimbursements, teaching assistantships with tuition reimbursements, career-related internships or fieldwork, Federal Work-Study, institutionally sponsored loans, scholarships/grants, tuition waivers (partial), and unspecified assistantships available. Support available to part-time students. Financial award applicants required to submit FAFSA. *Application contact:* Dr. Dorothy McAllen, Advisor, 734-487-4694, Fax: 734-487-0843, E-mail: dmcallen@emich.edu.

Embry-Riddle Aeronautical University–Worldwide, Department of Decision Sciences, Daytona Beach, FL 32114-3900. Offers aviation and aerospace (MSPM); aviation/aerospace management (MSEM); financial management (MSEM, MSPM); general management (MSPM); global management (MSPM); human resources management (MSPM); information systems (MSPM); leadership (MSEM, MSPM); logistics and supply chain management (MSEM, MSLSCM, MSPM); management (MSEM, MSPM); project management (MSEM); systems engineering (MSEM, MSPM); technical management (MSPM). *Program availability:* Part-time, evening/weekend, EagleVision Classroom (between classrooms), EagleVision Home (faculty and students at home), and a blend of Classroom or Home. *Degree requirements:* For master's, comprehensive exam (for some programs), thesis (for some programs). *Entrance requirements:* Additional exam requirements/recommendations for international students: required—TOEFL (minimum score 550 paper-based; 79 iBT), IELTS (minimum score 6). Electronic applications accepted. *Expenses:* Contact institution.

Embry-Riddle Aeronautical University–Worldwide, Department of Technology Management, Daytona Beach, FL 32114-3900. Offers information and security assurance (MS); management information systems (MS). *Program availability:* Part-time, evening/weekend, EagleVision Classroom (between classrooms), EagleVision Home (faculty and students at home), and a blend of Classroom or Home. *Entrance requirements:* Additional exam requirements/recommendations for international students: required—TOEFL (minimum score 550 paper-based; 79 iBT), IELTS (minimum score 6). Electronic applications accepted.

Fairfield University, School of Engineering, Fairfield, CT 06824. Offers database management (CAS); electrical and computer engineering (MS); information security (CAS); management of technology (MS); mechanical engineering (MS); network technology (CAS); software engineering (MS); Web application development (CAS). *Program availability:* Part-time, evening/weekend. *Faculty:* 10 full-time (2 women), 15 part-time/adjunct (1 woman). *Students:* 46 full-time (24 women), 57 part-time (10 women); includes 23 minority (5 Black or African American, non-Hispanic/Latino; 9 Asian, non-Hispanic/Latino; 9 Hispanic/Latino), 33 international. Average age 29. 68 applicants, 62% accepted, 30 enrolled. In 2019, 100 master's awarded. *Degree requirements:* For master's, capstone course. *Entrance requirements:* For master's, resume, 2 recommendations. Additional exam requirements/recommendations for international students: required—TOEFL (minimum score 550 paper-based; 80 iBT), IELTS (minimum score 6.5), TOEFL (minimum score 550 paper-based; 80 iBT) or IELTS (minimum score 6.5). *Application deadline:* For fall admission, 5/15 for international students; for spring admission, 10/15 for international students. Applications are processed on a rolling basis. Application fee: $60. Electronic applications accepted. *Expenses:* Tuition $900/credit hour; Registration Fee $50/semester; Graduate Student Activity Fee (Fall and Spring) $65/semester. *Financial support:* In 2019–20, 20 students received support. Scholarships/grants and unspecified assistantships available. Financial award applicants required to submit FAFSA. *Unit head:* Richard Heist, Dean, 203-254-4147, Fax: 203-254-4013, E-mail: rheist@fairfield.edu. *Application contact:* Melanie Rogers, Director of Graduate Admission, 203-254-4184, Fax: 203-254-4073, E-mail: gradadmis@fairfield.edu. Website: http://www.fairfield.edu/soe

Fairleigh Dickinson University, Florham Campus, Silberman College of Business, Departments of Management, Marketing, and Entrepreneurial Studies, Program in Management, Madison, NJ 07940-1099. Offers evolving technology (Certificate); management (MBA); MBA/MA.

Farmingdale State College, Program in Technology Management, Farmingdale, NY 11735. Offers construction management (MS); electrical and mechanical engineering (MS). *Degree requirements:* For master's, project or thesis.

George Mason University, School of Business, Program in Technology Management, Fairfax, VA 22030. Offers MS. *Entrance requirements:* For master's, GMAT/GRE,

resume; official transcripts; 2 professional letters of recommendation; professional essay; expanded goals statement; interview. Additional exam requirements/recommendations for international students: required—TOEFL (minimum score 575 paper-based; 93 iBT), IELTS (minimum score 7), PTE (minimum score 59). Electronic applications accepted. *Expenses:* Contact institution.

Georgetown University, Graduate School of Arts and Sciences, School of Continuing Studies, Washington, DC 20057. Offers American studies (MALS); applied intelligence (MPS); Catholic studies (MALS); classical civilizations (MALS); emergency and disaster management (MPS); ethics and the professions (MALS); global strategic communications (MPS); hospitality management (MPS); human resources management (MPS); humanities (MALS); individualized study (MALS); integrated marketing communications (MPS); international affairs (MALS); Islam and Muslim-Christian relations (MALS); journalism (MPS); liberal studies (DLS); literature and society (MALS); medieval and early modern European studies (MALS); public relations and corporate communications (MPS); real estate (MPS); religious studies (MALS); social and public policy (MALS); sports industry management (MPS); systems engineering management (MPS); technology management (MPS); the theory and practice of American democracy (MALS); urban and regional planning (MPS); visual culture (MALS). *Entrance requirements:* Additional exam requirements/recommendations for international students: required—TOEFL.

The George Washington University, School of Business, Department of Information Systems and Technology Management, Washington, DC 20052. Offers information and decision systems (PhD); information systems (MSIST); information systems development (MSIST); information systems management (MBA); information systems project management (MSIST); management information systems (MSIST); management of science, technology, and innovation (MBA, PhD). *Program availability:* Part-time, evening/weekend, online learning. *Entrance requirements:* For master's, GMAT. Additional exam requirements/recommendations for international students: required—TOEFL.

Golden Gate University, Ageno School of Business, San Francisco, CA 94105-2968. Offers accounting (MBA); adaptive leadership (MBA); advanced financial planning (MS); business administration (EMBA, MBA, DBA); business analytics (MBA, MS); entrepreneurship (MBA); finance (MBA, MS, Certificate); financial life planning (Certificate); financial planning (MS, Certificate); global supply chain management (MBA, Certificate); human resource management (MBA, MS, Certificate); information technology management (MBA, MS, Certificate); international business (MBA); marketing (MBA, MS, Certificate); project management (MBA, MS, Certificate); psychology (MA, Certificate); public administration (EMPA, MBA); public administration leadership (Certificate); JD/MBA. *Program availability:* Part-time, evening/weekend. *Degree requirements:* For doctorate, thesis/dissertation, qualifying examination. *Entrance requirements:* For master's, GMAT (for MBA), minimum GPA of 2.5 (MS). Additional exam requirements/recommendations for international students: required—TOEFL (minimum score 550 paper-based; 79 iBT). Electronic applications accepted. *Expenses:* Contact institution.

Grand Canyon University, Colangelo College of Business, Phoenix, AZ 85017-1097. Offers accounting (MBA, MS); business analytics (MS); disaster preparedness and executive fire service leadership (MS); finance (MBA); general management (MBA); health systems management (MBA); information technology management (MS); leadership (MBA, MS); marketing (MBA); organizational leadership and entrepreneurship (MS); project management (MBA); sports business (MBA); strategic human resource management (MBA). *Accreditation:* ACBSP. *Program availability:* Part-time, evening/weekend, online learning. *Entrance requirements:* For master's, equivalent of two years' full-time professional work experience. Additional exam requirements/recommendations for international students: required—TOEFL (minimum score 575 paper-based; 90 iBT), IELTS (minimum score 7). Electronic applications accepted.

Harrisburg University of Science and Technology, Program in Project Management, Harrisburg, PA 17101. Offers information technology (MS). *Program availability:* Part-time, evening/weekend. *Degree requirements:* For master's, thesis optional. *Entrance requirements:* For master's, baccalaureate degree. Additional exam requirements/recommendations for international students: required—TOEFL (minimum score 520 paper-based; 80 iBT); recommended—IELTS (minimum score 6). Electronic applications accepted. *Expenses: Tuition:* Full-time $15,900; part-time $7950 per credit hour.

Harvard University, Graduate School of Arts and Sciences, Program in Information, Technology and Management, Cambridge, MA 02138. Offers PhD.

Harvard University, Harvard Business School, Doctoral Programs in Management, Boston, MA 02163. Offers accounting and management (DBA); business economics (PhD); health policy management (PhD); management (DBA); marketing (DBA); organizational behavior (PhD); science, technology and management (PhD); strategy (DBA); technology and operations management (DBA). *Degree requirements:* For doctorate, comprehensive exam (for some programs), thesis/dissertation. *Entrance requirements:* For doctorate, GRE General Test or GMAT. Additional exam requirements/recommendations for international students: required—TOEFL.

Herzing University Online, Program in Business Administration, Menomonee Falls, WI 53051. Offers accounting (MBA); business administration (MBA); business management (MBA); healthcare management (MBA); human resources (MBA); marketing (MBA); project management (MBA); technology management (MBA). *Program availability:* Online learning.

Illinois State University, Graduate School, College of Applied Science and Technology, Department of Technology, Normal, IL 61790. Offers MS. *Faculty:* 20 full-time (2 women), 18 part-time/adjunct (3 women). *Students:* 42 full-time (22 women), 53 part-time (27 women). Average age 31. 87 applicants, 85% accepted, 12 enrolled. In 2019, 51 master's awarded. *Degree requirements:* For master's, thesis or alternative. *Entrance requirements:* For master's, GRE General Test, minimum GPA of 2.8. *Application deadline:* Applications are processed on a rolling basis. Application fee: $50. *Expenses: Tuition, area resident:* Full-time $7956. Tuition, nonresident: full-time $9233. *Required fees:* $1797. *Financial support:* In 2019–20, 22 research assistantships were awarded; tuition waivers (full) and unspecified assistantships also available. Financial award application deadline: 4/1. *Unit head:* Dr. Ted Branoff, Department Chair, 309-438-3661, E-mail: tjbrano@IllinoisState.edu. *Application contact:* Dr. Klaus Scmidt, Graduate Coordinator, 309-438-3502, E-mail: kschmid@ilstu.edu. Website: http://tec.illinoisstate.edu/

Indiana State University, College of Graduate and Professional Studies, College of Technology, Department of Applied Engineering and Technology Management, Terre Haute, IN 47809. Offers technology management (MS); MA/MS. *Accreditation:* NCATE (one or more programs are accredited). *Entrance requirements:* For master's, bachelor's degree in industrial technology or related field. Additional exam requirements/recommendations for international students: required—TOEFL. Electronic applications accepted.

Management of Technology

Indiana State University, College of Graduate and Professional Studies, Program in Technology Management, Terre Haute, IN 47809. Offers PhD. *Program availability:* Online learning. *Degree requirements:* For doctorate, thesis/dissertation. *Entrance requirements:* For doctorate, GRE or GMAT, minimum graduate GPA of 3.5, 6000 hours of occupational experience. Electronic applications accepted.

Indiana University-Purdue University Indianapolis, School of Engineering and Technology, MS in Technology Program, Indianapolis, IN 46202. Offers applied data management and analytics (MS); facilities management (MS); information security and assurance (MS); motorsports (MS); organizational leadership (MS); technical communication (MS). *Program availability:* Online learning.

Instituto Centroamericano de Administracion de Empresas, Graduate Programs, La Garita, Costa Rica. Offers agribusiness management (MIAM); business administration (EMBA); finance (MBA); real estate management (MGREM); sustainable development (MBA); technology (MBA). *Degree requirements:* For master's, comprehensive exam, essay. *Entrance requirements:* For master's, GMAT or GRE General Test, fluency in Spanish, interview, letters of recommendation, minimum 1 year of work experience. Additional exam requirements/recommendations for international students: recommended—TOEFL. Electronic applications accepted.

Instituto Tecnológico y de Estudios Superiores de Monterrey, Campus Cuernavaca, Programs in Information Science, Temixco, Mexico. Offers administration of information technology (MATI); computer science (MCC, DCC); information technology (MTI).

Instituto Tecnológico y de Estudios Superiores de Monterrey, Campus Irapuato, Graduate Programs, Irapuato, Mexico. Offers administration (MBA); administration of information technology (MAIT); administration of telecommunications (MAT); architecture (M Arch); computer science (MCS); education (M Ed); educational administration (MEA); educational innovation and technology (DEIT); educational technology (MET); electronic commerce (MBA); environmental administration and planning (MEAP); environmental systems (MES); finances (MBA); humanistic studies (MHS); international management for Latin American executives (MIMLAE); library and information science (MLIS); manufacturing quality management (MMQM); marketing research (MBA).

Iona College, School of Business, Department of Information Systems, New Rochelle, NY 10801-1890. Offers accounting and information systems (MS); business continuity and risk management (AC); information systems (MBA, MS, PMC); project management (MS). *Program availability:* Part-time, evening/weekend. *Faculty:* 6 full-time (0 women), 1 part-time/adjunct (0 women). *Students:* 9 full-time (3 women), 13 part-time (5 women); includes 12 minority (4 Black or African American, non-Hispanic/Latino; 2 Asian, non-Hispanic/Latino; 4 Hispanic/Latino; 2 Two or more races, non-Hispanic/Latino), 1 international. Average age 28. 9 applicants, 100% accepted, 4 enrolled. In 2019, 20 master's awarded. *Entrance requirements:* For master's, GMAT, 2 letters of recommendation, minimum GPA of 3.0; for other advanced degree, GMAT, minimum GPA of 3.0. Additional exam requirements/recommendations for international students: required—TOEFL (minimum score 550 paper-based; 80 iBT), IELTS (minimum score 6.5). *Application deadline:* For fall admission, 8/15 priority date for domestic students, 8/1 priority date for international students; for winter admission, 11/15 priority date for domestic students, 11/1 priority date for international students; for spring admission, 2/15 priority date for domestic students, 2/1 priority date for international students; for summer admission, 5/15 priority date for domestic students, 5/1 priority date for international students. Applications are processed on a rolling basis. Application fee: $50. Electronic applications accepted. *Expenses:* Contact institution. *Financial support:* In 2019–20, 15 students received support. Scholarships/grants, tuition waivers (partial), and unspecified assistantships available. Support available to part-time students. Financial award application deadline: 4/15; financial award applicants required to submit FAFSA. *Unit head:* Dr. Shoshana Altschuller, Department Chair, 914-637-7726, E-mail: saltschuller@iona.edu. *Application contact:* Kimberly Kelly, Director of Graduate Business Admissions, 914-633-2271, Fax: 914-633-2012, E-mail: kkelly@iona.edu. Website: http://www.iona.edu/Academics/Hagan-School-of-Business/Departments/Information-Systems/Graduate-Programs.aspx

John F. Kennedy University, College of Business and Professional Studies, Program in Business Administration, Pleasant Hill, CA 94523-4817. Offers business administration (MBA); finance (MBA); health care (MBA); human resources (MBA); information technology (MBA); management (MBA); sales management (MBA); strategic management (MBA). *Program availability:* Part-time, evening/weekend, online learning. *Degree requirements:* For master's, thesis or alternative. *Entrance requirements:* For master's, interview. Additional exam requirements/recommendations for international students: required—TOEFL.

Johns Hopkins University, Engineering Program for Professionals, Part-time Program in Technical Management, Baltimore, MD 21218. Offers MS, Graduate Certificate, Post-Master's Certificate. *Program availability:* Part-time, evening/weekend, 100% online, blended/hybrid learning. *Entrance requirements:* Additional exam requirements/recommendations for international students: required—TOEFL (minimum score 600 paper-based; 100 iBT). Electronic applications accepted.

Kansas State University, Graduate School, College of Technology and Aviation, Salina, KS 67401. Offers MT. *Program availability:* Part-time, evening/weekend, 100% online. *Entrance requirements:* For master's, GRE. Additional exam requirements/recommendations for international students: required—TOEFL (minimum score 550 paper-based; 79 iBT), IELTS (minimum score 6.5), TWE, or PTE. Electronic applications accepted.

Keiser University, Master of Business Administration Program, Fort Lauderdale, FL 33309. Offers accounting (MBA); health services administration (MBA); international business (MBA); management (MBA); marketing (MBA); technology management (MBA). *Program availability:* Part-time, online learning.

Kennesaw State University, Southern Polytechnic College of Engineering and Engineering Technology, Program in Quality Assurance, Kennesaw, GA 30144. Offers MS. *Program availability:* Online learning. *Students:* 7 full-time (4 women), 31 part-time (20 women); includes 15 minority (6 Black or African American, non-Hispanic/Latino; 3 Asian, non-Hispanic/Latino; 5 Hispanic/Latino; 1 Two or more races, non-Hispanic/Latino), 1 international. Average age 40. 17 applicants, 100% accepted, 12 enrolled. In 2019, 14 master's awarded. *Entrance requirements:* Additional exam requirements/recommendations for international students: required—TOEFL (minimum score 80 iBT), IELTS (minimum score 6.5). *Application deadline:* For fall admission, 7/1 for domestic and international students; for spring admission, 11/1 for domestic and international students. Applications are processed on a rolling basis. Application fee: $60. Electronic applications accepted. *Expenses: Tuition, area resident:* Full-time $7104; part-time $296 per credit hour. *Tuition, state resident:* full-time $7104; part-time $296 per credit hour. Tuition, nonresident: full-time $25,584; part-time $1066 per credit hour. *International tuition:* $25,584 full-time. *Required fees:* $2006; $1706 per unit. $853 per semester. *Financial support:* Applicants required to submit FAFSA. *Application contact:* Admissions Counselor, 470-578-4377, E-mail: ksugrad@kennesaw.edu. Website: http://engineering.kennesaw.edu/systems-industrial/degrees/ms-quality-assurance.php

La Salle University, School of Arts and Sciences, Program in Information Technology Leadership, Philadelphia, PA 19141-1199. Offers information technology leadership (MS); software project leadership (Certificate). *Program availability:* Part-time, evening/weekend, online only, 100% online. *Degree requirements:* For master's, capstone course. *Entrance requirements:* For master's, GRE, GMAT, or MAT, two letters of recommendation; background in computer science or equivalent other training; professional resume; interview; for Certificate, two letters of recommendation; background in computer science or equivalent other training; professional resume; interview. Additional exam requirements/recommendations for international students: required—TOEFL. Electronic applications accepted. Application fee is waived when completed online. *Expenses:* Contact institution.

Lewis University, College of Business, Program in Business Administration, Romeoville, IL 60446. Offers accounting (MBA); custom elective option (MBA); e-business (MBA); finance (MBA); healthcare management (MBA); human resources management (MBA); international business (MBA); management information systems (MBA); marketing (MBA); project management (MBA); technology and operations management (MBA). *Program availability:* Part-time, evening/weekend. *Students:* 96 full-time (65 women), 153 part-time (96 women); includes 100 minority (33 Black or African American, non-Hispanic/Latino; 14 Asian, non-Hispanic/Latino; 49 Hispanic/Latino; 4 Two or more races, non-Hispanic/Latino), 20 international. Average age 31. In 2019, 99 master's awarded. *Entrance requirements:* For master's, interview, bachelor's degree, resume, two recommendations. Additional exam requirements/recommendations for international students: required—TOEFL (minimum score 550 paper-based), IELTS. *Application deadline:* For fall admission, 5/1 priority date for international students; for spring admission, 11/15 priority date for international students. Applications are processed on a rolling basis. Application fee: $40. Electronic applications accepted. *Financial support:* Federal Work-Study and unspecified assistantships available. Financial award application deadline: 5/1; financial award applicants required to submit FAFSA. *Unit head:* Dr. Ryan Butt, Dean, 815-836-5348, E-mail: culleema@lewisu.edu. *Application contact:* Linda Campbell, Graduate Admission Counselor, 815-836-5610, E-mail: grad@lewisu.edu.

Lipscomb University, College of Computing and Technology, Nashville, TN 37204-3951. Offers data science (MS, Certificate); information technology (MS, Certificate), including data science (MS), information security (MS), information technology management (MS), software engineering (MS), software engineering (MS, Certificate). *Program availability:* Part-time, evening/weekend. *Degree requirements:* For master's, capstone project. *Entrance requirements:* For master's, GRE, 2 references, transcripts, resume, personal statement. Additional exam requirements/recommendations for international students: required—TOEFL (minimum score 570 paper-based; 80 iBT). Electronic applications accepted. *Expenses:* Contact institution.

London Metropolitan University, Graduate Programs, London, United Kingdom. Offers applied psychology (M Sc); architecture (MA); biomedical science (M Sc); blood science (M Sc); cancer pharmacology (M Sc); computer networking and cyber security (M Sc); computing and information systems (M Sc); conference interpreting (MA); counter-terrorism studies (M Sc); creative, digital and professional writing (MA); crime, violence and prevention (M Sc); criminology (M Sc); curating contemporary art (MA); data analytics (M Sc); digital media (MA); early childhood studies (MA); education (MA, Ed D); financial services law, regulation and compliance (LL M); food science (M Sc); forensic psychology (M Sc); health and social care management and policy (M Sc); human nutrition (M Sc); human resource management (MA); human rights and international conflict (MA); information technology (M Sc); intelligence and security studies (M Sc); international oil, gas and energy law (LL M); international relations (MA); interpreting (MA); learning and teaching in higher education (MA); legal practice (LL M); media and entertainment law (LL M); organizational and consumer psychology (M Sc); psychological therapy (M Sc); psychology of mental health (M Sc); public health (M Sc); public policy and management (MPA); security studies (M Sc); social work (M Sc); spatial planning and urban design (MA); sports therapy (M Sc); supporting older children and young people with dyslexia (MA); teaching languages (MA), including Arabic, English; translation (MA); woman and child abuse (MA).

Louisiana Tech University, Graduate School, College of Engineering and Science, Ruston, LA 71272. Offers applied physics (MS); biomedical engineering (PhD); computer science (MS); engineering (MS, PhD), including cyberspace engineering (PhD), engineering education (PhD), engineering physics (PhD), materials and infrastructure systems (PhD), micro/nanoscale systems (PhD); engineering and technology management (MS); mathematics (MS); molecular science and nanotechnology (MS, PhD). *Program availability:* Part-time-only. Terminal master's awarded for partial completion of doctoral program. *Degree requirements:* For master's, thesis (for some programs); for doctorate, thesis/dissertation. *Entrance requirements:* For master's and Graduate Certificate, GRE General Test, minimum GPA of 3.0 in last 60 hours. Additional exam requirements/recommendations for international students: required—TOEFL (minimum score 550 paper-based; 80 iBT), IELTS (minimum score 6.5). Electronic applications accepted. *Expenses: Tuition, area resident:* Full-time $6592; part-time $400 per credit. Tuition, state resident: full-time $6592; part-time $400 per credit. Tuition, nonresident: full-time $13,333; part-time $681 per credit. *International tuition:* $13,333 full-time. *Required fees:* $3011; $3011 per unit.

Marquette University, Graduate School, College of Engineering, Department of Biomedical Engineering, Milwaukee, WI 53201-1881. Offers biocomputing (ME); bioimaging (ME); bioinstrumentation (ME); bioinstrumentation/computers (MS, PhD); biomechanics (ME); biomechanics/biomaterials (MS, PhD); biorehabilitation (ME); functional imaging (PhD); healthcare technologies management (MS); rehabilitation bioengineering (PhD); systems physiology (MS, PhD). *Program availability:* Part-time, evening/weekend. Terminal master's awarded for partial completion of doctoral program. *Degree requirements:* For master's, comprehensive exam, thesis; for doctorate, comprehensive exam, thesis/dissertation, dissertation defense, qualifying exam. *Entrance requirements:* For master's, GRE General Test, minimum GPA of 3.0, official transcripts from all current and previous colleges/universities except Marquette, three letters of recommendation, brief statement of purpose that includes proposed area of research specialization, interview with program director (for ME), one year of post-baccalaureate professional work experience; for doctorate, GRE General Test, minimum GPA of 3.0, official transcripts from all current and previous colleges/universities except Marquette, three letters of recommendation, brief statement of purpose that includes proposed area of research specialization. Additional exam requirements/recommendations for international students: required—TOEFL (minimum score 530 paper-based). Electronic applications accepted.

Marshall University, Academic Affairs Division, College of Information Technology and Engineering, Division of Applied Science and Technology, Program in Technology Management, Huntington, WV 25755. Offers MS, Certificate. *Program availability:* Part-time, evening/weekend. *Degree requirements:* For master's, final project, oral exam. *Entrance requirements:* For master's, GRE General Test or GMAT, minimum undergraduate GPA of 2.5.

Mercer University, Graduate Studies, Macon Campus, School of Engineering, Macon, GA 31207. Offers biomedical engineering (MSE); computer engineering (MSE); electrical engineering (MSE); engineering management (MSE); environmental

engineering (MSE); environmental systems (MS); mechanical engineering (MSE); software engineering (MSE); software systems (MS); technical communications management (MS); technical management (MS). *Program availability:* Part-time-only, evening/weekend, online learning. *Faculty:* 27 full-time (9 women), 2 part-time/adjunct (0 women). *Students:* 38 full-time (10 women), 51 part-time (20 women); includes 22 minority (5 Black or African American, non-Hispanic/Latino; 11 Asian, non-Hispanic/Latino; 4 Hispanic/Latino; 2 Two or more races, non-Hispanic/Latino), 2 international. Average age 26. In 2019, 70 master's awarded. *Degree requirements:* For master's, thesis or alternative. *Entrance requirements:* For master's, GRE (minimum score 300), minimum undergraduate GPA of 3.0. Additional exam requirements/recommendations for international students: required—TOEFL (minimum score 550 paper-based; 80 iBT). *Application deadline:* For fall admission, 4/1 priority date for domestic and international students; for spring admission, 11/1 priority date for domestic and international students. Applications are processed on a rolling basis. Application fee: $75. *Expenses:* Tuition: $938.00 ($700.00 for Technical Communication Management program) per credit hour; Facility and Technology Fee: $17.00 per credit hour. *Financial support:* Federal Work-Study available. Financial award applicants required to submit FAFSA. *Unit head:* Dr. Laura W. Lackey, Dean, 478-301-4106, Fax: 478-301-5593, E-mail: lackey_l@mercer.edu. *Application contact:* Dr. Sinjae Hyun, Program Director, 478-301-2214, Fax: 478-301-5593, E-mail: hyun_s@mercer.edu.
Website: http://engineering.mercer.edu/

Montclair State University, The Graduate School, Feliciano School of Business, General MBA Program, Montclair, NJ 07043-1624. Offers accounting (MBA); business analytics (MBA); digital marketing (MBA); finance (MBA); general business administration (MBA); human resources management (MBA); management (MBA); management of information and technology (MBA); marketing (MBA); project management (MBA). *Program availability:* Part-time, evening/weekend. *Degree requirements:* For master's, culminating experience. *Entrance requirements:* For master's, GMAT or GRE General Test, 2 letters of recommendation, resume, essay. Additional exam requirements/recommendations for international students: required—TOEFL (minimum score 83 iBT), IELTS (minimum score 6.5). Electronic applications accepted.

National University, School of Engineering and Computing, La Jolla, CA 92037-1011. Offers computer science (MS), including advanced computing; cyber security and information assurance (MS); data analytics (MS); electrical engineering (MS); engineering management (MS); information technology management (MS); management information systems (MS); sustainability management (MS). *Program availability:* Part-time, evening/weekend, 100% online, blended/hybrid learning. *Degree requirements:* For master's, thesis (for some programs). *Entrance requirements:* For master's, interview, minimum GPA of 2.5. Additional exam requirements/recommendations for international students: required—TOEFL (minimum score 550 paper-based; 79 iBT), IELTS (minimum score 6). Electronic applications accepted. *Expenses: Tuition:* Full-time $442; part-time $442 per unit.

New Jersey Institute of Technology, Martin Tuchman School of Management, Newark, NJ 07102. Offers business data science (PhD); management (MS); management of technology (MBA, Certificate). *Accreditation:* AACSB. *Program availability:* Part-time, evening/weekend. *Faculty:* 35 full-time (9 women), 27 part-time/adjunct (7 women). *Students:* 148 full-time (43 women), 141 part-time (78 women); includes 146 minority (41 Black or African American, non-Hispanic/Latino; 55 Asian, non-Hispanic/Latino; 42 Hispanic/Latino; 8 Two or more races, non-Hispanic/Latino), 42 international. Average age 30. 336 applicants, 73% accepted, 91 enrolled. In 2019, 67 master's, 9 other advanced degrees awarded. Terminal master's awarded for partial completion of doctoral program. *Degree requirements:* For doctorate, thesis/dissertation. *Entrance requirements:* For master's, GRE General Test/GMAT, minimum GPA 2.8, personal statement, 1 letter of recommendation, transcripts, resume; for doctorate, GRE General Test/GMAT, minimum GPA 3.2, personal statement, 3 letters of recommendation, transcripts, CV. Additional exam requirements/recommendations for international students: required—TOEFL (minimum score 550 paper-based; 79 iBT), IELTS (minimum score 6.5). *Application deadline:* For fall admission, 6/1 priority date for domestic students, 5/1 priority date for international students; for spring admission, 11/15 priority date for domestic and international students. Applications are processed on a rolling basis. Application fee: $75. Electronic applications accepted. *Expenses:* $23,828 per year (in-state), $33,744 per year (out-of-state). *Financial support:* In 2019–20, 57 students received support, including 8 fellowships with full tuition reimbursements available (averaging $24,000 per year), 7 research assistantships with full tuition reimbursements available (averaging $24,000 per year), 13 teaching assistantships with full tuition reimbursements available (averaging $24,000 per year); career-related internships or fieldwork, Federal Work-Study, scholarships/grants, and unspecified assistantships also available. Financial award application deadline: 1/15. *Unit head:* Dr. Oya Tukel, Dean, 973-596-3248, Fax: 973-596-3074, E-mail: oya.i.tukel@njit.edu. *Application contact:* Stephen Eck, Executive Director of University Admissions, 973-596-3300, Fax: 973-596-3461, E-mail: admissions@njit.edu.
Website: http://management.njit.edu

New York University, Tandon School of Engineering, Department of Technology Management, Major in Management of Technology, New York, NY 10012-1019. Offers management of technology (MS). *Entrance requirements:* For master's, GMAT, minimum B average in undergraduate course work. Additional exam requirements/recommendations for international students: required—TOEFL (minimum score 550 paper-based; 90 iBT); recommended—IELTS (minimum score 7). Electronic applications accepted.

New York University, Tandon School of Engineering, Department of Technology Management, Major in Technology Management, New York, NY 10012-1019. Offers technology management (PhD). *Entrance requirements:* Additional exam requirements/recommendations for international students: required—TOEFL (minimum score 550 paper-based; 90 iBT); recommended—IELTS (minimum score 7). Electronic applications accepted.

North Carolina State University, Graduate School, Wilson College of Textiles, Department of Textile Engineering, Chemistry, and Science, Raleigh, NC 27695. Offers fiber and polymer science (PhD); textile chemistry (MS); textile engineering (MS); textile technology management (PhD). *Degree requirements:* For master's, thesis optional. Electronic applications accepted.

North Carolina State University, Graduate School, Wilson College of Textiles, Program in Textile Technology Management, Raleigh, NC 27695. Offers PhD. *Degree requirements:* For doctorate, one foreign language, thesis/dissertation, cumulative exams. *Entrance requirements:* For doctorate, GRE or GMAT. Electronic applications accepted.

Northern Kentucky University, Office of Graduate Programs, College of Informatics, Program in Computer Information Technology, Highland Heights, KY 41099. Offers MSCIT. *Program availability:* Part-time, evening/weekend. *Degree requirements:* For master's, comprehensive exam (for some programs), thesis or alternative. *Entrance requirements:* For master's, GRE (waived for undergraduates with GPA greater than 3.0 from a STEM discipline), resume, transcripts. Additional exam requirements/recommendations for international students: required—TOEFL (minimum score 79 iBT); recommended—IELTS (minimum score 6.5). Electronic applications accepted.

Pacific States University, College of Business, Los Angeles, CA 90010. Offers accounting (MBA, Certificate); beauty management (MBA); finance (MBA); international business (MBA); management of information technology (MBA); project management (Certificate); real estate management (MBA). *Program availability:* Part-time, evening/weekend, online learning. *Entrance requirements:* For master's, minimum undergraduate GPA of 2.5 during last 90 quarter units of course work, bachelor's degree in business administration or economics. Additional exam requirements/recommendations for international students: required—TOEFL (minimum score 500 paper-based; 61 iBT), IELTS (minimum score 5.5).

Pittsburg State University, Graduate School, College of Technology, Department of Technology and Workforce Learning, Pittsburg, KS 66762. Offers career and technical education (MS); human resource development (MS); technology (MS), including automotive technology, construction management, graphic design, graphics management, information technology, innovation in technology, personnel development, technology management, workforce learning; workforce development and education (Ed S). *Program availability:* Part-time, evening/weekend, 100% online, blended/hybrid learning. *Degree requirements:* For master's, thesis or alternative; for Ed S, thesis optional. *Entrance requirements:* Additional exam requirements/recommendations for international students: required—TOEFL (minimum score 520 paper-based; 68 iBT), IELTS (minimum score 6), PTE (minimum score 47). Electronic applications accepted. *Expenses:* Contact institution.

Polytechnic University of Puerto Rico, Graduate School, Hato Rey, PR 00918. Offers business administration (MBA), including computer information systems, general management, management of information systems, management of international enterprises; civil engineering (ME, MS); computer engineering (ME, MS); computer science (MCS, MS); electrical engineering (ME, MS); engineering management (MEM); environmental management (MEM); landscape architecture (M Land Arch); manufacturing competitiveness (MMC, MS); manufacturing engineering (ME, MS); mechanical engineering (M Mech E). *Accreditation:* ASLA. *Program availability:* Part-time, evening/weekend. *Entrance requirements:* For master's, 3 letters of recommendation.

Polytechnic University of Puerto Rico, Orlando Campus, Graduate School, Orlando, FL 32825. Offers accounting (MBA); business administration (MBA); construction management (MEM); engineering management (MEM); environmental management (MEM); finance (MBA); human resources management (MBA); management of international enterprises (MBA); management of technology (MBA); manufacturing management (MEM). *Program availability:* Part-time, evening/weekend, online learning. *Entrance requirements:* For master's, minimum GPA of 3.0. Additional exam requirements/recommendations for international students: recommended—TOEFL. Electronic applications accepted.

Polytechnique Montréal, Graduate Programs, Department of Mathematics and Industrial Engineering, Montréal, QC H3C 3A7, Canada. Offers ergonomy (M Eng, M Sc A, DESS); mathematical method in CA engineering (M Eng, M Sc A, PhD); operational research (M Eng, M Sc A, PhD); production (M Eng, M Sc A); technology management (M Eng, M Sc A). *Program availability:* Part-time. *Degree requirements:* For master's, one foreign language, thesis. *Entrance requirements:* For master's, minimum GPA of 2.75.

Portland State University, Graduate Studies, Maseeh College of Engineering and Computer Science, Department of Engineering and Technology Management, Portland, OR 97207-0751. Offers engineering and technology management (MS); technology management (PhD); MS/MBA; MS/MS. *Program availability:* Part-time, evening/weekend. *Faculty:* 4 full-time (1 woman), 6 part-time/adjunct (0 women). *Students:* 46 full-time (21 women), 68 part-time (18 women); includes 12 minority (2 Black or African American, non-Hispanic/Latino; 4 Asian, non-Hispanic/Latino; 5 Hispanic/Latino; 1 Two or more races, non-Hispanic/Latino), 62 international. Average age 36. 44 applicants, 80% accepted, 21 enrolled. In 2019, 33 master's, 4 doctorates awarded. *Degree requirements:* For master's, thesis or alternative, capstone; for doctorate, one foreign language, comprehensive exam, thesis/dissertation, oral and written exams. *Entrance requirements:* For master's, degree in engineering or related discipline; minimum GPA of 2.75 undergraduate or 3.0 graduate (at least 12 credits); minimum 4 years of experience in engineering or related discipline; 3 letters of recommendation; background in probability/statistics, differential equations, computer programming and linear algebra; for doctorate, GRE General Test (minimum combined score of 1100 for verbal and quantitative), minimum GPA of 3.0 undergraduate, 3.25 graduate. Additional exam requirements/recommendations for international students: required—TOEFL (minimum score 550 paper-based; 80 iBT). *Application deadline:* For fall admission, 4/1 for domestic students, 3/1 for international students; for winter admission, 9/1 for domestic students, 7/1 for international students; for spring admission, 11/1 for domestic students, 9/1 for international students; for summer admission, 2/1 for domestic students, 12/1 for international students. Application fee: $65. Electronic applications accepted. *Expenses:* Contact institution. *Financial support:* In 2019–20, 22 students received support, including 5 teaching assistantships with full and partial tuition reimbursements available (averaging $7,475 per year); research assistantships with full and partial tuition reimbursements available, career-related internships or fieldwork, Federal Work-Study, scholarships/grants, and unspecified assistantships also available. Support available to part-time students. Financial award application deadline: 3/1; financial award applicants required to submit FAFSA. *Unit head:* Dr. Timothy Anderson, Chair, 503-725-4668, Fax: 503-725-4667, E-mail: tim.anderson@pdx.edu. *Application contact:* Shawn Wall, Department Manager, E-mail: shawnw@pdx.edu.
Website: http://www.pdx.edu/engineering-technology-management/

Purdue University, Graduate School, Purdue Polytechnic Institute, Department of Technology Leadership and Innovation, West Lafayette, IN 47907. Offers leadership (MS, PhD); organizational leadership (MS); technology innovation (MS). *Program availability:* Part-time, evening/weekend, online learning. *Faculty:* 13 full-time (6 women), 2 part-time/adjunct (0 women). *Students:* 27 full-time (7 women), 19 part-time (8 women); includes 12 minority (4 Black or African American, non-Hispanic/Latino; 1 American Indian or Alaska Native, non-Hispanic/Latino; 3 Asian, non-Hispanic/Latino; 2 Hispanic/Latino; 2 Two or more races, non-Hispanic/Latino), 11 international. Average age 31. 30 applicants, 73% accepted, 12 enrolled. In 2019, 66 master's awarded. *Entrance requirements:* For master's, GRE General Test, minimum GPA of 3.0. Additional exam requirements/recommendations for international students: required—TOEFL (minimum score 550 paper-based; 77 iBT); recommended—TWE. *Application deadline:* For fall admission, 4/1 for domestic and international students; for spring admission, 10/1 for domestic students, 9/1 for international students. Applications are processed on a rolling basis. Application fee: $60 ($75 for international students). Electronic applications accepted. *Financial support:* Fellowships and teaching assistantships available. Support available to part-time students. Financial award applicants required to submit FAFSA. *Unit head:* Stephen John Elliott, Interim Department Head, 765-494-2311, E-mail: elliottb@purdue.edu. *Application contact:* Stephanie Schmidt, Graduate Contact, 765-496-6713, E-mail: sjschmid@purdue.edu.
Website: http://www.tech.purdue.edu/TLI/

Management of Technology

Rutgers University - Newark, Rutgers Business School–Newark and New Brunswick, Doctoral Programs in Management, Newark, NJ 07102. Offers accounting (PhD); accounting information systems (PhD); economics (PhD); finance (PhD); individualized study (PhD); information technology (PhD); international business (PhD); management science (PhD); marketing science (PhD); organizational management (PhD); science, technology and management (PhD); supply chain management (PhD). *Degree requirements:* For doctorate, comprehensive exam, thesis/dissertation. *Entrance requirements:* For doctorate, GRE or GMAT. Additional exam requirements/recommendations for international students: required—TOEFL (minimum score 550 paper-based; 79 iBT). Electronic applications accepted.

Ryerson University, School of Graduate Studies, Ted Rogers School of Management, Toronto, ON M5B 2K3, Canada. Offers global business administration (MBA); management (MSM); management of technology and innovation (MBA).

St. Ambrose University, College of Arts and Sciences, Program in Information Technology Management, Davenport, IA 52803-2898. Offers MSITM. *Program availability:* Part-time. *Degree requirements:* For master's, thesis (for some programs), practica. *Entrance requirements:* For master's, GRE or GMAT, minimum GPA of 2.8. Additional exam requirements/recommendations for international students: required—TOEFL. Electronic applications accepted.

Seton Hall University, Stillman School of Business, Programs in Business Administration, South Orange, NJ 07079-2697. Offers accounting (MBA); entrepreneurial studies (Certificate); finance (MBA); financial decision making (Certificate); information technology management (MBA); international business (MBA); management (MBA); marketing (MBA); sport management (MBA); supply chain management (MBA, Certificate). *Program availability:* Part-time, evening/weekend, 100% online, blended/hybrid learning. *Faculty:* 33 full-time (5 women), 19 part-time/adjunct (2 women). *Students:* 184 full-time (78 women), 273 part-time (110 women); includes 55 minority (19 Black or African American, non-Hispanic/Latino; 10 Asian, non-Hispanic/Latino; 18 Hispanic/Latino; 8 Two or more races, non-Hispanic/Latino; 253 international. Average age 31. 325 applicants, 61% accepted, 143 enrolled. In 2019, 161 master's awarded. *Degree requirements:* For master's, 20 hours of community service (Social Responsibility Project). *Entrance requirements:* For master's, GMAT or CPA, GRE (waived based on work experience or advanced degree from AACSB institution), MS in business discipline, professional degree or designation (MD, JD, PhD, DVM, DDS, CPA, etc.), minimum undergraduate GPA of 3.0. Additional exam requirements/recommendations for international students: required—TOEFL (minimum score 607 paper-based; 80 iBT), IELTS (minimum score 6), PTE, Duolingo English Test. *Application deadline:* For fall admission, 5/31 priority date for domestic students, 4/30 priority date for international students; for spring admission, 10/31 priority date for domestic students, 9/30 priority date for international students; for summer admission, 3/31 priority date for domestic students. Applications are processed on a rolling basis. Application fee: $75. Electronic applications accepted. Application fee is waived when completed online. *Expenses:* Tuition is currently $1,305 per credit hour. Our M.B.A. program is 40 credit hours. Fees for part-time students for the academic year is $550. Fees for full-time students for the academic year is $860. *Financial support:* In 2019–20, 29 students received support, including 22 research assistantships with partial tuition reimbursements available (averaging $3,644 per year); career-related internships or fieldwork, scholarships/grants, and unspecified assistantships also available. Financial award application deadline: 6/30; financial award applicants required to submit FAFSA. *Unit head:* Dr. Joyce Strawser, Dean, 973-761-9013, Fax: 973-761-9217, E-mail: joyce.strawser@shu.edu. *Application contact:* Alfred Ayoub, Director of Graduate Admissions, 973-761-9262, Fax: 973-761-9208, E-mail: alfred.ayoub@shu.edu. Website: http://www.shu.edu/business/mba-programs.cfm

Simon Fraser University, Office of Graduate Studies and Postdoctoral Fellows, Faculty of Business Administration, Vancouver, BC V6B 5K3, Canada. Offers business administration (EMBA, PhD, Graduate Diploma); finance (M Sc); management of technology (MBA); management of technology/biotechnology (MBA). *Program availability:* Online learning. *Degree requirements:* For master's, thesis (for some programs); for doctorate, comprehensive exam, thesis/dissertation. *Entrance requirements:* For master's, GMAT, minimum GPA of 3.0 (on scale of 4.33) or 3.33 based on last 60 credits of undergraduate courses; for doctorate, minimum GPA of 3.5 (on scale of 4.33); for Graduate Diploma, minimum GPA of 2.5 (on scale of 4.33) or 2.67 based on last 60 credits of undergraduate courses. Additional exam requirements/recommendations for international students: recommended—TOEFL (minimum score 580 paper-based; 93 iBT), IELTS (minimum score 7), TWE (minimum score 5). *Expenses:* Contact institution.

South Dakota School of Mines and Technology, Graduate Division, Program in Engineering Management, Rapid City, SD 57701-3995. Offers MS. *Program availability:* Part-time, online learning. *Entrance requirements:* For master's, GMAT. Additional exam requirements/recommendations for international students: required—TOEFL, TWE. Electronic applications accepted.

Southeast Missouri State University, School of Graduate Studies, Department of Engineering and Technology, Cape Girardeau, MO 63701-4799. Offers MS. *Program availability:* Part-time, evening/weekend, online learning. *Degree requirements:* For master's, comprehensive exam (for some programs), thesis or alternative. *Entrance requirements:* Additional exam requirements/recommendations for international students: required—TOEFL (minimum score 550 paper-based; 79 iBT), IELTS (minimum score 6), PTE (minimum score 53). Electronic applications accepted. *Expenses:* Contact institution.

State University of New York Polytechnic Institute, MBA Program in Technology Management, Utica, NY 13502. Offers accounting and finance (MBA); business management (MBA); health informatics (MBA); human resource management (MBA); marketing management (MBA). *Program availability:* Part-time, 100% online. *Degree requirements:* For master's, comprehensive exam, capstone project. *Entrance requirements:* For master's, GMAT or approved GMAT waiver, resume, letter of reference. Additional exam requirements/recommendations for international students: required—TOEFL (minimum score 79 iBT), IELTS (minimum score 6.5), PTE (minimum score 53), TOEFL, IELTS, or PTE; GMAT or approved GMAT waiver. Electronic applications accepted. *Expenses:* Contact institution.

Stevens Institute of Technology, Graduate School, School of Business, Program in Business Administration for Experienced Professionals, Hoboken, NJ 07030. Offers business administration (EMBA); technology management (EMBA). *Program availability:* Part-time, evening/weekend. *Faculty:* 59 full-time (11 women), 30 part-time/adjunct (5 women). *Students:* 1 full-time (0 women), 23 part-time (7 women); includes 7 minority (3 Black or African American, non-Hispanic/Latino; 3 Asian, non-Hispanic/Latino; 1 Hispanic/Latino). Average age 35. 16 applicants, 81% accepted, 9 enrolled. In 2019, 15 master's awarded. *Degree requirements:* For master's, thesis optional, minimum B average in major field and overall. *Entrance requirements:* For master's, International applicants must submit TOEFL/IELTS scores and fulfill the English Language Proficiency Requirement. Applicants to full-time programs who do not qualify for a score waiver are required to submit GRE/GMAT scores. Additional exam requirements/recommendations for international students: required—TOEFL (minimum

score 74 iBT), IELTS (minimum score 6). *Application deadline:* For fall admission, 7/1 for domestic students, 4/15 for international students; for spring admission, 12/1 for domestic and international students. Applications are processed on a rolling basis. Application fee: $60. Electronic applications accepted. *Expenses: Tuition:* Full-time $52,134. *Required fees:* $1880. Tuition and fees vary according to course load. *Financial support:* Fellowships, research assistantships, teaching assistantships, career-related internships or fieldwork, Federal Work-Study, scholarships/grants, and unspecified assistantships available. Financial award application deadline: 2/15; financial award applicants required to submit FAFSA. *Unit head:* Dr. Gregory Prastacos, Dean, 201-216-5366, E-mail: gprastac@stevens.edu. *Application contact:* Graduate Admissions, 888-783-8367, Fax: 888-511-1306, E-mail: graduate@stevens.edu. Website: https://www.stevens.edu/school-business/masters-programs/mbaemba

Stevens Institute of Technology, Graduate School, School of Business, Program in Management, Hoboken, NJ 07030. Offers general management (MS); global innovation management (MS); human resource management (MS); information management (MS); project management (MS); technology commercialization (MS); technology management (MS). *Program availability:* Part-time, evening/weekend. *Faculty:* 59 full-time (11 women), 30 part-time/adjunct (5 women). *Students:* 100 full-time (42 women), 75 part-time (41 women); includes 12 minority (4 Black or African American, non-Hispanic/Latino; 6 Asian, non-Hispanic/Latino; 2 Hispanic/Latino), 134 international. Average age 27. In 2019, 35 master's awarded. Terminal master's awarded for partial completion of doctoral program. *Degree requirements:* For master's, thesis optional, minimum B average in major field and overall. *Entrance requirements:* For master's, International applicants must submit TOEFL/IELTS scores and fulfill the English Language Proficiency Requirement. Applicants to full-time programs who do not qualify for a score waiver are required to submit GRE/GMAT scores. Additional exam requirements/recommendations for international students: required—TOEFL (minimum score 74 iBT), IELTS (minimum score 6). *Application deadline:* For fall admission, 4/1 for domestic and international students; for spring admission, 11/1 for domestic and international students; for summer admission, 5/1 for domestic students. Applications are processed on a rolling basis. Application fee: $60. Electronic applications accepted. *Expenses: Tuition:* Full-time $52,134. *Required fees:* $1880. Tuition and fees vary according to course load. *Financial support:* Fellowships, research assistantships, teaching assistantships, career-related internships or fieldwork, Federal Work-Study, scholarships/grants, and unspecified assistantships available. Financial award application deadline: 2/15; financial award applicants required to submit FAFSA. *Unit head:* Dr. Gregory Prascatos, Dean of SB, 201-216 8366, E-mail: gprastac@stevens.edu. *Application contact:* Graduate Admissions, 888-783-8367, Fax: 888-511-1306, E-mail: graduate@stevens.edu. Website: https://www.stevens.edu/school-business/masters-programs/management

Stevens Institute of Technology, Graduate School, School of Business, Program in Technology Management, Hoboken, NJ 07030. Offers information management (PhD); technology management (PhD); telecommunications management (PhD). *Program availability:* Part-time, evening/weekend, online learning. *Faculty:* 59 full-time (11 women), 30 part-time/adjunct (5 women). *Students:* 2 full-time (0 women), 18 part-time (4 women); includes 10 minority (4 Black or African American, non-Hispanic/Latino; 6 Asian, non-Hispanic/Latino), 2 international. Average age 40. Terminal master's awarded for partial completion of doctoral program. *Degree requirements:* For doctorate, comprehensive exam (for some programs), thesis/dissertation. *Entrance requirements:* Additional exam requirements/recommendations for international students: required—TOEFL (minimum score 74 iBT), IELTS (minimum score 6). *Application deadline:* For fall admission, 4/1 for domestic and international students; for spring admission, 11/1 for domestic and international students; for summer admission, 5/1 for domestic students. Applications are processed on a rolling basis. Application fee: $60. Electronic applications accepted. *Expenses: Tuition:* Full-time $52,134. *Required fees:* $1880. Tuition and fees vary according to course load. *Financial support:* Fellowships, research assistantships, teaching assistantships, career-related internships or fieldwork, Federal Work-Study, scholarships/grants, and unspecified assistantships available. Financial award application deadline: 2/15; financial award applicants required to submit FAFSA. *Unit head:* Dr. Gregory Prascatos, Dean of SB, 201-216 8366, Fax: 201-216-5385, E-mail: gprastac@stevens.edu. *Application contact:* Graduate Admissions, 888-783-8367, Fax: 888-511-1306, E-mail: graduate@stevens.edu. Website: https://www.stevens.edu/school-business/phd-business-administration

Stevens Institute of Technology, Graduate School, School of Business, Program in Telecommunications Management, Hoboken, NJ 07030. Offers business (MS); global innovation management (MS); management of wireless networks (MS); online security, technology and business (MS); project management (MS); technical management (MS); telecommunications management (PhD, Certificate). *Program availability:* Part-time, evening/weekend. *Faculty:* 59 full-time (11 women), 30 part-time/adjunct (5 women). *Students:* 1 part-time (0 women). Average age 47. In 2019, 3 master's awarded. *Degree requirements:* For master's, thesis optional, minimum B average in major field and overall; for doctorate, comprehensive exam (for some programs), thesis/dissertation; for Certificate, minimum B average. *Entrance requirements:* For master's, International applicants must submit TOEFL/IELTS scores and fulfill the English Language Proficiency Requirement. Applicants to full-time programs who do not qualify for a score waiver are required to submit GRE/GMAT scores. Additional exam requirements/recommendations for international students: required—TOEFL (minimum score 74 iBT), IELTS (minimum score 6). *Application deadline:* For fall admission, 4/1 for domestic and international students; for spring admission, 11/1 for domestic and international students; for summer admission, 5/1 for domestic students. Applications are processed on a rolling basis. Application fee: $60. Electronic applications accepted. *Expenses: Tuition:* Full-time $52,134. *Required fees:* $1880. Tuition and fees vary according to course load. *Financial support:* Fellowships, research assistantships, teaching assistantships, career-related internships or fieldwork, Federal Work-Study, scholarships/grants, health care benefits, and unspecified assistantships available. Financial award application deadline: 2/15; financial award applicants required to submit FAFSA. *Unit head:* Dr. Gregory Prastacos, Dean of SB, 201-216-8366, E-mail: gprastac@stevens.edu. *Application contact:* Graduate Admission, 888-783-8367, Fax: 888-511-1306, E-mail: graduate@stevens.edu. Website: https://www.stevens.edu/school-business/masters-programs/network-communication-management-services

Stevenson University, Program in Business and Technology Management, Stevenson, MD 21153. Offers emerging technology (MS); innovative leadership (MS). *Program availability:* Part-time, online only, 100% online. *Faculty:* 1 full-time (0 women), 10 part-time/adjunct (2 women). *Students:* 15 full-time (7 women), 43 part-time (25 women); includes 29 minority (20 Black or African American, non-Hispanic/Latino; 2 Asian, non-Hispanic/Latino; 3 Hispanic/Latino; 4 Two or more races, non-Hispanic/Latino). Average age 30. 21 applicants, 76% accepted, 11 enrolled. In 2019, 66 master's awarded. *Degree requirements:* For master's, capstone course. *Entrance requirements:* For master's, personal statement (3-5 paragraphs), bachelor's degree from a regionally accredited institution, official college transcript from degree-granting institution (additional transcripts may be required to demonstrate satisfaction of program-specific prerequisites), minimum cumulative GPA of 3.0 on a 4.0 scale in past academic work. *Application deadline:* For fall admission, 8/9 priority date for domestic students; for

spring admission, 1/11 priority date for domestic students; for summer admission, 5/1 priority date for domestic students. Applications are processed on a rolling basis. Application fee: $0. Electronic applications accepted. *Expenses:* $670 per credit. *Financial support:* Unspecified assistantships available. Financial award applicants required to submit FAFSA. *Unit head:* Steven Engorn, Graduate Program Director, 443-352-4220, Fax: 443-394-0538, E-mail: sengorn@stevenson.edu. *Application contact:* Amanda Millar, Director, Admissions, 443-352-4058, Fax: 443-394-0538, E-mail: amillar@stevenson.edu.
Website: https://www.stevenson.edu/online/academics/online-graduate-programs/business-and-technology-management/

Stony Brook University, State University of New York, Graduate School, College of Engineering and Applied Sciences, Department of Technology and Society, Program in Global Technology Management, Stony Brook, NY 11794. Offers MS. *Program availability:* Online learning. *Entrance requirements:* For master's, GRE. Additional exam requirements/recommendations for international students: required—TOEFL (minimum score 85 iBT), IELTS (minimum score 6.5). *Application deadline:* For fall admission, 7/2 for domestic students, 4/15 for international students; for spring admission, 12/3 for domestic students, 10/5 for international students; for summer admission, 4/15 for domestic students. Application fee: $100. Electronic applications accepted. *Expenses:* Contact institution. *Unit head:* Dr. Wolf Schafer, Chair, 631-632-7924, E-mail: wolf.schafer@stonybrook.edu. *Application contact:* Marypat Taveras, Coordinator, 631-632-8762, Fax: 631-632-7809, E-mail: marypat.taveras@stonybrook.edu.
Website: https://www.stonybrook.edu/commcms/est/masters/programs/msgtm

Stratford University, School of Graduate Studies, Falls Church, VA 22043. Offers accounting (MS); business administration (MBA, DBA); cyber security (MS); cyber security leadership and policy (MS); digital forensics (MS); healthcare administration (MS); information systems (MS); information technology (DIT); networking and telecommunications (MS); software engineering (MS). *Program availability:* Part-time, evening/weekend, 100% online, blended/hybrid learning. *Degree requirements:* For master's, comprehensive exam, capstone project. *Entrance requirements:* For master's, GRE or GMAT, baccalaureate degree. Additional exam requirements/recommendations for international students: required—TOEFL (minimum score 79 iBT), IELTS (minimum score 6.5), PTE (minimum score 5). Electronic applications accepted.

Texas A&M University–Commerce, College of Science and Engineering, Commerce, TX 75429. Offers biological sciences (MS); broadfield science biology (MS); broadfield science chemistry (MS); broadfield science physics (MS); chemistry (MS); computational linguistics (Graduate Certificate); computational science (MS); computer science (MS); environmental science (Graduate Certificate); mathematics (MS); physics (MS); technology management (MS). *Program availability:* Part-time. *Faculty:* 38 full-time (7 women), 6 part-time/adjunct (0 women). *Students:* 118 full-time (53 women), 197 part-time (86 women); includes 71 minority (18 Black or African American, non-Hispanic/Latino; 1 American Indian or Alaska Native, non-Hispanic/Latino; 12 Asian, non-Hispanic/Latino; 32 Hispanic/Latino; 8 Two or more races, non-Hispanic/Latino), 118 international. Average age 31. 303 applicants, 70% accepted, 99 enrolled. In 2019, 226 master's awarded. *Degree requirements:* For master's, comprehensive exam, thesis optional. *Entrance requirements:* For master's, GRE, official transcripts, letters of recommendation, resume, statement of goals. Additional exam requirements/recommendations for international students: required—TOEFL (minimum score 550 paper-based; 79 iBT), IELTS (minimum score 6), PTE (minimum score 53). *Application deadline:* For fall admission, 6/1 priority date for international students; for spring admission, 10/15 priority date for international students; for summer admission, 3/15 priority date for international students. Applications are processed on a rolling basis. Application fee: $50 ($75 for international students). Electronic applications accepted. *Expenses:* Contact institution. *Financial support:* In 2019–20, 56 students received support, including 47 research assistantships with partial tuition reimbursements available (averaging $3,080 per year), 130 teaching assistantships with partial tuition reimbursements available (averaging $3,359 per year); scholarships/grants, health care benefits, and unspecified assistantships also available. Financial award application deadline: 5/1; financial award applicants required to submit FAFSA. *Unit head:* Dr. Brent L. Donham, Dean, 903-886-5321, Fax: 903-886-5199, E-mail: brent.donham@tamuc.edu. *Application contact:* Dayla Burgin, Graduate Student Services Coordinator, 903-886-5134, E-mail: dayla.burgin@tamuc.edu.
Website: https://new.tamuc.edu/science-engineering/

Texas State University, The Graduate College, College of Science and Engineering, Program in Technology Management, San Marcos, TX 78666. Offers MS. *Program availability:* Part-time, evening/weekend. *Degree requirements:* For master's, comprehensive exam, thesis optional. *Entrance requirements:* For master's, baccalaureate degree from regionally-accredited university with minimum GPA of 2.75 on last 60 undergraduate semester hours, statement of purpose stating interest in technology management degree, and resume/CV. Additional exam requirements/recommendations for international students: required—TOEFL (minimum score 550 paper-based; 78 iBT), IELTS (minimum score 6.5). Electronic applications accepted.

Towson University, College of Business and Economics, Program in e-Business and Technology Management, Towson, MD 21252-0001. Offers project, program and portfolio management (Postbaccalaureate Certificate); supply chain management (MS). *Entrance requirements:* For master's and Postbaccalaureate Certificate, GRE or GMAT, bachelor's degree in relevant field and/or three years of post-bachelor's experience working in supply chain related areas; minimum cumulative GPA of 3.0; resume; 2 reference letters. Additional exam requirements/recommendations for international students: required—TOEFL (minimum score 550 paper-based). Electronic applications accepted. *Expenses:* Tuition, area resident: Full-time $7920; part-time $439 per credit. Tuition, nonresident: full-time $16,344; part-time $908 per credit. *International tuition:* $16,344 full-time. *Required fees:* $2628; $146 per credit. $876 per term.

University of Advancing Technology, Master of Science Program in Technology, Tempe, AZ 85283-1042. Offers advancing computer science (MS); emerging technologies (MS); game production and management (MS); information assurance (MS); technology leadership (MS). *Degree requirements:* For master's, project or thesis. *Entrance requirements:* Additional exam requirements/recommendations for international students: required—TOEFL (minimum score 550 paper-based). Electronic applications accepted.

The University of Alabama in Huntsville, School of Graduate Studies, College of Business Administration, Programs in Business and Management, Huntsville, AL 35899. Offers business analytics (MSMS); federal contracting and procurement management (Certificate); human resource management (MSM); management (MBA), including acquisition management, entrepreneurship, federal contract accounting, finance, human resource management, logistics and supply chain management, marketing, project management; supply chain management (Certificate); technology and innovation management (Certificate). *Accreditation:* AACSB. *Program availability:* Part-time. *Degree requirements:* For master's, comprehensive exam, thesis or alternative. *Entrance requirements:* For master's, GMAT (minimum score 500), minimum AACSB index of 1080. Additional exam requirements/recommendations for international students: required—TOEFL (minimum score 550 paper-based; 80 iBT), IELTS (minimum score 6.5). Electronic applications accepted.

University of Bridgeport, School of Engineering, Department of Technology Management, Bridgeport, CT 06604. Offers MS, PhD. *Degree requirements:* For master's, thesis optional. *Entrance requirements:* Additional exam requirements/recommendations for international students: recommended—TOEFL (minimum score 550 paper-based; 80 iBT), IELTS (minimum score 6.5). Electronic applications accepted. *Expenses:* Contact institution.

University of California, Los Angeles, Graduate Division, UCLA Anderson School of Management, Los Angeles, CA 90095-1481. Offers accounting (PhD); behavioral decision making (PhD); business administration (EMBA, MBA); business administration/computer science (MBA/MSCS); business administration/latin american studies (MBA/MLAS); business administration/law (MBA/JD); business administration/library science (MBA/MLIS); business administration/medicine (MBA/MD); business administration/nursing (MBA/MN); business administration/public health (MBA/MPH); business administration/public policy (MBA/MPP); business administration/urban and regional planning (MBA/MURP); business analytics (MSBA); decisions, operations, and technology management (PhD); finance (PhD); financial engineering (MFE); global economics and management (PhD); management and organizations (PhD); marketing (PhD); strategy and policy (PhD); DDS/MBA; MBA/JD; MBA/MD; MBA/MLAS; MBA/MLIS; MBA/MN; MBA/MPH; MBA/MPP; MBA/MSCS; MBA/MURP. *Accreditation:* AACSB. *Program availability:* Part-time, evening/weekend. *Faculty:* 81 full-time (21 women), 110 part-time/adjunct (21 women). *Students:* 1,033 full-time (377 women), 1,162 part-time (391 women); includes 768 minority (47 Black or African American, non-Hispanic/Latino; 3 American Indian or Alaska Native, non-Hispanic/Latino; 533 Asian, non-Hispanic/Latino; 105 Hispanic/Latino; 2 Native Hawaiian or other Pacific Islander, non-Hispanic/Latino; 78 Two or more races, non-Hispanic/Latino), 575 international. Average age 31. 6,394 applicants, 29% accepted, 932 enrolled. In 2019, 991 master's, 9 doctorates awarded. Terminal master's awarded for partial completion of doctoral program. *Degree requirements:* For master's, comprehensive exam, field consulting project (for MBA, FEMBA, EMBA, UCLA-NUS EMBA, MFE, and MSBA); internship (for MBA only); for doctorate, comprehensive exam, thesis/dissertation, oral and written qualifying exams. *Entrance requirements:* For master's, GMAT or GRE required (for MBA, MFE, MSBA); Executive Assessment (EA) also accepted for EMBA, UCLA-NUS EMBA, and FEMBA (only for candidates with 10+ years of work experience); STEM Master's degree, JD, MD, CPA, or extensive quantitative experience can waive exam requirement for EMBA, 4-year bachelor's degree or equivalent; 2 letters of recommendation; interview (invitation only); 1 essay (for MBA & FEMBA); 2 essays (for EMBA, MFE, MSBA); average 4-8 years of full-time work experience (for FEMBA); minimum 8 years of work experience with at least 5 years at management level (for EMBA & UCLA-NUS EMBA); for doctorate, GMAT or GRE, bachelor's degree from college or university of full-recognized standing with 3.0 minimum GPA, 3 letters of recommendation; statement of purpose. Additional exam requirements/recommendations for international students: required—TOEFL (minimum score 560 paper-based; 87 iBT), IELTS (minimum score 7), TOEFL with minimum iBT score of 100 (for MSBA program). *Application deadline:* For fall admission, 10/2 for domestic and international students; for winter admission, 1/8 for domestic and international students; for spring admission, 4/16 for domestic and international students. Applications are processed on a rolling basis. Application fee: $200. Electronic applications accepted. *Expenses:* $65,114 per year for MBA; $78,470 per year for MFE; $66,710 per year for MSBA; $32,474 per year for PhD; $83,996 per year for EMBA; $62,500 per year for UCLA-NUS EMBA (UC portion only); $42,853 per year for FEMBA. *Financial support:* Fellowships, research assistantships with partial tuition reimbursements, teaching assistantships with partial tuition reimbursements, career-related internships or fieldwork, institutionally sponsored loans, and scholarships/grants available. Support available to part-time students. *Unit head:* Dr. Antonio Bernardo, Dean and John E. Anderson Chair in Management, 310-825-7982, Fax: 310-206-2073, E-mail: a.bernardo@anderson.ucla.edu. *Application contact:* Alex Lawrence, Assistant Dean and Director of MBA Admissions, 310-825-6944, Fax: 310-825-8582, E-mail: mba.admissions@anderson.ucla.edu.
Website: http://www.anderson.ucla.edu/

University of California, Santa Barbara, Graduate Division, College of Engineering, Program in Technology Management, Santa Barbara, CA 93106-2014. Offers MTM.

University of Central Missouri, The Graduate School, Warrensburg, MO 64093. Offers accountancy (MA); accounting (MBA); applied mathematics (MS); aviation safety (MA); biology (MS); business administration (MBA); career and technology education (MS); college student personnel administration (MS); communication (MA); computer information systems and information technology (MS); computer science (MS); counseling (MS); criminal justice and criminology (MS); educational leadership (Ed S); educational leadership and policy analysis (Ed D); educational technology (MS, Ed S); elementary and early childhood education (MSE); English (MA); english language learners - teaching english as a second language (MA); environmental studies (MA); finance (MBA); history (MA); industrial hygiene (MS); industrial management (MS); information systems (MBA); kinesiology (MS); library science and information services (MS); literacy education (MSE); marketing (MBA); mathematics (MS); music (MA); occupational safety management (MS); professional leadership - adult, career, and technical education (Ed S); professional leadership - counseling (Ed S); psychology (MS); rural family nursing (MS); school administration (MSE); social gerontology (MS); sociology (MA); special education (MSE); speech language pathology (MS); teaching (MAT); technology (MS); technology management (PhD); theatre (MA). *Accreditation:* ASHA. *Program availability:* Part-time, 100% online, blended/hybrid learning. *Faculty:* 236 full-time (113 women), 97 part-time/adjunct (61 women). *Students:* 787 full-time (448 women), 1,459 part-time (997 women); includes 213 minority (72 Black or African American, non-Hispanic/Latino; 5 American Indian or Alaska Native, non-Hispanic/Latino; 27 Asian, non-Hispanic/Latino; 59 Hispanic/Latino; 50 Two or more races, non-Hispanic/Latino), 574 international. Average age 30. 1,477 applicants, 68% accepted, 664 enrolled. In 2019, 831 master's, 93 other advanced degrees awarded. *Degree requirements:* For master's and Ed S, comprehensive exam (for some programs), thesis (for some programs). *Entrance requirements:* For master's, A GRE or GMAT test score may be required by some of the programs, A minimum GPA, letters of recommendation, a statement of purpose may be required by some of the programs; for Ed S, A master's degree is required for the application of an Education Specialist's degree program. Additional exam requirements/recommendations for international students: required—TOEFL (minimum score 550 paper-based; 79 iBT). *Application deadline:* For fall admission, 6/1 priority date for domestic and international students; for spring admission, 10/15 priority date for domestic and international students; for summer admission, 4/1 priority date for domestic and international students. Applications are processed on a rolling basis. Application fee: $30 ($75 for international students). Electronic applications accepted. *Expenses:* Tuition, area resident: Full-time $7524; part-time $313.50 per credit hour. Tuition, state resident: full-time $7524; part-time $313.50 per credit hour. Tuition, nonresident: full-time $15,048; part-time $627 per credit hour. *International tuition:* $15,048 full-time. *Required fees:* $915; $30.50 per credit hour. *Financial support:* In 2019–20, 89 students received support. Research assistantships, teaching assistantships, career-related internships or fieldwork, Federal Work-Study, scholarships/grants, unspecified assistantships, and administrative and laboratory assistantships available. Support available to part-time students. Financial

award application deadline: 4/1; financial award applicants required to submit FAFSA. *Unit head:* Shellie Hewitt, Director of Graduate and International Student Services, 660-543-4621, Fax: 660-543-4778, E-mail: hewitt@ucmo.edu. *Application contact:* Shellie Hewitt, Director of Graduate and International Student Services, 660-543-4621, Fax: 660-543-4778, E-mail: hewitt@ucmo.edu.
Website: http://www.ucmo.edu/graduate/

University of Colorado Denver, Business School, Program in Information Systems, Denver, CO 80217. Offers accounting and information systems audit and control (MS); business intelligence systems (MS); digital health entrepreneurship (MS); enterprise risk management (MS); enterprise technology management (MS); geographic information systems (MS); health information technology (MS); technology innovation and entrepreneurship (MS); Web and mobile computing (MS). *Program availability:* Part-time, evening/weekend, online learning. *Degree requirements:* For master's, 30 credit hours. *Entrance requirements:* For master's, GMAT, resume, essay, two letters of recommendation, financial statements (for international applicants). Additional exam requirements/recommendations for international students: required—TOEFL (minimum score 525 paper-based; 71 iBT); recommended—IELTS (minimum score 6.5). Electronic applications accepted. *Expenses:* Contact institution.

University of Colorado Denver, Business School, Program in Management and Organization, Denver, CO 80217. Offers business strategy (MS); change and innovation (MS); enterprise technology management (MS); entrepreneurship and innovation (MS); global management (MS); leadership (MS); managing for sustainability (MS); managing human resources (MS); sports and entertainment (MS); strategic management (MS). *Accreditation:* AACSB. *Program availability:* Part-time, evening/weekend, online learning. *Degree requirements:* For master's, 30 semester hours (12 of required courses, 12 of management electives, and 6 of free electives). *Entrance requirements:* For master's, GMAT, resume, two letters of recommendation, essay, financial statements (for international applicants). Additional exam requirements/recommendations for international students: required—TOEFL (minimum score 525 paper-based; 71 iBT); recommended—IELTS (minimum score 6.5). Electronic applications accepted. *Expenses:* Contact institution.

University of Dallas, Satish and Yasmin Gupta College of Business, Irving, TX 75062. Offers accounting (MBA, MS); business administration (DBA); business analytics (MS); business management (MBA); corporate finance (MBA); cybersecurity (MS); finance (MS); financial services (MBA); global business (MBA, MS); health services management (MBA); human resource management (MBA); information and technology management (MS); information assurance (MBA); information technology (MBA); information technology service management (MBA); marketing management (MBA); organization development (MBA); project management (MBA); sports and entertainment management (MBA); strategic leadership (MBA); supply chain management (MBA). *Accreditation:* AACSB. *Program availability:* Part-time, evening/weekend, 100% online, blended/hybrid learning. *Students:* 120 full-time (53 women), 531 part-time (203 women); includes 353 minority (173 Black or African American, non-Hispanic/Latino; 1 American Indian or Alaska Native, non-Hispanic/Latino; 78 Asian, non-Hispanic/Latino; 92 Hispanic/Latino; 2 Native Hawaiian or other Pacific Islander, non-Hispanic/Latino; 7 Two or more races, non-Hispanic/Latino), 96 international. Average age 33. 291 applicants, 96% accepted, 141 enrolled. In 2019, 302 master's, 4 doctorates awarded. *Degree requirements:* For doctorate, thesis/dissertation. *Entrance requirements:* For master's and doctorate, U.S. bachelor's degree with a minimum cumulative GPA of 2.0 from a regionally accredited college or university (or comparable foreign degree); minimum 3.0 GPA in any graduate-level coursework completed; good academic standing with all colleges attended. Additional exam requirements/recommendations for international students: required—TOEFL (minimum score 80 iBT), IELTS (minimum score 6.5), PTE (minimum score 67). *Application deadline:* Applications are processed on a rolling basis. Application fee: $50. Electronic applications accepted. *Expenses:* $1,250 / Credit Hour, $160 Matriculation Fee, $100 Graduation Fee. *Financial support:* Research assistantships, teaching assistantships, scholarships/grants, and unspecified assistantships available. Support available to part-time students. Financial award application deadline: 2/15; financial award applicants required to submit FAFSA. *Unit head:* Brett J.L. Landry, Dean, 972-721-5356, E-mail: blandry@udallas.edu. *Application contact:* Breonna Collins, Director, Graduate Admissions, 972-7215304, E-mail: bcollins@udallas.edu.
Website: http://www.udallas.edu/cob/

University of Delaware, Alfred Lerner College of Business and Economics, Department of Accounting and Management Information Systems and Department of Electrical and Computer Engineering, Program in Information Systems and Technology Management, Newark, DE 19716. Offers MS. *Program availability:* Part-time, evening/weekend. *Entrance requirements:* For master's, GRE or GMAT, 2 letters of recommendation, resume, minimum GPA of 2.75. Additional exam requirements/recommendations for international students: required—TOEFL (minimum score 600 paper-based).

University of Illinois at Urbana-Champaign, Graduate College, College of Agricultural, Consumer and Environmental Sciences, Department of Agricultural and Biological Engineering, Champaign, IL 61820. Offers agricultural and biological engineering (MS, PhD); technical systems management (MS, PSM).

University of Illinois at Urbana-Champaign, Graduate College, Gies College of Business, Department of Business Administration, Champaign, IL 61820. Offers business administration (MS, PhD); technology management (MS). *Accreditation:* AACSB. *Expenses:* Contact institution.

University of Maryland, Baltimore County, The Graduate School, College of Engineering and Information Technology, Department of Computer Science and Electrical Engineering, Program in Technical Management, Baltimore, MD 21250. Offers MPS. *Program availability:* Part-time. *Students:* 3 full-time (2 women), 10 part-time (4 women); includes 4 minority (2 Black or African American, non-Hispanic/Latino; 2 Asian, non-Hispanic/Latino), 3 international. Average age 28. 6 applicants, 67% accepted, 2 enrolled. In 2019, 1 master's awarded. *Entrance requirements:* For master's, bachelor's degree in a science, technology, engineering, or mathematics related field; minimum undergraduate GPA of 3.0; minimum of two years' experience in a technical field; official transcripts; resume. Additional exam requirements/recommendations for international students: required—TOEFL (minimum score 550 paper-based; 80 iBT), IELTS. *Application deadline:* For fall admission, 8/1 for domestic students; for spring admission, 12/1 for domestic students. Applications are processed on a rolling basis. Application fee: $50. Electronic applications accepted. *Expenses:* $14,382 per year. *Unit head:* Dr. Toby Gouker, Director, 410-455-3445, E-mail: tgouker@umbc.edu. *Application contact:* Keara Fliggins, Program Management Specialist, 410-455-3000, Fax: 410-455-3969, E-mail: fliggins@umbc.edu.
Website: http://techm.umbc.edu/

University of Massachusetts Dartmouth, Graduate School, Charlton College of Business, Department of Decision and Information Sciences, North Dartmouth, MA 02747-2300. Offers healthcare management (MS); technology management (MS). *Program availability:* Part-time, 100% online, blended/hybrid learning. *Degree requirements:* For master's, thesis (for some programs), thesis or project (for healthcare management), e-portfolio for business administration. *Entrance requirements:* For

master's, GMAT (or waiver), statement of purpose (minimum 300 words), resume, official transcripts, 2 letters of recommendation. Additional exam requirements/recommendations for international students: required—TOEFL (minimum score 550 paper-based; 80 iBT), IELTS (minimum score 6.5). Electronic applications accepted.

University of Miami, Graduate School, College of Engineering, Department of Industrial Engineering, Coral Gables, FL 33124. Offers environmental health and safety (MS); ergonomics (PhD); industrial engineering (MSIE, PhD); management of technology (MS); occupational ergonomics and safety (MS, MSOES), including environmental health and safety (MS), occupational ergonomics and safety (MSOES); MBA/MSIE. *Program availability:* Part-time. *Degree requirements:* For master's, thesis (for some programs); for doctorate, comprehensive exam, thesis/dissertation. *Entrance requirements:* For master's and doctorate, GRE General Test, minimum GPA of 3.0. Additional exam requirements/recommendations for international students: required—TOEFL (minimum score 550 paper-based).

University of Minnesota, Twin Cities Campus, College of Science and Engineering, Technological Leadership Institute, Program in Management of Technology, Minneapolis, MN 55455-0213. Offers MSMOT. *Program availability:* Evening/weekend. *Degree requirements:* For master's, thesis, capstone project. *Entrance requirements:* For master's, 5 years of work experience in high-tech company, preferably in Twin Cities area; demonstrated technological leadership ability. Additional exam requirements/recommendations for international students: required—TOEFL (minimum score 580 paper-based; 90 iBT). Electronic applications accepted. *Expenses:* Contact institution.

University of New Mexico, Anderson School of Management, Finance, International and Innovation, Albuquerque, NM 87131. Offers entrepreneurship (MBA); finance (MBA); international management (MBA); international management in Latin America (MBA); management of technology (MBA). *Program availability:* Part-time. *Faculty:* 15 full-time (1 woman), 8 part-time/adjunct (2 women). In 2019, 29 master's awarded. *Degree requirements:* For master's, comprehensive exam. *Entrance requirements:* For master's, GMAT of 500 or higher, GRE conversion to GMAT of 500 or higher, LSAT of 155 or higher, PCAT or MCAT of 55 composite or higher, Minimum GPA of 3.0 in last 60 hours of coursework. We offer exam waivers for applicants with 3.5 GPA in upper division coursework. Additional exam requirements/recommendations for international students: required—TOEFL (minimum score 550 paper-based; 79 iBT), IELTS (minimum score 6.5). *Application deadline:* For fall admission, 4/1 priority date for domestic students, 5/1 priority date for international students; for spring admission, 10/1 priority date for domestic and international students; for summer admission, 2/1 priority date for domestic students, 2/1 for international students. Applications are processed on a rolling basis. Application fee: $100 ($70 for international students). Electronic applications accepted. *Expenses:* $542.36 is cost per credit hour, $6508.32 is cost per semester for full time study. *Financial support:* In 2019–20, 16 students received support, including 14 fellowships (averaging $18,720 per year), 10 research assistantships with partial tuition reimbursements available (averaging $15,291 per year); career-related internships or fieldwork, Federal Work-Study, scholarships/grants, and unspecified assistantships also available. Support available to part-time students. Financial award application deadline: 6/1; financial award applicants required to submit FAFSA. *Unit head:* Dr. Raj Mahto, Chair, 505-277-6471, E-mail: rmahto@unm.edu. *Application contact:* Lisa Beauchene-Lawson, Supervisor, Graduate Admissions & Advisement, 505-277-3290, E-mail: andersongrad@unm.edu.
Website: https://www.mgt.unm.edu/fii/contact.asp

University of Phoenix - Bay Area Campus, School of Business, San Jose, CA 95134-1805. Offers accountancy (MS); accounting (MBA); business administration (MBA, DBA); energy management (MBA); global management (MBA); health care management (MBA); human resource management (MBA); human resources management (MM); management (MM); marketing (MBA); organizational leadership (DM); project management (MBA); public administration (MPA); technology management (MBA). *Accreditation:* ACBSP. *Program availability:* Evening/weekend, online learning. *Degree requirements:* For master's, thesis (for some programs). *Entrance requirements:* For master's, minimum undergraduate GPA of 3.0, 3 years of work experience. Additional exam requirements/recommendations for international students: required—TOEFL (minimum score 550 paper-based; 79 iBT). Electronic applications accepted.

University of Phoenix - Central Valley Campus, College of Information Systems and Technology, Fresno, CA 93720-1552. Offers information systems (MIS); technology management (MBA).

University of Phoenix - Dallas Campus, College of Information Systems and Technology, Dallas, TX 75251. Offers e-business (MBA); information systems (MIS); technology management (MBA). *Program availability:* Evening/weekend. *Degree requirements:* For master's, thesis (for some programs). *Entrance requirements:* For master's, minimum undergraduate GPA of 3.0, 3 years of work experience. Additional exam requirements/recommendations for international students: required—TOEFL (minimum score 550 paper-based; 79 iBT). Electronic applications accepted.

University of Phoenix - Hawaii Campus, College of Information Systems and Technology, Honolulu, HI 96813-3800. Offers information systems (MIS); technology management (MBA). *Program availability:* Evening/weekend. *Degree requirements:* For master's, thesis (for some programs). *Entrance requirements:* For master's, minimum undergraduate GPA of 3.0, 3 years of work experience. Additional exam requirements/recommendations for international students: required—TOEFL (minimum score 550 paper-based; 79 iBT). Electronic applications accepted.

University of Phoenix - Houston Campus, College of Information Systems and Technology, Houston, TX 77079-2004. Offers e-business (MBA); information systems (MIS); technology management (MBA). *Program availability:* Evening/weekend, online learning. *Degree requirements:* For master's, comprehensive exam (for some programs), thesis. *Entrance requirements:* For master's, minimum undergraduate GPA of 3.0, 3 years of work experience. Additional exam requirements/recommendations for international students: required—TOEFL (minimum score 550 paper-based; 79 iBT). Electronic applications accepted.

University of Phoenix - Las Vegas Campus, College of Information Systems and Technology, Las Vegas, NV 89135. Offers information systems (MIS); technology management (MBA). *Program availability:* Evening/weekend. *Degree requirements:* For master's, thesis (for some programs). *Entrance requirements:* For master's, minimum undergraduate GPA of 3.0, 3 years of work experience. Additional exam requirements/recommendations for international students: required—TOEFL (minimum score 550 paper-based; 79 iBT). Electronic applications accepted.

University of Phoenix–Online Campus, School of Business, Phoenix, AZ 85034-7209. Offers accountancy (MS); accounting (MBA, Certificate); business administration (MBA); energy management (MBA); global management (MBA); health care management (MBA); human resource management (MBA, Certificate); human resources management (MM); management (MM); marketing (MBA, Certificate); project management (MBA, Certificate); public administration (MBA, MM); technology management (MBA). *Program availability:* Evening/weekend, online learning. *Entrance requirements:* Additional exam requirements/recommendations for international students: required—TOEFL, TOEIC (Test of English as an International

Communication), Berlitz Online English Proficiency Exam, PTE, or IELTS. Electronic applications accepted. *Expenses:* Contact institution.

University of Phoenix - Phoenix Campus, School of Business, Tempe, AZ 85282-2371. Offers accounting (MBA, MS, Certificate); business administration (MBA); energy management (MBA); global management (MBA); health care management (MBA); human resource management (MBA, Certificate); management (MM); marketing (MBA); project management (MBA); technology management (MBA). *Program availability:* Evening/weekend, online learning. *Entrance requirements:* Additional exam requirements/recommendations for international students: required—TOEFL, TOEIC (Test of English as an International Communication), Berlitz Online English Proficiency Exam, PTE, or IELTS. Electronic applications accepted. *Expenses:* Contact institution.

University of Phoenix - Sacramento Valley Campus, College of Information Systems and Technology, Sacramento, CA 95833-4334. Offers management (MIS); technology management (MBA). *Program availability:* Evening/weekend. *Degree requirements:* For master's, thesis (for some programs). *Entrance requirements:* For master's, minimum undergraduate GPA of 3.0, 3 years work experience. Additional exam requirements/recommendations for international students: required—TOEFL (minimum score 550 paper-based; 79 iBT). Electronic applications accepted.

University of Phoenix - San Antonio Campus, College of Information Systems and Technology, San Antonio, TX 78230. Offers information systems (MIS); technology management (MBA).

University of Phoenix - San Diego Campus, College of Information Systems and Technology, San Diego, CA 92123. Offers management (MIS); technology management (MBA). *Program availability:* Evening/weekend. *Degree requirements:* For master's, thesis (for some programs). *Entrance requirements:* For master's, minimum undergraduate GPA of 3.0, 3 years work experience. Additional exam requirements/recommendations for international students: required—TOEFL (minimum score 550 paper-based; 79 iBT). Electronic applications accepted.

University of Portland, Dr. Robert B. Pamplin, Jr. School of Business, Portland, OR 97203-5798. Offers entrepreneurship (MBA); finance (MBA, MS); health care management (MBA); marketing (MBA); nonprofit management (EMBA); operations and technology management (MBA, MS); sustainability (MBA). *Accreditation:* AACSB. *Program availability:* Part-time, evening/weekend. *Entrance requirements:* For master's, GMAT or GRE, minimum GPA of 3.0, resume, statement of goals, 2 letters of recommendation. Additional exam requirements/recommendations for international students: required—TOEFL (minimum score 88 iBT), IELTS (minimum score 7). Electronic applications accepted. *Expenses:* Contact institution.

University of St. Thomas, School of Engineering, St. Paul, MN 55105. Offers data science (MS); electrical engineering (MS); information technology (MS); manufacturing engineering (MS); manufacturing systems (Certificate); mechanical engineering (MS); medical device development (Certificate); regulatory science (MS); software engineering (MS); software management (MS); systems engineering (MS); technology leadership (Certificate); technology management (MS). *Program availability:* Part-time, evening/weekend. *Entrance requirements:* For master's, resume, official transcripts. Additional exam requirements/recommendations for international students: required—TOEFL (minimum score 80 iBT), IELTS (minimum score 6.5). Electronic applications accepted. *Expenses:* Contact institution.

University of South Florida, Innovative Education, Tampa, FL 33620-9951. Offers adult, career and higher education (Graduate Certificate), including college teaching, leadership in developing human resources, leadership in higher education; Africana studies (Graduate Certificate), including diasporas and health disparities, genocide and human rights; aging studies (Graduate Certificate), including gerontology; art research (Graduate Certificate), including museum studies; business foundations (Graduate Certificate); chemical and biomedical engineering (Graduate Certificate), including materials science and engineering, water, health and sustainability; child and family studies (Graduate Certificate), including positive behavior support; civil and industrial engineering (Graduate Certificate), including transportation systems analysis; community and family health (Graduate Certificate), including maternal and child health, social marketing and public health, violence and injury: prevention and intervention, women's health; criminology (Graduate Certificate), including criminal justice administration; data science for public administration (Graduate Certificate); digital humanities (Graduate Certificate); educational measurement and research (Graduate Certificate), including evaluation; English (Graduate Certificate), including comparative literary studies, creative writing, professional and technical communication; entrepreneurship (Graduate Certificate); environmental health (Graduate Certificate), including safety management; epidemiology and biostatistics (Graduate Certificate), including applied biostatistics, biostatistics, concepts and tools of epidemiology, epidemiology, epidemiology of infectious diseases; geography, environment and planning (Graduate Certificate), including community development, environmental policy and management, geographical information systems; geology (Graduate Certificate), including hydrogeology; global health (Graduate Certificate), including disaster management, global health and Latin American and Caribbean studies, global health practice, humanitarian assistance, infection control; government and international affairs (Graduate Certificate), including Cuban studies, globalization studies; health policy and management (Graduate Certificate), including health management and leadership, public health policy and programs; hearing specialist: early intervention (Graduate Certificate); industrial and management systems engineering (Graduate Certificate), including systems engineering, technology management; information studies (Graduate Certificate), including school library media specialist; information systems/decision sciences (Graduate Certificate), including analytics and business intelligence; instructional technology (Graduate Certificate), including distance education, Florida digital/virtual educator, instructional design, multimedia design, Web design; internal medicine, bioethics and medical humanities (Graduate Certificate), including biomedical ethics; Latin American and Caribbean studies (Graduate Certificate); leadership for coastal resiliency planning (Graduate Certificate); mass communications (Graduate Certificate), including multimedia journalism; mathematics and statistics (Graduate Certificate), including mathematics; medicine (Graduate Certificate), including aging and neuroscience, bioinformatics, biotechnology, brain fitness and memory management, clinical investigation, hand and upper limb rehabilitation, health informatics, health sciences, integrative weight management, intellectual property, medicine and gender, metabolic and nutritional medicine, metabolic cardiology, pharmacy sciences; national and competitive intelligence (Graduate Certificate); nursing (Graduate Certificate), including simulation based academic fellowship in advanced pain management; psychological and social foundations (Graduate Certificate), including career counseling, college teaching, diversity in education, mental health counseling, school counseling; public affairs (Graduate Certificate), including nonprofit management, public management, research administration; public health (Graduate Certificate), including assessing chemical toxicity and public health risks, health equity, pharmacoepidemiology, public health generalist, toxicology, translational research in adolescent behavioral health; public health practices (Graduate Certificate), including planning for healthy communities; rehabilitation and mental health counseling (Graduate Certificate), including integrative mental health care, marriage and family therapy, rehabilitation technology; secondary education (Graduate Certificate), including ESOL,

foreign language education: culture and content, foreign language education: professional; social work (Graduate Certificate), including geriatric social work/clinical gerontology; special education (Graduate Certificate), including autism spectrum disorder, disabilities education: severe/profound; world languages (Graduate Certificate), including teaching English as a second language (TESL) or foreign language. *Unit head:* Dr. Cynthia DeLuca, Associate Vice President and Assistant Vice Provost, 813-974-3077, Fax: 813-974-7061, E-mail: deluca@usf.edu. *Application contact:* Owen Hooper, Director, Summer and Alternative Calendar Programs, 813-974-6917, E-mail: hooper@usf.edu.
Website: http://www.usf.edu/innovative-education/

The University of Texas at Dallas, Naveen Jindal School of Management, Program in Information Systems, Richardson, TX 75080. Offers business analytics (MS); information technology and management (MS). *Program availability:* Part-time, evening/weekend. *Faculty:* 20 full-time (3 women), 30 part-time/adjunct (3 women). *Students:* 1,230 full-time (526 women), 563 part-time (214 women); includes 205 minority (17 Black or African American, non-Hispanic/Latino; 1 American Indian or Alaska Native, non-Hispanic/Latino; 150 Asian, non-Hispanic/Latino; 23 Hispanic/Latino; 14 Two or more races, non-Hispanic/Latino), 1,461 international. Average age 28. 2,695 applicants, 41% accepted, 611 enrolled. In 2019, 878 master's awarded. *Degree requirements:* For master's, thesis optional. *Entrance requirements:* For master's, GMAT. Additional exam requirements/recommendations for international students: required—TOEFL (minimum score 550 paper-based). *Application deadline:* For fall admission, 7/15 for domestic students, 5/1 priority date for international students; for spring admission, 11/15 for domestic students, 9/1 priority date for international students. Applications are processed on a rolling basis. Application fee: $50 ($100 for international students). Electronic applications accepted. *Expenses: Tuition, area resident:* Full-time $16,504. *Tuition, state resident:* full-time $16,504. *Tuition, nonresident:* full-time $34,266. Tuition and fees vary according to course load. *Financial support:* In 2019–20, 42 students received support, including 2 fellowships (averaging $1,000 per year), 2 research assistantships with partial tuition reimbursements available (averaging $17,800 per year), 38 teaching assistantships with partial tuition reimbursements available (averaging $10,050 per year); career-related internships or fieldwork, Federal Work-Study, institutionally sponsored loans, scholarships/grants, and unspecified assistantships also available. Support available to part-time students. Financial award application deadline: 4/30; financial award applicants required to submit FAFSA. *Unit head:* Dr. Syam Menon, Area Coordinator, 972-883-4779, E-mail: syam@utdallas.edu. *Application contact:* Dr. Syam Menon, Area Coordinator, 972-883-4779, E-mail: syam@utdallas.edu.
Website: https://jindal.utdallas.edu/information-systems/

The University of Texas at San Antonio, College of Business, Department of Information Systems and Cyber Security, San Antonio, TX 78249-0617. Offers cyber security (MSIT); information technology (MS, PhD); management of technology (MBA); technology entrepreneurship and management (Certificate). *Program availability:* Part-time, evening/weekend. *Degree requirements:* For master's, comprehensive exam (for some programs), thesis optional; for doctorate, comprehensive exam, thesis/dissertation. *Entrance requirements:* For master's and doctorate, GMAT/GRE, official transcripts, statement of purpose, letters of recommendation. Additional exam requirements/recommendations for international students: required—TOEFL (minimum score 550 paper-based; 79 iBT), IELTS (minimum score 6.5). Electronic applications accepted. *Expenses:* Contact institution.

University of Toronto, Faculty of Medicine, Program in Management of Innovation, Toronto, ON M5S 1A1, Canada. Offers MMI. *Entrance requirements:* For master's, GMAT, minimum B+ average, 2 reference letters, resume/curriculum vitae. Additional exam requirements/recommendations for international students: required—TOEFL (minimum score 580 paper-based; 93 iBT), TWE (minimum score 5). Electronic applications accepted.

University of Virginia, McIntire School of Commerce, M.S. in the Management of IT Program, Charlottesville, VA 22903. Offers MS. *Program availability:* Evening/weekend. *Entrance requirements:* For master's, 1 letter of recommendation, bachelor's degree, interview, essay. Additional exam requirements/recommendations for international students: required—TOEFL (minimum score 620 paper-based). Electronic applications accepted. *Expenses:* Contact institution.

University of Washington, Graduate School, Michael G. Foster School of Business, Seattle, WA 98195-3200. Offers auditing and assurance (MP Acc); business administration (MBA, PhD); entrepreneurship (MS); executive business administration (MBA); global executive business administration (MBA); information systems (MSIS); supply chain management (MSSCM); taxation (MP Acc); technology management (MBA); JD/MBA; MBA/MAIS; MBA/MHA. *Accreditation:* AACSB. *Program availability:* Part-time, evening/weekend, blended/hybrid learning. Terminal master's awarded for partial completion of doctoral program. *Degree requirements:* For doctorate, comprehensive exam, thesis/dissertation. *Entrance requirements:* For master's and doctorate, GMAT, GRE. Additional exam requirements/recommendations for international students: required—TOEFL (minimum score 600 paper-based; 100 iBT). Electronic applications accepted. *Expenses:* Contact institution.

University of Waterloo, Graduate Studies and Postdoctoral Affairs, Faculty of Engineering, Conrad School of Entrepreneurship and Business, Waterloo, ON N2L 3G1, Canada. Offers MBET. *Entrance requirements:* For master's, honors degree. Additional exam requirements/recommendations for international students: required—TOEFL (minimum score 90 iBT), IELTS (minimum score 7), PTE (minimum score 63). Electronic applications accepted.

University of Waterloo, Graduate Studies and Postdoctoral Affairs, Faculty of Engineering, Department of Management Sciences, Waterloo, ON N2L 3G1, Canada. Offers applied operations research (MA Sc, MMS, PhD); information systems (MA Sc, MMS, PhD); management of technology (MA Sc, MMS, PhD). *Program availability:* Part-time, online learning. *Degree requirements:* For master's, research paper or thesis; for doctorate, comprehensive exam, thesis/dissertation. *Entrance requirements:* For master's, GMAT or GRE, honors degree, minimum B average, resume; for doctorate, GMAT or GRE, master's degree, minimum A- average, resume. Additional exam requirements/recommendations for international students: required—TOEFL, IELTS, PTE. Electronic applications accepted.

University of Wisconsin–Madison, Graduate School, Wisconsin School of Business, Wisconsin Full-Time MBA Program, Madison, WI 53706-1380. Offers applied security analysis (MBA); arts administration (MBA); brand and product management (MBA); corporate finance and investment banking (MBA); marketing research (MBA); operations and technology management (MBA); real estate (MBA); risk management and insurance (MBA); strategic human resource management (MBA); supply chain management (MBA). *Faculty:* 131 full-time (35 women), 33 part-time/adjunct (11 women). *Students:* 146 full-time (51 women); includes 21 minority (2 Black or African American, non-Hispanic/Latino; 1 American Indian or Alaska Native, non-Hispanic/Latino; 6 Asian, non-Hispanic/Latino; 8 Hispanic/Latino; 4 Two or more races, non-Hispanic/Latino), 41 international. Average age 28. 314 applicants, 44% accepted, 67 enrolled. In 2019, 104 master's awarded. *Entrance requirements:* For master's, GMAT

or GRE, U.S. active military, U.S. veterans, candidates with terminal degrees (JD, PhD) or those with 5 years of work experience can apply for a GMAT or GRE waiver, bachelor's degree; standardized test scores (GMAT or GRE); English proficiency test (TOEFL, IELTS, or PTE for applicants whose native language is not English or whose undergraduate instruction was not in English); 2 years of work experience preferred; 1 completed recommendation; resume; essays (one required, one recommended, one optional). Additional exam requirements/recommendations for international students: required—TOEFL (minimum score 100 iBT), IELTS (minimum score 7.5), TOEFL is not required for international students whose undergraduate training was in English. *Application deadline:* For fall admission, 11/1 for domestic and international students; for winter admission, 1/10 for domestic and international students; for spring admission, 3/1 for domestic and international students; for summer admission, 4/27 for domestic students, 4/27 priority date for international students. Applications are processed on a rolling basis. Application fee: $75 ($81 for international students). Electronic applications accepted. *Expenses:* $43,061 resident (includes tuition and fees for 2-year program), $82,214 non-resident (includes tuition and fees for the 2-year program). *Financial support:* Fellowships, research assistantships, teaching assistantships, scholarships/grants, health care benefits, tuition waivers (full and partial), and unspecified assistantships available. Financial award application deadline: 1/10. *Unit head:* Dr. Enno Siemsen, Associate Dean of the MBA and Masters Programs, 608-890-3130, E-mail: esiemsen@wisc.edu. *Application contact:* Betsy Kacizak, Director of Admissions and Recruitment, Full-Time MBA and Masters Programs, 608-262-8948, E-mail: betsy.kacizak@wisc.edu.
Website: https://wsb.wisc.edu/

University of Wisconsin–Milwaukee, Graduate School, Lubar School of Business, Other Business Programs, Milwaukee, WI 53201-0413. Offers business analytics (Graduate Certificate); enterprise resource planning (Graduate Certificate); information technology management (MS); investment management (Graduate Certificate); nonprofit management (Graduate Certificate); nonprofit management and leadership (MS); state and local taxation (Graduate Certificate). *Entrance requirements:* Additional exam requirements/recommendations for international students: required—TOEFL (minimum score 550 paper-based; 79 iBT), IELTS (minimum score 6.5). Electronic applications accepted.

Walsh College of Accountancy and Business Administration, Graduate Programs, Program in Information Technology Leadership, Troy, MI 48083. Offers chief information officer (MS); chief security officer (MS); program management office (MS). *Program availability:* Part-time, evening/weekend. *Entrance requirements:* For master's, minimum overall cumulative GPA of 2.750 from all colleges previously attended. Additional exam requirements/recommendations for international students: required—TOEFL (minimum score 550 paper-based, 79-80 internet based), IELTS (6.5), Michigan Test of English Language Proficiency, or MTELP (80). Electronic applications accepted. *Expenses:* Contact institution.

Washington State University, Voiland College of Engineering and Architecture, Program in Engineering and Technology Management, Pullman, WA 99164-2785. Offers METM, Certificate. *Program availability:* Part-time, evening/weekend, online learning. *Degree requirements:* For master's, one foreign language, comprehensive exam (for some programs). *Entrance requirements:* Additional exam requirements/recommendations for international students: required—TOEFL. Electronic applications accepted.

Webster University, George Herbert Walker School of Business and Technology, Department of Management, St. Louis, MO 63119-3194. Offers business and organizational security management (MA); digital marketing management (Graduate Certificate); government contracting (Graduate Certificate); health administration (MHA); health care management (MA); health services management (MA); human resources development (MA); human resources management (MA); information technology management (MA, MS); management (D Mgt); management and leadership (MA); marketing (MA); nonprofit leadership (MA); nonprofit revenue development (Graduate Certificate); organizational development (Graduate Certificate); procurement and acquisitions management (MA); public administration (MPA); space systems operations management (MS). *Program availability:* Part-time, evening/weekend, online learning. *Degree requirements:* For master's, thesis (for some programs); for doctorate, thesis/dissertation, written exam. *Entrance requirements:* For doctorate, GMAT, 3 years of work experience, MBA. Additional exam requirements/recommendations for international students: required—TOEFL.

Wentworth Institute of Technology, Online Master of Science in Technology Management Program, Boston, MA 02115-5998. Offers MS. *Program availability:* Part-time-only, evening/weekend, online only, 100% online. *Degree requirements:* For master's, thesis optional, capstone. *Entrance requirements:* For master's, resume, official transcripts, two professional recommendations, BA or BS, one year of professional experience in a technical role and/or technical organization, statement of purpose, minimum GPA of 3.0. Additional exam requirements/recommendations for international students: recommended—TOEFL (minimum score 550 paper-based). Electronic applications accepted. *Expenses:* Contact institution.

Western Kentucky University, Graduate School, Ogden College of Science and Engineering, The School of Engineering and Applied Sciences, Bowling Green, KY 42101. Offers computer science (MS); engineering technology management (MS).

Wilfrid Laurier University, Faculty of Graduate and Postdoctoral Studies, Lazaridis School of Business and Economics, Department of Business, Waterloo, ON N2L 3C5, Canada. Offers accounting (PhD); finance (M Fin); financial economics (PhD); marketing (PhD); operations and supply chain management (PhD); organizational behavior and human resource management (M Sc); organizational behaviour and human resource management (PhD); supply chain management (M Sc); technology management (EMTM). *Accreditation:* AACSB. *Program availability:* Part-time, evening/weekend. *Degree requirements:* For master's, thesis optional; for doctorate, comprehensive exam, thesis/dissertation. *Entrance requirements:* For master's, GMAT, 4-year honors degree with minimum B+ average; for doctorate, GMAT, master's degree, minimum B+ average. Additional exam requirements/recommendations for international students: required—TOEFL (minimum score 89 iBT). Electronic applications accepted.

Operations Research

Air Force Institute of Technology, Graduate School of Engineering and Management, Department of Operational Sciences, Dayton, OH 45433-7765. Offers logistics management (MS); operations research (MS, PhD); space operations (MS). *Program availability:* Part-time. *Degree requirements:* For master's, thesis; for doctorate, thesis/dissertation. *Entrance requirements:* For doctorate, GRE General Test, minimum GPA of 3.0, U.S. citizenship.

Bowling Green State University, Graduate College, College of Arts and Sciences, Department of Computer Science, Bowling Green, OH 43403. Offers computer science (MS), including operations research, parallel and distributed computing, software engineering. *Program availability:* Part-time. *Degree requirements:* For master's, thesis or alternative. *Entrance requirements:* For master's, GRE General Test. Additional exam requirements/recommendations for international students: required—TOEFL. Electronic applications accepted.

Capella University, School of Business and Technology, Master's Programs in Business, Minneapolis, MN 55402. Offers accounting (MBA); business analysis (MS); business intelligence (MBA); entrepreneurship (MBA); finance (MBA); general business administration (MBA); general human resource management (MS); general leadership (MS); health care management (MBA); human resource management (MBA); marketing (MBA); project management (MBA, MS). *Accreditation:* ACBSP.

Carnegie Mellon University, Tepper School of Business, Program in Operations Research, Pittsburgh, PA 15213-3891. Offers PhD. *Degree requirements:* For doctorate, thesis/dissertation. *Entrance requirements:* For doctorate, GMAT or GRE General Test.

Case Western Reserve University, Weatherhead School of Management, Department of Operations, Cleveland, OH 44106. Offers operations and supply chain management (MSM); operations research (PhD); MBA/MSM. *Program availability:* Part-time. *Degree requirements:* For doctorate, thesis/dissertation. *Entrance requirements:* For master's, GRE General Test; for doctorate, GMAT, GRE General Test.

Claremont Graduate University, Graduate Programs, Institute of Mathematical Sciences, Claremont, CA 91711-6160. Offers computational and systems biology (PhD); computational mathematics and numerical analysis (MA, MS); computational science (PhD); engineering and industrial applied mathematics (PhD); mathematics (PhD); operations research and statistics (MA, MS); physical applied mathematics (MA, MS); pure mathematics (MA, MS); scientific computing (MA, MS); systems and control theory (MA, MS). *Program availability:* Part-time. Terminal master's awarded for partial completion of doctoral program. *Entrance requirements:* For master's and doctorate, GRE General Test. Additional exam requirements/recommendations for international students: required—TOEFL (minimum score 75 iBT). Electronic applications accepted.

Colorado School of Mines, Office of Graduate Studies, Department of Economics and Business, Golden, CO 80401. Offers engineering and technology management (MS); mineral and energy economics (MS, PhD); operations research and engineering (PhD); petroleum economics and management with mineral and energy economics (MS). *Program availability:* Part-time. *Degree requirements:* For master's, thesis (for some programs); for doctorate, comprehensive exam, thesis/dissertation. *Entrance requirements:* For master's and doctorate, GRE General Test. Additional exam requirements/recommendations for international students: required—TOEFL (minimum score 550 paper-based; 79 iBT). Electronic applications accepted. *Expenses:* Tuition, state resident: full-time $16,650; part-time $925 per credit hour. Tuition, nonresident: full-time $37,350; part-time $2075 per credit hour. *International tuition:* $37,350 full-time. *Required fees:* $2412.

Columbia University, Fu Foundation School of Engineering and Applied Science, Department of Industrial Engineering and Operations Research, New York, NY 10027. Offers financial engineering (MS); industrial engineering (MS); industrial engineering and operations research (PhD); management science and engineering (MS); operations research (MS); MS/MBA. *Program availability:* Part-time, evening/weekend, online learning. *Degree requirements:* For doctorate, thesis/dissertation, oral and written qualifying exams. *Entrance requirements:* For master's and doctorate, GRE General Test. Additional exam requirements/recommendations for international students: required—TOEFL, IELTS, PTE. Electronic applications accepted. *Expenses: Tuition:* Full-time $47,600; part-time $1880 per credit. One-time fee: $105.

Cornell University, Graduate School, Graduate Fields of Engineering, Field of Operations Research and Information Engineering, Ithaca, NY 14853. Offers applied probability and statistics (PhD); manufacturing systems engineering (PhD); mathematical programming (PhD); operations research and industrial engineering (M Eng). *Degree requirements:* For doctorate, comprehensive exam, thesis/dissertation. *Entrance requirements:* For master's and doctorate, GRE General Test, 3 letters of recommendation. Additional exam requirements/recommendations for international students: required—TOEFL (minimum score 600 paper-based; 100 iBT). Electronic applications accepted.

Florida Institute of Technology, Aberdeen Education Center (Maryland), Program in Management, Melbourne, FL 32901-6975. Offers acquisition and contract management (MS, PMBA); business administration (MS, PMBA); contracts management (PMBA); financial management (MPA); global management (PMBA); health management (MS); human resources management (MS, PMBA); information systems (PMBA); logistics management (MS); management (MS), including information systems, operations research; materials acquisition management (MS); operations research (MS); public administration (MPA); research (PMBA); space systems (MS); space systems management (MS).

Florida Institute of Technology, Aberdeen Education Center (Maryland), Program in Project Management - Operations Research, Melbourne, FL 32901-6975. Offers MS. Electronic applications accepted.

Florida Institute of Technology, College of Engineering and Science, Program in Operations Research, Melbourne, FL 32901-6975. Offers MS, PhD. *Program availability:* Part-time, evening/weekend. Terminal master's awarded for partial completion of doctoral program. *Degree requirements:* For master's, comprehensive exam (for some programs), thesis or final exam, 30 credit hours; for doctorate, comprehensive exam, thesis/dissertation, 42 credit hours after the masters, virtual written grant proposal and oral defense, written dissertation and oral defense, dissertation research, written qualifying exam. *Entrance requirements:* For master's, undergraduate degree in related field and strong math background. Additional exam requirements/recommendations for international students: required—TOEFL (minimum score 550 paper-based; 79 iBT). Electronic applications accepted.

George Mason University, Volgenau School of Engineering, Department of Systems Engineering and Operations Research, Fairfax, VA 22030. Offers operations research (MS); systems engineering and operations research (PhD, Certificate). *Program availability:* Evening/weekend, 100% online. *Degree requirements:* For master's, thesis optional; for doctorate, comprehensive exam, thesis/dissertation, qualifying exams. *Entrance requirements:* For master's, GRE General Test, BS in related field; minimum GPA of 3.0; 3 letters of recommendation; 2 official transcripts; expanded goals statement; proof of financial support; photocopy of passport; official bank statement; multivariable calculus, applied probability, statistics and a computer language course; self-evaluation form; for doctorate, GRE, MS with minimum GPA of 3.5; BS with minimum GPA of 3.0 in systems or operational research; 2 official transcripts; 3 letters of recommendation; resume; expanded goals statement; self evaluation form; photocopy of passport; official bank statement; proof of financial support; for Certificate, personal goals statement; 2 official transcripts; self-evaluation form; letter of recommendation; resume; official bank statement; photocopy of passport; proof of financial support; baccalaureate degree in related field. Additional exam requirements/recommendations for international students: required—TOEFL (minimum score 575 paper-based; 88 iBT), IELTS (minimum score 6.5), PTE (minimum score 59). Electronic applications accepted. *Expenses:* Contact institution.

Georgia Institute of Technology, Graduate Studies, College of Engineering, H. Milton Stewart School of Industrial and Systems Engineering, Atlanta, GA 30332. Offers health systems (MS); industrial and systems engineering (MS, PhD), including industrial engineering; international logistics (MS); operations research (MS, PhD). *Program availability:* Part-time, 100% online. *Faculty:* 54 full-time (11 women), 3 part-time/adjunct. *Students:* 416 full-time (140 women), 86 part-time (32 women); includes 63 minority (5 Black or African American, non-Hispanic/Latino; 36 Asian, non-Hispanic/Latino; 15 Hispanic/Latino; 7 Two or more races, non-Hispanic/Latino), 359 international. Average age 25. 1,533 applicants, 29% accepted, 206 enrolled. In 2019, 203 master's, 21 doctorates awarded. Terminal master's awarded for partial completion of doctoral program. *Degree requirements:* For doctorate, comprehensive exam, thesis/dissertation. *Entrance requirements:* For master's, GRE General Test, Must have an undergraduate Bachelor of Science degree or the equivalent. MS Analytics applicants may substitute Graduate Management Admission Test (GMAT) scores as a substitute, although the GRE is preferred. Should describe any relevant work experience in the personal statement.; for doctorate, GRE General Test, Transcripts of prior academic work are required, as is evidence of an earned bachelor's degree. Also need a statement of purpose, resume, and three credible letters of reference. Additional exam requirements/recommendations for international students: required—TOEFL (minimum score 577 paper-based; 90 iBT), IELTS (minimum score 7), TOEFL is the preferred method with the requirements shown on the programs. *Application deadline:* For fall admission, 1/1 for domestic students, 12/15 for international students; for spring admission, 2/1 for domestic and international students. Applications are processed on a rolling basis. Application fee: $75 ($85 for international students). Electronic applications accepted. *Expenses: Tuition, area resident:* Full-time $14,064; part-time $586 per credit hour. Tuition, state resident: full-time $14,064; part-time $586 per credit hour. Tuition, nonresident: full-time $29,140; part-time $1215 per credit hour. *International tuition:* $29,140 full-time. *Required fees:* $2024; $840 per semester. $2096. Tuition and fees vary according to course load. *Financial support:* In 2019–20, 10 fellowships, 140 research assistantships, 50 teaching assistantships were awarded; career-related internships or fieldwork, Federal Work-Study, institutionally sponsored loans, tuition waivers (full and partial), and unspecified assistantships also available. Support available to part-time students. Financial award application deadline: 7/1; financial award applicants required to submit FAFSA. *Unit head:* Edwin Romeijn, School Chair, 404-894-2300, Fax: 404-894-2301, E-mail: edwin.romeijn@isye.gatech.edu. *Application contact:* Marla Bruner, Director of Graduate Studies, 404-894-1610, Fax: 404-894-1609, E-mail: gradinfo@mail.gatech.edu.
Website: http://www.isye.gatech.edu

Georgia State University, J. Mack Robinson College of Business, Department of Managerial Sciences, Atlanta, GA 30302-3083. Offers business analysis (MBA, MS); entrepreneurship (MBA); human resources management (MBA, MS); operations management (MBA, MS); organization behavior/human resource management (PhD); organization management (MBA); organizational change (MS); strategic management (PhD). *Accreditation:* AACSB. *Program availability:* Part-time, evening/weekend. *Faculty:* 11 full-time (2 women), 1 part-time/adjunct (0 women). *Students:* 6 full-time (4 women); includes 2 minority (1 Black or African American, non-Hispanic/Latino; 1 Hispanic/Latino), 1 international. Average age 38. 23 applicants, 22% accepted, 2 enrolled. In 2019, 8 master's, 2 doctorates awarded. *Entrance requirements:* For master's, GRE or GMAT, transcripts from all institutions attended, resume, essays; for doctorate, GMAT, three letters of recommendation, personal statement, transcripts from all institutions attended, resume. Additional exam requirements/recommendations for international students: required—TOEFL (minimum score 610 paper-based; 101 iBT), IELTS (minimum score 7). *Application deadline:* For fall admission, 5/1 priority date for domestic students, 2/1 priority date for international students; for spring admission, 9/15 priority date for domestic students, 4/1 priority date for international students. Applications are processed on a rolling basis. Application fee: $50. Electronic applications accepted. *Expenses: Tuition, area resident:* Full-time $7164; part-time $398 per credit hour. Tuition, state resident: full-time $7164; part-time $398 per credit hour. Tuition, nonresident: full-time $22,662; part-time $1259 per credit hour. *International tuition:* $22,662 full-time. *Required fees:* $2128; $312 per credit hour. Tuition and fees vary according to course load and program. *Financial support:* Research assistantships, teaching assistantships, scholarships/grants, tuition waivers, and unspecified assistantships available. Financial award applicants required to submit FAFSA. *Unit head:* Dr. G. Peter Zhang, Chair, 404-413-7557. *Application contact:* Toby McChesney, Assistant Dean for Graduate Recruiting and Student Services, 404-413-7167, Fax: 404-413-7162, E-mail: rcbgradadmissions@gsu.edu.
Website: http://mgmt.robinson.gsu.edu/

HEC Montreal, School of Business Administration, Graduate Diploma Programs in Administration, Montréal, QC H3T 2A7, Canada. Offers business administration (Graduate Diploma); business analysis - information technology (Graduate Diploma); e-business (Graduate Diploma); entrepreneurship (Graduate Diploma); financial professions (Graduate Diploma); human resources (Graduate Diploma); management (Graduate Diploma); management and sustainable development (Graduate Diploma); management of cultural organizations (Graduate Diploma); marketing communication (Graduate Diploma); organizational development (Graduate Diploma); professional accounting (Graduate Diploma); supply chain management (Graduate Diploma); taxation (Graduate Diploma). *Entrance requirements:* For degree, bachelor's degree. Electronic applications accepted.

Idaho State University, Graduate School, College of Science and Engineering, Department of Mechanical Engineering, Pocatello, ID 83209-8060. Offers measurement and control engineering (MS); mechanical engineering (MS). *Program availability:* Part-time. *Degree requirements:* For master's, comprehensive exam (for some programs), 2 semesters of seminar; thesis or project. *Entrance requirements:* For master's, GRE. Additional exam requirements/recommendations for international students: required—TOEFL (minimum score 550 paper-based; 80 iBT). Electronic applications accepted.

Iowa State University of Science and Technology, Department of Industrial and Manufacturing Systems Engineering, Ames, IA 50011. Offers industrial engineering (M Eng, MS, PhD); operations research (MS); systems engineering (M Eng). *Degree requirements:* For master's, thesis or alternative; for doctorate, thesis/dissertation. *Entrance requirements:* For master's and doctorate, GRE General Test. Additional exam requirements/recommendations for international students: required—TOEFL (minimum

score 550 paper-based; 79 iBT), IELTS (minimum score 6.5). Electronic applications accepted.

Johns Hopkins University, G. W. C. Whiting School of Engineering, Department of Applied Mathematics and Statistics, Baltimore, MD 21218. Offers computational medicine (PhD); discrete mathematics (MA, MSE, PhD); financial mathematics (MSE); operations research/optimization (MA, MSE, PhD); statistics/probability (MA, MSE, PhD). Terminal master's awarded for partial completion of doctoral program. *Degree requirements:* For master's, thesis (for some programs); for doctorate, thesis/dissertation, oral exam, introductory exam. *Entrance requirements:* For master's and doctorate, GRE General Test, 3 letters of recommendation, statement of purpose, transcripts. Additional exam requirements/recommendations for international students: required—TOEFL (minimum score 600 paper-based; 100 iBT), IELTS (minimum score 7). Electronic applications accepted.

Johns Hopkins University, G. W. C. Whiting School of Engineering, Master of Science in Engineering Management Program, Baltimore, MD 21218. Offers biomaterials (MSEM); civil engineering (MSEM); communications science (MSEM); computer science (MSEM); environmental systems analysis, economics and public policy (MSEM); fluid mechanics (MSEM); materials science and engineering (MSEM); mechanical engineering (MSEM); mechanics and materials (MSEM); nano-biotechnology (MSEM); nanomaterials and nanotechnology (MSEM); operations research (MSEM); probability and statistics (MSEM); smart product and device design (MSEM). *Entrance requirements:* For master's, GRE, 3 letters of recommendation, statement of purpose, transcripts. Additional exam requirements/recommendations for international students: required—TOEFL (minimum score 600 paper-based, 100 iBT) or IELTS (7). Electronic applications accepted.

Kansas State University, Graduate School, College of Engineering, Department of Industrial and Manufacturing Systems Engineering, Manhattan, KS 66506. Offers engineering management (MEM); industrial engineering (MS); operations research (MS). *Program availability:* Part-time, online learning. *Degree requirements:* For master's, thesis or alternative; for doctorate, thesis/dissertation. *Entrance requirements:* For master's, GRE General Test (minimum score of 750 old version, 159 new format on Quantitative portion of exam), bachelor's degree in engineering, mathematics, or physical science; for doctorate, GRE General Test (minimum score of 770 old version, 164 new format on Quantitative portion of exam), master's degree in engineering or industrial manufacturing. Additional exam requirements/recommendations for international students: required—PTE (minimum score 58), TOEFL (minimum score 550 paper-based; 79 iBT) or IELTS (minimum score 6.5). Electronic applications accepted.

Massachusetts Institute of Technology, Operations Research Center, Cambridge, MA 02139. Offers SM, PhD. Terminal master's awarded for partial completion of doctoral program. *Degree requirements:* For master's, thesis; for doctorate, comprehensive exam, thesis/dissertation. *Entrance requirements:* For master's and doctorate, GRE General Test. Additional exam requirements/recommendations for international students: required—TOEFL, IELTS. Electronic applications accepted.

Mississippi State University, Bagley College of Engineering, Department of Industrial and Systems Engineering, Mississippi State, MS 39762. Offers human factors and ergonomics (MS); industrial and systems engineering (PhD); industrial systems (MS); management systems (MS); manufacturing systems (MS); operations research (MS). *Program availability:* Part-time, blended/hybrid learning. *Faculty:* 14 full-time (3 women). *Students:* 39 full-time (16 women), 64 part-time (18 women); includes 20 minority (7 Black or African American, non-Hispanic/Latino; 7 Asian, non-Hispanic/Latino; 5 Hispanic/Latino; 1 Two or more races, non-Hispanic/Latino), 28 international. Average age 36. 54 applicants, 44% accepted, 11 enrolled. In 2019, 14 master's, 6 doctorates awarded. *Degree requirements:* For master's, comprehensive exam (for some programs), thesis optional, comprehensive oral or written exam; for doctorate, comprehensive exam, thesis/dissertation, candidacy exam. *Entrance requirements:* For master's, GRE (for graduates from program not accredited by EAC/ABET), minimum GPA of 3.0 on junior and senior years; for doctorate, GRE (for graduates from program not accredited by EAC/ABET), minimum GPA of 3.5 on master's degree and junior and senior years of BS. Additional exam requirements/recommendations for international students: required—TOEFL (minimum score 550 paper-based; 79 iBT); recommended—IELTS (minimum score 6.5). *Application deadline:* For fall admission, 7/1 for domestic students, 5/1 for international students; for spring admission, 11/1 for domestic students, 9/1 for international students. Applications are processed on a rolling basis. Application fee: $60 ($80 for international students). Electronic applications accepted. *Expenses: Tuition, area resident:* Full-time $8880; part-time $456 per credit hour. Tuition, state resident: full-time $8880. Tuition, nonresident: full-time $23,840; part-time $1236 per credit hour. *Required fees:* $110; $11.12 per credit hour. Tuition and fees vary according to course load. *Financial support:* In 2019–20, 21 research assistantships with full tuition reimbursements (averaging $17,482 per year), 4 teaching assistantships with full tuition reimbursements (averaging $15,706 per year) were awarded; Federal Work-Study, institutionally sponsored loans, and unspecified assistantships also available. Financial award application deadline: 4/1; financial award applicants required to submit FAFSA. *Unit head:* Dr. Kari Babski-Reeves, Professor, Department Head and Associate Dean for Research and Graduate Studies, 662-325-8430, Fax: 662-325-7618, E-mail: kari@ise.msstate.edu. *Application contact:* Ryan King, Admissions and Enrollment Assistant, 662-325-8951, E-mail: rjk101@grad.msstate.edu.
Website: http://www.ise.msstate.edu/

Naval Postgraduate School, Departments and Academic Groups, Department of Operations Research, Monterey, CA 93943. Offers applied science (MS), including operations research; cost estimating analysis (MS); human systems integration (MS); operations research (MS, PhD); systems analysis (MS). *Program availability:* Part-time. *Degree requirements:* For master's, thesis (for some programs); for doctorate, thesis/dissertation.

Naval Postgraduate School, Departments and Academic Groups, Undersea Warfare Academic Group, Monterey, CA 93943. Offers applied mathematics (MS); applied physics (MS); applied science (MS), including acoustics, operations research, physical oceanography, signal processing; electrical engineering (MS); engineering acoustics (MS, PhD); engineering science (MS), including electrical engineering, mechanical engineering; mechanical engineer (ME); mechanical engineering (MS, MSME); meteorology (MS); operations research (MS); physical oceanography (MS). *Program availability:* Part-time. *Degree requirements:* For master's, thesis.

New Mexico Institute of Mining and Technology, Center for Graduate Studies, Department of Mathematics, Socorro, NM 87801. Offers applied and industrial mathematics (PhD); industrial mathematics (MS); mathematics (MS); operations research and statistics (MS). *Degree requirements:* For master's, thesis optional; for doctorate, thesis/dissertation. *Entrance requirements:* For master's, GRE General Test. Additional exam requirements/recommendations for international students: required—TOEFL (minimum score 540 paper-based).

North Carolina State University, Graduate School, College of Engineering and College of Sciences, Program in Operations Research, Raleigh, NC 27695. Offers MOR, MS, PhD. *Program availability:* Part-time. *Degree requirements:* For master's, thesis (MS); for doctorate, thesis/dissertation, comprehensive oral and written exams. *Entrance requirements:* For master's, GRE General Test, minimum GPA of 2.7; for doctorate, GRE General Test, minimum GPA of 3.0. Additional exam requirements/recommendations for international students: required—TOEFL. Electronic applications accepted.

Northeastern University, College of Engineering, Boston, MA 02115-5096. Offers bioengineering (MS, PhD); chemical engineering (MS, PhD); civil engineering (MS, PhD); computer engineering (PhD); computer systems engineering (MS); electrical and computer engineering (MS); electrical and computer engineering leadership (MS); electrical engineering (PhD); energy systems (MS); engineering and public policy (MS); engineering management (MS, Certificate); environmental engineering (MS); industrial engineering (MS, PhD); information assurance (PhD); information systems (MS); interdisciplinary engineering (PhD); mechanical engineering (PhD); operations research (MS); telecommunication systems management (MS). *Program availability:* Part-time, online learning. Electronic applications accepted. *Expenses:* Contact institution.

Northeastern University, College of Science, Boston, MA 02115-5096. Offers applied mathematics (MS); bioinformatics (MS); biology (PhD); biotechnology (MS); chemistry and chemical biology (MS, PhD); environmental science and policy (MS); marine and environmental sciences (PhD); marine biology (MS); mathematics (MS, PhD); operations research (MSOR); physics (MS, PhD); psychology (PhD). *Program availability:* Part-time. Terminal master's awarded for partial completion of doctoral program. *Degree requirements:* For master's, comprehensive exam (for some programs), thesis; for doctorate, comprehensive exam (for some programs), thesis/dissertation. *Entrance requirements:* For master's, GRE General Test. Electronic applications accepted. *Expenses:* Contact institution.

The Ohio State University, Graduate School, Max M. Fisher College of Business, Program in Business Operational Excellence, Columbus, OH 43210. Offers MBOE. *Program availability:* Online learning. *Entrance requirements:* For master's, GMAT if undergraduate GPA is below a 3.0, bachelor's degree from accredited university; at least 3-5 years of successful work experience in which managing processes are part of the job; recommendation by an executive sponsor. Additional exam requirements/recommendations for international students: required—TOEFL (minimum score 550 paper-based; 79 iBT), Michigan English Language Assessment Battery (minimum score 82); recommended—IELTS (minimum score 7).

Polytechnique Montréal, Graduate Programs, Department of Mathematics and Industrial Engineering, Montréal, QC H3C 3A7, Canada. Offers ergonomy (M Eng, M Sc A, DESS); mathematical method in CA engineering (M Eng, M Sc A, PhD); operational research (M Eng, M Sc A, PhD); production (M Eng, M Sc A); technology management (M Eng, M Sc A). *Program availability:* Part-time. *Degree requirements:* For master's, one foreign language, thesis. *Entrance requirements:* For master's, minimum GPA of 2.75.

Princeton University, Graduate School, School of Engineering and Applied Science, Department of Operations Research and Financial Engineering, Princeton, NJ 08544-1019. Offers M Eng, MSE, PhD. Terminal master's awarded for partial completion of doctoral program. *Degree requirements:* For master's, thesis (MSE); for doctorate, thesis/dissertation, general exam. *Entrance requirements:* For master's and doctorate, GRE General Test, official transcript(s), 3 letters of recommendation, personal statement. Additional exam requirements/recommendations for international students: required—TOEFL. Electronic applications accepted.

Purdue University Fort Wayne, College of Arts and Sciences, Department of Mathematical Sciences, Fort Wayne, IN 46805-1499. Offers applied mathematics (MS); applied statistics (Certificate); mathematics (MS); operations research (MS); teaching (MAT). *Program availability:* Part-time, evening/weekend. *Entrance requirements:* For master's, minimum GPA of 3.0, major or minor in mathematics, three letters of recommendation. Additional exam requirements/recommendations for international students: required—TOEFL (minimum score 550 paper-based; 79 iBT); recommended—TWE. Electronic applications accepted.

Rutgers University - New Brunswick, Graduate School-New Brunswick, Program in Operations Research, Piscataway, NJ 08854-8097. Offers PhD. *Program availability:* Part-time. *Degree requirements:* For doctorate, comprehensive exam, thesis/dissertation, qualifying exam. *Entrance requirements:* For doctorate, GRE General Test, GRE Subject Test. Electronic applications accepted.

Simon Fraser University, Office of Graduate Studies and Postdoctoral Fellows, Faculty of Science, Department of Mathematics, Burnaby, BC V5A 1S6, Canada. Offers applied and computational mathematics (M Sc, PhD); mathematics (M Sc, PhD); operations research (M Sc, PhD). *Degree requirements:* For master's, thesis or alternative; for doctorate, comprehensive exam, thesis/dissertation. *Entrance requirements:* For master's, GRE General Test, GRE Subject Test (mathematics), minimum GPA of 3.0 (on scale of 4.33) or 3.33 based on last 60 credits of undergraduate courses; for doctorate, GRE General Test, GRE Subject Test (mathematics), minimum GPA of 3.5 (on scale of 4.33). Additional exam requirements/recommendations for international students: recommended—TOEFL (minimum score 580 paper-based; 93 iBT), IELTS (minimum score 7), TWE (minimum score 5). Electronic applications accepted.

South Dakota State University, Graduate School, Jerome J. Lohr College of Engineering, Department of Construction and Operations Management, Brookings, SD 57007. Offers operations management (MS). *Degree requirements:* For master's, comprehensive exam, thesis (for some programs), oral exam. *Entrance requirements:* Additional exam requirements/recommendations for international students: required—TOEFL (minimum score 575 paper-based).

Southern Illinois University Edwardsville, Graduate School, College of Arts and Sciences, Department of Mathematics and Statistics, Program in Statistics and Operations Research, Edwardsville, IL 62026. Offers MS. *Program availability:* Part-time. *Degree requirements:* For master's, thesis (for some programs), special project. *Entrance requirements:* Additional exam requirements/recommendations for international students: required—TOEFL (minimum score 550 paper-based, 79 iBT), IELTS (minimum score 6.5), Michigan Test of English Language Proficiency or PTE. Electronic applications accepted.

Southern Methodist University, Lyle School of Engineering, Department of Engineering Management, Information, and Systems, Dallas, TX 75275. Offers engineering entrepreneurship (MS); engineering management (MS, DE); information engineering and management (MSIEM); operations research (MS, PhD); systems engineering (MS). *Program availability:* Part-time, evening/weekend, online learning. Terminal master's awarded for partial completion of doctoral program. *Degree requirements:* For master's, thesis optional; for doctorate, thesis/dissertation, oral and written qualifying exams. *Entrance requirements:* For master's, minimum GPA of 3.0 in last 2 years; bachelor's degree in engineering, mathematics, sciences, or technical area; for doctorate, GRE General Test (operations research, engineering management), bachelor's degree in related field. Additional exam requirements/recommendations for international students: required—TOEFL.

The University of Alabama in Huntsville, School of Graduate Studies, College of Engineering, Department of Industrial and Systems Engineering and Engineering Management, Huntsville, AL 35899. Offers engineering management (MSE, PhD); industrial engineering (MSE, PhD); operations research (MSOR); systems engineering (MSE, PhD). *Program availability:* Part-time. *Degree requirements:* For master's, comprehensive exam, thesis or alternative, oral and written exams; for doctorate, comprehensive exam, thesis/dissertation, oral and written exams. *Entrance requirements:* For master's and doctorate, GRE General Test, minimum GPA of 3.0. Additional exam requirements/recommendations for international students: required—TOEFL (minimum score 500 paper-based; 80 iBT), IELTS (minimum score 6.5). Electronic applications accepted.

University of California, Berkeley, Graduate Division, College of Engineering, Department of Industrial Engineering and Operations Research, Berkeley, CA 94720. Offers decision analytics (M Eng); industrial engineering and operations research (M Eng, MS, PhD). *Program availability:* Part-time, evening/weekend. Terminal master's awarded for partial completion of doctoral program. *Degree requirements:* For master's, comprehensive exam (for some programs), thesis (for some programs), comprehensive exam or thesis (MS); for doctorate, thesis/dissertation, qualifying exam. *Entrance requirements:* For master's and doctorate, GRE General Test, minimum GPA of 3.0, 3 letters of recommendation. Additional exam requirements/recommendations for international students: required—TOEFL (minimum score 570 paper-based; 90 iBT). Electronic applications accepted.

University of Colorado Denver, College of Liberal Arts and Sciences, Department of Mathematical and Statistical Sciences, Denver, CO 80217. Offers applied mathematics (MS, PhD), including applied mathematics, applied probability (MS), applied statistics (MS), computational biology (PhD), computational mathematics (PhD), discrete mathematics, finite geometry (PhD), mathematics education (PhD), mathematics of engineering and science (MS), numerical analysis, operations research (MS), optimization and operations research (PhD), probability (PhD), statistics (PhD). *Program availability:* Part-time. *Degree requirements:* For master's, comprehensive exam, thesis optional, 30 hours of course work with minimum GPA of 3.0; for doctorate, comprehensive exam, thesis/dissertation, 42 hours of course work with minimum GPA of 3.25. *Entrance requirements:* For master's, GRE General Test; GRE Subject Test in math (recommended), 30 hours of course work in mathematics (24 of which must be upper-division mathematics), bachelor's degree with minimum GPA of 3.0; for doctorate, GRE General Test; GRE Subject Test in math (recommended), 30 hours of course work in mathematics (24 of which must be upper-division mathematics), master's degree with minimum GPA of 3.25. Additional exam requirements/recommendations for international students: required—TOEFL (minimum score 537 paper-based; 75 iBT); recommended—IELTS (minimum score 6.5). Electronic applications accepted. Tuition and fees vary according to course load, program and reciprocity agreements.

University of Delaware, College of Agriculture and Natural Resources, Department of Food and Resource Economics, Operations Research Program, Newark, DE 19716. Offers MS. *Program availability:* Part-time. *Degree requirements:* For master's, thesis, oral exam. *Entrance requirements:* For master's, GRE General Test, 3 letters of recommendation, program language/s, engineering calculus. Additional exam requirements/recommendations for international students: required—TOEFL. Electronic applications accepted.

University of Illinois at Chicago, College of Engineering, Department of Mechanical and Industrial Engineering, Program in Industrial Engineering, Chicago, IL 60607-7128. Offers industrial engineering (MS); industrial engineering and operations research (PhD). *Program availability:* Part-time. *Degree requirements:* For doctorate, thesis/dissertation. *Entrance requirements:* For doctorate, GRE General Test, minimum GPA of 2.75. Additional exam requirements/recommendations for international students: required—TOEFL. Electronic applications accepted. *Expenses:* Contact institution.

The University of Iowa, Graduate College, College of Engineering, Department of Industrial Engineering, Iowa City, IA 52242-1316. Offers engineering design and manufacturing (MS, PhD); healthcare systems (MS, PhD); human factors (MS, PhD); information and engineering management (MS, PhD); operations research (MS, PhD); wind energy (MS, PhD). Terminal master's awarded for partial completion of doctoral program. *Degree requirements:* For master's, thesis optional, exam; for doctorate, comprehensive exam, thesis/dissertation, final defense exam. *Entrance requirements:* For master's and doctorate, GRE (minimum Verbal score of 153, Quantitative 151), minimum undergraduate GPA of 3.0. Additional exam requirements/recommendations for international students: required—TOEFL (minimum score 600 paper-based; 100 iBT), IELTS (minimum score 7). Electronic applications accepted.

University of Massachusetts Amherst, Graduate School, College of Engineering, Department of Mechanical and Industrial Engineering, Amherst, MA 01003. Offers industrial engineering and operations research (MS, PhD); mechanical engineering (MSME, PhD). *Program availability:* Part-time. Terminal master's awarded for partial completion of doctoral program. *Degree requirements:* For master's, thesis or alternative; for doctorate, comprehensive exam, thesis/dissertation. *Entrance requirements:* For master's and doctorate, GRE General Test. Additional exam requirements/recommendations for international students: required—TOEFL (minimum score 550 paper-based; 80 iBT), IELTS (minimum score 6.5). Electronic applications accepted.

University of Michigan, College of Engineering, Department of Industrial and Operations Engineering, Ann Arbor, MI 48109. Offers MS, MSE, PhD, MBA/MS, MBA/MSE. *Program availability:* Part-time. Terminal master's awarded for partial completion of doctoral program. *Degree requirements:* For doctorate, oral defense of dissertation, preliminary exams, qualifying exam. *Entrance requirements:* For master's and doctorate, GRE General Test. Additional exam requirements/recommendations for international students: required—TOEFL. Electronic applications accepted.

The University of North Carolina at Chapel Hill, Graduate School, College of Arts and Sciences, Department of Statistics and Operations Research, Chapel Hill, NC 27599. Offers operations research (MS, PhD); statistics (MS, PhD). *Degree requirements:* For master's, comprehensive exam, essay or thesis; for doctorate, comprehensive exam, thesis/dissertation. *Entrance requirements:* For master's and doctorate, GRE General Test, GRE Subject Test, minimum GPA of 3.0. Additional exam requirements/recommendations for international students: required—TOEFL.

University of Southern California, Graduate School, Viterbi School of Engineering, Daniel J. Epstein Department of Industrial and Systems Engineering, Los Angeles, CA 90089. Offers digital supply chain management (MS); engineering management (MS); engineering technology communication (Graduate Certificate); health systems operations (Graduate Certificate); industrial and systems engineering (MS, PhD, Engr); manufacturing engineering (MS); operations research engineering (MS); optimization and supply chain management (Graduate Certificate); product development engineering (MS); safety systems and security (MS); systems architecting and engineering (MS, Graduate Certificate); systems safety and security (Graduate Certificate); transportation systems (Graduate Certificate); MS/MBA. *Program availability:* Part-time, evening/weekend, online learning. Terminal master's awarded for partial completion of doctoral program. *Degree requirements:* For master's, thesis optional; for doctorate, thesis/dissertation. *Entrance requirements:* For master's and doctorate, GRE General Test.

Additional exam requirements/recommendations for international students: recommended—TOEFL. Electronic applications accepted.

The University of Texas at Austin, Graduate School, Cockrell School of Engineering, Department of Mechanical Engineering, Program in Operations Research and Industrial Engineering, Austin, TX 78712-1111. Offers MS, PhD. *Entrance requirements:* For master's and doctorate, GRE General Test. Additional exam requirements/recommendations for international students: required—TOEFL.

University of Waterloo, Graduate Studies and Postdoctoral Affairs, Faculty of Engineering, Department of Management Sciences, Waterloo, ON N2L 3G1, Canada.

Offers applied operations research (MA Sc, MMS, PhD); information systems (MA Sc, MMS, PhD); management of technology (MA Sc, MMS, PhD). *Program availability:* Part-time, online learning. *Degree requirements:* For master's, research paper or thesis; for doctorate, comprehensive exam, thesis/dissertation. *Entrance requirements:* For master's, GMAT or GRE, honors degree, minimum B average, resume; for doctorate, GMAT or GRE, master's degree, minimum A- average, resume. Additional exam requirements/recommendations for international students: required—TOEFL, IELTS, PTE. Electronic applications accepted.

Technology and Public Policy

Arizona State University at Tempe, College of Liberal Arts and Sciences, Program in Science and Technology Policy, Tempe, AZ 85287-6505. Offers MS. *Degree requirements:* For master's, thesis or alternative, internship, applied project, interactive Program of Study (iPOS) submitted before completing 50 percent of required credit hours. *Entrance requirements:* For master's, GRE, bachelor's degree (or equivalent) or graduate degree from regionally-accredited college or university or of recognized standing; minimum GPA of 3.0 or equivalent in last 2 years of work leading to bachelor's degree; 3 letters of recommendation; personal statement; current resume. Additional exam requirements/recommendations for international students: required—TOEFL, IELTS, or PTE. Electronic applications accepted. *Expenses:* Contact institution.

Carnegie Mellon University, Carnegie Institute of Technology, Department of Civil and Environmental Engineering, Pittsburgh, PA 15213. Offers advanced infrastructure systems (MS, PhD); advanced infrastructure systems technology development and application (MS); air quality engineering and science (MS); civil and environmental engineering (MS, PhD); civil and environmental engineering/engineering and public policy (PhD); civil engineering (MS, PhD); computational mechanics (MS, PhD); computational modeling and monitoring for resilient structural and material systems (MS); energy infrastructure systems (MS); environmental engineering (MS, PhD); environmental management and science (MS, PhD); IT-based sustainable global infrastructure and construction management (MS); sustainability and green design (MS); water quality engineering and science (MS). *Program availability:* Part-time. *Faculty:* 23 full-time (5 women), 12 part-time/adjunct (3 women). *Students:* 261 full-time (109 women); includes 19 minority (7 Black or African American, non-Hispanic/Latino; 8 Asian, non-Hispanic/Latino; 4 Hispanic/Latino), 214 international. Average age 25. 649 applicants, 57% accepted, 106 enrolled. In 2019, 80 master's, 12 doctorates awarded. Terminal master's awarded for partial completion of doctoral program. *Degree requirements:* For master's, thesis optional; for doctorate, comprehensive exam, thesis/dissertation, two-part qualifying exam, public defense of dissertation. *Entrance requirements:* For master's, GRE General Test, BS in engineering, science, or mathematics; for doctorate, GRE General Test, BS or MS in engineering, science, or mathematics. Additional exam requirements/recommendations for international students: required—TOEFL (minimum score 84 iBT), TOEFL (minimum score 84 iBT) or IELTS (7.0). *Application deadline:* For fall admission, 1/5 priority date for domestic and international students; for spring admission, 9/15 priority date for domestic and international students. Applications are processed on a rolling basis. Application fee: $75. Electronic applications accepted. *Financial support:* In 2019–20, 113 students received support. Fellowships with tuition reimbursements available, research assistantships with tuition reimbursements available, teaching assistantships, scholarships/grants, health care benefits, tuition waivers (full and partial), and unspecified assistantships available. Financial award application deadline: 1/5. *Unit head:* Dr. David A. Dzombak, Professor and Department Head, 412-268-2941, Fax: 412-268-7813, E-mail: dzombak@cmu.edu. *Application contact:* David A. Vey, Director of Graduate Programs, 412-268-2292, Fax: 412-268-7813, E-mail: dvey@andrew.cmu.edu.
Website: http://www.cmu.edu/cee/

Carnegie Mellon University, Carnegie Institute of Technology, Department of Engineering and Public Policy, Pittsburgh, PA 15213-3891. Offers PhD. *Degree requirements:* For doctorate, thesis/dissertation. *Entrance requirements:* For doctorate, GRE General Test, BS in physical sciences or engineering. Additional exam requirements/recommendations for international students: required—TOEFL.

Eastern Michigan University, Graduate School, College of Engineering and Technology, School of Technology and Professional Services Management, Program in Technology Studies, Ypsilanti, MI 48197. Offers MS. *Program availability:* Part-time, evening/weekend, online learning. *Students:* 11 full-time (2 women), 50 part-time (16 women); includes 15 minority (7 Black or African American, non-Hispanic/Latino; 1 American Indian or Alaska Native, non-Hispanic/Latino; 1 Asian, non-Hispanic/Latino; 3 Hispanic/Latino; 3 Two or more races, non-Hispanic/Latino), 3 international. Average age 40. 33 applicants, 76% accepted, 16 enrolled. In 2019, 14 master's awarded. *Entrance requirements:* For master's, GRE General Test, minimum GPA of 2.6. Additional exam requirements/recommendations for international students: required—TOEFL. *Application deadline:* Applications are processed on a rolling basis. Application fee: $45. *Financial support:* Fellowships, research assistantships with full tuition reimbursements, teaching assistantships with full tuition reimbursements, career-related internships or fieldwork, Federal Work-Study, institutionally sponsored loans, scholarships/grants, tuition waivers (partial), and unspecified assistantships available. Support available to part-time students. Financial award applicants required to submit FAFSA. *Application contact:* Dr. Denise Pilato, Program Coordinator, 734-487-1167, Fax: 734-487-7690, E-mail: cot_msts@emich.edu.

The George Washington University, Elliott School of International Affairs, Program in International Science and Technology Policy, Washington, DC 20052. Offers MA, Graduate Certificate. *Program availability:* Part-time. *Degree requirements:* For master's, one foreign language, capstone project. *Entrance requirements:* For master's, GRE General Test. Additional exam requirements/recommendations for international students: required—TOEFL (minimum score 100 iBT), IELTS (minimum score 7). Electronic applications accepted.

Massachusetts Institute of Technology, School of Engineering, Institute for Data, Systems, and Society, Cambridge, MA 02139. Offers social and engineering systems (PhD); technology and policy (SM). *Degree requirements:* For master's, thesis; for doctorate, comprehensive exam, thesis/dissertation. *Entrance requirements:* For doctorate, GRE General Test. Additional exam requirements/recommendations for international students: required—IELTS. Electronic applications accepted.

Massachusetts Institute of Technology, School of Humanities, Arts, and Social Sciences, Program in Science, Technology, and Society, Cambridge, MA 02139. Offers history, anthropology, and science, technology and society (PhD). *Degree requirements:* For doctorate, one foreign language, comprehensive exam, thesis/dissertation.

Entrance requirements: For doctorate, GRE General Test. Additional exam requirements/recommendations for international students: required—TOEFL, IELTS. Electronic applications accepted.

Rensselaer Polytechnic Institute, Graduate School, School of Humanities, Arts, and Social Sciences, Program in Science and Technology Studies, Troy, NY 12180-3590. Offers MS, PhD. *Faculty:* 15 full-time (5 women), 1 part-time/adjunct (0 women). *Students:* 18 full-time (9 women), 1 (woman) part-time; includes 3 minority (1 Asian, non-Hispanic/Latino; 1 Hispanic/Latino; 1 Two or more races, non-Hispanic/Latino), 5 international. Average age 29. 19 applicants, 63% accepted, 4 enrolled. In 2019, 2 master's, 5 doctorates awarded. Terminal master's awarded for partial completion of doctoral program. *Degree requirements:* For master's, thesis (for some programs); for doctorate, comprehensive exam, thesis/dissertation. *Entrance requirements:* For master's and doctorate, GRE, writing sample. Additional exam requirements/recommendations for international students: required—TOEFL (minimum score 600 paper-based; 100 iBT), IELTS (minimum score 7), PTE (minimum score 68). *Application deadline:* For fall admission, 1/1 priority date for domestic and international students; for spring admission, 8/15 priority date for domestic and international students. Applications are processed on a rolling basis. Application fee: $75. Electronic applications accepted. *Financial support:* In 2019–20, research assistantships (averaging $23,000 per year), teaching assistantships (averaging $23,000 per year) were awarded; fellowships also available. Financial award application deadline: 1/1. *Unit head:* Dr. Atsushi Akera, Graduate Program Director, 518-276-2314, E-mail: akeraa@rpi.edu. *Application contact:* Jarron Decker, Director of Graduate Admissions, 518-276-6216, Fax: 518-276-4072, E-mail: gradadmissions@rpi.edu.
Website: http://www.sts.rpi.edu/pl/graduate-programs-sts

Rochester Institute of Technology, Graduate Enrollment Services, College of Liberal Arts, Department of Public Policy, MS Program in Science, Technology and Public Policy, Rochester, NY 14623-5603. Offers MS. *Program availability:* Part-time. *Degree requirements:* For master's, thesis or alternative, thesis or comprehensive exam plus 2 graduate electives. *Entrance requirements:* For master's, GRE, minimum GPA of 3.0 (recommended), completed course work in calculus and statistics, two writing samples, two letters of recommendation. Additional exam requirements/recommendations for international students: required—TOEFL (minimum score 570 paper-based; 88 iBT), IELTS (minimum score 6.5), PTE (minimum score 61). Electronic applications accepted. *Expenses:* Contact institution.

University of Minnesota, Twin Cities Campus, Graduate School, Humphrey School of Public Affairs, Program in Science, Technology, and Environmental Policy, Minneapolis, MN 55455-0213. Offers MS, JD/MS. *Program availability:* Part-time. *Students:* 17 full-time (12 women), 4 part-time (all women), 1 international. Average age 26. 23 applicants, 87% accepted, 10 enrolled. In 2019, 7 master's awarded. *Degree requirements:* For master's, thesis. *Entrance requirements:* For master's, GRE General Test, undergraduate training in the biological or physical sciences or engineering. Additional exam requirements/recommendations for international students: required—TOEFL (minimum score 600 paper-based; 100 iBT), IELTS (minimum score 7). *Application deadline:* For fall admission, 4/1 for domestic and international students. Application fee: $75 ($95 for international students). Electronic applications accepted. *Expenses:* Contact institution. *Financial support:* In 2019–20, 6 students received support, including fellowships with tuition reimbursements available (averaging $15,000 per year); career-related internships or fieldwork, Federal Work-Study, scholarships/grants, health care benefits, tuition waivers (full and partial), and unspecified assistantships also available. Financial award application deadline: 1/15; financial award applicants required to submit FAFSA. *Unit head:* Laura Bloomberg, Associate Dean, 612-625-0608, Fax: 612-626-0002, E-mail: bloom004@umn.edu. *Application contact:* Jacob Merrifield, Admissions Program Manager, 612-624-3800, Fax: 612-626-0002, E-mail: jmerrifi@umn.edu.
Website: http://www.hhh.umn.edu/degrees/ms_step/

University of South Africa, College of Human Sciences, Pretoria, South Africa. Offers adult education (M Ed); African languages (MA, PhD); African politics (MA, PhD); Afrikaans (MA, PhD); ancient history (MA, PhD); ancient Near Eastern studies (MA, PhD); anthropology (MA, PhD); applied linguistics (MA); Arabic (MA, PhD); archaeology (MA); art history (MA); Biblical archaeology (MA); Biblical studies (M Th, D Th, PhD); Christian spirituality (M Th, D Th); church history (M Th, D Th); classical studies (MA, PhD); clinical psychology (MA); communication (MA, PhD); comparative education (M Ed, Ed D); consulting psychology (D Admin, D Com, PhD); curriculum studies (M Ed, Ed D); development studies (M Admin, MA, D Admin, PhD); didactics (M Ed, Ed D); education (M Tech); education management (M Ed, Ed D); educational psychology (M Ed); English (MA); environmental education (M Ed); French (MA, PhD); German (MA, PhD); Greek (MA); guidance and counseling (M Ed); health studies (MA, PhD), including health sciences education (MA), health services management (MA), medical and surgical nursing science (critical care general) (MA), midwifery and neonatal nursing science (MA), trauma and emergency care (MA); history (MA, PhD); history of education (Ed D); inclusive education (M Ed, Ed D); information and communications technology policy and regulation (MA); information science (MA, MIS, PhD); international politics (MA, PhD); Islamic studies (MA, PhD); Italian (MA, PhD); Judaica (MA, PhD); linguistics (MA, PhD); mathematical education (M Ed); mathematics education (MA); missiology (M Th, D Th); modern Hebrew (MA, PhD); musicology (MA, MMus, D Mus, PhD); natural science education (M Ed); New Testament (M Th, D Th); Old Testament (D Th); pastoral therapy (M Th, D Th); philosophy (MA); philosophy of education (M Ed, Ed D); politics (MA, PhD); Portuguese (MA, PhD); practical theology (M Th, D Th); psychology (MA, MS, PhD); psychology of education (M Ed, Ed D); public health (MA); religious studies (MA, D Th, PhD); Romance languages (MA); Russian (MA, PhD); Semitic languages (MA, PhD); social behavior studies in HIV/AIDS (MA); social science (mental health) (MA); social science in development studies (MA); social science in psychology (MA); social science in social work (MA); social science in sociology (MA); social work (MSW, DSW, PhD); socio-education (M Ed, Ed D); sociolinguistics (MA); sociology (MA, PhD); Spanish (MA, PhD); systematic theology (M Th, D Th); TESOL (teaching English to speakers of other languages) (MA); theological ethics (M Th, D Th); theory of literature (MA, PhD); urban ministries (D Th); urban ministry (M Th).

The University of Texas at Austin, Graduate School, McCombs School of Business, Program in Technology Commercialization, Austin, TX 78712-1111. Offers MS. *Program availability:* Evening/weekend, online learning. *Degree requirements:* For master's, year-long global teaming project. *Entrance requirements:* For master's, GRE General Test or GMAT. Additional exam requirements/recommendations for international students: required—TOEFL (minimum score 550 paper-based; 79 iBT). Electronic applications accepted. *Expenses:* Contact institution.

Section 16
Materials Sciences and Engineering

This section contains a directory of institutions offering graduate work in materials sciences and engineering, followed by an in-depth entry submitted by an institution that chose to prepare a detailed program description. Additional information about programs listed in the directory but not augmented by an in-depth entry may be obtained by writing directly to the dean of a graduate school or chair of a department at the address given in the directory.

For programs offering related work, see also in this book *Agricultural Engineering and Bioengineering, Biomedical Engineering and Biotechnology, Engineering and Applied Sciences,* and *Geological, Mineral/Mining, and Petroleum Engineering.* In another guide in this series:
Graduate Programs in the Physical Sciences, Mathematics, Agricultural Sciences, the Environment & Natural Resources

See *Chemistry* and *Geosciences*

CONTENTS

Program Directories

Ceramic Sciences and Engineering

Alfred University, Graduate School, College of Ceramics, Inamori School of Engineering, Alfred, NY 14802-1205. Offers biomaterials engineering (MS); ceramic engineering (MS, PhD); electrical engineering (MS); glass science (MS, PhD); materials science and engineering (MS, PhD); mechanical engineering (MS). *Program availability:* Part-time. *Faculty:* 27 full-time (4 women), 2 part-time/adjunct (both women). *Students:* 30 full-time (11 women), 15 part-time (5 women); includes 2 minority (both Asian, non-Hispanic/Latino), 12 international. Average age 28. 24 applicants, 83% accepted, 18 enrolled. In 2019, 8 master's, 5 doctorates awarded. *Degree requirements:* For master's, comprehensive exam, thesis; for doctorate, comprehensive exam, thesis/dissertation. *Entrance requirements:* Additional exam requirements/recommendations for international students: required—TOEFL (minimum score 590 paper-based; 90 iBT), IELTS (minimum score 6.5). *Application deadline:* For fall admission, 3/1 priority date for domestic students, 3/15 for international students; for spring admission, 10/1 priority date for domestic students, 10/1 for international students. Applications are processed on a rolling basis. Application fee: $60. Electronic applications accepted. Application fee is waived when completed online. *Expenses:* $23,530 per year. *Financial support:* In 2019–20, 31 students received support. Fellowships with full tuition reimbursements available, research assistantships with full tuition reimbursements available, teaching assistantships with full tuition reimbursements available, tuition waivers (full and partial), and unspecified assistantships available. Financial award application deadline: 3/15; financial award applicants required to submit FAFSA. *Unit head:* Dr. Gabrielle Gaustad, Dean, 607-871-2953, E-mail: gaustad@alfred.edu. *Application contact:* Lindsey Gertin, Assistant Director of Graduate Admissions, 607-871-2017, Fax: 607-871-2198, E-mail: gradinquiry@alfred.edu.
Website: http://engineering.alfred.edu/grad/

Missouri University of Science and Technology, Department of Materials Science and Engineering, Rolla, MO 65401. Offers ceramic engineering (MS, PhD); materials science and engineering (MS, PhD); metallurgical engineering (MS, PhD). *Degree requirements:* For master's, thesis optional; for doctorate, comprehensive exam. *Entrance requirements:* For master's, GRE (minimum combined score 1100, 600 verbal, 3.5 writing); for doctorate, GRE (minimum score: quantitative 600, writing 3.5). Additional exam requirements/recommendations for international students: required—TOEFL (minimum score 570 paper-based). Electronic applications accepted. *Expenses:* Tuition, state resident: full-time $7839; part-time $435.50 per credit hour. Tuition, nonresident: full-time $22,169; part-time $1231.60 per credit hour. *International tuition:* $18,156.60 full-time. *Required fees:* $649.76. One-time fee: $119. Tuition and fees vary according to course load and program.

Electronic Materials

Colorado School of Mines, Office of Graduate Studies, Department of Metallurgical and Materials Engineering, Golden, CO 80401. Offers materials science (MS, PhD); metallurgical and materials engineering (ME, MS, PhD). *Program availability:* Part-time. *Degree requirements:* For master's, thesis (for some programs); for doctorate, comprehensive exam, thesis/dissertation. *Entrance requirements:* For master's and doctorate, GRE General Test. Additional exam requirements/recommendations for international students: required—TOEFL (minimum score 550 paper-based; 79 iBT). Electronic applications accepted. *Expenses:* Tuition, state resident: full-time $16,650; part-time $925 per credit hour. Tuition, nonresident: full-time $37,350; part-time $2075 per credit hour. *International tuition:* $37,350 full-time. *Required fees:* $2412.

Princeton University, Princeton Institute for the Science and Technology of Materials (PRISM), Princeton, NJ 08544-1019. Offers materials (PhD).

University of Arkansas, Graduate School, Interdisciplinary Program in Microelectronics and Photonics, Fayetteville, AR 72701. Offers MS, PhD. *Students:* 31 full-time (10 women), 26 part-time (8 women); includes 7 minority (2 Black or African American, non-Hispanic/Latino; 1 Asian, non-Hispanic/Latino; 4 Hispanic/Latino), 31 international. 12 applicants, 100% accepted. In 2019, 5 master's, 8 doctorates awarded. *Application deadline:* For fall admission, 8/1 for domestic students, 4/1 for international students; for spring admission, 12/1 for domestic students, 10/1 for international students; for summer admission, 4/15 for domestic students, 3/1 for international students. Applications are processed on a rolling basis. Application fee: $60. Electronic applications accepted. *Financial support:* In 2019–20, 25 research assistantships, 4 teaching assistantships were awarded; fellowships with tuition reimbursements also available. Financial award application deadline: 4/1; financial award applicants required to submit FAFSA. *Unit head:* Dr. Rick Wise, Director, 479-575-2875, E-mail: rickwise@uark.edu. *Application contact:* Dr. Rick Wise, Director, 479-575-2875, E-mail: rickwise@uark.edu.
Website: https://microelectronics-photonics.uark.edu/

University of Memphis, Graduate School, Herff College of Engineering, Department of Engineering Technology, Memphis, TN 38152. Offers applied lean leadership (Graduate Certificate); engineering technology (MS). *Program availability:* Part-time, evening/weekend. *Students:* 2 full-time (1 woman), 4 part-time (0 women); includes 2 minority (both Black or African American, non-Hispanic/Latino). Average age 32. 3 applicants, 100% accepted, 1 enrolled. In 2019, 1 master's, 3 other advanced degrees awarded. *Degree requirements:* For master's, comprehensive exam, thesis optional. *Entrance requirements:* For master's, GRE General Test, GMAT, MAT, three letters of recommendation; for Graduate Certificate, letter of intent. Additional exam requirements/recommendations for international students: required—TOEFL (minimum score 550 paper-based; 70 iBT). *Application deadline:* For fall admission, 8/1 for domestic students; for spring admission, 12/1 for domestic students. Applications are processed on a rolling basis. Application fee: $35 ($60 for international students). Electronic applications accepted. *Expenses: Tuition, area resident:* Full-time $9216; part-time $512 per credit hour. Tuition, state resident: full-time $9216; part-time $512 per credit hour. Tuition, nonresident: full-time $12,672; part-time $704 per credit hour. *International tuition:* $16,128 full-time. *Required fees:* $1530; $85 per credit hour. Tuition and fees vary according to program. *Financial support:* Research assistantships with full tuition reimbursements, career-related internships or fieldwork, Federal Work-Study, scholarships/grants, and unspecified assistantships available. Financial award application deadline: 2/1; financial award applicants required to submit FAFSA. *Unit head:* Scott Southall, Chair, 901-678-3980, Fax: 901-678-4180, E-mail: ssouthll@memphis.edu. *Application contact:* Carl Williams, Graduate Program Coordinator, 901-678-3320, Fax: 901-678-4180, E-mail: crwillia@memphis.edu.
Website: http://www.memphis.edu/et

Wayne State University, College of Engineering, Division of Engineering Technology, Detroit, MI 48202. Offers MSET. *Faculty:* 5. *Students:* 8 full-time (0 women), 5 part-time (0 women); includes 4 minority (3 Black or African American, non-Hispanic/Latino; 1 Asian, non-Hispanic/Latino), 5 international. Average age 31. 13 applicants, 69% accepted, 2 enrolled. In 2019, 11 master's awarded. *Degree requirements:* For master's, thesis (for some programs), project. *Entrance requirements:* For master's, bachelor's degree in engineering technology or related field with minimum GPA of 3.0, 2 letters of recommendation, preliminary proposal for intended plan of study, resume (optional). Additional exam requirements/recommendations for international students: required—TOEFL (minimum score 550 paper-based; 79 iBT), TWE (minimum score 5.5), Michigan English Language Assessment Battery (minimum score 85); recommended—IELTS (minimum score 6.5). *Application deadline:* For fall admission, 6/1 priority date for domestic students, 5/1 priority date for international students; for winter admission, 10/1 priority date for domestic students, 9/1 priority date for international students; for spring admission, 2/1 priority date for domestic students, 1/1 priority date for international students. Applications are processed on a rolling basis. Application fee: $50. Electronic applications accepted. *Expenses:* $790 per credit hour in-state tuition, $1579 per credit hour out-of-state tuition. MS is 30 credit hours. *Financial support:* In 2019–20, 3 students received support. Career-related internships or fieldwork and scholarships/grants available. Financial award applicants required to submit FAFSA. *Unit head:* Dr. Ece Yaprak, Division Chair, 313-577-0875, E-mail: yaprak@eng.wayne.edu. *Application contact:* Rob Carlson, Graduate Program Coordinator, 313-577-9615, E-mail: rcarlson@wayne.edu.
Website: http://engineering.wayne.edu/et/

Materials Engineering

Alabama Agricultural and Mechanical University, School of Graduate Studies, College of Engineering, Technology, and Physical Sciences, Department of Mechanical and Civil Engineering, Huntsville, AL 35811. Offers material engineering (M Eng), including civil engineering, mechanical engineering.

Arizona State University at Tempe, Ira A. Fulton Schools of Engineering, School for Engineering of Matter, Transport and Energy, Tempe, AZ 85281. Offers aerospace engineering (MS, PhD); chemical engineering (MS, PhD); materials science and engineering (MS, PhD); mechanical engineering (MS, PhD); solar energy engineering and commercialization (PSM). *Program availability:* Part-time, evening/weekend, online learning. Terminal master's awarded for partial completion of doctoral program. *Degree requirements:* For master's, thesis and oral defense (MS); applied project or comprehensive exam (MSE); interactive Program of Study (iPOS) submitted before completing 50 percent of required credit hours; for doctorate, comprehensive exam, thesis/dissertation, interactive Program of Study (iPOS) submitted before completing 50 percent of required credit hours. *Entrance requirements:* For master's, GRE, minimum GPA of 3.0 or equivalent in last 2 years of work leading to bachelor's degree; for doctorate, GRE, minimum GPA of 3.0 in last 2 years of work leading to bachelor's degree. Additional exam requirements/recommendations for international students: required—TOEFL, IELTS, or PTE. Electronic applications accepted. *Expenses:* Contact institution.

Auburn University, Graduate School, Samuel Ginn College of Engineering, Department of Mechanical Engineering, Program in Materials Engineering, Auburn University, AL 36849. Offers M Mtl E, MS, PhD. *Faculty:* 42 full-time (1 woman), 4 part-time/adjunct (0 women). *Students:* 41 full-time (6 women), 15 part-time (6 women); includes 3 minority (2 Black or African American, non-Hispanic/Latino; 1 Hispanic/Latino), 41 international. Average age 30. 38 applicants, 71% accepted, 3 enrolled. In 2019, 19 master's, 2 doctorates awarded. *Degree requirements:* For master's, thesis, thesis (MS), oral exam; for doctorate, one foreign language, thesis/dissertation. *Entrance requirements:* For master's and doctorate, GRE General Test. Additional exam requirements/recommendations for international students: required—TOEFL (minimum score 550 paper-based; 79 iBT). *Application deadline:* Applications are processed on a rolling basis. Application fee: $60 ($70 for international students). Electronic applications accepted. *Expenses: Tuition, area resident:* Full-time $9828; part-time $546 per credit hour. Tuition, state resident: full-time $9828; part-time $546 per credit hour. Tuition, nonresident: full-time $29,484; part-time $1638 per credit hour. *International tuition:* $29,744 full-time. Tuition and fees vary according to course load, program and reciprocity agreements. *Financial support:* Fellowships, research assistantships, teaching assistantships, and Federal Work-Study available. Support available to part-time students. Financial award application deadline: 3/15; financial award applicants required to submit FAFSA. *Unit head:* Dr. Bart Prorok, Interim Program Chair, 334-844-4733, E-mail: prorobc@auburn.edu. *Application contact:* Dr. George Flowers, Dean of the Graduate School, 334-844-2125.
Website: http://www.eng.auburn.edu/matl/

Binghamton University, State University of New York, Graduate School, Materials Science and Engineering Program, Binghamton, NY 13902-6000. Offers MS, PhD. *Program availability:* Part-time, online learning. *Degree requirements:* For master's, thesis; for doctorate, comprehensive exam, thesis/dissertation. *Entrance requirements:* For master's and doctorate, GRE General Test. Additional exam requirements/

recommendations for international students: required—TOEFL (minimum score 550 paper-based; 80 iBT). Electronic applications accepted. *Expenses:* Contact institution.

Boise State University, College of Engineering, Micron School of Materials Science and Engineering, Boise, ID 83725-0399. Offers materials science and engineering (M Engr, MS, PhD). *Students:* 53 full-time (17 women), 11 part-time (3 women); includes 14 minority (1 Black or African American, non-Hispanic/Latino; 3 Asian, non-Hispanic/Latino; 7 Hispanic/Latino; 3 Two or more races, non-Hispanic/Latino), 9 international. Terminal master's awarded for partial completion of doctoral program. *Degree requirements:* For master's, comprehensive exam, thesis (for some programs). *Entrance requirements:* For master's, GRE General Test. Additional exam requirements/recommendations for international students: required—TOEFL, IELTS. Electronic applications accepted. *Expenses: Tuition, area resident:* Full-time $7110; part-time $470 per credit hour. Tuition, state resident: full-time $7110; part-time $470 per credit hour. Tuition, nonresident: full-time $24,030; part-time $827 per credit hour. *International tuition:* $827 full-time. *Required fees:* $2536. Tuition and fees vary according to course load and program. *Financial support:* Research assistantships, scholarships/grants, and unspecified assistantships available. Financial award applicants required to submit FAFSA. *Unit head:* Dr. Will Hughes, Director, 208-426-4859, E-mail: willhughes@boisestate.edu. *Application contact:* Jessica Economy, Academic Program Manager, 208-426-4896, E-mail: msegrad@boisestate.edu.
Website: https://www.boisestate.edu/coen-materials/

Boston University, College of Engineering, Division of Materials Science and Engineering, Brookline, MA 02215. Offers materials science and engineering (M Eng, MS, PhD). *Program availability:* Part-time. *Students:* 80 full-time (31 women), 21 part-time (6 women); includes 9 minority (1 Black or African American, non-Hispanic/Latino; 5 Asian, non-Hispanic/Latino; 3 Two or more races, non-Hispanic/Latino), 65 international. Average age 25. 379 applicants, 51% accepted, 35 enrolled. In 2019, 25 master's, 5 doctorates awarded. Terminal master's awarded for partial completion of doctoral program. *Degree requirements:* For master's, thesis (for some programs); for doctorate, comprehensive exam, thesis/dissertation. *Entrance requirements:* For master's and doctorate, GRE General Test. Additional exam requirements/recommendations for international students: required—TOEFL (minimum score 90 iBT), IELTS (minimum score 7). Application fee: $95. *Financial support:* Application deadline: 1/15. *Unit head:* Dr. David Bishop, Division Head, 617-353-8899, Fax: 617-353-5548, E-mail: djb1@bu.edu. *Application contact:* Dr. David Bishop, Division Head, 617-353-8899, Fax: 617-353-5548, E-mail: djb1@bu.edu.
Website: http://www.bu.edu/mse/

California State University, Northridge, Graduate Studies, College of Engineering and Computer Science, Department of Manufacturing Systems Engineering and Management, Northridge, CA 91330. Offers engineering automation (MS); engineering management (MS); manufacturing systems engineering (MS); materials engineering (MS). *Program availability:* Online learning. *Entrance requirements:* For master's, GRE (if cumulative undergraduate GPA less than 3.0).

Carleton University, Faculty of Graduate Studies, Faculty of Engineering and Design, Department of Mechanical and Aerospace Engineering, Ottawa, ON K1S 5B6, Canada. Offers aerospace engineering (M Eng, MA Sc, PhD); materials engineering (M Eng, MA Sc); mechanical engineering (M Eng, MA Sc, PhD). *Degree requirements:* For master's, thesis optional; for doctorate, thesis/dissertation. *Entrance requirements:* For master's, honors degree; for doctorate, MA Sc or M Eng. Additional exam requirements/recommendations for international students: required—TOEFL.

Carnegie Mellon University, Carnegie Institute of Technology, Department of Materials Science and Engineering, Pittsburgh, PA 15213-3891. Offers MS, PhD. *Program availability:* Part-time. Terminal master's awarded for partial completion of doctoral program. *Degree requirements:* For master's, exam; for doctorate, thesis/dissertation, qualifying exam. *Entrance requirements:* For master's and doctorate, GRE General Test. Additional exam requirements/recommendations for international students: required—TOEFL.

Case Western Reserve University, School of Graduate Studies, Case School of Engineering, Department of Materials Science and Engineering, Cleveland, OH 44106. Offers materials science and engineering (MS, PhD). *Program availability:* Part-time, online learning. Terminal master's awarded for partial completion of doctoral program. *Degree requirements:* For master's, thesis (for some programs); for doctorate, thesis/dissertation, qualifying exam, teaching experience. *Entrance requirements:* For master's and doctorate, GRE General Test. Additional exam requirements/recommendations for international students: required—TOEFL.

The Catholic University of America, School of Engineering, Department of Materials Science and Engineering, Washington, DC 20064. Offers MS. *Program availability:* Part-time. *Faculty:* 1 full-time (0 women), 3 part-time/adjunct (2 women). *Students:* 3 full-time (2 women), 5 part-time (3 women); includes 1 minority (Black or African American, non-Hispanic/Latino), 4 international. Average age 26. 9 applicants, 78% accepted, 3 enrolled. *Degree requirements:* For master's, thesis optional. *Entrance requirements:* For master's, GRE (minimum score 1250), minimum GPA of 3.0, statement of purpose, official copies of academic transcripts. Additional exam requirements/recommendations for international students: required—TOEFL (minimum score 550 paper-based; 80 iBT). *Application deadline:* For fall admission, 7/15 for domestic students, 7/1 for international students; for spring admission, 11/15 for domestic students, 11/1 for international students. Applications are processed on a rolling basis. Application fee: $55. Electronic applications accepted. *Expenses:* Contact institution. *Financial support:* Fellowships, research assistantships, teaching assistantships, Federal Work-Study, scholarships/grants, tuition waivers (full and partial), and unspecified assistantships available. Financial award application deadline: 2/1; financial award applicants required to submit FAFSA. *Unit head:* Mel Williams, Director, 202-319-5191, Fax: 202-319-4469, E-mail: williamsme@cua.edu. *Application contact:* Dr. Steven Brown, Director of Graduate Admissions, 202-319-5057, Fax: 202-319-6533, E-mail: cua-admissions@cua.edu.
Website: https://engineering.catholic.edu/materials-science/index.html

Clarkson University, Wallace H. Coulter School of Engineering, Program in Materials Science and Engineering, Potsdam, NY 13699. Offers PhD. *Students:* 5 full-time (1 woman); includes 1 minority (Asian, non-Hispanic/Latino), 3 international. 18 applicants, 50% accepted, 1 enrolled. In 2019, 2 doctorates awarded. *Degree requirements:* For doctorate, comprehensive exam, thesis/dissertation. *Entrance requirements:* For doctorate, GRE. Additional exam requirements/recommendations for international students: required—TOEFL (minimum score 550 paper-based, 80 iBT) or IELTS (6.5). *Application deadline:* Applications are processed on a rolling basis. Application fee: $50. Electronic applications accepted. *Expenses: Tuition:* Full-time $24,984; part-time $1388. *Required fees:* $225. Tuition and fees vary according to campus/location and program. *Financial support:* Scholarships/grants and unspecified assistantships available. *Unit head:* Dr. Silvana Andreescu, Professor / Egon Matijevic Chair of Chemistry / Co-Director of CAMP, 315-268-2394, E-mail: wjemison@clarkson.edu. *Application contact:* Daniel Capogna, Director of Graduate Admissions & Recruitment, 518-631-9910, E-mail: graduate@clarkson.edu.
Website: https://www.clarkson.edu/academics/graduate

Clemson University, Graduate School, College of Engineering, Computing and Applied Sciences, Department of Materials Science and Engineering, Clemson, SC 29634. Offers MS, PhD. *Faculty:* 20 full-time (4 women), 2 part-time/adjunct (0 women). *Students:* 61 full-time (20 women), 6 part-time (1 woman); includes 2 minority (1 Asian, non-Hispanic/Latino; 1 Hispanic/Latino), 38 international. Average age 26. 105 applicants, 82% accepted, 22 enrolled. In 2019, 6 master's, 8 doctorates awarded. *Expenses: Tuition, area resident:* Full-time $10,600; part-time $8688 per semester. Tuition, state resident: full-time $10,600; part-time $8688 per semester. Tuition, nonresident: full-time $22,050; part-time $17,412 per semester. *International tuition:* $22,050 full-time. *Required fees:* $1196; $617 per semester. $617 per semester. Tuition and fees vary according to course load, degree level, campus/location and program. *Financial support:* In 2019–20, 79 students received support, including 13 fellowships with full and partial tuition reimbursements available (averaging $3,877 per year), 43 research assistantships with full and partial tuition reimbursements available (averaging $20,249 per year); career-related internships or fieldwork and unspecified assistantships also available. *Unit head:* Dr. Kyle Brinkman, Department Chair, 864-656-1405, E-mail: ksbrink@clemson.edu. *Application contact:* Dr. Igor Luzinov, Graduate Program Coordinator, 864-656-5958, E-mail: luzinov@clemson.edu.
Website: https://www.clemson.edu/cecas/departments/mse/index.html

Colorado School of Mines, Office of Graduate Studies, Department of Metallurgical and Materials Engineering, Golden, CO 80401. Offers materials science (MS, PhD); metallurgical and materials engineering (ME, MS, PhD). *Program availability:* Part-time. *Degree requirements:* For master's, thesis (for some programs); for doctorate, comprehensive exam, thesis/dissertation. *Entrance requirements:* For master's and doctorate, GRE General Test. Additional exam requirements/recommendations for international students: required—TOEFL (minimum score 550 paper-based; 79 iBT). Electronic applications accepted. *Expenses:* Tuition, state resident: full-time $16,650; part-time $925 per credit hour. Tuition, nonresident: full-time $37,350; part-time $2075 per credit hour. *International tuition:* $37,350 full-time. *Required fees:* $2412.

Columbia University, Fu Foundation School of Engineering and Applied Science, Department of Applied Physics and Applied Mathematics, New York, NY 10027. Offers applied mathematics (MS, Eng Sc D, PhD); applied physics (MS, Eng Sc D, PhD); materials science and engineering (MS, Eng Sc D, PhD); medical physics (MS). *Program availability:* Part-time, online learning. Terminal master's awarded for partial completion of doctoral program. *Degree requirements:* For master's, comprehensive exam; for doctorate, thesis/dissertation, qualifying exam. *Entrance requirements:* For master's, GRE General Test, GRE Subject Test (strongly recommended); for doctorate, GRE General Test, GRE Subject Test (applied physics). Additional exam requirements/recommendations for international students: required—TOEFL, IELTS, PTE. Electronic applications accepted. *Expenses: Tuition:* Full-time $47,600; part-time $1880 per credit. One-time fee: $105.

Cornell University, Graduate School, Graduate Fields of Engineering, Field of Materials Science and Engineering, Ithaca, NY 14853. Offers materials engineering (M Eng, PhD); materials science (M Eng, PhD). *Degree requirements:* For doctorate, comprehensive exam, thesis/dissertation. *Entrance requirements:* For master's and doctorate, GRE General Test, 3 letters of recommendation. Additional exam requirements/recommendations for international students: required—TOEFL (minimum score 550 paper-based; 77 iBT). Electronic applications accepted.

Dartmouth College, Dartmouth Engineering - Thayer School of Engineering, Program in Materials Engineering, Hanover, NH 03755. Offers MS, PhD. Terminal master's awarded for partial completion of doctoral program. *Degree requirements:* For master's, thesis (for some programs); for doctorate, thesis/dissertation. *Entrance requirements:* For master's and doctorate, GRE General Test. Additional exam requirements/recommendations for international students: required—TOEFL, IELTS. *Application deadline:* For fall admission, 1/1 priority date for domestic students, 1/1 for international students. Applications are processed on a rolling basis. Application fee: $45. Electronic applications accepted. *Financial support:* Fellowships, research assistantships, teaching assistantships, career-related internships or fieldwork, institutionally sponsored loans, scholarships/grants, and tuition waivers (full and partial) available. Financial award application deadline: 2/15; financial award applicants required to submit CSS PROFILE. *Unit head:* Dr. Ian Baker, Sherman Fairchild Professor of Engineering, 603-646-2184, E-mail: ian.baker@dartmouth.edu. *Application contact:* Candace S. Potter, Graduate Admissions & Financial Aid Administrator, 603-646-3844, Fax: 603-646-1620, E-mail: candace.s.potter@dartmouth.edu.
Website: https://engineering.dartmouth.edu/

Drexel University, College of Engineering, Department of Materials Engineering, Philadelphia, PA 19104-2875. Offers MS, PhD. *Program availability:* Part-time, evening/weekend. Terminal master's awarded for partial completion of doctoral program. *Degree requirements:* For master's, thesis or alternative; for doctorate, thesis/dissertation. *Entrance requirements:* For master's, minimum GPA of 3.0; for doctorate, minimum GPA of 3.0, MS. Additional exam requirements/recommendations for international students: required—TOEFL. Electronic applications accepted.

Duke University, Graduate School, Pratt School of Engineering, Master of Engineering Program, Durham, NC 27708-0271. Offers biomedical engineering (M Eng); civil engineering (M Eng); computational mechanics and scientific computing (M Eng); electrical and computer engineering (M Eng); environmental engineering (M Eng); materials science and engineering (M Eng); mechanical engineering (M Eng); photonics and optical sciences (M Eng); risk engineering (M Eng). *Program availability:* Part-time. *Entrance requirements:* For master's, GRE General Test, resume, 3 letters of recommendation, statement of purpose, transcripts. Additional exam requirements/recommendations for international students: required—TOEFL. Electronic applications accepted.

Florida International University, College of Engineering and Computing, Department of Mechanical and Materials Engineering, Miami, FL 33199. Offers materials science and engineering (MS, PhD); mechanical engineering (MS, PhD). *Program availability:* Part-time, evening/weekend. *Faculty:* 22 full-time (5 women), 5 part-time/adjunct (1 woman). *Students:* 62 full-time (10 women), 11 part-time (4 women); includes 27 minority (4 Black or African American, non-Hispanic/Latino; 3 Asian, non-Hispanic/Latino; 17 Hispanic/Latino; 3 Two or more races, non-Hispanic/Latino), 43 international. Average age 29. 136 applicants, 51% accepted, 21 enrolled. In 2019, 11 master's, 8 doctorates awarded. Terminal master's awarded for partial completion of doctoral program. *Degree requirements:* For master's, thesis or alternative; for doctorate, comprehensive exam, thesis/dissertation. *Entrance requirements:* For master's, GRE (depending on program), 3 letters of recommendation, minimum undergraduate GPA of 3.0 in upper-level course work; for doctorate, GRE (minimum combined score of 1150, verbal 450, quantitative 650), minimum undergraduate GPA of 3.0 in upper-level coursework with BS, 3.3 with MS; 3 letters of recommendation; letter of intent. Additional exam requirements/recommendations for international students: required—TOEFL (minimum score 550 paper-based; 80 iBT) or IELTS (minimum score 6.5). *Application deadline:* For fall admission, 6/1 for domestic students, 4/1 for international students; for spring admission, 10/1 for domestic students, 9/1 for international students. Applications are processed on a rolling basis. Application fee: $30. Electronic applications accepted. *Expenses: Tuition, area resident:* Full-time $8912; part-time $446 per credit hour.

Tuition, state resident: full-time $8912; part-time $446 per credit hour. Tuition, nonresident: full-time $21,393; part-time $992 per credit hour. *Required fees:* $2194. *Financial support:* Institutionally sponsored loans, scholarships/grants, and unspecified assistantships available. Financial award application deadline: 3/1; financial award applicants required to submit FAFSA. *Unit head:* Dr. ARVIND AGARWAL, Chair, 305-348-1701, Fax: 305-348-1932, E-mail: Arvind.Agarwal@fiu.edu. *Application contact:* Nanett Rojas, Manager, Admissions Operations, 305-348-7464, Fax: 305-348-7441, E-mail: gradadm@fiu.edu.
Website: http://cec.fiu.edu

Florida State University, The Graduate School, Materials Science and Engineering Program, Tallahassee, FL 32310. Offers MS, PhD. *Faculty:* 34 full-time (5 women). *Students:* 14 full-time (7 women), 9 international. Average age 25. 48 applicants, 23% accepted, 2 enrolled. In 2019, 2 doctorates awarded. Terminal master's awarded for partial completion of doctoral program. *Degree requirements:* For master's, thesis; for doctorate, comprehensive exam, thesis/dissertation. *Entrance requirements:* For master's and doctorate, GRE General Test (minimum new format 55th percentile Verbal, 75th percentile Quantitative, old version 1100 combined Verbal and Quantitative), minimum GPA of 3.0, 3 letters of recommendation. Additional exam requirements/recommendations for international students: required—TOEFL (minimum score 80 iBT). *Application deadline:* For fall admission, 5/1 for domestic and international students; for spring admission, 9/1 for domestic and international students; for summer admission, 1/1 for domestic and international students. Applications are processed on a rolling basis. Application fee: $30. Electronic applications accepted. *Financial support:* In 2019–20, 13 students received support, including 12 research assistantships with full tuition reimbursements available (averaging $20,000 per year); partial payment of required health insurance also available. Financial award application deadline: 12/15. *Unit head:* Prof. Eric Hellstrom, Director, 850-645-7489, Fax: 850-645-7754, E-mail: hellstrom@asc.magnet.fsu.edu. *Application contact:* Stephanie Salters, Admissions Coordinator, 850-645-8980, Fax: 850-645-9123, E-mail: salters@eng.famu.fsu.edu.
Website: http://materials.fsu.edu

Georgia Institute of Technology, Graduate Studies, College of Engineering, School of Materials Science and Engineering, Atlanta, GA 30332. Offers MS, PhD. *Program availability:* Part-time. *Faculty:* 32 full-time (6 women), 1 part-time/adjunct. *Students:* 166 full-time (65 women), 20 part-time (3 women); includes 35 minority (3 Black or African American, non-Hispanic/Latino; 20 Asian, non-Hispanic/Latino; 7 Hispanic/Latino; 5 Two or more races, non-Hispanic/Latino), 71 international. Average age 26. 401 applicants, 22% accepted, 38 enrolled. In 2019, 10 master's, 28 doctorates awarded. Terminal master's awarded for partial completion of doctoral program. *Degree requirements:* For master's, thesis optional; for doctorate, comprehensive exam, thesis/dissertation, teaching assignment. *Entrance requirements:* For master's and doctorate, GRE General Test. Additional exam requirements/recommendations for international students: required—TOEFL (minimum score 100 iBT), IELTS, TOEFL is the preferred method with the requirements shown on the programs. *Application deadline:* For fall admission, 12/15 priority date for domestic students, 12/15 for international students; for spring admission, 10/1 for domestic students; for summer admission, 2/1 for domestic students. Applications are processed on a rolling basis. Application fee: $75 ($85 for international students). Electronic applications accepted. *Expenses: Tuition, area resident:* Full-time $14,064; part-time $586 per credit hour. Tuition, state resident: full-time $14,064; part-time $586 per credit hour. Tuition, nonresident: full-time $29,140; part-time $1215 per credit hour. *International tuition:* $29,140 full-time. *Required fees:* $2024; $840 per semester. $2096. Tuition and fees vary according to course load. *Financial support:* In 2019–20, 20 fellowships with tuition reimbursements, 123 research assistantships with tuition reimbursements were awarded; teaching assistantships, career-related internships or fieldwork, Federal Work-Study, institutionally sponsored loans, traineeships, tuition waivers (full and partial), and unspecified assistantships also available. Support available to part-time students. Financial award application deadline: 7/1; financial award applicants required to submit FAFSA. *Unit head:* Naresh Thadhani, School Chair, 404-894-2888, Fax: 404-894-9140, E-mail: naresh.thadhani@mse.gatech.edu. *Application contact:* Marla Bruner, Director of Graduate Studies, 404-894-1610, Fax: 404-894-1609, E-mail: gradinfo@mail.gatech.edu.
Website: http://www.mse.gatech.edu

Illinois Institute of Technology, Graduate College, Armour College of Engineering, Department of Mechanical, Materials and Aerospace Engineering, Chicago, IL 60616. Offers manufacturing engineering (MAS, MS); materials science and engineering (MAS, MS, PhD); mechanical and aerospace engineering (MAS, MS, PhD), including economics (MS), energy (MS), environment (MS). *Program availability:* Part-time, evening/weekend, online learning. Terminal master's awarded for partial completion of doctoral program. *Degree requirements:* For master's, comprehensive exam (for some programs), thesis (for some programs); for doctorate, comprehensive exam, thesis/dissertation. *Entrance requirements:* For master's and doctorate, GRE General Test (minimum score 1000 Quantitative and Verbal, 3.0 Analytical Writing), minimum undergraduate GPA of 3.0. Additional exam requirements/recommendations for international students: required—TOEFL (minimum score 550 paper-based; 80 iBT). Electronic applications accepted.

Instituto Tecnológico y de Estudios Superiores de Monterrey, Campus Estado de México, Professional and Graduate Division, Estado de Mexico, Mexico. Offers administration of information technologies (MITA); architecture (M Arch); business administration (GMBA, MBA); computer sciences (MCS, PhD); education (M Ed); educational institution administration (MAD); educational technology and innovation (PhD); electronic commerce (MEC); environmental systems (MS); finance (MAF); humanistic studies (MHS); information sciences and knowledge management (MISKM); information systems (MS); manufacturing systems (MS); marketing (MEM); quality systems and productivity (MS); science and materials engineering (PhD); telecommunications management (MTM). *Program availability:* Part-time, online learning. *Degree requirements:* For master's, one foreign language, thesis (for some programs); for doctorate, one foreign language, thesis/dissertation. *Entrance requirements:* For master's, E-PAEP 500, interview; for doctorate, E-PAEP 500, research proposal. Additional exam requirements/recommendations for international students: required—TOEFL (minimum score 550 paper-based).

Iowa State University of Science and Technology, Department of Materials Science and Engineering, Ames, IA 50011. Offers M Eng, MS, PhD. *Entrance requirements:* For master's and doctorate, GRE General Test. Additional exam requirements/recommendations for international students: required—TOEFL (minimum score 550 paper-based; 79 iBT), IELTS (minimum score 6.5). Electronic applications accepted.

Johns Hopkins University, Engineering Program for Professionals, Part-time Program in Materials Science and Engineering, Baltimore, MD 21218. Offers nanotechnology (M Mat SE). *Program availability:* Part-time, evening/weekend. *Entrance requirements:* Additional exam requirements/recommendations for international students: required—TOEFL (minimum score 600 paper-based; 100 iBT). Electronic applications accepted.

Johns Hopkins University, G. W. C. Whiting School of Engineering, Department of Materials Science and Engineering, Baltimore, MD 21218. Offers M Mat SE, MSE, PhD. Terminal master's awarded for partial completion of doctoral program. *Degree requirements:* For master's, thesis; for doctorate, thesis/dissertation, oral exam, thesis defense. *Entrance requirements:* For master's and doctorate, GRE General Test, 2 letters of recommendation, statement of purpose, transcripts. Additional exam requirements/recommendations for international students: required—TOEFL (minimum score 600 paper-based, 100 iBT) or IELTS (7). Electronic applications accepted.

Johns Hopkins University, G. W. C. Whiting School of Engineering, Master of Science in Engineering Management Program, Baltimore, MD 21218. Offers biomaterials (MSEM); civil engineering (MSEM); communications science (MSEM); computer science (MSEM); environmental systems analysis, economics and public policy (MSEM); fluid mechanics (MSEM); materials science and engineering (MSEM); mechanical engineering (MSEM); mechanics and materials (MSEM); nanobiotechnology (MSEM); nanomaterials and nanotechnology (MSEM); operations research (MSEM); probability and statistics (MSEM); smart product and device design (MSEM). *Entrance requirements:* For master's, GRE, 3 letters of recommendation, statement of purpose, transcripts. Additional exam requirements/recommendations for international students: required—TOEFL (minimum score 600 paper-based, 100 iBT) or IELTS (7). Electronic applications accepted.

Lehigh University, P.C. Rossin College of Engineering and Applied Science, Department of Materials Science and Engineering, Bethlehem, PA 18015. Offers materials science and engineering (M Eng, MS, PhD); photonics (MS); polymer science/engineering (M Eng, MS, PhD); MBA/E. *Program availability:* Part-time. *Faculty:* 14 full-time (4 women). *Students:* 30 full-time (6 women), 2 part-time (both women); includes 3 minority (1 Asian, non-Hispanic/Latino; 1 Hispanic/Latino; 1 Two or more races, non-Hispanic/Latino), 8 international. Average age 26. 91 applicants, 22% accepted, 10 enrolled. In 2019, 3 master's, 5 doctorates awarded. *Degree requirements:* For master's, thesis; for doctorate, comprehensive exam, thesis/dissertation. *Entrance requirements:* For master's and doctorate, GRE General Test, minimum GPA of 3.60. Additional exam requirements/recommendations for international students: required—TOEFL (minimum score 487 paper-based; 85 iBT), IELTS (minimum score 6.5), TOEFL or IELTS required. *Application deadline:* For fall admission, 1/15 priority date for domestic students, 1/15 for international students; for spring admission, 12/1 priority date for domestic students, 12/1 for international students. Application fee: $75. *Financial support:* In 2019–20, 26 students received support, including 12 fellowships with tuition reimbursements available (averaging $30,540 per year), 25 research assistantships with tuition reimbursements available (averaging $30,540 per year), 12 teaching assistantships with tuition reimbursements available (averaging $10,890 per year); scholarships/grants and health care benefits also available. Financial award application deadline: 1/15. *Unit head:* Dr. Wojciech Misiolek, Chairperson, 610-758-4252, Fax: 610-758-4244, E-mail: wzm2@lehigh.edu. *Application contact:* Lisa Carreras Arechiga, Graduate Administrative Coordinator, 610-758-4222, Fax: 610-758-4244, E-mail: lia4@lehigh.edu.
Website: https://engineering.lehigh.edu/matsci

Massachusetts Institute of Technology, School of Engineering, Department of Civil and Environmental Engineering, Cambridge, MA 02139. Offers biological oceanography (PhD, Sc D); chemical oceanography (PhD, Sc D); civil and environmental engineering (M Eng, SM, PhD, Sc D); civil and environmental systems (PhD, Sc D); civil engineering (PhD, Sc D, CE); civil engineering and computation (PhD); coastal engineering (PhD, Sc D); construction engineering and management (PhD, Sc D); environmental biology (PhD, Sc D); environmental chemistry (PhD, Sc D); environmental engineering (PhD, Sc D); environmental engineering and computation (PhD); environmental fluid mechanics (PhD, Sc D); geotechnical and geoenvironmental engineering (PhD, Sc D); hydrology (PhD, Sc D); information technology (PhD, Sc D); oceanographic engineering (PhD, Sc D); structures and materials (PhD, Sc D); transportation (PhD, Sc D); SM/MBA. *Degree requirements:* For master's, thesis; for doctorate, comprehensive exam, thesis/dissertation; for CE, comprehensive exam, thesis. *Entrance requirements:* For master's, doctorate, and CE, GRE General Test. Additional exam requirements/recommendations for international students: required—TOEFL, IELTS. Electronic applications accepted.

Massachusetts Institute of Technology, School of Engineering, Department of Materials Science and Engineering, Cambridge, MA 02139. Offers archaeological materials (PhD, Sc D); materials engineering (Mat E); materials science and engineering (SM, PhD, Sc D). *Degree requirements:* For master's, thesis; for doctorate, comprehensive exam, thesis/dissertation; for Mat E, comprehensive exam, thesis. *Entrance requirements:* For master's and doctorate, GRE General Test. Additional exam requirements/recommendations for international students: required—IELTS. Electronic applications accepted.

McGill University, Faculty of Graduate and Postdoctoral Studies, Faculty of Engineering, Department of Civil Engineering and Applied Mechanics, Montréal, QC H3A 2T5, Canada. Offers environmental engineering (M Eng, M Sc, PhD); fluid mechanics (M Sc); fluid mechanics and hydraulic engineering (M Eng, PhD); materials engineering (M Eng, PhD); rehabilitation of urban infrastructure (M Eng, PhD); soil behavior (M Eng, PhD); soil mechanics and foundations (M Eng, PhD); structures and structural mechanics (M Eng, PhD); water resources (M Sc); water resources engineering (M Eng, PhD).

McGill University, Faculty of Graduate and Postdoctoral Studies, Faculty of Engineering, Department of Mining and Materials Engineering, Montréal, QC H3A 2T5, Canada. Offers materials engineering (M Eng, PhD); mining engineering (M Eng, M Sc, PhD, Diploma).

McMaster University, School of Graduate Studies, Faculty of Engineering, Department of Materials Science and Engineering, Hamilton, ON L8S 4M2, Canada. Offers materials engineering (M Eng, MA Sc, PhD); materials science (M Eng, PhD). *Degree requirements:* For master's, thesis; for doctorate, comprehensive exam, thesis/dissertation. *Entrance requirements:* Additional exam requirements/recommendations for international students: required—TOEFL (minimum score 550 paper-based).

Michigan State University, The Graduate School, College of Engineering, Department of Chemical Engineering and Materials Science, East Lansing, MI 48824. Offers chemical engineering (MS, PhD); materials science and engineering (MS, PhD). *Entrance requirements:* Additional exam requirements/recommendations for international students: required—TOEFL. Electronic applications accepted.

Michigan Technological University, Graduate School, College of Engineering, Department of Materials Science and Engineering, Houghton, MI 49931. Offers MS, PhD. *Program availability:* Part-time, 100% online, blended/hybrid learning. *Faculty:* 30 full-time, 11 part-time/adjunct (3 women). *Students:* 31 full-time (10 women), 8 part-time (3 women); includes 2 minority (1 Hispanic/Latino; 1 Two or more races, non-Hispanic/Latino), 23 international. Average age 27. 140 applicants, 31% accepted, 9 enrolled. In 2019, 9 master's, 1 doctorate awarded. Terminal master's awarded for partial completion of doctoral program. *Degree requirements:* For master's, comprehensive exam (for some programs), thesis (for some programs); for doctorate, comprehensive exam, thesis/dissertation. *Entrance requirements:* For master's and doctorate, GRE (domestic students from ABET-accredited programs exempt), statement of purpose, personal statement, official transcripts, 3 letters of recommendation. Additional exam requirements/recommendations for international students: required—TOEFL (minimum score 79 iBT), IELTS (minimum score 6.5), TOEFL (minimum score 79 iBT) or IELTS (minimum score of 6.5). *Application deadline:* For fall admission, 2/1 priority date for

domestic and international students; for spring admission, 9/1 priority date for domestic and international students. Applications are processed on a rolling basis. Application fee: $0. Electronic applications accepted. *Expenses:* $1,212 per credit. *Financial support:* In 2019–20, 28 students received support, including 5 fellowships with tuition reimbursements available (averaging $16,590 per year), 17 research assistantships with tuition reimbursements available (averaging $16,590 per year); teaching assistantships, career-related internships or fieldwork, Federal Work-Study, scholarships/grants, health care benefits, unspecified assistantships, and cooperative program also available. Financial award applicants required to submit FAFSA. *Unit head:* Dr. Stephen L. Kampe, Chair, 906-487-2036, Fax: 906-487-2934, E-mail: kampe@mtu.edu. *Application contact:* Valentina O'Kane, Department Coordinator, 906-487-4326, Fax: 906-487-2934, E-mail: vokane@mtu.edu.
Website: http://www.mtu.edu/materials/

Missouri University of Science and Technology, Department of Materials Science and Engineering, Rolla, MO 65401. Offers ceramic engineering (MS, PhD); materials science and engineering (MS, PhD); metallurgical engineering (MS, PhD). *Degree requirements:* For master's, thesis optional; for doctorate, comprehensive exam. *Entrance requirements:* For master's, GRE (minimum combined score 1100, 600 verbal, 3.5 writing); for doctorate, GRE (minimum score: quantitative 600, writing 3.5). Additional exam requirements/recommendations for international students: required—TOEFL (minimum score 570 paper-based). Electronic applications accepted. *Expenses:* Tuition, state resident: full-time $7839; part-time $435.50 per credit hour. Tuition, nonresident: full-time $22,169; part-time $1231.60 per credit hour. *International tuition:* $18,156.60 full-time. *Required fees:* $649.76. One-time fee: $119. Tuition and fees vary according to course load and program.

New Jersey Institute of Technology, College of Science and Liberal Arts, Newark, NJ 07102. Offers applied mathematics (MS); applied physics (MS, PhD); applied statistics (MS, Certificate); biology (MS, PhD); biostatistics (MS); chemistry (MS, PhD); environmental and sustainability policy (MS); environmental science (MS, PhD); history (MA, MAT); materials science and engineering (MS, PhD); mathematical and computational finance (MS); mathematical sciences (PhD); pharmaceutical chemistry (MS); professional and technical communications (MS); technical communication essentials (Certificate). *Program availability:* Part-time, evening/weekend. *Faculty:* 159 full-time (42 women), 156 part-time/adjunct (61 women). *Students:* 197 full-time (80 women), 58 part-time (14 women); includes 58 minority (18 Black or African American, non-Hispanic/Latino; 22 Asian, non-Hispanic/Latino; 16 Hispanic/Latino; 2 Two or more races, non-Hispanic/Latino), 130 international. Average age 29. 401 applicants, 63% accepted, 73 enrolled. In 2019, 54 master's, 10 doctorates, 1 other advanced degree awarded. Terminal master's awarded for partial completion of doctoral program. *Degree requirements:* For master's, thesis (for some programs); for doctorate, thesis/dissertation. *Entrance requirements:* For master's and doctorate, GRE General Test, Minimum GPA of 3.0, personal statement, 3 letters of recommendation, and transcripts. Additional exam requirements/recommendations for international students: required—TOEFL (minimum score 550 paper-based; 79 iBT), IELTS (minimum score 6.5). *Application deadline:* For fall admission, 6/1 priority date for domestic students, 5/1 priority date for international students; for spring admission, 11/15 priority date for domestic and international students. Applications are processed on a rolling basis. Application fee: $75. Electronic applications accepted. *Expenses:* $23,828 per year (in-state), $33,744 per year (out-of-state). *Financial support:* In 2019–20, 147 students received support, including 13 fellowships with full tuition reimbursements available (averaging $24,000 per year), 41 research assistantships with full tuition reimbursements available (averaging $24,000 per year), 87 teaching assistantships with full tuition reimbursements available (averaging $24,000 per year); scholarships/grants, traineeships, health care benefits, and unspecified assistantships also available. Financial award application deadline: 1/15. *Unit head:* Dr. Kevin Belfield, Dean, 973-596-3676, Fax: 973-565-0586, E-mail: kevin.d.belfield@njit.edu. *Application contact:* Stephen Eck, Director of Admissions, 973-596-3300, Fax: 973-596-3461, E-mail: admissions@njit.edu.
Website: http://csla.njit.edu/

New Mexico Institute of Mining and Technology, Center for Graduate Studies, Department of Materials Engineering, Socorro, NM 87801. Offers MS, PhD. *Degree requirements:* For master's, thesis; for doctorate, thesis/dissertation. *Entrance requirements:* For master's, GRE General Test; for doctorate, GRE General Test, GRE Subject Test. Additional exam requirements/recommendations for international students: required—TOEFL (minimum score 540 paper-based).

North Carolina State University, Graduate School, College of Engineering, Department of Materials Science and Engineering, Raleigh, NC 27695. Offers MMSE, MNAE, MS, PhD. *Degree requirements:* For master's, thesis; for doctorate, thesis/dissertation. Electronic applications accepted.

Northwestern University, McCormick School of Engineering and Applied Science, Department of Materials Science and Engineering, Evanston, IL 60208. Offers integrated computational materials engineering (Certificate); materials science and engineering (MS, PhD). *Program availability:* Part-time. Terminal master's awarded for partial completion of doctoral program. *Degree requirements:* For master's, thesis optional, oral thesis defense; for doctorate, comprehensive exam, thesis/dissertation, oral defense of dissertation, preliminary evaluation, qualifying exam. *Entrance requirements:* For master's and doctorate, GRE General Test. Additional exam requirements/recommendations for international students: required—TOEFL (minimum score 577 paper-based; 90 iBT), IELTS (minimum score 7). Electronic applications accepted.

The Ohio State University, Graduate School, College of Engineering, Department of Materials Science and Engineering, Columbus, OH 43210. Offers materials science and engineering (MS, PhD); welding engineering (MS, PhD). *Entrance requirements:* For master's and doctorate, GRE (for graduates of foreign universities and holders of non-engineering degrees). Additional exam requirements/recommendations for international students: required—TOEFL (minimum score 550 paper-based; 79 iBT), Michigan English Language Assessment Battery (minimum score 82); recommended—IELTS (minimum score 7). Electronic applications accepted.

Oklahoma State University, College of Engineering, Architecture and Technology, School of Materials Science and Engineering, Stillwater, OK 74078. Offers MS, PhD. *Faculty:* 6 full-time (0 women). *Students:* 5 full-time (3 women), 15 part-time (2 women); includes 3 minority (1 American Indian or Alaska Native, non-Hispanic/Latino; 2 Two or more races, non-Hispanic/Latino), 9 international. Average age 29. 13 applicants, 38% accepted, 3 enrolled. In 2019, 2 master's awarded. *Entrance requirements:* Additional exam requirements/recommendations for international students: required—TOEFL. *Application deadline:* For fall admission, 3/1 for domestic students; for spring admission, 8/1 for domestic students. Application fee: $50 ($75 for international students). Electronic applications accepted. *Expenses: Tuition, area resident:* Full-time $4148.10; part-time $2765.40. Tuition, state resident: full-time $4148.10; part-time $2765.40. Tuition, nonresident: full-time $15,775; part-time $10,516.80. *International tuition:* $15,775.20 full-time. *Required fees:* $2196.90; $122.05 per credit hour. Tuition and fees vary according to course load, campus/location and program. *Financial support:* In 2019–20, 9 teaching assistantships (averaging $1,665 per year) were awarded;

research assistantships also available. *Unit head:* Dr. Raman P Singh, Head, 918-594-8155, E-mail: raman.singh@okstate.edu. *Application contact:* Dr. Sheryl Tucker, Dean, 405-744-6368, Fax: 405-744-0355, E-mail: gradi@okstate.edu.
Website: https://ceat.okstate.edu/mse/degrees.html

Penn State University Park, Graduate School, Intercollege Graduate Programs, Intercollege Graduate Program in Materials Science and Engineering, University Park, PA 16802. Offers MS, PhD.

Portland State University, Graduate Studies, Maseeh College of Engineering and Computer Science, Department of Mechanical and Materials Engineering, Portland, OR 97207-0751. Offers mechanical engineering (PhD). *Program availability:* Part-time, evening/weekend. *Faculty:* 16 full-time (1 woman), 5 part-time/adjunct (0 women). *Students:* 36 full-time (9 women), 62 part-time (23 women); includes 30 minority (1 Black or African American, non-Hispanic/Latino; 13 Asian, non-Hispanic/Latino; 11 Hispanic/Latino; 5 Two or more races, non-Hispanic/Latino), 15 international. Average age 31. 53 applicants, 79% accepted, 23 enrolled. In 2019, 37 master's, 4 doctorates awarded. *Degree requirements:* For master's, thesis or alternative; for doctorate, one foreign language, thesis/dissertation, oral and written exams. *Entrance requirements:* For master's, minimum GPA of 3.0 in upper-division course work, BS in mechanical engineering or allied field, 3 letters of recommendation, statement of purpose, resume/curriculum vitae; for doctorate, GRE General Test, GRE Subject Test, MS, minimum GPA of 3.0 in upper-division course work, 3 letters of recommendation. Additional exam requirements/recommendations for international students: required—TOEFL (minimum score 550 paper-based; 80 iBT). *Application deadline:* For fall admission, 1/15 priority date for domestic and international students; for winter admission, 9/1 for domestic students, 8/1 for international students; for spring admission, 11/1 for domestic students, 10/1 for international students. Applications are processed on a rolling basis. Application fee: $65. Electronic applications accepted. *Expenses:* Contact institution. *Financial support:* In 2019–20, 30 students received support, including 6 research assistantships with full and partial tuition reimbursements available (averaging $13,066 per year), 16 teaching assistantships with full and partial tuition reimbursements available (averaging $7,530 per year); Federal Work-Study, scholarships/grants, and unspecified assistantships also available. Support available to part-time students. Financial award application deadline: 3/1; financial award applicants required to submit FAFSA. *Unit head:* Sung Yi, Chair, 503-725-5470, Fax: 503-725-8255, E-mail: syi@pdx.edu. *Application contact:* Tricia Hutchins, Department Manager, 503-725-4291, Fax: 503-725-8255, E-mail: tricia.hutchins@pdx.edu.
Website: http://www.pdx.edu/mme/

Purdue University, College of Engineering, School of Materials Engineering, West Lafayette, IN 47907. Offers MSMSE, PhD. *Program availability:* Part-time. *Faculty:* 40. *Students:* 177. *Degree requirements:* For master's, thesis optional; for doctorate, thesis/dissertation. *Entrance requirements:* Additional exam requirements/recommendations for international students: required—GRE. *Application deadline:* For fall admission, 12/15 for domestic and international students; for spring admission, 10/15 for domestic and international students. Applications are processed on a rolling basis. Application fee: $60 ($75 for international students). Electronic applications accepted. *Financial support:* Fellowships with full and partial tuition reimbursements, research assistantships with full and partial tuition reimbursements, teaching assistantships with full and partial tuition reimbursements, career-related internships or fieldwork, scholarships/grants, health care benefits, and unspecified assistantships available. *Unit head:* Dr. David Bahr, Head and Professor of Materials Engineering, 765-494-4100, E-mail: dfbahr@purdue.edu. *Application contact:* Vicki Kline, 765-494-4103, E-mail: vicline@purdue.edu.
Website: https://engineering.purdue.edu/MSE

Queen's University at Kingston, School of Graduate Studies, Faculty of Engineering and Applied Science, Department of Mechanical and Materials Engineering, Kingston, ON K7L 3N6, Canada. Offers M Eng, M Sc, M Sc Eng, PhD. *Program availability:* Part-time. *Degree requirements:* For master's, thesis optional; for doctorate, comprehensive exam, thesis/dissertation. *Entrance requirements:* Additional exam requirements/recommendations for international students: required—TOEFL. Electronic applications accepted.

Rensselaer Polytechnic Institute, Graduate School, School of Engineering, Program in Materials Engineering, Troy, NY 12180. Offers M Eng, MS, D Eng, PhD. *Faculty:* 19 full-time (4 women). *Students:* 53 full-time (14 women); includes 6 minority (1 Asian, non-Hispanic/Latino; 1 Hispanic/Latino; 4 Two or more races, non-Hispanic/Latino), 29 international. Average age 25. 155 applicants, 38% accepted, 12 enrolled. In 2019, 5 master's, 6 doctorates awarded. Terminal master's awarded for partial completion of doctoral program. *Degree requirements:* For master's, thesis; for doctorate, comprehensive exam, thesis/dissertation. *Entrance requirements:* For master's and doctorate, GRE. Additional exam requirements/recommendations for international students: required—TOEFL (minimum score 600 paper-based; 100 iBT), IELTS (minimum score 7), PTE (minimum score 68). *Application deadline:* For fall admission, 1/1 priority date for domestic and international students; for spring admission, 8/15 priority date for domestic and international students. Applications are processed on a rolling basis. Application fee: $75. Electronic applications accepted. *Financial support:* In 2019–20, research assistantships with full tuition reimbursements (averaging $23,000 per year), teaching assistantships with full tuition reimbursements (averaging $23,000 per year) were awarded; fellowships also available. Financial award application deadline: 1/1. *Unit head:* Dr. Minoru Tomozawa, Graduate Program Director, 518-276-6659, E-mail: tomozm@rpi.edu. *Application contact:* Jarron Decker, Director of Graduate Admissions, 518-276-6216, Fax: 518-276-4072, E-mail: gradadmissions@rpi.edu.
Website: http://mse.rpi.edu/graduate

Rochester Institute of Technology, Graduate Enrollment Services, College of Science, School of Chemistry and Materials Science, MS Program in Materials Science and Engineering, Rochester, NY 14623-5603. Offers MS. *Program availability:* Part-time, evening/weekend. *Degree requirements:* For master's, thesis or project. *Entrance requirements:* For master's, minimum GPA of 3.0 (recommended), two letters of recommendation. Additional exam requirements/recommendations for international students: required—TOEFL (minimum score 575 paper-based; 90 iBT), IELTS (minimum score 6.5), PTE (minimum score 62). Electronic applications accepted.

Rutgers University - New Brunswick, Graduate School-New Brunswick, Program in Materials Science and Engineering, Piscataway, NJ 08854-8097. Offers MS, PhD. *Program availability:* Part-time. *Degree requirements:* For master's, thesis; for doctorate, comprehensive exam, thesis/dissertation. *Entrance requirements:* For master's and doctorate, GRE General Test. Additional exam requirements/recommendations for international students: recommended—TOEFL. Electronic applications accepted.

San Jose State University, Program in Chemical & Materials Engineering, San Jose, CA 95192-0082. Offers chemical engineering (MS); materials engineering (MS). *Program availability:* Part-time. *Faculty:* 2 full-time (both women), 5 part-time/adjunct (0 women). *Students:* 23 full-time (6 women), 68 part-time (16 women); includes 59 minority (32 Asian, non-Hispanic/Latino; 11 Hispanic/Latino; 16 Two or more races, non-Hispanic/Latino), 16 international. Average age 29. 68 applicants, 72% accepted, 27 enrolled. In 2019, 23 master's awarded. *Degree requirements:* For master's, thesis

optional, Research Project. *Entrance requirements:* For master's, Students with a US BS degree are admitted to classified standing if they have a GPA in the major of 3.0, or better or they are admitted to conditionally classified standing if they have a GPA in the major between 2.7 and 2.99. Additional exam requirements/recommendations for international students: required—TOEFL (minimum score 575 paper-based; 240 iBT), IELTS (minimum score 7.5). *Application deadline:* For fall admission, 7/1 for domestic students, 5/1 for international students; for spring admission, 12/1 for domestic students, 11/1 for international students. Applications are processed on a rolling basis. Application fee: $70. Electronic applications accepted. *Expenses: Tuition, area resident:* Full-time $7176; part-time $4164. Tuition, state resident: full-time $7176; part-time $4164. Tuition, nonresident: full-time $7176; part-time $4165 per credit hour. *International tuition:* $7176 full-time. *Required fees:* $2110; $2110. *Financial support:* In 2019–20, 16 students received support, including 1 fellowship (averaging $4,500 per year), 10 research assistantships (averaging $8,000 per year), 6 teaching assistantships (averaging $14,000 per year); scholarships/grants and health care benefits also available. Financial award application deadline: 5/1; financial award applicants required to submit FAFSA. *Unit head:* Dr. Richard Chung, Department Chair, 408-924-3927, E-mail: richard.chung@sjsu.edu. *Application contact:* Debi Fennern, Administrative Analyst, 408-924-4056, E-mail: debi.fennern@sjsu.edu.
Website: http://www.sjsu.edu/cme/

South Dakota School of Mines and Technology, Graduate Division, Doctoral Program in Materials Engineering and Science, Rapid City, SD 57701-3995. Offers PhD. *Program availability:* Part-time. *Degree requirements:* For doctorate, thesis/dissertation. *Entrance requirements:* For doctorate, GRE General Test, minimum graduate GPA of 3.0, 3 letters of recommendation. Additional exam requirements/recommendations for international students: required—TOEFL (minimum score 520 paper-based; 68 iBT), TWE. Electronic applications accepted.

South Dakota School of Mines and Technology, Graduate Division, Master's Program in Materials Engineering and Science, Rapid City, SD 57701-3995. Offers MS. *Degree requirements:* For master's, thesis (for some programs). *Entrance requirements:* For master's, GRE General Test. Additional exam requirements/recommendations for international students: required—TOEFL (minimum score 520 paper-based; 68 iBT), TWE. Electronic applications accepted.

Stanford University, School of Engineering, Department of Materials Science and Engineering, Stanford, CA 94305-2004. Offers MS, PhD, Engr. *Expenses: Tuition:* Full-time $52,479; part-time $34,110 per unit. *Required fees:* $672; $224 per quarter. Tuition and fees vary according to program and student level.
Website: https://mse.stanford.edu/

Stevens Institute of Technology, Graduate School, Charles V. Schaefer Jr. School of Engineering and Science, Department of Chemical Engineering and Materials Science, Program in Materials Science and Engineering, Hoboken, NJ 07030. Offers M Eng, PhD. *Program availability:* Part-time, evening/weekend. *Faculty:* 13 full-time (3 women), 2 part-time/adjunct. *Students:* 44 full-time (12 women), 1 (woman) part-time; includes 2 minority (both Asian, non-Hispanic/Latino), 40 international. Average age 26. In 2019, 23 master's, 7 doctorates awarded. Terminal master's awarded for partial completion of doctoral program. *Degree requirements:* For master's, thesis optional, minimum B average in major field and overall; for doctorate, comprehensive exam (for some programs), thesis/dissertation. *Entrance requirements:* For master's, International applicants must submit TOEFL/IELTS scores and fulfill the English Language Proficiency Requirement. Applicants to full-time programs who do not qualify for a score waiver are required to submit GRE/GMAT scores. Additional exam requirements/recommendations for international students: required—TOEFL (minimum score 74 iBT), IELTS (minimum score 6). *Application deadline:* For fall admission, 4/15 for domestic and international students; for spring admission, 11/1 for domestic and international students; for summer admission, 5/1 for domestic students. Applications are processed on a rolling basis. Application fee: $60. Electronic applications accepted. *Expenses: Tuition:* Full-time $52,134. *Required fees:* $1880. Tuition and fees vary according to course load. *Financial support:* Fellowships, research assistantships, teaching assistantships, career-related internships or fieldwork, Federal Work-Study, scholarships/grants, and unspecified assistantships available. Financial award application deadline: 2/15; financial award applicants required to submit FAFSA. *Unit head:* Dr. Jean Zu, Dean of SES, 201-216.8233, Fax: 201-216.8372, E-mail: Jean.Zu@stevens.edu. *Application contact:* Graduate Admissions, 888-783-8367, Fax: 888-511-1306, E-mail: graduate@stevens.edu.

Stony Brook University, State University of New York, Graduate School, College of Engineering and Applied Sciences, Department of Materials Science & Chemical Engineering, Stony Brook, NY 11794. Offers MS, PhD. *Faculty:* 18 full-time (5 women), 5 part-time/adjunct (2 women). *Students:* 78 full-time (19 women), 4 part-time (2 women); includes 15 minority (2 Black or African American, non-Hispanic/Latino; 8 Asian, non-Hispanic/Latino; 4 Hispanic/Latino; 1 Two or more races, non-Hispanic/Latino), 52 international. Average age 26. 102 applicants, 61% accepted, 20 enrolled. In 2019, 21 master's, 21 doctorates awarded. *Degree requirements:* For master's, thesis or alternative; for doctorate, comprehensive exam, thesis/dissertation. *Entrance requirements:* For master's and doctorate, GRE General Test, minimum undergraduate GPA of 3.0. Additional exam requirements/recommendations for international students: required—TOEFL (minimum score 90 iBT). *Application deadline:* For fall admission, 1/15 for domestic students; for spring admission, 10/1 for domestic students. Application fee: $100. *Expenses:* Contact institution. *Financial support:* In 2019–20, 6 fellowships, 35 research assistantships, 14 teaching assistantships were awarded. *Unit head:* Dr. Dilip Gersappe, Professor and Interim Chair, 631-632-8500, Fax: 631-632-8052, E-mail: dilip.gersappe@stonybrook.edu. *Application contact:* Chandrani Roy, 631-632-4174, Fax: 631-632-8052, E-mail: Chandrani.Roy@stonybrook.edu.
Website: http://www.stonybrook.edu/commcms/matscieng/index.html

Texas A&M University, College of Engineering, Department of Materials Science and Engineering, College Station, TX 77843. Offers materials science and engineering (M Eng). *Faculty:* 20. *Students:* 163 full-time (58 women), 12 part-time (2 women); includes 28 minority (1 Black or African American, non-Hispanic/Latino; 13 Asian, non-Hispanic/Latino; 11 Hispanic/Latino; 3 Two or more races, non-Hispanic/Latino), 109 international. Average age 28. 204 applicants, 53% accepted, 37 enrolled. In 2019, 15 master's, 15 doctorates awarded. *Degree requirements:* For master's, comprehensive exam (for some programs), thesis optional; for doctorate, comprehensive exam, thesis/dissertation. *Entrance requirements:* For master's and doctorate, GRE General Test, letters of recommendation. Additional exam requirements/recommendations for international students: required—TOEFL (minimum score 550 paper-based; 80 iBT), IELTS (minimum score 6), PTE (minimum score 53). *Application deadline:* For fall admission, 1/31 for domestic students, 1/15 for international students; for spring admission, 7/15 for domestic and international students. Application fee: $65 ($90 for international students). *Expenses:* Contact institution. *Financial support:* In 2019–20, 167 students received support, including 43 fellowships with tuition reimbursements available (averaging $12,117 per year), 130 research assistantships with tuition reimbursements available (averaging $16,448 per year), 17 teaching assistantships with tuition reimbursements available (averaging $13,115 per year); career-related internships or fieldwork, institutionally sponsored loans, scholarships/grants, traineeships, health care benefits, tuition waivers (full and partial), and unspecified assistantships also available. Support available to part-time students. Financial award application deadline: 3/15; financial award applicants required to submit FAFSA. *Unit head:* Ibrahim Karaman, Department Head, 979-862-3923, E-mail: ikaraman@tamu.edu. *Application contact:* Erin Bandza, Academic Advisor, Graduate Programs, 979-458-3180, E-mail: msen-advising@tamu.edu.
Website: http://engineering.tamu.edu/materials

Texas State University, The Graduate College, College of Science and Engineering, PhD Program in Materials Science, Engineering, and Commercialization, San Marcos, TX 78666. Offers PhD. *Degree requirements:* For doctorate, comprehensive exam, thesis/dissertation. *Entrance requirements:* For doctorate, GRE (for applicants who have not received a master's degree from a U.S. institution), baccalaureate and master's degrees from regionally-accredited college or university in biology, chemistry, engineering, materials science, physics, technology, or closely-related field with minimum GPA of 3.5 in graduate work; interviews with core doctoral faculty; statement of purpose; 3 letters of recommendation; curriculum vitae or resume. Additional exam requirements/recommendations for international students: required—TOEFL (minimum score 550 paper-based; 78 iBT); recommended—IELTS (minimum score 6.5). Electronic applications accepted.

Tuskegee University, Graduate Programs, College of Engineering, Department of Materials Science and Engineering, Tuskegee, AL 36088. Offers PhD. *Entrance requirements:* Additional exam requirements/recommendations for international students: required—TOEFL (minimum score 500 paper-based).

The University of Alabama, Graduate School, College of Engineering, Department of Metallurgical and Materials Engineering, Tuscaloosa, AL 35487. Offers MS Met E, PhD. *Faculty:* 14 full-time (4 women). *Students:* 35 full-time (9 women), 1 part-time (0 women); includes 4 minority (1 Black or African American, non-Hispanic/Latino; 3 Hispanic/Latino), 18 international. Average age 27. 19 applicants, 74% accepted, 6 enrolled. In 2019, 4 master's, 10 doctorates awarded. *Degree requirements:* For master's, thesis or alternative; for doctorate, thesis/dissertation. *Entrance requirements:* For master's, GRE General Test, minimum GPA of 3.0 in last 60 hours; for doctorate, GRE General Test, minimum graduate GPA of 3.0, graduate degree. Additional exam requirements/recommendations for international students: required—TOEFL (minimum score 550 paper-based). *Application deadline:* For fall admission, 7/1 for domestic students, 5/1 priority date for international students. Applications are processed on a rolling basis. Application fee: $50 ($60 for international students). Electronic applications accepted. *Expenses: Tuition, area resident:* Full-time $10,780; part-time $440 per credit hour. Tuition, nonresident: full-time $30,250; part-time $1550 per credit hour. *Financial support:* In 2019–20, 25 students received support. Fellowships, research assistantships, teaching assistantships, Federal Work-Study, and unspecified assistantships available. *Unit head:* Dr. Steven Daniewicz, Head/Professor, 205-348-2704, Fax: 205-348-2164, E-mail: srdaniewicz@eng.ua.edu. *Application contact:* Dr. Lin Li, Associate Professor, 205-348-4971, Fax: 205-348-2346, E-mail: lin.li@eng.ua.edu.
Website: http://www.eng.ua.edu/~mtedept/

The University of Alabama at Birmingham, School of Engineering, Program in Materials Engineering, Birmingham, AL 35294. Offers MS Mt E, PhD. *Faculty:* 6 full-time (2 women). *Students:* 29 full-time (6 women), 9 part-time (2 women); includes 7 minority (4 Black or African American, non-Hispanic/Latino; 1 American Indian or Alaska Native, non-Hispanic/Latino; 2 Hispanic/Latino), 20 international. 31 applicants, 52% accepted, 3 enrolled. In 2019, 13 master's, 4 doctorates awarded. *Degree requirements:* For master's, comprehensive exam, thesis (for some programs), project/thesis; for doctorate, comprehensive exam, thesis/dissertation. *Entrance requirements:* For master's, GRE general test is required for all applicants who did not receive a BS degree from a program accredited by the Engineering Accreditation Committee of ABET http://www.abet.org, or from other programs with reciprocal agreement under the Washington Accord http://www.ieagreements.org/accords/washington/., minimum GPA of 3.0 on all undergraduate degree major courses attempted; for doctorate, GRE General Test (minimum quantitative score of 156), minimum GPA of 3.0 on all undergraduate degree major courses attempted. Additional exam requirements/recommendations for international students: required—TOEFL (minimum score 80 iBT); recommended—IELTS (minimum score 6.5). *Application deadline:* For fall admission, 8/1 for domestic and international students; for spring admission, 12/1 for domestic and international students; for summer admission, 5/1 for domestic and international students. Applications are processed on a rolling basis. Application fee: $50 ($60 for international students). Electronic applications accepted. *Financial support:* In 2019–20, 21 students received support, including 9 fellowships with full tuition reimbursements available (averaging $27,432 per year), 7 research assistantships with full tuition reimbursements available (averaging $24,429 per year); unspecified assistantships also available. *Unit head:* Dr. Lee Moradi, Interim Chair, 205-934-8450, E-mail: moradi@uab.edu. *Application contact:* Jesse Keppley, Director of Academic and Student Services, 205-996-5696, E-mail: gradschool@uab.edu.
Website: https://www.uab.edu/engineering/home/departments-research/mse/grad

University of Alberta, Faculty of Graduate Studies and Research, Department of Chemical and Materials Engineering, Edmonton, AB T6G 2E1, Canada. Offers chemical engineering (M Eng, M Sc, PhD); materials engineering (M Eng, M Sc, PhD); process control (M Eng, M Sc, PhD); welding (M Eng). *Program availability:* Part-time, online learning. Terminal master's awarded for partial completion of doctoral program. *Degree requirements:* For master's, thesis; for doctorate, thesis/dissertation.

The University of Arizona, College of Engineering, Department of Materials Science and Engineering, Tucson, AZ 85721. Offers MS, PhD. *Program availability:* Part-time. *Degree requirements:* For master's, thesis (for some programs); for doctorate, comprehensive exam, thesis/dissertation. *Entrance requirements:* For master's and doctorate, GRE General Test, 3 letters of recommendation, statement of purpose. Additional exam requirements/recommendations for international students: required—TOEFL (minimum score 550 paper-based; 79 iBT). Electronic applications accepted.

The University of British Columbia, Faculty of Applied Science, Department of Materials Engineering, Vancouver, BC V6T 1Z4, Canada. Offers M Sc, MA Sc, PhD. *Degree requirements:* For master's, comprehensive exam, thesis; for doctorate, comprehensive exam, thesis/dissertation. *Entrance requirements:* Additional exam requirements/recommendations for international students: required—TOEFL. Electronic applications accepted. *Expenses:* Contact institution.

University of California, Berkeley, Graduate Division, College of Engineering, Department of Materials Science and Engineering, Berkeley, CA 94720. Offers engineering science (M Eng, MS, PhD). Terminal master's awarded for partial completion of doctoral program. *Degree requirements:* For master's, comprehensive exam (for some programs), thesis (for some programs), comprehensive exam or thesis (MS); for doctorate, comprehensive exam, thesis/dissertation, qualifying exam. *Entrance requirements:* For master's and doctorate, GRE General Test, minimum GPA of 3.0, 3 letters of recommendation. Additional exam requirements/recommendations for international students: required—TOEFL (minimum score 570 paper-based; 90 iBT). Electronic applications accepted.

University of California, Davis, College of Engineering, Program in Materials Science and Engineering, Davis, CA 95616. Offers MS, PhD. Terminal master's awarded for partial completion of doctoral program. *Degree requirements:* For master's, comprehensive exam (for some programs), thesis (for some programs); for doctorate, comprehensive exam, thesis/dissertation. *Entrance requirements:* Additional exam requirements/recommendations for international students: required—TOEFL (minimum score 550 paper-based).

University of California, Irvine, Samueli School of Engineering, Department of Chemical Engineering and Materials Science, Irvine, CA 92697. Offers chemical and biochemical engineering (MS, PhD); materials science and engineering (MS, PhD). *Program availability:* Part-time. *Students:* 139 full-time (58 women), 3 part-time (2 women); includes 40 minority (5 Black or African American, non-Hispanic/Latino; 28 Asian, non-Hispanic/Latino; 6 Hispanic/Latino; 1 Two or more races, non-Hispanic/Latino), 56 international. Average age 26. 435 applicants, 34% accepted, 48 enrolled. In 2019, 30 master's, 26 doctorates awarded. Terminal master's awarded for partial completion of doctoral program. *Entrance requirements:* For master's and doctorate, GRE General Test, minimum GPA of 3.0, 3 letters of recommendation. Additional exam requirements/recommendations for international students: required—TOEFL (minimum score 550 paper-based). *Application deadline:* For fall admission, 1/15 priority date for domestic students, 1/15 for international students. Applications are processed on a rolling basis. Application fee: $120 ($140 for international students). Electronic applications accepted. *Financial support:* Fellowships, research assistantships with full tuition reimbursements, teaching assistantships, institutionally sponsored loans, traineeships, health care benefits, and unspecified assistantships available. Financial award application deadline: 3/1; financial award applicants required to submit FAFSA. *Unit head:* Prof. Vasan Venugopalan, Chair, 949-824-5802, Fax: 949-824-2541, E-mail: vvenugop@uci.edu. *Application contact:* Grace Chau, Academic Program and Graduate Admission Coordinator, 949-824-3887, Fax: 949-824-2541, E-mail: chaug@uci.edu. Website: http://www.eng.uci.edu/dept/chems

University of California, Irvine, Samueli School of Engineering, Program in Materials and Manufacturing Technology, Irvine, CA 92697. Offers engineering (MS, PhD). *Program availability:* Part-time. *Students:* 18 full-time (5 women), 4 part-time (2 women); includes 5 minority (3 Asian, non-Hispanic/Latino; 2 Hispanic/Latino), 13 international. Average age 28. 21 applicants, 48% accepted, 5 enrolled. In 2019, 5 master's, 2 doctorates awarded. *Entrance requirements:* For master's and doctorate, GRE General Test, 3 letters of recommendation, minimum GPA of 3.0. Additional exam requirements/recommendations for international students: required—TOEFL (minimum score 550 paper-based). *Application deadline:* For fall admission, 1/15 priority date for domestic students, 1/15 for international students. Applications are processed on a rolling basis. Application fee: $120 ($140 for international students). Electronic applications accepted. *Financial support:* Fellowships, research assistantships with full tuition reimbursements, teaching assistantships, institutionally sponsored loans, traineeships, health care benefits, and unspecified assistantships available. Financial award application deadline: 3/1; financial award applicants required to submit FAFSA. *Application contact:* Connie Cheng, Assistant Director of Graduate Student Affairs, 949-824-3562, Fax: 949-824-8200, E-mail: connie.cheng@uci.edu. Website: http://www.eng.uci.edu/

University of California, Los Angeles, Graduate Division, Henry Samueli School of Engineering and Applied Science, Department of Materials Science and Engineering, Los Angeles, CA 90095-1595. Offers MS, PhD. *Degree requirements:* For master's, comprehensive exam or thesis; for doctorate, thesis/dissertation, qualifying exams. *Entrance requirements:* For master's, GRE General Test, minimum GPA of 3.0; for doctorate, GRE General Test, minimum GPA of 3.25. Additional exam requirements/recommendations for international students: required—TOEFL (minimum score 560 paper-based; 87 iBT), IELTS (minimum score 7). Electronic applications accepted.

University of California, Riverside, Graduate Division, Materials Science and Engineering Program, Riverside, CA 92521. Offers MS. *Entrance requirements:* For master's, GRE. Additional exam requirements/recommendations for international students: required—TOEFL (minimum score 550 paper-based; 80 iBT). Electronic applications accepted.

University of California, Santa Barbara, Graduate Division, College of Engineering, Department of Materials, Santa Barbara, CA 93106-5050. Offers MS, PhD, MS/PhD. Terminal master's awarded for partial completion of doctoral program. *Degree requirements:* For master's, variable foreign language requirement, comprehensive exam, thesis; for doctorate, variable foreign language requirement, comprehensive exam, thesis/dissertation. *Entrance requirements:* For master's and doctorate, GRE General Test. Additional exam requirements/recommendations for international students: required—TOEFL (minimum score 600 paper-based; 100 iBT), IELTS (minimum score 7). Electronic applications accepted.

University of Central Florida, College of Engineering and Computer Science, Department of Materials Science and Engineering, Orlando, FL 32816. Offers MSMSE, PhD. *Students:* 58 full-time (22 women), 19 part-time (9 women); includes 15 minority (1 Black or African American, non-Hispanic/Latino; 6 Asian, non-Hispanic/Latino; 5 Hispanic/Latino; 3 Two or more races, non-Hispanic/Latino), 34 international. Average age 28. 98 applicants, 42% accepted, 24 enrolled. In 2019, 4 master's, 8 doctorates awarded. *Degree requirements:* For master's, thesis or alternative; for doctorate, thesis/dissertation, candidacy exam, departmental qualifying exam. *Entrance requirements:* For master's, resume, goal statement; for doctorate, GRE, letters of recommendation, resume, goal statement. Additional exam requirements/recommendations for international students: required—TOEFL. *Application deadline:* For fall admission, 7/15 for domestic students; for spring admission, 12/1 for domestic students. Application fee: $30. Electronic applications accepted. *Financial support:* In 2019–20, 49 students received support, including 10 fellowships with tuition reimbursements available (averaging $12,980 per year), 52 research assistantships (averaging $7,696 per year), 7 teaching assistantships (averaging $8,566 per year); health care benefits also available. Financial award application deadline: 3/1; financial award applicants required to submit FAFSA. *Unit head:* Dr. Sudipta Seal, Chair, 407-823-5277, E-mail: sseal@ucf.edu. *Application contact:* Associate Director, Graduate Admissions, 407-823-2766, Fax: 407-823-6442, E-mail: gradadmissions@ucf.edu. Website: http://mse.ucf.edu/

University of Cincinnati, Graduate School, College of Engineering and Applied Science, Department of Mechanical and Materials Engineering, Program in Materials Science and Engineering, Cincinnati, OH 45221. Offers MS, PhD. *Program availability:* Evening/weekend. *Degree requirements:* For master's, thesis optional; for doctorate, one foreign language, comprehensive exam, thesis/dissertation, oral English proficiency exam. *Entrance requirements:* For master's and doctorate, GRE General Test, BS in related field, minimum undergraduate GPA of 3.0. Additional exam requirements/recommendations for international students: required—TOEFL. Electronic applications accepted.

University of Colorado Boulder, Graduate School, College of Engineering and Applied Science, Materials Science and Engineering Program, Boulder, CO 80309. Offers MS, PhD. Electronic applications accepted.

University of Connecticut, Graduate School, School of Engineering, Department of Materials Science and Engineering, Storrs, CT 06269. Offers M Eng. Terminal master's awarded for partial completion of doctoral program. *Degree requirements:* For master's, comprehensive exam, thesis or alternative. *Entrance requirements:* For master's, GRE General Test, GRE Subject Test. Additional exam requirements/recommendations for international students: required—TOEFL (minimum score 550 paper-based). Electronic applications accepted.

University of Dayton, Program in Materials Engineering, Dayton, OH 45469. Offers MS, DE, PhD. *Program availability:* Part-time, evening/weekend, blended/hybrid learning. Terminal master's awarded for partial completion of doctoral program. *Degree requirements:* For master's, thesis optional; for doctorate, comprehensive exam, thesis/dissertation, departmental qualifying exam. *Entrance requirements:* Additional exam requirements/recommendations for international students: required—TOEFL (minimum score 550 paper-based; 80 iBT). Electronic applications accepted.

University of Delaware, College of Engineering, Department of Materials Science and Engineering, Newark, DE 19716. Offers MMSE, PhD. Terminal master's awarded for partial completion of doctoral program. *Degree requirements:* For master's, thesis; for doctorate, thesis/dissertation. *Entrance requirements:* For master's and doctorate, GRE General Test, 3 letters of recommendation, minimum GPA of 3.2. Additional exam requirements/recommendations for international students: required—TOEFL. Electronic applications accepted.

University of Denver, Daniel Felix Ritchie School of Engineering and Computer Science, Department of Mechanical and Materials Engineering, Denver, CO 80208. Offers bioengineering (MS); engineering (MS, PhD), including management; materials science (MS, PhD); mechanical engineering (MS, PhD). *Program availability:* Part-time. *Faculty:* 12 full-time (2 women), 3 part-time/adjunct (1 woman). *Students:* 3 full-time (1 woman), 35 part-time (9 women); includes 3 minority (1 Black or African American, non-Hispanic/Latino; 1 Asian, non-Hispanic/Latino; 1 Hispanic/Latino), 16 international. Average age 27. 58 applicants, 81% accepted, 18 enrolled. In 2019, 16 master's, 4 doctorates awarded. Terminal master's awarded for partial completion of doctoral program. *Degree requirements:* For master's, thesis optional; for doctorate, comprehensive exam, thesis/dissertation. *Entrance requirements:* For master's, GRE General Test, bachelor's degree in engineering or closely related field, transcripts, personal statement, resume or curriculum vitae, two letters of recommendation; for doctorate, GRE General Test, master's degree in engineering or closely related field, transcripts, personal statement, resume or curriculum vitae, two letters of recommendation, recommended that applicants find a research advisor before submitting the application. Additional exam requirements/recommendations for international students: required—TOEFL (minimum score 550 paper-based; 80 iBT). *Application deadline:* For fall admission, 1/15 priority date for domestic and international students; for winter admission, 10/25 for domestic and international students; for spring admission, 2/7 for domestic and international students; for summer admission, 4/24 for domestic and international students. Applications are processed on a rolling basis. Application fee: $65. Electronic applications accepted. *Unit head:* Dr. Matt Gordon, Professor and Chair, 303-871-3580, E-mail: matthew.gordon@du.edu. *Application contact:* Chrissy Alexander, Assistant to the Chair, 303-871-3041, E-mail: Christine.Alexander@du.edu. Website: http://ritchieschool.du.edu/departments/mme/

University of Florida, Graduate School, Herbert Wertheim College of Engineering, Department of Materials Science and Engineering, Gainesville, FL 32611. Offers material science and engineering (MS), including clinical and translational science; materials science and engineering (ME, PhD); nuclear engineering (ME, PhD), including imaging science and technology (PhD), nuclear engineering sciences (ME, MS, PhD); nuclear engineering (MS), including nuclear engineering sciences (ME, MS, PhD); JD/MS. *Program availability:* Part-time, online learning. Terminal master's awarded for partial completion of doctoral program. *Degree requirements:* For master's, comprehensive exam, thesis; for doctorate, comprehensive exam, thesis/dissertation. *Entrance requirements:* For master's and doctorate, minimum GPA of 3.0. Additional exam requirements/recommendations for international students: required—TOEFL (minimum score 550 paper-based; 80 iBT), IELTS (minimum score 6). Electronic applications accepted.

University of Illinois at Chicago, College of Engineering, Department of Civil and Materials Engineering, Chicago, IL 60607-7128. Offers MS, PhD. *Program availability:* Evening/weekend. *Degree requirements:* For master's, thesis (for some programs); for doctorate, thesis/dissertation, preliminary and qualifying exams. *Entrance requirements:* For master's and doctorate, GRE General Test, minimum GPA of 3.0. Additional exam requirements/recommendations for international students: required—TOEFL. Electronic applications accepted. *Expenses:* Contact institution.

University of Illinois at Urbana-Champaign, Graduate College, College of Engineering, Department of Materials Science and Engineering, Champaign, IL 61820. Offers M Eng, MS, PhD, MS/MBA, PhD/MBA.

The University of Iowa, Graduate College, College of Engineering, Department of Mechanical Engineering, Iowa City, IA 52242-1316. Offers energy systems (MS, PhD); engineering design (MS, PhD); fluid dynamics (MS, PhD); materials and manufacturing (MS, PhD); wind energy (MS, PhD). Terminal master's awarded for partial completion of doctoral program. *Degree requirements:* For master's, oral exam or thesis; for doctorate, comprehensive exam, thesis/dissertation. *Entrance requirements:* For master's and doctorate, GRE (minimum Verbal score of 153, Quantitative 151), minimum undergraduate GPA of 3.0. Additional exam requirements/recommendations for international students: required—TOEFL (minimum score 600 paper-based; 100 iBT), IELTS (minimum score 7). Electronic applications accepted.

University of Kentucky, Graduate School, College of Engineering, Program in Materials Science and Engineering, Lexington, KY 40506-0032. Offers MS, PhD. *Degree requirements:* For master's, comprehensive exam, thesis optional; for doctorate, comprehensive exam, thesis/dissertation. *Entrance requirements:* For master's, GRE General Test, minimum undergraduate GPA of 2.75; for doctorate, GRE General Test, minimum undergraduate GPA of 3.0. Additional exam requirements/recommendations for international students: required—TOEFL (minimum score 550 paper-based). Electronic applications accepted.

University of Maryland, College Park, Academic Affairs, A. James Clark School of Engineering, Department of Materials Science and Engineering, Materials Science and Engineering Program, College Park, MD 20742. Offers MS, PhD. *Program availability:* Part-time, evening/weekend, online learning. *Degree requirements:* For master's, comprehensive exam, thesis optional, research paper; for doctorate, thesis/dissertation, oral exam. *Entrance requirements:* For master's and doctorate, GRE General Test, minimum B+ average in undergraduate course work. Additional exam requirements/recommendations for international students: required—TOEFL. Electronic applications accepted.

University of Maryland, College Park, Academic Affairs, A. James Clark School of Engineering, Department of Mechanical Engineering, College Park, MD 20742. Offers electronic packaging and reliability (MS, PhD); manufacturing and design (MS, PhD); mechanics and materials (MS, PhD); reliability engineering (M Eng, MS, PhD); thermal and fluid sciences (MS, PhD). *Program availability:* Part-time, evening/weekend, online learning. *Degree requirements:* For master's, thesis optional; for doctorate, thesis/dissertation, qualifying exam. *Entrance requirements:* For master's, GRE General Test, 3 letters of recommendation; for doctorate, GRE General Test, minimum GPA of 3.0. Additional exam requirements/recommendations for international students: required—TOEFL. Electronic applications accepted.

University of Michigan, College of Engineering, Department of Materials Science and Engineering, Ann Arbor, MI 48109. Offers MS, MSE, PhD. *Program availability:* Part-time. Terminal master's awarded for partial completion of doctoral program. *Degree requirements:* For master's, thesis, oral defense of thesis; for doctorate, thesis/dissertation, oral defense of dissertation, written exam. *Entrance requirements:* For master's and doctorate, GRE General Test. Additional exam requirements/recommendations for international students: required—TOEFL. Electronic applications accepted.

University of Minnesota, Twin Cities Campus, College of Science and Engineering, Department of Chemical Engineering and Materials Science, Program in Materials Science and Engineering, Minneapolis, MN 55455-0132. Offers M Mat SE, MS Mat SE, PhD. *Program availability:* Part-time. Terminal master's awarded for partial completion of doctoral program. *Degree requirements:* For master's, thesis; for doctorate, thesis/dissertation. *Entrance requirements:* For master's and doctorate, GRE General Test. Additional exam requirements/recommendations for international students: required—TOEFL. Electronic applications accepted.

University of Nebraska–Lincoln, Graduate College, College of Engineering, Department of Mechanical and Materials Engineering, Lincoln, NE 68588-0526. Offers biomedical engineering (PhD); engineering mechanics (MS); materials engineering (PhD); mechanical engineering (MS), including materials science engineering, metallurgical engineering; mechanical engineering and applied mechanics (PhD); MS/MS. *Degree requirements:* For master's, thesis optional; for doctorate, comprehensive exam, thesis/dissertation. *Entrance requirements:* For master's and doctorate, GRE General Test. Additional exam requirements/recommendations for international students: required—TOEFL (minimum score 550 paper-based). Electronic applications accepted.

University of Nevada, Las Vegas, Graduate College, Howard R. Hughes College of Engineering, Department of Mechanical Engineering, Las Vegas, NV 89154-4027. Offers aerospace engineering (MS); biomedical engineering (MS); materials and nuclear engineering (MS); mechanical engineering (MS, PhD); nuclear criticality safety engineering (Certificate); nuclear safeguards and security (Certificate). *Program availability:* Part-time. *Faculty:* 18 full-time (2 women), 1 (woman) part-time/adjunct. *Students:* 52 full-time (16 women), 26 part-time (7 women); includes 26 minority (5 Black or African American, non-Hispanic/Latino; 1 American Indian or Alaska Native, non-Hispanic/Latino; 7 Asian, non-Hispanic/Latino; 10 Hispanic/Latino; 3 Two or more races, non-Hispanic/Latino), 22 international. Average age 29. 45 applicants, 76% accepted, 14 enrolled. In 2019, 9 master's, 4 doctorates, 1 other advanced degree awarded. *Degree requirements:* For master's, thesis optional, design project; for doctorate, comprehensive exam, thesis/dissertation. *Entrance requirements:* For master's, GRE General Test, statement of purpose; 2 letters of recommendation; for doctorate, GRE General Test, 3 letters of recommendation; statement of purpose; bachelor's degree with minimum GPA of 3.5/master's degree with minimum GPA of 3.3. Additional exam requirements/recommendations for international students: required—TOEFL (minimum score 550 paper-based; 80 iBT), IELTS (minimum score 7). *Application deadline:* For fall admission, 8/1 for domestic students, 5/1 for international students; for spring admission, 12/1 for domestic students, 10/1 for international students. Application fee: $60 ($95 for international students). Electronic applications accepted. *Expenses:* Contact institution. *Financial support:* In 2019–20, 40 students received support, including 2 fellowships with full tuition reimbursements available (averaging $20,000 per year), 16 research assistantships with full tuition reimbursements available (averaging $16,738 per year), 26 teaching assistantships with full tuition reimbursements available (averaging $18,115 per year); institutionally sponsored loans, scholarships/grants, health care benefits, and unspecified assistantships also available. Financial award application deadline: 3/15; financial award applicants required to submit FAFSA. *Unit head:* Dr. Brendan O'Toole, Chair/Professor, 702-895-3885, Fax: 702-895-3936, E-mail: mechanical.chair@unlv.edu. *Application contact:* Dr. Hui Zhao, Graduate Coordinator, 702-895-1463, Fax: 702-895-3936, E-mail: mechanical.gradcoord@unlv.edu.
Website: http://me.unlv.edu/

University of Nevada, Reno, Graduate School, College of Engineering, Department of Chemical and Materials Engineering, Program in Materials Science and Engineering, Reno, NV 89557. Offers MS, PhD. Terminal master's awarded for partial completion of doctoral program. *Degree requirements:* For master's, thesis; for doctorate, one foreign language, thesis/dissertation. *Entrance requirements:* For master's, minimum GPA of 2.75; for doctorate, GRE, minimum GPA of 3.0. Additional exam requirements/recommendations for international students: required—TOEFL (minimum score 500 paper-based; 61 iBT), IELTS (minimum score 6). Electronic applications accepted.

University of New Hampshire, Graduate School, College of Engineering and Physical Sciences, Program in Materials Science, Durham, NH 03824. Offers materials science (MS); materials science and engineering (PhD). *Students:* 3 full-time (0 women), 4 part-time (1 woman), 4 international. Average age 29. 10 applicants, 40% accepted. *Entrance requirements:* For master's and doctorate, GRE. Additional exam requirements/recommendations for international students: required—TOEFL (minimum score 550 paper-based; 80 iBT), IELTS, PTE. *Application deadline:* For fall admission, 6/1 for domestic students, 4/1 for international students; for spring admission, 12/1 for domestic students. Application fee: $65. Electronic applications accepted. *Financial support:* In 2019–20, 6 students received support, including 2 research assistantships, 4 teaching assistantships; fellowships, Federal Work-Study, scholarships/grants, and tuition waivers (full and partial) also available. Support available to part-time students. Financial award application deadline: 2/15. *Unit head:* James Krzanowski, Director, 603-862-2315. *Application contact:* Katie Makem, Administrative Assistant, 603-862-2669, E-mail: materials.science@unh.edu.
Website: http://www.ceps.unh.edu/materials-science/

University of Pennsylvania, School of Engineering and Applied Science, Department of Materials Science and Engineering, Philadelphia, PA 19104. Offers MSE, PhD. *Program availability:* Part-time. *Faculty:* 22 full-time (4 women), 3 part-time/adjunct (1 woman). *Students:* 133 full-time (41 women), 4 part-time (1 woman); includes 18 minority (12 Asian, non-Hispanic/Latino; 4 Hispanic/Latino; 2 Two or more races, non-Hispanic/Latino), 90 international. Average age 24. 448 applicants, 36% accepted, 53 enrolled. In 2019, 45 master's, 8 doctorates awarded. *Degree requirements:* For master's, comprehensive exam, thesis optional; for doctorate, comprehensive exam, thesis/dissertation. *Entrance requirements:* For master's and doctorate, GRE, bachelor's degree, letters of recommendation, resume, personal statement. Additional exam requirements/recommendations for international students: required—TOEFL (minimum score 100 iBT), IELTS (minimum score 7). *Application deadline:* For fall admission, 12/15 priority date for domestic and international students. Application fee: $80. Electronic applications accepted. *Expenses:* Contact institution. *Application contact:* Associate Director of Graduate Admissions, 215-898-4542, Fax: 215-573-5577, E-mail: admissions1@seas.upenn.edu.
Website: http://www.mse.seas.upenn.edu/current-students/masters/index.php

University of Puerto Rico at Mayagüez, Graduate Studies, College of Engineering, Department of Engineering Sciences and Materials, Mayagüez, PR 00681-9000. Offers materials science and engineering (MS).

University of Puerto Rico at Mayagüez, Graduate Studies, College of Engineering, Department of Mechanical Engineering, Mayagüez, PR 00681-9000. Offers mechanical engineering (ME, MS, PhD), including aerospace and unmanned vehicles (ME), automation/mechatronics, bioengineering, fluid mechanics, heat transfer/energy systems, manufacturing, mechanics of materials, micro and nano engineering. *Program availability:* Part-time. Terminal master's awarded for partial completion of doctoral program. *Degree requirements:* For master's, one foreign language, comprehensive exam, thesis; for doctorate, one foreign language, comprehensive exam, thesis/dissertation. *Entrance requirements:* For master's, BS in mechanical engineering or its equivalent; for doctorate, GRE, BS or MS in mechanical engineering or its equivalent; minimum GPA of 3.0. Additional exam requirements/recommendations for international students: required—TOEFL (minimum score 80 iBT). Electronic applications accepted.

University of Southern California, Graduate School, Viterbi School of Engineering, Mork Family Department of Chemical Engineering and Materials Science, Los Angeles, CA 90089. Offers chemical engineering (MS, PhD, Engr); geoscience technologies (MS); materials engineering (MS); materials science (MS, PhD, Engr); petroleum engineering (MS, PhD, Engr); smart oilfield technologies (MS, Graduate Certificate). Terminal master's awarded for partial completion of doctoral program. *Degree requirements:* For master's, thesis optional; for doctorate, thesis/dissertation. *Entrance requirements:* For master's and doctorate, GRE General Test. Additional exam requirements/recommendations for international students: recommended—TOEFL. Electronic applications accepted. *Expenses:* Contact institution.

University of South Florida, College of Engineering, Department of Civil and Environmental Engineering, Tampa, FL 33620-9951. Offers civil engineering (MCE, MSCE), including geotechnical engineering, materials science and engineering, structures engineering, transportation engineering, water resources; environmental engineering (MEVE, MSEV, PhD), including engineering for international development (MSEV). *Program availability:* Part-time. *Faculty:* 19 full-time (5 women). *Students:* 144 full-time (46 women), 76 part-time (22 women); includes 35 minority (8 Black or African American, non-Hispanic/Latino; 5 Asian, non-Hispanic/Latino; 18 Hispanic/Latino; 4 Two or more races, non-Hispanic/Latino), 123 international. Average age 28. 220 applicants, 65% accepted, 59 enrolled. In 2019, 82 master's, 15 doctorates awarded. Terminal master's awarded for partial completion of doctoral program. *Degree requirements:* For master's, comprehensive exam, thesis (for some programs); for doctorate, comprehensive exam, thesis/dissertation. *Entrance requirements:* For master's, GRE required, bachelor's degree in appropriate field, minimum GPA of 3.0 in major, letters of reference, statement of purpose, resume, intake form; for doctorate, GRE with V (45th percentile), Q (75th percentile), and AW (55th percentile), letters of recommendation, statement of purpose, resume, intake form. Additional exam requirements/recommendations for international students: required—TOEFL, TOEFL (minimum score 550 paper-based; 79 iBT) or IELTS (minimum score 6.5). *Application deadline:* For fall admission, 2/15 for domestic students, 2/15 priority date for international students; for spring admission, 10/15 for domestic students, 9/15 priority date for international students. Application fee: $30. Electronic applications accepted. *Financial support:* In 2019–20, 45 students received support, including 44 research assistantships (averaging $14,123 per year), 21 teaching assistantships with tuition reimbursements available (averaging $15,329 per year). *Unit head:* Dr. Manjriker Gunaratne, Professor and Department Chair, 813-974-5818, Fax: 813-974-2957, E-mail: gunaratn@usf.edu. *Application contact:* Dr. Sarina J. Ergas, Professor and Graduate Program Coordinator, 813-974-1119, Fax: 813-974-2957, E-mail: sergas@usf.edu.
Website: http://www.usf.edu/engineering/cee/

University of South Florida, Innovative Education, Tampa, FL 33620-9951. Offers adult, career and higher education (Graduate Certificate), including college teaching, leadership in developing human resources, leadership in higher education; Africana studies (Graduate Certificate), including diasporas and health disparities, genocide and human rights; aging studies (Graduate Certificate), including gerontology; art research (Graduate Certificate), including museum studies; business foundations (Graduate Certificate); chemical and biomedical engineering (Graduate Certificate), including materials science and engineering, water, health and sustainability; child and family studies (Graduate Certificate), including positive behavior support; civil and industrial engineering (Graduate Certificate), including transportation systems analysis; community and family health (Graduate Certificate), including maternal and child health, social marketing and public health, violence and injury: prevention and intervention, women's health; criminology (Graduate Certificate), including criminal justice administration; data science for public administration (Graduate Certificate); digital humanities (Graduate Certificate); educational measurement and research (Graduate Certificate), including evaluation; English (Graduate Certificate), including comparative literary studies, creative writing, professional and technical communication; entrepreneurship (Graduate Certificate); environmental health (Graduate Certificate), including safety management; epidemiology and biostatistics (Graduate Certificate), including applied biostatistics, biostatistics, concepts and tools of epidemiology, epidemiology, epidemiology of infectious diseases; geography, environment and planning (Graduate Certificate), including community development, environmental policy and management, geographical information systems; geology (Graduate Certificate), including hydrogeology; global health (Graduate Certificate), including disaster management, global health and Latin American and Caribbean studies, global health practice, humanitarian assistance, infection control; government and international affairs (Graduate Certificate), including Cuban studies, globalization studies; health policy and management (Graduate Certificate), including health management and leadership, public health policy and programs; hearing specialist: early intervention (Graduate Certificate); industrial and management systems engineering (Graduate Certificate), including systems engineering, technology management; information studies (Graduate Certificate), including school library media specialist; information systems/decision sciences (Graduate Certificate), including analytics and business intelligence; instructional technology (Graduate Certificate), including distance education, Florida digital/virtual educator, instructional design, multimedia design, Web design; internal medicine, bioethics and medical humanities (Graduate Certificate), including biomedical ethics; Latin American and Caribbean studies (Graduate Certificate); leadership for coastal resiliency planning (Graduate Certificate); mass communications (Graduate Certificate), including multimedia journalism; mathematics and statistics (Graduate Certificate), including mathematics; medicine (Graduate Certificate), including aging and neuroscience, bioinformatics, biotechnology, brain fitness and memory management, clinical investigation, hand and upper limb rehabilitation, health informatics, health sciences, integrative weight management, intellectual property, medicine and gender, metabolic and nutritional medicine, metabolic cardiology, pharmacy sciences; national and competitive intelligence (Graduate Certificate); nursing (Graduate Certificate), including simulation based academic fellowship in advanced pain management; psychological and social foundations (Graduate Certificate), including career

counseling, college teaching, diversity in education, mental health counseling, school counseling; public affairs (Graduate Certificate), including nonprofit management, public management, research administration; public health (Graduate Certificate), including assessing chemical toxicity and public health risks, health equity, pharmacoepidemiology, public health generalist, toxicology, translational research in adolescent behavioral health; public health practices (Graduate Certificate), including planning for healthy communities; rehabilitation and mental health counseling (Graduate Certificate), including integrative mental health care, marriage and family therapy, rehabilitation technology; secondary education (Graduate Certificate), including ESOL, foreign language education: culture and content, foreign language education: professional; social work (Graduate Certificate), including geriatric social work/clinical gerontology; special education (Graduate Certificate), including autism spectrum disorder, disabilities education: severe/profound; world languages (Graduate Certificate), including teaching English as a second language (TESL) or foreign language. *Unit head:* Dr. Cynthia DeLuca, Associate Vice President and Assistant Vice Provost, 813-974-3077, Fax: 813-974-7061, E-mail: deluca@usf.edu. *Application contact:* Owen Hooper, Director, Summer and Alternative Calendar Programs, 813-974-6917, E-mail: hooper@usf.edu.
Website: http://www.usf.edu/innovative-education/

The University of Tennessee, Graduate School, Tickle College of Engineering, Department of Materials Science and Engineering, Knoxville, TN 37996-2200. Offers materials science and engineering (MS, PhD); reliability and maintainability engineering (MS); MS/MBA. *Program availability:* Part-time. *Faculty:* 26 full-time (5 women). *Students:* 78 full-time (28 women), 6 part-time (1 woman); includes 7 minority (2 Black or African American, non-Hispanic/Latino; 3 Asian, non-Hispanic/Latino; 2 Hispanic/Latino), 39 international. Average age 29. 85 applicants, 16% accepted, 11 enrolled. In 2019, 10 master's, 6 doctorates awarded. *Degree requirements:* For master's, thesis or alternative; for doctorate, comprehensive exam, thesis/dissertation. *Entrance requirements:* For master's, GRE General Test (for MS students pursuing research thesis), minimum GPA of 2.7 (for U.S. degree holders), 3.0 (for international degree holders); 3 references; for doctorate, GRE General Test, minimum GPA of 3.0 on previous graduate course work; 3 references. Additional exam requirements/recommendations for international students: required—TOEFL (minimum score 550 paper-based; 80 iBT), IELTS (minimum score 6.5). *Application deadline:* For fall admission, 2/1 priority date for domestic and international students; for spring admission, 6/15 for domestic and international students; for summer admission, 10/15 for domestic and international students. Applications are processed on a rolling basis. Application fee: $60. Electronic applications accepted. *Financial support:* In 2019–20, 103 students received support, including 17 fellowships with full tuition reimbursements available (averaging $11,364 per year), 65 research assistantships with full tuition reimbursements available (averaging $22,712 per year), 21 teaching assistantships with full tuition reimbursements available (averaging $21,410 per year); career-related internships or fieldwork, Federal Work-Study, institutionally sponsored loans, health care benefits, and unspecified assistantships also available. Financial award application deadline: 2/1; financial award applicants required to submit FAFSA. *Unit head:* Dr. Veerle Keppens, Head, 865-974-5336, Fax: 865-974-4115, E-mail: vkeppens@utk.edu. *Application contact:* Dr. Kurt Sickafus, Professor and Director of Graduate Studies, 865-974-4858, E-mail: kurt@utk.edu.
Website: http://www.engr.utk.edu/mse

The University of Texas at Arlington, Graduate School, College of Engineering, Department of Materials Science and Engineering, Arlington, TX 76019. Offers M Engr, MS, PhD. Terminal master's awarded for partial completion of doctoral program. *Degree requirements:* For master's, comprehensive exam (for some programs), thesis optional; for doctorate, comprehensive exam, thesis/dissertation optional. *Entrance requirements:* For master's, GRE General Test, minimum GPA of 3.0; for doctorate, GRE General Test, minimum GPA of 3.5. Additional exam requirements/recommendations for international students: required—TOEFL (minimum score 550 paper-based; 79 iBT), IELTS.

The University of Texas at Austin, Graduate School, Cockrell School of Engineering, Program in Materials Science and Engineering, Austin, TX 78712-1111. Offers MS, PhD. *Program availability:* Part-time. *Degree requirements:* For master's, thesis (for some programs); for doctorate, thesis/dissertation. *Entrance requirements:* For master's and doctorate, GRE General Test. Additional exam requirements/recommendations for international students: required—TOEFL (minimum score 550 paper-based). Electronic applications accepted.

The University of Texas at Dallas, Erik Jonsson School of Engineering and Computer Science, Department of Materials Science and Engineering, Richardson, TX 75080. Offers MS, PhD. *Program availability:* Part-time, evening/weekend. *Faculty:* 15 full-time (2 women). *Students:* 53 full-time (14 women), 4 part-time (0 women); includes 7 minority (3 Asian, non-Hispanic/Latino; 3 Hispanic/Latino; 1 Two or more races, non-Hispanic/Latino), 41 international. Average age 30. 90 applicants, 33% accepted, 11 enrolled. In 2019, 11 master's, 8 doctorates awarded. *Degree requirements:* For master's, thesis or major design project; for doctorate, thesis/dissertation. *Entrance requirements:* For master's, GRE General Test, minimum GPA of 3.0 in related bachelor's degree; for doctorate, GRE General Test, minimum GPA of 3.5. Additional exam requirements/recommendations for international students: required—TOEFL (minimum score 550 paper-based). *Application deadline:* For fall admission, 7/15 for domestic students, 5/1 priority date for international students; for spring admission, 11/15 for domestic students, 9/1 priority date for international students. Applications are processed on a rolling basis. Application fee: $50 ($100 for international students). Electronic applications accepted. *Expenses: Tuition, area resident:* Full-time $16,504. Tuition, state resident: full-time $16,504. Tuition, nonresident: full-time $34,266. Tuition and fees vary according to course load. *Financial support:* In 2019–20, 49 students received support, including 1 fellowship (averaging $7,500 per year), 43 research assistantships with partial tuition reimbursements available (averaging $26,121 per year), 4 teaching assistantships with partial tuition reimbursements available (averaging $18,338 per year); career-related internships or fieldwork, Federal Work-Study, institutionally sponsored loans, scholarships/grants, and unspecified assistantships also available. Support available to part-time students. Financial award application deadline: 4/30; financial award applicants required to submit FAFSA. *Unit head:* Dr. Amy Walker, Interim Department Head, 972-883-5780, Fax: 972-883-5725, E-mail: amy.walker@utdallas.edu. *Application contact:* Dr. Lev Gelb, Associate Department Head, 972-883-5644, Fax: 972-883-5725, E-mail: mseadmissions@utdallas.edu.
Website: http://mse.utdallas.edu/

The University of Texas at El Paso, Graduate School, College of Engineering, Department of Metallurgical and Materials Engineering, El Paso, TX 79968-0001. Offers materials science and engineering (PhD); metallurgical and materials engineering (MS). *Program availability:* Part-time, evening/weekend. *Degree requirements:* For master's, thesis. *Entrance requirements:* For master's, GRE General Test. Additional exam requirements/recommendations for international students: required—TOEFL. Electronic applications accepted.

The University of Texas at San Antonio, College of Engineering, Department of Electrical and Computer Engineering, San Antonio, TX 78249-0617. Offers advanced materials engineering (MS); computer engineering (MS); electrical engineering (MSEE, PhD). *Program availability:* Part-time. Terminal master's awarded for partial completion of doctoral program. *Degree requirements:* For master's, comprehensive exam, thesis (for some programs); for doctorate, comprehensive exam, thesis/dissertation. *Entrance requirements:* For master's, GRE General Test, bachelor's degree in electrical or computer engineering from ABET-accredited institution of higher education or related field; minimum GPA of 3.0 on the last 60 semester credit hours of undergraduate studies; for doctorate, GRE General Test, master's degree or minimum GPA of 3.3 in last 60 semester credit hours of undergraduate level coursework in electrical engineering; statement of purpose. Additional exam requirements/recommendations for international students: required—TOEFL (minimum score 550 paper-based; 79 iBT), IELTS (minimum score 6.5). Electronic applications accepted.

University of Toronto, School of Graduate Studies, Faculty of Applied Science and Engineering, Department of Materials Science and Engineering, Toronto, ON M5S 1A1, Canada. Offers M Eng, MA Sc, PhD. *Program availability:* Part-time. *Degree requirements:* For master's, thesis (for some programs), oral presentation/thesis defense (MA Sc), qualifying exam; for doctorate, thesis/dissertation. *Entrance requirements:* For master's, BA Sc or B Sc in materials science and engineering, 2 letters of reference; for doctorate, MA Sc or equivalent, 2 letters of reference, minimum B+ average in last 2 years. Additional exam requirements/recommendations for international students: required—TOEFL (minimum score 580 paper-based), TWE (minimum score 4). Electronic applications accepted.

University of Utah, Graduate School, College of Engineering, Department of Materials Science and Engineering, Salt Lake City, UT 84112. Offers MS, PhD. *Faculty:* 21 full-time (1 woman). *Students:* 43 full-time (12 women), 13 part-time (3 women); includes 5 minority (3 Asian, non-Hispanic/Latino; 1 Hispanic/Latino; 1 Native Hawaiian or other Pacific Islander, non-Hispanic/Latino), 25 international. Average age 28. 53 applicants, 28% accepted, 10 enrolled. In 2019, 19 master's, 13 doctorates awarded. *Degree requirements:* For master's, thesis (for some programs), Program of Study; for doctorate, comprehensive exam, thesis/dissertation, proposal defense, program of study. *Entrance requirements:* For master's and doctorate, GRE, BS in field or equivalent, from recognized institute of higher learning. Additional exam requirements/recommendations for international students: required—TOEFL (minimum score 550 paper-based; 80 iBT), IELTS (minimum score 6.5), Either TOEFL or IELTS. *Application deadline:* For fall admission, 1/15 for domestic and international students; for spring admission, 10/1 for domestic students, 9/1 for international students; for summer admission, 1/15 for domestic students, 12/15 for international students. Applications are processed on a rolling basis. Application fee: $45 ($65 for international students). Electronic applications accepted. *Expenses:* Tuition, state resident: full-time $7085; part-time $272.51 per credit hour. Tuition, nonresident: full-time $24,937; part-time $959.12 per credit hour. *Required fees:* $880.52; $880.52 per semester. Tuition and fees vary according to degree level, program and student level. *Financial support:* In 2019–20, 6 students received support, including 6 fellowships with full tuition reimbursements available (averaging $10,000 per year), 35 research assistantships with full tuition reimbursements available (averaging $15,727 per year). *Unit head:* Michael Simpson, Chair, 801-581-4013, E-mail: michael.simpson@utah.edu. *Application contact:* Sara Wilson, Administrative Manager, 801-581-4449, E-mail: sara.j.wilson@utah.edu.
Website: http://www.mse.utah.edu/

University of Washington, Graduate School, College of Engineering, Department of Materials Science and Engineering, Seattle, WA 98195-2120. Offers applied materials science and engineering (MS); materials science and engineering (MS, PhD); materials science and engineering and nanotechnology (PhD); materials science and engineering, nanotechnology, and molecular engineering (PhD). *Program availability:* Part-time. *Students:* 118 full-time (27 women), 26 part-time (8 women); includes 31 minority (1 Black or African American, non-Hispanic/Latino; 16 Asian, non-Hispanic/Latino; 9 Hispanic/Latino; 1 Native Hawaiian or other Pacific Islander, non-Hispanic/Latino; 4 Two or more races, non-Hispanic/Latino), 72 international. Average age 25. 435 applicants, 39% accepted, 57 enrolled. In 2019, 44 master's, 9 doctorates awarded. Terminal master's awarded for partial completion of doctoral program. *Degree requirements:* For master's, comprehensive exam, final paper or thesis and presentation; for doctorate, comprehensive exam, thesis/dissertation, qualifying evaluation, general and final exams. *Entrance requirements:* For master's and doctorate, GRE General Test, minimum GPA of 3.0, resume/curriculum vitae, letters of recommendation, statement of purpose, transcripts. Additional exam requirements/recommendations for international students: required—TOEFL (minimum score 92 iBT). *Application deadline:* For fall admission, 1/6 for domestic and international students. Application fee: $85. Electronic applications accepted. *Expenses:* Contact institution. *Financial support:* In 2019–20, 35 research assistantships with full tuition reimbursements (averaging $30,840 per year), 14 teaching assistantships with full tuition reimbursements (averaging $30,840 per year) were awarded; fellowships with full tuition reimbursements, Federal Work-Study, institutionally sponsored loans, scholarships/grants, health care benefits, tuition waivers, unspecified assistantships, and stipend supplements also available. Support available to part-time students. Financial award application deadline: 1/6. *Unit head:* Dr. Jihui Yang, Professor/Chair, 206-543-7090, Fax: 206-221-4934, E-mail: jihuiy@uw.edu. *Application contact:* Karen Wetterhahn, Academic Counselor, 206-543-2740, Fax: 206-543-3100, E-mail: karenlw@uw.edu.
Website: http://mse.washington.edu

The University of Western Ontario, School of Graduate and Postdoctoral Studies, Physical Sciences Division, Faculty of Engineering, London, ON N6A 3K7, Canada. Offers chemical and biochemical engineering (ME Sc, PhD); civil and environmental engineering (M Eng, ME Sc, PhD); electrical and computer engineering (M Eng, ME Sc, PhD); mechanical and materials engineering (M Eng, ME Sc, PhD). *Program availability:* Part-time. Terminal master's awarded for partial completion of doctoral program. *Degree requirements:* For master's, thesis; for doctorate, thesis/dissertation. *Entrance requirements:* For master's, minimum B average; for doctorate, minimum B+ average.

University of Windsor, Faculty of Graduate Studies, Faculty of Engineering, Department of Mechanical, Automotive, and Materials Engineering, Windsor, ON N9B 3P4, Canada. Offers engineering materials (M Eng, MA Sc, PhD); mechanical engineering (M Eng, MA Sc, PhD). *Program availability:* Part-time. *Degree requirements:* For master's, thesis; for doctorate, comprehensive exam, thesis/dissertation. *Entrance requirements:* For master's, minimum B average; for doctorate, master's degree, minimum B average. Additional exam requirements/recommendations for international students: required—TOEFL (minimum score 600 paper-based). Electronic applications accepted.

University of Wisconsin–Madison, Graduate School, College of Engineering, Department of Materials Science and Engineering, Madison, WI 53706-1380. Offers materials science and engineering (MS). *Program availability:* Part-time. Terminal master's awarded for partial completion of doctoral program. *Degree requirements:* For master's, thesis, minimum of 30 credits; minimum GPA of 3.0; for doctorate, comprehensive exam, thesis/dissertation, minimum of 51 credits; minimum GPA of 3.0. *Entrance requirements:* For master's and doctorate, GRE General Test, BS in physical sciences or engineering; minimum GPA of 3.0. Additional exam requirements/

recommendations for international students: required—TOEFL (minimum score 580 paper-based; 92 iBT), IELTS (minimum score 7). Electronic applications accepted.

University of Wisconsin–Milwaukee, Graduate School, College of Engineering and Applied Science, Program in Engineering, Milwaukee, WI 53201-0413. Offers biomedical engineering (MS); civil engineering (MS, PhD); computer science (PhD); electrical and computer engineering (MS); electrical engineering (PhD); engineering mechanics (MS); industrial and management engineering (MS); industrial engineering (PhD); manufacturing engineering (MS); materials (PhD); materials engineering (MS); mechanical engineering (MS). *Program availability:* Part-time. *Degree requirements:* For master's, comprehensive exam (for some programs), thesis or alternative; for doctorate, comprehensive exam, thesis/dissertation, internship. *Entrance requirements:* For master's, GRE, minimum GPA of 2.75; for doctorate, GRE, minimum GPA of 3.5. Additional exam requirements/recommendations for international students: required—TOEFL (minimum score 550 paper-based; 79 iBT), IELTS (minimum score 6.5).

Washington State University, Voiland College of Engineering and Architecture, School of Mechanical and Materials Engineering, Pullman, WA 99164-2920. Offers materials science and engineering (MS, PhD); mechanical engineering (MS, PhD). *Program availability:* Part-time. Terminal master's awarded for partial completion of doctoral program. *Degree requirements:* For master's, comprehensive exam, thesis; for doctorate, comprehensive exam, thesis/dissertation, preliminary exam. *Entrance requirements:* For master's, GRE, bachelor's degree, minimum GPA of 3.0, resume, statement of purpose, 3 letters of recommendation, official transcripts, Student Interest Profile form; for doctorate, GRE, bachelor's degree, minimum GPA of 3.4, resume, statement of purpose, 3 letters of recommendation, official transcripts, Student Interest Profile form. Additional exam requirements/recommendations for international students: required—TOEFL (minimum score 500 paper-based), IELTS. Electronic applications accepted.

West Virginia University, Statler College of Engineering and Mineral Resources, Morgantown, WV 26506. Offers aerospace engineering (MSAE, PhD); chemical engineering (MS Ch E, PhD); civil engineering (MSCE, PhD); computer engineering (PhD); computer science (MSCS, PhD); electrical engineering (MSEE, PhD); energy systems engineering (MSESE); engineering (MSE); industrial engineering (MSIE, PhD); industrial hygiene (MS); material science and engineering (MSMSE, PhD); mechanical engineering (MSME, PhD); mining engineering (MS Min E, PhD); petroleum and natural gas engineering (MSPNGE, PhD); safety management (MS); software engineering (MSSE). *Program availability:* Part-time. Terminal master's awarded for partial completion of doctoral program. *Degree requirements:* For master's, thesis optional; for doctorate, comprehensive exam, thesis/dissertation. *Entrance requirements:* Additional exam requirements/recommendations for international students: required—TOEFL (minimum score 550 paper-based). Electronic applications accepted. *Expenses:* Contact institution.

Worcester Polytechnic Institute, Graduate Admissions, Department of Mechanical Engineering, Program in Materials Science and Engineering, Worcester, MA 01609-2280. Offers materials science & engineering (MS). *Program availability:* Part-time, evening/weekend. Terminal master's awarded for partial completion of doctoral program. *Degree requirements:* For master's, thesis; for doctorate, comprehensive exam, thesis/dissertation. *Entrance requirements:* For master's and doctorate, Required for international applicants; recommended for all others., 3 letters of recommendation. Additional exam requirements/recommendations for international students: required—TOEFL (minimum score 563 paper-based; 84 iBT), IELTS (minimum score 7), GRE. Electronic applications accepted.

Wright State University, Graduate School, College of Engineering and Computer Science, Department of Mechanical and Materials Engineering, Dayton, OH 45435. Offers aerospace systems engineering (MS); materials science and engineering (MS); mechanical engineering (MS); renewable and clean energy (MS). *Degree requirements:* For master's, thesis or course option alternative. *Entrance requirements:* Additional exam requirements/recommendations for international students: required—TOEFL.

Materials Sciences

Air Force Institute of Technology, Graduate School of Engineering and Management, Department of Aeronautics and Astronautics, Dayton, OH 45433-7765. Offers aeronautical engineering (MS, PhD); astronautical engineering (MS, PhD); materials science (MS, PhD); space operations (MS); systems engineering (MS, PhD). *Accreditation:* ABET (one or more programs are accredited). *Program availability:* Part-time. *Degree requirements:* For master's, thesis; for doctorate, thesis/dissertation. *Entrance requirements:* For master's and doctorate, GRE General Test, minimum GPA of 3.0, U.S. citizenship.

Air Force Institute of Technology, Graduate School of Engineering and Management, Department of Engineering Physics, Dayton, OH 45433-7765. Offers applied physics (MS, PhD); electro-optics (MS, PhD); materials science (PhD); nuclear engineering (MS, PhD); space physics (MS). *Program availability:* Part-time. *Degree requirements:* For master's, thesis; for doctorate, thesis/dissertation. *Entrance requirements:* For master's and doctorate, GRE General Test, minimum GPA of 3.0, U.S. citizenship.

Alabama Agricultural and Mechanical University, School of Graduate Studies, College of Engineering, Technology, and Physical Sciences, Department of Physics, Chemistry and Mathematics, Huntsville, AL 35811. Offers physics (MS, PhD), including materials science (PhD), optics/lasers (PhD), space science (PhD). *Program availability:* Part-time, evening/weekend. *Degree requirements:* For doctorate, thesis/dissertation. *Entrance requirements:* For master's and doctorate, GRE General Test. Additional exam requirements/recommendations for international students: required—TOEFL (minimum score 500 paper-based; 61 iBT). Electronic applications accepted.

Alfred University, Graduate School, College of Ceramics, Inamori School of Engineering, Alfred, NY 14802-1205. Offers biomaterials engineering (MS); ceramic engineering (MS, PhD); electrical engineering (MS); glass science (MS, PhD); materials science and engineering (MS, PhD); mechanical engineering (MS). *Program availability:* Part-time. *Faculty:* 27 full-time (4 women), 2 part-time/adjunct (both women). *Students:* 30 full-time (11 women), 15 part-time (5 women); includes 2 minority (both Asian, non-Hispanic/Latino), 12 international. Average age 28. 24 applicants, 83% accepted, 18 enrolled. In 2019, 8 master's, 5 doctorates awarded. *Degree requirements:* For master's, comprehensive exam, thesis; for doctorate, comprehensive exam, thesis/dissertation. *Entrance requirements:* Additional exam requirements/recommendations for international students: required—TOEFL (minimum score 590 paper-based; 90 iBT), IELTS (minimum score 6.5). *Application deadline:* For fall admission, 3/1 priority date for domestic students, 3/15 for international students; for spring admission, 10/1 priority date for domestic students, 10/1 for international students. Applications are processed on a rolling basis. Application fee: $60. Electronic applications accepted. Application fee is waived when completed online. *Expenses:* $23,530 per year. *Financial support:* In 2019–20, 31 students received support. Fellowships with full tuition reimbursements available, research assistantships with full tuition reimbursements available, teaching assistantships with full tuition reimbursements available, tuition waivers (full and partial), and unspecified assistantships available. Financial award application deadline: 3/15; financial award applicants required to submit FAFSA. *Unit head:* Dr. Gabrielle Gaustad, Dean, 607-871-2953, E-mail: gaustad@alfred.edu. *Application contact:* Lindsey Gertin, Assistant Director of Graduate Admissions, 607-871-2017, Fax: 607-871-2198, E-mail: gradinquiry@alfred.edu.
Website: http://engineering.alfred.edu/grad/

Arizona State University at Tempe, Ira A. Fulton Schools of Engineering, School for Engineering of Matter, Transport and Energy, Tempe, AZ 85281. Offers aerospace engineering (MS, PhD); chemical engineering (MS, PhD); materials science and engineering (MS, PhD); mechanical engineering (MS, PhD); solar energy engineering and commercialization (PSM). *Program availability:* Part-time, evening/weekend, online learning. Terminal master's awarded for partial completion of doctoral program. *Degree requirements:* For master's, thesis and oral defense (MS); applied project or comprehensive exam (MSE); interactive Program of Study (iPOS) submitted before completing 50 percent of required credit hours; for doctorate, comprehensive exam, thesis/dissertation, interactive Program of Study (iPOS) submitted before completing 50 percent of required credit hours. *Entrance requirements:* For master's, GRE, minimum GPA of 3.0 or equivalent in last 2 years of work leading to bachelor's degree; for doctorate, GRE, minimum GPA of 3.0 in last 2 years of work leading to bachelor's degree. Additional exam requirements/recommendations for international students: required—TOEFL, IELTS, or PTE. Electronic applications accepted. *Expenses:* Contact institution.

Binghamton University, State University of New York, Graduate School, Materials Science and Engineering Program, Binghamton, NY 13902-6000. Offers MS, PhD.

Program availability: Part-time, online learning. *Degree requirements:* For master's, thesis; for doctorate, comprehensive exam, thesis/dissertation. *Entrance requirements:* For master's and doctorate, GRE General Test. Additional exam requirements/recommendations for international students: required—TOEFL (minimum score 550 paper-based; 80 iBT). Electronic applications accepted. *Expenses:* Contact institution.

Boston University, College of Engineering, Division of Materials Science and Engineering, Brookline, MA 02215. Offers materials science and engineering (M Eng, MS, PhD). *Program availability:* Part-time. *Students:* 80 full-time (31 women), 21 part-time (6 women); includes 9 minority (1 Black or African American, non-Hispanic/Latino; 5 Asian, non-Hispanic/Latino; 3 Two or more races, non-Hispanic/Latino), 65 international. Average age 25. 379 applicants, 51% accepted, 35 enrolled. In 2019, 25 master's, 5 doctorates awarded. Terminal master's awarded for partial completion of doctoral program. *Degree requirements:* For master's, thesis (for some programs); for doctorate, comprehensive exam, thesis/dissertation. *Entrance requirements:* For master's and doctorate, GRE General Test. Additional exam requirements/recommendations for international students: required—TOEFL (minimum score 90 iBT), IELTS (minimum score 7). Application fee: $95. *Financial support:* Application deadline: 1/15. *Unit head:* Dr. David Bishop, Division Head, 617-353-8899, Fax: 617-353-5548, E-mail: djb1@bu.edu. *Application contact:* Dr. David Bishop, Division Head, 617-353-8899, Fax: 617-353-5548, E-mail: djb1@bu.edu.
Website: http://www.bu.edu/mse/

Brown University, Graduate School, School of Engineering, Program in Materials Science and Engineering, Providence, RI 02912. Offers Sc M, PhD. *Degree requirements:* For doctorate, thesis/dissertation, preliminary exam.

California Institute of Technology, Division of Engineering and Applied Science, Option in Materials Science, Pasadena, CA 91125-0001. Offers MS, PhD. *Degree requirements:* For doctorate, thesis/dissertation.

Carnegie Mellon University, Carnegie Institute of Technology, Department of Materials Science and Engineering, Pittsburgh, PA 15213-3891. Offers MS, PhD. *Program availability:* Part-time. Terminal master's awarded for partial completion of doctoral program. *Degree requirements:* For master's, exam; for doctorate, thesis/dissertation, qualifying exam. *Entrance requirements:* For master's and doctorate, GRE General Test. Additional exam requirements/recommendations for international students: required—TOEFL.

Case Western Reserve University, School of Graduate Studies, Case School of Engineering, Department of Materials Science and Engineering, Cleveland, OH 44106. Offers materials science and engineering (MS, PhD). *Program availability:* Part-time, online learning. Terminal master's awarded for partial completion of doctoral program. *Degree requirements:* For master's, thesis (for some programs); for doctorate, thesis/dissertation, qualifying exam, teaching experience. *Entrance requirements:* For master's and doctorate, GRE General Test. Additional exam requirements/recommendations for international students: required—TOEFL.

The Catholic University of America, School of Engineering, Department of Materials Science and Engineering, Washington, DC 20064. Offers MS. *Program availability:* Part-time. *Faculty:* 1 full-time (0 women), 3 part-time/adjunct (2 women). *Students:* 3 full-time (2 women), 5 part-time (3 women); includes 1 minority (Black or African American, non-Hispanic/Latino), 4 international. Average age 26. 9 applicants, 78% accepted, 3 enrolled. *Degree requirements:* For master's, thesis optional. *Entrance requirements:* For master's, GRE (minimum score 1250), minimum GPA of 3.0, statement of purpose, official copies of academic transcripts. Additional exam requirements/recommendations for international students: required—TOEFL (minimum score 550 paper-based; 80 iBT). *Application deadline:* For fall admission, 7/15 for domestic students, 7/1 for international students; for spring admission, 11/15 for domestic students, 11/1 for international students. Applications are processed on a rolling basis. Application fee: $55. Electronic applications accepted. *Expenses:* Contact institution. *Financial support:* Fellowships, research assistantships, teaching assistantships, Federal Work-Study, scholarships/grants, tuition waivers (full and partial), and unspecified assistantships available. Financial award application deadline: 2/1; financial award applicants required to submit FAFSA. *Unit head:* Mel Williams, Director, 202-319-5191, Fax: 202-319-4469, E-mail: williamsme@cua.edu. *Application contact:* Dr. Steven Brown, Director of Graduate Admissions, 202-319-5057, Fax: 202-319-6533, E-mail: cua-admissions@cua.edu.
Website: https://engineering.catholic.edu/materials-science/index.html

Central Michigan University, College of Graduate Studies, College of Science and Engineering, Department of Physics, Program in the Science of Advanced Materials,

Mount Pleasant, MI 48859. Offers PhD. *Degree requirements:* For doctorate, comprehensive exam, thesis/dissertation. *Entrance requirements:* For doctorate, GRE. Electronic applications accepted. *Expenses: Tuition, area resident:* Full-time $12,267; part-time $8178 per year. Tuition, state resident: full-time $12,267; part-time $8178 per year. Tuition, nonresident: full-time $12,267; part-time $8178 per year. *International tuition:* $16,110 full-time. *Required fees:* $225 per semester. Tuition and fees vary according to degree level and program.

Clarkson University, Wallace H. Coulter School of Engineering, Program in Materials Science and Engineering, Potsdam, NY 13699. Offers PhD. *Students:* 5 full-time (1 woman); includes 1 minority (Asian, non-Hispanic/Latino), 3 international. 18 applicants, 50% accepted, 1 enrolled. In 2019, 2 doctorates awarded. *Degree requirements:* For doctorate, comprehensive exam, thesis/dissertation. *Entrance requirements:* For doctorate, GRE. Additional exam requirements/recommendations for international students: required—TOEFL (minimum score 550 paper-based, 80 iBT) or IELTS (6.5). *Application deadline:* Applications are processed on a rolling basis. Application fee: $50. Electronic applications accepted. *Expenses: Tuition:* Full-time $24,984; part-time $1388. *Required fees:* $225. Tuition and fees vary according to campus/location and program. *Financial support:* Scholarships/grants and unspecified assistantships available. *Unit head:* Dr. Silvana Andreescu, Professor / Egon Matijevic Chair of Chemistry / Co-Director of CAMP, 315-268-2394, E-mail: wjemison@clarkson.edu. *Application contact:* Daniel Capogna, Director of Graduate Admissions & Recruitment, 518-631-9910, E-mail: graduate@clarkson.edu.
Website: https://www.clarkson.edu/academics/graduate

Clemson University, Graduate School, College of Engineering, Computing and Applied Sciences, Department of Materials Science and Engineering, Clemson, SC 29634. Offers MS, PhD. *Faculty:* 20 full-time (4 women), 2 part-time/adjunct (0 women). *Students:* 61 full-time (20 women), 6 part-time (1 woman); includes 2 minority (1 Asian, non-Hispanic/Latino; 1 Hispanic/Latino), 38 international. Average age 26. 105 applicants, 82% accepted, 22 enrolled. In 2019, 6 master's, 8 doctorates awarded. *Expenses: Tuition, area resident:* Full-time $10,600; part-time $8688 per semester. Tuition, state resident: full-time $10,600; part-time $8688 per semester. Tuition, nonresident: full-time $22,050; part-time $17,412 per semester. *International tuition:* $22,050 full-time. *Required fees:* $1196; $617 per semester. $617 per semester. Tuition and fees vary according to course load, degree level, campus/location and program. *Financial support:* In 2019–20, 79 students received support, including 13 fellowships with full and partial tuition reimbursements available (averaging $3,877 per year), 43 research assistantships with full and partial tuition reimbursements available (averaging $20,249 per year); career-related internships or fieldwork and unspecified assistantships also available. *Unit head:* Dr. Kyle Brinkman, Department Chair, 864-656-1405, E-mail: ksbrink@clemson.edu. *Application contact:* Dr. Igor Luzinov, Graduate Program Coordinator, 864-656-5958, E-mail: luzinov@clemson.edu.
Website: https://www.clemson.edu/cecas/departments/mse/index.html

Colorado School of Mines, Office of Graduate Studies, Department of Metallurgical and Materials Engineering, Golden, CO 80401. Offers materials science (MS, PhD); metallurgical and materials engineering (ME, MS, PhD). *Program availability:* Part-time. *Degree requirements:* For master's, thesis (for some programs); for doctorate, comprehensive exam, thesis/dissertation. *Entrance requirements:* For master's and doctorate, GRE General Test. Additional exam requirements/recommendations for international students: required—TOEFL (minimum score 550 paper-based; 79 iBT). Electronic applications accepted. *Expenses:* Tuition, state resident: full-time $16,650; part-time $925 per credit hour. Tuition, nonresident: full-time $37,350; part-time $2075 per credit hour. *International tuition:* $37,350 full-time. *Required fees:* $2412.

Colorado State University, College of Natural Sciences, Programs in Natural Sciences Education, Fort Collins, CO 80523. Offers material science and engineering (PhD); natural science education (MNSE); zoo, aquarium, and animal shelter management (MS). *Program availability:* 100% online. *Degree requirements:* For master's, comprehensive exam (for some programs), thesis (for some programs); for doctorate, comprehensive exam (for some programs), thesis/dissertation. *Entrance requirements:* Additional exam requirements/recommendations for international students: required—TOEFL (minimum score 550 paper-based). Electronic applications accepted. *Expenses:* Contact institution.

Columbia University, Fu Foundation School of Engineering and Applied Science, Department of Applied Physics and Applied Mathematics, New York, NY 10027. Offers applied mathematics (MS, Eng Sc D, PhD); applied physics (MS, Eng Sc D, PhD); materials science and engineering (MS, Eng Sc D, PhD); medical physics (MS). *Program availability:* Part-time, online learning. Terminal master's awarded for partial completion of doctoral program. *Degree requirements:* For master's, comprehensive exam; for doctorate, thesis/dissertation, qualifying exam. *Entrance requirements:* For master's, GRE General Test, GRE Subject Test (strongly recommended); for doctorate, GRE General Test, GRE Subject Test (applied physics). Additional exam requirements/recommendations for international students: required—TOEFL, IELTS, PTE. Electronic applications accepted. *Expenses: Tuition:* Full-time $47,600; part-time $1880 per credit. One-time fee: $105.

Cornell University, Graduate School, Graduate Fields of Engineering, Field of Materials Science and Engineering, Ithaca, NY 14853. Offers materials engineering (M Eng, PhD); materials science (M Eng, PhD). *Degree requirements:* For doctorate, comprehensive exam, thesis/dissertation. *Entrance requirements:* For master's and doctorate, GRE General Test, 3 letters of recommendation. Additional exam requirements/recommendations for international students: required—TOEFL (minimum score 550 paper-based; 77 iBT). Electronic applications accepted.

Dartmouth College, Dartmouth Engineering - Thayer School of Engineering, Program in Materials Engineering, Hanover, NH 03755. Offers MS, PhD. Terminal master's awarded for partial completion of doctoral program. *Degree requirements:* For master's, thesis (for some programs); for doctorate, thesis/dissertation. *Entrance requirements:* For master's and doctorate, GRE General Test. Additional exam requirements/recommendations for international students: required—TOEFL, IELTS. *Application deadline:* For fall admission, 1/1 priority date for domestic students, 1/1 for international students. Applications are processed on a rolling basis. Application fee: $45. Electronic applications accepted. *Financial support:* Fellowships, research assistantships, teaching assistantships, career-related internships or fieldwork, institutionally sponsored loans, scholarships/grants, and tuition waivers (full and partial) available. Financial award application deadline: 2/15; financial award applicants required to submit CSS PROFILE. *Unit head:* Dr. Ian Baker, Sherman Fairchild Professor of Engineering, 603-646-2184, E-mail: ian.baker@dartmouth.edu. *Application contact:* Candace S. Potter, Graduate Admissions & Financial Aid Administrator, 603-646-3844, Fax: 603-646-1620, E-mail: candace.s.potter@dartmouth.edu.
Website: https://engineering.dartmouth.edu/

Duke University, Graduate School, Pratt School of Engineering, Department of Mechanical Engineering and Materials Science, Durham, NC 27708. Offers materials science (M Eng, MS, PhD); mechanical engineering (M Eng, MS, PhD); JD/MS. Terminal master's awarded for partial completion of doctoral program. *Degree requirements:* For master's, thesis optional; for doctorate, thesis/dissertation. *Entrance requirements:* For master's and doctorate, GRE General Test. Additional exam requirements/recommendations for international students: required—TOEFL (minimum score 90 iBT), IELTS (minimum score 7). Electronic applications accepted.

Duke University, Graduate School, Pratt School of Engineering, Master of Engineering Program, Durham, NC 27708-0271. Offers biomedical engineering (M Eng); civil engineering (M Eng); computational mechanics and scientific computing (M Eng); electrical and computer engineering (M Eng); environmental engineering (M Eng); materials science and engineering (M Eng); mechanical engineering (M Eng); photonics and optical sciences (M Eng); risk engineering (M Eng). *Program availability:* Part-time. *Entrance requirements:* For master's, GRE General Test, resume, 3 letters of recommendation, statement of purpose, transcripts. Additional exam requirements/recommendations for international students: required—TOEFL. Electronic applications accepted.

Florida International University, College of Engineering and Computing, Department of Mechanical and Materials Engineering, Miami, FL 33199. Offers materials science and engineering (MS, PhD); mechanical engineering (MS, PhD). *Program availability:* Part-time, evening/weekend. *Faculty:* 22 full-time (5 women), 5 part-time/adjunct (1 woman). *Students:* 62 full-time (10 women), 11 part-time (4 women); includes 27 minority (4 Black or African American, non-Hispanic/Latino; 3 Asian, non-Hispanic/Latino; 17 Hispanic/Latino; 3 Two or more races, non-Hispanic/Latino), 43 international. Average age 29. 136 applicants, 51% accepted, 21 enrolled. In 2019, 11 master's, 8 doctorates awarded. Terminal master's awarded for partial completion of doctoral program. *Degree requirements:* For master's, thesis or alternative; for doctorate, comprehensive exam, thesis/dissertation. *Entrance requirements:* For master's, GRE (depending on program), 3 letters of recommendation, minimum undergraduate GPA of 3.0 in upper-level course work; for doctorate, GRE (minimum combined score of 1150, verbal 450, quantitative 650), minimum undergraduate GPA of 3.0 in upper-level coursework with BS, 3.3 with MS; 3 letters of recommendation; letter of intent. Additional exam requirements/recommendations for international students: required—TOEFL (minimum score 550 paper-based; 80 iBT) or IELTS (minimum score 6.5). *Application deadline:* For fall admission, 6/1 for domestic students, 4/1 for international students; for spring admission, 10/1 for domestic students, 9/1 for international students. Applications are processed on a rolling basis. Application fee: $30. Electronic applications accepted. *Expenses: Tuition, area resident:* Full-time $8912; part-time $446 per credit hour. Tuition, state resident: full-time $8912; part-time $446 per credit hour. Tuition, nonresident: full-time $21,393; part-time $992 per credit hour. *Required fees:* $2194. *Financial support:* Institutionally sponsored loans, scholarships/grants, and unspecified assistantships available. Financial award application deadline: 3/1; financial award applicants required to submit FAFSA. *Unit head:* Dr. ARVIND AGARWAL, Chair, 305-348-1701, Fax: 305-348-1932, E-mail: Arvind.Agarwal@fiu.edu. *Application contact:* Nanett Rojas, Manager, Admissions Operations, 305-348-7464, Fax: 305-348-7441, E-mail: gradadm@fiu.edu.
Website: http://cec.fiu.edu

Florida State University, The Graduate School, Department of Anthropology, Department of Chemistry and Biochemistry, Tallahassee, FL 32306-4390. Offers analytical chemistry (MS, PhD); biochemistry (MS, PhD); inorganic chemistry (MS, PhD); materials chemistry (PhD); organic chemistry (MS, PhD); physical chemistry (MS, PhD). Terminal master's awarded for partial completion of doctoral program. *Degree requirements:* For master's, thesis (for some programs); for doctorate, thesis/dissertation. *Entrance requirements:* For master's and doctorate, GRE General Test (minimum scores: 150 verbal, 151 quantitative), minimum upper-division GPA of 3.1 in undergraduate course work. Additional exam requirements/recommendations for international students: required—TOEFL (minimum score 80 iBT). Electronic applications accepted.

Florida State University, The Graduate School, Department of Anthropology, Department of Scientific Computing, Tallahassee, FL 32306-4120. Offers computational science (MS, PhD), including atmospheric science (PhD), biochemistry (PhD), biological science (PhD), computational science (PhD), geological science (PhD), materials science (PhD), physics (PhD). *Program availability:* Part-time. *Faculty:* 9 full-time (1 woman), 2 part-time/adjunct (1 woman). *Students:* 34 full-time (6 women); includes 5 minority (2 Asian, non-Hispanic/Latino; 2 Hispanic/Latino; 1 Two or more races, non-Hispanic/Latino), 12 international. Average age 25. 65 applicants, 46% accepted, 8 enrolled. In 2019, 4 master's, 8 doctorates awarded. Terminal master's awarded for partial completion of doctoral program. *Degree requirements:* For master's, comprehensive exam (for some programs), thesis (for some programs); for doctorate, comprehensive exam, thesis/dissertation. *Entrance requirements:* For master's and doctorate, GRE General Test, knowledge of at least one object-oriented computing language, 3 letters of recommendation, resume, statement of purpose. Additional exam requirements/recommendations for international students: required—TOEFL (minimum score 550 paper-based; 80 iBT). *Application deadline:* For fall admission, 4/15 for domestic and international students. Applications are processed on a rolling basis. Application fee: $30. Electronic applications accepted. *Financial support:* In 2019–20, 30 students received support, including 6 research assistantships with full tuition reimbursements available (averaging $26,670 per year), 12 teaching assistantships with full tuition reimbursements available (averaging $23,000 per year); scholarships/grants, health care benefits, tuition waivers (full), and unspecified assistantships also available. Financial award application deadline: 1/15. *Unit head:* Dr. Gordon Erlebacher, Chair, 850-644-7024, E-mail: gerlebacher@fsu.edu. *Application contact:* Karey Fowler, Academic Program Specialist, 850-644-0143, Fax: 850-644-0098, E-mail: kgfowler@fsu.edu.
Website: http://www.sc.fsu.edu

Florida State University, The Graduate School, Materials Science and Engineering Program, Tallahassee, FL 32310. Offers MS, PhD. *Faculty:* 34 full-time (5 women). *Students:* 14 full-time (7 women), 9 international. Average age 25. 48 applicants, 23% accepted, 2 enrolled. In 2019, 2 doctorates awarded. Terminal master's awarded for partial completion of doctoral program. *Degree requirements:* For master's, thesis; for doctorate, comprehensive exam, thesis/dissertation. *Entrance requirements:* For master's and doctorate, GRE General Test (minimum new format 55th percentile Verbal, 75th percentile Quantitative, old version 1100 combined Verbal and Quantitative), minimum GPA of 3.0, 3 letters of recommendation. Additional exam requirements/recommendations for international students: required—TOEFL (minimum score 80 iBT). *Application deadline:* For fall admission, 5/1 for domestic and international students; for spring admission, 9/1 for domestic and international students; for summer admission, 1/1 for domestic and international students. Applications are processed on a rolling basis. Application fee: $30. Electronic applications accepted. *Financial support:* In 2019–20, 13 students received support, including 12 research assistantships with full tuition reimbursements available (averaging $20,000 per year); partial payment of required health insurance also available. Financial award application deadline: 12/15. *Unit head:* Prof. Eric Hellstrom, Director, 850-645-7489, Fax: 850-645-7754, E-mail: hellstrom@asc.magnet.fsu.edu. *Application contact:* Stephanie Salters, Admissions Coordinator, 850-645-8980, Fax: 850-645-9123, E-mail: salters@eng.famu.fsu.edu.
Website: http://materials.fsu.edu

Materials Sciences

Georgetown University, Graduate School of Arts and Sciences, Department of Chemistry, Washington, DC 20057. Offers analytical chemistry (PhD); biochemistry (PhD); computational chemistry (PhD); inorganic chemistry (PhD); materials chemistry (PhD); organic chemistry (PhD); theoretical chemistry (PhD). Terminal master's awarded for partial completion of doctoral program. *Degree requirements:* For doctorate, comprehensive exam, thesis/dissertation. *Entrance requirements:* For doctorate, GRE General Test. Additional exam requirements/recommendations for international students: required—TOEFL.

The George Washington University, Columbian College of Arts and Sciences, Department of Chemistry, Washington, DC 20052. Offers analytical chemistry (MS, PhD); inorganic chemistry (MS, PhD); materials science (MS, PhD); organic chemistry (MS, PhD); physical chemistry (MS, PhD). *Program availability:* Part-time, evening/weekend. Terminal master's awarded for partial completion of doctoral program. *Degree requirements:* For master's, comprehensive exam, thesis or alternative; for doctorate, thesis/dissertation, general exam. *Entrance requirements:* For master's and doctorate, GRE General Test, interview, minimum GPA of 3.0. Additional exam requirements/recommendations for international students: required—TOEFL (minimum score 550 paper-based; 80 iBT). Electronic applications accepted.

Harvard University, Graduate School of Arts and Sciences, Harvard John A. Paulson School of Engineering and Applied Sciences, Cambridge, MA 02138. Offers applied mathematics (PhD); applied physics (PhD); computational science and engineering (ME, SM); computer science (PhD); data science (SM); design engineering (MDE); engineering science (ME), including electrical engineering (ME, SM, PhD); engineering sciences (SM, PhD), including bioengineering (PhD), electrical engineering (ME, SM, PhD), environmental science and engineering (PhD), materials science and mechanical engineering (PhD). *Program availability:* Part-time. Terminal master's awarded for partial completion of doctoral program. *Degree requirements:* For master's, thesis (for ME); for doctorate, comprehensive exam, thesis/dissertation. *Entrance requirements:* For master's and doctorate, GRE General Test, GRE Subject Test (recommended), 3 letters of recommendation. Additional exam requirements/recommendations for international students: required—TOEFL (minimum score 80 iBT). Electronic applications accepted. *Expenses:* Contact institution.

Illinois Institute of Technology, Graduate College, Armour College of Engineering, Department of Mechanical, Materials and Aerospace Engineering, Chicago, IL 60616. Offers manufacturing engineering (MAS, MS); materials science and engineering (MAS, MS, PhD); mechanical and aerospace engineering (MAS, MS, PhD), including economics (MS), energy (MS), environment (MS). *Program availability:* Part-time, evening/weekend, online learning. Terminal master's awarded for partial completion of doctoral program. *Degree requirements:* For master's, comprehensive exam (for some programs), thesis (for some programs); for doctorate, comprehensive exam, thesis/dissertation. *Entrance requirements:* For master's and doctorate, GRE General Test (minimum score 1000 Quantitative and Verbal, 3.0 Analytical Writing), minimum undergraduate GPA of 3.0. Additional exam requirements/recommendations for international students: required—TOEFL (minimum score 550 paper-based; 80 iBT). Electronic applications accepted.

Illinois Institute of Technology, Graduate College, College of Science, Department of Chemistry, Chicago, IL 60616. Offers analytical chemistry (MAS); chemistry (MAS, MS, PhD); materials chemistry (MAS), including inorganic, organic, or polymeric materials. *Program availability:* Part-time, evening/weekend, online learning. Terminal master's awarded for partial completion of doctoral program. *Degree requirements:* For master's, comprehensive exam, thesis (for some programs); for doctorate, comprehensive exam, thesis/dissertation. *Entrance requirements:* For master's, GRE General Test (minimum score 300 Quantitative and Verbal, 2.5 Analytical Writing), minimum undergraduate GPA of 3.0; for doctorate, GRE General Test (minimum score 310 Quantitative and Verbal, 3.0 Analytical Writing), GRE Subject Test, minimum undergraduate GPA of 3.0. Additional exam requirements/recommendations for international students: required—TOEFL (minimum score 550 paper-based; 80 iBT); recommended—IELTS. Electronic applications accepted.

Indiana University Bloomington, University Graduate School, College of Arts and Sciences, Department of Chemistry, Bloomington, IN 47405. Offers analytical chemistry (PhD); chemical biology (PhD); chemistry (MAT); inorganic chemistry (PhD); materials chemistry (PhD); organic chemistry (PhD); physical chemistry (PhD); MSES/MS. Terminal master's awarded for partial completion of doctoral program. *Degree requirements:* For master's, thesis; for doctorate, thesis/dissertation. *Entrance requirements:* For master's and doctorate, GRE General Test, GRE Subject Test. Additional exam requirements/recommendations for international students: required—TOEFL. Electronic applications accepted.

Instituto Tecnológico y de Estudios Superiores de Monterrey, Campus Estado de México, Professional and Graduate Division, Estado de Mexico, Mexico. Offers administration of information technologies (MITA); architecture (M Arch); business administration (GMBA, MBA); computer sciences (MCS, PhD); education (M Ed); educational institution administration (MAD); educational technology and innovation (PhD); electronic commerce (MEC); environmental systems (MS); finance (MAF); humanistic studies (MHS); information sciences and knowledge management (MISKM); information systems (MS); manufacturing systems (MS); marketing (MEM); quality systems and productivity (MS); science and materials engineering (PhD); telecommunications management (MTM). *Program availability:* Part-time, online learning. *Degree requirements:* For master's, one foreign language, thesis (for some programs); for doctorate, one foreign language, thesis/dissertation. *Entrance requirements:* For master's, E-PAEP 500, interview; for doctorate, E-PAEP 500, research proposal. Additional exam requirements/recommendations for international students: required—TOEFL (minimum score 550 paper-based).

Iowa State University of Science and Technology, Department of Materials Science and Engineering, Ames, IA 50011. Offers M Eng, MS, PhD. *Entrance requirements:* For master's and doctorate, GRE General Test. Additional exam requirements/recommendations for international students: required—TOEFL (minimum score 550 paper-based; 79 iBT), IELTS (minimum score 6.5). Electronic applications accepted.

Jackson State University, Graduate School, College of Science, Engineering and Technology, Department of Civil and Environmental Engineering and Industrial Systems and Technology, Jackson, MS 39217. Offers civil engineering (MS, PhD); coastal engineering (MS, PhD); environmental engineering (MS, PhD); hazardous materials management (MS); technology education (MS Ed). *Program availability:* Part-time, evening/weekend. *Degree requirements:* For master's, comprehensive exam, thesis or alternative. *Entrance requirements:* For master's, GRE General Test. Additional exam requirements/recommendations for international students: required—TOEFL (minimum score 520 paper-based; 67 iBT).

Johns Hopkins University, Engineering Program for Professionals, Part-time Program in Materials Science and Engineering, Baltimore, MD 21218. Offers nanotechnology (M Mat SE). *Program availability:* Part-time, evening/weekend. *Entrance requirements:* Additional exam requirements/recommendations for international students: required—TOEFL (minimum score 600 paper-based; 100 iBT). Electronic applications accepted.

Johns Hopkins University, G. W. C. Whiting School of Engineering, Department of Materials Science and Engineering, Baltimore, MD 21218. Offers M Mat SE, MSE, PhD. Terminal master's awarded for partial completion of doctoral program. *Degree requirements:* For master's, thesis; for doctorate, thesis/dissertation, oral exam, thesis defense. *Entrance requirements:* For master's and doctorate, GRE General Test, 2 letters of recommendation, statement of purpose, transcripts. Additional exam requirements/recommendations for international students: required—TOEFL (minimum score 600 paper-based, 100 iBT) or IELTS (7). Electronic applications accepted.

Johns Hopkins University, G. W. C. Whiting School of Engineering, Master of Science in Engineering Management Program, Baltimore, MD 21218. Offers biomaterials (MSEM); civil engineering (MSEM); communications science (MSEM); computer science (MSEM); environmental systems analysis, economics and public policy (MSEM); fluid mechanics (MSEM); materials science and engineering (MSEM); mechanical engineering (MSEM); mechanics and materials (MSEM); nano-biotechnology (MSEM); nanomaterials and nanotechnology (MSEM); operations research (MSEM); probability and statistics (MSEM); smart product and device design (MSEM). *Entrance requirements:* For master's, GRE, 3 letters of recommendation, statement of purpose, transcripts. Additional exam requirements/recommendations for international students: required—TOEFL (minimum score 600 paper-based, 100 iBT) or IELTS (7). Electronic applications accepted.

Lehigh University, P.C. Rossin College of Engineering and Applied Science, Department of Materials Science and Engineering, Bethlehem, PA 18015. Offers materials science and engineering (M Eng, MS, PhD); photonics (MS); polymer science/engineering (M Eng, MS, PhD); MBA/E. *Program availability:* Part-time. *Faculty:* 14 full-time (4 women). *Students:* 30 full-time (6 women), 2 part-time (both women); includes 3 minority (1 Asian, non-Hispanic/Latino; 1 Hispanic/Latino; 1 Two or more races, non-Hispanic/Latino), 8 international. Average age 26. 91 applicants, 22% accepted, 10 enrolled. In 2019, 3 master's, 5 doctorates awarded. *Degree requirements:* For master's, thesis; for doctorate, comprehensive exam, thesis/dissertation. *Entrance requirements:* For master's and doctorate, GRE General Test, minimum GPA of 3.60. Additional exam requirements/recommendations for international students: required—TOEFL (minimum score 487 paper-based; 85 iBT), IELTS (minimum score 6.5), TOEFL or IELTS required. *Application deadline:* For fall admission, 1/15 priority date for domestic students, 1/15 for international students; for spring admission, 12/1 priority date for domestic students, 12/1 for international students. Application fee: $75. *Financial support:* In 2019–20, 26 students received support, including 12 fellowships with tuition reimbursements available (averaging $30,540 per year), 25 research assistantships with tuition reimbursements available (averaging $30,540 per year), 12 teaching assistantships with tuition reimbursements available (averaging $10,890 per year); scholarships/grants and health care benefits also available. Financial award application deadline: 1/15. *Unit head:* Dr. Wojciech Misiolek, Chairperson, 610-758-4252, Fax: 610-758-4244, E-mail: wzm2@lehigh.edu. *Application contact:* Lisa Carreras Arechiga, Graduate Administrative Coordinator, 610-758-4222, Fax: 610-758-4244, E-mail: lia4@lehigh.edu. Website: https://engineering.lehigh.edu/matsci

Louisiana Tech University, Graduate School, College of Engineering and Science, Ruston, LA 71272. Offers applied physics (MS); biomedical engineering (PhD); computer science (MS); engineering (MS, PhD), including cyberspace engineering (PhD), engineering education (PhD), engineering physics (PhD), materials and infrastructure systems (PhD), micro/nanoscale systems (PhD); engineering and technology management (MS); mathematics (MS); molecular science and nanotechnology (MS, PhD). *Program availability:* Part-time-only. Terminal master's awarded for partial completion of doctoral program. *Degree requirements:* For master's, thesis (for some programs); for doctorate, thesis/dissertation. *Entrance requirements:* For master's and Graduate Certificate, GRE General Test, minimum GPA of 3.0 in last 60 hours. Additional exam requirements/recommendations for international students: required—TOEFL (minimum score 550 paper-based; 80 iBT), IELTS (minimum score 6.5). Electronic applications accepted. *Expenses: Tuition, area resident:* Full-time $6592; part-time $400 per credit. Tuition, state resident: full-time $6592; part-time $400 per credit. Tuition, nonresident: full-time $13,333; part-time $681 per credit. *International tuition:* $13,333 full-time. *Required fees:* $3011; $3011 per unit.

Massachusetts Institute of Technology, School of Engineering, Department of Materials Science and Engineering, Cambridge, MA 02139. Offers archaeological materials (PhD, Sc D); materials engineering (Mat E); materials science and engineering (SM, PhD, Sc D). *Degree requirements:* For master's, thesis; for doctorate, comprehensive exam, thesis/dissertation; for Mat E, comprehensive exam, thesis. *Entrance requirements:* For master's and doctorate, GRE General Test. Additional exam requirements/recommendations for international students: required—IELTS. Electronic applications accepted.

McMaster University, School of Graduate Studies, Faculty of Engineering, Department of Materials Science and Engineering, Hamilton, ON L8S 4M2, Canada. Offers materials engineering (M Eng, MA Sc, PhD); materials science (M Eng, PhD). *Degree requirements:* For master's, thesis; for doctorate, comprehensive exam, thesis/dissertation. *Entrance requirements:* Additional exam requirements/recommendations for international students: required—TOEFL (minimum score 550 paper-based).

Michigan State University, The Graduate School, College of Engineering, Department of Chemical Engineering and Materials Science, East Lansing, MI 48824. Offers chemical engineering (MS, PhD); materials science and engineering (MS, PhD). *Entrance requirements:* Additional exam requirements/recommendations for international students: required—TOEFL. Electronic applications accepted.

Missouri State University, Graduate College, College of Natural and Applied Sciences, Department of Physics, Astronomy, and Materials Science, Springfield, MO 65897. Offers materials science (MS); natural and applied science (MNAS), including physics (MNAS, MS Ed); secondary education (MS Ed), including physics (MNAS, MS Ed). *Program availability:* Part-time. *Degree requirements:* For master's, comprehensive exam, thesis. *Entrance requirements:* For master's, GRE (MS, MNAS), minimum undergraduate GPA of 3.0 (MS and MNAS), 9-12 teaching certification (MS Ed). Additional exam requirements/recommendations for international students: required—TOEFL (minimum score 550 paper-based; 79 iBT), IELTS (minimum score 6). Electronic applications accepted. *Expenses: Tuition, area resident:* Full-time $2600; part-time $1735 per credit hour. Tuition, nonresident: full-time $5240; part-time $3495 per credit hour. *International tuition:* $5240 full-time. *Required fees:* $530; $438 per credit hour. Tuition and fees vary according to class time, course level, course load, degree level, campus/location and program.

Missouri University of Science and Technology, Department of Materials Science and Engineering, Rolla, MO 65401. Offers ceramic engineering (MS, PhD); materials science and engineering (MS, PhD); metallurgical engineering (MS, PhD). *Degree requirements:* For master's, thesis optional; for doctorate, comprehensive exam. *Entrance requirements:* For master's, GRE (minimum combined score 1100, 600 verbal, 3.5 writing); for doctorate, GRE (minimum score: quantitative 600, writing 3.5). Additional exam requirements/recommendations for international students: required—TOEFL (minimum score 570 paper-based). Electronic applications accepted. *Expenses:* Tuition, state resident: full-time $7839; part-time $435.50 per credit hour. Tuition, nonresident: full-time $22,169; part-time $1231.60 per credit hour. *International tuition:* $18,156.60 full-time. *Required fees:* $649.76. One-time fee: $119. Tuition and fees vary according to course load and program.

Montana Technological University, Materials Science Ph.D., Butte, MT 59701-8997. Offers PhD. *Faculty:* 14 full-time (4 women), 4 part-time/adjunct (1 woman). *Students:* 16 full-time (4 women), 1 (woman) part-time; includes 1 minority (Black or African American, non-Hispanic/Latino), 4 international. Average age 32. 10 applicants, 40% accepted, 4 enrolled. In 2019, 2 doctorates awarded. *Degree requirements:* For doctorate, thesis/dissertation optional. *Entrance requirements:* Additional exam requirements/recommendations for international students: required—TOEFL (minimum score 600 paper-based; 90 iBT), IELTS (minimum score 7). *Application deadline:* For fall admission, 4/1 for domestic students, 6/1 for international students; for spring admission, 9/1 for domestic and international students. Application fee: $50. *Financial support:* In 2019–20, 4 research assistantships with full tuition reimbursements (averaging $24,000 per year) were awarded; teaching assistantships, Federal Work-Study, health care benefits, tuition waivers (full), and unspecified assistantships also available. Financial award application deadline: 4/1; financial award applicants required to submit FAFSA. *Unit head:* Dr. Jerry Downey, Professor, Metallurgical and Materials Engineering, 406-496-4578, Fax: 406-496-4723, E-mail: jdowney@mtech.edu. *Application contact:* Daniel Stirling, Administrator, Graduate School, 406-496-4304, Fax: 406-496-4723, E-mail: gradschool@mtech.edu.
Website: http://www.mtmatsci.org/

New Jersey Institute of Technology, College of Science and Liberal Arts, Newark, NJ 07102. Offers applied mathematics (MS); applied physics (MS, PhD); applied statistics (MS, Certificate); biology (MS, PhD); biostatistics (MS); chemistry (MS, PhD); environmental and sustainability policy (MS); environmental science (MS, PhD); history (MA, MAT); materials science and engineering (MS, PhD); mathematical and computational finance (MS); mathematical sciences (PhD); pharmaceutical chemistry (MS); professional and technical communications (MS); technical communication essentials (Certificate). *Program availability:* Part-time, evening/weekend. *Faculty:* 159 full-time (42 women), 156 part-time/adjunct (61 women). *Students:* 197 full-time (80 women), 58 part-time (14 women); includes 58 minority (18 Black or African American, non-Hispanic/Latino; 22 Asian, non-Hispanic/Latino; 16 Hispanic/Latino; 2 Two or more races, non-Hispanic/Latino), 130 international. Average age 29. 401 applicants, 63% accepted, 73 enrolled. In 2019, 54 master's, 10 doctorates, 1 other advanced degree awarded. Terminal master's awarded for partial completion of doctoral program. *Degree requirements:* For master's, thesis (for some programs); for doctorate, thesis/dissertation. *Entrance requirements:* For master's and doctorate, GRE General Test, Minimum GPA of 3.0, personal statement, 3 letters of recommendation, and transcripts. Additional exam requirements/recommendations for international students: required—TOEFL (minimum score 550 paper-based; 79 iBT), IELTS (minimum score 6.5). *Application deadline:* For fall admission, 6/1 priority date for domestic students, 5/1 priority date for international students; for spring admission, 11/15 priority date for domestic and international students. Applications are processed on a rolling basis. Application fee: $75. Electronic applications accepted. *Expenses:* $23,828 per year (in-state), $33,744 per year (out-of-state). *Financial support:* In 2019–20, 147 students received support, including 13 fellowships with full tuition reimbursements available (averaging $24,000 per year), 41 research assistantships with full tuition reimbursements available (averaging $24,000 per year), 87 teaching assistantships with full tuition reimbursements available (averaging $24,000 per year); scholarships/grants, traineeships, health care benefits, and unspecified assistantships also available. Financial award application deadline: 1/15. *Unit head:* Dr. Kevin Belfield, Dean, 973-596-3676, Fax: 973-565-0586, E-mail: kevin.d.belfield@njit.edu. *Application contact:* Stephen Eck, Director of Admissions, 973-596-3300, Fax: 973-596-3461, E-mail: admissions@njit.edu.
Website: http://csla.njit.edu/

Norfolk State University, School of Graduate Studies, School of Science and Technology, Department of Chemistry, Norfolk, VA 23504. Offers materials science (MS). *Entrance requirements:* Additional exam requirements/recommendations for international students: required—TOEFL (minimum score 500 paper-based).

North Carolina State University, Graduate School, College of Engineering, Department of Materials Science and Engineering, Raleigh, NC 27695. Offers MMSE, MNAE, MS, PhD. *Degree requirements:* For master's, thesis; for doctorate, thesis/dissertation. Electronic applications accepted.

North Dakota State University, College of Graduate and Interdisciplinary Studies, Interdisciplinary Program in Materials and Nanotechnology, Fargo, ND 58102. Offers MS, PhD. *Entrance requirements:* For doctorate, GRE General Test. Additional exam requirements/recommendations for international students: required—TOEFL. Tuition and fees vary according to program and reciprocity agreements.

Northwestern University, McCormick School of Engineering and Applied Science, Department of Civil and Environmental Engineering, Evanston, IL 60208-3109. Offers environmental engineering and science (MS, PhD); geotechnical engineering (MS, PhD); mechanics of materials and solids (MS, PhD); project management (MS); structural engineering and materials (MS, PhD); transportation systems analysis and planning (MS, PhD). *Program availability:* Part-time. Terminal master's awarded for partial completion of doctoral program. *Degree requirements:* For master's, comprehensive exam (for some programs), thesis (for some programs); for doctorate, comprehensive exam, thesis/dissertation. *Entrance requirements:* For master's and doctorate, GRE General Test, minimum 2 letters of recommendation, transcripts from all academic institutions attended. Additional exam requirements/recommendations for international students: required—TOEFL (minimum score 577 paper-based; 90 iBT), IELTS (minimum score 7). Electronic applications accepted.

Northwestern University, McCormick School of Engineering and Applied Science, Department of Materials Science and Engineering, Evanston, IL 60208. Offers integrated computational materials engineering (Certificate); materials science and engineering (MS, PhD). *Program availability:* Part-time. Terminal master's awarded for partial completion of doctoral program. *Degree requirements:* For master's, thesis optional, oral thesis defense; for doctorate, comprehensive exam, thesis/dissertation, oral defense of dissertation, preliminary evaluation, qualifying exam. *Entrance requirements:* For master's and doctorate, GRE General Test. Additional exam requirements/recommendations for international students: required—TOEFL (minimum score 577 paper-based; 90 iBT), IELTS (minimum score 7). Electronic applications accepted.

The Ohio State University, Graduate School, College of Engineering, Department of Materials Science and Engineering, Columbus, OH 43210. Offers materials science and engineering (MS, PhD); welding engineering (MS, PhD). *Entrance requirements:* For master's and doctorate, GRE (for graduates of foreign universities and holders of non-engineering degrees). Additional exam requirements/recommendations for international students: required—TOEFL (minimum score 550 paper-based; 79 iBT), Michigan English Language Assessment Battery (minimum score 82); recommended—IELTS (minimum score 7). Electronic applications accepted.

Oklahoma State University, College of Engineering, Architecture and Technology, School of Materials Science and Engineering, Stillwater, OK 74078. Offers MS, PhD. *Faculty:* 6 full-time (0 women). *Students:* 5 full-time (3 women), 15 part-time (2 women); includes 3 minority (1 American Indian or Alaska Native, non-Hispanic/Latino; 2 Two or more races, non-Hispanic/Latino), 9 international. Average age 29. 13 applicants, 38% accepted, 3 enrolled. In 2019, 2 master's awarded. *Entrance requirements:* Additional exam requirements/recommendations for international students: required—TOEFL. *Application deadline:* For fall admission, 3/1 for domestic students; for spring admission, 8/1 for domestic students. Application fee: $50 ($75 for international students). Electronic applications accepted. *Expenses:* Tuition, area resident: Full-time $4148.10; part-time $2765.40. Tuition, state resident: full-time $4148.10; part-time $2765.40. Tuition, nonresident: full-time $15,775; part-time $10,516.80. *International tuition:* $15,775.20 full-time. *Required fees:* $2196.90; $122.05 per credit hour. Tuition and fees vary according to course load, campus/location and program. *Financial support:* In 2019–20, 9 teaching assistantships (averaging $1,665 per year) were awarded; research assistantships also available. *Unit head:* Dr. Raman P Singh, Head, 918-594-8155, E-mail: raman.singh@okstate.edu. *Application contact:* Dr. Sheryl Tucker, Dean, 405-744-6368, Fax: 405-744-0355, E-mail: gradi@okstate.edu.
Website: https://ceat.okstate.edu/mse/degrees.html

Oregon State University, College of Engineering, Program in Materials Science, Corvallis, OR 97331. Offers chemical engineering (MS, PhD); chemistry (MS, PhD); civil engineering (MS, PhD); electrical and computer engineering (MS, PhD); forest products (MS, PhD); mathematics (MS, PhD); mechanical engineering (MS, PhD); nuclear engineering (MS); physics (MS, PhD). *Entrance requirements:* For master's and doctorate, GRE. Additional exam requirements/recommendations for international students: required—TOEFL (minimum score 80 iBT), IELTS (minimum score 6.5). *Expenses:* Contact institution.

Penn State University Park, Graduate School, Intercollege Graduate Programs, Intercollege Graduate Program in Materials Science and Engineering, University Park, PA 16802. Offers MS, PhD.

Princeton University, Princeton Institute for the Science and Technology of Materials (PRISM), Princeton, NJ 08544-1019. Offers materials (PhD).

Rice University, Graduate Programs, George R. Brown School of Engineering, Department of Mechanical Engineering and Materials Science, Houston, TX 77251-1892. Offers materials science (MMS, MS, PhD); mechanical engineering (MME, MS, PhD); MBA/ME. *Program availability:* Part-time. Terminal master's awarded for partial completion of doctoral program. *Degree requirements:* For master's, comprehensive exam, thesis; for doctorate, comprehensive exam, thesis/dissertation. *Entrance requirements:* For master's and doctorate, GRE General Test, minimum GPA of 3.0. Additional exam requirements/recommendations for international students: required—TOEFL (minimum score 600 paper-based; 90 iBT), IELTS (minimum score 7). Electronic applications accepted.

Rochester Institute of Technology, Graduate Enrollment Services, College of Science, School of Chemistry and Materials Science, MS Program in Materials Science and Engineering, Rochester, NY 14623-5603. Offers MS. *Program availability:* Part-time, evening/weekend. *Degree requirements:* For master's, thesis or project. *Entrance requirements:* For master's, minimum GPA of 3.0 (recommended), two letters of recommendation. Additional exam requirements/recommendations for international students: required—TOEFL (minimum score 575 paper-based; 90 iBT), IELTS (minimum score 6.5), PTE (minimum score 62). Electronic applications accepted.

Rutgers University - New Brunswick, Graduate School-New Brunswick, Program in Materials Science and Engineering, Piscataway, NJ 08854-8097. Offers MS, PhD. *Program availability:* Part-time. *Degree requirements:* For master's, thesis; for doctorate, comprehensive exam, thesis/dissertation. *Entrance requirements:* For master's and doctorate, GRE General Test. Additional exam requirements/recommendations for international students: recommended—TOEFL. Electronic applications accepted.

South Dakota School of Mines and Technology, Graduate Division, Doctoral Program in Materials Engineering and Science, Rapid City, SD 57701-3995. Offers PhD. *Program availability:* Part-time. *Degree requirements:* For doctorate, thesis/dissertation. *Entrance requirements:* For doctorate, GRE General Test, minimum graduate GPA of 3.0, 3 letters of recommendation. Additional exam requirements/recommendations for international students: required—TOEFL (minimum score 520 paper-based; 68 iBT), TWE. Electronic applications accepted.

South Dakota School of Mines and Technology, Graduate Division, Master's Program in Materials Engineering and Science, Rapid City, SD 57701-3995. Offers MS. *Degree requirements:* For master's, thesis (for some programs). *Entrance requirements:* For master's, GRE General Test. Additional exam requirements/recommendations for international students: required—TOEFL (minimum score 520 paper-based; 68 iBT), TWE. Electronic applications accepted.

Stanford University, School of Engineering, Department of Materials Science and Engineering, Stanford, CA 94305-2004. Offers MS, PhD, Engr. *Expenses: Tuition:* Full-time $52,479; part-time $34,110 per unit. *Required fees:* $672; $224 per quarter. Tuition and fees vary according to program and student level.
Website: https://mse.stanford.edu/

State University of New York College of Environmental Science and Forestry, Department of Paper and Bioprocess Engineering, Syracuse, NY 13210-2779. Offers biomaterials engineering (MS, PhD); bioprocess engineering (MPS, MS, PhD); bioprocessing (Advanced Certificate); paper science and engineering (MPS, MS, PhD); sustainable engineering management (MPS). *Program availability:* Part-time. *Faculty:* 13 full-time (2 women), 1 part-time/adjunct (0 women). *Students:* 28 full-time (13 women), 3 part-time (0 women); includes 1 minority (Hispanic/Latino), 22 international. Average age 29. 19 applicants, 89% accepted, 10 enrolled. In 2019, 5 master's, 2 doctorates awarded. Terminal master's awarded for partial completion of doctoral program. *Degree requirements:* For master's, thesis; for doctorate, comprehensive exam, thesis/dissertation; for Advanced Certificate, 15 credit hours. *Entrance requirements:* For master's and doctorate, GRE General Test, minimum GPA of 3.0; for Advanced Certificate, BS, calculus plus science major. Additional exam requirements/recommendations for international students: required—TOEFL (minimum score 550 paper-based; 80 iBT), IELTS (minimum score 6). *Application deadline:* For fall admission, 2/1 priority date for domestic and international students; for spring admission, 11/1 priority date for domestic and international students. Applications are processed on a rolling basis. Application fee: $60. Electronic applications accepted. *Expenses:* Tuition, state resident: full-time $11,310; part-time $472 per credit hour. Tuition, nonresident: full-time $23,100; part-time $963 per credit hour. *Required fees:* $1890; $95.21 per credit hour. *Financial support:* In 2019–20, 17 students received support. Unspecified assistantships available. Financial award application deadline: 6/30; financial award applicants required to submit FAFSA. *Unit head:* Dr. Bandaru Ramarao, Chair, 315-470-6502, Fax: 315-470-6945, E-mail: bvramara@esf.edu. *Application contact:* Laura Payne, Office of Instruction and Graduate Studies, 315-470-6599, Fax: 315-470-6978, E-mail: esfgrad@esf.edu.
Website: http://www.esf.edu/pbe/

Materials Sciences

Stevens Institute of Technology, Graduate School, Charles V. Schaefer Jr. School of Engineering and Science, Department of Chemical Engineering and Materials Science, Program in Materials Science and Engineering, Hoboken, NJ 07030. Offers M Eng, PhD. *Program availability:* Part-time, evening/weekend. *Faculty:* 13 full-time (3 women), 2 part-time/adjunct. *Students:* 44 full-time (12 women), 1 (woman) part-time; includes 2 minority (both Asian, non-Hispanic/Latino), 40 international. Average age 26. In 2019, 23 master's, 7 doctorates awarded. Terminal master's awarded for partial completion of doctoral program. *Degree requirements:* For master's, thesis optional, minimum B average in major field and overall; for doctorate, comprehensive exam (for some programs), thesis/dissertation. *Entrance requirements:* For master's, International applicants must submit TOEFL/IELTS scores and fulfill the English Language Proficiency Requirement. Applicants to full-time programs who do not qualify for a score waiver are required to submit GRE/GMAT scores. Additional exam requirements/recommendations for international students: required—TOEFL (minimum score 74 iBT), IELTS (minimum score 6). *Application deadline:* For fall admission, 4/15 for domestic and international students; for spring admission, 11/1 for domestic and international students; for summer admission, 5/1 for domestic students. Applications are processed on a rolling basis. Application fee: $60. Electronic applications accepted. *Expenses: Tuition:* Full-time $52,134. *Required fees:* $1880. Tuition and fees vary according to course load. *Financial support:* Fellowships, research assistantships, teaching assistantships, career-related internships or fieldwork, Federal Work-Study, scholarships/grants, and unspecified assistantships available. Financial award application deadline: 2/15; financial award applicants required to submit FAFSA. *Unit head:* Dr. Jean Zu, Dean of SES, 201-216.8233, Fax: 201-216.8372, E-mail: Jean.Zu@stevens.edu. *Application contact:* Graduate Admissions, 888-783-8367, Fax: 888-511-1306, E-mail: graduate@stevens.edu.

Stony Brook University, State University of New York, Graduate School, College of Engineering and Applied Sciences, Department of Materials Science & Chemical Engineering, Stony Brook, NY 11794. Offers MS, PhD. *Faculty:* 18 full-time (5 women), 5 part-time/adjunct (2 women). *Students:* 78 full-time (19 women), 4 part-time (2 women); includes 15 minority (2 Black or African American, non-Hispanic/Latino; 8 Asian, non-Hispanic/Latino; 4 Hispanic/Latino; 1 Two or more races, non-Hispanic/Latino), 52 international. Average age 26. 102 applicants, 61% accepted, 20 enrolled. In 2019, 21 master's, 21 doctorates awarded. *Degree requirements:* For master's, thesis or alternative; for doctorate, comprehensive exam, thesis/dissertation. *Entrance requirements:* For master's and doctorate, GRE General Test, minimum undergraduate GPA of 3.0. Additional exam requirements/recommendations for international students: required—TOEFL (minimum score 90 iBT). *Application deadline:* For fall admission, 1/15 for domestic students; for spring admission, 10/1 for domestic students. Application fee: $100. *Expenses:* Contact institution. *Financial support:* In 2019–20, 6 fellowships, 35 research assistantships, 14 teaching assistantships were awarded. *Unit head:* Dr. Dilip Gersappe, Professor and Interim Chair, 631-632-8500, Fax: 631-632-8052, E-mail: dilip.gersappe@stonybrook.edu. *Application contact:* Chandrani Roy, 631-632-4174, Fax: 631-632-8052, E-mail: Chandrani.Roy@stonybrook.edu.
Website: http://www.stonybrook.edu/commcms/matscieng/index.html

Texas A&M University, College of Engineering, Department of Materials Science and Engineering, College Station, TX 77843. Offers materials science and engineering (M Eng). *Faculty:* 20. *Students:* 163 full-time (58 women), 12 part-time (2 women); includes 28 minority (1 Black or African American, non-Hispanic/Latino; 13 Asian, non-Hispanic/Latino; 11 Hispanic/Latino; 3 Two or more races, non-Hispanic/Latino), 109 international. Average age 28. 204 applicants, 53% accepted, 37 enrolled. In 2019, 15 master's, 15 doctorates awarded. *Degree requirements:* For master's, comprehensive exam (for some programs), thesis optional; for doctorate, comprehensive exam, thesis/dissertation. *Entrance requirements:* For master's and doctorate, GRE General Test, letters of recommendation. Additional exam requirements/recommendations for international students: required—TOEFL (minimum score 550 paper-based; 80 iBT), IELTS (minimum score 6), PTE (minimum score 53). *Application deadline:* For fall admission, 1/31 for domestic students, 1/15 for international students; for spring admission, 7/15 for domestic and international students. Application fee: $65 ($90 for international students). *Expenses:* Contact institution. *Financial support:* In 2019–20, 167 students received support, including 43 fellowships with tuition reimbursements available (averaging $12,117 per year), 130 research assistantships with tuition reimbursements available (averaging $16,448 per year), 17 teaching assistantships with tuition reimbursements available (averaging $13,115 per year); career-related internships or fieldwork, institutionally sponsored loans, scholarships/grants, traineeships, health care benefits, tuition waivers (full and partial), and unspecified assistantships also available. Support available to part-time students. Financial award application deadline: 3/15; financial award applicants required to submit FAFSA. *Unit head:* Ibrahim Karaman, Department Head, 979-862-3923, E-mail: ikaraman@tamu.edu. *Application contact:* Erin Bandza, Academic Advisor, Graduate Programs, 979-458-3180, E-mail: msen-advising@tamu.edu.
Website: http://engineering.tamu.edu/materials

Texas State University, The Graduate College, College of Science and Engineering, PhD Program in Materials Science, Engineering, and Commercialization, San Marcos, TX 78666. Offers PhD. *Degree requirements:* For doctorate, comprehensive exam, thesis/dissertation. *Entrance requirements:* For doctorate, GRE (for applicants who have not received a master's degree from a U.S. institution), baccalaureate and master's degrees from regionally-accredited college or university in biology, chemistry, engineering, materials science, physics, technology, or closely-related field with minimum GPA of 3.5 in graduate work; interviews with core doctoral faculty; statement of purpose; 3 letters of recommendation; curriculum vitae or resume. Additional exam requirements/recommendations for international students: required—TOEFL (minimum score 550 paper-based; 78 iBT); recommended—IELTS (minimum score 6.5). Electronic applications accepted.

Trent University, Graduate Studies, Program in Materials Science, Peterborough, ON K9J 7B8, Canada. Offers M Sc.

Université du Québec, Institut National de la Recherche Scientifique, Graduate Programs, Centre for Energie Materiaux Telecommunications, Varennes, QC J3X 1S2, Canada. Offers energy and materials science (M Sc, PhD); telecommunications (M Sc, PhD). *Program availability:* Part-time. *Faculty:* 38 full-time. *Students:* 208 full-time (61 women), 12 part-time (1 woman), 187 international. Average age 32. 36 applicants, 100% accepted, 29 enrolled. In 2019, 12 master's, 26 doctorates awarded. *Degree requirements:* For master's, thesis (for some programs); for doctorate, thesis/dissertation. *Entrance requirements:* For master's, appropriate bachelor's degree, proficiency in French; for doctorate, appropriate master's degree, proficiency in French. *Application deadline:* For fall admission, 3/30 for domestic and international students; for winter admission, 11/1 for domestic and international students; for spring admission, 3/1 for domestic and international students. Application fee: $45. Electronic applications accepted. *Financial support:* In 2019–20, fellowships (averaging $16,500 per year) were awarded; research assistantships and scholarships/grants also available. *Unit head:* Ana Tavares, Director, 514-228-6947, Fax: 450-929-8102, E-mail: ana.tavares@emt.inrs.ca. *Application contact:* Sean Otto, Registrar, 418-654-2518, Fax: 418-654-

3858, E-mail: sean.otto@inrs.ca.
Website: http://www.emt.inrs.ca

University at Buffalo, the State University of New York, Graduate School, School of Engineering and Applied Sciences, Department of Materials Design and Innovation, Buffalo, NY 14260. Offers MS, PhD. *Expenses: Tuition, area resident:* Full-time $11,310; part-time $471 per credit hour. Tuition, state resident: full-time $11,310; part-time $471 per credit hour. Tuition, nonresident: full-time $23,100; part-time $963 per credit hour. *International tuition:* $23,100 full-time. *Required fees:* $2820.

The University of Alabama in Huntsville, School of Graduate Studies, College of Engineering, Department of Chemical and Materials Engineering, Huntsville, AL 35899. Offers biotechnology science and engineering (PhD); chemical and materials engineering (MSE); materials science (PhD); mechanical engineering (PhD), including chemical engineering. *Program availability:* Part-time. *Degree requirements:* For master's, comprehensive exam, thesis or alternative, oral and written exams; for doctorate, comprehensive exam, thesis/dissertation. *Entrance requirements:* For master's, GRE General Test, appropriate bachelor's degree, minimum GPA of 3.0; for doctorate, GRE General Test, minimum GPA of 3.0. Additional exam requirements/recommendations for international students: required—TOEFL (minimum score 500 paper-based; 80 iBT), IELTS (minimum score 6.5). Electronic applications accepted.

The University of Alabama in Huntsville, School of Graduate Studies, College of Science, Department of Chemistry, Huntsville, AL 35899. Offers biotechnology science and engineering (PhD); chemistry (MS); education (MS); materials science (MS, PhD). *Program availability:* Part-time. *Degree requirements:* For master's, comprehensive exam, thesis or alternative, oral and written exams. *Entrance requirements:* For master's, GRE General Test, minimum GPA of 3.0. Additional exam requirements/recommendations for international students: required—TOEFL (minimum score 550 paper-based; 80 iBT), IELTS (minimum score 6.5). Electronic applications accepted.

The University of Arizona, College of Engineering, Department of Materials Science and Engineering, Tucson, AZ 85721. Offers MS, PhD. *Program availability:* Part-time. *Degree requirements:* For master's, thesis (for some programs); for doctorate, comprehensive exam, thesis/dissertation. *Entrance requirements:* For master's and doctorate, GRE General Test, 3 letters of recommendation, statement of purpose. Additional exam requirements/recommendations for international students: required—TOEFL (minimum score 550 paper-based; 79 iBT). Electronic applications accepted.

University of Calgary, Faculty of Graduate Studies, Schulich School of Engineering, Program in Civil Engineering, Calgary, AB T2N 1N4, Canada. Offers avalanche mechanics (M Sc, PhD); civil engineering (M Eng, M Sc, PhD); energy and environment engineering (M Eng, M Sc, PhD); environmental engineering (M Eng, M Sc, PhD); geotechnical engineering (M Eng, M Sc, PhD); materials science (M Eng, M Sc, PhD); project management (M Eng, M Sc, PhD); structures and solid mechanics (M Eng, M Sc, PhD); transportation engineering (M Eng, M Sc, PhD); water resources (M Eng, M Sc, PhD). *Program availability:* Part-time. *Degree requirements:* For master's, thesis; for doctorate, thesis/dissertation, written and oral candidacy exam. *Entrance requirements:* For master's, minimum GPA of 3.0; for doctorate, minimum GPA of 3.5. Additional exam requirements/recommendations for international students: required—TOEFL (minimum score 580 paper-based; 93 iBT), IELTS (minimum score 7). Electronic applications accepted.

University of California, Berkeley, Graduate Division, College of Engineering, Department of Materials Science and Engineering, Berkeley, CA 94720. Offers engineering science (M Eng, MS, PhD). Terminal master's awarded for partial completion of doctoral program. *Degree requirements:* For master's, comprehensive exam (for some programs), thesis (for some programs), comprehensive exam or thesis (MS); for doctorate, comprehensive exam, thesis/dissertation, qualifying exam. *Entrance requirements:* For master's and doctorate, GRE General Test, minimum GPA of 3.0, 3 letters of recommendation. Additional exam requirements/recommendations for international students: required—TOEFL (minimum score 570 paper-based; 90 iBT). Electronic applications accepted.

University of California, Davis, College of Engineering, Program in Materials Science and Engineering, Davis, CA 95616. Offers MS, PhD. Terminal master's awarded for partial completion of doctoral program. *Degree requirements:* For master's, comprehensive exam (for some programs), thesis (for some programs); for doctorate, comprehensive exam, thesis/dissertation. *Entrance requirements:* Additional exam requirements/recommendations for international students: required—TOEFL (minimum score 550 paper-based).

University of California, Irvine, Samueli School of Engineering, Department of Chemical Engineering and Materials Science, Irvine, CA 92697. Offers chemical and biochemical engineering (MS, PhD); materials science and engineering (MS, PhD). *Program availability:* Part-time. *Students:* 139 full-time (58 women), 3 part-time (2 women); includes 40 minority (5 Black or African American, non-Hispanic/Latino; 28 Asian, non-Hispanic/Latino; 6 Hispanic/Latino; 1 Two or more races, non-Hispanic/Latino), 56 international. Average age 26. 435 applicants, 34% accepted, 48 enrolled. In 2019, 30 master's, 26 doctorates awarded. Terminal master's awarded for partial completion of doctoral program. *Entrance requirements:* For master's and doctorate, GRE General Test, minimum GPA of 3.0, 3 letters of recommendation. Additional exam requirements/recommendations for international students: required—TOEFL (minimum score 550 paper-based). *Application deadline:* For fall admission, 1/15 priority date for domestic students, 1/15 for international students. Applications are processed on a rolling basis. Application fee: $120 ($140 for international students). Electronic applications accepted. *Financial support:* Fellowships, research assistantships with full tuition reimbursements, teaching assistantships, institutionally sponsored loans, traineeships, health care benefits, and unspecified assistantships available. Financial award application deadline: 3/1; financial award applicants required to submit FAFSA. *Unit head:* Prof. Vasan Venugopalan, Chair, 949-824-5802, Fax: 949-824-2541, E-mail: vvenugop@uci.edu. *Application contact:* Grace Chau, Academic Program and Graduate Admission Coordinator, 949-824-3887, Fax: 949-824-2541, E-mail: chaug@uci.edu.
Website: http://www.eng.uci.edu/dept/chems

University of California, Irvine, School of Physical Sciences, Program in Chemical and Materials Physics (CHAMP), Irvine, CA 92697. Offers MS, PhD. *Students:* 38 full-time (11 women); includes 9 minority (7 Asian, non-Hispanic/Latino; 2 Hispanic/Latino), 4 international. Average age 27. 28 applicants, 43% accepted, 10 enrolled. In 2019, 7 master's, 11 doctorates awarded. *Entrance requirements:* For master's and doctorate, GRE General Test, GRE Subject Test, minimum GPA of 3.0. *Application deadline:* For fall admission, 1/15 priority date for domestic students, 1/15 for international students. Applications are processed on a rolling basis. Application fee: $120 ($140 for international students). Electronic applications accepted. *Financial support:* Fellowships, research assistantships with full tuition reimbursements, teaching assistantships, institutionally sponsored loans, traineeships, health care benefits, and unspecified assistantships available. Financial award application deadline: 3/1; financial award applicants required to submit FAFSA. *Unit head:* A.J. Shaka, Co-Director, 949-824-8509, E-mail: ajshaka@uci.edu. *Application contact:* Jaime M. Albano, Student Affairs Manager, 949-824-4261, Fax: 949-824-8571, E-mail: jmalbano@uci.edu.

University of California, Los Angeles, Graduate Division, Henry Samueli School of Engineering and Applied Science, Department of Materials Science and Engineering, Los Angeles, CA 90095-1595. Offers MS, PhD. *Degree requirements:* For master's, comprehensive exam or thesis; for doctorate, thesis/dissertation, qualifying exams. *Entrance requirements:* For master's, GRE General Test, minimum GPA of 3.0; for doctorate, GRE General Test, minimum GPA of 3.25. Additional exam requirements/recommendations for international students: required—TOEFL (minimum score 560 paper-based; 87 iBT), IELTS (minimum score 7). Electronic applications accepted.

University of California, Riverside, Graduate Division, Materials Science and Engineering Program, Riverside, CA 92521. Offers MS. *Entrance requirements:* For master's, GRE. Additional exam requirements/recommendations for international students: required—TOEFL (minimum score 550 paper-based; 80 iBT). Electronic applications accepted.

University of California, San Diego, Graduate Division, Program in Materials Science and Engineering, La Jolla, CA 92093. Offers MS, PhD. *Students:* 183 full-time (50 women), 10 part-time (1 woman). 498 applicants, 56% accepted, 50 enrolled. In 2019, 44 master's, 24 doctorates awarded. *Degree requirements:* For master's, comprehensive exam (for some programs), thesis (for some programs), thesis or comprehensive exam; for doctorate, comprehensive exam, thesis/dissertation. *Entrance requirements:* For master's and doctorate, GRE General Test, minimum GPA of 3.2. Additional exam requirements/recommendations for international students: required—TOEFL (minimum score 550 paper-based; 80 iBT), IELTS (minimum score 7). *Application deadline:* For fall admission, 12/18 for domestic students. Application fee: $105 ($125 for international students). Electronic applications accepted. *Financial support:* Fellowships, research assistantships, and teaching assistantships available. Financial award applicants required to submit FAFSA. *Unit head:* Prabhakar Banderu, Director, 858-534-5325, E-mail: pbandaru@ucsd.edu. *Application contact:* Katie Hamilton, Graduate Coordinator, 858-246-5143, E-mail: mats-gradadm@eng.ucsd.edu. Website: http://matsci.ucsd.edu/

University of California, Santa Barbara, Graduate Division, College of Engineering, Department of Materials, Santa Barbara, CA 93106-5050. Offers MS, PhD, MS/PhD. Terminal master's awarded for partial completion of doctoral program. *Degree requirements:* For master's, variable foreign language requirement, comprehensive exam, thesis; for doctorate, variable foreign language requirement, comprehensive exam, thesis/dissertation. *Entrance requirements:* For master's and doctorate, GRE General Test. Additional exam requirements/recommendations for international students: required—TOEFL (minimum score 600 paper-based; 100 iBT), IELTS (minimum score 7). Electronic applications accepted.

University of Central Florida, College of Engineering and Computer Science, Department of Materials Science and Engineering, Orlando, FL 32816. Offers MSMSE, PhD. *Students:* 58 full-time (22 women), 19 part-time (9 women); includes 15 minority (1 Black or African American, non-Hispanic/Latino; 6 Asian, non-Hispanic/Latino; 5 Hispanic/Latino; 3 Two or more races, non-Hispanic/Latino), 34 international. Average age 28. 98 applicants, 42% accepted, 24 enrolled. In 2019, 4 master's, 8 doctorates awarded. *Degree requirements:* For master's, thesis or alternative; for doctorate, thesis/dissertation, candidacy exam, departmental qualifying exam. *Entrance requirements:* For master's, resume, goal statement; for doctorate, GRE, letters of recommendation, resume, goal statement. Additional exam requirements/recommendations for international students: required—TOEFL. *Application deadline:* For fall admission, 7/15 for domestic students; for spring admission, 12/1 for domestic students. Application fee: $30. Electronic applications accepted. *Financial support:* In 2019–20, 49 students received support, including 10 fellowships with tuition reimbursements available (averaging $12,980 per year), 52 research assistantships (averaging $7,696 per year), 7 teaching assistantships (averaging $8,566 per year); health care benefits also available. Financial award application deadline: 3/1; financial award applicants required to submit FAFSA. *Unit head:* Dr. Sudipta Seal, Chair, 407-823-5277, E-mail: sseal@ucf.edu. *Application contact:* Associate Director, Graduate Admissions, 407-823-2766, Fax: 407-823-6442, E-mail: gradadmissions@ucf.edu. Website: http://mse.ucf.edu/

University of Cincinnati, Graduate School, College of Engineering and Applied Science, Department of Mechanical and Materials Engineering, Program in Materials Science and Engineering, Cincinnati, OH 45221. Offers MS, PhD. *Program availability:* Evening/weekend. *Degree requirements:* For master's, thesis optional; for doctorate, one foreign language, comprehensive exam, thesis/dissertation, oral English proficiency exam. *Entrance requirements:* For master's and doctorate, GRE General Test, BS in related field, minimum undergraduate GPA of 3.0. Additional exam requirements/recommendations for international students: required—TOEFL. Electronic applications accepted.

University of Colorado Boulder, Graduate School, College of Engineering and Applied Science, Materials Science and Engineering Program, Boulder, CO 80309. Offers MS, PhD. Electronic applications accepted.

University of Connecticut, Graduate School, School of Engineering, Department of Materials Science and Engineering, Storrs, CT 06269. Offers M Eng. Terminal master's awarded for partial completion of doctoral program. *Degree requirements:* For master's, comprehensive exam, thesis or alternative. *Entrance requirements:* For master's, GRE General Test, GRE Subject Test. Additional exam requirements/recommendations for international students: required—TOEFL (minimum score 550 paper-based). Electronic applications accepted.

University of Connecticut, Institute of Materials Science, Storrs, CT 06269. Offers MS, PhD.

University of Delaware, College of Engineering, Department of Materials Science and Engineering, Newark, DE 19716. Offers MMSE, PhD. Terminal master's awarded for partial completion of doctoral program. *Degree requirements:* For master's, thesis; for doctorate, thesis/dissertation. *Entrance requirements:* For master's and doctorate, GRE General Test, 3 letters of recommendation, minimum GPA of 3.2. Additional exam requirements/recommendations for international students: required—TOEFL. Electronic applications accepted.

University of Denver, Daniel Felix Ritchie School of Engineering and Computer Science, Department of Mechanical and Materials Engineering, Denver, CO 80208. Offers bioengineering (MS); engineering (MS, PhD), including management; materials science (MS, PhD); mechanical engineering (MS, PhD). *Program availability:* Part-time. *Faculty:* 12 full-time (2 women), 3 part-time/adjunct (1 woman). *Students:* 3 full-time (1 woman), 35 part-time (9 women); includes 3 minority (1 Black or African American, non-Hispanic/Latino; 1 Asian, non-Hispanic/Latino; 1 Hispanic/Latino), 16 international. Average age 27. 58 applicants, 81% accepted, 18 enrolled. In 2019, 16 master's, 4 doctorates awarded. Terminal master's awarded for partial completion of doctoral program. *Degree requirements:* For master's, thesis optional; for doctorate, comprehensive exam, thesis/dissertation. *Entrance requirements:* For master's, GRE General Test, bachelor's degree in engineering or closely related field, transcripts, personal statement, resume or curriculum vitae, two letters of recommendation; for doctorate, GRE General Test, master's degree in engineering or closely related field, transcripts, personal statement, resume or curriculum vitae, two letters of

recommendation, recommended that applicants find a research advisor before submitting the application. Additional exam requirements/recommendations for international students: required—TOEFL (minimum score 550 paper-based; 80 iBT). *Application deadline:* For fall admission, 1/15 priority date for domestic and international students; for winter admission, 10/25 for domestic and international students; for spring admission, 2/7 for domestic and international students; for summer admission, 4/24 for domestic and international students. Applications are processed on a rolling basis. Application fee: $65. Electronic applications accepted. *Unit head:* Dr. Matt Gordon, Professor and Chair, 303-871-3580, E-mail: matthew.gordon@du.edu. *Application contact:* Chrissy Alexander, Assistant to the Chair, 303-871-3041, E-mail: Christine.Alexander@du.edu. Website: http://ritchieschool.du.edu/departments/mme/

University of Florida, Graduate School, Herbert Wertheim College of Engineering, Department of Materials Science and Engineering, Gainesville, FL 32611. Offers material science and engineering (MS), including clinical and translational science; materials science and engineering (ME, PhD); nuclear engineering (ME, PhD), including imaging science and technology (PhD), nuclear engineering sciences (ME, MS, PhD); nuclear engineering (MS), including nuclear engineering sciences (ME, MS, PhD); JD/MS. *Program availability:* Part-time, online learning. Terminal master's awarded for partial completion of doctoral program. *Degree requirements:* For master's, comprehensive exam, thesis; for doctorate, comprehensive exam, thesis/dissertation. *Entrance requirements:* For master's and doctorate, minimum GPA of 3.0. Additional exam requirements/recommendations for international students: required—TOEFL (minimum score 550 paper-based; 80 iBT), IELTS (minimum score 6). Electronic applications accepted.

University of Idaho, College of Graduate Studies, College of Engineering, Department of Chemical and Materials Engineering, Moscow, ID 83844-2282. Offers chemical engineering (M Engr, MS, PhD); materials science and engineering (PhD). *Faculty:* 14. *Students:* 23 full-time, 10 part-time. Average age 30. In 2019, 7 master's, 1 doctorate awarded. *Entrance requirements:* For master's and doctorate, GRE, minimum GPA of 3.0. Additional exam requirements/recommendations for international students: required—TOEFL (minimum score 79 iBT). *Application deadline:* For fall admission, 7/30 for domestic students; for spring admission, 12/1 for domestic students. Applications are processed on a rolling basis. Application fee: $60. Electronic applications accepted. *Expenses:* Tuition, state resident: full-time $7753.80; part-time $502 per credit hour. Tuition, nonresident: full-time $26,990; part-time $1571 per credit hour. *Required fees:* $2122.20; $47 per credit hour. *Financial support:* Fellowships, research assistantships, and teaching assistantships available. Financial award applicants required to submit FAFSA. Website: https://www.uidaho.edu/engr/departments/cme

University of Illinois at Urbana-Champaign, Graduate College, College of Engineering, Department of Materials Science and Engineering, Champaign, IL 61820. Offers M Eng, MS, PhD, MS/MBA, PhD/MBA.

University of Kentucky, Graduate School, College of Engineering, Program in Materials Science and Engineering, Lexington, KY 40506-0032. Offers MS, PhD. *Degree requirements:* For master's, comprehensive exam, thesis optional; for doctorate, comprehensive exam, thesis/dissertation. *Entrance requirements:* For master's, GRE General Test, minimum undergraduate GPA of 2.75; for doctorate, GRE General Test, minimum undergraduate GPA of 3.0. Additional exam requirements/recommendations for international students: required—TOEFL (minimum score 550 paper-based). Electronic applications accepted.

The University of Manchester, School of Chemistry, Manchester, United Kingdom. Offers biological chemistry (PhD); chemistry (M Ent, M Phil, M Sc, D Ent, PhD); inorganic chemistry (PhD); materials chemistry (PhD); nanoscience (PhD); nuclear fission (PhD); organic chemistry (PhD); physical chemistry (PhD); theoretical chemistry (PhD).

The University of Manchester, School of Materials, Manchester, United Kingdom. Offers advanced aerospace materials engineering (M Sc); advanced metallic systems (PhD); biomedical materials (M Phil, M Sc, PhD); ceramics and glass (M Phil, M Sc, PhD); composite materials (M Sc, PhD); corrosion and protection (M Phil, M Sc, PhD); materials (M Phil, PhD); metallic materials (M Phil, M Sc, PhD); nanostructural materials (M Phil, M Sc, PhD); paper science (M Phil, M Sc, PhD); polymer science and engineering (M Phil, M Sc, PhD); technical textiles (M Sc); textile design, fashion and management (M Phil, M Sc, PhD); textile science and technology (M Phil, M Sc, PhD); textiles (M Phil, PhD); textiles and fashion (M Ent).

University of Maryland, College Park, Academic Affairs, A. James Clark School of Engineering, Department of Materials Science and Engineering, Materials Science and Engineering Program, College Park, MD 20742. Offers MS, PhD. *Program availability:* Part-time, evening/weekend, online learning. *Degree requirements:* For master's, comprehensive exam, thesis optional, research paper; for doctorate, thesis/dissertation, oral exam. *Entrance requirements:* For master's and doctorate, GRE General Test, minimum B+ average in undergraduate course work. Additional exam requirements/recommendations for international students: required—TOEFL. Electronic applications accepted.

University of Michigan, College of Engineering, Department of Materials Science and Engineering, Ann Arbor, MI 48109. Offers MS, MSE, PhD. *Program availability:* Part-time. Terminal master's awarded for partial completion of doctoral program. *Degree requirements:* For master's, thesis, oral defense of thesis; for doctorate, thesis/dissertation, oral defense of dissertation, written exam. *Entrance requirements:* For master's and doctorate, GRE General Test. Additional exam requirements/recommendations for international students: required—TOEFL. Electronic applications accepted.

University of Michigan, Rackham Graduate School, College of Literature, Science, and the Arts, Department of Chemistry, Ann Arbor, MI 48109-1055. Offers analytical chemistry (PhD); chemical biology (PhD); chemical sciences (MS); inorganic chemistry (PhD); materials chemistry (PhD); organic chemistry (PhD); physical chemistry (PhD). *Program availability:* Part-time. *Degree requirements:* For doctorate, comprehensive exam, thesis/dissertation, oral defense of dissertation, organic cumulative proficiency exams. *Entrance requirements:* For master's, bachelor's degree, 3 letters of recommendation, personal statement; for doctorate, bachelor's degree, 3 letters of recommendation, personal statement, curriculum vitae/resume. Additional exam requirements/recommendations for international students: required—TOEFL (minimum score 560 paper-based; 84 iBT) or IELTS. Electronic applications accepted.

University of Minnesota, Twin Cities Campus, College of Science and Engineering, Department of Chemical Engineering and Materials Science, Program in Materials Science and Engineering, Minneapolis, MN 55455-0132. Offers M Mat SE, MS Mat SE, PhD. *Program availability:* Part-time. Terminal master's awarded for partial completion of doctoral program. *Degree requirements:* For master's, thesis; for doctorate, thesis/dissertation. *Entrance requirements:* For master's and doctorate, GRE General Test. Additional exam requirements/recommendations for international students: required—TOEFL. Electronic applications accepted.

Materials Sciences

University of Mississippi Medical Center, School of Graduate Studies in Health Sciences, Program in Biomedical Materials Science, Jackson, MS 39216-4505. Offers MS, PhD. Terminal master's awarded for partial completion of doctoral program. *Degree requirements:* For master's, thesis; for doctorate, comprehensive exam, thesis/dissertation. *Entrance requirements:* For master's, GRE, BS; for doctorate, GRE, BS, MS (preferred). Additional exam requirements/recommendations for international students: required—TOEFL (minimum score 105 iBT). Electronic applications accepted.

University of Nebraska–Lincoln, Graduate College, College of Arts and Sciences, Department of Chemistry, Lincoln, NE 68588. Offers analytical chemistry (PhD); biochemistry (PhD); chemistry (MS); inorganic chemistry (PhD); materials chemistry (PhD); organic chemistry (PhD); physical chemistry (PhD). *Degree requirements:* For master's, one foreign language, thesis optional, departmental qualifying exam; for doctorate, one foreign language, comprehensive exam, thesis/dissertation, departmental qualifying exams. *Entrance requirements:* For master's and doctorate, GRE. Additional exam requirements/recommendations for international students: required—TOEFL (minimum score 550 paper-based). Electronic applications accepted.

University of New Brunswick Fredericton, School of Graduate Studies, Faculty of Engineering, Department of Civil Engineering, Fredericton, NB E3B 5A3, Canada. Offers construction engineering and management (M Eng, M Sc E, PhD); environmental engineering (M Eng, M Sc E, PhD); environmental studies (M Eng); geotechnical engineering (M Eng, M Sc E, PhD); groundwater/hydrology (M Eng, M Sc E, PhD); materials (M Eng, M Sc E, PhD); pavements (M Eng, M Sc E, PhD); structures (M Eng, M Sc E, PhD); transportation (M Eng, M Sc E, PhD). *Program availability:* Part-time. *Faculty:* 17 full-time (2 women). *Students:* 31 full-time (6 women), 10 part-time (0 women), 12 international. Average age 27. In 2019, 11 master's awarded. *Degree requirements:* For master's, thesis; for doctorate, comprehensive exam, thesis/dissertation, qualifying exam; 27 credit hours of courses. *Entrance requirements:* For master's, minimum GPA of 3.0; B Sc E in civil engineering or related engineering degree; for doctorate, minimum GPA of 3.0; graduate degree in engineering or applied science. Additional exam requirements/recommendations for international students: required—IELTS (minimum score 7.5), TWE (minimum score 4), Michigan English Language Assessment Battery (minimum score 85) or CanTest (minimum score 4.5); recommended—TOEFL (minimum score 580 paper-based). *Application deadline:* For fall admission, 5/1 for domestic students; for winter admission, 11/1 for domestic students. Applications are processed on a rolling basis. Application fee: $50 Canadian dollars. Electronic applications accepted. *Expenses: Tuition, area resident:* Full-time $6975 Canadian dollars; part-time $3423 Canadian dollars per year. Tuition, state resident: full-time $6975 Canadian dollars; part-time $3423 Canadian dollars per year. Tuition, Canadian resident: full-time $6975 Canadian dollars; part-time $3423 Canadian dollars per year. *International tuition:* $12,435 Canadian dollars full-time. *Required fees:* $92.25 Canadian dollars per term. Full-time tuition and fees vary according to degree level, campus/location, program, reciprocity agreements and student level. *Financial support:* Fellowships, research assistantships, teaching assistantships, career-related internships or fieldwork, and scholarships/grants available. Financial award application deadline: 1/15. *Unit head:* Dr. Jeff Rankin, Chair, 506-453-4618, Fax: 506-453-3568, E-mail: ktm@unb.ca. *Application contact:* MaryBeth Nicholson, Graduate Secretary, 506-452-6127, Fax: 506-453-3568, E-mail: mbnich@unb.ca.
Website: http://go.unb.ca/gradprograms

University of New Hampshire, Graduate School, College of Engineering and Physical Sciences, Program in Materials Science, Durham, NH 03824. Offers materials science (MS); materials science and engineering (PhD). *Students:* 3 full-time (0 women), 4 part-time (1 woman), 4 international. Average age 29. 10 applicants, 40% accepted. *Entrance requirements:* For master's and doctorate, GRE. Additional exam requirements/recommendations for international students: required—TOEFL (minimum score 550 paper-based; 80 iBT), IELTS, PTE. *Application deadline:* For fall admission, 6/1 for domestic students, 4/1 for international students; for spring admission, 12/1 for domestic students. Application fee: $65. Electronic applications accepted. *Financial support:* In 2019–20, 6 students received support, including 2 research assistantships, 4 teaching assistantships; fellowships, Federal Work-Study, scholarships/grants, and tuition waivers (full and partial) also available. Support available to part-time students. Financial award application deadline: 2/15. *Unit head:* James Krzanowski, Director, 603-862-2315. *Application contact:* Katie Makem, Administrative Assistant, 603-862-2669, E-mail: materials.science@unh.edu.
Website: http://www.ceps.unh.edu/materials-science/

University of Pennsylvania, School of Engineering and Applied Science, Department of Materials Science and Engineering, Philadelphia, PA 19104. Offers MSE, PhD. *Program availability:* Part-time. *Faculty:* 22 full-time (4 women), 3 part-time/adjunct (1 woman). *Students:* 133 full-time (41 women), 4 part-time (1 woman); includes 18 minority (12 Asian, non-Hispanic/Latino; 4 Hispanic/Latino; 2 Two or more races, non-Hispanic/Latino), 90 international. Average age 24. 448 applicants, 36% accepted, 53 enrolled. In 2019, 45 master's, 8 doctorates awarded. *Degree requirements:* For master's, comprehensive exam, thesis optional; for doctorate, comprehensive exam, thesis/dissertation. *Entrance requirements:* For master's and doctorate, GRE, bachelor's degree, letters of recommendation, resume, personal statement. Additional exam requirements/recommendations for international students: required—TOEFL (minimum score 100 iBT), IELTS (minimum score 7). *Application deadline:* For fall admission, 12/15 priority date for domestic and international students. Application fee: $80. Electronic applications accepted. *Expenses:* Contact institution. *Application contact:* Associate Director of Graduate Admissions, 215-898-4542, Fax: 215-573-5577, E-mail: admissions1@seas.upenn.edu.
Website: http://www.mse.seas.upenn.edu/current-students/masters/index.php

University of Pittsburgh, Swanson School of Engineering, Department of Mechanical Engineering and Materials Science, Pittsburgh, PA 15260. Offers MSME, MSNE, PhD. *Program availability:* Part-time, 100% online. Terminal master's awarded for partial completion of doctoral program. *Degree requirements:* For doctorate, comprehensive exam, thesis/dissertation, final oral exams. *Entrance requirements:* For master's and doctorate, minimum GPA of 3.0. Additional exam requirements/recommendations for international students: required—TOEFL (minimum score 550 paper-based; 80 iBT). Electronic applications accepted. *Expenses:* Contact institution.

University of Puerto Rico at Mayagüez, Graduate Studies, College of Arts and Sciences, Department of Chemistry, Mayagüez, PR 00681-9000. Offers applied chemistry (MS, PhD), including biophysical chemistry (PhD), chemistry of materials (PhD), environmental chemistry (PhD). *Program availability:* Part-time. Terminal master's awarded for partial completion of doctoral program. *Degree requirements:* For master's, one foreign language, comprehensive exam, thesis; for doctorate, one foreign language, comprehensive exam, thesis/dissertation. *Entrance requirements:* For master's, GRE General Test or minimum GPA of 2.0, BS in chemistry or the equivalent; minimum GPA of 2.8; for doctorate, GRE General Test or minimum GPA of 2.0. Electronic applications accepted.

University of Puerto Rico at Mayagüez, Graduate Studies, College of Engineering, Department of Engineering Sciences and Materials, Mayagüez, PR 00681-9000. Offers materials science and engineering (MS).

University of Rochester, Hajim School of Engineering and Applied Sciences, Program in Materials Science, Rochester, NY 14627. Offers MS, PhD. *Students:* 33 full-time (9 women), 1 part-time (0 women); includes 3 minority (2 Black or African American, non-Hispanic/Latino; 1 American Indian or Alaska Native, non-Hispanic/Latino), 25 international. Average age 27. 97 applicants, 54% accepted, 11 enrolled. In 2019, 4 master's, 4 doctorates awarded. Terminal master's awarded for partial completion of doctoral program. *Degree requirements:* For master's, comprehensive exam, thesis (for some programs); for doctorate, comprehensive exam, thesis/dissertation, qualifying exam. *Entrance requirements:* For master's, personal statement, transcripts, resume/curriculum vitae, three letters of recommendation; for doctorate, GRE, personal statement, transcripts, resume/curriculum vitae, three letters of recommendation. Additional exam requirements/recommendations for international students: required—TOEFL (minimum score 95 iBT), IELTS (minimum score 7). *Application deadline:* For fall admission, 1/15 for domestic and international students. Application fee: $60. Electronic applications accepted. *Financial support:* In 2019–20, 18 students received support, including 4 fellowships (averaging $29,600 per year), 14 research assistantships (averaging $27,000 per year); scholarships/grants also available. Financial award application deadline: 1/15. *Unit head:* Danielle Benoit, Professor and Director of Materials Science Program, 585-273-2698, E-mail: benoit@bme.rochester.edu. *Application contact:* Gina Eagan, Administrative Assistant, 585-275-1626, E-mail: gina.eagan@rochester.edu.
Website: http://www.rochester.edu/college/matsci/

University of Southern California, Graduate School, Viterbi School of Engineering, Mork Family Department of Chemical Engineering and Materials Science, Los Angeles, CA 90089. Offers chemical engineering (MS, PhD, Engr); geoscience technologies (MS); materials engineering (MS); materials science (MS, PhD, Engr); petroleum engineering (MS, PhD, Engr); smart oilfield technologies (MS, Graduate Certificate). Terminal master's awarded for partial completion of doctoral program. *Degree requirements:* For master's, thesis optional; for doctorate, thesis/dissertation. *Entrance requirements:* For master's and doctorate, GRE General Test. Additional exam requirements/recommendations for international students: recommended—TOEFL. Electronic applications accepted. *Expenses:* Contact institution.

University of South Florida, Innovative Education, Tampa, FL 33620-9951. Offers adult, career and higher education (Graduate Certificate), including college teaching, leadership in developing human resources, leadership in higher education; Africana studies (Graduate Certificate), including diasporas and health disparities, genocide and human rights; aging studies (Graduate Certificate), including gerontology; art research (Graduate Certificate), including museum studies; business foundations (Graduate Certificate); chemical and biomedical engineering (Graduate Certificate), including materials science and engineering, water, health and sustainability; child and family studies (Graduate Certificate), including positive behavior support; civil and industrial engineering (Graduate Certificate), including transportation systems analysis; community and family health (Graduate Certificate), including maternal and child health, social marketing and public health, violence and injury: prevention and intervention, women's health; criminology (Graduate Certificate), including criminal justice administration; data science for public administration (Graduate Certificate); digital humanities (Graduate Certificate); educational measurement and research (Graduate Certificate), including evaluation; English (Graduate Certificate), including comparative literary studies, creative writing, professional and technical communication; entrepreneurship (Graduate Certificate); environmental health (Graduate Certificate), including safety management; epidemiology and biostatistics (Graduate Certificate), including applied biostatistics, biostatistics, concepts and tools of epidemiology, epidemiology, epidemiology of infectious diseases; geography, environment and planning (Graduate Certificate), including community development, environmental policy and management, geographical information systems; geology (Graduate Certificate), including hydrogeology; global health (Graduate Certificate), including disaster management, global health and Latin American and Caribbean studies, global health practice, humanitarian assistance, infection control; government and international affairs (Graduate Certificate), including Cuban studies, globalization studies; health policy and management (Graduate Certificate), including health management and leadership, public health policy and programs; hearing specialist: early intervention (Graduate Certificate); industrial and management systems engineering (Graduate Certificate), including systems engineering, technology management; information studies (Graduate Certificate), including school library media specialist; information systems/decision sciences (Graduate Certificate), including analytics and business intelligence; instructional technology (Graduate Certificate), including distance education, Florida digital/virtual educator, instructional design, multimedia design, Web design; internal medicine, bioethics and medical humanities (Graduate Certificate), including biomedical ethics; Latin American and Caribbean studies (Graduate Certificate); leadership for coastal resiliency planning (Graduate Certificate); mass communications (Graduate Certificate), including multimedia journalism; mathematics and statistics (Graduate Certificate), including mathematics; medicine (Graduate Certificate), including aging and neuroscience, bioinformatics, biotechnology, brain fitness and memory management, clinical investigation, hand and upper limb rehabilitation, health informatics, health sciences, integrative weight management, intellectual property, medicine and gender, metabolic and nutritional medicine, metabolic cardiology, pharmacy sciences; national and competitive intelligence (Graduate Certificate); nursing (Graduate Certificate), including simulation based academic fellowship in advanced pain management; psychological and social foundations (Graduate Certificate), including career counseling, college teaching, diversity in education, mental health counseling, school counseling; public affairs (Graduate Certificate), including nonprofit management, public management, research administration; public health (Graduate Certificate), including assessing chemical toxicity and public health risks, health equity, pharmacoepidemiology, public health generalist, toxicology, translational research in adolescent behavioral health; public health practices (Graduate Certificate), including planning for healthy communities; rehabilitation and mental health counseling (Graduate Certificate), including integrative mental health care, marriage and family therapy, rehabilitation technology; secondary education (Graduate Certificate), including ESOL, foreign language education: culture and content, foreign language education: professional; social work (Graduate Certificate), including geriatric social work/clinical gerontology; special education (Graduate Certificate), including autism spectrum disorder, disabilities education: severe/profound; world languages (Graduate Certificate), including teaching English as a second language (TESL) or foreign language. *Unit head:* Dr. Cynthia DeLuca, Associate Vice President and Assistant Vice Provost, 813-974-3077, Fax: 813-974-7061, E-mail: deluca@usf.edu. *Application contact:* Owen Hooper, Director, Summer and Alternative Calendar Programs, 813-974-6917, E-mail: hooper@usf.edu.
Website: http://www.usf.edu/innovative-education/

The University of Tennessee, Graduate School, Tickle College of Engineering, Department of Materials Science and Engineering, Knoxville, TN 37996-2200. Offers materials science and engineering (MS, PhD); reliability and maintainability engineering (MS); MS/MBA. *Program availability:* Part-time. *Faculty:* 26 full-time (5 women). *Students:* 78 full-time (28 women), 6 part-time (1 woman); includes 7 minority (2 Black or African American, non-Hispanic/Latino; 3 Asian, non-Hispanic/Latino; 2 Hispanic/

Latino), 39 international. Average age 29. 85 applicants, 16% accepted, 11 enrolled. In 2019, 10 master's, 6 doctorates awarded. *Degree requirements:* For master's, thesis or alternative; for doctorate, comprehensive exam, thesis/dissertation. *Entrance requirements:* For master's, GRE General Test (for MS students pursuing research thesis), minimum GPA of 2.7 (for U.S. degree holders), 3.0 (for international degree holders); 3 references; for doctorate, GRE General Test, minimum GPA of 3.0 on previous graduate course work; 3 references. Additional exam requirements/recommendations for international students: required—TOEFL (minimum score 550 paper-based; 80 iBT), IELTS (minimum score 6.5). *Application deadline:* For fall admission, 2/1 priority date for domestic and international students; for spring admission, 6/15 for domestic and international students; for summer admission, 10/15 for domestic and international students. Applications are processed on a rolling basis. Application fee: $60. Electronic applications accepted. *Financial support:* In 2019–20, 103 students received support, including 17 fellowships with full tuition reimbursements available (averaging $11,364 per year), 65 research assistantships with full tuition reimbursements available (averaging $22,712 per year), 21 teaching assistantships with full tuition reimbursements available (averaging $21,410 per year); career-related internships or fieldwork, Federal Work-Study, institutionally sponsored loans, health care benefits, and unspecified assistantships also available. Financial award application deadline: 2/1; financial award applicants required to submit FAFSA. *Unit head:* Dr. Veerle Keppens, Head, 865-974-5336, Fax: 865-974-4115, E-mail: vkeppens@utk.edu. *Application contact:* Dr. Kurt Sickafus, Professor and Director of Graduate Studies, 865-974-4858, E-mail: kurt@utk.edu.
Website: http://www.engr.utk.edu/mse

The University of Texas at Arlington, Graduate School, College of Engineering, Department of Materials Science and Engineering, Arlington, TX 76019. Offers M Engr, MS, PhD. Terminal master's awarded for partial completion of doctoral program. *Degree requirements:* For master's, comprehensive exam (for some programs), thesis optional; for doctorate, comprehensive exam, thesis/dissertation optional. *Entrance requirements:* For master's, GRE General Test, minimum GPA of 3.0; for doctorate, GRE General Test, minimum GPA of 3.5. Additional exam requirements/recommendations for international students: required—TOEFL (minimum score 550 paper-based; 79 iBT), IELTS.

The University of Texas at Austin, Graduate School, Cockrell School of Engineering, Program in Materials Science and Engineering, Austin, TX 78712-1111. Offers MS, PhD. *Program availability:* Part-time. *Degree requirements:* For master's, thesis (for some programs); for doctorate, thesis/dissertation. *Entrance requirements:* For master's and doctorate, GRE General Test. Additional exam requirements/recommendations for international students: required—TOEFL (minimum score 550 paper-based). Electronic applications accepted.

The University of Texas at Dallas, Erik Jonsson School of Engineering and Computer Science, Department of Materials Science and Engineering, Richardson, TX 75080. Offers MS, PhD. *Program availability:* Part-time, evening/weekend. *Faculty:* 15 full-time (2 women). *Students:* 53 full-time (14 women), 4 part-time (0 women); includes 7 minority (3 Asian, non-Hispanic/Latino; 3 Hispanic/Latino; 1 Two or more races, non-Hispanic/Latino), 41 international. Average age 30. 90 applicants, 33% accepted, 11 enrolled. In 2019, 11 master's, 8 doctorates awarded. *Degree requirements:* For master's, thesis or major design project; for doctorate, thesis/dissertation. *Entrance requirements:* For master's, GRE General Test, minimum GPA of 3.0 in related bachelor's degree; for doctorate, GRE General Test, minimum GPA of 3.5. Additional exam requirements/recommendations for international students: required—TOEFL (minimum score 550 paper-based). *Application deadline:* For fall admission, 7/15 for domestic students, 5/1 priority date for international students; for spring admission, 11/15 for domestic students, 9/1 priority date for international students. Applications are processed on a rolling basis. Application fee: $50 ($100 for international students). Electronic applications accepted. *Expenses: Tuition, area resident:* Full-time $16,504. Tuition, state resident: full-time $16,504. Tuition, nonresident: full-time $34,266. Tuition and fees vary according to course load. *Financial support:* In 2019–20, 49 students received support, including 1 fellowship (averaging $7,500 per year), 43 research assistantships with partial tuition reimbursements available (averaging $26,121 per year), 4 teaching assistantships with partial tuition reimbursements available (averaging $18,338 per year); career-related internships or fieldwork, Federal Work-Study, institutionally sponsored loans, scholarships/grants, and unspecified assistantships also available. Support available to part-time students. Financial award application deadline: 4/30; financial award applicants required to submit FAFSA. *Unit head:* Dr. Amy Walker, Interim Department Head, 972-883-5780, Fax: 972-883-5725, E-mail: amy.walker@utdallas.edu. *Application contact:* Dr. Lev Gelb, Associate Department Head, 972-883-5644, Fax: 972-883-5725, E-mail: mseadmissions@utdallas.edu.
Website: http://mse.utdallas.edu/

The University of Texas at El Paso, Graduate School, College of Engineering, Department of Metallurgical and Materials Engineering, El Paso, TX 79968-0001. Offers materials science and engineering (PhD); metallurgical and materials engineering (MS). *Program availability:* Part-time, evening/weekend. *Degree requirements:* For master's, thesis. *Entrance requirements:* For master's, GRE General Test. Additional exam requirements/recommendations for international students: required—TOEFL. Electronic applications accepted.

The University of Toledo, College of Graduate Studies, College of Natural Sciences and Mathematics, Department of Physics and Astronomy, Toledo, OH 43606-3390. Offers photovoltaics (PSM); physics (MS, PhD), including astrophysics (PhD), materials science, medical physics (PhD); MS/PhD. *Degree requirements:* For master's, thesis; for doctorate, thesis/dissertation, departmental qualifying exam. *Entrance requirements:* For master's and doctorate, GRE General Test, GRE Subject Test, minimum cumulative point-hour ratio of 2.7 for all previous academic work, three letters of recommendation, statement of purpose, transcripts from all prior institutions attended. Additional exam requirements/recommendations for international students: required—TOEFL (minimum score 550 paper-based; 80 iBT). Electronic applications accepted.

University of Toronto, School of Graduate Studies, Faculty of Applied Science and Engineering, Department of Materials Science and Engineering, Toronto, ON M5S 1A1, Canada. Offers M Eng, MA Sc, PhD. *Program availability:* Part-time. *Degree requirements:* For master's, thesis (for some programs), oral presentation/thesis defense (MA Sc), qualifying exam; for doctorate, thesis/dissertation. *Entrance requirements:* For master's, BA Sc or B Sc in materials science and engineering, 2 letters of reference; for doctorate, MA Sc or equivalent, 2 letters of reference, minimum B+ average in last 2 years. Additional exam requirements/recommendations for international students: required—TOEFL (minimum score 580 paper-based), TWE (minimum score 4). Electronic applications accepted.

University of Utah, Graduate School, College of Engineering, Department of Materials Science and Engineering, Salt Lake City, UT 84112. Offers MS, PhD. *Faculty:* 21 full-time (1 woman). *Students:* 43 full-time (12 women), 13 part-time (3 women); includes 5 minority (3 Asian, non-Hispanic/Latino; 1 Hispanic/Latino; 1 Native Hawaiian or other Pacific Islander, non-Hispanic/Latino), 25 international. Average age 28. 53 applicants, 28% accepted, 10 enrolled. In 2019, 19 master's, 13 doctorates awarded. *Degree requirements:* For master's, thesis (for some programs), Program of Study; for doctorate, comprehensive exam, thesis/dissertation, proposal defense, program of study. *Entrance requirements:* For master's and doctorate, GRE, BS in field or equivalent, from recognized institute of higher learning. Additional exam requirements/recommendations for international students: required—TOEFL (minimum score 550 paper-based; 80 iBT), IELTS (minimum score 6.5), Either TOEFL or IELTS. *Application deadline:* For fall admission, 1/15 for domestic and international students; for spring admission, 10/1 for domestic students, 9/1 for international students; for summer admission, 1/15 for domestic students, 12/15 for international students. Applications are processed on a rolling basis. Application fee: $45 ($65 for international students). Electronic applications accepted. *Expenses:* Tuition, state resident: full-time $7085; part-time $272.51 per credit hour. Tuition, nonresident: full-time $24,937; part-time $959.12 per credit hour. *Required fees:* $880.52; $880.52 per semester. Tuition and fees vary according to degree level, program and student level. *Financial support:* In 2019–20, 6 students received support, including 6 fellowships with full tuition reimbursements available (averaging $10,000 per year), 35 research assistantships with full tuition reimbursements available (averaging $15,727 per year). *Unit head:* Michael Simpson, Chair, 801-581-4013, E-mail: michael.simpson@utah.edu. *Application contact:* Sara Wilson, Administrative Manager, 801-581-4449, E-mail: sara.j.wilson@utah.edu.
Website: http://www.mse.utah.edu/

University of Vermont, Graduate College, Cross-College Interdisciplinary Program, Program in Materials Science, Burlington, VT 05405. Offers MS, PhD. *Degree requirements:* For master's, thesis or alternative; for doctorate, thesis/dissertation. *Entrance requirements:* For master's and doctorate, GRE General Test. Additional exam requirements/recommendations for international students: required—TOEFL (minimum score 550 paper-based; 90 iBT). Electronic applications accepted.

University of Virginia, School of Engineering and Applied Science, Department of Materials Science and Engineering, Charlottesville, VA 22903. Offers materials science (MMSE, MS, PhD). *Program availability:* Part-time, online learning. Terminal master's awarded for partial completion of doctoral program. *Degree requirements:* For master's, comprehensive exam, thesis (for some programs); for doctorate, comprehensive exam, thesis/dissertation. *Entrance requirements:* For master's and doctorate, GRE General Test, three recommendations. Additional exam requirements/recommendations for international students: required—TOEFL. Electronic applications accepted.

University of Washington, Graduate School, College of Engineering, Department of Materials Science and Engineering, Seattle, WA 98195-2120. Offers applied materials science and engineering (MS); materials science and engineering (MS, PhD); materials science and engineering and nanotechnology (PhD); materials science and engineering, nanotechnology, and molecular engineering (PhD). *Program availability:* Part-time. *Students:* 118 full-time (27 women), 26 part-time (8 women); includes 31 minority (1 Black or African American, non-Hispanic/Latino; 16 Asian, non-Hispanic/Latino; 9 Hispanic/Latino; 1 Native Hawaiian or other Pacific Islander, non-Hispanic/Latino; 4 Two or more races, non-Hispanic/Latino), 72 international. Average age 25. 435 applicants, 39% accepted, 57 enrolled. In 2019, 44 master's, 9 doctorates awarded. Terminal master's awarded for partial completion of doctoral program. *Degree requirements:* For master's, comprehensive exam, final paper or thesis and presentation; for doctorate, comprehensive exam, thesis/dissertation, qualifying evaluation, general and final exams. *Entrance requirements:* For master's and doctorate, GRE General Test, minimum GPA of 3.0, resume/curriculum vitae, letters of recommendation, statement of purpose, transcripts. Additional exam requirements/recommendations for international students: required—TOEFL (minimum score 92 iBT). *Application deadline:* For fall admission, 1/6 for domestic and international students. Application fee: $85. Electronic applications accepted. *Expenses:* Contact institution. *Financial support:* In 2019–20, 35 research assistantships with full tuition reimbursements (averaging $30,840 per year), 14 teaching assistantships with full tuition reimbursements (averaging $30,840 per year) were awarded; fellowships with full tuition reimbursements, Federal Work-Study, institutionally sponsored loans, scholarships/grants, health care benefits, tuition waivers, unspecified assistantships, and stipend supplements also available. Support available to part-time students. Financial award application deadline: 1/6. *Unit head:* Dr. Jihui Yang, Professor/Chair, 206-543-7090, Fax: 206-221-4934, E-mail: jihuiy@uw.edu. *Application contact:* Karen Wetterhahn, Academic Counselor, 206-543-2740, Fax: 206-543-3100, E-mail: karenlw@uw.edu.
Website: http://mse.washington.edu

Vanderbilt University, School of Engineering, Interdisciplinary Program in Materials Science, Nashville, TN 37240-1001. Offers M Eng, MS, PhD. *Program availability:* Part-time. Terminal master's awarded for partial completion of doctoral program. *Degree requirements:* For master's, thesis; for doctorate, thesis/dissertation. *Entrance requirements:* For master's and doctorate, GRE General Test. Electronic applications accepted. *Expenses: Tuition:* Full-time $51,018; part-time $2087 per hour. *Required fees:* $542. Tuition and fees vary according to program.

Washington State University, Voiland College of Engineering and Architecture, School of Mechanical and Materials Engineering, Pullman, WA 99164-2920. Offers materials science and engineering (MS, PhD); mechanical engineering (MS, PhD). *Program availability:* Part-time. Terminal master's awarded for partial completion of doctoral program. *Degree requirements:* For master's, comprehensive exam, thesis; for doctorate, comprehensive exam, thesis/dissertation, preliminary exam. *Entrance requirements:* For master's, GRE, bachelor's degree, minimum GPA of 3.0, resume, statement of purpose, 3 letters of recommendation, official transcripts, Student Interest Profile form; for doctorate, GRE, bachelor's degree, minimum GPA of 3.4, resume, statement of purpose, 3 letters of recommendation, official transcripts, Student Interest Profile form. Additional exam requirements/recommendations for international students: required—TOEFL (minimum score 500 paper-based), IELTS. Electronic applications accepted.

Washington University in St. Louis, School of Engineering and Applied Science, Department of Mechanical Engineering and Materials Science, St. Louis, MO 63130-4899. Offers aerospace engineering (MS, PhD); materials science (MS); mechanical engineering (M Eng, MS, PhD). *Program availability:* Part-time. Terminal master's awarded for partial completion of doctoral program. *Degree requirements:* For master's, thesis optional; for doctorate, thesis/dissertation optional. *Entrance requirements:* For master's, GRE; for doctorate, GRE General Test, departmental qualifying exam.

Wayne State University, College of Engineering, Department of Chemical Engineering and Materials Science, Detroit, MI 48202. Offers chemical engineering (MS, PhD); materials science and engineering (MS, PhD), including materials science and engineering; polymer engineering (Graduate Certificate), including polymer engineering. *Program availability:* Part-time. *Faculty:* 16. *Students:* 36 full-time (12 women), 20 part-time (5 women); includes 5 minority (1 Asian, non-Hispanic/Latino; 3 Hispanic/Latino; 1 Two or more races, non-Hispanic/Latino), 32 international. Average age 28. 128 applicants, 16% accepted, 9 enrolled. In 2019, 20 master's, 4 doctorates, 1 other advanced degree awarded. *Degree requirements:* For master's, thesis optional; for doctorate, comprehensive exam, thesis/dissertation. *Entrance requirements:* For master's, resume (optional); for doctorate, GRE, three letters of recommendation (at least two from the applicant's academic institution); personal statement; resume; for Graduate Certificate, bachelor's degree in engineering or other mathematics-based

sciences in exceptional cases. Additional exam requirements/recommendations for international students: required—TOEFL (minimum score 550 paper-based; 79 iBT), TWE (minimum score 5.5), Michigan English Language Assessment Battery (minimum score 85); recommended—IELTS (minimum score 6.5). *Application deadline:* For fall admission, 3/1 priority date for domestic and international students; for winter admission, 10/1 priority date for domestic students, 9/1 priority date for international students; for spring admission, 2/1 priority date for domestic and international students; for summer admission, 2/1 priority date for domestic and international students. Application fee: $50. Electronic applications accepted. *Expenses:* $790 per credit hour in-state tuition, $1579 per credit hour out-of-state tuition. 32 credits to complete the MS; 90 credits total to complete the PhD. *Financial support:* In 2019–20, 35 students received support, including 4 fellowships with tuition reimbursements available (averaging $20,000 per year), 18 research assistantships with tuition reimbursements available (averaging $21,856 per year), 6 teaching assistantships with tuition reimbursements available (averaging $20,792 per year); scholarships/grants, health care benefits, and unspecified assistantships also available. Support available to part-time students. Financial award applicants required to submit FAFSA. *Unit head:* Dr. Jeffrey Potoff, Professor and Interim Chair, 313-577-9357, E-mail: jpotoff@wayne.edu. *Application contact:* Rob Carlson, Graduate Program Coordinator, 313-577-9615, E-mail: rcarlson@wayne.edu.
Website: http://engineering.wayne.edu/che/

West Virginia University, Statler College of Engineering and Mineral Resources, Morgantown, WV 26506. Offers aerospace engineering (MSAE, PhD); chemical engineering (MS Ch E, PhD); civil engineering (MSCE, PhD); computer engineering (PhD); computer science (MSCS, PhD); electrical engineering (MSEE, PhD); energy systems engineering (MSESE); engineering (MSE); industrial engineering (MSIE, PhD); industrial hygiene (MS); material science and engineering (MSMSE, PhD); mechanical engineering (MSME, PhD); mining engineering (MS Min E, PhD); petroleum and natural gas engineering (MSPNGE, PhD); safety management (MS); software engineering (MSSE). *Program availability:* Part-time. Terminal master's awarded for partial completion of doctoral program. *Degree requirements:* For master's, thesis optional; for doctorate, comprehensive exam, thesis/dissertation. *Entrance requirements:* Additional exam requirements/recommendations for international students: required—TOEFL (minimum score 550 paper-based). Electronic applications accepted. *Expenses:* Contact institution.

Worcester Polytechnic Institute, Graduate Admissions, Department of Mechanical Engineering, Program in Materials Process Engineering, Worcester, MA 01609-2280. Offers materials process engineering (MS). *Program availability:* Part-time, evening/weekend. *Degree requirements:* For master's, thesis optional. *Entrance requirements:* For master's, Required for international applicants; recommended for all others., 3 letters of recommendation. Additional exam requirements/recommendations for international students: required—TOEFL (minimum score 563 paper-based; 84 iBT), IELTS (minimum score 7), GRE. Electronic applications accepted.

Worcester Polytechnic Institute, Graduate Admissions, Department of Mechanical Engineering, Program in Materials Science and Engineering, Worcester, MA 01609-2280. Offers materials science & engineering (MS). *Program availability:* Part-time, evening/weekend. Terminal master's awarded for partial completion of doctoral program. *Degree requirements:* For master's, thesis; for doctorate, comprehensive exam, thesis/dissertation. *Entrance requirements:* For master's and doctorate, Required for international applicants; recommended for all others., 3 letters of recommendation. Additional exam requirements/recommendations for international students: required—TOEFL (minimum score 563 paper-based; 84 iBT), IELTS (minimum score 7), GRE. Electronic applications accepted.

Wright State University, Graduate School, College of Engineering and Computer Science, Department of Mechanical and Materials Engineering, Dayton, OH 45435. Offers aerospace systems engineering (MS); materials science and engineering (MS); mechanical engineering (MS); renewable and clean energy (MS). *Degree requirements:* For master's, thesis or course option alternative. *Entrance requirements:* Additional exam requirements/recommendations for international students: required—TOEFL.

Metallurgical Engineering and Metallurgy

Colorado School of Mines, Office of Graduate Studies, Department of Metallurgical and Materials Engineering, Golden, CO 80401. Offers materials science (MS, PhD); metallurgical and materials engineering (ME, MS, PhD). *Program availability:* Part-time. *Degree requirements:* For master's, thesis (for some programs); for doctorate, comprehensive exam, thesis/dissertation. *Entrance requirements:* For master's and doctorate, GRE General Test. Additional exam requirements/recommendations for international students: required—TOEFL (minimum score 550 paper-based; 79 iBT). Electronic applications accepted. *Expenses:* Tuition, state resident: full-time $16,650; part-time $925 per credit hour. Tuition, nonresident: full-time $37,350; part-time $2075 per credit hour. *International tuition:* $37,350 full-time. *Required fees:* $2412.

Michigan Technological University, Graduate School, College of Engineering, Department of Materials Science and Engineering, Houghton, MI 49931. Offers MS, PhD. *Program availability:* Part-time, 100% online, blended/hybrid learning. *Faculty:* 30 full-time, 11 part-time/adjunct (3 women). *Students:* 31 full-time (10 women), 8 part-time (3 women); includes 2 minority (1 Hispanic/Latino; 1 Two or more races, non-Hispanic/Latino), 23 international. Average age 27. 140 applicants, 31% accepted, 9 enrolled. In 2019, 9 master's, 1 doctorate awarded. Terminal master's awarded for partial completion of doctoral program. *Degree requirements:* For master's, comprehensive exam (for some programs), thesis (for some programs); for doctorate, comprehensive exam, thesis/dissertation. *Entrance requirements:* For master's and doctorate, GRE (domestic students from ABET-accredited programs exempt), statement of purpose, personal statement, official transcripts, 3 letters of recommendation. Additional exam requirements/recommendations for international students: required—TOEFL (minimum score 79 iBT), IELTS (minimum score 6.5), TOEFL (minimum score 79 iBT) or IELTS (minimum score of 6.5). *Application deadline:* For fall admission, 2/1 priority date for domestic and international students; for spring admission, 9/1 priority date for domestic and international students. Applications are processed on a rolling basis. Application fee: $0. Electronic applications accepted. *Expenses:* $1,212 per credit. *Financial support:* In 2019–20, 28 students received support, including 5 fellowships with tuition reimbursements available (averaging $16,590 per year), 17 research assistantships with tuition reimbursements available (averaging $16,590 per year); teaching assistantships, career-related internships or fieldwork, Federal Work-Study, scholarships/grants, health care benefits, unspecified assistantships, and cooperative program also available. Financial award applicants required to submit FAFSA. *Unit head:* Dr. Stephen L. Kampe, Chair, 906-487-2036, Fax: 906-487-2934, E-mail: kampe@mtu.edu. *Application contact:* Valentina O'Kane, Department Coordinator, 906-487-4326, Fax: 906-487-2934, E-mail: vokane@mtu.edu.
Website: http://www.mtu.edu/materials/

Missouri University of Science and Technology, Department of Materials Science and Engineering, Rolla, MO 65401. Offers ceramic engineering (MS, PhD); materials science and engineering (MS, PhD); metallurgical engineering (MS, PhD). *Degree requirements:* For master's, thesis optional; for doctorate, comprehensive exam. *Entrance requirements:* For master's, GRE (minimum combined score 1100, 600 verbal, 3.5 writing); for doctorate, GRE (minimum score: quantitative 600, writing 3.5). Additional exam requirements/recommendations for international students: required—TOEFL (minimum score 570 paper-based). Electronic applications accepted. *Expenses:* Tuition, state resident: full-time $7839; part-time $435.50 per credit hour. Tuition, nonresident: full-time $22,169; part-time $1231.60 per credit hour. *International tuition:* $18,156.60 full-time. *Required fees:* $649.76. One-time fee: $119. Tuition and fees vary according to course load and program.

Montana Technological University, Department of Metallurgical/Mineral Processing Engineering, Butte, MT 59701-8997. Offers MS. *Program availability:* Part-time. *Faculty:* 6 full-time (0 women). *Students:* 7 full-time (1 woman), 3 international. Average age 27. 4 applicants, 75% accepted, 3 enrolled. In 2019, 2 master's awarded. *Degree requirements:* For master's, comprehensive exam (for some programs), thesis optional. *Entrance requirements:* For master's, GRE General Test, minimum GPA of 3.0. Additional exam requirements/recommendations for international students: required—TOEFL (minimum score 545 paper-based; 78 iBT), IELTS (minimum score 6.5). *Application deadline:* For fall admission, 4/1 priority date for domestic students, 3/1 priority date for international students; for spring admission, 10/1 priority date for domestic students, 6/1 priority date for international students. Applications are processed on a rolling basis. Application fee: $50. Electronic applications accepted. *Financial support:* In 2019–20, 4 students received support, including 2 teaching assistantships with partial tuition reimbursements available (averaging $5,000 per year); research assistantships with partial tuition reimbursements available, career-related internships or fieldwork, tuition waivers (full and partial), and unspecified assistantships also available. Financial award application deadline: 4/1; financial award applicants required to submit FAFSA. *Unit head:* Dr. Jerry Downey, Department Head, 406-496-4578, Fax: 406-496-4664, E-mail: jdowney@mtech.edu. *Application contact:* Daniel Stirling, Administrator, Graduate School, 406-496-4304, Fax: 406-496-4710, E-mail: gradschool@mtech.edu.
Website: http://www.mtech.edu/academics/gradschool/degreeprograms/degrees-metallurgical.htm

The Ohio State University, Graduate School, College of Engineering, Department of Materials Science and Engineering, Program in Welding Engineering, Columbus, OH 43210. Offers MS, PhD. *Program availability:* Part-time, online learning. *Entrance requirements:* For master's and doctorate, GRE General Test (for all with undergraduate GPA less than 3.0 or with a non-ABET accredited degree). Additional exam requirements/recommendations for international students: required—TOEFL (minimum score 550 paper-based; 79 iBT), Michigan English Language Assessment Battery (minimum score 82); recommended—IELTS (minimum score 7). Electronic applications accepted.

The University of Alabama, Graduate School, College of Engineering, Department of Metallurgical and Materials Engineering, Tuscaloosa, AL 35487. Offers MS Met E, PhD. *Faculty:* 14 full-time (4 women). *Students:* 35 full-time (9 women), 1 part-time (0 women); includes 4 minority (1 Black or African American, non-Hispanic/Latino; 3 Hispanic/Latino), 18 international. Average age 27. 19 applicants, 74% accepted, 6 enrolled. In 2019, 4 master's, 10 doctorates awarded. *Degree requirements:* For master's, thesis or alternative; for doctorate, thesis/dissertation. *Entrance requirements:* For master's, GRE General Test, minimum GPA of 3.0 in last 60 hours; for doctorate, GRE General Test, minimum graduate GPA of 3.0, graduate degree. Additional exam requirements/recommendations for international students: required—TOEFL (minimum score 550 paper-based). *Application deadline:* For fall admission, 7/1 for domestic students, 5/1 priority date for international students. Applications are processed on a rolling basis. Application fee: $50 ($60 for international students). Electronic applications accepted. *Expenses: Tuition, area resident:* Full-time $10,780; part-time $440 per credit hour. Tuition, nonresident: full-time $30,250; part-time $1550 per credit hour. *Financial support:* In 2019–20, 25 students received support. Fellowships, research assistantships, teaching assistantships, Federal Work-Study, and unspecified assistantships available. *Unit head:* Dr. Steven Daniewicz, Head/Professor, 205-348-2704, Fax: 205-348-2164, E-mail: srdaniewicz@eng.ua.edu. *Application contact:* Dr. Lin Li, Associate Professor, 205-348-4971, Fax: 205-348-2346, E-mail: lin.li@eng.ua.edu.
Website: http://www.eng.ua.edu/~mtedept/

The University of Manchester, School of Materials, Manchester, United Kingdom. Offers advanced aerospace materials engineering (M Sc); advanced metallic systems (PhD); biomedical materials (M Phil, M Sc, PhD); ceramics and glass (M Phil, M Sc, PhD); composite materials (M Sc, PhD); corrosion and protection (M Phil, M Sc, PhD); materials (M Phil, PhD); metallic materials (M Phil, M Sc, PhD); nanostructural materials (M Phil, M Sc, PhD); paper science (M Phil, M Sc, PhD); polymer science and engineering (M Phil, M Sc, PhD); technical textiles (M Sc); textile design, fashion and management (M Phil, M Sc, PhD); textile science and technology (M Phil, M Sc, PhD); textiles (M Phil, PhD); textiles and fashion (M Ent).

University of Nebraska–Lincoln, Graduate College, College of Engineering, Department of Mechanical and Materials Engineering, Lincoln, NE 68588-0526. Offers biomedical engineering (PhD); engineering mechanics (MS); materials engineering (PhD); mechanical engineering (MS), including materials science engineering, metallurgical engineering; mechanical engineering and applied mechanics (PhD); MS/MS. *Degree requirements:* For master's, thesis optional; for doctorate, comprehensive exam, thesis/dissertation. *Entrance requirements:* For master's and doctorate, GRE General Test. Additional exam requirements/recommendations for international students: required—TOEFL (minimum score 550 paper-based). Electronic applications accepted.

University of Nevada, Reno, Graduate School, College of Engineering, Department of Chemical and Materials Engineering, Program in Materials Science and Engineering, Reno, NV 89557. Offers MS, PhD. Terminal master's awarded for partial completion of doctoral program. *Degree requirements:* For master's, thesis; for doctorate, one foreign language, thesis/dissertation. *Entrance requirements:* For master's, minimum GPA of 2.75; for doctorate, GRE, minimum GPA of 3.0. Additional exam requirements/recommendations for international students: required—TOEFL (minimum score 500 paper-based; 61 iBT), IELTS (minimum score 6). Electronic applications accepted.

University of Nevada, Reno, Graduate School, College of Science, Mackay School of Earth Sciences and Engineering, Department of Mining and Metallurgical Engineering, Reno, NV 89557. Offers metallurgical engineering (MS); mining engineering (MS, PhD). *Degree requirements:* For master's, thesis optional. *Entrance requirements:* For master's, GRE, minimum GPA of 2.75. Additional exam requirements/recommendations for international students: required—TOEFL (minimum score 500 paper-based; 61 iBT), IELTS (minimum score 6). Electronic applications accepted.

The University of Texas at El Paso, Graduate School, College of Engineering, Department of Metallurgical and Materials Engineering, El Paso, TX 79968-0001. Offers materials science and engineering (PhD); metallurgical and materials engineering (MS). *Program availability:* Part-time, evening/weekend. *Degree requirements:* For master's, thesis. *Entrance requirements:* For master's, GRE General Test. Additional exam requirements/recommendations for international students: required—TOEFL. Electronic applications accepted.

Université Laval, Faculty of Sciences and Engineering, Department of Mining, Metallurgical and Materials Engineering, Programs in Metallurgical Engineering, Québec, QC G1K 7P4, Canada. Offers M Sc, PhD. Terminal master's awarded for partial completion of doctoral program. *Degree requirements:* For master's, thesis; for doctorate, comprehensive exam, thesis/dissertation. *Entrance requirements:* For master's and doctorate, knowledge of French and English. Electronic applications accepted.

Polymer Science and Engineering

California Polytechnic State University, San Luis Obispo, College of Science and Mathematics, Department of Chemistry and Biochemistry, San Luis Obispo, CA 93407. Offers polymers and coating science (MS). *Program availability:* Part-time. *Faculty:* 3 full-time (0 women). *Students:* 5 full-time (3 women), 5 part-time (0 women); includes 7 minority (2 Asian, non-Hispanic/Latino; 2 Hispanic/Latino; 3 Two or more races, non-Hispanic/Latino), 1 international. Average age 23. 10 applicants, 70% accepted, 4 enrolled. In 2019, 5 master's awarded. *Entrance requirements:* For master's, GRE. Additional exam requirements/recommendations for international students: required—TOEFL (minimum score 80 iBT). *Application deadline:* For fall admission, 4/1 for domestic and international students; for spring admission, 2/1 for domestic students. Applications are processed on a rolling basis. Application fee: $55. Electronic applications accepted. *Expenses:* Tuition, state resident: full-time $7176; part-time $4164 per year. Tuition, nonresident: full-time $18,690; part-time $8916 per year. *Required fees:* $4206; $3185 per unit. $1061 per term. *Financial support:* Fellowships, research assistantships, career-related internships or fieldwork, Federal Work-Study, and scholarships/grants available. Support available to part-time students. Financial award application deadline: 3/2; financial award applicants required to submit FAFSA. *Unit head:* Dr. Raymond Fernando, Graduate Coordinator, 805-756-2395, E-mail: rhfernan@calpoly.edu. *Application contact:* Dr. Raymond Fernando, Graduate Coordinator, 805-756-2395, E-mail: rhfernan@calpoly.edu. Website: http://www.chemistry.calpoly.edu/

Carnegie Mellon University, Carnegie Institute of Technology, Department of Chemical Engineering and Department of Chemistry, Program in Colloids, Polymers and Surfaces, Pittsburgh, PA 15213-3891. Offers MS. *Program availability:* Part-time, evening/weekend. *Entrance requirements:* For master's, GRE General Test, GRE Subject Test. Additional exam requirements/recommendations for international students: required—TOEFL.

Case Western Reserve University, School of Graduate Studies, Case School of Engineering, Department of Macromolecular Science and Engineering, Cleveland, OH 44106. Offers MS, PhD. *Program availability:* Part-time. Terminal master's awarded for partial completion of doctoral program. *Degree requirements:* For master's, thesis; for doctorate, thesis/dissertation, qualifying exam, teaching experience. *Entrance requirements:* For master's and doctorate, GRE General Test. Additional exam requirements/recommendations for international students: required—TOEFL.

Cornell University, Graduate School, Graduate Fields of Engineering, Field of Chemical Engineering, Ithaca, NY 14853. Offers advanced materials processing (M Eng, MS, PhD); applied mathematics and computational methods (M Eng, MS, PhD); biochemical engineering (M Eng, MS, PhD); chemical reaction engineering (M Eng, MS, PhD); classical and statistical thermodynamics (M Eng, MS, PhD); fluid dynamics, rheology and biorheology (M Eng, MS, PhD); heat and mass transfer (M Eng, MS, PhD); kinetics and catalysis (M Eng, MS, PhD); polymers (M Eng, MS, PhD); surface science (M Eng, MS, PhD). *Degree requirements:* For master's, thesis (MS); for doctorate, comprehensive exam, thesis/dissertation. *Entrance requirements:* For master's and doctorate, GRE General Test, 2 letters of recommendation. Additional exam requirements/recommendations for international students: required—TOEFL (minimum score 600 paper-based; 77 iBT). Electronic applications accepted.

Cornell University, Graduate School, Graduate Fields of Human Ecology, Field of Fiber Science and Apparel Design, Ithaca, NY 14853. Offers apparel design (MA, MPS); fiber science (MS, PhD); polymer science (MS, PhD); textile science (MS, PhD). *Degree requirements:* For master's, thesis (MA, MS), project paper (MPS); for doctorate, comprehensive exam, thesis/dissertation. *Entrance requirements:* For master's, GRE General Test, 2 letters of recommendation, portfolio (for functional apparel design); for doctorate, GRE General Test, 2 letters of recommendation. Additional exam requirements/recommendations for international students: required—TOEFL (minimum score 600 paper-based; 77 iBT). Electronic applications accepted.

DePaul University, College of Science and Health, Chicago, IL 60604-2287. Offers applied mathematics (MS); applied statistics (MS); biological sciences (MA, MS); chemistry (MS); environmental science (MS); mathematics education (MA); mathematics for teaching (MS); nursing (MS); nursing practice (DNP); physics (MS); polymer and coatings science (MS); psychology (MS); pure mathematics (MS); science education (MS); MA/PhD. *Accreditation:* AACN. Electronic applications accepted.

Eastern Michigan University, Graduate School, College of Engineering and Technology, School of Engineering, Programs in Polymers and Coatings Technology, Ypsilanti, MI 48197. Offers MS, Postbaccalaureate Certificate. *Program availability:* Part-time, evening/weekend, online learning. *Students:* 10 full-time (4 women), 13 part-time (4 women); includes 2 minority (both Asian, non-Hispanic/Latino), 11 international. Average age 28. 13 applicants, 92% accepted, 4 enrolled. In 2019, 5 master's awarded. *Entrance requirements:* For master's, GRE General Test, BS in chemistry, minimum GPA of 2.6. Additional exam requirements/recommendations for international students: required—TOEFL. *Application deadline:* Applications are processed on a rolling basis. Application fee: $45. *Financial support:* Fellowships, research assistantships with full tuition reimbursements, teaching assistantships with full tuition reimbursements, career-related internships or fieldwork, Federal Work-Study, institutionally sponsored loans, scholarships/grants, tuition waivers (partial), and unspecified assistantships available. Support available to part-time students. Financial award applicants required to submit FAFSA. *Application contact:* Dr. Vijay Mannari, Program Coordinator, 734-487-2040, Fax: 734-487-8755, E-mail: vmannari@emich.edu.

Lehigh University, P.C. Rossin College of Engineering and Applied Science, Center for Polymer Science and Engineering, Bethlehem, PA 18015. Offers M Eng, MS, PhD. *Program availability:* Part-time, evening/weekend, 100% online, blended/hybrid learning. *Faculty:* 5 full-time (3 women). *Students:* 6 full-time (4 women), 32 part-time (13 women); includes 13 minority (4 Black or African American, non-Hispanic/Latino; 5 Asian, non-Hispanic/Latino; 4 Hispanic/Latino), 3 international. Average age 31. 28

applicants, 43% accepted, 7 enrolled. In 2019, 9 master's awarded. Terminal master's awarded for partial completion of doctoral program. *Degree requirements:* For master's, thesis (for some programs); for doctorate, thesis/dissertation. *Entrance requirements:* For master's and doctorate, GRE General Test. Additional exam requirements/recommendations for international students: required—TOEFL (minimum score 487 paper-based; 85 iBT), IELTS (minimum score 6.5), TOEFL or IELTS required. *Application deadline:* For fall admission, 7/15 for domestic students, 1/15 for international students; for spring admission, 12/1 for domestic and international students; for summer admission, 4/30 for domestic and international students. Applications are processed on a rolling basis. Application fee: $75. Electronic applications accepted. *Financial support:* In 2019–20, 1 research assistantship with full tuition reimbursement (averaging $11,025 per year), 1 teaching assistantship with full tuition reimbursement (averaging $11,025 per year) were awarded; health care benefits also available. Financial award application deadline: 1/15. *Unit head:* Dr. Raymond A. Pearson, Director, 610-758-3857, Fax: 610-758-3526, E-mail: rp02@lehigh.edu. *Application contact:* James E. Roberts, Chair, Polymer Education Committee, 610-758-4841, Fax: 610-758-6536, E-mail: jer1@lehigh.edu. Website: http://www.lehihttps://engineering.lehigh.edu/academics/graduate/research-based/polymer-science-gh.edu/~inpcreng/academics/graduate/polymerscieng.html

Lehigh University, P.C. Rossin College of Engineering and Applied Science, Department of Materials Science and Engineering, Bethlehem, PA 18015. Offers materials science and engineering (M Eng, MS, PhD); photonics (MS); polymer science/engineering (M Eng, MS, PhD); MBA/E. *Program availability:* Part-time. *Faculty:* 14 full-time (4 women). *Students:* 30 full-time (6 women), 2 part-time (both women); includes 3 minority (1 Asian, non-Hispanic/Latino; 1 Hispanic/Latino; 1 Two or more races, non-Hispanic/Latino), 8 international. Average age 26. 91 applicants, 22% accepted, 10 enrolled. In 2019, 3 master's, 5 doctorates awarded. *Degree requirements:* For master's, thesis; for doctorate, comprehensive exam, thesis/dissertation. *Entrance requirements:* For master's and doctorate, GRE General Test, minimum GPA of 3.60. Additional exam requirements/recommendations for international students: required—TOEFL (minimum score 487 paper-based; 85 iBT), IELTS (minimum score 6.5), TOEFL or IELTS required. *Application deadline:* For fall admission, 1/15 priority date for domestic students, 1/15 for international students; for spring admission, 12/1 priority date for domestic students, 12/1 for international students. Application fee: $75. *Financial support:* In 2019–20, 26 students received support, including 12 fellowships with tuition reimbursements available (averaging $30,540 per year), 25 research assistantships with tuition reimbursements available (averaging $30,540 per year), 12 teaching assistantships with tuition reimbursements available (averaging $10,890 per year); scholarships/grants and health care benefits also available. Financial award application deadline: 1/15. *Unit head:* Dr. Wojciech Misiolek, Chairperson, 610-758-4252, Fax: 610-758-4244, E-mail: wzm2@lehigh.edu. *Application contact:* Lisa Carreras Arechiga, Graduate Administrative Coordinator, 610-758-4222, Fax: 610-758-4244, E-mail: lia4@lehigh.edu. Website: https://engineering.lehigh.edu/matsci

North Carolina State University, Graduate School, Wilson College of Textiles, Department of Textile Engineering, Chemistry, and Science, Raleigh, NC 27695. Offers fiber and polymer science (PhD); textile chemistry (MS); textile engineering (MS); textile technology management (PhD). *Degree requirements:* For master's, thesis optional. Electronic applications accepted.

North Carolina State University, Graduate School, Wilson College of Textiles, Program in Fiber and Polymer Science, Raleigh, NC 27695. Offers PhD. *Degree requirements:* For doctorate, one foreign language, thesis/dissertation, cumulative exams. *Entrance requirements:* For doctorate, GRE. Electronic applications accepted.

North Dakota State University, College of Graduate and Interdisciplinary Studies, College of Science and Mathematics, Department of Coatings and Polymeric Materials, Fargo, ND 58102. Offers MS, PhD. *Program availability:* Part-time. Terminal master's awarded for partial completion of doctoral program. *Degree requirements:* For master's, thesis, cumulative exams; for doctorate, comprehensive exam, thesis/dissertation, cumulative exams. *Entrance requirements:* For master's and doctorate, BS in chemistry or chemical engineering, minimum GPA of 3.0. Additional exam requirements/recommendations for international students: required—TOEFL (minimum score 550 paper-based). Electronic applications accepted. Tuition and fees vary according to program and reciprocity agreements.

Pittsburg State University, Graduate School, College of Arts and Sciences, Department of Chemistry, Pittsburg, KS 66762. Offers chemistry (MS); polymer chemistry (MS). *Degree requirements:* For master's, comprehensive exam (for some programs), thesis or alternative. *Entrance requirements:* Additional exam requirements/recommendations for international students: required—TOEFL (minimum score 520 paper-based; 68 iBT), IELTS (minimum score 6), PTE (minimum score 47). Electronic applications accepted. *Expenses:* Contact institution.

Pittsburg State University, Graduate School, College of Technology, Department of Engineering Technology, Pittsburg, KS 66762. Offers electrical engineering technology (MET); general engineering technology (MET); manufacturing engineering technology (MET); mechanical engineering technology (MET); plastics engineering technology (MET). *Program availability:* Part-time, 100% online, blended/hybrid learning. *Degree requirements:* For master's, thesis optional. *Entrance requirements:* Additional exam requirements/recommendations for international students: required—TOEFL (minimum score 550 paper-based; 79 iBT), IELTS (minimum score 6.5), PTE (minimum score 51). Electronic applications accepted. *Expenses:* Contact institution.

The University of Akron, Graduate School, College of Polymer Science and Polymer Engineering, Department of Polymer Engineering, Akron, OH 44325. Offers MS, PhD. *Program availability:* Part-time, evening/weekend. *Degree requirements:* For master's, thesis; for doctorate, one foreign language, thesis/dissertation, candidacy exam. *Entrance requirements:* For master's and doctorate, GRE, bachelor's degree in

Polymer Science and Engineering

engineering or physical science, minimum GPA of 3.0, three letters of recommendation, statement of purpose. Additional exam requirements/recommendations for international students: required—TOEFL (minimum score 79 iBT), IELTS (minimum score 6.5). Electronic applications accepted.

The University of Akron, Graduate School, College of Polymer Science and Polymer Engineering, Department of Polymer Science, Akron, OH 44325. Offers MS, PhD. *Program availability:* Part-time, evening/weekend. Terminal master's awarded for partial completion of doctoral program. *Degree requirements:* For master's, thesis; for doctorate, one foreign language, thesis/dissertation, cumulative exam, seminars. *Entrance requirements:* For master's and doctorate, GRE, minimum GPA of 3.0, three letters of recommendation, statement of purpose. Additional exam requirements/recommendations for international students: required—TOEFL (minimum score 79 iBT), IELTS (minimum score 6.5). Electronic applications accepted.

University of Connecticut, Institute of Materials Science, Polymer Program, Storrs, CT 06269-3136. Offers polymer science and engineering (MS, PhD). *Program availability:* Part-time. Terminal master's awarded for partial completion of doctoral program. *Degree requirements:* For master's, thesis (for some programs); for doctorate, one foreign language, comprehensive exam, thesis/dissertation. *Entrance requirements:* For master's and doctorate, GRE General Test. Additional exam requirements/recommendations for international students: required—TOEFL (minimum score 550 paper-based; 80 iBT), IELTS (minimum score 6.5). Electronic applications accepted.

The University of Manchester, School of Materials, Manchester, United Kingdom. Offers advanced aerospace materials engineering (M Sc); advanced metallic systems (PhD); biomedical materials (M Phil, M Sc, PhD); ceramics and glass (M Phil, M Sc, PhD); composite materials (M Sc, PhD); corrosion and protection (M Phil, M Sc, PhD); materials (M Phil, PhD); metallic materials (M Phil, M Sc, PhD); nanostructural materials (M Phil, M Sc, PhD); paper science (M Phil, M Sc, PhD); polymer science and engineering (M Phil, M Sc, PhD); technical textiles (M Sc); textile design, fashion and management (M Phil, M Sc, PhD); textile science and technology (M Phil, M Sc, PhD); textiles (M Phil, PhD); textiles and fashion (M Ent).

University of Massachusetts Amherst, Graduate School, College of Natural Sciences, Department of Polymer Science and Engineering, Amherst, MA 01003. Offers MS, PhD. Terminal master's awarded for partial completion of doctoral program. *Degree requirements:* For master's, thesis or alternative; for doctorate, comprehensive exam, thesis/dissertation. *Entrance requirements:* For master's and doctorate, GRE General Test. Additional exam requirements/recommendations for international students: required—TOEFL (minimum score 550 paper-based; 80 iBT), IELTS (minimum score 6.5). Electronic applications accepted.

University of Massachusetts Lowell, College of Sciences, Department of Chemistry, Program in Polymer Science, Lowell, MA 01854. Offers PhD. Electronic applications accepted.

University of Massachusetts Lowell, Francis College of Engineering, Department of Plastics Engineering, Lowell, MA 01854. Offers plastics engineering (MS Eng, PhD), including coatings and adhesives (MS Eng). *Program availability:* Part-time. Terminal master's awarded for partial completion of doctoral program. *Degree requirements:* For master's, thesis optional; for doctorate, comprehensive exam, thesis/dissertation. *Entrance requirements:* For master's and doctorate, GRE General Test. Additional exam requirements/recommendations for international students: required—TOEFL.

University of Missouri–Kansas City, College of Arts and Sciences, Department of Chemistry, Kansas City, MO 64110-2499. Offers analytical chemistry (PhD); inorganic chemistry (PhD); organic chemistry (PhD); physical chemistry (PhD); polymer chemistry (MS, PhD). *Program availability:* Part-time, evening/weekend. *Degree requirements:* For master's, thesis (for some programs); for doctorate, thesis/dissertation. *Entrance requirements:* For master's, equivalent of American Chemical Society approved bachelor's degree in chemistry; for doctorate, GRE General Test, equivalent of American Chemical Society approved bachelor's degree in chemistry. Additional exam

requirements/recommendations for international students: required—TOEFL (minimum score 550 paper-based; 80 iBT), TWE. Electronic applications accepted.

University of Southern Mississippi, College of Arts and Sciences, School of Polymer Science and Engineering, Hattiesburg, MS 39406-0001. Offers polymer science and engineering (MS, PhD), including polymer science and engineering (PhD). *Students:* 68 full-time (21 women), 5 part-time (2 women); includes 5 minority (2 Asian, non-Hispanic/Latino; 3 Hispanic/Latino), 15 international. 56 applicants, 52% accepted, 16 enrolled. In 2019, 6 master's, 13 doctorates awarded. Terminal master's awarded for partial completion of doctoral program. *Degree requirements:* For master's, comprehensive exam, thesis; for doctorate, comprehensive exam, thesis/dissertation, original proposal. *Entrance requirements:* For master's, GRE General Test, minimum GPA of 2.75; for doctorate, GRE General Test, minimum GPA of 3.5. Additional exam requirements/recommendations for international students: required—TOEFL, IELTS. *Application deadline:* For fall admission, 3/1 priority date for domestic students, 3/1 for international students. Applications are processed on a rolling basis. Application fee: $60. Electronic applications accepted. *Expenses: Tuition, area resident:* Full-time $4393; part-time $488 per credit hour. Tuition, nonresident: full-time $5393; part-time $600 per credit hour. *Required fees:* $6 per semester. *Financial support:* Fellowships, research assistantships with full tuition reimbursements, teaching assistantships with full tuition reimbursements, Federal Work-Study, scholarships/grants, health care benefits, and unspecified assistantships available. Financial award application deadline: 3/15; financial award applicants required to submit FAFSA. *Unit head:* Dr. Derek Patton, Director, 601-266-4229. *Application contact:* Dr. Derek Patton, Director, 601-266-4229. Website: https://www.usm.edu/polymer

Wayne State University, College of Engineering, Department of Chemical Engineering and Materials Science, Detroit, MI 48202. Offers chemical engineering (MS, PhD); materials science and engineering (MS, PhD), including materials science and engineering; polymer engineering (Graduate Certificate), including polymer engineering. *Program availability:* Part-time. *Faculty:* 16. *Students:* 36 full-time (12 women), 20 part-time (5 women); includes 5 minority (1 Asian, non-Hispanic/Latino; 3 Hispanic/Latino; 1 Two or more races, non-Hispanic/Latino), 32 international. Average age 28. 128 applicants, 16% accepted, 9 enrolled. In 2019, 20 master's, 4 doctorates, 1 other advanced degree awarded. *Degree requirements:* For master's, thesis optional; for doctorate, comprehensive exam, thesis/dissertation. *Entrance requirements:* For master's, resume (optional); for doctorate, GRE, three letters of recommendation (at least two from the applicant's academic institution); personal statement; resume; for Graduate Certificate, bachelor's degree in engineering or other mathematics-based sciences in exceptional cases. Additional exam requirements/recommendations for international students: required—TOEFL (minimum score 550 paper-based; 79 iBT), TWE (minimum score 5.5), Michigan English Language Assessment Battery (minimum score 85); recommended—IELTS (minimum score 6.5). *Application deadline:* For fall admission, 3/1 priority date for domestic and international students; for winter admission, 10/1 priority date for domestic students, 9/1 priority date for international students; for spring admission, 2/1 priority date for domestic and international students; for summer admission, 2/1 priority date for domestic and international students. Application fee: $50. Electronic applications accepted. *Expenses:* $790 per credit hour in-state tuition, $1579 per credit hour out-of-state tuition. 32 credits to complete the MS; 90 credits total to complete the PhD. *Financial support:* In 2019–20, 35 students received support, including 4 fellowships with tuition reimbursements available (averaging $20,000 per year), 18 research assistantships with tuition reimbursements available (averaging $21,856 per year), 6 teaching assistantships with tuition reimbursements available (averaging $20,792 per year); scholarships/grants, health care benefits, and unspecified assistantships also available. Support available to part-time students. Financial award applicants required to submit FAFSA. *Unit head:* Dr. Jeffrey Potoff, Professor and Interim Chair, 313-577-9357, E-mail: jpotoff@wayne.edu. *Application contact:* Rob Carlson, Graduate Program Coordinator, 313-577-9615, E-mail: rcarlson@wayne.edu. Website: http://engineering.wayne.edu/che/

Section 17
Mechanical Engineering and Mechanics

This section contains a directory of institutions offering graduate work in mechanical engineering and mechanics. Additional information about programs listed in the directory may be obtained by writing directly to the dean of a graduate school or chair of a department at the address given in the directory.

For programs offering related work, see also in this book *Engineering and Applied Sciences, Management of Engineering and Technology,* and *Materials Sciences and Engineering.* In another guide in this series: **Graduate Programs in the Physical Sciences, Mathematics, Agricultural Sciences, the Environment & Natural Resources**

See *Geosciences* and *Physics*

CONTENTS

Program Directories

Mechanical Engineering

Alfred University, Graduate School, College of Ceramics, Inamori School of Engineering, Alfred, NY 14802-1205. Offers biomaterials engineering (MS); ceramic engineering (MS, PhD); electrical engineering (MS); glass science (MS, PhD); materials science and engineering (MS, PhD); mechanical engineering (MS). *Program availability:* Part-time. *Faculty:* 27 full-time (4 women), 2 part-time/adjunct (both women). *Students:* 30 full-time (11 women), 15 part-time (5 women); includes 2 minority (both Asian, non-Hispanic/Latino), 12 international. Average age 28. 24 applicants, 83% accepted, 18 enrolled. In 2019, 8 master's, 5 doctorates awarded. *Degree requirements:* For master's, comprehensive exam, thesis; for doctorate, comprehensive exam, thesis/dissertation. *Entrance requirements:* Additional exam requirements/recommendations for international students: required—TOEFL (minimum score 590 paper-based; 90 iBT), IELTS (minimum score 6.5). *Application deadline:* For fall admission, 3/1 priority date for domestic students, 3/15 for international students; for spring admission, 10/1 priority date for domestic students, 10/1 for international students. Applications are processed on a rolling basis. Application fee: $60. Electronic applications accepted. Application fee is waived when completed online. *Expenses:* $23,530 per year. *Financial support:* In 2019–20, 31 students received support. Fellowships with full tuition reimbursements available, research assistantships with full tuition reimbursements available, teaching assistantships with full tuition reimbursements available, tuition waivers (full and partial), and unspecified assistantships available. Financial award application deadline: 3/15; financial award applicants required to submit FAFSA. *Unit head:* Dr. Gabrielle Gaustad, Dean, 607-871-2953, E-mail: gaustad@alfred.edu. *Application contact:* Lindsey Gertin, Assistant Director of Graduate Admissions, 607-871-2017, Fax: 607-871-2198, E-mail: gradinquiry@alfred.edu.
Website: http://engineering.alfred.edu/grad/

The American University in Cairo, School of Sciences and Engineering, Cairo, Egypt. Offers biotechnology (MS); chemistry (MS); computer science (MS); computing (M Comp); construction engineering (M Eng, MS); electronics and communications engineering (M Eng); environmental engineering (MS); environmental system design (M Eng); mechanical engineering (M Eng, MS); nanotechnology (MS); physics (MS); robotics, control and smart systems (MS); sciences and engineering (PhD); sustainable development (MS, Graduate Diploma). *Program availability:* Part-time, evening/weekend. *Degree requirements:* For master's, comprehensive exam (for some programs), thesis (for some programs); for doctorate, comprehensive exam (for some programs), thesis/dissertation. *Entrance requirements:* Additional exam requirements/recommendations for international students: required—TOEFL (minimum score 450 paper-based; 45 iBT), IELTS (minimum score 5). Electronic applications accepted.

American University of Sharjah, Graduate Programs, Sharjah, United Arab Emirates. Offers accounting (MS); biomedical engineering (MSBME); business administration (MBA); chemical engineering (MS Ch E); civil engineering (MSCE); computer engineering (MS); electrical engineering (MSEE); engineering systems management (MS, PhD); mathematics (MS); mechanical engineering (MSME); mechatronics engineering (MS); teaching English to speakers of other languages (MA); translation and interpreting (MA); urban planning (MUP). *Program availability:* Part-time, evening/weekend. *Degree requirements:* For master's, thesis (for some programs). *Entrance requirements:* For master's, GMAT (for MBA). Additional exam requirements/recommendations for international students: required—TOEFL (minimum score 550 paper-based; 80 iBT), TWE (minimum score 5); recommended—IELTS (minimum score 6.5). Electronic applications accepted.

Arizona State University at Tempe, Ira A. Fulton Schools of Engineering, The Polytechnic School, Program in Engineering Technology, Mesa, AZ 85212. Offers manufacturing engineering technology (MS). *Program availability:* Part-time, evening/weekend. *Degree requirements:* For master's, thesis or applied project and oral defense, final examination, interactive Program of Study (iPOS) submitted before completing 50 percent of required credit hours. *Entrance requirements:* For master's, bachelor's degree with minimum of 30 credit hours or equivalent in a technology area including course work applicable to the concentration being sought and minimum of 16 credit hours of math and science; industrial experience beyond bachelor's degree (recommended). Additional exam requirements/recommendations for international students: required—TOEFL, IELTS, or PTE. Electronic applications accepted.

Arizona State University at Tempe, Ira A. Fulton Schools of Engineering, School for Engineering of Matter, Transport and Energy, Tempe, AZ 85281. Offers aerospace engineering (MS, PhD); chemical engineering (MS, PhD); materials science and engineering (MS, PhD); mechanical engineering (MS, PhD); solar energy engineering and commercialization (PSM). *Program availability:* Part-time, evening/weekend, online learning. Terminal master's awarded for partial completion of doctoral program. *Degree requirements:* For master's, thesis and oral defense (MS); applied project or comprehensive exam (MSE); interactive Program of Study (iPOS) submitted before completing 50 percent of required credit hours; for doctorate, comprehensive exam, thesis/dissertation, interactive Program of Study (iPOS) submitted before completing 50 percent of required credit hours. *Entrance requirements:* For master's, GRE, minimum GPA of 3.0 or equivalent in last 2 years of work leading to bachelor's degree; for doctorate, GRE, minimum GPA of 3.0 in last 2 years of work leading to bachelor's degree. Additional exam requirements/recommendations for international students: required—TOEFL, IELTS, or PTE. Electronic applications accepted. *Expenses:* Contact institution.

Arkansas Tech University, College of Engineering and Applied Sciences, Russellville, AR 72801. Offers electrical engineering (M Engr); emergency management (MS); information technology (MS); mechanical engineering (M Engr). *Program availability:* Part-time, evening/weekend, 100% online, blended/hybrid learning. *Students:* 38 full-time (11 women), 45 part-time (22 women); includes 13 minority (10 Black or African American, non-Hispanic/Latino; 1 Asian, non-Hispanic/Latino; 1 Hispanic/Latino; 1 Two or more races, non-Hispanic/Latino), 24 international. Average age 32. In 2019, 26 master's awarded. *Degree requirements:* For master's, comprehensive exam (for some programs), thesis (for some programs). *Entrance requirements:* Additional exam requirements/recommendations for international students: required—TOEFL (minimum score 550 paper-based; 79 iBT), IELTS (minimum score 6.5), PTE (minimum score 58). *Application deadline:* For fall admission, 3/1 priority date for domestic students, 5/1 priority date for international students; for spring admission, 10/1 priority date for domestic and international students. Applications are processed on a rolling basis. Application fee: $40 ($90 for international students). Electronic applications accepted. *Expenses: Tuition, area resident:* Full-time $7008; part-time $292 per credit hour. *Tuition, state resident:* full-time $7008; part-time $292 per credit hour. *Tuition, nonresident:* full-time $14,016; part-time $584 per credit hour. *International tuition:* $14,016 full-time. *Required fees:* $343 per term. *Financial support:* In 2019–20, research assistantships with full and partial tuition reimbursements (averaging $4,800 per year), teaching assistantships with full and partial tuition reimbursements (averaging $4,800 per year) were awarded; career-related internships or fieldwork, Federal Work-

Study, scholarships/grants, health care benefits, and unspecified assistantships also available. Support available to part-time students. Financial award application deadline: 4/15; financial award applicants required to submit FAFSA. *Unit head:* Dr. Judy Cezeaux, Dean, 479-968-0353, E-mail: jcezeaux@atu.edu. *Application contact:* Dr. Richard Schoephoerster, Dean of Graduate College and Research, 479-968-0398, Fax: 479-964-0542, E-mail: gradcollege@atu.edu.
Website: http://www.atu.edu/appliedsci/

Auburn University, Graduate School, Samuel Ginn College of Engineering, Department of Mechanical Engineering, Auburn University, AL 36849. Offers M Mtl E, MME, MS, PhD. *Program availability:* Part-time. *Faculty:* 42 full-time (1 woman), 4 part-time/adjunct (0 women). *Students:* 124 full-time (22 women), 86 part-time (12 women); includes 14 minority (3 Black or African American, non-Hispanic/Latino; 3 Asian, non-Hispanic/Latino; 6 Hispanic/Latino; 2 Two or more races, non-Hispanic/Latino), 119 international. Average age 28. 163 applicants, 60% accepted, 32 enrolled. In 2019, 51 master's, 12 doctorates awarded. *Degree requirements:* For master's, thesis (for some programs); for doctorate, one foreign language, thesis/dissertation. *Entrance requirements:* For master's and doctorate, GRE General Test. Additional exam requirements/recommendations for international students: required—TOEFL (minimum score 550 paper-based; 79 iBT). *Application deadline:* Applications are processed on a rolling basis. Application fee: $60 ($70 for international students). *Expenses: Tuition, area resident:* Full-time $9828; part-time $546 per credit hour. *Tuition, state resident:* full-time $9828; part-time $546 per credit hour. *Tuition, nonresident:* full-time $29,484; part-time $1638 per credit hour. *International tuition:* $29,744 full-time. Tuition and fees vary according to course load, program and reciprocity agreements. *Financial support:* In 2019–20, 75 fellowships, 124 research assistantships (averaging $16,563 per year), 38 teaching assistantships (averaging $13,485 per year) were awarded; Federal Work-Study also available. Support available to part-time students. Financial award application deadline: 3/15; financial award applicants required to submit FAFSA. *Unit head:* Dr. Jeff Suhling, Chair, 334-844-3332, E-mail: suhlijc@auburn.edu. *Application contact:* Dr. George Flowers, Dean of the Graduate School, 334-844-2125.
Website: http://www.eng.auburn.edu/me/

Baylor University, Graduate School, School of Engineering and Computer Science, Department of Engineering, Waco, TX 76798. Offers biomedical engineering (MSBME); electrical and computer engineering (MSECE, PhD); engineering (ME); mechanical engineering (MSME).

Baylor University, Graduate School, School of Engineering and Computer Science, Department of Mechanical Engineering, Waco, TX 76798. Offers biomedical engineering (MSBME); engineering (ME); mechanical engineering (MS, PhD). *Program availability:* Part-time. *Degree requirements:* For master's, thesis (for some programs), 30 credits including 24 coursework and 6 research (for MS); 33 coursework credits or 6 project credits and 27 coursework credits (for ME); for doctorate, thesis/dissertation (for some programs), 48 semester hours of approved course work and research hours beyond the master's degree. *Entrance requirements:* For master's, GRE. Additional exam requirements/recommendations for international students: required—TOEFL (minimum score 550 paper-based; 80 iBT), IELTS (minimum score 6.5). Electronic applications accepted. *Expenses:* Contact institution.

Binghamton University, State University of New York, Graduate School, Thomas J. Watson School of Engineering and Applied Science, Department of Mechanical Engineering, Binghamton, NY 13902-6000. Offers M Eng, MS, PhD. *Program availability:* Part-time, evening/weekend, online learning. *Degree requirements:* For master's, thesis (for some programs); for doctorate, comprehensive exam, thesis/dissertation. *Entrance requirements:* For master's and doctorate, GRE General Test. Additional exam requirements/recommendations for international students: required—TOEFL (minimum score 550 paper-based; 80 iBT). Electronic applications accepted. *Expenses:* Contact institution.

Boise State University, College of Engineering, Department of Mechanical and Biomedical Engineering, Boise, ID 83725-0399. Offers mechanical engineering (M Engr, MS). *Program availability:* Part-time. *Students:* 15 full-time (2 women), 7 part-time (3 women); includes 2 minority (1 Asian, non-Hispanic/Latino; 1 Two or more races, non-Hispanic/Latino), 2 international. *Degree requirements:* For master's, comprehensive exam, thesis (for some programs). *Entrance requirements:* For master's, GRE General Test, minimum GPA of 3.0. Additional exam requirements/recommendations for international students: required—TOEFL, IELTS. Electronic applications accepted. *Expenses: Tuition, area resident:* Full-time $7110; part-time $470 per credit hour. *Tuition, state resident:* full-time $7110; part-time $470 per credit hour. *Tuition, nonresident:* full-time $24,030; part-time $827 per credit hour. *International tuition:* $827 full-time. *Required fees:* $2536. Tuition and fees vary according to course load and program. *Financial support:* Research assistantships, teaching assistantships, scholarships/grants, and unspecified assistantships available. Financial award applicants required to submit FAFSA. *Unit head:* Dr. Don Plumlee, Department Chair, 208-426-3575, E-mail: dplumlee@boisestate.edu. *Application contact:* Dr. John Gardner, Graduate Coordinator, 208-426-5702, E-mail: jgardner@boisestate.edu.
Website: https://www.boisestate.edu/coen-mbe/

Boston University, College of Engineering, Department of Mechanical Engineering, Boston, MA 02215. Offers manufacturing engineering (MS); mechanical engineering (PhD); MS/MBA. *Program availability:* Part-time, 100% online, blended/hybrid learning. *Students:* 174 full-time (43 women), 51 part-time (13 women); includes 39 minority (2 Black or African American, non-Hispanic/Latino; 14 Asian, non-Hispanic/Latino; 17 Hispanic/Latino; 6 Two or more races, non-Hispanic/Latino), 112 international. Average age 24. 773 applicants, 51% accepted, 78 enrolled. In 2019, 98 master's, 11 doctorates awarded. Terminal master's awarded for partial completion of doctoral program. *Degree requirements:* For master's, thesis (for some programs); for doctorate, comprehensive exam, thesis/dissertation. *Entrance requirements:* For master's and doctorate, GRE General Test. Additional exam requirements/recommendations for international students: required—TOEFL (minimum score 90 iBT), IELTS (minimum score 7). Application fee: $95. Application fee is waived when completed online. *Unit head:* Dr. Alice White, Chairperson, 617-353-2814, Fax: 617-353-5866, E-mail: aew1@bu.edu. *Application contact:* Dr. Alice White, Chairperson, 617-353-2814, Fax: 617-353-5866, E-mail: aew1@bu.edu.
Website: http://www.bu.edu/me/

Bradley University, The Graduate School, Caterpillar College of Engineering and Technology, Department of Mechanical Engineering, Peoria, IL 61625-0002. Offers MSME. *Program availability:* Part-time, evening/weekend. *Faculty:* 15 full-time (3 women), 1 part-time/adjunct. *Students:* 9 full-time (1 woman), 10 part-time (0 women), 16 international. Average age 26. 30 applicants, 60% accepted, 5 enrolled. In 2019, 8 master's awarded. *Degree requirements:* For master's, comprehensive exam, thesis optional. *Entrance requirements:* For master's, Minimum GPA of 2.5, Essays,

Admission, 203-254-4184, Fax: 203-254-4073, E-mail: gradadmis@fairfield.edu. Website: http://www.fairfield.edu/soe

Farmingdale State College, Program in Technology Management, Farmingdale, NY 11735. Offers construction management (MS); electrical and mechanical engineering (MS). *Degree requirements:* For master's, project or thesis.

Florida Agricultural and Mechanical University, Division of Graduate Studies, Research, and Continuing Education, FAMU-FSU College of Engineering, Department of Mechanical Engineering, Tallahassee, FL 32307-3200. Offers MS, PhD. *Degree requirements:* For master's, thesis optional; for doctorate, comprehensive exam, thesis/dissertation. *Entrance requirements:* For master's, GRE General Test, minimum GPA of 3.0. Additional exam requirements/recommendations for international students: required—TOEFL (minimum score 550 paper-based).

Florida Atlantic University, College of Engineering and Computer Science, Department of Ocean and Mechanical Engineering, Boca Raton, FL 33431-0991. Offers mechanical engineering (MS, PhD). *Program availability:* Part-time, evening/weekend. *Faculty:* 24 full-time (1 woman), 1 part-time/adjunct (0 women). *Students:* 38 full-time (8 women), 55 part-time (10 women); includes 13 minority (2 Black or African American, non-Hispanic/Latino; 2 Asian, non-Hispanic/Latino; 9 Hispanic/Latino), 34 international. Average age 30. 83 applicants, 57% accepted, 28 enrolled. In 2019, 27 master's, 10 doctorates awarded. Terminal master's awarded for partial completion of doctoral program. *Degree requirements:* For master's, thesis (for some programs); for doctorate, comprehensive exam, thesis/dissertation, qualifying exam. *Entrance requirements:* For master's and doctorate, GRE General Test, minimum GPA of 3.0. Additional exam requirements/recommendations for international students: required—TOEFL (minimum score 500 paper-based; 61 iBT), IELTS (minimum score 6). *Application deadline:* For fall admission, 7/1 priority date for domestic students, 2/15 for international students; for spring admission, 11/1 for domestic students, 7/15 for international students. Applications are processed on a rolling basis. Application fee: $30. *Expenses: Tuition:* Full-time $20,536; part-time $371.82 per credit hour. Tuition and fees vary according to program. *Financial support:* Research assistantships, career-related internships or fieldwork, Federal Work-Study, scholarships/grants, and unspecified assistantships available. Financial award application deadline: 1/10; financial award applicants required to submit FAFSA. *Unit head:* Manhar Dhanak, Chair, 561-297-2827, E-mail: dhanak@fau.edu. *Application contact:* Manhar Dhanak, Chair, 561-297-2827, E-mail: dhanak@fau.edu.
Website: http://www.ome.fau.edu/

Florida Institute of Technology, College of Engineering and Science, Program in Mechanical Engineering, Melbourne, FL 32901-6975. Offers MS, PhD. *Program availability:* Part-time. Terminal master's awarded for partial completion of doctoral program. *Degree requirements:* For master's, thesis, 30 credit hours; for doctorate, comprehensive exam, thesis/dissertation. *Entrance requirements:* For master's, GRE General Test, bachelor's degree from an ABET-accredited program, transcripts; for doctorate, GRE General Test, 3 letters of recommendation, minimum GPA of 3.5, resume, statement of objectives, master's degree. Additional exam requirements/recommendations for international students: required—TOEFL (minimum score 550 paper-based; 79 iBT). Electronic applications accepted.

Florida International University, College of Engineering and Computing, Department of Mechanical and Materials Engineering, Miami, FL 33199. Offers materials science and engineering (MS, PhD); mechanical engineering (MS, PhD). *Program availability:* Part-time, evening/weekend. *Faculty:* 22 full-time (5 women), 5 part-time/adjunct (1 woman). *Students:* 62 full-time (10 women), 11 part-time (4 women); includes 27 minority (4 Black or African American, non-Hispanic/Latino; 3 Asian, non-Hispanic/Latino; 17 Hispanic/Latino; 3 Two or more races, non-Hispanic/Latino), 43 international. Average age 29. 136 applicants, 51% accepted, 21 enrolled. In 2019, 11 master's, 8 doctorates awarded. Terminal master's awarded for partial completion of doctoral program. *Degree requirements:* For master's, thesis or alternative; for doctorate, comprehensive exam, thesis/dissertation. *Entrance requirements:* For master's, GRE (depending on program), 3 letters of recommendation, minimum undergraduate GPA of 3.0 in upper-level course work; for doctorate, GRE (minimum combined score of 1150, verbal 450, quantitative 650), minimum undergraduate GPA of 3.0 in upper-level coursework with BS, 3.3 with MS; 3 letters of recommendation; letter of intent. Additional exam requirements/recommendations for international students: required—TOEFL (minimum score 550 paper-based; 80 iBT) or IELTS (minimum score 6.5). *Application deadline:* For fall admission, 6/1 for domestic students, 4/1 for international students; for spring admission, 10/1 for domestic students, 9/1 for international students. Applications are processed on a rolling basis. Application fee: $30. Electronic applications accepted. *Expenses: Tuition, area resident:* Full-time $8912; part-time $446 per credit hour. Tuition, state resident: full-time $8912; part-time $446 per credit hour. Tuition, nonresident: full-time $21,393; part-time $992 per credit hour. *Required fees:* $2194. *Financial support:* Institutionally sponsored loans, scholarships/grants, and unspecified assistantships available. Financial award application deadline: 3/1; financial award applicants required to submit FAFSA. *Unit head:* Dr. ARVIND AGARWAL, Chair, 305-348-1701, Fax: 305-348-1932, E-mail: Arvind.Agarwal@fiu.edu. *Application contact:* Nanett Rojas, Manager, Admissions Operations, 305-348-7464, Fax: 305-348-7441, E-mail: gradadm@fiu.edu.
Website: http://cec.fiu.edu

Florida State University, The Graduate School, FAMU-FSU College of Engineering, Department of Mechanical Engineering, Tallahassee, FL 32310-6046. Offers mechanical engineering (MS, PhD); sustainable energy (MS). *Program availability:* Part-time. *Faculty:* 25 full-time (3 women), 2 part-time/adjunct (1 woman). *Students:* 85 full-time (10 women); includes 20 minority (3 Black or African American, non-Hispanic/Latino; 6 Asian, non-Hispanic/Latino; 10 Hispanic/Latino; 1 Two or more races, non-Hispanic/Latino), 34 international. Average age 25. 145 applicants, 50% accepted, 24 enrolled. In 2019, 15 master's, 4 doctorates awarded. Terminal master's awarded for partial completion of doctoral program. *Degree requirements:* For master's, thesis optional, 30 credit hours (24 coursework, 6 research); for doctorate, thesis/dissertation, 45 credit hours (21 coursework, 24 research). *Entrance requirements:* For master's and doctorate, GRE General Test (minimum scores: Verbal 150, Quantitative 155), minimum GPA of 3.0, official transcripts, resume, personal statement, 3 letters of recommendation. Additional exam requirements/recommendations for international students: required—TOEFL (minimum score 550 paper-based; 80 iBT), IELTS (minimum score 6.5). *Application deadline:* For fall admission, 4/1 for domestic and international students; for spring admission, 11/1 for domestic and international students. Applications are processed on a rolling basis. Application fee: $30. Electronic applications accepted. *Financial support:* In 2019–20, 77 students received support, including 1 fellowship with full tuition reimbursement available, 75 research assistantships with full tuition reimbursements available, 34 teaching assistantships with full tuition reimbursements available (averaging $4,364 per year); career-related internships or fieldwork, institutionally sponsored loans, tuition waivers (full), and unspecified assistantships also available. Support available to part-time students. Financial award application deadline: 3/1; financial award applicants required to submit FAFSA. *Unit head:* Dr. Emmanuel Collins, Chair, 850-410-6373, Fax: 850-410-6337, E-mail: ecollins@eng.famu.fsu.edu. *Application contact:* Breda Arnell, Coordinator of

Graduate Studies, 850-410-6196, Fax: 850-410-6337, E-mail: barnell@eng.famu.fsu.edu.
Website: http://www.eng.famu.fsu.edu/me/

Gannon University, School of Graduate Studies, College of Engineering and Business, School of Engineering and Computer Science, Program in Mechanical Engineering, Erie, PA 16541-0001. Offers MSME. *Program availability:* Part-time, evening/weekend. *Degree requirements:* For master's, comprehensive exam, thesis (for some programs), oral exam (for some programs), design project (for some programs). *Entrance requirements:* For master's, bachelor's degree in mechanical engineering from an ABET-accredited program or its equivalent with minimum GPA of 2.5, transcript, 3 letters of recommendation. Additional exam requirements/recommendations for international students: required—TOEFL (minimum score 79 iBT). Electronic applications accepted. Application fee is waived when completed online.

The George Washington University, School of Engineering and Applied Science, Department of Mechanical and Aerospace Engineering, Washington, DC 20052. Offers MS, PhD, App Sc, Engr, Graduate Certificate. *Program availability:* Part-time, evening/weekend. *Degree requirements:* For master's, thesis optional; for doctorate, thesis/dissertation, final and qualifying exams. *Entrance requirements:* For master's, appropriate bachelor's degree, minimum GPA of 3.0; for doctorate, GRE (if highest earned degree is BS), appropriate bachelor's or master's degree, minimum GPA of 3.4; for other advanced degree, appropriate master's degree, minimum GPA of 3.0. Additional exam requirements/recommendations for international students: required—TOEFL or The George Washington University English as a Foreign Language Test.

Georgia Institute of Technology, Graduate Studies, College of Engineering, George W. Woodruff School of Mechanical Engineering, Atlanta, GA 30332-0405. Offers mechanical engineering (MS, MSME, PhD); nuclear and radiological engineering and medical physics (MS, MSMP, MSNE, PhD), including medical physics (MS, MSMP), nuclear and radiological engineering (PhD), nuclear engineering (MSNE). *Program availability:* Part-time, 100% online. *Faculty:* 100 full-time (13 women), 5 part-time/adjunct (1 woman). *Students:* 608 full-time (110 women), 200 part-time (43 women); includes 205 minority (19 Black or African American, non-Hispanic/Latino; 1 American Indian or Alaska Native, non-Hispanic/Latino; 107 Asian, non-Hispanic/Latino; 47 Hispanic/Latino; 31 Two or more races, non-Hispanic/Latino), 231 international. Average age 26. 1,352 applicants, 32% accepted, 200 enrolled. In 2019, 229 master's, 56 doctorates awarded. Terminal master's awarded for partial completion of doctoral program. *Degree requirements:* For master's, thesis; for doctorate, comprehensive exam, thesis/dissertation. *Entrance requirements:* For master's, GRE General Test, minimum 3.0 for the MSNRE and MSMP; for doctorate, GRE General Test, minimum GPA of 3.3. Additional exam requirements/recommendations for international students: required—TOEFL (minimum score 94 iBT), IELTS (minimum score 7), TOEFL is the preferred method with the requirements shown on the programs. *Application deadline:* For fall admission, 2/1 for domestic and international students; for spring admission, 11/1 for domestic students, 10/1 for international students. Applications are processed on a rolling basis. Application fee: $75 ($85 for international students). Electronic applications accepted. *Expenses: Tuition, area resident:* Full-time $14,064; part-time $586 per credit hour. Tuition, state resident: full-time $14,064; part-time $586 per credit hour. Tuition, nonresident: full-time $29,140; part-time $1215 per credit hour. *International tuition:* $29,140 full-time. *Required fees:* $2024; $840 per semester. $2096. Tuition and fees vary according to course load. *Financial support:* In 2019–20, 41 fellowships, 395 research assistantships, 8 teaching assistantships were awarded; career-related internships or fieldwork, Federal Work-Study, institutionally sponsored loans, tuition waivers (full and partial), and unspecified assistantships also available. Support available to part-time students. Financial award application deadline: 7/1; financial award applicants required to submit FAFSA. *Unit head:* Samuel Graham, School Chair, 404-894-3200, Fax: 404-894-1658, E-mail: sgraham@gatech.edu. *Application contact:* Marla Bruner, Director of Graduate Studies, 404-894-1610, Fax: 404-894-1609, E-mail: gradinfo@mail.gatech.edu.
Website: http://www.me.gatech.edu

Georgia Southern University, Jack N. Averitt College of Graduate Studies, Allen E. Paulson College of Engineering and Computing, Department of Mechanical Engineering, Program in Engineering/Mechatronics, Statesboro, GA 30458. Offers MSAE. *Students:* 2 full-time (0 women), 2 part-time (0 women), 1 international. Average age 25. 1 applicant, 100% accepted. In 2019, 4 master's awarded. *Degree requirements:* For master's, thesis optional. *Entrance requirements:* Additional exam requirements/recommendations for international students: required—TOEFL (minimum score 80 iBT). *Application deadline:* For fall admission, 3/1 priority date for domestic and international students; for spring admission, 10/1 priority date for domestic students, 10/1 for international students. Applications are processed on a rolling basis. Electronic applications accepted. *Expenses: Tuition, area resident:* Full-time $4986; part-time $277 per credit hour. Tuition, nonresident: full-time $19,890; part-time $1105 per credit hour. *International tuition:* $19,890 full-time. *Required fees:* $2114; $1057 per semester. $1057 per semester. Tuition and fees vary according to course load, campus/location and program. *Financial support:* In 2019–20, 4 students received support. Unspecified assistantships available. *Unit head:* Dr. Biswanath Samanta, Program Coordinator, 912-478-0334, E-mail: bsamanta@georgiasouthern.edu. *Application contact:* Dr. Biswanath Samanta, Program Coordinator, 912-478-0334, E-mail: bsamanta@georgiasouthern.edu.

Grand Valley State University, Padnos College of Engineering and Computing, School of Engineering, Allendale, MI 49401-9403. Offers electrical and computer engineering (MSE); mechanical engineering (MSE); product design and manufacturing engineering (MSE). *Program availability:* Part-time, evening/weekend. *Faculty:* 22 full-time (6 women), 1 part-time/adjunct (0 women). *Students:* 23 full-time (2 women), 35 part-time (5 women); includes 4 minority (2 Asian, non-Hispanic/Latino; 1 Hispanic/Latino; 1 Two or more races, non-Hispanic/Latino), 25 international. Average age 27. 46 applicants, 78% accepted, 10 enrolled. In 2019, 32 master's awarded. *Degree requirements:* For master's, capstone experience. *Entrance requirements:* For master's, engineering degree, minimum GPA of 3.0, resume, 3 confidential letters of recommendation, 1-2 page essay, base of underlying relevant knowledge/evidence from academic records or relevant wok experience. Additional exam requirements/recommendations for international students: required—Michigan English Language Assessment Battery (minimum score 77), TOEFL (minimum iBT score of 80), or IELTS (6.5); GRE. *Application deadline:* Applications are processed on a rolling basis. Application fee: $30. Electronic applications accepted. *Expenses:* $733 per credit hour, 33 credit hours. *Financial support:* In 2019–20, 40 students received support, including 8 fellowships, 34 research assistantships with full and partial tuition reimbursements available (averaging $4,000 per year); career-related internships or fieldwork, Federal Work-Study, institutionally sponsored loans, scholarships/grants, and unspecified assistantships also available. *Unit head:* Dr. Wael Mokhtar, Director, 616-331-6015, Fax: 616-331-7215, E-mail: mokhtarw@gvsu.edu. *Application contact:* Dr. Shabbir Choudhuri, Graduate Program Director, 616-331-6845, Fax: 616-331-7215, E-mail: choudhus@gvsu.edu.
Website: http://www.engineer.gvsu.edu/

Harvard University, Graduate School of Arts and Sciences, Harvard John A. Paulson School of Engineering and Applied Sciences, Cambridge, MA 02138. Offers applied mathematics (PhD); applied physics (PhD); computational science and engineering (ME, SM); computer science (PhD); data science (SM); design engineering (MDE); engineering science (ME), including electrical engineering (ME, SM, PhD); engineering sciences (SM, PhD), including bioengineering (PhD), electrical engineering (ME, SM, PhD), environmental science and engineering (PhD), materials science and mechanical engineering (PhD). *Program availability:* Part-time. Terminal master's awarded for partial completion of doctoral program. *Degree requirements:* For master's, thesis (for ME); for doctorate, comprehensive exam, thesis/dissertation. *Entrance requirements:* For master's and doctorate, GRE General Test, GRE Subject Test (recommended), 3 letters of recommendation. Additional exam requirements/recommendations for international students: required—TOEFL (minimum score 80 iBT). Electronic applications accepted. *Expenses:* Contact institution.

Howard University, College of Engineering, Architecture, and Computer Sciences, School of Engineering and Computer Science, Department of Mechanical Engineering, Washington, DC 20059-0002. Offers M Eng, PhD. *Degree requirements:* For master's, comprehensive exam, thesis; for doctorate, one foreign language, comprehensive exam, thesis/dissertation, 2 terms of residency. *Entrance requirements:* For master's and doctorate, GRE General Test, minimum GPA of 3.0. Additional exam requirements/recommendations for international students: required—TOEFL. Electronic applications accepted.

Idaho State University, Graduate School, College of Science and Engineering, Department of Mechanical Engineering, Pocatello, ID 83209-8060. Offers measurement and control engineering (MS); mechanical engineering (MS). *Program availability:* Part-time. *Degree requirements:* For master's, comprehensive exam (for some programs), 2 semesters of seminar; thesis or project. *Entrance requirements:* For master's, GRE. Additional exam requirements/recommendations for international students: required—TOEFL (minimum score 550 paper-based; 80 iBT). Electronic applications accepted.

Illinois Institute of Technology, Graduate College, Armour College of Engineering, Department of Mechanical, Materials and Aerospace Engineering, Chicago, IL 60616. Offers manufacturing engineering (MAS, MS); materials science and engineering (MAS, MS, PhD); mechanical and aerospace engineering (MAS, MS, PhD), including economics (MS), energy (MS), environment (MS). *Program availability:* Part-time, evening/weekend, online learning. Terminal master's awarded for partial completion of doctoral program. *Degree requirements:* For master's, comprehensive exam (for some programs), thesis (for some programs); for doctorate, comprehensive exam, thesis/dissertation. *Entrance requirements:* For master's and doctorate, GRE General Test (minimum score 1000 Quantitative and Verbal, 3.0 Analytical Writing), minimum undergraduate GPA of 3.0. Additional exam requirements/recommendations for international students: required—TOEFL (minimum score 550 paper-based; 80 iBT). Electronic applications accepted.

Indiana University-Purdue University Indianapolis, School of Engineering and Technology, Department of Mechanical Engineering, Indianapolis, IN 46202. Offers engineering (MSE); mechanical engineering (MSME, PhD). *Program availability:* Part-time. *Degree requirements:* For master's, thesis optional; for doctorate, thesis/dissertation. *Entrance requirements:* For master's, GRE, minimum GPA of 3.0, three recommendation letters, statement of purpose/intent; for doctorate, GRE, minimum GPA of 3.0, three recommendation letters, statement of purpose/intent, curriculum vitae. Additional exam requirements/recommendations for international students: required—TOEFL (minimum score 550 paper-based; 79 iBT); recommended—IELTS (minimum score 6.5), TSE (minimum score 58). Electronic applications accepted. *Expenses:* Contact institution.

Instituto Tecnológico y de Estudios Superiores de Monterrey, Campus Chihuahua, Graduate Programs, Chihuahua, Mexico. Offers computer systems engineering (Ingeniero); electrical engineering (Ingeniero); electromechanical engineering (Ingeniero); electronic engineering (Ingeniero); engineering administration (MEA); industrial engineering (MIE, Ingeniero); international trade (MIT); mechanical engineering (Ingeniero).

Instituto Tecnológico y de Estudios Superiores de Monterrey, Campus Monterrey, Graduate and Research Division, Programs in Engineering, Monterrey, Mexico. Offers applied statistics (M Eng); artificial intelligence (PhD); automation engineering (M Eng); chemical engineering (M Eng); civil engineering (M Eng); electrical engineering (M Eng); electronic engineering (M Eng); environmental engineering (M Eng); industrial engineering (M Eng, PhD); manufacturing engineering (M Eng); mechanical engineering (M Eng); systems and quality engineering (M Eng). *Program availability:* Part-time, evening/weekend. Terminal master's awarded for partial completion of doctoral program. *Degree requirements:* For master's, one foreign language, thesis; for doctorate, one foreign language, thesis/dissertation. *Entrance requirements:* For master's, EXADEP; for doctorate, GRE, master's degree in related field. Additional exam requirements/recommendations for international students: required—TOEFL.

Inter American University of Puerto Rico, Bayamón Campus, Graduate School, Bayamón, PR 00957. Offers biology (MS), including environmental sciences and ecology, molecular biotechnology; electrical engineering (ME), including control system, potence system; human resources (MBA); mechanical engineering (ME, MS), including aerospace, energy. *Program availability:* Part-time, evening/weekend. *Degree requirements:* For master's, comprehensive exam, research project. *Entrance requirements:* For master's, EXADEP, GRE General Test, letters of recommendation. *Expenses: Tuition:* Full-time $3870; part-time $1935 per year. *Required fees:* $735; $642 per unit.

Iowa State University of Science and Technology, Department of Mechanical Engineering, Ames, IA 50011. Offers mechanical engineering (M Eng, MS, PhD); systems engineering (M Eng). *Degree requirements:* For master's, thesis or alternative; for doctorate, thesis/dissertation. *Entrance requirements:* For master's and doctorate, GRE General Test, resume. Additional exam requirements/recommendations for international students: required—TOEFL (minimum score 570 paper-based; 79 iBT), IELTS (minimum score 6.5). Electronic applications accepted.

Johns Hopkins University, Engineering Program for Professionals, Part-time Program in Mechanical Engineering, Baltimore, MD 21218. Offers MME, Post Master's Certificate. *Program availability:* Part-time, evening/weekend, 100% online, blended/hybrid learning. *Entrance requirements:* Additional exam requirements/recommendations for international students: required—TOEFL (minimum score 600 paper-based; 100 iBT). Electronic applications accepted.

Johns Hopkins University, G. W. C. Whiting School of Engineering, Department of Mechanical Engineering, Baltimore, MD 21218-2681. Offers MSE, PhD. Terminal master's awarded for partial completion of doctoral program. *Degree requirements:* For master's, thesis optional; for doctorate, comprehensive exam, thesis/dissertation, oral exam. *Entrance requirements:* For master's and doctorate, GRE General Test, 3 letters of recommendation, statement of purpose, transcripts. Additional exam requirements/recommendations for international students: required—TOEFL (minimum score 600 paper-based, 100 iBT) or IELTS (7). Electronic applications accepted.

Johns Hopkins University, G. W. C. Whiting School of Engineering, Master of Science in Engineering Management Program, Baltimore, MD 21218. Offers biomaterials

(MSEM); civil engineering (MSEM); communications science (MSEM); computer science (MSEM); environmental systems analysis, economics and public policy (MSEM); fluid mechanics (MSEM); materials science and engineering (MSEM); mechanical engineering (MSEM); mechanics and materials (MSEM); nano-biotechnology (MSEM); nanomaterials and nanotechnology (MSEM); operations research (MSEM); probability and statistics (MSEM); smart product and device design (MSEM). *Entrance requirements:* For master's, GRE, 3 letters of recommendation, statement of purpose, transcripts. Additional exam requirements/recommendations for international students: required—TOEFL (minimum score 600 paper-based, 100 iBT) or IELTS (7). Electronic applications accepted.

Kansas State University, Graduate School, College of Engineering, Department of Mechanical and Nuclear Engineering, Manhattan, KS 66506. Offers mechanical engineering (MS); nuclear engineering (PhD). *Degree requirements:* For master's, thesis optional; for doctorate, comprehensive exam, thesis/dissertation. *Entrance requirements:* For master's, GRE General Test; for doctorate, GRE General Test, master's degree in mechanical engineering; minimum GPA of 3.0 overall or last 60 hours in calculus-based engineering or related program. Additional exam requirements/recommendations for international students: required—TOEFL (minimum score 550 paper-based; 79 iBT). Electronic applications accepted.

Kennesaw State University, Southern Polytechnic College of Engineering and Engineering Technology, Program in Mechanical Engineering, Kennesaw, GA 30144. Offers MS. *Program availability:* Online learning. *Students:* 7 full-time (1 woman), 27 part-time (3 women); includes 6 minority (4 Black or African American, non-Hispanic/Latino; 2 Asian, non-Hispanic/Latino), 5 international. Average age 31. 15 applicants, 100% accepted, 7 enrolled. In 2019, 2 master's awarded. *Entrance requirements:* Additional exam requirements/recommendations for international students: required—TOEFL (minimum score 80 iBT), IELTS (minimum score 6.5). *Application deadline:* For fall admission, 7/1 for domestic and international students; for spring admission, 11/1 for domestic and international students. Applications are processed on a rolling basis. Application fee: $60. Electronic applications accepted. *Expenses: Tuition, area resident:* Full-time $7104; part-time $296 per credit hour. Tuition, state resident: full-time $7104; part-time $296 per credit hour. Tuition, nonresident: full-time $25,584; part-time $1066 per credit hour. *International tuition:* $25,584 full-time. *Required fees:* $2006; $1706 per unit. $853 per semester. *Financial support:* Applicants required to submit FAFSA. *Application contact:* Admissions Counselor, 470-578-4377, E-mail: ksugrad@kennesaw.edu. Website: http://engineering.kennesaw.edu/mechanical/degrees/ms-mechanical.php

Kettering University, Graduate School, Mechanical Engineering Department, Flint, MI 48504. Offers engineering (MS). *Program availability:* Part-time, evening/weekend, online learning. *Degree requirements:* For master's, thesis optional. *Entrance requirements:* Additional exam requirements/recommendations for international students: required—TOEFL (minimum score 550 paper-based; 79 iBT). Electronic applications accepted.

Lamar University, College of Graduate Studies, College of Engineering, Department of Mechanical Engineering, Beaumont, TX 77710. Offers ME, MES, DE. *Program availability:* Part-time. *Faculty:* 8 full-time (1 woman). *Students:* 17 full-time (0 women), 9 part-time (1 woman); includes 4 minority (all Asian, non-Hispanic/Latino), 21 international. Average age 27. 53 applicants, 87% accepted, 6 enrolled. In 2019, 25 master's awarded. Terminal master's awarded for partial completion of doctoral program. *Degree requirements:* For master's, comprehensive exam (for some programs), thesis (for some programs); for doctorate, thesis/dissertation. *Entrance requirements:* For master's and doctorate, GRE General Test. Additional exam requirements/recommendations for international students: required—TOEFL (minimum score 550 paper-based; 79 iBT), IELTS (minimum score 6.5). *Application deadline:* Applications are processed on a rolling basis. Application fee: $25 ($50 for international students). Electronic applications accepted. *Expenses: Tuition, area resident:* Full-time $6324; part-time $351 per credit. Tuition, state resident: full-time $6324; part-time $351 per credit. Tuition, nonresident: full-time $13,920; part-time $773 per credit. *International tuition:* $13,920 full-time. *Required fees:* $2462; $327 per credit. Tuition and fees vary according to course load, campus/location and reciprocity agreements. *Financial support:* In 2019–20, 2 students received support. Fellowships, research assistantships, teaching assistantships, and tuition waivers (partial) available. Financial award applicants required to submit FAFSA. *Unit head:* Dr. Kendrick Aung, Interim Chair, 409-880-8094, Fax: 409-880-8121. *Application contact:* Celeste Contreas, Director, Admissions and Academic Services, 409-880-8888, Fax: 409-880-7419, E-mail: gradmissions@lamar.edu. Website: http://engineering.lamar.edu/mechanical

Lawrence Technological University, College of Engineering, Southfield, MI 48075-1058. Offers architectural engineering (MS); automotive engineering (MS); biomedical engineering (MS); civil engineering (MA, MS, PhD), including environmental engineering (MS), geotechnical engineering (MS), structural engineering (MS), transportation engineering (MS), water resource engineering (MS); construction engineering management (MA); electrical and computer engineering (MS); engineering management (MEM); engineering technology (MS); fire engineering (MS); industrial engineering (MS), including healthcare systems; manufacturing systems (ME); mechanical engineering (MS, DE, PhD), including automotive engineering (MS), energy engineering (MS), manufacturing (DE), solid mechanics (MS), thermal/fluid systems (MS); mechatronic systems engineering (MS). *Program availability:* Part-time, evening/weekend. *Faculty:* 23 full-time (2 women), 20 part-time/adjunct (1 woman). *Students:* 14 full-time (5 women), 286 part-time (54 women); includes 26 minority (13 Black or African American, non-Hispanic/Latino; 8 Asian, non-Hispanic/Latino; 3 Hispanic/Latino; 2 Two or more races, non-Hispanic/Latino), 150 international. Average age 29. 384 applicants, 58% accepted, 74 enrolled. In 2019, 223 master's, 7 doctorates awarded. Terminal master's awarded for partial completion of doctoral program. *Degree requirements:* For master's, thesis optional; for doctorate, comprehensive exam, thesis/dissertation optional. *Entrance requirements:* Additional exam requirements/recommendations for international students: required—TOEFL (minimum score 550 paper-based; 79 iBT), IELTS (minimum score 6.5). *Application deadline:* For fall admission, 5/24 for international students; for spring admission, 10/13 for international students; for summer admission, 2/18 for international students. Applications are processed on a rolling basis. Application fee: $50. Electronic applications accepted. *Expenses: Tuition:* Full-time $16,618; part-time $8309 per year. *Required fees:* $600; $600. *Financial support:* In 2019–20, 21 students received support. Unspecified assistantships available. Financial award application deadline: 4/1; financial award applicants required to submit FAFSA. *Unit head:* Dr. Nabil Grace, Dean, 248-204-2500, Fax: 248-204-2509, E-mail: engrdean@ltu.edu. *Application contact:* Jane Rohrback, Director of Admissions, 248-204-3160, Fax: 248-204-2228, E-mail: admissions@ltu.edu. Website: http://www.ltu.edu/engineering/index.asp

Lehigh University, P.C. Rossin College of Engineering and Applied Science, Department of Mechanical Engineering and Mechanics, Bethlehem, PA 18015. Offers mechanical engineering (M Eng, MS, PhD); MBA/E. *Program availability:* Part-time, 100% online, blended/hybrid learning. *Faculty:* 27 full-time (4 women), 1 part-time/adjunct (0 women). *Students:* 113 full-time (10 women), 21 part-time (4 women);

includes 7 minority (2 Black or African American, non-Hispanic/Latino; 3 Hispanic/Latino; 1 Native Hawaiian or other Pacific Islander, non-Hispanic/Latino; 1 Two or more races, non-Hispanic/Latino), 88 international. Average age 27. 155 applicants, 56% accepted, 34 enrolled. In 2019, 28 master's, 13 doctorates awarded. Terminal master's awarded for partial completion of doctoral program. *Degree requirements:* For master's, thesis, there are 4 tracks for the MS degree, thesis; for doctorate, thesis/dissertation, general exam, proposal, dissertation. *Entrance requirements:* Additional exam requirements/recommendations for international students: required—TOEFL (minimum score 550 paper-based; 79 iBT), IELTS (minimum score 6.5), GRE. *Application deadline:* For fall admission, 7/15 for domestic students, 6/20 for international students; for spring admission, 12/1 for domestic and international students. Applications are processed on a rolling basis. Application fee: $75. Electronic applications accepted. *Financial support:* In 2019–20, 68 students received support, including 7 fellowships with full tuition reimbursements available (averaging $29,400 per year), 63 research assistantships with full tuition reimbursements available (averaging $28,200 per year), 13 teaching assistantships with full tuition reimbursements available (averaging $29,400 per year); unspecified assistantships also available. Support available to part-time students. Financial award application deadline: 1/15. *Unit head:* Dr. D. Gary Harlow, Chairman, 610-758-4102, Fax: 610-758-6224, E-mail: dgh0@lehigh.edu. *Application contact:* Allison B. Marsteller, Graduate Coordinator, 610-758-4107, Fax: 610-758-6224, E-mail: alm513@lehigh.edu.
Website: http://www.lehigh.edu/~inmem/

Louisiana State University and Agricultural & Mechanical College, Graduate School, College of Engineering, Department of Mechanical and Industrial Engineering, Baton Rouge, LA 70803. Offers MSME, PhD.

Loyola Marymount University, Frank R. Seaver College of Science and Engineering, Program in Mechanical Engineering, Los Angeles, CA 90045. Offers MSE. *Program availability:* Part-time, evening/weekend. *Students:* 29 full-time (4 women); includes 4 minority (2 Asian, non-Hispanic/Latino; 1 Hispanic/Latino; 1 Two or more races, non-Hispanic/Latino). Average age 25. 63 applicants, 49% accepted, 29 enrolled. In 2019, 5 master's awarded. *Entrance requirements:* For master's, graduate admissions application; undergrad GPA of at least 3.0; college-level calculus and general chemistry; 4 college-level life and physical science courses. Additional exam requirements/recommendations for international students: required—TOEFL, IELTS. *Application deadline:* Applications are processed on a rolling basis. Application fee: $50. Electronic applications accepted. *Financial support:* Research assistantships, teaching assistantships, Federal Work-Study, scholarships/grants, and unspecified assistantships available. Financial award applicants required to submit FAFSA. *Unit head:* Dr. Omar Es-Said, Graduate Program Director, Mechanical Engineering, 310-338-2829, E-mail: omar.es-said@lmu.edu. *Application contact:* Ammar Dalal, Assistant Vice Provost for Graduate Enrollment, 310-338-2721, Fax: 310-338-6086, E-mail: graduateadmission@lmu.edu.
Website: http://cse.lmu.edu/graduateprograms/mechanicalengineeringgraduateprogram

Manhattan College, Graduate Programs, School of Engineering, Program in Mechanical Engineering, Riverdale, NY 10471. Offers MS. *Program availability:* Part-time, evening/weekend. *Faculty:* 14 full-time (4 women), 3 part-time/adjunct (0 women). *Students:* 32 full-time (6 women), 18 part-time (4 women); includes 8 minority (3 Black or African American, non-Hispanic/Latino; 5 Hispanic/Latino). Average age 24. 31 applicants, 84% accepted, 20 enrolled. In 2019, 24 master's awarded. *Degree requirements:* For master's, thesis optional. *Entrance requirements:* For master's, GRE (recommended), minimum GPA of 3.0. Additional exam requirements/recommendations for international students: required—TOEFL (minimum score 550 paper-based; 80 iBT), IELTS (minimum score 6). *Application deadline:* For fall admission, 8/10 priority date for domestic students, 8/10 for international students; for spring admission, 1/7 for domestic and international students. Applications are processed on a rolling basis. Application fee: $60. Electronic applications accepted. *Financial support:* In 2019–20, 10 students received support, including 10 teaching assistantships with partial tuition reimbursements available (averaging $7,000 per year); career-related internships or fieldwork, Federal Work-Study, scholarships/grants, and unspecified assistantships also available. Support available to part-time students. Financial award application deadline: 2/1; financial award applicants required to submit FAFSA. *Unit head:* Dr. Bahman Litkouhi, Director, Graduate Program, 718-862-7927, Fax: 718-862-7163, E-mail: mechdept@manhattan.edu. *Application contact:* Kathy Balaj, Information Contact, 718-862-7145, Fax: 718-862-7163, E-mail: kathy.balaj@manhattan.edu.
Website: http://manhattan.edu/academics/engineering

Marquette University, Graduate School, College of Engineering, Department of Mechanical Engineering, Milwaukee, WI 53201-1881. Offers engineering innovation (Certificate); engineering management (MSEM); mechanical engineering (MS, PhD); new product and process development (Certificate). *Program availability:* Part-time, evening/weekend. Terminal master's awarded for partial completion of doctoral program. *Degree requirements:* For master's, comprehensive exam, thesis (for some programs); for doctorate, comprehensive exam, thesis/dissertation, qualifying exam. *Entrance requirements:* For master's, GRE General Test, minimum GPA of 3.0, official transcripts from all current and previous colleges/universities except Marquette, three letters of recommendation; for doctorate, GRE General Test, minimum GPA of 3.0, official transcripts from all current and previous colleges/universities except Marquette, three letters of recommendation, statement of purpose, copies of any published work. Additional exam requirements/recommendations for international students: required—TOEFL (minimum score 530 paper-based). Electronic applications accepted.

Marshall University, Academic Affairs Division, College of Information Technology and Engineering, Program in Mechanical Engineering, Huntington, WV 25755. Offers MSME.

Massachusetts Institute of Technology, School of Engineering, Department of Mechanical Engineering, Cambridge, MA 02139. Offers manufacturing (M Eng); mechanical engineering (SM, PhD, Sc D, Mech E); naval architecture and marine engineering (SM, PhD, Sc D); naval engineering (Naval E); ocean engineering (SM, PhD, Sc D); oceanographic engineering (SM, PhD, Sc D); SM/MBA. Terminal master's awarded for partial completion of doctoral program. *Degree requirements:* For master's, thesis; for doctorate, comprehensive exam, thesis/dissertation; for other advanced degree, comprehensive exam, thesis. *Entrance requirements:* For master's, doctorate, and other advanced degree, GRE General Test. Additional exam requirements/recommendations for international students: required—TOEFL, IELTS. Electronic applications accepted.

McGill University, Faculty of Graduate and Postdoctoral Studies, Faculty of Engineering, Department of Mechanical Engineering, Montréal, QC H3A 2T5, Canada. Offers aerospace (M Eng); manufacturing management (MMM); mechanical engineering (M Eng, M Sc, PhD).

McMaster University, School of Graduate Studies, Faculty of Engineering, Department of Mechanical Engineering, Hamilton, ON L8S 4M2, Canada. Offers M Eng, MA Sc, PhD. *Degree requirements:* For master's, thesis; for doctorate, comprehensive exam, thesis/dissertation. *Entrance requirements:* Additional exam requirements/recommendations for international students: required—TOEFL (minimum score 550 paper-based).

McNeese State University, Doré School of Graduate Studies, College of Engineering and Computer Science, Master of Engineering Program, Lake Charles, LA 70609. Offers chemical engineering (M Eng); civil engineering (M Eng); electrical engineering (M Eng); engineering management (M Eng); mechanical engineering (M Eng). *Program availability:* Part-time, evening/weekend. *Entrance requirements:* For master's, GRE, baccalaureate degree, minimum overall GPA of 3.0. Additional exam requirements/recommendations for international students: required—TOEFL (minimum score 560 paper-based; 83 iBT).

Memorial University of Newfoundland, School of Graduate Studies, Faculty of Engineering and Applied Science, St. John's, NL A1C 5S7, Canada. Offers civil engineering (M Eng, PhD); electrical and computer engineering (M Eng, PhD); mechanical engineering (M Eng, PhD); ocean and naval architecture engineering (M Eng, PhD). *Program availability:* Part-time. *Degree requirements:* For master's, thesis; for doctorate, comprehensive exam, thesis/dissertation, oral thesis defense. *Entrance requirements:* For master's, 2nd class degree; for doctorate, master's degree in engineering. Electronic applications accepted.

Mercer University, Graduate Studies, Macon Campus, School of Engineering, Macon, GA 31207. Offers biomedical engineering (MSE); computer engineering (MSE); electrical engineering (MSE); engineering management (MSE); environmental engineering (MSE); environmental systems (MS); mechanical engineering (MSE); software engineering (MSE); software systems (MS); technical communications management (MS); technical management (MS). *Program availability:* Part-time-only, evening/weekend, online learning. *Faculty:* 27 full-time (9 women), 2 part-time/adjunct (0 women). *Students:* 38 full-time (10 women), 51 part-time (20 women); includes 22 minority (5 Black or African American, non-Hispanic/Latino; 11 Asian, non-Hispanic/Latino; 4 Hispanic/Latino; 2 Two or more races, non-Hispanic/Latino), 2 international. Average age 26. In 2019, 70 master's awarded. *Degree requirements:* For master's, thesis or alternative. *Entrance requirements:* For master's, GRE (minimum score 300), minimum undergraduate GPA of 3.0. Additional exam requirements/recommendations for international students: required—TOEFL (minimum score 550 paper-based; 80 iBT). *Application deadline:* For fall admission, 4/1 priority date for domestic and international students; for spring admission, 11/1 priority date for domestic and international students. Applications are processed on a rolling basis. Application fee: $75. *Expenses:* Tuition: $938.00 ($700.00 for Technical Communication Management program) per credit hour; Facility and Technology Fee: $17.00 per credit hour. *Financial support:* Federal Work-Study available. Financial award applicants required to submit FAFSA. *Unit head:* Dr. Laura W. Lackey, Dean, 478-301-4106, Fax: 478-301-5593, E-mail: lackey_l@mercer.edu. *Application contact:* Dr. Sinjae Hyun, Program Director, 478-301-2214, Fax: 478-301-5593, E-mail: hyun_s@mercer.edu.
Website: http://engineering.mercer.edu/

Merrimack College, School of Science and Engineering, North Andover, MA 01845-5800. Offers civil engineering (MS); computer science (MS); data science (MS); engineering management (MS); mechanical engineering (MS), including engineering management. *Program availability:* Part-time, evening/weekend, 100% online. *Degree requirements:* For master's, comprehensive exam, thesis optional, internship or capstone (for some programs). *Entrance requirements:* For master's, official college transcripts, resume, personal statement, 2 recommendations. Additional exam requirements/recommendations for international students: required—TOEFL (minimum score 84 iBT), IELTS (minimum score 6.5), PTE (minimum score 56). Electronic applications accepted. Application fee is waived when completed online. *Expenses:* Contact institution.

Miami University, College of Engineering and Computing, Department of Mechanical and Manufacturing Engineering, Oxford, OH 45056. Offers MS.

Michigan State University, The Graduate School, College of Engineering, Department of Mechanical Engineering, East Lansing, MI 48824. Offers engineering mechanics (MS, PhD); mechanical engineering (MS, PhD). *Entrance requirements:* For master's, GRE General Test. Additional exam requirements/recommendations for international students: required—TOEFL. Electronic applications accepted.

Michigan Technological University, Graduate School, College of Engineering, Department of Mechanical Engineering-Engineering Mechanics, Houghton, MI 49931. Offers engineering mechanics (MS); hybrid electric drive vehicle engineering (Graduate Certificate); mechanical engineering-engineering mechanics (PhD). *Program availability:* Part-time, evening/weekend, 100% online, blended/hybrid learning. *Faculty:* 64 full-time, 36 part-time/adjunct. *Students:* 284 full-time, 79 part-time; includes 9 minority (2 Black or African American, non-Hispanic/Latino; 4 Asian, non-Hispanic/Latino; 3 Hispanic/Latino), 276 international. Average age 27. 862 applicants, 50% accepted, 127 enrolled. In 2019, 123 master's, 14 doctorates awarded. Terminal master's awarded for partial completion of doctoral program. *Degree requirements:* For master's, thesis (for some programs); for doctorate, comprehensive exam, thesis/dissertation. *Entrance requirements:* For master's, GRE (Michigan Tech and online students exempt), statement of purpose, personal statement, official transcripts, 2 letters of recommendation, resume/curriculum vitae; for doctorate, GRE (Michigan Tech and online students exempt), MS (preferred), statement of purpose, official transcripts, 2 letters of recommendation, resume/curriculum vitae; for Graduate Certificate, statement of purpose, official transcripts, BS in engineering. Additional exam requirements/recommendations for international students: required—TOEFL (minimum score 90 iBT) or IELTS (minimum score 7.0); recommended—TOEFL (minimum score 90 iBT), IELTS (minimum score 7). *Application deadline:* For fall admission, 3/1 priority date for domestic and international students; for spring admission, 8/1 priority date for domestic and international students. Applications are processed on a rolling basis. Application fee: $0. Electronic applications accepted. *Expenses:* $1,212 per credit. *Financial support:* In 2019–20, 255 students received support, including 25 fellowships with tuition reimbursements available (averaging $16,590 per year), 43 research assistantships with tuition reimbursements available (averaging $16,590 per year), 31 teaching assistantships with tuition reimbursements available (averaging $16,590 per year); career-related internships or fieldwork, Federal Work-Study, scholarships/grants, health care benefits, unspecified assistantships, and cooperative program also available. Financial award applicants required to submit FAFSA. *Unit head:* Dr. William W. Predebon, Chair, 906-487-2551, Fax: 906-487-2822, E-mail: wwpredeb@mtu.edu. *Application contact:* Cindy Wadaga, Graduate Program Assistant, 906-487-2551, Fax: 906-487-2822, E-mail: cawadaga@mtu.edu.
Website: http://www.mtu.edu/mechanical/

Mississippi State University, Bagley College of Engineering, Department of Mechanical Engineering, Mississippi State, MS 39762. Offers mechanical engineering (MS). *Program availability:* Part-time, blended/hybrid learning. *Faculty:* 23 full-time (4 women), 1 part-time/adjunct (0 women). *Students:* 51 full-time (12 women), 52 part-time (7 women); includes 15 minority (2 Black or African American, non-Hispanic/Latino; 7 Asian, non-Hispanic/Latino; 4 Hispanic/Latino; 2 Two or more races, non-Hispanic/Latino), 27 international. Average age 29. 70 applicants, 71% accepted, 21 enrolled. In 2019, 22 master's, 9 doctorates awarded. *Degree requirements:* For master's, thesis

optional, oral exam; for doctorate, thesis/dissertation, qualifying exam, preliminary exam, dissertation defense. *Entrance requirements:* For master's, GRE (for graduates from program not accredited by EAC/ABET), minimum GPA of 2.75; for doctorate, GRE, minimum GPA of 2.75. Additional exam requirements/recommendations for international students: required—TOEFL (minimum score 550 paper-based; 79 iBT); recommended—IELTS (minimum score 6.5). *Application deadline:* For fall admission, 7/1 for domestic students, 5/1 for international students; for spring admission, 11/1 for domestic students, 9/1 for international students. Applications are processed on a rolling basis. Application fee: $60 ($80 for international students). Electronic applications accepted. *Expenses: Tuition, area resident:* Full-time $8880; part-time $456 per credit hour. Tuition, state resident: full-time $8880. Tuition, nonresident: full-time $23,840; part-time $1236 per credit hour. *Required fees:* $110; $11.12 per credit hour. Tuition and fees vary according to course load. *Financial support:* In 2019–20, 8 research assistantships with full tuition reimbursements (averaging $15,154 per year), 2 teaching assistantships with full tuition reimbursements (averaging $16,934 per year) were awarded; career-related internships or fieldwork, Federal Work-Study, institutionally sponsored loans, scholarships/grants, and unspecified assistantships also available. Financial award application deadline: 4/1; financial award applicants required to submit FAFSA. *Unit head:* Dr. Haitham El Kadiri, Interim Department Head and Associate Professor, 662-325-4777, Fax: 662-325-7223, E-mail: elkadiri@me.msstate.edu. *Application contact:* Robbie Salters, Admissions and Enrollment Management Assistant and Coordinator, 662-325-5188, E-mail: rsalters@grad.msstate.edu.
Website: http://www.me.msstate.edu/

Missouri University of Science and Technology, Department of Mechanical and Aerospace Engineering, Rolla, MO 65401. Offers aerospace engineering (MS, PhD); manufacturing engineering (M Eng, MS); mechanical engineering (MS, PhD). *Program availability:* Part-time, evening/weekend. Terminal master's awarded for partial completion of doctoral program. *Degree requirements:* For master's, thesis optional; for doctorate, comprehensive exam, thesis/dissertation. *Entrance requirements:* For master's, GRE General Test (minimum score 1100 verbal and quantitative, writing 3.5), minimum GPA of 3.0; for doctorate, GRE General Test (minimum score: verbal and quantitative 1100, writing 3.5), minimum GPA of 3.5. Additional exam requirements/recommendations for international students: required—TOEFL (minimum score 550 paper-based). Electronic applications accepted. *Expenses:* Tuition, state resident: full-time $7839; part-time $435.50 per credit hour. Tuition, nonresident: full-time $22,169; part-time $1231.60 per credit hour. *International tuition:* $18,156.60 full-time. *Required fees:* $649.76. One-time fee: $119. Tuition and fees vary according to course load and program.

Montana State University, The Graduate School, College of Engineering, Department of Mechanical and Industrial Engineering, Bozeman, MT 59717. Offers engineering (PhD), including industrial engineering, mechanical engineering; industrial and management engineering (MS); mechanical engineering (MS). *Program availability:* Part-time. *Degree requirements:* For master's, comprehensive exam, thesis, oral exams; for doctorate, comprehensive exam, thesis/dissertation, qualifying exam. *Entrance requirements:* For master's, GRE, official transcript, minimum GPA of 3.0, demonstrated potential for success, statement of goals, three letters of recommendation, proof of funds affidavit; for doctorate, minimum undergraduate GPA of 3.0, 3.2 graduate; three letters of recommendation; statement of objectives. Additional exam requirements/recommendations for international students: required—TOEFL or IELTS. Electronic applications accepted.

Naval Postgraduate School, Departments and Academic Groups, Department of Mechanical and Aerospace Engineering, Monterey, CA 93943. Offers astronautical engineer (AstE); astronautical engineering (MS); engineering science (MS), including astronautical engineering, mechanical engineering; mechanical and aerospace engineering (PhD); mechanical engineering (MS). *Program availability:* Part-time, online learning. *Degree requirements:* For master's, thesis (for some programs), capstone or research/dissertation paper (for some programs); for doctorate, thesis/dissertation; for AstE, thesis.

Naval Postgraduate School, Departments and Academic Groups, Space Systems Academic Group, Monterey, CA 93943. Offers applied physics (MS); astronautical engineering (MS); computer science (MS); electrical engineering (MS); mechanical engineering (MS); space systems (Engr); space systems operations (MS). *Program availability:* Part-time. *Degree requirements:* For master's and Engr, thesis; for doctorate, thesis/dissertation.

Naval Postgraduate School, Departments and Academic Groups, Undersea Warfare Academic Group, Monterey, CA 93943. Offers applied mathematics (MS); applied physics (MS); applied science (MS), including acoustics, operations research, physical oceanography, signal processing; electrical engineering (MS); engineering acoustics (MS, PhD); engineering science (MS), including electrical engineering, mechanical engineering; mechanical engineer (ME); mechanical engineering (MS, MSME); meteorology (MS); operations research (MS); physical oceanography (MS). *Program availability:* Part-time. *Degree requirements:* For master's, thesis.

New Jersey Institute of Technology, Newark College of Engineering, Newark, NJ 07102. Offers biomedical engineering (MS, PhD); biopharmaceutical engineering (MS); chemical engineering (MS, PhD); civil engineering (MS, PhD); computer engineering (MS); critical infrastructure systems (MS); electrical engineering (MS, PhD); engineering management (MS); engineering science (MS); environmental engineering (MS, PhD); healthcare systems management (MS); industrial engineering (MS, PhD); internet engineering (MS); manufacturing systems engineering (MS); materials science & engineering (PhD); materials science and engineering (MS); mechanical engineering (MS, PhD); occupational safety and health engineering (MS). *Program availability:* Part-time, evening/weekend. *Faculty:* 151 full-time (29 women), 135 part-time/adjunct (15 women). *Students:* 576 full-time (161 women), 528 part-time (111 women); includes 366 minority (61 Black or African American, non-Hispanic/Latino; 1 American Indian or Alaska Native, non-Hispanic/Latino; 166 Asian, non-Hispanic/Latino; 115 Hispanic/Latino; 23 Two or more races, non-Hispanic/Latino), 450 international. Average age 28. 2,053 applicants, 67% accepted, 338 enrolled. In 2019, 474 master's, 30 doctorates awarded. Terminal master's awarded for partial completion of doctoral program. *Degree requirements:* For master's, thesis (for some programs); for doctorate, thesis/dissertation. *Entrance requirements:* For master's, GRE General Test, minimum GPA 2.8, personal statement, 1 letter of recommendation, transcripts; for doctorate, GRE General Test, minimum GPA of 3.5, personal statement, 3 letters of recommendation, transcripts. Additional exam requirements/recommendations for international students: required—TOEFL (minimum score 550 paper-based; 79 iBT), IELTS (minimum score 6.5). *Application deadline:* For fall admission, 6/1 priority date for domestic students, 5/1 priority date for international students; for spring admission, 11/15 priority date for domestic and international students. Applications are processed on a rolling basis. Application fee: $75. Electronic applications accepted. *Expenses:* $23,828 per year (in-state), $33,744 per year (out-of-state). *Financial support:* In 2019–20, 352 students received support, including 33 fellowships with full tuition reimbursements available (averaging $24,000 per year), 89 research assistantships with full tuition reimbursements available (averaging $24,000 per year), 112 teaching assistantships with full tuition reimbursements available (averaging $24,000 per year); career-related internships or fieldwork, Federal Work-Study, scholarships/grants, and unspecified assistantships also available. Financial award application deadline: 1/15. *Unit head:* Dr. Moshe Kam, Dean, 973-596-5534, Fax: 973-596-2316, E-mail: moshe.kam@njit.edu. *Application contact:* Stephen Eck, Executive Director of University Admissions, 973-596-3300, Fax: 973-596-3461, E-mail: admissions@njit.edu.
Website: http://engineering.njit.edu/

New Mexico Institute of Mining and Technology, Center for Graduate Studies, Department of Mechanical Engineering, Socorro, NM 87801. Offers explosives engineering (MS); fluid and thermal sciences (MS); mechatronics systems engineering (MS); solid mechanics (MS). *Degree requirements:* For master's, thesis (for some programs). *Entrance requirements:* For master's, GRE General Test. Additional exam requirements/recommendations for international students: required—TOEFL (minimum score 540 paper-based).

New York Institute of Technology, College of Engineering and Computing Sciences, Department of Mechanical Engineering, Old Westbury, NY 11568. Offers MS. *Program availability:* Part-time. *Faculty:* 7 full-time (2 women), 6 part-time/adjunct (0 women). *Students:* 38 full-time (3 women), 12 part-time (1 woman); includes 12 minority (4 Black or African American, non-Hispanic/Latino; 4 Asian, non-Hispanic/Latino; 3 Hispanic/Latino; 1 Two or more races, non-Hispanic/Latino), 29 international. Average age 25. 182 applicants, 53% accepted, 25 enrolled. In 2019, 28 master's awarded. *Degree requirements:* For master's, thesis. *Entrance requirements:* For master's, graduates of foreign universities are required to take the GRE and submit their scores; applicants with a GPA below 2.85 may, at the discretion of the dean, be asked to take the GRE or other diagnostic tests, bachelor's degree in Mechanical Engineering from an ABET-accredited program or bachelor's degree or its equivalent in a closely related field with appropriate prerequisite courses approved by the chairperson of the Mechanical Engineering department; minimum undergraduate GPA of 2.85; transcripts from all schools attended and proof of degree. Additional exam requirements/recommendations for international students: required—TOEFL (minimum score 79 iBT), IELTS (minimum score 6), PTE (minimum score 53), Duolingo English Test. *Application deadline:* For fall admission, 6/1 for international students; for spring admission, 12/1 for international students. Applications are processed on a rolling basis. Application fee: $50. Electronic applications accepted. *Expenses: Tuition:* Full-time $23,760; part-time $1320 per credit. *Required fees:* $260; $220 per unit. Full-time tuition and fees vary according to degree level and program. Part-time tuition and fees vary according to course load and program. *Financial support:* In 2019–20, 36 students received support. Fellowships, research assistantships, teaching assistantships, Federal Work-Study, scholarships/grants, and unspecified assistantships available. Support available to part-time students. Financial award application deadline: 2/15; financial award applicants required to submit FAFSA. *Unit head:* Dr. Xun Yu, Chair, 516-686-7829, E-mail: xyu@nyit.edu. *Application contact:* Alice Dolitsky, Director, Graduate Admissions, 800-345-6948, Fax: 516-686-1116, E-mail: grad@nyit.edu.
Website: https://www.nyit.edu/departments/mechanical_engineering

New York University, Tandon School of Engineering, Department of Mechanical and Aerospace Engineering, Major in Mechanical Engineering, New York, NY 10012-1019. Offers mechanical engineering (PhD). *Program availability:* Part-time, evening/weekend. *Degree requirements:* For master's, comprehensive exam (for some programs), thesis (for some programs); for doctorate, comprehensive exam, thesis/dissertation. *Entrance requirements:* For master's, BE or BS in engineering, physics, chemistry, mathematical sciences, or biological sciences or MBA. Additional exam requirements/recommendations for international students: required—TOEFL (minimum score 550 paper-based; 90 iBT); recommended—IELTS (minimum score 7). Electronic applications accepted.

North Carolina Agricultural and Technical State University, The Graduate College, College of Engineering, Department of Mechanical Engineering, Greensboro, NC 27411. Offers MSME, PhD. *Program availability:* Part-time. *Degree requirements:* For master's, thesis, qualifying exam, thesis defense; for doctorate, thesis/dissertation. *Entrance requirements:* For master's, BS in mechanical engineering from accredited institution with minimum overall GPA of 3.0; for doctorate, GRE, MS in mechanical engineering or closely-related field with minimum GPA of 3.3.

North Carolina State University, Graduate School, College of Engineering, Department of Mechanical and Aerospace Engineering, Program in Mechanical Engineering, Raleigh, NC 27695. Offers MS, PhD. *Program availability:* Part-time, online learning. *Degree requirements:* For master's, thesis optional, oral exam; for doctorate, thesis/dissertation, oral and preliminary exams. *Entrance requirements:* For master's and doctorate, GRE General Test. Additional exam requirements/recommendations for international students: required—TOEFL (minimum score 550 paper-based). Electronic applications accepted.

North Dakota State University, College of Graduate and Interdisciplinary Studies, College of Engineering, Department of Mechanical Engineering, Fargo, ND 58102. Offers MS, PhD. *Program availability:* Part-time. *Degree requirements:* For master's, thesis; for doctorate, comprehensive exam, thesis/dissertation. *Entrance requirements:* For master's and doctorate, minimum GPA of 3.0. Additional exam requirements/recommendations for international students: required—TOEFL (minimum score 550 paper-based). Electronic applications accepted. Tuition and fees vary according to program and reciprocity agreements.

Northeastern University, College of Engineering, Boston, MA 02115-5096. Offers bioengineering (MS, PhD); chemical engineering (MS, PhD); civil engineering (MS, PhD); computer engineering (PhD); computer systems engineering (MS); electrical and computer engineering (MS); electrical and computer engineering leadership (MS); electrical engineering (PhD); energy systems (MS); engineering and public policy (MS); engineering management (MS, Certificate); environmental engineering (MS); industrial engineering (MS, PhD); information assurance (PhD); information systems (MS); interdisciplinary engineering (PhD); mechanical engineering (PhD); operations research (MS); telecommunication systems management (MS). *Program availability:* Part-time, online learning. Electronic applications accepted. *Expenses:* Contact institution.

Northern Arizona University, College of Engineering, Informatics, and Applied Sciences, Department of Mechanical Engineering, Flagstaff, AZ 86011. Offers bioengineering (PhD); engineering (M Eng), including mechanical engineering. *Program availability:* Part-time. *Degree requirements:* For master's, variable foreign language requirement, comprehensive exam (for some programs), thesis (for some programs); for doctorate, variable foreign language requirement, comprehensive exam (for some programs), thesis/dissertation (for some programs). *Entrance requirements:* For master's and doctorate, GRE General Test. Additional exam requirements/recommendations for international students: required—TOEFL (minimum score 80 iBT), IELTS (minimum score 6.5). Electronic applications accepted.

Northern Illinois University, Graduate School, College of Engineering and Engineering Technology, Department of Mechanical Engineering, De Kalb, IL 60115-2854. Offers MS. *Program availability:* Part-time. *Faculty:* 9 full-time (0 women). *Students:* 25 full-time (5 women), 43 part-time (5 women); includes 10 minority (3 Asian, non-Hispanic/Latino; 5 Hispanic/Latino; 2 Two or more races, non-Hispanic/Latino), 19 international. Average age 28. 88 applicants, 51% accepted, 10 enrolled. In 2019, 43 master's awarded.

Degree requirements: For master's, comprehensive exam, thesis optional. *Entrance requirements:* For master's, GRE General Test, minimum GPA of 2.75. Additional exam requirements/recommendations for international students: required—TOEFL (minimum score 550 paper-based). *Application deadline:* For fall admission, 6/1 for domestic students, 5/1 for international students; for spring admission, 11/1 for domestic students, 10/1 for international students. Applications are processed on a rolling basis. Application fee: $40. Electronic applications accepted. *Financial support:* In 2019–20, 19 research assistantships with full tuition reimbursements, 31 teaching assistantships with full tuition reimbursements were awarded; fellowships with full tuition reimbursements, Federal Work-Study, scholarships/grants, tuition waivers (full), and staff assistantships also available. Support available to part-time students. Financial award applicants required to submit FAFSA. *Unit head:* Dr. Tariq Shamim, Chair, 815-753-9970, Fax: 815-753-0416, E-mail: sciammarella@niu.edu. *Application contact:* Graduate School Office, 815-753-0395, E-mail: gradsch@niu.edu.
Website: http://www.niu.edu/me/graduate/

Northwestern University, McCormick School of Engineering and Applied Science, Department of Mechanical Engineering, Evanston, IL 60208. Offers MS, PhD. *Program availability:* Part-time. Terminal master's awarded for partial completion of doctoral program. *Degree requirements:* For master's, thesis optional; for doctorate, comprehensive exam, thesis/dissertation. *Entrance requirements:* For master's and doctorate, GRE General Test. Additional exam requirements/recommendations for international students: required—TOEFL (minimum score 577 paper-based; 90 iBT), IELTS (minimum score 7). Electronic applications accepted.

Oakland University, Graduate Study and Lifelong Learning, School of Engineering and Computer Science, Department of Mechanical Engineering, Rochester, MI 48309-4401. Offers MS, PhD. *Program availability:* Part-time, evening/weekend. *Entrance requirements:* For master's, minimum GPA of 3.0. Additional exam requirements/recommendations for international students: required—TOEFL (minimum score 550 paper-based). Electronic applications accepted. *Expenses:* Contact institution.

The Ohio State University, Graduate School, College of Engineering, Department of Mechanical and Aerospace Engineering, Columbus, OH 43210. Offers aerospace engineering (MS, PhD); mechanical engineering (MS, PhD); nuclear engineering (MS, PhD). *Entrance requirements:* For master's and doctorate, GRE. Additional exam requirements/recommendations for international students: required—TOEFL (minimum score 550 paper-based; 79 iBT), Michigan English Language Assessment Battery (minimum score 82); recommended—IELTS (minimum score 7). Electronic applications accepted.

Ohio University, Graduate College, Russ College of Engineering and Technology, Department of Mechanical Engineering, Athens, OH 45701-2979. Offers biomedical engineering (MS); mechanical engineering (MS), including CAD/CAM, design, energy, manufacturing, materials, robotics, thermofluids. *Program availability:* Part-time. *Degree requirements:* For master's, comprehensive exam (for some programs), thesis. *Entrance requirements:* For master's, GRE, BS in engineering or science, minimum GPA of 2.8. Additional exam requirements/recommendations for international students: required—TOEFL (minimum score 550 paper-based; 80 iBT) or IELTS (minimum score 6.5). Electronic applications accepted.

Oklahoma Christian University, Graduate School of Engineering and Computer Science, Oklahoma City, OK 73136-1100. Offers electrical and computer engineering (MSE); engineering management (MSE); mechanical engineering (MSE); software engineering (MSCS, MSE). *Program availability:* Part-time. *Entrance requirements:* Additional exam requirements/recommendations for international students: required—TOEFL (minimum score 550 paper-based). Electronic applications accepted. *Expenses:* Contact institution.

Oklahoma State University, College of Engineering, Architecture and Technology, School of Mechanical and Aerospace Engineering, Stillwater, OK 74078. Offers mechanical and aerospace engineering (MS, PhD). *Program availability:* Online learning. *Faculty:* 30 full-time (1 woman), 1 part-time/adjunct (0 women). *Students:* 26 full-time (2 women), 100 part-time (9 women); includes 12 minority (1 Black or African American, non-Hispanic/Latino; 2 American Indian or Alaska Native, non-Hispanic/Latino; 3 Asian, non-Hispanic/Latino; 1 Hispanic/Latino; 5 Two or more races, non-Hispanic/Latino), 60 international. Average age 26. 134 applicants, 42% accepted, 45 enrolled. In 2019, 21 master's, 7 doctorates awarded. *Entrance requirements:* For master's and doctorate, GRE or GMAT. Additional exam requirements/recommendations for international students: required—TOEFL (minimum score 550 paper-based; 79 iBT). *Application deadline:* For fall admission, 3/1 priority date for international students; for spring admission, 8/1 priority date for international students. Applications are processed on a rolling basis. Application fee: $50 ($75 for international students). Electronic applications accepted. *Expenses: Tuition, area resident:* Full-time $4148.10; part-time $2765.40. *Tuition, state resident:* full-time $4148.10; part-time $2765.40. *Tuition, nonresident:* full-time $15,775; part-time $10,516.80. *International tuition:* $15,775.20 full-time. *Required fees:* $2196.90; $122.05 per credit hour. Tuition and fees vary according to course load, campus/location and program. *Financial support:* In 2019–20, 50 research assistantships (averaging $1,745 per year), 49 teaching assistantships (averaging $1,224 per year) were awarded; career-related internships or fieldwork, Federal Work-Study, scholarships/grants, health care benefits, tuition waivers (partial), and unspecified assistantships also available. Support available to part-time students. Financial award application deadline: 3/1; financial award applicants required to submit FAFSA. *Unit head:* Dr. Daniel E. Fisher, Department Head, 405-744-5900, Fax: 405-744-7873, E-mail: maehead@okstate.edu. *Application contact:* Dr. Charlotte Fore, Manager of Graduate Studies and Research Development, 405-744-5900, Fax: 405-744-7873, E-mail: charlotte.fore@okstate.edu.
Website: http://mae.okstate.edu

Old Dominion University, Frank Batten College of Engineering and Technology, Program in Mechanical Engineering, Norfolk, VA 23529. Offers ME, MS, D Eng, PhD. *Program availability:* Part-time, 100% online, blended/hybrid learning. *Degree requirements:* For master's, comprehensive exam (for some programs), thesis (for some programs); for doctorate, thesis/dissertation, diagnostic exam, candidacy exam. *Entrance requirements:* For master's, GRE, minimum GPA of 3.0; for doctorate, GRE, minimum GPA of 3.5. Additional exam requirements/recommendations for international students: required—TOEFL (minimum score 550 paper-based; 79 iBT), IELTS (minimum score 6.5). Electronic applications accepted.

Oregon State University, College of Engineering, Program in Materials Science, Corvallis, OR 97331. Offers chemical engineering (MS, PhD); chemistry (MS, PhD); civil engineering (MS, PhD); electrical and computer engineering (MS, PhD); forest products (MS, PhD); mathematics (MS, PhD); mechanical engineering (MS, PhD); nuclear engineering (MS); physics (MS, PhD). *Entrance requirements:* For master's and doctorate, GRE. Additional exam requirements/recommendations for international students: required—TOEFL (minimum score 80 iBT), IELTS (minimum score 6.5). *Expenses:* Contact institution.

Oregon State University, College of Engineering, Program in Mechanical Engineering, Corvallis, OR 97331. Offers M Eng, MS, PhD. *Program availability:* Part-time. *Entrance requirements:* For master's and doctorate, GRE. Additional exam requirements/

recommendations for international students: required—TOEFL (minimum score 80 iBT), IELTS (minimum score 6.5). *Expenses:* Contact institution.

Penn State Harrisburg, Graduate School, School of Science, Engineering and Technology, Middletown, PA 17057. Offers civil engineering (MS); computer science (MS); electrical engineering (M Eng, MS); engineering management (MPS); engineering science (M Eng); environmental engineering (M Eng); environmental pollution control (MEPC, MS); mechanical engineering (MS); structural engineering (Certificate). *Program availability:* Part-time, evening/weekend.

Penn State University Park, Graduate School, College of Engineering, Department of Mechanical and Nuclear Engineering, University Park, PA 16802. Offers additive manufacturing and design (MS); mechanical engineering (MS, PhD); nuclear engineering (M Eng, MS, PhD).

Pittsburg State University, Graduate School, College of Technology, Department of Engineering Technology, Pittsburg, KS 66762. Offers electrical engineering technology (MET); general engineering technology (MET); manufacturing engineering technology (MET); mechanical engineering technology (MET); plastics engineering technology (MET). *Program availability:* Part-time, 100% online, blended/hybrid learning. *Degree requirements:* For master's, thesis optional. *Entrance requirements:* Additional exam requirements/recommendations for international students: required—TOEFL (minimum score 550 paper-based; 79 iBT), IELTS (minimum score 6.5), PTE (minimum score 51). Electronic applications accepted. *Expenses:* Contact institution.

Polytechnic University of Puerto Rico, Graduate School, Hato Rey, PR 00918. Offers business administration (MBA), including computer information systems, general management, management of information systems, management of international enterprises; civil engineering (ME, MS); computer engineering (ME, MS); computer science (MCS, MS); electrical engineering (ME, MS); engineering management (MEM); environmental management (MEM); landscape architecture (M Land Arch); manufacturing competitiveness (MMC, MS); manufacturing engineering (ME, MS); mechanical engineering (M Mech E). *Accreditation:* ASLA. *Program availability:* Part-time, evening/weekend. *Entrance requirements:* For master's, 3 letters of recommendation.

Polytechnique Montréal, Graduate Programs, Department of Mechanical Engineering, Montréal, QC H3C 3A7, Canada. Offers aerothermics (M Eng, M Sc A, PhD); applied mechanics (M Eng, M Sc A, PhD); tool design (M Eng, M Sc A, PhD). *Program availability:* Part-time, evening/weekend. *Degree requirements:* For master's, one foreign language, thesis; for doctorate, one foreign language, thesis/dissertation. *Entrance requirements:* For master's, minimum GPA of 2.75; for doctorate, minimum GPA of 3.0.

Portland State University, Graduate Studies, College of Liberal Arts and Sciences, Systems Science Program, Portland, OR 97207-0751. Offers computational intelligence (Certificate); computer modeling and simulation (Certificate); systems science (MS); systems science/anthropology (PhD); systems science/business administration (PhD); systems science/civil engineering (PhD); systems science/economics (PhD); systems science/engineering management (PhD); systems science/general (PhD); systems science/mathematical sciences (PhD); systems science/mechanical engineering (PhD); systems science/psychology (PhD); systems science/sociology (PhD). *Program availability:* Part-time. *Faculty:* 2 full-time (0 women), 6 part-time/adjunct (1 woman). *Students:* 6 full-time (3 women), 25 part-time (8 women); includes 7 minority (2 Asian, non-Hispanic/Latino; 4 Hispanic/Latino; 1 Two or more races, non-Hispanic/Latino), 2 international. Average age 39. 25 applicants, 80% accepted, 15 enrolled. In 2019, 7 master's, 2 doctorates awarded. Terminal master's awarded for partial completion of doctoral program. *Degree requirements:* For master's, comprehensive exam (for some programs), thesis optional; for doctorate, variable foreign language requirement, comprehensive exam (for some programs), thesis/dissertation. *Entrance requirements:* For master's, GRE/GMAT (recommended), minimum GPA of 3.0 on undergraduate or graduate work, 2 letters of recommendation, statement of interest; for doctorate, GRE required, minimum GPA of 3.0 undergraduate, 3.25 graduate; 3 letters of recommendation; statement of interest. Additional exam requirements/recommendations for international students: required—TOEFL (minimum score 550 paper-based; 80 iBT). *Application deadline:* For fall admission, 3/15 priority date for domestic and international students. Application fee: $65. Electronic applications accepted. *Expenses: Tuition, area resident:* Full-time $13,020; part-time $6510 per year. Tuition, state resident: full-time $13,020; part-time $6510 per year. Tuition, nonresident: full-time $19,830; part-time $9915 per year. *International tuition:* $19,830 full-time. *Required fees:* $1226. One-time fee: $350. Tuition and fees vary according to course load, program and reciprocity agreements. *Financial support:* Research assistantships, teaching assistantships, career-related internships or fieldwork, Federal Work-Study, scholarships/grants, and unspecified assistantships available. Support available to part-time students. Financial award application deadline: 3/1; financial award applicants required to submit FAFSA. *Unit head:* Dr. Wayne Wakeland, Chair, 503-725-4975, E-mail: wakeland@pdx.edu. *Application contact:* Dr. Wayne Wakeland, Chair, 503-725-4975, E-mail: wakeland@pdx.edu.
Website: http://www.pdx.edu/sysc/

Portland State University, Graduate Studies, Maseeh College of Engineering and Computer Science, Department of Mechanical and Materials Engineering, Portland, OR 97207-0751. Offers mechanical engineering (PhD). *Program availability:* Part-time, evening/weekend. *Faculty:* 16 full-time (1 woman), 5 part-time/adjunct (0 women). *Students:* 36 full-time (9 women), 62 part-time (23 women); includes 30 minority (1 Black or African American, non-Hispanic/Latino; 13 Asian, non-Hispanic/Latino; 11 Hispanic/Latino; 5 Two or more races, non-Hispanic/Latino), 15 international. Average age 31. 53 applicants, 79% accepted, 23 enrolled. In 2019, 37 master's, 4 doctorates awarded. *Degree requirements:* For master's, thesis or alternative; for doctorate, one foreign language, thesis/dissertation, oral and written exams. *Entrance requirements:* For master's, minimum GPA of 3.0 in upper-division course work, BS in mechanical engineering or allied field, 3 letters of recommendation, statement of purpose, resume/curriculum vitae; for doctorate, GRE General Test, GRE Subject Test, MS, minimum GPA of 3.0 in upper-division course work, 3 letters of recommendation. Additional exam requirements/recommendations for international students: required—TOEFL (minimum score 550 paper-based; 80 iBT). *Application deadline:* For fall admission, 1/15 priority date for domestic and international students; for winter admission, 9/1 for domestic students, 8/1 for international students; for spring admission, 11/1 for domestic students, 10/1 for international students. Applications are processed on a rolling basis. Application fee: $65. Electronic applications accepted. *Expenses:* Contact institution. *Financial support:* In 2019–20, 30 students received support, including 6 research assistantships with full and partial tuition reimbursements available (averaging $13,066 per year), 16 teaching assistantships with full and partial tuition reimbursements available (averaging $7,530 per year); Federal Work-Study, scholarships/grants, and unspecified assistantships also available. Support available to part-time students. Financial award application deadline: 3/1; financial award applicants required to submit FAFSA. *Unit head:* Sung Yi, Chair, 503-725-5470, Fax: 503-725-8255, E-mail: syi@pdx.edu. *Application contact:* Tricia Hutchins, Department Manager, 503-725-4291, Fax: 503-725-8255, E-mail: tricia.hutchins@pdx.edu.
Website: http://www.pdx.edu/mme/

Mechanical Engineering

Princeton University, Graduate School, School of Engineering and Applied Science, Department of Mechanical and Aerospace Engineering, Princeton, NJ 08544. Offers M Eng, MSE, PhD. Terminal master's awarded for partial completion of doctoral program. *Degree requirements:* For master's, thesis (MSE); for doctorate, thesis/dissertation, general exam. *Entrance requirements:* For master's, GRE General Test, 3 letters of recommendation; for doctorate, GRE General Test, official transcript(s), 3 letters of recommendation, personal statement. Additional exam requirements/recommendations for international students: required—TOEFL. Electronic applications accepted.

Purdue University, College of Engineering, School of Mechanical Engineering, West Lafayette, IN 47907-2088. Offers MS, MSE, MSME, PhD, Certificate. *Program availability:* Part-time, online learning. *Faculty:* 84. *Students:* 624. Terminal master's awarded for partial completion of doctoral program. *Degree requirements:* For master's, thesis optional; for doctorate, thesis/dissertation. *Application deadline:* For fall admission, 12/15 for domestic and international students; for spring admission, 9/15 for domestic and international students. Applications are processed on a rolling basis. Application fee: $60 ($75 for international students). Electronic applications accepted. *Financial support:* Fellowships with full and partial tuition reimbursements, research assistantships with full and partial tuition reimbursements, teaching assistantships with full and partial tuition reimbursements, career-related internships or fieldwork, scholarships/grants, health care benefits, and unspecified assistantships available. *Unit head:* Eckhard Groll, Department Head, E-mail: groll@purdue.edu. *Application contact:* Xiaomin Qian, Graduate Administrator, 765-494-0231, E-mail: xiaomin@purdue.edu.
Website: https://engineering.purdue.edu/ME/

Purdue University Fort Wayne, College of Engineering, Technology, and Computer Science, Department of Civil and Mechanical Engineering, Fort Wayne, IN 46805-1499. Offers civil engineering (MSE); mechanical engineering (MSE). *Program availability:* Part-time. *Entrance requirements:* For master's, minimum GPA of 3.0, bachelor's degree in engineering discipline. Additional exam requirements/recommendations for international students: required—TOEFL (minimum score 550 paper-based; 79 iBT); recommended—TWE. Electronic applications accepted.

Purdue University Northwest, Graduate Studies Office, School of Engineering, Mathematics, and Science, Department of Engineering, Hammond, IN 46323-2094. Offers computer engineering (MSE); electrical engineering (MSE); engineering (MS); mechanical engineering (MSE). *Program availability:* Evening/weekend. *Entrance requirements:* Additional exam requirements/recommendations for international students: required—TOEFL.

Queen's University at Kingston, School of Graduate Studies, Faculty of Engineering and Applied Science, Department of Mechanical and Materials Engineering, Kingston, ON K7L 3N6, Canada. Offers M Eng, M Sc, M Sc Eng, PhD. *Program availability:* Part-time. *Degree requirements:* For master's, thesis optional; for doctorate, comprehensive exam, thesis/dissertation. *Entrance requirements:* Additional exam requirements/recommendations for international students: required—TOEFL. Electronic applications accepted.

Rensselaer at Hartford, Department of Engineering, Program in Mechanical Engineering, Hartford, CT 06120-2991. Offers ME, MS. *Program availability:* Part-time, evening/weekend. *Degree requirements:* For master's, thesis optional. *Entrance requirements:* For master's, GRE. Additional exam requirements/recommendations for international students: required—TOEFL (minimum score 600 paper-based; 100 iBT).

Rensselaer Polytechnic Institute, Graduate School, School of Engineering, Program in Mechanical Engineering, Troy, NY 12180-3590. Offers M Eng, MS, D Eng, PhD. *Faculty:* 55 full-time (6 women), 1 part-time/adjunct (0 women). *Students:* 118 full-time (23 women), 41 part-time (7 women); includes 28 minority (4 Black or African American, non-Hispanic/Latino; 13 Asian, non-Hispanic/Latino; 5 Hispanic/Latino; 6 Two or more races, non-Hispanic/Latino), 71 international. Average age 26. 211 applicants, 49% accepted, 46 enrolled. In 2019, 35 master's, 24 doctorates awarded. *Degree requirements:* For master's, thesis (for some programs); for doctorate, thesis/dissertation. *Entrance requirements:* For master's and doctorate, GRE. Additional exam requirements/recommendations for international students: required—TOEFL (minimum score 600 paper-based; 100 iBT), IELTS (minimum score 7), PTE (minimum score 68). *Application deadline:* For fall admission, 1/1 priority date for domestic and international students; for spring admission, 8/15 priority date for domestic and international students. Applications are processed on a rolling basis. Application fee: $75. Electronic applications accepted. *Financial support:* In 2019–20, research assistantships (averaging $23,000 per year), teaching assistantships (averaging $23,000 per year) were awarded; fellowships also available. Financial award application deadline: 1/1. *Unit head:* Dr. Theo Borca-Tasciuc, Graduate Program Director, 518-276-2627, E-mail: borcat@rpi.edu. *Application contact:* Jarron Decker, Director of Graduate Admissions, 518-276-6216, Fax: 518-276-4072, E-mail: gradadmissions@rpi.edu.
Website: http://mane.rpi.edu/

Rice University, Graduate Programs, George R. Brown School of Engineering, Department of Mechanical Engineering and Materials Science, Houston, TX 77251-1892. Offers materials science (MMS, MS, PhD); mechanical engineering (MME, MS, PhD); MBA/ME. *Program availability:* Part-time. Terminal master's awarded for partial completion of doctoral program. *Degree requirements:* For master's, comprehensive exam, thesis; for doctorate, comprehensive exam, thesis/dissertation. *Entrance requirements:* For master's and doctorate, GRE General Test, minimum GPA of 3.0. Additional exam requirements/recommendations for international students: required—TOEFL (minimum score 600 paper-based; 90 iBT), IELTS (minimum score 7). Electronic applications accepted.

Rochester Institute of Technology, Graduate Enrollment Services, College of Applied Science and Technology, School of Engineering Technology, MS Program in Manufacturing and Mechanical Systems Integration, Rochester, NY 14623-5603. Offers MS. *Program availability:* Part-time, evening/weekend. *Degree requirements:* For master's, thesis (for some programs). *Entrance requirements:* For master's, GRE required for applicants with degrees from international universities, minimum GPA of 3.0 (recommended). Additional exam requirements/recommendations for international students: required—TOEFL (minimum score 550 paper-based; 80 iBT), IELTS (minimum score 6.5), PTE (minimum score 58). Electronic applications accepted.

Rochester Institute of Technology, Graduate Enrollment Services, Kate Gleason College of Engineering, Mechanical Engineering Department, ME Program in Mechanical Engineering, Rochester, NY 14623-5603. Offers ME. *Program availability:* Part-time. *Degree requirements:* For master's, Internship or Project with paper options. *Entrance requirements:* For master's, GRE, minimum GPA of 3.0 (recommended), 2 letters of recommendation. Additional exam requirements/recommendations for international students: required—TOEFL (minimum score 550 paper-based; 79 iBT), IELTS (minimum score 6.5), PTE (minimum score 58). Electronic applications accepted.

Rochester Institute of Technology, Graduate Enrollment Services, Kate Gleason College of Engineering, Mechanical Engineering Department, MS Program in Mechanical Engineering, Rochester, NY 14623-5603. Offers MS. *Program availability:* Part-time. *Degree requirements:* For master's, thesis. *Entrance requirements:* For master's, GRE, minimum GPA of 3.0 (recommended), 2 letters of recommendation. Additional exam requirements/recommendations for international students: required—TOEFL (minimum score 550 paper-based; 79 iBT), IELTS (minimum score 6.5), PTE (minimum score 58). Electronic applications accepted.

Rose-Hulman Institute of Technology, Graduate Studies, Department of Mechanical Engineering, Terre Haute, IN 47803-3999. Offers M Eng, MS. *Program availability:* Part-time. *Faculty:* 27 full-time (6 women). *Students:* 2 applicants, 50% accepted. In 2019, 4 master's awarded. *Degree requirements:* For master's, thesis (for some programs). *Entrance requirements:* For master's, GRE, minimum GPA of 3.0. Additional exam requirements/recommendations for international students: required—TOEFL (minimum score 580 paper-based; 94 iBT), IELTS (minimum score 7). *Application deadline:* For fall admission, 2/1 priority date for domestic and international students; for winter admission, 10/1 for domestic students, 4/1 for international students; for spring admission, 1/15 for domestic students, 11/1 for international students. Applications are processed on a rolling basis. Application fee: $75. Electronic applications accepted. *Financial support:* Fellowships with tuition reimbursements, research assistantships with tuition reimbursements, institutionally sponsored loans, scholarships/grants, tuition waivers (full and partial), and unspecified assistantships available. *Unit head:* Dr. Richard Onyancha, Department Head, 812-877-8601, Fax: 812-877-3198, E-mail: onyancha@rose-hulman.edu. *Application contact:* Dr. Craig Downing, Associate Dean of Lifelong Learning, 812-877-8822, E-mail: downing@rose-hulman.edu.
Website: https://www.rose-hulman.edu/academics/academic-departments/mechanical-engineering/index.html

Rowan University, Graduate School, College of Engineering, Department of Mechanical Engineering, Glassboro, NJ 08028-1701. Offers MS. Electronic applications accepted. *Expenses: Tuition, area resident:* Part-time $715.50 per semester hour. Tuition, state resident: part-time $715.50 per semester hour. Tuition, nonresident: part-time $715.50 per semester hour. *Required fees:* $161.55 per semester hour.

Royal Military College of Canada, Division of Graduate Studies, Faculty of Engineering, Department of Mechanical Engineering, Kingston, ON K7K 7B4, Canada. Offers M Eng, MA Sc, PhD. *Degree requirements:* For master's, thesis; for doctorate, comprehensive exam, thesis/dissertation. *Entrance requirements:* For master's, honours degree with second-class standing; for doctorate, master's degree. Electronic applications accepted.

Rutgers University - New Brunswick, Graduate School-New Brunswick, Program in Mechanical and Aerospace Engineering, Piscataway, NJ 08854-8097. Offers design and control (MS, PhD); fluid mechanics (MS, PhD); solid mechanics (MS, PhD); thermal sciences (MS, PhD). *Program availability:* Part-time, evening/weekend. *Degree requirements:* For master's, thesis (for some programs); for doctorate, thesis/dissertation. *Entrance requirements:* For master's, GRE General Test, BS in mechanical/aerospace engineering or related field; for doctorate, GRE General Test, MS in mechanical/aerospace engineering or related field. Additional exam requirements/recommendations for international students: required—TOEFL. Electronic applications accepted.

Saint Martin's University, Office of Graduate Studies, Program in Mechanical Engineering, Lacey, WA 98503. Offers MME. *Program availability:* Part-time. *Students:* 7 full-time (1 woman), 2 part-time (0 women); includes 2 minority (1 Hispanic/Latino; 1 Two or more races, non-Hispanic/Latino), 2 international. Average age 30. In 2019, 5 master's awarded. *Degree requirements:* For master's, thesis optional. *Entrance requirements:* For master's, official transcripts from all colleges and universities attended, three letters of recommendation (preferably from professors, registered engineers or supervisors). Additional exam requirements/recommendations for international students: required—TOEFL (minimum score 550 paper-based; 79 iBT); recommended—IELTS (minimum score 6.5). *Application deadline:* For fall admission, 4/1 priority date for domestic and international students; for spring admission, 11/1 priority date for domestic and international students. Applications are processed on a rolling basis. Application fee: $50. Electronic applications accepted. *Expenses: Tuition:* Full-time $22,950; part-time $15,300 per year. Tuition and fees vary according to course level, course load, degree level, campus/location and program. *Financial support:* Unspecified assistantships available. Financial award application deadline: 3/1; financial award applicants required to submit FAFSA. *Unit head:* Dr. Shawn Duan, Chair, Mechanical Engineering, 360-688-2745, E-mail: sduan@stmartin.edu. *Application contact:* Timothy Greer, Graduate Admissions Recruiter, 360-412-6128, E-mail: tgreer@stmartin.edu.
Website: https://www.stmartin.edu

San Diego State University, Graduate and Research Affairs, College of Engineering, Department of Mechanical Engineering, San Diego, CA 92182. Offers engineering sciences and applied mechanics (PhD); manufacture and design (MS); mechanical engineering (MS). *Program availability:* Evening/weekend. *Degree requirements:* For master's, comprehensive exam (for some programs), thesis (for some programs); for doctorate, thesis/dissertation. *Entrance requirements:* For master's, GRE General Test; for doctorate, GRE, 3 letters of recommendation. Additional exam requirements/recommendations for international students: required—TOEFL. Electronic applications accepted.

San Jose State University, Program in Mechanical and Aerospace Engineering, San Jose, CA 95192-0087. Offers aerospace engineering (MS); mechanical engineering (MS). *Program availability:* Part-time, evening/weekend. *Faculty:* 15 full-time (4 women), 13 part-time/adjunct (0 women). *Students:* Average age 27. 113 applicants, 69% accepted, 51 enrolled. In 2019, 56 master's awarded. *Degree requirements:* For master's, thesis. *Entrance requirements:* For master's, GRE required only if undergraduate degree is not from an accredited U.S./Canadian university. Combined score in Verbal and Quantitative must be equal or greater than 310, and Analytical Writing Score must be 3.0 or above., BS in Mechanical Engineering or closely related STEM field. A 2.5 institutional GPA (from the 0.0-4.0 U.S. grading scale) in the last degree completed, or a 2.5 GPA in the last two years of full time study. Additional exam requirements/recommendations for international students: required—TOEFL (minimum score 550 paper-based; 80 iBT), IELTS (minimum score 6.5), PTE (minimum score 53), International students must only take one required test. *Application deadline:* For fall admission, 6/1 for domestic students, 5/1 for international students; for spring admission, 12/1 for domestic students, 11/1 for international students. Applications are processed on a rolling basis. Application fee: $150. Electronic applications accepted. *Expenses: Tuition, area resident:* Full-time $7176; part-time $4164. Tuition, state resident: full-time $7176; part-time $4164. Tuition, nonresident: full-time $7176; part-time $4165 per credit hour. *International tuition:* $7176 full-time. *Required fees:* $2110; $2110. *Financial support:* In 2019–20, 14 teaching assistantships with full and partial tuition reimbursements (averaging $6,400 per year) were awarded; scholarships/grants also available. *Unit head:* Dr. Nicole Okamoto, Department Chair, 408-924-4054, E-mail: nicole.okamoto@sjsu.edu. *Application contact:* Dr. Nicole Okamoto, Department Chair, 408-924-4054, E-mail: nicole.okamoto@sjsu.edu.
Website: http://www.sjsu.edu/me/

Santa Clara University, School of Engineering, Santa Clara, CA 95053. Offers applied mathematics (MS); bioengineering (MS); civil, environmental, and sustainable engineering (MS); computer science and engineering (MS, PhD, Engineer); electrical engineering (MS, PhD, Engineer); engineering management and leadership (MS); mechanical engineering (MS, PhD, Engineer); power systems and sustainable energy (MS); software engineering (MS). *Program availability:* Part-time. *Entrance requirements:* For master's, GRE, official transcript; for doctorate, GRE, Official transcript, 500 word statement of purpose, three letters of recommendation. Additional exam requirements/recommendations for international students: required—TOEFL (minimum score 79 iBT), IELTS (minimum score 6.5). Electronic applications accepted.

Simon Fraser University, Office of Graduate Studies and Postdoctoral Fellows, Faculty of Applied Sciences, School of Mechatronic Systems Engineering, Burnaby, BC V5A 1S6, Canada. Offers MA Sc, PhD. *Degree requirements:* For master's, one foreign language, thesis; for doctorate, one foreign language, comprehensive exam, thesis/dissertation. *Entrance requirements:* Additional exam requirements/recommendations for international students: required—TOEFL (minimum score 580 paper-based; 93 iBT), IELTS (minimum score 7), TWE (minimum score 5). Electronic applications accepted.

South Carolina State University, College of Graduate and Professional Studies, Department of Civil and Mechanical Engineering Technology, Orangeburg, SC 29117-0001. Offers transportation (MS). *Program availability:* Part-time, evening/weekend. *Degree requirements:* For master's, comprehensive exam, thesis, departmental qualifying exam. *Entrance requirements:* For master's, GRE. Additional exam requirements/recommendations for international students: recommended—TOEFL. Electronic applications accepted.

South Dakota School of Mines and Technology, Graduate Division, Department of Mechanical Engineering, Rapid City, SD 57701-3995. Offers MS, PhD. *Program availability:* Part-time. *Degree requirements:* For master's, thesis (for some programs); for doctorate, thesis/dissertation. *Entrance requirements:* For master's, GRE General Test. Additional exam requirements/recommendations for international students: required—TOEFL (minimum score 520 paper-based; 68 iBT), TWE. Electronic applications accepted.

South Dakota State University, Graduate School, Jerome J. Lohr College of Engineering, Department of Mechanical Engineering, Brookings, SD 57007. Offers agricultural, biosystems and mechanical engineering (PhD); mechanical engineering (MS). *Program availability:* Part-time. *Degree requirements:* For master's, thesis (for some programs), oral exam. *Entrance requirements:* Additional exam requirements/recommendations for international students: required—TOEFL (minimum score 525 paper-based; 71 iBT).

Southern Illinois University Carbondale, Graduate School, College of Engineering, Department of Mechanical Engineering and Energy Processes, Carbondale, IL 62901-4701. Offers engineering sciences (PhD), including mechanical engineering and energy processes; mechanical engineering (MS). *Degree requirements:* For master's, comprehensive exam, thesis or alternative. *Entrance requirements:* For master's, GRE General Test, minimum GPA of 2.7. Additional exam requirements/recommendations for international students: required—TOEFL.

Southern Illinois University Carbondale, Graduate School, College of Engineering, Program in Engineering Science, Carbondale, IL 62901-4701. Offers engineering science (PhD), including civil and environmental engineering, electrical and computer engineering, mechanical engineering and energy processes, mining and mineral resources engineering. *Degree requirements:* For doctorate, thesis/dissertation. *Entrance requirements:* For doctorate, GRE General Test, minimum GPA of 3.5. Additional exam requirements/recommendations for international students: required—TOEFL.

Southern Illinois University Edwardsville, Graduate School, School of Engineering, Department of Mechanical and Industrial Engineering, Program in Mechanical Engineering, Edwardsville, IL 62026. Offers MS. *Program availability:* Part-time, evening/weekend. *Degree requirements:* For master's, comprehensive exam (for some programs), thesis (for some programs). *Entrance requirements:* Additional exam requirements/recommendations for international students: required—TOEFL (minimum score 550 paper-based; 79 iBT), IELTS (minimum score 6.5). Electronic applications accepted.

Southern Methodist University, Lyle School of Engineering, Department of Mechanical Engineering, Dallas, TX 75205. Offers manufacturing systems management (MS); mechanical engineering (MS, PhD). *Program availability:* Part-time, evening/weekend, online learning. Terminal master's awarded for partial completion of doctoral program. *Degree requirements:* For master's, thesis optional; for doctorate, thesis/dissertation, oral and written qualifying exams, oral final exam. *Entrance requirements:* For master's, GRE General Test, minimum GPA of 3.0 in last 2 years; bachelor's degree in engineering, mathematics, or sciences; for doctorate, preliminary counseling exam, minimum graduate GPA of 3.0, bachelor's degree in related field. Additional exam requirements/recommendations for international students: required—TOEFL.

Stanford University, School of Engineering, Department of Mechanical Engineering, Stanford, CA 94305-2004. Offers mechanical engineering (MS, PhD). *Expenses: Tuition:* Full-time $52,479; part-time $34,110 per unit. *Required fees:* $672; $224 per quarter. Tuition and fees vary according to program and student level.
Website: http://me.stanford.edu/

Stevens Institute of Technology, Graduate School, Charles V. Schaefer Jr. School of Engineering and Science, Department of Mechanical Engineering, Program in Mechanical Engineering, Hoboken, NJ 07030. Offers M Eng, PhD, Eng. *Program availability:* Part-time, evening/weekend. *Faculty:* 29 full-time (3 women), 11 part-time/adjunct (0 women). *Students:* 120 full-time (17 women), 34 part-time (5 women); includes 18 minority (1 Black or African American, non-Hispanic/Latino; 14 Asian, non-Hispanic/Latino; 3 Hispanic/Latino), 80 international. Average age 26. In 2019, 75 master's, 5 doctorates, 9 other advanced degrees awarded. Terminal master's awarded for partial completion of doctoral program. *Degree requirements:* For master's, thesis optional, minimum B average in major field and overall; for doctorate, comprehensive exam (for some programs), thesis/dissertation; for Eng, minimum B average. *Entrance requirements:* For master's, International applicants must submit TOEFL/IELTS scores and fulfill the English Language Proficiency Requirement. Applicants to full-time programs who do not qualify for a score waiver are required to submit GRE/GMAT scores. Additional exam requirements/recommendations for international students: required—TOEFL (minimum score 74 iBT), IELTS (minimum score 6). *Application deadline:* For fall admission, 4/15 for domestic and international students; for spring admission, 11/1 for domestic and international students; for summer admission, 5/1 for domestic students. Applications are processed on a rolling basis. Application fee: $60. Electronic applications accepted. *Expenses: Tuition:* Full-time $52,134. *Required fees:* $1880. Tuition and fees vary according to course load. *Financial support:* Fellowships, research assistantships, teaching assistantships, career-related internships or fieldwork, Federal Work-Study, scholarships/grants, and unspecified assistantships available. Financial award application deadline: 2/15; financial award applicants required to submit FAFSA. *Unit head:* Dr. Jean Zu, Dean of SES, 201-216.8233, Fax: 201-216.8372, E-mail: Jean.Zu@stevens.edu. *Application contact:* Graduate Admissions, 888-783-8367, Fax: 888-511-1306, E-mail: graduate@stevens.edu.

Stony Brook University, State University of New York, Graduate School, College of Engineering and Applied Sciences, Department of Mechanical Engineering, Stony Brook, NY 11794. Offers MS, PhD. *Program availability:* Part-time, evening/weekend. *Faculty:* 18 full-time (0 women), 4 part-time/adjunct (1 woman). *Students:* 107 full-time (14 women), 17 part-time (3 women); includes 37 minority (5 Black or African American, non-Hispanic/Latino; 22 Asian, non-Hispanic/Latino; 6 Hispanic/Latino; 1 Native Hawaiian or other Pacific Islander, non-Hispanic/Latino; 3 Two or more races, non-Hispanic/Latino), 60 international. Average age 25. 156 applicants, 65% accepted, 42 enrolled. In 2019, 97 master's, 13 doctorates awarded. Terminal master's awarded for partial completion of doctoral program. *Degree requirements:* For master's, thesis or alternative; for doctorate, comprehensive exam, thesis/dissertation. *Entrance requirements:* For master's, GRE General Test, minimum GPA of 3.0; for doctorate, GRE General Test, minimum GPA of 3.5. Additional exam requirements/recommendations for international students: required—TOEFL (minimum score 90 iBT). *Application deadline:* For fall admission, 1/15 for domestic students; for spring admission, 10/1 for domestic students. Application fee: $100. *Expenses:* Contact institution. *Financial support:* In 2019–20, 1 fellowship, 14 research assistantships, 17 teaching assistantships were awarded. *Unit head:* Dr. Jeffrey Q. Ge, Chair, 631-632-8305, Fax: 631-632-8544, E-mail: qiaode.ge@stonybrook.edu. *Application contact:* Dianna Berger, Coordinator, 631-632-8340, Fax: 631-632-8544, E-mail: mechanicaengineeringgraduate@stonybrook.edu.
Website: http://me.eng.sunysb.edu/

Syracuse University, College of Engineering and Computer Science, Programs in Mechanical and Aerospace Engineering, Syracuse, NY 13244. Offers MS, PhD. *Program availability:* Part-time. *Degree requirements:* For master's, project or thesis; for doctorate, comprehensive exam, thesis/dissertation. *Entrance requirements:* For master's and doctorate, GRE General Test, official transcripts, personal statement, three letters of recommendation, resume. Additional exam requirements/recommendations for international students: required—TOEFL (minimum score 100 iBT). Electronic applications accepted.

Temple University, College of Engineering, Department of Mechanical Engineering, Philadelphia, PA 19122. Offers MSME. *Program availability:* Part-time, evening/weekend. *Faculty:* 23 full-time (4 women), 7 part-time/adjunct. *Students:* 31 full-time (3 women), 2 part-time (0 women); includes 3 minority (1 Black or African American, non-Hispanic/Latino; 1 Asian, non-Hispanic/Latino; 1 Hispanic/Latino), 22 international. 68 applicants, 46% accepted, 12 enrolled. In 2019, 3 master's awarded. Terminal master's awarded for partial completion of doctoral program. *Degree requirements:* For master's, thesis optional. *Entrance requirements:* For master's, GRE General Test. Waivers are considered on a case by case basis for master's applicants., Competitive applicants to the master's programs should have an undergraduate GPA of at least 3.0 and GREs of at least the 50th percentile in each section. Applicants should also possess an undergraduate degree in engineering from an ABET accredited or equivalent institution. Also required: letters of rec, resume, personal statement. Additional exam requirements/recommendations for international students: required—TOEFL (minimum score 79 iBT), IELTS (minimum score 6.5). *Application deadline:* For fall admission, 6/1 priority date for domestic students, 3/1 priority date for international students; for spring admission, 11/1 priority date for domestic students, 8/1 priority date for international students. Applications are processed on a rolling basis. Application fee: $60. Electronic applications accepted. *Financial support:* In 2019–20, 1 fellowship with full tuition reimbursement (averaging $30,000 per year), 28 research assistantships with full tuition reimbursements (averaging $19,739 per year), 20 teaching assistantships with full tuition reimbursements (averaging $19,739 per year) were awarded. Financial award applicants required to submit FAFSA. *Unit head:* Dr. Kurosh Darvish, Chair, 215-204-4307, Fax: 215-204-6936, E-mail: kurosh.darvish@temple.edu. *Application contact:* Colleen Baillie, Director of Enrollment, 215-204-7800, Fax: 215-204-6936, E-mail: gradengr@temple.edu.
Website: http://engineering.temple.edu/department/mechanical-engineering

Tennessee State University, The School of Graduate Studies and Research, College of Engineering, Nashville, TN 37209-1561. Offers biomedical engineering (ME); civil engineering (ME); computer and information systems engineering (MS, PhD); electrical engineering (ME); environmental engineering (ME); manufacturing engineering (ME); mathematical sciences (MS); mechanical engineering (ME). *Program availability:* Part-time, evening/weekend. *Degree requirements:* For master's, project; for doctorate, comprehensive exam, thesis/dissertation. *Entrance requirements:* For doctorate, minimum GPA of 3.3.

Tennessee Technological University, College of Graduate Studies, College of Engineering, Department of Mechanical Engineering, Cookeville, TN 38505. Offers MS. *Program availability:* Part-time. *Faculty:* 25 full-time (2 women). *Students:* 9 full-time (2 women), 27 part-time (1 woman); includes 2 minority (1 Black or African American, non-Hispanic/Latino; 1 Asian, non-Hispanic/Latino), 7 international. 32 applicants, 69% accepted, 8 enrolled. In 2019, 11 master's awarded. *Degree requirements:* For master's, thesis. *Entrance requirements:* For master's, GRE. Additional exam requirements/recommendations for international students: required—TOEFL (minimum score 550 paper-based; 79 iBT), IELTS (minimum score 5.5), PTE (minimum score 53), or TOEIC (Test of English as an International Communication). *Application deadline:* For fall admission, 8/1 for domestic students, 5/1 for international students; for spring admission, 12/1 for domestic students, 10/1 for international students; for summer admission, 5/1 for domestic students, 2/1 for international students. Applications are processed on a rolling basis. Application fee: $35 ($40 for international students). Electronic applications accepted. *Expenses: Tuition, area resident:* Part-time $597 per credit hour. Tuition, state resident: part-time $597 per credit hour. Tuition, nonresident: part-time $1323 per credit hour. *Financial support:* Fellowships, research assistantships, and teaching assistantships available. Financial award application deadline: 4/1. *Unit head:* Dr. Mohan Rao, Chairperson, 931-372-3254, Fax: 931-372-6340, E-mail: mrao@tntech.edu. *Application contact:* Shelia K. Kendrick, Coordinator of Graduate Studies, 931-372-3808, Fax: 931-372-3497, E-mail: skendrick@tntech.edu.

Texas A&M University, College of Engineering, J. Mike Walker '66 Department of Mechanical Engineering, College Station, TX 77843. Offers mechanical engineering (PhD). *Faculty:* 63. *Students:* 416 full-time (54 women), 82 part-time (10 women); includes 50 minority (6 Black or African American, non-Hispanic/Latino; 17 Asian, non-Hispanic/Latino; 22 Hispanic/Latino; 5 Two or more races, non-Hispanic/Latino), 329 international. Average age 27. 889 applicants, 44% accepted, 146 enrolled. In 2019, 88 master's, 47 doctorates awarded. *Degree requirements:* For master's, comprehensive exam (for some programs), thesis optional; for doctorate, comprehensive exam, thesis/dissertation. *Entrance requirements:* For master's and doctorate, GRE General Test, letters of recommendation. Additional exam requirements/recommendations for international students: required—TOEFL (minimum score 570 paper-based; 80 iBT), IELTS (minimum score 6), PTE (minimum score 53). *Application deadline:* For fall admission, 4/1 for domestic students, 3/1 for international students; for spring admission, 10/1 for domestic students, 9/1 for international students. Applications are processed on a rolling basis. Application fee: $65 ($90 for international students). Electronic applications accepted. *Expenses:* Contact institution. *Financial support:* In 2019–20, 408 students received support, including 92 fellowships with tuition

reimbursements available (averaging $6,492 per year), 260 research assistantships with tuition reimbursements available (averaging $15,249 per year), 123 teaching assistantships with tuition reimbursements available (averaging $12,148 per year); career-related internships or fieldwork, institutionally sponsored loans, scholarships/ grants, traineeships, health care benefits, tuition waivers (full and partial), and unspecified assistantships also available. Support available to part-time students. Financial award application deadline: 3/15; financial award applicants required to submit FAFSA. *Unit head:* Dr. Andreas A. Polycarpou, Department Head, 979-458-6631, E-mail: apolycarpou@tamu.edu. *Application contact:* Dr. Harry Hogan, Associate Dean for Graduate Programs, 979-845-1538, E-mail: hhogan@tamu.edu.
Website: http://engineering.tamu.edu/mechanical

Texas A&M University–Kingsville, College of Graduate Studies, Frank H. Dotterweich College of Engineering, Department of Mechanical and Industrial Engineering, Program in Mechanical Engineering, Kingsville, TX 78363. Offers ME, MS. *Degree requirements:* For master's, variable foreign language requirement, comprehensive exam, thesis (for some programs). *Entrance requirements:* For master's, GRE (minimum score quantitative and verbal 950 on old scale), MAT, GMAT, minimum GPA 2.6. Additional exam requirements/recommendations for international students: required—TOEFL (minimum score 550 paper-based; 79 iBT). Electronic applications accepted.

Texas State University, The Graduate College, College of Science and Engineering, Program in Engineering, San Marcos, TX 78666. Offers civil engineering (MS); electrical engineering (MS); industrial engineering (MS); mechanical and manufacturing engineering (MS). *Program availability:* Part-time. *Degree requirements:* For master's, comprehensive exam, thesis (for some programs), thesis or research project. *Entrance requirements:* For master's, official GRE (general test only) required with competitive scores in the verbal reasoning and quantitative reasoning sections, baccalaureate degree from regionally-accredited university in engineering, computer science, physics, technology, or closely-related field with minimum GPA of 3.0 on last 60 undergraduate semester hours; resume or curriculum vitae; 2 letters of recommendation; statement of purpose conveying research interest and professional aspirations. Additional exam requirements/recommendations for international students: required—TOEFL (minimum score 550 paper-based; 78 iBT), IELTS (minimum score 6.5). Electronic applications accepted.

Tufts University, School of Engineering, Department of Mechanical Engineering, Medford, MA 02155. Offers human factors (MS); mechanical engineering (MS, PhD); PhD/PhD. *Program availability:* Part-time. Terminal master's awarded for partial completion of doctoral program. *Degree requirements:* For master's, thesis; for doctorate, thesis/dissertation. *Entrance requirements:* For master's and doctorate, GRE General Test. Additional exam requirements/recommendations for international students: required—TOEFL (minimum score 550 paper-based; 80 iBT), IELTS (minimum score 6.5). Electronic applications accepted. Full-time tuition and fees vary according to degree level, program and student level. Part-time tuition and fees vary according to course load.

Tuskegee University, Graduate Programs, College of Engineering, Department of Mechanical Engineering, Tuskegee, AL 36088. Offers MSME. *Degree requirements:* For master's, thesis or alternative. *Entrance requirements:* For master's, GRE General Test, GRE Subject Test. Additional exam requirements/recommendations for international students: required—TOEFL (minimum score 500 paper-based).

Universidad del Turabo, Graduate Programs, School of Engineering, Gurabo, PR 00778-3030. Offers computer engineering (M Eng); electrical engineering (M Eng); mechanical engineering (M Eng); telecommunications and network systems administration (M Eng). *Entrance requirements:* For master's, GRE, EXADEP or GMAT, interview, essay, official transcript, recommendation letters. Electronic applications accepted.

Université de Moncton, Faculty of Engineering, Program in Mechanical Engineering, Moncton, NB E1A 3E9, Canada. Offers M Sc A. *Degree requirements:* For master's, thesis, proficiency in French.

Université de Sherbrooke, Faculty of Engineering, Department of Mechanical Engineering, Sherbrooke, QC J1K 2R1, Canada. Offers M Sc A, PhD. *Degree requirements:* For master's, one foreign language, thesis; for doctorate, comprehensive exam, thesis/dissertation. *Entrance requirements:* For master's, bachelor's degree in engineering or equivalent; for doctorate, master's degree in engineering or equivalent. Electronic applications accepted.

University at Buffalo, the State University of New York, Graduate School, School of Engineering and Applied Sciences, Department of Mechanical and Aerospace Engineering, Buffalo, NY 14260. Offers aerospace engineering (MS, PhD); mechanical engineering (MS, PhD). *Program availability:* Part-time. Terminal master's awarded for partial completion of doctoral program. *Degree requirements:* For master's, comprehensive exam, project or thesis; for doctorate, thesis/dissertation. *Entrance requirements:* For master's and doctorate, GRE General Test, GRE Subject Test. Additional exam requirements/recommendations for international students: required—TOEFL (minimum score 79 iBT). Electronic applications accepted. *Expenses: Tuition, area resident:* Full-time $11,310; part-time $471 per credit hour. Tuition, state resident: full-time $11,310; part-time $471 per credit hour. Tuition, nonresident: full-time $23,100; part-time $963 per credit hour. *International tuition:* $23,100 full-time. *Required fees:* $2820.

The University of Akron, Graduate School, College of Engineering, Department of Mechanical Engineering, Akron, OH 44325. Offers engineering (PhD); mechanical engineering (MS). *Program availability:* Part-time, evening/weekend. Terminal master's awarded for partial completion of doctoral program. *Degree requirements:* For master's, thesis optional; for doctorate, one foreign language, thesis/dissertation, candidacy exam, qualifying exam. *Entrance requirements:* For master's, GRE, minimum GPA of 2.75, baccalaureate degree in engineering, three letters of recommendation, statement of purpose; for doctorate, GRE, minimum GPA of 3.0 with bachelor's degree, 3.5 with master's degree; three letters of recommendation; statement of purpose; resume. Additional exam requirements/recommendations for international students: required—TOEFL (minimum score 79 iBT), IELTS (minimum score 6.5). Electronic applications accepted.

The University of Alabama, Graduate School, College of Engineering, Department of Mechanical Engineering, Tuscaloosa, AL 35487. Offers MS, PhD. *Program availability:* Part-time, online learning. *Faculty:* 27 full-time (0 women). *Students:* 92 full-time (13 women), 32 part-time (4 women); includes 13 minority (6 Black or African American, non-Hispanic/Latino; 4 Hispanic/Latino; 3 Two or more races, non-Hispanic/Latino), 34 international. Average age 28. 114 applicants, 75% accepted, 26 enrolled. In 2019, 20 master's, 8 doctorates awarded. Terminal master's awarded for partial completion of doctoral program. *Degree requirements:* For master's, comprehensive exam, thesis (for some programs); for doctorate, comprehensive exam, thesis/dissertation. *Entrance requirements:* For master's, GRE General Test, minimum GPA of 3.0; for doctorate, GRE General Test, minimum GPA of 3.0 with MS, 3.3 without MS. Additional exam requirements/recommendations for international students: required—TOEFL (minimum score 600 paper-based). *Application deadline:* Applications are processed on a rolling basis. Application fee: $50 ($60 for international students). Electronic applications accepted. *Expenses: Tuition, area resident:* Full-time $10,780; part-time $440 per credit hour. Tuition, nonresident: full-time $30,250; part-time $1550 per credit hour. *Financial support:* In 2019–20, 50 students received support. Fellowships with full tuition reimbursements available, research assistantships with full tuition reimbursements available, teaching assistantships with full tuition reimbursements available, career-related internships or fieldwork, health care benefits, and unspecified assistantships available. *Unit head:* Dr. Nader Jalili, Professor and Interim Head, 205-348-1645, Fax: 205-348-6419, E-mail: njalili@ua.edu. *Application contact:* Dr. Steve Shepard, Graduate Program Coordinator/Professor, 205-348-1650, Fax: 205-348-6419, E-mail: sshepard@eng.ua.edu.
Website: http://www.me.ua.edu

The University of Alabama at Birmingham, School of Engineering, Program in Mechanical Engineering, Birmingham, AL 35294. Offers mechanical engineering (MSME). *Faculty:* 5 full-time (0 women), 3 part-time/adjunct (1 woman). *Students:* 15 full-time (1 woman), 20 part-time (3 women); includes 4 minority (2 Black or African American, non-Hispanic/Latino; 1 Asian, non-Hispanic/Latino; 1 Hispanic/Latino), 23 international. 37 applicants, 49% accepted, 6 enrolled. In 2019, 23 master's awarded. *Degree requirements:* For master's, thesis (for some programs). *Entrance requirements:* For master's, GRE general test is required for all applicants who did not receive a BS degree from a program accredited by the Engineering Accreditation Committee of ABET http://www.abet.org, or from other programs with reciprocal agreement under the Washington Accord http://www.ieagreements.org/accords/washington/., minimum GPA of 3.0 overall or over last 60 semester hours of earned credit. Additional exam requirements/recommendations for international students: required—TOEFL (minimum score 80 iBT); recommended—IELTS (minimum score 6.5). *Application deadline:* For fall admission, 8/1 for domestic and international students; for spring admission, 12/1 for domestic and international students; for summer admission, 5/1 for domestic and international students. Applications are processed on a rolling basis. Application fee: $50 ($60 for international students). Electronic applications accepted. *Financial support:* In 2019–20, 12 students received support, including 1 fellowship with full tuition reimbursement available (averaging $29,004 per year), 3 research assistantships with full tuition reimbursements available (averaging $18,532 per year), 8 teaching assistantships. *Unit head:* Dr. David Littlefield, Graduate Program Director, 205-934-8460, E-mail: littlefield@uab.edu. *Application contact:* Jesse Keppley, Director of Academic and Student Services, 205-996-5696, E-mail: gradschool@uab.edu.
Website: http://www.uab.edu/engineering/home/departments-research/me/graduate

The University of Alabama in Huntsville, School of Graduate Studies, College of Engineering, Department of Chemical and Materials Engineering, Huntsville, AL 35899. Offers biotechnology science and engineering (PhD); chemical and materials engineering (MSE); materials science (PhD); mechanical engineering (PhD), including chemical engineering. *Program availability:* Part-time. *Degree requirements:* For master's, comprehensive exam, thesis or alternative, oral and written exams; for doctorate, comprehensive exam, thesis/dissertation. *Entrance requirements:* For master's, GRE General Test, appropriate bachelor's degree, minimum GPA of 3.0; for doctorate, GRE General Test, minimum GPA of 3.0. Additional exam requirements/ recommendations for international students: required—TOEFL (minimum score 500 paper-based; 80 iBT), IELTS (minimum score 6.5). Electronic applications accepted.

The University of Alabama in Huntsville, School of Graduate Studies, College of Engineering, Department of Mechanical and Aerospace Engineering, Huntsville, AL 35899. Offers aerospace systems engineering (MS, PhD). *Program availability:* Part-time. *Degree requirements:* For master's, comprehensive exam, thesis or alternative, oral and written exams; for doctorate, comprehensive exam, thesis/dissertation, oral and written exams. *Entrance requirements:* For master's, GRE General Test, BSE, minimum GPA of 3.0; for doctorate, GRE General Test, minimum GPA of 3.0. Additional exam requirements/recommendations for international students: required—TOEFL (minimum score 500 paper-based; 80 iBT), IELTS (minimum score 6.5). Electronic applications accepted.

University of Alaska Fairbanks, College of Engineering and Mines, Department of Mechanical Engineering, Fairbanks, AK 99775-5905. Offers MS. *Program availability:* Part-time. *Degree requirements:* For master's, comprehensive exam, oral defense of project or thesis. *Entrance requirements:* For master's, GRE General Test, bachelor's degree from accredited institution with minimum cumulative undergraduate and major GPA of 3.0. Additional exam requirements/recommendations for international students: required—TOEFL (minimum score 550 paper-based; 79 iBT), IELTS (minimum score 6.5). Electronic applications accepted. *Expenses:* Contact institution.

University of Alberta, Faculty of Graduate Studies and Research, Department of Mechanical Engineering, Edmonton, AB T6G 2E1, Canada. Offers engineering management (M Eng); mechanical engineering (M Eng, M Sc, PhD); MBA/M Eng. *Program availability:* Part-time. *Degree requirements:* For master's, thesis; for doctorate, thesis/dissertation. *Entrance requirements:* For master's and doctorate, minimum GPA of 7.0 on a 9.0 scale. Additional exam requirements/recommendations for international students: required—TOEFL (minimum score 580 paper-based).

The University of Arizona, College of Engineering, Department of Aerospace and Mechanical Engineering, Tucson, AZ 85721. Offers aerospace engineering (MS, PhD); mechanical engineering (MS, PhD). *Program availability:* Part-time. *Degree requirements:* For master's, thesis or alternative; for doctorate, thesis/dissertation. *Entrance requirements:* For master's, GRE General Test, 3 letters of recommendation; for doctorate, GRE General Test, 3 letters of recommendation, statement of purpose. Additional exam requirements/recommendations for international students: required—TOEFL (minimum score 550 paper-based; 79 iBT). Electronic applications accepted.

University of Arkansas, Graduate School, College of Engineering, Department of Mechanical Engineering, Fayetteville, AR 72701. Offers MSE, MSME, PhD. *Program availability:* Part-time, online learning. *Students:* 41 full-time (5 women), 5 part-time (0 women); includes 4 minority (1 Asian, non-Hispanic/Latino; 3 Hispanic/Latino), 24 international. 32 applicants, 56% accepted. In 2019, 8 master's, 3 doctorates awarded. *Degree requirements:* For master's, thesis optional; for doctorate, one foreign language, thesis/dissertation. *Application deadline:* For fall admission, 8/1 for domestic students, 4/1 for international students; for spring admission, 12/1 for domestic students, 10/1 for international students; for summer admission, 4/15 for domestic students, 3/1 for international students. Applications are processed on a rolling basis. Application fee: $60. Electronic applications accepted. *Financial support:* In 2019–20, 16 research assistantships, 1 teaching assistantship were awarded; fellowships, career-related internships or fieldwork, and Federal Work-Study also available. Support available to part-time students. Financial award application deadline: 4/1; financial award applicants required to submit FAFSA. *Unit head:* Dr. Darin Nutter, Department Head, 479-575-4503, E-mail: dnutter@uark.edu. *Application contact:* Dr. Steve Tung, Graduate Programs Coordinator and Curriculum Committee Chair, 479-575-5557, E-mail: chstung@uark.edu.
Website: https://mechanical-engineering.uark.edu/

University of Bridgeport, School of Engineering, Department of Mechanical Engineering, Bridgeport, CT 06604. Offers MS. *Degree requirements:* For master's, thesis optional. *Entrance requirements:* Additional exam requirements/

recommendations for international students: recommended—TOEFL (minimum score 550 paper-based; 80 iBT), IELTS (minimum score 6.5). Electronic applications accepted.

The University of British Columbia, Faculty of Applied Science, Department of Mechanical Engineering, Vancouver, BC V6T 1Z4, Canada. Offers M Eng, MA Sc, PhD. *Degree requirements:* For master's, thesis; for doctorate, comprehensive exam, thesis/dissertation. *Entrance requirements:* For master's, bachelor's degree, minimum B+ average; for doctorate, master's degree, minimum B+ average. Additional exam requirements/recommendations for international students: required—TOEFL (minimum score 93 iBT), IELTS; recommended—TWE. Electronic applications accepted. *Expenses:* Contact institution.

University of Calgary, Faculty of Graduate Studies, Schulich School of Engineering, Program in Mechanical and Manufacturing Engineering, Calgary, AB T2N 1N4, Canada. Offers M Eng, M Sc, PhD. *Program availability:* Part-time. *Degree requirements:* For master's, thesis (for some programs); for doctorate, thesis/dissertation, candidacy exam. *Entrance requirements:* For master's, minimum GPA of 3.0; for doctorate, minimum GPA of 3.3. Additional exam requirements/recommendations for international students: required—TOEFL (minimum score 550 paper-based; 80 iBT), IELTS (minimum score 7).

University of California, Berkeley, Graduate Division, College of Engineering, Department of Mechanical Engineering, Berkeley, CA 94720. Offers M Eng, MS, PhD. Terminal master's awarded for partial completion of doctoral program. *Degree requirements:* For master's, comprehensive exam (for some programs), thesis (for some programs), comprehensive exam or thesis (MS); for doctorate, thesis/dissertation, preliminary and qualifying exams. *Entrance requirements:* For master's and doctorate, GRE General Test, minimum GPA of 3.0, 3 letters of recommendation. Additional exam requirements/recommendations for international students: required—TOEFL (minimum score 570 paper-based; 90 iBT). Electronic applications accepted.

University of California, Davis, College of Engineering, Program in Mechanical and Aeronautical Engineering, Davis, CA 95616. Offers aeronautical engineering (M Engr, MS, D Engr, PhD, Certificate); mechanical engineering (M Engr, MS, D Engr, PhD, Certificate); M Engr/MBA. *Degree requirements:* For master's, comprehensive exam (for some programs), thesis (for some programs); for doctorate, thesis/dissertation. *Entrance requirements:* For master's and doctorate, GRE General Test, minimum GPA of 3.0. Additional exam requirements/recommendations for international students: required—TOEFL (minimum score 550 paper-based). Electronic applications accepted.

University of California, Irvine, Samueli School of Engineering, Department of Mechanical and Aerospace Engineering, Irvine, CA 92697. Offers MS, PhD. *Program availability:* Part-time. *Students:* 158 full-time (40 women), 9 part-time (3 women); includes 37 minority (4 Black or African American, non-Hispanic/Latino; 20 Asian, non-Hispanic/Latino; 10 Hispanic/Latino; 3 Two or more races, non-Hispanic/Latino), 88 international. Average age 27. 531 applicants, 29% accepted, 46 enrolled. In 2019, 29 master's, 5 doctorates awarded. Terminal master's awarded for partial completion of doctoral program. *Entrance requirements:* For master's and doctorate, GRE General Test, minimum GPA of 3.0, 3 letters of recommendation. Additional exam requirements/recommendations for international students: required—TOEFL (minimum score 550 paper-based). *Application deadline:* For fall admission, 1/15 priority date for domestic students, 1/15 for international students. Applications are processed on a rolling basis. Application fee: $120 ($140 for international students). Electronic applications accepted. *Financial support:* Fellowships, research assistantships with full tuition reimbursements, teaching assistantships, institutionally sponsored loans, traineeships, health care benefits, and unspecified assistantships available. Financial award application deadline: 3/1; financial award applicants required to submit FAFSA. *Unit head:* Prof. Kenneth Mease, Chair, 949-824-5855, Fax: 949-824-8585, E-mail: kmease@uci.edu. *Application contact:* Prof. Roger Rangel, Graduate Admissions Advisor, 949-824-4033, Fax: 949-824-8585, E-mail: rhrangel@uci.edu.
Website: http://mae.eng.uci.edu/

University of California, Los Angeles, Graduate Division, Henry Samueli School of Engineering and Applied Science, Department of Mechanical and Aerospace Engineering, Program in Mechanical Engineering, Los Angeles, CA 90095-1597. Offers MS, PhD. *Degree requirements:* For master's, comprehensive exam or thesis; for doctorate, thesis/dissertation, qualifying exams. *Entrance requirements:* For master's, GRE General Test, minimum GPA of 3.0; for doctorate, GRE General Test, minimum GPA of 3.25. Additional exam requirements/recommendations for international students: required—TOEFL (minimum score 560 paper-based; 87 iBT), IELTS (minimum score 7). Electronic applications accepted.

University of California, Merced, Graduate Division, School of Engineering, Merced, CA 95343. Offers biological engineering and small scale technologies (MS, PhD); electrical engineering and computer science (MS, PhD); environmental systems (MS, PhD); management of innovation, sustainability, and technology (MM); mechanical engineering (MS, PhD). *Faculty:* 60 full-time (16 women). *Students:* 244 full-time (83 women), 1 (woman) part-time; includes 56 minority (2 Black or African American, non-Hispanic/Latino; 20 Asian, non-Hispanic/Latino; 30 Hispanic/Latino; 1 Native Hawaiian or other Pacific Islander, non-Hispanic/Latino; 3 Two or more races, non-Hispanic/Latino), 153 international. Average age 28. 330 applicants, 32% accepted, 67 enrolled. In 2019, 30 master's, 17 doctorates awarded. Terminal master's awarded for partial completion of doctoral program. *Degree requirements:* For master's, variable foreign language requirement, comprehensive exam, thesis or alternative, oral defense; for doctorate, variable foreign language requirement, comprehensive exam, thesis/dissertation, oral defense. *Entrance requirements:* For master's and doctorate, GRE. Additional exam requirements/recommendations for international students: required—TOEFL (minimum score 550 paper-based; 80 iBT); recommended—IELTS (minimum score 6.5). *Application deadline:* For fall admission, 1/15 for domestic and international students. Application fee: $105 ($125 for international students). Electronic applications accepted. *Expenses: Tuition, area resident:* Full-time $11,442; part-time $5721. Tuition, state resident: full-time $11,442; part-time $5721. Tuition, nonresident: full-time $26,544; part-time $13,272. *International tuition:* $26,544 full-time. *Required fees:* $564 per semester. *Financial support:* In 2019–20, 205 students received support, including 6 fellowships with full tuition reimbursements available (averaging $22,005 per year), 76 research assistantships with full tuition reimbursements available (averaging $21,420 per year), 123 teaching assistantships with full tuition reimbursements available (averaging $21,911 per year); scholarships/grants, traineeships, and health care benefits also available. *Unit head:* Dr. Mark Matsumoto, Dean, 209-228-4047, Fax: 209-228-4047, E-mail: mmatsumoto@ucmerced.edu. *Application contact:* Tsu Ya, Director of Admissions and Academic Services, 209-228-4521, Fax: 209-228-6906, E-mail: tya@ucmerced.edu.

University of California, Riverside, Graduate Division, Department of Mechanical Engineering, Riverside, CA 92521. Offers MS, PhD. *Program availability:* Part-time. Terminal master's awarded for partial completion of doctoral program. *Degree requirements:* For master's, comprehensive exam or thesis, seminar in mechanical engineering; for doctorate, comprehensive exam, thesis/dissertation, seminar in mechanical engineering. *Entrance requirements:* Additional exam requirements/recommendations for international students: required—TOEFL (minimum score 550 paper-based; 80 iBT).

University of California, San Diego, Graduate Division, Department of Mechanical and Aerospace Engineering, Program in Mechanical Engineering, La Jolla, CA 92093. Offers MS, PhD. *Students:* 226 full-time (40 women), 20 part-time (5 women). 806 applicants, 40% accepted, 93 enrolled. In 2019, 64 master's, 18 doctorates awarded. *Degree requirements:* For master's, comprehensive exam (for some programs), thesis (for some programs), comprehensive exam or thesis; for doctorate, comprehensive exam, thesis/dissertation. *Entrance requirements:* For master's and doctorate, GRE General Test, minimum GPA of 3.0. Additional exam requirements/recommendations for international students: required—TOEFL (minimum score 550 paper-based; 80 iBT), IELTS (minimum score 7). *Application deadline:* For fall admission, 12/18 for domestic students. Application fee: $105 ($125 for international students). Electronic applications accepted. *Financial support:* Fellowships, research assistantships, teaching assistantships, scholarships/grants, and unspecified assistantships available. Financial award applicants required to submit FAFSA. *Unit head:* Carlos Coimbra, Chair, 858-534-4285, E-mail: mae-chair-l@ucsd.edu. *Application contact:* Jackie Tam, Graduate Coordinator, 858-534-4387, E-mail: mae-gradadm-l@ucsd.edu.
Website: http://maeweb.ucsd.edu/

University of California, Santa Barbara, Graduate Division, College of Engineering, Department of Mechanical Engineering, Santa Barbara, CA 93106-5070. Offers bioengineering (PhD); mechanical engineering (MS); MS/PhD. Terminal master's awarded for partial completion of doctoral program. *Degree requirements:* For master's, thesis optional; for doctorate, comprehensive exam, thesis/dissertation. *Entrance requirements:* For master's and doctorate, GRE. Additional exam requirements/recommendations for international students: required—TOEFL (minimum score 550 paper-based; 80 iBT), IELTS (minimum score 7). Electronic applications accepted.

University of Central Florida, College of Engineering and Computer Science, Department of Mechanical and Aerospace Engineering, Program in Mechanical Engineering, Orlando, FL 32816. Offers MSME, PhD. *Students:* 147 full-time (12 women), 93 part-time (3 women); includes 67 minority (4 Black or African American, non-Hispanic/Latino; 18 Asian, non-Hispanic/Latino; 37 Hispanic/Latino; 8 Two or more races, non-Hispanic/Latino), 86 international. Average age 28. 242 applicants, 49% accepted, 78 enrolled. In 2019, 44 master's, 18 doctorates awarded. *Degree requirements:* For master's, thesis or alternative; for doctorate, thesis/dissertation, candidacy exam, departmental qualifying exam. *Entrance requirements:* For master's, goal statement, resume; for doctorate, GRE, letters of recommendation, goal statement, resume. Additional exam requirements/recommendations for international students: required—TOEFL. *Application deadline:* For fall admission, 7/15 for domestic students; for spring admission, 12/1 for domestic students. Application fee: $30. Electronic applications accepted. *Financial support:* In 2019–20, 109 students received support, including 32 fellowships with partial tuition reimbursements available (averaging $125,081 per year), 70 research assistantships with partial tuition reimbursements available (averaging $8,970 per year), 39 teaching assistantships with partial tuition reimbursements available (averaging $8,330 per year); career-related internships or fieldwork, institutionally sponsored loans, scholarships/grants, health care benefits, tuition waivers (partial), and unspecified assistantships also available. Financial award application deadline: 3/1; financial award applicants required to submit FAFSA. *Unit head:* Dr. Jihua Gou, Program Coordinator, 407-823-2155, E-mail: jihua.gou@ucf.edu. *Application contact:* Associate Director, Graduate Admissions, 407-823-2766, Fax: 407-823-6442, E-mail: gradadmissions@ucf.edu.
Website: http://mae.ucf.edu/academics/graduate/

University of Central Oklahoma, The Jackson College of Graduate Studies, College of Mathematics and Science, Department of Engineering and Physics, Edmond, OK 73034-5209. Offers engineering physics (MS), including biomedical engineering, electrical engineering, mechanical systems, physics. *Program availability:* Part-time. *Degree requirements:* For master's, thesis optional. *Entrance requirements:* For master's, GRE, 24 hours of course work in physics or equivalent, mathematics through differential equations, minimum GPA of 2.75 overall and 3.0 in last 60 hours attempted, two letters of recommendation. Additional exam requirements/recommendations for international students: required—TOEFL (minimum score 550 paper-based; 79 iBT), IELTS (minimum score 6.5). Electronic applications accepted.

University of Cincinnati, Graduate School, College of Engineering and Applied Science, Department of Mechanical and Materials Engineering, Program in Mechanical Engineering, Cincinnati, OH 45221. Offers MS, PhD. *Program availability:* Evening/weekend. Terminal master's awarded for partial completion of doctoral program. *Degree requirements:* For master's, oral exam or thesis defense; for doctorate, variable foreign language requirement, thesis/dissertation. *Entrance requirements:* For master's and doctorate, GRE General Test. Additional exam requirements/recommendations for international students: required—TOEFL (minimum score 575 paper-based). Electronic applications accepted.

University of Colorado Boulder, Graduate School, College of Engineering and Applied Science, Department of Mechanical Engineering, Boulder, CO 80309. Offers ME, MS, PhD. Terminal master's awarded for partial completion of doctoral program. *Degree requirements:* For master's, comprehensive exam, thesis optional; for doctorate, comprehensive exam, thesis/dissertation, final and preliminary exams. *Entrance requirements:* For master's and doctorate, minimum undergraduate GPA of 3.0. Additional exam requirements/recommendations for international students: required—TOEFL. Electronic applications accepted. Application fee is waived when completed online.

University of Colorado Denver, College of Engineering, Design and Computing, Department of Mechanical Engineering, Denver, CO 80217. Offers mechanical engineering (MS); mechanics (MS); thermal sciences (MS). *Program availability:* Part-time, evening/weekend. *Degree requirements:* For master's, comprehensive exam, 30 credit hours, project or thesis. *Entrance requirements:* For master's, GRE, three letters of recommendation, personal statement. Additional exam requirements/recommendations for international students: required—TOEFL (minimum score 537 paper-based; 75 iBT); recommended—IELTS (minimum score 6.8). Tuition and fees vary according to course load, program and reciprocity agreements.

University of Colorado Denver, College of Engineering, Design and Computing, Master of Engineering Program, Denver, CO 80217-3364. Offers civil engineering (M Eng), including civil engineering, geographic information systems, transportation systems; electrical engineering (M Eng); mechanical engineering (M Eng). *Program availability:* Part-time. *Entrance requirements:* For master's, GRE (for those with GPA below 2.75), transcripts, references, statement of purpose. Tuition and fees vary according to course load, program and reciprocity agreements.

University of Connecticut, Graduate School, School of Engineering, Department of Mechanical Engineering, Storrs, CT 06269. Offers MS, PhD. Terminal master's awarded for partial completion of doctoral program. *Degree requirements:* For master's, comprehensive exam, thesis or alternative; for doctorate, thesis/dissertation. *Entrance requirements:* For master's and doctorate, GRE General Test, GRE Subject Test.

Additional exam requirements/recommendations for international students: required—TOEFL (minimum score 550 paper-based). Electronic applications accepted.

University of Dayton, Department of Mechanical and Aerospace Engineering, Dayton, OH 45469. Offers aerospace engineering (MSAE, PhD); mechanical engineering (MSME, PhD); renewable and clean energy (MS). *Program availability:* Part-time, 100% online, blended/hybrid learning. *Degree requirements:* For master's, variable foreign language requirement, comprehensive exam (for some programs), thesis; for doctorate, variable foreign language requirement, comprehensive exam, thesis/dissertation, departmental qualifying exam. *Entrance requirements:* For master's, BS in engineering, math, or physics; minimum GPA of 3.0; for doctorate, GRE. Additional exam requirements/recommendations for international students: required—TOEFL (minimum score 550 paper-based; 80 iBT), IELTS (minimum score 6.5). Electronic applications accepted.

University of Delaware, College of Engineering, Department of Mechanical Engineering, Newark, DE 19716. Offers MEM, MSME, PhD. *Program availability:* Part-time. Terminal master's awarded for partial completion of doctoral program. *Degree requirements:* For master's, thesis (for some programs); for doctorate, thesis/dissertation. *Entrance requirements:* For master's and doctorate, GRE General Test. Additional exam requirements/recommendations for international students: required—TOEFL (minimum score 600 paper-based). Electronic applications accepted.

University of Denver, Daniel Felix Ritchie School of Engineering and Computer Science, Department of Mechanical and Materials Engineering, Denver, CO 80208. Offers bioengineering (MS); engineering (MS, PhD), including management; materials science (MS, PhD); mechanical engineering (MS, PhD). *Program availability:* Part-time. *Faculty:* 12 full-time (2 women), 3 part-time/adjunct (1 woman). *Students:* 3 full-time (1 woman), 35 part-time (9 women); includes 3 minority (1 Black or African American, non-Hispanic/Latino; 1 Asian, non-Hispanic/Latino; 1 Hispanic/Latino), 16 international. Average age 27. 58 applicants, 81% accepted, 18 enrolled. In 2019, 16 master's, 4 doctorates awarded. Terminal master's awarded for partial completion of doctoral program. *Degree requirements:* For master's, thesis optional; for doctorate, comprehensive exam, thesis/dissertation. *Entrance requirements:* For master's, GRE General Test, bachelor's degree in engineering or closely related field, transcripts, personal statement, resume or curriculum vitae, two letters of recommendation; for doctorate, GRE General Test, master's degree in engineering or closely related field, transcripts, personal statement, resume or curriculum vitae, two letters of recommendation, recommended that applicants find a research advisor before submitting the application. Additional exam requirements/recommendations for international students: required—TOEFL (minimum score 550 paper-based; 80 iBT). *Application deadline:* For fall admission, 1/15 priority date for domestic and international students; for winter admission, 10/25 for domestic and international students; for spring admission, 2/7 for domestic and international students; for summer admission, 4/24 for domestic and international students. Applications are processed on a rolling basis. Application fee: $65. Electronic applications accepted. *Unit head:* Dr. Matt Gordon, Professor and Chair, 303-871-3580, E-mail: matthew.gordon@du.edu. *Application contact:* Chrissy Alexander, Assistant to the Chair, 303-871-3041, E-mail: Christine.Alexander@du.edu.
Website: http://ritchieschool.du.edu/departments/mme/

University of Detroit Mercy, College of Engineering and Science, Detroit, MI 48221. Offers chemistry (MS); civil and environmental engineering (DE); electrical and computer engineering (ME); electrical engineering (DE); engineering management (M Eng Mgt); environmental engineering (MEE); mechanical engineering (MME, DE); product development (MS); software engineering (MSSE); teaching of mathematics (MATM). *Program availability:* Part-time, evening/weekend. *Degree requirements:* For doctorate, thesis/dissertation. Electronic applications accepted. Application fee is waived when completed online. *Expenses:* Contact institution.

University of Florida, Graduate School, Herbert Wertheim College of Engineering, Department of Mechanical and Aerospace Engineering, Gainesville, FL 32611. Offers aerospace engineering (ME, MS, PhD); mechanical engineering (ME, MS, PhD). *Program availability:* Part-time, online learning. *Degree requirements:* For master's, thesis (for some programs); for doctorate, comprehensive exam, thesis/dissertation. *Entrance requirements:* For master's and doctorate, minimum GPA of 3.0. Additional exam requirements/recommendations for international students: required—TOEFL (minimum score 550 paper-based; 80 iBT), IELTS (minimum score 6). Electronic applications accepted.

University of Hawaii at Manoa, Office of Graduate Education, College of Engineering, Department of Mechanical Engineering, Honolulu, HI 96822. Offers MS, PhD. *Program availability:* Part-time. *Degree requirements:* For master's, comprehensive exam, thesis; for doctorate, comprehensive exam, thesis/dissertation. *Entrance requirements:* For master's and doctorate, GRE General Test. Additional exam requirements/recommendations for international students: required—TOEFL (minimum score 550 paper-based; 79 iBT), IELTS (minimum score 5).

University of Houston, Cullen College of Engineering, Department of Mechanical Engineering, Houston, TX 77204. Offers MME, MSME, PhD. *Program availability:* Part-time. Terminal master's awarded for partial completion of doctoral program. *Degree requirements:* For master's, thesis (for some programs); for doctorate, thesis/dissertation, departmental qualifying exam. *Entrance requirements:* For master's and doctorate, GRE General Test. Additional exam requirements/recommendations for international students: required—TOEFL.

University of Idaho, College of Graduate Studies, College of Engineering, Department of Mechanical Engineering, Moscow, ID 83844-2282. Offers M Engr, MS, PhD. *Faculty:* 21. *Students:* 38 full-time, 21 part-time. Average age 29. In 2019, 14 master's, 2 doctorates awarded. *Entrance requirements:* For master's and doctorate, minimum GPA of 3.0. Additional exam requirements/recommendations for international students: required—TOEFL (minimum score 79 iBT). *Application deadline:* For fall admission, 7/30 for domestic students; for spring admission, 12/1 for domestic students. Applications are processed on a rolling basis. Application fee: $60. Electronic applications accepted. *Expenses:* Tuition, state resident: full-time $7753.80; part-time $502 per credit hour. Tuition, nonresident: full-time $26,990; part-time $1571 per credit hour. *Required fees:* $2122.20; $47 per credit hour. *Financial support:* Research assistantships and teaching assistantships available. Financial award applicants required to submit FAFSA. *Unit head:* Dr. Steven Beyerlein, Chair, 208-885-6579, E-mail: medept@uidaho.edu. *Application contact:* Dr. Steven Beyerlein, Chair, 208-885-6579, E-mail: medept@uidaho.edu.
Website: https://www.uidaho.edu/engr/departments/me

University of Illinois at Chicago, College of Engineering, Department of Mechanical and Industrial Engineering, Program in Mechanical Engineering, Chicago, IL 60607-7128. Offers fluids engineering (MS, PhD); mechanical analysis and design (MS, PhD); thermomechanical and power engineering (MS, PhD). *Program availability:* Part-time. *Degree requirements:* For master's, thesis. *Entrance requirements:* For master's, GRE General Test, minimum GPA of 2.75. Additional exam requirements/recommendations for international students: required—TOEFL. Electronic applications accepted. *Expenses:* Contact institution.

University of Illinois at Urbana-Champaign, Graduate College, College of Engineering, Department of Mechanical Science and Engineering, Champaign, IL 61820. Offers mechanical engineering (MS, PhD); theoretical and applied mechanics (MS, PhD). Terminal master's awarded for partial completion of doctoral program. *Entrance requirements:* Additional exam requirements/recommendations for international students: required—TOEFL (minimum score 613 paper-based; 103 iBT), IELTS (minimum score 7).

The University of Iowa, Graduate College, College of Engineering, Department of Mechanical Engineering, Iowa City, IA 52242-1316. Offers energy systems (MS, PhD); engineering design (MS, PhD); fluid dynamics (MS, PhD); materials and manufacturing (MS, PhD); wind energy (MS, PhD). Terminal master's awarded for partial completion of doctoral program. *Degree requirements:* For master's, oral exam or thesis; for doctorate, comprehensive exam, thesis/dissertation. *Entrance requirements:* For master's and doctorate, GRE (minimum Verbal score of 153, Quantitative 151), minimum undergraduate GPA of 3.0. Additional exam requirements/recommendations for international students: required—TOEFL (minimum score 600 paper-based; 100 iBT), IELTS (minimum score 7). Electronic applications accepted.

The University of Kansas, Graduate Studies, School of Engineering, Department of Mechanical Engineering, Lawrence, KS 66045. Offers MS, PhD. *Program availability:* Part-time. *Students:* 41 full-time (7 women), 10 part-time (4 women); includes 9 minority (1 Asian, non-Hispanic/Latino; 4 Hispanic/Latino; 4 Two or more races, non-Hispanic/Latino), 18 international. Average age 33. 52 applicants, 50% accepted, 13 enrolled. In 2019, 7 master's, 1 doctorate awarded. Terminal master's awarded for partial completion of doctoral program. *Entrance requirements:* For master's, GRE, minimum GPA of 3.0, 3 letters of recommendation, official transcript, statement of purpose (one-page maximum); for doctorate, GRE, minimum GPA of 3.5, 3 letters of recommendation, official transcript, statement of purpose (one-page maximum). Additional exam requirements/recommendations for international students: required—TOEFL, IELTS. *Application deadline:* For fall admission, 12/15 priority date for domestic and international students; for spring admission, 11/1 for domestic students, 9/30 for international students; for summer admission, 5/1 for domestic and international students. Application fee: $65 ($85 for international students). Electronic applications accepted. *Expenses:* Tuition, state resident: full-time $9989. Tuition, nonresident: full-time $23,950. *International tuition:* $23,950 full-time. *Required fees:* $984; $81.99 per credit hour. Tuition and fees vary according to course load, campus/location and program. *Financial support:* Fellowships, research assistantships, teaching assistantships, career-related internships or fieldwork, and scholarships/grants available. Financial award application deadline: 12/15. *Unit head:* Theodore Bergman, Chair, 785-864-3181, E-mail: tlbergman@ku.edu. *Application contact:* Kate Maisch, Graduate Admissions Contact, 785-864-3181, E-mail: k223m620@ku.edu.
Website: http://www.me.engr.ku.edu/

University of Kentucky, Graduate School, College of Engineering, Program in Mechanical Engineering, Lexington, KY 40506-0032. Offers MSME, PhD. *Degree requirements:* For master's, comprehensive exam, thesis optional; for doctorate, comprehensive exam, thesis/dissertation. *Entrance requirements:* For master's, GRE General Test, minimum undergraduate GPA of 2.75; for doctorate, GRE General Test, minimum undergraduate GPA of 3.0. Additional exam requirements/recommendations for international students: required—TOEFL (minimum score 550 paper-based). Electronic applications accepted.

University of Louisiana at Lafayette, College of Engineering, Department of Mechanical Engineering, Lafayette, LA 70504. Offers MSE. *Program availability:* Evening/weekend. *Degree requirements:* For master's, comprehensive exam, thesis or alternative. *Entrance requirements:* For master's, GRE General Test, BS in mechanical engineering, minimum GPA of 2.85. Additional exam requirements/recommendations for international students: required—TOEFL (minimum score 550 paper-based). Electronic applications accepted. *Expenses: Tuition, area resident:* Full-time $5511. Tuition, state resident: full-time $5511. Tuition, nonresident: full-time $19,239. *Required fees:* $46,637.

University of Louisville, J. B. Speed School of Engineering, Department of Mechanical Engineering, Louisville, KY 40292-0001. Offers M Eng, MS, PhD. *Accreditation:* ABET (one or more programs are accredited). *Faculty:* 18 full-time (2 women), 3 part-time/adjunct (0 women). *Students:* 64 full-time (6 women), 52 part-time (13 women); includes 27 minority (7 Black or African American, non-Hispanic/Latino; 7 Asian, non-Hispanic/Latino; 6 Hispanic/Latino; 7 Two or more races, non-Hispanic/Latino), 24 international. Average age 27. 44 applicants, 55% accepted, 22 enrolled. In 2019, 39 master's, 4 doctorates awarded. *Degree requirements:* For master's, thesis optional; for doctorate, comprehensive exam, thesis/dissertation. *Entrance requirements:* For master's, two letters of recommendation, official transcripts; for doctorate, GRE, two letters of recommendation, official transcripts. Additional exam requirements/recommendations for international students: required—TOEFL (minimum score 550 paper-based; 80 iBT), IELTS (minimum score 6.5). *Application deadline:* For fall admission, 5/1 priority date for domestic and international students; for spring admission, 11/1 priority date for domestic and international students; for summer admission, 3/1 priority date for domestic and international students. Applications are processed on a rolling basis. Application fee: $65. Electronic applications accepted. *Expenses: Tuition, area resident:* Full-time $13,000; part-time $723 per credit hour. Tuition, state resident: full-time $13,000; part-time $723 per credit hour. Tuition, nonresident: full-time $27,114; part-time $1507 per credit hour. *International tuition:* $27,114 full-time. *Required fees:* $196. Tuition and fees vary according to program and reciprocity agreements. *Financial support:* In 2019–20, 48 students received support. Fellowships, research assistantships, teaching assistantships, scholarships/grants, health care benefits, and tuition waivers (full) available. Financial award application deadline: 1/1. *Unit head:* Dr. Kevin Murphy, Jr., Chair, Mechanical Engineering Department, 502-852-6332, E-mail: kevin.murphy@louisville.edu. *Application contact:* Peter Quesada, Director of Graduate Studies, 502-852-5981, E-mail: peter.quesada@louisville.edu.
Website: http://www.louisville.edu/speed/mechanical

University of Maine, Graduate School, College of Engineering, Department of Mechanical Engineering, Orono, ME 04469. Offers MS, PSM, PhD. *Program availability:* Part-time. *Faculty:* 18 full-time (2 women), 3 part-time/adjunct (0 women). *Students:* 40 full-time (4 women), 6 part-time (0 women); includes 1 minority (Hispanic/Latino), 20 international. Average age 27. 40 applicants, 93% accepted, 14 enrolled. In 2019, 8 master's awarded. *Degree requirements:* For master's, thesis (for some programs); for doctorate, comprehensive exam, thesis/dissertation. *Entrance requirements:* For master's and doctorate, GRE General Test. Additional exam requirements/recommendations for international students: required—TOEFL (minimum score 80 iBT), IELTS (minimum score 6.5), PTE (minimum score 60). *Application deadline:* For fall admission, 2/15 for domestic and international students; for spring admission, 7/31 for domestic and international students. Applications are processed on a rolling basis. Application fee: $65. Electronic applications accepted. *Expenses: Tuition, area resident:* Full-time $8100; part-time $450 per credit hour. Tuition, state resident: full-time $8100; part-time $450 per credit hour. Tuition, nonresident: full-time $26,388; part-time $1466 per credit hour. *International tuition:* $26,388 full-time. *Required fees:* $1257; $278 per semester. Tuition and fees vary according to course load. *Financial support:* In 2019–

20, 68 students received support, including 1 fellowship with full tuition reimbursement available (averaging $25,000 per year), 40 research assistantships with full tuition reimbursements available (averaging $16,250 per year), 8 teaching assistantships with full tuition reimbursements available (averaging $15,000 per year); Federal Work-Study, tuition waivers (full and partial), and unspecified assistantships also available. Financial award application deadline: 3/1; financial award applicants required to submit FAFSA. *Unit head:* Dr. Masoud Rais-Rohani, Chair, 207-581-4120, E-mail: masoud.raisrohani@maine.edu. *Application contact:* Scott G. Delcourt, Assistant Vice President for Graduate Studies and Senior Associate Dean, 207-581-3291, Fax: 207-581-3232, E-mail: graduate@maine.edu.
Website: http://umaine.edu/mecheng/

The University of Manchester, School of Mechanical, Aerospace and Civil Engineering, Manchester, United Kingdom. Offers advanced manufacturing technology (M Ent); aerospace engineering (M Phil, M Sc, PhD); civil engineering (M Phil, M Sc, PhD); environmental engineering (M Phil, PhD); management of projects (M Phil, M Sc, PhD); mechanical engineering (M Phil, M Sc, PhD); mechanical engineering design (M Ent); nuclear engineering (M Phil, D Eng, PhD).

University of Manitoba, Faculty of Graduate Studies, Faculty of Engineering, Department of Mechanical and Manufacturing Engineering, Winnipeg, MB R3T 2N2, Canada. Offers M Eng, M Sc, PhD. *Degree requirements:* For master's, thesis; for doctorate, thesis/dissertation.

University of Maryland, Baltimore County, The Graduate School, College of Engineering and Information Technology, Department of Mechanical Engineering, Program in Mechanical Engineering, Baltimore, MD 21250. Offers MS, PhD. *Program availability:* Part-time. *Faculty:* 17 full-time (4 women), 12 part-time/adjunct (0 women). *Students:* 46 full-time (11 women), 16 part-time (5 women); includes 13 minority (6 Black or African American, non-Hispanic/Latino; 4 Asian, non-Hispanic/Latino; 3 Hispanic/Latino), 25 international. Average age 29. 65 applicants, 72% accepted, 16 enrolled. In 2019, 7 master's, 8 doctorates awarded. *Degree requirements:* For master's, comprehensive exam (for some programs), thesis (for some programs); for doctorate, comprehensive exam, thesis/dissertation. *Entrance requirements:* For master's, GRE General Test (strongly recommended for applicants from ABET-accredited schools in U.S.), minimum GPA of 3.0; undergraduate degree in mechanical, aerospace, environmental, or chemical engineering (strongly recommended); for doctorate, GRE General Test (strongly recommended for applicants from ABET-accredited schools in U.S.), minimum overall GPA of 3.3; bachelor's degree in mechanical, aerospace, civil, industrial, or chemical engineering. Additional exam requirements/recommendations for international students: required—TOEFL (minimum score 550 paper-based; 80 iBT), GRE General Test. *Application deadline:* For fall admission, 6/1 for domestic students, 1/1 for international students; for spring admission, 11/1 for domestic students, 6/1 for international students. Applications are processed on a rolling basis. Application fee: $70. Electronic applications accepted. *Expenses:* $14,382 per year. *Financial support:* In 2019–20, 32 students received support, including 4 fellowships with full tuition reimbursements available, 11 research assistantships with full tuition reimbursements available, 17 teaching assistantships with full tuition reimbursements available; career-related internships or fieldwork, Federal Work-Study, scholarships/grants, health care benefits, tuition waivers (partial), and unspecified assistantships also available. Support available to part-time students. Financial award application deadline: 6/30; financial award applicants required to submit FAFSA. *Unit head:* Dr. Ruey -Hung Chen, Professor and Chair, 410-455-3313, Fax: 410-455-1052, E-mail: chenrh@umbc.edu. *Application contact:* Dr. Carlos Romero-Talamas, Graduate Program Director, 410-455-8049, Fax: 410-455-1052, E-mail: romero@umbc.edu.
Website: https://me.umbc.edu

University of Maryland, College Park, Academic Affairs, A. James Clark School of Engineering, Department of Mechanical Engineering, College Park, MD 20742. Offers electronic packaging and reliability (MS, PhD); manufacturing and design (MS, PhD); mechanics and materials (MS, PhD); reliability engineering (M Eng, MS, PhD); thermal and fluid sciences (MS, PhD). *Program availability:* Part-time, evening/weekend, online learning. *Degree requirements:* For master's, thesis optional; for doctorate, thesis/dissertation, qualifying exam. *Entrance requirements:* For master's, GRE General Test, 3 letters of recommendation; for doctorate, GRE General Test, minimum GPA of 3.0. Additional exam requirements/recommendations for international students: required—TOEFL. Electronic applications accepted.

University of Massachusetts Amherst, Graduate School, College of Engineering, Department of Mechanical and Industrial Engineering, Amherst, MA 01003. Offers industrial engineering and operations research (MS, PhD); mechanical engineering (MSME, PhD). *Program availability:* Part-time. Terminal master's awarded for partial completion of doctoral program. *Degree requirements:* For master's, thesis or alternative; for doctorate, comprehensive exam, thesis/dissertation. *Entrance requirements:* For master's and doctorate, GRE General Test. Additional exam requirements/recommendations for international students: required—TOEFL (minimum score 550 paper-based; 80 iBT), IELTS (minimum score 6.5). Electronic applications accepted.

University of Massachusetts Dartmouth, Graduate School, College of Engineering, Department of Mechanical Engineering, North Dartmouth, MA 02747-2300. Offers industrial and systems engineering (Postbaccalaureate Certificate); mechanical engineering (MS). *Program availability:* Part-time. *Degree requirements:* For master's, thesis, thesis or project. *Entrance requirements:* For master's, GRE unless UMass Dartmouth graduate in mechanical engineering, statement of purpose (minimum of 300 words), resume, 3 letters of recommendation, official transcripts; for Postbaccalaureate Certificate, statement of purpose (minimum of 300 words), resume, 3 letters of recommendation, official transcripts. Additional exam requirements/recommendations for international students: required—TOEFL (minimum score 533 paper-based; 72 iBT), IELTS (minimum score 6). Electronic applications accepted.

University of Massachusetts Lowell, Francis College of Engineering, Department of Mechanical Engineering, Lowell, MA 01854. Offers MS Eng, PhD. *Program availability:* Part-time. *Degree requirements:* For master's, thesis or alternative; for doctorate, 2 foreign languages, comprehensive exam, thesis/dissertation. *Entrance requirements:* For master's and doctorate, GRE General Test. Additional exam requirements/recommendations for international students: required—TOEFL (minimum score 560 paper-based). Electronic applications accepted.

University of Memphis, Graduate School, Herff College of Engineering, Department of Mechanical Engineering, Memphis, TN 38152. Offers power systems (MS). *Program availability:* Part-time. *Students:* 4 full-time (1 woman), 4 part-time (0 women), 2 international. Average age 30. 9 applicants, 78% accepted, 3 enrolled. In 2019, 6 master's awarded. Terminal master's awarded for partial completion of doctoral program. *Degree requirements:* For master's, comprehensive exam, thesis or alternative; for doctorate, comprehensive exam, thesis/dissertation. *Entrance requirements:* For master's, GRE General Test, MAT, GMAT, BS in mechanical engineering, minimum undergraduate GPA of 3.0, three letters of recommendation; for doctorate, GRE, BS in mechanical engineering, minimum undergraduate GPA of 3.0, three letters of recommendation; for Graduate Certificate, letter of intent, two letters of

recommendation. Additional exam requirements/recommendations for international students: required—TOEFL (minimum score 550 paper-based; 79 iBT). *Application deadline:* For fall admission, 8/1 for domestic students; for spring admission, 12/1 for domestic students. Application fee: $35 ($60 for international students). *Expenses: Tuition, area resident:* Full-time $9216; part-time $512 per credit hour. *Tuition, state resident:* full-time $9216; part-time $512 per credit hour. *Tuition, nonresident:* full-time $12,672; part-time $704 per credit hour. *International tuition:* $16,128 full-time. *Required fees:* $1530; $85 per credit hour. Tuition and fees vary according to program. *Financial support:* Fellowships with full tuition reimbursements, research assistantships with full tuition reimbursements, teaching assistantships with full tuition reimbursements, career-related internships or fieldwork, Federal Work-Study, scholarships/grants, and unspecified assistantships available. Financial award application deadline: 2/1; financial award applicants required to submit FAFSA. *Unit head:* Dr. Ali Fatemi, Chair, 901-678-2257, E-mail: afatemi@memphis.edu. *Application contact:* Dr. Teong Tan, Graduate Coordinator, 901-678-2701, Fax: 901-678-5459, E-mail: ttan@memphis.edu.
Website: http://www.memphis.edu/me/

University of Miami, Graduate School, College of Engineering, Department of Mechanical and Aerospace Engineering, Coral Gables, FL 33124. Offers MSME, PhD. *Program availability:* Part-time. *Degree requirements:* For master's, thesis (for some programs); for doctorate, comprehensive exam, thesis/dissertation. *Entrance requirements:* For master's and doctorate, GRE General Test, minimum GPA of 3.0. Additional exam requirements/recommendations for international students: required—TOEFL (minimum score 550 paper-based). Electronic applications accepted.

University of Michigan, College of Engineering, Department of Mechanical Engineering, Ann Arbor, MI 48109. Offers MSE, PhD. *Program availability:* Part-time. Terminal master's awarded for partial completion of doctoral program. *Degree requirements:* For master's, thesis optional; for doctorate, thesis/dissertation, oral defense of dissertation, preliminary and qualifying exams. *Entrance requirements:* For master's, GRE General Test, undergraduate degree in same or relevant field; for doctorate, GRE General Test. Additional exam requirements/recommendations for international students: required—TOEFL. Electronic applications accepted.

University of Michigan–Dearborn, College of Engineering and Computer Science, MSE Program in Mechanical Engineering, Dearborn, MI 48128. Offers MSE. *Program availability:* Part-time, evening/weekend, 100% online. *Faculty:* 24 full-time (4 women), 12 part-time/adjunct (2 women). *Students:* 35 full-time (7 women), 157 part-time (28 women); includes 32 minority (3 Black or African American, non-Hispanic/Latino; 16 Asian, non-Hispanic/Latino; 10 Hispanic/Latino; 3 Two or more races, non-Hispanic/Latino), 36 international. Average age 26. 208 applicants, 45% accepted, 37 enrolled. In 2019, 86 master's awarded. *Degree requirements:* For master's, thesis optional. *Entrance requirements:* For master's, BS in mechanical engineering or equivalent from accredited school with minimum GPA of 3.0. Additional exam requirements/recommendations for international students: required—TOEFL (minimum score 560 paper-based; 84 iBT), IELTS (minimum score 6.5). *Application deadline:* For fall admission, 8/1 priority date for domestic students, 5/1 for international students; for winter admission, 12/1 priority date for domestic students, 9/1 for international students; for spring admission, 4/1 priority date for domestic students, 1/1 for international students. Applications are processed on a rolling basis. Application fee: $60. Electronic applications accepted. *Financial support:* Research assistantships with full tuition reimbursements, teaching assistantships with full tuition reimbursements, health care benefits, unspecified assistantships, and non-resident tuition scholarships available. Financial award application deadline: 3/1; financial award applicants required to submit FAFSA. *Unit head:* Dr. Oleg Zikanov, Chair, 313-593-5241, E-mail: zikanov@umich.edu. *Application contact:* Office of Graduate Studies, 313-583-6321, E-mail: umd-graduatestudies@umich.edu.
Website: https://umdearborn.edu/cecs/departments/mechanical-engineering/graduate-programs/mse-mechanical-engineering

University of Michigan–Dearborn, College of Engineering and Computer Science, PhD Program in Mechanical Sciences and Engineering, Dearborn, MI 48128. Offers PhD. *Faculty:* 24 full-time (4 women), 12 part-time/adjunct (2 women). *Students:* 1 full-time (0 women), 17 part-time (1 woman), 16 international. Average age 27. 22 applicants, 32% accepted, 3 enrolled. *Degree requirements:* For doctorate, thesis/dissertation. *Entrance requirements:* For doctorate, GRE, bachelor's or master's degree in engineering, applied math, computer science, or physical science. Additional exam requirements/recommendations for international students: required—TOEFL (minimum score 560 paper-based; 84 iBT), IELTS (minimum score 6.5). *Application deadline:* For fall admission, 2/1 for domestic and international students. Application fee: $60. Electronic applications accepted. *Financial support:* Research assistantships with full tuition reimbursements, teaching assistantships with full tuition reimbursements, scholarships/grants, health care benefits, and unspecified assistantships available. Financial award application deadline: 2/1; financial award applicants required to submit FAFSA. *Unit head:* Dr. Dewey Dohoy Jung, Director, 313-436-9137, E-mail: dohoy@umich.edu. *Application contact:* Office of Graduate Studies Staff, 313-583-6321, E-mail: umd-graduatestudies@umich.edu.
Website: https://umdearborn.edu/cecs/departments/mechanical-engineering/graduate-programs/phd-mechanical-sciences-and-engineering

University of Michigan–Flint, College of Arts and Sciences, Program in Mechanical Engineering, Flint, MI 48502-1950. Offers MSE. *Program availability:* Part-time. *Faculty:* 6 full-time (2 women), 4 part-time/adjunct (1 woman). *Students:* 8 part-time (0 women), all international. Average age 25. 46 applicants, 30% accepted. *Degree requirements:* For master's, thesis optional. *Entrance requirements:* For master's, GRE, bachelor's degree in mechanical engineering from regionally-accredited college or university, minimum overall undergraduate GPA of 3.0 on 4.0 scale. Additional exam requirements/recommendations for international students: required—TOEFL (minimum score 84 iBT), IELTS (minimum score 6.5). *Application deadline:* For fall admission, 8/1 for domestic students, 5/1 for international students; for winter admission, 11/15 for domestic students, 10/1 for international students. Applications are processed on a rolling basis. Application fee: $55. Electronic applications accepted. *Expenses:* Contact institution. *Financial support:* Federal Work-Study, scholarships/grants, and unspecified assistantships available. Support available to part-time students. Financial award application deadline: 3/1; financial award applicants required to submit FAFSA. *Unit head:* Olanrewaju Aluko, DEPARTMENT CHAIR, 810-762-3181, E-mail: aluko@umich.edu. *Application contact:* Matt Bohlen, Associate Director of Graduate Programs, 810-762-3171, Fax: 810-766-6789, E-mail: mbohlen@umflint.edu.
Website: https://www.umflint.edu/graduateprograms/master-science-engineering-mse

University of Minnesota, Twin Cities Campus, College of Science and Engineering, Department of Mechanical Engineering, Minneapolis, MN 55455-0213. Offers MSME, PhD. *Program availability:* Part-time. *Degree requirements:* For doctorate, thesis/dissertation. *Entrance requirements:* For master's, GRE General Test, minimum GPA of 3.0; for doctorate, GRE General Test. Additional exam requirements/recommendations for international students: required—TOEFL. Electronic applications accepted.

University of Mississippi, Graduate School, School of Engineering, University, MS 38677. Offers aeroacoustics (MS, PhD); chemical engineering (MS, PhD); civil engineering (MS, PhD); computational hydroscience (MS, PhD); computer science (MS,

PhD); electrical engineering (MS, PhD); electromagnetics (MS, PhD); environmental engineering (MS, PhD); geology and geological engineering (MS, PhD); hydrology (MS); material science (MS); mechanical engineering (MS, PhD); telecommunications (MS). *Students:* 104 full-time (23 women), 19 part-time (5 women); includes 10 minority (3 Black or African American, non-Hispanic/Latino; 6 Asian, non-Hispanic/Latino; 1 Hispanic/Latino), 72 international. Average age 30. In 2019, 36 master's, 17 doctorates awarded. *Expenses:* Tuition, state resident: full-time $8718; part-time $484.25 per credit hour. Tuition, nonresident: full-time $24,990; part-time $1388.25 per credit hour. *Required fees:* $100; $4.16 per credit hour. *Unit head:* Dr. David Puleo, Dean, 662-915-5780, Fax: 662-915-5387, E-mail: engineer@olemiss.edu. *Application contact:* Temeka Smith, Graduate Activities Specialist for Admissions, 662-915-7474, Fax: 662-915-7577, E-mail: gschool@olemiss.edu.

University of Missouri, Office of Research and Graduate Studies, College of Engineering, Department of Mechanical and Aerospace Engineering, Columbia, MO 65211. Offers ME, MS, PhD. *Entrance requirements:* For master's and doctorate, GRE General Test, minimum GPA of 3.0.

University of Missouri–Kansas City, School of Computing and Engineering, Kansas City, MO 64110-2499. Offers civil engineering (MS); computer and electrical engineering (PhD); computer science (MS), including bioinformatics, software engineering, telecommunications networking; computer science and informatics (PhD); computing (PhD); electrical engineering (MS); engineering (PhD); engineering and construction management (Graduate Certificate); mechanical engineering (MS); telecommunications and computer networking (PhD). *Program availability:* Part-time. *Degree requirements:* For doctorate, thesis/dissertation. *Entrance requirements:* For master's, GRE General Test, minimum GPA of 3.0, 3 letters of recommendation from professors; for doctorate, GRE General Test, minimum GPA of 3.5. Additional exam requirements/recommendations for international students: required—TOEFL (minimum score 550 paper-based; 80 iBT).

University of Nebraska–Lincoln, Graduate College, College of Engineering, Department of Mechanical and Materials Engineering, Lincoln, NE 68588-0526. Offers biomedical engineering (PhD); engineering mechanics (MS); materials engineering (PhD); mechanical engineering (MS), including materials science engineering, metallurgical engineering; mechanical engineering and applied mechanics (PhD); MS/MS. *Degree requirements:* For master's, thesis optional; for doctorate, comprehensive exam, thesis/dissertation. *Entrance requirements:* For master's and doctorate, GRE General Test. Additional exam requirements/recommendations for international students: required—TOEFL (minimum score 550 paper-based). Electronic applications accepted.

University of Nevada, Reno, Graduate School, College of Engineering, Department of Mechanical Engineering, Reno, NV 89557. Offers MS, PhD. Terminal master's awarded for partial completion of doctoral program. *Degree requirements:* For master's, thesis optional; for doctorate, thesis/dissertation. *Entrance requirements:* For master's, GRE General Test, minimum GPA of 2.75; for doctorate, GRE General Test, minimum GPA of 3.0. Additional exam requirements/recommendations for international students: required—TOEFL (minimum score 500 paper-based; 61 iBT), IELTS (minimum score 6). Electronic applications accepted.

University of New Brunswick Fredericton, School of Graduate Studies, Faculty of Engineering, Department of Mechanical Engineering, Fredericton, NB E3B 5A3, Canada. Offers applied mechanics (M Eng, M Sc E, PhD); mechanical engineering (M Eng, M Sc E, PhD). *Program availability:* Part-time. *Faculty:* 15 full-time (0 women). *Students:* 55 full-time (9 women), 5 part-time (0 women), 31 international. Average age 28. In 2019, 16 master's, 3 doctorates awarded. *Degree requirements:* For master's, thesis; for doctorate, comprehensive exam, thesis/dissertation, qualifying exam. *Entrance requirements:* For master's, minimum GPA of 3.0; B Sc E; for doctorate, minimum GPA of 3.0; M Sc E. Additional exam requirements/recommendations for international students: required—TOEFL (minimum score 580 paper-based; 80 iBT), IELTS (minimum score 7), TWE (minimum score 4), Michigan English Language Assessment Battery (minimum score 85) or CanTest (minimum score 4.5). *Application deadline:* For fall admission, 3/1 for domestic students. Applications are processed on a rolling basis. Application fee: $50 Canadian dollars. Electronic applications accepted. *Expenses: Tuition, area resident:* Full-time $6975 Canadian dollars; part-time $3423 Canadian dollars per year. Tuition, state resident: full-time $6975 Canadian dollars; part-time $3423 Canadian dollars per year. Tuition, Canadian resident: full-time $6975 Canadian dollars; part-time $3423 Canadian dollars per year. *International tuition:* $12,435 Canadian dollars full-time. *Required fees:* $92.25 Canadian dollars per term. Full-time tuition and fees vary according to degree level, campus/location, program, reciprocity agreements and student level. *Financial support:* Fellowships, research assistantships, and teaching assistantships available. Financial award application deadline: 1/15. *Unit head:* Dr. Juan Carretero, Chair, 506-458 7454, Fax: 506-453-5025, E-mail: juan.carretero@unb.ca. *Application contact:* Ann Bye, Graduate Secretary, 506-453 4513, Fax: 506-453-5025, E-mail: A.Bye@unb.ca.
Website: http://go.unb.ca/gradprograms

University of New Hampshire, Graduate School, College of Engineering and Physical Sciences, Department of Mechanical Engineering, Durham, NH 03824. Offers mechanical engineering (M Engr, MS, PhD). *Program availability:* Part-time. *Students:* 23 full-time (4 women), 20 part-time (5 women); includes 2 minority (1 Asian, non-Hispanic/Latino; 1 Two or more races, non-Hispanic/Latino), 17 international. Average age 26. 39 applicants, 49% accepted, 10 enrolled. In 2019, 15 master's, 8 doctorates awarded. *Entrance requirements:* For master's and doctorate, GRE. Additional exam requirements/recommendations for international students: required—TOEFL (minimum score 550 paper-based; 80 iBT), IELTS, PTE. *Application deadline:* For fall admission, 7/1 for domestic students, 4/1 for international students; for spring admission, 12/1 for domestic students. Application fee: $65. Electronic applications accepted. *Financial support:* In 2019–20, 25 students received support, including 2 fellowships, 11 research assistantships, 12 teaching assistantships; Federal Work-Study, scholarships/grants, and tuition waivers (full and partial) also available. Support available to part-time students. Financial award application deadline: 2/15. *Unit head:* Chris White, Chair, 603-862-1495. *Application contact:* Pamela Lovejoy, Administrative Assistant, 603-862-1352, E-mail: pamela.lovejoy@unh.edu.
Website: http://www.ceps.unh.edu/mechanical-engineering

University of New Haven, Graduate School, Tagliatela College of Engineering, Program in Mechanical Engineering, West Haven, CT 06516. Offers MS. *Program availability:* Part-time, evening/weekend. *Students:* 34 full-time (4 women), 12 part-time (5 women); includes 4 minority (2 Asian, non-Hispanic/Latino; 2 Hispanic/Latino), 34 international. Average age 25. 104 applicants, 72% accepted, 13 enrolled. In 2019, 24 master's awarded. *Entrance requirements:* Additional exam requirements/recommendations for international students: required—TOEFL (minimum score 75 iBT), IELTS, PTE (minimum score 50). *Application deadline:* Applications are processed on a rolling basis. Application fee: $50. Electronic applications accepted. Application fee is waived when completed online. *Financial support:* Research assistantships with partial tuition reimbursements, teaching assistantships with partial tuition reimbursements, career-related internships or fieldwork, Federal Work-Study, scholarships/grants, and unspecified assistantships available. Support available to part-time students. Financial award applicants required to submit FAFSA. *Unit head:* Dr. Cheryl Li, Associate Professor, 203-932-7145, E-mail: CLi@newhaven.edu. *Application contact:* Selina O'Toole, Senior Associate Director of Graduate Admissions, 203-932-7337, E-mail: sotoole@newhaven.edu.
Website: https://www.newhaven.edu/engineering/graduate-programs/mechanical-engineering/

University of New Mexico, Graduate Studies, School of Engineering, Program in Mechanical Engineering, Albuquerque, NM 87131. Offers MS, PhD. *Program availability:* Part-time, 100% online, blended/hybrid learning. *Faculty:* 14 full-time (2 women), 5 part-time/adjunct (0 women). *Students:* 47 full-time (9 women), 54 part-time (7 women); includes 37 minority (2 American Indian or Alaska Native, non-Hispanic/Latino; 2 Asian, non-Hispanic/Latino; 30 Hispanic/Latino; 3 Two or more races, non-Hispanic/Latino), 17 international. 82 applicants, 65% accepted, 38 enrolled. In 2019, 34 master's, 3 doctorates awarded. *Degree requirements:* For master's, thesis optional; for doctorate, comprehensive exam, thesis/dissertation. *Entrance requirements:* For master's and doctorate, GRE. Additional exam requirements/recommendations for international students: required—TOEFL (minimum score 550 paper-based; 80 iBT), IELTS (minimum score 6.5), Toefl or IELTS, not both. *Application deadline:* For fall admission, 7/30 for domestic students, 3/1 for international students; for spring admission, 11/30 for domestic students, 8/1 for international students. Applications are processed on a rolling basis. Application fee: $50. Electronic applications accepted. *Expenses:* Tuition, state resident: full-time $7633; part-time $972 per year. Tuition, nonresident: full-time $22,586; part-time $3840 per year. *International tuition:* $23,292 full-time. *Required fees:* $8608. Tuition and fees vary according to course level, course load, degree level, program and student level. *Financial support:* In 2019–20, 1 fellowship, 21 research assistantships, 6 teaching assistantships were awarded; scholarships/grants, health care benefits, and unspecified assistantships also available. Financial award application deadline: 3/1; financial award applicants required to submit FAFSA. *Unit head:* Dr. Yu-Lin Shen, Chairperson, 505-277-1325, Fax: 505-277-1571, E-mail: shenyl@unm.edu. *Application contact:* Anna Mae Apodaca, Sr. Academic Advisor, 505-277-2762, Fax: 505-277-1571, E-mail: aapodaca@unm.edu.
Website: https://me.unm.edu/programs-and-degrees/graduate/

University of New Orleans, Graduate School, College of Engineering, Program in Engineering, New Orleans, LA 70148. Offers civil engineering (MS); electrical engineering (MS); mechanical engineering (MS); naval architecture and marine engineering (MS). *Degree requirements:* For master's, thesis optional. *Entrance requirements:* For master's, GRE General Test, minimum GPA of 3.0. Additional exam requirements/recommendations for international students: required—TOEFL (minimum score 550 paper-based; 79 iBT). Electronic applications accepted.

University of North Dakota, Graduate School, School of Engineering and Mines, Department of Mechanical Engineering, Grand Forks, ND 58202. Offers M Engr, MS, PhD. *Program availability:* Part-time. *Degree requirements:* For master's, comprehensive exam, thesis or alternative. *Entrance requirements:* For master's, GRE General Test, minimum GPA of 3.0 (MS), 2.5 (M Engr). Additional exam requirements/recommendations for international students: required—TOEFL (minimum score 550 paper-based; 79 iBT), IELTS (minimum score 6.5). Electronic applications accepted.

University of North Florida, College of Computing, Engineering, and Construction, School of Engineering, Jacksonville, FL 32224. Offers MSCE, MSEE, MSME. *Program availability:* Part-time.

University of North Texas, Toulouse Graduate School, Denton, TX 76203-5459. Offers accounting (MS); applied anthropology (MA, MS); applied behavior analysis (Certificate); applied geography (MA); applied technology and performance improvement (M Ed, MS); art education (MA); art history (MA); arts leadership (Certificate); audiology (Au D); behavior analysis (MS); behavioral science (PhD); biochemistry and molecular biology (MS); biology (MA, MS); biomedical engineering (MS); business analysis (MS); chemistry (MS); clinical health psychology (PhD); communication studies (MA, MS); computer engineering (MS); computer science (MS); counseling (M Ed, MS), including clinical mental health counseling (MS), college and university counseling, elementary school counseling, secondary school counseling; creative writing (MA); criminal justice (MS); curriculum and instruction (M Ed); decision sciences (MBA); design (MA, MFA), including fashion design (MFA), innovation studies, interior design (MFA); early childhood studies (MS); economics (MS); educational leadership (M Ed, Ed D); educational psychology (MS, PhD), including family studies (MS), gifted and talented (MS), human development (MS), learning and cognition (MS), research, measurement and evaluation (MS); electrical engineering (MS); emergency management (MPA); engineering technology (MS); English (MA); English as a second language (MA); environmental science (MS); finance (MBA, MS); financial management (MPA); French (MA); health services management (MBA); higher education (M Ed, Ed D); history (MA, MS); hospitality management (MS); human resources management (MPA); information science (MS); information systems (PhD); information technologies (MBA); interdisciplinary studies (MA, MS); international studies (MA); international sustainable tourism (MS); jazz studies (MM); journalism (MA, MJ, Graduate Certificate), including interactive and virtual digital communication (Graduate Certificate), narrative journalism (Graduate Certificate), public relations (Graduate Certificate); kinesiology (MS); linguistics (MA); local government management (MPA); logistics (PhD); logistics and supply chain management (MBA); long-term care, senior housing, and aging services (MA); management (PhD); marketing (MBA); mathematics (MA, MS); mechanical and energy engineering (MS, PhD); music (MA), including ethnomusicology, music theory, musicology, performance; music composition (PhD); music education (MM Ed, PhD); nonprofit management (MPA); operations and supply chain management (MBA); performance (MM, DMA); philosophy (MA); political science (MA); professional and technical communication (MA); radio, television and film (MA, MFA); rehabilitation counseling (Certificate); sociology (MA); Spanish (MA); special education (M Ed); speech-language pathology (MA); strategic management (MBA); studio art (MFA); teaching (M Ed); MBA/MS. *Program availability:* Part-time, evening/weekend, online learning. Terminal master's awarded for partial completion of doctoral program. *Degree requirements:* For master's, variable foreign language requirement, comprehensive exam (for some programs), thesis (for some programs); for doctorate, variable foreign language requirement, comprehensive exam (for some programs), thesis/dissertation; for other advanced degree, variable foreign language requirement, comprehensive exam (for some programs). *Entrance requirements:* For master's and doctorate, GRE, GMAT. Additional exam requirements/recommendations for international students: required—TOEFL (minimum score 550 paper-based; 79 iBT). Electronic applications accepted.

University of Notre Dame, The Graduate School, College of Engineering, Department of Aerospace and Mechanical Engineering, Notre Dame, IN 46556. Offers aerospace and mechanical engineering (M Eng, PhD); aerospace engineering (MS Aero E); mechanical engineering (MEME, MSME). Terminal master's awarded for partial completion of doctoral program. *Degree requirements:* For master's, comprehensive exam, thesis or alternative; for doctorate, thesis/dissertation, candidacy exam. *Entrance requirements:* For master's and doctorate, GRE General Test. Additional exam requirements/recommendations for international students: required—TOEFL (minimum score 600 paper-based; 80 iBT). Electronic applications accepted.

University of Oklahoma, Gallogly College of Engineering, School of Aerospace and Mechanical Engineering, Norman, OK 73019. Offers aerospace engineering (MS, PhD), including aerospace engineering-general; mechanical engineering (MS, PhD), including mechanical engineering-general. *Program availability:* Part-time. *Degree requirements:* For master's, comprehensive exam (for some programs), thesis (for some programs); for doctorate, comprehensive exam, thesis/dissertation, general exam. *Entrance requirements:* For master's and doctorate, GRE, letters of reference, resume, statement of purpose. Additional exam requirements/recommendations for international students: required—TOEFL (minimum score 79 iBT) or IELTS (minimum score 6.5). Electronic applications accepted. *Expenses:* Tuition, state resident: full-time $6583.20; part-time $274.30 per credit hour. Tuition, nonresident: full-time $21,242; part-time $885.10 per credit hour. *International tuition:* $21,242.40 full-time. *Required fees:* $1994.20; $72.55 per credit hour. $126.50 per semester. Tuition and fees vary according to course load and degree level.

University of Ottawa, Faculty of Graduate and Postdoctoral Studies, Faculty of Engineering, Ottawa-Carleton Institute for Mechanical and Aerospace Engineering, Ottawa, ON K1N 6N5, Canada. Offers M Eng, MA Sc, PhD. *Degree requirements:* For master's, thesis or alternative; for doctorate, thesis/dissertation, seminar series, qualifying exam. *Entrance requirements:* For master's, honors degree or equivalent, minimum B average; for doctorate, master's degree, minimum B+ average. Electronic applications accepted.

University of Pennsylvania, School of Engineering and Applied Science, Department of Mechanical Engineering and Applied Mechanics, Philadelphia, PA 19104. Offers MSE, PhD. *Program availability:* Part-time. *Faculty:* 39 full-time (7 women), 11 part-time/adjunct (2 women). *Students:* 185 full-time (37 women), 16 part-time (4 women); includes 28 minority (3 Black or African American, non-Hispanic/Latino; 12 Asian, non-Hispanic/Latino; 11 Hispanic/Latino; 2 Two or more races, non-Hispanic/Latino), 126 international. Average age 25. 612 applicants, 33% accepted, 109 enrolled. In 2019, 41 master's, 7 doctorates awarded. Terminal master's awarded for partial completion of doctoral program. *Degree requirements:* For master's, comprehensive exam, thesis optional; for doctorate, comprehensive exam, thesis/dissertation. *Entrance requirements:* For master's and doctorate, GRE, bachelor's degree, letters of recommendation, resume, personal statement. Additional exam requirements/recommendations for international students: required—TOEFL (minimum score 100 iBT), IELTS (minimum score 7). *Application deadline:* For fall admission, 12/15 priority date for domestic students, 12/15 for international students. Application fee: $80. Electronic applications accepted. *Expenses:* Contact institution. *Application contact:* Associate Director of Graduate Admissions, 215-898-4542, Fax: 215-573-5577, E-mail: admissions1@seas.upenn.edu.
Website: http://www.me.upenn.edu/prospective-students/masters/masters-degrees.php

University of Pittsburgh, Swanson School of Engineering, Department of Mechanical Engineering and Materials Science, Pittsburgh, PA 15260. Offers MSME, MSNE, PhD. *Program availability:* Part-time, 100% online. Terminal master's awarded for partial completion of doctoral program. *Degree requirements:* For doctorate, comprehensive exam, thesis/dissertation, final oral exams. *Entrance requirements:* For master's and doctorate, minimum GPA of 3.0. Additional exam requirements/recommendations for international students: required—TOEFL (minimum score 550 paper-based; 80 iBT). Electronic applications accepted. *Expenses:* Contact institution.

University of Portland, Shiley School of Engineering, Portland, OR 97203-5798. Offers biomedical engineering (MBME); civil engineering (ME); computer science (ME); electrical engineering (ME); mechanical engineering (ME). *Program availability:* Part-time, evening/weekend. *Degree requirements:* For master's, thesis optional. *Entrance requirements:* For master's, GRE General Test, minimum GPA of 3.0, 2 letters of recommendation, resume, statement of goals, official transcripts. Additional exam requirements/recommendations for international students: required—TOEFL (minimum score 80 iBT), IELTS (minimum score 7). Electronic applications accepted. *Expenses:* Contact institution.

University of Puerto Rico at Mayagüez, Graduate Studies, College of Engineering, Department of Mechanical Engineering, Mayagüez, PR 00681-9000. Offers mechanical engineering (ME, MS, PhD), including aerospace and unmanned vehicles (ME), automation/mechatronics, bioengineering, fluid mechanics, heat transfer/energy systems, manufacturing, mechanics of materials, micro and nano engineering. *Program availability:* Part-time. Terminal master's awarded for partial completion of doctoral program. *Degree requirements:* For master's, one foreign language, comprehensive exam, thesis; for doctorate, one foreign language, comprehensive exam, thesis/dissertation. *Entrance requirements:* For master's, BS in mechanical engineering or its equivalent; for doctorate, GRE, BS or MS in mechanical engineering or its equivalent; minimum GPA of 3.0. Additional exam requirements/recommendations for international students: required—TOEFL (minimum score 80 iBT). Electronic applications accepted.

University of Rochester, Hajim School of Engineering and Applied Sciences, Department of Mechanical Engineering, Rochester, NY 14627. Offers MS, PhD. *Faculty:* 16 full-time (3 women). *Students:* 48 full-time (8 women), 1 part-time (0 women); includes 2 minority (1 Asian, non-Hispanic/Latino; 1 Hispanic/Latino), 31 international. Average age 27. 95 applicants, 52% accepted, 11 enrolled. In 2019, 14 master's, 2 doctorates awarded. Terminal master's awarded for partial completion of doctoral program. *Degree requirements:* For master's, comprehensive exam, thesis (for some programs); for doctorate, comprehensive exam, thesis/dissertation, qualifying exam. *Entrance requirements:* For master's and doctorate, GRE, personal statement, official transcripts, three letters of recommendation. Additional exam requirements/recommendations for international students: required—TOEFL (minimum score 95 paper-based), IELTS (minimum score 6). *Application deadline:* For fall admission, 1/1 for domestic and international students. Application fee: $60. Electronic applications accepted. *Financial support:* In 2019–20, 37 students received support, including 19 fellowships with tuition reimbursements available (averaging $31,242 per year), 19 research assistantships with tuition reimbursements available (averaging $30,282 per year), 6 teaching assistantships with tuition reimbursements available (averaging $29,500 per year); tuition waivers (full and partial) and unspecified assistantships also available. *Unit head:* Renato Perucchio, Chair, 585-275-4071, E-mail: rlp@me.rochester.edu. *Application contact:* Sarah Ansini, Graduate Program Coordinator, 585-275-2849, E-mail: sarah.ansini@rochester.edu.
Website: http://www.hajim.rochester.edu/me/graduate/index.html

University of St. Thomas, School of Engineering, St. Paul, MN 55105. Offers data science (MS); electrical engineering (MS); information technology (MS); manufacturing engineering (MS); manufacturing systems (Certificate); mechanical engineering (MS); medical device development (Certificate); regulatory science (MS); software engineering (MS); software management (MS); systems engineering (MS); technology leadership (Certificate); technology management (MS). *Program availability:* Part-time, evening/weekend. *Entrance requirements:* For master's, resume, official transcripts. Additional exam requirements/recommendations for international students: required—TOEFL (minimum score 80 iBT), IELTS (minimum score 6.5). Electronic applications accepted. *Expenses:* Contact institution.

University of Saskatchewan, College of Graduate and Postdoctoral Studies, College of Engineering, Mechanical Engineering Program, Saskatoon, SK S7N 5E5, Canada. Offers M Eng, M Sc, PhD. *Program availability:* Part-time. *Degree requirements:* For master's, 30 credits (for M Eng); thesis and 12 credits (for MS); for doctorate, comprehensive exam, thesis/dissertation, qualifying exam, 18 credits. *Entrance requirements:* For master's and doctorate, GRE. Additional exam requirements/recommendations for international students: required—TOEFL (minimum iBT score of 80), IELTS (6.5), CanTEST (4.5), or PTE (59). Electronic applications accepted.

University of South Alabama, College of Engineering, Department of Mechanical, Aerospace, and Biomedical Engineering, Mobile, AL 36688-0002. Offers MSME. *Faculty:* 2 full-time (0 women), 1 part-time/adjunct (0 women). *Students:* 6 full-time (0 women), 5 part-time (0 women); includes 3 minority (2 Asian, non-Hispanic/Latino; 1 Two or more races, non-Hispanic/Latino), 1 international. Average age 25. 10 applicants, 90% accepted, 3 enrolled. In 2019, 7 master's awarded. *Degree requirements:* For master's, comprehensive exam, thesis optional. *Entrance requirements:* For master's, GRE. Additional exam requirements/recommendations for international students: required—TOEFL (minimum score 550 paper-based; 79 iBT), IELTS (minimum score 6.5). *Application deadline:* For fall admission, 7/1 priority date for domestic students, 6/15 priority date for international students; for spring admission, 12/1 priority date for domestic students, 11/1 priority date for international students; for summer admission, 5/1 priority date for domestic students, 4/1 priority date for international students. Applications are processed on a rolling basis. Application fee: $35. Electronic applications accepted. *Expenses:* Contact institution. *Financial support:* Fellowships, research assistantships, teaching assistantships, career-related internships or fieldwork, Federal Work-Study, institutionally sponsored loans, scholarships/grants, and unspecified assistantships available. Support available to part-time students. Financial award application deadline: 3/31; financial award applicants required to submit FAFSA. *Unit head:* Dr. David Nelson, Chair, Professor, Department of Mechanical Engineering, College of Engineering, 251-460-6168, Fax: 251-460-6549, E-mail: danelson@southalabama.edu. *Application contact:* Brenda Poole, Academic Records Specialist, 251-460-6140, Fax: 251-460-6343, E-mail: engineering@southalabama.edu.
Website: https://www.southalabama.edu/colleges/engineering/me/

University of South Carolina, The Graduate School, College of Engineering and Computing, Department of Mechanical Engineering, Columbia, SC 29208. Offers ME, MS, PhD. *Program availability:* Part-time, evening/weekend, online learning. *Degree requirements:* For master's, thesis (for some programs); for doctorate, thesis/dissertation. *Entrance requirements:* For master's and doctorate, GRE General Test. Additional exam requirements/recommendations for international students: required—TOEFL (minimum score 600 paper-based). Electronic applications accepted.

University of Southern California, Graduate School, Viterbi School of Engineering, Department of Aerospace and Mechanical Engineering, Los Angeles, CA 90089. Offers aerospace and mechanical engineering: computational fluid and solid mechanics (MS); aerospace and mechanical engineering: dynamics and control (MS); aerospace engineering (MS, PhD, Engr), including aerospace engineering (PhD, Engr); green technologies (MS); mechanical engineering (MS, PhD, Engr), including energy conversion (MS), mechanical engineering (PhD, Engr), nuclear power (MS); product development engineering (MS). *Program availability:* Part-time, evening/weekend, online learning. Terminal master's awarded for partial completion of doctoral program. *Degree requirements:* For master's, thesis optional; for doctorate, thesis/dissertation. *Entrance requirements:* For master's, doctorate, and Engr, GRE General Test. Additional exam requirements/recommendations for international students: recommended—TOEFL. Electronic applications accepted.

University of South Florida, College of Engineering, Department of Mechanical Engineering, Tampa, FL 33620-9951. Offers MSME, PhD. *Program availability:* Part-time. *Faculty:* 15 full-time (2 women). *Students:* 122 full-time (10 women), 37 part-time (3 women); includes 15 minority (2 Black or African American, non-Hispanic/Latino; 3 Asian, non-Hispanic/Latino; 8 Hispanic/Latino; 2 Two or more races, non-Hispanic/Latino), 118 international. Average age 25. 162 applicants, 46% accepted, 38 enrolled. In 2019, 83 master's, 11 doctorates awarded. Terminal master's awarded for partial completion of doctoral program. *Degree requirements:* For master's, comprehensive exam, thesis or alternative; for doctorate, comprehensive exam, thesis/dissertation, 2 tools of research as specified by dissertation committee. *Entrance requirements:* For master's, RE required, with minimum percentile rank of 50% on the quantitative portion and a minimum average percentile rank of 50% in verbal and quantitative., BS in Mechanical Eng or related field; 3.00 GPA for last 2 years of coursework from an ABET accredited engineering major. 2 letters of recommendation; statement of purpose; prerequisite coursework required.; for doctorate, GRE required, with minimum percentile rank of 60% on the quantitative portion and a minimum average percentile rank of 60% in verbal and quantitative., MS in mechanical engineering or closely-related field (preferred); one-page statement of purpose and research interests; 3 letters of recommendation; minimum of 3.00 GPA for last 2 years of coursework from an ABET accredited engineering major; prerequisite coursework required. Additional exam requirements/recommendations for international students: required—TOEFL, TOEFL (minimum score 550 paper-based; 79 iBT) or IELTS (minimum score 6.5). *Application deadline:* For fall admission, 2/15 for domestic and international students; for spring admission, 10/15 for domestic students, 9/15 for international students; for summer admission, 2/15 for domestic students, 1/15 for international students. Application fee: $30. Electronic applications accepted. *Financial support:* In 2019–20, 11 students received support, including 42 research assistantships with tuition reimbursements available (averaging $12,819 per year), 22 teaching assistantships with partial tuition reimbursements available (averaging $14,017 per year). Financial award applicants required to submit FAFSA. *Unit head:* Dr. Rajiv Dubey, Professor and Department Chair, 813-974-5619, Fax: 813-974-3539, E-mail: dubey@usf.edu. *Application contact:* Dr. Delcie Durham, Professor and Graduate Program Director, 813-974-5656, Fax: 813-974-3539, E-mail: drdurham@usf.edu.
Website: http://me.eng.usf.edu/

The University of Tennessee, Graduate School, Tickle College of Engineering, Department of Mechanical, Aerospace and Biomedical Engineering, Program in Mechanical Engineering, Knoxville, TN 37996-2210. Offers MS, PhD, MS/MBA. *Program availability:* Part-time, online learning. *Faculty:* 21 full-time (0 women), 1 part-time/adjunct (0 women). *Students:* 96 full-time (10 women), 20 part-time (2 women); includes 9 minority (4 Asian, non-Hispanic/Latino; 1 Hispanic/Latino; 4 Two or more races, non-Hispanic/Latino), 44 international. Average age 29. 103 applicants, 37% accepted, 25 enrolled. In 2019, 25 master's, 17 doctorates awarded. *Degree requirements:* For master's, thesis or alternative; for doctorate, comprehensive exam, thesis/dissertation. *Entrance requirements:* For master's, GRE General Test (for MS students pursuing research thesis), minimum GPA of 2.7 (for U.S. degree holders), 3.0 (for international degree holders); 3 references; statement of purpose; for doctorate, GRE General Test, minimum GPA of 3.0 on previous graduate course work; 3 references; statement of purpose. Additional exam requirements/recommendations for international students: required—TOEFL (minimum score 550 paper-based; 80 iBT), IELTS (minimum score 6.5). *Application deadline:* For fall admission, 2/1 priority date for

domestic and international students; for spring admission, 6/15 for domestic and international students; for summer admission, 10/15 for domestic and international students. Applications are processed on a rolling basis. Application fee: $60. Electronic applications accepted. *Financial support:* In 2019–20, 123 students received support, including 7 fellowships with full and partial tuition reimbursements available (averaging $28,704 per year), 77 research assistantships with full tuition reimbursements available (averaging $22,591 per year), 39 teaching assistantships with full tuition reimbursements available (averaging $21,894 per year); career-related internships or fieldwork, Federal Work-Study, institutionally sponsored loans, health care benefits, and unspecified assistantships also available. Financial award application deadline: 2/1; financial award applicants required to submit FAFSA. *Unit head:* Dr. Matthew Mench, Head, 865-974-5115, Fax: 865-974-5274, E-mail: mmench@utk.edu. *Application contact:* Dr. Kivanc Ekici, Professor/Graduate Program Director, 865-974-6016, Fax: 865-974-5274, E-mail: ekici@utk.edu.
Website: http://www.engr.utk.edu/mabe

The University of Tennessee at Chattanooga, Program in Engineering, Chattanooga, TN 37403. Offers automotive (MS Engr); chemical (MS Engr); civil (MS Engr); electrical (MS Engr); mechanical (MS Engr). *Program availability:* Part-time. *Students:* 29 full-time (4 women), 27 part-time (3 women); includes 9 minority (4 Black or African American, non-Hispanic/Latino; 2 Asian, non-Hispanic/Latino; 1 Hispanic/Latino; 1 Native Hawaiian or other Pacific Islander, non-Hispanic/Latino; 1 Two or more races, non-Hispanic/Latino), 19 international. Average age 29. 39 applicants, 74% accepted, 16 enrolled. In 2019, 22 master's awarded. *Degree requirements:* For master's, comprehensive exam, thesis or alternative, engineering project. *Entrance requirements:* For master's, GRE General Test, minimum undergraduate GPA of 2.7 or 3.0 in last two years of undergraduate coursework. Additional exam requirements/recommendations for international students: required—TOEFL (minimum score 550 paper-based; 79 iBT), IELTS (minimum score 6). *Application deadline:* For fall admission, 6/15 priority date for domestic students, 7/1 for international students; for spring admission, 11/1 priority date for domestic students, 11/1 for international students. Applications are processed on a rolling basis. Application fee: $35 ($40 for international students). Electronic applications accepted. *Financial support:* Research assistantships, teaching assistantships, career-related internships or fieldwork, scholarships/grants, health care benefits, and unspecified assistantships available. Support available to part-time students. Financial award application deadline: 7/1; financial award applicants required to submit FAFSA. *Unit head:* Dr. Daniel Pack, Dean, 423-425-2256, Fax: 423-425-5311, E-mail: daniel-pack@utc.edu. *Application contact:* Dr. Joanne Romagni, Dean of the Graduate School, 423-425-4478, Fax: 423-425-5223, E-mail: joanne-romagni@utc.edu.
Website: http://www.utc.edu/college-engineering-computer-science/graduate-programs/msengr.php

The University of Texas at Arlington, Graduate School, College of Engineering, Department of Mechanical and Aerospace Engineering, Program in Mechanical Engineering, Arlington, TX 76019. Offers M Engr, MS, PhD. *Program availability:* Part-time, evening/weekend, online learning. Terminal master's awarded for partial completion of doctoral program. *Degree requirements:* For master's, thesis optional; for doctorate, comprehensive exam, thesis/dissertation. *Entrance requirements:* For master's and doctorate, GRE General Test, minimum GPA of 3.0. Additional exam requirements/recommendations for international students: required—TOEFL (minimum score 550 paper-based).

The University of Texas at Austin, Graduate School, Cockrell School of Engineering, Department of Mechanical Engineering, Austin, TX 78712-1111. Offers mechanical engineering (MS, PhD); operations research and industrial engineering (MS, PhD); MBA/MSE; MP Aff/MSE. *Entrance requirements:* For master's and doctorate, GRE General Test. Additional exam requirements/recommendations for international students: required—TOEFL.

The University of Texas at Dallas, Erik Jonsson School of Engineering and Computer Science, Department of Mechanical Engineering, Richardson, TX 75080. Offers MS, PhD. *Program availability:* Part-time, evening/weekend. *Faculty:* 29 full-time (3 women), 1 part-time/adjunct (0 women). *Students:* 148 full-time (23 women), 25 part-time (4 women); includes 21 minority (1 Black or African American, non-Hispanic/Latino; 10 Asian, non-Hispanic/Latino; 9 Hispanic/Latino; 1 Two or more races, non-Hispanic/Latino), 113 international. Average age 28. 347 applicants, 24% accepted, 27 enrolled. In 2019, 38 master's, 8 doctorates awarded. *Degree requirements:* For master's, thesis or major design project; for doctorate, comprehensive exam, thesis/dissertation, final exam, research project, qualifying exam. *Entrance requirements:* For master's, GRE General Test, minimum GPA of 3.0 in related bachelor's degree; for doctorate, GRE General Test, essay. Additional exam requirements/recommendations for international students: required—TOEFL (minimum score 550 paper-based). *Application deadline:* For fall admission, 7/15 for domestic students, 5/1 priority date for international students; for spring admission, 11/15 for domestic students, 9/1 priority date for international students. Applications are processed on a rolling basis. Application fee: $50 ($100 for international students). Electronic applications accepted. *Expenses: Tuition, area resident:* Full-time $16,504. Tuition, state resident: full-time $16,504. Tuition, nonresident: full-time $34,266. Tuition and fees vary according to course load. *Financial support:* In 2019–20, 94 students received support, including 9 fellowships (averaging $2,667 per year), 62 research assistantships with partial tuition reimbursements available (averaging $23,613 per year), 31 teaching assistantships with partial tuition reimbursements available (averaging $17,245 per year); career-related internships or fieldwork, Federal Work-Study, institutionally sponsored loans, scholarships/grants, and unspecified assistantships also available. Support available to part-time students. Financial award application deadline: 4/30; financial award applicants required to submit FAFSA. *Unit head:* Dr. Mario Rotea, Department Head, 972-883-2720, Fax: 972-883-2813, E-mail: rotea@utdallas.edu. *Application contact:* Dr. Hongbing Lu, Associate Department Head, 972-883-4647, Fax: 972-883-2813, E-mail: hongbing.lu@utdallas.edu.
Website: http://me.utdallas.edu

The University of Texas at El Paso, Graduate School, College of Engineering, Department of Mechanical Engineering, El Paso, TX 79968-0001. Offers environmental science and engineering (PhD); mechanical engineering (MS). *Program availability:* Part-time. *Degree requirements:* For master's, thesis optional; for doctorate, thesis/dissertation. *Entrance requirements:* For master's, GRE, minimum GPA of 3.0, letter of reference; for doctorate, GRE, minimum GPA of 3.5, letters of reference, BS or equivalent. Additional exam requirements/recommendations for international students: required—TOEFL; recommended—IELTS. Electronic applications accepted.

The University of Texas at San Antonio, College of Engineering, Department of Mechanical Engineering, San Antonio, TX 78249-0617. Offers advanced manufacturing and enterprise engineering (MS); mechanical engineering (MS, PhD). *Program availability:* Part-time, evening/weekend. Terminal master's awarded for partial completion of doctoral program. *Degree requirements:* For master's, comprehensive exam, thesis; for doctorate, comprehensive exam, thesis/dissertation. *Entrance requirements:* For master's, GRE General Test, bachelor's degree in mechanical engineering or related field from accredited institution of higher education; for doctorate, GRE General Test, master's degree in mechanical engineering, or exceptionally

outstanding undergraduate record in mechanical engineering or related field; minimum GPA of 3.33. Additional exam requirements/recommendations for international students: required—TOEFL (minimum score 550 paper-based; 79 iBT), IELTS (minimum score 6.5). Electronic applications accepted. *Expenses:* Contact institution.

The University of Texas at Tyler, College of Engineering, Department of Mechanical Engineering, Tyler, TX 75799-0001. Offers MS. *Program availability:* Part-time, evening/weekend. *Faculty:* 8 full-time (1 woman). *Students:* 8 full-time (2 women), 6 part-time (0 women); includes 3 minority (1 Black or African American, non-Hispanic/Latino; 2 Hispanic/Latino), 3 international. Average age 29. 22 applicants, 45% accepted, 4 enrolled. In 2019, 4 master's awarded. *Entrance requirements:* For master's, GRE or GMAT, bachelor's degree in engineering. *Application deadline:* For fall admission, 10/30 for domestic students; for spring admission, 5/30 for domestic students. Applications are processed on a rolling basis. Application fee: $0 ($50 for international students). *Financial support:* Research assistantships with partial tuition reimbursements and scholarships/grants available. Financial award application deadline: 7/1; financial award applicants required to submit FAFSA. *Unit head:* Dr. Nael Barakat, Chair, 903-566-7003, E-mail: nbarakat@uttyler.edu. *Application contact:* Dr. Nael Barakat, Chair, 903-566-7003, E-mail: nbarakat@uttyler.edu.
Website: https://www.uttyler.edu/me/

The University of Texas Rio Grande Valley, College of Engineering and Computer Science, Department of Mechanical Engineering, Edinburg, TX 78539. Offers MSE. *Faculty:* 6 full-time. *Students:* 40 full-time (6 women), 20 part-time (3 women); includes 43 minority (1 Asian, non-Hispanic/Latino; 42 Hispanic/Latino), 14 international. Average age 25. 38 applicants, 84% accepted, 17 enrolled. In 2019, 21 master's awarded. *Expenses: Tuition, area resident:* Full-time $5959; part-time $440 per credit hour. Tuition, state resident: full-time $5959. Tuition, nonresident: full-time $5959. *International tuition:* $13,321 full-time. *Required fees:* $1169; $185 per credit hour.
Website: utrgv.edu/mece/

The University of Toledo, College of Graduate Studies, College of Engineering, Department of Mechanical, Industrial, and Manufacturing Engineering, Toledo, OH 43606-3390. Offers industrial engineering (MS, PhD); mechanical engineering (MS, PhD). *Program availability:* Part-time, online learning. *Degree requirements:* For master's, thesis optional; for doctorate, thesis/dissertation, qualifying exam. *Entrance requirements:* For master's, GRE General Test, minimum GPA of 3.0; for doctorate, GRE General Test, minimum GPA of 3.3. Additional exam requirements/recommendations for international students: required—TOEFL (minimum score 550 paper-based; 80 iBT). Electronic applications accepted.

University of Toronto, School of Graduate Studies, Faculty of Applied Science and Engineering, Department of Mechanical and Industrial Engineering, Toronto, ON M5S 1A1, Canada. Offers M Eng, MA Sc, PhD. *Program availability:* Part-time. *Degree requirements:* For master's, thesis (for some programs), oral exam/thesis defense (MA Sc); for doctorate, thesis/dissertation, thesis defense, qualifying examination. *Entrance requirements:* For master's, GRE (recommended), minimum B+ average in last 2 years of undergraduate study, 2 letters of reference, resume, Canadian citizenship or permanent residency (M Eng); for doctorate, GRE (recommended), minimum B+ average, 2 letters of reference, resume. Additional exam requirements/recommendations for international students: required—TOEFL (minimum score 580 paper-based), Michigan English Language Assessment Battery (minimum score 85), IELTS (minimum score 7), or COPE (minimum score 4). Electronic applications accepted.

The University of Tulsa, Graduate School, College of Engineering and Natural Sciences, Department of Mechanical Engineering, Tulsa, OK 74104-3189. Offers ME, MSE, PhD. *Program availability:* Part-time. Terminal master's awarded for partial completion of doctoral program. *Degree requirements:* For master's, thesis (MSE); for doctorate, comprehensive exam, thesis/dissertation. *Entrance requirements:* For master's and doctorate, GRE General Test. Additional exam requirements/recommendations for international students: required—TOEFL (minimum score 550 paper-based; 80 iBT), IELTS (minimum score 6). Electronic applications accepted. *Expenses: Tuition:* Full-time $22,896; part-time $1272 per credit hour. *Required fees:* $6 per credit hour. Tuition and fees vary according to course load and program.

University of Utah, Graduate School, College of Engineering, Department of Mechanical Engineering, Salt Lake City, UT 84112. Offers MS, PhD, MS/MBA. *Program availability:* Part-time, 100% online. *Faculty:* 37 full-time (6 women), 5 part-time/adjunct (1 woman). *Students:* 151 full-time (18 women), 84 part-time (9 women); includes 23 minority (2 Black or African American, non-Hispanic/Latino; 10 Asian, non-Hispanic/Latino; 5 Hispanic/Latino; 6 Two or more races, non-Hispanic/Latino), 57 international. Average age 28. 287 applicants, 37% accepted, 54 enrolled. In 2019, 65 master's, 27 doctorates awarded. Terminal master's awarded for partial completion of doctoral program. *Degree requirements:* For master's, thesis (for some programs); for doctorate, thesis/dissertation. *Entrance requirements:* For master's and doctorate, GRE General Test, Minimum GPA of 3.0, statement of purpose, 3 letters of recommendation, curriculum vitae/resume, transcripts. Additional exam requirements/recommendations for international students: required—TOEFL (minimum score 80 paper-based; 80 iBT), IELTS (minimum score 6.5). *Application deadline:* For fall admission, 1/1 priority date for domestic students, 1/15 priority date for international students; for spring admission, 11/1 priority date for domestic students; for summer admission, 3/15 priority date for domestic students. Applications are processed on a rolling basis. Application fee: $0 ($25 for international students). Electronic applications accepted. *Expenses:* Tuition, state resident: full-time $7085; part-time $272.51 per credit hour. Tuition, nonresident: full-time $24,937; part-time $959.12 per credit hour. *Required fees:* $880.52; $880.52 per semester. Tuition and fees vary according to degree level, program and student level. *Financial support:* In 2019–20, 132 students received support, including 10 fellowships with full tuition reimbursements available (averaging $25,000 per year), 79 research assistantships with full tuition reimbursements available (averaging $22,000 per year), 39 teaching assistantships with full and partial tuition reimbursements available (averaging $15,900 per year); scholarships/grants, traineeships, health care benefits, and unspecified assistantships also available. Financial award application deadline: 1/1; financial award applicants required to submit CSS PROFILE or FAFSA. *Unit head:* Mark Fehlberg, Director of Graduate Studies, Assistant Professor, 801-585-9293, E-mail: m.fehlberg@utah.edu. *Application contact:* Michelle Tarner, Graduate Advisor, 801-581-6441, E-mail: grad@mech.utah.edu.
Website: http://www.mech.utah.edu/

University of Vermont, Graduate College, College of Engineering and Mathematical Sciences, Department of Mechanical Engineering, Burlington, VT 05405-0156. Offers MS, PhD. *Degree requirements:* For master's, thesis; for doctorate, thesis/dissertation. *Entrance requirements:* For master's and doctorate, GRE General Test (for research assistant or teaching assistant funding). Additional exam requirements/recommendations for international students: required—TOEFL (minimum score 550 paper-based; 90 iBT), IELTS (minimum score 6.5). Electronic applications accepted.

University of Victoria, Faculty of Graduate Studies, Faculty of Engineering, Department of Mechanical Engineering, Victoria, BC V8W 2Y2, Canada. Offers M Eng, MA Sc, PhD. *Program availability:* Part-time. *Degree requirements:* For master's, thesis (for some programs); for doctorate, thesis/dissertation, candidacy exam. *Entrance requirements:* For master's, minimum B average in undergraduate course work. Additional exam requirements/recommendations for international students: required—TOEFL (minimum score 575 paper-based), IELTS (minimum score 7). Electronic applications accepted.

University of Virginia, School of Engineering and Applied Science, Department of Mechanical and Aerospace Engineering, Charlottesville, VA 22903. Offers ME, MS, PhD. *Program availability:* Online learning. *Degree requirements:* For master's, thesis (MS); for doctorate, comprehensive exam, thesis/dissertation. *Entrance requirements:* For master's and doctorate, GRE General Test, 3 letters of recommendation. Additional exam requirements/recommendations for international students: required—TOEFL (minimum score 650 paper-based; 90 iBT), IELTS (minimum score 7). Electronic applications accepted.

University of Washington, Graduate School, College of Engineering, Department of Mechanical Engineering, Seattle, WA 98195-2600. Offers MSE, MSME, PhD. *Program availability:* Part-time, blended/hybrid learning. *Students:* 274 full-time (58 women), 106 part-time (14 women); includes 47 minority (2 Black or African American, non-Hispanic/Latino; 26 Asian, non-Hispanic/Latino; 6 Hispanic/Latino; 1 Native Hawaiian or other Pacific Islander, non-Hispanic/Latino; 12 Two or more races, non-Hispanic/Latino), 192 international. Average age 26. 657 applicants, 67% accepted, 139 enrolled. In 2019, 123 master's, 20 doctorates awarded. *Degree requirements:* For master's, thesis optional; for doctorate, comprehensive exam, thesis/dissertation, qualifying, general, and final exams. *Entrance requirements:* For master's, GRE General Test, minimum GPA of 3.0 (overall undergraduate GPA of 3.3 preferred); 3 letters of recommendation; statement of purpose; for doctorate, GRE General Test, minimum GPA of 3.0 (overall undergraduate GPA of 3.3, graduate 3.5 preferred); letters of recommendation; statement of purpose. Additional exam requirements/recommendations for international students: required—TOEFL (minimum score 580 paper-based; 92 iBT). *Application deadline:* For fall admission, 12/15 priority date for domestic and international students; for winter admission, 11/1 for domestic students; for spring admission, 2/1 for domestic students; for summer admission, 4/1 for domestic students. Applications are processed on a rolling basis. Application fee: $85. Electronic applications accepted. *Expenses:* Contact institution. *Financial support:* In 2019–20, 11 fellowships with full tuition reimbursements (averaging $30,600 per year), 59 research assistantships with full tuition reimbursements (averaging $30,600 per year), 34 teaching assistantships with full tuition reimbursements (averaging $30,600 per year) were awarded; Federal Work-Study, institutionally sponsored loans, scholarships/grants, health care benefits, tuition waivers (full), and unspecified assistantships also available. Support available to part-time students. Financial award application deadline: 12/15. *Unit head:* Dr. Per Reinhall, Professor/Chair, 206-543-5090, Fax: 206-685-8047, E-mail: reinhall@uw.edu. *Application contact:* Wanwisa Kisalang, Graduate Academic Adviser, 206-543-7963, Fax: 206-685-8047, E-mail: megrad@uw.edu.
Website: http://www.me.washington.edu

University of Waterloo, Graduate Studies and Postdoctoral Affairs, Faculty of Engineering, Department of Mechanical and Mechatronics Engineering, Waterloo, ON N2L 3G1, Canada. Offers mechanical engineering (M Eng, MA Sc, PhD); mechanical engineering design and manufacturing (M Eng). *Program availability:* Part-time, evening/weekend. *Degree requirements:* For master's, research paper or thesis; for doctorate, comprehensive exam, thesis/dissertation. *Entrance requirements:* For master's, honors degree, minimum B average, resume; for doctorate, master's degree, minimum A- average, resume. Additional exam requirements/recommendations for international students: required—TOEFL, IELTS, PTE. Electronic applications accepted.

The University of Western Ontario, School of Graduate and Postdoctoral Studies, Physical Sciences Division, Faculty of Engineering, London, ON N6A 3K7, Canada. Offers chemical and biochemical engineering (ME Sc, PhD); civil and environmental engineering (M Eng, ME Sc, PhD); electrical and computer engineering (M Eng, ME Sc, PhD); mechanical and materials engineering (M Eng, ME Sc, PhD). *Program availability:* Part-time. Terminal master's awarded for partial completion of doctoral program. *Degree requirements:* For master's, thesis; for doctorate, thesis/dissertation. *Entrance requirements:* For master's, minimum B average; for doctorate, minimum B+ average.

University of Windsor, Faculty of Graduate Studies, Faculty of Engineering, Department of Mechanical, Automotive, and Materials Engineering, Windsor, ON N9B 3P4, Canada. Offers engineering materials (M Eng, MA Sc, PhD); mechanical engineering (M Eng, MA Sc, PhD). *Program availability:* Part-time. *Degree requirements:* For master's, thesis; for doctorate, comprehensive exam, thesis/dissertation. *Entrance requirements:* For master's, minimum B average; for doctorate, master's degree, minimum B average. Additional exam requirements/recommendations for international students: required—TOEFL (minimum score 600 paper-based). Electronic applications accepted.

University of Wisconsin–Madison, Graduate School, College of Engineering, Department of Mechanical Engineering, Madison, WI 53706. Offers mechanical engineering (MS, PhD), including automotive engineering (MS), modeling and simulation (MS). *Program availability:* Part-time. Terminal master's awarded for partial completion of doctoral program. *Degree requirements:* For master's, thesis (for some programs), 30 credits; minimum GPA of 3.0; for doctorate, thesis/dissertation, qualifying exam, preliminary exam, final oral defense, 42 formal course credits, 18 thesis credits, minimum GPA of 3.25. *Entrance requirements:* For master's, GRE, BS in mechanical engineering or related field, minimum GPA of 3.2 in last 60 hours of course work; for doctorate, GRE, BS in mechanical engineering or related field, minimum undergraduate GPA of 3.2 in last 60 hours of course work. Additional exam requirements/recommendations for international students: required—TOEFL (minimum score 580 paper-based; 92 iBT), IELTS (minimum score 7). Electronic applications accepted.

University of Wisconsin–Milwaukee, Graduate School, College of Engineering and Applied Science, Program in Engineering, Milwaukee, WI 53201-0413. Offers biomedical engineering (MS); civil engineering (MS, PhD); computer science (PhD); electrical and computer engineering (MS); electrical engineering (PhD); engineering mechanics (MS); industrial and management engineering (MS); industrial engineering (PhD); manufacturing engineering (MS); materials (PhD); materials engineering (MS); mechanical engineering (MS). *Program availability:* Part-time. *Degree requirements:* For master's, comprehensive exam (for some programs), thesis or alternative; for doctorate, comprehensive exam, thesis/dissertation, internship. *Entrance requirements:* For master's, GRE, minimum GPA of 2.75; for doctorate, GRE, minimum GPA of 3.5. Additional exam requirements/recommendations for international students: required—TOEFL (minimum score 550 paper-based; 79 iBT), IELTS (minimum score 6.5).

University of Wyoming, College of Engineering and Applied Science, Department of Mechanical and Energy Systems Engineering, Laramie, WY 82071. Offers MS, PhD. Terminal master's awarded for partial completion of doctoral program. *Degree requirements:* For master's, thesis; for doctorate, thesis/dissertation. *Entrance requirements:* For master's, GRE General Test (minimum score 900), minimum GPA of 3.0; for doctorate, GRE General Test (minimum score: 1000), minimum GPA of 3.0. Additional exam requirements/recommendations for international students: required—TOEFL (minimum score 550 paper-based). Electronic applications accepted.

Université Laval, Faculty of Sciences and Engineering, Department of Mechanical Engineering, Programs in Mechanical Engineering, Québec, QC G1K 7P4, Canada. Offers M Sc, PhD. *Program availability:* Part-time. Terminal master's awarded for partial completion of doctoral program. *Degree requirements:* For master's, thesis; for doctorate, comprehensive exam, thesis/dissertation. *Entrance requirements:* For master's and doctorate, knowledge of French. Electronic applications accepted.

Utah State University, School of Graduate Studies, College of Engineering, Department of Mechanical and Aerospace Engineering, Logan, UT 84322. Offers aerospace engineering (MS, PhD); mechanical engineering (ME, MS, PhD). Terminal master's awarded for partial completion of doctoral program. *Degree requirements:* For master's, thesis (for some programs); for doctorate, thesis/dissertation. *Entrance requirements:* For master's, GRE General Test, minimum GPA of 3.0; for doctorate, GRE General Test, minimum GPA of 3.3. Additional exam requirements/recommendations for international students: required—TOEFL.

Vanderbilt University, School of Engineering, Department of Mechanical Engineering, Nashville, TN 37240-1001. Offers M Eng, MS, PhD. *Program availability:* Part-time. Terminal master's awarded for partial completion of doctoral program. *Degree requirements:* For master's, comprehensive exam, thesis; for doctorate, comprehensive exam, thesis/dissertation. *Entrance requirements:* For master's and doctorate, GRE General Test. Additional exam requirements/recommendations for international students: required—TOEFL (minimum score 550 paper-based); recommended—TWE (minimum score 4). Electronic applications accepted. *Expenses: Tuition:* Full-time $51,018; part-time $2087 per hour. *Required fees:* $542. Tuition and fees vary according to program.

Villanova University, College of Engineering, Department of Electrical and Computer Engineering, Program in Electrical Engineering, Villanova, PA 19085-1699. Offers electric power systems (Certificate); electrical engineering (MSEE); electro mechanical systems (Certificate); high frequency systems (Certificate); intelligent control systems (Certificate); wireless and digital communications (Certificate). *Program availability:* Part-time, evening/weekend. *Degree requirements:* For master's, thesis optional. *Entrance requirements:* For master's, GRE General Test (for applicants with degrees from foreign universities), BEE, minimum GPA of 3.0. Additional exam requirements/recommendations for international students: required—TOEFL (minimum score 600 paper-based; 100 iBT).

Villanova University, College of Engineering, Department of Mechanical Engineering, Villanova, PA 19085-1699. Offers electro-mechanical systems (Certificate); machinery dynamics (Certificate); mechanical engineering (MSME); nonlinear dynamics and control (Certificate); thermofluid systems (Certificate). *Program availability:* Part-time, evening/weekend, online learning. *Degree requirements:* For master's, thesis optional. *Entrance requirements:* For master's, GRE General Test (for applicants with degrees from foreign universities), BME, minimum GPA of 3.0. Additional exam requirements/recommendations for international students: required—TOEFL (minimum score 600 paper-based; 100 iBT). Electronic applications accepted.

Virginia Commonwealth University, Graduate School, School of Engineering, Department of Mechanical and Nuclear Engineering, Richmond, VA 23284-9005. Offers MS, PhD. *Entrance requirements:* For master's and doctorate, GRE. Additional exam requirements/recommendations for international students: required—TOEFL (minimum score 600 paper-based; 100 iBT). Electronic applications accepted.

Washington State University, Voiland College of Engineering and Architecture, Engineering and Computer Science Programs, Vancouver Campus, Pullman, WA 99164. Offers MS. *Degree requirements:* For master's, comprehensive exam, thesis optional. *Entrance requirements:* For master's, official transcripts from all colleges and universities attended; one-page statement of purpose; three letters of recommendation. Additional exam requirements/recommendations for international students: required—TOEFL; recommended—IELTS. Electronic applications accepted.

Washington State University, Voiland College of Engineering and Architecture, School of Mechanical and Materials Engineering, Pullman, WA 99164-2920. Offers materials science and engineering (MS, PhD); mechanical engineering (MS, PhD). *Program availability:* Part-time. Terminal master's awarded for partial completion of doctoral program. *Degree requirements:* For master's, comprehensive exam, thesis; for doctorate, comprehensive exam, thesis/dissertation, preliminary exam. *Entrance requirements:* For master's, GRE, bachelor's degree, minimum GPA of 3.0, resume, statement of purpose, 3 letters of recommendation, official transcripts, Student Interest Profile form; for doctorate, GRE, bachelor's degree, minimum GPA of 3.4, resume, statement of purpose, 3 letters of recommendation, official transcripts, Student Interest Profile form. Additional exam requirements/recommendations for international students: required—TOEFL (minimum score 500 paper-based), IELTS. Electronic applications accepted.

Washington University in St. Louis, School of Engineering and Applied Science, Department of Mechanical Engineering and Materials Science, St. Louis, MO 63130-4899. Offers aerospace engineering (MS, PhD); materials science (MS); mechanical engineering (M Eng, MS, PhD). *Program availability:* Part-time. Terminal master's awarded for partial completion of doctoral program. *Degree requirements:* For master's, thesis optional; for doctorate, thesis/dissertation optional. *Entrance requirements:* For master's, GRE; for doctorate, GRE General Test, departmental qualifying exam.

Wayne State University, College of Engineering, Department of Mechanical Engineering, Detroit, MI 48202. Offers MS, PhD. *Faculty:* 14. *Students:* 110 full-time (15 women), 47 part-time (7 women); includes 17 minority (2 Black or African American, non-Hispanic/Latino; 9 Asian, non-Hispanic/Latino; 4 Hispanic/Latino; 2 Two or more races, non-Hispanic/Latino), 103 international. Average age 30. 253 applicants, 36% accepted, 22 enrolled. In 2019, 93 master's, 3 doctorates awarded. *Degree requirements:* For master's, thesis optional; for doctorate, thesis/dissertation. *Entrance requirements:* For master's, GRE (if BS is not from ABET-accredited university), minimum undergraduate GPA of 3.0, bachelor's degree in mechanical engineering or very similar field; resume (optional); for doctorate, GRE, minimum graduate or undergraduate upper-division GPA of 3.5, undergraduate major or substantial specialized work in proposed doctoral field; resume (optional). Additional exam requirements/recommendations for international students: required—TOEFL (minimum score 550 paper-based; 79 iBT), TWE (minimum score 5.5), Michigan English Language Assessment Battery (minimum score 85); recommended—IELTS (minimum score 6.5). *Application deadline:* For fall admission, 3/1 priority date for domestic and international students; for winter admission, 10/1 priority date for domestic students, 9/1 priority date for international students; for spring admission, 2/1 priority date for domestic students, 1/1 priority date for international students. Applications are processed on a rolling basis. Application fee: $50. Electronic applications accepted. *Expenses:* $790 per credit hour in-state tuition, $1579 per credit hour out-of-state tuition. MS degree is 30 credit hours; PhD degree is 90 credit hours. *Financial support:* In 2019–20, 76 students received support, including 3 fellowships with tuition reimbursements available (averaging $20,000 per year), 5 research assistantships with tuition reimbursements available (averaging $28,030 per year), 7 teaching assistantships with tuition reimbursements available (averaging $20,792 per year); scholarships/grants and unspecified assistantships also available. Financial award applicants required to submit FAFSA. *Unit*

Mechanical Engineering

head: Dr. Nabil Chalhoub, Chairman/Professor, 313-577-3753, E-mail: ab9714@wayne.edu. *Application contact:* Rob Carlson, Graduate Program Coordinator, 313-577-9615, E-mail: rcarlson@wayne.edu.
Website: http://engineering.wayne.edu/me/

Western Michigan University, Graduate College, College of Engineering and Applied Sciences, Department of Mechanical and Aerospace Engineering, Kalamazoo, MI 49008. Offers mechanical engineering (MSE, PhD). *Program availability:* Part-time. *Degree requirements:* For master's, thesis optional; for doctorate, thesis/dissertation.

Western New England University, College of Engineering, Department of Mechanical Engineering, Springfield, MA 01119. Offers MSME. *Program availability:* Part-time, evening/weekend. *Degree requirements:* For master's, comprehensive exam, thesis optional. *Entrance requirements:* For master's, official transcript, bachelor's degree in engineering or related field, two recommendations, resume. Additional exam requirements/recommendations for international students: required—TOEFL (minimum score 79 iBT). Electronic applications accepted. *Expenses:* Contact institution.

West Virginia University, Statler College of Engineering and Mineral Resources, Morgantown, WV 26506. Offers aerospace engineering (MSAE, PhD); chemical engineering (MS Ch E, PhD); civil engineering (MSCE, PhD); computer engineering (PhD); computer science (MSCS, PhD); electrical engineering (MSEE, PhD); energy systems engineering (MSESE); engineering (MSE); industrial engineering (MSIE, PhD); industrial hygiene (MS); material science and engineering (MSMSE, PhD); mechanical engineering (MSME, PhD); mining engineering (MS Min E, PhD); petroleum and natural gas engineering (MSPNGE, PhD); safety management (MS); software engineering (MSSE). *Program availability:* Part-time. Terminal master's awarded for partial completion of doctoral program. *Degree requirements:* For master's, thesis optional; for doctorate, comprehensive exam, thesis/dissertation. *Entrance requirements:* Additional exam requirements/recommendations for international students: required—TOEFL (minimum score 550 paper-based). Electronic applications accepted. *Expenses:* Contact institution.

Wichita State University, Graduate School, College of Engineering, Department of Mechanical Engineering, Wichita, KS 67260. Offers MS, PhD. *Program availability:* Part-time.

Widener University, Graduate Programs in Engineering, Program in Mechanical Engineering, Chester, PA 19013. Offers M Eng. *Program availability:* Part-time, evening/weekend. *Degree requirements:* For master's, thesis optional. Electronic applications accepted. *Expenses: Tuition:* Full-time $48,750; part-time $917 per credit hour. Tuition and fees vary according to class time, degree level, campus/location and program.

Worcester Polytechnic Institute, Graduate Admissions, Department of Mechanical Engineering, Worcester, MA 01609-2280. Offers manufacturing engineering (MS, PhD); materials process engineering (MS); materials science and engineering (PhD). *Program availability:* Part-time, evening/weekend, 100% online, blended/hybrid learning. Terminal master's awarded for partial completion of doctoral program. *Degree requirements:* For master's, thesis optional; for doctorate, comprehensive exam, thesis/dissertation. *Entrance requirements:* For master's and doctorate, GRE (recommended), 3 letters of recommendation, statement of purpose. Additional exam requirements/recommendations for international students: required—TOEFL (minimum score 563 paper-based; 84 iBT), IELTS (minimum score 7). Electronic applications accepted.

Wright State University, Graduate School, College of Engineering and Computer Science, Department of Mechanical and Materials Engineering, Dayton, OH 45435. Offers aerospace systems engineering (MS); materials science and engineering (MS); mechanical engineering (MS); renewable and clean energy (MS). *Degree requirements:* For master's, thesis or course option alternative. *Entrance requirements:* Additional exam requirements/recommendations for international students: required—TOEFL.

Yale University, Graduate School of Arts and Sciences, School of Engineering and Applied Science, Department of Mechanical Engineering, New Haven, CT 06520. Offers MS, PhD. Terminal master's awarded for partial completion of doctoral program. *Degree requirements:* For doctorate, thesis/dissertation, exam. *Entrance requirements:* For master's and doctorate, GRE General Test. Additional exam requirements/recommendations for international students: required—TOEFL.

Youngstown State University, College of Graduate Studies, College of Science, Technology, Engineering and Mathematics, Department of Mechanical, Industrial and Manufacturing Engineering, Youngstown, OH 44555-0001. Offers industrial and systems engineering (MSE); mechanical engineering (MSE). *Program availability:* Part-time, evening/weekend. *Degree requirements:* For master's, thesis optional. *Entrance requirements:* For master's, minimum GPA of 2.75 in field. Additional exam requirements/recommendations for international students: required—TOEFL.

Mechanics

Brown University, Graduate School, School of Engineering, Program in Mechanics of Solids and Structures, Providence, RI 02912. Offers Sc M, PhD. *Degree requirements:* For doctorate, thesis/dissertation, preliminary exam.

California Institute of Technology, Division of Engineering and Applied Science, Option in Applied Mechanics, Pasadena, CA 91125-0001. Offers MS, PhD. *Degree requirements:* For doctorate, thesis/dissertation.

Carnegie Mellon University, Carnegie Institute of Technology, Department of Civil and Environmental Engineering, Pittsburgh, PA 15213. Offers advanced infrastructure systems (MS, PhD); advanced infrastructure systems technology development and application (MS); air quality engineering and science (MS); civil and environmental engineering (MS, PhD); civil and environmental engineering/engineering and public policy (PhD); civil engineering (MS, PhD); computational mechanics (MS, PhD); computational modeling and monitoring for resilient structural and material systems (MS); energy infrastructure systems (MS); environmental engineering (MS, PhD); environmental management and science (MS, PhD); IT-based sustainable global infrastructure and construction management (MS); sustainability and green design (MS); water quality engineering and science (MS). *Program availability:* Part-time. *Faculty:* 23 full-time (5 women), 12 part-time/adjunct (3 women). *Students:* 261 full-time (109 women); includes 19 minority (7 Black or African American, non-Hispanic/Latino; 8 Asian, non-Hispanic/Latino; 4 Hispanic/Latino), 214 international. Average age 25. 649 applicants, 57% accepted, 106 enrolled. In 2019, 80 master's, 12 doctorates awarded. Terminal master's awarded for partial completion of doctoral program. *Degree requirements:* For master's, thesis optional; for doctorate, comprehensive exam, thesis/dissertation, two-part qualifying exam, public defense of dissertation. *Entrance requirements:* For master's, GRE General Test, BS in engineering, science, or mathematics; for doctorate, GRE General Test, BS or MS in engineering, science, or mathematics. Additional exam requirements/recommendations for international students: required—TOEFL (minimum score 84 iBT), TOEFL (minimum score 84 iBT) or IELTS (7.0). *Application deadline:* For fall admission, 1/5 priority date for domestic and international students; for spring admission, 9/15 priority date for domestic and international students. Applications are processed on a rolling basis. Application fee: $75. Electronic applications accepted. *Financial support:* In 2019–20, 113 students received support. Fellowships with tuition reimbursements available, research assistantships with tuition reimbursements available, teaching assistantships, scholarships/grants, health care benefits, tuition waivers (full and partial), and unspecified assistantships available. Financial award application deadline: 1/5. *Unit head:* Dr. David A. Dzombak, Professor and Department Head, 412-268-2941, Fax: 412-268-7813, E-mail: dzombak@cmu.edu. *Application contact:* David A. Vey, Director of Graduate Programs, 412-268-2292, Fax: 412-268-7813, E-mail: dvey@andrew.cmu.edu.
Website: http://www.cmu.edu/cee/

Columbia University, Fu Foundation School of Engineering and Applied Science, Department of Civil Engineering and Engineering Mechanics, New York, NY 10027. Offers civil engineering (MS, Eng Sc D, PhD); construction engineering and management (MS); engineering mechanics (MS, Eng Sc D, PhD). *Program availability:* Part-time, online learning. Terminal master's awarded for partial completion of doctoral program. *Degree requirements:* For doctorate, thesis/dissertation, qualifying exam. *Entrance requirements:* For master's and doctorate, GRE General Test. Additional exam requirements/recommendations for international students: required—TOEFL, IELTS, PTE. Electronic applications accepted. *Expenses: Tuition:* Full-time $47,600; part-time $1880 per credit. One-time fee: $105.

Cornell University, Graduate School, Graduate Fields of Engineering, Field of Theoretical and Applied Mechanics, Ithaca, NY 14853. Offers advanced composites and structures (M Eng); dynamics and space mechanics (MS, PhD); fluid mechanics (MS, PhD); mechanics of materials (MS, PhD); solid mechanics (MS, PhD). *Degree requirements:* For master's, thesis (MS); for doctorate, one foreign language, comprehensive exam, thesis/dissertation, teaching experience. *Entrance requirements:* For master's and doctorate, GRE General Test, 3 letters of recommendation. Additional exam requirements/recommendations for international students: required—TOEFL (minimum score 600 paper-based; 77 iBT). Electronic applications accepted.

Drexel University, College of Engineering, Department of Mechanical Engineering and Mechanics, Philadelphia, PA 19104-2875. Offers mechanical engineering (MS, PhD). *Program availability:* Part-time, evening/weekend. Terminal master's awarded for partial completion of doctoral program. *Degree requirements:* For master's, thesis optional; for doctorate, thesis/dissertation. *Entrance requirements:* For master's, minimum GPA of 3.0, BS in engineering or science; for doctorate, minimum GPA of 3.5, MS in engineering or science. Additional exam requirements/recommendations for international students: required—TOEFL. Electronic applications accepted.

Georgia Institute of Technology, Graduate Studies, College of Engineering, School of Civil and Environmental Engineering, Atlanta, GA 30332. Offers civil engineering (MS, PhD); engineering science and mechanics (MS, PhD); environmental engineering (MS, PhD). *Program availability:* Part-time. *Faculty:* 50 full-time (13 women), 3 part-time/adjunct (0 women). *Students:* 350 full-time (117 women), 46 part-time (16 women); includes 48 minority (8 Black or African American, non-Hispanic/Latino; 22 Asian, non-Hispanic/Latino; 16 Hispanic/Latino; 2 Two or more races, non-Hispanic/Latino), 260 international. Average age 26. 758 applicants, 55% accepted, 123 enrolled. In 2019, 150 master's, 32 doctorates awarded. Terminal master's awarded for partial completion of doctoral program. *Degree requirements:* For master's, thesis optional; for doctorate, comprehensive exam, thesis/dissertation. *Entrance requirements:* For master's and doctorate, GRE. Additional exam requirements/recommendations for international students: required—TOEFL (minimum score 577 paper-based; 90 iBT), IELTS (minimum score 7), TOEFL is the preferred method with the requirements shown on the programs. *Application deadline:* For fall admission, 12/15 for domestic and international students; for spring admission, 8/31 for domestic and international students; for summer admission, 12/15 for domestic and international students. Applications are processed on a rolling basis. Application fee: $75 ($85 for international students). Electronic applications accepted. *Expenses: Tuition, area resident:* Full-time $14,064; part-time $586 per credit hour. Tuition, state resident: full-time $14,064; part-time $586 per credit hour. Tuition, nonresident: full-time $29,140; part-time $1215 per credit hour. *International tuition:* $29,140 full-time. *Required fees:* $2024; $840 per semester. $2096. Tuition and fees vary according to course load. *Financial support:* In 2019–20, 16 fellowships, 166 research assistantships, 26 teaching assistantships were awarded; career-related internships or fieldwork, Federal Work-Study, institutionally sponsored loans, tuition waivers (full and partial), and unspecified assistantships also available. Support available to part-time students. Financial award application deadline: 7/1; financial award applicants required to submit FAFSA. *Unit head:* Donald Webster, School Chair, 404-894-2201, Fax: 404-894-2278, E-mail: dwebster@ce.gatech.edu. *Application contact:* Marla Bruner, Director of Graduate Studies, 404-894-1610, Fax: 404-894-1609, E-mail: gradinfo@mail.gatech.edu.
Website: https://ce.gatech.edu/

Iowa State University of Science and Technology, Program in Engineering Mechanics, Ames, IA 50011. Offers M Eng, MS, PhD. *Entrance requirements:* For master's and doctorate, GRE. Additional exam requirements/recommendations for international students: required—TOEFL (minimum score 550 paper-based; 80 iBT), IELTS (minimum score 6.5). Electronic applications accepted.

Johns Hopkins University, G. W. C. Whiting School of Engineering, Master of Science in Engineering Management Program, Baltimore, MD 21218. Offers biomaterials (MSEM); civil engineering (MSEM); communications science (MSEM); computer science (MSEM); environmental systems analysis, economics and public policy (MSEM); fluid mechanics (MSEM); materials science and engineering (MSEM); mechanical engineering (MSEM); mechanics and materials (MSEM); nano-biotechnology (MSEM); nanomaterials and nanotechnology (MSEM); operations research (MSEM); probability and statistics (MSEM); smart product and device design (MSEM). *Entrance requirements:* For master's, GRE, 3 letters of recommendation, statement of purpose, transcripts. Additional exam requirements/recommendations for international students: required—TOEFL (minimum score 600 paper-based, 100 iBT) or IELTS (7). Electronic applications accepted.

Lehigh University, P.C. Rossin College of Engineering and Applied Science, Department of Mechanical Engineering and Mechanics, Bethlehem, PA 18015. Offers mechanical engineering (M Eng, MS, PhD); MBA/E. *Program availability:* Part-time,

100% online, blended/hybrid learning. *Faculty:* 27 full-time (4 women), 1 part-time/adjunct (0 women). *Students:* 113 full-time (10 women), 21 part-time (4 women); includes 7 minority (2 Black or African American, non-Hispanic/Latino; 3 Hispanic/Latino; 1 Native Hawaiian or other Pacific Islander, non-Hispanic/Latino; 1 Two or more races, non-Hispanic/Latino), 88 international. Average age 27. 155 applicants, 56% accepted, 34 enrolled. In 2019, 28 master's, 13 doctorates awarded. Terminal master's awarded for partial completion of doctoral program. *Degree requirements:* For master's, thesis, there are 4 tracks for the MS degree, thesis; for doctorate, thesis/dissertation, general exam, proposal, dissertation. *Entrance requirements:* Additional exam requirements/recommendations for international students: required—TOEFL (minimum score 550 paper-based; 79 iBT), IELTS (minimum score 6.5), GRE. *Application deadline:* For fall admission, 7/15 for domestic students, 6/20 for international students; for spring admission, 12/1 for domestic and international students. Applications are processed on a rolling basis. Application fee: $75. Electronic applications accepted. *Financial support:* In 2019–20, 68 students received support, including 7 fellowships with full tuition reimbursements available (averaging $29,400 per year), 63 research assistantships with full tuition reimbursements available (averaging $28,200 per year), 13 teaching assistantships with full tuition reimbursements available (averaging $29,400 per year); unspecified assistantships also available. Support available to part-time students. Financial award application deadline: 1/15. *Unit head:* Dr. D. Gary Harlow, Chairman, 610-758-4102, Fax: 610-758-6224, E-mail: dgh0@lehigh.edu. *Application contact:* Allison B. Marsteller, Graduate Coordinator, 610-758-4107, Fax: 610-758-6224, E-mail: alm513@lehigh.edu.
Website: http://www.lehigh.edu/~inmem/

Louisiana State University and Agricultural & Mechanical College, Graduate School, College of Engineering, Department of Civil and Environmental Engineering, Baton Rouge, LA 70803. Offers environmental engineering (MSCE, PhD); geotechnical engineering (MSCE, PhD); structural engineering and mechanics (MSCE, PhD); transportation engineering (MSCE, PhD); water resources (MSCE, PhD).

McGill University, Faculty of Graduate and Postdoctoral Studies, Faculty of Engineering, Department of Civil Engineering and Applied Mechanics, Montréal, QC H3A 2T5, Canada. Offers environmental engineering (M Eng, M Sc, PhD); fluid mechanics (M Sc); fluid mechanics and hydraulic engineering (M Eng, PhD); materials engineering (M Eng, PhD); rehabilitation of urban infrastructure (M Eng, PhD); soil behavior (M Eng, PhD); soil mechanics and foundations (M Eng, PhD); structures and structural mechanics (M Eng, PhD); water resources (M Sc); water resources engineering (M Eng, PhD).

Michigan State University, The Graduate School, College of Engineering, Department of Mechanical Engineering, East Lansing, MI 48824. Offers engineering mechanics (MS, PhD); mechanical engineering (MS, PhD). *Entrance requirements:* For master's, GRE General Test. Additional exam requirements/recommendations for international students: required—TOEFL. Electronic applications accepted.

Michigan Technological University, Graduate School, College of Engineering, Department of Mechanical Engineering-Engineering Mechanics, Houghton, MI 49931. Offers engineering mechanics (MS); hybrid electric drive vehicle engineering (Graduate Certificate); mechanical engineering-engineering mechanics (PhD). *Program availability:* Part-time, evening/weekend, 100% online, blended/hybrid learning. *Faculty:* 64 full-time, 36 part-time/adjunct. *Students:* 284 full-time, 79 part-time; includes 9 minority (2 Black or African American, non-Hispanic/Latino; 4 Asian, non-Hispanic/Latino; 3 Hispanic/Latino), 276 international. Average age 27. 862 applicants, 50% accepted, 127 enrolled. In 2019, 123 master's, 14 doctorates awarded. Terminal master's awarded for partial completion of doctoral program. *Degree requirements:* For master's, thesis (for some programs); for doctorate, comprehensive exam, thesis/dissertation. *Entrance requirements:* For master's, GRE (Michigan Tech and online students exempt), statement of purpose, personal statement, official transcripts, 2 letters of recommendation, resume/curriculum vitae; for doctorate, GRE (Michigan Tech and online students exempt), MS (preferred), statement of purpose, official transcripts, 2 letters of recommendation, resume/curriculum vitae; for Graduate Certificate, statement of purpose, official transcripts, BS in engineering. Additional exam requirements/recommendations for international students: required—TOEFL (minimum score 90 iBT) or IELTS (minimum score 7.0); recommended—TOEFL (minimum score 90 iBT), IELTS (minimum score 7). *Application deadline:* For fall admission, 3/1 priority date for domestic and international students; for spring admission, 8/1 priority date for domestic and international students. Applications are processed on a rolling basis. Application fee: $0. Electronic applications accepted. *Expenses:* $1,212 per credit. *Financial support:* In 2019–20, 255 students received support, including 25 fellowships with tuition reimbursements available (averaging $16,590 per year), 43 research assistantships with tuition reimbursements available (averaging $16,590 per year), 31 teaching assistantships with tuition reimbursements available (averaging $16,590 per year); career-related internships or fieldwork, Federal Work-Study, scholarships/grants, health care benefits, unspecified assistantships, and cooperative program also available. Financial award applicants required to submit FAFSA. *Unit head:* Dr. William W. Predebon, Chair, 906-487-2551, Fax: 906-487-2822, E-mail: wwpredeb@mtu.edu. *Application contact:* Cindy Wadaga, Graduate Program Assistant, 906-487-2551, Fax: 906-487-2822, E-mail: cawadaga@mtu.edu.
Website: http://www.mtu.edu/mechanical/

Montana State University, The Graduate School, College of Engineering, Department of Civil Engineering, Bozeman, MT 59717. Offers civil engineering (MS); construction engineering management (MCEM); engineering (PhD), including applied mechanics option, civil engineering option. *Program availability:* Part-time. *Degree requirements:* For master's, comprehensive exam, thesis (for some programs); for doctorate, comprehensive exam, thesis/dissertation. *Entrance requirements:* For master's and doctorate, GRE General Test. Additional exam requirements/recommendations for international students: required—TOEFL (minimum score 550 paper-based). Electronic applications accepted.

New Mexico Institute of Mining and Technology, Center for Graduate Studies, Department of Mechanical Engineering, Socorro, NM 87801. Offers explosives engineering (MS); fluid and thermal sciences (MS); mechatronics systems engineering (MS); solid mechanics (MS). *Degree requirements:* For master's, thesis (for some programs). *Entrance requirements:* For master's, GRE General Test. Additional exam requirements/recommendations for international students: required—TOEFL (minimum score 540 paper-based).

Northwestern University, McCormick School of Engineering and Applied Science, Program in Theoretical and Applied Mechanics, Evanston, IL 60208. Offers MS, PhD. Terminal master's awarded for partial completion of doctoral program. *Degree requirements:* For master's, thesis optional; for doctorate, comprehensive exam, thesis/dissertation. *Entrance requirements:* For master's and doctorate, GRE General Test, minimum 2 letters of recommendation, transcripts from all academic institutions attended. Additional exam requirements/recommendations for international students: required—TOEFL (minimum score 577 paper-based; 90 iBT), IELTS (minimum score 7). Electronic applications accepted.

Ohio University, Graduate College, Russ College of Engineering and Technology, Department of Civil Engineering, Athens, OH 45701-2979. Offers civil engineering (PhD); construction engineering and management (MS); environmental (MS); geoenvironmental (MS); geotechnical (MS); mechanics (MS); structures (MS); transportation (MS); water resources (MS). *Program availability:* Part-time. *Degree requirements:* For master's, comprehensive exam (for some programs), thesis or alternative; for doctorate, comprehensive exam, thesis/dissertation. *Entrance requirements:* For master's, GRE General Test, minimum GPA of 3.0, 3 letters of recommendation; for doctorate, GRE General Test. Additional exam requirements/recommendations for international students: required—TOEFL (minimum score 550 paper-based; 80 iBT) or IELTS (minimum score 6.5). Electronic applications accepted.

Penn State University Park, Graduate School, College of Engineering, Department of Engineering Science and Mechanics, University Park, PA 16802. Offers engineering at the nano-scale (MS); engineering mechanics (M Eng); engineering science and mechanics (MS, PhD).

Polytechnique Montréal, Graduate Programs, Department of Mechanical Engineering, Montréal, QC H3C 3A7, Canada. Offers aerothermics (M Eng, M Sc A, PhD); applied mechanics (M Eng, M Sc A, PhD); tool design (M Eng, M Sc A, PhD). *Program availability:* Part-time, evening/weekend. *Degree requirements:* For master's, one foreign language, thesis; for doctorate, one foreign language, thesis/dissertation. *Entrance requirements:* For master's, minimum GPA of 2.75; for doctorate, minimum GPA of 3.0.

Rutgers University - New Brunswick, Graduate School-New Brunswick, Program in Mechanics, Piscataway, NJ 08854-8097. Offers MS, PhD. *Program availability:* Part-time. Terminal master's awarded for partial completion of doctoral program. *Degree requirements:* For master's, thesis optional, qualifying exam; for doctorate, thesis/dissertation, qualifying exam. *Entrance requirements:* For master's and doctorate, GRE General Test, GRE Subject Test (recommended). Additional exam requirements/recommendations for international students: required—TOEFL. Electronic applications accepted.

San Diego State University, Graduate and Research Affairs, College of Engineering, Department of Aerospace Engineering and Engineering Mechanics, San Diego, CA 92182. Offers aerospace engineering (MS); engineering mechanics (MS); engineering sciences and applied mechanics (PhD); flight dynamics (MS); fluid dynamics (MS). Terminal master's awarded for partial completion of doctoral program. *Degree requirements:* For master's, comprehensive exam (for some programs), thesis (for some programs); for doctorate, thesis/dissertation. *Entrance requirements:* For master's, GRE General Test; for doctorate, GRE, 3 letters of recommendation. Additional exam requirements/recommendations for international students: required—TOEFL. Electronic applications accepted.

Southern Illinois University Carbondale, Graduate School, College of Engineering, Department of Civil and Environmental Engineering, Carbondale, IL 62901-4701. Offers civil and environmental engineering (ME); civil engineering (MS). *Degree requirements:* For master's, comprehensive exam, thesis. *Entrance requirements:* For master's, GRE, minimum GPA of 2.7. Additional exam requirements/recommendations for international students: required—TOEFL.

Stanford University, School of Engineering, Department of Civil and Environmental Engineering, Stanford, CA 94305-2004. Offers atmosphere and energy (MS, PhD); construction (MS), including construction engineering and management, design-construction integration, sustainable design and construction; environmental engineering and science (MS, PhD); environmental fluid mechanics and hydrology (PhD); structural engineering (MS). *Expenses: Tuition:* Full-time $52,479; part-time $34,110 per unit. *Required fees:* $672; $224 per quarter. Tuition and fees vary according to program and student level.
Website: http://www-ce.stanford.edu/

The University of Alabama, Graduate School, College of Engineering, Department of Aerospace Engineering and Mechanics, Tuscaloosa, AL 35487. Offers aerospace engineering (MSAEM); engineering science and mechanics (PhD). *Program availability:* Part-time, online learning. *Faculty:* 23 full-time (4 women). *Students:* 46 full-time (6 women), 63 part-time (8 women); includes 16 minority (1 Black or African American, non-Hispanic/Latino; 2 Asian, non-Hispanic/Latino; 9 Hispanic/Latino; 4 Two or more races, non-Hispanic/Latino), 21 international. Average age 29. 105 applicants, 51% accepted, 25 enrolled. In 2019, 15 master's, 2 doctorates awarded. Terminal master's awarded for partial completion of doctoral program. *Degree requirements:* For master's, comprehensive exam (for some programs), thesis (for some programs), culminating expierence; for doctorate, comprehensive exam, thesis/dissertation, 1-year residency. *Entrance requirements:* For master's and doctorate, GRE (minimum score of 300), Minimum undergraduate GPA of 3.0. Additional exam requirements/recommendations for international students: required—TOEFL (minimum score 550 paper-based; 79 iBT); recommended—IELTS (minimum score 6.5). *Application deadline:* For fall admission, 7/15 priority date for domestic students, 4/30 priority date for international students; for spring admission, 12/1 priority date for domestic students, 9/30 priority date for international students. Applications are processed on a rolling basis. Application fee: $50 ($60 for international students). Electronic applications accepted. *Expenses: Tuition, area resident:* Full-time $10,780; part-time $440 per credit hour. Tuition, nonresident: full-time $30,250; part-time $1550 per credit hour. *Financial support:* In 2019–20, 33 students received support. Fellowships with full tuition reimbursements available, research assistantships with full tuition reimbursements available, teaching assistantships with full tuition reimbursements available, Federal Work-Study, institutionally sponsored loans, scholarships/grants, health care benefits, and unspecified assistantships available. Financial award application deadline: 1/31; financial award applicants required to submit FAFSA. *Unit head:* Dr. Mark Barkey, Professor/Department Head, 205-348-1621, Fax: 205-348-6959, E-mail: mbarkey@eng.ua.edu. *Application contact:* Dr. James Paul Hubner, Associate Professor, 205-348-1617, Fax: 208-348-7240, E-mail: phubner@eng.ua.edu.
Website: http://aem.eng.ua.edu/

University of Calgary, Faculty of Graduate Studies, Schulich School of Engineering, Program in Civil Engineering, Calgary, AB T2N 1N4, Canada. Offers avalanche mechanics (M Sc, PhD); civil engineering (M Eng, M Sc, PhD); energy and environment engineering (M Eng, M Sc, PhD); environmental engineering (M Eng, M Sc, PhD); geotechnical engineering (M Eng, M Sc, PhD); materials science (M Eng, M Sc, PhD); project management (M Eng, M Sc, PhD); structures and solid mechanics (M Eng, M Sc, PhD); transportation engineering (M Eng, M Sc, PhD); water resources (M Eng, M Sc, PhD). *Program availability:* Part-time. *Degree requirements:* For master's, thesis; for doctorate, thesis/dissertation, written and oral candidacy exam. *Entrance requirements:* For master's, minimum GPA of 3.0; for doctorate, minimum GPA of 3.5. Additional exam requirements/recommendations for international students: required—TOEFL (minimum score 580 paper-based; 93 iBT), IELTS (minimum score 7). Electronic applications accepted.

University of California, Berkeley, Graduate Division, College of Engineering, Department of Civil and Environmental Engineering, Berkeley, CA 94720. Offers engineering and project management (M Eng, MS, PhD); environmental engineering

(M Eng, MS, PhD); geoengineering (M Eng, MS, PhD); structural engineering, mechanics and materials (M Eng, MS, PhD); transportation engineering (M Eng, MS, PhD); M Arch/MS; MCP/MS; MPP/MS. Terminal master's awarded for partial completion of doctoral program. *Degree requirements:* For master's, comprehensive exam (for some programs), thesis (for some programs), comprehensive exam or thesis (MS); for doctorate, thesis/dissertation, qualifying exam. *Entrance requirements:* For master's, GRE General Test, minimum GPA of 3.0, 3 letters of recommendation; for doctorate, GRE General Test, minimum GPA of 3.5, 3 letters of recommendation. Additional exam requirements/recommendations for international students: required—TOEFL (minimum score 570 paper-based; 90 iBT). Electronic applications accepted.

University of California, Merced, Graduate Division, School of Engineering, Merced, CA 95343. Offers biological engineering and small scale technologies (MS, PhD); electrical engineering and computer science (MS, PhD); environmental systems (MS, PhD); management of innovation, sustainability, and technology (MM); mechanical engineering (MS, PhD). *Faculty:* 60 full-time (16 women). *Students:* 244 full-time (83 women), 1 (woman) part-time; includes 56 minority (2 Black or African American, non-Hispanic/Latino; 20 Asian, non-Hispanic/Latino; 30 Hispanic/Latino; 1 Native Hawaiian or other Pacific Islander, non-Hispanic/Latino; 3 Two or more races, non-Hispanic/Latino), 153 international. Average age 28. 330 applicants, 32% accepted, 67 enrolled. In 2019, 30 master's, 17 doctorates awarded. Terminal master's awarded for partial completion of doctoral program. *Degree requirements:* For master's, variable foreign language requirement, comprehensive exam, thesis or alternative, oral defense; for doctorate, variable foreign language requirement, comprehensive exam, thesis/dissertation, oral defense. *Entrance requirements:* For master's and doctorate, GRE. Additional exam requirements/recommendations for international students: required—TOEFL (minimum score 550 paper-based; 80 iBT); recommended—IELTS (minimum score 6.5). *Application deadline:* For fall admission, 1/15 for domestic and international students. Application fee: $105 ($125 for international students). Electronic applications accepted. *Expenses: Tuition, area resident:* Full-time $11,442; part-time $5721. Tuition, state resident: full-time $11,442; part-time $5721. Tuition, nonresident: full-time $26,544; part-time $13,272. *International tuition:* $26,544 full-time. *Required fees:* $564 per semester. *Financial support:* In 2019–20, 205 students received support, including 6 fellowships with full tuition reimbursements available (averaging $22,005 per year), 76 research assistantships with full tuition reimbursements available (averaging $21,420 per year), 123 teaching assistantships with full tuition reimbursements available (averaging $21,911 per year); scholarships/grants, traineeships, and health care benefits also available. *Unit head:* Dr. Mark Matsumoto, Dean, 209-228-4047, Fax: 209-228-4047, E-mail: mmatsumoto@ucmerced.edu. *Application contact:* Tsu Ya, Director of Admissions and Academic Services, 209-228-4521, Fax: 209-228-6906, E-mail: tya@ucmerced.edu.

University of California, San Diego, Graduate Division, Department of Mechanical and Aerospace Engineering, Program in Applied Mechanics, La Jolla, CA 92093. Offers MS, PhD. *Students:* 7 full-time (1 woman). 12 applicants, 17% accepted. In 2019, 3 doctorates awarded. *Degree requirements:* For master's, comprehensive exam (for some programs), thesis (for some programs), comprehensive exam or thesis; for doctorate, comprehensive exam, thesis/dissertation. *Entrance requirements:* For master's and doctorate, GRE General Test, minimum GPA of 3.0. Additional exam requirements/recommendations for international students: required—TOEFL (minimum score 550 paper-based; 80 iBT), IELTS (minimum score 7). *Application deadline:* For fall admission, 12/18 for domestic students. Application fee: $105 ($125 for international students). Electronic applications accepted. *Financial support:* Fellowships, research assistantships, teaching assistantships, scholarships/grants, and unspecified assistantships available. Financial award applicants required to submit FAFSA. *Unit head:* Carlos Coimbra, Chair, 858-534-4285, E-mail: mae-chair-l@ucsd.edu. *Application contact:* Jackie Tam, Graduate Coordinator, 858-534-4387, E-mail: mae-gradadm-l@ucsd.edu.
Website: http://maeweb.ucsd.edu/

University of Cincinnati, Graduate School, College of Engineering and Applied Science, Department of Aerospace Engineering and Engineering Mechanics, Cincinnati, OH 45221-0070. Offers M Eng, MS, PhD. *Program availability:* Part-time. Terminal master's awarded for partial completion of doctoral program. *Degree requirements:* For master's, thesis; for doctorate, thesis/dissertation. *Entrance requirements:* For master's and doctorate, GRE General Test. Additional exam requirements/recommendations for international students: required—TOEFL (minimum iBT score 90), IELTS (6.5), or PTE (47). Electronic applications accepted.

University of Colorado Denver, College of Engineering, Design and Computing, Department of Mechanical Engineering, Denver, CO 80217. Offers mechanical engineering (MS); mechanics (MS); thermal sciences (MS). *Program availability:* Part-time, evening/weekend. *Degree requirements:* For master's, comprehensive exam, 30 credit hours, project or thesis. *Entrance requirements:* For master's, GRE, three letters of recommendation, personal statement. Additional exam requirements/recommendations for international students: required—TOEFL (minimum score 537 paper-based; 75 iBT); recommended—IELTS (minimum score 6.8). Tuition and fees vary according to course load, program and reciprocity agreements.

University of Dayton, Department of Civil and Environmental Engineering and Engineering Mechanics, Dayton, OH 45469. Offers engineering mechanics (MSEM); environmental engineering (MSCE); geotechnical engineering (MSCE); structural engineering (MSCE); transportation engineering (MSCE); water resources engineering (MSCE). *Program availability:* Part-time, blended/hybrid learning. *Degree requirements:* For master's, thesis or alternative. *Entrance requirements:* For master's, minimum GPA of 3.0 in undergraduate work. Additional exam requirements/recommendations for international students: required—TOEFL (minimum score 550 paper-based; 80 iBT); recommended—IELTS (minimum score 6.5), TSE (minimum score 60). Electronic applications accepted.

University of Illinois at Urbana-Champaign, Graduate College, College of Engineering, Department of Mechanical Science and Engineering, Champaign, IL 61820. Offers mechanical engineering (MS, PhD); theoretical and applied mechanics (MS, PhD). Terminal master's awarded for partial completion of doctoral program. *Entrance requirements:* Additional exam requirements/recommendations for international students: required—TOEFL (minimum score 613 paper-based; 103 iBT), IELTS (minimum score 7).

University of Maryland, Baltimore County, The Graduate School, College of Engineering and Information Technology, Department of Mechanical Engineering, Post Baccalaureate Certificate Program in Computational Thermal Fluid Dynamics, Baltimore, MD 21250. Offers Postbaccalaureate Certificate. Application fee: $70. *Expenses:* Contact institution. *Unit head:* Dr. Carlos Romero-Talamas, Program Director, 410-455-8049, Fax: 410-455-1052, E-mail: romero@umbc.edu. *Application contact:* Dr. Carlos Romero-Talamas, Program Director, 410-455-8049, Fax: 410-455-1052, E-mail: romero@umbc.edu.
Website: https://me.umbc.edu/

University of Maryland, Baltimore County, The Graduate School, College of Engineering and Information Technology, Department of Mechanical Engineering, Post Baccalaureate Certificate Program in Mechatronics, Baltimore, MD 21250. Offers Postbaccalaureate Certificate. *Program availability:* Part-time. *Application deadline:* For fall admission, 7/1 for domestic and international students; for spring admission, 2/1 for domestic students, 12/1 for international students. Applications are processed on a rolling basis. Application fee: $70. Electronic applications accepted. *Expenses:* Contact institution. *Unit head:* Dr. Charles Eggleton, Professor and Chair, 410-455-3334, Fax: 410-455-1052, E-mail: eggleton@umbc.edu. *Application contact:* Dr. Charles Eggleton, Professor and Chair, 410-455-3330, Fax: 410-455-1052, E-mail: eggleton@umbc.edu.
Website: https://me.umbc.edu

University of Maryland, College Park, Academic Affairs, A. James Clark School of Engineering, Department of Mechanical Engineering, College Park, MD 20742. Offers electronic packaging and reliability (MS, PhD); manufacturing and design (MS, PhD); mechanics and materials (MS, PhD); reliability engineering (M Eng, MS, PhD); thermal and fluid sciences (MS, PhD). *Program availability:* Part-time, evening/weekend, online learning. *Degree requirements:* For master's, thesis optional; for doctorate, thesis/dissertation, qualifying exam. *Entrance requirements:* For master's, GRE General Test, 3 letters of recommendation; for doctorate, GRE General Test, minimum GPA of 3.0. Additional exam requirements/recommendations for international students: required—TOEFL. Electronic applications accepted.

University of Massachusetts Amherst, Graduate School, College of Engineering, Department of Civil and Environmental Engineering, Amherst, MA 01003. Offers civil engineering (MSCE, PhD); environmental and water resources engineering (MSCE); geotechnical engineering (MSCE); structural engineering and mechanics (MSCE); transportation engineering (MSCE). *Program availability:* Part-time. Terminal master's awarded for partial completion of doctoral program. *Degree requirements:* For master's, thesis or alternative; for doctorate, comprehensive exam, thesis/dissertation. *Entrance requirements:* For master's and doctorate, GRE General Test. Additional exam requirements/recommendations for international students: required—TOEFL (minimum score 550 paper-based; 80 iBT), IELTS (minimum score 6.5). Electronic applications accepted.

University of Minnesota, Twin Cities Campus, College of Science and Engineering, Department of Aerospace Engineering and Mechanics, Minneapolis, MN 55455-0213. Offers MS, PhD. *Program availability:* Part-time. *Degree requirements:* For doctorate, thesis/dissertation. *Entrance requirements:* Additional exam requirements/recommendations for international students: required—TOEFL (minimum score 550 paper-based). Electronic applications accepted.

University of Nebraska–Lincoln, Graduate College, College of Engineering, Department of Engineering Mechanics, Lincoln, NE 68588. Offers MS, PhD. *Degree requirements:* For master's, thesis optional; for doctorate, comprehensive exam, thesis/dissertation. *Entrance requirements:* For master's and doctorate, GRE. Additional exam requirements/recommendations for international students: required—TOEFL (minimum score 550 paper-based). Electronic applications accepted.

University of Nebraska–Lincoln, Graduate College, College of Engineering, Department of Mechanical and Materials Engineering, Lincoln, NE 68588-0526. Offers biomedical engineering (PhD); engineering mechanics (MS); materials engineering (PhD); mechanical engineering (MS), including materials science engineering, metallurgical engineering; mechanical engineering and applied mechanics (PhD); MS/MS. *Degree requirements:* For master's, thesis optional; for doctorate, comprehensive exam, thesis/dissertation. *Entrance requirements:* For master's and doctorate, GRE General Test. Additional exam requirements/recommendations for international students: required—TOEFL (minimum score 550 paper-based). Electronic applications accepted.

University of New Brunswick Fredericton, School of Graduate Studies, Faculty of Engineering, Department of Mechanical Engineering, Fredericton, NB E3B 5A3, Canada. Offers applied mechanics (M Eng, M Sc E, PhD); mechanical engineering (M Eng, M Sc E, PhD). *Program availability:* Part-time. *Faculty:* 15 full-time (0 women). *Students:* 55 full-time (9 women), 5 part-time (0 women), 31 international. Average age 28. In 2019, 16 master's, 3 doctorates awarded. *Degree requirements:* For master's, thesis; for doctorate, comprehensive exam, thesis/dissertation, qualifying exam. *Entrance requirements:* For master's, minimum GPA of 3.0; B Sc E; for doctorate, minimum GPA of 3.0; M Sc E. Additional exam requirements/recommendations for international students: required—TOEFL (minimum score 580 paper-based; 80 iBT), IELTS (minimum score 7), TWE (minimum score 4), Michigan English Language Assessment Battery (minimum score 85) or CanTest (minimum score 4.5). *Application deadline:* For fall admission, 3/1 for domestic students. Applications are processed on a rolling basis. Application fee: $50 Canadian dollars. Electronic applications accepted. *Expenses: Tuition, area resident:* Full-time $6975 Canadian dollars; part-time $3423 Canadian dollars per year. Tuition, state resident: full-time $6975 Canadian dollars; part-time $3423 Canadian dollars per year. Tuition, Canadian resident: full-time $6975 Canadian dollars; part-time $3423 Canadian dollars per year. *International tuition:* $12,435 Canadian dollars full-time. *Required fees:* $92.25 Canadian dollars per term. Full-time tuition and fees vary according to degree level, campus/location, program, reciprocity agreements and student level. *Financial support:* Fellowships, research assistantships, and teaching assistantships available. Financial award application deadline: 1/15. *Unit head:* Dr. Juan Carretero, Chair, 506-458 7454, Fax: 506-453-5025, E-mail: juan.carretero@unb.ca. *Application contact:* Ann Bye, Graduate Secretary, 506-453 4513, Fax: 506-453-5025, E-mail: A.Bye@unb.ca.
Website: http://go.unb.ca/gradprograms

University of Pennsylvania, School of Engineering and Applied Science, Department of Mechanical Engineering and Applied Mechanics, Philadelphia, PA 19104. Offers MSE, PhD. *Program availability:* Part-time. *Faculty:* 39 full-time (7 women), 11 part-time/adjunct (2 women). *Students:* 185 full-time (37 women), 16 part-time (4 women); includes 28 minority (3 Black or African American, non-Hispanic/Latino; 12 Asian, non-Hispanic/Latino; 11 Hispanic/Latino; 2 Two or more races, non-Hispanic/Latino), 126 international. Average age 25. 612 applicants, 33% accepted, 109 enrolled. In 2019, 41 master's, 7 doctorates awarded. Terminal master's awarded for partial completion of doctoral program. *Degree requirements:* For master's, comprehensive exam, thesis optional; for doctorate, comprehensive exam, thesis/dissertation. *Entrance requirements:* For master's and doctorate, GRE, bachelor's degree, letters of recommendation, resume, personal statement. Additional exam requirements/recommendations for international students: required—TOEFL (minimum score 100 iBT), IELTS (minimum score 7). *Application deadline:* For fall admission, 12/15 priority date for domestic students, 12/15 for international students. Application fee: $80. Electronic applications accepted. *Expenses:* Contact institution. *Application contact:* Associate Director of Graduate Admissions, 215-898-4542, Fax: 215-573-5577, E-mail: admissions1@seas.upenn.edu.
Website: http://www.me.upenn.edu/prospective-students/masters/masters-degrees.php

University of Southern California, Graduate School, Viterbi School of Engineering, Sonny Astani Department of Civil and Environmental Engineering, Los Angeles, CA 90089. Offers applied mechanics (MS); civil engineering (MS, PhD); computer-aided engineering (ME, Graduate Certificate); construction management (MCM); engineering technology commercialization (Graduate Certificate); environmental engineering (MS,

PhD); environmental quality management (ME); structural design (ME); sustainable cities (Graduate Certificate); transportation systems (MS, Graduate Certificate); water and waste management (MS). *Program availability:* Part-time, evening/weekend. Terminal master's awarded for partial completion of doctoral program. *Degree requirements:* For master's, thesis optional; for doctorate, thesis/dissertation. *Entrance requirements:* For master's and doctorate, GRE General Test. Additional exam requirements/recommendations for international students: recommended—TOEFL. Electronic applications accepted.

The University of Texas at Austin, Graduate School, Cockrell School of Engineering, Department of Aerospace Engineering and Engineering Mechanics, Program in Engineering Mechanics, Austin, TX 78712-1111. Offers MS, PhD. *Degree requirements:* For doctorate, one foreign language, thesis/dissertation, qualifying exam. *Entrance requirements:* For master's and doctorate, GRE General Test.

University of Washington, Graduate School, College of Engineering, Department of Civil and Environmental Engineering, Seattle, WA 98195-2700. Offers construction engineering (MSCE, PhD); environmental engineering (MSCE, PhD); geotechnical engineering (MSCE, PhD); hydrology and hydrodynamics (MSCE, PhD); structural engineering and mechanics (MSCE, PhD); transportation engineering (MSCE, PhD). *Program availability:* Part-time, 100% online. *Students:* 248 full-time (97 women), 174 part-time (63 women); includes 90 minority (8 Black or African American, non-Hispanic/Latino; 2 American Indian or Alaska Native, non-Hispanic/Latino; 46 Asian, non-Hispanic/Latino; 18 Hispanic/Latino; 16 Two or more races, non-Hispanic/Latino), 118 international. Average age 28. 756 applicants, 59% accepted, 164 enrolled. In 2019, 133 master's, 21 doctorates awarded. Terminal master's awarded for partial completion of doctoral program. *Degree requirements:* For master's, thesis optional; for doctorate, comprehensive exam, thesis/dissertation, qualifying, general and final exams; completion of degree within 10 years. *Entrance requirements:* For master's, GRE General Test, minimum GPA of 3.0, statement of purpose, letters of recommendation, transcripts; for doctorate, GRE General Test, minimum GPA of 3.5, statement of purpose, letters of recommendation, transcripts, resume. Additional exam requirements/recommendations for international students: required—TOEFL (minimum score 580 paper-based; 92 iBT). *Application deadline:* For fall admission, 12/15 for domestic and international students. Applications are processed on a rolling basis. Application fee: $85. Electronic applications accepted. *Expenses:* Contact institution. *Financial support:* In 2019–20, 21 fellowships with full tuition reimbursements (averaging $30,600 per year), 76 research assistantships with full tuition reimbursements (averaging $30,600 per year), 27 teaching assistantships with full tuition reimbursements (averaging $30,120 per year) were awarded; Federal Work-Study, institutionally sponsored loans, scholarships/grants, health care benefits, tuition waivers, and unspecified assistantships also available. Support available to part-time students. Financial award application deadline: 12/15. *Unit head:* Dr. Laura Lowes, Professor/Chair, 206-685-2563, Fax: 206-543-1543, E-mail: lowes@uw.edu. *Application contact:* Bryan Crockett, Director of Academic Services, 206-616-1891, Fax: 206-543-1543, E-mail: ceginfo@u.washington.edu.
Website: http://www.ce.washington.edu/

University of Wisconsin–Madison, Graduate School, College of Engineering, Department of Engineering Physics, Madison, WI 53706-1380. Offers engineering mechanics (MS, PhD), including fundamentals of applied mechanics (MS); nuclear engineering and engineering physics (MS, PhD). *Program availability:* Part-time. Terminal master's awarded for partial completion of doctoral program. *Degree requirements:* For master's, thesis optional, 30 credits of technical courses; oral exam; minimum GPA of 3.0; for doctorate, comprehensive exam, thesis/dissertation, minimum of 60 credits; minimum GPA of 3.0. *Entrance requirements:* For master's and doctorate, GRE General Test, minimum GPA of 3.0 in last 60 hours, appropriate bachelor's degree. Additional exam requirements/recommendations for international students: required—TOEFL (minimum score 580 paper-based; 92 iBT), IELTS (minimum score 7). Electronic applications accepted.

University of Wisconsin–Milwaukee, Graduate School, College of Engineering and Applied Science, Program in Engineering, Milwaukee, WI 53201-0413. Offers biomedical engineering (MS); civil engineering (MS, PhD); computer science (PhD); electrical and computer engineering (MS); electrical engineering (PhD); engineering mechanics (MS); industrial and management engineering (MS); industrial engineering (PhD); manufacturing engineering (MS); materials (PhD); materials engineering (MS); mechanical engineering (MS). *Program availability:* Part-time. *Degree requirements:* For master's, comprehensive exam (for some programs), thesis or alternative; for doctorate, comprehensive exam, thesis/dissertation, internship. *Entrance requirements:* For master's, GRE, minimum GPA of 2.75; for doctorate, GRE, minimum GPA of 3.5. Additional exam requirements/recommendations for international students: required—TOEFL (minimum score 550 paper-based; 79 iBT), IELTS (minimum score 6.5).

Section 18
Ocean Engineering

This section contains a directory of institutions offering graduate work in ocean engineering. Additional information about programs listed in the directory may be obtained by writing directly to the dean of a graduate school or chair of a department at the address given in the directory.

For programs offering related work, see also in this book *Civil and Environmental Engineering* and *Engineering and Applied Sciences*. In the other guides in this series:

Graduate Programs in the Biological/Biomedical Sciences & Health-Related Medical Professions
See *Marine Biology*

Graduate Programs in the Physical Sciences, Mathematics, Agricultural Sciences, the Environment & Natural Resources
See *Environmental Sciences and Management* and *Marine Sciences and Oceanography*

CONTENTS

Program Directory

Ocean Engineering

Florida Atlantic University, College of Engineering and Computer Science, Department of Ocean and Mechanical Engineering, Boca Raton, FL 33431-0991. Offers mechanical engineering (MS, PhD). *Program availability:* Part-time, evening/weekend. *Faculty:* 24 full-time (1 woman), 1 part-time/adjunct (0 women). *Students:* 38 full-time (8 women), 55 part-time (10 women); includes 13 minority (2 Black or African American, non-Hispanic/Latino; 2 Asian, non-Hispanic/Latino; 9 Hispanic/Latino), 34 international. Average age 30. 83 applicants, 57% accepted, 28 enrolled. In 2019, 27 master's, 10 doctorates awarded. Terminal master's awarded for partial completion of doctoral program. *Degree requirements:* For master's, thesis (for some programs); for doctorate, comprehensive exam, thesis/dissertation, qualifying exam. *Entrance requirements:* For master's and doctorate, GRE General Test, minimum GPA of 3.0. Additional exam requirements/recommendations for international students: required—TOEFL (minimum score 500 paper-based; 61 iBT), IELTS (minimum score 6). *Application deadline:* For fall admission, 7/1 priority date for domestic students, 2/15 for international students; for spring admission, 11/1 for domestic students, 7/15 for international students. Applications are processed on a rolling basis. Application fee: $30. *Expenses: Tuition:* Full-time $20,536; part-time $371.82 per credit hour. Tuition and fees vary according to program. *Financial support:* Research assistantships, career-related internships or fieldwork, Federal Work-Study, scholarships/grants, and unspecified assistantships available. Financial award application deadline: 1/10; financial award applicants required to submit FAFSA. *Unit head:* Manhar Dhanak, Chair, 561-297-2827, E-mail: dhanak@fau.edu. *Application contact:* Manhar Dhanak, Chair, 561-297-2827, E-mail: dhanak@fau.edu.
Website: http://www.ome.fau.edu/

Florida Institute of Technology, College of Engineering and Science, Program in Ocean Engineering, Melbourne, FL 32901-6975. Offers MS, PhD. *Program availability:* Part-time. Terminal master's awarded for partial completion of doctoral program. *Degree requirements:* For master's, comprehensive exam (for some programs), thesis optional, 30 credit hours (thesis), 33 credit hours (non-thesis) with technical paper; for doctorate, comprehensive exam, thesis/dissertation, research program and publication. *Entrance requirements:* For master's, GRE General Test, 3 letters of recommendation, resume, transcripts, statement of objectives, undergraduate degree in physical sciences or engineering, on-campus interview (highly recommended); for doctorate, GRE General Test, minimum GPA of 3.3, resume, 3 letters of recommendation, statement of objectives. Additional exam requirements/recommendations for international students: required—TOEFL (minimum score 550 paper-based; 79 iBT). Electronic applications accepted.

Massachusetts Institute of Technology, School of Engineering, Department of Mechanical Engineering, Cambridge, MA 02139. Offers manufacturing (M Eng); mechanical engineering (SM, PhD, Sc D, Mech E); naval architecture and marine engineering (SM, PhD, Sc D); naval engineering (Naval E); ocean engineering (SM, PhD, Sc D); oceanographic engineering (SM, PhD, Sc D); SM/MBA. Terminal master's awarded for partial completion of doctoral program. *Degree requirements:* For master's, thesis; for doctorate, comprehensive exam, thesis/dissertation; for other advanced degree, comprehensive exam, thesis. *Entrance requirements:* For master's, doctorate, and other advanced degree, GRE General Test. Additional exam requirements/recommendations for international students: required—TOEFL, IELTS. Electronic applications accepted.

Memorial University of Newfoundland, School of Graduate Studies, Faculty of Engineering and Applied Science, St. John's, NL A1C 5S7, Canada. Offers civil engineering (M Eng, PhD); electrical and computer engineering (M Eng, PhD); mechanical engineering (M Eng, PhD); ocean and naval architecture engineering (M Eng, PhD). *Program availability:* Part-time. *Degree requirements:* For master's, thesis; for doctorate, comprehensive exam, thesis/dissertation, oral thesis defense. *Entrance requirements:* For master's, 2nd class degree; for doctorate, master's degree in engineering. Electronic applications accepted.

Oregon State University, College of Engineering, Program in Civil Engineering, Corvallis, OR 97331. Offers civil engineering (M Eng, MS, PhD); coastal and ocean engineering (M Eng, MS, PhD); construction engineering management (M Eng, MS, PhD); engineering education (M Eng, MS, PhD); geomatics (M Eng, MS, PhD); geotechnical engineering (M Eng, MS, PhD); infrastructure materials (M Eng, MS, PhD); structural engineering (M Eng, MS, PhD); transportation engineering (M Eng). *Entrance requirements:* For master's and doctorate, GRE. Additional exam requirements/recommendations for international students: required—TOEFL (minimum score 80 iBT), IELTS (minimum score 6.5). *Expenses:* Contact institution.

Princeton University, Graduate School, Department of Geosciences, Princeton, NJ 80544. Offers atmospheric and oceanic sciences (PhD); geosciences (PhD); ocean sciences and marine biology (PhD). *Faculty:* 17 full-time (3 women). *Students:* 43 full-time (27 women); includes 5 minority (4 Asian, non-Hispanic/Latino; 1 Hispanic/Latino), 15 international. Average age 24. 58 applicants, 21% accepted, 7 enrolled. In 2019, 9 doctorates awarded. Terminal master's awarded for partial completion of doctoral program. *Degree requirements:* For doctorate, one foreign language, thesis/dissertation, General Qualifying Exam. *Entrance requirements:* Additional exam requirements/recommendations for international students: required—TOEFL (minimum score 600 paper-based). *Application deadline:* For fall admission, 12/31 for domestic and international students. Application fee: $95. Electronic applications accepted. *Financial support:* In 2019–20, 43 students received support, including 30 research assistantships with full tuition reimbursements available (averaging $30,000 per year), 20 teaching assistantships with full tuition reimbursements available (averaging $16,000 per year); fellowships with full tuition reimbursements available, Federal Work-Study, institutionally sponsored loans, and scholarships/grants also available. Financial award application deadline: 12/31. *Unit head:* Bess B Ward, Department Chair, 609-258-5150, Fax: 609-258-1274, E-mail: bbw@princeton.edu. *Application contact:* Graduate Admissions Office, 609-258-3034, Fax: 609-258-7262, E-mail: gsadmit@princeton.edu.
Website: https://geosciences.princeton.edu/

Stevens Institute of Technology, Graduate School, Charles V. Schaefer Jr. School of Engineering and Science, Department of Civil, Environmental, and Ocean Engineering, Program in Ocean Engineering, Hoboken, NJ 07030. Offers M Eng, PhD. *Program availability:* Part-time, evening/weekend. *Faculty:* 23 full-time (8 women), 21 part-time/adjunct (2 women). *Students:* 23 full-time (11 women), 5 part-time (1 woman); includes 1 minority (Asian, non-Hispanic/Latino), 16 international. Average age 28. In 2019, 6 master's, 2 doctorates awarded. Terminal master's awarded for partial completion of doctoral program. *Degree requirements:* For master's, thesis optional, minimum B average in major field and overall; for doctorate, comprehensive exam (for some programs), thesis/dissertation. *Entrance requirements:* For master's, International applicants must submit TOEFL/IELTS scores and fulfill the English Language Proficiency Requirement. Applicants to full-time programs who do not qualify for a score waiver are required to submit GRE/GMAT scores. Additional exam requirements/recommendations for international students: required—TOEFL (minimum score 74 iBT), IELTS (minimum score 6). *Application deadline:* For fall admission, 4/15 for domestic and international students; for spring admission, 11/1 for domestic and international students; for summer admission, 5/1 for domestic students. Applications are processed on a rolling basis. Application fee: $60. Electronic applications accepted. *Expenses: Tuition:* Full-time $52,134. *Required fees:* $1880. Tuition and fees vary according to course load. *Financial support:* Fellowships, research assistantships, teaching assistantships, career-related internships or fieldwork, Federal Work-Study, scholarships/grants, and unspecified assistantships available. Financial award application deadline: 2/15; financial award applicants required to submit FAFSA. *Unit head:* Dr. Jean Zu, Dean of SES, 201-216.8233, Fax: 201-216.8372, E-mail: Jean.Zu@stevens.edu. *Application contact:* Graduate Admission, 888-783-8367, Fax: 888-511-1306, E-mail: graduate@stevens.edu.

University of California, San Diego, Graduate Division, Department of Electrical and Computer Engineering, La Jolla, CA 92093. Offers applied ocean science (MS, PhD); applied physics (MS, PhD); communication theory and systems (MS, PhD); computer engineering (MS, PhD); electronic circuits and systems (MS, PhD); intelligent systems, robotics and control (MS, PhD); medical devices and systems (MS, PhD); nanoscale devices and systems (MS, PhD); photonics (MS, PhD); signal and image processing (MS, PhD). *Students:* 983 full-time (216 women), 80 part-time (15 women). 3,675 applicants, 33% accepted, 430 enrolled. In 2019, 287 master's, 50 doctorates awarded. Terminal master's awarded for partial completion of doctoral program. *Degree requirements:* For master's, comprehensive exam (for some programs), thesis (for some programs); for doctorate, comprehensive exam, thesis/dissertation. *Entrance requirements:* For master's and doctorate, GRE General Test, minimum GPA of 3.0, resume or curriculum vitae (recommended). Additional exam requirements/recommendations for international students: required—TOEFL (minimum score 550 paper-based; 80 iBT), IELTS (minimum score 7), PTE (minimum score 65). *Application deadline:* For fall admission, 12/18 for domestic students. Application fee: $105 ($125 for international students). Electronic applications accepted. *Financial support:* Fellowships, research assistantships, teaching assistantships, scholarships/grants, traineeships, and unspecified assistantships available. Financial award applicants required to submit FAFSA. *Unit head:* Bill Lin, Chair, 858-822-1383, E-mail: billin@ucsd.edu. *Application contact:* Sean Jones, Graduate Admissions Coordinator, 858-534-3213, E-mail: ecegradapps@ece.ucsd.edu.
Website: http://ece.ucsd.edu/

University of California, San Diego, Graduate Division, Department of Mechanical and Aerospace Engineering, Program in Applied Ocean Science, La Jolla, CA 92093. Offers MS, PhD. *Students:* 1 full-time (0 women). 4 applicants, 50% accepted. In 2019, 1 doctorate awarded. *Degree requirements:* For master's, comprehensive exam (for some programs), thesis (for some programs), comprehensive exam or thesis; for doctorate, comprehensive exam, thesis/dissertation. *Entrance requirements:* For master's and doctorate, GRE General Test, minimum GPA of 3.0. Additional exam requirements/recommendations for international students: required—TOEFL (minimum score 550 paper-based; 80 iBT), IELTS (minimum score 7). *Application deadline:* For fall admission, 12/18 for domestic students. Application fee: $105 ($125 for international students). Electronic applications accepted. *Financial support:* Fellowships, research assistantships, teaching assistantships, scholarships/grants, and unspecified assistantships available. Financial award applicants required to submit FAFSA. *Unit head:* Carlos Coimbra, Chair, 858-534-4285, E-mail: mae-chair-l@ucsd.edu. *Application contact:* Jackie Tam, Graduate Coordinator, 858-534-4387, E-mail: mae-gradadm-l@ucsd.edu.
Website: http://maeweb.ucsd.edu/

University of Delaware, College of Earth, Ocean, and Environment, School of Marine Science and Policy, Newark, DE 19716. Offers marine policy (MMP); marine studies (MS, PhD), including marine biosciences, oceanography, physical ocean science and engineering; oceanography (PhD).

University of Delaware, College of Engineering, Department of Civil and Environmental Engineering, Newark, DE 19716. Offers environmental engineering (MAS, MCE, PhD); geotechnical engineering (MAS, MCE, PhD); ocean engineering (MAS, MCE, PhD); structural engineering (MAS, MCE, PhD); transportation engineering (MAS, MCE, PhD); water resource engineering (MAS, MCE, PhD). *Program availability:* Part-time. Terminal master's awarded for partial completion of doctoral program. *Degree requirements:* For master's, thesis; for doctorate, thesis/dissertation. *Entrance requirements:* For master's and doctorate, GRE General Test. Additional exam requirements/recommendations for international students: required—TOEFL. Electronic applications accepted.

University of Florida, Graduate School, Herbert Wertheim College of Engineering, Department of Civil and Coastal Engineering, Gainesville, FL 32611. Offers civil engineering (ME, MS, PhD); coastal and oceanographic engineering (ME, MS, PhD); geographic information systems (ME, MS, PhD); hydrologic sciences (ME, MS, PhD); structural engineering (ME, MS); wetland sciences (ME, MS, PhD). *Program availability:* Part-time, online learning. Terminal master's awarded for partial completion of doctoral program. *Degree requirements:* For master's, thesis (for some programs); for doctorate, comprehensive exam, thesis/dissertation. *Entrance requirements:* For master's and doctorate, minimum GPA of 3.0. Additional exam requirements/recommendations for international students: required—TOEFL (minimum score 550 paper-based; 80 iBT), IELTS (minimum score 6). Electronic applications accepted.

University of Hawaii at Manoa, Office of Graduate Education, School of Ocean and Earth Science and Technology, Department of Ocean and Resources Engineering, Honolulu, HI 96822. Offers MS, PhD. *Accreditation:* ABET (one or more programs are accredited). *Program availability:* Part-time. *Degree requirements:* For master's, thesis optional, exams; for doctorate, comprehensive exam, thesis/dissertation, exams. *Entrance requirements:* For master's and doctorate, GRE General Test. Additional exam requirements/recommendations for international students: required—TOEFL (minimum score 560 paper-based; 83 iBT), IELTS (minimum score 5).

University of Michigan, College of Engineering, Department of Naval Architecture and Marine Engineering, Ann Arbor, MI 48109. Offers MS, MSE, PhD, Mar Eng, Nav Arch, MBA/MSE. *Program availability:* Part-time. Terminal master's awarded for partial completion of doctoral program. *Degree requirements:* For master's, thesis (for some programs); for doctorate, comprehensive exam, thesis/dissertation, oral defense of dissertation, written and oral preliminary exams; for other advanced degree, comprehensive exam, thesis, oral defense of thesis. *Entrance requirements:* For doctorate, GRE General Test, master's degree; for other advanced degree, GRE General Test. Additional exam requirements/recommendations for international students: required—TOEFL. Electronic applications accepted.

University of New Hampshire, Graduate School, School of Marine Science and Ocean Engineering, Durham, NH 03824. Offers ocean engineering (MS, PhD); ocean mapping

(MS, Postbaccalaureate Certificate). *Students:* 24 full-time (11 women), 5 part-time (1 woman); includes 1 minority (Hispanic/Latino), 10 international. Average age 29. 29 applicants, 62% accepted, 12 enrolled. In 2019, 4 master's, 1 doctorate, 6 other advanced degrees awarded. *Degree requirements:* For master's, thesis. *Entrance requirements:* Additional exam requirements/recommendations for international students: required—TOEFL (minimum score 550 paper-based; 80 iBT), IELTS, PTE. *Application deadline:* For fall admission, 7/1 for domestic students, 4/1 for international students; for spring admission, 12/1 for domestic students. Application fee: $65. Electronic applications accepted. *Financial support:* In 2019–20, 25 students received support, including 2 fellowships, 18 research assistantships, 5 teaching assistantships; Federal Work-Study, scholarships/grants, and tuition waivers (full and partial) also available. Support available to part-time students. Financial award application deadline: 2/15. *Unit head:* Martin Wosnik, Chair, 603-862-1891. *Application contact:* Laura Gustafson, Administrative Assistant, 603-862-0672, E-mail: laura.gustafson@unh.edu. Website: http://www.marine.unh.edu

University of Rhode Island, Graduate School, College of Engineering, Department of Ocean Engineering, Narragansett, RI 02882. Offers ocean engineering (MS, PhD), including acoustics, geomechanics (MS), hydrodynamics (MS), ocean instrumentation (MS), offshore energy (MS), offshore structures (MS), water wave mechanics (MS). *Program availability:* Part-time. *Faculty:* 9 full-time (1 woman). *Students:* 19 full-time (6 women), 16 part-time (5 women); includes 2 minority (1 Asian, non-Hispanic/Latino; 1 Two or more races, non-Hispanic/Latino), 9 international. 27 applicants, 89% accepted, 11 enrolled. In 2019, 18 master's, 4 doctorates awarded. *Entrance requirements:* Additional exam requirements/recommendations for international students: required—TOEFL. *Application deadline:* For fall admission, 7/15 for domestic students, 2/1 for international students; for spring admission, 11/15 for domestic students, 7/15 for international students; for summer admission, 4/15 for domestic students. Application fee: $65. Electronic applications accepted. *Expenses: Tuition, area resident:* Full-time $13,734; part-time $763 per credit. Tuition, state resident: full-time $13,734; part-time $763 per credit. Tuition, nonresident: full-time $26,512; part-time $1473 per credit. *International tuition:* $26,512 full-time. *Required fees:* $1780; $52 per credit. $35 per term. One-time fee: $165. *Financial support:* In 2019–20, 9 research assistantships with tuition reimbursements (averaging $8,915 per year), 3 teaching assistantships with tuition reimbursements (averaging $14,330 per year) were awarded. Financial award application deadline: 2/1; financial award applicants required to submit FAFSA. *Unit head:* Dr. Stephen Grilli, Chairman, 401-874-6636, E-mail: grilli@uri.edu. *Application contact:* Christopher Baxter, Graduate Program Director, 401-874-6575, E-mail: cbaxter@uri.edu. Website: http://www.oce.uri.edu/

Virginia Polytechnic Institute and State University, VT Online, Blacksburg, VA 24061. Offers advanced transportation systems (Certificate); aerospace engineering (MS); agricultural and life sciences (MSLFS); business information systems (Graduate Certificate); career and technical education (MS); civil engineering (MS); computer engineering (M Eng, MS); decision support systems (Graduate Certificate); eLearning leadership (MA); electrical engineering (M Eng, MS); engineering administration (MEA); environmental engineering (Certificate); environmental politics and policy (Graduate Certificate); environmental sciences and engineering (MS); foundations of political analysis (Graduate Certificate); health product risk management (Graduate Certificate); industrial and systems engineering (MS); information policy and society (Graduate Certificate); information security (Graduate Certificate); information technology (MIT); instructional technology (MA); integrative STEM education (MA Ed); liberal arts (Graduate Certificate); life sciences: health product risk management (MS); natural resources (MNR, Graduate Certificate); networking (Graduate Certificate); nonprofit and nongovernmental organization management (Graduate Certificate); ocean engineering (MS); political science (MA); security studies (Graduate Certificate); software development (Graduate Certificate). *Expenses:* Tuition, state resident: full-time $13,700; part-time $761.25 per credit hour. Tuition, nonresident: full-time $27,614; part-time $1534 per credit hour. *Required fees:* $886.50 per term. Tuition and fees vary according to campus/location and program.

Woods Hole Oceanographic Institution, MIT/WHOI Joint Program in Oceanography/ Applied Ocean Science and Engineering, Woods Hole, MA 02543-1541. Offers applied ocean science and engineering (PhD); biological oceanography (PhD); chemical oceanography (PhD); marine geology and geophysics (PhD); physical oceanography (PhD). *Degree requirements:* For doctorate, thesis/dissertation. *Entrance requirements:* For doctorate, GRE General Test. Additional exam requirements/recommendations for international students: required—TOEFL or IELTS. Electronic applications accepted.

Section 19
Paper and Textile Engineering

This section contains a directory of institutions offering graduate work in paper and textile engineering. Additional information about programs listed in the directory may be obtained by writing directly to the dean of a graduate school or chair of a department at the address given in the directory.

For programs offering related work, see also in this book *Engineering and Applied Sciences* and *Materials Sciences and Engineering*. In another guide in this series:

Graduate Programs in the Humanities, Arts & Social Sciences
See *Family and Consumer Sciences (Clothing and Textiles)*

CONTENTS

Program Directories

Paper and Pulp Engineering

State University of New York College of Environmental Science and Forestry, Department of Paper and Bioprocess Engineering, Syracuse, NY 13210-2779. Offers biomaterials engineering (MS, PhD); bioprocess engineering (MPS, MS, PhD); bioprocessing (Advanced Certificate); paper science and engineering (MPS, MS, PhD); sustainable engineering management (MPS). *Program availability:* Part-time. *Faculty:* 13 full-time (2 women), 1 part-time/adjunct (0 women). *Students:* 28 full-time (13 women), 3 part-time (0 women); includes 1 minority (Hispanic/Latino), 22 international. Average age 29. 19 applicants, 89% accepted, 10 enrolled. In 2019, 5 master's, 2 doctorates awarded. Terminal master's awarded for partial completion of doctoral program. *Degree requirements:* For master's, thesis; for doctorate, comprehensive exam, thesis/dissertation; for Advanced Certificate, 15 credit hours. *Entrance requirements:* For master's and doctorate, GRE General Test, minimum GPA of 3.0; for Advanced Certificate, BS, calculus plus science major. Additional exam requirements/recommendations for international students: required—TOEFL (minimum score 550 paper-based; 80 iBT), IELTS (minimum score 6). *Application deadline:* For fall admission, 2/1 priority date for domestic and international students; for spring admission, 11/1 priority date for domestic and international students. Applications are processed on a rolling basis. Application fee: $60. Electronic applications accepted. *Expenses:* Tuition, state resident: full-time $11,310; part-time $472 per credit hour. Tuition, nonresident: full-time $23,100; part-time $963 per credit hour. *Required fees:* $1890; $95.21 per credit hour. *Financial support:* In 2019–20, 17 students received support. Unspecified assistantships available. Financial award application deadline: 6/30; financial award applicants required to submit FAFSA. *Unit head:* Dr. Bandaru Ramarao, Chair, 315-470-6502, Fax: 315-470-6945, E-mail: bvramara@esf.edu. *Application contact:* Laura Payne, Office of Instruction and Graduate Studies, 315-470-6599, Fax: 315-470-6978, E-mail: esfgrad@esf.edu.
Website: http://www.esf.edu/pbe/

The University of Manchester, School of Materials, Manchester, United Kingdom. Offers advanced aerospace materials engineering (M Sc); advanced metallic systems (PhD); biomedical materials (M Phil, M Sc, PhD); ceramics and glass (M Phil, M Sc, PhD); composite materials (M Sc, PhD); corrosion and protection (M Phil, M Sc, PhD); materials (M Phil, PhD); metallic materials (M Phil, M Sc, PhD); nanostructural materials (M Phil, M Sc, PhD); paper science (M Phil, M Sc, PhD); polymer science and engineering (M Phil, M Sc, PhD); technical textiles (M Sc); textile design, fashion and management (M Phil, M Sc, PhD); textile science and technology (M Phil, M Sc, PhD); textiles (M Phil, PhD); textiles and fashion (M Ent).

University of Minnesota, Twin Cities Campus, Graduate School, College of Food, Agricultural and Natural Resource Sciences, Program in Natural Resources Science and Management, St. Paul, MN 55455-0213. Offers assessment, monitoring, and geospatial analysis (MS, PhD); economics, policy, management, and society (MS, PhD); forest hydrology and watershed management (MS, PhD); forest products (MS, PhD); forests: biology, ecology, conservation, and management (MS, PhD); natural resources science and management (MS, PhD); paper science and engineering (MS, PhD); recreation resources, tourism, and environmental education (MS, PhD). *Program availability:* Part-time. *Faculty:* 71 full-time (19 women), 61 part-time/adjunct (12 women). *Students:* 54 full-time (32 women), 34 part-time (17 women); includes 10 minority (1 Black or African American, non-Hispanic/Latino; 2 American Indian or Alaska Native, non-Hispanic/Latino; 5 Asian, non-Hispanic/Latino; 2 Hispanic/Latino), 11 international. Average age 30. 52 applicants, 33% accepted, 11 enrolled. In 2019, 22 master's, 2 doctorates awarded. Terminal master's awarded for partial completion of doctoral program. *Degree requirements:* For master's, comprehensive exam, thesis (for some programs); for doctorate, comprehensive exam, thesis/dissertation. *Entrance requirements:* For master's and doctorate, GRE General Test. Additional exam requirements/recommendations for international students: required—TOEFL (minimum score 550 paper-based; 79 iBT); recommended—IELTS (minimum score 6.5). *Application deadline:* For fall admission, 12/15 priority date for domestic and international students; for spring admission, 10/15 for domestic and international students. Applications are processed on a rolling basis. Application fee: $75 ($95 for international students). Electronic applications accepted. *Financial support:* In 2019–20, 6 students received support, including fellowships with full tuition reimbursements available (averaging $42,000 per year), research assistantships with full tuition reimbursements available (averaging $42,000 per year), teaching assistantships with full tuition reimbursements available (averaging $42,000 per year); scholarships/grants, health care benefits, and unspecified assistantships also available. *Unit head:* Dr. Matt Russell, Director of Graduate Studies, 612-626-4280, E-mail: russellm@umn.edu. *Application contact:* Jennifer Welsh, Graduate Program Coordinator, 612-624-7683, Fax: 612-625-5212, E-mail: nrsm@umn.edu.
Website: http://www.nrsm.umn.edu

Western Michigan University, Graduate College, College of Engineering and Applied Sciences, Department of Chemical and Paper Engineering, Kalamazoo, MI 49008. Offers MS, MSE, PhD. *Degree requirements:* For master's, thesis optional; for doctorate, one foreign language, comprehensive exam, thesis/dissertation.

Textile Sciences and Engineering

Cornell University, Graduate School, Graduate Fields of Human Ecology, Field of Fiber Science and Apparel Design, Ithaca, NY 14853. Offers apparel design (MA, MPS); fiber science (MS, PhD); polymer science (MS, PhD); textile science (MS, PhD). *Degree requirements:* For master's, thesis (MA, MS), project paper (MPS); for doctorate, comprehensive exam, thesis/dissertation. *Entrance requirements:* For master's, GRE General Test, 2 letters of recommendation, portfolio (for functional apparel design); for doctorate, GRE General Test, 2 letters of recommendation. Additional exam requirements/recommendations for international students: required—TOEFL (minimum score 600 paper-based; 77 iBT). Electronic applications accepted.

North Carolina State University, Graduate School, Wilson College of Textiles, Department of Textile and Apparel Technology and Management, Raleigh, NC 27695. Offers MS, MT. *Degree requirements:* For master's, thesis optional. *Entrance requirements:* For master's, GRE. Electronic applications accepted.

North Carolina State University, Graduate School, Wilson College of Textiles, Department of Textile Engineering, Chemistry, and Science, Program in Textile Chemistry, Raleigh, NC 27695. Offers MS. *Degree requirements:* For master's, thesis optional. *Entrance requirements:* For master's, GRE. Electronic applications accepted.

North Carolina State University, Graduate School, Wilson College of Textiles, Department of Textile Engineering, Chemistry, and Science, Program in Textile Engineering, Raleigh, NC 27695. Offers MS. *Degree requirements:* For master's, thesis optional. *Entrance requirements:* For master's, GRE. Electronic applications accepted.

North Carolina State University, Graduate School, Wilson College of Textiles, Program in Fiber and Polymer Science, Raleigh, NC 27695. Offers PhD. *Degree requirements:* For doctorate, one foreign language, thesis/dissertation, cumulative exams. *Entrance requirements:* For doctorate, GRE. Electronic applications accepted.

Thomas Jefferson University, Kanbar College of Design, Engineering and Commerce, PhD Program in Textile Engineering and Sciences, Philadelphia, PA 19107. Offers PhD.

Thomas Jefferson University, Kanbar College of Design, Engineering and Commerce, Program in Textile Engineering, Philadelphia, PA 19107. Offers MS. *Program availability:* Part-time. *Degree requirements:* For master's, thesis. *Entrance requirements:* For master's, GRE, minimum GPA of 2.8. Additional exam requirements/recommendations for international students: required—TOEFL (minimum score 550 paper-based; 79 iBT). Electronic applications accepted.

The University of Texas at Austin, Graduate School, College of Natural Sciences, School of Human Ecology, Program in Textile and Apparel Technology, Austin, TX 78712-1111. Offers MS.

Section 20
Telecommunications

This section contains a directory of institutions offering graduate work in tele-communications. Additional information about programs listed in the directory may be obtained by writing directly to the dean of a graduate school or chair of a department at the address given in the directory.

For programs offering related work, see also in this book *Computer Science and Information Technology* and *Engineering and Applied Sciences.* In the other guides in this series:

Graduate Programs in the Humanities, Arts & Social Sciences
See *Communication and Media*

Graduate Programs in Business, Education, Information Studies, Law & Social Work
See *Business Administration and Management*

CONTENTS

Program Directories

Telecommunications

Ball State University, Graduate School, College of Communication, Information, and Media, Department of Telecommunications, Muncie, IN 47306. Offers telecommunications (MA), including digital storytelling. *Program availability:* Part-time. *Entrance requirements:* For master's, minimum baccalaureate GPA of 2.75 or 3.0 in latter half of baccalaureate. Additional exam requirements/recommendations for international students: required—TOEFL (minimum score 550 paper-based; 79 iBT), IELTS (minimum score 6.5). Electronic applications accepted. *Expenses: Tuition, area resident:* Full-time $7506; part-time $417 per credit hour. Tuition, nonresident: full-time $20,610; part-time $1145 per credit hour. *Required fees:* $2126. Tuition and fees vary according to course load, campus/location and program.

Boston University, Metropolitan College, Department of Computer Science, Boston, MA 02215. Offers computer information systems (MS), including computer networks, data analytics, database management and business intelligence, health informatics, IT project management, security, Web application development; computer networks (Certificate); computer science (MS); data analytics (Certificate); digital forensics (Certificate); health informatics (Certificate); information technology project management (Certificate); software development (MS); software engineering in health care systems (Certificate); telecommunications (MS), including security. *Program availability:* Part-time, evening/weekend, online learning. *Faculty:* 16 full-time (3 women), 52 part-time/adjunct (5 women). *Students:* 253 full-time (80 women), 856 part-time (243 women); includes 246 minority (53 Black or African American, non-Hispanic/Latino; 1 American Indian or Alaska Native, non-Hispanic/Latino; 129 Asian, non-Hispanic/Latino; 48 Hispanic/Latino; 15 Two or more races, non-Hispanic/Latino), 418 international. Average age 30. 1,079 applicants, 72% accepted, 297 enrolled. In 2019, 513 master's awarded. *Entrance requirements:* For master's and Certificate, official transcripts from regionally-accredited bachelor's degree program, 3 letters of recommendation, professional resume, personal statement. Additional exam requirements/recommendations for international students: required—TOEFL (minimum score 84 iBT), IELTS. *Application deadline:* For fall admission, 8/1 priority date for domestic students, 6/1 priority date for international students; for spring admission, 12/1 priority date for domestic students, 11/15 priority date for international students; for summer admission, 4/1 priority date for domestic students, 3/1 priority date for international students. Applications are processed on a rolling basis. Application fee: $85. Electronic applications accepted. *Expenses:* Contact institution. *Financial support:* In 2019–20, 11 research assistantships (averaging $8,400 per year), 23 teaching assistantships (averaging $3,400 per year) were awarded; unspecified assistantships also available. Support available to part-time students. Financial award applicants required to submit FAFSA. *Unit head:* Dr. Anatoly Temkin, Chair, 617-353-2566, Fax: 617-353-2367, E-mail: csinfo@bu.edu. *Application contact:* Enrollment Services, 617-353-6004, E-mail: met@bu.edu.
Website: http://www.bu.edu/csmet/

California Miramar University, Program in Telecommunications Management, San Diego, CA 92108. Offers MST.

Claremont Graduate University, Graduate Programs, Center for Information Systems and Technology, Claremont, CA 91711-6160. Offers cybersecurity and networking (MS); data science and analytics (MS); electronic commerce (PhD); geographic information systems (MS); health informatics (MS); information systems (Certificate); IT strategy and innovation (MS); knowledge management (PhD); systems development (PhD); telecommunications and networking (PhD); MBA/MS. *Program availability:* Part-time. *Degree requirements:* For doctorate, comprehensive exam, thesis/dissertation, portfolio. *Entrance requirements:* For master's and doctorate, GMAT, GRE General Test. Additional exam requirements/recommendations for international students: required—TOEFL (minimum score 75 iBT). Electronic applications accepted.

Drexel University, College of Engineering, Department of Electrical and Computer Engineering, Program in Telecommunications Engineering, Philadelphia, PA 19104-2875. Offers MSEE. *Entrance requirements:* For master's, BS in electrical engineering or physics, minimum GPA of 3.0. Additional exam requirements/recommendations for international students: required—TOEFL. Electronic applications accepted.

Fairfield University, School of Engineering, Fairfield, CT 06824. Offers database management (CAS); electrical and computer engineering (MS); information security (CAS); management of technology (MS); mechanical engineering (MS); network technology (CAS); software engineering (MS); Web application development (CAS). *Program availability:* Part-time, evening/weekend. *Faculty:* 10 full-time (2 women), 15 part-time/adjunct (1 woman). *Students:* 46 full-time (24 women), 57 part-time (10 women); includes 23 minority (5 Black or African American, non-Hispanic/Latino; 9 Asian, non-Hispanic/Latino; 9 Hispanic/Latino), 33 international. Average age 29. 68 applicants, 62% accepted, 30 enrolled. In 2019, 100 master's awarded. *Degree requirements:* For master's, capstone course. *Entrance requirements:* For master's, resume, 2 recommendations. Additional exam requirements/recommendations for international students: required—TOEFL (minimum score 550 paper-based; 80 iBT), IELTS (minimum score 6.5), TOEFL (minimum score 550 paper-based; 80 iBT) or IELTS (minimum score 6.5). *Application deadline:* For fall admission, 5/15 for international students; for spring admission, 10/15 for international students. Applications are processed on a rolling basis. Application fee: $60. Electronic applications accepted. *Expenses:* Tuition $900/credit hour; Registration Fee $50/semester; Graduate Student Activity Fee (Fall and Spring) $65/semester. *Financial support:* In 2019–20, 20 students received support. Scholarships/grants and unspecified assistantships available. Financial award applicants required to submit FAFSA. *Unit head:* Richard Heist, Dean, 203-254-4147, Fax: 203-254-4013, E-mail: rheist@fairfield.edu. *Application contact:* Melanie Rogers, Director of Graduate Admission, 203-254-4184, Fax: 203-254-4073, E-mail: gradadmis@fairfield.edu.
Website: http://www.fairfield.edu/soe

Florida International University, College of Engineering and Computing, School of Computing and Information Sciences, Miami, FL 33199. Offers computer science (MS, PhD); cybersecurity (MS); data science (MS); information technology (MS); telecommunications and networking (MS). *Program availability:* Part-time, evening/weekend. *Faculty:* 53 full-time (14 women), 33 part-time/adjunct (9 women). *Students:* 162 full-time (39 women), 140 part-time (26 women); includes 160 minority (11 Black or African American, non-Hispanic/Latino; 1 American Indian or Alaska Native, non-Hispanic/Latino; 9 Asian, non-Hispanic/Latino; 132 Hispanic/Latino; 7 Two or more races, non-Hispanic/Latino), 120 international. Average age 30. 360 applicants, 49% accepted, 73 enrolled. In 2019, 89 master's, 13 doctorates awarded. *Degree requirements:* For master's, thesis or alternative; for doctorate, comprehensive exam, thesis/dissertation. *Entrance requirements:* For master's and doctorate, GRE General Test, 3 letters of recommendation, minimum GPA of 3.0. Additional exam requirements/recommendations for international students: required—TOEFL (minimum score 550 paper-based; 80 iBT). *Application deadline:* For fall admission, 6/1 for domestic students, 4/1 for international students; for spring admission, 10/1 for domestic students, 9/1 for international students. Applications are processed on a rolling basis. Application fee: $30. Electronic applications accepted. *Expenses: Tuition, area resident:* Full-time $8912; part-time $446 per credit hour. Tuition, state resident: full-time $8912; part-time $446 per credit hour. Tuition, nonresident: full-time $21,393; part-time $992 per credit hour. *Required fees:* $2194. *Financial support:* Research assistantships, teaching assistantships, institutionally sponsored loans, scholarships/grants, and unspecified assistantships available. Financial award application deadline: 3/1; financial award applicants required to submit FAFSA. *Unit head:* Dr. Sundararaj S. Iyengar, Director, 305-348-3947, Fax: 305-348-3549, E-mail: sundararaj.iyengar@fiu.edu. *Application contact:* Nanett Rojas, Manager, Admissions Operations, 305-348-7464, Fax: 305-348-7441, E-mail: gradadm@fiu.edu.

Franklin Pierce University, Graduate and Professional Studies, Rindge, NH 03461-0060. Offers curriculum and instruction (M Ed); elementary education (MS Ed); emerging network technologies (Graduate Certificate); energy and sustainability studies (MBA, Graduate Certificate); health administration (MBA, Graduate Certificate); human resource management (MBA, Graduate Certificate); information technology (MBA); leadership (MBA); nursing education (MS); nursing leadership (MS); physical therapy (DPT); physician assistant studies (MPAS); special education (M Ed); sports management (MBA). *Accreditation:* APTA. *Program availability:* Part-time, 100% online, blended/hybrid learning. *Degree requirements:* For master's, concentrated original research projects; student teaching; fieldwork and/or internship; leadership project; PRAXIS I and II (for M Ed); for doctorate, concentrated original research projects, clinical fieldwork and/or internship, leadership project. *Entrance requirements:* For master's, minimum GPA of 2.5, 3 letters of recommendation; competencies in accounting, economics, statistics, and computer skills through life experience or undergraduate coursework (for MBA); certification/e-portfolio, minimum C grade in all education courses (for M Ed); license to practice as RN (for MS); for doctorate, GRE, 80 hours of observation/work in PT settings; completion of anatomy, chemistry, physics, and statistics; minimum GPA of 3.0. Additional exam requirements/recommendations for international students: required—TOEFL (minimum score 550 paper-based; 61 iBT). Electronic applications accepted.

The George Washington University, School of Engineering and Applied Science, Department of Electrical and Computer Engineering, Washington, DC 20052. Offers electrical engineering (MS, PhD); telecommunication and computers (MS). *Program availability:* Part-time, evening/weekend. *Degree requirements:* For master's, thesis optional; for doctorate, comprehensive exam, thesis/dissertation, dissertation defense, qualifying exam. *Entrance requirements:* For master's, appropriate bachelor's degree, minimum GPA of 3.0; for doctorate, GRE (if highest earned degree is BS), appropriate bachelor's or master's degree, minimum GPA of 3.3; for other advanced degree, appropriate master's degree, minimum GPA of 3.0. Additional exam requirements/recommendations for international students: required—TOEFL or The George Washington University English as a Foreign Language Test.

Illinois Institute of Technology, Graduate College, Armour College of Engineering, Department of Electrical and Computer Engineering, Chicago, IL 60616. Offers biomedical imaging and signals (MAS); computer engineering (MS, PhD); electrical engineering (MS, PhD); electricity markets (MAS); network engineering (MAS); power engineering (MAS); telecommunications and software engineering (MAS); VLSI and microelectronics (MAS); MS/MS. *Program availability:* Part-time, evening/weekend, online learning. Terminal master's awarded for partial completion of doctoral program. *Degree requirements:* For master's, comprehensive exam (for some programs), thesis (for some programs); for doctorate, comprehensive exam, thesis/dissertation. *Entrance requirements:* For master's and doctorate, GRE General Test (minimum score 1100 Quantitative and Verbal, 3.5 Analytical Writing), minimum undergraduate GPA of 3.0. Additional exam requirements/recommendations for international students: required—TOEFL (minimum score 550 paper-based; 80 iBT); recommended—IELTS (minimum score 5.5). Electronic applications accepted.

Illinois Institute of Technology, Graduate College, College of Science, Department of Computer Science, Chicago, IL 60616. Offers business (MCS); computational intelligence (MCS); computer science (MCS, MS, PhD); cyber-physical systems (MCS); data analytics (MCS); data science (MAS); database systems (MCS); distributed and cloud computing (MCS); education (MCS); finance (MCS); information security and assurance (MCS); networking and communications (MCS); software engineering (MCS); telecommunications and software engineering (MAS); MS/MAS. *Program availability:* Part-time, evening/weekend, online learning. Terminal master's awarded for partial completion of doctoral program. *Degree requirements:* For master's, thesis optional; for doctorate, comprehensive exam, thesis/dissertation. *Entrance requirements:* For master's, GRE General Test with minimum scores of 298 Quantitative and Verbal, 3.0 Analytical Writing (for MS); GRE General Test with minimum scores of 292 Quantitative and Verbal, 2.5 Analytical Writing (for MAS), minimum undergraduate GPA of 3.0; for doctorate, GRE General Test (minimum scores: 304 Quantitative and Verbal, 3.5 Analytical Writing), minimum undergraduate GPA of 3.0. Additional exam requirements/recommendations for international students: required—TOEFL (minimum score 523 paper-based; 70 iBT). Electronic applications accepted.

Instituto Tecnologico de Santo Domingo, Graduate School, Area of Engineering, Santo Domingo, Dominican Republic. Offers construction administration (MS, Certificate); data telecommunications (M Eng, MS, Certificate); industrial engineering (M Eng, Certificate); industrial management (M Mgmt); information technology (Certificate); maintenance engineering (M Eng); occupational hazard prevention (M Mgmt); production management (Certificate); quantitative methods (Certificate); sanitary and environmental engineering (M Eng); structural engineering (M Eng); systems engineering and electronic data processing (Certificate); transportation (Certificate).

New Jersey Institute of Technology, Newark College of Engineering, Newark, NJ 07102. Offers biomedical engineering (MS, PhD); biopharmaceutical engineering (MS); chemical engineering (MS, PhD); civil engineering (MS, PhD); computer engineering (MS); critical infrastructure systems (MS); electrical engineering (MS, PhD); engineering management (MS); engineering science (MS); environmental engineering (MS, PhD); healthcare systems management (MS); industrial engineering (MS, PhD); internet engineering (MS); manufacturing systems engineering (MS); materials science & engineering (PhD); materials science and engineering (MS); mechanical engineering (MS, PhD); occupational safety and health engineering (MS). *Program availability:* Part-time, evening/weekend. *Faculty:* 151 full-time (29 women), 135 part-time/adjunct (15 women). *Students:* 576 full-time (161 women), 528 part-time (111 women); includes 366 minority (61 Black or African American, non-Hispanic/Latino; 1 American Indian or Alaska Native, non-Hispanic/Latino; 166 Asian, non-Hispanic/Latino; 115 Hispanic/Latino; 23 Two or more races, non-Hispanic/Latino), 450 international. Average age 28. 2,053 applicants, 67% accepted, 338 enrolled. In 2019, 474 master's, 30 doctorates awarded. Terminal master's awarded for partial completion of doctoral program. *Degree* *requirements:* For master's, thesis (for some programs); for doctorate, thesis/dissertation. *Entrance requirements:* For master's, GRE General Test, minimum GPA 2.8, personal statement, 1 letter of recommendation, transcripts; for doctorate, GRE General Test, minimum GPA of 3.5, personal statement, 3 letters of recommendation, transcripts. Additional exam requirements/recommendations for international students: required—TOEFL (minimum score 550 paper-based; 79 iBT), IELTS (minimum score 6.5). *Application deadline:* For fall admission, 6/1 priority date for domestic students, 5/1 priority date for international students; for spring admission, 11/15 priority date for domestic and international students. Applications are processed on a rolling basis. Application fee: $75. Electronic applications accepted. *Expenses:* $23,828 per year (in-state), $33,744 per year (out-of-state). *Financial support:* In 2019–20, 352 students received support, including 33 fellowships with full tuition reimbursements available (averaging $24,000 per year), 89 research assistantships with full tuition reimbursements available (averaging $24,000 per year), 112 teaching assistantships with full tuition reimbursements available (averaging $24,000 per year); career-related internships or fieldwork, Federal Work-Study, scholarships/grants, and unspecified assistantships also available. Financial award application deadline: 1/15. *Unit head:* Dr. Moshe Kam, Dean, 973-596-5534, Fax: 973-596-2316, E-mail: moshe.kam@njit.edu. *Application contact:* Stephen Eck, Executive Director of University Admissions, 973-596-3300, Fax: 973-596-3461, E-mail: admissions@njit.edu. Website: http://engineering.njit.edu/

Northeastern University, College of Engineering, Boston, MA 02115-5096. Offers bioengineering (MS, PhD); chemical engineering (MS, PhD); civil engineering (MS, PhD); computer engineering (PhD); computer systems engineering (MS); electrical and computer engineering (MS); electrical and computer engineering leadership (MS); electrical engineering (PhD); energy systems (MS); engineering and public policy (MS); engineering management (MS, Certificate); environmental engineering (MS); industrial engineering (MS, PhD); information assurance (PhD); information systems (MS); interdisciplinary engineering (PhD); mechanical engineering (PhD); operations research (MS); telecommunication systems management (MS). *Program availability:* Part-time, online learning. Electronic applications accepted. *Expenses:* Contact institution.

Ohio University, Graduate College, Scripps College of Communication, J. Warren McClure School of Information and Telecommunication Systems, Athens, OH 45701-2979. Offers MCTP. *Program availability:* Part-time. *Degree requirements:* For master's, comprehensive exam (for some programs), thesis (for some programs). *Entrance requirements:* For master's, GRE or GMAT, minimum cumulative GPA of 3.0. Additional exam requirements/recommendations for international students: required—TOEFL (minimum score 550 paper-based; 80 iBT) or IELTS (minimum score 6.5). Electronic applications accepted.

Pace University, Seidenberg School of Computer Science and Information Systems, New York, NY 10038. Offers chief information security officer (APC); computer science (MS, PhD); enterprise analytics (MS); information and communication technology strategy and innovation (APC); information systems (MS, APC); information technology (MS); professional studies in computing (DPS); secure software and information engineering (APC); security and information assurance (Certificate); software development and engineering (MS, Certificate); telecommunications systems and networks (MS, Certificate). *Program availability:* Part-time, evening/weekend, online only, 100% online, blended/hybrid learning. *Degree requirements:* For master's, thesis or alternative, capstone course; for doctorate, comprehensive exam (for some programs), thesis/dissertation. *Entrance requirements:* Additional exam requirements/recommendations for international students: required—TOEFL (minimum score 78 iBT), IELTS (minimum score 6.5) or PTE (minimum score 52). Electronic applications accepted. *Expenses:* Contact institution.

Rochester Institute of Technology, Graduate Enrollment Services, College of Applied Science and Technology, School of Engineering Technology, MS Program in Telecommunications Engineering Technology, Rochester, NY 14623-5603. Offers MS. *Program availability:* Part-time. *Degree requirements:* For master's, comprehensive exam (for some programs), thesis or alternative, Thesis, project, or exam options. *Entrance requirements:* For master's, GRE required for individuals with degrees from international universities, minimum GPA of 3.0 (recommended). Additional exam requirements/recommendations for international students: required—TOEFL (minimum score 570 paper-based; 88 iBT), IELTS (minimum score 6.5), PTE (minimum score 61). Electronic applications accepted. *Expenses:* Contact institution.

Southern Methodist University, Lyle School of Engineering, Department of Electrical Engineering, Dallas, TX 75275-0338. Offers electrical engineering (MS, PhD); telecommunications and network engineering (MS). *Program availability:* Part-time, evening/weekend, online learning. Terminal master's awarded for partial completion of doctoral program. *Degree requirements:* For master's, thesis optional; for doctorate, thesis/dissertation, oral and written qualifying exams, oral final exam. *Entrance requirements:* For master's, GRE General Test, minimum GPA of 3.0 in last 2 years; bachelor's degree in engineering, mathematics, or sciences; for doctorate, preliminary counseling exam, minimum GPA of 3.0, bachelor's degree in related field. Additional exam requirements/recommendations for international students: required—TOEFL. Electronic applications accepted.

Stevens Institute of Technology, Graduate School, School of Business, Program in Telecommunications Management, Hoboken, NJ 07030. Offers business (MS); global innovation management (MS); management of wireless networks (MS); online security, technology and business (MS); project management (MS); technical management (MS); telecommunications management (PhD, Certificate). *Program availability:* Part-time, evening/weekend. *Faculty:* 59 full-time (11 women), 30 part-time/adjunct (5 women). *Students:* 1 part-time (0 women). Average age 47. In 2019, 3 master's awarded. *Degree requirements:* For master's, thesis optional, minimum B average in major field and overall; for doctorate, comprehensive exam (for some programs), thesis/dissertation; for Certificate, minimum B average. *Entrance requirements:* For master's, International applicants must submit TOEFL/IELTS scores and fulfill the English Language Proficiency Requirement. Applicants to full-time programs who do not qualify for a score waiver are required to submit GRE/GMAT scores. Additional exam requirements/recommendations for international students: required—TOEFL (minimum score 74 iBT), IELTS (minimum score 6). *Application deadline:* For fall admission, 4/1 for domestic and international students; for spring admission, 11/1 for domestic and international students; for summer admission, 5/1 for domestic students. Applications are processed on a rolling basis. Application fee: $60. Electronic applications accepted. *Expenses:* Tuition: Full-time $52,134. *Required fees:* $1880. Tuition and fees vary according to course load. *Financial support:* Fellowships, research assistantships, teaching assistantships, career-related internships or fieldwork, Federal Work-Study, scholarships/grants, health care benefits, and unspecified assistantships available. Financial award application deadline: 2/15; financial award applicants required to submit FAFSA. *Unit head:* Dr. Gregory Prastacos, Dean of SB, 201-216-8366, E-mail: gprastac@stevens.edu. *Application contact:* Graduate Admission, 888-783-8367, Fax: 888-511-1306, E-mail: graduate@stevens.edu. Website: https://www.stevens.edu/school-business/masters-programs/network-communication-management-services

Stony Brook University, State University of New York, Graduate School, College of Engineering and Applied Sciences, Department of Electrical and Computer Engineering, Stony Brook, NY 11794. Offers computer engineering (MS, PhD); electrical engineering (MS, PhD); networking and wireless communications (Certificate). *Program availability:* Evening/weekend. *Faculty:* 29 full-time (6 women), 7 part-time/adjunct (2 women). *Students:* 157 full-time (25 women), 51 part-time (9 women); includes 29 minority (3 Black or African American, non-Hispanic/Latino; 19 Asian, non-Hispanic/Latino; 5 Hispanic/Latino; 2 Two or more races, non-Hispanic/Latino), 157 international. Average age 25. 346 applicants, 89% accepted, 81 enrolled. In 2019, 122 master's, 13 doctorates, 14 other advanced degrees awarded. *Degree requirements:* For master's, thesis or alternative; for doctorate, comprehensive exam, thesis/dissertation. *Entrance requirements:* For master's and doctorate, GRE General Test. Additional exam requirements/recommendations for international students: required—TOEFL (minimum score 90 iBT). *Application deadline:* For fall admission, 1/15 for domestic students; for spring admission, 10/1 for domestic students. Application fee: $100. *Expenses:* Contact institution. *Financial support:* In 2019–20, 2 fellowships, 33 research assistantships, 22 teaching assistantships were awarded. *Unit head:* Prof. Petar M. Djuric, Chair, 631-632-8420, Fax: 631-632-8494, E-mail: petar.djuric@stonybrook.edu. *Application contact:* Nicole Zinerco, Graduate Coordinator, 631-632-8401, E-mail: ecegradcoordinator@stonybrook.edu. Website: http://www.stonybrook.edu/commcms/electrical/

Stratford University, School of Graduate Studies, Falls Church, VA 22043. Offers accounting (MS); business administration (MBA, DBA); cyber security (MS); cyber security leadership and policy (MS); digital forensics (MS); healthcare administration (MS); information systems (MS); information technology (DIT); networking and telecommunications (MS); software engineering (MS). *Program availability:* Part-time, evening/weekend, 100% online, blended/hybrid learning. *Degree requirements:* For master's, comprehensive exam, capstone project. *Entrance requirements:* For master's, GRE or GMAT, baccalaureate degree. Additional exam requirements/recommendations for international students: required—TOEFL (minimum score 79 iBT), IELTS (minimum score 6.5), PTE (minimum score 5). Electronic applications accepted.

Universidad del Turabo, Graduate Programs, School of Engineering, Program in Telecommunications and Network Systems Administration, Gurabo, PR 00778-3030. Offers M Eng. *Entrance requirements:* For master's, GRE, EXADEP or GMAT, interview, essay, official transcript, recommendation letters. Electronic applications accepted.

Université du Québec, Institut National de la Recherche Scientifique, Graduate Programs, Centre for Energie Materiaux Telecommunications, Varennes, QC J3X 1S2, Canada. Offers energy and materials science (M Sc, PhD); telecommunications (M Sc, PhD). *Program availability:* Part-time. *Faculty:* 38 full-time. *Students:* 208 full-time (61 women), 12 part-time (1 woman), 187 international. Average age 32. 36 applicants, 100% accepted, 29 enrolled. In 2019, 12 master's, 26 doctorates awarded. *Degree requirements:* For master's, thesis (for some programs); for doctorate, thesis/dissertation. *Entrance requirements:* For master's, appropriate bachelor's degree, proficiency in French; for doctorate, appropriate master's degree, proficiency in French. *Application deadline:* For fall admission, 3/30 for domestic and international students; for winter admission, 11/1 for domestic and international students; for spring admission, 3/1 for domestic and international students. Application fee: $45. Electronic applications accepted. *Financial support:* In 2019–20, fellowships (averaging $16,500 per year) were awarded; research assistantships and scholarships/grants also available. *Unit head:* Ana Tavares, Director, 514-228-6947, Fax: 450-929-8102, E-mail: ana.tavares@emt.inrs.ca. *Application contact:* Sean Otto, Registrar, 418-654-2518, Fax: 418-654-3858, E-mail: sean.otto@inrs.ca. Website: http://www.emt.inrs.ca

University of Alberta, Faculty of Graduate Studies and Research, Department of Electrical and Computer Engineering, Edmonton, AB T6G 2E1, Canada. Offers communications (M Eng, M Sc, PhD); computer engineering (M Eng, M Sc, PhD); electromagnetics (M Eng, M Sc, PhD); nanotechnology and microdevices (M Eng, M Sc, PhD); power/power electronics (M Eng, M Sc, PhD); systems (M Eng, M Sc, PhD). Terminal master's awarded for partial completion of doctoral program. *Degree requirements:* For master's, thesis; for doctorate, thesis/dissertation. *Entrance requirements:* Additional exam requirements/recommendations for international students: required—TOEFL. Electronic applications accepted.

University of Arkansas, Graduate School, College of Engineering, Department of Electrical Engineering, Fayetteville, AR 72701. Offers electrical engineering (MSEE, PhD); telecommunications engineering (MS Tc E). *Students:* 48 full-time (12 women), 100 part-time (13 women); includes 20 minority (4 Black or African American, non-Hispanic/Latino; 8 Asian, non-Hispanic/Latino; 7 Hispanic/Latino; 1 Two or more races, non-Hispanic/Latino), 77 international. 27 applicants, 74% accepted. In 2019, 25 master's, 6 doctorates awarded. *Degree requirements:* For master's, thesis optional; for doctorate, one foreign language, thesis/dissertation. *Entrance requirements:* For master's and doctorate, GRE General Test. *Application deadline:* For fall admission, 8/1 for domestic students, 4/1 for international students; for spring admission, 12/1 for domestic students, 10/1 for international students; for summer admission, 4/15 for domestic students, 3/1 for international students. Applications are processed on a rolling basis. Application fee: $60. Electronic applications accepted. *Financial support:* In 2019–20, 48 research assistantships, 8 teaching assistantships were awarded; fellowships with tuition reimbursements, career-related internships or fieldwork, and Federal Work-Study also available. Support available to part-time students. Financial award application deadline: 4/1; financial award applicants required to submit FAFSA. *Unit head:* Dr. Juan Carlos Balda, Department Head, 479-575-3005, Fax: 479-575-7967, E-mail: jbalda@uark.edu. *Application contact:* Dr. Hameed Naseem, Graduate Coordinator, 479-575-6052, Fax: 479-575-7967, E-mail: hnaseem@uark.edu. Website: https://electrical-engineering.uark.edu/index.php

University of California, San Diego, Graduate Division, Department of Electrical and Computer Engineering, La Jolla, CA 92093. Offers applied ocean science (MS, PhD); applied physics (MS, PhD); communication theory and systems (MS, PhD); computer engineering (MS, PhD); electronic circuits and systems (MS, PhD); intelligent systems, robotics and control (MS, PhD); medical devices and systems (MS, PhD); nanoscale devices and systems (MS, PhD); photonics (MS, PhD); signal and image processing (MS, PhD). *Students:* 983 full-time (216 women), 80 part-time (15 women). 3,675 applicants, 33% accepted, 430 enrolled. In 2019, 287 master's, 50 doctorates awarded. Terminal master's awarded for partial completion of doctoral program. *Degree requirements:* For master's, comprehensive exam (for some programs), thesis (for some programs); for doctorate, comprehensive exam, thesis/dissertation. *Entrance requirements:* For master's and doctorate, GRE General Test, minimum GPA of 3.0, resume or curriculum vitae (recommended). Additional exam requirements/recommendations for international students: required—TOEFL (minimum score 550 paper-based; 80 iBT), IELTS (minimum score 7), PTE (minimum score 65). *Application deadline:* For fall admission, 12/18 for domestic students. Application fee: $105 ($125 for international students). Electronic applications accepted. *Financial support:* Fellowships, research assistantships, teaching assistantships, scholarships/grants, traineeships, and unspecified assistantships available. Financial award applicants

required to submit FAFSA. *Unit head:* Bill Lin, Chair, 858-822-1383, E-mail: billin@ucsd.edu. *Application contact:* Sean Jones, Graduate Admissions Coordinator, 858-534-3213, E-mail: ecegradapps@ece.ucsd.edu.
Website: http://ece.ucsd.edu/

University of California, San Diego, Graduate Division, Program in Wireless Embedded Systems, La Jolla, CA 92093. Offers MAS. *Program availability:* Part-time. *Students:* 20 part-time (2 women). 30 applicants, 73% accepted, 20 enrolled. In 2019, 21 master's awarded. *Degree requirements:* For master's, capstone project. *Entrance requirements:* For master's, GRE General Test (if applicant possesses fewer than 2 years' work experience), 3 letters of recommendation, statement of purpose, resume or curriculum vitae. Additional exam requirements/recommendations for international students: required—TOEFL (minimum score 550 paper-based; 80 iBT), IELTS (minimum score 7). *Application deadline:* For fall admission, 7/1 for domestic students. Application fee: $105 ($125 for international students). Electronic applications accepted. *Expenses:* Contact institution. *Financial support:* Applicants required to submit FAFSA. *Unit head:* Ryan Kastner, Director, 858- 534-8908, E-mail: rkastner@ucsd.edu. *Application contact:* Yvonne Wu, Graduate Coordinator, 858-246-1463, E-mail: wes-mas@ucsd.edu.
Website: http://maseng.ucsd.edu/wes

University of Colorado Boulder, Graduate School, College of Engineering and Applied Science, Technology, Cybersecurity and Policy Program, Boulder, CO 80309. Offers MS, JD/MS, MBA/MS. Terminal master's awarded for partial completion of doctoral program. *Degree requirements:* For master's, comprehensive exam, thesis or alternative. *Entrance requirements:* For master's, minimum undergraduate GPA of 3.0. Electronic applications accepted. Application fee is waived when completed online.

University of Florida, Graduate School, College of Journalism and Communications, Program in Mass Communication, Gainesville, FL 32611. Offers international/intercultural communication (MAMC); journalism (MAMC); mass communication (MAMC, PhD), including clinical translational science (MAMC); public relations (MAMC); science/health communication (MAMC); telecommunication (MAMC). *Entrance requirements:* For master's and doctorate, GRE General Test, minimum GPA of 3.0.

University of Hawaii at Manoa, Office of Graduate Education, College of Social Sciences, School of Communications, Program in Telecommunication and Information Resource Management, Honolulu, HI 96822. Offers Graduate Certificate. *Program availability:* Part-time. *Entrance requirements:* Additional exam requirements/recommendations for international students: required—TOEFL (minimum score 500 paper-based; 61 iBT), IELTS (minimum score 5).

University of Houston, College of Technology, Department of Engineering Technology, Houston, TX 77204. Offers construction management (MS); engineering technology (MS); network communications (M Tech). *Program availability:* Part-time. *Degree requirements:* For master's, project or thesis (most programs). *Entrance requirements:* For master's, GRE. Additional exam requirements/recommendations for international students: required—TOEFL (minimum score 550 paper-based; 79 iBT). Electronic applications accepted.

University of Maryland, College Park, Academic Affairs, A. James Clark School of Engineering, Department of Electrical and Computer Engineering, Program in Telecommunications, College Park, MD 20742. Offers MS. *Program availability:* Part-time, evening/weekend. *Degree requirements:* For master's, thesis or alternative. *Entrance requirements:* For master's, GRE General Test, minimum GPA of 3.0, professional experience. Additional exam requirements/recommendations for international students: required—TOEFL. Electronic applications accepted.

University of Massachusetts Dartmouth, Graduate School, College of Engineering, Department of Electrical and Computer Engineering, North Dartmouth, MA 02747-2300. Offers communications (Postbaccalaureate Certificate); computing infrastructure security (Postbaccalaureate Certificate); digital signal processing (Postbaccalaureate Certificate); electrical engineering (MS, PhD); electrical engineering systems (Postbaccalaureate Certificate). *Program availability:* Part-time. Terminal master's awarded for partial completion of doctoral program. *Degree requirements:* For master's, thesis, thesis or project; for doctorate, comprehensive exam, thesis/dissertation. *Entrance requirements:* For master's, GRE unless UMass Dartmouth graduate in computer engineering or electrical engineering, statement of purpose (minimum of 300 words), resume, 3 letters of recommendation, official transcripts; for doctorate, GRE unless UMass Dartmouth graduate in college of engineering major or about to receive electrical graduate certificate, statement of purpose (minimum of 300 words), resume, 3 letters of recommendation, official transcripts; for Postbaccalaureate Certificate, statement of purpose (minimum of 300 words), resume, official transcripts. Additional exam requirements/recommendations for international students: required—TOEFL (minimum score 550 paper-based; 79 iBT), IELTS (minimum score 6.5). Electronic applications accepted.

University of Mississippi, Graduate School, School of Engineering, University, MS 38677. Offers aeroacoustics (MS, PhD); chemical engineering (MS, PhD); civil engineering (MS, PhD); computational hydroscience (MS, PhD); computer science (MS, PhD); electrical engineering (MS, PhD); electromagnetics (MS, PhD); environmental engineering (MS, PhD); geology and geological engineering (MS, PhD); hydrology (MS); material science (MS); mechanical engineering (MS, PhD); telecommunications (MS). *Students:* 104 full-time (23 women), 19 part-time (5 women); includes 10 minority (3 Black or African American, non-Hispanic/Latino; 6 Asian, non-Hispanic/Latino; 1 Hispanic/Latino), 72 international. Average age 30. In 2019, 36 master's, 17 doctorates awarded. *Expenses:* Tuition, state resident: full-time $8718; part-time $484.25 per credit hour. Tuition, nonresident: full-time $24,990; part-time $1388.25 per credit hour. *Required fees:* $100; $4.16 per credit hour. *Unit head:* Dr. David Puleo, Dean, 662-915-5780, Fax: 662-915-5387, E-mail: engineer@olemiss.edu. *Application contact:* Temeka Smith, Graduate Activities Specialist for Admissions, 662-915-7474, Fax: 662-915-7577, E-mail: gschool@olemiss.edu.

University of Missouri–Kansas City, School of Computing and Engineering, Kansas City, MO 64110-2499. Offers civil engineering (MS); computer and electrical engineering (PhD); computer science (MS), including bioinformatics, software engineering, telecommunications networking; computer science and informatics (PhD); computing (PhD); electrical engineering (MS); engineering (PhD); engineering and construction management (Graduate Certificate); mechanical engineering (MS); telecommunications and computer networking (PhD). *Program availability:* Part-time. *Degree requirements:* For doctorate, thesis/dissertation. *Entrance requirements:* For master's, GRE General Test, minimum GPA of 3.0, 3 letters of recommendation from professors; for doctorate, GRE General Test, minimum GPA of 3.5. Additional exam requirements/recommendations for international students: required—TOEFL (minimum score 550 paper-based; 80 iBT).

The University of North Carolina at Chapel Hill, Graduate School, Hussman School of Journalism and Media, Chapel Hill, NC 27599. Offers digital communication (MA, Certificate); media and communication (MA, PhD), including interdisciplinary health communication (MA), journalism (MA), strategic communication (MA), theory and research (MA), visual communication (MA); JD/PhD; MA/JD. *Accreditation:* ACEJMC (one or more programs are accredited). *Program availability:* Part-time, all course instruction online, plus two on-campus experiences totaling seven days. *Faculty:* 30 full-time (15 women), 5 part-time/adjunct (4 women). *Students:* 68 full-time (45 women), 82 part-time (58 women); includes 35 minority (13 Black or African American, non-Hispanic/Latino; 1 American Indian or Alaska Native, non-Hispanic/Latino; 4 Asian, non-Hispanic/Latino; 1 Hispanic/Latino; 16 Two or more races, non-Hispanic/Latino), 9 international. Average age 34. 205 applicants, 49% accepted, 73 enrolled. In 2019, 32 master's, 5 doctorates, 24 other advanced degrees awarded. *Degree requirements:* For master's, comprehensive exam, thesis; for doctorate, comprehensive exam, thesis/dissertation. *Entrance requirements:* For master's, GRE General Test for online master's degree (waiver available); minimum GPA of 3.0 for residential master's degree; for doctorate, minimum GPA of 3.0. Additional exam requirements/recommendations for international students: required—TOEFL (minimum iBT score of 105) or IELTS (7.5). Application fee: $95. Electronic applications accepted. *Expenses:* Ph.D.: 7,550 per semester N.C. resident, 15,883 non-res; Residential M.A.: 8,425 per semester N.C., 16,708 non-res; Online M.A./certificate: 2,262 per semester N.C., 4,698 non-res. *Financial support:* In 2019–20, 60 students received support, including 41 fellowships with full tuition reimbursements available (averaging $17,901 per year), 4 research assistantships with full tuition reimbursements available (averaging $17,465 per year); scholarships/grants and health care benefits also available. Financial award application deadline: 12/15; financial award applicants required to submit FAFSA. *Unit head:* Susan King, Dean, 919-962-1204, Fax: 919-962-0620, E-mail: susanking@unc.edu. *Application contact:* Casey Hart, Assistant Director, Graduate Studies, 919-843-9471, Fax: 919-962-0620, E-mail: mjgrad@unc.edu.
Website: http://hussman.unc.edu

University of Oklahoma, Gallogly College of Engineering, School of Electrical and Computer Engineering, Norman, OK 73019. Offers electrical and computer engineering (MS, PhD); telecommunications engineering (MS). *Program availability:* Part-time. Terminal master's awarded for partial completion of doctoral program. *Degree requirements:* For master's, comprehensive exam (for some programs), thesis (for some programs); for doctorate, thesis/dissertation, general exam. *Entrance requirements:* For master's and doctorate, GRE, minimum GPA of 3.0. Additional exam requirements/recommendations for international students: required—TOEFL (minimum score 79 iBT) or IELTS (minimum score 6.5). Electronic applications accepted. *Expenses:* Tuition, state resident: full-time $6583.20; part-time $274.30 per credit hour. Tuition, nonresident: full-time $21,242; part-time $885.10 per credit hour. *International tuition:* $21,242.40 full-time. *Required fees:* $1994.20; $72.55 per credit hour. $126.50 per semester. Tuition and fees vary according to course load and degree level.

University of Southern California, Graduate School, Viterbi School of Engineering, Daniel J. Epstein Department of Industrial and Systems Engineering, Los Angeles, CA 90089. Offers digital supply chain management (MS); engineering management (MS); engineering technology communication (Graduate Certificate); health systems operations (Graduate Certificate); industrial and systems engineering (MS, PhD, Engr); manufacturing engineering (MS); operations research engineering (MS); optimization and supply chain management (Graduate Certificate); product development engineering (MS); safety systems and security (MS); systems architecting and engineering (MS, Graduate Certificate); systems safety and security (Graduate Certificate); transportation systems (Graduate Certificate); MS/MBA. *Program availability:* Part-time, evening/weekend, online learning. Terminal master's awarded for partial completion of doctoral program. *Degree requirements:* For master's, thesis optional; for doctorate, thesis/dissertation. *Entrance requirements:* For master's and doctorate, GRE General Test. Additional exam requirements/recommendations for international students: recommended—TOEFL. Electronic applications accepted.

University of Southern California, Graduate School, Viterbi School of Engineering, Ming Hsieh Department of Electrical Engineering, Los Angeles, CA 90089. Offers computer engineering (MS, PhD); electric power (MS); electrical engineering (MS, PhD, Engr); engineering technology commercialization (Graduate Certificate); multimedia and creative technologies (MS); telecommunications (MS); VLSI design (MS); wireless health technology (MS). *Program availability:* Part-time, online learning. Terminal master's awarded for partial completion of doctoral program. *Degree requirements:* For master's, thesis optional; for doctorate, thesis/dissertation. *Entrance requirements:* For master's and doctorate, GRE General Test. Additional exam requirements/recommendations for international students: recommended—TOEFL. Electronic applications accepted.

The University of Texas at Dallas, Erik Jonsson School of Engineering and Computer Science, Department of Electrical and Computer Engineering, Richardson, TX 75080. Offers computer engineering (MS, PhD); electrical engineering (MSEE, PhD); telecommunications engineering (MSTE, PhD). *Program availability:* Part-time, evening/weekend. *Faculty:* 41 full-time (3 women), 11 part-time/adjunct (2 women). *Students:* 383 full-time (96 women), 142 part-time (32 women); includes 46 minority (8 Black or African American, non-Hispanic/Latino; 28 Asian, non-Hispanic/Latino; 7 Hispanic/Latino; 3 Two or more races, non-Hispanic/Latino), 423 international. Average age 28. 1,343 applicants, 25% accepted, 125 enrolled. In 2019, 184 master's, 44 doctorates awarded. *Degree requirements:* For master's, thesis or major design project; for doctorate, thesis/dissertation. *Entrance requirements:* For master's, GRE General Test, minimum GPA of 3.0 in related bachelor's degree; for doctorate, GRE General Test, minimum GPA of 3.5. Additional exam requirements/recommendations for international students: required—TOEFL (minimum score 550 paper-based). *Application deadline:* For fall admission, 7/15 for domestic students, 5/1 priority date for international students; for spring admission, 11/15 for domestic students, 9/1 priority date for international students. Applications are processed on a rolling basis. Application fee: $50 ($100 for international students). Electronic applications accepted. *Expenses: Tuition, area resident:* Full-time $16,504. Tuition, state resident: full-time $16,504. Tuition, nonresident: full-time $34,266. Tuition and fees vary according to course load. *Financial support:* In 2019–20, 208 students received support, including 14 fellowships (averaging $4,096 per year), 140 research assistantships with partial tuition reimbursements available (averaging $22,844 per year), 70 teaching assistantships with partial tuition reimbursements available (averaging $16,888 per year); Federal Work-Study, institutionally sponsored loans, scholarships/grants, unspecified assistantships, and cooperative positions also available. Support available to part-time students. Financial award application deadline: 4/30; financial award applicants required to submit FAFSA. *Unit head:* Dr. Lawrence Overzet, Department Head, 972-883-2154, Fax: 972-883-2710, E-mail: overzet@utdallas.edu. *Application contact:* Dr. Aria Nosratinia, Associate Department Head, 972-883-2894, E-mail: aria@utdallas.edu.
Website: http://ece.utdallas.edu

Telecommunications Management

Alaska Pacific University, Graduate Programs, Business Administration Department, Programs in Information and Communication Technology, Anchorage, AK 99508-4672. Offers MBAICT. *Program availability:* Part-time, evening/weekend. *Degree requirements:* For master's, capstone course. *Entrance requirements:* For master's, GMAT or GRE General Test, minimum GPA of 3.0.

Boston University, Metropolitan College, Department of Computer Science, Boston, MA 02215. Offers computer information systems (MS), including computer networks, data analytics, database management and business intelligence, health informatics, IT project management, security, Web application development; computer networks (Certificate); computer science (MS); data analytics (Certificate); digital forensics (Certificate); health informatics (Certificate); information technology project management (Certificate); software development (MS); software engineering in health care systems (Certificate); telecommunications (MS), including security. *Program availability:* Part-time, evening/weekend, online learning. *Faculty:* 16 full-time (3 women), 52 part-time/adjunct (5 women). *Students:* 253 full-time (80 women), 856 part-time (243 women); includes 246 minority (53 Black or African American, non-Hispanic/Latino; 1 American Indian or Alaska Native, non-Hispanic/Latino; 129 Asian, non-Hispanic/Latino; 48 Hispanic/Latino; 15 Two or more races, non-Hispanic/Latino), 418 international. Average age 30. 1,079 applicants, 72% accepted, 297 enrolled. In 2019, 513 master's awarded. *Entrance requirements:* For master's and Certificate, official transcripts from regionally-accredited bachelor's degree program, 3 letters of recommendation, professional resume, personal statement. Additional exam requirements/recommendations for international students: required—TOEFL (minimum score 84 iBT), IELTS. *Application deadline:* For fall admission, 8/1 priority date for domestic students, 6/1 priority date for international students; for spring admission, 12/1 priority date for domestic students, 11/15 priority date for international students; for summer admission, 4/1 priority date for domestic students, 3/1 priority date for international students. Applications are processed on a rolling basis. Application fee: $85. Electronic applications accepted. *Expenses:* Contact institution. *Financial support:* In 2019–20, 11 research assistantships (averaging $8,400 per year), 23 teaching assistantships (averaging $3,400 per year) were awarded; unspecified assistantships also available. Support available to part-time students. Financial award applicants required to submit FAFSA. *Unit head:* Dr. Anatoly Temkin, Chair, 617-353-2566, Fax: 617-353-2367, E-mail: csinfo@bu.edu. *Application contact:* Enrollment Services, 617-353-6004, E-mail: met@bu.edu.
Website: http://www.bu.edu/csmet/

California Miramar University, Program in Telecommunications Management, San Diego, CA 92108. Offers MST.

Capitol Technology University, Graduate Programs, Laurel, MD 20708-9759. Offers business administration (MBA); computer science (MS); electrical engineering (MS); information and telecommunications systems management (MS); information architecture (MS); network security (MS). *Program availability:* Part-time, evening/weekend, online learning. *Entrance requirements:* For master's, minimum GPA of 3.0. Electronic applications accepted.

Carnegie Mellon University, Carnegie Institute of Technology, Information Networking Institute, Pittsburgh, PA 15213. Offers information networking (MS); information security (MS); information technology - information security (MS); information technology - mobility (MS); information technology - software management (MS). *Degree requirements:* For master's, thesis optional. *Entrance requirements:* For master's, GRE General Test, bachelor's degree in computer science, computer engineering, or electrical engineering, or related technology degree; programming skills (C/C++ fluency for some programs). Additional exam requirements/recommendations for international students: required—TOEFL.

Concordia University, School of Graduate Studies, Faculty of Engineering and Computer Science, Concordia Institute for Information Systems Engineering (CIISE), Montréal, QC H3G 1M8, Canada. Offers 3D graphics and game development (Certificate); information and systems engineering (PhD); information systems security (M Eng, MA Sc); quality systems engineering (M Eng, MA Sc); service engineering and network management (Certificate).

East Carolina University, Graduate School, College of Engineering and Technology, Department of Technology Systems, Greenville, NC 27858-4353. Offers computer network professional (Certificate); cyber security professional (Certificate); information assurance (Certificate); Lean Six Sigma Black Belt (Certificate); network technology (MS), including computer networking management, digital communications technology, information security, Web technologies; occupational safety (MS); technology management (MS, PhD), including industrial distribution and logistics (MS); Website developer (Certificate). *Application deadline:* For fall admission, 6/1 priority date for domestic students. *Expenses: Tuition, area resident:* Full-time $4749; part-time $185 per credit hour. Tuition, state resident: full-time $4749; part-time $185 per credit hour. Tuition, nonresident: full-time $17,898; part-time $864 per credit hour. *International tuition:* $17,898 full-time. *Required fees:* $2787. *Financial support:* Application deadline: 6/1. *Unit head:* Dr. Tijjani Mohammed, Chair, 252-328-9668, E-mail: mohammedt@ecu.edu. *Application contact:* Graduate School Admissions, 252-328-6012, Fax: 252-328-6071, E-mail: gradschool@ecu.edu.
Website: https://cet.ecu.edu/techsystems/

Instituto Tecnológico y de Estudios Superiores de Monterrey, Campus Ciudad de México, School of Design, Engineering and Architecture, Ciudad de Mexico, Mexico. Offers management (MA); telecommunications (MA). *Program availability:* Part-time, evening/weekend, online learning.

Instituto Tecnológico y de Estudios Superiores de Monterrey, Campus Ciudad Obregón, Program in Administration of Telecommunications, Ciudad Obregón, Mexico. Offers MAT.

Instituto Tecnológico y de Estudios Superiores de Monterrey, Campus Estado de México, Professional and Graduate Division, Estado de Mexico, Mexico. Offers administration of information technologies (MITA); architecture (M Arch); business administration (GMBA, MBA); computer sciences (MCS, PhD); education (M Ed); educational institution administration (MAD); educational technology and innovation (PhD); electronic commerce (MEC); environmental systems (MS); finance (MAF); humanistic studies (MHS); information sciences and knowledge management (MISKM); information systems (MS); manufacturing systems (MS); marketing (MEM); quality systems and productivity (MS); science and materials engineering (PhD); telecommunications management (MTM). *Program availability:* Part-time, online learning. *Degree requirements:* For master's, one foreign language, thesis (for some programs); for doctorate, one foreign language, thesis/dissertation. *Entrance requirements:* For master's, E-PAEP 500, interview; for doctorate, E-PAEP 500, research proposal. Additional exam requirements/recommendations for international students: required—TOEFL (minimum score 550 paper-based).

Instituto Tecnológico y de Estudios Superiores de Monterrey, Campus Irapuato, Graduate Programs, Irapuato, Mexico. Offers administration (MBA); administration of information technology (MAIT); administration of telecommunications (MAT); architecture (M Arch); computer science (MCS); education (M Ed); educational administration (MEA); educational innovation and technology (DEIT); educational technology (MET); electronic commerce (MBA); environmental administration and planning (MEAP); environmental systems (MES); finances (MBA); humanistic studies (MHS); international management for Latin American executives (MIMLAE); library and information science (MLIS); manufacturing quality management (MMQM); marketing research (MBA).

Murray State University, Jesse D. Jones College of Science, Engineering and Technology, Institute of Engineering, Program in Telecommunications Systems Management, Murray, KY 42071. Offers MS. *Program availability:* Part-time, evening/weekend, 100% online, blended/hybrid learning. *Entrance requirements:* For master's, GRE or GMAT, minimum university GPA of 2.75. Additional exam requirements/recommendations for international students: required—TOEFL (minimum score 527 paper-based; 71 iBT). Electronic applications accepted.

Oklahoma State University, Graduate College, Stillwater, OK 74078. Offers aerospace security (Graduate Certificate); bioenergy and sustainable technology (Graduate Certificate); business data mining (Graduate Certificate); business sustainability (Graduate Certificate); environmental science (MS); international studies (MS); non-profit management (Graduate Certificate); teaching English to speakers of other languages (Graduate Certificate); telecommunications management (MS). *Students:* 32 full-time (22 women), 203 part-time (114 women); includes 63 minority (12 Black or African American, non-Hispanic/Latino; 19 American Indian or Alaska Native, non-Hispanic/Latino; 12 Asian, non-Hispanic/Latino; 8 Hispanic/Latino; 12 Two or more races, non-Hispanic/Latino), 38 international. Average age 34. 301 applicants, 83% accepted, 173 enrolled. In 2019, 26 master's, 2 doctorates awarded. *Degree requirements:* For master's, thesis (for some programs); for doctorate, comprehensive exam, thesis/dissertation. *Entrance requirements:* For master's and doctorate, GRE or GMAT. Additional exam requirements/recommendations for international students: required—TOEFL (minimum score 550 paper-based; 79 iBT). *Application deadline:* For fall admission, 3/1 priority date for domestic and international students; for spring admission, 8/1 priority date for domestic and international students. Applications are processed on a rolling basis. Application fee: $50 ($75 for international students). Electronic applications accepted. *Expenses: Tuition, area resident:* Full-time $4148.10; part-time $2765.40. Tuition, state resident: full-time $4148.10; part-time $2765.40. Tuition, nonresident: full-time $15,775; part-time $10,516.80. *International tuition:* $15,775.20 full-time. *Required fees:* $2196.90; $122.05 per credit hour. Tuition and fees vary according to course load, campus/location and program. *Financial support:* Research assistantships, career-related internships or fieldwork, Federal Work-Study, scholarships/grants, health care benefits, tuition waivers (partial), and unspecified assistantships available. Support available to part-time students. Financial award application deadline: 3/1; financial award applicants required to submit FAFSA. *Unit head:* Dr. Sheryl Tucker, Dean, 405-744-6368, Fax: 405-744-0355, E-mail: gradi@okstate.edu. *Application contact:* Dr. Sheryl Tucker, Dean, 405-744-6368, Fax: 405-744-0355, E-mail: gradi@okstate.edu.
Website: http://gradcollege.okstate.edu/

Oklahoma State University, Spears School of Business, Department of Management Science and Information Systems, Stillwater, OK 74078. Offers management information systems (MS); management science and information systems (PhD); telecommunications management (MS). *Program availability:* Part-time, online learning. *Faculty:* 12 full-time (2 women), 2 part-time/adjunct (0 women). *Students:* 31 full-time (16 women), 60 part-time (15 women); includes 11 minority (2 Black or African American, non-Hispanic/Latino; 3 American Indian or Alaska Native, non-Hispanic/Latino; 3 Asian, non-Hispanic/Latino; 1 Hispanic/Latino; 2 Two or more races, non-Hispanic/Latino), 43 international. Average age 30. 109 applicants, 61% accepted, 23 enrolled. In 2019, 58 master's, 1 doctorate awarded. *Entrance requirements:* For master's and doctorate, GRE or GMAT. Additional exam requirements/recommendations for international students: required—TOEFL (minimum score 550 paper-based; 79 iBT). *Application deadline:* For fall admission, 3/1 priority date for international students; for spring admission, 8/1 priority date for international students. Applications are processed on a rolling basis. Application fee: $50 ($75 for international students). Electronic applications accepted. *Expenses: Tuition, area resident:* Full-time $4148.10; part-time $2765.40. Tuition, state resident: full-time $4148.10; part-time $2765.40. Tuition, nonresident: full-time $15,775; part-time $10,516.80. *International tuition:* $15,775.20 full-time. *Required fees:* $2196.90; $122.05 per credit hour. Tuition and fees vary according to course load, campus/location and program. *Financial support:* In 2019–20, 10 research assistantships (averaging $2,000 per year), 11 teaching assistantships (averaging $1,198 per year) were awarded; career-related internships or fieldwork, Federal Work-Study, scholarships/grants, health care benefits, tuition waivers (partial), and unspecified assistantships also available. Support available to part-time students. Financial award application deadline: 3/1; financial award applicants required to submit FAFSA. *Unit head:* Dr. Rick Wilson, Department Head, 405-744-3551, Fax: 405-744-5180, E-mail: rick.wilson@okstate.edu. *Application contact:* Dr. Sheryl Tucker, Vice Prov/Dean/Prof, 405-744-6368, E-mail: gradi@okstate.edu.
Website: https://business.okstate.edu/departments_programs/msis/index.html

San Diego State University, Graduate and Research Affairs, College of Professional Studies and Fine Arts, School of Communication, San Diego, CA 92182. Offers advertising and public relations (MA); critical-cultural studies (MA); interaction studies (MA); intercultural and international studies (MA); new media studies (MA); news and information studies (MA); telecommunications and media management (MA). *Degree requirements:* For master's, thesis. *Entrance requirements:* For master's, GRE General Test, 3 letters of recommendation. Additional exam requirements/recommendations for international students: required—TOEFL. Electronic applications accepted.

Stevens Institute of Technology, Graduate School, School of Business, Program in Business Administration, Hoboken, NJ 07030. Offers business intelligence and analytics (MBA); engineering management (MBA); finance (MBA); information systems (MBA); innovation and entrepreneurship (MBA); marketing (MBA); pharmaceutical management (MBA); project management (MBA, Certificate); technology management (MBA); telecommunications management (MBA). *Accreditation:* AACSB. *Program availability:* Part-time, evening/weekend. *Faculty:* 59 full-time (11 women), 30 part-time/adjunct (5 women). *Students:* 50 full-time (21 women), 242 part-time (112 women); includes 68 minority (13 Black or African American, non-Hispanic/Latino; 2 American Indian or Alaska Native, non-Hispanic/Latino; 51 Asian, non-Hispanic/Latino; 2 Hispanic/Latino), 55 international. Average age 36. In 2019, 60 master's awarded. Terminal master's awarded for partial completion of doctoral program. *Degree requirements:* For master's,

thesis optional, minimum B average in major field and overall; for Certificate, minimum B average. *Entrance requirements:* For master's, International applicants must submit TOEFL/IELTS scores and fulfill the English Language Proficiency Requirement. Applicants to full-time programs who do not qualify for a score waiver are required to submit GRE/GMAT scores. Additional exam requirements/recommendations for international students: required—TOEFL (minimum score 74 iBT), IELTS (minimum score 6). *Application deadline:* For fall admission, 4/1 for domestic and international students; for spring admission, 11/1 for domestic and international students; for summer admission, 5/1 for domestic students. Applications are processed on a rolling basis. Application fee: $60. Electronic applications accepted. *Expenses: Tuition:* Full-time $52,134. *Required fees:* $1880. Tuition and fees vary according to course load. *Financial support:* Fellowships, research assistantships, teaching assistantships, career-related internships or fieldwork, Federal Work-Study, scholarships/grants, and unspecified assistantships available. Financial award application deadline: 2/15; financial award applicants required to submit FAFSA. *Unit head:* Dr. Gregory Prastacos, Dean, 201-216-8366, E-mail: gprastac@stevens.edu. *Application contact:* Graduate Admissions, 888-783-8367, Fax: 888-511-1306, E-mail: graduate@stevens.edu.
Website: https://www.stevens.edu/school-business/masters-programs/mbaemba

Stevens Institute of Technology, Graduate School, School of Business, Program in Information Systems, Hoboken, NJ 07030. Offers computer science (MS); e-commerce (MS); enterprise systems (MS); entrepreneurial information technology (MS); information architecture (MS); information management (MS, Certificate); information security (MS); information technology in financial services industry (MS); information technology in the pharmaceutical industry (MS); information technology outsourcing management (MS); project management (MS, Certificate); software engineering (MS); telecommunications (MS). *Program availability:* Part-time, evening/weekend. *Faculty:* 59 full-time (11 women), 30 part-time/adjunct (5 women). *Students:* 221 full-time (80 women), 52 part-time (18 women); includes 24 minority (8 Black or African American, non-Hispanic/Latino; 16 Asian, non-Hispanic/Latino), 225 international. Average age 27. In 2019, 188 master's awarded. Terminal master's awarded for partial completion of doctoral program. *Degree requirements:* For master's, thesis optional, minimum B average in major field and overall; for Certificate, minimum B average. *Entrance requirements:* For master's, International applicants must submit TOEFL/IELTS scores and fulfill the English Language Proficiency Requirement. Applicants to full-time programs who do not qualify for a score waiver are required to submit GRE/GMAT scores. Additional exam requirements/recommendations for international students: required—TOEFL (minimum score 74 iBT), IELTS (minimum score 6). *Application deadline:* For fall admission, 4/1 for domestic and international students; for spring admission, 11/1 for domestic and international students; for summer admission, 5/1 for domestic students. Applications are processed on a rolling basis. Application fee: $60. Electronic applications accepted. *Expenses: Tuition:* Full-time $52,134. *Required fees:* $1880. Tuition and fees vary according to course load. *Financial support:* Fellowships, research assistantships, teaching assistantships, career-related internships or fieldwork, Federal Work-Study, scholarships/grants, and unspecified assistantships available. Financial award application deadline: 2/15; financial award applicants required to submit FAFSA. *Unit head:* Dr. Gregory Prastacos, Dean of SB, 201-216-8366, E-mail: gprastac@stevens.edu. *Application contact:* Graduate Admissions, 888-783-8367, Fax: 888-511-1306, E-mail: graduate@stevens.edu.
Website: https://www.stevens.edu/school-business/masters-programs/information-systems

Stevens Institute of Technology, Graduate School, School of Business, Program in Network and Communication Management and Services, Hoboken, NJ 07030. Offers MS. *Program availability:* Part-time, evening/weekend. *Faculty:* 59 full-time (11 women), 30 part-time/adjunct (5 women). *Students:* 11 full-time (2 women), 32 part-time (6 women); includes 10 minority (5 Black or African American, non-Hispanic/Latino; 1 American Indian or Alaska Native, non-Hispanic/Latino; 3 Asian, non-Hispanic/Latino; 1 Hispanic/Latino), 11 international. Average age 38. In 2019, 24 master's awarded. *Degree requirements:* For master's, thesis optional, minimum B average in major field and overall. *Entrance requirements:* For master's, International applicants must submit TOEFL/IELTS scores and fulfill the English Language Proficiency Requirement. Applicants to full-time programs who do not qualify for a score waiver are required to submit GRE/GMAT scores. Additional exam requirements/recommendations for international students: required—TOEFL (minimum score 74 iBT), IELTS (minimum score 6). *Application deadline:* For fall admission, 7/1 for domestic students, 4/1 for international students; for spring admission, 11/1 for domestic and international students; for summer admission, 5/1 for domestic students. Applications are processed on a rolling basis. Application fee: $60. Electronic applications accepted. *Expenses: Tuition:* Full-time $52,134. *Required fees:* $1880. Tuition and fees vary according to course load. *Financial support:* Fellowships, research assistantships, teaching assistantships, career-related internships or fieldwork, Federal Work-Study, scholarships/grants, and unspecified assistantships available. Financial award application deadline: 2/15; financial award applicants required to submit FAFSA. *Unit head:* Dr. Gregory Prastacos, Dean of SB, 201-216-8366, E-mail: gprastac@stevens.edu. *Application contact:* Graduate Admissions, 888-793-8367, Fax: 888-511-1306, E-mail: graduate@stevens.edu.
Website: http://www.stevens.edu/school-business/masters-programs/network-communication-management-services

Stevens Institute of Technology, Graduate School, School of Business, Program in Technology Management, Hoboken, NJ 07030. Offers information management (PhD); technology management (PhD); telecommunications management (PhD). *Program availability:* Part-time, evening/weekend, online learning. *Faculty:* 59 full-time (11 women), 30 part-time/adjunct (5 women). *Students:* 2 full-time (0 women), 18 part-time (4 women); includes 10 minority (4 Black or African American, non-Hispanic/Latino; 6 Asian, non-Hispanic/Latino), 2 international. Average age 40. Terminal master's awarded for partial completion of doctoral program. *Degree requirements:* For doctorate, comprehensive exam (for some programs), thesis/dissertation. *Entrance requirements:* Additional exam requirements/recommendations for international students: required—TOEFL (minimum score 74 iBT), IELTS (minimum score 6). *Application deadline:* For fall admission, 4/1 for domestic and international students; for spring admission, 11/1 for domestic and international students; for summer admission, 5/1 for domestic students. Applications are processed on a rolling basis. Application fee: $60. Electronic applications accepted. *Expenses: Tuition:* Full-time $52,134. *Required fees:* $1880. Tuition and fees vary according to course load. *Financial support:* Fellowships, research assistantships, teaching assistantships, career-related internships or fieldwork, Federal Work-Study, scholarships/grants, and unspecified assistantships available. Financial award application deadline: 2/15; financial award applicants required to submit FAFSA. *Unit head:* Dr. Gregory Prascatos, Dean of SB, 201-216 8366, Fax: 201-216-5385, E-mail: gprastac@stevens.edu. *Application contact:* Graduate Admissions, 888-783-8367, Fax: 888-511-1306, E-mail: graduate@stevens.edu.
Website: https://www.stevens.edu/school-business/phd-business-administration

Stevens Institute of Technology, Graduate School, School of Business, Program in Telecommunications Management, Hoboken, NJ 07030. Offers business (MS); global innovation management (MS); management of wireless networks (MS); online security, technology and business (MS); project management (MS); technical management (MS); telecommunications management (PhD, Certificate). *Program availability:* Part-time, evening/weekend. *Faculty:* 59 full-time (11 women), 30 part-time/adjunct (5 women). *Students:* 1 part-time (0 women). Average age 47. In 2019, 3 master's awarded. *Degree requirements:* For master's, thesis optional, minimum B average in major field and overall; for doctorate, comprehensive exam (for some programs), thesis/dissertation; for Certificate, minimum B average. *Entrance requirements:* For master's, International applicants must submit TOEFL/IELTS scores and fulfill the English Language Proficiency Requirement. Applicants to full-time programs who do not qualify for a score waiver are required to submit GRE/GMAT scores. Additional exam requirements/recommendations for international students: required—TOEFL (minimum score 74 iBT), IELTS (minimum score 6). *Application deadline:* For fall admission, 4/1 for domestic and international students; for spring admission, 11/1 for domestic and international students; for summer admission, 5/1 for domestic students. Applications are processed on a rolling basis. Application fee: $60. Electronic applications accepted. *Expenses: Tuition:* Full-time $52,134. *Required fees:* $1880. Tuition and fees vary according to course load. *Financial support:* Fellowships, research assistantships, teaching assistantships, career-related internships or fieldwork, Federal Work-Study, scholarships/grants, health care benefits, and unspecified assistantships available. Financial award application deadline: 2/15; financial award applicants required to submit FAFSA. *Unit head:* Dr. Gregory Prastacos, Dean of SB, 201-216-8366, E-mail: gprastac@stevens.edu. *Application contact:* Graduate Admission, 888-783-8367, Fax: 888-511-1306, E-mail: graduate@stevens.edu.
Website: https://www.stevens.edu/school-business/masters-programs/network-communication-management-services

Strayer University, Graduate Studies, Washington, DC 20005-2603. Offers accounting (MS); acquisition (MBA); business administration (MBA); communications technology (MS); educational management (M Ed); finance (MBA); health services administration (MHSA); hospitality and tourism management (MBA); human resource management (MBA); information systems (MS), including computer security management, decision support system management, enterprise resource management, network management, software engineering management, systems development management; management (MBA); management information systems (MS); marketing (MBA); professional accounting (MS), including accounting information systems, controllership, taxation; public administration (MPA); supply chain management (MBA); technology in education (M Ed). *Accreditation:* ACBSP. *Program availability:* Part-time, evening/weekend, online learning. *Degree requirements:* For master's, thesis. *Entrance requirements:* For master's, GMAT, GRE General Test, bachelor's degree from an accredited college or university, minimum undergraduate GPA of 2.75. Electronic applications accepted.

University of Colorado Boulder, Graduate School, College of Engineering and Applied Science, Technology, Cybersecurity and Policy Program, Boulder, CO 80309. Offers MS, JD/MS, MBA/MS. Terminal master's awarded for partial completion of doctoral program. *Degree requirements:* For master's, comprehensive exam, thesis or alternative. *Entrance requirements:* For master's, minimum undergraduate GPA of 3.0. Electronic applications accepted. Application fee is waived when completed online.

University of South Africa, College of Human Sciences, Pretoria, South Africa. Offers adult education (M Ed); African languages (MA, PhD); African politics (MA, PhD); Afrikaans (MA, PhD); ancient history (MA, PhD); ancient Near Eastern studies (MA, PhD); anthropology (MA, PhD); applied linguistics (MA); Arabic (MA, PhD); archaeology (MA); art history (MA); Biblical archaeology (MA); Biblical studies (M Th, D Th, PhD); Christian spirituality (M Th, D Th); church history (M Th, D Th); classical studies (MA, PhD); clinical psychology (MA); communication (MA, PhD); comparative education (M Ed, Ed D); consulting psychology (D Admin, D Com, PhD); curriculum studies (M Ed, Ed D); development studies (M Admin, MA, D Admin, PhD); didactics (M Ed, Ed D); education (M Tech); education management (M Ed, Ed D); educational psychology (M Ed); English (MA); environmental education (M Ed); French (MA, PhD); German (MA, PhD); Greek (MA); guidance and counseling (M Ed); health studies (MA, PhD), including health sciences education (MA), health services management (MA), medical and surgical nursing science (critical care general) (MA), midwifery and neonatal nursing science (MA), trauma and emergency care (MA); history (MA, PhD); history of education (Ed D); inclusive education (M Ed, Ed D); information and communications technology policy and regulation (MA); information science (MA, MIS, PhD); international politics (MA, PhD); Islamic studies (MA, PhD); Italian (MA, PhD); Judaica (MA, PhD); linguistics (MA, PhD); mathematical education (M Ed); mathematics education (MA); missiology (M Th, D Th); modern Hebrew (MA, PhD); musicology (MA, MMus, D Mus, PhD); natural science education (M Ed); New Testament (M Th, D Th); Old Testament (D Th); pastoral therapy (M Th, D Th); philosophy (MA); philosophy of education (M Ed, Ed D); politics (MA, PhD); Portuguese (MA, PhD); practical theology (M Th, D Th); psychology (MA, MS, PhD); psychology of education (M Ed, Ed D); public health (MA); religious studies (MA, D Th, PhD); Romance languages (MA); Russian (MA, PhD); Semitic languages (MA, PhD); social behavior studies in HIV/AIDS (MA); social science (mental health) (MA); social science in development studies (MA); social science in psychology (MA); social science in social work (MA); social science in sociology (MA); social work (MSW, DSW, PhD); socio-education (M Ed, Ed D); sociolinguistics (MA); sociology (MA, PhD); Spanish (MA, PhD); systematic theology (M Th, D Th); TESOL (teaching English to speakers of other languages) (MA); theological ethics (M Th, D Th); theory of literature (MA, PhD); urban ministries (D Th); urban ministry (M Th).

University of Wisconsin–Stout, Graduate School, College of Science, Technology, Engineering and Mathematics, Program in Information and Communication Technologies, Menomonie, WI 54751. Offers MS. *Program availability:* Part-time, online learning. *Degree requirements:* For master's, thesis. *Entrance requirements:* For master's, minimum GPA of 2.75. Additional exam requirements/recommendations for international students: required—TOEFL (minimum score 500 paper-based; 61 iBT). Electronic applications accepted.

APPENDIXES

Institutional Changes
Since the 2020 Edition (Graduate)

Following is an alphabetical listing of institutions that have recently closed, merged with other institutions, or changed their names or status. In the case of a name change, the former name appears first, followed by the new name.

Antioch University (Midwest Yellow Springs, OH): *closed.*

Argosy University, Atlanta (Atlanta, GA): *closed.*

Argosy University, Chicago (Chicago, IL): *closed.*

Argosy University, Hawaii (Honolulu, HI): *closed.*

Argosy University, Los Angeles (Los Angeles, CA): *closed.*

Argosy University, Northern Virginia (Arlington, VA): *closed.*

Argosy University, Orange County (Orange, CA): *closed.*

Argosy University, Phoenix (Phoenix, AZ): *closed.*

Argosy University, Seattle (Seattle, WA): *closed.*

Argosy University, Tampa (Tampa, FL): *closed.*

Argosy University, Twin Cities (Eagan, MN): *closed.*

College of Saint Elizabeth (Morristown, NJ): *name changed to Saint Elizabeth University.*

College of St. Joseph (Rutland, VT): *closed.*

Concordia University (Portland, OR): *closed.*

Elmhurst College (Elmhurst, IL): *name changed to Elmhurst University.*

The John Marshall Law School (Chicago, IL): *closed; acquired by University of Illinois at Chicago; name changed to UIC John Marshall Law School.*

Marygrove College (Detroit, MI): *closed.*

Nebraska Christian College of Hope International University (Papillion, NE): *closed.*

Northwest Christian University (Eugene, OR): *name changed to Bushnell University.*

Notre Dame de Namur University (Belmont, CA): *closed.*

Silver Lake College of the Holy Family (Manitowoc, WI): *closed.*

University of South Florida Sarasota-Manatee (Sarasota, FL): *to merge with University of South Florida Main Campus.*

University of South Florida, St. Petersburg (St. Petersburg, FL): *to merge with University of South Florida Main Campus.*

Watkins College of Art, Design, and Film (Nashville, TN): *to merge with Belmont University.*

Abbreviations Used in the Guides

The following list includes abbreviations of degree names used in the profiles in the 2021 edition of the guides. Because some degrees (e.g., Doctor of Education) can be abbreviated in more than one way (e.g., D.Ed. or Ed.D.), and because the abbreviations used in the guides reflect the preferences of the individual colleges and universities, the list may include two or more abbreviations for a single degree.

DEGREES

A Mus D	Doctor of Musical Arts
AC	Advanced Certificate
AD	Artist's Diploma
	Doctor of Arts
ADP	Artist's Diploma
Adv C	Advanced Certificate
AGC	Advanced Graduate Certificate
AGSC	Advanced Graduate Specialist Certificate
ALM	Master of Liberal Arts
AM	Master of Arts
AMBA	Accelerated Master of Business Administration
APC	Advanced Professional Certificate
APMPH	Advanced Professional Master of Public Health
App Sc	Applied Scientist
App Sc D	Doctor of Applied Science
AstE	Astronautical Engineer
ATC	Advanced Training Certificate
Au D	Doctor of Audiology
B Th	Bachelor of Theology
CAES	Certificate of Advanced Educational Specialization
CAGS	Certificate of Advanced Graduate Studies
CAL	Certificate in Applied Linguistics
CAPS	Certificate of Advanced Professional Studies
CAS	Certificate of Advanced Studies
CATS	Certificate of Achievement in Theological Studies
CE	Civil Engineer
CEM	Certificate of Environmental Management
CET	Certificate in Educational Technologies
CGS	Certificate of Graduate Studies
Ch E	Chemical Engineer
Clin Sc D	Doctor of Clinical Science
CM	Certificate in Management
CMH	Certificate in Medical Humanities
CMM	Master of Church Ministries
CMS	Certificate in Ministerial Studies
CNM	Certificate in Nonprofit Management
CPC	Certificate in Publication and Communication
CPH	Certificate in Public Health
CPS	Certificate of Professional Studies
CScD	Doctor of Clinical Science
CSD	Certificate in Spiritual Direction
CSS	Certificate of Special Studies
CTS	Certificate of Theological Studies
D Ac	Doctor of Acupuncture
D Admin	Doctor of Administration
D Arch	Doctor of Architecture
D Be	Doctor in Bioethics
D Com	Doctor of Commerce
D Couns	Doctor of Counseling
D Des	Doctorate of Design
D Div	Doctor of Divinity
D Ed	Doctor of Education
D Ed Min	Doctor of Educational Ministry
D Eng	Doctor of Engineering
D Engr	Doctor of Engineering

D Ent	Doctor of Enterprise
D Env	Doctor of Environment
D Law	Doctor of Law
D Litt	Doctor of Letters
D Med Sc	Doctor of Medical Science
D Mgt	Doctor of Management
D Min	Doctor of Ministry
D Miss	Doctor of Missiology
D Mus	Doctor of Music
D Mus A	Doctor of Musical Arts
D Phil	Doctor of Philosophy
D Prof	Doctor of Professional Studies
D Ps	Doctor of Psychology
D Sc	Doctor of Science
D Sc D	Doctor of Science in Dentistry
D Sc IS	Doctor of Science in Information Systems
D Sc PA	Doctor of Science in Physician Assistant Studies
D Th	Doctor of Theology
D Th P	Doctor of Practical Theology
DA	Doctor of Accounting
	Doctor of Arts
DACM	Doctor of Acupuncture and Chinese Medicine
DAIS	Doctor of Applied Intercultural Studies
DAOM	Doctorate in Acupuncture and Oriental Medicine
DAT	Doctorate of Athletic Training
	Professional Doctor of Art Therapy
DBA	Doctor of Business Administration
DBH	Doctor of Behavioral Health
DBL	Doctor of Business Leadership
DC	Doctor of Chiropractic
DCC	Doctor of Computer Science
DCD	Doctor of Communications Design
DCE	Doctor of Computer Engineering
DCJ	Doctor of Criminal Justice
DCL	Doctor of Civil Law
	Doctor of Comparative Law
DCM	Doctor of Church Music
DCN	Doctor of Clinical Nutrition
DCS	Doctor of Computer Science
DDN	Diplôme du Droit Notarial
DDS	Doctor of Dental Surgery
DE	Doctor of Education
	Doctor of Engineering
DED	Doctor of Economic Development
DEIT	Doctor of Educational Innovation and Technology
DEL	Doctor of Executive Leadership
DEM	Doctor of Educational Ministry
DEPD	Diplôme Études Spécialisées
DES	Doctor of Engineering Science
DESS	Diplôme Études Supérieures Spécialisées
DET	Doctor of Educational Technology
DFA	Doctor of Fine Arts
DGP	Diploma in Graduate and Professional Studies
DGS	Doctor of Global Security
DH Sc	Doctor of Health Sciences
DHA	Doctor of Health Administration
DHCE	Doctor of Health Care Ethics
DHL	Doctor of Hebrew Letters
DHPE	Doctorate of Health Professionals Education
DHS	Doctor of Health Science
DHSc	Doctor of Health Science
DIT	Doctor of Industrial Technology

	Doctor of Information Technology
DJS	Doctor of Jewish Studies
DLS	Doctor of Liberal Studies
DM	Doctor of Management
	Doctor of Music
DMA	Doctor of Musical Arts
DMD	Doctor of Dental Medicine
DME	Doctor of Manufacturing Management
	Doctor of Music Education
DMFT	Doctor of Marital and Family Therapy
DMH	Doctor of Medical Humanities
DML	Doctor of Modern Languages
DMP	Doctorate in Medical Physics
DMPNA	Doctor of Management Practice in Nurse Anesthesia
DN Sc	Doctor of Nursing Science
DNAP	Doctor of Nurse Anesthesia Practice
DNP	Doctor of Nursing Practice
DNP-A	Doctor of Nursing Practice - Anesthesia
DNS	Doctor of Nursing Science
DO	Doctor of Osteopathy
DOL	Doctorate of Organizational Leadership
DOM	Doctor of Oriental Medicine
DOT	Doctor of Occupational Therapy
DPA	Diploma in Public Administration
	Doctor of Public Administration
DPDS	Doctor of Planning and Development Studies
DPH	Doctor of Public Health
DPM	Doctor of Plant Medicine
	Doctor of Podiatric Medicine
DPPD	Doctor of Policy, Planning, and Development
DPS	Doctor of Professional Studies
DPT	Doctor of Physical Therapy
DPTSc	Doctor of Physical Therapy Science
Dr DES	Doctor of Design
Dr NP	Doctor of Nursing Practice
Dr OT	Doctor of Occupational Therapy
Dr PH	Doctor of Public Health
Dr Sc PT	Doctor of Science in Physical Therapy
DRSc	Doctor of Regulatory Science
DS	Doctor of Science
DS Sc	Doctor of Social Science
DScPT	Doctor of Science in Physical Therapy
DSI	Doctor of Strategic Intelligence
DSJS	Doctor of Science in Jewish Studies
DSL	Doctor of Strategic Leadership
DSNS	Doctorate of Statecraft and National Security
DSS	Doctor of Strategic Security
DSW	Doctor of Social Work
DTL	Doctor of Talmudic Law
	Doctor of Transformational Leadership
DV Sc	Doctor of Veterinary Science
DVM	Doctor of Veterinary Medicine
DWS	Doctor of Worship Studies
EAA	Engineer in Aeronautics and Astronautics
EASPh D	Engineering and Applied Science Doctor of Philosophy
ECS	Engineer in Computer Science
Ed D	Doctor of Education
Ed DCT	Doctor of Education in College Teaching
Ed L D	Doctor of Education Leadership
Ed M	Master of Education
Ed S	Specialist in Education
Ed Sp	Specialist in Education
EDB	Executive Doctorate in Business
EDM	Executive Doctorate in Management
EE	Electrical Engineer
EJD	Executive Juris Doctor
EMBA	Executive Master of Business Administration

EMFA	Executive Master of Forensic Accounting
EMHA	Executive Master of Health Administration
EMHCL	Executive Master in Healthcare Leadership
EMIB	Executive Master of International Business
EMIR	Executive Master in International Relations
EML	Executive Master of Leadership
EMPA	Executive Master of Public Administration
EMPL	Executive Master in Policy Leadership
	Executive Master in Public Leadership
EMS	Executive Master of Science
EMTM	Executive Master of Technology Management
Eng	Engineer
Eng Sc D	Doctor of Engineering Science
Engr	Engineer
Exec MHA	Executive Master of Health Administration
Exec Ed D	Executive Doctor of Education
Exec MBA	Executive Master of Business Administration
Exec MPA	Executive Master of Public Administration
Exec MPH	Executive Master of Public Health
Exec MS	Executive Master of Science
Executive MA	Executive Master of Arts
G Dip	Graduate Diploma
GBC	Graduate Business Certificate
GDM	Graduate Diploma in Management
GDPA	Graduate Diploma in Public Administration
GEMBA	Global Executive Master of Business Administration
GM Acc	Graduate Master of Accountancy
GMBA	Global Master of Business Administration
GP LL M	Global Professional Master of Laws
GPD	Graduate Performance Diploma
GSS	Graduate Special Certificate for Students in Special Situations
IEMBA	International Executive Master of Business Administration
IMA	Interdisciplinary Master of Arts
IMBA	International Master of Business Administration
IMES	International Master's in Environmental Studies
Ingeniero	Engineer
JCD	Doctor of Canon Law
JCL	Licentiate in Canon Law
JD	Juris Doctor
JM	Juris Master
JSD	Doctor of Juridical Science
	Doctor of Jurisprudence
	Doctor of the Science of Law
JSM	Master of the Science of Law
L Th	Licentiate in Theology
LL B	Bachelor of Laws
LL CM	Master of Comparative Law
LL D	Doctor of Laws
LL M	Master of Laws
LL M in Tax	Master of Laws in Taxation
LL M CL	Master of Laws in Common Law
M Ac	Master of Accountancy
	Master of Accounting
	Master of Acupuncture
M Ac OM	Master of Acupuncture and Oriental Medicine
M Acc	Master of Accountancy
	Master of Accounting
M Acct	Master of Accountancy
	Master of Accounting
M Accy	Master of Accountancy
M Actg	Master of Accounting
M Acy	Master of Accountancy
M Ad	Master of Administration
M Ad Ed	Master of Adult Education
M Adm	Master of Administration

M Adm Mgt	Master of Administrative Management
M Admin	Master of Administration
M ADU	Master of Architectural Design and Urbanism
M Adv	Master of Advertising
M Ag	Master of Agriculture
M Ag Ed	Master of Agricultural Education
M Agr	Master of Agriculture
M App Comp Sc	Master of Applied Computer Science
M App St	Master of Applied Statistics
M Appl Stat	Master of Applied Statistics
M Aq	Master of Aquaculture
M Ar	Master of Architecture
M Arch	Master of Architecture
M Arch I	Master of Architecture I
M Arch II	Master of Architecture II
M Arch E	Master of Architectural Engineering
M Arch H	Master of Architectural History
M Bioethics	Master in Bioethics
M Cat	Master of Catechesis
M Ch E	Master of Chemical Engineering
M Cl D	Master of Clinical Dentistry
M Cl Sc	Master of Clinical Science
M Comm	Master of Communication
M Comp	Master of Computing
M Comp Sc	Master of Computer Science
M Coun	Master of Counseling
M Dent	Master of Dentistry
M Dent Sc	Master of Dental Sciences
M Des	Master of Design
M Des S	Master of Design Studies
M Div	Master of Divinity
M E Sci	Master of Earth Science
M Ec	Master of Economics
M Econ	Master of Economics
M Ed	Master of Education
M Ed T	Master of Education in Teaching
M En	Master of Engineering
M En S	Master of Environmental Sciences
M Eng	Master of Engineering
M Eng Mgt	Master of Engineering Management
M Engr	Master of Engineering
M Ent	Master of Enterprise
M Env	Master of Environment
M Env Des	Master of Environmental Design
M Env E	Master of Environmental Engineering
M Env Sc	Master of Environmental Science
M Ext Ed	Master of Extension Education
M Fin	Master of Finance
M Geo E	Master of Geological Engineering
M Geoenv E	Master of Geoenvironmental Engineering
M Geog	Master of Geography
M Hum	Master of Humanities
M IDST	Master's in Interdisciplinary Studies
M Jur	Master of Jurisprudence
M Kin	Master of Kinesiology
M Land Arch	Master of Landscape Architecture
M Litt	Master of Letters
M Mark	Master of Marketing
M Mat SE	Master of Material Science and Engineering
M Math	Master of Mathematics
M Mech E	Master of Mechanical Engineering
M Med Sc	Master of Medical Science
M Mgmt	Master of Management
M Mgt	Master of Management
M Min	Master of Ministries
M Mtl E	Master of Materials Engineering
M Mu	Master of Music
M Mus	Master of Music
M Mus Ed	Master of Music Education
M Music	Master of Music
M Pet E	Master of Petroleum Engineering
M Pharm	Master of Pharmacy
M Phil	Master of Philosophy
M Phil F	Master of Philosophical Foundations
M Pl	Master of Planning
M Plan	Master of Planning
M Pol	Master of Political Science
M Pr Met	Master of Professional Meteorology
M Prob S	Master of Probability and Statistics
M Psych	Master of Psychology
M Pub	Master of Publishing
M Rel	Master of Religion
M Sc	Master of Science
M Sc A	Master of Science (Applied)
M Sc AC	Master of Science in Applied Computing
M Sc AHN	Master of Science in Applied Human Nutrition
M Sc BMC	Master of Science in Biomedical Communications
M Sc CS	Master of Science in Computer Science
M Sc E	Master of Science in Engineering
M Sc Eng	Master of Science in Engineering
M Sc Engr	Master of Science in Engineering
M Sc F	Master of Science in Forestry
M Sc FE	Master of Science in Forest Engineering
M Sc Geogr	Master of Science in Geography
M Sc N	Master of Science in Nursing
M Sc OT	Master of Science in Occupational Therapy
M Sc P	Master of Science in Planning
M Sc Pl	Master of Science in Planning
M Sc PT	Master of Science in Physical Therapy
M Sc T	Master of Science in Teaching
M SEM	Master of Sustainable Environmental Management
M Serv Soc	Master of Social Service
M Soc	Master of Sociology
M Sp Ed	Master of Special Education
M Stat	Master of Statistics
M Sys E	Master of Systems Engineering
M Sys Sc	Master of Systems Science
M Tax	Master of Taxation
M Tech	Master of Technology
M Th	Master of Theology
M Trans E	Master of Transportation Engineering
M U Ed	Master of Urban Education
M Urb	Master of Urban Planning
M Vet Sc	Master of Veterinary Science
MA	Master of Accounting
	Master of Administration
	Master of Arts
MA Comm	Master of Arts in Communication
MA Ed	Master of Arts in Education
MA Ed/HD	Master of Arts in Education and Human Development
MA Islamic	Master of Arts in Islamic Studies
MA Min	Master of Arts in Ministry
MA Miss	Master of Arts in Missiology
MA Past St	Master of Arts in Pastoral Studies
MA Ph	Master of Arts in Philosophy
MA Psych	Master of Arts in Psychology
MA Sc	Master of Applied Science
MA Sp	Master of Arts (Spirituality)
MA Th	Master of Arts in Theology
MA-R	Master of Arts (Research)
MAA	Master of Applied Anthropology
	Master of Applied Arts
	Master of Arts in Administration
MAAA	Master of Arts in Arts Administration

MAAD	Master of Advanced Architectural Design
MAAE	Master of Arts in Art Education
MAAPPS	Master of Arts in Asia Pacific Policy Studies
MAAS	Master of Arts in Aging and Spirituality
MAASJ	Master of Arts in Applied Social Justice
MAAT	Master of Arts in Applied Theology
MAB	Master of Agribusiness
	Master of Applied Bioengineering
	Master of Arts in Business
MABA	Master's in Applied Behavior Analysis
MABC	Master of Arts in Biblical Counseling
MABE	Master of Arts in Bible Exposition
MABL	Master of Arts in Biblical Languages
MABM	Master of Agribusiness Management
MABS	Master of Arts in Biblical Studies
MABT	Master of Arts in Bible Teaching
MAC	Master of Accountancy
	Master of Accounting
	Master of Arts in Communication
	Master of Arts in Counseling
MACC	Master of Arts in Christian Counseling
MACCT	Master of Accounting
MACD	Master of Arts in Christian Doctrine
MACE	Master of Arts in Christian Education
MACH	Master of Arts in Church History
MACI	Master of Arts in Curriculum and Instruction
MACIS	Master of Accounting and Information Systems
MACJ	Master of Arts in Criminal Justice
MACL	Master of Arts in Christian Leadership
	Master of Arts in Community Leadership
MACM	Master of Arts in Christian Ministries
	Master of Arts in Christian Ministry
	Master of Arts in Church Music
	Master of Arts in Counseling Ministries
MACML	Master of Arts in Christian Ministry and Leadership
MACN	Master of Arts in Counseling
MACO	Master of Arts in Counseling
MAcOM	Master of Acupuncture and Oriental Medicine
MACP	Master of Arts in Christian Practice
	Master of Arts in Church Planting
	Master of Arts in Counseling Psychology
MACS	Master of Applied Computer Science
	Master of Arts in Catholic Studies
	Master of Arts in Christian Studies
MACSE	Master of Arts in Christian School Education
MACT	Master of Arts in Communications and Technology
MAD	Master in Educational Institution Administration
	Master of Art and Design
MADR	Master of Arts in Dispute Resolution
MADS	Master of Applied Disability Studies
MAE	Master of Aerospace Engineering
	Master of Agricultural Economics
	Master of Agricultural Education
	Master of Applied Economics
	Master of Architectural Engineering
	Master of Art Education
	Master of Arts in Education
	Master of Arts in English
MAEd	Master of Arts Education
MAEE	Master of Agricultural and Extension Education
MAEL	Master of Arts in Educational Leadership
MAEM	Master of Arts in Educational Ministries
MAEP	Master of Arts in Economic Policy
	Master of Arts in Educational Psychology
MAES	Master of Arts in Environmental Sciences
MAET	Master of Arts in English Teaching

MAF	Master of Arts in Finance
MAFE	Master of Arts in Financial Economics
MAFM	Master of Accounting and Financial Management
MAFS	Master of Arts in Family Studies
MAG	Master of Applied Geography
MAGU	Master of Urban Analysis and Management
MAH	Master of Arts in Humanities
MAHA	Master of Arts in Humanitarian Assistance
MAHCM	Master of Arts in Health Care Mission
MAHG	Master of American History and Government
MAHL	Master of Arts in Hebrew Letters
MAHN	Master of Applied Human Nutrition
MAHR	Master of Applied Historical Research
MAHS	Master of Arts in Human Services
MAHSR	Master in Applied Health Services Research
MAIA	Master of Arts in International Administration
	Master of Arts in International Affairs
MAICS	Master of Arts in Intercultural Studies
MAIDM	Master of Arts in Interior Design and Merchandising
MAIH	Master of Arts in Interdisciplinary Humanities
MAIOP	Master of Applied Industrial/Organizational Psychology
MAIS	Master of Arts in Intercultural Studies
	Master of Arts in Interdisciplinary Studies
	Master of Arts in International Studies
MAIT	Master of Administration in Information Technology
MAJ	Master of Arts in Journalism
MAJCS	Master of Arts in Jewish Communal Service
MAJPS	Master of Arts in Jewish Professional Studies
MAJS	Master of Arts in Jewish Studies
MAL	Master of Athletic Leadership
MALA	Master of Arts in Liberal Arts
MALCM	Master in Arts Leadership and Cultural Management
MALD	Master of Arts in Law and Diplomacy
MALER	Master of Arts in Labor and Employment Relations
MALL	Master of Arts in Language Learning
MALLT	Master of Arts in Language, Literature, and Translation
MALP	Master of Arts in Language Pedagogy
MALS	Master of Arts in Liberal Studies
MAM	Master of Acquisition Management
	Master of Agriculture and Management
	Master of Applied Mathematics
	Master of Arts in Management
	Master of Arts in Ministry
	Master of Arts Management
	Master of Aviation Management
MAMC	Master of Arts in Mass Communication
	Master of Arts in Ministry and Culture
	Master of Arts in Ministry for a Multicultural Church
MAME	Master of Arts in Missions/Evangelism
MAMFC	Master of Arts in Marriage and Family Counseling
MAMFT	Master of Arts in Marriage and Family Therapy
MAMHC	Master of Arts in Mental Health Counseling
MAMS	Master of Applied Mathematical Sciences
	Master of Arts in Ministerial Studies
	Master of Arts in Ministry and Spirituality
MAMT	Master of Arts in Mathematics Teaching
MAN	Master of Applied Nutrition
MANT	Master of Arts in New Testament
MAOL	Master of Arts in Organizational Leadership
MAOM	Master of Acupuncture and Oriental Medicine
	Master of Arts in Organizational Management

MAOT	Master of Arts in Old Testament
MAP	Master of Applied Politics
	Master of Applied Psychology
	Master of Arts in Planning
	Master of Psychology
	Master of Public Administration
MAP Min	Master of Arts in Pastoral Ministry
MAPA	Master of Arts in Public Administration
MAPC	Master of Arts in Pastoral Counseling
MAPE	Master of Arts in Physics Education
MAPM	Master of Arts in Pastoral Ministry
	Master of Arts in Pastoral Music
	Master of Arts in Practical Ministry
MAPP	Master of Arts in Public Policy
MAPS	Master of Applied Psychological Sciences
	Master of Arts in Pastoral Studies
	Master of Arts in Public Service
MAPW	Master of Arts in Professional Writing
MAQRM	Master's of Actuarial and Quantitative Risk Management
MAR	Master of Arts in Reading
	Master of Arts in Religion
Mar Eng	Marine Engineer
MARC	Master of Arts in Rehabilitation Counseling
MARE	Master of Arts in Religious Education
MARL	Master of Arts in Religious Leadership
MARS	Master of Arts in Religious Studies
MAS	Master of Accounting Science
	Master of Actuarial Science
	Master of Administrative Science
	Master of Advanced Study
	Master of American Studies
	Master of Animal Science
	Master of Applied Science
	Master of Applied Statistics
	Master of Archival Studies
MASA	Master of Advanced Studies in Architecture
MASC	Master of Arts in School Counseling
MASD	Master of Arts in Spiritual Direction
MASE	Master of Arts in Special Education
MASF	Master of Arts in Spiritual Formation
MASJ	Master of Arts in Systems of Justice
MASLA	Master of Advanced Studies in Landscape Architecture
MASM	Master of Aging Services Management
	Master of Arts in Specialized Ministries
MASS	Master of Applied Social Science
MASW	Master of Aboriginal Social Work
MAT	Master of Arts in Teaching
	Master of Arts in Theology
	Master of Athletic Training
	Master's in Administration of Telecommunications
Mat E	Materials Engineer
MATCM	Master of Acupuncture and Traditional Chinese Medicine
MATDE	Master of Arts in Theology, Development, and Evangelism
MATDR	Master of Territorial Management and Regional Development
MATE	Master of Arts for the Teaching of English
MATESL	Master of Arts in Teaching English as a Second Language
MATESOL	Master of Arts in Teaching English to Speakers of Other Languages
MATF	Master of Arts in Teaching English as a Foreign Language/Intercultural Studies
MATFL	Master of Arts in Teaching Foreign Language
MATH	Master of Arts in Therapy

MATI	Master of Administration of Information Technology
MATL	Master of Arts in Teaching of Languages
	Master of Arts in Transformational Leadership
MATM	Master of Arts in Teaching of Mathematics
MATRN	Master of Athletic Training
MATS	Master of Arts in Theological Studies
	Master of Arts in Transforming Spirituality
MAUA	Master of Arts in Urban Affairs
MAUD	Master of Arts in Urban Design
MAURP	Master of Arts in Urban and Regional Planning
MAW	Master of Arts in Worship
MAWSHP	Master of Arts in Worship
MAYM	Master of Arts in Youth Ministry
MB	Master of Bioinformatics
MBA	Master of Business Administration
MBA-AM	Master of Business Administration in Aviation Management
MBA-EP	Master of Business Administration–Experienced Professionals
MBAA	Master of Business Administration in Aviation
MBAE	Master of Biological and Agricultural Engineering
	Master of Biosystems and Agricultural Engineering
MBAH	Master of Business Administration in Health
MBAi	Master of Business Administration–International
MBAICT	Master of Business Administration in Information and Communication Technology
MBC	Master of Building Construction
MBE	Master of Bilingual Education
	Master of Bioengineering
	Master of Bioethics
	Master of Biomedical Engineering
	Master of Business Economics
	Master of Business Education
MBEE	Master in Biotechnology Enterprise and Entrepreneurship
MBET	Master of Business, Entrepreneurship and Technology
MBI	Master in Business Informatics
MBIOT	Master of Biotechnology
MBiotech	Master of Biotechnology
MBL	Master of Business Leadership
MBLE	Master in Business Logistics Engineering
MBME	Master's in Biomedical Engineering
MBMSE	Master of Business Management and Software Engineering
MBOE	Master of Business Operational Excellence
MBS	Master of Biblical Studies
	Master of Biological Science
	Master of Biomedical Sciences
	Master of Bioscience
	Master of Building Science
	Master of Business and Science
	Master of Business Statistics
MBST	Master of Biostatistics
MBT	Master of Biomedical Technology
	Master of Biotechnology
	Master of Business Taxation
MBV	Master of Business for Veterans
MC	Master of Classics
	Master of Communication
	Master of Counseling
MC Ed	Master of Continuing Education
MC Sc	Master of Computer Science
MCA	Master of Commercial Aviation
	Master of Communication Arts
	Master of Criminology (Applied)

MCAM	Master of Computational and Applied Mathematics
MCC	Master of Computer Science
MCD	Master of Communications Disorders
	Master of Community Development
MCE	Master in Electronic Commerce
	Master of Chemistry Education
	Master of Christian Education
	Master of Civil Engineering
	Master of Control Engineering
MCEM	Master of Construction Engineering Management
MCEPA	Master of Chinese Economic and Political Affairs
MCHE	Master of Chemical Engineering
MCIS	Master of Communication and Information Studies
	Master of Computer and Information Science
	Master of Computer Information Systems
MCIT	Master of Computer and Information Technology
MCJ	Master of Criminal Justice
MCL	Master in Communication Leadership
	Master of Canon Law
	Master of Christian Leadership
	Master of Comparative Law
MCM	Master of Christian Ministry
	Master of Church Music
	Master of Communication Management
	Master of Community Medicine
	Master of Construction Management
	Master of Contract Management
MCMin	Master of Christian Ministry
MCMM	Master in Communications and Media Management
MCMP	Master of City and Metropolitan Planning
MCMS	Master of Clinical Medical Science
MCN	Master of Clinical Nutrition
MCOL	Master of Arts in Community and Organizational Leadership
MCP	Master of City Planning
	Master of Community Planning
	Master of Counseling Psychology
	Master of Cytopathology Practice
	Master of Science in Quality Systems and Productivity
MCPD	Master of Community Planning and Development
MCR	Master in Clinical Research
MCRP	Master of City and Regional Planning
	Master of Community and Regional Planning
MCRS	Master of City and Regional Studies
MCS	Master of Chemical Sciences
	Master of Christian Studies
	Master of Clinical Science
	Master of Combined Sciences
	Master of Communication Studies
	Master of Computer Science
	Master of Consumer Science
MCSE	Master of Computer Science and Engineering
MCSL	Master of Catholic School Leadership
MCSM	Master of Construction Science and Management
MCT	Master of Commerce and Technology
MCTM	Master of Clinical Translation Management
MCTP	Master of Communication Technology and Policy
MCTS	Master of Clinical and Translational Science
MCVS	Master of Cardiovascular Science
MD	Doctor of Medicine

MDA	Master of Dietetic Administration
MDB	Master of Design-Build
MDE	Master in Design Engineering
	Master of Developmental Economics
	Master of Distance Education
	Master of the Education of the Deaf
MDH	Master of Dental Hygiene
MDI	Master of Disruptive Innovation
MDM	Master of Design Methods
	Master of Digital Media
MDP	Master in Sustainable Development Practice
	Master of Development Practice
MDR	Master of Dispute Resolution
MDS	Master in Data Science
	Master of Dental Surgery
	Master of Design Studies
	Master of Digital Sciences
MDSPP	Master in Data Science for Public Policy
ME	Master of Education
	Master of Engineering
	Master of Entrepreneurship
ME Sc	Master of Engineering Science
ME-PD	Master of Education–Professional Development
MEA	Master of Educational Administration
	Master of Engineering Administration
MEAE	Master of Entertainment Arts and Engineering
MEAP	Master of Environmental Administration and Planning
MEB	Master of Energy Business
MEBD	Master in Environmental Building Design
MEBT	Master in Electronic Business Technologies
MEC	Master of Electronic Commerce
Mech E	Mechanical Engineer
MEDS	Master of Environmental Design Studies
MEE	Master in Education
	Master of Electrical Engineering
	Master of Energy Engineering
	Master of Environmental Engineering
MEECON	Master of Energy Economics
MEEM	Master of Environmental Engineering and Management
MEENE	Master of Engineering in Environmental Engineering
MEEP	Master of Environmental and Energy Policy
MEERM	Master of Earth and Environmental Resource Management
MEH	Master in Humanistic Studies
	Master of Environmental Health
	Master of Environmental Horticulture
MEHS	Master of Environmental Health and Safety
MEIM	Master of Entertainment Industry Management
	Master of Equine Industry Management
MEL	Master of Educational Leadership
	Master of Engineering Leadership
	Master of English Literature
MELP	Master of Environmental Law and Policy
MEM	Master of Engineering Management
	Master of Environmental Management
	Master of Marketing
MEME	Master of Engineering in Manufacturing Engineering
	Master of Engineering in Mechanical Engineering
MENR	Master of Environment and Natural Resources
MENVEGR	Master of Environmental Engineering
MEP	Master of Engineering Physics
MEPC	Master of Environmental Pollution Control
MEPD	Master of Environmental Planning and Design
MER	Master of Employment Relations

MERE	Master of Entrepreneurial Real Estate
MERL	Master of Energy Regulation and Law
MES	Master of Education and Science
	Master of Engineering Science
	Master of Environment and Sustainability
	Master of Environmental Science
	Master of Environmental Studies
	Master of Environmental Systems
MESM	Master of Environmental Science and Management
MET	Master of Educational Technology
	Master of Engineering Technology
	Master of Entertainment Technology
	Master of Environmental Toxicology
METM	Master of Engineering and Technology Management
MEVE	Master of Environmental Engineering
MF	Master of Finance
	Master of Forestry
MFA	Master of Financial Administration
	Master of Fine Arts
MFALP	Master of Food and Agriculture Law and Policy
MFAS	Master of Fisheries and Aquatic Science
MFC	Master of Forest Conservation
MFCS	Master of Family and Consumer Sciences
MFE	Master of Financial Economics
	Master of Financial Engineering
	Master of Forest Engineering
MFES	Master of Fire and Emergency Services
MFG	Master of Functional Genomics
MFHD	Master of Family and Human Development
MFM	Master of Financial Management
	Master of Financial Mathematics
MFPE	Master of Food Process Engineering
MFR	Master of Forest Resources
MFRC	Master of Forest Resources and Conservation
MFRE	Master of Food and Resource Economics
MFS	Master of Food Science
	Master of Forensic Sciences
	Master of Forest Science
	Master of Forest Studies
	Master of French Studies
MFST	Master of Food Safety and Technology
MFT	Master of Family Therapy
MFWCB	Master of Fish, Wildlife and Conservation Biology
MFYCS	Master of Family, Youth and Community Sciences
MGA	Master of Global Affairs
	Master of Government Administration
	Master of Governmental Administration
MGBA	Master of Global Business Administration
MGC	Master of Genetic Counseling
MGCS	Master of Genetic Counselor Studies
MGD	Master of Graphic Design
MGE	Master of Geotechnical Engineering
MGEM	Master of Geomatics for Environmental Management
	Master of Global Entrepreneurship and Management
MGIS	Master of Geographic Information Science
	Master of Geographic Information Systems
MGM	Master of Global Management
MGMA	Master of Greenhouse Gas Management and Accounting
MGP	Master of Gestion de Projet
MGPS	Master of Global Policy Studies
MGREM	Master of Global Real Estate Management
MGS	Master of Gender Studies
	Master of Gerontological Studies

	Master of Global Studies
MH	Master of Humanities
MH Sc	Master of Health Sciences
MHA	Master of Health Administration
	Master of Healthcare Administration
	Master of Hospital Administration
	Master of Hospitality Administration
MHB	Master of Human Behavior
MHC	Master of Mental Health Counseling
MHCA	Master of Health Care Administration
MHCD	Master of Health Care Design
MHCI	Master of Human-Computer Interaction
MHCL	Master of Health Care Leadership
MHCM	Master of Health Care Management
MHE	Master of Health Education
	Master of Higher Education
	Master of Human Ecology
MHE Ed	Master of Home Economics Education
MHEA	Master of Higher Education Administration
MHHS	Master of Health and Human Services
MHI	Master of Health Informatics
	Master of Healthcare Innovation
MHID	Master of Healthcare Interior Design
MHIHIM	Master of Health Informatics and Health Information Management
MHIIM	Master of Health Informatics and Information Management
MHK	Master of Human Kinetics
MHM	Master of Healthcare Management
MHMS	Master of Health Management Systems
MHP	Master of Health Physics
	Master of Heritage Preservation
	Master of Historic Preservation
MHPA	Master of Heath Policy and Administration
MHPCTL	Master of High Performance Coaching and Technical Leadership
MHPE	Master of Health Professions Education
MHR	Master of Human Resources
MHRD	Master in Human Resource Development
MHRIR	Master of Human Resources and Industrial Relations
MHRLR	Master of Human Resources and Labor Relations
MHRM	Master of Human Resources Management
MHS	Master of Health Science
	Master of Health Sciences
	Master of Health Studies
	Master of Hispanic Studies
	Master of Human Services
	Master of Humanistic Studies
MHSA	Master of Health Services Administration
MHSM	Master of Health Systems Management
MI	Master of Information
	Master of Instruction
MI Arch	Master of Interior Architecture
MIA	Master of Interior Architecture
	Master of International Affairs
MIAA	Master of International Affairs and Administration
MIAM	Master of International Agribusiness Management
MIAPD	Master of Interior Architecture and Product Design
MIB	Master of International Business
MIBS	Master of International Business Studies
MICLJ	Master of International Criminal Law and Justice
MICM	Master of International Construction Management
MID	Master of Industrial Design

	Master of Industrial Distribution
	Master of Innovation Design
	Master of Interior Design
	Master of International Development
MIDA	Master of International Development Administration
MIDP	Master of International Development Policy
MIDS	Master of Information and Data Science
MIE	Master of Industrial Engineering
MIF	Master of International Forestry
MIHTM	Master of International Hospitality and Tourism Management
MIJ	Master of International Journalism
MILR	Master of Industrial and Labor Relations
MIM	Master in Ministry
	Master of Information Management
	Master of International Management
	Master of International Marketing
MIMFA	Master of Investment Management and Financial Analysis
MIMLAE	Master of International Management for Latin American Executives
MIMS	Master of Information Management and Systems
	Master of Integrated Manufacturing Systems
MIP	Master of Infrastructure Planning
	Master of Intellectual Property
	Master of International Policy
MIPA	Master of International Public Affairs
MIPD	Master of Integrated Product Design
MIPER	Master of International Political Economy of Resources
MIPM	Master of International Policy Management
MIPP	Master of International Policy and Practice
	Master of International Public Policy
MIPS	Master of International Planning Studies
MIR	Master of Industrial Relations
	Master of International Relations
MIRD	Master of International Relations and Diplomacy
MIRHR	Master of Industrial Relations and Human Resources
MIS	Master of Imaging Science
	Master of Industrial Statistics
	Master of Information Science
	Master of Information Systems
	Master of Integrated Science
	Master of Interdisciplinary Studies
	Master of International Service
	Master of International Studies
MISE	Master of Industrial and Systems Engineering
MISKM	Master of Information Sciences and Knowledge Management
MISM	Master of Information Systems Management
MISW	Master of Indigenous Social Work
MIT	Master in Teaching
	Master of Industrial Technology
	Master of Information Technology
	Master of Initial Teaching
	Master of International Trade
MITA	Master of Information Technology Administration
MITM	Master of Information Technology and Management
MJ	Master of Journalism
	Master of Jurisprudence
MJ Ed	Master of Jewish Education
MJA	Master of Justice Administration
MJM	Master of Justice Management
MJS	Master of Judaic Studies

	Master of Judicial Studies
	Master of Juridical Studies
MK	Master of Kinesiology
MKM	Master of Knowledge Management
ML	Master of Latin
	Master of Law
ML Arch	Master of Landscape Architecture
MLA	Master of Landscape Architecture
	Master of Liberal Arts
MLAS	Master of Laboratory Animal Science
	Master of Liberal Arts and Sciences
MLAUD	Master of Landscape Architecture in Urban Development
MLD	Master of Leadership Development
	Master of Leadership Studies
MLE	Master of Applied Linguistics and Exegesis
MLER	Master of Labor and Employment Relations
MLI Sc	Master of Library and Information Science
MLIS	Master of Library and Information Science
	Master of Library and Information Studies
MLM	Master of Leadership in Ministry
MLPD	Master of Land and Property Development
MLRHR	Master of Labor Relations and Human Resources
MLS	Master of Leadership Studies
	Master of Legal Studies
	Master of Liberal Studies
	Master of Library Science
	Master of Life Sciences
	Master of Medical Laboratory Sciences
MLSCM	Master of Logistics and Supply Chain Management
MLT	Master of Language Technologies
MLTCA	Master of Long Term Care Administration
MLW	Master of Studies in Law
MLWS	Master of Land and Water Systems
MM	Master of Management
	Master of Mediation
	Master of Ministry
	Master of Music
MM Ed	Master of Music Education
MM Sc	Master of Medical Science
MM St	Master of Museum Studies
MMA	Master of Marine Affairs
	Master of Media Arts
	Master of Musical Arts
MMAL	Master of Maritime Administration and Logistics
MMAS	Master of Military Art and Science
MMB	Master of Microbial Biotechnology
MMC	Master of Manufacturing Competitiveness
	Master of Mass Communications
MMCM	Master of Music in Church Music
MMCSS	Master of Mathematical Computational and Statistical Sciences
MME	Master of Management in Energy
	Master of Manufacturing Engineering
	Master of Mathematics Education
	Master of Mathematics for Educators
	Master of Mechanical Engineering
	Master of Mining Engineering
	Master of Music Education
MMEL	Master's in Medical Education Leadership
MMF	Master of Mathematical Finance
MMFC/T	Master of Marriage and Family Counseling/ Therapy
MMFT	Master of Marriage and Family Therapy
MMG	Master of Management
MMH	Master of Management in Hospitality

Peterson's Graduate Programs in Engineering & Applied Sciences 2021

	Master of Medical Humanities		Master of Planning
MMI	Master of Management of Innovation	MP Ac	Master of Professional Accountancy
MMIS	Master of Management Information Systems	MP Acc	Master of Professional Accountancy
MML	Master of Managerial Logistics		Master of Professional Accounting
MMM	Master of Manufacturing Management		Master of Public Accounting
	Master of Marine Management	MP Aff	Master of Public Affairs
	Master of Medical Management	MP Th	Master of Pastoral Theology
MMP	Master of Marine Policy	MPA	Master of Performing Arts
	Master of Medical Physics		Master of Physician Assistant
	Master of Music Performance		Master of Professional Accountancy
MMPA	Master of Management and Professional Accounting		Master of Professional Accounting
			Master of Public Administration
MMQM	Master of Manufacturing Quality Management		Master of Public Affairs
MMR	Master of Marketing Research	MPAC	Master of Professional Accounting
MMRM	Master of Marine Resources Management	MPAID	Master of Public Administration and International Development
MMS	Master in Migration Studies		
	Master of Management Science	MPAP	Master of Physician Assistant Practice
	Master of Management Studies		Master of Public Administration and Policy
	Master of Manufacturing Systems		Master of Public Affairs and Politics
	Master of Marine Studies	MPAS	Master of Physician Assistant Science
	Master of Materials Science		Master of Physician Assistant Studies
	Master of Mathematical Sciences	MPC	Master of Professional Communication
	Master of Medical Science	MPD	Master of Product Development
	Master of Medieval Studies		Master of Public Diplomacy
MMSE	Master of Manufacturing Systems Engineering	MPDS	Master of Planning and Development Studies
MMSM	Master of Music in Sacred Music	MPE	Master of Physical Education
MMT	Master in Marketing	MPEM	Master of Project Engineering and Management
	Master of Math for Teaching		
	Master of Music Therapy	MPFM	Master of Public Financial Management
	Master's in Marketing Technology	MPH	Master of Public Health
MMus	Master of Music	MPHE	Master of Public Health Education
MN	Master of Nursing	MPHM	Master in Plant Health Management
	Master of Nutrition	MPHS	Master of Population Health Sciences
MN NP	Master of Nursing in Nurse Practitioner	MPHTM	Master of Public Health and Tropical Medicine
MNA	Master of Nonprofit Administration	MPI	Master of Public Informatics
	Master of Nurse Anesthesia	MPIA	Master of Public and International Affairs
MNAE	Master of Nanoengineering	MPL	Master of Pastoral Leadership
MNAL	Master of Nonprofit Administration and Leadership	MPM	Master of Pastoral Ministry
			Master of Pest Management
MNAS	Master of Natural and Applied Science		Master of Policy Management
MNCL	Master of Nonprofit and Civic Leadership		Master of Practical Ministries
MNCM	Master of Network and Communications Management		Master of Professional Management
			Master of Project Management
MNE	Master of Nuclear Engineering		Master of Public Management
MNL	Master in International Business for Latin America	MPNA	Master of Public and Nonprofit Administration
		MPNL	Master of Philanthropy and Nonprofit Leadership
MNM	Master of Nonprofit Management		
MNO	Master of Nonprofit Organization	MPO	Master of Prosthetics and Orthotics
MNPL	Master of Not-for-Profit Leadership	MPOD	Master of Positive Organizational Development
MNpS	Master of Nonprofit Studies	MPP	Master of Public Policy
MNR	Master of Natural Resources	MPPA	Master of Public Policy Administration
MNRD	Master of Natural Resources Development		Master of Public Policy and Administration
MNRES	Master of Natural Resources and Environmental Studies	MPPAL	Master of Public Policy, Administration and Law
		MPPGA	Master of Public Policy and Global Affairs
MNRM	Master of Natural Resource Management	MPPM	Master of Public Policy and Management
MNRMG	Master of Natural Resource Management and Geography	MPR	Master of Public Relations
		MPRTM	Master of Parks, Recreation, and Tourism Management
MNRS	Master of Natural Resource Stewardship		
MNS	Master of Natural Science	MPS	Master of Pastoral Studies
MNSE	Master of Natural Sciences Education		Master of Perfusion Science
MO	Master of Oceanography		Master of Planning Studies
MOD	Master of Organizational Development		Master of Political Science
MOGS	Master of Oil and Gas Studies		Master of Preservation Studies
MOL	Master of Organizational Leadership		Master of Prevention Science
MOM	Master of Organizational Management		Master of Professional Studies
	Master of Oriental Medicine		Master of Public Service
MOR	Master of Operations Research	MPSA	Master of Public Service Administration
MOT	Master of Occupational Therapy	MPSG	Master of Population and Social Gerontology
MP	Master of Physiology		

MPSIA	Master of Political Science and International Affairs
MPSL	Master of Public Safety Leadership
MPT	Master of Pastoral Theology
	Master of Physical Therapy
	Master of Practical Theology
MPVM	Master of Preventive Veterinary Medicine
MPW	Master of Professional Writing
	Master of Public Works
MQF	Master of Quantitative Finance
MQM	Master of Quality Management
	Master of Quantitative Management
MQS	Master of Quality Systems
MR	Master of Recreation
	Master of Retailing
MRA	Master in Research Administration
	Master of Regulatory Affairs
MRC	Master of Rehabilitation Counseling
MRCP	Master of Regional and City Planning
	Master of Regional and Community Planning
MRD	Master of Rural Development
MRE	Master of Real Estate
	Master of Religious Education
MRED	Master of Real Estate Development
MREM	Master of Resource and Environmental Management
MRLS	Master of Resources Law Studies
MRM	Master of Resources Management
MRP	Master of Regional Planning
MRRD	Master in Recreation Resource Development
MRS	Master of Religious Studies
MRSc	Master of Rehabilitation Science
MRUD	Master of Resilient Design
MS	Master of Science
MS Cmp E	Master of Science in Computer Engineering
MS Kin	Master of Science in Kinesiology
MS Acct	Master of Science in Accounting
MS Accy	Master of Science in Accountancy
MS Aero E	Master of Science in Aerospace Engineering
MS Ag	Master of Science in Agriculture
MS Arch	Master of Science in Architecture
MS Arch St	Master of Science in Architectural Studies
MS Bio E	Master of Science in Bioengineering
MS Bm E	Master of Science in Biomedical Engineering
MS Ch E	Master of Science in Chemical Engineering
MS Cp E	Master of Science in Computer Engineering
MS Eco	Master of Science in Economics
MS Econ	Master of Science in Economics
MS Ed	Master of Science in Education
MS Ed Admin	Master of Science in Educational Administration
MS El	Master of Science in Educational Leadership and Administration
MS En E	Master of Science in Environmental Engineering
MS Eng	Master of Science in Engineering
MS Engr	Master of Science in Engineering
MS Env E	Master of Science in Environmental Engineering
MS Exp Surg	Master of Science in Experimental Surgery
MS Mat SE	Master of Science in Material Science and Engineering
MS Met E	Master of Science in Metallurgical Engineering
MS Mgt	Master of Science in Management
MS Min	Master of Science in Mining
MS Min E	Master of Science in Mining Engineering
MS Mt E	Master of Science in Materials Engineering
MS Otol	Master of Science in Otolaryngology
MS Pet E	Master of Science in Petroleum Engineering
MS Sc	Master of Social Science

MS Sp Ed	Master of Science in Special Education
MS Stat	Master of Science in Statistics
MS Surg	Master of Science in Surgery
MS Tax	Master of Science in Taxation
MS Tc E	Master of Science in Telecommunications Engineering
MS-R	Master of Science (Research)
MSA	Master of School Administration
	Master of Science in Accountancy
	Master of Science in Accounting
	Master of Science in Administration
	Master of Science in Aeronautics
	Master of Science in Agriculture
	Master of Science in Analytics
	Master of Science in Anesthesia
	Master of Science in Architecture
	Master of Science in Aviation
	Master of Sports Administration
	Master of Surgical Assisting
MSAA	Master of Science in Astronautics and Aeronautics
MSABE	Master of Science in Agricultural and Biological Engineering
MSAC	Master of Science in Acupuncture
MSACC	Master of Science in Accounting
MSACS	Master of Science in Applied Computer Science
MSAE	Master of Science in Aeronautical Engineering
	Master of Science in Aerospace Engineering
	Master of Science in Applied Economics
	Master of Science in Applied Engineering
	Master of Science in Architectural Engineering
MSAEM	Master of Science in Aerospace Engineering and Mechanics
MSAF	Master of Science in Aviation Finance
MSAG	Master of Science in Applied Geosciences
MSAH	Master of Science in Allied Health
MSAL	Master of Sport Administration and Leadership
MSAM	Master of Science in Applied Mathematics
MSANR	Master of Science in Agriculture and Natural Resources
MSAS	Master of Science in Administrative Studies
	Master of Science in Applied Statistics
	Master of Science in Architectural Studies
MSAT	Master of Science in Accounting and Taxation
	Master of Science in Advanced Technology
	Master of Science in Athletic Training
MSB	Master of Science in Biotechnology
MSBA	Master of Science in Business Administration
	Master of Science in Business Analysis
MSBAE	Master of Science in Biological and Agricultural Engineering
	Master of Science in Biosystems and Agricultural Engineering
MSBCB	Master's in Bioinformatics and Computational Biology
MSBE	Master of Science in Biological Engineering
	Master of Science in Biomedical Engineering
MSBENG	Master of Science in Bioengineering
MSBH	Master of Science in Behavioral Health
MSBM	Master of Sport Business Management
MSBME	Master of Science in Biomedical Engineering
MSBMS	Master of Science in Basic Medical Science
MSBS	Master of Science in Biomedical Sciences
MSBTM	Master of Science in Biotechnology and Management
MSC	Master of Science in Commerce
	Master of Science in Communication
	Master of Science in Counseling
	Master of Science in Criminology
	Master of Strategic Communication

Peterson's Graduate Programs in Engineering & Applied Sciences 2021

MSCC	Master of Science in Community Counseling
MSCD	Master of Science in Communication Disorders
	Master of Science in Community Development
MSCE	Master of Science in Chemistry Education
	Master of Science in Civil Engineering
	Master of Science in Clinical Epidemiology
	Master of Science in Computer Engineering
	Master of Science in Continuing Education
MSCEE	Master of Science in Civil and Environmental Engineering
MSCF	Master of Science in Computational Finance
MSCH	Master of Science in Chemical Engineering
MSChE	Master of Science in Chemical Engineering
MSCI	Master of Science in Clinical Investigation
MSCID	Master of Science in Community and International Development
MSCIS	Master of Science in Computer and Information Science
	Master of Science in Computer and Information Systems
	Master of Science in Computer Information Science
	Master of Science in Computer Information Systems
MSCIT	Master of Science in Computer Information Technology
MSCJ	Master of Science in Criminal Justice
MSCJA	Master of Science in Criminal Justice Administration
MSCJS	Master of Science in Crime and Justice Studies
MSCLS	Master of Science in Clinical Laboratory Studies
MSCM	Master of Science in Church Management
	Master of Science in Conflict Management
	Master of Science in Construction Management
	Master of Supply Chain Management
MSCMP	Master of Science in Cybersecurity Management and Policy
MSCNU	Master of Science in Clinical Nutrition
MSCP	Master of Science in Clinical Psychology
	Master of Science in Community Psychology
	Master of Science in Computer Engineering
	Master of Science in Counseling Psychology
MSCPE	Master of Science in Computer Engineering
MSCPharm	Master of Science in Pharmacy
MSCR	Master of Science in Clinical Research
MSCRP	Master of Science in City and Regional Planning
	Master of Science in Community and Regional Planning
MSCS	Master of Science in Clinical Science
	Master of Science in Computer Science
	Master of Science in Cyber Security
MSCSD	Master of Science in Communication Sciences and Disorders
MSCSE	Master of Science in Computer Science and Engineering
MSCTE	Master of Science in Career and Technical Education
MSD	Master of Science in Dentistry
	Master of Science in Design
	Master of Science in Dietetics
MSDM	Master of Security and Disaster Management
MSE	Master of Science Education
	Master of Science in Economics
	Master of Science in Education
	Master of Science in Engineering
	Master of Science in Engineering Management
	Master of Software Engineering
	Master of Special Education
	Master of Structural Engineering

MSECE	Master of Science in Electrical and Computer Engineering
MSED	Master of Sustainable Economic Development
MSEE	Master of Science in Electrical Engineering
	Master of Science in Environmental Engineering
MSEH	Master of Science in Environmental Health
MSEL	Master of Science in Educational Leadership
MSEM	Master of Science in Engineering and Management
	Master of Science in Engineering Management
	Master of Science in Engineering Mechanics
	Master of Science in Environmental Management
MSENE	Master of Science in Environmental Engineering
MSEO	Master of Science in Electro-Optics
MSES	Master of Science in Embedded Software Engineering
	Master of Science in Engineering Science
	Master of Science in Environmental Science
	Master of Science in Environmental Studies
	Master of Science in Exercise Science
MSESE	Master of Science in Energy Systems Engineering
MSET	Master of Science in Educational Technology
	Master of Science in Engineering Technology
MSEV	Master of Science in Environmental Engineering
MSF	Master of Science in Finance
	Master of Science in Forestry
MSFA	Master of Science in Financial Analysis
MSFCS	Master of Science in Family and Consumer Science
MSFE	Master of Science in Financial Engineering
MSFM	Master of Sustainable Forest Management
MSFOR	Master of Science in Forestry
MSFP	Master of Science in Financial Planning
MSFS	Master of Science in Financial Sciences
	Master of Science in Forensic Science
MSFSB	Master of Science in Financial Services and Banking
MSFT	Master of Science in Family Therapy
MSGC	Master of Science in Genetic Counseling
MSH	Master of Science in Health
	Master of Science in Hospice
MSHA	Master of Science in Health Administration
MSHCA	Master of Science in Health Care Administration
MSHCPM	Master of Science in Health Care Policy and Management
MSHE	Master of Science in Health Education
MSHES	Master of Science in Human Environmental Sciences
MSHFID	Master of Science in Human Factors in Information Design
MSHFS	Master of Science in Human Factors and Systems
MSHI	Master of Science in Health Informatics
MSHP	Master of Science in Health Professions
MSHR	Master of Science in Human Resources
MSHRL	Master of Science in Human Resource Leadership
MSHRM	Master of Science in Human Resource Management
MSHROD	Master of Science in Human Resources and Organizational Development
MSHS	Master of Science in Health Science
	Master of Science in Health Services
	Master of Science in Homeland Security
MSHSR	Master of Science in Human Security and Resilience

MSI	Master of Science in Information	MSME	Master of Science in Mathematics Education
	Master of Science in Instruction		Master of Science in Mechanical Engineering
	Master of System Integration		Master of Science in Medical Ethics
MSIA	Master of Science in Industrial Administration	MSMHC	Master of Science in Mental Health Counseling
	Master of Science in Information Assurance	MSMIT	Master of Science in Management and Information Technology
MSIDM	Master of Science in Interior Design and Merchandising	MSMLS	Master of Science in Medical Laboratory Science
MSIE	Master of Science in Industrial Engineering	MSMOT	Master of Science in Management of Technology
MSIEM	Master of Science in Information Engineering and Management	MSMP	Master of Science in Medical Physics
MSIM	Master of Science in Industrial Management		Master of Science in Molecular Pathology
	Master of Science in Information Management	MSMS	Master of Science in Management Science
	Master of Science in International Management		Master of Science in Marine Science
MSIMC	Master of Science in Integrated Marketing Communications		Master of Science in Medical Sciences
MSIMS	Master of Science in Identity Management and Security	MSMSE	Master of Science in Manufacturing Systems Engineering
MSIS	Master of Science in Information Science		Master of Science in Material Science and Engineering
	Master of Science in Information Studies		Master of Science in Material Science Engineering
	Master of Science in Information Systems		Master of Science in Mathematics and Science Education
	Master of Science in Interdisciplinary Studies	MSMus	Master of Sacred Music
MSISE	Master of Science in Infrastructure Systems Engineering	MSN	Master of Science in Nursing
MSISM	Master of Science in Information Systems Management	MSNA	Master of Science in Nurse Anesthesia
MSISPM	Master of Science in Information Security Policy and Management	MSNE	Master of Science in Nuclear Engineering
		MSNS	Master of Science in Natural Science
MSIST	Master of Science in Information Systems Technology		Master of Science in Nutritional Science
MSIT	Master of Science in Industrial Technology	MSOD	Master of Science in Organization Development
	Master of Science in Information Technology		Master of Science in Organizational Development
	Master of Science in Instructional Technology	MSOEE	Master of Science in Outdoor and Environmental Education
MSITM	Master of Science in Information Technology Management	MSOES	Master of Science in Occupational Ergonomics and Safety
MSJ	Master of Science in Journalism	MSOH	Master of Science in Occupational Health
	Master of Science in Jurisprudence	MSOL	Master of Science in Organizational Leadership
MSJC	Master of Social Justice and Criminology	MSOM	Master of Science in Oriental Medicine
MSJFP	Master of Science in Juvenile Forensic Psychology	MSOR	Master of Science in Operations Research
MSJJ	Master of Science in Juvenile Justice	MSOT	Master of Science in Occupational Technology
MSJPS	Master of Science in Justice and Public Safety		Master of Science in Occupational Therapy
MSK	Master of Science in Kinesiology	MSP	Master of Science in Pharmacy
MSL	Master in the Study of Law		Master of Science in Planning
	Master of School Leadership		Master of Speech Pathology
	Master of Science in Leadership		Master of Sustainable Peacebuilding
	Master of Science in Limnology	MSPA	Master of Science in Physician Assistant
	Master of Sports Leadership	MSPAS	Master of Science in Physician Assistant Studies
	Master of Strategic Leadership	MSPC	Master of Science in Professional Communications
	Master of Studies in Law		
MSLA	Master of Science in Legal Administration	MSPE	Master of Science in Petroleum Engineering
MSLB	Master of Sports Law and Business	MSPH	Master of Science in Public Health
MSLFS	Master of Science in Life Sciences	MSPHR	Master of Science in Pharmacy
MSLP	Master of Speech-Language Pathology	MSPM	Master of Science in Professional Management
MSLS	Master of Science in Library Science		Master of Science in Project Management
MSLSCM	Master of Science in Logistics and Supply Chain Management	MSPNGE	Master of Science in Petroleum and Natural Gas Engineering
MSLT	Master of Second Language Teaching	MSPPM	Master of Science in Public Policy and Management
MSM	Master of Sacred Ministry	MSPS	Master of Science in Pharmaceutical Science
	Master of Sacred Music		Master of Science in Political Science
	Master of School Mathematics		Master of Science in Psychological Services
	Master of Science in Management	MSPT	Master of Science in Physical Therapy
	Master of Science in Medicine	MSRA	Master of Science in Recreation Administration
	Master of Science in Organization Management	MSRE	Master of Science in Real Estate
	Master of Security Management		Master of Science in Religious Education
	Master of Strategic Ministry	MSRED	Master of Science in Real Estate Development
	Master of Supply Management		Master of Sustainable Real Estate Development
MSMA	Master of Science in Marketing Analysis	MSRLS	Master of Science in Recreation and Leisure Studies
MSMAE	Master of Science in Materials Engineering		
MSMC	Master of Science in Management and Communications		
	Master of Science in Mass Communications		

MSRM	Master of Science in Risk Management	MTCM	Master of Traditional Chinese Medicine
MSRMP	Master of Science in Radiological Medical Physics	MTD	Master of Training and Development
		MTE	Master in Educational Technology
MSRS	Master of Science in Radiological Sciences		Master of Technological Entrepreneurship
	Master of Science in Rehabilitation Science	MTESOL	Master in Teaching English to Speakers of Other Languages
MSS	Master of Security Studies	MTHM	Master of Tourism and Hospitality Management
	Master of Social Science	MTI	Master of Information Technology
	Master of Social Services	MTID	Master of Tangible Interaction Design
	Master of Sports Science	MTL	Master of Talmudic Law
	Master of Strategic Studies	MTM	Master of Technology Management
	Master's in Statistical Science		Master of Telecommunications Management
MSSA	Master of Science in Social Administration		Master of the Teaching of Mathematics
MSSCM	Master of Science in Supply Chain Management		Master of Transformative Ministry
MSSD	Master of Arts in Software Driven Systems Design		Master of Translational Medicine
	Master of Science in Sustainable Design	MTMH	Master of Tropical Medicine and Hygiene
MSSE	Master of Science in Software Engineering	MTMS	Master in Teaching Mathematics and Science
	Master of Science in Special Education	MTOM	Master of Traditional Oriental Medicine
MSSEM	Master of Science in Systems and Engineering Management	MTPC	Master of Technical and Professional Communication
MSSI	Master of Science in Security Informatics	MTR	Master of Translational Research
	Master of Science in Strategic Intelligence	MTS	Master of Theatre Studies
MSSIS	Master of Science in Security and Intelligence Studies		Master of Theological Studies
MSSL	Master of Science in School Leadership	MTW	Master of Teaching Writing
MSSLP	Master of Science in Speech-Language Pathology	MTWM	Master of Trust and Wealth Management
		MUA	Master of Urban Affairs
MSSM	Master of Science in Sports Medicine	MUAP	Master's of Urban Affairs and Policy
	Master of Science in Systems Management	MUCD	Master of Urban and Community Design
MSSP	Master of Science in Social Policy	MUD	Master of Urban Design
MSSS	Master of Science in Safety Science	MUDS	Master of Urban Design Studies
	Master of Science in Systems Science	MUEP	Master of Urban and Environmental Planning
MSST	Master of Science in Security Technologies	MUP	Master of Urban Planning
MSSW	Master of Science in Social Work	MUPD	Master of Urban Planning and Development
MSSWE	Master of Science in Software Engineering	MUPP	Master of Urban Planning and Policy
MST	Master of Science and Technology	MUPRED	Master of Urban Planning and Real Estate Development
	Master of Science in Taxation	MURP	Master of Urban and Regional Planning
	Master of Science in Teaching		Master of Urban and Rural Planning
	Master of Science in Technology	MURPL	Master of Urban and Regional Planning
	Master of Science in Telecommunications	MUS	Master of Urban Studies
	Master of Science Teaching		Master of Music
MSTC	Master of Science in Technical Communication	Mus M	Master of Music
	Master of Science in Telecommunications	MUSA	Master of Urban Spatial Analytics
MSTCM	Master of Science in Traditional Chinese Medicine	MVP	Master of Voice Pedagogy
		MVS	Master of Visual Studies
MSTE	Master of Science in Telecommunications Engineering	MWBS	Master of Won Buddhist Studies
		MWC	Master of Wildlife Conservation
	Master of Science in Transportation Engineering	MWR	Master of Water Resources
		MWS	Master of Women's Studies
MSTL	Master of Science in Teacher Leadership		Master of Worship Studies
MSTM	Master of Science in Technology Management	MWSc	Master of Wildlife Science
	Master of Science in Transfusion Medicine	Nav Arch	Naval Architecture
MSTOM	Master of Science in Traditional Oriental Medicine	Naval E	Naval Engineer
		ND	Doctor of Naturopathic Medicine
MSUASE	Master of Science in Unmanned and Autonomous Systems Engineering		Doctor of Nursing
MSUD	Master of Science in Urban Design	NE	Nuclear Engineer
MSUS	Master of Science in Urban Studies	Nuc E	Nuclear Engineer
MSW	Master of Social Work	OD	Doctor of Optometry
MSWE	Master of Software Engineering	OTD	Doctor of Occupational Therapy
MSWREE	Master of Science in Water Resources and Environmental Engineering	PBME	Professional Master of Biomedical Engineering
		PC	Performer's Certificate
MT	Master of Taxation	PD	Professional Diploma
	Master of Teaching	PGC	Post-Graduate Certificate
	Master of Technology	PGD	Postgraduate Diploma
	Master of Textiles	Ph L	Licentiate of Philosophy
MTA	Master of Tax Accounting	Pharm D	Doctor of Pharmacy
	Master of Teaching Arts	PhD	Doctor of Philosophy
	Master of Tourism Administration	PhD Otol	Doctor of Philosophy in Otolaryngology
MTC	Master of Technical Communications	PhD Surg	Doctor of Philosophy in Surgery
		PhDEE	Doctor of Philosophy in Electrical Engineering

PMBA	Professional Master of Business Administration
PMC	Post Master Certificate
PMD	Post-Master's Diploma
PMS	Professional Master of Science
	Professional Master's
Post-Doctoral MS	Post-Doctoral Master of Science
Post-MSN Certificate	Post-Master of Science in Nursing Certificate
PPDPT	Postprofessional Doctor of Physical Therapy
Pro-MS	Professional Science Master's
Professional MA	Professional Master of Arts
Professional MBA	Professional Master of Business Administration
Professional MS	Professional Master of Science
PSM	Professional Master of Science
	Professional Science Master's
Psy D	Doctor of Psychology
Psy M	Master of Psychology
Psy S	Specialist in Psychology
Psya D	Doctor of Psychoanalysis
S Psy S	Specialist in Psychological Services
Sc D	Doctor of Science
Sc M	Master of Science
SCCT	Specialist in Community College Teaching
ScDPT	Doctor of Physical Therapy Science
SD	Specialist Degree
SJD	Doctor of Juridical Sciences
SLPD	Doctor of Speech-Language Pathology

SM	Master of Science
SM Arch S	Master of Science in Architectural Studies
SMACT	Master of Science in Art, Culture and Technology
SMBT	Master of Science in Building Technology
SP	Specialist Degree
Sp Ed	Specialist in Education
Sp LIS	Specialist in Library and Information Science
SPA	Specialist in Arts
Spec	Specialist's Certificate
Spec M	Specialist in Music
Spt	Specialist Degree
SSP	Specialist in School Psychology
STB	Bachelor of Sacred Theology
STD	Doctor of Sacred Theology
STL	Licentiate of Sacred Theology
STM	Master of Sacred Theology
tDACM	Transitional Doctor of Acupuncture and Chinese Medicine
TDPT	Transitional Doctor of Physical Therapy
Th D	Doctor of Theology
Th M	Master of Theology
TOTD	Transitional Doctor of Occupational Therapy
VMD	Doctor of Veterinary Medicine
WEMBA	Weekend Executive Master of Business Administration
XMA	Executive Master of Arts

INDEXES

Displays and Close-Ups

Directories and Subject Areas

Following is an alphabetical listing of directories and subject areas. Also listed are cross-references for subject area names not used in the directory structure of the guides, for example, "City and Regional Planning (*see* Urban and Regional Planning)."

Graduate Programs in the Humanities, Arts & Social Sciences

Addictions/Substance Abuse Counseling
Administration (*see* Arts Administration; Public Administration)
African-American Studies
African Languages and Literatures (*see* African Studies)
African Studies
Agribusiness (*see* Agricultural Economics and Agribusiness)
Agricultural Economics and Agribusiness
Alcohol Abuse Counseling (*see* Addictions/Substance Abuse Counseling)
American Indian/Native American Studies
American Studies
Anthropology
Applied Arts and Design—General
Applied Behavior Analysis
Applied Economics
Applied History (*see* Public History)
Applied Psychology
Applied Social Research
Arabic (*see* Near and Middle Eastern Languages)
Arab Studies (*see* Near and Middle Eastern Studies)
Archaeology
Architectural History
Architecture
Archives Administration (*see* Public History)
Area and Cultural Studies (*see* African-American Studies; African Studies; American Indian/Native American Studies; American Studies; Asian-American Studies; Asian Studies; Canadian Studies; Cultural Studies; East European and Russian Studies; Ethnic Studies; Folklore; Gender Studies; Hispanic Studies; Holocaust Studies; Jewish Studies; Latin American Studies; Near and Middle Eastern Studies; Northern Studies; Pacific Area/ Pacific Rim Studies; Western European Studies; Women's Studies)
Art/Fine Arts
Art History
Arts Administration
Arts Journalism
Art Therapy
Asian-American Studies
Asian Languages
Asian Studies
Behavioral Sciences (*see* Psychology)
Bible Studies (*see* Religion; Theology)
Biological Anthropology

Black Studies (*see* African-American Studies)
Broadcasting (*see* Communication; Film, Television, and Video Production)
Broadcast Journalism
Building Science
Canadian Studies
Celtic Languages
Ceramics (*see* Art/Fine Arts)
Child and Family Studies
Child Development
Chinese
Chinese Studies (*see* Asian Languages; Asian Studies)
Christian Studies (*see* Missions and Missiology; Religion; Theology)
Cinema (*see* Film, Television, and Video Production)
City and Regional Planning (*see* Urban and Regional Planning)
Classical Languages and Literatures (*see* Classics)
Classics
Clinical Psychology
Clothing and Textiles
Cognitive Psychology (*see* Psychology—General; Cognitive Sciences)
Cognitive Sciences
Communication—General
Community Affairs (*see* Urban and Regional Planning; Urban Studies)
Community Planning (*see* Architecture; Environmental Design; Urban and Regional Planning; Urban Design; Urban Studies)
Community Psychology (*see* Social Psychology)
Comparative and Interdisciplinary Arts
Comparative Literature
Composition (*see* Music)
Computer Art and Design
Conflict Resolution and Mediation/Peace Studies
Consumer Economics
Corporate and Organizational Communication
Corrections (*see* Criminal Justice and Criminology)
Counseling (*see* Counseling Psychology; Pastoral Ministry and Counseling)
Counseling Psychology
Crafts (*see* Art/Fine Arts)
Creative Arts Therapies (*see* Art Therapy; Therapies—Dance, Drama, and Music)
Criminal Justice and Criminology
Cultural Anthropology
Cultural Studies
Dance
Decorative Arts
Demography and Population Studies
Design (*see* Applied Arts and Design; Architecture; Art/Fine Arts; Environmental Design; Graphic Design; Industrial Design; Interior Design; Textile Design; Urban Design)
Developmental Psychology
Diplomacy (*see* International Affairs)
Disability Studies
Drama Therapy (*see* Therapies—Dance, Drama, and Music)
Dramatic Arts (*see* Theater)

Drawing (*see* Art/Fine Arts)
Drug Abuse Counseling (*see* Addictions/Substance Abuse Counseling)
Drug and Alcohol Abuse Counseling (*see* Addictions/Substance Abuse Counseling)
East Asian Studies (*see* Asian Studies)
East European and Russian Studies
Economic Development
Economics
Educational Theater (*see* Theater; Therapies—Dance, Drama, and Music)
Emergency Management
English
Environmental Design
Ethics
Ethnic Studies
Ethnomusicology (*see* Music)
Experimental Psychology
Family and Consumer Sciences—General
Family Studies (*see* Child and Family Studies)
Family Therapy (*see* Child and Family Studies; Clinical Psychology; Counseling Psychology; Marriage and Family Therapy)
Filmmaking (*see* Film, Television, and Video Production)
Film Studies (*see* Film, Television, and Video Production)
Film, Television, and Video Production
Film, Television, and Video Theory and Criticism
Fine Arts (*see* Art/Fine Arts)
Folklore
Foreign Languages (*see* specific language)
Foreign Service (*see* International Affairs; International Development)
Forensic Psychology
Forensic Sciences
Forensics (*see* Speech and Interpersonal Communication)
French
Gender Studies
General Studies (*see* Liberal Studies)
Genetic Counseling
Geographic Information Systems
Geography
German
Gerontology
Graphic Design
Greek (*see* Classics)
Health Communication
Health Psychology
Hebrew (*see* Near and Middle Eastern Languages)
Hebrew Studies (*see* Jewish Studies)
Hispanic and Latin American Languages
Hispanic Studies
Historic Preservation
History
History of Art (*see* Art History)
History of Medicine
History of Science and Technology
Holocaust and Genocide Studies
Home Economics (*see* Family and Consumer Sciences—General)
Homeland Security
Household Economics, Sciences, and Management (*see* Family and Consumer Sciences—General)
Human Development
Humanities
Illustration
Industrial and Labor Relations
Industrial and Organizational Psychology
Industrial Design
Interdisciplinary Studies
Interior Design
International Affairs
International Development
International Economics
International Service (*see* International Affairs; International Development)
International Trade Policy
Internet and Interactive Multimedia
Interpersonal Communication (*see* Speech and Interpersonal Communication)

Interpretation (*see* Translation and Interpretation)
Islamic Studies (*see* Near and Middle Eastern Studies; Religion)
Italian
Japanese
Japanese Studies (*see* Asian Languages; Asian Studies; Japanese)
Jewelry (*see* Art/Fine Arts)
Jewish Studies
Journalism
Judaic Studies (*see* Jewish Studies; Religion)
Labor Relations (*see* Industrial and Labor Relations)
Landscape Architecture
Latin American Studies
Latin (*see* Classics)
Law Enforcement (*see* Criminal Justice and Criminology)
Liberal Studies
Lighting Design
Linguistics
Literature (*see* Classics; Comparative Literature; specific language)
Marriage and Family Therapy
Mass Communication
Media Studies
Medical Illustration
Medieval and Renaissance Studies
Metalsmithing (*see* Art/Fine Arts)
Middle Eastern Studies (*see* Near and Middle Eastern Studies)
Military and Defense Studies
Mineral Economics
Ministry (*see* Pastoral Ministry and Counseling; Theology)
Missions and Missiology
Motion Pictures (*see* Film, Television, and Video Production)
Museum Studies
Music
Musicology (*see* Music)
Music Therapy (*see* Therapies—Dance, Drama, and Music)
National Security
Native American Studies (*see* American Indian/Native American Studies)
Near and Middle Eastern Languages
Near and Middle Eastern Studies
Northern Studies
Organizational Psychology (*see* Industrial and Organizational Psychology)
Oriental Languages (*see* Asian Languages)
Oriental Studies (*see* Asian Studies)
Pacific Area/Pacific Rim Studies
Painting (*see* Art/Fine Arts)
Pastoral Ministry and Counseling
Philanthropic Studies
Philosophy
Photography
Playwriting (*see* Theater; Writing)
Policy Studies (*see* Public Policy)
Political Science
Population Studies (*see* Demography and Population Studies)
Portuguese
Printmaking (*see* Art/Fine Arts)
Product Design (*see* Industrial Design)
Psychoanalysis and Psychotherapy
Psychology—General
Public Administration
Public Affairs
Public History
Public Policy
Public Speaking (*see* Mass Communication; Rhetoric; Speech and Interpersonal Communication)
Publishing
Regional Planning (*see* Architecture; Urban and Regional Planning; Urban Design; Urban Studies)
Rehabilitation Counseling
Religion
Renaissance Studies (*see* Medieval and Renaissance Studies)
Rhetoric
Romance Languages
Romance Literatures (*see* Romance Languages)
Rural Planning and Studies
Rural Sociology

Russian
Scandinavian Languages
School Psychology
Sculpture (*see* Art/Fine Arts)
Security Administration (*see* Criminal Justice and Criminology)
Slavic Languages
Slavic Studies (*see* East European and Russian Studies; Slavic Languages)
Social Psychology
Social Sciences
Sociology
Southeast Asian Studies (*see* Asian Studies)
Soviet Studies (*see* East European and Russian Studies; Russian)
Spanish
Speech and Interpersonal Communication
Sport Psychology
Studio Art (*see* Art/Fine Arts)
Substance Abuse Counseling (*see* Addictions/Substance Abuse Counseling)
Survey Methodology
Sustainable Development
Technical Communication
Technical Writing
Telecommunications (*see* Film, Television, and Video Production)
Television (*see* Film, Television, and Video Production)
Textile Design
Textiles (*see* Clothing and Textiles; Textile Design)
Thanatology
Theater
Theater Arts (*see* Theater)
Theology
Therapies—Dance, Drama, and Music
Translation and Interpretation
Transpersonal and Humanistic Psychology
Urban and Regional Planning
Urban Design
Urban Planning (*see* Architecture; Urban and Regional Planning; Urban Design; Urban Studies)
Urban Studies
Video (*see* Film, Television, and Video Production)
Visual Arts (*see* Applied Arts and Design; Art/Fine Arts; Film, Television, and Video Production; Graphic Design; Illustration; Photography)
Western European Studies
Women's Studies
World Wide Web (*see* Internet and Interactive Multimedia)
Writing

Graduate Programs in the Biological/Biomedical Sciences & Health-Related Medical Professions

Acupuncture and Oriental Medicine
Acute Care/Critical Care Nursing Administration (*see* Health Services Management and Hospital Administration; Nursing and Healthcare Administration; Pharmaceutical Administration)
Adult Nursing
Advanced Practice Nursing (*see* Family Nurse Practitioner Studies)
Allied Health—General
Allied Health Professions (*see* Clinical Laboratory Sciences/Medical Technology; Clinical Research; Communication Disorders; Dental Hygiene; Emergency Medical Services; Occupational Therapy; Physical Therapy; Physician Assistant Studies; Rehabilitation Sciences)
Allopathic Medicine
Anatomy
Anesthesiologist Assistant Studies
Animal Behavior
Bacteriology
Behavioral Sciences (*see* Biopsychology; Neuroscience; Zoology)
Biochemistry
Bioethics

Biological and Biomedical Sciences—General Biological Chemistry (*see* Biochemistry)
Biological Oceanography (*see* Marine Biology)
Biophysics
Biopsychology
Botany
Breeding (*see* Botany; Plant Biology; Genetics)
Cancer Biology/Oncology
Cardiovascular Sciences
Cell Biology
Cellular Physiology (*see* Cell Biology; Physiology)
Child-Care Nursing (*see* Maternal and Child/Neonatal Nursing)
Chiropractic
Clinical Laboratory Sciences/Medical Technology
Clinical Research
Community Health
Community Health Nursing
Computational Biology
Conservation (*see* Conservation Biology; Environmental Biology)
Conservation Biology
Crop Sciences (*see* Botany; Plant Biology)
Cytology (*see* Cell Biology)
Dental and Oral Surgery (*see* Oral and Dental Sciences)
Dental Assistant Studies (*see* Dental Hygiene)
Dental Hygiene
Dental Services (*see* Dental Hygiene)
Dentistry
Developmental Biology Dietetics (*see* Nutrition)
Ecology
Embryology (*see* Developmental Biology)
Emergency Medical Services
Endocrinology (*see* Physiology)
Entomology
Environmental Biology
Environmental and Occupational Health
Epidemiology
Evolutionary Biology
Family Nurse Practitioner Studies
Foods (*see* Nutrition)
Forensic Nursing
Genetics
Genomic Sciences
Gerontological Nursing
Health Physics/Radiological Health
Health Promotion
Health-Related Professions (*see* individual allied health professions)
Health Services Management and Hospital Administration
Health Services Research
Histology (*see* Anatomy; Cell Biology)
HIV/AIDS Nursing
Hospice Nursing
Hospital Administration (*see* Health Services Management and Hospital Administration)
Human Genetics
Immunology
Industrial Hygiene
Infectious Diseases
International Health
Laboratory Medicine (*see* Clinical Laboratory Sciences/Medical Technology; Immunology; Microbiology; Pathology)
Life Sciences (*see* Biological and Biomedical Sciences)
Marine Biology
Maternal and Child Health
Maternal and Child/Neonatal Nursing
Medical Imaging
Medical Microbiology
Medical Nursing (*see* Medical/Surgical Nursing)
Medical Physics
Medical/Surgical Nursing
Medical Technology (*see* Clinical Laboratory Sciences/Medical Technology)
Medical Sciences (*see* Biological and Biomedical Sciences)
Medical Science Training Programs (*see* Biological and Biomedical Sciences)
Medicinal and Pharmaceutical Chemistry
Medicinal Chemistry (*see* Medicinal and Pharmaceutical Chemistry)

Medicine (*see* Allopathic Medicine; Naturopathic Medicine; Osteopathic Medicine; Podiatric Medicine)
Microbiology
Midwifery (*see* Nurse Midwifery)
Molecular Biology
Molecular Biophysics
Molecular Genetics
Molecular Medicine
Molecular Pathogenesis
Molecular Pathology
Molecular Pharmacology
Molecular Physiology
Molecular Toxicology
Naturopathic Medicine
Neural Sciences (*see* Biopsychology; Neurobiology; Neuroscience)
Neurobiology
Neuroendocrinology (*see* Biopsychology; Neurobiology; Neuroscience; Physiology)
Neuropharmacology (*see* Biopsychology; Neurobiology; Neuroscience; Pharmacology)
Neurophysiology (*see* Biopsychology; Neurobiology; Neuroscience; Physiology)
Neuroscience
Nuclear Medical Technology (*see* Clinical Laboratory Sciences/ Medical Technology)
Nurse Anesthesia
Nurse Midwifery
Nurse Practitioner Studies (*see* Family Nurse Practitioner Studies)
Nursing Administration (*see* Nursing and Healthcare Administration)
Nursing and Healthcare Administration
Nursing Education
Nursing—General
Nursing Informatics
Nutrition
Occupational Health (*see* Environmental and Occupational Health; Occupational Health Nursing)
Occupational Health Nursing
Occupational Therapy
Oncology (*see* Cancer Biology/Oncology)
Oncology Nursing
Optometry
Oral and Dental Sciences
Oral Biology (*see* Oral and Dental Sciences)
Oral Pathology (*see* Oral and Dental Sciences)
Organismal Biology (*see* Biological and Biomedical Sciences; Zoology)
Oriental Medicine and Acupuncture (*see* Acupuncture and Oriental Medicine)
Orthodontics (*see* Oral and Dental Sciences)
Osteopathic Medicine
Parasitology
Pathobiology
Pathology
Pediatric Nursing
Pedontics (*see* Oral and Dental Sciences)
Perfusion
Pharmaceutical Administration
Pharmaceutical Chemistry (*see* Medicinal and Pharmaceutical Chemistry)
Pharmaceutical Sciences
Pharmacology
Pharmacy
Photobiology of Cells and Organelles (*see* Botany; Cell Biology; Plant Biology)
Physical Therapy
Physician Assistant Studies
Physiological Optics (*see* Vision Sciences)
Podiatric Medicine
Preventive Medicine (*see* Community Health and Public Health)
Physiological Optics (*see* Physiology)
Physiology
Plant Biology
Plant Molecular Biology
Plant Pathology
Plant Physiology
Pomology (*see* Botany; Plant Biology)
Psychiatric Nursing
Public Health—General

Public Health Nursing (*see* Community Health Nursing)
Psychiatric Nursing
Psychobiology (*see* Biopsychology)
Psychopharmacology (*see* Biopsychology; Neuroscience; Pharmacology)
Radiation Biology
Radiological Health (*see* Health Physics/Radiological Health)
Rehabilitation Nursing
Rehabilitation Sciences
Rehabilitation Therapy (*see* Physical Therapy)
Reproductive Biology
School Nursing
Sociobiology (*see* Evolutionary Biology)
Structural Biology
Surgical Nursing (*see* Medical/Surgical Nursing)
Systems Biology
Teratology
Therapeutics
Theoretical Biology (*see* Biological and Biomedical Sciences)
Therapeutics (*see* Pharmaceutical Sciences; Pharmacology; Pharmacy)
Toxicology
Transcultural Nursing
Translational Biology
Tropical Medicine (*see* Parasitology)
Veterinary Medicine
Veterinary Sciences
Virology
Vision Sciences
Wildlife Biology (*see* Zoology)
Women's Health Nursing
Zoology

Graduate Programs in the Physical Sciences, Mathematics, Agricultural Sciences, the Environment & Natural Resources

Acoustics
Agricultural Sciences
Agronomy and Soil Sciences
Analytical Chemistry
Animal Sciences
Applied Mathematics
Applied Physics
Applied Statistics
Aquaculture
Astronomy
Astrophysical Sciences (*see* Astrophysics; Atmospheric Sciences; Meteorology; Planetary and Space Sciences)
Astrophysics
Atmospheric Sciences
Biological Oceanography (*see* Marine Affairs; Marine Sciences; Oceanography)
Biomathematics
Biometry
Biostatistics
Chemical Physics
Chemistry
Computational Sciences
Condensed Matter Physics
Dairy Science (*see* Animal Sciences)
Earth Sciences (*see* Geosciences)
Environmental Management and Policy
Environmental Sciences
Environmental Studies (*see* Environmental Management and Policy)
Experimental Statistics (*see* Statistics)
Fish, Game, and Wildlife Management
Food Science and Technology
Forestry
General Science (*see* specific topics)
Geochemistry

Geodetic Sciences
Geological Engineering (*see* Geology)
Geological Sciences (*see* Geology)
Geology
Geophysical Fluid Dynamics (*see* Geophysics)
Geophysics
Geosciences
Horticulture
Hydrogeology
Hydrology
Inorganic Chemistry
Limnology
Marine Affairs
Marine Geology
Marine Sciences
Marine Studies (*see* Marine Affairs; Marine Geology; Marine Sciences; Oceanography)
Mathematical and Computational Finance
Mathematical Physics
Mathematical Statistics (*see* Applied Statistics; Statistics)
Mathematics
Meteorology
Mineralogy
Natural Resource Management (*see* Environmental Management and Policy; Natural Resources)
Natural Resources
Nuclear Physics (*see* Physics)
Ocean Engineering (*see* Marine Affairs; Marine Geology; Marine Sciences; Oceanography)
Oceanography
Optical Sciences
Optical Technologies (*see* Optical Sciences)
Optics (*see* Applied Physics; Optical Sciences; Physics)
Organic Chemistry
Paleontology
Paper Chemistry (*see* Chemistry)
Photonics
Physical Chemistry
Physics
Planetary and Space Sciences
Plant Sciences
Plasma Physics
Poultry Science (*see* Animal Sciences)
Radiological Physics (*see* Physics)
Range Management (*see* Range Science)
Range Science
Resource Management (*see* Environmental Management and Policy; Natural Resources)
Solid-Earth Sciences (*see* Geosciences)
Space Sciences (*see* Planetary and Space Sciences)
Statistics
Theoretical Chemistry
Theoretical Physics
Viticulture and Enology
Water Resources

Graduate Programs in Engineering & Applied Sciences

Aeronautical Engineering (*see* Aerospace/Aeronautical Engineering)
Aerospace/Aeronautical Engineering
Aerospace Studies (*see* Aerospace/Aeronautical Engineering)
Agricultural Engineering
Applied Mechanics (*see* Mechanics)
Applied Science and Technology
Architectural Engineering
Artificial Intelligence/Robotics
Astronautical Engineering (*see* Aerospace/Aeronautical Engineering)
Automotive Engineering
Aviation
Biochemical Engineering
Bioengineering
Bioinformatics
Biological Engineering (*see* Bioengineering)

Biomedical Engineering
Biosystems Engineering
Biotechnology
Ceramic Engineering (*see* Ceramic Sciences and Engineering)
Ceramic Sciences and Engineering
Ceramics (*see* Ceramic Sciences and Engineering)
Chemical Engineering
Civil Engineering
Computer and Information Systems Security
Computer Engineering
Computer Science
Computing Technology (*see* Computer Science)
Construction Engineering
Construction Management
Database Systems
Electrical Engineering
Electronic Materials
Electronics Engineering (*see* Electrical Engineering)
Energy and Power Engineering
Energy Management and Policy
Engineering and Applied Sciences
Engineering and Public Affairs (*see* Technology and Public Policy)
Engineering and Public Policy (*see* Energy Management and Policy; Technology and Public Policy)
Engineering Design
Engineering Management
Engineering Mechanics (*see* Mechanics)
Engineering Metallurgy (*see* Metallurgical Engineering and Metallurgy)
Engineering Physics
Environmental Design (*see* Environmental Engineering)
Environmental Engineering
Ergonomics and Human Factors
Financial Engineering
Fire Protection Engineering
Food Engineering (*see* Agricultural Engineering)
Game Design and Development
Gas Engineering (*see* Petroleum Engineering)
Geological Engineering
Geophysics Engineering (*see* Geological Engineering)
Geotechnical Engineering
Hazardous Materials Management
Health Informatics
Health Systems (*see* Safety Engineering; Systems Engineering)
Highway Engineering (*see* Transportation and Highway Engineering)
Human-Computer Interaction
Human Factors (*see* Ergonomics and Human Factors)
Hydraulics
Hydrology (*see* Water Resources Engineering)
Industrial Engineering (*see* Industrial/Management Engineering)
Industrial/Management Engineering
Information Science
Internet Engineering
Macromolecular Science (*see* Polymer Science and Engineering)
Management Engineering (*see* Engineering Management; Industrial/Management Engineering)
Management of Technology
Manufacturing Engineering
Marine Engineering (*see* Civil Engineering)
Materials Engineering
Materials Sciences
Mechanical Engineering
Mechanics
Medical Informatics
Metallurgical Engineering and Metallurgy
Metallurgy (*see* Metallurgical Engineering and Metallurgy)
Mineral/Mining Engineering
Modeling and Simulation
Nanotechnology
Nuclear Engineering
Ocean Engineering
Operations Research
Paper and Pulp Engineering
Petroleum Engineering
Pharmaceutical Engineering
Plastics Engineering (*see* Polymer Science and Engineering)

Graduate Programs in Business, Education, Information Studies, Law & Social Work

Accounting
Actuarial Science
Adult Education
Advertising and Public Relations
Agricultural Education
Alcohol Abuse Counseling (*see* Counselor Education)
Archival Management and Studies
Art Education
Athletics Administration (*see* Kinesiology and Movement Studies)
Athletic Training and Sports Medicine
Audiology (*see* Communication Disorders)
Aviation Management
Banking (*see* Finance and Banking)
Business Administration and Management—General
Business Education
Communication Disorders
Community College Education
Computer Education
Continuing Education (*see* Adult Education)
Counseling (*see* Counselor Education)
Counselor Education
Curriculum and Instruction
Developmental Education
Distance Education Development
Drug Abuse Counseling (*see* Counselor Education)
Early Childhood Education
Educational Leadership and Administration
Educational Measurement and Evaluation
Educational Media/Instructional Technology
Educational Policy
Educational Psychology
Education—General
Education of the Blind (*see* Special Education)
Education of the Deaf (*see* Special Education)
Education of the Gifted
Education of the Hearing Impaired (*see* Special Education)
Education of the Learning Disabled (*see* Special Education)
Education of the Mentally Retarded (*see* Special Education)
Education of the Physically Handicapped (*see* Special Education)
Education of Students with Severe/Multiple Disabilities
Education of the Visually Handicapped (*see* Special Education)
Electronic Commerce
Elementary Education
English as a Second Language
English Education
Entertainment Management
Entrepreneurship
Environmental Education
Environmental Law
Exercise and Sports Science
Exercise Physiology (*see* Kinesiology and Movement Studies)
Facilities and Entertainment Management
Finance and Banking
Food Services Management (*see* Hospitality Management)
Foreign Languages Education
Foundations and Philosophy of Education
Guidance and Counseling (*see* Counselor Education)
Health Education
Health Law
Hearing Sciences (*see* Communication Disorders)
Higher Education
Home Economics Education
Hospitality Management
Hotel Management (*see* Travel and Tourism)
Human Resources Development
Human Resources Management
Human Services
Industrial Administration (*see* Industrial and Manufacturing Management)
Industrial and Manufacturing Management

Industrial Education (*see* Vocational and Technical Education)
Information Studies
Instructional Technology (*see* Educational Media/Instructional Technology)
Insurance
Intellectual Property Law
International and Comparative Education
International Business
International Commerce (*see* International Business)
International Economics (*see* International Business)
International Trade (*see* International Business)
Investment and Securities (*see* Business Administration and Management; Finance and Banking; Investment Management)
Investment Management
Junior College Education (*see* Community College Education)
Kinesiology and Movement Studies
Law
Legal and Justice Studies
Leisure Services (*see* Recreation and Park Management)
Leisure Studies
Library Science
Logistics
Management (*see* Business Administration and Management)
Management Information Systems
Management Strategy and Policy
Marketing
Marketing Research
Mathematics Education
Middle School Education
Movement Studies (*see* Kinesiology and Movement Studies)
Multilingual and Multicultural Education
Museum Education
Music Education
Nonprofit Management
Nursery School Education (*see* Early Childhood Education)
Occupational Education (*see* Vocational and Technical Education)
Organizational Behavior
Organizational Management
Parks Administration (*see* Recreation and Park Management)
Personnel (*see* Human Resources Development; Human Resources Management; Organizational Behavior; Organizational Management; Student Affairs)
Philosophy of Education (*see* Foundations and Philosophy of Education)
Physical Education
Project Management
Public Relations (*see* Advertising and Public Relations)
Quality Management
Quantitative Analysis
Reading Education
Real Estate
Recreation and Park Management
Recreation Therapy (*see* Recreation and Park Management)
Religious Education
Remedial Education (*see* Special Education)
Restaurant Administration (*see* Hospitality Management)
Science Education
Secondary Education
Social Sciences Education
Social Studies Education (*see* Social Sciences Education)
Social Work
Special Education
Speech-Language Pathology and Audiology (*see* Communication Disorders)
Sports Management
Sports Medicine (*see* Athletic Training and Sports Medicine)
Sports Psychology and Sociology (*see* Kinesiology and Movement Studies)
Student Affairs
Substance Abuse Counseling (*see* Counselor Education)
Supply Chain Management
Sustainability Management
Systems Management (*see* Management Information Systems)
Taxation
Teacher Education (*see* specific subject areas)

Teaching English as a Second Language (*see* English as a Second Language)

Technical Education (*see* Vocational and Technical Education)

Transportation Management

Travel and Tourism

Urban Education

Vocational and Technical Education

Vocational Counseling (*see* Counselor Education)

Directories and Subject Areas in this Book